NCAA FOOTBALL RECORDS

OFFICIAL 2000

National Collegiate Athletic Association

THE NATIONAL COLLEGIATE ATHLETIC ASSOCIATION
P.O. Box 6222, Indianapolis, Indiana
46206-6222
www.ncaa.org

August 2000

Compiled By:
   Richard M. Campbell, *Statistics Coordinator.*
   John D. Painter, *Senior Statistics Coordinator.*
   Sean W. Straziscar, *Statistics Coordinator.*

Edited By:
   Scott Deitch, *Publications Editor.*

Typesetting/Production By:
   Toi Davis, *Graphic Technician II.*

Cover Design By:
   Wayne Davis, *Graphics Manager*

Distributed to sports information directors and conference publicity directors.

NCAA, NCAA logo and National Collegiate Athletic Association are registered marks of the Association and use in any manner is prohibited unless prior approval is obtained from the Association.

Copyright, 2000, by the National Collegiate Athletic Association.
Printed in the United States of America.
ISSN 0735-5475
NCAA 15135-8/00

Contents

Division I-A Records 5
Division I-AA Records 103
Division II Records 149
Division III Records 183
Individual Collegiate Records.................................215
Award Winners..235
Bowl/All-Star Game Records 283
Coaching Records...369
Added and Discontinued Programs 405
Championship Results...409
Attendance Records..437
1999 Statistical Leaders..449
Conference Standings and Champions..................469
2000 Schedules/1999 Results 487

Division I-A Records

Individual Records 6
Team Records 17
Annual Champions, All-Time Leaders 23
Team Champions 52
Toughest-Schedule Annual Leaders 55
Annual Most-Improved Teams 56
All-Time Team Won-Lost Records 57
National Poll Rankings 61
Bowl Coalition, Alliance and Bowl
Championship Series History 83
Streaks and Rivalries 87
Cliffhangers 89
1999 Overtime Games 91
Division I-A Stadiums 93
Famous Major-College Dynasties 94
Major-College Statistics Trends 95
College Football Rules Changes 100

Individual Records

Under a three-division reorganization plan adopted by the special NCAA Convention of August 1973, teams classified major-college in football on August 1, 1973, were placed in Division I. College-division teams were divided into Division II and Division III. At the NCAA Convention of January 1978, Division I was divided into Division I-A and Division I-AA for football only.

From 1937, when official national statistics rankings began, through 1969, individual rankings were by totals. Beginning in 1970, most season individual rankings were by per-game averages. In total offense, rushing and scoring, it is yards or points per game; in receiving, catches per game and yards per game; in interceptions, catches per game; and in punt and kickoff returns, yards per return. Punting always has been by average, and all team rankings have been per game. Beginning in 1979, passers were rated in all divisions on "efficiency rating points," which are derived from a formula that compares passers to the national averages for 14 seasons of two-platoon Division I football starting with the 1965 season. One hundred points equals the 14-year averages for all players in Division I. Those averages break down to 6.29 yards per attempt, 47.14 percent completions, 3.97 percent touchdown passes and 6.54 percent interceptions. The formula assumes that touchdowns are as good as interceptions are bad; therefore, these two figures offset each other for the average player. To determine efficiency rating points, multiply a passer's yards per attempt by 8.4, add his completion percentage, add his touchdown percentage times 3.3, then subtract his interception percentage times two.

Passers must have a minimum of 15 attempts per game to determine rating points because fewer attempts could allow a player to win the championship with fewer than 100 attempts in a season. A passer must play in at least 75 percent of his team's games to qualify for the rankings (e.g., a player on a team with a nine-game season could qualify by playing in seven games); thus, a passer with 105 attempts could qualify for the national rankings.

A pass efficiency rating comparison for each year since 1979 has been added to the passing section of all-time leaders.

All individual and team records and rankings include regular-season games only. Career records of players include only those years in which they competed in Division I-A.

Statistics in some team categories were not tabulated until the advent of the computerized statistics program in 1966. The records listed in those categories begin with the 1966 season and are so indicated.

In 1954, the regular-season schedule was limited to a maximum of 10 games, and in 1970, to a limit of 11 games, excluding postseason competition.

A player whose career includes statistics for parts of five seasons (or an active player who will play in five seasons) because he was granted an additional season of competition for reasons of hardship or a freshman redshirt are denoted by "$."

COLLEGIATE RECORDS

Individual collegiate records are determined by comparing the best records in all four divisions (I-A, I-AA, II and III) in comparable categories. Included are career records of players who played parts of their careers in different divisions (such as Dennis Shaw of San Diego State, Howard Stevens of Randolph-Macon and Louisville, and Doug Williams of Grambling). For individual collegiate career leaders, see page 216.

Total Offense

(Rushing Plus Passing)

MOST PLAYS
Quarter
41—Jason Davis, UNLV vs. Idaho, Sept. 17, 1994 (4th; 41 passes)
Half
57—Rusty LaRue, Wake Forest vs. Duke, Oct. 28, 1995 (2nd; 56 passes, 1 rush)
Game
94—Matt Vogler, TCU vs. Houston, Nov. 3, 1990 (696 yards)
Season
704—David Klingler, Houston, 1990 (5,221 yards)
2 Yrs
1,293—David Klingler, Houston, 1990-91 (8,447 yards)
3 Yrs
1,610—Ty Detmer, Brigham Young, 1989-91 (13,456 yards)
Career
(4 yrs.) 1,846—Chris Redman, Louisville, 1996-99 (12,129 yards)

MOST PLAYS PER GAME
Season
64.0—David Klingler, Houston, 1990 (704 in 11)
2 Yrs
61.6—David Klingler, Houston, 1990-91 (1,293 in 21)
Career
48.5—Doug Gaynor, Long Beach St., 1984-85 (1,067 in 22)

MOST PLAYS BY A FRESHMAN
Game
76—Sandy Schwab, Northwestern vs. Michigan, Oct. 23, 1982 (431 yards)
Season
594—Jon Denton, UNLV, 1996 (3,629 yards)
Also holds per-game record at 49.5 (594 in 12)

MOST YARDS GAINED
Quarter
347—Jason Davis, UNLV vs. Idaho, Sept. 17, 1994 (4th)
Half
510—Andre Ware, Houston vs. Southern Methodist, Oct. 21, 1989 (1st)
Game
732—David Klingler, Houston vs. Arizona St., Dec. 2, 1990 (16 rushing, 716 passing)
Season
5,221—David Klingler, Houston, 1990 (81 rushing, 5,140 passing)
2 Yrs
9,455—Ty Detmer, Brigham Young, 1989-90 (-293 rushing, 9,748 passing)
3 Yrs
13,456—Ty Detmer, Brigham Young, 1989-91 (-323 rushing, 13,779 passing)
Career
(4 yrs.) 14,665—Ty Detmer, Brigham Young, 1988-91 (-366 rushing, 15,031 passing)

MOST YARDS GAINED PER GAME
Season
474.6—David Klingler, Houston, 1990 (5,221 in 11)
2 Yrs
402.2—David Klingler, Houston, 1990-91 (8,447 in 21)
Career
382.4—Tim Rattay, Louisiana Tech, 1997-99 (12,618 in 33)

MOST YARDS GAINED, FIRST TWO SEASONS
8,808—Tim Rattay, Louisiana Tech, 1997-98
Also holds per-game record at 383.0

MOST SEASONS GAINING 4,000 YARDS OR MORE
3—Ty Detmer, Brigham Young, 1989-91

MOST SEASONS GAINING 3,000 YARDS OR MORE
3—Ty Detmer, Brigham Young, 1989-91; Chad Pennington, Marshall, 1997-99; Tim Rattay, Louisiana Tech, 1997-99

MOST SEASONS GAINING 2,500 YARDS OR MORE
3—John Elway, Stanford, 1980-82; Doug Flutie, Boston College, 1982-84; Randall Cunningham, UNLV, 1982-84; Brian McClure, Bowling Green, 1983-85; Erik Wilhelm, Oregon St., 1986-88; Shawn Moore, Virginia, 1988-90; Ty Detmer, Brigham Young, 1989-91; Shane Matthews, Florida, 1990-92; Stoney Case, New Mexico, 1992-94; Peyton Manning, Tennessee, 1995-97; Daunte Culpepper, UCF, 1996-98; Chris Redman, Louisville, 1997-99

MOST YARDS GAINED BY A FRESHMAN
Game
582—David Neill, Nevada vs. New Mexico St., Oct. 10, 1998 (61 plays)
Season
3,629—Jon Denton, UNLV, 1996 (594 plays)
Per-game record—372.3 by David Neill, Nevada, 1998

MOST YARDS GAINED BY A SOPHOMORE
Game
625—Scott Mitchell, Utah vs. Air Force, Oct. 15, 1988 (-6 rushing, 631 passing)
Season
4,433—Ty Detmer, Brigham Young, 1989 (12 games, 497 plays)
Per-game record—390.8, Scott Mitchell, Utah, 1988

MOST YARDS GAINED IN FIRST GAME OF CAREER
483—Billy Stevens, UTEP vs. North Texas, Sept. 18, 1965

MOST YARDS GAINED IN TWO, THREE AND FOUR CONSECUTIVE GAMES
2 Games
1,310—David Klingler, Houston, 1990 (578 vs. Eastern Wash., Nov. 17; 732 vs. Arizona St., Dec. 2)
3 Games
1,651—David Klingler, Houston, 1990 (341 vs. Texas, Nov. 10; 578 vs. Eastern Wash., Nov. 17; 732 vs. Arizona St., Dec. 2)
4 Games
2,276—David Klingler, Houston, 1990 (625 vs. TCU, Nov. 3; 341 vs. Texas, Nov. 10; 578 vs. Eastern Wash., Nov. 17; 732 vs. Arizona St., Dec. 2)

MOST GAMES GAINING 300 YARDS OR MORE
Season
12—Ty Detmer, Brigham Young, 1990
Career
33—Ty Detmer, Brigham Young, 1988-91

MOST CONSECUTIVE GAMES GAINING 300 YARDS OR MORE
Season
12—Ty Detmer, Brigham Young, 1990
Career
19—Ty Detmer, Brigham Young, 1989-90

MOST GAMES GAINING 400 YARDS OR MORE
Season
9—David Klingler, Houston, 1990
Career
13—Ty Detmer, Brigham Young, 1988-91

MOST CONSECUTIVE GAMES GAINING 400 YARDS OR MORE
Season
5—Ty Detmer, Brigham Young, 1990
Also holds career record at 5

MOST YARDS GAINED AGAINST ONE OPPONENT
Career
1,483—Ty Detmer, Brigham Young vs. San Diego St., 1988-91

INDIVIDUAL RECORDS—TOTAL OFFENSE

DIVISION I-A

MOST YARDS GAINED PER GAME AGAINST ONE OPPONENT
Career
(Min. 3 games) 399.0—Cody Ledbetter, New Mexico St. vs. UNLV, 1993-95 (1,197 yards)
(Min. 4 games) 370.8—Ty Detmer, Brigham Young vs. San Diego St., 1988-91 (1,483 yards)

MOST YARDS GAINED BY TWO OPPOSING PLAYERS
Game
1,321—Matt Vogler, TCU (696) & David Klingler, Houston (625), Nov. 3, 1990

GAINING 1,000 YARDS RUSHING AND 1,000 YARDS PASSING
Season
Johnny Bright (HB), Drake, 1950 (1,232 rushing, 1,168 passing); Reggie Collier (QB), Southern Miss., 1981 (1,005 rushing, 1,004 passing); Bart Weiss (QB), Air Force, 1985 (1,032 rushing, 1,449 passing); Darian Hagan (QB), Colorado, 1989 (1,004 rushing, 1,002 passing); Dee Dowis (QB), Air Force, 1989 (1,286 rushing, 1,285 passing); Brian Mitchell (QB), La.-Lafayette, 1989 (1,311 rushing, 1,966 passing); Michael Carter (QB), Hawaii, 1991 (1,092 rushing, 1,172 passing); Beau Morgan (QB), Air Force, 1995 (1,285 rushing, 1,165 passing); Beau Morgan (QB), Air Force, 1996 (1,494 rushing, 1,210 passing); Chris McCoy (QB), Navy, 1997 (1,370 rushing, 1,203 passing); Scott Frost (QB), Nebraska, 1997 (1,095 rushing, 1,237 passing)

A QUARTERBACK GAINING 2,000 YARDS RUSHING AND 4,000 YARDS PASSING
Career
Prince McJunkins, Wichita St., 1979-82 (2,047 rushing, 4,544 passing); John Bond, Mississippi St., 1980-83 (2,280 rushing, 4,621 passing); Rickey Foggie, Minnesota, 1984-87 (2,038 rushing, 4,903 passing); Brian Mitchell, La.-Lafayette, 1986-89 (3,335 rushing, 5,447 passing); Major Harris, West Virginia, 1987-89 (2,030 rushing, 4,834 passing)

A QUARTERBACK GAINING 3,000 YARDS RUSHING AND 3,000 YARDS PASSING
Career
Brian Mitchell, La.-Lafayette, 1986-89 (3,335 rushing, 5,447 passing); Beau Morgan, Air Force, 1994-96 (3,379 rushing, 3,248 passing)

A QUARTERBACK GAINING 300 YARDS PASSING AND 100 YARDS RUSHING
Game
Ned James, New Mexico vs. Wyoming, Nov. 1, 1986 (118 rushing, 406 passing); Randy Welniak, Wyoming vs. Air Force, Sept. 24, 1988 (108 rushing, 359 passing); Donald Douglas, Houston vs. Southern Methodist, Oct. 19, 1991 (103 rushing, 319 passing); Shaun King, Tulane vs. Army, Nov. 14, 1998 (133 rushing, 332 passing); Michael Bishop, Kansas St. vs. Nebraska, Nov. 14, 1998 (140 rushing, 306 passing); Michael Bishop, Kansas St. vs. Texas A&M, Dec. 5, 1998 (101 rushing, 341 passing)

A QUARTERBACK GAINING 300 YARDS PASSING AND 200 YARDS RUSHING
Game
Marques Tuiasosopo, Washington vs. Stanford, Oct. 30, 1999 (202 rushing, 307 passing)

A QUARTERBACK GAINING 200 YARDS RUSHING AND 200 YARDS PASSING
Game
Reds Bagnell, Pennsylvania vs. Dartmouth, Oct. 14, 1950 (214 rushing, 276 passing); Steve Gage, Tulsa vs. New Mexico, Nov. 8, 1986 (212 rushing, 209 passing); Brian Mitchell, La.-Lafayette vs. Colorado St., Nov. 21, 1987 (271 rushing, 205 passing)

TEAMS HAVING A 3,000-YARD PASSER, 1,000-YARD RUSHER AND 1,000-YARD RECEIVER IN THE SAME YEAR
19 teams. Most recent: Louisville, 1999 (Chris Redman [3,647 passer], Frank Moreau [1,298 rusher] and Arnold Jackson [1,209 receiver]); Nevada, 1999 (David Neill [3,402 passer], Chris Lemon [1,170 rusher], and Trevor Insley [2,060 receiver]); Western Mich., 1999 (Tim Lester [3,639 passer], Robert Stanford [1,092 rusher] and Steve Neal [1,113 receiver]); Louisville, 1998 (Chris Redman [4,042 passer], Leroy Collins [1,134 rusher] and Arnold Jackson [1,165 receiver]); Western Mich., 1998 (Tim Lester [3,311 passer], Darnell Fields [1,016 rusher] and Steve Neal [1,121 receiver]); Nevada, 1998 (David Neill [3,249 passer], Chris Lemon [1,154 rusher], Geoff Noisy [1,405 receiver] and Trevor Insley [1,220 receiver]); Nevada, 1997 (John Dutton [3,526 passer], Chris Lemon [1,055 rusher], Geoff Noisy [1,184 receiver] and Trevor Insley [1,151 receiver]); Tennessee, 1997 (Peyton Manning [3,819 passer], Jamal Lewis [1,364 rusher] and Marcus Nash [1,170 receiver]); Nevada, 1995 (Mike Maxwell [3,611 passer], Kim Minor [1,052 rusher] and Alex Van Dyke [1,854 receiver]); New Mexico St., 1995 (Cody Ledbetter [3,501 passer], Denvis Manns [1,120 rusher] and Lucious Davis [1,018 receiver]); Ohio St., 1995 (Bobby Hoying [3,023 passer], Eddie George [1,826 rusher] and Terry Glenn [1,316 receiver]); San Diego St., 1995 (Billy Blanton [3,300 passer], George Jones [1,842 rusher], Will Blackwell [1,207 receiver] and Az Hakim [1,022 receiver])

(Note: Nevada, 1997, 1998 and San Diego St., 1995, are the only teams to have two 1,000-yard receivers.)

TEAMS HAVING A 2,000-YARD RUSHER AND 2,000-YARD PASSER IN THE SAME YEAR
3—Oklahoma St., 1988 (Barry Sanders [2,628 rusher] and Mike Gundy [2,163 passer]); Colorado, 1994 (Rashaan Salaam [2,055 rusher] and Kordell Stewart [2,071 passer]); Texas, 1998 (Ricky Williams [2,124 rusher] and Major Applewhite [2,453 passer])

TEAMS HAVING A 2,000-YARD RUSHER, 2,000-YARD PASSER AND 1,000-YARD RECEIVER IN THE SAME YEAR
Oklahoma St., 1988 (Barry Sanders [2,628 rusher], Mike Gundy [2,163 passer] and Hart Lee Dykes [1,278 receiver]); Texas, 1998 (Ricky Williams [2,124 rusher], Major Applewhite [2,453 passer] and Wane McGarity [1,087 receiver])

TEAMS HAVING A 4,000-YARD PASSER AND 1,000-YARD RUSHER IN THE SAME YEAR
3—Houston, 1989 (Andre Ware [4,699 passer] and Chuck Weatherspoon [1,146 rusher]); Houston, 1990 (David Klingler [5,140 passer] and Chuck Weatherspoon [1,097 rusher]); Louisville, 1998 (Chris Redman [4,042 passer] and Leroy Collins [1,134 rusher])

HIGHEST AVERAGE GAIN PER PLAY
Game
(Min. 37-62 plays) 14.3—Jason Martin, Louisiana Tech vs. Toledo, Oct. 19, 1996 (37 for 529)
(Min. 63 plays) 9.9—David Klingler, Houston vs. TCU, Nov. 3, 1990 (63 for 625)
Season
(Min. 3,000 yards) 8.9—Ty Detmer, Brigham Young, 1989 (497 for 4,433)
Career
(Min. 7,500 yards) 8.2—Ty Detmer, Brigham Young, 1988-91 (1,795 for 14,665)

MOST TOUCHDOWNS RESPONSIBLE FOR (TDs Scored and Passed For)
Game
11—David Klingler, Houston vs. Eastern Wash., Nov. 17, 1990 (passed for 11)
Season
55—David Klingler, Houston, 1990 (scored 1, passed for 54)
2 Yrs
85—David Klingler, Houston, 1990-91 (scored 2, passed for 83)
3 Yrs
122—Ty Detmer, Brigham Young, 1989-91 (scored 14, passed for 108)
Career
(4 yrs) 135—Ty Detmer, Brigham Young, 1988-91 (scored 14, passed for 121)

MOST TOUCHDOWNS RESPONSIBLE FOR PER GAME
Season
5.0—David Klingler, Houston, 1990 (55 in 11)
2 Yrs
4.0—David Klingler, Houston, 1990-91 (85 in 21)
3 Yrs
3.5—Tim Rattay, Louisiana Tech, 1997-99 (117 in 33)
Career
(4 yrs) 2.9—Ty Detmer, Brigham Young, 1988-91 (135 in 46)
Collegiate record—3.6, Dennis Shaw, San Diego St., 1968-69 (72 in 20)

MOST POINTS RESPONSIBLE FOR (Points Scored and Passed For)
Game
66—David Klingler, Houston vs. Eastern Wash., Nov. 17, 1990 (passed for 11 TDs)
Season
334—David Klingler, Houston, 1990 (scored 1 TD, passed for 54 TDs, accounted for 2 two-point conversions)
2 Yrs
514—David Klingler, Houston, 1990-91 (scored 2 TDs, passed for 83 TDs, accounted for 2 two-point conversions)
3 Yrs
702—Tim Rattay, Louisiana Tech, 1997-99 (scored 2 TDs, passed for 115 TDs)
Career
820—Ty Detmer, Brigham Young, 1988-91 (scored 14 TDs, passed for 121 TDs, accounted for 5 two-point conversions)

MOST POINTS RESPONSIBLE FOR PER GAME
Season
30.4—David Klingler, Houston, 1990 (334 in 11)
2 Yrs
22.8—Jim McMahon, Brigham Young, 1980-81 (502 in 22)
3 Yrs
21.3—Tim Rattay, Louisiana Tech, 1997-99 (702 in 33)
Career
(4 yrs) 17.8—Ty Detmer, Brigham Young, 1988-91 (820 in 46)
Collegiate record—21.6, Dennis Shaw, San Diego St., 1968-69 (432 in 20)

SCORING 200 POINTS AND PASSING FOR 200 POINTS
Career
Rick Leach, Michigan, 1975-78 (scored 204, passed for 270)

Rushing

MOST RUSHES
Quarter
22—Alex Smith, Indiana vs. Michigan St., Nov. 11, 1995 (1st, 114 yards)
Half
34—Tony Sands, Kansas vs. Missouri, Nov. 23, 1991 (2nd, 240 yards)
Game
58—Tony Sands, Kansas vs. Missouri, Nov. 23, 1991 (396 yards)
Season
403—Marcus Allen, Southern California, 1981 (2,342 yards)
2 Yrs
757—Marcus Allen, Southern California, 1980-81 (3,905 yards)
Career
(3 yrs.) 994—Herschel Walker, Georgia, 1980-82 (5,259 yards)
(4 yrs.) 1,215—Steve Bartalo, Colorado St., 1983-86 (4,813 yards)

MOST RUSHES PER GAME
Season
39.6—Ed Marinaro, Cornell, 1971 (356 in 9)
2 Yrs
36.0—Marcus Allen, Southern California, 1980-81 (757 in 21)
Career
34.0—Ed Marinaro, Cornell, 1969-71 (918 in 27)

MOST RUSHES BY A FRESHMAN
Game
50—Ron Dayne, Wisconsin vs. Minnesota, Nov. 9, 1996 (297 yards)
Season
295—Ron Dayne, Wisconsin, 1996 (1,863 yards)

INDIVIDUAL RECORDS—RUSHING

MOST RUSHES PER GAME BY A FRESHMAN
Season
29.2—Steve Bartalo, Colorado St., 1983 (292 in 10)

MOST CONSECUTIVE RUSHES BY SAME PLAYER
Game
16—William Howard, Tennessee vs. Mississippi, Nov. 15, 1986 (during two possessions)

MOST RUSHES IN TWO CONSECUTIVE GAMES
Season
102—Lorenzo White, Michigan St., 1985 (53 vs. Purdue, Oct. 26; 49 vs. Minnesota, Nov. 2)

MOST CONSECUTIVE RUSHES WITHOUT LOSING A FUMBLE
Season
365—Travis Prentice, Miami (Ohio), 1998
Career
862—Travis Prentice, Miami (Ohio), 1997-99

MOST YARDS GAINED
Quarter
222—Corey Dillon, Washington vs. San Jose St., Nov. 16, 1996 (1st, 16 rushes)
Half
287—Stacey Robinson, Northern Ill. vs. Fresno St., Oct. 6, 1990 (1st; 114 in first quarter, 173 in second quarter; 20 rushes); LaDainian Tomlinson, TCU vs. UTEP, Nov. 20, 1999 (2nd; 121 in third quarter, 166 in fourth quarter; 28 rushes)
Game
406—LaDainian Tomlinson, TCU vs. UTEP, Nov. 20, 1999 (43 rushes) (59 yards in first quarter, 60 in second quarter, 121 in third quarter, 166 in fourth quarter)
Season
2,628—Barry Sanders, Oklahoma St., 1988 (344 rushes, 11 games)
2 Yrs
4,195—Troy Davis, Iowa St., 1995-96 (747 rushes)
Career
(3 yrs.) 5,259—Herschel Walker, Georgia, 1980-82 (994 rushes)
(4 yrs.) 6,397—Ron Dayne, Wisconsin, 1996-99 (1,115 rushes)

MOST YARDS GAINED PER GAME
Season
238.9—Barry Sanders, Oklahoma St., 1988 (2,628 in 11)
2 Yrs
190.7—Troy Davis, Iowa St., 1995-96 (4,195 in 22)
Career
174.6—Ed Marinaro, Cornell, 1969-71 (4,715 in 27)

MOST YARDS GAINED BY A FRESHMAN
Game
386—Marshall Faulk, San Diego St. vs. Pacific (Cal.), Sept. 14, 1991 (37 rushes)
Season
1,863—Ron Dayne, Wisconsin, 1996 (295 rushes)
Per-game record—158.8, Marshall Faulk, San Diego St., 1991 (1,429 in 9)

MOST YARDS GAINED BY A SOPHOMORE
Game
351—Scott Harley, East Caro. vs. North Carolina St., Nov. 30, 1996 (42 rushes)
Season
2,010—Troy Davis, Iowa St., 1995 (345 rushes)
Also holds per-game record at 182.7 (2,010 in 11)

FRESHMEN GAINING 1,000 YARDS OR MORE
Season
By 48 players (see chart after Annual Rushing Champions). Most recent: Avon Cobourne, West Virginia, 1999 (1,139); Derrick Nix, Southern Miss., 1998 (1,180); Ken Simonton, Oregon St., 1998 (1,028); Jamal Lewis, Tennessee, 1997 (1,364); Robert Sanford, Western Mich., 1997 (1,033); Ron Dayne, Wisconsin, 1996 (1,863); Demond Parker, Oklahoma, 1996 (1,184); Sedrick Irvin, Michigan St., 1996 (1,036).

TWO FRESHMEN, SAME TEAM, GAINING 1,000 YARDS OR MORE
Season
Mike Smith (1,062) & Gwain Durden (1,049), Chattanooga, 1977

EARLIEST GAME A FRESHMAN REACHED 1,000 YARDS
Season
7—Emmitt Smith, Florida, 1987 (1,011 vs. Temple, Oct. 17); Marshall Faulk, San Diego St., 1991 (1,157 vs. Colorado St., Nov. 9)

FIRST PLAYER TO GAIN 1,000 YARDS OR MORE
Season
Byron "Whizzer" White, Colorado, 1937 (1,121)
(Note: Before NCAA records began in 1937, Morley Drury of Southern California gained 1,163 yards in 1927.)

EARLIEST GAME GAINING 1,000 YARDS OR MORE
Season
5—Ed Marinaro, Cornell, 1971 (1,026); Ricky Bell, Southern California, 1976 (1,008); Marcus Allen, Southern California, 1981 (1,136); Ernest Anderson, Oklahoma St., 1982 (1,042); Barry Sanders, Oklahoma St., 1988 (1,002); Troy Davis, Iowa St., 1995 (1,001); Troy Davis, Iowa St., 1996 (1,047); Byron Hanspard, Texas Tech, 1996 (1,112); Ricky Williams, Texas, 1998 (1,086)

MOST YARDS GAINED BY A QUARTERBACK
Game
308—Stacey Robinson, Northern Ill. vs. Fresno St., Oct. 6, 1990 (22 rushes)
Season
1,494—Beau Morgan, Air Force, 1996 (225 rushes)
Also holds per-game record at 135.8 (1,494 in 11)
Career
3,612—Dee Dowis, Air Force, 1986-89 (543 rushes)
Per-game record—109.1, Stacey Robinson, Northern Ill., 1988-90 (2,727 in 25)

LONGEST GAIN BY A QUARTERBACK
Game
98—Mark Malone, Arizona St. vs. Utah St., Oct. 27, 1979 (TD)

MOST GAMES GAINING 100 YARDS OR MORE
Season
11—By 14 players. Most recent: Ahman Green, Nebraska, 1997; Troy Davis, Iowa St., 1996; Wasean Tait, Toledo, 1995; Darnell Autry, Northwestern, 1995
Career
33—Archie Griffin, Ohio St., 1972-75 (42 games); Tony Dorsett, Pittsburgh, 1973-76 (43 games)

MOST GAMES GAINING 100 YARDS OR MORE BY A FRESHMAN
Season
9—Ron "Po" James, New Mexico St., 1968; Tony Dorsett, Pittsburgh, 1973
James holds consecutive record at 8

MOST CONSECUTIVE GAMES GAINING 100 YARDS OR MORE
Career
31—Archie Griffin, Ohio St., began Sept. 15, 1973 (vs. Minnesota), ended Nov. 22, 1975 (vs. Michigan)

MOST GAMES GAINING 200 YARDS OR MORE
Season
8—Marcus Allen, Southern California, 1981
Career
11—Marcus Allen, Southern California, 1978-81 (in 21 games during 1980-81); Ricky Williams, Texas, 1995-98; Ron Dayne, Wisconsin, 1996-99

MOST GAMES GAINING 200 YARDS OR MORE BY A FRESHMAN
Season
4—Herschel Walker, Georgia, 1980; Ron Dayne, Wisconsin, 1996

MOST CONSECUTIVE GAMES GAINING 200 YARDS OR MORE
Season
5—Marcus Allen, Southern California, 1981 (210 vs. Tennessee, Sept. 12; 274 vs. Indiana, Sept. 19; 208 vs. Oklahoma, Sept. 26; 233 vs. Oregon St., Oct. 3; 211 vs. Arizona, Oct. 10); Barry Sanders, Oklahoma St., 1988 (320 vs. Kansas St., Oct. 29; 215 vs. Oklahoma, Nov. 5; 312 vs. Kansas, Nov. 12; 293 vs. Iowa St., Nov. 19; 332 vs. Texas Tech, Dec. 3)

MOST GAMES GAINING 300 YARDS OR MORE
Season
4—Barry Sanders, Oklahoma St., 1988
Also holds career record at 4

MOST CONSECUTIVE GAMES GAINING 300 YARDS OR MORE
Season
2—Ricky Williams, Texas, 1998 (318 vs. Rice, Sept. 26; 350 vs. Iowa St., Oct. 3)

MOST YARDS GAINED IN TWO, THREE, FOUR AND FIVE CONSECUTIVE GAMES
2 Games
668—Ricky Williams, Texas, 1998 (318 vs. Rice, Sept. 26; 350 vs. Iowa St., Oct. 3)
3 Games
937—Barry Sanders, Oklahoma St., 1988 (312 vs. Kansas, Nov. 12; 293 vs. Iowa St., Nov. 19; 332 vs. Texas Tech, Dec. 3)
4 Games
1,152—Barry Sanders, Oklahoma St., 1988 (215 vs. Oklahoma, Nov. 5; 312 vs. Kansas, Nov. 12; 293 vs. Iowa St., Nov. 19; 332 vs. Texas Tech, Dec. 3)
5 Games
1,472—Barry Sanders, Oklahoma St., 1988 (320 vs. Kansas St., Oct. 29; 215 vs. Oklahoma, Nov. 5; 312 vs. Kansas, Nov. 12; 293 vs. Iowa St., Nov. 19; 332 vs. Texas Tech, Dec. 3)

MOST SEASONS GAINING 1,500 YARDS OR MORE
Career
3—Tony Dorsett, Pittsburgh, 1973, 1975-76; Herschel Walker, Georgia, 1980-82; Travis Prentice, Miami (Ohio), 1997-99

MOST SEASONS GAINING 1,000 YARDS OR MORE
Career
4—Tony Dorsett, Pittsburgh, 1973-76; Amos Lawrence, North Carolina, 1977-80; Denvis Manns, New Mexico St., 1995-98; Ron Dayne, Wisconsin, 1996-99
Collegiate record tied by Howard Stevens, Randolph-Macon, 1968-69; Louisville, 1971-72

TWO PLAYERS, SAME TEAM, EACH GAINING 1,000 YARDS OR MORE
Season
25 times. Most recent: Nebraska, 1997—Ahman Green (1,698) & Scott Frost (1,016); Ohio, 1996—Steve Hookfin (1,125) & Kareem Wilson (1,072); Colorado St., 1996—Calvin Branch (1,279) & Damon Washington (1,075)

TWO PLAYERS, SAME TEAM, EACH GAINING 200 YARDS OR MORE
Game
Gordon Brown, 214 (23 rushes) & Steve Gage (QB), 206 (26 rushes), Tulsa vs. Wichita St., Nov. 2, 1985; Sedrick Irvin, 238 (28 rushes) & Marc Renaud, 203 (21 rushes), Michigan St. vs. Penn St., Nov. 29, 1997

TWO OPPOSING I-A PLAYERS EACH GAINING 200 YARDS OR MORE
Game
George Swarn, Miami (Ohio) (239) & Otis Cheatham, Western Mich. (219), Sept. 8, 1984; Barry Sanders, Oklahoma St. (215) & Mike Gaddis, Oklahoma (213), Nov. 5, 1988; Ricky Williams, Texas (249) & Michael Perry, Rice (211), Sept. 27, 1997; De'Mond Parker, Oklahoma (291) & Ricky Williams, Texas (223), Oct. 11, 1997

MOST YARDS GAINED BY TWO OPPOSING PLAYERS
Game
553—Marshall Faulk, San Diego St. (386) & Ryan Benjamin, Pacific (Cal.) (167), Sept. 14, 1991

MOST YARDS GAINED BY TWO PLAYERS, SAME TEAM
Game
476—Tony Sands (396) & Chip Hilleary (80), Kansas vs. Missouri, Nov. 23, 1991
Season
2,997—Barry Sanders (2,628) & Gerald Hudson (Sanders' backup, 369), Oklahoma St., 1988
Also hold per-game record at 272.5

INDIVIDUAL RECORDS—RUSHING

Career
8,193—Eric Dickerson (4,450) & Craig James (3,743), Southern Methodist, 1979-82 (alternated at the same position during the last 36 games)

MOST YARDS GAINED IN FIRST GAME OF CAREER
273—Chris McCoy (Soph.), Navy vs. Southern Methodist, Sept. 9, 1995

MOST YARDS GAINED BY A FRESHMAN IN FIRST GAME OF CAREER
212—Greg Hill, Texas A&M vs. LSU, Sept. 14, 1991 (30 carries)

LONGEST RUSH BY A FRESHMAN IN FIRST GAME OF CAREER
98—Jerald Sowell, Tulane vs. Alabama, Sept. 4, 1993

MOST YARDS GAINED IN OPENING GAME OF SEASON
343—Tony Jeffery, TCU vs. Tulane, Sept. 13, 1986 (16 rushes)

MOST YARDS GAINED AGAINST ONE OPPONENT
Career
(3 yrs.) 690—Mike Gaddis, Oklahoma vs. Oklahoma St., 1988-89, 1991 (82 rushes)
(4 yrs.) 754—Tony Dorsett, Pittsburgh vs. Notre Dame, 1973-76 (96 rushes)

MOST YARDS GAINED PER GAME AGAINST ONE OPPONENT
Career
(Min. 2 games) 292.0—Anthony Thompson, Indiana vs. Wisconsin, 1986, 89 (584 yards, 91 rushes)
(Min. 3 games) 230.0—Mike Gaddis, Oklahoma vs. Oklahoma St., 1988-89, 1991 (690 yards, 82 rushes)

MOST YARDS GAINED BY TWO BROTHERS
Season
3,690—Barry Sanders, Oklahoma St. (2,628) & Byron Sanders, Northwestern (1,062), 1988

HIGHEST AVERAGE GAIN PER RUSH
Game
(Min. 8-14 rushes) 30.2—Kevin Lowe, Wyoming vs. South Dakota St., Nov. 10, 1984 (10 for 302)
(Min. 15-25 rushes) 21.4—Tony Jeffery, TCU vs. Tulane, Sept. 13, 1986 (16 for 343)
(Min. 26 rushes) 13.7—Eddie Lee Ivery, Georgia Tech vs. Air Force, Nov. 11, 1978 (26 for 356)
Season
(Min. 75-100 rushes) 11.5—Glenn Davis, Army, 1945 (82 for 944)
(Min. 101-213 rushes) 9.6—Chuck Weatherspoon, Houston, 1989 (119 for 1,146)
(Min. 214-281 rushes) 7.8—Mike Rozier, Nebraska, 1983 (275 for 2,148)
(Min. 282 rushes) 7.6—Barry Sanders, Oklahoma St., 1988 (344 for 2,628)
Career
(Min. 300-413 rushes) 8.3—Glenn Davis, Army, 1943-46 (358 for 2,957)
(Min. 414-780 rushes) 7.2—Mike Rozier, Nebraska, 1981-83 (668 for 4,780)
(Min. 781 rushes) 6.21—Ricky Williams, Texas, 1995-98 (1,011 for 6,279)

MOST TOUCHDOWNS SCORED BY RUSHING
Quarter
4—Dick Felt, Brigham Young vs. San Jose St., Nov. 8, 1952 (4th); Howard Griffith, Illinois vs. Southern Ill., Sept. 22, 1990 (3rd); Frank Moreau, Louisville vs. East Caro., Nov. 1, 1997 (2nd)
Game
8—Howard Griffith, Illinois vs. Southern Ill., Sept. 22, 1990 (5, 51, 7, 41, 5, 18, 5, 3 yards; Griffith scored three touchdowns [51, 7, 41] on consecutive carries and scored four touchdowns in the third quarter)
Season
37—Barry Sanders, Oklahoma St., 1988 (11 games) Also holds per-game record at 3.4 (37 in 11)
Career
73—Travis Prentice, Miami (Ohio), 1996-99

MOST GAMES SCORING TWO OR MORE TOUCHDOWNS BY RUSHING
Season
11—Barry Sanders, Oklahoma St., 1988

MOST CONSECUTIVE GAMES SCORING TWO OR MORE TOUCHDOWNS BY RUSHING
Career
12—Barry Sanders, Oklahoma St. (last game of 1987, all 11 in 1988)

MOST TOUCHDOWNS SCORED BY RUSHING BY A FRESHMAN
Game
7—Marshall Faulk, San Diego St. vs. Pacific (Cal.), Sept. 14, 1991
Season
21—Marshall Faulk, San Diego St., 1991 Also holds per-game record at 2.3 (21 in 9)

MOST RUSHING TOUCHDOWNS SCORED BY A QUARTERBACK
Game
6—Dee Dowis, Air Force vs. San Diego St., Sept. 1, 1989 (55, 28, 12, 16, 60, 17 yards; 249 yards rushing on 13 carries)
Season
20—Chris McCoy, Navy, 1997
Career
49—Kareem Wilson, Ohio, 1995-98 (45 games)

MOST CONSECUTIVE RUSHES FOR A TOUCHDOWN IN A GAME
3—Howard Griffith, Illinois vs. Southern Ill., Sept. 22, 1990 (TDs of 51, 7 and 41 yards); Tiki Barber, Virginia vs. Texas, Sept. 28, 1996 (TDs of 16, 26 and 12 yards); Chris McCoy, Navy vs. Rutgers, Sept. 13, 1997 (TDs of 2, 9 and 2 yards)

MOST RUSHING TOUCHDOWNS SCORED BY A QUARTERBACK IN TWO CONSECUTIVE SEASONS
38—Stacey Robinson, Northern Ill., 1989-90 (19 and 19)

Passing

HIGHEST PASSING EFFICIENCY RATING POINTS
Game
(Min. 12-24 atts.) 403.4—Tim Clifford, Indiana vs. Colorado, Sept. 26, 1980 (14 attempts, 11 completions, 0 interceptions, 345 yards, 5 TD passes)
(Min. 25-49 atts.) 295.5—David Neill, Nevada vs. Idaho, Oct. 24, 1998 (26 attempts, 20 completions, 0 interceptions, 480 yards, 5 TD passes)
(Min. 50 atts.) 199.2—Chris Redman, Louisville vs. East Caro., Nov. 14, 1998 (56 attempts, 44 completions, 1 interception, 592 yards, 6 TD passes)
Season
(Min. 15 atts. per game) 183.3—Shaun King, Tulane, 1998 (328 attempts, 223 completions, 6 interceptions, 3,232 yards, 36 TD passes)
Career
(Min. 325 comps.) 163.6—Danny Wuerffel, Florida, 1993-96 (1,170 attempts, 708 completions, 42 interceptions, 10,875 yards, 114 TD passes)

HIGHEST PASSING EFFICIENCY RATING POINTS BY A FRESHMAN
Season
(Min. 15 atts. per game) 162.3—Donovan McNabb, Syracuse, 1995 (207 attempts, 128 completions, 6 interceptions, 1,991 yards, 16 TD passes)

MOST PASSES ATTEMPTED
Quarter
41—Jason Davis, UNLV vs. Idaho, Sept. 17, 1994 (4th, completed 28)
Half
56—Rusty LaRue, Wake Forest vs. Duke, Oct. 28, 1995 (2nd, completed 41)
Game
83—Drew Brees, Purdue vs. Wisconsin, Oct. 10, 1998 (completed 55)
Season
643—David Klingler, Houston, 1990 (11 games, completed 374)
2 Yrs
1,140—David Klingler, Houston, 1990-91 (completed 652)
3 Yrs
1,552—Tim Rattay, Louisiana Tech, 1997-99 (completed 1,015)
Career
(4 yrs.) 1,679—Chris Redman, Louisville, 1996-99 (completed 1,031)

MOST PASSES ATTEMPTED PER GAME
Season
58.5—David Klingler, Houston, 1990 (643 in 11)
Career
47.0—Tim Rattay, Louisiana Tech, 1997-99 (1,552 in 33)

MOST PASSES ATTEMPTED BY A FRESHMAN
Game
71—Sandy Schwab, Northwestern vs. Michigan, Oct. 23, 1982 (completed 45)
Season
506—Jon Denton, UNLV, 1996 (completed 277)

MOST PASSES COMPLETED
Quarter
28—Jason Davis, UNLV vs. Idaho, Sept. 17, 1994 (4th, attempted 41)
Half
41—Rusty LaRue, Wake Forest vs. Duke, Oct. 28, 1995 (2nd, attempted 56)
Game
55—Rusty LaRue, Wake Forest vs. Duke, Oct. 28, 1995 (attempted 78); Drew Brees, Purdue vs. Wisconsin, Oct. 10, 1998 (attempted 83)
Season
400—Tim Couch, Kentucky, 1998 (11 games, attempted 553)
2 Yrs
763—Tim Couch, Kentucky, 1997-98 (attempted 1,100)
Also holds per-game record at 34.7 (763 in 22)
3 Yrs
1,015—Tim Rattay, Louisiana Tech, 1997-99 (attempted 1,552)
Also holds per-game record at 30.8 (1,015 in 33)
Career
(4 yrs.) 1,031—Chris Redman, Louisville, 1996-99 (attempted 1,679)

MOST PASSES COMPLETED PER GAME
Season
36.4—Tim Couch, Kentucky, 1998 (400 in 11)
Career
30.8—Tim Rattay, Louisiana Tech, 1997-99 (1,015 in 33)

MOST PASSES COMPLETED BY A FRESHMAN
Game
45—Sandy Schwab, Northwestern vs. Michigan, Oct. 23, 1982 (attempted 71)
Season
282—Mike Romo, Southern Methodist, 1989 (attempted 503)
Also holds per-game record at 25.6 (282 in 11)

MOST CONSECUTIVE PASSES COMPLETED
Game
23—Tee Martin, Tennessee vs. South Carolina, Oct. 31, 1998
Season
24—Tee Martin, Tennessee, 1998 (completed last attempt vs. Alabama, Oct. 24 and first 23 vs. South Carolina, Oct. 31)

MOST PASSES COMPLETED IN TWO, THREE AND FOUR CONSECUTIVE GAMES
2 Games
96—Rusty LaRue, Wake Forest, 1995 (55 vs. Duke, Oct. 28; 41 vs. Georgia Tech, Nov. 4)
3 Games
146—Rusty LaRue, Wake Forest, 1995 (55 vs. Duke, Oct. 28; 41 vs. Georgia Tech, Nov. 4; 50 vs. North Carolina St., Nov. 18)
4 Games
166—Tim Rattay, Louisiana Tech, 1999 (41 vs. Middle Tenn. St., Oct. 16; 46 vs. UCF, Oct. 23; 44 vs. Toledo, Oct. 30; 35 vs. La.-Monroe, Nov. 6)

HIGHEST PERCENTAGE OF PASSES COMPLETED
Game
(Min. 20-29 comps.) 95.8%—Tee Martin, Tennessee vs. South Carolina, Oct. 31, 1998 (23 of 24)
(Min. 30-39 comps.) 91.2%—Steve Sarkisian, Brigham Young vs. Fresno St., Nov. 25, 1995 (31 of 34)
(Min. 40 comps.) 83.0%—Tim Couch, Kentucky vs. Vanderbilt, Nov. 14, 1998 (44 of 53)

INDIVIDUAL RECORDS—PASSING

Season
(Min. 150 atts.) 73.6%—Daunte Culpepper, UCF, 1998 (296 of 402)
Career
(Min. 875-999 atts.) 66.2%—Scott Milanovich, Maryland, 1992-95 (650 of 982)
(Min. 1,000 atts.) 67.1%—Tim Couch, Kentucky, 1996-98 (795 of 1,184)

HIGHEST PERCENTAGE OF PASSES COMPLETED BY A FRESHMAN
Season
(Min. 200 atts.) 66.2%—Grady Benton, Arizona St., 1992 (149 of 225)

MOST PASSES HAD INTERCEPTED
Game
9—John Reaves, Florida vs. Auburn, Nov. 1, 1969 (attempted 66)
Season
34—John Eckman, Wichita St., 1966 (attempted 458)
Also holds per-game record at 3.4 (34 in 10)
Career
(3 yrs.) 68—Zeke Bratkowski, Georgia, 1951-53 (attempted 734)
(4 yrs.) 73—Mark Herrmann, Purdue, 1977-80 (attempted 1,218)
Per-game record—2.3, Steve Ramsey, North Texas, 1967-69 (67 in 29)

LOWEST PERCENTAGE OF PASSES HAD INTERCEPTED
Season
(Min. 150-349 atts.) 0.0%—Matt Blundin, Virginia, 1991 (0 of 224)
(Min. 350 atts.) 0.85%—Billy Volek, Fresno St., 1999 (3 of 355)
Career
(Min. 600-1,049 atts.) 1.3%—Billy Volek, Fresno St., 1997-99 (12 of 934)
(Min. 1,050 atts.) 2.26%—Tim Rattay, Louisiana Tech, 1997-99 (35 of 1,552)

MOST PASSES ATTEMPTED WITHOUT AN INTERCEPTION
Game
68—David Klingler, Houston vs. Baylor, Oct. 6, 1990 (completed 35)
Entire Season
224—Matt Blundin, Virginia, 1991 (completed 135)

MOST CONSECUTIVE PASSES ATTEMPTED WITHOUT AN INTERCEPTION
Season
271—Trent Dilfer, Fresno St., 1993
Also holds career record at 271

MOST CONSECUTIVE PASSES ATTEMPTED WITH JUST ONE INTERCEPTION
Career
329—Damon Allen, Cal St. Fullerton, 1983-84 (during 16 games; began Oct. 8, 1983, vs. Nevada, ended Nov. 3, 1984, vs. Fresno St. Interception occurred vs. Idaho, Sept. 15, 1984)

MOST CONSECUTIVE PASSES ATTEMPTED WITHOUT AN INTERCEPTION AT THE START OF A CAREER BY A FRESHMAN
138—Mike Gundy, Oklahoma St., 1986 (during 8 games)

MOST CONSECUTIVE PASSES ATTEMPTED WITHOUT AN INTERCEPTION AT THE START OF A DIVISION I-A CAREER
202—Brad Otton, Southern California, 1994-95 (played 1993 at I-AA Weber St.)

MOST YARDS GAINED
Quarter
347—Jason Davis, UNLV vs. Idaho, Sept. 17, 1994 (4th)
Half
517—Andre Ware, Houston vs. Southern Methodist, Oct. 21, 1989 (1st, completed 25 of 41)
Game
716—David Klingler, Houston vs. Arizona St., Dec. 2, 1990 (completed 41 of 70)
Season
(11 games) 5,140—David Klingler, Houston, 1990 (completed 374 of 643)
(12 games) 5,188—Ty Detmer, Brigham Young, 1990 (completed 361 of 562)
2 Yrs
9,748—Ty Detmer, Brigham Young, 1989-90 (completed 626 of 974)
3 Yrs
13,779—Ty Detmer, Brigham Young, 1989-91 (completed 875 of 1,377)
Career
(4 yrs.) 15,031—Ty Detmer, Brigham Young, 1988-91 (completed 958 of 1,530)

MOST YARDS GAINED PER GAME
Season
467.3—David Klingler, Houston, 1990 (5,140 in 11)
2 Yrs
406.2—Ty Detmer, Brigham Young, 1989-90 (9,748 in 24)
3 Yrs
386.2—Tim Rattay, Louisiana Tech, 1997-99 (12,746 in 33)
Career
(3 yrs.) 386.2—Tim Rattay, Louisiana Tech, 1997-99 (12,746 in 33)
(4 yrs.) 326.8—Ty Detmer, Brigham Young, 1988-91 (15,031 in 46)

MOST YARDS GAINED BY A FRESHMAN
Game
611—David Neill, Nevada vs. New Mexico St., Oct. 10, 1998
Season
3,591—Jon Denton, UNLV, 1996
Per-game record—361.0, David Neill, Nevada, 1998 (3,249 in 9)

MOST YARDS GAINED BY A SOPHOMORE
Game
631—Scott Mitchell, Utah vs. Air Force, Oct. 15, 1988
Season
4,560—Ty Detmer, Brigham Young, 1989
Per-game record—392.9, Scott Mitchell, Utah, 1988 (4,322 in 11)

MOST SEASONS GAINING 2,000 YARDS OR MORE
Career
4—Kevin Sweeney, Fresno St., 1983-86 (2,359—3,259—2,604—2,363); Todd Santos, San Diego St., 1984-87 (2,063—2,877—2,553—3,932); Tom Hodson, LSU, 1986-89 (2,261—2,125—2,074—2,655); T. J. Rubley, Tulsa, 1987-89, 1991 (2,058—2,497—2,292—2,054); Alex Van Pelt, Pittsburgh, 1989-92 (2,527—2,427—2,796—3,163); Glenn Foley, Boston College, 1990-93 (2,189—2,225—2,231—3,397); Tim Lester, Western Mich., 1996-99 (2,189-2,160-3,311-3,639)

MOST YARDS GAINED IN TWO, THREE AND FOUR CONSECUTIVE GAMES
2 Games
1,288—David Klingler, Houston, 1990 (572 vs. Eastern Wash., Nov. 17; 716 vs. Arizona St., Dec. 2)
3 Games
1,798—David Klingler, Houston, 1990-91 (572 vs. Eastern Wash., Nov. 17, 1990; 716 vs. Arizona St., Dec. 2, 1990; 510 vs. Louisiana Tech, Aug. 31, 1991)
4 Games
2,150—David Klingler, Houston, 1990 (563 vs. TCU, Nov. 3; 299 vs. Texas, Nov. 10; 572 vs. Eastern Wash., Nov. 17; 716 vs. Arizona St., Dec. 2)

MOST GAMES GAINING 200 YARDS OR MORE
Season
12—Robbie Bosco, Brigham Young, 1985, 1984; Ty Detmer, Brigham Young, 1990, 1989; Chad Pennington, Marshall, 1999, 1997; Tim Rattay, Louisiana Tech, 1998
Career
38—Ty Detmer, Brigham Young, 1988-91

MOST CONSECUTIVE GAMES GAINING 200 YARDS OR MORE
Season
12—Robbie Bosco, Brigham Young, 1984; Ty Detmer, Brigham Young, 1990, 1989; Chad Pennington, Marshall, 1999, 1997; Tim Rattay, Louisiana Tech, 1998
Career
27—Ty Detmer, Brigham Young (from Sept. 2, 1989, to Sept. 21, 1991)

MOST GAMES GAINING 300 YARDS OR MORE
Season
12—Ty Detmer, Brigham Young, 1990, 1989
Career
33—Ty Detmer, Brigham Young, 1988-91

MOST CONSECUTIVE GAMES GAINING 300 YARDS OR MORE
Season
12—Ty Detmer, Brigham Young, 1990, 1989
Career
24—Ty Detmer, Brigham Young (from Sept. 2, 1989, to Dec. 1, 1990)

MOST GAMES GAINING 400 YARDS OR MORE
Season
9—David Klingler, Houston, 1990
Career
12—Ty Detmer, Brigham Young, 1988-91; Tim Rattay, Louisiana Tech, 1997-99

MOST YARDS GAINED BY TWO OPPOSING PLAYERS
Game
1,253—Matt Vogler, TCU (690) & David Klingler, Houston (563), Nov. 3, 1990

TWO PLAYERS, SAME TEAM, EACH PASSING FOR 250 YARDS OR MORE
Game
Steve Cottrell (311) & John Elway (270), Stanford vs. Arizona St., Oct. 24, 1981; Andre Ware (517) & David Klingler (254), Houston vs. Southern Methodist, Oct. 21, 1989; Jason Davis (381) & Jared Brown (254), UNLV vs. Idaho, Sept. 17, 1994

MOST YARDS GAINED IN OPENING GAME OF SEASON
590—Tim Rattay, Louisiana Tech vs. Nebraska, Aug. 29, 1998

MOST YARDS GAINED AGAINST ONE OPPONENT
Career
1,495—Ty Detmer, Brigham Young vs. New Mexico, 1988-91

MOST YARDS GAINED PER GAME AGAINST ONE OPPONENT
Career
(Min. 3 games) 410.7—Gary Schofield, Wake Forest vs. Maryland, 1981-83 (1,232 yards)
(Min. 4 games) 373.8—Ty Detmer, Brigham Young vs. New Mexico, 1988-91 (1,495 yards)

MOST YARDS GAINED PER ATTEMPT
Game
(Min. 25-39 atts.) 18.5—David Neill, Nevada vs. Idaho, Oct. 24, 1998 (26 for 480)
(Min. 40-59 atts.) 14.1—John Walsh, Brigham Young vs. Utah St., Oct. 30, 1993 (44 for 619)
(Min. 60 atts.) 10.5—Scott Mitchell, Utah vs. Air Force, Oct. 15, 1988 (60 for 631)
Season
(Min. 412 atts.) 11.1—Ty Detmer, Brigham Young, 1989 (412 for 4,560)
Career
(Min. 1,000 atts.) 9.8—Ty Detmer, Brigham Young, 1988-91 (1,530 for 15,031)

MOST YARDS GAINED PER COMPLETION
Game
(Min. 22-41 comps.) 22.9—John Walsh, Brigham Young vs. Utah St., Oct. 30, 1993 (27 for 619)
(Min. 42 comps.) 15.7—Matt Vogler, TCU vs. Houston, Nov. 3, 1990 (44 for 690)
Season
(Min. 109-204 comps.) 18.2—Doug Williams, Grambling, 1977 (181 for 3,286)
(Min. 205 comps.) 17.5—Danny Wuerffel, Florida, 1996 (207 for 3,625)
Career
(Min. 275-399 comps.) 17.3—J. J. Joe, Baylor, 1990-93 (347 for 5,995)
(Min. 400 comps.) 15.7—Shawn Moore, Virginia, 1987-90 (421 for 6,629)

MOST TOUCHDOWN PASSES
Quarter
6—David Klingler, Houston vs. Louisiana Tech, Aug. 31, 1991 (2nd)
Half
7—Dennis Shaw, San Diego St. vs. New Mexico St., Nov. 15, 1969 (1st); Terry Dean, Florida vs. New Mexico St., Sept. 3, 1994 (1st); Doug Johnson, Florida vs. Central Mich., Sept. 6, 1997 (1st)

INDIVIDUAL RECORDS—PASSING

Game
11—David Klingler, Houston vs. Eastern Wash., Nov. 17, 1990
Season
54—David Klingler, Houston, 1990 (11 games)
2 Yrs
83—David Klingler, Houston, 1990-91
Also holds per-game record at 4.0 (83 in 21)
3 Yrs
115—Tim Rattay, Louisiana Tech, 1997-99
Career
(3 yrs.) 115—Tim Rattay, Louisiana Tech, 1997-99
(4 yrs.) 121—Ty Detmer, Brigham Young, 1988-91

MOST TOUCHDOWN PASSES PER GAME
Season
4.9—David Klingler, Houston, 1990 (54 in 11)
Career
3.5—Tim Rattay, Louisiana Tech, 1997-99 (115 in 33)

HIGHEST PERCENTAGE OF PASSES FOR TOUCHDOWNS
Season
(Min. 175-374 atts.) 11.6%—Dennis Shaw, San Diego St., 1969 (39 of 335)
(Min. 375 atts.) 10.6%—Jim McMahon, Brigham Young, 1980 (47 of 445)
Career
(Min. 400-499 atts.) 9.7%—Rick Leach, Michigan, 1975-78 (45 of 462)
(Min. 500 atts.) 9.7%—Danny Wuerffel, Florida, 1993-96 (114 of 1,170)

MOST CONSECUTIVE GAMES THROWING A TOUCHDOWN PASS
Career
35—Ty Detmer, Brigham Young (from Sept. 7, 1989, to Nov. 23, 1991)

MOST CONSECUTIVE PASSES COMPLETED FOR TOUCHDOWNS
Game
6—Brooks Dawson, UTEP vs. New Mexico, Oct. 28, 1967 (first six completions of the game)

MOST TOUCHDOWN PASSES THROWN ON CONSECUTIVE PLAYS
Game
3—Jay Stuckey, UTEP vs. New Mexico St., Sept. 25, 1999 (9, 80, 33 yards in 1:53 of playing time in second quarter)

MOST TOUCHDOWN PASSES IN FIRST GAME OF CAREER
5—John Reaves, Florida vs. Houston, Sept. 20, 1969

MOST TOUCHDOWN PASSES BY A FRESHMAN
Game
6—Bob Hoernschemeyer, Indiana vs. Nebraska, Oct. 9, 1943
Season
29—David Neill, Nevada, 1998

MOST TOUCHDOWN PASSES IN FRESHMAN AND SOPHOMORE SEASONS
49—David Neill, Nevada, 1998 (29) & 1999 (20)

MOST TOUCHDOWN PASSES BY A SOPHOMORE
39—Chad Pennington, Marshall, 1997

MOST TOUCHDOWN PASSES AT CONCLUSION OF JUNIOR YEAR
86—Ty Detmer, Brigham Young, 1988 (13), 1989 (32) & 1990 (41)

MOST TOUCHDOWN PASSES, SAME PASSER AND RECEIVER
Season
24—Chad Pennington to Randy Moss, Marshall, 1997
Career
33—Troy Kopp to Aaron Turner, Pacific (Cal.), 1989-92

MOST PASSES ATTEMPTED WITHOUT A TOUCHDOWN PASS
Season
266—Stu Rayburn, Kent, 1984 (completed 125)

FEWEST TIMES SACKED ATTEMPTING TO PASS
Season
(Min. 300 atts.) 4—Steve Walsh, Miami (Fla.), 1988, in 390 attempts. Last 4 games of the season: Tulsa, 1 for -8 yards; LSU, 1 for -2; Arkansas, 1 for -12; Brigham Young, 1 for -9.

Receiving

MOST PASSES CAUGHT
Game
23—Randy Gatewood, UNLV vs. Idaho, Sept. 17, 1994 (363 yards)
Season
142—Manny Hazard, Houston, 1989 (1,689 yards)
Career
(2 yrs.) 227—Alex Van Dyke, Nevada, 1994-95 (3,100 yards)
(3 yrs.) 261—Howard Twilley, Tulsa, 1963-65 (3,343 yards)
(4 yrs.) 298—Trevor Insley, Nevada, 1996-99 (5,005 yards)

MOST PASSES CAUGHT PER GAME
Season
13.4—Howard Twilley, Tulsa, 1965 (134 in 10)
Career
10.5—Manny Hazard, Houston, 1989-90 (220 in 21)

MOST PASSES CAUGHT BY TWO PLAYERS, SAME TEAM
Season
212— Howard Twilley (134) & Neal Sweeney (78), Tulsa, 1965 (2,662 yards, 24 TDs); Damond Wilkins (114) & Geoff Noisy (98), Nevada, 1996 (2,556 yards, 13 TDs)
Career
453—Mark Templeton (262) & Charles Lockett (191), Long Beach St., 1983-86 (4,871 yards, 30 TDs)

MOST PASSES CAUGHT IN CONSECUTIVE GAMES
38—Manny Hazard, Houston, 1989 (19 vs. TCU, Nov. 4; 19 vs. Texas, Nov. 11)

MOST CONSECUTIVE GAMES CATCHING A PASS
Career
46—Carl Winston, New Mexico, 1990-93 (every game)

MOST PASSES CAUGHT BY A TIGHT END
Game
17—Emilio Vallez, New Mexico vs. UTEP, Oct. 27, 1967 (257 yards); Jon Harvey, Northwestern vs. Michigan, Oct. 23, 1982 (208 yards)
Season
90—James Whalen, Kentucky, 1999 (1,019 yards)
Career
217—Ibn Green, Louisville, 1996-99 (2,830 yards)

MOST PASSES CAUGHT PER GAME BY A TIGHT END
Season
8.2—James Whalen, Kentucky, 1999 (90 in 11)
Career
5.4—Gordon Hudson, Brigham Young, 1980-83 (178 in 33)

MOST PASSES CAUGHT BY A RUNNING BACK
Game
18—Mark Templeton, Long Beach St. vs. Utah St., Nov. 1, 1986 (173 yards)
Season
99—Mark Templeton, Long Beach St., 1986 (688 yards)
Career
262—Mark Templeton, Long Beach St., 1983-86 (1,969 yards)

MOST PASSES CAUGHT BY A FRESHMAN
Game
18—Richard Woodley (WR), TCU vs. Texas Tech, Nov. 10, 1990 (180 yards)
Season
75—Brandon Stokley, La.-Lafayette, 1995 (1,121 yards)
Also holds per-game record at 6.8 (75 in 11)

CATCHING AT LEAST 50 PASSES AND GAINING AT LEAST 1,000 YARDS RUSHING
Season
By 10 players. Most recent: Ryan Benjamin, Pacific (Cal.), 1991 (51 catches and 1,581 yards rushing)
Darrin Nelson, Stanford, holds record for most seasons at 3 (1977-78, 1981)

CATCHING AT LEAST 60 PASSES AND GAINING AT LEAST 1,000 YARDS RUSHING
Darrin Nelson, Stanford, 1981 (67 catches and 1,014 yards rushing); Brad Muster, Stanford, 1986 (61 catches and 1,053 yards rushing); Johnny Johnson, San Jose St., 1988 (61 catches and 1,219 yards rushing)

MOST YARDS GAINED
Game
405—Troy Edwards, Louisiana Tech vs. Nebraska, Aug. 29, 1998 (caught 21)
Season
2,060—Trevor Insley, Nevada, 1999 (caught 134)
Career
5,005—Trevor Insley, Nevada, 1996-99 (caught 298)

MOST YARDS GAINED PER GAME
Season
187.3—Trevor Insley, Nevada, 1999 (2,060 in 11)
Career
140.9—Alex Van Dyke, Nevada, 1994-95 (3,100 in 22)

MOST YARDS GAINED BY A TIGHT END
Game
259—Gordon Hudson, Brigham Young vs. Utah, Nov. 21, 1981 (caught 13)
Season
1,156—Chris Smith, Brigham Young, 1990 (caught 68)
Career
2,830—Ibn Green, Louisville, 1996-99 (caught 217)

MOST YARDS GAINED PER GAME BY A TIGHT END
Season
102.0—Mike Moore, Grambling, 1977 (1,122 in 11)
Career
75.3—Gordon Hudson, Brigham Young, 1980-83 (2,484 in 33)

MOST YARDS GAINED BY A FRESHMAN
Game
263—Corey Alston, Western Mich. vs. Eastern Mich., Nov. 1, 1997 (caught 9)
Season
1,121—Brandon Stokley, La.-Lafayette, 1995 (caught 75)
Also holds per-game record at 101.9 (1,121 in 11)

MOST GAMES GAINING 100 YARDS OR MORE
Season
11—Aaron Turner, Pacific (Cal.), 1991
Also holds consecutive record at 11
Career
26—Trevor Insley, Nevada, 1996-99
Consecutive record: 11, Aaron Turner, Pacific (Cal.), 1991 (all one season) and Keyshawn Johnson, Southern California, 1994-95 (over two seasons)

MOST GAMES GAINING 200 YARDS OR MORE
Season
6—Trevor Insley, Nevada, 1999
Consecutive record: 3, Howard Twilley, Tulsa, 1965 & Trevor Insley, Nevada, 1999

MOST YARDS GAINED BY TWO PLAYERS, SAME TEAM
Game
640—Rick Eber (322) & Harry Wood (318), Tulsa vs. Idaho St., Oct. 7, 1967 (caught 33, 6 TDs)
Season
2,774—Trevor Insley (2,060) & Cleavon Brooks (714), Nevada, 1999

TWO PLAYERS, SAME TEAM, EACH GAINING 1,000 YARDS
12 times. Jason Phillips (1,444; 108 catches) & James Dixon (1,103; 102 catches), Houston, 1988; Patrick Rowe (1,392; 71 catches) & Dennis Arey (1,118; 68 catches), San Diego St., 1990; Andy Boyce (1,241; 79 catches) & Chris Smith (1,156; 68 catches), Brigham Young, 1990; Charles Johnson (1,149; 57 catches) & Michael Westbrook (1,060; 76 catches), Colorado, 1992; Bryan Reeves (1,362; 91 catches) & Michael Stephens (1,062; 80 catches), Nevada, 1993; Will Blackwell (1,207; 86 catches) & Az Hakim (1,022; 57 catches), San Diego St., 1995; E. G. Green (1,007; 60 catches) & Andre Cooper

INDIVIDUAL RECORDS—RECEIVING

(1,002; 71 catches), Florida St., 1995; Chris Doering (1,045; 70 catches) & Ike Hilliard (1,008; 57 catches), Florida, 1995; Geoff Noisy (1,435; 98 catches) & Damond Wilkins (1,121; 114 catches), Nevada, 1996; Geoff Noisy (1,405; 94 catches) & Trevor Insley (1,220; 69 catches), Nevada, 1998; Geoff Noisy (1,184; 86 catches) & Trevor Insley (1,151; 59 catches), Nevada, 1997; Jajuan Dawson (1,051; 96 catches) & Adrian Burnette (1,095; 79 catches), Tulane, 1999

TWO PLAYERS, SAME TEAM, RANKED NO. 1 & NO. 2 IN FINAL RECEIVING RANKINGS
Season
Jason Phillips (No. 1, 9.8 catches per game) & James Dixon (No. 2, 9.3 catches per game), Houston, 1988

FOUR PLAYERS, SAME TEAM, EACH CATCHING 60 PASSES OR MORE
James Jordan (81), John Simon (79), Delwyn Daigre (77) & Sean Cangelosi (62), Louisiana Tech, 1999

THREE PLAYERS, SAME TEAM, EACH CATCHING 60 PASSES OR MORE
Patrick Rowe (71), Dennis Arey (68) & Jimmy Raye (62), San Diego St., 1990; Arnold Jackson (101), Ibn Green (60) & Lavell Boyd (60), Louisville, 1999

MOST 1,000-YARD RECEIVING SEASONS
3—Marc Zeno, Tulane, 1985-87 (1,137 in 1985; 1,033 in 1986; Clarkston Hines, Duke, 1987-89 (1,084 in 1987; 1,067 in 1988; 1,149 in 1989; 1,206 in 1987; Aaron Turner, Pacific (Cal.), 1990-92 (1,264 in 1990, 1,604 in 1991; 1,171 in 1992); Ryan Yarborough, Wyoming, 1991-93 (1,081 in 1991; 1,351 in 1992; 1,512 in 1993); Marcus Harris, Wyoming, 1993-96 (1,431 in 1994; 1,423 in 1995; 1,650 in 1996); Brandon Stokley, La.-Lafayette, 1995-96, 98 (1,121 in 1995; 1,160 in 1996; 1,175 in 1998); Geoff Noisy, Nevada, 1996-98 (1,435 in 1996; 1,184 in 1997; 1,405 in 1998); Trevor Insley, Nevada, 1997-99 (1,151 in 1997; 1,220 in 1998; 2,060 in 1999)

MOST RECEIVING SEASONS OVER 1,400 YARDS
3—Marcus Harris, Wyoming, 1993-96 (1,431 in 1994; 1,423 in 1995; 1,650 in 1996)

HIGHEST AVERAGE GAIN PER RECEPTION
Game
(Min. 3-4 receps.) 72.7—Terry Gallaher, East Caro. vs. Appalachian St., Sept. 13, 1975 (3 for 218; 82, 77, 59 yards)
(Min. 5-9 receps.) 52.6—Alexander Wright, Auburn vs. Pacific (Cal.), Sept. 9, 1989 (5 for 263; 78, 60, 41, 73, 11 yards)
(Min. 10 receps.) 34.9—Chuck Hughes, UTEP vs. North Texas, Sept. 18, 1965 (10 for 349)
Season
(Min. 30-49 receps.) 27.9—Elmo Wright, Houston, 1968 (43 for 1,198)
(Min. 50 receps.) 24.4—Henry Ellard, Fresno St., 1982 (62 for 1,510)
Career
(Min. 75-104 receps.) 25.7—Wesley Walker, California, 1973-76 (86 for 2,206)
(Min. 105 receps.) 22.0—Herman Moore, Virginia, 1988-90 (114 for 2,504)

HIGHEST AVERAGE GAIN PER RECEPTION BY A TIGHT END
Season
(Min. 30 receps.) 22.6—Jay Novacek, Wyoming, 1984 (33 for 745)
Career
(Min. 75 receps.) 19.2—Clay Brown, Brigham Young, 1978-80 (88 for 1,691)

MOST TOUCHDOWN PASSES CAUGHT
Game
6—Tim Delaney, San Diego St. vs. New Mexico St., Nov. 15, 1969 (16 receptions)
Season
27—Troy Edwards, Louisiana Tech, 1998 (140 receptions)
Per-game record—2.3, Tom Reynolds, San Diego St., 1969 (18 in 8); Troy Edwards, Louisiana Tech, 1998 (27 in 12)
Career
50—Troy Edwards, Louisiana Tech, 1996-98 (280 receptions)

MOST GAMES CATCHING A TOUCHDOWN PASS
Season
12—Randy Moss, Marshall, 1997
Career
27—Ryan Yarborough, Wyoming, 1990-93 (caught a total of 42 in 46 games)

MOST CONSECUTIVE GAMES CATCHING A TOUCHDOWN PASS
Season
12—Randy Moss, Marshall, 1997
Career
12—Desmond Howard, Michigan (last two games of 1990 and first 10 games of 1991); Aaron Turner, Pacific (Cal.) (last three games of 1990 and first nine games of 1991); Randy Moss, Marshall, 1997 (all in 1997)

MOST TOUCHDOWN PASSES CAUGHT BY A TIGHT END
Season
18—Dennis Smith, Utah, 1989 (73 receptions)
Career
33—Ibn Green, Louisville, 1996-99 (217 receptions)

HIGHEST PERCENTAGE OF PASSES CAUGHT FOR TOUCHDOWNS
Season
(Min. 10 TDs) 58.8%—Kevin Williams, Southern California, 1978 (10 of 17)
Career
(Min. 20 TDs) 35.3%—Kevin Williams, Southern California, 1977-80 (24 of 68)

HIGHEST AVERAGE YARDS PER TOUCHDOWN PASS
Season
(Min. 10 TDs) 56.1—Elmo Wright, Houston, 1968 (11 for 617 yards; 87, 50, 75, 2, 80, 79, 13, 67, 61, 43, 60 yards)
Career
(Min. 15 TDs) 46.5—Charles Johnson, Colorado, 1990-93 (15 for 697 yards)

MOST TOUCHDOWN PASSES CAUGHT, 50 YARDS OR MORE
Season
8—Elmo Wright, Houston, 1968 (87, 50, 75, 80, 79, 67, 61, 60 yards); Henry Ellard, Fresno St., 1982 (68, 51, 80, 61, 67, 72, 80, 72 yards)

MOST CONSECUTIVE PASSES CAUGHT FOR TOUCHDOWNS
6—Carlos Carson, LSU, 1977 (5 vs. Rice, Sept. 24; 1 vs. Florida, Oct. 1; first receptions of his career); Gerald Armstrong, Nebraska, 1992 (1 vs. Utah, Sept. 5; 1 vs. Arizona St., Sept. 26; 1 vs. Oklahoma St., Oct. 10; 1 vs. Colorado, Oct. 31; 2 vs. Kansas, Nov. 7)

MOST TOUCHDOWN PASSES CAUGHT BY A FRESHMAN
Season
10—Dwight Collins, Pittsburgh, 1980

Punting

MOST PUNTS
Game
36—Charlie Calhoun, Texas Tech vs. Centenary (La.), Nov. 11, 1939 (1,318 yards; 20 were returned, 8 went out of bounds, 6 were downed, 1 was blocked [blocked kicks counted against the punter until 1955] and 1 went into the end zone for a touchback. Thirty-three of the punts occurred on first down during a heavy downpour in the game played at Shreveport, Louisiana)
Season
101—Jim Bailey, VMI, 1969 (3,507 yards)
Career
(3 yrs.) 276—Jim Bailey, VMI, 1969-71 (10,127 yards)
(4 yrs.) 320—Cameron Young, TCU, 1976-79 (12,947 yards)

HIGHEST AVERAGE PER PUNT
Game
(Min. 5-9 punts) 60.4—Lee Johnson, Brigham Young vs. Wyoming, Oct. 8, 1983 (5 for 302; 53, 44, 63, 62, 80 yards)
(Min. 10 punts) 53.6—Jim Benien, Oklahoma St. vs. Colorado, Nov. 13, 1971 (10 for 536)
Season
(Min. 36-39 punts) 50.3—Chad Kessler, LSU, 1997 (39 for 1,961)
(Min. 40-49 punts) 49.8—Reggie Roby, Iowa, 1981 (44 for 2,193)
(Min. 50-74 punts) 48.4—Todd Sauerbrun, West Virginia, 1994 (72 for 3,486)
(Min. 75 punts) 46.6—Bill Marinangel, Vanderbilt, 1996 (77 for 3,586)
Career
(Min. 150-199 punts) 46.3—Todd Sauerbrun, West Virginia, 1991-94 (167 for 7,733)
(Min. 200-249 punts) 44.7—Ray Guy, Southern Miss., 1970-72 (200 for 8,934)
(Min. 250 punts) 44.7—Shane Lechler, Texas A&M, 1996-99 (268 for 11,977)

HIGHEST AVERAGE PER PUNT BY A FRESHMAN
Season
(Min. 40 punts) 47.0—Tom Tupa, Ohio St., 1984 (41 for 1,927)

MOST YARDS ON PUNTS
Game
1,318—Charlie Calhoun, Texas Tech vs. Centenary (La.), Nov. 11, 1939 (36 punts)
Season
4,138—Johnny Pingel, Michigan St., 1938 (99 punts)
Career
12,947—Cameron Young, TCU, 1976-79 (320 punts)

MOST GAMES WITH A 40-YARD AVERAGE OR MORE
Career
(Min. 4 punts) 37—Shane Lechler, Texas A&M, 1996-99 (punted in 48 games)

MOST PUNTS, 50 YARDS OR MORE
Season
32—Todd Sauerbrun, West Virginia, 1994 (72 punts)
Career
(2 yrs.) 51—Marv Bateman, Utah, 1970-71 (133 punts)
(3 yrs.) 61—Russ Henderson, Virginia, 1976-78 (226 punts)
(4 yrs.) 88—Bill Smith, Mississippi, 1983-86 (254 punts)

MOST CONSECUTIVE GAMES WITH AT LEAST ONE PUNT OF 50 YARDS OR MORE
Career
32—Bill Smith, Mississippi, 1983-86

MOST PUNTS IN A CAREER WITHOUT HAVING ONE BLOCKED
300—Tony DeLeone, Kent, 1981-84
Also holds consecutive record at 300

LONGEST PUNT
99—Pat Brady, Nevada vs. Loyola Marymount, Oct. 28, 1950

RANKING IN TOP 12 IN BOTH PUNTING AND FIELD GOALS
Steve Little, Arkansas, 1977 (No. 4 in punting, 44.3-yard average and No. 2 in field goals, 1.73 per game); Rob Keen, California, 1988 (No. 11 in punting, 42.6-yard average and No. 3 in field goals, 1.91 per game); Chris Gardocki, Clemson, 1990 (No. 4 in punting, 44.3-yard average and No. 4 in field goals, 1.73 per game), 1989 (No. 10 in punting, 42.7-yard average and No. 6 in field goals, 1.82 per game); Dan Eichloff, Kansas, 1991 (No. 12 in punting, 42.3-yard average and No. 3 in field goals, 1.64 per game); Daron Alcorn, Akron, 1992 (No. 11 in punting, 43.6-yard average and tied for No. 9 in field goals, 1.64 per game)

Interceptions

MOST PASSES INTERCEPTED
Game
5—Lee Cook, Oklahoma St. vs. Detroit, Nov. 28, 1942 (15 yards); Walt Pastuszak, Brown vs. Rhode Island, Oct. 8, 1949 (47 yards); Byron Beaver, Houston vs. Baylor, Sept. 22, 1962 (18 yards); Dan Rebsch, Miami (Ohio) vs. Western Mich., Nov. 4, 1972 (88 yards). Special note: Prior to NCAA College-division records, Dick Miller of Akron intercepted six passes vs. Baldwin-Wallace on Oct. 23, 1937.

INDIVIDUAL RECORDS—INTERCEPTIONS

Season
14—Al Worley, Washington, 1968 (130 yards)
Career
29—Al Brosky, Illinois, 1950-52 (356 yards)

MOST PASSES INTERCEPTED PER GAME
Season
1.4—Al Worley, Washington, 1968 (14 in 10)
Career
1.1—Al Brosky, Illinois, 1950-52 (29 in 27)

MOST PASSES INTERCEPTED BY A LINEBACKER
Game
3—Nate Kvamme, Colorado St. vs. San Jose St., Oct. 11, 1997; Aaron Humphrey, Texas vs. Rutgers, Sept. 6, 1997; Joseph Phipps, TCU vs. Oklahoma, Sept. 12, 1998; Lorenzo Ferguson, Virginia Tech vs. Clemson, Sept. 12, 1998
Season
9—Bill Sibley, Texas A&M, 1941 (57 yards)

MOST PASSES INTERCEPTED BY A FRESHMAN
Game
4—Mario Edwards, Florida St. vs. Wake Forest, Nov. 14, 1998 (60 yards)
Season
13—George Shaw, Oregon, 1951 (136 yards)
Also holds per-game record at 1.3 (13 in 10)

MOST YARDS ON INTERCEPTION RETURNS
Game
182—Ashley Lee, Virginia Tech vs. Vanderbilt, Nov. 12, 1983 (2 interceptions)
Season
302—Charles Phillips, Southern California, 1974 (7 interceptions)
Career
501—Terrell Buckley, Florida St., 1989-91 (21 interceptions)

MOST TOUCHDOWNS SCORED ON INTERCEPTION RETURNS
Game
3—Johnny Jackson, Houston vs. Texas, Nov. 7, 1987 (31, 53, 97 yards)
Season
4—Deltha O'Neal, California, 1999 (9 interceptions)
Career
5—Jackie Walker, Tennessee, 1969-71 (11 interceptions); Ken Thomas, San Jose St., 1979-82 (14 interceptions); Deltha O'Neal, California, 1996-99 (11 interceptions)

MOST TOUCHDOWNS SCORED ON INTERCEPTION RETURNS BY A LINEBACKER
Game
2—Tom Fisher, New Mexico St. vs. Lamar, Nov. 14, 1970 (52 & 28 yards in one quarter.); Randy Neal, Virginia vs. Virginia Tech, Nov. 21, 1992 (37 & 30 yards); Patrick Brown, Kansas vs. UAB, Aug. 28, 1997 (51 & 23 yards); Nate Kvamme, Colorado St. vs. San Jose St., Oct. 11, 1997 (15 & 57 yards)
Season
2—Tom Fisher, New Mexico St., 1970; Jerry Robinson, UCLA, 1976; Randy Neal, Virginia, 1994, 1992; Mike Rose, Purdue, 1997; Patrick Brown, Kansas, 1997; Nate Kvamme, Colorado St., 1997; Chris Claiborne, Southern California, 1998; Dustin Cohen, Miami (Ohio), 1998
Career
4—Randy Neal, Virginia, 1991-94; Dustin Cohen, Miami (Ohio), 1996-99

HIGHEST AVERAGE GAIN PER INTERCEPTION
Game
(Min. 2 ints.) 91.0—Ashley Lee, Virginia Tech vs. Vanderbilt, Nov. 12, 1983 (2 for 182)
Season
(Min. 5 ints.) 50.6—Norm Thompson, Utah, 1969 (5 for 253)
Career
(Min. 15 ints.) 26.5—Tom Pridemore, West Virginia, 1975-77 (15 for 398)

MOST CONSECUTIVE GAMES INTERCEPTING A PASS
15—Al Brosky, Illinois, began Nov. 11, 1950 (vs. Iowa), ended Oct. 18, 1952 (vs. Minnesota)

Punt Returns

MOST PUNT RETURNS
Game
20—Milton Hill, Texas Tech vs. Centenary (La.), Nov. 11, 1939 (110 yards)
Season
55—Dick Adams, Miami (Ohio), 1970 (578 yards)
Also holds per-game record at 5.5
Career
153—Vai Sikahema, Brigham Young, 1980-81, 1984-85 (1,312 yards)

MOST YARDS ON PUNT RETURNS
Game
225—Chris McCranie, Georgia vs. South Carolina, Sept. 2, 1995 (5 returns)
Season
791—Lee Nalley, Vanderbilt, 1948 (43 returns)
Also holds per-game record at 79.1
Career
1,695—Lee Nalley, Vanderbilt, 1947-49 (109 returns)

HIGHEST AVERAGE GAIN PER RETURN
Game
(Min. 3-4 rets.) 59.7—Chip Hough, Air Force vs. Southern Methodist, Oct. 9, 1971 (3 for 179)
(Min. 5 rets.) 45.0—Chris McCranie, Georgia vs. South Carolina, Sept. 2, 1995 (5 for 225)
Season
(Min. 1.2 rets. per game) 25.9—Bill Blackstock, Tennessee, 1951 (12 for 311)
(Min. 1.5 rets. per game) 25.0—George Sims, Baylor, 1948 (15 for 375)
Career
(Min. 1.2 rets. per game) 23.6—Jack Mitchell, Oklahoma, 1946-48 (39 for 922)
(Min. 1.5 rets. per game) 20.5—Gene Gibson, Cincinnati, 1949-50 (37 for 760)

MOST TOUCHDOWNS SCORED ON PUNT RETURNS
Game
2—By many players. Most recent: Steve Smith, Utah vs. New Mexico, Nov. 13, 1999 (70 & 52 yards)
Season
4—Golden Richards, Brigham Young, 1971; Cliff Branch, Colorado, 1971; James Henry, Southern Miss., 1987; Tinker Keck, Cincinnati, 1997; Quinton Spotwood, Syracuse, 1997; David Allen, Kansas St., 1998
Career
7—Jack Mitchell, Oklahoma, 1946-48 (3 in 1946, 1 in 1947, 3 in 1948); Johnny Rodgers, Nebraska, 1970-72 (2 in 1970, 3 in 1971, 2 in 1972); David Allen, Kansas St., 1997-99 (1 in 1997, 4 in 1998, 2 in 1999)

CONSECUTIVE GAMES WITH PUNT RETURN FOR A TOUCHDOWN
3—David Allen, Kansas St., 1998 (63 yards vs. Indiana St., Sept. 5; 69 yards vs. Northern Ill., Sept. 12; 93 yards vs. Texas, Sept. 19)
(Allen also returned punts for touchdowns in consecutive games in 1999 [94 yards vs. Iowa St., Sept. 25 & 74 yards vs. Texas, Oct.2])

Kickoff Returns

MOST KICKOFF RETURNS
Game
11—Trevor Cobb, Rice vs. Houston, Dec. 2, 1989 (166 yards)
Season
51—Deonce Whitaker, San Jose St., 1998 (1,214 yards)
Career
123—Jeff Liggon, Tulane, 1993-96 (2,922 yards)

MOST RETURNS PER GAME
Season
4.6—Dwayne Owens, Oregon St., 1990 (41 in 9)
Career
3.0—Steve Odom, Utah, 1971-73 (99 in 33)

MOST YARDS ON KICKOFF RETURNS
Game
248—Tyrone Watley, Iowa St. vs. Nebraska, Nov. 15, 1997 (10 returns)
Season
1,214—Deonce Whitaker, San Jose St., 1998 (51 returns)
Career
2,922—Jeff Liggon, Tulane, 1993-96 (123 returns)

MOST YARDS RETURNED PER GAME
Season
112.7—Dwayne Owens, Oregon St., 1990 (1,014 in 9)
Career
78.2—Steve Odom, Utah, 1971-73 (2,582 in 33)

HIGHEST AVERAGE GAIN PER RETURN
Game
(Min. 3 rets.) 72.7—Anthony Davis, Southern California vs. Notre Dame, Dec. 2, 1972 (3 for 218)
Season
(Min. 1.2 rets. per game) 40.1—Paul Allen, Brigham Young, 1961 (12 for 481)
(Min. 1.5 rets. per game) 38.2—Forrest Hall, San Francisco, 1946 (15 for 573)
Career
(Min. 1.2 rets. per game) 36.2—Forrest Hall, San Francisco, 1946-47 (22 for 796)
(Min. 1.5 rets. per game) 31.0—Overton Curtis, Utah St., 1957-58 (32 for 991)

MOST TOUCHDOWNS SCORED ON KICKOFF RETURNS
Game
2—Paul Copoulos, Marquette vs. Iowa Pre-Flight, Nov. 6, 1943 (85 & 82 yards); Ron Horwath, Detroit vs. Hillsdale, Sept. 22, 1950 (96 & 96 yards); Ollie Matson, San Francisco vs. Fordham, Oct. 20, 1951 (94 & 90 yards); Anthony Davis, Southern California vs. Notre Dame, Dec. 2, 1972 (97 & 96 yards); Raghib Ismail, Notre Dame vs. Rice, Nov. 5, 1988 (87 & 83 yards); *Raghib Ismail, Notre Dame vs. Michigan, Sept. 16, 1989 (88 & 92 yards); Stacey Corley, Brigham Young vs. Air Force, Nov. 11, 1989 (99 & 85 yards); Leeland McElroy, Texas A&M vs. Rice, Oct. 23, 1993 (93 & 88 yards); Tutu Atwell, Minnesota vs. Iowa St., Sept. 13, 1997 (89 & 93 yards)
Season
3—Forrest Hall, San Francisco, 1946; Stan Brown, Purdue, 1970; Anthony Davis, Southern California, 1974; Willie Gault, Tennessee, 1980; Terance Mathis, New Mexico, 1989; Leeland McElroy, Texas A&M, 1993
Career
6—Anthony Davis, Southern California, 1972-74

*Ismail is the only player in history to score twice in two games.

SCORING A TOUCHDOWN ON TEAM'S OPENING KICKOFF OF TWO SEASONS
Season
Barry Sanders, Oklahoma St., 1988 (100 yards vs. Miami [Ohio], Sept. 10) & 1987 (100 yards vs. Tulsa, Sept. 5)

Total Kick Returns

(Combined Punt and Kickoff Returns)

MOST KICK RETURNS
Game
20—Milton Hill, Texas Tech vs. Centenary (La.), Nov. 11, 1939 (20 punts, 110 yards)
Season
70—Keith Stephens, Louisville, 1986 (28 punts, 42 kickoffs, 1,162 yards); Dick Adams, Miami (Ohio), 1970 (55 punts, 15 kickoffs, 944 yards)
Career
203—Deltha O'Neal, California, 1996-99 (110 punts, 93 kickoffs, 3,455 yards)

MOST YARDS ON KICK RETURNS
Game
284—Tutu Atwell, Minnesota vs. Iowa St., Sept. 13, 1997 (59 punt returns, 225 kickoff returns)
Season
1,233—Deonce Whitaker, San Jose St., 1998 (19 punt returns, 1,214 kickoff returns)
Per-game record—116.2, Dion Johnson, East Caro., 1990 (1,046 yards, with 167 on punt returns and 879 on kickoff returns in 9 games)

Career
3,455—Deltha O'Neal, California, 1996-99 (1,169 on punts & 2,286 on kickoffs)

GAINING 1,000 YARDS ON PUNT RETURNS AND 1,000 YARDS ON KICKOFF RETURNS
Career
Troy Slade, Duke, 1973-75 (1,021 & 1,757); Devon Ford, Appalachian St., 1973-76 (1,197 & 1,761); Anthony Carter, Michigan, 1979-82 (1,095 & 1,504); Willie Drewrey, West Virginia, 1981-84 (1,072 & 1,302); Tony James, Mississippi St., 1989-92 (1,332 & 1,862); Thomas Bailey, Auburn, 1991-94 (1,170 & 1,520); Tim Dwight, Iowa, 1994-97 (1,051 & 1,133); Deltha O'Neal, California, 1996-99 (1,169 & 2,286)

HIGHEST AVERAGE PER KICK RETURN
(Min. 1.2 Punt Returns and 1.2 Kickoff Returns Per Game)
Season
27.2—Erroll Tucker, Utah, 1985 (40 for 1,087; 16 for 389 on punt returns, 24 for 698 on kickoff returns)
Career
22.0—Erroll Tucker, Utah, 1984-85 (79 for 1,741; 38 for 650 on punt returns, 41 for 1,091 on kickoff returns)

AVERAGING 20 YARDS EACH ON PUNT RETURNS AND KICKOFF RETURNS
(Min. 1.2 Returns Per Game Each)
Season
By 7 players. Most recent: Lee Gissendaner, Northwestern, 1992 (21.8 on punt returns, 15 for 327; 22.4 on kickoff returns, 17 for 381)

MOST TOUCHDOWNS SCORED ON KICK RETURNS
(Must Have at Least One Punt Return and One Kickoff Return)
Game
2—By 6 players. Most recent: Joe Rowe, Virginia vs. Central Mich., Sept. 7, 1996 (1 punt, 1 kickoff)
Season
5—Pinky Rohm, LSU, 1937 (3 punts, 2 kickoffs); Robert Woods, Grambling, 1977 (3 punts, 2 kickoffs)
Career
8—Cliff Branch, Colorado, 1970-71 (6 punts, 2 kickoffs); Johnny Rodgers, Nebraska, 1970-72 (7 punts, 1 kickoff)

WINNING BOTH PUNT RETURN AND KICKOFF RETURN CHAMPIONSHIPS
Season
Erroll Tucker, Utah, 1985
Career
Ira Matthews, Wisconsin, kickoff returns (1976) and punt returns (1978); Erroll Tucker, Utah, 1985

All Runbacks
(Combined Interceptions, Punt Returns and Kickoff Returns)

SCORING MORE THAN ONE TOUCHDOWN IN EACH CATEGORY
Season
Erroll Tucker, Utah, 1985 (3 interceptions, 2 punt returns, 2 kickoff returns)

SCORING ONE TOUCHDOWN IN EACH CATEGORY
Season
Dick Harris, South Carolina, 1970; Mark Haynes, Arizona St., 1974; Scott Thomas, Air Force, 1985; Joe Crocker, Virginia, 1994; Joe Walker, Nebraska, 1998; Deltha O'Neal, California, 1999

HIGHEST AVERAGE PER RUNBACK
Season
(Min. 40 rets.) 28.3—Erroll Tucker, Utah, 1985 (46 for 1,303; 6 for 216 on interceptions, 16 for 389 on punt returns, 24 for 698 on kickoff returns)

HIGHEST AVERAGE PER RUNBACK
(At Least 7 Interceptions and Min. 1.3 Punt Returns and 1.3 Kickoff Returns Per Game)
Career
22.6—Erroll Tucker, Utah, 1984-85 (87 for 1,965; 8 for 224 on interceptions, 38 for 650 on punt returns, 41 for 1,091 on kickoff returns)

MOST TOUCHDOWNS ON INTERCEPTIONS, PUNT RETURNS AND KICKOFF RETURNS
(Must Have at Least One Touchdown in Each Category)
Season
7—Erroll Tucker, Utah, 1985 (3 interceptions, 2 punt returns, 2 kickoff returns)
Career
9—Allen Rossum, Notre Dame, 1994-97 (3 interceptions, 3 punt returns, 3 kickoff returns)

Kicks Blocked

MOST PUNTS BLOCKED BY
Game
4—Ken Irvin, Memphis vs. Arkansas, Sept. 26, 1992
Season
8—Jimmy Lisko, Arkansas St., 1975 (11 games); James Francis (LB), Baylor, 1989 (11 games)

MOST PAT KICKS BLOCKED BY
Season
5—Ray Farmer, Duke, 1993
Career
8—Ray Farmer, Duke, 1992-95

MOST FIELD GOAL ATTEMPTS BLOCKED BY
Quarter
2—Jerald Henry, Southern California vs. California, Oct. 22, 1994 (1st, returned first one 60 yards for touchdown); Pat Larson, Wyoming vs. Fresno St., Nov. 18, 1995 (2nd)
Game
2—Jerald Henry, Southern California vs. California, Oct. 22, 1994; Pat Larson, Wyoming vs. Fresno St., Nov. 18, 1995; Kyle Vander Bosch, Nebraska vs. Texas A&M, Nov. 6, 1999

MOST TOTAL KICKS BLOCKED BY
(Includes Punts, PAT Attempts, FG Attempts)
Game
4—Ken Irvin, Memphis vs. Arkansas, Sept. 26, 1992 (4 punts)
Career
19—James Ferebee, New Mexico St., 1978-81 (5 punts, 6 PAT attempts, 8 FG attempts)

MOST TOUCHDOWNS SCORED ON BLOCKED PUNTS
Game
2—David Langner, Auburn vs. Alabama, Dec. 2, 1972 (2nd half); Frank Staine-Pyne, Air Force vs. Hawaii, Nov. 1, 1997 (1st half)
Season
3—Joe Wessel, Florida St., 1984

All-Purpose Yards
(Yardage Gained From Rushing, Receiving and All Runbacks)

MOST PLAYS
Game
58—Tony Sands, Kansas vs. Missouri, Nov. 23, 1991 (58 rushes)
Season
432—Marcus Allen, Southern California, 1981 (403 rushes, 29 receptions)
Career
(3 yrs.) 1,034—Herschel Walker, Georgia, 1980-82 (994 rushes, 26 receptions, 14 kickoff returns)
(4 yrs.) 1,347—Steve Bartalo, Colorado St., 1983-86 (1,215 rushes, 132 receptions)

MOST YARDS GAINED
Quarter
305—Corey Dillon, Washington vs. San Jose St., Nov. 16, 1996 (1st, 222 rushing, 83 receiving)
Game
435—Brian Pruitt, Central Mich. vs. Toledo, Nov. 5, 1994 (356 rushing, 79 kickoff returns)
Season
3,250—Barry Sanders, Oklahoma St., 1988 (2,628 rushing, 106 receiving, 95 punt returns, 421 kickoff returns; 11 games)
Career
(3 yrs.) 5,749—Herschel Walker, Georgia, 1980-82 (5,259 rushing, 243 receiving, 247 kickoff returns; 1,034 plays)
(4 yrs.) 7,206—Ricky Williams, Texas, 1995-98 (6,279 rushing, 927 receiving; 1,096 plays)

MOST YARDS GAINED PER GAME
Season
295.5—Barry Sanders, Oklahoma St., 1988 (3,250 in 11 games; 2,628 rushing, 106 receiving, 95 punt returns, 421 kickoff returns)
Career
237.8—Ryan Benjamin, Pacific (Cal.), 1990-92 (5,706 in 24 games; 3,119 rushing, 1,063 receiving, 100 punt returns, 1,424 kickoff returns)

MOST YARDS GAINED BY A FRESHMAN
Game
422—Marshall Faulk, San Diego St. vs. Pacific (Cal.), Sept. 14, 1991 (386 rushing, 11 receiving, 25 kickoff returns)
Season
2,026—Terrell Willis, Rutgers, 1993 (1,261 rushing, 61 receiving, 704 kickoff returns; 234 plays)
Per-game record—184.8, Marshall Faulk, San Diego St., 1991 (1,663 in 9)

MOST SEASONS WITH 2,000 OR MORE YARDS
2—Howard Stevens, Randolph-Macon, 1968 (2,115) & Louisville, 1972 (2,132); Napoleon McCallum, Navy, 1983 (2,385) & 1985 (2,330); Chuck Weatherspoon, Houston, 1989 (2,391) & 1990 (2,038); Sheldon Canley, San Jose St., 1989 (2,513) & 1990 (2,213); Glyn Milburn, Stanford, 1990 (2,222) & 1992 (2,121); Ryan Benjamin, Pacific (Cal.), 1991 (2,995) & 1992 (2,597); Troy Davis, Iowa St., 1995 (2,466) & 1996 (2,364); Kevin Faulk, LSU, 1996 (2,104) & 1998 (2,109); Ricky Williams, Texas, 1997 (2,043) & 1998 (2,386)

GAINED 1,000 YARDS RUSHING AND 1,000 YARDS RECEIVING
Career
By eight players. Most recent: Anthony White, Kentucky, 1996-99 (1,758 rushing & 1,520 receiving)

HIGHEST AVERAGE GAIN PER PLAY
Game
(Min. 300 yards, 25 plays) 16.8—Randy Gatewood, UNLV vs. Idaho, Sept. 17, 1994 (419 on 25)
Season
(Min. 1,500 yards, 100-124 plays) 18.5—Henry Bailey, UNLV, 1992 (1,883 on 102)
(Min. 1,500 yards, 125 plays) 16.8—Dennis Northcutt, Arizona, 1999 (2,249 on 134)
Career
(Min. 5,000 yards, 275-374 plays) 17.4—Anthony Carter, Michigan, 1979-82 (5,197 on 298)
(Min. 5,000 yards, 375 plays) 14.6—Terance Mathis, New Mexico, 1985-87, 1989 (6,691 on 457)

MOST YARDS GAINED BY TWO PLAYERS, SAME TEAM
Career
10,253—Marshall Faulk (5,595) & Darnay Scott (4,658), San Diego St., 1991-93

Scoring

MOST POINTS SCORED
(By Non-Kickers)
Game
48—Howard Griffith, Illinois vs. Southern Ill., Sept. 22, 1990 (8 TDs on runs of 5, 51, 7, 41, 5, 18, 5, 3 yards)
Game vs. Major-College Opponent
44—Marshall Faulk, San Diego St. vs. Pacific (Cal.), Sept. 14, 1991 (7 TDs, 1 two-point conversion)
Season
234—Barry Sanders, Oklahoma St., 1988 (39 TDs in 11 games)
2 Yrs
320—Ricky Williams, Texas, 1997-98 (53 TDs, 1 two-point conversion in 22 games)
3 Yrs
404—Ricky Williams, Texas, 1996-98 (67 TDs, 1 two-point conversion in 34 games)

INDIVIDUAL RECORDS—SCORING

Career
(4 yrs.) 468—Travis Prentice, Miami (Ohio), 1996-99 (78 TDs)

MOST POINTS SCORED PER GAME
Season
21.3—Barry Sanders, Oklahoma St., 1988 (234 in 11)
2 Yrs
14.5—Ricky Williams, Texas 1997-98 (320 in 22)
Career
12.1—Marshall Faulk, San Diego St., 1991-93 (376 in 31)

MOST POINTS SCORED BY A FRESHMAN
Game
44—Marshall Faulk, San Diego St. vs. Pacific (Cal.), Sept. 14, 1991 (7 TDs, 1 two-point conversion)
Season
140—Marshall Faulk, San Diego St., 1991 (23 TDs, 1 two-point conversion)
Also holds per-game record at 15.6 (140 in 9)

MOST TOUCHDOWNS SCORED
Quarter
4—Dick Felt, Brigham Young vs. San Jose St., Nov. 8, 1952 (all rushing, 4th); Howard Griffith, Illinois vs. Southern Ill., Sept. 22, 1990 (all rushing, 3rd); Corey Dillon, Washington vs. San Jose St., Nov. 16, 1996 (3 rushing, 1 receiving, 1st); Frank Moreau, Louisville vs. East Caro., Nov. 1, 1997 (all rushing, 2nd)
Game
8—Howard Griffith, Illinois vs. Southern Ill., Sept. 22, 1990 (all 8 by rushing on runs of 5, 51, 7, 41, 5, 18, 5, 3 yards)
Game vs. Major-College Opponent
7—Arnold "Showboat" Boykin, Mississippi vs. Mississippi St., Dec. 1, 1951; Marshall Faulk, San Diego St. vs. Pacific (Cal.), Sept. 14, 1991
Season
39—Barry Sanders, Oklahoma St., 1988 (11 games)
Also holds per-game record at 3.5 (39 in 11)
2 Yrs
53—Ricky Williams, Texas 1997-98 (22 games)
Also holds per-game record at 2.4 (53 in 22)
3 Yrs
67—Ricky Williams, Texas, 1996-98 (34 games)
Career
(4 yrs.) 78—Travis Prentice, Miami (Ohio) (73 rushing, 5 pass receptions)

MOST TOUCHDOWNS SCORED IN TWO AND THREE CONSECUTIVE GAMES
2 Games
11—Kelvin Bryant, North Carolina, 1981 (6 vs. East Caro., Sept. 12; 5 vs. Miami [Ohio], Sept. 19; Ricky Williams, Texas, 1998 (6 vs. Rice, Sept. 26; 5 vs. Iowa St., Oct. 3)
3 Games
15—Kelvin Bryant, North Carolina, 1981 (6 vs. East Caro., Sept. 12; 5 vs. Miami [Ohio], Sept. 19; 4 vs. Boston College, Sept. 26)

MOST TOUCHDOWNS SCORED BY A FRESHMAN
Game
7—Marshall Faulk, San Diego St. vs. Pacific (Cal.), Sept. 14, 1991 (all by rushing)
Season
23—Marshall Faulk, San Diego St., 1991 (21 rushing, 2 pass receptions)
Also holds per-game record at 2.6 (23 in 9)

MOST GAMES SCORING A TOUCHDOWN
Season
12—Randy Moss, Marshall, 1997
Career
35—Travis Prentice, Miami (Ohio), 1996-99

MOST CONSECUTIVE GAMES SCORING A TOUCHDOWN
Career
23—Bill Burnett, Arkansas (from Oct. 5, 1968, through Oct. 31, 1970; 47 touchdowns)

MOST GAMES SCORING TWO OR MORE TOUCHDOWNS
Season
11—Barry Sanders, Oklahoma St., 1988
Career
25—Travis Prentice, Miami (Ohio), 1996-99

MOST CONSECUTIVE GAMES SCORING TWO OR MORE TOUCHDOWNS
Season
11—Barry Sanders, Oklahoma St., 1988
Career
13—Barry Sanders, Oklahoma St. (from Nov. 14, 1987, through 1988)

MOST GAMES SCORING THREE OR MORE TOUCHDOWNS
Season
9—Barry Sanders, Oklahoma St., 1988

MOST CONSECUTIVE GAMES SCORING THREE OR MORE TOUCHDOWNS
Season
5—Paul Hewitt, San Diego St., 1987 (from Oct. 10 through Nov. 7); Barry Sanders, Oklahoma St., 1988 (from Sept. 10 through Oct. 15)

MOST TOUCHDOWNS AND POINTS SCORED BY TWO PLAYERS, SAME TEAM
Season
54 and 324—Barry Sanders (39-234) & Hart Lee Dykes (15-90), Oklahoma St., 1988
Career
97 and 585—Glenn Davis (59-354) & Doc Blanchard (38-231), Army, 1943-46

PASSING FOR A TOUCHDOWN AND SCORING TOUCHDOWNS BY RUSHING AND RECEIVING
Game
By many players. Most recent: Jacquez Green, Florida vs. Auburn, Oct. 18, 1997; Eric Crouch, Nebraska vs. California, Sept. 11, 1999 (all in 2nd quarter)

PASSING FOR A TOUCHDOWN AND SCORING ON A PASS RECEPTION AND PUNT RETURN
Game
By many players. Most recent: Tim Dwight, Iowa vs. Indiana, Oct. 25, 1997

PLAYER RETURNING A BLOCKED PUNT, FUMBLE RECOVERY AND INTERCEPTION RETURN FOR A TOUCHDOWN
Season
By many players. Most recent: Tim Curry, Air Force, 1997

MOST EXTRA POINTS ATTEMPTED BY KICKING
Game
14—Terry Leiweke, Houston vs. Tulsa, Nov. 23, 1968 (13 made)
Season
71—Kurt Gunther, Brigham Young, 1980 (64 made); Bart Edmiston, Florida, 1995 (71 made); Scott Bentley, Florida St., 1995 (67 made)
Career
222—Derek Mahoney, Fresno St., 1990-93 (216 made); Kris Brown, Nebraska, 1995-98 (217 made)

MOST EXTRA POINTS MADE BY KICKING
Game
13—Terry Leiweke, Houston vs. Tulsa, Nov. 23, 1968 (14 attempts); Derek Mahoney, Fresno St. vs. New Mexico, Oct. 5, 1991 (13 attempts)
Season
71—Bart Edmiston, Florida, 1995 (71 attempts)
Per-game record—6.1, Cary Blanchard, Oklahoma St., 1988, and Scott Bentley, Florida St., 1995 (67 in 11)
Career
217—Kris Brown, Nebraska, 1995-98 (222 attempts)
Per-game record—5.3, Bart Edmiston, Florida, 1993-96 (137 in 26)

BEST PERFECT RECORD OF EXTRA POINTS MADE
Season
71 of 71—Bart Edmiston, Florida, 1995

HIGHEST PERCENTAGE OF EXTRA POINTS MADE
Career
(Min. 100 atts.) 100%—Van Tiffin, Alabama, 1983-86 (135 of 135); Pete Stoyanovich, Indiana, 1985-88 (101 of 101); David Browndyke, LSU, 1986-89 (109 of 109); John Beckvoort, Tennessee, 1991-94 (161 of 161)

MOST CONSECUTIVE EXTRA POINTS MADE
Game
13—Derek Mahoney, Fresno St. vs. New Mexico, Oct. 5, 1991 (13 attempts)

Season
71—Bart Edmiston, Florida, 1995 (71 attempts)
Career
161—John Beckvoort, Tennessee, 1991-94

MOST POINTS SCORED BY KICKING
Game
24—Mike Prindle, Western Mich. vs. Marshall, Sept. 29, 1984 (7 FGs, 3 PATs)
Season
135—Martin Gramatica, Kansas St., 1998 (22 FGs, 69 PATs)
Per-game record: 11.9 by Roman Anderson, Houston, 1989 (131 in 11)
Career
423—Roman Anderson, Houston, 1988-91 (70 FGs, 213 PATs)
Also holds per-game record at 9.6 (423 in 44)

HIGHEST PERCENTAGE OF EXTRA POINTS AND FIELD GOALS MADE
Season
(Min. 20 PATS and 12 FGs made) 100.0%—Marc Primanti, North Carolina St., 1996 (24 of 24 PATs, 20 of 20 FGs); Ryan White, Memphis, 1998 (22 of 22 PATs, 16 of 16 FGs)
(Min. 30 PATs and 15 FGs made) 98.3%—Chuck Nelson, Washington, 1982 (34 of 34 PATs, 25 of 26 FGs)
(Min. 40 PATs and 20 FGs made) 97.3%—Chris Jacke, UTEP, 1988 (48 of 48 PATs, 25 of 27 FGs)
Career
(Min. 100 PATs and 50 FGs made) 93.3%—John Lee, UCLA, 1982-85 (116 of 117 PATs, 79 of 92 FGs)

MOST TWO-POINT ATTEMPTS MADE
Game
6—Jim Pilot, New Mexico St. vs. Hardin-Simmons, Nov. 25, 1961 (all by running, attempted 7)
Season
6—Pat McCarthy, Holy Cross, 1960 (all by running); Jim Pilot, New Mexico St., 1961 (all by running); Howard Twilley, Tulsa, 1964 (all on pass receptions)
Career
13—Pat McCarthy, Holy Cross, 1960-62 (all by running)

MOST SUCCESSFUL TWO-POINT PASSES
Season
12—John Hangartner, Arizona St., 1958 (attempted 21)
Career
19—Pat McCarthy, Holy Cross, 1960-62 (attempted 33)

Defensive Extra Points

MOST DEFENSIVE EXTRA POINTS RETURNED
Game
2—Corey Ivy, Oklahoma vs. California, Sept. 20, 1997; Tony Holmes, Texas vs. Iowa St., Oct. 3, 1998

MOST DEFENSIVE EXTRA POINTS SCORED
Game
2—Tony Holmes, Texas vs. Iowa St., Oct. 3, 1998
Season
2—Tony Holmes, Texas vs. Iowa St., Oct. 3, 1998

MOST DEFENSIVE EXTRA POINTS SCORED BY BOTH TEAMS
Game
2—Eric Kelly (fumbled snap return), Kentucky, and Mark Roman (blocked kick return), LSU, Oct. 17, 1998

LONGEST RETURN OF A DEFENSIVE EXTRA-POINT ATTEMPT
Game
100—Lee Ozmint (SS), Alabama vs. LSU, Nov. 11, 1989 (intercepted pass at Alabama goal line); Quintin Parker (DB), Illinois vs. Wisconsin, Oct. 28, 1989 (returned kick from Illinois goal line); Curt Newton (LB), Washington St. vs. Oregon St., Oct. 20, 1990 (intercepted pass from Washington St. goal line); William Price (CB), Kansas St. vs. Indiana St., Sept. 7, 1991 (intercepted pass three yards deep in Indiana St. end zone); Joe Crocker (CB), Virginia vs. North Carolina St., Nov. 25, 1994 (intercepted pass five yards deep in North Carolina St. end zone);

DIVISION I-A

Laymar Grant, Duke vs. Maryland, Oct. 26, 1996 (returned conversion pass attempt); Tony Holmes, Texas vs. Iowa St., Oct. 3, 1998 (intercepted pass)

FIRST DEFENSIVE EXTRA-POINT ATTEMPT
Season
Thomas King (S), La.-Lafayette vs. Cal St. Fullerton, Sept. 3, 1988 (returned blocked kick 6 yards)

MOST DEFENSIVE EXTRA-POINT KICKS BLOCKED
Game
2—Nigel Codrington (DB), Rice vs. Notre Dame, Nov. 5, 1988 (1 resulted in a score)
Also holds season record at 2

Fumble Returns
(Since 1992)

LONGEST FUMBLE RETURN FOR A TOUCHDOWN
100—Paul Rivers, Rutgers vs. Pittsburgh, Oct. 28, 1995; Dan Dawson, Rice vs. UNLV, Nov. 14, 1998; Kevin Thomas, UNLV vs. Baylor, Sept. 11, 1999

MOST FUMBLE RETURNS
Game
2—By many players.

MOST FUMBLE RETURNS RETURNED FOR TOUCHDOWNS
Game
2—Tyrone Carter, Minnesota vs. Syracuse, Sept. 21, 1996 (63 & 20 yards)

Field Goals

MOST FIELD GOALS ATTEMPTED
Game
9—Mike Prindle, Western Mich. vs. Marshall, Sept. 29, 1984 (7 made)
Season
38—Jerry DePoyster, Wyoming, 1966 (13 made)
Also holds per-game record at 3.8
Career
(3 yrs.) 93—Jerry DePoyster, Wyoming, 1965-67 (36 made)
Also holds per-game record at 3.1 (93 in 30)
(4 yrs.) 105—Luis Zendejas, Arizona St., 1981-84 (78 made); Philip Doyle, Alabama, 1987-90 (78 made)
Doyle holds per-game record at 2.4 (105 in 43)

MOST FIELD GOALS MADE
Quarter
4—By 5 players. Most recent: Jose Cortez, Oregon St. vs. California, Oct. 31, 1998 (2nd)
Half
5—Dale Klein, Nebraska vs. Missouri, Oct. 19, 1985 (1st); Dat Ly, New Mexico St. vs. Kansas, Oct. 1, 1988 (1st)
Game
7—Mike Prindle, Western Mich. vs. Marshall, Sept. 29, 1984 (32, 44, 42, 23, 48, 41, 27 yards), 9 attempts; Dale Klein, Nebraska vs. Missouri, Oct. 19, 1985 (32, 22, 43, 44, 29, 43, 43 yards), 7 attempts
Season
29—John Lee, UCLA, 1984 (33 attempts)
2 Yrs
50—John Lee, UCLA, 1984-85 (57 attempts)
Career
80—Jeff Jaeger, Washington, 1983-86 (99 attempts)

MOST FIELD GOALS MADE PER GAME
Season
2.6—John Lee, UCLA, 1984 (29 in 11)
Career
1.8—John Lee, UCLA, 1982-85 (79 in 43)

BEST PERFECT RECORD OF FIELD GOALS MADE
Game
7 of 7—Dale Klein, Nebraska vs. Missouri, Oct. 19, 1985
Season
20 of 20—Marc Primanti, North Carolina St., 1996

MOST FIELD GOALS MADE BY A FRESHMAN
Game
6—*Mickey Thomas, Virginia Tech vs. Vanderbilt, Nov. 4, 1989 (6 attempts)

Season
23—Collin Mackie, South Carolina, 1987 (30 attempts)

*Conventional-style kicker.

HIGHEST PERCENTAGE OF FIELD GOALS MADE
Season
(Min. 15 atts.) 100.0%—John Lee, UCLA, 1984 (16 of 16); Marc Primanti, North Carolina St., 1996 (20 of 20); Ryan White, Memphis, 1998 (16 of 16)
Career
(Min. 45-54 atts.) 87.8%—Bobby Raymond, Florida, 1983-84 (43 of 49)
(Min. 55 atts.) 85.9%—John Lee, UCLA, 1982-85 (79 of 92)

MOST CONSECUTIVE FIELD GOALS MADE
Season
25—Chuck Nelson, Washington, 1982 (first 25, missed last attempt of season vs. Washington St., Nov. 20)
Career
30—Chuck Nelson, Washington, 1981-82 (last 5 in 1981, from vs. Southern California, Nov. 14, and first 25 in 1982, ending with last attempt vs. Washington St., Nov. 20)

MOST GAMES KICKING A FIELD GOAL
Career
40—Gary Gussman, Miami (Ohio), 1984-87 (in 44 games played)

MOST CONSECUTIVE GAMES KICKING A FIELD GOAL
19—Larry Roach, Oklahoma St., 1983-84; Gary Gussman, Miami (Ohio), 1986-87

MOST FIELD GOALS MADE, 60 YARDS OR MORE
Game
2—Tony Franklin, Texas A&M vs. Baylor, Oct. 16, 1976 (65 & 64 yards)
Season
3—Russell Erxleben, Texas, 1977 (67 vs. Rice, Oct. 1; 64 vs. Baylor, Oct. 16; 60 vs. Texas Tech, Oct. 29) (4 attempts)
Career
3—Russell Erxleben, Texas, 1975-78 (see Season Record above)

MOST FIELD GOALS ATTEMPTED, 60 YARDS OR MORE
Season
5—Tony Franklin, Texas A&M, 1976 (2 made)
Career
11—Tony Franklin, Texas A&M, 1975-78 (2 made)

MOST FIELD GOALS MADE, 50 YARDS OR MORE
Game
3—Jerry DePoyster, Wyoming vs. Utah, Oct. 8, 1966 (54, 54, 52 yards); Sergio Lopez-Chavero, Wichita St. vs. Drake, Oct. 27, 1984 (54, 54, 51 yards); Tim Douglas, Iowa vs. Illinois, Sept. 26, 1998 (51, 58, 51 yards)
Season
8—Fuad Reveiz, Tennessee, 1982 (10 attempts)
Career
20—Jason Hanson, Washington St., 1988-91 (35 attempts)

MOST FIELD GOALS ATTEMPTED, 50 YARDS OR MORE
Season
17—Jerry DePoyster, Wyoming, 1966 (5 made)
Career
38—Tony Franklin, Texas A&M, 1975-78 (16 made)

HIGHEST PERCENTAGE OF FIELD GOALS MADE, 50 YARDS OR MORE
Season
(Min. 10 atts.) 80.0%—Fuad Reveiz, Tennessee, 1982 (8 of 10)
Career
(Min. 15 atts.) 60.9%—Max Zendejas, Arizona, 1982-85 (14 of 23)

MOST FIELD GOALS MADE, 40 YARDS OR MORE
Game
5—Alan Smith, Texas A&M vs. Arkansas St., Sept. 17, 1983 (44, 45, 42, 59, 57 yards)

Season
14—Chris Jacke, UTEP, 1988 (16 attempts)
Career
39—Jason Hanson, Washington St., 1988-91 (66 attempts) (19 of 31, 40-49 yards; 20 of 35, 50 or more yards)

MOST FIELD GOALS ATTEMPTED, 40 YARDS OR MORE
Season
25—Jerry DePoyster, Wyoming, 1966 (6 made)
Career
66—Jason Hanson, Washington St., 1988-91 (39 made)

HIGHEST PERCENTAGE OF FIELD GOALS MADE, 40 YARDS OR MORE
Season
(Min. 10 made) 90.9%—John Carney, Notre Dame, 1984 (10 of 11)
Career
(Min. 20 made) 69.4%—John Lee, UCLA, 1982-85 (25 of 36)

HIGHEST PERCENTAGE OF FIELD GOALS MADE, 40-49 YARDS
Season
(Min. 10 made) 100%—John Carney, Notre Dame, 1984 (10 of 10)
Career
(Min. 15 made) 82.6%—Jeff Jaeger, Washington, 1983-86 (19 of 23)

MOST CONSECUTIVE FIELD GOALS MADE, 40-49 YARDS
Career
12—John Carney, Notre Dame, 1984-85

HIGHEST PERCENTAGE OF FIELD GOALS MADE, UNDER 40 YARDS
Season
(Min. 16 made) 100%—Paul Woodside, West Virginia, 1982 (23 of 23); Randy Pratt, California, 1983 (16 of 16); John Lee, UCLA, 1984 (16 of 16); Bobby Raymond, Florida, 1984 (18 of 18); Scott Slater, Texas A&M, 1986 (16 of 16); Philip Doyle, Alabama, 1989 (19 of 19)
Career
(Min. 30-39 made) 97.0%—Bobby Raymond, Florida, 1983-84 (32 of 33)
(Min. 40 made) 96.4%—John Lee, UCLA, 1982-85 (54 of 56)

LONGEST AVERAGE DISTANCE FIELD GOALS MADE
Game
(Min. 4 made) 49.5—Jeff Heath, East Caro. vs. Texas-Arlington, Nov. 6, 1982 (58, 53, 42, 45 yards)
Season
(Min. 10 made) 50.9—Jason Hanson, Washington St., 1991 (10 made)
Career
(Min. 25 made) 42.4—Russell Erxleben, Texas, 1975-78 (49 made)

LONGEST AVERAGE DISTANCE FIELD GOALS ATTEMPTED
Season
(Min. 20 atts.) 51.2—Jason Hanson, Washington St., 1991 (22 attempts)
Career
(Min. 40 atts.) 44.7—Russell Erxleben, Texas, 1975-78 (78 attempts)

MOST TIMES KICKING TWO OR MORE FIELD GOALS IN A GAME
Season
10—Paul Woodside, West Virginia, 1982
Career
27—Kevin Butler, Georgia, 1981-84

MOST TIMES KICKING THREE OR MORE FIELD GOALS IN A GAME
Season
6—Luis Zendejas, Arizona St., 1983; Joe Allison, Memphis, 1992
Career
13—Luis Zendejas, Arizona St., 1981-84

INDIVIDUAL RECORDS—FIELD GOALS   17

MOST TIMES KICKING FOUR FIELD GOALS IN A GAME
Season
4—Matt Bahr, Penn St., 1978
Career
6—John Lee, UCLA, 1982-85

LONGEST FIELD GOAL MADE
67—Russell Erxleben, Texas vs. Rice, Oct. 1, 1977; Steve Little, Arkansas vs. Texas, Oct. 15, 1977; Joe Williams, Wichita St. vs. Southern Ill., Oct. 21, 1978

LONGEST INDOOR FIELD GOAL MADE
62—Chip Lohmiller, Minnesota vs. Iowa, Nov. 22, 1986 (in Minnesota's Metrodome)

LONGEST FIELD GOAL MADE WITHOUT USE OF A KICKING TEE
65—Martin Gramatica, Kansas St., vs. Northern Ill., Sept. 12, 1998

LONGEST FIELD GOAL MADE BY A FRESHMAN
61—Kyle Bryant, Texas A&M vs. Southern Miss., Sept. 24, 1994

LONGEST FIELD GOAL MADE ON FIRST ATTEMPT OF CAREER
61—Ralf Mojsiejenko, Michigan St. vs. Illinois, Sept. 11, 1982

MOST FIELD GOALS MADE IN FIRST GAME OF CAREER
5—Joe Liljenquist, Brigham Young vs. Colorado St., Sept. 20, 1969 (6 attempts); Nathan Ritter, North Carolina St. vs. East Caro., Sept. 9, 1978 (6 attempts); Jose Oceguera, Long Beach St. vs. Kansas St., Sept. 3, 1983 (5 attempts)

MOST GAMES IN WHICH FIELD GOAL(S) PROVIDED THE WINNING MARGIN
Season
6—Henrik Mike-Mayer, Drake, 1981
Career
10—Dan Miller, Miami (Fla.), 1978-81; John Lee, UCLA, 1982-85; Jeff Ward, Texas, 1983-86

Team Records

SINGLE GAME—Offense

Total Offense

MOST PLAYS
112—Montana vs. Montana St., Nov. 1, 1952 (475 yards)

MOST PLAYS, BOTH TEAMS
196—San Diego St. (99) & North Texas (97), Dec. 4, 1971 (851 yards)

FEWEST PLAYS
12—Texas Tech vs. Centenary (La.), Nov. 11, 1939 (10 rushes, 2 passes, -1 yard)

FEWEST PLAYS, BOTH TEAMS
33—Texas Tech (12) & Centenary (La.) (21), Nov. 11, 1939 (28 rushes, 5 passes, 30 yards)

MOST YARDS GAINED
1,021—Houston vs. Southern Methodist, Oct. 21, 1989 (250 rushing, 771 passing, 86 plays)

MOST YARDS GAINED, BOTH TEAMS
1,563—Houston (827) & TCU (736), Nov. 3, 1990 (187 plays)

FEWEST YARDS GAINED
Minus 47—Syracuse vs. Penn St., Oct. 18, 1947 (-107 rushing, gained 60 passing, 49 plays)

FEWEST YARDS GAINED, BOTH TEAMS
30—Texas Tech (-1) & Centenary (La.) (31), Nov. 11, 1939 (33 plays)

MOST YARDS GAINED BY A LOSING TEAM
736—TCU vs. Houston, Nov. 3, 1990 (lost 56-35)

BOTH TEAMS GAINING 600 YARDS OR MORE
In 22 games. Most recent: Nevada (653) & New Mexico St. (614), Oct. 10, 1998 (172 plays); Miami (Fla.) (689) & UCLA (670), Dec. 5, 1998 (152 plays); Tennessee (695) & Kentucky (634), Nov. 22, 1997; Kent (615) & UCF (612), Oct. 4, 1997 (154 plays); San Diego St. (670) & UNLV (627), Nov. 16, 1996 (166 plays); Nevada (727) & Louisiana Tech (607), Oct. 21, 1995 (180 plays); Idaho (707) & UNLV (614), Sept. 17, 1994 (181 plays); Maryland (649) & Virginia Tech (641), Sept. 25, 1993 (166 plays); Nevada (616) & Weber St. (615) Oct. 23, 1993 (180 plays)

FEWEST YARDS GAINED BY A WINNING TEAM
10—North Carolina St. vs. Virginia, Sept. 30, 1944 (won 13-0)

HIGHEST AVERAGE GAIN PER PLAY (Min. 75 Plays)
11.9—Houston vs. Southern Methodist, Oct. 21, 1989 (86 for 1,021)

MOST TOUCHDOWNS SCORED BY RUSHING AND PASSING
15—Wyoming vs. Northern Colo., Nov. 5, 1949 (9 rushing, 6 passing)

Rushing

MOST RUSHES
99—Missouri vs. Colorado, Oct. 12, 1968 (421 yards)

MOST RUSHES, BOTH TEAMS
141—Colgate (82) & Bucknell (59), Nov. 6, 1971 (440 yards)

FEWEST RUSHES
5—Houston vs. Texas Tech, Nov. 25, 1989 (36 yards)

FEWEST RUSHES, BOTH TEAMS
28—Texas Tech (10) & Centenary (La.) (18), Nov. 11, 1939 (23 yards)

MOST YARDS GAINED
768—Oklahoma vs. Kansas St., Oct. 15, 1988 (72 rushes)

MOST YARDS GAINED, BOTH TEAMS
1,039—Lenoir-Rhyne (837) & Davidson (202), Oct. 11, 1975 (111 rushes)

MOST YARDS GAINED, BOTH TEAMS, MAJOR-COLLEGE OPPONENTS
956—Oklahoma (711) & Kansas St. (245), Oct. 23, 1971 (111 rushes)

FEWEST YARDS GAINED
Minus 109—Northern Ill. vs. Toledo, Nov. 11, 1967 (33 rushes)

FEWEST YARDS GAINED, BOTH TEAMS
Minus 24—San Jose St. (-102) & UTEP (78), Oct. 22, 1966 (75 rushes)

MOST YARDS GAINED WITHOUT LOSS
677—Nebraska vs. New Mexico St., Sept. 18, 1982 (78 rushes)

MOST YARDS GAINED BY A LOSING TEAM
525—Air Force vs. New Mexico, Nov. 2, 1991 (70 rushes, lost 34-32)

HIGHEST AVERAGE GAIN PER RUSH (Min. 50 Rushes)
11.9—Alabama vs. Virginia Tech, Oct. 27, 1973 (63 for 748)

MOST PLAYERS ON ONE TEAM EACH GAINING 100 YARDS OR MORE
4—Arizona St. vs. Arizona, Nov. 10, 1951 (Bob Tarwater 140, Harley Cooper 123, Duane Morrison 118, Buzz Walker 113); Texas vs. Southern Methodist, Nov. 1, 1969 (Jim Bertelsen 137, Steve Worster 137, James Street 121, Ted Koy 111); Alabama vs. Virginia Tech, Oct. 27, 1973 (Jimmy Taylor 142, Wilbur Jackson 138, Calvin Culliver 127, Richard Todd 102); Army vs. Montana, Nov. 17, 1984 (Doug Black 183, Nate Sassaman 155, Clarence Jones 130, Jarvis Hollingsworth 124)

MOST TOUCHDOWNS SCORED BY RUSHING
12—UTEP vs. New Mexico St., Nov. 25, 1948

Passing

MOST PASSES ATTEMPTED
83—Purdue vs. Wisconsin, Oct. 10, 1998 (completed 55)

MOST PASSES ATTEMPTED, BOTH TEAMS
135—TCU (79) & Houston (56), Nov. 3, 1990 (completed 81)

FEWEST PASSES ATTEMPTED
0—By many teams. Most recent: Ohio vs. Akron, Oct. 25, 1997 (61 rushes; won 21-17)

FEWEST PASSES ATTEMPTED, BOTH TEAMS
1—Michigan St. (0) & Maryland (1), Oct. 20, 1944 (not completed)

MOST PASSES ATTEMPTED WITHOUT COMPLETION
18—West Virginia vs. Temple, Oct. 18, 1946

MOST PASSES ATTEMPTED WITHOUT INTERCEPTION
72—Houston vs. TCU, Nov. 4, 1989 (completed 47)

MOST PASSES ATTEMPTED WITHOUT INTERCEPTION, BOTH TEAMS
114—Illinois (67) & Purdue (47), Oct. 12, 1985 (completed 67)

MOST CONSECUTIVE PASSES ATTEMPTED WITHOUT A RUSHING PLAY
32—North Carolina St. vs. Duke, Nov. 11, 1989 (3rd & 4th quarters, completed 16)

MOST PASSES COMPLETED
55—Wake Forest vs. Duke, Oct. 28, 1995 (attempted 78); Purdue vs. Wisconsin, Oct. 10, 1998 (attempted 83)

MOST PASSES COMPLETED, BOTH TEAMS
81—TCU (44) & Houston (37), Nov. 3, 1990 (attempted 135)

BEST PERFECT GAME (100.0 Pct.)
11 of 11—Southern California vs. Washington, Oct. 9, 1965; Oregon St. vs. UCLA, Oct. 2, 1971; Air Force vs. Northwestern, Sept. 17, 1988; North Carolina vs. William & Mary, Oct. 5, 1991

HIGHEST PERCENTAGE OF PASSES COMPLETED
(Min. 15-24 comps.) 96.0%—Tennessee vs. South Carolina, Oct. 31, 1998 (24 of 25)
(Min. 25-34 comps.) 92.6%—UCLA vs. Washington, Oct. 29, 1983 (25 of 27)
(Min. 35 comps.) 87.0%—South Carolina vs. Mississippi St., Oct. 14, 1995 (40 of 46)

HIGHEST PERCENTAGE OF PASSES COMPLETED, BOTH TEAMS
(Min. 40 Completions)
84.6%—UCLA & Washington, Oct. 29, 1983 (44 of 52)

MOST PASSES HAD INTERCEPTED
10—Detroit vs. Oklahoma St., Nov. 28, 1942; California vs. UCLA, Oct. 21, 1978 (52 attempts)

MOST YARDS GAINED
771—Houston vs. Southern Methodist, Oct. 21, 1989 (completed 40 of 61)

MOST YARDS GAINED, BOTH TEAMS
1,253—TCU (690) & Houston (563), Nov. 3, 1990 (135 attempts)

FEWEST YARDS GAINED, BOTH TEAMS
Minus 13—North Carolina (-7 on 1 of 3 attempts) & Pennsylvania (-6 on 2 of 12 attempts), Nov. 13, 1943

MOST YARDS GAINED PER ATTEMPT
(Min. 30-39 atts.) 17.0—Nevada vs. Idaho, Oct. 24, 1998 (35 for 596)
(Min. 40 atts.) 15.9—UTEP vs. North Texas, Sept. 18, 1965 (40 for 634)

MOST YARDS GAINED PER COMPLETION
(Min. 15-24 comps.) 31.9—UTEP vs. New Mexico, Oct. 28, 1967 (16 for 510)
(Min. 25 comps.) 25.4—UTEP vs. North Texas, Sept. 18, 1965 (25 for 634)

MOST TOUCHDOWN PASSES
11—Houston vs. Eastern Wash., Nov. 17, 1990

DIVISION I-A

MOST TOUCHDOWN PASSES, MAJOR-COLLEGE OPPONENTS
10—Houston vs. Southern Methodist, Oct. 21, 1989; San Diego St. vs. New Mexico St., Nov. 15, 1969

MOST TOUCHDOWN PASSES, BOTH TEAMS
14—Houston (11) & Eastern Wash. (3), Nov. 17, 1990

MOST TOUCHDOWN PASSES, BOTH TEAMS, MAJOR-COLLEGE OPPONENTS
13—San Diego St. (10) & New Mexico St. (3), Nov. 15, 1969

Punting

MOST PUNTS
39—Texas Tech vs. Centenary (La.), Nov. 11, 1939 (1,377 yards)
38—Centenary (La.) vs. Texas Tech, Nov. 11, 1939 (1,248 yards)

MOST PUNTS, BOTH TEAMS
77—Texas Tech (39) & Centenary (La.) (38), Nov. 11, 1939 (2,625 yards) (The game was played in a heavy downpour in Shreveport, Louisiana. Forty-two punts were returned, 19 went out of bounds, 10 were downed, 1 went into the end zone for a touchback, 4 were blocked and 1 was fair caught. Sixty-seven punts [34 by Texas Tech and 33 by Centenary] occurred on first-down plays, including 22 consecutively in the third and fourth quarters. The game was a scoreless tie.)

FEWEST PUNTS
0—By many teams. Most recent: Fresno St. vs. San Jose St., Nov. 20, 1999 (won 63-12); Rice vs. San Jose St., Oct. 16, 1999 (won 49-7); Marshall vs. Liberty, Sept. 11, 1999 (won 63-3)

FEWEST PUNTS BY A LOSING TEAM
0—By many teams. Most recent: Idaho vs. Southwest Tex. St., Sept. 28, 1996 (lost 27-21)

HIGHEST AVERAGE PER PUNT
(Min. 5-9 punts) 60.4—Brigham Young vs. Wyoming, Oct. 8, 1983 (5 for 302)
(Min. 10 punts) 53.6—Oklahoma St. vs. Colorado, Nov. 13, 1971 (10 for 536)

HIGHEST AVERAGE PER PUNT, BOTH TEAMS
(Min. 10 Punts)
55.3—Brigham Young & Wyoming, Oct. 8, 1983 (11 for 608)

Punt Returns

MOST PUNT RETURNS
22—Texas Tech vs. Centenary (La.), Nov. 11, 1939 (112 yards)

MOST PUNT RETURNS, BOTH TEAMS
42—Texas Tech (22) & Centenary (La.) (20), Nov. 11, 1939 (233 yards)

MOST YARDS ON PUNT RETURNS
319—Texas A&M vs. North Texas, Sept. 21, 1946 (10 returns)

HIGHEST AVERAGE GAIN PER RETURN
(Min. 5 Returns)
45.0—Georgia vs. South Carolina, Sept. 2, 1995 (5 for 225)

MOST TOUCHDOWNS SCORED ON PUNT RETURNS
3—Wisconsin vs. Iowa, Nov. 8, 1947; Wichita St. vs. Northern St., Oct. 22, 1949; LSU vs. Mississippi, Dec. 5, 1970; Holy Cross vs. Brown, Sept. 21, 1974; Arizona St. vs. Pacific (Cal.), Nov. 15, 1975; Notre Dame vs. Pittsburgh, Nov. 16, 1996

Kickoff Returns

MOST KICKOFF RETURNS
14—Arizona St. vs. Nevada, Oct. 12, 1946 (290 yards)

MOST YARDS ON KICKOFF RETURNS
295—Cincinnati vs. Memphis, Oct. 30, 1971 (8 returns)

HIGHEST AVERAGE GAIN PER RETURN
(Min. 6 Returns)
46.2—Southern California vs. Washington St., Nov. 7, 1970 (6 for 277)

MOST TOUCHDOWNS SCORED ON KICKOFF RETURNS
2—By many teams. Most recent: Texas A&M vs. Rice, Oct. 23, 1993; Brigham Young vs. Air Force, Nov. 11, 1989; Notre Dame vs. Michigan, Sept. 16, 1989; New Mexico St. vs. Drake, Oct. 15, 1983 (consecutive returns)

TOUCHDOWNS SCORED ON BACK-TO-BACK KICKOFF RETURNS, BOTH TEAMS
2—By many teams. Most recent: Wisconsin & Northern Ill., Sept. 14, 1985

Total Kick Returns
(Combined Punt and Kickoff Returns)

MOST YARDS ON KICK RETURNS
376—Florida St. vs. Virginia Tech, Nov. 16, 1974 (9 returns)

HIGHEST AVERAGE GAIN PER RETURN
(Min. 7 Returns)
41.8—Florida St. vs. Virginia Tech, Nov. 16, 1974 (9 for 376)

Scoring

MOST POINTS SCORED
103—Wyoming vs. Northern Colo. (0), Nov. 5, 1949 (15 TDs, 13 PATs)

MOST POINTS SCORED AGAINST A MAJOR-COLLEGE OPPONENT
100—Houston vs. Tulsa (6), Nov. 23, 1968 (14 TDs, 13 PATs, 1 FG)

MOST POINTS SCORED, BOTH TEAMS
124—Oklahoma (82) & Colorado (42), Oct. 4, 1980

MOST POINTS SCORED BY A LOSING TEAM
56—Purdue vs. Minnesota (59), Oct. 9, 1993

MOST POINTS, BOTH TEAMS IN A TIE GAME
104—Brigham Young (52) & San Diego St. (52), Nov. 16, 1991

MOST POINTS SCORED IN ONE QUARTER
49—Houston vs. Tulsa, Nov. 23, 1968 (4th); Davidson vs. Furman, Sept. 27, 1969 (2nd); Fresno St. vs. New Mexico, Oct. 5, 1991 (2nd)

MOST POINTS SCORED IN ONE QUARTER, BOTH TEAMS
61—San Jose St. (34) vs. Hawaii (27), Nov. 6, 1999 (4th; Hawaii won, 62-41)

MOST POINTS SCORED IN ONE HALF
76—Houston vs. Tulsa, Nov. 23, 1968 (2nd)

MOST TOUCHDOWNS SCORED
15—Wyoming vs. Northern Colo., Nov. 5, 1949 (9 rushing, 6 passing)

MOST TOUCHDOWNS SCORED, BOTH TEAMS
18—Oklahoma (12) & Colorado (6), Oct. 4, 1980

MOST EXTRA POINTS MADE BY KICKING
13—Wyoming vs. Northern Colo., Nov. 5, 1949 (attempted 15); Houston vs. Tulsa, Nov. 23, 1968 (attempted 14); Fresno St. vs. New Mexico, Oct. 5, 1991 (attempted 13)

MOST TWO-POINT ATTEMPTS SCORED
7—Pacific (Cal.) vs. San Diego St., Nov. 22, 1958 (attempted 9)

MOST DEFENSIVE EXTRA-POINT ATTEMPTS
2—Rice vs. Notre Dame, Nov. 5, 1988 (2 kick returns; 1 scored); Northern Ill. vs. Akron, Nov. 3, 1990 (2 interception returns); Oklahoma vs. California, Sept. 20, 1997 (2 kick returns; 1 scored); Texas vs. Iowa St., Oct. 3, 1998 (2 kick returns; 2 scored)

MOST DEFENSIVE EXTRA POINTS SCORED
2—Texas vs. Iowa St., Oct. 3, 1998 (2 kick returns)

MOST FIELD GOALS MADE
7—Western Mich. vs. Marshall, Sept. 29, 1984 (attempted 9); Nebraska vs. Missouri, Oct. 19, 1985 (attempted 7)

MOST FIELD GOALS MADE, BOTH TEAMS
9—La.-Lafayette (5) & Central Mich. (4), Sept. 9, 1989 (attempted 11)

MOST FIELD GOALS ATTEMPTED
9—Western Mich. vs. Marshall, Sept. 29, 1984 (made 7)

MOST FIELD GOALS ATTEMPTED, BOTH TEAMS
12—Clemson (6) & Georgia (6), Sept. 17, 1983 (made 6)

MOST FIELD GOALS MISSED
7—LSU vs. Florida, Nov. 25, 1972 (attempted 8)

First Downs

MOST FIRST DOWNS
44—Nebraska vs. Utah St., Sept. 7, 1991 (33 rush, 10 pass, 1 penalty)

MOST FIRST DOWNS, BOTH TEAMS
72—New Mexico (37) & San Diego St. (35), Sept. 27, 1986

FEWEST FIRST DOWNS BY A WINNING TEAM
0—North Carolina St. vs. Virginia, Sept. 30, 1944 (won 13-0); Michigan vs. Ohio St., Nov. 25, 1950 (won 9-3)

MOST FIRST DOWNS BY RUSHING
36—Nebraska vs. New Mexico St., Sept. 18, 1982

MOST FIRST DOWNS BY PASSING
30—Tulsa vs. Idaho St., Oct. 7, 1967; Brigham Young vs. Colorado St., Nov. 7, 1981

Fumbles

MOST FUMBLES
17—Wichita St. vs. Florida St., Sept. 20, 1969 (lost 10)

MOST FUMBLES, BOTH TEAMS
27—Wichita St. (17) & Florida St. (10), Sept. 20, 1969 (lost 17)

MOST FUMBLES LOST
10—Wichita St. vs. Florida St., Sept. 20, 1969 (17 fumbles)

MOST FUMBLES LOST, BOTH TEAMS
17—Wichita St. (10) & Florida St. (7), Sept. 20, 1969 (27 fumbles)

MOST FUMBLES LOST IN A QUARTER
5—East Caro. vs. La.-Lafayette, Sept. 13, 1980 (3rd quarter on 5 consecutive possessions); San Diego St. vs. California, Sept. 18, 1982 (1st)

Penalties

MOST PENALTIES AGAINST
24—San Jose St. vs. Fresno St., Oct. 4, 1986 (199 yards)

MOST PENALTIES, BOTH TEAMS
36—San Jose St. (24) & Fresno St. (12), Oct. 4, 1986 (317 yards)

FEWEST PENALTIES, BOTH TEAMS
0—By many teams. Most recent: Army & Navy, Dec. 6, 1986

MOST YARDS PENALIZED
238—Arizona St. vs. UTEP, Nov. 11, 1961 (13 penalties)

MOST YARDS PENALIZED, BOTH TEAMS
421—Grambling (16 for 216 yards) & Texas Southern (17 for 205 yards), Oct. 29, 1977

Turnovers
(Number of Times Losing the Ball on Fumbles and Interceptions)

MOST TURNOVERS LOST
13—Georgia vs. Georgia Tech, Dec. 1, 1951 (5 fumbles, 8 interceptions)

TEAM RECORDS—TURNOVERS

MOST TURNOVERS, BOTH TEAMS
20—Wichita St. (12) & Florida St. (8), Sept. 20, 1969 (17 fumbles, 3 interceptions)

MOST TOTAL PLAYS WITHOUT A TURNOVER (Rushes, Passes, All Runbacks)
110—California vs. San Jose St., Oct. 5, 1968 (also did not fumble); Baylor vs. Rice, Nov. 13, 1976

MOST TOTAL PLAYS WITHOUT A TURNOVER, BOTH TEAMS
184—Arkansas (93) & Texas A&M (91), Nov. 2, 1968

MOST TOTAL PLAYS WITHOUT A TURNOVER OR A FUMBLE, BOTH TEAMS
158—Stanford (88) & Oregon (70), Nov. 2, 1957

MOST TURNOVERS BY A WINNING TEAM
11—Purdue vs. Illinois, Oct. 2, 1943 (9 fumbles, 2 interceptions; won 40-21)

MOST PASSES HAD INTERCEPTED BY A WINNING TEAM
7—Pittsburgh vs. Army, Nov. 15, 1980 (54 attempts; won 45-7); Florida vs. Kentucky, Sept. 11, 1993 (52 attempts; won 24-20)

MOST FUMBLES LOST BY A WINNING TEAM
9—Purdue vs. Illinois, Oct. 2, 1943 (10 fumbles; won 40-21); Arizona St. vs. Utah, Oct. 14, 1972 (10 fumbles; won 59-48)

Overtimes

MOST OVERTIME PERIODS
4—California (56) vs. Arizona (55), Nov. 2, 1996; Georgia (56) vs. Auburn (49), Nov. 16, 1996; North Ala. (Div. II) (48) vs. La.-Lafayette (42), Oct. 11, 1997; Kansas (39) vs. UAB (37), Sept. 26, 1998

MOST POINTS SCORED IN OVERTIME PERIODS
28—Georgia (56) vs. Auburn (49), Nov. 16, 1996 (4 overtime periods)

MOST POINTS SCORED IN OVERTIME PERIODS, BOTH TEAMS
49—Georgia (28) vs. Auburn (21), Nov. 16, 1996 (4 overtime periods; Georgia won, 56-49)

LARGEST WINNING MARGIN IN OVERTIME
13—Arizona St. (48) vs. Southern California (35), Oct. 19, 1996 (2 overtime periods); Central Mich. (36) vs. Eastern Mich. (23), Oct. 10, 1998 (one overtime period)

CONSECUTIVE OVERTIME GAMES (SEASON)
2—Southern California (41) vs. UCLA (48), Nov. 23, 1996 & Southern California (27) vs. Notre Dame (20), Nov. 30, 1996; Oklahoma St. (50) vs. Missouri (51), Oct. 25, 1997 & Oklahoma St. (25) vs. Texas A&M (28), Nov. 1, 1997; Cincinnati (38) vs. Houston (41), Oct. 18, 1997 & Cincinnati (34) vs. Miami (Ohio) (31), Oct. 25, 1997; San Diego St. (36) vs. New Mexico (33), Oct. 17, 1998 & San Diego St. (21) vs. Utah (20), Oct. 24, 1998; Mississippi (34) vs. Vanderbilt (37), Sept. 18, 1999 & Mississippi (24) vs. Auburn (17), Sept. 25, 1999

CONSECUTIVE OVERTIME GAMES WITH SAME OPPONENT
2—Cincinnati (34) vs. Miami (Ohio) (31), Oct. 25, 1997 & Cincinnati (30) vs. Miami (Ohio) (23), Sept. 28, 1996; Oregon (43) vs. Fresno St. (40), Sept. 20, 1997 & Oregon (30) vs. Fresno St. (27), Aug. 31, 1996; Missouri (51) vs. Oklahoma St. (50), Oct. 25, 1997 & Missouri (35) vs. Oklahoma St. (28), Oct. 26, 1996; Arizona (41) vs. California (38), Nov. 15, 1997 & Arizona (55) vs. California (56), Nov. 2, 1996

SINGLE GAME—Defense

Total Defense

FEWEST PLAYS ALLOWED
12—Centenary (La.) vs. Texas Tech, Nov. 11, 1939 (10 rushes, 2 passes; -1 yard)

FEWEST YARDS ALLOWED
Minus 47—Penn St. vs. Syracuse, Oct. 18, 1947 (-107 rushing, 60 passing; 49 plays)

MOST YARDS ALLOWED
1,021—Southern Methodist vs. Houston, Oct. 21, 1989 (250 rushing, 771 passing)

Rushing Defense

FEWEST RUSHES ALLOWED
5—Texas Tech vs. Houston, Nov. 25, 1989 (36 yards)

FEWEST RUSHING YARDS ALLOWED
Minus 109—Toledo vs. Northern Ill., Nov. 11, 1967 (33 rushes)

Pass Defense

FEWEST ATTEMPTS ALLOWED
0—By many teams. Most recent: Colorado vs. Oklahoma, Nov. 15, 1986

FEWEST COMPLETIONS ALLOWED
0—By many teams. Most recent: Brigham Young vs. Rice, Nov. 9, 1996 (5 attempts)

LOWEST COMPLETION PERCENTAGE ALLOWED (Min. 10 Attempts)
0.0%—North Carolina vs. Penn St., Oct. 2, 1943 (0 of 12 attempts); Temple vs. West Virginia, Oct. 18, 1946 (0 of 18 attempts); San Jose St. vs. Cal St. Fullerton, Oct. 10, 1992 (0 of 11 attempts)

FEWEST YARDS ALLOWED
Minus 16—VMI vs. Richmond, Oct. 5, 1957 (2 completions)

MOST PASSES INTERCEPTED BY
11—Brown vs. Rhode Island, Oct. 8, 1949 (136 yards)

MOST PASSES INTERCEPTED BY AGAINST A MAJOR-COLLEGE OPPONENT
10—Oklahoma St. vs. Detroit, Nov. 28, 1942; UCLA vs. California, Oct. 21, 1978

MOST PASSES INTERCEPTED BY A LOSING TEAM
7—Kentucky vs. Florida, Sept. 11, 1993 (52 attempts)

MOST YARDS ON INTERCEPTION RETURNS
240—Kentucky vs. Mississippi, Oct. 1, 1949 (6 returns)

MOST TOUCHDOWNS ON INTERCEPTION RETURNS
4—Houston vs. Texas, Nov. 7, 1987 (198 yards; 3 TDs in the 4th quarter)

First Downs

FEWEST FIRST DOWNS ALLOWED
0—By many teams. Most recent: North Carolina St. vs. Western Caro., Sept. 1, 1990

Opponent's Kicks Blocked

MOST OPPONENT'S PUNTS BLOCKED
4—Southern Methodist vs. Texas-Arlington, Sept. 30, 1944; Michigan vs. Ohio St., Nov. 25, 1950; Memphis vs. Arkansas, Sept. 26, 1992 (10 attempts)

MOST OPPONENT'S PUNTS BLOCKED, ONE QUARTER
3—Purdue vs. Northwestern, Nov. 11, 1989 (4 attempts)

BLOCKED OPPONENTS' FIELD GOAL, PUNT AND EXTRA-POINT KICK
Oregon St. blocked each type of kick against Southern California, Sept. 14, 1996.

MOST OPPONENT'S FIELD GOALS BLOCKED, ONE QUARTER
2—Southern California vs. California, Oct. 22, 1994; Wyoming vs. Fresno St., Nov. 18, 1995

Turnovers Gained

(Number of Times Gaining the Ball on Fumbles and Interceptions)

MOST TURNOVERS GAINED
13—Georgia Tech vs. Georgia, Dec. 1, 1951 (5 fumbles, 8 interceptions)

MOST CONSECUTIVE OPPONENT'S SERIES RESULTING IN TURNOVERS
7—Florida vs. Florida St., Oct. 7, 1972 (4 fumbles lost, 3 interceptions; first seven series of the game)

Fumble Returns

(Since 1992)

MOST TOUCHDOWNS ON FUMBLE RETURNS
2—Toledo vs. Arkansas St., Sept. 5, 1992; Arizona vs. Illinois, Sept. 18, 1993; Duke vs. Wake Forest, Oct. 22, 1994 (both occurred in 1st quarter); Iowa vs. Minnesota, Nov. 19, 1994; Minnesota vs. Syracuse, Sept. 21, 1996; Florida vs. La.-Lafayette, Aug. 31, 1996; Arizona St. vs. Washington St., Nov. 1, 1997

LONGEST RETURN OF A FUMBLE
100—Rutgers vs. Pittsburgh, Oct. 28, 1995; Rice vs. UNLV, Nov. 14, 1998; UNLV vs. Baylor, Sept. 11, 1999

Defensive Extra Points

MOST DEFENSIVE EXTRA POINTS SCORED AGAINST
1—By many teams. Most recent: Nevada vs. Utah St., Nov. 4, 1995 (interception return)

MOST DEFENSIVE EXTRA-POINT ATTEMPTS AGAINST
2—Notre Dame vs. Rice, Nov. 5, 1988 (2 blocked kick returns, 1 scored); Akron vs. Northern Ill., Nov. 3, 1990 (2 interception returns); California vs. Oklahoma, Sept. 20, 1997 (2 kick returns; 1 scored)

MOST DEFENSIVE EXTRA POINTS SCORED BY BOTH TEAM
2—Kentucky (fumbled snap return) vs. LSU (blocked kick return), Oct. 17, 1998

Safeties

MOST SAFETIES BY A DEFENSE
3—Arizona St. vs. Nebraska, Sept. 21, 1996

SEASON—Offense

Total Offense

MOST YARDS GAINED PER GAME
624.9—Houston, 1989 (6,874 in 11)

MOST YARDS GAINED
6,874—Houston, 1989 (11 games)

HIGHEST AVERAGE GAIN PER PLAY
7.9—Army, 1945 (526 for 4,164)

GAINING 300 YARDS OR MORE PER GAME RUSHING AND 200 YARDS OR MORE PER GAME PASSING
Houston, 1968 (361.7 rushing, 200.3 passing); Arizona St., 1973 (310.2 rushing, 255.3 passing)

MOST PLAYS PER GAME
92.4—Notre Dame, 1970 (924 in 10)

MOST TOUCHDOWNS RUSHING AND PASSING
84—Nebraska, 1983
Also holds per-game record at 7.0 (84 in 12)

TEAM RECORDS—RUSHING

Rushing

MOST YARDS GAINED PER GAME
472.4—Oklahoma, 1971 (5,196 in 11)

HIGHEST AVERAGE GAIN PER RUSH
7.6—Army, 1945 (424 for 3,238)

HIGHEST AVERAGE GAIN PER RUSH (Min. 500 Rushes)
7.0—Nebraska, 1995 (627 for 4,398)

MOST RUSHES PER GAME
73.9—Oklahoma, 1974 (813 in 11)

MOST TOUCHDOWNS RUSHING PER GAME
5.5—Nebraska, 1997 (66 in 12)

Passing

MOST YARDS GAINED PER GAME
511.3—Houston, 1989 (5,624 in 11)

MOST YARDS GAINED
5,624—Houston, 1989 (11 games)

HIGHEST AVERAGE GAIN PER ATTEMPT (Min. 350 Attempts)
10.9—Brigham Young, 1989 (433 for 4,732)

HIGHEST AVERAGE GAIN PER COMPLETION
(Min. 100-174 comps.) 19.1—Houston, 1968 (105 for 2,003)
(Min. 175-224 comps.) 18.0—Grambling, 1977 (187 for 3,360)
(Min. 225 comps.) 17.1—Florida, 1996 (234 for 4,007)

MOST PASSES ATTEMPTED PER GAME
63.1—Houston, 1989 (694 in 11)

MOST PASSES COMPLETED PER GAME
39.4—Houston, 1989 (434 in 11)

HIGHEST PERCENTAGE COMPLETED (Min. 150 Attempts)
73.5%—Central Fla., 1998 (302 of 411)

LOWEST PERCENTAGE HAD INTERCEPTED
(Min. 300-399 atts.) 0.84%—Fresno St., 1999 (3 of 359)
(Min. 400 atts.) 1.2%—Southern California, 1993 (5 of 432)

MOST TOUCHDOWN PASSES PER GAME
5.0—Houston, 1989 (55 in 11)

MOST TOUCHDOWN PASSES
55—Houston, 1989 (11 games)

FEWEST TOUCHDOWN PASSES
0—By 6 teams since 1975. Most recent: Vanderbilt, 1993 (11 games, 157 attempts)

HIGHEST PASSING EFFICIENCY RATING POINTS (Min. 150 Attempts)
184.4—Tulane, 1998 (339 attempts, 230 completions, 6 interceptions, 3,352 yards, 38 TD passes)

A TEAM WITH THE NO. 1 & NO. 2 RECEIVERS
Houston, 1988 (Jason Phillips, No. 1, 9.82 catches per game & James Dixon, No. 2, 9.27 catches per game)

MOST 100-YARD RECEIVING GAMES IN A SEASON, ONE TEAM
19—San Diego St., 1990 (Patrick Rowe 9, Dennis Arey 8 & Jimmy Raye 2)

Punting

MOST PUNTS PER GAME
13.9—Tennessee, 1937 (139 in 10)

FEWEST PUNTS PER GAME
2.0—Nevada, 1948 (18 in 9)

HIGHEST PUNTING AVERAGE
50.6—Brigham Young, 1983 (24 for 1,215 yards)

HIGHEST PUNTING AVERAGE (Min. 40 Punts)
47.7—North Carolina, 1999 (81 for 3,863)

HIGHEST NET PUNTING AVERAGE
45.0—Brigham Young, 1983 (24 for 1,215 yards, 134 yards in punts returned)

HIGHEST NET PUNTING AVERAGE (Min. 40 Punts)
44.9—San Diego St., 1996 (48 for 2,234, 77 in punts returned)

Punt Returns

MOST PUNT RETURNS PER GAME
6.9—Texas A&M, 1943 (69 in 10)

FEWEST PUNT RETURNS PER GAME
0.5—Iowa St., 1996 (5 in 11)

MOST PUNT-RETURN YARDS PER GAME
114.5—Colgate, 1941 (916 in 8)

HIGHEST AVERAGE GAIN PER RETURN
(Min. 15-29 rets.) 25.2—Arizona St., 1952 (18 for 454)
(Min. 30 rets.) 22.4—Oklahoma, 1948 (43 for 963)

MOST TOUCHDOWNS SCORED ON PUNT RETURNS (Since 1966)
7—Southern Miss., 1987 (on 46 returns)

Kickoff Returns

MOST KICKOFF RETURNS PER GAME
7.3—Cal St. Fullerton, 1990 (80 in 11)

FEWEST KICKOFF RETURNS PER GAME
0.7—Boston College, 1939 (7 in 10)

MOST KICKOFF-RETURN YARDS
1,588—Pittsburgh, 1996 (66 returns)

MOST KICKOFF-RETURN YARDS PER GAME
144.4—Pittsburgh, 1996 (1,588 in 11)

HIGHEST AVERAGE GAIN PER RETURN
(Min. 25-34 rets.) 30.3—Florida St., 1992 (27 for 819)
(Min. 35 rets.) 27.5—Rice, 1973 (39 for 1,074)

MOST TOUCHDOWNS SCORED ON KICKOFF RETURNS (Since 1966)
4—Dayton, 1974 (on 44 returns)

Scoring

MOST POINTS PER GAME
56.0—Army, 1944 (504 in 9)

MOST POINTS SCORED
624—Nebraska, 1983 (12 games)

HIGHEST SCORING MARGIN
52.1—Army, 1944 (scored 504 points for 56.0 average and allowed 35 points for 3.9 average in 9 games)

MOST POINTS SCORED, TWO CONSECUTIVE GAMES
177—Houston, 1968 (77-3 vs. Idaho, Nov. 16, and 100-6 vs. Tulsa, Nov. 23)

MOST TOUCHDOWNS PER GAME
8.2—Army, 1944 (74 in 9)

MOST TOUCHDOWNS
89—Nebraska, 1983 (12 games)

MOST EXTRA POINTS MADE BY KICKING
77—Nebraska, 1983 (77 in 12, attempted 85)
Also holds per-game record at 6.4

MOST CONSECUTIVE EXTRA POINTS MADE BY KICKING
71—Florida, 1995 (attempted 71); Nebraska, 1997 (attempted 71)

MOST TWO-POINT ATTEMPTS MADE PER GAME
2.2—Rutgers, 1958 (20 in 9, attempted 31)

MOST DEFENSIVE EXTRA-POINT ATTEMPTS
3—Rice, 1988 (1 vs. La.-Lafayette, Sept. 24, blocked kick return; 2 vs. Notre Dame, Nov. 5, 2 blocked kick returns, 1 scored)

MOST DEFENSIVE EXTRA POINTS SCORED
2—Texas, 1998 (2 vs. Iowa St., Oct. 3, 2 blocked kick returns)

MOST FIELD GOALS PER GAME
2.6—UCLA, 1984 (29 in 11)

First Downs

MOST FIRST DOWNS PER GAME
30.9—Brigham Young, 1983 (340 in 11)

MOST RUSHING FIRST DOWNS PER GAME
21.4—Oklahoma, 1974 (235 in 11)

MOST PASSING FIRST DOWNS PER GAME
19.8—Nevada, 1995 (218 in 11)

Fumbles

MOST FUMBLES
73—Cal St. Fullerton, 1992 (lost 41)

MOST FUMBLES LOST
41—Cal St. Fullerton, 1992 (73 fumbles)

FEWEST OWN FUMBLES LOST
1—Bowling Green, 1996; Miami (Ohio), 1998

FEWEST OWN FUMBLES LOST IN TWO CONSECUTIVE SEASONS
3—Miami (Ohio), 1998-99 (1 in 1998; 2 in 1999)

MOST CONSECUTIVE FUMBLES LOST
14—Oklahoma, 1983 (during 5 games, Oct. 8-Nov. 5)

Penalties

MOST PENALTIES PER GAME
12.9—Grambling, 1977 (142 in 11, 1,476 yards)

MOST YARDS PENALIZED PER GAME
134.2—Grambling, 1977 (1,476 in 11, 142 penalties)

Turnovers (Giveaways)

(Fumbles Lost and Passes Had Intercepted)

FEWEST TURNOVERS
8—Clemson, 1940 (2 fumbles lost, 6 interceptions); Miami (Ohio), 1966 (4 fumbles lost, 4 interceptions)

FEWEST TURNOVERS PER GAME
0.8—Miami (Ohio), 1966 (8 in 10 games)

MOST TURNOVERS
61—North Texas, 1971 (28 fumbles lost, 33 interceptions); Tulsa, 1976 (37 fumbles lost, 24 interceptions)

MOST TURNOVERS PER GAME
6.1—Mississippi St., 1949 (55 in 9 games; 30 fumbles lost, 25 interceptions)

SEASON—Defense

Total Defense

FEWEST YARDS ALLOWED PER GAME
69.9—Santa Clara, 1937 (559 in 8)

FEWEST RUSHING AND PASSING TOUCHDOWNS ALLOWED PER GAME
0.0—Duke, 1938; Tennessee, 1939

LOWEST AVERAGE YARDS ALLOWED PER PLAY
1.7—Texas A&M, 1939 (447 for 763)

LOWEST AVERAGE YARDS ALLOWED PER PLAY
(Min. 600-699 plays) 2.5—Nebraska, 1967 (627 for 1,576)
(Min. 700 plays) 2.7—Toledo, 1971 (734 for 1,795)

MOST YARDS ALLOWED PER GAME
553.0—Maryland, 1993 (6,083 in 11)

TEAM RECORDS—RUSHING DEFENSE

Rushing Defense

FEWEST YARDS ALLOWED PER GAME
17.0—Penn St., 1947 (153 in 9)

MOST YARDS LOST BY OPPONENTS PER GAME
70.1—Wyoming, 1968 (701 in 10, 458 rushes)

LOWEST AVERAGE YARDS ALLOWED PER RUSH
(Min. 240-399 rushes) 0.6—Penn St., 1947 (240 for 153)
(Min. 400-499 rushes) 1.3—North Texas, 1966 (408 for 513)
(Min. 500 rushes) 2.1—Nebraska, 1971 (500 for 1,031)

Pass Defense

FEWEST YARDS ALLOWED PER GAME
13.1—Penn St., 1938 (105 in 8)

FEWEST YARDS ALLOWED PER ATTEMPT
(Min. 200-299 atts.) 3.4—Toledo, 1970 (251 for 856)
(Min. 300 atts.) 3.8—Notre Dame, 1967 (306 for 1,158)

FEWEST YARDS ALLOWED PER COMPLETION
(Min. 100-149 comps.) 8.8—Michigan, 1997 (145 for 1,275)
(Min. 150 comps.) 9.5—Notre Dame, 1993 (263 for 2,502)

LOWEST COMPLETION PERCENTAGE ALLOWED
(Min. 150-199 atts.) 31.1%—Virginia, 1952 (50 of 161)
(Min. 200 atts.) 33.3%—Notre Dame, 1967 (102 of 306)

FEWEST TOUCHDOWNS ALLOWED BY PASSING
0—By many teams. Most recent: LSU, 1959; North Texas, 1959

LOWEST PASS EFFICIENCY DEFENSIVE RATING (Since 1990)
65.7—Kansas St., 1999 (315 attempts, 118 completions, 21 interceptions, 1,364 yards, 5 TDs)

MOST PASSES INTERCEPTED BY PER GAME
4.1—Pennsylvania, 1940 (33 in 8)

HIGHEST PERCENTAGE INTERCEPTED BY (Min. 200 Attempts)
17.9%—Army, 1944 (36 of 201)

MOST YARDS GAINED ON INTERCEPTION RETURNS
782—Tennessee, 1971 (25 interceptions)

MOST INTERCEPTION YARDS PER GAME
72.5—Texas, 1943 (580 in 8)

HIGHEST AVERAGE PER INTERCEPTION RETURN
(Min. 10-14 ints.) 36.3—Oregon St., 1959 (12 for 436)
(Min. 15 ints.) 31.3—Tennessee, 1971 (25 for 782)

MOST TOUCHDOWNS ON INTERCEPTION RETURNS
7—Tennessee, 1971 (25 interceptions; 287 pass attempts against)

Punting

MOST OPPONENT'S PUNTS BLOCKED BY
11—Arkansas St., 1975 (11 games, 95 punts against)

Punt Returns

FEWEST RETURNS ALLOWED
5—Notre Dame, 1968 (52 yards); Nebraska, 1995 (12 yards)

FEWEST YARDS ALLOWED
2—Miami (Fla.), 1989 (12 returns)

LOWEST AVERAGE YARDS ALLOWED PER PUNT RETURN
0.2—Miami (Fla.), 1989 (12 for 2 yards)

Kickoff Returns

LOWEST AVERAGE YARDS ALLOWED PER KICKOFF RETURN
8.3—Richmond, 1951 (23 for 192 yards)

Opponent's Kicks Blocked

MOST PAT KICKS BLOCKED
Season
6—Duke, 1993

Scoring

FEWEST POINTS ALLOWED PER GAME
0.0—Duke, 1938 (9 games); Tennessee, 1939 (10 games)

MOST POINTS ALLOWED
553—La.-Lafayette, 1997 (11 games)

MOST POINTS ALLOWED PER GAME
50.3—La.-Lafayette, 1997 (553 in 11)

Fumbles

MOST OPPONENT'S FUMBLES RECOVERED
36—North Texas, 1972; Brigham Young, 1977

MOST TOUCHDOWNS SCORED ON FUMBLE RETURNS
7—Georgia Tech, 1998

Turnovers (Takeaways)

(Opponent's Fumbles Recovered and Passes Intercepted)

MOST OPPONENT'S TURNOVERS
57—Tennessee, 1970 (21 fumbles recovered, 36 interceptions)

MOST OPPONENT'S TURNOVERS PER GAME
5.4—Wyoming, 1950 (49 in 9); Pennsylvania, 1950 (49 in 9); UCLA; 1952 (49 in 9); UCLA 1954 (49 in 9)

HIGHEST MARGIN OF TURNOVERS PER GAME OVER OPPONENTS
4.0—UCLA, 1952 (36 in 9; 13 giveaways vs. 49 takeaways)
Also holds total-margin record at 36

HIGHEST MARGIN OF TURNOVERS PER GAME BY OPPONENTS
3.1—Southern Miss., 1969 (31 in 10; 45 giveaways vs. 14 takeaways)

Defensive Extra Points

MOST DEFENSIVE EXTRA-POINT ATTEMPTS AGAINST
2—La.-Lafayette, 1988 (2 kick returns, none scored); Notre Dame, 1988 (2 kick returns, 1 scored); Akron, 1990 (2 interception returns, none scored); Oklahoma, 1992 (2 kick returns, 2 scored); Oklahoma, 1997 (2 kick returns, 1 scored); Texas, 1998 (2 kick returns, 2 scored)

MOST DEFENSIVE EXTRA POINTS SCORED AGAINST
2—Oklahoma, 1992 (vs. Texas Tech, Sept. 3, and vs. Oklahoma St., Nov. 14); Texas, 1998 (vs. Iowa St., Oct. 3)

Safeties

MOST SAFETIES BY A DEFENSE
4—Wisconsin, 1951

Consecutive Records

MOST CONSECUTIVE VICTORIES
47—Oklahoma, 1953-57

MOST CONSECUTIVE GAMES WITHOUT DEFEAT
48—Oklahoma, 1953-57 (1 tie)

MOST CONSECUTIVE LOSSES
34—Northwestern, from Sept. 22, 1979, vs. Syracuse through Sept. 18, 1982, vs. Miami (Ohio) (ended with 31-6 victory over Northern Ill., Sept. 25, 1982)

MOST CONSECUTIVE GAMES WITHOUT A VICTORY ON THE ROAD
46—Northwestern (including one tie), from Nov. 23, 1974, through Oct. 30, 1982

MOST CONSECUTIVE GAMES WITHOUT A TIE (Includes Bowl Games)
345—Miami (Fla.), from Nov. 11, 1968, through 1995 season (after 1995 tiebreaker used in Division I-A)

MOST CONSECUTIVE GAMES WITHOUT BEING SHUT OUT
312—Brigham Young (current), from Oct. 3, 1975

MOST CONSECUTIVE SHUTOUTS (Regular Season)
17—Tennessee, from Nov. 5, 1938, through Oct. 12, 1940

MOST CONSECUTIVE QUARTERS OPPONENTS HELD SCORELESS (Regular Season)
71—Tennessee, from 2nd quarter vs. LSU, Oct. 29, 1938, to 2nd quarter vs. Alabama, Oct. 19, 1940

MOST CONSECUTIVE VICTORIES AT HOME
58—Miami (Fla.) (Orange Bowl), from Oct. 12, 1985, to Sept. 24, 1994 (lost to Washington, 38-20)

MOST CONSECUTIVE WINNING SEASONS (All-Time)
42—Notre Dame, 1889-32 (no teams in 1890 & 1891)

MOST CONSECUTIVE WINNING SEASONS (Current)
38—Nebraska, from 1962

MOST CONSECUTIVE NON-LOSING SEASONS
49—Penn St., 1939-87

MOST CONSECUTIVE LOSING SEASONS
28—Oregon St., 1971-98

MOST CONSECUTIVE NON-WINNING SEASONS
28—Rice, 1964-91 (includes two .500 seasons)

MOST CONSECUTIVE SEASONS WINNING NINE OR MORE GAMES
31—Nebraska (current), from 1969

MOST CONSECUTIVE SEASONS PLAYING IN A BOWL GAME
31—Nebraska (current), from 1969

MOST CONSECUTIVE GAMES SCORING ON A PASS
62—Florida, from Oct. 1, 1992, to Oct. 4, 1997

MOST CONSECUTIVE GAMES PASSING FOR 200 YARDS OR MORE
64—Brigham Young, from Sept. 13, 1980, through Oct. 19, 1985

MOST CONSECUTIVE GAMES INTERCEPTING A PASS (Includes Bowl Games)
39—Virginia, from Nov. 6, 1993, through Nov. 29, 1996

MOST CONSECUTIVE GAMES WITHOUT POSTING A SHUTOUT
268—New Mexico St. (current), from Sept. 21, 1974

MOST CONSECUTIVE EXTRA POINTS MADE
262—Syracuse, from Nov. 18, 1978, to Sept. 9, 1989 (By the following kickers: Dave Jacobs, last PAT of 1978; Gary Anderson, 72 from 1979 through 1981; Russ Carpentieri, 17 in 1982; Don McAulay, 62 from 1983 through 1985; Tim Vesling, 71 in 1986

and 1987; Kevin Greene, 37 in 1988; John Biskup, 2 in 1989.)

MOST CONSECUTIVE STADIUM SELLOUTS
233—Nebraska (current), from 1962

Additional Records

HIGHEST-SCORING TIE GAME
52-52—Brigham Young & San Diego St., Nov. 16, 1991

MOST TIE GAMES IN A SEASON
4—Temple, 1937 (9 games); UCLA, 1939 (10 games); Central Mich., 1991 (11 games)

MOST SCORELESS TIE GAMES IN A SEASON
4—Temple, 1937 (9 games)

MOST CONSECUTIVE SCORELESS TIE GAMES
2—Georgia Tech, 1938, vs. Florida, Nov. 19 & vs. Georgia, Nov. 26; Alabama, 1954, vs. Georgia, Oct. 30 & vs. Tulane, Nov. 6

LAST TIE GAME
Nov. 25, 1995—Wisconsin 3, Illinois 3

LAST SCORELESS TIE GAME
Nov. 19, 1983—Oregon & Oregon St.

MOST POINTS OVERCOME TO WIN A GAME (Between Division I-A Teams)
31—Maryland (42) vs. Miami (Fla.) (40), Nov. 10, 1984 (trailed 31-0 with 12:35 remaining in 3rd quarter); Ohio St. (41) vs. Minnesota (37), Oct. 28, 1989 (trailed 31-0 with 4:29 remaining in 2nd quarter)
30—California (42) vs. Oregon (41), Oct. 2, 1993 (trailed 30-0 in 2nd quarter)

MOST POINTS SCORED IN FOURTH QUARTER TO WIN OR TIE A GAME
28—Utah (28) vs. Arizona (27), Nov. 4, 1972 (trailed 27-0 beginning 4th quarter); Washington St. (49) vs. Stanford (42), Oct. 20, 1984 (trailed 42-14 with 5:38 remaining in 3rd quarter and scored 35 consecutive points); Florida St. (31) vs. Florida (31), Nov. 26, 1994 (trailed 31-3 beginning 4th quarter)

MOST POINTS SCORED IN A BRIEF PERIOD OF TIME BY ONE TEAM
41 in 2:55 of possession time during six drives—Nebraska (69) vs. Colorado (19), Oct. 22, 1983 (6 TDs, 5 PATs in 3rd quarter. Drives occurred during 9:10 of total playing time in the period)
21 in 1:24 of total playing time—San Jose St. (42) vs. Fresno St. (7), Nov. 17, 1990 (3 TDs, 3 PATs in 2nd quarter; 1:17 of possession time on two drives and one intercepted pass returned for a TD)
15 in :10 of total playing time—Utah (22) vs. Air Force (21), Oct. 21, 1995 (2 TDs, 2-point conversion, 1 PAT. Drives occurred during :41 of 4th quarter)

MOST POINTS SCORED IN A BRIEF PERIOD OF TIME BY BOTH TEAMS
29 in 1:34 of possession time during four drives (4th quarter)—Hawaii (62) vs. San Jose St. (41), Nov. 6, 1999 (4 TDs, 1 PAT, two 2-point conversions). San Jose St. scores TDs on a blocked punt and pass reception (adds two 2-point conversions); Hawaii scores TDs on rush and interception return (adds PAT)

MOST IMPROVED WON-LOST RECORD
8½ games—Hawaii, 1999 (9-4-0, including a bowl win) from 1998 (0-12-0)

MOST IMPROVED WON-LOST RECORD AFTER WINLESS SEASON
8½ games—Hawaii, 1999 (9-4-0, including a bowl win) from 1998 (0-12-0)

ALL-TIME LEADERS—TOTAL OFFENSE

Annual Champions, All-Time Leaders

Total Offense

CAREER YARDS PER GAME
(Minimum 5,500 yards)

Player, Team	Years	G	Plays	Yards	TDR‡	Yd. PG
Tim Rattay, Louisiana Tech	1997-99	33	1,705	12,618	117	*382.4
Chris Vargas, Nevada	1992-93	20	872	6,417	48	320.9
Ty Detmer, Brigham Young	1988-91	46	1,795	*14,665	*135	318.8
Daunte Culpepper, UCF	1996-98	33	1,468	10,344	91	313.5
Mike Perez, San Jose St.	1986-87	20	875	6,182	37	309.1
Josh Wallwork, Wyoming	1995-96	22	845	6,753	60	307.0
Doug Gaynor, Long Beach St.	1984-85	22	1,067	6,710	45	305.0
Tony Eason, Illinois	1981-82	22	1,016	6,589	43	299.5
Chad Pennington, Marshall	1997-99	36	1,433	10,758	104	298.9
David Klingler, Houston	1988-91	32	1,439	9,363	93	292.6
Steve Sarkisian, Brigham Young	1995-96	25	953	7,253	56	290.1
Chris Redman, Louisville	1996-99	42	*1,846	12,129	87	288.8
Steve Young, Brigham Young	1981-83	31	1,177	8,817	74	284.4
Tim Couch, Kentucky	1996-98	29	1,338	8,160	78	281.4
Doug Flutie, Boston College	1981-84	42	1,558	11,317	74	269.5
Brent Snyder, Utah St.	1987-88	22	1,040	5,916	43	268.9
Scott Mitchell, Utah	1987-89	33	1,306	8,836	71	267.8
Mike Maxwell, Nevada	1993-95	27	946	7,226	66	267.6
Anthony Calvillo, Utah St.	1992-93	22	983	5,838	43	265.4
Shane Matthews, Florida	1989-92	35	1,397	9,241	82	264.0
Joe Hughes, Wyoming	1992-93	23	911	6,007	49	261.2
Larry Egger, Utah	1985-86	22	903	5,651	42	256.9
Jim Plunkett, Stanford	1968-70	31	1,174	7,887	62	254.4
Stoney Case, New Mexico	1991-94	42	1,673	10,651	98	253.6
Tim Lester, Western Mich.	1996-99	44	1,747	11,081	91	251.8
Troy Kopp, Pacific (Cal.)	1989-92	40	1,595	10,037	90	250.9
Peyton Manning, Tennessee	1994-97	44	1,534	11,020	101	250.5
Randall Cunningham, UNLV	1982-84	33	1,330	8,224	67	249.2
Michael Bishop, Kansas St.	1997-98	23	804	5,715	59	248.5
Joe Hamilton, Georgia Tech	1996-99	43	1,521	10,640	83	247.4
Eric Zeier, Georgia	1991-94	44	1,560	10,841	71	246.4
Erik Wilhelm, Oregon St.	1985-88	37	1,689	9,062	55	244.9
Todd Dillon, Long Beach St.	1982-83	23	1,031	5,588	38	243.0
Bernie Kosar, Miami (Fla.)	1983-84	23	847	5,585	48	242.8
Charlie Batch, Eastern Mich.	1994-97	32	1,179	7,715	58	241.1
Alex Van Pelt, Pittsburgh	1989-92	45	1,570	10,814	58	240.3
Steve Stenstrom, Stanford	1991-94	41	1,550	9,825	75	239.6
Cade McNown, UCLA	1995-98	44	1,429	10,487	74	238.3
Jack Trudeau, Illinois	1981, 83-85	34	1,318	8,096	56	238.1
Chuck Hixson, Southern Methodist	1968-70	29	1,358	6,884	50	237.4
Robbie Bosco, Brigham Young	1983-85	35	1,159	8,299	72	237.1
Dan Robinson, Hawaii	1997-99	25	1,058	5,920	45	236.8
Dan McGwire, Iowa/San Diego St.	1986-87, 89-90	32	1,067	7,557	50	236.2
Johnny Bright, Drake	1949-51	25	825	5,903	64	236.1
Kordell Stewart, Colorado	1991-94	33	1,087	7,770	48	235.5

*Record. ‡Touchdowns-responsible-for are player's TDs scored and passed for.

SEASON YARDS PER GAME

Player, Team	Year	G	Plays	Yards	TDR‡	Yd. PG
David Klingler, Houston	†1990	11	*704	*5,221	*55	*474.6
Andre Ware, Houston	†1989	11	628	4,661	49	423.7
Ty Detmer, Brigham Young	1990	12	635	5,022	45	418.5
Tim Rattay, Louisiana Tech	†1998	12	602	4,840	47	403.3
Mike Maxwell, Nevada	†1995	9	443	3,623	34	402.6
Chris Redman, Louisville	1998	10	513	4,009	31	400.9
Steve Young, Brigham Young	†1983	11	531	4,346	41	395.1
Chris Vargas, Nevada	†1993	11	535	4,332	35	393.8
Scott Mitchell, Utah	†1988	11	589	4,299	29	390.8
Jim McMahon, Brigham Young	†1980	12	540	4,627	53	385.6
Tim Rattay, Louisiana Tech	†1999	10	562	3,810	35	381.0
Daunte Culpepper, UCF	1998	11	543	4,153	40	377.5
Tim Couch, Kentucky	1998	11	617	4,151	37	377.4
David Neill, Nevada	1998	9	409	3,351	31	372.3
Ty Detmer, Brigham Young	1989	12	497	4,433	38	369.4
Troy Kopp, Pacific (Cal.)	1990	9	485	3,276	32	364.0
Tim Rattay, Louisiana Tech	1997	11	541	3,968	35	360.7
Josh Wallwork, Wyoming	†1996	12	525	4,209	35	350.8
Jim McMahon, Brigham Young	†1981	10	487	3,458	30	345.8
Joe Hamilton, Georgia Tech	1999	11	459	3,794	35	344.9
Jimmy Klingler, Houston	†1992	11	544	3,768	34	342.5
Shaun King, Tulane	1998	11	468	3,764	46	342.2
Tim Couch, Kentucky	1997	11	613	3,759	40	341.7
Cody Ledbetter, New Mexico St.	1995	11	543	3,724	32	338.6
Anthony Dilweg, Duke	1988	11	539	3,713	26	337.6

Louisiana Tech's Tim Rattay is Division I-A's total offense leader in career yards per game with 382.4. His 12,618 total yards ranks second behind Ty Detmer of Brigham Young.

ALL-TIME LEADERS—TOTAL OFFENSE

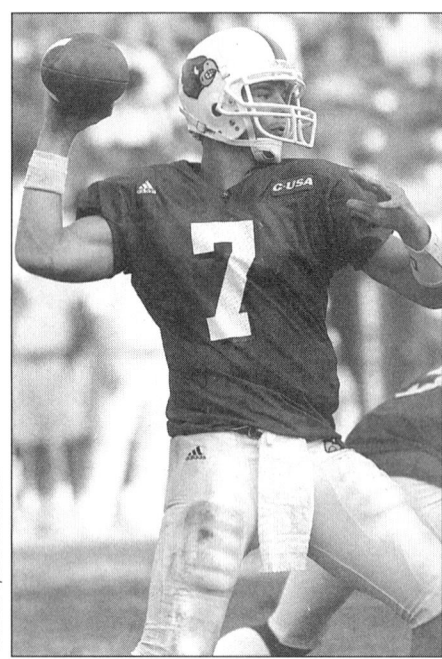

Chris Redman of Louisville racked up 12,129 total offense yards from 1996-99, placing him third on the Division I-A list.

Player, Team	Year	G	Plays	Yards	TDR‡	Yd. PG
Drew Brees, Purdue	1999	11	564	3,712	25	337.5
Bill Anderson, Tulsa	†1965	10	580	3,343	35	334.3
Ty Detmer, Brigham Young	†1991	12	478	4,001	39	333.4
Dan McGwire, San Diego St.	1990	11	484	3,664	28	333.1
Mike McCoy, Utah	1993	12	529	3,969	21	330.8

*Record. †National champion. ‡Touchdowns-responsible-for are player's TDs scored and passed for.

CAREER YARDS

Player, Team	Years	Plays	Rush	Pass	Total	Avg.
Ty Detmer, Brigham Young	1988-91	1,795	-366	*15,031	*14,665	#8.17
Tim Rattay, Louisiana Tech	1997-99	1,705	-128	12,746	12,618	7.40
Chris Redman, Louisville	1996-99	*1,846	-412	12,541	12,129	6.57
Doug Flutie, Boston College	1981-84	1,558	738	10,579	11,317	7.26
Tim Lester, Western Mich.	1996-99	1,747	-218	11,299	11,081	6.34
Peyton Manning, Tennessee	1994-97	1,534	-181	11,201	11,020	7.18
Eric Zeier, Georgia	1991-94	1,560	-312	11,153	10,841	6.95
Alex Van Pelt, Pittsburgh	1989-92	1,570	-99	10,913	10,814	6.89
Chad Pennington, Marshall	1997-99	1,433	60	10,698	10,758	7.51
Stoney Case, New Mexico	1991-94	1,673	1,191	9,460	10,651	6.37
Joe Hamilton, Georgia Tech	1996-99	1,521	1,758	8,882	10,640	7.00
Todd Santos, San Diego St.	1984-87	1,722	-912	11,425	10,513	6.11
Danny Wuerffel, Florida	1993-96	1,355	-375	10,875	10,500	7.75
Cade McNown, UCLA	1995-98	1,429	479	10,008	10,487	7.34
Daunte Culpepper, UCF	1996-98	1,468	1,003	9,341	10,344	7.05
Kevin Sweeney, Fresno St.	$1982-86	1,700	-371	10,623	10,252	6.03
Troy Kopp, Pacific (Cal.)	1989-92	1,595	-221	10,258	10,037	6.29
Donovan McNabb, Syracuse	1995-98	1,403	1,561	8,389	9,950	7.09
Steve Stenstrom, Stanford	1991-94	1,550	-706	10,531	9,825	6.34
Brian McClure, Bowling Green	1982-85	1,630	-506	10,280	9,774	6.00
Jim McMahon, Brigham Young	1977-78, 80-81	1,325	187	9,536	9,723	7.34
Glenn Foley, Boston College	1990-93	1,440	-340	10,042	9,702	6.74
Shaun King, Tulane	1995-98	1,516	1,046	8,419	9,468	6.25
Terrence Jones, Tulane	1985-88	1,620	1,761	7,684	9,445	5.83
David Klingler, Houston	1988-91	1,439	-103	9,466	9,363	6.51
Shawn Jones, Georgia Tech	1989-92	1,609	855	8,441	9,296	5.78
Shane Matthews, Florida	1989-92	1,397	-46	9,287	9,241	6.61
Spence Fischer, Duke	1992-95	1,612	89	9,021	9,110	5.65
T. J. Rubley, Tulsa	1987-89, 91	1,541	-244	9,324	9,080	5.89
Brad Tayles, Western Mich.	1989-92	1,675	354	8,717	9,071	5.42
John Elway, Stanford	1979-82	1,505	-279	9,349	9,070	6.03
Erik Wilhelm, Oregon St.	1985-88	1,689	-331	9,393	9,062	5.37
Ben Bennett, Duke	1980-83	1,582	-553	9,614	9,061	5.73
Chuck Long, Iowa	$1981-85	1,410	-176	9,210	9,034	6.41
Todd Ellis, South Carolina	1986-89	1,517	-497	9,519	9,022	5.95
Jason Martin, Louisiana Tech	1993-96	1,439	-127	9,066	8,939	6.21
Tom Hodson, LSU	1986-89	1,307	-177	9,115	8,938	6.84
Jake Delhomme, La.-Lafayette	1993-96	1,476	-340	9,216	8,876	6.01
Scott Mitchell, Utah	1987-89	1,306	-145	8,981	8,836	6.77
Steve Young, Brigham Young	1981-83	1,177	1,084	7,733	8,817	7.49
Brian Mitchell, La.-Lafayette	1986-89	1,521	3,335	5,447	8,782	5.77
Marvin Graves, Syracuse	1990-93	1,373	286	8,466	8,752	6.37
Jeremy Leach, New Mexico	1988-91	1,695	-762	9,382	8,620	5.09
Jake Plummer, Arizona St.	1993-96	1,375	-107	8,626	8,519	6.20
Robert Hall, Texas Tech	1990-93	1,341	581	7,908	8,489	6.33
Mark Herrmann, Purdue	1977-80	1,354	-744	9,188	8,444	6.24
Mike McCoy, Long Beach St./Utah	1991, 92-94	1,315	97	8,342	8,439	6.42
Robbie Bosco, Brigham Young	1983-85	1,158	-101	8,400	8,299	7.17
Troy Taylor, California	1986-89	1,490	110	8,126	8,236	5.53
Randall Cunningham, UNLV	1982-84	1,330	204	8,020	8,224	6.18
Cody Ledbetter, New Mexico St.	1991, 93-95	1,362	727	7,480	8,207	6.03
Steve Taneyhill, South Carolina	1992-95	1,423	-392	8,555	8,163	5.74
Tim Couch, Kentucky	1996-98	1,338	-275	8,435	8,160	6.10
Ryan Huzjak, Toledo	1993-96	1,478	1,480	6,672	8,152	5.52
Steve Slayden, Duke	1984-87	1,546	125	8,004	8,129	5.26
Jack Trudeau, Illinois	1981, 83-85	1,318	-50	8,146	8,096	6.14
Mark Barsotti, Fresno St.	1988-91	1,192	768	7,321	8,089	6.79
Gene Swick, Toledo	1972-75	1,579	807	7,267	8,074	5.11
Andre Ware, Houston	1987-89	1,194	-144	8,202	8,058	6.75
James Brown, Texas	1994-97	1,196	411	7,638	8,049	6.73
Len Williams, Northwestern	1990-93	1,614	542	7,486	8,028	4.97
Billy Blanton, San Diego St.	1993-96	1,108	-151	8,165	8,014	7.23

*Record. $See page 6 for explanation. #Record for minimum of 7,500 yards.

CAREER YARDS RECORD PROGRESSION
(Record Yards—Player, Team, Seasons Played)

3,481—Davey O'Brien, TCU, 1936-38; **3,882**—Paul Christman, Missouri, 1938-40; **4,602**—Frank Sinkwich, Georgia, 1940-42; **4,627**—Bob Fenimore, Oklahoma St., 1943-46; **4,871**—Charlie Justice, North Carolina, 1946-49; **5,903**—Johnny Bright, Drake, 1949-51; **6,354**—Virgil Carter, Brigham Young, 1964-66; **6,568**—Steve Ramsey, North Texas, 1967-69; **7,887**—Jim Plunkett, Stanford, 1968-70; **8,074**—Gene Swick, Toledo, 1972-75; **8,444**—Mark Herrmann, Purdue, 1977-80; **9,723**—Jim McMahon, Brigham Young, 1977-78, 1980-81; **11,317**—Doug Flutie, Boston College, 1981-84; **14,665**—Ty Detmer, Brigham Young, 1988-91.

ALL-TIME LEADERS—TOTAL OFFENSE

SEASON YARDS

Player, Team	Year	G	Plays	Rush	Pass	Total	Avg.
David Klingler, Houston	†1990	11	*704	81	5,140	*5,221	7.42
Ty Detmer, Brigham Young	1990	12	635	-106	*5,188	5,022	7.91
Tim Rattay, Louisiana Tech	†1998	12	602	-103	4,943	4,840	8.04
Andre Ware, Houston	†1989	11	628	-38	4,699	4,661	7.42
Jim McMahon, Brigham Young	†1980	12	540	56	4,571	4,627	8.57
Ty Detmer, Brigham Young	1989	12	497	-127	4,560	4,433	@8.92
Steve Young, Brigham Young	†1983	11	531	444	3,902	4,346	8.18
Chris Vargas, Nevada	†1993	11	535	67	4,265	4,332	8.10
Scott Mitchell, Utah	†1988	11	589	-23	4,322	4,299	7.30
Josh Wallwork, Wyoming	†1996	12	525	119	4,090	4,209	8.02
Daunte Culpepper, UCF	1998	11	543	463	3,690	4,153	7.65
Tim Couch, Kentucky	1998	11	617	-124	4,275	4,151	6.73
Robbie Bosco, Brigham Young	1985	13	578	-132	4,273	4,141	7.16
Chris Redman, Louisville	1998	10	513	-33	4,042	4,009	7.81
Ty Detmer, Brigham Young	†1991	12	478	-30	4,031	4,001	8.37
Steve Sarkisian, Brigham Young	1996	14	486	-44	4,027	3,983	8.20
Mike McCoy, Utah	1993	12	529	109	3,860	3,969	7.50
Tim Rattay, Louisiana Tech	†1997	11	541	87	3,881	3,968	7.33
Robbie Bosco, Brigham Young	†1984	12	543	57	3,875	3,932	7.24
Drew Brees, Purdue	1998	12	575	168	3,753	3,921	6.82
Chad Pennington, Marshall	1999	12	460	105	3,799	3,904	8.49
Tim Rattay, Louisiana Tech	†1999	10	562	-112	3,922	3,810	6.78
Joe Hamilton, Georgia Tech	1999	11	459	734	3,060	3,794	8.27
Peyton Manning, Tennessee	1997	12	526	-30	3,819	3,789	7.20
Jimmy Klingler, Houston	†1992	11	544	-50	3,818	3,768	6.93
Shaun King, Tulane	1998	11	468	532	3,232	3,764	8.04
Dan Robinson, Hawaii	1999	12	616	-91	3,853	3,762	6.11
Tim Couch, Kentucky	1997	11	613	-125	3,884	3,759	6.13
Cody Ledbetter, New Mexico St.	1995	11	543	223	3,501	3,724	6.86
Anthony Dilweg, Duke	1988	11	539	-111	3,824	3,713	6.89
Drew Brees, Purdue	1999	11	564	181	3,531	3,712	6.58
Todd Santos, San Diego St.	†1987	12	562	-244	3,932	3,688	6.56
Troy Kopp, Pacific (Cal.)	1991	12	496	-81	3,767	3,686	7.43
Dan McGwire, San Diego St.	1990	11	484	-169	3,833	3,664	7.57
Stoney Case, New Mexico	1994	12	549	532	3,117	3,649	6.65
Jon Denton, UNLV	1996	12	594	38	3,591	3,629	6.11
Mike Maxwell, Nevada	†1995	9	443	12	3,611	3,623	8.18
David Neill, Nevada	1999	11	523	209	3,402	3,611	6.90
Tim Lester, Western Mich.	1999	12	525	-35	3,639	3,604	6.86
Doug Flutie, Boston College	1984	11	448	149	3,454	3,603	8.04

*Record. †National champion. @ Record for minimum of 3,000 yards.

SINGLE-GAME YARDS

Yds.	Rush	Pass	Player, Team (Opponent)	Date
732	16	716	David Klingler, Houston (Arizona St.)	Dec. 2, 1990
696	6	690	Matt Vogler, TCU (Houston)	Nov. 3, 1990
625	62	563	David Klingler, Houston (TCU)	Nov. 3, 1990
625	-6	631	Scott Mitchell, Utah (Air Force)	Oct. 15, 1988
612	-1	613	Jimmy Klingler, Houston (Rice)	Nov. 28, 1992
603	4	599	Ty Detmer, Brigham Young (San Diego St.)	Nov. 16, 1991
601	37	564	Troy Kopp, Pacific (Cal.) (New Mexico St.)	Oct. 20, 1990
599	86	513	Virgil Carter, Brigham Young (UTEP)	Nov. 5, 1966
597	-22	619	John Walsh, Brigham Young (Utah St.)	Oct. 30, 1993
594	-28	622	Jeremy Leach, New Mexico (Utah)	Nov. 11, 1989
585	-36	621	Dave Wilson, Illinois (Ohio St.)	Nov. 8, 1980
582	-29	611	David Neill, Nevada (New Mexico St.)	Oct. 10, 1998
582	11	571	Marc Wilson, Brigham Young (Utah)	Nov. 5, 1977
578	-14	592	Chris Redman, Louisville (East Caro.)	Nov. 14, 1998
578	6	572	David Klingler, Houston (Eastern Wash.)	Nov. 17, 1990
568	-22	590	Tim Rattay, Louisiana Tech (Nebraska)	Aug. 29, 1998
568	11	557	John Dutton, Nevada (Boise St.)	Nov. 8, 1997
562	25	537	Ty Detmer, Brigham Young (Washington St.)	Sept. 7, 1989
559	13	546	Cody Ledbetter, New Mexico St. (UNLV)	Nov. 18, 1995
554	9	545	Rusty LaRue, Wake Forest (North Carolina St.)	Nov. 18, 1995
552	-13	565	Jim McMahon, Brigham Young (Utah)	Nov. 21, 1981
548	12	536	Dave Telford, Fresno St. (Pacific [Cal.])	Oct. 24, 1987
543	-9	552	Mike Maxwell, Nevada (UNLV)	Oct. 28, 1995
541	-20	561	Tim Rattay, Louisiana Tech (UCF)	Oct. 23, 1999
541	6	535	Mike Maxwell, Nevada (Louisiana Tech)	Oct. 21, 1995
540	-45	585	Robbie Bosco, Brigham Young (New Mexico)	Oct. 19, 1985
540	104	436	Archie Manning, Mississippi (Alabama)	Oct. 4, 1969
539	1	538	Jim McMahon, Brigham Young (Colorado St.)	Nov. 7, 1981
538	-1	539	Tim Rattay, Louisiana Tech (Boise St.)	Oct. 3, 1998
537	65	472	Anthony Calvillo, Utah St. (Brigham Young)	Oct. 30, 1993
537	-1	538	Chris Vargas, Nevada (UNLV)	Oct. 2, 1993
537	2	535	Shane Montgomery, North Carolina St. (Duke)	Nov. 11, 1989

DIVISION I-A

Yds.	Rush	Pass	Player, Team (Opponent)	Date
537	-24	561	Tony Adams, Utah St. (Utah)	Nov. 11, 1972
536	58	478	Tim Schade, Minnesota (Penn St.)	Sept. 4, 1993
536	28	508	Mike Perez, San Jose St. (Pacific [Cal.])	Oct. 25, 1986
534	-17	551	Jose Davis, Kent (Central Fla.)	Oct. 4, 1997
532	0	532	Jeff Van Raaphorst, Arizona St. (Florida St.)	Nov. 3, 1984
531	-11	542	Ryan Fien, Idaho (Wyoming)	Aug. 31, 1996
531	13	518	Jeff Graham, Long Beach St. (Hawaii)	Oct. 29, 1988

ANNUAL CHAMPIONS

Year	Player, Team	Class	Plays	Rush	Pass	Total
1937	Byron "Whizzer" White, Colorado	Sr.	224	1,121	475	1,596
1938	Davey O'Brien, TCU	Sr.	291	390	1,457	1,847
1939	Kenny Washington, UCLA	Sr.	259	811	559	1,370
1940	Johnny Knolla, Creighton	Sr.	298	813	607	1,420
1941	Bud Schwenk, Washington (Mo.)	Sr.	354	471	1,457	1,928
1942	Frank Sinkwich, Georgia	Sr.	341	795	1,392	2,187
1943	Bob Hoernschemeyer, Indiana	Fr.	355	515	1,133	1,648
1944	Bob Fenimore, Oklahoma St.	So.	241	897	861	1,758
1945	Bob Fenimore, Oklahoma St.	Jr.	203	1,048	593	1,641
1946	Travis Tidwell, Auburn	Fr.	339	772	943	1,715
1947	Fred Enke, Arizona	So.	329	535	1,406	1,941
1948	Stan Heath, Nevada	Sr.	233	-13	2,005	1,992
1949	Johnny Bright, Drake	So.	275	975	975	1,950
1950	Johnny Bright, Drake	Jr.	320	1,232	1,168	2,400
1951	Dick Kazmaier, Princeton	Sr.	272	861	966	1,827
1952	Ted Marchibroda, Detroit	Sr.	305	176	1,637	1,813
1953	Paul Larson, California	Jr.	262	141	1,431	1,572
1954	George Shaw, Oregon	Sr.	276	178	1,358	1,536
1955	George Welsh, Navy	Sr.	203	29	1,319	1,348
1956	John Brodie, Stanford	Sr.	295	9	1,633	1,642
1957	Bob Newman, Washington St.	Jr.	263	53	1,391	1,444
1958	Dick Bass, Pacific (Cal.)	Jr.	218	1,361	79	1,440
1959	Dick Norman, Stanford	Jr.	319	55	1,963	2,018
1960	Bill Kilmer, UCLA	Sr.	292	803	1,086	1,889
1961	Dave Hoppmann, Iowa St.	Jr.	320	920	718	1,638
1962	Terry Baker, Oregon St.	Sr.	318	538	1,738	2,276
1963	George Mira, Miami (Fla.)	Sr.	394	163	2,155	2,318
1964	Jerry Rhome, Tulsa	Sr.	470	258	2,870	3,128
1965	Bill Anderson, Tulsa	Sr.	580	-121	3,464	3,343
1966	Virgil Carter, Brigham Young	Sr.	388	363	2,182	2,545
1967	Sal Olivas, New Mexico St.	Sr.	368	-41	2,225	2,184
1968	Greg Cook, Cincinnati	Sr.	507	-62	3,272	3,210
1969	Dennis Shaw, San Diego St.	Sr.	388	12	3,185	3,197

Beginning in 1970, ranked on per-game (instead of total) yards

Year	Player, Team	Class	G	Plays	Rush	Pass	Total	Avg.
1970	Pat Sullivan, Auburn	Jr.	10	333	270	2,586	2,856	285.6
1971	Gary Huff, Florida St.	Jr.	11	386	-83	2,736	2,653	241.2
1972	Don Strock, Virginia Tech	Sr.	11	480	-73	3,243	3,170	288.2
1973	Jesse Freitas, San Diego St.	Sr.	11	410	-92	2,993	2,901	263.7
1974	Steve Joachim, Temple	Sr.	10	331	277	1,950	2,227	222.7
1975	Gene Swick, Toledo	Sr.	11	490	219	2,487	2,706	246.0
1976	Tommy Kramer, Rice	Sr.	11	562	-45	3,317	3,272	297.5
1977	Doug Williams, Grambling	Sr.	11	377	-57	3,286	3,229	293.5
1978	Mike Ford, Southern Methodist	So.	11	459	-50	3,007	2,957	268.8
1979	Marc Wilson, Brigham Young	Sr.	11	488	-140	3,720	3,580	325.5
1980	Jim McMahon, Brigham Young	Jr.	12	540	56	4,571	4,627	385.6
1981	Jim McMahon, Brigham Young	Sr.	10	487	-97	3,555	3,458	345.8
1982	Todd Dillon, Long Beach St.	Jr.	11	585	70	3,517	3,587	326.1
1983	Steve Young, Brigham Young	Sr.	11	531	444	3,902	4,346	395.1
1984	Robbie Bosco, Brigham Young	Jr.	12	543	57	3,875	3,932	327.7
1985	Jim Everett, Purdue	Sr.	11	518	-62	3,651	3,589	326.3
1986	Mike Perez, San Jose St.	Jr.	9	425	35	2,934	2,969	329.9
1987	Todd Santos, San Diego St.	Sr.	12	562	-244	3,932	3,688	307.3
1988	Scott Mitchell, Utah	So.	11	589	-23	4,322	4,299	390.8
1989	Andre Ware, Houston	Jr.	11	628	-38	4,699	4,661	423.7
1990	David Klingler, Houston	Jr.	11	*704	81	5,140	*5,221	*474.6
1991	Ty Detmer, Brigham Young	Sr.	12	478	-30	4,031	4,001	333.4
1992	Jimmy Klingler, Houston	So.	11	544	-50	3,818	3,768	342.5
1993	Chris Vargas, Nevada	Sr.	11	535	67	4,265	4,332	393.8
1994	Mike Maxwell, Nevada	Jr.	11	477	-39	3,537	3,498	318.0
1995	Mike Maxwell, Nevada	Sr.	9	443	12	3,611	3,623	402.6
1996	Josh Wallwork, Wyoming	Sr.	12	525	119	4,090	4,209	350.8
1997	Tim Rattay, Louisiana Tech	So.	11	541	87	3,881	3,968	360.7
1998	Tim Rattay, Louisiana Tech	Jr.	12	602	-103	4,943	4,840	403.3
1999	Tim Rattay, Louisiana Tech	Sr.	10	562	-112	3,922	3,810	381.0

*Record.

ALL-TIME LEADERS—RUSHING

Rushing

CAREER YARDS PER GAME
(Minimum 2,500 yards)

Player, Team	Years	G	Plays	Yards	TD	Yd. PG
Ed Marinaro, Cornell	1969-71	27	918	4,715	50	*174.6
O. J. Simpson, Southern California	1967-68	19	621	3,124	33	164.4
Herschel Walker, Georgia	1980-82	33	994	5,259	49	159.4
LeShon Johnson, Northern Ill.	1992-93	22	592	3,314	18	150.6
Ron Dayne, Wisconsin	1996-99	43	1,115	*6,397	63	148.8
Marshall Faulk, San Diego St.	1991-93	31	766	4,589	57	148.0
George Jones, San Diego St.	1995-96	19	486	2,810	34	147.9
Tony Dorsett, Pittsburgh	1973-76	43	1,074	6,082	55	141.4
Troy Davis, Iowa St.	1994-96	31	782	4,382	36	141.4
Mike Rozier, Nebraska	1981-83	35	668	4,780	50	136.6
Ricky Williams, Texas	1995-98	46	1,011	6,279	72	136.5
Howard Stevens, Louisville	1971-72	20	509	2,723	25	136.2
Jerome Persell, Western Mich.	1976-78	31	842	4,190	39	135.2
Rudy Mobley, Hardin-Simmons	1942,46	19	414	2,543	32	133.8
Alex Smith, Indiana	1994-96	27	723	3,492	21	129.3
Vaughn Dunbar, Indiana	1990-91	22	565	2,842	24	129.2
Steve Owens, Oklahoma	1967-69	30	905	3,867	56	128.9
Byron Hanspard, Texas Tech	1994-96	33	760	4,219	29	127.8
Charles White, Southern California	1976-79	44	1,023	5,598	46	127.2
Travis Prentice, Miami (Ohio)	1996-99	44	1,138	5,596	*73	127.2
Emmitt Smith, Florida	1987-89	31	700	3,928	36	126.7
Johnny Bright, Drake	1949-51	25	513	3,134	39	125.4
Woody Green, Arizona St.	1971-73	30	601	3,754	33	125.1
Archie Griffin, Ohio St.	1972-75	42	845	5,177	25	123.3
Anthony Thompson, Indiana	1986-89	41	1,089	4,965	64	121.1
Mark Kellar, Northern Ill.	1971-73	31	743	3,745	32	120.8
Paul Gipson, Houston	1966-68	23	447	2,769	25	120.4
John Cappelletti, Penn St.	‡1972-73	22	519	2,639	29	120.0
Brian Pruitt, Central Mich.	1992-94	31	671	3,693	31	119.1
Ahman Green, Nebraska	1995-97	33	574	3,880	42	117.6
Steve Bartalo, Colorado St.	1983-86	41	*1,215	4,813	46	117.4
Louie Giammona, Utah St.	1973-75	30	756	3,499	21	116.6
Paul Palmer, Temple	1983-86	42	948	4,895	39	116.5
Bill Marek, Wisconsin	1972-75	32	719	3,709	44	115.9
Toraino Singleton, UTEP	1994-95	23	560	2,635	19	114.6
Darren Lewis, Texas A&M	1987-90	44	909	5,012	44	113.9
Dick Jauron, Yale	1970-72	26	515	2,947	27	113.3
Bo Jackson, Auburn	1982-85	38	650	4,303	43	113.2
Rashaan Salaam, Colorado	1992-94	27	486	3,057	33	113.2
Joe Morris, Syracuse	1978-81	38	813	4,299	25	113.1
Darnell Autry, Northwestern	1994-96	32	738	3,617	30	113.0
Eugene "Mercury" Morris, West Tex. A&M	1966-68	30	541	3,388	34	112.9

*Record. ‡Defensive back in 1971.

SEASON YARDS PER GAME

Player, Team	Year	G	Plays	Yards	TD	Yd. PG
Barry Sanders, Oklahoma St.	†1988	11	344	*2,628	*37	*238.9
Marcus Allen, Southern California	†1981	11	*403	2,342	22	212.9
Ed Marinaro, Cornell	†1971	9	356	1,881	24	209.0
Troy Davis, Iowa St.	†1996	11	402	2,185	21	198.6
Ricky Williams, Texas	†1998	11	361	2,124	27	193.1
Byron Hanspard, Texas Tech	1996	11	339	2,084	13	189.5
Rashaan Salaam, Colorado	†1994	11	298	2,055	24	186.8
Troy Davis, Iowa St.	†1995	11	345	2,010	15	182.7
Charles White, Southern California	†1979	10	293	1,803	18	180.3
LeShon Johnson, Northern Ill.	†1993	11	327	1,976	12	179.6
Mike Rozier, Nebraska	†1983	12	275	2,148	29	179.0
Tony Dorsett, Pittsburgh	†1976	11	338	1,948	21	177.1
Ollie Matson, San Francisco	†1951	9	245	1,566	20	174.0
Lorenzo White, Michigan St.	†1985	11	386	1,908	17	173.5
Wasean Tait, Toledo	1995	11	357	1,905	20	173.2
Ricky Williams, Texas	†1997	11	279	1,893	25	172.1
Herschel Walker, Georgia	1981	11	385	1,891	18	171.9
Brian Pruitt, Central Mich.	1994	11	292	1,890	20	171.8
O. J. Simpson, Southern California	†1968	10	355	1,709	22	170.9
Ernest Anderson, Oklahoma St.	†1982	11	353	1,877	8	170.6
Ricky Bell, Southern California	†1975	11	357	1,875	13	170.5

*Record. †National champion.

CAREER YARDS

Player, Team	Years	Plays	Yards	Avg.	Long
Ron Dayne, Wisconsin	1996-99	1,115	*6,397	5.74	80
Ricky Williams, Texas	1995-98	1,011	6,279	††6.21	87
Tony Dorsett, Pittsburgh	1973-76	1,074	6,082	5.66	73
Charles White, Southern California	1976-79	1,023	5,598	5.47	79
Travis Prentice, Miami (Ohio)	1996-99	1,138	5,596	4.92	55
Herschel Walker, Georgia	1980-82	994	5,259	5.29	76
Archie Griffin, Ohio St.	1972-75	845	5,177	6.13	75
Darren Lewis, Texas A&M	1987-90	909	5,012	5.51	84
Anthony Thompson, Indiana	1986-89	1,089	4,965	4.56	52
George Rogers, South Carolina	1977-80	902	4,958	5.50	80
Trevor Cobb, Rice	1989-92	1,091	4,948	4.54	79
Paul Palmer, Temple	1983-86	948	4,895	5.16	78
Steve Bartalo, Colorado St.	1983-86	*1,215	4,813	3.96	39
Mike Rozier, Nebraska	1981-83	668	4,780	#7.16	93
Ed Marinaro, Cornell	1969-71	918	4,715	5.14	79
Denvis Manns, New Mexico St.	1995-98	889	4,692	5.28	73
Marcus Allen, Southern California	1978-81	893	4,682	5.24	45
Ted Brown, North Carolina St.	1975-78	860	4,602	5.35	95
Thurman Thomas, Oklahoma St.	1984-87	898	4,595	5.12	66
Marshall Faulk, San Diego St.	1991-93	766	4,589	5.99	71
Terry Miller, Oklahoma St.	1974-77	847	4,582	5.41	81
Kevin Faulk, LSU	1995-98	856	4,557	5.32	81
Darrell Thompson, Minnesota	1986-89	911	4,518	4.96	98
Lorenzo White, Michigan St.	1984-87	991	4,513	4.55	73
Eric Dickerson, Southern Methodist	1979-82	790	4,450	5.63	80
Earl Campbell, Texas	1974-77	765	4,443	5.81	‡‡83
Amos Lawrence, North Carolina	1977-80	881	4,391	4.98	62
Troy Davis, Iowa St.	1994-96	782	4,382	5.60	80
Deland McCullough, Miami (Ohio)	1992-95	949	4,368	4.60	51
David Thompson, Oklahoma St.	1993-96	846	4,318	5.10	91
Bo Jackson, Auburn	1982-85	650	4,303	6.62	80
Joe Morris, Syracuse	1978-81	813	4,299	5.29	75
Reggie Taylor, Cincinnati	1983-86	876	4,242	4.48	‡‡68
Byron Hanspard, Texas Tech	1994-96	760	4,219	5.55	72
Mike Mayweather, Army	1987-90	832	4,212	5.06	52
Jerome Persell, Western Mich.	1976-78	842	4,190	4.98	86
Napoleon McCallum, Navy	$1981-85	908	4,179	4.60	60
Tico Duckett, Michigan St.	1989-92	824	4,176	5.07	88
George Swarn, Miami (Ohio)	1983-86	881	4,172	4.74	98
Errict Rhett, Florida	$1989-93	873	4,163	4.77	49
Curtis Adams, Central Mich.	1981-84	761	4,162	5.47	87
Allen Pinkett, Notre Dame	1982-85	889	4,131	4.65	76
Robert Holcombe, Illinois	1994-97	943	4,105	4.35	67
Robert Lavette, Georgia Tech	1981-84	914	4,066	4.45	83
James Gray, Texas Tech	1986-89	742	4,066	5.48	72
Stump Mitchell, Citadel	1977-80	756	4,062	5.37	77
Dalton Hilliard, LSU	1982-85	882	4,050	4.59	66
Napoleon Kaufman, Washington	1991-94	710	4,041	5.69	91
Charles Alexander, LSU	1975-78	855	4,035	4.72	64
Darrin Nelson, Stanford	1977-78, 80-81	703	4,033	5.74	80

*Record. $See page 6 for explanation. ‡‡Did not score. ††Record for minimum 781 carries. #Record for minimum 414 carries. ¢Active player.

CAREER YARDS RECORD PROGRESSION
(Record Yards—Player, Team, Seasons Played)

1,961—Marshall Goldberg, Pittsburgh, 1936-38; **2,105**—Tom Harmon, Michigan, 1938-40; **2,271**—Frank Sinkwich, Georgia, 1940-42; **2,301**—Bill Daley, Minnesota, 1940-42, Michigan, 1943; **2,957**—Glenn Davis, Army, 1943-46; **3,095**—Eddie Price, Tulane, 1946-49; **3,238**—John Papit, Virginia, 1947-50; **3,381**—Art Luppino, Arizona, 1953-56; **3,388**—Eugene "Mercury" Morris, West Tex. A&M, 1966-68; **3,867**—Steve Owens, Oklahoma, 1967-69; **4,715**—Ed Marinaro, Cornell, 1969-71; **5,177**—Archie Griffin, Ohio St., 1972-75; **6,082**—Tony Dorsett, Pittsburgh, 1973-76; **6,279**—Ricky Williams, Texas, 1995-98; **6,397**—Ron Dayne, Wisconsin, 1996-99.

CAREER RUSHING TOUCHDOWNS

Player, Team	Years	G	TDs
Travis Prentice, Miami (Ohio)	1996-99	44	*73
Ricky Williams, Texas	1995-98	46	72
Anthony Thompson, Indiana	1986-89	41	64
Ron Dayne, Wisconsin	1996-99	43	63
Marshall Faulk, San Diego St.	1991-93	31	57
Steve Owens, Oklahoma	1967-69	30	56
Tony Dorsett, Pittsburgh	1973-76	43	55
Chris Lemon, Nevada	1996-99	44	52
Pete Johnson, Ohio St.	1973-76	41	51
Mike Rozier, Nebraska	1982-83	35	50
Billy Sims, Oklahoma	1975, 77-79	42	50
Ed Marinaro, Cornell	1969-71	27	50
Allen Pinkett, Notre Dame	1982-85	44	49
Herschel Walker, Georgia	1980-82	33	49
Ted Brown, North Carolina St.	1975-78	43	49
Skip Hicks, UCLA	$1993-97	40	48
Brian Mitchell, La.-Lafayette	1986-89	43	47
Barry Sanders, Oklahoma St.	1986-88	30	47
Eric Dickerson, Southern Methodist	1979-82	42	47
Kevin Faulk, LSU	1995-98	46	46
Steve Bartalo, Colorado St.	1983-86	41	46
Charles White, Southern California	1976-79	44	46
Bill Burnett, Arkansas	1968-70	28	46

DIVISION I-A

ALL-TIME LEADERS—RUSHING

Player, Team	Years	G	TDs
James Gray, Texas Tech	1986-89	44	45
Keith Byars, Ohio St.	1982-85	33	45
Robert Lavette, Georgia Tech	1981-84	43	45
Marcus Allen, Southern California	1978-81	44	45
Terry Miller, Oklahoma St.	1974-77	41	45

*Record. (Note: Howard Stevens of Louisville played two years at college division Randolph-Macon, 1968-69, with 33 touchdowns and two years at Louisville, 1971-72, with 25 touchdowns, scoring a total of 58 touchdowns in four years.) $ See page 6 for explanation.

SEASON YARDS

Player, Team	Year	G	Plays	Yards	Avg.
Barry Sanders, Oklahoma St.	†1988	11	344	*2,628	‡7.64
Marcus Allen, Southern California	†1981	11	*403	2,342	5.81
Troy Davis, Iowa St.	†1996	11	402	2,185	5.44
Mike Rozier, Nebraska	†1983	12	275	2,148	#7.81
Ricky Williams, Texas	†1998	11	361	2,124	5.88
Byron Hanspard, Texas Tech	1996	11	339	2,084	6.15
Rashaan Salaam, Colorado	†1994	11	298	2,055	6.90
Troy Davis, Iowa St.	1995	11	345	2,010	5.83
LeShon Johnson, Northern Ill.	†1993	11	327	1,976	6.04
Tony Dorsett, Pittsburgh	†1976	11	338	1,948	5.76
Lorenzo White, Michigan St.	†1985	11	386	1,908	4.94
Wasean Tait, Toledo	1995	11	357	1,905	5.34
Ricky Williams, Texas	†1997	11	279	1,893	6.78
Herschel Walker, Georgia	1981	11	385	1,891	4.91
Brian Pruitt, Central Mich.	1994	11	292	1,890	6.47
Ed Marinaro, Cornell	†1971	9	356	1,881	5.28
Ernest Anderson, Oklahoma St.	†1982	11	353	1,877	5.32
Ahman Green, Nebraska	1997	12	278	1,877	6.75
Ricky Bell, Southern California	†1975	11	357	1,875	5.25
Paul Palmer, Temple	†1986	11	346	1,866	5.39
Ron Dayne, Wisconsin	1996	12	295	1,863	6.32
LaDainian Tomlinson, TCU	†1999	11	268	1,850	6.90
George Jones, San Diego St.	1995	12	305	1,842	6.04
Ron Dayne, Wisconsin	1999	11	303	1,834	6.05
Eddie George, Ohio St.	1995	12	303	1,826	6.03
Charles White, Southern California	†1979	10	293	1,803	6.15
Thomas Jones, Virginia	1999	11	334	1,798	5.38
Anthony Thompson, Indiana	†1989	11	358	1,793	5.01
Obie Graves, Cal St. Fullerton	1978	12	275	1,789	6.51
Travis Prentice, Miami (Ohio)	1998	11	365	1,787	4.90
Bo Jackson, Auburn	1985	11	278	1,786	6.42
George Rogers, South Carolina	†1980	11	297	1,781	6.00
Billy Sims, Oklahoma	†1978	11	231	1,762	7.63
Charles White, Southern California	1978	11	342	1,760	5.15
Robert Newhouse, Houston	1971	11	277	1,757	6.34
Herschel Walker, Georgia	1982	11	335	1,752	5.23
Byron Morris, Texas Tech	1993	11	298	1,752	5.88
Scott Harley, East Caro.	1996	11	307	1,745	5.68
Earl Campbell, Texas	†1977	11	267	1,744	6.53
Mike Pringle, Cal St. Fullerton	1989	11	296	1,727	5.83

*Record. †National champion. ‡Record for minimum 282 carries. #Record for minimum 214 carries.

SINGLE-GAME YARDS

Yds.	Player, Team (Opponent)	Date
406	LaDainian Tomlinson, TCU (UTEP)	Nov. 20, 1999
396	Tony Sands, Kansas (Missouri)	Nov. 23, 1991
386	Marshall Faulk, San Diego St. (Pacific [Cal.])	Sept. 14, 1991
378	Troy Davis, Iowa St. (Missouri)	Sept. 28, 1996
377	Anthony Thompson, Indiana (Wisconsin)	Nov. 11, 1989
376	Travis Prentice, Miami (Ohio) (Akron)	Nov. 6, 1999
373	Astron Whatley, Kent (Eastern Mich.)	Sept. 20, 1997
357	Mike Pringle, Cal St. Fullerton (New Mexico St.)	Nov. 4, 1989
357	Rueben Mayes, Washington St. (Oregon)	Oct. 27, 1984
356	Brian Pruitt, Central Mich. (Toledo)	Nov. 5, 1994
356	Eddie Lee Ivery, Georgia Tech (Air Force)	Nov. 11, 1978
351	Scott Harley, East Caro. (North Carolina St.)	Nov. 30, 1996
350	Ricky Williams, Texas (Iowa St.)	Oct. 3, 1998
350	Eric Allen, Michigan St. (Purdue)	Oct. 30, 1971
349	Paul Palmer, Temple (East Caro.)	Oct. 11, 1986
347	Ricky Bell, Southern California (Washington St.)	Oct. 9, 1976
347	Ron Johnson, Michigan (Wisconsin)	Nov. 16, 1968
343	Tony Jeffery, TCU (Tulane)	Sept. 13, 1986
342	Roosevelt Leaks, Texas (Southern Methodist)	Nov. 3, 1973
342	Charlie Davis, Colorado (Oklahoma St.)	Nov. 13, 1971
340	Eugene "Mercury" Morris, West Tex. A&M (Montana St.)	Oct. 5, 1968
339	Ron Dayne, Wisconsin, (Hawaii)	Nov. 30, 1996
332	Barry Sanders, Oklahoma St. (Texas Tech)	Dec. 3, 1988
329	John Leach, Wake Forest (Maryland)	Nov. 20, 1993
328	Derrick Fenner, North Carolina (Virginia)	Nov. 15, 1986
326	George Swarn, Miami (Ohio) (Eastern Mich.)	Nov. 16, 1985
326	Fred Wendt, UTEP (New Mexico St.)	Nov. 25, 1948

Yds.	Player, Team (Opponent)	Date
325	Andre Davis, TCU (New Mexico)	Sept. 10, 1994
322	LeShon Johnson, Northern Ill. (Southern Ill.)	Oct. 2, 1993
322	Greg Allen, Florida St. (Western Caro.)	Oct. 31, 1981
321	David Thompson, Oklahoma St. (Baylor)	Nov. 23, 1996
321	Frank Mordica, Vanderbilt (Air Force)	Nov. 18, 1978
320	Barry Sanders, Oklahoma St. (Kansas St.)	Oct. 29, 1988
319	Devin West, Missouri (Kansas)	Sept. 12, 1998
319	Andre Herrera, Southern Ill. (Northern Ill.)	Oct. 23, 1976
319	Jim Pilot, New Mexico St. (Hardin-Simmons)	Nov. 25, 1961
318	Ricky Williams, Texas (Rice)	Sept. 26, 1998
317	Rashaan Salaam, Colorado (Texas)	Oct. 1, 1994
316	Emmitt Smith, Florida (New Mexico)	Oct. 21, 1989
316	Mike Adamle, Northwestern (Wisconsin)	Oct. 18, 1969
315	Robert Holcombe, Illinois (Minnesota)	Nov. 16, 1996
314	Eddie George, Ohio St. (Illinois)	Nov. 11, 1995
314	Tavian Banks, Iowa (Tulsa)	Sept. 13, 1997
313	Tim Biakabutuka, Michigan (Ohio St.)	Nov. 25, 1995
312	Mark Brus, Tulsa (New Mexico St.)	Oct. 27, 1990
312	Barry Sanders, Oklahoma St. (Kansas)	Nov. 12, 1988
310	Tony Alford, Colorado St. (Utah)	Oct. 28, 1989
310	Mitchell True, Pacific (Cal.) (UC Davis)	Nov. 18, 1972
308	Stacey Robinson (QB), Northern Ill. (Fresno St.)	Oct. 6, 1990
307	Curtis Kuykendall, Auburn (Miami [Fla.])	Nov. 24, 1944
306	Lamont Jordan, Maryland (Virginia)	Nov. 20, 1999
306	LeShon Johnson, Northern Ill. (Iowa)	Nov. 6, 1993
304	Casey McBeth, Toledo (Akron)	Oct. 22, 1994
304	Barry Sanders, Oklahoma St. (Tulsa)	Oct. 1, 1988
304	Sam Dejarnette, Southern Miss. (Florida St.)	Sept. 25, 1982
304	Bill Marek, Wisconsin (Minnesota)	Nov. 23, 1974
303	Tony Dorsett, Pittsburgh (Notre Dame)	Nov. 15, 1975
302	Troy Davis, Iowa St. (UNLV)	Sept. 23, 1995
302	Jason Davis, Louisiana Tech (La.-Lafayette)	Sept. 29, 1990
302	Kevin Lowe, Wyoming (South Dakota St.)	Nov. 10, 1984
300	LaDainian Tomlinson, TCU (San Jose St.)	Oct. 9, 1999
300	Marshall Faulk, San Diego St. (Hawaii)	Nov. 14, 1992

ANNUAL CHAMPIONS

Year	Player, Team	Class	Plays	Yards
1937	Byron "Whizzer" White, Colorado	Sr.	181	1,121
1938	Len Eshmont, Fordham	Sr.	132	831
1939	John Polanski, Wake Forest	So.	137	882
1940	Al Ghesquiere, Detroit	Sr.	146	957
1941	Frank Sinkwich, Georgia	Jr.	209	1,103
1942	Rudy Mobley, Hardin-Simmons	So.	187	1,281
1943	Creighton Miller, Notre Dame	Sr.	151	911
1944	Wayne "Red" Williams, Minnesota	Jr.	136	911
1945	Bob Fenimore, Oklahoma St.	Jr.	142	1,048
1946	Rudy Mobley, Hardin-Simmons	Sr.	227	1,262
1947	Wilton Davis, Hardin-Simmons	So.	193	1,173
1948	Fred Wendt, UTEP	Sr.	184	1,570
1949	John Dottley, Mississippi	Jr.	208	1,312
1950	Wilford White, Arizona St.	Sr.	199	1,502
1951	Ollie Matson, San Francisco	Sr.	245	1,566
1952	Howie Waugh, Tulsa	Sr.	164	1,372
1953	J. C. Caroline, Illinois	So.	194	1,256
1954	Art Luppino, Arizona	So.	179	1,359
1955	Art Luppino, Arizona	Jr.	209	1,313
1956	Jim Crawford, Wyoming	Sr.	200	1,104
1957	Leon Burton, Arizona St.	Sr.	117	1,126
1958	Dick Bass, Pacific (Cal.)	Jr.	205	1,361
1959	Pervis Atkins, New Mexico St.	Jr.	130	971
1960	Bob Gaiters, New Mexico St.	Sr.	197	1,338
1961	Jim Pilot, New Mexico St.	So.	191	1,278
1962	Jim Pilot, New Mexico St.	Jr.	208	1,247
1963	Dave Casinelli, Memphis	Sr.	219	1,016
1964	Brian Piccolo, Wake Forest	Sr.	252	1,044
1965	Mike Garrett, Southern California	Sr.	267	1,440
1966	Ray McDonald, Idaho	Sr.	259	1,329
1967	O. J. Simpson, Southern California	Jr.	266	1,415
1968	O. J. Simpson, Southern California	Sr.	355	1,709
1969	Steve Owens, Oklahoma	Sr.	358	1,523

Beginning in 1970, ranked on per-game (instead of total) yards

Year	Player, Team	Class	G	Plays	Yards	Avg.
1970	Ed Marinaro, Cornell	Jr.	9	285	1,425	158.3
1971	Ed Marinaro, Cornell	Sr.	9	356	1,881	209.0
1972	Pete VanValkenburg, Brigham Young	Sr.	10	232	1,386	138.6
1973	Mark Kellar, Northern Ill.	Sr.	11	291	1,719	156.3
1974	Louie Giammona, Utah St.	Jr.	10	329	1,534	153.4
1975	Ricky Bell, Southern California	Jr.	11	357	1,875	170.5
1976	Tony Dorsett, Pittsburgh	Sr.	11	338	1,948	177.1
1977	Earl Campbell, Texas	Sr.	11	267	1,744	158.5
1978	Billy Sims, Oklahoma	Jr.	11	231	1,762	160.2
1979	Charles White, Southern California	Sr.	10	293	1,803	180.3
1980	George Rogers, South Carolina	Sr.	11	297	1,781	161.9
1981	Marcus Allen, Southern California	Sr.	11	*403	2,342	212.9

ALL-TIME LEADERS—RUSHING

Year	Player, Team	Class	G	Plays	Yards	Avg.
1982	Ernest Anderson, Oklahoma St.	Jr.	11	353	1,877	170.6
1983	Mike Rozier, Nebraska	Sr.	12	275	2,148	179.0
1984	Keith Byars, Ohio St.	Jr.	11	313	1,655	150.5
1985	Lorenzo White, Michigan St.	So.	11	386	1,908	173.5
1986	Paul Palmer, Temple	Sr.	11	346	1,866	169.6
1987	Elbert "Ickey" Woods, UNLV	Sr.	11	259	1,658	150.7
1988	Barry Sanders, Oklahoma St.	Jr.	11	344	*2,628	*238.9
1989	Anthony Thompson, Indiana	Sr.	11	358	1,793	163.0
1990	Gerald Hudson, Oklahoma St.	Sr.	11	279	1,642	149.3
1991	Marshall Faulk, San Diego St.	Fr.	9	201	1,429	158.8
1992	Marshall Faulk, San Diego St.	So.	10	265	1,630	163.0
1993	LeShon Johnson, Northern Ill.	Sr.	11	327	1,976	179.6
1994	Rashaan Salaam, Colorado	Jr.	11	298	2,055	186.8
1995	Troy Davis, Iowa St.	So.	11	345	2,010	182.7
1996	Troy Davis, Iowa St.	Jr.	11	402	2,185	198.6
1997	Ricky Williams, Texas	Jr.	11	279	1,893	172.1
1998	Ricky Williams, Texas	Sr.	11	361	2,124	193.1
1999	LaDainian Tomlinson, TCU	Jr.	11	268	1,850	168.2

*Record.

FRESHMAN 1,000-YARD RUSHERS

Player, Team	Year	Yards
Ron "Po" James, New Mexico St.	1968	1,291
Tony Dorsett, Pittsburgh	1973	1,586
James McDougald, Wake Forest	1976	1,018
Mike Harkrader, Indiana	1976	1,003
Amos Lawrence, North Carolina	1977	1,211
Darrin Nelson, Stanford	1977	1,069
Mike Smith, Chattanooga	1977	1,062
Gwain Durden, Chattanooga	1977	1,049
Allen Ross, Northern Ill.	1977	1,043
Allen Harvin, Cincinnati	1978	1,238
Joe Morris, Syracuse	1978	1,001
Ron Lear, Marshall	1979	1,162
Herschel Walker, Georgia	1980	1,616
Kerwin Bell, Kansas	1980	1,114
Joe McIntosh, North Carolina St.	1981	1,190
Steve Bartalo, Colorado St.	1983	1,113
Spencer Tillman, Oklahoma	1983	1,047
D. J. Dozier, Penn St.	1983	1,002
Eddie Johnson, Utah	1984	1,021
Darrell Thompson, Minnesota	1986	1,240
Emmitt Smith, Florida	1987	1,341
Reggie Cobb, Tennessee	1987	1,197
Bernie Parmalee, Ball St.	1987	1,064
Curvin Richards, Pittsburgh	1988	1,228
Chuck Webb, Tennessee	1989	1,236
Robert Smith, Ohio St.	1990	1,064
Marshall Faulk, San Diego St.	1991	1,429
Greg Hill, Texas A&M	1991	1,216
David Small, Cincinnati	1991	1,004
Winslow Oliver, New Mexico	1992	1,063
Deland McCullough, Miami (Ohio)	1992	1,026
Terrell Willis, Rutgers	1993	1,261
June Henley, Kansas	1993	1,127
Marquis Williams, Arkansas St.	1993	1,060
Leon Johnson, North Carolina	1993	1,012
Alex Smith, Indiana	1994	1,475
Astron Whatley, Kent	1994	1,003
Denvis Manns, New Mexico St.	1995	1,120
Silas Massey, Central Mich.	1995	1,089
Ahman Green, Nebraska	1995	1,086
Ron Dayne, Wisconsin	1996	*1,863
Demond Parker, Oklahoma	1996	1,184
Sedrick Irvin, Michigan St.	1996	1,036
Jamal Lewis, Tennessee	1997	1,364
Robert Sanford, Western Mich.	1997	1,033
Derrick Nix, Southern Miss.	1998	1,180
Ken Simonton, Oregon St.	1998	1,028
Avon Cobourne, West Virginia	1999	1,139

*Record for freshman.

Quarterback Rushing

SEASON YARDS

Player, Team	Year	G	Plays	Yards	TD	Avg.
Beau Morgan, Air Force	1996	11	225	*1,494	18	6.64
Stacey Robinson, Northern Ill.	1989	11	223	1,443	19	6.47
Chris McCoy, Navy	1997	11	246	1,370	*20	5.57
Dee Dowis, Air Force	1987	12	194	1,315	10	6.78
Brian Mitchell, La.-Lafayette	1989	11	237	1,311	19	5.53
Fred Solomon, Tampa	1974	11	193	1,300	19	6.74
Dee Dowis, Air Force	1989	12	172	1,286	18	*7.48
Beau Morgan, Air Force	1995	12	229	1,285	19	5.61
Stacey Robinson, Northern Ill.	1990	11	193	1,238	19	6.41
Chris McCoy, Navy	1996	11	268	1,228	16	4.58
Rob Perez, Air Force	1991	12	233	1,157	10	4.97
Jack Mildren, Oklahoma	1971	11	193	1,140	17	5.91
Nolan Cromwell, Kansas	1975	11	218	1,124	9	5.16
Scott Frost, Nebraska	1997	12	176	1,095	19	6.22
Michael Carter, Hawaii	1991	12	221	1,092	16	4.94
Tory Crawford, Army	1986	11	*244	1,075	15	4.41
Kareem Wilson, Ohio	1996	12	275	1,072	14	3.90
Bart Weiss, Air Force	1985	12	180	1,032	12	5.73
Jimmy Sidle, Auburn	1963	10	185	1,006	10	5.44
Reggie Collier, Southern Miss.	1981	11	153	1,005	12	6.57
Darian Hagan, Colorado	1989	11	186	1,004	17	5.40
Nate Sassaman, Army	1984	11	189	1,002	7	5.30

*Record.

CAREER YARDS

Player, Team	Year	G	Plays	Yards	TD	Avg.
Dee Dowis, Air Force	1986-89	47	543	*3,612	41	76.9
Kareem Wilson, Ohio	1995-98	45	*885	3,597	*49	79.9
Chris McCoy, Navy	1995-97	32	682	3,401	43	106.3
Beau Morgan, Air Force	1994-96	35	594	3,379	42	96.5
Brian Mitchell, La.-Lafayette	1986-89	43	678	3,335	47	77.6
Fred Solomon, Tampa	1971-74	43	557	3,299	39	76.7
Stacey Robinson, Northern Ill.	1988-90	25	429	2,727	38	*109.1
Jamelle Holieway, Oklahoma	1985-88	38	505	2,699	30	71.0
Bill Hurley, Syracuse	1975-79	46	685	2,551	19	55.5
Michael Carter, Hawaii	1990-93	46	574	2,534	39	55.1
Corby Jones, Missouri	1995-98	39	559	2,533	38	64.9
Chad Nelson, Rice	1994-97	40	466	2,415	24	60.4
Bill Deery, William & Mary	1972-74	33	443	2,401	19	72.8
Reggie Collier, Southern Miss.	1979-82	39	446	2,304	26	59.1
John Bond, Mississippi St.	1980-83	44	572	2,280	24	51.8
Tory Crawford, Army	1984-87	31	495	2,255	34	72.7
Tom Parr, Colgate	1971-73	30	435	2,221	31	74.0
Alton Grizzard, Navy	1987-90	38	599	2,174	15	57.2
Gary Wood, Cornell	1961-63	27	433	2,156	19	79.9
Roy DeWalt, Texas-Arlington	1975, 77-79	38	468	2,136	27	56.2
Steve Taylor, Nebraska	1985-88	37	431	2,125	32	57.4
Bucky Richardson, Texas A&M	1987-88, 90-91	41	370	2,095	30	51.1
Rocky Long, New Mexico	1969-71	31	469	2,071	21	66.8
Steve Davis, Oklahoma	1973-75	33	515	2,069	33	62.7
Rick Leach, Michigan	1975-78	43	440	2,053	34	47.7
Prince McJunkins, Wichita St.	1979-82	44	613	2,047	27	46.5
Rickey Foggie, Minnesota	1984-87	42	517	2,038	24	48.5
Chris McCoy, Navy	1995-96	21	436	2,031	23	96.7
Major Harris, West Virginia	1987-89	33	386	2,030	18	51.5
Steve Gage, Tulsa	1983-84, 86	33	522	2,029	30	61.5
Harry Gilmer, Alabama	1944-47	40	390	2,025	19	50.6
Chad Richardson, Rice	1996-99	41	493	2,024	20	49.4
Darian Hagan, Colorado	1988-91	41	489	2,007	27	49.0

*Record.

Passing

SAMPLE COMPILATION OF NCAA PASSING EFFICIENCY RATING

Player	G	Att.	Cmp.	Yds.	TD	Int.
Danny Wuerffel, Florida	46	1,170	708	10,875	114	42

Completion Percentage:	60.51
Yards Per Attempted Pass:	9.29
Percent of Passes for TDs:	9.74
Percent of Passes Intercepted:	3.59

ADD the first three factors:

		Rating Points
Completion Percentage:	60.51	60.51
Yards Per Attempted Pass:	9.295 times 8.4	78.08
Percent of Passes for TDs:	9.74 times 3.3	32.14
		170.73

SUBTRACT the last factor:

Percent of Passes Intercepted:	3.59 times 2	-7.18
	Round off to:	**163.6**

DIVISION I-A PASSING EFFICIENCY RATING COMPARISON
1979-99

Passing statistics in Division I-A have increased dramatically since 1979, the first year that the NCAA official national statistics used the passing efficiency formula to rank passers in all divisions. Because passers have become more proficient every year, the average passing efficiency rating (based on final regular-season trends) also has risen at a similar rate. For historical purposes, the average passing efficiency rating for the division by year is presented below to show how any individual or team might rank in a particular season.

Year	Pass Effic. Rating	Year	Pass Effic. Rating
1979	104.49	1989	118.35
1980	106.63	1990	117.39
1981	107.00	1991	117.94
1982	110.77	1992	114.50
1983	113.56	1993	122.43
1984	113.02	1994	120.59
1985	114.58	1995	120.17
1986	115.00	1996	120.24
1987	112.67	1997	122.86
1988	114.32	1998	122.97
		1999	120.50

Chad Pennington of Marshall finished his career in 1999 with a passing efficiency rating of 156.2, the sixth-highest mark in Division I-A history.

CAREER PASSING EFFICIENCY
(Minimum 500 Completions)

Player, Team	Years	Att.	Cmp.	Int.	Pct.	Yds.	TD	Pts.
Danny Wuerffel, Florida	1993-96	1,170	708	42	.605	10,875	114	*163.6
Ty Detmer, Brigham Young	1988-91	1,530	958	65	.626	*15,031	*121	162.7
Steve Sarkisian, Brigham Young	1995-96	789	528	26	.669	7,464	53	162.0
Billy Blanton, San Diego St.	1993-96	920	588	25	.639	8,165	67	157.1
Jim McMahon, Brigham Young	1977-78, 80-81	1,060	653	34	.616	9,536	84	156.9
Chad Pennington, Marshall	1997-99	1,265	807	30	.638	10,698	100	156.2
Donovan McNabb, Syracuse	1995-98	938	548	26	.584	8,389	77	155.1
Tim Rattay, Louisiana Tech	1997-99	1,552	1,015	35	‡.654	12,746	115	154.3
Daunte Culpepper, UCF	1996-98	1,097	721	32	.657	9,341	72	153.1
Steve Young, Brigham Young	1981-83	908	592	33	.652	7,733	56	149.8
Robbie Bosco, Brigham Young	1983-85	997	638	36	.640	8,400	66	149.4
Mike Maxwell, Nevada	1993-95	881	560	33	.636	7,256	62	148.5
Joe Hamilton, Georgia Tech	1996-99	1,020	629	39	.617	8,882	65	148.2
Chuck Long, Iowa	$1981-85	1,072	692	46	.646	9,210	64	147.8
John Walsh, Brigham Young	1991-94	973	587	35	.603	8,375	66	147.8
Peyton Manning, Tennessee	1994-97	1,381	863	33	.625	11,201	89	147.1
Rob Johnson, Southern California	1991-94	963	623	24	.647	7,743	52	145.1
Andre Ware, Houston	1987-89	1,074	660	28	.615	8,202	75	143.3
Steve Stenstrom, Stanford	1991-94	1,320	833	36	.631	10,531	72	142.7
Marvin Graves, Syracuse	1990-93	943	563	45	.597	8,466	48	142.4
Tim Couch, Kentucky	1996-98	1,184	795	35	.671	8,435	74	141.7
Doug Gaynor, Long Beach St.	1984-85	837	569	35	.680	6,793	35	141.6
Danny Kanell, Florida St.	1992-95	851	529	26	.622	6,372	57	141.1
Kevin Feterik, Brigham Young	1996-99	1,004	609	27	.607	8,065	53	140.2
Dan McGwire, Iowa/San Diego St.	1986-87, 89-90	973	575	30	.591	8,164	49	140.0
Cade McNown, UCLA	1995-98	1,153	646	39	.560	10,008	61	139.6
Chris Vargas, Nevada	1992-93	806	502	34	.623	6,359	47	139.4
John Elway, Stanford	1979-82	1,246	774	39	.621	9,349	77	139.3
Mike McCoy, Long Beach St./Utah	1991, 92-94	1,069	650	26	.608	8,342	56	138.8
David Klingler, Houston	1988-91	1,268	732	38	.577	9,466	91	138.1
Scott Milanovich, Maryland	1992-95	982	650	35**	.662	7,301	49	138.0
Scott Mitchell, Utah	1987-89	1,165	669	38	.574	8,981	68	137.7
Shane Matthews, Florida	1989-92	1,202	722	46	.601	9,287	74	137.6
Marc Wilson, Brigham Young	1977-79	937	535	46	.571	7,637	61	137.2
Eric Zeier, Georgia	1991-94	1,402	838	37	.598	11,153	67	137.1
Randall Cunningham, UNLV	1982-84	1,029	597	29	.580	8,020	59	136.8
Kerwin Bell, Florida	1984-87	953	549	35	.576	7,585	56	136.5

ALL-TIME LEADERS—PASSING

DIVISION I-A

Player, Team	Years	Att.	Cmp.	Int.	Pct.	Yds.	TD	Pts.
Tom Hodson, LSU	1986-89	1,163	674	41	.580	9,115	69	136.3
Rodney Peete, Southern California	1985-88	972	571	32	.587	7,640	52	135.8
Ron Powlus, Notre Dame	1994-97	969	558	27	.576	7,602	52	135.6
Billy Volek, Fresno St.	1997-99	934	564	12	.604	6,385	57	135.4
Darrell Bevell, Wisconsin	1992-95	1,012	625	37	.618	7,429	58	135.0
Pat Barnes, California	1993-96	912	522	26	.572	7,047	51	134.9
Troy Kopp, Pacific (Cal.)	1989-92	1,374	798	47	.581	10,258	87	134.9
Chris Redman, Louisville	1996-99	*1,679	*1,031	51	.614	12,541	84	134.6
Joe Adams, Tennessee St.	1977-80	1,100	604	60	.549	8,649	81	134.4
Mike Gundy, Oklahoma St.	1986-89	1,037	606	37	.584	8,072	54	133.9
Todd Santos, San Diego St.	1984-87	1,484	910	57	.613	11,425	70	133.9
Tony Eason, Illinois	1981-82	856	526	29	.615	6,608	37	133.8
Jake Plummer, Arizona St.	1993-96	1,107	613	34	.554	8,626	64	133.8
Tim Lester, Western Mich.	1996-99	1,507	875	49	.581	11,299	87	133.6
Danny McCoin, Cincinnati	1984-87	899	544	26	.605	6,801	39	132.6
Rich Campbell, California	1977-80	891	574	42	.644	6,933	33	132.6
Jim Everett, Purdue	$1981-85	923	550	30	.596	7,158	40	132.5
Matt Rodgers, Iowa	1988-91	844	516	30	.611	6,308	40	132.5
Doug Flutie, Boston College	1981-84	1,270	677	54	.533	10,579	67	132.2
Gino Torretta, Miami (Fla.)	1989-92	991	555	24	.560	7,690	47	132.0
Robert Hall, Texas Tech	1990-93	997	548	28	.550	7,908	48	131.9
Jack Trudeau, Illinois	1981, 83-85	1,151	736	38	.639	8,146	51	131.4
Kevin Sweeney, Fresno St.	$1982-86	1,336	731	48	.547	10,623	66	130.6
Bill Musgrave, Oregon	1987-90	1,018	582	38	.572	7,631	55	130.6

(400-499 Completions)

Player, Team	Years	Att.	Cmp.	Int.	Pct.	Yds.	TD	Pts.
Vinny Testaverde, Miami (Fla.)	1982, 84-86	674	413	25	.613	6,058	48	152.9
Josh Wallwork, Wyoming	1995-96	729	449	28	.616	6,453	54	152.7
Trent Dilfer, Fresno St.	1991-93	774	461	21	.596	6,944	51	151.2
Troy Aikman, Oklahoma/UCLA	1984-85, 87-88	637	401	18	.630	5,436	40	149.7
Chuck Hartlieb, Iowa	1985-88	716	461	17	.643	6,269	34	148.9
Elvis Grbac, Michigan	1989-92	754	477	29	.633	5,859	64	148.9
Bobby Hoying, Ohio St.	1992-95	782	463	33	.592	6,751	54	146.1
Gifford Nielsen, Brigham Young	1975-77	708	415	29	.586	5,833	55	145.3
Tom Ramsey, UCLA	1979-82	691	411	33	.595	5,844	48	143.9
Shawn Moore, Virginia	1987-90	762	421	32	.552	6,629	55	143.8
Moses Moreno, Colorado St.	1994-97	787	457	28	.581	6,689	49	142.9
Jerry Rhome, Southern Methodist/Tulsa	1961, 63-64	713	448	23	.628	5,472	47	142.6
Thad Busby, Florida St.	1994-97	715	420	27	.587	5,916	46	141.9
Charlie Ward, Florida St.	1989, 91-93	759	474	21	.625	5,747	49	141.8
Ryan Leaf, Washington St.	1995-97	845	456	23	.540	7,102	58	141.8
Keith Smith, Arizona	1996-99	726	434	27	.598	5,972	42	140.5
Bernie Kosar, Miami (Fla.)	1983-84	743	463	29	.623	5,971	40	139.8
Craig Erickson, Miami (Fla.)	1987-90	752	420	22	.559	6,056	46	137.8
Mike Bobo, Georgia	1994-97	766	445	26	.581	6,334	38	137.1
Dave Yarema, Michigan St.	$1982-86	727	447	29	.615	5,569	41	136.5
Ryan Clement, Miami (Fla.)	1994-97	720	427	27	.593	5,730	35	134.7
Gary Huff, Florida St.	1970-72	796	436	42	.548	6,378	52	133.1
Joe Hughes, Wyoming	1992-93	744	424	25	.570	5,841	38	133.1
Jeff Francis, Tennessee	1985-88	768	476	26	.620	5,867	31	132.7
Mike Perez, San Jose St.	1986-87	792	471	30	.595	6,194	36	132.6
Cale Gundy, Oklahoma	1990-93	751	420	31	.559	6,142	36	132.2

(325-399 Completions)

Player, Team	Years	Att.	Cmp.	Int.	Pct.	Yds.	TD	Pts.
Joe Germaine, Ohio St.	1996-98	660	399	18	.605	5,844	52	155.4
Jim Harbaugh, Michigan	1983-86	582	368	19	.632	5,215	31	149.6
Danny White, Arizona St.	1971-73	649	345	36	.532	5,932	59	148.9
Koy Detmer, Colorado	1992, 94-96	594	350	25	.589	5,390	40	148.9
Tim Gutierrez, San Diego St.	1992-94	580	357	19	.616	4,740	36	144.1
Jim Karsatos, Ohio St.	1983-86	573	330	19	.576	4,698	36	140.6
Jerry Tagge, Nebraska	1969-71	581	348	19	.599	4,704	33	140.1
Mike Fouts, Utah	1995-96	625	356	19	.570	5,107	39	140.1
Garrett Gabriel, Hawaii	1987-90	661	356	31	.539	5,631	47	139.5
Rick Mirer, Notre Dame	1989-92	698	377	23	.540	5,996	41	139.0
Gary Sheide, Brigham Young	1973-74	594	358	31	.603	4,524	45	138.8
Dan Speltz, Cal St. Fullerton	1988-89	583	350	19	.600	4,595	33	138.4
Mike Moschetti, Colorado	1998-99	607	366	19	.603	4,797	33	138.4
Don McPherson, Syracuse	$1983-87	687	367	29	.534	5,812	46	138.1
Joe Youngblood, Central Mich.	1990-93	572	331	28	.579	4,718	35	137.6
Kerry Collins, Penn St.	1991-94	657	370	21	.563	5,304	39	137.3
Sam King, UNLV	1979-81	625	360	29	.576	5,393	30	136.6
J. J. Joe, Baylor	1990-93	665	347	28	.522	5,995	31	134.9
Jesse Freitas, Stanford/San Diego St.	1970, 72-73	547	338	33	.618	4,408	28	134.3
Jeff Blake, East Caro.	1988-91	667	360	20	.540	5,133	43	133.9

*Record. $See page 6 for explanation. **Record for minimum 875 attempts. ‡Record for minimum 1,000 attempts.

SEASON PASSING EFFICIENCY
(Minimum 15 Attempts Per Game)

Player, Team	Year	G	Att.	Cmp.	Int.	Pct.	Yds.	TD	Pts.
Shaun King, Tulane	†1998	11	328	223	6	.680	3,232	36	*183.3
Michael Vick, Virginia Tech	†1999	10	152	90	5	.592	1,840	12	180.4
Danny Wuerffel, Florida	†1995	11	325	210	10	.646	3,266	35	178.4
Jim McMahon, Brigham Young	#†1980	12	445	284	18	.638	4,571	47	176.9
Ty Detmer, Brigham Young	†1989	12	412	265	15	.643	4,560	32	175.6

ALL-TIME LEADERS—PASSING

Player, Team	Year	G	Att.	Cmp.	Int.	Pct.	Yds.	TD	Pts.
Joe Hamilton, Georgia Tech	1999	11	305	203	11	.666	3,060	29	175.0
Steve Sarkisian, Brigham Young	†1996	14	404	278	12	.688	4,027	33	173.6
Trent Dilfer, Fresno St.	†1993	11	333	217	4	.652	3,276	28	173.1
Kerry Collins, Penn St.	†1994	11	264	176	7	.667	2,679	21	172.9
Jerry Rhome, Tulsa	#†1964	10	326	224	4	.687	2,870	32	172.6
Chad Pennington, Marshall	1999	12	405	275	11	.679	3,799	37	171.4
Danny Wuerffel, Florida	1996	12	360	207	13	.575	3,625	39	170.6
Akili Smith, Oregon	1998	11	325	191	7	.588	3,307	30	170.4
Bobby Hoying, Ohio St.	1995	12	303	192	11	.634	3,023	28	170.4
Daunte Culpepper, UCF	1998	11	402	296	7	*.736	3,690	28	170.2
Billy Blanton, San Diego St.	1996	11	344	227	5	.660	3,221	29	169.6
Elvis Grbac, Michigan	†1991	11	228	152	5	.667	1,955	24	169.0
Cade McNown, UCLA	†1997	11	283	173	5	.611	2,877	22	168.6
Ty Detmer, Brigham Young	†1991	12	403	249	12	.618	4,031	35	168.5
Steve Young, Brigham Young	#†1983	11	429	306	10	.713	3,902	33	168.5
Vinny Testaverde, Miami (Fla.)	†1986	10	276	175	9	.634	2,557	26	165.8
Brian Dowling, Yale	1968	9	160	92	10	.575	1,554	19	165.8
Tim Rattay, Louisiana Tech	1998	12	559	380	13	.680	4,943	46	164.8
Dave Barr, California	1993	11	275	187	12	.680	2,619	21	164.5
Don McPherson, Syracuse	†1987	11	229	129	11	.563	2,341	22	164.3
Dave Wilson, Ball St.	1977	11	177	115	7	.650	1,589	17	164.2
Bob Berry, Oregon	1963	10	171	101	7	.591	1,675	16	164.0
Jim Harbaugh, Michigan	†1985	11	212	139	6	.656	1,913	18	163.7
Troy Aikman, UCLA	1987	11	243	159	6	.654	2,354	16	163.6
Turk Schonert, Stanford	†1979	11	221	148	6	.670	1,922	19	163.0
Donovan McNabb, Syracuse	1995	11	207	128	6	.618	1,991	16	162.3
Brian Broomell, Temple	1979	11	214	120	11	.561	2,103	22	162.3
Dennis Shaw, San Diego St.	†1969	10	335	199	26	.594	3,185	39	162.2
Timm Rosenbach, Washington St.	†1988	11	302	199	10	.659	2,791	23	162.0
Davey O'Brien, TCU	¢#†1938	10	167	93	4	.557	1,457	19	161.7
Chuck Hartlieb, Iowa	1987	12	299	196	8	.656	2,855	19	161.4
Ryan Leaf, Washington St.	1997	11	375	210	10	.560	3,637	33	161.2
Darrell Bevell, Wisconsin	1993	11	256	177	10	.691	2,294	19	161.1
David Brown, Duke	1989	9	163	104	6	.638	1,479	14	161.0
Shawn Moore, Virginia	†1990	10	241	144	8	.598	2,262	21	160.7
Joe Germaine, Ohio St.	1997	12	184	119	7	.647	1,674	15	160.4
Chuck Long, Iowa	1983	10	236	144	8	.610	2,434	14	160.4
Mike Maxwell, Nevada	#1995	9	409	277	17	.677	3,611	33	160.2
Jeff Garcia, San Jose St.	1991	9	160	99	5	.619	1,519	12	160.1
David Neill, Nevada	1998	9	344	199	9	.579	3,249	29	159.8
Michael Bishop, Kansas St.	1998	12	295	164	4	.556	2,844	23	159.6
Matt Blundin, Virginia	1991	9	224	135	0	.603	1,902	19	159.6
Kerwin Bell, Florida	1985	11	288	180	8	.625	2,687	21	159.4
Donovan McNabb, Syracuse	1998	11	251	157	5	.626	2,134	22	158.9
Mike Gundy, Oklahoma St.	1988	11	236	153	12	.648	2,163	19	158.2

*Record. †National pass-efficiency champion. #National total-offense champion. ¢Available records before 1946 do not include TD passes except for O'Brien and relatively few other passers; thus, passing efficiency points cannot be compiled for those players without TD passes.

ANNUAL PASSING EFFICIENCY LEADERS
(% Minimum 11 Attempts Per Game)

1946—Bill Mackrides, Nevada, 176.9; **1947**—Bobby Layne, Texas, 138.9; **1948**—Stan Heath, Nevada, 157.2 (#); **1949**—Bob Williams, Notre Dame, 159.1; **1950**—Claude Arnold, Oklahoma, 157.3; **1951**—Dick Kazmaier, Princeton, 155.3 (#); **1952**—Ron Morris, Tulsa, 177.4; **1953**—Bob Garrett, Stanford, 142.2; **1954**—Pete Vann, Army, 166.5; **1955**—George Welsh, Navy, 146.1 (#); **1956**—Tom Flores, Pacific (Cal.), 147.5; **1957**—Lee Grosscup, Utah, 175.5; **1958**—John Hangartner, Arizona St., 150.1; **1959**—Charley Johnson, New Mexico St., 135.7; **1960**—Eddie Wilson, Arizona, 140.8; **1961**—Ron DiGravio, Purdue, 140.1; **1962**—John Jacobs, Arizona St., 153.9; **1963**—Bob Berry, Oregon, 164.0; **1964**—Jerry Rhome, Tulsa, 172.6 (#).

(Minimum 15 Attempts Per Game)

1946—Ben Raimondi, Indiana, 117.0; **1947**—Charley Conerly, Mississippi, 125.8; **1948**—Stan Heath, Nevada, 157.2 (#); **1949**—Dick Doheny, Fordham, 153.3; **1950**—Dick Doheny, Fordham, 149.5; **1951**—Babe Parilli, Kentucky, 130.8; **1952**—Gene Rossi, Cincinnati, 149.7; **1953**—Bob Garrett, Stanford, 142.2; **1954**—Len Dawson, Purdue, 145.8; **1955**—George Welsh, Navy, 146.1 (#); **1956**—Bob Reinhart, San Jose St., 121.3; **1957**—Bob Newman, Washington St., 126.5 (#); **1958**—Randy Duncan, Iowa, 135.1; **1959**—Charley Johnson, New Mexico St., 135.7; **1960**—Charley Johnson, New Mexico St., 134.1; **1961**—Eddie Wilson, Arizona, 134.2; **1962**—Terry Baker, Oregon St., 146.5 (#); **1963**—Bob Berry, Oregon, 164.0; **1964**—Jerry Rhome, Tulsa, 172.6 (#).

(Minimum 15 Attempts Per Game)

Year	Player, Team	G	Att.	Cmp.	Int.	Pct.	Yds.	TD	Pts.
1965	Steve Sloan, Alabama	10	160	97	3	.606	1,453	10	153.8
1966	Dewey Warren, Tennessee	10	229	136	7	.594	1,716	18	142.2
1967	Bill Andrejko, Villanova	10	187	114	6	.610	1,405	13	140.6
1968	Brian Dowling, Yale	9	160	92	10	.575	1,554	19	165.8
1969	#Dennis Shaw, San Diego St.	10	335	199	26	.594	3,185	39	162.2
1970	Jerry Tagge, Nebraska	11	165	104	7	.630	1,383	12	149.0
1971	Jerry Tagge, Nebraska	12	239	143	4	.598	2,019	17	150.9
1972	John Hufnagel, Penn St.	11	216	115	8	.532	2,039	15	148.0
1973	Danny White, Arizona St.	11	265	146	12	.551	2,609	23	157.4
1974	#Steve Joachim, Temple	10	221	128	13	.579	1,950	20	150.1
1975	James Kubacki, Harvard	8	137	77	9	.562	1,273	11	147.6
1976	Steve Haynes, Louisiana Tech	10	216	120	11	.556	1,981	16	146.9
1977	Dave Wilson, Ball St.	11	177	115	7	.650	1,589	17	164.2
1978	Paul McDonald, Southern California	11	194	111	7	.572	1,667	18	152.8

(See page 37 for annual leaders beginning in 1979)

#National total-offense champion. %In many seasons during 1946-64, only a few passers threw as many as 15 passes per game; thus, a lower minimum was used.

ALL-TIME LEADERS—PASSING

CAREER YARDS

Player, Team	Years	Att.	Cmp.	Int.	Pct.	Yds.	TD	Long
Ty Detmer, Brigham Young	1988-91	1,530	958	65	.626	*15,031	*121	76
Tim Rattay, Louisiana Tech	1997-99	1,552	1,015	35	‡‡.654	12,746	115	94
Chris Redman, Louisville	1996-99	*1,679	*1,031	51	.614	12,541	84	86
Todd Santos, San Diego St.	1984-87	1,484	910	57	.613	11,425	70	84
Tim Lester, Western Mich.	1996-99	1,507	875	49	.581	11,299	87	82
Peyton Manning, Tennessee	1994-97	1,381	863	33	.625	11,201	89	80
Eric Zeier, Georgia	1991-94	1,402	838	37	.598	11,153	67	80
Alex Van Pelt, Pittsburgh	1989-92	1,463	845	59	.578	10,913	64	91
Danny Wuerffel, Florida	1993-96	1,170	708	42	.605	10,875	114	85
Chad Pennington, Marshall	1997-99	1,265	807	30	.638	10,698	100	92
Kevin Sweeney, Fresno St.	$1982-86	1,336	731	48	.547	10,623	66	95
Doug Flutie, Boston College	1981-84	1,270	677	54	.533	10,579	67	80
Steve Stenstrom, Stanford	1991-94	1,320	833	36	.631	10,531	72	92
Brian McClure, Bowling Green	1982-85	1,427	900	58	.631	10,280	63	90
Troy Kopp, Pacific (Cal.)	1989-92	1,374	798	47	.581	10,258	87	80
Glenn Foley, Boston College	1990-93	1,275	703	60	.551	10,042	72	78
Cade McNown, UCLA	1995-98	1,153	646	39	.560	10,008	61	88
Ben Bennett, Duke	1980-83	1,375	820	57	.596	9,614	55	88
Jim McMahon, Brigham Young	1977-78, 80-81	1,060	653	34	.616	9,536	84	80
Todd Ellis, South Carolina	1986-89	1,266	704	66	.556	9,519	49	97
David Klingler, Houston	1988-91	1,268	732	38	.577	9,466	91	95
Stoney Case, New Mexico	1991-94	1,237	677	39	.547	9,460	67	79
Erik Wilhelm, Oregon St.	1985-88	1,480	870	61	.588	9,393	52	‡74
Jeremy Leach, New Mexico	1988-91	1,432	735	62	.513	9,382	50	82
John Elway, Stanford	1979-82	1,246	774	39	.621	9,349	77	70
Daunte Culpepper, UCF	1996-98	1,097	721	32	.657	9,341	72	71
T. J. Rubley, Tulsa	1987-89, 91	1,336	682	54	.510	9,324	73	75
Shane Matthews, Florida	1989-92	1,202	722	46	.601	9,287	74	70
Jake Delhomme, La.-Lafayette	1993-96	1,246	655	57	.526	9,216	64	79
Chuck Long, Iowa	$1981-85	1,072	692	46	.646	9,210	64	89
Mark Herrmann, Purdue	1977-80	1,218	717	*73	.589	9,188	62	75
Tom Hodson, LSU	1986-89	1,163	674	41	.580	9,115	69	80
Jason Martin, Louisiana Tech	1993-96	1,320	705	55	.534	9,066	64	80
Spence Fischer, Duke	1992-95	1,369	786	46	.574	9,021	48	80
Scott Mitchell, Utah	1987-89	1,165	669	38	.574	8,981	68	72
Joe Hamilton, Georgia Tech	1996-99	1,020	629	39	.617	8,882	65	80
Brad Tayles, Western Mich.	1989-92	1,370	663	67	.484	8,717	49	84
Joe Adams, Tennessee St.	1977-80	1,100	604	60	.549	8,649	81	71
Jake Plummer, Arizona St.	1993-96	1,107	613	34	.554	8,626	64	83
Steve Taneyhill, South Carolina	1992-95	1,209	727	37	.601	8,555	61	93
Marvin Graves, Syracuse	1990-93	943	563	45	.597	8,466	48	84
Shawn Jones, Georgia Tech	1989-92	1,217	652	50	.536	8,441	51	82
Tim Couch, Kentucky	1996-98	1,184	795	35	.671	8,435	74	97
Shaun King, Tulane	1995-98	1,163	646	34	.555	8,419	70	79
Robbie Bosco, Brigham Young	1983-85	997	638	36	.640	8,400	66	‡89
Donovan McNabb, Syracuse	1995-98	938	548	26	.584	8,389	77	96
John Walsh, Brigham Young	1991-94	973	587	35	.603	8,375	66	93
Mike McCoy, Long Beach St./Utah	1991, 92-94	1,069	650	26	.608	8,342	56	87
Andre Ware, Houston	1987-89	1,074	660	28	.615	8,202	75	87
Billy Blanton, San Diego St.	1993-96	920	588	25	.639	8,165	67	85
Dan McGwire, Iowa/San Diego St.	1986-87, 89-90	973	575	30	.591	8,164	49	71
Jack Trudeau, Illinois	1981, 83-85	1,151	736	38	.639	8,146	51	83
Troy Taylor, California	1986-89	1,162	683	46	.588	8,126	51	79
Mike Gundy, Oklahoma St.	1986-89	1,037	606	37	.584	8,072	54	‡84
Kevin Feterik, Brigham Young	1996-99	1,004	609	27	.607	8,065	53	83
Jeff Graham, Long Beach St.	1985-88	1,175	664	42	.565	8,063	42	85
Randall Cunningham, UNLV	1982-84	1,029	597	29	.580	8,020	59	69
Brian Kuklich, Wake Forest	1994-98	1,230	665	49	.541	8,017	44	76
Stan White, Auburn	1990-93	1,231	659	52	.535	8,016	40	78
Steve Slayden, Duke	1984-87	1,204	699	53	.581	8,004	48	73

*Record. $See page 6 for explanation. ‡Did not score. ‡‡Record for minimum 1,000 attempts.

Western Michigan's Tim Lester threw for 11,299 yards in his career, third among Division I-A quarterbacks who completed their eligibility in 1999 and fifth in the history of the division.

CAREER YARDS RECORD PROGRESSION
(Record Yards—Player, Team, Seasons Played)

3,075—Billy Patterson, Baylor, 1936-38; **3,777**—Bud Schwenk, Washington (Mo.), 1939-41; **4,004**—Johnny Rauch, Georgia, 1945-48; **4,736**—John Ford, Hardin-Simmons, 1947-50; **4,863**—Zeke Bratkowski, Georgia, 1951-53; **5,472**—Jerry Rhome, Southern Methodist, 1961, Tulsa, 1963-64; **6,495**—Billy Stevens, UTEP, 1965-67; **7,076**—Steve Ramsey, North Texas, 1967-69; **7,544**—Jim Plunkett, Stanford, 1968-70; **7,549**—John Reaves, Florida, 1969-71; **7,818**—Jack Thompson, Washington St., 1975-78; **9,188**—Mark Herrmann, Purdue, 1977-80; **9,536**—Jim McMahon, Brigham Young, 1977-78, 1980-81; **9,614**—Ben Bennett, Duke, 1980-83; **10,579**—Doug Flutie, Boston College, 1981-84; **10,623**—Kevin Sweeney, Fresno St., $1982-86; **11,425**—Todd Santos, San Diego St., 1984-87; **15,031**—Ty Detmer, Brigham Young, 1988-91.

$See page 6 for explanation.

CAREER YARDS PER GAME
(Minimum 5,000 yards)

Player, Team	Years	G	Att.	Cmp.	Int.	Pct.	Yds.	TD	Yd.PG
Tim Rattay, Louisiana Tech	1997-99	33	1,552	1,015	35	.654	12,746	115	*386.2
Ty Detmer, Brigham Young	1988-91	46	1,530	958	65	.626	*15,031	*121	326.8
Chris Vargas, Nevada	1992-93	20	806	502	34	.623	6,359	47	318.0
Mike Perez, San Jose St.	1986-87	20	792	471	30	.595	6,194	36	309.7
Doug Gaynor, Long Beach St.	1984-85	22	837	569	35	.680	6,793	35	308.8

ALL-TIME LEADERS—PASSING

Player, Team	Years	G	Att.	Cmp.	Int.	Pct.	Yds.	TD	Yd.PG
Tony Eason, Illinois	1981-82	22	856	526	29	.614	6,608	37	300.4
Steve Sarkisian, Brigham Young	1995-96	25	789	528	26	.669	7,464	53	298.6
Chris Redman, Louisville	1996-99	42	*1,679	*1,031	51	.614	12,541	84	298.6
Chad Pennington, Marshall	1997-99	36	1,265	807	30	.638	10,698	100	297.2
David Klingler, Houston	1988-91	32	1,268	732	38	.577	9,466	91	295.8
Josh Wallwork, Wyoming	1995-96	22	729	449	28	.616	6,453	54	293.3
Tim Couch, Kentucky	1996-98	29	1,184	795	35	.671	8,435	74	290.9
Daunte Culpepper, UCF	1996-98	33	1,097	721	32	.657	9,341	72	283.1
Brent Snyder, Utah St.	1987-88	22	875	472	36	.539	6,105	39	277.5
Mike Maxwell, Nevada	1993-95	27	881	560	33	.636	7,256	62	268.7
Shane Matthews, Florida	1989-92	35	1,202	722	46	.601	9,287	74	265.3
Larry Egger, Utah	1985-86	22	799	470	31	.588	5,749	39	261.3

*Record.

CAREER TOUCHDOWN PASSES

Player, Team	Years	G	TD Passes
Ty Detmer, Brigham Young	1988-91	46	*121
Tim Rattay, Louisiana Tech	1997-99	33	115
Danny Wuerffel, Florida	1993-96	46	114
Chad Pennington, Marshall	1997-99	36	100
David Klingler, Houston	1988-91	32	91
Peyton Manning, Tennessee	1994-97	44	89
Tim Lester, Western Mich.	1996-99	44	87
Troy Kopp, Pacific (Cal.)	1989-92	40	87
Chris Redman, Louisville	1996-99	42	84
Jim McMahon, Brigham Young	1977-78, 80-81	44	84
Joe Adams, Tennessee St.	1977-80	41	81
Donovan McNabb, Syracuse	1995-98	45	77
John Elway, Stanford	1979-82	43	77
Andre Ware, Houston	1987-89	29	75
Tim Couch, Kentucky	1996-98	29	74
Shane Matthews, Florida	1989-92	35	74
Dan Marino, Pittsburgh	1979-82	40	74
T. J. Rubley, Tulsa	1987-89, 91	47	73
Daunte Culpepper, UCF	1996-98	33	72
Steve Stenstrom, Stanford	1991-94	41	72
Glenn Foley, Boston College	1990-93	44	72
Shaun King, Tulane	1995-98	41	70
Todd Santos, San Diego St.	1984-87	46	70
Tom Hodson, LSU	1986-89	44	69
Steve Ramsey, North Texas	1967-69	29	69
Scott Mitchell, Utah	1987-89	33	68
Billy Blanton, San Diego St.	1993-96	38	67
Stoney Case, New Mexico	1991-94	42	67
Eric Zeier, Georgia	1991-94	44	67
Doug Flutie, Boston College	1981-84	42	67
John Walsh, Brigham Young	1991-94	35	66
Kevin Sweeney, Fresno St.	1983-86	47	66
Robbie Bosco, Brigham Young	1983-85	35	66
Joe Hamilton, Georgia Tech	1996-99	43	65
Jake Delhomme, La.-Lafayette	1993-96	44	64
Jason Martin, Louisiana Tech	1993-96	41	64
Jake Plummer, Arizona St.	1993-96	42	64
Elvis Grbac, Michigan	1989-92	41	64
Alex Van Pelt, Pittsburgh	1989-92	45	64
Chuck Long, Iowa	$1981-85	45	64

*Record. $See page 6 for explanation.

SEASON YARDS

Player, Team	Year	G	Att.	Cmp.	Int.	Pct.	Yards	TD	Yds. Per Att.
Ty Detmer, Brigham Young	1990	12	562	361	28	.642	*5,188	41	9.23
David Klingler, Houston	1990	11	*643	*374	20	.582	5,140	*54	7.99
Tim Rattay, Louisiana Tech	1998	12	559	380	13	.680	4,943	46	8.84
Andre Ware, Houston	1989	11	578	365	15	.631	4,699	46	8.13
Jim McMahon, Brigham Young	†1980	12	445	284	18	.638	4,571	47	10.27
Ty Detmer, Brigham Young	†1989	12	412	265	15	.643	4,560	32	11.07
Scott Mitchell, Utah	1988	11	533	323	15	.606	4,322	29	8.11
Tim Couch, Kentucky	1998	11	553	400	15	.723	4,275	36	7.73
Robbie Bosco, Brigham Young	1985	13	511	338	24	.661	4,273	30	8.36
Chris Vargas, Nevada	1993	12	490	331	18	.676	4,265	34	8.70
Josh Wallwork, Wyoming	1996	12	458	286	15	.625	4,090	33	8.93
Chris Redman, Louisville	1998	10	473	309	15	.653	4,042	29	8.55
Ty Detmer, Brigham Young	1991	12	403	249	12	.618	4,031	35	10.00
Steve Sarkisian, Brigham Young	†1996	14	404	278	12	.688	4,027	33	9.97
Todd Santos, San Diego St.	1987	12	492	306	15	.622	3,932	26	7.99
Tim Rattay, Louisiana Tech	1999	10	516	342	12	.663	3,922	35	7.60
Steve Young, Brigham Young	†1983	11	429	306	10	.713	3,902	33	9.10
Tim Couch, Kentucky	1997	11	547	363	19	.664	3,884	37	7.10
Tim Rattay, Louisiana Tech	†1997	11	477	293	10	.614	3,881	34	8.14
Robbie Bosco, Brigham Young	1984	12	458	283	11	.618	3,875	33	8.46
Mike McCoy, Utah	1993	12	430	276	10	.642	3,860	21	8.98
Dan Robinson, Hawaii	1999	12	556	288	18	.518	3,853	28	6.93
Dan McGwire, San Diego St.	1990	11	449	270	7	.601	3,833	27	8.54

ALL-TIME LEADERS—PASSING

Player, Team	Year	G	Att.	Cmp.	Int.	Pct.	Yards	TD	Yds. Per Att.
Anthony Dilweg, Duke	1988	11	484	287	18	.593	3,824	24	7.90
Peyton Manning, Tennessee	1997	12	477	287	11	.602	3,819	36	8.01
Jimmy Klingler, Houston	1992	11	504	303	18	.601	3,818	32	7.58
Chad Pennington, Marshall	1999	12	405	275	11	.679	3,799	37	9.38
Sam King, UNLV	1981	12	433	255	19	.589	3,778	18	8.73
Troy Kopp, Pacific (Cal.)	1991	12	449	275	16	.612	3,767	37	8.39
Drew Brees, Purdue	1998	12	516	336	17	.651	3,753	36	7.27
John Walsh, Brigham Young	1993	11	397	244	15	.615	3,727	28	9.39
Marc Wilson, Brigham Young	1979	12	427	250	15	.585	3,720	29	8.71
John Walsh, Brigham Young	1994	12	463	284	14	.613	3,712	29	8.02
Daunte Culpepper, UCF	1998	11	402	296	7	*.736	3,690	28	9.18
Ryan Fien, Idaho	1996	11	455	267	12	.587	3,662	27	8.05
Dan McGwire, San Diego St.	1989	12	440	258	19	.586	3,651	16	8.30
Jim Everett, Purdue	1985	12	450	285	11	.633	3,651	23	8.11
Chris Redman, Louisville	1999	11	489	317	13	.648	3,647	29	7.46
Bernie Kosar, Miami (Fla.)	1984	12	416	262	16	.630	3,642	25	8.75

*Record. †National pass-efficiency champion.

SEASON YARDS PER GAME

Player, Team	Year	G	Att.	Cmp.	Int.	Pct.	Yards	TD	Yd.PG
David Klingler, Houston	1990	11	*643	*374	20	.582	5,140	*54	*467.3
Ty Detmer, Brigham Young	1990	12	562	361	28	.642	*5,188	41	432.3
Andre Ware, Houston	1989	11	578	365	15	.631	4,699	46	427.2
Tim Rattay, Louisiana Tech	1998	12	559	380	13	.680	4,943	46	411.9
Chris Redman, Louisville	1998	10	473	309	15	.653	4,042	29	404.2
Mike Maxwell, Nevada	1995	9	409	277	17	.677	3,611	33	401.2
Scott Mitchell, Utah	1988	11	533	323	15	.606	4,322	29	392.9
Tim Rattay, Louisiana Tech	1999	10	516	342	12	.663	3,922	35	392.2
Tim Couch, Kentucky	1998	11	553	400	15	.723	4,275	36	388.6
Chris Vargas, Nevada	1993	11	490	331	18	.676	4,265	34	387.7
Jim McMahon, Brigham Young	†1980	12	445	284	18	.638	4,571	47	380.9
Ty Detmer, Brigham Young	†1989	12	412	265	15	.643	4,560	32	380.0
Troy Kopp, Pacific (Cal.)	1990	9	428	243	14	.568	3,311	31	367.9
Tim Rattay, Louisville Tech	1999	10	516	342	12	.663	3,922	35	392.2
David Neill, Nevada	1998	9	344	199	9	.578	3,249	29	361.0
Jim McMahon, Brigham Young	†1981	10	423	272	7	.643	3,555	30	355.5
Steve Young, Brigham Young	†1983	11	429	306	10	.713	3,902	33	354.7
Tim Couch, Kentucky	1997	11	547	363	19	.664	3,884	37	353.1
Tim Rattay, Louisiana Tech	†1997	11	477	293	10	.614	3,881	34	352.8
Dan McGwire, San Diego St.	1990	11	449	270	7	.601	3,833	27	348.5
Anthony Dilweg, Duke	1988	11	484	287	18	.593	3,824	24	347.6
Jimmy Klingler, Houston	1992	11	504	303	18	.601	3,818	32	347.1
Bill Anderson, Tulsa	†1965	10	509	296	14	.582	3,464	30	346.4
Josh Wallwork, Wyoming	1996	12	458	286	15	.625	4,090	33	340.8
David Klingler, Houston	1991	10	497	278	17	.559	3,388	29	338.8
Marc Wilson, Brigham Young	1979	12	427	250	15	.585	3,720	29	338.2

*Record. †National pass-efficiency champion.

SEASON TOUCHDOWN PASSES

Player, Team	Year	G	TD Passes
David Klingler, Houston	1990	11	*54
Jim McMahon, Brigham Young	1980	12	47
Tim Rattay, Louisiana Tech	1998	12	46
Andre Ware, Houston	1989	11	46
Ty Detmer, Brigham Young	1990	12	41
Chad Pennington, Marshall	1997	12	39
Danny Wuerffel, Florida	1996	12	39
Dennis Shaw, San Diego St.	1969	10	39
Doug Williams, Grambling	1977	11	38
Tim Couch, Kentucky	1997	11	37
Troy Kopp, Pacific (Cal.)	1991	12	37
Chad Pennington, Marshall	1999	12	37
Peyton Manning, Tennessee	1997	12	36
Shaun King, Tulane	1998	11	36
Tim Couch, Kentucky	1998	11	36
Drew Brees, Purdue	1998	12	36
Danny Wuerffel, Florida	1995	11	35
Ty Detmer, Brigham Young	1991	12	35
Tim Rattay, Louisiana Tech	1999	10	35
Dan Marino, Pittsburgh	1981	11	34
Chris Vargas, Nevada	1993	11	34
Tim Rattay, Louisiana Tech	1997	11	34
Tim Lester, Western Mich.	1999	12	34
Robbie Bosco, Brigham Young	1984	12	33
Mike Maxwell, Nevada	1995	9	33
Josh Wallwork, Wyoming	1996	12	33
Steve Sarkisian, Brigham Young	1996	14	33
Ryan Leaf, Washington St.	1997	11	33
Steve Young, Brigham Young	1983	11	33
Jerry Rhome, Tulsa	1964	10	32

Player, Team	Year	G	Passes
Ty Detmer, Brigham Young	1989	12	32
Jimmy Klingler, Houston	1992	11	32
Danny Kanell, Florida St.	1995	11	32
Jason Martin, Louisiana Tech	1996	11	32
Jose Davis, Kent	1997	10	32
Troy Kopp, Pacific (Cal.)	1990	9	31
Pat Barnes, California	1996	11	31

*Record.

CAREER YARDS PER ATTEMPT
(Minimum 900 Attempts)

Player, Team	Years	Att.	Cmp.	Pct.	Yards	Yards Per Cmp.	Yards Per Att.
Ty Detmer, Brigham Young	1988-91	1,530	958	.626	*15,031	*15.69	*9.82
Danny Wuerffel, Florida	1993-96	1,170	708	.605	10,875	15.36	9.29
Jim McMahon, Brigham Young	1977-78, 80-81	1,060	653	.616	9,536	14.60	9.00
Marvin Graves, Syracuse	1990-93	943	563	.597	8,466	15.04	8.98
Donovan McNabb, Syracuse	1995-98	938	548	.584	8,389	15.31	8.94
Billy Blanton, San Diego St.	1993-96	920	588	.639	8,165	13.89	8.88
Joe Hamilton, Georgia Tech	1996-99	1,020	629	.617	8,882	14.12	8.71
Cade McNown, UCLA	1995-98	1,153	646	.560	10,008	15.49	8.68
John Walsh, Brigham Young	1991-94	973	587	.603	8,375	14.27	8.61
Chuck Long, Iowa	$1981-85	1,072	692	.646	9,210	13.31	8.59
Steve Young, Brigham Young	1981-83	908	592	.652	7,733	13.06	8.52
Daunte Culpepper, UCF	1996-98	1,097	721	.657	9,341	12.96	8.52
Chad Pennington, Marshall	1997-99	1,265	807	.638	10,698	13.26	8.45
Robbie Bosco, Brigham Young	1983-85	997	638	.640	8,400	13.17	8.43
Dan McGwire, Iowa/San Diego St.	1986-87, 89-90	973	575	.591	8,164	14.20	8.39
Doug Flutie, Boston College	1981-84	1,270	677	.533	10,579	15.63	8.33
Tim Rattay, Louisiana Tech	1997-99	1,552	1,015	#.654	12,746	12.56	8.21
Marc Wilson, Brigham Young	1977-79	937	535	.571	7,637	14.27	8.15
Peyton Manning, Tennessee	1994-97	1,381	863	.625	11,201	12.98	8.11
Rob Johnson, Southern California	1991-94	963	623	.647	7,743	12.43	8.04
Kevin Feterik, Brigham Young	1996-99	1,004	609	.607	8,065	13.24	8.03
Steve Stenstrom, Stanford	1991-94	1,320	833	.631	10,531	12.64	7.98
Kerwin Bell, Florida	1984-87	953	549	.576	7,585	13.82	7.96
Eric Zeier, Georgia	1991-94	1,402	838	.598	11,153	13.31	7.96
Kevin Sweeney, Fresno St.	$1982-86	1,336	731	.547	10,623	14.53	7.95
Robert Hall, Texas Tech	1990-93	997	548	.550	7,908	14.43	7.93
Glenn Foley, Boston College	1990-93	1,275	703	.551	10,042	14.28	7.88
Joe Adams, Tennessee St.	1977-80	1,100	604	.549	8,649	14.32	7.86
Rodney Peete, Southern California	1985-88	972	571	.587	7,640	13.38	7.86
Ron Powlus, Notre Dame	1994-97	969	558	.576	7,602	13.62	7.85
Tom Hodson, LSU	1986-89	1,163	674	.580	9,115	13.52	7.84
Jim Plunkett, Stanford	1968-70	962	530	.551	7,544	14.23	7.84

*Record. $See page 6 for explanation. #Record for minimum 1,000 attempts.

SINGLE-GAME YARDS

Yds.	Player, Team (Opponent)	Date
716	David Klingler, Houston (Arizona St.)	Dec. 2, 1990
690	Matt Vogler, TCU (Houston)	Nov. 3, 1990
631	Scott Mitchell, Utah (Air Force)	Oct. 15, 1988
622	Jeremy Leach, New Mexico (Utah)	Nov. 11, 1989
621	Dave Wilson, Illinois (Ohio St.)	Nov. 8, 1980
619	John Walsh, Brigham Young (Utah St.)	Oct. 30, 1993
613	Jimmy Klingler, Houston (Rice)	Nov. 28, 1992
611	David Neill, Nevada (New Mexico St.)	Oct. 10, 1998
599	Ty Detmer, Brigham Young (San Diego St.)	Nov. 16, 1991
592	Chris Redman, Louisville (East Caro.)	Nov. 14, 1998
590	Tim Rattay, Louisiana Tech (Nebraska)	Aug. 29, 1998
585	Robbie Bosco, Brigham Young (New Mexico)	Oct. 19, 1985
572	David Klingler, Houston (Eastern Wash.)	Nov. 17, 1990
571	Marc Wilson, Brigham Young (Utah)	Nov. 5, 1977
568	David Lowery, San Diego St. (Brigham Young)	Nov. 16, 1991
565	Jim McMahon, Brigham Young (Utah)	Nov. 21, 1981
564	Troy Kopp, Pacific (Cal.) (New Mexico St.)	Oct. 20, 1990
563	David Klingler, Houston (TCU)	Nov. 3, 1990
561	Tim Rattay, Louisiana Tech (UCF)	Oct. 23, 1999
561	Tony Adams, Utah St. (Utah)	Nov. 11, 1972
560	Ty Detmer, Brigham Young (Utah St.)	Nov. 24, 1990
558	Chuck Hartlieb, Iowa (Indiana)	Oct. 29, 1988
557	John Dutton, Nevada (Boise St.)	Nov. 8, 1997
554	Greg Cook, Cincinnati (Ohio)	Nov. 16, 1968
552	Mike Maxwell, Nevada (UNLV)	Oct. 28, 1995
551	Jose Davis, Kent St. (UCF)	Oct. 4, 1997
546	Cody Ledbetter, New Mexico St. (UNLV)	Nov. 18, 1995
545	Rusty LaRue, Wake Forest (North Carolina St.)	Nov. 18, 1995
544	Eric Zeier, Georgia (Southern Miss.)	Oct. 9, 1993
542	Jason Martin, Louisiana Tech (Toledo)	Oct. 19, 1996
542	Ryan Fien, Idaho (Wyoming)	Aug. 31, 1996
539	Tim Rattay, Louisiana Tech (Boise St.)	Oct. 3, 1998

ALL-TIME LEADERS—PASSING

Yds.	Player, Team (Opponent)	Date
538	Chris Vargas, Nevada (UNLV)	Oct. 2, 1993
538	Jim McMahon, Brigham Young (Colorado St.)	Nov. 7, 1981
537	Ty Detmer, Brigham Young (Washington St.)	Sept. 7, 1989
536	Steve Sarkisian, Brigham Young (Texas A&M)	Aug. 24, 1996
536	Dave Telford, Fresno St. (Pacific [Cal.])	Oct. 24, 1987
536	Todd Santos, San Diego St. (Stanford)	Oct. 17, 1987
536	David Spriggs, New Mexico St. (Southern Ill.)	Sept. 30, 1978

SINGLE-GAME ATTEMPTS

No.	Player, Team (Opponent)	Date
83	Drew Brees, Purdue (Wisconsin)	Oct. 10, 1998
79	Matt Vogler, TCU (Houston)	Nov. 3, 1990
78	Rusty LaRue, Wake Forest (Duke)	Oct. 28, 1995
76	David Klingler, Houston (Southern Methodist)	Oct. 20, 1990
75	Chris Vargas, Nevada (McNeese St.)	Sept. 19, 1992
73	Jeff Handy, Missouri (Oklahoma St.)	Oct. 17, 1992
73	Troy Kopp, Pacific (Cal.) (Hawaii)	Oct. 27, 1990
73	Shane Montgomery, North Carolina St. (Duke)	Nov. 11, 1989
72	Matt Vogler, TCU (Texas Tech)	Nov. 10, 1990
71	Jimmy Klingler, Houston (Rice)	Nov. 28, 1992
71	Sandy Schwab, Northwestern (Michigan)	Oct. 23, 1982
70	David Klingler, Houston (Texas Tech)	Nov. 30, 1991
70	David Klingler, Houston (Arizona St.)	Dec. 2, 1990
70	Dave Telford, Fresno St. (Utah St.)	Nov. 14, 1987
69	Dave Wilson, Illinois (Ohio St.)	Nov. 8, 1980
69	Chuck Hixson, Southern Methodist (Ohio St.)	Sept. 28, 1968
68	Tim Rattay, Louisiana Tech (Southern California)	Nov. 26, 1999
68	Tim Rattay, Louisiana Tech (Nebraska)	Aug. 29, 1998
68	David Klingler, Houston (Baylor)	Oct. 6, 1990
68	Jeremy Leach, New Mexico (Utah)	Nov. 11, 1989
68	Steve Smith, Stanford (Notre Dame)	Oct. 7, 1989
68	Andre Ware, Houston (Arizona St.)	Sept. 23, 1989
67	Tim Couch, Kentucky (Arkansas)	Oct. 3, 1998
67	Rusty LaRue, Wake Forest (North Carolina St.)	Nov. 18, 1995
67	Danny Kanell, Florida St. (Virginia)	Nov. 2, 1995
67	Mike Hohensee, Minnesota (Ohio St.)	Nov. 7, 1981
66	Tim Rattay, Louisiana Tech (Toledo)	Oct. 30, 1999
66	Tim Couch, Kentucky (LSU)	Nov. 1, 1997
66	Chuck Clements, Houston (Cincinnati)	Nov. 13, 1993
66	Tim Schade, Minnesota (Penn St.)	Sept. 4, 1993
66	Drew Bledsoe, Washington St. (Montana)	Sept. 5, 1992
66	Jack Trudeau, Illinois (Purdue)	Oct. 12, 1985
66	John Reaves, Florida (Auburn)	Nov. 1, 1969
65	Tim Rattay, Louisiana Tech (Texas A&M)	Sept. 4, 1999
65	Peyton Manning, Tennessee (Florida)	Sept. 21, 1996
65	Rusty LaRue, Wake Forest (Georgia Tech)	Nov. 4, 1995
65	Jason Martin, Louisiana Tech (Nevada)	Oct. 21, 1995
65	Eric Zeier, Georgia (Florida)	Oct. 30, 1993
65	Jimmy Klingler, Houston (TCU)	Oct. 31, 1992
65	Scott Mitchell, Utah (UTEP)	Oct. 1, 1988
65	Mike Bates, Miami, Ohio (Toledo)	Oct. 24, 1987
65	Craig Burnett, Wyoming (San Diego St.)	Nov. 15, 1986
65	Gary Schofield, Wake Forest (Maryland)	Oct. 16, 1982
65	Jim McMahon, Brigham Young (Colorado St.)	Nov. 7, 1981
65	Brooks Dawson, UTEP (UC Santa Barb.)	Sept. 14, 1968
65	Bill Anderson, Tulsa (Southern Ill.)	Oct. 30, 1965
65	Bill Anderson, Tulsa (Memphis)	Oct. 9, 1965

SINGLE-GAME COMPLETIONS

No.	Player, Team (Opponent)	Date
55	Drew Brees, Purdue (Wisconsin)	Oct. 10, 1998
55	Rusty LaRue, Wake Forest (Duke)	Oct. 28, 1995
50	Rusty LaRue, Wake Forest (North Carolina St.)	Nov. 18, 1995
48	David Klingler, Houston (Southern Methodist)	Oct. 20, 1990
47	Tim Couch, Kentucky (Arkansas)	Oct. 3, 1998
46	Tim Rattay, Louisiana Tech (UCF)	Oct. 23, 1999
46	Scott Milanovich, Maryland (Florida St.)	Nov. 18, 1995
46	Tim Rattay, Louisiana Tech (Nebraska)	Aug. 29, 1998
46	Jimmy Klingler, Houston (Rice)	Nov. 28, 1992
45	Tim Rattay, Louisiana Tech (Texas A&M)	Sept. 4, 1999
45	Sandy Schwab, Northwestern (Michigan)	Oct. 23, 1982
44	Tim Rattay, Louisiana Tech (Toledo)	Oct. 30, 1999
44	Chris Redman, Louisville (East Caro.)	Nov. 14, 1998
44	Tim Couch, Kentucky (Vanderbilt)	Nov. 14, 1998
44	Matt Vogler, TCU (Houston)	Nov. 3, 1990
44	Chuck Hartlieb, Iowa (Indiana)	Oct. 29, 1988
44	Jim McMahon, Brigham Young (Colorado St.)	Nov. 7, 1981
43	Tim Rattay, Louisiana Tech (UCF)	Sept. 5, 1998
43	Jeff Handy, Missouri (Oklahoma St.)	Oct. 17, 1992
43	Chris Vargas, Nevada (McNeese St.)	Sept. 19, 1992
43	Gary Schofield, Wake Forest (Maryland)	Oct. 17, 1981
43	Dave Wilson, Illinois (Ohio St.)	Nov. 8, 1980
43	Rich Campbell, California (Florida)	Sept. 13, 1980

ALL-TIME LEADERS—PASSING

No.	Player, Team (Opponent)	Date
42	Jimmy Klingler, Houston (TCU)	Oct. 31, 1992
42	Troy Kopp, Pacific (Cal.) (Hawaii)	Oct. 27, 1990
42	Andre Ware, Houston (TCU)	Nov. 4, 1989
42	Dan Speltz, Cal St. Fullerton (Utah St.)	Oct. 7, 1989
42	Robbie Bosco, Brigham Young (New Mexico)	Oct. 19, 1985
42	Bill Anderson, Tulsa (Southern Ill.)	Oct. 30, 1965
41	Tim Rattay, Louisiana Tech (Middle Tenn. St.)	Oct. 16, 1999
41	Tim Couch, Kentucky (Georgia)	Oct. 25, 1997
41	Tim Couch, Kentucky (LSU)	Nov. 1, 1997
41	Rusty LaRue, Wake Forest (Georgia Tech)	Nov. 4, 1995
41	Mike Maxwell, Nevada (UNLV)	Oct. 28, 1995
41	Danny Kanell, Florida St. (Georgia Tech)	Oct. 21, 1995
41	David Klingler, Houston (Texas Tech)	Nov. 30, 1991
41	David Klingler, Houston (Arizona St.)	Dec. 2, 1990
41	David Klingler, Houston (Eastern Wash.)	Nov. 17, 1990
41	Jeremy Leach, New Mexico (Utah)	Nov. 11, 1989
41	Scott Mitchell, Utah (UTEP)	Oct. 1, 1988
41	Doug Gaynor, Long Beach St. (Utah St.)	Sept. 7, 1985
40	Drew Brees, Purdue (Michigan St.)	Oct. 16, 1999
40	Tim Couch, Kentucky (Florida)	Sept. 26, 1998
40	Danny Kanell, Florida St. (Florida)	Nov. 26, 1994
40	Mike Romo, Southern Methodist (Rice)	Nov. 10, 1990
40	Andre Ware, Houston (Arizona St.)	Sept. 23, 1989
40	Dave Telford, Fresno St. (Utah St.)	Nov. 14, 1987
40	Todd Santos, San Diego St. (Stanford)	Oct. 17, 1987
40	Larry Egger, Utah (UTEP)	Nov. 29, 1986
40	John Paye, Stanford (San Diego St.)	Oct. 5, 1985
40	Gary Schofield, Wake Forest (Maryland)	Oct. 16, 1982
40	Jim McMahon, Brigham Young (North Texas)	Nov. 8, 1980

ANNUAL CHAMPIONS

Year	Player, Team	Class	Att.	Cmp.	Int.	Pct.	Yds.	TD
1937	Davey O'Brien, TCU	Jr.	234	94	18	.402	969	—
1938	Davey O'Brien, TCU	Sr.	167	93	4	.557	1,457	—
1939	Kay Eakin, Arkansas	Sr.	193	78	18	.404	962	—
1940	Billy Sewell, Washington St.	Sr.	174	86	17	.494	1,023	—
1941	Bud Schwenk, Washington (Mo.)	Sr.	234	114	19	.487	1,457	—
1942	Ray Evans, Kansas	Jr.	200	101	9	.505	1,117	—
1943	Johnny Cook, Georgia	Fr.	157	73	20	.465	1,007	—
1944	Paul Rickards, Pittsburgh	So.	178	84	20	.472	997	—
1945	Al Dekdebrun, Cornell	Sr.	194	90	15	.464	1,227	—
1946	Travis Tidwell, Auburn	Fr.	158	79	10	.500	943	5
1947	Charlie Conerly, Mississippi	Sr.	233	133	7	.571	1,367	18
1948	Stan Heath, Nevada	Sr.	222	126	9	.568	2,005	22
1949	Adrian Burk, Baylor	Sr.	191	110	6	.576	1,428	14
1950	Don Heinrich, Washington	Jr.	221	134	9	.606	1,846	14
1951	Don Klosterman, Loyola Marymount	Sr.	315	159	21	.505	1,843	9
1952	Don Heinrich, Washington	Sr.	270	137	17	.507	1,647	13
1953	Bob Garrett, Stanford	Sr.	205	118	10	.576	1,637	17
1954	Paul Larson, California	Sr.	195	125	8	.641	1,537	10
1955	George Welsh, Navy	Sr.	150	94	6	.627	1,319	8
1956	John Brodie, Stanford	Sr.	240	139	14	.579	1,633	12
1957	Ken Ford, Hardin-Simmons	Sr.	205	115	11	.561	1,254	14
1958	Buddy Humphrey, Baylor	Sr.	195	112	8	.574	1,316	7
1959	Dick Norman, Stanford	Jr.	263	152	12	.578	1,963	11
1960	Harold Stephens, Hardin-Simmons	Sr.	256	145	14	.566	1,254	3
1961	Chon Gallegos, San Jose St.	Sr.	197	117	13	.594	1,480	14
1962	Don Trull, Baylor	Jr.	229	125	12	.546	1,627	11
1963	Don Trull, Baylor	Sr.	308	174	12	.565	2,157	12
1964	Jerry Rhome, Tulsa	Sr.	326	224	4	.687	2,870	32
1965	Bill Anderson, Tulsa	Sr.	509	296	14	.582	3,464	30
1966	John Eckman, Wichita St.	Jr.	458	195	*34	.426	2,339	7
1967	Terry Stone, New Mexico	Jr.	336	160	19	.476	1,946	9
1968	Chuck Hixson, Southern Methodist	So.	468	265	23	.566	3,103	21
1969	John Reaves, Florida	So.	396	222	19	.561	2,896	24

Beginning in 1970, ranked on per-game (instead of total) completions

Year	Player, Team	Class	G	Att.	Cmp.	Avg.	Int.	Pct.	Yds.	TD
1970	Sonny Sixkiller, Washington	So.	10	362	186	18.6	22	.514	2,303	15
1971	Brian Sipe, San Diego St.	Sr.	11	369	196	17.8	21	.531	2,532	17
1972	Don Strock, Virginia Tech	Sr.	11	427	228	20.7	27	.534	3,243	16
1973	Jesse Freitas, San Diego St.	Sr.	11	347	227	20.6	17	.654	2,993	21
1974	Steve Bartkowski, California	Sr.	11	325	182	16.5	7	.560	2,580	12
1975	Craig Penrose, San Diego St.	Sr.	11	349	198	18.0	24	.567	2,660	15
1976	Tommy Kramer, Rice	Sr.	11	501	269	24.5	19	.537	3,317	21
1977	Guy Benjamin, Stanford	Sr.	10	330	208	20.8	15	.630	2,521	19
1978	Steve Dils, Stanford	Sr.	11	391	247	22.5	15	.632	2,943	22

Beginning in 1979, ranked on passing efficiency rating points (instead of per-game completions)

Year	Player, Team	Class	G	Att.	Cmp.	Int.	Pct.	Yds.	TD	Pts.
1979	Turk Schonert, Stanford	Sr.	11	221	148	6	.670	1,922	19	163.0
1980	Jim McMahon, Brigham Young	Jr.	12	445	284	18	.638	4,571	47	176.9
1981	Jim McMahon, Brigham Young	Sr.	10	423	272	7	.643	3,555	30	155.0
1982	Tom Ramsey, UCLA	Sr.	11	311	191	10	.614	2,824	21	153.5
1983	Steve Young, Brigham Young	Sr.	11	429	306	10	*.713	3,902	33	168.5

ALL-TIME LEADERS—PASSING

Year	Player, Team	Class	G	Att.	Cmp.	Int.	Pct.	Yds.	TD	Pts.
1984	Doug Flutie, Boston College	Sr.	11	386	233	11	.604	3,454	27	152.9
1985	Jim Harbaugh, Michigan	Jr.	11	212	139	6	.656	1,913	18	163.7
1986	Vinny Testaverde, Miami (Fla.)	Sr.	10	276	175	9	.634	2,557	26	165.8
1987	Don McPherson, Syracuse	Sr.	11	229	129	11	.563	2,341	22	164.3
1988	Timm Rosenbach, Washington St.	Jr.	11	302	199	10	.659	2,791	23	162.0
1989	Ty Detmer, Brigham Young	So.	12	412	265	15	.643	4,560	32	175.6
1990	Shawn Moore, Virginia	Sr.	10	241	144	8	.598	2,262	21	160.7
1991	Elvis Grbac, Michigan	Jr.	11	228	152	5	.667	1,955	24	169.0
1992	Elvis Grbac, Michigan	Sr.	9	169	112	12	.663	1,465	15	154.2
1993	Trent Dilfer, Fresno St.	Jr.	11	333	217	4	.652	3,276	28	173.1
1994	Kerry Collins, Penn St.	Sr.	11	264	176	7	.667	2,679	21	172.9
1995	Danny Wuerffel, Florida	Jr.	11	325	210	10	.646	3,266	35	178.4
1996	Steve Sarkisian, Brigham Young	Sr.	14	404	278	12	.688	4,027	33	173.6
1997	Cade McNown, UCLA	Jr.	11	283	173	5	.611	2,877	22	168.6
1998	Shaun King, Tulane	Sr.	11	328	223	6	.680	3,232	36	183.3
1999	Michael Vick, Virginia Tech	So.	10	152	90	5	.592	1,840	12	180.4

*Record.

Nevada's Trevor Insley grabbed 298 career receptions, edging former Wolf Pack teammate Geoff Noisy by three catches for the top spot in Division I-A.

Receiving

CAREER RECEPTIONS PER GAME
(Minimum 125 Receptions)

Player, Team	Years	G	Rec.	Yards	TD	Rec.PG
Manny Hazard, Houston	1989-90	21	220	2,635	31	*10.5
Alex Van Dyke, Nevada	1994-95	22	227	3,100	26	10.3
Howard Twilley, Tulsa	1963-65	26	261	3,343	32	10.0
Jason Phillips, Houston	1987-88	22	207	2,319	18	9.4
Troy Edwards, Louisiana Tech	1996-98	34	280	4,352	*50	8.2
Bryan Reeves, Nevada	1992-93	21	172	2,476	27	8.2
Siaha Burley, UCF	1997-98	22	165	2,248	15	7.5
David Williams, Illinois	1983-85	33	245	3,195	22	7.4
Geoff Noisy, Nevada	1995-98	40	295	4,249	21	7.4
James Dixon, Houston	1987-88	22	161	1,762	14	7.3
John Love, North Texas	1965-66	20	144	2,124	17	7.2
Fred Gilbert, UCLA/Houston	1989, 91-92	22	158	1,672	14	7.2
Arnold Jackson, Louisville	1997-99	33	237	3,061	26	7.2
Ron Sellers, Florida St.	1966-68	30	212	3,598	23	7.1
Keyshawn Johnson, Southern California	1994-95	21	148	2,358	12	7.1
Barry Moore, North Texas	1968-69	20	140	2,183	12	7.0
Nakia Jenkins, Utah St.	1996-97	22	155	2,483	14	7.0
Mike Kelly, Davidson	1967-69	23	156	2,114	17	6.8
Guy Liggins, San Jose St.	1986-87	22	149	2,191	16	6.8
Trevor Insley, Nevada	1996-99	44	*298	*5,005	35	6.8
Dave Petzke, Northern Ill.	1977-78	22	148	1,960	16	6.7
Loren Richey, Utah	1985-86	21	140	1,746	13	6.7
Chris Penn, Tulsa	1991, 93	22	142	2,370	17	6.5
Antonio Wilson, Idaho	1996-97	22	142	2,113	17	6.5
Brandon Stokley, La.-Lafayette	1995-98	37	241	3,702	25	6.5
Tim Delaney, San Diego St.	1968-70	29	180	2,535	22	6.2
Larry Willis, Fresno St.	1983-84	23	142	2,260	14	6.2
Phil Odle, Brigham Young	1965-67	30	183	2,548	25	6.1
Randy Gatewood, UNLV	1993-94	21	128	1,832	13	6.1
Mike Mikolayunas, Davidson	1989	29	175	1,768	14	6.0
Terance Mathis, New Mexico	1985-87, 89	44	263	4,254	36	6.0
Aaron Turner, Pacific (Cal.)	1989-92	44	266	4,345	43	6.0
Michael Stephens, Nevada	1992-93	21	125	1,712	15	6.0
Chad Mackey, Louisiana Tech	1993-96	44	264	3,789	22	6.0

*Record.

SEASON RECEPTIONS PER GAME

Player, Team	Year	G	Rec.	Yards	TD	Rec.PG
Howard Twilley, Tulsa	†1965	10	134	1,779	16	*13.4
Manny Hazard, Houston	†1989	11	*142	1,689	22	12.9
Trevor Insley, Nevada	†1999	11	134	*2,060	13	12.2
Alex Van Dyke, Nevada	†1995	11	129	1,854	16	11.7
Troy Edwards, Louisiana Tech	†1998	12	140	1,996	*27	11.7
Damond Wilkins, Nevada	†1996	11	114	1,121	4	10.4
Chris Daniels, Purdue	1999	11	109	1,133	5	9.9
Jason Phillips, Houston	†1988	11	108	1,444	15	9.8
Fred Gilbert, Houston	†1991	11	106	957	7	9.6
Jajuan Dawson, Tulane	1999	10	96	1,051	8	9.6
Howard Twilley, Tulsa	†1964	10	95	1,178	13	9.5
Jerry Hendren, Idaho	†1969	10	95	1,452	12	9.5
Chris Penn, Tulsa	†1993	11	105	1,578	12	9.5
Sherman Smith, Houston	†1992	11	103	923	6	9.4
Eugene Baker, Kent St.	†1997	11	103	1,549	18	9.4
Troy Edwards, Louisiana Tech	1997	11	102	1,707	13	9.3
James Dixon, Houston	1988	11	102	1,103	11	9.3
David Williams, Illinois	†1984	11	101	1,278	8	9.2
Arnold Jackson, Louisville	1999	11	101	1,209	9	9.2
Glenn Meltzer, Wichita St.	†1966	10	91	1,115	4	9.1

Player, Team	Year	G	Rec.	Yards	TD	Rec.PG
Jay Miller, Brigham Young	†1973	11	100	1,181	8	9.1
Bryan Reeves, Nevada	1993	10	91	1,362	17	9.1
Marcus Harris, Wyoming	1996	12	109	1,650	13	9.1
Dameane Douglas, California	1998	11	100	1,150	4	9.1

*Record. †National champion.

CAREER RECEPTIONS

Player, Team	Years	Rec.	Yards	Avg.	TD
Trevor Insley, Nevada	1996-99	*298	*5,005	16.8	35
Geoff Noisy, Nevada	1995-98	295	4,249	14.4	21
Troy Edwards, Louisiana Tech	1996-98	280	4,352	15.5	*50
Aaron Turner, Pacific (Cal.)	1989-92	266	4,345	16.3	43
Chad Mackey, Louisiana Tech	1993-96	264	3,789	14.4	22
Terance Mathis, New Mexico	1985-87, 89	263	4,254	16.2	36
Mark Templeton, Long Beach St. (RB)	1983-86	262	1,969	7.5	11
Howard Twilley, Tulsa	1963-65	261	3,343	12.8	32
Marcus Harris, Wyoming	1993-96	259	4,518	17.4	38
David Williams, Illinois	1983-85	245	3,195	13.0	22
Troy Walters, Stanford	1996-99	244	3,986	16.3	26
Brandon Stokley, La.-Lafayette	1995-98	241	3,702	15.4	25
Arnold Jackson, Louisville	1997-99	237	3,061	12.9	26
Marc Zeno, Tulane	1984-87	236	3,725	15.8	25
Jason Wolf, Southern Methodist	1989-92	235	2,232	9.5	17
Ryan Yarborough, Wyoming	1990-93	229	4,357	‡19.0	42
Eugene Baker, Kent St.	1995-98	229	3,513	15.3	35
Alex Van Dyke, Nevada	1994-95	227	3,100	13.7	26
Dennis Northcutt, Arizona	1996-99	223	3,252	14.5	24
Manny Hazard, Houston	1989-90	220	2,635	12.0	31
Kevin Lockett, Kansas St.	1993-96	217	3,032	14.0	26
Ibn Green, Louisville (TE)	1996-99	217	2,830	13.0	33
Desmond Clark, Wake Forest	1995-98	216	2,834	13.1	20
Darrin Nelson, Stanford (RB)	1977-78, 80-81	214	2,368	11.1	16
Ron Sellers, Florida St.	1966-68	212	3,598	17.0	23
Craig Yeast, Kentucky	1995-98	208	2,899	13.9	28
Jason Phillips, Houston	1987-88	207	2,319	11.2	18
Peter Warrick, Florida St.	1996-99	207	3,517	17.0	32
Hart Lee Dykes, Oklahoma St.	1985-88	203	3,171	15.6	29
Carl Winston, New Mexico	1990-93	202	2,972	14.7	14
Keith Edwards, Vanderbilt	1980, 82-84	200	1,757	8.8	3
Bobby Slaughter, Louisiana Tech	1987-90	198	2,544	12.9	14
Gerald Harp, Western Caro.	1977-80	197	3,305	16.8	26
Richard Buchanan, Northwestern	1987-90	197	2,474	12.6	22
Brad Muster, Stanford (FB)	1984-87	196	1,669	8.5	6
Matt Bellini, Brigham Young (RB)	1987-90	196	2,544	13.0	13
Anthony White, Kentucky (RB)	1996-99	194	1,520	7.8	8
Jermaine Lewis, Maryland	1992-95	193	2,932	15.2	21
Greg Primus, Colorado St.	1989-92	192	3,200	16.7	16
Charles Lockett, Long Beach St.	1983-86	191	2,902	15.1	19
Torry Holt, North Carolina St.	1995-98	191	3,379	17.7	31
Pete Mitchell, Boston College (TE)	1991-94	190	2,389	12.6	20
Clarkston Hines, Duke	1986-89	189	3,318	17.6	38
Lloyd Hill, Texas Tech	1990-93	189	3,059	16.2	20
Kez McCorvey, Florida St.	1991-94	189	2,660	14.1	16
Boo Mitchell, Vanderbilt	1985-88	188	2,964	15.8	9
Ricky Proehl, Wake Forest	1986-89	188	2,949	15.7	25
Wil Ursin, Tulane	1990-93	188	2,466	13.1	17
Brian Roberson, Fresno St.	1993-96	188	2,956	15.7	15
Monty Gilbreath, San Diego St.	1986-89	187	2,241	12.0	8
Damon Williams, UNLV	1995-98	187	2,558	13.7	9
Eric Henley, Rice	1988-91	186	2,200	11.8	6
Mick Rossley, Southern Methodist	1991-94	186	1,911	10.3	10
Johnnie Morton, Southern California	1990-93	185	2,957	16.0	21
Geroy Simon, Maryland	1993-96	185	2,059	11.1	10
Jeff Champine, Colorado St.	1980-83	184	2,811	15.3	21

ALL-TIME LEADERS—RECEIVING

Player, Team	Years	Rec.	Yards	Avg.	TD
Phil Odle, Brigham Young	1965-67	183	2,548	13.9	25
Wendell Davis, LSU	1984-85	183	2,708	14.8	19
Joey Kent, Tennessee	1993-96	183	2,814	15.4	25
Mark Szlachcic, Bowling Green	1989-92	182	2,507	13.8	18
Brice Hunter, Georgia	1992-95	182	2,373	13.0	19
Kelly Blackwell, TCU (TE)	1988-91	181	2,155	11.9	13
Charlie Jones, Fresno St.	1992-95	181	3,260	18.0	25
Duane Gregory, New Mexico St.	1994-97	181	2,641	14.6	14
Tim Delaney, San Diego St.	1968-70	180	2,535	14.1	22

*Record. ‡Record for minimum of 200 catches.

SEASON RECEPTIONS

Player, Team	Year	G	Rec.	Yards	TD
Manny Hazard, Houston	†1989	11	*142	1,689	22
Troy Edwards, Louisiana Tech	†1998	12	140	1,996	*27
Trevor Insley, Nevada	†1999	11	134	*2,060	13
Howard Twilley, Tulsa	†1965	10	134	1,779	16
Alex Van Dyke, Nevada	†1995	11	129	1,854	16
Damond Wilkins, Nevada	1996	11	114	1,121	4
Chris Daniels, Purdue	1999	11	109	1,133	5
Marcus Harris, Wyoming	1996	12	109	1,650	13
Jason Phillips, Houston	†1988	11	108	1,444	15
Fred Gilbert, Houston	†1991	11	106	957	7
Chris Penn, Tulsa	†1993	11	105	1,578	12
Eugene Baker, Kent St.	†1997	11	103	1,549	18
Sherman Smith, Houston	†1992	11	103	923	6
Troy Edwards, Louisiana Tech	1997	11	102	1,707	13
James Dixon, Houston	1988	11	102	1,103	11
Arnold Jackson, Louisville	1999	11	101	1,209	9
David Williams, Illinois	†1984	11	101	1,278	8
Kwame Cavil, Texas	1999	13	100	1,188	6
Dameane Douglas, California	1998	11	100	1,150	4
Jay Miller, Brigham Young	†1973	11	100	1,181	8
Jason Phillips, Houston	†1987	11	99	875	3
Mark Templeton, Long Beach St. (RB)	†1986	11	99	688	2
Geoff Noisy, Nevada	1996	11	98	1,435	9
Alex Van Dyke, Nevada	†1994	11	98	1,246	10
Rodney Carter, Purdue	†1985	11	98	1,099	4
Keith Edwards, Vanderbilt	†1983	11	97	909	0
Jajuan Dawson, Tulane	1999	10	96	1,051	8
Jerry Hendren, Idaho	†1969	10	95	1,452	12
Howard Twilley, Tulsa	†1964	10	95	1,178	13
Geoff Noisy, Nevada	1998	11	94	1,405	7
Richard Buchanan, Northwestern	1989	11	94	1,115	9
Kevin Alexander, Utah St.	1995	11	92	1,400	6
Aaron Turner, Pacific (Cal.)	1991	11	92	1,604	18
Bryan Reeves, Nevada	1993	10	91	1,362	17
Dave Petzke, Northern Ill.	†1978	11	91	1,217	11
Glenn Meltzer, Wichita St.	†1966	10	91	1,115	4

*Record. †National champion.

SEASON TOUCHDOWN RECEPTIONS

Player, Team	Year	G	TD
Troy Edwards, Louisiana Tech	1998	12	*27
Randy Moss, Marshall	1997	12	25
Manny Hazard, Houston	1989	11	22
Desmond Howard, Michigan	1991	11	19
Eugene Baker, Kent St.	1997	11	18
Reidel Anthony, Florida	1996	12	18
Aaron Turner, Pacific (Cal.)	1991	11	18
Dennis Smith, Utah	1989	12	18
Tom Reynolds, San Diego St.	1971	10	18
Terry Glenn, Ohio St.	1995	11	17
Chris Doering, Florida	1995	12	17
Bryan Reeves, Nevada	1993	10	17
J. J. Stokes, UCLA	1993	11	17
Mario Bailey, Washington	1991	11	17
Clarkston Hines, Duke	1989	11	17
Torry Holt, North Carolina St.	1997	11	16
Alex Van Dyke, Nevada	1995	11	16
Ryan Yarborough, Wyoming	1993	11	16
Dan Bitson, Tulsa	1989	11	16
Howard Twilley, Tulsa	1965	10	16
Andre Cooper, Florida St.	1995	11	15
Ike Hilliard, Florida	1995	11	15
Jack Jackson, Florida	1994	12	15
Jason Phillips, Houston	1988	11	15
Henry Ellard, Fresno St.	1982	11	15

*Record.

SINGLE-GAME RECEPTIONS

Rec.	Player, Team (Opponent)	Date
23	Randy Gatewood, UNLV (Idaho)	Sept. 17, 1994
22	Jay Miller, Brigham Young (New Mexico)	Nov. 3, 1973
21	Chris Daniels, Purdue (Michigan St.)	Oct. 16, 1999
21	Troy Edwards, Louisiana Tech (Nebraska)	Aug. 29, 1998
20	Rick Eber, Tulsa (Idaho St.)	Oct. 7, 1967
19	Manny Hazard, Houston (Texas)	Nov. 11, 1989
19	Manny Hazard, Houston (TCU)	Nov. 4, 1989
19	Ron Fair, Arizona St. (Washington St.)	Oct. 28, 1989
19	Howard Twilley, Tulsa (Colorado St.)	Nov. 27, 1965
18	Randall Lane, Purdue (Wisconsin)	Oct. 10, 1998
18	Geoff Noisy, Nevada (Oregon)	Sept. 13, 1997
18	Geoff Noisy, Nevada (Arkansas St.)	Nov. 16, 1996
18	Albert Connell, Texas A&M (Colorado)	Sept. 28, 1996
18	Alex Van Dyke, Nevada (UNLV)	Oct. 28, 1995
18	Alex Van Dyke, Nevada (Toledo)	Sept. 23, 1995
18	Richard Woodley, TCU (Texas Tech)	Nov. 10, 1990
18	Mark Templeton (RB), Long Beach St. (Utah St.)	Nov. 1, 1986
18	Howard Twilley, Tulsa (Southern Ill.)	Oct. 30, 1965
17	Trevor Insley, Nevada (Colorado St.)	Sept. 11, 1999
17	Willie Gosha, Auburn (Arkansas)	Oct. 28, 1995
17	Chad Mackey, Louisiana Tech (Nevada)	Oct. 21, 1995
17	Curtis Shearer, San Diego St. (Air Force)	Oct. 1, 1994
17	Loren Richey, Utah (UTEP)	Nov. 29, 1986
17	Keith Edwards, Vanderbilt (Georgia)	Oct. 15, 1983
17	Jon Harvey, Northwestern (Michigan)	Oct. 23, 1982
17	Don Roberts, San Diego St. (California)	Sept. 18, 1982
17	Tom Reynolds, San Diego St. (Utah St.)	Oct. 22, 1971
17	Mike Mikolayunas, Davidson (Richmond)	Oct. 11, 1969
17	Jerry Hendren, Idaho (Southern Miss.)	Oct. 4, 1969
17	Emilio Vallez, New Mexico (New Mexico St.)	Oct. 27, 1967
17	Chuck Hughes, UTEP (Arizona St.)	Oct. 30, 1965

CAREER YARDS

Player, Team	Years	Rec.	Yards	Avg.	TD
Trevor Insley, Nevada	1996-99	*298	*5,005	16.8	35
Marcus Harris, Wyoming	1993-96	259	4,518	17.4	38
Ryan Yarborough, Wyoming	1990-93	229	4,357	#19.0	42
Troy Edwards, Louisiana Tech	1996-98	280	4,352	15.5	*50
Aaron Turner, Pacific (Cal.)	1989-92	266	4,345	16.3	43
Terance Mathis, New Mexico	1985-87, 89	263	4,254	16.2	36
Geoff Noisy, Nevada	1995-98	295	4,249	14.4	21
Troy Walters, Stanford	1996-99	244	3,986	16.3	26
Chad Mackey, Louisiana Tech	1993-96	264	3,789	14.4	22
Marc Zeno, Tulane	1984-87	236	3,725	15.8	5
Brandon Stokley, La.-Lafayette	1995-98	241	3,702	15.4	25
Ron Sellers, Florida St.	1966-68	212	3,598	17.0	23
Peter Warrick, Florida St.	1996-99	207	3,517	17.0	32
Eugene Baker, Kent St.	1995-98	229	3,513	15.3	35
Torry Holt, North Carolina St.	1995-98	191	3,379	17.7	31
Elmo Wright, Houston	1968-70	153	3,347	21.9	34
Howard Twilley, Tulsa	1963-65	261	3,343	12.8	32
Clarkston Hines, Duke	1986-89	189	3,318	17.6	38
Gerald Harp, Western Caro.	1977-80	197	3,305	16.8	26
Dan Bitson, Tulsa	1987-89, 91	163	3,300	20.2	29
Charlie Jones, Fresno St.	1992-95	181	3,260	18.0	25
Dennis Northcutt, Arizona	1996-99	223	3,252	14.5	24
Greg Primus, Colorado St.	1989-92	192	3,200	16.7	16
David Williams, Illinois	1983-85	245	3,195	13.0	22
Hart Lee Dykes, Oklahoma St.	1985-88	203	3,171	15.6	29
Bryan Rowley, Utah	$1989-93	177	3,143	17.8	25
Darnay Scott, San Diego St.	1991-93	178	3,139	17.6	25
Rick Beasley, Appalachian St.	1978-80	178	3,124	17.6	23
Alex Van Dyke, Nevada	1994-95	227	3,100	13.7	26
Eric Drage, Brigham Young	1990-93	162	3,065	18.9	29
Arnold Jackson, Louisville	1997-99	237	3,061	12.9	26
Lloyd Hill, Texas Tech	1990-93	189	3,059	16.2	20
Mike Adams, Texas	1992-93, 95-96	177	3,032	17.1	16
Kevin Lockett, Kansas St.	1993-96	217	3,032	14.0	26
Bobby Engram, Penn St.	1991, 93-95	167	3,026	18.1	31
Carl Winston, New Mexico	1990-93	202	2,972	14.7	14
Brian Alford, Purdue	1994-97	160	2,968	18.6	30
Boo Mitchell, Vanderbilt	1985-88	188	2,964	15.8	9
Johnnie Morton, Southern California	1990-93	185	2,957	16.0	21
Brian Roberson, Fresno St.	1993-96	188	2,956	15.7	15
Ricky Proehl, Wake Forest	1986-89	188	2,949	15.7	25
Henry Ellard, Fresno St.	1979-82	138	2,947	21.4	25
Kendal Smith, Utah St.	1985-88	169	2,943	17.4	25
Jermaine Lewis, Maryland	1992-95	193	2,932	15.2	21
E. G. Green, Florida St.	1994-97	166	2,920	17.6	29
Charles Lockett, Long Beach St.	1983-86	191	2,902	15.1	19

*Record. $See page 6 for explanation. #Record for minimum 200 catches.

ALL-TIME LEADERS—RECEIVING

CAREER YARDS PER GAME
(Minimum 2,200 Yards)

Player, Team	Years	G	Yards	Yd.PG
Alex Van Dyke, Nevada	1994-95	22	3,100	*140.9
Troy Edwards, Louisiana Tech	1996-98	34	4,352	128.0
Manny Hazard, Houston	1989-90	21	2,635	125.5
Ron Sellers, Florida St.	1966-68	30	3,598	119.9
Bryan Reeves, Nevada	1992-93	21	2,476	117.9
Trevor Insley, Nevada	1996-99	44	*5,005	113.8
Nakia Jenkins, Utah St.	1996-97	22	2,483	112.9
Keyshawn Johnson, Southern California	1994-95	21	2,358	112.3
Elmo Wright, Houston	1968-70	30	3,347	111.6
Howard Twilley, Tulsa	1963-65	30	3,343	111.4
Chris Penn, Tulsa	1991, 93	22	2,370	107.7
Goeff Noisy, Nevada	1995-98	40	4,249	106.2
Jason Phillips, Houston	1987-88	22	2,319	105.4
Siaha Burley, UCF	1997-98	22	2,248	102.2
Brandon Stokley, La.-Lafayette	1995-98	37	3,702	100.1
Aaron Turner, Pacific (Cal.)	1989-92	44	4,345	98.8
Marcus Harris, Wyoming	1993-96	46	4,518	98.2
Rick Beasley, Appalachian St.	†1977-80	32	3,124	97.6
David Williams, Illinois	1982-85	33	3,195	96.8
Terance Mathis, New Mexico	1985-87,89	44	4,254	96.7
Troy Walters, Stanford	1996-99	42	3,986	94.9
Ryan Yarborough, Wyoming	1990-93	46	4,357	94.7
Arnold Jackson, Louisville	1997-99	33	3,061	92.8
Darnay Scott, San Diego St.	1991-93	34	3,139	92.3
Eugene Baker, Kent	1995-98	39	3,513	90.1
Lloyd Hill, Texas Tech	1990-93	34	3,059	90.0

*Record. †Played defensive back in 1977.

CAREER TOUCHDOWN RECEPTIONS

Player, Team	Years	G	TD
Troy Edwards, Louisiana Tech	1996-98	34	*50
Aaron Turner, Pacific (Cal.)	1989-92	44	43
Ryan Yarborough, Wyoming	1990-93	46	42
Marcus Harris, Wyoming	1993-96	46	38
Clarkston Hines, Duke	1986-89	44	38
Terance Mathis, New Mexico	1985-87, 89	44	36
Trevor Insley, Nevada	1996-99	44	35
Eugene Baker, Kent	1995-98	39	35
Elmo Wright, Houston	1968-70	30	34
Ibn Green, Louisville (TE)	1996-99	43	33
Peter Warrick, Florida St.	1996-99	43	32
David Boston, Ohio St.	1996-98	34	32
Steve Largent, Tulsa	1973-75	30	32
Howard Twilley, Tulsa	1963-65	30	32
Torry Holt, North Carolina St.	1995-98	40	31
Chris Doering, Florida	1992-95	40	31
Lucious Davis, New Mexico St.	1992-95	42	31
Bobby Engram, Penn St.	1991, 93-95	42	31
Manny Hazard, Houston	1989-90	21	31
Brian Alford, Purdue	1994-97	38	30
Sean Dawkins, California	1990-92	33	30
Desmond Howard, Michigan	1989-91	33	30
Jade Butcher, Indiana	1967-69	30	30
E. G. Green, Florida St.	1994-97	44	29
Ike Hilliard, Florida	1994-96	32	29
Jack Jackson, Florida	1992-94	34	29
Eric Drage, Brigham Young	1990-93	46	29
Dan Bitson, Tulsa	1987-89, 91	44	29
Hart Lee Dykes, Oklahoma St.	1985-88	41	29

*Record.

SEASON YARDS

Player, Team	Year	Rec.	Yards	Avg.	TD
Trevor Insley, Nevada	†1999	134	*2,060	15.4	13
Troy Edwards, Louisiana Tech	†1998	140	1,996	14.3	*27
Alex Van Dyke, Nevada	†1995	129	1,854	14.4	16
Howard Twilley, Tulsa	1965	134	1,779	13.3	16
Troy Edwards, Louisiana Tech	†1997	102	1,707	16.7	13
Manny Hazard, Houston	1989	*142	1,689	11.9	22
Marcus Harris, Wyoming	†1996	109	1,650	15.1	13
Randy Moss, Marshall	1997	90	1,647	18.3	25
Aaron Turner, Pacific (Cal.)	†1991	92	1,604	17.4	19
Torry Holt, North Carolina St.	1998	88	1,604	18.2	11
Chris Penn, Tulsa	†1993	105	1,578	15.0	12
Eugene Baker, Kent	1997	103	1,549	15.0	18
Chuck Hughes, UTEP	1965	80	1,519	19.0	12
Ryan Yarborough, Wyoming	1993	67	1,512	22.6	16
Henry Ellard, Fresno St.	1982	62	1,510	††24.4	15
Ron Sellers, Florida St.	1968	86	1,496	17.4	12
Chad Mackey, Louisiana Tech	1996	85	1,466	17.3	10

Player, Team	Year	Rec.	Yards	Avg.	TD
Troy Walters, Stanford	1999	74	1,456	19.7	10
Jerry Hendren, Idaho	1969	95	1,452	15.3	12
Jason Phillips, Houston	1988	108	1,444	13.4	15

*Record. †National champion. ††Record for minimum 50 catches.

SINGLE-GAME YARDS

Yds.	Player, Team (Opponent)	Date
405	Troy Edwards, Louisiana Tech (Nebraska)	Aug. 29, 1998
363	Randy Gatewood, UNLV (Idaho)	Sept. 17, 1994
349	Chuck Hughes, UTEP (North Texas)	Sept. 18, 1965
322	Rick Eber, Tulsa (Idaho St.)	Oct. 7, 1967
318	Harry Wood, Tulsa (Idaho St.)	Oct. 7, 1967
316	Jeff Evans, New Mexico St. (Southern Ill.)	Sept. 30, 1978
314	Alex Van Dyke, Nevada (San Jose St.)	Nov. 18, 1995
310	Chad Mackey, Louisiana Tech (Toledo)	Oct. 19, 1996
301	Chris Daniels, Purdue (Michigan St.)	Oct. 16, 1999
297	Brian Oliver, Ball St. (Toledo)	Oct. 9, 1993
296	Geoffery Noisy, Nevada (Utah St.)	Nov. 9, 1996
290	Tom Reynolds, San Diego St. (Utah St.)	Oct. 22, 1971
289	Wesley Walker, California (San Jose St.)	Oct. 2, 1976
288	Mike Siani, Villanova (Xavier [Ohio])	Oct. 30, 1971
285	Thomas Lewis, Indiana (Penn St.)	Nov. 6, 1993
284	Don Clune, Pennsylvania (Harvard)	Oct. 30, 1971
284	Lennie Johnson, Arkansas St. (Southwest Mo. St.)	Nov. 8, 1997
283	Chris Castor, Duke (Wake Forest)	Nov. 6, 1982
283	Jeremy McDaniel, Arizona (California)	Nov. 2, 1996
283	Geoff Noisy, Nevada (New Mexico St.)	Oct. 10, 1998
282	Larry Willis, Fresno St. (Montana St.)	Nov. 17, 1984
280	Will Blackwell, San Diego St. (California)	Sept. 14, 1996

ANNUAL CHAMPIONS

Year	Player, Team	Class	Rec.	Yards	TD
1937	Jim Benton, Arkansas	Sr.	48	814	7
1938	Sam Boyd, Baylor	Sr.	32	537	—
1939	Ken Kavanaugh, LSU	Sr.	30	467	—
1940	Eddie Bryant, Virginia	So.	30	222	2
1941	Hank Stanton, Arizona	Sr.	50	820	—
1942	Bill Rogers, Texas A&M	Sr.	39	432	—
1943	Neil Armstrong, Oklahoma St.	Fr.	39	317	—
1944	Reid Moseley, Georgia	So.	32	506	—
1945	Reid Moseley, Georgia	Jr.	31	662	—
1946	Neil Armstrong, Oklahoma St.	Sr.	32	479	1
1947	Barney Poole, Mississippi	Jr.	52	513	8
1948	Johnny "Red" O'Quinn, Wake Forest	Jr.	39	605	7
1949	Art Weiner, North Carolina	Sr.	52	762	7
1950	Gordon Cooper, Denver	Jr.	46	569	8
1951	Dewey McConnell, Wyoming	Sr.	47	725	9
1952	Ed Brown, Fordham	Sr.	57	774	6
1953	John Carson, Georgia	Sr.	45	663	4
1954	Jim Hanifan, California	Sr.	44	569	7
1955	Hank Burnine, Missouri	Sr.	44	594	2
1956	Art Powell, San Jose St.	So.	40	583	5
1957	Stuart Vaughan, Utah	Sr.	53	756	5
1958	Dave Hibbert, Arizona	Jr.	61	606	4
1959	Chris Burford, Stanford	Sr.	61	756	6
1960	Hugh Campbell, Washington St.	So.	66	881	10
1961	Hugh Campbell, Washington St.	Jr.	53	723	5
1962	Vern Burke, Oregon St.	Jr.	69	1,007	10
1963	Lawrence Elkins, Baylor	Jr.	70	873	8
1964	Howard Twilley, Tulsa	Jr.	95	1,178	13
1965	Howard Twilley, Tulsa	Sr.	134	1,779	16
1966	Glenn Meltzer, Wichita St.	So.	91	1,115	4
1967	Bob Goodridge, Vanderbilt	Sr.	79	1,114	6
1968	Ron Sellers, Florida St.	Sr.	86	1,496	12
1969	Jerry Hendren, Idaho	Sr.	95	1,452	12

Beginning in 1970, ranked on per-game (instead of total) catches

Year	Player, Team	Class	G	Rec.	Avg.	Yards	TD
1970	Mike Mikolayunas, Davidson	Sr.	10	87	8.7	1,128	8
1971	Tom Reynolds, San Diego St.	Sr.	10	67	6.7	1,070	7
1972	Tom Forzani, Utah St.	Sr.	11	85	7.7	1,169	8
1973	Jay Miller, Brigham Young	So.	11	100	9.1	1,181	8
1974	Dwight McDonald, San Diego St.	Sr.	11	86	7.8	1,157	7
1975	Bob Farnham, Brown	Jr.	9	56	6.2	701	2
1976	Billy Ryckman, Louisiana Tech	Sr.	11	77	7.0	1,382	10
1977	Wayne Tolleson, Western Caro.	Sr.	11	73	6.6	1,101	7
1978	Dave Petzke, Northern Ill.	Sr.	11	91	8.3	1,217	11
1979	Rick Beasley, Appalachian St.	Jr.	11	74	6.7	1,205	12
1980	Dave Young, Purdue	Sr.	11	67	6.1	917	8
1981	Pete Harvey, North Texas	Sr.	9	57	6.3	743	3
1982	Vincent White, Stanford	Sr.	10	68	6.8	677	8
1983	Keith Edwards, Vanderbilt	Jr.	11	97	8.8	909	8
1984	David Williams, Illinois	Jr.	11	101	9.2	1,278	8

All-Time Leaders—Receiving

Year	Player, Team	Class	G	Rec.	Avg.	Yards	TD
1985	Rodney Carter, Purdue	Sr.	11	98	8.9	1,099	4
1986	Mark Templeton, Long Beach St. (RB)	Sr.	11	99	9.0	688	2
1987	Jason Phillips, Houston	Jr.	11	99	9.0	875	3
1988	Jason Phillips, Houston	Sr.	11	108	9.8	1,444	15
1989	Manny Hazard, Houston	Jr.	11	*142	12.9	1,689	*22

Beginning in 1990, ranked on both per-game catches and yards per game

PER-GAME CATCHES

Year	Player, Team	Class	G	Rec.	Avg.	Yards	TD
1990	Manny Hazard, Houston	Sr.	10	78	7.8	946	9
1991	Fred Gilbert, Houston	Jr.	11	106	9.6	957	7
1992	Sherman Smith, Houston	Jr.	11	103	9.4	923	6
1993	Chris Penn, Tulsa	Sr.	11	105	9.6	1,578	12
1994	Alex Van Dyke, Nevada	Jr.	11	98	8.9	1,246	10
1995	Alex Van Dyke, Nevada	Sr.	11	129	11.7	1,854	16
1996	Damond Wilkins, Nevada	Sr.	11	114	10.4	1,121	4
1997	Eugene Baker, Kent	Jr.	11	103	9.4	1,549	18
1998	Troy Edwards, Louisiana Tech	Sr.	12	140	11.7	1,996	*27
1999	Trevor Insley, Nevada	Sr.	11	134	12.2	*2,060	13

YARDS PER GAME

Year	Player, Team	Class	G	Rec.	Yards	Avg.	TD
1990	Patrick Rowe, San Diego St.	Jr.	11	71	1,392	126.6	8
1991	Aaron Turner, Pacific (Cal.)	Jr.	11	92	1,604	145.8	18
1992	Lloyd Hill, Texas Tech	Jr.	11	76	1,261	114.6	12
1993	Chris Penn, Tulsa	Sr.	11	105	1,578	143.5	12
1994	Marcus Harris, Wyoming	So.	12	71	1,431	119.3	11
1995	Alex Van Dyke, Nevada	Sr.	11	129	1,854	168.6	16
1996	Marcus Harris, Wyoming	Sr.	12	109	1,650	137.5	13
1997	Troy Edwards, Louisiana Tech	Jr.	11	102	1,707	155.2	13
1998	Troy Edwards, Louisiana Tech	Sr.	12	140	1,996	166.3	*27
1999	Trevor Insley, Nevada	Sr.	11	134	*2,060	*187.3	13

*Record.

Scoring

CAREER POINTS PER GAME
(Minimum 225 Points)

Player, Team	Years	G	TD	XPt.	FG	Pts.	Pt.PG
Marshall Faulk, San Diego St.	1991-93	31	‡62	4	0	‡376	*12.1
Ed Marinaro, Cornell	1969-71	27	52	6	0	318	11.8
Bill Burnett, Arkansas	1968-70	26	49	0	0	294	11.3
Steve Owens, Oklahoma	1967-69	30	56	0	0	336	11.2
Eddie Talboom, Wyoming	1948-50	28	34	99	0	303	10.8
Travis Prentice, Miami (Ohio)	1996-99	44	*78	0	0	*468	10.6
Troy Edwards, Louisiana Tech	1996-98	34	57	2	0	344	10.1
Howard Twilley, Tulsa	1963-65	26	32	67	0	259	10.0
Tom Harmon, Michigan	1938-40	24	33	33	2	237	9.9
Ricky Williams, Texas	1995-98	46	75	2	0	452	9.8
Glenn Davis, Army	1943-46	37	59	0	0	354	9.6
Johnny Bright, Drake	1949-51	25	40	0	0	240	9.6
Anthony Thompson, Indiana	1986-89	41	65	4	0	394	9.6
Roman Anderson, Houston	1988-91	44	0	213	70	423	9.6
Stacey Robinson, Northern Ill. (QB)	1988-90	25	38	6	0	234	9.4
Floyd Little, Syracuse	1964-66	30	46	2	0	278	9.3
Anthony Davis, Southern California	1972-74	33	50	2	0	302	9.2
Felix "Doc" Blanchard, Army	1944-46	25	38	3	0	231	9.2

*Record. ‡Three-year totals record.

SEASON POINTS PER GAME

Player, Team	Year	G	TD	XPt.	FG	Pts.	Pt.PG
Barry Sanders, Oklahoma St.	†1988	11	*39	0	0	*234	*21.3
Bobby Reynolds, Nebraska	†1950	9	22	25	0	157	17.4
Art Luppino, Arizona	†1954	10	24	22	0	166	16.6
Ed Marinaro, Cornell	†1971	9	24	4	0	148	16.4
Lydell Mitchell, Penn St.	1971	11	29	0	0	174	15.8
Troy Edwards, Louisiana Tech	†1998	12	31	2	0	188	15.7
Marshall Faulk, San Diego St.	†1991	9	23	2	0	140	15.6
Byron "Whizzer" White, Colorado	†1937	8	16	23	1	122	15.3
Ricky Williams, Texas	1998	11	28	0	0	168	15.3

*Record. †National champion.

CAREER POINTS
(Non-Kickers)

Player, Team	Years	TD	XPt.	FG	Pts.
Travis Prentice, Miami (Ohio)	1996-99	*78	0	0	*468
Ricky Williams, Texas	1995-98	75	2	0	452
Anthony Thompson, Indiana	1986-89	65	4	0	394
Ron Dayne, Wisconsin	1996-99	63	0	0	378
Marshall Faulk, San Diego St.	1991-93	‡62	4	0	‡376
Tony Dorsett, Pittsburgh	1973-76	59	2	0	356
Glenn Davis, Army	1943-46	59	0	0	354
Troy Edwards, Louisiana Tech	1995-98	57	2	0	344
Art Luppino, Arizona	1953-56	48	49	0	337
Chris Lemon, Nevada	1996-99	56	0	0	336
Steve Owens, Oklahoma	1967-69	56	0	0	336
Wilford White, Arizona St.	1947-50	48	27	4	327
Skip Hicks, UCLA	$1993-97	54	0	0	324
Barry Sanders, Oklahoma St.	1986-88	54	0	0	324
Allen Pinkett, Notre Dame	1982-85	53	2	0	320
Kevin Faulk, LSU	1995-98	53	0	0	318
Pete Johnson, Ohio St.	1973-76	53	0	0	318
Ed Marinaro, Cornell	1969-71	52	6	0	318
Herschel Walker, Georgia	1980-82	52	2	0	314
James Gray, Texas Tech	1986-89	52	0	0	312
Mike Rozier, Nebraska	1981-83	52	0	0	312
Ted Brown, North Carolina St.	1975-78	51	6	0	312
Leon Johnson, North Carolina	1993-96	50	3	0	306
John Harvey, UTEP	1985-88	51	0	0	306
Eddie Talboom, Wyoming	1948-50	34	99	0	303
Shaun Alexander, Alabama	1996-99	50	2	0	302
Anthony Davis, Southern California	1972-74	50	2	0	302
Dalton Hilliard, LSU	1982-85	50	0	0	300
Billy Sims, Oklahoma	$1975-79	50	0	0	300
Charles White, Southern California	1976-79	49	2	0	296
Nolan Jones, Arizona St.	1958-61	30	77	13	296
Warrick Dunn, Florida St.	1993-96	49	0	0	294
Steve Bartalo, Colorado St.	1983-86	49	0	0	294
Bill Burnett, Arkansas	1968-70	49	0	0	294
Brian Mitchell, La.-Lafayette	1986-89	47	4	0	286
Rick Badanjek, Maryland	1982-85	46	10	0	286
Keith Byars, Ohio St.	1982-85	48	0	0	286

*Record. $See page 6 for explanation. ‡Three-year totals record. ¢Active player.

CAREER POINTS
(Kickers)

Player, Team	Years	PAT	PAT Att.	FG	FG Att.	Pts.
Roman Anderson, Houston	1988-91	213	217	70	101	423
Carlos Huerta, Miami (Fla.)	1988-91	178	181	73	91	397
Jason Elam, Hawaii	$1988-92	158	161	79	100	395
Derek Schmidt, Florida St.	1984-87	174	178	73	102	393
Kris Brown, Nebraska	1995-98	*217	*222	57	77	388
Shayne Graham, Virginia Tech	1996-99	167	169	68	93	371
Jeff Hall, Tennessee	1995-98	188	202	61	89	371
Luis Zendejas, Arizona St.	1981-84	134	135	78	*105	368
Jeff Jaeger, Washington	1983-86	118	123	*80	99	358
John Lee, UCLA	1982-85	116	117	79	92	353
Max Zendejas, Arizona	1982-85	122	124	77	104	353
Kevin Butler, Georgia	1981-84	122	125	77	98	353
Derek Mahoney, Fresno St.	1990-93	216	*222	45	63	351
Martin Gramatica, Kansas St.	1994-95, 1997-98	187	192	54	70	349
Philip Doyle, Alabama	1987-90	105	108	78	*105	†345
Phil Dawson, Texas	1994-97	162	170	59	79	339
Andy Trakas, San Diego St.	1989-92	170	178	56	82	338
Nathan Trout, Syracuse	1996-99	187	195	49	65	334
Scott Bentley, Florida St.	1993-96	200	215	42	61	326
Michael Proctor, Alabama	1992-95	131	132	65	91	326
Barry Belli, Fresno St.	1984-87	116	123	70	99	326
Kyle Bryant, Texas A&M	1994-97	145	152	60	85	325
Sebastian Janikowski, Florida St.	1997-99	125	128	66	83	323
Jason Hanson, Washington St.	1988-91	136	141	62	95	322
R. D. Lashar, Oklahoma	1987-90	194	200	42	60	320
Collin Mackie, South Carolina	1987-90	112	113	69	95	319
John Becksvoort, Tennessee	1991-94	161	161	52	75	317
Cary Blanchard, Oklahoma St.	1987-90	150	151	54	73	#314
Fuad Reveiz, Tennessee	1981-84	101	103	71	95	314
Sean Fleming, Wyoming	1988-91	150	155	54	92	312
Van Tiffin, Alabama	1983-86	135	135	59	87	312
Jess Atkinson, Maryland	1981-84	128	131	60	82	308
Gary Gussman, Miami (Ohio)	1984-87	102	104	68	94	306
Greg Cox, Miami (Fla.)	1984-87	162	169	47	64	303
Peter Holt, San Diego St.	1993-96	158	169	48	72	302
Dan Eichloff, Kansas	1990-93	116	119	62	87	302
Cory Wedel, Wyoming	1994-97	139	140	54	73	301

*Record. $See page 6 for explanation. †Includes one TD reception. #Includes one two-point conversion.

SEASON POINTS

Player, Team	Year	TD	XPt.	FG	Pts.
Barry Sanders, Oklahoma St.	†1988	*39	0	0	*234
Troy Edwards, Louisiana Tech	†1998	31	2	0	188
Mike Rozier, Nebraska	†1983	29	0	0	174
Lydell Mitchell, Penn St.	1971	29	0	0	174
Ricky Williams, Texas	1998	28	0	0	168

… ALL-TIME LEADERS—SCORING

Player, Team	Year	TD	XPt.	FG	Pts.
Art Luppino, Arizona	†1954	24	22	0	166
Bobby Reynolds, Nebraska	†1950	22	25	0	157
Anthony Thompson, Indiana	†1989	25	4	0	154
Ricky Williams, Texas	†1997	25	2	0	152
Randy Moss, Marshall	1997	25	2	0	152
Fred Wendt, UTEP	†1948	20	32	0	152
Skip Hicks, UCLA	1997	25	0	0	150
Travis Prentice, Miami (Ohio)	1997	25	0	0	150
Pete Johnson, Ohio St.	†1975	25	0	0	150

*Record. †National champion.

SINGLE-GAME POINTS

No.	Player, Team (Opponent)	Date
48	Howard Griffith, Illinois (Southern Ill.)	Sept. 22, 1990
44	Marshall Faulk, San Diego St. (Pacific [Cal.])	Sept. 14, 1991
43	Jim Brown, Syracuse (Colgate)	Nov. 17, 1956
42	Arnold "Showboat" Boykin, Mississippi (Mississippi St.)	Dec. 1, 1951
42	Fred Wendt, UTEP (New Mexico St.)	Nov. 25, 1948
38	Dick Bass, Pacific, Cal. (San Diego St.)	Nov. 22, 1958
37	Jimmy Nutter, Wichita St. (Northern St.)	Oct. 22, 1949
36	LaDainian Tomlinson, TCU (UTEP)	Nov. 20, 1999
36	Ricky Williams, Texas (Rice)	Sept. 26, 1998
36	Ricky Williams, Texas (New Mexico St.)	Sept. 5, 1998
36	Scott Harley, East Caro. (Ohio)	Nov. 16, 1996
36	Antowain Smith, Houston (Southern Miss.)	Nov. 9, 1996
36	Madre Hill, Arkansas (South Carolina)	Sept. 9, 1995
36	Calvin Jones, Nebraska (Kansas)	Nov. 9, 1991
36	Blake Ezor, Michigan St. (Northwestern)	Nov. 18, 1989
36	Dee Dowis, Air Force (San Diego St.)	Sept. 2, 1989
36	Kelvin Bryant, North Carolina (East Caro.)	Sept. 12, 1981
36	Andre Herrera, Southern Ill. (Northern Ill.)	Oct. 23, 1976
36	Anthony Davis, Southern California (Notre Dame)	Dec. 2, 1972
36	Tim Delaney, San Diego St. (New Mexico St.)	Nov. 15, 1969
36	Tom Francisco, Virginia Tech (VMI)	Nov. 24, 1966
36	Howard Twilley, Tulsa (Louisville)	Nov. 6, 1965
36	Pete Pedro, West Tex. A&M (UTEP)	Sept. 30, 1961
36	Tom Powers, Duke (Richmond)	Oct. 21, 1950

ANNUAL CHAMPIONS

Year	Player, Team	Class	TD	XPt.	FG	Pts.
1937	Byron "Whizzer" White, Colorado	Sr.	16	23	1	122
1938	Parker Hall, Mississippi	Sr.	11	7	0	73
1939	Tom Harmon, Michigan	Jr.	14	15	1	102
1940	Tom Harmon, Michigan	Sr.	16	18	1	117
1941	Bill Dudley, Virginia	Sr.	18	23	1	134
1942	Bob Steuber, Missouri	Sr.	18	13	0	121
1943	Steve Van Buren, LSU	Sr.	14	14	0	98
1944	Glenn Davis, Army	So.	20	0	0	120
1945	Felix "Doc" Blanchard, Army	Jr.	19	1	0	115
1946	Gene Roberts, Chattanooga	Sr.	18	9	0	117
1947	Lou Gambino, Maryland	Jr.	16	0	0	96
1948	Fred Wendt, UTEP	Sr.	20	32	0	152
1949	George Thomas, Oklahoma	Sr.	19	3	0	117
1950	Bobby Reynolds, Nebraska	So.	22	25	0	157
1951	Ollie Matson, San Francisco	Sr.	21	0	0	126
1952	Jackie Parker, Mississippi St.	Jr.	16	24	0	120
1953	Earl Lindley, Utah St.	Sr.	13	3	0	81
1954	Art Luppino, Arizona	So.	24	22	0	166
1955	Jim Swink, TCU	Jr.	20	5	0	125
1956	Clendon Thomas, Oklahoma	Jr.	18	0	0	108
1957	Leon Burton, Arizona St.	Jr.	16	0	0	96
1958	Dick Bass, Pacific (Cal.)	Jr.	18	8	0	116
1959	Pervis Atkins, New Mexico St.	Jr.	17	5	0	107
1960	Bob Gaiters, New Mexico St.	Sr.	23	7	0	145
1961	Jim Pilot, New Mexico St.	So.	21	12	0	138
1962	Jerry Logan, West Tex. A&M	Sr.	13	32	0	110
1963	Cosmo Iacavazzi, Princeton	Jr.	14	0	0	84
	Dave Casinelli, Memphis	Sr.	14	0	0	84
1964	Brian Piccolo, Wake Forest	Sr.	17	9	0	111
1965	Howard Twilley, Tulsa	Sr.	16	31	0	127
1966	Ken Hebert, Houston	Jr.	11	41	2	113
1967	Leroy Keyes, Purdue	Jr.	19	0	0	114
1968	Jim O'Brien, Cincinnati	Jr.	12	31	13	142
1969	Steve Owens, Oklahoma	Sr.	23	0	0	138

Beginning in 1970, ranked on per-game (instead of total) points

Year	Player, Team	Class	G	TD	XPt.	FG	Pts.	Avg.
1970	Brian Bream, Air Force	Jr.	10	20	0	0	120	12.0
	Gary Kosins, Dayton	Jr.	9	18	0	0	108	12.0
1971	Ed Marinaro, Cornell	Sr.	9	24	4	0	148	16.4
1972	Harold Henson, Ohio St.	So.	10	20	0	0	120	12.0
1973	Jim Jennings, Rutgers	Sr.	11	21	2	0	128	11.6
1974	Bill Marek, Wisconsin	Jr.	9	19	0	0	114	12.7
1975	Pete Johnson, Ohio St.	Jr.	11	25	0	0	150	13.6
1976	Tony Dorsett, Pittsburgh	Sr.	11	22	2	0	134	12.2
1977	Earl Campbell, Texas	Sr.	11	19	0	0	114	10.4

Year	Player, Team	Class	G	TD	XPt.	FG	Pts.	Avg.
1978	Billy Sims, Oklahoma	Jr.	11	20	0	0	120	10.9
1979	Billy Sims, Oklahoma	Sr.	11	22	0	0	132	12.0
1980	Sammy Winder, Southern Miss.	Jr.	11	20	0	0	120	10.9
1981	Marcus Allen, Southern California	Sr.	11	23	0	0	138	12.5
1982	Greg Allen, Florida St.	So.	11	21	0	0	126	11.5
1983	Mike Rozier, Nebraska	Sr.	12	29	0	0	174	14.5
1984	Keith Byars, Ohio St.	Jr.	11	24	0	0	144	13.1
1985	Bernard White, Bowling Green	Sr.	11	19	0	0	114	10.4
1986	Steve Bartalo, Colorado St.	Sr.	11	19	0	0	114	10.4
1987	Paul Hewitt, San Diego St.	Jr.	12	24	0	0	144	12.0
1988	Barry Sanders, Oklahoma St.	Jr.	11	*39	0	0	*234	*21.3
1989	Anthony Thompson, Indiana	Sr.	11	25	4	0	154	14.0
1990	Stacey Robinson, Northern Ill. (QB)	Sr.	11	19	6	0	120	10.9
1991	Marshall Faulk, San Diego St.	Fr.	9	23	2	0	140	15.6
1992	Garrison Hearst, Georgia	Jr.	11	21	0	0	126	11.5
1993	Byron Morris, Texas Tech	Jr.	11	22	2	0	134	12.2
1994	Rashaan Salaam, Colorado	Jr.	11	24	0	0	144	13.1
1995	Eddie George, Ohio St.	Sr.	12	24	0	0	144	12.0
1996	Corey Dillon, Washington	Jr.	11	23	0	0	138	12.6
1997	Ricky Williams, Texas	Jr.	11	25	2	0	152	13.8
1998	Troy Edwards, Louisiana Tech	Sr.	12	31	2	0	188	15.7
1999	Shaun Alexander, Alabama	Sr.	11	24	0	0	144	13.1

*Record.

Interceptions

CAREER INTERCEPTIONS

Player, Team	Years	No.	Yards	Avg.
Al Brosky, Illinois	1950-52	*29	356	12.3
Martin Bayless, Bowling Green	1980-83	27	266	9.9
John Provost, Holy Cross	1972-75	27	470	17.4
Tracy Saul, Texas Tech	1989-92	25	425	17.0
Tony Thurman, Boston College	1981-84	25	221	8.8
Tom Curtis, Michigan	1967-69	25	440	17.6
Jeff Nixon, Richmond	1975-78	23	377	16.4
Bennie Blades, Miami (Fla.)	1984-87	22	355	16.1
Jim Bolding, East Caro.	1973-76	22	143	6.5
Terrell Buckley, Florida St.	1989-91	21	*501	23.9
Chuck Cecil, Arizona	1984-87	21	241	11.5
Barry Hill, Iowa St.	1972-74	21	202	9.6
Mike Sensibaugh, Ohio St.	1968-70	21	226	10.8
Kevin Smith, Texas A&M	1988-91	20	289	14.5
Mark Collins, Cal St. Fullerton	1982-85	20	193	9.7
Anthony Young, Temple	1981-84	20	230	11.5
Chris Williams, LSU	1977-80	20	91	4.6
Charles Jefferson, McNeese St.	1975-78	20	95	4.8
Artimus Parker, Southern California	1971-73	20	268	13.4
Dave Atkinson, Brigham Young	1971-73	20	222	11.1
Jackie Wallace, Arizona	1970-72	20	250	12.5
Tom Wilson, Colgate	1964-66	20	215	10.8
Lynn Chandnois, Michigan St.	1946-49	20	410	20.5
Bobby Wilson, Mississippi	1946-49	20	369	18.5

*Record.

SEASON INTERCEPTIONS

Player, Team	Year	No.	Yards
Al Worley, Washington	†1968	*14	130
George Shaw, Oregon	†1951	13	136
Terrell Buckley, Florida St.	†1991	12	238
Cornelius Price, Houston	†1989	12	187
Bob Navarro, Eastern Mich.	†1989	12	73
Tony Thurman, Boston College	†1984	12	99
Terry Hoage, Georgia	†1982	12	51
Frank Polito, Villanova	†1971	12	261
Bill Albrecht, Washington	1951	12	140
Hank Rich, Arizona St.	†1950	12	135

*Record. †National champion.

ANNUAL CHAMPIONS

Year	Player, Team	Class	No.	Yards
1938	Elmer Tarbox, Texas Tech	Sr.	11	89
1939	Harold Van Every, Minnesota	Sr.	8	59
1940	Dick Morgan, Tulsa	Jr.	7	210
1941	Bobby Robertson, Southern California	Sr.	9	126
1942	Ray Evans, Kansas	Jr.	10	76
1943	Jay Stoves, Washington	Sr.	7	139
1944	Jim Hardy, Southern California	Sr.	8	73
1945	Jake Leicht, Oregon	So.	9	195
1946	Larry Hatch, Washington	So.	8	114
1947	John Bruce, William & Mary	Jr.	9	78
1948	Jay Van Noy, Utah St.	Jr.	8	228
1949	Bobby Wilson, Mississippi	Sr.	10	70

ALL-TIME LEADERS—INTERCEPTIONS

Year	Player, Team	Class	No.	Yards
1950	Hank Rich, Arizona St.	Sr.	12	135
1951	George Shaw, Oregon	Fr.	13	136
1952	Cecil Ingram, Alabama	Jr.	10	163
1953	Bob Garrett, Stanford	Sr.	9	80
1954	Gary Glick, Colorado St.	Jr.	8	168
1955	Sam Wesley, Oregon St.	Jr.	7	61
1956	Jack Hill, Utah St.	Sr.	7	132
1957	Ray Toole, North Texas	Sr.	7	133
1958	Jim Norton, Idaho	Jr.	9	222
1959	Bud Whitehead, Florida St.	Jr.	6	111
1960	Bob O'Billovich, Montana	Jr.	7	71
1961	Joe Zuger, Arizona St.	Sr.	10	121
1962	Byron Beaver, Houston	Sr.	10	56
1963	Dick Kern, William & Mary	Sr.	8	116
1964	Tony Carey, Notre Dame	Jr.	8	121
1965	Bob Sullivan, Maryland	Sr.	10	61
1966	Henry King, Utah St.	Sr.	11	180
1967	Steve Haterius, West Tex. A&M	Sr.	11	90
1968	Al Worley, Washington	Sr.	*14	130
1969	Seth Miller, Arizona St.	Sr.	11	63

Beginning in 1970, ranked on per-game (instead of total) number

Year	Player, Team	Class	G	No.	Avg.	Yards
1970	Mike Sensibaugh, Ohio St.	Sr.	8	8	1.00	40
1971	Frank Polito, Villanova	So.	10	12	1.20	261
1972	Mike Townsend, Notre Dame	Jr.	10	10	1.00	39
1973	Mike Gow, Illinois	Jr.	11	10	0.91	142
1974	Mike Haynes, Arizona St.	Jr.	11	10	0.91	115
1975	Jim Bolding, East Caro.	Jr.	10	10	1.00	51
1976	Anthony Francis, Houston	Jr.	11	10	0.91	118
1977	Paul Lawler, Colgate	Sr.	9	7	0.78	53
1978	Pete Harris, Penn St.	Jr.	11	10	0.91	155
1979	Joe Callan, Ohio	Sr.	9	9	1.00	110
1980	Ronnie Lott, Southern California	Sr.	11	8	0.73	166
	Steve McNamee, William & Mary	Sr.	11	8	0.73	125
	Greg Benton, Drake	Sr.	11	8	0.73	119
	Jeff Hipp, Georgia	Sr.	11	8	0.73	104
	Mike Richardson, Arizona St.	So.	11	8	0.73	89
	Vann McElroy, Baylor	Jr.	11	8	0.73	73
1981	Sam Shaffer, Temple	Sr.	10	9	0.90	76
1982	Terry Hoage, Georgia	Jr.	10	12	1.20	51
1983	Martin Bayless, Bowling Green	Sr.	11	10	0.91	64
1984	Tony Thurman, Boston College	Sr.	11	12	1.09	99
1985	Chris White, Tennessee	Sr.	11	9	0.82	168
	Kevin Walker, East Caro.	Sr.	11	9	0.82	155
1986	Bennie Blades, Miami (Fla.)	Jr.	11	10	0.91	128
1987	Keith McMeans, Virginia	Fr.	10	9	0.90	35
1988	Kurt Larson, Michigan St. (LB)	Sr.	11	8	0.73	78
	Andy Logan, Kent	Sr.	11	8	0.73	54
1989	Cornelius Price, Houston	Jr.	11	12	1.09	187
	Bob Navarro, Eastern Mich.	Jr.	11	12	1.09	73
1990	Jerry Parks, Houston	Jr.	11	8	0.73	124
1991	Terrell Buckley, Florida St.	Jr.	12	12	1.00	238
1992	Carlton McDonald, Air Force	Sr.	11	8	0.73	109
1993	Orlanda Thomas, La.-Lafayette	Jr.	11	9	0.82	84
1994	Aaron Beasley, West Virginia	Jr.	12	10	0.83	133
1995	Willie Smith, Louisiana Tech	Jr.	10	8	0.80	65
1996	Dre' Bly, North Carolina	Fr.	11	11	1.00	141
1997	Brian Lee, Wyoming	Sr.	11	8	0.73	103
1998	Jamar Fletcher, Wisconsin	Fr.	9	6	0.67	99
1999	Deltha O'Neal, California	Sr.	11	9	0.82	280
	Deon Grant, Tennessee	Jr.	11	9	0.82	167
	Rodregis Brooks, UAB	Jr.	11	9	0.82	152

*Record.

Punting

CAREER AVERAGE
(Minimum 250 Punts)

Player, Team	Years	No.	Yards	Avg.	Long
Shane Lechler, Texas A&M	1996-99	268	11,977	*44.7	76
Bill Smith, Mississippi	1983-86	254	11,260	44.3	92
Jim Arnold, Vanderbilt	1979-82	277	12,171	43.9	79
Ralf Mojsiejenko, Michigan St.	1981-84	275	11,997	43.6	72
Jim Miller, Mississippi	1976-79	266	11,549	43.4	82
Russ Henderson, Virginia	1975-78	276	11,957	43.3	74
Maury Buford, Texas Tech	1978-81	293	12,670	43.2	75
Nate Cochran, Pittsburgh	1993-96	252	10,851	43.1	80
Chris Becker, TCU	1985-88	265	11,407	43.0	77
James Gargus, TCU	1981-84	255	10,862	42.6	74
Ron Keller, New Mexico	1983-86	252	10,737	42.6	77

(Minimum 150-249 Punts)

Player, Team	Years	No.	Yards	Avg.	Long
Todd Sauerbrun, West Virginia	1991-94	167	7,733	*46.3	90
Reggie Roby, Iowa	1979-82	172	7,849	45.6	69
Greg Montgomery, Michigan St.	1985-87	170	7,721	45.4	86
Tom Tupa, Ohio St.	1984-87	196	8,854	45.2	75
Barry Helton, Colorado	1984-87	153	6,873	44.9	68
Aron Langley, Wyoming	1996-98	171	7,649	44.7	72
Ray Guy, Southern Miss.	1970-72	200	8,934	44.7	93
Bucky Scribner, Kansas	1980-82	217	9,670	44.6	70
Terry Daniel, Auburn	1992-94	169	7,522	44.5	71
Greg Horne, Arkansas	1983-86	180	8,002	44.5	72
Ray Criswell, Florida	1982-85	161	7,153	44.4	73
Mark Simon, Air Force	1984-86	164	7,283	44.4	64
Brian Schmitz, North Carolina	1996-99	208	9,233	44.4	72
Russell Erxleben, Texas	1975-78	214	9,467	44.2	80
Brad Maynard, Ball St.	1993-96	242	10,702	44.2	76
Chuck Ramsey, Wake Forest	1971-73	205	9,010	44.0	70
Johnny Evans, North Carolina St.	1974-77	185	8,143	44.0	81
Jimmy Colquitt, Tennessee	1981-84	201	8,816	43.9	70
John Teltschik, Texas	1982-85	217	9,496	43.8	81

*Record.

SEASON AVERAGE
(Qualifiers for Championship)

Player, Team	Year	No.	Yards	Avg.
Chad Kessler, LSU	†1997	39	1,961	*50.3
Reggie Roby, Iowa	†1981	44	2,193	49.8
Kirk Wilson, UCLA	†1956	30	1,479	49.3
Todd Sauerbrun, West Virginia	†1994	72	3,486	‡48.4
Zack Jordan, Colorado	†1950	38	1,830	48.2
Ricky Anderson, Vanderbilt	†1984	58	2,793	48.2
Marv Bateman, Utah	†1971	68	3,269	48.1
Reggie Roby, Iowa	†1982	52	2,501	48.1
Andrew Bayes, East Caro.	†1999	47	2,259	48.1
Owen Price, UTEP	†1940	30	1,440	48.0
Jack Jacobs, Oklahoma	1940	31	1,483	47.8
Brian Schmitz, North Carolina	1999	74	3,538	47.8
Bill Smith, Mississippi	1984	44	2,099	47.7
Ed Bunn, UTEP	†1992	41	1,955	47.7

*Record. †National champion. ‡Record for minimum 50 punts.

ANNUAL CHAMPIONS

Year	Player, Team	Class	No.	Yards	Avg.
1937	Johnny Pingel, Michigan St.	Jr.	49	2,101	42.9
1938	Jerry Dowd, St. Mary's (Cal.)	Sr.	62	2,711	43.7
1939	Harry Dunkle, North Carolina	So.	37	1,725	46.6
1940	Owen Price, UTEP	Jr.	30	1,440	48.0
1941	Owen Price, UTEP	Sr.	40	1,813	45.3
1942	Bobby Cifers, Tennessee	Jr.	37	1,586	42.9
1943	Harold Cox, Arkansas	Fr.	37	1,518	41.0
1944	Bob Waterfield, UCLA	Sr.	60	2,575	42.9
1945	Howard Maley, Southern Methodist	Sr.	59	2,458	41.7
1946	Johnny Galvin, Purdue	Sr.	30	1,286	42.9
1947	Leslie Palmer, North Carolina St.	Sr.	65	2,816	43.3
1948	Charlie Justice, North Carolina	Sr.	62	2,728	44.0
1949	Paul Stombaugh, Furman	Sr.	57	2,550	44.7
1950	Zack Jordan, Colorado	So.	38	1,830	48.2
1951	Chuck Spaulding, Wyoming	Jr.	37	1,610	43.5
1952	Des Koch, Southern California	Jr.	47	2,043	43.5
1953	Zeke Bratkowski, Georgia (QB)	Sr.	50	2,132	42.6
1954	A. L. Terpening, New Mexico	Sr.	41	1,869	45.6
1955	Don Chandler, Florida	Sr.	22	975	44.3
1956	Kirk Wilson, UCLA	So.	30	1,479	49.3
1957	Dave Sherer, Southern Methodist	Jr.	36	1,620	45.0
1958	Bobby Walden, Georgia	So.	44	1,991	45.3
1959	John Hadl, Kansas	So.	43	1,960	45.6
1960	Dick Fitzsimmons, Denver	So.	25	1,106	44.2
1961	Joe Zuger, Arizona St.	Sr.	31	1,305	42.1
1962	Joe Don Looney, Oklahoma	Jr.	34	1,474	43.4
1963	Danny Thomas, Southern Methodist	Jr.	48	2,110	44.0
1964	Frank Lambert, Mississippi	Sr.	50	2,205	44.1
1965	Dave Lewis, Stanford	Jr.	29	1,302	44.9
1966	Ron Widby, Tennessee	Sr.	48	2,104	43.8
1967	Zenon Andrusyshyn, UCLA	So.	34	1,502	44.2
1968	Dany Pitcock, Wichita St.	Sr.	71	3,068	43.2
1969	Ed Marsh, Baylor	Jr.	68	2,965	43.6
1970	Marv Bateman, Utah	Jr.	65	2,968	45.7
1971	Marv Bateman, Utah	Sr.	68	3,269	48.1
1972	Ray Guy, Southern Miss.	Sr.	58	2,680	46.2
1973	Chuck Ramsey, Wake Forest	Jr.	87	3,896	44.8
1974	Joe Parker, Appalachian St.	So.	63	2,788	44.3
1975	Tom Skladany, Ohio St.	Jr.	36	1,682	46.7
1976	Russell Erxleben, Texas	So.	61	2,842	46.6

ALL-TIME LEADERS—PUNTING

Year	Player, Team	Class	No.	Yards	Avg.
1977	Jim Miller, Mississippi	So.	66	3,029	45.9
1978	Maury Buford, Texas Tech	Fr.	71	3,131	44.1
1979	Clay Brown, Brigham Young	Jr.	43	1,950	45.3

Beginning in 1980, ranked on minimum 3.6 punts per game

Year	Player, Team	Class	No.	Yards	Long	Avg.
1980	Steve Cox, Arkansas	Sr.	47	2,186	86	46.5
1981	Reggie Roby, Iowa	Jr.	44	2,193	68	49.8
1982	Reggie Roby, Iowa	Sr.	52	2,501	66	48.1
1983	Jack Weil, Wyoming	Sr.	52	2,369	86	45.6
1984	Ricky Anderson, Vanderbilt	Sr.	58	2,793	82	48.2
1985	Mark Simon, Air Force	Jr.	53	2,506	71	47.3
1986	Greg Horne, Arkansas	Sr.	49	2,313	65	47.2
1987	Tom Tupa, Ohio St. (QB)	Sr.	63	2,963	72	47.0
1988	Keith English, Colorado	Sr.	51	2,297	77	45.0
1989	Tom Rouen, Colorado	So.	36	1,651	63	45.8
1990	Cris Shale, Bowling Green	Sr.	66	3,087	81	46.8
1991	Mark Bounds, Texas Tech	Sr.	53	2,481	78	46.8
1992	Ed Bunn, UTEP	Sr.	41	1,955	73	47.7
1993	Chris MacInnis, Air Force	Sr.	49	2,303	74	47.0
1994	Todd Sauerbrun, West Virginia	Sr.	72	3,486	90	‡48.4
1995	Brad Maynard, Ball St.	Jr.	66	3,071	67	46.5
1996	Bill Marinangel, Vanderbilt	Sr.	77	3,586	79	46.6
1997	Chad Kessler, LSU	Sr.	39	1,961	66	*50.3
1998	Joe Kristosik, UNLV	Sr.	76	3,509	69	46.2
1999	Andrew Bayes, East Caro.	Sr.	47	2,259	78	48.1

*Record. ‡Record for minimum of 50 punts.

Punt Returns

CAREER AVERAGE
(Minimum 1.2 Returns Per Game; Minimum 30 Returns)

Player, Team	Years	No.	Yards	TD	Long	Avg.
Jack Mitchell, Oklahoma	1946-48	39	922	**7	70	*23.6
Gene Gibson, Cincinnati	1949-50	37	760	4	75	‡20.5
Eddie Macon, Pacific (Cal.)	1949-51	48	907	4	**100	18.9
Jackie Robinson, UCLA	1939-40	37	694	2	89	18.8
Bobby Dillon, Texas	1949-51	47	830	1	84	17.7
Mike Fuller, Auburn	1972-74	50	883	3	63	17.7
James Dye, Brigham Young/Utah St.	1992-93, 95-96	61	1,046	5	90	17.2
George Hoey, Michigan	1966-68	31	529	1	60	17.1
Erroll Tucker, Utah	1984-85	38	650	3	89	17.1
Henry Pryor, Rutgers	1948-49	37	625	1	85	16.9
Jack Christiansen, Colorado St.	1948-50	37	626	2	89	16.9
Adolph Bellizeare, Pennsylvania	1972-74	33	557	3	73	16.9
Ken Hatfield, Arkansas	1962-64	70	1,135	5	95	16.2
Gene Rossides, Columbia	1945-48	53	851	3	70	16.1
Bill Hillenbrand, Indiana	1941-42	65	1,042	2	88	16.0

*Record. **Record tied. ‡Record for minimum 1.5 returns per game.

SEASON AVERAGE
(Minimum 1.2 Returns Per Game)

Player, Team	Year	No.	Yards	Avg.
Bill Blackstock, Tennessee	1951	12	311	*25.9
George Sims, Baylor	1948	15	375	25.0
Gene Derricotte, Michigan	1947	14	347	24.8
George Hoey, Michigan	1967	12	291	24.3
Erroll Tucker, Utah	†1985	16	389	24.3
Floyd Little, Syracuse	1965	18	423	23.5

*Record. †National champion. ‡Ranked for minimum 1.5 returns per game.

ANNUAL CHAMPIONS
(Ranked on Total Yards Until 1970)

Year	Player, Team	Class	No.	Yards	Avg.
1939	Bosh Pritchard, VMI	So.	42	583	13.9
1940	Junie Hovious, Mississippi	Sr.	33	498	15.1
1941	Bill Geyer, Colgate	Sr.	33	616	18.7
1942	Bill Hillenbrand, Indiana	Jr.	23	481	20.9
1943	Marion Flanagan, Texas A&M	Jr.	49	475	9.7
1944	Joe Stuart, California	Jr.	39	372	9.5
1945	Jake Leicht, Oregon	So.	28	395	14.1
1946	Harry Gilmer, Alabama	Jr.	37	436	11.8
1947	Lindy Berry, TCU	So.	42	493	11.7
1948	Lee Nalley, Vanderbilt	Jr.	43	*791	18.4
1949	Lee Nalley, Vanderbilt	Sr.	35	498	14.2
1950	Dave Waters, Wash. & Lee	Jr.	30	445	14.8
1951	Tom Murphy, Holy Cross	So.	25	533	21.3
1952	Horton Nesrsta, Rice	Jr.	44	536	12.2
1953	Paul Giel, Minnesota	Sr.	17	288	16.9
1954	Dicky Maegle, Rice	Sr.	15	293	19.5
1955	Mike Sommer, George Washington	So.	24	330	13.8
1956	Bill Stacy, Mississippi St.	Jr.	24	290	12.1
1957	Bobby Mulgado, Arizona St.	Sr.	14	267	19.1
1958	Howard Cook, Colorado	Sr.	24	242	10.1
1959	Pervis Atkins, New Mexico St.	Jr.	16	241	15.1
1960	Lance Alworth, Arkansas	Jr.	18	307	17.1
1961	Lance Alworth, Arkansas	Sr.	28	336	12.0
1962	Darrell Roberts, Utah St.	Sr.	16	333	20.8
1963	Ken Hatfield, Arkansas	Jr.	21	350	16.7
1964	Ken Hatfield, Arkansas	Sr.	31	518	16.7
1965	Nick Rassas, Notre Dame	Sr.	24	459	19.1
1966	Vic Washington, Wyoming	Jr.	34	443	13.0
1967	Mike Battle, Southern California	Jr.	47	570	12.1
1968	Roger Wehrli, Missouri	Sr.	41	478	11.7
1969	Chris Farasopoulous, Brigham Young	Jr.	35	527	15.1

Beginning in 1970, ranked on average per return (instead of total yards)‡

Year	Player, Team	Class	No.	Yards	TD	Long	Avg.
1970	Steve Holden, Arizona St.	So.	17	327	2	94	19.2
1971	Golden Richards, Brigham Young	Jr.	33	624	**4	87	18.9
1972	Randy Rhino, Georgia Tech	So.	25	441	1	96	17.6
1973	Gary Hayman, Penn St.	Sr.	23	442	1	83	19.2
1974	John Provost, Holy Cross	Sr.	13	238	2	85	18.3
1975	Donnie Ross, New Mexico St.	Sr.	21	338	1	#81	16.1
1976	Henry Jenkins, Rutgers	Sr.	30	449	0	#40	15.0
1977	Robert Woods, Grambling	Sr.	††11	279	3	72	25.4
1978	Ira Matthews, Wisconsin	Sr.	16	270	3	78	16.9
1979	Jeffrey Shockley, Tennessee St.	Sr.	27	456	1	79	16.9
1980	Scott Woerner, Georgia	Sr.	31	488	1	67	15.7
1981	Glen Young, Mississippi St.	Jr.	19	307	2	87	16.2
1982	Lionel James, Auburn	Jr.	25	394	0	#63	15.8
1983	Jim Sandusky, San Diego St.	Sr.	20	381	1	90	19.0
1984	Ricky Nattiel, Florida	So.	22	346	1	67	15.7
1985	Erroll Tucker, Utah	Sr.	16	389	2	89	24.3
1986	Rod Smith, Nebraska	Jr.	‡‡12	227	1	63	18.9
1987	Alan Grant, Stanford	Jr.	27	446	2	77	16.5
1988	Deion Sanders, Florida St.	Sr.	33	503	1	76	15.2
1989	Larry Hargrove, Ohio	Sr.	17	309	1	83	18.2
1990	Dave McCloughan, Colorado	Sr.	32	524	2	90	16.4
1991	Bo Campbell, Virginia Tech	Jr.	15	273	0	45	18.2
1992	Lee Gissendaner, Northwestern	Sr.	15	327	1	72	21.8
1993	Aaron Glenn, Texas A&M	Sr.	17	339	2	76	19.9
1994	Steve Clay, Eastern Mich.	Jr.	14	278	1	65	19.9
1995	James Dye, Brigham Young	Jr.	20	438	2	90	21.9
1996	Allen Rossum, Notre Dame	Jr.	15	344	3	83	22.9
1997	Tim Dwight, Iowa	Sr.	19	367	3	—	19.3
1998	David Allen, Kansas St.	So.	33	730	**4	93	22.1
1999	Dennis Northcutt, Arizona	Sr.	23	436	2	81	19.0

*Record. **Record tied. #Did not score. ‡Ranked on minimum 1.5 returns per game, 1970-73; 1.2 from 1974. ††Declared champion; with three more returns (making 1.3 per game) for zero yards still would have highest average. ‡‡Declared champion; with two more returns (making 1.2 per game) for zero yards still would have highest average.

ANNUAL PUNT RETURN LEADERS (1939-69)
BASED ON AVERAGE PER RETURN
(Minimum 1.2 Returns Per Game)

1939—Jackie Robinson, UCLA, 20.0; **1940**—Jackie Robinson, UCLA, 21.0; **1941**—Walt Slater, Tennessee, 20.4; **1942**—Billy Hillenbrand, Indiana, 20.9; **1943**—Otto Graham, Northwestern, 19.7; **1944**—Glenn Davis, Army, 18.4; **1945**—Jake Leicht, Oregon, 14.8; **1946**—Harold Griffin, Florida, 20.1; **1947**—Gene Derricotte, Michigan, 24.8; **1948**—George Sims, Baylor, ‡25.0; **1949**—Gene Evans, Wisconsin, 21.8; **1950**—Lindy Hanson, Boston U., 22.5; **1951**—Bill Blackstock, Tennessee, *25.9; **1952**—Gil Reich, Kansas, 17.2; **1953**—Bobby Lee, New Mexico, 19.4; **1954**—Dicky Maegle, Rice, 19.5; **1955**—Ron Lind, Drake, 21.1; **1956**—Ron Lind, Drake, 19.1; **1957**—Bobby Mulgado, Arizona St., 19.1; **1958**—Herb Hallas, Yale, 23.4; **1959**—Jacque MacKinnon, Colgate, 17.5; **1960**—Pat Fischer, Nebraska, 21.2; **1961**—Tom Larscheid, Utah St., 23.4; **1962**—Darrell Roberts, Utah St., 20.8; **1963**—Rickie Harris, Arizona, 17.4; **1964**—Ken Hatfield, Arkansas, 16.7; **1965**—Floyd Little, Syracuse, 23.5; **1966**—Don Bean, Houston, 20.2; **1967**—George Hoey, Michigan, 24.3; **1968**—Rob Bordley, Princeton, 20.5; **1969**—George Hannen, Davidson, 22.4.

*Record. ‡Record for minimum 1.5 returns per game.

Kickoff Returns

CAREER AVERAGE
(Minimum 1.2 Returns Per Game; Minimum 30 Returns)

Player, Team	Years	No.	Yards	Avg.
Anthony Davis, Southern California	1972-74	37	1,299	*35.1
Eric Booth, Southern Miss.	1994-97	35	1,135	32.4
Overton Curtis, Utah St.	1957-58	32	991	‡31.0
Fred Montgomery, New Mexico St.	1991-92	39	1,191	30.5
Altie Taylor, Utah St.	1966-68	40	1,170	29.3

ALL-TIME LEADERS—KICKOFF RETURNS

Player, Team	Years	No.	Yards	Avg.
Stan Brown, Purdue	1968-70	49	1,412	28.8
Henry White, Colgate	1974-77	41	1,180	28.8
Kevin Johnson, Syracuse	1995-98	50	1,437	28.7
Pat Johnson, Oregon	1994-97	36	1,023	28.4
Paul Loughran, Temple	1970-72	40	1,123	28.1
Jim Krieg, Washington	1970-71	31	860	27.7

*Record. ‡Record for minimum 1.5 returns per game.

SEASON AVERAGE
(Minimum 1.2 Returns Per Game)

Player, Team	Year	No.	Yards	Avg.
Paul Allen, Brigham Young	1961	12	481	*40.1
Tremain Mack, Miami (Fla.)	†1996	13	514	39.5
Leeland McElroy, Texas A&M	†1993	15	590	39.3
Forrest Hall, San Francisco	†1946	15	573	‡38.2
Tony Ball, Chattanooga	†1977	13	473	36.4
George Marinkov, North Carolina St.	1954	13	465	35.8
Bob Baker, Cornell	1964	11	386	35.1

*Record. †National champion. ‡Record for minimum 1.5 returns per game.

ANNUAL CHAMPIONS
(Ranked on Total Yards Until 1970)

Year	Player, Team	Class	No.	Yards	Avg.
1939	Nile Kinnick, Iowa	Sr.	15	377	25.1
1940	Jack Emigh, Montana	Sr.	18	395	21.9
1941	Earl Ray, Wyoming	So.	23	496	21.6
1942	Frank Porto, California	Sr.	17	483	28.4
1943	Paul Copoulos, Marquette	So.	11	384	34.9
1944	Paul Copoulos, Marquette	Jr.	14	337	24.1
1945	Al Dekdebrun, Cornell	Sr.	14	321	22.9
1946	Forrest Hall, San Francisco	Jr.	15	573	**38.2
1947	Doak Walker, Southern Methodist	So.	10	387	38.7
1948	Bill Gregus, Wake Forest	Jr.	19	503	26.5
1949	Johnny Subda, Nevada	Sr.	18	444	24.7
1950	Chuck Hill, New Mexico	Jr.	27	729	27.0
1951	Chuck Hill, New Mexico	Sr.	17	504	29.6
1952	Curly Powell, VMI	Sr.	27	517	19.1
1953	Max McGee, Tulane	Sr.	17	371	21.8
1954	Art Luppino, Arizona	So.	20	632	31.6
1955	Sam Woolwine, VMI	Jr.	22	471	21.4
1956	Sam Woolwine, VMI	Sr.	18	503	27.9
1957	Overton Curtis, Utah St.	Jr.	23	695	30.2
1958	Sonny Randle, Virginia	Sr.	21	506	24.1
1959	Don Perkins, New Mexico	Sr.	15	520	34.7
1960	Bruce Samples, Brigham Young	Sr.	23	577	25.1
1961	Dick Mooney, Idaho	Sr.	23	494	21.5
1962	Donnie Frederick, Wake Forest	Sr.	29	660	22.8
1963	Gary Wood, Cornell	Sr.	19	618	32.5
1964	Dan Bland, Mississippi St.	Jr.	20	558	27.9
1965	Eric Crabtree, Pittsburgh	Sr.	25	636	25.4
1966	Marcus Rhoden, Mississippi St.	Sr.	26	572	22.0
1967	Joe Casas, New Mexico	Sr.	23	602	26.2
1968	Mike Adamle, Northwestern	So.	34	732	21.5
1969	Stan Brown, Purdue	Jr.	26	698	26.8

Beginning in 1970, ranked on average per return (instead of total yards)‡

Year	Player, Team	Class	No.	Yards	Avg.
1970	Stan Brown, Purdue	Sr.	19	638	33.6
1971	Paul Loughran, Temple	Jr.	15	502	33.5
1972	Larry Williams, Texas Tech	So.	16	493	30.8
1973	Steve Odom, Utah	Sr.	21	618	29.4
1974	Anthony Davis, Southern California	Sr.	††11	467	42.5
1975	John Schultz, Maryland	Sr.	13	403	31.0
1976	Ira Matthews, Wisconsin	So.	14	415	29.6
1977	Tony Ball, Chattanooga	Fr.	13	473	36.4
1978	Drew Hill, Georgia Tech	Sr.	19	570	30.0
1979	Stevie Nelson, Ball St.	Fr.	18	565	31.4
1980	Mike Fox, San Diego St.	So.	†11	361	32.8
1981	Frank Minnifield, Louisville	Jr.	11	334	30.4
1982	Carl Monroe, Utah	Sr.	14	421	30.1
1983	Henry Williams, East Caro.	Jr.	19	591	31.1
1984	Keith Henderson, Texas Tech	Fr.	13	376	28.9
1985	Erroll Tucker, Utah	Sr.	24	698	29.1
1986	Terrance Roulhac, Clemson	Sr.	17	561	33.0
1987	Barry Sanders, Oklahoma St.	So.	14	442	31.6
1988	Raghib Ismail, Notre Dame	Fr.	#12	433	36.1
1989	Tony Smith, Southern Miss.	So.	14	455	32.5
1990	Dale Carter, Tennessee	Jr.	17	507	29.8
1991	Fred Montgomery, New Mexico St.	Jr.	25	734	29.4
1992	Fred Montgomery, New Mexico St.	Sr.	14	457	32.6
1993	Leeland McElroy, Texas A&M	Fr.	15	590	39.3
1994	Eric Moulds, Mississippi St.	Jr.	†13	426	32.8
1995	Robert Tate, Cincinnati	Jr.	15	515	34.3
1996	Tremain Mack, Miami (Fla.)	Jr.	13	514	39.5
1997	Eric Booth, Southern Miss.	Sr.	22	766	34.8
1998	Broderick McGrew, North Texas	Jr.	18	587	32.6
1999	James Williams, Marshall	Sr.	15	493	32.9

**Record for minimum 1.5 returns per game. #Declared champion; with two more returns (making 1.3 per game) for zero yards still would have highest average. †Declared champion; with one more return (making 1.2 per game) for zero yards still would have highest average. ††Declared champion; with three more returns (making 1.3 per game) for zero yards still would have highest average. ‡Ranked on minimum 1.5 returns per game, 1970-73; 1.2 from 1974.

ANNUAL KICKOFF RETURN LEADERS (1939-69) BASED ON AVERAGE PER RETURN
(Minimum 1.2 Returns Per Game)

1939—Nile Kinnick, Iowa, 25.1; **1940**—Bill Geyer, Colgate, 27.0; **1941**—Vern Lockard, Colorado, 24.4; **1942-45**—Not compiled; **1946**—Forrest Hall, San Francisco, ‡38.2; **1947**—Skippy Minisi, Pennsylvania, 28.8; **1948**—Jerry Williams, Washington St., 29.9; **1949**—Billy Conn, Georgetown, 31.1; **1950**—Johnny Turco, Holy Cross, 27.4; **1951**—Bob Mischak, Army, 31.3; **1952**—Carroll Hardy, Colorado, 32.2; **1953**—Carl Bolt, Wash. & Lee, 27.1; **1954**—George Marinkov, North Carolina St., 35.8; **1955**—Jim Brown, Syracuse, 32.0; **1956**—Paul Hornung, Notre Dame, 31.0; **1957**—Overton Curtis, Utah St., 30.2; **1958**—Marshall Starks, Illinois, 26.3; **1959**—Don Perkins, New Mexico, 34.7; **1960**—Tom Hennessey, Holy Cross, 33.4; **1961**—Paul Allen, Brigham Young, *40.1; **1962**—Larry Coyer, Marshall, 30.2; **1963**—Gary Wood, Cornell, 32.5; **1964**—Bob Baker, Cornell, 35.1; **1965**—Tom Barrington, Ohio St., 34.3; **1966**—Frank Moore, Louisville, 27.9; **1967**—Altie Taylor, Utah St., 31.9; **1968**—Kerry Reardon, Iowa, 32.1; **1969**—Chris Farasopoulous, Brigham Young, 32.2.

*Record. ‡Record for minimum 1.5 returns per game.

All-Purpose Yards

CAREER YARDS PER GAME
(Minimum 3,500 Yards)

Player, Team	Years	G	Rush	Rcv.	Int.	PR	KOR	Yds.	Yd.PG
Ryan Benjamin, Pacific (Cal.)	1990-92	24	3,119	1,063	0	100	1,424	5,706	*237.8
Sheldon Canley, San Jose St.	1988-90	25	2,513	828	0	5	1,800	5,146	205.8
Howard Stevens, Louisville	1971-72	20	2,723	389	0	401	360	3,873	193.7
O. J. Simpson, Southern California	1967-68	19	3,124	235	0	0	307	3,666	192.9
Alex Van Dyke, Nevada	1994-95	22	7	3,100	0	5	1,034	4,146	188.5
Ed Marinaro, Cornell	1969-71	27	4,715	225	0	0	0	4,940	183.0
Marshall Faulk, San Diego St.	1991-93	31	4,589	973	0	0	33	5,595	180.5
Troy Edwards, Louisiana Tech	1996-98	34	447	4,352	0	241	991	6,031	177.4
Herschel Walker, Georgia	1980-82	33	5,259	243	0	0	247	5,749	174.2
Louie Giammona, Utah St.	1973-75	30	3,499	171	0	188	1,345	5,203	173.4

*Record.

SEASON YARDS PER GAME

Player, Team	Years	Rush	Rcv.	Int.	PR	KOR	Yds.	Yd.PG
Barry Sanders, Oklahoma St.	†1988	*2,628	106	0	95	421	*3,250	*295.5
Ryan Benjamin, Pacific (Cal.)	†1991	1,581	612	0	4	798	2,995	249.6

ALL-TIME LEADERS—ALL-PURPOSE YARDS

Player, Team	Years	Rush	Rcv.	Int.	PR	KOR	Yds.	Yd.PG
Byron "Whizzer" White, Colorado	†1937	1,121	0	103	587	159	1,970	246.3
Mike Pringle, Cal St. Fullerton	†1989	1,727	249	0	0	714	2,690	244.6
Paul Palmer, Temple	†1986	1,866	110	0	0	657	2,633	239.4
Ryan Benjamin, Pacific (Cal.)	†1992	1,441	434	0	96	626	2,597	236.1
Marcus Allen, Southern California	†1981	2,342	217	0	0	0	2,559	232.6
Troy Edwards, Louisiana Tech	†1998	227	*1,996	0	235	326	2,784	232.0
Sheldon Canley, San Jose St.	1989	1,201	353	0	0	959	2,513	228.5
Ollie Matson, San Francisco	†1951	1,566	58	18	115	280	2,037	226.3
Troy Davis, Iowa St.	†1995	2,010	159	0	0	297	2,466	224.2
Alex Van Dyke, Nevada	1995	6	1,854	0	0	583	2,443	222.1
Art Luppino, Arizona	†1954	1,359	50	84	68	632	2,193	219.3
Chuck Weatherspoon, Houston	1989	1,146	735	0	715	95	2,391	217.4
Anthony Thompson, Indiana	1989	1,793	201	0	0	394	2,388	217.1
Ricky Williams, Texas	1998	2,124	262	0	0	0	2,386	216.9
Napoleon McCallum, Navy	†1983	1,587	166	0	272	360	2,385	216.8
Troy Davis, Iowa St.	†1996	2,185	61	0	0	118	2,364	214.9
Ed Marinaro, Cornell	†1971	1,881	51	0	0	0	1,932	214.7
Rashaan Salaam, Colorado	†1994	2,055	294	0	0	0	2,349	213.6
Howard Stevens, Louisville	†1972	1,294	221	0	337	240	2,132	213.2
Napoleon McCallum, Navy	†1985	1,327	358	0	157	488	2,330	211.8
Brian Pruitt, Central Mich.	1994	1,890	69	0	0	330	2,289	208.1
Keith Byars, Ohio St.	†1984	1,655	453	0	0	176	2,284	207.6
Mike Rozier, Nebraska	1983	2,148	106	0	0	232	2,486	207.2

*Record. †National champion.

Barry Sanders remains the only Division I-A player to compile over 3,000 all-purpose yards in a season, after totaling 3,250 as an Oklahoma State junior in 1988.

CAREER YARDS

Player, Team	Years	Rush	Rcv.	Int.	PR	KOR	Yds.	Yd.PP
Ricky Williams, Texas	1995-98	6,279	927	0	0	0	*7,206	6.6
Napoleon McCallum, Navy	$1981-85	4,179	796	0	858	1,339	7,172	6.3
Darrin Nelson, Stanford	1977-78, 80-81	4,033	2,368	0	471	13	6,885	7.1
Kevin Faulk, LSU	1995-98	4,557	600	0	857	819	6,833	6.8
Ron Dayne, Wisconsin	1996-99	*6,397	304	0	0	0	6,701	5.8
Terance Mathis, New Mexico	1985-87, 89	329	4,254	0	115	1,993	6,691	**14.6
Tony Dorsett, Pittsburgh	1973-76	6,082	406	0	0	127	6,615	5.9
Paul Palmer, Temple	1983-86	4,895	705	0	12	997	6,609	6.1
Charles White, Southern California	1976-79	5,598	507	0	0	440	6,545	6.0
Trevor Cobb, Rice	1989-92	4,948	892	0	21	651	6,512	5.3
Glyn Milburn, Oklahoma/Stanford	1988, 90-92	2,302	1,495	0	1,145	1,246	6,188	8.1
Travis Prentice, Miami (Ohio)	1996-99	5,596	527	0	0	0	6,123	5.1
Anthony Thompson, Indiana	1986-89	4,965	713	0	0	412	6,090	5.1
Troy Edwards, Louisiana Tech	1996-98	447	4,352	0	241	991	6,031	15.8
Archie Griffin, Ohio St.	1972-75	5,177	286	0	0	540	6,003	6.7
Ron "Po" James, New Mexico St.	1968-71	3,884	217	0	8	1,870	5,979	6.5
Eric Wilkerson, Kent	1985-88	3,830	506	0	0	1,638	5,974	7.0
Steve Bartalo, Colorado St.	1983-86	4,813	1,079	0	0	0	5,892	4.4
Wilford White, Arizona St.	1947-50	3,173	892	212	798	791	5,866	9.2
Leon Johnson, North Carolina	1993-96	3,693	1,288	0	390	457	5,828	5.9
Joe Washington, Oklahoma	1972-75	3,995	253	0	807	726	5,781	7.3
Herschel Walker, Georgia	1980-82	5,259	243	0	0	247	‡5,749	5.6
George Swarn, Miami (Ohio)	1983-86	4,172	1,057	0	0	498	5,727	5.6
Chuck Weatherspoon, Houston	1987-90	3,247	1,375	0	611	482	5,715	9.7
Ryan Benjamin, Pacific (Cal.)	1990-92	3,119	1,063	0	100	1,424	‡5,706	8.8
Eric Metcalf, Texas	1985-88	2,661	1,394	0	1,076	574	5,705	6.7
Denvis Manns, New Mexico St.	1995-98	4,692	620	0	0	384	5,696	5.9
George Rogers, South Carolina	1977-80	4,958	371	0	0	339	5,668	5.9
Napoleon Kaufman, Washington	1991-94	4,041	424	0	368	825	5,658	6.7
Jamie Morris, Michigan	1984-87	3,944	703	0	0	984	5,631	6.4
Joe Morris, Syracuse	1978-81	4,299	278	0	0	1,023	5,600	6.3
James Brooks, Auburn	1977-80	3,523	219	0	128	1,726	5,596	7.6
Marshall Faulk, San Diego St.	1991-93	4,589	973	0	0	33	‡5,595	6.6
Johnny Rodgers, Nebraska	1970-72	745	2,479	0	1,515	847	‡5,586	13.8

*Record. $See page 6 for explanation. ‡Three-year totals. **Record for minimum 375 plays.

SEASON YARDS

Player, Team	Year	Rush	Rcv.	Int.	PR	KOR	Yds.	Yd.PP
Barry Sanders, Oklahoma St.	†1988	*2,628	106	0	95	421	*3,250	8.3
Ryan Benjamin, Pacific (Cal.)	†1991	1,581	612	0	4	798	2,995	9.6
Troy Edwards, Louisiana Tech	†1998	227	1,996	0	235	326	2,784	14.7
Mike Pringle, Cal St. Fullerton	†1989	1,727	249	0	0	714	2,690	7.6
Paul Palmer, Temple	†1986	1,866	110	0	0	657	2,633	6.8
Ryan Benjamin, Pacific (Cal.)	†1992	1,441	434	0	96	626	2,597	8.1
Marcus Allen, Southern California	†1981	2,342	217	0	0	0	2,559	5.9
Sheldon Canley, San Jose St.	1989	1,201	353	0	0	959	2,513	7.4
Mike Rozier, Nebraska	1983	2,148	106	0	0	232	2,486	8.4
Troy Davis, Iowa St.	†1995	2,010	159	0	0	297	2,466	6.7
Alex Van Dyke, Nevada	1995	6	1,854	0	0	583	2,443	15.7
Chuck Weatherspoon, Houston	1989	1,146	735	0	415	95	2,391	10.7
Anthony Thompson, Indiana	1989	1,793	201	0	0	394	2,388	5.8
Ricky Williams, Texas	1998	2,124	262	0	0	0	2,386	6.2
Napoleon McCallum, Navy	†1983	1,587	166	0	272	360	2,385	6.1
Troy Davis, Iowa St.	†1996	2,185	61	0	0	118	2,364	5.7
Rashaan Salaam, Colorado	†1994	2,055	294	0	0	0	2,349	7.3
Napoleon McCallum, Navy	†1985	1,327	358	0	157	488	2,330	6.3
Brian Pruitt, Central Mich.	1994	1,890	69	0	0	330	2,289	7.3

ALL-TIME LEADERS—ALL-PURPOSE YARDS

Travis Prentice of Miami (Ohio) is 12th in Division I-A in career all-purpose yards with 6,123. He gained 411 of those yards vs. Akron on November 6, 1999.

Player, Team	Year	Rush	Rcv.	Int.	PR	KOR	Yds.	Yd.PP
Keith Byars, Ohio St.	†1984	1,655	453	0	0	176	2,284	6.4
Byron Hanspard, Texas Tech	1996	2,084	192	0	0	0	2,276	6.4
Dennis Northcutt, Arizona	1999	200	1,422	0	436	191	2,249	16.8
Eddie George, Ohio St.	1995	1,826	399	0	0	0	2,225	6.4
Glyn Milburn, Stanford	†1990	729	632	0	267	594	2,222	8.4
Sheldon Canley, San Jose St.	1990	1,248	386	0	5	574	2,213	6.3
Vaughn Dunbar, Indiana	1991	1,699	252	0	0	262	2,213	5.9
Johnny Johnson, San Jose St.	1988	1,219	668	0	0	315	2,202	7.1
Art Luppino, Arizona	†1954	1,359	50	84	68	632	2,193	10.4
Corey Dillon, Washington	1996	1,555	273	0	0	357	2,185	7.2
Rick Calhoun, Cal St. Fullerton	1986	1,398	125	0	138	522	2,183	7.0
Randy Moss, Marshall	1997	2	1,647	0	266	263	2,178	‡16.9
Trevor Insley, Nevada	†1999	5	*2,060	0	111	0	2,176	14.7
Marshall Faulk, San Diego St.	1993	1,530	644	0	0	0	2,174	6.3
Troy Edwards, Louisiana Tech	1997	190	1,707	0	6	241	2,144	16.5
Terance Mathis, New Mexico	1989	38	1,315	0	0	785	2,138	15.7
Howard Stevens, Louisville	†1972	1,294	221	0	377	240	2,132	6.4

*Record. †National champion. ‡Record for minimum 125 plays.

ALL-PURPOSE SINGLE-GAME HIGHS

Yds.	Player, Team (Opponent)	Date
435	Brian Pruitt, Central Mich. (Toledo)	Nov. 5, 1994
429	Moe Williams, Kentucky (South Carolina)	Sept. 23, 1995
426	LaDainian Tomlinson, TCU (UTEP)	Nov. 20, 1999
424	Troy Edwards, Louisiana Tech (Nebraska)	Aug. 29, 1998
422	Marshall Faulk, San Diego St. (Pacific [Cal.])	Sept. 14, 1991
419	Randy Gatewood, UNLV (Idaho)	Sept. 17, 1994
417	Paul Palmer, Temple (East Caro.)	Nov. 10, 1986
417	Greg Allen, Florida St. (Western Caro.)	Oct. 31, 1981
416	Anthony Thompson, Indiana (Wisconsin)	Nov. 11, 1989
411	Travis Prentice, Miami (Ohio) (Akron)	Nov. 6, 1999
411	John Leach, Wake Forest (Maryland)	Nov. 20, 1993
402	Ryan Benjamin, Pacific (Cal.) (Utah St.)	Nov. 21, 1992
401	Chuck Hughes, UTEP (North Texas)	Sept. 18, 1965
397	Eric Allen, Michigan St. (Purdue)	Oct. 30, 1971
388	Astron Whatley, Kent St. (Eastern Mich.)	Sept. 20, 1997
388	Ryan Benjamin, Pacific (Cal.) (Cal St. Fullerton)	Oct. 5, 1991
387	Kendal Smith, Utah St. (San Jose St.)	Oct. 22, 1988
387	Ron Johnson, Michigan (Wisconsin)	Nov. 16, 1968
386	Barry Sanders, Oklahoma St. (Kansas)	Nov. 12, 1988
379	Glyn Milburn, Stanford (California)	Nov. 17, 1990
377	Robert Kilow, Arkansas St. (Mississippi)	Sept. 11, 1999
376	Kevin Faulk, LSU (Houston)	Sept. 7, 1996
375	Alex Van Dyke, Nevada (Toledo)	Sept. 23, 1995
375	Rueben Mayes, Washington St. (Oregon St.)	Nov. 3, 1984
374	Troy Davis, Iowa St. (Missouri)	Sept. 28, 1996
374	Tony Dorsett, Pittsburgh (Penn St.)	Nov. 22, 1975
373	Barry Sanders, Oklahoma St. (Oklahoma)	Nov. 5, 1988
372	Peter Warrick, Florida St. (Clemson)	Sept. 20, 1997
372	Chuck Weatherspoon, Houston (Eastern Wash.)	Nov. 17, 1990

ANNUAL CHAMPIONS

Year	Player, Team	Class	Rush	Rcv.	Int.	PR	KOR	Yds.	Yd.PG
1937	Byron "Whizzer" White, Colorado	Sr.	1,121	0	103	587	159	1,970	246.3
1938	Parker Hall, Mississippi	Sr.	698	0	128	0	594	1,420	129.1
1939	Tom Harmon, Michigan	Jr.	868	110	98	0	132	1,208	151.0
1940	Tom Harmon, Michigan	Sr.	844	0	20	244	204	1,312	164.0
1941	Bill Dudley, Virginia	Sr.	968	60	76	481	89	1,674	186.0
1942	records not available	—	—	—	—	—	—	—	—
1943	Stan Koslowski, Holy Cross	Fr.	784	63	50	438	76	1,411	176.4
1944	Red Williams, Minnesota	Jr.	911	0	0	242	314	1,467	163.0
1945	Bob Fenimore, Oklahoma St.	Jr.	1,048	12	129	157	231	1,577	197.1
1946	Rudy Mobley, Hardin-Simmons	Sr.	1,262	13	79	273	138	1,765	176.5
1947	Wilton Davis, Hardin-Simmons	So.	1,173	79	0	295	251	1,798	179.8
1948	Lou Kusserow, Columbia	Sr.	766	463	19	130	359	1,737	193.0
1949	Johnny Papit, Virginia	Jr.	1,214	0	0	0	397	1,611	179.0
1950	Wilford White, Arizona St.	Sr.	1,502	225	0	64	274	2,065	206.5
1951	Ollie Matson, San Francisco	Sr.	1,566	58	18	115	280	2,037	226.3
1952	Billy Vessels, Oklahoma	Sr.	1,072	165	10	120	145	1,512	151.2
1953	J. C. Caroline, Illinois	So.	1,256	52	0	129	33	1,470	163.3
1954	Art Luppino, Arizona	So.	1,359	50	84	68	632	2,193	219.3
1955	Jim Swink, TCU	Jr.	1,283	111	46	64	198	1,702	170.2
	Art Luppino, Arizona	Jr.	1,313	74	0	62	253	1,702	170.2
1956	Jack Hill, Utah St.	Sr.	920	215	132	21	403	1,691	169.1
1957	Overton Curtis, Utah St.	Jr.	616	193	60	44	695	1,608	160.8
1958	Dick Bass, Pacific (Cal.)	Jr.	1,361	121	5	164	227	1,878	187.8
1959	Pervis Atkins, New Mexico St.	Jr.	971	301	23	241	264	1,800	180.0
1960	Pervis Atkins, New Mexico St.	Sr.	611	468	23	218	293	1,613	161.3
1961	Jim Pilot, New Mexico St.	So.	1,278	20	0	161	147	1,606	160.6
1962	Gary Wood, Cornell	Jr.	889	7	0	69	430	1,395	155.0
1963	Gary Wood, Cornell	Sr.	818	15	0	57	618	1,508	167.6
1964	Donny Anderson, Texas Tech	Jr.	966	396	0	28	320	1,710	171.0
1965	Floyd Little, Syracuse	Jr.	1,065	248	0	423	254	1,990	199.0

ALL-TIME LEADERS—ALL-PURPOSE YARDS

DIVISION I-A

Year	Player, Team	Class	Rush	Rcv.	Int.	PR	KOR	Yds.	Yd.PG
1966	Frank Quayle, Virginia	So.	727	420	0	30	439	1,616	161.6
1967	O. J. Simpson, Southern California	Jr.	1,415	109	0	0	176	1,700	188.9
1968	O. J. Simpson, Southern California	Sr.	1,709	126	0	0	131	1,966	196.6
1969	Lynn Moore, Army	Sr.	983	44	0	223	545	1,795	179.5
1970	Don McCauley, North Carolina	Sr.	1,720	235	0	0	66	2,021	183.7
1971	Ed Marinaro, Cornell	Sr.	1,881	51	0	0	0	1,932	214.7
1972	Howard Stevens, Louisville	Sr.	1,294	221	0	377	240	2,132	213.2
1973	Willard Harrell, Pacific (Cal.)	Jr.	1,319	18	0	88	352	1,777	177.7
1974	Louie Giammona, Utah St.	Jr.	1,534	79	0	16	355	1,984	198.4
1975	Louie Giammona, Utah St.	Sr.	1,454	33	0	124	434	2,045	185.9
1976	Tony Dorsett, Pittsburgh	Sr.	1,948	73	0	0	0	2,021	183.7
1977	Earl Campbell, Texas	Sr.	1,744	111	0	0	0	1,855	168.6
1978	Charles White, Southern California	Jr.	1,760	191	0	0	145	2,096	174.7
1979	Charles White, Southern California	Sr.	1,803	138	0	0	0	1,941	194.1
1980	Marcus Allen, Southern California	Jr.	1,563	231	0	0	0	1,794	179.4
1981	Marcus Allen, Southern California	Sr.	2,342	217	0	0	0	2,559	232.6
1982	Carl Monroe, Utah	Sr.	1,507	108	0	0	421	2,036	185.1
1983	Napoleon McCallum, Navy	Jr.	1,587	166	0	272	360	2,385	216.8
1984	Keith Byars, Ohio St.	Jr.	1,655	453	0	0	176	2,284	207.6
1985	Napoleon McCallum, Navy	Sr.	1,327	358	0	157	488	2,330	211.8
1986	Paul Palmer, Temple	Sr.	1,866	110	0	0	657	2,633	239.4
1987	Eric Wilkerson, Kent St.	Jr.	1,221	269	0	0	584	2,074	188.6
1988	Barry Sanders, Oklahoma St.	Jr.	*2,628	106	0	95	421	*3,250	*295.5
1989	Mike Pringle, Cal St. Fullerton	Sr.	1,727	249	0	0	714	2,690	244.6
1990	Glyn Milburn, Stanford	So.	729	632	0	267	594	2,222	202.0
1991	Ryan Benjamin, Pacific (Cal.)	Jr.	1,581	612	0	4	798	2,995	249.6
1992	Ryan Benjamin, Pacific (Cal.)	Sr.	1,441	434	0	96	626	2,597	236.1
1993	LeShon Johnson, Northern Ill.	Sr.	1,976	106	0	0	0	2,082	189.3
1994	Rashaan Salaam, Colorado	Jr.	2,055	294	0	0	0	2,349	213.6
1995	Troy Davis, Iowa St.	So.	2,010	159	0	0	297	2,466	224.2
1996	Troy Davis, Iowa St.	Jr.	2,185	61	0	0	118	2,364	214.9
1997	Troy Edwards, Louisiana Tech	Jr.	190	1,707	0	6	241	2,144	194.9
1998	Troy Edwards, Louisiana Tech	Sr.	227	1,996	0	235	326	2,784	232.0
1999	Trevor Insley, Nevada	Sr.	5	*2,060	0	111	0	2,176	197.8

*Record.

Field Goals

CAREER FIELD GOALS

(One-inch tees were permitted in 1949, two-inch tees were permitted in 1965, and use of tees was eliminated in 1989. The goal posts were widened from 18 feet, 6 inches to 23 feet, 4 inches in 1959 and were narrowed back to 18 feet, 6 inches in 1991. In 1993, the hash marks were moved 6 feet, 8 inches closer to the center of the field, to 60 feet from each sideline.)

Player, Team	Years	Total	Pct.	Under 40 Yds.	40 Plus	Long	‡Won
Jeff Jaeger, Washington (S)	1983-86	*80-99	.808	59-68	21-31	52	5
John Lee, UCLA (S)	1982-85	79-92	@.859	54-56	25-36	52	**10
Jason Elam, Hawaii (S)	$1988-92	79-100	.790	50-55	29-45	56	3
Philip Doyle, Alabama (S)	1987-90	78-*105	.743	57-61	21-44	53	6
Luis Zendejas, Arizona St. (S)	1981-84	78-*105	.743	53-59	25-46	55	1
Kevin Butler, Georgia (S)	1981-84	77-98	.786	50-56	27-42	60	7
Max Zendejas, Arizona (S)	1982-85	77-104	.740	47-53	30-51	57	7
Carlos Huerta, Miami (Fla.) (S)	1988-91	73-91	.802	56-60	17-31	52	3
Derek Schmidt, Florida St. (S)	1984-87	73-104	.702	44-55	29-49	54	1
Fuad Reveiz, Tennessee (S)	1981-84	71-95	.747	45-53	26-42	60	7
Barry Belli, Fresno St. (S)	1984-87	70-99	.707	47-53	23-46	55	5
Nelson Welch, Clemson (S)	1991-94	70-100	.700	49-64	21-36	53	7
Roman Anderson, Houston (S)	1988-91	70-101	.693	*61-*72	9-29	53	3
Collin Mackie, South Carolina (S)	1987-90	69-95	.726	48-57	21-38	52	5
Shayne Graham, Virginia Tech (S)	1996-99	68-93	.731	48-57	20-36	53	5
Larry Roach, Oklahoma St. (S)	1981-84	68-101	.673	46-54	22-47	56	5
Gary Gusman, Miami (Ohio) (S)	1984-87	68-94	.723	50-57	18-37	53	2
Rusty Hanna, Toledo (S)	1989-92	68-99	.687	51-58	17-41	51	3
Sebastian Janikowski, Florida St. (S)	1997-99	66-83	.795	46-51	20-32	56	4
Paul Woodside, West Virginia (S)	1981-84	65-81	.802	45-49	20-32	55	5
Michael Proctor, Alabama (S)	1992-95	65-91	.714	48-64	17-27	53	5
John Diettrich, Ball St. (S)	1983-86	63-90	.700	42-50	21-40	62	5
Jason Hanson, Washington St. (S)	1988-91	63-96	.656	24-30	*39-*66	62	4
Kenny Stucker, Ball St. (S)	1988-91	62-87	.713	45-51	17-36	52	4
Dan Eichloff, Kansas (S)	1990-93	62-87	.713	40-50	22-37	61	5
Jeff Hall, Tennessee (S)	1995-98	61-89	.685	43-56	18-33	53	4
David Browndyke, LSU (S)	1986-89	61-75	.813	49-53	12-22	52	3
Todd Gregoire, Wisconsin (S)	1984-87	61-81	.753	48-56	13-25	54	6
Kanon Parkman, Georgia (S)	1991, 93-95	61-85	.718	52-61	9-24	48	1
Todd Wright, Arkansas (S)	1989-92	60-79	.759	41-47	19-32	50	2
Jess Atkinson, Maryland (S)	1981-84	60-82	.732	40-48	20-34	50	5
Kyle Bryant, Texas A&M (S)	1994-97	60-85	.706	38-48	22-37	61	3
Scott Sisson, Georgia Tech (S)	1989-92	60-88	.682	45-53	15-35	51	6
Obed Ariri, Clemson (S)	1977-80	60-92	.652	47-55	13-37	57	5
Chuck Nelson, Washington (S)	1980-82	59-72	.819	47-53	12-19	51	5

ALL-TIME LEADERS—FIELD GOALS

Player, Team	Years	Total	Pct.	Under 40 Yds.	40 Plus	Long	‡Won
Phil Dawson, Texas (S)	1994-97	59-79	.747	33-38	26-41	54	3
Van Tiffin, Alabama (S)	1983-86	59-87	.678	32-38	27-49	57	5
John Hopkins, Stanford (S)	1987-90	59-88	.670	43-50	16-38	54	4
Rafael Garcia, Virginia (S)	1994-96	58-76	.763	42-50	16-26	56	5
Remy Hamilton, Michigan (S)	1993-96	58-76	.763	49-60	9-16	49	3
Jeff Ward, Texas (S)	1983-86	58-78	.744	36-41	22-37	57	**10
Jeff Shudak, Iowa St. (S)	1987-90	58-79	.734	38-45	20-34	55	5
Brian Gowins, Northwestern (S)	1995-98	58-85	.682	36-46	22-39	52	3

*Record. $See page 6 for explanation. **Record tied. @Record for minimum 55 attempts. ‡Number of games in which his field goal(s) provided the winning margin. (S) Soccer-style kicker.

SEASON FIELD GOALS

Player, Team	Years	Total	Pct.	Under 40 Yds.	40 Plus	Long	‡Won
John Lee, UCLA (S)	†1984	*29-33	.879	16-16	13-17	51	5
Paul Woodside, West Virginia (S)	†1982	28-31	.903	23-23	5-8	45	2
Luis Zendejas, Arizona St. (S)	†1983	28-37	.757	19-22	9-15	52	1
Fuad Reveiz, Tennessee (S)	1982	27-31	.871	14-14	13-17	60	2
Sebastian Janikowski, Florida St. (S)	†1998	27-32	.844	17-19	10-13	53	1
Chuck Nelson, Washington (S)	1982	25-26	*.962	22-23	3-3	49	1
Chris Jacke, UTEP (S)	1988	25-27	.926	11-11	*14-16	52	2
John Diettrich, Ball St. (S)	†1985	25-29	.862	16-17	9-12	54	2
Kendall Trainor, Arkansas (S)	†1988	24-27	.889	14-15	10-12	58	4
Brad Bohn, Utah St. (S)	1998	24-28	.857	21-22	3-6	51	2
Carlos Reveiz, Tennessee (S)	1985	24-28	.857	12-14	12-14	52	2
Chris White, Illinois (S)	1984	24-28	.857	16-17	8-11	52	1
Remy Hamilton, Michigan (S)	1994	24-29	.828	23-27	1-2	42	2
Philip Doyle, Alabama (S)	†1990	24-29	.828	16-17	8-12	47	2
Bruce Kallmeyer, Kansas (S)	1983	24-29	.828	13-14	11-15	57	1
Mike Prindle, Western Mich. (S)	1984	24-30	.800	17-20	7-10	56	1
Michael Reeder, TCU (S)	†1995	23-25	.920	19-19	4-6	47	3
Joe Allison, Memphis (S)	†1992	23-25	.920	13-14	10-11	51	1
Bobby Raymond, Florida (S)	1984	23-26	.885	18-18	5-8	51	1
Mike Bass, Illinois (S)	1982	23-26	.885	12-13	11-13	53	1
Brad Palazzo, Tulane (S)	†1997	23-28	.821	15-15	8-13	52	0
Kevin Butler, Georgia (S)	1984	23-28	.821	12-14	11-14	60	2
Steve McLaughlin, Arizona (S)	1994	23-29	.793	11-13	12-16	54	4
Sebastian Janikowski, Florida St. (S)	†1999	23-30	.767	15-18	8-12	54	0
Collin Mackie, South Carolina (S)	†1987	23-30	.767	17-21	6-9	49	0
Obed Ariri, Clemson (S)	†1980	23-30	.767	18-19	5-11	52	3
Derek Schmidt, Florida St. (S)	†1987	23-31	.742	16-21	7-10	53	0

*Record. †National champion. ‡Number of games in which his field goal(s) provided the winning margin. (S) Soccer-style kicker.

SINGLE-GAME FIELD GOALS

No.	Player, Team (Opponent)	Date
7	Dale Klein, Nebraska (Missouri)	Oct. 19, 1985
7	Mike Prindle, Western Mich. (Marshall)	Sept. 29, 1984
6	Josh McGee, North Carolina (Duke)	Nov. 20, 1999
6	Cory Wedel, Wyoming (Idaho)	Aug. 31, 1996
6	Rusty Hanna, Toledo (Northern Ill.)	Nov. 21, 1992
6	Philip Doyle, Alabama (La.-Lafayette)	Oct. 6, 1990
6	Sean Fleming, Wyoming (Arkansas St.)	Sept. 15, 1990
6	Bobby Raymond, Florida (Kentucky)	Nov. 17, 1984
6	John Lee, UCLA (San Diego St.)	Sept. 8, 1984
6	Bobby Raymond, Florida (Florida St.)	Dec. 3, 1983
6	Alan Smith, Texas A&M (Arkansas St.)	Sept. 17, 1983
6	Al Del Greco, Auburn (Kentucky)	Oct. 9, 1982
6	Vince Fusco, Duke (Clemson)	Oct. 16, 1976
6	Frank Nester, West Virginia (Villanova)	Sept. 9, 1972
6	Charley Gogolak, Princeton (Rutgers)	Sept. 25, 1965

ANNUAL CHAMPIONS

(From 1959-90, goal posts were 23 feet, 4 inches; and from 1991, narrowed to 18 feet, 6 inches)

Year	Player, Team	Total	PG	Pct.	Under 40 Yds.	40 Plus	Long	‡Won
1959	Karl Holzwarth, Wisconsin (C)	7-8	0.8	.875	7-8	0-0	29	4
1960	Ed Dyas, Auburn (C)	13-18	1.3	.722	13-17	0-1	37	2
1961	Greg Mather, Navy (C)	11-15	1.1	.733	9-12	2-3	45	1
1962	Bob Jencks, Miami (Ohio) (C)	8-11	0.8	.727	7-9	1-2	52	3
	Al Woodall, Auburn (C)	8-20	0.8	.400	8-13	0-7	35	0
1963	Billy Lothridge, Georgia Tech (C)	12-16	1.2	.750	10-14	2-2	41	3
1964	Doug Moreau, LSU (C)	13-20	1.3	.650	13-20	0-0	36	0
1965	Charley Gogolak, Princeton (S)	16-23	1.8	.696	7-10	9-13	54	0
1966	Jerry DePoyster, Wyoming (C)	13-*38	1.3	.342	7-13	6-*25	54	1
1967	Gerald Warren, North Carolina St. (C)	17-22	1.7	.773	13-14	4-8	47	1
1968	Bob Jacobs, Wyoming (C)	14-29	1.4	.483	10-15	4-14	51	2
1969	Bob Jacobs, Wyoming (C)	18-27	1.8	.667	13-16	5-11	43	2

ALL-TIME LEADERS—FIELD GOALS

Beginning in 1970, ranked on per-game (instead of total) made

Year	Player, Team	Total	PG	Pct.	Under 40 Yds.	40 Plus	Long	‡Won
1970	Kim Braswell, Georgia (C)	13-17	1.3	.765	11-14	2-3	43	0
1971	Nick Mike-Mayer, Temple (S)	12-17	1.3	.706	8-10	4-7	48	1
1972	Nick Mike-Mayer, Temple (S)	13-20	1.4	.650	10-11	3-9	44	3
1973	Rod Garcia, Stanford (S)	18-29	1.6	.621	10-14	8-15	59	2
1974	Dave Lawson, Air Force (C)	19-31	1.7	.613	13-14	6-17	60	1
1975	Don Bitterlich, Temple (S)	21-31	1.9	.677	13-14	8-17	56	0
1976	Tony Franklin, Texas A&M (S)	17-26	1.6	.654	9-12	8-14	65	0
1977	Paul Marchese, Kent St. (S)	18-27	1.8	.667	13-15	5-12	51	2
1978	Matt Bahr, Penn St. (S)	22-27	2.0	.815	19-20	3-7	50	3
1979	Ish Ordonez, Arkansas (S)	18-22	1.6	.818	12-14	6-8	50	1
1980	Obed Ariri, Clemson (S)	23-30	2.1	.767	18-19	5-11	52	3
1981	Bruce Lahay, Arkansas (S)	19-24	1.7	.792	12-15	7-9	49	4
	Kevin Butler, Georgia (S)	19-26	1.7	.731	11-14	8-12	52	0
	Larry Roach, Oklahoma (S)	19-28	1.7	.679	12-14	7-14	56	3
1982	Paul Woodside, West Virginia (S)	28-31	2.6	.903	23-23	5-8	45	2
1983	Luis Zendejas, Arizona St. (S)	28-37	2.6	.757	19-22	9-15	52	1
1984	John Lee, UCLA (S)	*29-33	*2.6	.879	16-16	13-17	51	5
1985	John Diettrich, Ball St. (S)	25-29	2.1	.862	16-17	9-12	54	2
1986	Chris Kinzer, Virginia Tech (C)	22-27	2.0	.815	14-17	8-10	50	5
1987	Collin Mackie, South Carolina (S)	23-30	2.1	.767	17-21	6-9	49	0
	Derek Schmidt, Florida St. (S)	23-31	2.1	.742	16-21	7-10	53	0
1988	Kendall Trainor, Arkansas (S)	24-27	2.2	.889	14-15	10-12	58	4
1989	Philip Doyle, Alabama (S)	22-25	2.0	.880	19-19	3-6	44	2
	Gregg McCallum, Oregon (S)	22-29	2.0	.759	15-15	7-14	47	2
	Roman Anderson, Houston (S)	22-34	2.0	.647	17-20	5-14	51	0
1990	Philip Doyle, Alabama (S)	24-29	2.2	.828	16-17	8-12	47	2
1991	Doug Brien, California (S)	19-28	1.7	.679	15-20	4-8	50	2
1992	Joe Allison, Memphis (S)	23-25	2.1	.920	13-14	10-11	51	1
1993	Michael Proctor, Alabama (S)	22-29	1.8	.759	15-20	7-9	53	0
1994	Remy Hamilton, Michigan (S)	24-29	2.2	.828	23-27	1-2	42	2
1995	Michael Reeder, TCU (S)	23-25	2.1	.920	19-19	4-6	47	3
1996	Rafael Garcia, Virginia (S)	21-27	1.9	.778	16-17	5-10	46	1
1997	Brad Palazzo, Tulane (S)	23-28	2.1	.821	15-15	8-15	52	0
1998	Sebastian Janikowski, Florida St. (S)	27-32	2.3	.844	17-19	10-13	53	1
1999	Sebastian Janikowski, Florida St. (S)	23-30	2.1	.767	15-18	8-12	54	0

*Record. ‡Number of games in which his field goal(s) provided the winning margin. (C) Conventional kicker. (S) Soccer-style kicker.

All-Time Longest Plays

Since 1941, official maximum length of all plays fixed at 100 yards.

RUSHING

Yds.	Player, Team (Opponent)	Year
99	Eric Vann, Kansas (Oklahoma)	1997
99	Kelsey Finch, Tennessee (Florida)	1977
99	Ralph Thompson, West Tex. A&M (Wichita St.)	1970
99	Max Anderson, Arizona St. (Wyoming)	1967
99	Gale Sayers, Kansas (Nebraska)	1963
98	Jerald Sowell, Tulane (Alabama)	1993
98	Darrell Thompson, Minnesota (Michigan)	1987
98	George Swarn, Miami, Ohio (Western Mich.)	1984
98	Mark Malone, Arizona St. (Utah St.)	1979
98	Stanley Howell, Mississippi St. (Southern Miss.)	1979
98	Steve Atkins, Maryland (Clemson)	1978
98	Granville Amos, VMI (William & Mary)	1964
98	Jim Thacker, Davidson (George Washington)	1952
98	Bill Powell, California (Oregon St.)	1951
98	Al Yannelli, Bucknell (Delaware)	1946
98	Meredith Warner, Iowa St. (Iowa Pre-Flight)	1943

PASSING

Yds.	Passer-Receiver, Team (Opponent)	Year
99	Drew Brees-Vinny Sutherland, Purdue (Northwestern)	1999
99	Troy DeGar-Wes Caswell, Tulsa (Oklahoma)	1996
99	John Paci-Thomas Lewis, Indiana (Penn St.)	1993
99	Gino Torretta-Horace Copeland, Miami (Fla.) (Arkansas)	1991
99	Scott Ankrom-James Maness, TCU (Rice)	1984
99	Cris Collinsworth-Derrick Gaffney, Florida (Rice)	1977
99	Terry Peel-Robert Ford, Houston (San Diego St.)	1972
99	Terry Peel-Robert Ford, Houston (Syracuse)	1970
99	Colin Clapton-Eddie Jenkins, Holy Cross (Boston U.)	1970
99	Bo Burris-Warren McVea, Houston (Washington St.)	1966
99	Fred Owens-Jack Ford, Portland (St. Mary's [Cal.])	1947
98	Jose Davis-Eugene Baker, Kent (Central Fla.)	1997
98	Mike Neu-Brian Oliver, Ball St. (Toledo)	1993
98	Tom Dubs-Richard Hill, Ohio (Kent)	1991
98	Paul Oates-Sean Foster, Long Beach St. (San Diego St.)	1989
98	Barry Garrison-Al Owens, New Mexico (Brigham Young)	1987
98	Kelly Donohoe-Willie Vaughn, Kansas (Colorado)	1987
98	Jeff Martin-Mark Flaker, Drake (New Mexico St.)	1976
98	Pete Woods-Joe Stewart, Missouri (Nebraska)	1976
98	Dan Hagemann-Jack Steptoe, Utah (New Mexico)	1976
98	Bruce Shaw-Pat Kenney, North Carolina St. (Penn St.)	1972
98	Jerry Rhome-Jeff Jordan, Tulsa (Wichita St.)	1963
98	Bob Dean-Norman Dawson, Cornell (Navy)	1947

INTERCEPTION RETURNS

Since 1941, 69 players have returned interceptions 100 yards. The most recent:

Yds.	Player, Team (Opponent)	Year
100	Deltha O'Neal, California (Oregon)	1999
100	Pat Dennis, La.-Monroe (Nicholls St.)	1998
100	Steve Rosga, Colorado (Oklahoma St.)	1996
100	Michael Hicks, UTEP (Brigham Young)	1996
100	Mario Smith, Kansas St. (Missouri)	1996
100	Keion Carpenter, Virginia Tech (Miami [Fla.])	1996
100	Reggie Love, North Carolina (Tulane)	1994
100	Harold Lusk, Utah (Colorado St.)	1994
100	Marlon Kerner, Ohio St. (Purdue)	1993
100	Ray Jackson, Colorado St. (UTEP)	1993
100	John Hardy, California (Wisconsin)	1990
100	Ed Givens, Army (Lafayette)	1990

PUNT RETURNS

Yds.	Player, Team (Opponent)	Year
100	Courtney Davis, Bowling Green (Kent St.)	1996
100	Eddie Kennison, LSU (Mississippi St.)	1994
100‡	Richie Luzzi, Clemson (Georgia)	1968
100‡	Don Guest, California (Washington St.)	1966
100	Jimmy Campagna, Georgia (Vanderbilt)	1952

Yds.	Player, Team (Opponent)	Year
100	Hugh McElhenny, Washington (Southern California)	1951
100	Frank Brady, Navy (Maryland)	1951
100	Bert Rechichar, Tennessee (Wash. & Lee)	1950
100	Eddie Macon, Pacific (Cal.) (Boston U.)	1950

‡Return of field goal attempt.

KICKOFF RETURNS

Since 1941, 203 players have returned kickoffs 100 yards. The most recent:

Yds.	Player, Team (Opponent)	Year
100	Leonard Scott, Tennessee (Georgia)	1999
100	Bo Carroll, Florida (LSU)	1999
100	Ben Kelly, Colorado (Missouri)	1999
100	Lincoln Dupree, Eastern Mich. (Northern Ill.)	1999
100	Deltha O'Neal, California (Stanford)	1999
100	Deuce McAllister, Mississippi (Arkansas)	1999
100	Kevin Johnson, Syracuse (Miami [Fla.])	1998
100	Tim Alexander, Oregon St. (Southern California)	1998
100	Craig Yeast, Kentucky (Florida)	1998
100	Peerless Price, Tennessee (Alabama)	1998
100	Derin Graham, Indiana (Wisconsin)	1998
100	Chris McAlister, Arizona (Hawaii)	1998
100	Dez White, Georgia Tech (Maryland)	1998
100	Eric Vann, Kansas (Oklahoma)	1997
100	Nate Terry, West Virginia (East Caro.)	1997
100	Michael Wiley, Ohio St. (Bowling Green)	1997
100	John Avery, Mississippi (Alabama)	1997
100	Boo Williams, South Carolina (Vanderbilt)	1997

PUNTS

Yds.	Player, Team (Opponent)	Year
99	Pat Brady, Nevada (Loyola Marymount)	1950
96	George O'Brien, Wisconsin (Iowa)	1952
94	John Hadl, Kansas (Oklahoma)	1959
94	Carl Knox, TCU (Oklahoma St.)	1947
94	Preston Johnson, Southern Methodist (Pittsburgh)	1940

FUMBLE RETURNS

(Since 1992)

Yds.	Player, Team (Opponent)	Year
100	Kevin Thomas, UNLV (Baylor)	1999
100	Dan Dawson, Rice (UNLV)	1998
100	Paul Rivers, Rutgers (Pittsburgh)	1995
99	David Williams, Houston (East Caro.)	1998
99	Dennis Gibbs, Idaho (Boise St.)	1997
99	Izell McGill, Mississippi St. (Memphis)	1996
98	Cornelius Pearson, Eastern Mich. (Western Mich.)	1996
97	Chris Martin, Northwestern (Air Force)	1994
97	Mike Collins, West Virginia (Missouri)	1993
97	Ernie Lewis, East Caro. (West Virginia)	1992

Yds.	Player, Team (Opponent)	Year
96	Ben Kelly, Colorado (Kansas)	1999
96	Jeff Arneson, Illinois (Ohio St.)	1992
95	Ben Hanks, Florida (Arkansas)	1995
94	Dorian Boose, Washington St. (Colorado)	1996

FIELD GOALS

Yds.	Player, Team (Opponent)	Year
67	Joe Williams, Wichita St. (Southern Ill.)	1978
67	Steve Little, Arkansas (Texas)	1977
67	Russell Erxleben, Texas (Rice)	1977
65†	Martin Gramatica, Kansas St. (Northern Ill.)	1998
65	Tony Franklin, Texas A&M (Baylor)	1976
64	Russell Erxleben, Texas (Oklahoma)	1977
64	Tony Franklin, Texas A&M (Baylor)	1976
63	Morten Andersen, Michigan St. (Ohio St.)	1981
63	Clark Kemble, Colorado St. (Arizona)	1975
62	Terance Kitchens, Texas A&M (Southern Miss.)	1999
62	Jason Hanson, Washington St. (UNLV)	1991
62	John Diettrich, Ball St. (Ohio)	1986
62#	Chip Lohmiller, Minnesota (Iowa)	1986
62	Tom Whelihan, Missouri (Colorado)	1986
62	Dan Christopulos, Wyoming (Colorado St.)	1977
62	Iseed Khoury, North Texas (Richmond)	1977
62	Dave Lawson, Air Force (Iowa St.)	1975
61	Garret Courtney, North Texas (Idaho)	1998
61$	Kyle Bryant, Texas A&M (Southern Miss.)	1994
61	Dan Eichloff, Kansas (Ball St.)	1992
61	Mark Porter, Kansas St. (Nebraska)	1988
61	Ralf Mojsiejenko, Michigan St. (Illinois)	1982
61	Steve Little, Arkansas (Tulsa)	1976
61	Wayne Latimer, Virginia Tech (Florida St.)	1975
61	Ray Guy, Southern Miss. (Utah St.)	1972
60	Derek Schorejs, Bowling Green (Toledo)	1995
60	John Hall, Wisconsin (Minnesota)	1995
60	Joe Nedney, San Jose St. (Wyoming)	1992
60	Don Shafer, Southern California (Notre Dame)	1986
60	Steve DeLine, Colorado St. (Air Force)	1985
60	Kevin Butler, Georgia (Clemson)	1984
60	Chris Perkins, Florida (Tulane)	1984
60	Fuad Reveiz, Tennessee (Georgia Tech)	1982
60	Russell Erxleben, Texas (Texas Tech)	1977
60	Bubba Hicks, Baylor (Rice)	1975
60	Dave Lawson, Air Force (Colorado)	1974
60	Tony Di Rienzo, Oklahoma (Kansas)	1973
60	Bill McClard, Arkansas (Southern Methodist)	1970

†Longest collegiate field goal without use of a kicking tee; all kicks after 1988 season were without the use of a tee. Also longest field goal with narrower (18'6") goal posts. $Longest field goal made by a freshman. #Longest field goal made indoors.

Team Champions

Annual Offense Champions

TOTAL OFFENSE

Year	Team	Avg.
1937	Colorado	375.4
1938	Fordham	341.6
1939	Ohio St.	309.3
1940	Lafayette	368.2
1941	Duke	372.2
1942	Georgia	429.5
1943	Notre Dame	418.0
1944	Tulsa	434.7
1945	Army	462.7
1946	Notre Dame	441.3
1947	Michigan	412.7
1948	Nevada	487.0
1949	Notre Dame	434.8
1950	Arizona St.	470.4
1951	Tulsa	480.1
1952	Tulsa	466.6
1953	Cincinnati	409.5
1954	Army	448.7
1955	Oklahoma	410.7

Year	Team	Avg.
1956	Oklahoma	481.7
1957	Arizona St.	444.9
1958	Iowa	405.9
1959	Syracuse	451.5
1960	New Mexico St.	419.6
1961	Mississippi	418.7
1962	Arizona St.	384.4
1963	Utah St.	395.3
1964	Tulsa	461.8
1965	Tulsa	427.8
1966	Houston	437.2
1967	Houston	427.9
1968	Houston	562.0
1969	San Diego St.	532.2
1970	Arizona St.	514.5
1971	Oklahoma	566.5
1972	Arizona St.	516.5
1973	Arizona St.	565.5
1974	Oklahoma	507.7
1975	California	458.5
1976	Michigan	448.1
1977	Colgate	486.1
1978	Nebraska	501.4

Year	Team	Avg.
1979	Brigham Young	521.4
1980	Brigham Young	535.0
1981	Arizona St.	498.7
1982	Nebraska	518.6
1983	Brigham Young	584.3
1984	Brigham Young	486.5
1985	Brigham Young	500.2
1986	San Jose St.	481.4
1987	Oklahoma	499.7
1988	Utah	526.8
1989	Houston	*624.9
1990	Houston	586.8
1991	Fresno St.	541.9
1992	Houston	519.5
1993	Nevada	569.1
1994	Penn St.	520.2
1995	Nevada	569.4
1996	Nevada	527.3
1997	Nebraska	513.7
1998	Louisville	559.9
1999	Georgia Tech	509.0

*Record.

TEAM CHAMPIONS—ANNUAL OFFENSE

RUSHING OFFENSE

Year	Team	Avg.
1937	Colorado	310.0
1938	Fordham	297.1
1939	Wake Forest	290.3
1940	Lafayette	306.4
1941	Missouri	307.7
1942	Hardin-Simmons	307.4
1943	Notre Dame	313.7
1944	Army	298.6
1945	Army	359.8
1946	Notre Dame	340.1
1947	Detroit	319.7
1948	UTEP	378.3
1949	UTEP	333.2
1950	Arizona St.	347.0
1951	Arizona St.	334.8
1952	Tulsa	321.5
1953	Oklahoma	306.9
1954	Army	322.0
1955	Oklahoma	328.9
1956	Oklahoma	391.0
1957	Colorado	322.4
1958	Pacific (Cal.)	259.6
1959	Syracuse	313.6
1960	Utah St.	312.0
1961	New Mexico St.	299.1
1962	Ohio St.	278.9
1963	Nebraska	262.6
1964	Syracuse	251.0
1965	Nebraska	290.0
1966	Harvard	269.0
1967	Houston	270.9
1968	Houston	361.7
1969	Texas	363.0
1970	Texas	374.5
1971	Oklahoma	*472.4
1972	Oklahoma	368.8
1973	UCLA	400.3
1974	Oklahoma	438.8
1975	Arkansas St.	340.5
1976	Michigan	362.6
1977	Oklahoma	328.9
1978	Oklahoma	427.5
1979	East Caro.	368.5
1980	Nebraska	378.3
1981	Oklahoma	334.3
1982	Nebraska	394.3
1983	Nebraska	401.7
1984	Army	345.3
1985	Nebraska	374.3
1986	Oklahoma	404.7
1987	Oklahoma	428.8
1988	Nebraska	382.3
1989	Nebraska	375.3
1990	Northern Ill.	344.6
1991	Nebraska	353.2
1992	Nebraska	328.2
1993	Army	298.5
1994	Nebraska	340.0
1995	Nebraska	399.8
1996	Army	346.5
1997	Nebraska	392.6
1998	Army	293.8
1999	Navy	292.2

*Record.

PASSING OFFENSE

Year	Team	Avg.
1937	Arkansas	185.0
1938	TCU	164.1
1939	TCU	148.5
1940	Cornell	186.3
1941	Arizona	177.7
1942	Tulsa	233.9
1943	Brown	133.1
1944	Tulsa	206.3
1945	St. Mary's (Cal.)	161.3
1946	Nevada	198.1
1947	Michigan	173.9
1948	Nevada	255.0
1949	Fordham	183.4
1950	Southern Methodist	214.6
1951	Loyola Marymount	210.6
1952	Fordham	225.8
1953	Stanford	179.5
1954	Purdue	177.3
1955	Navy	185.1
1956	Washington St.	206.8
1957	Utah	195.2
1958	Army	172.2
1959	Stanford	227.8
1960	Washington St.	185.5
1961	Wisconsin	188.4
1962	Tulsa	199.3
1963	Tulsa	244.8
1964	Tulsa	317.9
1965	Tulsa	346.4
1966	Tulsa	272.0
1967	UTEP	301.1
1968	Cincinnati	335.8
1969	San Diego St.	374.2
1970	Auburn	288.5
1971	San Diego St.	251.4
1972	Virginia Tech	304.4
1973	San Diego St.	305.0
1974	Colorado St.	261.8
1975	San Diego St.	291.3
1976	Brigham Young	307.8
1977	Brigham Young	341.6
1978	Southern Methodist	276.2
1979	Brigham Young	368.3
1980	Brigham Young	409.8
1981	Brigham Young	356.9
1982	Long Beach St.	326.8
1983	Brigham Young	381.2
1984	Brigham Young	346.2
1985	Brigham Young	354.5
1986	San Jose St.	312.5
1987	San Jose St.	338.1
1988	Utah	395.9
1989	Houston	*511.3
1990	Houston	473.9
1991	Houston	372.8
1992	Houston	407.1
1993	Nevada	397.5
1994	Georgia	338.3
1995	Nevada	416.3
1996	Wyoming	359.2
1997	Nevada	370.2
1998	Louisiana Tech	432.1
1999	Louisiana Tech	403.1

*Record.

SCORING OFFENSE

Year	Team	Avg.
1937	Colorado	31.0
1938	Dartmouth	28.2
1939	Utah	28.4
1940	Boston College	32.0
1941	Texas	33.8
1942	Tulsa	42.7
1943	Duke	37.2
1944	Army	*56.0
1945	Army	45.8
1946	Georgia	37.2
1947	Michigan	38.3
1948	Nevada	44.4
1949	Army	39.3
1950	Princeton	38.8
1951	Maryland	39.2
1952	Oklahoma	40.7
1953	Texas Tech	38.9
1954	UCLA	40.8
1955	Oklahoma	36.5
1956	Oklahoma	46.6
1957	Arizona St.	39.7
1958	Rutgers	33.4
1959	Syracuse	39.0
1960	New Mexico St.	37.4
1961	Utah St.	38.7
1962	Wisconsin	31.7
1963	Utah St.	31.7
1964	Tulsa	38.4
1965	Arkansas	32.4
1966	Notre Dame	36.2
1967	UTEP	35.9

DIVISION I-A

Year	Team	Avg.
1968	Houston	42.5
1969	San Diego St.	46.4
1970	Texas	41.2
1971	Oklahoma	44.9
1972	Arizona St.	46.6
1973	Arizona St.	44.6
1974	Oklahoma	43.0
1975	Ohio St.	34.0
1976	Michigan	38.7
1977	Grambling	42.0
1978	Oklahoma	40.0
1979	Brigham Young	40.6
1980	Brigham Young	46.7
1981	Brigham Young	38.7
1982	Nebraska	41.1
1983	Nebraska	52.0
1984	Boston College	36.7
1985	Fresno St.	39.1
1986	Oklahoma	42.4
1987	Oklahoma	43.5
1988	Oklahoma St.	47.5
1989	Houston	53.5
1990	Houston	46.5
1991	Fresno St.	44.2
1992	Fresno St.	40.5
1993	Florida St.	43.2
1994	Penn St.	47.8
1995	Nebraska	52.4
1996	Florida	46.6
1997	Nebraska	47.1
1998	Kansas St.	48.0
1999	Virginia Tech	41.4

*Record.

Annual Defense Champions

TOTAL DEFENSE

Year	Team	Avg.
1937	Santa Clara	*69.9
1938	Alabama	77.9
1939	Texas A&M	76.3
1940	Navy	96.0
1941	Duquesne	110.6
1942	Texas	117.3
1943	Duke	121.7
1944	Virginia	96.8
1945	Alabama	109.9
1946	Notre Dame	141.7
1947	Penn St.	76.8
1948	Georgia Tech	151.3
1949	Kentucky	153.8
1950	Wake Forest	163.2
1951	Wisconsin	154.8
1952	Tennessee	166.7
1953	Cincinnati	184.3
1954	Mississippi	172.3
1955	Army	160.7
1956	Miami (Fla.)	189.4
1957	Auburn	133.0
1958	Auburn	157.5
1959	Syracuse	96.2
1960	Wyoming	149.6
1961	Alabama	132.6
1962	Mississippi	142.2
1963	Southern Miss.	131.2
1964	Auburn	164.7
1965	Southern Miss.	161.1
1966	Southern Miss.	163.7
1967	Nebraska	157.6
1968	Wyoming	206.8
1969	Toledo	209.1
1970	Toledo	185.8
1971	Toledo	179.5
1972	Louisville	202.5
1973	Miami (Ohio)	177.4
1974	Notre Dame	195.2
1975	Texas A&M	183.8
1976	Rutgers	179.2
1977	Jackson St.	207.0
1978	Penn St.	203.9
1979	Yale	175.4
1980	Pittsburgh	205.5

TEAM CHAMPIONS—ANNUAL DEFENSE

Year	Team	Avg.
1981	Pittsburgh	224.8
1982	Arizona St.	228.9
1983	Texas	212.0
1984	Nebraska	203.3
1985	Oklahoma	193.5
1986	Oklahoma	169.6
1987	Oklahoma	208.1
1988	Auburn	218.1
1989	Miami (Fla.)	216.5
1990	Clemson	216.9
1991	Texas A&M	222.4
1992	Alabama	194.2
1993	Mississippi	234.5
1994	Miami (Fla.)	220.9
1995	Kansas St.	250.8
1996	West Virginia	217.5
1997	Michigan	206.9
1998	Florida St.	214.8
1999	Mississippi St.	222.5

*Record.

RUSHING DEFENSE

Year	Team	Avg.
1937	Santa Clara	25.3
1938	Oklahoma	43.3
1939	Texas A&M	41.5
1940	Texas A&M	44.3
1941	Duquesne	56.0
1942	Boston College	48.9
1943	Duke	39.4
1944	Navy	53.8
1945	Alabama	33.9
1946	Oklahoma	58.0
1947	Penn St.	*17.0
1948	Georgia Tech	74.9
1949	Oklahoma	55.6
1950	Ohio St.	64.0
1951	San Francisco	51.6
1952	Michigan St.	83.9
1953	Maryland	83.9
1954	UCLA	73.2
1955	Maryland	75.9
1956	Miami (Fla.)	106.9
1957	Auburn	67.4
1958	Auburn	79.6
1959	Syracuse	19.3
1960	Wyoming	82.4
1961	Utah St.	50.8
1962	Minnesota	52.2
1963	Mississippi	77.3
1964	Washington	61.3
1965	Michigan St.	45.6
1966	Wyoming	38.5
1967	Wyoming	42.3
1968	Arizona St.	57.0
1969	LSU	38.9
1970	LSU	52.2
1971	Michigan	63.3
1972	Louisville	82.1
1973	Miami (Ohio)	77.0
1974	Notre Dame	102.8
1975	Texas A&M	80.3
1976	Rutgers	83.9
1977	Jackson St.	67.8
1978	Penn St.	54.5
1979	Yale	75.0
1980	Pittsburgh	65.3
1981	Pittsburgh	62.4
1982	Virginia Tech	49.5
1983	Virginia Tech	69.4
1984	Oklahoma	68.8
1985	UCLA	70.3
1986	Oklahoma	60.7
1987	Michigan St.	61.5
1988	Auburn	63.2
1989	Southern California	61.5
1990	Washington	66.8
1991	Clemson	53.4
1992	Alabama	55.0
1993	Arizona	30.1
1994	Virginia	63.6
1995	Virginia Tech	77.4
1996	Florida St.	59.0
1997	Florida St.	51.9

Year	Team	Avg.
1998	Ohio St.	67.4
1999	Mississippi St.	66.9

*Record.

PASSING DEFENSE

Year	Team	$Avg.
1937	Harvard	31.0
1938	Penn St.	*13.1
1939	Kansas	34.1
1940	Harvard	33.3
1941	Purdue	27.1
1942	Harvard	45.4
1943	North Carolina	36.5
1944	Michigan St.	26.7
1945	Holy Cross	37.7
1946	Holy Cross	53.7
1947	North Carolina St.	39.3
1948	Northwestern	54.1
1949	Miami (Fla.)	54.7
1950	Tennessee	67.5
1951	Wash. & Lee	67.9
1952	Virginia	50.3
1953	Richmond	40.3
1954	Alabama	45.8
1955	Florida	42.0
1956	Villanova	43.8
1957	Georgia Tech	33.4
1958	Iowa St.	39.0
1959	Alabama	45.7
1960	Iowa St.	30.2
1961	Pennsylvania	56.9
1962	New Mexico	56.8
1963	UTEP	43.8
1964	Kent St.	53.6
1965	Toledo	69.8
1966	Toledo	70.4
1967	Nebraska	90.1
1968	Kent St.	107.6
1969	Dayton	90.0
1970	Toledo	77.8
1971	Texas Tech	60.1
1972	Vanderbilt	80.3
1973	Nebraska	39.9
1974	Iowa	65.7
1975	VMI	51.1
1976	Western Mich.	78.5
1977	Tennessee St.	67.9
1978	Boston College	65.1
1979	Western Caro.	77.5
1980	Kansas St.	91.4
1981	Nebraska	100.1
1982	Missouri	123.5
1983	Ohio	115.3
1984	Texas Tech	114.8
1985	Oklahoma	103.6
1986	Oklahoma	108.9
1987	Oklahoma	102.4
1988	Baylor	117.8
1989	Kansas St.	129.3
1990	Alabama	82.5
1991	Texas	77.4
1992	Western Mich.	83.2
1993	Texas A&M	75.0
1994	Miami (Fla.)	81.3
1995	Miami (Ohio)	85.5
1996	Ohio St.	81.3
1997	Michigan	75.8
1998	Florida St.	79.9
1999	Kansas St.	65.7

*Record. $Beginning in 1990, ranked on passing-efficiency defense rating points instead of per-game yardage allowed.

SCORING DEFENSE

Year	Team	Avg.
1937	Santa Clara	1.1
1938	Duke	**0.0
1939	Tennessee	**0.0
1940	Tennessee	2.6
1941	Duquesne	2.9
1942	Tulsa	3.2
1943	Duke	3.8
1944	Army	3.9
1945	St. Mary's (Cal.)	4.0

Year	Team	Avg.
1946	Notre Dame	2.7
1947	Penn St.	3.0
1948	Michigan	4.9
1949	Kentucky	4.8
1950	Army	4.4
1951	Wisconsin	5.9
1952	Southern California	4.7
1953	Maryland	3.1
1954	UCLA	4.4
1955	Georgia Tech	4.6
1956	Georgia Tech	3.3
1957	Auburn	2.8
1958	Oklahoma	4.9
1959	Mississippi	2.1
1960	LSU	5.0
1961	Alabama	2.2
1962	LSU	3.4
1963	Mississippi	3.7
1964	Arkansas	5.7
1965	Michigan St.	6.2
1966	Alabama	3.7
1967	Oklahoma	6.8
1968	Georgia	9.8
1969	Arkansas	7.6
1970	Dartmouth	4.7
1971	Michigan	6.4
1972	Michigan	5.2
1973	Ohio St.	4.3
1974	Michigan	6.8
1975	Alabama	6.0
1976	Michigan	7.4
	Rutgers	7.4
1977	North Carolina	7.4
1978	Ball St.	7.5
1979	Alabama	5.3
1980	Florida St.	7.7
1981	Southern Miss.	8.1
1982	Arkansas	10.5
1983	Virginia Tech	8.3
1984	Nebraska	9.5
1985	Michigan	6.8
1986	Oklahoma	6.6
1987	Oklahoma	7.5
1988	Auburn	7.2
1989	Miami (Fla.)	9.3
1990	Central Mich.	8.9
1991	Miami (Fla.)	9.1
1992	Arizona	8.9
1993	Florida St.	9.4
1994	Miami (Fla.)	10.8
1995	Northwestern	12.7
1996	North Carolina	10.0
1997	Michigan	8.9
1998	Wisconsin	10.2
1999	Virginia Tech	10.5

**Record tied.

Other Annual Team Champions

PUNTING

Year	Team	#Avg.
1937	Iowa	43.0
1938	Arkansas	41.6
1939	Auburn	43.3
1940	Auburn	42.3
1941	Clemson	42.3
1942	Tulsa	41.3
1943	Michigan	39.2
1944	UCLA	43.0
1945	Miami (Fla.)	39.9
1946	UTEP	41.2
1947	Duke	41.9
1948	North Carolina	44.0
1949	Furman	44.7
1950	Colorado	45.1
1951	Alabama	41.8
1952	Colorado	43.3
1953	Georgia	41.2
1954	New Mexico	42.6
1955	Michigan St.	41.2
1956	Colorado St.	42.2
1957	Utah St.	40.1

TEAM CHAMPIONS—OTHER ANNUAL

DIVISION I-A

Year	Team	Avg.
1958	Georgia	41.9
1959	Brigham Young	43.2
1960	Georgia	43.7
1961	Arizona St.	42.1
1962	Wyoming	42.6
1963	Southern Methodist	41.4
1964	Mississippi	44.1
1965	Arizona St.	44.0
1966	Tennessee	43.4
1967	Houston	44.4
1968	Wichita St.	43.2
1969	Georgia	43.5
1970	Utah	45.0
1971	Utah	46.7
1972	Southern Miss.	45.1
1973	Wake Forest	44.1
1974	Ohio St.	44.9
1975	Ohio St.	44.1
1976	Colorado St.	**44.4
1977	Mississippi	43.4
1978	Texas	41.7
1979	Mississippi	42.4
1980	Florida St.	42.6
1981	Michigan	43.1
1982	Vanderbilt	42.1
1983	Brigham Young	*45.0
1984	Ohio St.	44.0
1985	Colorado	43.6
1986	Michigan	43.1
1987	Ohio St.	40.7
1988	Brigham Young	42.9
1989	Colorado	43.8
1990	Pittsburgh	41.2
1991	Texas Tech	40.6
1992	Nebraska	41.7
1993	New Mexico	41.8
1994	Ball St.	42.2
1995	Ball St.	41.3
1996	San Diego St.	44.9
1997	LSU	43.3
1998	UNLV	41.4
1999	Texas A&M	42.7

#Beginning in 1975, ranked on net punting average.
*Record for net punting average. **Record for net punting average, minimum 40 punts.

PUNT RETURNS

Year	Team	Avg.
1937	—	—
1938	—	—
1939	UCLA	16.3
1940	UCLA	16.2
1941	Colgate	18.7
1942	—	—
1943	Columbia	20.9
1944	New York U.	22.0
1945	—	—
1946	Columbia	16.8
1947	Florida	19.7
1948	Oklahoma	*22.4
1949	Wichita St.	18.3
1950	Texas A&M	17.6
1951	Holy Cross	18.1
1952	Arizona St.	**25.2
1953	Kansas St.	23.8
1954	Miami (Fla.)	19.7
1955	North Carolina	22.5
1956	Cincinnati	17.7
1957	North Texas	17.5
1958	Notre Dame	17.6
1959	Wyoming	16.6
1960	Arizona	17.7
1961	Memphis	17.4
1962	West Tex. A&M	18.4
1963	Army	18.1
1964	UTEP	16.9
1965	Georgia Tech	23.0
1966	Brown	21.0
1967	Memphis	16.3
1968	Army	17.4
1969	Davidson	21.3
1970	Wichita St.	28.5
1971	Mississippi St.	20.8
1972	Georgia Tech	17.3
1973	Utah	23.4
1974	Auburn	16.6
1975	New Mexico St.	15.3
1976	Wichita St.	15.0
1977	Grambling	16.9
1978	McNeese St.	15.7
1979	Tennessee St.	16.9
1980	Georgia	16.5
1981	North Carolina St.	13.4
1982	Auburn	15.8
1983	San Diego St.	17.0
1984	Florida	13.8
1985	Utah	20.7
1986	Arizona St.	17.9
1987	Stanford	15.4
1988	Florida St.	15.5
1989	Ohio	18.2
1990	Michigan	15.6
1991	Alabama	16.9
1992	Northwestern	21.8
1993	Texas A&M	17.9
1994	Ball St.	19.9
1995	Eastern Mich.	20.8
1996	Kansas	19.5
1997	Iowa	18.2
1998	Kansas St.	21.3
1999	UAB	19.1

*Record for minimum 30 punt returns. **Record for minimum 15 punt returns.

KICKOFF RETURNS

Year	Team	Avg.
1937	—	—
1938	—	—
1939	Wake Forest	32.9
1940	Minnesota	36.4
1941	Tulane	32.1
1942	—	—
1943	Navy	28.8
1944	—	—
1945	—	—
1946	William & Mary	31.7
1947	Southern Methodist	31.4
1948	Wyoming	27.4
1949	Army	34.1
1950	Wyoming	29.3
1951	Marquette	25.0
1952	Wake Forest	25.1
1953	Texas Tech	23.8
1954	Arizona	26.1
1955	Southern California	25.8
1956	Georgia Tech	24.6
1957	Notre Dame	27.6
1958	Tulsa	25.8
1959	Auburn	25.8
1960	Yale	26.7
1961	Harvard	25.9
1962	Alabama	28.9
1963	Memphis	27.7
1964	Cornell	27.1
1965	Dartmouth	28.7
1966	Notre Dame	29.6
1967	Air Force	25.3
1968	Louisville	25.7
1969	Brigham Young	28.7
1970	South Carolina	26.5
1971	Miami (Fla.)	24.1
1972	Michigan	26.9
1973	Rice	*27.5
1974	Southern California	25.7
1975	Maryland	**29.5
1976	South Carolina	27.0
1977	Miami (Ohio)	24.6
1978	Utah St.	26.7
1979	Brigham Young	26.3
1980	Oklahoma	33.2
1981	Iowa	29.1
1982	Utah	25.5
1983	Tennessee	28.8
1984	Texas Tech	25.2
1985	Air Force	27.0
1986	Clemson	26.1
1987	Oklahoma St.	23.7
1988	Notre Dame	24.2
1989	Colorado	26.1
1990	Nebraska	27.8
1991	New Mexico St.	25.2
1992	Florida St.	30.3
1993	Texas A&M	31.2
1994	Texas A&M	27.8
1995	New Mexico	27.1
1996	Miami (Fla.)	28.9
1997	Southern Miss.	28.2
1998	Utah	27.1
1999	TCU	27.5

*Record for minimum 35 kickoff returns. **Record for minimum 25 kickoff returns.

Toughest-Schedule Annual Leaders

The NCAA's toughest-schedule program (which began in 1977) is based on what all Division I-A teams opponents did against other Division I-A teams when not playing the team in question. Games against non-I-A teams are deleted, and nine intradivision games are required to qualify. (Bowl games are not included.) The leaders:

Year	Team (†Record)	Opponents' Record W	L	T	Pct.
1977	Miami (Fla.) (3-8-0)	66	42	2	.609
	Penn St. (10-1-0)	61	39	2	.608
1978	Notre Dame (8-3-0)	77	31	2	.709
	Southern California (11-1-0)	79	40	1	.663
1979	UCLA (5-6-0)	71	37	2	.655
	South Carolina (8-3-0)	69	38	2	.642
1980	Florida St. (10-1-0)	70	34	0	.673
	Miami (Fla.) (8-3-0)	64	33	1	.658
1981	Penn St. (9-2-0)	71	33	2	.679
	Temple (5-5-0)	71	33	2	.669
1982	Penn St. (10-1-0)	63	34	2	.646
	Kentucky (0-10-1)	63	34	5	.642
1983	Auburn (10-1-0)	70	31	3	.688
	UCLA (6-4-1)	68	37	5	.641
1984	Penn St. (6-5-0)	58	36	3	.613
	Georgia (7-4-0)	60	39	4	.602
1985	Notre Dame (5-6-0)	72	29	3	.707
	Alabama (8-2-1)	65	32	5	.662
1986	Florida (6-5-0)	64	29	3	.682
	LSU (9-2-0)	67	36	2	.648
1987	Notre Dame (8-3-0)	71	34	2	.673
	Florida St. (10-1-0)	60	29	4	.667
1988	Virginia Tech (3-8-0)	74	36	0	.673
	Arizona (7-4-0)	70	37	3	.650
1989	Notre Dame (11-1-0)	74	38	4	.655
	LSU (4-7-0)	67	41	1	.619
1990	Colorado (10-1-1)	72	42	3	.628
	Stanford (5-6-0)	67	39	4	.627

TOUGHEST-SCHEDULE ANNUAL LEADERS

Year	Team (†Record)	Opponents' Record W-L-T	Pct.
1991	South Carolina (3-6-2)	57-31-2	.644
	Florida (10-2-0)	66-37-1	.639
1992	Southern California (6-5-1)	68-38-4	.636
	Stanford (10-3-0)	73-43-4	.625
1993	LSU (5-6-0)	67-38-5	.632
	Purdue (1-10-0)	66-38-3	.631
1994	Michigan (8-4-0)	67-38-6	.631
	Oklahoma (6-6-0)	66-39-4	.624

†Not including bowl games. ¢When not playing the team listed.

Top 10 Toughest-Schedule Leaders for 1995-99

1995

	Team	¢Opp. Record	Pct.
1.	Notre Dame	67-37-5	.638
2.	Illinois	69-40-2	.631
3.	Minnesota	64-38-5	.621
4.	Cincinnati	66-40-2	.620
5.	Vanderbilt	68-42-1	.617
6.	Indiana	66-41-3	.614
7.	Washington	64-40-2	.613
8.	Purdue	67-42-2	.613
9.	Houston	66-42-3	.608
	Northwestern	65-41-5	.608

1996

	Team	¢Opp. Record	Pct.
1.	Florida	70-41	.631
2.	UCLA	66-41	.617
3.	Purdue	68-44	.607
4.	Washington	68-46	.596
5.	Arkansas	62-42	.596
6.	Tulane	63-43	.594
7.	Minnesota	63-44	.589
8.	Nebraska	70-49	.588
9.	Rutgers	57-40	.588
10.	Iowa St.	59-42	.584

1997

	Team	¢Opp. Record	Pct.
1.	Colorado	76-37	.673
2.	Auburn	80-39	.672
3.	Florida	72-40	.643
4.	Arkansas	71-40	.640
5.	Tennessee	77-44	.636
6.	Washington	70-42	.625
7.	Mississippi	68-43	.613
8.	Bowling Green	67-43	.609
9.	South Carolina	66-44	.600
10.	Alabama	67-45	.598

1998

	Team	¢Opp. Record	Pct.
1.	Auburn	74-34	.685
2.	Missouri	66-36	.647
3.	Florida St.	74-43	.632
4.	Southern California	76-46	.623
5.	LSU	65-41	.613
6.	Baylor	68-43	.613
7.	Washington	69-44	.611
8.	Alabama	67-43	.609
9.	Texas A&M	79-51	.608
10.	Michigan St.	73-49	.598

1999

	Team	¢Opp. Record	Pct.
1.	Alabama	80-38	.678
2.	Auburn	62-36	.633
3.	Notre Dame	74-46	.617
4.	South Carolina	66-43	.606
5.	Florida St.	65-43	.602
6.	Miami (Fla.)	66-44	.600
7.	Ohio St.	70-47	.598
8.	Michigan	67-45	.598
9.	Penn St.	72-49	.595
10.	Temple	63-44	.589
	Clemson	63-44	.589

¢When not playing the team listed.

Annual Most-Improved Teams

Year	Team	$Games Improved	From		To		Coach
1937	California	4½	1936	6-5-0	1937	*10-0-1	Stub Allison
	Syracuse	4½	1936	1-7-0	1937	5-2-1	#Ossie Solem
1938	TCU	5½	1937	4-4-2	1938	*11-0-0	Dutch Meyer
1939	Texas A&M	5½	1938	4-4-1	1939	*11-0-0	Homer Norton
1940	Stanford	8	1939	1-7-1	1940	*10-0-0	#Clark Shaughnessy
1941	Vanderbilt	4½	1940	3-6-1	1941	8-2-0	Red Sanders
1942	Utah St.	5½	1941	0-8-0	1942	6-3-1	Dick Romney
1943	Purdue	8	1942	1-8-0	1943	9-0-0	Elmer Burnham
1944	Ohio St.	6	1943	3-6-0	1944	9-0-0	#Carroll Widdoes
1945	Miami (Fla.)	7	1944	1-7-1	1945	*9-1-0	Jack Harding
1946	Illinois	5	1945	2-6-1	1946	*8-2-0	Ray Eliot
	Kentucky	5	1945	2-8-0	1946	7-3-0	#Paul "Bear" Bryant
1947	California	6½	1946	2-7-0	1947	9-1-0	#Lynn "Pappy" Waldorf
1948	Clemson	6	1947	4-5-0	1948	*11-0-0	Frank Howard
1949	Tulsa	5	1948	0-9-1	1949	5-4-1	J. O. Brothers
1950	Brigham Young	5	1949	0-11-0	1950	4-5-1	Chick Atkinson
	Texas A&M	5	1949	1-8-1	1950	*7-4-0	Harry Stiteler
1951	Georgia Tech	6	1950	5-6-0	1951	*11-0-1	Bobby Dodd
1952	Alabama	4½	1951	5-6-0	1952	*10-2-0	Harold "Red" Drew
1953	Texas Tech	7	1952	3-7-1	1953	*11-1-0	DeWitt Weaver
1954	Denver	5	1953	3-5-2	1954	9-1-0	Bob Blackman
1955	Texas A&M	6½	1954	1-9-0	1955	7-2-1	Paul "Bear" Bryant
1956	Iowa	5	1955	3-5-1	1956	*9-1-0	Forest Evashevski
1957	Notre Dame	5	1956	2-8-0	1957	7-3-0	Terry Brennan
	Texas	5	1956	1-9-0	1957	†6-4-1	#Darrell Royal
1958	Air Force	6	1957	3-6-1	1958	‡9-0-1	#Ben Martin
1959	Washington	6½	1958	3-7-0	1959	*10-1-0	Jim Owens
1960	Minnesota	5½	1959	2-7-0	1960	†8-2-0	Murray Warmath
	North Carolina St.	5½	1959	1-9-0	1960	6-3-1	Earle Edwards
1961	Villanova	6	1960	2-8-0	1961	*8-2-0	Alex Bell
1962	Southern California	6	1961	4-5-1	1962	*11-0-0	John McKay
1963	Illinois	6	1962	2-7-0	1963	*8-1-1	Pete Elliott
1964	Notre Dame	6½	1963	2-7-0	1964	9-1-0	#Ara Parseghian
1965	UTEP	6½	1964	0-8-2	1965	*8-3-0	#Bobby Dobbs
1966	Dayton	6½	1965	1-8-1	1966	8-2-0	John McVay
1967	Indiana	7	1966	1-8-1	1967	†9-2-0	John Pont
1968	Arkansas	5	1967	4-5-1	1968	*10-1-0	Frank Broyles
1969	UCLA	5½	1968	3-7-0	1969	8-1-1	Tommy Prothro
1970	Tulsa	5	1969	1-9-0	1970	6-4-0	#Claude Gibson
1971	Army	5	1970	1-9-1	1971	6-4-0	Tom Cahill
	Georgia	5	1970	5-5-0	1971	*11-1-0	Vince Dooley
1972	Pacific (Cal.)	5	1971	3-8-0	1972	8-3-0	Chester Caddas
	Southern California	5	1971	6-4-1	1972	*12-0-0	John McKay
	UCLA	5	1971	2-7-1	1972	8-3-0	Pepper Rodgers

ANNUAL MOST-IMPROVED TEAMS

DIVISION I-A

Year	Team	$Games Improved	From		To		Coach
1973	Pittsburgh	5	1972	1-10-0	1973	†6-5-1	#Johnny Majors
1974	Baylor	5½	1973	2-9-0	1974	†8-4-0	Grant Teaff
1975	Arizona St.	5	1974	7-5-0	1975	*12-0-0	Frank Kush
1976	Houston	7	1975	2-8-0	1976	*10-2-0	Bill Yeoman
1977	Miami (Ohio)	7	1976	3-8-0	1977	10-1-0	Dick Crum
1978	Tulsa	6	1977	3-8-0	1978	9-2-0	John Cooper
1979	Wake Forest	6½	1978	1-10-0	1979	†8-4-0	John Mackovic
1980	Florida	7	1979	0-10-1	1980	*8-4-0	Charley Pell
1981	Clemson	5½	1980	6-5-0	1981	*12-0-0	Danny Ford
1982	New Mexico	6	1981	4-7-1	1982	10-1-0	Joe Morrison
	La.-Lafayette	6	1981	1-9-1	1982	7-3-1	Sam Robertson
1983	Kentucky	5½	1982	0-10-1	1983	†6-5-1	Jerry Claiborne
	Memphis	5½	1982	1-10-0	1983	6-4-1	Rex Dockery
1984	Army	6	1983	2-9-0	1984	*8-3-1	Jim Young
1985	Colorado	5½	1984	1-10-0	1985	†7-5-0	Bill McCartney
	Fresno St.	5½	1984	6-6-0	1985	*11-0-1	Jim Sweeney
1986	San Jose St.	7	1985	2-8-1	1986	*10-2-0	Claude Gilbert
1987	Syracuse	6	1986	5-6-0	1987	‡11-0-1	Dick MacPherson
1988	West Virginia	5	1987	6-6-0	1988	†11-1-0	Don Nehlen
	Washington St.	5	1987	3-7-1	1988	*9-3-0	Dennis Erickson
1989	Tennessee	5½	1988	5-6-0	1989	*11-1-0	Johnny Majors
1990	Temple	6	1989	1-10-0	1990	7-4-0	Jerry Berndt
1991	Tulsa	6½	1990	3-8-0	1991	*10-2-0	Dave Rader
1992	Hawaii	6	1991	4-7-1	1992	*11-2-0	Bob Wagner
1993	La.-Lafayette	6	1992	2-9-0	1993	8-3-0	Nelson Stokley
	Virginia Tech	6	1992	2-8-1	1993	*9-3-0	Frank Beamer
1994	Colorado St.	4½	1993	5-6-0	1994	†10-2-0	Sonny Lubick
	Duke	4½	1993	3-8-0	1994	†8-4-0	#Fred Goldsmith
	East Caro.	4½	1993	2-9-0	1994	†7-5-0	Steve Logan
1995	Northwestern	6	1994	3-7-1	1995	†10-2-0	Gary Barnett
1996	Brigham Young	5	1995	7-4-0	1996	*14-1-0	LaVell Edwards
1997	Western Mich.	6	1996	2-9-0	1997	8-3-0	Gary Darnell
1998	Louisville	5½	1997	1-10-0	1998	7-5-0	#John L. Smith
	TCU	5½	1997	1-10-0	1998	7-5-0	#Dennis Franchione
1999	Hawaii	8½	1998	0-12-0	1999	*9-4-0	#June Jones

$To determine games improved, add the difference in victories between the two seasons to the difference in losses, then divide by two; ties not counted. Bowl victory (*), loss (†), tie (‡) included in record. #First year as head coach at that college.

June Jones' first season as a collegiate head coach was dramatically successful, as he directed Hawaii to an 9-4 record in 1999 after the Rainbow Warriors went 0-12 the previous year. The 8½-game improvement is a Division I-A record.

All-Time Most-Improved Teams

Games	Team (Year)	Games	Team (Year)
8½	Hawaii (1999)	6½	Tulsa (1991)
8	Purdue (1943)	6½	Wake Forest (1979)
8	Stanford (1940)	6½	Toledo (1967)
7	San Jose St. (1986)	6½	Dayton (1966)
7	Florida (1980)	6½	UTEP (1965)
7	Miami (Ohio) (1977)	6½	Notre Dame (1964)
7	Houston (1976)	6½	Washington (1959)
7	Indiana (1967)	6½	Texas A&M (1955)
7	Texas Tech (1953)	6½	California (1947)
7	Miami (Fla.) (1945)		

1999 Most-Improved Teams

College (Coach)	1999	1998	$Games Improved
Hawaii (June Jones)	9-4-0	0-12-0	8½
Illinois (Ron Turner)	8-4-0	3-8-0	4½
Stanford (Tyrone Willingham)	8-4-0	3-8-0	4½
Michigan St. (Nick Saban)	10-2-0	6-6-0	4
Houston (Kim Helton)	7-4-0	3-8-0	4
Boston College (Tom O'Brien)	8-4-0	4-7-0	3½
Wake Forest (Jim Caldwell)	7-5-0	3-8-0	3½
Nebraska (Frank Solich)	12-1-0	9-4-0	3
Boise St. (Dirk Koetter)	10-3-0	6-5-0	3
Akron (Lee Owens)	7-4-0	4-7-0	3
New Mexico St. (Tony Samuel)	6-5-0	3-8-0	3
Memphis (Rip Scherer)	5-6-0	2-9-0	3
Northern Ill. (Joe Novak)	5-6-0	2-9-0	3
Pittsburgh (Walt Harris)	5-6-0	2-9-0	3
Vanderbilt (Woody Widenhofer)	5-6-0	2-9-0	3
UNLV (John Robinson)	3-8-0	0-11-0	3

$To determine games improved, add the difference in victories between the two seasons to the difference in losses, then divide by two, ties not counted. Includes bowl games.

All-Time Team Won-Lost Records

PERCENTAGE
Includes records as senior college only. Bowl and playoff games are included, and each tie game is computed as half won and half lost. Teams listed with years in parentheses indicates reclassification within the past 10 years. The year in parentheses is the first year of Division I-A membership. Note: Tiebreaker rule began with 1996 season.

Team	Yrs.	Won	Lost	Tied	Pct.	Total Games
Notre Dame	111	767	238	42	.753	1047
Michigan	120	796	259	36	.746	1091
Alabama	105	734	268	43	.723	1045
Nebraska	110	743	297	40	.706	1080
Ohio St.	110	716	283	53	.706	1052
Texas	107	735	299	33	.704	1067
Oklahoma	105	689	278	53	.701	1020
Penn St.	113	734	305	41	.699	1080
Tennessee	103	699	288	52	.698	1039
Southern California	107	673	281	54	.694	1008
Florida St.	53	381	183	17	.670	581
Boise St. (1996)	32	241	127	2	.654	370
Miami (Ohio)	111	591	327	44	.637	962
Washington	110	606	336	50	.636	992
Georgia	106	633	358	54	.632	1045
Central Mich.	99	510	292	36	.630	838
Arizona St.	87	484	284	24	.626	792
LSU	106	610	356	47	.625	1013
Army	110	617	364	51	.623	1032
Auburn	107	601	361	47	.619	1009
Colorado	110	608	368	36	.619	1012
Miami (Fla.)	73	461	281	19	.618	761
Florida	93	554	344	40	.612	938
Texas A&M	105	602	381	48	.607	1031
Syracuse	110	632	406	49	.604	1087

ALL-TIME TEAM WON-LOST RECORDS

Team	Yrs.	Won	Lost	Tied	Pct.+	Total Games
UCLA	81	478	308	37	.603	823
Michigan St.	103	556	363	44	.600	963
Arkansas	106	588	393	40	.595	1021
Bowling Green	81	420	277	52	.595	749
Middle Tenn. St. (1999)	83	461	309	28	.595	798
Southern Miss.	83	462	311	26	.594	799
Arizona	95	503	340	33	.593	876
Georgia Tech	107	592	401	43	.592	1036
Fresno St.	78	464	318	29	.590	811
West Virginia	107	596	411	45	.588	1052
Minnesota	116	581	401	43	.588	1025
Clemson	104	562	390	45	.586	997
San Diego St.	77	437	305	32	.585	774
Virginia Tech	106	568	397	46	.585	1011
Louisiana Tech	96	491	344	37	.584	872
North Carolina	109	594	420	54	.581	1068
Stanford	93	513	363	49	.581	925
Pittsburgh	110	589	429	42	.575	1060
Boston College	101	529	388	36	.574	953
Tulsa	95	493	366	27	.572	886
Utah	106	520	386	31	.572	937
Mississippi	105	552	410	35	.571	997
Western Mich.	94	451	338	24	.569	813
California	104	555	421	51	.565	1027
Hawaii	84	435	338	26	.561	799
Brigham Young	75	424	330	26	.560	780
Navy	119	578	461	57	.553	1096
Wisconsin	110	527	422	53	.552	1002
Texas Tech	75	426	350	32	.547	808
Nevada (1992)	89	429	360	32	.542	821
UAB (1996)	9	51	43	3	.541	97
Air Force	44	260	220	13	.541	493
Duke	87	434	368	31	.540	833
Ball St.	75	350	298	32	.538	680
North Texas (1995)	84	425	364	33	.537	822
Houston	54	305	262	15	.537	582
Purdue	112	508	437	48	.536	993
Illinois	109	521	449	50	.535	1020
Missouri	109	537	463	52	.535	1052
Toledo	79	391	343	24	.532	758
Virginia	110	549	483	48	.531	1080
Oregon	104	481	429	46	.527	956
East Caro.	64	326	294	12	.525	632
UCF (1996)	21	118	107	1	.524	226
Maryland	107	530	479	42	.524	1051
San Jose St.	81	399	362	38	.523	799
Baylor	97	491	446	43	.523	980
Vanderbilt	110	522	474	50	.523	1046
Utah St.	102	443	406	31	.521	880
Northern Ill.	98	433	404	51	.516	888
Akron	99	434	406	36	.516	876
Iowa	111	498	467	39	.515	1004
Kentucky	109	517	486	44	.515	1047
Kansas	110	511	487	58	.511	1056
Southern Methodist	83	413	397	54	.509	864
Rutgers	130	547	531	42	.507	1120
UNLV	32	178	174	4	.506	356
Wyoming	103	442	434	28	.504	904
Marshall (1997)	96	449	443	44	.503	936
North Carolina St.	108	468	468	55	.500	991
Ohio	104	447	447	48	.500	942
Arkansas St. (1992)	85	368	369	37	.499	774
Washington St.	103	433	435	45	.499	913
La.-Lafayette	92	428	430	32	.499	890
TCU	103	473	482	56	.496	1011
Mississippi St.	100	448	457	39	.495	944
South Carolina	106	468	478	44	.495	990
Memphis	84	379	389	32	.494	800
Oklahoma St.	98	440	464	48	.487	952
Cincinnati	112	468	495	51	.487	1014
Eastern Mich.	107	393	420	46	.484	859
Louisville	81	358	384	17	.483	759
Colorado St.	101	409	455	33	.474	897
Tulane	106	446	497	38	.474	981
Idaho (1996)	102	402	453	25	.471	880
New Mexico	101	392	458	31	.463	881
Oregon St.	103	414	486	50	.462	950
Temple	101	378	446	52	.461	876
Iowa St.	108	434	512	46	.461	992
La.-Monroe (1994)	49	230	275	8	.456	513
Buffalo (1999)	86	304	376	29	.449	709
New Mexico St.	104	382	475	32	.448	889
Rice	88	382	476	32	.447	890
Indiana	112	404	532	44	.435	980
Northwestern	112	405	558	43	.424	1006
Kansas St.	104	387	549	42	.417	978
UTEP	82	310	447	30	.413	787
Wake Forest	98	348	533	23	.398	904
Kent St.	77	267	414	28	.396	709

ALPHABETICAL LISTING

Team	Yrs.	Won	Lost	Tied	Pct.	Total Games
Air Force	44	260	220	13	.541	493
Akron	99	434	406	36	.516	876
Alabama	105	734	268	43	.723	1045
UAB (1996)	9	51	43	3	.541	97
Arizona	95	503	340	33	.593	876
Arizona St.	87	484	284	24	.626	792
Arkansas	106	588	393	40	.595	1021
Arkansas St. (1992)	85	368	369	37	.499	774
Army	110	617	364	51	.623	1032
Auburn	107	601	361	47	.619	1009
Ball St.	75	350	298	32	.538	680
Baylor	97	491	446	43	.523	980
Boise St. (1996)	32	241	127	2	.654	370
Boston College	101	529	388	36	.574	953
Bowling Green	81	420	277	52	.595	749
Brigham Young	75	424	330	26	.560	780
Buffalo (1999)	86	304	376	29	.449	709
California	104	555	421	51	.565	1027
UCF (1996)	21	118	107	1	.524	226
Central Mich.	99	510	292	36	.630	838
Cincinnati	112	468	495	51	.487	1014
Clemson	104	562	390	45	.586	997
Colorado	110	608	368	36	.619	1012
Colorado St.	101	409	455	33	.474	897
Duke	87	434	368	31	.540	833
East Caro.	64	326	294	12	.525	632
Eastern Mich.	107	393	420	46	.484	859
Florida	93	554	344	40	.612	938
Florida St.	53	381	183	17	.670	581
Fresno St.	78	464	318	29	.590	811
Georgia	106	633	358	54	.632	1045
Georgia Tech	107	592	401	43	.592	1036
Hawaii	84	435	338	26	.561	799
Houston	54	305	262	15	.537	582
Idaho (1996)	102	402	453	25	.471	880
Illinois	109	521	449	50	.535	1020
Indiana	112	404	532	44	.435	980
Iowa	111	498	467	39	.515	1004
Iowa St.	108	434	512	46	.461	992
Kansas	110	511	487	58	.511	1056
Kansas St.	104	387	549	42	.417	978
Kent St.	77	267	414	28	.396	709
Kentucky	109	517	486	44	.515	1047
La.-Lafayette	92	428	430	32	.499	890
La.-Monroe (1994)	49	230	275	8	.456	513
LSU	106	610	356	47	.625	1013
Louisiana Tech	96	491	344	37	.584	872
Louisville	81	358	384	17	.483	759
Marshall (1997)	96	449	443	44	.503	936
Maryland	107	530	479	42	.524	1051
Memphis	84	379	389	32	.494	800
Miami (Fla.)	73	461	281	19	.618	761
Miami (Ohio)	111	591	327	44	.637	962
Michigan	120	796	259	36	.746	1091
Michigan St.	103	556	363	44	.600	963
Middle Tenn. St. (1999)	83	461	309	28	.595	798
Minnesota	116	581	401	43	.588	1025
Mississippi	105	552	410	35	.571	997
Mississippi St.	100	448	457	39	.495	944
Missouri	109	537	463	52	.535	1052
Navy	119	578	461	57	.553	1096
Nebraska	110	743	297	40	.706	1080
UNLV	32	178	174	4	.506	356
Nevada (1992)	89	429	360	32	.542	821
New Mexico	101	392	458	31	.463	881
New Mexico St.	104	382	475	32	.448	889
North Carolina	109	594	420	54	.581	1068
North Carolina St.	108	468	468	55	.500	991
North Texas (1995)	84	425	364	33	.537	822
Northern Ill.	98	433	404	51	.516	888

ALL-TIME TEAM WON-LOST RECORDS

Team	Yrs.	Won	Lost	Tied	Pct.+	Total Games
Northwestern	112	405	558	43	.424	1006
Notre Dame	111	767	238	42	.753	1047
Ohio	104	447	447	48	.500	942
Ohio St.	110	716	283	53	.706	1052
Oklahoma	105	689	278	53	.701	1020
Oklahoma St.	98	440	464	48	.487	952
Oregon	104	481	429	46	.527	956
Oregon St.	103	414	486	50	.462	950
Penn St.	113	734	305	41	.699	1080
Pittsburgh	110	589	429	42	.575	1060
Purdue	112	508	437	48	.536	993
Rice	88	382	476	32	.447	890
Rutgers	130	547	531	42	.507	1120
San Diego St.	77	437	305	32	.585	774
San Jose St.	81	399	362	38	.523	799
South Carolina	106	468	478	44	.495	990
Southern California	107	673	281	54	.694	1008
Southern Methodist	83	413	397	54	.509	864
Southern Miss.	83	462	311	26	.594	799
Stanford	93	513	363	49	.581	925
Syracuse	110	632	406	49	.604	1087
Temple	101	378	446	52	.461	876
Tennessee	103	699	288	52	.698	1039

Team	Yrs.	Won	Lost	Tied	Pct.+	Total Games
Texas	107	735	299	33	.704	1067
Texas A&M	105	602	381	48	.607	1031
TCU	103	473	482	56	.496	1011
UTEP	82	310	447	30	.413	787
Texas Tech	75	426	350	32	.547	808
Toledo	79	391	343	24	.532	758
Tulane	106	446	497	38	.474	981
Tulsa	95	493	366	27	.572	886
UCLA	81	478	308	37	.603	823
Utah	106	520	386	31	.572	937
Utah St.	102	443	406	31	.521	880
Vanderbilt	110	522	474	50	.523	1046
Virginia	110	549	483	48	.531	1080
Virginia Tech	106	568	397	46	.585	1011
Wake Forest	98	348	533	23	.398	904
Washington	110	606	336	50	.636	992
Washington St.	103	433	435	45	.499	913
West Virginia	107	596	411	45	.588	1052
Western Mich.	94	451	338	24	.569	813
Wisconsin	110	527	422	53	.552	1002
Wyoming	103	442	434	28	.504	904

BY VICTORIES

Team	Wins
Michigan	796
Notre Dame	767
Nebraska	743
Texas	735
Alabama	734
Penn St.	734
Ohio St.	716
Tennessee	699
Oklahoma	689
Southern California	673
Georgia	633
Syracuse	632
Army	617
LSU	610
Colorado	608
Washington	606
Texas A&M	602
Auburn	601
West Virginia	596
North Carolina	594
Georgia Tech	592
Miami (Ohio)	591
Pittsburgh	589
Arkansas	588
Minnesota	581
Navy	578
Virginia Tech	568
Clemson	562
Michigan St.	556
California	555
Florida	554
Mississippi	552
Virginia	549
Rutgers	547
Missouri	537
Maryland	530
Boston College	529
Wisconsin	527
Vanderbilt	522
Illinois	521
Utah	520
Kentucky	517
Stanford	513
Kansas	511
Central Mich.	510
Purdue	508
Arizona	503
Iowa	498
Tulsa	493
Louisiana Tech	491
Baylor	491
Arizona St.	484
Oregon	481
UCLA	478
TCU	473
North Carolina St.	468
South Carolina	468
Cincinnati	468
Fresno St.	464
Southern Miss.	462
Miami (Fla.)	461
Middle Tenn. St. (1999)	461
Western Mich.	451
Marshall (1997)	449
Mississippi St.	448
Ohio	447
Tulane	446
Utah St.	443
Wyoming	442
Oklahoma St.	440
San Diego St.	437
Hawaii	435
Duke	434
Akron	434
Iowa St.	434
Northern Ill.	433
Washington St.	433
Nevada (1992)	429
La.-Lafayette	428
Texas Tech	426
North Texas (1995)	425
Brigham Young	424
Bowling Green	420
Oregon St.	414
Southern Methodist	413
Colorado St.	409
Northwestern	405
Indiana	404
Idaho (1996)	402
San Jose St.	399
Eastern Mich.	393
New Mexico	392
Toledo	391
Kansas St.	387
New Mexico St.	382
Rice	382
Florida St.	381
Memphis	379
Temple	378
Arkansas St. (1992)	368
Louisville	358
Ball St.	350
Wake Forest	348
East Caro.	326
UTEP	310
Houston	305
Buffalo (1999)	304
Kent	267
Air Force	260
Boise St. (1996)	241
La.-Monroe (1994)	230
UNLV	178
UCF (1996)	118
UAB (1996)	51

DIVISION I-A

Records in the 1990s

(1990-91-92-93-94-95-96-97-98-99, Including Bowls and Playoffs; Tiebreaker Began 1996)

PERCENTAGE

Team	W-L-T	*Pct.
Florida St.	109-13-1	.890
Nebraska	108-16-1	.868
Marshall	114-25-0	.820
Florida	102-22-1	.820
Tennessee	99-22-2	.813
Penn St.	97-26-0	.789
Michigan	93-26-3	.775
Miami (Fla.)	92-27-0	.773
Texas A&M	94-28-2	.766
Ohio St.	91-29-3	.752
Colorado	87-29-4	.742
Kansas St.	87-30-1	.742
Notre Dame	84-35-2	.702
Washington	82-35-1	.699
Syracuse	82-35-3	.696
Brigham Young	86-39-2	.685
Alabama	83-40-0	.675
Nevada	80-39-0	.672
North Carolina	78-39-1	.665
Virginia Tech	77-39-1	.662
Virginia	78-40-1	.660
Idaho	77-41-0	.653
Toledo	72-38-3	.650
Air Force	78-44-0	.639
Auburn	72-40-3	.639
Georgia	72-43-1	.625
Texas	74-44-2	.625
Colorado St.	74-46-0	.617
Miami (Ohio)	65-40-5	.614
Utah	71-46-0	.607
Arizona	71-46-1	.606
Wisconsin	69-45-4	.602
UCLA	69-46-0	.600
Wyoming	70-47-1	.597
Middle Tenn. St.	68-46-1	.596
Western Mich.	65-44-2	.595
Clemson	69-47-1	.594
Oregon	70-48-0	.593
UCF	67-46-0	.593
Southern Miss.	67-46-1	.592
East Caro.	67-47-0	.588
Mississippi	67-48-0	.583
Southern California	68-49-4	.579
Fresno St.	68-50-2	.575
Georgia Tech	66-49-1	.573
West Virginia	65-49-2	.569
Bowling Green	61-46-4	.568
North Carolina St.	66-51-1	.564
Mississippi St.	64-50-2	.560
Boise St.	67-53-0	.558
Louisiana Tech	61-48-3	.558
Arizona St.	62-51-0	.549
Oklahoma	61-51-3	.543
San Diego St.	62-52-2	.543
UAB	51-43-2	.542
Texas Tech	62-53-0	.539
Iowa	62-53-2	.538

Team	W-L-T	*Pct.
Michigan St.	62-53-2	.538
Stanford	60-54-2	.526
Louisville	59-54-1	.522
La.-Monroe	58-56-1	.509
Central Mich.	54-53-5	.504
Boston College	57-57-2	.500
Kansas	56-57-1	.496
Arkansas	55-58-2	.487
California	55-59-1	.483
LSU	54-58-1	.482
Rice	52-57-1	.477
Ball St.	52-58-2	.473
Washington St.	53-61-0	.465
TCU	51-61-1	.456
Army	50-60-1	.455
Illinois	50-63-2	.443
Baylor	49-63-1	.438
Utah St.	48-63-1	.433
Purdue	47-64-3	.425
Indiana	47-64-2	.425
Memphis	45-64-1	.414
Hawaii	49-71-1	.410
San Jose St.	44-66-2	.402
Missouri	43-67-3	.394
Cincinnati	43-67-1	.392
South Carolina	42-66-3	.392
Kentucky	44-69-0	.389
New Mexico	45-71-0	.388
Navy	43-69-0	.384
Houston	42-68-1	.383
Northwestern	43-70-1	.382
Oklahoma St.	41-68-3	.379
Akron	40-68-2	.373
North Texas	40-69-2	.369
Tulsa	40-70-1	.365
La.-Lafayette	39-70-1	.359
Minnesota	40-72-0	.357
Maryland	38-72-1	.347
Rutgers	37-72-1	.341
Tulane	38-74-0	.339
Wake Forest	38-74-0	.339
Pittsburgh	37-74-1	.335
Eastern Mich.	35-74-1	.323
Ohio	34-74-3	.320
Vanderbilt	34-76-0	.309
Duke	33-77-1	.302
New Mexico St.	33-77-0	.300
Southern Methodist	31-76-3	.295
UNLV	33-79-0	.295
Northern Ill.	32-78-0	.291
Buffalo	30-77-0	.280
Oregon St.	29-81-1	.266
Arkansas St.	28-80-2	.264
Iowa St.	27-80-3	.259
UTEP	28-84-2	.254
Temple	22-88-0	.200
Kent St.	15-94-1	.141

*Ties counted as half won and half lost.

BY VICTORIES

Team	Wins
Marshall	114
Florida St.	109
Nebraska	108
Florida	102
Tennessee	99
Penn St.	97
Texas A&M	94
Michigan	93
Miami (Fla.)	92
Ohio St.	91
Colorado	87
Kansas St.	87
Brigham Young	86

Team	Wins
Notre Dame	84
Alabama	83
Syracuse	82
Washington	82
Nevada	80
Air Force	78
North Carolina	78
Virginia	78
Idaho	77
Virginia Tech	77
Colorado St.	74
Texas	74
Auburn	72

Team	Wins
Georgia	72
Toledo	72
Arizona	71
Utah	71
Oregon	70
Wyoming	70
Clemson	69
UCLA	69
Wisconsin	69
Fresno St.	68
Middle Tenn. St.	68
Southern California	68
Boise St.	67
UCF	67
East Caro.	67
Mississippi	67
Southern Miss.	67
Georgia Tech	66
North Carolina St.	66
Miami (Ohio)	65
West Virginia	65
Western Mich.	65
Mississippi St.	64
Arizona St.	62
Iowa	62
Michigan St.	62
San Diego St.	62
Texas Tech	62
Bowling Green	61
Louisiana Tech	61
Oklahoma	61
Stanford	60
Louisville	59
La.-Monroe	58
Boston College	57
Kansas	56
Arkansas	55
California	55
Central Mich.	54
LSU	54
Washington St.	53
Ball St.	52
Rice	52
UAB	51

Team	Wins
TCU	51
Army	50
Illinois	50
Baylor	49
Hawaii	49
Utah St.	48
Indiana	47
Purdue	47
Memphis	45
New Mexico	45
Kentucky	44
San Jose St.	44
Cincinnati	43
Missouri	43
Navy	43
Northwestern	43
Houston	42
South Carolina	42
Oklahoma St.	41
Akron	40
Minnesota	40
North Texas	40
Tulsa	40
La.-Lafayette	39
Maryland	38
Tulane	38
Wake Forest	38
Pittsburgh	37
Rutgers	37
Eastern Mich.	35
Ohio	34
Vanderbilt	34
Duke	33
UNLV	33
New Mexico St.	33
Northern Ill.	32
Southern Methodist	31
Buffalo	30
Oregon St.	29
Arkansas St.	28
UTEP	28
Iowa St.	27
Temple	22
Kent St.	15

Winningest Teams by Decade

(By Percentage; Bowls and Playoffs Included, Unless Noted)

1980-89

Rank	Team	W-L-T	Pct.†	Rank	Team	W-L-T	Pct.†
1.	Nebraska	103-20-0	.837	11.	Alabama	85-32-2	.723
2.	Miami (Fla.)	98-20-0	.831		Arkansas	85-32-2	.723
3.	Brigham Young	102-26-0	.797	13.	UCLA	81-30-6	.718
4.	Oklahoma	91-25-2	.780	14.	Washington	83-33-1	.714
5.	Clemson	86-25-4	.765	15.	Fresno St.	80-34-1	.700
6.	Penn St.	89-27-2	.763	16.	Ohio St.	82-35-2	.697
7.	Georgia	88-27-4	.756	17.	Southern Methodist	63-28-1	.690
8.	Florida St.	87-28-3	.750	18.	Southern California	78-35-3	.685
	Michigan	89-29-2	.750	19.	Florida	76-37-3	.668
10.	Auburn	86-31-1	.733	20.	Arizona St.	73-36-4	.664

1970-79

Rank	Team	W-L-T	Pct.†	Rank	Team	W-L-T	Pct.†
1.	Oklahoma	102-13-3	.877	11.	Arizona St.	90-28-0	.763
2.	Alabama	103-16-1	.863	12.	Yale@	67-21-2	.756
3.	Michigan	96-16-3	.848	13.	San Diego St.	82-26-2	.755
4.	Tennessee St.	85-17-2	.827	14.	Miami (Ohio)	80-26-2	.750
5.	Nebraska	98-20-4	.820	15.	Central Mich.	80-27-3	.741
6.	Penn St.	96-22-0	.814	16.	Arkansas	79-31-5	.709
7.	Ohio St.	91-20-3	.811	17.	Houston	80-33-2	.704
8.	Notre Dame	91-22-0	.805	18.	Louisiana Tech	77-34-2	.690
9.	Southern California	93-21-5	.803	19.	McNeese St.@	75-33-4	.688
10.	Texas	88-26-1	.770	20.	Dartmouth@	60-27-3	.683

1960-69

(By Percentage; Bowls and Playoffs Not Included)

Rank	Team	W-L-T	Pct.†	Rank	Team	W-L-T	Pct.†
1.	Alabama	85-12-3	.865	5.	Bowling Green	71-22-2	.758
2.	Texas	80-18-2	.810	6.	Dartmouth@	68-22-0	.756
3.	Arkansas	80-19-1	.805		Ohio St.	67-21-2	.756
4.	Mississippi	72-20-6	.765	8.	Missouri	72-22-6	.750

WINNINGEST TEAMS BY DECADE

Rank	Team	W-L-T	Pct.†	Rank	Team	W-L-T	Pct.†
	Southern California	73-23-4	.750	15.	Wyoming	69-26-4	.717
10.	Penn St.	73-26-0	.737	16.	Princeton@	64-26-0	.711
11.	Memphis	70-25-1	.734	17.	Utah St.	68-29-3	.695
12.	Arizona St.	72-26-1	.732	18.	Purdue	64-28-3	.689
13.	LSU	70-25-5	.725	19.	Syracuse	68-31-0	.687
	Nebraska	72-27-1	.725	20.	Florida	66-30-4	.680
					Miami (Ohio)	66-30-4	.680
					Tennessee	65-29-6	.680

1950-59

Rank	Team	W-L-T	Pct.†	Rank	Team	W-L-T	Pct.†
1.	Oklahoma	93-10-2	.895	11.	Syracuse	62-29-2	.677
2.	Mississippi	80-21-5	.778	12.	Army	58-27-5	.672
3.	Michigan St.	70-21-1	.766	13.	Cincinnati	64-30-7	.668
4.	Princeton@	67-22-1	.750	14.	Notre Dame	64-31-4	.667
5.	Georgia Tech	79-26-6	.739	15.	Clemson	64-32-5	.658
6.	UCLA	68-26-3	.716	16.	Wisconsin	57-28-7	.658
7.	Ohio St.	63-24-5	.712	17.	Colorado	62-33-6	.644
8.	Tennessee	71-31-4	.692	18.	Duke	62-33-7	.642
9.	Penn St.	62-28-4	.681	19.	Navy	55-30-8	.634
10.	Maryland	67-31-3	.678	20.	Yale@	54-30-6	.633

†Ties computed as half won and half lost. @Now a member of I-AA.

DIVISION I-A

Winningest Teams of Last Five Years

(By Percentage and Wins; Bowls included)

PERCENTAGE

Team	W-L	*Pct.	Team	W-L	*Pct.
Florida St.	55-6-0	.902	Southern Miss.	39-19-0	.672
Marshall	62-7-0	.899	Oregon	39-20-0	.661
Nebraska	57-7-0	.891	Wyoming	38-20-0	.655
Tennessee	54-8-0	.871	Alabama	39-21-0	.650
Kansas St.	52-9-0	.852	Virginia	39-21-0	.650
Florida	53-10-0	.841	East Caro.	37-20-0	.649
Michigan	49-13-0	.790	Utah	37-20-0	.649
Ohio St.	49-13-0	.790	Georgia	38-21-0	.644
Virginia Tech	47-13-0	.783	North Carolina	38-21-0	.644
Penn St.	48-14-0	.774	Texas	40-22-1	.643
Miami (Ohio)	39-15-1	.718	Arizona St.	37-21-0	.638
Brigham Young	44-19-0	.698	Notre Dame	38-22-0	.633
Toledo	40-17-1	.698	Washington	37-22-1	.625
Air Force	42-19-0	.689	Georgia Tech	36-22-0	.621
Colorado St.	42-19-0	.689	UCLA	36-22-0	.621
Syracuse	42-19-0	.689	Arizona	36-23-0	.610
Wisconsin	41-18-2	.689	Louisiana Tech	34-22-0	.607
Texas A&M	43-20-0	.683	Texas Tech	35-23-0	.603
Colorado	40-19-0	.678	Michigan St.	35-24-1	.592
Miami (Fla.)	40-19-0	.678	Southern California	35-24-1	.592

*Ties computed as half won and half lost.

BY VICTORIES

Team	Wins	Team	Wins
Marshall	62	Miami (Ohio)	39
Nebraska	57	Oregon	39
Florida St.	55	Southern Miss.	39
Tennessee	54	Virginia	39
Florida	53	Georgia	38
Kansas St.	52	North Carolina	38
Michigan	49	Notre Dame	38
Ohio St.	49	Wyoming	38
Penn St.	48	Arizona St.	37
Virginia Tech	47	East Caro.	37
Brigham Young	44	Utah	37
Texas A&M	43	Washington	37
Air Force	42	Arizona	36
Colorado St.	42	Georgia Tech	36
Syracuse	42	UCLA	36
Wisconsin	41	Michigan St.	35
Colorado	40	Southern California	35
Miami (Fla.)	40	Texas Tech	35
Texas	40	Auburn	34
Toledo	40	Louisiana Tech	34
Alabama	39	Mississippi	34

National Poll Rankings

National Champion Major Selectors (1869 to Present)

Selector	Selection Format	Active Seasons First	Last	Total	Predated Seasons	Total Rankings
Frank Dickinson	Math	1926	1940	15	1924-25	17
Deke Houlgate	Math	1927	1958	32	1885-1926	72
Dunkel*	Math	1929	1999	71		71
William Boand	Math	1930	1960	31	1919-29	42
Paul Williamson	Math	1932	1963	32		32
Parke Davis	Research	1933	1933	1	1869-1932	65
Edward Litkenhous	Math	1934	1984	51		51
Richard Poling	Math	1935	1984	50	1924-34	61
Associated Press*	Poll	1936	1999	64		64
Helms Athletic Foundation	Poll	1941	1982	42	1883-1940	100
Harry DeVold	Math	1945	1999	55	1939-44	61
United Press International	Poll	1950	1995	44		44
International News Service	Poll	1952	1957	6		6
Football Writers Association	Poll	1954	1999	46		46
Football News	Poll	1958	1999	42		42
National Football Foundation	Poll	1959	1999	37		37
Billingsley*	Math	1970	1999	30	1869-70, 1872-1969	130
Herman Matthews*	Math	1966	1999	34		34
FACT*	Math	1968	1999	32		32
Sporting News	Poll	1975	1999	25		25
Sagarin*	Math	1978	1999	22	1938, 56-77	45
New York Times*	Math	1979	1999	21		21
National Championship Foundation	Poll	1980	1999	20	1869-70, 1872-1979	130
College Football Researchers Association	Poll	1982	1992	11	1919-81	74
USA Today/CNN	Poll	1982	1996	15		15
Berryman	Math	1990	1999	10	1940-89	60
UPI/National Football Foundation	Poll	1991	1992	2		2
USA Today/National Football Foundation	Poll	1993	1994	2		2
Alderson	Math	1994	1998	5		5
Massey*	Math	1995	1999	5		5
USA Today/ESPN*	Poll	1997	1999	3		3
Seattle Times*	Math	1997	1999	3		3

*Poll utilized in Bowl Championship Series Rankings for 1999.

POLL SYSTEMS HISTORY

Alderson System (1994-98), a mathematical rating system based strictly on a point value system reflecting competition as well as won-lost record. Developed by Bob Alderson of Muldrow, Oklahoma.

Associated Press (1936-present), the first major nationwide poll for ranking college football teams was voted on by sportswriters and broadcasters. It continues to this day and is probably the most well-known and widely circulated among all of history's polls. The Associated Press annual national champions were awarded the Williams Trophy and the Reverend J. Hugh O'Donnell Trophy. In 1947, Notre Dame retired the Williams Trophy (named after Henry L. Williams, Minnesota coach, and sponsored by the M Club of Minnesota). In 1956, Oklahoma retired the O'Donnell Trophy (named for Notre Dame's president and sponsored by Notre Dame alumni). Beginning with the 1957 season, the award was known as the AP Trophy, and since 1983, has been known as the Paul "Bear" Bryant Trophy.

Berryman (QPRS) (1990-present), a mathematical rating system based on a quality point rating formula developed by Clyde P. Berryman of Washington, D.C. Predated national champions from 1940-1989.

Billingsley Report (1970-present), a mathematically based power rating system developed by Richard Billingsley of Nashville, Tennessee. His work is published annually as the Billingsley Report through his own company, the College Football Research Center. In 1996, he finished his three-year research project ranking the national champions from 1869-95. The research is located on the World Wide Web at www.CFRC.com. Predated national champions from 1869-1970.

Boand System (1930-60), known as the Azzi Ratem System developed by William Boand of Tucson, Arizona. He moved to Chicago in 1932. Appeared in many newspapers as well as Illustrated Football Annual (1932-42) and weekly in Football News (1942-44, 1951-60). Predated national champions from 1919-29.

College Football Researchers Association (1982-92), founded by Anthony Cusher of Reeder, North Dakota, and Robert Kirlin of Spokane, Washington. Announced its champion in its monthly bulletin and No. 1 team determined by top-10 vote of membership on a point system. Predated national champions from 1919-81, conducted on a poll by Harry Carson Frye.

DeVold System (1945-present), a mathematical rating system developed by Harry DeVold from Minneapolis, Minnesota, a former football player at Cornell. He eventually settled in the Detroit, Michigan, area and worked in the real estate business. The ratings have appeared in The Football News since 1962. Predated national champions from 1939-44.

Dickinson System (1926-40), a mathematical point system devised by Frank Dickinson, a professor of economics at Illinois. The annual Dickinson ratings were emblematic of the national championship and the basis for awarding the Rissman National Trophy and the Knute K. Rockne Intercollegiate Memorial Trophy. Notre Dame gained permanent possession of the Rissman Trophy (named for Jack F. Rissman, a Chicago clothing manufacturer) after its third victory in 1930. Minnesota retired the Rockne Trophy (named in honor of the famous Notre Dame coach) after winning it for a third time in 1940.

Dunkel System (1929-present), a power index system devised by Dick Dunkel Sr. (1929-71); by Dick Dunkel Jr. (1972-95); and by John Duck (1996-present), systems director of the Daytona (Fla.) Beach News-Journal.

FACT (1968-present), a computerized mathematical ranking system developed by David Rothman of Hawthorne, California. FACT is the Foundation for the Analysis of Competitions and Tournaments, which began selecting a national champion in 1968. Rothman is a semiretired defense and aerospace statistician and was cochair of the Committee on Statistics in Sports and Competition of the American Statistical Association in the 1970s.

Football News (1958-present), weekly poll of its staff writers has named a national champion since 1958.

Football Writers Association of America (1954-present), the No. 1 team of the year is determined by a five-person panel representing the nation's football writers. The national championship team named receives the Grantland Rice Award.

Helms Athletic Foundation (1941-82), originally known by this name from 1936-69 and established by the founding sponsor, Paul H. Helms, Los Angeles sportsman and philanthropist. After Helms' death in 1957, United Savings & Loan Association became its benefactor during 1970-72. A merger of United Savings and Citizen Savings was completed in 1973, and the Athletic Foundation became known as Citizens Savings Athletic Foundation. In 1982, First Interstate Bank assumed sponsorship for its final rankings. In 1941, Bill Schroeder, managing director of the Helms Athletic Foundation, retroactively selected the national football champions for the period beginning in 1883 (the first year of a scoring system) through 1940. Thereafter, Schroeder, who died in 1988, then chose, with the assistance of a Hall Board, the annual national champion after the bowl games.

Houlgate System (1927-58), a mathematical rating system developed by Deke Houlgate of Los Angeles, California. His ratings were syndicated in newspapers and published in Illustrated Football and the Football Thesaurus (1946-58).

International News Service (1952-57), a poll conducted for six years by members of the International News Service (INS) before merger with United Press in 1958.

Litkenhous (1934-84), a difference-by-score formula developed by Edward E. Litkenhous, a professor of chemical engineering at Vanderbilt, and his brother, Frank.

Massey College Football Ratings (1995-present), a mathematical rating system developed by Kenneth Massey, a graduate student at Virginia Tech in mathematics. His ratings, which account for homefield advantage, joined the BCS panel in 1999.

Matthews Grid Ratings (1966-present), a mathematical rating system developed by college mathematics professor Herman Matthews of Middlesboro, Kentucky. Has appeared in newspapers and The Football News.

National Championship Foundation (1980-present), established by Mike Riter of Hudson, New York. Issues annual report. Predated national champions from 1869-1979.

National Football Foundation (1959-present), the National Football Foundation and Hall of Fame named its first national champion in 1959. Headquartered in Larchmont, New York, the present National Football Foundation was established in 1947 to promote amateur athletics in America. The national champion was awarded the MacArthur Bowl from 1959-90. In 1991 and 1992, the NFF/HOF joined with UPI to award the MacArthur Bowl, and in 1993, the NFF/HOF joined with USA Today to award the MacArthur Bowl.

New York Times (1979-present), a mathematical rating system introduced by this major newspaper.

Parke Davis (1933), a noted college football historian and former Princeton lineman, Parke H. Davis went back and named the championship teams from 1869 through the 1932 season. He also named a national champion at the conclusion of the 1933 season. Interestingly, the years 1869-75 were identified by Davis as the Pioneer Period; the years 1876-93 were called the Period of the American Intercollegiate Football Association, and the years 1894-1933 were referred to as the Period of Rules Committees and Conferences. He also coached at Wisconsin, Amherst and Lafayette.

Poling System (1935-84), a mathematical rating system for college football teams developed by Richard Poling from Mansfield, Ohio, a former football player at Ohio Wesleyan. Poling's football ratings were published annually in the Football Review Supplement and in various newspapers. Predated national champions from 1924-34.

Sagarin Ratings (1978-present), a mathematical rating system developed by Jeff Sagarin of Bloomington, Indiana, a 1970 MIT mathematics graduate. Runs annually in USA Today newspaper. Predated national champions from 1938 and 1956-1977.

Seattle Times (1997-present), a mathematical rating system developed by Jeff Anderson and Chris Hester. Runs weekly in The Seattle Times. Published since 1993.

Sporting News (1975-present), voted on annually by the staff of this St. Louis-based nationally circulated sports publication.

United Press International (1950-90, 1993-95), in 1950, the United Press news service began its poll of football coaches (replaced as coaches' poll after 1990 season). When the United Press merged with the International News Service in 1958, it became known as United Press International. The weekly UPI rankings were featured in newspapers and on radio and television nationwide. UPI and the National Football Foundation formed a coalition for 1991 and 1992 to name the MacArthur Bowl national champion. Returned to single poll in 1994-95.

USA Today/Cable News Network and ESPN (1982-1996;1997-present), introduced a weekly poll of sportswriters in 1982 and ranked the top 25 teams in the nation with a point system. The poll results were featured in USA Today, a national newspaper, and on the Cable News Network, a national cable television network. Took over as the coaches' poll in 1991. USA Today also formed a coalition with the National Football Foundation in 1993 to name the MacArthur Bowl national champion. Combined with ESPN in 1997 to distribute the coaches' poll nationally.

Williamson System (1932-63), a power rating system chosen by Paul Williamson of New Orleans, Louisiana, a geologist and member of the Sugar Bowl committee.

Thanks from the NCAA Statistics Service to Robert A. Rosiek of Dearborn, Michigan, who researched much of the former polls' history, and to Tex Noel of Bedford, Indiana, who provided information about Parke H. Davis.

National Poll Champions

Over the last 130 years, there have been nearly 30 selectors of national champions using polls, historical research and mathematical rating systems. Beginning in 1936, The Associated Press began the best-known and most widely circulated poll of sportswriters and broadcasters. Before 1936, national champions were determined by historical research and retroactive ratings and polls.

*Note: * indicates selectors that chose multiple schools. The national champion was selected before bowl games as follows: AP (1936-64 and 1966-67); UP-UPI (1950-73); FWAA (1954); NFF-HOF (1959-70). In all other latter-day polls, champions were selected after bowl games.*

1869
Princeton: Billingsley, National Championship Foundation, Parke Davis*
Rutgers: Parke Davis*

1870
Princeton: Billingsley, National Championship Foundation, Parke Davis

1871
No national champions selected.

1872
Princeton: Billingsley, National Championship Foundation, Parke Davis*
Yale: Parke Davis*

1873
Princeton: Billingsley, National Championship Foundation, Parke Davis

1874
Harvard: Parke Davis*
Princeton: Billingsley, Parke Davis*
Yale: National Championship Foundation, Parke Davis*

1875
Colgate: Parke Davis*
Harvard: National Championship Foundation, Parke Davis*
Princeton: Billingsley, Parke Davis*

1876
Yale: Billingsley, National Championship Foundation, Parke Davis

1877
Princeton: Parke Davis*
Yale: Billingsley, National Championship Foundation, Parke Davis*

1878
Princeton: Billingsley, National Championship Foundation, Parke Davis

1879
Princeton: Billingsley, National Championship Foundation, Parke Davis
Yale: Parke Davis*

1880
Princeton: National Championship Foundation*, Parke Davis*
Yale: Billingsley, National Championship Foundation*, Parke Davis*

1881
Princeton: Billingsley, Parke Davis*
Yale: National Championship Foundation, Parke Davis*

NATIONAL POLL CHAMPIONS

1882
Yale: Billingsley, National Championship Foundation, Parke Davis

1883
Yale: Billingsley, Helms, National Championship Foundation, Parke Davis

1884
Princeton: Parke Davis*
Yale: Billingsley, Helms, National Championship Foundation, Parke Davis*

1885
Princeton: Billingsley, Helms, Houlgate, National Championship Foundation, Parke Davis

1886
Princeton: Parke Davis*
Yale: Billingsley, Helms, National Championship Foundation, Parke Davis*

1887
Yale: Billingsley, Helms, Houlgate, National Championship Foundation, Parke Davis

1888
Yale: Billingsley, Helms, Houlgate, National Championship Foundation, Parke Davis

1889
Princeton: Billingsley, Helms, Houlgate, National Championship Foundation, Parke Davis

1890
Harvard: Billingsley, Helms, Houlgate, National Championship Foundation, Parke Davis

1891
Yale: Billingsley, Helms, Houlgate, National Championship Foundation, Parke Davis

1892
Yale: Billingsley, Helms, Houlgate, National Championship Foundation, Parke Davis

1893
Princeton: Billingsley, Helms, Houlgate, National Championship Foundation
Yale: Parke Davis

1894
Pennsylvania: Parke Davis*
Princeton: Houlgate
Yale: Billingsley, Helms, National Championship Foundation, Parke Davis*

1895
Pennsylvania: Billingsley, Helms, Houlgate, National Championship Foundation, Parke Davis*
Yale: Parke Davis*

1896
Lafayette: National Championship Foundation*, Parke Davis*
Princeton: Billingsley, Helms, Houlgate, National Championship Foundation*, Parke Davis*

1897
Pennsylvania: Billingsley, Helms, Houlgate, National Championship Foundation, Parke Davis*
Yale: Parke Davis*

1898
Harvard: Billingsley, Helms, Houlgate, National Championship Foundation
Princeton: Parke Davis

1899
Harvard: Billingsley, Helms, Houlgate, National Championship Foundation
Princeton: Parke Davis

1900
Yale: Billingsley, Helms, Houlgate, National Championship Foundation, Parke Davis

1901
Harvard: Billingsley
Michigan: Helms, Houlgate, National Championship Foundation
Yale: Parke Davis

1902
Michigan: Billingsley, Helms, Houlgate, National Championship Foundation, Parke Davis*
Yale: Parke Davis*

1903
Michigan: Billingsley, National Championship Foundation*
Princeton: Helms, Houlgate, National Championship Foundation*, Parke Davis

1904
Michigan: Billingsley, National Championship Foundation*
Pennsylvania: Helms, Houlgate, National Championship Foundation*, Parke Davis

1905
Chicago: Billingsley, Helms, Houlgate, National Championship Foundation
Yale: Parke Davis

1906
Princeton: Helms, National Championship Foundation
Vanderbilt: Billingsley
Yale: Parke Davis

1907
Pennsylvania: Billingsley
Yale: Helms, Houlgate, National Championship Foundation, Parke Davis

1908
LSU: National Championship Foundation*
Pennsylvania: Billingsley, Helms, Houlgate, National Championship Foundation*, Parke Davis

1909
Yale: Billingsley, Helms, Houlgate, National Championship Foundation, Parke Davis

1910
Harvard: Helms, Houlgate, National Championship Foundation*
Michigan: Billingsley
Pittsburgh: National Championship Foundation*

1911
Penn St.: National Championship Foundation*
Princeton: Helms, Houlgate, National Championship Foundation*, Parke Davis
Vanderbilt: Billingsley

1912
Harvard: Billingsley, Helms, Houlgate, National Championship Foundation*, Parke Davis
Penn St.: National Championship Foundation*

1913
Auburn: Billingsley
Chicago: Parke Davis*
Harvard: Helms, Houlgate, National Championship Foundation, Parke Davis*

1914
Army: Helms, Houlgate, National Championship Foundation, Parke Davis*
Illinois: Billingsley, Parke Davis*

1915
Cornell: Helms, Houlgate, National Championship Foundation, Parke Davis*
Nebraska: Billingsley
Pittsburgh: Parke Davis*

1916
Army: Parke Davis*
Pittsburgh: Billingsley, Helms, Houlgate, National Championship Foundation, Parke Davis*

1917
Georgia Tech: Billingsley, Helms, Houlgate, National Championship Foundation

1918
Michigan: Billingsley, National Championship Foundation*
Pittsburgh: Helms, Houlgate, National Championship Foundation*

1919
Harvard: Football Research*, Helms, Houlgate, National Championship Foundation*, Parke Davis*
Illinois: Billingsley, Boand, Football Research*, Parke Davis*
Notre Dame: National Championship Foundation*, Parke Davis*
Texas A&M: National Championship Foundation*

1920
California: Billingsley, Football Research, Helms, Houlgate, National Championship Foundation
Harvard: Boand*
Notre Dame: Parke Davis*
Princeton: Boand*, Parke Davis*

1921
California: Boand*, Football Research
Cornell: Helms, Houlgate, National Championship Foundation, Parke Davis*
Iowa: Billingsley, Parke Davis*
Lafayette: Boand*, Parke Davis*
Wash. & Jeff.: Boand*

1922
California: Houlgate, National Championship Foundation*
Cornell: Helms, Parke Davis*
Iowa: Billingsley
Princeton: Boand, Football Research, National Championship Foundation*, Parke Davis*

1923
California: Houlgate
Illinois: Boand, Football Research, Helms, National Championship Foundation*, Parke Davis
Michigan: Billingsley, National Championship Foundation*

1924
Notre Dame: Billingsley, Boand, Dickinson, Football Research, Helms, Houlgate, National Championship Foundation, Poling
Pennsylvania: Parke Davis

1925
Alabama: Billingsley, Boand, Football Research, Helms, Houlgate, National Championship Foundation, Poling
Dartmouth: Dickinson, Parke Davis

1926
Alabama: Billingsley, Football Research, Helms*, National Championship Foundation*, Poling
Lafayette: Parke Davis
Navy: Boand, Houlgate
Stanford: Dickinson, Helms*, National Championship Foundation*

1927
Georgia: Boand, Poling
Illinois: Billingsley, Dickinson, Helms, National Championship Foundation, Parke Davis
Notre Dame: Houlgate
Yale: Football Research

1928
Detroit: Parke Davis*
Georgia Tech: Billingsley, Boand, Football Research, Helms, Houlgate, National Championship Foundation, Parke Davis*, Poling
Southern California: Dickinson

1929
Notre Dame: Billingsley, Boand, Dickinson, Dunkel, Football Research, Helms, National Championship Foundation, Poling
Pittsburgh: Parke Davis
Southern California: Houlgate

1930
Alabama: Football Research, Parke Davis*
Notre Dame: Billingsley, Boand, Dickinson, Dunkel, Helms, Houlgate, National Championship Foundation, Parke Davis*, Poling

NATIONAL POLL CHAMPIONS

1931
Pittsburgh: Parke Davis*
Purdue: Parke Davis*
Southern California: Billingsley, Boand, Dickinson, Dunkel, Helms, Houlgate, Football Research, National Championship Foundation, Poling, Williamson

1932
Colgate: Parke Davis*
Michigan: Dickinson, Parke Davis*
Southern California: Billingsley, Boand, Dunkel, Football Research, Helms, Houlgate, National Championship Foundation, Parke Davis*, Poling, Williamson

1933
Michigan: Billingsley, Boand, Dickinson, Helms, Houlgate, Football Research, National Championship Foundation, Parke Davis*, Poling
Ohio St.: Dunkel
Princeton: Parke Davis*
Southern California: Williamson

1934
Alabama: Dunkel, Houlgate, Poling, Williamson
Minnesota: Billingsley, Boand, Dickinson, Football Research, Helms, Litkenhous, National Championship Foundation

1935
LSU: Williamson*
Minnesota: Billingsley, Boand, Football Research, Helms, Litkenhous, National Championship Foundation, Poling
Princeton: Dunkel
Southern Methodist: Dickinson, Houlgate
TCU: Williamson*

1936
LSU: Williamson
Minnesota: AP, Billingsley, Dickinson, Dunkel, Helms, Litkenhous, National Championship Foundation, Poling
Pittsburgh: Boand, Football Research, Houlgate

1937
California: Dunkel, Helms
Pittsburgh: AP, Billingsley, Boand, Dickinson, Football Research, Houlgate, Litkenhous, National Championship Foundation, Poling, Williamson

1938
Notre Dame: Dickinson
Tennessee: Billingsley, Boand, Dunkel, Football Research, Houlgate, Litkenhous, Poling, Sagarin
TCU: AP, Helms, National Championship Foundation, Williamson

1939
Cornell: Billingsley, Litkenhous
Southern California: Dickinson
Texas A&M: AP, Boand, DeVold, Dunkel, Football Research, Helms, Houlgate, National Championship Foundation, Poling, Williamson

1940
Minnesota: AP, Berryman, Billingsley, Boand, DeVold, Dickinson, Football Research, Houlgate, Litkenhous, National Championship Foundation
Stanford: Helms, Poling
Tennessee: Dunkel, Williamson

1941
Alabama: Houlgate
Minnesota: AP, Billingsley, Boand, DeVold, Dunkel, Football Research, Helms, Litkenhous, National Championship Foundation, Poling
Texas: Berryman, Williamson

1942
Georgia: Berryman, DeVold, Houlgate, Litkenhous, Poling, Williamson
Ohio St.: AP, Billingsley, Boand, Dunkel, Football Research, National Championship Foundation
Wisconsin: Helms

1943
Notre Dame: AP, Berryman, Billingsley, Boand, DeVold, Dunkel, Football Research, Helms, Houlgate, Litkenhous, National Championship Foundation, Poling, Williamson

1944
Army: AP, Berryman, Billingsley, Boand, DeVold, Dunkel, Football Research, Helms, Houlgate, Litkenhous, National Championship Foundation*, Poling, Sagarin, Williamson
Ohio St.: National Championship Foundation*

1945
Alabama: National Championship Foundation*
Army: AP, Berryman, Billingsley, Boand, DeVold, Dunkel, Football Research, Helms, Houlgate, Litkenhous, National Championship Foundation*, Poling, Sagarin, Williamson

1946
Army: Boand*, Football Research, Helms*, Houlgate, Poling*
Georgia: Williamson
Notre Dame: AP, Berryman, Billingsley, Boand*, DeVold, Dunkel, Helms*, Litkenhous, National Championship Foundation, Poling*, Sagarin

1947
Michigan: Berryman, Billingsley, Boand, DeVold, Dunkel, Football Research, Helms*, Houlgate, Litkenhous, National Championship Foundation, Poling, Sagarin
Notre Dame: AP, Helms*, Williamson

1948
Michigan: AP, Berryman, Billingsley, Boand, DeVold, Dunkel, Football Research, Helms, Houlgate, Litkenhous, National Championship Foundation, Poling, Sagarin, Williamson

1949
Notre Dame: AP, Berryman, Billingsley, Boand, DeVold, Dunkel, Helms; Houlgate, Litkenhous, National Championship Foundation, Poling, Sagarin, Williamson
Oklahoma: Football Research

1950
Kentucky: Sagarin
Oklahoma: AP, Berryman, Helms, Litkenhous, UPI, Williamson
Princeton: Boand, Poling
Tennessee: Billingsley, DeVold, Dunkel, Football Research, National Championship Foundation

1951
Georgia Tech: Berryman, Boand*
Illinois: Boand*
Maryland: DeVold, Dunkel, Football Research, National Championship Foundation, Sagarin
Michigan St.: Billingsley, Helms, Poling
Tennessee: AP, Litkenhous, UPI, Williamson

1952
Georgia Tech: Berryman, INS, Poling
Michigan St.: AP, Billingsley, Boand, DeVold, Dunkel, Football Research, Helms, Litkenhous, National Championship Foundation, Sagarin, UPI, Williamson

1953
Maryland: AP, INS, UPI
Notre Dame: Billingsley, Boand, DeVold, Dunkel, Helms, Litkenhous, National Championship Foundation, Poling, Sagarin, Williamson
Oklahoma: Berryman, Football Research

1954
Ohio St.: AP, Berryman, Boand, DeVold, Football Research*, Helms*, INS, National Championship Foundation*, Poling, Sagarin, Williamson
UCLA: Billingsley, Dunkel, Football Research*, FW, Helms*, Litkenhous, National Championship Foundation*, UPI

1955
Michigan St.: Boand
Oklahoma: AP, Berryman, Billingsley, DeVold, Dunkel, Football Research, FW, Helms, INS, Litkenhous, National Championship Foundation, Poling, Sagarin, UPI, Williamson

1956
Georgia Tech: Berryman
Iowa: Football Research
Oklahoma: AP, Billingsley, Boand, DeVold, Dunkel, FW, Helms, INS, Litkenhous, National Championship Foundation, Sagarin, UPI, Williamson
Tennessee: Sagarin

1957
Auburn: AP, Football Research, Helms, National Championship Foundation, Poling, Williamson
Michigan St.: Billingsley, Dunkel, Sagarin
Ohio St.: Boand, DeVold, FW, INS, Litkenhous, UPI
Oklahoma: Berryman

1958
Iowa: FW
LSU: AP, Berryman, Billingsley, Boand, DeVold, Dunkel, FB News, Football Research, Helms, Litkenhous, National Championship Foundation, Poling, Sagarin, UPI, Williamson

1959
Mississippi: Berryman, Billingsley, Dunkel, Sagarin
Syracuse: AP, Boand, DeVold, FB News, Football Research, FW, Helms, Litkenhous, National Championship Foundation, NFF, Poling, UPI, Williamson

1960
Iowa: Berryman, Boand, Litkenhous, Sagarin
Minnesota: AP, FB News, NFF, UPI
Mississippi: Billingsley, DeVold, Dunkel, Football Research, FW, National Championship Foundation, Williamson
Missouri: Poling
Washington: Helms

1961
Alabama: AP, Berryman, Billingsley, DeVold, Dunkel, FB News, Football Research, Helms, Litkenhous, National Championship Foundation, NFF, Sagarin, UPI, Williamson
Ohio St.: FW, Poling

1962
Alabama: Billingsley
LSU: Berryman*
Southern California: AP, Berryman*, DeVold, Dunkel, FB News, Football Research, FW, Helms, National Championship Foundation, NFF, Poling, Sagarin, UPI, Williamson
Mississippi: Litkenhous

1963
Texas: AP, Berryman, Billingsley, DeVold, Dunkel, FB News, Football Research, FW, Helms, Litkenhous, National Championship Foundation, NFF, Poling, Sagarin, UPI, Williamson

1964
Alabama: AP, Berryman, Litkenhous, UPI
Arkansas: Billingsley, Football Research, FW, Helms, National Championship Foundation, Poling
Michigan: Dunkel
Notre Dame: DeVold, FB News, NFF, Sagarin

1965
Alabama: AP, Billingsley, Football Research, FW*, National Championship Foundation
Michigan St.: Berryman, DeVold, Dunkel, FB News, FW*, Helms, Litkenhous, NFF, Poling, Sagarin, UPI

1966
Alabama: Berryman
Michigan St.: Football Research, Helms*, NFF*, Poling*
Notre Dame: AP, Billingsley, DeVold, Dunkel, FB News, FW, Helms*, Litkenhous, Matthews, National Championship Foundation, NFF*, Poling*, Sagarin, UPI

1967
Notre Dame: Dunkel
Oklahoma: Poling
Southern California: AP, Berryman, Billingsley, DeVold, FB News, Football Research, FW, Helms, Matthews, National Championship Foundation, NFF, Sagarin, UPI
Tennessee: Litkenhous

1968
Georgia: Litkenhous
Ohio St.: AP, Berryman, Billingsley, Dunkel, FACT, FB News, Football Research, FW, Helms, National Championship Foundation, NFF, Poling, UPI
Texas: DeVold, Matthews, Sagarin

1969
Ohio St.: Matthews
Penn St.: FACT*

NATIONAL POLL CHAMPIONS

Texas: AP, Berryman, Billingsley, DeVold, Dunkel, FACT*, FB News, Football Research, FW, Helms, Litkenhous, National Championship Foundation, NFF, Poling, Sagarin, UPI

1970
Arizona St.: Poling
Nebraska: AP, Billingsley, DeVold, Dunkel, FACT*, FB News, Football Research, FW, Helms, National Championship Foundation
Notre Dame: FACT*, Matthews
Ohio St.: NFF*
Texas: Berryman, FACT*, Litkenhous, NFF*, Sagarin, UPI

1971
Nebraska: AP, Berryman, Billingsley, DeVold, Dunkel, FACT, FB News, Football Research, FW, Helms, Litkenhous, Matthews, National Championship Foundation, NFF, Poling, Sagarin, UPI

1972
Southern California: AP, Berryman, Billingsley, DeVold, Dunkel, FACT, FB News, Football Research, FW, Helms, Litkenhous, Matthews, National Championship Foundation, NFF, Poling, Sagarin, UPI

1973
Alabama: Berryman, UPI
Michigan: National Championship Foundation*, Poling*
Notre Dame: AP, FB News, FW, Helms, National Championship Foundation*, NFF
Ohio St.: FACT, National Championship Foundation*, Poling*
Oklahoma: Billingsley, DeVold, Dunkel, Football Research, Sagarin

1974
Ohio St.: Matthews
Oklahoma: AP, Berryman, Billingsley, DeVold, Dunkel, FACT, FB News, Football Research, Helms*, Litkenhous, National Championship Foundation*, Poling, Sagarin
Southern California: FW, Helms*, National Championship Foundation*, NFF, UPI

1975
Alabama: Matthews*
Arizona St.: National Championship Foundation*, Sporting News
Ohio St.: Berryman, FACT*, Helms*, Matthews*, Poling
Oklahoma: AP, Billingsley, DeVold, Dunkel, FACT*, FB News, Football Research, FW, Helms*, National Championship Foundation*, NFF, Sagarin, UPI

1976
Pittsburgh: AP, FACT, FB News, FW, Helms, National Championship Foundation, NFF, Poling, Sagarin, Sporting News, UPI
Southern California: Berryman, Billingsley, DeVold, Dunkel, Football Research, Matthews

1977
Alabama: Football Research*
Arkansas: FACT*
Notre Dame: AP, Billingsley, DeVold, Dunkel, FACT*, FB News, Football Research*, FW, Helms, Matthews, National Championship Foundation, NFF, Poling, Sagarin, Sporting News, UPI
Texas: Berryman, FACT*

1978
Alabama: AP, FACT*, Football Research, FW, Helms*, National Championship Foundation*, NFF
Oklahoma: Billingsley, DeVold, Dunkel, FACT*, Helms*, Litkenhous, Matthews, Poling, Sagarin
Southern California: Berryman, FACT*, FB News, Helms*, National Championship Foundation*, Sporting News, UPI

1979
Alabama: AP, Berryman, Billingsley, DeVold, Dunkel, FACT, FB News, FW, Helms, Matthews, National Championship Foundation, NFF, NY Times, Poling, Sagarin, Sporting News, UPI
Southern California: Football Research

1980
Florida St.: FACT*
Georgia: AP, Berryman, FACT*, FB News, FW, Helms, National Championship Foundation, NFF, Poling, Sporting News, UPI
Nebraska: FACT*, Sagarin
Oklahoma: Billingsley, Dunkel, Matthews
Pittsburgh: DeVold, FACT*, Football Research, NY Times

1981
Clemson: AP, Berryman, Billingsley, DeVold, FACT, FB News, Football Research, FW, Helms, Litkenhous, Matthews, National Championship Foundation*, NFF, NY Times, Poling, Sagarin, Sporting News, UPI
Nebraska: National Championship Foundation*
Penn St.: Dunkel
Pittsburgh: National Championship Foundation*
Texas: National Championship Foundation*
Southern Methodist: National Championship Foundation*

1982
Nebraska: Berryman
Penn St.: AP, Billingsley, DeVold, Dunkel, FACT, FB News, Football Research, FW, Helms*, Litkenhous, Matthews, National Championship Foundation, NFF, NY Times, Poling, Sagarin, Sporting News, UPI, USA/CNN
Southern Methodist: Helms*

1983
Auburn: FACT*, Football Research, NY Times
Miami (Fla.): AP, Billingsley, Dunkel, FB News, FW, National Championship Foundation, NFF, Sporting News, UPI, USA/CNN
Nebraska: Berryman, DeVold, FACT*, Litkenhous, Matthews, Poling, Sagarin

1984
Brigham Young: AP, Football Research, FW, National Championship Foundation*, NFF, Poling, UPI, USA/CNN
Florida: Billingsley, Dunkel, FACT, Matthews, NY Times, Sagarin, Sporting News
Nebraska: Litkenhous
Washington: Berryman, FB News, National Championship Foundation*

1985
Michigan: Matthews, Sagarin
Oklahoma: AP, Berryman, Billingsley, DeVold, Dunkel, FACT, FB News, Football Research, FW, National Championship Foundation, NFF, NY Times, Sporting News, UPI, USA/CNN

1986
Miami (Fla.): FACT*
Oklahoma: Berryman, DeVold, Dunkel, Football Research, NY Times, Sagarin
Penn St.: AP, Billingsley, FACT*, FB News, FW, Matthews, National Championship Foundation, NFF, Sporting News, UPI, USA/CNN

1987
Florida St.: Berryman, Sagarin
Miami (Fla.): AP, Billingsley, DeVold, Dunkel, FACT, FB News, Football Research, FW, Matthews, National Championship Foundation, NFF, NY Times, Sporting News, UPI, USA/CNN

1988
Miami (Fla.): Berryman
Notre Dame: AP, Billingsley, DeVold, Dunkel, FACT, FB News, Football Research, FW, Matthews, National Championship Foundation, NFF, NY Times, Sagarin, Sporting News, UPI, USA/CNN

1989
Miami (Fla.): AP, Billingsley, DeVold, Dunkel, FACT*, FB News, Football Research, FW, Matthews, National Championship Foundation, NFF, NY Times, Sporting News, UPI, USA/CNN
Notre Dame: Berryman, FACT*, Sagarin

1990
Colorado: AP, Berryman, DeVold, FACT*, FB News, Football Research, FW, Matthews, National Championship Foundation*, NFF, Sporting News, USA/CNN

Georgia Tech: Dunkel, FACT*, National Championship Foundation*, UPI
Miami (Fla.): Billingsley, FACT*, NY Times, Sagarin
Washington: FACT*

1991
Miami (Fla.): AP, Football Research, National Championship Foundation*, NY Times, Sporting News
Washington: Berryman, Billingsley, DeVold, Dunkel, FACT, FB News, FW, Matthews, National Championship Foundation*, Sagarin, UPI/NFF, USA/CNN

1992
Alabama: AP, Berryman, Billingsley, DeVold, Dunkel, FACT, FB News, Football Research, FW, Matthews, National Championship Foundation, NY Times, Sporting News, UPI/NFF, USA/CNN
Florida St.: Sagarin

1993
Auburn: National Championship Foundation*
Florida St.: AP, Berryman, Billingsley, DeVold, Dunkel, FACT, FB News, FW, National Championship Foundation*, NY Times, Sagarin, Sporting News, UPI, USA/CNN, USA/NFF
Nebraska: National Championship Foundation*
Notre Dame: Matthews, National Championship Foundation*

1994
Florida St.: Dunkel
Nebraska: Alderson, AP, Berryman, Billingsley, FACT*, FB News, FW, National Championship Foundation*, Sporting News, UPI, USA/CNN, USA/NFF
Penn St.: DeVold, FACT*, Matthews, National Championship Foundation*, NY Times, Sagarin

1995
Nebraska: Alderson, AP, Berryman, Billingsley, DeVold, Dunkel, FACT, FB News, FW, Matthews, National Championship Foundation, NFF, NY Times, Sagarin, Sporting News, UPI, USA/CNN

1996
Florida: AP, Berryman, Billingsley, FACT, FB News, FW, NFF, Sagarin, Sporting News, USA/CNN, NY Times, National Championship Foundation, Dunkel, Matthews, DeVold
Florida St.: Alderson

1997
Michigan: AP, FB News, FW, National Championship Foundation*, NFF, Sporting News
Nebraska: Alderson, Berryman, Billingsley, DeVold, Dunkel, FACT, Matthews, National Championship Foundation*, NY Times, Sagarin, Seattle Times, USA/ESPN

1998
Ohio St.: Sagarin
Tennessee: Alderson, AP, Berryman, Billingsley, DeVold, Dunkel, FACT, FB News, FW, Matthews, National Championship Foundation, NFF, NY Times, Seattle Times, Sporting News, USA/ESPN

1999
Florida St.: AP, Berryman, Billingsley, DeVold, Dunkel, FACT, FB News, FW, Massey, Matthews, National Championship Foundation, NFF, NY Times, Sagarin, Seattle Times, Sporting News, USA/ESPN

(**Legend of Present Major Selectors:** Associated Press (AP) from 1936-present; Football Writers Association of America (FW) from 1954-present; National Football Foundation and Hall of Fame (NFF) from 1959-90 and 1995 to present; USA Today/Cable News Network (USA/CNN) from 1982-96; USA Today/ESPN (USA/ESPN) from 1997-present; USA Today/National Football Foundation and Hall of Fame (USA/NFF) from 1993-94 to present. The Associated Press has been the designated media poll since 1936. United Press International served as the coaches' poll from 1950 to 1991 when it was taken over by USA Today/Cable News Network and in 1997 became USA Today/ESPN. In 1991-92, the No. 1 team in the final UPI/NFF ratings received the MacArthur Bowl as the national champion by the NFF. In 1993-94 and again in 1996, the No. 1 team in the USA Today/NFF final poll received the MacArthur Bowl.)

Major Selectors Since 1936

ASSOCIATED PRESS

Year	Team	Record
1936	Minnesota	7-1-0
1937	Pittsburgh	9-0-1
1938	TCU	11-0-0
1939	Texas A&M	11-0-0
1940	Minnesota	8-0-0
1941	Minnesota	8-0-0
1942	Ohio St.	9-1-0
1943	Notre Dame	9-1-0
1944	Army	9-0-0
1945	Army	9-0-0
1946	Notre Dame	8-0-1
1947	Notre Dame	9-0-0
1948	Michigan	9-0-0
1949	Notre Dame	10-0-0
1950	Oklahoma	10-1-0
1951	Tennessee	10-0-0
1952	Michigan St.	9-0-0
1953	Maryland	10-1-0
1954	Ohio St.	10-0-0
1955	Oklahoma	11-0-0
1956	Oklahoma	10-0-0
1957	Auburn	10-0-0
1958	LSU	11-0-0
1959	Syracuse	11-0-0
1960	Minnesota	8-2-0
1961	Alabama	11-0-0
1962	Southern California	11-0-0
1963	Texas	11-0-0
1964	Alabama	10-1-0
1965	Alabama	9-1-1
1966	Notre Dame	9-0-1
1967	Southern California	10-1-0
1968	Ohio St.	10-0-0
1969	Texas	11-0-0
1970	Nebraska	11-0-1
1971	Nebraska	13-0-0
1972	Southern California	12-0-0
1973	Notre Dame	11-0-0
1974	Oklahoma	11-0-0
1975	Oklahoma	11-1-0
1976	Pittsburgh	12-0-0
1977	Notre Dame	11-1-0
1978	Alabama	12-1-0
1979	Alabama	12-0-0
1980	Georgia	12-0-0
1981	Clemson	12-0-0
1982	Penn St.	11-1-0
1983	Miami (Fla.)	11-1-0
1984	Brigham Young	13-0-0
1985	Oklahoma	11-1-0
1986	Penn St.	12-0-0
1987	Miami (Fla.)	12-0-0
1988	Notre Dame	12-0-0
1989	Miami (Fla.)	11-1-0
1990	Colorado	11-1-1
1991	Miami (Fla.)	12-0-0
1992	Alabama	13-0-0
1993	Florida St.	12-1-0
1994	Nebraska	13-0-0
1995	Nebraska	12-0-0
1996	Florida	12-1-0
1997	Michigan	12-0-0
1998	Tennessee	13-0-0
1999	Florida St.	12-0-0

NATIONAL FOOTBALL FOUNDATION AND COLLEGE FOOTBALL HALL OF FAME
(MacArthur Bowl)

Year	Team	Record
1959	Syracuse	11-0-0
1960	Minnesota	8-2-0
1961	Alabama	11-0-0
1962	Southern California	11-0-0
1963	Texas	11-0-0
1964	Notre Dame	9-1-0
1965	Michigan St.	10-1-0
1966	Michigan St. 9-0-1/Notre Dame 9-0-1	
1967	Southern California	10-1-0
1968	Ohio St.	10-0-0
1969	Texas	11-0-0
1970	Ohio St. 10-1-0/Texas	10-1-0
1971	Nebraska	13-0-0
1972	Southern California	12-0-0
1973	Notre Dame	11-0-0
1974	Southern California	10-1-1
1975	Oklahoma	11-1-0
1976	Pittsburgh	12-0-0
1977	Notre Dame	11-1-0
1978	Alabama	11-1-0
1979	Alabama	12-0-0
1980	Georgia	12-0-0
1981	Clemson	12-0-0
1982	Penn St.	11-1-0
1983	Miami (Fla.)	11-1-0
1984	Brigham Young	13-0-0
1985	Oklahoma	11-1-0
1986	Penn St.	12-0-0
1987	Miami (Fla.)	12-0-0
1988	Notre Dame	12-0-0
1989	Miami (Fla.)	11-1-0
1990	Colorado	11-1-1
1991	Wash. (UPI/NFF)	12-0-0
1992	Alabama (UPI/NFF)	13-0-0
1993	Florida St. (USA/NFF)	12-1-0
1994	Nebraska (USA/NFF)	13-0-0
1995	Nebraska (USA/NFF)	12-0-0
1996	Florida (USA/NFF)	12-1-0
1997	Michigan	12-0-0
1998	Tennessee	13-0-0
1999	Florida St.	12-0-0

UNITED PRESS

Year	Team	Record
1950	Oklahoma	10-1-0
1951	Tennessee	10-0-0
1952	Michigan St.	9-0-0
1953	Maryland	10-1-0
1954	UCLA	9-0-0
1955	Oklahoma	11-0-0
1956	Oklahoma	10-0-0
1957	Ohio St.	9-1-0
1958	LSU	11-0-0
1959	Syracuse	11-0-0
1960	Minnesota	8-2-0
1961	Alabama	11-0-0
1962	Southern California	11-0-0
1963	Texas	11-0-0
1964	Alabama	10-1-0
1965	Michigan St.	10-1-0
1966	Notre Dame	9-0-1
1967	Southern California	10-1-0
1968	Ohio St.	10-0-0
1969	Texas	11-0-0
1970	Texas	10-1-0
1971	Nebraska	13-0-0
1972	Southern California	12-0-0
1973	Alabama	11-1-0
1974	Southern California	10-1-1
1975	Oklahoma	11-1-0
1976	Pittsburgh	12-0-0
1977	Notre Dame	11-1-0
1978	Southern California	12-1-0
1979	Alabama	12-0-0
1980	Georgia	12-0-0
1981	Clemson	12-0-0
1982	Penn St.	11-1-0
1983	Miami (Fla.)	11-1-0
1984	Brigham Young	13-0-0
1985	Oklahoma	11-1-0
1986	Penn St.	12-0-0
1987	Miami (Fla.)	12-0-0
1988	Notre Dame	12-0-0
1989	Miami (Fla.)	11-1-0
1990	Georgia Tech	11-0-1
1991	Washington	12-0-0
1992	Alabama	13-0-0
1993	Florida St.	12-1-0
1994	Nebraska	13-0-0
1995	Nebraska	12-0-0

FOOTBALL WRITERS'

Year	Team	Record
1954	UCLA	9-0-0
1955	Oklahoma	11-0-0
1956	Oklahoma	10-0-0
1957	Ohio St.	9-1-0
1958	Iowa	8-1-1
1959	Syracuse	11-0-0
1960	Mississippi	10-0-1
1961	Ohio St.	8-0-1
1962	Southern California	11-0-0
1963	Texas	11-0-0
1964	Arkansas	11-0-0
1965	Alabama 9-1-1/ Michigan St.	10-1-0
1966	Notre Dame	9-0-1
1967	Southern California	10-1-0
1968	Ohio St.	10-0-0
1969	Texas	11-0-0
1970	Nebraska	11-0-1
1971	Nebraska	13-0-0
1972	Southern California	12-0-0
1973	Notre Dame	11-0-0
1974	Southern California	10-1-1
1975	Oklahoma	11-1-0
1976	Pittsburgh	12-0-0
1977	Notre Dame	11-1-0
1978	Alabama	11-1-0
1979	Alabama	12-0-0
1980	Georgia	12-0-0
1981	Clemson	12-0-0
1982	Penn St.	11-1-0
1983	Miami (Fla.)	11-1-0
1984	Brigham Young	13-0-0
1985	Oklahoma	11-1-0
1986	Penn St.	12-0-0
1987	Miami (Fla.)	12-0-0
1988	Notre Dame	12-0-0
1989	Miami (Fla.)	11-1-0
1990	Colorado	11-1-1
1991	Washington	12-0-0
1992	Alabama	13-0-0
1993	Florida St.	12-1-0
1994	Nebraska	13-0-0
1995	Nebraska	12-0-0
1996	Florida	12-1-0
1997	Michigan	12-0-0
1998	Tennessee	13-0-0
1999	Florida St.	12-0-0

USA TODAY/ESPN

Year	Team	Record
1982	Penn St.	11-1-0
1983	Miami (Fla.) (CNN)	11-1-0
1984	Brigham Young (CNN)	13-0-0
1985	Oklahoma (CNN)	11-1-0
1986	Penn St. (CNN)	12-0-0
1987	Miami (Fla.) (CNN)	12-0-0
1988	Notre Dame (CNN)	12-0-0
1989	Miami (Fla.) (CNN)	11-1-0
1990	Colorado (CNN)	11-1-1
1991	Washington (CNN)	12-0-0
1992	Alabama (CNN)	13-0-0
1993	Florida St. (CNN)	12-1-0
1994	Nebraska (CNN)	13-0-0
1995	Nebraska (CNN)	12-0-0
1996	Florida (CNN)	12-1-0
1997	Nebraska (ESPN)	13-0-0
1998	Tennessee (ESPN)	13-0-0
1999	Florida St. (ESPN)	12-0-0

NATIONAL POLL CHAMPIONS IN BOWL GAMES

National Poll Champions in Bowl Games

Year	Team	Coach (Years†)	Record	Bowl (Result)
1900	Yale	Malcolm McBride	12-0-0	None
1901	Michigan	Fielding Yost	11-0-0	Rose (beat Stanford, 49-0)
	Harvard	William Reid	12-0-0	None
1902	Michigan	Fielding Yost	11-0-0	None
	Yale	Joseph Swan	11-0-1	None
1903	Princeton	Art Hillebrand	11-0-0	None
1904	Pennsylvania	Carl Williams	12-0-0	None
1905	Chicago	Amos Alonzo Stagg	11-0-0	None
	Yale	J. E. Owsley	10-0-0	None
1906	Princeton	Bill Roper	9-0-1	None
	Yale	Foster Rockwell	9-0-1	None
1907	Yale	William Knox	9-0-1	None
1908	Pennsylvania	Sol Metzger	11-0-1	None
	Harvard	Percy Haughton	9-0-1	None
1909	Yale	Howard Jones	10-0-0	None
1910	Harvard	Percy Haughton	8-0-1	None
1911	Princeton	Bill Roper	8-0-2	None
1912	Harvard	Percy Haughton	9-0-0	None
1913	Harvard	Percy Haughton	9-0-0	None
1914	Army	Charley Daly	9-0-0	None
	Harvard	Percy Haughton	7-0-2	None
1915	Cornell	Al Sharpe	9-0-0	None
1916	Pittsburgh	Glenn "Pop" Warner	8-0-0	None
1917	Georgia Tech	John Heisman	9-0-0	None
1918	Pittsburgh	Glenn "Pop" Warner	4-1-0	None
1919	Harvard	Robert Fisher	9-0-1	Rose (beat Oregon, 7-6)
	Penn St.	Hugo Bezdek	7-1-0	None
1920	California	Andy Smith	9-0-0	Rose (beat Ohio St., 28-0)
	Princeton	Bill Roper	6-0-1	None
1921	Cornell	Gil Dobie	8-0-0	None
	Penn St.	Hugo Bezdek	8-0-2	None
1922	Cornell	Gil Dobie	8-0-0	None
	Princeton	Bill Roper	8-0-0	None
1923	Illinois	Robert Zuppke	8-0-0	None
1924	Notre Dame	Knute Rockne	10-0-0	Rose (beat Stanford, 27-10)
1925	Alabama	Wallace Wade	10-0-0	Rose (beat Washington, 20-19)
	Dartmouth	Jesse Hawley	8-0-0	None
1926	Alabama	Wallace Wade	9-0-1	Rose (tied Stanford, 7-7)
	Stanford	Glenn "Pop" Warner	10-0-1	Rose (tied Alabama, 7-7)
1927	Illinois	Robert Zuppke	7-0-1	None
1928	Georgia Tech	Bill Alexander	10-0-0	Rose (beat California, 8-7)
	Southern California	Howard Jones	9-0-1	None
1929	Notre Dame	Knute Rockne	9-0-0	None
1930	Notre Dame	Knute Rockne	10-0-0	None
1931	Southern California	Howard Jones	10-1-0	Rose (beat Tulane, 21-12)
1932	Michigan	Harry Kipke	8-0-0	None
	Southern California	Howard Jones	10-0-0	Rose (beat Pittsburgh, 35-0)
1933	Michigan	Harry Kipke	7-0-1	None
1934	Minnesota	Bernie Bierman	8-0-0	None
1935	Minnesota	Bernie Bierman	8-0-0	None
	Southern Methodist	Matty Bell	12-1-0	Rose (lost to Stanford, 7-0)
1936	Minnesota	Bernie Bierman (5-15)	7-1-0	None
1937	Pittsburgh	Jock Sutherland (13-18)	9-0-1	None
1938	TCU	Dutch Meyer (5-5)	11-0-0	Sugar (beat Carnegie Mellon, 15-7)
1939	Texas A&M	Homer Norton (6-16)	11-0-0	Sugar (beat Tulane, 14-13)
1940	Minnesota	Bernie Bierman (9-19)	8-0-0	None
1941	Minnesota	Bernie Bierman (10-20)	8-0-0	None
1942	Ohio St.	Paul Brown (2-2)	9-1-0	None
1943	Notre Dame	Frank Leahy (3-5)	9-1-0	None
1944	Army	Earl "Red" Blaik (4-11)	9-0-0	None
1945	Army	Earl "Red" Blaik (5-12)	9-0-0	None
1946	Notre Dame	Frank Leahy (4-6)	8-0-1	None
1947	Notre Dame	Frank Leahy (5-7)	9-0-0	None
1948	Michigan	Bennie Oosterbaan (1-1)	9-0-0	None
1949	Notre Dame	Frank Leahy (7-9)	10-0-0	None
1950	Oklahoma	Bud Wilkinson (4-4)	10-1-0	Sugar (lost to Kentucky, 13-7)
1951	Tennessee	Robert Neyland (20-20)	10-0-0	Sugar (lost to Maryland, 28-13)
1952	Michigan St.	Clarence "Biggie" Munn (6-9)	9-0-0	None
1953	Maryland	Jim Tatum (7-9)	10-1-0	Orange (lost to Oklahoma, 7-0)
1954	Ohio St.	Woody Hayes (4-9)	10-0-0	Rose (beat Southern California, 20-7)
	UCLA	Red Sanders (6-12)	9-0-0	None
1955	Oklahoma	Bud Wilkinson (9-9)	11-0-0	Orange (beat Maryland, 20-6)
1956	Oklahoma	Bud Wilkinson (10-10)	10-0-0	None
1957	Auburn	Ralph "Shug" Jordan (7-7)	10-0-0	None
	Ohio St.	Woody Hayes (7-12)	9-1-0	Rose (beat Oregon, 10-7)
1958	LSU	Paul Dietzel (4-4)	11-0-0	Sugar (beat Clemson, 7-0)
	Iowa	Forest Evashevski (5-8)	8-1-1	Rose (beat California, 38-12)
1959	Syracuse	Ben Schwartzwalder (11-14)	11-0-0	Cotton (beat Texas, 23-14)
1960	Minnesota	Murray Warmath (7-9)	8-2-0	Rose (lost to Washington, 17-7)
	Mississippi	Johnny Vaught (14-14)	10-0-1	Sugar (beat Rice, 14-6)

CONSENSUS NATIONAL CHAMPIONS

SINCE 1950

AP — Associated Press
UPI — United Press International
FWAA — Football Writers Association of America
NFF — National Football Foundation/College Football Hall of Fame
USA/CNN — USA Today/CNN
USA/ESPN — USA Today/ESPN

Year	Champion (Selectors)
1950	Oklahoma (AP, UPI)
1951	Tennessee (AP, UPI)
1952	Michigan St. (AP, UPI)
1953	Maryland (AP, UPI)
1954	UCLA (FWAA, UPI)
	Ohio St. (AP
1955	Oklahoma (AP, FWAA, UPI)
1956	Oklahoma (AP, FWAA, UPI)
1957	Ohio St. (FWAA, UPI)
	Auburn (AP)
1958	LSU (AP, UPI)
	Iowa (FWAA)
1959	Syracuse (AP, FWAA, NFF, UPI)
1960	Minnesota (AP, NFF, UPI)
	Mississippi (FWAA)
1961	Alabama (AP, NFF, UPI)
	Ohio St. (FWAA)
1962	Southern California (AP, FWAA, NFF, UPI)
1963	Texas (AP, FWAA, NFF, UPI)
1964	Alabama (AP, UPI)
	Arkansas (FWAA)
	Notre Dame (NFF)
1965	Michigan St. (FWAA, NFF, UPI)
	Alabama (AP, FWAA)
1966	Notre Dame (AP, FWAA, NFF, UPI)
	Michigan St. (NFF)
1967	Southern California (AP, FWAA, NFF, UPI)
1968	Ohio St. (AP, FWAA, NFF, UPI)
1969	Texas (AP, FWAA, NFF, UPI)
1970	Nebraska (AP, FWAA)
	Texas (NFF, UPI)
	Ohio St. (NFF)
1971	Nebraska (AP, FWAA, NFF, UPI)
1972	Southern California (AP, FWAA, NFF, UPI)
1973	Notre Dame (AP, FWAA, NFF)
	Alabama (UPI)
1974	Southern California (FWAA, NFF, UPI)
	Oklahoma (AP)
1975	Oklahoma (AP, FWAA, NFF, UPI)
1976	Pittsburgh (AP, FWAA, NFF, UPI)
1977	Notre Dame (AP, FWAA, NFF, UPI)
1978	Alabama (AP, FWAA, NFF)
	Southern California (UPI)
1979	Alabama (AP, FWAA, NFF, UPI)
1980	Georgia (AP, FWAA, NFF, UPI)
1981	Clemson (AP, FWAA, NFF, UPI)
1982	Penn St. (AP, FWAA, NFF, UPI, USA/CNN)
1983	Miami (Fla.) (AP, FWAA, NFF, UPI, USA/CNN)
1984	Brigham Young (AP, FWAA, NFF, UPI, USA/CNN)
1985	Oklahoma (AP, FWAA, NFF, UPI, USA/CNN)
1986	Penn St. (AP, FWAA, NFF, UPI, USA/CNN)
1987	Miami (Fla.) (AP, FWAA, NFF, UPI, USA/CNN)
1988	Notre Dame (AP, FWAA, NFF, UPI, USA/CNN)
1989	Miami (Fla.) (AP, FWAA, NFF, UPI, USA/CNN)
1990	Colorado (AP, FWAA, NFF, USA/CNN)
	Georgia Tech (UPI)
1991	Washington (FWAA, NFF, USA/CNN, UPI)
	Miami (Fla.) (AP)
1992	Alabama (AP, FWAA, NFF, USA/CNN, UPI)
1993	Florida St. (AP, FWAA, NFF, USA/CNN, UPI)
1994	Nebraska (AP, FWAA, NFF, USA/CNN, UPI)
1995	Nebraska (AP, FWAA, NFF, USA/CNN, UPI)
1996	Florida (AP, FWAA, NFF, USA/CNN)
1997	Michigan (AP, FWAA, NFF)
	Nebraska (USA/ESPN)
1998	Tennessee (AP, FWAA, NFF, USA/ESPN)
1999	Florida St. (AP, FWAA, NFF, USA/ESPN)

DIVISION I-A

NATIONAL CHAMPIONS IN BOWL GAMES

Year	Team	Coach (Years†)	Record	Bowl (Result)
1961	Alabama	Paul "Bear" Bryant (4-17)	11-0-0	Sugar (beat Arkansas, 10-3)
	Ohio St.	Woody Hayes (11-16)	8-0-1	None
1962	Southern California	John McKay (3-3)	11-0-0	Rose (beat Wisconsin, 42-37)
1963	Texas	Darrell Royal (7-10)	11-0-0	Cotton (beat Navy, 28-6)
1964	Alabama	Paul "Bear" Bryant (7-20)	10-1-0	Orange (lost to Texas, 21-17)
	Arkansas	Frank Broyles (3-4)	11-0-0	Cotton (beat Nebraska, 10-7)
	Notre Dame	Ara Parseghian (1-14)	9-1-0	None
1965	Alabama	Paul "Bear" Bryant (8-21)	9-1-1	Orange (beat Nebraska, 39-28)
	Michigan St.	Duffy Daugherty (12-12)	10-1-0	Rose (lost to UCLA, 14-12)
1966	Michigan St.	Duffy Daugherty (13-13)	9-0-1	None
	Notre Dame	Ara Parseghian (3-17)	9-0-1	None
1967	Southern California	John McKay (8-8)	10-1-0	Rose (beat Indiana, 14-3)
1968	Ohio St.	Woody Hayes (18-23)	10-0-0	Rose (beat Southern California, 27-16)
1969	Texas	Darrell Royal (13-16)	11-0-0	Cotton (beat Notre Dame, 21-17)
1970	Nebraska	Bob Devaney (9-14)	11-0-1	Orange (beat LSU, 17-12)
	Ohio St.	Woody Hayes (20-25)	9-1-0	Rose (lost to Stanford, 27-17)
	Texas	Darrell Royal (14-17)	10-1-0	Cotton (lost to Notre Dame, 24-11)
1971	Nebraska	Bob Devaney (10-15)	13-0-0	Orange (beat Alabama, 38-6)
1972	Southern California	John McKay (13-13)	12-0-0	Rose (beat Ohio St., 42-17)
1973	Alabama	Paul "Bear" Bryant (16-29)	11-1-0	Sugar (lost to Notre Dame, 24-23)
	Notre Dame	Ara Parseghian (10-23)	11-0-0	Sugar (beat Alabama, 24-23)
1974	Oklahoma	Barry Switzer (2-2)	11-0-0	None
	Southern California	John McKay (15-15)	10-1-1	Rose (beat Ohio St., 18-17)
1975	Oklahoma	Barry Switzer (3-3)	11-1-0	Orange (beat Michigan, 14-6)
1976	Pittsburgh	Johnny Majors (4-9)	12-0-0	Sugar (beat Georgia, 27-3)
1977	Notre Dame	Dan Devine (3-19)	11-1-0	Cotton (beat Texas, 38-10)
1978	Alabama	Paul "Bear" Bryant (21-34)	11-1-0	Sugar (beat Penn St., 14-7)
	Southern California	John Robinson (3-3)	12-1-0	Rose (beat Michigan, 17-10)
1979	Alabama	Paul "Bear" Bryant (22-35)	12-0-0	Sugar (beat Arkansas, 24-9)
1980	Georgia	Vince Dooley (17-17)	12-0-0	Sugar (beat Notre Dame, 17-10)
1981	Clemson	Danny Ford (4-4#)	12-0-0	Orange (beat Nebraska, 22-15)
1982	Penn St.	Joe Paterno (17-17)	11-1-0	Sugar (beat Georgia, 27-23)
1983	Miami (Fla.)	Howard Schnellenberger (5-5)	11-1-0	Orange (beat Nebraska, 31-30)
1984	Brigham Young	LaVell Edwards (13-13)	13-0-0	Holiday (beat Michigan, 24-17)
1985	Oklahoma	Barry Switzer (13-13)	11-1-0	Orange (beat Penn St., 25-10)
1986	Penn St.	Joe Paterno (21-21)	12-0-0	Fiesta (beat Miami [Fla.], 14-10)
1987	Miami (Fla.)	Jimmy Johnson (3-9)	12-0-0	Orange (beat Oklahoma, 20-14)
1988	Notre Dame	Lou Holtz (3-19)	12-0-0	Fiesta (beat West Virginia, 34-21)
1989	Miami (Fla.)	Dennis Erickson (1-8)	11-1-0	Sugar (beat Alabama, 33-25)
1990	Colorado	Bill McCartney (9-9)	11-1-1	Orange (beat Notre Dame, 10-9)
	Georgia Tech	Bobby Ross (4-14)	11-0-1	Fla. Citrus (beat Nebraska, 45-21)
1991	Miami (Fla.)	Dennis Erickson (3-10)	12-0-0	Orange (beat Nebraska, 22-0)
	Washington	Don James (17-21)	12-0-0	Rose (beat Michigan, 34-14)
1992	Alabama	Gene Stallings (3-10)	13-0-0	Sugar (beat Miami [Fla.], 34-13)
1993	Florida St.	Bobby Bowden (18-28)	12-1-0	Orange (beat Nebraska, 18-16)
1994	Nebraska	Tom Osborne (22-22)	13-0-0	Orange (beat Miami [Fla.], 24-17)
1995	Nebraska	Tom Osborne (23-23)	12-0-0	Fiesta (beat Florida, 62-24)
1996	Florida	Steve Spurrier (7-10)	12-1-0	Sugar (beat Florida St., 52-20)
1997	Michigan	Lloyd Carr (3-3)	12-0-0	Rose (beat Washington St., 21-16)
	Nebraska	Tom Osborne (25-25)	13-0-0	Orange (beat Tennessee, 42-17)
1998*	Tennessee	Phillip Fulmer (7-7)	13-0-0	Fiesta (beat Florida St., 23-16)
1999	Florida St.	Bobby Bowden (25-35)	12-0-0	Sugar (beat Virginia Tech, 46-29)

†Years head coach at that college and total years at four-year colleges. #Includes last game of 1978 season. *First year of BCS ranking system.

Associated Press Weekly Poll Leaders

The weekly dates are for Monday or Tuesday, the most frequent release dates of the poll, except when the final poll was taken after January 1-2 bowl games. A team's record includes its last game before the weekly poll. A new weekly leader's rank the previous week is indicated in parentheses after its record. Final poll leaders (annual champions) are in bold face. (Note: Only 10 teams were ranked in the weekly polls during 1962, 1963, 1964, 1965, 1966 and 1967; 20 were ranked in all other seasons until 1989, when 25 were ranked.)

1936
10-20	Minnesota	(3-0-0)
10-27	Minnesota	(4-0-0)
11-3	Northwestern	(5-0-0) (3)
11-10	Northwestern	(6-0-0)
11-17	Northwestern	(7-0-0)
11-24	Minnesota	(7-1-0) (2)
12-1	**Minnesota**	**(7-1-0)**

1937
10-20	California	(5-0-0)
10-27	California	(6-0-0)
11-2	California	(7-0-0)
11-9	Pittsburgh	(6-0-1) (3)
11-16	Pittsburgh	(7-0-1)
11-23	Pittsburgh	(8-0-1)
11-30	**Pittsburgh**	**(9-0-1)**

1938
10-18	Pittsburgh	(4-0-0)
10-25	Pittsburgh	(5-0-0)
11-1	Pittsburgh	(6-0-0)
11-8	TCU	(7-0-0) (2)
11-15	Notre Dame	(7-0-0) (2)
11-22	Notre Dame	(8-0-0)
11-29	Notre Dame	(8-0-0)
12-6	**TCU**	**(10-0-0) (2)**

1939
10-17	Pittsburgh	(3-0-0)
10-24	Tennessee	(4-0-0) (5)
10-31	Tennessee	(5-0-0)
11-7	Tennessee	(6-0-0)
11-14	Tennessee	(7-0-0)
11-21	Texas A&M	(9-0-0) (2)
11-28 (tie)	Texas A&M	(9-0-0)
(tie)	Southern California	(6-0-1) (4)
12-5	Texas A&M	(10-0-0)
12-12	**Texas A&M**	**(10-0-0)**

1940
10-15	Cornell	(2-0-0)
10-22	Cornell	(3-0-0)
10-29	Cornell	(4-0-0)
11-5	Cornell	(5-0-0)
11-12	Minnesota	(6-0-0) (2)
11-19	Minnesota	(7-0-0)
11-26	Minnesota	(8-0-0)
12-3	**Minnesota**	**(8-0-0)**

1941
10-14	Minnesota	(2-0-0)
10-21	Minnesota	(3-0-0)
10-28 (tie)	Minnesota	(4-0-0)
(tie)	Texas	(5-0-0) (2)
11-4	Texas	(6-0-0)
11-11	Minnesota	(6-0-0) (2)
11-18	Minnesota	(7-0-0)
11-25	Minnesota	(8-0-0)
12-2	**Minnesota**	**(8-0-0)**

1942
10-13	Ohio St.	(3-0-0)
10-20	Ohio St.	(4-0-0)
10-27	Ohio St.	(5-0-0)
11-3	Georgia	(7-0-0) (2)
11-10	Georgia	(8-0-0)
11-17	Georgia	(9-0-0)
11-24	Boston College	(8-0-0) (3)
12-1	**Ohio St.**	**(9-1-0) (3)**

1943
10-5	Notre Dame	(2-0-0)
10-12	Notre Dame	(3-0-0)
10-19	Notre Dame	(4-0-0)
10-26	Notre Dame	(5-0-0)
11-2	Notre Dame	(6-0-0)
11-9	Notre Dame	(7-0-0)
11-16	Notre Dame	(8-0-0)
11-23	Notre Dame	(9-0-0)
11-30	**Notre Dame**	**(9-1-0)**

ASSOCIATED PRESS WEEKLY POLL LEADERS

1944
10-10	Notre Dame	(2-0-0)
10-17	Notre Dame	(3-0-0)
10-24	Notre Dame	(4-0-0)
10-31	Army	(5-0-0) (2)
11-7	Army	(6-0-0)
11-14	Army	(7-0-0)
11-21	Army	(8-0-0)
11-28	Army	(8-0-0)
12-5	**Army**	**(9-0-0)**

1945
10-9	Army	(2-0-0)
10-16	Army	(3-0-0)
10-23	Army	(4-0-0)
10-30	Army	(5-0-0)
11-6	Army	(6-0-0)
11-13	Army	(7-0-0)
11-20	Army	(8-0-0)
11-27	Army	(8-0-0)
12-4	**Army**	**(9-0-0)**

1946
10-8	Texas	(3-0-0)
10-15	Army	(4-0-0) (2)
10-22	Army	(5-0-0)
10-29	Army	(6-0-0)
11-5	Army	(7-0-0)
11-12	Army	(7-0-1)
11-19	Army	(8-0-1)
11-26	Army	(8-0-1)
12-3	**Notre Dame**	**(8-0-1) (2)**

1947*
10-7	Notre Dame	(1-0-0)
10-14	Michigan	(3-0-0) (2)
10-21	Michigan	(4-0-0)
10-28	Notre Dame	(4-0-0) (2)
11-4	Notre Dame	(5-0-0)
11-11	Notre Dame	(6-0-0)
11-18	Michigan	(8-0-0) (2)
11-25	Notre Dame	(8-0-0) (2)
12-2	Notre Dame	(8-0-0)
12-9	**Notre Dame**	**(9-0-0)**

1948
10-5	Notre Dame	(2-0-0)
10-12	North Carolina	(3-0-0) (2)
10-19	Michigan	(4-0-0) (4)
10-26	Michigan	(5-0-0)
11-2	Notre Dame	(6-0-0) (2)
11-9	Michigan	(7-0-0) (2)
11-16	Michigan	(8-0-0)
11-23	Michigan	(9-0-0)
11-30	**Michigan**	**(9-0-0)**

1949
10-4	Michigan	(2-0-0)
10-11	Notre Dame	(3-0-0) (2)
10-18	Notre Dame	(4-0-0)
10-25	Notre Dame	(4-0-0)
11-1	Notre Dame	(5-0-0)
11-8	Notre Dame	(6-0-0)
11-15	Notre Dame	(7-0-0)
11-22	Notre Dame	(8-0-0)
11-29	**Notre Dame**	**(9-0-0)**

1950
10-3	Notre Dame	(1-0-0)
10-10	Army	(2-0-0) (4)
10-17	Army	
10-24	Southern Methodist	(5-0-0) (3)
10-31	Southern Methodist	(5-0-0)
11-7	Army	(6-0-0) (2)
11-14	Ohio St.	(6-1-0) (4)
11-21	Oklahoma	(8-0-0) (2)
11-28	**Oklahoma**	**(9-0-0)**

1951
10-2	Michigan St.	(2-0-0)
10-9	Michigan St.	(3-0-0)
10-16	California	(4-0-0) (2)
10-23	Tennessee	(4-0-0) (2)
10-30	Tennessee	(5-0-0)
11-6	Tennessee	(6-0-0)
11-13	Michigan St.	(7-0-0)(5)
11-20	Tennessee	(8-0-0) (2)
11-27	Tennessee	(9-0-0)
12-4	**Tennessee**	**(10-0-0)**

1952
9-30	Michigan St.	(1-0-0)
10-7	Wisconsin	(2-0-0) (8)
10-14	Michigan St.	(3-0-0)(2)
10-21	Michigan St.	(4-0-0)
10-28	Michigan St.	(5-0-0)
11-4	Michigan St.	(6-0-0)
11-11	Michigan St.	(7-0-0)
11-18	Michigan St.	(8-0-0)
11-25	Michigan St.	(9-0-0)
12-1	**Michigan St.**	**(9-0-0)**

1953
9-29	Notre Dame	(1-0-0)
10-6	Notre Dame	(2-0-0)
10-13	Notre Dame	(2-0-0)
10-20	Notre Dame	(3-0-0)
10-27	Notre Dame	(4-0-0)
11-3	Notre Dame	(5-0-0)
11-10	Notre Dame	(6-0-0)
11-17	Notre Dame	(7-0-0)
11-24	Maryland	(10-0-0) (2)
12-1	**Maryland**	**(10-0-0)**

1954
9-21	Oklahoma	(1-0-0)
9-28	Notre Dame	(1-0-0) (2)
10-5	Oklahoma	(2-0-0) (2)
10-12	Oklahoma	(3-0-0)
10-19	Oklahoma	(4-0-0)
10-26	Ohio St.	(5-0-0) (4)
11-2	UCLA	(7-0-0) (3)
11-9	UCLA	(8-0-0)
11-16	Ohio St.	(8-0-0) (2)
11-23	Ohio St.	(9-0-0)
11-30	**Ohio St.**	**(9-0-0)**

1955
9-20	UCLA	(1-0-0)
9-27	Maryland	(2-0-0) (5)
10-4	Maryland	(3-0-0)
10-11	Michigan	(3-0-0) (2)
10-18	Michigan	(4-0-0)
10-25	Maryland	(6-0-0) (2)
11-1	Maryland	(7-0-0)
11-8	Oklahoma	(7-0-0) (4)
11-15	Oklahoma	(8-0-0)
11-22	Oklahoma	(9-0-0)
11-29	**Oklahoma**	**(10-0-0)**

1956
9-25	Oklahoma	(0-0-0)
10-2	Oklahoma	(1-0-0)
10-9	Oklahoma	(2-0-0)
10-16	Oklahoma	(3-0-0)
10-23	Michigan St.	(4-0-0) (2)
10-30	Oklahoma	(5-0-0) (2)
11-6	Oklahoma	(6-0-0)
11-13	Tennessee	(7-0-0) (3)
11-20	Oklahoma	(8-0-0) (2)
11-27	Oklahoma	(9-0-0)
12-4	**Oklahoma**	**(10-0-0)**

1957
9-24	Oklahoma	(1-0-0)
10-1	Oklahoma	(1-0-0)
10-8	Oklahoma	(2-0-0)
10-15	Michigan St.	(3-0-0) (2)
10-22	Oklahoma	(4-0-0) (2)
10-29	Texas A&M	(6-0-0) (2)
11-5	Texas A&M	(7-0-0) (2)
11-12	Texas A&M	(8-0-0)
11-19	Michigan St.	(7-1-0)(4)
11-26	Auburn	(9-0-0) (2)
12-3	**Auburn**	**(10-0-0)**

1958
9-23	Ohio St.	(0-0-0)
9-30	Oklahoma	(1-0-0) (2)
10-7	Auburn	(2-0-0) (2)
10-14	Army	(3-0-0) (3)
10-21	Army	(4-0-0)
10-28	LSU	(6-0-0) (3)
11-4	LSU	(7-0-0)
11-11	LSU	(8-0-0)
11-18	LSU	(9-0-0)
11-25	LSU	(10-0-0)
12-2	**LSU**	**(10-0-0)**

1959
9-22	LSU	(1-0-0)
9-29	LSU	(2-0-0)
10-6	LSU	(3-0-0)
10-13	LSU	(4-0-0)
10-20	LSU	(5-0-0)
10-27	LSU	(6-0-0)
11-3	LSU	(7-0-0)
11-10	Syracuse	(7-0-0) (4)
11-17	Syracuse	(8-0-0)
11-24	Syracuse	(9-0-0)
12-1	Syracuse	(9-0-0)
12-8	**Syracuse**	**(10-0-0)**

1960
9-20	Mississippi	(1-0-0)
9-27	Mississippi	(2-0-0)
10-4	Syracuse	(2-0-0) (2)
10-11	Mississippi	(4-0-0) (2)
10-18	Iowa	(4-0-0) (2)
10-25	Iowa	(5-0-0)
11-1	Iowa	(6-0-0)
11-8	Minnesota	(7-0-0) (3)
11-15	Missouri	(9-0-0) (3)
11-22	Minnesota	(8-1-0) (4)
11-29	**Minnesota**	**(8-1-0)**

1961
9-26	Iowa	(0-0-0)
10-3	Iowa	(1-0-0)
10-10	Mississippi	(3-0-0) (2)
10-17	Michigan St.	(3-0-0) (5)
10-24	Michigan St.	(4-0-0) (2)
10-31	Michigan St.	(5-0-0)
11-7	Texas	(7-0-0) (3)
11-14	Texas	(8-0-0)
11-21	Alabama	(9-0-0) (2)
11-28	Alabama	(9-0-0)
12-5	**Alabama**	**(10-0-0)**

1962
9-25	Alabama	(1-0-0)
10-2	Ohio St.	(1-0-0) (2)
10-9	Alabama	(3-0-0) (2)
10-16	Texas	(4-0-0) (2)
10-23	Texas	(5-0-0)
10-30	Northwestern	(5-0-0) (3)
11-6	Northwestern	(6-0-0)
11-13	Alabama	(8-0-0) (3)
11-20	Southern California	(8-0-0) (2)
11-27	Southern California	(9-0-0)
12-4	**Southern California**	**(10-0-0)**

1963
9-24	Southern California	(1-0-0)
10-1	Oklahoma	(1-0-0) (3)
10-8	Oklahoma	(2-0-0)
10-15	Texas	(4-0-0) (3)
10-22	Texas	(5-0-0)
10-29	Texas	(6-0-0)
11-5	Texas	(7-0-0)
11-12	Texas	(8-0-0)
11-19	Texas	(9-0-0)
11-26	Texas	(9-0-0)
12-3	Texas	(10-0-0)
12-10	**Texas**	**(10-0-0)**

1964
9-29	Texas	(2-0-0)
10-6	Texas	(3-0-0)
10-13	Texas	(4-0-0)
10-20	Ohio St.	(4-0-0)(2)
10-27	Ohio St.	(5-0-0)
11-3	Notre Dame	(6-0-0)
11-10	Notre Dame	(7-0-0)
11-17	Notre Dame	(8-0-0)
11-24	Notre Dame	(9-0-0)
12-1	**Alabama**	**(10-0-0) (2)**

1965
9-21	Notre Dame	(1-0-0)
9-28	Texas	(2-0-0) (3)
10-5	Texas	(3-0-0)
10-12	Texas	(4-0-0)
10-19	Arkansas	(5-0-0) (3)
10-26	Michigan St.	(6-0-0) (3)
11-2	Michigan St.	(7-0-0)
11-9	Michigan St.	(8-0-0)
11-16	Michigan St.	(9-0-0)
11-23	Michigan St.	(10-0-0)
11-30	Michigan St.	(10-0-0)
1-4	**Alabama**	**(9-1-1) (4)**

DIVISION I-A

1966
9-20	Michigan St.	(1-0-0)
9-27	Michigan St.	(2-0-0)
10-4	Michigan St.	(3-0-0)
10-11	Michigan St.	(4-0-0)
10-18	Notre Dame	(4-0-0) (2)
10-25	Notre Dame	(5-0-0)
11-1	Notre Dame	(6-0-0)
11-8	Notre Dame	(7-0-0)
11-15	Notre Dame	(8-0-0)
11-22	Notre Dame	(8-0-1)
11-29	Notre Dame	(9-0-1)
12-5	**Notre Dame**	**(9-0-1)**

1967
9-19	Notre Dame	(0-0-0)
9-26	Notre Dame	(1-0-0)
10-3	Southern California	(3-0-0) (2)
10-10	Southern California	(4-0-0)
10-17	Southern California	(5-0-0)
10-24	Southern California	(6-0-0)
10-31	Southern California	(7-0-0)
11-7	Southern California	(8-0-0)
11-14	UCLA	(7-0-1) (2)
11-21	Southern California	(9-1-0) (4)
11-28	**Southern California**	**(9-1-0)**

1968
9-17	Purdue	(0-0-0)
9-24	Purdue	(1-0-0)
10-1	Purdue	(2-0-0)
10-8	Purdue	(3-0-0)
10-15	Southern California	(4-0-0) (2)
10-22	Southern California	(5-0-0)
10-29	Southern California	(5-0-0)
11-5	Southern California	(6-0-0)
11-12	Southern California	(7-0-0)
11-19	Southern California	(8-0-0)
11-26	Ohio St.	(9-0-0) (2)
12-2	Ohio St.	(9-0-0)
12-9	**Ohio St.**	**(10-0-0)**

1969
9-23	Ohio St.	(0-0-0)
9-30	Ohio St.	(1-0-0)
10-7	Ohio St.	(2-0-0)
10-14	Ohio St.	(3-0-0)
10-21	Ohio St.	(4-0-0)
10-28	Ohio St.	(5-0-0)
11-4	Ohio St.	(6-0-0)
11-11	Ohio St.	(7-0-0)
11-18	Ohio St.	(8-0-0)
11-25	Texas	(8-0-0) (2)
12-2	Texas	(9-0-0)
12-9	Texas	(10-0-0)
1-4	**Texas**	**(11-0-0)**

1970
9-15	Ohio St.	(0-0-0)
9-22	Ohio St.	(0-0-0)
9-29	Ohio St.	(1-0-0)
10-6	Ohio St.	(2-0-0)
10-13	Ohio St.	(3-0-0)
10-20	Ohio St.	(4-0-0)
10-27	Texas	(5-0-0) (2)
11-3	Texas	(6-0-0)
11-10	Texas	(7-0-0)
11-17	Texas	(8-0-0)
11-24	Texas	(8-0-0)
12-1	Texas	(9-0-0)
12-8	Texas	(10-0-0)
1-6	**Nebraska**	**(11-0-1) (3)**

1971
9-14	Nebraska	(1-0-0)
9-21	Nebraska	(2-0-0)
9-28	Nebraska	(3-0-0)
10-5	Nebraska	(4-0-0)
10-12	Nebraska	(5-0-0)
10-19	Nebraska	(6-0-0)
10-26	Nebraska	(7-0-0)
11-2	Nebraska	(8-0-0)
11-9	Nebraska	(9-0-0)
11-16	Nebraska	(10-0-0)
11-23	Nebraska	(10-0-0)
11-30	Nebraska	(11-0-0)
12-7	Nebraska	(12-0-0)
1-4	**Nebraska**	**(13-0-0)**

1972
9-12	Southern California	(1-0-0)
9-19	Southern California	(2-0-0)
9-26	Southern California	(3-0-0)
10-3	Southern California	(4-0-0)
10-10	Southern California	(5-0-0)
10-17	Southern California	(6-0-0)
10-24	Southern California	(7-0-0)
10-31	Southern California	(8-0-0)
11-7	Southern California	(9-0-0)
11-14	Southern California	(9-0-0)
11-21	Southern California	(10-0-0)
11-28	Southern California	(10-0-0)
12-5	Southern California	(11-0-0)
1-3	**Southern California**	**(12-0-0)**

1973
9-11	Southern California	(0-0-0)
9-18	Southern California	(1-0-0)
9-25	Southern California	(2-0-0)
10-2	Ohio St.	(2-0-0) (3)
10-9	Ohio St.	(3-0-0)
10-16	Ohio St.	(4-0-0)
10-23	Ohio St.	(5-0-0)
10-30	Ohio St.	(6-0-0)
11-6	Ohio St.	(7-0-0)
11-13	Ohio St.	(8-0-0)
11-20	Ohio St.	(9-0-0)
11-27	Alabama	(10-0-0) (2)
12-4	Alabama	(11-0-0)
1-3	**Notre Dame**	**(11-0-0) (3)**

1974
9-10	Oklahoma	(0-0-0)
9-17	Notre Dame	(1-0-0) (2)
9-24	Ohio St.	(2-0-0) (2)
10-1	Ohio St.	(3-0-0)
10-8	Ohio St.	(4-0-0)
10-15	Ohio St.	(5-0-0)
10-22	Ohio St.	(6-0-0)
10-29	Ohio St.	(7-0-0)
11-5	Ohio St.	(8-0-0)
11-12	Oklahoma	(8-0-0) (2)
11-19	Oklahoma	(9-0-0)
11-26	Oklahoma	(10-0-0)
12-3	Oklahoma	(11-0-0)
1-3	**Oklahoma**	**(11-0-0)**

1975
9-9	Oklahoma	(0-0-0)
9-16	Oklahoma	(1-0-0)
9-23	Oklahoma	(2-0-0)
9-30	Oklahoma	(3-0-0)
10-7	Ohio St.	(4-0-0) (2)
10-14	Ohio St.	(5-0-0)
10-21	Ohio St.	(6-0-0)
10-28	Ohio St.	(7-0-0)
11-4	Ohio St.	(8-0-0)
11-11	Ohio St.	(9-0-0)
11-18	Ohio St.	(10-0-0)
11-25	Ohio St.	(11-0-0)
12-2	Ohio St.	(11-0-0)
1-3	**Oklahoma**	**(11-1-0) (3)**

1976
9-14	Michigan	(1-0-0)
9-21	Michigan	(2-0-0)
9-28	Michigan	(3-0-0)
10-5	Michigan	(4-0-0)
10-12	Michigan	(5-0-0)
10-19	Michigan	(6-0-0)
10-26	Michigan	(7-0-0)
11-2	Michigan	(8-0-0)
11-9	Pittsburgh	(9-0-0) (2)
11-16	Pittsburgh	(10-0-0)
11-23	Pittsburgh	(10-0-0)
11-30	Pittsburgh	(11-0-0)
1-5	**Pittsburgh**	**(12-0-0)**

1977
9-13	Michigan	(1-0-0)
9-20	Michigan	(2-0-0)
9-27	Oklahoma	(3-0-0) (3)
10-4	Southern California	(4-0-0) (2)
10-11	Michigan	(5-0-0) (3)
10-18	Michigan	(6-0-0)
10-25	Texas	(6-0-0) (2)
11-1	Texas	(7-0-0)
11-8	Texas	(8-0-0)
11-15	Texas	(9-0-0)
11-22	Texas	(10-0-0)
11-29	Texas	(11-0-0)
1-4	**Notre Dame**	**(11-1-0) (5)**

1978
9-12	Alabama	(1-0-0)
9-19	Alabama	(2-0-0)
9-26	Oklahoma	(3-0-0) (tie 3)
10-3	Oklahoma	(4-0-0)
10-10	Oklahoma	(5-0-0)
10-17	Oklahoma	(6-0-0)
10-24	Oklahoma	(7-0-0)
10-31	Oklahoma	(8-0-0)
11-7	Oklahoma	(9-0-0)
11-14	Penn St.	(10-0-0) (2)
11-21	Penn St.	(10-0-0)
11-28	Penn St.	(11-0-0)
12-5	Penn St.	(11-0-0)
1-4	**Alabama**	**(11-1-0) (2)**

1979
9-11	Southern California	(1-0-0)
9-18	Southern California	(2-0-0)
9-25	Southern California	(3-0-0)
10-2	Southern California	(4-0-0)
10-9	Southern California	(5-0-0)
10-16	Alabama	(5-0-0) (2)
10-23	Alabama	(6-0-0)
10-30	Alabama	(7-0-0)
11-6	Alabama	(8-0-0)
11-13	Alabama	(9-0-0)
11-20	Alabama	(10-0-0)
11-27	Alabama	(10-0-0)
12-4	Ohio St.	(11-0-0) (3)
1-3	**Alabama**	**(12-0-0) (2)**

1980
9-9	Ohio St.	(0-0-0)
9-16	Alabama	(1-0-0) (2)
9-23	Alabama	(2-0-0)
9-30	Alabama	(3-0-0)
10-7	Alabama	(4-0-0)
10-14	Alabama	(5-0-0)
10-21	Alabama	(6-0-0)
10-28	Alabama	(7-0-0)
11-4	Notre Dame	(7-0-0) (3)
11-11	Georgia	(9-0-0) (2)
11-18	Georgia	(10-0-0)
11-25	Georgia	(10-0-0)
12-2	Georgia	(11-0-0)
12-9	Georgia	(11-0-0)
1-4	**Georgia**	**(12-0-0)**

1981
9-8	Michigan	(0-0-0)
9-15	Notre Dame	(1-0-0) (4)
9-22	Southern California	(2-0-0) (2)
9-29	Southern California	(3-0-0)
10-6	Southern California	(4-0-0)
10-13	Texas	(4-0-0) (3)
10-20	Penn St.	(5-0-0) (2)
10-27	Penn St.	(6-0-0)
11-3	Pittsburgh	(7-0-0) (2)
11-10	Pittsburgh	(8-0-0)
11-17	Pittsburgh	(9-0-0)
11-24	Pittsburgh	(10-0-0)
12-1	Clemson	(11-0-0) (2)
1-3	**Clemson**	**(12-0-0)**

1982
9-7	Pittsburgh	(0-0-0)
9-14	Washington	(1-0-0) (2)
9-21	Washington	(2-0-0)
9-28	Washington	(3-0-0)
10-5	Washington	(4-0-0)
10-12	Washington	(5-0-0)
10-19	Washington	(6-0-0)
10-26	Pittsburgh	(6-0-0) (2)
11-2	Pittsburgh	(7-0-0)
11-9	Georgia	(9-0-0) (3)
11-16	Georgia	(10-0-0)
11-23	Georgia	(10-0-0)
11-30	Georgia	(11-0-0)
12-7	Georgia	(11-0-0)
1-3	**Penn St.**	**(11-1-0) (2)**

1983
9-6	Nebraska	(1-0-0)
9-13	Nebraska	(2-0-0)
9-20	Nebraska	(3-0-0)
9-27	Nebraska	(4-0-0)
10-4	Nebraska	(5-0-0)
10-11	Nebraska	(6-0-0)
10-18	Nebraska	(7-0-0)

ASSOCIATED PRESS WEEKLY POLL LEADERS

Date	Team	Record
10-25	Nebraska	(8-0-0)
11-1	Nebraska	(9-0-0)
11-8	Nebraska	(10-0-0)
11-15	Nebraska	(11-0-0)
11-22	Nebraska	(11-0-0)
11-29	Nebraska	(12-0-0)
12-6	Nebraska	(12-0-0)
1-3	**Miami (Fla.)**	**(11-1-0) (5)**

1984
Date	Team	Record
9-4	Miami (Fla.)	(2-0-0)
9-11	Nebraska	(1-0-0) (2)
9-18	Nebraska	(2-0-0)
9-25	Nebraska	(3-0-0)
10-2	Texas	(2-0-0) (2)
10-9	Texas	(3-0-0)
10-16	Washington	(6-0-0) (2)
10-23	Washington	(7-0-0)
10-30	Washington	(8-0-0)
11-6	Washington	(9-0-0)
11-13	Nebraska	(9-1-0) (2)
11-20	Brigham Young	(11-0-0) (3)
11-27	Brigham Young	(12-0-0)
12-4	Brigham Young	(12-0-0)
1-3	**Brigham Young**	**(13-0-0)**

1985
Date	Team	Record
9-3	Oklahoma	(0-0-0)
9-10	Auburn	(1-0-0) (2)
9-17	Auburn	(2-0-0)
9-24	Auburn	(2-0-0)
10-1	Iowa	(3-0-0) (3)
10-8	Iowa	(4-0-0)
10-15	Iowa	(5-0-0)
10-22	Iowa	(6-0-0)
10-29	Iowa	(7-0-0)
11-5	Florida	(7-0-1) (2)
11-12	Penn St.	(9-0-0) (2)
11-19	Penn St.	(10-0-0)
11-26	Penn St.	(11-0-0)
12-3	Penn St.	(11-0-0)
1-3	**Oklahoma**	**(11-1-0) (4)**

1986
Date	Team	Record
9-9	Oklahoma	(1-0-0)
9-16	Oklahoma	(1-0-0)
9-23	Oklahoma	(2-0-0)
9-30	Miami (Fla.)	(4-0-0) (2)
10-7	Miami (Fla.)	(5-0-0)
10-14	Miami (Fla.)	(6-0-0)
10-21	Miami (Fla.)	(7-0-0)
10-28	Miami (Fla.)	(7-0-0)
11-4	Miami (Fla.)	(8-0-0)
11-11	Miami (Fla.)	(9-0-0)
11-18	Miami (Fla.)	(10-0-0)
11-25	Miami (Fla.)	(10-0-0)
12-2	Miami (Fla.)	(11-0-0)
1-4	**Penn St.**	**(12-0-0) (2)**

1987
Date	Team	Record
9-8	Oklahoma	(1-0-0)
9-15	Oklahoma	(2-0-0)
9-22	Oklahoma	(2-0-0)
9-29	Oklahoma	(3-0-0)
10-6	Oklahoma	(4-0-0)
10-13	Oklahoma	(5-0-0)
10-20	Oklahoma	(6-0-0)
10-27	Oklahoma	(7-0-0)
11-3	Oklahoma	(8-0-0)
11-10	Oklahoma	(9-0-0)
11-17	Nebraska	(9-0-0) (2)
11-24	Oklahoma	(11-0-0) (2)
12-1	Oklahoma	(11-0-0)
12-8	Oklahoma	(11-0-0)
1-3	**Miami (Fla.)**	**(12-0-0) (2)**

1988
Date	Team	Record
9-6	Miami (Fla.)	(1-0-0)
9-13	Miami (Fla.)	(1-0-0)
9-20	Miami (Fla.)	(2-0-0)
9-27	Miami (Fla.)	(3-0-0)
10-4	Miami (Fla.)	(4-0-0)
10-11	Miami (Fla.)	(4-0-0)
10-18	UCLA	(6-0-0) (2)
10-25	UCLA	(7-0-0)
11-1	Notre Dame	(8-0-0) (2)
11-8	Notre Dame	(9-0-0)
11-15	Notre Dame	(9-0-0)
11-22	Notre Dame	(10-0-0)
11-29	Notre Dame	(11-0-0)
12-6	Notre Dame	(11-0-0)
1-3	**Notre Dame**	**(12-0-0)**

1989
Date	Team	Record
9-5	Notre Dame	(1-0-0)
9-12	Notre Dame	(1-0-0)
9-19	Notre Dame	(2-0-0)
9-26	Notre Dame	(3-0-0)
10-3	Notre Dame	(4-0-0)
10-10	Notre Dame	(5-0-0)
10-17	Notre Dame	(6-0-0)
10-24	Notre Dame	(7-0-0)
10-31	Notre Dame	(8-0-0)
11-7	Notre Dame	(9-0-0)
11-14	Notre Dame	(10-0-0)
11-21	Notre Dame	(11-0-0)
11-28	Colorado	(11-0-0) (2)
12-5	Colorado	(11-0-0)
1-2	**Miami (Fla.)**	**(11-1-0) (2)**

1990
Date	Team	Record
9-4	Miami (Fla.)	(0-0-0)
9-11	Notre Dame	(0-0-0) (2)
9-18	Notre Dame	(1-0-0)
9-25	Notre Dame	(2-0-0)
10-2	Notre Dame	(3-0-0)
10-9	Michigan	(3-1-0) (3)
10-16	Virginia	(6-0-0) (2)
10-23	Virginia	(7-0-0)
10-30	Virginia	(7-0-0)
11-6	Notre Dame	(7-1-0) (2)
11-13	Notre Dame	(8-1-0)
11-20	Colorado	(10-1-1) (2)
11-27	Colorado	(10-1-1)
12-4	Colorado	(10-1-1)
1-2	**Colorado**	**(11-1-1)**

1991
Date	Team	Record
9-3	Florida St.	(1-0-0)
9-10	Florida St.	(2-0-0)
9-17	Florida St.	(3-0-0)
9-23	Florida St.	(3-0-0)
9-30	Florida St.	(4-0-0)
10-7	Florida St.	(5-0-0)
10-14	Florida St.	(6-0-0)
10-21	Florida St.	(7-0-0)
10-28	Florida St.	(8-0-0)
11-4	Florida St.	(9-0-0)
11-11	Florida St.	(10-0-0)
11-18	Miami (Fla.)	(9-0-0) (2)
11-25	Miami (Fla.)	(10-0-0)
12-2	Miami (Fla.)	(11-0-0)
1-2	**Miami (Fla.)**	**(12-0-0)**

1992
Date	Team	Record
9-8	Miami (Fla.)	(1-0-0)
9-15	Miami (Fla.)	(1-0-0)
9-22	Miami (Fla.)	(2-0-0)
9-29	Washington	(3-0-0) (2)
10-6	Washington	(4-0-0)
10-13	Washington	(5-0-0)
10-20	Miami (Fla.)†	(6-0-0) (2)
10-27	Miami (Fla.)	(7-0-0)
11-3	Washington	(8-0-0) (2)
11-10	Miami (Fla.)	(8-0-0) (2)
11-17	Miami (Fla.)	(9-0-0)
11-24	Miami (Fla.)	(10-0-0)
12-1	Miami (Fla.)	(11-0-0)
12-8	Miami (Fla.)	(11-0-0)
1-2	**Alabama**	**(13-0-0) (2)**

1993
Date	Team	Record
8-31	Florida St.	(1-0-0)
9-7	Florida St.	(2-0-0)
9-14	Florida St.	(3-0-0)
9-21	Florida St.	(4-0-0)
9-28	Florida St.	(4-0-0)
10-5	Florida St.	(5-0-0)
10-12	Florida St.	(6-0-0)
10-19	Florida St.	(7-0-0)
10-26	Florida St.	(7-0-0)
11-2	Florida St.	(8-0-0)
11-9	Florida St.	(9-0-0)
11-16	Notre Dame	(10-0-0) (2)
11-23	Florida St.	(10-1-0) (2)
11-30	Florida St.	(11-1-0)
12-7	Florida St.	(11-1-0)
1-3	**Florida St.**	**(12-1-0)**

1994
Date	Team	Record
8-31	Florida	(0-0-0)
9-6	Nebraska	(1-0-0) (2)
9-13	Florida	(2-0-0) (2)
9-20	Florida	(3-0-0)
9-27	Florida	(3-0-0)
10-4	Florida	(4-0-0)
10-11	Florida	(5-0-0)
10-18	Penn St.	(6-0-0) (3)
10-25	Penn St.	(6-0-0)
11-1	Nebraska	(9-0-0) (3)
11-8	Nebraska	(10-0-0)
11-15	Nebraska	(11-0-0)
11-22	Nebraska	(11-0-0)
11-29	Nebraska	(12-0-0)
12-6	Nebraska	(12-0-0)
1-3	**Nebraska**	**(13-0-0)**

1995
Date	Team	Record
8-29	Florida St.	(0-0-0)
9-5	Florida St.	(1-0-0)
9-12	Florida St.	(2-0-0)
9-19	Florida St.	(3-0-0)
9-26	Florida St.	(4-0-0)
10-3	Florida St.	(4-0-0)
10-10	Florida St.	(5-0-0)
10-17	Florida St.	(6-0-0)
10-24	Florida St.	(7-0-0)
10-31	Nebraska	(8-0-0) (2)
11-7	Nebraska	(9-0-0)
11-14	Nebraska	(10-0-0)
11-21	Nebraska	(10-0-0)
11-28	Nebraska	(11-0-0)
12-5	Nebraska	(11-0-0)
1-3	**Nebraska**	**(12-0-0)**

1996
Date	Team	Record
8-26	Nebraska	(0-0-0)
9-2	Nebraska	(0-0-0)
9-9	Nebraska	(1-0-0)
9-16	Nebraska	(1-0-0)
9-23	Florida	(3-0-0) (4)
9-30	Florida	(4-0-0)
10-7	Florida	(5-0-0)
10-14	Florida	(6-0-0)
10-21	Florida	(7-0-0)
10-28	Florida	(7-0-0)
11-4	Florida	(8-0-0)
11-11	Florida	(9-0-0)
11-18	Florida	(10-0-0)
11-25	Florida	(10-0-0)
12-2	Florida St.	(11-0-0) (2)
12-9	Florida St.	(11-0-0)
1-3	**Florida**	**(12-1-0)**

1997
Date	Team	Record
8-25	Penn St.	(0-0-0)
9-2	Penn St.	(0-0-0)
9-8	Penn St.	(1-0-0)
9-15	Penn St.	(2-0-0)
9-22	Florida	(3-0-0) (3)
9-29	Florida	(4-0-0)
10-6	Florida	(5-0-0)
10-13	Penn St.	(5-0-0) (2)
10-20	Nebraska	(6-0-0) (2)
10-27	Nebraska	(7-0-0)
11-3	Nebraska	(8-0-0)
11-10	Michigan	(9-0-0) (4)
11-17	Michigan	(10-0-0)
11-24	Michigan	(11-0-0)
12-1	Michigan	(11-0-0)
12-8	Michigan	(11-0-0)
1-3	**Michigan**	**(12-0-0)**

1998
Date	Team	Record
9-7	Ohio St.	(1-0-0)
9-14	Ohio St.	(2-0-0)
9-21	Ohio St.	(3-0-0)
9-28	Ohio St.	(3-0-0)
10-5	Ohio St.	(4-0-0)
10-12	Ohio St.	(5-0-0)
10-19	Ohio St.	(6-0-0)
10-26	Ohio St.	(7-0-0)
11-2	Ohio St.	(7-0-0)
11-9	Tennessee	(8-0-0) (2)
11-16	Tennessee	(9-0-0)
11-23	Tennessee	(10-0-0)
11-30	Tennessee	(11-0-0)
12-7	Tennessee	(12-0-0)
1-5	**Tennessee**	**(13-0-0)**

1999
Date	Team	Record
8-30	Florida St.	(1-0-0)
9-6	Florida St.	(1-0-0)

DIVISION I-A

Date			
9-13	Florida St.	(2-0-0)
9-20	Florida St.	(3-0-0)
9-27	Florida St.	(4-0-0)
10-4	Florida St.	(5-0-0)
10-11	Florida St.	(6-0-0)
10-18	Florida St.	(7-0-0)
10-25	Florida St.	(8-0-0)
11-1	Florida St.	(9-0-0)
11-8	Florida St.	(9-0-0)
11-15	Florida St.	(10-0-0)
11-22	Florida St.	(11-0-0)
11-29	Florida St.	(11-0-0)
12-6	Florida St.	(11-0-0)
1-5	**Florida St.**	**(12-0-0)**

*On January 6, 1948, in a special postseason poll after the Rose Bowl, The Associated Press voted Michigan No. 1 and Notre Dame No. 2. However, the postseason poll did not supersede the final regular-season poll of December 9, 1947. †Miami (Fla.) and Washington actually tied for first place in The Associated Press poll for the first time in 51 years, but Miami (Fla.) had one more first-place vote, 31-30, than Washington.

1999 Associated Press Week-By-Week Polls

Preseason 8/15	A30	S6	S13	S20	S27	O4	O11	O18	O25	N1	N8	N15	N22	N29	D6	J5
1. Florida St.	1	1	1	1	1	1	1	1	1	1	1	1	1	1	1	1
2. Tennessee	3	3	2	7	7	6	6	5	4	4	3	7	6	6	6	9
3. Penn St.	2	2	3	2	2	2	2	2	2	2	6	13	15	14	13	11
4. Arizona	15	19	19	NR	NR	NR	NR	NR	NR	NR	NR	NR	NR	NR	NR	NR
5. Florida	4	4	4t	3	3	8	7	6	5	5	4	3	5	5	10	12
6. Nebraska	5	5	4t	6	6	4	3	3	8T	9	7	4	3	3	3	3
7. Texas A&M	6	7	7	5	5	13	13	13	22	21	NR	24	24	18	18	23
8. Michigan	7	6	6	4	4	3	10	9	15	16	16	10	10	9	8	5
9. Ohio St.	13	13	13	12	12	21	18	22	21	20	25	NR	NR	NR	NR	NR
10. Wisconsin	9	9	9	20	NR	20	17	17	11	10	9	5	4	4	4	4
11. Georgia Tech	10	10	12	10	9	7	8	8	7	7	13	14	20	17	17	20
12. Miami (Fla.)	8	8	8	9	18	19	24	23	23	22	19	NR	NR	23	23	15
13. Virginia Tech	11	11	10	8	8	5	4	4	3	3	2	2	2	2	2	2
14. Georgia	12	12	11	11	10	10	14	14	10	14	14	21	16	21	21	16
15. Colorado	14	NR	NR	NR	NR	NR	NR	NR	NR	NR	NR	NR	NR	NR	NR	NR
16. UCLA	17	14	21	18	NR	NR	NR	NR	NR	NR	NR	NR	NR	NR	NR	NR
17. Texas	NR	NR	NR	22	15	23	19	18	12	11	10	6	7	12	14	21
18. Notre Dame	16	16	24	NR	NR	NR	NR	NR	NR	24	NR	NR	NR	NR	NR	NR
19. Southern California	21	18	17	16	NR	22	NR	NR	NR	NR	NR	NR	NR	NR	NR	NR
20T. Alabama	20	21	18	NR	21	12	11	10	14	12	11	8	8	7	5	8
20T. Kansas St.	19	17	16	15	13	9	9	7	6	6	5	9	9	8	7	6
22. Arkansas	18	15	15	14	20	NR	NR	NR	NR	NR	NR	22	17	24	24	17
23. Purdue	22	20	14	13	11	17	20	16	18	17	22	19T	19	19	19	25
24. Virginia	23	22	NR	NR	24	NR	NR	NR	NR	NR	NR	NR	NR	NR	NR	NR
25. Arizona St.	25	25	22	NR	NR	NR	NR	NR	NR	NR	NR	NR	NR	NR	NR	NR
NR North Carolina St.	24	23	20	25	NR	NR	NR	NR	NR	NR	NR	NR	NR	NR	NR	NR
NR Colorado St.	NR	24	23	NR	NR	NR	NR	NR	NR	NR	NR	NR	NR	NR	NR	NR
NR Brigham Young	NR	NR	25	17	NR	24	21	19	16	15	15	19T	NR	NR	NR	NR
NR Michigan St.	NR	NR	NR	19	14	11	5	11	19	19	17	15	11	10	9	7
NR Marshall	NR	NR	NR	21	17	15	15	15	13	13	12	11	12	11	11	10
NR Mississippi St.	NR	NR	NR	23	16	14	12	12	8T	8	8	12	18	16	15	13
NR Air Force	NR	NR	NR	24	NR	NR	NR	NR	NR	NR	NR	NR	NR	NR	NR	NR
NR East Caro.	NR	NR	NR	NR	19	16	23	20	17	18	24	23	21	20	20	NR
NR Syracuse	NR	NR	NR	NR	22	18	16	24	NR	NR	NR	NR	NR	NR	NR	NR
NR Oklahoma	NR	NR	NR	NR	23	NR	NR	NR	24	NR	NR	NR	NR	NR	NR	NR
NR Oregon	NR	NR	NR	25	NR	NR	NR	NR	NR	NR	NR	NR	NR	NR	NR	19
NR Minnesota	NR	NR	NR	NR	25	NR	NR	NR	NR	NR	20	17	13	13	12	18
NR Mississippi	NR	NR	NR	NR	NR	22	25	25	23	18	16	23	NR	NR	NR	22
NR Southern Miss.	NR	NR	NR	NR	NR	25	21	20	25	21	18	14	15	16	16	14
NR Washington	NR	NR	NR	NR	NR	NR	NR	NR	NR	23	NR	NR	NR	NR	NR	NR
NR Boston College	NR	NR	NR	NR	NR	NR	NR	NR	NR	NR	25	22	25	25	25	NR
NR Louisiana Tech	NR	NR	NR	NR	NR	NR	NR	NR	NR	NR	NR	NR	25	NR	NR	NR
NR Stanford	NR	NR	NR	NR	NR	NR	NR	NR	NR	NR	NR	NR	NR	22	22	NR
NR Illinois	NR	NR	NR	NR	NR	NR	NR	NR	NR	NR	NR	NR	NR	NR	NR	24

No. 1 vs. No. 2

The No. 1 and No. 2 teams in The Associated Press poll (begun in 1936) have faced each other 33 times (20 in regular-season games and 13 in bowl games). The No. 1 team has won 20, with two games ending in ties.

Date	Score	Stadium (Site)
10-9-43	No. 1 Notre Dame 35, No. 2 Michigan 12	Michigan Stadium (Ann Arbor)
11-20-43	No. 1 Notre Dame 14, No. 2 Iowa Pre-Flight 13	Notre Dame (South Bend)
12-2-44	No. 1 Army 23, No. 2 Navy 7	Municipal (Baltimore)
11-10-45	No. 1 Army 48, No. 2 Notre Dame 0	Yankee (New York)
12-1-45	No. 1 Army 32, No. 2 Navy 13	Municipal (Philadelphia)
11-9-46	No. 1 Army 0, No. 2 Notre Dame 0 (tie)	Yankee (New York)
1-1-63	No. 1 Southern California 42, No. 2 Wisconsin 37 (Rose Bowl)	Rose Bowl (Pasadena)
10-12-63	No. 2 Texas 28, No. 1 Oklahoma 7	Cotton Bowl (Dallas)
1-1-64	No. 1 Texas 28, No. 2 Navy 6 (Cotton Bowl)	Cotton Bowl (Dallas)

NO. 1 vs. NO. 2

Date	Score	Stadium (Site)
11-19-66	No. 1 Notre Dame 10, No. 2 Michigan St. 10 (tie)	Spartan (East Lansing)
9-28-68	No. 1 Purdue 37, No. 2 Notre Dame 22	Notre Dame (South Bend)
1-1-69	No. 1 Ohio St. 27, No. 2 Southern California 16 (Rose Bowl)	Rose Bowl (Pasadena)
12-6-69	No. 1 Texas 15, No. 2 Arkansas 14	Razorback (Fayetteville)
11-25-71	No. 1 Nebraska 35, No. 2 Oklahoma 31	Owen Field (Norman)
1-1-72	No. 1 Nebraska 38, No. 2 Alabama 6 (Orange Bowl)	Orange Bowl (Miami)
1-1-79	No. 2 Alabama 14, No. 1 Penn St. 7 (Sugar Bowl)	Sugar Bowl (New Orleans)
9-26-81	No. 1 Southern California 28, No. 2 Oklahoma 24	Coliseum (Los Angeles)
1-1-83	No. 2 Penn St. 27, No. 1 Georgia 23 (Sugar Bowl)	Sugar Bowl (New Orleans)
10-19-85	No. 1 Iowa 12, No. 2 Michigan 10	Kinnick (Iowa City)
9-27-86	No. 2 Miami (Fla.) 28, No. 1 Oklahoma 16	Orange Bowl (Miami)
1-2-87	No. 2 Penn St. 14, No. 1 Miami (Fla.) 10 (Fiesta Bowl)	Sun Devil (Tempe)
11-21-87	No. 2 Oklahoma 17, No. 1 Nebraska 7	Memorial (Lincoln)
1-1-88	No. 2 Miami (Fla.) 20, No. 1 Oklahoma 14 (Orange Bowl)	Orange Bowl (Miami)
11-26-88	No. 1 Notre Dame 27, No. 2 Southern California 10	Coliseum (Los Angeles)
9-16-89	No. 1 Notre Dame 24, No. 2 Michigan 19	Michigan (Ann Arbor)
11-16-91	No. 2 Miami (Fla.) 17, No. 1 Florida St. 16	Doak Campbell (Tallahassee)
1-1-93	No. 2 Alabama 34, No. 1 Miami (Fla.) 13 (Sugar Bowl)	Superdome (New Orleans)
11-13-93	No. 2 Notre Dame 31, No. 1 Florida St. 24	Notre Dame (South Bend)
1-1-94	No. 1 Florida St. 18, No. 2 Nebraska 16 (Orange Bowl)	Orange Bowl (Miami)
1-2-96	No. 1 Nebraska 62, No. 2 Florida 24 (Fiesta Bowl)	Sun Devil (Tempe)
11-30-96	No. 2 Florida St. 24, No. 1 Florida 21	Doak Campbell (Tallahassee)
1-4-99	No. 1 Tennessee 23, No. 2 Florida St. 16 (Fiesta Bowl)	Sun Devil (Tempe)
1-4-00	No. 1 Florida St. 46, No. 2 Virginia Tech 29	Superdome (New Orleans)

Games in Which a No. 1-Ranked Team Was Defeated or Tied

Listed here are 112 games in which the No. 1-ranked team in The Associated Press poll was defeated or tied. An asterisk (*) indicates the home team, an (N) a neutral site. In parentheses after the winning or tying team is its rank in the previous week's poll (NR indicates it was not ranked), its won-lost record entering the game and its score. The defeated or tied No. 1-ranked team follows with its score, and in parentheses is its rank in the poll the following week. Before 1965, the polls were final before bowl games. (Note: Only 10 teams were ranked in the weekly polls during 1962, 1963, 1964, 1965, 1966 and 1967; 20 teams all other seasons until 1989, when 25 teams were ranked.)

Date	Game
10-31-36	*Northwestern (3, 4-0-0) 6, Minnesota 0 (2)
11-21-36	*Notre Dame (11, 5-2-0) 26, Northwestern 6 (7)
10-30-37	(Tie) Washington (NR, 3-2-1) 0, *California 0 (2)
10-29-38	Carnegie Mellon (T19, 4-1-0) 20, *Pittsburgh 10 (3)
12-2-38	*Southern California (8, 7-2-0) 13, Notre Dame 0 (5)
10-14-39	Duquesne (NR, 3-0-0) 21, *Pittsburgh 13 (18)
11-8-41	(Tie) Baylor (NR, 3-0-0) 7, *Texas 7 (2)
10-31-42	*Wisconsin (6, 5-0-1) 17, Ohio St. 7 (6)
11-21-42	(N) Auburn (NR, 4-4-1) 27, Georgia 13 (5)
11-28-42	Holy Cross (NR, 4-4-1) 55, *Boston College 12 (8)
11-27-43	*Great Lakes NTS (NR, 9-2-0) 19, Notre Dame 14 (1)
11-9-46	(Tie) (N) Notre Dame (2, 5-0-0) 0, Army 0 (1)
10-8-49	Army (7, 2-0-0) 21, *Michigan 7 (7)
10-7-50	Purdue (NR, 0-1-0) 28, *Notre Dame 14 (10)
11-4-50	*Texas (7, 4-1-0) 23, Southern Methodist 20 (7)
11-18-50	*Illinois (10, 6-1-0) 14, Ohio St. 7 (8)
1-1-51	(Sugar Bowl) Kentucky (7, 10-1-0) 13, Oklahoma 7 (1)
10-20-51	Southern California (11, 4-1-0) 21, *California 14 (9)
1-1-52	(Sugar Bowl) Maryland (3, 9-0-0) 28, Tennessee 13 (1)
10-11-52	*Ohio St. (NR, 1-1-0) 23, Wisconsin 14 (12)
11-21-53	(Tie) Iowa (20, 5-3-0) 14, *Notre Dame 14 (2)
1-1-54	(Orange Bowl) Oklahoma (4, 8-1-1) 7, Maryland 0 (1)
10-2-54	Purdue (19, 1-0-0) 27, *Notre Dame 14 (8)
9-24-55	*Maryland (5, 1-0-0) 7, UCLA 0 (7)
10-27-56	*Illinois (NR, 1-3-0) 20, Michigan St. 13 (4)
10-19-57	Purdue (NR, 0-3-0) 20, *Michigan St. 13 (8)
11-16-57	*Rice (20, 4-3-0) 7, Texas A&M 6 (4)
10-25-58	(Tie) *Pittsburgh (NR, 4-1-0) 14, Army 14 (3)
11-7-59	*Tennessee (13, 4-1-1) 14, LSU 13 (3)
11-5-60	*Minnesota (3, 6-0-0) 27, Iowa 10 (5)
11-12-60	Purdue (NR, 2-4-1) 23, *Minnesota 14 (4)
11-19-60	Kansas (NR, 6-2-1) 23, *Missouri 7 (5)
1-1-61	(Rose Bowl) Washington (6, 9-1-0) 17, Minnesota 7 (1)
11-4-61	*Minnesota (NR, 4-1-0) 13, Michigan St. 0 (6)
11-18-61	TCU (NR, 2-4-1) 6, *Texas 0 (5)
10-6-62	*UCLA (NR, 0-0-0) 9, Ohio St. 7 (10)
10-27-62	(Tie) *Rice (NR, 0-3-1) 14, Texas 14 (5)
11-10-62	*Wisconsin (8, 5-1-0) 37, Northwestern 6 (9)
11-17-62	*Georgia Tech (NR, 5-2-1) 7, Alabama 6 (6)
9-28-63	Oklahoma (3, 1-0-0) 17, *Southern California 12 (8)
10-12-63	(N) Texas (2, 3-0-0) 28, Oklahoma 7 (6)
10-17-64	Arkansas (8, 4-0-0) 14, *Texas 13 (6)
11-28-64	*Southern California (NR, 6-3-0) 20, Notre Dame 17 (3)
1-1-65	(Orange Bowl) Texas (5, 9-1-0) 21, Alabama 17 (1)
9-25-65	*Purdue (6, 1-0-0) 25, Notre Dame 21 (8)
10-16-65	*Arkansas (3, 4-0-0) 27, Texas 24 (5)
1-1-66	(Rose Bowl) UCLA (5, 7-2-1) 14, Michigan St. 12 (2)
11-19-66	(Tie) *Michigan St. (2, 9-0-0) 10, Notre Dame 10 (1)
9-30-67	*Purdue (10, 1-0-0) 28, Notre Dame 21 (6)
11-11-67	*Oregon St. (NR, 5-2-1) 3, Southern California 0 (4)
11-18-67	*Southern California (4, 8-1-0) 21, UCLA 20 (4)
10-12-68	*Ohio St. (4, 2-0-0) 13, Purdue 0 (5)
11-22-69	*Michigan (12, 7-2-0) 24, Ohio St. 12 (4)
1-1-71	(Cotton Bowl) Notre Dame (6, 8-1-1) 24, Texas 11 (3)
9-29-73	(Tie) Oklahoma (8, 1-0-0) 7, *Southern California 7 (4)
11-24-73	(Tie) *Michigan (4, 10-0-0) 10, Ohio St. 10 (3)
12-31-73	(Sugar Bowl) Notre Dame (3, 10-0-0) 24, Alabama 23 (4)
11-9-74	*Michigan St. (NR, 4-3-1) 16, Ohio St. 13 (4)
1-1-76	(Rose Bowl) UCLA (11, 8-2-1) 23, Ohio St. 10 (4)
11-6-76	*Purdue (NR, 3-5-0) 16, Michigan 14 (4)
10-8-77	Alabama (T7, 3-1-0) 21, *Southern California 20 (6)
10-22-77	*Minnesota (NR, 4-2-0) 16, Michigan 0 (6)
1-2-78	(Cotton Bowl) Notre Dame (5, 10-1-0) 38, Texas 10 (4)
9-23-78	(N) Southern California (7, 2-0-0) 24, Alabama 14 (3)
11-11-78	*Nebraska (4, 8-1-0) 17, Oklahoma 14 (2)
1-1-79	(Sugar Bowl) Alabama (2, 10-1-0) 14, Penn St. 7 (4)
10-13-79	(Tie) Stanford (NR, 3-2-0) 21, *Southern California 21 (4)
1-1-80	(Rose Bowl) Southern California (3, 10-0-1) 17, Ohio St. 16 (4)
11-1-80	(N) Mississippi St. (NR, 6-2-0) 6, Alabama 3 (6)
11-8-80	(Tie) *Georgia Tech (NR, 1-7-0) 3, Notre Dame 3 (6)
9-12-81	*Wisconsin (NR, 0-0-0) 21, Michigan 14 (11)
9-19-81	*Michigan (11, 0-1-0) 25, Notre Dame 7 (13)
10-10-81	Arizona (NR, 2-2-0) 13, *Southern California 10 (7)
10-17-81	Arkansas (NR, 4-1-0) 42, Texas 11 (10)
10-31-81	*Miami (Fla.) (NR, 4-2-0) 17, Penn St. 14 (5)
11-28-81	Penn St. (11, 8-2-0) 48, *Pittsburgh 14 (10)
11-6-82	Notre Dame (NR, 5-1-1) 31, *Pittsburgh 16 (8)
1-1-83	(Sugar Bowl) Penn St. (2, 10-1-0) 27, Georgia 23 (4)
1-2-84	(Orange Bowl) Miami (Fla.) (5, 10-1-0) 31, Nebraska 30 (4)
9-8-84	*Michigan (14, 0-0-0) 22, Miami (Fla.) 14 (5)
9-29-84	*Syracuse (NR, 2-1-0) 17, Nebraska 9 (8)
10-13-84	(N) (Tie) Oklahoma (3, 4-0-0) 15, Texas 15 (3)
11-10-84	*Southern California (12, 7-1-0) 16, Washington 7 (5)
11-17-84	Oklahoma (6, 7-1-0) 17, *Nebraska 7 (7)
9-28-85	*Tennessee (NR, 0-0-1) 38, Auburn 20 (14)
11-2-85	*Ohio St. (7, 6-1-0) 22, Iowa 13 (6)
11-9-85	(N) Georgia (17, 6-1-1) 24, Florida 3 (11)
1-1-86	(Orange Bowl) Oklahoma (4, 9-1-0) 25, Penn St. 10 (3)
9-27-86	*Miami (Fla.) (2, 3-0-0) 28, Oklahoma 16 (6)
1-2-87	(Fiesta Bowl) Penn St. (2, 11-0-0) 14, Miami (Fla.) 10 (2)
11-21-87	Oklahoma (2, 11-0-0) 17, *Nebraska 7 (5)
1-1-88	(Orange Bowl) Miami (Fla.) (2, 11-1-0) 20, Oklahoma 14 (3)
10-15-88	*Notre Dame (4, 5-0-0) 31, Miami (Fla.) 30 (4)
10-29-88	Washington St. (NR, 4-3-0) 34, *UCLA 30 (4)
11-25-89	*Miami (Fla.) (7, 9-1-0) 27, Notre Dame 10 (5)
1-1-90	(Orange Bowl) Notre Dame (4, 11-1-0) 21, Colorado 6 (4)
9-8-90	*Brigham Young (16, 1-0-0) 28, Miami (Fla.) 21 (10)
10-6-90	Stanford (NR, 1-3-0) 36, *Notre Dame 31 (8)
10-13-90	Michigan St. (NR, 1-2-1) 28, *Michigan 27 (10)

DIVISION I-A

74 GAMES IN WHICH NO. 1 RANKED TEAM WAS DEFEATED OR TIED

Date	Game
11-3-90	Georgia Tech (16, 6-0-1) 41, *Virginia 38 (11)
11-17-90	Penn St. (18, 7-2-0) 24, *Notre Dame 21 (7)
11-16-91	Miami (Fla.) (2, 8-0-0) 17, *Florida St. 16 (3)
11-7-92	*Arizona (12, 5-2-1) 16, Washington 3 (6)
1-1-93	(Sugar Bowl) Alabama (2, 12-0) 34, Miami (Fla.) 13 (3)
11-13-93	*Notre Dame (2, 9-0-0) 31, Florida St. 24 (2)
11-20-93	Boston College (17, 7-2-0) 41, *Notre Dame 39 (4)
10-15-94	Auburn (6, 6-0-0) 36, *Florida 33 (5)
9-21-96	*Arizona St. (17, 2-0-0) 19, Nebraska 0 (8)
11-30-96	*Florida St. (2, 10-0-0) 24, Florida 21 (4)
1-2-97	(Sugar Bowl) Florida (3, 11-1-0) 52, Florida St. 20 (3)
10-11-97	LSU (14, 4-1-0) 28, Florida 21 (7)
11-7-98	Michigan St. (NR, 4-4) 28, *Ohio St. 24 (7)

Associated Press Preseason No. 1 Teams

(The No. 1-ranked team in the annual Associated Press preseason college football poll. The preseason poll started in 1950.)

Year	Team+
1950	Notre Dame
1951	Tennessee+
1952	Michigan St.+
1953	Notre Dame
1954	Notre Dame
1955	UCLA
1956	Oklahoma+
1957	Oklahoma
1958	Ohio St.
1959	LSU
1960	Syracuse
1961	Iowa
1962	Ohio St.
1963	Southern California
1964	Mississippi
1965	Nebraska
1966	Alabama
1967	Notre Dame
1968	Purdue
1969	Ohio St.
1970	Ohio St.
1971	Notre Dame
1972	Nebraska
1973	Southern California
1974	Oklahoma+
1975	Oklahoma+
1976	Nebraska
1977	Oklahoma
1978	Alabama+
1979	Southern California
1980	Ohio St.
1981	Michigan
1982	Pittsburgh
1983	Nebraska
1984	Auburn
1985	Oklahoma+
1986	Oklahoma
1987	Oklahoma
1988	Florida St.
1989	Michigan
1990	Miami (Fla.)
1991	Florida St.
1992	Miami (Fla.)
1993	Florida St.+
1994	Florida
1995	Florida St.
1996	Nebraska
1997	Penn St.
1998	Ohio St.
1999	Florida St.+

+Indicated eventual national champion.

Associated Press (Writers and Broadcasters) Final Polls

1936
Team
1. Minnesota
2. LSU
3. Pittsburgh
4. Alabama
5. Washington
6. Santa Clara
7. Northwestern
8. Notre Dame
9. Nebraska
10. Pennsylvania
11. Duke
12. Yale
13. Dartmouth
14. Duquesne
15. Fordham
16. TCU
17. Tennessee
18. Arkansas
    Navy
20. Marquette

1937
Team
1. Pittsburgh
2. California
3. Fordham
4. Alabama
5. Minnesota
6. Villanova
7. Dartmouth
8. LSU
9. Notre Dame
    Santa Clara
11. Nebraska
12. Yale
13. Ohio St.
14. Holy Cross
    Arkansas
16. TCU
17. Colorado
18. Rice
19. North Carolina
20. Duke

1938
Team
1. TCU
2. Tennessee
3. Duke
4. Oklahoma
5. Notre Dame
6. Carnegie Mellon
7. Southern California
8. Pittsburgh
9. Holy Cross
10. Minnesota
11. Texas Tech
12. Cornell
13. Alabama
14. California
15. Fordham
16. Michigan
17. Northwestern
18. Villanova
19. Tulane
20. Dartmouth

1939
Team
1. Texas A&M
2. Tennessee
3. Southern California
4. Cornell
5. Tulane
6. Missouri
7. UCLA
8. Duke
9. Iowa
10. Duquesne
11. Boston College
12. Clemson
13. Notre Dame
14. Santa Clara
15. Ohio St.
16. Georgia Tech
17. Fordham
18. Nebraska
19. Oklahoma
20. Michigan

1940
Team
1. Minnesota
2. Stanford
3. Michigan
4. Tennessee
5. Boston College
6. Texas A&M
7. Nebraska
8. Northwestern
9. Mississippi St.
10. Washington
11. Santa Clara
12. Fordham
13. Georgetown
14. Pennsylvania
15. Cornell
16. Southern Methodist
17. Hardin-Simmons
18. Duke
19. Lafayette

1941
Team
1. Minnesota
2. Duke
3. Notre Dame
4. Texas
5. Michigan
6. Fordham
7. Missouri
8. Duquesne
9. Texas A&M
10. Navy
11. Northwestern
12. Oregon St.
13. Ohio St.
14. Georgia
15. Pennsylvania
16. Mississippi St.
17. Mississippi
18. Tennessee
19. Washington St.
20. Alabama

1942
Team
1. Ohio St.
2. Georgia
3. Wisconsin
4. Tulsa
5. Georgia Tech
6. Notre Dame
7. Tennessee
8. Boston College
9. Michigan
10. Alabama
11. Texas
12. Stanford
13. UCLA
14. William & Mary
15. Santa Clara
16. Auburn
17. Washington St.
18. Mississippi St.
19. Minnesota
    Holy Cross
    Penn St.

1943
Team
1. Notre Dame
2. Iowa Pre-Flight
3. Michigan
4. Navy
5. Purdue
6. Great Lakes
7. Duke
8. Del Monte P-F
9. Northwestern
10. March Field
11. Army
12. Washington
13. Georgia Tech
14. Texas
15. Tulsa
16. Dartmouth
17. Bainbridge NTS
18. Colorado Col.
19. Pacific (Cal.)
20. Pennsylvania

1944
Team
1. Army
2. Ohio St.
3. Randolph Field
4. Navy
5. Bainbridge NTS
6. Iowa Pre-Flight
7. Southern California
8. Michigan
9. Notre Dame
10. March Field
11. Duke
12. Tennessee
13. Georgia Tech
    Norman Pre-Flight
15. Illinois
16. El Toro Marines
17. Great Lakes
18. Fort Pierce
19. St. Mary's Pre-Flight
20. Second Air Force

1945
Team
1. Army
2. Alabama
3. Navy
4. Indiana
5. Oklahoma St.
6. Michigan
7. St. Mary's (Cal.)
8. Pennsylvania
9. Notre Dame
10. Texas
11. Southern California
12. Ohio St.
13. Duke
14. Tennessee
15. LSU
16. Holy Cross
17. Tulsa
18. Georgia
19. Wake Forest
20. Columbia

1946
Team
1. Notre Dame
2. Army
3. Georgia
4. UCLA
5. Illinois
6. Michigan
7. Tennessee
8. LSU
9. North Carolina
10. Rice
11. Georgia Tech
12. Yale
13. Pennsylvania
14. Oklahoma
15. Texas
16. Arkansas
17. Tulsa
18. North Carolina St.
19. Delaware
20. Indiana

*1947
Team
1. Notre Dame
2. Michigan
3. Southern Methodist
4. Penn St.
5. Texas
6. Alabama
7. Pennsylvania
8. Southern California
9. North Carolina
10. Georgia Tech
11. Army
12. Kansas
13. Mississippi
14. William & Mary
15. California
16. Oklahoma
17. North Carolina St.
18. Rice
19. Duke
20. Columbia

DIVISION I-A — ASSOCIATED PRESS FINAL POLLS

1948
Team
1. Michigan
2. Notre Dame
3. North Carolina
4. California
5. Oklahoma
6. Army
7. Northwestern
8. Georgia
9. Oregon
10. Southern Methodist
11. Clemson
12. Vanderbilt
13. Tulane
14. Michigan St.
15. Mississippi
16. Minnesota
17. William & Mary
18. Penn St.
19. Cornell
20. Wake Forest

1949
Team
1. Notre Dame
2. Oklahoma
3. California
4. Army
5. Rice
6. Ohio St.
7. Michigan
8. Minnesota
9. LSU
10. Pacific (Cal.)
11. Kentucky
12. Cornell
13. Villanova
14. Maryland
15. Santa Clara
16. North Carolina
17. Tennessee
18. Princeton
19. Michigan St.
20. Missouri
    Baylor

1950
Team
1. Oklahoma
2. Army
3. Texas
4. Tennessee
5. California
6. Princeton
7. Kentucky
8. Michigan St.
9. Michigan
10. Clemson
11. Washington
12. Wyoming
13. Illinois
14. Ohio St.
15. Miami (Fla.)
16. Alabama
17. Nebraska
18. Wash. & Lee
19. Tulsa
20. Tulane

1951
Team
1. Tennessee
2. Michigan St.
3. Maryland
4. Illinois
5. Georgia Tech
6. Princeton
7. Stanford
8. Wisconsin
9. Baylor
10. Oklahoma
11. TCU
12. California
13. Virginia
14. San Francisco
15. Kentucky
16. Boston U.
17. UCLA
18. Washington St.
19. Holy Cross
20. Clemson

1952
Team
1. Michigan St.
2. Georgia Tech
3. Notre Dame
4. Oklahoma
5. Southern California
6. UCLA
7. Mississippi
8. Tennessee
9. Alabama
10. Texas
11. Wisconsin
12. Tulsa
13. Maryland
14. Syracuse
15. Florida
16. Duke
17. Ohio St.
18. Purdue
19. Princeton
20. Kentucky

1953
Team
1. Maryland
2. Notre Dame
3. Michigan St.
4. Oklahoma
5. UCLA
6. Rice
7. Illinois
8. Georgia Tech
9. Iowa
10. West Virginia
11. Texas
12. Texas Tech
13. Alabama
14. Army
15. Wisconsin
16. Kentucky
17. Auburn
18. Duke
19. Stanford
20. Michigan

1954
Team
1. Ohio St.
2. UCLA
3. Oklahoma
4. Notre Dame
5. Navy
6. Mississippi
7. Army
8. Maryland
9. Wisconsin
10. Arkansas
11. Miami (Fla.)
12. West Virginia
13. Auburn
14. Duke
15. Michigan
16. Virginia Tech
17. Southern California
18. Baylor
19. Rice
20. Penn St.

1955
Team
1. Oklahoma
2. Michigan St.
3. Maryland
4. UCLA
5. Ohio St.
6. TCU
7. Georgia Tech
8. Auburn
9. Notre Dame
10. Mississippi
11. Pittsburgh
12. Michigan
13. Southern California
14. Miami (Fla.)
15. Miami (Ohio)
16. Stanford
17. Texas A&M
18. Navy
19. West Virginia
20. Army

1956
Team
1. Oklahoma
2. Tennessee
3. Iowa
4. Georgia Tech
5. Texas A&M
6. Miami (Fla.)
7. Michigan
8. Syracuse
9. Michigan St.
10. Oregon St.
11. Baylor
12. Minnesota
13. Pittsburgh
14. TCU
15. Ohio St.
16. Navy
17. George Washington
18. Southern California
19. Clemson
20. Colorado

1957
Team
1. Auburn
2. Ohio St.
3. Michigan St.
4. Oklahoma
5. Navy
6. Iowa
7. Mississippi
8. Rice
9. Texas A&M
10. Notre Dame
11. Texas
12. Arizona St.
13. Tennessee
14. Mississippi St.
15. North Carolina St.
16. Duke
17. Florida
18. Army
19. Wisconsin
20. VMI

1958
Team
1. LSU
2. Iowa
3. Army
4. Auburn
5. Oklahoma
6. Air Force
7. Wisconsin
8. Ohio St.
9. Syracuse
10. TCU
11. Mississippi
12. Clemson
13. Purdue
14. Florida
15. South Carolina
16. California
17. Notre Dame
18. Southern Methodist
19. Oklahoma St.
20. Rutgers

1959
Team
1. Syracuse
2. Mississippi
3. LSU
4. Texas
5. Georgia
6. Wisconsin
7. TCU
8. Washington
9. Arkansas
10. Alabama
11. Clemson
12. Penn St.
13. Illinois
14. Southern California
15. Oklahoma
16. Wyoming
17. Notre Dame
18. Missouri
19. Florida
20. Pittsburgh

1960
Team
1. Minnesota
2. Mississippi
3. Iowa
4. Navy
5. Missouri
6. Washington
7. Arkansas
8. Ohio St.
9. Alabama
10. Duke
11. Kansas
12. Baylor
13. Auburn
14. Yale
15. Michigan St.
16. Penn St.
17. New Mexico St.
18. Florida
19. Syracuse
    Purdue

1961
Team
1. Alabama
2. Ohio St.
3. Texas
4. LSU
5. Mississippi
6. Minnesota
7. Colorado
8. Michigan St.
9. Arkansas
10. Utah St.
11. Missouri
12. Purdue
13. Georgia Tech
14. Syracuse
15. Rutgers
16. UCLA
17. Rice
    Penn St.
    Arizona
20. Duke

1962
Team
1. Southern California
2. Wisconsin
3. Mississippi
4. Texas
5. Alabama
6. Arkansas
7. LSU
8. Oklahoma
9. Penn St.
10. Minnesota
Only 10 ranked

1963
Team
1. Texas
2. Navy
3. Illinois
4. Pittsburgh
5. Auburn
6. Nebraska
7. Mississippi
8. Alabama
9. Oklahoma
10. Michigan St.
Only 10 ranked

1964
Team
1. Alabama
2. Arkansas
3. Notre Dame
4. Michigan
5. Texas
6. Nebraska
7. LSU
8. Oregon St.
9. Ohio St.
10. Southern California
Only 10 ranked

1965
Team
1. Alabama
2. Michigan St.
3. Arkansas
4. UCLA
5. Nebraska
6. Missouri
7. Tennessee
8. LSU
9. Notre Dame
10. Southern California
Only 10 ranked

1966
Team
1. Notre Dame
2. Michigan St.
3. Alabama
4. Georgia
5. UCLA
6. Nebraska
7. Purdue
8. Georgia Tech
9. Miami (Fla.)
10. Southern Methodist

Only 10 ranked

1967
Team
1. Southern California
2. Tennessee
3. Oklahoma
4. Indiana
5. Notre Dame
6. Wyoming
7. Oregon St.
8. Alabama
9. Purdue
10. Penn St.

Only 10 ranked

1968
Team
1. Ohio St.
2. Penn St.
3. Texas
4. Southern California
5. Notre Dame
6. Arkansas
7. Kansas
8. Georgia
9. Missouri
10. Purdue
11. Oklahoma
12. Michigan
13. Tennessee
14. Southern Methodist
15. Oregon St.
16. Auburn
17. Alabama
18. Houston
19. LSU
20. Ohio

1969
Team
1. Texas
2. Penn St.
3. Southern California
4. Ohio St.
5. Notre Dame
6. Missouri
7. Arkansas
8. Mississippi
9. Michigan
10. LSU
11. Nebraska
12. Houston
13. UCLA
14. Florida
15. Tennessee
16. Colorado
17. West Virginia
18. Purdue
19. Stanford
20. Auburn

1970
Team
1. Nebraska
2. Notre Dame
3. Texas
4. Tennessee
5. Ohio St.
6. Arizona St.
7. LSU
8. Stanford
9. Michigan
10. Auburn
11. Arkansas
12. Toledo
13. Georgia Tech
14. Dartmouth
15. Southern California
16. Air Force
17. Tulane
18. Penn St.
19. Houston
20. Oklahoma
    Mississippi

1971
Team
1. Nebraska
2. Oklahoma
3. Colorado
4. Alabama
5. Penn St.
6. Michigan
7. Georgia
8. Arizona St.
9. Tennessee
10. Stanford
11. LSU
12. Auburn
13. Notre Dame
14. Toledo
15. Mississippi
16. Arkansas
17. Houston
18. Texas
19. Washington
20. Southern California

1972
Team
1. Southern California
2. Oklahoma
3. Texas
4. Nebraska
5. Auburn
6. Michigan
7. Alabama
8. Tennessee
9. Ohio St.
10. Penn St.
11. LSU
12. North Carolina
13. Arizona St.
14. Notre Dame
15. UCLA
16. Colorado
17. North Carolina St.
18. Louisville
19. Washington St.
20. Georgia Tech

1973
Team
1. Notre Dame
2. Ohio St.
3. Oklahoma
4. Alabama
5. Penn St.
6. Michigan
7. Nebraska
8. Southern California
9. Arizona St.
   Houston
11. Texas Tech
12. UCLA
13. LSU
14. Texas
15. Miami (Ohio)
16. North Carolina St.
17. Missouri
18. Kansas
19. Tennessee
20. Maryland
    Tulane

1974
Team
1. Oklahoma
2. Southern California
3. Michigan
4. Ohio St.
5. Alabama
6. Notre Dame
7. Penn St.
8. Auburn
9. Nebraska
10. Miami (Ohio)
11. North Carolina St.
12. Michigan St.
13. Maryland
14. Baylor
15. Florida
16. Texas A&M
17. Mississippi St.
    Texas
19. Houston
20. Tennessee

1975
Team
1. Oklahoma
2. Arizona St.
3. Alabama
4. Ohio St.
5. UCLA
6. Texas
7. Arkansas
8. Michigan
9. Nebraska
10. Penn St.
11. Texas A&M
12. Miami (Ohio)
13. Maryland
14. California
15. Pittsburgh
16. Colorado
17. Southern California
18. Arizona
19. Georgia
20. West Virginia

1976
Team
1. Pittsburgh
2. Southern California
3. Michigan
4. Houston
5. Oklahoma
6. Ohio St.
7. Texas A&M
8. Maryland
9. Nebraska
10. Georgia
11. Alabama
12. Notre Dame
13. Texas Tech
14. Oklahoma St.
15. UCLA
16. Colorado
17. Rutgers
18. Kentucky
19. Iowa St.
20. Mississippi St.

1977
Team
1. Notre Dame
2. Alabama
3. Arkansas
4. Texas
5. Penn St.
6. Kentucky
7. Oklahoma
8. Pittsburgh
9. Michigan
10. Washington
11. Ohio St.
12. Nebraska
13. Southern California
14. Florida St.
15. Stanford
16. San Diego St.
17. North Carolina
18. Arizona St.
19. Clemson
20. Brigham Young

1978
Team
1. Alabama
2. Southern California
3. Oklahoma
4. Penn St.
5. Michigan
6. Clemson
7. Notre Dame
8. Nebraska
9. Texas
10. Houston
11. Arkansas
12. Michigan St.
13. Purdue
14. UCLA
15. Missouri
16. Georgia
17. Stanford
18. North Carolina St.
19. Texas A&M
20. Maryland

1979
Team
1. Alabama
2. Southern California
3. Oklahoma
4. Ohio St.
5. Houston
6. Florida St.
7. Pittsburgh
8. Arkansas
9. Nebraska
10. Purdue
11. Washington
12. Texas
13. Brigham Young
14. Baylor
15. North Carolina
16. Auburn
17. Temple
18. Michigan
19. Indiana
20. Penn St.

1980
Team
1. Georgia
2. Pittsburgh
3. Oklahoma
4. Michigan
5. Florida St.
6. Alabama
7. Nebraska
8. Penn St.
9. Notre Dame
10. North Carolina
11. Southern California
12. Brigham Young
13. UCLA
14. Baylor
15. Ohio St.
16. Washington
17. Purdue
18. Miami (Fla.)
19. Mississippi St.
20. Southern Methodist

1981
Team
1. Clemson
2. Texas
3. Penn St.
4. Pittsburgh
5. Southern Methodist
6. Georgia
7. Alabama
8. Miami (Fla.)
9. North Carolina
10. Washington
11. Nebraska
12. Michigan
13. Brigham Young
14. Southern California
15. Ohio St.
16. Arizona St.
17. West Virginia
18. Iowa
19. Missouri
20. Oklahoma

1982
Team
1. Penn St.
2. Southern Methodist
3. Nebraska
4. Georgia
5. UCLA
6. Arizona St.
7. Washington
8. Clemson
9. Arkansas
10. Pittsburgh
11. LSU
12. Ohio St.
13. Florida St.
14. Auburn
15. Southern California
16. Oklahoma
17. Texas
18. North Carolina
19. West Virginia
20. Maryland

1983
Team
1. Miami (Fla.)
2. Nebraska
3. Auburn
4. Georgia
5. Texas
6. Florida
7. Brigham Young
8. Michigan
9. Ohio St.
10. Illinois
11. Clemson
12. Southern Methodist
13. Air Force
14. Iowa
15. Alabama
16. West Virginia
17. UCLA
18. Pittsburgh
19. Boston College
20. East Caro.

ASSOCIATED PRESS FINAL POLLS

1984
Team
1. Brigham Young
2. Washington
3. Florida
4. Nebraska
5. Boston College
6. Oklahoma
7. Oklahoma St.
8. Southern Methodist
9. UCLA
10. Southern California
11. South Carolina
12. Maryland
13. Ohio St.
14. Auburn
15. LSU
16. Iowa
17. Florida St.
18. Miami (Fla.)
19. Kentucky
20. Virginia

1985
Team
1. Oklahoma
2. Michigan
3. Penn St.
4. Tennessee
5. Florida
6. Texas A&M
7. UCLA
8. Air Force
9. Miami (Fla.)
10. Iowa
11. Nebraska
12. Arkansas
13. Alabama
14. Ohio St.
15. Florida St.
16. Brigham Young
17. Baylor
18. Maryland
19. Georgia Tech
20. LSU

1986
Team
1. Penn St.
2. Miami (Fla.)
3. Oklahoma
4. Arizona St.
5. Nebraska
6. Auburn
7. Ohio St.
8. Michigan
9. Alabama
10. LSU
11. Arizona
12. Baylor
13. Texas A&M
14. UCLA
15. Arkansas
16. Iowa
17. Clemson
18. Washington
19. Boston College
20. Virginia Tech

1987
Team
1. Miami (Fla.)
2. Florida St.
3. Oklahoma
4. Syracuse
5. LSU
6. Nebraska
7. Auburn
8. Michigan St.
9. UCLA
10. Texas A&M
11. Oklahoma St.
12. Clemson
13. Georgia
14. Tennessee
15. South Carolina
16. Iowa
17. Notre Dame
18. Southern California
19. Michigan
20. Arizona St.

1988
Team
1. Notre Dame
2. Miami (Fla.)
3. Florida St.
4. Michigan
5. West Virginia
6. UCLA
7. Southern California
8. Auburn
9. Clemson
10. Nebraska
11. Oklahoma St.
12. Arkansas
13. Syracuse
14. Oklahoma
15. Georgia
16. Washington St.
17. Alabama
18. Houston
19. LSU
20. Indiana

†1989
Team
1. Miami (Fla.)
2. Notre Dame
3. Florida St.
4. Colorado
5. Tennessee
6. Auburn
7. Michigan
8. Southern California
9. Alabama
10. Illinois
11. Nebraska
12. Clemson
13. Arkansas
14. Houston
15. Penn St.
16. Michigan St.
17. Pittsburgh
18. Virginia
19. Texas Tech
20. Texas A&M
21. West Virginia
22. Brigham Young
23. Washington
24. Ohio St.
25. Arizona

1990
Team
1. Colorado
2. Georgia Tech
3. Miami (Fla.)
4. Florida St.
5. Washington
6. Notre Dame
7. Michigan
8. Tennessee
9. Clemson
10. Houston
11. Penn St.
12. Texas
13. Florida
14. Louisville
15. Texas A&M
16. Michigan St.
17. Oklahoma
18. Iowa
19. Auburn
20. Southern California
21. Mississippi
22. Brigham Young
23. Virginia
24. Nebraska
25. Illinois

1991
Team
1. Miami (Fla.)
2. Washington
3. Penn St.
4. Florida St.
5. Alabama
6. Michigan
7. Florida
8. California
9. East Caro.
10. Iowa
11. Syracuse
12. Texas A&M
13. Notre Dame
14. Tennessee
15. Nebraska
16. Oklahoma
17. Georgia
18. Clemson
19. UCLA
20. Colorado
21. Tulsa
22. Stanford
23. Brigham Young
24. North Carolina St.
25. Air Force

1992
Team
1. Alabama
2. Florida St.
3. Miami (Fla.)
4. Notre Dame
5. Michigan
6. Syracuse
7. Texas A&M
8. Georgia
9. Stanford
10. Florida
11. Washington
12. Tennessee
13. Colorado
14. Nebraska
15. Washington St.
16. Mississippi
17. North Carolina St.
18. Ohio St.
19. North Carolina
20. Hawaii
21. Boston College
22. Kansas
23. Mississippi St.
24. Fresno St.
25. Wake Forest

1993
Team
1. Florida St.
2. Notre Dame
3. Nebraska
4. Auburn
5. Florida
6. Wisconsin
7. West Virginia
8. Penn St.
9. Texas A&M
10. Arizona
11. Ohio St.
12. Tennessee
13. Boston College
14. Alabama
15. Miami (Fla.)
16. Colorado
17. Oklahoma
18. UCLA
19. North Carolina
20. Kansas St.
21. Michigan
22. Virginia Tech
23. Clemson
24. Louisville
25. California

1994
Team
1. Nebraska
2. Penn St.
3. Colorado
4. Florida St.
5. Alabama
6. Miami (Fla.)
7. Florida
8. Texas A&M
9. Auburn
10. Utah
11. Oregon
12. Michigan
13. Southern California
14. Ohio St.
15. Virginia
16. Colorado St.
17. North Carolina St.
18. Brigham Young
19. Kansas St.
20. Arizona
21. Washington St.
22. Tennessee
23. Boston College
24. Mississippi St.
25. Texas

1995
Team
1. Nebraska
2. Florida
3. Tennessee
4. Florida St.
5. Colorado
6. Ohio St.
7. Kansas St.
8. Northwestern
9. Kansas
10. Virginia Tech
11. Notre Dame
12. Southern California
13. Penn St.
14. Texas
15. Texas A&M
16. Virginia
17. Michigan
18. Oregon
19. Syracuse
20. Miami (Fla.)
21. Alabama
22. Auburn
23. Texas Tech
24. Toledo
25. Iowa

1996
Team
1. Florida (12-1)
2. Ohio St. (11-1)
3. Florida St. (11-1)
4. Arizona St. (11-1)
5. Brigham Young (14-1)
6. Nebraska (11-2)
7. Penn St. (11-2)
8. Colorado (10-2)
9. Tennessee (10-2)
10. North Carolina (10-2)
11. Alabama (10-3)
12. LSU (10-2)
13. Virginia Tech (10-2)
14. Miami (Fla.) (9-3)
15. Northwestern (9-3)
16. Washington (9-3)
17. Kansas St. (9-3)
18. Iowa (9-3)
19. Notre Dame (8-3)
20. Michigan (8-4)
21. Syracuse (9-3)
22. Wyoming (10-2)
23. Texas (8-5)
24. Auburn (8-4)
25. Army (10-2)

1997
Team
1. Michigan (12-0)
2. Nebraska (13-0)
3. Florida St. (11-1)
4. Florida (10-2)
5. UCLA (10-2)
6. North Carolina (11-1)
7. Tennessee (11-2)
8. Kansas St. (11-1)
9. Washington St. (10-2)
10. Georgia (10-2)
11. Auburn (10-3)
12. Ohio St. (10-3)
13. LSU (9-3)
14. Arizona St. (9-3)
15. Purdue (9-3)
16. Penn St. (9-3)
17. Colorado St. (11-2)
18. Washington (8-4)
19. Southern Miss. (9-3)
20. Texas A&M (9-4)
21. Syracuse (9-4)
22. Mississippi (8-4)
23. Missouri (7-5)
24. Oklahoma St. (8-4)
25. Georgia Tech (7-5)

1998
Team
1. Tennessee (13-0)
2. Ohio St. (11-1)
3. Florida St. (11-2)
4. Arizona (12-1)
5. Florida (10-2)
6. Wisconsin (11-1)
7. Tulane (12-0)
8. UCLA (10-2)
9. Georgia Tech (10-2)
10. Kansas St. (11-2)
11. Texas A&M (11-3)
12. Michigan (10-3)
13. Air Force (12-1)
14. Georgia (9-3)
15. Texas (9-3)
16. Arkansas (9-3)
17. Penn St. (9-3)
18. Virginia (9-3)
19. Nebraska (9-4)
20. Miami (Fla.) (9-3)
21. Missouri (8-4)
22. Notre Dame (9-3)
23. Virginia Tech (9-3)
24. Purdue (9-4)
25. Syracuse (8-4)

1999
Team
1. Florida St. (12-0)
2. Virginia Tech (11-1)
3. Nebraska (12-1)
4. Wisconsin (10-2)
5. Michigan (10-2)
6. Kansas St. (11-1)
7. Michigan St. (10-2)
8. Alabama (10-3)
9. Tennessee (9-3)
10. Marshall (13-0)
11. Penn St. (10-3)
12. Florida (9-4)
13. Mississippi St. (10-2)
14. Southern Miss. (9-3)
15. Miami (Fla.) (9-4)
16. Georgia (8-4)
17. Arkansas (8-4)
18. Minnesota (8-4)
19. Oregon (9-3)
20. Georgia Tech (8-4)
21. Texas (9-5)
22. Mississippi (8-4)
23. Texas A&M (8-4)
24. Illinois (8-4)
25. Purdue (7-5)

*On January 6, 1948, in a special postseason poll after the Rose Bowl, the Associated Press voted Michigan No. 1 and Notre Dame No. 2. However, the postseason poll did not supersede the final regular-season poll of December 6, 1947. †Beginning in 1989 season, AP selected top 25 teams instead of 20.

DIVISION I-A

United Press International Final Polls

United Press (UP), 1950-57; United Press International (UPI) from 1958-95 after merger with International News Service (INS). Served as the coaches' poll until 1991, when it was taken over by USA Today/Cable News Network (CNN)/ESPN poll.

1950
Team
1. Oklahoma
2. Texas
3. Tennessee
4. California
5. Army
6. Michigan
7. Kentucky
8. Princeton
9. Michigan St.
10. Ohio St.
11. Illinois
12. Clemson
13. Miami (Fla.)
14. Wyoming
15. Washington
    Baylor
17. Alabama
18. Wash. & Lee
19. Navy
20. Nebraska
    Wisconsin
    Cornell

1951
Team
1. Tennessee
2. Michigan St.
3. Illinois
4. Maryland
5. Georgia Tech
6. Princeton
7. Stanford
8. Wisconsin
9. Baylor
10. TCU
11. Oklahoma
12. California
13. Notre Dame
14. San Francisco
    Purdue
    Washington St.
17. Holy Cross
    UCLA
    Kentucky
20. Kansas

1952
Team
1. Michigan St.
2. Georgia Tech
3. Notre Dame
4. Oklahoma
   Southern California
6. UCLA
7. Mississippi
8. Tennessee
9. Alabama
10. Wisconsin
11. Alabama
12. Purdue
13. Maryland
14. Princeton
15. Ohio St.
    Pittsburgh
17. Navy
18. Duke
19. Houston
    Kentucky

1953
Team
1. Maryland
2. Notre Dame
3. Michigan St.
4. UCLA
5. Oklahoma
6. Rice
7. Illinois
8. Texas
9. Georgia Tech
10. Iowa
11. Alabama
12. Texas Tech
13. West Virginia
14. Wisconsin
15. Kentucky
16. Army
17. Stanford
18. Duke
19. Michigan
20. Ohio St.

1954
Team
1. UCLA
2. Ohio St.
3. Oklahoma
4. Notre Dame
5. Navy
6. Mississippi
7. Army
8. Arkansas
9. Miami (Fla.)
10. Wisconsin
11. Southern California
    Maryland
    Georgia Tech
14. Duke
15. Michigan
16. Penn St.
17. Southern Methodist
18. Denver
19. Rice
20. Minnesota

1955
Team
1. Oklahoma
2. Michigan St.
3. Maryland
4. UCLA
5. Ohio St.
6. TCU
7. Georgia Tech
8. Auburn
9. Mississippi
10. Notre Dame
11. Pittsburgh
12. Southern California
13. Michigan
14. Texas A&M
15. Army
16. Duke
17. West Virginia
18. Miami (Fla.)
19. Iowa
20. Navy
    Stanford
    Miami (Ohio)

1956
Team
1. Oklahoma
2. Tennessee
3. Iowa
4. Georgia Tech
5. Texas A&M
6. Miami (Fla.)
7. Michigan
8. Syracuse
9. Minnesota
10. Michigan St.
11. Baylor
12. Pittsburgh
13. Oregon St.
14. TCU
15. Southern California
16. Wyoming
17. Yale
18. Colorado
19. Navy
20. Duke

1957
Team
1. Ohio St.
2. Auburn
3. Michigan St.
4. Oklahoma
5. Iowa
6. Navy
7. Rice
8. Mississippi
9. Notre Dame
10. Texas A&M
11. Texas
12. Arizona St.
13. Army
14. Duke
    Wisconsin
16. Tennessee
17. Oregon
18. Clemson
    UCLA
20. North Carolina St.

1958
Team
1. LSU
2. Iowa
3. Army
4. Auburn
5. Oklahoma
6. Wisconsin
7. Ohio St.
8. Air Force
9. TCU
10. Syracuse
11. Purdue
12. Mississippi
13. Clemson
14. Notre Dame
15. Florida
16. California
17. Northwestern
18. Southern Methodist
(Only 18 teams received votes)

1959
Team
1. Syracuse
2. Mississippi
3. LSU
4. Texas
5. Georgia
6. Wisconsin
7. Washington
8. TCU
9. Arkansas
10. Penn St.
11. Clemson
12. Illinois
13. Alabama
    Southern California
15. Auburn
16. Michigan St.
17. Oklahoma
18. Notre Dame
19. Pittsburgh
    Missouri
    Florida

1960
Team
1. Minnesota
2. Iowa
3. Mississippi
4. Missouri
5. Wisconsin
6. Navy
7. Arkansas
8. Ohio St.
9. Kansas
10. Alabama
11. Duke
    Baylor
    Michigan St.
14. Auburn
15. Purdue
16. Florida
17. Texas
18. Yale
19. New Mexico St.
    Tennessee

1961
Team
1. Alabama
2. Ohio St.
3. LSU
4. Texas
5. Mississippi
6. Minnesota
7. Colorado
8. Arkansas
9. Michigan St.
10. Utah St.
11. Purdue
    Missouri
13. Georgia Tech
14. Duke
15. Kansas
16. Syracuse
17. Wyoming
18. Wisconsin
19. Miami (Fla.)
    Penn St.

1962
Team
1. Southern California
2. Wisconsin
3. Mississippi
4. Texas
5. Alabama
6. Arkansas
7. Oklahoma
8. LSU
9. Penn St.
10. Minnesota
11. Georgia Tech
12. Missouri
13. Ohio St.
14. Duke
    Washington
16. Northwestern
    Oregon St.
18. Arizona St.
    Illinois
    Miami (Fla.)

1963
Team
1. Texas
2. Navy
3. Pittsburgh
4. Illinois
5. Nebraska
6. Auburn
7. Mississippi
8. Oklahoma
9. Alabama
10. Michigan St.
11. Mississippi St.
12. Syracuse
13. Arizona St.
14. Memphis
15. Washington
16. Penn St.
    Southern California
    Missouri
19. North Carolina
20. Baylor

1964
Team
1. Alabama
2. Arkansas
3. Notre Dame
4. Michigan
5. Texas
6. Nebraska
7. LSU
8. Oregon St.
9. Ohio St.
10. Southern California
11. Florida St.
12. Syracuse
13. Princeton
14. Penn St.
    Utah
16. Illinois
    New Mexico
18. Tulsa
    Missouri
20. Mississippi
    Michigan St.

1965
Team
1. Michigan St.
2. Arkansas
3. Nebraska
4. Alabama
5. UCLA
6. Missouri
7. Tennessee
8. Notre Dame
9. Southern California
10. Texas Tech
11. Ohio St.
12. Florida
13. Purdue
14. LSU
15. Georgia
16. Tulsa
17. Mississippi
18. Kentucky
19. Syracuse
20. Colorado

1966
Team
1. Notre Dame
2. Michigan St.
3. Alabama
4. Georgia
5. UCLA
6. Purdue
7. Nebraska
8. Georgia Tech
9. Southern Methodist
10. Miami (Fla.)
11. Florida
12. Mississippi
13. Arkansas
14. Tennessee
15. Wyoming
16. Syracuse
17. Houston
18. Southern California
19. Oregon St.
20. Virginia Tech

1967
Team
1. Southern California
2. Tennessee
3. Oklahoma
4. Notre Dame
5. Wyoming
6. Indiana
7. Alabama
8. Oregon St.
9. Purdue
10. UCLA
11. Penn St.
12. Syracuse
13. Colorado
14. Minnesota
15. Florida St.
16. Miami (Fla.)
17. North Carolina St.
18. Georgia
19. Houston
20. Arizona St.

UNITED PRESS INTERNATIONAL FINAL POLLS

1968
Team
1. Ohio St.
2. Southern California
3. Penn St.
4. Georgia
5. Texas
6. Kansas
7. Tennessee
8. Notre Dame
9. Arkansas
10. Oklahoma
11. Purdue
12. Alabama
13. Oregon St.
14. Florida St.
15. Michigan
16. Southern Methodist
17. Missouri
18. Ohio
    Minnesota
20. Houston
    Stanford

1969
Team
1. Texas
2. Penn St.
3. Arkansas
4. Southern California
5. Ohio St.
6. Missouri
7. LSU
8. Michigan
9. Notre Dame
10. UCLA
11. Tennessee
12. Nebraska
13. Mississippi
14. Stanford
15. Auburn
16. Houston
17. Florida
18. Purdue
    San Diego St.
    West Virginia

1970
Team
1. Texas
2. Ohio St.
3. Nebraska
4. Tennessee
5. Notre Dame
6. LSU
7. Michigan
8. Arizona St.
9. Auburn
10. Stanford
11. Air Force
12. Arkansas
13. Houston
    Dartmouth
15. Oklahoma
16. Colorado
17. Georgia Tech
    Toledo
19. Penn St.
    Southern California

1971
Team
1. Nebraska
2. Alabama
3. Oklahoma
4. Michigan
5. Auburn
6. Arizona St.
7. Colorado
8. Georgia
9. Tennessee
10. LSU
11. Penn St.
12. Texas
13. Toledo
14. Houston
15. Notre Dame
16. Stanford
17. Iowa St.
18. North Carolina
19. Florida St.
20. Arkansas
    Mississippi

1972
Team
1. Southern California
2. Oklahoma
3. Ohio St.
4. Alabama
5. Texas
6. Michigan
7. Auburn
8. Penn St.
9. Nebraska
10. LSU
11. Tennessee
12. Notre Dame
13. Arizona St.
14. Colorado
    North Carolina
16. Louisville
17. UCLA
    Washington St.
19. Utah St.
20. San Diego St.

1973
Team
1. Alabama
2. Oklahoma
3. Ohio St.
4. Notre Dame
5. Penn St.
6. Michigan
7. Southern California
8. Texas
9. UCLA
10. Arizona St.
11. Nebraska
    Texas Tech
13. Houston
14. LSU
15. Kansas
    Tulane
17. Miami (Ohio)
18. Maryland
19. San Diego St.
    Florida

*1974
Team
1. Southern California
2. Alabama
3. Ohio St.
4. Notre Dame
5. Michigan
6. Auburn
7. Penn St.
8. Nebraska
9. North Carolina St.
10. Miami (Ohio)
11. Houston
12. Florida
13. Maryland
14. Baylor
15. Texas A&M
    Tennessee
17. Mississippi St.
18. Michigan St.
19. Tulsa

1975
Team
1. Oklahoma
2. Arizona St.
3. Alabama
4. Ohio St.
5. UCLA
6. Arkansas
7. Texas
8. Michigan
9. Nebraska
10. Penn St.
11. Maryland
12. Texas A&M
13. Arizona
    Pittsburgh
15. California
16. Miami (Ohio)
17. Notre Dame
    West Virginia
19. Georgia
    Southern California

1976
Team
1. Pittsburgh
2. Southern California
3. Michigan
4. Houston
5. Ohio St.
6. Oklahoma
7. Nebraska
8. Texas A&M
9. Alabama
10. Georgia
11. Maryland
12. Notre Dame
13. Texas Tech
14. Oklahoma St.
15. UCLA
16. Colorado
17. Rutgers
18. Iowa St.
19. Baylor
    Kentucky

1977
Team
1. Notre Dame
2. Alabama
3. Arkansas
4. Penn St.
5. Texas
6. Oklahoma
7. Pittsburgh
8. Michigan
9. Washington
10. Nebraska
11. Florida St.
12. Ohio St.
    Southern California
14. North Carolina
15. Stanford
16. North Texas
    Brigham Young
18. Arizona St.
19. San Diego St.
    North Carolina St.

1978
Team
1. Southern California
2. Alabama
3. Oklahoma
4. Penn St.
5. Michigan
6. Notre Dame
7. Clemson
8. Nebraska
9. Texas
10. Arkansas
11. Houston
12. UCLA
13. Purdue
14. Missouri
15. Georgia
16. Stanford
17. Navy
18. Texas A&M
19. Arizona St.
    North Carolina St.

1979
Team
1. Alabama
2. Southern California
3. Oklahoma
4. Ohio St.
5. Houston
6. Pittsburgh
7. Nebraska
8. Florida St.
9. Arkansas
10. Purdue
11. Washington
12. Brigham Young
13. Texas
14. North Carolina
15. Baylor
16. Indiana
17. Temple
18. Penn St.
19. Michigan
20. Missouri

1980
Team
1. Georgia
2. Pittsburgh
3. Oklahoma
4. Michigan
5. Florida St.
6. Alabama
7. Nebraska
8. Penn St.
9. North Carolina
10. Notre Dame
11. Brigham Young
12. Southern California
13. Baylor
14. UCLA
15. Ohio St.
16. Purdue
17. Washington
18. Miami (Fla.)
19. Florida
20. Southern Methodist

1981
Team
1. Clemson
2. Pittsburgh
3. Penn St.
4. Texas
5. Georgia
6. Alabama
7. Washington
8. North Carolina
9. Nebraska
10. Michigan
11. Brigham Young
12. Ohio St.
13. Southern California
14. Oklahoma
15. Iowa
16. Arkansas
17. Mississippi St.
18. West Virginia
19. Southern Miss.
20. Missouri

1982
Team
1. Penn St.
2. Southern Methodist
3. Nebraska
4. Georgia
5. UCLA
6. Arizona St.
7. Washington
8. Arkansas
9. Pittsburgh
10. Florida St.
11. LSU
12. Ohio St.
13. North Carolina
14. Auburn
15. Michigan
16. Oklahoma
17. Alabama
18. Texas
19. West Virginia
20. Maryland

1983
Team
1. Miami (Fla.)
2. Nebraska
3. Auburn
4. Georgia
5. Texas
6. Florida
7. Brigham Young
8. Ohio St.
9. Michigan
10. Illinois
11. Southern Methodist
12. Alabama
13. UCLA
14. Iowa
15. Air Force
16. West Virginia
17. Penn St.
18. Oklahoma St.
19. Pittsburgh
20. Boston College

1984
Team
1. Brigham Young
2. Washington
3. Nebraska
4. Boston College
5. Oklahoma St.
6. Oklahoma
7. Florida
8. Southern Methodist
9. Southern California
10. UCLA
11. Maryland
12. Ohio St.
13. South Carolina
14. Auburn
15. Iowa
16. LSU
17. Virginia
18. West Virginia
19. Kentucky
    Florida St.

1985
Team
1. Oklahoma
2. Michigan
3. Penn St.
4. Tennessee
5. Air Force
6. UCLA
7. Texas A&M
8. Miami (Fla.)
9. Iowa
10. Nebraska
11. Ohio St.
12. Arkansas
13. Florida St.
14. Alabama
15. Baylor
16. Fresno St.
17. Brigham Young
18. Georgia Tech
19. Maryland
20. LSU

DIVISION I-A

UNITED PRESS INTERNATIONAL FINAL POLLS

1986
Team
1. Penn St.
2. Miami (Fla.)
3. Oklahoma
4. Nebraska
5. Arizona St.
6. Ohio St.
7. Michigan
8. Auburn
9. Alabama
10. Arizona
11. LSU
12. Texas A&M
13. Baylor
14. UCLA
15. Iowa
16. Arkansas
17. Washington
18. Boston College
19. Clemson
20. Florida St.

1987
Team
1. Miami (Fla.)
2. Florida St.
3. Oklahoma
4. Syracuse
5. LSU
6. Nebraska
7. Auburn
8. Michigan St.
9. Texas A&M
10. Clemson
11. UCLA
12. Oklahoma St.
13. Tennessee
14. Georgia
15. South Carolina
16. Iowa
17. Southern California
18. Michigan
19. Texas
20. Indiana

1988
Team
1. Notre Dame
2. Miami (Fla.)
3. Florida St.
4. Michigan
5. West Virginia
6. UCLA
7. Auburn
8. Clemson
9. Southern California
10. Nebraska
11. Oklahoma St.
12. Syracuse
13. Arkansas
14. Oklahoma
15. Georgia
16. Washington St.
17. North Carolina St.
    Alabama
19. Indiana
20. Wyoming

1989
Team
1. Miami (Fla.)
2. Florida St.
3. Notre Dame
4. Colorado
5. Tennessee
6. Auburn
7. Alabama
8. Michigan
9. Southern California
10. Illinois
11. Clemson
12. Nebraska
13. Arkansas
14. Penn St.
15. Virginia
16. Texas Tech
    Michigan St.
18. Brigham Young
19. Pittsburgh
20. Washington

#1990
Team
1. Georgia Tech
2. Colorado
3. Miami (Fla.)
4. Florida St.
5. Washington
6. Notre Dame
7. Tennessee
8. Michigan
9. Clemson
10. Penn St.
11. Texas
12. Louisville
13. Texas A&M
14. Michigan St.
15. Virginia
16. Iowa
17. Brigham Young
    Nebraska
19. Auburn
20. San Jose St.
21. Syracuse
22. Southern California
23. Mississippi
24. Illinois
25. Virginia Tech

¢1991
Team
1. Washington
2. Miami (Fla.)
3. Penn St.
4. Florida St.
5. Alabama
6. Michigan
7. Florida
8. California
9. East Caro.
10. Iowa
11. Syracuse
12. Notre Dame
13. Texas A&M
14. Tennessee
15. Nebraska
16. Oklahoma
17. Clemson
18. Colorado
19. UCLA
20. Georgia
21. Tulsa
22. Stanford
23. North Carolina St.
24. Brigham Young
25. Ohio St.

1992
Team
1. Alabama
2. Florida St.
3. Miami (Fla.)
4. Notre Dame
5. Michigan
6. Syracuse
7. Texas A&M
8. Georgia
9. Stanford
10. Florida
11. Washington
12. Tennessee
13. Colorado
14. Nebraska
15. Washington St.
16. Mississippi
17. North Carolina St.
18. North Carolina
19. Ohio St.
20. Hawaii
21. Boston College
22. Kansas
23. Fresno St.
24. Penn St.
25. Mississippi St.

1993
Team
1. Florida St.
2. Notre Dame
3. Nebraska
4. Florida
5. Wisconsin
6. Texas A&M
7. Penn St.
8. West Virginia
9. Ohio St.
10. Arizona
11. Boston College
12. Tennessee
13. Alabama
14. Miami (Fla.)
15. Oklahoma
16. Colorado
17. UCLA
18. Kansas St.
19. Michigan
20. North Carolina
21. Virginia Tech
22. Louisville
23. Clemson
24. California
25. Southern California

1994
Team
1. Nebraska
2. Penn St.
3. Colorado
4. Florida St.
5. Alabama
6. Miami (Fla.)
7. Florida
8. Utah
9. Michigan
10. Ohio St.
11. Oregon
12. Brigham Young
13. Southern California
14. Colorado St.
15. Virginia
16. Kansas St.
17. North Carolina St.
18. Tennessee
19. Washington St.
20. Arizona
21. North Carolina
22. Boston College
23. Texas
24. Virginia Tech
25. Mississippi St.

1995
Team
1. Nebraska
2. Florida
3. Tennessee
4. Colorado
5. Florida St.
6. Ohio St.
7. Kansas St.
8. Northwestern
9. Virginia Tech
10. Kansas
11. Southern California
12. Penn St.
13. Notre Dame
14. Texas A&M
15. Texas
16. Virginia
17. Syracuse
18. Oregon
19. Michigan
20. Texas Tech
21. Auburn
22. Toledo
23. Iowa
24. East Caro.
25. LSU

*Beginning in 1974, by agreement with the American Football Coaches Association, teams on probation by the NCAA were ineligible for ranking and national championship consideration by the UPI Board of Coaches. #Beginning in 1990 season, UPI selected top 25 teams instead of 20. ¢In 1991-92, the No. 1 team in the final UPI/NFF poll received the MacArthur Bowl, awarded by the NFF since 1959 to recognize its national champion. Beginning in 1993, the No. 1 team in the USA Today/Hall of Fame poll was awarded the MacArthur Bowl. The National Football Foundation and Hall of Fame MacArthur Bowl national champions before 1991 are listed in national polls section.

USA Today/ESPN (Coaches) Weekly Poll Leaders

1992
9-8	Miami (Fla.)	(1-0-0)
9-15	Miami (Fla.)	(1-0-0)
9-22	Miami (Fla.)	(2-0-0)
9-29	Washington	(3-0-0) (2)
10-6	Washington	(4-0-0)
10-13	Miami (Fla.)	(5-0-0) (2)
10-20	Miami (Fla.)	(6-0-0)
10-27	Miami (Fla.)	(7-0-0)
11-3	Miami (Fla.)	(8-0-0)
11-10	Miami (Fla.)	(8-0-0)
11-17	Miami (Fla.)	(9-0-0)
11-24	Miami (Fla.)	(10-0-0)
12-1	Miami (Fla.)	(11-0-0)
12-8	Miami (Fla.)	(11-0-0)
1-2	**Alabama**	**(13-0-0) (2)**

1993
8-31	Florida St.	(1-0-0)
9-7	Florida St.	(2-0-0)
9-14	Florida St.	(3-0-0)
9-21	Florida St.	(4-0-0)
9-28	Florida St.	(4-0-0)
10-5	Florida St.	(5-0-0)
10-12	Florida St.	(6-0-0)
10-19	Florida St.	(7-0-0)
10-26	Florida St.	(7-0-0)
11-2	Florida St.	(8-0-0)
11-9	Florida St.	(9-0-0)
11-16	Notre Dame	(10-0-0) (2)
11-23	Nebraska	(10-0-0) (2)
11-30	Nebraska	(11-0-0)
12-7	Nebraska	(11-0-0)
1-3	**Florida St.**	**(12-1-0) (3)**

1994
9-6	Nebraska	(1-0-0)
9-13	Nebraska	(2-0-0)
9-20	Nebraska	(3-0-0)
9-27	Nebraska	(4-0-0)
10-4	Florida	(4-0-0) (2)
10-11	Florida	(5-0-0)
10-18	Penn St.	(6-0-0) (3)
10-25	Penn St.	(6-0-0)
11-1	Penn St.	(7-0-0)
11-8	Nebraska	(10-0-0) (2)
11-15	Nebraska	(11-0-0)
11-22	Nebraska	(11-0-0)
11-29	Nebraska	(12-0-0)
12-6	Nebraska	(12-0-0)
1-3	**Nebraska**	**(13-0-0)**

1995
9-5	Florida St.	(1-0-0)
9-12	Florida St.	(2-0-0)
9-19	Florida St.	(3-0-0)
9-26	Florida St.	(4-0-0)
10-3	Florida St.	(4-0-0)
10-10	Florida St.	(5-0-0)
10-17	Florida St.	(6-0-0)
10-24	Florida St.	(7-0-0)
10-31	Nebraska	(8-0-0) (2)
11-7	Nebraska	(9-0-0)
11-14	Nebraska	(10-0-0)
11-21	Nebraska	(10-0-0)
11-28	Nebraska	(11-0-0)
12-5	Nebraska	(11-0-0)
1-3	**Nebraska**	**(12-0-0)**

1996
9-2	Nebraska	(0-0-0)
9-9	Nebraska	(1-0-0)
9-16	Nebraska	(1-0-0)
9-23	Florida	(3-0-0) (4)
9-30	Florida	(4-0-0)
10-7	Florida	(5-0-0)
10-14	Florida	(6-0-0)
10-21	Florida	(7-0-0)
10-28	Florida	(7-0-0)
11-4	Florida	(8-0-0)
11-11	Florida	(9-0-0)
11-18	Florida	(10-0-0)
11-25	Florida	(10-0-0)
12-2	Florida St.	(11-0-0) (2)
12-9	Florida St.	(11-0-0)
1-3	**Florida**	**(12-1-0)**

1997
9-2	Florida	(1-0-0)
9-8	Florida	(2-0-0)
9-15	Florida	(2-0-0)
9-22	Florida	(3-0-0)
9-29	Florida	(4-0-0)
10-6	Florida	(5-0-0)
10-13	Penn St.	(5-0-0) (2)
10-20	Nebraska	(6-0-0) (2)
10-27	Nebraska	(7-0-0)
11-3	Nebraska	(8-0-0)
11-10	Florida St.	(9-0-0) (2)
11-17	Florida St.	(10-0-0)
11-24	Michigan	(11-0-0) (2)
12-1	Michigan	(11-0-0)
12-8	Michigan	(11-0-0)
1-3	**Nebraska**	**(13-0-0) (2)**

1998
9-7	Ohio St.	(1-0-0)
9-14	Ohio St.	(2-0-0)
9-21	Ohio St.	(3-0-0)
9-28	Ohio St.	(3-0-0)
10-5	Ohio St.	(4-0-0)
10-12	Ohio St.	(5-0-0)
10-19	Ohio St.	(6-0-0)
10-26	Ohio St.	(7-0-0)
11-2	Ohio St.	(8-0-0)
11-9	Tennessee (8-0-0) (3) & Kansas St.	(9-0-0) (2)
11-16	Kansas St.	(10-0-0)
11-23	Kansas St.	(11-0-0)
11-30	Kansas St.	(11-0-0)
12-7	Tennessee	(12-0-0) (2)
1-5	**Tennessee**	**(13-0-0)**

1999
8-30	Florida St.	(1-0-0)
9-6	Florida St.	(1-0-0)
9-13	Florida St.	(2-0-0)
9-20	Florida St.	(3-0-0)
9-27	Florida St.	(4-0-0)
10-4	Florida St.	(5-0-0)
10-11	Florida St.	(6-0-0)
10-18	Florida St.	(7-0-0)
10-25	Florida St.	(8-0-0)
11-1	Florida St.	(9-0-0)
11-8	Florida St.	(9-0-0)
11-15	Florida St.	(10-0-0)
11-22	Florida St.	(11-0-0)
11-29	Florida St.	(11-0-0)
12-6	Florida St.	(11-0-0)
1-5	**Florida St.**	**(12-0-0)**

1999 USA Today/ESPN Week-by-Week Polls

	Preseason 8/6	A30	S6	S13	S20	S27	O4	O11	O18	O25	N1	N6	N15	N22	N29	D6	J5
1. Florida St.	1	1	1	1	1	1	1	1	1	1	1	1	1	1	1	1	1
2. Tennessee	2	3	2	7	8	6	5	5	4	4	3	7	7	6	5	9	9
3. Arizona	3	15	17	NR	NR	NR	NR	NR	NR	NR	NR	NR	NR	NR	NR	NR	NR
4. Penn St.	4	2	3	2	2	2	2	2	2	2	8	13	15	17	17	11	11
5. Florida	5	4	4	3	3	7	6	6	5	5	4	3	6	5	10	14	14
6. Nebraska	6	6	6	5	5	4	3	3	9	9	6	4	3	3	3	2	2
7. Michigan	7	5	5	4	4	3	10	9	14	15	15	10	10	9	8	5	5
8. Texas A&M	8	7	7	6	6	12	11	10	18	18	23	20	17	14	13	20	20
9. Ohio St.	9	14	12	10	9	19	17	22	21	20	NR	NR	NR	NR	NR	NR	NR
10. Wisconsin	10	8	8	17	NR	20	18	16	11	10	9	5	4	4	4	4	4
11. Georgia Tech	11	10	13	12	12	8	9	8	7	7	14	12	16	16	15	21	21
12. Miami (Fla.)	12	9	9	13	20	21	24	23	23	22	19	NR	NR	24	23	15	15
13. Georgia	13	12	11	9	11	9	14	14	10	16	16	23	21	23	24	16	16
14. Virginia Tech	14	11	10	8	7	5	4	4	3	3	2	2	2	2	2	3	3
15. UCLA	15	13	21	18	NR	NR	NR	NR	NR	NR	NR	NR	NR	NR	NR	NR	NR
16. Texas	16	23	22	20	15	23	19	18	12	11	10	6	5	12	18	23	23
17. Colorado	17	NR	NR	NR	NR	NR	NR	NR	NR	NR	NR	NR	NR	NR	NR	NR	NR
18. Notre Dame	18	21	NR	NR	NR	NR	NR	NR	NR	NR	NR	NR	NR	NR	NR	NR	NR
19. Kansas St.	19	18	16	15	13	10	8	7	6	6	5	9	8	7	7	6	6
20. Alabama	20	22	18	NR	22	14	13	12	16	14	13	8	9	8	6	8	8
21. Southern California	21	20	19	16	23	22	NR	NR	NR	NR	NR	NR	NR	NR	NR	NR	NR
22. Arkansas	22	17	15	14	18	NR	NR	NR	24	NR	24	22	NR	NR	NR	19	19
23. Purdue	23	16	14	11	10	15T	21	17	22	21	NR	25	23	20	20	NR	NR
24. Virginia	24	19	NR	NR	24	NR	NR	NR	NR	NR	NR	NR	NR	NR	NR	NR	NR
25. Arizona St.	25	25	23	NR	NR	NR	NR	NR	NR	NR	NR	NR	NR	NR	NR	NR	NR
NR North Carolina St.	NR	24	20	24	NR	NR	NR	NR	NR	NR	NR	NR	NR	NR	NR	NR	NR
NR Colorado St.	NR	NR	24	NR	NR	NR	NR	NR	NR	NR	NR	NR	NR	NR	NR	NR	NR
NR Marshall	NR	NR	25	22	17	15T	16	15	13	12	11	11	12	11	11	10	10
NR Brigham Young	NR	NR	NR	19	NR	24	20	19	15	13	12	19	NR	25	25	NR	NR
NR Michigan St.	NR	NR	NR	NR	21	11	7	13	20	19	17	14	11	10	9	7	7
NR Mississippi St.	NR	NR	NR	23	16	13	12	11	8	8	7	15	19	18	16	12	12
NR Air Force	NR	NR	NR	25	NR	NR	25	NR	NR	NR	NR	NR	NR	NR	NR	NR	NR
NR Syracuse	NR	NR	NR	NR	19	17	15	24	24	NR	NR	NR	NR	NR	NR	NR	NR

Preseason 8/6		A30	S6	S13	S20	S27	O4	O11	O18	O25	N1	N6	N15	N22	N29	D6	J5
NR	East Caro.	NR	NR	NR	NR	21	18	23	20	17	17	24	21	18	19	19	NR
NR	Oklahoma	NR	NR	NR	NR	25	NR	NR	NR	NR	NR	NR	NR	NR	NR	NR	NR
NR	Mississippi	NR	NR	NR	NR	NR	25	22	25	NR	23	18	16	24	NR	NR	22
NR	Southern Miss.	NR	NR	NR	NR	NR	NR	NR	21	19	25	20	17	13	15	14	13
NR	Stanford	NR	NR	NR	NR	NR	NR	NR	NR	25	NR	NR	NR	25	21	21	24
NR	Minnesota	NR	NR	NR	NR	NR	NR	NR	NR	NR	NR	21	18	14	13	12	17
NR	Washington	NR	NR	NR	NR	NR	NR	NR	NR	NR	NR	22	NR	NR	NR	NR	NR
NR	Boston College	NR	NR	NR	NR	NR	NR	NR	NR	NR	NR	25	22	20	22	22	NR
NR	Oregon	NR	NR	NR	NR	NR	NR	NR	NR	NR	NR	NR	NR	NR	NR	NR	18
NR	Illinois	NR	NR	NR	NR	NR	NR	NR	NR	NR	NR	NR	NR	NR	NR	NR	25

USA Today/ESPN Final Polls (Coaches)

Took over as coaches poll in 1991. (Cable News Network, 1982-96; ESPN 1997-)

1982
Team
1. Penn St.
2. Southern Methodist
3. Nebraska
4. Georgia
5. UCLA
6. Arizona St.
7. Pittsburgh
8. Arkansas
9. Clemson
10. Washington
11. LSU
12. Florida St.
13. Ohio St.
14. Southern California
15. Oklahoma
16. Auburn
17. West Virginia
18. Maryland
19. North Carolina
20. Texas
21. Michigan
22. Alabama
23. Tulsa
24. Iowa
25. Florida

1983
Team
1. Miami (Fla.)
2. Auburn
3. Nebraska
4. Georgia
5. Texas
6. Brigham Young
7. Michigan
8. Ohio St.
9. Florida
10. Clemson
11. Illinois
12. Southern Methodist
13. Alabama
14. Air Force
15. West Virginia
16. Iowa
17. Tennessee
18. UCLA
19. Pittsburgh
20. Penn St.
21. Oklahoma
22. Boston College
23. Oklahoma St.
24. Maryland
25. East Caro.

1984
Team
1. Brigham Young
2. Washington
3. Florida
4. Nebraska
5. Oklahoma
6. Boston College
7. Oklahoma St.
8. Southern Methodist
9. Maryland
10. South Carolina
11. Southern California
12. UCLA
13. LSU
14. Ohio St.
15. Auburn
16. Miami (Fla.)
17. Florida St.
18. Virginia
19. Kentucky
20. Iowa
21. West Virginia
22. Army
23. Georgia
24. Air Force
25. Notre Dame

1985
Team
1. Oklahoma
2. Penn St.
3. Michigan
4. Tennessee
5. Florida
6. Miami (Fla.)
7. Air Force
8. Texas A&M
9. UCLA
10. Iowa
11. Nebraska
12. Alabama
13. Ohio St.
14. Florida St.
15. Arkansas
16. Brigham Young
17. Maryland
18. Georgia Tech
19. Baylor
20. Auburn
21. LSU
22. Army
23. Fresno St.
24. Georgia
25. Oklahoma St.

1986
Team
1. Penn St.
2. Miami (Fla.)
3. Oklahoma
4. Nebraska
5. Arizona St.
6. Ohio St.
7. Auburn
8. Michigan
9. Alabama
10. LSU
11. Arizona
12. Texas A&M
13. UCLA
14. Baylor
15. Boston College
16. Iowa
17. Arkansas
18. Clemson
19. Washington
20. Virginia Tech
21. Florida St.
22. Stanford
23. Georgia
24. North Carolina St.
25. San Diego St.

1987
Team
1. Miami (Fla.)
2. Florida St.
3. Oklahoma
4. Syracuse
5. Nebraska
6. LSU
7. Auburn
8. Michigan St.
9. Texas A&M
10. UCLA
11. Clemson
12. Oklahoma St.
13. Georgia
14. Tennessee
15. Iowa
16. Notre Dame
17. Southern California
18. South Carolina
19. Michigan
20. Texas
21. Pittsburgh
22. Indiana
23. Penn St.
24. Ohio St.
25. Alabama

1988
Team
1. Notre Dame
2. Miami (Fla.)
3. Florida St.
4. UCLA
5. Michigan
6. West Virginia
7. Southern California
8. Nebraska
9. Auburn
10. Clemson
11. Oklahoma St.
12. Syracuse
13. Oklahoma
14. Arkansas
15. Washington St.
16. Georgia
17. Alabama
18. North Carolina St.
19. Houston
20. Indiana
21. Wyoming
22. LSU
23. Colorado
24. Southern Miss.
25. Brigham Young

1989
Team
1. Miami (Fla.)
2. Notre Dame
3. Florida St.
4. Colorado
5. Tennessee
6. Auburn
7. Southern California
8. Michigan
9. Alabama
10. Illinois
11. Nebraska
12. Clemson
13. Arkansas
14. Houston
15. Penn St.
16. Virginia
17. Michigan St.
18. Texas Tech
19. Pittsburgh
20. Texas A&M
21. West Virginia
22. Brigham Young
23. Syracuse
24. Ohio St.
25. Washington

1990
Team
1. Colorado
2. Georgia Tech
3. Miami (Fla.)
4. Florida St.
5. Washington
6. Notre Dame
7. Tennessee
8. Michigan
9. Clemson
10. Texas
11. Penn St.
12. Houston
13. Florida
14. Louisville
15. Michigan St.
16. Texas A&M
17. Oklahoma
18. Iowa
19. Auburn
20. Brigham Young
21. Mississippi
22. Southern California
23. Nebraska
24. Illinois
25. Virginia

1991
Team
1. Washington
2. Miami (Fla.)
3. Penn St.
4. Florida St.
5. Alabama
6. Michigan
7. California
8. Florida
9. East Caro.
10. Iowa
11. Syracuse
12. Notre Dame
13. Texas A&M
14. Oklahoma
15. Tennessee
16. Nebraska
17. Clemson
18. UCLA
19. Georgia
20. Colorado
21. Tulsa
22. Stanford
23. Brigham Young
24. Air Force
25. North Carolina St.

1992
Team
1. Alabama
2. Florida St.
3. Miami (Fla.)
4. Notre Dame
5. Michigan
6. Texas A&M
7. Syracuse
8. Georgia
9. Stanford
10. Washington
11. Florida
12. Tennessee
13. Colorado
14. Nebraska
15. North Carolina St.
16. Mississippi
17. Washington St.
18. North Carolina
19. Ohio St.
20. Hawaii
21. Boston College
22. Fresno St.
23. Kansas
24. Penn St.
25. Wake Forest

1993
Team
1. Florida St.
2. Notre Dame
3. Nebraska
4. Florida
5. Wisconsin
6. West Virginia
7. Penn St.
8. Texas A&M
9. Arizona
10. Ohio St.
11. Tennessee
12. Boston College
13. Alabama
14. Oklahoma
15. Miami (Fla.)
16. Colorado
17. UCLA
18. Kansas St.
19. Michigan
20. Virginia Tech
21. North Carolina
22. Clemson
23. Louisville
24. California
25. Southern California

USA TODAY/ESPN FINAL POLLS

1994
Team
1. Nebraska
2. Penn St.
3. Colorado
4. Alabama
5. Florida St.
6. Miami (Fla.)
7. Florida
8. Utah
9. Ohio St.
10. Brigham Young
11. Oregon
12. Michigan
13. Virginia
14. Colorado St.
15. Southern California
16. Kansas St.
17. North Carolina St.
18. Tennessee
19. Washington St.
20. Arizona
21. North Carolina
22. Boston College
23. Texas
24. Virginia Tech
25. Mississippi St.

1995
Team
1. Nebraska
2. Tennessee
3. Florida
4. Colorado
5. Florida St.
6. Kansas St.
7. Northwestern
8. Ohio St.
9. Virginia Tech
10. Kansas
11. Southern California
12. Penn St.
13. Notre Dame
14. Texas
15. Texas A&M
16. Syracuse
17. Virginia
18. Oregon
19. Michigan
20. Texas Tech
21. Auburn
22. Iowa
23. East Caro.
24. Toledo
25. LSU

1996
Team
1. Florida (12-1)
2. Ohio St. (11-1)
3. Florida St. (11-1)
4. Arizona St. (11-1)
5. Brigham Young (14-1)
6. Nebraska (11-2)
7. Penn St. (11-2)
8. Colorado (10-2)
9. Tennessee (10-2)
10. North Carolina (10-2)
11. Alabama (10-3)
12. Virginia Tech (10-2)
13. LSU (10-2)
14. Miami (Fla.) (9-3)
15. Washington (9-3)
16. Northwestern (9-3)
17. Kansas St. (9-3)
18. Iowa (9-3)
19. Syracuse (9-3)
20. Michigan (8-4)
21. Notre Dame (8-3)
22. Wyoming (10-2)
23. Texas (8-5)
24. Army (10-2)
25. Auburn (8-4)

1997
Team
1. Nebraska (13-0)
2. Michigan (12-0)
3. Florida St. (11-1)
4. North Carolina (11-1)
5. UCLA (10-2)
6. Florida (10-2)
7. Kansas St. (11-1)
8. Tennessee (11-2)
9. Washington St. (10-2)
10. Georgia (10-2)
11. Auburn (10-3)
12. Ohio St. (10-3)
13. LSU (9-3)
14. Arizona St. (9-3)
15. Purdue (9-3)
16. Colorado St. (11-2)
17. Penn St. (9-3)
18. Washington (8-4)
19. Southern Miss. (9-3)
20. Syracuse (9-4)
21. Texas A&M (9-4)
22. Mississippi (8-4)
23. Missouri (7-5)
24. Oklahoma St. (8-4)
25. Air Force (10-3)

1998
Team
1. Tennessee (13-0)
2. Ohio St. (11-1)
3. Florida St. (11-2)
4. Arizona (12-1)
5. Wisconsin (11-1)
6. Florida (10-2)
7. Tulane (12-0)
8. UCLA (10-2)
9. Kansas St. (11-2)
10. Air Force (12-1)
11. Georgia Tech (10-2)
12. Michigan (10-3)
13. Texas A&M (11-3)
14. Georgia (9-3)
15. Penn St. (9-3)
16. Texas (9-3)
17. Arkansas (9-3)
18. Virginia (9-3)
19. Virginia Tech (9-3)
20. Nebraska (9-4)
21. Miami (Fla.) (9-3)
22. Notre Dame (9-3)
23. Purdue (9-4)
24. Syracuse (8-4)
25. Missouri (8-4)

1999
Team
1. Florida St. (12-0)
2. Nebraska (12-1)
3. Virginia Tech (11-1)
4. Wisconsin (10-2)
5. Michigan (10-2)
6. Kansas St. (11-1)
7. Michigan St. (10-2)
8. Alabama (10-3)
9. Tennessee (9-3)
10. Marshall (13-0)
11. Penn St. (10-3)
12. Mississippi St. (10-2)
13. Southern Miss. (9-3)
14. Florida (9-4)
15. Miami (Fla.) (9-4)
16. Georgia (8-4)
17. Minnesota (8-4)
18. Oregon (9-3)
19. Arkansas (8-4)
20. Texas A&M (8-4)
21. Georgia Tech (8-4)
22. Mississippi (8-4)
23. Texas (9-5)
24. Stanford (8-4)
25. Illinois (8-4)

BOWL COALITION, ALLIANCE AND BOWL CHAMPIONSHIP SERIES HISTORY

BOWL COALITION

The history of the College Football Bowl Coalition began in 1992 and lasted for three years through the 1994 season. The Bowl Coalition featured four games – the Orange, Sugar, Cotton and Fiesta Bowls – with conference champions locked into the Orange (Big Eight), Sugar (Southeastern) and Cotton (Southwest) Bowls and the Fiesta Bowl pairing two at-large teams.

The Fiesta Bowl had the ability to select one Coalition-eligible team, that was not a conference champion, before the national selection date. The original Coalition also involved champions from the Big East and Atlantic Coast Conferences, as well as Notre Dame.

Selections were made on the basis of how the champions of the Big Eight, Southeastern and Southwest Conferences finished in the final regular-season poll, which was a combination of the Associated Press and CNN/USA Today rankings. All selections were made by the Coalition as a group on the first Sunday in December following the final weekend of the regular season.

All teams had to have at least six wins against Division I-A opponents and Notre Dame was guaranteed a spot with seven wins and could still qualify with six wins given mutual agreement between the bowls.

There were 56 Division I-A members that were members of the original Coalition, which also included original involvement with the Gator and Hancock Bowls. The remainder of the bowls remained in place, many with predetermined conference tie-ins. A second layer of bowls eventually was identified and came to be known as the Tier Two bowls.

BOWL COALITION (1992-94)

1992 SEASON

SUGAR BOWL
Alabama 34, Miami (Fla.) 13

(Had first selection, but had automatic matchup between SEC champion Alabama, which was ranked No. 2 in final regular-season AP poll, against Big East champion Miami (Florida), which was ranked No. 1.)

COTTON BOWL
Notre Dame 28, Texas A&M 3

(Has second selection based on SWC champion Texas A&M being ranked No. 4 at end of regular season and chose at-large selection Notre Dame.)

ORANGE BOWL
Florida St. 27, Nebraska 14

(Had third selection based on Big Eight champion Nebraska being ranked No. 11 at end of regular season and chose ACC champion Florida State.)

FIESTA BOWL
Syracuse 26, Colorado 22

(Had fourth selection and chose at-large selection Syracuse and at-large selection Colorado.)

1993 SEASON

ORANGE BOWL
Florida St. 18, Nebraska 14

(Had first selection, but had automatic matchup between Big Eight champion Nebraska, which was ranked No. 1 in final regular-season coalition poll, against ACC champion Florida State, which was ranked No. 2.)

SUGAR BOWL
Florida 41, West Virginia 7

(Had second selection based on Big East champion West Virginia being ranked No. 3 at end of regular season and chose SEC champion Florida.)

COTTON BOWL
Notre Dame 24, Texas A&M 21

(Had third selection based on SWC champion Texas A&M being ranked No. 7 at end of regular season and chose at-large selction Notre Dame.)

FIESTA BOWL
Arizona 29, Miami (Fla.) 0

(Had fourth selection and chose at-large selection Miami (Florida) and also picked at-large Arizona.)

1994 SEASON

ORANGE BOWL
Nebraska 24, Miami (Fla.) 17

(Had first selection based on Big Eight champion Nebraska being ranked No. 1 at end of regular season in coalition poll and chose Big East champion Miami [Florida].)

SUGAR BOWL
Florida St. 23, Florida 17

(Had second selection based on SEC champion Florida being ranked No. 5 and chose ACC champion Florida State.)

COTTON BOWL
Southern California 55, Texas Tech 14

(Had third selection based on SWC champion Texas Tech being unranked and chose at-large Southern California.)

FIESTA BOWL
Colorado 41, Notre Dame 24

(Had fourth selection and chose at-large Notre Dame and at-large Colorado.)

BOWL ALLIANCE

The Bowl Alliance lasted three seasons, 1995 through 1997, and involved three games – the Fiesta, Orange and Sugar Bowls. A predetermined rotation created a situation in which each year a different bowl had the first two choices, while a second bowl chose third and fifth and the third bowl chose fourth and sixth.

Conferences that were a part of the Alliance were the Big 12, Atlantic Coast, Big East and Southeastern, leaving two at-large slots.

The most noteworthy change from the Coalition to the Alliance was the elimination of the conference tie-ins which had been in existence for years. The goal was to provide the best opportunity to match the top two teams and provide the greatest flexibility in creating the postseason matchups between Alliance partners.

In 1995, the first season of the Alliance, there was only one at-large position since the merger of the Big Eight and Southwest Conferences into the Big 12 had not yet taken place, providing five guaranteed conference champions that season.

Notre Dame was guaranteed the at-large slot in 1995 by finishing in the top ten of either the Associated Press or CNN/USA Today poll.

BOWL ALLIANCE (1995-97)

1995 SEASON

FIESTA BOWL
Nebraska 62, Florida 24

(Had first and second selections and picked Big Eight champion Nebraska, which was ranked No. 1 in the regular-season AP poll, against SEC champion Florida, which was ranked No. 2. This pick was required through mandatory No. 1 vs. No. 2 matchup rules.)

ORANGE BOWL
Florida St. 31, Notre Dame 26

(Had third and fifth selections and picked ACC champion Florida State against at-large Notre Dame.)

SUGAR BOWL
Virginia Tech 28, Texas 10

(Had fourth and sixth selections and picked Big East champion Virginia Tech against SWC champion Texas.)

1996 SEASON

SUGAR BOWL
Florida 52, Florida St. 20

(Had first and second selections and picked SEC champion Florida and ACC champion Florida State.)

FIESTA BOWL
Penn State 38, Texas 15

(Had third and fifth selections and picked at-large Penn State and Big 12 champion Texas.)

ORANGE BOWL
Nebraska 41, Virginia Tech 21

(Had fourth and sixth selections and picked at-large selection Nebraska and Big East champion Virginia Tech.)

1997 SEASON

ORANGE BOWL
Nebraska 42, Tennessee 17

(Had first and second selections and picked Big 12 champion Nebraska and SEC champion Tennessee.)

SUGAR BOWL
Florida St. 31, Ohio St. 14

(Had third and fifth selections and picked ACC champion Florida State and at-large Ohio State.)

FIESTA BOWL
Kansas St. 35, Syracuse 18

(Had fourth and sixth selections and picked at-large Kansas State and Big East champion Syracuse.)

BOWL CHAMPIONSHIP SERIES RANKINGS

The Bowl Championship Series (BCS) was launched in 1998 to match the No. 1 and No. 2 teams in a bowl game to determine the national champion.

In 1999, the BCS saw its second year of determining the national Division I collegiate football champion. The BCS consisted of the Sugar Bowl, Rose Bowl, Orange Bowl and Fiesta Bowl. The Sugar Bowl hosted the national championship between No. 1 Florida State and No. 2 Virginia Tech on January 4 in New Orleans. Florida State was crowned the national champion by the BCS after a 46-29 victory.

The ranking system utilized by the BCS consists of four major elements: polls, computer rankings, strength of schedule and losses.

The poll component is calculated on the average of the ranking of each team in the Associated Press media poll and the USA Today/ESPN coaches poll. The rankings of each team is added and divided by two. Others receiving votes are calculated in order received.

The second component consists of eight computer rankings. These rankings include the three used in 1998 (New York Times, Jeff Sagarin's USA Today and The Anderson/Hester/Seattle Times) along with five additional rankings: Richard Billingsley, Dunkel Index, Kenneth Massey, David Rothman and the Matthews/Scripps-Howard rankings. The lowest computer ranking will be disregarded.

The third component will be the team's strength of schedule. This component is calculated by determining the cumulative won-loss records of the team's opponents (weighted 66 2/3 percent) and the cumulative won-loss records of the opponents' opponents (33 1/3 percent). The team's schedule strength shall be calculated to determine in which quartile it will rank: 1-25, 26-50, 51-75, or 76-100, and shall be further quantified by its ranking within each quartile (divided by 25).

The final component shall evaluate the team's won-loss record. Each loss during the season will represent one point in this component.

BCS RANKING: All four components described above shall be added together for a total rating. The team with the lowest point total shall rank first in the BCS standings.

NOTE: The NCAA football certification subcommittee has not enacted, adopted or otherwise approved of the process described above. The NCAA has no role in the selection of the institutions that participate in postseason bowl games and does not sponsor a Division I-A football championship.

1999 FINAL BOWL CHAMPIONSHIP SERIES RANKINGS
(Games Through December 4)

Rk	Team	AP	USA/ESPN	Poll Avg.	Bill	Dunk	MASS	NYT	Roth	SAG	SH	ST	Comp. Avg.	SSch	SRk	L	TOTAL
1.	Florida St.	1	1	1.0	1	1	1	1	1	1	1	1	1.00	6	0.24	0	2.24
2.	Virginia Tech	2	2	2.0	2	2	2	2	2	2	2	3	2.00	53	2.12	0	6.12
3.	Nebraska	3	3	3.0	3	3	3	4	3	3	3	2	2.86	14	0.56	1	7.42
4.	Alabama	5	6	5.5	5	7	6	3	4	6	4	4	4.57	1	0.04	2	12.11
5.	Tennessee	6	5	5.5	7	6	5	5	6	5	5	8	5.57	16	0.64	2	13.71
6.	Kansas St.	7	7	7.0	4	5	4	6	5	4	6	5	4.71	63	2.52	1	15.23
7.	Wisconsin	4	4	4.0	8	4	7	8	9	7	11	12	7.71	75	3.00	2	16.71
8.	Michigan	8	8	8.0	10	9	8	7	10	9	7	6	8.00	2	0.08	2	18.08
9.	Michigan St.	9	9	9.0	6	8	9	10	8	8	7	8	7.71	10	0.40	2	19.11
10.	Florida	10	10	10.0	9	12	12	16	7	11	9	9	9.86	5	0.20	3	23.06
11.	Penn St.	13	17	15.0	11	10	10	20	11	10	10	11	10.43	8	0.32	3	28.75
12.	Marshall	11	11	11.0	33	31	11	11	12	13	22	15	16.43	93	3.72	0	31.15
13.	Minnesota	12	12	12.0	14	19	17	21.5	15	15	15	21	16.57	51	2.04	3	33.61
14.	Texas A&M	18	13	15.5	13	16	15	15	16	17	19	14	15.14	28	1.12	3	34.76
15.	Texas	14	18	16.0	17	13	16	21.5	13	14	14	13	14.29	13	0.52	4	34.81

Key: AP (Associated Press poll); USA/ESPN (USA Today/ESPN coaches poll); Poll Avg. (Average of two polls); Bill (Richard Billingsley); Dunk (Dunkel Index); Mass (Kenneth Massey); NYT (New York Times); Roth (David Rothman); SAG (Jeff Sagarin); SH (Scripps-Howard); ST (Seattle Times); Comp Avg. (Computer Services Average); SSch (Schedule Strength); SRk (Schedule Rank); L (Losses).

BCS PAIRINGS FOR 1999-00:
Sugar Bowl—#1 Florida St. (11-0) vs. #2 Virginia Tech (11-0)
Fiesta Bowl—#3 Nebraska (11-1) vs. #6 Tennessee (9-2)
Orange Bowl—#8 Michigan (9-2) vs. #5 Alabama (10-2)
Rose Bowl—#22 Stanford (8-3) vs. #4 Wisconsin (9-2)

1999-00 RESULTS:
Sugar Bowl—Florida St. 46, Virginia Tech 29
Fiesta Bowl—Nebraska 31, Tennessee 21
Orange Bowl—Michigan 35, Alabama 34 (ot)
Rose Bowl—Wisconsin 17, Stanford 9

BOWL CHAMPIONSHIP SERIES RANKINGS

FINAL 1998 BCS RANKINGS

Team	Total Score
1. Tennessee	3.47
2. Florida St.	4.91
3. Kansas St.	9.96
4. Ohio St.	10.37
5. UCLA	10.90
6. Texas A&M	15.70
7. Arizona	16.49
8. Florida	19.95
9. Wisconsin	21.61
10. Tulane	26.67
11. Nebraska	29.06
12. Virginia	32.22
13. Arkansas	32.28
14. Georgia Tech	32.76
15. Syracuse	34.80

1998 SEASON

FIESTA BOWL
Tennessee 23, Florida St. 16
(Had first and second selections and picked SEC champion Tennessee and ACC champion Florida State)

SUGAR BOWL
Ohio St. 24, Texas A&M 14
(Had third and fifth selections and picked Big Ten Ohio State and Big 12 champion Texas A&M)

ORANGE BOWL
Florida 31, Syracuse 10
(Had fourth and sixth selections and chose SEC Florida and Big East champion Syracuse)

ROSE BOWL
Wisconsin 38, UCLA 31
(Selected Big Ten Wisconsin and Pacific-10 champion UCLA)

FUTURE SEASONS

2000 SEASON
National Championship—Orange Bowl, January 3, 2001
Rose Bowl, January 1, 2001
Fiesta Bowl, January 1, 2001
Sugar Bowl, January 2, 2001

2001 SEASON
National Championship—Rose Bowl, January 3, 2002
Fiesta Bowl, January 1, 2002
Sugar Bowl, January 1, 2002
Orange Bowl, January 2, 2002

Undefeated, Untied Teams

(Regular-Season Games Only)

Minimum of five games played against opponents above the high-school level. Subsequent bowl win is indicated by (†), loss (‡) and tie ($). Unscored-on teams are indicated by (•).

(Note: Following are undefeated, untied teams in regular-season games not included with major colleges at the time—Centre, 1919 & 1921; Lafayette, 1921, 1926 & 1937; Wash. & Jeff., 1921; Marquette, 1923; Louisville, 1925; Centenary (La.), 1927; Memphis, 1938; San Jose St., 1939; Hardin-Simmons, 1940; Arizona, 1945; Pacific [Cal.], 1949; Fresno St., 1961; and San Diego St., 1966.)

Year	College	Wins
1878	Princeton	6
1882	Yale	8
1883	Yale	8
1885	Princeton	9
1887	Yale	9
1888	Yale	•13
1889	Princeton	10
1890	Harvard	11
1891	Yale	•13
1892	Minnesota	5
	Purdue	8
	Yale	•13
1893	Minnesota	6
	Princeton	11
1894	Pennsylvania	12
	VMI	5
	Yale	16
1895	Pennsylvania	14
1896	LSU	6
1897	Pennsylvania	15
1898	Harvard	11
	Kentucky	•7
	Michigan	10
	North Carolina	9
1899	Kansas	10
	Sewanee	12
1900	Clemson	6
	Texas	6
	Tulane	•5
	Yale	12
1901	Harvard	12
	Michigan	†•10
	Wisconsin	9
1902	Arizona	•5
	California	8
	Michigan	11
	Nebraska	•9
1903	Nebraska	10
	Princeton	11
1904	Auburn	5
	Michigan	10
	Minnesota	13
	Pennsylvania	12
	Pittsburgh	10
	Vanderbilt	9
1905	Chicago	10
	Stanford	8
	Yale	10
1906	New Mexico St.	5
	Washington St.	•6
	Wisconsin	5

Year	College	Wins
1907	Oregon St.	•6
1908	Kansas	9
	LSU	10
1909	Arkansas	7
	Colorado	•6
	Washington	7
	Yale	•10
1910	Colorado	6
	Illinois	•7
	Pittsburgh	•9
	Washington	6
1911	Colorado	6
	Oklahoma	8
	Utah St.	•5
	Washington	7
1912	Harvard	9
	Notre Dame	7
	Penn St.	8
	Washington	6
	Wisconsin	7
1913	Auburn	8
	Chicago	7
	Harvard	9
	Michigan St.	7
	Nebraska	8
	Notre Dame	7
	Washington	7
1914	Army	9
	Illinois	7
	Tennessee	9
	Texas	8
	Wash. & Lee	9
1915	Colorado St.	7
	Columbia	5
	Cornell	9
	Nebraska	8
	Oklahoma	10
	Pittsburgh	8
	Washington	7
	Washington St.	†•6
1916	Army	9
	Ohio St.	7
	Pittsburgh	8
	Tulsa	10
1917	Denver	9
	Georgia Tech	9
	Pittsburgh	9
	Texas A&M	•8
	Washington	6
1918	Michigan	5
	Oklahoma	6
	Texas	9
	Virginia Tech	7
	Washington (Mo.)	6
1919	Notre Dame	9
	Texas A&M	•10
1920	Boston College	8
	California	†8
	Notre Dame	9
	Ohio St.	‡7
	Southern California	6
	Texas	9
	VMI	9
1921	California	$9
	Cornell	8
	Iowa	7
1922	California	9

Year	College	Wins
	Cornell	8
	Drake	7
	Iowa	7
	Princeton	8
	Tulsa	7
1923	Colorado	9
	Cornell	8
	Illinois	8
	Michigan	8
	Southern Methodist	9
	Yale	8
1924	Notre Dame	†9
1925	Alabama	†9
	Dartmouth	8
1926	Alabama	$9
	Stanford	$10
	Utah	7
1927	(None)	
1928	Boston College	9
	Detroit	9
	Georgia Tech	†9
1929	Notre Dame	9
	Pittsburgh	‡9
	Purdue	8
	Tulane	9
	Utah	7
1930	Alabama	†9
	Notre Dame	10
	Utah	8
	Washington St.	‡9
1931	Tulane	‡11
1932	Colgate	•9
	Michigan	8
	Southern California	†9
1933	Princeton	9
1934	Alabama	†9
	Minnesota	8
1935	Minnesota	8
	Princeton	9
	Southern Methodist	‡12
1936	(None)	
1937	Alabama	‡9
	Colorado	‡8
	Santa Clara	†8
1938	Duke	‡•9
	Georgetown	8
	Oklahoma	‡10
	Tennessee	†10
	TCU	†10
	Texas Tech	‡10
1939	Cornell	8
	Tennessee	‡•10
	Texas A&M	†10
1940	Boston College	†10
	Lafayette	9
	Minnesota	8
	Stanford	†9
	Tennessee	‡10
1941	Duke	‡9
	Duquesne	8
	Minnesota	8
1942	Tulsa	‡10
1943	Purdue	9
1944	Army	9
	Ohio St.	9
1945	Alabama	†9
	Army	9

Year	College	Wins
	Oklahoma St.	†8
1946	Georgia	†10
	Hardin-Simmons	10
	UCLA	‡10
1947	Michigan	†9
	Notre Dame	9
	Penn St.	$9
1948	California	‡10
	Clemson	†10
	Michigan	9
1949	Army	9
	California	‡10
	Notre Dame	10
	Oklahoma	†10
1950	Oklahoma	‡10
	Princeton	9
	Wyoming	†9
1951	Maryland	†9
	Michigan St.	9
	Princeton	9
	San Francisco	9
	Tennessee	‡10
1952	Georgia Tech	†11
	Michigan St.	9
1953	Maryland	‡10
1954	Ohio St.	†9
	Oklahoma	10
	UCLA	9
1955	Maryland	‡10
	Oklahoma	†10
1956	Oklahoma	10
	Tennessee	‡10
	Wyoming	10
1957	Arizona St.	10
	Auburn	10
1958	LSU	†10
1959	Syracuse	†10
1960	New Mexico St.	†10
	Yale	9
1961	Alabama	†10
	Rutgers	9
1962	Dartmouth	9
	Mississippi	†9

Year	College	Wins
	Southern California	†10
1963	Texas	†10
1964	Alabama	‡10
	Arkansas	†10
	Princeton	9
1965	Arkansas	‡10
	Dartmouth	9
	Michigan St.	‡10
	Nebraska	†10
1966	Alabama	†10
1967	Wyoming	‡10
1968	Ohio	‡10
	Ohio St.	†9
	Penn St.	†10
1969	Penn St.	†10
	San Diego St.	†10
	Texas	†10
	Toledo	†10
1970	Arizona St.	†10
	Dartmouth	9
	Ohio St.	†9
	Texas	†10
	Toledo	†11
1971	Alabama	‡11
	Michigan	‡11
	Nebraska	†12
	Toledo	‡11
1972	Southern California	†11
1973	Alabama	‡11
	Miami (Ohio)	†10
	Notre Dame	†10
	Penn St.	†11
1974	Alabama	‡11
	Oklahoma	11
1975	Arizona St.	†11
	Arkansas St.	11
	Ohio St.	‡11
1976	Maryland	‡11
	Pittsburgh	†11
	Rutgers	11
1977	Texas	‡11
1978	Penn St.	‡11
1979	Alabama	†11

Year	College	Wins
	Brigham Young	‡11
	Florida St.	‡11
	McNeese St.	‡11
	Ohio St.	‡11
1980	Georgia	†11
1981	Clemson	‡11
1982	Georgia	‡11
1983	Nebraska	‡12
	Texas	‡11
1984	Brigham Young	†12
1985	Bowling Green	‡11
	Penn St.	‡11
1986	Miami (Fla.)	‡11
	Penn St.	‡11
1987	Miami (Fla.)	‡11
	Oklahoma	‡11
	Syracuse	$11
1988	Notre Dame	†11
	West Virginia	‡11
1989	Colorado	‡11
1990	(None)	
1991	Miami (Fla.)	†11
	Washington	†11
1992	Alabama	†12
	Miami (Fla.)	‡11
	Texas A&M	‡12
1993	Auburn	11
	Nebraska	‡11
	West Virginia	‡11
1994	Nebraska	†12
	Penn St.	†11
1995	Florida	‡12
	Nebraska	‡11
1996	Arizona St.	‡11
	Florida St.	‡11
1997	Michigan	†12
	Nebraska	†13
1998	Tennessee	†12
	Tulane	‡11
1999	Florida St.	†11
	Marshall	†12

The Spoilers

(From 1937 Season)

Following is a list of the spoilers of major-college teams that lost their perfect (undefeated, untied) record in their **final** game of the season, including a bowl game (in parentheses). Confrontations of two undefeated, untied teams at the time are in bold face. An asterisk (*) indicates the home team in a regular-season game, a dagger (†) indicates a neutral site.

Date	Spoiler	Victim	Score
1-1-38	California	Alabama (Rose)	13-0
1-1-38	Rice	Colorado (Cotton)	28-14
12-3-38	*Southern California	Notre Dame	13-0
1-2-39	Southern California	Duke (Rose)	7-3
1-2-39	**Tennessee**	**Oklahoma (Orange)**	17-0
1-2-39	St. Mary's (Cal.)	Texas Tech (Cotton)	20-13
12-2-39	*Duquesne	Detroit	tie 10-10
1-1-40	Southern California	Tennessee (Rose)	14-0
1-1-41	**Boston College**	**Tennessee (Sugar)**	19-13
1-1-42	Oregon St.	Duke (Rose)	20-16
11-27-43	*Great Lakes	Notre Dame	19-14
1-1-44	Southern California	Washington (Rose)	29-0
11-25-44	*Virginia	Yale	tie 6-6
1-1-47	Illinois	UCLA (Rose)	45-14
1-1-48	Southern Methodist	Penn St. (Cotton)	tie 13-13
11-27-48	†Navy	Army	tie 21-21
12-2-48	*Southern California	Notre Dame	tie 14-14
1-1-49	Northwestern	California (Rose)	20-14
1-2-50	Ohio St.	California (Rose)	17-14
12-2-50	†Navy	Army	14-2
1-1-51	Kentucky	Oklahoma (Sugar)	13-7
1-1-52	**Maryland**	**Tennessee (Sugar)**	28-13
11-22-52	Southern California	*UCLA	14-12
1-1-54	Oklahoma	Maryland (Orange)	7-0
1-2-56	**Oklahoma**	**Maryland (Orange)**	20-6
1-1-57	Baylor	Tennessee (Sugar)	13-7
11-28-64	*Southern California	Notre Dame	20-17
1-1-65	Texas	Alabama (Orange)	21-17
11-20-65	**Dartmouth**	***Princeton**	28-14
1-1-66	UCLA	Michigan St. (Rose)	14-12
1-1-66	Alabama	Nebraska (Orange)	39-28
1-1-66	LSU	Arkansas (Cotton)	14-7
11-19-66	**Notre Dame**	***Michigan St.**	tie 10-10
1-1-68	LSU	Wyoming (Sugar)	20-13
11-23-68	***Harvard**	***Yale**	tie 29-29
12-27-68	Richmond	Ohio (Tangerine)	49-42
11-22-69	*Michigan	Ohio St.	24-12
11-22-69	*Princeton	Dartmouth	35-7
11-21-70	***Ohio St.**	**Michigan**	20-9
1-1-71	Stanford	Ohio St. (Rose)	27-17
1-1-71	Notre Dame	Texas (Cotton)	24-11
1-1-72	Stanford	Michigan (Rose)	13-12
1-1-72	**Nebraska**	**Alabama (Orange)**	38-6
11-25-72	*Ohio St.	Michigan	14-11
11-24-73	**Ohio St.**	***Michigan**	tie 10-10
12-31-73	**Notre Dame**	**Alabama (Sugar)**	24-23
11-23-74	*Ohio St.	Michigan	12-10
11-23-74	*Harvard	Yale	21-16
1-1-75	Notre Dame	Alabama (Orange)	13-11
1-1-76	UCLA	Ohio St. (Rose)	23-10
1-1-77	Houston	Maryland (Cotton)	30-21
11-19-77	*Delaware	Colgate	21-3
1-2-78	Notre Dame	Texas (Cotton)	38-10
1-1-79	Alabama	Penn St. (Sugar)	14-7
11-17-79	Harvard	*Yale	22-7
12-15-79	Syracuse	McNeese St. (Independence)	31-7
12-21-79	Indiana	Brigham Young (Holiday)	38-37
1-1-80	Southern California	Ohio St. (Rose)	17-16
1-1-80	Oklahoma	Florida St. (Orange)	24-7
1-1-83	Penn St.	Georgia (Sugar)	27-23
1-2-84	Georgia	Texas (Cotton)	10-9
1-2-84	Miami (Fla.)	Nebraska (Orange)	31-30
12-14-85	Fresno St.	Bowling Green (California)	51-7
1-1-86	Oklahoma	Penn St. (Orange)	25-10
1-2-87	**Penn St.**	**Miami (Fla.) (Fiesta)**	14-10
1-1-88	Auburn	Syracuse (Sugar)	tie 16-16
1-1-88	**Miami (Fla.)**	**Oklahoma (Orange)**	20-14
1-2-89	**Notre Dame**	**West Virginia (Fiesta)**	34-21
1-1-90	Notre Dame	Colorado (Orange)	21-6
1-1-93	Notre Dame	Texas A&M (Cotton)	28-3

THE SPOILERS

Date	Spoiler	Victim	Score
1-1-93	**Alabama**	Miami (Fla.) (Sugar)	34-13
1-1-94	Florida St.	Nebraska (Orange)	18-16
1-1-94	Florida	West Virginia (Sugar)	41-7
1-2-96	**Nebraska**	**Florida (Fiesta)**	62-24
1-1-97	Ohio St.	Arizona St. (Rose)	20-17
1-2-97	Florida	Florida St. (Sugar)	52-20
1-4-00	**Florida St.**	**Virginia Tech (Sugar)**	**46-29**

Streaks and Rivalries

Longest Winning Streaks

(Includes Bowl Games)

Wins	Team	Years	Ended by	Score
47	Oklahoma	1953-57	Notre Dame	7-0
39	Washington	1908-14	Oregon St.	0-0
37	Yale	1890-93	Princeton	6-0
37	Yale	1887-89	Princeton	10-0
35	Toledo	1969-71	Tampa	21-0
34	Pennsylvania	1894-96	Lafayette	6-4
31	Oklahoma	1948-50	Kentucky	*13-7
31	Pittsburgh	1914-18	Cleveland Naval Reserve	10-9
31	Pennsylvania	1896-98	Harvard	10-0
30	Texas	1968-70	Notre Dame	*24-11
29	Miami (Fla.)	1990-93	Alabama	*34-13
29	Michigan	1901-03	Minnesota	6-6
28	Alabama	1991-93	Tennessee	17-17
28	Alabama	1978-80	Mississippi St.	6-3
28	Oklahoma	1973-75	Kansas	23-3
28	Michigan St.	1950-53	Purdue	6-0
26	Nebraska	1994-96	Arizona St.	19-0
26	Cornell	1921-24	Williams	14-7
26	Michigan	1903-05	Chicago	2-0
25	Brigham Young	1983-85	UCLA	27-24
25	San Diego St.	1965-67	Utah St.	31-25
25	Michigan	1946-49	Army	21-7
25	Army	1944-46	Notre Dame	0-0
25	Southern California	1931-33	Oregon St.	0-0
24	Princeton	1949-52	Pennsylvania	13-7
24	Minnesota	1903-05	Wisconsin	16-12
24	Nebraska	1901-04	Colorado	6-0
24	Yale	1894-95	Boston AC	0-0
24	Harvard	1890-91	Yale	10-0
24	Yale	1882-84	Princeton	0-0
23	Alabama	1991-92	#	
23	Notre Dame	1988-89	Miami (Fla.)	27-10
23	Nebraska	1970-71	UCLA	20-17
23	Penn St.	1968-70	Colorado	41-13
23	Tennessee	1937-39	Southern California	*14-0
23	Harvard	1901-02	Yale	23-0
22	Washington	1990-92	Arizona	16-3
22	Nebraska	1982-83	Miami (Fla.)	*31-30
22	Ohio St.	1967-69	Michigan	24-12
22	Arkansas	1963-65	LSU	*14-7
22	Harvard	1912-14	Penn St.	13-13
22	Yale	1904-06	Princeton	0-0
21	Arizona St.	1969-71	Oregon St.	24-18
21	San Diego St.	1968-70	Long Beach St.	27-11
21	Notre Dame	1946-48	Southern California	14-14
21	Minnesota	1933-36	Northwestern	6-0
21	Colorado	1908-12	Colorado St.	21-0
21	Pennsylvania	1903-05	Lafayette	6-6
21	Yale	1900-01	Army	5-5
21	Harvard	1898-99	Yale	0-0
20	UCLA	1997-98	Miami (Fla.)	49-45
20	Penn St.	1993-95	Wisconsin	17-9
20	Auburn	1993-94	Georgia	23-23
20	Oklahoma	1986-87	Miami (Fla.)	*20-14
20	Tennessee	1950-51	Maryland	*28-13
20	Texas A&M	1938-40	Texas	7-0
20	Notre Dame	1929-31	Northwestern	0-0
20	Alabama	1924-26	Stanford	*7-7
20	Iowa	1920-23	Illinois	9-6
20	Notre Dame	1919-21	Iowa	10-7

*Streak ended in bowl game. #Eight victories and one tie in 1993 forfeited by action of the NCAA Committee on Infractions.

Longest Unbeaten Streaks

(Includes Bowl Games; May Include Ties)

No.	Wins	Ties	Team	Years	Ended by	Score
63	59	4	Washington	1907-17	California	27-0
56	55	1	Michigan	1901-05	Chicago	2-0
50	46	4	California	1920-25	Olympic Club	15-0
48	47	1	Oklahoma	1953-57	Notre Dame	7-0
48	47	1	Yale	1885-89	Princeton	10-0
47	42	5	Yale	1879-85	Princeton	6-5
44	42	2	Yale	1894-96	Princeton	24-6
42	39	3	Yale	1904-08	Harvard	4-0
39	37	2	Notre Dame	1946-50	Purdue	28-14
37	37	0	Yale	1890-93	Princeton	6-0
37	36	1	Oklahoma	1972-75	Kansas	23-3
35	35	0	Toledo	1969-71	Tampa	21-0
35	34	1	Minnesota	1903-05	Wisconsin	16-12
34	34	0	Pennsylvania	1894-96	Lafayette	6-4
34	33	1	Nebraska	1912-16	Kansas	7-3
34	32	2	Princeton	1884-87	Harvard	12-0
34	29	5	Princeton	1877-82	Harvard	1-0
33	31	2	Georgia Tech	1914-18	Pittsburgh	32-0
33	30	3	Tennessee	1926-30	Alabama	18-6
33	30	3	Harvard	1911-15	Cornell	10-0
32	31	1	Nebraska	1969-71	UCLA	20-17
32	31	1	Harvard	1898-00	Yale	28-0
32	30	2	Army	1944-47	Columbia	21-20
31	31	0	Oklahoma	1948-50	Kentucky	13-7
31	31	0	Pittsburgh	1914-18	Cleveland Naval	10-9
31	31	0	Pennsylvania	1896-98	Harvard	10-0
31	30	1	Penn St.	1967-70	Colorado	41-13
31	30	1	San Diego St.	1967-70	Long Beach St.	27-11
31	29	2	Georgia Tech	1950-53	Notre Dame	27-14
30	30	0	Texas	1968-70	Notre Dame	24-11
30	28	2	Pennsylvania	1903-06	Swarthmore	4-0
30	25	5	Penn St.	1919-22	Navy	14-0
29	29	0	Miami (Fla.)	1990-93	Alabama	34-13
28	28	0	Alabama	1978-80	Mississippi St.	6-3
28	28	0	Michigan St.	1950-53	Purdue	6-0
28	26	2	Southern California	1978-80	Washington	20-10
28	26	2	Army	1947-50	Navy	14-2
28	26	2	Tennessee	1930-33	Duke	10-2
28	24	4	Minnesota	1933-36	Northwestern	6-0
27	26	1	Southern California	1931-33	Stanford	13-7
27	24	3	Notre Dame	1910-14	Yale	28-0

Longest Home Winning Streaks

(Includes Bowl Games)

Wins	Team	Years	Ended by	Score
58	Miami (Fla.)	1985-94	Washington	38-20
57	Alabama	1963-82	Southern Miss.	38-29
56	Harvard	1890-95	Boston AA	0-0
50	Michigan	1901-07	Pennsylvania	6-0
47	Nebraska	1991-98	Texas	20-16
42	Texas	1968-76	Houston	30-0
40	Notre Dame	1907-18	Great Lakes	7-7
38	Notre Dame	1919-27	Minnesota	7-7
37	Yale	1904-08	Brown	10-10
37	Yale	1900-03	Princeton	11-6
33	Nebraska	1901-06	Iowa St.	14-2
33	Harvard	1900-03	Amherst	5-0
31	Marshall	1995-99	Current	
31	Texas A&M	1990-95	Texas	16-6
31	Yale	1890-93	Princeton	6-0
30	Florida	1994-99	Alabama	40-39 (ot)
30	Auburn	1952-61	Kentucky	14-12
30	Tennessee	1928-33	Alabama	12-6
29	Yale	1885-89	Princeton	10-0
28	Michigan	1969-73	Ohio St.	0-0
28	Notre Dame	1942-50	Purdue	28-14
27	Vanderbilt	1903-07	Michigan	8-0
26	Utah	1928-34	Oregon	8-7
26	California	1919-23	Nevada	0-0
25	Ohio St.	1972-76	Missouri	22-21
25	Oklahoma	1947-53	Notre Dame	28-21
25	Wisconsin	1900-03	Chicago	15-6
24	Georgia	1980-83	Auburn	13-7
24	Georgia Tech	1916-19	Wash. & Lee	3-0
24	Virginia	1899-04	Navy	5-0
23	Florida	1990-93	Florida St.	33-21

Streaks and Rivalries — Longest Home Winning Streaks

Wins	Team	Years	Ended by	Score
23	Nebraska	1969-72	Oklahoma	17-14
23	Tulane	1929-32	Vanderbilt	6-6
23	Michigan St.	1904-08	Michigan	0-0
23	Michigan	1897-00	Ohio St.	0-0
23	Harvard	1887-89	Princeton	41-15
22	Kansas St.	1996-99	Current	
22	Wyoming	1965-70	Air Force	41-17
22	Navy	1953-64	Syracuse	14-6
22	Minnesota	1933-37	Notre Dame	7-6
22	LSU	1907-12	Mississippi	10-7
22	Notre Dame	1901-05	Wabash	5-0
21	Nebraska	1981-84	Oklahoma	17-7
21	Arizona St.	1969-72	Air Force	39-31
21	Mississippi	1952-60	LSU	6-6
21	Oklahoma	1953-57	Notre Dame	7-0
21	Miami (Ohio)	1942-48	Xavier (Ohio)	27-19
21	North Carolina	1893-00	Virginia Tech	0-0
20	Fresno St.	1987-90	Utah St.	24-24
20	Rutgers	1974-78	Colgate	14-9
20	Nebraska	1963-67	Colorado	21-16
20	Mississippi St.	1939-45	Mississippi	7-6
20	Missouri	1938-43	Oklahoma	20-13
20	Southern California	1927-29	California	15-7
20	Southern California	1919-23	California	13-7
20	Iowa	1918-23	Illinois	9-6
20	Harvard	1912-14	Penn St.	13-13

Longest Losing Streaks

Losses	Team	Years	Ended with	Score
34	Northwestern	1979-82	Northern Ill.	31-6
28	Virginia	1958-61	William & Mary	21-6
28	Kansas St.	1945-48	Arkansas St.	37-6
27	New Mexico St.	1988-90	Cal St. Fullerton	43-9
27	Eastern Mich.	1980-82	Kent	9-7
26	Colorado St.	1960-63	Pacific (Cal.)	20-0
23	Northern Ill.	1996-98	Central Mich.	16-6
21	South Carolina	1998-99	Current	
21	Kent	1981-83	Eastern Mich.	37-13
21	New Mexico	1967-69	Kansas	16-7
20	TCU	1974-75	Rice	28-21
20	Florida St.	1972-74	Miami (Fla.)	21-14
19	Hawaii	1997-99	Eastern Ill.	31-27
18	Illinois	1996-98	Middle Tenn. St.	48-20
18	Rice	1987-89	Southern Methodist	35-6
18	Wisconsin	1967-69	Iowa	23-17
18	Wake Forest	1962-63	South Carolina	20-19
18	Kansas St.	1961-62	Brigham Young	24-7
17	Ball St.	1998-99	Current	
17	Kent	1992-94	Akron	32-16
17	Kent	1989-90	Ohio	44-15
17	Memphis	1981-82	Arkansas St.	12-0
17	Kansas St.	1964-66	Kansas	3-3
17	Tulane	1961-63	South Carolina	20-7
17	Alabama	1954-56	Mississippi St.	13-12
17	Kansas	1953-55	Washington St.	13-0
16	UNLV	1997-98	North Texas	26-3
16	Kansas St.	1987-89	North Texas	20-17
16	Indiana	1983-85	Louisville	41-28
16	Vanderbilt	1961-62	Tulane	20-0
16	Iowa St.	1929-30	Simpson	6-0

Most Consecutive Winning Seasons

(All-Time and Current) (.500 percentage and above)

No.	School	Years
46	Penn St.	1939-87
42	Notre Dame	1889-32#
40	Texas	1893-32
38	Alabama	1911-50†
38	Nebraska	1962-99*
32	Michigan	1968-99*
29	Oklahoma	1966-94
29	Texas	1957-85
28	Virginia	1888-15
27	Michigan	1892-18
26	Virginia Tech	1894-19
25	Brigham Young	1974-99*
23	Syracuse	1913-35
23	Ohio St.	1899-21
23	Florida St.	1977-99*

No.	School	Years
23	Washington	1977-99*
21	Northern Ill.	1929-49
21	Ohio St.	1967-87
21	Southern California	1962-82
21	Vanderbilt	1915-35
21	Wyoming	1949-69
20	Florida	1980-99*
19	Wisconsin	1891-09
18	Ohio St.	1925-42
18	Nebraska	1920-37
17	San Diego St.	1961-77
17	Miami (Ohio)	1943-59
17	Miami (Fla.)	1980-96
17	Texas A&M	1983-99*
16	Texas A&M	1914-29
16	Purdue	1889-05
16	LSU	1958-73
16	Marshall	1984-99*
15	Miami (Ohio)	1961-75
15	Bowling Green	1955-69
15	Utah	1928-42
15	Texas	1939-53
15	Southern California	1919-33
15	Georgia Tech	1908-22
14	Kentucky	1903-16
14	Virginia Tech	1901-14
14	Purdue	1926-39
13	Arkansas	1977-89
13	Purdue	1957-69
13	Central Mich.	1973-85
13	Wyoming	1949-61
13	Missouri	1957-69
13	Georgia	1964-76
13	Navy	1889-01
13	Virginia	1987-99*
13	Syracuse	1987-99*
12	Notre Dame	1987-98
12	Colorado	1985-96
12	Georgia	1978-89
12	Auburn	1953-64
12	Colorado	1950-61
12	Ohio St.	1928-39
12	Tulane	1928-39
12	TCU	1925-36
12	West Virginia	1914-26@

*Current streak. #No teams in 1890 and 1891. †No teams in 1918 and 1943. @No team in 1918.

Most-Played Rivalries

(Ongoing Unless Indicated)

Games	Opponents (Series leader listed first)	Rivalry Record	First Game
109	Minnesota-Wisconsin	57-44-8	1890
108	Missouri-Kansas	50-49-9	1891
106	Nebraska-Kansas	82-21-3	1892
106	Texas-Texas A&M	67-34-5	1894
104	Miami (Ohio)-Cincinnati	55-42-7	1888
104	North Carolina-Virginia	*55-45-4	1892
103	Auburn-Georgia	49-46-8	1892
103	%Baylor-TCU	49-47-7	1899
103	Oregon-Oregon St.	52-41-10	1894
102	Purdue-Indiana	62-34-6	1891
102	Stanford-California	52-39-11	1892
100	Army-Navy	48-45-7	1890
99	Utah-Utah St.	67-28-4	1892
97	Clemson-South Carolina	58-35-4	1896
97	Kansas-Kansas St.	61-31-5	1902
96	North Carolina-Wake Forest	64-30-2	1888
96	Michigan-Ohio St.	55-35-6	1897
96	Mississippi-Mississippi St.	54-36-6	1901
95	Penn St.-Pittsburgh	50-41-4	1893
95	Tennessee-Kentucky	63-23-9	1893
95	^Oklahoma-Kansas	62-27-6	1903
94	Georgia-Georgia Tech	52-37-5	1893
94	Nebraska-Iowa St.	78-14-2	1896
94	Texas-Oklahoma	55-34-5	1900
94	Oklahoma-Oklahoma St.	73-14-7	1904
93	Illinois-Northwestern	49-39-5	1892
93	Nebraska-Missouri	58-32-3	1892
93	Tennessee-Vanderbilt	62-26-5	1892
93	LSU-Tulane	¢64-22-7	1893
93	North Carolina St.-Wake Forest	56-31-6	1895
93	Washington-Oregon	56-32-5	1900
92	Pittsburgh-West Virginia	56-33-3	1895

MOST-PLAYED RIVALRIES

Games	Opponents (Series leader listed first)	Record	Game
92	Michigan-Michigan St.	60-27-5	1898
92	Washington-Washington St.	59-27-6	1900
90	#Auburn-Georgia Tech	47-39-4	1892

*Disputed series record: Virginia claims North Carolina leads the series 54-46-4, based on a forfeit game in 1956. ¢Disputed series record: Tulane claims 23-61-7 record; LSU and Tulane have not met since 1996. #Have not met since 1989. %Have not met since 1995. ^Have not met since 1997.

Additional Records

Longest Uninterrupted Series (Must have played every year)
- 95 games—Kansas-Oklahoma (1903-97)
- 94 games—Kansas-Nebraska (from 1906)
- 93 games—Minnesota-Wisconsin (from 1907)
- 91 games—Clemson-South Carolina (from 1909)
- 90 games—Wake Forest-North Carolina St. (from 1910)
- 89 games—Kansas-Kansas St. (from 1911)
- 88 games—North Carolina-Virginia (from 1910)*
- 86 games—Illinois-Ohio St. (from 1914)
- 85 games—Texas-Texas A&M (from 1915)
- 84 games—Mississippi-Mississippi St. (from 1915)**
- 82 games—Michigan-Ohio St. (from 1918)
- 81 games—Kansas-Missouri (from 1919)
- 81 games—Missouri-Iowa St. (from 1919)
- 80 games—Indiana-Purdue (from 1920)
- 78 games—Missouri-Nebraska (from 1922)
- 78 games—North Carolina-Duke (from 1922)
- 77 games—Missouri-Oklahoma (1919-95)
- 77 games—Tulane-LSU (1919-94)
- 76 games—Southern Methodist-Texas A&M (1920-95)
- 74 games—Michigan-Illinois (1924-97)
- 72 games—Rice-TCU (from 1928)
- 72 games—Southern Methodist-Texas (1924-95)

*Neither school fielded a team in 1917-18 due to World War I. **Neither school fielded a team in 1943 due to World War II.

Most Consecutive Wins Over a Major Opponent in an Uninterrupted Series (Must have played in consecutive years)
- 36—Notre Dame over Navy, 1964-99 (current)
- 32—Oklahoma over Kansas St., 1937-68
- 31—Nebraska over Kansas, 1969-99 (current)
- 29—Nebraska over Kansas St., 1969-97
- 28—Texas over Rice, 1966-93
- 26—Syracuse over Hobart, 1906-31
- 25—Penn St. over West Virginia, 1959-83
- 22—Nebraska over Oklahoma St. 1974-95
- 22—Arkansas over TCU, 1959-80
- 22—Alabama over Mississippi St., 1958-79
- 21—Nebraska over Missouri, 1979-99 (current)
- 20—Purdue over Iowa, 1961-80
- 18—UCLA over California, 1972-89
- 17—New Mexico over UTEP, 1970-86
- 17—Arizona St. over UTEP, 1957-73
- 17—LSU over Tulane, 1956-72
- 16—Virginia over Wake Forest, 1984-99 (current)
- 16—Michigan over Illinois, 1967-82
- 16—North Carolina over Wake Forest, 1908-23
- 15—Southern Methodist over TCU, 1972-86
- 15—Iowa over Iowa St., 1983-97

Most Consecutive Wins Over a Major Opponent in a Nonconsecutive Series (Did not play in consecutive years)
- 29—Clemson over Virginia, 1955-90 (over 36-year period)
- 26—Southern California over Oregon St., 1968-99 (32-year period)
- 24—Nebraska over Oklahoma St., 1974-99 (26-year period)
- 21—Ohio St. over Northwestern, 1972-98 (27-year period)
- 19—Michigan over Northwestern, 1966-92 (27-year period)
- 19—Vanderbilt over Mississippi, 1894-38 (45-year period)
- 17—Washington over California, 1977-99 (23-year period)
- 17—Tulsa over Drake, 1939-85 (47-year period)
- 17—Mississippi over Memphis, 1921-62 (42-year period)
- 17—North Carolina over Wake Forest, 1893-23 (29-year period)

Most Consecutive Current Wins Over a Major Opponent in a Series (Must have played every year)
- 36—Notre Dame over Navy, 1964-99 (63-9-1 in rivalry)
- 31—Nebraska over Kansas, 1969-99 (82-21-3 in rivalry)
- 16—Virginia over Wake Forest, 1984-99 (27-11-0 in rivalry)
- 16—Colorado over Iowa St., 1984-99 (42-11-1 in rivalry)
- 14—Iowa over Iowa St., 1983-96 (32-12-0 in rivalry)
- 13—Florida over Kentucky, 1987-99 (33-17-0 in rivalry)
- 13—San Diego St. over New Mexico, 1984-96 (18-5-0 in rivalry)

Most Consecutive Games Without a Loss Against a Major Opponent
- 36—Notre Dame over Navy, 1964-99 (0 ties)
- 34—Oklahoma over Kansas St., 1935-68 (1 tie)

Cliffhangers

Regular-season Division I-A games won on the final play (since 1971, when first recorded). The extra point is listed when it provided the margin of victory after the winning touchdown on the game's final play. Overtime games are not included but follow Cliffhangers.

Date	Opponents, Score	Game-Winning Play
9-25-71	Marshall 15, Xavier (Ohio) 13	Terry Gardner 13 pass from Reggie Oliver
10-9-71	California 30, Oregon St. 27	Steve Sweeney 7 pass from Jay Cruze
10-23-71	Washington St. 24, Stanford 23	Don Sweet 27 FG
11-6-71	Kentucky 14, Vanderbilt 7	Darryl Bishop 43 interception return
11-4-72	LSU 17, Mississippi 16	Brad Davis 10 pass from Bert Jones (Rusty Jackson kick)
11-18-72	California 24, Stanford 21	Steve Sweeney 7 pass from Vince Ferragamo
9-15-73	Lamar 21, Howard Payne 17	Larry Spears 14 pass from Jabo Leonard
9-22-73	Hawaii 13, Fresno St. 10	Reinhold Stuprich 29 FG
11-17-73	New Mexico 23, Wyoming 21	Bob Berg 43 FG
11-23-74	Stanford 22, California 20	Mike Langford 50 FG
9-20-75	Indiana St. 23, Southern Ill. 21	Dave Vandercook 50 FG
10-18-75	Cal St. Fullerton 32, UC Riverside 31	John Choukair 52 FG
11-1-75	Yale 16, Dartmouth 14	Randy Carter 46 FG
11-8-75	West Virginia 17, Pittsburgh 14	Bill McKenzie 38 FG
11-8-75	Stanford 13, Southern California 10	Mike Langford 37 FG
11-15-75	North Carolina 17, Tulane 15	Tom Biddle 40 FG
11-6-76	Eastern Mich. 30, Central Mich. 27	Ken Dudal 38 FG
9-30-78	Virginia Tech 22, William & Mary 19	Ron Zollicoffer 50 pass from David Lamie
10-21-78	Arkansas St. 6, McNeese St. 3	Doug Dobbs 42 FG
11-9-78	San Jose St. 33, Pacific (Cal.) 31	Rick Parma 5 pass from Ed Luther
10-6-79	Stanford 27, UCLA 24	Ken Naber 56 FG
10-20-79	UNLV 43, Utah 41	Todd Peterson 49 FG
10-27-79	Michigan 27, Indiana 21	Anthony Carter 45 pass from John Wangler
11-10-79	Penn St. 9, North Carolina St. 7	Herb Menhardt 54 FG
11-17-79	Air Force 30, Vanderbilt 29	Andy Bark 14 pass from Dave Ziebart
11-24-79	Arizona 27, Arizona St. 24	Brett Weber 27 FG
9-13-80	Southern California 20, Tennessee 17	Eric Hipp 47 FG
9-13-80	Illinois 20, Michigan St. 17	Mike Bass 38 FG
9-20-80	Notre Dame 29, Michigan 27	Harry Oliver 51 FG
9-27-80	Tulane 26, Mississippi 24	Vince Manalla 29 FG

Date	Opponents, Score	Game-Winning Play
10-18-80	Connecticut 18, Holy Cross 17	Ken Miller 4 pass from Ken Sweitzer (Keith Hugger pass from Sweitzer)
10-18-80	Washington 27, Stanford 24	Chuck Nelson 25 FG
11-1-80	Tulane 24, Kentucky 22	Vince Manalla 22 FG
11-15-80	Florida 17, Kentucky 15	Brian Clark 34 FG
10-16-82	Arizona 16, Notre Dame 13	Max Zendejas 48 FG
10-23-82	Illinois 29, Wisconsin 28	Mike Bass 46 FG
11-20-82	California 25, Stanford 20	57 (5 laterals) kickoff return involving, in order: Kevin Moen, Richard Rodgers, Dwight Garner, Rodgers, Mariet Ford and Moen
10-8-83	Iowa St. 38, Kansas 35	Marc Bachrodt 47 FG
10-29-83	Bowling Green 15, Central Mich. 14	Stan Hunter 8 pass from Brian McClure
11-5-83	Baylor 24, Arkansas 21	Marty Jimmerson 24 FG
11-12-83	Pacific (Cal.) 30, San Jose St. 26	Ron Woods 85 pass from Mike Pitz
11-12-83	Miami (Fla.) 17, Florida St. 16	Jeff Davis 19 FG
11-26-83	Arizona 17, Arizona St. 15	Max Zendejas 45 FG
9-8-84	La.-Lafayette 17, Louisiana Tech 16	Patrick Broussard 21 FG
9-15-84	Syracuse 13, Northwestern 12	Jim Tait 2 pass from Todd Norley (Don McAulay kick)
10-13-84	UCLA 27, Washington St. 24	John Lee 47 FG
11-17-84	La.-Lafayette 18, Tulsa 17	Patrick Broussard 45 FG
11-17-84	Temple 19, West Virginia 17	Jim Cooper 36 FG
11-23-84	Boston College 47, Miami (Fla.) 45	Gerard Phelan 48 pass from Doug Flutie
9-14-85	Clemson 20, Virginia Tech 17	David Treadwell 36 FG
9-14-85	Oregon St. 23, California 20	Jim Nielsen 20 FG
9-14-85	Utah 29, Hawaii 27	Andre Guardi 19 FG
9-21-85	New Mexico St. 22, UTEP 20	Andy Weiler 32 FG
10-5-85	Mississippi St. 31, Memphis 28	Artie Cosby 54 FG
10-5-85	Illinois 31, Ohio St. 28	Chris White 38 FG
10-12-85	Tulsa 37, Long Beach St. 35	Jason Staurovsky 46 FG
10-19-85	Northwestern 17, Wisconsin 14	John Duvic 42 FG
10-19-85	Iowa 12, Michigan 10	Rob Houghtlin 29 FG
10-19-85	Utah 39, San Diego St. 37	Andre Guardi 42 FG
11-30-85	Alabama 25, Auburn 23	Van Tiffin 52 FG
9-13-86	Oregon 32, Colorado 30	Matt MacLeod 35 FG
9-13-86	Wyoming 23, Pacific (Cal.) 20	Greg Worker 38 FG
9-20-86	Clemson 31, Georgia 28	David Treadwell 46 FG
9-20-86	Southern California 17, Baylor 14	Don Shafer 32 FG
10-18-86	Michigan 20, Iowa 17	Mike Gillette 34 FG
10-25-86	Syracuse 27, Temple 24	Tim Vesling 32 FG
11-1-86	North Carolina St. 23, South Carolina 22	Danny Peebles 33 pass from Erik Kramer
11-1-86	North Carolina 32, Maryland 30	Lee Gliarmis 28 FG
11-8-86	Southern Miss. 23, East Caro. 21	Rex Banks 31 FG
11-15-86	Minnesota 20, Michigan 17	Chip Lohmiller 30 FG
11-29-86	Notre Dame 38, Southern California 37	John Carney 19 FG
9-12-87	Youngstown St. 20, Bowling Green 17	John Dowling 36 FG
9-19-87	Utah 31, Wisconsin 28	Scott Lieber 39 FG
10-10-87	Marshall 34, Louisville 31	Keith Baxter 31 pass from Tony Petersen
10-17-87	Texas 16, Arkansas 14	Tony Jones 18 pass from Bret Stafford
11-12-88	New Mexico 24, Colorado St. 23	Tony Jones 28 pass from Jeremy Leach
9-16-89	Southern Methodist 31, Connecticut 30	Mike Bowen 4 pass from Mike Romo
9-30-89	Kansas St. 20, North Texas 17	Frank Hernandez 12 pass from Carl Straw
10-7-89	Florida 16, LSU 13	Arden Czyzewski 41 FG
10-14-89	Southern Miss. 16, Louisville 10	Darryl Tillman 79 pass from Brett Favre
10-28-89	Virginia 16, Louisville 15	Jake McInerney 37 FG
11-4-89	Toledo 19, Western Mich. 18	Romauldo Brown 9 pass from Kevin Meger
11-4-89	Northern Ill. 23, La.-Lafayette 20	Stacey Robinson 7 run
9-8-90	Utah 35, Minnesota 29	Lavon Edwards 91 run of blocked FG
9-29-90	North Carolina St. 12, North Carolina 9	Damon Hartman 56 FG
10-6-90	Colorado 33, Missouri 31	Charles S. Johnson 1 run
10-20-90	Alabama 9, Tennessee 6	Philip Doyle 47 FG
11-3-90	Southern Miss. 14, La.-Lafayette 13	Michael Welch 11 pass from Brett Favre (Jim Taylor kick)
11-10-90	Ohio St. 27, Iowa 26	Bobby Olive 3 pass from Greg Frey
11-17-90	Stanford 27, California 25	John Hopkins 39 FG
11-24-90	Michigan 16, Ohio St. 13	J. D. Carlson 37 FG
9-7-91	Central Mich. 27, La.-Lafayette 24	L. J. Muddy 2 pass from Jeff Bender
9-21-91	California 23, Arizona 21	Doug Brien 33 FG
9-21-91	Georgia Tech 24, Virginia 21	Scott Sisson 33 FG
9-21-91	Louisiana Tech 17, Eastern Mich. 14	Chris Bonoil 54 FG
10-12-91	Ball St. 10, Eastern Mich. 8	Kenny Stucker 41 FG
11-2-91	Kentucky 20, Cincinnati 17	Doug Pelphrey 53 FG
11-2-91	Tulsa 13, Southern Miss. 10	Eric Lange 24 FG
9-5-92	Louisiana Tech 10, Baylor 9	Chris Bonoil 30 FG
9-19-92	Miami (Ohio) 17, Cincinnati 14	Chad Seitz 21 FG
9-19-92	Southern Miss. 16, Louisiana Tech 13	Johnny Lomoro 46 FG
10-3-92	Texas A&M 19, Texas Tech 17	Terry Venetoulias 21 FG
10-3-92	Georgia Tech 16, North Carolina St. 13	Scott Sisson 29 FG
10-3-92	San Jose St. 26, Wyoming 24	Joe Nedney 60 FG
10-24-92	Maryland 27, Duke 25	Marcus Badgett 38 pass from John Kaleo
10-31-92	Rutgers 50, Virginia Tech 49	Chris Brantley 15 pass from Bryan Fortay
11-14-92	UCLA 9, Oregon 6	Louis Perez 40 FG
10-2-93	Tulane 27, Navy 25	Bart Baldwin 43 FG
10-9-93	Ball St. 31, Toledo 30	Eric McCray 6 pass from Mike Neu (Matt Swart kick)
10-9-93	North Carolina St. 36, Texas Tech 34	Gary Downs 11 pass from Robert Hinton
10-16-93	Arizona 27, Stanford 24	Steve McLaughlin 27 FG
10-30-93	Missouri 37, Iowa St. 34	Kyle Pooler 40 FG
11-20-93	Maryland 33, Wake Forest 32	Russ Weaver 8 pass from Scott Milanovich (John Milligan kick)

CLIFFHANGERS   91

Date	Opponents, Score	Game-Winning Play
11-20-93	Boston College 41, Notre Dame 39	David Gordon 41 FG
11-20-93	Arkansas St. 23, Nevada 21	Reginald Murphy 30 pass from Johnny Covington
9-10-94	Tulane 15, Rice 13	Bart Baldwin 47 FG
9-10-94	San Diego St. 22, California 20	Peter Holt 32 FG
9-24-94	Colorado 27, Michigan 26	Michael Westbrook 64 pass from Kordell Stewart
10-22-94	Central Mich. 32, Miami (Ohio) 30	Terrance McMillan 19 pass from Erik Timpf
10-22-94	Army 25, Citadel 24	Kurt Heiss 24 FG
11-19-94	Eastern Mich. 40, Toledo 37	Ontario Pryor 16 pass from Charlie Batch
8-26-95	Michigan 18, Virginia 17	Mercury Hayes 15 pass from Scott Dreisbach
9-9-95	Kansas St. 23, Cincinnati 21	Kevin Lockett 22 pass from Matt Miller
10-21-95	Texas 17, Virginia 16	Phil Dawson 50 FG
10-28-95	East Caro. 36, Southern Miss. 34	Chad Holcomb 29 FG
8-31-96	Boston College 24, Hawaii 21	John Matich 42 FG
9-7-96	Arizona St. 45, Washington 42	Robert Nycz 38 FG
9-21-96	Notre Dame 27, Texas 24	Jim Sanson 39 FG
9-21-96	Navy 19, Southern Methodist 17	Tom Vanderhorst 38 FG
10-12-96	Louisville 23, Tulane 20	David Akers 39 FG
9-27-97	Colorado 20, Wyoming 19	Jeremy Aldrich 18 FG
9-5-98	Tennessee 34, Syracuse 33	Jeff Hall 27 FG
9-5-98	Minnesota 17, Arkansas St. 14	Adam Bailey 17 FG
9-19-98	Marshall 24, South Carolina 21	Billy Malashevich 37 FG
9-19-98	Stanford 37, North Carolina 34	Kevin Miller 20 FG
10-17-98	Kentucky 39, LSU 36	Seth Hanson 33 FG
11-14-98	Syracuse 28, Virginia Tech 26	Stephen Brominski 13 pass from Donovan McNabb
9-11-99	UNLV 27, Baylor 24	Kevin Thomas 100 fumble return
9-25-99	Western Mich. 24, Northern Ill. 21	Brad Selent 37 FG
9-25-99	Arizona 30, Washington St. 24	Bobby Wade 42 pass from Keith Smith
10-30-99	Texas 44, Iowa St. 41	Kris Stockton 18 FG
11-6-99	Minnesota 24, Penn St. 23	Dan Nystrom 32 FG
11-6-99	Virginia Tech 22, West Virginia 20	Shayne Graham 44 FG
11-27-99	Stanford 40, Notre Dame 37	Mike Biselli 22 FG

"CARDIAC SEASONS"
(From 1937; Won-Lost Record in Parentheses)

Games Decided by Two Points or Less
6—Kansas, 1973 (3-2-1): Tennessee 27-28, Nebraska 9-10, Iowa St. 22-20, Oklahoma St. 10-10, Colorado 17-15, Missouri 14-13 (season record: 7-3-1)
5—Illinois, 1992 (2-2-1): Minnesota 17-18, Ohio St. 18-16, Northwestern 26-27, Wisconsin 13-12, Michigan 22-22 (season record: 6-4-1)
5—Columbia, 1971 (4-1-0): Princeton 22-20, Harvard 19-21, Yale 15-14, Rutgers 17-16, Dartmouth 31-29 (season record: 6-3-0)
5—Missouri, 1957 (2-2-1): Vanderbilt 7-7, Southern Methodist 7-6, Nebraska 14-13, Kansas St. 21-23, Kansas 7-9 (season record: 5-4-1)

Games Decided by Three Points or Less
7—Bowling Green, 1980 (2-5-0): Ohio 20-21, Ball St. 24-21, Western Mich. 17-14, Kentucky 20-21, Long Beach St. 21-23, Eastern Mich. 16-18, Richmond 17-20 (season record: 4-7-0)
7—Columbia, 1971 (4-3-0): Lafayette 0-3, Princeton 22-20, Harvard 19-21, Yale 15-14, Rutgers 17-16, Cornell 21-24, Dartmouth 31-29 (season record: 6-3-0)
6—Illinois, 1992 (3-2-1): Minnesota 17-18, Ohio St. 18-16, Northwestern 26-27, Wisconsin 13-12, Purdue 20-17, Michigan 22-22 (season record: 6-4-1)
6—Central Mich., 1991 (2-0-4): Ohio 17-17, La.-Lafayette 27-24, Akron 31-29, Toledo 16-16, Miami (Ohio) 10-10, Eastern Mich. 14-14 (season record: 6-1-4)
6—Kansas, 1973 (3-2-1): Tennessee 27-28, Nebraska 9-10, Iowa St. 22-20, Oklahoma St. 10-10, Colorado 17-15, Missouri 14-13 (season record: 7-3-1)
6—Air Force, 1967 (2-2-2): Oklahoma St. 0-0, California 12-14, North Carolina 10-8, Tulane 13-10, Colorado St. 17-17, Army 7-10 (season record: 2-6-2)
6—Missouri, 1957 (3-2-1): Vanderbilt 7-7, Southern Methodist 7-6, Nebraska 14-13, Colorado 9-6, Kansas St. 21-23, Kansas 7-9 (season record: 5-4-1)

1999 DIVISION I-A OVERTIME FOOTBALL GAMES

Date	Winner's Conf.	Score (Loser's Conf.)	OT Periods	Reg. Score	Team With Choice	Choice
9-4	Big East	Boston College 30, Baylor (Big 12) 29	1OT	23-23	Baylor	Defense
9-18	Big Ten	Northwestern 15, Duke (ACC) 12	1OT	9-9	Northwestern	Defense
9-18	SEC	Vanderbilt 37, Mississippi (SEC) 34	1OT	34-34	Vanderbilt	Defense
9-25	Pac-10	Oregon 33, Southern California (Pac-10) 30	3OT	23-23	Oregon	Defense
9-25	SEC	Mississippi 24, Auburn (SEC) 17	1OT	17-17	Auburn	Defense
10-2	Big Ten	Indiana 34, Illinois (Big Ten) 31	2OT	28-28	Indiana	Defense
10-2	SEC	Alabama 40, Florida (SEC) 39	1OT	33-33	Alabama	Defense
10-7	Conf. USA	Army 59, Louisville (CUSA) 52	2OT	45-45	Army	Defense
10-9	ACC	Duke 24, Virginia 17 (ACC) 17	2OT	17-17	Duke	Defense
10-9	ACC	Georgia Tech 31, North Carolina (ACC) 24	1OT	24-24	North Carolina	Defense
10-9	Big Ten	Wisconsin 20, Minnesota (Big Ten) 17	1OT	14-14	Wisconsin	Defense
10-9	Big 12	Colorado 46, Missouri (Big 12) 39	1OT	39-39	Missouri	Defense
10-9	MAC	Western Mich. 40, Eastern Mich. (MAC) 37	1OT	37-37	Eastern Mich.	Defense
10-16	Big West	Idaho 30, Arkansas St. (Big West) 24	1OT	24-24	Idaho	Defense
10-23	ACC	North Carolina St. 31, Duke (ACC) 24	1OT	24-24	Duke	Defense

DIVISION I-A OVERTIME FOOTBALL GAMES

Date	Winner's Conf.	Score (Loser's Conf.)	OT Periods	Reg. Score	Team With Choice	Choice
10-23	WAC	Fresno St. 24, UTEP (WAC) 23	1OT	17-17	UTEP	Defense
11-13	Big East	Rutgers 24, Syracuse (Big East) 21	1OT	21-21	Rutgers	Defense
11-13	Pac-10	UCLA 23, Washington (Pac-10) 20	1OT	20-20	UCLA	Defense
11-13	WAC	Hawaii 31, Fresno St. (WAC) 24	2OT	21-21	Hawaii	Defense
11-20	MAC	Bowling Green 33, UCF (Indep.) 30	1OT	27-27	Bowling Green	Defense
11-26	Big 12	Nebraska 33, Colorado (Big 12) 30	1OT	27-27	Nebraska	Defense
11-27	SEC	Georgia Tech 51, Georgia (SEC) 48	1OT	48-48	Georgia	Defense
1-1-00	SEC	Georgia 28, Purdue (Big Ten) 25 (Outback)	1OT	25-25	Georgia	Defense
1-1-00	Big Ten	Michigan 35, Alabama (SEC) 34 (Orange)	1OT	28-28	Alabama	Defense

All-Time Division I-A Won-Lost Records in Overtime Games 1996-99

Team	1996	1997	1998	1999	Overall W-L
Air Force	2-0	1-0	0-0	0-0	3-0
Alabama	0-0	0-1	1-0	1-1	2-2
UAB	0-0	0-0	0-1	0-0	0-1
Arizona	0-1	1-1	0-0	0-0	1-2
Arizona St.	1-0	0-0	1-0	0-0	2-0
Arkansas	1-0	0-0	0-0	0-0	1-0
Arkansas St.	0-0	0-0	1-0	0-1	1-1
Army	0-0	0-0	0-0	1-0	1-0
Auburn	0-1	0-0	0-0	0-1	0-2
Ball St.	1-0	1-0	0-0	0-0	2-0
Baylor	0-1	0-0	0-0	0-1	0-2
Boise St.	0-0	1-0	0-1	0-0	1-1
Boston College	0-0	0-1	0-0	1-0	1-1
Bowling Green	0-1	0-0	0-0	1-0	1-1
Brigham Young	1-0	1-0	0-0	0-0	2-0
California	2-0	0-1	0-0	0-0	2-1
UCF	0-0	0-1	0-0	0-1	0-2
Central Mich.	0-0	0-1	1-0	0-0	1-1
Clemson	0-0	1-0	0-0	0-0	1-0
Cincinnati	1-0	1-1	0-0	0-0	2-1
Colorado	0-0	0-0	0-0	1-1	1-1
Duke	0-0	0-1	0-1	1-2	1-4
Eastern Mich.	0-0	0-0	0-1	0-1	0-2
Florida	0-0	0-0	0-0	0-1	0-1
Fresno St.	0-2	0-1	0-0	1-1	1-4
Georgia	1-0	0-0	0-0	1-1	2-1
Georgia Tech	0-0	0-0	0-0	2-0	2-0
Hawaii	0-0	0-1	0-0	1-0	1-1
Houston	2-0	1-0	0-0	0-0	3-0
Idaho	0-0	0-1	1-0	1-0	2-1
Illinois	1-0	0-0	0-0	0-1	1-1
Indiana	0-1	0-0	0-1	1-0	1-2
Iowa St.	0-1	0-0	0-0	0-0	0-1
Kansas	0-0	0-0	1-0	0-0	1-0
Kansas St.	0-0	0-0	0-1	0-0	0-1
Kentucky	0-0	1-0	0-0	0-0	1-0
La.-Lafayette	0-0	0-2	0-0	0-0	0-2
La.-Monroe	1-0	2-0	0-0	0-0	3-0
LSU	0-0	0-0	0-1	0-0	0-1
Louisville	0-0	0-0	0-0	0-1	0-1
Miami (Fla.)	0-0	1-0	0-1	0-0	1-1
Miami (Ohio)	0-1	0-0	0-0	0-1	0-2
Michigan	0-0	0-0	0-0	1-0	1-0
Michigan St.	0-0	0-0	1-0	0-0	1-0
Minnesota	0-0	0-0	0-0	0-1	0-1
Mississippi	0-0	1-0	2-1	1-1	4-2
Mississippi St.	0-1	0-0	0-0	0-0	0-1
Missouri	2-0	1-1	0-0	0-1	3-2
UNLV	0-0	0-2	0-1	0-0	0-3
Nebraska	0-0	1-0	0-0	1-0	2-0
New Mexico	0-0	0-0	1-1	0-0	1-1
New Mexico St.	0-0	0-1	0-2	0-0	0-3

Team	1996	1997	1998	1999	Overall W-L
North Carolina	0-0	0-0	1-0	0-1	1-1
North Carolina St.	0-0	1-0	0-1	1-0	2-1
Northwestern	0-0	0-0	0-0	1-0	1-0
Notre Dame	0-2	0-0	0-0	0-0	0-2
Ohio	0-1	0-0	0-0	0-0	0-1
Oklahoma	1-0	0-0	0-0	0-0	1-0
Oklahoma St.	1-1	0-2	0-0	0-0	1-3
Oregon	1-1	1-0	0-2	1-0	3-3
Oregon St.	0-1	0-0	1-0	0-0	1-1
Pittsburgh	0-1	2-0	0-0	0-0	2-1
Purdue	0-0	0-0	0-0	0-1	0-1
Rice	0-0	0-0	1-0	0-0	1-0
Rutgers	0-0	0-1	0-0	1-0	1-1
San Diego St.	0-0	1-1	2-0	0-0	3-1
San Jose St.	0-0	1-0	0-0	0-0	1-0
Southern California	1-2	0-0	0-0	0-1	1-3
Southern Methodist	0-0	0-1	0-2	0-0	0-3
Southern Miss.	0-1	0-0	0-0	0-0	0-1
Stanford	1-0	0-0	0-1	0-0	1-1
Syracuse	0-0	0-1	0-0	0-1	0-2
Tennessee	0-0	0-0	1-0	0-0	1-0
Texas	0-1	0-0	0-0	0-0	0-1
Texas A&M	0-0	0-0	1-0	1-0	2-0
TCU	0-0	0-0	1-0	0-0	1-0
UTEP	0-0	0-0	0-1	0-1	0-2
Toledo	1-0	0-0	0-0	0-0	1-0
UCLA	1-0	0-0	1-0	1-0	3-0
Utah	0-0	1-0	0-0	0-1	1-1
Utah St.	0-0	0-0	1-1	0-0	1-1
Vanderbilt	0-0	0-0	1-1	0-0	1-1
Virginia	0-0	0-0	0-0	0-1	0-1
Virginia Tech	0-0	0-0	1-0	1-0	2-0
Washington	1-0	0-0	0-0	0-1	1-1
Washington St.	0-1	1-0	0-0	0-0	1-1
West Virginia	0-0	0-1	0-0	0-0	0-1
Western Mich.	1-1	0-0	0-0	1-0	2-1
Wisconsin	0-0	0-0	0-0	1-0	1-0
Wyoming	1-1	0-0	1-0	0-0	2-1
I-AA, II Opponents	0-2	2-0	0-0	0-0	2-2
Totals	**26-26**	**25-25**	**24-24**	**24-24**	**99-99**

BY CONFERENCE

Conference	1996	1997	1998	1999	Overall W-L
Atlantic Coast	0-0	2-1	1-2	3-4	6-7
Big East	0-1	3-4	1-2	2-1	6-8
Big Ten	1-1	0-0	1-1	4-3	6-5
Big 12	4-4	3-3	2-1	2-3	11-11
Big West	0-0	1-2	3-4	1-1	5-7
Conference USA	3-1	2-1	0-0	1-1	6-3
Mid-American	3-4	1-2	0-0	2-1	7-7
Mountain West	0-0	0-0	0-0	0-0	0-0
Pacific-10	8-6	3-2	3-3	2-2	16-13
Southeastern	2-2	2-1	5-4	5-5	14-12
Western Athletic	4-3	4-6	7-6	2-2	17-17
I-A Independents	1-2	2-3	0-1	0-1	3-7
I-AA, II Opponents	0-2	2-0	0-0	0-0	2-2
Totals	**26-26**	**25-25**	**24-24**	**24-24**	**99-99**

Division I-A Stadiums

STADIUMS LISTED ALPHABETICALLY BY SCHOOL

School	Stadium	Conference	Year Built	Cap.	Surface* (Year)
Air Force	Falcon	Mountain West	1962	52,480	Grass
Akron	Rubber Bowl	Mid-American-E	1940	35,202	AstroTurf (94)
Alabama	Bryant-Denny	Southeastern-W	1929	83,818	PAT (S91)
UAB	^Legion Field	Conference USA	1927	83,091	Grass (S95)
Arizona	Arizona	Pacific-10	1928	57,803	Grass
Arizona St.	Sun Devil	Pacific-10	1959	73,656	Grass
Arkansas	Razorback	Southeastern-W	1938	50,019	Grass (S95)
	^War Memorial	Southeastern-W	1948	53,727	Grass (S94)
Arkansas St.	Indian	Big West	1974	33,410	Grass
Army	Michie	Conference USA	1924	39,929	AstroTurf (92)
Auburn	Jordan-Hare	Southeastern-W	1939	85,214	Grass
Ball St.	Ball State	Mid-American-W	1967	21,581	Grass
Baylor	Floyd Casey	Big 12-S	1950	50,000	SportGrass (S98)
Boise St.	Bronco	Big West	1970	30,000	Blue AstroTurf
Boston College	Alumni	Big East	1957	44,500	AstroTurf (97)
Bowling Green	Doyt Perry	Mid-American-E	1966	30,599	Grass
Brigham Young	Cougar	Mountain West	1964	65,000	Grass
Buffalo	UB Stadium	Mid-American-E	1993	30,000	Grass
California	Memorial	Pacific-10	1923	75,662	Grass (S95)
UCF	^Florida Citrus	Independent	1936	70,188	Grass
Central Mich.	Kelly-Shorts	Mid-American-W	1972	30,087	AstroTurf (97)
Cincinnati	Nippert	Conference USA	1916	35,000	AstroTurf 8 (92)
Clemson	Memorial	Atlantic Coast	1942	81,473	Grass
Colorado	Folsom	Big 12-N	1924	51,655	Grass (S99)
Colorado St.	Hughes	Mountain West	1968	30,000	Grass
Duke	Wallace Wade	Atlantic Coast	1929	33,941	Grass
East Caro.	Dowdy-Ficklen	Conference USA	1963	43,000	Grass (83)
Eastern Mich.	Rynearson	Mid-American-W	1969	30,200	StadiaTurf (91)
Florida	Florida Field	Southeastern-E	1929	83,000	Grass (S90)
Florida St.	Doak S. Campbell	Atlantic Coast	1950	80,000	PAT (88)
Fresno St.	Bulldog	Western Athletic	1980	41,031	Grass
Georgia	Sanford	Southeastern-E	1929	86,117	Grass
Georgia Tech	Bobby Dodd/Grant Field	Atlantic Coast	1913	46,000	Grass (S95)
Hawaii	^Aloha	Western Athletic	1975	50,000	AstroTurf (85)
Houston	Robertson	Conference USA	1942	22,000	Grass
Idaho	#Kibbie Dome	Big West	1975	16,000	AstroTurf
Illinois	Memorial	Big Ten	1923	70,904	AstroTurf (89)
Indiana	Memorial	Big Ten	1960	52,354	Grass (S98)
Iowa	Kinnick	Big Ten	1929	70,397	PAT (S89)
Iowa St.	Cyclone-Jack Trice	Big 12-N	1975	43,000	Gras (S96)
Kansas	Memorial	Big 12-N	1921	50,250	AstroTurf (90)
Kansas St.	K S U-Wagner Field	Big 12-N	1968	51,000	AstroTurf-8 (91)
Kent St.	Dix	Mid-American-E	1969	30,520	AstroTurf (S97)
Kentucky	Commonwealth	Southeastern-E	1973	67,530	Grass
La.-Lafayette	Cajun Field	Independent	1971	31,000	Grass
La.-Monroe	Malone	Independent	1978	30,427	Grass
LSU	Tiger	Southeastern-W	1924	91,600	Grass
Louisiana Tech	Joe Aillet	Independent	1968	30,600	Grass
Louisville	Papa John's Cardinal	Conference USA	1998	42,000	SportGrass (98)
Marshall	Marshall University	Mid-American-E	1991	30,000	PolyTurf
Maryland	Byrd	Atlantic Coast	1950	48,055	Grass
Memphis	^Liberty Bowl	Conference USA	1965	62,380	Grass (87)
Miami (Fla.)	^Orange Bowl	Big East	1935	74,476	PAT (S77)
Miami (Ohio)	Fred C. Yager	Mid-American-E	1983	30,012	Grass
Michigan	Michigan	Big Ten	1927	107,501	PAT (S91)
Michigan St.	Spartan	Big Ten	1957	72,027	Turf (94)
Middle Tenn. St.	Floyd/Jones Field	Independent	1998	31,000	AstroTurf
Minnesota	^#Metrodome	Big Ten	1982	63,669	AstrTurf-8
Mississippi	Vaught-Hemingway	Southeastern-W	1941	50,577	Grass
Mississippi St.	Scott Field	Southeastern-W	1914	40,656	PAT (86)
Missouri	Memorial/Faurot Field	Big 12-N	1926	62,000	Grass (S95)
Navy	Navy-Marine Corps Mem.	Independent	1959	30,000	Grass
Nebraska	Memorial/Osborne Field	Big 12-N	1923	74,056	FieldTurf (S99)
UNLV	^Sam Boyd	Mountain West	1971	40,000	Grass (S99)
Nevada	Mackay	Big West	1967	31,545	Grass
New Mexico	University	Mountain West	1960	31,218	Grass
New Mexico St.	Aggie Memorial	Big West	1978	30,343	Grass
North Carolina	Kenan Memorial	Atlantic Coast	1927	60,000	Grass
North Carolina St.	^Carter-Finley	Atlantic Coast	1966	50,000	Grass
North Texas	Fouts Field	Big West	1952	30,500	All-Pro Turf
Northern Ill.	Huskie	Mid-American-W	1965	31,000	AstroTurf (89)
Northwestern	Ryan Field	Big Ten	1926	47,129	Grass (S97)
Notre Dame	Notre Dame	Independent	1930	80,012	Grass
Ohio	Peden	Mid-American-E	1929	20,000	Grass
Ohio St.	Ohio	Big Ten	1922	91,470	PAT (90)
Oklahoma	Memorial	Big 12-S	1923	72,422	Grass (S94)
Oklahoma St.	Lewis	Big 12-S	1920	50,614	AstroTurf (87)
Oregon	Autzen	Pacific-10	1967	41,698	Omni-Turf (91)
Oregon St.	Parker	Pacific-10	1953	35,362	Grass (S99)
Penn St.	Beaver	Big Ten	1960	93,967	Grass
Pittsburgh	Three Rivers (temporary)	Big East	NA	59,600	AstroTurf
Purdue	Ross-Ade	Big Ten	1924	67,861	PAT (75)

DIVISION I-A STADIUMS

School	Stadium	Conference	Year Built	Cap.	Surface* (Year)
Rice	Rice	Western Athletic	1950	70,000	AstroTurf-12 (97)
Rutgers	Rutgers	Big East	1994	41,500	Grass
San Diego St.	^Qualcomm	Mountain West	1967	71,400	Grass
San Jose St.	Spartan	Western Athletic	1933	31,218	Grass
South Carolina	Williams-Brice	Southeastern-E	1934	80,250	Grass
Southern California	^L.A. Mem. Coliseum	Pacific-10	1923	92,000	Grass
Southern Methodist	Cotton Bowl	Western Athletic	1930	68,252	Grass (S93)
Southern Miss.	Roberts	Conference USA	1976	33,000	Grass
Stanford	Stanford	Pacific-10	1921	85,500	Grass
Syracuse	#Carrier Dome	Big East	1980	50,000	AstroTurf
Temple	Veterans	Big East	1971	66,592	Astro-Turf-8
Tennessee	Neyland	Southeastern-E	1921	102,854	Grass (S94)
Texas	Royal-Memorial	Big 12-S	1924	80,082	PAT (S99)
Texas A&M	Kyle Field	Big 12-S	1925	80,200	Grass (S96)
TCU	Amon G. Carter	Western Athletic	1929	46,000	Grass (S92)
UTEP	^Sun Bowl	Western Athletic	1963	52,000	AstroTurf (97)
Texas Tech	Jones	Big 12-S	1947	50,500	AstroTurf-8 (88)
Toledo	Glass Bowl	Mid-American-W	1937	26,248	AstroTurf (90)
Tulane	^#Superdome	Conference USA	1975	70,892	AstroTurf (95)
Tulsa	Skelly	Western Athletic	1930	40,385	Stadia Turf (91)
UCLA	^Rose Bowl	Pacific-10	1922	89,000	Grass
Utah	Robert Rice	Mountain West	1927	32,500	SportGrass (S95)
Utah St.	E.L. Romney	Big West	1968	30,257	Grass
Vanderbilt	Vanderbilt	Southeastern-E	1981	41,448	Grass (S99)
Virginia	Scott/Harrison Field	Atlantic Coast	1931	61,500	PAT (S95)
Virginia Tech	Lane	Big East	1965	50,000	Grass
Wake Forest	Groves	Atlantic Coast	1968	31,500	Grass
Washington	Husky	Pacific-10	1920	72,500	AstroTurf (95)
Washington St.	Clarence D. Martin	Pacific-10	1972	37,600	Omni-Turf (90)
West Virginia	Mountaineer Field	Big East	1980	63,500	AstroTurf-12 (97)
Western Mich.	Waldo	Mid-American-W	1939	30,200	PAT (S99)
Wisconsin	Camp Randall	Big Ten	1917	76,129	AstroTurf (98)
Wyoming	War Memorial	Mountain West	1950	33,500	Grass

^Not located on campus. #Indoor facility.

STADIUMS LISTED BY CAPACITY (70,000 AND ABOVE)

School	Stadium	Surface* (Year)	Capacity
Michigan	Michigan	PAT (S91)	107,501
Tennessee	Neyland	Grass (S94)	102,854
Penn St.	Beaver	Grass	93,967
Southern California	^L.A. Mem. Coliseum	Grass	92,000
LSU	Tiger	Grass	91,600
Ohio St.	Ohio	PAT (90)	91,470
UCLA	^Rose Bowl	Grass	89,000
Georgia	Sanford	Grass	86,117
Stanford	Stanford	Grass	85,500
Auburn	Jordan-Hare	Grass	85,214
Alabama	Bryant-Denny	PAT (S91)	83,818
UAB	^Legion Field	Grass (S95)	83,091
Florida	Florida Field	Grass (S90)	83,000
Clemson	Memorial	Grass	81,473
South Carolina	Williams-Brice	Grass	80,250
Texas A&M	Kyle Field	Grass (S96)	80,200
Texas	Royal-Memorial	PAT (S99)	80,082
Notre Dame	Notre Dame	Grass	80,012
Florida St.	Doak S. Campbell	PAT (88)	80,000
Wisconsin	Camp Randall	AstroTurf (98)	76,129
California	Memorial	Grass (S95)	75,662
Miami (Fla.)	^Orange Bowl	PAT (S77)	74,476
Nebraska	Memorial/Osborne Field	FieldTurf (S99)	74,056
Arizona St.	Sun Devil	Grass	73,656
Washington	Husky	AstroTurf (95)	72,500
Oklahoma	Memorial	Grass (S94)	72,422
Michigan St.	Spartan	Turf (94)	72,027
San Diego St.	^Qualcomm	Grass	71,400
Illinois	Memorial	AstroTurf (89)	70,904
Tulane	^#Superdome	AstroTurf (95)	70,892
Iowa	Kinnick	PAT (S89)	70,397
UCF	^Florida Citrus	Grass	70,188
Rice	Rice	AstroTurf-12 (97)	70,000

^Not located on campus. @ Indoor facility.

Surface Notes: *This column indicates the type of surface (either artificial or natural grass) present this year in the stadium. The brand name of the artificial turf, if known, is listed as well as the year the last installation occurred. The "S" preceding the year indicates that the school has switched either from natural grass to artificial turf or vice-versa. Legend: Turf—Any of several types of artificial turfs (name brands include AstroTurf, All-Pro, Omni-Turf, SuperTurf, etc.); Grass—Natural grass surface; PAT—Prescription Athletic Turf (a "natural-artificial" surface featuring a network of pipes connected to pumps capable of sucking water from the natural turf or watering it. The pipes are located 18 inches from the surface and covered with a mixture of sand and filler. The turf also is lined with heating coils to keep it from freezing in temperatures below 32 degrees). SportGrass–Combines natural grass with a below-the-surface system of synthetic elements.

Division I-A Stadium Facts: Houston and Tulsa claim to be the first college football teams to play in an indoor stadium (the Astrodome on September 11, 1965). But actually, Utah and West Virginia met December 19, 1964, in the Liberty Bowl in the Atlantic City Convention Hall. Technically, the Astrodome was the first indoor stadium built specially for football and baseball. The first major-college football game ever played on artificial turf was between Houston and Washington State on September 23, 1966.

Famous Major-College Dynasties

The following are singled out because of their historical significance, and all represent an outstanding record as well as at least one national championship.

NOTRE DAME (1918-30)

Under Knute Rockne, the Fighting Irish posted an overall record of 105-12-5 (.881 winning percentage) and captured three national titles during this 13-year period. Rockne, who died in an airplane crash in 1931, did not accomplish this by himself, with athletes like George Gipp and the legendary Four Horsemen (Harry Stuhldreher, Elmer Layden, Jim Crowley and Don Miller) around. The longest unbeaten streak was 22 games, which began in 1918 under Gipp, but the South Benders had three other streaks of at least 15 games in the period.

MINNESOTA (1933-41)

Bernie Bierman, known as "The Silver Fox" for his prematurely gray hair, led the Golden Gophers through their best era. In the nine-year span, Minnesota posted a 58-9-5 (.840) record and won five national titles (1934, 1936, 1940 and 1941 outright and 1935 shared). Bierman oversaw five undefeated teams in the span, and the longest unbeaten streak was 28 games. Defense was a trademark of the Gophers, who notched 23 shutouts in the 72 games. The top offensive player was 1941 Heisman Trophy winner Bruce Smith.

NOTRE DAME (1946-53)

Under head coach Frank Leahy, Notre Dame began another streak almost as successful as the Rockne era. Leahy led the Irish to a national title in 1943, and beginning in 1946, Notre Dame set off on a 63-8-6 (.857) journey that yielded three more national championships (1946, 1947 and 1949) in four years. The longest unbeaten streak stretched to 39 games. The top players were Heisman Trophy winners Johnny Lujack (1947), Leon Hart (1949) and John Lattner (1953).

OKLAHOMA (1948-58)

Many felt this particular span featured the greatest accomplishment in modern-day collegiate football—Oklahoma's Bud Wilkinson-led 47-game winning streak from 1953-57.

FAMOUS MAJOR-COLLEGE DYNASTIES

The Sooners posted a 107-8-2 (.923) mark during the 11-year stretch that included three consensus national titles (1950, 1955 and 1956). Halfback Billy Vessels, the 1952 Heisman winner, was the outstanding individual player in the streak, but Wilkinson's teams were typified by overall speed and quickness.

ALABAMA (1959-67)

Paul "Bear" Bryant's return to his alma mater started a chain of events that eventually yielded one of the greatest dynasties in history. During the nine-year span, Bryant's teams fashioned an 83-10-6 (.869) record and captured three national prizes (1961, 1964 and 1965). His players included Joe Namath, Ken Stabler, Pat Trammell, Ray Perkins, Steve Sloan and Lee Roy Jordan, an eclectic group that featured no Heisman winners. All his players knew how to do was win football games, and the 1963-67 teams never lost a home game.

SOUTHERN CALIFORNIA (1967-79)

Two coaches—John McKay and John Robinson—shared this dynasty, which posted a 122-23-7 (.826) record and four national titles (1967, 1972 and 1974 under McKay and 1978 under Robinson). The longest unbeaten streak was 28 games. Southern California had two Heisman winners—O. J. Simpson (1968) and Charles White (1979)—and 18 consensus all-Americans in the 13-year period.

ALABAMA (1971-80)

This was the second great run for the Crimson Tide under Bryant. Alabama reeled off a 28-game unbeaten streak and posted a 107-13-0 (.892) record during the 10-year span, including national championships in 1973, 1978 and 1979. Again, there were no Heisman winners for Bryant, but he had a list of players like John Hannah, Steadman Shealy, Jeff Rutledge, Tony Nathan and Major Ogilvie. Bryant died in 1983 as the winningest college coach.

OKLAHOMA (1971-80)

Barry Switzer led the Sooner dynasty to a 102-14-2 (.873) record that included a 37-game unbeaten string and 10 Big Eight championships. Back-to-back national titles in 1974 and 1975 were the result of enormous talent and Switzer's coaching. Some of the Sooner all-Americans during the 10-year period included Jack Mildren, Greg Pruitt, Lucious Selmon, Rod Shoate, Tinker Owens, Dewey Selmon, Lee Roy Selmon, Joe Washington, Billy Brooks and George Cumby. Heisman Trophy winner Billy Sims (1978) was the biggest name in a Sooner rushing attack that was virtually unstoppable.

MIAMI (FLA.) (1983-92)

The loss to Alabama in the 1993 Sugar Bowl ended a real streak for the Hurricanes, going for a fifth national title since 1983. Few would argue that during the 1980s under three different coaches—Howard Schnellenberger, Jimmy Johnson and Dennis Erickson—the Hurricanes were the most successful team in America. With a 107-14-0 (.884) record that included national titles in 1983, 1987, 1989 and 1991, the Hurricanes served notice that an undefeated season was a possibility every year.

FLORIDA ST. (1987-95)

Under Bobby Bowden, Florida State fashioned one of the most remarkable regular-season and postseason records over this nine-year period. The Seminoles did what no other Division I school ever accomplished—win at least 10 games in all nine seasons. In fact, Florida State posted a 96-13-1 mark during the streak, which also includes an unprecedented 11 straight bowl victories. Bowden led teams that finished in the top five of The Associated Press poll for nine consecutive years. Florida State captured Bowden's first national title in 1993.

NEBRASKA (1988-97)

Some suggest that Nebraska under Tom Osborne was on a 25-year dynasty streak, beginning with the fact that every one of his first 25 teams posted at least nine victories. But that aside, these 10 years were a remarkable run for the Cornhuskers, with an 108-15-1 (.875) record including back-to-back national championships in 1994 and 1995 and a co-championship in 1997. The Huskers' 26-game win streak was the nation's longest through 1996, and the 29-year consecutive bowl string was a collegiate record. Actually, the Huskers were just a last-second field goal away from four national titles in the 1990s, losing to Florida State, 18-16, in the 1994 FedEx Orange Bowl.

FLORIDA (1990-99)

The beginning of Steve Spurrier's career at Florida also marked the start of a terrific dynasty in Gatorland. Not only did the Gators win at least nine games every season in the 1990s, but they won at least 10 games for six straight seasons (1993-98). Florida's record was 102-22-1 (.820) during the 10-year stretch. The Gators captured the 1996 national championship trophy with a 52-20 victory over state rival Florida State in the Sugar Bowl.

Other College Football Dynasties

(Listed Because of Their Historical Significance)

School (Years)	W-L-T	Pct.	Duration	Titles*
Yale (1876-1909)	315-14-18	.934	34 years	19
Princeton (1877-1903)	233-21-11	.900	27 years	12
Pennsylvania (1894-1908)	168-21-7	.875	15 years	4
Michigan (1901-09)	75-6-2	.916	9 years	2
Harvard (1908-15)	64-4-5	.911	8 years	5
Pittsburgh (1913-20)	55-5-4	.891	8 years	3
Southern California (1919-33)	129-18-3	.870	15 years	2
Tennessee (1938-46)#	72-9-2	.880	9 years	2
Michigan (1940-48)	68-13-2	.831	9 years	2
Army (1943-50)	64-5-5	.899	8 years	3
Michigan St. (1950-66)	117-37-4	.753	17 years	4
Ohio St. (1954-61)	56-14-4	.784	8 years	3
Texas (1961-72)	107-21-2	.831	12 years	3
Nebraska (1969-76)	79-14-4	.835	8 years	2
Penn St. (1980-87)	76-19-1	.797	8 years	2

*Some titles were shared. #No team in 1943 due to World War II.
(Special thanks to Bob Kirlin of Spokane, Wash., for his compilations.)

Major-College Statistics Trends†

(Average Per Game, One Team)

Year	Rushing Plays	Yds.	Avg.	Passing Att.	Cmp.	Pct.	Yds.	Av. Att.	Total Offense Plays	Yds.	Avg.	Scoring TD	FG	Pts.
1937	–	133.8	–	13.0	5.0	.381	64.5	4.96	–	198.4	–	–	–	10.1
1938	40.8	140.1	3.43	14.0	5.2	.371	70.1	5.01	54.8	210.2	3.85	1.75	0.06	11.8
1939	40.8	135.9	3.33	13.8	5.2	.374	66.4	4.81	54.6	202.3	3.70	1.66	0.09	11.4
1940	41.9	140.5	3.35	14.8	5.8	.386	77.8	5.26	56.7	218.5	3.85	1.97	0.08	13.3
1941	42.2	141.2	3.35	15.0	5.9	.392	80.7	5.38	57.2	221.8	3.88	2.03	0.06	13.8
1946	42.3	152.4	3.60	15.5	6.1	.389	88.2	5.69	57.8	240.7	4.16	2.39	0.04	16.1
1947	42.3	158.7	3.75	15.3	6.3	.414	90.3	5.91	57.6	248.8	4.32	2.37	0.04	15.9
1948	43.7	162.2	3.71	15.9	6.7	.423	94.6	5.95	59.5	256.5	4.31	2.52	0.05	17.1
1949	47.2	180.6	3.83	17.7	7.6	.431	110.4	6.24	64.9	290.7	4.48	2.86	0.04	19.4
1950	47.0	180.2	3.83	17.5	7.7	.438	108.5	6.19	64.5	288.6	4.47	2.79	0.04	18.9
1951	48.6	182.5	3.76	18.9	8.4	.446	113.7	6.02	67.5	296.1	4.39	2.86	0.05	19.4
1952	48.3	176.4	3.65	18.4	8.1	.441	111.9	6.09	66.7	288.2	4.32	2.68	0.07	18.4
1953	45.1	176.6	3.92	15.2	6.5	.428	91.7	6.03	60.3	268.2	4.45	2.54	0.05	17.1
1954	45.5	184.1	*4.05	14.9	6.5	.437	91.1	6.14	60.3	225.1	4.56	2.59	0.05	17.4
1955	46.1	176.7	3.83	13.6	5.9	.435	84.7	6.24	59.6	261.3	4.38	2.37	0.05	16.1
1956	49.2	193.1	3.93	14.1	6.2	.437	85.9	6.09	63.3	279.0	4.41	2.45	0.05	16.5
1957	49.3	177.5	3.60	14.4	6.4	.444	85.5	5.94	63.6	263.0	4.14	2.31	0.06	15.6
1958	47.1	170.7	3.62	16.1	7.4	.458	97.7	6.06	63.2	268.4	4.24	2.31	0.09	16.0
1959	46.2	166.0	3.59	16.5	7.5	.451	98.5	5.96	62.7	264.5	4.21	2.25	0.17	15.9
1960	45.3	169.9	3.75	15.8	7.2	.454	93.6	5.94	61.1	263.4	4.31	2.19	0.19	15.6
1961	45.6	166.7	3.66	15.9	7.2	.448	94.7	5.95	61.5	261.4	4.25	2.23	0.23	16.0
1962	45.3	164.0	3.63	17.2	8.0	.463	105.0	6.10	62.5	269.0	4.31	2.30	0.21	16.4
1963	44.1	160.0	3.63	17.6	8.1	.461	105.3	5.98	61.7	265.3	4.30	2.19	0.27	15.8
1964	43.7	149.7	3.43	17.9	8.5	.472	110.0	6.14	61.6	259.6	4.21	2.07	0.29	15.1
1965	45.1	149.4	3.31	20.8	9.7	.464	123.2	5.93	65.9	272.5	4.14	2.26	0.42	16.7
1966	44.3	148.7	3.36	22.0	10.3	.470	133.2	6.07	66.2	281.8	4.26	2.35	0.42	17.5
1967	47.3	154.7	3.27	22.9	10.7	.467	139.8	6.10	70.2	294.5	4.19	2.48	0.46	18.4

MAJOR-COLLEGE STATISTICS TRENDS

Year	Rushing Plays	Rushing Yds.	Rushing Avg.	Att.	Cmp.	Pct.	Yds.	Av. Att.	Total Offense Plays	Total Offense Yds.	Total Offense Avg.	TD	FG	Pts.
1968	49.7	170.8	3.44	25.4	12.1	.474	157.7	6.22	*75.1	328.5	4.38	2.89	0.46	21.2
1969	49.5	171.8	3.47	25.5	12.0	.471	157.1	6.17	74.9	328.9	4.39	2.90	0.54	21.6
1970	49.3	175.7	3.57	25.0	11.7	.467	152.7	6.12	74.2	328.3	4.42	2.83	0.57	21.3
1971	49.7	182.2	3.67	21.7	10.1	.463	132.3	6.10	71.3	314.5	4.41	2.69	0.54	20.2
1972	49.8	184.5	3.70	22.0	10.2	.462	136.9	6.24	71.8	321.4	4.48	2.71	0.61	20.6
1973	50.1	192.8	3.85	20.4	9.6	.472	130.9	6.41	70.5	323.6	4.59	2.75	0.65	21.0
1974	51.8	201.8	3.89	18.8	8.9	.474	122.3	6.50	70.7	324.1	4.59	2.64	0.63	20.2
1975	*51.9	*204.5	3.94	18.4	8.7	.473	119.6	6.52	70.3	324.1	4.61	2.57	0.74	20.1
1976	51.4	198.8	3.87	19.1	9.1	.474	123.5	6.49	70.4	322.2	4.58	2.57	0.75	20.0
1977	51.3	194.6	3.80	20.2	9.8	.483	134.5	6.67	71.5	329.1	4.61	2.67	0.73	20.8
1978	50.9	192.6	3.79	21.2	10.3	.486	138.9	6.55	72.1	331.5	4.60	2.64	0.76	20.6
1979	49.1	187.9	3.83	21.6	10.6	.491	139.3	6.47	70.6	327.2	4.63	2.55	0.77	20.7
1980	47.7	178.3	3.74	23.3	11.6	.500	151.9	6.52	71.0	330.2	4.65	2.61	0.81	20.5
1981	46.3	169.4	3.66	25.3	12.7	.502	164.7	6.51	71.6	334.1	4.67	2.57	0.87	20.5
1982	45.1	169.3	3.75	27.6	14.5	.522	182.4	6.61	72.7	351.7	4.84	2.71	1.02	21.9
1983	44.6	169.5	3.80	27.0	14.4	.536	182.8	6.79	71.6	352.3	4.92	2.73	1.06	22.1
1984	44.7	168.1	3.76	26.8	14.1	.527	181.1	6.77	71.5	349.2	4.89	2.66	1.15	22.1
1985	44.6	169.2	3.80	27.3	14.7	.537	186.1	6.82	71.8	355.3	4.95	2.74	1.09	22.4
1986	44.2	167.9	3.80	27.2	14.6	.537	185.1	6.81	71.4	353.0	4.95	2.80	1.07	22.7
1987	44.4	174.2	3.92	27.1	14.2	.526	183.6	6.78	71.5	357.8	5.01	2.83	1.13	23.1
1988	44.0	174.6	3.97	27.1	14.3	.529	185.8	6.87	71.1	360.3	5.07	2.91	*1.16	23.8
1989	42.7	166.4	3.90	28.5	15.4	.540	200.9	7.05	71.2	367.3	5.16	2.97	1.13	24.1
1990	43.1	167.7	3.90	28.3	15.1	.534	197.2	6.96	71.4	364.8	5.11	3.04	1.08	24.4
1991	43.3	169.7	3.91	27.2	14.6	.535	189.6	6.98	70.5	359.4	5.10	2.95	0.89	23.1
1992	42.7	165.6	3.89	28.1	14.9	.530	190.5	6.77	70.8	356.1	5.03	2.84	1.04	22.9
1993	41.8	166.3	3.98	28.7	15.9	*.551	204.9	7.13	70.5	371.2	5.27	3.09	0.97	24.4
1994	41.8	166.8	3.99	28.5	15.6	.547	198.3	6.96	70.3	365.1	5.19	3.11	0.99	24.6
1995	41.5	167.3	4.03	29.7	16.3	.547	205.5	6.92	71.2	*372.8	5.24	3.21	0.93	25.1
1996	41.5	164.4	3.97	28.9	15.4	.533	202.0	6.99	70.4	366.3	5.21	*3.26	0.94	25.48
1997	40.2	158.7	3.94	29.2	15.8	.543	207.6	7.12	69.4	366.3	*5.28	3.25	0.97	25.52
1998	40.7	158.6	3.89	29.1	15.7	.540	209.5	*7.19	69.9	368.1	5.27	3.20	1.05	25.46
1999	39.8	152.8	3.83	*30.6	*16.7	.544	*212.5	6.94	70.4	365.3	5.18	3.23	1.05	*25.63

*Record. +Records not compiled in 1942-45 except for Scoring Points Per Game: 1942 (15.7); 1943 (15.7); 1944 (16.3); 1945 (16.1).

Additional Major-College Statistics Trends†

Rules changes and statistics changes affecting trends: PUNTING—Beginning in 1965, 20 yards not deducted from a punt into the end zone for a touchback. INTERCEPTIONS—Interception yards not compiled, 1958-65. KICKOFF RETURNS—During 1937-45, if a kickoff went out of bounds, the receiving team put the ball in play on its 35-yard line instead of a second kickoff; in 1984 (rescinded in 1985), a 30-yard-line touchback for kickoffs crossing the goal line in flight and first touching the ground out of the end zone; in 1986, kickoffs from the 35-yard line. PUNT RETURNS—In 1967, interior linemen restricted from leaving until the ball is kicked.

(Average Per Game, One Team)

Year	Punting No.	Punting Avg.	Net Avg.	Interceptions No.	Interceptions Avg. Ret.	Interceptions Yds.	Punt Returns No.	Punt Returns Avg. Ret.	Punt Returns Yds.	Kickoff Returns No.	Kickoff Returns Avg. Ret.	Kickoff Returns Yds.	Pct. Ret'd
1937	9.2	36.3	–	1.68	–	–	–	–	–	–	–	–	–
1938	9.3	37.2	–	1.70	9.19	15.8	–	–	–	–	–	–	–
1939	*9.4	36.7	–	1.67	9.84	16.5	*4.42	9.40	41.6	2.14	19.3	41.3	.764
1940	9.1	36.6	–	1.79	10.05	18.0	4.21	10.58	44.5	2.32	20.4	47.5	.753
1941	8.9	36.1	–	*1.81	11.28	20.4	4.27	11.10	*47.4	*2.41	20.2	48.6	.768
1946	7.3	35.7	–	1.75	11.79	20.6	3.70	11.32	41.9	3.01	18.9	56.9	.870
1947	6.7	36.4	30.3	1.61	11.93	19.2	3.47	11.73	40.7	3.04	18.9	57.3	.884
1948	6.3	36.3	30.2	1.60	12.59	20.2	3.09	*12.16	37.6	3.17	18.5	58.6	.873
1949	6.3	36.6	30.3	1.69	*13.23	*22.3	3.21	12.13	38.9	3.51	17.9	62.8	.885
1950	6.0	36.3	30.8	1.61	11.99	19.3	3.04	10.72	32.6	3.46	16.6	57.4	.889
1951	6.4	35.9	30.7	1.67	12.00	20.1	3.10	10.58	32.8	3.53	17.0	59.9	.884
1952	6.3	36.4	31.6	1.60	11.60	18.5	3.07	9.95	30.5	3.45	17.6	60.7	.908
1953	5.2	34.9	29.7	1.37	12.12	16.6	2.57	10.66	27.4	3.27	17.8	58.2	.903
1954	4.9	34.9	29.4	1.36	12.48	16.9	2.42	11.16	27.0	3.32	18.4	61.0	*.910
1955	4.9	34.9	29.8	1.26	12.96	16.8	2.39	10.54	25.2	3.09	18.5	57.2	.892
1956	5.0	35.1	30.1	1.29	12.86	16.6	2.49	10.07	25.1	3.19	18.0	57.4	.906
1957	5.3	34.8	30.2	1.26	11.95	15.0	2.53	9.57	24.2	3.05	18.7	57.1	.897
1958	5.6	35.4	30.9	1.33	–	–	2.57	9.70	24.9	3.02	18.9	57.0	.880
1959	5.5	35.9	31.5	1.33	–	–	2.67	9.06	24.2	3.09	18.7	57.8	.892
1960	5.1	36.0	31.4	1.24	–	–	2.39	9.73	23.3	3.05	18.8	57.3	.890
1961	5.2	35.5	35.5	1.22	–	–	2.43	9.44	22.9	3.06	18.3	56.1	.873
1962	5.2	35.7	35.7	1.25	–	–	2.36	9.66	22.8	3.10	19.6	60.7	.876
1963	5.2	36.3	32.5	1.19	–	–	2.34	9.71	22.7	3.08	20.1	61.9	.880
1964	5.3	36.4	32.5	1.20	–	–	2.33	8.99	20.9	2.93	19.6	57.3	.862
1965	5.9	38.5	38.5	1.42	–	–	2.73	9.99	27.3	3.15	18.8	59.3	.849
1966	5.9	37.5	33.5	1.50	12.07	18.1	2.63	8.82	23.2	3.24	18.7	60.8	.849
1967	6.5	36.8	31.6	1.52	11.39	17.3	3.42	9.92	33.9	3.31	18.7	61.7	.831
1968	6.7	37.4	33.3	1.61	11.51	18.6	3.01	8.95	26.9	3.64	19.1	69.6	.829
1969	6.6	37.5	33.4	1.70	11.07	18.8	3.00	9.00	27.0	3.67	18.9	69.4	.818
1970	6.3	37.4	37.4	1.66	11.65	19.4	2.89	9.28	26.9	3.69	19.0	70.1	.828
1971	6.2	37.6	33.4	1.49	11.75	17.5	2.89	9.04	26.2	3.57	19.2	68.6	.834
1972	6.1	37.2	33.4	1.54	11.54	17.7	2.72	8.61	23.4	3.50	19.0	66.4	.803
1973	5.8	37.8	34.1	1.36	11.30	15.4	2.52	8.65	21.8	3.54	19.6	69.2	.797
1974	5.6	37.4	34.2	1.23	11.30	13.9	2.40	7.92	19.0	3.38	19.1	64.3	.784
1975	5.4	38.1	35.0	1.21	11.26	13.6	2.39	7.19	17.2	3.20	19.3	61.7	.733
1976	5.7	38.0	35.1	1.23	11.44	14.0	2.42	6.83	16.5	3.14	18.3	57.4	.722
1977	5.8	38.0	35.0	1.26	11.05	13.9	2.45	7.10	17.3	3.16	18.4	58.1	.711
1978	6.0	38.0	34.9	1.34	10.83	14.5	2.51	7.39	18.6	3.18	18.7	59.6	.665
1979	5.8	37.7	34.8	1.31	10.66	14.0	2.38	7.09	16.9	3.02	18.8	56.9	.637

ADDITIONAL MAJOR-COLLEGE STATISTICS TRENDS

(Average Per Game, One Team)

Year	Punting No.	Avg.	Net Avg.	Interceptions No.	Avg. Ret.	Yds.	Punt Returns No.	Avg. Ret.	Yds.	Kickoff Returns No.	Avg. Ret.	Yds.	Pct. Ret'd
1980	5.8	38.3	35.4	1.37	10.85	14.9	2.44	7.01	17.1	2.91	19.0	55.1	.651
1981	6.0	38.9	35.9	1.38	10.22	14.1	2.45	7.22	17.7	2.86	18.8	53.9	.636
1982	5.9	39.8	*36.5	1.39	10.70	14.9	2.40	8.00	19.2	2.69	19.3	51.9	.561
1983	5.5	39.5	35.9	1.37	10.43	14.3	2.47	7.95	19.7	2.65	19.2	50.8	.549
1984	5.6	39.7	36.3	1.31	10.07	13.2	2.47	7.61	18.8	3.03	18.6	56.2	.621
1985	5.5	39.6	36.1	1.30	10.47	13.6	2.45	7.92	19.4	2.94	19.4	57.0	.603
1986	5.4	39.2	35.4	1.30	10.99	14.3	2.51	8.23	20.7	3.78	19.8	74.6	.770
1987	5.4	38.6	34.7	1.32	10.82	14.3	2.48	8.31	20.6	3.89	19.1	74.5	.780
1988	5.2	38.4	34.7	1.24	11.17	14.0	2.39	7.96	19.1	*3.97	19.4	77.1	.778
1989	5.2	38.5	34.3	1.28	10.75	13.8	2.36	8.46	20.0	3.92	19.7	*77.2	.776
1990	5.3	38.6	34.3	1.23	11.40	14.0	2.45	9.33	22.9	3.79	19.6	74.5	.738
1991	5.3	38.4	34.3	1.18	11.30	13.3	2.50	8.74	21.9	3.43	19.4	66.6	.741
1992	5.6	39.0	34.9	1.20	11.00	13.2	2.63	9.04	23.8	3.30	20.1	66.4	.732
1993	5.2	38.8	35.1	1.14	11.00	12.5	2.28	8.28	18.9	3.43	20.0	68.7	.679
1994	5.3	39.2	35.3	1.10	12.10	13.3	2.38	8.64	20.5	3.50	20.0	69.8	.714
1995	5.3	38.7	34.9	1.12	11.67	13.1	2.23	8.98	20.0	3.57	19.5	69.7	.848
1996	5.5	40.0	35.8	1.04	12.83	13.4	2.39	9.56	22.8	3.34	20.4	68.0	.783
1997	5.4	*40.5	36.2	1.05	12.45	13.0	2.47	9.49	23.4	3.47	20.3	70.5	.816
1998	5.5	39.8	35.5	1.05	12.80	13.4	2.53	9.45	23.9	3.52	*20.6	72.4	.837
1999	5.6	39.8	35.3	1.12	13.00	14.5	2.61	9.61	25.1	3.36	20.3	68.2	.901

*Record. †Records not compiled in 1942-45.

Field Goal Trends (1938-1968)

Year	Made	Year	Made	Year	Made	Atts.	Pct.
1938	47	1951	53	1961	277		
1939	80	1952	83	1962	261		
1940	84	1953	50	1963	314		
1941	59	1954	48	1964	368		
1942-45	*	1955	57	1965	484	1,035	.468
1946	44	1956	53	1966	522	1,125	.464
1947	38	1957	64	1967	555	1,266	.438
1948	53	1958	103	1968	566	1,287	.440
1949	46	1959	†199				
1950	46	1960	224				

*Records not compiled. †Goal posts widened from 18 feet, 6 inches to 23 feet, 4 inches in 1959.

Field Goal Trends (From 1969)

(Includes Field Goal Attempts by Divisions I-AA, II and III Opponents)

Year	Made	Atts.	Pct.	16-39	Pct.	16-49	Pct.	40-49	Pct.	50-59	Pct.	60 Plus
1969	669	1,402	.477	538-872	.617	654-1,267	.516	116-395	.294	15-135	.111	0-8
1970	754	1,548	.487	614-990	.620	740-1,380	.536	126-390	.323	14-168	.083	1-9
1971	780	1,625	.480	607-1,022	.594	760-1,466	.518	153-444	.345	20-159	.126	0-11
1972	876	1,828	.479	705-1,150	.613	855-1,641	.521	150-491	.305	21-187	.112	1-12
1973	958	1,920	.499	728-1,139	.639	914-1,670	.547	186-531	.350	44-250	.176	1-21
1974	947	1,905	.497	706-1,096	.644	906-1,655	.547	200-559	.358	41-250	.164	1-17
1975	1,164	2,237	.520	849-1,255	.676	1,088-1,896	.574	239-641	.373	76-341	.223	4-32
1976	1,187	2,330	.509	854-1,301	.656	1,131-1,997	.566	277-696	.398	56-333	.168	3-24
1977	1,238	2,514	.492	882-1,315	.671	1,160-2,088	.556	278-773	.360	78-426	.183	6-40
1978	1,229	2,113	.582	938-1,361	.689	1,193-1,982	.602	255-621	.411	36-131	.275	1-4

Year	Made	Atts.	Pct.	Under 20		20-29		30-39		40-49		50-59		60 Plus	
1979	1,241	2,129	.583	34-43	.791	455-601	.757	425-706	.602	286-600	.477	41-173	.237	0-6	.000
1980	1,245	2,128	.585	31-39	.795	408-529	.771	452-696	.649	317-682	.465	37-175	.211	0-7	.000
1981	1,368	2,254	.607	42-48	.875	471-598	.788	461-731	.631	335-698	.480	58-169	.343	1-10	.100
1982	1,224	1,915	.639	31-34	.912	384-475	.808	415-597	.695	319-604	.528	73-190	.384	2-15	.133
1983	1,329	2,025	.656	34-37	.919	417-508	.821	477-636	.750	329-628	.524	72-201	.358	0-15	.000
1984	1,442	2,112	.683	44-49	.898	450-532	.846	503-681	.739	363-630	.576	80-206	.388	2-14	.143
1985	1,360	2,106	.646	40-47	.851	416-511	.814	478-657	.728	341-647	.527	84-227	.370	1-17	.059
1986	1,326	2,034	.652	45-48	.938	445-525	.848	448-641	.699	340-629	.541	44-182	.242	4-9	.444
1987	1,381	2,058	.671	45-48	.938	484-559	.866	469-638	.735	311-604	.515	72-200	.360	0-9	.000
1988	1,421	2,110	.673	33-35	.943	487-573	.850	495-664	.745	337-610	.552	68-217	.313	1-11	.091
1989#	1,389	2,006	*.692	50-53	.943	497-565	.880	471-655	.719	319-573	.557	52-154	.338	0-6	.000
1990	1,348	2,011	.670	39-42	.929	477-546	.874	454-626	.725	319-625	.510	59-167	.353	0-5	.000
1991$	1,092	1,831	.596	31-32	.969	395-519	.761	366-612	.598	254-531	.478	45-132	.341	1-5	.200
1992	1,288	1,986	.649	32-38	.842	464-569	.815	447-673	.664	294-577	.510	49-126	.389	2-3	.667
1993§	1,182	1,832	.645	23-25	.920	490-599	.818	407-617	.660	224-488	.459	38-98	.388	0-5	.000
1994	1,220	1,877	.650	39-40	.975	458-528	.867	419-626	.669	263-547	.481	40-128	.313	1-8	.125
1995	1,150	1,759	.654	32-32	1.000	468-549	.852	373-587	.635	244-489	.499	31-100	.310	2-2	1.000
1996	1,207	1,899	.636	28-29	.966	431-509	.847	422-632	.668	277-581	.477	49-147	.333	0-1	.000
1997	1,255	1,895	.662	47-48	.979	445-524	.849	446-659	.677	272-540	.504	45-122	.369	0-2	.000
1998	1,376	2,075	.663	50-60	.833	475-563	.844	466-681	.684	336-622	.540	48-144	.333	1-5	.200
1999	1,387	2,074	.669	36-38	.947	499-608	.821	480-671	.715	321-611	.525	50-142	.352	1-4	.250

*Record. #First year after kicking tee became illegal. $First year after goal-post width narrowed back to 18'6" from 23'4". §First year after hash marks narrowed to 60 feet from each sideline.

Field Goal Trends by Soccer-Style and Conventional Kickers

(Division I-A Kickers Only)
(Pete Gogolak of Cornell was documented as the first soccer-style kicker in college football history. The Hungarian-born kicker played at Cornell from 1961 through 1963. He set a national major-college record of 44 consecutive extra-point conversions and finished 54 of 55 for his career. His younger brother, Charley, also a soccer-styler, kicked at Princeton from 1963 through 1965.)

SOCCER-STYLE

Year	†No.	Made	Atts.	Pct.	16-39	Pct.	16-49	Pct.	40-49	Pct.	50-59	Pct.	60 Plus
1975	70	528	1,012	.522	370-540	.685	479-816	.587	109-276	.395	49-196	.250	1-17
1976	84	517	1,019	.507	350-517	.677	477-831	.574	127-314	.404	40-188	.213	3-16
1977	96	665	1,317	.505	450-649	.693	615-1,047	.587	165-398	.415	50-270	.185	2-27
1978	98	731	1,244	.588	540-768	.703	703-1,148	.612	163-380	.429	28-96	.292	1-3

Year	†No.	Made	Atts.	Pct.	Under 20	20-29	30-39	40-49	50-59	60 Plus
1979	116	839	1,413	.594	23-28	288-380	282-455	214-419	32-126	0-5
1980	121	988	1,657	.596	26-32	327-416	342-522	261-540	32-147	0-5
1981	138	1,108	1,787	.620	32-36	377-476	376-576	279-551	43-142	1-6
1982	105	1,026	1,548	.663	26-27	317-375	346-482	273-495	62-156	2-13
1983	110	1,139	1,724	.661	29-31	345-416	403-541	294-543	68-179	0-14
1984	127	1,316	1,898	*.694	43-47	414-480	438-589	341-572	78-197	2-13
1985	133	1,198	1,838	.652	35-41	369-452	415-578	306-560	72-191	1-16
1986	128	1,201	1,829	.657	37-40	398-467	410-575	313-576	39-162	4-9
1987	122	1,275	1,892	.674	40-43	458-523	424-574	290-566	63-177	0-9
1988	140	1,317	1,947	.676	31-33	445-521	468-630	311-562	61-201	1-11
1989	138	1,313	1,897	.692	49-52	462-526	441-612	310-551	51-150	0-6
1990	135	1,282	1,890	.678	36-38	450-515	432-589	308-590	56-154	0-4
1991	132	1,048	1,763	.594	30-31	381-500	349-589	243-512	44-130	1-1
1992	135	1,244	1,926	.646	31-37	447-554	429-647	288-561	47-124	2-3
1993	132	1,153	1,776	.649	23-25	475-578	398-600	219-475	38-93	0-5
1994	138	1,203	1,856	.648	38-39	452-522	410-617	263-543	39-127	1-8
1995	148	1,150	1,759	.654	32-32	468-549	373-587	244-489	31-100	2-2
1996	149	1,207	1,899	.636	28-29	431-509	422-632	277-581	49-147	0-1
1997	146	1,255	1,895	.662	47-48	445-524	446-659	272-540	45-122	0-2
1998	149	1,376	2,075	.663	50-60	475-563	466-681	336-622	48-144	1-5
1999	153	1,387	2,074	.669	36-38	499-608	480-671	321-611	50-142	1-4

CONVENTIONAL

Year	†No.	Made	Atts.	Pct.	16-39	Pct.	16-49	Pct.	40-49	Pct.	50-59	Pct.	60 Plus
1975	116	564	1,085	.520	427-640	.667	541-959	.564	114-319	.357	23-126	.183	3-13
1976	101	608	1,192	.510	460-720	.639	594-1,065	.558	134-345	.388	14-127	.110	0-7
1977	98	513	1,054	.487	384-586	.655	487-916	.532	103-330	.312	26-138	.188	4-14
1978	86	440	761	.578	352-516	.682	434-729	.595	82-213	.385	6-32	.188	0-0

Year	†No.	Made	Atts.	Pct.	Under 20	20-29	30-39	40-49	50-59	60 Plus
1979	70	333	585	.569	10-14	140-185	111-198	63-150	9-37	0-1
1980	62	258	471	.548	5-7	81-113	110-174	56-142	6-33	0-2
1981	50	195	367	.531	8-9	70-97	69-126	41-112	7-22	0-1
1982	25	103	195	.528	3-4	36-50	34-62	25-59	5-18	0-2
1983	23	112	181	.619	4-5	40-55	46-58	22-50	0-12	0-1
1984	10	44	76	.579	0-1	17-26	20-33	7-15	0-1	0-0
1985	12	81	138	.587	3-4	22-29	29-40	19-44	8-20	0-1
1986	8	58	89	.652	4-4	21-28	17-27	14-24	2-6	0-0
1987	4	35	50	.700	4-4	10-14	14-16	6-9	1-7	0-0
1988	5	26	40	.650	0-0	17-21	5-7	4-10	0-2	0-0
1989	2	37	47	.787	1-1	19-20	12-16	5-9	0-1	0-0
1990	2	23	38	.605	1-1	8-10	8-9	4-13	2-5	0-0
1991	2	16	24	.667	0-0	5-9	6-7	5-7	0-1	0-0
1992	1	12	18	.667	0-0	5-6	6-8	1-4	0-0	0-0
1993	1	6	11	.545	0-0	4-5	2-3	0-3	0-0	0-0
1994	1	17	21	*.810	1-1	6-6	9-9	0-4	1-1	0-0
1995	0	0	0	.000	0-0	0-0	0-0	0-0	0-0	0-0
1996	0	0	0	.000	0-0	0-0	0-0	0-0	0-0	0-0
1997	0	0	0	.000	0-0	0-0	0-0	0-0	0-0	0-0
1998	0	0	0	.000	0-0	0-0	0-0	0-0	0-0	0-0
1999	0	0	0	.000	0-0	0-0	0-0	0-0	0-0	0-0

*Record. †Number of kickers attempting at least one field goal.

Average Yardage of Field Goals

(Division I-A Kickers Only)

Year	Soccer-Style Made	Missed	Total	Conventional Made	Missed	Total	Nation Made	Missed	Total
1975	35.1	43.2	39.0	33.1	41.3	37.0	34.1	42.2	37.9
1976	35.0	43.1	39.0	33.2	40.7	36.9	34.0	41.8	37.9
1977	34.7	44.3	39.5	33.3	41.9	37.7	34.1	43.2	38.7
1978	34.0	39.9	36.4	31.9	38.3	34.6	33.2	39.3	35.7
1979	33.7	39.9	36.2	31.9	38.0	34.5	33.2	39.3	35.7
1980	34.0	40.7	36.7	33.4	39.6	36.2	33.8	40.4	36.6
1981	33.9	40.1	36.2	33.2	38.6	35.7	33.8	39.8	36.1
1982	34.8	41.8	37.2	34.0	39.8	36.7	34.7	41.5	37.1
1983	34.7	42.1	37.2	32.3	40.5	35.5	34.5	41.9	37.0
1984	34.4	41.8	36.7	32.3	34.9	33.4	34.3	41.5	36.5
1985	34.5	41.3	36.8	35.4	41.7	38.0	34.5	41.3	36.9
1986	33.9	41.6	36.6	32.5	38.6	34.7	33.9	41.4	36.5
1987	33.5	41.8	36.2	32.3	41.4	35.1	33.5	41.8	36.2
1988	33.9	41.7	36.4	30.0	37.6	32.7	32.0	39.3	34.4
1989	33.5	41.2	35.9	30.5	39.6	32.4	33.4	41.2	35.8
1990	33.4	41.3	36.0	33.4	42.0	36.7	33.4	41.3	36.0
1991	33.2	40.7	35.8	28.6	31.9	40.7	35.9	40.4	36.1
1992	34.1	41.2	36.7	30.1	37.8	32.7	34.1	41.3	37.2
1993	32.4	38.9	34.7	26.8	38.0	31.9	32.3	38.9	34.6
1994	32.9	40.6	35.6	31.4	45.5	34.0	32.9	40.7	35.6
1995	32.4	40.1	35.0	—	—	—	32.4	40.1	35.0
1996	33.4	40.5	36.0	—	—	—	33.4	40.5	36.0
1997	33.2	40.1	35.5	—	—	—	33.2	40.1	35.5
1998	33.4	40.6	36.1	—	—	—	33.4	40.6	36.1
1999	34.0	40.9	36.8	—	—	—	34.0	40.9	36.8

Division I-A Extra-Point Trends

(From Start of Two-Point Attempts)

Year	Games	Percent Total Tries Kick	Percent Total Tries 2-Pt.	Kick Attempts Atts.	Kick Attempts Made	Kick Attempts Pct.	Two-Point Attempts Atts.	Two-Point Attempts Made	Two-Point Attempts Pct.
1958	578	#.486	*.514	1,295	889	.686	*1,371	*613	.447
1959	578	.598	.402	1,552	1,170	.754	1,045	421	.403
1960	596	.701	.299	1,849	1,448	.783	790	345	.437
1961	574	.723	.277	1,842	1,473	.800	706	312	.442
1962	602	.724	.276	1,987	1,549	.780	757	341	.450
1963	605	.776	.224	2,057	1,659	.807	595	256	.430
1964	613	.814	.186	2,053	1,704	.830	469	189	.403
1965	619	.881	.119	2,460	2,083	.847	331	134	.405
1966	626	.861	.139	2,530	2,167	.857	410	165	.402
1967	611	.869	.131	2,629	2,252	.857	397	160	.403
1968	615	.871	.129	3,090	2,629	.851	456	181	.397
1969	621	.880	.120	3,168	2,781	.878	432	170	.394
1970	667	.862	.138	3,255	2,875	.883	522	246	*.471
1971	726	.889	.111	3,466	3,081	.889	433	173	.400
1972	720	.872	.128	3,390	3,018	.890	497	219	.441
1973	741	.893	.107	3,637	3,258	.896	435	180	.414
1974	749	.885	.115	3,490	3,146	.901	455	211	.464
1975	785	.891	.109	3,598	3,266	.908	440	171	.389
1976	796	.877	.123	3,579	3,241	.906	502	203	.404
1977	849	.891	.109	*4,041	*3,668	.908	495	209	.422
1978	816	.884	.116	3,808	3,490	.916	498	208	.418
1979	811	.897	.103	3,702	3,418	.923	424	176	.415
1980	810	.895	.105	3,785	3,480	.919	442	170	.384
1981	788	.901	.099	3,655	3,387	.927	403	172	.427
1982	599	.901	.099	2,920	2,761	.946	320	120	.375
1983	631	.896	.104	3,080	2,886	.937	356	151	.424
1984	626	.889	.111	2,962	2,789	.942	370	173	.468
1985	623	.899	.101	3,068	2,911	.949	345	121	.351
1986	619	.905	.095	3,132	2,999	.958	330	131	.397
1987	615	.892	.108	3,094	2,935	.949	375	163	.435
1988	616	.899	.101	3,215	3,074	.956	363	156	.430
1989	614	.888	.112	3,233	3,090	.956	409	179	.438
1990	623	.911	.089	3,429	3,291	*.960	335	138	.412
1991	617	.906	.094	3,279	3,016	.920	342	128	.374
1992	619	.899	.101	3,156	2,967	.940	353	159	.450
1993	613	.912	#.088	3,455	3,251	.941	333	143	.429
1994	617	.897	.103	3,433	3,207	.934	395	163	.413
1995	622	.902	.098	3,594	3,354	.933	389	173	.445
1996	644	*.923	.077	3,862	3,630	.940	322	144	.447
1997	646	.913	.087	3,828	3,572	.933	367	155	.422
1998	652	.919	.081	3,826	3,590	.938	339	146	.431
1999	663	.926	.074	3,957	3,725	.941	315	128	.406

*Record high. #Record low.

Division I-A Extra-Point Kick Attempts (1938-1957)

Year	Pct. Made	Year	Pct. Made	Year	Pct. Made	Year	Pct. Made
1938	.608	1946	.657	1951	.711	1956	.666
1939	.625	1947	.657	1952	.744	1957	.653
1940	.607	1948	.708	1953	.650		
1941	.638	1949	.738	1954	.656		
1942-45	*	1950	.713	1955	.669		

*Not compiled.

Division I-A Defensive Extra-Point Trends

In 1988, the NCAA Football Rules Committee adopted a rule that gave defensive teams an opportunity to score two points on point-after-touchdown tries. The two points were awarded for returning an interception or advancing a blocked kick for a touchdown on point-after tries.

DIVISION I-A

Year	Games	Kick Ret./TDs	Int. Ret./TDs	Total Ret./TDs
1988	616	8/2	6/0	14/2
1989	614	12/3	9/2	21/5
1990	623	9/3	5/2	14/5
1991	617	9/3	10/3	19/6
1992	619	8/5	1/0	9/5
1993	613	5/2	6/1	11/3
1994	617	4/0	8/3	12/3
1995	622	12/5	5/3	17/8
1996	644	9/4	7/3	16/7
1997	646	13/3	6/1	19/4
1998	652	11/4	7/4	18/8
1999	663	8/2	3/0	11/2
Totals	7,546	108/36	73/22	181/58

Division I-A Fumble-Recovery Returns

In 1990, the NCAA Football Rules Committee adopted a rule that gave the defense an opportunity to advance fumbles that occur beyond the neutral zone (or line of scrimmage). In 1992, the rule was changed to allow defenses to advance any fumble regardless of position behind or beyond the line of scrimmage. Here are the number of fumble recoveries by division that were advanced, and the number that resulted in a score.

DIVISION I-A

Year	Games	Fumble Rec./TDs
1990	623	51/17
1991	617	60/16
1992	619	126/34
1993	613	117/24
1994	617	131/43
1995	622	148/49
1996	644	195/86
1997	646	206/76
1998	652	136/73
1999	663	150/84
Total	6,316	1,320/502

Major-College Tie Games

The record for most tie games in a single week is six—on October 27, 1962; September 28, 1963; and October 9, 1982.

Note: Tiebreaker procedures added for 1996 season.

Year	No.	Games	Pct.	Scoreless
1954	15	551	2.72	2
1955	22	536	4.10	1
1956	28	558	5.02	2
1957	24	570	4.21	4
1958*	19	578	3.29	2
1959	13	578	2.25	4
1960	23	596	3.86	4
1961	11	574	1.92	1
1962	20	602	3.32	2
1963	25	605	4.13	4
1964	19	613	3.10	2
1965	19	619	3.07	4
1966	13	626	2.08	0
1967	14	611	2.29	1
1968	17	615	2.76	1
1969	9	621	1.45	0
1970	7	667	1.05	0
1971	12	726	1.65	1
1972	14	720	1.94	1
1973	18	741	2.43	2
1974	18	749	2.40	0
1975	16	785	2.04	0
1976	13	796	1.63	1
1977	16	849	1.88	1
1978	16	816	1.96	1
1979	17	811	2.10	1
1980	12	810	1.48	0
1981	17	788	2.16	0
1982	14	599	2.34	0
1983	13	631	2.06	†1
1984	15	626	2.40	0
1985	13	623	2.09	0
1986	10	619	1.62	0
1987	13	615	2.11	0
1988	12	616	1.95	0
1989	15	614	2.44	0
1990	15	623	2.41	0
1991	14	617	2.27	0
1992	13	619	2.10	0
1993	11	613	1.79	0
1994	13	617	2.11	0
1995	9	622	1.45	0
1996	0	644	0.00	0
1997	0	646	0.00	0
1998	0	652	0.00	0
1999	0	663	0.00	0

*First year of two-point conversion rule. †Last scoreless tie game: Nov. 19, 1983, Oregon vs. Oregon St.

Highest-Scoring Tie Games

(Home Team Listed First; Both Teams Classified Major-College or Division I-A at Time)

Note: Tiebreaker procedures added for 1996 season.

Score	Date	Opponents
52-52	11-16-91	San Diego St.-Brigham Young
48-48	9-8-79	San Jose St.-Utah St.
43-43	11-12-88	Duke-North Carolina St.
41-41	9-10-94	Northwestern-Stanford
41-41	9-23-89	San Diego St.-Cal St. Fullerton

HIGHEST-SCORING TIE GAMES

Score	Date	Opponents
40-40	11-8-75	Idaho-Weber St.
39-39	11-7-82	Texas Tech-TCU
37-37	9-23-67	*Alabama-Florida St.
36-36	9-30-72	Georgia Tech-Rice
35-35	9-23-95	Michigan St.-Purdue
35-35	11-16-91	San Jose St.-Hawaii
35-35	12-9-89	Hawaii-Air Force
35-35	9-23-89	Colorado St.-Eastern Mich.
35-35	10-7-78	Ohio St.-Southern Methodist
35-35	10-19-74	Idaho-Montana
35-35	10-9-71	New Mexico-New Mexico St.
35-35	9-27-69	Minnesota-Ohio
35-35	9-21-68	Washington-Rice
35-35	11-18-67	Navy-Vanderbilt
35-35	12-11-48	†Pacific (Cal.)—Hardin-Simmons
34-34	10-6-90	Iowa St.-Kansas
33-33	10-1-83	California-Arizona
33-33	9-24-49	TCU-Oklahoma St.
33-33	10-31-31	Yale-Dartmouth

*At Birmingham. †Grape Bowl, Lodi, Calif.

Home-Field Records
(Includes Host Teams at Neutral-Site Games)

Year	Games	Won	Lost	Tied	Pct.
1966	626	365	248	13	.594
1967	611	333	264	14	.557
1968	615	348	250	17	.580
1969	621	366	246	9	.596
1970	667	399	261	7	.603
1971	726	416	298	12	.581
1972	720	441	265	14	.622
1973	741	439	284	18	.605
1974	749	457	274	18	.622
1975	785	434	335	16	.563
1976	796	463	320	13	.590
1977	849	501	332	16	.600
1978	816	482	318	16	.601
1979	811	460	334	17	.578
1980	809	471	327	12	.589
1981	788	457	314	17	.591
1982	599	368	217	14	.626
1983	631	364	254	13	.587
1984	626	371	240	15	.605
1985	623	371	239	13	.606
1986	619	363	246	10	.595
1987	615	387	215	13	*.640
1988	616	370	234	12	.610
1989	614	365	234	15	.607
1990	623	373	235	15	.611
1991	617	362	241	14	.598
1992	619	388	218	13	.637
1993	613	375	227	11	.621
1994	617	357	247	13	.589
1995	622	354	259	9	.576
1996	644	389	255	0	.604
1997	646	392	254	0	.607
1998	652	399	253	0	.612
1999	663	403	260	0	.608

* Record.

I-A Members Since 1978

The following list shows years of active membership for current and former Division I-A football-playing institutions. The lists are from 1978, the year Division I was divided into I-A and I-AA.

Active Members
Air Force	1978-99
Akron	1987-99
Alabama	1978-99
UAB	1996-99
Arizona	1978-99
Arizona St.	1978-99
Arkansas	1978-99
Arkansas St.	1978-81, 92-99
Army	1978-99
Auburn	1978-99
Ball St.	1978-81, 83-99
Baylor	1978-99
Boise St.	1996-99
Boston College	1978-99
Bowling Green	1978-81, 83-99
Brigham Young	1978-99
Buffalo	1999
California	1978-99

Active Members
UCF	1996-99
Central Mich.	1978-99
Cincinnati	1978-81, 83-99
Clemson	1978-99
Colorado	1978-99
Colorado St.	1978-99
Duke	1978-99
East Caro.	1978-99
Eastern Mich.	1978-81, 83-99
Florida	1978-99
Florida St.	1978-99
Fresno St.	1978-99
Georgia	1978-99
Georgia Tech	1978-99
Hawaii	1978-99
Houston	1978-99
Idaho	1997-99
Illinois	1978-99

Active Members
Indiana	1978-99
Iowa	1978-99
Iowa St.	1978-99
Kansas	1978-99
Kansas St.	1978-99
Kent St.	1978-81, 83-99
Kentucky	1978-99
La.-Lafayette	1978-99
La.-Monroe	1978-81, 94-99
LSU	1978-99
Louisiana Tech	1978-81, 89-99
Louisville	1978-99
Marshall	1978-81, 98-99
Maryland	1978-99
Memphis	1978-99
Miami (Fla.)	1978-99
Miami (Ohio)	1978-81, 83-99
Michigan	1978-99
Michigan St.	1978-99
Middle Tenn. St.	1999-00
Minnesota	1978-99
Mississippi	1978-99
Mississippi St.	1978-99
Missouri	1978-99
Navy	1978-99
Nebraska	1978-99

Active Members
UNLV	1978-99
Nevada	1992-99
New Mexico	1978-99
New Mexico St.	1978-99
North Carolina	1978-99
North Carolina St.	1978-99
North Texas	1978-81, 95-99
Northern Ill.	1978-81, 83-99
Northwestern	1978-99
Notre Dame	1978-99
Ohio	1978-81, 83-99
Ohio St.	1978-99
Oklahoma	1978-99
Oklahoma St.	1978-99
Oregon	1978-99
Oregon St.	1978-99
Penn St.	1978-99
Pittsburgh	1978-99
Purdue	1978-99
Rice	1978-99
Rutgers	1978-99
San Diego St.	1978-99
San Jose St.	1978-99
South Carolina	1978-99
Southern Calif.	1978-99
Southern Methodist	1978-86, 89-99
Southern Miss.	1978-99

Active Members
Stanford	1978-99
Syracuse	1978-99
Temple	1978-99
Tennessee	1978-99
Texas	1978-99
Texas A&M	1978-99
TCU	1978-99
UTEP	1978-99
Texas Tech	1978-99
Toledo	1978-99
Tulane	1978-99
Tulsa	1978-99
UCLA	1978-99
Utah	1978-99
Utah St.	1978-99
Vanderbilt	1978-99
Virginia	1978-99
Virginia Tech	1978-99
Wake Forest	1978-99
Washington	1978-99
Washington St.	1978-99
West Virginia	1978-99
Western Mich.	1978-81, 83-99
Wisconsin	1978-99
Wyoming	1978-99

Former Members
Appalachian St.	1978-81
Brown	1978-81
Cal St. Fullerton	1978-92

Former Members
Chattanooga	1978-81
Citadel	1978-81
Colgate	1978-81
Columbia	1978-81
Cornell	1978-81
Dartmouth	1978-81
Drake	1978-80
East Tenn. St.	1978-81
Furman	1978-81
Harvard	1978-81
Holy Cross	1978-81
Illinois St.	1978-81
Indiana St.	1978-81
Lamar	1978-81
Long Beach St.	1978-91
McNeese St.	1978-81
Pacific (Cal.)	1978-95
Pennsylvania	1978-81
Princeton	1978-81
Richmond	1978-81
Southern Ill.	1978-81
Tennessee St.	1978-80
Texas-Arlington	1978-81
Villanova	1978-80
VMI	1978-81
West Tex. A&M	1978-80
Western Caro.	1978-81
Wichita St.	1978-86
William & Mary	1978-81
Yale	1978-81

College Football Rules Changes

The Ball

1869—Round, rubber Association ball.
1875—Egg-shaped, leather-covered Rugby ball.
1896—Prolate spheroid, without specific measurements.
1912—28-28 1/2 inches around ends, 22 1/2-23 inches around middle, weight 14-15 ounces.
1929—28-28 1/2 inches around ends, 22-22 1/2 inches around middle, weight 14-15 ounces.
1934—28-28 1/2 inches around ends, 21 1/4-21 1/2 inches around middle, weight 14-15 ounces.
1941—For night games, a white ball or other colored ball with two black stripes around the ball may be used at the discretion of the referee.
1952—Ball may be inclined no more than 45 degrees by snapper.
1956—Rubber-covered ball permitted.
1973—Teams allowed to use ball of their choice while in possession.
1978—Ball may not be altered, and new or nearly new balls added.
1982—10 7/8 to 11 7/16 inches long, 20 3/4 to 21 1/4 inches around middle, and 27 3/4 to 28 1/2 inches long-axis circumference.
1993—Rubber or composition ball ruled illegal.

The Field

1869—120 yards by 75 yards; uprights 24 feet apart.
1871—166 2/3 yards by 100 yards.
1872—133 1/3 yards by 83 1/3 yards.
1873—Uprights 25 feet apart.
1876—110 yards by 53 1/3 yards. Uprights 18 1/2 feet apart; crossbar 10 feet high.
1882—Field marked with transverse lines every five yards. This distance to be gained in three downs to retain possession.
1912—Field 120 yards by 53 1/3 yards, including two 10-yard end zones.
1927—Goal posts moved back 10 yards, to end line.
1957—Team area at 35-yard lines.
1959—Uprights widened to 23 feet, 4 inches apart.
1966—Pylons placed in corners of end zone and at goal lines mandatory in 1974.
1991—Uprights moved back to 18 feet, 6 inches apart.
1993—Hash marks moved six feet, eight inches closer to center of field to 60 feet from each sideline (40 feet apart).

Scoring

1869—All goals count 1 each.
1883—Safety 1, touchdown 4, goal after TD 4, goal from field 5.
1884—Safety 2, touchdown 4, goal from field 5.
1897—Touchdown 4, field goal 5, touchdown failing goal 5, safety 2.
1902—Teams change goals after every try at goal following a touchdown, after every goal from the field and also at the beginning of the half.
1904—Goal from field 4.
1909—Goal from field 3.
1912—Touchdown 4.
1921—Ball put in play at 30-yard line after a safety, 20-yard line after a touchback.
1922—Try-for-point by scrimmage play from 5-yard line.
1924—Try-for-point by scrimmage play from 3-yard line.
1927—Goal posts placed on end lines.
1929—Try-for-point by scrimmage play from 2-yard line.
1958—One-point & two-point conversion (from 3-yard line). One-point safety added.
1974—Ball must go between the uprights for a successful field goal, over the uprights previously scored.
1976—Forfeit score changed from 1-0 to score at time of forfeit if the offended team is ahead at time of forfeit.

COLLEGE FOOTBALL RULES CHANGES—SCORING

1984—Try may be eliminated at end of game if both captains agree.
1995—Try at end of game mandatory unless team behind in score leaves field.

Scoring Values

1882—Touchdown 2 points; field goal 5 points; extra points 4 points
1883-87—Touchdown 4 points; field goal 5 points; extra points 4 points
1888-97—Touchdown 4 points; field goal 5 points; extra points 2 points
1898-1903—Touchdown 5 points; field goal 5 points; extra points 1 point
1904-08—Touchdown 5 points; field goal 4 points; extra points 1 point
1909-11—Touchdown 5 points; field goal 3 points; extra points 1 point
1912-57—Touchdown 6 points; field goal 3 points; extra points 1 point
1958-present—Touchdown 6 points; field goal 3 points; extra points 1 point/kick, 2 points/run or pass.
1988-present—Extra points 2 points/defense.

Note: Safety worth 1 point from 1882-1883, 2 points in all seasons since 1884.

Players

1869—Each team consisted of 25 players.
1873—Each team consisted of 20 players.
1876—Each team consisted of 15 players.
1880—Each team consisted of 11 players.
1895—Only one man in motion forward before the snap. No more than three players behind the line. One player permitted in motion toward own goal line.
1910—Seven players required on line.
1911—Illegal to conceal ball beneath a player's clothing.
1947—All players urged to be numbered in a uniform manner. Ends to wear numbers in the 80s; tackles, 70s; guards, 60s; centers, 50s; and backs, 10-49.
1966—Mandatory numbering of five players on the line 50-79.
1970—All players numbered 1-99.

Equipment

1894—No one wearing projecting nails or iron plates on his shoes, or any metal substance upon his person, is allowed to play. No greasy or sticky substance shall be used on the person of players.
1903—If head protectors are worn, there can be no sole leather or other hard or unyielding substances in their construction. Leather cleats on shoes allowed.
1908—First documented jersey numbers used by Washington & Jefferson.
1915—Numbers added to jerseys.
1927—Rubber cleats allowed, but under no conditions are cleats to be dangerously sharp.
1930—No player shall wear equipment that endangers players. The committee forbids the use of head protectors or jerseys that are so similar in color to the ball that they give the wearer an unfair and unsportsmanlike advantage over the opponent. Stripes may be used to break up the solid colors.
1933—Head protectors or helmets recommended to be worn by all players.
1937—All players must wear minimum 6-inch Arabic numerals on the front and minimum 8-inch Arabic numerals on the back of jerseys.
1939—All players must wear helmets.
1946—All players must wear minimum 8-inch Arabic numerals on front (changed from 6 inches) and minimum 10-inch Arabic numerals on back of jerseys (changed from 8 inches), of a single color which must be in sharp contrast with the color of the jerseys.
1948—One-inch kicking tees permitted.
1951—Any circular or ring cleat prohibited unless it has rounded edges and a wall at least 3/16-inch thick. Face masks added to helmet. Must be made of non-breakable, molded plastic with rounded edges.
1962—All players recommended to wear properly fitted mouth protectors.
1965—Two-inch kicking tees permitted.
1966—Players prohibited from wearing equipment with electronic, mechanical or other signal devices for the purpose of communicating with any source.
1968—Metal face masks having surfaces with material as resilient as rubber are allowed.
1970—Shoe cleats more than one-half inch in length (changed from three-quarters inch) prohibited.
1972—All players must wear mouth protectors, beginning with 1973 season.
1973—All players shall wear head protectors with a secured chin strap.
1974—All players shall wear shoulder pads.
1976—All players shall wear hip pads and thigh guards.
1979—Beginning in 1981, one team shall wear white jerseys.
1982—Tearaway jersey eliminated by charging a timeout.
1983—Mandatory white jersey for visiting teams.
1986—Therapeutic or preventive knee braces must be worn under the pants.
1989—Kicking tees eliminated for field goals and extra-point attempts.
1991—Rib and back pad covering mandatory.
1994—Standards established to limit glove stickiness. Jerseys that extend below the top of the pants must be tucked into the pants.
1995—Home team may wear white jerseys if both teams agree before the season.
1996—Cleats limited to one-half inch in length (see 1970). Violators disqualified for remainder of game and entire next game. Rule a dead ball when a ball carrier's helmet comes completely off, with the ball belonging to runner's team at that spot. Jerseys must extend to top of pants and must be tucked in if longer.
1997—Require all players on the same team to wear white or team-colored socks of the same design and length. Leg coverings, such as tights, if worn, must be in team colors and of a uniform design for all players on the same team.
1998—All eye shields, if worn, must be clear (transparent) and made from molded and rigid material. NCAA member institutions can, in the case of a death or catastrophic injury or illness, memorialize a player or person with a patch or decal not greater than 1 1/2 inches in diameter that displays the number, name or initials of the individual on the uniform or helmet.
1999—Visible bandanas are ruled an illegal uniform attachment.
2000—A maximum of two defensive players are allowed to wear 4-inch by 12-inch white towels without markings attached to the front belt.

Substitutions

1876—Fifteen players to a team and few if any substitutions.
1882—Replacements for disqualified or injured players.
1897—Substitutions may enter the game any time at discretion of captains.
1922—Players withdrawn during the first half may be returned during the second half. A player withdrawn in the second half may not return.
1941—A player may substitute any time but may not be withdrawn and the outgoing player returned to the game until one play had intervened. Platoon football made possible.
1948—Unlimited substitution on change of team possession.
1953—Two-platoon abolished and players allowed to enter the game only once in each quarter.
1954-64—Changes each year toward more liberalized substitution rule and platoon football.
1965—Platoon football returns. Unlimited substitutions between periods, after a score or try.
1974—Substitutes must be in for one play and replaced players out for one play.
1993—Players who are bleeding or whose uniforms are saturated with blood must come out of the game until their return has been approved by medical personnel.
2000—Offensive teams, while in the process of substitution or simulated substitution, are now prohibited from pushing quickly to the line of scrimmage and snapping the ball with the obvious attempt to create a defensive disadvantage.

Passing Game

1906—One forward pass legalized behind the line if made five yards right or left of center. Ball went to opponents if it failed to touch a player of either side before touching the ground. Either team could recover a pass touched by an opponent. One pass each scrimmage down.
1910—Pass interference does not apply 20 yards beyond the line of scrimmage. Passer must be five yards behind the line of scrimmage. One forward pass permitted during each down.
1914—Roughing the passer added.
1923—Handing the ball forward is an illegal forward pass and receivers going out of bounds and returning prohibited.
1934—Three changes encourage use of pass. (1) First forward pass in series of downs can be incomplete in the end zone without loss of ball except on fourth down. (2) Circumference of ball reduced, making it easier to throw. (3) Five-yard penalty for more than one incomplete pass in same series of downs eliminated.
1941—Fourth-down forward pass incomplete in end zone no longer a touchback. Ball goes to opponent at spot where put in play.
1945—Forward pass may be thrown from anywhere behind the line, encouraging use of modern T formation.
1949—Intentional grounding of a pass shall result in a loss of down and a five-yard penalty from the spot of the foul.
1966—Compulsory numbering system makes only players numbered other than 50-79 eligible forward-pass receivers.
1976—Offensive blocking changed to provide half extension of arms to assist pass blocking.
1980—Retreat blocking added with full arm extension to assist pass blocking, and illegal use of hands reduced to five yards.
1982—Pass interference only on a catchable forward pass. Forward pass intentionally grounded to conserve time permitted.
1983—First down added to roughing the passer.
1985—Retreat block deleted and open hands and extended arms permitted anywhere on the field.
1990—Pass thrown immediately to the ground to conserve time legal.
1994—Ball must be catchable for offensive player to be charged with pass interference.
1996—Principle of "reasonable opportunity to catch the pass" applied to intentional grounding situations.
1998—A backward pass can be recovered and advanced by the defense.
1999—Intentional grounding of a pass shall result in a loss of down at the spot of the foul.
2000—Allowing a passer, who is five yards or more toward the sideline from the original position of the ball at the snap, to throw the ball so that it lands beyond the neutral zone to avoid loss of yardage without penalty.

General Changes

1876—Holding and carrying the ball permitted.
1880—Eleven players on a side and a scrimmage line established.
1882—Downs and yards to gain enter the rules.
1883—Scoring system established.
1906—Forward passes permitted. Ten yards for first down.
1920—Clipping defined.
1922—Try-for-point introduced. Ball brought out five yards from goal line for scrimmage, allowing try for extra point by place kick, drop kick, run or forward pass.
1925—Kickoff returned to 40-yard line. Clipping made a violation, with penalty of 25 yards.
1927—One-second pause imposed on shift. Thirty seconds allowed for putting ball in play. Huddle limited to 15 seconds. To encourage use of lateral pass, missed backward pass other than from center declared dead ball when it hits the ground and cannot be recovered by opponents.
1929—All fumbles ruled dead at point of recovery.
1932—Most far-reaching changes in nearly a quarter of a century set up safeguards against hazards of game. (1) Ball declared dead when any portion of player in possession, except his hands or feet, touches ground. (2) Use of flying block and flying tackle barred under penalty of five yards. (3) Players on defense forbidden to strike opponents on head, neck or face. (4) Hard and dangerous equipment must be covered with padding.

College Football Rules Changes—General Changes

1941—Legal to hand ball forward behind the neutral zone.
1949—Blockers required to keep hands against their chest.
1951—Fair catch restored.
1952—Penalty for striking with forearm, elbow or locked hands, or for flagrantly rough play or unsportsmanlike conduct, changed from 15 yards to mandatory suspension.
1957—Penalty for grabbing face mask.
1959—Distance penalties limited to one-half distance to offending team's goal line.
1967—Coaching from sideline permitted.
1971—Crack-back block (blocking below waist) illegal.
1972—Freshman eligibility restored.
1977—Clock started on snap after a penalty.
1978—Unsuccessful field goal returned to the previous spot.
1983—Offensive encroachment changed...no offensive player permitted in or beyond the neutral zone after snapper touches ball.
1985—One or both feet on ground required for blocking below waist foul.
1986—Kickoff from the 35-yard line.
1988—Defensive team allowed to score two points on return of blocked extra-point kick attempt or interception of extra-point pass attempt.
1990—Defense allowed to advance fumbles that occur beyond the neutral zone.
1991—Width between goal-post uprights reduced from 23 feet, 4 inches to 18 feet, 6 inches. Kickoffs out of bounds allow receiving team to elect to take ball 30 yards beyond yard line where kickoff occurred. Holding behind the neutral zone penalized 10 yards from the spot of the foul.
1992—Defense allowed to advance fumbles regardless of where they occur. Changes ruling of 1990 fumble advancement.
1993—Guard-around or "fumblerooski" play ruled illegal.
1994—Players involved in a fight after half time disqualified for first half of next game; substitutes and coaches who participate in a fight in their team area or leave the team area to join a fight disqualified for entire next game; squad members and coaches involved in a fight during half time disqualified for first half of next game.
1995—Defense penalized five yards for entering neutral zone before snap and causing offensive player to react immediately. Players prohibited from removing helmets on the field. Players disqualified after second unsportsmanlike-conduct foul in one game. Fight suspensions allowed to carry over to next season.
1996—NCAA tiebreaker system to be used in all games tied after four periods.
1997—In overtime tiebreaker system, require a team that scores a touchdown to attempt a two-point conversion in the third overtime period. Approved a rule requiring a game to be declared a tie if it is in overtime but cannot be finished due to weather, darkness or other conditions. Chop block redefined to be penalized if "obviously delayed" and added restrictions to the "crack-back" block to make it illegal up to five yards beyond line of scrimmage regardless of position of the ball. Officials prompted to enforce mouthpiece rule, charging a timeout to offending team if clock is stopped and player does not have mouthpiece in place. To prevent opponents from leveling punt returners with unnecessarily vicious hits, the penalty was increased from five to 15 yards.
1998—For the first time in history, a backward pass can be recovered and advanced by the defense. It is now consistent with the application of the rules similar to how the defense is allowed to advance a fumble.
1999—Holding behind the neutral zone will be penalized 10 yards from the previous line of scrimmage. Dead-ball fouls by both teams which are part of continuing action or of a retaliatory nature and reported at the same time will be canceled and the penalties disregarded. However, any disqualified player must leave the game. Teams may not break the huddle with 12 or more players.
2000—An illegal block shall now include any high-low, low-high or low-low combination block by any two offensive players beyond the neutral zone regardless of simultaneous contact by both. Also, blocking below the waist by offensive players ("crack-back block") now includes not only wide receivers or players in motion but any player in motion in any direction at the snap and the area is expanded to included the neutral zone and 10 yards beyond. Also, prohibiting a defensive player(s) aligned in a stationary position within one yard of the line of scrimmage from making quick or abrupt actions that are not part of normal player movement in an obvious attempt to cause an offensive player(s) to foul.

Division I-AA Records

Individual Records	104
Team Records	110
Annual Champions, All-Time Leaders	114
Team Champions	132
Toughest-Schedule Annual Leaders	133
Annual Most-Improved Teams	134
All-Time Team Won-Lost Records	135
National Poll Rankings	137
Streaks and Rivalries	140
Cliffhangers	141
Division I-AA Stadiums	143
Division I-AA Statistics Trends	145
Black College National Champions	147

Individual Records

Total Offense

(Rushing Plus Passing)

MOST PLAYS
Quarter
33—Mickey Fein, Maine vs. Connecticut, Oct. 11, 1997 (4th)
Half
59—Joe Walland, Yale vs. Harvard, Nov. 20, 1999 (2nd)
Game
89—Thomas Leonard, Mississippi Val. vs. Texas Southern, Oct. 25, 1986 (440 yards)
Season
649—Steve McNair, Alcorn St., 1994 (5,799 yards)
Career
2,055—Steve McNair, Alcorn St., 1991-94 (16,823 yards)

MOST PLAYS PER GAME
Season
59.0—Steve McNair, Alcorn St., 1994 (649 in 11)
Career
49.5—Tom Proudian, Iona, 1993-95 (1,337 in 27)

MOST PLAYS BY A FRESHMAN
Game
81—Kevin Glenn, Illinois St. vs. Western Ill., Nov. 8, 1997 (470 yards)
Season
507—Marcus Brady, Cal St. Northridge, 1998 (2,942 yards)
Per-game record—48.9, James Lopusznick, Fairfield, 1996 (440 in 9)

MOST YARDS GAINED
Quarter
278—Willie Totten, Mississippi Val. vs. Kentucky St., Sept. 1, 1984 (2nd)
Half
404—Todd Hammel, Stephen F. Austin vs. La.-Monroe, Nov. 11, 1989 (1st)
Game
649—Steve McNair, Alcorn St. vs. Samford, Oct. 29, 1994 (587 passing, 62 rushing)
Season
5,799—Steve McNair, Alcorn St., 1994 (4,863 passing, 936 rushing)
2 Yrs
9,629—Steve McNair, Alcorn St., 1993-94 (8,060 passing, 1,569 rushing)
3 Yrs
13,686—Steve McNair, Alcorn St., 1992-94 (11,601 passing, 2,085 rushing)
Career
(4 yrs.) 16,823—Steve McNair, Alcorn St., 1991-94 (14,496 passing, 2,327 rushing)

MOST YARDS GAINED PER GAME
Season
527.2—Steve McNair, Alcorn St., 1994 (5,799 in 11)
Career
400.5—Steve McNair, Alcorn St., 1991-94 (16,823 in 42)

MOST SEASONS GAINING 3,000 YARDS OR MORE
4—Steve McNair, Alcorn St., 1991-94

MOST YARDS GAINED BY A FRESHMAN
Game
536—Brad Otton, Weber St. vs. Northern Ariz., Nov. 6, 1993 (48 plays)
Season
3,336—Travis Brown, Northern Ariz., 1996
Per-game record—313.7, Steve McNair, Alcorn St., 1991 (3,137 in 10)

MOST YARDS GAINED IN TWO, THREE AND FOUR CONSECUTIVE GAMES
2 Games
1,280—Steve McNair, Alcorn St., 1994 (633 vs. Grambling, Sept. 3; 647 vs. Chattanooga, Sept. 10)
3 Games
1,859—Steve McNair, Alcorn St., 1994 (649 vs. Samford, Oct. 29; 624 vs. Mississippi Val., Nov. 5; 586 vs. Troy St., Nov. 12)
4 Games
2,423—Steve McNair, Alcorn St., 1994 (649 vs. Samford, Oct. 29; 624 vs. Mississippi Val., Nov. 5; 586 vs. Troy St., Nov. 12; 564 vs. Jackson St., Nov. 19)

MOST GAMES GAINING 300 YARDS OR MORE
Season
11—Steve McNair, Alcorn St., 1994
Career
32—Steve McNair, Alcorn St., 1991-94

MOST CONSECUTIVE GAMES GAINING 300 YARDS OR MORE
Season
11—Steve McNair, Alcorn St., 1994
Career
13—Neil Lomax, Portland St., 1979-80; Willie Totten, Mississippi Val., 1984-85; Steve McNair, Alcorn St., 1992-93

MOST GAMES GAINING 400 YARDS OR MORE
Season
9—Steve McNair, Alcorn St., 1994
Career
15—Steve McNair, Alcorn St., 1991-94

MOST CONSECUTIVE GAMES GAINING 400 YARDS OR MORE
Season
5—Willie Totten, Mississippi Val., 1984; Steve McNair, Alcorn St., 1994

MOST GAMES GAINING 500 YARDS OR MORE
Season
6—Steve McNair, Alcorn St., 1994
Career
9—Steve McNair, Alcorn St., 1991-94

MOST YARDS GAINED AGAINST ONE OPPONENT
Career
1,772—Steve McNair, Alcorn St. vs. Jackson St., 1991-94
Also holds per-game record at 443.0 (1,772 in 4)

GAINING 1,000 YARDS RUSHING AND 1,000 YARDS PASSING
Season
Tracy Ham (QB), Ga. Southern, 1986 (1,048 rushing, 1,772 passing); Alcede Surtain (QB), Alabama St., 1995 (1,024 rushing, 1,224 passing); David Dinkins (QB), Morehead St., 1998 (1,169 rushing, 1,812 passing); Greg Hill (QB), Ga. Southern, 1998 (1,061 rushing, 1,193 passing); Greg Hill, Ga. Southern, 1999 (1,084 rushing, 1,262 passing)

GAINING 1,000 YARDS RUSHING AND 1,000 YARDS RECEIVING
Season
Brian Westbrook (TB), Villanova, 1998 (1,046 rushing, 1,144 receiving) (first NCAA player to accomplish this feat)

GAINING 2,000 YARDS RUSHING AND 4,000 YARDS PASSING
Career
Tracy Ham (QB), Ga. Southern, 1984-86 (2,506 rushing, 4,871 passing); Bill Vergantino (QB), Delaware, 1989-92 (2,287 rushing, 6,177 passing); Steve McNair (QB), Alcorn St., 1991-94 (2,327 rushing, 14,496 passing); Ryan Vena (QB), Colgate, 1996-99 (2,008 rushing, 7,427 passing)

GAINING 3,000 YARDS RUSHING AND 3,000 YARDS PASSING
Career
Willie Taggart (QB), Western Ky., 1995-98 (3,957 rushing, 3,029 passing); Greg Hill (QB), Ga. Southern, 1996-99 (3,309 rushing, 3,369 passing)

HIGHEST AVERAGE GAIN PER PLAY
Game
(Min. 39-49 plays) 12.4—John Whitcomb, UAB vs. Prairie View, Nov. 19, 1994 (43 for 533)
(Min. 50-59 plays) 11.4—Steve McNair, Alcorn St. vs. Chattanooga, Sept. 10, 1994 (57 for 647)
(Min. 60 plays) 9.7—Steve McNair, Alcorn St. vs. Grambling, Sept. 3, 1994 (65 for 633)
Season
(Min. 2,500-3,299 yards) 9.6—Frank Baur, Lafayette, 1988 (285 for 2,727)
(Min. 3,300 yards) 8.9—Steve McNair, Alcorn St., 1994 (649 for 5,799)
Career
(Min. 4,000 yards) 8.2—Steve McNair, Alcorn St., 1991-94 (2,055 for 16,823)

MOST TOUCHDOWNS RESPONSIBLE FOR
(TDs Scored and Passed For)
Game
9—Neil Lomax, Portland St. vs. Delaware St., Nov. 8, 1980 (passed for 8, scored 1); Willie Totten, Mississippi Val. vs. Prairie View, Oct. 27, 1984 (passed for 8, scored 1) & vs. Kentucky St., Sept. 1, 1984 (passed for 9)
Season
61—Willie Totten, Mississippi Val., 1984 (passed for 56, scored 5)
Also holds per-game record at 6.1 (61 in 10)
Career
157—Willie Totten, Mississippi Val., 1982-85 (passed for 139, scored 18)
Also holds per-game record at 3.9 (157 in 40)

MOST POINTS RESPONSIBLE FOR
(Points Scored and Passed For)
Game
56—Willie Totten, Mississippi Val. vs. Kentucky St., Sept. 1, 1984 (passed for 9 TDs and 1 two-point conversion)
Season
368—Willie Totten, Mississippi Val., 1984 (passed for 56 TDs, scored 5 TDs and passed for 1 two-point conversion)
Also holds per-game record at 36.8 (368 in 10)
Career
946—Willie Totten, Mississippi Val., 1982-85 (passed for 139 TDs, scored 18 TDs and passed for 1 two-point conversion)
Also holds per-game record at 23.7 (946 in 40)

Rushing

MOST RUSHES
Quarter
20—Arnold Mickens, Butler vs. Dayton, Oct. 15, 1994 (4th)
Half
32—David Clark, Dartmouth vs. Pennsylvania, Nov. 18, 1989 (2nd); Arnold Mickens, Butler vs. Valparaiso, Oct. 8, 1994 (1st)
Game
56—Arnold Mickens, Butler vs. Valparaiso, Oct. 8, 1994 (295 yards)
Season
409—Arnold Mickens, Butler, 1994 (2,255 yards)
Career
1,044—Jerry Azumah, New Hampshire, 1995-98 (6,193 yards)

MOST RUSHES PER GAME
Season
40.9—Arnold Mickens, Butler, 1994 (409 in 10)
Career
38.2—Arnold Mickens, Butler, 1994-95 (763 in 20)

MOST RUSHES IN TWO CONSECUTIVE GAMES
110—Arnold Mickens, Butler, 1994 (56 vs. Valparaiso, Oct. 8; 54 vs. Dayton, Oct. 15)

MOST CONSECUTIVE CARRIES BY SAME PLAYER
Game
26—Arnold Mickens, Butler vs. Valparaiso, Oct. 8, 1994 (during 6 series)

MOST YARDS GAINED
Quarter
194—Otto Kelly, Nevada vs. Idaho, Nov. 12, 1983 (3rd, 8 rushes)

INDIVIDUAL RECORDS—RUSHING

Half
272—Tony Vinson, Towson vs. Morgan St., Nov. 20, 1993 (1st, 26 rushes)
Game
409—Charles Roberts, Cal St. Sacramento vs. Idaho St., Nov. 6, 1999 (39 rushes)
Season
2,260—Charles Roberts, Cal St. Sacramento, 1998 (386 rushes)
Career
6,193—Jerry Azumah, New Hampshire, 1995-98 (1,044 rushes)

MOST YARDS GAINED PER GAME
Season
225.5—Arnold Mickens, Butler, 1994 (2,255 in 10)
Career
(2 yrs.) 190.7—Arnold Mickens, Butler, 1994-95 (3,813 in 20)
(3 yrs.) 149.4—Charles Roberts, Cal St. Sacramento, 1997-99 (4,929 in 33)
(4 yrs.) 151.0—Jerry Azumah, New Hampshire, 1995-98 (6,193 in 41)

MOST YARDS GAINED BY A FRESHMAN
Game
324—John Campbell, Wagner vs. Jacksonville, Nov. 14, 1998 (39 rushes)
Season
1,932—Adrian Peterson, Ga. Southern, 1998 (257 rushes)
Also holds per-game record—175.6 (1,932 in 11)

MOST YARDS GAINED BY A QUARTERBACK
Game
309—Eddie Thompson, Western Ky. vs. Southern Ill., Oct. 31, 1992 (28 rushes)
Season
1,553—Matt Cannon, Southern Utah, 1998 (199 rushes)
Also holds per-game record—141.2 (1,553 in 11)
Career
3,957—Willie Taggart, Western Ky., 1995-98 (684 rushes)

MOST GAMES GAINING 100 YARDS OR MORE
Season
11—Frank Hawkins, Nevada, 1980; Rich Lemon, Bucknell, 1994; Charles Roberts, Cal St. Sacramento, 1998; Adrian Peterson, Ga. Southern, 1998-99
Career
29—Frank Hawkins, Nevada, 1977-80 (43 games); Kenny Gamble, Colgate, 1984-87 (42 games)

MOST CONSECUTIVE GAMES GAINING 100 YARDS OR MORE
Season
11—Frank Hawkins, Nevada, 1980; Rich Lemon, Bucknell, 1994; Charles Roberts, Cal St. Sacramento, 1998; Adrian Peterson, Ga. Southern, 1998-99
Career
22—¢Adrian Peterson, Ga. Southern, 1998-99
¢Active Player.

MOST GAMES GAINING 100 YARDS OR MORE BY A FRESHMAN
11—Adrian Peterson, Ga. Southern, 1998

MOST GAMES GAINING 200 YARDS OR MORE
Season
8—Arnold Mickens, Butler, 1994
Career
11—Charles Roberts, Cal St. Sacramento, 1997-99

MOST CONSECUTIVE GAMES GAINING 200 YARDS OR MORE
Season
8—Arnold Mickens, Butler, 1994

MOST YARDS GAINED IN TWO, THREE AND FOUR CONSECUTIVE GAMES
2 Games
691—Tony Vinson, Towson, 1993 (364 vs. Bucknell, Nov. 13; 327 vs. Morgan St., Nov. 20)
3 Games
876—Arnold Mickens, Butler, 1994 (288 vs. Wis.-Stevens Point, Sept. 24; 293 vs. Drake, Oct. 1; 295 vs. Valparaiso, Oct. 8)
4 Games
1,109—Arnold Mickens, Butler, 1994 (233 vs. Georgetown [Ky.], Sept. 17; 288 vs. Wis.-Stevens Point, Sept. 24; 293 vs. Drake, Oct. 1; 295 vs. Valparaiso, Oct. 8)

MOST SEASONS GAINING 1,000 YARDS OR MORE
Career
4—Jerry Azumah, New Hampshire, 1995-98

TWO PLAYERS, SAME TEAM, EACH GAINING 1,000 YARDS OR MORE
Jackson St., 1978—Perry Harrington (1,105) & Jeffrey Moore (1,094); Nevada, 1983—Otto Kelly (1,090) & Tony Corley (1,006); Eastern Ky., 1985—James Crawford (1,282) & Elroy Harris (1,134); Eastern Ky., 1986—Elroy Harris (1,152) & James Crawford (1,070); Citadel, 1988—Adrian Johnson (1,091) & Gene Brown (1,006); William & Mary, 1990—Robert Green (1,185) & Tyrone Shelton (1,020); Yale, 1991—Chris Kouri (1,101) & Nick Crawford (1,024); La.-Monroe, 1992—Greg Robinson (1,011) & Roosevelt Potts (1,004); Eastern Ky., 1993—Mike Penman (1,139) & Leon Brown (1,046); South Carolina St., 1994—Michael Hicks (1,368) & Marvin Marshall (1,201); Massachusetts, 1995—Frank Alessio (1,276) & Rene Ingoglia (1,178); Southern Utah, 1996—Brook Madsen (1,405) & Joe Dupaix (1,246); Colgate, 1997—Ed Weiss (1,069) & Daymon Smith (1,012); Cal Poly, 1997—Antonio Warren (1,151) & Craig Young (1,038); Southern Utah, 1997—Brook Madsen (1,214) & Matt Cannon (1,024); Ga. Southern, 1998—Adrian Peterson (1,932) & Greg Hill (1,061); Texas Southern, 1998—D.J. Bradley (1,219) & Thomas Sieh (1,202); Southern Utah, 1999—Matt Cannon (1,310) & Brook Madsen (1,046); Ga. Southern, 1999—Adrian Peterson (1,807) & Greg Hill (1,084)

MOST YARDS GAINED BY TWO PLAYERS, SAME TEAM
Game
473—Jovan Griffith (262) & Jesse Chatman (211), Eastern Wash. vs. Cal St. Northridge, Sept. 25, 1999
Season
2,993—Adrian Peterson, (1,932) & Greg Hill (1,061), Ga. Southern, 1998

EARLIEST GAME GAINING 1,000 YARDS OR MORE
Season
5—Arnold Mickens, Butler, 1994 (1,106)

MOST YARDS GAINED IN OPENING GAME OF SEASON
304—Tony Citizen, McNeese St. vs. Prairie View, Sept. 6, 1986 (30 rushes)

MOST YARDS GAINED IN FIRST GAME OF CAREER
304—Tony Citizen, McNeese St. vs. Prairie View, Sept. 6, 1986 (30 rushes)

HIGHEST AVERAGE GAIN PER RUSH
Game
(Min. 15-19 rushes) 19.1—Gene Brown, Citadel vs. VMI, Nov. 12, 1988 (15 for 286)
(Min. 20 rushes) 17.3—Russell Davis, Idaho vs. Portland St., Oct. 3, 1981 (20 for 345)
Season
(Min. 150-199 rushes) 8.7—Tim Hall, Robert Morris, 1994 (154 for 1,336)
(Min. 200 rushes) 7.5—Adrian Peterson, Ga. Southern, 1998 (257 for 1,932)
Career
(Min. 350-599 rushes) 7.4—Tim Hall, Robert Morris, 1994-95 (393 for 2,908)
(Min. 600 rushes) 6.6—Markus Thomas, Eastern Ky., 1989-92 (784 for 5,149)

MOST TOUCHDOWNS SCORED BY RUSHING
Game
7—Archie Amerson, Northern Ariz. vs. Weber St., Oct. 5, 1996
Season
28—Adrian Peterson, Ga. Southern, 1999
Career
60—Jerry Azumah, New Hampshire, 1995-98

MOST TOUCHDOWNS SCORED PER GAME BY RUSHING
Season
2.5—Adrian Peterson, Ga. Southern, 1999 (28 in 11)
Career
1.8—Aaron Stecker, Western Ill., 1997-98 (36 in 20)

MOST TOUCHDOWNS SCORED BY RUSHING BY A QUARTERBACK
Season
23—Matt Cannon, Southern Utah, 1999
Career
49—Greg Hill, Ga. Southern, 1996-99
Also holds per-game record—1.2 (49 in 41)

LONGEST PLAY
99—Hubert Owens, Mississippi Val. vs. Ark.-Pine Bluff, Sept. 20, 1980; Pedro Bacon, Western Ky. vs. West Ala., Sept. 13, 1986 (only rush of the game); Phillip Collins, Southwest Mo. St. vs. Western Ill., Sept. 16, 1989; Jim Varick, Monmouth vs. Sacred Heart, Oct. 29, 1994; Jermaine Creighton, St. John's (N.Y.) vs. Siena, Nov. 2, 1996

Passing

HIGHEST PASSING EFFICIENCY RATING POINTS
Game
(Min. 15-24 atts.) 389.9—Mark Washington, Jackson St. vs. Alcorn St., Nov. 20, 1999 (17 attempts, 16 completions, 0 interceptions, 363 yards, 6 TD passes)
(Min. 25-44 atts.) 287.2—Doug Turner, Morehead St. vs. Miles, Oct. 18, 1997 (26 attempts, 20 completions, 0 interceptions, 415 yards, 6 TD passes)
(Min. 45 atts.) 220.8—Todd Hammel, Stephen F. Austin vs. La.-Monroe, Nov. 11, 1989 (45 attempts, 31 completions, 3 interceptions, 571 yards, 8 TD passes)
Season
(Min. 15 atts. per game) 204.6—Shawn Knight, William & Mary, 1993 (177 attempts, 125 completions, 4 interceptions, 2,055 yards, 22 TD passes)
Career
(Min. 300-399 comps.) 170.8—Shawn Knight, William & Mary, 1991-94 (558 attempts, 367 completions, 15 interceptions, 5,527 yards, 46 TD passes)
(Min. 400 comps.) 166.3—Dave Dickenson, Montana, 1992-95 (1,208 attempts, 813 completions, 26 interceptions, 11,080 yards, 96 TD passes)

MOST PASSES ATTEMPTED
Quarter
33—Joe Walland, Yale vs. Harvard, Nov. 20, 1999 (3rd, completed 20)
Half
51—Joe Walland, Yale vs. Harvard, Nov. 20, 1999 (2nd, completed 33)
Game
77—Neil Lomax, Portland St. vs. Northern Colo., Oct. 20, 1979 (completed 44)
Season
577—Joe Lee, Towson, 1999 (completed 322)
Also holds per-game record—52.5 (577 in 11)
Career
1,680—Steve McNair, Alcorn St., 1991-94 (completed 927)
Per-game record—42.9, Stan Greene, Boston U., 1989-90 (944 in 22)

MOST PASSES ATTEMPTED BY A FRESHMAN
Game
66—Chris Swartz, Morehead St. vs. Tennessee Tech, Oct. 17, 1987 (completed 35); Kevin Glenn, Illinois St. vs. Western Ill., Nov. 8, 1997 (completed 41)
Season
411—Travis Brown, Northern Ariz., 1996 (completed 223)
Per-game record—37.8, Jason Whitmer, Idaho St., 1987 (340 in 9)

MOST PASSES COMPLETED
Quarter
20—Joe Walland, Yale vs. Harvard, Nov. 20, 1999 (3rd, attempted 33)
Half
33—Joe Walland, Yale vs. Harvard, Nov. 20, 1999 (2nd, attempted 51)
Game
48—Clayton Millis, Cal St. Northridge vs. St. Mary's (Cal.), Nov. 11, 1995 (attempted 65)
Season
324—Willie Totten, Mississippi Val., 1984 (attempted 518)
Also holds per-game record—32.4 (324 in 10)

DIVISION I-AA

INDIVIDUAL RECORDS—PASSING

Career
934—Jamie Martin, Weber St., 1989-92 (attempted 1,544)
Per-game record—25.1, Aaron Flowers, Cal St. Northridge, 1996-97 (502 in 20)

MOST PASSES COMPLETED BY A FRESHMAN
Game
42—Travis Brown, Northern Ariz. vs. Montana, Oct. 26, 1996 (attempted 65)
Season
255—Marcus Brady, Cal St. Northridge, 1998 (attempted 376)
Also holds per-game record—23.2 (255 in 11)

MOST PASSES COMPLETED IN FRESHMAN AND SOPHOMORE SEASONS
518—Greg Wyatt, Northern Ariz., 1986-87 (attempted 804)

MOST CONSECUTIVE PASSES COMPLETED
Game
19—Kirk Schulz, Villanova vs. Central Conn. St., Oct. 10, 1987

MOST CONSECUTIVE PASSES COMPLETED TO START GAME
18—Scott Auchenbach, Bucknell vs. Colgate, Nov. 11, 1989; Jeff Lewis, Northern Ariz. vs. Cal St. Northridge, Sept. 23, 1995

MOST CONSECUTIVE PASSES COMPLETED TO START FIRST GAME AS A FRESHMAN
12—Daunte Culpepper, UCF vs. Eastern Ky., Aug. 31, 1995

HIGHEST PERCENTAGE OF PASSES COMPLETED
Game
(Min. 20-29 comps.) 95.7%—Butch Mosby, Murray St. vs. Tenn.-Martin, Oct. 2, 1993 (22 of 23)
(Min. 30 comps.) 85.0%—Marcus Brady, Cal St. Northridge vs. Southwest Mo. St., Nov. 14, 1998 (34 of 40)
Season
(Min. 200 atts.) 70.6%—Giovanni Carmazzi, Hofstra, 1997 (288 of 408)
Career
(Min. 750 atts.) 67.3%—Dave Dickenson, Montana, 1992-95 (813 of 1,208)

MOST PASSES HAD INTERCEPTED
Game
7—Mick Spoon, Idaho St. vs. Montana, Oct. 21, 1978 (attempted 35); Charles Hebert, Southeastern La. vs. Northwestern St., Nov. 12, 1983 (23 attempts); Carlton Jenkins, Mississippi Val. vs. Prairie View, Oct. 31, 1987 (34 attempts); Dan Crowley, Towson vs. Maine, Nov. 16, 1991 (53 attempts)
Season
29—Willie Totten, Mississippi Val., 1985 (492 attempts)
Also holds per-game record—2.6 (29 in 11)
Career
75—Willie Totten, Mississippi Val., 1982-85
Per-game record—2.0, John Witkowski, Columbia, 1981-83 (60 in 30)

LOWEST PERCENTAGE OF PASSES HAD INTERCEPTED
Season
(Min. 175-324 atts.) 0.6%—Kharon Brown, Hofstra, 1995 (2 of 320)
(Min. 325 atts.) 0.84%—Jimmy Blanchard, Portland St., 1999 (3 of 355)
Career
(Min. 500-749 atts.) 1.8%—Jason Garrett, Princeton, 1987-88 (10 of 550)
(Min. 750 atts.) 1.8%—Jeff Lewis, Northern Ariz., 1992-95 (24 of 1,315)

MOST PASSES ATTEMPTED WITHOUT INTERCEPTION
Regulation Game
68—Tony Petersen, Marshall vs. Western Caro., Nov. 14, 1987 (completed 34)
Overtime Game
69—Chris Boden, Villanova vs. Connecticut, Oct. 16, 1999 (completed 43) (3 ot)

MOST CONSECUTIVE PASSES ATTEMPTED WITHOUT INTERCEPTION
Season
342—Jimmy Blanchard, Portland St., 1999 (in 11 games, from Sept. 4 through Nov. 13)
Career
342—Jimmy Blanchard, Portland St., began Sept. 4, 1999, ended Nov. 13, 1999

MOST YARDS GAINED
Quarter
278—Willie Totten, Mississippi Val. vs. Kentucky St., Sept. 1, 1984 (2nd)
Half
383—Michael Payton, Marshall vs. VMI, Nov. 16, 1991 (1st)
Game
624—Jamie Martin, Weber St. vs. Idaho St., Nov. 23, 1991
Season
4,863—Steve McNair, Alcorn St., 1994
Career
14,496—Steve McNair, Alcorn St., 1991-94

MOST YARDS GAINED PER GAME
Season
455.7—Willie Totten, Mississippi Val., 1984 (4,557 in 10)
Career
350.0—Neil Lomax, Portland St., 1978-80 (11,550 in 33)

MOST YARDS GAINED BY A FRESHMAN
Game
540—Brad Otton, Weber St. vs. Northern Ariz., Nov. 6, 1993
Season
3,398—Travis Brown, Northern Ariz., 1996
Also holds per-game record—308.9 (3,398 in 11)

MOST YARDS GAINED IN FRESHMAN AND SOPHOMORE SEASONS
6,793—Travis Brown, Northern Ariz., 1996-97

MOST YARDS GAINED IN TWO, THREE AND FOUR CONSECUTIVE GAMES
2 Games
1,150—Steve McNair, Alcorn St., 1994 (587 vs. Samford, Oct. 29; 563 vs. Mississippi Val., Nov. 5)
3 Games
1,626—Steve McNair, Alcorn St., 1994 (587 vs. Samford, Oct. 29; 563 vs. Mississippi Val., Nov. 5; 476 vs. Troy St., Nov. 12)
4 Games
2,159—Steve McNair, Alcorn St., 1994 (587 vs. Samford, Oct. 29; 563 vs. Mississippi Val., Nov. 5; 476 vs. Troy St., Nov. 12; 533 vs. Jackson St., Nov. 19)

MOST GAMES GAINING 200 YARDS OR MORE
Season
11—By 15 players. Most recent: Chris Sanders, Chattanooga, 1999; Joe Lee, Towson, 1999; Steve McNair, Alcorn St., 1994; Chris Hakel, William & Mary, 1991; Jamie Martin, Weber St., 1991
Career
41—Steve McNair, Alcorn St., 1991-94 (42 games)

MOST CONSECUTIVE GAMES GAINING 200 YARDS OR MORE
Season
11—By 12 players. Most recent: Chris Sanders, Chattanooga, 1999; Steve McNair, Alcorn St., 1994; Chris Hakel, William & Mary, 1991; Jamie Martin, Weber St., 1991
Career
28—Steve McNair, Alcorn St., 1991-93; Neil Lomax, Portland St., 1978-80

MOST GAMES GAINING 300 YARDS OR MORE
Season
10—Willie Totten, Mississippi Val., 1984; John Friesz, Idaho, 1989; Steve McNair, Alcorn St., 1994
Career
28—Neil Lomax, Portland St., 1978-80

MOST CONSECUTIVE GAMES GAINING 300 YARDS OR MORE
Season
10—Willie Totten, Mississippi Val., 1984; John Friesz, Idaho, 1989

Career
13—Neil Lomax, Portland St., 1979-80

MOST YARDS GAINED AGAINST ONE OPPONENT
Career
1,675—Willie Totten, Mississippi Val. vs. Prairie View, 1982-85
Also holds per-game record—418.8 (1,675 in 4)

MOST YARDS PER ATTEMPT
Game
(Min. 30-44 atts.) 16.1—Gilbert Renfroe, Tennessee St. vs. Dist. Columbia, Nov. 5, 1983 (30 for 484)
(Min. 45 atts.) 12.7—Todd Hammel, Stephen F. Austin vs. La.-Monroe, Nov. 11, 1989 (45 for 571)
Season
(Min. 250-324 atts.) 10.3—Mike Smith, Northern Iowa, 1986 (303 for 3,125)
(Min. 325 atts.) 9.5—John Friesz, Idaho, 1989 (425 for 4,041)
Career
(Min. 500-999 atts.) 9.5—Jay Johnson, Northern Iowa, 1989-92 (744 for 7,049)
(Min. 1,000 atts.) 9.2—Dave Dickenson, Montana, 1992-95 (1,208 for 11,080)

MOST YARDS GAINED PER COMPLETION
Game
(Min. 15-19 comps.) 28.5—Kendrick Nord, Grambling vs. Alcorn St., Sept. 3, 1994 (17 for 485)
(Min. 20 comps.) 24.2—Matt Nagy, Delaware vs. Connecticut, Nov. 7, 1998 (23 for 556)
Season
(Min. 200 comps.) 16.4—Todd Hammel, Stephen F. Austin, 1989 (238 for 3,914)
Career
(Min. 350-399 comps.) 17.8—Jay Johnson, Northern Iowa, 1989-92 (397 for 7,049)
(Min. 400 comps.) 16.0—Shane Stafford, Connecticut, 1995-98 (522 for 8,368)

MOST TOUCHDOWN PASSES
Quarter
7—Neil Lomax, Portland St. vs. Delaware St., Nov. 8, 1980 (1st)
Half
7—Neil Lomax, Portland St. vs. Delaware St., Nov. 8, 1980 (1st)
Game
9—Willie Totten, Mississippi Val. vs. Kentucky St., Sept. 1, 1984
Season
56—Willie Totten, Mississippi Val., 1984
Also holds per-game record—5.6 (56 in 10)
Career
139—Willie Totten, Mississippi Val., 1982-85
Also holds per-game record—3.5 (139 in 40)

MOST TOUCHDOWN PASSES BY A FRESHMAN
Season
25—Marcus Brady, Cal St. Northridge, 1998

MOST CONSECUTIVE GAMES THROWING A TOUCHDOWN PASS
Career
36—Steve McNair, Alcorn St., 1991-94

MOST TOUCHDOWN PASSES, SAME PASSER AND RECEIVER
Season
27—Willie Totten to Jerry Rice, Mississippi Val., 1984
Career
47—Willie Totten to Jerry Rice, Mississippi Val., 1982-84

HIGHEST PERCENTAGE OF PASSES FOR TOUCHDOWNS
Season
(Min. 200-299 atts.) 12.5%—Ted White, Howard, 1996 (36 of 289)
(Min. 300 atts.) 10.9%—Doug Nussmeier, Idaho, 1993 (33 of 304)
Career
(Min. 500-749 atts.) 8.5%—Mike Williams, Grambling, 1977-80 (44 of 520)
(Min. 750 atts.) 7.9%—Dave Dickenson, Montana, 1992-95 (96 of 1,208)

INDIVIDUAL RECORDS—RECEIVING

Receiving

MOST PASSES CAUGHT
Game
24—Jerry Rice, Mississippi Val. vs. Southern U., Oct. 1, 1983 (219 yards)
Season
115—Brian Forster, Rhode Island, 1985 (1,617 yards)
Also holds per-game record—11.5 (115 in 10)
Career
301—Jerry Rice, Mississippi Val., 1981-84 (4,693 yards)
Also holds per-game record—7.3 (301 in 41)

MOST PASSES CAUGHT BY A TIGHT END
Game
18—Brian Forster, Rhode Island vs. Brown, Sept. 28, 1985 (327 yards)
Season
115—Brian Forster, Rhode Island, 1985 (1,617 yards)
Also holds per-game record—11.5 (115 in 10)
Career
245—Brian Forster, Rhode Island, 1983-85, 1987 (3,410 yards)

MOST PASSES CAUGHT BY A RUNNING BACK
Game
21—David Pandt, Montana St. vs. Eastern Wash., Sept. 21, 1985 (169 yards)
Season
89—Brian Westbrook, Villanova, 1998 (1,144 yards)
2 Yrs
135—Gordie Lockbaum, Holy Cross, 1986-87 (2,012 yards)
Also holds per-game record—6.1 (135 in 22)
Career
188—Jason Corle, Towson, 1996-99 (1,725 yards)

MOST PASSES CAUGHT BY A FRESHMAN
Game
15—Emerson Foster, Rhode Island vs. Northeastern, Nov. 9, 1985 (205 yards); Drew Amerson, Cal St. Northridge vs. Weber St., Oct. 30, 1999 (147 yards)
Season
71—Drew Amerson, Cal St. Northridge, 1999 (897 yards)

MOST PASSES CAUGHT BY TWO PLAYERS, SAME TEAM
Season
183—Jerry Rice (103 for 1,682 yards and 27 TDs) & Joe Thomas (80 for 1,119 yards and 11 TDs), Mississippi Val., 1984
Career
420—Darrell Colbert (217 for 3,177 yards and 33 TDs) & Donald Narcisse (203 for 2,429 yards and 26 TDs), Texas Southern, 1983-86

MOST YARDS GAINED
Game
370—Michael Lerch, Princeton vs. Brown, Oct. 12, 1991 (caught 9)
Season
1,712—Eddie Conti, Delaware, 1998 (caught 91)
Career
4,693—Jerry Rice, Mississippi Val., 1981-84 (caught 301)

MOST YARDS GAINED PER GAME
Season
168.2—Jerry Rice, Mississippi Val., 1984 (1,682 in 10)
Career
(Min. 2,000-2,999 yds.) 116.9—Derrick Ingram, UAB, 1993-94 (2,572 in 22)
(Min. 3,000 yds.) 114.5—Jerry Rice, Mississippi Val., 1981-84 (4,693 in 41)

MOST YARDS GAINED BY A TIGHT END
Game
327—Brian Forster, Rhode Island vs. Brown, Sept. 28, 1985 (caught 18)
Season
1,617—Brian Forster, Rhode Island, 1985 (caught 115)
Also holds per-game record—161.7 (1,617 in 10)
Career
3,410—Brian Forster, Rhode Island, 1983-85, 1987 (caught 245)

MOST YARDS GAINED BY A RUNNING BACK
Game
220—Alvin Atkinson, Davidson vs. Furman, Nov. 3, 1979 (caught 9)

Season
1,152—Gordie Lockbaum, Holy Cross, 1987 (caught 78)
Also holds per-game record—104.7 (1,152 in 11)

MOST YARDS GAINED BY A FRESHMAN
Game
284—Jacquay Nunnally, Florida A&M vs. N.C. A&T, Oct. 11, 1997 (caught 13)
Season
1,073—Randy Moss, Marshall, 1996 (55 catches)

MOST YARDS GAINED BY TWO PLAYERS, SAME TEAM
Season
2,801—Jerry Rice (1,682, 103 caught and 27 TDs) & Joe Thomas (1,119, 80 caught and 11 TDs), Mississippi Val., 1984
Career
5,806—Roy Banks (3,177, 184 caught and 38 TDs) & Cal Pierce (2,629, 163 caught and 13 TDs), Eastern Ill., 1983-86

HIGHEST AVERAGE GAIN PER RECEPTION
Game
(Min. 5-9 receps.) 44.6—John Taylor, Delaware St. vs. St. Paul's, Sept. 21, 1985 (5 for 223)
(Min. 10 receps.) 29.0—Jason Cristino, Lehigh vs. Lafayette, Nov. 21, 1992 (11 for 319)
Season
(Min. 35-59 receps.) 28.9—Mikhael Ricks, Stephen F. Austin, 1997 (47 for 1,358)
(Min. 60 receps.) 20.7—Golden Tate, Tennessee St., 1983 (63 for 1,307)
Career
(Min. 90-124 receps.) 24.3—John Taylor, Delaware St., 1982-85 (100 for 2,426)
(Min. 125 receps.) 22.0—Dedric Ward, Northern Iowa, 1993-96 (176 for 3,876)

MOST GAMES GAINING 100 YARDS OR MORE
Career
23—Jerry Rice, Mississippi Val., 1981-84 (41 games)

MOST TOUCHDOWN PASSES CAUGHT
Game
5—Jerry Rice, Mississippi Val. vs. Prairie View, Oct. 27, 1984 & vs. Kentucky St., Sept. 1, 1984; Rennie Benn, Lehigh vs. Indiana (Pa.), Sept. 14, 1985 (266 yards); Wayne Chrebet, Hofstra vs. Delaware, Nov. 12, 1994 (245 yards); Rod Marshall, Northern Ariz. vs. Abilene Christian, Sept. 16, 1995 (154 yards); Sylvester Morris, Jackson St. vs. Grambling, Oct. 24, 1998 (201 yards)
Season
27—Jerry Rice, Mississippi Val., 1984
Career
50—Jerry Rice, Mississippi Val., 1981-84

MOST TOUCHDOWN PASSES CAUGHT BY A FRESHMAN
Season
19—Randy Moss, Marshall, 1996

MOST TOUCHDOWN PASSES CAUGHT PER GAME
Season
2.7—Jerry Rice, Mississippi Val., 1984 (27 in 10)
Career
1.2—Jerry Rice, Mississippi Val., 1981-84 (50 in 41)

MOST GAMES CATCHING A TOUCHDOWN PASS
Season
11—Randy Moss, Marshall, 1996
Also holds consecutive record—11 (1996)
Career
26—Jerry Rice, Mississippi Val., 1981-84
Also holds consecutive record—17 (1983-84)

Punting

MOST PUNTS
Game
16—Matt Stover, Louisiana Tech vs. La.-Monroe, Nov. 18, 1988 (567 yards)

Season
98—Barry Hickingbotham, Louisiana Tech, 1987 (3,821 yards)
Career
301—Barry Bowman, Louisiana Tech, 1983-86 (11,441 yards)

HIGHEST AVERAGE PER PUNT
Game
(Min. 5-9 punts) 55.7—Harold Alexander, Appalachian St. vs. Citadel, Oct. 3, 1992 (6 for 334); Jody Farmer, Montana vs. Nevada, Oct. 1, 1988 (9 for 501)
(Min. 10 punts) 52.2—Stuart Dodds, Montana St. vs. Northern Ariz., Oct. 20, 1979 (10 for 522)
Season
(Min. 60 punts) 47.0—Harold Alexander, Appalachian St., 1991 (64 for 3,009)
Career
(Min. 150 punts) 44.4—Pumpy Tudors, Chattanooga, 1989-91 (181 for 8,041)

LONGEST PUNT
91—Bart Helsley, North Texas vs. La.-Monroe, Nov. 17, 1990

Interceptions

MOST PASSES INTERCEPTED
Game
5—Karl Johnson, Jackson St. vs. Grambling, Oct. 23, 1982 (29 yards); Michael Richardson, Northwestern St. vs. Southeastern La., Nov. 12, 1983 (128 yards); Mark Cordes, Eastern Wash. vs. Boise St., Sept. 6, 1986 (48 yards)
Season
12—Dean Cain, Princeton, 1987 (98 yards)
Also holds per-game record—1.2 (12 in 10)
Career
28—Dave Murphy, Holy Cross, 1986-89 (309 yards)
Per-game record—0.73, Dean Cain, Princeton, 1985-87 (22 in 30)

MOST YARDS ON INTERCEPTION RETURNS
Game
216—Keiron Bigby, Brown vs. Yale, Sept. 29, 1984 (3 interceptions) (first career game)
Season
280—William Hampton, Murray St., 1995 (8 interceptions)
Career
488—Darren Sharper, William & Mary, 1993-96 (24 interceptions)

MOST TOUCHDOWNS SCORED ON INTERCEPTION RETURNS
Game
2—By 11 players. Most recent: Tom Lennon, Marist vs. Iona, Nov. 13, 1999; Kunle Williams, Pennsylvania vs. Princeton, Nov. 6, 1999; Corey Cobb, Tenn.-Martin vs. Austin Peay, Nov. 15, 1997; Cedric Allen, Western Ky. vs. Ky. Wesleyan, Aug. 29, 1996
Season
4—Robert Turner, Jackson St., 1990 (9 interceptions, 212 yards); Joseph Vaughn, Cal St. Northridge, 1994 (9 interceptions, 265 yards); William Hampton, Murray St., 1995 (8 interceptions, 280 yards)
Career
6—William Hampton, Murray St., 1993-96 (20 interceptions)

HIGHEST AVERAGE GAIN PER INTERCEPTION
Game
(Min. 3 ints.) 72.0—Keiron Bigby, Brown vs. Yale, Sept. 29, 1984 (3 for 216)
Season
(Min. 3 ints.) 72.0—Keiron Bigby, Brown, 1984 (3 for 216)
Career
(Min. 12 ints.) 25.8—Zack Bronson, McNeese St., 1993-96 (16 for 413)

Punt Returns

MOST PUNT RETURNS
Game
9—By 16 players. Most recent: Joey Jamison, Texas Southern vs. Southern U., Nov. 13, 1999 (54 yards)

INDIVIDUAL RECORDS—PUNT RETURNS

Season
55—Tommy Houk, Murray St., 1980 (442 yards)
Also holds per-game record—5.0 (55 in 11)
Career
123—Chuck Calhoun, Southwest Mo. St., 1990-93 (978 yards)
Per-game record—3.8, Tommy Houk, Murray St., 1979-80 (84 in 22)

MOST YARDS ON PUNT RETURNS
Game
216—Willie Ware, Mississippi Val. vs. Washburn, Sept. 15, 1984 (7 returns); Gary Harrell, Howard vs. Morgan St., Nov. 3, 1990 (7 returns); Ricky Pearsall, Northern Ariz. vs. Western N.M., Aug. 29, 1996 (5 returns)
Season
575—Joey Jamison, Texas Southern, 1999 (41 returns)
Per-game record—54.7, Joe Rosato, Duquesne, 1996 (547 in 10)
Career
1,230—David McCrary, Chattanooga, 1982-85 (117 returns)

HIGHEST AVERAGE GAIN PER RETURN
Game
(Min. 5 rets.) 43.2—Ricky Pearsall, Northern Ariz. vs. Western N.M., Aug. 29, 1996 (5 for 216)
Season
(Min. 1.2 rets. per game) 23.0—Tim Egerton, Delaware St., 1988 (16 for 368)
Career
(Min. 1.2 rets. per game) 16.4—Willie Ware, Mississippi Val., 1982-85 (61 for 1,003)

MOST TOUCHDOWNS SCORED ON PUNT RETURNS
Game
3—Aaron Fix, Canisius vs. Siena, Sept. 24, 1994 (5 returns)
Season
4—Howard Huckaby, Florida A&M, 1988 (26 returns); Kenny Shedd, Northern Iowa, 1992 (27 returns); Aaron Fix, Canisius, 1994 (34 returns)
Career
7—Kenny Shedd, Northern Iowa, 1989-92

LONGEST PUNT RETURN
98—Barney Bussey, South Carolina St. vs. Johnson Smith, Oct. 10, 1981; Willie Ware, Mississippi Val. vs. Bishop, Sept. 21, 1985

MOST CONSECUTIVE GAMES RETURNING PUNT FOR TOUCHDOWN
3—Troy Jones, McNeese St., 1989 (vs. Mississippi Col., Sept. 2; vs. Samford, Sept. 9; vs. La.-Monroe, Sept. 16)

Kickoff Returns

MOST KICKOFF RETURNS
Game
10—Merril Hoge, Idaho St. vs. Weber St., Oct. 25, 1986 (179 yards); Ryan Steen, Cal Poly vs. Eastern Wash., Sept. 10, 1994 (203 yards)
Season
50—David Primus, Samford, 1989 (1,411 yards)
Also holds per-game record—4.5 (50 in 11)
Career
118—Clarence Alexander, Mississippi Val., 1986-89 (2,439 yards)
Per-game record—3.0, Lorenza Rivers, Tennessee Tech, 1985, 1987 (62 in 21)

MOST YARDS ON KICKOFF RETURNS
Game
326—Bashir Levingston, Eastern Wash. vs. Cal St. Sacramento, Oct. 31, 1998 (5 returns)
Season
1,411—David Primus, Samford, 1989 (50 returns)
Also holds per-game record—128.3 (1,411 in 11)
Career
2,535—Carlos Frank, Citadel, 1996-99 (108 returns)
Also holds per-game record—63.4 (2,535 in 40)

HIGHEST AVERAGE GAIN PER RETURN
Game
(Min. 5 rets.) 65.2—Bashir Levingston, Eastern Wash. vs. Cal St. Sacramento, Oct. 31, 1998 (5 for 326)
Season
(Min. 1.2 rets. per game) 37.3—David Fraterrigo, Canisius, 1993 (13 for 485)
Career
(Min. 1.2 Returns Per Game)
(Min. 30-44 rets.) 29.7—Troy Brown, Marshall, 1991-92 (32 for 950)
(Min. 45 rets.) 29.3—Charles Swann, Indiana St., 1989-91 (45 for 1,319)

MOST TOUCHDOWNS SCORED ON KICKOFF RETURNS
Game
3—Bashir Levingston, Eastern Wash. vs. Cal St. Sacramento, Oct. 31, 1998
Season
4—Ryan Zimpleman, Butler, 1998
Career
5—Kerry Hayes, Western Caro., 1991-94; Ryan Zimpleman, Butler, 1997-99

Total Kick Returns

(Combined Punt and Kickoff Returns)

MOST KICK RETURNS
Game
12—Craig Hodge, Tennessee St. vs. Morgan St., Oct. 24, 1987 (8 punts, 4 kickoffs; 319 yards)
Season
64—Joe Markus, Connecticut, 1981 (34 punts, 30 kickoffs; 939 yards)
Career
199—Herman Hunter, Tennessee St., 1981-84 (103 punts, 96 kickoffs; 3,232 yards)

MOST YARDS ON KICK RETURNS
Game
349—Bashir Levingston, Eastern Wash. vs. Cal St. Sacramento, Oct. 31, 1998 (8 returns, 23 on punt returns, 326 on kickoff returns)
Season
1,469—David Primus, Samford, 1989 (1,411 on kickoffs, 58 on punts)
Also holds per-game record—133.5 (1,469 in 11)
Career
3,232—Herman Hunter, Tennessee St., 1981-84 (974 on punts, 2,258 on kickoffs)
Per-game record—80.2, Carlos Frank, Citadel, 1996-99 (3,209 in 40)

GAINING 1,000 YARDS ON PUNT RETURNS AND 1,000 YARDS ON KICKOFF RETURNS
Career
Joe Markus, Connecticut, 1979-82 (1,012 on punts and 1,185 on kickoffs); Kenny Shedd, Northern Iowa, 1989-92 (1,081 on punts and 1,359 on kickoffs); Joe Rosato, Duquesne, 1994-97 (1,036 on punt returns and 1,661 on kickoffs)

HIGHEST AVERAGE PER KICK RETURN
Game
(Min. 6 rets.) 44.7—Jay Jones, James Madison vs. Richmond, Oct. 19, 1996 (6 for 268)
Season
(Min. 40 rets.) 26.7—David Primus, Samford, 1989 (55 for 1,469)
Career
(Min. 60 rets.) 20.9—Bill LaFreniere, Northeastern, 1978-81 (112 for 2,336)

MOST TOUCHDOWNS SCORED ON KICK RETURNS
Game
3—Aaron Fix, Canisius vs. Siena, Sept. 24, 1994 (3 punt returns); Bashir Levingston, Eastern Wash. vs. Cal St. Sacramento, Oct. 31, 1998 (3 kickoffs)
Season
6—Bashir Levingston, Eastern Wash., 1998 (3 punt returns and 3 kickoff returns)
Career
7—Willie Ware, Mississippi Val., 1982-85 (5 punts and 2 kickoffs); Kenny Shedd, Northern Iowa, 1989-92 (7 punts); Kerry Hayes, Western Caro., 1991-94 (2 punts and 5 kickoffs); Joe Rosato, Duquesne, 1994-97 (4 punts and 3 kickoffs)

All-Purpose Yards

(Yardage Gained From Rushing, Receiving and All Runbacks; Must Have One Attempt From at Least Two Categories)

MOST PLAYS
Game
54—Ron Darby, Marshall vs. Western Caro., Nov. 12, 1988 (47 rushes, 4 receptions, 3 kickoff returns; 329 yards)
(Note: 56—Arnold Mickens, Butler vs. Valparaiso, Oct. 8, 1994; all rushes)
Season
411—Arnold Mickens, Butler, 1994 (409 rushes, 2 receptions; 2,262 yards)
Career
1,147—Rich Lemon, Bucknell, 1993-96 (994 rushes, 129 receptions, 16 punt returns, 8 kickoff returns; 5,952 yards)

MOST YARDS GAINED
Game
467—Joey Stockton, Western Ky. vs. Austin Peay, Sept. 16, 1995 (29 rushing, 276 receiving, 18 punt returns, 144 kickoff returns; 14 plays)
Season
3,026—Brian Westbrook, Villanova, 1998 (1,046 rushing, 1,144 receiving, 192 punt returns, 644 kickoff returns; 329 plays)
Also holds per-game record—275.1 (3,026 in 11)
Career
8,376—Jerry Azumah, New Hampshire, 1995-98 (6,193 rushing, 1,153 receiving, 5 punt returns, 1,025 kickoff returns; 1,126 plays)
Also holds per-game record—204.3 (8,376 in 41)

MOST YARDS GAINED BY A FRESHMAN
Season
2,014—David Wright, Indiana St., 1992 (1,313 rushing, 108 receiving, 593 kickoff returns; 254 plays)

HIGHEST AVERAGE GAIN PER PLAY
Game
(Min. 20 plays) 20.6—Herman Hunter, Tennessee St. vs. Mississippi Val., Nov. 13, 1982 (453 on 22)
Season
(Min. 1,000 yards, 100 plays) 19.7—Otis Washington, Western Caro., 1988 (2,086 on 106)
Career
(Min. 4,000 yards, 350 plays) 15.7—Sean Morey, Brown, 1995-98 (5,726 on 364)

GAINING 1,000 YARDS RUSHING AND 1,000 YARDS RECEIVING
Season
Brian Westbrook, Villanova, 1998 (1,046 rushing, 1,144 receiving)

Scoring

MOST POINTS SCORED
Game
42—Archie Amerson, Northern Ariz. vs. Weber St., Oct. 5, 1996 (7 TDs); Jessie Burton, McNeese St. vs. Southern Utah, Sept. 19, 1998 (7 TDs)
Season
174—Adrian Peterson, Ga. Southern, 1999 (29 TDs)
Career
418—Jerry Azumah, New Hampshire, 1995-98 (69 TDs, 4 PATs)

MOST POINTS SCORED PER GAME
Season
16.2—Jerry Rice, Mississippi Val., 1984 (162 in 10)
Career
(Min. 200-299 pts.) 11.7—Aaron Stecker, Western Ill., 1997-98 (234 in 20)
(Min. 300 pts.) 10.7—Keith Elias, Princeton, 1991-93 (320 in 30)

MOST TOUCHDOWNS SCORED
Game
7—Archie Amerson, Northern Ariz. vs. Weber St., Oct. 5, 1996; Jessie Burton, McNeese St. vs. Southern Utah, Sept. 19, 1998
Season
29—Adrian Peterson, Ga. Southern, 1999

INDIVIDUAL RECORDS—SCORING

Career
69—Jerry Azumah, New Hampshire, 1995-98

MOST TOUCHDOWNS SCORED PER GAME
Season
2.7—Jerry Rice, Mississippi Val., 1984 (27 in 10)
Career
(Min. 18-29 games) 1.95—Aaron Stecker, Western Ill., 1997-98 (39 in 20)
(Min. 30 games) 1.7—Keith Elias, Princeton, 1991-93 (52 in 30)

MOST TOUCHDOWNS SCORED BY A FRESHMAN
Season
26—Adrian Peterson, Ga. Southern, 1998
Also holds per-game record—2.4 (26 in 11)

PASSING FOR A TOUCHDOWN AND SCORING TOUCHDOWNS BY RUSHING, RECEIVING AND PUNT RETURN
WR Sean Beckton, UCF, threw a 33-yard touchdown pass, rushed for an 11-yard touchdown, caught a 17-yard touchdown pass and returned a punt 60 yards for a touchdown vs. Texas Southern, Nov. 17, 1990

MOST EXTRA POINTS ATTEMPTED BY KICKING
Game
15—John Kincheloe, Portland St. vs. Delaware St., Nov. 8, 1980 (15 made)
Season
74—John Kincheloe, Portland St., 1980 (70 made)
Per-game record—7.2, Jonathan Stokes, Mississippi Val., 1984 (72 in 10)
Career
194—Gilad Landau, Grambling, 1991-94 (181 made)

MOST EXTRA POINTS MADE BY KICKING
Game
15—John Kincheloe, Portland St. vs. Delaware St., Nov. 8, 1980 (15 attempts)
Season
70—John Kincheloe, Portland St., 1980 (74 attempts)
Per-game record—6.8, Jonathan Stokes, Mississippi Val., 1984 (68 in 10)
Career
181—Gilad Landau, Grambling, 1991-94 (194 attempts)
Per-game record—4.8, Tim Openlander, Marshall, 1994-96 (159 in 33)

BEST PERFECT RECORD OF EXTRA POINTS MADE
Season
68 of 68—Mike Hollis, Idaho, 1993

HIGHEST PERCENTAGE OF EXTRA POINTS MADE
Season
(Min. 50 atts.) 100.0—Billy Hayes, Sam Houston St., 1987 (50 of 50); Jim Hodson, Lafayette, 1988 (51 of 51); Mike Hollis, Idaho, 1993 (68 of 68); Chris Dill, Murray St., 1995 (56 of 56); Tim Openlander, Marshall, 1996 (58 of 58)
Career
(Min. 100-119 atts.) 100%—Anders Larsson, Montana St., 1985-88 (101 of 101)
(Min. 120 atts.) 99.2%—Brian Mitchell, Marshall/ Northern Iowa, 1987, 1989-91 (130 of 131)

MOST CONSECUTIVE EXTRA POINTS MADE
Game
15—John Kincheloe, Portland St. vs. Delaware St., Nov. 8, 1980
Season
68—Mike Hollis, Idaho, 1993
Career
121—Brian Mitchell, Marshall/Northern Iowa, 1987, 1989-91

MOST POINTS SCORED BY KICKING
Game
24—Goran Lingmerth, Northern Ariz. vs. Idaho, Oct. 25, 1986 (8 FGs)
Season
112—Rob Hart, Murray St., 1996 (22 FGs, 46 PATs)
Career
385—Marty Zendejas, Nevada, 1984-87 (72 FGs, 169 PATs)

MOST POINTS SCORED BY KICKING PER GAME
Season
10.1—Rob Hart, Murray St., 1996 (112 in 11)
Career
9.1—Tony Zendejas, Nevada, 1981-83 (300 in 33)

MOST DEFENSIVE EXTRA-POINT RETURNS, ONE GAME, SINGLE PLAYER
2—Joe Lee Johnson, Western Ky. vs. Indiana St., Nov. 10, 1990 (both kick returns, scored on neither)

MOST DEFENSIVE EXTRA POINTS SCORED
Game
1—By many players
Season
2—Jackie Kellogg, Eastern Wash. vs. Weber St., Oct. 6, 1990 (90-yard interception return) & vs. Portland St., Oct. 27, 1990 (94-yard interception return)

LONGEST RETURN OF A DEFENSIVE EXTRA POINT
100—Morgan Ryan (DB), Montana St. vs. Sam Houston St., Sept. 7, 1991 (interception return); Rich Kinsman (DB), William & Mary vs. Lehigh, Nov. 14, 1992

FIRST DEFENSIVE EXTRA-POINT ATTEMPTS
Mike Rogers (DB), Davidson vs. Lehigh, Sept. 10, 1988 (30-yard interception return); Dave Benna (LB), Towson vs. Northeastern, Sept. 10, 1988 (35-yard interception return)

MOST TWO-POINT ATTEMPTS
Season
11—Brent Woods, Princeton, 1982; Jamie Martin, Weber St., 1990

MOST SUCCESSFUL TWO-POINT PASSES
Game
3—Brent Woods, Princeton vs. Lafayette, Nov. 6, 1982 (attempted 3)
Season
7—Jamie Martin, Weber St., 1992 (attempted 7)
Career
15—Jamie Martin, Weber St., 1989-92 (attempted 28)

Opponent's Kicks Blocked

MOST OPPONENT'S TOTAL KICKS BLOCKED BY (Includes Punts, PAT Attempts, FG Attempts)
Game
3—Ben Duhon, McNeese St. vs. Ark.-Monticello, 1998 (3 punts); Adrian Hardy, Northwestern St. vs. Arkansas St., Oct. 3, 1992 (2 PATs, 1 FG)
Season
6—Murphy Edwards, Nicholls St., 1998 (4 PATs, 2 FGs)
Career
12—Trey Woods, Sam Houston St., 1992-95 (8 punts, 2 PATs, 2 FGs)

Field Goals

MOST FIELD GOALS ATTEMPTED
Game
8—Goran Lingmerth, Northern Ariz. vs. Idaho, Oct. 25, 1986 (made 8)
Season
33—Tony Zendejas, Nevada, 1982 (made 26); David Ettinger, Hofstra, 1995 (made 22)
Career
102—Kirk Roach, Western Caro., 1984-87 (made 71)

MOST FIELD GOALS MADE
Quarter
4—Tony Zendejas, Nevada vs. Northern Ariz., Oct. 16, 1982 (4th); Ryan Weeks, Tennessee Tech vs. Chattanooga, Sept. 9, 1989 (3rd)
Half
5—Dean Biasucci, Western Caro. vs. Mars Hill, Sept. 18, 1982 (1st); Tony Zendejas, Nevada vs. Northern Ariz., Oct. 16, 1982 (2nd); Ryan Weeks, Tennessee Tech vs. Chattanooga, Sept. 9, 1989 (2nd)
Game
8—Goran Lingmerth, Northern Ariz. vs. Idaho, Oct. 25, 1986 (39, 18, 20, 33, 46, 27, 22, 35 yards; by quarters—1, 3, 2, 2), 8 attempts
Season
26—Tony Zendejas, Nevada, 1982 (33 attempts); Brian Mitchell, Northern Iowa, 1990 (27 attempts)
Also share per-game record—2.4 (26 in 11)
Career
72—Marty Zendejas, Nevada, 1984-87 (90 attempts)
Per-game record—2.1, Tony Zendejas, Nevada, 1981-83 (70 in 33)

HIGHEST PERCENTAGE OF FIELD GOALS MADE
Season
(Min. 20 atts.) 96.3%—Brian Mitchell, Northern Iowa, 1990 (26 of 27)
Career
(Min. 50 atts.) 82.0%—Juan Toro, Florida A&M, 1995-98 (41 of 50)

BEST PERFECT RECORD OF FIELD GOALS MADE
Season
100.0%—John Coursey, James Madison, 1995 (14 of 14)

MOST CONSECUTIVE FIELD GOALS MADE
Game
8—Goran Lingmerth, Northern Ariz. vs. Idaho, Oct. 25, 1986
Season
21—Brian Mitchell, Northern Iowa, 1990
Career
26—Brian Mitchell, Northern Iowa, 1990-91

MOST CONSECUTIVE GAMES KICKING A FIELD GOAL
Career
33—Tony Zendejas, Nevada, 1981-83 (at least one in every game played)

MOST FIELD GOALS MADE, 50 YARDS OR MORE
Game
3—Jesse Garcia, La.-Monroe vs. McNeese St., Oct. 29, 1983 (52, 56, 53 yards); Terry Belden, Northern Ariz. vs. Cal St. Northridge, Sept. 18, 1993 (60, 50, 54 yards)
Season
7—Jesse Garcia, La.-Monroe, 1983 (12 attempts); Kirk Roach, Western Caro., 1987 (12 attempts)
Career
11—Kirk Roach, Western Caro., 1984-87 (26 attempts); Pete Garces, Idaho St., 1998-99 (16 attempts)

HIGHEST PERCENTAGE OF FIELD GOALS MADE, 50 YARDS OR MORE
Season
(Min. 5 atts.) 100.0%—Wayne Boyer, Southwest Mo. St., 1996 (5 of 5)
Career
(Min. 10 atts.) 90.9%—Tim Foley, Ga. Southern, 1984-87 (10 of 11)

MOST FIELD GOALS MADE, 40 YARDS OR MORE
Season
12—Marty Zendejas, Nevada, 1985 (15 attempts)
Career
30—Marty Zendejas, Nevada, 1984-87 (45 attempts)

HIGHEST PERCENTAGE OF FIELD GOALS MADE, 40 YARDS OR MORE
Season
(Min. 8 made) 100.0%—Tim Foley, Ga. Southern, 1985 (8 of 8)
Career
(Min. 15 made) 72.0%—Tim Foley, Ga. Southern, 1984-87 (18 of 25)

HIGHEST PERCENTAGE OF FIELD GOALS MADE, 40-49 YARDS
Season
(Min. 8 made) 90.0%—Marty Zendejas, Nevada, 1985 (9 of 10)
Career
(Min. 12 made) 72.0%—Tony Zendejas, Nevada, 1981-83 (18 of 25)

HIGHEST PERCENTAGE OF FIELD GOALS MADE, UNDER 40 YARDS
Season
(Min. 15 made) 100.0%—Matt Stover, Louisiana Tech, 1986 (15 of 15); Kirk Roach, Western Caro., 1986 (17 of 17); Brian Mitchell, Northern Iowa, 1990 (23 of 23)
Career
(Min. 25 made) 93.3%—Marty Zendejas, Nevada, 1984-87 (42 of 45)

MOST TIMES KICKING TWO OR MORE FIELD GOALS IN A GAME
Season
10—Brian Mitchell, Northern Iowa, 1991
Career
25—Kirk Roach, Western Caro., 1984-87

DIVISION I-AA

INDIVIDUAL RECORDS—FIELD GOALS

MOST TIMES KICKING THREE OR MORE FIELD GOALS IN A GAME
Season
7—Brian Mitchell, Northern Iowa, 1991
Career
11—Brian Mitchell, Marshall/Northern Iowa, 1987, 1989-91

MOST CONSECUTIVE QUARTERS KICKING A FIELD GOAL
Season
7—Scott Roper, Arkansas St., 1986 (last 3 vs. McNeese St., Oct. 25; all 4 vs. North Texas, Nov. 1)

LONGEST AVERAGE DISTANCE FIELD GOALS MADE
Game
(Min. 3 made) 54.7—Terry Belden, Northern Ariz. vs. Cal St. Northridge, Sept. 18, 1993 (60, 50, 54 yards)
Season
(Min. 14 made) 45.0—Jesse Garcia, La.-Monroe, 1983 (15 made)
Career
(Min. 35 made) 37.5—Roger Ruzek, Weber St., 1979-82 (46 made)

LONGEST AVERAGE DISTANCE FIELD GOALS ATTEMPTED
Season
(Min. 20 atts.) 45.9—Jesse Garcia, La.-Monroe, 1983 (26 attempts)
Career
(Min. 60 atts.) 40.5—Kirk Roach, Western Caro., 1984-87 (102 attempts)

LONGEST FIELD GOAL MADE
63—Scott Roper, Arkansas St. vs. North Texas, Nov. 7, 1987; Tim Foley, Ga. Southern vs. James Madison, Nov. 7, 1987

LONGEST FIELD GOAL MADE BY A FRESHMAN
60—David Cool, Ga. Southern vs. James Madison, Nov. 5, 1988

MOST FIELD GOALS MADE BY A FRESHMAN
Game
5—Mike Powers, Colgate vs. Army, Sept. 10, 1983 (6 attempts); Marty Zendejas, Nevada vs. Idaho St., Nov. 17, 1984 (5 attempts); Chuck Rawlinson, Stephen F. Austin vs. Prairie View, Sept. 10, 1988 (5 attempts)
Season
22—Marty Zendejas, Nevada, 1984 (27 attempts)

MOST FIELD GOALS MADE IN FIRST GAME OF CAREER
5—Mike Powers, Colgate vs. Army, Sept. 10, 1983 (6 attempts)

MOST GAMES IN WHICH FIELD GOAL(S) PROVIDED WINNING MARGIN
Career
11—John Dowling, Youngstown St., 1984-87

LONGEST RETURN OF A MISSED FIELD GOAL
89—Pat Bayers, Western Ill. vs. Youngstown St., Nov. 6, 1982 (TD)

Team Records

SINGLE GAME—Offense

Total Offense

MOST PLAYS
115—Buffalo vs. Connecticut, Oct. 4, 1997 (437 yards)

MOST PLAYS, BOTH TEAMS
196—Villanova (113) & Connecticut (83), Oct. 7, 1989 (904 yards)

MOST YARDS GAINED
876—Weber St. vs. Idaho St., Nov. 23, 1991 (252 rushing, 624 passing)

MOST YARDS GAINED, BOTH TEAMS
1,418—Howard (740) & Bethune-Cookman (678), Sept. 19, 1987 (161 plays)

MOST YARDS GAINED BY A LOSING TEAM
756—Alcorn St. vs. Grambling, Sept. 3, 1994 (lost 62-56)

FEWEST YARDS GAINED BY A WINNING TEAM
31—Middle Tenn. St. vs. Murray St., Oct. 17, 1981 (won 14-9)

HIGHEST AVERAGE GAIN PER PLAY
(Min. 55 Plays)
12.7—Marshall vs. VMI, Nov. 16, 1991 (62 for 789)

MOST TOUCHDOWNS SCORED BY RUSHING AND PASSING
14—Portland St. vs. Delaware St., Nov. 8, 1980 (10 passing, 4 rushing)

Rushing

MOST RUSHES
90—VMI vs. East Tenn. St., Nov. 17, 1990 (311 yards)

MOST RUSHES, BOTH TEAMS
127—Western Ky. (73) & Elon (54), Oct. 24, 1998 (718 yards)

FEWEST RUSHES
11—Mississippi Val. vs. Kentucky St., Sept. 1, 1984 (17 yards); Western Ill. vs. Northern Iowa, Oct. 24, 1987 (-11 yards)

MOST YARDS GAINED
681—Southwest Mo. St. vs. Mo. Southern St., Sept. 10, 1988 (83 rushes)

MOST YARDS GAINED, BOTH TEAMS
775—Southern Utah (535) & Eastern Wash. (240), Nov. 21, 1998 (108 rushes)

MOST YARDS GAINED BY A LOSING TEAM
448—Western Ky. vs. Southern Ill., Nov. 4, 1995 (lost 30-28)
(Note: Western Ky. rushed for 469 yards vs. Division I-A Louisville on Oct. 31, 1998, but lost, 63-34)

HIGHEST AVERAGE GAIN PER RUSH
(Min. 45 Rushes)
11.22—Southwest Mo. St. vs. Truman, Oct. 5, 1985 (45 for 505)
(Note: Ga. Southern rushed for 591 yards in 53 carries vs. Western Caro. on Oct. 9, 1999, for an 11.15 average)

MOST TOUCHDOWNS SCORED BY RUSHING
10—Arkansas St. vs. Tex. A&M-Commerce, Sept. 26, 1987

Passing

MOST PASSES ATTEMPTED
78—Towson vs. Lehigh, Oct. 30, 1999 (completed 47 for 567 yards)

MOST PASSES ATTEMPTED, BOTH TEAMS
122—Idaho (62) & Idaho St. (60), Sept. 24, 1983 (completed 48 for 639 yards)

FEWEST PASSES ATTEMPTED
1—By many teams. Most recent: Northeastern vs. Towson, Sept. 9, 1989 (completed 1)

FEWEST PASSES ATTEMPTED, BOTH TEAMS
11—Memphis (3) & Arkansas St. (8), Nov. 27, 1982 (completed 6); N.C. A&T (5) & Western Ky. (6), Nov. 19, 1988 (completed 2); Citadel (3) & Ga. Southern (8), Nov. 19, 1994 (completed 6)

MOST PASSES ATTEMPTED WITHOUT INTERCEPTION
72—Marshall vs. Western Caro., Nov. 14, 1987 (completed 35)

MOST PASSES COMPLETED
50—Mississippi Val. vs. Southern U., Sept. 29, 1984 (attempted 70 for 633 yards); Mississippi Val. vs. Prairie View, Oct. 27, 1984 (attempted 66 for 642 yards)

MOST PASSES COMPLETED, BOTH TEAMS I-AA
77—La.-Monroe (46) & Stephen F. Austin (31), Nov. 11, 1989 (attempted 116 for 1,190 yards)

MOST PASSES COMPLETED, BOTH TEAMS
80—Hofstra (50) & Fordham (30), Oct. 19, 1991 (attempted 120 for 987 yards)

FEWEST PASSES COMPLETED
0—By many teams. Most recent: Western Ky. vs. Eastern Ky., Oct. 9, 1999

FEWEST PASSES COMPLETED, BOTH TEAMS
2—N.C. A&T (0) & Western Ky. (2), Nov. 19, 1988 (attempted 11)

HIGHEST PERCENTAGE COMPLETED
(Min. 30-44 atts.) 85.4%—Cal St. Northridge vs. Southwest Mo. St., Nov. 14, 1998 (35 of 41)
(Min. 45 atts.) 79.2%—Montana vs. Weber St., Oct. 7, 1995 (38 of 48)

LOWEST PERCENTAGE COMPLETED
(Min. 20 Attempts)
9.5%—Florida A&M vs. Central St., Oct. 11, 1986 (2 of 21)

MOST PASSES HAD INTERCEPTED
10—Mississippi Val. vs. Grambling, Oct. 17, 1987 (47 attempts); Boise St. vs. Montana, Oct. 28, 1989 (55 attempts)

MOST YARDS GAINED
699—Mississippi Val. vs. Kentucky St., Sept. 1, 1984

MOST YARDS GAINED, BOTH TEAMS
1,190—La.-Monroe (619) & Stephen F. Austin (571), Nov. 11, 1989

MOST YARDS GAINED PER ATTEMPT
(Min. 25 Attempts)
20.1—Delaware vs. Connecticut, Nov. 7, 1998 (29 for 584)

MOST YARDS GAINED PER COMPLETION
(Min. 10-24 comps.) 33.0—Jackson St. vs. Southern U., Oct. 13, 1990 (14 for 462)
(Min. 25 comps.) 22.9—Marshall vs. VMI, Nov. 16, 1991 (28 for 642)

MOST TOUCHDOWN PASSES
11—Mississippi Val. vs. Kentucky St., Sept. 1, 1984

MOST TOUCHDOWN PASSES, BOTH TEAMS
14—Mississippi Val. (8) & Texas Southern (6), Oct. 26, 1985

Punting

MOST PUNTS
16—Louisiana Tech vs. La.-Monroe, Nov. 19, 1988 (567 yards)

MOST PUNTS, BOTH TEAMS
26—Hofstra (14) vs. Buffalo (12), Nov. 2, 1996

HIGHEST AVERAGE PER PUNT
(Min. 5-9 punts) 55.7—Montana vs. Nevada, Oct. 1, 1988 (9 for 501); Appalachian St. vs. Citadel, Oct. 3, 1992 (6 for 334)

TEAM RECORDS—PUNTING

(Min. 10 punts) 52.2—Montana St. vs. Northern Ariz., Oct. 20, 1979 (10 for 522)

FEWEST PUNTS
0—By many teams. Most recent: Ga. Southern vs. Chattanooga, Sept. 25, 1999; Delaware vs. James Madison, Nov. 21, 1995; Connecticut vs. Central Conn. St., Sept. 16, 1995

FEWEST PUNTS, BOTH TEAMS
0—Ga. Southern & James Madison, Nov. 15, 1986

MOST OPPONENT'S PUNTS BLOCKED BY
4—Montana vs. Montana St., Oct. 31, 1987 (13 punts); Middle Tenn. St. vs. Mississippi Val., Oct. 8, 1988 (7 punts)

Punt Returns

MOST PUNT RETURNS
12—Northern Iowa vs. Youngstown St., Oct. 20, 1984 (83 yards)

MOST YARDS ON PUNT RETURNS
322—Northern Ariz. vs. Western N.M., Aug. 29, 1996 (10 returns)

HIGHEST AVERAGE GAIN PER RETURN
(Min. 6 Returns)
32.2—Northern Ariz. vs. Western N.M., Aug. 29, 1996 (10 for 322, 2 TDs)

MOST TOUCHDOWNS SCORED ON PUNT RETURNS
3—Canisius vs. Siena, Sept. 24, 1994; Northern Ariz. vs. Western N.M., Aug. 29, 1996

Kickoff Returns

MOST KICKOFF RETURNS
15—Delaware St. vs. Portland St., Nov. 8, 1980 (209 yards)

MOST YARDS ON KICKOFF RETURNS
326—Eastern Wash. vs. Cal St. Sacramento, Oct. 31, 1998 (5 returns)

HIGHEST AVERAGE GAIN PER RETURN
(Min. 3-5 rets.) 65.2—Eastern Wash. vs. Cal St. Sacramento, Oct. 31, 1998 (5 for 326)
(Min. 6 rets.) 46.3—Western Caro. vs. VMI, Oct. 10, 1992 (6 for 278)

MOST TOUCHDOWNS SCORED ON KICKOFF RETURNS
3—Eastern Wash. vs. Cal St. Sacramento, Oct. 31, 1998

Total Kick Returns

(Combined Punt and Kickoff Returns)

MOST YARDS ON KICK RETURNS
349—Eastern Wash. vs. Cal St. Sacramento, Oct. 31, 1998 (23 punt returns, 326 kickoff returns)

HIGHEST AVERAGE GAIN PER RETURN
(Min. 6 Returns)
46.8—Connecticut vs. Yale, Sept. 24, 1983 (6 for 281)

Scoring

MOST POINTS SCORED
105—Portland St. vs. Delaware St., Nov. 8, 1980 (15 TDs, 15 PATs)

MOST POINTS SCORED, BOTH TEAMS
122—Weber St. (63) & Eastern Wash. (59), Sept. 28, 1991 (17 TDs, 14 PATs, 2 FGs)

MOST POINTS SCORED BY A LOSING TEAM
59—Eastern Wash. vs. Weber St. (63), Sept. 28, 1991

MOST POINTS SCORED EACH QUARTER
1st: 49—Portland St. vs. Delaware St., Nov. 8, 1980
2nd: 50—Alabama St. vs. Prairie View, Oct. 26, 1991
3rd: 35—Portland St. vs. Delaware St., Nov. 8, 1980; La.-Monroe vs. Arkansas St., Nov. 6, 1993
4th: 39—Montana vs. South Dakota St., Sept. 4, 1993

MOST POINTS SCORED EACH HALF
1st: 73—Montana St. vs. Eastern Ore., Sept. 14, 1985
2nd: 56—Brown vs. Columbia, Nov. 19, 1994

MOST TOUCHDOWNS SCORED
15—Portland St. vs. Delaware St., Nov. 8, 1980

MOST POINTS SCORED IN FOURTH QUARTER, BOTH TEAMS
58—Brown (30) vs. Pennsylvania (28), Oct. 10, 1998

MOST TOUCHDOWNS SCORED, BOTH TEAMS
17—Furman (9) & Davidson (8), Nov. 3, 1979; Weber St. (9) & Eastern Wash. (8), Sept. 28, 1991; Grambling (9) & Alcorn St. (8), Sept. 3, 1994

MOST EXTRA POINTS MADE BY KICKING
15—Portland St. vs. Delaware St., Nov. 8, 1980 (15 attempts)

MOST TWO-POINT ATTEMPTS MADE
5—Weber St. vs. Eastern Wash., Oct. 6, 1990 (5 passes attempted)

MOST FIELD GOALS MADE
8—Northern Ariz. vs. Idaho, Oct. 25, 1986 (8 attempts)

MOST FIELD GOALS ATTEMPTED
8—Northern Ariz. vs. Idaho, Oct. 25, 1986 (made 8)

MOST FIELD GOALS MADE, BOTH TEAMS
9—Nevada (5) & Northern Ariz. (4), Oct. 9, 1982 (12 attempts); Nevada (5) & Weber St. (4), Nov. 6, 1982 (11 attempts, 3 ot)

MOST SAFETIES SCORED
3—Alabama St. vs. Albany St. (Ga.), Oct. 15, 1988

MOST DEFENSIVE EXTRA POINTS SCORED
2—VMI vs. Davidson, Nov. 4, 1989 (Jeff Barnes, 95-yard interception return, and Wayne Purcell, 90-yard interception return)

MOST DEFENSIVE EXTRA-POINT ATTEMPTS
2—VMI vs. Davidson, Nov. 4, 1989 (2 interception returns); Western Ky. vs. Indiana St., Nov. 10, 1990 (2 interception returns)

First Downs

MOST FIRST DOWNS
46—Weber St. vs. Idaho St., Nov. 23, 1991 (12 rushing, 31 passing, 3 penalty)

MOST FIRST DOWNS, BOTH TEAMS
72—Bethune-Cookman (40) & Howard (32), Sept. 19, 1987

MOST FIRST DOWNS BY RUSHING
31—Ga. Southern vs. Glenville St., Nov. 12, 1994

MOST FIRST DOWNS BY PASSING
32—Montana vs. Weber St., Sept. 25, 1999

MOST FIRST DOWNS BY PENALTY
11—Towson vs. Liberty, Oct. 21, 1990

Fumbles

MOST FUMBLES
16—Delaware St. vs. Portland St., Nov. 8, 1980 (lost 6)

MOST FUMBLES, BOTH TEAMS
21—N.C. A&T (15) & Lane (6), Nov. 11, 1995 (lost 12)

MOST FUMBLES LOST
9—N.C. A&T vs. Lane, Nov. 11, 1995 (15 fumbles)

MOST FUMBLES LOST, BOTH TEAMS
12—Virginia St. (7) & Howard (5), Oct. 13, 1979 (16 fumbles); Austin Peay (8) & Mars Hill (4), Nov. 17, 1979 (18 fumbles); N.C. A&T (9) & Lane (3), Nov. 11, 1995 (21 fumbles)

Penalties

MOST PENALTIES AGAINST
23—Idaho vs. Idaho St., Oct. 10, 1992 (204 yards)

MOST PENALTIES, BOTH TEAMS
39—In four games. Most recent: Jackson St. (22) & Grambling (17), Oct. 24, 1987 (370 yards)

MOST YARDS PENALIZED
260—Southern U. vs. Howard, Nov. 4, 1978 (22 penalties)

MOST YARDS PENALIZED, BOTH TEAMS
423—Southern U. (260) & Howard (163), Nov. 4, 1978 (37 penalties)

Turnovers

(Passes Had Intercepted and Fumbles Lost)

MOST TURNOVERS
12—Texas Southern vs. Lamar, Sept. 6, 1980 (4 interceptions, 8 fumbles lost)

MOST TURNOVERS, BOTH TEAMS
15—Bucknell (8) & Hofstra (7), Sept. 8, 1990 (10 interceptions, 5 fumbles lost); Stephen F. Austin (8) & Nicholls St. (7), Sept. 22, 1990 (8 interceptions, 7 fumbles lost)

Overtimes

MOST OVERTIME PERIODS
6—Rhode Island (58) vs. Maine (55), Sept. 18, 1982; Villanova (41) vs. Connecticut (35), Oct. 7, 1989; Florida A&M (59) vs. Hampton (58), Oct. 5, 1996

MOST POINTS SCORED IN OVERTIME PERIODS
39—Florida A&M (59) vs. Hampton (58), Oct. 5, 1996 (6 overtime periods)

MOST POINTS SCORED IN OVERTIME PERIODS, BOTH TEAMS
77—Florida A&M (39) vs. Hampton (38), Oct. 5, 1996 (6 overtime periods; Florida A&M won, 59-58)

LARGEST WINNING MARGIN IN OVERTIME
13—Nicholls St. (49) vs. Southwest Tex. St. (36), Oct. 26, 1996 (5 overtime periods)

MOST CONSECUTIVE OVERTIME GAMES PLAYED
2—Maine, 1982 (Rhode Island 58, Maine 55, 6 ot, Sept. 18; and Boston U. 48, Maine 45, 4 ot, Sept. 25); Connecticut, 1989 (Villanova 41, Connecticut 35, 6 ot, Oct. 7; and Connecticut 39, Massachusetts 33, Oct. 14); Montana, 1991 (Nevada 35, Montana 28, 2 ot, Nov. 9; and Montana 35, Idaho 34, Nov. 16); Tennessee Tech, 1998 (Tennessee Tech 31, Tenn.-Martin 24, Oct. 17 and Tennessee Tech 31, Eastern Ky. 29, 3 ot, Oct. 24)

SINGLE GAME—Defense

Total Defense

FEWEST PLAYS ALLOWED
31—Howard vs. Dist. Columbia, Sept. 2, 1989 (32 yards)

FEWEST YARDS ALLOWED
Minus 12—Eastern Ill. vs. Kentucky St., Nov. 13, 1982 (-67 rushing, 55 passing)

Rushing Defense

FEWEST RUSHES ALLOWED
9—Mississippi Val. vs. Alcorn St., Nov. 6, 1999 (4 yards)

FEWEST RUSHING YARDS ALLOWED
Minus 88—Austin Peay vs. Morehead St., Oct. 8, 1983 (31 rushes)

Pass Defense

FEWEST ATTEMPTS ALLOWED
1—By six teams. Most recent: Western Caro. vs. Wofford, Oct. 17, 1998

DIVISION I-AA

FEWEST COMPLETIONS ALLOWED
  0—By many teams. Most recent: Western Caro. vs. Wofford, Oct. 17, 1998 (1 attempt); South Fla. vs. Cumberland, Nov. 8, 1997 (4 attempts)

LOWEST COMPLETION PERCENTAGE ALLOWED (Min. 30 Attempts)
  11.8%—Southern U. vs. Nicholls St., Oct. 11, 1980 (4 of 34)

FEWEST YARDS ALLOWED
  Minus 2—Florida A&M vs. Albany St. (Ga.), Oct. 16, 1982

MOST PASSES INTERCEPTED BY
  10—Grambling vs. Mississippi Val., Oct. 17, 1987 (47 attempts); Montana vs. Boise St., Oct. 28, 1989 (55 attempts)

MOST TIMES OPPONENT TACKLED FOR LOSS ATTEMPTING TO PASS
  14—Duquesne vs. Iona, Oct. 31, 1998 (92 yards)

MOST INTERCEPTIONS RETURNED FOR TOUCHDOWNS
  3—Chattanooga vs. La.-Lafayette, Sept. 17, 1983 (4 for 122 yards); Montana vs. Eastern Wash., Nov. 12, 1983 (4 for 134 yards); Delaware St. vs. Akron, Oct. 17, 1987 (5 for 124 yards); Canisius vs. Siena, Sept. 16, 1995 (6 for 120 yards); Nicholls St. vs. Southwest Tex. St., Oct. 26, 1996 (4 for 166 yards)

Opponent's Kicks Blocked

MOST OPPONENT'S PUNTS BLOCKED
  4—Montana vs. Montana St., Oct. 31, 1987 (13 punts); Middle Tenn. St. vs. Mississippi Val., Oct. 8, 1988 (7 punts)

MOST OPPONENT'S TOTAL KICKS BLOCKED (Includes punts, field goals, PATs)
  4—Montana vs. Montana St., Oct. 31, 1987 (all punts); Middle Tenn. St. vs. Mississippi Val., Oct. 8, 1988 (all punts)

Fumble Returns

(Since 1992)

MOST FUMBLES RETURNED FOR TOUCHDOWNS
  2—Marshall vs. VMI, Oct. 9, 1993; Idaho vs. Weber St., Nov. 12, 1994

Safeties

MOST SAFETIES BY A DEFENSE
  2—By several teams. Most recent: Duquesne vs. St. Francis (Pa.), Sept. 12, 1998

SEASON—Offense

Total Offense

MOST YARDS GAINED PER GAME
  640.1—Mississippi Val., 1984 (6,401 in 10)

HIGHEST AVERAGE GAIN PER PLAY
  7.8—Alcorn St., 1994 (848 for 6,577)

MOST PLAYS PER GAME
  89.6—Weber St., 1991 (986 in 11)

MOST TOUCHDOWNS BY RUSHING AND PASSING PER GAME
  8.4—Mississippi Val., 1984 (84 in 10)

Rushing

MOST YARDS GAINED PER GAME
  419.0—Ga. Southern, 1999 (4,609 in 11)

HIGHEST AVERAGE GAIN PER RUSH
  7.0—Ga. Southern, 1999 (654 for 4,609)

MOST RUSHES PER GAME
  69.8—Northeastern, 1986 (698 in 10)

MOST TOUCHDOWNS BY RUSHING PER GAME
  5.5—Ga. Southern, 1999 (61 in 11)

Passing

MOST YARDS GAINED PER GAME
  496.8—Mississippi Val., 1984 (4,968 in 10)

HIGHEST AVERAGE GAIN PER ATTEMPT
  (Min. 250-399 atts.) 10.7—Northern Iowa, 1996 (252 for 2,700)
  (Min. 400 atts.) 9.3—Montana, 1999 (438 for 4,070)

HIGHEST AVERAGE GAIN PER COMPLETION
  (Min. 125-199 comps.) 19.3—Jackson St., 1990 (156 for 3,006)
  (Min. 200 comps.) 16.6—Stephen F. Austin, 1989 (240 for 3,985)

MOST PASSES ATTEMPTED PER GAME
  55.8—Mississippi Val., 1984 (558 in 10)

MOST PASSES COMPLETED PER GAME
  35.1—Mississippi Val., 1984 (351 in 10)

HIGHEST PERCENTAGE COMPLETED
  (Min. 200-449 atts.) 70.6%—Hofstra, 1997 (293 of 415)
  (Min. 450 atts.) 67.2%—Montana, 1995 (336 of 500)

LOWEST PERCENTAGE HAD INTERCEPTED
  (Min. 200-399 atts.) 0.78%—Portland St., 1999 (3 of 383)
  (Min. 400 atts.) 1.2%—Lamar, 1988 (5 of 411)

MOST CONSECUTIVE PASSES ATTEMPTED WITHOUT AN INTERCEPTION
  275—Lamar, 1988 (during 8 games, Sept. 3 to Oct. 29)

MOST TOUCHDOWN PASSES PER GAME
  6.4—Mississippi Val., 1984 (64 in 10)

HIGHEST PASSING EFFICIENCY RATING POINTS
  190.6—William & Mary, 1993 (232 attempts, 161 completions, 4 interceptions, 2,499 yards, 24 TDs)

Punting

MOST PUNTS PER GAME
  9.6—Louisiana Tech, 1987 (106 in 11)

FEWEST PUNTS PER GAME
  2.1—Ga. Southern, 1999 (23 in 11)

HIGHEST PUNTING AVERAGE
  47.0—Appalachian St., 1991 (64 for 3,009)

HIGHEST NET PUNTING AVERAGE
  44.5—Marshall, 1996 (38 for 1,739; 47 yards returned)

MOST PUNTS HAD BLOCKED
  8—Western Ky., 1982

Punt Returns

MOST PUNT RETURNS PER GAME
  5.4—Murray St., 1980 (59 in 11)

FEWEST PUNT RETURNS PER GAME
  0.6—Youngstown St., 1990 (7 in 11); Prairie View, 1991 (7 in 11); Southern Ill., 1991 (7 in 11)

MOST PUNT-RETURN YARDS PER GAME
  64.8—Duquesne, 1996 (648 in 10)

HIGHEST AVERAGE GAIN PER PUNT RETURN
  (Min. 20-29 rets.) 19.5—Towson, 1994 (27 for 526)
  (Min. 30 rets.) 18.1—Mississippi Val., 1985 (31 for 561)

MOST TOUCHDOWNS SCORED ON PUNT RETURNS
  5—Southern Ill., 1985

Kickoff Returns

MOST KICKOFF RETURNS PER GAME
  7.7—Morehead St., 1994 (85 in 11; 1,582 yards)

FEWEST KICKOFF RETURNS PER GAME
  1.2—McNeese St., 1997 (13 in 11)

MOST KICKOFF-RETURN YARDS PER GAME
  143.8—Morehead St., 1994 (1,582 in 11; 85 returns)

HIGHEST AVERAGE GAIN PER KICKOFF RETURN (Min. 20 Returns)
  29.5—Eastern Ky., 1986 (34 for 1,022)

Combined Returns

(Interceptions, Punt Returns and Kickoff Returns)

MOST TOUCHDOWNS SCORED
  9—Delaware St., 1987 (5 interceptions, 3 punt returns, 1 kickoff return)

Scoring

MOST POINTS PER GAME
  60.9—Mississippi Val., 1984 (609 in 10)

MOST TOUCHDOWNS PER GAME
  8.7—Mississippi Val., 1984 (87 in 10)

MOST EXTRA POINTS MADE BY KICKING PER GAME
  7.7—Mississippi Val., 1984 (77 in 10)

MOST CONSECUTIVE EXTRA POINTS MADE BY KICKING
  56—Murray St., 1995

MOST TWO-POINT ATTEMPTS MADE
  9—Weber St., 1992 (11 attempts)

MOST DEFENSIVE EXTRA-POINT ATTEMPTS
  2—VMI, 1989; Eastern Wash., 1990; Western Ky., 1990

MOST DEFENSIVE EXTRA POINTS SCORED
  2—VMI, 1989 (2 interception returns); Eastern Wash., 1990 (2 interception returns)

MOST FIELD GOALS MADE PER GAME
  2.4—Nevada, 1982 (26 in 11); Northern Iowa, 1990 (26 in 11)

MOST SAFETIES SCORED
  5—Jackson St., 1986

First Downs

MOST FIRST DOWNS PER GAME
  31.7—Mississippi Val., 1984 (317 in 10)

MOST RUSHING FIRST DOWNS PER GAME
  18.6—Ga. Southern, 1999 (205 in 11)

MOST PASSING FIRST DOWNS PER GAME
  21.4—Mississippi Val., 1984 (214 in 10)

MOST FIRST DOWNS BY PENALTY PER GAME
  3.7—Alabama St., 1984 (41 in 11; 109 penalties by opponents); Texas Southern, 1987 (41 in 11; 134 penalties by opponents)

Fumbles

MOST FUMBLES PER GAME
  5.3—Prairie View, 1984 (58 in 11)

MOST FUMBLES LOST PER GAME
  3.1—Idaho, 1978 (31 in 10); Delaware St., 1980 (31 in 10)

FEWEST OWN FUMBLES LOST
  1—Yale, 1999 (5 fumbles)

Penalties

MOST PENALTIES PER GAME
  13.7—Grambling, 1984 (151 in 11; 1,206 yards)

MOST YARDS PENALIZED PER GAME
  125.5—Tennessee St., 1982 (1,255 in 10; 132 penalties)

TEAM RECORDS—TURNOVERS

Turnovers

FEWEST TURNOVERS
9—Hofstra, 1995 (6 fumbles, 3 interceptions); Yale, 1999 (1 fumble, 8 interceptions)

MOST TURNOVERS
59—Texas Southern, 1980 (27 fumbles, 32 interceptions)

HIGHEST TURNOVER MARGIN PER GAME OVER OPPONENTS
2.5—Florida A&M, 1981; Appalachian St., 1985

SEASON—Defense

Total Defense

FEWEST YARDS ALLOWED PER GAME
149.9—Florida A&M, 1978 (1,649 in 11)

FEWEST RUSHING AND PASSING TOUCHDOWNS ALLOWED PER GAME
0.7—Western Mich., 1982 (8 in 11)

LOWEST AVERAGE YARDS ALLOWED PER PLAY
2.4—South Carolina St., 1978 (719 for 1,736)

Rushing Defense

FEWEST YARDS ALLOWED PER GAME
40.4—Marist, 1997 (404 in 10)

LOWEST AVERAGE YARDS ALLOWED PER RUSH
1.3—Marist, 1997 (319 for 404)

FEWEST RUSHING TOUCHDOWNS ALLOWED PER GAME
0.3—Florida A&M, 1978 (3 in 11)

Pass Defense

FEWEST YARDS ALLOWED PER GAME
59.9—Bethune-Cookman, 1981 (659 in 11)

FEWEST YARDS ALLOWED PER ATTEMPT (Min. 200 Attempts)
4.0—Middle Tenn. St., 1988 (251 for 999)

FEWEST YARDS ALLOWED PER COMPLETION (Min. 100 Completions)
9.1—Middle Tenn. St., 1988 (110 for 999)

LOWEST COMPLETION PERCENTAGE ALLOWED
(Min. 200-299 atts.) 32.3%—Alcorn St., 1979 (76 of 235)
(Min. 300 atts.) 34.2%—Tennessee St., 1986 (107 of 313)

FEWEST TOUCHDOWNS ALLOWED BY PASSING
1—Nevada, 1978; Middle Tenn. St., 1990; Pennsylvania, 1994

LOWEST PASSING EFFICIENCY DEFENSE RATING (Since 1990)
63.1—Pennsylvania, 1994 (235 attempts, 90 completions, 15 interceptions, 1,013 yards, 1 TD)

MOST PASSES INTERCEPTED BY, PER GAME
3.2—Florida A&M, 1981 (35 in 11)

HIGHEST PERCENTAGE INTERCEPTED BY
13.4%—Florida A&M, 1981 (35 of 262)

MOST YARDS GAINED ON INTERCEPTIONS
551—Weber St., 1996 (26 interceptions)

MOST YARDS GAINED PER GAME ON INTERCEPTIONS
51.3—Canisius, 1996 (462 in 9)

HIGHEST AVERAGE PER INTERCEPTION RETURN (Min. 15 Returns)
24.7—Marist, 1997 (16 for 395)

MOST TOUCHDOWNS ON INTERCEPTION RETURNS
7—Jackson St., 1985; Northeastern, 1996

Opponents' Kicks Blocked

MOST OPPONENTS' TOTAL KICKS BLOCKED (Includes punts, field goals, PATs)
13—Davidson, 1999 (6 punts, 4 field goals, 3 PATs)

Punting

MOST OPPONENTS' PUNTS BLOCKED BY
9—Middle Tenn. St., 1988 (73 punts)

Punt Returns

LOWEST AVERAGE YARDS ALLOWED PER PUNT RETURN
1.0—Yale, 1988 (24 for 23)

FEWEST RETURNS ALLOWED
7—Furman, 1984 (11 games, 8 yards); Cal Poly, 1997 (11 games, 108 yards)

Kickoff Returns

LOWEST AVERAGE YARDS ALLOWED PER KICKOFF RETURN
10.6—Southern Utah, 1996 (33 for 350)

Scoring

FEWEST POINTS ALLOWED PER GAME
6.5—South Carolina St., 1978 (72 in 11)

Fumbles

MOST OPPONENTS' FUMBLES RECOVERED
29—Western Ky., 1982 (43 fumbles)

Fumble Returns

(Since 1992)

MOST FUMBLES RETURNED FOR TOUCHDOWNS
2—Citadel, 1992 (vs. Arkansas, Sept. 5 & vs. Western Caro., Oct. 24); Marshall, 1993 (both vs. VMI, Oct. 9)

Turnovers

MOST OPPONENTS' TURNOVERS PER GAME
4.9—Canisius, 1996 (44 in 9)

Additional Records

MOST CONSECUTIVE VICTORIES
24—Pennsylvania, from Nov. 14, 1992, through Sept. 30, 1995 (ended Oct. 7, 1995, with 24-14 loss to Columbia)

MOST CONSECUTIVE HOME VICTORIES
38—Ga. Southern, from Oct. 5, 1985, through Sept. 22, 1990 (includes 10 I-AA playoff games)

MOST CONSECUTIVE LOSSES
80—Prairie View, from Nov. 4, 1989, until Sept. 26, 1998

MOST CONSECUTIVE GAMES WITHOUT A WIN
80—Prairie View, from Nov. 4, 1989, until Sept. 26, 1998

MOST CONSECUTIVE GAMES WITHOUT BEING SHUT OUT
263—Dayton, from Oct. 23, 1976, through present
(Note: Dayton has been a I-AA member since 1993. Boise State had a 193-game streak from Sept. 21, 1968, through Nov. 10, 1984)

MOST SHUTOUTS IN A SEASON
5—South Carolina St., 1978

MOST CONSECUTIVE QUARTERS HOLDING OPPONENTS SCORELESS
15—Robert Morris, 1996

MOST CONSECUTIVE GAMES WITHOUT A TIE
343—Richmond, from Nov. 2, 1963, to Oct. 14, 1995 (ended Oct. 21, 1995, with 3-3 tie with Fordham)

LAST TIE GAME
Nov. 18, 1995—Dartmouth 10, Princeton 10

LAST SCORELESS-TIE GAME
Oct. 26, 1985—McNeese St. & North Texas

MOST CONSECUTIVE PASSES ATTEMPTED WITHOUT AN INTERCEPTION
370—Portland St. (in 11 games from Sept 4, 1999, to Nov. 13, 1999)

MOST POINTS OVERCOME IN SECOND HALF TO WIN A GAME
35—Nevada (55) vs. Weber St. (49), Nov. 2, 1991 (trailed 49-14 with 12:16 remaining in 3rd quarter)
32—Morehead St. (36) vs. Wichita St. (35), Sept. 20, 1986 (trailed 35-3 with 9:03 remaining in 3rd quarter)
31—Montana (52) vs. South Dakota St. (48), Sept. 4, 1993 (trailed 38-7 with 8:12 remaining in 3rd quarter)

MOST POINTS OVERCOME IN FOURTH QUARTER TO WIN A GAME
28—Delaware St. (38) vs. Liberty (37), Oct. 6, 1990 (trailed 37-9 with 13:00 remaining in 4th quarter)

MOST POINTS SCORED IN FOURTH QUARTER TO WIN A GAME
39—Montana (52) vs. South Dakota St. (48), Sept. 4, 1993 (trailed 38-13 to begin 4th quarter)
33—Southwest Mo. St. (40) vs. Illinois St. (28), Oct. 9, 1993 (trailed 21-7 with 11:30 remaining in 4th quarter)

MOST CONSECUTIVE EXTRA-POINT KICKS MADE
134—Boise St. (began Oct. 27, 1984; ended Nov. 12, 1988)

MOST CONSECUTIVE WINNING SEASONS
27—Grambling (1960-86)

MOST IMPROVED WON-LOST RECORD
9 1/2 games—Montana St., 1984 (12-2-0, including 3 Division I-AA playoff games) from 1983 (1-10-0)

DIVISION I-AA

Annual Champions, All-Time Leaders

Total Offense

CAREER YARDS PER GAME
(Minimum 5,500 Yards)

Player, Team	Years	G	Plays	Yards	TDR‡	Yd. PG
Steve McNair, Alcorn St.	1991-94	42	*2,055	*16,823	152	*400.5
Neil Lomax, Portland St.	1978-80	33	1,680	11,647	100	352.9
Aaron Flowers, Cal St. Northridge	1996-97	20	944	6,754	60	337.7
Dave Dickenson, Montana	1992-95	35	1,539	11,523	116	329.2
Willie Totten, Mississippi Val.	1982-85	40	1,812	13,007	*157	325.2
Tom Ehrhardt, Rhode Island	1984-85	21	1,010	6,492	66	309.1
Doug Nussmeier, Idaho	1990-93	39	1,556	12,054	109	309.1
Oteman Sampson, Florida A&M	1996-97	22	906	6,751	57	306.9
Jamie Martin, Weber St.	1989-92	41	1,838	12,287	93	299.7
Tom Proudian, Iona	1993-95	27	1,337	7,939	61	294.0
Robert Dougherty, Boston U.	1993-94	21	918	6,135	56	292.1
Stan Greene, Boston U.	1989-90	22	1,167	6,408	49	291.3
John Friesz, Idaho	1986-89	35	1,459	10,187	79	291.1
Travis Brown, Northern Ariz.	1996-99	41	1,732	11,267	95	274.8
Grady Bennett, Montana	1988-90	31	1,389	8,304	69	267.9
Sean Payton, Eastern Ill.	1983-86	39	1,690	10,298	91	264.1
James Perry, Brown	1996-99	35	1,408	9,225	75	263.6
Giovanni Carmazzi, Hofstra	1996-99	40	1,564	10,416	103	260.4
Brian Ah Yat, Montana	1995-98	36	1,365	9,319	98	258.9
John Witkowski, Columbia	1981-83	30	1,330	7,748	58	258.3
John Whitcomb, UAB	1993-94	22	800	5,683	43	258.3
Ken Hobart, Idaho	1980-83	44	1,847	11,127	105	252.9
Tony Hilde, Boise St.	1993-95	29	1,175	7,284	64	251.2
Jeff Wiley, Holy Cross	1985-88	40	1,428	9,877	76	246.9
Doug Butler, Princeton	1983-85	29	1,137	7,157	52	246.8
Tom Ciaccio, Holy Cross	1988-91	37	1,283	9,066	87	245.0
Greg Wyatt, Northern Ariz.	1986-89	42	1,753	10,277	75	244.7
Jeff Lewis, Northern Ariz.	1992-95	40	1,654	9,769	82	244.2
Jay Fiedler, Dartmouth	1991-93	30	1,063	7,249	73	241.6
Chris Boden, Villanova	1996-99	39	1,514	9,369	94	240.2
Chris Hakel, William & Mary	1988-91	28	915	6,458	56	239.2
Bob Jean, New Hampshire	1985-88	32	1,287	7,621	59	238.2
Ryan Vena, Colgate	1996-99	40	1,404	9,435	94	235.9
Ted White, Howard	1995-98	41	1,377	9,669	98	235.8
Michael Proctor, Murray St.	1986-89	43	1,577	9,886	66	230.0

*Record. ‡Touchdowns-responsible-for are player's TDs scored and passed for.

SEASON YARDS PER GAME

Player, Team	Years	G	Plays	Yards	TDR‡	Yd. PG
Steve McNair, Alcorn St.	†1994	11	*649	*5,799	53	*527.2
Willie Totten, Mississippi Val.	†1984	10	564	4,572	*61	457.2
Steve McNair, Alcorn St.	†1992	10	519	4,057	39	405.7
Jamie Martin, Weber St.	†1991	11	591	4,337	37	394.3
Dave Dickenson, Montana	†1995	11	544	4,209	41	382.6
Neil Lomax, Portland St.	†1980	11	550	4,157	42	377.9
Joe Lee, Towson	†1999	11	608	4,031	22	366.5
Dave Dickenson, Montana	†1993	11	530	3,978	46	361.6
Neil Lomax, Portland St.	†1979	11	611	3,966	31	360.5
John Friesz, Idaho	†1989	11	464	3,853	31	350.3
Steve McNair, Alcorn St.	1993	11	493	3,830	30	348.2
Aaron Flowers, Cal St. Northridge	†1997	9	456	3,132	26	348.0
Todd Hammel, Stephen F. Austin	1989	11	487	3,822	38	347.5
Tom Ehrhardt, Rhode Island	†1985	10	529	3,460	35	346.0
Ken Hobart, Idaho	†1983	11	578	3,800	37	345.5
Dave Dickenson, Montana	1994	9	431	3,108	27	345.3
Dave Stireman, Weber St.	1985	11	502	3,759	33	341.7
Brian Ah Yat, Montana	†1996	11	501	3,744	45	340.4
Willie Totten, Mississippi Val.	1985	11	561	3,742	43	340.2
Jeff Wiley, Holy Cross	†1987	11	445	3,722	34	338.4
Jamie Martin, Weber St.	†1990	11	508	3,713	25	337.6
Giovanni Carmazzi, Hofstra	1997	11	524	3,707	36	337.0
Sean Payton, Eastern Ill.	1984	11	584	3,661	31	332.8
Tod Mayfield, West Tex. A&M	1985	10	526	3,328	21	332.8
Tom Proudian, Iona	1993	10	521	3,322	30	332.2

*Record. †National champion. ‡Touchdowns-responsible-for are player's TDs scored and passed for.

CAREER YARDS

Player, Team	Years	Plays	Yards	Avg.
Steve McNair, Alcorn St.	1991-94	*2,055	*16,823	*8.19
Willie Totten, Mississippi Val.	1982-85	1,812	13,007	7.18
Jamie Martin, Weber St.	1989-92	1,838	12,287	6.68
Doug Nussmeier, Idaho	1990-93	1,556	12,054	7.75
Neil Lomax, Portland St.	1978-80	1,680	11,647	6.93
Dave Dickenson, Montana	1992-95	1,539	11,523	7.49
Travis Brown, Northern Ariz.	1996-99	1,732	11,267	6.51
Ken Hobart, Idaho	1980-83	1,847	11,127	6.02
Giovanni Carmazzi, Hofstra	1996-99	1,564	10,416	6.66
Sean Payton, Eastern Ill.	1983-86	1,690	10,298	6.09
Greg Wyatt, Northern Ariz.	1986-89	1,753	10,277	5.86
John Friesz, Idaho	1986-89	1,459	10,187	6.98
Michael Proctor, Murray St.	1986-89	1,577	9,886	6.27
Jeff Wiley, Holy Cross	1985-88	1,428	9,877	6.92
Jeff Lewis, Northern Ariz.	1992-95	1,654	9,769	5.91
Ted White, Howard	1995-98	1,377	9,669	7.02
Ryan Vena, Colgate	1996-99	1,404	9,435	6.72
Chris Boden, Villanova	1996-99	1,514	9,369	6.19
Brian Ah Yat, Montana	1995-98	1,365	9,319	6.83
Matt DeGennaro, Connecticut	1987-90	1,619	9,269	5.73
Phil Stambaugh, Lehigh	1996-99	1,430	9,245	6.47
James Perry, Brown	1996-99	1,408	9,225	6.55
Tom Ciaccio, Holy Cross	1988-91	1,283	9,066	7.07
Eric Beavers, Nevada	1983-86	1,307	9,025	6.91
Marty Horn, Lehigh	1982-85	1,612	8,956	5.56
Kirk Schulz, Villanova	1986-89	1,534	8,900	5.80
Darin Hinshaw, UCF	1991-94	1,266	8,841	6.98
Robbie Justino, Liberty	1989-92	1,469	8,803	5.99
Dan Crowley, Towson	1991-94	1,263	8,797	6.97
Mitch Maher, North Texas	1991-94	1,417	8,735	6.16
Chris Swartz, Morehead St.	1987-90	1,559	8,648	5.55
Frank Baur, Lafayette	1985, 87-89	1,312	8,579	6.54
Steve Calabria, Colgate	1981-84	1,342	8,532	6.36
Mike Buck, Maine	1986-89	1,288	8,457	6.57
Jason Whitmer, Idaho St.	1987-90	1,618	8,449	5.22
Scott Davis, North Texas	1987-90	1,548	8,436	5.45
Grady Bennett, Montana	1988-90	1,389	8,304	5.98
Bill Vergantino, Delaware	1989-92	1,459	8,225	5.64
Shane Stafford, Connecticut	1995-98	1,127	8,193	7.27
Stan Yagiello, William & Mary	$1981-85	1,492	8,168	5.47
Mike Smith, Northern Iowa	1984-87	1,163	8,145	7.00

*Record. $See page 6 for explanation.

SEASON YARDS

Player, Team	Year	G	Plays	Yards	Avg.
Steve McNair, Alcorn St.	†1994	11	*649	*5,799	*8.94
Willie Totten, Mississippi Val.	†1984	10	564	4,572	8.11
Jamie Martin, Weber St.	†1991	11	591	4,337	7.34
Dave Dickenson, Montana	†1995	11	544	4,209	7.74
Neil Lomax, Portland St.	†1980	11	550	4,157	7.56
Steve McNair, Alcorn St.	†1992	10	519	4,057	7.82
Joe Lee, Towson	†1999	11	608	4,031	6.63
Dave Dickenson, Montana	†1993	11	530	3,978	7.51
Neil Lomax, Portland St.	†1979	11	611	3,966	6.49
John Friesz, Idaho	†1989	11	464	3,853	8.30
Steve McNair, Alcorn St.	1993	11	493	3,830	7.77
Todd Hammel, Stephen F. Austin	1989	11	487	3,822	7.85
Ken Hobart, Idaho	†1983	11	578	3,800	6.57
Dave Stireman, Weber St.	1985	11	502	3,759	7.49
Brian Ah Yat, Montana	†1996	11	501	3,744	7.47
Willie Totten, Mississippi Val.	1985	11	561	3,742	6.67
Jeff Wiley, Holy Cross	†1987	11	445	3,722	8.36
Jamie Martin, Weber St.	†1990	11	508	3,713	7.31
Giovanni Carmazzi, Hofstra	1997	11	524	3,707	7.07
Sean Payton, Eastern Ill.	1984	11	584	3,661	6.27
Todd Brunner, Lehigh	1989	11	504	3,639	7.22
Oteman Sampson, Florida A&M	1997	11	492	3,625	7.37
Aaron Flowers, Cal St. Northridge	†1996	11	488	3,622	7.42
Patrick Bonner, Florida A&M	†1998	11	488	3,568	7.31
Scott Semptimphelter, Lehigh	1993	11	515	3,528	6.85
Neil Lomax, Portland St.	†1978	11	519	3,524	6.79
Doug Nussmeier, Idaho	1993	11	400	3,514	8.79
Glenn Kempa, Lehigh	1991	11	513	3,511	6.84
Chris Sanders, Chattanooga	1999	11	524	3,491	6.67
John Friesz, Idaho	1987	11	543	3,489	6.43

*Record. †National champion.

SINGLE-GAME YARDS

Yds.	Player, Team (Opponent)	Date
649	Steve McNair, Alcorn St. (Southern U.)	Oct. 22, 1994
647	Steve McNair, Alcorn St. (Chattanooga)	Sept. 10, 1994
643	Jamie Martin, Weber St. (Idaho St.)	Nov. 23, 1991
633	Steve McNair, Alcorn St. (Grambling)	Sept. 3, 1994
624	Steve McNair, Alcorn St. (Samford)	Oct. 29, 1994
621	Willie Totten, Mississippi Val. (Prairie View)	Oct. 27, 1984

ALL-TIME LEADERS—TOTAL OFFENSE

Yds.	Player, Team (Opponent)	Date
614	Bryan Martin, Weber St. (Cal Poly)	Sept. 23, 1995
604	Steve McNair, Alcorn St. (Jackson St.)	Nov. 21, 1992
595	Doug Pederson, La.-Monroe (Stephen F. Austin)	Nov. 11, 1989
587	Vern Harris, Idaho St. (Montana)	Oct. 12, 1985
586	Steve McNair, Alcorn St. (Troy St.)	Nov. 12, 1994
574	Dave Dickenson, Montana (Idaho)	Oct. 21, 1995
570	Steve McNair, Alcorn St. (Texas Southern)	Sept. 11, 1993
569	Jimmy Blanchard, Portland St. (Montana)	Oct. 2, 1999
566	Tom Ehrhardt, Rhode Island (Connecticut)	Nov. 16, 1985
566	Brian Ah Yat, Montana (Eastern Wash.)	Oct. 19, 1996
564	Steve McNair, Alcorn St. (Jackson St.)	Nov. 19, 1994
563	Joe Lee, Towson (Lehigh)	Oct. 30, 1999
562	Todd Hammel, Stephen F. Austin (La.-Monroe)	Nov. 11, 1989
561	Willie Totten, Mississippi Val. (Southern U.)	Sept. 29, 1984
555	Bobby Townsend, Howard (Morgan St.)	Nov. 13, 1999
549	Steve McNair, Alcorn St. (Jacksonville St.)	Oct. 31, 1992
549	Brian Ah Yat, Montana (Northern Ariz.)	Oct. 26, 1996
548	Ryan Helming, Northern Iowa (Western Ill.)	Nov. 13, 1999
547	Tod Mayfield, West Tex. A&M (New Mexico St.)	Nov. 16, 1985
546	Dave Stireman, Weber St. (Montana)	Nov. 2, 1985
543	Ken Hobart, Idaho (Southern Colo.)	Sept. 10, 1983
539	Jamie Martin, Weber St. (Montana St.)	Sept. 26, 1992
539	Dave Dickenson, Montana (Idaho)	Nov. 6, 1993
537	Matt Nagy, Delaware (Connecticut)	Nov. 7, 1998
536	Willie Totten, Mississippi Val. (Kentucky St.)	Sept. 1, 1984
536	Brad Otton, Weber St. (Northern Ariz.)	Nov. 6, 1993

ANNUAL CHAMPIONS

Year	Player, Team	Class	G	Plays	Yards	Avg.
1978	Neil Lomax, Portland St.	So.	11	519	3,524	320.4
1979	Neil Lomax, Portland St.	Jr.	11	611	3,966	360.5
1980	Neil Lomax, Portland St.	Sr.	11	550	4,157	377.9
1981	Mike Machurek, Idaho St.	Sr.	9	363	2,645	293.9
1982	Brent Woods, Princeton	Sr.	10	577	3,079	307.9
1983	Ken Hobart, Idaho	Sr.	11	578	3,800	345.5
1984	Willie Totten, Mississippi Val.	Jr.	10	564	4,572	457.2
1985	Tom Ehrhardt, Rhode Island	Sr.	10	529	3,460	346.0
1986	Brent Pease, Montana	Sr.	11	499	3,094	309.4
1987	Jeff Wiley, Holy Cross	Jr.	11	445	3,722	338.4
1988	John Friesz, Idaho	Jr.	10	424	2,751	275.1
1989	John Friesz, Idaho	Sr.	11	464	3,853	350.3
1990	Jamie Martin, Weber St.	So.	11	508	3,713	337.6
1991	Jamie Martin, Weber St.	Jr.	11	591	4,337	394.3
1992	Steve McNair, Alcorn St.	So.	10	519	4,057	405.7
1993	Dave Dickenson, Montana	So.	11	530	3,978	361.6
1994	Steve McNair, Alcorn St.	Sr.	11	*649	*5,799	*527.2
1995	Dave Dickenson, Montana	Sr.	11	544	4,209	382.6
1996	Brian Ah Yat, Montana	So.	11	501	3,744	340.4
1997	Aaron Flowers, Cal St. Northridge	Sr.	9	456	3,132	348.0
1998	Patrick Bonner, Florida A&M	Sr.	11	488	3,568	324.4
1999	Joe Lee, Towson	Sr.	11	608	4,031	366.5

*Record.

Rushing

CAREER YARDS PER GAME
(Minimum 2,500 Yards)

Player, Team	Years	G	Plays	Yards	TD	Yd. PG
Arnold Mickens, Butler	1994-95	20	763	3,813	29	*190.7
Aaron Stecker, Western Ill.	1997-98	20	550	3,081	36	154.1
Tim Hall, Robert Morris	1994-95	19	393	2,908	27	153.1
Jerry Azumah, New Hampshire	1995-98	41	*1,044	*6,193	*60	151.0
Reggie Greene, Siena	1994-97	36	890	5,415	45	150.4
Archie Amerson, Northern Ariz.	1995-96	22	526	3,196	37	145.3
Keith Elias, Princeton	1991-93	30	736	4,208	49	140.3
Mike Clark, Akron	1984-86	32	804	4,257	24	133.0
Rick Sarille, Wagner	$1995-99	41	965	5,290	50	129.0
Michael Hicks, South Carolina St.	1993-95	32	701	4,093	51	127.9
Rich Erenberg, Colgate	1982-83	21	464	2,618	22	124.7
Kenny Gamble, Colgate	1984-87	42	963	5,220	55	124.3
Frank Hawkins, Nevada	1977-80	43	945	5,333	39	124.0
Curtis Keaton, James Madison	1998-99	22	513	2,723	29	123.8
Elroy Harris, Eastern Ky.	1985, 87-88	31	648	3,829	47	123.5
Chad Levitt, Cornell	1993-96	38	922	4,657	44	122.6
Thomas Haskins, VMI	1993-96	44	899	5,355	50	121.7
Gill Fenerty, Holy Cross	1983-85	30	622	3,618	26	120.6
Markus Thomas, Eastern Ky.	1989-92	43	784	5,149	51	119.7
Destry Wright, Jackson St.	1997-99	34	726	4,049	30	119.1
Marquette Smith, UCF	1994-95	22	467	2,569	19	116.8
Erik Marsh, Lafayette	1991-94	42	1,027	4,834	35	115.1
Sherriden May, Idaho	1992-94	33	689	3,748	50	113.6

Player, Team	Years	G	Plays	Yards	TD	Yd. PG
Jason Grove, Drake	1995-98	37	853	4,182	42	113.0
Rene Ingoglia, Massachusetts	1992-95	41	905	4,623	54	112.8
Rabih Abdullah, Lehigh	1994-97	33	672	3,696	33	112.0
Willie High, Eastern Ill.	1992-95	38	913	4,231	37	111.3
Rich Lemon, Bucknell	1993-96	43	994	4,742	35	110.3
Derrick Harmon, Cornell	1981-83	28	545	3,074	26	109.8
Paul Lewis, Boston U.	1982-84	37	878	3,995	50	108.0
Eric Gant, Grambling	1990-93	34	617	3,667	32	107.9
Derrick Franklin, Indiana St.	1989-91	30	710	3,231	23	107.7
Charvez Foger, Nevada	1985-88	42	864	4,484	52	106.8
Claude Mathis, Southwest Tex. St.	1994-97	44	882	4,691	45	106.6
James Crawford, Eastern Ky.	1985-87	32	661	3,404	22	106.4
Eion Hu, Harvard	1994-96	29	714	3,073	26	106.0
Bryan Keys, Pennsylvania	1987-89	30	609	3,137	34	104.6
Judd Garrett, Princeton	1987-89	30	687	3,109	32	103.6

*Record. $See page 6 for explanation.

SEASON YARDS PER GAME

Player, Team	Year	G	Plays	Yards	TD	Yd. PG
Arnold Mickens, Butler	†1994	10	*409	2,255	18	*225.5
Charles Roberts, Cal St. Sacramento	†1998	11	386	*2,260	19	205.5
Tony Vinson, Towson	†1993	10	293	2,016	23	201.6
Jerry Azumah, New Hampshire	1998	11	342	2,195	22	199.6
Reggie Greene, Siena	†1997	9	256	1,778	18	197.6
Reggie Greene, Siena	†1996	9	280	1,719	12	191.0
Charles Roberts, Cal St. Sacramento	†1999	11	303	2,082	22	189.3
Archie Amerson, Northern Ariz.	1996	11	333	2,079	25	189.0
Aaron Stecker, Western Ill.	1997	11	298	1,957	24	177.9
Marcel Shipp, Massachusetts	1998	11	319	1,949	13	177.2
Adrian Peterson, Ga. Southern	1998	11	257	1,932	25	175.6
Keith Elias, Princeton	1993	10	305	1,731	19	173.1
Gene Lake, Delaware St.	†1984	10	238	1,722	20	172.2
Karlton Carpenter, Southern Ill.	1998	11	323	1,892	16	172.0
Rich Erenberg, Colgate	†1983	11	302	1,883	20	171.2
Sean Bennett, Evansville	1997	10	235	1,668	16	166.8
Kenny Gamble, Colgate	†1986	11	307	1,816	21	165.1
Kenny Bynum, South Carolina St.	1996	10	236	1,649	14	164.9
J. J. Allen, Marist	1998	11	279	1,646	21	164.6
Adrian Peterson, Ga. Southern	1999	11	248	1,807	*28	164.3
Mike Clark, Akron	1986	11	245	1,786	8	162.4
Reggie Greene, Siena	†1995	9	273	1,461	11	162.3
Randall Joseph, Colgate	1999	9	193	1,446	15	160.7
Derrick Cullors, Murray St.	1995	11	269	1,765	16	160.5
Chad Levitt, Cornell	1996	9	267	1,435	13	159.4
Keith Elias, Princeton	†1992	10	245	1,575	18	157.5
Tim Hall, Robert Morris	1995	10	239	1,572	16	157.2
Frank Hawkins, Nevada	†1980	11	307	1,719	9	156.3
Arnold Mickens, Butler	1995	10	354	1,558	11	155.8
Brad Baxter, Alabama St.	1986	11	302	1,705	13	155.0
Thomas Haskins, VMI	1996	11	287	1,704	15	154.9
Elroy Harris, Eastern Ky.	1988	10	277	1,543	21	154.3
Corey Holmes, Mississippi Val.	1999	11	331	1,692	11	153.8
Richard Johnson, Butler	1993	10	322	1,535	10	153.5

*Record. †National champion.

Wagner's Rick Sarille finished his career in 1999 with 5,290 rushing yards, good for fifth place on the Division I-AA list.

ALL-TIME LEADERS—RUSHING

CAREER YARDS

Player, Team	Years	Plays	Yards	Avg.	Long
Jerry Azumah, New Hampshire	1995-98	*1,044	*6,193	5.93	96
Reggie Greene, Siena	1994-97	890	5,415	6.08	82
Thomas Haskins, VMI	1993-96	899	5,355	5.96	80
Frank Hawkins, Nevada	1977-80	945	5,333	5.64	50
Rick Sarille, Wagner	$1995-99	965	5,290	5.48	80
Kenny Gamble, Colgate	1984-87	963	5,220	5.42	91
Markus Thomas, Eastern Ky.	1989-92	784	5,149	‡6.57	90
¢Charles Roberts, Cal St. Sacramento	1997-99	828	4,929	5.95	70
Erik Marsh, Lafayette	1991-94	1,027	4,834	4.71	62
Rich Lemon, Bucknell	1993-96	994	4,742	4.77	83
Claude Mathis, Southwest Tex. St.	1994-97	882	4,691	5.32	79
Chad Levitt, Cornell	1993-96	922	4,657	5.05	88
Rene Ingoglia, Massachusetts	1992-95	905	4,623	5.11	84
Chris Parker, Marshall	1992-95	780	4,571	5.86	89
Cedric Minter, Boise St.	1977-80	752	4,475	5.95	77
John Settle, Appalachian St.	1983-86	891	4,409	4.95	88
¢Marcel Shipp, Massachusetts	1997-99	785	4,277	5.45	82
Jermaine Creighton, St. John's (N.Y.)	1994-97	948	4,271	4.51	99
Mike Clark, Akron	1984-86	804	4,257	5.29	†65
Willie High, Eastern Ill.	1992-95	913	4,231	4.63	55
¢Charles Dunn, Portland St.	1997-99	796	4,215	5.30	63
Keith Elias, Princeton	1991-93	736	4,208	5.72	69
Jason Grove, Drake	1995-98	853	4,182	4.90	50
David Wright, Indiana St.	1992-95	784	4,181	5.33	75
Warren Marshall, James Madison	$1982-86	737	4,168	5.66	59
Carl Tremble, Furman	1989-92	696	4,149	5.96	65
Harvey Reed, Howard	1984-87	635	4,142	6.52	85
Michael Hicks, South Carolina St.	1993-95	701	4,093	5.84	82
Destry Wright, Jackson St.	1997-99	726	4,049	5.58	68
Paul Lewis, Boston U.	1981-84	878	3,995	4.55	80
Willie Taggart, Western Ky. (QB)	1995-98	684	3,957	5.79	74
Daryl Brown, Delaware	1991-94	678	3,932	5.80	71
¢Matt Cannon, Southern Utah (QB)	1997-99	538	3,887	7.22	47
Joe Ross, Ga. Southern	1987-90	687	3,876	5.64	75
Garry Pearson, Massachusetts	1979-82	808	3,859	4.78	71
Elroy Harris, Eastern Ky.	1985, 87-88	648	3,829	5.91	64
Lorenzo Bouier, Maine	1979-82	879	3,827	4.35	77
Lewis Tillman, Jackson St.	$1984-88	779	3,824	4.91	39
Joe Campbell, Middle Tenn. St.	1988-91	638	3,823	5.99	81
Carl Smith, Maine	1988-91	759	3,815	5.03	89
Arnold Mickens, Butler	1994-95	763	3,813	5.00	70
Damon Scott, Appalachian St.	1993-96	745	3,800	5.10	49

*Record. †Did not score. $See page 6 for explanation. ‡Record for minimum 600 carries. ¢Active player.

CAREER RUSHING TOUCHDOWNS

Player, Team	Years	G	TDs
Jerry Azumah, New Hampshire	1995-98	41	*60
Kenny Gamble, Colgate	1984-87	42	55
Rene Ingoglia, Massachusetts	1992-95	41	54
¢Adrian Peterson, Ga. Southern	1998-99	22	53
Charvez Foger, Nevada	1985-88	42	52
Michael Hicks, South Carolina St.	1993-95	32	51
Markus Thomas, Eastern Ky.	1989-92	43	51
Rick Sarille, Wagner	$1995-99	41	50
Thomas Haskins, VMI	1993-96	44	50
Sherriden May, Idaho	1992-94	33	50
Paul Lewis, Boston U.	1981-84	37	50
Greg Hill, Ga. Southern (QB)	1996-99	43	49
Chris Parker, Marshall	1992-95	45	49
Keith Elias, Princeton	1991-93	30	49
¢Matt Cannon, Southern Utah (QB)	1997-99	33	47
Elroy Harris, Eastern Ky.	1985, 87-88	31	47
Harvey Reed, Howard	1984-87	41	47

*Record. (Note: Anthony Russo of St. John's, N.Y., scored 16 TDs in 1993 at I-AA level but had 57 total touchdowns during 1990-94.) ¢Active player. $See page 6 for explanation.

SEASON YARDS

Player, Team	Year	G	Plays	Yards	Avg.
Charles Roberts, Cal St. Sacramento	†1998	11	386	*2,260	5.85
Arnold Mickens, Butler	†1994	10	*409	2,255	5.51
Jerry Azumah, New Hampshire	1998	11	342	2,195	6.42
Charles Roberts, Cal St. Sacramento	†1999	11	303	2,082	6.87
Archie Amerson, Northern Ariz.	1996	11	333	2,079	6.24
Tony Vinson, Towson	†1993	10	293	2,016	6.89
Aaron Stecker, Western Ill.	1997	11	298	1,957	6.57
Marcel Shipp, Massachusetts	1998	11	319	1,949	6.11
Adrian Peterson, Ga. Southern	1998	11	257	1,932	7.52
Karlton Carpenter, Southern Ill.	1998	11	323	1,892	5.86
Rich Erenberg, Colgate	†1983	11	302	1,883	6.24
Kenny Gamble, Colgate	†1986	11	307	1,816	5.92
Adrian Peterson, Ga. Southern	1999	11	248	1,807	7.29
Mike Clark, Akron	1986	11	245	1,786	‡7.29
Reggie Greene, Siena	†1997	9	256	1,778	6.95
Derrick Cullors, Murray St.	1995	11	269	1,765	6.56
Keith Elias, Princeton	1993	10	305	1,731	5.68
Gene Lake, Delaware St.	†1984	10	238	1,722	7.24
Frank Hawkins, Nevada	†1980	11	307	1,719	5.60
Reggie Greene, Siena	†1996	9	280	1,719	6.14
Brad Baxter, Alabama St.	1986	11	302	1,705	5.65
Thomas Haskins, VMI	1996	11	287	1,704	5.94
Corey Holmes, Mississippi Val.	1999	11	331	1,692	5.11
Frank Hawkins, Nevada	†1979	11	293	1,683	5.74
Carl Smith, Maine	†1989	11	305	1,680	5.51
Sean Bennett, Evansville	1997	10	235	1,668	7.10
Brad Hoover, Western Caro.	1998	11	331	1,663	5.02
John Settle, Appalachian St.	1986	11	317	1,661	5.24
Curtis Keaton, James Madison	1999	11	290	1,659	5.72
Kenny Bynum, South Carolina St.	1996	10	236	1,649	6.99
J. J. Allen, Marist	1998	10	279	1,646	5.90
Destry Wright, Jackson St.	1999	12	296	1,643	5.55
Garry Pearson, Massachusetts	†1982	11	312	1,631	5.23
Morgan Welch, Weber St.	1998	11	305	1,629	5.34
Lorenzo Bouier, Maine	1980	11	349	1,622	4.65
Markus Thomas, Eastern Ky.	1989	11	232	1,620	6.98

*Record. †National champion. ‡Record for minimum of 200 carries.

SINGLE-GAME YARDS

Yds.	Player, Team (Opponent)	Date
409	Charles Roberts, Cal St. Sacramento (Idaho St.)	Nov. 6, 1999
379	Reggie Greene, Siena (St. John's [N.Y.])	Nov. 2, 1996
364	Tony Vinson, Towson (Bucknell)	Nov. 13, 1993
346	William Arnold, Jackson St. (Texas Southern)	Nov. 6, 1993
345	Russell Davis, Idaho (Portland St.)	Oct. 3, 1981
337	Frank Alessio, Massachusetts (Boston U.)	Nov. 11, 1995
337	Gill Fenerty, Holy Cross (Columbia)	Oct. 29, 1983
336	Gene Lake, Delaware St. (Liberty)	Nov. 10, 1984
329	Jerry Azumah, New Hampshire (Hofstra)	Nov. 7, 1998
327	Tony Vinson, Towson (Morgan St.)	Nov. 20, 1993
324	John Campbell, Wagner (Jacksonville)	Nov. 14, 1998
324	Robert Vaughn, Alabama St. (Tuskegee)	Nov. 24, 1994
323	Matt Johnson, Harvard (Brown)	Nov. 9, 1991
316	J.J. Allen, Marist (St. Francis [Pa.])	Oct. 31, 1998
315	Angelo Todd, Norfolk St. (Delaware St.)	Sept. 19, 1998
313	Sean Bennett, Evansville (San Diego)	Oct. 19, 1996
313	Rene Ingoglia, Massachusetts (Rhode Island)	Oct. 1, 1994
312	Surkano Edwards, Samford (Tenn.-Martin)	Nov. 14, 1992
310	Claude Mathis, Southwest Tex. St. (Stephen F. Austin)	Nov. 16, 1996
309	Eddie Thompson, Western Ky. (Southern Ill.)	Oct. 29, 1992
308	Claude Mathis, Southwest Tex. St. (Jacksonville St.)	Nov. 15, 1997
307	Kenny Bynum, South Carolina St. (N.C. A&T)	Nov. 23, 1996
305	Lawrence Worthington, Liberty (Charleston So.)	Nov. 19, 1994
305	Lucius Floyd, Nevada (Montana St.)	Sept. 27, 1986
304	Tony Citizen, McNeese St. (Prairie View)	Sept. 6, 1986
302	Lorenzo Bouier, Maine (Northeastern)	Nov. 1, 1980
301	Jovan Rhodes, Marist (Siena)	Nov. 12, 1994
300	Jerry Azumah, New Hampshire (Boston U.)	Nov. 15, 1997
300	Markus Thomas, Eastern Ky. (Marshall)	Oct. 21, 1989

ANNUAL CHAMPIONS

Year	Player, Team	Class	G	Plays	Yards	Avg.
1978	Frank Hawkins, Nevada	So.	10	259	1,445	144.5
1979	Frank Hawkins, Nevada	Jr.	11	293	1,683	153.0
1980	Frank Hawkins, Nevada	Sr.	11	307	1,719	156.3
1981	Gregg Drew, Boston U.	Jr.	10	309	1,257	125.7
1982	Garry Pearson, Massachusetts	Sr.	11	312	1,631	148.3
1983	Rich Erenberg, Colgate	Sr.	11	302	1,883	171.2
1984	Gene Lake, Delaware St.	Jr.	10	238	1,722	172.2
1985	Burton Murchison, Lamar	So.	11	265	1,547	140.6
1986	Kenny Gamble, Colgate	Jr.	11	307	1,816	165.1
1987	Harvey Reed, Howard	Sr.	10	211	1,512	151.2
1988	Elroy Harris, Eastern Ky.	Jr.	10	277	1,543	154.3
1989	Carl Smith, Maine	So.	11	305	1,680	152.7
1990	Walter Dean, Grambling	Sr.	11	221	1,401	127.4
1991	Al Rosier, Dartmouth	Sr.	10	258	1,432	143.2
1992	Keith Elias, Princeton	Jr.	10	245	1,575	157.5
1993	Tony Vinson, Towson	Sr.	10	293	2,016	201.6
1994	Arnold Mickens, Butler	Jr.	10	*409	2,255	*225.5
1995	Reggie Greene, Siena	So.	9	273	1,461	162.3
1996	Reggie Greene, Siena	Jr.	9	280	1,719	191.0
1997	Reggie Greene, Siena	Sr.	9	256	1,778	197.6
1998	Charles Roberts, Cal St. Sacramento	So.	11	386	*2,260	205.5
1999	Charles Roberts, Cal St. Sacramento	Jr.	11	303	2,082	189.3

*Record.

ALL-TIME LEADERS—QUARTERBACK RUSHING

Quarterback Rushing

CAREER YARDS
(Since 1978)

Player, Team	Years	G	Plays	Yards	TD	Yd. PG
Willie Taggart, Western Ky.	1995-98	41	684	*3,957	46	*96.5
Jack Douglas, Citadel	1989-92	44	*832	3,674	48	83.5
Greg Hill, Ga. Southern	1996-99	41	575	3,309	*49	80.7
¢Matt Cannon, Southern Utah	1997-99	33	456	3,250	42	98.5
Tracy Ham, Ga. Southern	1984-86	33	511	2,506	32	75.9
Tony Scales, VMI	1989-92	44	561	2,475	19	56.3
Eddie Thompson, Western Ky.	1991-93	27	387	2,349	19	87.0
Steve McNair, Alcorn St.	1991-94	42	375	2,327	33	55.4
Eriq Williams, James Madison	1989-92	43	642	2,321	32	54.0
Raymond Gross, Ga. Southern	1987-90	42	695	2,290	20	54.5
Bill Vergantino, Delaware	1989-92	44	656	2,287	34	52.0
Dwane Brown, Arkansas St.	1984-87	42	595	2,192	33	52.2
Roy Johnson, Arkansas St.	1988-91	43	558	2,182	22	50.7
DeAndre Smith, Southwest Mo. St.	1987-90	42	558	2,140	36	50.9
Ryan Vena, Colgate	1996-99	40	585	2,008	33	50.2
Ken Hobart, Idaho	1980-83	44	628	1,827	26	41.5
Darin Kehler, Yale	1987-90	28	402	1,643	13	58.7

*Record. ¢Active player.

SEASON YARDS
(Since 1978)

Player, Team	Year	G	Plays	Yards	TD	Avg.
Matt Cannon, Southern Utah	1998	11	199	*1,533	14	7.80
Willie Taggart, Western Ky.	1998	11	210	1,313	15	6.25
Matt Cannon, Southern Utah	1999	11	203	1,310	*23	6.45
Joe Dupaix, Southern Utah	1996	11	*271	1,246	12	4.60
Willie Taggart, Western Ky.	1997	10	152	1,217	15	*8.01
Marvin Marshall, South Carolina St.	1994	11	160	1,201	10	7.51
David Dinkins, Morehead St.	1998	11	147	1,169	20	7.95
Jack Douglas, Citadel	1991	11	266	1,152	13	4.33
David Dinkins, Morehead St.	1999	10	200	1,138	20	5.69
Tony Scales, VMI	1991	11	185	1,105	8	5.97
Pa'tel Troutman, Bethune-Cookman	1999	11	220	1,089	9	4.95
Greg Hill, Ga. Southern	1999	11	152	1,084	16	7.13
Greg Hill, Ga. Southern	1998	11	202	1,061	16	5.25
Pa'tel Troutman, Bethune-Cookman	1998	10	183	1,054	15	5.76
Tracy Ham, Ga. Southern	1986	11	207	1,048	18	5.06
Sheraton Fox, Indiana St.	1999	11	228	1,034	8	4.54
Matt Cannon, Southern Utah	1997	11	137	1,024	10	7.47
Alcede Surtain, Alabama St.	1995	11	178	1,024	21	5.75
Nick Crawford, Yale	1991	10	210	1,024	8	4.98
Gene Brown, Citadel	1988	9	152	1,006	13	6.62
Willie Taggart, Western Ky.	1996	10	167	997	8	5.97
Kharon Brown, Hofstra	1995	11	151	977	7	6.47
Corey Thomas, Nicholls St.	1994	11	158	962	8	6.09
Steve McNair, Alcorn St.	1994	11	119	936	9	7.87
Jack Douglas, Citadel	1992	11	178	926	13	5.20
Roy Johnson, Arkansas St.	1989	11	193	925	6	4.79
Darin Kehler, Yale	1989	10	210	903	6	4.30

*Record.

Passing

CAREER PASSING EFFICIENCY
(Minimum 300 Completions)

Player, Team	Years	Att.	Cmp.	Int.	Pct.	Yards	TD	Pts.
Shawn Knight, William & Mary	1991-94	558	367	15	.658	5,527	46	*170.8
Dave Dickenson, Montana	1992-95	1,208	813	26	*.673	11,080	96	166.3
Doug Nussmeier, Idaho	1990-93	1,225	746	32	.609	10,824	91	154.4
Mark Washington, Jackson St.	1996-99	724	384	24	.530	6,561	68	153.5
Mike Simpson, Eastern Ill.	1996-97	493	331	15	.671	3,901	32	148.9
Jay Johnson, Northern Iowa	1989-92	744	397	25	.534	7,049	51	148.9
Ryan Vena, Colgate	1996-99	819	482	46	.589	7,427	61	148.4
Mike Cook, William & Mary	1995-98	804	495	21	.616	6,644	55	148.3
Michael Payton, Marshall	1989-92	876	542	32	.619	7,530	57	148.2
Bryan Martin, Weber St.	1992-95	606	365	14	.602	5,211	37	148.0
Aaron Flowers, Cal St. Northridge	1996-97	819	502	21	.613	6,766	54	147.3
Willie Totten, Mississippi Val.	1982-85	1,555	907	*75	.583	12,711	*139	146.8
Kenneth Biggles, Tennessee St.	1981-84	701	397	28	.566	5,933	57	146.6
Shane Stafford, Connecticut	1995-98	951	522	29	.549	8,368	67	146.0
Oteman Sampson, Florida A&M	1996-97	686	387	26	.564	6,104	46	145.7
Brian Ah Yat, Montana	1995-98	1,190	735	39	.618	9,315	89	145.6
Giovanni Carmazzi, Hofstra	1996-99	1,187	764	32	.644	9,371	71	145.0
Ted White, Howard	1995-98	1,163	635	34	.546	9,611	92	144.3
Steve McNair, Alcorn St.	1991-94	*1,680	927	58	.552	*14,496	119	144.1
Mike Smith, Northern Iowa	1984-87	943	557	43	.591	8,219	58	143.5
Braniff Bonaventure, Furman	1993-96	672	413	17	.615	5,361	39	142.6
Tom Ciaccio, Holy Cross	1988-91	1,073	658	46	.613	8,603	72	142.2
Jim Zaccheo, Nevada	1987-88	554	326	27	.588	4,750	35	142.0
Todd Donnan, Marshall	1991-94	712	425	25	.597	5,566	51	142.0
Mike Cherry, Murray St.	1995-96	526	305	24	.580	4,490	34	141.9
Eric Beavers, Nevada	1983-86	1,094	646	37	.591	8,626	77	141.8
Scott Semptimphelter, Lehigh	1990-93	823	493	27	.599	6,668	50	141.5
John Whitcomb, UAB	1993-94	738	448	28	.607	6,043	43	141.1
Harry Leons, Eastern Wash.	1995-97	523	307	23	.587	4,363	33	140.8
Jason Garrett, Princeton	1987-88	550	368	10	.669	4,274	20	140.6
Phil Stambaugh, Lehigh	1996-99	1,284	816	43	.636	9,669	78	140.2
Neil Lomax, Portland St.	1978-80	1,425	836	50	.587	11,550	88	140.1
Chris Boden, Villanova	1996-99	1,338	818	30	.611	9,538	93	139.5
Jamie Martin, Weber St.	1989-92	1,544	*934	56	.605	12,207	87	138.2
Darin Hinshaw, UCF	1991-94	1,113	614	52	.552	9,000	82	138.1
Ricky Jones, Alabama St.	1988-91	644	324	30	.503	5,472	49	137.5
Jeff Carlson, Weber St.	1984, 86-88	723	384	33	.531	6,147	47	136.9
Chris Hakel, William & Mary	1988-91	812	489	26	.602	6,447	40	136.7
Jeff Wiley, Holy Cross	1985-88	1,208	723	63	.599	9,698	71	136.3
Robert Dougherty, Boston U.	1993-94	705	405	26	.574	5,608	41	136.1
Eriq Williams, James Madison	1989-92	617	326	35	.528	5,356	40	135.8
Chad Barnhardt, South Fla.	1997-98	519	300	16	.578	4,138	27	135.8
Rob Compson, Montana St.	1995-98	901	516	27	.573	6,838	55	135.2
Tom Ehrhardt, Rhode Island	1984-85	919	526	35	.572	6,722	66	134.8
Tony Hilde, Boise St.	1993-95	842	459	23	.545	6,634	49	134.4

Mark Washington of Jackson State threw 68 career touchdown passes and only 24 interceptions from 1996-99, a ratio which contributed to his 153.5 passing efficiency rating. He is fourth in that category in Division I-AA history.

ALL-TIME LEADERS—PASSING

Player, Team	Years	Att.	Cmp.	Int.	Pct.	Yards	TD	Pts.
Jeff Lewis, Northern Ariz.	1992-95	1,316	785	24	.597	9,655	67	134.4
Todd Bankhead, Massachusetts	1998-99	731	438	29	.599	5,502	42	134.2
Tom Kirchoff, Lafayette	1989-92	878	510	36	.581	6,721	53	134.1
Dan Sabella, Monmouth	1994-97	868	500	17	.576	6,229	52	133.7
Mike Buck, Maine	1986-89	1,134	637	41	.562	8,721	68	133.4
Frankie DeBusk, Furman	1987-90	634	333	29	.525	5,414	35	133.3
Frank Novak, Lafayette	1981-83	834	478	36	.573	6,378	51	133.1
Robbie Justino, Liberty	1989-92	1,267	769	51	.607	9,548	64	132.6
Rick Worman, Eastern Wash.	1984-85	672	381	23	.567	5,004	41	132.5
Glenn Kempa, Lehigh	1989-91	901	520	27	.577	6,722	49	132.3
Jay Walker, Howard	1991-93	718	377	23	.525	5,671	42	131.8
James Ritchey, Stephen F. Austin	1992-95	613	325	25	.530	4,766	40	131.7
Gilbert Renfroe, Tennessee St.	1982-85	721	370	23	.513	5,556	48	131.6
James Perry, Brown	1996-99	1,310	790	48	.603	9,293	74	131.2
Tracy Ham, Ga. Southern	1984-86	568	301	31	.530	4,881	29	131.1

*Record.

SEASON PASSING EFFICIENCY
(Minimum 15 Attempts Per Game)

Player, Team	Year	G	Att.	Cmp.	Int.	Pct.	Yards	TD	Pts.
Shawn Knight, William & Mary	†1993	10	177	125	4	.706	2,055	22	*204.6
Michael Payton, Marshall	†1991	9	216	143	5	.622	2,333	19	181.3
Alli Abrew, Cal Poly	†1997	11	191	130	4	.681	1,961	17	179.5
Doug Turner, Morehead St.	1997	10	290	190	6	.655	2,869	29	177.5
Ted White, Howard	†1996	11	289	174	10	.602	2,814	36	176.2
Doug Nussmeier, Idaho	1993	11	304	185	5	.609	2,960	33	175.2
Brian Kadel, Dayton	†1995	11	183	115	6	.628	1,880	18	175.0
Chris Boden, Villanova	1997	11	345	231	4	.670	3,079	36	174.0
Kelvin Simmons, Troy St.	1993	11	224	143	6	.638	2,144	23	172.8
Frank Baur, Lafayette	†1988	10	256	164	11	.641	2,621	23	171.1
Bobby Lamb, Furman	†1985	11	181	106	6	.586	1,856	18	170.9
Harry Leons, Eastern Wash.	1997	11	257	159	5	.619	2,588	21	169.5
Steven Beard, Northern Iowa	1996	11	238	140	9	.588	2,526	21	169.5
Jay Fiedler, Dartmouth	†1992	10	273	175	13	.641	2,748	25	169.4
Dave Dickenson, Montana	1995	11	455	309	9	.679	4,176	38	168.6
Drew Miller, Montana	†1999	10	368	240	8	.652	3,461	32	168.6
Mike Smith, Northern Iowa	†1986	11	303	190	16	.627	3,125	27	168.2
Dave Dickenson, Montana	1993	11	390	262	9	.672	3,640	32	168.0
Simon Fuentes, Eastern Ky.	1997	11	189	116	2	.614	1,932	13	167.8
Jim Blanchard, Portland St.	†1998	9	169	112	1	.663	1,512	14	167.6
Willie Totten, Mississippi Val.	†1983	9	279	174	9	.624	2,566	29	167.5
Lonnie Galloway, Western Caro.	1992	11	211	128	12	.607	2,181	20	167.4
Leo Hamlett, Delaware	1995	11	174	95	6	.546	1,849	15	165.4
Eriq Williams, James Madison	1991	11	192	107	7	.557	1,914	19	164.5
Dave Dickenson, Montana	†1994	9	336	229	6	.682	3,053	24	164.5
Willie Totten, Mississippi Val.	†1984	10	518	*324	22	.626	4,557	*56	163.6
Jeff Wiley, Holy Cross	†1987	11	400	265	17	.663	3,677	34	163.0
Todd Hammel, Stephen F. Austin	†1989	11	401	238	13	.594	3,914	34	162.8
Mike Williams, Grambling	†1980	11	239	127	5	.531	2,116	28	162.0
Giovanni Carmazzi, Hofstra	1997	11	408	288	8	.706	3,554	27	161.7
Dan Crowley, Towson	1993	10	217	125	4	.576	1,882	23	161.7
Mike Stadler, San Diego	1997	11	262	152	10	.580	2,287	30	161.5
John Friesz, Idaho	1989	11	425	260	8	.612	4,041	31	161.4
Wendal Lowrey, La.-Monroe	1992	11	227	147	9	.648	2,190	16	161.1
Donny Simmons, Western Ill.	1992	11	281	182	11	.648	2,496	25	160.9
Chris Berg, Northern Iowa	1995	10	206	113	6	.549	2,144	15	160.5
Sean Laird, St. Mary's (Cal.)	1996	10	256	161	4	.629	2,199	22	160.3
David Charpia, Furman	1983	9	155	99	4	.635	1,419	12	160.1
Todd Donnan, Marshall	1994	11	288	182	8	.632	2,403	28	159.8
Joe Aliotti, Boise St.	†1979	11	219	144	7	.658	1,870	19	159.7
Gilbert Renfroe, Tennessee St.	1984	11	165	95	5	.576	1,458	17	159.7
Mike Buck, Maine	1989	11	264	170	3	.644	2,315	19	159.4
Bobby Lamb, Furman	1984	11	191	106	7	.555	1,781	19	159.3

*Record. †National champion.

CAREER YARDS

Player, Team	Years	Att.	Cmp.	Int.	Pct.	Yards	TD
Steve McNair, Alcorn St.	1991-94	*1,680	927	58	.552	*14,496	119
Willie Totten, Mississippi Val.	1982-85	1,555	907	*75	.583	12,711	*139
Jamie Martin, Weber St.	1989-92	1,544	*934	56	.605	12,207	87
Neil Lomax, Portland St.	1978-80	1,425	836	50	.587	11,550	88
Travis Brown, Northern Ariz.	1996-99	1,577	888	42	.563	11,400	86
Dave Dickenson, Montana	1992-95	1,208	813	26	*.673	11,080	96
Doug Nussmeier, Idaho	1990-93	1,225	746	32	.609	10,824	91
John Friesz, Idaho	1986-89	1,350	801	40	.593	10,697	77
Greg Wyatt, Northern Ariz.	1986-89	1,510	926	49	.613	10,697	70
Sean Payton, Eastern Ill.	1983-86	1,408	756	55	.537	10,655	75
Jeff Wiley, Holy Cross	1985-88	1,208	723	63	.599	9,698	71
Phil Stambaugh, Lehigh	1996-99	1,284	816	43	.636	9,669	78
Jeff Lewis, Northern Ariz.	1992-95	1,316	785	24	.597	9,655	67
Ted White, Howard	1995-98	1,163	635	34	.546	9,611	92
Robbie Justino, Liberty	1989-92	1,267	769	51	.607	9,548	64
Chris Boden, Villanova	1996-99	1,338	818	30	.611	9,538	93
Giovanni Carmazzi, Hofstra	1996-99	1,187	764	32	.644	9,371	71
Brian Ah Yat, Montana	1995-98	1,190	735	39	.618	9,315	89

ALL-TIME LEADERS—PASSING

Player, Team	Years	Att.	Cmp.	Int.	Pct.	Yards	TD
Kirk Schulz, Villanova	1986-89	1,297	774	70	.597	9,305	70
Ken Hobart, Idaho	1980-83	1,219	629	42	.516	9,300	79
James Perry, Brown	1996-99	1,309	789	48	.603	9,294	74
Matt DeGennaro, Connecticut	1987-90	1,319	803	49	.609	9,288	73
Marty Horn, Lehigh	1982-85	1,390	744	64	.535	9,120	62
Jason Whitmer, Idaho St.	1987-90	1,349	721	53	.534	9,081	55
Chris Swartz, Morehead St.	1987-90	1,408	774	47	.550	9,027	56
Darin Hinshaw, UCF	1991-94	1,114	614	52	.551	9,000	82
Dan Crowley, Towson	1991-94	1,170	617	54	.527	8,900	81
Michael Proctor, Murray St.	1986-89	1,148	578	45	.503	8,682	52
Eric Beavers, Nevada	1983-86	1,094	646	37	.590	8,626	77
Tom Ciaccio, Holy Cross	1988-91	1,073	658	46	.613	8,603	72
Steve Calabria, Colgate	1981-84	1,143	626	68	.548	8,555	54
Mike Buck, Maine	1986-89	1,102	619	39	.562	8,491	67
Jeff Cesarone, Western Ky.	1984-87	1,339	714	39	.533	8,404	45
Frank Baur, Lafayette	1985, 87-89	1,103	636	46	.577	8,399	62
Shane Stafford, Connecticut	1995-98	951	522	29	.549	8,368	67
Mitch Maher, North Texas	1991-94	1,100	610	47	.555	8,252	66
Stan Yagiello, William & Mary	$1981-85	1,247	737	36	.591	8,249	51
Mike Smith, Northern Iowa	1984-87	943	557	43	.591	8,219	58
Kelly Bradley, Montana St.	1983-86	1,238	714	45	.577	8,152	60
Jim Lopusznick, Fairfield	1996-99	1,227	657	59	.535	8,092	83
Tom Proudian, Iona	1993-95	1,134	656	48	.578	8,088	58
Bob Bleier, Richmond	1983-86	1,169	672	56	.575	8,057	54
Chris Goetz, Towson	1987-90	1,172	648	51	.553	7,882	42
Mickey Fein, Maine	1995-98	1,203	644	43	.535	7,856	66
Paul Singer, Western Ill.	1985-88	1,171	646	43	.552	7,850	61
John Witkowski, Columbia	1981-83	1,176	613	60	.521	7,849	56
Greg Ryan, East Tenn. St.	1993-96	1,148	694	49	.605	7,826	56
Grady Bennett, Montana	1987-90	1,097	641	42	.584	7,778	55
Bernard Hawk, Bethune-Cookman	1982-85	1,120	554	51	.495	7,737	56
Bob Jean, New Hampshire	1985-88	1,126	567	49	.504	7,704	51

*Record. $See page 6 for explanation.

CAREER YARDS PER GAME
(Minimum 5,000 Yards)

Player, Team	Years	G	Att.	Cmp.	Yards	TD	Yd. PG
Neil Lomax, Portland St.	1978-80	33	1,425	836	11,550	88	*350.0
Steve McNair, Alcorn St.	1991-94	42	*1,680	927	*14,496	119	345.1
Aaron Flowers, Cal St. Northridge	1996-97	20	819	502	6,766	54	338.3
Willie Totten, Mississippi Val.	1982-85	40	1,555	907	12,711	*139	317.8
Dave Dickenson, Montana	1992-95	35	1,208	813	11,080	96	316.6
John Friesz, Idaho	1986-89	35	1,350	801	10,697	77	305.6
James Perry, Brown	1996-99	31	1,309	789	9,294	74	299.8
Tom Proudian, Iona	1993-95	27	1,134	656	8,088	58	299.6
Jamie Martin, Weber St.	1989-92	41	1,544	*934	12,207	87	297.7
Sean Payton, Eastern Ill.	1983-86	37	1,408	756	10,655	75	288.0
Travis Brown, Northern Ariz.	1996-99	41	1,577	888	11,400	86	278.0
Doug Nussmeier, Idaho	1990-93	39	1,225	746	10,824	91	277.5
Oteman Sampson, Florida A&M	1996-97	22	686	387	6,104	46	277.5
Robert Dougherty, Boston U.	1993-94	21	705	405	5,608	41	267.0
Brian Ah Yat, Montana	1995-98	36	1,190	735	9,315	89	258.8
Scott Semptimphelter, Lehigh	1990-93	26	823	493	6,668	50	256.5
Greg Wyatt, Northern Ariz.	1986-89	42	1,510	926	10,697	70	254.7

*Record.

CAREER TOUCHDOWN PASSES

Player, Team	Years	G	TD Passes
Willie Totten, Mississippi Val.	1982-85	40	*139
Steve McNair, Alcorn St.	1991-94	42	119
Dave Dickenson, Montana	1992-95	35	96
Chris Boden, Villanova	1996-99	39	93
Ted White, Howard	1995-98	41	92
Doug Nussmeier, Idaho	1990-93	39	91
Brian Ah Yat, Montana	1995-98	36	89
Neil Lomax, Portland St.	1978-80	33	88
Jamie Martin, Weber St.	1989-92	41	87
Travis Brown, Northern Ariz.	1996-99	41	86
Jim Lopusznick, Fairfield	1996-99	39	83
Darin Hinshaw, UCF	1991-94	40	82
Dan Crowley, Towson	1991-94	40	81
Ken Hobart, Idaho	1980-83	44	79
Phil Stambaugh, Lehigh	1996-99	44	78
Eric Beavers, Nevada	1983-86	40	77
John Friesz, Idaho	1986-89	35	77
Sean Payton, Eastern Ill.	1983-86	39	75
James Perry, Brown	1996-99	31	74
Matt DeGennaro, Connecticut	1987-90	43	73
Tom Ciaccio, Holy Cross	1988-91	37	72
Jeff Wiley, Holy Cross	1985-88	41	71
Giovanni Carmazzi, Hofstra	1996-99	40	71
Kirk Schulz, Villanova	1986-89	42	70
Greg Wyatt, Northern Ariz.	1986-89	42	70

*Record.

Northern Arizona's Travis Brown is fifth in Division I-AA history in career passing yards (11,400), 10th in career touchdown passes (86) and 11th in career passing yards per game (278.0).

DIVISION I-AA

SEASON YARDS

Player, Team	Year	G	Att.	Cmp.	Int.	Pct.	Yards	TD
Steve McNair, Alcorn St.	1994	11	530	304	17	.574	*4,863	44
Willie Totten, Mississippi Val.	†1984	10	518	*324	22	.626	4,557	*56
Dave Dickenson, Montana	1995	11	455	309	9	.679	4,176	38
Joe Lee, Towson	1999	11	*577	322	13	.558	4,168	22
Jamie Martin, Weber St.	1991	11	500	310	17	.620	4,125	35
Neil Lomax, Portland St.	1980	11	473	296	12	.626	4,094	37
John Friesz, Idaho	1989	11	425	260	8	.612	4,041	31
Neil Lomax, Portland St.	1979	11	516	299	16	.579	3,950	26
Todd Hammel, Stephen F. Austin	†1989	11	401	238	13	.594	3,914	34
Sean Payton, Eastern Ill.	1984	11	473	270	15	.571	3,843	28
Jamie Martin, Weber St.	1990	11	428	256	15	.598	3,700	23
Willie Totten, Mississippi Val.	1985	11	492	295	*29	.600	3,698	39
Jeff Wiley, Holy Cross	†1987	11	400	265	17	.663	3,677	34
John Friesz, Idaho	1987	11	502	311	14	.620	3,677	28
Dave Dickenson, Montana	1993	11	390	262	9	.672	3,640	32
Ken Hobart, Idaho	1983	11	477	268	19	.562	3,618	32
Brian Ah Yat, Montana	1996	11	432	265	16	.613	3,615	42
Glenn Kempa, Lehigh	1991	11	474	286	15	.603	3,565	31
Giovanni Carmazzi, Hofstra	1997	11	408	288	8	.706	3,554	27
Tom Ehrhardt, Rhode Island	1985	10	497	283	19	.569	3,542	35
Steve McNair, Alcorn St.	1992	10	427	231	11	.541	3,541	29
Aaron Flowers, Cal St. Northridge	1996	11	415	247	11	.595	3,540	30
Chris Sanders, Chattanooga	1999	11	490	297	14	.606	3,539	27
Tony Petersen, Marshall	1987	11	466	251	25	.539	3,529	22
Todd Brunner, Lehigh	1989	11	450	273	19	.607	3,516	26
Kelly Bradley, Montana St.	1984	11	499	289	20	.579	3,508	30
Neil Lomax, Portland St.	†1978	11	436	241	22	.553	3,506	25

*Record. †National pass-efficiency champion.

SEASON YARDS PER GAME

Player, Team	Year	G	Att.	Cmp.	Int.	Pct.	Yards	TD	Yd.PG
Willie Totten, Mississippi Val.	†1984	10	518	*324	22	.626	4,557	*56	*455.7
Steve McNair, Alcorn St.	1994	11	530	304	17	.574	*4,863	44	442.1
Dave Dickenson, Montana	1995	11	455	309	9	.679	4,176	38	379.6
Joe Lee, Towson	1999	11	*577	322	13	.558	4,168	22	378.9
Jamie Martin, Weber St.	1991	11	500	310	17	.620	4,125	35	375.0
Neil Lomax, Portland St.	1980	11	473	296	12	.626	4,094	37	372.2
John Friesz, Idaho	1989	11	425	260	8	.612	4,041	31	367.4
Neil Lomax, Portland St.	1979	11	516	299	16	.579	3,950	26	359.1
Aaron Flowers, Cal St. Northridge	1997	9	404	255	10	.631	3,226	24	358.4
Todd Hammel, Stephen F. Austin	†1989	11	401	238	13	.594	3,914	34	355.8
Tom Ehrhardt, Rhode Island	1985	10	497	283	19	.569	3,542	35	354.2
Steve McNair, Alcorn St.	1992	10	427	231	11	.541	3,541	29	354.1
Sean Payton, Eastern Ill.	1984	11	473	270	15	.571	3,843	28	349.4
Drew Miller, Montana	1999	10	368	240	8	.652	3,461	32	346.1
Dave Dickenson, Montana	†1994	9	336	229	6	.682	3,053	24	339.2
Tom Proudian, Iona	1993	10	440	262	13	.595	3,368	29	336.8
Jamie Martin, Weber St.	1990	11	428	256	15	.598	3,700	23	336.4
Willie Totten, Mississippi Val.	1985	11	492	295	*29	.600	3,698	39	336.2

*Record. †National pass-efficiency champion.

SEASON TOUCHDOWN PASSES

Player, Team	Years	G	TD Passes
Willie Totten, Mississippi Val.	1984	10	*56
Steve McNair, Alcorn St.	1994	11	44
Brian Ah Yat, Montana	1996	11	42
Willie Totten, Mississippi Val.	1985	11	39
Dave Dickenson, Montana	1995	11	38
Patrick Bonner, Florida A&M	1998	11	37
Neil Lomax, Portland St.	1980	11	37
Chris Boden, Villanova	1997	11	36
Ted White, Howard	1996	11	36
Jamie Martin, Weber St.	1991	11	35
Tom Ehrhardt, Rhode Island	1985	10	35
Todd Hammel, Stephen F. Austin	1989	11	34
Jeff Wiley, Holy Cross	1987	11	34
Doug Nussmeier, Idaho	1993	11	33
Drew Miller, Montana	1999	10	32
Dave Dickenson, Montana	1993	11	32
Doug Hudson, Nicholls St.	1986	11	32
Ken Hobart, Idaho	1983	11	32
Ryan Helming, Northern Iowa	1999	11	31
Travis Brown, Northern Ariz.	1999	11	31
Ted White, Howard	1998	11	31
Chris Boden, Villanova	1998	11	31
Glenn Kempa, Lehigh	1991	11	31
John Friesz, Idaho	1989	11	31
Lionel Hayes, Grambling	1999	11	30
Mike Stadler, San Diego	1997	11	30
Aaron Flowers, Cal St. Northridge	1996	11	30
Scott Semptimphelter, Lehigh	1993	11	30
Brent Pease, Montana	1986	11	30
Kelly Bradley, Montana St.	1984	11	30

*Record.

ALL-TIME LEADERS—PASSING

SINGLE-GAME YARDS

Yds.	Player, Team (Opponent)	Date
624	Jamie Martin, Weber St. (Idaho St.)	Nov. 23, 1991
619	Doug Pederson, La.-Monroe (Stephen F. Austin)	Nov. 11, 1989
599	Willie Totten, Mississippi Val. (Prairie View)	Oct. 27, 1984
589	Vern Harris, Idaho St. (Montana)	Oct. 12, 1985
587	Steve McNair, Alcorn St. (Southern U.)	Oct. 22, 1994
571	Todd Hammel, Stephen F. Austin (La.-Monroe)	Nov. 11, 1989
567	Joe Lee, Towson (Lehigh)	Oct. 30, 1999
566	Tom Ehrhardt, Rhode Island (Connecticut)	Nov. 16, 1985
563	Steve McNair, Alcorn St. (Samford)	Oct. 29, 1994
560	Brian Ah Yat, Montana (Eastern Wash.)	Oct. 19, 1996
558	Dave Dickenson, Montana (Idaho)	Oct. 21, 1995
556	Matt Nagy, Delaware (Connecticut)	Nov. 7, 1998
553	Willie Totten, Mississippi Val. (Southern U.)	Sept. 29, 1984
553	Justin Fuente, Murray St. (Southern Ill.)	Sept. 11, 1999
553	Kevin McCarthy, Idaho St. (Southern Utah)	Oct. 23, 1999
550	Jimmy Blanchard, Portland St. (Montana)	Oct. 2, 1999
547	Jamie Martin, Weber St. (Montana St.)	Sept. 26, 1992
545	Willie Totten, Mississippi Val. (Grambling)	Oct. 13, 1984
541	Ryan Helming, Northern Iowa (Western Ill.)	Nov. 13, 1999
540	Brad Otten, Weber St. (Northern Ariz.)	Nov. 6, 1993
539	John Whitcomb, UAB (Prairie View)	Nov. 19, 1994
537	Tod Mayfield, West Tex. A&M (New Mexico St.)	Nov. 16, 1985
536	Willie Totten, Mississippi Val. (Kentucky St.)	Sept. 1, 1984
534	Todd Hammel, Stephen F. Austin (Sam Houston St.)	Nov. 4, 1989
534	Steve McNair, Alcorn St. (Grambling)	Sept. 3, 1994
533	Steve McNair, Alcorn St. (Jackson St.)	Nov. 19, 1994

SINGLE-GAME ATTEMPTS

No.	Player, Team (Opponent)	Date
77	Neil Lomax, Portland St. (Northern Colo.)	Oct. 20, 1979
76	Joe Lee, Towson (Lehigh)	Oct. 30, 1999
74	Paul Peterson, Idaho St. (Nevada)	Oct. 1, 1983
72	Dave Dickenson, Montana (Idaho)	Oct. 21, 1995
71	Doug Pederson, La.-Monroe (Stephen F. Austin)	Nov. 11, 1989
71	Bobby Townsend, Howard (Morgan St.)	Nov. 13, 1999
70	Greg Farland, Rhode Island (Boston U.)	Oct. 18, 1986
70	Joe Lee, Towson (Dayton)	Nov. 6, 1999
69	Chris Boden, Villanova (Connecticut)	Oct. 16, 1999
69	Ryan Helming, Northern Iowa (Western Ill.)	Nov. 13, 1999
69	Aaron Flowers, Cal St. Northridge (Cal St. Sacramento)	Oct. 25, 1997
69	Steve McNair, Alcorn St. (Jacksonville St.)	Oct. 31, 1992
68	Tony Petersen, Marshall (Western Caro.)	Nov. 14, 1987
68	Kevin McCarthy, Idaho St. (Southern Utah)	Oct. 23, 1999
67	Joe Walland, Yale (Harvard)	Nov. 20, 1999
67	Tom Proudian, Iona (Siena)	Oct. 1, 1994
67	Michael Payton, Marshall (Western Caro.)	Oct. 31, 1992
67	Vern Harris, Idaho St. (Montana)	Oct. 12, 1985
67	Rick Worman, Eastern Wash. (Nevada)	Oct. 12, 1985
67	Tod Mayfield, West Tex. A&M (Indiana St.)	Oct. 5, 1985
67	Tom Ehrhardt, Rhode Island (Brown)	Sept. 28, 1985

SINGLE-GAME COMPLETIONS

No.	Player, Team (Opponent)	Date
48	Clayton Millis, Cal St. Northridge (St. Mary's [Cal.])	Nov. 11, 1995
47	Jamie Martin, Weber St. (Idaho St.)	Nov. 23, 1991
47	Joe Lee, Towson (Lehigh)	Oct. 30, 1999
46	Doug Pederson, La.-Monroe (Stephen F. Austin)	Nov. 11, 1989
46	Willie Totten, Mississippi Val. (Southern U.)	Sept. 29, 1984
45	Willie Totten, Mississippi Val. (Prairie View)	Oct. 27, 1984
44	Neil Lomax, Portland St. (Northern Colo.)	Oct. 20, 1979
43	Chris Boden, Villanova (Connecticut)	Oct. 16, 1999
43	Aaron Flowers, Cal St. Northridge (Cal St. Sacramento)	Oct. 25, 1997
43	Dave Dickenson, Montana (Idaho)	Oct. 21, 1995
42	Joe Walland, Yale (Harvard)	Nov. 20, 1999
42	James Perry, Brown (Princeton)	Oct. 9, 1999
42	Travis Brown, Northern Ariz. (Montana)	Oct. 26, 1996
42	Tod Mayfield, West Tex. A&M (Indiana St.)	Oct. 5, 1985
42	Kelly Bradley, Montana St. (Eastern Wash.)	Sept. 21, 1985
42	Rusty Hill, North Texas (Tulsa)	Nov. 20, 1982

Joe Lee of Towson threw the ball 76 times against Lehigh Oct. 30, 1999, completing 47. The number of attempts and completions were just one shy of the Division I-AA single-game records.

ANNUAL CHAMPIONS

Year	Player, Team	Class	G	Att.	Cmp.	Avg.	Int.	Pct.	Yds.	TD
1978	Neil Lomax, Portland St.	So.	11	436	241	21.9	22	.553	3,506	25

Beginning in 1979, ranked on passing efficiency rating points (instead of per-game completions)

Year	Player, Team	Class	G	Att.	Cmp.	Int.	Pct.	Yds.	TD	Pts.
1979	Joe Aliotti, Boise St.	Jr.	11	219	144	7	.658	1,870	19	159.7
1980	Mike Williams, Grambling	Sr.	11	239	127	5	.531	2,116	28	162.0
1981	Mike Machurek, Idaho St.	Sr.	9	313	188	11	.601	2,752	22	150.1
1982	Frank Novak, Lafayette	Jr.	10	257	154	12	.599	2,257	20	150.0
1983	Willie Totten, Mississippi Val.	So.	9	279	174	9	.624	2,566	29	167.5
1984	Willie Totten, Mississippi Val.	Jr.	10	518	*324	22	.626	4,557	*56	163.6
1985	Bobby Lamb, Furman	Sr.	11	181	106	6	.586	1,856	18	170.9
1986	Mike Smith, Northern Iowa	Jr.	11	303	190	16	.627	3,125	27	168.2

DIVISION I-AA

ALL-TIME LEADERS—PASSING

Year	Player, Team	Class	G	Att.	Cmp.	Int.	Pct.	Yds.	TD	
1987	Jeff Wiley, Holy Cross	Jr.	11	400	265	17	.663	3,677	34	163.0
1988	Frank Baur, Lafayette	Jr.	10	256	164	11	.641	2,621	23	171.1
1989	Todd Hammel, Stephen F. Austin	Sr.	11	401	238	13	.594	3,914	34	162.8
1990	Connell Maynor, N.C. A&T	Jr.	11	191	123	10	.644	1,699	16	156.3
1991	Michael Payton, Marshall	Jr.	9	216	143	5	.662	2,333	19	181.3
1992	Jay Fiedler, Dartmouth	Jr.	10	273	175	13	.641	2,748	25	169.4
1993	Shawn Knight, William & Mary	Jr.	10	177	125	4	.706	2,055	22	*204.6
1994	Dave Dickenson, Montana	Jr.	9	336	229	6	.682	3,053	24	164.5
1995	Brian Kadel, Dayton	Sr.	11	183	115	6	.628	1,880	18	175.0
1996	Ted White, Howard	So.	11	289	174	10	.602	2,814	36	176.2
1997	Alli Abrew, Cal Poly	Sr.	11	191	130	4	.681	1,961	17	179.5
1998	Jim Blanchard, Portland St.	So.	9	169	112	1	.663	1,512	14	167.6
1999	Drew Miller, Montana	Jr.	10	368	240	8	.652	3,461	32	168.6

*Record.

Receiving

CAREER RECEPTIONS PER GAME
(Minimum 125 Receptions)

Player, Team	Years	G	Rec.	Yards	TD	Rec. PG
Jerry Rice, Mississippi Val.	1981-84	41	*301	*4,693	*50	*7.3
Mike Furrey, Northern Iowa	1997-99	33	242	3,544	27	7.3
Derrick Ingram, UAB	1993-94	22	159	2,572	21	7.2
Jeff Johnson, East Tenn. St.	1993-94	20	142	1,772	19	7.1
Miles Macik, Pennsylvania	1993-95	29	200	2,364	26	6.9
Kevin Guthrie, Princeton	1981-83	28	193	2,645	16	6.9
Eric Yarber, Idaho	1984-85	19	129	1,920	17	6.8
Joe Douglass, Montana	1995-96	22	145	2,301	25	6.6
Brian Forster, Rhode Island (TE)	1983-85, 87	38	245	3,410	31	6.5
Kasey Dunn, Idaho	1988-91	42	268	3,847	25	6.4
Sean Morey, Brown	1995-98	40	251	3,850	39	6.3
Gordie Lockbaum, Holy Cross (RB)	‡1986-87	22	135	2,012	17	6.1
Derek Graham, Princeton	1981, 83-84	29	176	2,819	19	6.1
Stuart Gaussoin, Portland St.	1978-80	23	135	1,909	14	5.9
Don Lewis, Columbia	1981-83	30	176	2,207	11	5.9
Mike Barber, Marshall	1985-88	36	209	3,520	20	5.8
Rennie Benn, Lehigh	1982-85	41	237	3,662	44	5.8
Daren Altieri, Boston U.	1987-90	39	225	2,518	15	5.8
Bill Reggio, Columbia	1981-83	30	170	2,384	26	5.7

*Record. ‡Defensive back in 1984-85.

SEASON RECEPTIONS PER GAME

Player, Team	Years	G	Rec.	Yards	TD	Rec. PG
Brian Forster, Rhode Island (TE)	†1985	10	*115	1,617	12	*11.5
Jerry Rice, Mississippi Val.	†1984	10	103	1,682	*27	10.3
Jerry Rice, Mississippi Val.	†1983	10	102	1,450	14	10.2
Stuart Gaussoin, Portland St.	†1979	9	90	1,132	8	10.0
Eric Krawczyk, Cornell	†1997	10	89	1,042	11	8.9
Murle Sango, Villanova	†1999	11	98	1,064	10	8.9
Stephen Campbell, Brown	1999	10	89	1,107	11	8.9
Kevin Guthrie, Princeton	1983	10	88	1,259	9	8.8
David Romines, Cal St. Northridge	†1996	10	87	1,300	12	8.7
Jacquay Nunnally, Florida A&M	†1998	11	93	1,316	12	8.5
Alfred Pupunu, Weber St. (TE)	†1991	11	93	1,204	12	8.5
Derek Graham, Princeton	1983	10	84	1,363	11	8.4
Don Lewis, Columbia	†1982	10	84	1,000	6	8.4
Peter Macon, Weber St.	†1989	11	92	1,047	6	8.4
Sean Morey, Brown	1998	10	83	1,023	10	8.3
Eddie Conti, Delaware	1998	11	91	*1,712	10	8.3
Marvin Walker, North Texas	1982	11	91	934	11	8.3

*Record. †National champion.

CAREER RECEPTIONS

Player, Team	Years	Rec.	Yards	Avg.	TD
Jerry Rice, Mississippi Val.	1981-84	*301	*4,693	15.6	*50
Kasey Dunn, Idaho	1988-91	268	3,847	14.4	25
Sean Morey, Brown	1995-98	251	3,850	15.3	39
Brian Forster, Rhode Island	1983-85, 87	245	3,410	13.9	31
Mike Furrey, Northern Iowa	1997-99	242	3,544	14.6	27
Mark Didio, Connecticut	1988-91	239	3,535	14.8	21
Rennie Benn, Lehigh	1982-85	237	3,662	15.5	44
Daren Altieri, Boston U.	1987-90	225	2,518	11.2	15
Darrell Colbert, Texas Southern	1983-86	217	3,177	14.6	33
Deron Braswell, Lehigh	1995-98	217	3,292	15.2	28
David Rhodes, UCF	1991-94	213	3,618	17.0	29
Corey Hill, Colgate	1995-98	212	3,434	16.2	34
Eric Wise, Fairfield	1996-99	211	2,139	10.1	20
Robert Wilson, Florida A&M	1993-96	209	2,949	14.1	24
Mike Barber, Marshall	1985-88	209	3,520	16.8	20

Player, Team	Years	Rec.	Yards	Avg.	TD
Cornell Craig, Southern Ill.	1996-99	207	3,550	17.1	37
Trevor Shaw, Weber St.	1989-90, 92-93	206	2,383	11.6	17
William Brooks, Boston U.	1982-85	204	3,154	15.5	26
Donald Narcisse, Texas Southern	1983-86	203	2,429	12.0	26
Alex Davis, Connecticut	1989-92	202	2,567	12.7	24
Shawn Collins, Northern Ariz.	1985-88	201	2,764	13.8	24
Miles Macik, Pennsylvania	1993-95	200	2,364	11.8	26
Leland Melvin, Richmond	1982-85	198	2,669	13.5	16
Mike Wilson, Boise St.	1990-93	196	3,017	15.4	13
Aaron Arnold, Cal St. Northridge	1996-99	195	2,660	13.6	24
Blake Tuffli, St. Mary's (Cal.)	1993-96	194	2,990	15.4	25
Curtis Olds, New Hampshire	1985-88	193	3,028	15.7	23
Kevin Guthrie, Princeton	1981-83	193	2,645	13.7	16
Raul Pacheco, Montana	1995-96	192	2,527	13.2	21
Dylan Ching, San Diego	1996-99	189	3,111	16.5	32
Matt Wells, Montana	1992-95	189	2,733	14.5	19
Sergio Hebra, Maine	1984-87	189	2,612	13.8	17
Jason Corle, Towson (RB)	1996-99	188	1,725	9.2	14
John Perry, New Hampshire	1989-92	186	2,798	15.0	19
Glenn Antrum, Connecticut	1985-88	186	2,552	13.7	14
Joe Thomas, Mississippi Val.	1982-85	186	2,816	15.1	36
Gary Harrell, Howard	1990-93	184	2,619	14.2	19
Roy Banks, Eastern Ill.	1983-86	184	3,177	17.3	38
Merril Hoge, Idaho St. (RB)	1983-86	182	1,734	9.5	13
Eddie Conti, Delaware	1994-98	181	3,496	19.3	28
George Delaney, Colgate	1988-91	181	2,938	16.2	25
Sylvester Morris, Jackson St.	1996-99	180	3,324	18.5	34
Robert Brady, Villanova	1986-89	180	2,725	15.1	28

*Record.

SEASON RECEPTIONS

Player, Team	Year	G	Rec.	Yards	TD
Brian Forster, Rhode Island (TE)	†1985	10	*115	1,617	12
Jerry Rice, Mississippi Val.	†1984	10	103	1,682	*27
Jerry Rice, Mississippi Val.	†1983	10	102	1,450	14
Murle Sango, Villanova	†1999	11	98	1,064	10
Jacquay Nunnally, Florida A&M	†1998	11	93	1,316	12
Alfred Pupunu, Weber St. (TE)	†1991	11	93	1,204	12
Peter Macon, Weber St.	†1989	11	92	1,047	6
Eddie Conti, Delaware	1998	11	91	*1,712	10
Marvin Walker, North Texas	1982	11	91	934	11
Stuart Gaussoin, Portland St.	†1979	9	90	1,132	8
Stephen Campbell, Brown	1999	10	89	1,107	11
Brian Westbrook, Villanova	1998	11	89	1,144	15
Eric Krawczyk, Cornell	†1997	10	89	1,042	11
Dave Cecchini, Lehigh	†1993	11	88	1,318	16
Rameck Wright, Maine	1997	11	88	1,176	7
Mark Didio, Connecticut	1991	11	88	1,354	6
Kasey Dunn, Idaho	†1990	11	88	1,164	7
Donald Narcisse, Texas Southern	†1986	11	88	1,074	15
Kevin Guthrie, Princeton	1983	10	88	1,259	9
David Romines, Cal St. Northridge	†1996	10	87	1,300	12
Mike Furrey, Northern Iowa	1998	11	86	1,074	10
Kasey Dunn, Idaho	1991	11	85	1,263	6
Elijah Thurman, Howard	1999	11	84	1,366	9
Derek Graham, Princeton	1983	10	84	1,363	11
Don Lewis, Columbia	†1982	10	84	1,000	6

*Record. †National champion.

SEASON TOUCHDOWN RECEPTIONS

Player, Team	Year	G	TD
Jerry Rice, Mississippi Val.	1984	10	*27
Randy Moss, Marshall	1996	11	19
Joe Douglass, Montana	1996	11	18
Sylvester Morris, Jackson St.	1995	11	17

ALL-TIME LEADERS—RECEIVING

Player, Team	Year	G	TD
Brian Finneran, Villanova	1997	11	17
Mark Carrier, Nicholls St.	1986	11	17
Dameon Reilly, Rhode Island	1985	11	17
Joe Thomas, Mississippi Val.	1985	11	17
Roy Banks, Eastern Ill.	1984	11	17
Drew O'Connor, Maine	1998	11	16
Wayne Chrebet, Hofstra	1994	10	16
Dave Cecchini, Lehigh	1993	11	16
Cornell Craig, Southern Ill.	1999	11	15
Scotty Anderson, Grambling	1999	11	15
Dave Klemic, Northeastern	1998	11	15
Brian Westbrook, Villanova	1998	11	15
Tarig Qaiyam, Florida A&M	1998	11	15
Sean Morey, Brown	1997	10	15
Donald Narcisse, Texas Southern	1986	11	15
Rennie Benn, Lehigh	1983	11	15
Terrance Tillman, Murray St.	1999	11	14
Jimmy Moore, Massachusetts	1998	11	14
Macey Brooks, James Madison	1996	11	14
Dedric Ward, Northern Iowa	1996	11	14
Rennie Benn, Lehigh	1985	11	14
Jerry Rice, Mississippi Val.	1983	10	14
Bill Reggio, Columbia	1982	10	14

*Record.

SINGLE-GAME RECEPTIONS

No.	Player, Team (Opponent)	Date
24	Jerry Rice, Mississippi Val. (Southern U.)	Oct. 1, 1983
22	Marvin Walker, North Texas (Tulsa)	Nov. 20, 1982
21	David Pandt, Montana St. (Eastern Wash.)	Sept. 21, 1985
21	Eric Johnson, Yale (Harvard)	Nov. 20, 1999
20	Tim Hilton, Cal St. Northridge (St. Mary's [Cal.])	Nov. 11, 1995
18	Jeremy Nunamaker, St. Francis (Pa.) (Sacred Heart)	Oct. 2, 1999
18	David Romines, Cal St. Northridge (UC Davis)	Sept. 14, 1996
18	Jerome Williams, Morehead St. (Eastern Ky.)	Nov. 18, 1989
18	Brian Forster, Rhode Island (Brown)	Sept. 28, 1985
17	Damon Hodge, Alabama St. (Alabama A&M)	Oct. 31, 1998
17	Rameek Wright, Maine (Buffalo)	Nov. 16, 1996
17	Elliot Miller, St. Francis (Pa.) (Central Conn. St.)	Oct. 2, 1993
17	Lifford Jackson, Louisiana Tech (Kansas St.)	Oct. 1, 1988
17	Brian Forster, Rhode Island (Lehigh)	Oct. 12, 1985
17	Jerry Rice, Mississippi Val. (Southern U.)	Sept. 29, 1984
17	Jerry Rice, Mississippi Val. (Kentucky St.)	Sept. 1, 1984

CAREER YARDS

Player, Team	Years	Rec.	Yards	Avg.	TD
Jerry Rice, Mississippi Val.	1981-84	*301	*4,693	15.6	*50
Dedric Ward, Northern Iowa	1993-96	176	3,876	22.0	41
Sean Morey, Brown	1995-98	251	3,850	15.3	39
Kasey Dunn, Idaho	1988-91	268	3,847	14.4	25
Rennie Benn, Lehigh	1982-85	237	3,662	15.5	44
David Rhodes, UCF	1991-94	213	3,618	17.0	29
Correll Craig, Southern Ill.	1996-99	207	3,550	17.1	37
Mike Furrey, Northern Iowa	1997-99	242	3,544	14.6	27
Mark Didio, Connecticut	1988-91	239	3,535	14.8	21
Mike Barber, Marshall	1985-88	209	3,520	16.8	20
Eddie Conti, Delaware	1994-98	181	3,496	19.3	28
Corey Hill, Colgate	1995-98	212	3,434	16.2	34
Brian Forster, Rhode Island (TE)	1983-85, 87	245	3,410	13.9	31
Sylvester Morris, Jackson St.	1996-99	180	3,324	18.5	34
Deron Braswell, Lehigh	1995-98	217	3,292	15.2	28
Tracy Singleton, Howard	1979-82	159	3,187	20.0	16
Courtney Batts, Delaware	1994-97	153	3,181	20.8	26
Roy Banks, Eastern Ill.	1983-86	184	3,177	17.3	38
Darrell Colbert, Texas Southern	1983-86	217	3,177	14.6	33
William Brooks, Boston U.	1982-85	204	3,154	15.5	26

*Record.

CAREER YARDS PER GAME
(Minimum 2,000 Yards)

Player, Team	Years	G	Yards	Yds. PG
Derrick Ingram, UAB	1993-94	22	2,572	*116.9
Jerry Rice, Mississippi Val.	1981-84	41	*4,693	114.5
Mike Furrey, Northern Iowa	1997-99	33	3,544	107.4
Joe Douglass, Montana	1995-96	22	2,301	104.6
Eddie Conti, Delaware	1994-98	35	3,496	99.9
Derek Graham, Princeton	1981, 83-84	29	2,819	97.2
Sean Morey, Brown	1995-98	40	3,850	96.3
Kevin Guthrie, Princeton	1981-83	28	2,645	94.5
Tracy Singleton, Howard	1979-82	34	3,187	93.7
David Rhodes, UCF	1991-94	39	3,618	92.8
Kasey Dunn, Idaho	1988-91	42	3,847	91.6

Player, Team	Years	G	Yards	Yds. PG
Gordie Lockbaum, Holy Cross	‡1986-87	22	2,012	91.5
Bryan Calder, Nevada	1984-86	28	2,559	91.4
Mike Barber, Marshall	1985-88	36	3,250	90.3
Dedric Ward, Northern Iowa	1993-96	43	3,876	90.1
Brian Forster, Rhode Island	1983-85, 87	38	3,410	89.7

*Record. ‡Defensive back in 1984-85.

CAREER TOUCHDOWN RECEPTIONS

Player, Team	Year	G	TD
Jerry Rice, Mississippi Val.	1981-84	41	*50
Rennie Benn, Lehigh	1982-85	41	44
Dedric Ward, Northern Iowa	1993-96	43	41
Sean Morey, Brown	1995-98	40	39
Roy Banks, Eastern Ill.	1983-86	38	38
Mike Jones, Tennessee St.	1979-82	42	38
Cornell Craig, Southern Ill.	1996-99	44	37
Joe Thomas, Mississippi Val.	1982-85	41	36
Dameon Reilly, Rhode Island	1983-85	32	35
Sylvester Morris, Jackson St.	1996-99	45	34
Corey Hill, Colgate	1995-98	43	34
Darrell Colbert, Texas Southern	1983-86	43	33
John Taylor, Delaware St.	1982-85	43	33
Dylan Ching, San Diego	1996-99	41	32
Trumaine Johnson, Grambling	1979-82	44	32
Brian Forster, Rhode Island	1983-85, 87	38	31
David Rhodes, UCF	1991-94	39	29
Tom Stenglein, Colgate	1983-85	32	29

*Record.

SEASON YARDS

Player, Team	Year	Rec.	Yards	Avg.	TD
Eddie Conti, Delaware	†1998	91	*1,712	18.8	10
Jerry Rice, Mississippi Val.	1984	103	1,682	16.3	*27
Brian Forster, Rhode Island	1985	*115	1,617	14.1	12
Joe Douglass, Montana	1996	82	1,469	17.9	18
Derrick Ingram, UAB	1994	83	1,457	17.6	13
Jerry Rice, Mississippi Val.	1983	102	1,450	14.2	14
Sean Morey, Brown	†1997	73	1,427	19.6	15
Cornell Craig, Southern Ill.	†1999	77	1,419	18.4	15
B. J. Adigun, East Tenn. St.	1997	68	1,389	20.4	12
Elijah Thurmon, Howard	1999	84	1,366	16.3	9
Derek Graham, Princeton	1983	84	1,363	16.2	11
Mikhael Ricks, Stephen F. Austin	1997	47	1,358	28.9	13
Mark Didio, Connecticut	†1991	88	1,354	15.4	8
Gerald Foster, Duquesne	1999	72	1,340	16.8	10
Jamal White, Towson	1999	82	1,322	16.1	8
Dave Cecchini, Lehigh	†1993	88	1,318	15.0	16
Jacquay Nunnally, Florida A&M	1998	93	1,316	14.2	12
Golden Tate, Tennessee St.	1983	63	1,307	20.7	13

*Record. †National champion.

SINGLE-GAME YARDS

Yds.	Player, Team (Opponent)	Date
370	Michael Lerch, Princeton (Brown)	Oct. 12, 1991
354	Eddie Conti, Delaware (Connecticut)	Nov. 7, 1998
330	Nate Singleton, Grambling (Virginia Union)	Sept. 14, 1991
327	Brian Forster, Rhode Island (Brown)	Sept. 28, 1985
319	Jason Cristino, Lehigh (Lafayette)	Nov. 21, 1992
316	Marcus Hinton, Alcorn St. (Chattanooga)	Sept. 10, 1994
299	Brian Forster, Rhode Island (Lehigh)	Oct. 12, 1985
299	Treamelle Taylor, Nevada (Montana)	Oct. 14, 1989
294	Jerry Rice, Mississippi Val. (Kentucky St.)	Sept. 1, 1984
289	Derrick Ingram, UAB (Prairie View)	Nov. 19, 1994
286	Mike Furrey, Northern Iowa (Western Ill.)	Nov. 13, 1999
285	Jerry Rice, Mississippi Val. (Jackson St.)	Sept. 22, 1984
284	Jacquay Nunnally, Florida A&M (N.C. A&T)	Oct. 11, 1997
280	Rondel Menendez, Eastern Ky. (Eastern Ill.)	Nov. 22, 1997
279	Joe Douglass, Montana (Eastern Wash.)	Oct. 19, 1996
279	Jerry Rice, Mississippi Val. (Southern U.)	Oct. 1, 1983
276	Joey Stockton, Western Ky. (Austin Peay)	Sept. 16, 1995
276	Terry Charles, Portland St. (Montana)	Oct. 2, 1999
274	Corey Hill, Colgate (Navy)	Oct. 17, 1998

ANNUAL CHAMPIONS

Year	Player, Team	Class	G	Rec.	Avg.	Yards	TD
1978	Dan Ross, Northeastern	Sr.	11	68	6.2	988	7
1979	Stuart Gaussoin, Portland St.	Jr.	9	90	10.0	1,132	8
1980	Kenny Johnson, Portland St.	So.	11	72	6.5	1,011	11
1981	Ken Harvey, Northern Iowa	Sr.	11	78	7.1	1,161	15
1982	Don Lewis, Columbia	Jr.	10	84	8.4	1,000	6
1983	Jerry Rice, Mississippi Val.	Jr.	10	102	10.2	1,450	14
1984	Jerry Rice, Mississippi Val.	Sr.	10	103	10.3	1,682	*27

DIVISION I-AA

Year	Player, Team	Class	G	Rec.	Avg.	Yards	TD
1985	Brian Forster, Rhode Island (TE)	Jr.	10	*115	*11.5	1,617	12
1986	Donald Narcisse, Texas Southern	Sr.	11	88	8.0	1,074	11
1987	Mike Barber, Marshall	Jr.	11	78	7.1	1,237	7
	Gordie Lockbaum, Holy Cross (RB)	Sr.	11	78	7.1	1,152	9
1988	Glenn Antrum, Connecticut	Sr.	11	77	7.0	1,130	7
1989	Peter Macon, Weber St.	Sr.	11	92	8.4	1,047	6

Beginning in 1990, ranked on both per-game catches and yards per game.

PER-GAME RECEPTIONS

Year	Player, Team	Class	G	Rec.	Avg.	Yards	TD
1990	Kasey Dunn, Idaho	Jr.	11	88	8.0	1,164	7
1991	Alfred Pupunu, Weber St. (TE)	Sr.	11	93	8.5	1,204	12
1992	Glenn Krupa, Southeast Mo. St.	Sr.	11	77	7.0	773	4
1993	Dave Cecchini, Lehigh	Sr.	11	88	8.0	1,318	16
1994	Jeff Johnson, East Tenn. St.	Sr.	9	73	8.1	857	8
1995	Ed Mantie, Boston U.	Sr.	11	81	7.4	943	1
1996	David Romines, Cal St. Northridge	Sr.	10	87	8.7	1,300	12
1997	Eric Krawczyk, Cornell	Sr.	10	89	8.9	1,042	11
1998	Jacquay Nunnally, Florida A&M	So.	11	93	8.5	1,316	12
1999	Murle Sango, Villanova	So.	11	98	8.9	1,064	10

YARDS PER GAME

Year	Player, Team	Class	G	Rec.	Avg.	Yards	TD
1990	Kasey Dunn, Idaho	Jr.	11	88	105.8	1,164	7
1991	Mark Didio, Connecticut	Sr.	11	88	123.1	1,354	8
1992	Jason Cristino, Lehigh	Sr.	11	65	116.5	1,282	9
1993	Dave Cecchini, Lehigh	Sr.	11	88	119.8	1,318	16
1994	Mark Orlando, Towson	Sr.	9	55	135.9	1,223	12
1995	Dedric Ward, Northern Iowa	Jr.	10	44	116.4	1,164	12
1996	Joe Douglass, Montana	Sr.	11	82	133.6	1,469	18
1997	Sean Morey, Brown	Jr.	10	73	142.7	1,427	15
1998	Eddie Conti, Delaware	Sr.	11	91	*155.6	*1,712	10
1999	Cornell Craig, Southern Ill.	Sr.	11	77	129.0	1,419	15

*Record.

Scoring

CAREER POINTS PER GAME

(Minimum 225 Points)

Player, Team	Years	G	TD	XPt.	FG	Pts.	Pt. PG
Aaron Stecker, Western Ill.	1997-98	20	39	0	0	234	*11.7
Keith Elias, Princeton	1991-93	30	52	8	0	320	10.7
Archie Amerson, Northern Ariz.	1995-96	22	38	0	0	228	10.4
Jerry Azumah, New Hampshire	1995-98	41	*69	4	0	*418	10.2
Michael Hicks, South Carolina St.	1993-95	32	52	4	0	316	9.9
Elroy Harris, Eastern Ky.	1985, 87-88	31	47	6	0	288	9.3
Joel Sigel, Portland St.	1978-80	30	46	2	0	278	9.3
Tony Zendejas, Nevada	1981-83	33	0	90	70	300	9.1
Gerald Harris, Ga. Southern	1984-86	31	45	2	0	272	8.8
Marty Zendejas, Nevada	1984-87	44	0	169	*72	385	8.8
Charvez Foger, Nevada	1985-88	42	60	2	0	362	8.6
Paul Lewis, Boston U.	1981-84	37	51	2	0	308	8.3
Sherriden May, Idaho	1991-94	44	61	0	0	366	8.3
Judd Garrett, Princeton	1987-89	30	41	1	0	248	8.3
Andre Garron, New Hampshire	1982-85	30	41	0	0	246	8.2
Kenny Gamble, Colgate	1984-87	42	57	0	0	342	8.1
Rene Ingoglia, Massachusetts	1992-95	41	55	2	0	332	8.1
Reggie Greene, Siena	1994-97	36	48	2	0	290	8.1
Rick Sarille, Wagner	$1995-99	41	55	4	0	334	8.1
Barry Bourassa, New Hampshire	1989-92	39	51	0	0	306	7.8
Tim Openlander, Marshall	1994-96	33	0	159	32	255	7.7
Dave Ettinger, Hofstra	1994-97	43	0	140	62	326	7.6
Chad Levitt, Cornell	1993-96	39	48	4	0	292	7.5
Markus Thomas, Eastern Ky.	1989-92	43	53	4	0	322	7.5
Kris Heppner, Montana	1997-99	33	0	138	36	246	7.5
Jerry Rice, Mississippi Val.	1981-84	41	50	2	0	302	7.4
Brian Mitchell, Marshall/ Northern Iowa	1987, 89-91	44	0	130	64	322	7.3
David Ettinger, Hofstra	1994-96	32	0	98	45	233	7.3
Stan House, Central Conn. St.	1994-97	40	48	2	0	290	7.3
Scott Shields, Weber St.	1995-98	44	2	109	67	322	7.3
Ronald Jean, Lehigh	1997-99	33	40	0	0	240	7.3
Harvey Reed, Howard	1984-87	41	48	6	0	294	7.2
Jason Corle, Towson	1996-99	39	47	0	0	282	7.2
Greg Hill, Ga. Southern	1996-99	41	49	0	0	294	7.2
Thayne Doyle, Idaho	1988-91	43	0	160	49	307	7.1
Chris Parker, Marshall	1992-95	44	52	2	0	314	7.1

*Record. $See page 6 for explanation.

SEASON POINTS PER GAME

Player, Team	Year	G	TD	XPt.	FG	Pts.	Pt. PG
Jerry Rice, Mississippi Val.	†1984	10	27	0	0	162	*16.2
Adrian Peterson, Ga. Southern	†1999	11	29	0	0	174	15.8
Geoff Mitchell, Weber St.	†1991	11	*28	1	0	*170	15.5
Brian Westbrook, Villanova	†1998	11	26	4	0	160	14.6
Tony Vinson, Towson	†1993	10	24	0	0	144	14.4
Ronald Jean, Lehigh	1999	11	26	0	0	156	14.2
Adrian Peterson, Ga. Southern	1998	11	26	0	0	156	14.2
Archie Amerson, Northern Ariz.	†1996	11	26	0	0	156	14.2
Aaron Stecker, Western Ill.	†1997	11	25	0	0	150	13.6
Sherriden May, Idaho	†1992	11	25	0	0	150	13.6
Chris Reed, Monmouth	1998	10	22	0	0	132	13.2
Keith Elias, Princeton	1993	10	21	4	0	130	13.0
Elroy Harris, Eastern Ky.	†1988	10	21	2	0	128	12.8
Jerry Azumah, New Hampshire	1998	11	23	2	0	140	12.7
Jessie Burton, McNeese St.	1998	9	19	0	0	114	12.7
Charles Roberts, Cal St. Sacramento	1999	11	22	6	0	138	12.6
Matt Cannon, Southern Utah	1999	11	23	0	0	138	12.6
J. J. Allen, Marist	1998	10	21	0	0	126	12.6
Sean Sanders, Weber St.	†1987	10	21	0	0	126	12.6
Rich Erenberg, Colgate	†1983	11	21	10	0	136	12.4
David Dinkins, Morehead St.	1999	10	20	2	0	122	12.2
Reggie Greene, Siena	1997	9	18	2	0	110	12.2
Sean Bennett, Evansville	1997	10	20	2	0	122	12.2
Harvey Reed, Howard	1987	10	20	2	0	122	12.2
Paul Lewis, Boston U.	1983	10	20	2	0	122	12.2
Stan House, Central Conn. St.	1996	10	20	0	0	120	12.0
Alcede Surtain, Alabama St.	†1995	11	21	6	0	132	12.0
Tim Hall, Robert Morris	†1995	10	20	0	0	120	12.0
Michael Hicks, South Carolina St.	†1994	11	22	0	0	132	12.0
Sherriden May, Idaho	1993	11	22	0	0	132	12.0
Gordie Lockbaum, Holy Cross	1987	11	22	0	0	132	12.0
Gordie Lockbaum, Holy Cross	†1986	11	22	0	0	132	12.0
Gene Lake, Delaware St.	1984	10	20	0	0	120	12.0
Sean Bennett, Evansville	1996	10	19	4	0	118	11.8
Ernest Thompson, Ga. Southern	1988	10	19	2	0	116	11.6
Marcel Shipp, Massachusetts	1999	11	21	0	0	126	11.5
Jerry Azumah, New Hampshire	1996	11	21	0	0	126	11.5
Barry Bourassa, New Hampshire	1991	11	21	0	0	126	11.5
Kenny Gamble, Colgate	1986	11	21	0	0	126	11.5

*Record. †National champion.

CAREER POINTS

(Non-Kickers)

Player, Team	Years	TD	XPt.	Pts.
Jerry Azumah, New Hampshire	1995-98	*69	4	*418
Sherriden May, Idaho	1991-94	61	0	366
Charvez Foger, Nevada	1985-88	60	2	362
Kenny Gamble, Colgate	1984-87	57	0	342
Rick Sarille, Wagner	$1995-99	55	4	334
Rene Ingoglia, Massachusetts	1992-95	55	2	332
¢Adrian Peterson, Ga. Southern	1998-99	55	0	330
Markus Thomas, Eastern Ky.	1989-92	53	4	322
Keith Elias, Princeton	1991-93	52	8	320
Michael Hicks, South Carolina St.	1993-95	52	4	316
Chris Parker, Marshall	1992-95	52	2	314
Thomas Haskins, VMI	1993-96	50	8	308
Paul Lewis, Boston U.	1981-84	51	2	308
Barry Bourassa, New Hampshire	1989-92	51	0	306
Erick Torain, Lehigh	1987-90	50	6	306
Jerry Rice, Mississippi Val.	1981-84	50	2	302
Greg Hill, Ga. Southern (QB)	1996-99	49	0	294
Claude Mathis, Southwest Tex. St.	1994-97	49	0	294
Harvey Reed, Howard	1984-87	48	6	294
Chad Levitt, Cornell	1993-96	48	4	292
¢Matt Cannon, Southern Utah (QB)	1997-99	48	2	290
Reggie Greene, Siena	1994-97	48	2	290
Stan House, Central Conn. St.	1994-97	48	2	290
Jack Douglas, Citadel (QB)	1989-92	48	0	288
Elroy Harris, Eastern Ky.	1985, 87-88	47	6	288
Jason Corle, Towson	1996-99	47	0	282
Willie Taggart, Western Ky. (QB)	1995-98	46	2	278
Joel Sigel, Portland St.	1978-80	46	2	278
Joe Campbell, Middle Tenn. St.	1988-91	45	2	272
Gerald Harris, Ga. Southern	1984-86	45	2	272
Carl Tremble, Furman	1989-92	45	0	270
Norm Ford, New Hampshire	1986-89	45	0	270
John Settle, Appalachian St.	1983-86	44	4	268
¢Charles Roberts, Cal St. Sacramento	1997-99	43	8	266
Ernest Thompson, Ga. Southern	1985, 87-89	44	2	266
Rennie Benn, Lehigh	1982-85	44	2	266
Joe Segreti, Holy Cross	1987-90	44	0	264
Gordie Lockbaum, Holy Cross	1984-87	44	0	264
Frank Hawkins, Nevada	1977-80	44	0	264

*Record. ¢Active player. $See page 6 for explanation.

ALL-TIME LEADERS—SCORING

CAREER POINTS
(Kickers)

Player, Team	Years	PAT	PAT Att.	FG	FG Att.	Pts.
Marty Zendejas, Nevada	1984-87	169	175	*72	90	*385
Dave Ettinger, Hofstra	1994-97	140	155	62	93	326
Scott Shields, Weber St.	1995-98	109	118	67	90	#322
Brian Mitchell, Marshall/ Northern Iowa	1987, 89-91	130	131	64	81	322
Thayne Doyle, Idaho	1988-91	160	174	49	75	307
Jose Larios, McNeese St.	1992-95	133	136	57	89	304
Kirk Roach, Western Caro.	1984-87	89	91	71	*102	302
Tim Foley, Ga. Southern	1984-87	151	156	50	62	301
Dewey Klein, Marshall	1988-91	156	165	48	66	300
Tony Zendejas, Nevada	1981-83	90	96	70	86	300
Jeff Wilkins, Youngstown St.	1990-93	134	136	50	73	286
Garth Petrilli, Middle Tenn. St.	1991-94	166	170	38	60	280
Steve Christie, William & Mary	1986-89	108	116	57	83	279
Franco Grilla, UCF	1989-92	141	147	45	69	278
Gilad Landau, Grambling	1991-94	*181	*194	32	50	277
Shonz Lafrenz, McNeese St.	1996-99	120	128	52	78	276
Mike Black, Boise St.	1988-91	122	127	51	75	275
Juan Toro, Florida A&M	1995-98	151	169	41	50	274
Kirk Duce, Montana	1988-91	131	141	47	78	272
Todd Kurz, Illinois St.	1993-96	89	94	59	87	266
Jeff Poisel, Western Ky.	1996-99	170	180	31	53	263
Paul Hickert, Murray St.	1984-87	116	121	49	79	263
Dean Biasucci, Western Caro.	1980-83	101	106	54	80	263
Andy Larson, Montana	1993-96	177	188	28	45	261
Kelly Potter, Middle Tenn. St.	1981-84	105	109	52	78	261
Steve Largent, Eastern Ill.	1992-95	122	126	46	73	260
Brian Shallcross, William & Mary	1994-97	117	131	47	73	258
Billy Hayes, Sam Houston St.	1985-88	117	120	47	71	258
Michael O'Neal, Samford	1989-92	142	152	38	60	256
Tim Openlander, Marshall	1994-96	159	162	32	42	255
Jason McLaughlin, Lafayette	1991-94	131	138	41	74	254
Jim Hodson, Lafayette	1987-90	134	140	40	66	254
Dave Parkinson, Delaware St.	1985-88	134	143	40	77	254
Chuck Rawlinson, Stephen F. Austin	1988-91	106	110	49	69	253
Paul Politi, Illinois St.	1983-86	101	103	50	78	251
Wayne Boyer, Southwest Mo. St.	1993-96	100	104	49	71	247
Kris Heppner, Montana	1997-99	138	149	36	58	246
Teddy Garcia, La.-Monroe	1984-87	78	81	56	88	246

*Record. #Includes 2 TDs.

SEASON POINTS

Player, Team	Year	TD	XPt.	FG	Pts.
Adrian Peterson, Ga. Soutern	†1999	*29	0	0	*174
Geoff Mitchell, Weber St.	†1991	28	2	0	170
Jerry Rice, Mississippi Val.	†1984	27	0	0	162
Brian Westbrook, Villanova	†1998	26	4	0	160
Ronald Jean, Lehigh	1999	26	0	0	156
Adrian Peterson, Ga. Southern	1998	26	0	0	156
Archie Amerson, Northern Ariz.	†1996	26	0	0	156
Aaron Stecker, Western Ill.	†1997	25	0	0	150
Sherriden May, Idaho	†1992	25	0	0	150
Tony Vinson, Towson	†1993	24	0	0	144
Jerry Azumah, New Hampshire	1998	23	2	0	140
Charles Roberts, Cal St. Sacramento	1999	22	6	0	138
Matt Cannon, Southern Utah	1999	23	0	0	138
Rich Erenberg, Colgate	†1983	21	10	0	136
Chris Reed, Monmouth	1998	22	0	0	132
Alcede Surtain, Alabama St.	†1995	21	6	0	132
Michael Hicks, South Carolina St.	†1994	22	0	0	132
Sherriden May, Idaho	1993	22	0	0	132
Gordie Lockbaum, Holy Cross	1987	22	0	0	132
Gordie Lockbaum, Holy Cross	†1986	22	0	0	132
Keith Elias, Princeton	1993	21	4	0	130
Elroy Harris, Eastern Ky.	†1988	21	1	0	128
Marcel Shipp, Massachusetts	1999	21	0	0	126
J. J. Allen, Marist	1998	21	0	0	126
Jerry Azumah, New Hampshire	1996	21	0	0	126
Barry Bourassa, New Hampshire	1991	21	0	0	126
Sean Sanders, Weber St.	†1987	21	0	0	126
Kenny Gamble, Colgate	1986	21	0	0	126
David Dinkins, Morehead St.	1999	20	2	0	122
Charles Roberts, Cal St. Sacramento	1998	20	2	0	122
David Dinkins, Morehead St.	1998	20	2	0	122
Sean Bennett, Evansville	1997	20	2	0	122
Harvey Reed, Howard	1987	20	2	0	122
Paul Lewis, Boston U.	1983	20	2	0	122

*Record. †National champion.

ANNUAL CHAMPIONS

Year	Player, Team	Class	G	TD	XPt.	FG	Pts.	Avg.
1978	Frank Hawkins, Nevada	So.	10	17	0	0	102	10.2
1979	Joel Sigel, Portland St.	Jr.	10	16	0	0	96	9.6
1980	Ken Jenkins, Bucknell	Jr.	10	16	0	0	96	9.6
1981	Paris Wicks, Youngstown St.	Jr.	11	17	2	0	104	9.5
1982	Paul Lewis, Boston U.	So.	10	18	0	0	108	10.8
1983	Rich Erenberg, Colgate	Sr.	11	21	10	0	136	12.4
1984	Jerry Rice, Mississippi Val.	Sr.	10	27	0	0	162	*16.2
1985	Charvez Foger, Nevada	Fr.	10	18	0	0	108	10.8
1986	Gordie Lockbaum, Holy Cross	Jr.	11	22	0	0	132	12.0
1987	Sean Sanders, Weber St.	Sr.	10	21	0	0	126	12.6
1988	Elroy Harris, Eastern Ky.	Jr.	10	21	1	0	128	12.8
1989	Carl Smith, Maine	So.	11	20	0	0	120	10.9
1990	Barry Bourassa, New Hampshire	So.	9	16	0	0	96	10.7
1991	Geoff Mitchell, Weber St.	Sr.	11	28	1	0	170	15.5
1992	Sherriden May, Idaho	So.	11	25	0	0	150	13.6
1993	Tony Vinson, Towson	Sr.	10	24	0	0	144	14.4
1994	Michael Hicks, South Carolina St.	Jr.	11	22	0	0	132	12.0
1995	Alcede Surtain, Alabama St.	Sr.	11	21	6	0	132	12.0
	Tim Hall, Robert Morris	Sr.	10	20	0	0	120	12.0
1996	Archie Amerson, Northern Ariz.	Sr.	11	26	0	0	156	14.2
1997	Aaron Stecker, Western Ill.	Jr.	11	25	0	0	150	13.6
1998	Brian Westbrook, Villanova	So.	11	26	4	0	160	14.6
1999	Adrian Peterson, Ga. Southern	So.	11	*29	0	0	*174	15.8

*Record.

Interceptions

CAREER INTERCEPTIONS

Player, Team	Years	No.	Yards	Avg.
Dave Murphy, Holy Cross	1986-89	*28	309	11.0
Cedric Walker, Stephen F. Austin	1990-93	25	230	9.2
Issiac Holt, Alcorn St.	1981-84	24	319	13.3
Bill McGovern, Holy Cross	1981-84	24	168	7.0
Darren Sharper, William & Mary	1993-96	24	488	20.3
Scott Shields, Weber St.	1995-98	23	278	12.1
Adrion Smith, Southwest Mo. St.	1990-93	23	219	9.5
William Carroll, Florida A&M	1989-92	23	328	14.3
Kevin Smith, Rhode Island	1987-90	23	287	12.5
Mike Prior, Illinois St.	1981-84	23	211	9.2
Robert Taylor, Tennessee Tech	1993-96	22	267	12.1
Chris Helon, Boston U.	1991-94	22	110	5.0
Morgan Ryan, Montana St.	1990-93	22	245	11.1
Dave Roberts, Youngstown St.	1989-92	22	131	6.0
Frank Robinson, Boise St.	1988-91	22	203	9.2
Dean Cain, Princeton	1985-87	22	203	9.2
Paul Serie, Siena	1995-98	21	107	5.1
Derek Carter, Maine	1994-97	21	301	14.3
Brian Randall, Delaware St.	1990-93	21	367	17.4
Kevin Dent, Jackson St.	1985-88	21	280	13.3
Mark Seals, Boston U.	1985-88	21	169	8.0
Jeff Smith, Illinois St.	1985-88	21	152	7.2
Chris Demarest, Northeastern	1984-87	21	255	12.1
Greg Greely, Nicholls St.	1981-84	21	218	10.4
George Floyd, Eastern Ky.	1978-81	21	318	15.1
Eric Kenesie, Valparaiso	1996-99	20	183	9.2
William Hampton, Murray St.	1993-96	20	409	20.5
Rick Harris, East Tenn. St.	1986-88	20	452	22.6
Mark Kelso, William & Mary	1981-84	20	171	8.6
Leslie Frazier, Alcorn St.	1977-80	20	269	13.5
Bob Jordan, New Hampshire	1990-93	19	96	5.1
Ricky Thomas, South Carolina St.	1988-91	19	374	19.7
Dwayne Harper, South Carolina St.	1984-87	19	163	8.6
Joe Burton, Delaware St.	1983-86	19	248	13.1
Michael Richardson, Northwestern St.	1981-84	19	344	18.1
Mike Genetti, Northeastern	1980-83	19	296	15.6
George Schmitt, Delaware	1980-82	19	280	14.7

*Record.

SEASON INTERCEPTIONS

Player, Team	Year	No.	Yards
Dean Cain, Princeton	†1987	*12	98
Aeneas Williams, Southern U.	‡1990	11	173
Claude Pettaway, Maine	‡1990	11	161
Bill McGovern, Holy Cross	†1984	11	102
Everson Walls, Grambling	†1980	11	145
Anthony Young, Jackson St.	†1978	11	108
Darren Sharper, William & Mary	1996	10	228
Scott Shields, Weber St.	1996	10	101
Chris Helon, Boston U.	†1993	10	42

DIVISION I-AA

… ALL-TIME LEADERS—INTERCEPTIONS

Player, Team	Year	No.	Yards
Cedric Walker, Stephen F. Austin	1990	10	11
Chris Demarest, Northeastern	1987	10	129
Kevin Dent, Jackson St.	‡1986	10	192
Eric Thompson, New Hampshire	‡1986	10	94
Anthony Anderson, Grambling	†1986	10	37
Mike Armentrout, Southwest Mo. St.	†1983	10	42
George Schmitt, Delaware	†1982	10	186
Mike Genetti, Northeastern	†1981	10	144
Bob Mahr, Lafayette	1981	10	48
Neale Henderson, Southern U.	†1979	10	151

*Record. †National champion. ‡National championship shared.

ANNUAL CHAMPIONS
(Ranked on Per-Game Average)

Year	Player, Team	Class	G	No.	Avg.	Yards
1978	Anthony Young, Jackson St.	Sr.	11	11	1.00	108
1979	Neale Henderson, Southern U.	Sr.	11	10	0.91	151
1980	Everson Walls, Grambling	Sr.	11	11	1.00	145
1981	Mike Genetti, Northeastern	So.	10	10	1.00	144
1982	George Schmitt, Delaware	Sr.	11	10	0.91	186
1983	Mike Armentrout, Southwest Mo. St.	Jr.	11	10	0.91	42
1984	Bill McGovern, Holy Cross	Sr.	11	11	1.00	102
1985	Mike Cassidy, Rhode Island	Sr.	10	9	0.90	169
	George Duarte, Northern Ariz.	Jr.	10	9	0.90	150
1986	Kevin Dent, Jackson St.	So.	11	10	0.91	192
	Eric Thompson, New Hampshire	Sr.	11	10	0.91	94
	Anthony Anderson, Grambling	Sr.	11	10	0.91	37
1987	Dean Cain, Princeton	Sr.	10	*12	*1.20	98
1988	Kevin Smith, Rhode Island	So.	10	9	0.90	94
1989	Mike Babb, Weber St.	Sr.	11	9	0.82	90
1990	Aeneas Williams, Southern U.	Sr.	11	11	1.00	173
	Claude Pettaway, Maine	Sr.	11	11	1.00	161
1991	Warren McIntire, Delaware	Jr.	11	9	0.82	208
1992	Dave Roberts, Youngstown St.	Sr.	11	9	0.82	39
1993	Chris Helon, Boston U.	Jr.	11	10	0.91	42
1994	Joseph Vaughn, Cal St. Northridge	Sr.	10	9	0.90	265
	Brian Clark, Hofstra	Jr.	10	9	0.90	56
1995	Picasso Nelson, Jackson St.	Sr.	9	8	0.89	101
1996	Shane Hurd, Canisius	Jr.	7	7	1.00	198
1997	Roderic Parson, Brown	Sr.	8	8	1.00	93
1998	Ken Krapf, St. John's (N.Y.)	Jr.	11	9	0.82	144
	Eric Kenesie, Valparaiso	Jr.	11	9	0.82	88
1999	Ryan Crawford, Davidson	Jr.	11	8	0.73	63

*Record.

Punting

CAREER AVERAGE
(Minimum 150 Punts)

Player, Team	Years	No.	Yards	Long	Avg.
Pumpy Tudors, Chattanooga	1989-91	181	8,041	79	*44.4
Case de Bruijn, Idaho St.	1978-81	256	11,184	76	43.7
Terry Belden, Northern Ariz.	1990-93	225	9,760	76	43.4
Chad Stanley, Stephen F. Austin	1996-98	178	7,709	79	43.3
George Cimadevilla, East Tenn. St.	1983-86	225	9,676	72	43.0
Harold Alexander, Appalachian St.	1989-92	259	11,100	78	42.9
Ken Hinsley, Western Caro.	1995-98	199	8,512	85	42.8
Brad Costello, Boston U.	1995-97	193	8,206	73	42.5
John Christopher, Morehead St.	1979-82	298	12,633	62	42.4
Colin Godfrey, Tennessee St.	1989-92	213	9,012	69	42.3
Bret Wright, Southeastern La.	1981-83	165	6,963	66	42.2
Jeff Kaiser, Idaho St.	1982-84	156	6,571	88	42.1
Greg Davis, Citadel	1983-86	263	11,076	81	42.1
Mark Royals, Appalachian St.	1983-85	223	9,372	67	42.0

*Record.

SEASON AVERAGE
(Qualifiers for Championship)

Player, Team	Year	No.	Yards	Avg.
Harold Alexander, Appalachian St.	†1991	64	3,009	*47.0
Chad Stanley, Stephen F. Austin	†1998	58	2,703	46.6
Terry Belden, Northern Ariz.	†1993	59	2,712	46.0
Case de Bruijn, Idaho St.	†1981	42	1,928	45.9
Colin Godfrey, Tennessee St.	†1990	57	2,614	45.9
Barry Cantrell, Fordham	†1997	65	2,980	45.9
Matthew Peot, Montana St.	†1999	48	2,195	45.7
Stuart Dodds, Montana St.	†1979	59	2,689	45.6
Pumpy Tudors, Chattanooga	1991	53	2,414	45.5
Matt Bushart, Southern U.	1998	50	2,260	45.2
Mark Gagliano, Southern Ill.	†1996	54	2,432	45.0
Paul Asbury, Southwest Tex. St.	1990	39	1,749	44.9
Brian Bivens, Murray St.	1999	43	1,926	44.8
Tom Sugg, Idaho	1991	53	2,371	44.7
Chad Stanley, Stephen F. Austin	1997	62	2,771	44.7
Mike Rice, Montana	†1985	62	2,771	44.7
Case de Bruijn, Idaho St.	1979	73	3,261	44.7
George Cimadevilla, East Tenn. St.	1985	66	2,948	44.7
Greg Davis, Citadel	†1986	61	2,723	44.6
Pumpy Tudors, Chattanooga	1990	63	2,810	44.6
Pat Velarde, Marshall	†1983	64	2,852	44.6
Ken Hinsley, Western Caro.	1998	57	2,536	44.5
Bart Bradley, Sam Houston St.	1986	44	1,957	44.5
Harold Alexander, Appalachian St.	†1992	55	2,445	44.5
Curtis Moody, Texas Southern	1985	64	2,844	44.4
Mike Leach, William & Mary	1998	45	1,997	44.4
Terry Belden, Northern Ariz.	1991	43	1,908	44.4
Brad Costello, Boston U.	1997	73	3,239	44.4
Terry Belden, Northern Ariz.	1992	59	2,614	44.3
Bret Wright, Southeastern La.	1983	66	2,923	44.3
George Cimadevilla, East Tenn. St.	1986	65	2,876	44.2
Ryan Klaus, Sam Houston St.	1998	72	3,182	44.2
Ken Hinsley, Western Caro.	1997	46	2,032	44.2
Steve Thorns, Cal St. Sacramento	1997	66	2,907	44.1
Matt Evans, Princeton	1998	54	2,377	44.0

*Record. †National champion.

ANNUAL CHAMPIONS

Year	Player, Team	Class	No.	Yards	Avg.
1978	Nick Pavich, Nevada	So.	47	1,939	41.3
1979	Stuart Dodds, Montana St.	Sr.	59	2,689	45.6
1980	Case de Bruijn, Idaho St.	Jr.	67	2,945	43.9
1981	Case de Bruijn, Idaho St.	Sr.	42	1,928	45.9
1982	John Christopher, Morehead St.	Sr.	93	4,084	43.9
1983	Pat Velarde, Marshall	Sr.	64	2,852	44.6
1984	Steve Kornegay, Western Caro.	Jr.	49	2,127	43.4
1985	Mike Rice, Montana	Jr.	62	2,771	44.7
1986	Greg Davis, Citadel	Sr.	61	2,723	44.6
1987	Eric Stein, Eastern Wash.	Sr.	74	3,193	43.2
1988	Mike McCabe, Illinois St.	Sr.	69	3,042	44.1
1989	Pumpy Tudors, Chattanooga	So.	65	2,817	43.3
1990	Colin Godfrey, Tennessee St.	So.	57	2,614	45.9
1991	Harold Alexander, Appalachian St.	Jr.	64	3,009	*47.0
1992	Harold Alexander, Appalachian St.	Sr.	55	2,445	44.5
1993	Terry Belden, Northern Ariz.	Sr.	59	2,712	46.0
1994	Scott Holmes, Samford	Jr.	49	2,099	42.8
1995	Kevin O'Leary, Northern Ariz.	Sr.	44	1,881	42.8
1996	Mark Gagliano, Southern Ill.	Sr.	54	2,432	45.0
1997	Barry Cantrell, Fordham	Sr.	65	2,980	45.9
1998	Chad Stanley, Stephen F. Austin	Sr.	58	2,703	46.6
1999	Matthew Peot, Montana St.	Jr.	48	2,195	45.7

*Record.

Punt Returns

CAREER AVERAGE
(Minimum 1.2 Returns Per Game; Minimum 30 Returns)

Player, Team	Years	No.	Yards	Avg.
Willie Ware, Mississippi Val.	1982-85	61	1,003	*16.4
Buck Phillips, Western Ill.	1994-95	40	656	16.4
Tim Egerton, Delaware St.	1986-89	59	951	16.1
Mark Orlando, Towson	1991-94	41	644	15.7
John Armstrong, Richmond	1984-85	31	449	14.5
Darrick Brown, Maine	1995-98	56	807	14.4
Joey Jamison, Texas Southern	1997-99	88	1,269	14.4
Ricky Pearsall, Northern Ariz.	1994-97	39	546	14.0
Undre Williams, Florida A&M	1995-97	31	429	13.8
Kenny Shedd, Northern Iowa	1989-92	79	1,081	13.7
Chris Berry, Morehead St.	1994-97	37	505	13.7
Dejuan Alfonzo, Indiana St.	1997-99	40	539	13.5
Dione Tyler, Southeast Mo. St.	1994-95	39	523	13.4
Reggie Barlow, Alabama St.	1992-95	49	645	13.2
Joe Fuller, Northern Iowa	1982-85	69	888	12.9
Eric Yarber, Idaho	1984-85	32	406	12.7
Troy Brown, Marshall	1991-92	36	455	12.6
Trumaine Johnson, Grambling	1979-82	53	662	12.5
Kerry Hayes, Western Caro.	1991-94	70	876	12.5
Goree White, Alcorn St.	1993-96	70	902	12.5
Tony Merriwether, North Texas	1982-83	41	507	12.4
Eric Alden, Idaho St.	1992-93	31	383	12.4
Thaylen Armstead, Grambling	1989-91	44	540	12.3
Trevor Bell, Idaho St.	1995-97	38	461	12.3

ALL-TIME LEADERS—PUNT RETURNS

Player, Team	Years	No.	Yards	Avg.
Barney Bussey, South Carolina St.	1980-83	47	573	12.2
Mike Furrey, Northern Iowa	1997-99	52	632	12.2
Cornell Johnson, Southern U.	1990-92	40	482	12.1
John Taylor, Delaware St.	1982-85	48	576	12.0
Ricky Ellis, St. Mary's (Cal.)	1994-96	32	384	12.0

*Record.

SEASON AVERAGE
(Minimum 1.2 Returns Per Game and Qualifiers for Championship)

Player, Team	Year	No.	Yards	Avg.
Tim Egerton, Delaware St.	†1988	16	368	*23.0
Ryan Priest, Lafayette	†1982	12	271	22.6
Craig Hodge, Tennessee St.	†1987	19	398	21.0
Chris Berry, Morehead St.	†1997	13	273	21.0
Reggie Barlow, Alabama St.	†1995	12	249	20.8
Bashir Levingston, Eastern Wash.	†1998	16	333	20.8
John Armstrong, Richmond	†1985	19	391	20.6
KaRon Coleman, Stephen F. Austin	†1999	17	348	20.5
Mark Orlando, Towson	†1994	19	377	19.8
Willie Ware, Mississippi Val.	†1984	19	374	19.7
Buck Phillips, Western Ill.	1994	24	464	19.3
Mark Hurt, Alabama St.	1988	10	185	18.5
Howard Huckaby, Florida A&M	1988	26	478	18.4
Ashley Ambrose, Mississippi Val.	†1991	28	514	18.4
Quincy Miller, South Carolina St.	†1992	17	311	18.3
Barney Bussey, South Carolina St.	†1981	14	255	18.2
Willie Ware, Mississippi Val.	1985	31	*561	18.1
Chris Darrington, Weber St.	†1986	16	290	18.1
Kerry Lawyer, Boise St.	1992	18	325	18.1
Drew Hadded, Buffalo	1998	23	410	17.8
Kenny Shedd, Northern Iowa	1992	27	477	17.7
Claude Mathis, Southwest Tex. St.	1995	20	352	17.6
Clarence Alexander, Mississippi Val.	1986	22	380	17.3
Henry Richard, La.-Monroe	†1989	15	258	17.2
Ray Marshall, St. Peter's	†1993	10	171	17.1
Delvin Joyce, James Madison	1997	17	289	17.0
Ricky Pearsall, Northern Ariz.	†1996	29	490	16.9
Carl Williams, Texas Southern	1981	16	269	16.8
Jerome Bledsoe, Massachusetts	1988	17	285	16.8

*Record. †National champion.

ANNUAL CHAMPIONS

Year	Player, Team	Class	No.	Yards	Avg.
1978	Ray Smith, Northern Ariz.	Sr.	13	181	13.9
1979	Joseph Markus, Connecticut	Fr.	17	219	12.9
1980	Trumaine Johnson, Grambling	So.	††13	226	17.4
1981	Barney Bussey, South Carolina St.	So.	14	255	18.2
1982	Ryan Priest, Lafayette	Fr.	12	271	22.6
1983	Joe Fuller, Northern Iowa	So.	22	344	15.6
1984	Willie Ware, Mississippi Val.	Jr.	19	374	19.7
1985	John Armstrong, Richmond	Sr.	19	391	20.6
1986	Chris Darrington, Weber St.	Sr.	16	290	18.1
1987	Craig Hodge, Tennessee St.	Sr.	19	398	21.0
1988	Tim Egerton, Delaware St.	Jr.	16	368	*23.0
1989	Henry Richard, La.-Monroe	Jr.	15	258	17.2
1990	Gary Harrell, Howard	Fr.	26	417	16.0
1991	Ashley Ambrose, Mississippi Val.	Sr.	28	514	18.4
1992	Quincy Miller, South Carolina St.	Jr.	17	311	18.3
1993	Ray Marshall, St. Peter's	Jr.	10	171	17.1
1994	Mark Orlando, Towson	Sr.	19	377	19.8
1995	Reggie Barlow, Alabama St.	Sr.	12	249	20.8
1996	Ricky Pearsall, Northern Ariz.	Jr.	29	490	16.9
1997	Chris Berry, Morehead St.	Sr.	13	273	21.0
1998	Bashir Levingston, Eastern Wash.	Sr.	16	333	20.8
1999	KaRon Coleman, Stephen F. Austin	Sr.	17	348	20.5

*Record. ††Declared champion; with one more return (making 1.3 per game) for zero yards, still would have highest average.

Kickoff Returns

CAREER AVERAGE
(Minimum 1.2 Returns Per Game; Minimum 30 Returns)

Player, Team	Years	No.	Yards	Avg.
Troy Brown, Marshall	1991-92	32	950	*29.7
Charles Swann, Indiana St.	1989-91	45	1,319	29.3
Craig Richardson, Eastern Wash.	1983-86	71	2,021	28.5
Kenyatta Sparks, Southern U.	1992-95	39	1,100	28.2
Kerry Hayes, Western Caro.	1991-94	73	2,058	28.2
Daryl Holcombe, Eastern Ill.	1986-89	49	1,379	28.1
Dwight Robinson, James Madison	1990-93	51	1,434	28.1
Curtis Chappell, Howard	1984-87	42	1,177	28.0
Leon Brown, Eastern Ky.	1990-93	44	1,230	28.0
Josh Cole, Furman	1993-96	65	1,808	27.8
Tyree Talton, Northern Iowa	1995-98	72	1,999	27.8
Joe Rosato, Duquesne	1994-97	60	1,661	27.7
Marcus Durgin, Samford	1990-93	44	1,218	27.7
Cornelius Turner, Mississippi Val.	1992-94	50	1,379	27.6
Anthony Taylor, Northern Iowa	1992-95	30	821	27.4
Jerry Parrish, Eastern Ky.	1978-81	61	1,668	27.3
Tony James, Eastern Ky.	1982-84	57	1,552	27.2
Ricky Ellis, St. Mary's (Cal.)	1994-96	31	836	27.0
Frank Selto, Idaho St.	1986-87	30	803	26.8
Chris Hickman, La.-Monroe	1991-92	30	798	26.6
Chris Pollard, Dartmouth	1986-88	52	1,376	26.5
Tyrone Butterfield, Tennessee St.	1997-98	44	1,164	26.5
John Jarvis, Howard	1986-88	39	1,031	26.4
Ronald Scott, Southern U.	1982-85	38	1,003	26.4
Vernon Williams, Eastern Wash.	1986-88	40	1,052	26.3
Rob Tesch, Montana St.	1989-92	50	1,317	26.3
Rick Sarille, Wagner	$1995-99	64	1,682	26.3
Steve Ortman, Pennsylvania	1982-84	31	808	26.1
John Armstrong, Richmond	1984-85	32	826	25.8
Renard Coleman, Montana	1985-88	57	1,465	25.7
Michael Haynes, Northern Ariz.	1986-87	36	925	25.7
Jeb Dougherty, San Diego	1993-96	62	1,589	25.6
Kevin Gainer, Bethune-Cookman	1988-90	42	1,070	25.5
Mareno Philyaw, Troy St.	1996-99	32	816	25.5
Archie Herring, Youngstown St.	1987-90	79	2,005	25.4
Joey Jamison, Texas Southern	1997-99	50	1,266	25.3
Kenny Shedd, Northern Iowa	1989-92	54	1,359	25.2
Damon Boddie, Montana	1993-94	49	1,232	25.1
Jerry Azumah, New Hampshire	1995-98	41	1,025	25.0
Joey Stockton, Western Ky.	1994-97	87	2,175	25.0
Michael High, North Texas	1991-93	47	1,171	24.9
David Smith, Northeastern	1994-97	60	1,484	24.7
Andy Swafford, Troy St.	1995-97	31	764	24.7
Jerome Stelly, Western Ill.	1981-82	42	1,024	24.4
Kino Carson, Northern Ariz.	1996-97	32	778	24.3

*Record. $See page 6 for explanation.

SEASON AVERAGE
(Minimum 1.2 Returns Per Game and Qualifiers for Championship)

Player, Team	Year	No.	Yards	Avg.
David Fraterrigo, Canisius	†1993	13	485	*37.3
Kerry Hayes, Western Caro.	1993	16	584	36.5
Cordell Roane, Richmond	†1999	13	470	36.2
Ryan Zimpleman, Butler	†1998	28	972	34.7
Craig Richardson, Eastern Wash.	†1984	21	729	34.7
Randy Moss, Marshall	†1996	14	484	34.6
Avion Black, Tennessee St.	1999	23	786	34.2
Lamont Brightful, Eastern Wash.	1999	26	882	33.9
Errin Hatwood, St. John's (N.Y.)	†1994	12	401	33.4
Marcus Durgin, Samford	†1992	15	499	33.3
Rory Lee, Western Ill.	1993	16	527	32.9
Dave Meggett, Towson	†1988	13	418	32.2
Josh Cole, Furman	†1995	17	546	32.1
Charles Swann, Indiana St.	†1990	20	642	32.1
Tyree Talton, Northern Iowa	1996	22	703	32.0
Archie Herring, Youngstown St.	1990	18	575	31.9
Dwight Robinson, James Madison	1994	16	510	31.9
Davlin Mullen, Western Ky.	†1982	18	574	31.9
Todd Cleveland, UCF	1994	15	476	31.7
Naylon Albritton, South Carolina St.	1993	15	475	31.7
Jermine Sharp, Southern U.	1995	16	504	31.5
Andy Swafford, Troy St.	†1997	14	440	31.4
Ozzie Young, Valparaiso	1994	17	533	31.4
Danny Copeland, Eastern Ky.	†1986	26	812	31.2
Chris Chappell, Howard	1986	17	528	31.1
Thomas Haskins, VMI	1994	15	464	30.9
Dave Loehle, New Hampshire	†1978	15	460	30.7
Paul Ashby, Alabama St.	†1991	17	520	30.6
Juan Jackson, N.C. A&T	1986	16	487	30.4
Kevin Gainer, Bethune-Cookman	1990	21	635	30.2
Robert Thomas, Hofstra	1998	26	784	30.2
Ed Williams, St. Mary's (Cal.)	1996	16	482	30.1
Howard Huckaby, Florida A&M	†1987	20	602	30.1
Tony James, Eastern Ky.	†1983	17	511	30.1

*Record. †National champion.

ANNUAL CHAMPIONS

Year	Player, Team	Class	No.	Yards	Avg.
1978	Dave Loehle, New Hampshire	Jr.	15	460	30.7
1979	Garry Pearson, Massachusetts	Fr.	12	348	29.0

ALL-TIME LEADERS—KICKOFF RETURNS

Year	Player, Team	Class	No.	Yards	Avg.
1980	Danny Thomas, N.C. A&T	Fr.	15	381	25.4
1981	Jerry Parrish, Eastern Ky.	Sr.	18	534	29.7
1982	Davlin Mullen, Western Ky.	Sr.	18	574	31.9
1983	Tony James, Eastern Ky.	Jr.	17	511	30.1
1984	Craig Richardson, Eastern Wash.	So.	21	729	34.7
1985	Rodney Payne, Murray St.	Fr.	16	464	29.0
1986	Danny Copeland, Eastern Ky.	Jr.	26	812	31.2
1987	Howard Huckaby, Florida A&M	So.	20	602	30.1
1988	Dave Meggett, Towson	Sr.	13	418	32.2
1989	Scott Thomas, Liberty	Fr.	13	373	28.7
1990	Charles Swann, Indiana St.	Jr.	20	642	32.1
1991	Paul Ashby, Alabama St.	Jr.	17	520	30.6
1992	Marcus Durgin, Samford	Jr.	15	499	33.3
1993	David Fraterrigo, Canisius	Sr.	13	485	*37.3
1994	Errin Hatwood, St. John's (N.Y.)	Sr.	12	401	33.4
1995	Josh Cole, Furman	Jr.	17	546	32.1
1996	Randy Moss, Marshall	Fr.	14	484	34.6
1997	Andy Swafford, Troy St.	Sr.	14	440	31.4
1998	Ryan Zimpleman, Butler	So.	28	972	34.7
1999	Cordell Roane, Richmond	Fr.	13	470	36.2

*Record.

New Hampshire's Jerry Azumah is the Division I-AA career leader in all-purpose yards (8,376) and career yards per game (204.3).

All-Purpose Yards

CAREER YARDS PER GAME
(Minimum 3,200 Yards)

Player, Team	Years	G	Rush	Rcv.	Int.	PR	KOR	Yds.	Yd. PG
Jerry Azumah, New Hampshire	1995-98	41	*6,193	1,153	0	5	1,025	*8,376	*204.3
Arnold Mickens, Butler	1994-95	20	3,813	47	0	0	87	3,947	197.4
Tim Hall, Robert Morris	1994-95	19	2,908	793	0	0	0	3,701	194.8
Reggie Greene, Siena	1994-97	36	5,415	274	0	53	1,217	6,959	193.3
Dave Meggett, Towson	1987-88	18	1,658	788	0	212	745	3,403	189.1
Archie Amerson, Northern Ariz.	1995-96	22	3,196	484	0	0	382	4,062	184.6
Kenny Gamble, Colgate	1984-87	42	5,220	536	0	104	1,763	7,623	181.5
Rick Sarille, Wagner	$1995-99	41	5,290	365	0	0	1,682	7,337	179.0
Aaron Stecker, Western Ill.	1997-98	20	3,081	427	0	0	0	3,508	175.4
Rich Erenberg, Colgate	1982-83	21	2,618	423	0	268	315	3,624	172.6
Claude Mathis, Southwest Tex. St.	1994-97	44	4,691	744	0	635	1,353	7,423	168.7
Thomas Haskins, VMI	1993-96	44	5,355	179	0	216	1,661	7,411	168.4
Ozzie Young, Valparaiso	1993-95	29	1,576	1,123	0	418	1,728	4,845	167.1
Fine Unga, Weber St.	1987-88	22	2,298	391	0	7	967	3,663	166.5
Gill Fenerty, Holy Cross	1983-85	30	3,618	477	0	1	731	4,827	160.9
Keith Elias, Princeton	1991-93	30	4,208	508	0	0	25	4,741	158.0
Don Wilkerson, Southwest Tex. St.	1993-94	22	2,356	255	0	83	757	3,451	156.9
Kito Lockwood, Wagner	1993-95	25	2,576	891	0	0	420	3,887	155.5
Tyrone Butterfield, Tennessee St.	1997-98	22	12	2,182	0	44	1,164	3,402	154.6
Barry Bourassa, New Hampshire	1989-92	39	2,960	1,307	0	306	1,370	5,943	152.4
Judd Garrett, Princeton	1987-89	30	3,109	1,385	0	0	10	4,510	150.3
Treamelle Taylor, Nevada	1987-90	22	0	1,926	0	662	687	3,275	148.9
Troy Brown, Marshall	1991-92	22	138	1,716	0	455	950	3,259	148.1
Andre Garron, New Hampshire	1982-85	30	2,901	809	0	8	651	4,369	145.6
Carl Boyd, Northern Iowa	1983, 85-87	34	2,735	1,987	0	0	183	4,905	144.3
Sean Morey, Brown	1995-98	40	131	3,850	0	9	1,736	5,726	143.2
Merril Hoge, Idaho St.	1983-86	39	2,713	1,734	0	1	1,005	5,453	139.8
Rich Lemon, Bucknell	1993-96	43	4,742	961	0	99	150	5,952	138.4
Jason Corle, Towson	1996-99	39	3,601	1,725	0	26	30	5,382	138.0
Pete Mandley, Northern Ariz.	1979-80, 82-83	43	436	2,598	11	901	1,979	5,925	137.8
Erik Marsh, Lafayette	1991-94	42	4,834	383	0	76	490	5,783	137.7
Joey Stockton, Western Ky.	1994-97	36	248	1,878	0	627	2,175	4,928	136.9
Kerry Hayes, Western Caro.	1991-94	41	75	2,594	0	876	2,058	5,603	136.7
Destry Wright, Jackson St.	1997-99	34	4,049	323	0	121	148	4,641	136.5
Frank Hawkins, Nevada	1977-80	43	5,333	519	0	0	0	5,852	136.1
Derrick Harmon, Cornell	1981-83	28	3,074	679	0	5	42	3,800	135.7
Dorron Hunter, Morehead St.	1977-80	38	1,336	1,320	0	510	1,970	5,136	135.2

*Record. $See page 6 for explanation.

SEASON YARDS PER GAME

Player, Team	Year	Rush	Rcv.	Int.	PR	KOR	Yds.	Yd. PG
Brian Westbrook, Villanova	†1998	1,046	1,144	0	192	644	*3,026	*275.1
Jerry Azumah, New Hampshire	1998	2,195	218	0	5	308	2,726	247.8
Reggie Greene, Siena	†1996	1,719	50	0	0	337	2,106	234.0
Arnold Mickens, Butler	†1994	2,255	7	0	0	0	2,262	226.2
Reggie Greene, Siena	†1997	1,719	50	0	0	158	2,009	223.2
Charles Roberts, Cal St. Sacramento	1998	*2,260	79	0	0	91	2,430	220.9
Archie Amerson, Northern Ariz.	1996	2,079	262	0	0	88	2,429	220.8
Kenny Gamble, Colgate	†1986	1,816	178	0	40	391	2,425	220.5
Reggie Greene, Siena	†1995	1,461	77	0	53	363	1,954	217.1
Eddie Conti, Delaware	1998	-2	*1,712	0	156	502	2,368	215.3
Marcel Shipp, Massachusetts	1998	1,949	288	0	0	100	2,337	212.5
Michael Clemons, William & Mary	1986	1,065	516	0	330	423	2,334	212.2
Rick Sarille, Wagner	†1999	1,373	226	0	0	475	2,074	207.4
Tony Vinson, Towson	†1993	2,016	57	0	0	0	2,073	207.3
Derrick Cullors, Murray St.	1995	1,765	312	0	0	201	2,278	207.1
Clarence Matthews, Northwestern St.	1995	1,384	194	0	145	554	2,277	207.0
Claude Mathis, Southwest Tex. St.	1995	1,286	315	0	352	308	2,261	205.6
Anthony Jordan, Samford	1994	924	400	0	169	767	2,260	205.5
Sean Bennett, Evansville	1997	1,668	260	0	81	34	2,043	204.3
Aaron Stecker, Western Ill.	1997	1,957	288	0	0	0	2,245	204.1
Rich Erenberg, Colgate	†1983	1,883	214	0	126	18	2,241	203.7
Kenny Bynum, South Carolina St.	1996	1,649	118	0	1	255	2,023	202.3

ALL-TIME LEADERS—ALL-PURPOSE YARDS

Player, Team	Year	Rush	Rcv.	Int.	PR	KOR	Yds.	Yd. PG
Jerry Azumah, New Hampshire	1997	1,572	297	0	0	351	2,220	201.8
Charles Roberts, Cal St. Sacramento	1999	2,082	108	0	12	0	2,202	200.2
Tim Hall, Robert Morris	1994	1,336	460	0	0	0	1,796	199.6
Dave Meggett, Towson	†1987	814	572	0	78	327	1,791	199.0
Joey Stockton, Western Ky.	1995	46	863	0	147	934	1,990	199.0
Gordie Lockbaum, Holy Cross	1986	827	860	34	0	452	2,173	197.6
Gill Fenerty, Holy Cross	†1985	1,368	187	0	1	414	1,970	197.0
Barry Bourassa, New Hampshire	†1991	1,130	426	0	0	596	2,152	195.6
Sean Bennett, Evansville	1996	1,189	740	0	0	27	1,956	195.6
Karlton Carpenter, Southern Ill.	1998	1,892	75	0	0	175	2,142	194.7
Thomas Haskins, VMI	1995	1,548	33	0	0	553	2,134	194.0
Keith Elias, Princeton	1993	1,731	193	0	0	15	1,939	193.9
Rick Sarille, Wagner	1996	1,475	36	0	0	427	1,938	193.8
Barry Bourassa, New Hampshire	†1990	957	276	0	133	368	1,734	192.7
Sean Morey, Brown	1997	10	1,427	0	15	470	1,922	192.2
Merril Hoge, Idaho St.	1985	1,041	708	0	0	364	2,113	192.1
Jerry Azumah, New Hampshire	1996	1,308	521	0	0	280	2,109	191.7
Andre Garron, New Hampshire	1983	1,009	539	0	0	359	1,907	190.7
Thomas Haskins, VMI	1996	1,704	66	0	216	112	2,098	190.7
Kenny Gamble, Colgate	1987	1,411	151	0	64	471	2,097	190.6
Tim Hall, Robert Morris	1995	1,572	333	0	0	0	1,905	190.5
Kito Lockwood, Wagner	1995	1,018	187	0	0	127	1,332	190.3

*Record. †National champion.

CAREER YARDS

Player, Team	Years	Rush	Rcv.	Int.	PR	KOR	Yds.	Yd. PP
Jerry Azumah, New Hampshire	1995-98	*6,193	1,153	0	5	1,025	*8,376	7.4
Kenny Gamble, Colgate	1984-87	5,220	536	0	104	1,763	7,623	7.0
Claude Mathis, Southwest Tex. St.	1994-97	4,691	744	0	635	1,353	7,423	7.0
Thomas Haskins, VMI	1993-96	5,355	179	0	216	1,661	7,411	7.2
Rick Sarille, Wagner	$1995-99	5,290	365	0	0	1,682	7,337	6.9
Reggie Greene, Siena	1994-97	5,415	274	0	53	1,217	6,959	7.1
Rich Lemon, Bucknell	1993-96	4,742	961	0	99	150	5,952	5.2
Barry Bourassa, New Hampshire	1989-92	2,960	1,307	0	306	1,370	5,943	7.5
Pete Mandley, Northern Ariz.	1979-80, 82-83	436	2,598	11	901	1,979	5,925	14.8
Frank Hawkins, Nevada	1977-80	5,333	519	0	0	0	5,852	5.8
Erik Marsh, Lafayette	1991-94	4,834	383	0	76	490	5,783	5.2
Eddie Conti, Delaware	1994-98	-7	3,496	0	802	1,446	5,737	17.1
Sean Morey, Brown	1995-98	131	3,850	0	9	1,736	5,726	15.7
Kerry Hayes, Western Caro.	1991-94	5	2,594	0	876	2,058	5,603	*19.1
Jamie Jones, Eastern Ill.	1988-91	3,466	816	0	66	1,235	5,583	6.2
Chris Parker, Marshall	1992-95	4,571	838	0	0	133	5,542	6.5
Sherriden May, Idaho	1991-94	3,748	926	0	153	646	5,473	6.9
Merril Hoge, Idaho St.	1983-86	2,713	1,734	0	1	1,005	5,453	6.6
Herman Hunter, Tennessee St.	1981-84	1,049	1,129	0	974	*2,258	5,410	10.5
Jason Corle, Towson	1996-99	3,601	1,725	0	26	30	5,382	5.5
¢Marcel Shipp, Massachusetts	1997-99	4,277	702	0	0	392	5,371	6.0
David Wright, Indiana St.	1992-95	4,181	255	0	0	904	5,340	6.2
Cedric Minter, Boise St.	1977-80	4,475	525	0	49	267	5,316	6.5
Charvez Foger, Nevada	1985-88	4,484	821	0	0	0	5,305	5.7
¢Charles Roberts, Cal St. Sacramento	1997-99	4,929	246	0	0	112	5,287	6.2
Garry Pearson, Massachusetts	1979-82	3,859	466	0	0	952	5,277	5.9
John Settle, Appalachian St.	1983-86	4,409	526	0	0	319	5,254	5.3
Joe Rosato, Duquesne	1994-97	80	2,360	0	1,036	1,661	5,137	15.6
Dorron Hunter, Morehead St.	1977-80	1,336	1,320	0	510	1,970	5,136	9.6

*Record. ¢Active player. $See page 6 for explanation.

SEASON YARDS

Player, Team	Years	Rush	Rcv.	Int.	PR	KOR	Yds.	Yd. PP
Brian Westbrook, Villanova	†1998	1,046	1,144	0	192	644	*3,026	9.2
Jerry Azumah, New Hampshire	1998	2,195	218	0	5	308	2,726	7.3
Charles Roberts, Cal St. Sacramento	1998	*2,260	79	0	0	91	2,430	6.1
Archie Amerson, Northern Ariz.	1996	2,079	262	0	0	88	2,429	6.9
Kenny Gamble, Colgate	†1986	1,816	178	0	40	391	2,425	7.1
Eddie Conti, Delaware	1998	-2	*1,712	0	156	502	2,368	18.2
Marcel Shipp, Massachusetts	1998	1,949	288	0	0	100	2,337	6.6
Michael Clemons, William & Mary	1986	1,065	516	0	330	423	2,334	6.7
Derrick Cullors, Murray St.	1995	1,765	312	0	0	201	2,278	7.6
Clarence Matthews, Northwestern St.	1995	1,384	194	0	145	554	2,277	7.7
Arnold Mickens, Butler	†1994	2,255	7	0	0	0	2,262	5.5
Claude Mathis, Southwest Tex. St.	1995	1,286	315	0	352	308	2,261	7.3
Anthony Jordan, Samford	1994	924	400	0	169	767	2,260	10.8
Aaron Stecker, Western Ill.	1997	1,957	288	0	0	0	2,245	6.9
Rich Erenberg, Colgate	†1983	1,883	214	0	126	18	2,241	6.7
Jerry Azumah, New Hampshire	1997	1,572	297	0	0	351	2,220	7.2
Charles Roberts, Cal St. Sacramento	1999	2,082	108	0	12	0	2,202	6.9
Gordie Lockbaum, Holy Cross	1986	827	860	34	0	452	2,173	9.7
Barry Bourassa, New Hampshire	†1991	1,130	426	0	0	596	2,152	7.5
Karlton Carpenter, Southern Ill.	1998	1,892	75	0	0	175	2,142	6.3
Thomas Haskins, VMI	1995	1,548	33	0	0	553	2,134	7.6
Merril Hoge, Idaho St.	1985	1,041	708	0	0	364	2,113	7.4
Jerry Azumah, New Hampshire	1996	1,308	521	0	0	280	2,109	7.0
Reggie Greene, Siena	1996	1,719	50	0	0	337	2,106	6.9

DIVISION I-AA

ALL-TIME LEADERS—ALL-PURPOSE YARDS

Player, Team	Years	Rush	Rcv.	Int.	PR	KOR	Yds.	Yd. PP
Thomas Haskins, VMI	1996	1,704	66	0	216	112	2,098	6.4
Kenny Gamble, Colgate	1987	1,411	151	0	64	471	2,097	6.5
Otis Washington, Western Caro.	†1988	66	907	0	0	1,113	2,086	*19.7
Rick Sarille, Wagner	†1999	1,373	226	0	0	475	2,074	6.8
Tony Vinson, Towson	†1993	2,016	57	0	0	0	2,073	6.8
Don Wilkerson, Southwest Tex. St.	1994	1,569	131	0	21	327	2,048	6.2
Kenny Gamble, Colgate	1985	1,361	162	0	0	520	2,043	7.3
Sean Bennett, Evansville	1997	1,668	260	0	81	34	2,043	7.7
Gordie Lockbaum, Holy Cross	1987	403	1,152	0	209	277	2,041	10.4
Thomas Haskins, VMI	1994	1,509	50	0	0	464	2,023	7.2
Kenny Bynum, South Carolina St.	1996	1,649	118	0	1	255	2,023	7.7
Jerome Bledsoe, Massachusetts	1991	1,545	178	0	0	293	2,016	6.7
David Wright, Indiana St.	†1992	1,313	108	0	0	593	2,014	7.9
Mark Stock, VMI	1988	90	1,161	0	260	500	2,011	14.0
Reggie Greene, Siena	†1997	1,778	73	0	0	158	2,009	7.4
Michael Cosey, Southwest Mo. St.	†1996	1,453	555	0	0	0	2,008	5.9
Jamie Jones, Eastern Ill.	1991	1,403	299	0	0	305	2,007	7.2

*Record. †National champion.

ALL-PURPOSE SINGLE-GAME HIGHS

Yds.	Player, Team (Opponent)	Date
467	Joey Stockton, Western Ky. (Austin Peay)	Sept. 16, 1995
463	Michael Lerch, Princeton (Brown)	Oct. 12, 1991
453	Herman Hunter, Tennessee St. (Mississippi Val.)	Nov. 13, 1982
428	Brian Westbrook, Villanova (Pittsburgh)	Sept. 5, 1998
420	Reggie Greene, Siena (St. John's [N.Y.])	Nov. 2, 1996
409	Charles Roberts, Cal St. Sacramento (Idaho St.)	Nov. 6, 1999
401	Eddie Conti, Delaware (Northeastern)	Oct. 3, 1998
401	Eddie Conti, Delaware (Connecticut)	Nov. 7, 1998
395	Scott Oliaro, Cornell (Yale)	Nov. 3, 1990
386	Gill Fenerty, Holy Cross (Columbia)	Oct. 29, 1983
378	Joe Delaney, Northwestern St. (Nicholls St.)	Oct. 28, 1978
373	Aaron Stecker, Western Ill. (Southern Ill.)	Nov. 1, 1997
373	William Arnold, Jackson St. (Texas Southern)	Nov. 6, 1993
372	Gary Harrell, Howard (Morgan St.)	Nov. 3, 1990
372	Treamelle Taylor, Nevada (Montana)	Oct. 14, 1989
370	Ronald Jean, Lehigh (Bucknell)	Nov. 13, 1999
369	Flip Johnson, McNeese St. (La.-Lafayette)	Nov. 15, 1986
367	Chris Darrington, Weber St. (Idaho St.)	Oct. 25, 1986
365	Erwin Matthews, Richmond (Delaware)	Sept. 26, 1987
361	Patrick Robinson, Tennessee St. (Jackson St.)	Sept. 12, 1992
358	Claude Mathis, Southwest Tex. St. (Eastern Wash.)	Sept. 7, 1995
357	Tony Vinson, Towson (Bucknell)	Nov. 13, 1993
353	Bashir Levingston, Eastern Wash. (Cal St. Sacramento)	Oct. 31, 1998
352	Jason Anderson, Eastern Wash. (Montana)	Sept. 17, 1994
352	Andre Garron, New Hampshire (Lehigh)	Oct. 15, 1983
349	Jerry Azumah, New Hampshire (Lehigh)	Oct. 12, 1996
347	Tony Vinson, Towson (Morgan St.)	Nov. 20, 1993
345	Kenny Bynum, South Carolina St. (N.C. A&T)	Nov. 23, 1996
345	Russell Davis, Idaho (Weber St.)	Oct. 2, 1982

ANNUAL CHAMPIONS

Year	Player, Team	Class	Rush	Rcv.	Int.	PR	KOR	Yds.	Yd. PG
1978	Frank Hawkins, Nevada	So.	1,445	211	0	0	0	1,656	165.6
1979	Frank Hawkins, Nevada	Jr.	1,683	123	0	0	0	1,806	164.2
1980	Ken Jenkins, Bucknell	Jr.	1,270	293	0	65	256	1,884	188.4
1981	Garry Pearson, Massachusetts	Jr.	1,026	105	0	0	450	1,581	175.7
1982	Pete Mandley, Northern Ariz.	Jr.	36	1,067	0	344	532	1,979	179.9
1983	Rich Erenberg, Colgate	Sr.	1,883	214	0	126	18	2,241	203.7
1984	Gene Lake, Delaware St.	Jr.	1,722	37	0	0	0	1,759	175.9
1985	Gill Fenerty, Holy Cross	Sr.	1,368	187	0	1	414	1,970	197.0
1986	Kenny Gamble, Colgate	Jr.	1,816	178	0	40	391	2,425	220.5
1987	Dave Meggett, Towson	Jr.	814	572	0	78	327	1,791	199.0
1988	Otis Washington, Western Caro.	Sr.	66	907	0	0	1,113	2,086	189.6
1989	Dominic Corr, Eastern Wash.	Sr.	796	52	0	0	807	1,655	183.9
1990	Barry Bourassa, New Hampshire	So.	957	276	0	133	368	1,734	192.7
1991	Barry Bourassa, New Hampshire	Jr.	1,130	426	0	0	596	2,152	195.6
1992	David Wright, Indiana St.	Fr.	1,313	108	0	0	593	2,014	183.1
1993	Tony Vinson, Towson	Sr.	2,016	57	0	0	0	2,073	207.3
1994	Arnold Mickens, Butler	Jr.	2,255	7	0	0	0	2,262	226.2
1995	Reggie Greene, Siena	So.	1,461	77	0	53	363	1,954	217.1
1996	Reggie Greene, Siena	Jr.	1,719	50	0	0	337	2,106	234.0
1997	Reggie Greene, Siena	Sr.	1,778	73	0	0	158	2,009	223.2
1998	Brian Westbrook, Villanova	So.	1,046	1,144	0	192	644	*3,026	*275.1
1999	Rick Sarille, Wagner	Sr.	1,373	226	0	0	475	2,074	207.4

*Record.

Field Goals

CAREER FIELD GOALS

Player, Team	Years	Total	Pct.	Under 40 Yds.	40 Plus	Long
Marty Zendejas, Nevada (S)	1984-87	*72-90	.800	42-45	30-45	54
Kirk Roach, Western Caro. (S)	1984-87	71-*102	.696	45-49	26-53	57

ALL-TIME LEADERS—FIELD GOALS

Player, Team	Years	Total	Pct.	40 Yds.	Plus	Long
Tony Zendejas, Nevada (S)	1981-83	70-86	*.814	45-49	25-37	58
Scott Shields, Weber St. (S)	1995-98	67-90	.744	48-55	19-35	55
Brian Mitchell, Marshall/Northern Iowa (S)	1987, 89-91	64-81	.790	48-55	16-26	57
Dave Ettinger, Hofstra (S)	1994-97	62-93	.667	37-48	24-45	54
Todd Kurz, Illinois St. (S)	1993-96	59-87	.678	40-53	19-34	51
Jose Larios, McNeese St. (S)	1992-95	57-89	.640	47-57	10-32	47
Steve Christie, William & Mary (S)	1986-89	57-83	.686	39-49	18-34	53
Teddy Garcia, La.-Monroe (S)	1984-87	56-88	.636	35-43	21-45	55
Bjorn Nittmo, Appalachian St. (S)	1985-88	55-74	.743	35-40	20-34	54
Shonz LaFrenz, McNeese St. (S)	1996-99	52-78	.667	44-65	8-13	46
Kelly Potter, Middle Tenn. St. (S)	1981-84	52-78	.667	37-49	15-29	57
Paul McFadden, Youngstown St. (S)	1980-83	52-90	.578	28-42	24-48	54
Mike Black, Boise St. (S)	1988-91	51-75	.680	35-43	16-32	48
Jeff Wilkins, Youngstown St. (S)	1990-93	50-73	.685	33-38	17-35	54
Tim Foley, Ga. Southern (S)	1984-87	50-62	.806	32-37	18-25	**63
Paul Politi, Illinois St. (S)	1983-86	50-78	.641	34-48	16-30	50
Wayne Boyer, Southwest Mo. St. (S)	1993-96	49-71	.690	36-45	13-26	57
Chuck Rawlinson, Stephen F. Austin (S)	1988-91	49-69	.710	34-43	15-26	58
Thayne Doyle, Idaho (S)	1988-91	49-75	.653	35-51	14-24	52
Matt Stover, Louisiana Tech (S)	1986-88	49-68	.721	29-34	20-34	57
Scott Roper, Texas-Arlington/Arkansas St. (S)	1985, 86-87	49-75	.653	35-43	14-32	**63
Paul Hickert, Murray St. (S)	1984-87	49-79	.620	34-48	15-31	62
Dewey Klein, Marshall (S)	1988-91	48-66	.727	37-47	11-19	54
John Dowling, Youngstown St. (S)	1984-87	48-76	.632	36-44	12-32	49
Brian Shallcross, William & Mary (S)	1994-97	47-73	.644	41-54	6-19	49
Kirk Duce, Montana (S)	1988-91	47-78	.603	37-51	10-27	51
Billy Hayes, Sam Houston St. (S)	1985-88	47-71	.662	37-55	10-16	54
Steve Largent, Eastern Ill. (S)	1992-95	46-73	.630	30-38	16-35	53
Roger Ruzek, Weber St. (S)	1979-82	46-78	.590	28-37	18-41	51

*Record. **Record tied. (S)Soccer-style kicker.

SEASON FIELD GOALS

Player, Team	Year	Total	Pct.	Under 40 Yds.	40 Plus	Long
Tony Zendejas, Nevada (S)	†1982	**26-**33	.788	18-20	8-13	52
Brian Mitchell, Northern Iowa (S)	†1990	**26-27	*.963	23-23	3-4	45
Wayne Boyer, Southwest Mo. St. (S)	†1996	25-30	.833	16-18	9-12	57
George Benyola, Louisiana Tech (S)	†1985	24-31	.774	15-18	9-13	53
Kirk Roach, Western Caro. (S)	1986	24-28	.857	17-17	7-11	52
Tony Zendejas, Nevada (S)	†1983	23-29	.793	14-15	9-14	58
Goran Lingmerth, Northern Ariz. (S)	1986	23-29	.793	16-19	7-10	55
Marty Zendejas, Nevada (S)	†1984	22-27	.815	12-13	10-14	52
Mike Dodd, Boise St. (S)	†1992	22-31	.710	16-21	6-10	50
Jose Larios, McNeese St. (S)	†1993	22-28	.786	19-21	3-7	47
David Ettinger, Hofstra (S)	†1995	22-**33	.667	17-22	5-11	54
Rob Hart, Murray St. (S)	1996	22-27	.815	18-20	4-7	52
Tony Zendejas, Nevada (S)	†1981	21-24	.875	13-14	8-10	55
Scott Roper, Arkansas St. (S)	1986	21-28	.750	15-17	6-11	50
Matt Stover, Louisiana Tech (S)	1986	21-25	.840	15-15	6-10	53
Kevin McKelvie, Nevada (S)	1990	21-24	.875	16-17	5-7	52
Travis Brawner, Southwest Mo. St. (S)	†1997	21-28	.750	15-17	6-11	52
Teddy Garcia, La.-Monroe (S)	1987	20-28	.714	10-11	10-17	55
Steve Christie, William & Mary (S)	†1989	20-29	.690	16-17	4-12	53
Darren Goodman, Idaho St. (S)	1990	20-28	.714	12-14	8-14	53

*Record. **Record tied. †National champion. (S) Soccer-style kicker.

ANNUAL CHAMPIONS
(Ranked on Per-Game Average)

Year	Player, Team	Total	PG	Pct.
1978	Tom Sarette, Boise St. (S)	12-20	1.2	.600
1979	Wilfredo Rosales, Alcorn St. (S)	13-20	1.3	.650
	Sandro Vitiello, Massachusetts (S)	13-22	1.3	.591
1980	Scott Norwood, James Madison (S)	15-21	1.5	.714
1981	Tony Zendejas, Nevada (S)	21-24	1.9	.875
1982	Tony Zendejas, Nevada (S)	**26-**33	**2.4	.788
1983	Tony Zendejas, Nevada (S)	23-29	2.1	.793
1984	Marty Zendejas, Nevada (S)	22-27	2.0	.815
1985	George Benyola, Louisiana Tech (S)	24-31	2.2	.774
1986	Kirk Roach, Western Caro. (S)	24-28	2.2	.857
1987	Micky Penaflor, Northern Ariz. (S)	19-27	1.9	.704
1988	Chris Lutz, Princeton (S)	19-24	1.9	.792
1989	Steve Christie, William & Mary (S)	20-29	1.8	.690
1990	Brian Mitchell, Northern Iowa (S)	**26-27	**2.4	*.963
1991	Brian Mitchell, Northern Iowa (S)	19-24	1.7	.792
1992	Mike Dodd, Boise St. (S)	22-31	2.0	.710
1993	Jose Larios, McNeese St. (S)	22-28	2.0	.786
1994	Andy Glockner, Pennsylvania (S)	14-20	1.6	.700
1995	David Ettinger, Hofstra (S)	22-**33	2.0	.667
1996	Wayne Boyer, Southwest Mo. St. (S)	25-30	2.3	.833
1997	Travis Brawner, Southwest Mo. St. (S)	21-28	1.9	.750
1998	Mike Goldstein, Northern Ariz. (S)	16-23	1.5	.696
	Scott Shields, Weber St. (S)	16-23	1.5	.696
	Bill Gramatica, South Fla. (S)	16-24	1.5	.667
	Chad Johnson, Hofstra (S)	16-27	1.5	.593

Year	Player, Team	Total	PG	Pct.
	Joe Lopez, Western Ill. (S)	16-28	1.5	.571
1999	Brett Sterba, William & Mary (S)	18-23	1.6	.783

*Record. **Record tied. (S) Soccer-style kicker.

All-Time Longest Plays

Since 1941, official maximum length of all plays fixed at 100 yards.

RUSHING

Yds.	Player, Team (Opponent)	Year
99	Jermaine Creighton, St. John's (N. Y.) (Siena)	1996
99	Jim Varick, Monmouth (Sacred Heart)	1994
99	Phillip Collins, Southwest Mo. St. (Western Ill.)	1989
99	Pedro Bacon, Western Ky. (West Ala.)	1986
99	Hubert Owens, Mississippi Val. (Ark.-Pine Bluff)	1980
98	Jon Underhill, Jacksonville (Greensboro)	1998
98	Johnny Gordon, Nevada (Montana St.)	1984
97	Pat Williams, Delaware (West Chester)	1995
97	Norman Bradford, Grambling (Prairie View)	1992
97	David Clark, Dartmouth (Harvard)	1989
97	David Clark, Dartmouth (Princeton)	1988
96	Jerry Azumah, New Hampshire (Connecticut)	1996
96	Jim Pizano, Massachusetts (Rhode Island)	1996
96	Kelvin Anderson, Southeast Mo. St. (Murray St.)	1992
96	Andre Lockhart, Chattanooga (East Tenn. St.)	1986
95	Corey Hill, Colgate (Brown)	1996

DIVISION I-AA

ALL-TIME LEADERS—ALL-TIME LONGEST PLAYS

Yds.	Player, Team (Opponent)	Year
95	Brett Chappell, Western Caro. (Elon)	1995
95	Tim Hall, Robert Morris (Gannon)	1994
95	Jeff Sawulski, Siena (Iona)	1993
95	Jerry Ellison, Chattanooga (Boise St.)	1992
95	John McNiff, Cornell (Columbia)	1990
95	Joe Sparksman, James Madison (William & Mary)	1990
94	Kenny Bynum, South Carolina St. (Delaware St.)	1996
94	Mark Vigil, Idaho (Simon Fraser)	1980

PASSING

Yds.	Passer-Receiver, Team (Opponent)	Year
99	Jimmy Blanchard-Terry Charles, Portland St. (Eastern Wash.)	1999
99	Michael Moore-Otis Covington, Morgan St. (Florida A&M)	1995
99	Todd Bennett-Jason Anderson, Eastern Wash. (Montana)	1994
99	Aaron Garcia-Greg Ochoa, Cal St. Sacramento (Cal Poly)	1993
99	Todd Donnan-Troy Brown, Marshall (East Tenn. St.)	1991
99	Antoine Ezell-Tyrone Davis, Florida A&M (Bethune-Cookman)	1991
99	Jay Johnson-Kenny Shedd, Northern Iowa (Oklahoma St.)	1990
99	John Bonds-Hendricks Johnson, Northern Ariz. (Boise St.)	1990
99	Scott Stoker-Victor Robinson, Northwestern St. (La.-Monroe)	1989
98	Ben Anderson-Courtney Freeman, Liberty (Charleston So.)	1996
98	Derek Jensen-Jason Cannon, Southwest Mo. St. (Eastern Ill.)	1995
98	Jonathan Quinn-Dee Mostiller, Middle Tenn. St. (Tennessee Tech)	1995
98	Antoine Ezell-Tim Daniel, Florida A&M (Delaware St.)	1991
98	John Friesz-Lee Allen, Idaho (Northern Ariz.)	1989
98	Fred Gatlin-Treamelle Taylor, Nevada (Montana)	1989
98	Steve Monaco-Emerson Foster, Rhode Island (Holy Cross)	1988
98	Frank Baur-Maurice Caldwell, Lafayette (Columbia)	1988
98	David Gabianelli-Craig Morton, Dartmouth (Columbia)	1986
98	Joe Pizzo-Bryan Calder, Nevada (Eastern Wash.)	1984
98	Bobby Hebert-Randy Liles, Northwestern St. (Southeastern La.)	1980
97	Brad Smith-Sullivan Beard, Nicholls St. (Jacksonville St.)	1999
97	Peyton Jones-Mikhael Ricks, Stephen F. Austin (Troy St.)	1997
97	Lester Anderson-Kevin Glenn, Illinois St. (Ball St.)	1993
97	Nate Harrison-Brian Thomas, Southern U. (Dist. Columbia)	1989
97	Jerome Baker-John Taylor, Delaware St. (St. Paul's)	1985
97	John McKenzie-Chris Burkett, Jackson St. (Mississippi Val.)	1983
96	Chris Berg-Dedric Ward, Northern Iowa (Western Ill.)	1995
96	Damon Williams-Ryan Blakely, Alabama St. (Texas Southern)	1994
96	Greg Wyatt-Shawn Collins, Northern Ariz. (Montana St.)	1988
96	Rick Fahnestock-Albert Brown, Western Ill. (Northern Iowa)	1986
96	Jeff Cesarone-Keith Paskett, Western Ky. (Akron)	1985
96	Mike Williams-Trumaine Johnson, Grambling (Jackson St.)	1980

INTERCEPTION RETURNS

Yds.	Player, Team (Opponent)	Year
100	Tehran Hunter, Massachusetts (Buffalo)	1997
100	Derek Grier, Marshall (East Tenn. St.)	1991
100	Ricky Fields, Samford (Concord [W.Va.])	1990
100	Warren Smith, Stephen F. Austin (Nicholls St.)	1990
100	Rob Pouliot, Montana St. (Boise St.)	1988
100	Rick Harris, East Tenn. St. (Davidson)	1986
100	Bruce Alexander, Stephen F. Austin (Lamar)	1986
100	Guy Carbone, Rhode Island (Lafayette)	1985
100	Moses Aimable, Northern Iowa (Western Ill.)	1985
100	Kervin Fontenette, Southeastern La. (Nicholls St.)	1985
100	Jim Anderson, Princeton (Cornell)	1984
100	Keiron Bigby, Brown (Yale)	1984
100	Vencie Glenn, Indiana St. (Wayne St. [Mich.])	1984

Yds.	Player, Team (Opponent)	Year
100	George Floyd, Eastern Ky. (Youngstown St.)	1980

PUNT RETURNS

Yds.	Player, Team (Opponent)	Year
98	Willie Ware, Mississippi Val. (Bishop)	1985
98	Barney Bussey, South Carolina St. (Johnson Smith)	1981
96	Carl Williams, Texas Southern (Grambling)	1981
95	Clarence Weathers, Delaware St. (Salisbury St.)	1980
94	Drew Haddad, Buffalo (Cornell)	1998
94	Brad Friedman, Towson (St. Francis [Pa.])	1996
93	Andrew McFadden, Liberty (Delaware St.)	1995
93	Patrick Plott, Jacksonville St. (Southwest Mo. St.)	1995
93	Joe Fuller, Northern Iowa (Wis.-Whitewater)	1984

KICKOFF RETURNS

Forty-four players have returned kickoffs 100 yards. The most recent:

Yds.	Player, Team (Opponent)	Year
100	Joey Hamilton, Jacksonville St. (Samford)	1999
100	Lamont Brightful, Eastern Wash. (Central Wash.)	1999
100	Corey Joyner, Ga. Southern (East Tenn. St.)	1998
100	Darriel Ruffin, Tenn.-Martin (Murray St.)	1997
100	Clemente Sainten, Weber St. (Western St.)	1996
100	Robert Davis, Fordham (Brown)	1996
100	Joey Stockton, Western Ky. (Southern Ill.)	1996
100	Goree White, Alcorn St. (Ark.-Pine Bluff)	1995
100	Joe Rosato, Duquesne (Robert Morris)	1995
100	Chris Watson, Eastern Ill. (Northern Iowa)	1995
100	Todd Cleveland, UCF (Bethune-Cookman)	1994
100	Montrel Williams, Idaho (Eastern Wash.)	1994
100	Len Raney, Northern Ariz. (Idaho St.)	1994
100	Jason Anderson, Eastern Wash. (Cal Poly)	1994

PUNTS

Yds.	Player, Team (Opponent)	Year
91	Bart Helsley, North Texas (La.-Monroe)	1990
89	Jim Carriere, Connecticut (Maine)	1987
88	Jeff Kaiser, Idaho St. (UTEP)	1983
87	John Starnes, North Texas (Texas-Arlington)	1983
86	Andy Dorsey, Tennessee Tech (Eastern Ill.)	1998
85	Ken Hinsley, Western Caro. (Chattanooga)	1998
85	Don Alonzo, Nicholls St. (Northwestern St.)	1980
84	Billy Smith, Chattanooga (Appalachian St.)	1988
83	Jason Harkins, Appalachian St. (Citadel)	1986
82	Scott White, Delaware (Maine)	1996
82	Scott Shields, Weber St. (Cal St. Northridge)	1996
82	Tim Healy, Delaware (Boston U.)	1987
82	John Howell, Chattanooga (Vanderbilt)	1982

FIELD GOALS

Yds.	Player, Team (Opponent)	Year
63	Scott Roper, Arkansas St. (North Texas)	1987
63	Tim Foley, Ga. Southern (James Madison)	1987
62	Paul Hickert, Murray St. (Eastern Ky.)	1986
60	Pete Garces, Idaho St. (Cal St. Northridge)	1998
60	David Cool, Ga. Southern (James Madison)	1988
60	Terry Belden, Northern Ariz. (Cal St. Northridge)	1993
58	Rich Emke, Eastern Ill. (Northern Iowa)	1986
58	Tony Zendejas, Nevada (Boise St.)	1983

Team Champions

Annual Offense Champions

TOTAL OFFENSE

Year	Team	Avg.
1978	Portland St.	477.4
1979	Portland St.	460.7
1980	Portland St.	504.3
1981	Idaho	438.8
1982	Drake	444.8
1983	Idaho	479.5
1984	Mississippi Val.	*640.1
1985	Weber St.	516.1
1986	Nevada	492.0
1987	Holy Cross	552.2
1988	Lehigh	485.6
1989	Idaho	495.9
1990	William & Mary	498.7
1991	Weber St.	581.4
1992	Alcorn St.	502.9
1993	Idaho	532.0
1994	Alcorn St.	597.9
1995	Montana	512.5
1996	Northern Ariz.	522.8
1997	Eastern Wash.	505.6
1998	Florida A&M	535.7
1999	Ga. Southern	551.7

*Record.

RUSHING OFFENSE

Year	Team	Avg.
1978	Jackson St.	314.5
1979	Jackson St.	288.4
1980	N.C. A&T	322.1
1981	Idaho	266.3
1982	Delaware	258.4
1983	Furman	287.1
1984	Delaware St.	377.3
1985	Southwest Mo. St.	298.7
1986	Northeastern	336.0
1987	Howard	381.6
1988	Eastern Ky.	303.0
1989	Ga. Southern	329.2
1990	Delaware St.	298.7
1991	VMI	316.9
1992	Citadel	345.5
1993	Western Ky.	300.1
1994	Citadel	382.0
1995	Massachusetts	302.5
1996	Southern Utah	330.8
1997	Western Ky.	366.0
1998	Southern Utah	386.0
1999	Ga. Southern	*419.0

*Record.

TEAM CHAMPIONS—ANNUAL OFFENSE CHAMPIONS

PASSING OFFENSE

Year	Team	Avg.
1978	Portland St.	367.1
1979	Portland St.	368.9
1980	Portland St.	434.9
1981	Idaho St.	325.7
1982	West Tex. A&M	313.7
1983	Idaho	336.1
1984	Mississippi Val.	*496.8
1985	Rhode Island	384.3
1986	Eastern Ill.	326.1
1987	Holy Cross	358.4
1988	Lehigh	330.1
1989	Idaho	374.3
1990	Weber St.	342.2
1991	Weber St.	389.1
1992	Alcorn St.	360.5
1993	Montana	359.0
1994	Alcorn St.	442.3
1995	Montana	408.2
1996	Montana	339.6
1997	Cal. St. Northridge	358.1
1998	Florida A&M	400.6
1999	Towson	381.2

*Record.

SCORING OFFENSE

Year	Team	Avg.
1978	Nevada	35.6
1979	Portland St.	34.3
1980	Portland St.	49.2
1981	Delaware	34.1
1982	Delaware	34.1
1983	Mississippi Val.	39.2
1984	Mississippi Val.	*60.9
1985	Mississippi Val.	41.5
1986	Nevada	39.4
1987	Holy Cross	46.5
1988	Lafayette	38.2
1989	Grambling	37.1
1990	Jackson St.	38.0
1991	Nevada	45.1
1992	Marshall	42.4
1993	Idaho	47.5
1994	Alcorn St.	45.7
1995	Montana	42.5
1996	Northern Ariz.	43.2
1997	Morehead St.	41.9
1998	Florida A&M	49.6
1999	Ga. Southern	50.0

*Record.

Annual Defense Champions

TOTAL DEFENSE

Year	Team	Avg.
1978	Florida A&M	*149.9
1979	Alcorn St.	166.3
1980	Massachusetts	193.5
1981	South Carolina St.	204.0
1982	South Carolina St.	191.4
1983	Grambling	206.0
1984	Tennessee St.	187.0
1985	Arkansas St.	258.8
1986	Tennessee St.	178.5
1987	Southern U.	202.8
1988	Alcorn St.	215.4
1989	Howard	220.0
1990	Middle Tenn. St.	244.8
1991	South Carolina St.	208.9
1992	South Carolina St.	250.9
1993	McNeese St.	249.5
1994	Pennsylvania	218.9
1995	Georgetown	216.4
1996	Georgetown	218.2
1997	Marist	213.6
1998	Fairfield	213.8
1999	St. John's (N.Y.)	199.7

*Record.

RUSHING DEFENSE

Year	Team	Avg.
1978	Florida A&M	48.6
1979	Alcorn St.	56.7
1980	South Carolina St.	61.8
1981	South Carolina St.	60.8
1982	South Carolina St.	59.4
1983	Jackson St.	79.2
1984	Grambling	44.5
1985	Jackson St.	63.0
1986	Eastern Ky.	62.8
1987	Southern U.	64.5
1988	Stephen F. Austin	83.5
1989	Montana	70.2
1990	Delaware St.	77.2
1991	Boise St.	84.4
1992	Villanova	77.8
1993	Wagner	87.0
1994	Idaho	65.3
1995	McNeese St.	60.9
1996	Georgetown	53.2
1997	Marist	*40.4
1998	Fairfield	61.7
1999	Jackson St.	67.8

*Record.

PASSING DEFENSE

Year	Team	$Avg.
1978	Southern U.	85.6
1979	Mississippi Val.	64.2
1980	Howard	93.8
1981	Bethune-Cookman	*59.9
1982	Northeastern	98.8
1983	Louisiana Tech	111.4
1984	Louisiana Tech	105.5
1985	Dartmouth	110.3
1986	Bethune-Cookman	99.8
1987	Alcorn St.	101.3
1988	Middle Tenn. St.	90.8
1989	Chattanooga	104.4
1990	Middle Tenn. St.	78.83
1991	South Carolina St.	70.01
1992	Middle Tenn. St.	76.93
1993	Georgetown	76.92
1994	Pennsylvania	*63.15
1995	Canisius	69.13
1996	Canisius	71.99
1997	McNeese St.	79.05
1998	Davidson	74.64
1999	Robert Morris	80.80

*Record. $Beginning in 1990, ranked on passing-efficiency defense rating points instead of per-game yardage allowed.

SCORING DEFENSE

Year	Team	Avg.
1978	South Carolina St.	*6.5
1979	Lehigh	7.2
1980	Murray St.	9.1
1981	Jackson St.	9.4
1982	Western Mich.	7.1
1983	Grambling	8.6
1984	Northwestern St.	9.0
1985	Appalachian St.	9.9
1986	Tennessee St.	8.3
1987	Holy Cross	10.0
1988	Furman	9.7
1989	Howard	10.5
1990	Middle Tenn. St.	9.2
1991	Villanova	12.0
1992	Citadel	13.0
1993	Marshall	11.2
1994	Pennsylvania	7.6
1995	McNeese St.	8.9
1996	Duquesne	10.1
1997	McNeese St.	10.5
1998	Western Ill.	9.4
1999	St. John's (N.Y.)	12.9

*Record.

DIVISION I-AA

Toughest-Schedule Annual Leaders

The Division I-AA toughest-schedule program, which began in 1982, is based on what all Division I-AA opponents did against other Division I-AA and Division I-A teams when *not* playing the team in question. Games against non-I-AA and I-A teams are deleted. (Playoff or postseason games are not included.) The top two leaders by year:

Year	Team (Record†)	¢Opponents' Record W	L	T	Pct.
1982	Massachusetts (5-6-0)	50	30	1	.623
	Lehigh (4-6-0)	44	31	0	.587
1983	Florida A&M (7-4-0)	42	23	3	.640
	Grambling (8-1-2)	49	31	0	.613
1984	North Texas (2-9-0)	55	35	2	.609
	VMI (1-9-0)	53	37	2	.587
1985	South Carolina St. (5-6-0)	43	20	1	.680
	Lehigh (5-6-0)	47	33	1	.586
1986	James Madison (5-5-1)	46	28	1	.620
	Bucknell (3-7-0)	43	27	0	.614
1987	Ga. Southern (8-3-0)	47	31	0	.603
	Northeastern (6-5-0)	50	37	0	.575

Year	Team (Record†)	¢Opponents' Record W	L	T	Pct.
1988	Northwestern St. (9-2-0)	54	36	2	.598
	Ga. Southern (9-2-0)	43	31	1	.580
1989	Liberty (7-3-0)	39	22	2	.635
	Western Caro. (3-7-1)	46	34	2	.573
1990	Ga. Southern (8-3-0)	53	25	1	.677
	Western Ky. (2-8-0)	55	36	1	.603
1991	Bucknell (1-9-0)	53	29	1	.645
	William & Mary (5-6-0)	62	43	0	.590
1992	VMI (3-8-0)	46	36	0	.561
	Harvard (3-7-0)	51	40	0	.560
1993	Samford (5-6-0)	55	26	0	.679
	Delaware St. (6-5-0)	44	30	0	.595
1994	Montana (9-2-0)	46	30	1	.604
	McNeese St. (9-2-0)	44	29	5	.596
1995	Western Ky. (2-8-0)	59	32	0	.648
	Nicholls St. (0-11-0)	61	38	0	.616
1996	Indiana (6-5)	50	32	0	.610
	Towson (6-4)	42	29	0	.592
1997	Lehigh (4-7)	65	39	0	.625
	William & Mary (7-4)	65	42	0	.607
1998	Connecticut (9-2)	66	41	0	.617
	New Hampshire (4-7)	54	40	0	.596

Year	Team (Record†)	¢Opponents' Record W	L	T	Pct.
1999	Elon (9-2)	50	26	0	.658
	Cal Poly (3-8)	52	32	0	.619

†Not including playoff or postseason games. ¢When not playing the team listed.

Top 10 Toughest-Schedule Leaders for 1995-99†

1995

Team	¢Opp. Record	Pct.
1. Western Ky.	59-32-0	.648
2. Nicholls St.	61-38-0	.616
3. William & Mary	65-43-1	.601
4. Northwestern St.	48-33-0	.593
5. UCF	55-38-0	.591
6. East Tenn. St.	62-43-1	.590
7. Western Ill.	52-38-0	.578
8. Columbia	49-37-2	.568
9. Rhode Island	60-46-0	.566
10. VMI	58-46-1	.557

TOUGHEST-SCHEDULE ANNUAL LEADERS—TOP 10 TOUGHEST-SCHEDULE LEADERS FOR 1995-99

1996

Team	¢Opp. Record	Pct.
1. Indiana St.	50-32	.610
2. Towson	42-29	.592
3. McNeese St.	47-33	.587
4. Fordham	56-40	.583
5. Alcorn St.	47-34	.580
6. Rhode Island	50-38	.568
7. Jacksonville St.	47-37	.560
8. Sam Houston St.	45-36	.556
9. Yale	51-41	.554
10. Marshall	52-42	.553

1997

Team	¢Opp. Record	Pct.
1. Lehigh	65-39	.625
2. William & Mary	65-42	.607
3. Dayton	32-21	.604
4. Florida A&M	59-39	.589
5. Yale	52-37	.584
6. Howard	45-33	.577
7. Tennessee St.	60-45	.571
8. New Hampshire	60-46	.566
9. Holy Cross	57-46	.553
10. Northern Iowa	48-39	.552

1998

Team	¢Opp. Record	Pct.
1. Connecticut	66-41	.617
2. New Hampshire	59-40	.596
3. Fordham	63-44	.589
4. Rhode Island	62-45	.579
5. Massachusetts	61-45	.575
6. Delaware	55-41	.573
7. Florida A&M	56-42	.571
8. Wofford	59-45	.567
9. Holy Cross	60-47	.561
10. Citadel	58-46	.558

1999

Team	¢Opp. Record	Pct.
1. Elon	50-26	.658
2. Cal Poly	52-32	.619
3. Dartmouth	57-36	.613
Columbia	57-36	.613
5. Holy Cross	63-41	.606
6. Jackson St.	60-40	.600
7. Florida A&M	60-41	.594
8. South Fla.	55-39	.585
9. Alabama St.	52-37	.584
10. James Madison	62-45	.579

†Not including playoff or postseason games. ¢When not playing the team listed.

Annual Most-Improved Teams

Year	Team	$Games Improved	From		To		Coach
1978	Western Ky.	6½	1977	1-8-1	1978	8-2-0	Jimmy Feix
1979	Murray St.	5	1978	4-7-0	1979	*9-2-1	Mike Gottfried
1980	Idaho St.	6	1979	0-11-0	1980	6-5-0	#Dave Kragthorpe
1981	Lafayette	5½	1980	3-7-0	1981	9-2-0	#Bill Russo
1982	Pennsylvania	6	1981	1-9-0	1982	7-3-0	Jerry Berndt
1983	North Texas	5½	1982	2-9-0	1983	*8-4-0	Corky Nelson
	Southern Ill.	5½	1982	6-5-0	1983	*13-1-0	Rey Dempsey
1984	Montana St.	9½	1983	1-10-0	1984	*12-2-0	Dave Arnold
1985	Appalachian St.	4	1984	4-7-0	1985	8-3-0	Sparky Woods
	Massachusetts	4	1984	3-8-0	1985	7-4-0	Bob Stull
	West Tex. A&M	4	1984	3-8-0	1985	6-3-1	#Bill Kelly
1986	Morehead St.	6	1985	1-10-0	1986	7-4-0	Bill Baldridge
1987	Weber St.	6	1986	3-8-0	1987	*10-3-0	Mike Price
1988	Stephen F. Austin	5½	1987	3-7-1	1988	*10-3-0	Jim Hess
1989	Yale	4½	1988	3-6-1	1989	8-2-0	Carmen Cozza
1990	Nevada	4	1989	7-4-0	1990	*13-2-0	Chris Ault
	N.C. A&T	4	1989	5-6-0	1990	9-2-0	Bill Hayes
1991	Alcorn St.	5	1990	2-7-0	1991	7-2-1	#Cardell Jones
	Austin Peay	5	1990	0-11-0	1991	5-6-0	#Roy Gregory
	Princeton	5	1990	3-7-0	1991	8-2-0	Steve Tosches
	Southern Ill.	5	1990	2-9-0	1991	7-4-0	Bob Smith
1992	Howard	5	1991	2-9-0	1992	7-4-0	Steve Wilson
	Pennsylvania	5	1991	2-8-0	1992	7-3-0	#Al Bagnoli
	Richmond	5	1991	2-9-0	1992	7-4-0	Jim Marshall
	Tennessee Tech	5	1991	2-9-0	1992	7-4-0	Jim Ragland
	Western Caro.	5	1991	2-9-0	1992	7-4-0	Steve Hodgin
1993	Boston U.	8	1992	3-8-0	1993	*12-1-0	Dan Allen
1994	Boise St.	8	1993	3-8-0	1994	*13-2-0	Pokey Allen
1995	Murray St.	5½	1994	5-6-0	1995	*11-1-0	Houston Nutt
1996	Nicholls St.	7½	1995	0-11	1996	*8-4	Darren Barbier
1997	McNeese St.	8	1996	3-8	1997	*13-2	Bobby Keasler
1998	Massachusetts	8	1997	2-9	1998	*12-3	#Mark Whipple
1999	Stephen F. Austin	5	1998	3-8	1999	8-3	#Mike Santiago

$To determine games improved, add the difference in victories between the two seasons to the difference in losses, then divide by two; ties not counted. *I-AA playoff included. #First year as head coach at that college.

ALL-TIME MOST-IMPROVED TEAMS

Games	Team (Year)
9½	Montana St. (1984)
8	Massachusetts (1998)
8	McNeese St. (1997)
8	Boise St. (1994)
8	Boston U. (1993)
7½	Nicholls St. (1996)
7	Lehigh (1998)
6½	Western Ky. (1978)
6	Jacksonville St. (1998)
6	Colgate (1996)
6	Weber St. (1987)
6	Morehead St. (1986)
6	Pennsylvania (1982)
6	Idaho St. (1980)
5½	Davidson (1998)
5½	Illinois St. (1998)
5½	Fairfield (1997)
5½	Murray St. (1995)
5½	Southern U. (1993)
5½	Stephen F. Austin (1988)
5½	East Tenn. St. (1986)
5½	Holy Cross (1986)
5½	Yale (1984)
5½	North Texas (1983)
5½	Southern Ill. (1983)
5½	Lafayette (1981)

1999 MOST-IMPROVED TEAMS
(Includes Playoff Games)

College (Coach)	1999	1998	$Games Improved
Stephen F. Austin (Mike Santiago)	8-3	3-8	5
James Madison (Mickey Matthews)	8-4	3-8	4½
Elon (Al Seagraves)	9-2	5-6	4
Valparaiso (Tom Horne)	9-2	5-6	4
Youngstown St. (Jim Tressel)	12-3	6-5	4
Robert Morris (Joe Walton)	8-2	4-6	4
Delaware St. (John McKenzie)	4-7	0-11	4
Furman (Bobby Johnson)	9-3	5-6	3½

$To determine games improved, add the difference in victories between the two seasons to the difference in losses, then divide by two, ties not counted.

All-Time Team Won-Lost Records

PERCENTAGE (TOP 25)

Includes records as senior college only. Bowl and playoff games are included, and each tie game is computed as half won and half lost. Note: Tiebreaker rule began with 1996 season.

Team	Yrs.	Won	Lost	Tied	Pct.	Total Games
Yale	127	799	298	55	.717	1152
Florida A&M	67	474	188	18	.710	680
Tennessee St.	72	458	184	30	@.704	672
Grambling	57	420	175	15	.701	610
Robert Morris	6	42	18	1	.697	61
Princeton	130	737	317	50	.690	1104
Harvard	125	729	354	50	.665	1133
Jackson St.	54	355	187	13	.651	555
Ga. Southern	31	219	122	7	.639	348
Southern U.	78	469	265	25	.634	759
Dartmouth	118	624	350	46	.634	1020
Fairfield	4	26	15	0	.634	41
Fordham	101	686	387	53	.633	1126
Eastern Ky.	76	464	265	27	.632	756
Pennsylvania	123	734	428	42	.627	1204
Hofstra	59	347	208	11	.623	566
Dayton	92	525	319	26	.618	870
Albany (N.Y.)	27	165	102	0	.618	267
South Carolina St.	72	398	241	27	.618	666
Appalachian St.	70	438	267	29	.616	734
McNeese St.	49	318	197	14	.614	529
South Fla.	3	20	13	0	.606	33
Youngstown St.	59	352	232	17	.600	601
Delaware	108	559	366	43	.600	968
Georgetown	88	433	284	31	.600	748

@Tennessee State's participation in the 1981 and 1982 Division I-AA championships (1-2 record) voided.

ALPHABETICAL LISTING

Team	Yrs.	Won	Lost	Tied	Pct.+	Total Games
Alabama A&M	62	287	261	26	.523	574
Alabama St.	94	380	375	43	.503	798
Albany (N.Y.)	27	165	102	0	.618	267
Alcorn St.	76	372	256	39	.587	667
Appalachian St.	70	438	267	29	.616	734
Ark.-Pine Bluff	68	292	324	42	.476	658
Austin Peay	63	231	386	16	.378	633
Bethune-Cookman	61	324	231	22	.581	577
Brown	114	515	496	40	.509	1051
Bucknell	114	517	468	51	.524	1036
Butler	110	500	348	35	.586	883
Cal Poly	59	315	248	9	.559	572
Cal St. Northridge	38	175	216	4	.448	395
Cal St. Sacramento	46	203	255	8	.444	466
Canisius	54	225	206	24	.521	455
Central Conn. St.	61	227	271	22	.458	520
Charleston So.	9	19	73	0	.207	92
Chattanooga	92	443	409	33	.519	885
Citadel	92	414	440	32	.485	886
Colgate	109	514	408	50	.555	972
Columbia	109	339	537	43	.392	919
Connecticut	101	410	439	38	.484	887
Cornell	112	580	405	34	.586	1019
Dartmouth	118	624	350	46	.634	1020
Davidson	102	357	498	45	.422	900
Dayton	92	525	319	26	.618	870
Delaware	108	559	366	43	.600	968
Delaware St.	54	235	276	8	.461	519
Drake	106	489	438	29	.527	956
Duquesne	52	238	213	18	.527	469
East Tenn. St.	76	321	373	27	.464	721
Eastern Ill.	99	396	428	44	.482	868
Eastern Ky.	76	464	265	27	.632	756
Eastern Wash.	89	392	328	23	.543	743
Elon	78	420	322	18	.564	760
Fairfield	4	26	15	0	.634	41
Florida A&M	67	474	188	18	.710	680
Fordham	101	686	387	53	.633	1126
Furman	86	473	367	37	.560	877
Georgetown	88	433	284	31	.600	748
Ga. Southern	31	219	122	7	.639	348
Grambling	57	420	175	15	.701	610
Hampton	98	447	336	34	.568	817
Harvard	125	729	354	50	.665	1133
Hofstra	59	347	208	11	.623	566
Holy Cross	104	537	411	55	.563	1003
Howard	103	428	336	42	.557	806
Idaho St.	95	402	377	20	.516	799
Illinois St.	100	385	444	65	.467	894
Indiana St.	83	323	368	20	.468	711
Iona	22	90	124	3	.422	217
Jackson St.	54	355	187	13	.651	555
Jacksonville	3	7	11	0	.389	18
Jacksonville St.	67	350	261	27	.570	638
James Madison	27	161	131	3	.551	295
La Salle	3	7	20	0	.259	27
Lafayette	118	588	490	39	.544	1117
Lehigh	116	553	524	45	.513	1122
Liberty	27	137	136	4	.502	277
Maine	108	422	404	38	.510	864
Marist	22	92	110	3	.456	205
Massachusetts	117	468	473	51	.497	992
McNeese St.	49	318	197	14	.614	529
Mississippi Val.	47	190	247	11	.436	448
Monmouth	6	33	25	0	.569	58
Montana	100	411	439	26	.484	876
Montana St.	96	376	392	34	.490	802
Morehead St.	70	250	368	22	.408	640
Morgan St.	79	366	300	30	.547	696
Murray St.	75	399	308	34	.561	741
New Hampshire	103	435	379	54	.532	868
Nicholls St.	28	132	174	4	.432	310
Norfolk St.	39	189	184	7	.507	380
N.C. A&T	76	385	302	39	.557	726
Northeastern	64	242	298	17	.450	557
Northern Ariz.	75	335	335	22	.500	692
Northern Iowa	101	513	340	47	.596	900
Northwestern St.	91	435	349	33	.553	817
Pennsylvania	123	734	428	42	.627	1204
Portland St.	48	247	244	7	.503	498
Prairie View	73	330	367	31	.475	728
Princeton	130	737	317	50	.690	1104
Rhode Island	99	336	456	41	.428	833
Richmond	116	418	549	53	.436	1020
Robert Morris	6	42	18	1	.697	61
Sacred Heart	9	23	64	0	.264	87
St. Francis (Pa.)	51	152	251	13	.381	416
St. John's (N.Y.)	31	168	120	7	.581	295
St. Mary's (Cal.)	71	348	258	20	.572	626
St. Peter's	28	54	174	1	.238	229
Sam Houston St.	83	341	344	47	.498	732
Samford	84	383	377	34	.504	794
San Diego	32	148	149	8	.498	305
Siena	12	27	83	0	.245	110
South Carolina St.	72	398	241	27	.618	666
South Fla.	3	20	13	0	.606	33
Southeast Mo. St.	87	368	379	37	.493	784
Southern Ill.	84	330	421	33	.442	784
Southern U.	78	469	265	25	.634	759
Southern Utah	37	181	178	6	.504	365
Southwest Mo. St.	88	391	377	40	.509	808
Southwest Tex. St.	85	418	331	27	.556	776
Stephen F. Austin%	73	303	399	30	.434	732
Stony Brook	17	78	80	2	.494	160
Tenn.-Martin	43	181	259	5	.412	445
Tennessee St.@	72	458	184	30	.704	672
Tennessee Tech	78	334	390	31	.463	755
Texas Southern	54	259	276	27	.485	562
Towson	31	176	139	4	.558	319
Troy St.	69	372	282	15	.567	669
Valparaiso	79	321	358	24	.474	703
Villanova	102	484	397	41	.547	922
VMI	109	428	536	43	.446	1007
Wagner	69	314	259	17	.547	590
Weber St.	38	196	204	3	.490	403
Western Caro.	66	273	361	23	.433	657
Western Ill.	96	420	355	37	.540	812
Western Ky.	81	440	296	31	.594	767
William & Mary	104	469	462	37	.504	968
Wofford	91	389	425	36	.479	850
Yale	127	799	298	55	.717	1152
Youngstown St.	59	352	232	17	.600	601

*Also includes any participation in major bowl games. +Ties computed as half won and half lost. %Stephen F. Austin's participation in 1989 Division I-AA championships (3-1 record) voided. @Tennessee State's participation in 1981 and 1982 Division I-AA championships (1-2 record) voided.

DIVISION I-AA

ALL-TIME TEAM WON-LOST RECORDS

VICTORIES

Team	Wins
Yale	799
Princeton	737
Pennsylvania	734
Harvard	729
Fordham	686
Dartmouth	624
Lafayette	588
Cornell	580
Delaware	559
Lehigh	553
Holy Cross	537
Dayton	525
Bucknell	517
Brown	515
Colgate	514
Northern Iowa	513
Butler	500
Drake	489
Villanova	484
Florida A&M	474
Furman	473
Southern U.	469
William & Mary	469
Massachusetts	468
Eastern Ky.	464
Tennessee St.	458
Hampton	447
Chattanooga	443
Western Ky.	440
Appalachian St.	438
New Hampshire	435
Northwestern St.	435
Georgetown	433
Howard	428
VMI	428
Maine	422
Elon	420
Grambling	420
Western Ill.	420
Richmond	418
Southwest Tex. St.	418
Citadel	414
Montana	411
Connecticut	410
Idaho St.	402
Murray St.	399
South Carolina St.	398
Eastern Ill.	396
Eastern Wash.	392
Southwest Mo. St.	391
Wofford	389
Illinois St.	385
N.C. A&T	385
Samford	383
Alabama St.	380
Montana St.	376
Alcorn St.	372
Troy St.	372
Southeast Mo. St.	368
Morgan St.	366
Davidson	357

Team	Wins
Jackson St.	355
Youngstown St.	352
Jacksonville St.	350
St. Mary's (Cal.)	348
Hofstra	347
Sam Houston St.	341
Columbia	339
Rhode Island	336
Northern Ariz.	335
Tennessee Tech	334
Prairie View	330
Southern Ill.	330
Bethune-Cookman	324
Indiana St.	323
East Tenn. St.	321
Valparaiso	321
McNeese St.	318
Cal Poly	315
Wagner	314
Stephen F. Austin	303
Ark.-Pine Bluff	292
Alabama A&M	287
Western Caro.	273
Texas Southern	259
Morehead St.	250
Portland St.	247
Northeastern	242
Duquesne	238
Delaware St.	235
Austin Peay	231
Central Conn. St.	227
Canisius	225
Ga. Southern	219
Cal St. Sacramento	203
Weber St.	196
Mississippi Val.	190
Norfolk St.	189
Southern Utah	181
Tenn.-Martin	181
Towson	176
Cal St. Northridge	175
St. John's (N.Y.)	168
Albany (N.Y.)	165
James Madison	161
St. Francis (Pa.)	152
San Diego	148
Liberty	137
Nicholls St.	132
Marist	92
Iona	90
Stony Brook	78
St. Peter's	54
Robert Morris	42
Monmouth	33
Siena	27
Fairfield	26
Sacred Heart	23
South Fla.	20
Charleston So.	19
Jacksonville	7
La Salle	7

Records in the 1990s

(1990-91-92-93-94-95-96-97-98-99, including playoffs; tiebreaker began in 1996)

PERCENTAGE

Team	W-L-T	*Pct.
Dayton	92-17-0	.844
Youngstown St.	103-30-2	.770
Montana	93-32-0	.744
Hofstra	81-29-2	.732
Troy St.	87-32-1	.729
Delaware	88-33-1	.725
Northern Iowa	89-34-0	.724
Ga. Southern	92-36-0	.719
Eastern Ky.	85-35-0	.708
Robert Morris	42-18-1	.697
N.C. A&T	79-35-0	.693
Drake	70-31-2	.689

Team	W-L-T	*Pct.
Hampton	78-36-1	.683
McNeese St.	84-39-2	.680
William & Mary	78-37-0	.678
Jackson St.	76-37-1	.671
Appalachian St.	79-40-0	.664
Florida A&M	79-40-0	.664
Ark.-Pine Bluff	56-31-0	.644
Dartmouth	62-35-3	.635
Fairfield	26-15-0	.634
Georgetown	63-37-0	.630
Southern Utah	66-39-0	.629
Pennsylvania	62-37-0	.626
Lehigh	70-42-1	.624
Wagner	63-38-0	.624

Team	W-L-T	*Pct.
St. John's (N.Y.)	65-40-0	.619
Marist	61-38-2	.614
Samford	69-43-2	.614
Western Ill.	71-45-1	.611
Albany (N.Y.)	62-40-0	.608
South Fla.	20-13-0	.606
Villanova	69-46-0	.600
Portland St.	70-47-0	.598
New Hampshire	65-45-2	.589
Massachusetts	67-47-1	.587
South Carolina St.	64-45-0	.587
Princeton	58-41-0	.585
Duquesne	59-42-1	.583
Howard	65-47-0	.580
Furman	66-48-1	.578
San Diego	57-42-1	.575
Southwest Mo. St.	57-43-1	.569
Monmouth	33-25-0	.569
Elon	61-47-0	.565
James Madison	65-51-0	.560
Grambling	62-50-0	.554
Northern Ariz.	62-50-0	.554
Northwestern St.	63-51-0	.553
Cornell	55-45-0	.550
Eastern Wash.	61-51-0	.545
Liberty	60-50-0	.545
St. Mary's (Cal.)	54-46-1	.540
Wofford	59-51-1	.536
Cal Poly	57-50-1	.532
Weber St.	59-52-0	.532
Stephen F. Austin	58-52-3	.527
Butler	53-48-1	.525
Bucknell	57-52-0	.523
Murray St.	59-54-0	.522
Alabama St.	55-51-4	.518
Connecticut	57-54-0	.514
Jacksonville St.	58-55-1	.513
Eastern Ill.	57-55-1	.509
Stony Brook	50-49-2	.505
Alcorn St.	52-52-3	.500
Davidson	49-49-1	.500
Western Ky.	54-54-0	.500
Illinois St.	55-57-2	.491
Towson	51-53-0	.490
Citadel	55-58-0	.487
Tennessee St.	54-58-0	.482
Alabama A&M	52-57-1	.477
Sam Houston St.	51-56-3	.477
Tennessee Tech	51-58-0	.468

Team	W-L-T	*Pct.
Norfolk St.	48-55-1	.466
Colgate	52-60-1	.465
Cal St. Northridge	49-57-0	.462
Brown	46-54-0	.460
Delaware St.	50-59-0	.459
Yale	45-55-0	.450
East Tenn. St.	50-62-0	.446
Lafayette	47-59-3	.445
Harvard	43-56-1	.435
Cal St. Sacramento	45-59-1	.433
Iona	42-56-1	.429
Richmond	47-63-1	.428
Montana St.	47-63-0	.427
Texas Southern	46-62-1	.427
Valparaiso	43-59-1	.422
Chattanooga	46-64-0	.418
Indiana St.	46-64-0	.418
Morehead St.	44-62-0	.415
Bethune-Cookman	44-64-0	.407
Holy Cross	44-65-1	.405
Mississippi Val.	40-62-3	.395
Western Caro.	43-66-0	.394
Maine	43-67-0	.391
Jacksonville	7-11-0	.389
Southern U.	38-63-1	.377
Southeast Mo. St.	40-70-0	.364
Northeastern	39-70-1	.359
Morgan St.	20-37-0	.351
Canisius	34-64-1	.348
Columbia	33-65-2	.340
Southern Ill.	37-73-0	.336
Idaho St.	36-73-1	.332
Central Conn. St.	31-66-1	.321
Nicholls St.	35-75-1	.320
Rhode Island	34-75-0	.312
St. Francis (Pa.)	29-70-1	.295
Tenn.-Martin	31-79-0	.282
Sacred Heart	23-64-0	.264
La Salle	7-20-0	.259
Southwest Tex. St.	23-68-0	.253
Siena	22-69-0	.242
St. Peter's	21-70-0	.231
Austin Peay	24-85-0	.220
Charleston So.	19-73-0	.207
VMI	22-88-0	.200
Fordham	20-85-1	.193
Prairie View	3-93-0	.031

*Ties counted as half won and half lost.

VICTORIES

(Minimum 55 victories; Playoffs Included)

Team	Wins
Youngstown St.	103
Montana	93
Dayton	92
Ga. Southern	92
Northern Iowa	89
Delaware	88
Troy St.	87
Eastern Ky.	85
McNeese St.	84
Hofstra	81
Appalachian St.	79
Florida A&M	79
N.C. A&T	79
Hampton	78
William & Mary	78
Jackson St.	76
Western Ill.	71
Drake	70
Lehigh	70
Portland St.	70
Samford	69
Villanova	69
Massachusetts	67
Furman	66
Southern Utah	66
Howard	65
James Madison	65
New Hampshire	65
St. John's (N.Y.)	65
South Carolina St.	64

Team	Wins
Georgetown	63
Northwestern St.	63
Wagner	63
Albany (N.Y.)	62
Dartmouth	62
Grambling	62
Northern Ariz.	62
Pennsylvania	62
Eastern Wash.	61
Elon	61
Marist	61
Liberty	60
Duquesne	59
Murray St.	59
Weber St.	59
Wofford	59
Jacksonville St.	58
Princeton	58
Stephen F. Austin	58
Bucknell	57
Cal Poly	57
Connecticut	57
Eastern Ill.	57
San Diego	57
Southwest Mo. St.	57
Ark.-Pine Bluff	56
Alabama St.	55
Citadel	55
Cornell	55
Illinois St.	55

ALL-TIME TEAM WON-LOST RECORDS

Records in the Last Five Years (1995-99)

(Playoffs Included; tiebreaker began in 1996)

PERCENTAGE

Team	W-L-T	*Pct.
Southern U.	49-12-0	.803
Duquesne	43-11-0	.796
Dayton	41-11-0	.788
Montana	52-14-0	.788
Florida A&M	48-15-0	.762
Troy St.	47-15-0	.758
Appalachian St.	45-15-0	.750
Georgetown	39-13-0	.750
Ga. Southern	50-17-0	.746
Jackson St.	44-15-0	.746
Murray St.	43-15-0	.741
Delaware	45-16-0	.738
Albany (N.Y.)	38-14-0	.731
Hofstra	43-16-0	.729
Drake	38-14-1	.726
Northern Iowa	42-18-0	.700
McNeese St.	44-19-0	.698
Hampton	40-18-0	.690
Western Ill.	42-19-0	.689
Robert Morris	35-17-0	.673
Lehigh	39-19-0	.672
N.C. A&T	38-19-0	.667
Youngstown St.	42-21-0	.667
Bucknell	36-19-0	.655
Stephen F. Austin	37-20-0	.649
William & Mary	37-20-0	.649
Brown	32-18-0	.640
Fairfield	26-15-0	.634
Eastern Ky.	36-21-0	.632
Northern Ariz.	36-21-0	.632
Marist	32-19-0	.627
Howard	35-21-0	.625
Ark.-Pine Bluff	33-20-0	.623
Furman	36-22-0	.621
Villanova	36-22-0	.621
Pennsylvania	31-19-0	.620
Wagner	31-19-0	.620
South Fla.	20-13-0	.606
Samford	33-22-0	.600
Northwestern St.	35-24-0	.593
Dartmouth	29-20-1	.590
Connecticut	33-23-0	.589
Eastern Ill.	34-24-0	.586
St. John's (N.Y.)	31-22-0	.585
Western Ky.	32-23-0	.582
Massachusetts	35-26-0	.574
Eastern Wash.	33-25-0	.569
Morehead St.	29-22-0	.569
Liberty	31-24-0	.564
Alabama A&M	30-25-0	.545
East Tenn. St.	31-26-0	.544
James Madison	31-26-0	.544
Colgate	31-27-0	.534
Monmouth	26-23-0	.531
South Carolina St.	28-25-0	.528
Elon	29-26-0	.527
Richmond	29-26-1	.527
Tennessee St.	30-27-0	.526
Cornell	26-24-0	.520
Towson	27-25-0	.519
Davidson	26-25-1	.510

Team	W-L-T	*Pct.
New Hampshire	28-27-0	.509
Weber St.	28-27-0	.509
Stony Brook	25-25-0	.500
Valparaiso	26-26-0	.500
Illinois St.	29-30-0	.492
Portland St.	28-29-0	.491
Cal St. Northridge	27-28-0	.491
Montana St.	27-28-0	.491
Princeton	24-25-1	.490
Texas Southern	26-28-0	.481
Harvard	24-26-0	.480
Cal Poly	26-29-0	.473
Southwest Mo. St.	26-29-0	.473
San Diego	24-27-0	.471
Columbia	23-26-1	.470
Maine	25-30-0	.455
Northeastern	25-30-0	.455
St. Mary's (Cal.)	23-28-0	.451
Bethune-Cookman	2 4-31-0	.436
Chattanooga	24-31-0	.436
Indiana St.	24-31-0	.436
Southern Utah	24-31-0	.436
Sam Houston St.	23-31-0	.426
Tennessee Tech	23-31-0	.426
Wofford	23-31-0	.426
Yale	21-29-0	.420
Grambling	23-32-0	.418
Butler	20-30-0	.400
Norfolk St.	21-32-0	.396
Jacksonville	7-11-0	.389
Southern Ill.	21-34-0	.382
Southwest Tex. St.	21-34-0	.382
Alcorn St.	20-33-1	.380
Alabama St.	20-34-1	.373
Lafayette	19-34-1	.361
Central Conn. St.	18-32-0	.360
Western Caro.	19-35-0	.352
Citadel	19-36-0	.345
Idaho St.	19-36-0	.345
Jacksonville St.	18-36-0	.333
Southeast Mo. St.	18-37-0	.327
Nicholls St.	18-38-0	.321
Canisius	16-34-0	.320
Cal St. Sacramento	17-37-1	.318
Mississippi Val.	17-37-0	.315
Rhode Island	17-37-0	.315
Siena	14-32-0	.304
Delaware St.	16-39-0	.291
Fordham	15-38-1	.287
Iona	13-36-0	.265
La Salle	7-20-0	.259
Sacred Heart	12-39-0	.235
Holy Cross	12-43-0	.218
Charleston So.	11-41-0	.212
Morgan St.	11-42-0	.208
Austin Peay	11-43-0	.204
VMI	9-46-0	.164
Tenn.-Martin	8-47-0	.145
St. Francis (Pa.)	7-45-0	.135
St. Peter's	6-43-0	.122
Prairie View	3-49-0	.058

*Ties counted as half won and half lost.

VICTORIES

(Minimum 30 victories; Playoffs Included)

Team	Wins
Montana	52
Ga. Southern	50
Southern U.	49
Florida A&M	48
Troy St.	47
Appalachian St.	45
Delaware	45
Jackson St.	44
McNeese St.	44
Duquesne	43
Hofstra	43
Murray St.	43
Northern Iowa	42

Team	Wins
Western Ill.	42
Youngstown St.	42
Dayton	41
Hampton	40
Georgetown	39
Lehigh	39
Albany (N.Y.)	38
Drake	38
N.C. A&T	38
Stephen F. Austin	37
William & Mary	37
Bucknell	36
Eastern Ky.	36

Team	Wins
Northern Ariz.	36
Furman	36
Villanova	36
Howard	35
Massachusetts	35
Northwestern St.	35
Robert Morris	35
Eastern Ill.	34
Ark.-Pine Bluff	33
Connecticut	33
Eastern Wash.	33
Samford	33

Team	Wins
Brown	32
Marist	32
Western Ky.	32
Colgate	31
East Tenn. St.	31
James Madison	31
Liberty	31
Pennsylvania	31
St. John's (N.Y.)	31
Wagner	31
Alabama A&M	30
Tennessee St.	30

Records in the 1980s

(Playoffs Included)

PERCENTAGE

Team	W-L-T	Pct.†
Eastern Ky.	88-24-2	.781
Furman	83-23-4	.773
Ga. Southern	68-22-1	*.753
Jackson St.	71-25-5	.728
Grambling	68-30-3	.688
Nevada	71-35-1	.668
Holy Cross	67-33-2	.667
Tennessee St.	64-32-4	.660
Eastern Ill.	70-36-1	.659
Idaho	69-36-0	.657

Team	W-L-T	Pct.†
Delaware	68-36-0	.654
Middle Tenn. St.	65-36-0	.644
Boise St.	66-38-0	.635
Southwest Tex. St.	66-39-0	.629
Murray St.	61-36-2	.626
Northern Iowa	64-38-2	.625
Towson	60-36-2	.622
Alcorn St.	56-34-0	.622
La.-Monroe	64-39-0	.621
South Carolina St.	55-34-1	.617

†Ties counted as half won and half lost. *Includes two nonvarsity seasons and five varsity seasons; varsity record, 55-14-0 for .797.

National Poll Rankings

Final Poll Leaders

(Released Before Division Championship Playoffs)

Year	Team, Record*	Coach	Record in Championship†
1978	Nevada (10-0-0)	Chris Ault	0-1 Lost in semifinals
1979	Grambling (8-2-0)	Eddie Robinson	Did not compete
1980	Lehigh (9-0-2)	John Whitehead	0-1 Lost in semifinals
1981	Eastern Ky. (9-1-0)	Roy Kidd	2-1 Lost in championship
1982	Eastern Ky. (10-0-0)	Roy Kidd	3-0 Champion
1983	Southern Ill. (10-1-0)	Rey Dempsey	3-0 Champion
1984	Alcorn St. (9-0-0)	Marino Casem	0-1 Lost in quarterfinals
1985	Middle Tenn. St. (11-0-0)	James Donnelly	0-1 Lost in quarterfinals
1986	Nevada (11-0-0)	Chris Ault	2-1 Lost in semifinals
1987	Holy Cross (11-0-0)	Mark Duffner	Did not compete
1988	Idaho (9-1-0)	Keith Gilbertson	2-1 Lost in semifinals
1989	Ga. Southern (11-0-0)	Erk Russell	4-0 Champion
1990	Middle Tenn. St. (10-0-0)	James Donnelly	1-1 Lost in quarterfinals
1991	Nevada (11-0-0)	Chris Ault	1-1 Lost in quarterfinals
1992	(tie) Citadel (10-1-0)	Charlie Taaffe	1-1 Lost in quarterfinals
	La.-Monroe (9-2-0)	Dave Roberts	1-1 Lost in quarterfinals
1993	Troy St. (10-0-1)	Larry Blakeney	2-1 Lost in semifinals
1994	Youngstown St. (10-0-1)	Jim Tressel	4-0 Champion
1995	McNeese St. (11-0-0)	Bobby Keasler	2-1 Lost in semifinals
1996	Marshall (11-0)	Bob Pruett	4-0 Champion
1997	Villanova (11-0)	Andy Talley	1-1 Lost in quarterfinals
1998	Ga. Southern (11-0)	Paul Johnson	3-1 Lost in championship
1999	Tennessee St. (11-0)	L. C. Cole	0-1 Lost in first round

*Final poll record; in some cases, a team had one or two games remaining before the championship playoffs. †Number of teams in the championship: 4 (1978-80); 8 (1981); 12 (1982-85); 16 (1986-present).

DIVISION I-AA

Final Regular-Season Polls

1978 (NCAA)
Team
1. Nevada
2. Jackson St.
3. Florida A&M
4. Massachusetts
5. Western Ky.
6. South Carolina St.
7. Northern Ariz.
   Montana St.
   Eastern Ky.
   Lehigh
   Rhode Island

1979 (NCAA)
Team
1. Grambling
2. Murray St.
3. Eastern Ky.
   Lehigh
5. Nevada
6. Alcorn St.
7. Boston U.
8. Jackson St.
9. Montana St.
10. Northern Ariz.
    Southern U.

1980 (NCAA)
Team
1. Lehigh
2. Grambling
3. Eastern Ky.
4. South Carolina St.
5. Western Ky.
6. Delaware
7. Boise St.
8. Northwestern St.
9. Boston U.
10. Connecticut
    Massachusetts
    Murray St.

1981 (NCAA)
Team
1. Eastern Ky.
2. Idaho St.
3. South Carolina St.
4. Jackson St.
5. Boise St.
6. Tennessee St.
7. Delaware
8. Lafayette
9. Murray St.
10. New Hampshire

1982 (NCAA)
Team
1. Eastern Ky.
2. Louisiana Tech
3. Delaware
4. Tennessee St.
5. Eastern Ill.
6. Furman
7. South Carolina St.
8. Jackson St.
9. Colgate
10. Grambling
11. Idaho
12. Northern Ill.
13. Holy Cross
14. Bowling Green
15. Boise St.
16. Western Mich.
17. Chattanooga
18. Northwestern St.
19. Montana
20. Lafayette

1983 (NCAA)
Team
1. Southern Ill.
2. Furman
3. Holy Cross
4. North Texas
5. Indiana St.
6. Eastern Ill.
7. Colgate
8. Eastern Ky.
9. Western Caro.
10. Grambling
11. Nevada
12. Idaho St.
13. Boston U.
    La.-Monroe
15. Jackson St.
16. Middle Tenn. St.
17. Tennessee St.
18. South Carolina St.
19. Mississippi Val.
20. New Hampshire

1984 (NCAA)
Team
1. Alcorn St.
2. Montana St.
   Rhode Island
4. Boston U.
5. Indiana St.
6. Middle Tenn. St.
   Mississippi Val.
8. Eastern Ky.
9. Louisiana Tech
10. Arkansas St.
11. New Hampshire
12. Richmond
13. Murray St.
14. Western Caro.
15. Holy Cross
16. Furman
17. Chattanooga
18. Northern Iowa
19. Delaware
20. McNeese St.

1985 (NCAA)
Team
1. Middle Tenn. St.
2. Furman
   Nevada
4. Northern Iowa
5. Idaho
6. Arkansas St.
7. Rhode Island
8. Grambling
9. Ga. Southern
10. Akron
11. Eastern Wash.
12. Appalachian St.
    Delaware St.
14. Louisiana Tech
15. Jackson St.
16. William & Mary
17. Murray St.
18. Richmond
19. Eastern Ky.
20. Alcorn St.

1986 (NCAA)
Team
1. Nevada
2. Arkansas St.
3. Eastern Ill.
4. Ga. Southern
5. Holy Cross
6. Appalachian St.
7. Pennsylvania
8. William & Mary
9. Jackson St.
10. Eastern Ky.
11. Sam Houston St.
12. Nicholls St.
13. Delaware
14. Tennessee St.
15. Furman
16. Idaho
17. Southern Ill.
18. Murray St.
19. Connecticut
20. N.C. A&T

1987 (NCAA)
Team
1. Holy Cross
2. Appalachian St.
3. La.-Monroe
4. Northern Iowa
5. Idaho
6. Ga. Southern
7. Eastern Ky.
8. James Madison
9. Jackson St.
10. Weber St.
11. Western Ky.
12. Arkansas St.
13. Maine
14. Marshall
15. Youngstown St.
16. North Texas
17. Richmond
18. Howard
19. Sam Houston St.
20. Delaware St.

1988 (NCAA)
Team
1. Stephen F. Austin
2. Idaho
3. Ga. Southern
4. Western Ill.
5. Furman
6. Jackson St.
7. Marshall
8. Eastern Ky.
9. Citadel
10. Northwestern St.
11. Massachusetts
12. North Texas
13. Boise St.
14. Florida A&M
    Pennsylvania
16. Western Ky.
17. Connecticut
18. Grambling
19. Montana
20. New Hampshire

1989 (NCAA)
Team
1. Ga. Southern
2. Furman
3. Stephen F. Austin
4. Holy Cross
   Idaho
6. Montana
7. Appalachian St.
8. Maine
9. Southwest Mo. St.
10. Middle Tenn. St.
    William & Mary
12. Eastern Ky.
13. Grambling
14. Youngstown St.
15. Eastern Ill.
16. Villanova
17. Jackson St.
18. Connecticut
19. Nevada
20. Northern Iowa

1990 (NCAA)
Team
1. Middle Tenn. St.
2. Youngstown St.
3. Ga. Southern
4. Nevada
5. Eastern Ky.
6. Southwest Mo. St.
7. William & Mary
8. Holy Cross
9. Massachusetts
10. Boise St.
11. Northern Iowa
12. Furman
13. Idaho
14. La.-Monroe
15. Citadel
16. Jackson St.
17. Dartmouth
18. UCF
19. New Hampshire
    N.C. A&T

1991 (NCAA)
Team
1. Nevada
2. Eastern Ky.
3. Holy Cross
4. Northern Iowa
5. Alabama St.
6. Delaware
7. Villanova
8. Marshall
9. Middle Tenn. St.
10. Samford
11. New Hampshire
12. Sam Houston St.
13. Youngstown St.
14. Western Ill.
15. Weber St.
16. James Madison
17. Appalachian St.
18. La.-Monroe
19. McNeese St.
20. Citadel
    Furman

1992 (NCAA)
Team
1. Citadel
   La.-Monroe
3. Northern Iowa
4. Middle Tenn. St.
5. Idaho
6. Marshall
7. Youngstown St.
8. Delaware
9. Samford
10. Villanova
11. McNeese St.
12. Eastern Ky.
13. William & Mary
14. Eastern Wash.
15. Florida A&M
16. Appalachian St.
17. N.C. A&T
18. Alcorn St.
19. Liberty
20. Western Ill.

1993 (Sports Network)
Team
1. Troy St.
2. Ga. Southern
3. Montana
4. La.-Monroe
5. McNeese St.
6. Boston U.
7. Youngstown St.
8. Howard
9. Marshall
10. William & Mary
11. Idaho
12. UCF
13. Northern Iowa
14. Stephen F. Austin
15. Southern U.
16. Pennsylvania
17. Eastern Ky.
18. Delaware
19. Western Ky.
20. Eastern Wash.
21. N.C. A&T
22. Tennessee Tech
23. Alcorn St.
24. Towson
25. Massachusetts

1994 (Sports Network)
Team
1. Youngstown St.
2. Marshall
3. Boise St.
4. Eastern Ky.
5. McNeese St.
6. Idaho
7. Grambling
8. Montana
9. Boston U.
10. Troy St.
11. Northern Iowa
12. New Hampshire
13. James Madison
14. Pennsylvania
15. Alcorn St.
16. Middle Tenn. St.
17. Appalachian St.
18. North Texas
19. William & Mary
20. UCF
21. Stephen F. Austin
22. South Carolina St.
23. Hofstra
24. Western Ill.
25. Northern Ariz.

1995 (Sports Network)
Team
1. McNeese St.
2. Appalachian St.
3. Troy St.
4. Murray St.
5. Stephen F. Austin
6. Marshall
7. Delaware
8. Montana
9. Hofstra
10. Eastern Ky.
11. Southern U.
12. Eastern Ill.
13. James Madison
14. Jackson St.
15. Ga. Southern
16. Florida A&M
17. Idaho
18. Northern Iowa
19. William & Mary
20. Richmond
21. Boise St.
22. Northern Ariz.
23. Connecticut
24. Indiana St.
25. Middle Tenn. St.

FINAL REGULAR-SEASON POLLS

1996
(Sports Network)

Team
1. Marshall
2. Montana
3. Northern Iowa
4. Murray St.
5. Troy St.
6. Northern Ariz.
7. William & Mary
8. Jackson St.
(tie) East Tenn. St.
10. Western Ill.
11. Delaware
12. Florida A&M
13. Furman
14. Villanova
15. Youngstown St.
16. Eastern Ill.
17. Dartmouth
18. New Hampshire
19. Nicholls St.
20. Howard
21. Southwest Mo. St.
22. Stephen F. Austin
23. James Madison
24. Dayton
25. Appalachian St.

1997
(Sports Network)

Team
1. Villanova
2. Western Ill.
3. Delaware
4. Eastern Wash.
5. Western Ky.
6. McNeese St.
7. Hampton
8. Ga. Southern
9. Youngstown St.
10. Florida A&M
11. Montana
12. Southern U.
13. Jackson St.
14. Hofstra
15. Eastern Ky.
16. Cal Poly
17. Northwestern St.
18. Stephen F. Austin
19. South Carolina St.
20. Liberty
21. Eastern Ill.
22. Appalachian St.
23. Dayton
24. Northeastern
25. Colgate

1997
(USA Today/ESPN)

Team
1. Youngstown St.
2. McNeese St.
3. Delaware
4. Eastern Wash.
5. Villanova
6. Western Ill.
7. Western Ky.
8. Ga. Southern
9. Montana
10. Hampton
11. Southern U.
12. Florida A&M
13. Jackson St.
14. Northwestern St.
15. Eastern Ky.
16. Hofstra
17. Cal Poly
18. Stephen F. Austin
19. Liberty
20. South Carolina St.
21. Colgate
22. Eastern Ill.
23. Appalachian St.
24. Northeastern
25. Dayton

1998
(USA Today/ESPN)
(After Playoffs)

Team
1. Massachusetts
2. Ga. Southern
3. Northwestern St.
4. Western Ill.
5. Florida A&M
6. Appalachian St.
7. Connecticut
8. McNeese St.
9. Richmond
10. Hampton
11. Troy St.
12. Lehigh
13. Tennessee St.
14. Montana
15. Illinois St.
16. Southern U.
17. South Fla.
18. Hofstra
19. William & Mary
20. Murray St.
21. Colgate
22. Western Ky.
23. Bethune-Cookman
24. Delaware
25. Montana St.

1998
(Sports Network)

Team
1. Ga. Southern
2. Northwestern St.
3. Florida A&M
4. Western Ill.
5. Richmond
6. McNeese St.
7. Appalachian St.
8. Connecticut
9. Hampton
10. Tennessee St.
11. Troy St.
12. Massachusetts
13. Lehigh
14. Montana
15. Southern U.
16. William & Mary
17. Western Ky.
18. Hofstra
19. South Fla.
20. Bethune-Cookman
21. Illinois St.
22. Delaware
23. Murray St.
24. Montana St.
25. Northern Iowa

1999
(USA Today/ESPN)

Team (Record)
1. Tennessee St. (11-0)
2. Ga. Southern (9-2)
3. Appalachian St. (8-2)
4. Hofstra (10-1)
5. Illinois St. (9-2)
6. Troy St. (10-1)
7. Montana (9-2)
8. Furman (9-2)
9. Youngstown St. (9-2)
10. Southern U. (9-1)
11. Massachusetts (8-3)
12. James Madison (8-3)
13. Lehigh (10-1)
14. Jackson St. (9-2)
15. Florida A&M (8-3)
16. N.C. A&T (10-1)
17. Northern Iowa (8-3)
18. Colgate (10-1)
19. Northern Ariz. (8-3)
20. Elon (9-2)
21. Portland St. (8-3)
22. Stephen F. Austin (8-3)
23. South Fla. (7-4)
24. Southern Utah (8-3)
25. Villanova (7-4)

1999
(Sports Network)
(After Playoffs)

Team (Record)
1. Ga. Southern (13-2)
2. Youngstown St. (12-3)
3. Illinois St. (11-3)
4. Florida A&M (10-4)
5. Hofstra (11-2)
6. Troy St. (11-2)
7. Massachusetts (9-4)
8. Montana (9-3)
9. Appalachian St. (9-3)
10. (tie) N.C. A&T (11-2)
11. Tennessee St. (11-1)
12. Furman (9-3)
13. James Madison (8-4)
14. Lehigh (10-2)
15. Northern Iowa (8-3)
16. Northern Ariz. (8-4)
17. Southern U. (11-2)
18. Colgate (10-2)
19. Jackson St. (9-3)
20. Portland St. (8-3)
21. Elon (9-2)
22. Stephen F. Austin (8-3)
23. South Fla. (7-4)
24. Villanova (7-4)
25. Brown (9-1)

DIVISION I-AA

Undefeated, Untied Teams

Regular-season games only, from 1978. Subsequent loss in Division I-AA championship is indicated by (††).

Year	Team	Wins
1978	Nevada	††11
1979	(None)	
1980	(None)	
1981	(None)	
1982	*Eastern Ky.	10
1983	(None)	
1984	Tennessee St.	11
	Alcorn St.	††9
1985	Middle Tenn. St.	††11
1986	Nevada	††11
	Pennsylvania	10
1987	Holy Cross	11
1988	(None)	
1989	*Ga. Southern	11
1990	Youngstown St.	††11
1991	Holy Cross	11
	Nevada	††11
1992	(None)	
1993	Boston U.	††11
	Howard	††11
	Pennsylvania	10
1994	Pennsylvania	9
1995	Appalachian St.	††11
	McNeese St.	††11
	Murray St.	††11
	Troy St.	††11
1996	Dartmouth	10
	Dayton	11
	*Marshall	11
	Montana	††11
1997	Villanova	††11
1998	Lehigh	††11
	Ga. Southern	††11
1999	(None)	

*Won Division I-AA championship.

The Spoilers

(From 1978 Season)

Following is a list of the spoilers of Division I-AA teams that lost their perfect (undefeated, untied) record in their **season-ending** game, including the Division I-AA championship playoffs. An asterisk (*) indicates a championship playoff game and a dagger (†) indicates the home team in a regular-season game.

Date	Spoiler	Victim	Score
12-9-78	*Massachusetts	Nevada	44-21
11-15-80	†Grambling	South Carolina St.	26-3
11-22-80	†Murray St.	Western Ky.	49-0
12-1-84	*Louisiana Tech	Alcorn St.	44-21
12-7-85	*Ga. Southern	Middle Tenn. St.	28-21
11-22-86	Boston College	†Holy Cross	56-26
12-19-86	*Ga. Southern	Nevada	48-38
11-19-88	*Cornell	Pennsylvania	19-6
11-24-90	*UCF	Youngstown St.	20-17
12-7-91	*Youngstown St.	Nevada	30-28
11-27-93	*Marshall	Howard	28-14
12-4-93	*Idaho	Boston U.	21-14
11-25-95	*Ga. Southern	Troy St.	24-21
11-25-95	*Northern Iowa	Murray St.	35-34
12-2-95	*Stephen F. Austin	Appalachian St.	27-17
12-9-95	*Marshall	McNeese St.	25-13
11-23-96	Robert Morris	Duquesne	28-26
12-21-96	*Marshall	Montana	49-29
11-22-97	†Colgate	Bucknell	48-14
12-6-97	*Youngstown St.	Villanova	37-34
12-5-98	*Massachusetts	Lehigh	27-21
12-19-98	*Massachusetts	Ga. Southern	55-43
11-27-99	*N.C. A&T	Tennessee St.	24-10

Streaks and Rivalries

Because Division I-AA began in 1978, only those streaks from the period (1978-present) are listed. Only schools that have been I-AA members for five years are eligible for inclusion.

Longest Winning Streaks

(From 1978; Includes Playoff Games)

Wins	Team	Years	Ended by	Score
24	Pennsylvania	1992-95	Columbia	14-24
21	Montana	1995-96	Marshall	49-29
20	Dayton	1996-97	Cal Poly	24-44
20	Holy Cross	1990-92	Army	7-17
19	Duquesne	1995-96	Robert Morris	28-26
18	Eastern Ky.	1982-83	Western Ky.	10-10
16	Ga. Southern	1989-90	Middle Tenn. St.	13-16
15	Dartmouth	1996-97	Lehigh	26-46
15	Marshall	1996	Moved to Division I-A	
14	Ga. Southern	1998	Massachusetts	55-43
14	Youngstown St.	1994	Kent St.	14-17
14	Delaware	1979-80	Lehigh	20-27
13	Fairfield	1998-99	Holy Cross	23-24
13	Lehigh	1997-98	Massachusetts	27-21
13	McNeese St.	1995	Marshall	13-25
13	Holy Cross	1988-89	Army	9-45
13	Nevada	1986	Ga. Southern	38-48
13	Tennessee St.	1983-85	Western Ky.	17-22
13	Eastern Ill.	1978-79	Western Ill.	7-10
12	Bucknell	1996-97	Colgate	14-48
12	Appalachian St.	1995	Stephen F. Austin	17-27
12	Nevada	1989-90	Boise St.	14-30
12	Furman	1989	Stephen F. Austin	19-21
12	Holy Cross	1987-88	Army	3-23
12	Southern Ill.	1982-83	Wichita St.	6-28
12	Florida A&M	1978-79	Tennessee St.	3-20

Longest Unbeaten Streaks

(From 1978; Includes Playoff Games and Ties)

No.	Wins	Ties	Team	Years	Ended by
24	24	0	Pennsylvania	1992-95	Columbia
22	21	1	Dartmouth	1995-97	Lehigh
21	21	0	Montana	1995-96	Marshall
20	20	0	Dayton	1996-97	Cal Poly
20	20	0	Holy Cross	1990-92	Army
20	19	1	Youngstown St.	1993-94	Kent
19	19	0	Duquesne	1995-96	Robert Morris
19	18	1	Eastern Ky.	1982-83	Murray St.
17	16	1	Alabama St.	1990-92	Alcorn St.
17	16	1	Grambling	1977-78	Florida A&M
16	16	0	Ga. Southern	1989-90	Middle Tenn. St.
15	15	0	Marshall	1996	Moved to Division I-A
15	14	1	Delaware	1994-95	Navy
14	14	0	Ga. Southern	1998	Massachusetts
14	14	0	Delaware	1979-80	Lehigh
13	13	0	Fairfield	1998-99	Holy Cross
13	13	0	Lehigh	1997-98	Massachusetts
13	13	0	McNeese St.	1995	Marshall
13	13	0	Holy Cross	1988-89	Army
13	13	0	Nevada	1986	Ga. Southern
13	13	0	Tennessee St.	1983-85	Western Ky.
13	13	0	Eastern Ill.	1978-79	Western Ill.
13	12	1	Mississippi Val.	1983-84	Alcorn St.
13	12	1	Eastern Ill.	1981-82	Tennessee St.
12	12	0	Bucknell	1996-97	Colgate
12	12	0	Appalachian St.	1995	Stephen F. Austin
12	12	0	Nevada	1989-90	Boise St.
12	12	0	Furman	1989	Stephen F. Austin
12	12	0	Holy Cross	1987-88	Army
12	12	0	Southern Ill.	1982-83	Wichita St.
12	12	0	Florida A&M	1978-79	Tennessee St.
12	11	1	Tennessee St.	1985-86	Alabama St.
12	11	1	Tennessee St.	1981-83	Jackson St.
11	11	0	Tennessee St.	1999	N.C. A&T
11	11	0	Florida A&M	1998	Western Ill.
11	11	0	Murray St.	1996	Troy St.
11	11	0	Pennsylvania	1985-87	Cornell
10	9	1	Stephen F. Austin	1989	Ga. Southern
10	9	1	Holy Cross	1983	Boston College
10	9	1	Jackson St.	1980	Grambling

Longest Home Winning Streaks

(From 1978; Includes Playoff Games)

Wins	Team	Years	Ended by
38	Ga. Southern	1985-90	Eastern Ky.
34	Eastern Ky.	1978-83	Western Ky.
31	Middle Tenn. St.	1987-94	Eastern Ky.
30	Montana	1994-97	Eastern Wash.
25	Northern Iowa	1989-92	Youngstown St.
23	Ga. Southern	1997-99	Current
23	Northern Iowa	1983-87	Montana
22	Nevada	1989-91	Youngstown St.
20	Arkansas St.	1984-87	Northwestern St.
16	Pennsylvania	1992-95	Princeton
16	Southwest Tex. St.	1981-83	Central St.
16	Citadel	1980-82	East Tenn. St.
15	Holy Cross	1987-89	Massachusetts
14	Delaware	1994-97	Villanova
14	William & Mary	1991-94	Massachusetts
13	Youngstown St.	1992-93	Stephen F. Austin
13	William & Mary	1988-91	Delaware
13	Idaho	1987-89	Eastern Ill.
13	Sam Houston St.	1986-88	Stephen F. Austin

LONGEST HOME WINNING STREAKS

Wins	Team	Years	Ended by
13	Delaware St.	1983-86	Northeastern
12	Rhode Island	1984-85	Towson
12	Eastern Ill.	1981-83	Indiana St.

Longest Losing Streaks

(From 1978; Can Include Playoff Games)

Losses	Team	Years	Ended Against
80	Prairie View	1989-98	Langston
44	Columbia	1983-88	Princeton
19	Delaware St.	1997-99	Norfolk St.
19	Charleston So.	1993-95	Morehead St.
19	Idaho St.	1978-80	Portland St.
17	Davidson	1985-87	Wofford
17	Tennessee Tech	1984-85	Morehead St.
16	Colgate	1994-96	Brown
16	Siena	1994-96	Iona
16	Middle Tenn. St.	1978-79	Tennessee Tech
14	St. Francis (Pa.)	1998-99	Sacred Heart
14	St. Peter's	1997-99	Canisius
14	Nicholls St.	1994-96	Jacksonville St.
14	Fordham	1993-95	Marist
12	Tenn.-Martin	1998-99	Lambuth
12	St. Francis (Pa.)	1994-96	Waynesburg
12	Fordham	1991-92	Bucknell
12	UCF	1981-82	Elizabeth City St.

Most-Played Rivalries

(Ongoing Unless Indicated)

Games	Opponents (Series leader listed first)	Rivalry Record	First Game
135	Lafayette-Lehigh	71-59-5	1884
122	Yale-Princeton	66-46-10	1873
116	Yale-Harvard	63-45-8	1875
109	William & Mary-Richmond	56-48-5	1898
106	Pennsylvania-Cornell	59-42-5	1893
104	Yale-Brown	73-26-5	1880
103	Harvard-Dartmouth	55-43-5	1882
99	Montana-Montana St.	62-32-5	1897
99	Harvard-Brown	69-28-2	1893
92	Princeton-Harvard	49-36-7	1877
91	Princeton-Pennsylvania	60-30-1	1876
89	Connecticut-Rhode Island	48-33-8	1897
88	Illinois St.-Eastern Ill.	43-36-9	1901
87	New Hampshire-Maine	40-39-8	1903
87	Cornell-Columbia	55-29-3	1889
83	Western Ill.-Illinois St.	42-36-5	1904
82	Cornell-Colgate	47-32-3	1896

Additional Rivalry Records

LONGEST UNINTERRUPTED SERIES
(Must have played every year; current unless indicated)
110 games—Lafayette-Lehigh (from 1897)$
106 games—Cornell-Pennsylvania (from 1893)
81 games—Cornell-Dartmouth (from 1919)
74 games—Dartmouth-Yale (from 1926)
68 games—Brown-Yale (from 1932)
67 games—Dartmouth-Princeton (from 1933)
58 games—Columbia-Dartmouth (from 1942)
57 games—Columbia-Yale (from 1943)
56 games—Richmond-William & Mary (from 1944)
56 games—VMI-William & Mary (from 1944)
55 games—Brown-Harvard (from 1945)
55 games—Bucknell-Lafayette (from 1945)
55 games—Harvard-Yale (from 1945)
55 games—Princeton-Yale (from 1945)
54 games—Dartmouth-Holy Cross (1942-93)
54 games—Eastern Ky.-Western Ky. (from 1946)
54 games—Harvard-Princeton (from 1946)
54 games—Sam Houston St.-Southwest Tex. St. (from 1946)
54 games—Southwest Tex. St.-Stephen F. Austin (from 1946)
54 games—Montana-Montana St. (from 1946)

$Played twice in 1897-1901 and 1943-44.

MOST CONSECUTIVE WINS OVER AN OPPONENT IN AN UNINTERRUPTED SERIES
(Must have played in consecutive years)
23—Grambling over Prairie View, 1977-99 (current)
22—Eastern Ky. over Tennessee Tech, 1976-97
20—Eastern Ky. over Austin Peay, 1978-97
18—Eastern Ky. over Morehead St., 1972-89
18—Southeast Mo. St. over Lincoln (Mo.), 1972-89
17—Princeton over Columbia, 1954-70
16—Western Ill. over Southern Ill., 1984-99 (current)
16—Harvard over Columbia, 1979-94
16—Middle Tenn. St. over Morehead St., 1951-66
15—Delaware over West Chester, 1968-82
15—Dartmouth over Brown, 1960-74
15—Evansville over Ky. Wesleyan, 1983-97
14—Montana over Montana St., 1986-99 (current)
14—Yale over Princeton, 1967-80
14—Marshall over VMI, 1983-96
14—Dartmouth over Columbia, 1984-97
13—Duquesne over St. Francis (Pa.), 1977-89
13—Massachusetts over Northeastern, 1984-96
12—Idaho over Boise St., 1982-93
12—Cornell over Columbia, 1977-88
11—Wofford over Newberry, 1960-70
11—Tennessee Tech over Morehead St., 1951-61
11—William & Mary over Richmond, 1944-54

MOST CONSECUTIVE WINS OVER AN OPPONENT IN A SERIES
(Did not have to play in consecutive years)
46—Yale over Wesleyan (Conn.), 1875-1913
30—Harvard over Williams, 1883-1920
23—Harvard over Bates, 1899-1944
23—Brown over Rhode Island, 1909-34
21—Grambling over Mississippi Val., 1957-77
17—Harvard over Columbia, 1979-95
16—Yale over Connecticut, 1948-64
14—Delaware over Massachusetts, 1958-89
14—Massachusetts over Northwestern, 1984-99 (current)
12—Idaho over Ricks College, 1919-33
12—Yale over Pennsylvania, 1879-92

MOST CONSECUTIVE CURRENT WINS OVER AN OPPONENT IN AN UNINTERRUPTED SERIES
(Must have played in consecutive years)
23—Grambling over Prairie View, 1977-99
16—Western Ill. over Southern Ill., 1984-99

Cliffhangers

Regular-season Division I-AA games won on the final play in regulation time. The extra point is listed when it provided the margin of victory after the winning touchdown on the game's final play.

Date	Opponents, Score	Game-Winning Play
10-21-78	Western Ky. 17, Eastern Ky. 16	Kevin McGrath 25 FG
9-8-79	Northern Ariz. 22, Portland St. 21	Ken Fraser 15 pass from Brian Potter (Mike Jenkins pass from Potter)
11-15-80	Morris Brown 19, Bethune-Cookman 18	Ray Mills 1 run (Carlton Johnson kick)
9-26-81	Abilene Christian 41, Northwestern St. 38	David Russell 17 pass from Loyal Proffitt
10-10-81	C. W. Post 37, James Madison 36	Tom DeBona 10 pass from Tom Ehrhardt
11-13-82	Pennsylvania 23, Harvard 21	Dave Shulman 27 FG
10-1-83	Connecticut 9, New Hampshire 7	Larry Corn 7 run
9-8-84	La.-Lafayette 17, Louisiana Tech 16	Patrick Broussard 21 FG
9-15-84	Lehigh 10, Connecticut 7	Dave Melick 45 FG
9-15-84	William & Mary 23, Delaware 21	Jeff Sanders 18 pass from Stan Yagiello
10-13-84	Lafayette 20, Connecticut 13	Ryan Priest 2 run
10-20-84	UCF 28, Illinois St. 24	Jeff Farmer 30 punt return
10-27-84	Western Ky. 33, Morehead St. 31	Arnold Grier 50 pass from Jeff Cesarone
9-7-85	UCF 39, Bethune-Cookman 37	Ed O'Brien 55 FG
10-26-85	VMI 39, William & Mary 38	Al Comer 3 run (James Wright run)

Date	Opponents, Score	Game-Winning Play
8-30-86	Texas Southern 38, Prairie View 35	Don Espinoza 23 FG
9-20-86	Delaware 33, West Chester 31	Fred Singleton 3 run
10-4-86	Northwestern St. 17, La.-Monroe 14	Keith Hodnett 27 FG
10-11-86	Eastern Ill. 31, Northern Iowa 30	Rich Ehmke 58 FG
9-12-87	Youngstown St. 20, Bowling Green 17	John Dowling 36 FG
10-3-87	La.-Monroe 33, Northwestern St. 31	Jackie Harris 48 pass from Stan Humphries
10-10-87	Marshall 34, Louisville 31	Keith Baxter 31 pass from Tony Petersen
10-17-87	Princeton 16, Lehigh 15	Rob Goodwin 38 FG
11-12-87	South Carolina St. 15, Grambling 13	William Wrighten 23 FG
9-24-88	Holy Cross 30, Princeton 26	70 kickoff return; Tim Donovan 55 on lateral from Darin Cromwell (15)
10-15-88	Weber St. 37, Nevada 31	Todd Beightol 57 pass from Jeff Carlson
10-29-88	Nicholls St. 13, Southwest Tex. St. 10	Jim Windham 33 FG
9-2-89	Alabama St. 16, Troy St. 13	Reggie Brown 28 pass from Antonius Smith
9-16-89	Western Caro. 26, Chattanooga 20	Terrell Wagner 68 interception return
9-23-89	Northwestern St. 18, McNeese St. 17	Chris Hamler 25 FG
10-14-89	East Tenn. St. 24, Chattanooga 23	George Searcy 1 run
9-29-90	Southwest Tex. St. 33, Nicholls St. 30	Robbie Roberson 32 FG
10-6-90	Grambling 27, Alabama A&M 20	Dexter Butcher 28 pass from Shawn Burras
11-2-91	Grambling 30, Texas Southern 27	Gilad Landau 37 FG
9-19-92	Eastern Ky. 26, La.-Monroe 21	Sean Little recovered fumble in end zone
10-10-92	Appalachian St. 27, James Madison 21	Craig Styron 44 pass from D. J. Campbell
11-14-92	Towson 33, Northeastern 32	Mark Orlando 10 pass from Dan Crowley
9-4-93	Delaware St. 31, Fayetteville St. 28	Jon Jensen 17 FG
9-11-93	Connecticut 24, New Hampshire 23	Wilbur Gilliard 14 run (Nick Sosik kick)
10-16-93	Howard 44, Towson 41	Germaine Kohn 9 pass from Jay Walker
10-7-95	Valparaiso 44, Butler 42	Cameron Hatten 27 FG
10-14-95	Montana 24, Northern Ariz. 21	Andy Larson 29 FG
10-14-95	Connecticut 31, Maine 30	David DeArmas 38 FG
10-28-95	Northern Iowa 19, Southwest Mo. St. 17	Matt Waller 39 FG
10-28-95	William & Mary 18, Villanova 15	Brian Shallcross 49 FG
9-7-96	Valparaiso 23, Hope 22	Cameron Hatten 37 FG
9-21-96	Charleston So. 17, West Virginia St. 14	Clint Kelly 20 FG
11-2-96	Butler 33, Evansville 31	Shawn Wood 32 FG
11-2-96	Wagner 38, Robert Morris 35	Carl Franke 41 FG
11-9-96	Murray St. 17, Eastern Ky. 14	Rob Hart 36 FG
9-6-97	Butler 10, Howard Payne 9	Jeremy Harkin 26 pass from Eli Stoddard (Shawn Wood kick)
9-13-97	Southern U. 36, Ark.-Pine Bluff 33	Chris Diaz 23 FG
9-20-97	Dayton 16, Robert Morris 13	Ryan Hulme 18 FG
10-4-97	Southwest Mo. St. 36, Southern Ill. 35	Travis Brawner 32 FG
11-8-97	Cal Poly 20, Montana St. 19	Alan Beilke 50 FG
11-15-97	James Madison 39, Rhode Island 37	Lindsay Fleshman 3 pass from Greg Maddox
11-22-97	Montana 27, Montana St. 25	Kris Heppner 37 FG
9-19-98	South Fla. 24, Liberty 21	Bill Gramatica 44 FG
9-19-98	Yale 30, Brown 28	Jake Borden 27 pass from Joe Walland (run failed)
10-2-99	Robert Morris 23, Wagner 21	J. T. Kirk 14 pass from Steve Tryon
11-6-99	Ga. Southern 41, Furman 38	Chris Chambers 28 FG

Regular-Season Overtime Games Prior to 1996

In 1981, the NCAA Football Rules Committee approved an overtime tiebreaker system to decide a tie game for the purpose of determining a conference champion. The following conferences used the tiebreaker system to decide conference-only tie games. (Beginning in 1996, all college football games used the tiebreaker if the score was tied after four periods.) In an overtime period, one end of the field is used and each team gets an offensive possession beginning at the 25-yard line. Each team shall have possession until it has scored, failed to gain a first down or lost possession. The team scoring the greater number of points after completion of both possessions is declared the winner. The periods continue until a winner is determined.

NUMBER OF DIVISION I-AA OVERTIME GAMES SINCE 1981

1981	2	1986	4	1991	5	*1996	23
1982	4	1987	6	1992	2	*1997	23
1983	0	1988	6	1993	4	*1998	25
1984	4	1989	2	1994	6	*1999	21
1985	2	1990	6	1995	8		

*All games tied at end of four periods use tiebreaker system.

BIG SKY CONFERENCE

Date	Opponents, Score	No. OTs	Score, Reg.
10-31-81	‡Weber St. 24, Northern Ariz. 23	1	17-17
11-21-81	‡Idaho 33, Weber St. 30	3	23-23
10-2-82	‡Montana St. 30, Idaho 27	3	17-17
11-6-82	Nevada 46, ‡Weber St. 43	3	30-30
10-13-84	‡Montana 44, Nevada 41	4	21-21
9-17-88	Boise St. 24, ‡Northern Ariz. 21	2	14-14
10-15-88	‡Montana 33, Northern Ariz. 26	2	26-26
9-15-90	‡Weber St. 45, Idaho 38	2	31-31
9-29-90	‡Nevada 31, Idaho 28	1	28-28
11-3-90	Eastern Wash. 33, ‡Idaho St. 26	1	26-26

Date	Opponents, Score	No. OTs	Score, Reg.
11-10-90	Montana St. 28, ‡Eastern Wash. 25	1	25-25
10-26-91	Eastern Wash. 34, ‡Idaho 31	2	24-24
11-16-91	Montana 35, ‡Idaho 34	1	28-28
10-29-94	‡Eastern Wash. 34, Montana St. 31	3	31-31

GATEWAY CONFERENCE

Date	Opponents, Score	No. OTs	Score, Reg.
9-24-94	Western Ill. 31, ‡Southwest Mo. St. 24	1	24-24
9-30-95	Illinois St. 20, ‡Southwest Mo. St. 17	1	17-17
10-14-95	‡Southern Ill. 33, Southwest Mo. St. 30	1	30-30

MID-EASTERN ATHLETIC CONFERENCE

Date	Opponents, Score	No. OTs	Score, Reg.
11-1-86	‡N.C. A&T 30, Bethune-Cookman 24	1	24-24
10-22-93	Howard 41, ‡N.C. A&T 35	1	35-35
11-20-93	‡South Carolina St. 58, N.C. A&T 52	1	52-52

OHIO VALLEY CONFERENCE

Date	Opponents, Score	No. OTs	Score, Reg.
10-13-84	Youngstown St. 17, ‡Austin Peay 13	1	10-10
11-3-84	‡Murray St. 20, Austin Peay 13	2	10-10
10-19-85	‡Middle Tenn. St. 31, Murray St. 24	2	17-17
11-2-85	‡Middle Tenn. St. 28, Youngstown St. 21	2	14-14
10-4-86	‡Austin Peay 7, Middle Tenn. St. 0	1	0-0
10-10-87	‡Austin Peay 20, Morehead St. 13	1	13-13
11-7-87	‡Youngstown St. 20, Murray St. 13	1	13-13
10-1-88	Tennessee Tech 16, Murray St. 13	1	10-10
10-29-88	Eastern Ky. 31, ‡Murray St. 24	1	24-24
11-18-89	Eastern Ky. 38, ‡Morehead St. 31	3	24-24
11-10-90	‡Tennessee Tech 20, Austin Peay 14	1	14-14
11-17-90	Murray St. 31, ‡Austin Peay 24	3	24-24
11-7-92	‡Eastern Ky. 21, Murray St. 18	1	18-18

REGULAR-SEASON OVERTIME GAMES

Date	Opponents, Score	No. OTs	Score, Reg.
10-2-93	Murray St. 28, ‡Tenn.-Martin 21	1	21-21
11-20-93	Tenn.-Martin 39, ‡Austin Peay 33	2	26-26

PATRIOT LEAGUE

Date	Opponents, Score	No. OTs	Score, Reg.
11-11-95	Bucknell 21, ‡Colgate 14	1	14-14
11-11-95	‡Lafayette 24, Fordham 21	2	21-21
11-18-95	‡Lehigh 37, Lafayette 30	2	30-30

SOUTHERN CONFERENCE

Date	Opponents, Score	No. OTs	Score, Reg.
10-19-91	Appalachian St. 26, Furman 23	3	20-20
11-2-91	Marshall 27, Western Caro. 24	3	20-20
11-21-92	VMI 37, Chattanooga 34	1	34-34
11-19-94	VMI 26, Appalachian St. 23	1	20-20

YANKEE CONFERENCE

Date	Opponents, Score	No. OTs	Score, Reg.
9-18-82	Rhode Island 58, ‡Maine 55	6	21-21
9-25-82	‡Boston U. 48, Maine 45	4	24-24
10-27-84	Maine 13, ‡Connecticut 10	1	10-10
9-13-86	New Hampshire 28, ‡Delaware 21	1	21-21
11-15-86	‡Connecticut 21, Rhode Island 14	1	14-14
9-19-87	‡Richmond 52, Massachusetts 51	4	28-28
9-19-87	New Hampshire 27, ‡Boston U. 20	3	17-17
10-31-87	Maine 59, ‡Delaware 56	2	49-49
11-21-87	‡Delaware 17, Boston U. 10	1	10-10
9-24-88	Villanova 31, ‡Boston U. 24	1	24-24
10-8-88	‡Richmond 23, New Hampshire 17	1	17-17
10-7-89	‡Villanova 41, Connecticut 35	6	21-21
11-16-91	Boston U. 29, ‡Connecticut 26	2	23-23
9-11-93	‡Connecticut 24, New Hampshire 23	1	17-17
10-16-93	Maine 26, ‡Rhode Island 23	2	17-17
9-17-94	Delaware 38, ‡Villanova 31	1	31-31
11-19-94	Northeastern 9, ‡James Madison 6	1	6-6
9-23-95	James Madison 28, ‡Villanova 27	1	21-21
10-7-95	‡Richmond 26, Northeastern 23	1	23-23
11-4-95	‡Maine 24, Massachusetts 21	1	21-21
11-19-94	New Hampshire 52, ‡Boston U. 51	2	45-45

‡Home team.

1999 DIVISION I-AA OVERTIME FOOTBALL GAMES

Date	Winner Conf.	Score (Loser's Conference)	OT Periods	Reg. Score	Team With Choice	Choice
9-4	NAIA	McKendree 38, Dayton (Pioneer) 31	2OT	24-24	Dayton	Defense
9-4	Pioneer	Butler 27, Albion (Div. III) 20	1OT	20-20	Butler	Defense
9-4	NAIA	Azusa Pacific 26, San Diego (Pioneer) 19	1OT	19-19	San Diego	Defense
9-11	Big Sky	Montana 41, Cal St. Sacramento (Big Sky) 38	2OT	31-31	Montana	Defense
9-11	Ohio Valley	Tenn.-Martin 25, Lambuth (NAIA) 19	1OT	19-19	Tenn.-Martin	Defense
10-2	Independent	Charleston So. 14, Lenoir-Rhyne (Div. II) 7	1OT	7-7	Charleston So.	Defense
10-2	Independent	Jacksonville 28, Austin Peay (Ind.) 21	2OT	21-21	Jacksonville	Defense
10-2	Big Sky	Portland St. 51, Montana (Big Sky) 48	1OT	45-45	Portland St.	Offense
10-9	MAAC	Georgetown 41, Marist (MAAC) 40	1OT	34-34	Marist	Defense
10-9	MEAC	Florida A&M 40, Howard (MEAC) 34	1OT	34-34	Florida A&M	Defense
10-9	Gateway	Youngstown St. 43, Southern Ill. (Gateway) 37	1OT	37-37	Youngstown St.	Defense
10-16	Atlantic 10	Villanova 48, Connecticut (Atlantic 10) 45	3OT	28-28	Villanova	Defense
10-16	Independent	Jacksonville 48, Greensboro (Non) 41	2OT	41-41	Jacksonville	Defense
10-16	Southland	McNeese St. 39, Jacksonville St. (Southland) 36	2OT	29-29	Jacksonville St.	Defense
10-23	Gateway	Indiana St. 39, Western Ill. (Gateway) 36	2OT	29-29	Western Ill.	Defense
10-31	Atlantic 10	Delaware 37, Northeastern (Atlantic 10) 34	1OT	34-34	Delaware	Defense
10-31	Atlantic 10	Richmond 28, Connecticut (Atlantic 10) 21	1OT	21-21	Connecticut	Defense
11-6	MEAC	Bethune-Cookman 34, Hampton (MEAC) 27	1OT	27-27	Hampton	Defense
11-6	Independent	Samford 35, Western Carolina (Southern) 32	1OT	29-29	Samford	Defense
11-6	Southern	Chattanooga 30, Citadel (Southern) 27	1OT	24-24	Chattanooga	Defense
11-20	Atlantic 10	Villanova 51, Delaware (Atlantic 10) 45	1OT	45-45	Villanova	Defense

Division I-AA Stadiums

STADIUMS LISTED ALPHABETICALLY BY SCHOOL

School	Stadium	Conference	Year Built	Cap.	Surface*
Alabama A&M	Louis Crews	SWAC-E	1996	21,000	Grass
Alabama St.	^Cramton	SWAC-E	1922	24,600	Grass
Albany St. (N.Y.)	University Field	Independent	1967	10,000	Grass
Alcorn St.	Jack Spinks	SWAC-E	1992	25,000	Grass
Appalachian St.	Kidd Brewer	Southern	1962	16,650	AstroTurf
Ark.-Pine Bluff	Pumphrey	SWAC-W	1951	6,000	Grass
Austin Peay	Governors	Independent	1946	10,000	Stadia Turf
Bethune-Cookman	Municipal	MEAC	NA	10,000	Grass
Brown	Brown	Ivy	1925	20,000	Grass
Bucknell	Christy Mathewson	Patriot	1924	13,100	Grass
Butler	Butler Bowl	Pioneer	1927	19,000	Grass
Cal Poly	Mustang	Independent	1935	8,500	Grass
Cal St. Northridge	North Campus	Big Sky	1971	6,000	Grass
Cal St. Sacramento	Hornet Field	Big Sky	1964	21,418	Grass
Canisius	Demske	MAAC	1989	1,000	AstroTurf
Central Conn. St.	Arute Field	Northeast	1969	5,000	Grass
Charleston So.	CSU	Independent	1970	3,000	Grass
Chattanooga	^Finley	Southern	1997	20,000	Grass
Citadel	Johnson Hagood	Southern	1948	22,500	Grass
Colgate	Andy Kerr	Patriot	1937	10,221	Grass
Columbia	Lawrence A. Wien	Ivy	1984	17,000	Grass
Connecticut	Memorial	Independent	1953	16,200	Grass
Cornell	Schoellkopf	Ivy	1915	27,000	All-Pro Turf
Dartmouth	Memorial Field	Ivy	1923	20,416	Grass
Davidson	Richardson Field	Independent	1924	5,200	Grass

DIVISION I-AA STADIUMS

School	Stadium	Conference	Year Built	Cap.	Surface*
Dayton	Welcome	Pioneer	1949	11,000	AstroTurf
Delaware	Delaware	Atlantic 10	1952	23,000	Grass
Delaware St.	Alumni Field	MEAC	1957	5,000	Grass
Drake	Drake	Pioneer	1925	18,000	Grass
Duquesne	Arthur J. Rooney Field	MAAC	1993	4,500	AstroTurf
East Tenn. St.	#Memorial	Southern	1977	12,000	AstroTurf
Eastern Ill.	O'Brien	Ohio Valley	1970	10,000	Grass
Eastern Ky.	Roy Kidd	Ohio Valley	1969	20,000	Grass
Eastern Wash.	Woodward	Big Sky	1967	6,000	Grass
Elon	Burlington Mem.	Independent	1949	10,000	Grass
Fairfield	Alumni	MAAC	1980	3,000	Grass
Florida A&M	Bragg Memorial	MEAC	1957	25,500	Grass
Fordham	Jack Coffey Field	Patriot	1930	7,000	Grass
Furman	Paladin	Southern	1981	16,000	Grass
Georgetown	Kehoe Field	MAAC	NA	2,400	AstroTurf
Ga. Southern	Paulson	Southern	1984	18,000	PAT
Grambling	Robinson	SWAC-W	1983	19,600	Grass
Hampton	Armstrong Field	MEAC	1928	11,000	Grass
Harvard	Harvard	Ivy	1903	37,289	Grass
Hofstra	Hofstra	Independent	1963	15,000	AstroTurf
Holy Cross	Fitton Field	Patriot	1924	23,500	Grass
Howard	Greene	MEAC	1986	8,890	AstroTurf
Idaho St.	#Holt Arena	Big Sky	1970	12,000	AstroTurf
Illinois St.	Hancock	Gateway	1967	15,000	AstroTurf
Indiana St.	Memorial	Gateway	1970	20,500	All-Pro Turf
Iona	Mazzella Field	MAAC	1989	1,200	AstroTurf
Jackson St.	^Mississippi Mem.	SWAC-E	1949	62,512	Grass
Jacksonville	Milne Field	Independent	1998	4,500	Grass
Jacksonville St.	Paul Snow	Southland	1947	15,000	Grass
James Madison	Bridgeforth	Atlantic 10	1974	12,500	AstroTurf
La Salle	McCarthy	Independent	1936	7,500	Grass
Lafayette	Fisher Field	Patriot	1926	13,750	Grass
Lehigh	Goodman	Patriot	1988	16,000	Grass
Liberty	Williams	Independent	1989	12,000	OmniTurf
Maine	Alumni	Atlantic 10	1942	10,000	Grass
Marist	Leonidoff Field	MAAC	1972	2,500	Grass
Massachusetts	Warren McGuirk	Atlantic 10	1965	17,000	Grass
McNeese St.	Cowboy	Southland	1965	17,500	Grass
Mississippi Val.	Magnolia	SWAC-E	1958	10,500	Grass
Monmouth	Kessler Field	Northeast	1993	4,600	Grass
Montana	Washington-Grizzly	Big Sky	1986	18,845	Grass
Montana St.	Reno H. Sales	Big Sky	1973	15,197	Grass
Morehead St.	Jayne	Independent	1964	10,000	OmniTurf
Morgan St.	Hughes	MEAC	1934	10,000	Grass
Murray St.	Stewart	Ohio Valley	1973	16,800	AstroTurf
New Hampshire	Cowell	Atlantic 10	1936	9,571	Grass
Nicholls St.	John L. Guidry	Southland	1972	12,800	Grass
Norfolk St.	Price	MEAC	1997	27,700	Grass
N.C. A&T	Aggie	MEAC	1981	21,000	Grass
Northeastern	E.S. Parsons	Atlantic 10	1933	7,000	AstroTurf
Northern Ariz.	#Walkup Skydome	Big Sky	1977	15,300	AstroTurf
Northern Iowa	#U.N.I.-Dome	Gateway	1976	16,324	AstroTurf
Northwestern St.	Turpin	Southland	1976	15,971	AstroTurf
Pennsylvania	Franklin Field	Ivy	1895	53,000	AstroTurf
Portland St.	^Civic	Big Sky	1928	23,150	AstroTurf
Prairie View	Blackshear	SWAC-W	1960	6,000	Grass
Princeton	Princeton	Ivy	1998	30,000	Grass
Rhode Island	Meade	Atlantic 10	1928	8,000	Grass
Richmond	Richmond	Atlantic 10	1929	21,319	SuperTurf
Robert Morris	Moon	Northeast	1950	7,000	Grass
Sacred Heart	Campus Field	Independent	1993	2,000	AstroTurf
St. Francis (Pa.)	Pine Bowl	Northeast	1979	1,500	Grass
St. John's (N.Y.)	Da Silva Memorial	MAAC	1961	3,000	OmniTurf
St. Mary's (Cal.)	St. Mary's	Independent	1973	5,000	Grass
St. Peter's	Cochrane	MAAC	1990	4,000	AstroTurf
Sam Houston St.	Bowers	Southland	1986	14,000	All-Pro Turf
Samford	Seibert	Independent	1960	6,700	Grass
San Diego	USD Torero	Pioneer	1955	4,000	Grass
Siena	Heritage Park	MAAC	NA	5,500	Grass
South Carolina St.	Dawson Bulldog	MEAC	1955	22,000	Grass
South Fla.	^Raymond James	Independent	1998	41,441	Grass
Southeast Mo. St.	Houck	Ohio Valley	1930	10,000	Grass
Southern Ill.	McAndrew	Gateway	1975	17,324	OmniTurf
Southern U.	A.W. Mumford	SWAC-W	1928	24,000	Grass
Southern Utah	Col. of Southern Utah	Independent	1967	6,500	Grass
Southwest Mo. St.	Plaster Field	Gateway	1941	16,300	OmniTurf
Southwest Tex. St.	Bobcat	Southland	1981	14,104	Grass
Stephen F. Austin	Homer Bryce	Southland	1973	14,575	All-Pro Turf
Stony Brook	Seawolves Field	Independent	1978	2,000	Grass
Tenn.-Martin	Skyhawk	Ohio Valley	1964	7,500	Grass
Tennessee St.	W.J. Hale	Ohio Valley	1953	16,000	Grass
Tennessee Tech	Tucker	Ohio Valley	1966	16,500	Stadia Turf
Texas Southern	^Robertson	SWAC-W	1965	22,000	Grass

DIVISION I-AA STADIUMS

School	Stadium	Conference	Year Built	Cap.	Surface*
Towson	Minnegan	Patriot	1978	5,000	Grass
Troy St.	Memorial	Southland	1950	12,000	Grass
Valparaiso	Brown Field	Pioneer	1947	5,000	Grass
Villanova	Villanova	Atlantic 10	1927	12,000	AstroTurf
VMI	Alumni Field	Southern	1962	10,000	Grass
Wagner	Fischer Mem. Field	Northeast	1967	5,000	Grass
Weber St.	Eilzabeth Dee Shaw Stewart	Big Sky	1966	17,500	Grass
Western Caro.	E.J. Whitmire	Southern	1974	12,000	AstroTurf
Western Ill.	Hanson Field	Gateway	1948	15,000	Grass
Western Ky.	L.T. Smith	Independent	1968	17,500	Grass
William & Mary	Walter Zable	Atlantic 10	1935	15,000	Grass
Wofford	Gibbs	Southern	1996	13,000	Grass
Yale	Yale Bowl	Ivy	1914	64,269	Grass
Youngstown St.	Arnold D. Stambaugh	Gateway	1982	20,360	Turf

^Not located on campus. #Indoor facility.

STADIUMS LISTED BY CAPACITY (TOP 30)

School	Stadium	Capacity
Yale	Yale Bowl	64,269
Jackson St.	^Mississippi Mem.	62,512
Pennsylvania	Franklin Field	53,000
South Fla.	^Raymond James	41,441
Harvard	Harvard	37,289
Princeton	Princeton	30,000
Norfolk St.	Price	27,700
Cornell	Schoellkopf	27,000
Florida A&M	Bragg Memorial	25,500
Alcorn St.	Jack Spinks	25,000
Alabama St.	^Cramton	24,600
Southern U.	A.W. Mumford	24,000
Holy Cross	Fitton Field	23,500
Portland St.	^Civic	23,150
Delaware	Delaware	23,000
Citadel	Johnson Hagood	22,500
South Carolina St.	Dawson Bulldog	22,000
Texas Southern	^Robertson	22,000
Cal St. Sacramento	Hornet Field	21,418
Richmond	Richmond	21,319
Alabama A&M	Louis Crews	21,000
N.C. A&T	Aggie	21,000
Indiana St.	Memorial	20,500
Dartmouth	Memorial Field	20,416
Youngstown St.	Arnold D. Stambaugh	20,360
Brown	Brown	20,000
Chattanooga	^Finley	20,000
Eastern Ky.	Roy Kidd	20,000
Grambling	Robinson	19,600
Butler	Butler Bowl	19,000

^Not located on campus. #Indoor facility.

Division I-AA Statistics Trends

(Average Per Game, One Team)

Year	Plays	Rushing Yds.	Avg.	Att.	Cmp.	Passing Pct.	Yds.	Av. Att.	Plays	Total Offense Yds.	Avg.	TD	Scoring FG	Pts.
1978	*48.4	*171.8	3.55	20.7	9.5	46.2	129.3	6.24	69.1	301.1	4.36	2.60	0.52	19.5
1979	47.1	164.7	3.50	20.5	9.2	45.0	125.2	6.13	67.5	289.9	4.30	2.40	0.62	18.5
1980	45.2	164.8	3.65	22.4	10.4	46.5	144.4	6.45	67.6	309.2	4.58	2.58	0.59	19.6
1981	44.3	155.0	3.50	24.9	11.9	47.7	161.5	6.49	69.1	316.4	4.58	2.71	0.69	20.9
1982	44.4	156.6	3.53	26.1	12.8	48.9	166.0	6.35	70.5	322.6	4.57	2.62	0.80	20.5
1983	43.9	155.2	3.54	26.2	13.0	49.4	167.3	6.38	70.1	322.4	4.60	2.69	0.79	21.1
1984	42.9	152.6	3.56	27.9	14.0	50.0	181.0	6.49	70.7	333.5	4.72	2.80	0.80	21.8
1985	42.4	157.6	3.72	*28.9	14.6	50.4	187.3	6.49	*71.2	344.9	4.84	2.84	0.81	22.1
1986	42.4	157.9	3.72	28.3	14.1	49.7	186.4	6.60	70.7	344.3	4.87	2.90	0.86	22.7
1987	43.1	158.6	3.68	27.1	13.6	50.1	175.6	6.48	70.2	334.2	4.76	2.78	0.91	22.0
1988	43.2	161.3	3.74	26.5	13.3	50.2	172.7	6.53	69.6	334.0	4.80	2.80	*0.92	22.1
1989	42.5	160.2	3.77	27.7	14.2	51.3	186.0	6.71	70.2	346.2	4.93	2.72	0.75	22.8
1990	42.7	161.5	3.79	27.8	14.1	50.6	187.0	6.73	70.5	348.5	4.95	2.98	0.84	23.2
1991	43.2	170.6	3.95	26.9	14.0	51.9	184.7	6.87	70.1	355.3	5.07	3.19	0.67	24.1
1992	43.0	171.4	3.99	26.0	13.5	51.7	179.4	6.89	69.0	350.8	5.08	3.16	0.68	23.9
1993	42.4	168.3	3.97	27.0	14.0	51.8	186.4	6.90	69.4	354.7	5.11	3.20	0.70	24.2
1994	41.6	164.1	3.95	27.5	14.3	51.9	188.1	6.85	69.0	352.1	5.10	3.18	0.70	24.1
1995	42.0	165.1	3.94	27.1	13.9	51.3	177.7	6.57	69.0	342.8	4.97	3.06	0.68	23.2
1996	42.0	162.0	3.86	26.9	13.7	51.1	177.6	6.62	68.8	339.6	4.94	3.05	0.72	23.2
1997	40.2	153.2	3.81	27.8	14.3	51.3	185.2	6.67	68.0	338.4	4.98	3.06	0.72	23.3
1998	40.8	162.7	3.98	27.2	14.3	*52.6	187.8	*6.91	68.0	350.5	5.15	3.26	0.71	24.7
1999	40.8	162.9	*4.02	28.8	*15.1	52.5	*197.1	6.83	69.4	*360.0	*5.19	*3.45	0.71	*25.9

*Record.

Additional Division I-AA Statistics Trends

(Average Per Game, One Team)

Year	Punting No.	Punting Avg.	Punting Net Avg.	Int. No.	Int. Avg. Ret.	Int. Yds.	PR No.	PR Avg. Ret.	PR Yds.	KR No.	KR Avg. Ret.	KR Yds.
1978	*6.1	36.5	33.6	1.42	11.92	17.0	2.39	7.49	17.9	3.23	18.4	59.2
1979	6.0	36.5	33.4	1.44	11.39	16.4	2.41	7.46	18.0	3.06	18.4	56.2
1980	5.8	37.0	33.7	1.37	10.06	13.8	2.44	7.94	19.4	3.09	17.4	53.7
1981	5.9	37.2	33.9	*1.60	10.63	*17.0	2.50	7.77	19.4	3.27	18.4	60.1
1982	6.0	37.1	34.0	1.50	10.15	15.2	2.44	7.63	18.6	3.08	19.0	58.4
1983	6.0	37.3	34.1	1.52	9.99	15.1	*2.59	7.58	19.6	3.06	18.6	56.9
1984	5.8	37.3	33.9	1.53	10.40	15.9	2.55	7.84	20.0	3.23	18.6	60.0
1985	5.7	37.6	*34.2	1.51	10.56	16.0	2.55	7.52	19.2	3.20	18.1	57.9
1986	5.6	37.6	34.0	1.51	10.90	16.4	2.55	7.92	20.2	*4.02	19.4	*77.9
1987	5.6	36.8	33.4	1.40	10.57	14.9	2.48	7.51	18.7	3.96	19.0	74.6
1988	5.5	36.3	32.8	1.34	10.61	14.2	2.40	7.96	19.2	3.95	18.8	74.3
1989	5.5	36.1	32.8	1.31	10.40	13.7	2.32	7.93	18.4	3.96	18.9	74.7
1990	5.4	36.7	32.7	1.38	11.94	16.5	2.49	8.46	21.0	4.02	18.9	75.9
1991	5.3	36.6	32.6	1.35	10.81	14.6	2.46	8.57	21.1	3.84	19.1	73.4
1992	5.3	36.6	32.2	1.21	10.24	12.3	2.53	9.35	*23.6	3.82	19.5	74.4
1993	5.2	36.0	32.3	1.23	10.79	13.2	2.35	8.26	19.5	3.72	19.3	71.7
1994	5.2	36.3	32.1	1.27	10.94	13.8	2.38	9.20	21.9	3.83	*19.9	76.0
1995	5.4	35.8	32.0	1.16	12.20	14.1	2.36	8.57	20.2	3.73	18.6	69.4
1996	5.5	36.6	32.8	1.22	12.25	15.0	2.44	8.54	20.9	3.60	19.0	68.4
1997	5.6	37.3	33.3	1.18	12.32	14.5	2.53	8.90	22.5	3.60	19.1	68.8
1998	5.3	*37.6	33.3	1.12	12.33	13.8	2.54	8.98	22.8	3.90	19.5	75.9
1999	5.4	37.2	32.8	1.18	*12.55	14.8	2.46	*9.40	23.1	3.91	19.1	74.7

*Record.

Rules changes and statistics changes affecting trends: PUNTING–Beginning in 1965, 20 yards not deducted from a punt into the end zone for a touchback. INTERCEPTIONS–Interceptions yards not compiled, 1958-65. KICKOFF RETURNS–During 1937-45, if a kickoff went out of bounds, the receiving team put the ball in play on its 35-yard line instead of a second kickoff; in 1984 (rescinded in 1985), a 30-yard-line touchback for kickoffs crossing the goal line in flight and first touching the ground out of the end zone; in 1986, kickoffs from the 35-yard line. PUNT RETURNS–In 1967, interior linemen restricted from leaving until the ball is kicked.

Division I-AA Defensive Extra-Point Trends

Year	Games	Ret./TDs	Ret./TDs	Ret./TDs
1988	553	4/1	7/1	11/2
1989	554	11/4	4/2	15/6
1990	548	7/3	4/2	11/5
1991	560	12/3	9/2	21/5
1992	553	9/5	8/5	17/10
1993	725	11/5	19/3	30/8
1994	733	4/1	5/1	9/2
1995	736	9/2	9/4	18/6
1996	723	8/3	3/0	11/3
1997	723	11/1	7/5	18/6
1998	733	18/4	8/2	26/6
1999	742	19/5	6/2	25/7
Totals	7,883	123/37	89/29	212/66

Division I-AA Fumble-Recovery Returns

Year	Games	Fumble Rec./TDs
1990	548	34/16
1991	560	42/13
1992	553	96/42
1993	725	86/25
1994	733	99/23
1995	736	164/58
1996	723	169/63
1997	723	149/63
1998	733	121/66
1999	742	136/68
Total	6,776	1,096/437

DIVISION I-AA CLASSIFICATION HISTORY

Classification History

SINCE 1978

The following lists show years of active membership for current and former Division I-AA football-playing institutions. The lists are from 1978, the year that Division I was divided into I-A and I-AA.

ACTIVE MEMBERS (122)

Institution	Years
Alabama A&M	1999
Alabama St.	1992-99
Albany (N.Y.)	1999
Alcorn St.	1978-99
Appalachian St.	1992-99
Ark.-Pine Bluff	1998-99
Austin Peay	1978-99
Bethune-Cookman	1980-99
Brown	1982-99
Bucknell	1978-99
Butler	1993-99
Cal Poly	1994-99
Cal St. Northridge	1993-99
Cal St. Sacramento	1993-99
Canisius	1993-99
Central Conn. St.	1993-99
Charleston So.	1993-99
Chattanooga	1982-99
Citadel	1982-99
Colgate	1982-99
Columbia	1982-99
Connecticut	1978-99
Cornell	1982-99
Dartmouth	1982-99
Davidson	1978-90, 93-99
Dayton	1993-99
Delaware	1980-99
Delaware St.	1978, 80-99
Drake	1992-85, 93-99
Duquesne	1993-99
East Tenn. St.	1982-99
Eastern Ill.	1981-99
Eastern Ky.	1978-99
Eastern Wash.	1984-99
Elon	1999
Fairfield	1997-99
Florida A&M	1979-99
Fordham	1989-99
Furman	1982-99
Georgetown	1993-99
Ga. Southern	1984-99
Grambling	1978-99
Hampton	1997-99
Harvard	1982-99
Hofstra	1993-99
Holy Cross	1982-99
Howard	1978, 80-99
Idaho St.	1978-99
Illinois St.	1982-99
Indiana St.	1982-99
Iona	1993-99
Jackson St.	1978-99
Jacksonville	1998-99
Jacksonville St.	1997-99
James Madison	1980-99
La Salle	1997-99
Lafayette	1978-99
Lehigh	1978-99
Liberty	1989-99
Maine	1978-99
Marist	1993-99
Massachusetts	1978-99
McNeese St.	1982-99
Mississippi Val.	1980-99
Monmouth	1994-99
Montana	1978-99
Montana St.	1978-99
Morehead St.	1978-99
Morgan St.	1986-99
Murray St.	1978-99
New Hampshire	1978-99
Nicholls St.	1980-99
Norfolk St.	1997-99
N.C. A&T	1978, 80-99
Northeastern	1978-99
Northern Ariz.	1978-99
Northern Iowa	1981-99
Northwestern St.	1978-99
Pennsylvania	1982-99
Portland St.	1978-80, 98-99
Prairie View	1990-89, 92-99
Princeton	1982-99
Rhode Island	1978-99
Richmond	1982-99
Robert Morris	1998-99
St. Francis (Pa.)	1993-99
St. John's (N.Y.)	1993-99
St. Mary's (Cal.)	1993-99
St. Peter's	1993-99
Sacred Heart	1999
Samford	1989-99
Sam Houston St.	1986-99
San Diego	1993-99
Siena	1993-99
South Carolina St.	1978, 80-99
South Fla.	1997-99
Southeast Mo. St.	1990-99
Southern Ill.	1982-99
Southern U.	1978-99
Southern Utah	1993-99
Southwest Mo. St.	1982-99
Southwest Tex. St.	1984-99
Stephen F. Austin	1986-99
Stony Brook	1999
Tenn.-Martin	1992-99
Tennessee St.	1981-99
Tennessee Tech	1978-99
Texas Southern	1978-99
Towson	1987-99
Troy St.	1993-99
Valparaiso	1993-99
Villanova	1987-99
VMI	1982-99
Wagner	1993-99
Weber St.	1978-99
Western Caro.	1982-99
Western Ill.	1981-99
Western Ky.	1978-99
William & Mary	1982-99
Wofford	1997-99
Yale	1982-99
Youngstown St.	1981-99

FORMER MEMBERS

Institution	Years
UAB	1993-95
Akron	1980-86
Arkansas St.	1982-91
Ball St.	1982
Boise St.	1978-98
Boston U.	1978-97
Bowling Green	1982
Buffalo	1993-98
UCF	1990-95
Eastern Mich.	1982
Evansville	1993-97
Idaho	1978-96
Kent St.	1982
Lamar	1982-89
La.-Monroe	1982-93
Louisiana Tech	1982-88
Marshall	1982-96
Middle Tenn. St.	1978-98
Nevada	1978-91
North Texas	1982-94
Northern Ill.	1982
Ohio	1982
Southeastern La.	1980-85
Texas-Arlington	1982-85
West Tex. A&M	1982-85

Black College National Champions

Sheridan Poll

Selected by the Pittsburgh Courier, 1920-1980, and compiled by Collie Nicholson, former Grambling sports information director; William Nunn Jr., Pittsburgh Courier sports editor; and Eric "Ric" Roberts, Pittsburgh Courier sports writer and noted black college sports historian. Selected from 1981 by the Sheridan Broadcasting Network, 411 Seventh Ave., Suite 1500, Pittsburgh, Pa. 15219-1905. Records include postseason games.

Year	Team	Won	Lost	Tied	Coach
1920	Howard	7	0	0	Edward Morrison
	Talladega	5	0	1	Jubie Bragg
1921	Talladega	6	0	1	Jubie Bragg
	Wiley	7	0	1	Jason Grant
1922	Hampton	6	1	0	Gideon Smith
1923	Virginia Union	6	0	1	Harold Martin
1924	Tuskegee	9	0	1	Cleve Abbott
	Wiley	8	0	1	Fred Long
1925	Tuskegee	8	0	1	Cleve Abbott
	Howard	6	0	2	Louis Watson
1926	Tuskegee	10	0	0	Cleve Abbott
	Howard	7	0	0	Louis Watson
1927	Tuskegee	9	0	1	Cleve Abbott
	Bluefield St.	8	0	1	Harry Jefferson
1928	Bluefield St.	8	0	1	Harry Jefferson
	Wiley	8	0	1	Fred Long
1929	Tuskegee	10	0	0	Cleve Abbott
1930	Tuskegee	11	0	1	Cleve Abbott
1931	Wilberforce	9	0	0	Harry Graves
1932	Wiley	9	0	0	Fred Long
1933	Morgan St.	9	0	0	Edward Hurt
1934	Kentucky St.	9	0	0	Henry Kean
1935	Texas College	9	0	0	Arnett Mumford
1936	West Virginia St.	8	0	0	Adolph Hamblin
	Virginia St.	7	0	2	Harry Jefferson
1937	Morgan St.	7	0	0	Edward Hurt
1938	Florida A&M	8	0	0	Bill Bell
1939	Langston	9	0	0	Felton "Zip" Gayles
1940	Morris Brown	9	1	0	Artis Graves
1941	Morris Brown	8	1	0	William Nicks
1942	Florida A&M	9	0	0	Bill Bell
1943	Morgan St.	5	0	0	Edward Hurt
1944	Morgan St.	6	1	0	Edward Hurt

Black College National Champions

Year	Team	Won	Lost	Tied	Coach
1945	Wiley	10	0	0	Fred Long
1946	Tennessee St.	10	1	0	Henry Kean
	Morgan St.	8	0	0	Edward Hurt
1947	Tennessee St.	10	0	0	Henry Kean
	Shaw	10	0	0	Brutus Wilson
1948	Southern U.	12	0	0	Arnett Mumford
1949	Southern U.	10	0	1	Arnett Mumford
	Morgan St.	8	0	0	Edward Hurt
1950	Southern U.	10	0	1	Arnett Mumford
	Florida A&M	8	1	1	Alonzo "Jake" Gaither
1951	Morris Brown	10	1	0	Edward "Ox" Clemons
1952	Florida A&M	8	2	0	Alonzo "Jake" Gaither
	Texas Southern	10	0	1	Alexander Durley
	Lincoln (Mo.)	8	0	1	Dwight Reed
	Virginia St.	8	1	0	Sylvester "Sal" Hall
1953	Prairie View	12	0	0	William Nicks
1954	Tennessee St.	10	1	0	Henry Kean
	Southern U.	10	1	0	Arnett Mumford
	Florida A&M	8	1	0	Alonzo "Jake" Gaither
	Prairie View	10	1	0	William Nicks
1955	Grambling	10	0	0	Eddie Robinson
1956	Tennessee St.	10	0	0	Howard Gentry
1957	Florida A&M	9	0	0	Alonzo "Jake" Gaither
1958	Prairie View	10	0	1	William Nicks
1959	Florida A&M	10	0	0	Alonzo "Jake" Gaither
1960	Southern U.	9	1	0	Arnett Mumford
1961	Florida A&M	10	0	0	Alonzo "Jake" Gaither
1962	Jackson St.	10	1	0	John Merritt
1963	Prairie View	10	1	0	William Nicks
1964	Prairie View	9	0	0	William Nicks
1965	Tennessee St.	9	0	1	John Merritt
1966	Tennessee St.	10	0	0	John Merritt
1967	Morgan St.	8	0	0	Earl Banks
	Grambling	9	1	0	Eddie Robinson
1968	Alcorn St.	9	1	0	Marino Casem
	N.C. A&T	8	1	0	Hornsby Howell
1969	Alcorn St.	8	0	1	Marino Casem
1970	Tennessee St.	11	0	0	John Merritt
1971	Tennessee St.	9	1	0	John Merritt
1972	Grambling	11	2	0	Eddie Robinson
1973	Tennessee St.	10	0	0	John Merritt
1974	Grambling	11	1	0	Eddie Robinson
	Alcorn St.	9	2	0	Marino Casem
1975	Grambling	10	2	0	Eddie Robinson
1976	South Carolina St.	10	1	0	Willie Jeffries
1977	South Carolina St.	9	1	1	Willie Jeffries
	Grambling	10	1	0	Eddie Robinson
	Florida A&M	11	0	0	Rudy Hubbard
1978	Florida A&M	12	1	0	Rudy Hubbard
1979	Tennessee St.	8	3	0	John Merritt
1980	Grambling	10	2	0	Eddie Robinson
1981	South Carolina St.	10	3	0	Bill Davis
1982	*Tennessee St.	9	0	1	John Merritt
1983	Grambling	8	1	2	Eddie Robinson
1984	Alcorn St.	9	1	0	Marino Casem
1985	Jackson St.	8	3	0	W. C. Gorden
1986	Central St.	10	1	1	Billy Joe
1987	Central St.	10	1	1	Billy Joe
1988	Central St.	11	2	0	Billy Joe
1989	Central St.	10	2	0	Billy Joe
1990	# Central St.	11	1	0	Billy Joe
1991	Alabama St.	11	0	1	Houston Markham
1992	Grambling	10	2	0	Eddie Robinson
1993	Southern U.	11	1	0	Pete Richardson
1994	Hampton	10	1	0	Joe Taylor
1995	Southern U.	11	1	0	Pete Richardson
1996	Jackson St.	10	2	0	James Carson
1997	Southern U.	11	1	0	Pete Richardson
1998	Florida A&M	11	2	0	Billy Joe
1999	N.C. A&T	11	2	0	Bill Hayes

*Tennessee State's participation in the 1982 Division I-AA championship (1-1 record) voided. #NAIA Division I national champion.

American Sports Wire

Selected by American Sports Wire and compiled by Dick Simpson, Executive Director. Selected from 1990 by the American Sports Wire, P.O. Box 802031, Santa Clarita, Calif. 91380-2031. Record includes postseason games.

Year	Team	Won	Lost	Tied	Coach
1990	N.C. A&T	9	2	0	Bill Hayes
1991	Alabama St.	11	0	1	Houston Markham
1992	Grambling	10	2	0	Eddie Robinson
1993	Southern U.	11	1	0	Pete Richardson
1994	Hampton	10	1	0	Joe Taylor
1995	Southern U.	11	1	0	Pete Richardson
1996	Jackson St.	10	2	0	James Carson
1997	Southern U.	11	1	0	Pete Richardson
1998	Florida A&M	11	2	0	Billy Joe
1999	N.C. A&T	11	2	0	Bill Hayes

Heritage Bowl

The first bowl game matching historically black schools in Division I-AA. The champion of the Southwestern Athletic Conference meets the champion of the Mid-Eastern Athletic Conference.

Date	Score (Attendance)	Site
12-21-91	Alabama St. 36, N.C. A&T 13 (7,724)	Miami, Fla.
1-2-93	Grambling 45, Florida A&M 15 (11,273)	Tallahassee, Fla.
1-1-94	Southern U. 11, South Carolina St. 0 (36,128)	Atlanta, Ga.
12-30-94	South Carolina St. 31, Grambling 27 (22,179)	Atlanta, Ga.
12-29-95	Southern U. 30, Florida A&M 25 (25,164)	Atlanta, Ga.
12-31-96	Howard 27, Southern U. 24 (18,126)	Atlanta, Ga.
12-27-97	Southern U. 34, South Carolina St. 28 (32,629)	Atlanta, Ga.
12-26-98	Southern U. 28, Bethune-Cookman 2 (32, 955)	Atlanta, Ga.
12-18-99	Hampton 24, Southern U. 3 (29,561)	Atlanta, Ga.

All-Time Black College Football Team

(Selected by the Sheridan Broadcasting Network in 1993)

OFFENSE

QB	Doug Williams	Grambling
RB	Walter Payton	Jackson St.
RB	Tank Younger	Grambling
WR	Jerry Rice	Mississippi Val.
WR	John Stallworth	Alabama A&M
WR	Charlie Joiner	Grambling
OL	Art Shell	Md.-East. Shore
OL	Rayfield Wright	Fort Valley St.
OL	Jackie Slater	Jackson St.
OL	Larry Little	Bethune-Cookman
OL	Ernie Barnes	N.C. Central

DEFENSE

DL	Willie Davis	Grambling
DL	Ed "Too Tall" Jones	Tennessee St.
DL	Deacon Jones	South Carolina St.
DL	L. C. Greenwood	Ark.-Pine Bluff
LB	Robert Brazile	Jackson St.
LB	Harry Carson	South Carolina St.
LB	Willie Lanier	Morgan St.
DB	Mel Blount	Southern U.
DB	Lem Barney	Jackson St.
DB	Donnie Shell	South Carolina St.
DB	Everson Walls	Grambling

Division II Records

Individual Records 150
Team Records 155
Annual Champions, All-Time Leaders 157
Team Champions 170
All-Time Team Won-Lost Records 173
National Poll Rankings 174
Undefeated, Untied Teams 175
Streaks and Rivalries 177
Cliffhangers 178
Division II Stadiums 179
Division II Statistics Trends 180

Individual Records

Official national statistics for all nonmajor four-year colleges began in 1946 with a limited post-season survey. In 1948, the service was expanded to include weekly individual and team statistics rankings in all categories except interceptions, field goals, punt returns and kickoff returns; these categories were added to official individual rankings and records in 1970. In 1992, statistics compilations for individual all-purpose yards and team net punting, punt returns, kickoff returns and turnover margin were begun.

From 1946, individual rankings were by totals. Beginning in 1970, most season individual rankings were by per-game averages. In total offense, receiving yards, all-purpose yards, rushing and scoring, yards or points per game determine rankings; in receiving and interceptions, catches per game; in punt and kickoff returns, yards per return; and in field goals, number made per game. Punting always has been by average, and all team rankings have been per game.

Beginning in 1979, passers were ranked in all divisions on efficiency rating points, and team pass defense rankings changed to the same rating system in 1990 (see page 6 for explanation).

Before 1967, rankings and records included all four-year colleges that reported their statistics to the NCAA. Beginning with the 1967 season, rankings and records included only members of the NCAA.

In 1973, College Division teams were divided into Division II and Division III under a three-division reorganization plan adopted by the special NCAA Convention on August 1, 1973. Career records of players include only those years in which they competed in Division II.

Collegiate records for all NCAA divisions can be determined by comparing records for all four divisions.

All individual and team statistics rankings include regular-season games only.

Total Offense

(Rushing Plus Passing)

MOST PLAYS
Game
  88—Jarrod DeGeorgia, Wayne St. (Neb.) vs. Drake, Nov. 9, 1996 (594 yards)
Season
  599—Matt Kissell, Mercyhurst, 1999 (3,070 yards)
  Also holds per-game record with 59.9 (599 in 10)
Career
  2,045—Earl Harvey, N.C. Central, 1985-88 (10,667 yards)
  Also holds per-game record with 49.9 (2,045 in 41)

MOST PLAYS BY A FRESHMAN
Season
  538—Earl Harvey, N.C. Central, 1985 (3,008 yards)
  Also holds per-game record with 53.8 (538 in 10)

MOST YARDS GAINED
Game
  651—Wilkie Perez, Glenville St. vs. Concord, Oct. 25, 1997 (9 rushing, 642 passing)
Season
  4,301—Wilkie Perez, Glenville St., 1997 (112 rushing, 4,189 passing)
  Per-game record—411.0, Grady Benton, West Tex. A&M, 1994 (3,699 in 9)

Career
  11,227—Vernon Buck, Wingate, 1991-94 (1,343 rushing, 9,884 passing)
  Per-game record—323.9, Grady Benton, West Tex. A&M, 1994-95 (5,831 in 18)

MOST SEASONS GAINING 3,000 YARDS OR MORE
  2—Pat Brennan, Franklin, 1983 (3,239) & 1984 (3,248); Chris Hatcher, Valdosta St., 1993 (3,532) & 1994 (3,512); Lance Funderburk, Valdosta St., 1995 (3,549) & 1996 (3,676)

MOST SEASONS GAINING 2,500 YARDS OR MORE
  3—Jim Lindsey, Abilene Christian, 1968 (2,740), 1969 (2,646) & 1970 (2,654); Thad Trujillo, Fort Lewis, 1992 (3,047), 1993 (2,784) & 1994 (2,535); Bob McLaughlin, Lock Haven, 1993 (2,928), 1994 (2,996) & 1995 (3,092)

GAINING 1,000 YARDS RUSHING AND 1,000 YARDS PASSING
Season
  Ed Thompson, Neb.-Omaha, 1997 (1,075 rushing, 1,164 passing) & 1998 (1,191 rushing, 1,027 passing); Kwanzi Watts, Neb.-Omaha, 1999 (1,119 rushing, 1,324 passing)

GAINING 2,000 YARDS RUSHING AND 4,000 YARDS PASSING
Career
  Brad Cornelson, Mo. Southern St., 1995-97 (2,134 rushing, 4,186 passing)

GAINING 2,500 YARDS RUSHING AND 3,000 YARDS PASSING
Career
  Jeff Bentrim, North Dakota St., 1983-86 (2,946 rushing, 3,453 passing)

MOST YARDS GAINED BY A FRESHMAN
Game
  482—Matt Montgomery, Hampton vs. Tuskegee, Oct. 26, 1991
Season
  3,008—Earl Harvey, N.C. Central, 1985 (538 plays)
  Per-game record—318.1, Shawn Dupris, Southwest St., 1993 (2,863 in 9)

MOST GAMES GAINING 300 YARDS OR MORE
Season
  8—Chris Hegg, Truman, 1985
Career
  16—Thad Trujillo, Fort Lewis, 1991-94

HIGHEST AVERAGE GAIN PER PLAY
Season
  (Min. 350 plays) 8.8—Brett Salisbury, Wayne St. (Neb.), 1993 (424 for 3,732)
Career
  (Min. 950 plays) 7.4—Donald Smith, Langston, 1958-61 (998 for 7,376)

MOST TOUCHDOWNS RESPONSIBLE FOR
(TDs Scored and Passed For)
Game
  10—Bruce Swanson, North Park vs. North Central, Oct. 12, 1968 (passed for 10)
  Also holds Most Points Responsible For record with 60
Season
  50—Chris Hatcher, Valdosta St., 1994 (passed for 50)
  Also holds Most Points Responsible For record with 300
Career
  120—Chris Hatcher, Valdosta St., 1991-94 (scored 4, passed for 116)
  Also holds Most Points Responsible For record with 722

Rushing

MOST RUSHES
Game
  62—Nelson Edmonds, Northern Mich. vs. Wayne St. (Mich.), Oct. 26, 1991 (291 yards)

Season
  385—Joe Gough, Wayne St. (Mich.), 1994 (1,593 yards)
  Per-game record—38.6, Mark Perkins, Hobart, 1968 (309 in 8)
Career
  1,072—Bernie Peeters, Luther, 1968-71 (4,435 yards)
  Also holds per-game record with 29.8 (1,072 in 36)

MOST CONSECUTIVE RUSHES BY SAME PLAYER
Game
  21—Roger Graham, New Haven vs. Knoxville, Oct. 29, 1994 (during six possessions)

MOST RUSHES BY A QUARTERBACK
Career
  730—Shawn Graves, Wofford, 1989-92

MOST YARDS GAINED
Half
  226—Brian Shay, Emporia St. vs. Central Mo. St., Nov. 16, 1996 (28 rushes)
Game
  403—Rob Davidson, Fairmont St. vs. Concord, Nov. 14, 1998 (48 rushes)
Season
  2,653—Kavin Gailliard, American Int'l, 1999 (320 rushes)
  Per-game record—222.0, Anthony Gray, Western N.M, 1997 (277 rushes)
Career
  6,958—Brian Shay, Emporia St., 1995-98 (1,007 rushes)
  Per-game record—183.4, Anthony Gray, Western N.M., 1997-98 (3,484 in 19)

MOST YARDS GAINED BY A FRESHMAN
Game
  370—Jim Hissam, Marietta vs. Bethany (W.Va.), Nov. 15, 1958 (22 rushes)
Season
  2,011—Johnny Bailey, Tex. A&M-Kingsville, 1986 (271 rushes)
  Also holds per-game record with 182.8 (2,011 in 11)

MOST YARDS GAINED IN FIRST GAME OF CAREER
  238—Johnny Bailey, Tex. A&M-Kingsville vs. Texas Southern, Sept. 6, 1986

MOST YARDS GAINED AGAINST ONE OPPONENT
Career
  1,010—Brian Shay, Emporia St. vs. Washburn, 1995-98 (112 rushes)

MOST YARDS GAINED BY TWO PLAYERS, SAME TEAM
Game
  514—Thelbert Withers (333) & Derrick Ray (181), N.M. Highlands vs. Fort Lewis, Oct. 17, 1992
Season
  3,526—Johnny Bailey (2,011) & Heath Sherman (1,515), Tex. A&M-Kingsville, 1986
  Also hold per-game record with 320.5 (3,526 in 11)
Career
  8,594—Johnny Bailey (5,051) & Heath Sherman (3,543), Tex. A&M-Kingsville, 1986-88 (1,317 rushes)

TWO PLAYERS, SAME TEAM, EACH GAINING 200 YARDS OR MORE
Game
  Five times. Most recent: Thad Variance (204) & Pat Norris (203), N.M. Highlands vs. Colorado Mines, Oct. 10, 1998

TWO PLAYERS, SAME TEAM, EACH GAINING 1,000 YARDS OR MORE
Season
  17 times. Most recent: Terrance Wilson (1,039) & Aamir Dew (1,002), Indiana (Pa.), 1999; Kwanzi Watts (1,119) & Adam Wright (1,056), Neb.-Omaha, 1999; Dorrian Glenn (1,067) & Stan Kennedy (1,021), Slippery Rock, 1999

MOST GAMES GAINING 100 YARDS OR MORE
Season
  11—Johnny Bailey, Tex. A&M-Kingsville, 1986; Ronald Moore, Pittsburg St., 1992; Brian Shay, Emporia St., 1996 & 1998; Kavin Gailliard, American Int'l, 1999
  Bailey also holds freshman record with 11

INDIVIDUAL RECORDS—RUSHING

Career
34—Damian Beane, Shepherd, 1996-99 (38 games)

MOST CONSECUTIVE GAMES GAINING 100 YARDS OR MORE
Season
11—Johnny Bailey, Tex. A&M-Kingsville, 1986; Ronald Moore, Pittsburg St., 1992; Brian Shay, Emporia St., 1996 & 1998
Bailey also holds freshman record with 11
Career
25—Roger Graham, New Haven, 1992-94

MOST GAMES GAINING 200 YARDS OR MORE
Season
10—Kavin Gailliard, American Int'l, 1999
Career
15—Brian Shay, Emporia St., 1995-98 (44 games)

MOST GAMES GAINING 200 YARDS OR MORE BY A FRESHMAN
Season
5—Johnny Bailey, Tex. A&M-Kingsville, 1986

MOST CONSECUTIVE GAMES GAINING 200 YARDS OR MORE
Season
8—Kavin Gailliard, American Int'l, 1999

MOST GAMES GAINING 300 YARDS OR MORE
Season
4—Anthony Gray, Western N.M., 1997

MOST YARDS GAINED BY A QUARTERBACK
Game
323—Shawn Graves, Wofford vs. Lenoir-Rhyne, Sept. 15, 1990 (23 rushes)
Season
1,483—Shawn Graves, Wofford, 1989 (241 rushes)
Career
5,128—Shawn Graves, Wofford, 1989-92 (730 rushes)

MOST SEASONS GAINING 1,000 YARDS OR MORE
Career
4—Johnny Bailey, Tex. A&M-Kingsville, 1986-89; Jeremy Monroe, Michigan Tech, 1990-93; Jarrett Anderson, Truman, 1993-96; Damian Beane, Shepherd, 1996-99

HIGHEST AVERAGE GAIN PER RUSH
Game
(Min. 20 rushes) 17.5—Don Polkinghorne, Washington (Mo.) vs. Wash. & Lee, Nov. 23, 1957 (21 for 367)
Season
(Min. 140 rushes) 10.5—Billy Johnson, Widener, 1972 (148 for 1,556)
(Min. 200 rushes) 8.6—Roger Graham, New Haven, 1992 (200 for 1,717)
(Min. 250 rushes) 8.3—Kavin Gailliard, American Int'l, 1999 (320 for 2,653)
Career
(Min. 500 rushes) 8.5—Bill Rhodes, Western St., 1953-56 (506 for 4,294)
(Min. 750 rushes) 7.3—Roger Graham, New Haven, 1991-94 (821 for 5,953)

MOST RUSHING TOUCHDOWNS SCORED
Game
8—Junior Wolf, Okla. Panhandle vs. St. Mary (Kan.), Nov. 8, 1958
Season
32—Kavin Gailliard, American Int'l, 1999
Career
81—Brian Shay, Emporia St., 1995-98
Also holds per-game record with 1.8 (81 in 44)

MOST RUSHING TOUCHDOWNS SCORED BY A FRESHMAN
Season
24—Shawn Graves, Wofford, 1989
Also holds per-game record with 2.2 (24 in 11)

MOST RUSHING TOUCHDOWNS SCORED BY A QUARTERBACK
Season
24—Shawn Graves, Wofford, 1989
Per-game record—2.3, Jeff Bentrim, North Dakota St., 1986 (23 in 10)

Career
72—Shawn Graves, Wofford, 1989-92
Per-game record—1.8, Jeff Bentrim, North Dakota St., 1983-86 (64 in 35)

MOST RUSHING TOUCHDOWNS SCORED BY TWO PLAYERS, SAME TEAM
Season
41—Heath Sherman (23) & Johnny Bailey (18), Tex. A&M-Kingsville, 1986; Roger Graham (22) & A. J. Livingston (19), New Haven, 1992
Per-game record—4.1, Roger Graham & A. J. Livingston, New Haven, 1992 (41 in 10)
Career
106—Heath Sherman (55) & Johnny Bailey (51), Tex. A&M-Kingsville, 1985-88

LONGEST PLAY
99 yards—21 times. Most recent: Ronaie Maye, Carson-Newman vs. Lenoir-Rhyne, Oct. 30, 1999

Passing

HIGHEST PASSING EFFICIENCY RATING POINTS
Season
(Min. 15 atts. per game) 210.1—Boyd Crawford, Col. of Idaho, 1953 (120 attempts, 72 completions, 6 interceptions, 1,462 yards, 21 TD passes)
(Min. 100 comps.) 189.0—Chuck Green, Wittenberg, 1963 (182 attempts, 114 completions, 8 interceptions, 2,181 yards, 19 TD passes)
(Min. 200 comps.) 179.0—Chris Hatcher, Valdosta St., 1994 (430 attempts, 321 completions, 9 interceptions, 3,591 yards, 50 TD passes)
Career
(Min. 375 comps.) 167.0—Wilkie Perez, Glenville St., 1997-98 (567 attempts, 376 completions, 17 interceptions, 5,240 yards, 50 TD passes)
(Min. 750 comps.) 153.1—Chris Hatcher, Valdosta St., 1991-94 (1,451 attempts, 1,001 completions, 38 interceptions, 10,878 yards, 116 TD passes)

MOST PASSES ATTEMPTED
Game
76—Jarrod DeGeorgia, Wayne St. (Neb.) vs. Drake, Nov. 9, 1996 (completed 56)
Season
544—Lance Funderburk, Valdosta St., 1995 (completed 356)
Per-game record—50.5, Marty Washington, West Ala., 1993 (404 in 8)
Career
1,719—Bob McLaughlin, Lock Haven, 1992-95 (completed 910)
Per-game record—46.2, Tim Von Dulm, Portland St., 1969-70 (924 in 20)

MOST PASSES COMPLETED
Game
56—Jarrod DeGeorgia, Wayne St. (Neb.) vs. Drake, Nov. 9, 1996 (attempted 76)
Season
356—Lance Funderburk, Valdosta St., 1995 (attempted 544)
Also holds per-game record with 32.4 (356 in 11)
Career
1,001—Chris Hatcher, Valdosta St., 1991-94 (attempted 1,451)
Also holds per-game record with 25.7 (1,001 in 39)

MOST PASSES COMPLETED BY A FRESHMAN
Game
41—Neil Lomax, Portland St. vs. Montana St., Nov. 19, 1977 (attempted 59)

MOST CONSECUTIVE PASSES COMPLETED
Game
20—Rod Bockwoldt, Weber St. vs. South Dakota St., Nov. 6, 1976; Chris Hatcher, Valdosta St. vs. New Haven, Oct. 8, 1994
Season
23—Mike Ganey, Allegheny, 1967 (completed last 16 attempts vs. Carnegie Mellon, Oct. 9, and first 7 vs. Oberlin, Oct. 16)

HIGHEST PERCENTAGE OF PASSES COMPLETED
Game
(Min. 20 comps.) 90.9%—Rod Bockwoldt, Weber St. vs. South Dakota St., Nov. 6, 1976 (20 of 22)
(Min. 35 comps.) 88.6%—Chris Hatcher, Valdosta St. vs. New Haven, Oct. 8, 1994 (39 of 44)
Season
(Min. 225 atts.) 74.7%—Chris Hatcher, Valdosta St., 1994 (321 of 430)
Career
(Min. 500 atts.) 69.6%—Chris Petersen, UC Davis, 1985-86 (385 of 553)
(Min. 1,000 atts.) 69.0%—Chris Hatcher, Valdosta St., 1991-94 (1,001 of 1,451)

MOST PASSES HAD INTERCEPTED
Game
9—Henry Schafer, Johns Hopkins vs. Haverford, Oct. 16, 1965; Pat Brennan, Franklin vs. Saginaw Valley, Sept. 24, 1983
Season
32—Joe Stetser, Cal St. Chico, 1967 (attempted 464)
Career
88—Bob McLaughlin, Lock Haven, 1992-95 (attempted 1,719)

LOWEST PERCENTAGE OF PASSES HAD INTERCEPTED
Season
(Min. 200 atts.) 0.4%—James Weir, New Haven, 1993 (1 of 266)
(Min. 300 atts.) 1.0%—Jesse Showerda, New Haven, 1996 (3 of 300)
Career
(Min. 500 atts.) 2.1%—Jeff Fox, Grand Valley St., 1995-98 (22 of 1,031)

MOST PASSES ATTEMPTED WITHOUT INTERCEPTION
Game
70—Tim Von Dulm, Portland St. vs. Eastern Wash., Nov. 21, 1970
Season
113—Jeff Allen, New Hampshire, 1975

MOST CONSECUTIVE PASSES ATTEMPTED WITHOUT INTERCEPTION
280—Jesse Showerda, New Haven, during 10 games from Sept. 7 to Nov. 16, 1996

MOST YARDS GAINED
Game
642—Wilkie Perez, Glenville St. vs. Concord, Oct. 25, 1997
Season
4,189—Wilkie Perez, Glenville St., 1997
Per-game record—393.4, Grady Benton, West Tex. A&M, 1994 (3,541 in 9)
Career
10,878—Chris Hatcher, Valdosta St., 1991-94
Per-game record—312.1, Grady Benton, West Tex. A&M, 1994-95 (5,618 in 18)

MOST YARDS GAINED BY A FRESHMAN
Game
469—Neil Lomax, Portland St. vs. Montana St., Nov. 19, 1977
Season
3,190—Earl Harvey, N.C. Central, 1985

MOST GAMES GAINING 200 YARDS OR MORE
Season
11—Six times. Most recent: Mike Mitros, West Chester, 1998
Career
31—Chris Hatcher, Valdosta St., 1991-94

MOST CONSECUTIVE GAMES GAINING 200 YARDS OR MORE
Career
28—Chris Hatcher, Valdosta St., 1992-94 (last 6 in 1992, all 11 in 1993 and 1994)

MOST GAMES GAINING 300 YARDS OR MORE
Season
10—Brett Salisbury, Wayne St. (Neb.), 1993
Career
16—Chris Hatcher, Valdosta St., 1991-94

INDIVIDUAL RECORDS—PASSING

MOST CONSECUTIVE GAMES GAINING 300 YARDS OR MORE
Season
10—Brett Salisbury, Wayne St. (Neb.), 1993

MOST YARDS GAINED PER ATTEMPT
Season
(Min. 300 atts.) 11.3—Jayson Merrill, Western St., 1991 (309 for 3,484)
Career
(Min. 500 atts.) 10.6—John Charles, Portland St., 1991-92 (510 for 5,389)
(Min. 700 atts.) 9.0—Bruce Upstill, Col. of Emporia, 1960-63 (769 for 6,935)

MOST YARDS GAINED PER COMPLETION
Season
(Min. 125 comps.) 18.7—Matt Cook, Mo. Southern St., 1991 (141 for 2,637)
(Min. 175 comps.) 17.9—Damian Poalucci, East Stroudsburg, 1996 (214 for 3,831)
Career
(Min. 300 comps.) 17.8—Jayson Merrill, Western St., 1990-91 (328 for 5,830)
(Min. 600 comps.) 15.4—Earl Harvey, N.C. Central, 1985-88 (690 for 10,621)

MOST TOUCHDOWN PASSES
Quarter
5—Kevin Russell, Calif. (Pa.) vs. Frostburg St., Nov. 5, 1983 (2nd quarter)
Game
10—Bruce Swanson, North Park vs. North Central, Oct. 12, 1968
Season
50—Chris Hatcher, Valdosta St., 1994
Also holds per-game record with 4.5 (50 in 11)
Career
116—Chris Hatcher, Valdosta St., 1991-94
Also holds per-game record with 3.0 (116 in 39)

MOST TOUCHDOWN PASSES BY A FRESHMAN
Game
6—Earl Harvey, N.C. Central vs. Johnson Smith, Nov. 9, 1985; Todd Cunningham, Presbyterian vs. Newberry, Nov. 14, 1998
Season
29—Justin Coleman, Neb.-Kearney, 1997

HIGHEST PERCENTAGE OF PASSES FOR TOUCHDOWNS
Season
(Min. 150 atts.) 16.0%—John Ford, Hardin-Simmons, 1949 (26 of 163)
(Min. 300 atts.) 11.6%—Chris Hatcher, Valdosta St., 1994 (50 of 430)
Career
(Min. 500 atts.) 12.2%—Al Niemela, West Chester, 1985-88 (73 of 600)

MOST CONSECUTIVE GAMES THROWING A TOUCHDOWN PASS
Career
24—Matt Cook, Mo. Southern St., 1990-93 (last 2 in 1990, all 11 in 1991, 1 in 1992, all 10 in 1993)

MOST GAMES THROWING A TOUCHDOWN PASS
Career
41—John Craven, Gardner-Webb, 1991-94 (played in 43)

LONGEST COMPLETION
99 yards—20 times. Most recent: Justin Coleman to Mike Smith, Neb.-Kearney vs. Wayne St. (Neb.), Oct. 25, 1997

Receiving

MOST PASSES CAUGHT
Game
23—Barry Wagner, Alabama A&M vs. Clark Atlanta, Nov. 4, 1989 (370 yards); Chris George, Glenville St. vs. West Va. Wesleyan, Oct. 15, 1994 (303 yards)
Season
119—Brad Bailey, West Tex. A&M, 1994 (1,552 yards)
Per-game record—11.7, Chris George, Glenville St., 1993 (117 in 10)
Career
262—Carlos Ferralls, Glenville St., 1994-97 (3,835 yards)
Per-game record—11.5, Chris George, Glenville St., 1993-94 (230 in 20)

MOST CONSECUTIVE GAMES CATCHING A PASS
Career
44—Mitch Allner, Morningside, 1996-99 (all 44 played)

MOST PASSES CAUGHT BY A TIGHT END
Game
15—Six times. Most recent: Mark Martin, Cal St. Chico vs. San Fran. St., Oct. 21, 1989 (223 yards)
Season
77—Bob Tucker, Bloomsburg, 1967 (1,325 yards)
Career
199—Barry Naone, Portland St., 1985-88 (2,237 yards)

MOST PASSES CAUGHT BY A RUNNING BACK
Season
94—Billy Joe Masters, Evansville, 1987 (960 yards)
Also holds per-game record with 9.4 (94 in 10)
Career
200—Mark Steinmeyer, Kutztown, 1988-91 (2,118 yards)
Per-game record—5.4, Mark Marana, Northern Mich., 1979-80 (107 in 20)

MOST PASSES CAUGHT BY A FRESHMAN
Season
94—Jarett Vito, Emporia St., 1995 (932 yards)

MOST PASSES CAUGHT BY TWO PLAYERS, SAME TEAM
Career
399—Jon Spinosa (218) & Bryan McGinty (181), Lock Haven, 1993-95 (4,615 yards)

MOST YARDS GAINED
Game
401—Kevin Ingram, West Chester, vs. Clarion, Oct. 31, 1998 (caught 13)
Season
1,876—Chris George, Glenville St., 1993 (caught 117)
Also holds per-game record with 187.6 (1,876 in 10)
Career
4,468—James Roe, Norfolk St., 1992-95 (caught 239)
Per-game record—160.8, Chris George, Glenville St., 1993-94 (3,215 in 20)

MOST YARDS GAINED BY A TIGHT END
Game
290—Bob Tucker, Bloomsburg vs. Susquehanna, Oct. 7, 1967 (caught 15)
Season
1,325—Bob Tucker, Bloomsburg, 1967 (caught 77)
Career
2,494—Dan Anderson, Northwest Mo. St., 1982-85 (caught 186)

MOST YARDS GAINED BY A RUNNING BACK
Game
209—Don Lenhard, Bucknell vs. Delaware, Nov. 19, 1966 (caught 11)
Season
1,202—Larry Bales, Emory & Henry, 1968 (caught 62)
Also holds per-game record with 120.2 (1,202 in 10)
Career
2,118—Mark Steinmeyer, Kutztown, 1988-91 (caught 200)

MOST YARDS GAINED BY TWO PLAYERS, SAME TEAM
Career
6,528—Robert Clark (4,231) & Robert Green (2,297), N.C. Central, 1983-86 (caught 363)

HIGHEST AVERAGE GAIN PER RECEPTION
Season
(Min. 30 receps.) 32.5—Tyrone Johnson, Western St., 1991 (32 for 1,039)
(Min. 40 receps.) 27.6—Chris Harkness, Ashland, 1987 (41 for 1,131)
(Min. 55 receps.) 24.0—Rod Smith, Mo. Southern St., 1991 (60 for 1,439)
Career
(Min. 135 receps.) 22.8—Tyrone Johnson, Western St., 1990-93 (163 for 3,717)
(Min. 180 receps.) 20.1—Robert Clark, N.C. Central, 1983-86 (210 for 4,231)

HIGHEST AVERAGE GAIN PER RECEPTION BY A RUNNING BACK
Season
(Min. 40 receps.) 19.4—Larry Bales, Emory & Henry, 1968 (62 for 1,202)
Career
(Min. 80 receps.) 18.1—John Smith, Boise St., 1972-75 (89 for 1,608)

MOST TOUCHDOWN PASSES CAUGHT
Quarter
3—Colby Cloude, Shepherd vs. West Liberty St., Nov. 14, 1998
Game
8—Paul Zaeske, North Park vs. North Central, Oct. 12, 1968 (caught 11)
Season
21—Chris Perry, Adams St., 1995 (caught 88); Kevin Ingram, West Chester, 1998 (caught 115)
Perry also holds per-game record with 2.1 (21 in 10)
Career
49—Bruce Cerone, Yankton/Emporia St., 1965-66, 1968-69 (caught 241)
Per-game record—1.6, Ed Bell, Idaho St., 1968-69 (30 in 19)

MOST TOUCHDOWN PASSES CAUGHT BY A TIGHT END
Game
5—Alex Preuss, Grand Valley St. vs. Winona St., Sept. 17, 1988; Mike Palomino, Portland St. vs. Cal Poly, Nov. 16, 1991
Season
13—Bob Tucker, Bloomsburg, 1967

MOST TOUCHDOWN PASSES CAUGHT BY A RUNNING BACK
Season
12—Larry Bales, Emory & Henry, 1968
Career
24—John Smith, Boise St., 1972-75

MOST TOUCHDOWN PASSES CAUGHT BY A FRESHMAN
Season
13—Sean Scott, Millersville, 1997

HIGHEST PERCENTAGE OF PASSES CAUGHT FOR TOUCHDOWNS
Season
(Min. 10 TDs) 68.8%—Jim Callahan, Temple, 1966 (11 of 16)
Career
(Min. 20 TDs) 30.0%—Bob Cherry, Wittenberg, 1960-63 (27 of 90)

MOST CONSECUTIVE PASSES CAUGHT FOR TOUCHDOWNS
Game
5—Jim Callahan, Temple vs. Bucknell, Oct. 8, 1966
Season
10—Jim Callahan, Temple, 1966 (first 5 games of career)

MOST CONSECUTIVE GAMES CATCHING A TOUCHDOWN PASS
Career
20—Brian Penecale, West Chester, from Oct. 30, 1993, through Oct. 7, 1995

MOST GAMES CATCHING A TOUCHDOWN PASS
Career
27—James Roe, Norfolk St., 1992-95 (in 41 games)

LONGEST RECEPTION
99 yards—20 times. Most recent: Mike Smith from Justin Coleman, Neb.-Kearney vs. Wayne St. (Neb.), Oct. 25, 1997

INDIVIDUAL RECORDS—PUNTING

Punting

MOST PUNTS
Game
32—Jan Jones, Sam Houston St. vs. Tex. A&M-Commerce, Nov. 2, 1946 (1,203 yards)
Season
98—John Tassi, Lincoln (Mo.), 1981 (3,163 yards)
Career
328—Dan Brown, Nicholls St., 1976-79 (12,883 yards)

HIGHEST AVERAGE PER PUNT
Game
(Min. 5 punts) 57.5—Tim Baer, Colorado Mines vs. Fort Lewis, Oct. 25, 1986 (8 for 460)
Season
(Min. 20 punts) 49.1—Steve Ecker, Shippensburg, 1965 (32 for 1,570)
(Min. 40 punts) 46.3—Mark Bounds, West Tex. A&M, 1990 (69 for 3,198)
Career
(Min. 100 punts) 44.3—Jason Van Dyke, Adams St., 1995-98 (242 for 10,720)

LONGEST PUNT
97 yards—Earl Hurst, Emporia St. vs. Central Mo. St., Oct. 3, 1964

Interceptions

(From 1970)

MOST PASSES INTERCEPTED
Quarter
3—Mike McDonald, La.-Lafayette vs. Lamar, Oct. 24, 1970 (4th; 25 yards); Anthony Devine, Millersville vs. Cheyney, Oct. 13, 1990 (3rd; 90 yards); Nate Neuhaus, Neb.-Kearney vs. Wayne St. (Neb.), Oct. 25, 1997 (3rd)
Half
4—Nate Neuhaus, Neb.-Kearney vs. Wayne St. (Neb.), Oct. 25, 1997 (2nd)
Game
5—Five times. Most recent: Gary Evans, Truman vs. Mo.-Rolla, Oct. 18, 1975
Season
14—Five times. Most recent: Luther Howard, Delaware St., 1972 (99 yards); Eugene Hunter, Fort Valley St., 1972 (211 yards)
Per-game record—1.6, Tom Rezzuti, Northeastern, 1971 (14 in 9); Eugene Hunter, Fort Valley St., 1972 (14 in 9); Luther Howard, Delaware St., 1972 (14 in 9)
Career
37—Tom Collins, Indianapolis, 1982-85 (390 yards)

MOST CONSECUTIVE GAMES INTERCEPTING A PASS
Career
8—Darin Nix, Mo.-Rolla, 1993-94

MOST YARDS ON INTERCEPTION RETURNS
Game
152—Desmond Brown, Tuskegee vs. Morris Brown, Sept. 15, 1990 (2 interceptions)
Season
300—Mike Brim, Virginia Union, 1986 (8 interceptions)
Career
504—Anthony Leonard, Virginia Union, 1973-76 (17 interceptions)

HIGHEST AVERAGE GAIN PER INTERCEPTION
Season
(Min. 6 ints.) 44.7—Ray Cannon, Bowie St., 1997 (6 for 268)
Career
(Min. 10 ints.) 37.4—Greg Anderson, Montana, 1974-76 (11 for 411)
(Min. 15 ints.) 29.6—Anthony Leonard, Virginia Union, 1973-76 (17 for 504)

MOST TOUCHDOWNS SCORED ON INTERCEPTIONS
Season
4—Clay Blalack, Tenn.-Martin, 1976 (8 interceptions)

LONGEST INTERCEPTION RETURN
100 yards—Many times. Most recent: Tonmar Johnson, Eastern N.M. vs. Midwestern St., Nov. 13, 1999

Punt Returns

(From 1970)

MOST PUNT RETURNS
Game
12—David Nelson, Ferris St. vs. Northern Mich., Oct. 2, 1993 (240 yards)
Season
61—Armin Anderson, UC Davis, 1984 (516 yards)
Career
153—Armin Anderson, UC Davis, 1983-85 (1,207 yards)

MOST YARDS ON PUNT RETURNS
Game
265—Billy Johnson, Widener vs. St. John's (N.Y.), Sept. 23, 1972 (4 returns)
Season
604—David Nelson, Ferris St., 1993 (50 returns)
Career
1,228—Brian Pinks, Northern Mich., 1994-97 (111 returns)

HIGHEST AVERAGE GAIN PER RETURN
Game
(Min. 4 rets.) 66.3—Billy Johnson, Widener vs. St. John's (N.Y.), Sept. 23, 1972 (4 for 265)
Season
(Min. 1.2 rets. per game) 34.1—Billy Johnson, Widener, 1972 (15 for 511)
Career
(Min. 1.2 rets. per game) 26.2—Billy Johnson, Widener, 1971-72 (29 for 759)

MOST OPPONENT'S PUNTS BLOCKED
Season
6—Tim Bowie, Northern Colo., 1995

MOST TOUCHDOWNS SCORED ON PUNT RETURNS
Game
3—Bobby Ahu, Hawaii vs. Linfield, Nov. 15, 1969; Billy Johnson, Widener vs. St. John's (N.Y.), Sept. 23, 1972; Virgil Seay, Troy St. vs. West Ala., Sept. 29, 1979
Season
5—James Rooths, Shepherd, 1998
Career
8—James Rooths, Shepherd, 1997-99

LONGEST PUNT RETURN
100 yards—Many times. Most recent: Randy Ladson, Fayetteville St. vs. St. Paul's, Sept. 19, 1987

Kickoff Returns

(From 1970)

MOST KICKOFF RETURNS
Game
12—Johnny Cox, Fort Lewis vs. Mesa St., Nov. 3, 1990
Season
48—Matt Kacanda, East Stroudsburg, 1999 (1,210 yards)
Career
116—Johnny Cox, Fort Lewis, 1990-93 (2,476 yards)

MOST YARDS ON KICKOFF RETURNS
Game
276—Tom Dufresne, Hamline vs. Minn.-Duluth, Sept. 30, 1972 (7 returns); Matt Pericolosi, Central Conn. St. vs. Hofstra, Sept. 14, 1991 (6 returns)
Season
1,210—Matt Kacanda, East Stroudsburg, 1999 (48 returns)

Career
2,630—Dave Ludy, Winona St., 1991-9.

HIGHEST AVERAGE GAIN PER RETURN
Game
(Min. 3 rets.) 71.7—Clarence Martin, Cal Po Poly Pomona, Nov. 20, 1982 (3 for 215)
Season
(Min. 1.2 rets. per game) 39.4—LaVon Reis, V St., 1993 (14 for 552)
Career
(Min. 1.2 rets. per game) 34.0—Glen Prin Southern Colo., 1973-74 (25 for 851)

MOST TOUCHDOWNS SCORED ON KICKOFF RETURNS
Game
2—Four times. Most recent: Lamart Cooper, Wayne St. (Neb.) vs. Moorhead St., Oct. 29, 1994
Season
3—Eight times. Most recent: Billy Cook, Grand Valley St., 1998
Career
8—Dave Ludy, Winona St., 1991-94

LONGEST KICKOFF RETURN
100 yards—Many times. Most recent: Derrick Foster, Tex. A&M-Kingsville vs. Angelo St., Nov. 13, 1999

Total Kick Returns

(Combined Punt and Kickoff Returns)

MOST KICK RETURNS
Season
63—Bobby Yates, Central Mo. St., 1990 (32 punts, 31 kickoffs, 840 yards)

MOST KICK-RETURN YARDS
Career
3,219—Sean Smith, Bloomsburg, 1993-96 (1,049 on punt returns, 2,170 on kickoff returns, 171 returns)

MOST TOUCHDOWNS
Career
10—Anthony Leonard, Virginia Union, 1973-76 (6 punt returns, 4 kickoff returns)

MOST CONSECUTIVE TOUCHDOWNS ON KICK RETURNS
Game
3—Bootsie Washington, Shepherd vs. West Va. Tech, Oct. 18, 1997 (89-yard kickoff return, 60-yard punt return, 59-yard punt return)

All Runbacks

(Combined Interceptions, Punt Returns and Kick-off Returns)

MOST TOUCHDOWNS
Season
6—Anthony Leonard, Virginia Union, 1974 (2 interceptions, 2 punt returns, 2 kickoff returns); Terry Guess, Gardner-Webb, 1994 (3 punt returns, 3 kickoff returns); Bootsie Washington, Shepherd, 1997 (1 interception, 4 punt returns, 1 kickoff return)
Career
13—Anthony Leonard, Virginia Union, 1973-76 (3 interceptions, 6 punt returns, 4 kickoff returns)

LONGEST RETURN OF A MISSED FIELD GOAL
100—Kalvin Simmons, Clark Atlanta vs. Morris Brown, Sept. 5, 1987 (actually from 6 yards in end zone)

Kicks Blocked

MOST TOTAL KICKS BLOCKED BY
Season
9—Clinton Washington, West Ala., 1997
Career
22—Clinton Washington, West Ala., 1996-99

DIVISION II

INDIVIDUAL RECORDS—ALL-PURPOSE YARDS

All-Purpose Yards
(Yardage Gained From Rushing, Receiving and Runbacks)

MOST PLAYS
Season
415—Steve Roberts, Butler, 1989 (325 rushes, 49 receptions, 21 punt returns, 20 kickoff returns; 2,669 yards)
Career
1,195—Steve Roberts, Butler, 1986-89 (1,026 rushes, 120 receptions, 21 punt returns, 28 kickoff returns; 6,674 yards)

MOST YARDS GAINED
Game
525—Andre Johnson, Ferris St. vs. Clarion, Sept. 16, 1989 (19 rushing, 235 receiving, 10 punt returns, 261 kickoff returns; 17 plays)
Season
3,064—Kavin Gailliard, American Int'l, 1999 (2,653 rushing, 289 receiving, 122 kickoff returns)
Per-game record—266.9, Steve Roberts, Butler, 1989 (2,669 in 10)
Career
9,301—Brian Shay, Emporia St., 1995-98 (6,958 rushing, 1,032 receiving, 104 punt returns, 1,207 kickoff returns)
Per-game record—234.0, Chris George, Glenville St., 1993-94 (4,679 in 20)

MOST YARDS GAINED BY A FRESHMAN
Season
2,425—Johnny Bailey, Tex. A&M-Kingsville, 1986 (2,011 rushing, 54 receiving, 20 punt returns, 340 kickoff returns; 296 plays)
Also holds per-game record with 220.5 (2,425 in 11)

MOST YARDS GAINED BY TWO PLAYERS, SAME TEAM
Season
4,112—Brian Shay (2,738) & Chet Pobolish (1,374), Emporia St., 1996
Also hold per-game record with 373.8 (4,112 in 11)

HIGHEST AVERAGE GAIN PER PLAY
Game
(Min. 15 plays) 30.9—Andre Johnson, Ferris St. vs. Clarion, Sept. 16, 1989 (17 for 525)
Season
(Min. 150 plays, 1,500 yards) 12.9—Billy Johnson, Widener, 1972 (175 for 2,265)
Career
(Min. 300 plays, 4,000 yards) 15.2—Chris George, Glenville St., 1993-94 (307 for 4,679)

Scoring

MOST POINTS SCORED
Game
48—Junior Wolf, Okla. Panhandle vs. St. Mary (Kan.), Nov. 8, 1958 (8 TDs); Paul Zaeske, North Park vs. North Central, Oct. 12, 1968 (8 TDs)
Season
206—Kavin Gailliard, American Int'l, 1999 (34 TDs, 2 PATs)
Per-game record—21.0, Carl Herakovich, Rose-Hulman, 1958 (168 in 8)
Career
544—Brian Shay, Emporia St., 1995-98 (88 TDs, 8 PATs)
Per-game record—13.4, Ole Gunderson, St. Olaf, 1969-71 (362 in 27)

MOST POINTS SCORED BY A FRESHMAN
Season
144—Shawn Graves, Wofford, 1989 (24 TDs)
Also holds per-game record with 13.1 (144 in 11)

MOST POINTS SCORED BY A QUARTERBACK
Season
144—Shawn Graves, Wofford, 1989 (24 TDs)
Per-game record—13.8, Jeff Bentrim, North Dakota St., 1986 (138 in 10)
Career
438—Shawn Graves, Wofford, 1989-92
Per-game record—11.0, Jeff Bentrim, North Dakota St., 1983-86 (386 in 35)

MOST POINTS SCORED BY TWO PLAYERS, SAME TEAM
Season
266—Brian Shay (198) & Jarett Vito (68), Emporia St., 1997
Career
666—Heath Sherman (336) & Johnny Bailey (330), Tex. A&M-Kingsville, 1986-88

MOST TOUCHDOWNS SCORED
Game
8—Junior Wolf, Okla. Panhandle vs. St. Mary (Kan.), Nov. 8, 1958 (all by rushing); Paul Zaeske, North Park vs. North Central, Oct. 12, 1968 (all on pass receptions)
Season
34—Kavin Gailliard, American Int'l, 1999
Per-game record—3.1, Carl Herakovich, Rose-Hulman, 1958 (25 in 8)
Career
88—Brian Shay, Emporia St., 1995-98
Per-game record—2.2, Ole Gunderson, St. Olaf, 1969-71 (60 in 27)

MOST TOUCHDOWNS SCORED BY A FRESHMAN
Season
24—Shawn Graves, Wofford, 1989
Also holds per-game record with 2.2 (24 in 11)

MOST TOUCHDOWNS SCORED BY A QUARTERBACK
Season
24—Shawn Graves, Wofford, 1989
Per-game record—2.3, Jeff Bentrim, North Dakota St., 1986 (23 in 10)
Career
72—Shawn Graves, Wofford, 1989-92
Per-game record—1.8, Jeff Bentrim, North Dakota St., 1983-86 (64 in 35)

MOST TOUCHDOWNS SCORED BY TWO PLAYERS, SAME TEAM
Season
42—Heath Sherman (23) & Johnny Bailey (19), Tex. A&M-Kingsville, 1986; Brian Shay (32) & Jarett Vito (10), Emporia St., 1997
Career
110—Heath Sherman (56) & Johnny Bailey (54), Tex. A&M-Kingsville, 1986-88

MOST CONSECUTIVE GAMES SCORING A TOUCHDOWN
Career
22—Billy Johnson, Widener, 1971-72

MOST EXTRA POINTS MADE BY KICKING
Game
14—Matt Johnson, Connecticut vs. Newport Naval Training, Oct. 22, 1949 (attempted 17); Art Anderson, North Park vs. North Central, Oct. 12, 1968 (attempted 15)
Season
71—John O'Riordan, New Haven, 1993 (attempted 78)
Career
203—David Purnell, Northwest Mo. St., 1996-99 (attempted 215)

MOST EXTRA POINTS ATTEMPTED BY KICKING
Game
17—Matt Johnson, Connecticut vs. Newport Naval Training, Oct. 22, 1949 (made 14)
Season
78—John O'Riordan, New Haven, 1993 (made 71)
Career
215—David Purnell, Northwest Mo. St., 1996-99 (made 203)

HIGHEST PERCENTAGE OF EXTRA POINTS MADE BY KICKING
Season
(Best perfect season) 100.0%—David Purnell, Northwest Mo. St., 1999 (56 of 56)
Career
(Min. 90 atts.) 98.9%—Mark DeMoss, Liberty, 1980-83 (92 of 93)
(Min. 150 atts.) 94.4%—David Purnell, Northwest Mo. St., 1996-99 (203 of 215)

MOST CONSECUTIVE EXTRA POINTS MADE BY KICKING
Season
56—David Purnell, Northwest Mo. St., 1999 (entire season)
Career
82—Mark DeMoss, Liberty (from Sept. 13, 1980, to Oct. 1, 1983; ended with missed PAT vs. Central St., Oct. 1, 1983)

MOST POINTS SCORED BY KICKING
Game
20—Clarence Joseph, Central St. vs. Kentucky St., Oct. 16, 1982 (5 FGs, 5 PATs)
Season
96—David Purnell, Northwest Mo. St., 1997 (14 FGs, 54 PATs); Jason Williams, Southern Ark., 1998 (20 FGs, 36 PATs)
Williams also holds per-game record with 9.6 (96 in 10)
Career
326—David Purnell, Northwest Mo. St., 1996-99 (41 FGs, 203 PATs)
Per-game record (min. 145 pts.)—8.3, Dave Austinson, Truman, 1981-82 (149 in 18)
Per-game record (min. 200 pts.)—7.8, David Purnell, Northwest Mo. St., 1996-99 (326 in 42)

Defensive Extra Points

MOST DEFENSIVE EXTRA POINTS SCORED
Game and Season
1—Many times

LONGEST DEFENSIVE EXTRA POINT BLOCKED-KICK RETURN
99—Robert Fair (DB), Carson-Newman vs. Mars Hill, Oct. 15, 1994 (scored)

LONGEST DEFENSIVE EXTRA POINT FUMBLE RETURN
90—Kyle Hinshaw (LB), Elon vs. Catawba, Oct. 25, 1997

LONGEST DEFENSIVE EXTRA POINT INTERCEPTION RETURN
100—Morice Mabry (DB), UC Davis vs. St. Mary's (Cal.), Sept. 28, 1991 (scored); Brian Muldrow (CB), St. Francis (Ill.) vs. Northwood, Oct. 8, 1994 (scored); Jonathan Mitchell (DB), Central Ark. vs. Delta St., Sept. 27, 1997

FIRST DEFENSIVE EXTRA POINT SCORED
Herman Rice (DB), Springfield vs. Worcester Tech, Sept. 9, 1988 (80-yard blocked kick return)

Fumble Returns

LONGEST FUMBLE RETURN
100—Sam Durst, Gardner-Webb vs. West Virginia St., Sept. 19, 1998 (scored)

Field Goals

MOST FIELD GOALS MADE
Game
6—Steve Huff, Central Mo. St. vs. Southeast Mo. St., Nov. 2, 1985 (37, 45, 37, 24, 32, 27 yards; 6 attempts)
Season
20—Four times. Most recent: Jason Williams, Southern Ark., 1998 (24 attempts)
Williams holds per-game record with 2.0 (20 in 10)
Career
64—Mike Wood, Southeast Mo. St., 1974-77 (109 attempts)
Also holds per-game record with 1.5 (64 in 44)

MOST CONSECUTIVE FIELD GOALS MADE
Career
17—Greg Payne, Catawba (from Oct. 5, 1996, to Sept. 20, 1997; ended with missed FG vs. Charleston So., Sept. 27, 1997)

INDIVIDUAL RECORDS—FIELD GOALS

MOST FIELD GOALS ATTEMPTED
Game
7—Jim Turcotte, Mississippi Col. vs. Troy St., Oct. 3, 1981 (made 2)
Season
35—Mike Wood, Southeast Mo. St., 1977 (made 16)
Per-game record—3.3, Skipper Butler, Texas-Arlington, 1968 (33 in 10)
Career
109—Mike Wood, Southeast Mo. St., 1974-77 (made 64)

Per-game record—2.7, Jaime Nunez, Weber St., 1969-71 (83 in 31)

HIGHEST PERCENTAGE OF FIELD GOALS MADE
Season
(Min. 15 atts.) 88.2%—Kurt Seibel, South Dakota, 1983 (15 of 17); Howie Guarini, Shippensburg, 1990 (15 of 17)
(Min. 20 atts.) 86.4%—Dennis Hochman, Sonoma St., 1986 (19 of 22)

Career
(Min. 35 made) 80.0%—Bill May, Clarion, 1977-80 (48 of 60)

LONGEST FIELD GOAL
67 yards—Tom Odle, Fort Hays St. vs. Washburn, Nov. 5, 1988

Team Records

Single Game—Offense

Total Offense

MOST YARDS GAINED
910—Hanover vs. Franklin, Oct. 30, 1948 (426 rushing, 484 passing; 75 plays)

MOST YARDS GAINED, BOTH TEAMS
1,328—Northwood (688) vs. Saginaw Valley (640), Oct. 24, 1998

MOST PLAYS
117—Tex. A&M-Kingsville vs. Angelo St., Oct. 30, 1982 (96 rushes, 21 passes; 546 yards)

HIGHEST AVERAGE GAIN PER PLAY
12.1—Hanover vs. Franklin, Oct. 30, 1948 (75 for 910)

MOST TOUCHDOWNS SCORED BY RUSHING AND PASSING
15—North Park vs. North Central, Oct. 12, 1968 (4 by rushing, 11 by passing)

MOST TOUCHDOWNS SCORED BY RUSHING AND PASSING, BOTH TEAMS
20—North Park (15) & North Central (5), Oct. 12, 1968

MOST YARDS GAINED BY A LOSING TEAM
736—East Stroudsburg vs. New Haven, Sept. 14, 1996 (lost 59-56)

Rushing

MOST YARDS GAINED
719—Coe vs. Beloit, Oct. 16, 1971 (73 rushes)

MOST RUSHES
97—Hobart vs. Union (N.Y.), Oct. 23, 1971 (444 yards)

HIGHEST AVERAGE GAIN PER RUSH
(Min. 50 Rushes)
11.2—Wofford vs. Charleston So., Nov. 12, 1994 (53 for 595)

MOST TOUCHDOWNS SCORED BY RUSHING
12—Coe vs. Beloit, Oct. 16, 1971

MOST PLAYERS, ONE TEAM, EACH GAINING 100 YARDS OR MORE
5—South Dakota vs. St. Cloud St., Nov. 1, 1986 (James Hambrick 125, Darryl Colvin 123, Tony Higgins 118, Dave Elle 109, Joe Longueville [QB] 106; team gained 581)

Passing

MOST PASSES ATTEMPTED
85—West Tex. A&M vs. Eastern N.M., Nov. 5, 1994 (completed 47)

MOST PASSES ATTEMPTED, BOTH TEAMS
121—Franklin (68) & Saginaw Valley (53), Sept. 22, 1984 (completed 63)

MOST PASSES COMPLETED
56—Wayne St. (Neb.) vs. Drake, Nov. 9, 1996 (attempted 76)

MOST PASSES COMPLETED, BOTH TEAMS
72—Western N.M. (39) & West Tex. A&M (33), Oct. 8, 1994 (attempted 111)

MOST PASSES HAD INTERCEPTED
11—Hamline vs. Concordia-M'head, Nov. 5, 1955; Rhode Island vs. Brown, Oct. 8, 1949

MOST PASSES ATTEMPTED WITHOUT INTERCEPTION
63—Hamline vs. St. John's (Minn.), Oct. 8, 1955 (completed 34)

HIGHEST PERCENTAGE OF PASSES COMPLETED
(Min. 20 Attempts)
90.9%—Northwestern St. vs. La.-Lafayette, Nov. 12, 1966 (20 of 22)

MOST YARDS GAINED
678—Portland St. vs. Mont. St.-Billings, Nov. 20, 1976

MOST YARDS GAINED, BOTH TEAMS
1,065—Western N.M. (614) & West Tex. A&M (451), Oct. 8, 1994

MOST TOUCHDOWN PASSES
11—North Park vs. North Central, Oct. 12, 1968

MOST TOUCHDOWN PASSES, BOTH TEAMS
14—North Park (11) & North Central (3), Oct. 12, 1968

Punting

MOST PUNTS
32—Sam Houston St. vs. Tex. A&M-Commerce, Nov. 2, 1946 (1,203 yards)

MOST PUNTS, BOTH TEAMS
63—Sam Houston St. (32) & Tex. A&M-Commerce (31), Nov. 2, 1946

HIGHEST AVERAGE PER PUNT
(Min. 5 Punts)
57.5—Colorado Mines vs. Fort Lewis, Oct. 21, 1989 (8 for 460)

Punt Returns

MOST YARDS ON PUNT RETURNS
265—Widener vs. St. John's (N.Y.), Sept. 23, 1972 (4 returns)

MOST TOUCHDOWNS SCORED ON PUNT RETURNS
3—Hawaii vs. Linfield, Nov. 15, 1969; Widener vs. St. John's (N.Y.), Sept. 23, 1972; Troy St. vs. West Ala., Sept. 29, 1979

Scoring

MOST POINTS SCORED
125—Connecticut vs. Newport Naval Training, Oct. 22, 1949

MOST POINTS SCORED AGAINST A COLLEGE OPPONENT
106—Fort Valley St. vs. Knoxville, Oct. 11, 1969 (14 TDs, 2 PATs, 9 two-point conversions, 1 safety)

MOST POINTS SCORED BY A LOSING TEAM
60—New Haven vs. Southern Conn. St. (64), Oct. 25, 1991

MOST POINTS SCORED, BOTH TEAMS
136—North Park (104) & North Central (32), Oct. 12, 1968

MOST POINTS SCORED IN TWO CONSECUTIVE GAMES
172—Tuskegee, 1966 (93-0 vs. Morehouse, Oct. 14; 79-0 vs. Lane, Oct. 22)

MOST POINTS OVERCOME TO WIN A GAME
28—Ferris St. (46) vs. Saginaw Valley (42), Nov. 11, 1995 (trailed 28-0 with 11:17 remaining in 2nd quarter)

MOST POINTS SCORED IN A BRIEF PERIOD OF TIME
21 in 1:20—Winona St. vs. Bemidji St., Oct. 15, 1994 (turned 14-0 game into 35-0 in 1st quarter)

MOST TOUCHDOWNS SCORED
17—Connecticut vs. Newport Naval Training, Oct. 22, 1949

MOST TOUCHDOWNS SCORED AGAINST A COLLEGE OPPONENT
15—Iowa Wesleyan vs. William Penn, Oct. 31, 1953; Alcorn St. vs. Paul Quinn, Sept. 9, 1967; North Park vs. North Central, Oct. 12, 1968

MOST SAFETIES SCORED
3—Fort Valley St. vs. Miles, Oct. 16, 1993

MOST POINTS AFTER TOUCHDOWN MADE BY KICKING
14—Connecticut vs. Newport Naval Training, Oct. 22, 1949 (attempted 17); North Park vs. North Central, Oct. 12, 1968 (attempted 15)

MOST TWO-POINT ATTEMPTS
11—Fort Valley St. vs. Knoxville, Oct. 11, 1969 (made 9)

MOST TWO-POINT ATTEMPTS MADE
9—Fort Valley St. vs. Knoxville, Oct. 11, 1969 (attempted 11)

MOST FIELD GOALS MADE
6—Central Mo. St. vs. Southeast Mo. St., Nov. 2, 1985 (6 attempts)

MOST DEFENSIVE EXTRA POINTS SCORED
1—By many teams

MOST DEFENSIVE EXTRA-POINT OPPORTUNITIES
2—North Dakota St. vs. Augustana (S.D.), Sept. 24, 1988 (2 interceptions; none scored); Mo. Southern St. vs. Central Mo. St., Sept. 28, 1996 (2 interceptions; none scored)

First Downs

MOST TOTAL FIRST DOWNS
42—Delaware vs. Baldwin-Wallace, Oct. 6, 1973

MOST FIRST DOWNS BY PENALTY
14—La Verne vs. Northern Ariz., Oct. 11, 1958

MOST TOTAL FIRST DOWNS, BOTH TEAMS
66—Ferris St. (33) & Northwood (33), Oct. 26, 1985; North Dakota (36) & Tex. A&M-Kingsville (30), Sept. 13, 1986

Penalties

MOST PENALTIES
28—Northern Ariz. vs. La Verne, Oct. 11, 1958 (155 yards)

MOST PENALTIES, BOTH TEAMS
42—N.C. Central (23) & St. Paul's (19), Sept. 13, 1986 (453 yards)

MOST YARDS PENALIZED
293—Cal Poly vs. Portland St., Oct. 31, 1981 (26 penalties)

MOST YARDS PENALIZED, BOTH TEAMS
453—N.C. Central (256) & St. Paul's (197), Sept. 13, 1986 (42 penalties)

Fumbles

MOST FUMBLES
16—Carthage vs. North Park, Nov. 14, 1970 (lost 7)

SINGLE GAME—Defense

Total Defense

FEWEST TOTAL OFFENSE PLAYS ALLOWED
29—North Park vs. Concordia (Ill.), Sept. 26, 1964

FEWEST TOTAL OFFENSE YARDS ALLOWED
Minus 69—Fort Valley St. vs. Miles, Oct. 16, 1993 (39 plays)

FEWEST RUSHES ALLOWED
7—Indianapolis vs. Valparaiso, Oct. 30, 1982 (-57 yards)

FEWEST RUSHING YARDS ALLOWED
Minus 95—San Diego St. vs. U.S. Int'l, Nov. 27, 1965 (35 plays)

FEWEST PASS COMPLETIONS ALLOWED
0—By many teams. Most recent: Winona St. vs. Wis.-River Falls, Sept. 6, 1997 (attempted 7)

FEWEST PASSING YARDS ALLOWED
Minus 19—Ashland vs. Heidelberg, Sept. 25, 1948 (completed 4)

Punting

MOST OPPONENT'S PUNTS BLOCKED
5—Southeastern La. vs. Troy St., Oct. 7, 1978 (holds record for most consecutive punts blocked with 4); Winston-Salem vs. N.C. Central, Oct. 4, 1986

MOST TOUCHDOWNS SCORED ON BLOCKED PUNT RETURNS
2—Northern Colo. vs. Western St., Sept. 7, 1996; Fairmont St. vs. West Va. Tech, Oct. 12, 1996

Interceptions

MOST PASSES INTERCEPTED BY
11—St. Cloud St. vs. Bemidji St., Oct. 31, 1970 (45 attempts); Concordia-M'head vs. Hamline, Nov. 5, 1955 (37 attempts)

MOST TOUCHDOWNS ON INTERCEPTION RETURNS
3—By many teams. Most recent: Bloomsburg vs. East Stroudsburg, Oct. 31, 1998

SEASON—Offense

Total Offense

MOST YARDS GAINED
6,284—West Tex. A&M, 1994 (931 plays, 11 games)
Per-game record—624.1, Hanover, 1948 (4,993 in 8)

HIGHEST AVERAGE GAIN PER PLAY
(Min. 500 plays) 9.2—Hanover, 1948 (543 for 4,993)
(Min. 800 plays) 6.9—American Int'l, 1998 (805 for 5,562)

MOST PLAYS PER GAME
88.7—Cal St. Chico, 1967 (887 in 10)

Rushing

MOST YARDS GAINED
4,347—Tex. A&M-Kingsville, 1986 (689 rushes, 11 games)
Per-game record—404.8, Col. of Emporia, 1954 (3,643 in 9)

HIGHEST AVERAGE GAIN PER RUSH
(Min. 300 rushes) 8.4—Hanover, 1948 (382 for 3,203)
(Min. 600 rushes) 6.9—Saginaw Valley, 1998 (615 for 4,240)

MOST RUSHES PER GAME
78.9—Okla. Panhandle, 1963 (789 in 10)

Passing

MOST YARDS GAINED
5,000—West Tex. A&M, 1994 (363 completions, 11 games)
Also holds per-game record with 454.5 (5,000 in 11)

HIGHEST AVERAGE GAIN PER ATTEMPT (Min. 175 Attempts)
10.8—Western St., 1991 (330 for 3,574)

HIGHEST AVERAGE GAIN PER COMPLETION
(Min. 100 comps.) 19.4—Calif. (Pa.), 1966 (116 for 2,255)
(Min. 200 comps.) 18.0—East Stroudsburg, 1996 (224 for 4,041)

MOST PASSES ATTEMPTED
623—Emporia St., 1995 (completed 322)
Also holds per-game record with 56.6 (623 in 11)

MOST PASSES COMPLETED
373—Valdosta St., 1995 (attempted 570)
Also holds per-game record with 33.9 (373 in 11)

FEWEST PASSES COMPLETED PER GAME
0.4—Hobart, 1971 (4 in 9)

HIGHEST PERCENTAGE COMPLETED (Min. 200 Attempts)
70.8%—Valdosta St., 1993 (363 of 513)

LOWEST PERCENTAGE OF PASSES HAD INTERCEPTED (Min. 275 Attempts)
0.7%—New Haven, 1993 (2 of 296)

MOST TOUCHDOWN PASSES PER GAME
4.9—San Fran. St., 1967 (49 in 10)

HIGHEST PASSING EFFICIENCY RATING POINTS
(Min. 200 atts.) 183.8—Wittenberg, 1963 (216 attempts, 138 completions, 10 interceptions, 2,457 yards, 22 TDs)
(Min. 300 atts.) 180.2—Western St., 1991 (330 attempts, 203 completions, 12 interceptions, 3,574 yards, 35 TDs)

Punting

MOST PUNTS PER GAME
10.0—Wash. & Lee, 1968 (90 in 9)

FEWEST PUNTS PER GAME
1.8—Emporia St., 1997 (20 in 11)

HIGHEST PUNTING AVERAGE
48.0—Adams St., 1966 (36 for 1,728)

Punt Returns

MOST PUNT RETURNS
64—UC Davis, 1984 (557 yards)

MOST TOUCHDOWNS SCORED ON PUNT RETURNS
6—Northern Colo., 1996 (52 returns); Shepherd, 1998 (33 returns)

Kickoff Returns

MOST KICKOFF RETURNS
78—Ark.-Monticello, 1998 (1,634 yards)

Scoring

MOST POINTS PER GAME
54.7—New Haven, 1993 (547 in 10)

MOST TOUCHDOWNS PER GAME
7.8—New Haven, 1993 (78 in 10)

MOST CONSECUTIVE EXTRA POINTS MADE BY KICKING
56—Northwest Mo. St., 1999 (entire season)

MOST CONSECUTIVE FIELD GOALS MADE
13—UC Davis, 1976

MOST TWO-POINT ATTEMPTS PER GAME
6.8—Florida A&M, 1961 (61 in 9, made 32)

MOST TWO-POINT ATTEMPTS MADE PER GAME
3.6—Florida A&M, 1961 (32 in 9, attempted 61)

MOST FIELD GOALS MADE
20—Four times. Most recent: Southern Ark., 1998 (attempted 24)

MOST DEFENSIVE EXTRA POINTS SCORED
2—UC Davis, 1991 (1 blocked kick return, 1 interception); Wingate, 1997 (2 blocked kick returns)

MOST DEFENSIVE EXTRA-POINT OPPORTUNITIES
3—Northern Colo., 1988 (2 blocked kick returns, 1 interception; none scored); Central Okla., 1989 (2 blocked kick returns, 1 interception; one scored); UC Davis, 1991 (2 interceptions, 1 blocked kick return; two scored)

Penalties

MOST PENALTIES AGAINST
146—Gardner-Webb, 1992 (1,344 yards); Portland St., 1994 (1,340 yards)
Per-game record—14.6, Portland St., 1994 (146 in 10)

MOST YARDS PENALIZED
1,356—Hampton, 1977 (124 penalties, 11 games)

Turnovers (Giveaways)

(From 1985)

FEWEST TURNOVERS
8—Lenoir-Rhyne, 1994 (4 interceptions, 4 fumbles lost)
Also holds per-game record with 0.8 (8 in 10)

MOST TURNOVERS
61—Cheyney, 1990 (36 interceptions, 25 fumbles lost)
Per-game record—5.8, Livingstone, 1986 (58 in 10)

FEWEST FUMBLES LOST
2—Michigan Tech, 1995 (9 fumbles); Western St., 1998 (11 fumbles)

SEASON—Defense

Total Defense

FEWEST YARDS ALLOWED PER GAME
44.4—John Carroll, 1962 (311 in 7)

LOWEST AVERAGE YARDS ALLOWED PER PLAY
(Min. 300 plays) 1.0—John Carroll, 1962 (310 for 311 yards)
(Min. 600 plays) 1.8—Alcorn St., 1976 (603 for 1,089)

TEAM RECORDS—RUSHING DEFENSE 157

Rushing Defense

FEWEST YARDS ALLOWED PER GAME
Minus 16.7—Tennessee St., 1967 (-150 in 9)

LOWEST AVERAGE YARDS ALLOWED PER RUSH
(Min. 250 rushes) Minus 0.5—Tennessee St., 1967 (296 for -150 yards)
(Min. 400 rushes) 1.3—Luther, 1971 (414 for 518)

Pass Defense

FEWEST YARDS ALLOWED PER GAME
10.1—Ashland, 1948 (91 in 9)

FEWEST YARDS ALLOWED PER ATTEMPT
(Min. 200 atts.) 3.1—Virginia St., 1971 (205 for 630)
(Min. 300 atts.) 3.2—Southwest Mo. St., 1966 (315 for 996)

FEWEST YARDS ALLOWED PER COMPLETION
(Min. 100 comps.) 8.8—Long Beach St., 1965 (144 for 1,264)

LOWEST COMPLETION PERCENTAGE ALLOWED
(Min. 250 atts.) 24.1%—Southwest Mo. St., 1966 (76 of 315)

MOST PASSES INTERCEPTED PER GAME
3.9—Delaware, 1946 (35 in 9); Whitworth, 1959 (35 in 9)

FEWEST PASSES INTERCEPTED
(Min. 150 atts.) 1—Gettysburg, 1972 (175 attempts; 0 yards returned)

HIGHEST PERCENTAGE INTERCEPTED
(Min. 150 atts.) 21.7%—Stephen F. Austin, 1949 (35 of 161)
(Min. 275 atts.) 11.8%—Mo.-Rolla, 1978 (35 of 297)

MOST TOUCHDOWNS ON INTERCEPTION RETURNS
7—Virginia Union, 1986 (31 interceptions); Fort Valley St., 1991 (15 interceptions); Gardner-Webb, 1992 (35 interceptions)

LOWEST PASSING EFFICIENCY RATING ALLOWED
(Min. 250 atts.) 41.7—Fort Valley St., 1985 (allowed 283 attempts, 90 completions, 1,039 yards, 2 TDs and intercepted 33)

Blocked Kicks

MOST BLOCKED KICKS
27—Winston-Salem, 1986 (16 punts, 7 field goal attempts, 4 PAT kicks)

Scoring

FEWEST POINTS ALLOWED PER GAME
0.0—Albany St. (Ga.), 1960 (0 in 9 games)

MOST POINTS ALLOWED PER GAME
64.5—Rose-Hulman, 1961 (516 in 8)

Turnovers (Takeaways)
(From 1985)

HIGHEST TURNOVER MARGIN PER GAME
2.7—Hillsdale, 1993 (plus 30 in 11; 11 giveaways vs. 41 takeaways)

MOST TAKEAWAYS
56—Gardner-Webb, 1992 (35 interceptions, 21 fumble recoveries)
Also holds per-game record with 5.1 (56 in 11)

Additional Records

MOST CONSECUTIVE VICTORIES
34—Hillsdale (from Oct. 2, 1954, to Nov. 16, 1957; ended with 27-26 loss to Pittsburg St., Dec. 21, 1957)

MOST CONSECUTIVE VICTORIES OVER DIVISION II OPPONENT
40—North Ala. (from Sept. 4, 1993, to Dec. 9, 1995; ended with 17-10 loss to Albany St. [Ga.], Aug. 31, 1996)

MOST CONSECUTIVE HOME VICTORIES
28—North Dakota St. (from Sept. 12, 1964, to Nov. 1, 1969; ended with 14-14 tie vs. Eastern Mich., Sept. 12, 1970); North Ala. (from Sept. 4, 1993, to Sept. 14, 1996; ended with 38-35 loss to Arkansas Tech, Sept. 28, 1996)

MOST CONSECUTIVE GAMES UNBEATEN
54—Morgan St. (from Nov. 5, 1931, to Nov. 18, 1938; ended with 15-0 loss to Virginia St., Nov. 30, 1938)

MOST CONSECUTIVE VICTORIES OVER ONE OPPONENT
40—West Chester vs. Millersville (from Nov. 18, 1922, to Oct. 5, 1974; ended with 17-12 loss Oct. 4, 1975)

MOST CONSECUTIVE VICTORIES OVER ONE OPPONENT IN AN UNINTERRUPTED SERIES
(Must have played in consecutive years)
25—UC Davis vs. San Fran. St. (from Sept. 26, 1970, to Nov. 12, 1994; San Fran. St. dropped football program after 1994 season)

MOST CONSECUTIVE GAMES WITHOUT BEING SHUT OUT
178—North Dakota (from Oct. 7, 1967, to Nov. 10, 1984; ended with 41-0 loss to Northern Ariz., Aug. 31, 1985)

MOST CONSECUTIVE WINNING SEASONS
31—West Chester (from 1940-72; ended with 5-5-0 record in 1973)

MOST CONSECUTIVE NON-LOSING SEASONS
33—West Chester (from 1940-74; ended with 4-5-0 record in 1975)

MOST CONSECUTIVE LOSSES
39—St. Paul's (from Oct. 23, 1948, to Oct. 24, 1953; ended with 7-6 win over Delaware St., Oct. 31, 1953); Cheyney (from Sept. 3, 1994, to Oct. 24, 1998; ended with 40-13 win over Mansfield, Oct. 31, 1998)

MOST CONSECUTIVE GAMES WITHOUT A VICTORY
49—Paine (1954-61, includes 1 tie)

MOST CONSECUTIVE GAMES WITHOUT A TIE
329—West Chester (from Oct. 26, 1945, to Oct. 31, 1980; ended with 24-24 tie vs. Cheyney, Nov. 8, 1980)

MOST TIE GAMES IN A SEASON
5—Wofford, 1948 (Sept. 25 to Oct. 23, consecutive)

HIGHEST-SCORING TIE GAME
54-54—Norfolk St. vs. Winston-Salem, Oct. 9, 1993

MOST CONSECUTIVE QUARTERS WITHOUT YIELDING A RUSHING TOUCHDOWN
51—Butler (from Sept. 25, 1982, to Oct. 15, 1983)

MOST CONSECUTIVE POINT-AFTER-TOUCHDOWN KICKS MADE
123—Liberty (from 1976 to Sept. 10, 1983; ended with missed PAT vs. Saginaw Valley, Sept. 10, 1983)

MOST IMPROVED WON-LOST RECORD
11 games—Northern Mich., 1975 (13-1, including three Division II playoff victories, from 0-10 in 1974)

DIVISION II

Annual Champions, All-Time Leaders

Total Offense

CAREER YARDS PER GAME
(Minimum 5,000 Yards)

Player, Team	Years	G	Plays	Yards	Yd. PG
Grady Benton, West Tex. A&M	1994-95	18	844	5,831	*323.9
Wilkie Perez, Glenville St.	1997-98	17	702	5,447	320.4
Marty Washington, West Ala.	1992-93	17	773	5,212	306.6
Scott Otis, Glenville St.	1994-95	20	755	5,911	295.6
Jarrod DeGeorgia, Wayne St. (Neb.)	1995-96	18	753	5,145	285.8
Jayson Merrill, Western St.	1990-91	20	641	5,619	281.0
Jermaine Whitaker, N.M. Highlands	1992-94	31	1,374	8,650	279.0
Chris Petersen, UC Davis	1985-86	20	735	5,532	276.6
Tim Von Dulm, Portland St.	1969-70	20	989	5,501	275.1
Vernon Buck, Wingate	1991-94	41	1,761	*11,227	273.8
Chris Hatcher, Valdosta St.	1991-94	39	1,557	10,588	271.5
Chris Hegg, Truman	1984-85	20	930	5,418	270.9
Pat Graham, Augustana (S.D.)	1995-96	21	948	5,672	270.1
June Jones, Portland St.	1975-76	21	760	5,590	266.2
Jeff Fox, Grand Valley St.	1995-98	34	1,341	8,941	263.0
Troy Mott, Wayne St. (Neb.)	1991-92	20	943	5,212	260.6
Earl Harvey, N.C. Central	1985-88	41	*2,045	10,667	260.2
Jim Zorn, Cal Poly Pomona	1973-74	21	946	5,364	255.4
Steve Wray, Franklin	1979, 81-82	26	1,178	6,564	252.5
Bob McLaughlin, Lock Haven	1992-95	44	2,007	11,041	250.9
Thad Trujillo, Fort Lewis	1991-94	41	1,787	10,209	249.0
Lance Funderburk, Valdosta St.	1993-96	30	1,126	7,469	249.0
Matt McCarthy, Ferris St.	1996-99	32	1,188	7,942	248.2
Rob Tomlinson, Cal St. Chico	1988-91	40	1,656	9,921	248.0
Matt Kissell, Mercyhurst	1996-99	29	1,286	7,087	244.4

*Record.

SEASON YARDS PER GAME

Player, Team	Years	G	Plays	Yards	Yd. PG
Grady Benton, West Tex. A&M	†1994	9	505	3,699	*411.0
Perry Klein, C. W. Post	†1993	10	499	4,052	405.2
Marty Washington, West Ala.	1993	8	453	3,146	393.3
Wilkie Perez, Glenville St.	†1997	11	509	*4,301	391.0
Damian Poalucci, East Stroudsburg	†1996	10	505	3,883	388.3
Brett Salisbury, Wayne St. (Neb.)	1993	10	424	3,732	373.2
Jed Drenning, Glenville St.	1993	10	473	3,593	359.3
Alfred Montez, Western N.M.	1994	6	244	2,130	355.0
Rob Tomlinson, Cal St. Chico	†1989	10	534	3,525	352.5

ALL-TIME LEADERS—TOTAL OFFENSE

Player, Team	Years	G	Plays	Yards	Yd. PG
Chris Hegg, Truman	†1985	11	*594	3,782	343.8
Jarrod DeGeorgia, Wayne St. (Neb.)	1996	10	495	3,416	341.6
Rod Smith, Glenville St.	1996	10	472	3,410	341.0
Bob Toledo, San Fran. St.	†1967	10	409	3,407	340.7
Jayson Merrill, Western St.	†1991	10	337	3,400	340.0
John Charles, Portland St.	†1992	8	303	2,708	338.5
Lance Funderburk, Valdosta St.	1996	11	490	3,676	334.2
Aaron Sparrow, Norfolk St.	†1995	10	464	3,300	330.0
George Bork, Northern Ill.	†1963	9	413	2,945	327.2
Richard Strasser, San Fran. St.	1985	10	536	3,259	325.9
Pat Brennan, Franklin	†1984	10	583	3,248	324.8

*Record. †National champion.

CAREER YARDS

Player, Team	Years	Plays	Yards
Vernon Buck, Wingate	1991-94	1,761	*11,227
Bob McLaughlin, Lock Haven	1992-95	2,007	11,041
Earl Harvey, N.C. Central	1985-88	*2,045	10,667
Chris Hatcher, Valdosta St.	1991-94	1,557	10,588
Thad Trujillo, Fort Lewis	1991-94	1,787	10,209
Rob Tomlinson, Cal St. Chico	1988-91	1,656	9,921
John Hebgen, Minn. St.-Mankato	1993-96	1,545	9,772
Mike Mitros, West Chester	1996-99	1,716	9,714
Jarrod Fergason, Fairmont St.	$1993-97	1,583	9,638
John Craven, Gardner-Webb	1991-94	1,666	9,630
Sam Mannery, Calif. (Pa.)	1987-90	1,669	9,125
Trevor Moon, Chadron St.	1995-98	1,395	9,044
Andy Breault, Kutztown	1989-92	1,459	8,975
Jeff Fox, Grand Valley St.	1995-98	1,341	8,941
Jermaine Whitaker, N.M. Highlands	1992-95	1,374	8,650
Damian Poalucci, East Stroudsburg	1994-97	1,365	8,569
Dave MacDonald, West Chester	1991-94	1,257	8,453
Mike Lazo, Concord	1995-98	1,222	8,390
Jim Lindsey, Abilene Christian	1967-70	1,510	8,385
Dave Walter, Michigan Tech	1983-86	1,660	8,345
Maurice Heard, Tuskegee	1988-91	1,289	8,321
Aaron Sparrow, Norfolk St.	1992-95	1,345	8,301
Jack Hull, Grand Valley St.	1988-91	1,196	8,221
Dave DenBraber, Ferris St.	1984-87	1,522	8,115
Tracy Kendall, Alabama A&M	1988-91	1,480	8,112

*Record. $See page 6 for explanation.

SEASON YARDS

Player, Team	Year	G	Plays	Yards
Wilkie Perez, Glenville St.	†1997	11	509	*4,301
Perry Klein, C. W. Post	†1993	10	499	4,052
Damian Poalucci, East Stroudsburg	†1996	10	505	3,883
Chris Hegg, Truman	†1985	11	*594	3,782
Brett Salisbury, Wayne St. (Neb.)	1993	10	424	3,732
Grady Benton, West Tex. A&M	†1994	9	505	3,699
Lance Funderburk, Valdosta St.	1996	11	490	3,676
Jed Drenning, Glenville St.	1993	10	473	3,593
Lance Funderburk, Valdosta St.	1995	11	581	3,549
Jamie Pass, Minn. St.-Mankato	1993	11	543	3,537
Tod Mayfield, West Tex. A&M	†1986	11	555	3,533
Chris Hatcher, Valdosta St.	1993	11	495	3,532
Rob Tomlinson, Cal St. Chico	†1989	10	534	3,525
Chris Hatcher, Valdosta St.	1994	11	452	3,512
Ted Larkin, Bentley	†1999	11	545	3,490
Mike Mitros, West Chester	†1998	11	537	3,478
Jeff Fox, Grand Valley, St.	1998	11	481	3,472
June Jones, Portland St.	†1976	11	465	3,463
Jarrod DeGeorgia, Wayne St. (Neb.)	1996	10	495	3,416
Rod Smith, Glenville St.	1996	10	472	3,410

*Record. †National champion.

SINGLE-GAME YARDS

Yds.	Player, Team (Opponent)	Date
651	Wilkie Perez, Glenville St. (Concord)	Oct. 25, 1997
631	Jayce Goree, Glenville St. (Concord)	Oct. 24, 1998
623	Perry Klein, C. W. Post (Salisbury St.)	Nov. 6, 1993
614	Alfred Montez, Western N.M. (West Tex. A&M)	Oct. 8, 1994
597	Damian Poalucci, East Stroudsburg (Mansfield)	Nov. 2, 1996
594	Jarrod DeGeorgia, Wayne St. (Neb.) (Drake)	Nov. 9, 1996
591	Marty Washington, West Ala. (Nicholls St.)	Sept. 11, 1993
584	Tracy Kendall, Alabama A&M (Clark Atlanta)	Nov. 4, 1989
580	Grady Benton, West Tex. A&M (Howard Payne)	Sept. 17, 1994
575	Scott Otis, Glenville St. (West Va. Wesleyan)	Oct. 15, 1994
573	Pat Graham, Augustana (S.D.) (Minn.-Mankato)	Oct. 28, 1995
571	John Charles, Portland St. (Cal Poly)	Nov. 16, 1991
569	Bob McLaughlin, Lock Haven (Calif. [Pa.])	Oct. 29, 1994
562	Bob Toledo, San Fran. St. (Cal St. Hayward)	Oct. 21, 1967
555	A. J. Vaughn, Wayne St. (Mich.) (Wis.-Milwaukee)	Sept. 30, 1967

ANNUAL CHAMPIONS

Year	Player, Team	Class	Plays	Yards
1946	Buster Dixon, Abilene Christian	Sr.	170	960
1947	Jim Peterson, Hanover	So.	108	1,449
1948	Jim Peterson, Hanover	Jr.	130	1,589
1949	Connie Callahan, Morningside	Sr.	311	2,006
1950	Bob Heimerdinger, Northern Ill.	Jr.	286	1,782
1951	Bob Heimerdinger, Northern Ill.	Sr.	292	1,775
1952	Don Gottlob, Sam Houston St.	Sr.	303	2,470
1953	Ralph Capitani, Northern Iowa	Jr.	317	1,755
1954	Bill Engelhardt, Neb.-Omaha	So.	243	1,645
1955	Jim Stehlin, Brandeis	Sr.	222	1,455
1956	Dick Jamieson, Bradley	So.	240	1,925
1957	Stan Jackson, Cal Poly Pomona	Jr.	301	2,145
1958	Stan Jackson, Cal Poly Pomona	Sr.	334	2,478
1959	Gary Campbell, Whittier	Sr.	309	2,383
1960	Charles Miller, Austin	Sr.	287	1,966
1961	Denny Spurlock, Whitworth	Sr.	224	1,684
1962	George Bork, Northern Ill.	Jr.	397	2,398
1963	George Bork, Northern Ill.	Sr.	413	2,945
1964	Jerry Bishop, Austin	Jr.	332	2,152
1965	Ron Christian, Northern Ill.	Sr.	377	2,307
1966	Joe Stetser, Cal St. Chico	Jr.	406	2,382
1967	Bob Toledo, San Fran. St.	Sr.	409	3,407
1968	Terry Bradshaw, Louisiana Tech	Jr.	426	2,987
1969	Tim Von Dulm, Portland St.	Jr.	462	2,736

Beginning in 1970, ranked on per-game (instead of total) yards

Year	Player, Team	Class	G	Plays	Yards	Avg.
1970	Jim Lindsey, Abilene Christian	Sr.	9	440	2,654	294.9
1971	Randy Mattingly, Evansville	Jr.	9	402	2,234	248.2
1972	Bob Biggs, UC Davis	Sr.	9	381	2,356	261.8
1973	Jim Zorn, Cal Poly Pomona	Jr.	11	499	3,000	272.7
1974	Jim McMillan, Boise St.	Sr.	10	403	3,101	310.1
1975	Lynn Hieber, Indiana (Pa.)	Sr.	10	402	2,503	250.3
1976	June Jones, Portland St.	Sr.	11	465	3,463	314.8
1977	Steve Mariucci, Northern Mich.	Sr.	8	270	1,780	222.5
1978	Charlie Thompson, Western St.	Jr.	9	304	2,138	237.6
1979	Phil Kessel, Northern Mich.	Jr.	9	368	2,164	240.4
1980	Curt Strasheim, Southwest St.	Jr.	10	501	2,565	256.5
1981	Steve Wray, Franklin	Jr.	10	488	2,726	272.6
1982	Steve Wray, Franklin	Sr.	8	382	2,114	264.3
1983	Pat Brennan, Franklin	Jr.	10	524	3,239	323.9
1984	Pat Brennan, Franklin	Sr.	10	583	3,248	324.8
1985	Chris Hegg, Truman	Sr.	11	*594	3,782	343.8
1986	Tod Mayfield, West Tex. A&M	Sr.	11	555	3,533	312.2
1987	Randy Hobson, Evansville	Sr.	10	457	2,964	296.4
1988	Mark Sedinger, Northern Colo.	Sr.	10	413	2,828	282.8
1989	Rob Tomlinson, Cal St. Chico	So.	10	534	3,525	352.5
1990	Andy Breault, Kutztown	Jr.	11	562	3,173	288.5
1991	Jayson Merrill, Western St.	Sr.	10	337	3,400	340.0
1992	John Charles, Portland St.	Sr.	8	303	2,708	338.5
1993	Perry Klein, C. W. Post	Sr.	10	499	4,052	405.2
1994	Grady Benton, West Tex. A&M	Jr.	9	505	3,699	*411.0
1995	Aaron Sparrow, Norfolk St.	Sr.	10	464	3,300	330.0
1996	Damian Poalucci, East Stroudsburg	Jr.	10	505	3,883	388.3
1997	Wilkie Perez, Glenville St.	Jr.	11	509	*4,301	391.0
1998	Mike Mitros, West Chester	Jr.	11	537	3,478	316.2
1999	Ted Larkin, Bentley	Jr.	11	545	3,490	317.3

*Record.

Rushing

CAREER YARDS PER GAME
(Minimum 2,500 Yards)

Player, Team	Years	G	Plays	Yards	Yd. PG
Anthony Gray, Western N.M.	1997-98	19	503	3,484	*183.4
Damian Beane, Shepherd	1996-99	38	1,065	6,346	167.0
Johnny Bailey, Tex. A&M-Kingsville	1986-89	39	885	6,320	162.1
Brian Shay, Emporia St.	1995-98	44	1,007	*6,958	158.1
Kavin Gailliard, American Int'l	1996-99	43	950	6,523	151.7
Fred Lane, Lane	1994-96	29	700	4,433	152.9
Ole Gunderson, St. Olaf	1969-71	27	639	4,060	150.4
Richard Huntley, Winston-Salem	1992-95	42	932	6,286	149.7
Roger Graham, New Haven	1991-94	40	821	5,953	148.8
Brad Hustad, Luther	1957-59	27	655	3,943	146.0
Rashaan Dumas, Southern Conn. St.	1996-99	37	977	5,396	145.8
Jarrett Anderson, Truman	1993-96	43	979	6,166	143.4
Quincy Tillmon, Emporia St.	1990-92, 94	29	790	4,141	142.8
Joe Iacone, West Chester	1960-62	27	565	3,767	139.5
Leonard Davis, Lenoir-Rhyne	$1990-94	35	839	4,853	138.7
Phillip Moore, North Dakota	1995-98	40	1,060	5,467	136.7
Don Aleksiewicz, Hobart	1969-72	34	819	4,525	133.1

ALL-TIME LEADERS—RUSHING

Player, Team	Years	G	Plays	Yards	Yd. PG
Jim VanWagner, Michigan Tech	1973-76	36	958	4,788	133.0
Steve Roberts, Butler	1986-89	35	1,026	4,623	132.1

*Record. $See page 6 for explanation.

SEASON YARDS PER GAME

Player, Team	Year	G	Plays	Yards	TD	Yd. PG
Anthony Gray, Western N.M.	†1997	10	277	2,220	12	*222.0
Kavin Gailliard, American Int'l	†1999	12	320	*2,653	*32	221.1
Brian Shay, Emporia St.	†1998	11	293	2,265	29	205.9
Irv Sigler, Bloomsburg	1997	10	299	2,038	20	203.8
Jarrett Anderson, Truman	†1996	11	321	2,140	27	194.5
Brian Shay, Emporia St.	1996	11	342	2,103	18	191.2
Richard Huntley, Winston-Salem	†1995	10	273	1,889	16	188.9
Josh Ranek, South Dakota St.	1999	11	329	2,055	25	186.8
Fred Lane, Lane	1995	10	273	1,833	19	183.3
Johnny Bailey, Tex. A&M-Kingsville	†1986	11	271	2,011	18	182.8
Bob White, Western N.M.	†1951	9	202	1,643	20	182.6
Kevin Mitchell, Saginaw Valley	†1989	8	236	1,460	6	182.5
Rashaan Dumas, Southern Conn. St.	1996	9	291	1,639	18	182.1
Don Aleksiewicz, Hobart	†1971	9	276	1,616	19	179.6
Kavin Gailliard, American Int'l	1998	11	269	1,971	23	179.2
Jim Holder, Okla. Panhandle	†1963	10	275	1,775	9	177.5
Damian Beane, Shepherd	1998	10	299	1,775	17	177.5
Phillip Moore, North Dakota	1997	10	293	1,771	14	177.1
Wilmont Perry, Livingstone	1997	10	195	1,770	20	177.0
Jim Baier, Wis.-River Falls	†1966	9	240	1,587	17	176.3

*Record. †National champion.

CAREER YARDS

Player, Team	Years	Plays	Yards	Avg.
Brian Shay, Emporia St.	1995-98	1,007	*6,958	6.91
Kavin Gailliard, American Int'l	1996-99	950	6,523	6.87
Damian Beane, Shepherd	1996-99	1,065	6,346	5.96
Johnny Bailey, Tex. A&M-Kingsville	1986-89	885	6,320	7.14
Richard Huntley, Winston-Salem	1992-95	932	6,286	6.74
Jarrett Anderson, Truman	1993-96	979	6,166	6.30
Roger Graham, New Haven	1991-94	821	5,953	+7.25
Phillip Moore, North Dakota	1995-98	1,060	5,467	5.16
Rashaan Dumas, Southern Conn. St.	1996-99	977	5,396	5.52
Antonio Leroy, Albany St. (Ga.)	1993-96	973	5,152	5.29
Shawn Graves, Wofford	1989-92	730	5,128	7.02
Chris Cobb, Eastern Ill.	1976-79	930	5,042	5.42
Irv Sigler, Bloomsburg	1994-97	820	5,034	6.14
Harry Jackson, St. Cloud St.	1986-89	915	4,890	5.34
Leonard Davis, Lenoir-Rhyne	$1990-94	839	4,853	5.78
Jerry Linton, Okla. Panhandle	1959-62	648	4,839	7.47
Jim VanWagner, Michigan Tech	1973-76	958	4,788	5.00
Jeremy Monroe, Michigan Tech	1990-93	666	4,661	7.00
Heath Sherman, Tex. A&M-Kingsville	1985-88	804	4,654	5.79
Steve Roberts, Butler	1986-89	1,026	4,623	4.51
Randy Martin, St. Cloud St.	1993-96	814	4,618	5.67
Don Aleksiewicz, Hobart	1969-72	819	4,525	5.53
Dale Mills, Truman	1957-60	751	4,502	5.99
Scott Schulte, Hillsdale	1990-93	879	4,495	5.11
Leo Lewis, Lincoln (Mo.)	1951-54	623	4,458	7.16

*Record. +Record for minimum 750 rushes. $See page 6 for explanation.

SEASON YARDS

Player, Team	Year	G	Plays	Yards	Avg.
Kavin Gailliard, American Int'l	†1999	12	320	*2,653	‡8.29
Brian Shay, Emporia St.	†1998	11	293	2,265	7.73
Anthony Gray, Western N.M.	†1997	10	277	2,220	8.01
Jarrett Anderson, Truman	†1996	11	321	2,140	6.67
Brian Shay, Emporia St.	1996	11	342	2,103	6.15
Josh Ranek, South Dakota St.	1999	11	329	2,055	6.25
Irv Sigler, Bloomsburg	1997	10	299	2,038	6.82
Johnny Bailey, Tex. A&M-Kingsville	†1986	11	271	2,011	7.42
Kavin Gailliard, American Int'l	1998	11	269	1,971	7.33
Wesley Cates, Calif. (Pa.)	1999	11	298	1,935	6.49
Brian Shay, Emporia St.	1997	11	269	1,912	7.11
Richard Huntley, Winston-Salem	†1995	10	273	1,889	6.92
Josh Ranek, South Dakota St.	1998	11	302	1,881	6.23
Ronald Moore, Pittsburg St.	1992	11	239	1,864	7.80
Tyrone Morgan, Northern St.	1998	11	318	1,838	5.78
Fred Lane, Lane	1995	10	273	1,833	6.71
Zed Robinson, Southern Utah	1991	11	254	1,828	7.20
Richard Huntley, Winston-Salem	1994	11	251	1,815	7.23
Jamel White, South Dakota	1999	11	316	1,807	5.72
Fred Lane, Lane	1994	11	280	1,779	6.35

*Record. †National champion. ‡Record for minimum 250 rushes.

SINGLE-GAME YARDS

Yds.	Player, Team (Opponent)	Date
403	Rob Davidson, Fairmont St. (Concord)	Nov. 14, 1998
382	Kelly Ellis, Northern Iowa (Western Ill.)	Oct. 13, 1979
373	Dallas Garber, Marietta (Wash. & Jeff.)	Nov. 7, 1959
370	Jim Hissam, Marietta (Bethany [W.Va.])	Nov. 15, 1958
370	Jim Baier, Wis.-River Falls (Wis.-Stevens Point)	Nov. 5, 1966
367	Don Polkinghorne, Washington (Mo.) (Wash. & Lee)	Nov. 23, 1957
363	Richie Weaver, Widener (Moravian)	Oct. 17, 1970
361	Richard Huntley, Winston-Salem (Virginia Union)	Nov. 5, 1994
361	Brian Shay, Emporia St. (Washburn)	Oct. 5, 1996
359	Anthony Gray, Western N.M. (Hardin-Simmons)	Oct. 4, 1997
356	Ole Gunderson, St. Olaf (Monmouth [Ill.])	Oct. 11, 1969
350	Ricke Stonewall, Millersville (New Haven)	Nov. 13, 1982
349	Alvon Brown, Kentucky St. (Morris Brown)	Nov. 7, 1998
348	Carlton Booe, Northeastern St. (Southeastern Okla.)	Oct. 31, 1998
347	Kavin Gailliard, American Int'l (Bryant)	Nov. 6, 1999

ANNUAL CHAMPIONS

Year	Player, Team	Class	Plays	Yards
1946	V. T. Smith, Abilene Christian	So.	99	733
1947	John Williams, Jacksonville St.	Jr.	150	931
1948	Hank Treesh, Hanover	Jr.	100	1,383
1949	Odie Posey, Southern U.	Jr.	121	1,399
1950	Meriel Michelson, Eastern Wash.	Sr.	180	1,234
1951	Bob White, Western N.M.	Jr.	202	1,643
1952	Al Conway, William Jewell	Sr.	134	1,325
1953	Elroy Payne, McMurry	So.	183	1,274
1954	Lem Harkey, Col. of Emporia	Sr.	121	1,146
1955	Gene Scott, Centre	Sr.	107	1,138
1956	Bill Rhodes, Western St.	Sr.	130	1,200
1957	Brad Hustad, Luther	So.	219	1,401
1958	Dale Mills, Truman	So.	186	1,358
1959	Dale Mills, Truman	Jr.	248	1,385
1960	Joe Iacone, West Chester	So.	199	1,438
1961	Bobby Lisa, St. Mary (Kan.)	Jr.	156	1,082
1962	Jerry Linton, Okla. Panhandle	Sr.	272	1,483
1963	Jim Holder, Okla. Panhandle	Sr.	275	1,775
1964	Jim Allison, San Diego St.	Sr.	174	1,186
1965	Allen Smith, Findlay	Jr.	207	1,240
1966	Jim Baier, Wis.-River Falls	Sr.	240	1,587
1967	Dickie Moore, Western Ky.	Jr.	208	1,444
1968	Howard Stevens, Randolph-Macon	Fr.	191	1,468
1969	Leon Burns, Long Beach St.	Jr.	350	1,659

Beginning in 1970, ranked on per-game (instead of total) yards

Year	Player, Team	Class	G	Plays	Yards	Avg.
1970	Dave Kiarsis, Trinity (Conn.)	Sr.	8	201	1,374	171.8
1971	Don Aleksiewicz, Hobart	Jr.	9	276	1,616	179.6
1972	Billy Johnson, Widener	So.	9	148	1,556	172.9
1973	Mike Thomas, UNLV	Jr.	11	274	1,741	158.3
1974	Jim VanWagner, Michigan Tech	So.	9	246	1,453	161.4
1975	Jim VanWagner, Michigan Tech	Jr.	9	289	1,331	147.9
1976	Ted McKnight, Minn.-Duluth	Sr.	10	220	1,482	148.2
1977	Bill Burnham, New Hampshire	Sr.	10	281	1,422	142.2
1978	Mike Harris, Truman	Sr.	11	329	1,598	145.3
1979	Chris Cobb, Eastern Ill.	Sr.	11	293	1,609	146.3
1980	Louis Jackson, Cal Poly	Sr.	10	287	1,424	142.4
1981	Rick Porter, Slippery Rock	Sr.	9	208	1,179	131.0
1982	Ricke Stonewall, Millersville	So.	10	191	1,387	138.7
1983	Mark Corbin, Central St.	So.	10	208	1,502	150.2
1984	Charles Sanders, Slippery Rock	Jr.	10	269	1,280	128.0
1985	Dan Sonnek, South Dakota St.	So.	11	303	1,518	138.0
1986	Johnny Bailey, Tex. A&M-Kingsville	Fr.	11	271	2,011	182.8
1987	Johnny Bailey, Tex. A&M-Kingsville	So.	10	217	1,598	159.8
1988	Johnny Bailey, Tex. A&M-Kingsville	Jr.	10	229	1,442	144.2
1989	Kevin Mitchell, Saginaw Valley	Jr.	8	236	1,460	182.5
1990	David Jones, Chadron St.	Sr.	10	225	1,570	157.0
1991	Quincy Tillmon, Emporia St.	So.	9	259	1,544	171.6
1992	Roger Graham, New Haven	So.	10	200	1,717	171.7
1993	Keith Higdon, Cheyney	Sr.	10	330	1,742	174.2
1994	Leonard Davis, Lenoir-Rhyne	Sr.	9	216	1,559	173.2
1995	Richard Huntley, Winston-Salem	Sr.	10	273	1,889	188.9
1996	Jarrett Anderson, Truman	Sr.	11	321	2,140	194.5
1997	Anthony Gray, Western N.M.	Jr.	10	277	2,220	*222.0
1998	Brian Shay, Emporia St.	Sr.	11	293	2,265	205.9
1999	Kavin Gailliard, American Int'l	Sr.	12	320	*2,653	221.1

*Record.

DIVISION II

ALL-TIME LEADERS—PASSING

Passing

CAREER PASSING EFFICIENCY
(Minimum 375 Completions)

Player, Team	Years	Att.	Cmp.	Int.	Pct.	Yards	TD	Pts.
Wilkie Perez, Glenville St.	1997-98	567	376	17	.663	5,240	50	*167.0
Corte McGuffey, Northern Colo.	1996-99	768	484	23	.630	6,975	75	165.6
Chris Petersen, UC Davis	1985-86	553	385	13	*.696	4,988	39	164.0
Rick Hebert, American Int'l	1996-99	699	423	16	.605	5,990	55	153.9
Chris Hatcher, Valdosta St.	1991-94	1,451	*1,001	38	‡.690	*10,878	*116	+153.1
Jim McMillan, Boise St.	1971-74	640	382	29	.597	5,508	58	152.8
Chris Greisen, Northwest Mo. St.	1995-98	653	379	22	.580	5,741	51	150.9
Jack Hull, Grand Valley St.	1988-91	835	485	22	.581	7,120	64	149.7
Scott Otis, Glenville St.	1994-95	693	421	21	.608	5,563	56	148.8
Jesse Showerda, New Haven	1993-96	675	402	15	.596	5,175	57	147.4
Grady Benton, West Tex. A&M	1994-95	686	421	22	.614	5,618	49	147.3
Bruce Upstill, Col. of Emporia	1960-63	769	438	36	.570	6,935	48	144.0
Jarrod DeGeorgia, Wayne St. (Neb.)	1995-96	645	428	18	.664	5,161	31	143.9
Jeff Fox, Grand Valley St.	1995-98	1,031	626	22	.607	8,197	62	143.1
Lance Funderburk, Valdosta St.	1993-96	1,054	689	23	.654	7,698	64	142.4
George Bork, Northern Ill.	1960-63	902	577	33	.640	6,782	60	141.8
June Jones, Portland St.	1975-76	658	375	34	.570	5,798	41	141.2
Steve Mariucci, Northern Mich.	1974-77	678	380	33	.561	6,022	41	140.9
Scott Barry, UC Davis	1982-84	588	377	16	.641	4,421	33	140.4
Kevin Daft, UC Davis	1995-98	805	459	23	.570	6,197	54	138.1
Matt Cook, Mo. Southern St.	$1989-93	816	411	29	.504	6,715	63	137.9
Aaron Sparrow, Norfolk St.	1992-95	1,117	615	38	.551	8,758	79	137.5
Chris Crawford, Portland St.	1985-88	954	588	35	.616	7,543	48	137.3
Trevor Spradley, Southwest Baptist	1990-92	712	441	27	.619	5,881	29	137.2
Matt McCarthy, Ferris St.	1996-99	1,077	620	26	.576	8,174	64	136.1
Dan Miles, Southern Ore.	1964-67	871	577	56	.662	6,531	52	136.1

*Record. ‡Record for minimum 1,000 attempts. +Record for minimum 750 completions. $See page 6 for explanation.

SEASON PASSING EFFICIENCY
(Minimum 15 Attempts Per Game)

Player, Team	Year	G	Att.	Cmp.	Int.	Pct.	Yards	TD	Pts.
Boyd Crawford, Col. of Idaho	†1953	8	120	72	6	.600	1,462	21	*210.1
Chuck Green, Wittenberg	†1963	9	182	114	8	.626	2,181	19	+189.0
Jayson Merrill, Western St.	†1991	10	309	195	11	.631	3,484	35	188.1
Rick Hebert, American Int'l	†1999	12	234	166	4	.709	2,351	25	187.2
Jim Feely, Johns Hopkins	†1967	7	110	69	5	.627	1,264	12	186.2
John Charles, Portland St.	1991	11	247	147	7	.595	2,619	32	185.7
Steve Smith, Western St.	†1992	10	271	180	5	.664	2,719	30	183.5
Jim Peterson, Hanover	†1948	8	125	81	12	.648	1,571	12	182.9
John Wristen, Southern Colo.	†1982	8	121	68	2	.562	1,358	13	182.6
John Charles, Portland St.	1992	8	263	179	7	.681	2,770	24	181.3
Richard Basil, Savannah St.	†1989	9	211	120	7	.569	2,148	29	181.1
Chris Hatcher, Valdosta St.	†1994	11	430	321	9	*.747	3,591	*50	‡179.0
Wilkie Perez, Glenville St.	†1997	11	425	280	12	.658	*4,189	45	178.0
Jim Cahoon, Ripon	†1964	8	127	74	7	.583	1,206	19	176.4
Ken Suhl, New Haven	1992	10	239	148	5	.619	2,336	26	175.7
Corte McGuffey, Northern Colo.	1999	11	296	189	11	.639	2,893	31	173.0
Tony Aliucci, Indiana (Pa.)	1990	10	181	111	10	.613	1,801	21	172.2
James Weir, New Haven	†1993	10	266	161	1	.605	2,336	31	172.0
Shawn Behr, Fort Hays St.	†1995	11	318	191	6	.600	3,158	31	171.9
John Costello, Widener	†1956	9	149	74	10	.497	1,702	17	169.8

*Record. †National champion. +Record for minimum 100 completions. ‡Record for minimum 200 completions.

CAREER YARDS PER GAME
(Minimum 4,500 Yards)

Player, Team	Years	G	Att.	Cmp.	Int.	Pct.	Yards	TD	Avg.
Grady Benton, West Tex. A&M	1994-95	18	686	421	22	.614	5,618	49	*312.1
Wilkie Perez, Glenville St.	1997-98	17	567	376	17	.663	5,240	50	308.2
Tim Von Dulm, Portland St.	1969-70	20	924	500	41	.541	5,967	51	298.4
Marty Washington, West Ala.	1992-93	17	690	379	25	.549	5,018	40	295.2
Jayson Merrill, Western St.	1990-91	20	580	328	25	.566	5,830	56	291.5
Jarrod DeGeorgia, Wayne St. (Neb.)	1995-96	18	645	428	18	.664	5,161	31	286.7
John Charles, Portland St.	1991-92	19	510	326	14	.639	5,389	56	283.6
Chris Hatcher, Valdosta St.	1991-94	39	1,451	*1,001	38	‡.690	*10,878	*116	278.9
Scott Otis, Glenville St.	1994-95	20	693	421	21	.608	5,563	56	278.2
June Jones, Portland St.	1975-76	21	658	375	34	.570	5,798	41	276.1
Jermaine Whitaker, N.M. Highlands	1992-94	31	1,150	625	45	.543	8,532	71	275.2
Steve Wray, Franklin	1979, 81-82	26	1,070	511	40	.478	7,019	56	270.0
Pat Graham, Augustana (S.D.)	1995-96	21	820	469	26	.572	5,636	43	268.4
Earl Harvey, N.C. Central	1985-88	40	1,442	690	81	.479	10,621	86	265.5
Chris Hegg, Truman	1984-85	20	771	410	32	.532	5,306	44	265.3
Brad Norris, Adams St.	1998-99	20	653	327	18	.501	5,171	44	258.6
Pat Brennan, Franklin	1981-84	30	1,123	535	62	.476	7,717	53	257.2
Jay McLucas, New Haven	1989-90	20	699	370	30	.529	5,139	37	257.0
Lance Funderburk, Valdosta St.	1993-96	30	1,054	689	23	.654	7,698	64	256.6
Matt McCarthy, Ferris St.	1996-99	32	1,077	620	26	.576	8,174	64	255.4

Corte McGuffey of Northern Colorado is second in Division II history in passing efficiency with a 165.6 rating.

ALL-TIME LEADERS—PASSING

Player, Team	Years	G	Att.	Cmp.	Int.	Pct.	Yards	TD	Avg.
Troy Mott, Wayne St. (Neb.)	1991-92	20	757	437	37	.577	5,003	25	250.2
Chris Petersen, UC Davis	1985-86	20	553	385	13	*.696	4,988	39	249.4
Rich Ingold, Indiana (Pa.)	1983-85	26	852	499	36	.586	6,454	48	248.2
Matt McCarthy, Ferris St.	1996-98	22	720	410	19	.569	5,453	33	247.9
Jeff Phillips, Central Mo. St.	1986-88	26	892	496	54	.556	6,294	46	242.1

*Record. ‡Record for minimum 1,000 attempts.

SEASON YARDS PER GAME

Player, Team	Year	G	Att.	Cmp.	Int.	Pct.	Yards	TD	Avg.
Grady Benton, West Tex. A&M	1994	9	409	258	13	.631	3,541	30	*393.4
Damian Poalucci, East Stroudsburg	1996	10	393	214	13	.545	3,831	40	383.1
Marty Washington, West Ala.	1993	8	404	221	13	.547	3,062	26	382.8
Wilkie Perez, Glenville St.	†1997	11	425	280	12	.658	*4,189	45	380.8
Perry Klein, C. W. Post	1993	10	407	248	18	.609	3,757	38	375.7
Brett Salisbury, Wayne St. (Neb.)	1993	10	395	276	14	.699	3,729	29	372.9
Alfred Montez, Western N.M.	1994	6	231	133	7	.576	2,182	18	363.7
Bob Toledo, San Fran. St.	1967	10	396	211	24	.533	3,513	45	351.3
Pat Brennan, Franklin	1983	10	458	226	30	.493	3,491	25	349.1
Jayson Merrill, Western St.	†1991	10	309	195	11	.631	3,484	35	348.4
John Charles, Portland St.	1992	8	263	179	7	.681	2,770	24	346.3
Rod Smith, Glenville St.	1996	10	409	249	14	.609	3,455	29	345.5
Aaron Sparrow, Norfolk St.	1995	10	409	238	14	.581	3,434	32	343.4
George Bork, Northern Ill.	†1963	9	374	244	12	.652	3,077	32	341.9
Chris Hegg, Truman	†1985	11	503	284	20	.565	3,741	32	340.1
Lance Funderburk, Valdosta St.	1996	11	459	300	10	.654	3,732	35	339.3
Jed Drenning, Glenville St.	1993	10	390	244	12	.626	3,391	25	339.1
Jarrod DeGeorgia, Wayne St. (Neb.)	1996	10	420	286	12	.681	3,388	19	338.8
Lance Funderburk, Valdosta St.	1995	11	*544	*356	12	.654	3,706	26	336.9
Pat Brennan, Franklin	1984	10	502	238	20	.474	3,340	18	334.0

*Record. †National champion.

CAREER YARDS

Player, Team	Years	Att.	Cmp.	Int.	Pct.	Yards	TD
Chris Hatcher, Valdosta St.	1991-94	1,451	*1,001	38	‡.690	*10,878	*116
Bob McLaughlin, Lock Haven	1992-95	*1,719	910	*88	.529	10,640	60
Earl Harvey, N.C. Central	1985-88	1,442	690	81	.479	10,621	86
John Craven, Gardner-Webb	1991-94	1,535	828	82	.539	9,934	80
Vernon Buck, Wingate	1991-94	1,393	728	61	.523	9,884	72
Thad Trujillo, Fort Lewis	1991-94	1,455	760	57	.522	9,873	78
Jarrod Furgason, Fairmont St.	$1993-97	1,392	798	44	.573	9,856	101
Mike Mitros, West Chester	1996-99	1,402	819	48	.584	9,834	94
Rob Tomlinson, Cal St. Chico	1988-91	1,328	748	43	.563	9,434	52
John Hebgen, Minn. St.-Mankato	1993-96	1,268	727	38	.573	9,410	71
Trevor Moon, Chadron St.	1995-98	1,241	635	36	.512	9,333	63
Andy Breault, Kutztown	1989-92	1,259	733	63	.582	9,096	86
Aaron Sparrow, Norfolk St.	1992-95	1,117	615	38	.551	8,758	79
Sam Mannery, Calif. (Pa.)	1987-90	1,283	649	68	.506	8,680	64
Damian Poalucci, East Stroudsburg	1994-97	1,067	583	47	.546	8,654	69
¢Justin Coleman, Neb.-Kearney	1997-99	902	527	31	.548	8,568	73
Dave DenBraber, Ferris St.	1984-87	1,254	661	45	.527	8,536	52
Jermaine Whitaker, N.M. Highlands	1992-94	1,150	625	45	.543	8,532	71
Jim Lindsey, Abilene Christian	1967-70	1,237	642	69	.519	8,521	61
Dave MacDonald, West Chester	1991-94	1,123	604	46	.538	8,449	82
Maurice Heard, Tuskegee	1988-91	1,134	556	54	.490	8,434	87
Jeff Fox, Grand Valley St.	1995-98	1,031	626	22	.607	8,197	62
Matt McCarthy, Ferris St.	1996-99	1,077	620	26	.576	8,174	64
John St. Jacques, Santa Clara	1988-89, 91-92	1,060	543	36	.512	7,968	68
Rex Lamberti, Abilene Christian	1984-86, 93	1,133	595	44	.525	7,934	84

*Record. ‡Record for minimum 1,000 attempts. $See page 6 for explanation. ¢Active player.

SEASON YARDS

Player, Team	Year	G	Att.	Cmp.	Int.	Pct.	Yards	TD
Wilkie Perez, Glenville St.	†1997	11	425	280	12	.658	*4,189	45
Damian Poalucci, East Stroudsburg	1996	10	393	214	13	.545	3,831	40
Perry Klein, C. W. Post	1993	10	407	248	18	.609	3,757	38
Chris Hegg, Truman	1985	11	503	284	20	.565	3,741	32
Lance Funderburk, Valdosta St.	1996	11	459	300	10	.654	3,732	35
Brett Salisbury, Wayne St. (Neb.)	1993	10	395	276	14	.699	3,729	29
Lance Funderburk, Valdosta St.	1995	11	*544	*356	12	.654	3,706	26
Tod Mayfield, West Tex. A&M	1986	11	515	317	20	.616	3,664	31
Chris Hatcher, Valdosta St.	1993	11	471	335	11	.711	3,651	37
Chris Hatcher, Valdosta St.	†1994	11	430	321	9	*.747	3,591	*50
Grady Benton, West Tex. A&M	1994	9	409	258	13	.631	3,541	30
June Jones, Portland St.	†1976	11	423	238	24	.563	3,518	25
Bob Toledo, San Fran. St.	1967	10	396	211	24	.533	3,513	45
Pat Brennan, Franklin	1983	10	458	226	30	.493	3,491	25
Jayson Merrill, Western St.	†1991	10	309	195	11	.631	3,484	35
Rod Smith, Glenville St.	1996	10	409	249	14	.609	3,455	29
Gregory Clark, Virginia St.	1993	11	380	227	11	.597	3,437	38
Mike Mitros, West Chester	1998	11	457	267	12	.584	3,437	32
Aaron Sparrow, Norfolk St.	1995	10	409	238	14	.581	3,434	32
Jed Drenning, Glenville St.	1993	10	390	244	12	.626	3,391	25

*Record. †National champion.

DIVISION II

ALL-TIME LEADERS—PASSING

West Chester's Mike Mitros concluded his career in 1999 in third place in touchdown passes with 94 and eighth in career passing yards with 9,834.

CAREER TOUCHDOWN PASSES

Player, Team	Years	Att.	Cmp.	Int.	Pct.	Yds.	TD
Chris Hatcher, Valdosta St.	1991-94	1,451	*1,001	38	‡.690	*10,878	*116
Jarrod Furgason, Fairmont St.	$1993-97	1,392	798	44	.573	9,856	101
Mike Mitros, West Chester	1996-99	1,402	819	48	.584	9,834	94
Maurice Heard, Tuskegee	1988-91	1,134	556	54	.490	8,434	87
Earl Harvey, N.C. Central	1985-88	1,442	690	82	.479	10,621	86
Andy Breault, Kutztown	1989-92	1,259	733	63	.582	9,086	86
Rex Lamberti, Abilene Christian	1984-86, 93	1,133	595	44	.525	7,934	84
Dave MacDonald, West Chester	1991-94	1,123	604	46	.538	8,449	82
John Craven, Gardner-Webb	1991-94	1,535	828	82	.539	9,934	80
Aaron Sparrow, Norfolk St.	1992-95	1,117	615	38	.551	8,758	79

*Record. ‡Record for minimum 1,000 attempts. $See page 6 for explanation.

SEASON TOUCHDOWN PASSES

Player, Team	Years	Att.	Cmp.	Int.	Pct.	Yds.	TD
Chris Hatcher, Valdosta St.	†1994	430	321	9	*.747	3,591	*50
Wilkie Perez, Glenville St.	†1997	425	280	12	.658	*4,189	45
Bob Toledo, San Fran. St.	1967	396	211	24	.533	3,513	45
Damian Poalucci, East Stroudsburg	1996	393	214	13	.545	3,831	40
Perry Klein, C. W. Post	1993	407	248	18	.609	3,757	38
Chris Hatcher, Valdosta St.	1993	471	335	11	.711	3,651	37
Andy Breault, Kutztown	1991	360	225	20	.625	2,927	37
Lance Funderburk, Valdosta St.	1996	459	300	10	.654	3,732	35
Jarrod Furgason, Fairmont St.	1995	349	222	8	.636	2,696	35
Dave MacDonald, West Chester	1994	458	251	18	.548	3,308	35
Jason Merrill, Western St.	1991	309	195	11	.631	3,484	35

*Record. †National champion.

SINGLE-GAME YARDS

Yds.	Player, Team (Opponent)	Date
642	Wilkie Perez, Glenville St. (Concord)	Oct. 25, 1997
616	Damian Poalucci, East Stroudsburg (Mansfield)	Nov. 2, 1996
614	Alfred Montez, Western N.M. (West Tex. A&M)	Oct. 8, 1994
614	Perry Klein, C. W. Post (Salisbury St.)	Nov. 6, 1993
613	Jayce Goree, Glenville St. (Concord)	Oct. 24, 1998
599	Jarrod DeGeorgia, Wayne St. (Neb.) (Drake)	Nov. 9, 1996
592	John Charles, Portland St. (Cal Poly)	Nov. 16, 1991
568	Scott Otis, Glenville St. (West Va. Wesleyan)	Oct. 15, 1994
568	Bob Toledo, San Fran. St. (Cal St. Hayward)	Oct. 21, 1967
564	Pat Graham, Augustana (S.D.) (Minn. St.-Mankato)	Oct. 28, 1995
551	Jamie Sander, N.M. Highlands (Neb.-Kearney)	Nov. 9, 1996
550	Earl Harvey, N.C. Central (Jackson St.)	Aug. 30, 1986
549	Matt LaTour, Northern Mich. (Ashland)	Nov. 5, 1994
541	Arnold Marcha, West Tex. A&M (Okla. Panhandle)	Nov. 12, 1994
539	Maurice Heard, Tuskegee (Alabama A&M)	Nov. 10, 1990

SINGLE-GAME ATTEMPTS

No.	Player, Team (Opponent)	Date
76	Jarrod DeGeorgia, Wayne St. (Neb.) (Drake)	Nov. 9, 1996
74	Jamie Sander, N.M. Highlands (Neb.-Kearney)	Nov. 9, 1996
74	Jermaine Whitaker, N.M. Highlands (Western St.)	Nov. 5, 1994
72	Kurt Otto, North Dakota (Tex. A&M-Kingsville)	Sept. 13, 1986
72	Kaipo Spencer, Santa Clara (Portland St.)	Oct. 11, 1975
72	Joe Stetser, Cal St. Chico (Oregon Tech)	Sept. 23, 1967
71	Pat Brennan, Franklin (Ashland)	Nov. 3, 1984

SINGLE-GAME COMPLETIONS

No.	Player, Team (Opponent)	Date
56	Jarrod DeGeorgia, Wayne St. (Neb.) (Drake)	Nov. 9, 1996
45	Chris Hatcher, Valdosta St. (Mississippi Col.)	Oct. 23, 1993
45	Chris Hatcher, Valdosta St. (West Ga.)	Oct. 16, 1993
44	Wilkie Perez, Glenville St. (Concord)	Oct. 25, 1997
44	Tom Bonds, Cal Lutheran (St. Mary's [Cal.])	Nov. 22, 1986
43	George Bork, Northern Ill. (Central Mich.)	Nov. 9, 1963
42	Luke Cullins, Harding (Central Okla.)	Oct. 16, 1999
42	Lance Funderburk, Valdosta St. (West Ga.)	Nov. 11, 1995
42	Jermaine Whitaker, N.M. Highlands (Western St.)	Nov. 5, 1994
42	Marty Washington, West Ala. (Jacksonville St.)	Nov. 7, 1992
42	Chris Teal, West Ga. (Valdosta St.)	Oct. 19, 1991
42	Tim Von Dulm, Portland St. (Eastern Wash.)	Nov. 21, 1970

ANNUAL CHAMPIONS

Year	Player, Team	Class	Att.	Cmp.	Int.	Pct.	Yds.	TD
1946	Hank Caver, Presbyterian	Sr.	128	59	13	.461	790	7
1947	James Batchelor, Tex. A&M-Commerce	Sr.	184	94	10	.511	1,114	9
1948	Sam Gary, Swarthmore	Jr.	153	93	11	.608	1,218	16
1949	Sam McGowan, New Mexico St.	Sr.	219	112	22	.511	1,712	12
1950	Andy MacDonald, Central Mich.	Jr.	200	109	12	.545	1,577	15
1951	Andy MacDonald, Central Mich.	Sr.	183	114	7	.623	1,560	12
1952	Wes Bair, Illinois St.	So.	242	135	18	.558	1,375	14
1953	Pence Dacus, Southwest Tex. St.	Sr.	207	113	10	.546	1,654	11
1954	Tommy Egan, Brandeis	Sr.	144	87	8	.604	1,050	11

ALL-TIME LEADERS—PASSING

Year	Player, Team	Class	Att.	Cmp.	Int.	Pct.	Yds.	TD
1955	Jerry Foley, Hamline	Fr.	167	87	8	.521	1,034	6
1956	James Stehlin, Brandeis	Sr.	206	116	11	.563	1,155	6
1957	Jay Roelen, Pepperdine	Sr.	214	106	16	.495	1,428	13
1958	Stan Jackson, Cal Poly Pomona	Sr.	256	123	14	.480	1,994	16
1959	Gary Campbell, Whittier	Sr.	183	111	4	.607	1,717	12
1960	Denny Spurlock, Whitworth	Jr.	257	135	16	.525	1,892	14
1961	Tom Gryzwinski, Defiance	Jr.	258	127	17	.492	1,684	14
1962	George Bork, Northern Ill.	Jr.	356	232	11	.652	2,506	22
1963	George Bork, Northern Ill.	Sr.	374	244	12	.652	3,077	32
1964	Jerry Bishop, Austin	Jr.	300	182	16	.607	2,246	17
1965	Bob Caress, Bradley	Sr.	393	210	21	.534	2,167	24
1966	Paul Krause, Dubuque	Sr.	318	179	22	.563	2,210	16
1967	Joe Stetser, Cal St. Chico	Sr.	464	220	*32	.474	2,446	14
1968	Jim Lindsey, Abilene Christian	So.	396	204	19	.515	2,717	18
1969	Tim Von Dulm, Portland St.	Jr.	434	241	18	.555	2,926	26

Beginning in 1970, ranked on per-game (instead of total) completions

Year	Player, Team	Class	G	Att.	Cmp.	Avg.	Int.	Pct.	Yds.	TD
1970	Tim Von Dulm, Portland St.	Sr.	10	490	259	25.9	23	.529	3,041	25
1971	Bob Baron, Rensselaer	Sr.	9	302	168	18.7	13	.556	2,105	15
1972	Bob Biggs, UC Davis	Sr.	9	327	186	20.7	16	.569	2,291	15
1973	Kim McQuilken, Lehigh	Sr.	11	326	196	17.8	13	.601	2,603	19
1974	Jim McMillan, Boise St.	Sr.	10	313	192	19.2	15	.613	2,900	13
1975	Dan Hayes, UC Riverside	Sr.	10	316	171	17.1	20	.541	2,215	21
1976	June Jones, Portland St.	Sr.	11	423	238	21.6	24	.563	3,518	25
1977	Ed Schultz, Moorhead St.	Sr.	10	304	187	18.7	16	.615	1,943	21
1978	Jeff Knapple, Northern Colo.	Sr.	10	349	178	17.8	21	.510	2,191	16

Beginning in 1979, ranked on passing efficiency rating points (instead of per-game completions)

Year	Player, Team	Class	G	Att.	Cmp.	Int.	Pct.	Yds.	TD	Pts.
1979	Dave Alfaro, Santa Clara	Jr.	9	168	110	9	.655	1,721	13	166.3
1980	Willie Tullis, Troy St.	Sr.	10	203	108	8	.532	1,880	15	147.5
1981	Steve Michuta, Grand Valley St.	Sr.	8	173	114	11	.659	1,702	17	168.3
1982	John Wristen, Southern Colo.	Jr.	8	121	68	2	.562	1,358	13	182.6
1983	Kevin Parker, Fort Valley St.	Jr.	9	168	87	8	.518	1,539	18	154.6
1984	Brian Quinn, Northwest Mo. St.	Sr.	10	178	96	2	.539	1,561	14	151.3
1985	Chris Petersen, UC Davis	Jr.	10	242	167	6	.690	2,366	17	169.4
1986	Chris Petersen, UC Davis	Sr.	10	311	218	7	.701	2,622	22	159.7
1987	Dave Biondo, Ashland	Jr.	10	177	95	11	.537	1,828	14	154.1
1988	Al Niemela, West Chester	Sr.	10	217	138	9	.636	1,932	21	162.0
1989	Richard Basil, Savannah St.	Sr.	9	211	120	7	.569	2,148	29	181.1
1990	Tony Aliucci, Indiana (Pa.)	Jr.	10	181	111	10	.613	1,801	21	172.2
1991	Jayson Merrill, Western St.	Sr.	10	309	195	11	.631	3,484	35	188.1
1992	Steve Smith, Western St.	Sr.	10	271	180	5	.664	2,719	30	183.5
1993	James Weir, New Haven	Jr.	10	266	161	1	.605	2,336	31	172.0
1994	Chris Hatcher, Valdosta St.	Sr.	11	430	321	9	*.747	3,591	*50	‡179.0
1995	Shawn Behr, Fort Hays St.	Sr.	11	318	191	6	.600	3,158	31	171.9
1996	Jesse Showerda, New Haven	Sr.	10	300	180	3	.600	2,625	31	165.6
1997	Wilkie Perez, Glenville St.	Jr.	11	425	280	12	.658	*4,189	45	178.0
1998	Sleepie Tollie, Northwood	Fr.	10	148	80	7	.540	1,862	18	††190.4
1999	Rick Hebert, American Int'l	Sr.	12	234	166	4	.709	2,351	25	187.2

*Record. ‡Record for minimum 200 completions. ††Declared champion; with two more pass attempts (Making 15 per game), both interceptions, still would have the highest efficiency rating (185.2).

ANNUAL PASSING EFFICIENCY LEADERS BEFORE 1979
(Minimum 11 Attempts Per Game)

1948—Jim Peterson, Hanover, 182.9; **1949**—John Ford, Hardin-Simmons, 179.6; **1950**—Edward Ludorf, Trinity (Conn.), 167.8; **1951**—Vic Lesch, Western Ill., 182.4; **1952**—Jim Gray, Tex. A&M-Commerce, 205.5; **1953**—Boyd Crawford, Col. of Idaho, *210.1; **1954**—Bill Englehardt, Neb.-Omaha, 170.7; **1955**—Robert Alexander, Trinity (Conn.), 208.7; **1956**—John Costello, Widener, 169.8; **1957**—Doug Maison, Hillsdale, 200.0; **1958**—Kurt Duecker, Ripon, 161.7; **1959**—Fred Whitmire, Humboldt St., 188.7; **1960**—Larry Cline, Otterbein, 195.2.

(Minimum 15 Attempts Per Game)

Year	Player, Team	G	Att.	Cmp.	Int.	Pct.	Yds.	TD	Pts.
1961	Denny Spurlock, Whitworth	10	189	115	16	.608	1,708	26	165.2
1962	Roy Curry, Jackson St.	10	194	104	8	.536	1,862	15	151.5
1963	Chuck Green, Wittenberg	9	182	114	8	.626	2,181	19	+189.0
1964	Jim Cahoon, Ripon	8	127	74	7	.583	1,206	19	176.4
1965	Ed Buzzell, Ottawa	9	238	118	5	.496	2,170	31	165.0
1966	Jim Alcorn, Clarion	9	199	107	4	.538	1,714	19	161.9
1967	Jim Feely, Johns Hopkins	7	110	69	5	.627	1,264	12	186.2
1968	Larry Green, Doane	9	182	97	7	.533	1,592	22	159.0
1969	George Kaplan, Northern Colo.	9	155	92	5	.594	1,396	16	162.6
1970	Gary Wichard, C. W. Post	9	186	100	5	.538	1,527	12	138.6
1971	Peter Mackey, Middlebury	8	180	101	4	.561	1,597	19	161.0
1972	David Hamilton, Fort Valley St.	9	180	99	9	.550	1,571	24	162.3
1973	Jim McMillan, Boise St.	11	179	110	5	.615	1,525	17	158.8
1974	Jim McMillan, Boise St.	10	313	192	15	.613	2,900	33	164.4
1975	Joe Sterrett, Lehigh	11	228	135	13	.592	2,114	22	157.5
1976	Mike Makings, Western St.	10	179	90	6	.503	1,617	14	145.3
1977	Mike Rieker, Lehigh	11	230	137	14	.596	2,431	23	169.2
1978	Mike Moroski, UC Davis	10	205	119	9	.580	1,689	17	145.9

*Record. +Record for minimum 100 completions.

DIVISION II

Receiving

CAREER RECEPTIONS PER GAME
(Minimum 125 Receptions)

Player, Team	Years	G	Rec.	Yards	TD	Rec. PG
Chris George, Glenville St.	1993-94	20	230	3,215	30	*11.5
Ed Bell, Idaho St.	1968-69	19	163	2,608	30	8.6
Byron Chamberlain, Wayne St. (Neb.)	1993-94	19	161	1,941	14	8.3
Carlos Ferralls, Glenville St.	1994-97	32	262	3,835	43	8.2
Jerry Hendren, Idaho	1967-69	30	230	3,435	27	7.7
Gary Garrison, San Diego St.	1964-65	20	148	2,188	26	7.4
Brad Bailey, West Tex. A&M	1992-94	30	221	2,677	22	7.4
Chris Myers, Kenyon	1967-70	35	253	3,897	33	7.2

*Record.

SEASON RECEPTIONS PER GAME

Player, Team	Year	G	Rec.	Yards	TD	Rec. PG
Chris George, Glenville St.	†1993	10	117	*1,876	15	*11.7
Chris George, Glenville St.	1994	10	113	1,339	15	11.3
Brad Bailey, West Tex. A&M	1994	11	*119	1,552	16	10.8
Kevin Ingram, West Chester	†1998	11	115	1,673	**21	10.5
Carlos Ferralls, Glenville St.	†1996	8	81	965	6	10.1
Bruce Cerone, Emporia St.	1968	9	91	1,479	15	10.1
Mike Healey, Valparaiso	†1985	10	101	1,279	11	10.1
Sean Pender, Valdosta St.	†1995	11	111	983	2	10.1
Barry Wagner, Alabama A&M	†1989	11	106	1,812	17	9.6
Ed Bell, Idaho St.	†1969	10	96	1,522	20	9.6
Jerry Hendren, Idaho	1968	9	86	1,457	14	9.6
Dick Hewins, Drake	†1968	10	95	1,316	13	9.5
Carlos Ferralls, Glenville St.	†1997	10	94	1,566	19	9.4
Jarett Vito, Emporia St.	1995	10	+94	932	7	9.4
Billy Joe Masters, Evansville	†1987	10	‡94	‡960	4	‡9.4
Joe Dittrich, Southwest St.	†1980	9	83	974	7	9.2
Mark DeBrito, Bentley	†1999	11	101	1,637	19	9.2
Manley Sarnowsky, Drake	†1966	10	92	1,114	7	9.2

*Record. **Record tied. †National champion. +Record for a freshman. ‡Record for a running back.

CAREER RECEPTIONS

Player, Team	Years	Rec.	Yards	TD
Carlos Ferralls, Glenville St.	1994-97	*262	3,835	43
Jon Spinosa, Lock Haven	1992-95	261	2,710	12
Chris Myers, Kenyon	1967-70	253	3,897	33
Bruce Cerone, Yankton/Emporia St.	1965-66, 68-69	241	4,354	*49
James Roe, Norfolk St.	1992-95	239	*4,468	46
Mark DeBrito, Bentley	1996-99	238	3,711	41
Bryan McGinty, Lock Haven	1993-96	238	3,100	18
Kevin Ingram, West Chester	1995-96, 98-99	235	3,159	45
"Red" Roberts, Austin Peay	1967-70	232	3,005	31
Chris George, Glenville St.	1993-94	230	3,215	30
Jerry Hendren, Idaho	1967-69	230	3,435	27
Mike Healey, Valparaiso	1982-85	228	3,212	26
Jarett Vito, Emporia St.	1995-98	226	2,608	25
William Mackall, Tenn.-Martin	1985-88	224	2,488	16
Mike McFetridge, Millersville	1995-98	224	2,778	27
Brad Bailey, West Tex. A&M	1992-94	221	2,677	22
Johnny Cox, Fort Lewis	1990-93	220	3,611	33
Tywan Mitchell, Minn. St.-Mankato	1995-98	216	3,342	30
Greg Hopkins, Slippery Rock	1991-94	215	3,382	28
Robert Clark, N.C. Central	1983-86	210	4,231	38
¢Damien Hoffman, Minn.-Morris	1997-99	209	2,360	18
Neal Mozdzierz, Ferris St.	1996-99	206	2,563	22
Terry Fredenberg, Wis.-Milwaukee	1965-68	206	2,789	24
Dan Bogar, Valparaiso	1981-84	204	2,816	26
¢Damon Thompson, Virginia St.	1997-99	203	3,284	28

*Record. ¢Active player.

SEASON RECEPTIONS

Player, Team	Year	G	Rec.	Yards	TD
Brad Bailey, West Tex. A&M	1994	11	*119	1,552	16
Chris George, Glenville St.	†1993	10	117	*1,876	15
Kevin Ingram, West Chester	†1998	11	115	1,673	**21
Chris George, Glenville St.	†1994	10	113	1,339	15
Sean Pender, Valdosta St.	†1995	11	111	983	2
Barry Wagner, Alabama A&M	†1989	11	106	1,812	17
Mark DeBrito, Bentley	†1999	11	101	1,637	19
Mike Healey, Valparaiso	†1985	10	101	1,279	11
Ed Bell, Idaho St.	†1969	10	96	1,522	20
Dick Hewins, Drake	†1968	10	95	1,316	13
Carlos Ferralls, Glenville St.	†1997	10	94	1,566	19
Jarett Vito, Emporia St.	1995	10	+94	932	7
Billy Joe Masters, Evansville	†1987	10	‡94	‡960	4

Player, Team	Year	G	Rec.	Yards	TD
Stan Carraway, West Tex. A&M	†1986	11	94	1,175	9
Manley Sarnowsky, Drake	†1966	10	92	1,114	7
Rus Bailey, N.M. Highlands	1993	10	91	1,192	12
Bruce Cerone, Emporia St.	1968	9	91	1,479	15
Damon Thompson, Virginia St.	1999	10	90	1,517	10
Rodney Robinson, Gardner-Webb	1992	11	89	1,496	16

*Record. **Record tied. †National champion. +Record for a freshman. ‡Record for a running back.

SINGLE-GAME RECEPTIONS

No.	Player, Team (Opponent)	Date
23	Chris George, Glenville St. (West Va. Wesleyan)	Oct. 15, 1994
23	Barry Wagner, Alabama A&M (Clark Atlanta)	Nov. 4, 1989
21	Kevin Swayne, Wayne St. (Neb.) (Drake)	Nov. 9, 1996
21	Jarett Vito, Emporia St. (Truman)	Nov. 4, 1995
20	Sean Pender, Valdosta St. (Mississippi Col.)	Nov. 4, 1995
20	Keylie Martin, N.M. Highlands (Western St.)	Nov. 5, 1994
20	"Red" Roberts, Austin Peay (Murray St.)	Nov. 8, 1969
19	Preston Cunningham, Southwest St. (Mo. Western St.)	Sept. 3, 1994
19	Matt Carman, West Ala. (Jacksonville St.)	Nov. 7, 1992
19	Aaron Marsh, Eastern Ky. (Northwood)	Oct. 14, 1967
19	Donnie Pruitt, Emory & Henry (Carson-Newman)	Sept. 23, 1967
19	George LaPorte, Union (N.Y.) (Rensselaer)	Oct. 16, 1965

CAREER YARDS PER GAME
(Minimum 2,200 yards)

Player, Team	Years	G	Rec.	Yards	Avg.
Chris George, Glenville St.	1993-94	20	230	3,215	*160.8
Ed Bell, Idaho St.	1968-69	19	163	2,608	137.3
Bruce Cerone, Yankton/Emporia St.	1965-66, 68-69	36	241	4,354	120.9
Carlos Ferralls, Glenville St.	1994-97	32	*262	3,835	119.8
Jerry Hendren, Idaho	1967-69	30	230	3,435	114.5
Chris Myers, Kenyon	1967-70	35	253	3,897	111.3
James Roe, Norfolk St.	1992-95	41	239	*4,468	109.0

*Record.

SEASON YARDS PER GAME

Player, Team	Years	G	Rec.	Yards	Avg.
Chris George, Glenville St.	†1993	10	117	*1,876	*187.6
Chris Perry, Adams St.	†1995	10	88	1,719	171.9
Barry Wagner, Alabama A&M	†1989	11	106	1,812	164.7
Bruce Cerone, Emporia St.	1968	9	91	1,479	164.3
Jerry Hendren, Idaho	†1969	9	86	1,457	161.9
Carlos Ferralls, Glenville St.	†1997	10	94	1,566	156.6
Ed Bell, Idaho St.	†1969	10	96	1,522	152.2
Kevin Ingram, West Chester	†1998	11	115	1,673	152.1
Damon Thompson, Virginia St.	†1999	10	90	1,517	151.7
Mark DeBrito, Bentley	1999	11	101	1,637	148.8
James Roe, Norfolk St.	†1994	10	77	1,454	145.4
Dan Fulton, Neb.-Omaha	1976	11	67	1,581	143.7
Brad Bailey, West Tex. A&M	1994	11	*119	1,552	141.1

*Record. †National champion.

CAREER YARDS

Player, Team	Years	Rec.	Yards	Avg.	TD
James Roe, Norfolk St.	1992-95	239	*4,468	18.7	46
Bruce Cerone, Yankton/Emporia St.	1965-66, 68-69	241	4,354	18.1	*49
Robert Clark, N.C. Central	1983-86	210	4,231	‡20.1	38
Chris Myers, Kenyon	1967-70	253	3,897	15.4	33
Carlos Ferralls, Glenville St.	1994-97	*262	3,835	14.6	43
Shannon Sharpe, Savannah St.	1986-89	192	3,744	19.5	40
Tyrone Johnson, Western St.	1990-93	163	3,717	*22.8	35
Mark DeBrito, Bentley	1996-99	238	3,711	15.6	41
Jeff Tiefenthaler, South Dakota St.	1983-86	173	3,621	20.9	31
Willie Richardson, Jackson St.	1959-62	166	3,616	21.8	36
Johnny Cox, Fort Lewis	1990-93	220	3,611	16.4	33

*Record. ‡Record for minimum 180 catches.

SEASON YARDS

Player, Team	Year	Rec.	Yards	Avg.	TD
Chris George, Glenville St.	†1993	117	*1,876	16.0	15
Barry Wagner, Alabama A&M	1989	106	1,812	17.1	17
Chris Perry, Adams St.	1995	88	1,719	19.5	**21
Kevin Ingram, West Chester	†1998	115	1,673	14.5	**21
Mark DeBrito, Bentley	1999	101	1,637	16.2	19
Dan Fulton, Neb.-Omaha	1976	67	1,581	23.6	16
Carlos Ferralls, Glenville St.	†1997	94	1,566	16.6	19
Brad Bailey, West Tex. A&M	1994	*119	1,552	13.0	16
Jeff Tiefenthaler, South Dakota St.	1986	73	1,534	21.0	11
Ed Bell, Idaho St.	1969	96	1,522	15.9	20
Damon Thompson, Virginia St.	†1999	90	1,517	16.9	10

ALL-TIME LEADERS—RECEIVING

Player, Team	Year	Rec.	Yards	Avg.	TD
Rodney Robinson, Gardner-Webb	†1992	89	1,496	16.8	16
Bruce Cerone, Emporia St.	1968	91	1,479	16.3	15
Jerry Hendren, Idaho	1968	86	1,457	16.9	14

*Record. **Record tied. †National champion.

SINGLE-GAME YARDS

No.	Player, Team (Opponent)	Date
401	Kevin Ingram, West Chester (Clarion)	Oct. 31, 1998
370	Barry Wagner, Alabama A&M (Clark Atlanta)	Nov. 4, 1989
363	Tom Nettles, San Diego St. (Southern Miss.)	Nov. 9, 1968
354	Robert Clark, N.C. Central (Jackson St.)	Aug. 30, 1986
325	Paul Zaeske, North Park (North Central)	Oct. 12, 1968
317	Dan Fulton, Neb.-Omaha (South Dakota)	Sept. 4, 1976
310	Mike Collodi, Colorado Mines (Westminster [Utah])	Oct. 3, 1970

CAREER TOUCHDOWN RECEPTIONS

Player, Team	Year	G	TD
Bruce Cerone, Yankton/Emporia St.	1965-66,68-69	36	*49
James Roe, Norfolk St.	1992-95	41	46
Kevin Ingram, West Chester	1995-96,98-99	39	45
Carlos Ferralls, Glenville St.	1994-97	35	43
Sedrick Robinson, Ky. Wesleyan	1993-96	38	42
Mark DeBrito, Bentley	1996-99	39	41
Shannon Sharpe, Savannah St.	1986-89	42	40
Robert Clark, N.C. Central	1983-86	40	38
Tony Willis, New Haven	1990-93	40	38
Willie Richardson, Jackson St.	1959-62	38	36

*Record.

SEASON TOUCHDOWN RECEPTIONS

Player, Team	Year	G	TD
Kevin Ingram, West Chester	1998	11	**21
Chris Perry, Adams St.	1995	10	**21
Ed Bell, Idaho St.	1969	10	20
Mark DeBrito, Bentley	1999	11	19
Carlos Ferralls, Glenville St.	1997	10	19
Stanley Flanders, Valdosta St.	1994	11	19
Jamar Nailor, N.M. Highlands	1996	10	18
Wayne Thomas, Miles	1996	10	18
Brian Penecale, West Chester	1997	11	18
James Roe, Norfolk St.	1997	10	17
Robert Williams, Valdosta St.	1997	11	17
Barry Wagner, Alabama A&M	1989	11	17

**Record tied.

ANNUAL CHAMPIONS

Year	Player, Team	Class	Rec.	Yards	TD
1946	Hugh Taylor, Oklahoma City	Jr.	23	457	8
1947	Bill Klein, Hanover	So.	52	648	12
1948	Bill Klein, Hanover	Jr.	43	812	6
1949	Cliff Coggin, Southern Miss.	Sr.	53	1,087	9
1950	Jack Bighead, Pepperdine	Jr.	38	551	6
1951	Jim Stefoff, Kalamazoo	Jr.	45	680	5
1952	Jim McKinzie, Northern Ill.	Sr.	44	703	6
1953	Dick Beetsch, Northern Iowa	So.	54	837	9
1954	R. C. Owens, Col. of Idaho	Sr.	48	905	7
1955	Dick Donlin, Hamline	Sr.	41	480	2
1956	Tom Rychlec, American Int'l	Sr.	40	353	3
1957	Tom Whitaker, Nevada	Jr.	40	527	4
1958	Bruce Shenk, Nevada	Sr.	39	580	9
1959	Fred Tunnicliffe, UC Santa Barb.	So.	48	1,087	11
1960	Ken Gregory, Whittier	Sr.	74	1,018	4
1961	Marty Baumhower, Defiance	Jr.	57	708	4
1962	Hugh Rohrschneider, Northern Ill.	Jr.	76	795	5
1963	Hugh Rohrschneider, Northern Ill.	Sr.	75	1,036	14
1964	Steve Gilliatt, Parsons	So.	81	984	12
1965	George LaPorte, Union (N.Y.)	Sr.	74	724	5
1966	Manley Sarnowsky, Drake	Sr.	92	1,114	7
1967	Harvey Tanner, Murray St.	Jr.	88	1,019	3
1968	Dick Hewins, Drake	Sr.	95	1,316	13
1969	Ed Bell, Idaho St.	Sr.	96	1,522	20

Beginning in 1970, ranked on per-game (instead of total) catches

Year	Player, Team	Class	G	Rec.	Avg.	Yards	TD
1970	Steve Mahaffey, Wash. & Lee	Sr.	9	74	8.2	897	2
1971	Kalle Kontson, Rensselaer	Sr.	9	69	7.7	1,031	7
1972	Freddie Scott, Amherst	Jr.	8	66	8.3	936	12
1973	Ron Gustafson, North Dakota	Jr.	10	67	6.7	1,210	10
1974	Andy Sanchez, Cal Poly Pomona	Sr.	10	62	6.2	903	0
1975	Butch Johnson, UC Riverside	Sr.	8	67	8.4	1,027	8
1976	Bo Darden, Shaw	So.	9	57	6.3	863	4
1977	Jeff Tesch, Moorhead St.	Sr.	10	67	6.7	760	9
1978	Mike Chrobot, Butler	Sr.	10	55	5.5	628	6
	Tom Ferguson, Cal St. Hayward	Jr.	10	55	5.5	698	6
	Mark McDaniel, Northern Colo.	Sr.	10	55	5.5	761	6

Mark DeBrito of Bentley led Division II in receptions per game in 1999 with 9.2, and he is among the top 10 in career receptions, career yards, and career touchdown receptions.

Year	Player, Team	Class	G	Rec.	Avg.	Yards	TD
1979	Robbie Ray, Franklin	Sr.	10	63	6.3	987	3
1980	Joe Dittrich, Southwest St.	Sr.	9	83	9.2	974	7
1981	Paul Choudek, Southwest St.	Sr.	10	70	7.0	747	5
1982	Jay Barnett, Evansville	Sr.	10	81	8.1	1,181	12
1983	Perry Kemp, Calif. (Pa.)	Sr.	10	74	7.4	1,101	9
1984	Dan Bogar, Valparaiso	Sr.	10	73	7.3	861	11
1985	Mike Healey, Valparaiso	Sr.	10	101	10.1	1,279	11
1986	Stan Carraway, West Tex. A&M	Sr.	11	94	8.5	1,175	9
1987	Billy Joe Masters, Evansville	Sr.	10	‡94	‡9.4	‡960	4
1988	Todd Smith, Morningside	Sr.	11	86	7.8	1,006	8
1989	Barry Wagner, Alabama A&M	Sr.	11	106	9.6	1,812	17

Beginning in 1990, ranked on both per-game catches and yards per game.

PER-GAME RECEPTIONS

Year	Player, Team	Class	G	Rec.	Avg.	Yards	TD
1990	Mark Steinmeyer, Kutztown	Jr.	11	86	7.8	940	5
1991	Jesse Lopez, Cal St. Hayward	Sr.	10	86	8.6	861	4
1992	Randy Bartosh, Southwest Baptist	Sr.	8	65	8.1	860	2
1993	Chris George, Glenville St.	Jr.	10	117	*11.7	*1,876	15
1994	Chris George, Glenville St.	Sr.	10	113	11.3	1,339	15
1995	Sean Pender, Valdosta St.	Jr.	11	111	10.1	983	2
1996	Carlos Ferralls, Glenville St.	Jr.	8	81	10.1	965	6
1997	Carlos Ferralls, Glenville St.	Sr.	10	94	9.4	1,566	19
1998	Kevin Ingram, West Chester	Jr.	11	115	10.5	1,673	**21
1999	Mark DeBrito, Bentley	Sr.	11	101	9.2	1,637	19

YARDS PER GAME

Year	Player, Team	Class	G	Rec.	Yards	Avg.	TD
1990	Ernest Priester, Edinboro	Sr.	8	45	1,060	132.5	14
1991	Rod Smith, Mo. Southern St.	Jr.	11	60	1,439	130.8	15
1992	Rodney Robinson, Gardner-Webb	Sr.	11	89	1,496	136.0	16
1993	Chris George, Glenville St.	Jr.	10	117	*1,876	*187.6	15
1994	James Roe, Norfolk St.	Jr.	10	77	1,454	145.4	17
1995	Chris Perry, Adams St.	Sr.	10	88	1,719	171.9	**21
1996	Ron Lelko, Bloomsburg	Jr.	11	87	1,455	132.3	15
1997	Carlos Ferralls, Glenville St.	Sr.	10	94	1,566	156.6	19
1998	Kevin Ingram, West Chester	Jr.	11	115	1,673	152.1	**21
1999	Damon Thompson, Virginia St.	Jr.	10	90	1,517	151.7	10

*Record. **Record tied. ‡Record for a running back.

Scoring

CAREER POINTS PER GAME
(Minimum 225 Points)

Player, Team	Years	G	TD	XPt.	FG	Pts.	Pt. PG
Ole Gunderson, St. Olaf	1969-71	27	60	2	0	362	*13.4
Leon Burns, Long Beach St.	1969-70	22	47	2	0	284	12.9
Brian Shay, Emporia St.	1995-98	44	*88	16	0	*544	12.4
Billy Johnson, Widener	1971-72	19	39	0	0	234	12.3
Rashaan Dumas, Southern Conn. St.	1996-99	37	72	0	0	432	11.7
Dale Mills, Truman	1957-60	36	64	23	0	407	11.3
Kavin Gailliard, American Int'l	1996-99	43	78	8	0	476	11.1
Walter Payton, Jackson St.	1971-74	42	66	53	5	464	11.0
Jeff Bentrim, North Dakota St.	1983-86	35	64	2	0	386	11.0
Steve Roberts, Butler	1986-89	35	63	4	0	386	11.0

DIVISION II

ALL-TIME LEADERS—SCORING

Player, Team	Years	G	TD	XPt.	FG	Pts.	Pt. PG
Shawn Graves, Wofford	1989-92	40	72	3	0	438	11.0
Johnny Bailey, Tex. A&M-Kingsville	1986-89	39	70	3	0	426	10.9
Garney Henley, Huron	1956-59	37	63	16	0	394	10.6
Roger Graham, New Haven	1991-94	40	70	2	0	424	10.6

*Record.

SEASON POINTS PER GAME

Player, Team	Years	G	TD	XPt.	FG	Pts.	Pt. PG
Carl Herakovich, Rose-Hulman	†1958	8	25	18	0	168	*21.0
Jim Switzer, Col. of Emporia	†1963	9	28	0	0	168	18.7
Billy Johnson, Widener	†1972	9	27	0	0	162	18.0
Brian Shay, Emporia St.	†1997	11	32	6	0	198	18.0
Carl Garrett, N.M. Highlands	†1966	9	26	2	0	158	17.6
Kavin Gailliard, Amerian Int'l	†1999	12	*34	2	0	*206	17.2
Ted Scown, Sul Ross St.	†1948	10	28	0	0	168	16.8
Travis Walch, Winona St.	1997	11	30	2	0	182	16.5
Larry Ras, Michigan Tech	†1971	9	24	0	0	144	16.0
Brian Shay, Emporia St.	†1998	11	29	2	0	176	16.0

*Record. †National champion.

CAREER POINTS

Player, Team	Years	TD	XPt.	FG	Pts.
Brian Shay, Emporia St.	1995-98	*88	16	0	*544
Kavin Gailliard, American Int'l	1996-99	78	8	0	476
Walter Payton, Jackson St.	1971-74	66	53	5	464
Jarrett Anderson, Truman	1993-96	73	2	0	440
Shawn Graves, Wofford	1989-92	72	3	0	438
Rashaan Dumas, Southern Conn. St.	1996-99	72	0	0	432
Johnny Bailey, Tex. A&M-Kingsville	1986-89	70	3	0	426
Roger Graham, New Haven	1991-94	70	2	0	424
Dale Mills, Truman	1957-60	64	23	0	407
Jeremy Monroe, Michigan Tech	1990-93	67	0	0	402
Garney Henley, Huron	1956-59	63	16	0	394
Jeff Bentrim, North Dakota St.	1983-86	64	2	0	386
Steve Roberts, Butler	1986-89	63	4	0	386
Leo Lewis, Lincoln (Mo.)	1951-54	64	0	0	384
Bob Miller, Emory & Henry	1948-51	63	0	1	379
Heath Sherman, Tex. A&M-Kingsville	1985-88	63	0	0	378
Antonio Leroy, Albany St. (Ga.)	1993-96	62	6	0	378
Damian Beane, Shepherd	1996-99	60	10	0	370
Tank Younger, Grambling	1945-48	60	9	0	369
Richard Huntley, Winston-Salem	1992-95	60	8	0	368
Bill Cooper, Muskingum	1957-60	54	37	1	364
Ole Gunderson, St. Olaf	1969-71	60	2	0	362
Mike Joseph, Fairmont St.	1994-97	57	14	0	356

*Record.

SEASON POINTS

Player, Team	Year	TD	XPt.	FG	Pts.
Kavin Gailliard, American Int'l	†1999	*34	2	0	*206
Brian Shay, Emporia St.	†1997	32	6	0	198
Travis Walch, Winona St.	1997	30	2	0	182
Terry Metcalf, Long Beach St.	1971	29	4	0	178
Brian Shay, Emporia St.	†1998	29	2	0	176
Josh Ranek, South Dakota St.	1999	28	2	0	170
Jarrett Anderson, Truman	†1996	28	0	0	168
Jim Switzer, Col. of Emporia	†1963	28	0	0	168
Carl Herakovich, Rose-Hulman	†1958	25	18	0	168
Ted Scown, Sul Ross St.	†1948	28	0	0	168
Ronald Moore, Pittsburg St.	1992	27	4	0	166
Leon Burns, Long Beach St.	†1969	27	2	0	164
Mike Deutsch, North Dakota	1972	27	0	0	162
Billy Johnson, Widener	†1972	27	0	0	162

*Record. †National champion.

ANNUAL CHAMPIONS

Year	Player, Team	Class	TD	XPt.	FG	Pts.
1946	Joe Carter, Florida N&I	So.	21	26	0	152
1947	Darwin Horn, Pepperdine	Jr.	19	1	0	115
	Chuck Schoenherr, Wheaton (Ill.)	So.	19	1	0	115
1948	Ted Scown, Sul Ross St.	So.	28	0	0	168
1949	Sylvester Polk, Md.-East. Shore	Jr.	19	15	0	129
1950	Carl Taseff, John Carroll	Sr.	23	0	0	138
1951	Paul Yackey, Heidelberg	Jr.	22	0	0	132
1952	Al Conway, William Jewell	Sr.	22	1	0	133
1953	Leo Lewis, Lincoln (Mo.)	Jr.	22	0	0	132
1954	Jim Podoley, Central Mich.	Jr.	18	1	0	109
	Dick Nyers, Indianapolis	Sr.	16	13	0	109
1955	Nate Clark, Hillsdale	Jr.	24	0	0	144
1956	Larry Houdek, Kan. Wesleyan	Sr.	19	0	0	114
1957	Lenny Lyles, Louisville	Sr.	21	6	0	132
1958	Carl Herakovich, Rose-Hulman	Sr.	25	18	0	168

Year	Player, Team	Class	TD	XPt.	FG	Pts.
1959	Garney Henley, Huron	Sr.	22	9	0	141
1960	Bill Cooper, Muskingum	Sr.	23	14	0	152
1961	John Murio, Whitworth	Jr.	15	33	2	129
1962	Mike Goings, Bluffton	So.	22	0	0	132
1963	Jim Switzer, Col. of Emporia	Sr.	28	0	0	168
1964	Henry Dyer, Grambling	Jr.	17	2	0	104
	Dunn Marteen, Cal St. Los Angeles	Sr.	11	38	0	104
1965	Allen Smith, Findlay	Jr.	24	2	0	146
1966	Carl Garrett, N.M. Highlands	So.	26	2	0	158
1967	Bert Nye, West Chester	Jr.	19	13	0	127
1968	Howard Stevens, Randolph-Macon	Fr.	23	4	0	142
1969	Leon Burns, Long Beach St.	Jr.	27	2	0	164

Beginning in 1970, ranked on per-game (instead of total) points

Year	Player, Team	Class	G	TD	XPt.	FG	Pts.	Avg.
1970	Mike DiBlasi, Mount Union	Sr.	9	22	0	0	132	14.7
1971	Larry Ras, Michigan Tech	Sr.	9	24	0	0	144	16.0
1972	Billy Johnson, Widener	Jr.	9	27	0	0	162	18.0
1973	Walter Payton, Jackson St.	Jr.	11	24	13	1	160	14.5
1974	Walter Payton, Jackson St.	Sr.	10	19	6	1	123	12.3
1975	Dale Kasowski, North Dakota	Sr.	7	16	4	0	100	14.3
1976	Ted McKnight, Minn.-Duluth	Sr.	10	24	0	0	144	14.4
1977	Bill Burnham, New Hampshire	Sr.	10	22	0	0	132	13.2
1978	Marschell Brunfield, Youngstown St.	Sr.	9	14	0	0	84	9.3
	Charlie Thompson, Western St.	Sr.	9	14	0	0	84	9.3
1979	Robby Robson, Youngstown St.	Jr.	10	20	0	0	120	12.0
1980	Amory Bodin, Minn.-Duluth	Sr.	10	19	2	0	116	11.6
1981	George Works, Northern Mich.	Jr.	10	21	0	0	126	12.6
1982	George Works, Northern Mich.	Sr.	10	23	0	0	138	13.8
1983	Clarence Johnson, North Ala.	Jr.	10	16	0	0	96	9.6
1984	Jeff Bentrim, North Dakota St.	So.	9	14	0	0	84	9.3
1985	Jeff Bentrim, North Dakota St.	Jr.	8	18	2	0	110	††13.8
1986	Jeff Bentrim, North Dakota St.	Sr.	10	23	0	0	138	13.8
1987	Johnny Bailey, Tex. A&M-Kingsville	So.	10	20	0	0	120	12.0
1988	Steve Roberts, Butler	Jr.	10	23	4	0	142	14.2
1989	Jimmy Allen, St. Joseph's (Ind.)	Jr.	10	23	0	0	138	13.8
1990	Ernest Priester, Edinboro	Sr.	8	16	0	0	96	12.0
1991	Quincy Tillmon, Emporia St.	So.	9	19	0	0	114	12.7
1992	David McCartney, Chadron St.	Jr.	10	25	4	0	154	15.4
1993	Roger Graham, New Haven	Jr.	10	23	0	0	138	13.8
1994	Leonard Davis, Lenoir-Rhyne	Sr.	9	19	0	0	114	12.7
1995	Antonio Leroy, Albany St. (Ga.)	Jr.	11	24	0	0	144	13.1
1996	Jarrett Anderson, Truman	Sr.	11	28	0	0	168	15.3
1997	Brian Shay, Emporia St.	Jr.	11	32	6	0	198	18.0
1998	Brian Shay, Emporia St.	Sr.	11	29	2	0	176	16.0
1999	Kavin Gailliard, American Int'l	Sr.	12	*34	2	0	*206	17.2

††Declared champion; with one more game (to meet 75 percent of games played minimum) for zero points, still would have highest per-game average (12.2).

Interceptions

CAREER INTERCEPTIONS

Player, Team	Years	No.	Yards	Avg.
Tom Collins, Indianapolis	1982-85	*37	390	10.5
Dean Diaz, Humboldt St.	1980-83	31	328	10.6
Bill Grantham, Mo.-Rolla	1977-80	29	263	9.1
Jason Johnson, Shepherd	1991-94	28	321	11.5
Tony Woods, Bloomsburg	1982-85	26	105	4.0
Buster West, Gust. Adolphus	1967-70	26	192	7.4
Nate Gruber, Winona St.	1991-94	25	275	11.0
Gary Rubeling, Towson	1980-83	25	122	4.9
Greg Mercier, Ripon	1968-70	25	243	9.7

*Record.

SEASON INTERCEPTIONS

Player, Team	Year	No.	Yards
Eugene Hunter, Fort Valley St.	†1972	**14	211
Luther Howard, Delaware St.	†1972	**14	99
Tom Rezzuti, Northeastern	†1971	**14	153
Jim Blackwell, Southern U.	†1970	**14	196
Carl Ray Harris, Fresno St.	1970	**14	98

**Record tied. †National champion.

ANNUAL CHAMPIONS

Year	Player, Team	Class	G	No.	Avg.	Yards
1970	Jim Blackwell, Southern U.	Sr.	11	**14	1.27	196
1971	Tom Rezzuti, Northeastern	Jr.	9	**14	**1.56	153
1972	Eugene Hunter, Fort Valley St.	So.	9	**14	**1.56	211
	Luther Howard, Delaware St.	Sr.	9	**14	**1.56	99
1973	Mike Pierce, Northern Colo.	Sr.	7	7	1.00	158
	James Smith, Shaw	So.	8	8	1.00	94
1974	Terry Rusin, Wayne St. (Mich.)	Fr.	10	10	1.00	62

ALL-TIME LEADERS—INTERCEPTIONS

Year	Player, Team	Class	G	No.	Avg.	Yards
1975	Jim Poettgen, Cal Poly Pomona	Jr.	11	12	1.09	156
1976	Johnny Tucker, Tennessee Tech	Sr.	11	10	0.91	74
1977	Mike Ellis, Norfolk St.	So.	11	12	1.09	257
	Cornelius Washington, Winston-Salem	Sr.	11	12	1.09	128
1978	Bill Grantham, Mo.-Rolla	So.	11	11	1.00	109
1979	Jeff Huffman, Michigan Tech	Sr.	10	11	1.10	97
1980	Mike Lush, East Stroudsburg	Sr.	10	12	1.20	208
1981	Bobby Futrell, Elizabeth City St.	So.	9	11	1.22	159
1982	Greg Maack, Central Mo. St.	Sr.	10	11	1.10	192
1983	Matt Didio, Wayne St. (Mich.)	Sr.	10	13	1.30	131
1984	Bob Jahelka, C. W. Post	Sr.	8	9	1.13	83
1985	Duvaal Callaway, Fort Valley St.	Sr.	11	10	0.91	175
	Tony Woods, Bloomsburg	Sr.	11	10	0.91	10
1986	Doug Smart, Winona St.	Jr.	8	10	1.25	56
1987	Mike Petrich, Minn.-Duluth	Jr.	11	9	0.82	151
1988	Pete Jaros, Augustana (S.D.)	Jr.	11	13	1.18	120
1989	Jacque DeMatteo, Clarion	Jr.	8	6	0.75	21
1990	Eric Turner, Tex. A&M-Commerce	So.	11	10	0.91	105
1991	Jeff Fickes, Shippensburg	Sr.	11	12	1.09	154
1992	Pat Williams, Tex. A&M-Commerce	Sr.	11	13	1.18	145
1993	Troy Crissman, Ky. Wesleyan	So.	10	9	0.90	39
1994	Keith Hawkins, Humboldt St.	Sr.	10	11	1.10	159
	Elton Rhoades, Central Okla.	Sr.	10	11	1.10	126
1995	Chenelle Jones, Western N.M.	Sr.	8	7	0.88	61
1996	Britt Henderson, Savannah St.	Sr.	11	12	1.09	180
1997	Jamey Hutchinson, Winona St.	Jr.	11	11	1.00	125
	Tim Bednarski, Mercyhurst	Jr.	9	9	1.00	59
1998	Jermel Johnson, Fayetteville St.	Sr.	10	9	0.90	95
1999	Tommie Dawson, Virginia Union	Jr.	8	8	1.00	79

**Record tied.

Punting

CAREER AVERAGE
(Minimum 100 Punts)

Player, Team	Years	No.	Yards	Avg.
Jason Van Dyke, Adams St.	1995-98	242	10,720	*44.30
Tim Baer, Colorado Mines	1986-89	235	10,406	44.28
Brian Moorman, Pittsburg St.	1995-98	157	6,903	44.0
Jeff Guy, Western St.	1983-85	113	4,967	44.0
Russ Pilcher, Carroll (Mont.)	1964-66	124	5,424	43.7
Russell Gonzales, Morris Brown	1976-77	111	4,833	43.5
Gerald Circo, Cal St. Chico	1964-65	103	4,470	43.4
Trent Morgan, Cal St. Northridge	1987-88	128	5,531	43.2
Bryan Wagner, Cal St. Northridge	1981-84	203	8,762	43.2
Tom Kolesar, Nevada	1973-74	140	6,032	43.1
Jimmy Morris, Angelo St.	1991-92	101	4,326	42.8
Don Geist, Northern Colo.	1981-84	263	11,247	42.8
Jan Chapman, San Diego	1958-60	106	4,533	42.8
Warner Robertson, Md.-East. Shore	1968-70	131	5,578	42.6

*Record.

SEASON AVERAGE
(Qualifiers for Championship)

Player, Team	Year	No.	Yards	Avg.
Steve Ecker, Shippensburg	†1965	32	1,570	*49.1
Don Cockroft, Adams St.	†1966	36	1,728	48.0
Jack Patterson, William Jewell	1965	29	1,377	47.5
Art Calandrelli, Canisius	†1949	25	1,177	47.1
Grover Perkins, Southern U.	†1961	22	1,034	47.0
Erskine Valrie, Alabama A&M	1966	36	1,673	46.5
Mark Bounds, West Tex. A&M	†1990	69	3,198	+46.3
Bruce Swanson, North Park	†1967	53	2,455	46.3
Jason Van Dyke, Adams St.	†1998	59	2,727	46.2
Lyle Johnston, Weber St.	1965	29	1,340	46.2

*Record. †National champion. +Record for minimum 40 punts.

ANNUAL CHAMPIONS

Year	Player, Team	Class	No.	Yards	Avg.
1948	Arthur Teixeira, Central Mich.	Sr.	42	1,867	44.5
1949	Art Calandrelli, Canisius	Jr.	25	1,177	47.1
1950	Flavian Weidekamp, Butler	Sr.	41	1,762	43.0
1951	Curtiss Harris, Savannah St.	Sr.	42	1,854	44.1
1952	Virgil Stan, Western St.	Sr.	37	1,622	43.8
1953	Bill Bradshaw, Bowling Green	Jr.	50	2,199	44.0
1954	Bill Bradshaw, Bowling Green	Sr.	28	1,228	43.9
1955	Don Baker, North Texas	Sr.	30	1,349	45.0
1956	Marion Zody, Ashland	Jr.	34	1,475	43.4
1957	Lawson Persley, Mississippi Val.	Sr.	36	1,659	46.1
1958	Tom Lewis, Lake Forest	Jr.	24	1,089	45.4
1959	Buck Grover, Salem-Teikyo	Fr.	27	1,203	44.6
1960	Joe Roy, N.M. Highlands	So.	40	1,744	43.6
1961	Grover Perkins, Southern U.	Fr.	22	1,034	47.0
1962	Ron Crouse, Catawba	Jr.	37	1,653	44.7
1963	Steve Bailey, Kentucky St.	Sr.	39	1,747	44.8
1964	Russ Pilcher, Carroll (Mont.)	So.	34	1,545	45.4
1965	Steve Ecker, Shippensburg	Sr.	32	1,570	*49.1
1966	Don Cockroft, Adams St.	Sr.	36	1,728	48.0
1967	Bruce Swanson, North Park	Jr.	53	2,455	46.3
1968	Warner Robertson, Md.-East. Shore	Fr.	61	2,699	44.2
1969	Warner Robertson, Md.-East. Shore	So.	37	1,629	44.0
1970	John Bonner, Chattanooga	Sr.	73	3,243	44.4
1971	Ken Gamble, Fayetteville St.	Sr.	47	2,092	44.5
1972	Raymond Key, Jackson St.	Jr.	44	1,883	42.8
1973	Jerry Pope, Louisiana Tech	Fr.	48	2,064	43.0
1974	Mike Shawen, Middle Tenn. St.	Sr.	62	2,720	43.9
1975	Mike Wood, Southeast Mo. St.	Jr.	40	1,729	43.2
1976	Russell Gonzales, Morris Brown	So.	54	2,474	45.8
1977	Jeff Gossett, Eastern Ill.	Jr.	62	2,668	43.0
1978	Bill Moats, South Dakota	Sr.	77	3,377	43.9
1979	Bob Fletcher, Truman	Sr.	79	3,409	43.2
1980	Sean Landeta, Towson	So.	47	2,038	43.4
1981	Gregg Lowery, Jacksonville St.	Jr.	64	2,787	43.5
1982	Don Geist, Northern Colo.	So.	66	2,966	44.4
1983	Jeff Guy, Western St.	So.	39	1,734	44.5
1984	Jeff Guy, Western St.	Jr.	46	2,012	43.7
1985	Jeff Williams, Slippery Rock	Sr.	46	1,977	43.0
1986	Tim Baer, Colorado Mines	Fr.	62	2,797	45.1
1987	Jeff McComb, Southern Utah	Sr.	42	1,863	44.4
1988	Tim Baer, Colorado Mines	Jr.	65	2,880	43.9
1989	Tim Baer, Colorado Mines	Sr.	55	2,382	43.3
1990	Mark Bounds, West Tex. A&M	Jr.	69	3,198	+46.3
1991	Doug O'Neill, Cal Poly	Sr.	42	1,895	45.1
1992	Jimmy Morris, Angelo St.	So.	45	2,001	44.5
1993	Chris Carter, Henderson St.	Sr.	53	2,305	43.5
1994	Pat Hogelin, Colorado Mines	Sr.	48	2,167	45.1
1995	Jon Mason, West Tex. A&M	Sr.	54	2,459	45.5
1996	Tom O'Brien, South Dakota St.	So.	60	2,671	44.5
1997	Brian Moorman, Pittsburg St.	Jr.	36	1,657	46.0
1998	Jason Van Dyke, Adams St.	Sr.	59	2,727	46.2
1999	Nathan White, Fairmont St.	So.	43	1,930	44.9

*Record. +Record for minimum 40 punts.

Punt Returns

CAREER AVERAGE
(Minimum 1.2 Returns Per Game)

Player, Team	Years	No.	Yards	Avg.
Billy Johnson, Widener	1971-72	29	759	*26.2
Bootsie Washington, Shepherd	1996-97	26	512	19.7
Chuck Goehl, Monmouth (Ill.)	1970-72	48	911	19.0
Robbie Martin, Cal Poly	1978-80	69	1,168	16.9
Roscoe Word, Jackson St.	1970-73	35	554	15.8
Darryl Skinner, Hampton	1983-86	53	835	15.8
Michael Fields, Mississippi Col.	1984-85	50	695	13.9

*Record.

SEASON AVERAGE
(Minimum 1.2 Returns Per Game)

Player, Team	Year	No.	Yards	Avg.
Billy Johnson, Widener	†1972	15	511	*34.1
William Williams, Livingstone	1976	16	453	28.3
Terry Egerdahl, Minn.-Duluth	†1975	13	360	27.7
Ennis Thomas, Bishop	†1971	18	450	25.0
Chuck Goehl, Monmouth (Ill.)	1972	17	416	24.5
Doug Grant, Savannah St.	†1992	15	366	24.4
James Rooths, Shepherd	†1999	15	366	24.4
Bootsie Washington, Shepherd	†1997	19	461	24.3

*Record. †National champion.

ANNUAL CHAMPIONS

Year	Player, Team	Class	No.	Yards	Avg.
1970	Kevin Downs, Benedictine (Ill.)	Jr.	11	255	23.2
1971	Ennis Thomas, Bishop	So.	18	450	25.0
1972	Billy Johnson, Widener	Jr.	15	511	*34.1
1973	Roscoe Word, Jackson St.	Sr.	19	316	16.6
1974	Greg Anderson, Montana	So.	13	263	20.2
1975	Terry Egerdahl, Minn.-Duluth	Sr.	13	360	27.7
1976	William Williams, Livingstone	So.	16	453	28.3
1977	Armando Olivieri, New York Tech	So.	14	270	19.3
1978	Dwight Walker, Nicholls St.	Fr.	16	284	17.8
1979	Ricky Eberhart, Morris Brown	Fr.	18	401	22.3
1980	Ron Bagby, Puget Sound	So.	16	242	15.1

DIVISION II

ALL-TIME LEADERS—PUNT RETURNS

Year	Player, Team	Class	No.	Yards	Avg.
1981	Ron Trammell, Tex. A&M-Commerce	Jr.	29	467	16.1
1982	Darrell Green, Tex. A&M-Kingsville	Sr.	19	392	20.6
1983	Steve Carter, Albany St. (Ga.)	Sr.	27	511	18.9
1984	Michael Fields, Mississippi Col.	Jr.	23	487	21.2
1985	Darryl Skinner, Hampton	Jr.	19	426	22.4
1986	Ben Frazier, Cheyney	So.	14	246	17.6
1987	Ronald Day, Savannah St.	Sr.	12	229	19.1
1988	Donnie Morris, Norfolk St.	Jr.	12	283	23.6
1989	Dennis Mailhot, East Stroudsburg	Jr.	16	284	17.8
1990	Ron West, Pittsburg St.	Jr.	23	388	16.9
1991	Doug Grant, Savannah St.	So.	19	331	17.4
1992	Doug Grant, Savannah St.	Jr.	15	366	24.4
1993	Jerry Garrett, Wayne St. (Neb.)	Jr.	26	498	19.2
1994	Terry Guess, Gardner-Webb	So.	16	312	19.5
1995	Kevin Cannon, Millersville	Sr.	16	277	17.3
1996	Sean Smith, Bloomsburg	Sr.	25	481	19.2
1997	Bootsie Washington, Shepherd	Sr.	19	461	24.3
1998	James Rooths, Shepherd	So.	21	451	21.5
1999	James Rooths, Shepherd	Jr.	15	366	24.4

*Record.

Kickoff Returns

CAREER AVERAGE
(Minimum 1.2 Returns Per Game)

Player, Team	Years	No.	Yards	Avg.
Glen Printers, Southern Colo.	1973-74	25	851	*34.0
Karl Evans, Mo. Southern St.	1991-92	32	959	30.0
Kevin Cannon, Millersville	1992-95	67	1,999	29.8
Dave Ludy, Winona St.	1991-94	89	*2,630	29.6
Doug Parrish, San Fran. St.	1990	35	1,002	28.6
Clarence Chapman, Eastern Mich.	1973-75	45	1,278	28.4
Greg Wilson, East Tenn. St.	1975-77	34	952	28.0
Bernie Rose, North Ala.	1974-76	62	1,681	27.1
Roscoe Word, Jackson St.	1970-73	74	1,980	26.8

*Record.

SEASON AVERAGE
(Minimum 1.2 Returns Per Game)

Player, Team	Year	No.	Yards	Avg.
LaVon Reis, Western St.	†1993	14	552	*39.43
Danny Lee, Jacksonville St.	†1992	12	473	39.42
Fran DeFalco, Assumption	1993	12	461	38.4
Kendall James, Carson-Newman	1993	15	549	36.6
Roscoe Word, Jackson St.	†1973	18	650	36.1
Steve Levenseller, Puget Sound	†1978	17	610	35.9
Winston Horshaw, Shippensburg	†1991	15	536	35.7

Player, Team	Year	No.	Yards	Avg.
Boobie Thornton, Midwestern St.	†1997	12	426	35.5
Anthony Rivera, Western St.	1991	18	635	35.3
Dave Ludy, Winona St.	1992	25	881	35.2
Mike Scullin, Baldwin-Wallace	†1970	14	492	35.1
Billy Cook, Grand Valley St.	†1998	17	597	35.1
Rufus Smith, Eastern N.M.	†1985	11	386	35.1
Rebert Mack, West Tex. A&M	†1996	14	489	34.9
Brian Polk, Slippery Rock	†1999	15	513	34.2
Norman Miller, Tex. A&M-Kingsville	1995	12	405	33.8
Greg Anderson, Montana	†1974	10	335	33.5
Kevin Cannon, Millersville	1995	14	463	33.1
Kevin McDevitt, Butler	†1975	12	395	32.9

*Record. †National champion.

ANNUAL CHAMPIONS

Year	Player, Team	Class	No.	Yards	Avg.
1970	Mike Scullin, Baldwin-Wallace	So.	14	492	35.1
1971	Joe Brockmeyer, Western Md.	Jr.	16	500	31.3
1972	Rick Murphy, Indiana St.	Jr.	22	707	32.1
1973	Roscoe Word, Jackson St.	Sr.	18	650	36.1
1974	Greg Anderson, Montana	So.	10	335	33.5
1975	Kevin McDevitt, Butler	Jr.	12	395	32.9
1976	Henry Vereen, UNLV	So.	20	628	31.4
1977	Dickie Johnson, Southern Colo.	Jr.	13	385	29.6
1978	Steve Levenseller, Puget Sound	Sr.	17	610	35.9
1979	Otha Hill, Central St.	Sr.	18	526	29.2
1980	Charlie Taylor, Southeast Mo. St.	Sr.	13	396	30.5
1981	Willie Canady, Fort Valley St.	Jr.	13	415	31.9
1982	Clarence Martin, Cal Poly	So.	11	360	32.7
1983	David Anthony, Southern Ore.	Jr.	14	436	31.1
1984	Larry Winters, St. Paul's	Sr.	20	644	32.2
1985	Rufus Smith, Eastern N.M.	Fr.	11	386	35.1
1986	John Barron, Butler	So.	21	653	31.1
1987	Albert Fann, Cal St. Northridge	Fr.	16	468	29.3
1988	Pierre Fils, New Haven	So.	12	378	31.5
1989	Dennis Mailhot, East Stroudsburg	Jr.	11	359	32.6
1990	Alfred Banks, West Ala.	Sr.	17	529	31.1
1991	Winston Horshaw, Shippensburg	Jr.	15	536	35.7
1992	Danny Lee, Jacksonville St.	Sr.	12	473	39.4
1993	LaVon Reis, Western St.	Sr.	14	552	*39.4
1994	Darell Whitaker, Eastern N.M.	Sr.	20	642	32.1
1995	Melvin German, Southwest St.	Sr.	9	413	††45.9
1996	Rebert Mack, West Tex. A&M	Jr.	14	489	34.9
1997	Boobie Thornton, Midwestern St.	Fr.	12	426	35.5
1998	Billy Cook, Grand Valley St.	Sr.	17	597	35.1
1999	Brian Polk, Slippery Rock	Sr.	15	513	34.2

*Record. ††Declared champion; with two more returns (to make 1.2 per game minimum) for zero yards, still would have highest average (37.5).

Brian Shay, who played for Division II Emporia State from 1995-98, is the all-divisions career leader in all-purpose yards (9,301) and rushing yards (6,958).

All-Purpose Yards

CAREER YARDS PER GAME
(Minimum 3,500 Yards)

Player, Team	Years	G	Rush	Rcv.	Int.	PR	KOR	Yds.	Yd. PG
Chris George, Glenville St.	1993-94	20	23	3,215	0	391	1,050	4,679	*234.0
Brian Shay, Emporia St.	1995-98	44	*6,958	1,032	0	104	1,207	*9,301	211.4
Anthony Gray, Western N.M.	1997-98	19	3,484	499	0	0	8	3,991	210.1
Kavin Gailliard, American Int'l	1996-99	43	6,523	1,049	0	472	814	8,858	206.0
Howard Stevens, Randolph-Macon	1968-69	18	2,574	349	0	380	388	3,691	205.1
Johnny Bailey, Tex. A&M-Kingsville	1986-89	39	6,320	452	0	20	1,011	7,803	200.1
Steve Roberts, Butler	1986-89	35	4,623	1,201	0	272	578	6,674	190.7
Billy Johnson, Widener	1971-72	19	2,241	242	43	759	251	3,536	186.1

*Record.

SEASON YARDS PER GAME

Player, Team	Year	G	Rush	Rcv.	Int.	PR	KOR	Yds.	Yd. PG
Steve Roberts, Butler	1989	10	1,450	532	0	272	415	2,669	*266.9
Bobby Felix, Western N.M.	†1994	8	439	853	0	150	667	2,109	263.6
Chris George, Glenville St.	†1993	10	23	*1,876	0	157	562	2,618	261.8
Brian Shay, Emporia St.	†1998	11	2,265	165	0	0	389	2,819	256.3
Kavin Gailliard, American Int'l	†1999	12	*2,653	289	0	0	122	*3,064	255.3
Damon Thompson, Virginia St.	1998	10	127	1,330	0	292	770	2,519	251.9
Billy Johnson, Widener	1972	9	1,556	40	43	511	115	2,265	251.7
Brian Shay, Emporia St.	†1996	11	2,103	247	0	48	340	2,738	248.9
Damon Thompson, Virginia St.	1999	10	88	1,517	0	410	465	2,480	248.0
Brian Shay, Emporia St.	†1997	11	1,912	277	0	56	478	2,723	247.5
Kavin Gailliard, American Int'l	1998	11	1,971	270	0	151	196	2,588	235.3
Roger Graham, New Haven	1993	10	1,687	116	0	0	516	2,319	231.9
Anthony Gray, Western N.M.	1997	10	2,220	78	0	0	0	2,298	229.8

ALL-TIME LEADERS—ALL-PURPOSE YARDS

Player, Team	Year	G	Rush	Rcv.	Int.	PR	KOR	Yds.	Yd. PG
Larry Jackson, Edinboro	1994	10	1,660	237	0	0	387	2,284	228.4
Jamel White, South Dakota	1999	11	1,807	640	0	0	0	2,447	222.5
Johnny Bailey, Tex. A&M-Kingsville	1986	11	2,011	54	0	20	340	2,425	220.5
Johnny Cox, Fort Lewis	†1992	10	95	1,331	0	80	679	2,185	218.5
Steve Papin, Portland St.	†1995	11	1,619	525	0	1	252	2,397	217.9
Ronald Moore, Pittsburg St.	1992	11	1,864	141	0	0	388	2,393	217.6
Karl Evans, Mo. Southern St.	1992	10	1,586	10	0	0	571	2,167	216.7

*Record. †National champion.

CAREER YARDS

Player, Team	Years	Rush	Rcv.	Int.	PR	KOR	Yds.
Brian Shay, Emporia St.	1995-98	*6,958	1,032	0	104	1,207	*9,301
Kavin Gailliard, American Int'l	1996-99	6,523	1,049	0	472	814	8,858
Johnny Bailey, Tex. A&M-Kingsville	1986-89	6,320	452	0	20	1,011	7,803
Roger Graham, New Haven	1991-94	5,953	393	0	0	870	7,216
Dave Ludy, Winona St.	1991-94	3,501	906	0	34	*2,630	7,071
Albert Fann, Cal St. Northridge	1987-90	4,090	803	0	0	2,141	7,032
Curtis Delgardo, Portland St.	$1986-90	4,178	1,258	0	318	1,188	6,942
Jarrett Anderson, Truman	1993-96	6,166	633	0	0	127	6,926
Damian Beane, Shepherd	1996-99	6,346	416	0	0	0	6,762
Johnny Cox, Fort Lewis	1990-93	112	3,611	0	495	2,476	6,694
Steve Roberts, Butler	1986-89	4,623	1,201	0	272	578	6,674
Richard Huntley, Winston-Salem	1992-95	6,286	333	0	0	0	6,619
Mike Smith, Neb.-Kearney	1994-97	348	2,975	0	932	2,255	6,510
Chris Cobb, Eastern Ill.	1976-79	5,042	520	0	37	478	6,077
Don Aleksiewicz, Hobart	1969-72	4,525	470	0	320	748	6,063

*Record. $See page 6 for explanation.

SEASON YARDS

Player, Team	Year	Rush	Rcv.	Int.	PR	KOR	Yds.
Kavin Gailliard, American Int'l	†1999	*2,653	289	0	0	122	*3,064
Brian Shay, Emporia St.	†1998	2,265	165	0	0	389	2,819
Brian Shay, Emporia St.	†1996	2,103	247	0	48	340	2,738
Brian Shay, Emporia St.	†1997	1,912	277	0	56	478	2,723
Steve Roberts, Butler	1989	1,450	532	0	272	415	2,669
Chris George, Glenville St.	†1993	23	*1,876	0	157	562	2,618
Kavin Gailliard, American Int'l	1998	1,971	270	0	151	196	2,588
Damon Thompson, Virginia St.	1998	127	1,330	0	292	770	2,519
Damon Thompson, Virginia St.	1999	88	1,517	0	410	465	2,480
Jamel White, South Dakota	1999	1,807	640	0	0	0	2,447
Johnny Bailey, Tex. A&M-Kingsville	1986	2,011	54	0	20	340	2,425
Rick Wegher, South Dakota St.	1984	1,317	264	0	0	824	2,405
Steve Papin, Portland St.	†1995	1,619	525	0	1	252	2,397
Ronald Moore, Pittsburg St.	1992	1,864	141	0	0	388	2,393
Roger Graham, New Haven	1993	1,687	116	0	0	516	2,319
Josh Ranek, South Dakota St.	1999	2,055	258	0	0	0	2,313
Jarrett Anderson, Truman	1996	2,140	167	0	0	0	2,307
Anthony Gray, Western N.M.	1997	2,220	78	0	0	0	2,298
Larry Jackson, Edinboro	1994	1,660	237	0	0	387	2,284
Dave Ludy, Winona St.	1994	1,553	153	0	0	568	2,274

*Record. †National champion.

ANNUAL CHAMPIONS

Year	Player, Team	Cl.	G	Rush	Rcv.	Int.	PR	KOR	Yds.	Yd. PG
1992	Johnny Cox, Fort Lewis	Jr.	10	95	1,331	0	80	679	2,185	218.5
1993	Chris George, Glenville St.	Jr.	10	23	1,876	0	157	562	2,618	261.8
1994	Bobby Felix, Western N.M.	Jr.	8	439	853	0	150	667	2,109	263.6
1995	Steve Papin, Portland St.	Sr.	11	1,619	525	0	1	252	2,397	217.9
1996	Brian Shay, Emporia St.	So.	11	2,103	247	0	48	340	2,738	248.9
1997	Brian Shay, Emporia St.	Jr.	11	1,912	277	0	56	478	2,723	247.5
1998	Brian Shay, Emporia St.	Sr.	11	2,265	165	0	0	389	2,819	256.3
1999	Kavin Gailliard, American Int'l	Sr.	12	*2,653	289	0	0	122	3,064	255.3

Field Goals

CAREER FIELD GOALS

Player, Team	Years	Made	Atts.	Pct.
Mike Wood, Southeast Mo. St. (S)	1974-77	*64	*109	.587
Pat Beaty, North Dakota (S)	1985-88	52	82	.634
Ed O'Brien, UCF (S)	1984-87	50	77	.649
Bob Gilbreath, Eastern N.M. (S)	1986-89	50	77	.649
Shane Meyer, Central Mo. St. (S)	1995-98	49	77	.636
Billy Watkins, Tex. A&M-Commerce (S)	1990-93	49	84	.583
Bill May, Clarion (C)	1977-80	48	60	*.800
Ed Detwiler, East Stroudsburg (S)	1989-92	48	87	.552
Steve Huff, Central Mo. St. (C)	1982-85	47	80	.588
Phil Brandt, Central Mo. St. (S)	1987-90	46	66	.697
Scott Doyle, Chadron St. (S)	1992-95	46	69	.667
Howie Guarini, Shippensburg (S)	1988-91	45	62	.726
Eric Myers, West Va. Wesleyan (S)	1993-96	45	67	.672
Mike Schauer, Northern Colo.	1996-99	45	70	.643
Ed Hotz, Southeast Mo. St. (S)	1978-81	45	77	.584
James Knowles, North Ala. (C)	1982-85	45	77	.584
Kurt Seibel, South Dakota (C)	1980-83	44	62	.710
Jason Monday, Lenoir-Rhyne (S)	1989-92	44	64	.688
Pat Bolton, Montana St. (C)	1972-75	44	76	.579
Skipper Butler, Texas-Arlington (C)	1966-69	44	101	.436

*Record. (C) Conventional kicker. (S) Soccer-style kicker.

SEASON FIELD GOALS

Player, Team	Years	Made	Atts.	Pct.
Jason Williams, Southern Ark. (S)	†1998	**20	24	.833
Pat Beaty, North Dakota (S)	1988	**20	26	.769
Raul De la Flor, Humboldt St. (S)	†1993	**20	26	.769
Tom Jurich, Northern Ariz. (C)	†1977	**20	29	.690
Dennis Hochman, Sonoma St. (S)	1986	19	22	+.864
Cory Solberg, North Dakota (S)	1989	19	27	.704
Jaime Nunez, Weber St. (S)	1971	19	32	.594
Jon Ruff, Indiana (Pa.) (S)	†1995	18	22	.818

DIVISION II

ALL-TIME LEADERS—FIELD GOALS

Player, Team	Years	Made	Atts.	Pct.
Shane Meyer, Central Mo. St. (S)	†1997	18	25	.720
Bernard Henderson, Albany St. (Ga.) (S)	†1985	18	26	.692
Milan Smado, Southeastern Okla. (S)	†1999	17	19	.895
Ki Tok Chu, Tenn.-Martin (S)	1988	17	22	.773
Jack McTyre, Valdosta St. (S)	1990	17	23	.739
Dino Beligrinis, Winston-Salem (S)	1988	17	23	.739
Ed O'Brien, UCF (S)	†1987	17	26	.654
David Dell, Tex. A&M-Commerce (S)	1995	17	26	.654
Mike Wood, Southeast Mo. St. (S)	1976	17	33	.515

**Record tied. +Record for minimum 20 attempts. (C) Conventional kicker. (S) Soccer-style kicker.

ANNUAL CHAMPIONS

Year	Player, Team	Class	Made	Atts.	Pct.	PG
1970	Chris Guerrieri, Alfred (S)	Sr.	11	21	.524	1.38
1971	Jaime Nunez, Weber St. (S)	Sr.	19	32	.594	1.90
1972	Randy Walker, Northwestern St. (C)	Jr.	13	19	.684	1.30
1973	Reinhold Struprich, Hawaii (S)	Jr.	15	23	.652	1.36
1974	Mike Wood, Southeast Mo. St. (S)	Fr.	16	23	.696	1.45
1975	Wolfgang Taylor, Western St. (S)	Sr.	14	21	.667	1.56
1976	Rolf Benirschke, UC Davis (S)	Sr.	14	19	.737	1.56
1977	Tom Jurich, Northern Ariz. (C)	Sr.	**20	29	.690	1.81
1978	Frank Friedman, Cal St. Northridge (S)	Jr.	15	22	.682	1.50
1979	Bill May, Clarion (C)	Jr.	16	21	.762	1.60
1980	Nelson McMurain, North Ala. (S)	Jr.	14	22	.636	1.40
	Sean Landeta, Towson (S)	So.	14	28	.500	1.40
1981	Russ Meier, South Dakota St. (S)	Fr.	16	21	.762	1.60
1982	Joey Malone, Alabama A&M (C)	Fr.	15	21	.714	1.36
	Rick Ruszkiewicz, Edinboro (S)	Sr.	15	24	.625	1.36
1983	Mike Thomas, Angelo St. (S)	Sr.	16	22	.727	1.45
1984	Terry Godfrey, South Dakota (S)	Jr.	16	26	.615	1.60
1985	Bernard Henderson, Albany St. (Ga.) (S)	Sr.	18	26	.692	1.64
1986	Dennis Hochman, Sonoma St. (S)	Sr.	19	22+	.864	1.90
1987	Ed O'Brien, UCF (S)	Sr.	17	26	.654	1.70
1988	Pat Beaty, North Dakota (S)	Sr.	**20	26	.769	1.82
1989	Cory Solberg, North Dakota (S)	Jr.	19	27	.704	1.73
1990	Jack McTyre, Valdosta St. (S)	Sr.	17	23	.739	1.70
1991	Billy Watkins, Tex. A&M-Commerce (S)	So.	15	24	.625	1.36
1992	Mike Estrella, St. Mary's (Cal.) (S)	Jr.	15	27	.556	1.67
1993	Raul De la Flor, Humboldt St. (S)	Sr.	**20	26	.769	1.82
1994	Matt Seagreaves, East Stroudsburg (S)	So.	15	26	.577	1.50
1995	Jon Ruff, Indiana (Pa.) (S)	Sr.	18	23	.783	1.64
1996	Juan Gomez-Tagle, North Dakota (S)	Sr.	15	20	.750	1.50
1997	Shane Meyer, Central Mo. St. (S)	Jr.	18	25	.720	1.64
1998	Jason Williams, Southern Ark. (S)	So.	**20	24	.833	*2.00
1999	Milan Smado, Southeastern Okla. (S)	So.	17	19	.895	1.55

*Record. +Record for minimum 20 attempts. (C) Conventional kicker. (S) Soccer-style kicker.

All-Time Longest Plays

Since 1941, official maximum length of all plays fixed at 100 yards.

RUSHING

Rushing plays have covered 99 yards 21 times. The most recent:

Yds.	Player, Team (Opponent)	Year
99	Ronaie Maye, Carson-Newman (Lenoir-Rhyne)	1999

Yds.	Player, Team (Opponent)	Year
99	Thelbert Withers, N.M. Highlands (Fort Lewis)	1992
99	Lester Frye, Edinboro (Calif. [Pa.])	1991
99	Kelvin Minefee, Southern Utah (Mesa St.)	1988
99	Fred Deutsch, Springfield (Wagner)	1977
99	Sammy Croom, San Diego (Azusa Pacific)	1972
99	John Stenger, Swarthmore (Widener)	1970
99	Jed Knuttila, Hamline (St. Thomas [Minn.])	1968
99	Dave Lanoha, Colorado Col. (Texas Lutheran)	1967
99	Tom Pabst, UC Riverside (Cal Tech)	1965

PASSING

Pass plays have resulted in 99-yard completions 21 times. The most recent:

Yds.	Passer-Receiver, Team (Opponent)	Year
99	Justin Coleman-Mike Smith, Neb.-Kearney (Wayne St. [Neb.])	1997
99	Antonio Hawkins-Jovelle Tillman, Virgina St. (Fayetteville St.)	1997
99	Matt Morris-Casey Cowan, Tex. A&M-Commerce (Midwestern St.)	1997
99	Rod Smith-Scott Hammond, Glenville St. (Concord)	1996
99	Ken Collums-Jerome Davis, Central Ark. (Delta St.)	1994
99	Greg Younger-Marty Walsh, Hillsdale (St. Francis [Ill.])	1994
99	Ray Morrow-Jeff Williamson, Cal St. Hayward (Redlands)	1993
99	Bob McLaughlin-Eric Muldowney, Lock Haven (Mansfield)	1993
99	Rob Rayl-John Unger, Valparaiso (Hillsdale)	1992
99	Bret Comp-Ken Kopetchny, East Stroudsburg (Mansfield)	1990

PUNTS

Yds.	Player, Team (Opponent)	Year
97	Earl Hurst, Emporia St. (Central Mo. St.)	1964
96	Alex Campbell, Morris Brown (Clark Atlanta)	1994
96	Gary Frens, Hope (Olivet)	1966
96	Jim Jarrett, North Dakota (South Dakota)	1957
93	Elliot Mills, Carleton (Monmouth [Ill.])	1970
93	Kaspar Fitins, Taylor (Georgetown [Ky.])	1966
93	Leeroy Sweeney, Pomona-Pitzer (UC Riverside)	1960

FIELD GOALS

Yds.	Player, Team (Opponent)	Year
67	Tom Odle, Fort Hays St. (Washburn)	1988
63	Joe Duren, Arkansas St. (McNeese St.)	1974
62	Doc Proctor, Ferris St. (Michigan Tech)	1999
62	Mike Flater, Colorado Mines (Western St.)	1973
61	Duane Christian, Cameron (Southwestern Okla.)	1976
61	Mike Wood, Southeast Mo. St. (Lincoln [Mo.])	1975
61	Bill Shear, Cortland St. (Hobart)	1966
60	Mike Panasuk, Ferris St. (St. Joseph's [Ind.])	1990
60	Ed Beaulac, Sonoma St. (St. Mary's [Cal.])	1989
60	Roger McCoy, Grand Valley St. (Grand Rapids)	1976
60	Skipper Butler, Texas-Arlington (Tex. A&M-Commerce)	1968

Since 1941, many players have returned interceptions, punts and kickoffs 100 yards. For the 1999 season leaders, see pages .

Team Champions

Annual Offense Champions

TOTAL OFFENSE

Year	Team	Avg.
1948	Hanover	*624.1
1949	Pacific (Cal.)	505.3
1950	West Tex. A&M	465.3
1951	Western Ill.	473.6
1952	Sam Houston St.	448.2
1953	Col. of Idaho	476.3
1954	Col. of Emporia	469.7
1955	Centre	431.0
1956	Florida A&M	475.0
1957	Denison	430.8
1958	Missouri Valley	449.6
1959	Whittier	461.3
1960	Muskingum	456.4
1961	Florida A&M	413.6
1962	Baker	438.4
1963	Col. of Emporia	517.1
1964	San Diego St.	422.6
1965	Long Beach St.	439.5
1966	Weber St.	460.1
1967	San Fran. St.	490.0
1968	Louisiana Tech	459.1
1969	Delaware	488.9
1970	Grambling	457.7
1971	Delaware	515.6
1972	Hobart	457.3
1973	Boise St.	466.5
1974	Boise St.	516.9
1975	Portland St.	472.4
1976	Portland St.	497.5
1977	Portland St.	506.7
1978	Western St.	487.0
1979	Delaware	450.5
1980	Southwest Tex. St.	423.0
1981	Southwest Tex. St.	482.3
1982	Northern Mich.	450.4
1983	Central St.	491.1
1984	North Dakota St.	455.3
1985	Truman	471.4
1986	Tex. A&M-Kingsville	542.6
1987	Tex. A&M-Kingsville	486.4
1988	Cal St. Sacramento	486.0
1989	Grand Valley St.	480.8
1990	Chadron St.	479.6
1991	Western St.	549.8
1992	New Haven	587.7
1993	Wayne St. (Neb.)	581.5
1994	West Tex. A&M	571.3
1995	Portland St.	472.0
1996	East Stroudsburg	509.1
1997	Emporia St.	531.5

TEAM CHAMPIONS—TOTAL OFFENSE

Year	Team	Avg.
1998	American Int'l	505.6
1999	Ferris St.	534.5

*Record.

RUSHING OFFENSE

Year	Team	Avg.
1948	Hanover	400.4
1949	Southern U.	382.9
1950	St. Lawrence	356.1
1951	Western N.M.	379.2
1952	William Jewell	345.0
1953	McPherson	375.9
1954	Col. of Emporia	*404.8
1955	Centre	373.4
1956	Tufts	359.9
1957	Denison	372.1
1958	Huron	353.3
1959	Bemidji St.	326.6
1960	Muskingum	355.2
1961	Huron	313.1
1962	Northern St.	355.3
1963	Luther	356.0
1964	Cal St. Los Angeles	325.9
1965	Huron	303.3
1966	Neb.-Kearney	370.1
1967	North Dakota St.	299.6
1968	Delaware	315.8
1969	St. Olaf	369.1
1970	Delaware	385.9
1971	Delaware	371.2
1972	Hobart	380.7
1973	Bethune-Cookman	308.8
1974	Central Mich.	324.6
1975	North Dakota	344.4
1976	Montana St.	287.5
1977	South Carolina St.	321.5
1978	Western St.	320.2
1979	Mississippi Col.	314.5
1980	Minn.-Duluth	307.3
1981	Millersville	322.9
1982	Mississippi Col.	297.0
1983	Jamestown	297.7
1984	North Dakota St.	334.7
1985	Saginaw Valley	300.4
1986	Tex. A&M-Kingsville	395.2
1987	Tex. A&M-Kingsville	330.5
1988	North Dakota St.	373.1
1989	Wofford	373.7
1990	North Dakota St.	364.2
1991	Wofford	347.9
1992	Pittsburg St.	353.8
1993	North Ala.	371.5
1994	Moorhead St.	375.0
1995	Pittsburg St.	318.8
1996	North Dakota St.	325.9
1997	Saginaw Valley	334.8
1998	Saginaw Valley	385.5
1999	Neb.-Omaha	335.2

*Record.

PASSING OFFENSE

Year	Team	Avg.
1948	Hanover	223.8
1949	Baldwin-Wallace	196.9
1950	Northern Ill.	187.0
1951	Central Mich.	213.8
1952	Sam Houston St.	263.0
1953	Southern Conn. St.	193.5
1954	Northern Iowa	206.1
1955	Hamline	210.7
1956	Widener	207.7
1957	Cal Poly Pomona	236.0
1958	Cal Poly Pomona	217.6
1959	Whittier	199.3
1960	Whitworth	213.6
1961	Cal Poly Pomona	244.1
1962	Northern Ill.	285.6
1963	Northern Ill.	349.3
1964	Parsons	301.3
1965	Southern Ore. St.	268.9
1966	San Diego St.	268.1
1967	San Fran. St.	387.0
1968	Louisiana Tech	316.4
1969	Portland St.	308.6
1970	Portland St.	313.8
1971	C. W. Post	262.5
1972	Maryville (Tenn.)	277.8
1973	Lehigh	275.0
1974	Boise St.	334.5
1975	Portland St.	361.7
1976	Portland St.	404.1
1977	Portland St.	378.5
1978	Northern Mich.	242.3
1979	Northern Mich.	284.2
1980	Northern Mich.	269.6
1981	Franklin	306.5
1982	Evansville	313.0
1983	Franklin	358.0
1984	Franklin	334.0
1985	Truman	345.1
1986	West Tex. A&M	345.5
1987	Evansville	306.6
1988	UCF	292.2
1989	Cal St. Chico	328.8
1990	New Haven	335.4
1991	Western St.	357.4
1992	Gardner-Webb	367.8
1993	C. W. Post	409.0
1994	West Tex. A&M	*454.5
1995	Norfolk St.	367.4
1996	East Stroudsburg	404.1
1997	Glenville St.	381.9
1998	West Chester	313.8
1999	Neb.-Kearney	338.6

*Record.

SCORING OFFENSE

Year	Team	Avg.
1948	Sul Ross St.	43.1
1949	Pacific (Cal.)	50.0
1950	West Tex. A&M	37.2
1951	Western Ill.	42.1
1952	Tex. A&M-Commerce	49.6
1953	Col. of Idaho	42.4
1954	Col. of Emporia	43.2
1955	Central Mich.	36.3
1956	Florida A&M	45.9
1957	Denison	38.6
1958	West Chester	51.4
1959	Florida A&M	42.6
1960	Florida A&M	52.8
1961	Florida A&M	54.7
1962	Florida A&M	42.0
1963	Col. of Emporia	42.4
1964	San Diego St.	42.3
1965	Ottawa	43.2
1966	N.M. Highlands	48.1
1967	Waynesburg	53.7
1968	Doane	52.9
1969	St. Olaf	45.2
1970	Wittenberg	40.0
1971	Michigan Tech	42.4
1972	Fort Valley St.	45.0
1973	Western Ky.	37.7
1974	Boise St.	44.6
1975	Bethune-Cookman	37.9
1976	Northern Mich.	43.0
1977	South Carolina St.	38.4
1978	Western St.	45.2
1979	Delaware	35.5
1980	Minn.-Duluth	35.4
1981	Southwest Tex. St.	37.5
1982	Truman	40.0
1983	Central St.	43.6
1984	North Dakota St.	39.0
1985	UC Davis	37.6
1986	Tex. A&M-Kingsville	43.1
1987	UCF	34.5
	West Chester	34.5
1988	North Dakota St.	39.6
	Tex. A&M-Kingsville	39.6
1989	Grand Valley St.	44.5
1990	Indiana (Pa.)	44.2
1991	Western St.	46.1
1992	New Haven	50.5
1993	New Haven	*54.7
1994	Hampton	46.4

Year	Team	Avg.
1995	Tex. A&M-Kingsville	40.1
1996	Clarion	43.5
1997	New Haven	43.3
1998	Northwest Mo. St.	46.4
1999	Ferris St.	47.3

*Record.

Annual Defense Champions

TOTAL DEFENSE

Year	Team	Avg.
1948	Morgan St.	104.4
1949	Southern Conn. St.	95.6
1950	Southern Conn. St.	93.6
1951	Southern Conn. St.	84.3
1952	West Chester	128.4
1953	Shippensburg	81.9
1954	Geneva	106.3
1955	Col. of Emporia	102.0
1956	Tennessee St.	118.9
1957	West Chester	90.2
1958	Rose-Hulman	95.8
1959	Md.-East. Shore	75.3
1960	Md.-East. Shore	104.8
1961	Florida A&M	85.3
1962	John Carroll	*44.4
1963	West Chester	100.8
1964	Morgan St.	126.4
1965	Morgan St.	91.5
1966	Tennessee St.	85.7
1967	Tennessee St.	61.6
1968	Alcorn St.	103.4
1969	Livingstone	148.5
1970	Delaware St.	103.5
1971	Hampden-Sydney	115.6
1972	Wis.-Whitewater	143.8
1973	Livingstone	114.9
1974	Livingstone	120.5
1975	South Carolina St.	100.6
1976	Alcorn St.	108.9
1977	Virginia Union	160.3
1978	East Stroudsburg	153.8
1979	Virginia Union	138.2
1980	Concordia-M'head	191.7
1981	Fort Valley St.	148.3
1982	Jamestown	187.9
1983	Virginia Union	143.7
1984	Virginia St.	180.6
1985	Fort Valley St.	162.2
1986	Virginia Union	163.5
1987	Alabama A&M	167.1
1988	Alabama A&M	175.8
1989	Winston-Salem	185.7
1990	Sonoma St.	218.5
1991	Ashland	195.5
1992	Ashland	211.5
1993	Bentley	188.3
1994	Bentley	195.5
1995	Kentucky St.	205.1
1996	Stonehill	194.0
1997	Livingstone	171.5
1998	Savannah St.	166.3
1999	Northeastern St.	180.6

*Record.

RUSHING DEFENSE

Year	Team	Avg.
1948	Morgan St.	44.8
1949	Hanover	43.5
1950	Lewis & Clark	50.3
1951	Southern Conn. St.	17.1
1952	Tex. A&M-Commerce	48.5
1953	Shippensburg	53.6
1954	Tennessee St.	29.2
1955	Muskingum	52.5
1956	Hillsdale	51.1
1957	West Chester	27.9
1958	Ithaca	48.4
1959	Md.-East. Shore	36.3
1960	West Chester	41.4
1961	Florida A&M	20.1

DIVISION II

TEAM CHAMPIONS—RUSHING DEFENSE

Year	Team	Avg.
1962	John Carroll	-1.0
1963	St. John's (Minn.)	12.9
1964	Fort Valley St.	39.7
1965	Morgan St.	15.0
1966	Tennessee St.	13.9
1967	Tennessee St.	*-16.7
1968	Alcorn St.	8.8
1969	Merchant Marine	16.2
1970	Delaware St.	4.9
1971	Northern Colo.	27.5
1972	Alcorn St.	49.8
1973	Alcorn St.	45.9
1974	Livingstone	53.0
1975	Alcorn St.	15.9
1976	Alcorn St.	32.5
1977	Virginia Union	63.6
1978	East Stroudsburg	52.2
1979	Virginia Union	41.0
1980	Mo.-Rolla	34.6
1981	Fort Valley St.	46.9
1982	Butler	71.1
1983	Butler	38.2
1984	Norfolk St.	53.8
1985	Norfolk St.	50.9
1986	Central St.	44.5
1987	West Chester	67.2
1988	Cal Poly	56.4
1989	Tex. A&M-Kingsville	60.7
1990	Sonoma St.	58.3
1991	Sonoma St.	63.6
1992	Ashland	64.4
1993	Albany St. (Ga.)	59.1
1994	Hampton	66.0
1995	North Ala.	56.8
1996	Livingstone	66.9
1997	Livingstone	52.8
1998	Savannah St.	48.8
1999	Catawba	53.4

*Record.

PASSING DEFENSE

Year	Team	$Avg.
1948	Ashland	*10.1
1949	Wilmington (Ohio)	39.8
1950	Vermont	34.4
1951	Alfred	52.0
1952	Cortland St.	45.9
1953	Shippensburg	28.3
1954	St. Augustine's	26.5
1955	Ithaca	15.5
1956	West Va. Tech	29.1
1957	Lake Forest	25.0
1958	Coast Guard	25.4
1959	Huron	21.9
1960	Susquehanna	27.3
1961	Westminster (Utah)	24.8
1962	Principia	27.8
1963	Western Caro.	39.3
1964	Mont. St.-Billings	44.1
1965	Minot St.	44.5
1966	Manchester	54.7
1967	Mount Union	61.4
1968	Bridgeport	47.6
1969	Wabash	72.0
1970	Hampden-Sydney	62.9
1971	Western Ky.	57.7
1972	Howard	48.8
1973	East Stroudsburg	37.6
1974	Tennessee St.	52.6
1975	N.C. Central	60.2
1976	Morris Brown	60.8
1977	Delaware St.	64.3
1978	Concordia-M'head	55.8
1979	Kentucky St.	62.3
1980	Norfolk St.	71.5
1981	Bowie St.	75.7
1982	Elizabeth City St.	49.0
1983	Elizabeth City St.	65.0
1984	Virginia St.	80.4
1985	Fort Valley St.	94.5
1986	Virginia Union	84.7
1987	Alabama A&M	72.5
1988	Alabama A&M	84.3
1989	Mo. Southern St.	93.0
1990	Angelo St.	65.4
1991	Carson-Newman	64.9
1992	Tex. A&M-Commerce	61.8
1993	Alabama A&M	71.5
1994	Bentley	55.6
1995	Savannah St.	72.4
1996	N.C. Central	62.1
1997	Kentucky St.	64.4
1998	Central Okla.	72.3
1999	Northeastern St.	59.2

*Record. $Beginning in 1990, based on pass efficiency ranking instead of yards per game.

SCORING DEFENSE

Year	Team	Avg.
1959	Huron	2.1
1960	Albany St. (Ga.)	*0.0
1961	Florida A&M	2.8
1962	John Carroll	2.9
1963	Massachusetts	1.3
1964	Central (Iowa)	4.8
1965	St. John's (Minn.)	2.2
1966	Morgan St.	3.6
1967	Waynesburg	4.3
1968	Central Conn. St.	4.4
1969	Carthage	6.0
1970	Hampden-Sydney	2.8
1971	Hampden-Sydney	3.4
1972	Ashland	5.6
1973	Virginia Union	3.8
1974	Minn.-Duluth	5.5
1975	South Carolina St.	2.9
1976	South Carolina St.	3.4
1977	Minn.-Duluth	7.8
1978	La.-Lafayette	7.1
1979	Virginia Union	6.1
1980	Minn.-Duluth	7.6
1981	Moorhead St.	5.0
1982	Jamestown	5.9
1983	Towson	5.8
1984	Cal Poly	9.0
1985	Fort Valley St.	6.3
1986	North Dakota St.	6.8
1987	Tuskegee	9.1
1988	Alabama A&M	7.5
1989	Jacksonville St.	7.0
1990	Cal Poly	11.3
1991	Butler	7.1
1992	Ferris St.	10.5
1993	Albany St. (Ga.)	8.7
1994	Bentley	6.0
1995	North Ala.	10.6
1996	Carson-Newman	10.7
1997	Albany St. (Ga.)	7.3
1998	Central Okla.	7.7
1999	Pittsburg St.	9.5

*Record.

Other Annual Team Champions

NET PUNTING

Year	Team	Avg.
1992	Fort Lewis	37.9
1993	North Ala.	39.5
1994	Colorado Mines	42.9
1995	New Haven	38.7
1996	Adams St.	40.2
1997	North Ala.	39.5
1998	Adams St.	41.8
1999	Fairmont St.	40.1

PUNT RETURNS

Year	Team	Avg.
1992	Savannah St.	21.2
1993	Wayne St. (Neb.)	19.1
1994	Adams St.	16.7
1995	Elizabeth City St.	23.1
1996	Angelo St.	14.7
1997	Gardner-Webb	19.8
1998	Morehouse	19.5
1999	Northwest Mo. St.	18.0

KICKOFF RETURNS

Year	Team	Avg.
1992	Jacksonville St.	34.0
1993	Adams St.	27.5
1994	Western N.M.	31.8
1995	Millersville	26.0
1996	Northern Colo.	27.5
1997	Carson-Newman	30.4
1998	Central Okla.	28.9
1999	Northeastern St.	28.4

TURNOVER MARGIN

Year	Team	Avg.
1992	Hillsdale	2.2
1993	Hillsdale	2.7
1994	Lenoir-Rhyne	2.6
1995	Central Okla.	2.6
1996	Central Okla.	2.3
1997	North Dakota St.	2.0
1998	Presbyterian	2.3
1999	American Int'l	*2.8

MOST IMPROVED

Year	Team	From	To	Imp.
1996	St. Joseph's (Ind.)	1-9	9-2	7½
1997	Carson-Newman	2-9	8-3	6
1998	Fort Valley St.	5-6	11-2	5
1999	Mars Hill	1-10	7-4	6

*Record.

1999 Most-Improved Teams

School (Coach)	1998	1999	$Games Improved
Mars Hill (Tim Clifton)	1-10	7-4	6
Hillsdale (Dave Dye)	3-8	8-3	5
Southwestern Okla. (Paul Sharp)	0-10	5-5	5
Ky. Wesleyan (John Johnson)	2-7	7-4	4
Ark.-Monticello (Clarence Holley)	0-11	4-7	4
Catawba (David Bennett)	6-4	11-2	3½
Merrimack (Tom Caito)	3-6	7-3	3½
Moorhead St. (Ralph Micheli)	3-7	7-4	3½
Fairmont St. (Doug Sams)	5-5	8-2	3
Arkansas Tech (Steve Mullins)	5-5	9-3	3
Virginia St. (Lou Anderson)	3-7	6-4	3
Morris Brown (Joseph Crosby)	3-8	6-5	3
Lenoir-Rhyne (Bill Hart)	2-9	5-6	3
American Int'l (Art Wilkins)	7-4	10-2	2½
Western Wash. (Rob Smith)	5-5	8-3	2½
Winston-Salem (Kermit Blount)	5-5	8-3	2½
Ferris St. (Jeff Pierce)	5-6	7-3	2½
Southwest St. (Ron Flowers)	3-7	6-5	2½
West Virginia St. (Carl Lee)	3-8	5-5	2½
Assumption (Sean Mahoney)	0-9	3-7	2½
Morehouse (Anthony Jones)	0-11	2-8	2½

$To determine games improved, add the difference in victories between the two seasons to the difference in losses, then divide by two. Includes postseason.

All-Time Team Won-Lost Records

Includes records as a senior college only, minimum 20 seasons of competition since 1937. Postseason games are included, and each tie game is computed as half won and half lost.

PERCENTAGE (TOP 25)

Team	Yrs.	Won	Lost	Tied	Pct.
West Chester	71	458	196	17	.695
Tex. A&M-Kingsville	71	495	217	16	.691
Indiana (Pa.)	71	409	215	23	.650
Central Okla.	94	535	284	47	.645
Grand Valley St.	29	192	105	3	.645
Pittsburg St.	92	542	293	47	.641
Carson-Newman	76	460	255	30	.638
Neb.-Kearney	76	425	248	27	.626
North Dakota St.	103	531	320	34	.619
Angelo St.	36	234	144	7	.617
Northern St.	94	472	289	32	.615
Truman	92	480	300	34	.611
Tuskegee	104	519	325	50	.609
Minn.-Duluth	67	346	219	24	.608
Hillsdale	107	526	332	46	.607
Virginia St.	88	448	281	48	.607
North Dakota	103	508	327	30	.605
North Ala.	51	314	203	16	.604
Arkansas Tech	85	453	291	41	.603
Fort Valley St.	54	305	197	21	.603
Westminster (Pa.)	105	515	332	53	.602
C. W. Post	43	247	164	5	.600
Virginia Union	99	453	296	47	.599
East Stroudsburg	72	365	248	19	.593
Slippery Rock	72	369	256	28	.587

VICTORIES (TOP 26)

Team	Yrs.	Won	Lost	Tied	Pct.
Pittsburg St.	92	542	293	47	.641
Central Okla.	94	535	284	47	.645
North Dakota St.	103	531	320	34	.619
Hillsdale	107	526	332	46	.607
Tuskegee	104	519	325	50	.609
Westminster (Pa.)	105	515	332	53	.602
North Dakota	103	508	327	30	.605
Tex. A&M-Kingsville	71	495	217	16	.691
Truman	92	480	300	34	.611
Northern St.	94	472	289	32	.615
South Dakota St.	102	461	379	38	.547
Carson-Newman	76	460	255	30	.638
West Chester	71	458	196	17	.695
Arkansas Tech	85	453	291	41	.603
Virginia Union	99	453	296	47	.599
Virginia St.	88	448	281	48	.607
South Dakota	104	444	422	34	.512
Washburn	108	439	488	40	.475
Central Ark.	88	438	312	42	.580
Tex. A&M-Commerce	82	428	329	31	.563
Neb.-Kearney	76	425	248	27	.626
Presbyterian	87	417	392	35	.515
Ouachita Baptist	93	412	359	42	.533
Emporia St.	102	410	438	44	.484
Central Mo. St.	103	409	448	51	.479
Indiana (Pa.)	71	409	215	23	.650

ALPHABETICAL LISTING
(No Minimum Seasons of Competition)

Team	Yrs.	Won	Lost	Tied	Pct.
Abilene Christian	78	390	328	32	.541
Adams St.	65	279	269	17	.509
Albany St. (Ga.)	54	274	219	21	.554
American Int'l	63	265	267	20	.498
Angelo St.	36	234	144	7	.617
Ark.-Monticello	82	308	387	25	.445
Arkansas Tech	85	453	291	41	.603
Ashland	77	364	293	29	.552
Assumption	12	36	74	1	.329
Augustana (S.D.)	79	308	372	14	.454
Bemidji St.	74	240	356	23	.406
Bentley	12	84	30	1	.735
Bloomsburg	72	300	296	21	.503
Bowie St.	28	95	169	6	.363
Bryant	1	5	4	0	.556
C. W. Post	43	247	164	5	.600
UC Davis	81	406	311	33	.563
Calif. (Pa.)	70	256	320	19	.446
Carson-Newman	76	460	255	30	.638
Catawba	80	394	361	26	.521
Central Ark.	88	438	312	42	.580
Central Mo. St.	103	409	448	51	.479
Central Okla.	94	535	284	47	.645
Central Wash.	81	374	262	23	.585
Chadron St.	85	389	305	15	.559
Cheyney	46	84	329	5	.207
Clarion	71	329	264	17	.553
Clark Atlanta	61	197	299	23	.402
Colorado Mines	110	323	480	32	.406
Concord	77	331	320	27	.508
Delta St.	70	323	323	23	.500
East Central	87	394	386	38	.505
East Stroudsburg	72	365	248	19	.593
Eastern N.M.	56	283	265	15	.516
Edinboro	71	268	306	24	.468
Elizabeth City St.	58	245	267	18	.479
Emporia St.	102	410	438	44	.484
Fairmont St.	86	375	308	44	.546
Fayetteville St.	54	179	299	26	.381
Ferris St.	71	274	306	34	.474
Findlay	95	396	313	25	.557
Fort Hays St.	78	354	366	49	.492
Fort Lewis	37	119	228	3	.344
Fort Valley St.	54	305	197	21	.603
Gannon	12	58	55	2	.513
Gardner-Webb	30	150	167	2	.473
Glenville St.	87	282	338	37	.457
Grand Valley St.	29	192	105	3	.645
Harding	46	208	221	16	.485
Henderson St.	92	392	358	44	.521
Hillsdale	107	526	332	46	.607
Humboldt St.	72	322	290	20	.525
Indiana (Pa.)	71	409	215	23	.650
Indianapolis	62	266	284	23	.484
Johnson Smith	72	285	332	34	.464
Kentucky St.	71	304	360	26	.459
Ky. Wesleyan	39	123	168	16	.427
Kutztown	69	236	325	21	.424
Lane	76	199	365	26	.359
Lenoir-Rhyne	80	400	344	34	.536
Livingstone	51	210	253	15	.455
Lock Haven	71	258	367	25	.416
Mansfield	70	213	355	30	.381
Mars Hill	36	162	191	10	.460
Mass.-Lowell	20	83	106	2	.440
Mercyhurst	19	95	76	4	.554
Merrimack	4	18	19	0	.486
Mesa St.	24	137	112	5	.549
Michigan Tech	77	272	276	17	.496
Midwestern St.	23	100	131	6	.435
Miles	30	66	200	7	.255
Millersville	68	317	249	21	.558
Minn.-Duluth	67	346	219	24	.608
Minn.-Morris	38	168	193	10	.466
Minn. St.-Mankato	74	323	304	27	.515
Mo.-Rolla	94	345	440	36	.442
Mo. Southern St.	32	174	144	7	.546
Mo. Western St.	30	145	162	9	.473
Moorhead St.	82	362	302	31	.543
Morehouse	100	340	384	49	.472
Morningside	98	337	465	37	.424
Morris Brown	74	327	319	37	.506
Neb.-Kearney	76	425	248	27	.626
Neb.-Omaha	83	355	349	30	.504
New Haven	27	156	112	5	.581
N.M. Highlands	73	268	320	27	.458
Newberry	86	324	465	33	.414
North Ala.	51	314	203	16	.604
N.C. Central	69	349	273	24	.559
North Dakota	103	508	327	30	.605
North Dakota St.	103	531	320	34	.619
Northeastern St.	77	382	295	30	.562
Northern Colo.	87	371	339	24	.522
Northern Mich.	86	366	270	26	.573
Northern St.	94	472	289	32	.615
Northwest Mo. St.	82	365	364	32	.501
Northwood	38	154	187	8	.453

DIVISION II

Team	Yrs.	Won	Lost	Tied	Pct.
Okla. Panhandle	76	275	415	25	.402
Ouachita Baptist	93	412	359	42	.533
Pace	22	85	123	2	.410
Pittsburg St.	92	542	293	47	.641
Presbyterian	87	417	392	35	.515
Quincy	13	56	66	1	.459
Saginaw Valley	25	138	119	3	.537
St. Anselm	31	90	79	11	.531
St. Cloud St.	72	333	282	21	.540
St. Joseph's (Ind.)	80	259	324	24	.446
Savannah St.	47	171	237	15	.422
Shepherd	76	337	281	26	.543
Shippensburg	70	336	284	21	.541
Slippery Rock	72	369	256	28	.587
South Dakota	104	444	422	34	.512
South Dakota St.	102	461	379	38	.547
Southeastern Okla.	88	370	382	44	.492
Southern Ark.	80	361	301	27	.544
Southern Conn. St.	52	280	198	11	.584
Southwest Baptist	17	47	120	2	.284
Southwest St.	32	122	195	5	.387
Southwestern Okla.	90	395	368	37	.517
Stonehill	12	56	49	3	.532
Tarleton St.	39	160	229	3	.412
Tex. A&M-Commerce	82	430	329	31	.564
Tex. A&M-Kingsville	71	495	217	16	.691
Texas Lutheran	64	235	274	12	.463
Truman	92	480	300	34	.611
Tusculum	50	104	216	24	.337
Tuskegee	104	519	325	50	.609
Valdosta St.	18	112	79	3	.585
Virginia St.	88	448	281	48	.607
Virginia Union	99	453	296	47	.599
Washburn	108	439	488	40	.475
Wayne St. (Mich.)	82	282	383	29	.427
Wayne St. (Neb.)	84	333	368	40	.476
West Ala.	58	218	304	15	.420
West Chester	71	458	196	17	.695
West Ga.	21	113	106	0	.516
West Liberty St.	73	353	290	35	.546
West Tex. A&M	88	390	417	22	.484
West Virginia St.	76	275	345	40	.447
West Va. Tech	80	265	369	35	.422
West Va. Wesleyan	94	349	412	30	.460
Western N.M.	63	235	297	15	.443
Western St.	77	331	323	14	.506
Western Wash.	83	325	320	32	.504
Westminster (Pa.)	105	515	332	53	.602
Wingate	14	61	82	0	.427
Winona St.	99	296	427	32	.413
Winston-Salem	56	292	231	22	.556

Winningest Teams of the 1990s

BY PERCENTAGE
Minimum seven years in Division II

School	Years*	Won	Lost	Tied	Pct.
Pittsburg St.	10	103	18	2	.846
Carson-Newman	9	91	18	1	.832
Indiana (Pa.)	10	94	26	1	.781
Bentley	7	56	17	0	.767
North Dakota St.	10	88	27	0	.765
Northern Colo.	10	92	31	0	.748
North Dakota	10	81	27	1	.748

School	Years*	Won	Lost	Tied	Pct.
North Ala.	10	87	31	1	.735
Albany St. (Ga.)	10	79	30	1	.723
UC Davis	10	81	31	2	.719
Millersville	10	73	28	2	.718
Grand Valley St.	10	80	31	2	.717
New Haven	10	79	31	1	.716
Tex. A&M-Kingsville	10	85	34	0	.714
Chadron St.	10	77	31	1	.711
C. W. Post	7	50	22	0	.694
Ferris St.	10	78	34	3	.691
Slippery Rock	10	77	35	1	.686
Shepherd	10	71	34	1	.675
Central Okla.	10	72	35	1	.671
Glenville St.	7	52	26	0	.667
Western St.	10	72	36	1	.665
Ashland	10	68	37	1	.646
Angelo St.	10	66	36	2	.644
Saginaw Valley	10	66	40	0	.623

Fewer than seven years in Division II and still active

School	Years*	Won	Lost	Tied	Pct.
Southern Ark.	3	25	6	0	.806
Northeastern St.	2	18	6	0	.750
#Albany (N.Y.)	4	31	12	0	.721
#Butler	3	22	9	1	.703
#Southeast Mo. St.	1	7	3	0	.700
Central Wash.	2	15	7	0	.682
#Hampton	5	38	18	1	.675
#Jacksonville St.	5	40	19	0	.675
#Wofford	5	36	20	1	.640
#Cal St. Sacramento	3	19	11	0	.633
#Troy St.	3	20	12	0	.625

Years of NCAA Division II active membership. #No longer Division II member. Records include postseason.

BY VICTORIES

School	Years*	Won	Lost	Tied	Pct.
Pittsburg St.	10	103	18	2	.846
Indiana (Pa.)	10	94	26	1	.781
Northern Colo.	10	92	31	0	.748
Carson-Newman	9	91	18	1	.832
North Dakota St.	10	88	27	0	.765
North Ala.	10	87	31	1	.735
Tex. A&M-Kingsville	10	85	34	0	.714
UC Davis	10	81	31	2	.719
North Dakota	10	81	27	1	.748
Grand Valley St.	10	80	31	2	.717
Albany St. (Ga.)	10	79	30	1	.723
New Haven	10	79	31	1	.716
Ferris St.	10	78	34	3	.691
Chadron St.	10	77	31	1	.711
Slippery Rock	10	77	35	1	.686
Northwest Mo. St.	10	74	47	1	.611
Millersville	10	73	28	2	.718
Central Okla.	10	72	35	1	.671
Western St.	10	72	36	1	.665
Shepherd	10	71	34	1	.675
Ashland	10	68	37	1	.646
Angelo St.	10	66	36	2	.644
Saginaw Valley	10	66	40	0	.623
Truman	10	66	44	0	.600
West Chester	10	66	41	1	.616
West Ga.	10	66	43	0	.606
Valdosta St.	10	66	43	2	.604

Years of NCAA Division II active membership. Records include postseason.

National Poll Rankings

Wire Service National Champions

(1958-74)
(For what was then known as College Division teams. Selections by United Press International from 1958 and Associated Press from 1960.)

Year	Team	Coach	Record*
1958	Southern Miss.	Thad "Pie" Vann	9-0-0
1959	Bowling Green	Doyt Perry	9-0-0
1960	Ohio	Bill Hess	10-0-0
1961	Pittsburg St.	Carnie Smith	9-0-0
1962	Southern Miss. (UPI)	Thad "Pie" Vann	9-1-0
	Florida A&M (AP)	Jake Gaither	9-0-0
1963	Delaware (UPI)	Dave Nelson	8-0-0
	Northern Ill. (AP)	Howard Fletcher	9-0-0
1964	Cal St. Los Angeles (UPI)	Homer Beatty	9-0-0
	Wittenberg (AP)	Bill Edwards	8-0-0
1965	North Dakota. St.	Darrell Mudra	10-0-0
1966	San Diego St.	Don Coryell	10-0-0
1967	San Diego St.	Don Coryell	9-1-0
1968	San Diego St. (UPI)	Don Coryell	9-0-1
	North Dakota St. (AP)	Ron Erhardt	9-0-0
1969	North Dakota St.	Ron Erhardt	9-0-0
1970	Arkansas St.	Bennie Ellender	10-0-0

NATIONAL POLL RANKINGS—WIRE SERVICE NATIONAL CHAMPIONS

Year	Team	Coach	Record*
1971	Delaware	"Tubby" Raymond	9-1-0
1972	Delaware	"Tubby" Raymond	10-0-0
1973	Tennessee St.	John Merritt	10-0-0
1974	Louisiana Tech (UPI)	Maxie Lambright	10-0-0
	Central Mich. (AP)	Roy Kramer	9-1-0

*Regular season.

Final Poll Leaders

(Released Before Division Championship Playoffs)

Year	Team (Record*)	Coach	Record in Championship†
1975	North Dakota (9-0)	Jerry Olson	0-1 Lost in first round
1976	Northern Mich. (10-0)	Gil Krueger	1-1 Lost in semifinals
1977	North Dakota St. (8-1-1)	Jim Wacker	1-1 Lost in semifinals
1978	Winston-Salem (10-0)	Bill Hayes	Did not compete
1979	Delaware (9-1)	"Tubby" Raymond	3-0 Champion
1980	Eastern Ill. (8-2)	Darrell Mudra	2-1 Runner-up
1981	Southwest Tex. St. (9-0)	Jim Wacker	3-0 Champion
1982	Southwest Tex. St. (11-0)	Jim Wacker	3-0 Champion
1983	UC Davis (9-0)	Jim Sochor	1-1 Lost in semifinals
1984	North Dakota St. (9-1)	Don Morton	2-1 Runner-up
1985	UC Davis (9-1)	Jim Sochor	0-1 Lost in first round
1986	North Dakota St. (10-0)	Earle Solomonson	3-0 Champion
1987	Tex. A&M-Kingsville (9-1)	Ron Harms	Did not compete
1988	North Dakota St. (10-0)	Rocky Hager	4-0 Champion
1989	Tex. A&M-Kingsville (10-0)	Ron Harms	0-1 Lost in first round
1990	North Dakota St. (10-0)	Rocky Hager	4-0 Champion
1991	Indiana (Pa.) (10-0)	Frank Cignetti	2-1 Lost in semifinals
1992	Pittsburg St. (11-0)	Chuck Broyles	3-1 Runner-up
1993	North Ala. (10-0)	Bobby Wallace	4-0 Champion
1994	North Ala. (8-1)	Bobby Wallace	4-0 Champion
1995	North Ala. (9-0)	Bobby Wallace	4-0 Champion
1996	Tex. A&M-Kingsville (7-2)	Ron Harms	0-1 Lost in first round
1997	Carson-Newman (9-0)	Ken Sparks	2-1 Lost in semifinals
1998	Central Okla. (10-0)	Gary Howard	1-1 Lost in quarterfinals
1999	Carson-Newman (10-0)	Ken Sparks	3-1 Runner-up

*Final poll record; in some cases, a team had one game remaining before the championship playoffs. †Number of teams in the championship: 8 (1975-87); 16 (1988-present).

Weekly Poll Leaders

Poll conducted by the NCAA Division II Football Committee. Information for 1982-96 researched and submitted by Jeff Hodges, SID, University of North Alabama. Information on missing weekly polls should be submitted to NCAA Statistics Service.

1982
- 9-30..........Southwest Tex. St.
- Final..........Southwest Tex. St.

1983
- 9-26..........Southwest Tex. St.
- 10-10..........Southwest Tex. St.
- 10-24..........Mississippi Col.
- 10-31..........UC Davis
- 11-7..........UC Davis
- Final..........UC Davis

1984
- 9-17..........Troy St.
- 9-24..........Central St.
- 10-8..........Central St.
- 10-15..........Central St.
- 10-29..........North Dakota St.
- Final..........North Dakota St.

1985
- 9-23..........South Dakota
- 9-30..........South Dakota
- 10-14..........South Dakota
- 10-21..........Central St.
- 10-28..........Central St.
- 11-11..........UC Davis
- 11-18..........UC Davis
- Final..........UC Davis

1986
- 9-15..........North Dakota St.
- 9-22..........North Dakota St.
- 9-29..........North Dakota St.
- 10-6..........North Dakota St.
- 10-13..........North Dakota St.
- 10-20..........North Dakota St.
- 10-27..........North Dakota St.
- 11-3..........North Dakota St.
- 11-10..........North Dakota St.
- Final..........North Dakota St.

1987
- 9-15..........South Dakota
- 9-29..........South Dakota
- 10-5..........South Dakota
- 10-19..........Northern Mich.
- 10-26..........Northern Mich.
- 11-8..........Tex. A&M-Kingsville
- Final..........Tex. A&M-Kingsville

1988
- Pre..........Troy St.
- 9-12..........Troy St.
- 9-19..........North Dakota St.
- 9-26..........North Dakota St.
- 10-3..........North Dakota St.
- 10-10..........North Dakota St.
- 10-17..........North Dakota St.
- 10-24..........North Dakota St.
- 10-31..........North Dakota St.
- Final..........North Dakota St.

1989
- Pre..........North Dakota St.
- 9-11..........North Dakota St.
- 9-18..........North Dakota St.
- 9-25..........North Dakota St.
- 10-2..........North Dakota St.
- 10-9..........North Dakota St.
- 10-16..........North Dakota St.
- 10-23..........Tex. A&M-Kingsville
- 10-30..........Tex. A&M-Kingsville
- 11-6..........Tex. A&M-Kingsville

1990
- 9-17..........North Dakota St.
- 9-24..........North Dakota St.
- 10-1..........North Dakota St.
- 10-8..........North Dakota St.
- 10-15..........North Dakota St.
- 10-22..........North Dakota St.
- 10-29..........North Dakota St.
- Final..........North Dakota St.

1991
- Pre..........North Dakota St.
- 9-16..........Indiana (Pa.)
- 9-23..........Indiana (Pa.)
- 9-30..........Indiana (Pa.)
- 10-7..........Indiana (Pa.)
- 10-14..........Indiana (Pa.)
- 10-21..........Indiana (Pa.)
- 10-28..........Indiana (Pa.)
- 11-4..........Indiana (Pa.)
- Final..........Indiana (Pa.)

1992
- Pre..........Pittsburg St.
- 9-14..........Pittsburg St.
- 9-21..........Pittsburg St.
- 9-28..........Pittsburg St.
- 10-5..........Pittsburg St.
- 10-12..........Pittsburg St.
- 10-19..........Pittsburg St.
- 10-26..........Pittsburg St.
- 11-2..........Pittsburg St.
- Final..........Pittsburg St.

1993
- Pre..........North Dakota St.
- 9-20..........North Dakota St.
- 9-27..........North Dakota St.
- 10-4..........North Dakota St.
- 10-11..........North Ala.
- 10-18..........North Ala.
- 10-25..........North Ala.
- 11-1..........North Ala.
- 11-8..........North Ala.
- Final..........North Ala.

1994
- Pre..........North Ala.
- 9-12..........North Ala.
- 9-19..........North Ala.
- 9-26..........North Ala.
- 10-3..........North Ala.
- 10-10..........North Ala.
- 10-17..........North Ala.
- 10-24..........North Ala.
- 10-31..........North Ala.
- Final..........North Ala.

1995
- Pre..........North Ala.
- 9-11..........North Ala.
- 9-18..........North Ala.
- 9-25..........North Ala.
- 10-2..........North Ala.
- 10-9..........North Ala.
- 10-16..........North Ala.
- 10-23..........North Ala.
- 10-30..........North Ala.
- Final..........North Ala.

1996
- Pre..........North Ala.
- 9-9..........Ferris St.
- 9-16..........Ferris St.
- 9-23..........North Dakota St.
- 9-30..........Carson-Newman
- 10-7..........Indiana (Pa.)
- 10-14..........Indiana (Pa.)
- 10-21..........Valdosta St.
- 10-28..........Valdosta St.
- 11-4..........Tex. A&M-Kingsville
- Final..........Tex. A&M-Kingsville

1997
- 9-8..........Northern Colo.
- 9-15..........Carson-Newman
- 9-22..........Carson-Newman
- 9-29..........Carson-Newman
- 10-6..........Carson-Newman
- 10-13..........Carson-Newman
- 10-20..........Carson-Newman
- 10-27..........Carson-Newman
- 11-3..........Carson-Newman
- 11-10..........Carson-Newman
- Final..........Carson-Newman

1998
- Pre..........Northern Colo.
- 9-21..........Northern Colo.
- 9-28..........Northern Colo.
- 10-5..........Northern Colo.
- 10-12..........Northern Colo.
- 10-19..........Northern Colo.
- 10-26..........Central Okla.
- 11-2..........Central Okla.
- Final..........Central Okla.

1999
- Pre..........Northwest Mo. St.
- 9-20..........Carson-Newman
- 9-27..........Carson-Newman
- 10-4..........Carson-Newman
- 10-11..........Carson-Newman
- 10-18..........Carson-Newman
- 10-25..........Carson-Newman
- 11-1..........Carson-Newman
- Final..........Carson-Newman

Undefeated, Untied Teams

(Regular-Season Games Only)

In 1948, official national statistics rankings began to include all nonmajor four-year colleges. Until the 1967 season, rankings and records included all four-year colleges that reported their statistics to the NCAA. Beginning with the 1967 season, statistics (and won-lost records) included only members of the NCAA.

Since 1981, conference playoff games have been included in a team's regular-season statistics and won-lost record (previously, such games were considered postseason contests).

The regular-season list includes games in which a home team served as a predetermined, preseason host of a "bowl game" regardless of its record and games scheduled before the season, thus eliminating postseason designation for the Orange Blossom Classic, annually hosted by Florida A&M, and the Prairie View Bowl, annually hosted by Prairie View, for example.

Figures are regular-season wins only. A subsequent postseason win(s) is indicated by (*), a loss by (†) and a tie by (‡).

UNDEFEATED, UNTIED TEAMS

Year	College	Wins
1948	Alma	8
	Bloomsburg	9
	Denison	8
	Heidelberg	9
	Michigan Tech	7
	Missouri Valley	†‡9
	Occidental	*8
	Southern U.	*11
	Sul Ross St.	‡10
	Wesleyan (Conn.)	8
1949	Ball St.	8
	Emory & Henry	*†10
	Gannon	8
	Hanover	†8
	Lewis	8
	Md.-East. Shore	8
	Morgan St.	8
	Pacific (Cal.)	11
	St. Ambrose	8
	St. Vincent	*9
	Trinity (Conn.)	8
	Wayne St. (Neb.)	9
	Wofford	11
1950	Abilene Christian	*10
	Canterbury	8
	Florida St.	8
	Frank. & Marsh.	9
	Lehigh	9
	Lewis & Clark	*8
	Md.-East. Shore	8
	Mission House	6
	New Hampshire	8
	St. Lawrence	8
	St. Norbert	7
	Thiel	7
	Valparaiso	†9
	West Liberty St.	*8
	Wis.-La Crosse	*9
	Wis.-Whitewater	6
1951	Bloomsburg	8
	Bucknell	9
	Col. of Emporia	8
	Ill. Wesleyan	8
	Lawrence	7
	Northern Ill.	9
	Principia	6
	St. Michael's	6
	South Dakota Tech	8
	Susquehanna	6
	Col. of New Jersey	6
	Valparaiso	9
	Western Md.	8
1952	Beloit	8
	Clarion	*8
	Tex. A&M-Commerce	*10
	Fairmont St.	6
	Idaho St.	8
	Lenoir-Rhyne	†8
	Northeastern St.	†9
	Peru St.	10
	Rochester	8
	St. Norbert	6
	Shippensburg	7
	West Chester	7
1953	Cal Poly	9
	Col. of Emporia	8
	Col. of Idaho	†8
	Defiance	8
	Tex. A&M-Commerce	‡10
	Florida A&M	10
	Indianapolis	8
	Iowa Wesleyan	†9
	Juniata	7
	Northern St.	8
	Martin Luther	6
	Peru St.	8
	Prairie View	10
	St. Olaf	8
	Shippensburg	8
	Westminster (Pa.)	8
	Wis.-La Crosse	‡9
	Wis.-Platteville	6
1954	Ashland	7
	Carleton	8
	Central Conn. St.	6
	Col. of Emporia	†9
	Delta St.	8
	Hastings	*8
	Hobart	8
	Juniata	8
	Luther	9

Year	College	Wins
	Miles	8
	Neb.-Omaha	*9
	Martin Luther	6
	Pomona-Pitzer	8
	Principia	7
	Southeastern La.	9
	Tennessee St.	†10
	Trinity (Conn.)	7
	Trinity (Tex.)	9
	Whitworth	8
	Widener	7
	Worcester Tech	6
1955	Alfred	8
	Centre	8
	Coe	8
	Col. of Emporia	9
	Drexel	8
	Grambling	10
	Heidelberg	9
	Hillsdale	9
	Juniata	‡8
	Md.-East. Shore	9
	Miami (Ohio)	9
	Muskingum	8
	Northern St.	†9
	Parsons	8
	Shepherd	8
	Southeast Mo. St.	9
	Trinity (Conn.)	7
	Whitworth	9
	Wis.-Stevens Point	8
1956	Alfred	7
	Central Mich.	9
	Hillsdale	9
	Lenoir-Rhyne	10
	Milton	6
	Montana St.	‡9
	Neb.-Kearney	9
	Redlands	9
	St. Thomas (Minn.)	8
	Sam Houston St.	*9
	Southern Conn. St.	9
	Tennessee St.	10
	Westminster (Pa.)	8
1957	Elon	6
	Fairmont St.	7
	Florida A&M	9
	Hillsdale	†9
	Hobart	6
	Idaho St.	9
	Jamestown	7
	Juniata	7
	Lock Haven	8
	Middle Tenn. St.	10
	Pittsburg St.	*10
	Ripon	8
	St. Norbert	8
	West Chester	9
1958	Calif. (Pa.)	8
	Chadron St.	8
	Gust. Adolphus	†8
	Missouri Valley	†8
	Neb.-Kearney	9
	Northeastern St.	**9
	Northern Ariz.	*†10
	Rochester	8
	Rose-Hulman	8
	St. Benedict's	†10
	Sewanee	8
	Southern Miss.	9
	Wheaton (Ill.)	8
1959	Bowling Green	9
	Butler	9
	Coe	8
	Fairmont St.	9
	Florida A&M	10
	Hofstra	9
	John Carroll	7
	Lenoir-Rhyne	*†9
	San Fran. St.	10
	Western Ill.	9
1960	Albright	9
	Arkansas Tech	†10
	Humboldt St.	*†10
	Langston	9
	Lenoir-Rhyne	*‡10
	Montclair St.	8
	Muskingum	9
	Northern Iowa	†9
	Ohio	10
	Ottawa	9

Year	College	Wins
	Wagner	9
	West Chester	9
	Whitworth	9
	Willamette	8
1961	Albion	9
	Baldwin-Wallace	9
	Butler	9
	Central Okla.	9
	Florida A&M	10
	Fresno St.	*9
	Linfield	*†10
	Mayville St.	8
	Millikin	9
	Northern St.	9
	Ottawa	9
	Pittsburg St.	**9
	Wash. & Lee	9
	Wheaton (Ill.)	8
	Whittier	†9
1962	Carthage	8
	Central Okla.	**9
	Col. of Emporia	†10
	Earlham	8
	East Stroudsburg	†8
	John Carroll	7
	Kalamazoo	8
	Lenoir-Rhyne	*†10
	Northern St.	†9
	Parsons	9
	St. John's (Minn.)	9
	Susquehanna	9
	Wittenberg	9
1963	Alabama A&M	8
	Central Wash.	9
	Coast Guard	†8
	Col. of Emporia	10
	Delaware	8
	John Carroll	9
	Lewis & Clark	8
	Luther	8
	McNeese St.	8
	Neb.-Kearney	†9
	Northeastern	†8
	Northeastern St.	*10
	Northern Ill.	*9
	Prairie View	*†9
	Ripon	8
	St. John's (Minn.)	**8
	Sewanee	8
	Southwest Mo. St.	†9
	Southwest Tex. St.	10
	Wis.-Eau Claire	7
1964	Albion	8
	Amherst	8
	Cal St. Los Angeles	9
	Concordia-M'head	*‡9
	Frank. & Marsh.	8
	Montclair St.	7
	Prairie View	9
	Wagner	10
	Western St.	†9
	Westminster (Pa.)	8
	Wittenberg	8
1965	Ball St.	*9
	East Stroudsburg	†8
	Fairmont St.	9
	Georgetown (Ky.)	9
	Ill. Wesleyan	8
	Ithaca	8
	Middle Tenn. St.	10
	Morgan St.	9
	North Dakota St.	*10
	Northern Ill.	†9
	Ottawa	9
	St. John's (Minn.)	**9
	Springfield	9
	Sul Ross St.	†10
	Tennessee St.	‡9
1966	Central (Iowa)	†9
	Clarion	*9
	Defiance	9
	Morgan St.	*8
	Muskingum	†9
	Northwestern St.	9
	San Diego St.	*10
	Tennessee St.	*9
	Waynesburg	**9
	Wilkes	8
	Wis.-Whitewater	*†9

UNDEFEATED, UNITED TEAMS

Beginning in 1967, NCAA members only.

Year	College	Wins
1967	Alma	8
	Central (Iowa)	9
	Doane	‡8
	Lawrence	8
	Morgan St.	8
	North Dakota St.	†9
	Northern Mich.	†9
	Wagner	9
	West Chester	*†9
	Wilkes	8
1968	Alma	8
	Doane	*9
	East Stroudsburg	‡8
	Indiana (Pa.)	†9
	North Dakota St.	*9
	Randolph-Macon	9
1969	Albion	8
	Carthage	9
	Defiance	9
	Doane	8
	Montana	†10
	North Dakota St.	*9
	Northern Colo.	10
	Wesleyan (Conn.)	8
	Wittenberg	*9
1970	Arkansas St.	*10
	Jacksonville St.	10
	Montana	†10
	St. Olaf	9
	Tennessee St.	*10
	Westminster (Pa.)	**8
	Wittenberg#	9
1971	Alfred	8
	Hampden-Sydney	†10
	Westminster (Pa.)	†‡8
1972	Ashland	11

Year	College	Wins
	Bridgeport	*10
	Delaware	10
	Doane	†10
	Frank. & Marsh.	9
	Heidelberg	**9
	Louisiana Tech	*11
	Middlebury	8
	Monmouth (Ill.)	9
1973	Tennessee St.	10
	Western Ky.	**†10
1974	Louisiana Tech	*†10
	Michigan Tech	9
	UNLV	*†11
1975	East Stroudsburg	*9
	North Dakota	†9
1976	East Stroudsburg	‡9
1977	UC Davis	*†10
	Florida A&M	11
	Winston-Salem	†11
1978	Western St.	*9
	Winston-Salem	*10
1979	(None)	
1980	Minn.-Duluth	10
	Mo.-Rolla	10
1981	Northern Mich.	*†10
	Shippensburg	*†11
	Virginia Union	†11
1982	UC Davis	**†10
	North Dakota St.	*†11
	Southwest Tex. St.	***†11
1983	UC Davis	**†10
	Central St.	**†10
1984	(None)	
1985	Bloomsburg	*†11
1986	UC Davis	†10
	North Dakota St.	***10
	Virginia Union	†11

Year	College	Wins
1987	(None)	
1988	North Dakota St.	****10
	St. Mary's (Cal.)	10
1989	Grand Valley St.	†11
	Jacksonville St.	***†10
	Pittsburg St.	*†11
	Tex. A&M-Kingsville	†10
1990	North Dakota St.	****10
	Pittsburg St.	**†10
1991	Carson-Newman	†10
	Indiana (Pa.)	**†10
	Jacksonville St.	***†9
1992	New Haven	**†10
	Pittsburg St.	***†11
1993	Albany St. (Ga.)	†11
	Bentley	10
	Hampton	*†11
	Indiana (Pa.)	***†10
	New Haven	*†10
	North Ala.	****10
	Quincy	9
1994	Bentley	*10
	Ferris St.	*†10
	Pittsburg St.	†10
1995	Ferris St.	**†10
	North Ala.	****10
1996	(None)	
1997	Albany St. (Ga.)	*†10
	Carson-Newman	**†9
	Livingstone##	10
	Northwest Mo. St.	*†10
1998	Central Okla.	*†11
	Northwest Mo. St.	****11
1999	Carson-Newman	***†10

#Later forfeited all games. ## Later forfeited two games.

The Spoilers

Compiled since 1973, when the three-division reorganization plan was adopted by the special NCAA Convention. Following is a list of the spoilers of Division II teams that lost their perfect (undefeated, untied) record in their season-ending game, including the Division II championship playoffs. An asterisk (*) indicates an NCAA championship playoff game, a pound sign (#) indicates an NAIA championship playoff game, a dagger (†) indicates the home team in a regular-season game, and (@) indicates a neutral-site game. A game involving two undefeated, untied teams is in **bold** face.

Date	Spoiler	Victim	Score
12-15-73	* Louisiana Tech	Western Ky.	34-0
11-30-74	* Louisiana Tech	Western Caro.	10-7
11-15-75	† C. W. Post	American Int'l	21-0
11-15-75	Eastern N.M.	† Northern Colo.	16-14
11-29-75	* West Ala.	North Dakota	34-14
11-20-76	† Shippensburg	East Stroudsburg	tie 14-14
12-3-77	‡ South Carolina St.	Winston-Salem	10-7
12-3-77	* Lehigh	UC Davis	39-30
12-2-78	* Delaware	Winston-Salem	41-0
11-28-81	* Shippensburg	Virginia Union	40-27
12-5-81	* North Dakota St.	Shippensburg	18-6
12-5-81	* Southwest Tex. St.	Northern Mich.	62-0
12-4-82	* UC Davis	North Dakota St.	19-14
12-11-82	**Southwest Tex. St.**	**UC Davis**	34-9
12-3-83	* North Dakota St.	UC Davis	26-17
12-10-83	* North Dakota St.	Central St.	41-21
12-7-85	* North Ala.	Bloomsburg	34-0
11-15-86	West Chester	† Millersville	7-3
11-29-86	* Troy St.	Virginia Union	31-7
11-29-86	* South Dakota	UC Davis	26-23
12-10-88	# Adams St.	Pittsburg St.	13-10
11-18-89	* Mississippi Col.	Tex. A&M-Kingsville	34-19
11-18-89	* Indiana (Pa.)	Grand Valley St.	34-24
11-25-89	* Angelo St.	Pittsburg St.	24-21
12-9-89	* Mississippi Col.	Jacksonville St.	3-0
12-1-90	* **North Dakota St.**	**Pittsburg St.**	39-29
11-23-91	# Western St.	Carson-Newman	38-21
12-7-91	* **Jacksonville St.**	**Indiana (Pa.)**	27-20
12-14-91	* Pittsburg St.	Jacksonville St.	23-6
11-14-92	@Moorhead St.	Michigan Tech	36-35
12-5-92	* Jacksonville St.	New Haven	46-35
12-12-92	* Jacksonville St.	Pittsburg St.	17-13
11-13-93	@Minn.-Duluth	Wayne St. (Neb.)	29-28
11-20-93	* **Hampton**	**Albany St. (Ga.)**	33-7
11-27-93	* **Indiana (Pa.)**	**New Haven**	38-35
11-27-93	* North Ala.	Hampton	45-20
12-11-93	* North Ala.	Indiana (Pa.)	41-34
11-19-94	* North Dakota St.	Pittsburg St.	(3 ot) 18-12
11-26-94	* Indiana (Pa.)	Ferris St.	21-17
12-2-95	* **North Ala.**	**Ferris St.**	45-7
11-29-97	* Carson-Newman	Albany St. (Ga.)	23-22
11-29-97	* Northern Colo.	Northwest Mo. St.	35-28
12-6-97	* Northern Colo.	Carson-Newman	30-29
11-28-98	* Tex. A&M-Kingsville	Central Okla.	(ot) 24-21
12-11-99	@* Northwest Mo. St.	Carson-Newman	(4 ot) 58-52

‡Gold Bowl.

Streaks and Rivalries

Longest Winning Streaks

(From 1931; Includes Postseason Games)

Wins	Team	Years
34	Hillsdale	1954-57
32	Wilkes	1965-69
31	Morgan St.	1965-68
31	Missouri Valley	1946-48
30	Bentley	1993-95
29	Tex. A&M-Commerce	1951-53
27	Truman	1931-35
25	Pittsburg St.	1991-92
25	San Diego St.	1965-67
25	Peru St.	1951-54
25	Md.-East. Shore	1948-51
24	North Dakota St.	1964-66
24	Wesleyan (Conn.)	1945-48

Longest Unbeaten Streaks

(From 1931; Includes Postseason Games)

No.	Wins	Ties	Team	Years
54	47	7	Morgan St.	1931-38
38	36	2	Doane	1965-70
37	35	2	Southern U.	1947-51
35	34	1	North Dakota St.	1968-71
34	34	0	Hillsdale	1954-57

DIVISION II

No.	Wins	Ties	Team	Years
32	32	0	Wilkes	1965-69
31	31	0	Morgan St.	1965-68
31	31	0	Missouri Valley	1946-48
31	29	2	St. Ambrose	1935-38
30	30	0	Bentley	1993-95
30	29	1	Wittenberg	1961-65
30	29	1	Tex. A&M-Commerce	1951-53
28	27	1	Wesleyan (Conn.)	†1942-48
28	27	1	Case Reserve	1934-37
27	26	1	Pittsburg St.	1991-92
27	26	1	Juniata	1956-59
27	27	0	Truman	1931-35

†Did not field teams in 1943-44.

Most-Played Rivalries

Games	Opponents (Series leader listed first)	Series Record	First Game
106	North Dakota-North Dakota St.	59-44-3	1894
100	South Dakota-South Dakota St.	49-44-7	1889
96	Emporia St.-Washburn	48-42-6	1899
90	South Dakota-Morningside	56-29-5	1898
88	Colorado Mines-Colorado Col.	46-37-5	1889
88	Presbyterian-Newberry	52-31-5	1913
88	Tuskegee-Morehouse	55-25-8	1902
84	North Dakota St.-South Dakota St.	46-34-5	1903
83	Virginia Union-Hampton	41-39-3	1906

Trophy Games

Following is a list of the current Division II football trophy games. The games are listed alphabetically by the trophy-object name. The date refers to the season the trophy was first exchanged and is not necessarily the start of competition between the participants. All games involving a Division II team are listed.

Trophy	Date	Colleges
Axe Bowl	1975	Northwood-Saginaw Valley
Backyard Bowl	1987	Cheyney-West Chester
Battle Axe	1948	Bemidji St.-Moorhead St.
Battle of the Ravine	1976	Henderson St.-Ouachita Baptist
Bishop's	1970	Lenoir-Rhyne—Newberry
Bronze Derby	1946	Newberry-Presbyterian
Chennault Cup	1990	Tex. A&M-Commerce—Tex. A&M-Kingsville
Eagle-Rock	1980	Chadron St.-Black Hills St.
East Meets West	1987	Chadron St.-Peru St.
Elm City	1983	New Haven-Southern Conn. St.
Field Cup	1983	Ky. Wesleyan-Evansville
Governor's	1979	Southern Conn. St.-Central Conn. St.
Great Valley	1998	Shepherd-Shippensburg
Heritage Bell	1979	Delta St.-Mississippi Col.
John Wesley	1984	Ky. Wesleyan-Union (Ky.)
Miner's Bowl	1986	Mo. Southern St.-Pittsburg St.
Nickel	1938	North Dakota-North Dakota St.
Old Hickory Stick	1931	Northwest Mo. St.-Truman
Old Settler's Musket	1975	Adams St.-Fort Lewis
President's Cup	1998	Central Okla.-Northeastern St.
Sitting Bull	1953	North Dakota-South Dakota
Springfield Mayor's	1941	American Int'l-Springfield
Textile	1960	Clark Atlanta-Fort Valley St.
Top Dog	1971	Indianapolis-Butler
Traveling	1976	Ashland-Hillsdale
Traveling	1997	Harding-Ouachita Baptist
Traveling Training Kit	1978	Minn. St.-Mankato–St. Cloud St.
Victory Carriage	1960	UC Davis-Cal St. Sacramento
Wagon Wheel	1986	Eastern N.M.-West Tex. A&M
Wooden Shoes	1977	Grand Valley St.-Wayne St. (Mich.)

Cliffhangers

Regular-season games won by Division II teams on the final play of the game (from 1973). The extra point is listed when it provided the margin of victory after the winning touchdown.

Date	Opponents, Score	Game-Winning Play
9-22-73	South Dakota 9, North Dakota St. 7	Kelly Higgins 5 pass from Mark Jenkins
11-23-74	Arkansas St. 22, McNeese St. 20	Joe Duren 56 FG
10-11-75	Indiana (Pa.) 16, Westminster (Pa.) 14	Tom Alper 37 FG
9-25-76	Portland St. 50, Montana 49	Dave Stief 2 pass from June Jones
10-30-76	South Dakota St. 16, Northern Iowa 13	Monte Mosiman 53 pass from Dick Weikert
10-27-77	Albany (N.Y.) 42, Maine 39	Larry Leibowitz 19 FG
10-6-79	Indiana (Pa.) 31, Shippensburg 24	Jeff Heath 4 run
10-20-79	North Dakota 23, South Dakota 22	Tom Biolo 6 run
9-6-80	Ferris St. 20, St. Joseph's (Ind.) 15	Greg Washington 17 pass from (holder) John Gibson (after bad snap on 34 FG attempt)
11-15-80	Morris Brown 19, Bethune-Cookman 18	Ray Mills 1 run (Carlton Jackson kick)
11-15-80	Tuskegee 23, Alabama A&M 21	Korda Joseph 45 FG
9-26-81	Abilene Christian 41, Northwestern St. 38	David Russell 17 pass from Loyal Proffitt
9-26-81	Cal St. Chico 10, Santa Clara 7	Mike Sullivan 46 FG
10-10-81	C. W. Post 37, James Madison 36	Tom DeBona 10 pass from Tom Ehrhardt (Ehrhardt run)
10-9-82	Grand Valley St. 38, Ferris St. 35	Randy Spangler 20 FG
11-6-82	South Dakota 30, Augustana (S.D.) 28	Kurt Seibel 47 FG
9-17-83	Central Mo. St. 13, Sam Houston St. 10	Steve Huff 27 FG
9-22-84	Clarion 16, Shippensburg 13	Eric Fairbanks 26 FG
9-29-84	Angelo St. 18, Eastern N.M. 17	Ned Cox 3 run
10-13-84	UC Davis 16, Cal St. Chico 13	Ray Sullivan 48 FG
10-13-84	Northwest Mo. St. 35, Central Mo. St. 34	Pat Johnson 20 FG
11-3-84	Bloomsburg 34, West Chester 31	Curtis Still 50 pass from Jay Dedea
9-7-85	UCF 39, Bethune-Cookman 37	Ed O'Brien 55 FG
10-12-85	South Dakota 40, Morningside 38	Scott Jones 2 run
9-13-86	Michigan Tech 34, St. Norbert 30	Jim Wallace 41 pass from Dave Walter
10-18-86	Indianapolis 25, Evansville 24	Ken Bruce 18 FG
10-24-87	Indianapolis 27, Evansville 24	Doug Sabotin 2 pass from Tom Crowell
11-7-87	Central Mo. St. 35, Truman 33	Phil Brandt 25 FG
9-3-88	Alabama A&M 17, North Ala. 16	Edmond Allen 30 FG
9-17-88	Michigan Tech 17, Hope 14	Pete Weiss 22 FG
9-17-89	Morehouse 22, Fort Valley St. 21	David Boone 18 pass from Jimmie Davis
11-11-89	East Stroudsburg 22, Central Conn. St. 19	Frank Magolon 4 pass from Tom Taylor
10-13-90	East Stroudsburg 23, Bloomsburg 21	Ken Kopetchny 3 pass from Bret Comp
11-10-90	Southern Conn. St. 12, Central Conn. St. 10	Paul Boulanger 48 FG
9-21-91	West Ala. 22, Albany St. (Ga.) 21	Matt Carman 24 pass from Deon Timmons (Anthony Armstrong kick)
10-26-91	Central Mo. St. 38, Truman 37	Chris Pyatt 45 FG
10-26-91	Eastern N.M. 17, Tex. A&M-Commerce 14	Jodie Peterson 35 FG
10-9-93	Delta St. 20, Henderson St. 19	Greg Walker 3 run (Stephen Coker kick)

CLIFFHANGERS

Date	Opponents, Score	Game-Winning Play
11-6-93	Henderson St. 46, West Ala. 44	Craig Moses 44 FG
9-24-94	Mo.-Rolla 15, Emporia St. 14	Jason Politte 1 run
9-24-94	St. Cloud St. 18, North Dakota 17	Todd Bouman 1 run
9-16-95	West Va. Wesleyan 16, Kutztown 14	Eric Myers 42 FG
9-30-95	Michigan Tech 37, Saginaw Valley 35	Matt Johnson 46 FG
11-23-96	Northwest Mo. St. 22, Neb.-Omaha 21	Jesse Haynes 17 pass from Greg Teale
9-6-97	Bemidji St. 25, St. John's (Minn.) 21	Ty Houglum 47 pass from Pat O'Connor
11-8-97	Harding 31, Ouachita Baptist 28	Jeremy Thompson 34 FG
10-10-98	Slippery Rock 27, Indiana (Pa.) 21	D. J. Flick 52 pass from Randy McKavish
9-18-99	Central Okla. 37, Angelo St. 34	Evan Luttrell 41 FG

Stadiums

LISTED ALPHABETICALLY

School	Stadium	Year Built	Capacity	Surface
Abilene Christian	Shotwell	1959	15,000	Grass
Adams St.	Rex Field	1949	2,800	Grass
Albany St. (Ga.)	Mills Memorial	1957	11,000	Grass
American Int'l	J.H. Miller Field	1964	5,000	Grass
Angelo St.	San Angelo	1962	17,500	Grass
Ark.-Monticello	Cotton Boll	NA	6,500	Grass
Arkansas Tech	Buerkle Field	1970	6,000	Grass
Ashland	Community	1963	5,700	Grass
Assumption	Rocheleau Field	1961	1,200	Grass
Augustana (S.D.)	Howard Wood	1957	10,000	Grass
Bemidji St.	BSU	1937	4,000	Grass
Bentley	Bentley College	1990	3,200	Grass
Bloomsburg	Redman	1974	5,000	Grass
Bowie St.	Bulldog	1992	6,000	Grass
Bryant	Bulldog	NA	3,000	Grass
C. W. Post	Hickox Field	1966	5,000	Grass
UC Davis	Toomey Field	1949	10,111	Grass
Calif. (Pa.)	Adamson	1970	5,000	Grass
Carson-Newman	Burke-Tarr	1966	5,000	Grass
Catawba	Shuford Field	1926	4,000	Grass
Central Ark.	Estes	1939	8,500	Grass
Central Mo. St.	Audrey J. Walton	1995	10,000	Grass
Central Okla.	Wantland	1965	10,000	Grass
Central Wash.	Tomlinson	NA	4,000	Grass
Chadron St.	Elliott Field	1930	2,500	Grass
Cheyney	O'Shield-Stevenson	NA	3,500	Grass
Clarion	Memorial Field	1965	5,000	Grass
Clark Atlanta	Georgia Dome#	1992	71,000	AstroTurf
Colorado Mines	Brooks Field	1922	5,000	Grass
Concord	Callahan	NA	5,000	Grass
Delta St.	Travis E. Parker Field	1970	8,000	Grass
East Central	Norris Field	NA	5,000	Grass
East Stroudsburg	Eiler-Martin	1969	6,000	Grass
Eastern N.M.	Greyhound	1969	6,500	Grass
Edinboro	Sox Harrison	1965	5,000	Grass
Elizabeth City St.	Roebuck	NA	6,500	Grass
Emporia St.	Welch	1937	7,000	Grass
Fairmont St.	Rosier Field	1929	6,000	Grass
Fayetteville St.	Jeralds Ath. Complex	1993	6,100	Grass
Ferris St.	Top Taggart Field	1957	9,100	Grass
Findlay	Donnell	NA	7,500	Grass
Fort Hays St.	Lewis Field	1936	6,362	Stadia-Turf
Fort Lewis	Ray Dennison Memorial	1958	4,000	Grass
Fort Valley St.	Wildcat	1957	7,500	Grass
Gannon	Erie Veterans Memorial	1958	10,500	AstroTurf
Gardner-Webb	Spangler	1969	5,000	Grass
Glenville St.	Pioneer	1977	5,000	Grass
Grand Valley St.	Arend D. Lubbers	1979	4,146	Grass
Harding	Alumni	1959	4,500	Grass
Henderson St.	Carpenter-Haygood	1968	9,600	Grass
Hillsdale	Frank Waters	1982	8,500	Grass
Humboldt St.	Redwood Bowl	1946	7,000	Grass
Indiana (Pa.)	Miller	1962	6,500	AstroTurf
Indianapolis	Key	1971	5,500	Grass
Johnson Smith	Memorial	1990	26,000	Grass
Kentucky St.	Alumni Field	1978	6,000	Grass
Ky. Wesleyan	Apollo	1989	3,000	Grass
Kutztown	University Field	1987	5,600	Grass
Lane	Rothrock	1930	3,500	Grass
Lenoir-Rhyne	Moretz	1923	8,500	Grass
Livingstone	Alumni	NA	4,000	Grass
Lock Haven	Hubert Jack	NA	3,000	Turf
Mansfield	Van Norman Field	NA	4,000	Grass
Mars Hill	Meares	1965	5,000	Grass
Mass.-Lowell	LeLacheur Park	NA	4,800	Grass
Mercyhurst	Louis J. Tullio Field	1996	2,300	Astro Turf
Merrimack	Merrimack	NA	2,000	Grass
Mesa St.	Stocker	1949	8,000	Grass

School	Stadium	Year Built	Capacity	Surface
Michigan Tech	Sherman Field	1954	3,000	Grass
Midwestern St.	Memorial	NA	14,000	Turf
Miles	Alumni	NA	3,400	Grass
Millersville	Biemesderfer	1970	6,500	Grass
Minn.-Duluth	Griggs Field	1966	4,000	SuperTurf II
Minn.-Morris	UMM Field	NA	5,000	Grass
Minn. St.-Mankato	Blakeslee Field	1962	7,500	Grass
Mo.-Rolla	Jackling Field	1967	8,000	Grass
Mo. Southern St.	Fred G. Hughes	1975	7,000	Turf
Mo. Western St.	Spratt	1979	6,000	Grass
Moorhead St.	Alex Nemzek	1960	5,000	Grass
Morehouse	B. T. Harvey	1983	9,850	Grass
Morningside	Roberts	1939	9,000	Grass
Morris Brown	A. F. Herndon	1996	15,000	Grass
Neb.-Kearney	Foster Field	1929	6,500	Grass
Neb.-Omaha	Al F. Caniglia Field	1949	9,500	AstroTurf
New Haven	Robert B. Dodds	NA	3,500	Grass
N.M. Highlands	Perkins	1941	5,000	Grass
Newberry	Setzler Field	1930	4,000	Grass
North Ala.	Braly Municipal	1940	13,000	PAT
N.C. Central	O'Kelly-Riddick	1975	11,500	Grass
North Dakota	Memorial	1927	10,000	Turf
North Dakota St.	FargoDome#	1992	18,700	AstroTurf
Northeastern St.	Gable Field	NA	12,000	Grass
Northern Colo.	Nottingham Field	1995	7,000	Grass
Northern Mich.	Superior Dome#	1991	8,000	Turf
Northern St.	Swisher	1975	6,000	Grass
Northwest Mo. St.	Rickenbrode	1917	7,500	Grass
Northwood	Louis Juillerat	1964	2,500	Grass
Okla. Panhandle	Carl Wooten	NA	5,000	Grass
Ouachita Baptist	A. U. Williams Field	NA	5,200	Grass
Pace	Finnerty Field	1969	1,500	Grass
Pittsburg St.	Carnie Smith	1924	5,600	Grass
Presbyterian	Bailey Memorial	1928	5,000	Grass
Quincy	QU	1938	2,500	Grass
Saginaw Valley	Harvey R. Wickes	1975	4,028	PAT
St. Anselm	Grappone	1999	4,500	Grass
St. Cloud St.	Selke Field	1937	4,000	Grass
St. Joseph's (Ind.)	Alumni Field	1947	4,000	Grass
Savannah St.	Ted Wright	1967	7,500	Grass
Shepherd	Ram	1959	3,000	Grass
Shippensburg	Grove	1972	7,700	Grass
Slippery Rock	N. Kerr Thompson	1974	10,000	Grass
South Dakota	DakotaDome#	1979	10,000	Monsanto
South Dakota St.	Coughlin-Alumni	1962	16,000	Grass
Southeastern Okla.	Paul Laird Field	NA	4,000	Grass
Southern Ark.	Wilkins	1949	6,000	Grass
Southern Conn. St.	Jess Dow Field	1988	6,000	Balsam
Southwest Baptist	Plaster	1986	2,500	Grass
Southwest St.	Mattke Field	1974	5,000	Grass
Southwestern Okla.	Milam	NA	9,000	Grass
Stonehill	Chieftain	1980	2,000	Grass
Tarleton St.	Memorial	1976	6,784	Grass
Tex. A&M-Commerce	Memorial	1950	10,000	Grass
Tex. A&M-Kingsville	Javelina	1950	15,000	Grass
Texas Lutheran	Matador	1959	9,500	Grass
Truman	Stokes	1962	4,000	Grass
Tusculum	Pioneer Field	1991	3,000	Grass
Tuskegee	Alumni Bowl	1925	10,000	Grass
Valdosta St.	Cleveland Field	1922	11,500	Grass
Virginia St.	Rogers	1950	13,500	Grass
Virginia Union	Hovey Field	NA	10,000	Grass
Washburn	Moore Bowl	1928	7,200	Grass
Wayne St. (Mich.)	Wayne State	1968	6,000	Grass
Wayne St. (Neb.)	Memorial	1931	3,500	Grass
West Ala.	Tiger	1952	7,000	Grass
West Chester	Farrell	1970	7,500	Grass
West Ga.	Grisham	1966	6,500	Grass
West Liberty St.	Russek Field	1960	4,000	Grass
West Tex. A&M	Kimbrough	1959	20,000	Grass
West Va. St.	Lakin Field	1964	5,000	Grass
West Va. Tech	Martin Field	NA	2,500	Turf
West Va. Wesleyan	Cebe Ross Field	1957	3,500	Grass

School	Stadium	Year Built	Capacity	Surface
Western N.M.	Silver Sports Complex	1969	2,000	Grass
Western St.	Mountaineer Bowl	1950	2,400	Grass
Western Wash.	Bellingham Civic	NA	4,500	Grass
Westminster (Pa.)	Memorial Field	NA	4,500	Grass
Wingate	Irwin Belk	NA	3,000	Grass
Winona St.	Maxwell Field	NA	3,500	Grass
Winston-Salem	Bowman-Gray	1940	18,000	Grass

LISTED BY CAPACITY (TOP 16)

School	Stadium	Surface	Capacity
Clark Atlanta	Georgia Dome#	AstroTurf	71,000
Johnson Smith	Memorial	Grass	26,000
West Tex. A&M	Kimbrough	Grass	20,000
North Dakota St.	FargoDome#	AstroTurf	18,700
Winston-Salem	Bowman-Gray	Grass	18,000
Angelo St.	San Angelo	Grass	17,500
South Dakota St.	Coughlin-Alumni	Grass	16,000
Abilene Christian	Shotwell	Grass	15,000
Morris Brown	A. F. Herndon	Turf	15,000
Tex. A&M-Kingsville	Javelina	Grass	15,000
Midwestern St.	Memorial	Turf	14,000
Virginia St.	Rogers	Grass	13,500
North Ala.	Braly Municipal	PAT	13,000
Northeastern St.	Gable Field	Grass	12,000
N.C. Central	O'Kelly Riddick	Grass	11,500
Valdosta St.	Cleveland Field	Grass	11,500

#Indoor facility. PAT=Prescription Athletic Turf.

Statistics Trends

For valid comparisons from 1973, when College Division teams were divided into Division II and Division III.

(Average Per Game, Per Team)

	Rushing			Passing				Total Offense			Scoring		
Year	Plays	Yds.	Avg.	Att.	Cmp.	Pct.	Yds.	Av. Att.	Plays	Yds.	Avg.	TD	FG	Pts.
1973	47.6	169.6	3.57	20.0	8.8	.442	121.5	6.08	67.6	291.1	4.31	2.53	0.42	18.2
1974	47.6	156.3	3.29	19.5	8.7	.445	122.4	6.28	67.1	278.7	4.16	2.55	0.43	19.0
1975	47.3	168.6	3.56	19.5	8.7	.448	120.6	6.21	66.8	289.2	4.33	2.49	0.45	18.6
1976	47.4	165.7	3.50	19.9	9.1	.457	125.9	6.32	67.3	291.6	4.34	2.52	0.47	18.7
1977	*48.4	173.8	3.59	20.3	9.2	.453	126.2	6.21	68.7	300.0	4.37	2.58	0.46	19.1
1978	48.0	169.3	3.52	20.6	9.2	.448	124.3	6.05	68.6	293.6	4.29	2.56	0.49	19.3
1979	45.8	154.7	3.38	21.0	9.5	.450	125.8	6.00	66.8	280.5	4.20	2.37	0.52	17.9
1980	45.3	153.8	3.40	22.4	10.4	.463	137.6	6.16	67.7	291.4	4.31	2.51	0.52	18.9
1981	44.6	146.6	3.29	24.0	11.0	.457	145.9	6.09	68.6	292.5	4.27	2.48	0.54	18.7
1982	43.3	144.1	3.32	26.1	12.3	.469	161.0	6.17	69.4	305.1	4.40	2.63	0.62	19.8
1983	43.2	145.4	3.37	26.1	12.5	.479	164.5	6.31	69.3	309.9	4.48	2.64	0.62	19.6
1984	41.9	142.2	3.39	26.0	12.5	.481	164.8	6.33	67.9	307.0	4.52	2.63	0.62	19.4
1985	41.7	144.0	3.46	27.4	13.2	.483	170.6	6.23	69.1	314.6	4.56	2.73	0.65	20.9
1986	41.8	148.9	3.56	26.9	13.0	.484	168.4	6.27	68.7	317.3	4.62	2.89	0.64	22.0
1987	42.8	151.9	3.55	24.6	11.9	.483	155.5	6.31	67.4	307.4	4.56	2.65	0.64	20.2
1988	43.9	159.4	3.64	24.6	11.9	.484	159.8	6.49	68.5	319.2	4.66	2.92	0.65	22.1
1989	43.7	166.0	3.80	25.1	12.2	.485	161.5	6.45	68.8	327.5	4.77	2.97	0.62	22.6
1990	43.7	168.3	3.86	26.4	12.8	.485	173.3	6.57	70.1	341.6	4.88	3.10	0.63	23.4
1991	43.7	167.8	3.84	26.4	12.8	.484	172.4	6.54	70.1	340.2	4.86	3.05	*0.66	23.2
1992	44.1	167.6	3.80	25.6	12.4	.484	171.4	6.70	69.7	339.0	4.87	3.01	0.65	23.1
1993	42.7	167.3	3.92	*27.4	*13.6	.495	*180.2	6.11	*70.1	347.5	4.96	3.28	0.53	24.0
1994	42.6	*174.5	*4.10	26.3	13.2	.503	178.0	6.79	68.9	*352.5	*5.13	*3.42	0.54	*25.1
1995	41.6	164.0	3.95	26.8	13.4	.501	176.9	6.61	68.4	340.9	4.99	3.22	0.56	23.7
1996	41.9	161.5	3.86	26.0	12.9	.495	173.1	6.65	67.9	334.6	4.93	3.15	0.58	23.4
1997	42.2	167.6	3.97	25.0	12.2	.489	166.3	6.66	67.2	333.9	4.97	3.24	0.58	24.0
1998	41.6	165.9	3.98	25.7	12.8	.499	174.9	*6.81	67.3	340.8	5.06	3.27	0.65	24.5
1999	41.3	165.2	4.00	26.1	13.3	*.511	176.8	6.77	67.4	342.1	5.08	3.29	0.61	24.5

*Record.

Additional Statistics Trends

(Average Per Game, Per Team)

			Punting		PAT Kick Attempts		Two-Point Attempts		Field Goals
Year	Teams†	Games	No.	Avg.	Pct. Made	Pct. of Total Tries	Pct. Made	Pct. of Total Tries	Pct. Made
1973	131	1,326	5.8	36.0	.833	.876	.419	.124	.439
1974	136	1,388	5.7	*36.8	.830	.859	.432	.141	.472
1975	126	1,282	5.5	36.3	.837	.874	.464	.126	.476
1976	122	1,244	5.8	36.2	.841	.878	.419	.122	.461
1977	124	1,267	5.9	36.1	.832	.874	.436	.126	.442
1978	91	921	6.0	35.9	.830	.880	.452	.120	.519
1979	99	1,016	6.1	35.2	.854	.861	.459	.139	.543
1980	103	1,040	5.9	35.6	.852	.864	.438	.136	.512
1981	113	1,138	*6.1	35.6	.856	.861	.440	.139	.531
1982	118	1,196	6.1	36.4	.862	.877	.431	.123	.560
1983	115	1,175	6.0	36.1	.866	.847	.428	.153	.564
1984	112	1,150	5.9	36.4	.876	.875	.448	.125	.567
1985	107	1,098	5.8	35.9	*.905	.864	.414	.136	.549
1986	109	1,124	5.6	36.5	.870	.865	.466	.135	*.576
1987	105	1,100	5.7	35.7	.857	.865	.435	.135	.547
1988	111	1,114	5.6	35.6	.886	.868	.399	.132	.555
1989	106	1,084	5.5	36.7	.873	.845	.376	.155	.567
1990	105	1,065	5.7	35.7	.876	*.885	*.474	.115	.568
1991	114	1,150	5.5	36.1	.882	.880	.426	.120	.572
1992	115	1,145	5.5	35.9	.888	.870	.442	.130	.575
1993	136	1,354	5.3	35.2	.839	.853	.438	.147	.528
1994	128	1,325	5.1	36.0	.850	.840	.439	.160	.559

STATISTICS TRENDS—ADDITIONAL STATISTICS TRENDS

			Punting		PAT Kick Attempts		Two-Point Attempts		Field Goals
Year	Teams†	Games	No.	Avg.	Pct. Made	Pct. of Total Tries	Pct. Made	Pct. of Total Tries	Pct. Made
1995	131	1,362	5.3	34.9	.835	.837	.473	*.163	.552
1996	137	1,434	5.5	35.6	.837	.846	.473	.154	.560
1997	129	1,357	5.4	36.2	.841	.879	.425	.121	.561
1998	134	1,412	5.4	36.7	.862	.877	.387	.123	.575
1999	147	1,550	5.4	36.4	.859	.883	.419	.117	.571

*Record. †Teams reporting statistics, not the total number of teams in the division.

Classification History (1973-00)

The following lists show years of active membership for current and former Division II football-playing institutions. Provisional members also are shown, along with the year in which they will become active members.

ACTIVE MEMBERS (148)

Abilene Christian 1981-00
Adams St. 1983, 90-00
Albany St. (Ga.) 1976-00
American Int'l 1974-00
Angelo St. 1981-00

Ark.-Monticello 1997-00
Arkansas Tech 1997-00
Ashland 1980-00
Assumption 1993-00
Augustana (S.D.) 1973-00

Bemidji St. 1979-00
Bentley 1993-00
Bloomsburg 1980-00
Bowie St. 1980-00
Bryant 1999-00

C. W. Post 1973, 78-84, 93-00
UC Davis 1973-00
Calif. (Pa.) 1973-00
Carson-Newman 1991-00
Catawba 1991-00

Central Ark. 1992-00
Central Mo. St. 1973-00
Central Okla. 1976-78, 88-00
Central Wash. 1973-75, 82-83, 98-00
Chadron St. 1990-00

Cheyney 1980-00
Clarion 1973-00
Clark Atlanta 1980-00
Colorado Mines 1974-00
Concord 1993-00

Delta St. 1973-00
East Central 1998-00
East Stroudsburg 1973-00
Eastern N.M. 1985-00
Edinboro 1973-00

Elizabeth City St. 1973-00
Emporia St. 1990-00
Fairmont St. 1978-79, 93-00
Fayetteville St. 1973-00
Ferris St. 1977-00

Findlay 2000
Fort Hays St. 1988-00
Fort Lewis 1973-84, 90-00
Fort Valley St. 1981-00
Gannon 1993-00

Gardner-Webb 1991-00
Glenville St. 1993-00
Grand Valley St. 1976-00
Harding 1997-00
Henderson St. 1992-00

Hillsdale 1976-78, 84-00
Humboldt St. 1973, 80-00
Indiana (Pa.) 1973-00
Indianapolis 1976-00
Johnson Smith 1973-00

Kentucky St. 1973-00
Ky. Wesleyan 1993-00
Kutztown 1980-00
Lane 1993-00
Lenoir-Rhyne 1989-00

Livingstone 1973-00
Lock Haven 1980-00
Mansfield 1980-00

Mars Hill 1991-00
Mass.-Lowell 1993-00

Mercyhurst 1993-00
Merrimack 1996-00
Mesa St. 1982-83, 90-00
Michigan Tech 1973-00
Midwestern St. 1997-00

Miles 1988-00
Millersville 1980-00
Minn.-Duluth 1973-00
Minn.-Morris 1993-00
Minn. St.-Mankato 1973-76, 78-00

Mo.-Rolla 1973-00
Mo. Southern St. 1988-00
Mo. Western St. 1988-00
Moorhead St. 1973-82, 93-00
Morehouse 1981-00

Morningside 1973-00
Morris Brown 1973-00
Neb.-Kearney 1988-00
Neb.-Omaha 1973-00
New Haven 1975-76, 81-00

N.M. Highlands 1982-84, 91-00
Newberry 1990-00
North Ala. 1973-00
N.C. Central 1973-00
North Dakota 1973-00

North Dakota St. 1973-00
Northeastern St. 1998-00
Northern Colo. 1973-00
Northern Mich. 1973-00
Northern St. 1980-81, 93-00

Northwest Mo. St. 1973-00
Northwood 1981-87, 92-00
Okla. Panhandle 1999-00
Ouachita Baptist 1997-00
Pace 1993-00

Pittsburg St. 1988-00
Presbyterian 1991-00
Quincy 1993-94, 96-00
Saginaw Valley 1981-00
St. Anselm 1999-00

St. Cloud St. 1973-00
St. Joseph's (Ind.) 1979-00
Savannah St. 1981-00
Shepherd 1990-00
Shippensburg 1976-00

Slippery Rock 1979-00
South Dakota 1973-00
South Dakota St. 1973-00
Southeastern Okla. 1998-00
Southern Ark. 1997-00

Southern Conn. St. 1973-00
Southwest Baptist 1986-00
Southwest St. 1978-83, 93-00
Southwestern Okla. 1998-00
Stonehill 1993-00

Tarleton St. 1994-00
Tex. A&M-Commerce 1981-00
Tex. A&M-Kingsville 1980-00
Texas Lutheran 1983, 98-00
Truman 1973-00

Tusculum 1998-00

Tuskegee 1973-00
Valdosta St. 1982-00
Virginia St. 1973-00
Virginia Union 1973-00

Washburn 1988-00
Wayne St. (Mich.) 1973-00
Wayne St. (Neb.) 1988-00
West Ala. 1974-00
West Chester 1973-00

West Ga. 1983-00
West Liberty St. 1991-00
West Tex. A&M 1986-90, 92-00
West Virginia St. 1997-00
West Va. Tech 1993-00

West Va. Wesleyan 1973-80, 93-00
Western N.M. 1983, 94-00
Western St. 1973-78, 82-85, 90-00

Western Wash. 1998-00
Westminster (Pa.) 1998-00

Wingate 1991-00
Winona St. 1978-00
Winston-Salem 1973-00

PROVISIONAL MEMBERS (7)*

Benedict 2002
Concordia-St. Paul 2002
Minn.-Crookston 2002
North Greenville 2003
Tiffin 2002

Va.-Wise 2003
Western Ore. 2002

FORMER MEMBERS (127)

Akron 1973-79
Alabama A&M 1973-98
Alabama St. 1973-81
Albany (N.Y.) 1995-98
Alcorn St. 1973-76

Ark.-Pine Bluff 1973-82
Arkansas St. 1973-74
Austin Peay 1973-74
Ball St. 1973-74
Bethune-Cookman 1973-79

Boise St. 1973-77
Boston U. 1973-77
Bucknell 1973-77
Butler 1973-92
UC Riverside 1973-75

UC Santa Barb. 1991
Cal Lutheran 1985-90
Cal Poly 1973-93
Cal Poly Pomona 1973-82
Cal St. Chico 1978-96

Cal St. Fullerton 1973-74
Cal St. Hayward 1973-93
Cal St. Los Angeles 1973-74
Cal St. Northridge 1973-92
Cal St. Sacramento 1973-92

Cameron 1988-92
Central Conn. St. 1973-92
UCF 1982-89
Central Mich. 1973-74
Central St. 1973-87

DIVISION II

School	Years
Chattanooga	1973-76
Connecticut	1973-77
Davidson	1977
Delaware	1973-79
Dist. Columbia	1973-75
East Tenn. St.	1973-77
Eastern Ill.	1973-80
Eastern Ky.	1973-77
Eastern Mich.	1973-75
Eastern Wash.	1978-83
Elon	1991-98
Evansville	1978-88
Florida A&M	1973-77
Franklin	1979-85
Georgetown (Ky.)	1980-82
Grambling	1973-76
Hampton	1973-94
Hardin-Simmons	1993
Howard	1973-77
Howard Payne	1981-86
Idaho St.	1973-77
Illinois St.	1973-75
Indiana St.	1973-75
Jackson St.	1973-76
Jacksonville St.	1973-94
James Madison	1974-76
Jamestown	1982-83
Knoxville	1989
Lafayette	1973-77
Lehigh	1973-77
Liberty	1981-87
La.-Monroe	1973-74
Louisiana Tech	1973-74
Maine	1973-77
Md.-East. Shore	1973-79
Massachusetts	1973-77
McNeese St.	1973-74
Merchant Marine	1978-81
Middle Tenn. St.	1973-77
Mississippi Col.	1973-96
Mississippi Val.	1973-79
Montana	1973-77
Montana St.	1973-77
Morehead St.	1973-77
Morgan St.	1973-85
Murray St.	1973-77
Nevada	1973-77
UNLV	1973-77
New Hampshire	1973-77
New York Tech	1974-83
Nicholls St.	1973-79
Norfolk St.	1973-96
N.C. A&T	1973-77
Northeastern	1973-77
Northern Ariz.	1973-77
Northern Iowa	1973-80
Northwestern St.	1973-75
Portland St.	1973-77, 81-97
Prairie View	1973-79
Puget Sound	1973-88
Rhode Island	1973-77
St. Francis (Ill.)	1993-98
St. Mary's (Cal.)	1981-92
St. Paul's	1973-87
Sam Houston St.	1981-85
San Fran. St.	1979-94
Santa Clara	1973-92
Sacred Heart	1993-98
Sonoma St.	1984-96
South Carolina St.	1973-77
Southeast Mo. St.	1973-90
Southeastern La.	1973-79
Southern U.	1973-76
Southern Ore.	1981-83
Southern Utah	1982-92
Southwest Mo. St.	1973-81
Southwest Tex. St.	1978-83
Springfield	1973-94
Stephen F. Austin	1981-85
Stony Brook	1995-98
Tenn.-Martin	1973-91
Tennessee St.	1973-76
Tennessee Tech	1973-77
Texas Southern	1973-76
Towson	1980-86
Troy St.	1973-92
Valparaiso	1979-92
Vermont	1973-74
Weber St.	1973-77
Western Caro.	1973-76
Western Ill.	1973-80
Western Ky.	1973-77
Wis.-Milwaukee	1973-74
Wis.-La Crosse	1975
Wis.-Oshkosh	1973-74
Wofford	1988-94
Youngstown St.	1973-80

* Provisional members are not active members of the Association and are not eligible for NCAA statistics, records and championship play. The end of the four-year provisional status and first season of active membership in Division II football is listed to the right of the school name.

Division III Records

Individual Records	184
Team Records	188
Annual Champions, All-Time Leaders	190
Team Champions	204
All-Time Team Won-Lost Records	205
Winningest Football Teams of 1990s	207
National Poll Rankings	207
Undefeated, Untied Teams	208
Streaks and Rivalries	210
Trophy Games	210
Cliffhangers	210
Division III Stadiums	212
Statistics Trends	213

Individual Records

Division III football records are based on the performances of Division III teams since the three-division reorganization plan was adopted by the special NCAA Convention in August 1973.

Total Offense

(Rushing Plus Passing)

MOST PLAYS
Quarter
  37—Justin Peery, Westminster (Mo.) vs. MacMurray, Nov. 14, 1998 (4th)
Half
  59—Justin Peery, Westminster (Mo.) vs. Bethel (Tenn.), Nov. 8, 1997 (2nd); Mike Wallace, Ohio Wesleyan vs. Denison, Oct. 3, 1981 (2nd)
Game
  98—Justin Peery, Westminster (Mo.) vs. MacMurray, Nov. 14, 1998 (21 rushes, 77 passes; 628 yards)
Season
  645—Justin Peery, Westminster (Mo.), 1998 (4,651 yards)
  Per-game record—64.9, Jordan Poznick, Principia, 1992 (519 in 8)
Career
  2,007—Kirk Baumgartner, Wis.-Stevens Point, 1986-89 (12,767 yards)
  Per-game record—51.3, Justin Peery, Westminster (Mo.), 1996-99 (2,001 in 39)

MOST PLAYS BY A FRESHMAN
Season
  491—Mark Novara, Lakeland, 1994 (2,572 yards)
  Also holds per-game record with 54.6 (491 in 9)

MOST YARDS GAINED
Half
  517—Justin Peery, Westminster (Mo.) vs. Bethel (Tenn.), Nov. 8, 1997 (497 passing, 20 rushing)
Game
  630—Justin Peery, Westminster (Mo.) vs. Colorado Col., Oct. 30, 1999 (79 rushing, 551 passing)
Season
  4,651—Justin Peery, Westminster (Mo.), 1998 (150 rushing, 4,501 passing)
  Also holds per-game record with 465.1 (4,651 in 10)
Career
  13,645—Justin Peery, Westminster (Mo.), 1996-99 (383 rushing, 13,262 passing)
  Also holds per-game record with 349.9 (13,645 in 39)

MOST YARDS GAINED BY A FRESHMAN
Season
  2,780—Jake Knott, Wabash, 1999 (485 plays)
  Per-game record—285.8, Mark Novara, Lakeland, 1994 (2,572 in 9)

MOST GAMES GAINING 300 YARDS OR MORE
Season
  9—Justin Peery, Westminster (Mo.), 1999
Career
  26—Kirk Baumgartner, Wis.-Stevens Point, 1986-89

MOST CONSECUTIVE GAMES GAINING 300 YARDS OR MORE
Season
  8—Danny Ragsdale, Redlands, 1999

GAINING 4,000 YARDS RUSHING AND 2,000 YARDS PASSING
Career
  Chris Spriggs, Denison, 1983-86 (4,248 rushing & 2,799 passing)
  Also holds record for yards gained by a running back with 7,047

GAINING 3,000 YARDS RUSHING AND 3,000 YARDS PASSING
Career
  Clay Sampson (TB), Denison, 1977-80 (3,726 rushing & 3,194 passing)

HIGHEST AVERAGE GAIN PER PLAY
Season
  (Min. 2,500 yards) 12.4—Adam Ryan, Wilmington (Ohio), 1999 (280 for 3,478)

Career
  (Min. 6,000 yards) 8.4—Bill Borchert, Mount Union, 1994-97 (1,274 for 10,639)

MOST TOUCHDOWNS RESPONSIBLE FOR
(TDs Scored and Passed For)
Career
  166—Justin Peery, Westminster (Mo.), 1996-99 (148 passing, 18 rushing)
  Also holds per-game record with 4.3 (166 in 39)

Rushing

MOST RUSHES
Game
  58—Bill Kaiser, Wabash vs. DePauw, Nov. 9, 1985 (211 yards)
Season
  380—Mike Birosak, Dickinson, 1989 (1,798 yards)
  Also holds per-game record with 38.0 (380 in 10)
Career
  1,190—Steve Tardif, Maine Maritime, 1996-99 (6,093 yards)
  Per-game record—32.7, Chris Sizemore, Bridgewater (Va.), 1972-74 (851 in 26)

MOST RUSHES BY A QUARTERBACK
Season
  231—Jeff Saueressig, Wis.-River Falls, 1988 (1,095 yards)
  Also holds per-game record with 25.7 (231 in 9)

MOST CONSECUTIVE RUSHES BY THE SAME PLAYER
Game
  46—Dan Walsh, Montclair St. vs. Ramapo, Sept. 30, 1989 (during 13 possessions)
Season
  51—Dan Walsh, Montclair St., 1989 (Sept. 23 to Sept. 30)

MOST YARDS GAINED
Half
  310—Leroy Horn, Montclair St. vs. New Jersey City, Nov. 9, 1985 (21 rushes)
Game
  441—Dante Brown, Marietta vs. Baldwin-Wallace, Oct. 5, 1996
Season
  2,385—Dante Brown, Marietta, 1996 (314 rushes)
  Also holds per-game record with 238.5 (2,385 in 10)
Career
  6,125—Carey Bender, Coe, 1991-94 (926 rushes)
  Per-game record—175.1, Ricky Gales, Simpson, 1988-89 (3,326 in 19)

MOST YARDS GAINED BY A FRESHMAN
Season
  1,380—Fredrick Nanhed, Cal Lutheran, 1995 (242 rushes)
  Also holds per-game record with 153.3 (1,380 in 9)

MOST RUSHING YARDS GAINED BY A QUARTERBACK
Game
  235—Mark Cota, Wis.-River Falls vs. Minn.-Morris, Sept. 13, 1986 (27 rushes)
Season
  1,279—Mark Cota, Wis.-River Falls, 1986 (227 rushes)
  Also holds per-game record with 127.9 (1,279 in 10)
Career
  3,315—Eric Hyten, Rose-Hulman, 1996-99 (796 rushes)

LONGEST GAIN BY A QUARTERBACK
Game
  98 yards—Jon Hinds, Principia vs. Illinois Col., Sept. 20, 1986 (TD)

MOST GAMES GAINING 100 YARDS OR MORE
Career
  31—Steve Tardif, Maine Maritime, 1996-99 (39 games)

MOST CONSECUTIVE GAMES GAINING 100 YARDS OR MORE
Career
  19—Brandon Steinheim, Wesley, Sept. 9, 1995-Nov. 16, 1996

MOST GAMES GAINING 200 YARDS OR MORE
Season
  8—Ricky Gales, Simpson, 1989 (consecutive)
Career
  11—Ricky Gales, Simpson, 1988-89; Rob Marchitello, Maine Maritime, 1993-95

MOST SEASONS GAINING 1,000 YARDS OR MORE
Career
  4—Rich Kowalski, Hobart, 1972-75; Joe Dudek, Plymouth St., 1982-85; Jim Romagna, Loras, 1989-92; Steve Dixon, Beloit, 1990-93; Carey Bender, Coe, 1991-94; Steve Tardif, Maine Maritime, 1996-99

TWO PLAYERS, SAME TEAM, EACH GAINING 1,000 YARDS OR MORE
Season
  By 11 teams. Most recent: Grove City, 1997—Doug Steiner (RB) 1,490 & R. J. Bowers (RB) 1,239

MOST YARDS GAINED RUSHING BY TWO PLAYERS, SAME TEAM
Game
  519—Carey Bender (417) & Jason Whitaker (102), Coe vs. Grinnell, Oct. 9, 1993
Season
  2,738—Dante Brown (RB) 2,385 & Aaron Conte (QB) 353, Marietta, 1996 (10 games)

HIGHEST AVERAGE GAIN PER RUSH
Game
  (Min. 15 rushes) 19.1—Billy Johnson, Widener vs. Swarthmore, Nov. 10, 1973 (15 for 286)
  (Min. 24 rushes) 15.9—Pete Baranek, Carthage vs. North Central, Oct. 5, 1985 (24 for 382)
Season
  (Min. 140 rushes) 8.9—Billy Johnson, Widener, 1973 (168 for 1,494)
  (Min. 200 rushes) 7.9—Jamie Lee, MacMurray, 1997 (207 for 1,639)
  (Min. 250 rushes) 7.6—Carey Bender, Coe, 1994 (295 for 2,243)
Career
  (Min. 500 rushes) 7.1—Joe Dudek, Plymouth St., 1982-85 (785 for 5,570)

MOST TOUCHDOWNS SCORED BY RUSHING
Game
  8—Carey Bender, Coe vs. Beloit, Nov. 12, 1994
Season
  34—R. J. Bowers, Grove City, 1998
  Also holds per-game record with 3.4 (34 in 10)
Career
  76—Joe Dudek, Plymouth St., 1982-85
  Also holds per-game record with 1.9 (76 in 41)

MOST RUSHING TOUCHDOWNS SCORED BY A QUARTERBACK
Season
  17—Mark Reed, Monmouth (Ill.), 1987
  Also holds per-game record with 1.7 (17 in 10)

Passing

HIGHEST PASSING EFFICIENCY RATING POINTS
Season
  (Min. 15 atts. per game) 225.0—Mike Simpson, Eureka, 1994 (158 attempts, 116 completions, 5 interceptions, 1,988 yards, 25 TDs)
  (Min. 25 atts. per game) 216.7—Bill Borchert, Mount Union, 1997 (272 attempts, 190 completions, 1 interception, 2,933 yards, 47 TDs)
Career
  (Min. 650 comps.) 194.2—Bill Borchert, Mount Union, 1994-97 (1,009 attempts, 671 completions, 17 interceptions, 10,201 yards, 141 TDs)

MOST PASSES ATTEMPTED
Quarter
  31—Mike Wallace, Ohio Wesleyan vs. Denison, Oct. 3, 1981 (4th)

INDIVIDUAL RECORDS—PASSING

Half
57—Mike Wallace, Ohio Wesleyan vs. Denison, Oct. 3, 1981 (2nd); Justin Peery, Westminster (Mo.) vs. Bethel (Tenn.), Nov. 8, 1997 (2nd)

Game
81—Jordan Poznick, Principia vs. Blackburn, Oct. 10, 1992 (completed 48)

Season
527—Kirk Baumgartner, Wis.-Stevens Point, 1988 (completed 276)
Per-game record—56.4, Jordan Poznick, Principia, 1992 (451 in 8)

Career
1,696—Kirk Baumgartner, Wis.-Stevens Point, 1986-89 (completed 883)
Per-game record—42.8, Justin Peery, Westminster (Mo.), 1996-99 (1,669 in 39)

MOST PASSES ATTEMPTED BY A FRESHMAN
Season
453—Mark Novara, Lakeland, 1994 (completed 227)
Also holds per-game record with 50.3 (453 in 9)

MOST PASSES COMPLETED
Quarter
21—Rob Bristow, Pomona-Pitzer vs. Whittier, Oct. 19, 1985 (4th)

Half
36—Mike Wallace, Ohio Wesleyan vs. Denison, Oct. 3, 1981 (2nd)

Game
50—Tim Lynch, Hofstra vs. Fordham, Oct. 19, 1991 (attempted 69); Justin Peery, Westminster (Mo.) vs. MacMurray, Nov. 14, 1998 (attempted 77)

Season
329—Justin Peery, Westminster (Mo.), 1999 (attempted 498)
Also holds per-game record with 32.9 (329 in 10)

Career
1,012—Justin Peery, Westminster (Mo.), 1996-99 (attempted 1,669)
Also holds per-game record with 25.9 (1,012 in 39)

MOST PASSES COMPLETED BY A FRESHMAN
Season
227—Mark Novara, Lakeland, 1994 (attempted 453)
Also holds per-game record with 25.2 (227 in 9)

HIGHEST PERCENTAGE OF PASSES COMPLETED
Game
(Min. 20 comps.) 91.3%—Chris Esterley, St. Thomas (Minn.) vs. St. Olaf, Sept. 23, 1995 (21 of 23)
(Min. 35 comps.) 83.3%—Scott Driggers, Colorado Col. vs. Neb. Wesleyan, Sept. 10, 1983 (35 of 42)

Season
(Min. 250 atts.) 72.9%—Jim Ballard, Mount Union, 1993 (229 of 314)

Career
(Min. 750 atts.) 66.5%—Bill Borchert, Mount Union, 1994-97 (671 of 1,009)

MOST CONSECUTIVE PASSES COMPLETED
Game
17—William Snyder, Carnegie Mellon vs. Wooster, Oct. 20, 1990; Jim Ballard, Mount Union vs. Ill. Wesleyan, Nov. 28, 1992

Season
25—Ty Grovesteen, Wis.-Whitewater, 1997 (1 vs. Wis.-Oshkosh, Oct. 11; 9 vs. Wis.-Stout, Oct. 18; 15 vs. Wis.-Platteville, Oct. 25)

MOST CONSECUTIVE PASSES COMPLETED BY TWO PLAYERS, SAME TEAM
Game
20—Kevin Keefe (16) & David Skarupa (4), Baldwin-Wallace vs. Moravian, Sept. 10, 1994

MOST PASSES HAD INTERCEPTED
Game
8—Kevin Karwath, Canisius vs. Liberty, Nov. 19, 1979; Dennis Bogacz, Wis.-Oshkosh vs. Wis.-Stevens Point, Oct. 29, 1988; Jim Higgins, Brockport St. vs. Buffalo St., Sept. 29, 1990; Jason Clark, Ohio Northern vs. John Carroll, Nov. 9, 1991

Season
43—Steve Hendry, Wis.-Superior, 1982 (attempted 480)
Also holds per-game record with 3.9 (43 in 11)

Career
117—Steve Hendry, Wis.-Superior, 1980-83 (attempted 1,343)
Per-game record—3.2, Willie Martinez, Oberlin, 1973-74 (58 in 18)

LOWEST PERCENTAGE OF PASSES HAD INTERCEPTED
Season
(Min. 150 atts.) 0.4%—Bill Borchert, Mount Union, 1997 (1 of 272)

Career
(Min. 600 atts.) 1.7%—Bill Borchert, Mount Union 1994-97 (17 of 1,009)

MOST PASSES ATTEMPTED WITHOUT INTERCEPTION
Game
77—Justin Peery, Westminster (Mo.) vs. MacMurray, Nov. 14, 1998 (completed 50)

Season
124—Tim Tenhet, Sewanee, 1982

MOST CONSECUTIVE PASSES ATTEMPTED WITHOUT AN INTERCEPTION
Season
221—Bill Borchert, Mount Union, 1997 (during 8 games; began Sept. 27 vs. Otterbein, ended Nov. 15 vs. Hiram)

MOST YARDS GAINED
Half
497—Justin Peery, Westminster (Mo.) vs. Bethel (Tenn.), Nov. 8, 1997 (2nd)

Game
619—Justin Perry, Westminster (Mo.) vs. MacMurray, Nov. 14, 1998

Season
4,501—Justin Peery, Westminster (Mo.), 1998
Also holds per-game record with 450.1 (4,501 in 10)

Career
13,262—Justin Peery, Westminster (Mo.), 1996-99
Also holds per-game record with 340.1 (13,262 in 39)

MOST YARDS GAINED BY A FRESHMAN
Season
2,612—Jake Knott, Wabash, 1999 (10 games)
Per-game record—286.2, Mark Novara, Lakeland, 1994 (2,576 in 9)

MOST GAMES PASSING FOR 200 YARDS OR MORE
Season
10—Kirk Baumgartner, Wis.-Stevens Point, 1989, 1988, 1987; Troy Dougherty, Grinnell, 1998; Justin Peery, Westminster (Mo.), 1998, 1999

Career
32—Kirk Baumgartner, Wis.-Stevens Point, 1986-89; Justin Peery, Westminster (Mo.), 1996-99

MOST CONSECUTIVE GAMES PASSING FOR 200 YARDS OR MORE
Season
10—Kirk Baumgartner, Wis.-Stevens Point, 1989 (entire season); Troy Dougherty, Grinnell, 1998 (entire season); Justin Peery, Westminster (Mo.), 1998 (entire season); Justin Peery, Westminster (Mo.), 1999 (entire season)

Career
27—Keith Bishop, Ill. Wesleyan/Wheaton (Ill.), 1981, 1983-85

MOST GAMES PASSING FOR 300 YARDS OR MORE
Season
9—Kirk Baumgartner, Wis.-Stevens Point, 1989; Justin Peery, Westminster (Mo.), 1999

Career
24—Kirk Baumgartner, Wis.-Stevens Point, 1986-89

MOST CONSECUTIVE GAMES PASSING FOR 300 YARDS OR MORE
Season
9—Kirk Baumgartner, Wis.-Stevens Point, 1989 (began Sept. 9 vs. St. Norbert, through Nov. 4 vs. Wis.-Superior)

Career
13—Kirk Baumgartner, Wis.-Stevens Point, 1988-89 (began Oct. 22, 1988, vs. Wis.-Stout, through Nov. 4, 1989, vs. Wis.-Superior)

MOST YARDS GAINED BY TWO OPPOSING PLAYERS
Game
1,020—Josh Wakefield, Alma (569) & Travis McMahen, Franklin (451), Sept. 25, 1999 (completed 60 of 109)

MOST YARDS GAINED PER ATTEMPT
Season
(Min. 175 atts.) 12.9—Willie Seiler, St. John's (Minn.), 1993 (205 for 2,648)
(Min. 275 atts.) 11.3—Troy Dougherty, Grinnell, 1998 (293 for 3,310)

Career
(Min. 950 atts.) 10.1—Bill Borchert, Mount Union, 1994-97 (1,009 for 10,201)

MOST YARDS GAINED PER COMPLETION
Season
(Min. 100 comps.) 19.7—David Parker, Bishop, 1981 (114 for 2,242)
(Min. 200 comps.) 16.1—John Furmaniak, Eureka, 1995 (210 for 3,372)

Career
(Min. 300 comps.) 18.3—David Parker, Bishop, 1981-84 (378 for 6,934)
(Min. 425 comps.) 15.2—Bill Borchert, Mount Union, 1994-97 (671 for 10,201)

MOST TOUCHDOWN PASSES
Quarter
5—David Sullivan, Williams vs. Hamilton, Oct. 30, 1993 (2nd)

Game
9—Joe Zarlinga, Ohio Northern vs. Capital, Nov. 14, 1998

Season
54—Justin Peery, Westminster (Mo.), 1999
Also holds per-game record with 5.4 (54 in 10)

Career
148—Justin Peery, Westminster (Mo.), 1996-99
Also holds per-game record with 3.8 (148 in 39)

HIGHEST PERCENTAGE OF PASSES FOR TOUCHDOWNS
Season
(Min. 200 atts.) 17.3%—Bill Borchert, Mount Union, 1997 (47 of 272)
(Min. 300 atts.) 11.8%—Jim Ballard, Mount Union, 1993 (37 of 314)

Career
(Min. 800 atts.) 14.0%—Bill Borchert, Mount Union, 1994-97 (141 of 1,009)

MOST TOUCHDOWN PASSES BY A FRESHMAN
Season
26—Bill Borchert, Mount Union, 1994
Also holds per-game record with 2.6 (26 in 10)

MOST CONSECUTIVE GAMES THROWING A TOUCHDOWN PASS
Career
40—Bill Borchert, Mount Union (from Sept. 10, 1994, through Nov. 15, 1997)

Receiving

MOST PASSES CAUGHT
Game
23—Sean Munroe, Mass.-Boston vs. Mass. Maritime, Oct. 10, 1992 (332 yards)

Season
136—Scott Pingel, Westminster (Mo.), 1999 (1,648 yards)
Also holds per-game record with 13.6 (136 in 10)

Career
436—Scott Pingel, Westminster (Mo.), 1996-99 (6,108 yards)
Also holds per-game record with 11.2 (436 in 39)

MOST PASSES CAUGHT BY A TIGHT END
Game
17—Matt Surette, Worcester Tech vs. Springfield, Oct. 25, 1997

Season
75—Ryan Davis, St. Thomas (Minn.), 1994 (1,164 yards); Matt Surette, Worcester Tech, 1997 (1,287 yards)

Career
185—Hanz Hoag, Evansville, 1991-93 (2,173 yards)

MOST PASSES CAUGHT BY A RUNNING BACK
Game
17—Tim Mowery, Wis.-Superior vs. Wis.-Stevens Point, Oct. 17, 1981 (154 yards); Theo Blanco, Wis.-Stevens Point vs. Wis.-Oshkosh, Oct. 31, 1987 (271 yards)
Season
106—Theo Blanco, Wis.-Stevens Point, 1987 (1,616 yards)
Career
169—Mike Christman, Wis.-Stevens Point, 1983-86 (2,190 yards)

MOST PASSES CAUGHT BY A FRESHMAN
Season
92—Darryl DeShields, Greenville, 1999 (1,515 yards)

MOST PASSES CAUGHT BY TWO PLAYERS, SAME TEAM
Season
203—Scott Pingel (WR) 130 & Logan Stanley (TE) 73, Westminster (Mo.), 1998 (3,168 yards, 33 TDs)

MOST PASSES CAUGHT BY THREE PLAYERS, SAME TEAM
Season
270—Scott Pingel (WR) 130, Logan Stanley (TE) 73 & John Squires (WR) 67, Westminster (Mo.), 1998 (3,996 yards, 33 TDs; team totals: 319 recepts., 4,501 yards, 51 TDs)

MOST CONSECUTIVE GAMES CATCHING A PASS
Career
40—Brandon Good, Wooster, 1995-98

MOST YARDS GAINED
Game
397—Matt Eisenberg, Juniata vs. Widener, Nov. 13, 1999 (caught 13)
Season
2,157—Scott Pingel, Westminster (Mo.), 1998 (caught 130)
Also holds per-game record with 215.7 (2,157 in 10)
Career
6,108—Scott Pingel, Westminster (Mo.), 1996-99 (caught 436)
Also holds per-game record with 156.6 (6,108 in 39)

MOST YARDS GAINED BY A TIGHT END
Game
362—Matt Surette, Worcester Tech vs. Springfield, Oct. 25, 1997 (caught 17)
Season
1,290—Don Moehling, Wis.-Stevens Point, 1988 (caught 72)
Career
2,663—Don Moehling, Wis.-Stevens Point, 1986-89 (caught 152)

MOST YARDS GAINED BY A RUNNING BACK
Game
271—Theo Blanco, Wis.-Stevens Point vs. Wis.-Oshkosh, Oct. 31, 1987 (caught 17)
Season
1,616—Theo Blanco, Wis.-Stevens Point, 1987 (caught 106)
Career
2,190—Mike Christman, Wis.-Stevens Point, 1983-86 (caught 169)

MOST YARDS GAINED BY TWO PLAYERS, SAME TEAM
Season
3,168—Scott Pingel (WR) 2,157 & Logan Stanley (TE) 1,011, Westminster (Mo.), 1998 (caught 203, 33 TDs)

HIGHEST AVERAGE GAIN PER RECEPTION
Game
(Min. 3 receps.) 68.3—Paul Jaeckel, Elmhurst vs. Ill. Wesleyan, Oct. 8, 1983 (3 for 205)
(Min. 5 receps.) 56.8—Tom Casperson, Col. of New Jersey vs. Ramapo, Nov. 15, 1980 (5 for 284)
Season
(Min. 35 receps.) 26.9—Marty Redlawsk, Concordia (Ill.), 1985 (38 for 1,022)
(Min. 50 receps.) 23.5—Evan Elkington, Worcester Tech, 1989 (52 for 1,220)
Career
(Min. 125 receps.) 22.9—Kirk Aikens, Hartwick, 1995-98 (127 for 2,902)

HIGHEST AVERAGE GAIN PER RECEPTION BY A RUNNING BACK
Season
(Min. 50 receps.) 17.5—Barry Rose, Wis.-Stevens Point, 1989 (67 for 1,171)

MOST TOUCHDOWN PASSES CAUGHT
Game
7—Matt Perceval, Wesleyan (Conn.) vs. Middlebury, Sept. 26, 1998
Season
26—Scott Pingel, Westminster (Mo.), 1998
Also holds per-game record with 2.6 (26 in 10)
Career
75—Scott Pingel, Westminster (Mo.), 1996-99 (caught 436)
Also holds per-game record with 1.9 (75 in 39)

MOST TOUCHDOWN PASSES CAUGHT BY A FRESHMAN
Season
12—Chris Bisaillon, Ill. Wesleyan, 1989; Matt Plummer, Dubuque, 1996

HIGHEST PERCENTAGE OF PASSES CAUGHT FOR TOUCHDOWNS
Season
(Min. 12 TDs) 55.6%—Kirk Aikens, Hartwick, 1998 (20 of 36)
Career
(Min. 20 TDs) 33.9%—Kirk Aikens, Hartwick, 1995-98 (43 of 127)

MOST CONSECUTIVE PASSES CAUGHT FOR TOUCHDOWNS
9—Keith Gilliam, Randolph-Macon, 1984 (during four games)

Punting

MOST PUNTS
Game
17—Jerry Williams, Frostburg St. vs. Salisbury St., Sept. 30, 1978
Season
106—Bob Blake, Wis.-Superior, 1977 (3,404 yards)
Per-game record—11.0, Mark Roedelbronn, FDU-Madison, 1990 (99 in 9)
Career
263—Chris Gardner, Loras, 1987-90 (9,394 yards)

HIGHEST AVERAGE PER PUNT
Season
(Min. 40 punts) 45.5—Justin Shively, Anderson (Ind.), 1997 (55 for 2,502)
Career
(Min. 100 punts) 43.4—Jeff Shea, Cal Lutheran, 1994-97 (183 for 7,939)

Interceptions

MOST PASSES INTERCEPTED
Game
5—By nine players. Most recent: Freeman Perry, Howard Payne vs. Hardin-Simmons, Oct. 23, 1999
Season
15—Mark Dorner, Juniata, 1987 (202 yards)
Also holds per-game record with 1.5 (15 in 10)
Career
29—Ralph Gebhardt, Rochester, 1973-75 (384 yards)

MOST CONSECUTIVE GAMES INTERCEPTING A PASS
Season
9—Brent Sands, Cornell College, 1992
Also holds career record with 9

MOST YARDS ON INTERCEPTION RETURNS
Game
164—Rick Conner, Western Md. vs. Dickinson, Oct. 15, 1983 (89-yard interception and 75-yard lateral after an interception)
Season
358—Rod Pesek, Whittier, 1987 (10 interceptions)
Career
443—Mark Dorner, Juniata, 1984-87 (26 interceptions)

HIGHEST AVERAGE GAIN PER INTERCEPTION
Season
(Min. 7 ints.) 38.4—Randy Ames, Hope, 1996 (7 for 269)
Career
(Min. 20 ints.) 20.4—Todd Schoelzel, Wis.-Oshkosh, 1985-88 (22 for 448)

MOST TOUCHDOWNS SCORED ON INTERCEPTIONS
Game
3—By many players
Season
3—By many players. Most recent: Will Hall, Millsaps, 1992 (6 interceptions); Mike Sikma, Carroll (Wis.), 1992 (4 interceptions)

Punt Returns

MOST PUNT RETURNS
Game
10—Ellis Wangelin, Wis.-River Falls vs. Wis.-Platteville, Oct. 12, 1985 (87 yards)
Season
48—Rick Bealer, Lycoming, 1989 (492 yards)
Career
126—Mike Caterbone, Frank. & Marsh., 1980-83 (1,141 yards)

MOST YARDS ON PUNT RETURNS
Game
212—Melvin Dillard, Ferrum vs. Newport News App., Oct. 13, 1990 (6 returns)
Season
688—Melvin Dillard, Ferrum, 1990 (25 returns)
Career
1,239—Charles Warren, Dickinson, 1993-96 (117 returns)

HIGHEST AVERAGE GAIN PER RETURN
Season
(Min. 1.2 rets. per game) 31.2—Chuck Downey, Stony Brook, 1986 (17 for 530)
Career
(Min. 1.2 rets. per game) 22.9—Keith Winston, Knoxville, 1986-87 (30 for 686)
(Min. 50 rets.) 20.3—Chuck Downey, Stony Brook, 1984-87 (59 for 1,198)

MOST TOUCHDOWNS SCORED ON PUNT RETURNS
Game
2—By nine players. Most recent: LaVant King, Ohio Northern vs. Otterbein, Oct. 7, 1995 (50 & 73 yards)
Season
4—Keith Winston, Knoxville, 1986 (14 returns); Chuck Downey, Stony Brook, 1986 (17 returns); Matt Pekarske, Wis.-La Crosse, 1986 (37 returns); Chris Warren, Ferrum, 1989 (18 returns)
Career
7—Chuck Downey, Stony Brook, 1984-87 (59 returns)

Kickoff Returns

MOST KICKOFF RETURNS
Game
11—Mason Tootell, Swarthmore vs. Johns Hopkins, Sept. 19, 1997 (197 yards)
Season
48—Mason Tootell, Swarthmore, 1997 (944 yards)
Career
104—Simeon Henderson, Elmhurst, 1991-94 (2,063 yards)

MOST YARDS ON KICKOFF RETURNS
Game
279—Chuck Downey, Stony Brook vs. Col. of New Jersey, Oct. 5, 1984 (7 returns)
Season
981—Joshua Carter, Muhlenberg, 1999 (28 returns)
Career
2,075—Ryan Kuttler, Claremont-M-S, 1993-96 (98 returns)

HIGHEST AVERAGE GAIN PER RETURN
Game
(Min. 3 rets.) 68.0—Victor Johnson, Elmhurst vs. Wheaton (Ill.), Sept. 15, 1979 (3 for 204)
Season
(Min. 1.2 rets. per game) 42.2—Brandon Steinheim, Wesley, 1994 (10 for 422)
Career
(Min. 1.2 rets. per game) 34.9—David Ziegler, John Carroll, 1996-99 (30 for 1,047)

INDIVIDUAL RECORDS—KICKOFF RETURNS

MOST TOUCHDOWNS SCORED ON KICKOFF RETURNS
Game
2—By many players. Most recent: Homer Atkins, Muskingum vs. Mount Union, Oct. 26, 1996
Season
4—Byron Womack, Iona, 1989
Career
6—Byron Womack, Iona, 1988-91

Total Kick Returns

(Combined Punt and Kickoff Returns)

MOST YARDS ON KICK RETURNS
Game
354—Chuck Downey, Stony Brook vs. Col. of New Jersey, Oct. 5, 1984 (7 kickoff returns for 279 yards, 1 punt return for 75 yards)

GAINING 1,000 YARDS ON PUNT RETURNS AND 1,000 YARDS ON KICKOFF RETURNS
Career
Chuck Downey, Stony Brook, 1984-87 (1,198 on punt returns, 1,281 on kickoff returns); LaVant King, Ohio Northern, 1991, 93-95 (1,074 on punt returns, 1,298 on kickoff returns); Charles Warren, Dickinson, 1993-96 (1,239 on punt returns, 1,021 on kickoff returns); David Ziegler, John Carroll, 1996-99 (1,063 on punt returns, 1,047 on kickoff returns)

MOST TOUCHDOWNS ON KICK RETURNS
Game
3—Chuck Downey, Stony Brook vs. Col. of New Jersey, Oct. 5, 1984 (2 kickoff returns, 98 & 95 yards; 1 punt return, 75 yards)
Season
5—Chuck Downey, Stony Brook, 1986 (4 punt returns, 1 kickoff return); Chris Warren, Ferrum, 1989 (4 punt returns, 1 kickoff return); Charles Jordan, Occidental, 1993 (2 punt returns, 3 kickoff returns)
Career
10—Chuck Downey, Stony Brook, 1984-87 (7 punt returns, 3 kickoff returns)

HIGHEST AVERAGE PER KICK RETURN
(Min. 1.2 Returns Per Game Each)
Career
23.6—Chuck Downey, Stony Brook, 1984-87 (59 for 1,198 on punt returns, 46 for 1,281 on kickoff returns)

AVERAGING 20 YARDS EACH ON PUNT RETURNS AND KICKOFF RETURNS
(Min. 1.2 Returns Per Game Each)
Career
Chuck Downey, Stony Brook, 1984-87 (20.3 on punt returns, 59 for 1,198; 27.8 on kickoff returns, 46 for 1,281)

All Runbacks

(Combined Interceptions, Punt Returns and Kickoff Returns)

MOST TOUCHDOWNS ON INTERCEPTIONS, PUNT RETURNS AND KICKOFF RETURNS
Season
6—Chuck Downey, Stony Brook, 1986 (1 interception return, 4 punt returns, 1 kickoff return)
Career
11—Chuck Downey, Stony Brook, 1984-87 (1 interception return, 7 punt returns, 3 kickoff returns)

Punts Blocked By

MOST PUNTS BLOCKED BY
Game
3—Jim Perryman, Millikin vs. Carroll (Wis.), Nov. 1, 1980
Season
9—Jim Perryman, Millikin, 1980
Career
13—Frank Lyle, Millsaps, 1979-82
Note: Daryl Hobson, Benedictine (Ill.) DB, blocked 9 punts during 17 games in 1987-88

All-Purpose Yards

(Yardage Gained From Rushing, Receiving and All Runbacks)

MOST PLAYS
Season
383—Mike Birosak, Dickinson, 1989 (380 rushes, 3 receptions)
Career
1,313—Steve Tardif, Maine Maritime, 1996-99 (1,190 rushing, 58 receptions, 1 interception, 10 punt returns, 55 kickoff returns)

MOST YARDS GAINED
Game
527—Paul Smith, Gettysburg vs. Muhlenberg, Oct. 23, 1999 (390 rushing, 137 receiving)
Season
2,973—Dante Brown, Marietta, 1996 (2,385 rushing, 174 receiving, 46 punt returns, 368 kickoff returns; 338 plays)
Also holds per-game record with 297.3 (2,973 in 10)
Career
9,104—Paul Smith, Gettysburg, 1996-99 (5,205 rushing, 758 receiving, 959 punt returns, 2,182 kickoff returns; 1,135 plays)
Also holds per-game record with 227.6 (9,104 in 40)

HIGHEST AVERAGE GAIN PER PLAY
Season
(Min. 1,500 yards, 125 plays) 16.9—Matt Eisenberg, Juniata, 1999 (2,113 in 125)
Career
(Min. 4,000 yards, 300 plays) 16.0—Chris Wiesehan, Wabash, 1990-93 (4,825 in 301)

Scoring

MOST POINTS SCORED
Game
48—Carey Bender, Coe vs. Beloit, Nov. 12, 1994
Season
206—R. J. Bowers, Grove City, 1998 (34 TDs & 2 PATs)
Per-game record—20.8, James Regan, Pomona-Pitzer, 1997 (166 in 8)
Career
528—Carey Bender, Coe, 1991-94 (86 TDs & 12 PATs)
Per-game record—14.4, Ricky Gales, Simpson, 1988-89 (274 in 19)

TWO PLAYERS, SAME TEAM, EACH SCORING 100 POINTS OR MORE
Season
Theo Blanco (102) & Aatron Kenney (102), Wis.-Stevens Point, 1987; Denis McDermott (126) & Manny Tsantes (102), St. John's (N.Y.), 1989; Steve Harris (122) & R. J. Hoppe (106), Carroll (Wis.), 1994; Andrew Notarfrancesco (130) & Jeff Clay (120), Catholic, 1997; Jamie Lee (160) & Troy Austin (108), MacMurray, 1998; Richard Wemer (134) & David Snider (126), Grinnell, 1998; Chuck Moore (132) & Adam Marino (116), Mount Union, 1999

MOST TOUCHDOWNS SCORED
Season
34—R. J. Bowers, Grove City, 1998
Also holds per-game record with 3.4 (34 in 10)
Career
86—Carey Bender, Coe, 1991-94
Also holds per-game record with 2.2 (86 in 39)

MOST GAMES SCORING A TOUCHDOWN
Career
36—Carey Bender, Coe, 1991-94 (39 games)

MOST GAMES SCORING TWO OR MORE TOUCHDOWNS
Career
24—Joe Dudek, Plymouth St., 1982-85 (41 games)

MOST EXTRA POINTS ATTEMPTED BY KICKING
Game
14—Kurt Christenson, Concordia-M'head vs. Macalester, Sept. 24, 1977 (made 13)
Season
70—Greg Poulin, St. John's (Minn.), 1993 (made 63); Bill Andrea, Mount Union, 1997 (made 67)
Career
194—Tim Mercer, Ferrum, 1987-90 (made 183)

MOST EXTRA POINTS MADE BY KICKING
Game
13—Kurt Christenson, Concordia-M'head vs. Macalester, Sept. 24, 1977 (attempted 14)
Season
67—Bill Andrea, Mount Union, 1997 (attempted 70)
Career
183—Tim Mercer, Ferrum, 1987-90 (attempted 194)

HIGHEST PERCENTAGE OF EXTRA POINTS MADE (Best Perfect Season)
100.0%—Mike Duvic, Dayton, 1989 (46 of 46)

HIGHEST PERCENTAGE OF EXTRA POINTS MADE
Career
(Min. 80 atts.) 100.0%—Mike Farrell, Adrian, 1983-85 (84 of 84)
(Min. 100 atts.) 98.5%—Rims Roof, Coe, 1982-85 (135 of 137)

MOST CONSECUTIVE EXTRA POINTS MADE BY KICKING
Game
13—Kurt Christenson, Concordia-M'head vs. Macalester, Sept. 24, 1977
Career
102—Rims Roof, Coe (from Sept. 24, 1983, through Nov. 9, 1985)

MOST POINTS SCORED BY KICKING
Game
20—Jim Hever, Rhodes vs. Millsaps, Sept. 22, 1984 (6 FGs, 2 PATs)
Season
102—Ken Edelman, Mount Union, 1990 (20 FGs, 42 PATs)
Also holds per-game record with 10.2 (102 in 10)
Career
274—Ken Edelman, Mount Union, 1987-90 (52 FGs, 118 PATs)
Also holds per-game record with 6.9 (274 in 40)

MOST SUCCESSFUL TWO-POINT PASS ATTEMPTS
Game
4—Dave Geissler, Wis.-Stevens Point vs. Wis.-La Crosse, Sept. 21, 1985 (all in 4th quarter); Rob Bristow, Pomona-Pitzer vs. Whittier, Oct. 19, 1985 (all in 4th quarter)
Season
10—Justin Peery, Westminster (Mo.), 1997 (14 attempts)
Career
25—Justin Peery, Westminster (Mo.), 1996-99 (44 attempts)
Note: Rob Bristow, Pomona-Pitzer, 1983-86, holds record for highest percentage of successful two-point pass attempts (best perfect record) at 9 of 9

MOST TWO-POINT PASSES CAUGHT
Season
8—Scott Pingel, Westminster (Mo.), 1997
Career
17—Scott Pingel, Westminster (Mo.), 1996-99

Defensive Extra Points

MOST DEFENSIVE EXTRA POINTS SCORED
Game
1—By many players
Season
2—Dan Fichter, Brockport St., 1990 (2 blocked kick returns)

LONGEST DEFENSIVE EXTRA POINT BLOCKED KICK RETURN
97—Keith Mottram (CB), Colorado Col. vs. Austin, Oct. 10, 1992 (scored)

LONGEST DEFENSIVE EXTRA POINT INTERCEPTION
100—By many players. Most recent: Mike Ortiz (DB), FDU-Madison vs. Widener, Sept. 11, 1999

FIRST DEFENSIVE EXTRA POINT SCORED
Steve Nieves (DB), St. John's (N.Y.) vs. Iona, Sept. 10, 1988 (83-yard blocked kick return)

Field Goals

MOST FIELD GOALS MADE
Game
6—Jim Hever, Rhodes vs. Millsaps, Sept. 22, 1984 (30, 24, 42, 44, 46, 30 yards; attempted 8)
Season
20—Ken Edelman, Mount Union, 1990 (attempted 27)
Also holds per-game record with 2.0 (20 in 10)
Career
52—Ken Edelman, Mount Union, 1987-90 (attempted 71)
Also holds per-game record (Min. 30) with 1.3 (52 in 40)

MOST FIELD GOALS ATTEMPTED
Game
8—Jim Hever, Rhodes vs. Millsaps, Sept. 22, 1984 (made 6)
Season
29—Scott Ryerson, UCF, 1981 (made 18)
Career
71—Doug Hart, Grove City, 1985-88 (made 40); Ken Edelman, Mount Union, 1987-90 (made 52)

HIGHEST PERCENTAGE OF FIELD GOALS MADE
Season
(Min. 15 atts.) 93.8%—Steve Graeca, John Carroll, 1988 (15 of 16)

Career
(Min. 50 atts.) *77.6%—Mike Duvic, Dayton, 1986-89 (38 of 49)
*Declared champion; with one more attempt (making 50), failed, still would have highest percentage (76.0).

LONGEST FIELD GOAL MADE
62—Dom Antonini, Rowan vs. Salisbury St., Sept. 18, 1976

MOST FIELD GOALS ATTEMPTED WITHOUT SUCCESS
Season
11—Scott Perry, Moravian, 1986

Team Records

Single Game—Offense

Total Offense

MOST PLAYS
112—Gust. Adolphus vs. Bethel (Minn.), Nov. 2, 1985 (47 rushes, 65 passes; 493 yards)

MOST PLAYS, BOTH TEAMS
214—Gust. Adolphus (112) & Bethel (Minn.) (102), Nov. 2, 1985 (71 rushes, 143 passes; 930 yards)

MOST YARDS GAINED
823—Westminster (Mo.) vs. Principia, Oct. 17, 1998 (176 rushing, 647 passing)

MOST YARDS GAINED, BOTH TEAMS
1,395—Occidental (753) & Claremont-M-S (642), Oct. 30, 1993 (136 plays)

MOST TOUCHDOWNS SCORED BY RUSHING AND PASSING
14—Concordia-M'head vs. Macalester, Sept. 24, 1977 (12 rushing, 2 passing)

Rushing

MOST RUSHES
92—Wis.-River Falls vs. Wis.-Platteville, Oct. 21, 1989 (464 yards)

MOST YARDS GAINED
642—Wis.-River Falls vs. Wis.-Superior, Oct. 14, 1989 (88 rushes)

MOST TOUCHDOWNS SCORED BY RUSHING
12—Concordia-M'head vs. Macalester, Sept. 24, 1977

Passing

MOST PASSES ATTEMPTED
81—Principia vs. Blackburn, Oct. 10, 1992 (completed 48)

MOST PASSES ATTEMPTED, BOTH TEAMS
143—Bethel (Minn.) (78) & Gust. Adolphus (65), Nov. 2, 1985 (completed 65)

MOST PASSES ATTEMPTED WITHOUT AN INTERCEPTION
77—Westminster (Mo.) vs. MacMurray, Nov. 14, 1998 (completed 50)

MOST PASSES COMPLETED
50—Hofstra vs. Fordham, Oct. 19, 1991 (attempted 69); Westminster (Mo.) vs. MacMurray, Nov. 14, 1998 (attempted 77)

MOST PASSES COMPLETED, BOTH TEAMS
72—Wis.-Superior (41) & Wis.-Stevens Point (31), Oct. 17, 1981 (attempted 131)

HIGHEST PERCENTAGE OF PASSES COMPLETED (Min. 35 Attempts)
78.9%—Wheaton (Ill.) vs. North Park, Oct. 8, 1983 (30 of 38)

MOST YARDS GAINED
647—Westminster (Mo.) vs. Principia, Oct. 17, 1998

MOST YARDS GAINED, BOTH TEAMS
1,100—St. Thomas (Minn.) (602) & Bethel (Minn.) (498), Nov. 13, 1993 (attempted 113, completed 69)

MOST TOUCHDOWN PASSES
9—Westminster (Mo.) vs. Principia, Oct. 17, 1998; Ohio Northern vs. Capital, Nov. 14, 1998

MOST TOUCHDOWN PASSES, BOTH TEAMS
12—St. Thomas (Minn.) (6) & Bethel (Minn.) (6), Nov. 13, 1993

Punt Returns

MOST TOUCHDOWNS SCORED ON PUNT RETURNS
3—Emory & Henry vs. Tenn. Wesleyan, Sept. 27, 1986

Kickoff Returns

MOST YARDS ON KICKOFF RETURNS
302—MacMurray vs. Greenville, Sept. 4, 1999

Scoring

MOST POINTS SCORED
97—Concordia-M'head vs. Macalester, Sept. 24, 1977

MOST POINTS SCORED, BOTH TEAMS
123—Westminster (Mo.) (62) vs. Greenville (61), Sept. 19, 1998; Susquehanna (62) vs. Juniata (61), Oct. 24, 1998

MOST POINTS SCORED BY A LOSING TEAM
61—Greenville vs. Westminster (Mo.), Sept. 19, 1998; Juniata vs. Susquehanna, Oct. 24, 1998

MOST POINTS OVERCOME TO WIN A GAME
33—Wis.-Platteville vs. Wis.-Eau Claire, Nov. 8, 1980 (trailed 33-0 with 7:00 left in 2nd quarter; won 52-43); Salisbury St. vs. Randolph-Macon, Sept. 15, 1984 (trailed 33-0 with 14:18 left in 2nd quarter; won 34-33); Lakeland vs. Concordia (Wis.), Oct. 11, 1997 (trailed 33-0 with 7:53 left in 3rd quarter; won 41-33)

MOST POINTS SCORED IN A BRIEF PERIOD OF TIME
21 in 33 seconds—Mount Union vs. Defiance, Sept. 14, 1996 (turned 13-3 game into 34-3 in 2nd quarter, won 62-10)

32 in 4:04—Wis.-Stevens Point vs. Wis.-La Crosse, Sept. 21, 1985 (trailed 27-3 and 35-11 in 4th quarter; ended in 35-35 tie)

MOST POINTS SCORED IN FIRST VARSITY GAME
63—Bentley vs. Brooklyn (26), Sept. 24, 1988

MOST TOUCHDOWNS SCORED
14—Concordia-M'head vs. Macalester, Sept. 24, 1977

MOST PLAYERS SCORING TOUCHDOWNS
10—Johns Hopkins vs. Swarthmore, Sept. 19, 1997

MOST EXTRA POINTS MADE BY KICKING
13—Concordia-M'head vs. Macalester, Sept. 24, 1977 (attempted 14)

MOST FIELD GOALS MADE
6—Rhodes vs. Millsaps, Sept. 22, 1984 (attempted 8)

MOST FIELD GOALS ATTEMPTED
8—Rhodes vs. Millsaps, Sept. 22, 1984 (made 6)

MOST DEFENSIVE EXTRA-POINT RETURNS SCORED
1—By many teams

MOST DEFENSIVE EXTRA-POINT OPPORTUNITIES
2—Buffalo St. vs. Brockport St., Oct. 1, 1988 (1 interception & 1 kick return; none scored); Wis.-Platteville vs. Wis.-Oshkosh, Oct. 15, 1988 (2 interceptions; none scored); Wis.-River Falls vs. Wis.-La Crosse, Nov. 11, 1989 (2 kick returns; 1 scored); Frank. & Marsh. vs. Johns Hopkins, Nov. 7, 1992 (1 interception & 1 kick return; none scored)

Turnovers

(Most Times Losing the Ball on Interceptions and Fumbles)

MOST TURNOVERS
13—Albany (N.Y.) vs. Rochester Inst., Oct. 1, 1977; Mercyhurst vs. Buffalo St., Oct. 23, 1982 (1 interception, 12 fumbles); St. Olaf vs. St. Thomas (Minn.), Oct. 12, 1985 (10 interceptions, 3 fumbles)

MOST TURNOVERS, BOTH TEAMS
24—Albany (N.Y.) (13) & Rochester Inst. (11), Oct. 1, 1977

First Downs

MOST TOTAL FIRST DOWNS
40—Upper Iowa vs. Loras, Nov. 7, 1992 (19 rushing, 17 passing, 4 by penalty)

Penalties

MOST PENALTIES AGAINST
25—Norwich vs. Coast Guard, Sept. 29, 1985 (192 yards)

SINGLE GAME—Defense

Total Defense

FEWEST YARDS ALLOWED
Minus 52—Worcester St. vs. Maine Maritime, Sept. 28, 1996 (-71 rushing, 19 passing)

Rushing Defense

FEWEST RUSHES ALLOWED
9—Wis.-La Crosse vs. Huron, Sept. 21, 1996 (-63 yards)

FEWEST YARDS ALLOWED
Minus 112—Coast Guard vs. Wesleyan (Conn.), Oct. 7, 1989 (23 plays)

Pass Defense

FEWEST ATTEMPTS ALLOWED
0—By many teams. Most recent: Concordia-M'head vs. Macalester, Oct. 12, 1991

FEWEST COMPLETIONS ALLOWED
0—By many teams. Most recent: Hartwick vs. Rensselaer, Oct. 26, 1996 (8 attempts)

FEWEST YARDS ALLOWED
Minus 6—Central (Iowa) vs. Simpson, Oct. 19, 1985 (1 completion)

MOST PASSES INTERCEPTED BY
10—St. Thomas (Minn.) vs. St. Olaf, Oct. 12, 1985 (91 yards; 50 attempts)

MOST PLAYERS INTERCEPTING A PASS
8—Samford vs. Anderson (S.C.), Oct. 11, 1986 (8 interceptions in the game)

MOST TOUCHDOWNS ON INTERCEPTION RETURNS
4—Millikin vs. Ill. Wesleyan, Nov. 6, 1999

Punts Blocked By

MOST OPPONENT'S PUNTS BLOCKED BY
4—Benedictine (Ill.) vs. Olivet Nazarene, Oct. 22, & vs. Aurora, Oct. 29, 1988 (consecutive games, resulting in 4 TDs and 1 safety). Blocked 9 punts in three consecutive games, vs. MacMurray, Oct. 15, Olivet Nazarene and Aurora, resulting in 4 TDs and 2 safeties

First Downs

FEWEST FIRST DOWNS ALLOWED
0—Case Reserve vs. Wooster, Sept. 21, 1985

SEASON—Offense

Total Offense

MOST YARDS GAINED PER GAME
561.2—Westminster (Mo.), 1998 (5,612 in 10)

HIGHEST AVERAGE GAIN PER PLAY
8.1—Ferrum, 1990 (534 for 4,350)

MOST PLAYS PER GAME
85.6—Hampden-Sydney, 1978 (856 in 10)

MOST TOUCHDOWNS SCORED PER GAME BY RUSHING AND PASSING
8.4—St. John's (Minn.), 1993 (84 in 10; 44 rushing, 40 passing)

Rushing

MOST YARDS GAINED PER GAME
434.7—Ferrum, 1990 (3,912 in 9)

HIGHEST AVERAGE GAIN PER RUSH
8.3—Ferrum, 1990 (470 for 3,912)

MOST RUSHES PER GAME
71.4—Wis.-River Falls, 1988 (714 in 10)

MOST TOUCHDOWNS SCORED PER GAME BY RUSHING
5.4—Ferrum, 1990 (49 in 9)

Passing

MOST YARDS GAINED PER GAME
488.8—Westminster (Mo.), 1998 (4,888 in 10)

FEWEST YARDS GAINED PER GAME
18.4—Wis.-River Falls, 1983 (184 in 10)

HIGHEST AVERAGE GAIN PER ATTEMPT
(Min. 250 atts.) 11.1—Grinnell, 1998 (301 for 3,354)
(Min. 350 atts.) 9.3—Redlands, 1999 (406 for 3,796)

HIGHEST AVERAGE GAIN PER COMPLETION (Min. 200 Completions)
16.5—Grinnell, 1998 (203 for 3,354)

MOST PASSES ATTEMPTED PER GAME
58.5—Hofstra, 1991 (585 in 10)

FEWEST PASSES ATTEMPTED PER GAME
4.0—Wis.-River Falls, 1988 (40 in 10)

MOST PASSES COMPLETED PER GAME
34.4—Hofstra, 1991 (344 in 10)

FEWEST PASSES COMPLETED PER GAME
1.3—Wis.-River Falls, 1983 (13 in 10)

HIGHEST PERCENTAGE COMPLETED (Min. 200 Attempts)
70.7%—Mount Union, 1993 (244 of 345)

LOWEST PERCENTAGE OF PASSES HAD INTERCEPTED (Min. 150 Attempts)
0.7%—San Diego, 1990 (1 of 153)

MOST TOUCHDOWN PASSES PER GAME
5.7—Westminster (Mo.), 1998 (57 in 10)

HIGHEST PASSING EFFICIENCY RATING POINTS
(Min. 15 atts. per game) 211.3—Eureka, 1994 (205 attempts, 142 completions, 8 interceptions, 2,478 yards, 30 TDs)
(Min. 300 atts.) 202.8—Mount Union, 1997 (311 attempts, 212 completions, 3 interceptions, 3,171 yards, 48 TDs)

Punting

MOST PUNTS PER GAME
11.0—FDU-Madison, 1990 (99 in 9)

FEWEST PUNTS PER GAME
2.2—Mount Union, 1997 (22 in 10)

HIGHEST PUNTING AVERAGE
45.3—Ohio Northern, 1999 (43 for 1,950)

Scoring

MOST POINTS PER GAME
61.5—St. John's (Minn.), 1993 (615 in 10)

MOST TOUCHDOWNS PER GAME
8.9—St. John's (Minn.), 1993 (89 in 10)

BEST PERFECT RECORD ON EXTRA POINTS MADE BY KICKING
49 of 49—Dayton, 1989

MOST TWO-POINT ATTEMPTS PER GAME
2.8—Martin Luther, 1990 (17 in 6)

MOST FIELD GOALS MADE PER GAME
2.0—Mount Union, 1990 (20 in 10)

HIGHEST SCORING MARGIN
51.8—St. John's (Minn.), 1993 (averaged 61.5 and allowed 9.7 in 10 games)

MOST TOUCHDOWNS ON BLOCKED PUNT RETURNS
5—Widener, 1990

MOST SAFETIES
4—Wis.-Stevens Point, 1990; Westfield St., 1992; Central (Iowa), 1992; Alfred, 1992; Upper Iowa, 1995

MOST DEFENSIVE EXTRA-POINT RETURNS SCORED
2—Brockport St., 1990; Eureka, 1991; Springfield, 1998

MOST DEFENSIVE EXTRA POINT BLOCKED KICK RETURNS
3—Brockport St., 1990 (2 scored); Ohio Wesleyan, 1991 (none scored); Assumption, 1992 (1 scored)

MOST DEFENSIVE EXTRA POINT INTERCEPTIONS
2—Wis.-Platteville, 1988 (none scored); Swarthmore, 1989 (1 scored)

Penalties

MOST PENALTIES PER GAME
13.3—Kean, 1990 (133 in 10, 1,155 yards)

MOST YARDS PENALIZED PER GAME
121.9—Hofstra, 1991 (1,219 in 10, 124 penalties)

Turnovers (Giveaways)

(Passes Had Intercepted and Fumbles Lost, From 1985)

FEWEST TURNOVERS
6—Mount Union, 1995 (4 interceptions, 2 fumbles lost); Western Md., 1999 (4 interceptions, 2 fumbles lost)
Also share per-game record with 0.6 (6 in 10)

MOST TURNOVERS
52—William Penn, 1985 (19 interceptions, 33 fumbles lost)
Also holds per-game record with 5.2 (52 in 10)

SEASON—Defense

Total Defense

FEWEST YARDS ALLOWED PER GAME
94.0—Knoxville, 1977 (940 in 10)

LOWEST AVERAGE YARDS ALLOWED PER PLAY
(Min. 500 plays) 1.8—Bowie St., 1978 (576 for 1,011)
(Min. 650 plays) 2.0—Plymouth St., 1987 (733 for 1,488)

FEWEST RUSHING AND PASSING TOUCHDOWNS ALLOWED PER GAME
0.3—Montclair St., 1984 (3 in 10)

Rushing Defense

FEWEST YARDS ALLOWED PER GAME
Minus 2.3—Knoxville, 1977 (-23 in 10 games)

LOWEST AVERAGE YARDS ALLOWED PER RUSH
(Min. 275 rushes) Minus 0.1—Knoxville, 1977 (333 for -23)
(Min. 400 rushes) 1.0—Lycoming, 1976 (400 for 399)

FEWEST TOUCHDOWNS ALLOWED BY RUSHING
0—New Haven, 1978 (9 games); Union (N.Y.), 1983 (9 games)

Pass Defense

FEWEST YARDS ALLOWED PER GAME
48.5—Mass. Maritime, 1976 (388 in 8)

FEWEST YARDS ALLOWED PER ATTEMPT
(Min. 150 atts.) 2.9—Plymouth St., 1982 (170 for 488)
(Min. 225 atts.) 3.3—Plymouth St., 1987 (281 for 919)

FEWEST YARDS ALLOWED PER COMPLETION (Min. 100 Completions)
8.6—Baldwin-Wallace, 1990 (151 for 1,305)

TEAM RECORDS—PASS DEFENSE

LOWEST COMPLETION PERCENTAGE ALLOWED
(Min. 150 atts.) 24.3%—Doane, 1973 (41 of 169)
(Min. 250 atts.) 33.5%—Plymouth St., 1987 (94 of 281)

HIGHEST PERCENTAGE INTERCEPTED BY (Min. 200 Attempts)
15.2%—Rose-Hulman, 1977 (32 of 210)

MOST PASSES INTERCEPTED BY
35—Plymouth St., 1987 (12 games, 281 attempts against, 348 yards returned)
Per-game record—3.4, Montclair St., 1981 (34 in 10)

FEWEST PASSES INTERCEPTED BY (Min. 125 Attempts)
1—Bates, 1987 (134 attempts against in 8 games, 0 yards returned)

MOST YARDS ON INTERCEPTION RETURNS
576—Emory & Henry, 1987 (31 interceptions)

MOST TOUCHDOWNS SCORED ON INTERCEPTIONS
6—Augustana (Ill.), 1987 (23 interceptions, 229 passes against); Coe, 1992 (22 interceptions, 272 passes against)

FEWEST TOUCHDOWN PASSES ALLOWED
0—By many teams. Most recent: Dayton, 1980 (11 games)

LOWEST PASSING EFFICIENCY RATING POINTS ALLOWED OPPONENTS
(Min. 150 atts.) 27.8—Plymouth St., 1982 (allowed 170 attempts, 53 completions, 488 yards, 1 TD & intercepted 25 passes)
(Min. 275 atts.) 43.1—Plymouth St., 1987 (allowed 281 attempts, 94 completions, 919 yards, 6 TDs & intercepted 35 passes)

Punting

MOST PUNTS BLOCKED BY
11—Benedictine (Ill.) 1987 (78 punts against in 10 games). Blocked 17 punts in 18 games during 1987-88, resulting in 5 TDs and 3 safeties

Scoring

FEWEST POINTS ALLOWED PER GAME
3.4—Millsaps, 1980 (31 in 9)

FEWEST TOUCHDOWNS ALLOWED
4—Millsaps, 1980 (9 games); Baldwin-Wallace, 1981 (10 games); Bentley, 1990 (8 games)

MOST SHUTOUTS
6—Plymouth St., 1982 (consecutive); Cortland St., 1989

MOST CONSECUTIVE SHUTOUTS
6—Plymouth St., 1982

MOST POINTS ALLOWED PER GAME
59.1—Macalester, 1977 (532 in 9; 76 TDs, 64 PATs, 4 FGs)

MOST DEFENSIVE EXTRA-POINT ATTEMPTS BY OPPONENTS
5—Norwich, 1992 (4 blocked kick returns, 1 interception; none scored)

Turnovers (Takeaways)

(Opponent's Passes Intercepted and Fumbles Recovered, From 1985)

HIGHEST MARGIN OF TURNOVERS PER GAME OVER OPPONENTS
2.9—Macalester, 1986 (29 in 10; 29 giveaways vs. 58 takeaways)

MOST TAKEAWAYS
58—Macalester, 1986 (28 interceptions, 30 fumbles gained)
Also holds per-game record with 5.8 (58 in 10)

Additional Records

MOST CONSECUTIVE VICTORIES
54—Mount Union (from Sept. 14, 1996, to Dec. 4, 1999)

MOST CONSECUTIVE REGULAR-SEASON VICTORIES
52—Mount Union (from Sept. 14, 1996, to present)

MOST CONSECUTIVE GAMES WITHOUT DEFEAT
60—Augustana (Ill.), (from Sept. 17, 1983, through Nov. 22, 1987; ended with 38-36 loss to Dayton, Nov. 29, 1987, in Division III playoffs and included one tie)

MOST CONSECUTIVE REGULAR-SEASON GAMES WITHOUT DEFEAT
70—Augustana (Ill.) (from Oct. 25, 1980, through Oct. 1, 1988; ended with 24-21 loss to Carroll [Wis.], Oct. 8, 1988)

MOST CONSECUTIVE WINNING SEASONS
39—Central (Iowa) (from 1961 to present)

MOST CONSECUTIVE GAMES WITHOUT BEING SHUT OUT
224—Carnegie Mellon (from Sept. 30, 1972, through Nov. 4, 1995; ended with 3-0 loss to Case Reserve, Nov. 11, 1995)

MOST CONSECUTIVE LOSSES
50—Macalester (from Oct. 5, 1974, to Nov. 10, 1979; ended with 17-14 win over Mount Senario, Sept. 6, 1980)

MOST CONSECUTIVE GAMES WITHOUT A TIE
371—Widener (from Oct. 29, 1949, to Nov. 11, 1989; ended with 14-14 tie against Gettysburg, Sept. 8, 1990)

HIGHEST-SCORING TIE GAME
50-50—Catholic & Randolph-Macon, Sept. 16, 1995

LAST SCORELESS GAME
Sept. 10, 1988—Wis.-Oshkosh & Valparaiso

MOST CONSECUTIVE QUARTERS WITHOUT YIELDING A TOUCHDOWN BY RUSHING
61—Union (N.Y.) (in 16 games from Oct. 23, 1982, to Sept. 29, 1984); Augustana (Ill.) (in 16 games from Sept. 27, 1986, to Nov. 7, 1987; 77 including four 1986 Division III playoff games)

MOST CONSECUTIVE QUARTERS WITHOUT YIELDING A TOUCHDOWN BY PASSING
44—Swarthmore (from Oct. 31, 1981, to Nov. 13, 1982)

MOST IMPROVED WON-LOST RECORD (Including Postseason Games)
7 games—Maryville (Tenn.), 1976 (7-2-0) from 1975 (0-9-0); Susquehanna, 1986 (11-1-0) from 1985 (3-7-0); Catholic, 1994 (8-2-0) from 1993 (1-9-0)

Annual Champions, All-Time Leaders

Total Offense

CAREER YARDS PER GAME
(Minimum 5,000 Yards)

Player, Team	Years	G	Plays	Yards	Yd. PG
Justin Peery, Westminster (Mo.)	1996-99	39	2,001	*13,645	*349.9
Terry Peebles, Hanover	1992-95	23	1,140	7,672	333.6
Kirk Baumgartner, Wis.-Stevens Point	1986-89	41	*2,007	12,767	311.4
Willie Reyna, La Verne	1991-92	17	551	4,996	293.9
Keith Bishop, Ill. Wesleyan/ Wheaton (Ill.)	1981, 83-85	31	1,467	9,052	292.0
Mark Novara, Lakeland	1994-97	38	1,653	10,801	284.2
Jordan Poznick, Principia	1990-93	32	1,757	8,983	280.7
Troy Dougherty, Grinnell	1994, 97-99	37	1,520	10,314	278.8
John Rooney, Ill. Wesleyan	1982-84	27	1,260	7,393	273.8
Sean Hoolihan, Wis.-Eau Claire	1996-98	28	972	7,650	273.2
Tim Peterson, Wis.-Stout	1986-89	36	1,558	9,701	269.5
Gregg McDonald, Kalamazoo	1994-96	27	1,155	7,273	269.4
Bill Borchert, Mount Union	1994-97	40	1,274	10,639	266.0
Jim Ballard, Wilmington (Ohio)/ Mount Union	1990, 91-93	40	1,328	10,545	263.6
Kevin Ricca, Catholic	1994-97	38	1,533	9,982	262.7
Robert Farra, Claremont-M-S	1978-79	16	690	4,179	261.2
Chris Ings, Wabash	1992-95	37	1,532	9,608	259.7
Jack Ramirez, Pomona-Pitzer	1994-97	34	1,328	8,721	256.5
Eric Noble, Wilmington (Ohio)	1992-95	38	1,513	9,731	256.0
Brian Partlow, Randolph-Macon	1997-99	20	882	5,111	255.6
Chris Stormer, Hanover	1995-98	27	1,104	6,879	254.8
Brian Tomalak, Wis.-Oshkosh	1994-98	36	1,313	9,022	250.6
Matt D'Orazio, Otterbein	1996-99	38	1,625	9,364	246.4
Brian Van Deusen, Western Md.	1992-95	30	1,415	7,172	239.1
Kurt Ramler, St. John's (Minn.)	1994-96	28	958	6,639	237.1
Jason VanDerMaas, Alma	1995-98	23	891	5,452	237.0

*Record.

SEASON YARDS PER GAME

Player, Team	Year	G	Plays	Yards	Yd. PG
Justin Peery, Westminster (Mo.)	†1998	10	*645	*4,651	*465.1
Justin Peery, Westminster (Mo.)	†1999	10	599	4,419	441.9
Danny Ragsdale, Redlands	1999	9	464	3,855	428.3
Terry Peebles, Hanover	†1995	10	572	3,981	398.1
Keith Bishop, Wheaton (Ill.)	†1983	9	421	3,193	354.8
Kirk Baumgartner, Wis.-Stevens Point	†1989	10	530	3,540	354.0
Bill Nietzke, Alma	†1996	9	468	3,185	353.9
John Furmaniak, Eureka	1995	10	414	3,503	350.3
Adam Ryan, Wilmington (Ohio)	1999	10	280	3,478	347.8
Chris Stormer, Hanover	1998	10	507	3,470	347.0
Gregg McDonald, Kalamazoo	1996	9	415	3,101	344.6
Kirk Baumgartner, Wis.-Stevens Point	†1988	11	604	3,790	344.5
Terry Peebles, Hanover	†1994	10	520	3,441	344.1
Jordan Poznick, Principia	†1992	8	519	2,747	343.4
Eric Noble, Wilmington (Ohio)	1994	9	460	3,072	341.3
Brian Partlow, Randolph-Macon	1999	10	566	3,400	340.0

ANNUAL CHAMPIONS, ALL-TIME LEADERS—TOTAL OFFENSE 191

Player, Team	Year	G	Plays	Yards	Yd. PG
Jordan Poznick, Principia	†1993	8	488	2,705	338.1
Kirk Baumgartner, Wis.-Stevens Point	1987	11	561	3,712	337.5
Jim Ballard, Mount Union	1993	10	372	3,371	337.1
Steve Austin, Mass.-Boston	1992	9	466	3,003	333.7
Josh Wakefield, Alma	1999	9	476	2,990	332.2
Troy Dougherty, Grinnell	1998	10	375	3,296	329.6
Willie Reyna, La Verne	†1991	8	220	2,633	329.1
Keith Bishop, Wheaton (Ill.)	†1985	9	521	2,951	327.9
Eric Bruns, Hanover	1999	10	488	3,252	325.2

*Record. †National champion.

CAREER YARDS

Player, Team	Years	Plays	Yards
Justin Peery, Westminster (Mo.)	1996-99	2,001	*13,645
Kirk Baumgartner, Wis.-Stevens Point	1986-89	*2,007	12,767
Mark Novara, Lakeland	1994-97	1,653	10,801
Bill Borchert, Mount Union	1994-97	1,274	10,639
Jim Ballard, Wilmington (Ohio)/Mount Union	1990, 91-93	1,328	10,545
Troy Dougherty, Grinnell	1994, 97-99	1,520	10,314
Kevin Ricca, Catholic	1994-97	1,533	9,982
Eric Noble, Wilmington (Ohio)	1992-95	1,513	9,731
Tim Peterson, Wis.-Stout	1986-89	1,558	9,701
Chris Ings, Wabash	1992-95	1,532	9,608
Matt D'Orazio, Otterbein	1996-99	1,625	9,364
Keith Bishop, Ill. Wesleyan/Wheaton (Ill.)	1981, 83-85	1,467	9,052
Brian Tomalak, Wis.-Oshkosh	1994-98	1,313	9,022
Dave Geissler, Wis.-Stevens Point	1982-85	1,695	8,990
Jordan Poznick, Principia	1990-93	1,757	8,983
Mike Burton, Trinity (Tex.)	1996-99	1,250	8,883
Dennis Bogacz, Wis.-Oshkosh/Wis.-Whitewater	1988-89, 90-91	1,394	8,850
John Clark, Wis.-Eau Claire	1987-90	1,354	8,838
Jack Ramirez, Pomona-Pitzer	1994-97	1,328	8,721
Ron Sermarini, Western Md.	1996-99	1,491	8,627
Matt Bunyan, Wis.-Stout	1995-98	1,231	8,237
Matt Jozokos, Plymouth St.	1987-90	1,234	8,188
Nick Caserio, John Carroll	1995-98	1,260	7,976
Troy Dougherty, Grinnell	1994, 97-98	1,151	7,906
Darryl Kosut, William Penn	1983-86	1,583	7,817

*Record.

SEASON YARDS

Player, Team	Year	G	Plays	Yards
Justin Peery, Westminster (Mo.)	†1998	10	*645	*4,651
Justin Peery, Westminster (Mo.)	†1999	10	599	4,419
Terry Peebles, Hanover	†1995	10	572	3,981
Danny Ragsdale, Redlands	1999	9	464	3,855
Kirk Baumgartner, Wis.-Stevens Point	†1988	11	604	3,790
Kirk Baumgartner, Wis.-Stevens Point	1987	11	561	3,712
Kirk Baumgartner, Wis.-Stevens Point	†1989	10	530	3,540
John Furmaniak, Eureka	1995	10	414	3,503
Adam Ryan, Wilmington (Ohio)	1999	10	280	3,478
Chris Stormer, Hanover	1998	10	507	3,470
Terry Peebles, Hanover	†1994	10	520	3,441
Brian Partlow, Randolph-Macon	1999	10	566	3,400
Jim Ballard, Mount Union	1993	10	372	3,371
Troy Dougherty, Grinnell	1998	10	375	3,296
Eric Bruns, Hanover	1999	10	488	3,252
Mark Novara, Lakeland	†1996	10	454	3,250
Tim Peterson, Wis.-Stout	1989	10	614	3,244
Brad Boyd, Hardin-Simmons	1999	10	381	3,236
Travis McMahen, Franklin	1999	10	536	3,220
Matt Bunyan, Wis.-Stout	†1997	10	422	3,216
Kevin Ricca, Catholic	1997	10	392	3,200
Keith Bishop, Wheaton (Ill.)	†1983	9	421	3,193
Bill Nietzke, Alma	1996	9	468	3,185
Tom Stallings, St. Thomas (Minn.)	1993	10	438	3,158
Scott Isphording, Hanover	1992	10	484	3,150

*Record. †National champion.

SINGLE-GAME YARDS

Yds.	Player, Team (Opponent)	Date
630	Justin Peery, Westminster (Mo.) (Colorado Col.)	Oct. 30, 1999
628	Justin Peery, Westminster (Mo.) (MacMurray)	Nov. 14, 1998
617	Justin Peery, Westminster (Mo.) (Principia)	Oct. 17, 1998
596	John Love, North Park (Elmhurst)	Oct. 13, 1990
590	Tom Stallings, St. Thomas (Minn.) (Bethel [Minn.])	Nov. 13, 1993
590	Danny Ragsdale, Redlands (Azusa Pacific)	Sept. 25, 1999
588	Danny Ragsdale, Redlands (Cal Lutheran)	Nov. 13, 1999
580	Joe Montrella, Juniata (Widener)	Nov. 13, 1999
577	Eric Noble, Wilmington (Ohio) (Urbana)	Nov. 5, 1994
567	Jim Newland, Heidelberg (Ohio Northern)	Nov. 12, 1994
564	Tim Lynch, Hofstra (Fordham)	Oct. 19, 1991
563	Justin Peery, Westminster (Mo.) (Greenville)	Sept. 19, 1998
555	Bill Nietzke, Alma (Hope)	Oct. 26, 1996
549	Danny Ragsdale, Redlands (Chapman)	Oct. 9, 1999
547	Josh Wakefield, Alma (Franklin)	Sept. 25, 1999
545	Terry Peebles, Hanover (Franklin)	Nov. 12, 1994
541	Michael Kornblau, Greenville (Blackburn)	Oct. 9, 1999
539	Justin Peery, Westminster (Mo.) (Bethel [Tenn.])	Nov. 8, 1997
538	Jordan Poznick, Principia (Blackburn)	Oct. 10, 1992
538	Justin Peery, Westminster (Mo.) (Cent. Methodist)	Sept. 11, 1999

ANNUAL CHAMPIONS

Year	Player, Team	Class	G	Plays	Yards	Avg.
1973	Bob Dulich, San Diego	Jr.	11	340	2,543	231.2
1974	Larry Cenotto, Pomona-Pitzer	Sr.	9	436	2,127	236.3
1975	Ricky Haygood, Millsaps	Jr.	9	332	2,176	241.8
1976	Rollie Wiebers, Buena Vista	So.	9	353	2,198	244.2
1977	Tom Hamilton, Occidental	Sr.	9	358	2,050	227.8
1978	Robert Farra, Claremont-M-S	Jr.	9	427	2,685	298.3
1979	Clay Sampson, Denison	Jr.	9	412	2,255	250.6
1980	Jeff Beer, Bethany (W.Va.)	Sr.	9	372	2,331	259.0
1981	Brion Demski, Wis.-Stevens Point	Sr.	10	503	2,895	289.5
1982	Dave McCarrell, Wheaton (Ill.)	Sr.	9	387	2,503	278.1
1983	Keith Bishop, Wheaton (Ill.)	So.	9	421	3,193	354.8
1984	Keith Bishop, Wheaton (Ill.)	Jr.	9	479	2,777	308.6
1985	Keith Bishop, Wheaton (Ill.)	Sr.	9	521	2,951	327.9
1986	Larry Barretta, Lycoming	Sr.	10	453	2,875	287.5
1987	Todde Greenough, Willamette	Jr.	9	436	2,567	285.2
1988	Kirk Baumgartner, Wis.-Stevens Point	Jr.	11	604	3,790	344.5
1989	Kirk Baumgartner, Wis.-Stevens Point	Sr.	10	530	3,540	354.0
1990	Rhory Moss, Hofstra	Jr.	9	372	2,775	308.3
1991	Willie Reyna, La Verne	Jr.	8	220	2,633	329.1
1992	Jordan Poznick, Principia	Jr.	8	519	2,747	343.4
1993	Jordan Poznick, Principia	Sr.	8	488	2,705	338.1
1994	Terry Peebles, Hanover	Jr.	10	520	3,441	344.1
1995	Terry Peebles, Hanover	Sr.	10	572	3,981	398.1
1996	Bill Nietzke, Alma	Sr.	9	468	3,185	353.9
1997	Matt Bunyan, Wis.-Stout	Jr.	10	422	3,216	321.6
1998	Justin Peery, Westminster (Mo.)	Jr.	10	*645	*4,651	*465.1
1999	Justin Peery, Westminster (Mo.)	Sr.	10	599	4,419	441.9

*Record.

Rushing

CAREER YARDS PER GAME
(Minimum 2,200 Yards)

Player, Team	Years	G	Plays	Yards	Yd. PG
Ricky Gales, Simpson	1988-89	19	530	3,326	*175.1
Rob Marchitello, Maine Maritime	1993-95	26	879	4,300	165.4
Kelvin Gladney, Millsaps	1993-94	19	510	3,085	162.4
Carey Bender, Coe	1991-94	39	926	*6,125	157.1
Brad Olson, Lawrence	1994-97	34	792	5,325	156.6
Steve Tardif, Maine Maritime	1996-99	39	*1,190	6,093	156.2
Kirk Matthieu, Maine Maritime	$1989-93	33	964	5,107	154.8
Terry Underwood, Wagner	1985-88	33	742	5,010	151.8
D'Andra Freeman, Fitchburg St.	1997-99	27	789	3,957	146.6
Anthony Russo, St. John's (N.Y.)	1990-92	30	841	4,276	142.5
Joe Dudek, Plymouth St.	1982-85	41	785	5,570	135.9
Jason Brader, Muhlenberg	1997-98	20	548	2,684	134.2
Mark Kacmarynski, Central (Iowa)	$1992-96	41	854	5,434	132.5
Rich Kowalski, Hobart	1973-75	27	762	3,574	132.4
Eric Frees, Western Md.	1988-91	40	1,059	5,281	132.0
Rick Etienne, Franklin	1994-96	30	676	3,952	131.7
Paul Smith, Gettysburg	1996-99	40	881	5,205	130.1
Tim Barrett, John Carroll	1973-74	19	457	2,469	129.9
Heath Butler, Martin Luther	1990-93	31	767	4,000	129.0
Scott Reppert, Lawrence	1979-82	33	757	4,211	127.6
Dan McGovern, Rensselaer	1994-97	28	665	3,572	127.6

*Record. $See page 6 for explanation.

SEASON YARDS PER GAME

Player, Team	Year	G	Plays	Yards	TD	Yd. PG
Dante Brown, Marietta	†1996	10	314	*2,385	25	*238.5
R. J. Bowers, Grove City	†1998	10	329	2,283	*34	228.3
Carey Bender, Coe	†1994	10	295	2,243	29	224.3
R. J. Bowers, Grove City	†1999	10	344	2,098	25	209.8
Jamie Lee, MacMurray	†1997	8	207	1,639	11	204.9
Ricky Gales, Simpson	1989	10	297	2,035	26	203.5
Terry Underwood, Wagner	†1988	9	245	1,809	21	201.0
Kenneth Sasu, Marietta	1999	9	332	1,770	15	196.7
Brad Olson, Lawrence	†1995	9	242	1,760	16	195.6
Kirk Matthieu, Maine Maritime	†1992	9	327	1,733	16	192.6
Kelvin Gladney, Millsaps	1994	10	307	1,882	19	188.2

DIVISION III

Maine Maritime's Steve Tardif became only the second rusher in Division III history to surpass 6,000 career yards in 1999.

Player, Team	Year	G	Plays	Yards	TD	Yd. PG
Brandon Steinheim, Wesley	1996	9	319	1,684	20	187.1
D'Andra Freeman, Fitchburg St.	1999	10	365	1,871	14	187.1
Krishaun Gilmore, Rensselaer	1998	9	228	1,670	22	185.6
Jon Warga, Wittenberg	†1990	10	254	1,836	15	183.6
Jamie Lee, MacMurray	1998	10	252	1,818	25	181.8
Anthony Jones, La Verne	1995	8	200	1,453	19	181.6
Hank Wineman, Albion	†1991	9	307	1,629	14	181.0
Eric Grey, Hamilton	1991	8	217	1,439	13	179.9
Mike Birosak, Dickinson	1989	10	*380	1,798	18	179.8
Guy Leman, Simpson	1998	10	333	1,788	31	178.8
Shane Davis, Loras	1997	10	267	1,774	18	177.4
Rob Marchitello, Maine Maritime	1995	8	292	1,413	19	176.6
Chris Babirad, Wash. & Jeff.	1992	9	243	1,589	22	176.6
Mark Kacmarynski, Central (Iowa)	1994	10	236	1,741	21	174.1

*Record. †National champion.

CAREER YARDS

Player, Team	Years	Plays	Yards	Avg.
Carey Bender, Coe	1991-94	926	*6,125	6.61
Steve Tardif, Maine Maritime	1996-99	*1,190	6,093	5.12
#R. J. Bowers, Grove City	1997-99	836	5,620	6.72
Joe Dudek, Plymouth St.	1982-85	785	5,570	‡7.10
Mark Kacmarynski, Central (Iowa)	$1992-96	854	5,434	6.36
Brad Olson, Lawrence	1994-97	792	5,325	6.72
Eric Frees, Western Md.	1988-91	1,059	5,281	4.99
Paul Smith, Gettysburg	1996-99	881	5,205	5.91
Kirk Matthieu, Maine Maritime	$1989-93	964	5,107	5.30
Terry Underwood, Wagner	1985-88	742	5,010	6.75
Steve Dixon, Beloit	1990-93	986	4,792	4.86
Shane Davis, Loras	1994-97	694	4,738	6.83
Mike Birosak, Dickinson	1986-89	1,112	4,662	4.19
Jamie Lee, MacMurray	1994-95, 97-98	742	4,586	6.18
Dante Brown, Marietta	1994-97	712	4,512	6.34
Jim Romagna, Loras	1989-92	983	4,493	4.57
Chris Babirad, Wash. & Jeff.	1989-92	683	4,419	6.47
Petie Davis, Wesley	1991-94	741	4,414	5.96
Mike Hankins, Wilkes	1996-99	874	4,399	5.03
Tim Lightfoot, Westfield St.	1992-95	876	4,380	5.00
Willie Beers, John Carroll	1989-92	848	4,332	5.11
Rob Marchitello, Maine Maritime	1993-95	879	4,300	4.89
Bob Beatty, Wartburg	1991-94	875	4,292	4.91
Trevor Shannon, Wartburg	1995-98	832	4,292	5.16
Frank Baker, Chicago	1990-93	855	4,283	5.01

*Record. #Active player. $See page 6 for explanation. ‡Record for minimum 500 carries.

SEASON YARDS

Player, Team	Year	G	Plays	Yards	Avg.
Dante Brown, Marietta	†1996	10	314	*2,385	7.60
R. J. Bowers, Grove City	†1998	10	329	2,283	6.94
Carey Bender, Coe	†1994	10	295	2,243	7.60
R. J. Bowers, Grove City	†1999	10	344	2,098	6.10
Ricky Gales, Simpson	†1989	10	297	2,035	6.85
Kelvin Gladney, Millsaps	1994	10	307	1,882	6.13
D'Andra Freeman, Fitchburg St.	1999	10	365	1,871	5.13
Jon Warga, Wittenberg	†1990	10	254	1,836	7.23
Jamie Lee, MacMurray	1998	10	252	1,818	7.21
Terry Underwood, Wagner	†1988	9	245	1,809	6.75
Mike Birosak, Dickinson	1989	10	*380	1,798	4.73
Guy Leman, Simpson	1998	10	333	1,788	5.37
Shane Davis, Loras	1997	10	267	1,774	6.64
Kenneth Sasu, Marietta	1999	9	332	1,770	5.33
Brad Olson, Lawrence	†1995	9	242	1,760	7.27
Mark Kacmarynski, Central (Iowa)	1994	10	236	1,741	7.38
Kirk Matthieu, Maine Maritime	†1992	9	327	1,733	5.30
Sandy Rogers, Emory & Henry	†1986	11	231	1,730	7.49
Carey Bender, Coe	†1993	10	261	1,718	6.58
Spencer Johnson, Wis.-Whitewater	1994	10	290	1,697	5.85
Anthony Russo, St. John's (N.Y.)	†1991	10	287	1,685	5.87
Brandon Steinheim, Wesley	1996	9	319	1,684	5.28
Krishaun Gilmore, Rensselaer	1998	9	228	1,670	7.32
John Bernatavitz, Dickinson	1990	10	266	1,666	6.26
Jamie Lee, MacMurray	†1997	8	207	1,639	‡7.92
Casey Donaldson, Wittenberg	1998	10	234	1,639	7.00

*Record. †National champion. ‡Record for minimum 195 carries.

SINGLE-GAME YARDS

Yds.	Player, Team (Opponent)	Date
441	Dante Brown, Marietta (Baldwin-Wallace)	Oct. 5, 1996
436	A. J. Pittorino, Hartwick (Waynesburg)	Nov. 2, 1996
417	Carey Bender, Coe (Grinnell)	Oct. 9, 1993
413	Dante Brown, Marietta (Heidelberg)	Nov. 9, 1996
390	Paul Smith, Gettysburg (Muhlenberg)	Oct. 23, 1999
382	Pete Baranek, Carthage (North Central)	Oct. 5, 1985
382	Shane Davis, Loras (Dubuque)	Nov. 8, 1997
363	Terry Underwood, Wagner (Hofstra)	Oct. 15, 1988
361	Guy Leman, Simpson (Luther)	Nov. 14, 1998
354	Terry Underwood, Wagner (Western Conn. St.)	Oct. 3, 1986
352	Steve Tardif, Maine Maritime (Westfield St.)	Nov. 16, 1996
348	Carey Bender, Coe (Beloit)	Nov. 12, 1994
347	Chuck Wotkowicz, Johns Hopkins (Georgetown)	Oct. 22, 1993
342	Dave Bednarek, Wis.-River Falls (Wis.-Stevens Point)	Oct. 29, 1983
342	Trevor Shannon, Wartburg (Loras)	Oct. 5, 1996
337	Eric Hamilton, Concordia (Wis.)(Concordia [Ill.])	Oct. 30, 1999
337	Kirk Matthieu, Maine Maritime (Curry)	Oct. 27, 1990
337	Ted Helsel, St. Francis (Pa.) (Gallaudet)	Nov. 3, 1979
335	Paul Smith, Gettysburg (St. Lawrence)	Oct. 30, 1999
334	Oliver Bridges, Stony Brook (Pace)	Nov. 16, 1991

ANNUAL CHAMPIONS

Year	Player, Team	Class	G	Plays	Yards	Avg.
1973	Billy Johnson, Widener	Sr.	9	168	1,494	166.0
1974	Tim Barrett, John Carroll	Sr.	9	256	1,409	156.6
1975	Ron Baker, Monmouth (Ill.)	Sr.	8	200	1,116	139.5
1976	Chuck Evans, Ferris St.	Jr.	10	224	1,509	150.9
1977	Don Taylor, Central (Iowa)	Sr.	9	267	1,329	147.7
1978	Dino Hall, Rowan	Sr.	10	239	1,330	133.0
1979	Clay Sampson, Denison	Jr.	9	323	1,517	168.6
1980	Scott Reppert, Lawrence	So.	8	223	1,223	152.9
1981	Scott Reppert, Lawrence	Jr.	9	250	1,410	156.7
1982	Scott Reppert, Lawrence	Sr.	8	254	1,323	165.4
1983	John Franco, Wagner	Sr.	8	175	1,166	145.8
1984	Gary Errico, Mass.-Lowell	Sr.	9	165	1,404	156.0
1985	Bruce Montella, Chicago	Sr.	9	265	1,372	152.4
1986	Sandy Rogers, Emory & Henry	Sr.	11	231	1,730	157.3
1987	Chris Dabrow, Claremont-M-S	Sr.	9	265	1,486	165.1
1988	Terry Underwood, Wagner	Sr.	9	245	1,809	201.0
1989	Ricky Gales, Simpson	Sr.	10	297	2,035	203.5
1990	Jon Warga, Wittenberg	Sr.	10	254	1,836	183.6
1991	Hank Wineman, Albion	Sr.	9	307	1,629	181.0
1992	Kirk Matthieu, Maine Maritime	Jr.	9	327	1,733	192.6
1993	Carey Bender, Coe	Jr.	10	261	1,718	171.8
1994	Carey Bender, Coe	Sr.	10	295	2,243	224.3
1995	Brad Olson, Lawrence	So.	9	242	1,760	195.6
1996	Dante Brown, Marietta	Jr.	10	314	*2,385	*238.5
1997	Jamie Lee, MacMurray	Sr.	8	207	1,639	204.9
1998	R. J. Bowers, Grove City	So.	10	329	2,283	228.3
1999	R. J. Bowers, Grove City	Jr.	10	344	2,098	209.8

*Record.

Passing

CAREER PASSING EFFICIENCY
(Minimum 325 Completions)

Player, Team	Years	Att.	Cmp.	Int.	Pct.	Yards	TD	Pts.
Bill Borchert, Mount Union	1994-97	1,009	671	17	‡.665	10,201	141	*194.2
Kurt Ramler, St. John's (Minn.)	1994-96	722	420	16	.582	6,475	75	163.4
Matt Wheeler, Wartburg	1996-99	595	362	21	.608	5,390	59	162.6
Danny Ragsdale, Redlands	1997-99	610	386	17	.633	5,560	51	161.9
Kyle Adamson, Allegheny	1995-97	608	388	18	.638	5,506	48	160.0
Craig Kusick, Wis.-La Crosse	1993-95	537	327	14	.609	4,767	48	159.8
Jim Ballard, Wilmington (Ohio)/Mount Union	1990, 91-93	1,199	743	41	.620	10,379	115	159.5
Troy Dougherty, Grinnell	1994, 97-99	1,192	734	33	.616	10,140	109	157.7
Jason Baer, Wash. & Jeff.	1993-96	671	406	24	.605	5,632	66	156.3
Joel Parrett, Bluffton	1996-99	633	412	28	.651	5,684	43	154.1
Joe Blake, Simpson	1987-90	672	399	15	.594	6,183	43	153.3
Mike Burton, Trinity (Tex.)	1996-99	1,067	631	29	.591	9,008	92	153.1
Sean Hoolihan, Wis.-Eau Claire	1996-98	686	413	23	.602	6,301	46	152.8
Willie Reyna, La Verne	1991-92	542	346	19	.638	4,712	37	152.4
Greg Lister, Rowan	1994-97	773	454	29	.587	6,553	66	150.6
Justin Peery, Westminster (Mo.)	1996-99	1,669	*1,012	57	.606	*13,262	*148	149.8
Geoff Hemlinger, Baldwin-Wallace	1995-98	592	348	14	.588	4,936	46	149.7
Gary Collier, Emory & Henry	1984-87	738	386	33	.523	6,103	80	148.6
John Koz, Baldwin-Wallace	1990-93	981	609	28	.621	7,724	71	146.4
Ron Sermarini, Western Md.	1996-99	970	617	20	.636	7,197	68	144.9
Greg Kaiser, St. Thomas (Minn.)	1996-99	810	498	23	.615	6,439	54	144.6
Greg Heeres, Hope	1981-84	630	347	21	.537	5,120	53	144.4
Jeff Brown, Wheaton (Ill.)	1992-95	767	441	30	.575	6,219	60	143.6
Lon Erickson, Ill. Wesleyan	1993-96	786	461	24	.587	6,108	58	142.2
Chris Esterley, St. Thomas (Minn.)	1993-96	1,012	615	30	.608	7,709	71	142.0
Kevin Ricca, Catholic	1994-97	1,109	713	56	.643	9,469	89	142.0

*Record. ‡Record for minimum 750 attempts.

SEASON PASSING EFFICIENCY
(Minimum 15 Attempts Per Game)

Player, Team	Year	G	Att.	Cmp.	Int.	Pct.	Yards	TD	Pts.
Mike Simpson, Eureka	†1994	10	158	116	5	.734	1,988	25	*225.0
Willie Seiler, St. John's (Minn.)	†1993	10	205	141	6	.687	2,648	33	224.6
Bill Borchert, Mount Union	†1997	10	272	190	1	.698	2,933	*47	‡216.7
Bill Borchert, Mount Union	†1996	10	240	165	6	.687	2,655	38	208.9
Gary Smeck, Mount Union	†1999	10	199	131	3	.658	2,274	30	208.6
Matt LeFever, Western Conn. St.	1999	10	158	95	7	.601	1,874	25	203.1
Troy Dougherty, Grinnell	†1998	10	293	198	5	.675	3,310	36	199.6
Bill Borchert, Mount Union	†1995	10	225	160	4	.711	2,270	30	196.3
Jim Ballard, Mount Union	1993	10	314	229	11	*.729	3,304	37	193.2
Jason Baer, Wash. & Jeff.	1995	8	146	95	3	.650	1,536	19	192.3
Greg Lister, Rowan	1997	9	162	111	4	.685	1,688	20	191.9
Ty Grovesteen, Wis.-Whitewater	1998	9	180	103	5	.572	2,074	22	188.8
Kurt Ramler, St. John's (Minn.)	1994	9	154	93	4	.603	1,560	22	187.4
Mike Bajakian, Williams	1994	8	141	92	1	.652	1,382	17	186.0
Kevin Ricca, Catholic	1997	10	306	208	6	.679	2,990	35	183.9
Mitch Sanders, Bridgeport	1973	10	151	84	7	.556	1,551	23	182.9
Pat Mayew, St. John's (Minn.)	†1991	9	247	154	4	.623	2,408	30	181.0
Guy Simons, Coe	1993	10	185	110	9	.594	1,979	21	177.1
Kyle Adamson, Allegheny	1996	10	182	119	3	.653	1,761	18	176.0
Jimbo Fisher, Samford	†1987	10	252	139	5	.551	2,394	34	175.4
Gary Collier, Emory & Henry	1987	11	249	152	10	.610	2,317	33	174.8
Paul Bell, Allegheny	1994	10	215	142	2	.660	2,137	17	173.8
Greg Lister, Rowan	1996	8	167	94	2	.562	1,711	17	173.6
James Grant, Ramapo	1989	9	147	91	7	.619	1,441	17	172.7
Chris Adams, Gettysburg	1994	10	211	139	2	.658	1,977	19	172.4

*Record. †National champion. ‡Record for minimum 25 attempts per game.

CAREER YARDS

Player, Team	Years	Att.	Cmp.	Int.	Pct.	Yards	TD
Justin Peery, Westminster (Mo.)	1996-99	1,669	*1,012	57	.606	*13,262	*148
Kirk Baumgartner, Wis.-Stevens Point	1986-89	*1,696	883	57	.521	13,028	110
Mark Novara, Lakeland	1994-97	1,586	882	63	.556	11,101	100
Jim Ballard, Wilmington (Ohio)/Mount Union	1990, 91-93	1,199	743	41	.620	10,379	115
Bill Borchert, Mount Union	1994-97	1,009	671	17	.665	10,201	141
Troy Dougherty, Grinnell	1994, 97-99	1,192	734	33	.616	10,140	109
Bryan Snyder, Albright	1994-97	1,294	763	49	.590	9,865	92
Keith Bishop, Ill. Wesleyan/Wheaton (Ill.)	1981, 83-85	1,311	772	65	.589	9,579	71
Dennis Bogacz, Wis.-Oshkosh/Wis.-Whitewater	1988-89, 90-91	1,275	654	59	.513	9,536	66
Dave Geissler, Wis.-Stevens Point	1982-85	1,346	789	57	.586	9,518	65
Kevin Ricca, Catholic	1994-97	1,190	713	56	.643	9,469	89
Eric Noble, Wilmington (Ohio)	1992-95	1,264	682	62	.540	9,260	62
John Clark, Wis.-Eau Claire	1987-90	1,119	645	42	.576	9,196	63
Mike Burton, Trinity (Tex.)	1996-99	1,067	631	29	.591	9,008	92
Brian Tomalak, Wis.-Oshkosh	1994-98	1,129	607	32	.538	8,983	83
Tim Peterson, Wis.-Stout	1986-89	1,185	653	62	.551	8,881	59
Matt D'Orazio, Otterbein	1996-99	1,224	680	35	.556	8,770	73

Grinnell's Troy Dougherty is sixth in Division III in career passing yards (10,140) and fifth in career touchdown passes (109).

Mike Burton threw 92 touchdown passes for Trinity (Texas) from 1996-99, placing him in a tie for eighth on the Division III list.

Player, Team	Years	Att.	Cmp.	Int.	Pct.	Yards	TD
Jordan Poznick, Principia	1990-93	1,480	765	68	.517	8,485	55
Matt Bunyan, Wis.-Stout	1995-98	1,119	624	36	.558	8,462	85
Brad Hensley, Kenyon	1991-94	1,439	718	61	.499	8,154	65
Nick Caserio, John Carroll	1995-98	1,093	653	35	.597	8,050	77
Troy Dougherty, Grinnell	1994, 97-98	894	554	22	.620	7,817	80
John Koz, Baldwin-Wallace	1990-93	981	609	28	.621	7,724	71
Luke Hanks, Otterbein	1990-93	1,267	715	62	.564	7,718	47
Chris Esterley, St. Thomas (Minn.)	1993-96	1,012	615	30	.608	7,709	71

*Record.

CAREER YARDS PER GAME
(Minimum 4,500 yards)

Player, Team	Years	G	Att.	Cmp.	Int.	Pct.	Yards	TD	Avg.
Justin Peery, Westminster (Mo.)	1996-99	39	1,669	*1,012	57	.606	*13,262	*148	*340.1
Kirk Baumgartner, Wis.-Stevens Point	1986-89	41	*1,696	883	57	.521	13,028	110	317.8
Keith Bishop, Ill. Wesleyan/Wheaton (Ill.)	1981, 83-85	31	1,311	772	65	.589	9,579	71	309.0
Mark Novara, Lakeland	1994-97	38	1,586	882	63	.556	11,101	100	292.1
Bryan Snyder, Albright	1994-97	35	1,294	763	49	.590	9,865	92	281.9
Willie Reyna, La Verne	1991-92	17	542	346	19	.638	4,712	37	277.2
Troy Dougherty, Grinnell	1994, 97-99	37	1,192	734	33	.616	10,140	109	274.1
Gregg McDonald, Kalamazoo	1994-96	27	1,019	593	41	.582	7,339	50	271.8
Troy Dougherty, Grinnell	1994, 97-98	29	894	554	22	.620	7,817	80	269.6
Jordan Poznick, Principia	1990-93	32	1,480	765	68	.517	8,485	55	265.2
Jim Ballard, Wilmington (Ohio)/Mount Union	1990, 91-93	40	1,199	743	41	.620	10,379	115	259.5
Travis McMahen, Franklin	1997-99	26	962	530	32	.551	6,737	59	259.1
Brian Partlow, Randolph-Macon	1997-99	20	786	421	29	.536	5,179	46	259.0
Bill Borchert, Mount Union	1994-97	40	1,009	671	17	‡.665	10,201	*141	255.0
Chris Stormer, Hanover	1995-98	27	950	619	29	.652	6,814	58	252.4
Dennis Bogacz, Wis.-Oshkosh/Wis.-Whitewater	1988-89, 90-91	38	1,275	654	59	.513	9,536	66	250.9
Brian Tomalak, Wis.-Oshkosh	1994-98	36	1,129	607	32	.538	8,983	83	249.5
Tim Peterson, Wis.-Stout	1986-89	36	1,185	653	62	.551	8,881	59	246.7
Braxton Shaver, McMurry	1997-99	29	1,026	560	33	.546	7,147	84	246.4
Rob Bristow, Pomona-Pitzer	1983-86	29	1,155	628	60	.544	7,120	27	245.5
Eric Noble, Wilmington (Ohio)	1992-95	38	1,264	682	62	.540	9,260	62	243.7
John Rooney, Ill. Wesleyan	1982-84	27	986	489	47	.496	6,576	55	243.6
John Clark, Wis.-Eau Claire	1987-90	38	1,119	645	42	.576	9,196	63	242.0
Brian Van Deusen, Western Md.	1992-95	30	1,129	621	40	.550	7,239	51	241.3
Matt Bunyan, Wis.-Stout	1995-98	36	1,119	624	36	.558	8,462	85	235.1

*Record. ‡Record for minimum 750 attempts.

CAREER TOUCHDOWN PASSES

Player, Team	Years	G	TD
Justin Peery, Westminster (Mo.)	1996-99	39	*148
Bill Borchert, Mount Union	1994-97	40	141
Jim Ballard, Wilmington (Ohio)/Mount Union	1990, 91-93	40	115
Kirk Baumgartner, Wis.-Stevens Point	1986-89	41	110
Troy Dougherty, Grinnell	1994, 97-99	37	109
Mark Novara, Lakeland	1994-97	38	100
Matt Jozokos, Plymouth St.	1987-90	40	95
Bryan Snyder, Albright	1994-97	35	92
Mike Burton, Trinity (Tex.)	1996-99	39	92
Kevin Ricca, Catholic	1994-97	34	89
Matt Bunyan, Wis.-Stout	1995-98	36	85
Braxton Shaver, McMurry	1997-99	29	84
Brian Tomalak, Wis.-Oshkosh	1994-98	36	83
Gary Collier, Emory & Henry	1984-87	41	80
Terry Peebles, Hanover	1992-95	23	79

*Record.

SEASON YARDS

Player, Team	Year	G	Att.	Cmp.	Int.	Pct.	Yards	TD
Justin Peery, Westminster (Mo.)	1998	10	526	319	21	.606	*4,501	51
Justin Peery, Westminster (Mo.)	1999	10	498	*329	15	.660	4,092	*54
Kirk Baumgartner, Wis.-Stevens Point	1988	11	*527	276	16	.524	3,828	25
Kirk Baumgartner, Wis.-Stevens Point	1987	11	466	243	22	.521	3,755	31
Kirk Baumgartner, Wis.-Stevens Point	1989	10	455	247	9	.542	3,692	39
Danny Ragsdale, Redlands	1999	9	380	247	7	.650	3,639	33
Travis McMahen, Franklin	1999	10	486	264	15	.543	3,554	28
Terry Peebles, Hanover	1995	10	488	283	10	.579	3,521	39
Mark Novara, Lakeland	1996	10	410	258	12	.629	3,405	40
John Furmaniak, Eureka	1995	10	361	210	11	.581	3,372	34
Adam Ryan, Wilmington (Ohio)	1999	10	372	212	10	.569	3,343	34
Troy Dougherty, Grinnell	1998	10	293	198	5	.675	3,310	36
Jim Ballard, Mount Union	1993	10	314	229	11	*.729	3,304	37
Keith Bishop, Wheaton (Ill.)	1983	9	375	236	19	.629	3,274	24
Chris Stormer, Hanover	1998	10	424	286	8	.674	3,265	31
Matt Bunyon, Wis.-Stout	1997	10	399	223	12	.558	3,221	33
Matt Bunyan, Wis.-Stout	1998	10	389	227	9	.583	3,220	38
Tom Stallings, St. Thomas (Minn.)	1993	10	395	219	20	.554	3,210	22

ANNUAL CHAMPIONS, ALL-TIME LEADERS—PASSING

Player, Team	Year	G	Att.	Cmp.	Int.	Pct.	Yards	TD
Terry Peebles, Hanover	1994	10	445	252	17	.566	3,197	37
Bill Nietzke, Alma	1996	9	440	248	21	.563	3,197	28
Keith Bishop, Wheaton (Ill.)	1985	9	457	262	22	.573	3,171	25
Brad Boyd, Hardin-Simmons	1999	10	315	192	17	.609	3,134	27
Scott Isphording, Hanover	1992	10	359	207	19	.576	3,098	24
Mark Novara, Lakeland	1997	10	427	252	6	.590	3,098	23
Gregg McDonald, Kalamazoo	1996	9	367	237	10	.645	3,089	23

*Record.

SEASON YARDS PER GAME

Player, Team	Year	G	Att.	Cmp.	Int.	Pct.	Yards	TD	Avg.
Justin Peery, Westminster (Mo.)	1998	10	526	319	21	.606	*4,501	51	*450.1
Justin Peery, Westminster (Mo.)	1999	10	498	*329	15	.660	4,092	*54	409.2
Danny Ragsdale, Redlands	1999	9	380	247	7	.650	3,639	33	404.3
Kirk Baumgartner, Wis.-Stevens Point	1989	10	455	247	9	.543	3,692	39	369.2
Keith Bishop, Wheaton (Ill.)	1983	9	375	236	19	.629	3,274	24	363.8
Travis McMahen, Franklin	1999	10	486	264	15	.543	3,554	28	355.4
Bill Nietzke, Alma	1996	9	440	248	21	.563	3,197	28	355.2
Keith Bishop, Wheaton (Ill.)	1985	9	457	262	22	.573	3,171	25	352.3
Terry Peebles, Hanover	1995	10	488	283	10	.579	3,521	39	352.1
Kirk Baumgartner, Wis.-Stevens Point	1988	11	*527	276	16	.524	3,828	25	348.0
Gregg McDonald, Kalamazoo	1996	9	367	237	10	.645	3,089	23	343.2
Kirk Baumgartner, Wis.-Stevens Point	1987	11	466	243	22	.521	3,755	31	341.4
Mark Novara, Lakeland	1996	10	410	258	12	.629	3,405	40	340.5
Eric Noble, Wilmington (Ohio)	1994	9	398	221	17	.555	3,058	22	339.8
John Furmaniak, Eureka	1995	10	361	210	11	.581	3,372	34	337.2
Adam Ryan, Wilmington (Ohio)	1999	10	372	212	10	.569	3,343	34	334.3
Steve Austin, Mass.-Boston	1992	9	396	181	25	.457	2,991	29	332.3
Chris Stormer, Hanover	1997	8	352	235	14	.667	2,654	20	331.8
Troy Dougherty, Grinnell	1998	10	293	198	5	.675	3,310	36	331.0
Jim Ballard, Mount Union	1993	10	314	229	11	*.729	3,304	37	330.4
Keith Bishop, Wheaton (Ill.)	1984	9	440	259	16	.589	2,968	21	329.8
Jordan Poznick, Principia	1992	8	451	241	13	.534	2,618	21	327.3
Chris Stormer, Hanover	1998	10	424	286	8	.674	3,265	31	326.5
Matt Bunyan, Wis.-Stout	1997	10	399	223	12	.558	3,221	33	322.1
Matt Bunyon, Wis.-Stout	1998	10	389	227	9	.583	3,220	38	322.0

*Record.

SEASON TOUCHDOWN PASSES

Player, Team	Year	G	TD
Justin Peery, Westminster (Mo.)	1999	10	*54
Justin Peery, Westminster (Mo.)	1998	10	51
Bill Borchert, Mount Union	1997	10	47
Mark Novara, Lakeland	1996	10	40
Terry Peebles, Hanover	1995	10	39
Kirk Baumgartner, Wis.-Stevens Point	1989	10	39
Bryan Snyder, Albright	1996	10	39
Matt Bunyan, Wis.-Stout	1998	10	38
Bill Borchert, Mount Union	1996	10	38
Terry Peebles, Hanover	1994	10	37
Jim Ballard, Mount Union	1993	10	37
Matt D'Orazio, Otterbein	1999	10	36
Troy Dougherty, Grinnell	1998	10	36
Kevin Ricca, Catholic	1997	10	35

*Record.

SINGLE-GAME YARDS

Yds.	Player, Team (Opponent)	Date
619	Justin Peery, Westminster (Mo.) (MacMurray)	Nov. 24, 1998
618	Justin Peery, Westminster (Mo.) (Principia)	Oct. 17, 1998
602	Danny Ragsdale, Redlands (Azusa Pacific)	Sept. 25, 1999
602	Tom Stallings, St. Thomas (Minn.) (Bethel [Minn.])	Nov. 13, 1993
589	Joe Montrella, Juniata (Widener)	Nov. 13, 1999
585	Tim Lynch, Hofstra (Fordham)	Oct. 19, 1991
575	Eric Noble, Wilmington (Ohio) (Urbana)	Nov. 5, 1994
569	Josh Wakefield, Alma (Franklin)	Sept. 25, 1999
563	Justin Peery, Westminster (Mo.) (Greenville)	Sept. 19, 1998
551	Justin Peery, Westminster (Mo.) (Colorado Col.)	Oct. 30, 1999
548	Danny Ragsdale, Redlands (Claremont-M-S)	Oct. 30, 1999
546	Danny Ragsdale, Redlands (Cal Lutheran)	Nov. 13, 1999
546	Bill Nietzke, Alma (Hope)	Oct. 26, 1996
543	Michael Kornblau, Greenville (Blackburn)	Oct. 9, 1999
533	John Love, North Park (Elmhurst)	Oct. 13, 1990
532	Bob Monroe, Knox (Cornell College)	Oct. 11, 1986
529	Justin Peery, Westminster (Mo.) (Bethel [Tenn.])	Nov. 7, 1998
526	Jon DeVille, Menlo (Claremont-M-S)	Nov. 1, 1997
525	Justin Peery, Westminster (Mo.) (Cent. Methodist)	Sept. 11, 1999
525	Chris Stormer, Hanover (Manchester)	Oct. 4, 1997

SINGLE-GAME ATTEMPTS

Att.	Player, Team (Opponent)	Date
81	Jordan Poznick, Principia (Blackburn)	Oct. 10, 1992
79	Mike Wallace, Ohio Wesleyan (Denison)	Oct. 3, 1981
78	Shawn Wheeler, Capital (Ohio Northern)	Nov. 13, 1999
72	Bob Lockhart, Millikin (Franklin)	Nov. 12, 1977

Redlands' Danny Ragsdale threw for more than 500 yards three times in 1999 and averaged 404.3 passing yards per game for the season.

SINGLE-GAME COMPLETIONS

Cmp.	Player, Team (Opponent)	Date
50	Justin Peery, Westminster (Mo.) (MacMurray)	Nov. 14, 1998
50	Tim Lynch, Hofstra (Fordham)	Oct. 19, 1991
48	Jordan Poznick, Principia (Blackburn)	Oct. 10, 1992
47	Mike Wallace, Ohio Wesleyan (Denison)	Oct. 3, 1981
44	Chris Stormer, Hanover (Franklin)	Nov. 14, 1998
43	Chris Czernek, Cal Lutheran (Menlo)	Nov. 6, 1999
43	Bill Nietzke, Alma (Hope)	Oct. 26, 1996
43	Bill Nietzke, Alma (Olivet Nazarene)	Sept. 21, 1996
43	Terry Peebles, Hanover (Franklin)	Nov. 12, 1994
42	Mark Novara, Lakeland (Concordia [Wis.])	Oct. 15, 1994
42	Tim Lynch, Hofstra (Towson)	Nov. 2, 1991
42	Keith Bishop, Wheaton (Ill.) (Millikin)	Sept. 14, 1985
41	Justin Peery, Westminster (Mo.) (Colorado Col.)	Oct. 30, 1999
41	Troy Dougherty, Grinnell (Lawrence)	Oct. 1, 1994
41	Michael Doto, Hofstra (Central Conn. St.)	Sept. 21, 1991
41	Todd Monken, Knox (Cornell College)	Oct. 8, 1988
40	Brian Partlow, Randolph-Macon (Davidson)	Oct. 23, 1999
40	James Parker, Oberlin (Kenyon)	Sept. 20, 1997
40	Chris Stormer, Hanover (Otterbein)	Sept. 6, 1997
40	Dave Geissler, Wis.-Stevens Point (Wis.-Eau Claire)	Nov. 12, 1983

ANNUAL CHAMPIONS

Year	Player, Team	Class	G	Att.	Cmp.	Avg.	Int.	Pct.	Yds.	TD
1973	Pat Clements, Kenyon	Jr.	9	239	133	14.8	17	.556	1,738	12
1974	Larry Cenotto, Pomona-Pitzer	Sr.	9	294	147	16.3	23	.500	2,024	15
1975	Ron Miller, Elmhurst	Sr.	8	205	118	14.8	15	.576	1,398	7
1976	Tom Hamilton, Occidental	Jr.	8	235	131	16.4	10	.557	1,988	10
1977	Tom Hamilton, Occidental	Sr.	9	323	171	19.0	17	.529	2,132	13
1978	Robert Farra, Claremont-M-S	Jr.	9	359	196	21.8	15	.546	2,770	20

Beginning in 1979, ranked on passing efficiency rating points, minimum 15 attempts per game (instead of per-game completions)

Year	Player, Team	Class	G	Att.	Cmp.	Int.	Pct.	Yds.	TD	Pts.
1979	David Broecker, Wabash	Fr.	9	145	81	9	.559	1,311	13	149.0
1980	George Muller, Hofstra	Sr.	10	189	115	14	.608	1,983	15	160.4
1981	Larry Atwater, Coe	Sr.	9	172	92	10	.535	1,615	15	147.2
1982	Mike Bennett, Cornell College	Sr.	9	154	83	8	.539	1,436	17	158.3
1983	Joe Shield, Trinity (Conn.)	Jr.	8	238	135	13	.567	2,185	19	149.1
1984	Cody Dearing, Randolph-Macon	Sr.	10	226	125	12	.553	2,139	27	163.4
1985	Robb Disbennett, Salisbury St.	Sr.	10	153	94	6	.614	1,462	16	168.4
1986	Gary Collier, Emory & Henry	Jr.	11	171	88	6	.514	1,509	21	158.9
1987	Jimbo Fisher, Samford	Sr.	10	252	139	5	.551	2,394	34	175.4
1988	Steve Flynn, Central (Iowa)	Jr.	8	133	82	6	.616	1,190	10	152.5
1989	Joe Blake, Simpson	††Jr.	10	144	93	3	.645	1,705	19	203.3
1990	Dan Sharley, Dayton	†††Sr.	10	149	95	2	.637	1,377	12	165.1
1991	Pat Mayew, St. John's (Minn.)	Sr.	9	247	154	4	.623	2,408	30	181.0
1992	Steve Keller, Dayton	Sr.	10	153	99	5	.647	1,350	17	168.9
1993	Willie Seiler, St. John's (Minn.)	Sr.	10	205	141	6	.687	2,648	33	224.6
1994	Mike Simpson, Eureka	So.	10	158	116	5	.734	1,988	25	*225.0
1995	Bill Borchert, Mount Union	So.	10	225	160	4	.711	2,270	30	196.3
1996	Bill Borchert, Mount Union	Jr.	10	240	165	6	.687	2,655	38	208.9
1997	Bill Borchert, Mount Union	Sr.	10	272	190	1	.698	2,933	47	216.7
1998	Troy Dougherty, Grinnell	Jr.	10	293	198	5	.675	3,310	36	199.6
1999	Gary Smeck, Mount Union	Jr.	10	199	131	5	.658	2,274	30	208.6

*Record. ††Declared champion; with six more pass attempts (making 15 per game), all interceptions, still would have highest efficiency rating (187.3). †††Declared champion; with one more attempt (making 15 per game), an interception, still would have highest efficiency rating (162.8).

ANNUAL PASSING EFFICIENCY LEADERS BEFORE 1979
(Minimum 15 Attempts Per Game)

Year	Player, Team	G	Att.	Cmp.	Int.	Pct.	Yds.	TD	Pts.
1973	Mitch Sanders, Bridgeport	10	151	84	7	.556	1,551	23	182.9
1974	Tom McGuire, Benedictine (Ill.)	10	221	142	16	.643	2,206	16	157.5
1975	Jim Morrow, Wash. & Jeff.	9	137	82	7	.599	1,283	11	154.8
1976	Aaron Van Dyke, Cornell College	9	154	91	12	.591	1,611	14	161.4
1977	Matt Winslow, Middlebury	8	130	79	5	.608	919	17	155.6
1978	Matt Dillon, Cornell College	9	166	98	7	.590	1,567	16	161.7

Receiving

CAREER RECEPTIONS PER GAME
(Minimum 120 Receptions)

Player, Team	Years	G	Rec.	Yards	TD	Rec.PG
Scott Pingel, Westminster (Mo.)	1996-99	39	*436	*6,108	*75	*11.2
Matt Newton, Principia	1990-93	33	287	3,646	32	8.7
Todd Bloom, Hardin-Simmons	1995-97	28	233	2,621	14	8.3
Jeff Clay, Catholic	1994-97	36	269	4,101	44	7.5
Bill Stromberg, Johns Hopkins	1978-81	36	258	3,776	39	7.2
Scott Hvistendahl, Augsburg	1995-98	40	285	4,697	40	7.1
Tarrik Wilson, Hanover	1996-99	34	240	2,897	30	7.1
Tim McNamara, Trinity (Conn.)	1981-84	21	146	2,313	19	7.0
Ron Severance, Otterbein	1989-91	30	207	2,378	17	6.9
Chuck Braun, Wis.-Stevens Point	1980-81	18	124	1,914	19	6.9
Jim Jorden, Wheaton (Ill.)	1982-85	33	225	3,022	22	6.8
Ryan Ditze, Albright	1993-96	33	224	3,169	29	6.8
Mike Groll, Defiance	1996-99	34	231	2,812	20	6.8
Matt Plummer, Dubuque	1996-99	40	271	4,049	42	6.8
Mike Whitehouse, St. Norbert	1986-89	35	230	3,480	37	6.6
Eric Nemec, Albright	1995-98	39	256	3,300	35	6.6
Kurt Barth, Eureka	1994-97	39	256	4,311	51	6.6
Joe Rettler, Ripon	1997-99	29	189	3,100	27	6.5
Dan Daley, Pomona-Pitzer	1985-88	35	227	2,598	10	6.5
Rich Johnson, Pace	1985-87	29	188	2,614	8	6.5
Steve Wilkerson, Catholic	1993-94	19	120	1,966	17	6.3
Chris Bisaillon, Ill. Wesleyan	1989-92	36	223	3,670	55	6.2
Rick Fry, Occidental	1974-77	33	200	3,073	18	6.1
Zac Williams, Ill. Wesleyan	1996-99	23	139	1,765	24	6.0
Chris Hanratty, Concordia (Wis.)	1997-98	20	120	1,702	17	6.0
Mike Funk, Wabash	1985, 87-89	38	228	2,858	33	6.0

*Record.

SEASON RECEPTIONS PER GAME

Player, Team	Year	G	Rec.	Yards	TD	Rec.PG
Scott Pingel, Westminster (Mo.)	†1999	10	*136	1,648	24	*13.6
Scott Pingel, Westminster (Mo.)	†1998	10	130	*2,157	*26	13.0
Matt Newton, Principia	†1992	8	98	1,487	14	12.3
Matt Newton, Principia	†1993	8	96	1,080	11	12.0
Jeff Clay, Catholic	†1997	10	112	1,625	20	11.2
Scott Hvistendahl, Augsburg	1998	10	112	1,860	15	11.2
Ben Fox, Hanover	†1995	9	95	1,087	15	10.6
Sean Munroe, Mass.-Boston	1992	9	95	1,693	17	10.6
Scott Faessler, Framingham St.	†1990	9	92	916	5	10.2
Scott Pingel, Westminster (Mo.)	1997	10	98	1,420	17	9.8
Mike Funk, Wabash	†1989	9	87	1,169	12	9.7
Jim Jorden, Wheaton (Ill.)	†1985	9	87	1,011	8	9.7
Theo Blanco, Wis.-Stevens Point	1987	11	106	1,616	8	9.6
Todd Bloom, Hardin-Simmons	†1996	10	96	1,019	6	9.6
Eric Nemec, Albright	1997	9	86	1,147	15	9.6
Sean Eaton, Randolph-Macon	1999	10	95	1,289	15	9.5
Jason Tincher, Wilmington (Ohio)	†1994	9	85	1,298	9	9.4
Mike Groll, Defiance	1999	9	84	1,010	11	9.3
Rick Fry, Occidental	†1976	8	74	1,214	8	9.3
Tarrik Wilson, Hanover	1999	9	83	974	7	9.2
Darryl DeShields, Greenville	1999	10	92	1,515	12	9.2
Mike Cook, Claremont-M-S	1995	9	83	993	7	9.2
Ron Severance, Otterbein	1990	10	92	1,049	8	9.2
Matt Perceval, Wesleyan (Conn.)	1999	8	73	1,137	13	9.1
Rick Fry, Occidental	†1977	9	82	1,222	5	9.1
Jim Myers, Kenyon	†1974	9	82	1,483	12	9.1

*Record. †National champion.

CAREER RECEPTIONS

Player, Team	Years	Rec.	Yards	TD
Scott Pingel, Westminster (Mo.)	1996-99	*436	*6,108	*75
Matt Newton, Principia	1990-93	287	3,646	32
Scott Hvistendahl, Augsburg	1995-98	285	4,696	40
Matt Plummer, Dubuque	1996-99	271	4,049	42
Jeff Clay, Catholic	1994-97	269	4,101	44
Bill Stromberg, Johns Hopkins	1978-81	258	3,776	39
Eric Nemec, Albright	1995-98	256	3,300	35
Kurt Barth, Eureka	1994-97	256	4,311	51
Tarrik Wilson, Hanover	1996-99	240	2,897	30
Todd Bloom, Hardin-Simmons	1995-97	233	2,621	14
Dale Amos, Frank. & Marsh.	1986-89	233	3,846	35
Scott Fredrickson, Wis.-Stout	1986-89	233	3,390	23
Mike Groll, Defiance	1996-99	231	2,812	20
Mike Whitehouse, St. Norbert	1986-89	230	3,480	37
Mike Funk, Wabash	1985, 87-89	228	2,858	33
Dan Daley, Pomona-Pitzer	1985-88	227	2,598	10
Jim Jorden, Wheaton (Ill.)	1982-85	225	3,022	22
Brandon Good, Wooster	1995-98	224	2,838	30
Ryan Ditze, Albright	1993-96	224	3,169	29
Chris Bisaillon, Ill. Wesleyan	1989-92	223	3,670	55
Theo Blanco, Wis.-Stevens Point	1985-88	223	3,139	18
Ed Brady, Ill. Wesleyan	1981-84	220	2,907	22
Richard Wemer, Grinnell	1995-98	219	3,133	40
Walter Kalinowski, Catholic	1983-86	219	2,430	16
Jim Bradford, Carleton	1988-91	212	3,719	32
Mike Cottle, Juniata	1985-88	212	2,607	36
John Ward, Cornell College	1979-82	211	3,085	30

*Record.

SEASON RECEPTIONS

Player, Team	Year	G	Rec.	Yards	TD
Scott Pingel, Westminster (Mo.)	†1999	10	*136	1,648	24
Scott Pingel, Westminster (Mo.)	†1998	10	130	*2,157	*26
Scott Hvistendahl, Augsburg	1998	10	112	1,860	15
Jeff Clay, Catholic	†1997	10	112	1,625	20
Theo Blanco, Wis.-Stevens Point	1987	11	106	1,616	8
Scott Pingel, Westminster (Mo.)	1997	10	98	1,420	17
Matt Newton, Principia	†1992	8	98	1,487	14
Todd Bloom, Hardin-Simmons	†1996	10	96	1,019	6
Matt Newton, Principia	†1993	8	96	1,080	11
Sean Eaton, Randolph-Macon	1999	10	95	1,289	15
Ben Fox, Hanover	†1995	9	95	1,087	15
Sean Munroe, Mass.-Boston	1992	9	95	1,693	17
Darryl DeShields, Greenville	1999	10	92	1,515	12
Ron Severance, Otterbein	1990	10	92	1,049	8
Scott Faessler, Framingham St.	†1990	9	92	916	5
Steve Wilkerson, Catholic	1994	10	90	1,457	13
Vince Annel, Knox	1999	10	87	1,062	6
Mike Hunter, Catholic	1998	10	87	1,279	12
Greg Lehrer, Heidelberg	1993	10	87	1,202	8
Mike Funk, Wabash	†1989	9	87	1,169	12
Ted Taggart, Kenyon	1989	10	87	1,004	7
Jim Jorden, Wheaton (Ill.)	†1985	9	87	1,011	8
Eric Nemec, Albright	1997	9	86	1,147	15
Matt Plummer, Dubuque	1996	10	86	1,237	12
Tarrik Wilson, Hanover	1998	10	85	1,014	15
Jason Tincher, Wilmington (Ohio)	†1994	9	85	1,298	9
Ron Severance, Otterbein	†1991	10	85	929	4

*Record. †National champion.

SEASON TOUCHDOWN RECEPTIONS

Player, Team	Year	G	TD
Scott Pingel, Westminster (Mo.)	1998	10	*26
Scott Pingel, Westminster (Mo.)	1999	10	24

Scott Pingel of Division III Westminster (Missouri) is the all-divisions leader in career receptions (436), career yards (6,108) and career touchdown catches (75).

ANNUAL CHAMPIONS, ALL-TIME LEADERS—RECEIVING

Player, Team	Year	G	TD
David Snider, Grinnell	1998	10	21
Steve Vagades, Ohio Northern	1998	10	20
Kirk Aikens, Hartwick	1998	10	20
Jeff Clay, Catholic	1997	10	20
John Aromando, Col. of New Jersey	1983	10	20
Matt Eisenberg, Juniata	1999	10	19
Adam Marino, Mount Union	1999	10	19
Ben Streby, Otterbein	1999	10	19
Chad Hustead, Redlands	1999	9	18
Ryan Hinske, Wis.-Oshkosh	1997	10	18
Kurt Barth, Eureka	1995	10	18
Scott Pingel, Westminster (Mo.)	1997	10	17
Junior Lord, Guilford	1997	9	17
Jeremy Loretz, St. John's (Minn.)	1994	10	17
Sean Munroe, Mass.-Boston	1992	9	17
Chris Bisaillon, Ill. Wesleyan	1991	9	17
Jon May, Wis.-Oshkosh	1998	10	16
Matt Surette, Worcester Tech	1997	10	16
Wesley Bell, Upper Iowa	1996	10	16
Jeff Clay, Catholic	1996	10	16
Ryan Ditze, Albright	1996	10	16
Evan Elkington, Worcester Tech	1989	10	16

*Record.

SINGLE-GAME RECEPTIONS

No.	Player, Team (Opponent)	Date
23	Sean Munroe, Mass.-Boston (Mass. Maritime)	Oct. 10, 1992
20	Scott Pingel, Westminster (Mo.) (Colorado Col.)	Oct. 30, 1999
20	Todd Bloom, Hardin-Simmons (Mississippi Col.)	Oct. 12, 1996
20	Kurt Barth, Eureka (Concordia [Wis.])	Sept. 28, 1996
20	Rich Johnson, Pace (Fordham)	Nov. 7, 1987
20	Pete Thompson, Carroll (Wis.) (Augustana [Ill.])	Nov. 4, 1978
18	Darryl DeShields, Greenville (Lakeland)	Oct. 2, 1999
18	Scott Hvistendahl, Augsburg (Concordia-M'head)	Nov. 13, 1998
18	Scott Pingel, Westminster (Mo.) (Greenville)	Sept. 19, 1998
18	Richard Wemer, Grinnell (Beloit)	Nov. 20, 1997
18	Adam Herbst, St. John's (Minn.) (St. Thomas [Minn.])	Nov. 7, 1997
18	Jeff Clay, Catholic (Albright)	Nov. 16, 1996
18	Matt Plummer, Dubuque (Buena Vista)	Oct. 12, 1996
18	Craig Antonio, Waynesburg (Bethany [W.Va.])	Oct. 16, 1993
18	Ed Sullivan, Catholic (Carnegie Mellon)	Nov. 7, 1992

CAREER YARDS

Player, Team	Years	Rec.	Yards	Avg.	TD
Scott Pingel, Westminster (Mo.)	1996-99	*436	*6,108	14.0	*75
Scott Hvistendahl, Augsburg	1995-98	285	4,696	16.5	40
Kurt Barth, Eureka	1994-97	256	4,311	16.8	51
Jeff Clay, Catholic	1994-97	269	4,101	15.2	44
Matt Plummer, Dubuque	1996-99	271	4,049	14.9	42
Dale Amos, Frank. & Marsh.	1986-89	233	3,846	16.5	35
Bill Stromberg, Johns Hopkins	1978-81	258	3,776	14.6	39
Jim Bradford, Carleton	1988-91	212	3,719	17.5	32
Chris Bisaillon, Ill. Wesleyan	1989-92	223	3,670	16.5	*55
Matt Newton, Principia	1990-93	287	3,646	12.7	32
Mike Gundersdorf, Wilkes	1993-96	205	3,603	17.6	34
Mike Whitehouse, St. Norbert	1986-89	230	3,480	15.1	37
Scott Fredrickson, Wis.-Stout	1986-89	233	3,390	14.5	23
Eric Nemec, Albright	1995-98	256	3,300	12.9	35
R. J. Hoppe, Carroll (Wis.)	1993-96	152	3,295	21.7	49
John Aromando, Col. of New Jersey	1981-84	165	3,197	19.4	39
Todd Stoner, Kenyon	1981-84	197	3,191	16.2	31
Rodd Patten, Framingham St.	1990-93	154	3,170	20.6	38
Ryan Ditze, Albright	1993-96	224	3,169	14.1	29
Mark Loeffler, Wheaton (Ill.)	1993-96	205	3,163	15.4	43
Theo Blanco, Wis.-Stevens Point	1985-88	223	3,139	14.1	18
Richard Wemer, Grinnell	1995-98	219	3,133	14.3	40
Joe Rettler, Ripon	1997-99	189	3,100	16.4	27
Junior Lord, Guilford	1994-97	201	3,089	15.4	33
John Ward, Cornell College	1979-82	211	3,085	14.6	30

*Record.

CAREER YARDS PER GAME
(Minimum 2,200 Yards)

Player, Team	Years	G	Yards	Yd. PG
Scott Pingel, Westminster (Mo.)	1996-99	39	*6,108	*156.6
Scott Hvistendahl, Augsburg	1995-98	40	4,696	117.4
Jeff Clay, Catholic	1994-97	36	4,101	113.9
Kurt Barth, Eureka	1994-97	39	4,311	110.5
Matt Newton, Principia	1990-93	33	3,646	110.5
Tim McNamara, Trinity (Conn.)	1981-84	21	2,313	110.1
Joe Rettler, Ripon	1997-99	29	3,100	106.9
Bill Stromberg, Johns Hopkins	1978-81	36	3,776	104.9
Chris Bisaillon, Ill. Wesleyan	1989-92	36	3,670	101.9
Matt Plummer, Dubuque	1996-99	40	4,049	101.2
Steve Vagedes, Ohio Northern	1997-99	30	3,036	101.2

*Record.

CAREER TOUCHDOWN RECEPTIONS

Player, Team	Years	G	TD
Scott Pingel, Westminster (Mo.)	1996-99	39	*75
Chris Bisaillon, Ill. Wesleyan	1989-92	36	55
Kurt Barth, Eureka	1994-97	39	51
R. J. Hoppe, Carroll (Wis.)	1993-96	37	49
Jeff Clay, Catholic	1994-97	36	44
Mark Loeffler, Wheaton (Ill.)	1993-96	38	43
Kirk Aikens, Hartwick	1995-98	38	43
Matt Plummer, Dubuque	1996-99	40	42
Scott Hvistendahl, Augsburg	1995-98	40	40
Richard Wemer, Grinnell	1995-98	38	40
Adam Herbst, St. John's (Minn.)	1995-98	39	40
Bill Stromberg, Johns Hopkins	1978-81	40	39
John Aromando, Col. of New Jersey	1981-84	40	39

*Record.

SEASON YARDS

Player, Team	Years	Rec.	Yards	Avg.	TD
Scott Pingel, Westminster (Mo.)	1998	130	*2,157	16.6	*26
Scott Hvistendahl, Augsburg	1998	112	1,860	16.6	15
Sean Munroe, Mass.-Boston	†1992	95	1,693	17.8	17
Scott Pingel, Westminster (Mo.)	†1999	*136	1,648	12.1	24
Jeff Clay, Catholic	†1997	112	1,625	14.5	20
Theo Blanco, Wis.-Stevens Point	1987	106	1,616	15.2	8
Matt Eisenberg, Juniata	1999	76	1,547	20.4	19
Darryl DeShields, Greenville	1999	92	1,515	16.5	12
Matt Newton, Principia	1992	98	1,487	15.2	14
Jim Myers, Kenyon	1974	82	1,483	18.1	12
Jeff Clay, Catholic	†1996	81	1,460	18.0	16
Steve Wilkerson, Catholic	†1994	90	1,457	16.2	13
Adam Marino, Mount Union	1999	73	1,456	19.9	19
Scott Pingel, Westminster (Mo.)	1997	98	1,420	14.5	17
David Snider, Grinnell	1998	63	1,383	22.0	21
Beau Almodobar, Norwich	1984	71	1,375	19.4	10
Stacy Seidl, Lawrence	1999	60	1,343	22.4	12
Kurt Barth, Eureka	†1995	68	1,337	19.7	18
Scott Hvistendahl, Augsburg	1997	84	1,328	15.8	15
Chris Vogel, Knox	1987	78	1,326	17.0	15
Dale Amos, Frank. & Marsh.	1989	72	1,302	18.1	15
Jason Tincher, Wilmington (Ohio)	1994	85	1,298	15.3	9
Don Moehling, Wis.-Stevens Point	1988	72	1,290	17.9	7
Sean Eaton, Randolph-Macon	1999	95	1,289	13.6	15
Matt Surette, Worcester Tech	1997	75	1,287	17.2	16

*Record. †National champion.

SINGLE-GAME YARDS

Yds.	Player, Team (Opponent)	Date
397	Matt Eisenberg, Juniata (Widener)	Nov. 13, 1999
395	Scott Pingel, Westminster (Mo.) (Bethel [Tenn.])	Nov. 7, 1998
364	Jeff Clay, Catholic (Albright)	Nov. 16, 1996
362	Matt Surette, Worcester Tech (Springfield)	Oct. 25, 1997
332	Ryan Pifer, Heidelberg (Marietta)	Nov. 8, 1997
332	Sean Munroe, Mass.-Boston (Mass. Maritime)	Oct. 10, 1992
314	Matt Eisenberg, Juniata (Albright)	Oct. 2, 1999
310	Jeff Clay, Catholic (LaSalle)	Oct. 11, 1997
309	Dale Amos, Frank. & Marsh. (Western Md.)	Oct. 24, 1987
306	Scott Pingel, Westminster (Mo.) (Greenville)	Sept. 19, 1998
303	Chuck Braun, Wis.-Stevens Point (Wis.-Superior)	Oct. 17, 1981
303	Rick Fry, Occidental (Claremont-M-S)	Oct. 30, 1976
301	Jeremy Snyder, Whittier (Occidental)	Nov. 15, 1997
301	Greg Holmes, Carroll (Wis.) (North Central)	Nov. 7, 1981
297	Adam Marino, Mount Union (Ohio Northern)	Sept. 25, 1999
296	Tim Jordain, Rensselaer (St. Lawrence)	Nov. 7, 1998
296	Joe Richards, Johns Hopkins (Georgetown)	Oct. 26, 1991
296	Vince Hull, Minn.-Morris (Bemidji St.)	Oct. 10, 1981
295	Aatron Kenney, Wis.-Stevens Point (Wis.-Stout)	Oct. 24, 1987
293	Mike Stotz, Catholic (Bridgewater [Va.])	Nov. 15, 1980
292	Darryl DeShields, Greenville (Concordia [Ill.])	Nov. 13, 1999
292	Andy Steckel, Western Md. (Gettysburg)	Sept. 15, 1990

ANNUAL CHAMPIONS
RECEPTIONS PER GAME

Year	Player, Team	Class	G	Rec.	Avg.	Yards	TD
1973	Ron Duckett, Trinity (Conn.)	Sr.	8	57	7.1	834	7
1974	Jim Myers, Kenyon	Sr.	9	82	9.1	1,483	12
1975	C. J. DeWitt, Bridgewater (Va.)	Sr.	9	64	7.1	836	2
1976	Rick Fry, Occidental	Jr.	8	74	9.3	1,214	8
1977	Rick Fry, Occidental	Sr.	9	82	9.1	1,222	5
1978	Pat McNamara, Trinity (Conn.)	Jr.	8	67	8.4	1,024	11
1979	Theodore Anderson, Fisk	Jr.	7	49	7.0	699	2
1980	Bill Stromberg, Johns Hopkins	Jr.	9	66	7.3	907	11
1981	Bill Stromberg, Johns Hopkins	Sr.	9	78	8.7	924	10

ANNUAL CHAMPIONS, ALL-TIME LEADERS—RECEIVING

Year	Player, Team	Class	G	Rec.	Avg.	Yards	TD
1982	Jim Gustafson, St. Thomas (Minn.)	Jr.	10	72	7.2	990	5
1983	Ed Brady, Ill. Wesleyan	Jr.	9	80	8.9	873	7
1984	Tim McNamara, Trinity (Conn.)	Sr.	8	67	8.4	1,004	10
1985	Jim Jorden, Wheaton (Ill.)	Sr.	9	87	9.7	1,011	8
1986	John Tucci, Amherst	Sr.	8	70	8.8	1,025	8
1987	Chris Vogel, Knox	So.	9	78	8.7	1,326	15
1988	Theo Blanco, Wis.-Stevens Point	Sr.	10	80	8.0	1,009	7
1989	Mike Funk, Wabash	Sr.	9	87	9.7	1,169	12
1990	Scott Faessler, Framingham St.	So.	9	92	10.2	916	5
1991	Ron Severance, Otterbein	Sr.	10	85	8.5	929	4
1992	Matt Newton, Principia	Jr.	8	98	12.3	1,487	14
1993	Matt Newton, Principia	Sr.	8	96	12.0	1,080	11
1994	Jason Tincher, Wilmington (Ohio)	Sr.	9	85	9.4	1,298	9
1995	Ben Fox, Hanover	Sr.	9	95	10.6	1,087	15
1996	Todd Bloom, Hardin-Simmons	Jr.	10	96	9.6	1,019	6
1997	Jeff Clay, Catholic	Sr.	10	112	11.2	1,625	20
1998	Scott Pingel, Westminster (Mo.)	Jr.	10	130	13.0	*2,157	*26
1999	Scott Pingel, Westminster (Mo.)	Sr.	10	*136	*13.6	1,648	24

YARDS PER GAME

Year	Player, Team	Class	G	Rec.	Yards	TD	Avg.
1990	Ray Shelley, Juniata	Sr.	10	54	1,147	12	114.7
1991	Rodd Patten, Framingham St.	So.	8	49	956	13	119.5
1992	Sean Munroe, Mass.-Boston	Sr.	9	95	1,693	17	188.1
1993	Rob Lokerson, Muhlenberg	Jr.	9	76	1,275	6	141.7
1994	Steve Wilkerson, Catholic	Sr.	10	90	1,457	13	145.7
1995	Kurt Barth, Eureka	So.	10	68	1,337	18	133.7
1996	Jeff Clay, Catholic	Jr.	9	81	1,460	16	162.2
1997	Jeff Clay, Catholic	Sr.	10	112	1,625	20	162.5
1998	Scott Pingel, Westminster (Mo.)	Jr.	10	130	*2,157	*26	*215.7
1999	Scott Pingel, Westminster (Mo.)	Sr.	10	*136	1,648	24	164.8

*Record.

Scoring

CAREER POINTS PER GAME
(Minimum 225 Points)

Player, Team	Years	G	TD	XPt.	FG	Pts.	Pt. PG
Ricky Gales, Simpson	1988-89	19	44	10	0	274	*14.4
Cory Christensen, Simpson	1996-97	19	44	0	0	264	13.9
Rob Marchitello, Maine Maritime	1993-95	26	59	4	0	358	13.8
Carey Bender, Coe	1991-94	39	*86	12	0	*528	13.5
Trevor Shannon, Wartburg	1995-98	39	79	10	0	484	12.4
Scott Pingel, Westminster (Mo.)	1996-99	39	75	34	0	484	12.4
Jim Regan, Pomona-Pitzer	1995-98	30	37	93	15	360	12.0
Chad Hoiska, Wis.-Eau Claire	1995-97	30	58	2	0	350	11.7
Joe Dudek, Plymouth St.	1982-85	41	79	0	0	474	11.6
Chris Babirad, Wash. & Jeff.	1989-92	35	62	2	0	374	10.7
Terry Underwood, Wagner	1985-88	33	58	0	0	348	10.5
Chris Bisaillon, Ill. Wesleyan	1989-92	36	61	12	0	378	10.5
Stanley Drayton, Allegheny	1989-92	32	56	0	0	336	10.5
Greg Novarro, Bentley	1990-92	24	42	0	0	252	10.5
Mark Kacmarynski, Central (Iowa)	$1992-96	41	70	2	0	422	10.3
Ryan Kolpin, Coe	1987-90	28	48	0	0	288	10.3
Anthony Rice, La Verne	1994-96	27	46	0	0	276	10.2
Andrew Notarfrancesco, Catholic	1996-99	39	65	8	0	398	10.2
Trent Nauholz, Simpson	1990-93	31	49	4	0	298	9.6
Dan McGovern, Rensselaer	1994-97	28	44	4	0	268	9.4
Guy Leman, Simpson	1995-98	34	52	0	0	312	9.2
Jason Wooley, Worcester Tech	1990-93	37	55	8	0	338	9.1
R. J. Hoppe, Carroll (Wis.)	1993-96	37	54	12	0	336	9.1
Paul Smith, Gettysburg	1996-99	40	60	2	0	362	9.1
A. J. Pagano, Wash. & Jeff.	1984-87	36	53	5	0	323	9.0
Heath Butler, Martin Luther	1990-93	31	44	14	0	278	9.0

*Record. $See page 6 for explanation.

SEASON POINTS PER GAME

Player, Team	Years	G	TD	XPt.	FG	Pts.	Pt. PG
James Regan, Pomona-Pitzer	†1997	8	21	34	2	166	*20.8
R. J. Bowers, Grove City	†1998	10	*34	2	0	*206	20.6
Guy Leman, Simpson	1998	10	33	0	0	198	19.8
Carey Bender, Coe	†1994	10	32	2	0	194	19.4
Chad Hoiska, Wis.-Eau Claire	1997	10	29	2	0	176	17.6
Jim Mormino, Allegheny	1997	10	29	0	0	174	17.4
Doug Steiner, Grove City	1997	10	29	0	0	174	17.4
Rob Marchitello, Maine Maritime	1994	9	25	4	0	154	17.1
Stanley Drayton, Allegheny	†1991	10	28	0	0	168	16.8
Dante Brown, Marietta	†1996	10	27	4	0	166	16.6
Ricky Gales, Simpson	†1989	10	26	10	0	166	16.6
Matt Malmberg, St. John's (Minn.)	†1993	10	27	2	0	164	16.4
Scott Pingel, Westminster (Mo.)	1998	10	26	6	0	162	16.2

Player, Team	Years	G	TD	XPt.	FG	Pts.	Pt. PG
Trevor Shannon, Wartburg	1998	10	26	6	0	162	16.2
Jamie Lee, MacMurray	1998	10	26	4	0	160	16.0
Chris Babirad, Wash. & Jeff.	†1992	9	24	0	0	144	16.0
Trent Nauholz, Simpson	†1992	8	21	2	0	128	16.0
R. J. Bowers, Grove City	†1999	10	25	4	0	154	15.4
Krishaun Gilmore, Rensselaer	1998	9	23	0	0	138	15.3
Billy Johnson, Widener	†1973	9	23	0	0	138	15.3
Cory Christensen, Simpson	1997	10	25	0	0	150	15.0
Greg Novarro, Bentley	1992	10	25	0	0	150	15.0
Bruce Naszimento, New Jersey City	1973	10	25	0	0	150	15.0
Chris Babirad, Wash. & Jeff.	1991	9	22	2	0	134	14.9
Scott Pingel, Westminster (Mo.)	1999	10	24	4	0	148	14.8
Anthony Jones, La Verne	†1995	8	19	4	0	118	14.8

*Record. †National champion.

CAREER POINTS

Player, Team	Years	TD	XPt.	FG	Pts.
Carey Bender, Coe	1991-94	*86	12	0	528
Scott Pingel, Westminster (Mo.)	1996-99	75	34	0	484
Trevor Shannon, Wartburg	1995-98	79	10	0	484
Joe Dudek, Plymouth St.	1982-85	79	0	0	474
#R. J. Bowers, Grove City	1997-99	73	6	0	444
Mark Kacmarynski, Central (Iowa)	$1992-96	70	2	0	422
Andrew Notarfrancesco, Catholic	1996-99	65	8	0	398
Chris Bisaillon, Ill. Wesleyan	1989-92	61	12	0	378
Chris Babirad, Wash. & Jeff.	1989-92	62	2	0	374
Paul Smith, Gettysburg	1996-99	60	2	0	362
Jim Regan, Pomona-Pitzer	1995-98	40	93	15	360
Rob Marchitello, Maine Maritime	1993-95	59	4	0	358
Chad Hoiska, Wis.-Eau Claire	1995-97	58	2	0	350
Terry Underwood, Wagner	1985-88	58	0	0	348
Jim Romagna, Loras	1989-92	57	2	0	344
Jason Wooley, Worcester Tech	1990-93	55	8	0	338
R. J. Hoppe, Carroll (Wis.)	1993-96	54	12	0	336
Stanley Drayton, Allegheny	1989-92	56	0	0	336
Scott Tumilty, Augustana (Ill.)	1992-95	55	0	0	330
Cary Osborn, Wis.-Eau Claire	1987-90	55	0	0	330
Dante Brown, Marietta	1994-97	54	0	0	328
Matt Taylor, Catholic	1993-96	54	4	0	328
Kurt Barth, Eureka	1994-97	51	21	0	327
Steve Tardif, Maine Maritime	1996-99	53	6	0	324
Tim McDaniel, Centre	1988-91	54	0	0	324

*Record. $See page 6 for explanation. #Active player.

SEASON POINTS

Player, Team	Year	TD	XPt.	FG	Pts.
R. J. Bowers, Grove City	†1998	*34	2	0	*206
Guy Leman, Simpson	1998	33	0	0	198
Carey Bender, Coe	†1994	32	2	0	194
Chad Hoiska, Wis.-Eau Claire	1997	29	2	0	176
Jim Mormino, Allegheny	1997	29	0	0	174
Doug Steiner, Grove City	1997	29	0	0	174
Stanley Drayton, Allegheny	†1991	28	0	0	168
James Regan, Pomona-Pitzer	†1997	21	34	2	166
Dante Brown, Marietta	†1996	27	4	0	166
Ricky Gales, Simpson	†1989	26	10	0	166
Matt Malmberg, St. John's (Minn.)	†1993	27	2	0	164
Scott Pingel, Westminster (Mo.)	1998	26	6	0	162
Trevor Shannon, Wartburg	1998	26	6	0	162
Jamie Lee, MacMurray	1998	26	4	0	160
R. J. Bowers, Grove City	†1999	25	4	0	154
Rob Marchitello, Maine Maritime	1994	25	4	0	154
Cory Christensen, Simpson	1997	25	0	0	150
Greg Novarro, Bentley	1992	25	0	0	150
Joe Dudek, Plymouth St.	1985	25	0	0	150
Bruce Naszimento, New Jersey City	1973	25	0	0	150
Scott Pingel, Westminster (Mo.)	1999	24	4	0	148
Chris Babirad, Wash. & Jeff.	†1992	24	0	0	144
Trevor Shannon, Wartburg	1996	23	4	0	142
Kirk Aikens, Hartwick	1998	23	2	0	140
Andrew Notarfrancesco, Catholic	1999	23	0	0	138
Krishaun Gilmore, Rensselaer	1998	23	0	0	138
Scott Barnyak, Carnegie Mellon	†1990	22	6	0	138
Ryan Kolpin, Coe	†1990	23	0	0	138
Ron Corbett, Cornell College	1982	23	0	0	138
Billy Johnson, Widener	†1973	23	0	0	138

* Record. †National champion.

ANNUAL CHAMPIONS

Year	Player, Team	Class	G	TD	XPt.	FG	Pts.	Avg.
1973	Billy Johnson, Widener	Sr.	9	23	0	0	138	15.3
1974	Joe Thompson, Augustana (Ill.)	So.	9	17	0	0	102	11.3
1975	Ron Baker, Monmouth (Ill.)	Sr.	8	15	2	0	92	11.5

ANNUAL CHAMPIONS, ALL-TIME LEADERS—SCORING

Year	Player, Team	Class	G	TD	XPt.	FG	Pts.	Avg.
1976	Chris Hipsley, Cornell College	So.	9	14	42	2	132	14.7
1977	Chip Zawoiski, Widener	Sr.	9	18	0	0	108	12.0
1978	Roger Andrachik, Baldwin-Wallace	Sr.	8	16	0	0	96	12.0
1979	Jay Wessler, Illinois Col.	Jr.	8	16	4	0	100	12.5
1980	Daryl Johnson, Wabash	Jr.	9	20	0	0	120	13.3
1981	Scott Reppert, Lawrence	Jr.	9	15	0	0	90	10.0
	Daryl Johnson, Wabash	Sr.	9	15	0	0	90	10.0
1982	Rick Bell, St. John's (Minn.)	Sr.	9	21	2	0	128	14.2
1983	John Aromando, Col. of New Jersey	Jr.	10	20	0	0	120	12.0
1984	Joe Dudek, Plymouth St.	Jr.	10	21	0	0	126	12.6
1985	Kevin Weaver, Wash. & Lee	Jr.	8	17	8	0	110	13.8
1986	Jim Korfonta, Hamilton	Sr.	8	16	0	0	96	12.0
	Russ Kring, Mount Union	Jr.	10	20	0	0	120	12.0
1987	Michael Waithe, Curry	Sr.	8	19	0	0	114	14.3
1988	Terry Underwood, Wagner	Sr.	9	21	0	0	126	14.0
1989	Ricky Gales, Simpson	Sr.	10	26	10	0	166	16.6
1990	Scott Barnyak, Carnegie Mellon	Sr.	10	22	6	0	138	13.8
	Ryan Kolpin, Coe	Sr.	10	23	0	0	138	13.8
1991	Stanley Drayton, Allegheny	Jr.	10	28	0	0	168	16.8
1992	Chris Babirad, Wash. & Jeff.	Sr.	9	24	0	0	144	16.0
	Trent Nauholz, Simpson	Jr.	8	21	2	0	128	16.0
1993	Matt Malmberg, St. John's (Minn.)	Jr.	10	27	2	0	164	16.4
1994	Carey Bender, Coe	Sr.	10	32	2	0	194	19.4
1995	Anthony Jones, La Verne	Sr.	8	19	4	0	118	14.8
1996	Dante Brown, Marietta	Jr.	10	27	4	0	166	16.6
1997	James Regan, Pomona-Pitzer	Jr.	8	21	34	2	166	*20.8
1998	R. J. Bowers, Grove City	So.	10	*34	2	0	*206	20.6
1999	R. J. Bowers, Grove City	Jr.	10	25	4	0	154	15.4

*Record.

Interceptions

CAREER INTERCEPTIONS

Player, Team	Years	No.	Yards	Avg.
Ralph Gebhardt, Rochester	1973-75	*29	384	13.2
Brian Fetterolf, Aurora	1986-89	28	390	13.9
Rick Bealer, Lycoming	1987-90	28	279	10.0
Andrew Ostrand, Carroll (Wis.)	1990-93	27	258	9.6
Tim Lennon, Curry	1986-89	27	190	7.0
Mike Hintz, Wis.-Platteville	1983-86	27	183	6.8
Scott Stanitous, Moravian	1985-88	27	178	6.6
Mark Dorner, Juniata	1984-87	26	*443	17.0
Cory Mabry, Susquehanna	1988-91	26	400	15.4
Jeff Hughes, Ripon	1975-78	26	333	12.8
Jon Dunham, Denison	1996-99	25	333	13.3
Neal Guggemos, St. Thomas (Minn.)	1982-85	25	377	15.1
Dave Adams, Carleton	1984-87	25	327	13.1
Will Hill, Bishop	1983-86	25	261	10.4
Tom Devine, Juniata	1979-82	25	248	9.9
Gary Ellis, Rose-Hulman	1974-77	25	226	9.1

*Record.

SEASON INTERCEPTIONS

Player, Team	Year	No.	Yards
Mark Dorner, Juniata	†1987	*15	202
Steve Nappo, Buffalo	†1986	13	155
Antonio Moore, Widener	†1994	13	116
Chris McMahon, Catholic	†1984	13	105
Ralph Gebhardt, Rochester	†1973	13	105
Brian Barr, Gettysburg	†1985	12	144
John Bernard, Buffalo	†1983	12	143
Mick McConkey, Neb. Wesleyan	†1982	12	111
Chris Butts, Worcester St.	†1992	12	109
Tom Devine, Juniata	†1981	12	91

*Record. †National champion.

ANNUAL CHAMPIONS
(Ranked on Average Per Game)

Year	Player, Team	Class	G	No.	Avg.	Yards
1973	Ralph Gebhardt, Rochester	So.	9	13	1.44	105
1974	Kevin Birkholz, Carleton	Jr.	9	11	1.22	137
1975	Mark Persichetti, Wash. & Jeff.	So.	9	10	1.11	97
1976	Gary Jantzer, Southern Ore. St.	Sr.	9	10	1.11	63
1977	Greg Jones, FDU-Madison	So.	9	10	1.11	106
	Mike Jones, Norwich	So.	9	10	1.11	98
1978	Don Sutton, San Fran. St.	Fr.	8	10	1.25	43
1979	Greg Holland, Simpson	Fr.	9	11	1.22	150
1980	Tim White, Lawrence	Sr.	8	10	1.25	131
1981	Tom Devine, Juniata	Sr.	9	12	1.33	91
1982	Mick McConkey, Neb. Wesleyan	Sr.	9	12	1.33	111
1983	John Bernard, Buffalo	Sr.	10	12	1.20	143
1984	Chris McMahon, Catholic	Sr.	9	13	1.44	140
1985	Kim McManis, Lane	Sr.	9	11	1.22	165
1986	Steve Nappo, Buffalo	Sr.	11	13	1.18	155
1987	Mark Dorner, Juniata	Sr.	10	*15	*1.50	202
1988	Tim Lennon, Curry	Jr.	9	11	1.22	86
1989	Ron Davies, Coast Guard	So.	9	11	1.22	90
1990	Craig Garritano, FDU-Madison	Jr.	9	10	1.11	158
	Brad Bohn, Neb. Wesleyan	So.	9	10	1.11	90
	Frank Greer, Sewanee	So.	9	10	1.11	67
	Harold Krebs, Merchant Marine	Sr.	9	10	1.11	19
1991	Murray Meadows, Millsaps	Sr.	9	11	1.22	46
1992	Chris Butts, Worcester St.	Jr.	9	12	1.33	109
1993	Ricky Webb, Emory & Henry	Sr.	8	8	1.00	56
1994	Antonio Moore, Widener	So.	10	13	1.30	116
1995	Mike Susi, Lebanon Valley	Sr.	8	8	1.00	153
	LeMonde Zachary, St. Lawrence	Fr.	7	7	1.00	109
1996	Peter Hinkle, Ursinus	So.	10	11	1.10	247
1997	Joel Feuerstahler, Martin Luther	Sr.	9	10	1.10	222
1998	Mike Cotton, Mass.-Dartmouth	Jr.	10	11	1.10	206
1999	Steve Cella, Trinity (Conn.)	Jr.	8	9	1.10	106
	Eric Newsome, Hobart	Jr.	8	9	1.10	148

*Record.

Punting

CAREER AVERAGE
(Minimum 100 Punts)

Player, Team	Years	No.	Yards	Avg.
Jeff Shea, Cal Lutheran	1994-97	183	7,939	*43.4
Phil Barry, St. John's (Minn.)	1996-99	126	5,327	42.3
Mike Manson, Benedictine (Ill.)	1975-78	120	5,056	42.1
Dan Osborn, Occidental	1981-83	157	6,528	41.6
Jim Allshouse, Adrian	1973-75	163	6,718	41.2
Thomas Murray, Catholic	1983-84	122	5,028	41.2
Ryan Haley, John Carroll	1991-94	151	6,208	41.1
Mario Acosta, Chapman	1994-96, 98	164	6,695	40.8
Scott Lanz, Bethany (W.Va.)	1975-78	235	9,592	40.8
Mitch Holloway, Millsaps	1992-93	105	4,283	40.8
Richard Harr, Ferrum	1996-99	219	8,914	40.7

*Record.

SEASON AVERAGE
(Qualifiers for Championship)

Player, Team	Year	No.	Yards	Avg.
Steve Vagedes, Ohio Northern	†1999	37	1,708	*46.2
Justin Shively, Anderson (Ind.)	†1997	55	2,502	45.5
Jeff Shea, Cal Lutheran	†1996	53	2,402	45.3
Jeff Shea, Cal Lutheran	†1995	43	1,933	45.0
Mario Acosta, Chapman	1996	34	1,528	44.9
Bob Burwell, Rose-Hulman	†1978	61	2,740	44.9
Charles McPherson, Clark Atlanta	1978	50	2,237	44.7
Dan Osborn, Occidental	†1982	55	2,454	44.6
Jeff Shea, Cal Lutheran	1997	43	1,910	44.4
Phil Barry, St. John's (Minn.)	1999	49	2,176	44.4
Mike Manson, Benedictine (Ill.)	†1976	36	1,587	44.1
Linc Welles, Bloomsburg	†1973	39	1,708	43.8
Matt George, Chapman	1997	38	1,663	43.8
Kirk Seufert, Rhodes	†1983	44	1,921	43.7
Kelvin Albert, Knoxville	†1987	30	1,308	43.6

*Record. †National champion.

ANNUAL CHAMPIONS

Year	Player, Team	Class	No.	Yards	Avg.
1973	Linc Welles, Bloomsburg	Sr.	39	1,708	43.8
1974	Sylvester Cunningham, Fort Valley St.	So.	40	1,703	42.6
1975	Larry Hersh, Shepherd	Jr.	58	2,519	43.4
1976	Mike Manson, Benedictine (Ill.)	So.	36	1,587	44.1
1977	Scott Lanz, Bethany (W.Va.)	Jr.	78	3,349	42.9
1978	Bob Burwell, Rose-Hulman	Sr.	61	2,740	44.9
1979	Jay Lenstrom, Neb. Wesleyan	Sr.	64	2,641	41.3
1980	Duane Harrison, Bridgewater (Va.)	Sr.	43	1,792	41.7
1981	Dan Paro, Denison	Jr.	54	2,223	41.2
1982	Dan Osborn, Occidental	Jr.	55	2,454	44.6
1983	Kirk Seufert, Rhodes	Jr.	44	1,921	43.7
1984	Thomas Murray, Catholic	Sr.	59	2,550	43.2
1985	Dave Lewis, Muhlenberg	So.	55	2,290	41.6
	Mike Matzen, Coe	Sr.	55	2,290	41.6
1986	Darren Estes, Millsaps	Jr.	45	1,940	43.1
1987	Kelvin Albert, Knoxville	So.	30	1,308	43.6
1988	Bobby Graves, Sewanee	So.	57	2,445	42.9
1989	Paul Becker, Kenyon	Sr.	57	2,307	40.5

ANNUAL CHAMPIONS, ALL-TIME LEADERS—PUNTING

Year	Player, Team	Class	No.	Yards	Avg.
1990	Bill Nolan, Carroll (Wis.)	Sr.	33	1,322	40.1
1991	Jeff Stolte, Chicago	So.	54	2,295	42.5
1992	Robert Ray, San Diego	So.	44	1,860	42.3
1993	Mitch Holloway, Millsaps	Sr.	45	1,910	42.4
1994	Ryan Haley, John Carroll	Sr.	54	2,311	42.8
1995	Jeff Shea, Cal Lutheran	So.	43	1,933	45.0
1996	Jeff Shea, Cal Lutheran	Jr.	53	2,402	45.3
1997	Justin Shively, Anderson (Ind.)	Sr.	55	2,502	45.5
1998	Chris Morehouse, Albright	Jr.	52	2,247	43.2
1999	Steve Vagedes, Ohio Northern	Sr.	37	1,708	*46.2

*Record.

Punt Returns

CAREER AVERAGE
(Minimum 1.2 Returns Per Game)

Player, Team	Years	No.	Yards	Avg.
Keith Winston, Knoxville	1986-87	30	686	*22.9
Robert Middlebrook, Knoxville	1984-85	21	473	22.5
Kevin Doherty, Mass. Maritime	1976-78, 80	45	939	20.9
Chuck Downey, Stony Brook	1984-87	59	*1,198	+20.3
Mike Askew, Kean	1980-81	28	555	19.8
Willie Canady, Fort Valley St.	1979-82	41	772	18.8

*Record. +Record for minimum 50 returns.

SEASON AVERAGE
(Minimum 1.2 Returns Per Game)

Player, Team	Year	No.	Yards	Avg.
Chuck Downey, Stony Brook	†1986	17	530	*31.2
Kevin Doherty, Mass. Maritime	†1976	11	332	30.2
Robert Middlebrook, Knoxville	†1984	9	260	28.9
Joe Troise, Kean	†1974	12	342	28.5
Melvin Dillard, Ferrum	†1990	25	*688	27.5
Eric Green, Benedictine (Ill.)	†1993	13	346	26.6
Chris Warren, Ferrum	†1989	18	421	23.4
Matt Buddenhagen, Ithaca	†1998	29	667	23.0
Kevin Doherty, Mass. Maritime	1978	11	246	22.4

*Record. †National champion.

ANNUAL CHAMPIONS

Year	Player, Team	Class	No.	Yards	‡Avg.
1973	Al Shepherd, Monmouth (Ill.)	Sr.	18	347	19.3
1974	Joe Troise, Kean	Fr.	12	342	28.5
1975	Mitch Brown, St. Lawrence	So.	25	430	17.2
1976	Kevin Doherty, Mass. Maritime	Fr.	11	332	30.2
1977	Charles Watkins, Knoxville	Sr.	15	278	18.5
1978	Dennis Robinson, Wesleyan (Conn.)	Sr.	††9	263	29.2
1979	Steve Moffett, Maryville (Tenn.)	Jr.	19	357	18.8
1980	Mike Askew, Kean	Jr.	16	304	19.0
1981	Mike Askew, Kean	Sr.	12	251	20.9
1982	Tom Southall, Colorado Col.	So.	13	281	21.6
1983	Edmond Donald, Millsaps	Jr.	15	320	21.3
1984	Robert Middlebrook, Knoxville	So.	9	260	28.9
1985	Dan Schone, Illinois Col.	Fr.	11	231	21.0
1986	Chuck Downey, Stony Brook	Jr.	17	530	*31.2
1987	Keith Winston, Knoxville	Sr.	16	343	21.4
1988	Dennis Tarr, Framingham St.	Jr.	9	178	19.8
1989	Chris Warren, Ferrum	Sr.	18	421	23.4
1990	Melvin Dillard, Ferrum	Sr.	25	*688	27.5
1991	Jordan Nixon, Augustana (Ill.)	Sr.	27	473	17.5
1992	Vic Moncato, FDU-Madison	So.	††††10	243	24.3
1993	Eric Green, Benedictine (Ill.)	Sr.	13	346	26.6
1994	Ariel Bell, Frostburg St.	Sr.	19	329	17.3
1995	Jim Wallace, Ripon	Jr.	17	305	17.9
1996	Tyrone Brown, Howard Payne	Sr.	21	415	19.8
1997	Seth Wallace, Coe	Fr.	††††10	301	30.1
1998	Matt Buddenhagen, Ithaca	Sr.	29	667	23.0
1999	Jake Wolter, Wis.-Whitewater	Jr.	12	230	19.2

*Record. ‡Ranked on minimum of 1.5 returns per game in 1973; 1.2 from 1974. ††Declared champion; with one more return (making 1.25 per game) for zero yards, still would have highest average (26.3). †††Declared champion; with one more return (making 1.22 per game) for zero yards, still would have highest average (22.1). ††††Declared champion; with one more return (making 1.22 per game) for zero yards, still would have highest average (27.4).

Kickoff Returns

CAREER AVERAGE
(Minimum 1.2 Returns Per Game)

Player, Team	Years	No.	Yards	Avg.
David Ziegler, John Carroll	1996-99	30	1,047	$34.9
Daryl Brown, Tufts	1974-76	38	1,111	29.2
Darnell Rubin, Chapman	1994, 96	17	485	28.5
Mike Askew, Kean	1980-81	33	938	28.4
Chuck Downey, Stony Brook	1984-87	46	1,281	27.8
R. J. Hoppe, Carroll (Wis.)	1993-96	59	1,632	27.7
Ryan Reynolds, Thomas More	1991-94	49	1,311	26.8
LaVant King, Ohio Northern	1991, 93-95	50	1,298	26.0
Scott Reppert, Lawrence	1979-82	44	1,134	25.8
Lamont Rhim, Buffalo St.	1994-96	47	1,210	25.7
Jerome Porter, Kean	1996-98	51	1,286	25.2
Rick Rosenfeld, Western Md.	1973-76	69	1,732	25.1

*Record. $Declared record; with 5 more returns (making 35), for zero yards, still would have highest average (29.9).

SEASON AVERAGE
(Minimum 1.2 Returns Per Game)

Player, Team	Year	No.	Yards	Avg.
Brandon Steinheim, Wesley	†1994	10	422	*42.2
Jason Martin, Coe	†1992	11	438	39.8
Tony Hill, Salisbury St.	†1998	14	549	39.2
Nate Kirtman, Pomona-Pitzer	†1990	14	515	36.8
Tom Myers, Coe	†1983	11	401	36.5
Ron Scott, Occidental	1983	10	363	36.3
Alan Hill, DePauw	1980	12	434	36.2
Trevor Shannon, Wartburg	1996	14	501	35.8
David Ziegler, John Carroll	†1999	11	393	35.7
Al White, Wm. Paterson	1990	12	427	35.6
Byron Womack, Iona	†1989	15	531	35.4
Derrick Brooms, Chicago	†1995	12	422	35.2
Darnell Marshall, Carroll (Wis.)	1989	17	586	34.5
Daryl Brown, Tufts	†1976	11	377	34.3
Rich Jinnette, Methodist	1992	15	514	34.3
Jeff Higgins, Ithaca	1995	12	407	33.9
Oscar Ford, Chapman	1995	11	373	33.9
Sean Healy, Coe	1989	11	372	33.8
Anthony Drakeford, Ferrum	†1987	15	507	33.8
Ryan Reynolds, Thomas More	1992	14	473	33.8
Glenn Koch, Tufts	†1986	14	472	33.7

*Record. †National champion.

ANNUAL CHAMPIONS

Year	Player, Team	Class	No.	Yards	‡Avg.
1973	Greg Montgomery, Wis.-Whitewater	So.	17	518	30.5
1974	Tom Oleksa, Muhlenberg	Sr.	15	467	31.1
1975	Jeff Levant, Beloit	Jr.	15	434	28.9
1976	Daryl Brown, Tufts	Sr.	11	377	34.3
1977	Charlie Black, Marietta	Jr.	14	465	33.2
1978	Russ Atchison, Centre	So.	11	284	25.8
1979	Jim Iannone, Rochester	Jr.	13	411	31.6
1980	Mike Askew, Kean	So.	††10	415	41.5
1981	Gene Cote, Wesleyan (Conn.)	Sr.	16	521	32.6
1982	Jim Hachey, Bri'water (Mass.)	Jr.	16	477	29.8
1983	Tom Myers, Coe	So.	11	401	36.5
1984	Mike Doetsch, Trinity (Conn.)	Jr.	13	434	33.4
1985	Gary Newsom, Lane	So.	10	319	31.9
1986	Glenn Koch, Tufts	Sr.	14	472	33.7
1987	Anthony Drakeford, Ferrum	Sr.	15	507	33.8
1988	Harold Owens, Wis.-La Crosse	Jr.	10	508	29.9
1989	Byron Womack, Iona	Sr.	15	531	35.4
1990	Nate Kirtman, Pomona-Pitzer	Jr.	14	515	36.8
1991	Tom Reason, Albion	So.	13	423	32.5
1992	Jason Martin, Coe	So.	11	438	39.8
1993	Eric Green, Benedictine (Ill.)	Sr.	19	628	33.1
1994	Brandon Steinheim, Wesley	Fr.	10	422	*42.2
1995	Derrick Brooms, Chicago	Sr.	12	422	35.2
1996	Trevor Shannon, Wartburg	So.	14	501	35.8
1997	Qasim Ward, Mass.-Boston	Fr.	10	314	31.4
1998	Tony Hill, Salisbury St.	Sr.	14	549	39.2
1999	David Ziegler, John Carroll	Sr.	11	393	35.7

*Record. ‡Ranked on minimum of 1.5 returns per game in 1973; 1.2 from 1974. ††Declared champion; with one more return (making 1.2 per game) for zero yards, still would have highest average (37.7).

DIVISION III

With over 5,000 rushing yards and 2,000 kickoff return yards, Gettysburg's Paul Smith wound up with Division III records of 9,104 career all-purpose yards and 227.6 yards per game.

All-Purpose Yards

CAREER YARDS PER GAME
(Minimum 3,500 Yards)

Player, Team	Years	G	Rush	Rcv.	Int.	PR	KOR	Yds.	Yd. PG
Paul Smith, Gettysburg	1996-99	40	5,205	758	0	959	2,182	*9,104	*227.6
Kirk Matthieu, Maine Maritime	$1989-93	33	5,107	315	0	254	1,279	6,955	210.8
Carey Bender, Coe	1991-94	39	*6,125	1,751	0	7	87	7,970	204.4
Steve Tardif, Maine Maritime	1996-99	39	6,093	643	8	65	1,151	7,960	204.1
Gary Trettel, St. Thomas (Minn.)	1988-90	29	3,483	834	0	0	1,407	5,724	197.4

*Record. $See page 6 for explanation.

SEASON YARDS PER GAME

Player, Team	Year	G	Rush	Rcv.	Int.	PR	KOR	Yds.	Yd. PG
Dante Brown, Marietta	†1996	10	*2,385	174	0	46	368	*2,973	*297.3
R. J. Bowers, Grove City	†1998	10	2,283	51	0	4	538	2,876	287.6
Paul Smith, Gettysburg	†1999	10	1,546	301	0	255	615	2,717	271.7
Carey Bender, Coe	†1994	10	2,243	319	0	7	87	2,656	265.6
Kenneth Sasu, Marietta	1999	9	1,770	82	0	0	374	2,226	247.3
Steve Tardif, Maine Maritime	1999	9	1,567	149	8	0	479	2,203	244.8
Paul Smith, Gettysburg	1998	10	1,515	178	0	191	554	2,438	243.8
Kirk Matthieu, Maine Maritime	†1992	9	1,733	91	0	56	308	2,188	243.1
Guy Leman, Simpson	1998	10	1,788	210	0	0	408	2,406	240.6
Ray Neosh, Coe	1996	9	1,472	273	0	0	403	2,148	238.7
Ricky Gales, Simpson	1989	10	2,035	102	0	0	248	2,385	238.5
R. J. Bowers, Grove City	1999	10	2,098	34	0	0	240	2,372	237.2
Paul Smith, Gettysburg	†1997	10	1,256	102	0	199	805	2,362	236.2
Gary Trettel, St. Thomas (Minn.)	1989	10	1,502	337	0	0	496	2,335	233.5
Kirk Matthieu, Maine Maritime	1990	9	1,428	77	0	99	495	2,099	233.2
Gary Trettel, St. Thomas (Minn.)	1990	10	1,620	388	0	0	319	2,327	232.7
Carey Bender, Coe	†1993	10	1,718	601	0	0	0	2,319	231.9

*Record. †National champion.

CAREER YARDS

Player, Team	Years	Rush	Rcv.	Int.	PR	KOR	Yds.
Paul Smith, Gettysburg	1996-99	5,205	758	0	959	2,182	*9,104
Carey Bender, Coe	1991-94	*6,125	1,751	0	7	87	7,970
Steve Tardif, Maine Maritime	1996-99	6,093	643	8	65	1,151	7,960
#R. J. Bowers, Grove City	1997-99	5,620	338	0	50	1,266	7,274
Kirk Matthieu, Maine Maritime	$1989-93	5,107	315	0	254	1,279	6,955
Eric Frees, Western Md.	1988-91	5,281	392	0	47	1,158	6,878
Joe Dudek, Plymouth St.	1982-85	5,570	348	0	0	243	6,509
Richard Wemer, Grinnell	1995-98	1,016	3,133	7	674	1,657	6,487
Trevor Shannon, Wartburg	1995-98	4,292	1,037	0	0	964	6,293
Dante Brown, Marietta	1994-97	4,512	425	0	202	1,040	6,179
Scott Pingel, Westminster (Mo.)	1996-99	5	*6,108	0	0	0	6,113
Adam Henry, Carleton	1990-93	3,482	601	0	186	1,839	6,108
Brad Olson, Lawrence	1994-97	5,325	590	0	14	145	6,074
Mark Kacmarnyski, Central (Iowa)	$1992-96	5,434	211	0	45	364	6,054
Gary Trettel, St. Thomas (Minn.)	1988-90	3,724	853	0	0	1,467	6,044

*Record. $See page 6 for explanation. #Active player.

SEASON YARDS

Player, Team	Year	Rush	Rcv.	Int.	PR	KOR	Yds.
Dante Brown, Marietta	†1996	*2,385	174	0	46	368	*2,973
R. J. Bowers, Grove City	†1998	2,283	51	0	4	538	2,876
Paul Smith, Gettysburg	†1999	1,546	301	0	255	615	2,717
Carey Bender, Coe	†1994	2,243	319	0	7	87	2,656
Paul Smith, Gettysburg	1998	1,515	178	0	191	554	2,438
Theo Blanco, Wis.-Stevens Point	1987	454	1,616	0	245	103	2,418
Guy Leman, Simpson	1998	1,788	210	0	0	408	2,406
Ricky Gales, Simpson	1989	2,035	102	0	0	248	2,385
R. J. Bowers, Grove City	1999	2,098	34	0	0	240	2,372
Paul Smith, Gettsburg	†1997	1,256	102	0	199	805	2,362
Gary Trettel, St. Thomas (Minn.)	1989	1,502	337	0	0	496	2,335
Gary Trettel, St. Thomas (Minn.)	1990	1,620	388	0	0	319	2,327
Carey Bender, Coe	†1993	1,718	601	0	0	0	2,319

*Record. †National champion.

ANNUAL CHAMPIONS

Year	Player, Team	Cl.	Rush	Rcv.	Int.	PR	KOR	Yds.	Yd. PG
1992	Kirk Matthieu, Maine Matime	Jr.	1,733	91	0	56	308	2,188	243.1
1993	Carey Bender, Coe	Jr.	1,718	601	0	0	0	2,319	231.9
1994	Carey Bender, Coe	Sr.	2,243	319	0	7	87	2,656	265.6
1995	Brad Olson, Lawrence	So.	1,760	279	0	0	0	2,039	226.6
1996	Dante Brown, Marietta	Jr.	*2,385	174	0	46	368	*2,973	*297.3
1997	Paul Smith, Gettysburg	So.	1,256	102	0	199	805	2,362	236.2
1998	R. J. Bowers, Grove City	So.	2,283	51	0	4	538	2,876	287.6
1999	Paul Smith, Gettysburg	Sr.	1,546	301	0	255	615	2,717	271.7

*Record.

Field Goals

CAREER FIELD GOALS

Player, Team	Years	Made	Atts.	Pct.
Ken Edelman, Mount Union (S)	1987-90	*52	*71	.732
Ted Swan, Colorado Col. (S)	1973-76	43	57	.754
Jim Hever, Rhodes (S)	1982-85	42	66	.636
Manny Matsakis, Capital (C)	1980-83	40	66	.606
Doug Hart, Grove City (S)	1985-88	40	*71	.563
Mike Duvic, Dayton (S)	1986-89	38	49	$.776
Jeff Reitz, Lawrence (C)	1974-77	37	60	.617
Dan Deneher, Montclair St. (S)	1978-79, 81-82	37	65	.569
Jim Flynn, Gettysburg (S)	1982-85	37	68	.544

*Record. $Declared record; with one more attempt (making 50), failed, still would have highest percentage (.760). (C) Conventional kicker. (S) Soccer-style kicker.

SEASON FIELD GOALS

Player, Team	Year	Made	Atts.	Pct.
Ken Edelman, Mount Union (S)	†1990	*20	27	.741
Scott Ryerson, UCF (S)	†1981	18	*29	.621
Dennis Unger, Albright (S)	†1995	16	20	.800
Haakon Nelson, St. Olaf (S)	†1999	15	20	.750
Steve Graeca, John Carroll (S)	†1988	15	16	*.938
Ken Edelman, Mount Union (S)	1988	15	17	.882
Gary Potter, Hamline (C)	†1984	15	21	.714
Jeff Reitz, Lawrence (C)	†1975	15	26	.577

*Record. †National champion. (C) Conventional kicker. (S) Soccer-style kicker.

ANNUAL CHAMPIONS

Year	Player, Team	Class	Made	Atts.	Pct.	PG
1973	Chuck Smeltz, Susquehanna (C)	Jr.	10	14	.714	1.11
1974	Ted Swan, Colorado Col. (S)	So.	13	15	.867	1.44
1975	Jeff Reitz, Lawrence (C)	So.	15	26	.577	1.67
1976	Mark Sniegocki, Bethany (W.Va.) (C)	So.	11	14	.786	1.22
1977	Bob Unruh, Wheaton (Ill.) (S)	Jr.	11	14	.786	1.22
1978	Craig Walker, Western Md. (C)	So.	13	24	.542	1.44
1979	Jeff Holter, Concordia-M'head (S)	Jr.	12	15	.800	1.33
1980	Jeff Holter, Concordia-M'head (S)	Sr.	13	19	.684	1.30
1981	Scott Ryerson, UCF (S)	So.	18	*29	.621	1.80
1982	Manny Matsakis, Capital (C)	Jr.	13	20	.650	1.44
1983	Mike Farrell, Adrian (S)	So.	12	21	.571	1.33
1984	Gary Potter, Hamline (C)	Jr.	15	21	.714	1.50
1985	Joe Bevelhimer, Wabash (C)	Sr.	14	22	.636	1.40
	Jim Hever, Rhodes (S)	Sr.	14	23	.609	1.40
1986	Tim Dewberry, Occidental (C)	Sr.	13	21	.619	1.44
1987	Doug Dickason, John Carroll (S)	Sr.	13	21	.619	1.44
1988	Steve Graeca, John Carroll (S)	Fr.	15	16	*.938	1.67
1989	Dave Bergmann, San Diego (S)	So.	14	18	.778	1.56
	Rich Egal, Merchant Marine (S)	Fr.	14	22	.636	1.56
1990	Ken Edelman, Mount Union (S)	Sr.	*20	27	.741	*2.00
1991	Greg Harrison, Union (N.Y.) (S)	So.	12	16	.750	1.33
1992	Todd Holthaus, Rose-Hulman (S)	Jr.	13	19	.684	1.30
1993	Steve Milne, Brockport St. (S)	Sr.	13	16	.813	1.30
1994	Chris Kondik, Baldwin-Wallace (S)	Fr.	13	17	.765	1.30
1995	Dennis Unger, Albright (S)	So.	16	20	.800	1.60
1996	Roger Egbert, Union (N.Y.) (S)	Sr.	11	15	.733	1.22
1997	Ryan Boutwell, Gust. Adolphus (S)	Jr.	13	18	.722	1.30
1998	David Vitatoe, John Carroll (S)	Jr.	13	16	.813	1.30
	Michael Padgett, Bridgewater (Va.)	Sr.	13	23	.565	1.30
1999	Ryan Geisler, Cal Lutheran (S)	Jr.	14	18	.778	1.56

*Record. (C) Conventional kicker. (S) Soccer-style kicker.

All-Time Longest Plays

Since 1941, official maximum length of all plays fixed at 100 yards.

RUSHING

Yds.	Player, Team (Opponent)	Year
99	Bill Casey, Mass.-Dartmouth (Norwich)	1995
99	Kelly Wilkinson, Principia (Trinity Bible)	1995
99	Arnie Boigner, Ohio Northern (Muskingum)	1992
99	Reese Wilson, MacMurray (Eureka)	1986
99	Don Patria, Rensselaer (Mass.-Lowell)	1981
99	Kevin Doherty, Mass. Maritime (New Haven)	1980
99	Sam Halliston, Albany (N.Y.) (Norwich)	1977
98	Rich Vargas, Wis.-Stout (Wis.-Oshkosh)	1992
98	Ted Pretasky, Wis.-La Crosse (Wis.-River Falls)	1987
98	Jon Hinds, Principia (Illinois Col.)	1986
98	Alex Schmidt, Muhlenberg (Lebanon Valley)	1984
98	Eric Batt, Ohio Northern (Ohio Wesleyan)	1982
98	Mike Shannon, Centre (Sewanee)	1978

PASSING

Yds.	Passer-Receiver, Team (Opponent)	Year
99	Dan Pincelli-John Nowak, Hartwick (Union [N.Y.])	1999
99	Greg Kaiser-Mark Warder, St. Thomas (Minn.) (Augsburg)	1998
99	Brian Partlow-Sean Eaton, Randolph-Macon (Catholic)	1998
99	Tim Vinyard-L. C. Lewis, Coe (Loras)	1998
99	Eric Block-R. J. Hoppe, Carroll (Wis.) (Lake Forest)	1996
99	Mike Schultz-R. J. Hoppe, Carroll (Wis.) (Ripon)	1995
99	Mike Magistrelli-Jason Martin, Coe (Quincy)	1994
99	Jim Connolley-Duane Martin, Wesley (FDU-Madison)	1993
99	Marc Klausner-Eric Frink, Pace (Hobart)	1992
99	Carlos Nazario-Ray Marshall, St. Peter's (Georgetown)	1991
99	Mike Jones-Warren Tweedy, Frostburg St. (Waynesburg)	1990
99	Chris Etzler-Andy Nowlin, Bluffton (Urbana)	1990
99	John Clark-Pete Balistrieri, Wis.-Eau Claire (Minn.-Duluth)	1989
99	Kelly Sandidge-Mark Green, Centre (Sewanee)	1988
99	Mike Francis-John Winter, Carleton (Trinity [Tex.])	1983
99	Rich Boling-Lewis Borsellino, DePauw (Valparaiso)	1976
99	John Wicinski-Donnell Lipford, John Carroll (Allegheny)	1975
99	Jack Berry-Mercer West, Wash. & Lee (Hampden-Sydney)	1974
99	Gary Shope-Rick Rudolph, Juniata (Moravian)	1973

INTERCEPTION RETURNS

Thirty players have returned interceptions 100 yards. The most recent:

Yds.	Player, Team (Opponent)	Year
100	Jeremy Jones, Mississippi Col. (Austin)	1999
100	Duane Manson, Wesley (Stonehill)	1998
100	Michael Turner, Chicago (Rose-Hulman)	1998
100	Terrance Oliver, Delaware Valley (Lebanon Valley)	1997
100	Randy Ames, Hope (Adrian)	1996
100	Dan Gilson, Curry (Stonehill)	1995
100	Tony Hinkle, Rose-Hulman (Millsaps)	1995
100	Mike Gerhart, Susquehanna (Moravian)	1994
100	Bruce Pritchett, Kean (Widener)	1994
100	Adam Smith, Heidelberg (Capital)	1994
100	Jason Pass, Hamline (St. John's [Minn.])	1994
100	Guy Nardulli, Elmhurst (North Central)	1994

PUNT RETURNS

Yds.	Player, Team (Opponent)	Year
99	Robert Middlebrook, Knoxville (Miles)	1985
98	Mark Griggs, Wooster (Oberlin)	1980
98	Ron Mabry, Emory & Henry (Maryville [Tenn.])	1973
97	Rob Allard, Nichols (Curry)	1991
97	Leon Kornegaey, Carthage (Millikin)	1985
96	Marvin Robbins, Salisbury St. (Wesley)	1987
96	Gary Martin, Muskingum (Wooster)	1976
95	Tyrone Croom, Susquehanna (Delaware Valley)	1993
95	Brian Sarver, William Penn (Dubuque)	1992
95	Stan Thompson, Knoxville (Livingstone)	1982

KICKOFF RETURNS

Forty-six players have returned kickoffs 100 yards. The most recent:

Yds.	Player, Team (Opponent)	Year
100	Paul Sage, Colorado Col. (Pomona-Pitzer)	1999
100	Greg Ortberg, Dubuque (Upper Iowa)	1999
100	Michael Kirtman, Pomona-Pitzer (Colorado Col.)	1999
100	Scott Meinerz, Concordia (Ill.) (Principia)	1998
100	Lamar Wilson, Buffalo St. (Rochester)	1998
100	Jeff Rogers, Albright (Wm. Paterson)	1998
100	Eric Green, Benedictine (Ill.) (Carthage)	1992

PUNTS

Yds.	Player, Team (Opponent)	Year
90	Dan Heeren, Coe (Lawrence)	1974
88	Steve Vagedes, Ohio Northern (Capital)	1999
86	David Anastasi, Buffalo (John Carroll)	1989
86	Dana Loucks, Buffalo (Frostburg St.)	1987
86	John Pavlik, Wabash (Centre)	1978
85	Jeff Shea, Cal Lutheran (Azusa Pacific)	1996
84	Todd Whitehurst, Menlo (Cal Lutheran)	1997
84	Rob Sarvis, Norwich (Western Conn. St.)	1995
83	Jeff Shooks, Albion (Alma)	1994
83	Geoff Hansen, Gust. Adolphus (Augustana [S.D.])	1992

FIELD GOALS

Yds.	Player, Team (Opponent)	Year
62	Dom Antonini, Rowan (Salisbury St.)	1976
60	Rick Brands, Alma (Franklin)	1998
59	Chris Gustafson, Carroll (Wis.) (North Park)	1985
59	Hartmut Strecker, Dayton (Iowa St.)	1977
57	Scott Fritz, Wartburg (Simpson)	1982
57	Kevin Shea, St. Mary's (Cal.) (Oregon Tech)	1976

Team Champions

Annual Offense Champions

TOTAL OFFENSE

Year	Team	Avg.
1973	San Diego	441.0
1974	Ithaca	487.9
1975	Frank. & Marsh.	439.4
1976	St. John's (Minn.)	451.8
1977	St. John's (Minn.)	437.5
1978	Lawrence	432.6
1979	Norwich	465.2
1980	Widener	459.0
1981	Middlebury	446.5
1982	West Ga.	470.6
1983	Elmhurst	483.3
1984	Alma	465.1
1985	St. Thomas (Minn.)	446.9
1986	Mount Union	452.8
1987	Samford	523.1
1988	Wagner	465.9
1989	Simpson	514.0
1990	Hofstra	505.7
1991	St. John's (Minn.)	503.8
1992	Mount Union	463.7
1993	St. John's (Minn.)	549.7
1994	Allegheny	543.8
1995	Mount Union	495.8
1996	Albion	538.0
1997	Simpson	*565.3
1998	Westminster (Mo.)	561.2
1999	Mount Union	559.5

*Record.

RUSHING OFFENSE

Year	Team	Avg.
1973	Widener	361.7
1974	Albany (N.Y.)	361.6
1975	Widener	345.8
1976	St. John's (Minn.)	348.9
1977	St. John's (Minn.)	315.3
1978	Ithaca	320.1
1979	Norwich	383.1
1980	Widener	317.5
1981	Augustana (Ill.)	313.6
1982	West Ga.	319.6
1983	Augustana (Ill.)	345.7
1984	Augustana (Ill.)	338.4
1985	Denison	351.0
1986	Wis.-River Falls	361.4
1987	Augustana (Ill.)	369.1
1988	Tufts	369.0
1989	Wis.-River Falls	388.5
1990	Ferrum	*434.7
1991	Ferrum	361.4
1992	Wis.-River Falls	315.6
1993	Chicago	324.8
1994	Wis.-River Falls	336.7
1995	Lawrence	344.0
1996	Springfield	351.2
1997	Wis.-River Falls	365.6
1998	Wis.-River Falls	393.9
1999	Springfield	375.3

*Record.

PASSING OFFENSE

Year	Team	Avg.
1973	San Diego	231.7
1974	Benedictine (Ill.)	255.4
1975	St. Norbert	227.7
1976	Occidental	255.4
1977	Southwestern	257.8
1978	Claremont-M-S	331.7
1979	Claremont-M-S	250.1
1980	Occidental	255.9
1981	Wis.-Stevens Point	288.9
1982	Wheaton (Ill.)	308.7
1983	Wheaton (Ill.)	380.4
1984	Wheaton (Ill.)	351.6
1985	Wheaton (Ill.)	371.6
1986	Pace	286.9
1987	Wis.-Stout	314.6
1988	Wis.-Stevens Point	356.7
1989	Wis.-Stevens Point	380.4
1990	Hofstra	342.2
1991	St. John's (Minn.)	302.8
1992	Mass.-Boston	337.0
1993	Mount Union	352.8
1994	Hanover	351.3
1995	Hanover	362.8
1996	Alma	368.3
1997	Lakeland	357.3
1998	Westminster (Mo.)	*488.8
1999	Redlands	421.8

*Record.

SCORING OFFENSE

Year	Team	Avg.
1973	San Diego	40.1
1974	Frank. & Marsh.	45.1
1975	Frank. & Marsh.	38.2
1976	St. John's (Minn.)	42.5
1977	Lawrence	38.2
1978	Georgetown	36.5
1979	Wittenberg	39.7
1980	Widener	43.3
1981	Lawrence	35.3
1982	West Ga.	42.1
1983	Elmhurst	38.1
1984	Hope	40.3
1985	Salisbury St.	39.5
1986	Dayton	40.8
1987	Samford	51.7
1988	Central (Iowa)	37.6
1989	Ferrum	46.7
1990	Ferrum	47.3
1991	Union (N.Y.)	46.1
1992	Coe	46.4
1993	St. John's (Minn.)	*61.5
1994	St. John's (Minn.)	47.1
1995	Chapman	47.2
1996	Albion	50.8
1997	Mount Union	54.5
1998	MacMurray	48.2
1999	Mount Union	53.4

*Record.

Annual Defense Champions

TOTAL DEFENSE

Year	Team	Avg.
1973	Doane	144.3
1974	Alfred	153.6
1975	Lycoming	133.1
1976	Albion	129.9
1977	Knoxville	*94.0
1978	Bowie St.	112.3
1979	Catholic	116.9
1980	Maine Maritime	127.2
1981	Millsaps	147.6
1982	Plymouth St.	122.2
1983	Lycoming	154.5
1984	Swarthmore	159.2
1985	Augustana (Ill.)	149.1
1986	Augustana (Ill.)	136.2
1987	Plymouth St.	135.3
1988	Plymouth St.	143.6
1989	Frostburg St.	119.7
1990	Bentley	139.8
1991	Wash. & Jeff.	143.0
1992	Bentley	184.5
1993	Wash. & Jeff.	142.4
1994	Wash. & Jeff.	165.3
1995	Mass. Maritime	161.2
1996	Worcester St.	125.8
1997	Salve Regina	146.0
1998	St. John's (Minn.)	182.6
1999	Washington (Mo.)	192.1

*Record.

RUSHING DEFENSE

Year	Team	Avg.
1973	Oregon Col.	61.2
1974	Millersville	57.2
1975	Cal Lutheran	62.4
1976	Lycoming	44.3
1977	Knoxville	*-2.3
1978	Western Md.	43.4
1979	Catholic	46.4
1980	Maine Maritime	3.2
1981	Augustana (Ill.)	30.7
1982	Lycoming	34.2
1983	DePauw	41.6
1984	Swarthmore	40.0
1985	Augustana (Ill.)	35.1
1986	Dayton	13.5
1987	Lycoming	35.4
1988	Worcester St.	43.9
1989	Frostburg St.	49.7
1990	Ohio Wesleyan	18.9
1991	Wash. & Jeff.	64.6
1992	Bri'water (Mass.)	43.2
1993	Wash. & Jeff.	19.1
1994	Wash. & Jeff.	23.7
1995	Marietta	46.2
1996	Worcester St.	20.3
1997	Mount Union	48.6
1998	Widener	31.4
1999	Rowan	35.9

*Record.

PASSING DEFENSE

Year	Team	$Avg.
1973	Nichols	53.0
1974	Findlay	49.2
1975	Wash. & Jeff.	56.0
1976	Mass. Maritime	*48.5
1977	Hofstra	49.4
1978	Bowie St.	64.7
1979	Wagner	59.5
1980	Williams	63.8
1981	Plymouth St.	66.9
1982	Plymouth St.	48.8
1983	Muhlenberg	76.4
1984	Bri'water (Mass.)	68.7
1985	Bri'water (Mass.)	77.3
1986	Knoxville	83.2
1987	New Jersey City	67.0
1988	Colorado Col.	78.9
1989	Frostburg St.	70.0
1990	Bentley	47.4
1991	Wash. & Jeff.	50.3
1992	St. Peter's	51.7
1993	Worcester St.	50.0
1994	Worcester St.	69.2
1995	Union (N.Y.)	54.6
1996	Worcester St.	50.6
1997	Salve Regina	57.3
1998	Wittenberg	64.7
1999	Union (N.Y.)	69.7

*Record. $Beginning in 1990, ranked on passing efficiency defense rating points instead of per-game yardage allowed.

SCORING DEFENSE

Year	Team	Avg.
1973	Fisk	6.4
	Slippery Rock	6.4
1974	Central (Iowa)	6.9
	Rhodes	6.9
1975	Millsaps	5.0
1976	Albion	5.4
1977	Central (Iowa)	5.0
1978	Minn.-Morris	5.9
1979	Carnegie Mellon	4.9
1980	Millsaps	*3.4
1981	Baldwin-Wallace	3.9
1982	West Ga.	4.6
1983	Carnegie Mellon	5.3
1984	Union (N.Y.)	4.6
1985	Augustana (Ill.)	4.7

TEAM CHAMPIONS—SCORING DEFENSE

Year	Team	Avg.
1986	Augustana (Ill.)	5.1
1987	Plymouth St.	6.2
1988	Plymouth St.	6.5
1989	Millikin	4.8
1990	Bentley	4.5
1991	Mass.-Lowell	5.4
1992	Dayton	6.7
1993	Wash. & Jeff.	6.1
1994	Trinity (Tex.)	6.2
1995	Wash. & Jeff.	5.6
	Williams	5.6
1996	Amherst	8.4
1997	Mount Union	5.6
1998	Wittenberg	5.3
1999	Lycoming	6.0

*Record.

Other Annual Team Champions

NET PUNTING

Year	Team	Avg.
1992	San Diego	39.2
1993	Benedictine (Ill.)	38.9
1994	Redlands	37.9
1995	Hardin-Simmons	37.9
1996	Cal Lutheran	39.0
1997	John Carroll	40.7
1998	Chapman	39.8
1999	Ohio Northern	41.3

PUNT RETURNS

Year	Team	Avg.
1992	Occidental	18.7
1993	Curry	17.9
	Wheaton (Ill.)	17.9
1994	Frostburg St.	15.2
1995	Ohio Northern	16.5
1996	Howard Payne	17.4
1997	Juniata	18.4
1998	Ithaca	22.5
1999	Westminster (Mo.)	20.1

KICKOFF RETURNS

Year	Team	Avg.
1992	Thomas More	27.7
1993	St. John's (Minn.)	28.9
1994	Buffalo St.	26.8
1995	Howard Payne	29.5
1996	Trinity (Conn.)	30.1
1997	Western Md.	29.2
1998	John Carroll	29.5
1999	Muhlenberg	28.7

TURNOVER MARGIN

Year	Team	Avg.
1992	Illinois Col.	2.44
1993	Trinity (Conn.)	2.87
1994	Dickinson	2.70
1995	Thomas More	2.80
1996	DePauw	2.50
1997	Rensselaer	2.22
1998	Wartburg	2.30
	Western Md.	2.30
1999	Rensselaer	2.44

MOST IMPROVED

Year	Team	Imp.
1996	DePauw	6
1997	Grove City	6½
1998	Curry	6
1999	Ursinus	6

1999 Most-Improved Teams

School (Coach)	1999	1998	$Games Improved
Ursinus (Paul Guenther)	10-2	3-7	6
Bridgewater (Va.) (Michael Clark)	5-5	0-10	5
Wilmington (Ohio) (Mike Wallace)	9-1	4-6	5
MIT (Dwight Smith)	6-4	1-8	4½
Western Conn. St. (John Cervino)	10-1	5-5	4½
Thomas More (Dean Paul)	7-3	3-7	4
Wis.-Platteville (Mike Emendorfer)	5-5	1-9	4
Menlo (Ken Margerum)	5-4	2-8	3½
St. Norbert (Jim Purtill)	9-2	5-5	3½
Sewanee (John Windham)	6-4	2-7	3½

14 schools tied with an improvement of three games

All-Time Leaders

School (Coach)	Year	W-L-T	Pvs.	$Games Improved
Catholic (Tom Clark)	1994	8-2-0	1-9-0	7
Susquehanna (Rocky Rees)	1986	11-1-0	3-7-0	7
Maryville (Tenn.) (Jim Jordan)	1976	7-2-0	0-9-0	7

$To determine games improved, add the difference in victories between the two seasons to the difference in losses, then divide by two; ties not counted. Includes postseason.

All-Time Team Won-Lost Records

Won-lost-tied record includes postseason games

BY PERCENTAGE (TOP 25)
(Minimum 20 seasons of competition)

Team	Yrs.	Won	Lost	Tied	Pct.
Plymouth St.	30	201	83	7	.703
Wis.-La Crosse	75	463	192	40	.695
St. John's (Minn.)	89	460	206	24	.684
Ithaca	67	359	189	11	.652
Wittenberg	106	603	319	32	.649
Linfield	85	431	229	31	.646
Pacific Lutheran	65	378	202	29	.644
Augustana (Ill.)	87	448	249	28	.637
Wis.-Whitewater	75	393	220	21	.636
Baldwin-Wallace	95	476	278	30	.626
Concordia-M'head	80	409	237	38	.626
Central (Iowa)	91	471	278	26	.625
Montclair St.	69	350	208	20	.623
Concordia (Wis.)	20	114	69	2	.622
Williams	114	551	329	47	.620
Cal Lutheran	38	224	139	7	.615
Wash. & Jeff.	108	567	353	40	.611
Millikin	94	464	293	28	.609
Widener	119	564	358	38	.607
Gust. Adolphus	84	409	262	21	.606
St. Thomas (Minn.)	94	457	291	32	.606
Albion	113	511	328	43	.604
Lycoming	50	267	173	11	.604
Wis.-River Falls	74	365	235	32	.603
Hardin-Simmons	63	320	216	35	.591

BY VICTORIES (TOP 25)
(Minimum 20 seasons of competition)

Team	Yrs.	Won	Lost	Tied	Pct.
Wittenberg	106	603	319	32	.649
Wash. & Jeff.	108	567	353	40	.611
Widener	119	564	358	38	.607
Williams	114	551	329	47	.620
Frank. & Marsh.	112	534	396	47	.571
Amherst	120	527	382	54	.575
Mount Union	103	527	382	34	.577
Wabash	113	517	351	59	.590
Albion	113	511	328	43	.604
Ohio Wesleyan	109	500	418	44	.543
Gettysburg	107	489	423	42	.535
Centre	107	481	362	38	.568
Coe	107	480	335	38	.585
Denison	110	478	396	57	.544
Baldwin-Wallace	95	476	278	30	.626
Central (Iowa)	91	471	278	26	.625
DePauw	112	464	428	41	.519
Ill. Wesleyan	108	464	340	41	.573
Millikin	94	464	293	28	.609
Wis.-La Crosse	75	463	192	40	.695
Muskingum	105	462	361	39	.559
Trinity (Conn.)	115	462	328	42	.581
Lawrence	106	460	332	29	.578
St. John's (Minn.)	89	460	206	24	.684
Cornell College	109	458	367	33	.553

ALPHABETICAL
(No minimum seasons of competition)

Team	Yrs.	Won	Lost	Tied	Pct.
Adrian	97	314	397	17	.443
Albion	113	511	328	43	.604
Albright	87	359	402	22	.473
Alfred	101	396	315	45	.554
Allegheny	105	427	346	44	.550
Alma	103	419	349	27	.544
Amherst	120	527	382	54	.575
Anderson (Ind.)	53	230	239	12	.491
Augsburg	68	173	373	18	.323

DIVISION III

ALL-TIME TEAM WON-LOST RECORDS

Team	Yrs.	Won	Lost	Tied	Pct.
Augustana (Ill.)	87	448	249	28	.637
Aurora	14	72	50	1	.589
Austin	103	393	400	40	.496
Baldwin-Wallace	95	476	278	30	.626
Bates	104	284	444	46	.397
Beloit	109	376	439	47	.463
Benedictine (Ill.)	78	253	312	24	.450
Bethany (W.Va.)	99	305	470	34	.398
Bethel (Minn.)	47	162	253	8	.392
Blackburn	11	26	72	0	.265
Bluffton	77	252	347	23	.424
Bowdoin	106	358	416	44	.465
Bri'water (Mass.)	40	180	165	6	.521
Bridgewater (Va.)	55	131	314	11	.299
Brockport St.	53	152	273	4	.359
Buena Vista	95	370	347	28	.515
Buffalo St.	19	101	82	0	.552
Cal Lutheran	38	224	139	7	.615
Capital	76	286	316	27	.476
Carleton	105	430	342	25	.555
Carnegie Mellon	90	428	314	29	.574
Carroll (Wis.)	96	384	293	38	.564
Carthage	103	372	365	42	.504
Case Reserve	30	107	168	4	.391
Catholic	54	234	212	13	.524
Central (Iowa)	91	471	278	26	.625
Centre	107	481	362	38	.568
Chapman	6	32	21	1	.602
Chicago	80	351	325	33	.518
Claremont-M-S	42	134	232	5	.368
Coast Guard	76	264	345	49	.438
Coe	107	480	335	38	.585
Colby	106	307	426	33	.422
Colorado Col.	114	440	409	35	.518
Concordia (Ill.)	61	174	295	19	.376
Concordia-M'head	80	409	237	38	.626
Concordia (Wis.)	20	114	69	2	.622
Cornell College	109	458	367	33	.553
Cortland St.	73	307	260	28	.539
Curry	35	114	183	6	.386
Defiance	77	302	328	20	.480
Delaware Valley	52	189	251	10	.431
Denison	110	478	396	57	.544
DePauw	112	464	428	41	.519
Dickinson	111	417	475	55	.469
Dubuque	77	268	353	25	.434
Earlham	109	322	486	23	.401
Eastern Ore.	67	191	362	14	.349
Elmhurst	80	243	394	24	.386
Emory & Henry	84	449	333	19	.572
Eureka	66	163	341	26	.332
FDU-Madison	26	71	160	1	.308
Ferrum	15	90	62	1	.592
Fitchburg St.	16	23	131	1	.152
Framingham St.	26	85	147	2	.368
Franklin	99	359	427	31	.458
Frank. & Marsh.	112	534	396	47	.571
Frostburg St.	39	189	173	8	.522
Gettysburg	107	489	423	42	.535
Greensboro	3	6	22	0	.214
Grinnell	109	362	476	33	.435
Grove City	105	414	412	60	.501
Guilford	94	257	492	25	.348
Gust. Adolphus	84	409	262	21	.606
Hamilton	106	337	412	47	.453
Hamline	108	379	375	30	.503
Hampden-Sydney	105	427	401	28	.515
Hanover	107	392	356	29	.523
Hardin-Simmons	63	320	216	35	.591
Hartwick	28	84	128	11	.401
Heidelberg	104	413	419	41	.497
Hiram	101	246	506	32	.334
Hobart	106	379	432	40	.469
Hope	90	351	283	38	.551
Howard Payne	94	416	381	41	.521
Illinois Col.	103	350	418	36	.458
Ill. Wesleyan	108	464	340	41	.573
Ithaca	67	359	189	11	.652
John Carroll	77	369	266	37	.577
Johns Hopkins	115	384	437	57	.470
Juniata	77	324	298	22	.520
Kalamazoo	105	350	413	41	.461
Kean	28	103	158	9	.398
Kenyon	110	316	510	47	.389
King's (Pa.)	7	17	51	1	.254

Team	Yrs.	Won	Lost	Tied	Pct.
Knox	106	370	456	43	.451
La Verne	74	293	309	18	.487
Lake Forest	107	354	409	55	.466
Lakeland	65	262	254	13	.508
Lawrence	106	460	332	29	.578
Lebanon Valley	99	346	462	36	.431
Lewis & Clark	58	229	234	12	.495
Linfield	85	431	229	31	.646
Loras	71	309	249	31	.551
Luther	86	367	316	21	.536
Lycoming	50	267	173	11	.604
Macalester	97	233	462	29	.342
MacMurray	15	73	71	1	.507
Maine Maritime	54	229	198	9	.536
Manchester	74	228	366	20	.388
Maranatha Baptist	40	111	139	5	.445
Marietta	105	366	462	36	.444
Martin Luther	101	320	322	31	.499
Maryville (Tenn.)	102	394	419	35	.485
Mass.-Boston	12	26	83	1	.241
Mass.-Dartmouth	12	63	51	0	.553
MIT	12	39	59	1	.399
Mass. Maritime	27	139	106	1	.567
McMurry	74	304	366	36	.456
Menlo	14	50	76	2	.398
Merchant Marine	55	245	248	13	.497
Methodist	11	41	69	0	.373
Middlebury	103	350	361	42	.493
Millikin	94	464	293	28	.609
Millsaps	77	321	309	36	.509
Mississippi Col.	87	415	323	37	.559
Monmouth (Ill.)	107	426	423	39	.502
Montclair St.	69	350	208	20	.623
Moravian	66	284	267	21	.515
Mt. St. Joseph	10	34	63	1	.352
Mount Union	103	527	382	34	.577
Muhlenberg	100	399	449	42	.472
Muskingum	105	462	361	39	.559
Neb. Wesleyan	91	398	360	42	.524
Col. of New Jersey	75	284	278	32	.505
New Jersey City	32	107	191	3	.360
Nichols	41	162	168	6	.491
North Central	95	329	382	36	.465
North Park	41	84	279	7	.236
Norwich	101	297	440	31	.407
Oberlin	109	352	499	39	.417
Occidental	98	396	356	26	.526
Ohio Northern	101	395	407	35	.493
Ohio Wesleyan	109	500	418	44	.543
Olivet	99	274	457	33	.380
Otterbein	110	352	516	43	.410
Pacific Lutheran	65	378	202	29	.644
Plymouth St.	30	201	83	7	.703
Pomona-Pitzer	102	355	377	31	.486
Principia	66	180	319	16	.365
Puget Sound	90	365	304	36	.543
Randolph-Macon	112	423	398	57	.514
Redlands	90	403	358	28	.529
Rensselaer	110	322	485	46	.404
Rhodes	88	316	339	38	.483
Ripon	106	439	309	46	.582
Rochester	111	441	415	38	.515
Rose-Hulman	104	350	450	29	.440
Rowan	40	221	158	8	.581
St. John Fisher	12	34	96	0	.262
St. John's (Minn.)	89	460	206	24	.684
St. Lawrence	105	345	390	29	.471
St. Norbert	66	298	250	20	.542
St. Olaf	82	360	298	20	.546
St. Thomas (Minn.)	94	457	291	32	.606
Salisbury St.	28	140	125	4	.528
Salve Regina	7	52	12	0	.813
Sewanee	105	434	396	39	.522
Simpson	94	395	425	37	.482
Springfield	106	445	394	55	.529
Susquehanna	119	438	456	36	.480
Swarthmore	119	438	456	36	.490
Thiel	95	299	403	36	.430
Thomas More	10	68	32	0	.680
Trinity (Conn.)	115	462	328	42	.581
Trinity (Tex.)	95	369	410	49	.475
Tufts	118	451	451	46	.500
Union (N.Y.)	112	431	394	62	.521
Upper Iowa	97	307	385	25	.446
Ursinus	107	330	506	54	.401

ALL-TIME TEAM WON-LOST RECORDS

Team	Yrs.	Won	Lost	Tied	Pct.
Wabash	113	517	351	59	.590
Wartburg	64	280	265	12	.513
Washington (Mo.)	102	416	410	28	.504
Wash. & Jeff.	108	567	353	40	.611
Wash. & Lee	106	410	452	39	.477
Waynesburg	96	363	341	37	.515
Wesley	14	74	59	1	.556
Wesleyan (Conn.)	118	457	436	42	.511
Western Conn. St.	28	101	164	3	.382
Western Md.	105	454	394	49	.533
Western New Eng.	19	62	105	1	.372
Westfield St.	18	77	94	1	.451
Westminster (Mo.)	37	132	108	17	.547
Wheaton (Ill.)	87	371	309	29	.544
Whittier	90	420	328	36	.559
Whitworth	84	257	346	20	.429
Widener	119	564	358	38	.607
Wilkes	54	218	242	8	.474
Willamette	99	425	331	40	.559
Wm. Paterson	28	106	167	4	.390
William Penn	99	264	490	15	.357
Williams	114	551	329	47	.620
Wilmington (Ohio)	67	266	290	14	.479
Wis.-Eau Claire	81	307	324	34	.487
Wis.-La Crosse	75	463	192	40	.695
Wis.-Oshkosh	73	234	335	30	.416
Wis.-Platteville	91	306	324	31	.486
Wis.-River Falls	74	365	235	32	.603
Wis.-Stevens Point	100	400	320	43	.552
Wis.-Stout	80	222	409	33	.359
Wis.-Whitewater	75	393	220	21	.636
Wittenberg	106	603	319	32	.649
Wooster	101	433	376	41	.534
Worcester St.	15	81	62	0	.566
Worcester Tech	110	269	426	30	.392

Winningest Football Teams of 1990s

Won-lost-tied record includes postseason games

BY PERCENTAGE (TOP 25)
(Minimum seven seasons as Division III member)

School	Yrs.	Won	Lost	Tied	Pct.
Mount Union	10	120	7	1	.941
Williams	10	70	8	2	.888
Central (Iowa)	10	91	15	0	.858
Allegheny	10	93	16	1	.850
Albion	10	83	14	2	.848
St. John's (Minn.)	10	97	17	1	.848
Salve Regina	7	53	10	0	.841
Wittenberg	10	86	17	1	.832
Lycoming	10	91	19	1	.824
Wis.-La Crosse	10	93	20	1	.820
Union (N.Y.)	10	80	18	0	.816
Rowan	10	99	23	1	.809
Wash. & Jeff.	10	89	21	0	.809
Emory & Henry	10	81	22	0	.786
Wartburg	10	81	23	0	.779
Ill. Wesleyan	10	72	21	1	.771
Carnegie Mellon	10	77	23	0	.770
John Carroll	10	76	22	4	.765
Baldwin-Wallace	10	76	24	1	.757
Augustana (Ill.)	10	71	23	0	.755
Buffalo St.	10	78	26	0	.750
Hanover	8	62	21	0	.747
Coe	10	73	25	0	.745
Dickinson	10	75	25	2	.745
Ithaca	10	79	27	0	.745

BY VICTORIES (TOP 28)

School	Yrs.	Won	Lost	Tied	Pct.
Mount Union	10	120	7	1	.941
Rowan	10	99	23	1	.809
St. John's (Minn.)	10	97	17	1	.848
Allegheny	10	93	16	1	.850
Wis.-La Crosse	10	93	20	1	.820
Central (Iowa)	10	91	15	0	.858
Lycoming	10	91	19	1	.824
Wash. & Jeff.	10	89	21	0	.809
Wittenberg	10	86	17	1	.832
Albion	10	83	14	2	.848
Emory & Henry	10	81	22	0	.786
Wartburg	10	81	23	0	.779
Union (N.Y.)	10	80	18	0	.816
Ithaca	10	79	27	0	.745
Buffalo St.	10	78	26	0	.750
Carnegie Mellon	10	77	23	0	.770
Baldwin-Wallace	10	76	24	1	.757
Frostburg St.	10	76	26	2	.740
John Carroll	10	76	22	4	.765
Simpson	10	76	27	1	.736
Dickinson	10	75	25	2	.745
Coe	10	73	25	0	.745
Ill. Wesleyan	10	72	21	1	.771
Wis.-Whitewater	10	72	28	0	.720
Augustana (Ill.)	10	71	23	0	.755
Hardin-Simmons	10	71	27	0	.724
Plymouth St.	10	71	29	2	.706
Wesley	10	71	30	1	.701

National Poll Rankings

Final Poll Leaders
(Released Before Division Championship Playoffs)

Year	Team (Record*)	Coach	Record in Championship†
1975	Ithaca (8-0-0)	Jim Butterfield	2-1 Runner-up
1976	St. John's (Minn.) (7-0-1)	John Gagliardi	3-0 Champion
1977	Wittenberg (8-0-0)	Dave Maurer	Did not compete
1978	Minn.-Morris (9-0-0)	Al Molde	1-1 Lost in semifinals
1979	Wittenberg (8-0-0)	Dave Maurer	2-1 Runner-up
1980	Ithaca (10-0-0)	Jim Butterfield	2-1 Runner-up
1981	Widener (9-0-0)	Bill Manlove	3-0 Champion
1982	Baldwin-Wallace (10-0-0)	Bob Packard	0-1 Lost in first round
1983	Augustana (Ill.) (9-0-0)	Bob Reade	3-0 Champion
1984	Augustana (Ill.) (9-0-0)	Bob Reade	3-0 Champion
1985	Augustana (Ill.) (9-0-0)	Bob Reade	4-0 Champion
1986	Dayton (10-0-0)	Mike Kelly	0-1 Lost in first round
1987	Augustana (Ill.) (9-0-0)	Bob Reade	1-1 Lost in quarterfinals
1988	**East Region**		
	Cortland St. (9-0-0)	Dennis Kayser	1-1 Lost in quarterfinals
	North Region		
	Dayton (9-1-0)	Mike Kelly	0-1 Lost in first round
	South Region		
	Ferrum (9-0-0)	Hank Norton	2-1 Lost in semifinals
	West Region		
	Central (Iowa) (8-0-0)	Ron Schipper	3-1 Runner-up
1989	**East Region**		
	Union (N.Y.) (9-0-0)	Al Bagnoli	3-1 Runner-up
	North Region		
	Dayton (8-0-1)	Mike Kelly	4-0 Champion
	South Region		
	Rhodes (7-0-0)	Mike Clary	Did not compete
	West Region		
	Central (Iowa) (8-0-0)	Ron Schipper	1-1 Lost in quarterfinals
1990	**East Region**		
	Hofstra (9-0-0)	Joe Gardi	2-1 Lost in semifinals
	North Region		
	Dayton (9-0-0)	Mike Kelly	1-1 Lost in quarterfinals
	South Region		
	Ferrum (8-0-0)	Hank Norton	0-1 Lost in first round
	West Region		
	Wis.-Whitewater (9-0-0)	Bob Berezowitz	0-1 Lost in first round
1991	**East Region**		
	Ithaca (7-1-0)	Jim Butterfield	4-0 Champion
	North Region		
	Allegheny (10-0-0)	Ken O'Keefe	1-1 Lost in quarterfinals
	South Region		
	Lycoming (8-0-0)	Frank Girardi	1-1 Lost in quarterfinals
	West Region		
	St. John's (Minn.) (9-0-0)	John Gagliardi	2-1 Lost in semifinals
1992	**East Region**		
	Rowan (9-0-0)	John Bunting	2-1 Lost in semifinals
	North Region		
	Dayton (9-0-0)	Mike Kelly	0-1 Lost in first round
	South Region		
	Wash. & Jeff. (8-0-0)	John Luckhardt	3-1 Runner-up
	West Region		
	Central (Iowa) (9-0-0)	Ron Schipper	1-1 Lost in quarterfinals

Year	Team (Record*)	Coach	Record in Championship†
1993	**East Region** Rowan (7-1-0)	K. C. Keeler	3-1 Runner-up
	North Region Mount Union (9-0-0)	Larry Kehres	4-0 Champion
	South Region Wash. & Jeff. (8-0-0)	John Luckhardt	2-1 Lost in semifinals
	West Region Wis.-La Crosse (9-0-0)	Roger Harring	1-1 Lost in quarterfinals
1994	**East Region** Plymouth St. (9-0-0)	Don Brown	1-1 Lost in quarterfinals
	North Region Allegheny (9-0-0)	Ken O'Keefe	0-1 Lost in first round
	South Region Dickinson (9-0-0)	Darwin Breaux	0-1 Lost in first round
	West Region Central (Iowa) (9-0-0)	Ron Schipper	0-1 Lost in first round
1995	**East Region** Buffalo St. (8-1-0)	Jerry Boyes	0-1 Lost in first round
	North Region Mount Union (9-0-0)	Larry Kehres	2-1 Lost in semifinals
	South Region Wash. & Jeff. (7-0-0)	John Luckhardt	2-1 Lost in semifinals
	West Region Wis.-La Crosse (9-0-0)	Roger Harring	4-0 Champion

Year	Team (Record*)	Coach	Record in Championship†
1996	**East Region** Buffalo St. (7-1)	Jerry Boyes	0-1 Lost in first round
	North Region Mount Union (9-0)	Larry Kehres	4-0 Champion
	South Region Lycoming (8-0)	Frank Girardi	2-1 Lost in semifinals
	West Region Wis.-La Crosse (9-0)	Roger Harring	2-1 Lost in semifinals
1997	**East Region** Rowan (8-0)	K.C. Keeler	2-1 Lost in semifinals
	North Region Mount Union (9-0)	Larry Kehres	4-0 Champion
	South Region Lycoming (8-0)	Frank Girardi	3-1 Runner-up
	West Region Wis.-Whitewater (9-0)	Bob Berezowitz	0-1 Lost in first round
1998	**East Region** Springfield (9-0)	Mike DeLong	0-1 Lost in first round
	North Region Mount Union (10-0)	Larry Kehres	4-0 Champion
	South Region Lycoming (8-0)	Frank Girardi	1-1 Lost in quarterfinals
	West Region Central (Iowa) (9-0)	Rich Kacmarynski	0-1 Lost in first round

*Final poll record. †Number of teams in the championship: 8 (1975-84); 16 (1985-98). Beginning in 1999, regional polls were no longer conducted.

Undefeated, Untied Teams

(Regular-Season Games Only)

Following is a list of undefeated and untied teams since 1973, when College Division teams were divided into Division II and Division III under a three-division reorganization plan adopted by the special NCAA Convention in August 1973. Since 1981, conference playoff games have been included in a team's won-lost record (previously, such games were considered postseason contests). Figures indicate the regular-season wins (minimum seven games against four-year varsity opponents). A subsequent postseason win(s) in the Division III championship or a conference playoff game (before 1981) is indicated by (*), a loss by (†) and a tie by (‡).

Year	College	Wins
1973	Fisk	9
	Wittenberg	***9
1974	Albany (N.Y.)	9
	Central (Iowa)	**9
	Frank. & Marsh.	9
	Ithaca	*†9
	Towson	10
1975	Cal Lutheran	*†9
	Ithaca	**†8
	Widener	*†9
	Wittenberg	†***9
1976	Albion	9
1977	Central (Iowa)	†9
	Cornell College	†8
	Wittenberg	†9
1978	Baldwin-Wallace	‡***8
	Illinois Col.	9
	Minn.-Morris	*†10
	Wittenberg	‡***8
1979	Carnegie Mellon	*†9
	Dubuque	†9
	Jamestown	7
	Tufts	8
	Widener	*†9
	Wittenberg	***8
1980	Adrian	9
	Baldwin-Wallace	†9
	Bethany (W.Va.)	†9
	Dayton	***11
	Ithaca	**†10
	Millsaps	9
	Widener	*†10
1981	Alfred	†10
	Augustana (Ill.)	†9
	Lawrence	*†9
	West Ga.	†9

Year	College	Wins
	Widener	***10
1982	Augustana (Ill.)	**†9
	Baldwin-Wallace	†10
	Plymouth St.	10
	St. John's (Minn.)	9
	St. Lawrence	*†9
	Wabash	10
	West Ga.	***9
1983	Augustana (Ill.)	***9
	Carnegie Mellon	†9
	Hofstra	†10
	Worcester Tech	8
1984	Amherst	8
	Augustana (Ill.)	***9
	Case Reserve	9
	Central (Iowa)	**†9
	Dayton	†10
	Hope	9
	Occidental	†10
	Plymouth St.	†10
1985	Augustana (Ill.)	****9
	Carnegie Mellon	†8
	Central (Iowa)	**†9
	Denison	†10
	Lycoming	†10
	Mount Union	*†10
	Union (N.Y.)	†9
1986	Central (Iowa)	*†10
	Dayton	†10
	Ithaca	**†9
	Mount Union	*†10
	Salisbury St.	***10
	Susquehanna	*†10
	Union (N.Y.)	†9
1987	Augustana (Ill.)	*†9
	Gust. Adolphus	†10
	Wash. & Jeff.	*†9
1988	Cortland St.	*†10
	Ferrum	**†9
1989	Central (Iowa)	*†9
	Millikin	*†9
	Union (N.Y.)	***†10
	Williams	8
1990	Carnegie Mellon	†10
	Dayton	*†10
	Hofstra	†10
	Lycoming	***†9
	Mount Union	†10
	Wash. & Jeff.	*†9
	Williams	8
	Wis.-Whitewater	†10
1991	Allegheny	*†10
	Baldwin-Wallace	†10
	Dayton	***†10
	Dickinson	†10
	Eureka	10

Year	College	Wins
	Lycoming	*†9
	Mass.-Lowell	†10
	St. John's (Minn.)	**†9
	Simpson	†10
	Thomas More	10
	Union (N.Y.)	*†9
1992	Aurora	†9
	Central (Iowa)	*†9
	Cornell College	10
	Dayton	†10
	Emory & Henry	*†9
	Ill. Wesleyan	*†9
	Mount Union	**†10
	Rowan	**†10
1993	Albion	*†9
	Anderson (Ind.)	†10
	Coe	†9
	Mount Union	****10
	St. John's (Minn.)	**†10
	Trinity (Conn.)	8
	Union (N.Y.)	†9
	Wash. & Jeff.	**†9
	Wilkes	†10
	Wis.-La Crosse	*†10
1994	Albion	****9
	Allegheny	†10
	Central (Iowa)	†10
	Dickinson	†10
	La Verne	†9
	Plymouth St.	*†9
	Trinity (Tex.)	†10
	Williams	8
1995	Central (Iowa)	†10
	Hanover	†10
	La Verne	9
	Mount Union	**†10
	Plymouth St.	†9
	Thomas More	10
	Wash. & Jeff.	**†8
	Wheaton (Ill.)	*†9
	Wis.-La Crosse	****10
	Wittenberg	†10
1996	Albion	†9
	Allegheny	†10
	Ill. Wesleyan	*†9
	Lycoming	**†9
	Mount Union	****10
	St. John's (Minn.)	*†10
	Salve Regina	9
	Simpson	†9
	Worcester St.	9
1997	Catholic	†10
	Hanover	†10
	Lakeland	10
	Lycoming	***†9
	Mount Union	****10

UNDEFEATED UNTIED TEAMS

Year	College	Wins
	Rowan	**†9
	Simpson	**†10
	Trinity (Tex.)	*†9
	Western Md.	†10
	Wis.-Whitewater	†9
1998	Catholic	†10
	Central (Iowa)	†10
	Emory & Henry	10
	Grinnell	10

Year	College	Wins
	Lycoming	*†9
	Mount Union	****†10
	St. John's (Minn.)	*†10
	Trinity (Tex.)	**†10
	Western Md.	†10
	Williams	8
1999	Bri'water (Mass.)	†10
	Hanover	†10
	Hardin-Simmons	**†10

Year	College	Wins
	Lycoming	†9
	Mount Union	**†10
	Rensselaer	†9
	Trinity (Tex.)	**†10
	Wartburg	†10
	Western Conn. St.	†10
	Western Md.	*†10
	Wittenberg	*†10

The Spoilers

(Since 1973, when the three-division reorganization plan was adopted by the special NCAA Convention, creating Divisions II and III.)

Following is a list of the spoilers of Division III teams that lost their perfect (undefeated, untied) record in their **season-ending** game, including the Division III championship playoffs. An asterisk (*) indicates a Division III championship playoff game and a dagger (†) indicates the home team in a regular-season game or a conference playoff. A game involving two undefeated, untied teams is in bold face.

Date	Spoiler	Victim	Score
11-17-73	† Williams	Amherst	30-14
12-7-74	* Central (Iowa)	Ithaca	10-8
11-8-75	Cornell College	† Lawrence	17-16
11-22-75	* **Ithaca**	**Widener**	23-14
12-6-75	* Wittenberg	Ithaca	28-0
11-12-77	Norwich	† Middlebury	34-20
11-12-77	Ripon	† Cornell College	10-7
11-19-77	† Baldwin-Wallace	Wittenberg	14-7
11-19-77	* Widener	Central (Iowa)	19-0
11-25-78	* Wittenberg	Minn.-Morris	35-14
11-17-79	* Ithaca	Dubuque	27-7
11-17-79	‡ Findlay	Jamestown	41-15
11-24-79	* **Wittenberg**	**Widener**	17-14
11-24-79	* Ithaca	Carnegie Mellon	15-6
12-1-79	* Ithaca	Wittenberg	14-10
11-8-80	DePauw	† Wabash	tie 22-22
11-22-80	* **Widener**	**Bethany (W.Va.)**	43-12
11-22-80	* Dayton	Baldwin-Wallace	34-0
11-29-80	* Dayton	Widener	28-24
12-6-80	#* Dayton	Ithaca	63-0
11-14-81	† DePauw	Wabash	21-14
11-14-81	† St. Mary's (Cal.)	San Diego	31-14
11-21-81	* Widener	West Ga.	10-3
11-21-81	* Dayton	Augustana (Ill.)	19-7
11-21-81	* Montclair St.	Alfred	13-12
11-28-81	* Dayton	Lawrence	38-0
11-13-82	† Widener	Swarthmore	24-7
11-20-82	‡ Northwestern (Iowa)	St. John's (Minn.)	33-28
11-20-82	* **Augustana (Ill.)**	**Baldwin-Wallace**	28-22
11-27-82	* **Augustana (Ill.)**	**St. Lawrence**	14-0
12-4-82	* **West Ga.**	**Augustana (Ill.)**	14-0
11-19-83	* Salisbury St.	Carnegie Mellon	16-14
11-19-83	* Union (N.Y.)	Hofstra	51-19
11-10-84	St. John's (N.Y.)	† Hofstra	19-16
11-10-84	† St. Olaf	Hamline	tie 7-7
11-17-84	* Union (N.Y.)	Plymouth St.	26-14
11-17-84	* Central (Iowa)	Occidental	23-22
11-17-84	* Augustana (Ill.)	Dayton	14-13
12-8-84	* **Augustana (Ill.)**	**Central (Iowa)**	21-12
11-23-85	* Gettysburg	Lycoming	14-10
11-23-85	* **Mount Union**	**Denison**	35-3
11-23-85	* Salisbury St.	Carnegie Mellon	35-22
11-23-85	* Ithaca	Union (N.Y.)	13-12
11-30-85	* **Augustana (Ill.)**	**Mount Union**	21-14
12-7-85	* **Augustana (Ill.)**	**Central (Iowa)**	14-7
11-15-86	† Lawrence	Coe	14-10
11-22-86	* **Mount Union**	**Dayton**	42-36
11-22-86	* **Ithaca**	**Union (N.Y.)**	(ot) 24-17
11-29-86	* Concordia-M'head	Central (Iowa)	17-14
11-29-86	* **Salisbury St.**	**Susquehanna**	31-17
11-29-86	* **Augustana (Ill.)**	**Mount Union**	16-7
12-6-86	* **Salisbury St.**	**Ithaca**	44-40
12-13-86	* **Augustana (Ill.)**	**Salisbury St.**	31-3
11-11-87	St. John's	† Monmouth (Ill.)	20-15
11-21-87	* St. John's (Minn.)	Gust. Adolphus	7-3
11-28-87	* Emory & Henry	Wash. & Jeff.	23-16
11-28-87	$* Dayton	Augustana (Ill.)	38-36
12-12-88	† St. Norbert	Monmouth (Ill.)	12-0
11-19-88	Coast Guard	† Plymouth St.	28-19
11-26-88	* Ithaca	Cortland St.	24-17
12-3-88	* Ithaca	Ferrum	62-28
11-11-89	† Baldwin-Wallace	John Carroll	25-19
11-11-89	† **Bri'water (Mass.)**	**Mass.-Lowell**	14-10

Date	Spoiler	Victim	Score
11-11-89	† Centre	Rhodes	13-10
11-18-89	† Alfred	Bri'water (Mass.)	30-27
11-25-89	* St. John's (Minn.)	Central (Iowa)	27-24
11-25-89	* Dayton	Millikin	28-16
12-9-89	* Dayton	Union (N.Y.)	17-7
11-10-90	Col. of New Jersey	† Ramapo	9-0
11-10-90	† Waynesburg	Frostburg St.	28-18
11-17-90	* Allegheny	Mount Union	26-15
11-17-90	* **Lycoming**	**Carnegie Mellon**	17-7
11-17-90	* St. Thomas (Minn.)	Wis.-Whitewater	24-23
11-24-90	* Allegheny	Dayton	31-23
11-24-90	* **Lycoming**	**Wash. & Jeff.**	24-0
12-1-90	* **Lycoming**	**Hofstra**	20-10
12-8-90	* Allegheny	Lycoming	(ot) 21-14
11-9-91	† Coe	Beloit	26-10
11-23-91	* **Union (N.Y.)**	**Mass.-Lowell**	55-16
11-23-91	* **Dayton**	**Baldwin-Wallace**	27-10
11-30-91	* **Dayton**	**Allegheny**	(ot) 28-25
11-30-91	* Ithaca	Union (N.Y.)	35-23
11-30-91	* Susquehanna	Lycoming	31-24
12-7-91	* **Dayton**	**St. John's (Minn.)**	19-7
12-14-91	* Ithaca	Dayton	34-20
11-7-92	Cornell College	† Coe	37-20
11-7-92	Union (N.Y.)	† Rochester	14-10
11-21-92	* **Ill. Wesleyan**	**Aurora**	21-12
11-21-92	* **Mount Union**	**Dayton**	27-10
11-28-92	* **Mount Union**	**Ill. Wesleyan**	49-27
11-28-92	* Wash. & Jeff.	Emory & Henry	51-15
11-28-92	* Wis.-La Crosse	Central (Iowa)	34-9
12-5-92	* Wash. & Jeff.	Rowan	18-13
12-5-92	* Wis.-La Crosse	Mount Union	29-24
10-30-93	Mount Senario	† Martin Luther	21-20
11-13-93	Hastings	† Colorado Col.	22-21
11-20-93	* **Albion**	**Anderson (Ind.)**	41-21
11-20-93	* **St. John's (Minn.)**	**Coe**	32-14
11-20-93	* Frostburg St.	Wilkes	26-25
11-20-93	* Wm. Paterson	Union (N.Y.)	17-7
11-27-93	* **Mount Union**	**Albion**	30-16
11-27-93	* **St. John's (Minn.)**	**Wis.-La Crosse**	47-25
12-5-93	* **Mount Union**	**St. John's (Minn.)**	56-8
12-5-93	* Rowan	Wash. & Jeff.	23-16
11-12-94	John Carroll	† Baldwin-Wallace	9-0
11-19-94	* Mount Union	Allegheny	28-19
11-19-94	* Wartburg	Central (Iowa)	22-21
11-19-94	* St. John's (Minn.)	La Verne	51-12
11-19-94	* Widener	Dickinson	14-0
11-19-94	* Wash. & Jeff.	Trinity (Tex.)	28-0
11-26-94	* Ithaca	Plymouth St.	22-7
11-11-95	Amherst	† Williams	0-0
11-18-95	* **Mount Union**	**Hanover**	52-18
11-18-95	* **Wheaton (Ill.)**	**Wittenberg**	63-41
11-18-95	* Wis.-River Falls	Central (Iowa)	10-7
11-18-95	* Union (N.Y.)	Plymouth St.	24-7
11-25-95	* **Mount Union**	**Wheaton (Ill.)**	40-14
12-2-95	* **Wis.-La Crosse**	**Mount Union**	20-17
12-2-95	* Rowan	Wash. & Jeff.	28-15
11-9-96	Williams	† Amherst	19-13
11-23-96	Ithaca	Worcester St.	27-21
11-23-96	* **Mount Union**	**Allegheny**	31-26
11-23-96	* Ill. Wesleyan	Albion	23-20
11-23-96	* **St. John's (Minn.)**	**Simpson**	21-18
11-30-96	* **Mount Union**	**Ill. Wesleyan**	49-14
11-30-96	* Wis.-La Crosse	St. John's (Minn.)	37-30
12-7-96	* Rowan	Lycoming	33-14
11-1-97	† Cornell College	Coe	28-21
11-8-97	† Williams	Amherst	48-46
11-15-97	† **Catholic**	**Albright**	44-22
11-22-97	* John Carroll	Hanover	30-20
11-22-97	* **Simpson**	**Wis.-Whitewater**	34-31
11-22-97	* **Lycoming**	**Western Md.**	27-13
11-22-97	* **Trinity (Tex.)**	**Catholic**	44-33
11-29-97	* Lycoming	Trinity (Tex.)	46-26

DIVISION III

THE SPOILERS

Date	Spoiler	Victim	Score
12-6-97	* Mount Union	Simpson	54-7
12-6-97	* Lycoming	Rowan	28-20
12-13-97	* Mount Union	Lycoming	61-12
11-14-98	DePauw	† Wabash	42-7
11-14-98	MacMurray	† Westminster (Mo.)	52-51
11-21-98	* Lycoming	Catholic	49-14
11-21-98	* Wis.-Eau Claire	Central (Iowa)	28-21
11-21-98	* Trinity (Tex.)	Western Md.	30-20
11-28-98	* Trinity (Tex.)	Lycoming	37-21
11-28-98	* Wis.-Eau Claire	St. John's (Minn.)	10-7
11-28-98	* Mount Union	Wittenberg	21-19
12-5-98	* Mount Union	Trinity (Tex.)	34-29
11-13-99	Montclair St.	†Rowan	28-24
11-20-99	* Ohio Northern	Hanover	56-14
11-20-99	* Rowan	Rensselaer	29-10
11-20-99	* Ursinus	Bri'water (Mass.)	43-38
11-20-99	* Wash. & Jeff.	Lycoming	14-7
11-27-99	* Ohio Northern	Wittenberg	58-24
11-27-99	* Montclair St.	Western Conn. St.	32-24
11-27-99	* Pacific Lutheran	Wartburg	49-14
11-27-99	* Trinity (Tex.)	Western Md.	20-16
12-4-99	* Trinity (Tex.)	Hardin-Simmons	40-33
12-11-99	* Rowan	Mount Union	(ot) 24-17
12-11-99	* Pacific Lutheran	Trinity (Tex.)	49-28

‡NAIA championship playoff game. #Defeated three consecutive perfect-record teams in the Division III championship playoffs. $Ended Augustana's (Illinois) 60-game undefeated streak.

Streaks and Rivalries

Longest Winning Streaks

(Minimum Two Seasons in Division III; Includes Postseason Games)

Wins	Team	Years
54	Mount Union	1996-99
37	Augustana (Ill.)	1983-85
24	Allegheny	1990-91
23	Wis.-La Crosse	1995-96
23	Williams	1988-91
22	Dayton	1989-90
22	Augustana (Ill.)	1986-87
21	Dayton	1979-81
20	Plymouth St.	1987-88
19	Mount Union	1993-94
19	Wis.-La Crosse	1992-93
19	Plymouth St.	1981-82
18	Lawrence	1980-81
18	Ithaca	1979-80

Longest Unbeaten Streaks

(Minimum Two Seasons in Division III; Includes Postseason Games)

No.	Wins	Ties	Team	Years
60	59	1	Augustana (Ill.)	1983-87
54	54	0	Mount Union	1996-99
25	24	1	Dayton	1989-90
24	24	0	Allegheny	1990-91
24	23	1	Wis.-La Crosse	1992-93
24	23	1	Wabash	1979-81
23	23	0	Wis.-La Crosse	1995-96
23	23	0	Williams	1988-91
22	21	1	Dayton	1979-81
21	20	1	Baldwin-Wallace	1977-79
20	20	0	Plymouth St.	1987-88
20	18	2	St. John's (Minn.)	1975-76

Longest Division III Series

Games	Opponents (Series leader listed first)	Series Record	First Game
114	Williams-Amherst	64-45-5	1884
113	Albion-Kalamazoo	75-34-4	1896
111	Bowdoin-Colby	62-40-9	1892
110	Knox-Monmouth (Ill.)	50-50-10	1891
109	Coe-Cornell College	53-52-4	1891
106	DePauw-Wabash	49-48-9	1890
105	Williams-Wesleyan (Conn.)	63-37-5	1881
105	Amherst-Wesleyan (Conn.)	56-40-9	1882
105	Hampden-Sydney—Randolph-Macon	51-43-11	1893
102	Bowdoin-Bates	60-35-7	1889
102	Colby-Bates	54-40-8	1893
101	Occidental—Pomona-Pitzer	52-46-3	1895
99	Wesleyan (Conn.)-Trinity (Conn.)	51-47-1	1885
99	Lawrence-Ripon	47-45-7	1893
98	Albion-Alma	54-39-5	1894

Trophy Games

Following is a list of the current Division III football trophy games. The games are listed alphabetically by the trophy-object name. The date refers to the season the trophy was first exchanged and is not necessarily the start of the competition between the participants.

Trophy	Date	Colleges
Academic Bowl	1986	Carnegie Mellon-Case Reserve
Admiral's Cup	1980	Maine Maritime-Mass. Maritime
Baird Bros. Golden Stringer	1984	Case Reserve-Wooster
Bell	1931	Franklin-Hanover
Bill Edwards Trophy	1989	Case Reserve-Wittenberg
Bridge Bowl	1990	Mt. St. Joseph-Thomas More
Bronze Turkey	1929	Knox-Monmouth (Ill.)
CBB	1966	Bates, Bowdoin, Colby
Conestoga Wagon	1963	Dickinson-Frank. & Marsh.
Cortaca Jug	1959	Cortland St.-Ithaca
Cranberry Bowl	1979	Bri'water (Mass.)-Mass. Maritime
Doehling-Heselton Helmet	1988	Lawrence-Ripon
Drum	1940	Occidental—Pomona-Pitzer
Dutchman's Shoes	1950	Rensselaer-Union (N.Y.)
Edumund Orgill	1954	Rhodes-Sewanee
Founder's	1987	Chicago-Washington (Mo.)
Goat	1931	Carleton-St. Olaf
John Wesley	1984	Ky. Wesleyan-Union (Ky.)
Keystone Cup	1981	Delaware Valley-Widener
Little Brass Bell	1947	North Central-Wheaton (Ill.)
Little Brown Bucket	1938	Dickinson-Gettysburg
Little Three	1971	Amherst, Wesleyan (Conn.), Williams
Mercer County Cup	1984	Grove City-Thiel
Monon Bell	1932	DePauw-Wabash
Mug	1931	Coast Guard-Norwich
Old Goal Post	1953	Juniata-Susquehana
Old Musket	1964	Carroll (Wis.)-Carthage
Old Rocking Chair	1980	Hamilton-Middlebury
Old Tin Cup	1954	Gettysburg-Muhlenberg
Old Water Bucket	1989	Maranatha Baptist-Martin Luther
Paint Bucket	1965	Hamline-Macalester
Pella Corporation Classic	1988	Central (Iowa)-William Penn
President's Cup	1971	Case Reserve-John Carroll
Rhine River Cup	1992	Heidelberg-Otterbein
Secretary's Cup	1981	Coast Guard-Merchant Marine
Shoes	1946	Occidental-Whittier
Shot Glass	1938	Coast Guard-Rensselaer
Soup Bowl	1997	Guilford-Greensboro
Steve Dean Memorial	1976	Catholic-Georgetown
Totem Pole	1950	Pacific Lutheran-Puget Sound
Transit	1980	Rensselaer-Worcester Tech
Victory Bell	1946	Loras-St. Thomas (Minn.)
Victory Bell	1949	Upper Iowa-Wartburg
Wadsworth	1977	Middlebury-Norwich
Wilson Brothers Cup	1986	Hamline-St. Thomas (Minn.)
Wooden Shoes	1946	Hope-Kalamazoo

Cliffhangers

Regular-season games won by Division III teams on the final play of the game in regulation time (from 1973). The extra point is listed when it provided the margin of victory after the winning touchdown.

Date	Opponents, Score	Game-Winning Play
9-22-73	Hofstra 21, Seton Hall 20	Tom Calder 15 pass from Steve Zimmer (Jim Hogan kick)
9-18-76	Ohio Wesleyan 23, DePauw 20	Tom Scurfield 48 pass from Bob Mauck
10-27-77	Albany (N.Y.) 42, Maine 39	Larry Leibowitz 19 FG
9-22-79	Augustana (Ill.) 19, Carthage 18	John Stockton 14 pass from Mark Schick

CLIFFHANGERS

Date	Opponents, Score	Game-Winning Play
10-6-79	Carleton 17, Lake Forest 14	Tim Schoonmaker 46 FG
11-10-79	Dayton 24, St. Norbert 22	Jim Fullenkamp 21 FG
9-13-80	Cornell College 14, Lawrence 13	John Bryant 8 pass from Matt Dillon (Keith Koehler kick)
9-27-80	Muhlenberg 41, Johns Hopkins 38	Mickey Mottola 1 run
10-25-80	Mass.-Lowell 15, Marist 13	Ed Kulis 3 run
10-17-81	Carleton 22, Ripon 21	John Winter 23 pass from Billy Ford (Dave Grein kick)
10-2-82	Frostburg St. 10, Mercyhurst 7	Mike Lippold 34 FG
11-6-82	Williams 27, Wesleyan (Conn.) 24	Marc Hummon 33 pass from Robert Connolly
10-7-83	Johns Hopkins 19, Ursinus 17	John Tucker 10 pass from Mark Campbell
10-8-83	Susquehanna 17, Widener 14	Todd McCarthy 20 FG
10-29-83	Frank. & Marsh. 16, Swarthmore 15	Billy McLean 51 pass from Niall Rosenzweig
9-24-84	Muhlenberg 3, Frank. & Marsh. 0	Tom Mulroy 26 FG
9-14-85	Principia 26, Illinois Col. 22	Dan Sellers 48 pass from Jon Hinds
10-26-85	Buffalo 13, Brockport St. 11	Dan Friedman 37 FG
11-9-85	Frank. & Marsh. 29, Johns Hopkins 28	Brad Ramsey 1 run (Ken Scalet pass from John Travagline)
9-18-86	Beloit 16, Lakeland 13	Sean Saturnio 38 pass from Ed Limon
9-20-86	Susquehanna 43, Lycoming 42	Rob Sochovka 40 pass from Todd Coolidge (Randy Pozsar kick)
10-18-86	Ill. Wesleyan 25, Elmhurst 23	Dave Anderson 11 pass from Doug Moews
9-5-87	Wash. & Jeff. 17, Ohio Wesleyan 16	John Ivory 28 FG
9-26-87	Gust. Adolphus 19, Macalester 17	Dave Fuecker 8 pass from Dean Kraus
10-3-87	Wis.-Whitewater 10, Wis.-Platteville 7	Dave Emond 25 FG
10-24-87	Geneva 9, St. Francis (Pa.) 7	John Moores 19 FG
10-1-88	Canisius 17, Rochester 14	Jim Ehrig 34 FG
10-1-88	Cortland St. 24, Western Conn. St. 21	Ted Nagengast 35 FG
10-8-88	UC Santa Barb. 20, Sonoma St. 18	Harry Konstantinopoulos 52 FG
10-8-88	Hamilton 13, Bowdoin 10	Nate O'Steen 19 FG
11-5-88	Colby 20, Middlebury 18	Eric Aulenback 1 run
11-12-88	Wis.-River Falls 24, Wis.-Stout 23	Andy Feil 45 FG
10-7-89	Moravian 13, Juniata 10	Mike Howey 75 pass from Rob Light
10-21-89	Western New Eng. 17, Bentley 14	Leo Coughlin 17 FG
10-21-89	Thiel 19, Carnegie Mellon 14	Bill Barber 4 pass from Jeff Sorenson
9-8-90	Emory & Henry 22, Wash. & Lee 21	Todd Woodall 26 pass from Pat Walker
9-15-90	Otterbein 20, Capital 17	Korey Brown 39 FG
10-27-90	Hamline 26, Gust. Adolphus 24	Mike Sunnarborg 2 pass from Bob Hackney
11-10-90	Colby 23, Bowdoin 20	Paul Baisley 10 pass from Bob Ward
9-7-91	Central (Iowa) 26, Gust. Adolphus 25	Brian Krob 1 pass from Shad Flynn
9-13-91	St. John's (N.Y.) 30, Iona 27	John Ledwith 42 FG
10-5-91	Trinity (Conn.) 30, Williams 27	John Mullaney 5 pass from James Lane
10-26-91	DePauw 12, Anderson (Ind.) 7	Steve Broderick 65 pass from Brian Goodman
9-19-92	Lake Forest 9, North Park 7	Dave Mills 2 pass from Jim DeLisa
10-17-92	Elmhurst 30, North Central 28	Eric Ekstrom 2 pass from Jack Lamb
10-16-93	Union (N.Y.) 16, Rensselaer 13	Greg Harrison 38 FG
10-16-93	North Central 24, Elmhurst 22	Bryce Cann 35 FG
10-23-93	Stony Brook 21, Merchant Marine 20	Brian Hughes 44 FG
10-30-93	Thomas More 24, Defiance 18	Greg Stotko 6 blocked field goal return
9-10-94	Colorado Col. 16, Buena Vista 14	Josh Vitt 4 run
9-8-95	FDU-Madison 20, Johns Hopkins 17	Jason Herrick 37 FG
10-12-96	Defiance 20, Mt. St. Joseph 19	Randy Weldman 40 pass from Jeff Edred
9-13-97	Adrian 10, Heidelberg 7	Mike Hirvela 24 FG
10-25-97	Carthage 22, Millikin 17	Kris Norton 45 pass from Eric Corbett
11-15-97	Worcester Tech 9, Plymouth St. 7	Matt Surette 2 pass from John Riccio
9-12-98	Elmhurst 12, Ripon 10	Brendon Lyons 5 pass from Rasand Hall
9-19-98	Wis.-Oshkosh 41, Menlo 38	David Gaulke 31 FG
10-10-98	Baldwin-Wallace 38, Ohio Northern 35	Brian Hegnauer 44 FG

Regular-Season Overtime Games

In 1981, the NCAA Football Rules Committee approved an overtime tiebreaker system to decide a tie game for the purpose of determining a conference champion. The following conferences used the tiebreaker system to decide conference-only tie games. (In 1996, the tiebreaker became mandatory in all games tied after four periods.) The number of overtimes is indicated in parentheses.

EASTERN COLLEGIATE FOOTBALL CONFERENCE

Date	Opponents, Score
10-28-95	Western New Eng. 6, Nichols 0 (4 ot)

IOWA INTERCOLLEGIATE ATHLETIC CONFERENCE

Date	Opponents, Score
9-26-81	William Penn 24, Wartburg 21 (1 ot)
9-25-82	Dubuque 16, Buena Vista 13 (1 ot)
10-2-82	Luther 25, Dubuque 22 (1 ot)
10-30-82	Wartburg 27, Dubuque 24 (3 ot)
10-4-86	Luther 28, Wartburg 21 (1 ot)
9-26-87	William Penn 19, Upper Iowa 13 (2 ot)
11-7-87	William Penn 17, Loras 10 (1 ot)
10-10-92	Simpson 20, Loras 14 (1 ot)
11-14-92	Luther 17, Buena Vista 10 (1 ot)

MIDWEST CONFERENCE

Date	Opponents, Score
10-25-86	Lake Forest 30, Chicago 23 (1 ot)
10-26-86	Lawrence 7, Beloit 0 (1 ot)
9-30-89	Illinois Col. 26, Ripon 20 (3 ot)
10-27-90	Beloit 16, St. Norbert 10 (1 ot)
11-2-91	Monmouth (Ill.) 13, Knox 7 (1 ot)
10-14-95	Beloit 20, Carroll (Wis.) 14 (1 ot)

NEW ENGLAND FOOTBALL CONFERENCE
(From 1987)

Date	Opponents, Score
10-31-87	Nichols 21, Mass.-Lowell 20 (1 ot)
9-17-88	Mass.-Lowell 22, Worcester St. 19 (2 ot)
9-30-89	Worcester St. 23, Mass.-Dartmouth 20 (1 ot)
10-27-89	Westfield St. 3, Mass.-Dartmouth 0 (3 ot)
10-28-89	Worcester St. 27, Nichols 20 (1 ot)
11-7-92	Mass.-Dartmouth 21, Westfield St. 14 (3 ot)
9-25-93	Mass. Maritime 28, Westfield St. 21 (1 ot)
11-5-94	Mass.-Dartmouth 21, Westfield St. 14 (1 ot)

SOUTHERN CALIFORNIA INTERCOLLEGIATE ATHLETIC CONFERENCE

Date	Opponents, Score
10-18-86	La Verne 53, Occidental 52 (1 ot)
9-26-87	Claremont-M-S 33, Occidental 30 (1 ot)
10-27-90	Occidental 47, Claremont-M-S 41 (1 ot)
10-17-92	Cal Lutheran 17, Occidental 14 (1 ot)
10-30-93	Redlands 23, Cal Lutheran 17 (2 ot)

Stadiums

STADIUMS LISTED ALPHABETICALLY

School	Stadium	Year Built	Capacity	Surface
Adrian	Maple	1960	5,000	Grass
Albion	Sprankle-Sprandel	1976	5,010	Grass
Albright	Eugene L. Shirk	1925	7,000	Grass
Alfred	Merrill Field	1926	5,000	Turf
Allegheny	Robertson Field	1948	5,000	Grass
Alma	Bahlke Field	1986	4,000	Turf
Amherst	Pratt Field	1891	8,000	Grass
Anderson (Ind.)	Macholtz	NA	4,200	Grass
Augsburg	Anderson-Nelson Field	1984	2,000	AstroTurf
Augustana (Ill.)	Ericson Field	1938	3,200	Grass
Aurora	Aurora Field	NA	1,500	Grass
Baldwin-Wallace	George Finnie	1971	8,100	StadiaTurf
Bates	Garcelon Field	1900	3,000	Grass
Beloit	Strong	1934	3,500	Grass
Benedictine (Ill.)	Alumni	1951	3,000	Grass
Bethany (W.Va.)	Bethany Field	1938	1,000	Grass
Bethel (Minn.)	Bremer Field	1972	3,000	Grass
Blackburn	Blackburn College	NA	1,500	Grass
Bluffton	Salzman	1993	3,000	Grass
Bowdoin	Whittier Field	NA	9,000	Grass
Bri'water (Mass.)	Swenson Field	1974	3,000	Grass
Bridgewater (Va.)	Jopson Field	1971	3,000	Grass
Brockport St.	Special Olympics	1979	10,000	Grass
Buena Vista	J. Leslie Rollins	1980	3,500	Grass
Buffalo St.	Coyer Field	NA	3,000	Grass
Cal Lutheran	Mt. Clef	1962	2,000	Grass
Capital	Bernlohr	1928	2,000	Grass
Carleton	Laird	1926	7,500	Grass
Carnegie Mellon	Gesling	1990	3,500	Omni-Turf
Carroll (Wis.)	Van Male Field	1976	4,200	Grass
Carthage	Art Keller Field	1965	3,100	Grass
Case Reserve	E. L. Finningan Field	1968	3,000	Grass
Catholic	Cardinal Field	1985	3,500	Grass
Central (Iowa)	A. N. Kuyper	1977	5,000	Grass
Centre	Farris	1925	2,500	Grass
Chapman	Ernie Chapman	NA	3,000	Grass
Chicago	Stagg Field	1969	1,500	Grass
Claremont-M-S	Zinda Field	1955	3,000	Grass
Coast Guard	Cadet Memorial Field	1932	4,500	Grass
Coe	Clark Field	1989	2,200	Grass
Colby	Seaverns	1948	5,000	Grass
Colorado Col.	Washburn Field	1898	2,000	Grass
Concordia (Ill.)	Concordia	NA	1,500	Grass
Concordia-M'head	Jake Christiansen	NA	7,500	Grass
Cornell College	Ash Park Field	1922	2,500	Grass
Cortland St.	Davis Field	1959	5,000	Grass
Curry	D. Forbes Will Field	NA	1,500	Grass
Defiance	Justin F. Coressel	1994	4,000	Grass
Delaware Valley	James Work Memorial	1978	4,500	Grass
Denison	Deeds Field	1922	5,000	Grass
DePauw	Blackstock	1941	4,000	Grass
Dickinson	Biddle Field	1909	2,577	Grass
Dubuque	Chalmers Field	1942	2,800	PAT
Earlham	M. O. Ross Field	1975	1,500	Grass
Elmhurst	Langhorst Field	1920	2,500	Grass
Emory & Henry	Fullerton Field	NA	5,500	Grass
Eureka	McKinzie	1913	3,000	Grass
FDU-Madison	Robert T. Shields	1973	4,000	Grass
Ferrum	W. B. Adams	1970	5,500	Grass
Fitchburg St.	Robert Elliot	1984	1,200	Grass
Framingham St.	Maple Street Field	NA	1,500	Grass
Franklin	Goodell Field	1889	2,000	Grass
Frank. & Marsh.	Sponaugle-Williamson Field	1920	4,000	Grass
Frostburg St.	Bobcat	1974	4,000	Grass
Gettysburg	Musselman	1965	6,176	Grass
Grinnell	Rosenbloom Field	1911	1,750	Grass
Grove City	Thorn Field	1981	3,500	Grass
Guilford	Armfield Athletic Center	1960	3,500	Grass
Gust. Adolphus	Hollingsworth Field	1929	4,500	Grass
Hamilton	Steuben Field	NA	2,500	Grass
Hamline	Norton	1921	2,000	Grass
Hampden-Sydney	Hundley	1964	2,400	Grass
Hanover	L. S. Ayers Field	1973	4,000	Grass
Hardin-Simmons	Shelton	1993	4,000	Grass
Hartwick	All-Weather Field	1985	1,200	AstroTurf
Heidelberg	Frost-Kalnow	1941	7,500	Grass
Hiram	Charles Henry Field	1958	3,000	Grass
Hobart	Boswell Field	1975	4,500	Grass
Hope	Holland Municipal	1979	5,322	Grass
Howard Payne	Gordon Wood	NA	7,600	Grass
Illinois Col.	England Field	1960	2,500	Grass
Ill. Wesleyan	Ill. Wesleyan	1893	3,500	Grass
Ithaca	Jim Butterfield	1958	5,000	Grass
John Carroll	Wasmer Field	1968	3,500	Turf
Johns Hopkins	Homewood Field	1906	8,000	Turf
Juniata	Chuck Knox	1988	3,000	Grass
Kalamazoo	Angell Field	1946	3,000	Grass
Kean	Zweidinger Field	NA	2,200	Grass
Kenyon	McBride Field	1962	2,500	Grass
King's (Pa.)	Monarch Field	NA	3,000	Grass
Knox	Knox Bowl	1968	6,000	Grass
La Verne	Ortmayer	1991	1,500	Grass
Lake Forest	Farwell Field	NA	2,000	Grass
Lakeland	John Taylor Field	1958	1,500	Grass
Lawrence	Banta Bowl	1965	5,255	Grass
Lebanon Valley	Arnold Field	1969	2,500	Grass
Linfield	Maxwell Field	1922	4,000	Grass
Loras	Rock Bowl	1945	3,000	Grass
Luther	Carlson	1966	5,000	Grass
Lycoming	Person Field	1962	2,500	Grass
Macalester	Macalester	1965	4,000	Grass
MacMurray	MacMurray Field	1984	5,000	Grass
Maine Maritime	Ritchie	1965	3,500	Turf
Manchester	Burt Memorial	NA	4,500	Grass
Marietta	Don Drumm Field	1935	7,000	Grass
Martin Luther	Northwestern	1953	2,000	Grass
Maryville (Tenn.)	Thornton-Honaker Field	1951	2,500	Grass
Mass.-Boston	Clark Ath. Center	1981	750	Grass
Mass.-Dartmouth	University	NA	1,850	Grass
MIT	Henry G. Steinbrenner	1980	1,600	Grass
Mass. Maritime	Edward Ellis Field	1972	3,000	Grass
Menlo	Conner Field	1972	1,000	Grass
Merchant Marine	Captain Tomb Field	1945	5,840	Grass
Methodist	Monarch Field	1989	1,500	Grass
Middlebury	Alumni	1991	3,500	Grass
Millikin	Frank M. Lindsay Field	1987	4,000	Grass
Millsaps	Alumni Field	NA	4,000	Grass
Mississippi Col.	Robinson-Hale	1985	8,500	Grass
Monmouth (Ill.)	Bobby Woll Memorial Field	1981	3,000	Grass
Montclair St.	Sprague Field	1934	6,000	AstroTurf
Moravian	Steel Field	1932	2,200	Grass
Mount Union	Mount Union	1915	5,000	Grass
Muhlenberg	Scotty Wood Stadium	1998	3,000	AstroTurf
Muskingum	McConagha	1925	5,000	Grass
Neb. Wesleyan	Abel	1986	2,000	Grass
New Jersey City	Tidelands Ath. Complex	1986	2,500	Grass
College of New Jersey	Lions	1984	5,000	AstroTurf
Nichols	Bison Bowl	1961	3,000	Grass
North Central	Kroehler Field	NA	3,000	Grass
North Park	Hedstrand Field	1955	2,500	Grass
Norwich	Sabine Field	1921	5,000	Grass
Oberlin	Dill Field	1925	3,500	Grass
Occidental	Patterson Field	1900	4,000	Grass
Ohio Northern	Ada War Memorial	1948	4,000	Grass
Ohio Wesleyan	Selby	1929	9,600	Grass
Olivet	Griswold Field	1972	3,500	Grass
Otterbein	Memorial	1946	4,000	Grass
Pacific Lutheran	Sparles Stadium	1935	4,500	Turf
Plymouth St.	Currier Memorial Field	1970	1,000	Grass
Pomona-Pitzer	Merritt Field	1991	2,000	Grass
Principia	Clark Field	1937	1,000	Grass
Randolph-Macon	Day Field	1953	5,000	Grass
Redlands	Ted Runner	1968	7,000	Grass
Rensselaer	86 Field	1912	3,000	Grass
Rhodes	Fargason Field	NA	5,000	Grass
Ripon	Ingalls Field	1888	2,500	Grass
Rochester	Edwin Fauver	1930	5,000	All-Pro Turf
Rose-Hulman	Phil Brown Field	NA	2,500	Grass
Rowan	John Page	1969	5,000	Grass
St. John Fisher	Growney Stadium	1999	2,100	AstroTurf
St. John's (Minn.)	St. John's	1908	5,000	Grass
St. Lawrence	Weeks Field	1906	3,000	Grass
St. Norbert	Minahan	1937	3,100	Grass
St. Olaf	Manitou Field	1930	5,000	Grass
St. Thomas (Minn.)	O'Shaughnessy	1948	5,025	Grass
Salisbury St.	Sea Gull	1980	2,500	Grass
Salve Regina	Toppa	NA	2,500	Grass
Sewanee	McGee Field	1935	1,500	Grass
Simpson	Simpson/Indianola Field	1990	5,000	Grass
Springfield	Benedum Field	1971	2,500	All-Pro Plus
Susquehanna	Amos Alonzo Stagg Field	1892	4,600	Grass
Swarthmore	Clothier	1950	2,000	Grass

STADIUMS

School	Stadium	Year Built	Capacity	Surface
Thiel	Stewart Field	1954	5,000	Grass
Thomas More	Lockland	1945	6,500	Grass
Trinity (Conn.)	Dan Jessee Field	1900	6,500	Grass
Trinity (Tex.)	E. M. Stevens	1972	3,500	Grass
Tufts	Ellis Oval	1923	6,000	Grass
Union (N.Y.)	Frank Bailey Field	1981	2,000	AstroTurf
Upper Iowa	Eischeid	1993	3,500	Grass
Ursinus	Patterson Field	1923	2,500	Grass
Wabash	Little Giant	1967	4,200	Grass
Wartburg	Schield	1956	2,500	Grass
Washington (Mo.)	Francis Field	1904	4,000	Grass
Wash. & Jeff.	College Field	1958	5,000	Grass
Wash. & Lee	Wilson Field	1930	7,000	Grass
Waynesburg	College Field	1904	1,300	Grass
Wesley	Wolverine	1989	2,000	Grass
Wesleyan (Conn.)	Andrus Field	1881	8,000	Grass
Western Conn. St.	Midtown Campus Field	NA	2,500	Turf
Western Md.	Scott S. Bair	1981	4,000	Grass
Western New Eng.	WNEC	NA	1,500	Grass
Westfield St.	Alumni Field	1982	4,800	AstroTurf
Westminster (Mo.)	Priest Field	1906	1,500	Grass
Wheaton (Ill.)	McCully Field	1956	7,000	Grass
Whittier	Memorial	NA	7,000	Grass
Widener	Leslie C. Quick Jr.	1994	4,000	Grass
Wilkes	Ralston Field	1965	4,000	Grass
Wm. Paterson	Wrightman	NA	2,000	Grass
William Penn	Community	NA	5,000	Grass
Williams	Weston Field	1875	10,000	Grass
Wilmington (Ohio)	Williams	1983	3,250	Grass
Wis.-Eau Claire	Carson Park	NA	6,500	Grass
Wis.-La Crosse	Veterans Memorial	1924	4,349	Grass
Wis.-Oshkosh	Titan	1970	9,800	Grass
Wis.-Platteville	Ralph E. Davis Pioneer	1972	10,000	Grass
Wis.-River Falls	Ramer Field	1966	4,800	Grass
Wis.-Stevens Point	Goerke Field	1932	4,000	Grass
Wis.-Stout	Nelson Field	1936	5,000	Grass
Wis.-Whitewater	Forrest Perkins	1970	11,000	Grass
Wittenberg	Edwards-Maurer	1995	2,400	StadiaTurf
Wooster	John P. Papp	1991	4,500	Grass
Worcester St.	John Coughlin Memorial	1976	2,500	AstroTurf
Worcester Tech	Alumni Field	1916	2,800	Omni-Turf

STADIUMS LISTED BY CAPACITY (Top 35)

School	Stadium	Surface	Capacity
Wis.-Whitewater	Forrest Perkins	Grass	11,000
Brockport St.	Special Olympics	Grass	10,000
Williams	Weston Field	Grass	10,000
Wis.-Platteville	Ralph E. Davis Pioneer	Grass	10,000
Wis.-Oshkosh	Titan	Grass	9,800
Ohio Wesleyan	Selby	Grass	9,600
Bowdoin	Whittier Field	Grass	9,000
Mississippi Col.	Robinson-Hale	Grass	8,500
Baldwin-Wallace	George Finnie	StadiaTurf	8,100
Amherst	Pratt Field	Grass	8,000
Johns Hopkins	Homewood Field	Turf	8,000
Wesleyan (Conn.)	Andrus Field	Grass	8,000
Howard Payne	Gordon Wood	Grass	7,600
Carleton	Laird	Grass	7,500
Concordia-M'head	Jake Christiansen	Grass	7,500
Heidelberg	Frost-Kalnow	Grass	7,500
Albright	Eugene L. Shirk	Grass	7,000
Marietta	Don Drumm Field	Grass	7,000
Redlands	Ted Runner	Grass	7,000
Wash. & Lee	Wilson Field	Grass	7,000
Wheaton (Ill.)	McCully Field	Grass	7,000
Whittier	Memorial	Grass	7,000
Thomas More	Lockland	Grass	6,500
Trinity (Conn.)	Dan Jessee Field	Grass	6,500
Wis.-Eau Claire	Carson Park	Grass	6,500
Gettysburg	Musselman	Grass	6,176
Knox	Knox Bowl	Grass	6,000
Montclair St.	Sprague Field	AstroTurf	6,000
Tufts	Ellis Oval	Grass	6,000
Merchant Marine	Captain Tomb Field	Grass	5,840
Ferrum	W. B. Adams	Grass	5,500
Emory & Henry	Fullerton Field	Grass	5,500
Hope	Holland Municipal	Grass	5,322
Lawrence	Banta Bowl	Grass	5,255
St. Thomas (Minn.)	O'Shaughnessy Field	Grass	5,025

PAT=Prescription Athletic Turf.

Statistics Trends

(Average Per Game, One Team)

	Rushing			Passing					Total Off.			Scoring		
Year	Plays	Yds.	Avg.	Att.	Cmp.	Pct.	Yds.	Avg. Att.	Plays	Yds.	Avg.	TD	FG	Pts.
1995	42.8	159.9	3.74	25.5	12.5	49.1	159.3	6.24	68.3	319.2	4.67	3.01	0.41	21.
1996	42.8	166.9	3.90	25.9	12.8	49.4	167.8	6.48	68.7	334.7	4.87	3.21	0.43	23.3
1997	41.8	159.1	3.81	26.6	13.2	49.7	175.3	6.58	68.4	334.4	4.89	3.26	0.43	23.6
1998	41.6	159.8	3.84	26.9	13.6	50.5	181.4	6.75	68.5	341.2	4.98	3.37	0.46	24.5
1999	41.0	155.0	3.78	28.9	14.6	50.5	191.8	6.64	69.9	346.8	4.96	3.36	0.47	24.4

Additional Statistics Trends

(Average Per Game, Both Teams)

		Avg.	Punting		PAT Kick Attempts		Two-Point Attempts		Field Goals
Year	Teams	Games	No.	Avg.	Pct. Made	Pct. of Total Tries	Pct. Made	Pct. of Total Tries	Pct. Made
1995	187	9.48	5.6	33.3	.818	.854	.456	.146	.533
1996	197	9.52	5.4	34.3	.850	.862	.483	.138	.528
1997	199	9.43	5.5	35.0	.824	.859	.476	.141	.542
1998	198	9.63	5.4	35.0	.854	.867	.461	.133	.544
1999	206	9.65	5.6	34.9	.838	.877	.419	.123	.557

Classification History

The following lists show years of active membership for current and former Division III football-playing institutions. Provisional members also are shown along with the year in which they will become active members.

ACTIVE MEMBERS (219)

Adrian 1973-00	Alma 1973-00	Aurora 1988-00	Benedictine (Ill.) 1973-00
Albion 1973-00	Amherst 1973-00	Austin 1973-77, 97-00	Bethany (W.Va.) 1973-00
Albright 1973-00	Anderson (Ind.) 1992-00	Baldwin-Wallace 1973-00	Bethel (Minn.) 1983-00
Alfred 1973-00	Augsburg 1982-00	Bates 1973-00	Blackburn 1990-00
Allegheny 1973-00	Augustana (Ill.) 1973-00	Beloit 1973-00	Bluffton 1990, 92-00

School	Years
Bowdoin	1973-00
Bri'water (Mass.)	1973-00
Bridgewater (Va.)	1973-00
Brockport St.	1973-00
Buena Vista	1976-00
Buffalo St.	1981-00
Cal Lutheran	1975-77, 91-00
Capital	1973-00
Carleton	1973-00
Carnegie-Mellon	1973-00
Carroll (Wis.)	1976-00
Carthage	1976-00
Case Reserve	1973-00
Catholic	1978-00
Central (Iowa)	1973-00
Centre	1973-00
Chapman	1994-00
Chicago	1973-00
Chowan	1997-00
Claremont-M-S	1973-00
Coast Guard	1973-00
Coe	1973-00
Colby	1973-00
Colorado Col.	1973-00
Concordia (Ill.)	1973-75, 81-00
Concordia-M'head	1977-00
Concordia (Wis.)	1997-00
Cornell College	1973-00
Cortland St.	1973-00
Curry	1973-00
Defiance	1973-75, 91-00
Delaware Valley	1973-00
Denison	1973-00
DePauw	1973-00
Dickinson	1973-00
Dubuque	1976-00
Earlham	1982-00
Eastern Ore.	1999-00
Elmhurst	1973-00
Emory & Henry	1973-00
Eureka	1978-00
FDU-Madison	1973-00
Ferrum	1985-00
Fitchburg St.	1984-00
Framingham St.	1973-00
Franklin	1992-00
Frank. & Marsh.	1973-00
Frostburg St.	1977-00
Gettysburg	1973-00
Greensboro	1997-00
Greenville	1997-00
Grinnell	1973-00
Grove City	1973-00
Guilford	1990-00
Gust. Adolphus	1973-00
Hamilton	1973-00
Hamline	1973-00
Hampden-Sydney	1973-00
Hanover	1992-00
Hardin-Simmons	1990-92, 94-00
Hartwick	1992-00
Heidelberg	1973-00
Hiram	1973-00
Hobart	1973-00
Hope	1973-00
Howard Payne	1994-00
Illinois Col.	1978-00
Ill. Wesleyan	1978-00
Ithaca	1973-00
John Carroll	1973-00
Johns Hopkins	1973-00
Juniata	1973-00
Kalamazoo	1973-00
Kean	1973-00
Kenyon	1973-00
King's (Pa.)	1994-00
Knox	1973-00
La Verne	1982-00
Lake Forest	1973-00
Lakeland	1994-00
Lawrence	1973-00
Lebanon Valley	1973-00
Lewis & Clark	1998-00
Linfield	1998-00
Loras	1986-00
Luther	1973-00
Lycoming	1973-00
Macalester	1973-00
MacMurray	1984-00
Maine Maritime	1973-00
Manchester	1992-00
Maranatha Baptist	1999-00
Marietta	1973-00
Martin Luther	1991-00
Mary Hardin-Baylor	2000
Maryville (Tenn.)	1973-00
Mass.-Boston	1988-00
Mass.-Dartmouth	1988-00
MIT	1988-00
Mass. Maritime	1973-00
McMurry	1997-00
Menlo	1986-00
Merchant Marine	1973-77, 82-00
Methodist	1989-00
Middlebury	1973-00
Millikin	1976-00
Millsaps	1973-00
Mississippi Col.	1997-00
Monmouth (Ill.)	1973-00
Montclair St.	1973-00
Moravian	1973-00
Mt. St. Joseph	1998-00
Mount Union	1973-00
Muhlenberg	1973-00
Muskingum	1973-00
Neb. Wesleyan	1973-00
Col. of New Jersey	1973-00
New Jersey City	1973-00
Nichols	1973-00
North Central	1973-00
North Park	1973-00
Norwich	1973-00
Oberlin	1973-00
Occidental	1973-00
Ohio Northern	1973-00
Ohio Wesleyan	1973-00
Olivet	1973-00
Otterbein	1973-00
Pacific Lutheran	1998-00
Plymouth St.	1973-00
Pomona-Pitzer	1973-00
Principia	1973-00
Puget Sound	1999-00
Randolph-Macon	1973-00
Redlands	1973-78, 82-00
Rensselaer	1973-00
Rhodes	1984-00
Ripon	1973-00
Rochester	1973-00
Rose-Hulman	1973-00
Rowan	1973-00
St. John Fisher	1988-00
St. John's (Minn.)	1973-00
St. Lawrence	1973-00
St. Norbert	1973-00
St. Olaf	1973-00
St. Thomas (Minn.)	1973-00
Salisbury St.	1973-00
Salve Regina	1993-00
Sewanee	1973-00
Simpson	1973-00
Springfield	1995-00
Stillman	1999-00
Sul Ross St.	1997-00
Susquehanna	1973-00
Swarthmore	1973-00
Thiel	1973-00
Thomas More	1990-00
Trinity (Conn.)	1973-00
Trinity (Tex.)	1973-00
Tufts	1973-00
Union (N.Y.)	1973-00
Upper Iowa	1976-00
Ursinus	1973-00
Wabash	1973-00
Wartburg	1973-00
Washington (Mo.)	1973-00
Wash. & Jeff.	1973-00
Wash. & Lee	1973-00
Waynesburg	1990-00
Wesley	1986-00
Wesleyan (Conn.)	1973-00
Western Conn. St.	1977-00
Western Md.	1973-00
Western New Eng.	1981-00
Westfield St.	1982-00
Westminster (Mo.)	1997-00
Wheaton (Ill.)	1973-00
Whittier	1973-00
Whitworth	1998-00
Widener	1973-00
Wilkes	1973-00
Willamette	1998-00
Wm. Paterson	1973-00
William Penn	1976-00
Williams	1973-00
Wilmington (Ohio)	1977-80, 90-00
Wis.-Eau Claire	1986-00
Wis.-La Crosse	1983-00
Wis.-Oshkosh	1975-00
Wis.-Platteville	1980-00
Wis.-River Falls	1977, 82-00
Wis.-Stevens Point	1980-00
Wis.-Stout	1980-00
Wis.-Whitewater	1973-77, 80-00
Wittenberg	1973-00
Wooster	1973-00
Worcester St.	1985-00
Worcester Tech	1973-00

PROVISIONAL MEMBER (1)*

School	Years
Mount Ida	2003

FORMER MEMBERS

Ala.-Birmingham	1991-92
Albany (N.Y.)	1973-94
Albany St. (Ga.)	1973-75
American Int'l	1973
Ashland	1973-79
Assumption	1988-92
Bentley	1988-92
Bloomsburg	1973-79
Bowie St.	1973-79
Bridgeport	1973
Brooklyn	1978-91
Buffalo	1978-92
UC Santa Barb.	1986-90
Cal St. Chico	1973-77
Cal Tech	1973-77
Cameron	1973
Canisius	1975-92
UCF	1980-81
Charleston So.	1991-92
Cheyney	1973-79
Clark Atlanta	1973-79
Colorado Mines	1973
C.W. Post	1975-77, 84, 89-92
Davidson	1990-92
Dayton	1976-92
Delaware St.	1973-77
Dist. Columbia	1978
Drake	1987-92
Duquesne	1979-92
Evansville	1973-77, 89-92
Ferris St.	1975-76
Fisk	1973-83
Fordham	1973-88
Fort Valley St.	1973-80
Gallaudet	1973-79, 86-94
Gannon	1989-92
Georgetown	1973-92
Hillsdale	1975
Hofstra	1973-92
Humboldt St.	1975-79
Ill.-Chicago	1973
Iona	1978-92
James Madison	1977-79
Ky. Wesleyan	1983-92
Knoxville	1973-88
Kutztown	1973-79
Lane	1973-87
Livingston	1973
Lock Haven	1973-79
Mansfield	1973-79
Marist	1978-92
Maritime (N.Y.)	1985, 88
Mass.-Lowell	1981-92
Mercyhurst	1982-92
Merrimack	1989
Miles	1973-87
Millersville	1973-79
Minn.-Morris	1978-84
Minn. St.-Mankato	1977
Morehouse	1973-80
New Haven	1973, 77-80
New York Tech	1973
Oswego St.	1976
Pace	1978-92
Plattsburgh St.	1973-78
Quincy	1987-92
Ramapo	1981-92
Rochester Inst.	1973-77
Sacred Heart	1991-92
St. Francis (Pa.)	1978-92
St. John's (N.Y.)	1978-92
St. Joseph's (Ind.)	1973-78
St. Mary's (Cal.)	1973-80
St. Peter's	1973-92
Samford	1985-88
San Diego	1973-92
San Fran. St.	1973-78
Savannah St.	1973-80
Seton Hall	1973-76, 78-80
Shepherd	1973-75
Shippensburg	1973-75
Siena	1988-92
Slippery Rock	1973-78
Sonoma St.	1980-83
Stonehill	1989-00
Stony Brook	1983-94
Tarleton St.	1977
Towson	1973-79
Upsala	1973-96
Valparaiso	1973-78
Villanova	1985-86
Wagner	1973-92
West Ga.	1981-82
Winona St.	1975
Wis.-Superior	1973-92

*Provisional members are not active members of the Association and, thus are not eligible for NCAA statistics, records and championship play. The end of the three-year provisional status and first season of active membership in Division III football is listed to the right of the school name.

Individual Collegiate Records

Individual Collegiate Records...............................216

Individual Collegiate Records

Individual collegiate records are determined by comparing the best records in all four divisions (I-A, I-AA, II and III) in comparable categories. Included are career records of players who played in two divisions (e.g., Dennis Shaw of San Diego St., Howard Stevens of Randolph-Macon and Louisville, and Tom Ehrhardt of C. W. Post and Rhode Island). Players who played seasons other than in the NCAA will have statistics only including NCAA seasons.

Total Offense

CAREER YARDS PER GAME

(Minimum 5,500 Yards)

Player, Team (Division[s])	Years	G	Plays	Yards	TDR‡	Yd. PG
Steve McNair, Alcorn St. (I-AA)	1991-94	42	*2,055	*16,823	152	*400.5
Tim Rattay, Louisiana Tech (I-A)	1997-99	33	1,705	12,618	117	382.4
Justin Peery, Westminster (Mo.) (III)	1996-99	39	2,001	13,645	*166	349.9
Aaron Flowers, Cal St. Northridge (I-AA)	1996-97	20	944	6,754	60	337.7
Terry Peebles, Hanover (III)	1992-95	23	1,140	7,672	89	333.6
Dave Dickenson, Montana (I-AA)	1992-95	35	1,539	11,523	116	329.2
Willie Totten, Mississippi Val. (I-AA)	1982-85	40	1,812	13,007	157	325.2
Grady Benton, West Tex. A&M (II)	1994-95	18	844	5,831	55	323.9
Ty Detmer, Brigham Young (I-A)	1988-91	46	1,795	14,665	135	318.8
Neil Lomax, Portland St. (II; I-AA)	1977; 78-80	42	1,901	13,345	120	317.7
Kirk Baumgartner, Wis.-Stevens Point (III)	1986-89	41	2,007	12,767	110	311.4
Mike Perez, San Jose St. (I-A)	1986-87	20	875	6,182	37	309.1
Doug Nussmeier, Idaho (I-AA)	1990-93	39	1,556	12,054	109	309.1
Josh Wallwork, Wyoming (I-A)	1995-96	22	845	6,753	60	307.0
Oteman Sampson, Florida A&M (I-AA)	1996-97	22	906	6,751	57	306.9
Doug Gaynor, Long Beach St. (I-A)	1984-85	22	1,067	6,710	45	305.0
Tod Mayfield, West Tex. A&M (I-AA; II)	1984-85; 86	24	1,165	7,316	58	304.8
Jamie Martin, Weber St. (I-AA)	1989-92	41	1,838	12,287	93	299.7
Tony Eason, Illinois (I-A)	1981-82	22	1,016	6,589	43	299.5
Scott Otis, Glenville St. (II)	1994-95	20	755	5,911	66	295.6
Tom Proudian, Iona (I-AA)	1993-95	27	1,337	7,939	61	294.0
Robert Dougherty, Boston U. (I-AA)	1993-94	21	918	6,135	56	292.1
Keith Bishop, Ill. Wesleyan/Wheaton (Ill.) (III)	1981, 83-85	31	1,467	9,052	77	292.0
David Klingler, Houston (I-A)	1988-91	32	1,431	9,327	93	291.5
Stan Greene, Boston U. (I-AA)	1989-90	22	1,167	6,408	49	291.3
John Friesz, Idaho (I-AA)	1986-89	35	1,459	10,187	79	291.1
Steve Sarkisian, Brigham Young (I-A)	1995-96	25	953	7,253	56	290.1
Chris Redman, Louisville (I-A)	1996-99	42	1,846	12,129	87	288.8
Steve Young, Brigham Young (I-A)	1981-83	31	1,177	8,817	74	284.4
Mark Novara, Lakeland (III)	1994-97	38	1,653	10,801	112	284.2
Daunte Culpepper, UCF (I-AA; I-A)	1995-98	44	1,847	12,432	108	282.5
Tim Couch, Kentucky (I-A)	1996-98	29	1,338	8,160	78	281.4
Jayson Merrill, Western St. (II)	1990-91	20	641	5,619	57	281.0
Jordan Poznick, Principia (III)	1990-93	32	1,757	8,983	71	280.7

*Record. ‡Touchdowns-responsible-for are player's TDs scored and passed for.

SEASON YARDS PER GAME

Player, Team (Division)	Year	G	Plays	Yards	TDR‡	Yd. PG
Steve McNair, Alcorn St. (I-AA)	†1994	11	649	*5,799	53	*527.2
David Klingler, Houston (I-A)	†1990	11	*704	5,221	55	474.6
Justin Peery, Westminster (Mo.) (III)	†1998	10	645	4,651	57	465.1
Willie Totten, Mississippi Val. (I-AA)	†1984	10	564	4,572	*61	457.2
Justin Peery, Westminster (Mo.) (III)	†1999	10	599	4,419	60	441.9
Danny Ragsdale, Redlands (III)	1999	9	464	3,855	35	428.3
Andre Ware, Houston (I-A)	†1989	11	628	4,661	49	423.7
Ty Detmer, Brigham Young (I-A)	1990	12	635	5,022	45	418.5
Grady Benton, West Tex. A&M (II)	†1994	9	505	3,699	35	411.0
Steve McNair, Alcorn St. (I-AA)	†1992	10	519	4,057	39	405.7
Perry Klein, C. W. Post (II)	†1993	10	499	4,052	41	405.2
Tim Rattay, Louisiana Tech (I-A)	†1998	12	602	4,840	47	403.3
Mike Maxwell, Nevada (I-A)	†1995	9	443	3,623	34	402.6
Chris Redman, Louisville (I-A)	1998	10	513	4,009	31	400.9
Terry Peebles, Hanover (III)	†1995	10	572	3,981	43	398.1
Steve Young, Brigham Young (I-A)	†1983	11	531	4,346	41	395.1
Jamie Martin, Weber St. (I-AA)	†1991	11	591	4,337	37	394.3
Chris Vargas, Nevada (I-A)	†1993	11	535	4,332	35	393.8
Marty Washington, West Ala. (II)	1993	8	453	3,146	29	393.8
Wilkie Perez, Glenville St. (II)	†1997	11	509	4,301	45	391.0
Scott Mitchell, Utah (I-A)	†1988	11	589	4,299	29	390.8
Damian Poalucci, East Stroudsburg (II)	†1996	10	505	3,883	41	388.3
Jim McMahon, Brigham Young (I-A)	†1980	12	540	4,627	53	385.6
Dave Dickenson, Montana (I-AA)	†1995	11	544	4,209	41	382.6
Tim Rattay, Louisiana Tech (I-A)	†1999	10	562	3,810	35	381.0
Neil Lomax, Portland St. (I-AA)	†1980	11	550	4,157	42	377.9
Daunte Culpepper, UCF (I-A)	1998	11	543	4,153	40	377.5
Tim Couch, Kentucky (I-A)	1998	11	617	4,151	37	377.4
Brett Salisbury, Wayne St. (Neb.) (II)	1993	10	424	3,732	32	373.2
David Neill, Nevada (I-A)	1998	9	409	3,351	31	372.3

Steve McNair played for Alcorn State from 1991-94 and remains the only player in NCAA history to average over 400 yards per game in total offense in a career.

INDIVIDUAL COLLEGIATE RECORDS—TOTAL OFFENSE

Player, Team (Division)	Year	G	Plays	Yards	TDR‡	Yd. PG
Ty Detmer, Brigham Young (I-A)	1989	12	497	4,433	38	369.4
Joe Lee, Towson (I-AA)	†1999	11	608	4,031	22	366.5
Troy Kopp, Pacific (Cal.) (I-A)	1990	9	485	3,276	32	364.0
Dave Dickenson, Montana (I-AA)	†1993	11	530	3,978	46	361.6
Tim Rattay, Louisiana Tech (I-A)	†1997	11	541	3,968	35	360.7
Neil Lomax, Portland St. (I-AA)	†1979	11	611	3,966	31	360.5
Jed Drenning, Glenville St. (II)	1993	10	473	3,593	32	359.3
Alfred Montez, Western N.M. (II)	1994	6	244	2,130	18	355.0
Keith Bishop, Wheaton (Ill.) (III)	†1983	9	421	3,193	24	354.8
Kirk Baumgartner, Wis.-Stevens Point (III)	†1989	10	530	3,540	39	354.0
Bill Nietzke, Alma (III)	†1996	9	468	3,185	29	353.9
Rob Tomlinson, Cal St. Chico (II)	†1989	10	534	3,525	26	352.5
Josh Wallwork, Wyoming (I-A)	†1996	12	525	4,209	35	350.8
John Furmaniak, Eureka (III)	1995	10	414	3,503	35	350.3
John Friesz, Idaho (I-AA)	†1989	11	464	3,853	31	350.3

*Record. †National total-offense champion. ‡Touchdowns-responsible-for are player's TDs scored and passed for.

CAREER YARDS

Player, Team (Division[s])	Years	Plays	Yards	Avg.
Steve McNair, Alcorn St. (I-AA)	1991-94	*2,055	*16,823	8.19
Ty Detmer, Brigham Young (I-A)	1988-91	1,795	14,665	8.17
Justin Peery, Westminster (Mo.) (III)	1996-99	2,001	13,645	6.82
Neil Lomax, Portland St. (II; I-AA)	1977; 78-80	1,901	13,345	7.02
Willie Totten, Mississippi Val. (I-AA)	1982-85	1,812	13,007	7.18
Kirk Baumgartner, Wis.-Stevens Point (III)	1986-89	2,007	12,767	6.36
Tim Rattay, Louisiana Tech (I-A)	1997-99	1,705	12,618	7.40
Daunte Culpepper, UCF (I-AA; I-A)	1995-98	1,847	12,432	6.73
Chad Pennington, Marshall (I-AA, I-A)	1995, 97-99	1,719	12,313	7.16
Jamie Martin, Weber St. (I-AA)	1989-92	1,838	12,287	6.68
Chris Redman, Louisville (I-A)	1996-99	1,846	12,129	6.57
Doug Nussmeier, Idaho (I-AA)	1990-93	1,556	12,054	7.75
Dave Dickenson, Montana (I-AA)	1992-95	1,539	11,523	7.49
Doug Flutie, Boston College (I-A)	1981-84	1,558	11,317	7.26
Travis Brown, Northern Ariz. (I-AA)	1996-99	1,732	11,267	6.51
Vernon Buck, Wingate (II)	1991-94	1,761	11,227	6.38
Ken Hobart, Idaho (I-AA)	1980-83	1,847	11,127	6.02
Tim Lester, Western Mich. (I-A)	1996-99	1,747	11,081	6.34
Bob McLaughlin, Lock Haven (II)	1992-95	2,007	11,041	5.50
Peyton Manning, Tennessee (I-A)	1994-97	1,534	11,020	7.18
Eric Zeier, Georgia (I-A)	1991-94	1,560	10,841	6.95
Alex Van Pelt, Pittsburgh (I-A)	1989-92	1,570	10,814	6.89
Mark Novara, Lakeland (III)	1994-97	1,653	10,801	6.53
Earl Harvey, N.C. Central (II)	1985-88	2,045	10,667	5.22
Stoney Case, New Mexico (I-A)	1991-94	1,673	10,651	6.37
Joe Hamilton, Georgia Tech (I-A)	1996-99	1,758	10,640	7.00
Bill Borchert, Mount Union (III)	1994-97	1,274	10,639	*8.35
Chris Hatcher, Valdosta St. (II)	1991-94	1,557	10,588	6.80
Jim Ballard, Wilmington (Ohio)/Mount Union (III)	1990, 91-93	1,328	10,545	7.94
Todd Santos, San Diego St. (I-A)	1984-87	1,722	10,513	6.11
Danny Wuerffel, Florida (I-A)	1993-96	1,355	10,500	7.75
Cade McNown, UCLA (I-A)	1995-98	1,429	10,487	7.34
Giovanni Carmazzi, Hofstra (I-AA)	1996-99	1,564	10,416	6.66
Troy Dougherty, Grinnell (III)	1994, 97-99	1,520	10,314	6.79
Sean Payton, Eastern Ill. (I-AA)	1983-86	1,690	10,298	6.09
Greg Wyatt, Northern Ariz. (I-AA)	1986-89	1,753	10,277	5.86
Kevin Sweeney, Fresno St. (I-A)	$1982-86	1,700	10,252	6.03
Thad Trujillo, Fort Lewis (II)	1991-94	1,787	10,209	5.71
John Friesz, Idaho (I-AA)	1986-89	1,459	10,187	6.98
Troy Kopp, Pacific (Cal.) (I-A)	1989-92	1,595	10,037	6.29
Kevin Ricca, Catholic (III)	1994-97	1,533	9,982	6.51
Donovan McNabb, Syracuse (I-A)	1995-98	1,403	9,950	7.09
Rob Tomlinson, Cal St. Chico (II)	1988-91	1,656	9,921	5.99
Michael Proctor, Murray St. (I-AA)	1986-89	1,577	9,886	6.27
Jeff Wiley, Holy Cross (I-AA)	1985-88	1,428	9,877	6.92
Tom Ehrhardt, C. W. Post (II); Rhode Island (I-AA)	1981-82; 84-85	1,674	9,793	5.85
Brian McClure, Bowling Green (I-A)	1982-85	1,630	9,774	6.00
John Hebgen, Minn. St.-Mankato (II)	1993-96	1,545	9,772	6.32
Jeff Lewis, Northern Ariz. (I-A)	1992-95	1,654	9,769	5.91
Eric Noble, Wilmington (Ohio) (III)	1992-95	1,513	9,731	6.43
Jim McMahon, Brigham Young (I-A)	1977-78, 80-81	1,325	9,723	7.34
Mike Mitros, West Chester (II)	1996-99	1,716	9,714	5.66
Glenn Foley, Boston College (I-A)	1990-93	1,440	9,702	6.74
Tim Peterson, Wis.-Stout (III)	1986-89	1,558	9,701	6.23
Ted White, Howard (I-AA)	1995-98	1,377	9,669	7.02
Jarrod Furgason, Fairmont St. (II)	$1993-97	1,583	9,638	6.09
John Craven, Gardner-Webb (II)	1991-94	1,666	9,630	5.78
Chris Ings, Wabash (III)	1992-95	1,532	9,608	6.27
Shaun King, Tulane (I-A)	1995-98	1,516	9,468	6.25
Terrence Jones, Tulane (I-A)	1985-88	1,620	9,445	5.83
Ryan Vena, Colgate (I-AA)	1996-99	1,404	9,435	6.72
Chris Boden, Villanova (I-AA)	1996-99	1,514	9,369	6.19
Matt D'Orazio, Otterbein (III)	1996-99	1,625	9,364	5.76
David Klingler, Houston (I-A)	1988-91	1,431	9,327	6.52
Brian Ah Yat, Montana (I-AA)	1995-98	1,365	9,319	6.83

*Record. $See page 6 for explanation.

SEASON YARDS

Player, Team (Division)	Year	G	Plays	Yards	Avg.
Steve McNair, Alcorn St. (I-AA)	†1994	11	649	*5,799	@8.94
David Klingler, Houston (I-A)	†1990	11	*704	5,221	7.42
Ty Detmer, Brigham Young (I-A)	1990	12	635	5,022	7.91
Tim Rattay, Louisiana Tech (I-A)	†1998	12	602	4,840	8.04
Andre Ware, Houston (I-A)	†1989	11	628	4,661	7.42
Justin Peery, Westminster (Mo.) (III)	†1998	10	645	4,651	6.58
Jim McMahon, Brigham Young (I-A)	1980	12	540	4,627	8.57
Willie Totten, Mississippi Val. (I-AA)	†1984	10	564	4,572	8.11
Ty Detmer, Brigham Young (I-A)	1989	12	497	4,433	8.92
Justin Peery, Westminster (Mo.) (III)	†1999	10	599	4,419	7.38
Steve Young, Brigham Young (I-A)	†1983	11	531	4,346	8.18
Jamie Martin, Weber St. (I-AA)	†1991	11	591	4,337	7.34
Chris Vargas, Nevada (I-A)	†1993	11	535	4,332	8.10
Wilkie Perez, Glenville St. (II)	†1997	11	509	4,301	8.45
Scott Mitchell, Utah (I-A)	†1988	11	589	4,299	7.30
Dave Dickenson, Montana (I-AA)	†1995	11	544	4,209	7.74
Josh Wallwork, Wyoming (I-A)	†1996	12	525	4,209	8.02
Neil Lomax, Portland St. (I-AA)	†1980	11	550	4,157	7.56
Daunte Culpepper, UCF (I-A)	1998	11	543	4,153	7.65
Tim Couch, Kentucky (I-A)	1998	11	617	4,151	6.73
Robbie Bosco, Brigham Young (I-A)	1985	13	578	4,141	7.16
Steve McNair, Alcorn St. (I-AA)	1992	10	519	4,057	7.82
Perry Klein, C. W. Post (II)	†1993	10	499	4,052	8.12
Joe Lee, Towson (I-AA)	†1999	11	608	4,031	6.63
Chris Redman, Louisville (I-A)	1998	10	513	4,009	7.81
Ty Detmer, Brigham Young (I-A)	†1991	12	478	4,001	8.37
Steve Sarkisian, Brigham Young (I-A)	1996	14	486	3,983	8.20
Terry Peebles, Hanover (III)	†1995	10	572	3,981	6.96
Dave Dickenson, Montana (I-AA)	†1993	11	530	3,978	7.51
Tim Rattay, Louisiana Tech (I-A)	†1997	11	541	3,968	7.33
Neil Lomax, Portland St. (I-AA)	†1979	11	611	3,966	6.49
Robbie Bosco, Brigham Young (I-A)	†1984	12	543	3,932	7.24
Drew Brees, Purdue (I-A)	1998	12	575	3,921	6.82
Chad Pennington, Marshall (I-A)	1999	12	460	3,904	8.49
Damian Poalucci, East Stroudsburg (II)	†1996	10	505	3,883	7.69
Mike McCoy, Utah (I-A)	1993	12	529	3,860	7.50
Danny Ragsdale, Redlands (III)	1999	9	464	3,855	8.31
John Friesz, Idaho (I-AA)	†1989	11	464	3,853	8.30
Steve McNair, Alcorn St. (I-AA)	1993	11	493	3,830	7.77
Todd Hammel, Stephen F. Austin (I-AA)	1989	11	487	3,822	7.85
Tim Rattay, Louisiana Tech (I-A)	†1999	10	562	3,810	6.78
Ken Hobart, Idaho (I-AA)	1983	11	578	3,800	6.57
Joe Hamilton, Georgia Tech (I-A)	1999	11	459	3,794	8.27
Kirk Baumgartner, Wis.-Stevens Point (III)	†1988	11	604	3,790	6.27
Peyton Manning, Tennessee (I-A)	1997	12	526	3,789	7.20
Chris Hegg, Truman (II)	†1985	11	594	3,782	6.37
Jimmy Klingler, Houston (I-A)	†1992	11	544	3,768	6.93
Shaun King, Tulane (I-A)	1998	11	468	3,764	8.04
Dan Robinson, Hawaii (I-A)	1999	12	616	3,762	6.11
Dave Stireman, Weber St. (I-AA)	1985	11	502	3,759	7.49
Tim Couch, Kentucky (I-A)	1997	11	613	3,759	6.13
Brian Ah Yat, Montana (I-AA)	1996	11	501	3,744	7.47
Willie Totten, Mississippi Val. (I-AA)	1985	11	561	3,742	6.67
Brett Salisbury, Wayne St. (Neb.) (II)	1993	10	424	3,732	8.80
Jeff Wiley, Holy Cross (I-AA)	†1987	11	445	3,722	8.36

*Record. †National total-offense champion. @ Record for minimum 3,000 yards.

SINGLE-GAME YARDS

Yds.	Div.	Player, Team (Opponent)	Date
732	I-A	David Klingler, Houston (Arizona St.)	Dec. 2, 1990
696	I-A	Matt Vogler, TCU (Houston)	Nov. 3, 1990
651	II	Wilkie Perez, Glenville St. (Concord)	Oct. 25, 1997
649	I-AA	Steve McNair, Alcorn St. (Southern U.)	Oct. 22, 1994
647	I-AA	Steve McNair, Alcorn St. (Chattanooga)	Sept. 10, 1994
643	I-AA	Jamie Martin, Weber St. (Idaho St.)	Nov. 23, 1991
633	I-AA	Steve McNair, Alcorn St. (Grambling)	Sept. 3, 1994
631	II	Jayce Goree, Glenville St. (Concord)	Oct. 24, 1998
630	III	Justin Peery, Westminster (Mo.) (Colorado Col.)	Oct. 30, 1999
628	III	Justin Peery, Westminster (Mo.) (MacMurray)	Nov. 14, 1998
625	I-A	David Klingler, Houston (TCU)	Nov. 3, 1990
625	I-A	Scott Mitchell, Utah (Air Force)	Oct. 15, 1988
624	I-AA	Steve McNair, Alcorn St. (Samford)	Oct. 29, 1994
623	II	Perry Klein, C. W. Post (Salisbury St.)	Nov. 6, 1993
621	I-AA	Willie Totten, Mississippi Val. (Prairie View)	Oct. 27, 1984
617	III	Justin Peery, Westminster (Mo.) (Principia)	Oct. 17, 1998
614	I-AA	Bryan Martin, Weber St. (Cal Poly)	Sept. 23, 1995
614	II	Alfred Montez, Western N.M. (West Tex. A&M)	Oct. 8, 1994
612	I-A	Jimmy Klingler, Houston (Rice)	Nov. 28, 1992
604	I-AA	Steve McNair, Alcorn St. (Jackson St.)	Nov. 21, 1992
603	I-A	Ty Detmer, Brigham Young (San Diego St.)	Nov. 16, 1991
601	I-A	Troy Kopp, Pacific (Cal.) (New Mexico St.)	Oct. 20, 1990
599	I-A	Virgil Carter, Brigham Young (UTEP)	Nov. 5, 1966
597	II	Damian Poalucci, East Stroudsburg (Mansfield)	Nov. 2, 1996
597	I-A	John Walsh, Brigham Young (Utah St.)	Oct. 30, 1993
596	III	John Love, North Park (Elmhurst)	Oct. 13, 1990
595	I-AA	Doug Pederson, La.-Monroe (Stephen F. Austin)	Nov. 11, 1989
594	II	Jarrod DeGeorgia, Wayne St. (Neb.) (Drake)	Nov. 9, 1996
594	I-A	Jeremy Leach, New Mexico (Utah)	Nov. 11, 1989
591	II	Marty Washington, West Ala. (Nicholls St.)	Sept. 11, 1993
590	III	Danny Ragsdale, Redlands (Azusa Pacific)	Sept. 25, 1999
590	III	Tom Stallings, St. Thomas (Minn.) (Bethel [Minn.])	Nov. 13, 1993
588	III	Danny Ragdale, Redlands (Cal Lutheran)	Nov. 13, 1999
587	I-AA	Vern Harris, Idaho St. (Montana)	Oct. 12, 1985
586	I-AA	Steve McNair, Alcorn St. (Troy St.)	Nov. 12, 1994
585	I-A	Dave Wilson, Illinois (Ohio St.)	Nov. 8, 1980

Rushing

CAREER YARDS PER GAME

(Minimum 2,500 Yards)

Player, Team (Division[s])	Years	G	Plays	Yards	TD	Yd. PG
Arnold Mickens, Butler (I-AA)	1994-95	20	763	3,813	29	*190.7
Anthony Gray, Western N.M. (II)	1997-98	19	503	3,484	19	183.4
Ed Marinaro, Cornell (I-A)	1969-71	27	918	4,715	50	174.6
Damian Beane, Shepherd (II)	1996-99	38	1,065	6,346	58	167.0
Rob Marchitello, Maine Maritime (III)	1993-95	26	879	4,300	59	165.4
O. J. Simpson, Southern California (I-A)	1967-68	19	621	3,214	33	164.4
Kelvin Gladney, Millsaps (III)	1993-94	19	510	3,085	36	162.4
Johnny Bailey, Tex. A&M-Kingsville (III)	1986-89	39	885	6,320	66	162.1
Herschel Walker, Georgia (I-A)	1980-82	33	994	5,259	49	159.4
Brian Shay, Emporia St. (II)	1995-98	44	1,007	*6,958	81	158.1
Carey Bender, Coe (III)	1991-94	39	926	6,125	71	157.1
Brad Olson, Lawrence (III)	1994-97	34	792	5,325	44	156.6
Steve Tardif, Maine Maritime (III)	1996-99	39	1,190	6,093	50	156.2
Kirk Matthieu, Maine Maritime (III)	$1989-93	33	964	5,107	41	154.8
Aaron Stecker, Western Ill. (I-AA)	1997-98	20	550	3,081	36	154.1
Tim Hall, Robert Morris (I-AA)	1994-95	19	393	2,908	27	153.1
Fred Lane, Lane (II)	1994-96	29	700	4,433	41	152.9
Terry Underwood, Wagner (III)	1985-88	33	742	5,010	52	151.8
Kavin Gailliard, American Int'l (II)	1996-99	43	950	6,523	69	151.7
Jerry Azumah, New Hampshire (I-AA)	1995-98	41	1,044	6,193	60	151.0
LeShon Johnson, Northern Ill. (I-A)	1992-93	22	592	3,314	18	150.6
Reggie Greene, Siena (I-AA)	1994-97	36	890	5,415	45	150.4
Ole Gunderson, St. Olaf (II)	1969-71	27	639	4,060	56	150.4
Richard Huntley, Winston-Salem (II)	1992-95	42	932	6,286	57	149.7
Roger Graham, New Haven (II)	1991-94	40	821	5,953	66	148.8
Ron Dayne, Wisconsin (I-A)	1996-99	43	1,115	6,397	63	148.8
Marshall Faulk, San Diego St. (I-A)	1991-93	31	766	4,589	57	148.0
George Jones, San Diego St. (I-A)	1995-96	19	486	2,810	34	147.9
D'Andra Freeman, Fitchburg St. (III)	1997-99	27	789	3,957	29	146.6
Brad Hustad, Luther (II)	1957-59	27	655	3,943	25	146.0
Rashaan Dumas, Southern Conn. St. (II)	1996-99	37	977	5,396	71	145.8
Archie Amerson, Northern Ariz. (I-AA)	1995-96	22	526	3,196	37	145.3
Jarrett Anderson, Truman (II)	1993-96	43	979	6,166	69	143.4
Quincy Tillmon, Emporia St. (II)	1990-92, 94	29	790	4,141	37	142.8
Anthony Russo, St. John's (N.Y.) (III)	1990-93	41	1,152	5,834	57	142.3
Tony Dorsett, Pittsburgh (I-A)	1973-76	43	1,074	6,082	55	141.4
Troy Davis, Iowa St. (I-A)	1994-96	31	782	4,382	36	141.4

Player, Team (Division[s])	Years	G	Plays	Yards	TD	Yd. PG
Keith Elias, Princeton (I-AA)	1991-93	30	736	4,208	49	140.3
Joe Iacone, West Chester (II)	1960-62	27	565	3,767	40	139.5

*Record. $See page 6 for explanation.

SEASON YARDS PER GAME

Player, Team (Division)	Year	G	Plays	Yards	TD	Yd. PG
Barry Sanders, Oklahoma St. (I-A)	†1988	11	344	2,628	*37	*238.9
Dante Brown, Marietta (III)	†1996	10	314	2,385	25	238.5
R. J. Bowers, Grove City (III)	†1998	10	329	2,283	34	228.3
Arnold Mickens, Butler (I-AA)	†1994	10	*409	2,255	18	225.5
Carey Bender, Coe (III)	1994	10	295	2,243	29	224.3
Anthony Gray, Western N.M. (II)	†1997	10	277	2,220	12	222.0
Kavin Gailliard, American Int'l (II)	†1999	12	320	*2,653	32	221.1
Marcus Allen, Southern California (I-A)	†1981	11	403	2,342	22	212.9
R. J. Bowers, Grove City (III)	1999	10	344	2,098	25	209.8
Ed Marinaro, Cornell (I-A)	†1971	9	356	1,881	24	209.0
Brian Shay, Emporia St. (II)	†1998	11	293	2,265	29	205.9
Charles Roberts, Cal St. Sacramento (I-AA)	†1998	11	386	2,260	19	205.5
Irv Sigler, Bloomsburg (II)	1997	10	299	2,038	20	203.8
Ricky Gales, Simpson (III)	†1989	10	297	2,035	26	203.5
Tony Vinson, Towson (I-AA)	†1993	10	293	2,016	23	201.6
Terry Underwood, Wagner (III)	†1988	9	245	1,809	21	201.0
Jerry Azumah, New Hampshire (I-AA)	1998	11	342	2,195	22	199.6
Troy Davis, Iowa St. (I-A)	†1996	11	402	2,185	21	198.6
Reggie Greene, Siena (I-AA)	†1997	9	256	1,778	18	197.6
Kenneth Sasu, Marietta (III)	1999	9	332	1,770	15	196.7
Brad Olson, Lawrence (III)	†1995	9	242	1,760	16	195.6
Jarrett Anderson, Truman (II)	†1996	11	321	2,140	27	194.5
Ricky Williams, Texas (I-A)	†1998	11	361	2,124	27	193.1
Kirk Matthieu, Maine Maritime (III)	†1992	9	327	1,733	16	192.6
Brian Shay, Emporia St. (II)	1996	11	342	2,103	18	191.2
Reggie Greene, Siena (I-AA)	†1996	9	280	1,719	12	191.0
Kenneth Sasu, Marietta (III)	1999	9	332	1,770	15	196.7
Byron Hanspard, Texas Tech (I-A)	1996	11	339	2,084	13	189.5
Charles Roberts, Cal St. Sacramento (I-AA)	1999	11	303	2,082	22	189.3
Archie Amerson, Northern Ariz. (I-AA)	1996	11	333	2,079	25	189.0
Richard Huntley, Winston-Salem (II)	†1995	10	273	1,889	16	188.9
Kelvin Gladney, Millsaps (III)	1994	10	307	1,882	19	188.2
Brandon Steinheim, Wesley (III)	1996	9	319	1,684	20	187.1
D'Andra Freeman, Fitchburg St. (III)	1999	10	365	1,871	14	187.1
Rashaan Salaam, Colorado (I-A)	†1994	11	298	2,055	24	186.8
Josh Ranek, South Dakota St. (II)	1999	11	329	2,055	25	186.8
Krishaun Gilmore, Rensselaer (III)	1998	9	228	1,670	22	185.6
Jon Warga, Wittenberg (III)	†1990	10	254	1,836	15	183.6
Fred Lane, Lane (II)	1995	10	273	1,833	19	183.3
Johnny Bailey, Tex. A&M-Kingsville (II)	1986	11	271	2,011	18	182.8
Troy Davis, Iowa St. (I-A)	1995	11	345	2,010	15	182.7
Bob White, Western N.M. (II)	†1951	9	202	1,643	20	182.6
Kevin Mitchell, Saginaw Valley (II)	1989	8	236	1,460	6	182.5
Rashaan Dumas, Southern Conn. St. (II)	1996	9	291	1,639	18	182.1
Jamie Lee, MacMurray (III)	1998	10	252	1,818	25	181.8
Anthony Jones, La Verne (III)	1995	8	200	1,453	19	181.6
Hank Wineman, Albion (III)	†1991	9	307	1,629	14	181.0
Charles White, Southern California (I-A)	†1979	10	293	1,803	18	180.3

*Record. †National champion.

CAREER YARDS

Player, Team (Division[s])	Years	Plays	Yards	Avg.
Brian Shay, Emporia St. (II)	1995-98	1,007	*6,958	6.91
Kavin Gailliard, American Int'l (II)	1996-99	950	6,523	6.87
Ron Dayne, Wisconsin (I-A)	1996-99	1,115	6,397	5.74
Damian Beane, Shepherd (II)	1996-99	1,065	6,346	5.96
Johnny Bailey, Tex. A&M-Kingsville (II)	1986-89	885	6,320	7.14
Richard Huntley, Winston-Salem (II)	1992-95	932	6,286	6.74
Ricky Williams, Texas (I-A)	1995-98	1,011	6,279	6.21
Jerry Azumah, New Hampshire (I-AA)	1995-98	1,044	6,193	5.93
Jarrett Anderson, Truman St. (II)	1993-96	979	6,166	6.30
Carey Bender, Coe (III)	1991-94	926	6,125	6.61
Steve Tardif, Maine Maritime (III)	1996-99	1,190	6,093	5.12
Tony Dorsett, Pittsburgh (I-A)	1973-76	1,074	6,082	5.66
Roger Graham, New Haven (II)	1991-94	821	5,953	7.25
Anthony Russo, St. John's (N.Y.) (III)	1990-93	1,152	5,834	5.06
¢R. J. Bowers, Grove City (III)	1997-99	836	5,620	6.72
Charles White, Southern California (I-A)	1976-79	1,023	5,598	5.47
Travis Prentice, Miami (Ohio) (I-A)	1996-99	1,138	5,596	4.92
Joe Dudek, Plymouth St. (II)	1982-85	785	5,570	7.10
Phillip Moore, North Dakota (II)	1995-98	1,060	5,467	5.16
Mark Kacmarynski, Central (Iowa) (III)	$1992-96	854	5,434	6.36
Reggie Greene, Siena (I-AA)	1994-97	890	5,415	6.08
Rashaan Dumas, Southern Conn. St. (II)	1996-99	977	5,396	5.52
Thomas Haskins, VMI (I-AA)	1993-96	899	5,355	5.96
Frank Hawkins, Nevada (I-AA)	1977-80	945	5,333	5.64
Howard Stevens, Randolph-Macon (II); Louisville (I-A)	1968-69; 71-72	891	5,297	5.95

INDIVIDUAL COLLEGIATE RECORDS—RUSHING

Player, Team (Division[s])	Years	Plays	Yards	Avg.
Rick Sarille, Wagner (I-AA)	$1995-99	965	5,290	5.48
Eric Frees, Western Md. (III)	1988-91	1,059	5,281	4.99
Herschel Walker, Georgia (I-A)	1980-82	994	5,259	5.29
Kenny Gamble, Colgate (I-AA)	1984-87	963	5,220	5.42
Paul Smith, Gettysburg (III)	1996-99	881	5,205	5.91
Archie Griffin, Ohio St. (I-A)	1972-75	845	5,177	6.13
Antonio Leroy, Albany St. (Ga.) (II)	1993-96	973	5,152	5.29
Markus Thomas, Eastern Ky. (I-AA)	1989-92	784	5,149	6.57
Shawn Graves, Wofford (QB) (I-AA)	1989-92	730	5,128	7.02
Kirk Matthieu, Maine Maritime (III)	$1989-93	964	5,107	5.30
Chris Cobb, Eastern Ill. (II)	1976-79	930	5,042	5.42
Irv Sigler, Bloomsburg (II)	1994-97	820	5,034	6.14
Darren Lewis, Texas A&M (I-A)	1987-90	909	5,012	5.51
Terry Underwood, Wagner (III)	1985-88	742	5,010	6.75
Anthony Thompson, Indiana (I-A)	1986-89	1,089	4,965	4.56
George Rogers, South Carolina (I-A)	1977-80	902	4,958	5.50
Trevor Cobb, Rice (I-A)	1989-92	1,091	4,948	4.54
¢Charles Roberts, Cal St. Sacramento (I-AA)	1997-99	828	4,929	5.95
Paul Palmer, Temple (I-A)	1983-86	948	4,895	5.16
Harry Jackson, St. Cloud St. (II)	1986-89	915	4,890	5.34
Leonard Davis, Lenoir-Rhyne (II)	$1990-94	839	4,853	5.78
Jerry Linton, Okla. Panhandle (II)	1959-62	648	4,839	‡7.47
Erik Marsh, Lafayette (I-AA)	1991-94	1,027	4,834	4.71

*Record. ‡Record for minimum 600 carries. $See page 6 for explanation. ¢Active player.

SEASON YARDS

Player, Team (Division)	Year	G	Plays	Yards	Avg.
Kavin Gailliard, American Int'l (II)	†1999	12	320	*2,653	††8.29
Barry Sanders, Oklahoma St. (I-A)	†1988	11	344	2,628	7.64
Dante Brown, Marietta (III)	†1996	10	314	2,385	7.60
Marcus Allen, Southern California (I-A)	†1981	11	403	2,342	5.81
R. J. Bowers, Grove City (III)	†1998	10	329	2,283	6.94
Brian Shay, Emporia St. (II)	†1998	11	293	2,265	7.73
Charles Roberts, Cal St. Sacramento (I-AA)	†1998	11	386	2,260	5.85
Arnold Mickens, Butler (I-AA)	†1994	10	*409	2,255	5.51
Carey Bender, Coe (III)	†1994	11	295	2,243	7.60
Anthony Gray, Western N.M. (II)	†1997	10	277	2,220	8.01
Jerry Azumah, New Hampshire (I-AA)	1998	11	342	2,195	6.42
Troy Davis, Iowa St. (I-A)	†1996	11	402	2,185	5.44
Mike Rozier, Nebraska (I-A)	†1983	12	275	2,148	7.81
Jarrett Anderson, Truman (II)	†1996	11	321	2,140	6.67
Ricky Williams, Texas (I-A)	†1998	11	361	2,124	5.88
Brian Shay, Emporia St. (II)	1996	11	342	2,103	6.15
R. J. Bowers, Grove City (III)	†1999	10	344	2,098	6.10
Byron Hanspard, Texas Tech (I-A)	1996	11	339	2,084	6.15
Charles Roberts, Cal St. Sacramento (I-AA)	†1999	11	303	2,082	6.87
Archie Amerson, Northern Ariz. (I-AA)	1996	11	333	2,079	6.24
Rashaan Salaam, Colorado (I-A)	†1994	11	298	2,055	6.90
Josh Ranek, South Dakota St. (II)	1999	11	329	2,055	6.25
Irv Sigler, Bloomsburg (II)	1997	10	299	2,038	6.82
Ricky Gales, Simpson (III)	†1989	10	297	2,035	6.85
Tony Vinson, Towson (I-AA)	†1993	10	293	2,016	6.89
Johnny Bailey, Tex. A&M-Kingsville (II)	†1986	11	271	2,011	7.42
Troy Davis, Iowa St. (I-A)	†1995	11	345	2,010	5.83
LeShon Johnson, Northern Ill. (I-A)	†1993	11	327	1,976	6.04
Kavin Gailliard, American Int'l (II)	1998	11	269	1,971	7.33
Aaron Stecker, Western Ill. (I-AA)	1997	11	298	1,957	6.57
Marcel Shipp, Massachusetts (I-AA)	1998	11	319	1,949	6.11
Tony Dorsett, Pittsburgh (I-A)	†1976	11	338	1,948	5.76
Wesley Cates, Calif. (Pa.) (II)	1999	11	298	1,935	6.49
Adrian Peterson, Ga. Southern (I-AA)	1998	11	257	1,932	7.52
Brian Shay, Emporia St. (II)	1997	11	269	1,912	7.11

Player, Team (Division)	Year	G	Plays	Yards	Avg.
Lorenzo White, Michigan St. (I-A)	†1985	11	386	1,908	4.94
Wasean Tait, Toledo (I-A)	1995	11	357	1,905	5.34
Ricky Williams, Texas (I-A)	†1997	11	279	1,893	6.78
Karlton Carpenter, Southern III. (I-AA)	1998	11	323	1,892	5.86
Herschel Walker, Georgia (I-A)	†1981	11	385	1,891	4.91
Brian Pruitt, Central Mich. (I-AA)	1994	11	292	1,890	6.47
Richard Huntley, Winston-Salem (II)	†1995	10	273	1,889	6.92
Rich Erenberg, Colgate (I-AA)	†1983	11	302	1,883	6.24
Kelvin Gladney, Millsaps (III)	1994	10	307	1,882	6.13
Ed Marinaro, Cornell (I-A)	†1971	9	356	1,881	5.28
Josh Ranek, South Dakota St. (II)	1998	11	302	1,881	6.23
Ernest Anderson, Oklahoma St. (I-A)	†1982	11	353	1,877	5.32
Ahman Green, Nebraska (I-A)	1997	12	278	1,877	6.75
Ricky Bell, Southern California (I-A)	†1975	11	357	1,875	5.25
D'Andra Freeman, Fitchburg St. (III)	1999	10	365	1,871	5.13
Paul Palmer, Temple (I-A)	†1986	11	346	1,866	5.39
Ronald Moore, Pittsburg St. (II)	1992	11	239	1,864	7.80
Ron Dayne, Wisconsin (I-A)	1996	12	295	1,863	6.32
LaDainian Tomlinson, TCU (I-A)	†1999	11	268	1,850	6.90

*Record. †National champion. ††Record for minimum 214 carries.

SINGLE-GAME YARDS

Yds.	Div.	Player, Team (Opponent)	Date
441	III	Dante Brown, Marietta (Baldwin-Wallace)	Oct. 5, 1996
436	III	A. J. Pittorino, Hartwick (Waynesboro)	Nov. 2, 1996
417	III	Carey Bender, Coe (Grinnell)	Oct. 9, 1993
413	III	Dante Brown, Marietta (Heidelberg)	Nov. 9, 1996
409	I-AA	Charles Roberts, Cal St. Sacramento (Idaho St.)	Nov. 6, 1999
406	I-A	LaDainian Tomlinson, TCU (UTEP)	Nov. 20, 1999
403	II	Rob Davidson, Fairmont St. (Concord)	Nov. 14, 1998
396	I-A	Tony Sands, Kansas (Missouri)	Nov. 23, 1991
390	III	Paul Smith, Gettysburg (Muhlenberg)	Oct. 23, 1999
386	I-A	Marshall Faulk, San Diego St. (Pacific [Cal.])	Sept. 14, 1991
382	III	Shane Davis, Loras (Dubuque)	Nov. 8, 1997
382	III	Pete Baranek, Carthage (North Central)	Oct. 5, 1985
382	II	Kelly Ellis, Northern Iowa (Western Ill.)	Oct. 13, 1979
379	I-AA	Reggie Greene, Siena (St. John's [N.Y.])	Nov. 2, 1996
378	I-A	Troy Davis, Iowa St. (Missouri)	Sept. 28, 1996
377	I-A	Anthony Thompson, Indiana (Wisconsin)	Nov. 11, 1989
376	I-A	Travis Prentice, Miami (Ohio) (Akron)	Nov. 6, 1999
373	I-A	Astron Whatley, Kent (Eastern Mich.)	Sept. 20, 1997
373	II	Dallas Garber, Marietta (Wash. & Jeff.)	Nov. 7, 1959
370	III	Jim Baier, Wis.-River Falls (Wis.-Stevens Point)	Nov. 5, 1966
370	II	Jim Hissam, Marietta (Bethany [W.Va.])	Nov. 15, 1958
367	II	Don Polkinghorne, Washington (Mo.) (Wash. & Lee)	Nov. 23, 1957
364	I-AA	Tony Vinson, Towson (Bucknell)	Nov. 13, 1993
363	III	Terry Underwood, Wagner (Hofstra)	Oct. 15, 1988
363	II	Richie Weaver, Widener (Moravian)	Oct. 17, 1970
361	III	Guy Leman, Simpson (Luther)	Nov. 14, 1998
361	II	Brian Shay, Emporia St. (Washburn)	Oct. 5, 1996
361	II	Richard Huntley, Winston-Salem (Virginia Union)	Nov. 5, 1994
359	II	Anthony Gray, Western N.M. (Hardin-Simmons)	Oct. 4, 1997
357	I-A	Mike Pringle, Cal St. Fullerton (New Mexico St.)	Nov. 4, 1989
357	I-A	Rueben Mayes, Washington St. (Oregon)	Oct. 27, 1984
356	I-A	Brian Pruitt, Central Mich. (Toledo)	Nov. 5, 1994
356	I-A	Eddie Lee Ivery, Georgia Tech (Air Force)	Nov. 11, 1978
356	II	Ole Gunderson, St. Olaf (Monmouth [Ill.])	Oct. 11, 1969
354	II	Terry Underwood, Wagner (Western Conn. St.)	Oct. 3, 1986
352	III	Steve Tardif, Maine Maritime (Westfield St.)	Nov. 16, 1996
351	I-A	Scott Harley, East Caro. (North Carolina St.)	Nov. 30, 1996
350	II	Ricke Stonewall, Millersville (New Haven)	Nov. 13, 1982
350	I-A	Eric Allen, Michigan St. (Purdue)	Oct. 30, 1971

Passing

CAREER PASSING EFFICIENCY

(Minimum 475 Completions)

Player, Team (Division[s])	Years	Att.	Cmp.	Int.	Pct.	Yds.	TD	Pts.
Bill Borchert, Mount Union (III)	1994-97	1,009	671	17	.665	10,201	141	*194.2
Dave Dickenson, Montana (I-AA)	1992-95	1,208	813	26	.673	11,080	96	166.3
Corte McGuffey, Northern Colo. (II)	1996-99	768	484	23	.630	6,975	75	165.6
Danny Wuerffel, Florida (I-A)	1993-96	1,170	708	42	.605	10,875	114	163.6
Ty Detmer, Brigham Young (I-A)	1988-91	1,530	958	65	.626	*15,031	121	162.7
Steve Sarkisian, Brigham Young (I-A)	1995-96	789	528	26	.669	7,464	53	162.0
Mike Simpson, Eureka (III)/ Eastern Ill. (I-AA)	1993-94, 96-97	724	481	25	.664	6,402	58	160.3
Jim Ballard, Wilmington (Ohio)/ Mount Union (III)	1990, 91-93	1,199	743	41	.620	10,379	115	159.5
Troy Dougherty, Grinnell (III)	1994, 97-99	1,192	734	33	.616	10,140	109	157.7
Billy Blanton, San Diego St. (I-A)	1993-96	920	588	25	.639	8,165	67	157.1
Jim McMahon, Brigham Young (I-A)	1977-78, 80-81	1,060	653	34	.616	9,536	84	156.9

Mount Union's Bill Borchert has a lead of nearly 28 points on the all-divisions career passing efficiency list.

Player, Team (Division[s])	Years	Att.	Cmp.	Int.	Pct.	Yds.	TD	Pts.
Donovan McNabb, Syracuse (I-A)	1995-98	938	548	26	.584	8,389	77	155.1
Doug Nussmeier, Idaho (I-AA)	1990-93	1,225	746	32	.609	10,824	91	154.4
Tim Rattay, Louisiana Tech (I-A)	1997-99	1,552	1,015	35	.654	12,746	115	154.3
Chris Hatcher, Valdosta St. (II)	1991-94	1,451	1,001	38	.690	10,878	116	153.1
Mike Burton, Trinity (Tex.) (III)	1996-99	1,067	631	29	.591	9,008	92	153.1
Chad Pennington, Marshall (I-AA; I-A)	1995, 97-99	1,501	947	39	.631	12,348	110	151.2
Steve Young, Brigham Young (I-A)	1981-83	908	592	33	.652	7,733	56	149.8
Justin Peery, Westminster (Mo.) (III)	1996-99	1,669	1,012	57	.606	13,262	*148	149.8
Jack Hull, Grand Valley St. (II)	1988-91	835	485	22	.581	7,120	64	149.7
Robbie Bosco, Brigham Young (I-A)	1983-85	997	638	36	.640	8,400	66	149.4
Elvis Grbac, Michigan (I-A)	1989-92	754	477	29	.633	5,859	64	148.9
Mike Maxwell, Nevada (I-A)	1993-95	881	560	33	.636	7,256	62	148.5
Ryan Vena, Colgate (I-AA)	1996-99	819	482	46	.589	7,427	61	148.4
Mike Cook, William & Mary (I-AA)	1995-98	804	495	21	.616	6,644	55	148.3
Michael Payton, Marshall (I-AA)	1989-92	876	542	32	.619	7,530	57	148.2
Joe Hamilton, Georgia Tech (I-A)	1996-99	1,020	629	39	.617	8,882	65	148.2
Chuck Long, Iowa (I-A)	$1981-85	1,072	692	46	.646	9,210	64	147.8
John Walsh, Brigham Young (I-A)	1991-94	973	587	35	.603	8,375	66	147.8
Aaron Flowers, Cal St. Northridge (I-AA)	1996-97	819	502	21	.613	6,766	54	147.3
Peyton Manning, Tennessee (I-A)	1994-97	1,381	863	33	.625	11,201	89	147.1
Willie Totten, Mississippi Val. (I-AA)	1982-85	1,555	907	75	.583	12,711	139	146.8
Daunte Culpepper, UCF (I-AA; I-A)	1995-98	1,391	889	42	.639	11,412	84	146.7
John Koz, Baldwin-Wallace (III)	1990-93	981	609	28	.621	7,724	71	146.4
Shane Stafford, Connecticut (I-AA)	1995-98	951	522	29	.549	8,368	67	146.0
Brian Ah Yat, Montana (I-AA)	1995-98	1,190	735	39	.618	9,315	89	145.6
Rob Johnson, Southern California (I-A)	1991-94	963	623	24	.647	7,743	52	145.1
Giovanni Carmazzi, Hofstra (I-AA)	1996-99	1,187	764	32	.644	9,371	71	145.0
Ron Sermarini, Western Md. (III)	1996-99	970	617	20	.636	7,197	68	144.9
Greg Kaiser, St. Thomas (Minn.) (III)	1996-99	810	498	23	.615	6,439	54	144.6
Ted White, Howard (I-AA)	1995-98	1,163	635	34	.546	9,611	92	144.3
Steve McNair, Alcorn St. (I-AA)	1991-94	1,680	929	58	.553	14,496	119	144.3
Mike Smith, Northern Iowa (I-AA)	1984-87	943	557	43	.591	8,219	58	143.5
Jeff Fox, Grand Valley St. (II)	1995-98	1,031	626	22	.607	8,197	62	143.1
Steve Stenstrom, Stanford (I-A)	1991-94	1,320	833	36	.631	10,531	72	142.7
Neil Lomax, Portland St. (II; I-AA)	1977, 78-80	1,606	938	55	.584	13,220	106	142.5
Lance Funderburk, Valdosta St. (II)	1993-96	1,054	689	23	.654	7,698	64	142.4
Marvin Graves, Syracuse (I-A)	1990-93	943	563	45	.597	8,466	48	142.4
Tom Ciaccio, Holy Cross (I-AA)	1988-91	1,073	658	46	.613	8,603	72	142.2
Kevin Ricca, Catholic (III)	1994-97	1,109	713	56	.643	9,469	89	142.0
Chris Esterley, St. Thomas (Minn.) (III)	1993-96	1,012	615	30	.608	7,709	71	142.0
George Bork, Northern Ill. (II)	1960-63	902	577	33	.640	6,782	60	141.8
Eric Beavers, Nevada (I-AA)	1983-86	1,094	646	37	.591	8,626	77	141.8
Tim Couch, Kentucky (I-A)	1996-98	1,184	795	35	.671	8,435	74	141.7
Doug Gaynor, Long Beach St. (I-A)	1984-85	837	569	35	.680	6,793	35	141.6
Scott Semptimphelter, Lehigh (I-AA)	1990-93	823	493	27	.599	6,668	50	141.5
Ed Hesson, Rowan (III)	1990-93	895	504	26	.563	7,053	67	141.2
Danny Kanell, Florida St. (I-A)	1992-95	851	529	26	.622	6,372	57	141.1
Jack Ramirez, Pomona-Pitzer (III)	1994-97	959	558	39	.582	7,523	71	140.3
Matt Jozokos, Plymouth St. (III)	1987-90	1,003	527	39	.525	7,658	95	140.2
Kevin Feterik, Brigham Young (I-A)	1996-99	1,004	609	27	.607	8,065	53	140.2
Phil Stambaugh, Lehigh (I-AA)	1996-99	1,284	816	43	.636	9,669	78	140.2
Dan McGwire, Iowa/San Diego St. (I-A)	1986-87, 89-90	973	575	30	.591	8,164	49	140.0

*Record. $See page 6 for explanation.

CAREER PASSING EFFICIENCY

(Minimum 375-474 Completions)

Player, Team (Division)	Years	Att.	Cmp.	Int.	Pct.	Yds.	TD	Pts.
Chris Petersen, UC Davis (II)	1985-86	553	385	13	*.696	4,988	39	164.0
Kurt Ramler, St. John's (Minn.) (III)	1994-96	722	420	16	.582	6,475	75	163.4
Danny Ragsdale, Redlands (III)	1997-99	610	386	17	.633	5,560	51	161.9
Kyle Adamson, Allegheny (III)	1995-97	608	388	18	.638	5,506	48	160.0
Jason Baer, Wash. & Jeff. (III)	1993-96	671	406	24	.605	5,632	66	156.3
Joe Germaine, Ohio St. (I-A)	1996-98	660	399	18	.605	5,844	52	155.4
Joel Parrett, Bluffton (III)	1996-99	633	412	28	.651	5,684	43	154.1
Rick Hebert, American Int'l (II)	1996-99	699	423	16	.605	5,990	55	153.9
Mark Washington, Jackson St. (I-AA)	1996-99	724	384	24	.530	6,561	68	153.5
Joe Blake, Simpson (III)	1987-90	672	399	15	.594	6,183	43	153.3
Vinny Testaverde, Miami (Fla.) (I-A)	1982, 84-86	674	413	25	.613	6,058	48	152.9
Jim McMillan, Boise St. (II)	1971-74	640	382	29	.597	5,508	53	152.8
Sean Hoolihan, Wis.-Eau Claire (III)	1996-98	686	413	23	.602	6,301	46	152.8
Josh Wallwork, Wyoming (I-A)	1995-96	729	449	28	.616	6,453	54	152.7
Trent Dilfer, Fresno St. (I-A)	1991-93	774	461	21	.596	6,944	51	151.2
Chris Greisen, Northwest Mo. St. (II)	1995-98	653	379	22	.580	5,741	51	150.9
Greg Lister, Rowan (III)	1994-97	773	454	29	.587	6,553	66	150.6
Troy Aikman, Oklahoma/UCLA (I-A)	1984-85, 87-88	637	401	18	.630	5,436	40	149.7
Chuck Hartlieb, Iowa (I-A)	1985-88	716	461	17	.643	6,269	34	148.9
Jay Johnson, Northern Iowa (I-AA)	1989-92	744	397	25	.534	7,049	51	148.9
Scott Otis, Glenville St. (II)	1994-95	693	421	21	.608	5,563	56	148.8
Gary Collier, Emory & Henry (III)	1984-87	738	386	33	.523	6,103	80	148.6
Jesse Showerda, New Haven (II)	1993-96	675	402	15	.596	5,175	57	147.4
Grady Benton, West Tex. A&M (II)	1994-95	686	421	22	.614	5,618	49	147.3
Kenneth Biggles, Tennessee St. (I-AA)	1981-84	701	397	28	.566	5,933	57	146.6

INDIVIDUAL COLLEGIATE RECORDS—PASSING

Player, Team (Division)	Years	Att.	Cmp.	Int.	Pct.	Yds.	TD	Pts.
Bobby Hoying, Ohio St. (I-A)	1992-95	782	463	33	.592	6,751	54	146.1
Oteman Sampson, Florida A&M (I-AA)	1996-97	686	387	26	.564	6,104	46	145.7
Gifford Nielsen, Brigham Young (I-A)	1975-77	708	415	29	.586	5,833	55	145.3
Bruce Upstill, Col. of Emporia (II)	1960-63	769	438	36	.570	6,935	48	144.0
Tom Ramsey, UCLA (I-A)	1979-82	691	411	33	.595	5,844	48	143.9
Jarrod DeGeorgia, Wayne St. (Neb.) (II)	1995-96	645	428	18	.664	5,161	31	143.9
Shawn Moore, Virginia (I-A)	1987-90	762	421	32	.552	6,629	55	143.8
Jeff Brown, Wheaton (Ill.) (III)	1992-95	767	441	30	.575	6,219	60	143.6
Moses Moreno, Colorado St. (I-A)	1994-97	787	457	28	.581	6,689	49	142.9
Jerry Rhome, Southern Methodist/Tulsa (I-A)	1961, 63-64	713	448	23	.628	5,472	47	142.6
Braniff Bonaventure, Furman (I-AA)	1993-96	672	413	17	.615	5,361	39	142.6
Lon Erickson, Ill. Wesleyan (III)	1993-96	786	461	24	.587	6,108	58	142.2
Todd Donnan, Marshall (I-AA)	1991-94	712	425	25	.597	5,566	51	142.0

*Record.

SEASON PASSING EFFICIENCY
(Minimum 30 Attempts Per Game)

Player, Team (Division)	Year	G	Att.	Cmp.	Int.	Pct.	Yds.	TD	Pts.
Jim Ballard, Mount Union (III)	1993	10	314	229	11	.729	3,304	37	*193.2
Jayson Merrill, Western St. (II)	†1991	10	309	195	11	.631	3,484	35	188.1
Kevin Ricca, Catholic (III)	1997	10	306	208	6	.679	2,990	35	183.9
John Charles, Portland St. (II)	1992	8	263	179	7	.681	2,770	24	181.3
Chris Hatcher, Valdosta St. (II)	†1994	11	430	321	9	*.747	3,591	50	179.0
Wilkie Perez, Glenville St. (II)	†1997	11	425	280	12	.658	4,189	45	178.0
Jim McMahon, Brigham Young (I-A)	1980	12	445	284	18	.638	4,571	47	176.9
Ty Detmer, Brigham Young (I-A)	†1989	12	412	265	15	.643	4,560	32	175.6
Chris Boden, Villanova (I-AA)	1997	11	345	231	4	.670	3,079	36	174.0
Trent Dilfer, Fresno St. (I-A)	†1993	11	333	217	4	.652	3,276	28	173.1
Jerry Rhome, Tulsa (I-A)	†1964	10	326	224	4	.687	2,870	32	172.6
Danny Wuerffel, Florida (I-A)	1996	12	360	207	13	.575	3,625	39	170.6
Daunte Culpepper, UCF (I-A)	1998	11	402	296	7	.736	3,690	28	170.2
Billy Blanton, San Diego St. (I-A)	1996	11	344	227	5	.660	3,221	29	169.6
Dave Dickenson, Montana (I-AA)	1995	11	455	309	9	.679	4,176	38	168.6
Drew Miller, Montana (I-AA)	†1999	10	368	240	8	.652	3,461	32	168.6
Ty Detmer, Brigham Young (I-A)	1991	12	403	249	12	.618	4,031	35	168.5
Steve Young, Brigham Young (I-A)	1983	11	429	306	10	.713	3,902	33	168.5
Willie Totten, Mississippi Val. (I-AA)	†1983	9	279	174	9	.624	2,566	29	167.5
Dave Dickenson, Montana (I-AA)	†1994	9	336	229	6	.682	3,053	24	164.5
Jim McMillan, Boise St. (II)	1974	10	313	192	15	.613	2,900	33	164.4
Willie Totten, Mississippi Val. (I-AA)	†1984	10	518	324	22	.626	4,557	*56	163.6
Jeff Wiley, Holy Cross (I-AA)	†1987	11	400	265	17	.663	3,677	34	163.0
Todd Hammel, Stephen F. Austin (I-AA)	†1989	11	401	238	13	.594	3,914	34	162.8
Dennis Shaw, San Diego St. (I-A)	†1969	10	335	199	26	.594	3,185	39	162.2
Giovanni Carmazzi, Hofstra (I-AA)	1997	11	408	288	8	.706	3,554	27	161.7
John Friesz, Idaho (I-AA)	1989	11	425	260	8	.612	4,041	31	161.4
Willie Reyna, La Verne (III)	1991	8	267	170	6	.636	2,543	16	158.8
Charlie Ward, Florida St. (I-A)	1993	11	380	264	4	.695	3,032	27	157.8
Glenn Foley, Boston College (I-A)	1993	11	363	222	10	.612	3,395	25	157.0
Chris Vargas, Nevada (I-A)	1993	11	490	331	18	.676	4,265	34	156.2
George Bork, Northern Ill. (II)	1963	9	374	244	12	.652	3,077	32	156.2
John Walsh, Brigham Young (I-A)	1993	11	397	244	15	.615	3,727	28	156.0
Neil Lomax, Portland St. (I-AA)	1980	11	473	296	12	.626	4,094	37	156.0
Ty Detmer, Brigham Young (I-A)	1990	12	562	361	28	.642	*5,188	41	155.9
Rob Johnson, Southern California (I-A)	1993	12	405	278	5	.686	3,285	26	155.5
Doug Williams, Grambling (I-A)	1977	11	352	181	18	.514	3,286	38	155.2
Jim McMahon, Brigham Young (I-A)	†1981	10	423	272	7	.643	3,555	30	155.0
Josh Wallwork, Wyoming (I-A)	1996	12	458	286	15	.625	4,090	33	154.7
John Dutton, Nevada (I-A)	1996	11	334	222	6	.665	2,750	22	153.8
Andy Breault, Kutztown (II)	1991	10	360	225	20	.625	2,927	37	153.4
Chuck Long, Iowa (I-A)	1985	11	351	231	15	.658	2,978	26	153.0
Doug Flutie, Boston College (I-A)	1984	11	386	233	11	.604	3,454	27	152.9

*Record. †National pass-efficiency champion.

Chris Hatcher of Valdosta State completed a record 74.7 percent of his passes and threw for 50 touchdowns in 1994. His 179.0 passing efficiency rating is fifth in NCAA history for players with a minimum of 30 attempts per game.

SEASON PASSING EFFICIENCY
(Minimum 15 Attempts Per Game)

Player, Team (Division)	Year	G	Att.	Cmp.	Int.	Pct.	Yds.	TD	Pts.
Mike Simpson, Eureka (III)	†1994	10	158	116	5	.734	1,988	25	*225.0
Willie Seiler, St. John's (Minn.) (III)	†1993	10	205	141	6	.687	2,648	33	224.6
Bill Borchert, Mount Union (III)	†1997	10	272	190	1	.698	2,933	47	216.7
Boyd Crawford, Col. of Idaho (II)	†1953	8	120	72	6	.600	1,462	21	210.1
Bill Borchert, Mount Union (III)	†1996	10	240	165	6	.687	2,655	38	208.9
Gary Smeck, Mount Union (III)	†1999	10	199	131	3	.658	2,274	30	208.6
Shawn Knight, William & Mary (I-AA)	†1993	10	177	125	4	.706	2,055	22	204.6
Matt LeFever, Western Conn. St. (III)	1999	10	158	95	7	.601	1,874	25	203.1
Troy Dougherty, Grinnell (III)	1998	10	293	198	5	.675	3,310	36	199.6
Bill Borchert, Mount Union (III)	†1995	10	225	160	4	.711	2,270	30	196.3
Jason Baer, Wash. & Jeff. (III)	1995	8	146	95	3	.650	1,536	19	192.3
Greg Lister, Rowan (III)	1997	9	162	111	4	.685	1,688	20	191.9
Chuck Green, Wittenberg (II)	†1963	9	182	114	8	.626	2,181	19	189.0
Ty Grovesteen, Wis.-Whitewater (III)	1998	9	180	103	5	.572	2,074	22	188.8
Kurt Ramler, St. John's (Minn.) (III)	1994	9	154	93	4	.603	1,560	22	187.4
Rick Hebert, American Int'l (II)	†1999	12	234	166	4	.709	2,351	25	187.2

Ty Detmer's all-divisions record of 15,031 passing yards has stood for nearly a decade since his final season at Brigham Young in 1991.

Player, Team (Division)	Year	G	Att.	Cmp.	Int.	Pct.	Yds.	TD	Pts.
Jim Feeley, Johns Hopkins (II)	†1967	7	110	69	5	.627	1,264	12	186.2
Mike Bajakian, Williams (III)	1994	8	141	92	1	.652	1,382	17	186.0
John Charles, Portland St. (II)	1991	11	247	147	7	.595	2,619	32	185.7
Steve Smith, Western St. (II)	†1992	10	271	180	5	.664	2,719	30	183.5
Shaun King, Tulane (I-A)	†1998	11	328	223	6	.680	3,232	36	183.3
Mitch Sanders, Bridgeport (III)	†1973	10	151	84	7	.556	1,551	23	182.9
Jim Peterson, Hanover (II)	†1948	8	125	81	12	.648	1,571	12	182.9
John Wristen, Southern Colo. (II)	†1982	8	121	68	2	.562	1,358	13	182.6
Michael Payton, Marshall (I-AA)	†1991	9	216	143	5	.622	2,333	19	181.3
Richard Basil, Savannah St. (II)	†1989	9	211	120	7	.568	2,148	29	181.1
Pat Mayew, St. John's (Minn.) (III)	†1991	9	247	154	4	.623	2,408	30	181.0
Michael Vick, Virginia Tech (I-A)	†1999	10	152	90	5	.592	1,840	12	180.4
Alli Abrew, Cal Poly (I-AA)	†1997	11	191	130	4	.681	1,961	17	179.5
Danny Wuerffel, Florida (I-A)	†1995	11	325	210	10	.646	3,266	35	178.4
Doug Turner, Morehead St. (I-AA)	1997	10	290	190	6	.655	2,869	29	177.5
Guy Simons, Coe (III)	1993	10	185	110	9	.594	1,979	21	177.1
Jim Cahoon, Ripon (II)	†1964	8	127	74	7	.583	1,206	19	176.4
Ted White, Howard (I-AA)	†1996	11	289	174	10	.602	2,814	36	176.2
Kyle Adamson, Allegheny (III)	1996	10	182	119	3	.653	1,761	18	176.0
Ken Suhl, New Haven (II)	1992	10	239	148	5	.619	2,336	26	175.7
Jimbo Fisher, Samford (III)	†1987	10	252	139	5	.551	2,394	34	175.4
Doug Nussmeier, Idaho (I-AA)	1993	11	304	185	5	.609	2,960	33	175.2
Joe Hamilton, Georgia Tech (I-A)	1999	11	305	203	11	.666	3,060	29	175.0
Brian Kadel, Dayton (I-AA)	†1995	11	183	115	6	.628	1,880	18	175.0
Gary Collier, Emory & Henry (III)	1987	11	249	152	10	.610	2,317	33	174.8
Paul Bell, Allegheny (III)	1994	10	215	142	2	.660	2,137	17	173.8
Steve Sarkisian, Brigham Young (I-A)	†1996	14	404	278	12	.688	4,027	33	173.6
Greg Lister, Rowan (III)	1996	8	167	94	2	.562	1,711	17	173.6
Corte McGuffey, Northern Colo. (II)	1999	11	296	189	11	.639	2,893	31	173.0
Kerry Collins, Penn St. (I-A)	†1994	11	264	176	7	.667	2,679	21	172.9
Kelvin Simmons, Troy St. (I-AA)	1993	11	224	143	6	.638	2,144	23	172.8
James Grant, Ramapo (III)	1989	9	147	91	7	.619	1,441	17	172.7
Tony Aliucci, Indiana (Pa.) (II)	†1990	10	181	111	10	.613	1,801	21	172.7
Chris Adams, Gettysburg (III)	1994	10	211	139	2	.658	1,977	19	172.4
Matt Wheeler, Wartburg (III)	1998	9	227	152	9	.669	2,150	23	172.0
James Weir, New Haven (II)	†1993	10	266	161	1	.605	2,336	31	172.0
Shawn Behr, Fort Hays St. (II)	†1995	11	318	191	6	.600	3,158	31	171.9
Chad Pennington, Marshall (I-A)	1999	12	405	275	11	.679	3,799	37	171.4
Frank Baur, Lafayette (I-AA)	†1988	10	256	164	11	.641	2,621	23	171.1
Mike Donnelly, Wittenberg (III)	1995	10	153	92	2	.601	1,480	15	171.1

*Record. †National pass-efficiency champion.

CAREER YARDS

Player, Team (Division[s])	Years	Att.	Cmp.	Int.	Pct.	Yds.	TD
Ty Detmer, Brigham Young (I-A)	1988-91	1,530	958	65	.626	*15,031	121
Steve McNair, Alcorn St. (I-AA)	1991-94	1,680	929	58	.553	14,496	119
Justin Peery, Westminster (Mo.) (III)	1996-99	1,669	1,012	57	.606	13,262	*148
Neil Lomax, Portland St. (II; I-AA)	1977, 78-80	1,606	938	55	.584	13,220	106
Kirk Baumgartner, Wis.-Stevens Point (III)	1986-89	1,696	883	57	.521	13,028	110
Tim Rattay, Louisiana Tech (I-A)	1997-99	1,552	1,015	35	.654	12,746	115
Willie Totten, Mississippi Val. (I-AA)	1982-85	1,555	907	75	.583	12,711	139
Chris Redman, Louisville (I-A)	1996-99	1,679	*1,031	51	.614	12,541	84
Chad Pennington, Marshall (I-AA; I-A)	1995, 97-99	1,501	947	39	.631	12,348	110
Jamie Martin, Weber St. (I-AA)	1989-92	1,544	934	56	.605	12,207	87
Todd Santos, San Diego St. (I-A)	1984-87	1,484	910	57	.613	11,425	70
Daunte Culpepper, UCF (I-AA; I-A)	1995-98	1,391	889	42	.639	11,412	84
Travis Brown, Northern Ariz. (I-AA)	1996-99	1,577	888	42	.563	11,400	86
Tim Lester, Western Mich. (I-A)	1996-99	1,507	875	49	.581	11,299	87
Peyton Manning, Tennessee (I-A)	1994-97	1,381	863	33	.625	11,201	89
Eric Zeier, Georgia (I-A)	1991-94	1,402	838	37	.598	11,153	67
Mark Novara, Lakeland (III)	1994-97	1,586	882	63	.556	11,101	100
Dave Dickenson, Montana (I-AA)	1992-95	1,208	813	26	.673	11,080	96
Alex Van Pelt, Pittsburgh (I-A)	1989-92	1,463	845	59	.578	10,913	64
Chris Hatcher, Valdosta St. (II)	1991-94	1,451	1,001	38	.690	10,878	116
Danny Wuerffel, Florida (I-A)	1993-96	1,170	708	42	.605	10,875	114
Doug Nussmeier, Idaho (I-AA)	1990-93	1,225	746	32	.609	10,824	91
John Friesz, Idaho (I-AA)	1986-89	1,350	801	40	.593	10,697	77
Greg Wyatt, Northern Ariz. (I-AA)	1986-89	1,510	926	49	.613	10,697	70
Sean Payton, Eastern Ill. (I-AA)	1983-86	1,408	756	55	.537	10,655	75
Bob McLaughlin, Lock Haven (II)	1992-95	*1,719	910	*88	.529	10,640	60
Kevin Sweeney, Fresno St. (I-A)	$1982-86	1,336	731	48	.547	10,623	66
Earl Harvey, N.C. Central (II)	1985-88	1,442	690	81	.479	10,621	86
Doug Flutie, Boston College (I-A)	1981-84	1,270	677	54	.533	10,579	67
Jim Ballard, Wilmington (Ohio)/Mount Union (III)	1990, 91-93	1,199	743	41	.620	10,379	115
Tom Ehrhardt, C. W. Post (II); Rhode Island (I-AA)	1981-82, 84-85	1,489	833	63	.559	10,325	92
Brian McClure, Bowling Green (I-A)	1982-85	1,427	900	58	.631	10,280	63
Troy Kopp, Pacific (Cal.) (I-A)	1989-92	1,374	798	47	.581	10,258	87
Bill Borchert, Mount Union (III)	1994-97	1,009	671	17	.665	10,201	141
Troy Dougherty, Grinnell (III)	1994, 97-99	1,192	734	33	.616	10,140	109
Glenn Foley, Boston College (I-A)	1990-93	1,275	703	60	.551	10,042	72
Cade McNown, UCLA (I-A)	1995-98	1,153	646	39	.560	10,008	61
John Craven, Gardner-Webb (II)	1991-94	1,535	828	82	.539	9,934	80

INDIVIDUAL COLLEGIATE RECORDS—PASSING

Player, Team (Division[s])	Years	Att.	Cmp.	Int.	Pct.	Yds.	TD
Vernon Buck, Wingate (II)	1991-94	1,393	728	61	.523	9,884	72
Thad Trujillo, Fort Lewis (II)	1991-94	1,455	760	57	.522	9,873	78
Bryan Snyder, Albright (III)	1994-97	1,294	763	49	.590	9,865	92
Jarrod Furgason, Fairmont St. (II)	$1993-97	1,392	798	44	.573	9,856	101
Mike Mitros, West Chester (II)	1996-99	1,402	819	48	.584	9,834	94
Jeff Wiley, Holy Cross (I-AA)	1985-88	1,208	723	63	.599	9,698	71
Phil Stambaugh, Lehigh (I-AA)	1996-99	1,284	816	43	.636	9,669	78
Jeff Lewis, Northern Ariz. (I-AA)	1992-95	1,316	785	24	.597	9,655	67
Ben Bennett, Duke (I-A)	1980-83	1,375	820	57	.596	9,614	53
Ted White, Howard (I-AA)	1995-98	1,163	635	34	.546	9,611	92
Keith Bishop, Ill. Wesleyan/Wheaton (III.) (III)	1981, 83-85	1,311	772	65	.589	9,579	71
Robbie Justino, Liberty (I-AA)	1989-92	1,267	769	51	.607	9,548	64
Chris Boden, Villanova (I-AA)	1996-99	1,338	818	30	.611	9,538	93
Jim McMahon, Brigham Young (I-A)	1977-78, 80-81	1,060	653	34	.616	9,536	84
Dennis Bogacz, Wis.-Oshkosh/Wis.-Whitewater (III)	1988-89, 90-91	1,275	654	59	.513	9,536	66
Todd Ellis, South Carolina (I-A)	1986-89	1,266	704	66	.556	9,519	97
Dave Geissler, Wis.-Stevens Point (III)	1982-85	1,346	789	57	.586	9,518	65
Kevin Ricca, Catholic (III)	1994-97	1,190	713	56	.643	9,469	89
Stoney Case, New Mexico (I-A)	1991-94	1,237	677	39	.547	9,460	67
Rob Tomlinson, Cal St. Chico (II)	1988-91	1,328	748	43	.563	9,434	52
David Klingler, Houston (I-A)	1988-91	1,261	726	38	.576	9,430	91
John Hebgen, Minn. St.-Mankato (II)	1993-96	1,268	727	38	.573	9,410	71

*Record. $See page 6 for explanation.

CAREER YARDS PER GAME

(Minimum 5,000 Yards)

Player, Team (Division[s])	Years	G	Att.	Cmp.	Int.	Pct.	Yds.	TD	Yd. PG
Tim Rattay, Louisiana Tech (I-A)	1997-99	33	1,552	1,015	35	.654	12,746	115	*386.2
Steve McNair, Alcorn St. (I-AA)	1991-94	42	1,680	929	58	.553	14,496	119	345.1
Justin Peery, Westminster (Mo.) (III)	1996-99	39	1,669	1,012	57	.606	13,262	*148	340.1
Aaron Flowers, Cal St. Northridge (I-AA)	1996-97	20	819	502	21	.613	6,766	54	338.3
Ty Detmer, Brigham Young (I-A)	1988-91	46	1,530	958	65	.626	*15,031	121	326.8
Willie Totten, Mississippi Val. (I-AA)	1982-85	40	1,555	907	75	.583	12,711	139	317.8
Kirk Baumgartner, Wis.-Stevens Point (III)	1986-89	41	1,696	883	57	.521	13,028	110	317.8
Dave Dickenson, Montana (I-AA)	1992-95	35	1,208	813	26	.673	11,080	96	316.6
Neil Lomax, Portland St. (II; I-AA)	1977; 78-80	42	1,606	938	55	.584	13,220	106	314.8
Grady Benton, West Tex. A&M (II)	1994-95	18	686	421	22	.614	5,618	49	312.1
Mike Perez, San Jose St. (I-A)	1986-87	20	792	471	30	.595	6,194	36	309.7
Keith Bishop, Ill. Wes./Wheaton (III.) (III)	1981, 83-85	31	1,311	772	65	.589	9,579	71	309.0
Doug Gaynor, Long Beach St. (I-A)	1984-85	22	837	569	35	.680	6,793	35	308.8
John Friesz, Idaho (I-AA)	1986-89	35	1,350	801	40	.593	10,697	77	305.6
Tony Eason, Illinois (I-A)	1981-82	22	856	526	29	.615	6,608	37	300.4

*Record.

CAREER TOUCHDOWN PASSES

Player, Team (Division[s])	Years	Att.	Cmp.	Int.	Pct.	Yds.	TD
Justin Peery, Westminster (Mo.) (III)	1996-99	1,669	1,012	57	.606	13,262	*148
Bill Borchert, Mount Union (III)	1994-97	1,009	671	17	.665	10,201	141
Willie Totten, Mississippi Val. (I-AA)	1982-85	1,555	907	75	.583	12,711	139
Ty Detmer, Brigham Young (I-A)	1988-91	1,530	958	65	.626	*15,031	121
Steve McNair, Alcorn St. (I-AA)	1991-94	1,680	929	58	.553	14,496	119
Chris Hatcher, Valdosta St. (II)	1991-94	1,451	1,001	38	.690	10,878	116
Jim Ballard, Wilmington (Ohio)/Mount Union (III)	1990, 91-93	1,199	743	41	.620	10,379	115
Tim Rattay, Louisiana Tech (I-A)	1997-99	1,552	1,015	35	.654	12,746	115
Danny Wuerffel, Florida (I-A)	1993-96	1,170	708	42	.605	10,875	114
Kirk Baumgartner, Wis.-Stevens Point (III)	1986-89	1,696	883	57	.521	13,028	110
Chad Pennington, Marshall (I-AA; I-A)	1995, 97-99	1,501	947	39	.631	12,348	110
Troy Dougherty, Grinnell (III)	1994, 97-99	1,192	734	33	.616	10,140	109
Neil Lomax, Portland St. (II; I-AA)	1977; 78-80	1,606	938	55	.584	13,220	106
Jarrod Furgason, Fairmont St. (II)	$1993-97	1,392	798	44	.573	9,856	101
Mark Novara, Lakeland (III)	1994-97	1,586	882	63	.556	11,101	100
Dave Dickenson, Montana (I-AA)	1992-95	1,208	813	26	.673	11,080	96
Matt Jozokos, Plymouth St. (III)	1987-90	1,003	527	39	.525	7,658	95
Mike Mitros, West Chester (II)	1996-99	1,402	819	48	.584	9,834	94
Doug Williams, Grambling (II; I-A)	1974-76; 77	1,009	484	52	.480	8,411	93
Chris Boden, Villanova (I-AA)	1996-99	1,338	818	30	.611	9,538	93
Mike Burton, Trinity (Tex.) (III)	1996-99	1,067	631	29	.591	9,008	92
Ted White, Howard (I-AA)	1995-98	1,163	635	34	.546	9,611	92
Bryan Snyder, Albright (III)	1994-97	1,294	763	49	.590	9,865	92
Tom Ehrhardt, C. W. Post (II); Rhode Island (I-AA)	1981-82; 84-85	1,489	833	63	.559	10,325	92
Doug Nussmeier, Idaho (I-AA)	1990-93	1,225	746	32	.609	10,824	91
David Klingler, Houston (I-A)	1988-91	1,261	726	38	.576	9,430	91
Brian Ah Yat, Montana (I-AA)	1995-98	1,190	735	39	.618	9,315	89
Peyton Manning, Tennessee (I-A)	1994-97	1,381	863	33	.625	11,201	89
Kevin Ricca, Catholic (III)	1994-97	1,190	713	56	.643	9,469	89
Maurice Heard, Tuskegee (II)	1988-91	1,134	556	54	.490	8,434	87
Tim Lester, Western Mich. (I-A)	1996-99	1,507	875	49	.581	11,299	87
Troy Kopp, Pacific (Cal.) (I-A)	1989-92	1,374	798	47	.581	10,258	87
Jamie Martin, Weber St. (I-AA)	1989-92	1,544	934	56	.605	12,207	87
Travis Brown, Northern Ariz. (I-AA)	1996-99	1,577	888	42	.563	11,400	86
Andy Breault, Kutztown (II)	1989-92	1,259	733	63	.582	9,086	86
Earl Harvey, N.C. Central (II)	1985-88	1,442	690	81	.479	10,621	86
Matt Bunyan, Wis.-Stout (III)	1995-98	1,119	624	36	.558	8,462	85

Player, Team (Division[s])	Years	Att.	Cmp.	Int.	Pct.	Yds.	TD
Braxton Shaver, McMurry (III)	1997-99	1,026	560	33	.546	7,147	84
Chris Redman, Louisville (I-A)	1996-99	1,679	1,031	51	.614	12,541	84
Daunte Culpepper, UCF (I-AA; I-A)	1995-98	1,391	889	42	.639	11,412	84
Rex Lamberti, Abilene Christian (II)	1984-86, 93	1,133	595	44	.525	7,934	84
Jim McMahon, Brigham Young (I-A)	1977-78, 80-81	1,060	653	34	.616	9,536	84
Brian Tomalak, Wis.-Oshkosh (III)	1995-98	1,129	607	32	.538	8,983	83
Jim Lopusznick, Fairfield (I-AA)	1996-99	1,227	657	59	.535	8,092	83
Darin Hinshaw, UCF (I-AA)	1991-94	1,113	614	52	.552	9,000	82
Dave MacDonald, West Chester (II)	1991-94	1,123	604	46	.538	8,449	82
Dan Crowley, Towson (I-AA)	1991-94	1,170	617	54	.527	8,900	81
Joe Adams, Tennessee St. (I-A)	1977-80	1,100	604	60	.549	8,649	81
Troy Dougherty, Grinnell (III)	1994, 97-98	894	554	22	.620	7,817	80
John Craven, Gardner-Webb (II)	1991-94	1,535	828	82	.539	9,934	80
Gary Collier, Emory & Henry (III)	1984-87	738	386	33	.523	6,103	80

*Record.

SEASON YARDS

Player, Team (Division)	Year	G	Att.	Cmp.	Int.	Pct.	Yds.	TD
Ty Detmer, Brigham Young (I-A)	†1990	12	562	361	28	.642	*5,188	41
David Klingler, Houston (I-A)	1990	11	*643	*374	20	.582	5,140	54
Tim Rattay, Louisiana Tech (I-A)	1998	12	559	380	13	.680	4,943	46
Steve McNair, Alcorn St. (I-AA)	1994	11	530	304	17	.574	4,863	44
Andre Ware, Houston (I-A)	†1989	11	578	365	15	.631	4,699	46
Jim McMahon, Brigham Young (I-A)	†1980	12	445	284	18	.638	4,571	47
Ty Detmer, Brigham Young (I-A)	1989	12	412	265	15	.643	4,560	32
Willie Totten, Mississippi Val. (I-AA)	†1984	10	518	324	22	.626	4,557	*56
Justin Peery, Westminster (Mo.) (III)	1998	10	526	319	21	.606	4,501	51
Scott Mitchell, Utah (I-A)	1988	11	533	323	15	.606	4,322	29
Tim Couch, Kentucky (I-A)	1998	11	553	400	15	.723	4,275	36
Chris Vargas, Nevada (I-A)	1993	11	490	331	18	.676	4,265	34
Robbie Bosco, Brigham Young (I-A)	1985	13	511	338	24	.661	4,257	30
Wilkie Perez, Glenville St. (II)	†1997	11	425	280	12	.658	4,189	45
Dave Dickenson, Montana (I-AA)	1995	11	455	309	9	.679	4,176	38
Joe Lee, Towson (I-AA)	1999	11	577	322	13	.558	4,168	22
Jamie Martin, Weber St. (I-AA)	1991	11	500	310	17	.620	4,125	35
Neil Lomax, Portland St. (I-AA)	1980	11	473	296	12	.626	4,094	37
Justin Peery, Westminster (Mo.) (III)	1999	10	498	329	15	.660	4,092	54
Josh Wallwork, Wyoming (I-A)	1996	12	458	286	15	.625	4,090	33
Chris Redman, Louisville (I-A)	1998	10	473	309	15	.653	4,042	29
John Friesz, Idaho (I-AA)	†1989	11	425	260	8	.612	4,041	31
Ty Detmer, Brigham Young (I-A)	1991	12	403	249	12	.618	4,031	35
Steve Sarkisian, Brigham Young (I-A)	†1996	14	404	278	12	.688	4,027	33
Neil Lomax, Portland St. (I-AA)	1979	11	516	299	16	.579	3,950	26
Todd Santos, San Diego St. (I-A)	1987	12	492	306	15	.622	3,932	26
Tim Rattay, Louisiana Tech (I-A)	1999	10	516	342	12	.663	3,922	35
Todd Hammel, Stephen F. Austin (I-AA)	1989	11	401	238	13	.594	3,914	34
Steve Young, Brigham Young (I-A)	†1983	11	429	306	10	.713	3,902	33
Tim Couch, Kentucky (I-A)	1997	11	547	363	19	.664	3,884	37
Tim Rattay, Louisiana Tech (I-A)	1997	11	477	293	10	.614	3,881	34
Robbie Bosco, Brigham Young (I-A)	1984	12	458	283	11	.618	3,875	33
Mike McCoy, Utah (I-A)	1993	12	430	276	10	.642	3,860	21
Dan Robinson, Hawaii (I-A)	1999	12	556	288	18	.518	3,853	28
Sean Payton, Eastern Ill. (I-AA)	1984	11	473	270	15	.571	3,843	28
Dan McGwire, San Diego St. (I-A)	1990	11	449	270	7	.601	3,833	27
Damian Poalucci, East Stroudsburg (II)	1996	11	393	214	13	.545	3,831	40
Kirk Baumgartner, Wis.-Stevens Point (III)	1988	11	527	276	16	.524	3,828	25
Anthony Dilweg, Duke (I-A)	1988	11	484	287	18	.593	3,824	24
Peyton Manning, Tennessee (I-A)	1997	12	477	287	11	.602	3,819	36
Jimmy Klingler, Houston (I-A)	1992	11	504	303	18	.601	3,818	32
Chad Pennington, Marshall (I-A)	1999	12	405	275	11	.679	3,799	37
Sam King, UNLV (I-A)	1981	12	433	255	19	.589	3,778	18
Troy Kopp, Pacific (Cal.) (I-A)	1991	12	449	275	16	.612	3,767	37
Perry Klein, C. W. Post (II)	1993	10	407	248	18	.609	3,757	38
Kirk Baumgartner, Wis.-Stevens Point (III)	1987	11	466	243	22	.521	3,755	31
Drew Brees, Purdue (I-A)	1998	12	516	336	17	.651	3,753	36
Chris Hegg, Truman (II)	1985	11	503	284	20	.565	3,741	32
Lance Funderburk, Valdosta St. (II)	1996	11	459	300	10	.654	3,732	35
Brett Salisbury, Wayne St. (Neb.) (II)	1993	10	395	276	14	.699	3,729	29
John Walsh, Brigham Young (I-A)	1993	11	397	244	15	.615	3,727	28
Marc Wilson, Brigham Young (I-A)	1979	12	427	250	15	.585	3,720	29

*Record. †National pass-efficiency champion.

SEASON YARDS PER GAME

Player, Team (Division)	Year	G	Att.	Cmp.	Int.	Pct.	Yds.	TD	Yd. PG
David Klingler, Houston (I-A)	1990	11	*643	*374	20	.582	5,140	54	*467.3
Willie Totten, Mississippi Val. (I-AA)	1984	10	518	324	22	.626	4,557	*56	455.7
Justin Peery, Westminster (Mo.) (III)	1998	10	526	319	21	.606	4,501	51	450.1
Steve McNair, Alcorn St. (I-AA)	1994	11	530	304	17	.574	4,863	44	442.1
Ty Detmer, Brigham Young (I-A)	1990	12	562	361	28	.642	*5,188	41	432.3
Andre Ware, Houston (I-A)	1989	11	578	365	15	.631	4,699	46	427.2
Tim Rattay, Louisiana Tech (I-A)	1998	12	559	380	13	.680	4,943	46	411.9
Justin Peery, Westminster (Mo.) (III)	1999	10	498	329	15	.660	4,092	54	409.2
Danny Ragsdale, Redlands (III)	1999	9	380	247	7	.650	3,639	33	404.3

INDIVIDUAL COLLEGIATE RECORDS—PASSING 225

Player, Team (Division)	Year	G	Att.	Cmp.	Int.	Pct.	Yds.	TD	Yd. PG
Chris Redman, Louisville (I-A)	1998	10	473	309	15	.653	4,042	29	404.2
Mike Maxwell, Nevada (I-A)	1995	9	409	277	17	.677	3,611	33	401.2
Grady Benton, West Tex. A&M (II)	1994	9	409	258	13	.631	3,541	30	393.4
Scott Mitchell, Utah (I-A)	1988	11	533	323	15	.606	4,322	29	392.9
Tim Rattay, Louisiana Tech (I-A)	1999	10	516	342	12	.663	3,922	35	392.2
Tim Couch, Kentucky (I-A)	1998	11	553	400	15	.723	4,275	36	388.6
Chris Vargas, Nevada (I-A)	1993	11	490	331	18	.676	4,265	34	387.7
Damian Poalucci, East Stroudsburg (II)	1996	10	393	214	13	.545	3,831	40	383.1
Marty Washington, West Ala. (II)	1993	8	404	221	13	.547	3,062	26	382.8
Jim McMahon, Brigham Young (I-A)	1980	12	445	284	18	.638	4,571	47	380.9
Wilkie Perez, Glenville St. (II)	1997	11	425	280	12	.658	4,189	45	380.8
Ty Detmer, Brigham Young (I-A)	1989	12	412	265	15	.643	4,560	32	380.0

*Record.

SEASON TOUCHDOWN PASSES

Player, Team (Division)	Year	Att.	Cmp.	Int.	Pct.	Yds.	TD
Willie Totten, Mississippi Val. (I-AA)	1984	518	324	22	.626	4,557	*56
Justin Peery, Westminster (Mo.) (III)	1999	498	329	15	.660	4,092	54
David Klingler, Houston (I-A)	1990	*643	*374	20	.582	5,140	54
Justin Peery, Westminster (Mo.) (III)	1998	526	319	21	.606	4,501	51
Chris Hatcher, Valdosta St. (II)	1994	430	321	9	*.747	3,591	50
Bill Borchert, Mount Union (III)	†1997	272	190	1	.698	2,933	47
Jim McMahon, Brigham Young (I-A)	1980	445	284	18	.638	4,571	47
Tim Rattay, Louisiana Tech (I-A)	1998	559	380	13	.680	4,943	46
Andre Ware, Houston (I-A)	1989	578	365	15	.631	4,699	46
Wilkie Perez, Glenville St. (II)	†1997	425	280	12	.658	4,189	45
Bob Toledo, San Fran. St. (II)	1967	396	211	24	.533	3,513	45
Steve McNair, Alcorn St. (I-AA)	1994	530	304	17	.574	4,863	44
Brian Ah Yat, Montana (I-AA)	1996	432	265	16	.613	3,615	42
Ty Detmer, Brigham Young (I-A)	1990	562	361	28	.642	*5,188	41
Damian Poalucci, East Stroudsburg (II)	1996	393	214	13	.545	3,831	40
Mark Novara, Lakeland (III)	1996	410	258	12	.629	3,405	40
Chad Pennington, Marshall (I-A)	1997	428	253	12	.591	3,480	39
Danny Wuerffel, Florida (I-A)	1996	360	207	13	.575	3,625	39
Terry Peebles, Hanover (III)	1995	488	283	10	.579	3,521	39
Kirk Baumgartner, Wis.-Stevens Point (III)	1989	455	247	9	.542	3,692	39
Willie Totten, Mississippi Val. (I-AA)	1985	492	295	29	.600	3,698	39
Dennis Shaw, San Diego St. (I-A)	1969	335	199	26	.594	3,185	39
Matt Bunyan, Wis.-Stout (III)	1998	389	227	9	.583	3,220	38
Bryan Snyder, Albright (III)	1996	358	223	9	.622	2,983	38
Bill Borchert, Mount Union (III)	†1996	240	165	6	.687	2,655	38
Dave Dickenson, Montana (I-AA)	1995	455	309	9	.679	4,176	38
Perry Klein, C. W. Post (II)	1993	407	248	18	.609	3,757	38
Doug Williams, Grambling (I-A)	1977	352	181	18	.514	3,286	38
Chad Pennington, Marshall (I-A)	1999	405	275	11	.679	3,799	37
Patrick Bonner, Florida A&M (I-AA)	1998	426	265	7	.622	3,473	37
Tim Couch, Kentucky (I-A)	1997	547	363	19	.664	3,884	37
Terry Peebles, Hanover (III)	1994	445	252	17	.566	3,197	37
Jim Ballard, Mount Union (III)	1993	314	229	11	.729	3,304	37
Chris Hatcher, Valdosta St. (II)	1993	471	335	11	.711	3,651	37
Andy Breault, Kutztown (II)	1991	360	225	20	.625	2,927	37
Troy Kopp, Pacific (Cal.) (I-A)	1991	449	275	16	.613	3,767	37
Neil Lomax, Portland St. (I-AA)	1980	473	296	12	.626	4,094	37

*Record. †National pass-efficiency champion.

SINGLE-GAME YARDS

Yds.	Div.	Player, Team (Opponent)	Date
716	I-A	David Klingler, Houston (Arizona St.)	Dec. 2, 1990
690	I-A	Matt Vogler, TCU (Houston)	Nov. 3, 1990
642	II	Wilkie Perez, Glenville St. (Concord)	Oct. 25, 1997
631	I-A	Scott Mitchell, Utah (Air Force)	Oct. 15, 1988
624	I-AA	Jamie Martin, Weber St. (Idaho St.)	Nov. 23, 1991
622	I-A	Jeremy Leach, New Mexico (Utah)	Nov. 11, 1989
621	I-A	Dave Wilson, Illinois (Ohio St.)	Nov. 8, 1980
619	III	Justin Peery, Westminster (Mo.) (MacMurray)	Nov. 14, 1998
619	I-A	John Walsh, Brigham Young (Utah St.)	Oct. 30, 1993
619	I-AA	Doug Pederson, La.-Monroe (Stephen F. Austin)	Nov. 11, 1989
618	III	Justin Peery, Westminster (Mo.) (Principia)	Oct. 17, 1998
616	II	Damian Poalucci, East Stroudsburg (Mansfield)	Nov. 2, 1996
614	II	Alfred Montez, Western N.M. (West Tex. A&M)	Oct. 8, 1994
614	II	Perry Klein, C. W. Post (Salisbury St.)	Nov. 6, 1993
613	II	Jayce Goree, Glenville St. (Concord)	Oct. 24, 1998
613	I-A	Jimmy Klingler, Houston (Rice)	Nov. 28, 1992
611	I-A	David Neill, Nevada (New Mexico St.)	Oct. 10, 1999
602	III	Danny Ragsdale, Redlands (Azusa Pacific)	Sept. 25, 1999
602	III	Tom Stallings, St. Thomas (Minn.) (Bethel [Minn.])	Nov. 13, 1993
599	II	Jarrod DeGeorgia, Wayne St. (Neb.) (Drake)	Nov. 9, 1996
599	I-A	Ty Detmer, Brigham Young (San Diego St.)	Nov. 16, 1991
599	I-AA	Willie Totten, Mississippi Val. (Prairie View)	Oct. 27, 1984

Yds.	Div.	Player, Team (Opponent)	Date
592	I-A	Chris Redman, Louisville (East Caro.)	Nov. 14, 1998
592	II	John Charles, Portland St. (Cal Poly)	Nov. 16, 1991
590	I-A	Tim Rattay, Louisiana Tech (Nebraska)	Aug. 29, 1998
589	III	Joe Montrella, Juniata (Widener)	Nov. 13, 1999
589	I-AA	Vern Harris, Idaho St. (Montana)	Oct. 12, 1985
587	I-AA	Steve McNair, Alcorn St. (Southern U.)	Oct. 22, 1994
585	III	Tim Lynch, Hofstra (Fordham)	Oct. 19, 1991
585	I-A	Robbie Bosco, Brigham Young (New Mexico)	Oct. 19, 1985
575	III	Eric Noble, Wilmington (Ohio) (Urbana)	Nov. 5, 1994
572	I-A	David Klingler, Houston (Eastern Wash.)	Nov. 17, 1990
571	I-AA	Todd Hammel, Stephen F. Austin (Northeast La.)	Nov. 11, 1989
571	I-A	Marc Wilson, Brigham Young (Utah)	Nov. 5, 1977

SINGLE-GAME ATTEMPTS

Atts.	Div.	Player, Team (Opponent)	Date
83	I-A	Drew Brees, Purdue (Wisconsin)	Oct. 10, 1998
81	III	Jordan Poznick, Principia (Blackburn)	Oct. 10, 1992
79	I-A	Matt Vogler, TCU (Houston)	Nov. 3, 1990
79	III	Mike Wallace, Ohio Wesleyan (Denison)	Oct. 3, 1981
78	III	Shawn Wheeler, Capital (Ohio Northern)	Nov. 13, 1999
78	I-A	Rusty LaRue, Wake Forest (Duke)	Oct. 28, 1995
77	III	Justin Peery, Westminster (Mo.) (MacMurray)	Nov. 14, 1998
77	I-AA	Neil Lomax, Portland St. (Northern Colo.)	Oct. 20, 1979
76	I-AA	Joe Lee, Towson (Lehigh)	Oct. 30, 1999
76	II	Jarrod DeGeorgia, Wayne St. (Neb.) (Drake)	Nov. 9, 1996
76	I-A	David Klingler, Houston (Southern Methodist)	Oct. 20, 1990
75	I-A	Chris Vargas, Nevada (McNeese St.)	Sept. 19, 1992
74	II	Jamie Sander, N.M. Highlands (Neb.-Kearney)	Nov. 9, 1996
74	II	Jermaine Whitaker, N.M. Highlands (Western St.)	Nov. 5, 1994
74	I-AA	Paul Peterson, Idaho St. (Nevada)	Oct. 1, 1983
73	I-A	Jeff Handy, Missouri (Oklahoma St.)	Oct. 17, 1992
73	I-A	Troy Kopp, Pacific (Cal.) (Hawaii)	Oct. 27, 1990
73	I-A	Shane Montgomery, North Carolina St. (Duke)	Nov. 11, 1989
72	I-AA	Dave Dickenson, Montana (Idaho)	Oct. 21, 1995
72	I-A	Matt Vogler, TCU (Texas Tech)	Nov. 10, 1990
72	II	Kurt Otto, North Dakota (Tex. A&M-Kingsville)	Sept. 13, 1986
72	III	Bob Lockhart, Millikin (Franklin)	Nov. 12, 1977
72	II	Kaipo Spencer, Santa Clara (Portland St.)	Oct. 11, 1975
72	II	Joe Stetser, Cal St. Chico (Oregon Tech)	Sept. 23, 1967

SINGLE-GAME COMPLETIONS

Cmp.	Div.	Player, Team (Opponent)	Date
56	II	Jarrod DeGeorgia, Wayne St. (Neb.) (Drake)	Nov. 9, 1996
55	I-A	Drew Brees, Purdue (Wisconsin)	Oct. 10, 1998
55	I-A	Rusty LaRue, Wake Forest (Duke)	Oct. 28, 1995
50	III	Justin Peery, Westminster (Mo.) (MacMurray)	Nov. 14, 1998
50	I-A	Rusty LaRue, Wake Forest (North Carolina St.)	Nov. 18, 1995
50	III	Tim Lynch, Hofstra (Fordham)	Oct. 19, 1991
48	I-AA	Clayton Millis, Cal St. Northridge (St. Mary's [Cal.])	Nov. 11, 1995
48	III	Jordan Poznick, Principia (Blackburn)	Oct. 10, 1992
48	I-A	David Klingler, Houston (Southern Methodist)	Oct. 20, 1990
47	I-AA	Joe Lee, Towson (Lehigh)	Oct. 30, 1999
47	I-A	Tim Couch, Kentucky (Arkansas)	Oct. 3, 1998
47	I-AA	Jamie Martin, Weber St. (Idaho St.)	Nov. 23, 1991
47	III	Mike Wallace, Ohio Wesleyan (Denison)	Oct. 3, 1981
46	I-A	Tim Rattay, Louisiana Tech (UCF)	Oct. 23, 1999
46	I-A	Tim Rattay, Louisiana Tech (Nebraska)	Aug. 29, 1998
46	I-A	Scott Milanovich, Maryland (Florida St.)	Nov. 18, 1995
46	I-A	Jimmy Klingler, Houston (Rice)	Nov. 28, 1992
46	I-AA	Doug Pederson, Northeast La. (Stephen F. Austin)	Nov. 11, 1989
46	I-AA	Willie Totten, Mississippi Val. (Southern U.)	Sept. 29, 1984
45	I-A	Tim Rattay, Louisiana Tech (Texas A&M)	Sept. 4, 1999
45	II	Chris Hatcher, Valdosta St. (Mississippi Col.)	Oct. 23, 1993
45	II	Chris Hatcher, Valdosta St. (West Ga.)	Oct. 16, 1993
45	I-AA	Willie Totten, Mississippi Val. (Prairie View)	Oct. 27, 1984

Cmp.	Div.	Player, Team (Opponent)	Date
45	I-A	Sandy Schwab, Northwestern (Michigan)	Oct. 23, 1982
44	I-A	Tim Rattay, Louisiana Tech (Toledo)	Oct. 30, 1999
44	III	Chris Stormer, Hanover (Franklin)	Nov. 14, 1998
44	I-A	Chris Redman, Louisville (East Caro.)	Nov. 14, 1998
44	I-A	Tim Couch, Kentucky (Vanderbilt)	Nov. 14, 1998
44	II	Wilkie Perez, Glenville St. (Concord)	Oct. 25, 1997
44	I-A	Matt Vogler, TCU (Houston)	Nov. 3, 1990
44	I-A	Chuck Hartlieb, Iowa (Indiana)	Oct. 29, 1988
44	II	Tom Bonds, Cal Lutheran (St. Mary's [Cal.])	Nov. 22, 1986
44	I-A	Jim McMahon, Brigham Young (Colorado St.)	Nov. 7, 1981
44	I-AA	Neil Lomax, Portland St. (Northern Colo.)	Oct. 20, 1979

Receiving

CAREER RECEPTIONS

Player, Team (Division)	Years	Rec.	Yards	Avg.	TD
Scott Pingel, Westminster (Mo.) (III)	1996-99	*436	*6,108	14.0	*75
Jerry Rice, Mississippi Val. (I-AA)	1981-84	301	4,693	15.6	50
Trevor Insley, Nevada (I-A)	1996-99	298	5,005	16.8	35
Geoff Noisy, Nevada (I-A)	1995-98	295	4,249	14.4	21
Matt Newton, Principia (III)	1990-93	287	3,646	12.7	32
Scott Hvistendahl, Augsburg (III)	1995-98	285	4,696	16.5	40
Carlos Ferralls, Glenville St. (II)	1994-97	282	4,091	14.5	53
Troy Edwards, Louisiana Tech (I-A)	1996-98	280	4,352	15.5	50
Matt Plummer, Dubuque (III)	1996-99	271	4,049	14.9	42
Jeff Clay, Catholic (III)	1994-97	269	4,101	15.2	44
Kasey Dunn, Idaho (I-A)	1988-91	268	3,847	14.4	25
Aaron Turner, Pacific (Cal.) (I-A)	1989-92	266	4,345	16.3	43
Chad Mackey, Louisiana Tech (I-A)	1993-96	264	3,789	14.4	22
Terance Mathis, New Mexico (I-A)	1985-87, 89	263	4,254	16.2	36
Mark Templeton, Long Beach St. (I-A) (RB)	1983-86	¢262	1,969	7.5	11
Jon Spinosa, Lock Haven (II)	1992-95	261	2,710	10.4	12
Howard Twilley, Tulsa (I-A)	1963-65	261	3,343	12.8	32
Marcus Harris, Wyoming (I-A)	1993-96	259	4,518	17.4	38
Bill Stromberg, Johns Hopkins (III)	1978-81	258	3,776	14.6	39
Eric Nemec, Albright (III)	1995-98	256	3,300	12.9	35
Kurt Barth, Eureka (III)	1994-97	256	4,311	16.8	51
Chris Myers, Kenyon (II)	1967-70	253	3,897	15.4	33
Sean Morey, Brown (I-AA)	1995-98	251	3,850	15.3	39
Brian Forster, Rhode Island (I-AA) (TE)	1983-85, 87	#245	#3,410	13.9	31
David Williams, Illinois (I-A)	1983-85	245	3,195	13.0	22
Troy Walters, Stanford (I-A)	1996-99	244	3,986	16.3	26
Mike Furrey, Northern Iowa (I-AA)	1997-99	242	3,544	14.6	27
Brandon Stokley, La.-Lafayette (I-A)	1995-98	241	3,702	15.4	25
Bruce Cerone, Yankton/Emporia St. (II)	1965-66, 68-69	241	4,354	18.1	49
James Roe, Norfolk St. (II)	1992-95	239	4,468	18.7	46
Mark Didio, Connecticut (I-AA)	1988-91	239	3,535	14.8	21
Mark DeBrito, Bentley (II)	1996-99	238	3,711	15.6	41
Bryan McGinty, Lock Haven (II)	1993-96	238	3,100	13.0	18
Arnold Jackson, Louisville (I-A)	1997-99	237	3,061	12.9	26
Rennie Benn, Lehigh (I-AA)	1982-85	237	3,662	15.5	44
Marc Zeno, Tulane (I-A)	1984-87	236	3,725	15.8	25
Kevin Ingram, West Chester (II)	1995-96, 98-99	235	3,159	13.4	45
Jason Wolf, Southern Methodist (I-A)	1989-92	235	2,232	9.5	17

*Record. ¢Record for a running back. #Record for a tight end.

CAREER RECEPTIONS PER GAME

(Minimum 125 Receptions)

Player, Team (Division[s])	Years	G	Rec.	Yards	TD	Rec. PG
Chris George, Glenville St. (II)	1993-94	20	230	3,215	30	*11.5
Scott Pingel, Westminster (Mo.) (III)	1996-99	39	*436	*6,108	*75	11.2
Manny Hazard, Houston (I-A)	1989-90	21	220	2,635	31	10.5
Alex Van Dyke, Nevada (I-A)	1994-95	22	227	3,100	26	10.3
Howard Twilley, Tulsa (I-A)	1963-65	26	261	3,343	32	10.0
Jason Phillips, Houston (I-A)	1987-88	22	207	2,319	18	9.4
Matt Newton, Principia (III)	1990-93	33	287	3,646	32	8.7
Ed Bell, Idaho St. (II)	1968-69	19	163	2,608	30	8.6
Byron Chamberlain, Wayne St. (Neb.) (II)	1993-94	19	161	1,941	14	8.5
Todd Bloom, Hardin-Simmons (III)	1995-97	28	233	2,621	14	8.3
Troy Edwards, Louisiana Tech (I-A)	1996-98	34	280	4,352	50	8.2
Carlos Ferralls, Glenville St. (II)	1994-97	35	282	4,091	53	8.1
Jerry Hendren, Idaho (II)	1967-69	30	230	3,435	27	7.7
Bryan Reeves, Nevada (I-AA; I-A)	1991; 92-93	31	234	3,407	32	7.6
Siaha Burley, UCF (I-A)	1997-98	22	165	2,248	15	7.5
Jeff Clay, Catholic (III)	1994-97	36	269	4,101	44	7.5
Geoff Noisy, Nevada (I-A)	1995-98	40	295	4,249	21	7.4
David Williams, Illinois (I-A)	1983-85	33	245	3,195	22	7.4
Gary Garrison, San Diego St. (II)	1964-65	20	148	2,188	26	7.4
Brad Bailey, West Tex. A&M (II)	1992-94	30	221	2,677	22	7.4
Jerry Rice, Mississippi Val. (I-AA)	1981-84	41	301	4,693	50	7.3
James Dixon, Houston (I-A)	1987-88	22	161	1,762	14	7.3
Mike Furrey, Northern Iowa (I-AA)	1997-99	33	242	3,544	27	7.3

*Record.

CAREER TOUCHDOWN RECEPTIONS

Player, Team (Division[s])	Years	G	TD
Scott Pingel, Westminster (Mo.) (III)	1996-99	39	*75
Chris Bisaillon, Ill. Wesleyan (III)	1989-92	36	55
Kurt Barth, Eureka (III)	1994-97	39	51
Troy Edwards, Louisiana Tech (I-A)	1996-98	34	50
Jerry Rice, Mississippi Val. (I-AA)	1981-84	41	50
Bruce Cerone, Yankton/Emporia St. (II)	1965-66, 68-69	36	49
R. J. Hoppe, Carroll (Wis.) (III)	1993-96	37	49
James Roe, Norfolk St. (II)	1992-95	41	46
Kevin Ingram, West Chester (II)	1995-96, 98-99	39	45
Randy Moss, Marshall (I-AA; I-A)	1996-97	23	44
Jeff Clay, Catholic (III)	1994-97	36	44
Rennie Benn, Lehigh (I-AA)	1982-85	41	44
Aaron Turner, Pacific (Cal.) (I-A)	1989-92	44	43
Carlos Ferralls, Glenville St. (II)	1994-97	35	43
Mark Loeffler, Wheaton (Ill.) (III)	1993-96	38	43
Matt Plummer, Dubuque (III)	1996-99	40	42
Sedrick Robinson, Ky. Wesleyan (II)	1993-96	38	42
Ryan Yarborough, Wyoming (I-A)	1990-93	46	42
Mark DeBrito, Bentley (II)	1996-99	39	41
Dedric Ward, Northern Iowa (I-AA)	1993-96	43	41
Richard Wemer, Grinnell (III)	1995-98	38	40
Scott Hvistendahl, Augsburg (III)	1995-98	40	40
Shannon Sharpe, Savannah St. (II)	1986-89	42	40
Sean Morey, Brown (I-AA)	1995-98	40	39
John Aromando, Col. of New Jersey (III)	1981-84	40	39
Bill Stromberg, Johns Hopkins (III)	1978-81	40	39
Marcus Harris, Wyoming (I-A)	1993-96	46	38
Kurt Barth, Eureka (III)	1994-96	29	38
Rodd Patten, Framingham St. (III)	1990-93	35	38
Tony Willis, New Haven (II)	1990-93	40	38
Clarkston Hines, Duke (I-A)	1986-89	44	38
Roy Banks, Eastern Ill. (I-AA)	1983-86	38	38
Robert Clark, N.C. Central (II)	1983-86	40	38
Mike Jones, Tennessee St. (I-AA)	1979-82	42	38
Cornell Craig, Southern Ill. (I-AA)	1996-99	44	37
Chris Holder, Tuskegee (II)	1988-91	40	37
Mike Whitehouse, St. Norbert (III)	1986-89	38	37
Terance Mathis, New Mexico (I-A)	1985-87, 89	44	36
Mike Cottle, Juniata (III)	1985-88	37	36
Joe Thomas, Mississippi Val. (I-AA)	1982-85	41	36
Willie Richardson, Jackson St. (II)	1959-62	38	36

*Record.

SEASON RECEPTIONS

Player, Team (Division)	Year	G	Rec.	Yards	TD
Manny Hazard, Houston (I-A)	†1989	11	*142	1,689	22
Troy Edwards, Louisiana Tech (I-A)	†1998	12	140	1,996	*27
Scott Pingel, Westminster (Mo.) (III)	†1999	10	136	1,648	24
Trevor Insley, Nevada (I-A)	†1999	11	134	2,060	13
Howard Twilley, Tulsa (I-A)	†1965	10	134	1,779	16
Scott Pingel, Westminster (Mo.) (III)	†1998	10	130	*2,157	26
Alex Van Dyke, Nevada (I-A)	†1995	11	129	1,854	16
Brad Bailey, West Tex. A&M (II)	1994	11	119	1,552	16
Chris George, Glenville St. (II)	†1993	10	117	1,876	15
Kevin Ingram, West Chester (II)	†1998	11	115	1,673	21
Brian Forster, Rhode Island (I-AA) (TE)	†1985	10	115	1,617	12
Damond Wilkins, Nevada (I-A)	†1996	11	114	1,121	4
Chris George, Glenville St. (II)	†1994	10	113	1,339	15
Scott Hvistendahl, Augsburg (III)	1998	10	112	1,860	15
Jeff Clay, Catholic (III)	†1997	10	112	1,625	20
Sean Pender, Valdosta St. (II)	†1995	11	111	983	2
Chris Daniels, Purdue (I-A)	1999	11	109	1,133	5
Marcus Harris, Wyoming (I-A)	1996	12	109	1,650	13
Fred Gilbert, Houston (I-A)	†1991	11	106	957	7
Barry Wagner, Alabama A&M (II)	†1989	11	106	1,812	17
Theo Blanco, Wis.-Stevens Point (III) (RB)	1987	11	#106	#1,616	8
Chris Penn, Tulsa (I-A)	†1993	11	105	1,578	12
Eugene Baker, Kent (I-A)	†1997	11	103	1,549	18
Sherman Smith, Houston (I-A)	†1992	11	103	923	6
Jerry Rice, Mississippi Val. (I-AA)	†1984	10	103	1,682	*27
Troy Edwards, Louisiana Tech (I-A)	1997	11	102	1,707	13
James Dixon, Houston (I-A)	1988	11	102	1,103	11
Jerry Rice, Mississippi Val. (I-AA)	†1983	11	102	1,450	14
Mark DeBrito, Bentley (II)	1999	11	101	1,637	19
Arnold Jackson, Louisville (I-A)	1999	11	101	1,209	9
Mike Healey, Valparaiso (II)	†1985	10	101	1,279	11
David Williams, Illinois (I-A)	†1984	11	101	1,278	8
Kwame Cavil, Texas (I-A)	1999	13	100	1,188	6
Dameane Douglas, California (I-A)	1998	11	100	1,150	4
Jay Miller, Brigham Young (I-A)	†1973	11	100	1,181	8
Jason Phillips, Houston (I-A)	†1987	11	99	875	3
Mark Templeton, Long Beach St. (I-A) (RB)	†1986	11	99	688	2
Murle Sango, Villanova (I-AA)	†1999	11	98	1,064	10

INDIVIDUAL COLLEGIATE RECORDS—RECEIVING

Player, Team (Division)	Year	G	Rec.	Yards	TD
Scott Pingel, Westminster (Mo.) (III)	1997	10	98	1,420	17
Geoffery Noisy, Nevada (I-A)	1996	11	98	1,435	9
Alex Van Dyke, Nevada (I-A)	†1994	11	98	1,246	10
Matt Newton, Principia (III)	†1992	8	98	1,487	14
Rodney Carter, Purdue (I-A)	†1985	11	98	1,099	4

*Record. †National champion. #Record for a running back.

SEASON RECEPTIONS PER GAME

Player, Team (Division)	Year	G	Rec.	Yards	TD	Rec. PG
Scott Pingel, Westminster (Mo.) (III)	†1999	10	136	1,648	24	*13.6
Howard Twilley, Tulsa (I-A)	†1965	10	134	1,779	16	13.4
Scott Pingel, Westminster (Mo.) (III)	†1998	10	130	*2,157	26	13.0
Manny Hazard, Houston (I-A)	†1989	11	*142	1,689	22	12.9
Matt Newton, Principia (III)	†1992	8	98	1,487	14	12.3
Trevor Insley, Nevada (I-A)	†1999	11	134	2,060	13	12.2
Matt Newton, Principia (III)	†1993	8	96	1,080	11	12.0
Alex Van Dyke, Nevada (I-A)	†1995	11	129	1,854	16	11.7
Chris George, Glenville St. (II)	†1993	10	117	1,876	15	11.7
Troy Edwards, Louisiana Tech (I-A)	†1998	12	140	1,996	*27	11.7
Brian Forster, Rhode Island (I-AA) (TE)	†1985	10	115	1,617	12	11.5
Chris George, Glenville St. (II)	†1994	10	113	1,339	15	11.3
Scott Hvistendahl, Augsburg (III)	1998	10	112	1,860	15	11.2
Jeff Clay, Catholic (III)	†1997	10	112	1,625	20	11.2
Brad Bailey, West Tex. A&M (II)	1994	11	119	1,552	16	10.8
Ben Fox, Hanover (III)	†1995	9	95	1,087	15	10.6
Sean Munroe, Mass.-Boston (III)	1992	9	95	1,693	17	10.6
Kevin Ingram, West Chester (II)	†1998	11	115	1,673	21	10.5
Damond Wilkins, Nevada (I-A)	†1996	11	114	1,121	4	10.4
Jerry Rice, Mississippi Val. (I-AA)	†1984	10	103	1,682	*27	10.3
Scott Faessler, Framingham St. (III)	†1990	9	92	916	5	10.2
Jerry Rice, Mississippi Val. (I-AA)	†1983	10	102	1,450	14	10.2
Bruce Cerone, Emporia St. (II)	†1968	9	91	1,479	15	10.1
Mike Healy, Valparaiso (II)	†1985	10	101	1,279	11	10.1
Sean Pender, Valdosta St. (II)	†1995	11	111	983	2	10.1
Carlos Ferralls, Glenville St. (II)	†1996	8	81	965	6	10.1
Stuart Gaussoin, Portland St. (I-AA)	†1979	9	90	1,132	8	10.0

*Record. †National champion.

SINGLE-GAME RECEPTIONS

No.	Div.	Player, Team (Opponent)	Date
24	I-AA	Jerry Rice, Mississippi Val. (Southern U.)	Oct. 1, 1983
23	II	Chris George, Glenville St. (West Va. Wesleyan)	Oct. 15, 1994
23	I-A	Randy Gatewood, UNLV (Idaho)	Sept. 17, 1994
23	III	Sean Munroe, Mass.-Boston (Mass. Maritime)	Oct. 10, 1992
23	II	Barry Wagner, Alabama A&M (Clark Atlanta)	Nov. 4, 1989
22	I-AA	Marvin Walker, North Texas (Tulsa)	Nov. 20, 1982
22	I-A	Jay Miller, Brigham Young (New Mexico)	Nov. 3, 1973
21	I-A	Chris Daniels, Purdue (Michigan St.)	Oct. 16, 1999
21	I-AA	Eric Johnson, Yale (Harvard)	Nov. 20, 1999
21	I-A	Troy Edwards, Louisiana Tech (Nebraska)	Aug. 29, 1998
21	II	Kevin Swayne, Wayne St. (Neb.) (Drake)	Nov. 9, 1996
21	II	Jarett Vito, Emporia St. (Truman)	Nov. 4, 1995
21#	I-AA	David Pandt, Montana St. (Eastern Wash.)	Sept. 21, 1985
20	III	Scott Pingel, Westminster (Mo.) (Colorado Col.)	Oct. 30, 1999
20	III	Todd Bloom, Hardin-Simmons (Mississippi Col.)	Oct. 12, 1996
20	III	Kurt Barth, Eureka (Concordia [Wis.])	Sept. 28, 1996
20	I-AA	Tim Hilton, Cal St. Northridge (St. Mary's [Cal.])	Nov. 11, 1995
20	II	Sean Pender, Valdosta St. (Mississippi Col.)	Nov. 4, 1995
20	III	Keylie Martin, N.M. Highlands (Western St.)	Nov. 5, 1994
20	III	Rich Johnson, Pace (Fordham)	Nov. 7, 1987
20	III	Pete Thompson, Carroll (Wis.) (Augustana [Ill.])	Nov. 4, 1978
20	II	Harold "Red" Roberts, Austin Peay (Murray St.)	Nov. 8, 1969
20	I-A	Rick Eber, Tulsa (Idaho St.)	Oct. 7, 1967

#Record for a running back.

CAREER YARDS

Player, Team (Division)	Years	Rec.	Yards	Avg.	TD
Scott Pingel, Westminster (Mo.) (III)	1996-99	*436	*6,108	14.0	*75
Trevor Insley, Nevada (I-A)	1996-99	298	5,005	16.8	35
Scott Hvistendahl, Augsburg (III)	1995-98	285	4,696	16.5	40
Jerry Rice, Mississippi Val. (I-AA)	1981-84	301	4,693	15.6	50
Marcus Harris, Wyoming (I-A)	1993-96	259	4,518	17.4	38
James Roe, Norfolk St. (II)	1992-95	239	4,468	18.7	46
Ryan Yarborough, Wyoming (I-A)	1990-93	229	4,357	19.0	42
Bruce Cerone, Yankton/Emporia St. (II)	1965-66, 68-69	241	4,354	18.1	49
Troy Edwards, Louisiana Tech (I-A)	1996-98	280	4,352	15.5	50
Aaron Turner, Pacific (Cal.) (I-A)	1989-92	266	4,345	16.3	43
Kurt Barth, Eureka (III)	1994-97	256	4,311	16.8	51
Terance Mathis, New Mexico (I-A)	1985-87, 89	263	4,254	16.2	36
Geoff Noisy, Nevada (I-A)	1995-98	295	4,249	14.4	21
Robert Clark, N.C. Central (II)	1983-86	210	4,231	‡20.1	38
Jeff Clay, Catholic (III)	1994-97	269	4,101	15.2	44

Player, Team (Division)	Years	Rec.	Yards	Avg.	TD
Carlos Ferralls, Glenville St. (II)	1994-97	282	4,091	14.5	53
Matt Plummer, Dubuque (III)	1996-99	271	4,049	14.9	42
Troy Walters, Stanford (I-A)	1996-99	244	3,986	16.3	26
Chris Myers, Kenyon (II)	1967-70	253	3,897	15.4	33
Dedric Ward, Northern Iowa (I-AA)	1993-96	176	3,876	22.0	41
Sean Morey, Brown (I-AA)	1995-98	251	3,850	15.3	39
Kasey Dunn, Idaho (I-AA)	1988-91	268	3,847	14.4	25
Dale Amos, Frank. & Marsh. (III)	1986-89	233	3,846	16.5	35
Chad Mackey, Louisiana Tech (I-A)	1993-96	264	3,789	14.4	22
Bill Stromberg, Johns Hopkins (III)	1978-81	258	3,776	14.6	39
Shannon Sharpe, Savannah St. (II)	1986-89	192	3,744	19.5	40
Marc Zeno, Tulane (I-A)	1984-87	236	3,725	15.8	25
Jim Bradford, Carleton (III)	1988-91	212	3,719	17.5	32
Tyrone Johnson, Western St. (II)	1990-93	163	3,717	22.8	35
Mark DeBrito, Bentley (II)	1996-99	238	3,711	15.6	41
Brandon Stokley, La.-Lafayette (I-A)	1995-98	241	3,702	15.4	25
Chris Bisaillon, Ill. Wesleyan (III)	1989-92	223	3,670	16.5	*55
Rennie Benn, Lehigh (I-AA)	1982-85	237	3,662	15.5	44
Matt Newton, Principia (III)	1990-93	287	3,646	12.7	32
Jeff Tiefenthaler, South Dakota St. (II)	1983-86	173	3,621	20.9	31
David Rhodes, UCF (I-AA)	1991-94	213	3,618	17.0	29
Willie Richardson, Jackson St. (II)	1959-62	166	3,616	21.8	36
Johnny Cox, Fort Lewis (II)	1990-93	220	3,611	16.4	33
Mike Gundersdorf, Wilkes (III)	1993-96	205	3,603	17.6	34
Ron Sellers, Florida St. (I-A)	1966-68	212	3,598	17.0	23

*Record. ‡Record for minimum 180 catches.

CAREER YARDS PER GAME

(Minimum 2,200 Yards)

Player, Team (Division[s])	Years	G	Yards	Yd. PG
Chris George, Glenville St. (II)	1993-94	20	3,215	*160.8
Scott Pingel, Westminster (Mo.) (III)	1996-99	39	*6,108	156.6
Alex Van Dyke, Nevada (I-A)	1994-95	22	3,100	140.9
Ed Bell, Idaho St. (II)	1968-69	19	2,608	137.3
Troy Edwards, Louisiana Tech (I-A)	1996-98	34	4,352	128.0
Manny Hazard, Houston (I-A)	1989-90	21	2,635	125.5
Bruce Cerone, Yankton/Emporia St. (II)	1965-66, 68-69	36	4,354	120.9
Ron Sellers, Florida St. (I-A)	1966-68	30	3,598	119.9
Randy Moss, Marshall (I-AA; I-A)	1996-97	23	2,720	118.3
Scott Hvistendahl, Augsburg (III)	1995-98	40	4,696	117.4
Derrick Ingram, UAB (I-AA)	1993-94	22	2,572	116.9
Carlos Ferralls, Glenville St. (II)	1994-97	35	4,091	116.9
Jerry Rice, Mississippi Val. (I-AA)	1981-84	41	4,693	114.5
Jerry Hendren, Idaho (II)	1967-69	30	3,435	114.5
Jeff Clay, Catholic (III)	1994-97	36	4,101	113.9
Trevor Insley, Nevada (I-A)	1996-99	44	5,005	113.8
Nakia Jenkins, Utah St. (I-A)	1996-97	22	2,483	112.9
Elmo Wright, Houston (I-A)	1968-70	30	3,347	111.6
Howard Twilley, Tulsa (I-A)	1963-65	30	3,343	111.4
Chris Myers, Kenyon (II)	1967-70	35	3,897	111.3
Kurt Barth, Eureka (III)	1994-97	39	4,311	110.5
Matt Newton, Principia (III)	1990-93	33	3,646	110.5
Tim McNamara, Trinity (Conn.) (III)	1981-84	21	2,313	110.1
Bryan Reeves, Nevada (I-AA; I-A)	1991; 92-93	31	3,407	109.9
James Roe, Norfolk St. (II)	1992-95	41	4,468	109.0
Chris Penn, Tulsa (I-A)	1991, 93	22	2,370	107.7
Mike Furrey, Northern Iowa (I-AA)	1997-99	33	3,544	107.4
Joe Rettler, Ripon (III)	1997-99	29	3,100	106.9
Geoff Noisy, Nevada (I-A)	1995-98	40	4,249	106.2
Jason Phillips, Houston (I-A)	1987-88	22	2,319	105.4
Bill Stromberg, Johns Hopkins (III)	1978-81	36	3,776	104.9
Joe Douglass, Montana (I-AA)	1995-96	22	2,301	104.6
Siaha Burley, UCF (I-A)	1997-98	22	2,248	102.2
Chris Bisaillon, Ill. Wesleyan (III)	1989-92	36	3,670	101.9

*Record.

SEASON YARDS

Player, Team (Division)	Year	Rec.	Yards	Avg.	TD
Scott Pingel, Westminster (Mo.) (III)	†1998	130	*2,157	16.6	26
Trevor Insley, Nevada (I-A)	†1999	134	2,060	15.4	13
Troy Edwards, Louisiana Tech (I-A)	†1998	140	1,996	14.3	*27
Chris George, Glenville St. (II)	†1993	117	1,876	16.0	15
Scott Hvistendahl, Augsburg (III)	1998	112	1,860	16.6	15
Alex Van Dyke, Nevada (I-A)	†1995	129	1,854	14.4	16
Barry Wagner, Alabama A&M (II)	†1989	106	1,812	17.1	17
Howard Twilley, Tulsa (I-A)	1965	134	1,779	13.3	16
Chris Perry, Adams St. (II)	1995	88	1,719	19.5	21
Eddie Conti, Delaware (I-AA)	†1998	91	1,712	18.8	10
Troy Edwards, Louisiana Tech (I-A)	1997	102	1,707	16.7	13
Sean Munroe, Mass.-Boston (III)	†1992	95	1,693	17.8	17
Manny Hazard, Houston (I-A)	†1989	*142	1,689	11.9	22
Jerry Rice, Mississippi Val. (I-AA)	†1984	103	1,682	16.3	*27
Kevin Ingram, West Chester (II)	†1998	115	1,673	14.5	21

INDIVIDUAL COLLEGIATE RECORDS—RECEIVING

Player, Team (Division)	Year	Rec.	Yards	Avg.	TD
Marcus Harris, Wyoming (I-A)	†1996	109	1,650	15.1	13
Scott Pingel, Westminster (Mo.) (III)	†1999	136	1,648	12.1	24
Randy Moss, Marshall (I-A)	1997	90	1,647	18.3	25
Mark DeBrito, Bentley (II)	1999	101	1,637	16.2	19
Jeff Clay, Catholic (III)	†1997	112	1,625	14.5	25
Brian Forster, Rhode Island (I-AA) (TE)	†1985	115	1,617	14.1	12
Theo Blanco, Wis.-Stevens Point (III) (RB)	1987	#106	#1,616	15.2	8
Aaron Turner, Pacific (Cal.) (I-A)	†1991	92	1,604	17.4	18
Torry Holt, North Carolina St. (I-A)	1998	88	1,604	18.2	11
Dan Fulton, Neb.-Omaha (II)	1976	67	1,581	23.6	16
Chris Penn, Tulsa (I-A)	†1993	105	1,578	15.0	12
Carlos Ferralls, Glenville St. (II)	†1997	94	1,566	16.6	19
Brad Bailey, West Tex. A&M (II)	1994	119	1,552	13.0	16
Eugene Baker, Kent (I-A)	†1997	103	1,547	15.0	18
Matt Eisenberg, Juniata (III)	1999	76	1,547	20.4	19
Jeff Tiefenthaler, South Dakota St. (II)	1986	73	1,534	21.0	11
Ed Bell, Idaho St. (II)	†1969	96	1,522	15.9	20
Chuck Hughes, UTEP (I-A)	1965	80	1,519	19.0	12
Damon Thompson, Virginia St. (II)	†1999	90	1,517	16.9	10
Darryl DeShields, Greenville (III)	1999	92	1,515	16.5	12
Ryan Yarborough, Wyoming (I-A)	1993	67	1,512	22.6	16

*Record. †National champion. #Record for a running back.

SEASON YARDS PER GAME

Player, Team (Division)	Year	G	Rec.	Yards	Yd. PG
Scott Pingel, Westminster (Mo.) (III)	†1998	10	130	*2,157	*215.7
Sean Munroe, Mass.-Boston (III)	†1992	9	95	1,693	188.1
Chris George, Glenville St. (II)	†1993	10	117	1,876	187.6
Trevor Insley, Nevada (I-A)	†1999	11	134	2,060	187.3
Scott Hvistendahl, Augsburg (III)	1998	10	112	1,860	186.0
Matt Newton, Principia (III)	†1992	8	98	1,487	185.9
Howard Twilley, Tulsa (I-A)	†1965	10	134	1,779	177.9
Chris Perry, Adams St. (II)	†1995	10	88	1,719	171.9
Alex Van Dyke, Nevada (I-A)	†1995	11	129	1,854	168.5
Jerry Rice, Mississippi Val. (I-AA)	†1984	10	103	1,682	168.2
Troy Edwards, Louisiana Tech (I-A)	†1998	12	140	1,996	166.3
Scott Pingel, Westminster (Mo.) (III)	†1999	10	136	1,648	164.8
Barry Wagner, Alabama A&M (II)	†1989	11	106	1,812	164.7
Bruce Cerone, Emporia St. (II)	†1968	9	91	1,479	164.3
Jeff Clay, Catholic (III)	†1997	10	112	1,625	162.5
Jeff Clay, Catholic (III)	†1996	9	81	1,460	162.2
Brian Forster, Rhode Island (I-AA)	†1985	10	115	1,617	161.7

*Record. †National champion.

SEASON TOUCHDOWN RECEPTIONS

Player, Team (Division)	Year	G	TD
Troy Edwards, Louisiana Tech (I-A)	1998	12	*27
Jerry Rice, Mississippi Val. (I-AA)	1984	10	*27
Scott Pingel, Westminster (Mo.) (III)	1998	10	26
Randy Moss, Marshall (I-A)	1997	12	25
Scott Pingel, Westminster (Mo.) (III)	1999	10	24
Manny Hazard, Houston (I-A)	1989	11	22
David Snider, Grinnell (III)	1998	10	21
Chris Perry, Adams St. (II)	1995	10	21
Kirk Aikens, Hartwick (III)	1998	10	20
Steve Vagades, Ohio Northern (III)	1998	10	20
Jeff Clay, Catholic (III)	1997	10	20
John Aromando, Col. of New Jersey (III)	1983	10	20
Ed Bell, Idaho St. (II)	1969	10	20
Mark DeBrito, Bentley (II)	1999	11	19
Matt Eisenberg, Juniata (III)	1999	10	19
Adam Marino, Mount Union (III)	1999	10	19
Ben Streby, Otterbein (III)	1999	10	19
Carlos Ferralls, Glenville St. (II)	1997	10	19
Randy Moss, Marshall (I-AA)	1996	11	19
Stanley Flanders, Valdosta St. (II)	1994	11	19
Desmond Howard, Michigan (I-A)	1991	11	19
Chad Hustead, Redlands (III)	1999	9	18
Eugene Baker, Kent (I-A)	1997	11	18
Ryan Hinske, Wis.-Oshkosh (III)	1997	10	18
Joe Douglass, Montana (I-AA)	1996	11	18
Jamar Nailor, N.M. Highlands (II)	1996	10	18
Wayne Thomas, Miles (II)	1996	10	18
Kurt Barth, Eureka (III)	1995	10	18
Brian Penecale, West Chester (II)	1994	11	18
Aaron Turner, Pacific (Cal.) (I-A)	1991	11	18
Dennis Smith, Utah (I-A)	1989	12	18
Tom Reynolds, San Diego St. (I-A)	1971	10	18

*Record.

SINGLE-GAME YARDS

Yds.	Div.	Player, Team (Opponent)	Date
405	I-A	Troy Edwards, Louisiana Tech (Nebraska)	Aug. 29, 1998
401	II	Kevin Ingram, West Chester (Clarion)	Oct. 31, 1998
397	III	Matt Eisenberg, Juniata (Widener)	Nov. 13, 1999
395	III	Scott Pingel, Westminster (Mo.) (Bethel [Tenn.])	Nov. 7, 1998
370	I-AA	Michael Lerch, Princeton (Brown)	Oct. 12, 1991
370	II	Barry Wagner, Alabama A&M (Clark Atlanta)	Nov. 4, 1989
364	III	Jeff Clay, Catholic (Albright)	Nov. 16, 1996
363	I-A	Randy Gatewood, UNLV (Idaho)	Sept. 17, 1994
363	II	Tom Nettles, San Diego St. (Southern Miss.)	Nov. 9, 1968
362	III	Matt Surette, Worcester Tech (Springfield)	Oct. 25, 1997
354	I-AA	Eddie Conti, Delaware (Connecticut)	Nov. 7, 1998
354	II	Robert Clark, N.C. Central (Jackson St.)	Aug. 30, 1986
349	I-A	Chuck Hughes, UTEP (North Texas)	Sept. 18, 1965
332	III	Ryan Pifer, Heidelberg (Marietta)	Nov. 8, 1997
332	III	Sean Munroe, Mass.-Boston (Mass. Maritime)	Oct. 10, 1992
330	I-AA	Nate Singleton, Grambling (Virginia Union)	Sept. 14, 1991
327@	I-AA	Brian Forster, Rhode Island (Brown)	Sept. 28, 1985
325	II	Paul Zaeske, North Park (North Central)	Oct. 12, 1968
322	I-A	Rick Eber, Tulsa (Idaho St.)	Oct. 7, 1967
319	I-AA	Jason Cristino, Lehigh (Lafayette)	Nov. 21, 1992
318	I-A	Harry Wood, Tulsa (Idaho St.)	Oct. 7, 1967
317	II	Dan Fulton, Neb.-Omaha (South Dakota)	Sept. 4, 1976
316	I-AA	Marcus Hinton, Alcorn St. (Chattanooga)	Sept. 10, 1994
316	I-A	Jeff Evans, New Mexico St. (Southern Ill.)	Sept. 30, 1978
314	III	Matt Eisenberg, Juniata (Albright)	Oct. 2, 1999
314	I-A	Alex Van Dyke, Nevada (San Jose St.)	Nov. 18, 1995
310	III	Jeff Clay, Catholic (La Salle)	Oct. 11, 1997
310	I-A	Chad Mackey, Louisiana Tech (Toledo)	Oct. 19, 1996
310	II	Mike Collodi, Colorado Mines (Westminster [Utah])	Oct. 3, 1970
309	III	Dale Amos, Frank. & Marsh. (Western Md.)	Oct. 24, 1987

@Record for a tight end.

Interceptions

CAREER INTERCEPTIONS

Player, Team (Division[s])	Years	No.	Yards	Avg.
Tom Collins, Indianapolis (II)	1982-85	*37	390	10.5
Ralph Gebhardt, Rochester (II; III)	1972; 73-75	34	406	11.9
Dean Diaz, Humboldt St. (II)	1980-83	31	328	10.6
Bill Grantham, Mo.-Rolla (II)	1977-80	29	263	9.1
Eugene Hunter, Fort Valley St. (II; III)	1972; 73-74	29	479	16.5
Al Brosky, Illinois (I-A)	1950-52	29	356	12.3
Jason Johnson, Shepherd (II)	1991-94	28	321	11.5
Rick Bealer, Lycoming (III)	1987-90	28	279	10.0
Brian Fetterolf, Aurora (III)	1986-89	28	390	13.9
Dave Murphy, Holy Cross (I-AA)	1986-89	28	309	11.0
Tim Lennon, Curry (III)	1986-89	27	190	7.0
Scott Stanitous, Moravian (III)	1985-88	27	178	6.6
Mike Hintz, Wis.-Platteville (III)	1983-86	27	183	6.8
Martin Bayless, Bowling Green (I-A)	1980-83	27	266	9.9
John Provost, Holy Cross (I-A)	1972-74	27	470	17.4
Cory Mabry, Susquehanna (III)	1988-91	26	400	15.4
Tony Woods, Bloomsburg (II)	1982-85	26	105	4.0
Jeff Hughes, Ripon (III)	1975-78	26	333	12.8
Buster West, Gust. Adolphus (II)	1967-70	26	192	7.4

*Record.

SEASON INTERCEPTIONS

Player, Team (Division)	Year	No.	Yards
Mark Dorner, Juniata (III)	†1987	*15	202
Eugene Hunter, Fort Valley St. (II)	†1972	14	211
Luther Howard, Delaware St. (II)	†1972	14	99
Tom Rezzuti, Northeastern (II)	†1971	14	153
Jim Blackwell, Southern U. (II)	†1970	14	196
Carl Ray Harris, Fresno St. (II)	†1970	14	98
Al Worley, Washington (I-A)	†1968	14	130

*Record. †National champion.

Punt Returns

CAREER AVERAGE

(Minimum 1.2 Returns Per Game; Minimum 30 Returns)

Player, Team (Division[s])	Years	No.	Yards	Avg.
Billy Johnson, Widener (II; III)	1971-72; 73	40	989	*24.7
Jack Mitchell, Oklahoma (I-A)	1946-48	39	922	23.6

INDIVIDUAL COLLEGIATE RECORDS—PUNT RETURNS 229

Player, Team (Division[s])	Years	No.	Yards	Avg.
Keith Winston, Knoxville (III)	1986-87	30	686	22.9
Kevin Doherty, Mass. Maritime (III)	1976-78, 80	45	939	20.9
Chuck Downey, Stony Brook (III)	1984-87	59	1,198	**20.3
Chuck Goehl, Monmouth (Ill.) (II)	1970-72	48	911	19.0
Eddie Macon, Pacific (Cal.) (I-A)	1949-51	48	907	18.9
Jackie Robinson, UCLA (I-A)	1939-40	37	694	18.8
Willie Canady, Fort Valley St. (III)	1979-82	41	772	18.8

*Record. **Record for minimum 50 returns.

SEASON AVERAGE

(Minimum 1.2 Returns Per Game and Qualifiers for Championship)

Player, Team (Division)	Year	No.	Yards	Avg.
Billy Johnson, Widener (II)	†1972	15	511	*34.1
Chuck Downey, Stony Brook (III)	†1986	17	530	31.2
Kevin Doherty, Mass. Maritime (III)	†1976	11	332	30.2
Dennis Robinson, Wesleyan (Conn.) (III)	†1978	9	263	29.2
Robert Middlebrook, Knoxville (III)	†1984	9	260	28.9
Joe Troise, Kean (III)	†1974	12	342	28.5
William Williams, Livingstone (II)	†1976	16	453	28.3
Terry Egerdahl, Minn.-Duluth (II)	†1975	13	360	27.7
Melvin Dillard, Ferrum (III)	†1990	25	688	27.5
Eric Green, Benedictine (Ill.) (III)	†1993	13	346	26.6
Bill Blackstock, Tennessee (I-A)	1951	12	311	25.9
George Sims, Baylor (I-A)	1948	15	375	25.0
Ennis Thomas, Bishop (II)	†1971	18	450	25.0

*Record. †National champion.

Kickoff Returns

CAREER AVERAGE

(Minimum 1.2 Returns Per Game; Minimum 30 Returns)

Player, Team (Division)	Years	No.	Yards	Avg.
Anthony Davis, Southern California (I-A)	1972-74	37	1,299	*35.1
Eric Booth, Southern Miss. (I-A)	1994	35	1,135	32.4
Overton Curtis, Utah St. (I-A)	1957-58	32	991	31.0
Fred Montgomery, New Mexico St. (I-A)	1991-92	39	1,191	30.5
Karl Evans, Mo. Southern St. (II)	1991-92	32	959	30.0
Kevin Cannon, Millersville (II)	1992-95	67	1,999	29.8
Troy Brown, Marshall (I-AA)	1991-92	32	950	29.7
Dave Ludy, Winona St. (II)	1991-94	89	2,630	29.6
Charles Swann, Indiana St. (I-AA)	1989-91	45	1,319	29.3
Altie Taylor, Utah St. (I-A)	1966-68	40	1,170	29.3
Daryl Brown, Tufts (III)	1974-76	38	1,111	29.2
Stan Brown, Purdue (I-A)	1968-70	49	1,412	28.8
Henry White, Colgate (I-A)	1974-77	41	1,180	28.8
Kevin Johnson, Syracuse (I-A)	1995-98	50	1,437	28.7
Doug Parrish, San Fran. St. (II)	1990	35	1,002	28.6
Craig Richardson, Eastern Wash. (I-AA)	1983-86	71	2,021	28.5

*Record.

SEASON AVERAGE

(Minimum 1.2 Returns Per Game and Qualifiers for Championship)

Player, Team (Division)	Year	No.	Yards	Avg.
Brandon Steinheim, Wesley (III)	†1994	10	422	*42.2
Paul Allen, Brigham Young (I-A)	1961	12	481	40.1
Jason Martin, Coe (III)	†1992	11	438	39.8
Tremain Mack, Miami (Fla.) (I-A)	†1996	13	514	39.5
LaVon Reis, Western St. (II)	†1993	14	552	39.4
Danny Lee, Jacksonville St. (II)	†1992	12	473	39.4
Leeland McElroy, Texas A&M (I-A)	†1993	15	590	39.3
Tony Hill, Salisbury St. (III)	†1998	14	549	39.2
Fran DeFalco, Assumption (II)	1993	12	461	38.4
Forrest Hall, San Francisco (I-A)	1946	15	573	@38.2
David Fraterrigo, Canisius (I-AA)	†1993	13	485	37.3
Nate Kirtman, Pomona-Pitzer (III)	†1990	14	515	36.8
Kendall James, Carson-Newman (II)	1993	15	549	36.6
Kerry Hayes, Western Caro. (I-AA)	1993	16	584	36.5
Tom Myers, Coe (III)	†1983	11	401	36.5
Tony Ball, Chattanooga (I-A)	†1977	13	473	36.4
Ron Scott, Occidental (III)	1983	10	363	36.3
Alan Hill, DePauw (III)	1980	12	434	36.2
Cordell Roane, Richmond (I-AA)	†1999	13	470	36.2
Roscoe Word, Jackson St. (II)	†1973	18	650	36.1
Steve Levenseller, Puget Sound (II)	1978	17	610	35.9
Trevor Shannon, Wartburg (III)	†1996	14	501	35.8
George Marinkov, North Carolina St. (I-A)	1954	13	465	35.8

*Record. †National champion. @ Record for minimum 1.5 returns per game.

Field Goals

(One-inch tees were permitted in 1949, two-inch tees were permitted in 1965, and use of tees was eliminated before the 1989 season. The goal posts were widened from 18 feet, 6 inches to 23 feet, 4 inches in 1959 and were narrowed back to 18 feet, 6 inches before the 1991 season. The hash marks were moved six feet, eight inches closer to the center of the field to 60 feet from each sideline in 1993.)

CAREER FIELD GOALS

Player, Team (Division)	Years	FGM	FGA	Pct.
Jeff Jaeger, Washington (S) (I-A)	1983-86	*80	99	.808
John Lee, UCLA (S) (I-A)	1982-85	79	92	*.859
Philip Doyle, Alabama (S) (I-A)	1987-90	78	*105	.743
Luis Zendejas, Arizona St. (S) (I-A)	1981-84	78	*105	.743
Max Zendejas, Arizona (S) (I-A)	1982-85	77	104	.740
Kevin Butler, Georgia (S) (I-A)	1981-84	77	98	.786
Carlos Huerta, Miami (Fla.) (S) (I-A)	1988-91	73	91	.802
Derek Schmidt, Florida St. (S) (I-A)	1984-87	73	104	.702
Marty Zendejas, Nevada (S) (I-A)	1984-87	72	90	.800
Kirk Roach, Western Caro. (S) (I-AA)	1984-87	71	102	.696
Fuad Reveiz, Tennessee (S) (I-A)	1981-84	71	95	.747
Roman Anderson, Houston (S) (I-A)	1988-91	70	101	.693
Barry Belli, Fresno St. (S) (I-A)	1984-87	70	99	.707
Tony Zendejas, Nevada (S) (I-AA)	1981-83	70	86	.814
Collin Mackie, South Carolina (S) (I-A)	1987-90	69	95	.726
Shayne Graham, Virginia Tech (S) (I-A)	1996-99	68	93	.731
Gary Gussman, Miami (Ohio) (S) (I-A)	1984-87	68	94	.723
Larry Roach, Oklahoma St. (S) (I-A)	1981-84	68	101	.673
Scott Shields, Weber St. (S) (I-AA)	1995-98	67	90	.744

*Record. (S) Soccer-style kicker.

SEASON FIELD GOALS

Player, Team (Division)	Year	FGM	FGA	Pct.
John Lee, UCLA (S) (I-A)	1984	*29	33	.879
Luis Zendejas, Arizona St. (S) (I-A)	1983	28	37	.757
Paul Woodside, West Virginia (S) (I-A)	1982	28	31	.903
Sebastian Janikowski, Florida St. (S) (I-A)	1998	27	32	.844
Fuad Reveiz, Tennessee (S) (I-A)	1982	27	31	.871
Brian Mitchell, Northern Iowa (S) (I-AA)	1990	26	27	*.963
Tony Zendejas, Nevada (S) (I-AA)	1982	26	33	.788
Wayne Boyer, Southwest Mo. St. (S) (I-AA)	1996	25	30	.833
Chris Jacke, UTEP (S) (I-A)	1988	25	27	.926
John Diettrich, Ball St. (S) (I-A)	1985	25	29	.862
Chuck Nelson, Washington (S) (I-A)	1982	25	26	.962
Brad Bohn, Utah St. (S) (I-A)	1998	24	28	.857
Remy Hamilton, Michigan (S) (I-A)	1994	24	29	.828
Philip Doyle, Alabama (S) (I-A)	1990	24	29	.828
Kendall Trainor, Arkansas (S) (I-A)	1988	24	27	.889
Kirk Roach, Western Caro. (S) (I-AA)	1986	24	28	.857
Carlos Reveiz, Tennessee (S) (I-A)	1985	24	28	.857
George Benyola, Louisiana Tech (S) (I-AA)	1985	24	31	.774
Chris White, Illinois (S) (I-A)	1984	24	28	.857
Mike Prindle, Western Mich. (S) (I-A)	1984	24	30	.800
Bruce Kallmeyer, Kansas (S) (I-A)	1983	24	29	.828

*Record. (S) Soccer-style kicker. (Record for attempts is 38)

LONGEST FIELD GOALS

Yds.	Div.	Player, Team (Opponent)	Year
67	II	Tom Odle, Fort Hays St. (Washburn)	1988
67	I-A	Joe Williams, Wichita St. (Southern Ill.)	1978
67	I-A	Russell Erxleben, Texas (Rice)	1977
67	I-A	Steve Little, Arkansas (Texas)	1977
65*	I-A	Martin Gramatica, Kansas St. (Northern Ill.)	1998
65	I-A	Tony Franklin, Texas A&M (Baylor)	1976
64	I-A	Russell Erxleben, Texas (Oklahoma)	1977
64	I-A	Tony Franklin, Texas A&M (Baylor)	1976
63	I-AA	Tim Foley, Ga. Southern (James Madison)	1987
63	I-AA	Scott Roper, Arkansas St. (North Texas)	1987
63	I-A	Morten Andersen, Michigan St. (Ohio St.)	1981
63	I-A	Clark Kemble, Colorado St. (Arizona)	1975
63	II	Joe Duren, Arkansas St. (McNeese St.)	1974
62	I-A	Terance Kitchens, Texas A&M (Southern Miss.)	1999
62	II	Doc Proctor, Ferris St. (Michigan Tech)	1999
62	I-A	Jason Hanson, Washington St. (UNLV)	1991
62	I-A	John Diettrich, Ball St. (Ohio)	1986
62	I-AA	Paul Hickert, Murray St. (Eastern Ky.)	1986
62#	I-A	Chip Lohmiller, Minnesota (Iowa)	1986
62	I-A	Tom Whelihan, Missouri (Colorado)	1986
62	I-A	Dan Christopulos, Wyoming (Colorado St.)	1977
62	I-A	Iseed Khoury, North Texas (Richmond)	1977

INDIVIDUAL COLLEGIATE RECORDS—FIELD GOALS

Yds.	Div.	Player, Team (Opponent)	Year
62	III	Dom Antonini, Rowan (Salisbury St.)	1976
62	I-A	Dave Lawson, Air Force (Iowa St.)	1975
62	II	Mike Flater, Colorado Mines (Western St.)	1973

*Longest collegiate field goal without use of a tee and also longest collegiate field goal with narrower goal posts (18 feet, 6 inches). #Longest field goal made indoors.

Special Reference: Ove Johannson, Abilene Christian (not an NCAA-member college at the time), kicked a 69-yard field goal against East Texas State, Oct. 16, 1976, the longest collegiate field goal.

Punting

CAREER PUNTING AVERAGE
(Minimum 150 Punts)

Player, Team (Division)	Years	No.	Yards	Avg.
Todd Sauerbrun, West Virginia (I-A)	1991-94	167	7,733	*46.3
Reggie Roby, Iowa (I-A)	1979-82	172	7,849	45.6
Greg Montgomery, Michigan St. (I-A)	1985-87	170	7,721	45.4
Tom Tupa, Ohio St. (I-A)	1984-87	196	8,854	45.2
Barry Helton, Colorado (I-A)	1984-87	153	6,873	44.9
Aron Langley, Wyoming (I-A)	1996-98	171	7,649	44.7
Shane Lechler, Texas A&M (I-A)	1996-99	268	11,977	44.7
Ray Guy, Southern Miss. (I-A)	1970-72	200	8,934	44.7
Bucky Scribner, Kansas (I-A)	1980-82	217	9,670	44.6
Terry Daniel, Auburn (I-A)	1992-94	169	7,522	44.5
Greg Horne, Arkansas (I-A)	1983-86	180	8,002	44.5
Ray Criswell, Florida (I-A)	1982-85	161	7,153	44.4
Pumpy Tudors, Chattanooga (I-AA)	1988-91	181	8,041	44.4
Mark Simon, Air Force (I-A)	1984-86	164	7,283	44.4
Brian Schmitz, North Carolina (I-A)	1996-99	208	9,233	44.4
Bill Smith, Mississippi (I-A)	1983-86	254	11,260	44.3
Jason Van Dyke, Adams St. (II)	1995-98	242	10,720	44.3
Tim Baer, Colorado Mines (II)	1986-89	235	10,406	44.3
Russell Erxleben, Texas (I-A)	1975-78	214	9,467	44.2
Brad Maynard, Ball St. (I-A)	1993-96	242	10,702	44.2
Mark Simon, Air Force (I-A)	1984-86	156	6,898	44.2
Johnny Evans, North Carolina St. (I-A)	1974-77	185	8,143	44.0
Brian Moorman, Pittsburg St. (II)	1995-98	157	6,903	44.0
Chuck Ramsey, Wake Forest (I-A)	1971-73	205	9,010	44.0

*Record.

SEASON PUNTING AVERAGE
(Qualifiers for Championship)

Player, Team (Division)	Year	No.	Yards	Avg.
Chad Kessler, LSU (I-A)	†1997	39	1,961	*50.3
Reggie Roby, Iowa (I-A)	†1981	44	2,193	49.8
Kirk Wilson, UCLA (I-A)	†1956	30	1,479	49.3
Steve Ecker, Shippensburg (II)	†1965	32	1,570	49.1
Todd Sauerbrun, West Virginia (I-A)	†1994	72	3,486	48.4
Zack Jordan, Colorado (I-A)	†1950	38	1,830	48.2
Ricky Anderson, Vanderbilt (I-A)	†1984	58	2,793	48.2
Reggie Roby, Iowa (I-A)	†1982	52	2,501	48.1
Marv Bateman, Utah (I-A)	†1971	68	3,269	48.1
Andrew Bayes, East Caro. (I-A)	†1999	47	2,259	48.1
Don Cockroft, Adams St. (II)	†1966	36	1,728	48.0
Owen Price, UTEP (I-A)	†1940	30	1,440	48.0
Jack Jacobs, Oklahoma (I-A)	1940	31	1,483	47.8
Brian Schmitz, North Carolina (I-A)	1999	74	3,538	47.8
Bill Smith, Mississippi (I-A)	1984	44	2,099	47.7

*Record. †National champion.

LONGEST PUNTS

Yds.	Div.	Player, Team (Opponent)	Year
99	I-A	Pat Brady, Nevada (Loyola Marymount)	1950
97	II	Earl Hurst, Emporia St. (Central Mo. St.)	1964
96	II	Alex Campbell, Morris Brown (Clark Atlanta)	1994
96	II	Gary Frens, Hope (Olivet)	1966
96	II	Jim Jarrett, North Dakota (South Dakota)	1957
96	I-A	George O'Brien, Wisconsin (Iowa)	1952
94	I-A	John Hadl, Kansas (Oklahoma)	1959
94	I-A	Carl Knox, TCU (Oklahoma St.)	1947
94	I-A	Preston Johnson, Southern Methodist (Pittsburgh)	1940
93	II	Elliot Mills, Carleton (Monmouth [Ill.])	1970
93	II	Kasper Fitins, Taylor (Georgetown [Ky.])	1966
93	II	Leeroy Sweeney, Pomona-Pitzer (UC Riverside)	1960
93	I-A	Bob Handke, Drake (Wichita St.)	1949

All-purpose yardage is the combined net yards gained by rushing, receiving, interception (and fumble) returns, punt returns, kickoff returns and runbacks of field goal attempts. All-purpose yardage does not include forward passing yardage.

Total offense is the total of net gain rushing and net gain forward passing. Receiving and runback yards are not included in total offense.

All-Purpose Yards

CAREER YARDS

Player, Team (Division[s])	Years	Rush	Rcv.	Int.	PR	KO	Yds.
Brian Shay, Emporia St. (II)	1995-98	*6,958	1,032	0	104	1,207	*9,301
Paul Smith, Gettysburg (III)	1996-99	5,205	758	0	959	2,182	9,104
Kavin Gailliard, American Int'l (II)	1996-99	6,523	1,049	0	472	814	8,858
Jerry Azumah, New Hampshire (I-AA)	1995-98	6,193	1,153	0	5	1,025	8,376
Carey Bender, Coe (III)	1991-94	6,125	1,751	0	7	87	7,970
Steve Tardif, Maine Maritime (III)	1996-99	6,093	643	8	65	1,151	7,960
Johnny Bailey, Tex. A&M-Kingsville (II)	1986-89	6,320	452	0	20	1,011	7,803
Kenny Gamble, Colgate (I-AA)	1984-87	5,220	536	0	104	1,763	7,623
Howard Stevens, Randolph-Macon (II); Louisville (I-A)	1968-69; 71-72	5,297	738	0	781	748	7,564
Claude Mathis, Southwest Tex. St. (I-AA)	1994-97	4,691	744	0	635	1,353	7,423
Thomas Haskins, VMI (I-AA)	1993-96	5,355	179	0	216	1,661	7,411
Rick Sarille, Wagner (I-AA)	$1995-99	5,290	365	0	0	1,682	7,337
¢R. J. Bowers, Grove City (III)	1997-99	5,620	338	0	50	1,266	7,274
Roger Graham, New Haven (II)	1991-94	5,953	393	0	0	870	7,216
Ricky Williams, Texas (I-A)	1995-98	6,279	927	0	0	0	7,206
Napoleon McCallum, Navy (I-A)	$1981-85	4,179	796	0	858	1,339	7,172
Dave Ludy, Winona St. (II)	1991-94	3,501	906	0	34	2,630	7,071
Albert Fann, Cal St. Northridge (II)	1987-90	4,090	803	0	0	2,141	7,032
Reggie Greene, Siena (I-AA)	1994-97	5,415	274	0	53	1,217	6,959
Kirk Matthieu, Maine Maritime (III)	$1989-93	5,107	315	0	254	1,279	6,955
Curtis Delgardo, Portland St. (II)	$1986-90	4,178	1,258	0	318	1,188	6,942
Jarrett Anderson, Truman (II)	1993-96	6,166	633	0	0	127	6,926
Darrin Nelson, Stanford (I-A)	1977-78, 80-81	4,033	2,368	0	471	13	6,885
Eric Frees, Western Md. (III)	1988-91	5,281	392	0	47	1,158	6,878
Kevin Faulk, LSU (I-A)	1995-98	4,557	600	0	857	819	6,833
Damian Beane, Shepherd (II)	1996-99	6,346	416	0	0	0	6,762
Ron Dayne, Wisconsin (I-A)	1996-99	6,397	304	0	0	0	6,701
Johnny Cox, Fort Lewis (II)	1990-93	112	3,611	0	495	2,476	6,694
Steve Roberts, Butler (II)	1986-89	4,623	1,201	0	272	578	6,674
Anthony Russo, St. John's (N.Y.) (III; I-AA)	1990-92; 93	5,834	405	0	25	379	6,643

INDIVIDUAL COLLEGIATE RECORDS—ALL-PURPOSE YARDS

Player, Team (Division[s])	Years	Rush	Rcv.	Int.	PR	KO	Yds.
Richard Huntley, Winston-Salem (II)	1992-95	6,286	333	0	0	0	6,619
Tony Dorsett, Pittsburgh (I-A)	1973-76	6,082	406	0	0	127	6,615
Paul Palmer, Temple (I-A)	1983-86	4,895	705	0	0	997	6,609
Charles White, Southern California (I-A)	1976-79	5,598	507	0	0	440	6,545
Trevor Cobb, Rice (I-A)	1989-92	4,948	892	0	21	651	6,512
Mike Smith, Neb.-Kearney (II)	1994-97	348	2,975	0	932	2,255	6,510
Joe Dudek, Plymouth St. (III)	1982-85	5,570	348	0	0	243	6,509
Richard Wemer, Grinnell (III)	1995-98	1,016	3,133	7	674	1,657	6,487
Glyn Milburn, Oklahoma/Stanford (I-A)	1988, 90-92	2,302	1,495	0	1,145	1,246	6,188
Dante Brown, Marietta (III)	1994-97	4,512	425	0	202	1,040	6,179
Travis Prentice, Miami (Ohio) (I-A)	1996-99	5,596	527	0	0	0	6,123
Adam Henry, Carleton (III)	1990-93	3,482	601	0	186	1,839	6,108
Chris Cobb, Eastern Ill. (II)	1976-79	5,042	520	0	37	478	6,077
Brad Olson, Lawrence (III)	1994-97	5,325	590	0	14	145	6,074
Don Aleksiewicz, Hobart (III)	1969-72	4,525	470	0	320	748	6,063
Mark Kacmarynski, Central (Iowa) (III)	$1992-96	5,434	211	0	45	364	6,054
Gary Trettel, St. Thomas (Minn.) (III)	1988-90	3,724	853	0	0	1,467	6,044
Troy Edwards, Louisiana Tech (I-A)	1996-98	447	4,352	0	241	991	6,031
Archie Griffin, Ohio St. (I-A)	1972-75	5,177	286	0	0	540	6,003

*Record. $See page 6 for explanation. ¢Active player.

CAREER YARDS PER GAME

(Minimum 3,500 Yards)

Player, Team (Division[s])	Years	G	Rush	Rcv.	Int.	PR	KO	Yds.	Yd. PG
Ryan Benjamin, Pacific (Cal.) (I-A)	1990-92	24	3,119	1,063	0	100	1,424	5,706	*237.8
Chris George, Glenville St. (II)	1993-94	20	23	3,215	0	391	1,050	4,679	234.0
Paul Smith, Gettysburg (III)	1996-99	40	5,205	758	0	959	2,182	9,104	227.6
Brian Shay, Emporia St. (II)	1995-98	44	*6,958	1,032	0	104	1,207	*9,301	211.4
Kirk Matthieu, Maine Maritime (III)	$1989-93	33	5,107	315	0	254	1,279	6,955	210.8
Anthony Gray, Western N.M. (II)	1997-98	19	3,484	499	0	0	8	3,991	210.1
Kavin Gailliard, American Int'l (II)	1996-99	43	6,523	1,049	0	472	814	8,858	206.0
Sheldon Canley, San Jose St. (I-A)	1988-90	25	2,513	828	0	5	1,800	5,146	205.8
Carey Bender, Coe (III)	1991-94	39	6,125	1,751	0	7	87	7,970	204.4
Jerry Azumah, New Hampshire (I-AA)	1995-98	41	6,193	1,153	0	5	1,025	8,376	204.3
Steve Tardif, Maine Maritime (III)	1996-99	39	6,093	643	8	65	1,151	7,960	204.1
Johnny Bailey, Tex. A&M-Kingsville (II)	1986-89	39	6,320	452	0	20	1,011	7,803	200.1
Howard Stevens, Randolph-Macon (II); Louisville (I-A)	1968-69; 71-72	38	5,297	738	0	781	748	7,564	199.1
Gary Trettel, St. Thomas (Minn.) (III)	1988-90	29	3,483	834	0	0	1,407	5,724	197.4
Arnold Mickens, Butler (I-AA)	1994-95	22	3,813	47	0	0	87	3,947	197.4
Tim Hall, Robert Morris (I-AA)	1994-95	19	2,908	793	0	0	0	3,701	194.8
Reggie Greene, Siena (I-AA)	1994-97	36	5,415	274	0	53	1,217	6,959	193.3
Billy Johnson, Widener (II; III)	1971-72; 73	28	3,737	27	0	43	989	5,404	193.0
O. J. Simpson, Southern California (I-A)	1967-68	19	3,124	235	0	0	307	3,666	192.9
Steve Roberts, Butler (II)	1986-89	35	4,623	1,201	0	272	578	6,674	190.7

*Record. $See page 6 for explanation.

SEASON YARDS

Player, Team (Division)	Year	Rush	Rcv.	Int.	PR	KO	Yds.
Barry Sanders, Oklahoma St. (I-A)	†1988	2,628	106	0	95	421	*3,250
Kavin Gailliard, American Int'l (II)	†1999	*2,653	289	0	0	122	3,064
Brian Westbrook, Villanova (I-AA)	1998	1,046	1,144	0	192	644	3,026
Ryan Benjamin, Pacific (Cal.) (I-A)	†1991	1,581	612	0	4	798	2,995
Dante Brown, Marietta (III)	†1996	2,385	174	0	46	368	2,973
R. J. Bowers, Grove City (III)	†1998	2,283	51	0	4	538	2,876
Brian Shay, Emporia St. (II)	†1998	2,265	165	0	0	389	2,819
Troy Edwards, Louisiana Tech (I-A)	†1998	227	1,996	0	235	326	2,784
Brian Shay, Emporia St. (II)	†1996	2,103	247	0	48	340	2,738
Jerry Azumah, New Hampshire (I-AA)	1998	2,195	218	0	5	308	2,726
Brian Shay, Emporia St. (II)	†1997	1,912	277	0	56	478	2,723
Paul Smith, Gettysburg (III)	†1999	1,546	301	0	255	615	2,717
Mike Pringle, Cal St. Fullerton (I-A)	†1989	1,727	249	0	0	714	2,690
Steve Roberts, Butler (II)	†1989	1,450	532	0	272	415	2,669
Carey Bender, Coe (III)	†1994	2,243	319	0	7	87	2,656
Paul Palmer, Temple (I-A)	†1986	1,866	110	0	0	657	2,633
Chris George, Glenville St. (II)	†1993	23	1,876	0	157	562	2,618
Ryan Benjamin, Pacific (Cal.) (I-A)	†1992	1,441	434	0	96	626	2,597
Kavin Gailliard, American Int'l (II)	1998	1,971	270	0	151	196	2,588
Marcus Allen, Southern California (I-A)	†1981	2,342	217	0	0	0	2,559
Damon Thompson, Virginia St. (II)	1998	127	1,330	0	292	770	2,519
Sheldon Canley, San Jose St. (I-A)	1989	1,201	353	0	0	959	2,513
Mike Rozier, Nebraska (I-A)	1983	2,148	106	0	0	232	2,486
Damon Thompson, Virginia St. (II)	1999	88	1,517	0	410	465	2,480
Troy Davis, Iowa St. (I-A)	†1995	2,010	159	0	0	297	2,466
Jamel White, South Dakota (II)	1999	1,807	640	0	0	0	2,447
Alex Van Dyke, Nevada (I-A)	1995	6	1,854	0	0	583	2,443
Paul Smith, Gettysburg (III)	1998	1,515	178	0	191	554	2,438
Charles Roberts, Cal St. Sacramento (I-AA)	1998	2,260	79	0	0	91	2,430
Archie Amerson, Northern Ariz. (I-AA)	1996	2,079	262	0	0	88	2,429
Johnny Bailey, Tex. A&M-Kingsville (II)	†1986	2,011	54	0	20	340	2,425
Kenny Gamble, Colgate (I-AA)	†1986	1,816	198	0	40	391	2,425
Theo Blanco, Wis.-Stevens Point (III)	1987	454	1,616	0	245	103	2,418
Guy Leman, Simpson (III)	1998	1,788	210	0	0	408	2,406
Rick Wegher, South Dakota St. (II)	1984	1,317	264	0	0	824	2,405

INDIVIDUAL COLLEGIATE RECORDS—ALL PURPOSE YARDS

Player, Team (Division)	Year	Rush	Rcv.	Int.	PR	KO	Yds.
Steve Papin, Portland St. (II)	†1995	1,619	525	0	1	252	2,397
Ronald Moore, Pittsburg St. (II)	1992	1,864	141	0	0	388	2,393
Chuck Weatherspoon, Houston (I-A)	1989	1,146	735	0	415	95	2,391
Anthony Thompson, Indiana (I-A)	1989	1,793	201	0	0	394	2,388
Ricky Williams, Texas (I-A)	1998	2,124	262	0	0	0	2,386
Napoleon McCallum, Navy (I-A)	†1983	1,587	166	0	272	360	2,385
Ricky Gales, Simpson (III)	†1989	2,035	102	0	0	248	2,385
R. J. Bowers, Grove City (III)	1999	2,098	34	0	0	240	2,372
Eddie Conti, Delaware (I-AA)	1998	-2	1,712	0	156	502	2,368
Troy Davis, Iowa St. (I-A)	†1996	2,185	61	0	0	118	2,364
Paul Smith, Gettysburg (III)	†1997	1,256	102	0	199	805	2,362
Rashaan Salaam, Colorado (I-A)	†1994	2,055	294	0	0	0	2,349
Marcel Shipp, Massachusetts (I-AA)	1998	1,949	288	0	0	100	2,337
Gary Trettel, St. Thomas (Minn.) (III)	1989	1,502	337	0	0	496	2,335
Michael Clemons, William & Mary (I-AA)	1986	1,065	516	0	330	423	2,334
Napoleon McCallum, Navy (I-A)	†1985	1,327	358	0	157	488	2,330

*Record. †National champion.

SEASON YARDS PER GAME

Player, Team (Division)	Year	G	Rush	Rcv.	Int.	PR	KO	Yds.	Yd.PG
Dante Brown, Marietta (III)	†1996	10	2,385	174	0	46	368	2,973	*297.3
Barry Sanders, Oklahoma St. (I-A)	†1988	11	2,628	106	0	0	95	*3,250	295.5
R. J. Bowers, Grove City (III)	†1998	10	2,283	51	0	4	538	2,876	287.6
Brian Westbrook, Villanova (I-AA)	†1998	11	1,046	1,144	0	192	644	3,026	275.1
Paul Smith, Gettysburg (III)	†1999	10	1,546	301	0	255	615	2,717	271.7
Steve Roberts, Butler (II)	†1989	10	1,450	532	0	272	415	2,669	266.9
Carey Bender, Coe (III)	†1994	10	2,243	319	0	7	87	2,656	265.6
Bobby Felix, Western N.M. (II)	†1994	8	439	853	0	150	667	2,109	263.6
Chris George, Glenville St. (II)	†1993	10	23	1,876	0	157	562	2,618	261.8
Brian Shay, Emporia St. (II)	†1998	11	2,265	165	0	0	389	2,819	256.3
Kavin Gailliard, American Int'l (II)	†1999	12	*2,653	289	0	0	122	3,064	255.3
Damon Thompson, Virginia St. (II)	1998	10	127	1,330	0	292	770	2,519	251.9
Billy Johnson, Widener (II)	1972	9	1,556	40	43	511	115	2,265	251.7
Ryan Benjamin, Pacific (Cal.) (I-A)	†1991	12	1,581	612	0	4	798	2,995	249.6
Brian Shay, Emporia St. (II)	†1996	11	2,103	247	0	48	340	2,738	248.9
Damon Thompson, Virginia St. (II)	1999	10	88	1,517	0	410	465	2,480	248.0
Jerry Azumah, New Hampshire (I-AA)	1998	11	2,195	218	0	5	308	2,726	247.8
Brian Shay, Emporia St. (II)	†1997	11	1,912	277	0	56	478	2,723	247.5
Kenneth Sasu, Marietta (III)	1999	9	1,770	82	0	0	374	2,226	247.3
Byron "Whizzer" White, Colorado (I-A)	†1937	8	1,121	0	103	587	159	1,970	246.3
Steve Tardif, Maine Maritime (III)	1999	9	1,567	149	8	0	479	2,203	244.8
Mike Pringle, Cal St. Fullerton (I-A)	†1989	11	1,727	249	0	0	714	2,690	244.6
Paul Smith, Gettysburg (III)	1998	10	1,515	178	0	191	554	2,438	243.8
Kirk Matthieu, Maine Maritime (III)	†1992	9	1,733	91	0	56	308	2,188	243.1
Guy Leman, Simpson (III)	1998	10	1,788	210	0	0	408	2,406	240.6
Paul Palmer, Temple (I-A)	†1986	11	1,866	110	0	0	657	2,633	239.4
Ray Neosh, Coe (III)	1996	9	1,472	273	0	0	403	2,148	238.7
Ricky Gales, Simpson (III)	†1989	10	2,035	102	0	0	248	2,385	238.5
R. J. Bowers, Grove City (III)	1999	10	2,098	34	0	0	240	2,372	237.2
Paul Smith, Gettysburg (III)	†1997	10	1,256	102	0	199	805	2,362	236.2
Ryan Benjamin, Pacific (Cal.) (I-A)	†1992	11	1,441	434	0	96	626	2,597	236.1
Kavin Gailliard, American Int'l (II)	1998	11	1,971	270	0	151	196	2,588	235.3
Reggie Greene, Siena (I-AA)	†1996	9	1,719	50	0	0	337	2,106	234.0
Gary Trettel, St. Thomas (Minn.) (III)	1989	10	1,502	337	0	0	496	2,335	233.5
Kirk Matthieu, Maine Maritime (III)	1990	9	1,428	77	0	99	495	2,099	233.2

*Record. †National champion.

With 2,973 all-purpose yards in 10 games, Marietta's Dante Brown set the all-divisions season yards per game record in 1996.

Scoring

CAREER POINTS

Player, Team (Division[s])	Years	TD	XPt.	FG	Pts.
Brian Shay, Emporia St. (II)	1995-98	*88	16	0	*544
Carey Bender, Coe (III)	1991-94	86	12	0	528
Scott Pingel, Westminster (Mo.) (III)	1996-99	75	34	0	484
Trevor Shannon, Wartburg (III)	1995-98	79	10	0	484
Kavin Gailliard, American Int'l (II)	1996-99	78	8	0	476
Joe Dudek, Plymouth St. (III)	1982-85	79	0	0	474
Travis Prentice, Miami (Ohio) (I-A)	1996-99	78	0	0	468
Walter Payton, Jackson St. (II)	1971-74	66	53	5	464
Ricky Williams, Texas (I-A)	1995-98	75	2	0	452
¢R. J. Bowers, Grove City (III)	1997-99	73	6	0	444
Jarrett Anderson, Truman (II)	1993-96	73	2	0	440
Shawn Graves, Wofford (QB) (II)	1989-92	72	3	0	438
Rashaan Dumas, Southern Conn. St. (II)	1996-99	72	0	0	432
Johnny Bailey, Tex. A&M-Kingsville (II)	1986-89	70	3	0	426
Roger Graham, New Haven (II)	1991-94	70	2	0	424
Roman Anderson, Houston (I-A)	1988-91	0	213	70	423
Mark Kacmarynski, Central (Iowa) (III)	$1992-96	70	2	0	422
Jerry Azumah, New Hampshire (I-AA)	1995-98	69	4	0	418

Player, Team (Division[s])	Years	TD	XPt.	FG	Pts.
Howard Stevens, Randolph-Macon (II); Louisville (I-A)	1968-69; 71-72	69	4	0	418
Dale Mills, Truman (II)	1957-60	64	23	0	407
Jeremy Monroe, Michigan Tech (II)	1990-93	67	0	0	402
Andrew Notarfrancesco, Catholic (III)	1996-99	65	8	0	398
Carlos Huerta, Miami (Fla.) (I-A)	1988-91	0	178	73	397
Jason Elam, Hawaii (I-A)	$1988-92	0	158	79	395
Anthony Thompson, Indiana (I-A)	1986-89	65	4	0	394
Garney Henley, Huron (II)	1956-59	63	16	0	394
Derek Schmidt, Florida St. (I-A)	1984-87	0	174	73	393
Kris Brown, Nebraska (I-A)	1995-98	0	217	57	388
Steve Roberts, Butler (II)	1986-89	63	4	0	386
Jeff Bentrim, North Dakota St. (QB) (II)	1983-86	64	2	0	386
Marty Zendejas, Nevada (I-AA)	1984-87	0	169	72	385
Leo Lewis, Lincoln (Mo.) (II)	1951-54	64	0	0	384
Ron Dayne, Wisconsin (I-A)	1996-99	63	0	0	378
Chris Bisaillon, Ill. Wesleyan (III)	1989-92	61	12	0	378
Heath Sherman, Tex. A&M-Kingsville (II)	1985-88	63	0	0	378
Marshall Faulk, San Diego St. (I-A)	1991-93	62	4	0	376
Chris Babirad, Wash. & Jeff. (III)	1989-92	62	2	0	374
Billy Johnson, Widener (II; III)	1971-72; 73	62	0	0	372
Shayne Graham, Virginia Tech (I-A)	1996-99	0	167	68	371
Jeff Hall, Tennessee (I-A)	1995-98	0	188	61	371

*Record. $See page 6 for explanation. ¢Active player.

INDIVIDUAL COLLEGIATE RECORDS—SCORING

CAREER POINTS PER GAME

(Minimum 225 Points)

Player, Team (Division[s])	Years	G	TD	XPt.	FG	Pts.	Pt.PG
Cory Christensen, Simpson (III)	1996-97	19	44	0	0	264	*13.9
Rob Marchitello, Maine Maritime (III)	1993-95	26	59	4	0	358	13.8
Carey Bender, Coe (III)	1991-94	39	86	12	0	528	13.5
Ole Gunderson, St. Olaf (II)	1969-71	27	60	2	0	362	13.4
Billy Johnson, Widener (II; III)	1971-72; 73	28	62	0	0	372	13.3
Leon Burns, Long Beach St. (II)	1969-70	22	47	2	0	284	12.9
Trevor Shannon, Wartburg (III)	1995-98	39	79	10	0	484	12.4
Brian Shay, Emporia St. (II)	1995-98	44	*88	16	0	*544	12.4
Scott Pingel, Westminster (Mo.) (III)	1996-99	39	75	34	0	484	12.4
Marshall Faulk, San Diego St. (I-A)	1991-93	31	62	4	0	376	12.1
Jim Regan, Pomona-Pitzer (III)	1995-98	30	37	93	15	360	12.0
Ed Marinaro, Cornell (I-A)	1969-71	27	52	6	0	318	11.8
Aaron Stecker, Western Ill. (I-AA)	1997-98	20	39	0	0	234	11.7
Rashaan Dumas, Southern Conn. St. (II)	1996-99	37	72	0	0	432	11.7
Chad Hoiska, Wis.-Eau Claire (III)	1995-97	30	58	2	0	350	11.7
Joe Dudek, Plymouth St. (III)	1982-85	41	79	0	0	474	11.6
Bill Burnett, Arkansas (I-A)	1968-70	26	49	0	0	294	11.3
Dale Mills, Truman (II)	1957-60	36	64	23	0	407	11.3
Steve Owens, Oklahoma (I-A)	1967-69	30	56	0	0	336	11.2
Kavin Gailliard, American Int'l (II)	1996-99	43	78	8	0	476	11.1
Walter Payton, Jackson St. (II)	1971-74	42	66	53	5	464	11.0
Steve Roberts, Butler (II)	1986-89	35	63	4	0	386	11.0
Jeff Bentrim, North Dakota St. (II)	1983-86	35	64	2	0	386	11.0
Shawn Graves, Wofford (II)	1989-92	40	72	3	0	438	11.0
Johnny Bailey, Tex. A&M-Kingsville (II)	1986-89	39	70	3	0	426	10.9
Eddie Talboom, Wyoming (I-A)	1948-50	28	34	99	0	303	10.8
Chris Babirad, Wash. & Jeff. (III)	1989-92	35	62	2	0	374	10.7
Keith Elias, Princeton (I-AA)	1991-93	30	52	8	0	320	10.7

*Record.

SEASON POINTS

Player, Team (Division)	Year	TD	XPt	FG	Pts.
Barry Sanders, Oklahoma St. (I-A)	†1988	*39	0	0	*234
Kavin Gailliard, American Int'l (II)	†1999	34	2	0	206
R. J. Bowers, Grove City (III)	†1998	34	2	0	206
Brian Shay, Emporia St. (II)	†1997	32	6	0	198
Guy Leman, Simpson (III)	1998	33	0	0	198
Carey Bender, Coe (III)	†1994	32	2	0	194
Troy Edwards, Louisiana Tech (I-A)	†1998	31	2	0	188
Travis Walch, Winona St. (II)	1997	30	2	0	182
Terry Metcalf, Long Beach St. (I)	1971	29	4	0	178
Brian Shay, Emporia St. (II)	†1998	29	2	0	176
Chad Hoiska, Wis.-Eau Claire (III)	1997	29	2	0	176
Adrian Peterson, Ga. Southern (I-AA)	†1999	29	0	0	174
Jim Mormino, Allegheny (III)	1997	29	0	0	174
Doug Steiner, Grove City (III)	1997	29	0	0	174
Mike Rozier, Nebraska (I-A)	†1983	29	0	0	174
Lydell Mitchell, Penn St. (I-A)	1971	29	0	0	174
Josh Ranek, South Dakota St. (II)	1999	28	2	0	170
Geoff Mitchell, Weber St. (I-AA)	†1991	28	2	0	170
Ricky Williams, Texas (I-A)	1998	28	0	0	168
Jarrett Anderson, Truman (II)	†1996	28	0	0	168
Stanley Drayton, Allegheny (III)	†1991	28	0	0	168
Jim Switzer, Col. of Emporia (II)	†1963	28	0	0	168
Carl Herakovich, Rose-Hulman (II)	†1958	25	18	0	168
Ted Scown, Sul Ross St. (II)	†1948	28	0	0	168
James Regan, Pomona-Pitzer (III)	†1997	21	34	2	166
Dante Brown, Marietta (III)	†1996	27	4	0	166
Ronald Moore, Pittsburg St. (II)	1992	27	4	0	166

Player, Team (Division)	Year	TD	XPt.	FG	Pts.
Ricky Gales, Simpson (III)	†1989	26	10	0	166
Art Luppino, Arizona (I-A)	†1954	24	22	0	166
Matt Malmberg, St. John's (Minn.) (III)	†1993	27	2	0	164
Leon Burns, Long Beach St. (II)	†1969	27	2	0	164
Scott Pingel, Westminster (Mo.) (III)	1998	26	6	0	162
Trevor Shannon, Wartburg (III)	1998	26	6	0	162
Jerry Rice, Mississippi Val. (I-AA)	†1984	27	0	0	162
Mike Deutsch, North Dakota (II)	1972	27	0	0	162
Billy Johnson, Widener (II)	†1972	27	0	0	162

*Record. †National champion.

SEASON POINTS PER GAME

Player, Team (Division)	Year	G	TD	XPt.	FG	Pts.	Pt.PG
Barry Sanders, Oklahoma St. (I-A)	†1988	11	*39	0	0	*234	*21.3
Carl Herakovich, Rose-Hulman (II)	†1958	8	25	18	0	168	21.0
James Regan, Pomona-Pitzer (III)	†1997	8	21	34	2	166	20.8
R. J. Bowers, Grove City (III)	†1998	10	34	2	0	206	20.6
Guy Leman, Simpson (III)	1998	10	33	0	0	198	19.8
Carey Bender, Coe (III)	†1994	10	32	2	0	194	19.4
Jim Switzer, Col. of Emporia (II)	†1963	9	28	0	0	168	18.7
Brian Shay, Emporia St. (II)	†1997	11	32	6	0	198	18.0
Billy Johnson, Widener (II)	†1972	9	27	0	0	162	18.0
Chad Hoiska, Wis.-Eau Claire (III)	1997	10	29	2	0	176	17.6
Carl Garrett, N.M. Highlands (II)	†1966	9	26	2	0	158	17.6
Jim Mormino, Allegheny (III)	1997	10	29	0	0	174	17.4
Doug Steiner, Grove City (III)	1997	10	29	0	0	174	17.4
Bobby Reynolds, Nebraska (I-A)	†1950	9	22	25	0	157	17.4
Kavin Gailliard, American Int'l (II)	†1999	12	34	2	0	206	17.2
Rob Marchitello, Maine Maritime (III)	1994	9	25	4	0	154	17.1
Stanley Drayton, Allegheny (III)	†1991	10	28	0	0	168	16.8
Ted Scown, Sul Ross St. (II)	†1948	10	28	0	0	168	16.8
Dante Brown, Marietta (III)	†1996	10	27	4	0	166	16.6
Ricky Gales, Simpson (III)	†1989	10	26	10	0	166	16.6
Art Luppino, Arizona (I-A)	†1954	10	24	22	0	166	16.6
Travis Walch, Winona St. (II)	1997	11	30	2	0	182	16.5
Ed Marinaro, Cornell (I-A)	1971	9	24	4	0	148	16.4
Matt Malmberg, St. John's (Minn.) (III)	†1993	10	27	2	0	164	16.4
Scott Pingel, Westminster (Mo.) (III)	1998	10	26	6	0	162	16.2
Jerry Rice, Mississippi Val. (I-AA)	†1984	10	27	0	0	162	16.2
Trevor Shannon, Wartburg (III)	1998	10	26	6	0	162	16.2
Jamie Lee, MacMurray (III)	1998	10	26	4	0	160	16.0
Brian Shay, Emporia St. (II)	†1998	11	29	2	0	176	16.0
Chris Babirad, Wash. & Jeff. (III)	†1992	9	24	0	0	144	16.0
Larry Ras, Michigan Tech (II)	†1971	9	24	0	0	144	16.0
Trent Nauholz, Simpson (III)	†1992	8	21	2	0	128	16.0
Adrian Peterson, Ga. Southern (I-AA)	†1999	11	29	0	0	174	15.8
Lydell Mitchell, Penn St. (I-A)	1971	11	29	0	0	174	15.8
Troy Edwards, Louisiana Tech (I-A)	†1998	12	31	2	0	188	15.7
Marshall Faulk, San Diego St. (I-A)	†1991	9	23	2	0	140	15.6

*Record. †National champion.

SINGLE-GAME POINTS

Pts.	Div.	Player, Team (Opponent)	Date
48	III	Carey Bender, Coe (Beloit)	Nov. 12, 1994
48	I-A	Howard Griffith, Illinois (Southern Ill.)	Sept. 22, 1990
48	II	Paul Zaeske, North Park (North Central)	Oct. 12, 1968
48	II	Junior Wolf, Okla. Panhandle (St. Mary [Kan.])	Nov. 8, 1958
44	I-A	Marshall Faulk, San Diego St. (Pacific [Cal.])	Sept. 14, 1991
43	I-A	Jim Brown, Syracuse (Colgate)	Nov. 17, 1956
42	I-A	Arnold "Showboat" Boykin, Mississippi (Mississippi St.)	Dec. 1, 1951
42	I-A	Fred Wendt, UTEP (New Mexico St.)	Nov. 25, 1948

Award Winners

Consensus All-America Selections, 1889-1999......236
Special Awards 251
First-Team All-Americans Below Division I-A.........258
NCAA Postgraduate Scholarship Winners............269
Academic All-America Hall of Fame......................274
Academic All-Americans by School......................274

Consensus All-America Selections, 1889-1999

In 1950, the National Collegiate Athletic Bureau (the NCAA's service bureau) compiled the first official comprehensive roster of all-time all-Americans. The compilation of the all-American roster was supervised by a panel of analysts working in large part with the historical records contained in the files of the Dr. Baker Football Information Service.

The roster consists of only those players who were first-team selections on one or more of the all-America teams that were selected for the national audience and received nationwide circulation. Not included are the thousands of players who received mention on all-America second or third teams, nor the numerous others who were selected by newspapers or agencies with circulations that were not primarily national and with viewpoints, therefore, that were not normally nationwide in scope.

The following chart indicates, by year (in left column), which national media and organizations selected all-America teams. The headings at the top of each column refer to the selector (see legend after chart)

All-America Selectors

	AA	AP	C	COL	CP	FBW	FC	FN	FW	INS	L	LIB	M	N	NA	NEA	SN	UP	UPI	W	WCF
1889	-	-	-	-	-	-	-	-	-	-	-	-	-	-	-	-	-	-	-	√	-
1890	-	-	-	-	-	-	-	-	-	-	-	-	-	-	-	-	-	-	-	√	-
1891	-	-	-	-	-	-	-	-	-	-	-	-	-	-	-	-	-	-	-	√	-
1892	-	-	-	-	-	-	-	-	-	-	-	-	-	-	-	-	-	-	-	√	-
1893	-	-	-	-	-	-	-	-	-	-	-	-	-	-	-	-	-	-	-	√	-
1894	-	-	-	-	-	-	-	-	-	-	-	-	-	-	-	-	-	-	-	√	-
1895	-	-	-	-	-	-	-	-	-	-	-	-	-	-	-	-	-	-	-	√	-
1896	-	-	-	-	-	-	-	-	-	-	-	-	-	-	-	-	-	-	-	√	-
1897	-	-	-	-	-	-	-	-	-	-	-	-	-	-	-	-	-	-	-	√	-
1898	-	-	√	-	-	-	-	-	-	-	-	-	-	-	-	-	-	-	-	√	-
1899	-	-	√	-	-	-	-	-	-	-	-	-	-	-	-	-	-	-	-	√	-
1900	-	-	√	-	-	-	-	-	-	-	-	-	-	-	-	-	-	-	-	√	-
1901	-	-	√	-	-	-	-	-	-	-	-	-	-	-	-	-	-	-	-	√	-
1902	-	-	√	-	-	-	-	-	-	-	-	-	-	-	-	-	-	-	-	√	-
1903	-	-	√	-	-	-	-	-	-	-	-	-	-	-	-	-	-	-	-	√	-
1904	-	-	√	-	-	-	-	-	-	-	-	-	-	-	-	-	-	-	-	√	-
1905	-	-	√	-	-	-	-	-	-	-	-	-	-	-	-	-	-	-	-	√	-
1906	-	-	√	-	-	-	-	-	-	-	-	-	-	-	-	-	-	-	-	√	-
1907	-	-	√	-	-	-	-	-	-	-	-	-	-	-	-	-	-	-	-	√	-
1908	-	-	√	-	-	-	-	-	-	-	-	-	-	-	-	-	-	-	-	√	-
1909	-	-	√	-	-	-	-	-	-	-	-	-	-	-	-	-	-	-	-	-	-
1910	-	-	√	-	-	-	-	-	-	-	-	-	-	-	-	-	-	-	-	-	-
1911	-	-	√	-	-	-	-	-	-	-	-	-	-	-	-	-	-	-	-	-	-
1912	-	-	√	-	-	-	-	-	-	-	-	-	-	-	-	-	-	-	-	-	-
1913	-	-	√	-	-	-	-	-	-	√	-	-	-	-	-	-	-	-	-	-	-
1914	-	-	√	-	-	-	-	-	-	√	-	-	-	-	-	-	-	-	-	-	-
1915	-	-	√	-	-	-	-	-	-	√	-	-	-	-	-	-	-	-	-	-	-
1916	-	-	√	-	-	-	-	-	-	√	-	-	-	-	√	-	-	-	-	-	-
1917	-	-	(*)	-	-	-	-	-	-	√	-	-	-	-	√	-	√	-	-	-	-
1918	-	-	√	-	-	-	-	-	-	-	-	-	-	-	√	-	-	-	-	-	-
1919	-	-	√	-	-	-	-	-	-	-	-	-	-	-	√	-	-	-	-	-	-
1920	-	-	√	-	-	√	-	-	-	√	-	-	-	-	√	-	-	-	-	-	-
1921	-	-	√	-	-	-	-	-	-	-	-	-	-	-	-	-	-	-	-	-	-
1922	-	-	√	-	-	-	-	-	-	-	-	-	-	-	-	-	-	-	-	-	-
1923	-	-	√	-	-	√	-	-	-	-	-	-	-	-	-	-	-	-	-	-	-
1924	√	-	√	-	-	√	-	-	-	√	-	√	-	-	-	√	-	-	-	-	-
1925	√	√	-	√	-	√	-	-	-	√	-	√	-	-	-	√	-	-	√	-	-
1926	√	√	-	√	-	-	-	-	-	√	-	-	-	-	-	√	-	-	√	-	-
1927	√	√	-	√	-	-	-	-	-	√	-	-	-	-	-	√	√	-	√	-	-
1928	√	√	-	-	-	-	-	-	-	√	-	-	-	-	-	√	√	-	√	-	-
1929	√	√	-	√	-	-	-	-	-	√	-	-	-	-	-	√	√	-	√	-	-
1930	√	√	-	√	-	-	-	-	-	√	-	-	-	-	-	√	√	-	√	-	-
1931	√	√	-	√	-	-	-	-	-	√	-	-	-	-	-	√	√	-	√	-	-
1932	√	√	-	√	-	-	-	-	-	√	-	-	-	-	-	√	√	-	√	-	-
1933	√	√	-	√	-	-	-	-	-	√	-	-	-	-	-	√	√	-	√	-	-
1934	√	√	-	√	-	-	-	-	-	√	-	-	-	-	-	√	√	√	√	-	-
1935	√	√	-	√	-	-	-	-	-	√	-	-	-	-	-	√	√	√	√	-	-
1936	√	√	-	√	-	-	-	-	-	√	-	-	-	-	-	√	√	√	√	-	-
1937	√	√	-	√	-	-	-	-	-	√	-	-	-	√	-	√	√	√	√	-	-
1938	√	√	-	√	-	-	-	-	-	√	-	-	-	√	-	√	√	√	√	-	-
1939	-	√	-	√	-	-	-	-	-	√	-	-	-	√	-	√	√	√	√	-	-
1940	√	√	-	√	-	-	-	-	-	√	-	-	-	√	-	√	√	√	√	-	-
1941	√	√	-	√	-	-	-	-	-	√	-	-	-	√	-	√	√	√	√	-	-
1942	√	√	-	√	-	-	-	-	-	√	√	-	-	√	-	√	√	√	√	-	-
1943	√	√	-	√	-	-	√	-	√	√	√	-	-	√	-	√	√	√	√	-	-
1944	√	√	-	√	-	-	√	√	√	√	-	-	-	√	-	√	√	√	√	-	-
1945	√	√	-	√	-	-	√	-	√	√	√	-	-	√	-	√	√	√	√	-	-
1946	√	√	-	√	-	-	√	-	√	√	(†)	-	-	√	-	√	√	√	√	-	-
1947	-	√	-	√	-	-	√	-	√	√	-	-	-	√	-	√	√	√	√	-	-
1948	-	√	-	(§)	-	-	√	-	√	(#)√	-	-	-	√	-	√	√	√	√	-	-
1949	√	√	-	√	-	-	√	-	√	√	-	-	-	√	-	√	√	√	√	-	-
1950	√	√	-	√	-	-	√	-	√	√	-	-	-	√	-	√	√	√	√	-	-
1951	√	√	-	√	-	-	√	-	√	√	-	-	-	√	-	√	√	√	√	-	-
1952	√	√	-	√	-	-	√	-	√	√	-	-	-	√	-	√	√	√	√	-	-
1953	√	√	-	√	-	-	√	-	√	√	-	-	-	√	-	√	√	√	√	-	-

ALL-AMERICA SELECTORS

	AA	AP	C	COL	CP	FBW	FC	FN	FW	INS	L	LIB	M	N	NA	NEA	SN	UP	UPI	W	WCF
1954	√	√	-	-	-	-	√	-	√	√	-	-	-	-	-	√	√	√	-	-	-
1955	√	√	-	-	-	-	√	-	√	√	-	-	-	-	-	√	√	√	-	-	-
1956	-	√	-	-	-	-	√	-	√	√	-	-	-	-	-	√	√	√	-	-	-
1957	-	√	-	-	-	-	√	-	√	√	-	-	-	-	-	√	√	√	-	-	-
1958	-	√	-	-	-	-	√	-	√	-	-	-	-	-	-	√	√	-	√	-	-
1959	-	√	-	-	-	-	√	-	√	-	-	-	-	-	-	√	√	-	√	-	-
1960	-	√	-	-	-	-	√	-	√	-	-	-	-	-	-	√	√	-	√	-	-
1961	-	√	-	-	-	-	√	-	√	-	-	-	-	-	-	√	√	-	√	-	-
1962	-	√	-	-	-	-	√	-	√	-	-	-	-	-	-	√	√	-	√	-	-
1963	-	√	-	-	√	-	√	-	√	-	-	-	-	-	-	√	√	-	√	-	-
1964	-	√	-	-	√	-	√	-	√	-	-	-	-	-	-	√	-	-	√	-	-
1965	-	√	-	-	√	-	√	-	√	-	-	-	-	-	-	√	-	-	√	-	-
1966	-	√	-	-	√	-	√	-	√	-	-	-	-	-	-	√	-	-	√	-	-
1967	-	√	-	-	√	-	√	-	√	-	-	-	-	-	-	√	-	-	√	-	-
1968	-	√	-	-	√	-	√	-	√	-	-	-	-	-	-	√	-	-	√	-	-
1969	-	√	-	-	√	-	√	-	√	-	-	-	-	-	-	√	-	-	√	-	-
1970	-	√	-	-	√	-	√	-	√	-	-	-	-	-	-	√	-	-	√	-	-
1971	-	√	-	-	-	-	√	-	√	-	-	-	-	-	-	√	-	-	√	-	-
1972	-	√	-	-	-	-	√	-	√	-	-	-	-	-	-	√	-	-	√	-	-
1973	-	√	-	-	-	-	√	-	√	-	-	-	-	-	-	√	-	-	√	-	√
1974	-	√	-	-	-	-	√	-	√	-	-	-	-	-	-	-	-	-	√	-	√
1975	-	√	-	-	-	-	√	-	√	-	-	-	-	-	-	-	-	-	√	-	√
1976	-	√	-	-	-	-	√	-	√	-	-	-	-	-	-	-	-	-	√	-	√
1977	-	√	-	-	-	-	√	-	√	-	-	-	-	-	-	-	-	-	√	-	√
1978	-	√	-	-	-	-	√	-	√	-	-	-	-	-	-	-	-	-	√	-	√
1979	-	√	-	-	-	-	√	-	-	-	-	-	-	-	-	-	-	-	√	-	√
1980	-	√	-	-	-	-	√	-	-	-	-	-	-	-	-	-	-	-	√	-	√
1981	-	√	-	-	-	-	√	-	-	-	-	-	-	-	-	-	-	-	√	-	√
1982	-	√	-	-	-	-	√	-	-	-	-	-	-	-	-	-	-	-	√	-	√
1983	-	√	-	-	-	-	√	-	-	-	-	-	-	-	-	-	-	-	√	-	√
1984	-	√	-	-	-	-	√	-	-	-	-	-	-	-	-	-	-	-	√	-	√
1985	-	√	-	-	-	-	√	-	-	-	-	-	-	-	-	-	-	-	√	-	√
1986	-	√	-	-	-	-	√	-	-	-	-	-	-	-	-	-	-	-	√	-	√
1987	-	√	-	-	-	-	√	-	-	-	-	-	-	-	-	-	-	-	√	-	√
1988	-	√	-	-	-	-	√	-	-	-	-	-	-	-	-	-	-	-	√	-	√
1989	-	√	-	-	-	-	√	-	-	-	-	-	-	-	-	-	-	-	√	-	√
1990	-	√	-	-	-	-	√	-	-	-	-	-	-	-	-	-	-	-	√	-	√
1991	-	√	-	-	-	-	√	-	-	-	-	-	-	-	-	-	-	-	√	-	√
1992	-	√	-	-	-	-	√	-	-	-	-	-	-	-	-	-	-	-	√	-	√
1993	-	√	-	-	-	-	√	√	-	-	-	-	-	-	-	-	√	-	√	-	√
1994	-	√	-	-	-	-	-	√	-	-	-	-	-	-	-	-	-	-	√	-	√
1995	-	√	-	-	-	-	-	√	-	-	-	-	-	-	-	-	-	-	√	-	√
1996	-	√	-	-	-	-	-	√	-	-	-	-	-	-	-	-	-	-	√	-	√
1997	-	√	-	-	-	-	-	√	-	-	-	-	-	-	-	-	-	-	√	-	√
1998	-	√	-	-	-	-	√	√	-	-	-	-	-	-	-	-	-	-	-	-	√
1999	-	√	-	-	-	-	-	√	√	-	-	-	-	-	-	√	-	-	-	-	√

*In 1917, Walter Camp selected an all-Service, all-America team composed of military personnel. †During 1946-70, Look Magazine published the Football Writers Association of America's selections, listed under FW. §During 1948-56, Collier's Magazine published the American Football Coaches Association's selections, listed under FC. #International News Service was the first to select offensive and defensive teams.

LEGEND FOR SELECTORS
AA—All-America Board
AP—Associated Press
C—Walter Camp (published in Harper's Weekly, 1897; in Collier's Magazine, 1898-1924)
COL—Collier's Magazine (selections by Grantland Rice, 1925-47; published American Football Coaches Association teams, 1948-56, listed under FC)
CP—Central Press
FBW—Football World Magazine
FC—American Football Coaches Association (published in Saturday Evening Post Magazine, 1945-47; in Collier's Magazine, 1948-56; sponsored by General Mills in 1957-59 and by Eastman Kodak from 1960-93)
FN—Football News
FW—Football Writers Association of America (published in Look Magazine, 1946-70)
INS—International News Service (merged with United Press in 1958 to form UPI)
L—Look Magazine (published Football Writers Association of America teams, 1946-70, listed under FW)
LIB—Liberty Magazine
M—Frank Menke Syndicate
N—Newsweek
NA—North American Newspaper Alliance
NEA—Newspaper Enterprise Association
SN—Sporting News
UP—United Press (merged with International News Service in 1958 to form UPI)
UPI—United Press International
W—Caspar Whitney (published in The Week's Sport in association with Walter Camp, 1889-90; published in Harper's Weekly, 1891-96, and in Outing Magazine, which he owned, 1898-1908; Walter Camp substituted for Whitney, who was on a world sports tour, and selected Harper's Weekly's team for 1897)
WCF—Walter Camp Foundation

All-America Selections

Listed on the following pages are the consensus all-Americans (i.e., the players who were accorded a majority of votes at their positions by the selectors). Included are the selections of 1889-97, 1909-12 and 1921-22 when there was only one selector.

1889
E—Amos Alonzo Stagg, Yale; Arthur Cumnock, Harvard; T—Hector Cowan, Princeton; Charles Gill, Yale; G—Pudge Heffelfinger, Yale; John Cranston, Harvard; C—William George, Princeton; B—Edgar Allan Poe, Princeton; Roscoe Channing, Princeton; Knowlton Ames, Princeton; James Lee, Harvard.

1890
E—Frank Hallowell, Harvard; Ralph Warren, Princeton; T—Marshall Newell, Harvard; William Rhodes, Yale; G—Pudge Heffelfinger, Yale; Jesse Riggs, Princeton; C—John Cranston, Harvard; B—Thomas McClung, Yale; Sheppard Homans, Princeton; Dudley Dean, Harvard; John Corbett, Harvard.

1891
E—Frank Hinkey, Yale; John Hartwell, Yale; T—Wallace Winter, Yale; Marshall Newell, Harvard; G—Pudge Heffelfinger, Yale; Jesse Riggs, Princeton; C—John Adams, Pennsylvania; B—Philip King, Princeton; Everett Lake, Harvard; Thomas McClung, Yale; Sheppard Homans, Princeton.

1892
E—Frank Hinkey, Yale; Frank Hallowell, Harvard; T—Marshall Newell, Harvard; A. Hamilton Wallis, Yale; G—Arthur Wheeler, Princeton; Bertram Waters, Harvard; C—William Lewis, Harvard; B—Charles Brewer, Harvard; Vance McCormick, Yale; Philip King, Princeton; Harry Thayer, Pennsylvania.

1893
E—Frank Hinkey, Yale; Thomas Trenchard, Princeton; T—Langdon Lea, Princeton; Marshall Newell, Harvard; G—Arthur Wheeler, Princeton; William Hickok, Yale; C—William Lewis, Harvard; B—Philip King, Princeton; Charles Brewer, Harvard; Franklin Morse, Princeton; Frank Butterworth, Yale.

1894
E—Frank Hinkey, Yale; Charles Gelbert, Pennsylvania; T—Bertram Waters, Harvard; Langdon Lea, Princeton; G—Arthur Wheeler, Princeton; William Hickok, Yale; C—Philip Stillman, Yale; B—George Adee, Yale; Arthur Knipe, Pennsylvania; George Brooke, Pennsylvania; Frank Butterworth, Yale.

1895
E—Norman Cabot, Harvard; Charles Gelbert, Pennsylvania; T—Langdon Lea, Princeton; Fred Murphy, Yale; G—Charles Wharton, Pennsylvania; Dudley Riggs, Princeton; C—Alfred Bull, Pennsylvania; B—Clinton Wyckoff, Cornell; Samuel Thorne, Yale; Charles Brewer, Harvard; George Brooke, Pennsylvania.

1896
E—Norman Cabot, Harvard; Charles Gelbert, Pennsylvania; T—William Church, Princeton; Fred Murphy, Yale; G—Charles Wharton, Pennsylvania; Wylie Woodruff, Pennsylvania; C—Robert Gailey, Princeton; B—Clarence Fincke, Yale; Edgar Wrightington, Harvard; Addison Kelly, Princeton; John Baird, Princeton.

1897
E—Garrett Cochran, Princeton; John Hall, Yale; T—Burr Chamberlain, Yale; John Outland, Pennsylvania; G—T. Truxton Hare, Pennsylvania; Gordon Brown, Yale; C—Alan Doucette, Harvard; B—Charles DeSaulles, Yale; Benjamin Dibblee, Harvard; Addison Kelly, Princeton; John Minds, Pennsylvania.

1898
E—Lew Palmer, Princeton; John Hallowell, Harvard; T—Arthur Hillebrand, Princeton; Burr Chamberlain, Yale; G—T. Truxton Hare, Pennsylvania; Gordon Brown, Yale; Walter Boal, Harvard; C—Pete Overfield, Pennsylvania; William Cunningham, Michigan; B—Charles Daly, Harvard; Benjamin Dibblee, Harvard; John Outland, Pennsylvania; Clarence Herschberger, Chicago; Malcolm McBride, Yale; Charles Romeyn, Army.

1899
E—David Campbell, Harvard; Arthur Poe, Princeton; T—Arthur Hillebrand, Princeton; George Stillman, Yale; G—T. Truxton Hare, Pennsylvania; Gordon Brown, Yale; C—Pete Overfield, Pennsylvania; B—Charles Daly, Harvard; Josiah McCracken, Pennsylvania; Malcolm McBride, Yale; Isaac Seneca, Carlisle; Albert Sharpe, Yale; Howard Reiter, Princeton.

1900
E—John Hallowell, Harvard; David Campbell, Harvard; William Smith, Army; T—George Stillman, Yale; James Bloomer, Yale; G—Gordon Brown, Yale; T. Truxton Hare, Pennsylvania; C—Herman Olcott, Yale; Walter Bachman, Lafayette; B—Bill Morley, Columbia; George Chadwick, Yale; Perry Hale, Yale; William Fincke, Yale; Charles Daly, Harvard; Raymond Starbuck, Cornell.

1901
E—David Campbell, Harvard; Ralph Davis, Princeton; Edward Bowditch, Harvard; Neil Snow, Michigan; T—Oliver Cutts, Harvard; Paul Bunker, Army; Crawford Blagden, Harvard; G—William Warner, Cornell; William Lee, Harvard; Charles Barnard, Harvard; Sanford Hunt, Cornell; C—Henry Holt, Yale; Walter Bachman, Lafayette; B—Robert Kernan, Harvard; Charles Daly, Army; Thomas Graydon, Harvard; Harold Weekes, Columbia; Bill Morley, Columbia.

1902
E—Thomas Shevlin, Yale; Edward Bowditch, Harvard; T—Ralph Kinney, Yale; James Hogan, Yale; Paul Bunker, Army; G—Edgar Glass, Yale; John DeWitt, Princeton; William Warner, Cornell; C—Henry Holt, Yale; Robert Boyers, Army; B—Foster Rockwell, Yale; George Chadwick, Yale; Thomas Graydon, Harvard; Thomas Barry, Brown.

1903
E—Howard Henry, Princeton; Charles Rafferty, Yale; T—Daniel Knowlton, Harvard; James Hogan, Yale; Fred Schacht, Minnesota; G—John DeWitt, Princeton; Andrew Marshall, Harvard; James Bloomer, Yale; C—Henry Hooper, Dartmouth; B—Willie Heston, Michigan; J. Dana Kafer, Princeton; James Johnson, Carlisle; Richard Smith, Columbia; Myron Witham, Dartmouth; W. Ledyard Mitchell, Yale.

1904
E—Thomas Shevlin, Yale; Fred Speik, Chicago; T—James Hogan, Yale; James Cooney, Princeton; G—Frank Piekarski, Pennsylvania; Joseph Gilman, Dartmouth; Ralph Kinney, Yale; C—Arthur Tipton, Army; B—Daniel Hurley, Harvard; Walter Eckersall, Chicago; Vincent Stevenson, Pennsylvania; Willie Heston, Michigan; Andrew Smith, Pennsylvania; Foster Rockwell, Yale; Henry Torney, Army.

1905
E—Thomas Shevlin, Yale; Ralph Glaze, Dartmouth; Mark Catlin, Chicago; T—Otis Lamson, Pennsylvania; Beaton Squires, Harvard; Karl Brill, Yale; G—Roswell Tripp, Yale; Francis Burr, Harvard; C—Robert Torrey, Pennsylvania; B—Walter Eckersall, Chicago; Howard Roome, Yale; John Hubbard, Amherst; James McCormick, Princeton; Guy Hutchinson, Yale; Daniel Hurley, Harvard; Henry Torney, Army.

1906
E—Robert Forbes, Yale; L. Casper Wister, Princeton; T—L. Horatio Biglow, Yale; James Cooney, Princeton; Charles Osborne, Harvard; G—Francis Burr, Harvard; Elmer Thompson, Cornell; August Ziegler, Pennsylvania; C—William Dunn, Penn St.; William Newman, Cornell; B—Walter Eckersall, Chicago; Hugh Knox, Yale; Edward Dillon, Princeton; John Mayhew, Brown; William Hollenback, Pennsylvania; Paul Veeder, Yale.

1907
E—Bill Dague, Navy; Clarence Alcott, Yale; Albert Exendine, Carlisle; L. Casper Wister, Princeton; T—Dexter Draper, Pennsylvania; L. Horatio Biglow, Yale; G—August Ziegler, Pennsylvania; William Erwin, Army; C—Adolph Schulz, Michigan; Patrick Grant, Harvard; B—John Wendell, Harvard; Thomas A. D. Jones, Yale; Edwin Harlan, Princeton; James McCormick, Harvard; Edward Coy, Yale; Peter Hauser, Carlisle.

1908
E—Hunter Scarlett, Pennsylvania; George Schildmiller, Dartmouth; T—Hamilton Fish, Harvard; Frank Horr, Syracuse; Percy Northcroft, Navy; G—Clark Tobin, Dartmouth; William Goebel, Yale; Hamlin Andrus, Yale; Bernard O'Rourke, Cornell; C—Charles Nourse, Harvard; B—Edward Coy, Yale; Frederick Tibbott, Princeton; William Hollenback, Pennsylvania; Walter Steffen, Chicago; Ed Lange, Navy; Hamilton Corbett, Harvard.

1909
E—Adrian Regnier, Brown; John Kilpatrick, Yale; T—Hamilton Fish, Harvard; Henry Hobbs, Yale; G—Albert Benbrook, Michigan; Hamlin Andrus, Yale; C—Carroll Cooney, Yale; B—Edward Coy, Yale; John McGovern, Minnesota; Stephen Philbin, Yale; Wayland Minot, Harvard.

1910
E—John Kilpatrick, Yale; Stanfield Wells, Michigan; T—Robert McKay, Harvard; James Walker, Minnesota; G—Robert Fisher, Harvard; Albert Benbrook, Michigan; C—Ernest Cozens, Pennsylvania; B—E. LeRoy Mercer, Pennsylvania; Percy Wendell, Harvard; Earl Sprackling, Brown; Talbot Pendleton, Princeton.

1911
E—Douglass Bomeisler, Yale; Sanford White, Princeton; T—Edward Hart, Princeton; Leland Devore, Army; G—Robert Fisher, Harvard; Joseph Duff, Princeton; C—Henry Ketcham, Yale; B—Jim Thorpe, Carlisle; Percy Wendell, Harvard; Arthur Howe, Yale; Jack Dalton, Navy.

1912
E—Samuel Felton, Harvard; Douglass Bomeisler, Yale; T—Wesley Englehorn, Dartmouth; Robert Butler, Wisconsin; G—Stanley Pennock, Harvard; John Logan, Princeton; C—Henry Ketcham, Yale; B—Charles Brickley, Harvard; Jim Thorpe, Carlisle; George Crowther, Brown; E. LeRoy Mercer, Pennsylvania.

1913
E—Robert Hogsett, Dartmouth; Louis Merrillat, Army; T—Harold Ballin, Princeton; Nelson Talbott, Yale; Miller Pontius, Michigan; Harvey Hitchcock, Harvard; G—John Brown, Navy; Stanley Pennock, Harvard; Ray Keeler, Wisconsin; C—Paul Des Jardien, Chicago; B—Charles Brickley, Harvard; Edward Mahan, Harvard; Jim Craig, Michigan; Ellery Huntington, Colgate; Gus Dorais, Notre Dame.

1914
E—Huntington Hardwick, Harvard; John O'Hearn, Cornell; Perry Graves, Illinois; T—Harold Ballin, Princeton; Walter Trumbull, Harvard; G—Stanley Pennock, Harvard; Ralph Chapman, Illinois; Clarence Spears, Dartmouth; C—John McEwan, Army; B—John Maulbetsch, Michigan; Edward Mahan, Harvard; Charles Barrett, Cornell; John Spiegel, Wash. & Jeff.; Harry LeGore, Yale.

1915
E—Murray Shelton, Cornell; Guy Chamberlin, Nebraska; T—Joseph Gilman, Harvard; Howard Buck, Wisconsin; G—Clarence Spears, Dartmouth; Harold White, Syracuse; C—Robert Peck, Pittsburgh; B—Charles Barrett, Cornell; Edward Mahan, Harvard; Richard King, Harvard; Bart Macomber, Illinois; Eugene Mayer, Virginia; Neno Jerry DaPrato, Michigan St.

1916
E—Bert Baston, Minnesota; James Herron, Pittsburgh; T—Clarence Horning, Colgate; D. Belford West, Colgate; G—Clinton Black, Yale; Harrie Dadmun, Harvard; Frank Hogg, Princeton; C—Robert Peck, Pittsburgh; B—Elmer Oliphant, Army; Oscar Anderson, Colgate; Fritz Pollard, Brown; Charles Harley, Ohio St.

1917
E—Charles Bolen, Ohio St.; Paul Robeson, Rutgers; Henry Miller, Pennsylvania; T—Alfred Cobb, Syracuse; George Hauser, Minnesota; G—Dale Seis, Pittsburgh; John Sutherland, Pittsburgh; Eugene Neely, Dartmouth; C—Frank Rydzewski, Notre Dame; B—Elmer Oliphant, Army; Ben Boynton, Williams; Everett Strupper, Georgia Tech; Charles Harley, Ohio St.

1918
E—Paul Robeson, Rutgers; Bill Fincher, Georgia Tech; T—Wilbur Henry, Wash. & Jeff.; Leonard Hilty, Pittsburgh; Lou Usher, Syracuse; Joe Guyon, Georgia Tech; G—Joe Alexander, Syracuse; Lyman Perry, Navy; C—Ashel Day, Georgia Tech; John Depler, Illinois; B—Frank Murrey, Princeton; Tom Davies, Pittsburgh; Wolcott Roberts, Navy; George McLaren, Pittsburgh.

1919
E—Bob Higgins, Penn St.; Henry Miller, Pennsylvania; Lester Belding, Iowa; T—Wilbur Henry, Wash. & Jeff.; D. Belford West, Colgate; G—Joe Alexander, Syracuse; Adolph Youngstrom, Dartmouth; C—James Weaver, Centre; Charles Carpenter, Wisconsin; B—Charles Harley, Ohio State; Ira Rodgers, West Virginia; Edward Casey, Harvard; Bo McMillin, Centre; Ben Boynton, Williams.

1920
E—Luke Urban, Boston College; Charles Carney, Illinois; Bill Fincher, Georgia Tech; T—Stan Keck, Princeton; Ralph Scott, Wisconsin; G—Tim Callahan, Yale; Tom Woods, Harvard; Iolas Huffman, Ohio St.; C—Herb Stein, Pittsburgh; B—George Gipp, Notre Dame; Donold Lourie, Princeton; Gaylord Stinchcomb, Ohio St.; Charles Way, Penn St.

1921
E—Brick Muller, California; Eddie Anderson, Notre Dame; T—Dan McMillan, California; Iolas Huffman, Ohio St.; G—Frank Schwab, Lafayette; John Brown, Harvard; Stan Keck, Princeton; C—Herb Stein, Pittsburgh; B—Aubrey Devine, Iowa; Glenn Killinger, Penn St.; Bo McMillin, Centre; Malcolm Aldrich, Yale; Edgar Kaw, Cornell.

1922
E—Brick Muller, California; Wendell Taylor, Navy; T—C. Herbert Treat, Princeton; John Thurman, Pennsylvania; G—Frank Schwab, Lafayette; Charles Hubbard, Harvard; C—Ed Garbisch, Army; B—Harry Kipke, Michigan; Gordon Locke, Iowa; John Thomas, Chicago; Edgar Kaw, Cornell.

1923
E—Pete McRae, Syracuse; Ray Ecklund, Minnesota; Lynn Bomar, Vanderbilt; T—Century Milstead, Yale; Marty Below, Wisconsin; G—Charles Hubbard, Harvard; James McMillen, Illinois; C—Jack Blott, Michigan; B—George Pfann, Cornell; Red Grange, Illinois; William Mallory, Yale; Harry Wilson, Penn St.

Beginning in 1924, unanimous selections are indicated by (*).

1924
E—Jim Lawson, Stanford, 5-11, 190, Long Beach, Calif.; (tie) E—Dick Luman, Yale, 6-1, 176, Pinedale, Wyo.; E—Henry Wakefield, Vanderbilt, 5-10, 160, Petersburg, Tenn.; T—Ed McGinley, Pennsylvania, 5-11, 185, Swarthmore, Pa.; T—Ed Weir, Nebraska, 6-1, 194, Superior, Neb.; G—Joe Pondelik, Chicago, 5-11, 215, Cicero, Ill.; G—Carl Diehl, Dartmouth, 6-1, 205, Chicago, Ill.; C—Edwin Horrell, California, 5-11, 185, Pasadena, Calif.; B—*Red Grange, Illinois, 5-10, 170, Wheaton, Ill.; B—Harry Stuhldreher, Notre Dame, 5-7, 151, Massillon, Ohio; B—Jimmy Crowley, Notre Dame, 5-11, 162, Green Bay, Wis.; B—Elmer Layden, Notre Dame, 6-0, 162, Davenport, Iowa.

1925
E—Bennie Oosterbaan, Michigan, 6-0, 180, Muskegon, Mich.; E—George Tully, Dartmouth, 5-10, 175, Orange, N.J.; T—Ed Weir, Nebraska, 6-1, 194, Superior, Neb.; T—Ralph Chase, Pittsburgh, 6-3, 202, Easton, Pa.; G—Carl Diehl, Dartmouth, 6-1, 205, Chicago, Ill.; G—Ed Hess, Ohio St., 6-1, 190, Cincinnati, Ohio; C—Ed McMillan, Princeton, 6-0, 208, Pittsburgh, Pa.; B—*Andy Oberlander, Dartmouth, 6-0, 197, Everett, Mass.; B—Red Grange, Illinois, 5-10, 170, Wheaton, Ill.; B—Ernie Nevers, Stanford, 6-0, 200, Superior, Wis.; (tie) B—Benny Friedman, Michigan, 5-8, 170, Cleveland, Ohio; B—George Wilson, Washington, 5-11, 190, Everett, Wash.

1926
E—Bennie Oosterbaan, Michigan, 6-0, 186, Muskegon, Mich.; E—Vic Hanson, Syracuse, 5-10, 174, Syracuse, N.Y.; T—Frank Wickhorst, Navy, 6-0, 218, Oak Park, Ill.; T—Bud Sprague, Army, 6-2, 210, Dallas, Texas; G—Harry Connaughton, Georgetown, 6-2, 275, Philadelphia, Pa.; G—Bernie Shively, Illinois, 6-4, 208, Oliver, Ill.; C—Bud Boeringer, Notre Dame, 6-1, 186, St. Paul, Minn.; B—Benny Friedman, Michigan, 5-8, 172, Cleveland, Ohio; B—Mort Kaer, Southern California, 5-11, 167, Red Bluff, Calif.; B—Ralph Baker, Northwestern, 5-10, 172, Rockford, Ill.; B—Herb Joesting, Minnesota, 6-1, 192, Owatonna, Minn.

1927
E—*Bennie Oosterbaan, Michigan, 6-0, 186, Muskegon, Mich.; E—Tom Nash, Georgia, 6-3, 200, Washington, Ga.; T—Jesse Hibbs, Southern California, 5-11, 185, Glendale, Calif.; T—Ed Hake, Pennsylvania, 6-0, 190, Philadelphia, Pa.; G—Bill Webster, Yale, 6-0, 200, Shelton, Conn.; G—John Smith, Notre Dame, 5-9, 164, Hartford, Conn.; (tie) C—Larry Bettencourt, St. Mary's (Cal.), 5-10, 187, Centerville, Calif.; C—John Charlesworth, Yale, 5-11, 198, North Adams, Mass.; B—*Gibby Welch, Pittsburgh, 5-11, 170, Parkersburg, W. Va.; B—Morley Drury, Southern California, 6-0, 185, Long Beach, Calif.; B—Red Cagle, Army, 5-9, 167, Merryville, La.; B—Herb Joesting, Minnesota, 6-1, 192, Owatonna, Minn.

1928
E—Irv Phillips, California, 6-1, 188, Salinas, Calif.; E—Wes Fesler, Ohio St., 6-0, 173, Youngstown, Ohio; T—Otto Pommerening, Michigan, 6-0, 178, Ann Arbor, Mich.; T—Mike Getto, Pittsburgh, 6-2, 198, Jeannette, Pa.; G—Seraphim Post, Stanford, 6-0, 190, Berkeley, Calif.; (tie) G—Don Robesky, Stanford, 5-11, 198, Bakersfield, Calif.; G—Edward Burke, Navy, 6-0, 180, Larksville, Pa.; C—Pete Pund, Georgia Tech, 6-0, 195, Augusta, Ga.; B—*Red Cagle, Army, 5-9, 167, Merryville, La.; B—Paul Scull, Pennsylvania, 5-8, 187, Bala, Pa.; B—(tie) Ken Strong, New York U., 6-0, 201, West Haven, Conn.; Howard Harpster, Carnegie Mellon, 6-1, 160, Akron, Ohio; B—Charles Carroll, Washington, 6-0, 190, Seattle, Wash.

1929
E—*Joe Donchess, Pittsburgh, 6-0, 175, Youngstown, Ohio; E—Wes Fesler, Ohio St., 6-0, 183, Youngstown, Ohio; T—Bronko Nagurski, Minnesota, 6-2, 217, International Falls, Minn.; T—Elmer Sleight, Purdue, 6-2, 193, Morris, Ill.; G—Jack Cannon, Notre Dame, 5-11, 193, Columbus, Ohio; G—Ray Montgomery, Pittsburgh, 6-1, 188, Wheeling, W.Va.; C—Ben Ticknor, Harvard, 6-2, 193, New York, N.Y.; B—*Frank Carideo, Notre Dame, 5-7, 175, Mount Vernon, N.Y.; B—Ralph Welch, Purdue, 6-1, 189, Whitesboro, Texas; B—Red Cagle, Army, 5-9, 167, Merryville, La.; B—Gene McEver, Tennessee, 5-10, 185, Bristol, Va.

1930
E—*Wes Fesler, Ohio St., 6-0, 185, Youngstown, Ohio; E—Frank Baker, Northwestern, 6-2, 175, Cedar Rapids, Iowa; T—*Fred Sington, Alabama, 6-2, 215, Birmingham, Ala.; T—Milo Lubratovich, Wisconsin, 6-2, 216, Duluth, Minn.; G—Ted Beckett, California, 6-1, 190, Oroville, Calif.; G—Barton Koch, Baylor, 5-10, 195, Temple, Texas; C—*Ben Ticknor, Harvard, 6-2, 193, New York, N.Y.; B—*Frank Carideo, Notre Dame, 5-7, 175, Mount Vernon, N.Y.; B—Marchy Schwartz, Notre Dame, 5-11, 172, Bay St. Louis, Miss.; B—Erny Pinckert, Southern California, 6-0, 189, San Bernardino, Calif.; B—Leonard Macaluso, Colgate, 6-2, 210, East Aurora, N.Y.

1931
E—*Jerry Dalrymple, Tulane, 5-10, 175, Arkadelphia, Ark.; E—Vernon Smith, Georgia, 6-2, 190, Macon, Ga.; T—Jesse Quatse, Pittsburgh, 5-8, 198, Greensburg, Pa.; (tie) T—Jack Riley, Northwestern, 6-2, 218, Wilmette, Ill.; T—Dallas Marvil, Northwestern, 6-3, 227, Laurel, Del.; G—Biggie Munn, Minnesota, 6-0, 217, Minneapolis, Minn.; G—John Baker, Southern California, 6-0, 185, Kingsburg, Calif.; C—Tommy Yarr, Notre Dame, 5-11, 197, Chimacum, Wash.; B—Gus Shaver, Southern California, 5-11, 185, Covina, Calif.; B—Marchy Schwartz, Notre Dame, 5-11, 178, Bay St. Louis, Miss.; B—Pug Rentner, Northwestern, 6-1, 185, Joliet, Ill.; B—Barry Wood, Harvard, 6-1, 173, Milton, Mass.

1932
E—*Paul Moss, Purdue, 6-2, 185, Terre Haute, Ind.; E—Joe Skladany, Pittsburgh, 5-10, 185, Larksville, Pa.; T—*Joe Kurth, Notre Dame, 6-2, 204, Madison, Wis.; T—*Ernie Smith, Southern California, 6-2, 215, Los Angeles, Calif.; G—Milt Summerfelt, Army, 6-0, 181, Benton Harbor, Mich.; G—Bill Corbus, Stanford, 5-11, 188, Vallejo, Calif.; C—Pete Gracey, Vanderbilt, 6-0, 188, Franklin, Tenn.; B—*Harry Newman, Michigan, 5-7, 175, Detroit, Mich.; B—*Warren Heller, Pittsburgh, 6-0, 170, Steelton, Pa.; B—Don Zimmerman, Tulane, 5-10, 190, Lake Charles, La.; B—Jimmy Hitchcock, Auburn, 5-11, 172, Union Springs, Ala.

1933
E—Joe Skladany, Pittsburgh, 5-10, 190, Larksville, Pa.; E—Paul Geisler, Centenary (La.), 6-2, 189, Berwick, La.; T—Fred Crawford, Duke, 6-2, 195, Waynesville, N.C.; T—Francis Wistert, Michigan, 6-2, 212, Chicago, Ill.; G—Bill Corbus, Stanford, 5-11, 195, Vallejo, Calif.; G—Aaron Rosenberg, Southern California, 6-0, 210, Los Angeles, Calif.; C—*Chuck Bernard, Michigan, 6-2, 215, Benton Harbor, Mich.; B—*Cotton Warburton, Southern California, 5-7, 147, San Diego, Calif.; B—George Sauer, Nebraska, 6-2, 195, Lincoln, Neb.; B—Beattie Feathers, Tennessee, 5-10, 180, Bristol, Va.; B—Duane Purvis, Purdue, 6-1, 190, Mattoon, Ill.

1934
E—Don Hutson, Alabama, 6-1, 185, Pine Bluff, Ark.; E—Frank Larson, Minnesota, 6-3, 190, Duluth, Minn.; T—Bill Lee, Alabama, 6-2, 225, Eutaw, Ala.; T—Bob Reynolds, Stanford, 6-4, 220, Okmulgee, Okla.; G—Chuck Hartwig, Pittsburgh, 6-0, 190, Benwood, W.Va.; G—Bill Bevan, Minnesota, 5-11, 194, St. Paul, Minn.; C—Jack Robinson, Notre Dame, 6-3, 195, Huntington, N.Y.; B—Bobby Grayson, Stanford, 5-11, 186, Portland, Ore.; B—Pug Lund, Minnesota, 5-11, 185, Rice Lake, Wis.; B—Dixie Howell, Alabama, 5-10, 164, Hartford, Ala.; B—Fred Borries, Navy, 6-0, 175, Louisville, Ky.

1935
E—Wayne Millner, Notre Dame, 6-0, 184, Salem, Mass.; (tie) E—James Moscrip, Stanford, 6-0, 186, Adena, Ohio; E—Gaynell Tinsley, LSU, 6-0, 188, Homer, La.; T—Ed Widseth, Minnesota, 6-2, 220, McIntosh, Minn.; T—Larry Lutz, California, 6-0, 201, Santa Ana, Calif.; G—John Weller, Princeton, 6-0, 195, Wynnewood, Pa.; (tie) G—Sidney Wagner, Michigan St., 5-11, 186, Lansing, Mich.; G—J. C. Wetsel, Southern Methodist, 5-10, 185, Dallas, Texas; (tie) C—Gomer Jones, Ohio St., 5-8, 210, Cleveland, Ohio; C—Darrell Lester, TCU, 6-4, 218, Jacksboro, Texas; B—*Jay Berwanger, Chicago, 6-0, 195, Dubuque, Iowa; B—*Bobby Grayson, Stanford, 5-11, 190, Portland, Ore.; B—Bobby Wilson, Southern Methodist, 5-10, 147, Corsicana, Texas; B—Riley Smith, Alabama, 6-1, 195, Columbus, Miss.

1936
E—*Larry Kelley, Yale, 6-1, 190, Williamsport, Pa.; E—*Gaynell Tinsley, LSU, 6-0, 196, Homer, La.; T—*Ed Widseth, Minnesota, 6-2, 220, McIntosh, Minn.; T—Averell Daniell, Pittsburgh, 6-3, 200, Mt. Lebanon, Pa.; G—Steve Reid, Northwestern, 5-9, 192, Chicago, Ill.; G—Max Starcevich, Washington, 5-10, 198, Duluth, Minn.; (tie) C—Alex Wojciechowicz, Fordham, 6-0, 192, South River, N.J.; C—Mike Basrak, Duquesne, 6-1, 210, Bellaire, Ohio; B—Sammy Baugh, TCU, 6-2, 180, Sweetwater, Texas; B—Ace Parker, Duke, 5-11, 175, Portsmouth, Va.; B—Ray Buivid, Marquette, 6-1, 193, Port Washington, Wis.; B—Sam Francis, Nebraska, 6-1, 207, Oberlin, Kan.

1937
E—Chuck Sweeney, Notre Dame, 6-0, 190, Bloomington, Ill.; E—Andy Bershak, North Carolina, 6-0, 190, Clairton, Pa.; T—Ed Franco, Fordham, 5-8, 196, Jersey City, N.J.; T—Tony Matisi, Pittsburgh, 6-0, 224, Endicott, N.Y.; G—Joe Routt, Texas A&M, 6-0, 193, Chappel Hill, Texas; G—Leroy Monsky, Alabama, 6-0, 198, Montgomery, Ala.; C—Alex Wojciechowicz, Fordham, 6-0, 196, South River, N.J.; B—*Clint Frank, Yale, 5-10, 190, Evanston, Ill.; B—Marshall Goldberg, Pittsburgh, 5-11, 185, Elkins, W.Va.; B—Byron "Whizzer" White, Colorado, 6-1, 185, Wellington, Colo.; B—Sam Chapman, California, 6-0, 190, Tiburon, Calif.

1938
E—Waddy Young, Oklahoma, 6-2, 203, Ponca City, Okla.; (tie) E—Brud Holland, Cornell, 6-1, 205, Auburn, N.Y.; E—Bowden Wyatt, Tennessee, 6-1, 190, Kingston, Tenn.; T—*Ed Beinor, Notre Dame, 6-2, 207, Harvey, Ill.; T—Alvord Wolff, Santa Clara, 6-2, 220, San Francisco, Calif.; G—*Ralph Heikkinen, Michigan, 5-10, 185, Ramsey, Mich.; G—Ed Bock, Iowa St., 6-0, 202, Fort Dodge, Iowa; C—Ki Aldrich, TCU, 5-11, 195, Temple, Texas; B—*Davey O'Brien, TCU, 5-7, 150, Dallas, Texas; B—*Marshall Goldberg, Pittsburgh, 6-0, 190, Elkins, W.Va.; B—Bob MacLeod, Dartmouth, 6-0, 190, Glen Ellyn, Ill.; B—Vic Bottari, California, 5-9, 182, Vallejo, Calif.

1939
E—Esco Sarkkinen, Ohio St., 6-0, 192, Fairport Harbor, Ohio; E—Ken Kavanaugh, LSU, 6-3, 203, Little Rock, Ark.; T—Nick Drahos, Cornell, 6-3, 200, Cedarhurst, N.Y.; T—Harley McCollum, Tulane, 6-4, 235, Wagoner, Okla.; G—*Harry Smith, Southern California, 5-11, 218, Ontario, Calif.; G—Ed Molinski, Tennessee, 5-10, 190, Massillon, Ohio; C—John Schiechl, Santa Clara, 6-2,

220, San Francisco, Calif.; B—Nile Kinnick, Iowa, 5-8, 167, Omaha, Neb.; B—Tom Harmon, Michigan, 6-0, 195, Gary, Ind.; B—John Kimbrough, Texas A&M, 6-2, 210, Haskell, Texas; B—George Cafego, Tennessee, 6-0, 174, Scarbro, W.Va.

1940

E—Gene Goodreault, Boston College, 5-10, 184, Haverhill, Mass.; E—Dave Rankin, Purdue, 6-1, 190, Warsaw, Ind.; T—Nick Drahos, Cornell, 6-3, 212, Cedarhurst, N.Y.; (tie) T—Alf Bauman, Northwestern, 6-1, 210, Chicago, Ill.; T—Urban Odson, Minnesota, 6-3, 247, Clark, S.D.; G—*Bob Suffridge, Tennessee, 6-0, 190, Knoxville, Tenn.; G—Marshall Robnett, Texas A&M, 6-1, 205, Klondike, Texas; C—Rudy Mucha, Washington, 6-2, 210, Chicago, Ill.; B—*Tom Harmon, Michigan, 6-0, 195, Gary, Ind.; B—*John Kimbrough, Texas A&M, 6-2, 221, Haskell, Texas; B—Frank Albert, Stanford, 5-9, 170, Glendale, Calif.; B—George Franck, Minnesota, 6-0, 175, Davenport, Iowa.

1941

E—Holt Rast, Alabama, 6-1, 185, Birmingham, Ala.; E—Bob Dove, Notre Dame, 6-2, 195, Youngstown, Ohio; T—Dick Wildung, Minnesota, 6-0, 210, Luverne, Minn.; T—Ernie Blandin, Tulane, 6-3, 245, Keighley, Kan.; G—*Endicott Peabody, Harvard, 6-0, 181, Syracuse, N.Y.; G—Ray Frankowski, Washington, 5-10, 210, Hammond, Ind.; C—Darold Jenkins, Missouri, 6-0, 195, Higginsville, Mo.; B—Bob Westfall, Michigan, 5-8, 190, Ann Arbor, Mich.; B—Bruce Smith, Minnesota, 6-0, 193, Faribault, Minn.; B—Frank Albert, Stanford, 5-9, 173, Glendale, Calif.; (tie) B—Bill Dudley, Virginia, 5-10, 175, Bluefield, Va.; B—Frank Sinkwich, Georgia, 5-8, 180, Youngstown, Ohio.

1942

E—*Dave Schreiner, Wisconsin, 6-2, 198, Lancaster, Wis.; E—Bob Dove, Notre Dame, 6-2, 195, Youngstown, Ohio; T—Dick Wildung, Minnesota, 6-0, 215, Luverne, Minn.; T—Albert Wistert, Michigan, 6-2, 205, Chicago, Ill.; G—Chuck Taylor, Stanford, 5-11, 200, San Jose, Calif.; (tie) G—Harvey Hardy, Georgia Tech, 5-10, 185, Thomaston, Ga.; G—Julie Franks, Michigan, 6-0, 187, Hamtramck, Mich.; C—Joe Domnanovich, Alabama, 6-1, 200, South Bend, Ind.; B—*Frank Sinkwich, Georgia, 5-8, 185, Youngstown, Ohio; B—Paul Governali, Columbia, 5-11, 186, New York, N.Y.; B—Mike Holovak, Boston College, 6-2, 214, Lansford, Pa.; B—Billy Hillenbrand, Indiana, 6-0, 195, Evansville, Ind.

1943

E—Ralph Heywood, Southern California, 6-2, 195, Huntington Park, Calif.; E—John Yonakor, Notre Dame, 6-4, 220, Dorchester, Mass.; T—Jim White, Notre Dame, 6-2, 210, Edgewater, N.J.; T—Don Whitmire, Navy, 5-11, 215, Decatur, Ala.; G—Alex Agase, Purdue, 5-10, 190, Evanston, Ill.; G—Pat Filley, Notre Dame, 5-8, 175, South Bend, Ind.; C—*Casimir Myslinski, Army, 5-11, 186, Steubenville, Ohio; B—*Bill Daley, Michigan, 6-2, 206, St. Cloud, Minn.; B—Angelo Bertelli, Notre Dame, 6-1, 173, West Springfield, Mass.; B—Creighton Miller, Notre Dame, 6-0, 185, Wilmington, Del.; B—Bob Odell, Pennsylvania, 5-11, 182, Sioux City, Iowa.

1944

E—Phil Tinsley, Georgia Tech, 6-1, 188, Bessemer, Ala.; (tie) E—Paul Walker, Yale, 6-3, 203, Oak Park, Ill.; E—Jack Dugger, Ohio St., 6-3, 210, Canton, Ohio; T—*Don Whitmire, Navy, 5-11, 215, Decatur, Ala.; T—John Ferraro, Southern California, 6-3, 235, Maywood, Calif.; G—Bill Hackett, Ohio St., 5-9, 191, London, Ohio; G—Ben Chase, Navy, 6-1, 195, San Diego, Calif.; C—John Tavener, Indiana, 6-0, 220, Granville, Ohio; B—*Les Horvath, Ohio St., 5-10, 167, Parma, Ohio; B—Glenn Davis, Army, 5-9, 170, Claremont, Calif.; B—Doc Blanchard, Army, 6-0, 205, Bishopville, S.C.; B—Bob Jenkins, Navy, 6-1, 195, Talladega, Ala.

1945

E—Dick Duden, Navy, 6-2, 203, New York, N.Y.; (tie) E—Hubert Bechtol, Texas, 6-2, 190, Lubbock, Texas; E—Bob Ravensberg, Indiana, 6-1, 180, Bellevue, Ky.; E—Max Morris, Northwestern, 6-2, 195, West Frankfort, Ill.; T—Tex Coulter, Army, 6-3, 220, Fort Worth, Texas; T—George Savitsky, Pennsylvania, 6-3, 250, Camden, N.J.; G—*Warren Amling, Ohio St., 6-0, 197, Pana, Ill.; G—John Green, Army, 5-11, 190, Shelbyville, Ky.; C—Vaughn Mancha, Alabama, 6-0, 235, Birmingham, Ala.; B—*Glenn Davis, Army, 5-9, 170, Claremont, Calif.; B—*Doc Blanchard, Army, 6-0, 205, Bishopville, S.C.; B—*Herman Wedemeyer, St. Mary's (Cal.), 5-10, 173,

Honolulu, Hawaii; B—Bob Fenimore, Oklahoma St., 6-2, 188, Woodward, Okla.

1946

E—*Burr Baldwin, UCLA, 6-1, 196, Bakersfield, Calif.; E—(tie) Hubert Bechtol, Texas, 6-2, 201, Lubbock, Texas; Hank Foldberg, Army, 6-1, 200, Dallas, Texas; T—George Connor, Notre Dame, 6-3, 225, Chicago, Ill.; (tie) T—Warren Amling, Ohio St., 6-0, 197, Pana, Ill.; T—Dick Huffman, Tennessee, 6-2, 230, Charleston, W.Va.; G—Alex Agase, Illinois, 5-10, 191, Evanston, Ill.; G—Weldon Humble, Rice, 6-1, 214, San Antonio, Texas; C—Paul Duke, Georgia Tech, 6-1, 210, Atlanta, Ga.; B—*John Lujack, Notre Dame, 6-0, 180, Connellsville, Pa.; B—*Charley Trippi, Georgia, 5-11, 185, Pittston, Pa.; B—*Glenn Davis, Army, 5-9, 170, Claremont, Calif.; B—*Doc Blanchard, Army, 6-0, 205, Bishopville, S.C.

1947

E—Paul Cleary, Southern California, 6-1, 195, Santa Ana, Calif.; E—Bill Swiacki, Columbia, 6-2, 198, Southbridge, Mass.; T—Bob Davis, Georgia Tech, 6-4, 220, Columbus, Ga.; T—George Connor, Notre Dame, 6-3, 225, Chicago, Ill.; G—Joe Steffy, Army, 5-11, 190, Chattanooga, Tenn.; G—Bill Fischer, Notre Dame, 6-2, 230, Chicago, Ill.; C—Chuck Bednarik, Pennsylvania, 6-3, 220, Bethlehem, Pa.; B—*John Lujack, Notre Dame, 6-0, 180, Connellsville, Pa.; B—*Bob Chappuis, Michigan, 6-0, 180, Toledo, Ohio; B—Doak Walker, Southern Methodist, 5-11, 170, Dallas, Texas; (tie) B—Charley Conerly, Mississippi, 6-0, 184, Clarksdale, Miss.; B—Bobby Layne, Texas, 6-0, 191, Dallas, Texas.

1948

E—Dick Rifenburg, Michigan, 6-3, 197, Saginaw, Mich.; E—Leon Hart, Notre Dame, 6-4, 225, Turtle Creek, Pa.; T—Leo Nomellini, Minnesota, 6-2, 248, Chicago, Ill.; T—Alvin Wistert, Michigan, 6-3, 218, Chicago, Ill.; G—Buddy Burris, Oklahoma, 5-11, 214, Muskogee, Okla.; G—Bill Fischer, Notre Dame, 6-2, 233, Chicago, Ill.; C—Chuck Bednarik, Pennsylvania, 6-3, 220, Bethlehem, Pa.; B—*Doak Walker, Southern Methodist, 5-11, 168, Dallas, Texas; B—Charlie Justice, North Carolina, 5-10, 165, Asheville, N.C.; B—Jackie Jensen, California, 5-11, 195, Oakland, Calif.; (tie) B—Emil Sitko, Notre Dame, 5-8, 180, Fort Wayne, Ind.; B—Clyde Scott, Arkansas, 6-0, 175, Smackover, Ark.

1949

E—*Leon Hart, Notre Dame, 6-5, 260, Turtle Creek, Pa.; E—James Williams, Rice, 6-0, 197, Waco, Texas; T—Leo Nomellini, Minnesota, 6-2, 255, Chicago, Ill.; T—Alvin Wistert, Michigan, 6-3, 223, Chicago, Ill.; G—*Rod Franz, California, 6-1, 198, San Francisco, Calif.; G—Ed Bagdon, Michigan St., 5-10, 200, Dearborn, Mich.; C—*Clayton Tonnemaker, Minnesota, 6-3, 240, Minneapolis, Minn.; B—*Emil Sitko, Notre Dame, 5-8, 180, Fort Wayne, Ind.; B—Doak Walker, Southern Methodist, 5-11, 170, Dallas, Texas; B—Arnold Galiffa, Army, 6-2, 190, Donora, Pa.; B—Bob Williams, Notre Dame, 6-1, 180, Baltimore, Md.

1950

E—*Dan Foldberg, Army, 6-1, 185, Dallas, Texas; E—Bill McColl, Stanford, 6-4, 225, San Diego, Calif.; T—Bob Gain, Kentucky, 6-3, 230, Weirton, W.Va.; T—Jim Weatherall, Oklahoma, 6-4, 220, White Deer, Texas; G—Bud McFadin, Texas, 6-3, 225, Iraan, Texas; G—Les Richter, California, 6-2, 220, Fresno, Calif.; C—Jerry Groom, Notre Dame, 6-3, 215, Des Moines, Iowa; B—*Vic Janowicz, Ohio St., 5-9, 189, Elyria, Ohio; B—Kyle Rote, Southern Methodist, 6-0, 190, San Antonio, Texas; B—Babe Parilli, Kentucky, 6-1, 183, Rochester, Pa.; B—Leon Heath, Oklahoma, 6-1, 195, Hollis, Okla.

1951

E—*Bill McColl, Stanford, 6-4, 225, San Diego, Calif.; E—Bob Carey, Michigan St., 6-5, 215, Charlevoix, Mich.; T—*Don Coleman, Michigan St., 5-10, 185, Flint, Mich.; T—*Jim Weatherall, Oklahoma, 6-4, 230, White Deer, Texas; G—*Bob Ward, Maryland, 5-10, 185, Elizabeth, N.J.; G—Les Richter, California, 6-2, 230, Fresno, Calif.; C—Dick Hightower, Southern Methodist, 6-1, 215, Tyler, Texas; B—*Dick Kazmaier, Princeton, 5-11, 171, Maumee, Ohio; B—*Hank Lauricella, Tennessee, 5-10, 169, New Orleans, La.; B—Babe Parilli, Kentucky, 6-1, 188, Rochester, Pa.; B—Johnny Karras, Illinois, 5-11, 171, Argo, Ill.

1952

E—Frank McPhee, Princeton, 6-3, 203, Youngstown, Ohio; E—Bernie Flowers, Purdue, 6-1, 189, Erie, Pa.; T—

Dick Modzelewski, Maryland, 6-0, 235, West Natrona, Pa.; T—Hal Miller, Georgia Tech, 6-4, 235, Kingsport, Tenn.; G—John Michels, Tennessee, 5-10, 195, Philadelphia, Pa.; G—Elmer Wilhoite, Southern California, 6-2, 216, Winton, Calif.; C—Donn Moomaw, UCLA, 6-4, 220, Santa Ana, Calif.; B—*Jack Scarbath, Maryland, 6-1, 190, Baltimore, Md.; B—*Johnny Lattner, Notre Dame, 6-1, 190, Chicago, Ill.; B—Billy Vessels, Oklahoma, 6-0, 185, Cleveland, Okla.; B—Jim Sears, Southern California, 5-9, 167, Inglewood, Calif.

1953

E—Don Dohoney, Michigan St., 6-1, 193, Ann Arbor, Mich.; E—Carlton Massey, Texas, 6-4, 210, Rockwall, Texas; T—*Stan Jones, Maryland, 6-0, 235, Lemoyne, Pa.; T—Art Hunter, Notre Dame, 6-2, 226, Akron, Ohio; G—J. D. Roberts, Oklahoma, 5-10, 210, Dallas, Texas; G—Crawford Mims, Mississippi, 5-10, 200, Greenwood, Miss.; C—Larry Morris, Georgia Tech, 6-0, 205, Decatur, Ga.; B—*Johnny Lattner, Notre Dame, 6-1, 190, Chicago, Ill.; B—*Paul Giel, Minnesota, 5-11, 185, Winona, Minn.; B—Paul Cameron, UCLA, 6-0, 185, Burbank, Calif.; B—J. C. Caroline, Illinois, 6-0, 184, Columbia, S.C.

1954

E—Max Boydston, Oklahoma, 6-2, 207, Muskogee, Okla.; E—Ron Beagle, Navy, 6-0, 185, Covington, Ky.; T—Jack Ellena, UCLA, 6-3, 214, Susanville, Calif.; T—Sid Fournet, LSU, 5-11, 225, Baton Rouge, La.; G—*Bud Brooks, Arkansas, 5-11, 200, Wynne, Ark.; G—Calvin Jones, Iowa, 6-0, 200, Steubenville, Ohio; C—Kurt Burris, Oklahoma, 6-1, 209, Muskogee, Okla.; B—*Ralph Guglielmi, Notre Dame, 6-0, 185, Columbus, Ohio; B—*Howard Cassady, Ohio St., 5-10, 177, Columbus, Ohio; B—*Alan Ameche, Wisconsin, 6-0, 215, Kenosha, Wis.; B—Dicky Maegle, Rice, 6-0, 175, Taylor, Texas.

1955

E—*Ron Beagle, Navy, 6-0, 186, Covington, Ky.; E—Ron Kramer, Michigan, 6-3, 218, East Detroit, Mich.; T—Norman Masters, Michigan St., 6-2, 225, Detroit, Mich.; T—Bruce Bosley, West Virginia, 6-2, 225, Green Bank, W.Va.; G—Bo Bolinger, Oklahoma, 5-10, 206, Muskogee, Okla.; (tie) G—Calvin Jones, Iowa, 6-0, 220, Steubenville, Ohio; G—Hardiman Cureton, UCLA, 6-0, 213, Duarte, Calif.; C—*Bob Pellegrini, Maryland, 6-2, 225, Yatesboro, Pa.; B—*Howard Cassady, Ohio St., 5-10, 172, Columbus, Ohio; B—*Jim Swink, TCU, 6-1, 180, Rusk, Texas; B—Earl Morrall, Michigan St., 6-1, 180, Muskegon, Mich.; B—Paul Hornung, Notre Dame, 6-2, 205, Louisville, Ky.

1956

E—*Joe Walton, Pittsburgh, 5-11, 205, Beaver Falls, Pa.; E—*Ron Kramer, Michigan, 6-3, 220, East Detroit, Mich.; T—John Witte, Oregon St., 6-2, 232, Klamath Falls, Ore.; T—Lou Michaels, Kentucky, 6-2, 229, Swoyersville, Pa.; G—*Jim Parker, Ohio St., 6-2, 251, Toledo, Ohio; C—*Bill Glass, Baylor, 6-4, 220, Corpus Christi, Texas; C—*Jerry Tubbs, Oklahoma, 6-2, 205, Breckenridge, Texas; B—*Jim Brown, Syracuse, 6-2, 212, Manhasset, N.Y.; B—*John Majors, Tennessee, 5-10, 162, Huntland, Tenn.; B—Tommy McDonald, Oklahoma, 5-9, 169, Albuquerque, N.M.; B—John Brodie, Stanford, 6-1, 190, Oakland, Calif.

1957

E—*Jimmy Phillips, Auburn, 6-2, 205, Alexander City, Ala.; E—Dick Wallen, UCLA, 6-0, 185, Alhambra, Calif.; T—Lou Michaels, Kentucky, 6-2, 235, Swoyersville, Pa.; T—Alex Karras, Iowa, 6-2, 233, Gary, Ind.; G—Bill Krisher, Oklahoma, 6-1, 213, Midwest City, Okla.; G—Al Ecuyer, Notre Dame, 5-10, 190, New Orleans, La.; C—Dan Currie, Michigan St., 6-3, 225, Detroit, Mich.; B—*John David Crow, Texas A&M, 6-2, 214, Springhill, La.; B—Walt Kowalczyk, Michigan St., 6-0, 205, Westfield, Mass.; B—Bob Anderson, Army, 6-2, 200, Cocoa, Fla.; B—Clendon Thomas, Oklahoma, 6-2, 188, Oklahoma City, Okla.

1958

E—Buddy Dial, Rice, 6-1, 185, Magnolia, Texas; E—Sam Williams, Michigan St., 6-5, 225, Dansville, Mich.; T—Ted Bates, Oregon St., 6-2, 215, Los Angeles, Calif.; T—Brock Strom, Air Force, 6-0, 217, Ironwood, Mich.; G—John Guzik, Pittsburgh, 6-2, 223, Lawrence, Pa.; (tie) G—Zeke Smith, Auburn, 6-2, 210, Uniontown, Ala.; G—George Deiderich, Vanderbilt, 6-1, 198, Toronto, Ohio; C—Bob Harrison, Oklahoma, 6-2, 206, Stamford, Texas; B—*Randy Duncan, Iowa, 6-0, 180, Des Moines, Iowa;

CONSENSUS ALL-AMERICA SELECTIONS

B—*Pete Dawkins, Army, 6-1, 197, Royal Oak, Mich.; B—*Billy Cannon, LSU, 6-1, 200, Baton Rouge, La.; B—Bob White, Ohio St., 6-2, 212, Covington, Ky.

1959
E—Bill Carpenter, Army, 6-2, 210, Springfield, Pa.; E—Monty Stickles, Notre Dame, 6-4, 225, Poughkeepsie, N.Y.; T—*Dan Lanphear, Wisconsin, 6-2, 214, Madison, Wis.; T—Don Floyd, TCU, 6-3, 215, Midlothian, Texas; G—*Roger Davis, Syracuse, 6-2, 228, Solon, Ohio; G—Bill Burrell, Illinois, 6-0, 210, Chebanse, Ill.; C—Maxie Baughan, Georgia Tech, 6-1, 212, Bessemer, Ala.; B—Richie Lucas, Penn St., 6-1, 185, Glassport, Pa.; B—Billy Cannon, LSU, 6-1, 208, Baton Rouge, La.; B—Charlie Flowers, Mississippi, 6-0, 198, Marianna, Ark.; B—Ron Burton, Northwestern, 5-9, 185, Springfield, Ohio.

1960
E—*Mike Ditka, Pittsburgh, 6-3, 215, Aliquippa, Pa.; E—*Danny LaRose, Missouri, 6-4, 220, Crystal City, Mo.; T—*Bob Lilly, TCU, 6-5, 250, Throckmorton, Texas; T—Ken Rice, Auburn, 6-3, 250, Bainbridge, Ga.; G—*Tom Brown, Minnesota, 6-0, 225, Minneapolis, Minn.; G—Joe Romig, Colorado, 5-10, 197, Lakewood, Colo.; C—E. J. Holub, Texas Tech, 6-4, 215, Lubbock, Texas; B—*Jake Gibbs, Mississippi, 6-0, 185, Grenada, Miss.; B—*Joe Bellino, Navy, 5-9, 181, Winchester, Mass.; B—*Bob Ferguson, Ohio St., 6-0, 217, Troy, Ohio; B—Ernie Davis, Syracuse, 6-2, 205, Elmira, N.Y.

1961
E—Gary Collins, Maryland, 6-3, 205, Williamstown, Pa.; E—Bill Miller, Miami (Fla.), 6-0, 188, McKeesport, Pa.; T—*Billy Neighbors, Alabama, 5-11, 229, Tuscaloosa, Ala.; T—Merlin Olsen, Utah St., 6-5, 265, Logan, Utah; G—*Roy Winston, LSU, 6-1, 225, Baton Rouge, La.; G—Joe Romig, Colorado, 5-10, 199, Lakewood, Colo.; C—Alex Kroll, Rutgers, 6-2, 228, Leechburg, Pa.; B—Ernie Davis, Syracuse, 6-2, 210, Elmira, N.Y.; B—*Bob Ferguson, Ohio St., 6-0, 217, Troy, Ohio; B—*Jimmy Saxton, Texas, 5-11, 160, Palestine, Texas; B—Sandy Stephens, Minnesota, 6-0, 215, Uniontown, Pa.

1962
E—Hal Bedsole, Southern California, 6-5, 225, Northridge, Calif.; E—Pat Richter, Wisconsin, 6-5, 229, Madison, Wis.; T—*Bobby Bell, Minnesota, 6-4, 214, Shelby, N.C.; T—Jim Dunaway, Mississippi, 6-4, 260, Columbia, Miss.; G—*Johnny Treadwell, Texas, 6-1, 194, Austin, Texas; G—Jack Cvercko, Northwestern, 6-0, 230, Campbell, Ohio; C—*Lee Roy Jordan, Alabama, 6-2, 207, Monroeville, Ala.; B—*Terry Baker, Oregon St., 6-3, 191, Portland, Ore.; B—*Jerry Stovall, LSU, 6-2, 195, West Monroe, La.; B—Mel Renfro, Oregon, 5-11, 190, Portland, Ore.; B—George Saimes, Michigan St., 5-10, 186, Canton, Ohio.

1963
E—Vern Burke, Oregon St., 6-4, 195, Bakersfield, Calif.; E—Lawrence Elkins, Baylor, 6-1, 187, Brownwood, Texas; T—*Scott Appleton, Texas, 6-3, 235, Brady, Texas; T—Carl Eller, Minnesota, 6-6, 241, Winston-Salem, N.C.; G—*Bob Brown, Nebraska, 6-5, 259, Cleveland, Ohio; G—Rick Redman, Washington, 5-11, 210, Seattle, Wash.; C—*Dick Butkus, Illinois, 6-3, 234, Chicago, Ill.; B—*Roger Staubach, Navy, 6-2, 190, Cincinnati, Ohio; B—Sherman Lewis, Michigan St., 5-8, 154, Louisville, Ky.; B—Jim Grisham, Oklahoma, 6-2, 205, Olney, Texas; (tie) B—Gale Sayers, Kansas, 6-0, 196, Omaha, Neb.; B—Paul Martha, Pittsburgh, 6-1, 180, Wilkinsburg, Pa.

1964
E—Jack Snow, Notre Dame, 6-2, 210, Long Beach, Calif.; E—Fred Biletnikoff, Florida St., 6-1, 186, Erie, Pa.; T—*Larry Kramer, Nebraska, 6-2, 240, Austin, Minn.; T—Ralph Neely, Oklahoma, 6-5, 243, Farmington, N.M.; G—Rick Redman, Washington, 5-11, 215, Seattle, Wash.; G—Glenn Ressler, Penn St., 6-2, 230, Dornsife, Pa.; C—Dick Butkus, Illinois, 6-3, 237, Chicago, Ill.; B—John Huarte, Notre Dame, 6-0, 180, Anaheim, Calif.; B—Gale Sayers, Kansas, 6-0, 194, Omaha, Neb.; B—Lawrence Elkins, Baylor, 6-1, 187, Brownwood, Texas; B—Tucker Frederickson, Auburn, 6-2, 210, Hollywood, Fla.

Beginning in 1965, offense and defense selected.

1965
Offense E—*Howard Twilley, Tulsa, 5-10, 180, Galena Park, Texas; E—Freeman White, Nebraska, 6-5, 220, Detroit, Mich.; T—Sam Ball, Kentucky, 6-4, 241, Henderson, Ky.; T—Glen Ray Hines, Arkansas, 6-5, 235, El Dorado, Ark.; G—*Dick Arrington, Notre Dame, 5-11, 232, Erie, Pa.; G—Stas Maliszewski, Princeton, 6-1, 215, Davenport, Iowa; C—Paul Crane, Alabama, 6-2, 188, Prichard, Ala.; B—*Mike Garrett, Southern California, 5-9, 185, Los Angeles, Calif.; B—*Jim Grabowski, Illinois, 6-2, 211, Chicago, Ill.; B—Bob Griese, Purdue, 6-1, 185, Evansville, Ind.; B—Donny Anderson, Texas Tech, 6-3, 210, Stinnett, Texas.

Defense E—Aaron Brown, Minnesota, 6-4, 230, Port Arthur, Texas; E—Bubba Smith, Michigan St., 6-7, 268, Beaumont, Texas; T—Walt Barnes, Nebraska, 6-3, 235, Chicago, Ill.; T—Loyd Phillips, Arkansas, 6-3, 221, Longview, Texas; T—Bill Yearby, Michigan, 6-3, 222, Detroit, Mich.; LB—Carl McAdams, Oklahoma, 6-3, 215, White Deer, Texas; LB—Tommy Nobis, Texas, 6-2, 230, San Antonio, Texas; LB—Frank Emanuel, Tennessee, 6-3, 228, Newport News, Va.; B—George Webster, Michigan St., 6-4, 204, Anderson, S.C.; B—Johnny Roland, Missouri, 6-2, 198, Corpus Christi, Texas; B—Nick Rassas, Notre Dame, 6-0, 185, Winnetka, Ill.

1966
Offense E—*Jack Clancy, Michigan, 6-1, 192, Detroit, Mich.; E—*Ray Perkins, Alabama, 6-0, 184, Petal, Miss.; T—*Cecil Dowdy, Alabama, 6-0, 206, Cherokee, Ala.; T—Ron Yary, Southern California, 6-6, 265, Bellflower, Calif.; G—Tom Regner, Notre Dame, 6-1, 245, Kenosha, Wis.; G—LaVerne Allers, Nebraska, 6-0, 209, Davenport, Iowa; C—Jim Breland, Georgia Tech, 6-2, 223, Blacksburg, Va.; B—*Steve Spurrier, Florida, 6-2, 203, Johnson City, Tenn.; B—*Nick Eddy, Notre Dame, 6-0, 195, Lafayette, Calif.; B—Mel Farr, UCLA, 6-2, 208, Beaumont, Texas; B—Clint Jones, Michigan St., 6-0, 206, Cleveland, Ohio.

Defense E—*Bubba Smith, Michigan St., 6-7, 283, Beaumont, Texas; E—Alan Page, Notre Dame, 6-5, 238, Canton, Ohio; T—*Loyd Phillips, Arkansas, 6-3, 230, Longview, Texas; T—Tom Greenlee, Washington, 6-0, 195, Seattle, Wash.; MG—Wayne Meylan, Nebraska, 6-0, 239, Bay City, Mich.; MG—John LaGrone, Southern Methodist, 5-10, 232, Borger, Texas; LB—*Jim Lynch, Notre Dame, 6-1, 225, Lima, Ohio; LB—Paul Naumoff, Tennessee, 6-1, 209, Columbus, Ohio; B—*George Webster, Michigan St., 6-4, 218, Anderson, S.C.; B—Tom Beier, Miami (Fla.), 5-11, 197, Fremont, Ohio; B—Nate Shaw, Southern California, 6-2, 205, San Diego, Calif.

1967
Offense E—Dennis Homan, Alabama, 6-0, 182, Muscle Shoals, Ala.; E—Ron Sellers, Florida St., 6-4, 187, Jacksonville, Fla.; T—*Ron Yary, Southern California, 6-6, 245, Bellflower, Calif.; T—Ed Chandler, Georgia, 6-2, 222, Cedartown, Ga.; G—Harry Olszewski, Clemson, 5-11, 237, Baltimore, Md.; G—Rich Stotter, Houston, 5-11, 225, Shaker Heights, Ohio; C—*Bob Johnson, Tennessee, 6-4, 232, Cleveland, Tenn.; B—Gary Beban, UCLA, 6-0, 191, Redwood City, Calif.; B—Leroy Keyes, Purdue, 6-3, 199, Newport News, Va.; B—*O. J. Simpson, Southern California, 6-2, 205, San Francisco, Calif.; B—*Larry Csonka, Syracuse, 6-3, 230, Stow, Ohio.

Defense E—*Ted Hendricks, Miami (Fla.), 6-8, 222, Miami Springs, Fla.; E—Tim Rossovich, Southern California, 6-5, 235, Mountain View, Calif.; T—Dennis Byrd, North Carolina St., 6-4, 250, Lincolnton, N.C.; MG—*Granville Liggins, Oklahoma, 5-11, 216, Tulsa, Okla.; MG—Wayne Meylan, Nebraska, 6-0, 231, Bay City, Mich.; LB—Adrian Young, Southern California, 6-1, 210, La Puente, Calif.; LB—Don Manning, UCLA, 6-2, 204, Culver City, Calif.; B—Tom Schoen, Notre Dame, 5-11, 178, Euclid, Ohio; B—Frank Loria, Virginia Tech, 5-9, 174, Clarksburg, W.Va.; B—Bobby Johns, Alabama, 6-1, 180, Birmingham, Ala.; B—Dick Anderson, Colorado, 6-2, 204, Boulder, Colo.

1968
Offense E—*Ted Kwalick, Penn St., 6-4, 230, McKees Rocks, Pa.; E—Jerry LeVias, Southern Methodist, 5-10, 170, Beaumont, Texas; T—*Dave Foley, Ohio St., 6-5, 246, Cincinnati, Ohio; T—George Kunz, Notre Dame, 6-5, 240, Arcadia, Calif.; G—*Charles Rosenfelder, Tennessee, 6-1, 220, Humboldt, Tenn.; (tie) G—Jim Barnes, Arkansas, 6-4, 227, Pine Bluff, Ark.; G—Mike Montler, Colorado, 6-4, 235, Columbus, Ohio; C—*John Didion, Oregon St., 6-4, 242, Woodland, Calif.; B—*O. J. Simpson, Southern California, 6-2, 205, San Francisco, Calif.; B—*Leroy Keyes, Purdue, 6-3, 205, Newport News, Va.; B—Terry Hanratty, Notre Dame, 6-1, 200, Butler, Pa.; B—Chris Gilbert, Texas, 5-11, 176, Spring, Texas.

Defense E—*Ted Hendricks, Miami (Fla.), 6-8, 222, Miami Springs, Fla.; E—John Zook, Kansas, 6-4, 230, Larned, Kan.; T—Bill Stanfill, Georgia, 6-5, 245, Cairo, Ga.; T—Joe Greene, North Texas, 6-4, 274, Temple, Texas; MG—Ed White, California, 6-3, 245, Palm Desert, Calif.; MG—Chuck Kyle, Purdue, 6-1, 225, Fort Thomas, Ky.; LB—Steve Kiner, Tennessee, 6-1, 205, Tampa, Fla.; LB—Dennis Onkotz, Penn St., 6-2, 205, Northampton, Pa.; B—Jake Scott, Georgia, 6-1, 188, Arlington, Va.; B—Roger Wehrli, Missouri, 6-0, 184, King City, Mo.; B—Al Worley, Washington, 6-0, 175, Wenatchee, Wash.

1969
Offense E—Jim Mandich, Michigan, 6-3, 222, Solon, Ohio; (tie) E—Walker Gillette, Richmond, 6-5, 200, Capron, Va.; E—Carlos Alvarez, Florida, 5-11, 180, Miami, Fla.; T—Bob McKay, Texas, 6-6, 245, Crane, Texas; T—John Ward, Oklahoma St., 6-5, 248, Tulsa, Okla.; G—Chip Kell, Tennessee, 6-0, 255, Decatur, Ga.; G—Bill Bridges, Houston, 6-2, 230, Carrollton, Texas; C—Rodney Brand, Arkansas, 6-2, 218, Newport, Ark.; B—*Mike Phipps, Purdue, 6-3, 206, Columbus, Ind.; B—*Steve Owens, Oklahoma, 6-2, 215, Miami, Okla.; B—Jim Otis, Ohio St., 6-0, 214, Celina, Ohio; B—Bob Anderson, Colorado, 6-0, 208, Boulder, Colo.

Defense E—Jim Gunn, Southern California, 6-1, 210, San Diego, Calif.; E—Phil Olsen, Utah St., 6-5, 255, Logan, Utah; T—*Mike Reid, Penn St., 6-3, 240, Altoona, Pa.; T—*Mike McCoy, Notre Dame, 6-5, 274, Erie, Pa.; MG—Jim Stillwagon, Ohio St., 6-0, 216, Mount Vernon, Ohio; LB—*Steve Kiner, Tennessee, 6-1, 215, Tampa, Fla.; LB—Dennis Onkotz, Penn St., 6-2, 212, Northampton, Pa.; LB—Mike Ballou, UCLA, 6-3, 230, Los Angeles, Calif.; B—Jack Tatum, Ohio St., 6-0, 204, Passaic, N.J.; B—Buddy McClinton, Auburn, 5-11, 190, Montgomery, Ala.; B—Tom Curtis, Michigan, 6-1, 190, Aurora, Ohio.

1970
Offense E—Tom Gatewood, Notre Dame, 6-2, 208, Baltimore, Md.; E—Ernie Jennings, Air Force, 6-0, 172, Kansas City, Mo.; E—Elmo Wright, Houston, 6-0, 195, Brazoria, Texas; T—Dan Dierdorf, Michigan, 6-4, 250, Canton, Ohio; (tie) T—Bobby Wuensch, Texas, 6-3, 230, Houston, Texas; T—Bob Newton, Nebraska, 6-4, 248, LaMirada, Calif.; G—*Chip Kell, Tennessee, 6-0, 240, Decatur, Ga.; G—Larry DiNardo, Notre Dame, 6-1, 235, New York, N.Y.; C—Don Popplewell, Colorado, 6-2, 240, Raytown, Mo.; QB—Jim Plunkett, Stanford, 6-3, 204, San Jose, Calif.; RB—Steve Worster, Texas, 6-0, 210, Bridge City, Texas; RB—Don McCauley, North Carolina, 6-0, 211, Garden City, N.Y.

Defense E—Bill Atessis, Texas, 6-3, 255, Houston, Texas; E—Charlie Weaver, Southern California, 6-2, 214, Richmond, Calif.; T—Rock Perdoni, Georgia Tech, 5-11, 236, Wellesley, Mass.; T—Dick Bumpas, Arkansas, 6-1, 225, Fort Smith, Ark.; MG—*Jim Stillwagon, Ohio St., 6-0, 220, Mount Vernon, Ohio; LB—Jack Ham, Penn St., 6-3, 212, Johnstown, Pa.; LB—Mike Anderson, LSU, 6-3, 225, Baton Rouge, La.; B—*Jack Tatum, Ohio St., 6-0, 208, Passaic, N.J.; B—Larry Willingham, Auburn, 6-1, 185, Birmingham, Ala.; B—Dave Elmendorf, Texas A&M, 6-1, 190, Houston, Texas; B—Tommy Casanova, LSU, 6-1, 191, Crowley, La.

1971
Offense E—*Terry Beasley, Auburn, 5-11, 184, Montgomery, Ala.; E—Johnny Rodgers, Nebraska, 5-10, 171, Omaha, Neb.; T—*Jerry Sisemore, Texas, 6-4, 255, Plainview, Texas; T—Dave Joyner, Penn St., 6-0, 235, State College, Pa.; G—*Royce Smith, Georgia, 6-3, 240, Savannah, Ga.; G—Reggie McKenzie, Michigan, 6-4, 232, Highland Park, Mich.; C—Tom Brahaney, Oklahoma, 6-2, 231, Midland, Texas; QB—*Pat Sullivan, Auburn, 6-0, 191, Birmingham, Ala.; RB—*Ed Marinaro, Cornell, 6-3, 210, New Milford, N.J.; RB—*Greg Pruitt, Oklahoma, 5-9, 176, Houston, Texas; RB—Johnny Musso, Alabama, 5-11, 194, Birmingham, Ala.

Defense E—*Walt Patulski, Notre Dame, 6-5, 235, Liverpool, N.Y.; E—Willie Harper, Nebraska, 6-3, 207, Toledo, Ohio; T—Larry Jacobson, Nebraska, 6-6, 250, Sioux Falls, S.D.; T—Mel Long, Toledo, 6-1, 230, Toledo, Ohio; T—Sherman White, California, 6-5, 250, Portsmouth, N.H.; T—Mike Taylor, Michigan, 6-2, 224, Detroit, Mich.; LB—Jeff Siemon, Stanford, 6-2, 225, Bakersfield, Calif.; B—*Bobby Majors, Tennessee, 6-1, 197, Sewanee, Tenn.; B—Clarence Ellis, Notre Dame,

6-0, 178, Grand Rapids, Mich.; B—Ernie Jackson, Duke, 5-10, 170, Hopkins, S.C.; B—Tommy Casanova, LSU, 6-2, 195, Crowley, La.

1972
Offense WR—*Johnny Rodgers, Nebraska, 5-9, 173, Omaha, Neb.; TE—*Charles Young, Southern California, 6-4, 228, Fresno, Calif.; T—*Jerry Sisemore, Texas, 6-4, 260, Plainview, Texas; T—Paul Seymour, Michigan, 6-5, 250, Berkley, Mich.; G—*John Hannah, Alabama, 6-3, 282, Albertville, Ala.; G—Ron Rusnak, North Carolina, 6-1, 223, Prince George, Va.; C—Tom Brahaney, Oklahoma, 6-2, 227, Midland, Texas; QB—Bert Jones, LSU, 6-3, 205, Ruston, La.; RB—*Greg Pruitt, Oklahoma, 5-9, 177, Houston, Texas; RB—Otis Armstrong, Purdue, 5-11, 197, Chicago, Ill.; RB—Woody Green, Arizona St., 6-1, 190, Portland, Ore.

Defense E—Willie Harper, Nebraska, 6-2, 207, Toledo, Ohio; E—Bruce Bannon, Penn St., 6-3, 224, Rockaway, N.J.; T—*Greg Marx, Notre Dame, 6-5, 265, Redford, Mich.; T—Dave Butz, Purdue, 6-7, 279, Park Ridge, Ill.; MG—*Rich Glover, Nebraska, 6-1, 234, Jersey City, N.J.; LB—Randy Gradishar, Ohio St., 6-3, 232, Champion, Ohio; LB—John Skorupan, Penn St., 6-2, 208, Beaver, Pa.; B—*Brad VanPelt, Michigan St., 6-5, 221, Owosso, Mich.; B—Cullen Bryant, Colorado, 6-2, 215, Colorado Springs, Colo.; B—Robert Popelka, Southern Methodist, 6-1, 190, Temple, Texas; B—Randy Logan, Michigan, 6-2, 192, Detroit, Mich.

1973
Offense WR—Lynn Swann, Southern California, 6-0, 180, Foster City, Calif.; TE—Dave Casper, Notre Dame, 6-3, 252, Chilton, Wis.; T—*John Hicks, Ohio St., 6-3, 258, Cleveland, Ohio; T—Booker Brown, Southern California, 6-3, 270, Santa Barbara, Calif.; G—Buddy Brown, Alabama, 6-2, 242, Tallahassee, Fla.; G—Bill Yoest, North Carolina St., 6-0, 235, Pittsburgh, Pa.; C—Bill Wyman, Texas, 6-2, 235, Spring, Texas; QB—Dave Jaynes, Kansas, 6-2, 212, Bonner Springs, Kan.; RB—*John Cappelletti, Penn St., 6-1, 206, Upper Darby, Pa.; RB—Roosevelt Leaks, Texas, 5-11, 209, Brenham, Texas; RB—Woody Green, Arizona St., 6-1, 202, Portland, Ore.; RB—Kermit Johnson, UCLA, 6-0, 185, Los Angeles, Calif.

Defense L—*John Dutton, Nebraska, 6-7, 248, Rapid City, S.D.; L—Dave Gallagher, Michigan, 6-4, 245, Piqua, Ohio; L—*Lucious Selmon, Oklahoma, 5-11, 236, Eufaula, Okla.; L—Tony Cristiani, Miami (Fla.), 5-10, 215, Brandon, Fla.; LB—*Randy Gradishar, Ohio St., 6-3, 236, Champion, Ohio; LB—Rod Shoate, Oklahoma, 6-1, 214, Spiro, Okla.; LB—Richard Wood, Southern California, 6-2, 217, Elizabeth, N.J.; B—Mike Townsend, Notre Dame, 6-3, 183, Hamilton, Ohio; B—Artimus Parker, Southern California, 6-3, 215, Sacramento, Calif.; B—Dave Brown, Michigan, 6-1, 188, Akron, Ohio; B—Randy Rhino, Georgia Tech, 5-10, 179, Charlotte, N.C.

1974
Offense WR—Pete Demmerle, Notre Dame, 6-1, 190, New Canaan, Conn.; TE—Bennie Cunningham, Clemson, 6-5, 252, Seneca, S.C.; T—Kurt Schumacher, Ohio St., 6-4, 250, Lorain, Ohio; T—Marvin Crenshaw, Nebraska, 6-6, 240, Toledo, Ohio; G—Ken Huff, North Carolina, 6-4, 261, Coronado, Calif.; G—John Roush, Oklahoma, 6-0, 252, Arvada, Colo.; G—Gerry DiNardo, Notre Dame, 6-1, 237, New York, N.Y.; C—Steve Myers, Ohio St., 6-2, 244, Kent, Ohio; QB—Steve Bartkowski, California, 6-4, 215, Santa Clara, Calif.; RB—*Archie Griffin, Ohio St., 5-9, 184, Columbus, Ohio; RB—Joe Washington, Oklahoma, 5-10, 178, Port Arthur, Texas; RB—*Anthony Davis, Southern California, 5-9, 183, San Fernando, Calif.

Defense L—*Randy White, Maryland, 6-4, 238, Wilmington, Del.; L—Mike Hartenstine, Penn St., 6-4, 233, Bethlehem, Pa.; L—Pat Donovan, Stanford, 6-5, 240, Helena, Mont.; L—Jimmy Webb, Mississippi St., 6-5, 245, Florence, Miss.; L—Leroy Cook, Alabama, 6-4, 205, Abbeville, Ala.; MG—Louie Kelcher, Southern Methodist, 6-5, 275, Beaumont, Texas; MG—Rubin Carter, Miami (Fla.), 6-3, 260, Ft. Lauderdale, Fla.; LB—*Rod Shoate, Oklahoma, 6-1, 213, Spiro, Okla.; LB—Richard Wood, Southern California, 6-2, 213, Elizabeth, N.J.; LB—Ken Bernich, Auburn, 6-2, 240, Gretna, La.; LB—Woodrow Lowe, Alabama, 6-0, 211, Phenix City, Ala.; B—*Dave Brown, Michigan, 6-1, 188, Akron, Ohio; B—Pat Thomas, Texas A&M, 5-9, 180, Plano, Texas; B—John Provost, Holy Cross, 5-10, 180, Quincy, Mass.

1975
Offense E—Steve Rivera, California, 6-0, 185, Wilmington, Calif.; E—Larry Seivers, Tennessee, 6-4, 198, Clinton, Tenn.; T—Bob Simmons, Texas, 6-5, 245, Temple, Texas; T—Dennis Lick, Wisconsin, 6-3, 262, Chicago, Ill.; G—Randy Johnson, Georgia, 6-2, 250, Rome, Ga.; G—Ted Smith, Ohio St., 6-1, 242, Gibsonburg, Ohio; C—*Rik Bonness, Nebraska, 6-4, 223, Bellevue, Neb.; QB—John Sciarra, UCLA, 5-10, 178, Alhambra, Calif.; RB—*Archie Griffin, Ohio St., 5-9, 182, Columbus, Ohio; RB—*Ricky Bell, Southern California, 6-2, 215, Los Angeles, Calif.; RB—Chuck Muncie, California, 6-3, 220, Uniontown, Pa.

Defense E—*Leroy Cook, Alabama, 6-4, 205, Abbeville, Ala.; E—Jimbo Elrod, Oklahoma, 6-0, 210, Tulsa, Okla.; T—*Lee Roy Selmon, Oklahoma, 6-2, 256, Eufaula, Okla.; T—*Steve Niehaus, Notre Dame, 6-5, 260, Cincinnati, Ohio; MG—Dewey Selmon, Oklahoma, 6-1, 257, Eufaula, Okla.; LB—*Ed Simonini, Texas A&M, 6-0, 215, Las Vegas, Nev.; LB—Greg Buttle, Penn St., 6-3, 220, Linwood, N.J.; LB—Sammy Green, Florida, 6-2, 228, Ft. Meade, Fla.; B—*Chet Moeller, Navy, 6-0, 189, Kettering, Ohio; B—Tim Fox, Ohio St., 6-0, 186, Canton, Ohio; B—Pat Thomas, Texas A&M, 5-10, 180, Plano, Texas.

1976
Offense SE—Larry Seivers, Tennessee, 6-4, 200, Clinton, Tenn.; TE—Ken MacAfee, Notre Dame, 6-4, 251, Brockton, Mass.; T—Mike Vaughan, Oklahoma, 6-5, 275, Ada, Okla.; T—Chris Ward, Ohio St., 6-4, 274, Dayton, Ohio; G—Joel Parrish, Georgia, 6-3, 232, Douglas, Ga.; G—Mark Donahue, Michigan, 6-3, 245, Oak Lawn, Ill.; C—Derrel Gofourth, Oklahoma St., 6-2, 250, Parsons, Kan.; QB—Tommy Kramer, Rice, 6-2, 190, San Antonio, Texas; RB—*Tony Dorsett, Pittsburgh, 5-11, 192, Aliquippa, Pa.; RB—*Ricky Bell, Southern California, 6-2, 218, Los Angeles, Calif.; RB—Rob Lytle, Michigan, 6-1, 195, Fremont, Ohio; PK—Tony Franklin, Texas A&M, 5-10, 170, Fort Worth, Texas.

Defense E—*Ross Browner, Notre Dame, 6-3, 248, Warren, Ohio; E—Bob Brudzinski, Ohio St., 6-4, 228, Fremont, Ohio; T—Wilson Whitley, Houston, 6-3, 268, Brenham, Texas; T—Gary Jeter, Southern California, 6-5, 255, Cleveland, Ohio; T—Joe Campbell, Maryland, 6-6, 255, Wilmington, Del.; MG—Al Romano, Pittsburgh, 6-3, 230, Solvay, N.Y.; LB—*Robert Jackson, Texas A&M, 6-2, 228, Houston, Texas; LB—Jerry Robinson, UCLA, 6-3, 208, Santa Rosa, Calif.; B—*Bill Armstrong, Wake Forest, 6-4, 205, Randolph, N.J.; B—Gary Green, Baylor, 5-11, 182, San Antonio, Texas; B—Dennis Thurman, Southern California, 5-11, 170, Santa Monica, Calif.; B—Dave Butterfield, Nebraska, 5-10, 182, Kersey, Colo.

1977
Offense WR—John Jefferson, Arizona St., 6-1, 184, Dallas, Texas; WR—Ozzie Newsome, Alabama, 6-4, 210, Leighton, Ala.; TE—*Ken MacAfee, Notre Dame, 6-4, 250, Brockton, Mass.; T—*Chris Ward, Ohio St., 6-4, 272, Dayton, Ohio; T—Dan Irons, Texas Tech, 6-7, 260, Lubbock, Texas; G—*Mark Donahue, Michigan, 6-3, 245, Oak Lawn, Ill.; G—Leotis Harris, Arkansas, 6-1, 254, Little Rock, Ark.; C—Tom Brzoza, Pittsburgh, 6-3, 240, New Castle, Pa.; QB—Guy Benjamin, Stanford, 6-4, 202, Sepulveda, Calif.; RB—*Earl Campbell, Texas, 6-1, 220, Tyler, Texas; RB—*Terry Miller, Oklahoma St., 6-0, 196, Colorado Springs, Colo.; RB—Charles Alexander, LSU, 6-1, 215, Galveston, Texas; K—Steve Little, Arkansas, 6-0, 179, Overland Park, Kan.

Defense L—*Ross Browner, Notre Dame, 6-3, 247, Warren, Ohio; L—*Art Still, Kentucky, 6-8, 247, Camden, N.J.; L—*Brad Shearer, Texas, 6-4, 255, Austin, Texas; L—Randy Holloway, Pittsburgh, 6-6, 228, Sharon, Pa.; L—Dee Hardison, North Carolina, 6-4, 252, Newton Grove, N.C.; LB—*Jerry Robinson, UCLA, 6-3, 208, Santa Rosa, Calif.; LB—Tom Cousineau, Ohio St., 6-3, 228, Fairview Park, Ohio; LB—Gary Spani, Kansas St., 6-2, 222, Manhattan, Kan.; B—*Dennis Thurman, Southern California, 5-11, 173, Santa Monica, Calif.; B—*Zac Henderson, Oklahoma, 6-1, 184, Burkburnett, Texas; B—Luther Bradley, Notre Dame, 6-2, 204, Muncie, Ind.; B—Bob Jury, Pittsburgh, 6-0, 190, Library, Pa.

1978
Offense WR—Emanuel Tolbert, Southern Methodist, 5-10, 180, Little Rock, Ark.; TE—Kellen Winslow, Missouri, 6-6, 235, East St. Louis, Ill.; T—*Keith Dorney, Penn St., 6-5, 257, Allentown, Pa.; T—Kelvin Clark, Nebraska, 6-4, 275, Odessa, Texas; G—*Pat Howell, Southern California, 6-6, 255, Fresno, Calif.; G—*Greg Roberts, Oklahoma, 6-3, 238, Nacogdoches, Texas; C—Dave Huffman, Notre Dame, 6-5, 245, Dallas, Texas; C—Jim Ritcher, North Carolina St., 6-3, 242, Hinckley, Ohio; QB—*Chuck Fusina, Penn St., 6-1, 195, McKees Rocks, Pa.; RB—*Billy Sims, Oklahoma, 6-0, 205, Hooks, Texas; RB—*Charles White, Southern California, 5-11, 183, San Fernando, Calif.; RB—Ted Brown, North Carolina St., 5-10, 195, High Point, N.C.; RB—Charles Alexander, LSU, 6-1, 214, Galveston, Texas.

Defense L—*Al Harris, Arizona St., 6-5, 240, Wheeler AFB, Hawaii; L—*Bruce Clark, Penn St., 6-3, 246, New Castle, Pa.; L—Hugh Green, Pittsburgh, 6-2, 215, Natchez, Miss.; L—Mike Bell, Colorado St., 6-5, 265, Wichita, Kan.; L—Marty Lyons, Alabama, 6-6, 250, St. Petersburg, Fla.; LB—*Bob Golic, Notre Dame, 6-3, 244, Willowick, Ohio; LB—*Jerry Robinson, UCLA, 6-3, 209, Santa Rosa, Calif.; LB—Tom Cousineau, Ohio St., 6-3, 227, Fairview Park, Ohio; B—*Johnnie Johnson, Texas, 6-2, 183, LaGrange, Texas; B—Kenny Easley, UCLA, 6-2, 202, Chesapeake, Va.; B—Jeff Nixon, Richmond, 6-4, 195, Glendale, Ariz.

1979
Offense WR—Ken Margerum, Stanford, 6-1, 175, Fountain Valley, Calif.; TE—*Junior Miller, Nebraska, 6-4, 222, Midland, Texas; T—*Greg Kolenda, Arkansas, 6-1, 258, Kansas City, Kan.; T—Jim Bunch, Alabama, 6-2, 240, Mechanicsville, Va.; G—*Brad Budde, Southern California, 6-5, 253, Kansas City, Mo.; G—Ken Fritz, Ohio St., 6-3, 238, Ironton, Ohio; C—*Jim Ritcher, North Carolina St., 6-3, 245, Hinckley, Ohio; QB—*Marc Wilson, Brigham Young, 6-5, 204, Seattle, Wash.; RB—*Charles White, Southern California, 6-0, 185, San Fernando, Calif.; RB—*Billy Sims, Oklahoma, 6-0, 205, Hooks, Texas; RB—Vagas Ferguson, Notre Dame, 6-1, 194, Richmond, Ind.; PK—Dale Castro, Maryland, 6-1, 170, Shady Side, Md.

Defense L—*Hugh Green, Pittsburgh, 6-2, 220, Natchez, Miss.; L—*Steve McMichael, Texas, 6-2, 250, Freer, Texas; L—Bruce Clark, Penn St., 6-3, 255, New Castle, Pa.; L—Jim Stuckey, Clemson, 6-5, 241, Cayce, S.C.; MG—Ron Simmons, Florida St., 6-1, 235, Warner Robins, Ga.; LB—*George Cumby, Oklahoma, 6-0, 205, Tyler, Texas; LB—Ron Simpkins, Michigan, 6-2, 220, Detroit, Mich.; LB—Mike Singletary, Baylor, 6-1, 224, Houston, Texas; B—*Kenny Easley, UCLA, 6-3, 204, Chesapeake, Va.; B—*Johnnie Johnson, Texas, 6-2, 190, LaGrange, Texas; B—Roland James, Tennessee, 6-2, 182, Jamestown, Ohio; P—Jim Miller, Mississippi, 5-11, 183, Ripley, Miss.

1980
Offense WR—*Ken Margerum, Stanford, 6-1, 175, Fountain Valley, Calif.; TE—*Dave Young, Purdue, 6-6, 242, Akron, Ohio; L—*Mark May, Pittsburgh, 6-6, 282, Oneonta, N.Y.; L—Keith Van Horne, Southern California, 6-7, 265, Fullerton, Calif.; L—Nick Eyre, Brigham Young, 6-5, 276, Las Vegas, Nev.; L—Louis Oubre, Oklahoma, 6-3, 262, New Orleans, La.; L—Randy Schleusener, Nebraska, 6-7, 242, Rapid City, S.D.; C—*John Scully, Notre Dame, 6-5, 255, Huntington, N.Y.; QB—Mark Herrmann, Purdue, 6-4, 187, Carmel, Ind.; RB—*George Rogers, South Carolina, 6-2, 220, Duluth, Ga.; RB—*Herschel Walker, Georgia, 6-2, 220, Wrightsville, Ga.; RB—Jarvis Redwine, Nebraska, 5-11, 204, Inglewood, Calif.

Defense L—*Hugh Green, Pittsburgh, 6-2, 222, Natchez, Miss.; L—*E. J. Junior, Alabama, 6-3, 227, Nashville, Tenn.; L—Kenneth Sims, Texas, 6-6, 265, Groesbeck, Texas; L—Leonard Mitchell, Houston, 6-7, 270, Houston, Texas; MG—Ron Simmons, Florida St., 6-1, 230, Warner Robins, Ga.; LB—*Mike Singletary, Baylor, 6-1, 232, Houston, Texas; LB—Lawrence Taylor, North Carolina, 6-3, 237, Williamsburg, Va.; LB—David Little, Florida, 6-1, 228, Miami, Fla.; LB—Bob Crable, Notre Dame, 6-3, 222, Cincinnati, Ohio; B—*Kenny Easley, UCLA, 6-3, 206, Chesapeake, Va.; B—*Ronnie Lott, Southern California, 6-2, 200, Rialto, Calif.; B—John Simmons, Southern Methodist, 5-11, 188, Little Rock, Ark.

1981
Offense WR—*Anthony Carter, Michigan, 5-11, 161, Riviera Beach, Fla.; TE—*Tim Wrightman, UCLA, 6-3, 237, San Pedro, Calif.; L—*Sean Farrell, Penn St., 6-3, 266, Westhampton Beach, N.Y.; L—Roy Foster, Southern California, 6-4, 265, Overland Park, Kan.; L—Terry Crouch, Oklahoma, 6-1, 275, Dallas, Texas; L—Ed Muransky, Michigan, 6-7, 275, Youngstown, Ohio; L—Terry Tausch, Texas, 6-4, 265, New Braunfels, Texas; L—Kurt Becker, Michigan, 6-6, 260, Aurora, Ill.; C—*Dave Rimington, Nebraska, 6-3, 275, Omaha, Neb.; QB—

CONSENSUS ALL-AMERICA SELECTIONS

*Jim McMahon, Brigham Young, 6-0, 185, Roy, Utah; RB—*Marcus Allen, Southern California, 6-2, 202, San Diego, Calif.; RB—*Herschel Walker, Georgia, 6-2, 222, Wrightsville, Ga.

Defense L—*Billy Ray Smith, Arkansas, 6-4, 228, Plano, Texas; L—*Kenneth Sims, Texas, 6-6, 265, Groesbeck, Texas; L—Andre Tippett, Iowa, 6-4, 235, Newark, N.J.; L—Tim Krumrie, Wisconsin, 6-3, 237, Mondovi, Wis.; LB—Bob Crable, Notre Dame, 6-3, 225, Cincinnati, Ohio; LB—Jeff Davis, Clemson, 6-0, 223, Greensboro, N.C.; LB—Sal Sunseri, Pittsburgh, 6-0, 220, Pittsburgh, Pa.; DB—Tommy Wilcox, Alabama, 5-11, 187, Harahan, La.; DB—Mike Richardson, Arizona St., 6-1, 192, Compton, Calif.; DB—Terry Kinard, Clemson, 6-1, 183, Sumter, S.C.; DB—Fred Marion, Miami (Fla.), 6-3, 194, Gainesville, Fla.; P—Reggie Roby, Iowa, 6-3, 215, Waterloo, Iowa.

1982

Offense WR—*Anthony Carter, Michigan, 5-11, 161, Riviera Beach, Fla.; TE—*Gordon Hudson, Brigham Young, 6-4, 224, Salt Lake City, Utah; L—*Don Mosebar, Southern California, 6-7, 270, Visalia, Calif.; L—*Steve Korte, Arkansas, 6-2, 270, Littleton, Colo.; L—Jimbo Covert, Pittsburgh, 6-5, 279, Conway, Pa.; L—Bruce Matthews, Southern California, 6-5, 265, Arcadia, Calif.; C—*Dave Rimington, Nebraska, 6-3, 290, Omaha, Neb.; QB—*John Elway, Stanford, 6-4, 202, Northridge, Calif.; RB—*Herschel Walker, Georgia, 6-2, 222, Wrightsville, Ga.; RB—*Eric Dickerson, Southern Methodist, 6-2, 215, Sealy, Texas; RB—Mike Rozier, Nebraska, 5-11, 210, Camden, N.J.; PK—*Chuck Nelson, Washington, 5-11, 178, Everett, Wash.

Defense L—*Billy Ray Smith, Arkansas, 6-3, 228, Plano, Texas; L—Vernon Maxwell, Arizona St., 6-2, 225, Carson, Calif.; L—Mike Pitts, Alabama, 6-5, 255, Baltimore, Md.; L—Wilber Marshall, Florida, 6-1, 230, Titusville, Fla.; L—Gabriel Rivera, Texas Tech, 6-3, 270, San Antonio, Texas; L—Rick Bryan, Oklahoma, 6-4, 260, Coweta, Okla.; MG—George Achica, Southern California, 6-5, 260, San Jose, Calif.; LB—*Darryl Talley, West Virginia, 6-4, 210, East Cleveland, Ohio; LB—Ricky Hunley, Arizona, 6-1, 230, Petersburg, Va.; LB—Marcus Marek, Ohio St., 6-2, 224, Masury, Ohio; DB—*Terry Kinard, Clemson, 6-1, 189, Sumter, S.C.; DB—Mike Richardson, Arizona St., 6-0, 190, Compton, Calif.; DB—Terry Hoage, Georgia, 6-3, 196, Huntsville, Texas; P—*Jim Arnold, Vanderbilt, 6-3, 205, Dalton, Ga.

1983

Offense WR—*Irving Fryar, Nebraska, 6-0, 200, Mount Holly, N.J.; TE—*Gordon Hudson, Brigham Young, 6-4, 231, Salt Lake City, Utah; L—*Bill Fralic, Pittsburgh, 6-5, 270, Penn Hills, Pa.; L—Terry Long, East Carolina, 6-0, 280, Columbia, S.C.; L—Dean Steinkuhler, Nebraska, 6-3, 270, Burr, Neb.; L—Doug Dawson, Texas, 6-3, 263, Houston, Texas; C—Tony Slaton, Southern California, 6-4, 260, Merced, Calif.; QB—*Steve Young, Brigham Young, 6-1, 198, Greenwich, Conn.; RB—*Mike Rozier, Nebraska, 5-11, 210, Camden, N.J.; RB—Bo Jackson, Auburn, 6-1, 222, Bessemer, Ala.; RB—Greg Allen, Florida St., 6-0, 200, Milton, Fla.; RB—Napoleon McCallum, Navy, 6-2, 208, Milford, Ohio; PK—Luis Zendejas, Arizona St., 5-9, 186, Chino, Calif.

Defense L—*Rick Bryan, Oklahoma, 6-4, 260, Coweta, Okla.; L—*Reggie White, Tennessee, 6-5, 264, Chattanooga, Tenn.; L—William Perry, Clemson, 6-3, 320, Aiken, S.C.; L—William Fuller, North Carolina, 6-4, 250, Chesapeake, Va.; LB—*Ricky Hunley, Arizona, 6-2, 230, Petersburg, Va.; LB—*Wilber Marshall, Florida, 6-1, 230, Titusville, Fla.; LB—Ron Rivera, California, 6-3, 225, Monterey, Calif.; LB—Jeff Leiding, Texas, 6-4, 240, Tulsa, Okla.; DB—*Russell Carter, Southern Methodist, 6-3, 193, Ardmore, Pa.; DB—Jerry Gray, Texas, 6-1, 183, Lubbock, Texas; DB—Terry Hoage, Georgia, 6-3, 196, Huntsville, Texas; DB—Don Rogers, UCLA, 6-2, 208, Sacramento, Calif.; P—Jack Weil, Wyoming, 5-11, 171, Northglenn, Colo.

1984

Offense WR—*David Williams, Illinois, 6-3, 195, Los Angeles, Calif.; WR—Eddie Brown, Miami (Fla.), 6-0, 185, Miami, Fla.; TE—Jay Novacek, Wyoming, 6-4, 211, Gothenburg, Neb.; T—*Bill Fralic, Pittsburgh, 6-5, 285, Penn Hills, Pa.; T—Lomas Brown, Florida, 6-5, 277, Miami, Fla.; G—Del Wilkes, South Carolina, 6-3, 255, Columbia, S.C.; G—Jim Lachey, Ohio St., 6-6, 274, St. Henry, Ohio; G—Bill Mayo, Tennessee, 6-3, 280, Dalton, Ga.; C—*Mark Traynowicz, Nebraska, 6-5, 265, Bellevue, Neb.; QB—*Doug Flutie, Boston College, 5-9, 177, Natick, Mass.; RB—*Keith Byars, Ohio St., 6-2, 233, Dayton, Ohio; RB—*Kenneth Davis, TCU, 5-11, 205, Temple, Texas; RB—Rueben Mayes, Washington St., 6-0, 200, North Battleford, Saskatchewan, Canada; PK—Kevin Butler, Georgia, 6-1, 190, Stone Mountain, Ga.

Defense DL—Bruce Smith, Virginia Tech, 6-4, 275, Norfolk, Va.; DL—Tony Degrate, Texas, 6-4, 280, Snyder, Texas; DL—Ron Holmes, Washington, 6-4, 255, Lacey, Wash.; DL—Tony Casillas, Oklahoma, 6-3, 272, Tulsa, Okla.; LB—Gregg Carr, Auburn, 6-2, 215, Birmingham, Ala.; LB—Jack Del Rio, Southern California, 6-4, 235, Hayward, Calif.; LB—Larry Station, Iowa, 5-11, 233, Omaha, Neb.; DB—*Jerry Gray, Texas, 6-1, 183, Lubbock, Texas; DB—Tony Thurman, Boston College, 6-0, 179, Lynn, Mass.; DB—Jeff Sanchez, Georgia, 6-0, 183, Yorba Linda, Calif.; DB—David Fulcher, Arizona St., 6-3, 220, Los Angeles, Calif.; DB—Rod Brown, Oklahoma St., 6-3, 188, Gainesville, Texas; P—*Ricky Anderson, Vanderbilt, 6-2, 190, St. Petersburg, Fla.

1985

Offense WR—*David Williams, Illinois, 6-3, 195, Los Angeles, Calif.; WR—Tim McGee, Tennessee, 5-10, 181, Cleveland, Ohio; TE—*Willie Smith, Miami (Fla.), 6-2, 230, Jacksonville, Fla.; L—*Jim Dombrowski, Virginia, 6-5, 290, Williamsville, N.Y.; L—Jeff Bregel, Southern California, 6-4, 280, Granada Hills, Calif.; L—Brian Jozwiak, West Virginia, 6-6, 290, Catonsville, Md.; L—John Rienstra, Temple, 6-4, 280, Colorado Springs, Colo.; L—J. D. Maarleveld, Maryland, 6-5, 300, Rutherford, N.J.; L—Jamie Dukes, Florida St., 6-0, 272, Orlando, Fla.; C—Pete Anderson, Georgia, 6-3, 264, Glen Ridge, N.J.; QB—*Chuck Long, Iowa, 6-4, 213, Wheaton, Ill.; RB—*Bo Jackson, Auburn, 6-1, 222, Bessemer, Ala.; RB—*Lorenzo White, Michigan St., 5-11, 205, Fort Lauderdale, Fla.; RB—Thurman Thomas, Oklahoma St., 5-11, 186, Missouri City, Texas; RB—Reggie Dupard, Southern Methodist, 6-0, 201, New Orleans, La.; RB—Napoleon McCallum, Navy, 6-2, 214, Milford, Ohio; PK—*John Lee, UCLA, 5-11, 187, Downey, Calif.

Defense L—*Tim Green, Syracuse, 6-2, 246, Liverpool, N.Y.; L—*Leslie O'Neal, Oklahoma St., 6-4, 245, Little Rock, Ark.; L—Tony Casillas, Oklahoma, 6-3, 280, Tulsa, Okla.; L—Mike Ruth, Boston College, 6-2, 250, Norristown, Pa.; L—Mike Hammerstein, Michigan, 6-4, 240, Wapakoneta, Ohio; LB—*Brian Bosworth, Oklahoma, 6-2, 234, Irving, Texas; LB—*Larry Station, Iowa, 5-11, 227, Omaha, Neb.; LB—Johnny Holland, Texas A&M, 6-2, 219, Hempstead, Texas; DB—David Fulcher, Arizona St., 6-3, 228, Los Angeles, Calif.; DB—Brad Cochran, Michigan, 6-3, 219, Royal Oak, Mich.; DB—Scott Thomas, Air Force, 6-0, 185, San Antonio, Texas; P—Barry Helton, Colorado, 6-3, 195, Simla, Colo.

1986

Offense WR—Cris Carter, Ohio St., 6-3, 194, Middletown, Ohio; TE—Keith Jackson, Oklahoma, 6-3, 241, Little Rock, Ark.; L—Jeff Bregel, Southern California, 6-4, 280, Granada Hills, Calif.; L—Randy Dixon, Pittsburgh, 6-4, 286, Clewiston, Fla.; L—Danny Villa, Arizona St., 6-5, 284, Nogales, Ariz.; L—John Clay, Missouri, 6-5, 285, St. Louis, Mo.; C—*Ben Tamburello, Auburn, 6-3, 268, Birmingham, Ala.; QB—*Vinny Testaverde, Miami (Fla.), 6-5, 218, Elmont, N.Y.; RB—*Brent Fullwood, Auburn, 5-11, 209, St. Cloud, Fla.; RB—*Paul Palmer, Temple, 5-10, 180, Potomac, Md.; RB—Terrence Flagler, Clemson, 6-1, 200, Fernandina Beach, Fla.; RB—Brad Muster, Stanford, 6-3, 226, Novato, Calif.; RB—D. J. Dozier, Penn St., 6-1, 204, Virginia Beach, Va.; PK—Jeff Jaeger, Washington, 5-11, 191, Kent, Wash.

Defense L—*Jerome Brown, Miami (Fla.), 6-2, 285, Brooksville, Fla.; L—*Danny Noonan, Nebraska, 6-4, 280, Lincoln, Neb.; L—Tony Woods, Pittsburgh, 6-4, 240, Newark, N.J.; L—Jason Buck, Brigham Young, 6-6, 270, St. Anthony, Idaho; L—Reggie Rogers, Washington, 6-6, 260, Sacramento, Calif.; LB—*Cornelius Bennett, Alabama, 6-4, 235, Birmingham, Ala.; LB—Shane Conlan, Penn St., 6-3, 225, Frewsburg, N.Y.; LB—Brian Bosworth, Oklahoma, 6-2, 240, Irving, Texas; LB—Chris Spielman, Ohio St., 6-2, 227, Massillon, Ohio; DB—*Thomas Everett, Baylor, 5-9, 180, Daingerfield, Texas; DB—Tim McDonald, Southern California, 6-3, 205, Fresno, Calif.; DB—Bennie Blades, Miami (Fla.), 6-0, 207, Ft. Lauderdale, Fla.; DB—Rod Woodson, Purdue, 6-0, 195, Fort Wayne, Ind.; DB—Garland Rivers, Michigan, 6-1, 187, Canton, Ohio; P—Barry Helton, Colorado, 6-4, 200, Simla, Colo.

1987

Offense WR—*Tim Brown, Notre Dame, 6-0, 195, Dallas, Texas; WR—Wendell Davis, LSU, 6-0, 186, Shreveport, La.; TE—*Keith Jackson, Oklahoma, 6-3, 248, Little Rock, Ark.; L—*Mark Hutson, Oklahoma, 6-4, 282, Fort Smith, Ark.; L—Dave Cadigan, Southern California, 6-5, 280, Newport Beach, Calif.; L—John Elliott, Michigan, 6-7, 306, Lake Ronkonkoma, N.Y.; L—Randall McDaniel, Arizona St., 6-5, 261, Avondale, Ariz.; C—*Nacho Albergamo, LSU, 6-2, 257, Marrera, La.; QB—*Don McPherson, Syracuse, 6-0, 182, West Hempstead, N.Y.; RB—Lorenzo White, Michigan St., 5-11, 211, Fort Lauderdale, Fla.; RB—Craig Heyward, Pittsburgh, 6-0, 260, Passaic, N.J.; PK—David Treadwell, Clemson, 6-1, 165, Jacksonville, Fla.

Defense L—*Daniel Stubbs, Miami (Fla.), 6-4, 250, Red Bank, N.J.; L—*Chad Hennings, Air Force, 6-5, 260, Elboron, Iowa; L—Tracy Rocker, Auburn, 6-3, 258, Atlanta, Ga.; L—Ted Gregory, Syracuse, 6-1, 260, East Islip, N.Y.; L—John Roper, Texas A&M, 6-2, 215, Houston, Texas; LB—*Chris Spielman, Ohio St., 6-2, 236, Massillon, Ohio; LB—Aundray Bruce, Auburn, 6-6, 236, Montgomery, Ala.; LB—Dante Jones, Oklahoma, 6-2, 235, Dallas, Texas; DB—*Bennie Blades, Miami (Fla.), 6-0, 215, Fort Lauderdale, Fla.; DB—*Deion Sanders, Florida St., 6-0, 192, Fort Myers, Fla.; DB—Rickey Dixon, Oklahoma, 5-10, 184, Dallas, Texas; DB—Chuck Cecil, Arizona, 6-0, 185, Red Bluff, Calif.; P—*Tom Tupa, Ohio St., 6-5, 215, Brecksville, Ohio.

1988

Offense WR—Jason Phillips, Houston, 5-9, 175, Houston, Texas; WR—Hart Lee Dykes, Oklahoma St., 6-4, 220, Bay City, Texas; TE—Marv Cook, Iowa, 6-4, 243, West Branch, Iowa; L—*Tony Mandarich, Michigan St., 6-6, 315, Oakville, Ontario, Canada; L—*Anthony Phillips, Oklahoma, 6-3, 286, Tulsa, Okla.; L—Mike Utley, Washington St., 6-6, 302, Seattle, Wash.; L—Mark Stepnoski, Pittsburgh, 6-3, 265, Erie, Pa.; C—Jake Young, Nebraska, 6-5, 260, Midland, Texas; C—John Vitale, Michigan, 6-1, 273, Detroit, Mich.; QB—Steve Walsh, Miami (Fla.), 6-3, 195, St. Paul, Minn.; QB—Troy Aikman, UCLA, 6-4, 217, Henryetta, Okla.; RB—*Barry Sanders, Oklahoma St., 5-8, 197, Wichita, Kan.; RB—Anthony Thompson, Indiana, 6-0, 205, Terre Haute, Ind.; RB—Tim Worley, Georgia, 6-2, 216, Lumberton, N.C.; PK—Kendall Trainor, Arkansas, 6-2, 205, Fredonia, Kan.

Defense L—*Mark Messner, Michigan, 6-3, 244, Hartland, Mich.; L—*Tracy Rocker, Auburn, 6-3, 278, Atlanta, Ga.; L—Wayne Martin, Arkansas, 6-5, 263, Cherry Valley, Ark.; L—Frank Stams, Notre Dame, 6-4, 237, Akron, Ohio; L—Bill Hawkins, Miami (Fla.), 6-6, 260, Hollywood, Fla.; LB—*Derrick Thomas, Alabama, 6-4, 230, Miami, Fla.; LB—*Broderick Thomas, Nebraska, 6-3, 235, Houston, Texas; LB—Michael Stonebreaker, Notre Dame, 6-1, 228, River Ridge, La.; DB—*Deion Sanders, Florida St., 6-0, 195, Fort Myers, Fla.; DB—Donnell Woolford, Clemson, 5-10, 195, Fayetteville, N.C.; DB—Louis Oliver, Florida, 6-2, 222, Bell Glade, Fla.; DB—Darryl Henley, UCLA, 5-10, 165, Ontario, Calif.; P—Keith English, Colorado, 6-3, 215, Greeley, Colo.

1989

Offense WR—*Clarkston Hines, Duke, 6-1, 170, Chapel Hill, N.C.; WR—Terance Mathis, New Mexico, 5-9, 167, Stone Mountain, Ga.; TE—Mike Busch, Iowa St., 6-5, 252, Donahue, Iowa; L—Jim Mabry, Arkansas, 6-4, 262, Memphis, Tenn.; L—Bob Kula, Michigan St., 6-4, 282, West Bloomfield, Mich.; L—Mohammed Elewonibi, Brigham Young, 6-5, 290, Kamloops, British Columbia, Canada; L—Joe Garten, Colorado, 6-3, 280, Placentia, Calif.; L—*Eric Still, Tennessee, 6-3, 283, Germantown, Tenn.; C—Jake Young, Nebraska, 6-4, 270, Midland, Texas; QB—Andre Ware, Houston, 6-2, 205, Dickinson, Texas; RB—*Anthony Thompson, Indiana, 6-0, 209, Terre Haute, Ind.; RB—*Emmitt Smith, Florida, 5-10, 201, Pensacola, Fla.; PK—*Jason Hanson, Washington St., 6-0, 164, Spokane, Wash.

Defense L—Chris Zorich, Notre Dame, 6-1, 268, Chicago, Ill.; L—Greg Mark, Miami (Fla.), 6-4, 255, Pennsauken, N.J.; L—Tim Ryan, Southern California, 6-5, 260, San Jose, Calif.; L—*Moe Gardner, Illinois, 6-2, 250, Indianapolis, Ind.; LB—*Percy Snow, Michigan St., 6-3, 241, Canton, Ohio; LB—*Keith McCants, Alabama, 6-5, 256, Mobile, Ala.; LB—Alfred Williams, Colorado, 6-6, 230, Houston, Texas; DB—*Todd Lyght, Notre Dame, 6-1, 181, Flint, Mich.; DB—*Mark Carrier, Southern California, 6-1, 185, Long Beach, Calif.; DB—*Tripp Welborne, Michigan, 6-1, 193, Greensboro,

AWARD WINNERS

N.C.; DB—LeRoy Butler, Florida St., 6-0, 194, Jacksonville, Fla.; P—Tom Rouen, Colorado, 6-3, 220, Littleton, Colo.

1990

Offense WR—*Raghib Ismail, Notre Dame, 5-10, 175, Wilkes-Barre, Pa.; WR—Herman Moore, Virginia, 6-5, 197, Danville, Va.; TE—*Chris Smith, Brigham Young, 6-4, 230, La Canada, Calif.; OL—*Antone Davis, Tennessee, 6-4, 310, Fort Valley, Ga.; OL—*Joe Garten, Colorado, 6-3, 280, Placentia, Calif.; OL—*Ed King, Auburn, 6-4, 284, Phenix City, Ala.; OL—Stacy Long, Clemson, 6-2, 275, Griffin, Ga.; C—John Flannery, Syracuse, 6-4, 301, Pottsville, Pa.; QB—Ty Detmer, Brigham Young, 6-0, 175, San Antonio, Texas; RB—*Eric Bieniemy, Colorado, 5-7, 195, West Covina, Calif.; RB—Darren Lewis, Texas A&M, 6-0, 220, Dallas, Texas; PK—*Philip Doyle, Alabama, 6-1, 190, Birmingham, Ala.

Defense DL—*Russell Maryland, Miami (Fla.), 6-2, 273, Chicago, Ill.; DL—*Chris Zorich, Notre Dame, 6-1, 266, Chicago, Ill.; DL—Moe Gardner, Illinois, 6-2, 258, Indianapolis, Ind.; DL—David Rocker, Auburn, 6-4, 264, Atlanta, Ga.; LB—*Alfred Williams, Colorado, 6-6, 236, Houston, Texas; LB—*Michael Stonebreaker, Notre Dame, 6-1, 228, River Ridge, La.; LB—Maurice Crum, Miami (Fla.), 6-0, 222, Tampa, Fla.; DB—*Tripp Welborne, Michigan, 6-1, 201, Greensboro, N.C.; DB—*Darryll Lewis, Arizona, 5-9, 186, West Covina, Calif.; DB—Ken Swilling, Georgia Tech, 6-3, 230, Toccoa, Ga.; DB—Todd Lyght, Notre Dame, 6-1, 184, Flint, Mich.; P—Brian Greenfield, Pittsburgh, 6-1, 210, Sherman Oaks, Calif.

1991

Offense WR—*Desmond Howard, Michigan, 5-9, 176, Cleveland, Ohio; WR—Mario Bailey, Washington, 5-9, 167, Seattle, Wash.; TE—Kelly Blackwell, TCU, 6-2, 242, Fort Worth, Texas; OL—*Greg Skrepenak, Michigan, 6-8, 322, Wilkes-Barre, Pa.; OL—Bob Whitfield, Stanford, 6-7, 300, Carson, Calif.; OL—Jeb Flesch, Clemson, 6-3, 266, Morrow, Ga.; OL—(tie) Jerry Ostroski, Tulsa, 6-4, 305, Collegeville, Pa.; Mirko Jurkovic, Notre Dame, 6-4, 289, Calumet City, Ill.; C—*Jay Leeuwenburg, Colorado, 6-3, 265, Kirkwood, Mo.; QB—Ty Detmer, Brigham Young, 6-0, 175, San Antonio, Texas; RB—*Vaughn Dunbar, Indiana, 6-0, 207, Fort Wayne, Ind.; RB—(tie) Trevor Cobb, Rice, 5-9, 180, Houston, Texas; Russell White, California, 6-0, 210, Van Nuys, Calif.; PK—Carlos Huerta, Miami (Fla.), 5-9, 186, Miami, Fla.

Defense DL—*Steve Emtman, Washington, 6-4, 280, Cheney, Wash.; DL—*Santana Dotson, Baylor, 6-5, 264, Houston, Texas; DL—Brad Culpepper, Florida, 6-2, 263, Tallahassee, Fla.; DL—Leroy Smith, Iowa, 6-2, 214, Sicklerville, N.J.; LB—*Robert Jones, East Carolina, 6-3, 234, Blackstone, Va.; LB—*Marvin Jones, Florida St., 6-2, 220, Miami, Fla.; LB—Levon Kirkland, Clemson, 6-2, 245, Lamar, S.C.; DB—*Terrell Buckley, Florida St., 5-10, 175, Pascagoula, Miss.; DB—Dale Carter, Tennessee, 6-2, 182, Oxford, Ga.; DB—Kevin Smith, Texas A&M, 6-0, 180, Orange, Texas; DB—Darryl Williams, Miami (Fla.), 6-2, 190, Miami, Fla.; P—*Mark Bounds, Texas Tech, 5-11, 185, Stamford, Texas.

1992

Offense WR—O. J. McDuffie, Penn St., 5-11, 185, Warrensville Heights, Ohio; WR—Sean Dawkins, California, 6-4, 205, Sunnyvale, Calif.; TE—*Chris Gedney, Syracuse, 6-5, 256, Liverpool, N.Y.; OL—*Lincoln Kennedy, Washington, 6-7, 325, San Diego, Calif.; OL—*Will Shields, Nebraska, 6-1, 305, Lawton, Okla.; OL—Aaron Taylor, Notre Dame, 6-4, 294, Concord, Calif.; OL—(tie) Willie Roaf, Louisiana Tech, 6-5, 300, Pine Bluff, Ark.; Everett Lindsay, Mississippi, 6-5, 290, Raleigh, N.C.; C—Mike Compton, West Virginia, 6-7, 289, Richlands, Va.; QB—*Gino Torretta, Miami (Fla.), 6-3, 205, Pinole, Calif.; RB—*Marshall Faulk, San Diego St., 5-10, 200, New Orleans, La.; RB—*Garrison Hearst, Georgia, 5-11, 202, Lincolnton, Ga.; PK—Joe Allison, Memphis, 6-0, 184, Atlanta, Ga.

Defense DL—Eric Curry, Alabama, 6-6, 265, Thomasville, Ga.; DL—John Copeland, Alabama, 6-3, 261, Lanett, Ala.; DL—Chris Slade, Virginia, 6-5, 235, Tabb, Va.; DL—Rob Waldrop, Arizona, 6-2, 265, Phoenix, Ariz.; LB—*Marcus Buckley, Texas A&M, 6-4, 230, Fort Worth, Texas; LB—*Marvin Jones, Florida St., 6-2, 235, Miami, Fla.; LB—Micheal Barrow, Miami (Fla.), 6-2, 230, Homestead, Fla.; DB—*Carlton McDonald, Air Force, 6-0, 185, Jacksonville, Fla.; DB—Carlton Gray, UCLA, 6-0, 194, Cincinnati, Ohio; DB—Deon Figures,

Colorado, 6-1, 195, Compton, Calif.; DB—Ryan McNeil, Miami (Fla.), 6-2, 185, Fort Pierce, Fla.; P—Sean Snyder, Kansas St., 6-1, 190, Greenville, Texas.

1993

Offense WR—*J. J. Stokes, UCLA, 6-5, 214, San Diego, Calif.; WR—Johnnie Morton, Southern California, 6-0, 190, Torrance, Calif.; OL—Mark Dixon, Virginia, 6-4, 283, Jamestown, N.C.; OL—Stacy Seegars, Clemson, 6-4, 320, Kershaw, S.C.; OL—*Aaron Taylor, Notre Dame, 6-4, 299, Concord, Calif.; OL—Wayne Gandy, Auburn, 6-5, 275, Haines City, Fla.; C—*Jim Pyne, Virginia Tech, 6-2, 280, Milford, Mass.; QB—*Charlie Ward, Florida St., 6-2, 190, Thomasville, Ga.; RB—*Marshall Faulk, San Diego St., 5-10, 200, New Orleans, La.; RB—*LeShon Johnson, Northern Ill., 6-0, 201, Haskell, Okla.; PK—Bjorn Merten, UCLA, 6-0, 203, Centreville, Va.; KR—David Palmer, Alabama, 5-9, 170, Birmingham, Ala.

Defense DL—*Rob Waldrop, Arizona, 6-2, 275, Phoenix, Ariz.; DL—Dan Wilkinson, Ohio St., 6-5, 300, Dayton, Ohio; DL—Sam Adams, Texas A&M, 6-4, 269, Cypress, Texas; LB—*Trev Alberts, Nebraska, 6-4, 240, Cedar Falls, Iowa; LB—*Derrick Brooks, Florida St., 6-1, 225, Pensacola, Fla.; LB—Jamir Miller, UCLA, 6-4, 233, El Cerrito, Calif.; DB—*Antonio Langham, Alabama, 6-1, 170, Town Creek, Ala.; DB—Aaron Glenn, Texas A&M, 5-10, 182, Aldine, Texas; DB—Jeff Burris, Notre Dame, 6-0, 204, Rock Hill, S.C.; DB—Corey Sawyer, Florida St., 5-11, 171, Key West, Fla.; P—Terry Daniel, Auburn, 6-1, 226, Valley, Ala.

1994

Offense WR—Jack Jackson, Florida, 5-9, 171, Moss Point, Miss.; WR—Michael Westbrook, Colorado, 6-4, 210, Detroit, Mich.; TE—Pete Mitchell, Boston College, 6-2, 238, Bloomfield Hills, Mich.; OL—*Zach Wiegert, Nebraska, 6-5, 300, Fremont, Neb.; OL—Tony Boselli, Southern California, 6-8, 305, Boulder, Colo.; OL—Korey Stringer, Ohio St., 6-5, 320, Warren, Ohio; OL—Brenden Stai, Nebraska, 6-4, 300, Yorba Linda, Calif.; C—Cory Raymer, Wisconsin, 6-4, 290, Fond du Lac, Wis.; QB—Kerry Collins, Penn St., 6-5, 235, West Lawn, Pa.; RB—*Rashaan Salaam, Colorado, 6-1, 210, San Diego, Calif.; RB—*Ki-Jana Carter, Penn St., 5-10, 212, Westerville, Ohio; PK—Steve McLaughlin, Arizona, 6-1, 175, Tucson, Ariz.; KR—Leeland McElroy, Texas A&M, 5-11, 200, Beaumont, Texas.

Defense DL—*Warren Sapp, Miami (Fla.), 6-3, 284, Plymouth, Fla.; DL—Tedy Bruschi, Arizona, 6-1, 255, Roseville, Calif.; DL—Luther Elliss, Utah, 6-6, 288, Mancos, Colo.; DL—Kevin Carter, Florida, 6-6, 265, Tallahassee, Fla.; LB—*Dana Howard, Illinois, 6-0, 235, East St. Louis, Ill.; LB—Ed Stewart, Nebraska, 6-1, 215, Chicago, Ill.; LB—Derrick Brooks, Florida St., 6-1, 226, Pensacola, Fla.; DB—Clifton Abraham, Florida St., 5-9, 185, Dallas, Texas; DB—Bobby Taylor, Notre Dame, 6-3, 201, Longview, Texas; DB—Chris Hudson, Colorado, 5-11, 195, Houston, Texas; DB—Brian Robinson, Auburn, 6-3, 194, Fort Lauderdale, Fla.; DB—Tony Bouie, Arizona, 5-10, 183, New Orleans, La.; P—*Todd Sauerbrun, West Virginia, 6-0, 205, Setauket, N.Y.

1995

Offense WR—Terry Glenn, Ohio St., 5-11, 185, Columbus, Ohio; WR—*Keyshawn Johnson, Southern California, 6-4, 210, Los Angeles, Calif.; TE—*Marco Battaglia, Rutgers, 6-3, 240, Queens, N.Y.; OL—*Jonathan Ogden, UCLA, 6-8, 310, Washington, D.C.; OL—*Jason Odom, Florida, 6-5, 291, Bartow, Fla.; OL—*Orlando Pace, Ohio St., 6-6, 320, Sandusky, Ohio; OL—Jeff Hartings, Penn St., 6-3, 278, St. Henry, Ohio; C—(tie) Clay Shiver, Florida St., 6-2, 285, Tifton, Ga.; Bryan Stoltenberg, Colorado, 6-2, 280, Sugarland, Texas; QB—Tommie Frazier, Nebraska, 6-2, 205, Bradenton, Fla.; RB—*Eddie George, Ohio St., 6-3, 230, Philadelphia, Pa.; RB—Troy Davis, Iowa St., 5-8, 182, Miami, Fla.; PK—Michael Reeder, TCU, 6-0, 160, Sulphur, La.

Defense DL—*Tedy Bruschi, Arizona, 6-1, 253, Roseville, Calif.; DL—Cornell Brown, Virginia Tech, 6-2, 240, Lynchburg, Va.; DL—Marcus Jones, North Carolina, 6-6, 270, Jacksonville, N.C.; DL—Tony Brackens, Texas, 6-4, 250, Fairfield, Texas; LB—*Zach Thomas, Texas Tech, 6-0, 232, Pampa, Texas; LB—Kevin Hardy, Illinois, 6-4, 243, Evansville, Ind.; LB—Pat Fitzgerald, Northwestern, 6-4, 228, Orland Park, Ill.; DB—Chris Canty, Kansas St., 5-10, 190, Voorhees, N.J.; DB—*Lawyer Milloy, Washington, 6-2, 200, Tacoma, Wash.; DB—Aaron Beasley, West Virginia, 6-0, 190, Pottstown,

Pa.; DB—Greg Myers, Colorado St., 6-2, 191, Windsor, Colo.; P—Brad Maynard, Ball St., 6-1, 175, Atlanta, Ind.

1996

Offense WR—Marcus Harris, Wyoming, 6-2, 216, Senior, Minneapolis, Minn.; WR—(tie) Ike Hilliard, Florida, 5-11, 182, Junior, Patterson, La.; Reidel Anthony, Florida, 6-0, 181, Junior, South Bay, Fla.; TE—Tony Gonzalez, California, 6-6, 235, Junior, Huntington Beach, Calif.; OL—*Orlando Pace, Ohio St., 6-6, 330, Junior, Sandusky, Ohio; OL—Juan Roque, Arizona St., 6-8, 319, Senior, Ontario, Calif.; OL—Chris Naeole, Colorado, 6-4, 310, Senior, Kaaava, Hawaii; OL—Dan Neil, Texas, 6-2, 283, Senior, Cypress Creek, Texas; OL—Benji Olson, Washington, 6-4, 310, Sophomore, Port Orchard, Wash.; C—Aaron Taylor, Nebraska, 6-1, 305, Junior, Wichita Falls, Texas; QB—Danny Wuerffel, Florida, 6-2, 209, Senior, Fort Walton Beach, Fla.; RB—*Byron Hanspard, Texas Tech, 6-0, 193, Junior, DeSoto, Texas; RB—Troy Davis, Iowa St., 5-8, 185, Junior, Miami, Fla.; PK—Marc Primanti, North Carolina St., 5-7, 171, Senior, Thorndale, Pa.

Defense DL—Grant Wistrom, Nebraska, 6-5, 250, Junior, Webb City, Mo.; DL—Peter Boulware, Florida St., 6-5, 255, Junior, Columbia, S.C.; DL—*Reinard Wilson, Florida St., 6-2, 255, Senior, Lake City, Fla.; DL—(tie) Derrick Rodgers, Arizona St., 6-2, 220, Junior, Cordova, Tenn.; Mike Vrabel, Ohio St., 6-4, 260, Senior, Akron, Ohio; LB—#Canute Curtis, West Virginia, 6-2, 250, Senior, Amityville, N.Y.; LB—Pat Fitzgerald, Northwestern, 6-2, 243, Senior, Orland Park, Ill.; LB—Matt Russell, Colorado, 6-2, 245, Senior, Fairview Heights, Ill.; LB—Jarrett Irons, Michigan, 6-2, 234, Senior, The Woodlands, Texas; DB—*Chris Canty, Kansas St., 5-10, 190, Junior, Voorhees, N.J.; DB—*Kevin Jackson, Alabama, 6-2, 206, Senior, Dothan, Ala.; DB—Dre' Bly, North Carolina, 5-10, 180, Freshman, Chesapeake, Va.; DB—Shawn Springs, Ohio St., 6-0, 188, Junior, Silver Spring, Md.; P—Brad Maynard, Ball St., 6-1, 176, Senior, Atlanta, Ind.

1997

Offense WR—*Randy Moss, Marshall, 6-5, 210, Sophomore, Rand, W.Va.; WR—Jacquez Green, Florida, 5-9, 168, Junior, Ft. Valley, Ga.; TE—Alonzo Mayes, Oklahoma St., 6-6, 265, Senior, Oklahoma City, Okla.; OL—*Aaron Taylor, Nebraska, 6-1, 305, Senior, Wichita Falls, Texas; OL—Alan Faneca, LSU, 6-5, 310, Junior, Rosenberg, Texas; OL—Kyle Turley, San Diego St., 6-6, 305, Senior, Moreno Valley, Calif.; OL—Chad Overhauser, UCLA, 6-6, 304, Senior, Sacramento, Calif.; C—Olin Kreutz, Washington, 6-4, 290, Junior, Honolulu, Hawaii; QB—Peyton Manning, Tennessee, 6-5, 222, Senior, New Orleans, La.; RB—*Ricky Williams, Texas, 6-0, 220, Junior, San Diego, Calif.; RB—Curtis Enis, Penn St., 6-1, 233, Junior, Union City, Ohio; PK—Martin Gramatica, Kansas St., 5-9, 170, Junior, Buenos Aires, Argentina; KR—Tim Dwight, Iowa, 5-9, 185, Senior, Iowa City, Iowa.

Defense DL—Grant Wistrom, Nebraska, 6-5, 255, Senior, Webb City, Mo.; DL—Andre Wadsworth, Florida St., 6-4, 282, Senior, Miami, Fla.; DL—Greg Ellis, North Carolina, 6-6, 265, Senior, Wendell, N.C.; DL—Jason Peter, Nebraska, 6-5, 285, Senior, Locust, N.J.; LB—Andy Katzenmoyer, Ohio St., 6-4, 260, Sophomore, Westerville, Ohio; LB—Sam Cowart, Florida St., 6-3, 239, Senior, Jacksonville, Fla.; LB—Anthony Simmons, Clemson, 6-1, 225, Junior, Spartanburg, S.C.; LB—Brian Simmons, North Carolina, 6-4, 230, Senior, New Bern, N.C.; DB—*Charles Woodson, Michigan, 6-1, 198, Junior, Fremont, Ohio; DB—Dre' Bly, North Carolina, 5-10, 185, Sophomore, Chesapeake, Va.; DB—Fred Weary, Florida, 5-10, 180, Senior, Jacksonville, Fla.; DB—Brian Lee, Wyoming, 6-2, 200, Senior, Arvada, Colo.; P—Chad Kessler, LSU, 6-1, 197, Senior, Longwood, Fla.

1998

Offense WR—Torry Holt, North Carolina St., 6-2, 188, Senior, Gibsonville, N.C. (Eastern Guilford HS); WR—Peter Warrick, Florida St., 6-0, 190, Junior, Bradenton, Fla. (Southeast HS); WR—Troy Edwards, Louisiana Tech, 5-10, 195, Senior, Shreveport, La. (Huntington HS); TE—*Rufus French, Mississippi, 6-4, 245, Junior, Amory, Miss. (Amory HS); OL—Kris Farris, UCLA, 6-9, 310, Junior, Mission Viejo, Calif. (Santa Margarita HS); OL—Aaron Gibson, Wisconsin, 6-7, 372, Senior, Indianapolis, Ind. (Decatur Central HS); OL—Matt Stinchcomb, Georgia, 6-6, 291, Senior, Lilburn, Ga. (Lilburn HS); OL—Rob Murphy, Ohio St., 6-5, 300, Junior, Cincinnati, Ohio

CONSENSUS ALL-AMERICA SELECTIONS

(Moeller HS); C—Craig Page, Georgia Tech, 6-3, 288, Senior, Jupiter, Fla. (Jupiter HS); QB—Cade McNown, UCLA, 6-1, 214, Senior, West Linn, Ore. (West Linn HS); Michael Bishop, Kansas St., 6-1, 205, Senior, Willis, Texas (Willis HS); QB—Tim Couch, Kentucky, 6-5, 225, Junior, Hyden, Ky. (Leslie County HS); RB—*Ricky Williams, Texas, 6-0, 225, Senior, San Diego, Calif. (Patrick Henry HS); RB—Mike Cloud, Boston College, 5-11, 201, Senior, Portsmouth, R.I. (Portsmouth HS); PK—Sebastian Janikowski, Florida St., 6-2, 255, Sophomore, Daytona Beach, Fla. (Seabreeze HS); KR—David Allen, Kansas St., 5-9, 185, Sophomore, Liberty, Mo. (Liberty HS).

Defense DL—*Tom Burke, Wisconsin, 6-4, 249, Senior, Poplar, Wis. (Northwestern HS); DL—Montae Reagor, Texas Tech, 6-2, 254, Senior, Waxahachie, Texas (Waxahachie HS); DL—Jared DeVries, Iowa, 6-4, 284, Senior, Aplington, Iowa (Aplington-Parkersburg HS); LB—*Chris Claiborne, Southern California, 6-3, 250, Junior, Riverside, Calif. (North HS); LB—*Dat Nguyen, Texas A&M, 6-0, 216, Senior, Rockport, Texas (Rockport-Fulton HS); LB—Jeff Kelly, Kansas St., 6-0, 250, Senior, LaGrange, Texas (LaGrange HS); LB—Al Wilson, Tennessee, 6-0, 226, Senior, Jackson, Tenn. (Central Merry HS); DB—*Chris McAlister, Arizona, 6-2, 185, Senior, Pasadena, Calif. (Pasadena HS); DB—*Antoine Winfield, Ohio St., 5-9, 180, Senior, Akron, Ohio (Garfield HS); DB—Champ Bailey, Georgia, 6-1, 186, Junior, Folkston, Ga. (Folkston HS); DB—Anthony Poindexter, Virginia, 6-1, 220, Senior, Forest, Va. (Jefferson Forest HS); P—Joe Kristosik, UNLV, 6-3, 220, Junior, Las Vegas, Nev. (Bishop Gorman HS).

1999

The 26-man NCAA Consensus All-America Football Team features 14 players on offense and 12 on defense. The players listed had the majority of votes competing against players at that position only. Three first-team votes were considered the minimum number required of the six teams. The only tie was at center where two players tied with two votes each of the five votes available, so both were listed. Eight players were unanimous choices by all six teams used in the consensus chart—Associated Press, Football Writers Association of America, American Football Coaches Association, Walter Camp Foundation, The Football News and The Sporting News.

Offense WR—Troy Walters, Stanford, 5-8, 170, Senior, College Station, Texas (A&M Consolidated HS); WR—*Peter Warrick, Florida St., 6-0, 195, Senior, Bradenton, Fla. (Southeast HS); TE—James Whalen, Kentucky, 6-4, 231, Senior, Portland, Ore. (LaSalle HS); OL—*Chris McIntosh, Wisconsin, 6-7, 310, Senior, Pewaukee, Wis. (Pewaukee HS); OL—*Chris Samuels, Alabama, 6-6, 291, Senior, Mobile, Ala. (Shaw HS); OL—Cosey Coleman, Tennessee, 6-5, 315, Junior, Clarkston, Ga. (Southwest DeKalb HS); OL—Jason Whitaker, Florida St., 6-5, 300, Senior, Panama City, Fla. (Moseley HS); C—Ben Hamilton, Minnesota, 6-5, 271, Junior, Plymouth, Minn. (Wayzata HS); C—Rob Riti, Missouri, 6-3, 289, Senior, Florissant, Mo. (Hazelwood West HS); QB—Joe Hamilton, Georgia Tech, 5-10, 189, Senior, Alvin, S.C. (Macedonia HS); RB—*Ron Dayne, Wisconsin, 5-10, 254, Senior, Berlin, N.J. (Overbrook HS); RB—Thomas Jones, Virginia, 5-10, 205, Senior, Big Stone Gap, Va. (Powell Valley HS); PK—*Sebastian Janikowski, Florida St., 6-2, 255, Junior, Daytona Beach, Fla. (Seabreeze HS); AP—Dennis Northcutt, Arizona, 5-11, 178, Senior, Los Angeles, Calif. (Dorsey HS)#.

Defense DL—*Courtney Brown, Penn St., 6-5, 270, Senior, Alvin, S.C. (Macedonia HS); DL—*Corey Moore, Virginia Tech, 6-0, 225, Senior, Brownsville, Tenn. (Haywood HS); DL—Corey Simon, Florida St., 6-4, 275, Senior, Pompano Beach, Fla. (Ely HS); LB—*LaVar Arrington, Penn St., 6-3, 242, Junior, Pittsburgh, Pa. (North Hills HS); LB—Mark Simoneau, Kansas St., 6-0, 240, Senior, Smith Center, Kan. (Smith Center HS); LB—Brandon Short, Penn St., 6-3, 252, Senior, McKeesport, Pa. (McKeesport HS); DB—Tyrone Carter, Minnesota, 5-9, 184, Senior, Pompano Beach, Fla. (Ely HS); DB—Brian Urlacher, New Mexico, 6-4, 240, Senior, Lovington, N.M. (Lovington HS); DB—Ralph Brown, Nebraska, 5-10, 180, Senior, Hacienda Heights, Calif. (Bishop Amat HS); DB—Deon Grant, Tennessee, 6-3, 205, Junior, Augusta, Ga. (Josey HS); DB—Deltha O'Neal, California, 5-11, 195, Senior, Milpitas, Calif. (Milpitas HS)@; P—Andrew Bayes, East Caro., 6-3, 200, Senior, Hyattsville, Md. (DeMatha HS).

*—Indicates unanimous selection. #Received one vote at wide receiver. @Received one vote on offense.

Consensus All-Americans by College

Beginning in 1924, unanimous selections are indicated by (*).

AIR FORCE
58— Brock Strom, T
70— Ernie Jennings, E
85— Scott Thomas, DB
87— *Chad Hennings, DL
92— *Carlton McDonald, DB

ALABAMA
30— *Fred Sington, T
34— Don Hutson, E
Bill Lee, T
Dixie Howell, B
35— Riley Smith, B
37— Leroy Monsky, G
41— Holt Rast, E
42— Joe Domnanovich, C
45— Vaughn Mancha, C
61— *Billy Neighbors, T
62— *Lee Roy Jordan, C
65— Paul Crane, C
66— Ray Perkins, E
*Cecil Dowdy, T
67— Dennis Homan, E
Bobby Johns, DB
71— Johnny Musso, B
72— *John Hannah, G
73— Buddy Brown, G
74— Leroy Cook, DL
Woodrow Lowe, LB
75— *Leroy Cook, DE
77— Ozzie Newsome, WR
78— Marty Lyons, DL
79— Jim Bunch, T
80— E. J. Junior, DL
81— Tommy Wilcox, DB
82— Mike Pitts, DL
86— *Cornelius Bennett, LB
88— *Derrick Thomas, LB
89— *Keith McCants, LB
90— *Philip Doyle, PK
92— John Copeland, DL
Eric Curry, DL
93— David Palmer, KR
Antonio Langham, DB
96— *Kevin Jackson, DB
99— *Chris Samuels, OL

AMHERST
05— John Hubbard, B

ARIZONA
82— Ricky Hunley, LB
83— *Ricky Hunley, LB
87— Chuck Cecil, DB
90— *Darryll Lewis, DB
92— Rob Waldrop, DL
93— Rob Waldrop, DL
94— Steve McLaughlin, PK
Tedy Bruschi, DL
Tony Bouie, DB
95— *Tedy Bruschi, DL
98— *Chris McAlister, DB
99— Dennis Northcutt, AP

ARIZONA ST.
72— Woody Green, B
73— Woody Green, B
77— John Jefferson, WR
78— *Al Harris, DL
81— Mike Richardson, DB
82— Mike Richardson, DB
Vernon Maxwell, DL
83— Luis Zendejas, PK
84— David Fulcher, DB
85— David Fulcher, DB
86— Danny Villa, OL
87— Randall McDaniel, OL
96— Juan Rogue, OL
Derrick Rodgers, DL
99— Dennis Northcutt, AP

ARKANSAS
48— Clyde Scott, B
54— *Bud Brooks, G
65— Glen Ray Hines, T
Loyd Phillips, DT
66— *Loyd Phillips, DT
68— Jim Barnes, G
69— Rodney Brand, C
70— Dick Bumpas, DT
77— Leotis Harris, G
Steve Little, K
79— *Greg Kolenda, T
81— *Billy Ray Smith, DL
82— *Billy Ray Smith, DL
*Steve Korte, OL
88— Kendall Trainor, PK
Wayne Martin, DL
89— Jim Mabry, OL

ARMY
1898— Charles Romeyn, B
00— William Smith, E
01— Paul Bunker, T
Charles Daly, B
02— Paul Bunker, T-B
Robert Boyers, C
04— Arthur Tipton, C
Henry Torney, B
05— Henry Torney, B
07— William Erwin, G
11— Leland Devore, T
13— Louis Merillat, E
14— John McEwan, C
16— Elmer Oliphant, B
17— Elmer Oliphant, B
22— Ed Garbisch, C
26— Bud Sprague, T
27— Red Cagle, B
28— *Red Cagle, B
29— Red Cagle, B
32— Milt Summerfelt, G
43— *Casimir Myslinski, C
44— Glenn Davis, B
Doc Blanchard, B
45— Tex Coulter, T
John Green, G
*Glenn Davis, B
*Doc Blanchard, B
46— Hank Foldberg, E
*Glenn Davis, B
*Doc Blanchard, B
47— Joe Steffy, G
49— Arnold Galiffa, B
50— *Dan Foldberg, E
57— Bob Anderson, B
58— *Pete Dawkins, B
59— Bill Carpenter, E

AUBURN
32— Jimmy Hitchcock, B
57— *Jimmy Phillips, E
58— Zeke Smith, G
60— Ken Rice, T
64— Tucker Frederickson, B
69— Buddy McClinton, DB
70— Larry Willingham, DB
71— *Pat Sullivan, QB
*Terry Beasley, E
74— Ken Bernich, LB
83— Bo Jackson, RB
84— Gregg Carr, LB
85— *Bo Jackson, RB
86— *Ben Tamburello, C
*Brent Fullwood, RB
87— Tracy Rocker, DL
Aundray Bruce, LB
88— *Tracy Rocker, DL
90— *Ed King, OL
David Rocker, DL
93— Wayne Gandy, OL
Terry Daniel, P
94— Brian Robinson, DB

BALL ST.
95— Brad Maynard, P
96— Brad Maynard, P

BAYLOR
30— Barton Koch, G
56— *Bill Glass, G
63— Lawrence Elkins, E
64— Lawrence Elkins, B
76— Gary Green, DB
79— Mike Singletary, LB
80— *Mike Singletary, LB
86— *Thomas Everett, DB
91— *Santana Dotson, DL

BOSTON COLLEGE
20— Luke Urban, E
40— Gene Goodreault, E
42— Mike Holovak, B
84— *Doug Flutie, QB
Tony Thurman, DB
85— Mike Ruth, DL
94— Pete Mitchell, TE
98— Mike Cloud, RB

BRIGHAM YOUNG
79— *Marc Wilson, QB
80— Nick Eyre, OL
81— *Jim McMahon, QB
82— *Gordon Hudson, TE
83— *Gordon Hudson, TE
*Steve Young, QB
86— Jason Buck, DL
89— Mohammed Elewonibi, OL
90— Ty Detmer, QB
*Chris Smith, TE
91— Ty Detmer, QB

BROWN
02— Thomas Barry, B
06— John Mayhew, B
09— Adrian Regnier, E
10— Earl Sprackling, B
12— George Crowther, B
16— Fritz Pollard, B

CALIFORNIA
21— Brick Muller, E
Dan McMillan, T
22— Brick Muller, E

24— Edwin Horrell, C
28— Irv Phillips, E
30— Ted Beckett, G
35— Larry Lutz, T
37— Sam Chapman, B
38— Vic Bottari, B
48— Jackie Jensen, B
49— *Rod Franz, G
50— Les Richter, G
51— Les Richter, G
68— Ed White, MG
71— Sherman White, DT
74— Steve Bartkowski, QB
75— Chuck Muncie, RB
     Steve Rivera, E
83— Ron Rivera, LB
91— Russell White, RB
92— Sean Dawkins, WR
96— Tony Gonzalez, TE
99— Deltha O'Neal, DB

CARLISLE
1899— Isaac Seneca, B
03— James Johnson, B
07— Albert Exendine, E
     Peter Hauser, B
11— Jim Thorpe, B
12— Jim Thorpe, B

CARNEGIE MELLON
28— Howard Harpster, B

CENTENARY (LA.)
33— Paul Geisler, E

CENTRE
19— James Weaver, C
     Bo McMillin, B
21— Bo McMillin, B

CHICAGO
1898— Clarence Herschberger, B
04— Fred Speik, E
     Walter Eckersall, B
05— Mark Catlin, E
     Walter Eckersall, B
06— Walter Eckersall, B
08— Walter Steffen, B
13— Paul Des Jardien, C
22— John Thomas, B
24— Joe Pondelik, G
35— *Jay Berwanger, B

CLEMSON
67— Harry Olszewski, G
74— Bennie Cunningham, TE
79— Jim Stuckey, DL
81— Jeff Davis, LB
     Terry Kinard, DB
82— *Terry Kinard, DB
83— William Perry, DL
86— Terrence Flagler, RB
87— David Treadwell, PK
88— Donnell Woolford, DB
90— Stacy Long, OL
91— Jeb Flesch, OL
     Levon Kirkland, LB
93— Stacy Seegars, OL
97— Anthony Simmons, LB

COLGATE
13— Ellery Huntington, B
16— Clarence Horning, T
     D. Belford West, T
     Oscar Anderson, B
19— D. Belford West, T
30— Leonard Macaluso, B

COLORADO
37— Byron White, B
60— Joe Romig, G
61— Joe Romig, G
67— Dick Anderson, DB
68— Mike Montler, G
69— Bob Anderson, B
70— Don Popplewell, C
72— Cullen Bryant, DB
85— Barry Helton, P
86— Barry Helton, P
88— Keith English, P
89— Joe Garten, OL
     Alfred Williams, LB
     Tom Rouen, P
90— *Eric Bieniemy, RB
     *Joe Garten, OL
     *Alfred Williams, LB

91— *Jay Leeuwenburg, OL
92— Deon Figures, DB
94— Michael Westbrook, WR
     *Rashaan Salaam, RB
     Chris Hudson, DB
95— Bryan Stoltenberg, C
96— Matt Russell, LB
     Chris Naeole, OL

COLORADO ST.
78— Mike Bell, DL
95— Greg Myers, DB

COLUMBIA
00— Bill Morley, B
01— Harold Weekes, B
     Bill Morley, B
03— Richard Smith, B
42— Paul Governali, B
47— Bill Swiacki, E

CORNELL
1895— Clinton Wyckoff, B
00— Raymond Starbuck, B
01— William Warner, G
     Sanford Hunt, G
02— William Warner, G
06— Elmer Thompson, G
     William Newman, C
08— Bernard O'Rourke, G
14— John O'Hearn, E
     Charles Barrett, B
15— Murray Shelton, E
     Charles Barrett, B
21— Edgar Kaw, B
22— Edgar Kaw, B
23— George Pfann, B
38— Brud Holland, E
39— Nick Drahos, T
40— Nick Drahos, T
71— *Ed Marinaro, B

DARTMOUTH
03— Henry Hooper, C
     Myron Witham, B
04— Joseph Gilman, G
05— Ralph Glaze, E
08— George Schildmiller, E
     Clark Tobin, G
12— Wesley Englehorn, T
13— Robert Hogsett, E
14— Clarence Spears, G
15— Clarence Spears, G
17— Eugene Neely, G
19— Adolph Youngstrom, G
24— Carl Diehl, G
25— Carl Diehl, G
     George Tully, E
     *Andy Oberlander, B
38— Bob MacLeod, B

DUKE
33— Fred Crawford, T
36— Ace Parker, B
71— Ernie Jackson, DB
89— *Clarkston Hines, WR

DUQUESNE
36— Mike Basrak, C

EAST CARO.
83— Terry Long, OL
91— *Robert Jones, LB
99— Andrew Bayes, P

FLORIDA
66— *Steve Spurrier, B
69— Carlos Alvarez, E
75— Sammy Green, LB
80— David Little, LB
82— Wilber Marshall, DL
83— Wilber Marshall, LB
84— Lomas Brown, OT
88— Louis Oliver, DB
89— *Emmitt Smith, RB
91— Brad Culpepper, DL
94— Jack Jackson, WR
     Kevin Carter, DL
95— Jason Odom, OL
96— Danny Wuerffel, QB
     Ike Hilliard, WR
     Reidel Anthony, WR
97— Jacquez Green, WR
     Fred Weary, DB

FLORIDA ST.
64— Fred Biletnikoff, E
67— Ron Sellers, E
79— Ron Simmons, MG
80— Ron Simmons, MG
83— Greg Allen, RB
85— Jamie Dukes, OL
87— *Deion Sanders, DB
88— *Deion Sanders, DB
89— LeRoy Butler, DB
91— *Terrell Buckley, DB
     Marvin Jones, LB
92— *Marvin Jones, LB
93— *Charlie Ward, QB
     *Derrick Brooks, LB
     Corey Sawyer, DB
94— Derrick Brooks, LB
     Clifton Abraham, DB
95— Clay Shiver, C
96— Peter Boulware, DL
     Reinard Wilson, DL
97— Andre Wadsworth, DL
     Sam Cowart, LB
98— Peter Warrick, WR
     Sebastian Janikowski, PK
99— *Sebastian Janikowski, PK
     *Peter Warrick, WR
     Jason Whitaker, OL
     Corey Simon, DL

FORDHAM
36— Alex Wojciechowicz, C
37— Ed Franco, T
     Alex Wojciechowicz, C

GEORGETOWN
26— Harry Connaughton, G

GEORGIA
27— Tom Nash, E
31— Vernon Smith, E
41— Frank Sinkwich, B
42— *Frank Sinkwich, B
46— *Charley Trippi, B
67— Ed Chandler, T
68— Bill Stanfill, DT
     Jake Scott, DB
71— *Royce Smith, G
75— Randy Johnson, G
76— Joel Parrish, G
80— Herschel Walker, RB
81— *Herschel Walker, RB
82— *Herschel Walker, RB
     Terry Hoage, DB
83— Terry Hoage, DB
84— Kevin Butler, PK
     Jeff Sanchez, DB
85— Pete Anderson, C
88— Tim Worley, RB
92— *Garrison Hearst, RB
98— Champ Bailey, DB
     Matt Stinchcomb, OL

GEORGIA TECH
17— Everett Strupper, B
18— Bill Fincher, E
     Joe Guyon, T
     Ashel Day, C
20— Bill Fincher, E
28— Pete Pund, C
42— Harvey Hardy, G
44— Phil Tinsley, E
46— Paul Duke, C
47— Bob Davis, T
52— Hal Miller, T
53— Larry Morris, C
59— Maxie Baughan, C
66— Jim Breland, C
70— Rock Perdoni, DT
73— Randy Rhino, DB
90— Ken Swilling, DB
98— Craig Page, C
99— Joe Hamilton, QB

HARVARD
1889— Arthur Cumnock, E
     John Cranston, G
     James Lee, B
1890— Frank Hallowell, E
     Marshall Newell, T
     John Cranston, C
     Dudley Dean, B
     John Corbett, B
1891— Marshall Newell, T
     Everett Lake, B
1892— Frank Hallowell, E
     Marshall Newell, T
     Bertram Waters, G
     William Lewis, C
     Charles Brewer, B
1893— Marshall Newell, T
     William Lewis, C
     Charles Brewer, B
1894— Bertram Waters, T
1895— Norman Cabot, E
     Charles Brewer, B
1896— Norman Cabot, E
     Edgar Wrightington, B
1897— Alan Doucette, C
     Benjamin Dibblee, B
1898— John Hallowell, E
     Walter Boal, G
     Charles Daly, B
     Benjamin Dibblee, B
1899— David Campbell, E
     Charles Daly, B
1900— John Hallowell, E
     David Campbell, E
     Charles Daly, B
01— David Campbell, E
     Edward Bowditch, E
     Oliver Cutts, T
     Crawford Blagden, T
     William Lee, G
     Charles Barnard, G
     Robert Kernan, B
     Thomas Graydon, B
02— Edward Bowditch, E
     Thomas Graydon, B
03— Daniel Knowlton, T
     Andrew Marshall, G
04— Daniel Hurley, B
05— Beaton Squires, T
     Karl Brill, T
     Francis Burr, G
     Daniel Hurley, B
06— Charles Osborne, T
     Francis Burr, G
07— Patrick Grant, C
     John Wendell, B
08— Hamilton Fish, T
     Charles Nourse, C
     Hamilton Corbett, B
09— Hamilton Fish, T
     Wayland Minot, B
10— Robert McKay, T
     Robert Fisher, G
     Percy Wendell, B
11— Robert Fisher, G
     Percy Wendell, B
12— Samuel Felton, E
     Stanley Pennock, G
     Charles Brickley, B
13— Harvey Hitchcock, E
     Stanley Pennock, G
     Charles Brickley, B
     Edward Mahan, B
14— Huntington Hardwick, E
     Walter Trumbull, T
     Stanley Pennock, G
     Edward Mahan, B
15— Joseph Gilman, T
     Edward Mahan, B
     Richard King, B
16— Harrie Dadmun, T
19— Edward Casey, B
20— Tom Woods, G
21— John Brown, G
22— Charles Hubbard, G
23— Charles Hubbard, G
29— Ben Ticknor, C
30— *Ben Ticknor, C
31— Barry Wood, B
41— *Endicott Peabody, G

HOLY CROSS
74— John Provost, DB

CONSENSUS ALL-AMERICANS BY COLLEGE

HOUSTON
67— Rich Stotter, G
69— Bill Bridges, G
70— Elmo Wright, E
76— Wilson Whitley, DT
80— Leonard Mitchell, DL
88— Jason Phillips, WR
89— Andre Ware, QB

ILLINOIS
14— Perry Graves, E
     Ralph Chapman, G
15— Bart Macomber, B
18— John Depler, C
20— Charles Carney, E
23— James McMillen, G
     Red Grange, B
24— *Red Grange, B
25— *Red Grange, B
26— Bernie Shively, G
46— Alex Agase, G
51— Johnny Karras, B
53— J. C. Caroline, B
59— Bill Burrell, G
63— *Dick Butkus, C
64— Dick Butkus, C
65— *Jim Grabowski, B
84— *David Williams, WR
85— *David Williams, WR
89— *Moe Gardner, DL
90— Moe Gardner, DL
94— *Dana Howard, LB
95— Kevin Hardy, LB

INDIANA
42— Billy Hillenbrand, B
44— John Tavener, C
45— Bob Ravensberg, E
88— Anthony Thompson, RB
89— *Anthony Thompson, RB
91— *Vaughn Dunbar, RB

IOWA
19— Lester Belding, E
21— Aubrey Devine, B
22— Gordon Locke, B
39— Nile Kinnick, B
54— Calvin Jones, G
55— Calvin Jones, G
57— Alex Karras, T
58— *Randy Duncan, B
81— Andre Tippett, DL
     Reggie Roby, P
84— Larry Station, LB
85— *Chuck Long, QB
     *Larry Station, LB
88— Marv Cook, TE
91— Leroy Smith, DL
97— Tim Dwight, KR
98— Jared DeVries, DL

IOWA ST.
38— Ed Bock, G
89— Mike Busch, TE
95— Troy Davis, RB
96— Troy Davis, RB

KANSAS
63— Gale Sayers, B
64— Gale Sayers, B
68— John Zook, DE
73— David Jaynes, QB

KANSAS ST.
77— Gary Spani, LB
92— Sean Snyder, P
95— Chris Canty, DB
96— *Chris Canty, DB
97— Martin Gramatica, PK
98— Jeff Kelly, LB
     Michael Bishop, QB
     David Allen, KR
99— Mark Simoneau, LB

KENTUCKY
50— Bob Gain, T
     Babe Parilli, B
51— Babe Parilli, B
56— Lou Michaels, T
57— Lou Michaels, T
65— Sam Ball, T
77— *Art Still, DL
98— Tim Couch, QB
99— James Whalen, TE

LAFAYETTE
00— Walter Bachman, C
01— Walter Bachman, C
21— Frank Schwab, G
22— Frank Schwab, G

LSU
35— Gaynell Tinsley, E
36— *Gaynell Tinsley, E
39— Ken Kavanaugh, E
54— Sid Fournet, T
58— *Billy Cannon, B
59— Billy Cannon, B
61— *Roy Winston, G
62— *Jerry Stovall, B
70— Mike Anderson, LB
     Tommy Casanova, DB
71— Tommy Casanova, DB
72— Bert Jones, QB
77— Charles Alexander, RB
78— Charles Alexander, RB
87— Wendell Davis, WR
     *Nacho Albergamo, C
97— Alan Faneca, OL
     Chad Kessler, P

LOUISIANA TECH
92— Willie Roaf, OL
98— Troy Edwards, WR

MARQUETTE
36— Ray Buivid, B

MARSHALL
97— *Randy Moss, WR

MARYLAND
51— *Bob Ward, G
52— Dick Modzelewski, T
     *Jack Scarbath, B
53— *Stan Jones, T
55— *Bob Pellegrini, C
61— Gary Collins, E
74— *Randy White, DL
76— Joe Campbell, DT
79— Dale Castro, PK
85— J. D. Maarleveld, OL

MEMPHIS
92— Joe Allison, PK

MIAMI (FLA.)
61— Bill Miller, E
66— Tom Beier, DB
67— *Ted Hendricks, DE
68— *Ted Hendricks, DE
73— Tony Cristiani, DL
74— Rubin Carter, MG
81— Fred Marion, DB
84— Eddie Brown, WR
85— Willie Smith, TE
86— *Vinny Testaverde, QB
     *Jerome Brown, DL
     Bennie Blades, DB
87— *Daniel Stubbs, DL
     *Bennie Blades, DB
88— Steve Walsh, QB
     Bill Hawkins, DL
89— Greg Mark, DL
90— Maurice Crum, LB
     *Russell Maryland, DL
91— Carlos Huerta, PK
     Darryl Williams, DB
92— *Gino Torretta, QB
     Micheal Barrow, LB
     Ryan McNeil, DB
94— *Warren Sapp, DL

MICHIGAN
1898— William Cunningham, C
01— Neil Snow, E
03— Willie Heston, B
04— Willie Heston, B
07— Adolph Schulz, C
09— Albert Benbrook, G
10— Stanfield Wells, E
     Albert Benbrook, G
13— Miller Pontius, T
     Jim Craig, B
14— John Maulbetsch, B
22— Harry Kipke, B
23— Jack Blott, C
25— Bennie Oosterbaan, E
     Benny Friedman, B
26— Bennie Oosterbaan, E
     Benny Friedman, B
27— *Bennie Oosterbaan, E
28— Otto Pommerening, T
32— Harry Newman, B
33— Francis Wistert, T
     *Chuck Bernard, C
38— Ralph Heikkinen, G
39— Tom Harmon, B
40— *Tom Harmon, B
41— Bob Westfall, B
42— Albert Wistert, T
     Julie Franks, G
43— *Bill Daley, B
47— Bob Chappuis, B
48— Dick Rifenburg, E
     Alvin Wistert, T
49— Alvin Wistert, T
55— Ron Kramer, E
56— *Ron Kramer, E
65— Bill Yearby, DT
66— *Jack Clancy, E
69— *Jim Mandich, E
     Tom Curtis, DB
70— Dan Dierdorf, T
71— Reggie McKenzie, G
     *Mike Taylor, LB
72— Paul Seymour, T
     Randy Logan, DB
73— Dave Gallagher, DL
     Dave Brown, DB
74— *Dave Brown, DB
76— Rob Lytle, RB
     Mark Donahue, G
77— *Mark Donahue, G
79— Ron Simpkins, LB
81— Anthony Carter, WR
     Ed Muransky, OL
     Kurt Becker, OL
82— *Anthony Carter, WR
85— Mike Hammerstein, DL
     Brad Cochran, DB
86— Garland Rivers, DB
87— John Elliott, OL
88— John Vitale, C
     *Mark Messner, DL
89— *Tripp Welborne, DB
90— *Tripp Welborne, DB
91— *Desmond Howard, WR
     *Greg Skrepenak, OL
96— Jarrett Irons, LB
97— *Charles Woodson, DB

MICHIGAN ST.
15— Neno Jerry DaPrato, B
35— Sidney Wagner, G
49— Ed Bagdon, G
51— Bob Carey, E
     *Don Coleman, T
53— Don Dohoney, E
55— Norman Masters, T
     Earl Morrall, B
57— Dan Currie, C
     Walt Kowalczyk, B
58— Sam Williams, E
62— George Saimes, B
63— Sherman Lewis, B
65— Bubba Smith, DE
     *George Webster, DB
66— Clint Jones, B
     *Bubba Smith, DE
     *George Webster, DB
72— *Brad VanPelt, DB
85— *Lorenzo White, RB
87— Lorenzo White, RB
88— Tony Mandarich, OL
89— *Percy Snow, LB
     Bob Kula, OL

MINNESOTA
03— Fred Schacht, T
09— John McGovern, B
10— James Walker, T
16— Bert Baston, E
17— George Hauser, T
23— Ray Ecklund, E
26— Herb Joesting, B
27— Herb Joesting, B
29— Bronko Nagurski, T
31— Biggie Munn, G
34— Frank Larson, E
     Bill Bevan, G
     Pug Lund, B
35— Ed Widseth, T

36— *Ed Widseth, T
40— Urban Odson, T
     George Franck, B
41— Dick Wildung, T
     Bruce Smith, B
42— Dick Wildung, T
48— Leo Nomellini, T
49— Leo Nomellini, T
     *Clayton Tonnemaker, C
53— *Paul Giel, B
60— Tom Brown, G
61— Sandy Stephens, B
62— *Bobby Bell, T
63— Carl Eller, T
65— Aaron Brown, DE
99— Tyrone Carter, DB
     Ben Hamilton, C

MISSISSIPPI
47— Charley Conerly, B
53— Crawford Mims, G
59— Charlie Flowers, B
60— *Jake Gibbs, B
62— Jim Dunaway, T
79— Jim Miller, P
92— Everett Lindsay, OL
98— Rufus French, TE

MISSISSIPPI ST.
74— Jimmy Webb, DL

MISSOURI
41— Darold Jenkins, C
60— *Danny LaRose, E
65— Johnny Roland, DB
68— Roger Wehrli, DB
78— Kellen Winslow, TE
86— John Clay, OL
99— Rob Riti, C

NAVY
07— Bill Dague, E
08— Percy Northcroft, T
     Ed Lange, B
11— Jack Dalton, B
13— John Brown, G
18— Lyman Perry, G
     Wolcott Roberts, B
22— Wendell Taylor, T
26— *Frank Wickhorst, T
28— Edward Burke, G
34— Fred Borries, B
43— Don Whitmire, T
44— *Don Whitmire, T
     Ben Chase, G
     Bob Jenkins, B
45— Dick Duden, E
54— Ron Beagle, E
55— Ron Beagle, E
60— *Joe Bellino, B
63— *Roger Staubach, B
75— *Chet Moeller, DB
83— Napoleon McCallum, RB
85— Napoleon McCallum, RB

NEBRASKA
15— Guy Chamberlin, E
24— Ed Weir, T
25— *Ed Weir, T
33— George Sauer, B
36— Sam Francis, B
63— *Bob Brown, G
64— *Larry Kramer, T
65— Freeman White, E
     Walt Barnes, DT
66— LaVerne Allers, G
     Wayne Meylan, MG
67— Wayne Meylan, MG
70— Bob Newton, T
71— Johnny Rodgers, FL
     Willie Harper, DE
     Larry Jacobson, DT
72— *Johnny Rodgers, FL
     Willie Harper, DE
     *Rich Glover, MG
73— *John Dutton, DL
74— Marvin Crenshaw, OT
75— *Rik Bonness, C
76— Dave Butterfield, DB
78— Kelvin Clark, OT
79— *Junior Miller, TE
80— Randy Schleusener, OL
     Jarvis Redwine, RB
81— *Dave Rimington, C

AWARD WINNERS

82— *Dave Rimington, C
      Mike Rozier, RB
83— *Irving Fryar, WR
      Dean Steinkuhler, OL
      *Mike Rozier, RB
84— *Mark Traynowicz, C
86— *Danny Noonan, DL
88— Jake Young, C
      *Broderick Thomas, LB
89— Jake Young, C
92— *Will Shields, OL
93— *Trev Alberts, LB
94— *Zach Wiegert, OL
      Brenden Stai, OL
      Ed Stewart, LB
95— Tommie Frazier, QB
96— Aaron Taylor, C
      Grant Wistrom, DL
97— *Aaron Taylor, OL
      Grant Wistrom, DL
      Jason Peter, DL
99— Ralph Brown, DB

UNLV
98— Joe Kristosik, P

NEW MEXICO
89— Terance Mathis, WR
99— Brian Urlacher, DB

NEW YORK U.
28— Ken Strong, B

NORTH CAROLINA
37— Andy Bershak, E
48— Charlie Justice, B
70— Don McCauley, B
72— Ron Rusnak, G
74— Ken Huff, G
77— Dee Hardison, DL
80— *Lawrence Taylor, LB
83— William Fuller, DL
95— Marcus Jones, DL
96— Dre' Bly, DB
97— Greg Ellis, DL
      Brian Simmons, LB
      Dre' Bly, DB

NORTH CAROLINA ST.
67— Dennis Byrd, DT
73— Bill Yoest, G
78— Jim Ritcher, C
      Ted Brown, RB
79— *Jim Ritcher, C
96— Marc Primanti, PK
98— Torry Holt, WR

NORTH TEXAS
68— Joe Greene, DT

NORTHERN ILL.
93— *LeShon Johnson, RB

NORTHWESTERN
26— Ralph Baker, B
30— Frank Baker, E
31— Jack Riley, T
      Dallas Marvil, T
      Pug Rentner, B
36— Steve Reid, G
40— Alf Bauman, T
45— Max Morris, E
59— Ron Burton, B
62— Jack Cvercko, G
95— Pat Fitzgerald, LB
96— Pat Fitzgerald, LB

NOTRE DAME
13— Gus Dorais, B
17— Frank Rydzewski, C
20— George Gipp, B
21— Eddie Anderson, E
24— Harry Stuhldreher, B
      Jimmy Crowley, B
      Elmer Layden, B
26— Bud Boeringer, C
27— John Smith, G
29— Jack Cannon, G
      *Frank Carideo, B
30— *Frank Carideo, B
      Marchy Schwartz, B
31— Tommy Yarr, C
      Marchy Schwartz, B
32— *Joe Kurth, T
34— Jack Robinson, C
35— Wayne Millner, E
37— Chuck Sweeney, E

38— *Ed Beinor, T
41— Bob Dove, E
42— Bob Dove, E
43— John Yonakor, E
      Jim White, T
      Pat Filley, G
      Angelo Bertelli, B
      Creighton Miller, B
46— George Connor, T
      *John Lujack, B
47— George Connor, T
      Bill Fischer, G
      *John Lujack, B
48— Leon Hart, E
      Bill Fischer, G
      Emil Sitko, B
49— *Leon Hart, E
      *Emil Sitko, B
      Bob Williams, B
50— Jerry Groom, C
52— *Johnny Lattner, B
53— Art Hunter, T
      *Johnny Lattner, B
54— *Ralph Guglielmi, B
55— Paul Hornung, B
57— Al Ecuyer, G
59— Monty Stickles, E
64— Jack Snow, E
      John Huarte, B
65— *Dick Arrington, G
      Nick Rassas, B
66— Tom Regner, G
      *Nick Eddy, B
      Alan Page, DE
      *Jim Lynch, LB
67— Tom Schoen, DB
68— George Kunz, T
      Terry Hanratty, QB
69— *Mike McCoy, DT
70— Tom Gatewood, E
      Larry DiNardo, G
71— *Walt Patulski, DE
      Clarence Ellis, DB
72— *Greg Marx, DT
73— Dave Casper, TE
      Mike Townsend, DB
74— Pete Demmerle, WR
      Gerry DiNardo, G
75— *Steve Niehaus, DT
76— Ken MacAfee, TE
      *Ross Browner, DE
77— *Ken MacAfee, TE
      *Ross Browner, DL
      Luther Bradley, DB
78— Dave Huffman, C
      *Bob Golic, LB
79— Vagas Ferguson, RB
80— *John Scully, C
      Bob Crable, LB
81— Bob Crable, LB
87— *Tim Brown, WR
88— Frank Stams, DL
      Michael Stonebreaker, LB
89— *Todd Lyght, DB
      Chris Zorich, DL
90— *Raghib Ismail, WR
      Todd Lyght, DB
      *Michael Stonebreaker, LB
      *Chris Zorich, DL
91— Mirko Jurkovic, OL
92— Aaron Taylor, OL
93— *Aaron Taylor, OL
      Jeff Burris, DB
94— Bobby Taylor, DB

OHIO ST.
16— Charles Harley, B
17— Charles Bolen, E
      Charles Harley, B
19— Charles Harley, B
20— *Iolas Huffman, G
      Gaylord Stinchcomb, B
21— Iolas Huffman, T
25— Ed Hess, G
28— Wes Fesler, E
29— Wes Fesler, E
30— *Wes Fesler, E
35— Gomer Jones, C
39— Esco Sarkkinen, E
44— Jack Dugger, E
      Bill Hackett, G
      *Les Horvath, B

45— *Warren Amling, G
46— Warren Amling, T
50— *Vic Janowicz, B
54— *Howard Cassady, B
55— *Howard Cassady, B
56— *Jim Parker, G
58— Bob White, B
60— *Bob Ferguson, B
61— *Bob Ferguson, B
68— Dave Foley, T
69— Jim Otis, B
      Jim Stillwagon, MG
      Jack Tatum, DB
70— *Jim Stillwagon, MG
      *Jack Tatum, DB
72— Randy Gradishar, LB
73— *John Hicks, OT
      *Randy Gradishar, LB
74— Kurt Schumacher, OT
      Steve Myers, C
      *Archie Griffin, RB
75— *Archie Griffin, RB
      Ted Smith, G
      Tim Fox, DB
76— Chris Ward, T
      Bob Brudzinski, DE
77— *Chris Ward, T
      Tom Cousineau, LB
78— Tom Cousineau, LB
79— Ken Fritz, G
82— Marcus Marek, LB
84— Jim Lachey, OG
      *Keith Byars, RB
86— Cris Carter, WR
      Chris Spielman, LB
87— *Chris Spielman, LB
      *Tom Tupa, P
93— Dan Wilkinson, DL
94— Korey Stringer, OL
95— Terry Glenn, WR
      *Orlando Pace, OL
      *Eddie George, RB
96— *Orlando Pace, OL
      Mike Vrabel, DL
      Shawn Springs, DB
97— Andy Katzenmoyer, LB
98— *Antoine Winfield, DB
      Rob Murphy, OL

OKLAHOMA
38— Waddy Young, E
48— Buddy Burris, G
50— Jim Weatherall, T
      Leon Heath, B
51— *Jim Weatherall, T
52— Billy Vessels, B
53— J. D. Roberts, G
54— Max Boydston, E
      Kurt Burris, C
55— Bo Bolinger, G
56— *Jerry Tubbs, C
      Tommy McDonald, B
57— Bill Krisher, G
      Clendon Thomas, B
58— Bob Harrison, C
63— Jim Grisham, B
64— Ralph Neely, T
65— Carl McAdams, LB
67— *Granville Liggins, MG
69— *Steve Owens, B
71— *Greg Pruitt, B
      Tom Brahaney, C
72— *Greg Pruitt, B
      Tom Brahaney, C
73— *Lucious Selmon, DL
      Rod Shoate, LB
74— John Roush, G
      *Joe Washington, RB
      *Rod Shoate, LB
75— *Lee Roy Selmon, DT
      Dewey Selmon, MG
      Jimbo Elrod, DE
76— *Mike Vaughan, OT
77— *Zac Henderson, DB
78— *Greg Roberts, G
      *Billy Sims, RB
79— *Billy Sims, RB
      *George Cumby, LB
80— Louis Oubre, OL
81— Terry Crouch, OL
82— Rick Bryan, DL
83— *Rick Bryan, DL
84— Tony Casillas, DL
85— Tony Casillas, DL
      *Brian Bosworth, LB

86— *Keith Jackson, TE
      *Brian Bosworth, LB
87— *Keith Jackson, TE
      *Mark Hutson, OL
      Dante Jones, LB
      Rickey Dixon, DB
88— *Anthony Phillips, OL

OKLAHOMA ST.
45— Bob Fenimore, B
69— John Ward, T
76— Derrel Gofourth, C
77— *Terry Miller, RB
84— Rod Brown, DB
85— Thurman Thomas, RB
      *Leslie O'Neal, DL
88— Hart Lee Dykes, WR
      *Barry Sanders, RB
97— Alonzo Mayes, TE

OREGON
62— Mel Renfro, B

OREGON ST.
56— John Witte, T
58— Ted Bates, T
62— *Terry Baker, B
63— Vern Burke, E
68— *John Didion, C

PENNSYLVANIA
1891— John Adams, C
1892— Harry Thayer, B
1894— Charles Gelbert, E
      Arthur Knipe, B
      George Brooke, B
1895— Charles Gelbert, E
      Charles Wharton, G
      Alfred Bull, C
      George Brooke, B
1896— Charles Gelbert, E
      Charles Wharton, G
      Wylie Woodruff, G
1897— John Outland, T
      T. Truxton Hare, G
      John Minds, B
1898— T. Truxton Hare, G
      Pete Overfield, C
      John Outland, B
1899— T. Truxton Hare, G
      Pete Overfield, C
      Josiah McCracken, B
00—   T. Truxton Hare, G
04—   Frank Piekarski, G
      Vincent Stevenson, B
      Andrew Smith, B
05—   Otis Lamson, T
      Robert Torrey, C
06—   August Ziegler, G
      William Hollenback, B
07—   Dexter Draper, T
      August Ziegler, G
08—   Hunter Scarlett, E
      William Hollenback, B
10—   Ernest Cozens, C
      E. LeRoy Mercer, B
12—   E. LeRoy Mercer, B
17—   Henry Miller, E
19—   Henry Miller, E
22—   John Thurman, T
24—   Ed McGinley, T
27—   Ed Hake, T
28—   Paul Scull, B
43—   Bob Odell, B
45—   George Savitsky, T
47—   Chuck Bednarik, C
48—   Chuck Bednarik, C

PENN ST.
06—   William Dunn, C
19—   Bob Higgins, E
20—   Charles Way, B
21—   Glenn Killinger, B
23—   Harry Wilson, B
59—   Richie Lucas, B
64—   Glenn Ressler, G
68— *Ted Kwalick, E
      Dennis Onkotz, LB
69— *Mike Reid, DT
      Dennis Onkotz, LB
70—   Jack Ham, LB
71—   Dave Joyner, T
72—   Bruce Bannon, DE
      John Skorupan, LB

CONSENSUS ALL-AMERICANS BY COLLEGE

73—*John Cappelletti, B
74— Mike Hartenstine, DL
75— Greg Buttle, LB
78—*Keith Dorney, OT
  *Chuck Fusina, QB
  *Bruce Clark, DL
79— Bruce Clark, DL
81—*Sean Farrell, OL
86— D. J. Dozier, RB
  Shane Conlan, LB
92— O. J. McDuffie, WR
94— Kerry Collins, QB
  *Ki-Jana Carter, RB
95— Jeff Hartings, OL
97— Curtis Enis, RB
99—*LaVar Arrington, LB
  *Courtney Brown, DL
  Brandon Short, LB

PITTSBURGH
15— Robert Peck, C
16— James Herron, E
  Robert Peck, C
17— Dale Seis, G
  John Sutherland, G
18— Leonard Hilty, T
  Tom Davies, B
  George McLaren, B
20— Herb Stein, C
21— Herb Stein, C
25— Ralph Chase, T
27—*Gibby Welch, B
28— Mike Getto, T
29—*Joe Donchess, E
  Ray Montgomery, G
31— Jesse Quatse, T
32— Joe Skladany, E
  *Warren Heller, B
33— Joe Skladany, E
34— Chuck Hartwig, G
36— Averell Daniell, T
37— Tony Matisi, T
  Marshall Goldberg, B
38—*Marshall Goldberg, B
56—*Joe Walton, E
58— John Guzik, G
60—*Mike Ditka, E
63— Paul Martha, B
76—*Tony Dorsett, RB
  Al Romano, MG
77— Tom Brzoza, C
  Randy Holloway, DL
  Bob Jury, DB
78— Hugh Green, DL
79— Hugh Green, DL
80— Hugh Green, DL
  *Mark May, OL
81— Sal Sunseri, LB
82— Jimbo Covert, OL
83—*Bill Fralic, OL
84—*Bill Fralic, OT
86— Randy Dixon, OL
  Tony Woods, DL
87— Craig Heyward, RB
88— Mark Stepnoski, OL
90— Brian Greenfield, P

PRINCETON
1889— Hector Cowan, T
  William George, C
  Edgar Allan Poe, B
  Roscoe Channing, B
  Knowlton Ames, B
1890— Ralph Warren, E
  Jesse Riggs, G
  Sheppard Homans, B
1891— Jesse Riggs, G
  Philip King, B
  Sheppard Homans, B
1892— Arthur Wheeler, G
  Philip King, B
1893— Thomas Trenchard, E
  Langdon Lea, T
  Arthur Wheeler, G
  Philip King, B
  Franklin Morse, B
1894— Langdon Lea, T
  Arthur Wheeler, G
1895— Langdon Lea, T
  Dudley Riggs, G
1896— William Church, T
  Robert Gailey, C

Addison Kelly, B
  John Baird, B
1897— Garrett Cochran, E
  Addison Kelly, B
1898— Lew Palmer, E
  Arthur Hillebrand, T
1899— Arthur Hillebrand, T
  Arthur Poe, E
  Howard Reiter, B
01— Ralph Davis, E
02— John DeWitt, G
03— Howard Henry, E
  John DeWitt, G
  J. Dana Kafer, B
04— James Cooney, T
05— James McCormick, B
06— L. Casper Wister, E
  James Cooney, T
  Edward Dillon, B
07— L. Casper Wister, E
  Edwin Harlan, B
  James McCormick, B
08— Frederick Tibbott, B
10— Talbot Pendleton, B
11— Sanford White, E
  Edward Hart, T
  Joseph Duff, G
12— John Logan, G
13— Harold Ballin, T
14— Harold Ballin, T
16— Frank Hogg, G
18— Frank Murrey, B
20— Stan Keck, T
  Donold Lourie, B
21— Stan Keck, G
22— C. Herbert Treat, T
25— Ed McMillan, C
35— John Weller, G
51—*Dick Kazmaier, B
52— Frank McPhee, E
65— Stas Maliszewski, G

PURDUE
29— Elmer Sleight, T
  Ralph Welch, B
32—*Paul Moss, E
33— Duane Purvis, B
40— Dave Rankin, E
43— Alex Agase, G
52— Bernie Flowers, E
65— Bob Griese, QB
67—*Leroy Keyes, B
68—*Leroy Keyes, B
  Chuck Kyle, MG
69—*Mike Phipps, QB
72— Otis Armstrong, B
  Dave Butz, DT
80—*Dave Young, TE
  *Mark Herrmann, QB
86— Rod Woodson, DB

RICE
46— Weldon Humble, G
49— James Williams, E
54— Dicky Maegle, B
58— Buddy Dial, E
76— Tommy Kramer, QB
91— Trevor Cobb, RB

RICHMOND
69— Walker Gillette, E
78— Jeff Nixon, DB

RUTGERS
17— Paul Robeson, E
18— Paul Robeson, E
61— Alex Kroll, C
95—*Marco Battaglia, TE

ST. MARY'S (CAL.)
27— Larry Bettencourt, C
45—*Herman Wedemeyer, B

SAN DIEGO ST.
92—*Marshall Faulk, RB
93—*Marshall Faulk, RB
97— Kyle Turley, OL

SANTA CLARA
38— Alvord Wolff, T
39— John Schiechl, C

SOUTH CAROLINA
80—*George Rogers, RB
84— Del Wilkes, OG

SOUTHERN CALIFORNIA
26— Mort Kaer, B
27— Jesse Hibbs, T
  Morley Drury, B
30— Erny Pinckert, B
31— John Baker, G
  Gus Shaver, B
32—*Ernie Smith, T
33— Aaron Rosenberg, G
  *Cotton Warburton, B
39—*Harry Smith, G
43— Ralph Heywood, E
44— John Ferraro, T
47— Paul Cleary, E
52— Elmer Willhoite, G
  Jim Sears, B
62— Hal Bedsole, E
65—*Mike Garrett, B
66— Ron Yary, T
  Nate Shaw, DB
67—*Ron Yary, T
  *O. J. Simpson, B
  Tim Rossovich, DE
  Adrian Young, LB
68—*O. J. Simpson, B
69— Jim Gunn, DE
70— Charlie Weaver, DE
72—*Charles Young, TE
73— Lynn Swann, WR
  Booker Brown, OT
  Richard Wood, LB
  Artimus Parker, DB
74—*Anthony Davis, RB
  Richard Wood, LB
75—*Ricky Bell, RB
76—*Ricky Bell, RB
  Gary Jeter, DT
  Dennis Thurman, DB
77—*Dennis Thurman, DB
78—*Pat Howell, G
  *Charles White, RB
79—*Brad Budde, G
  *Charles White, RB
80— Keith Van Horne, OL
  *Ronnie Lott, DB
81— Roy Foster, OL
  *Marcus Allen, RB
82—*Don Mosebar, OL
  Bruce Matthews, OL
  George Achica, MG
83— Tony Slaton, C
84— Jack Del Rio, LB
85— Jeff Bregel, OL
86— Jeff Bregel, OL
  Tim McDonald, DB
87— Dave Cadigan, OL
89—*Mark Carrier, DB
  Tim Ryan, DL
93— Johnnie Morton, WR
94— Tony Boselli, OL
95—*Keyshawn Johnson, WR
98—*Chris Claiborne, LB

SOUTHERN METHODIST
35— J. C. Wetsel, G
  Bobby Wilson, B
47—*Doak Walker, B
48—*Doak Walker, B
49—*Doak Walker, B
50— Kyle Rote, B
51— Dick Hightower, C
66— John LaGrone, MG
68— Jerry LeVias, E
72— Robert Popelka, DB
74— Louie Kelcher, G
78— Emanuel Tolbert, WR
80— John Simmons, DB
82—*Eric Dickerson, RB
83—*Russell Carter, DB
85— Reggie Dupard, RB

STANFORD
24— Jim Lawson, E
25— Ernie Nevers, B
28— Seraphim Post, G
  Don Robesky, G
32— Bill Corbus, G
33— Bill Corbus, G
34— Bob Reynolds, T
  Bobby Grayson, B
35— James Moscrip, E
  *Bobby Grayson, B

40— Frank Albert, B
41— Frank Albert, B
42— Chuck Taylor, G
50— Bill McColl, E
51—*Bill McColl, E
56— John Brodie, QB
70— Jim Plunkett, QB
71— Jeff Siemon, LB
74— Pat Donovan, DL
77— Guy Benjamin, QB
79— Ken Margerum, WR
80—*Ken Margerum, WR
82—*John Elway, QB
86— Brad Muster, RB
91— Bob Whitfield, OL
99— Troy Walters, WR

SYRACUSE
08— Frank Horr, T
15— Harold White, G
17— Alfred Cobb, T
18— Lou Usher, T
  Joe Alexander, G
19— Joe Alexander, G
23— Pete McRae, E
26— Vic Hanson, E
56—*Jim Brown, B
59—*Roger Davis, G
60— Ernie Davis, B
61—*Ernie Davis, B
67—*Larry Csonka, B
85—*Tim Green, DL
87—*Don McPherson, QB
  Ted Gregory, DL
90— John Flannery, C
92—*Chris Gedney, TE

TEMPLE
85— John Rienstra, OL
86—*Paul Palmer, RB

TENNESSEE
29— Gene McEver, B
33— Beattie Feathers, B
38— Bowden Wyatt, E
39— Ed Molinski, G
  George Cafego, B
40—*Bob Suffridge, G
46— Dick Huffman, T
51—*Hank Lauricella, B
52— John Michels, G
56—*John Majors, B
65— Frank Emanuel, LB
66— Paul Naumoff, LB
67—*Bob Johnson, C
68—*Charles Rosenfelder, G
  Steve Kiner, LB
69— Chip Kell, G
  *Steve Kiner, LB
70—*Chip Kell, G
71—*Bobby Majors, DB
75— Larry Seivers, E
76— Larry Seivers, SE
79— Roland James, DB
83—*Reggie White, DL
84— Bill Mayo, OG
85— Tim McGee, WR
89—*Eric Still, OL
90—*Antone Davis, OL
91— Dale Carter, DB
97— Peyton Manning, QB
98— Al Wilson, LB
99— Cosey Coleman, OL
  Deon Grant, DB

TEXAS
45— Hubert Bechtol, E
46— Hubert Bechtol, E
47— Bobby Layne, B
50—*Bud McFadin, G
53— Carlton Massey, E
61—*Jimmy Saxton, B
62— Johnny Treadwell, G
63—*Scott Appleton, T
65— Tommy Nobis, LB
68— Chris Gilbert, B
69— Bob McKay, T
70— Bobby Wuensch, T
  Steve Worster, B
  Bill Atessis, DE
71—*Jerry Sisemore, T
72—*Jerry Sisemore, T
73—*Bill Wyman, C

AWARD WINNERS

Roosevelt Leaks, B
75— Bob Simmons, T
77— *Earl Campbell, RB
   *Brad Shearer, DL
78— *Johnnie Johnson, DB
79— *Steve McMichael, DL
   *Johnnie Johnson, DB
80— Kenneth Sims, DL
81— Terry Tausch, OL
   *Kenneth Sims, DL
83— Doug Dawson, OL
   Jeff Leiding, LB
   Jerry Gray, DB
84— Tony Degrate, DL
   *Jerry Gray, DB
95— Tony Brackens, DL
96— Dan Neil, OL
97— *Ricky Williams, RB
98— *Ricky Williams, RB

TEXAS A&M
37— Joe Routt, G
39— John Kimbrough, B
40— Marshall Robnett, G
   *John Kimbrough, B
57— *John David Crow, B
70— Dave Elmendorf, DB
74— Pat Thomas, DB
75— *Ed Simonini, LB
   Pat Thomas, DB
76— Tony Franklin, PK
   *Robert Jackson, LB
85— Johnny Holland, LB
87— John Roper, DL
90— Darren Lewis, RB
91— Kevin Smith, DB
92— *Marcus Buckley, LB
93— Aaron Glenn, DB
   Sam Adams, DL
94— Leeland McElroy, KR
98— *Dat Nguyen, LB

TCU
35— Darrell Lester, C
36— Sammy Baugh, B
38— Ki Aldrich, C
   *Davey O'Brien, B
55— *Jim Swink, B
59— Don Floyd, T
60— *Bob Lilly, T
84— *Kenneth Davis, RB
91— Kelly Blackwell, TE
95— Michael Reeder, PK

TEXAS TECH
60— E. J. Holub, C
65— Donny Anderson, B
77— Dan Irons, T
82— Gabriel Rivera, DL
91— *Mark Bounds, P
95— *Zach Thomas, LB
96— *Byron Hanspard, RB
98— Montae Reagor, DL

TOLEDO
71— Mel Long, DT

TULANE
31— *Jerry Dalrymple, E
32— Don Zimmerman, B
39— Harley McCollum, T
41— Ernie Blandin, T

TULSA
65— *Howard Twilley, E
91— Jerry Ostroski, OL

UCLA
46— *Burr Baldwin, E
52— Donn Moomaw, C
53— Paul Cameron, B
54— Jack Ellena, T
55— Hardiman Cureton, G
57— Dick Wallen, E
66— Mel Farr, B
67— *Gary Beban, B
   Don Manning, LB
69— Mike Ballou, LB
73— Kermit Johnson, B
75— John Sciarra, QB
76— Jerry Robinson, LB
77— *Jerry Robinson, LB
78— *Jerry Robinson, LB
   Kenny Easley, DB
79— Kenny Easley, DB
80— *Kenny Easley, DB

81— *Tim Wrightman, TE
83— Don Rogers, DB
85— John Lee, PK
88— Troy Aikman, QB
   Darryl Henley, DB
92— Carlton Gray, DB
93— *J. J. Stokes, WR
   Bjorn Merten, PK
   Jamir Miller, LB
95— *Jonathan Ogden, OL
97— Chad Overhauser, OL
98— Cade McNown, QB
   Kris Farris, OL

UTAH
94— Luther Elliss, DL

UTAH ST.
61— Merlin Olsen, T
69— Phil Olsen, DE

VANDERBILT
23— Lynn Bomar, E
24— Henry Wakefield, E
32— Pete Gracey, C
58— George Deiderich, G
82— *Jim Arnold, P
84— *Ricky Anderson, P

VIRGINIA
15— Eugene Mayer, B
41— Bill Dudley, B
85— *Jim Dombrowski, OL
90— Herman Moore, WR
92— Chris Slade, DL
93— Mark Dixon, OL
98— Anthony Poindexter, DB
99— Thomas Jones, RB

VIRGINIA TECH
67— Frank Loria, DB
84— Bruce Smith, DL
93— *Jim Pyne, C
95— Cornell Brown, DL
99— *Corey Moore, DL

WAKE FOREST
76— *Bill Armstrong, DB

WASH. & JEFF.
14— John Spiegel, B
18— Wilbur Henry, T
19— Wilbur Henry, T

WASHINGTON
25— George Wilson, B
28— Charles Carroll, B
36— Max Starcevich, G
40— Rudy Mucha, C
41— Ray Frankowski, G
63— Rick Redman, G
64— Rick Redman, G
66— Tom Greenlee, DT
68— Al Worley, DB
82— *Chuck Nelson, PK
84— Ron Holmes, DL
86— Jeff Jaeger, PK
   Reggie Rogers, DL
91— *Steve Emtman, DL
   Mario Bailey, WR
92— *Lincoln Kennedy, OL
95— *Lawyer Milloy, DB
96— Benji Olson, OL
97— Olin Kreutz, C

WASHINGTON ST.
84— Rueben Mayes, RB
88— Mike Utley, OL
89— *Jason Hanson, PK

WEST VIRGINIA
19— Ira Rodgers, B
55— Bruce Bosley, T
82— *Darryl Talley, LB
85— Brian Jozwiak, OL
92— Mike Compton, C
94— *Todd Sauerbrun, P
95— Aaron Beasley, DB
96— Canute Curtis, LB

WILLIAMS
17— Ben Boynton, B
19— Ben Boynton, B

WISCONSIN
12— Robert Butler, T
13— Ray Keeler, G
15— Howard Buck, T
19— Charles Carpenter, C

20— Ralph Scott, T
23— Marty Below, T
30— Milo Lubratovich, T
42— *Dave Schreiner, E
54— *Alan Ameche, B
59— *Dan Lanphear, T
62— Pat Richter, E
75— Dennis Lick, T
81— Tim Krumrie, DL
94— Cory Raymer, C
98— Aaron Gibson, OL
   *Tom Burke, DL
99— *Chris McIntosh, OL
   *Ron Dayne, RB

WYOMING
83— Jack Weil, P
84— Jay Novacek, TE
96— Marcus Harris, WR
97— Brian Lee, DB

YALE
1889— Amos Alonzo Stagg, E
   Charles Gill, T
   Pudge Heffelfinger, G
1890— William Rhodes, T
   Pudge Heffelfinger, G
   Thomas McClung, B
1891— Frank Hinkey, E
   John Hartwell, E
   Wallace Winter, T
   Pudge Heffelfinger, G
   Thomas McClung, B
1892— Frank Hinkey, E
   A. Hamilton Wallis, T
   Vance McCormick, B
1893— Frank Hinkey, E
   William Hickok, G
   Frank Butterworth, B
1894— Frank Hinkey, E
   William Hickok, G
   Philip Stillman, C
   George Adee, B
   Frank Butterworth, B
1895— Fred Murphy, T
   Samuel Thorne, B
1896— Fred Murphy, T
   Clarence Fincke, B
1897— John Hall, E
   Burr Chamberlin, T
   Gordon Brown, G
   Charles DeSaulles, B
1898— Burr Chamberlin, T
   Gordon Brown, G
   Malcolm McBride, B
1899— George Stillman, T
   Gordon Brown, G
   Malcolm McBride, B
   Albert Sharpe, B
00— George Stillman, T
   James Bloomer, T
   Gordon Brown, G
   Herman Olcott, C
   George Chadwick, B
   Perry Hale, B
   William Fincke, B
01— Henry Holt, C
02— Thomas Shevlin, E
   Ralph Kinney, T
   James Hogan, T
   Edgar Glass, G
   Henry Holt, C
   Foster Rockwell, B
   George Chadwick, B
03— Charles Rafferty, E
   James Hogan, T
   James Bloomer, G
   W. Ledyard Mitchell, B
04— Thomas Shevlin, E
   James Hogan, T
   Ralph Kinney, G
   Foster Rockwell, B
05— Thomas Shevlin, E
   Roswell Tripp, G
   Howard Roome, B
   Guy Hutchinson, B
06— Robert Forbes, E
   L. Horatio Biglow, T
   Hugh Knox, B
   Paul Veeder, B
07— Clarence Alcott, E
   L. Horatio Biglow, T

Thomas A. D. Jones, B
Edward Coy, B
08— William Goebel, G
   Hamlin Andrus, G
   Edward Coy, B
09— John Kilpatrick, E
   Henry Hobbs, T
   Hamlin Andrus, G
   Carroll Cooney, C
   Edward Coy, B
   Stephen Philbin, B
10— John Kilpatrick, E
11— Douglass Bomeisler, E
   Henry Ketcham, C
   Arthur Howe, B
12— Douglass Bomeisler, E
   Henry Ketcham, C
13— Nelson Talbott, T
14— Harry LeGore, B
16— Clinton Black, G
20— Tim Callahan, T
21— Malcolm Aldrich, B
23— Century Milstead, T
   William Mallory, B
24— Dick Luman, E
27— Bill Webster, G
   John Charlesworth, C
36— Larry Kelley, E
37— *Clint Frank, B
44— Paul Walker, E

Team Leaders in Consensus All-Americans

(Ranked on Total Number of Selections)

Team	No.	Players
Yale	100	69
Notre Dame	93	77
Harvard	89	59
Michigan	67	55
Princeton	65	49
Ohio St.	64	49
Southern California	61	54
Oklahoma	52	43
Nebraska	50	41
Pittsburgh	46	39
Pennsylvania	46	32
Alabama	38	37
Army	37	28
Texas	36	31
Penn St.	33	31
Tennessee	32	24
Minnesota	31	27
UCLA	30	26
Florida St.	28	22
Stanford	26	21
Miami (Fla.)	25	23
Colorado	25	21
Michigan St.	24	21
Auburn	23	21
Navy	23	20
Georgia	23	19
Illinois	23	18
California	22	20
Texas A&M	20	18
Georgia Tech	19	18
Washington	19	18
Cornell	19	15
Wisconsin	18	18
Florida	18	17
Syracuse	18	16
LSU	18	14
Purdue	17	16
Arkansas	17	15
Dartmouth	17	15
Iowa	17	15
Southern Methodist	16	14
Clemson	15	14
Arizona St.	14	11
North Carolina	13	13
Northwestern	12	12
Arizona	12	9
Brigham Young	11	9

TEAM LEADERS IN CONSENSUS ALL-AMERICANS

Team	No.	Players
Chicago	11	9
Maryland	10	10
Oklahoma St.	10	10
TCU	10	10
Kansas St.	9	8
Baylor	9	7

Team	No.	Players
Kentucky	9	7
Boston College	8	8
Mississippi	8	8
Texas Tech	8	8
Virginia	8	8
West Virginia	8	8

Team	No.	Players
Houston	7	7
Missouri	7	7
North Carolina St.	7	6
Brown	6	6
Rice	6	6
Vanderbilt	6	6

Team	No.	Players
Carlisle	6	5
Colgate	6	5
Columbia	6	5
Indiana	6	5
Air Force	5	5
Oregon St.	5	5
Virginia Tech	5	5

Special Awards

HEISMAN MEMORIAL TROPHY

Originally presented in 1935 as the DAC Trophy by the Downtown Athletic Club of New York City to the best college player east of the Mississippi River. In 1936, players across the country were eligible and the award was renamed the Heisman Memorial Trophy to honor former college coach and DAC athletics director John W. Heisman. The award now goes to the outstanding college football player in the United States. The bronze trophy was sculpted by Frank Eliscu, with the aid of Jim Crowley, one of Notre Dame's famed Four Horsemen. Crowley was then coach at Fordham, and some of his players posed as models for the trophy.

Year / Player (Winner Bold), School, Position / Points

1935 **Jay Berwanger,** Chicago, HB 84
2nd—Monk Meyer, Army 29
3rd—Bill Shakespeare, Notre Dame, HB 23
4th—Pepper Constable, Princeton, FB 20

1936 **Larry Kelley,** Yale, E 219
2nd—Sam Francis, Nebraska, FB 47
3rd—Ray Buivid, Marquette, HB 43
4th—Sammy Baugh, TCU, HB 39

1937 **Clint Frank,** Yale, HB 524
2nd—Byron White, Colorado, HB 264
3rd—Marshall Goldberg, Pittsburgh, HB 211
4th—Alex Wojciechowicz, Fordham, C 85

1938 **Davey O'Brien,** TCU, QB 519
2nd—Marshall Goldberg, Pittsburgh, HB 294
3rd—Sid Luckman, Columbia, QB 154
4th—Bob MacLeod, Dartmouth, HB 78

1939 **Nile Kinnick,** Iowa, HB 651
2nd—Tom Harmon, Michigan, HB 405
3rd—Paul Christman, Missouri, QB 391
4th—George Cafego, Tennessee, QB 296

1940 **Tom Harmon,** Michigan, HB 1,303
2nd—John Kimbrough, Texas A&M, FB 841
3rd—George Franck, Minnesota, HB 102
4th—Frankie Albert, Stanford, QB 90

1941 **Bruce Smith,** Minnesota, HB 554
2nd—Angelo Bertelli, Notre Dame, QB 345
3rd—Frankie Albert, Stanford, QB 336
4th—Frank Sinkwich, Georgia, HB 249

1942 **Frank Sinkwich,** Georgia, HB 1,059
2nd—Paul Governali, Columbia, QB 218
3rd—Clint Castleberry, Georgia Tech, HB 99
4th—Mike Holovak, Boston College, FB 95

1943 **Angelo Bertelli,** Notre Dame, QB 648
2nd—Bob Odell, Pennsylvania, HB 177
3rd—Otto Graham, Northwestern, QB 140
4th—Creighton Miller, Notre Dame, HB 134

1944 **Les Horvath,** Ohio St., QB/HB 412
2nd—Glenn Davis, Army, HB 287
3rd—Doc Blanchard, Army, FB 237
4th—Don Whitmire, Navy, T 115

1945 *****Doc Blanchard,** Army, FB 860
2nd—Glenn Davis, Army, HB 638
3rd—Bob Fenimore, Oklahoma St., HB 187
4th—Herman Wedemeyer, St. Mary's (Cal.), HB 152

1946 **Glenn Davis,** Army, HB 792
2nd—Charlie Trippi, Georgia, HB 435
3rd—Johnny Lujack, Notre Dame, QB 379
4th—Doc Blanchard, Army, FB 267

1947 **Johnny Lujack,** Notre Dame, QB 742
2nd—Bob Chappuis, Michigan, HB 555
3rd—Doak Walker, Southern Methodist, HB 196
4th—Charlie Conerly, Mississippi, QB 186

1948 *****Doak Walker,** Southern Methodist, HB 778
2nd—Charlie Justice, North Carolina, HB 443
3rd—Chuck Bednarik, Pennsylvania, C 336
4th—Jackie Jensen, California, HB 143

1949 **Leon Hart,** Notre Dame, E 995
2nd—Charlie Justice, North Carolina, HB 272
3rd—Doak Walker, Southern Methodist, HB 229
4th—Arnold Galiffa, Army, QB 196

1950 *****Vic Janowicz,** Ohio St., HB 633
2nd—Kyle Rote, Southern Methodist, HB 280
3rd—Reds Bagnell, Pennsylvania, HB 231
4th—Babe Parilli, Kentucky, QB 214

1951 **Dick Kazmaier,** Princeton, HB 1,777
2nd—Hank Lauricella, Tennessee, HB 424
3rd—Babe Parilli, Kentucky, QB 344
4th—Bill McColl, Stanford, E 313

1952 **Billy Vessels,** Oklahoma, HB 525
2nd—Jack Scarbath, Maryland, QB 367
3rd—Paul Giel, Minnesota, HB 329
4th—Donn Moomaw, UCLA, C 257

1953 **Johnny Lattner,** Notre Dame, HB 1,850
2nd—Paul Giel, Minnesota, HB 1,794
3rd—Paul Cameron, UCLA, HB 444
4th—Bernie Faloney, Maryland, QB 258

1954 **Alan Ameche,** Wisconsin, FB 1,068
2nd—Kurt Burris, Oklahoma, C 838
3rd—Howard Cassady, Ohio St., HB 810
4th—Ralph Guglielmi, Notre Dame, QB 691

1955 **Howard Cassady,** Ohio St., HB 2,219
2nd—Jim Swink, TCU, HB 742
3rd—George Welsh, Navy, QB 383
4th—Earl Morrall, Michigan St., QB 323

1956 **Paul Hornung,** Notre Dame, QB 1,066
2nd—Johnny Majors, Tennessee, HB 994
3rd—Tommy McDonald, Oklahoma, HB 973
4th—Jerry Tubbs, Oklahoma, C 724

1957 **John David Crow,** Texas A&M, HB 1,183
2nd—Alex Karras, Iowa, T 693
3rd—Walt Kowalczyk, Michigan St., HB 630
4th—Lou Michaels, Kentucky, T 330

1958 **Pete Dawkins,** Army, HB 1,394
2nd—Randy Duncan, Iowa, QB 1,021
3rd—Billy Cannon, LSU, HB 975
4th—Bob White, Ohio St., HB 365

1959 **Billy Cannon,** LSU, HB 1,929
2nd—Richie Lucas, Penn St., QB 613
3rd—Don Meredith, Southern Meth., QB 286
4th—Bill Burrell, Illinois, G 196

1960 **Joe Bellino,** Navy, HB 1,793
2nd—Tom Brown, Minnesota, G 731
3rd—Jake Gibbs, Mississippi, QB 453
4th—Ed Dyas, Auburn, HB 319

1961 **Ernie Davis,** Syracuse, HB 824
2nd—Bob Ferguson, Ohio St., HB 771
3rd—Jimmy Saxton, Texas, HB 551
4th—Sandy Stephens, Minnesota, QB 543

1962 **Terry Baker,** Oregon St., QB 707
2nd—Jerry Stovall, LSU, HB 618
3rd—Bobby Bell, Minnesota, T 429
4th—Lee Roy Jordan, Alabama, C 321

1963 *****Roger Staubach,** Navy, QB 1,860
2nd—Billy Lothridge, Georgia Tech, QB 504
3rd—Sherman Lewis, Michigan St., HB 369
4th—Don Trull, Baylor, QB 253

1964 **John Huarte,** Notre Dame, QB 1,026
2nd—Jerry Rhome, Tulsa, QB 952
3rd—Dick Butkus, Illinois, C 505
4th—Bob Timberlake, Michigan, QB 361

1965 **Mike Garrett,** Southern California, HB 926
2nd—Howard Twilley, Tulsa, E 528
3rd—Jim Grabowski, Illinois, FB 481
4th—Donny Anderson, Texas Tech, HB 408

1966 **Steve Spurrier,** Florida, QB 1,679
2nd—Bob Griese, Purdue, QB 816
3rd—Nick Eddy, Notre Dame, HB 456
4th—Gary Beban, UCLA, QB 318

1967 **Gary Beban,** UCLA, QB 1,968
2nd—O. J. Simpson, Southern California, HB 1,722
3rd—Leroy Keyes, Purdue, HB 1,366
4th—Larry Csonka, Syracuse, FB 136

1968 **O. J. Simpson,** Southern California, HB 2,853
2nd—Leroy Keyes, Purdue, HB 1,103
3rd—Terry Hanratty, Notre Dame, QB 387
4th—Ted Kwalik, Penn St., TE 254

1969 **Steve Owens,** Oklahoma, HB 1,488
2nd—Mike Phipps, Purdue, QB 1,344
3rd—Rex Kern, Ohio St., QB 856
4th—Archie Manning, Mississippi, QB 582

1970 **Jim Plunkett,** Stanford, QB 2,229
2nd—Joe Theismann, Notre Dame, QB 1,410
3rd—Archie Manning, Mississippi, QB 849
4th—Steve Worster, Texas, RB 398

1971 **Pat Sullivan,** Auburn, QB 1,597
2nd—Ed Marinaro, Cornell, RB 1,445
3rd—Greg Pruitt, Oklahoma, RB 586
4th—Johnny Musso, Alabama, RB 365

1972 **Johnny Rodgers,** Nebraska, WR 1,310
2nd—Greg Pruitt, Oklahoma, RB 966
3rd—Rich Glover, Nebraska, MG 652
4th—Bert Jones, LSU, QB 351

1973 **John Cappelletti,** Penn St., RB 1,057
2nd—John Hicks, Ohio St., OT 524
3rd—Roosevelt Leaks, Texas, RB 482
4th—David Jaynes, Kansas, QB 394

1974 *****Archie Griffin,** Ohio St., RB 1,920
2nd—Anthony Davis, Southern California, RB 819
3rd—Joe Washington, Oklahoma, RB 661
4th—Tom Clements, Notre Dame, QB 244

1975 **Archie Griffin,** Ohio St., RB 1,800
2nd—Chuck Muncie, California, RB 730
3rd—Ricky Bell, Southern California, RB 708
4th—Tony Dorsett, Pittsburgh, RB 616

1976 **Tony Dorsett,** Pittsburgh, RB 2,357
2nd—Ricky Bell, Southern California, RB 1,346
3rd—Rob Lytle, Michigan, RB 413
4th—Terry Miller, Oklahoma St., RB 197

1977 **Earl Campbell,** Texas, RB 1,547
2nd—Terry Miller, Oklahoma St., RB 812
3rd—Ken MacAfee, Notre Dame, TE 343
4th—Doug Williams, Grambling, QB 266

1978 *****Billy Sims,** Oklahoma, RB 827
2nd—Chuck Fusina, Penn St., QB 750
3rd—Rick Leach, Michigan, QB 435
4th—Charles White, Southern California, RB 354

1979 **Charles White,** Southern California, RB 1,695
2nd—Billy Sims, Oklahoma, RB 773
3rd—Marc Wilson, Brigham Young, QB 589
4th—Art Schlichter, Ohio St., QB 251

1980 **George Rogers,** South Carolina, RB 1,128
2nd—Hugh Green, Pittsburgh, DE 861
3rd—Herschel Walker, Georgia, RB 683
4th—Mark Hermann, Purdue, QB 405

AWARD WINNERS

Year	Player (Winner Bold), School, Position	Points
1981	**Marcus Allen,** Southern California, RB	1,797
	2nd—Herschel Walker, Georgia, RB	1,199
	3rd—Jim McMahon, Brigham Young, QB	706
	4th—Dan Marino, Pittsburgh, QB	256
1982	***Herschel Walker,** Georgia, RB	1,926
	2nd—John Elway, Stanford, QB	1,231
	3rd—Eric Dickerson, Southern Meth., RB	465
	4th—Anthony Carter, Michigan, WR	142
1983	**Mike Rozier,** Nebraska, RB	1,801
	2nd—Steve Young, Brigham Young, QB	1,172
	3rd—Doug Flutie, Boston College, QB	253
	4th—Turner Gill, Nebraska, QB	190
1984	**Doug Flutie,** Boston College, QB	2,240
	2nd—Keith Byars, Ohio St., RB	1,251
	3rd—Robbie Bosco, Brigham Young, QB	443
	4th—Bernie Kosar, Miami (Fla.), QB	320
1985	**Bo Jackson,** Auburn, RB	1,509
	2nd—Chuck Long, Iowa, QB	1,464
	3rd—Robbie Bosco, Brigham Young, QB	459
	4th—Lorenzo White, Michigan St., RB	391
1986	**Vinny Testaverde,** Miami (Fla.), QB	2,213
	2nd—Paul Palmer, Temple, RB	672
	3rd—Jim Harbaugh, Michigan, QB	458
	4th—Brian Bosworth, Oklahoma, LB	395
1987	**Tim Brown,** Notre Dame, WR	1,442
	2nd—Don McPherson, Syracuse, QB	831
	3rd—Gordie Lockbaum, Holy Cross, WR/DB	657
	4th—Lorenzo White, Michigan St., RB	632
1988	***Barry Sanders,** Oklahoma St., RB	1,878
	2nd—Rodney Peete, Southern California, QB	912
	3rd—Troy Aikman, UCLA, QB	582
	4th—Steve Walsh, Miami (Fla.), QB	341
1989	***Andre Ware,** Houston, QB	1,073
	2nd—Anthony Thompson, Indiana, RB	1,003
	3rd—Major Harris, West Virginia, QB	709
	4th—Tony Rice, Notre Dame, QB	523
1990	***Ty Detmer,** Brigham Young, QB	1,482
	2nd—Raghib Ismail, Notre Dame, WR	1,177
	3rd—Eric Bieniemy, Colorado, RB	798
	4th—Shawn Moore, Virginia, QB	465
1991	#**Desmond Howard,** Michigan, WR	2,077
	2nd—Casey Weldon, Florida St., QB	503
	3rd—Ty Detmer, Brigham Young, QB	445
	4th—Steve Emtman, Washington, DT	357
1992	**Gino Torretta,** Miami (Fla.), QB	1,400
	2nd—Marshall Faulk, San Diego St., RB	1,080
	3rd—Garrison Hearst, Georgia, RB	982
	4th—Marvin Jones, Florida St., LB	392
1993	**Charlie Ward,** Florida St., QB	2,310
	2nd—Heath Shuler, Tennessee, QB	688
	3rd—David Palmer, Alabama, RB	292
	4th—Marshall Faulk, San Diego St., RB	250
1994	***Rashaan Salaam,** Colorado, RB	1,743
	2nd—Ki-Jana Carter, Penn St., RB	901
	3rd—Steve McNair, Alcorn St., QB	655
	4th—Kerry Collins, Penn St., QB	639
1995	**Eddie George,** Ohio St., RB	1,460
	2nd—Tommie Frazier, Nebraska, QB	1,196
	3rd—Danny Wuerffel, Florida, QB	987
	4th—Darnell Autry, Northwestern, RB	535
1996	**Danny Wuerffel,** Florida, QB	1,363
	2nd—Troy Davis, Iowa St., RB	1,174
	3rd—Jake Plummer, Arizona St., QB	685
	4th—Orlando Pace, Ohio St., OL	599
1997	***Charles Woodson,** Michigan, DB	1,815
	2nd—Peyton Manning, Tennessee, QB	1,543
	3rd—Ryan Leaf, Washington St., QB	861
	4th—Randy Moss, Marshall, WR	253
1998	***Ricky Williams,** Texas, RB	2,355
	2nd—Michael Bishop, Kansas St., QB	792
	3rd—Cade McNown, UCLA, QB	696
	4th—Tim Couch, Kentucky, QB	527

*Winner as junior (all others seniors). #Had one year of eligibility remaining.

1999 Heisman Voting

(Voting on a 3-2-1 basis)	1st	2nd	3rd	Total
1. Ron Dayne, RB, Wisconsin	586	121	42	2,042
2. Joe Hamilton, QB, Georgia Tech	96	285	136	994
3. #Michael Vick, QB, Virginia Tech	25	72	100	319
4. *Drew Brees, QB, Purdue	3	89	121	308
5. Chad Pennington, QB, Marshall	21	45	94	247
6. Peter Warrick, WR, Florida St.	14	50	61	203
7. Shaun Alexander, RB, Alabama	11	43	52	171
8. Thomas Jones, RB, Virginia	10	32	46	140
9. *LaVar Arrington, LB, Penn St.	3	14	17	54
10. Tim Rattay, QB, Louisiana Tech	1	5	16	29

#Freshman. *Junior. All others seniors.

OUTLAND TROPHY

Honoring the outstanding interior lineman in the nation, first presented in 1946 by the Football Writers Association of America. The award is named for its benefactor, Dr. John H. Outland.

Year	Player, College, Position
1946	George Connor, Notre Dame, T
1947	Joe Steffy, Army, G
1948	Bill Fischer, Notre Dame, G
1949	Ed Bagdon, Michigan St., G
1950	Bob Gain, Kentucky, T
1951	Jim Weatherall, Oklahoma, T
1952	Dick Modzelewski, Maryland, T
1953	J. D. Roberts, Oklahoma, G
1954	Bill Brooks, Arkansas, G
1955	Calvin Jones, Iowa, G
1956	Jim Parker, Ohio St., G
1957	Alex Karras, Iowa, T
1958	Zeke Smith, Auburn, G
1959	Mike McGee, Duke, T
1960	Tom Brown, Minnesota, G
1961	Merlin Olsen, Utah St., T
1962	Bobby Bell, Minnesota, T
1963	Scott Appleton, Texas, T
1964	Steve DeLong, Tennessee, T
1965	Tommy Nobis, Texas, G
1966	Loyd Phillips, Arkansas, T
1967	Ron Yary, Southern California, T
1968	Bill Stanfill, Georgia, T
1969	Mike Reid, Penn St., DT
1970	Jim Stillwagon, Ohio St., MG
1971	Larry Jacobson, Nebraska, DT
1972	Rich Glover, Nebraska, MG
1973	John Hicks, Ohio St., OT
1974	Randy White, Maryland, DE
1975	Lee Roy Selmon, Oklahoma, DT
1976	*Ross Browner, Notre Dame, DE
1977	Brad Shearer, Texas, DT
1978	Greg Roberts, Oklahoma, G
1979	Jim Ritcher, North Carolina St., C
1980	Mark May, Pittsburgh, OT
1981	*Dave Rimington, Nebraska, C
1982	Dave Rimington, Nebraska, C
1983	Dean Steinkuhler, Nebraska, G
1984	Bruce Smith, Virginia Tech, DT
1985	Mike Ruth, Boston College, NG
1986	Jason Buck, Brigham Young, DT
1987	Chad Hennings, Air Force, DT
1988	Tracy Rocker, Auburn, DT
1989	Mohammed Elewonibi, Brigham Young, G
1990	Russell Maryland, Miami (Fla.), DT
1991	*Steve Emtman, Washington, DT
1992	Will Shields, Nebraska, G
1993	Rob Waldrop, Arizona, NG
1994	Zach Wiegert, Nebraska, OT
1995	Jonathan Ogden, UCLA, OT
1996	*Orlando Pace, Ohio St., OT
1997	Aaron Taylor, Nebraska, OG
1998	*Kris Farris, UCLA, OT
1999	Chris Samuels, Alabama, OT

*Junior (all others seniors).

VINCE LOMBARDI/ROTARY AWARD

Honoring the outstanding college lineman of the year, first presented in 1970 by the Rotary Club of Houston, Texas. The award is named after professional football coach Vince Lombardi, a member of the legendary "Seven Blocks of Granite" at Fordham in the 1930s.

Year	Player, College, Position
1970	Jim Stillwagon, Ohio St., MG
1971	Walt Patulski, Notre Dame, DE
1972	Rich Glover, Nebraska, MG
1973	John Hicks, Ohio St., OT
1974	Randy White, Maryland, DT
1975	Lee Roy Selmon, Oklahoma, DT
1976	Wilson Whitley, Houston, DT
1977	Ross Browner, Notre Dame, DE
1978	Bruce Clark, Penn St., DT
1979	Brad Budde, Southern California, G
1980	Hugh Green, Pittsburgh, DE
1981	Kenneth Sims, Texas, DT
1982	Dave Rimington, Nebraska, C
1983	Dean Steinkuhler, Nebraska, G
1984	Tony Degrate, Texas, DT
1985	Tony Casillas, Oklahoma, NG
1986	Cornelius Bennett, Alabama, LB
1987	Chris Spielman, Ohio St., LB
1988	Tracy Rocker, Auburn, DT
1989	Percy Snow, Michigan St., LB
1990	Chris Zorich, Notre Dame, NT
1991	Steve Emtman, Washington, DT
1992	Marvin Jones, Florida St., LB
1993	Aaron Taylor, Notre Dame, OT
1994	Warren Sapp, Miami (Fla.), DT
1995	Orlando Pace, Ohio St., OT
1996	Orlando Pace, Ohio St., OT
1997	Grant Wistrom, Nebraska, DE
1998	Dat Nguyen, Texas A&M, LB
1999	Corey Moore, Virginia Tech, DE

WALTER CAMP AWARD

Honoring the nation's outstanding college football player, first presented in 1967 by the Walter Camp Foundation in balloting by Division I-A coaches and sports information directors. The award is named after Walter Camp, one of the founders of modern American football.

Year	Player, College, Position
1967	O. J. Simpson, Southern California, RB
1968	O. J. Simpson, Southern California, RB
1969	Steve Owens, Oklahoma, RB
1970	Jim Plunkett, Stanford, QB
1971	Pat Sullivan, Auburn, QB
1972	Johnny Rodgers, Nebraska, WR
1973	John Cappelletti, Penn St., RB
1974	Archie Griffin, Ohio St., RB
1975	Archie Griffin, Ohio St., RB
1976	Tony Dorsett, Pittsburgh, RB
1977	Ken MacAfee, Notre Dame, TE
1978	Billy Sims, Oklahoma, RB
1979	Charles White, Southern California, RB
1980	Hugh Green, Pittsburgh, DE
1981	Marcus Allen, Southern California, RB
1982	Herschel Walker, Georgia, RB
1983	Mike Rozier, Nebraska, RB
1984	Doug Flutie, Boston College, QB
1985	Bo Jackson, Auburn, RB
1986	Vinny Testaverde, Miami (Fla.), QB
1987	Tim Brown, Notre Dame, WR
1988	Barry Sanders, Oklahoma St., RB
1989	Andre Ware, Houston, QB
1990	Raghib Ismail, Notre Dame, RB/WR
1991	Desmond Howard, Michigan, WR
1992	Gino Torretta, Miami (Fla.), QB
1993	Charlie Ward, Florida St., QB
1994	Rashaan Salaam, Colorado, RB
1995	Eddie George, Ohio St., RB
1996	Danny Wuerffel, Florida, QB
1997	Charles Woodson, Michigan, DB
1998	Ricky Williams, Texas, RB
1999	Ron Dayne, Wisconsin, RB

MAXWELL AWARD

Honoring the nation's outstanding college football player, first presented in 1937 by the Maxwell Memorial Football Club of Philadelphia. The award is named after Robert "Tiny" Maxwell, a Philadelphia native who played at the University of Chicago as a lineman near the turn of the century.

Year	Player, College, Position
1937	Clint Frank, Yale, HB
1938	Davey O'Brien, TCU, QB
1939	Nile Kinnick, Iowa, HB
1940	Tom Harmon, Michigan, HB

SPECIAL AWARDS

Year	Player, College, Position
1941	Bill Dudley, Virginia, HB
1942	Paul Governali, Columbia, QB
1943	Bob Odell, Pennsylvania, HB
1944	Glenn Davis, Army, HB
1945	Doc Blanchard, Army, FB
1946	Charley Trippi, Georgia, HB
1947	Doak Walker, Southern Methodist, HB
1948	Chuck Bednarik, Pennsylvania, C
1949	Leon Hart, Notre Dame, E
1950	Reds Bagnell, Pennsylvania, HB
1951	Dick Kazmaier, Princeton, HB
1952	Johnny Lattner, Notre Dame, HB
1953	Johnny Lattner, Notre Dame, HB
1954	Ron Beagle, Navy, E
1955	Howard Cassady, Ohio St., HB
1956	Tommy McDonald, Oklahoma, HB
1957	Bob Reifsnyder, Navy, T
1958	Pete Dawkins, Army, HB
1959	Rich Lucas, Penn St., QB
1960	Joe Bellino, Navy, HB
1961	Bob Ferguson, Ohio St., FB
1962	Terry Baker, Oregon St., QB
1963	Roger Staubach, Navy, QB
1964	Glenn Ressler, Penn St., C
1965	Tommy Nobis, Texas, LB
1966	Jim Lynch, Notre Dame, LB
1967	Gary Beban, UCLA, QB
1968	O. J. Simpson, Southern California, RB
1969	Mike Reid, Penn St., DT
1970	Jim Plunkett, Stanford, QB
1971	Ed Marinaro, Cornell, RB
1972	Brad VanPelt, Michigan St., DB
1973	John Cappelletti, Penn St., RB
1974	Steve Joachim, Temple, QB
1975	Archie Griffin, Ohio St., RB
1976	Tony Dorsett, Pittsburgh, RB
1977	Ross Browner, Notre Dame, DE
1978	Chuck Fusina, Penn St., QB
1979	Charles White, Southern California, RB
1980	Hugh Green, Pittsburgh, DE
1981	Marcus Allen, Southern California, RB
1982	Herschel Walker, Georgia, RB
1983	Mike Rozier, Nebraska, RB
1984	Doug Flutie, Boston College, QB
1985	Chuck Long, Iowa, QB
1986	Vinny Testaverde, Miami (Fla.), QB
1987	Don McPherson, Syracuse, QB
1988	Barry Sanders, Oklahoma St., RB
1989	Anthony Thompson, Indiana, RB
1990	Ty Detmer, Brigham Young, QB
1991	Desmond Howard, Michigan, WR
1992	Gino Torretta, Miami (Fla.), QB
1993	Charlie Ward, Florida St., QB
1994	Kerry Collins, Penn St., QB
1995	Eddie George, Ohio St., RB
1996	Danny Wuerffel, Florida, QB
1997	Peyton Manning, Tennessee, QB
1998	Ricky Williams, Texas, RB
1999	Ron Dayne, Wisconsin, RB

JOHNNY UNITAS GOLDEN ARM AWARD

Presented for the first time in 1987 to honor the nation's top senior quarterback. Sponsored by the Kentucky Chapter of the National Football Foundation and College Football Hall of Fame, Inc. Each year, a committee composed of NFL executives, coaches, scouts and media members selects the winner based on citizenship, scholarship, leadership and athletic accomplishments. The award is named after NFL Hall of Fame quarterback Johnny Unitas.

Year	Player, College
1987	Don McPherson, Syracuse
1988	Rodney Peete, Southern California
1989	Tony Rice, Notre Dame
1990	Craig Erickson, Miami (Fla.)
1991	Casey Weldon, Florida St.
1992	Gino Torretta, Miami (Fla.)
1993	Charlie Ward, Florida St.
1994	Jay Barker, Alabama
1995	Tommy Frazier, Nebraska
1996	Danny Wuerffel, Florida
1997	Peyton Manning, Tennessee

Year	Player, College, Position
1998	Cade McNown, UCLA
1999	Chris Redman, Louisville

BUTKUS AWARD

First presented in 1985 to honor the nation's best collegiate linebacker by the Downtown Athletic Club of Orlando, Fla. The award is named after Dick Butkus, two-time consensus all-American at Illinois and six-time all-pro linebacker with the Chicago Bears.

Year	Player, College
1985	Brian Bosworth, Oklahoma
1986	Brian Bosworth, Oklahoma
1987	Paul McGowan, Florida St.
1988	Derrick Thomas, Alabama
1989	Percy Snow, Michigan St.
1990	Alfred Williams, Colorado
1991	Erick Anderson, Michigan
1992	Marvin Jones, Florida St.
1993	Trev Alberts, Nebraska
1994	Dana Howard, Illinois
1995	Kevin Hardy, Illinois
1996	Matt Russell, Colorado
1997	Andy Katzenmoyer, Ohio St.
1998	Chris Claiborne, Southern California
1999	LaVar Arrington, Penn St.

JIM THORPE AWARD

First presented in 1986 to honor the nation's best defensive back by the Jim Thorpe Athletic Club of Oklahoma City. The award is named after Jim Thorpe, Olympic champion, two-time consensus all-American halfback at Carlisle and professional football player.

Year	Player, College
1986	Thomas Everett, Baylor
1987	Bennie Blades, Miami (Fla.)
	Rickey Dixon, Oklahoma
1988	Deion Sanders, Florida St.
1989	Mark Carrier, Southern California
1990	Darryll Lewis, Arizona
1991	Terrell Buckley, Florida St.
1992	Deon Figures, Colorado
1993	Antonio Langham, Alabama
1994	Chris Hudson, Colorado
1995	Greg Myers, Colorado St.
1996	Lawrence Wright, Florida
1997	Charles Woodson, Michigan
1998	Antoine Winfield, Ohio St.
1999	Tyrone Carter, Minnesota

DAVEY O'BRIEN NATIONAL QUARTERBACK AWARD

First presented in 1977 as the O'Brien Memorial Trophy to the outstanding player in the Southwest. In 1981, the Davey O'Brien Educational and Charitable Trust of Fort Worth, Texas, renamed the award the Davey O'Brien National Quarterback Award, and it now honors the nation's best quarterback.

MEMORIAL TROPHY

Year	Player, College, Position
1977	Earl Campbell, Texas, RB
1978	Billy Sims, Oklahoma, RB
1979	Mike Singletary, Baylor, LB
1980	Mike Singletary, Baylor, LB

NATIONAL QB AWARD

Year	Player, College
1981	Jim McMahon, Brigham Young
1982	Todd Blackledge, Penn St.
1983	Steve Young, Brigham Young
1984	Doug Flutie, Boston College
1985	Chuck Long, Iowa
1986	Vinny Testaverde, Miami (Fla.)
1987	Don McPherson, Syracuse
1988	Troy Aikman, UCLA
1989	Andre Ware, Houston
1990	Ty Detmer, Brigham Young
1991	Ty Detmer, Brigham Young
1992	Gino Torretta, Miami (Fla.)
1993	Charlie Ward, Florida St.
1994	Kerry Collins, Penn St.
1995	Danny Wuerffel, Florida
1996	Danny Wuerffel, Florida
1997	Peyton Manning, Tennessee
1998	Michael Bishop, Kansas St.
1999	Joe Hamilton, Georgia Tech

After rushing for 1,834 yards and leading Wisconsin to the Big Ten Conference title and a Rose Bowl victory, Ron Dayne was the recipient of the Doak Walker National Running Back Award, the Walter Camp Award, the Maxwell Award and the Heisman Trophy.

DOAK WALKER NATIONAL RUNNING BACK AWARD

Presented for the first time in 1990 to honor the nation's best running back among Division I-A juniors or seniors who combine outstanding achievements on the field, in the classroom and in the community. Presented by the GTE/Southern Methodist Athletic Forum in Dallas, Texas, and sponsored by Dr. Pepper, a $10,000 scholarship is donated to the recipient's university in his name. It is voted on by a 16-member panel of media and former college football standouts. The award is named after Doak Walker, Southern Methodist's three-time consensus all-American halfback and 1948 Heisman Trophy winner.

Year	Player, College
1990	Greg Lewis, Washington
1991	Trevor Cobb, Rice
1992	Garrison Hearst, Georgia
1993	Byron Morris, Texas Tech
1994	Rashaan Salaam, Colorado
1995	Eddie George, Ohio St.
1996	Byron Hanspard, Texas Tech
1997	Ricky Williams, Texas
1998	Ricky Williams, Texas
1999	Ron Dayne, Wisconsin

LOU GROZA COLLEGIATE PLACE-KICKER AWARD

Presented for the first time in 1992 to honor the nation's top collegiate place-kicker. Sponsored by the Palm Beach County Sports Authority in conjunction with the Orange Bowl Committee. The award is named after NFL Hall of Fame kicker Lou Groza.

Year	Player, College
1992	Joe Allison, Memphis
1993	Judd Davis, Florida
1994	Steve McLaughlin, Arizona
1995	Michael Reeder, TCU
1996	Marc Primanti, North Carolina St.
1997	Martin Gramatica, Kansas St.
1998	Sebastian Janikowski, Florida St.
1999	Sebastian Janikowski, Florida St.

FRED BILETNIKOFF RECEIVER AWARD

First presented in 1994 to honor the nation's top collegiate pass receiver. Sponsored by the Tallahassee Quarterback Club of Tallahassee, Fla. The award is named after Fred Biletnikoff, former Florida State all-American and NFL Oakland Raider receiver, a member of both the College Football Hall of Fame and Pro Football Hall of Fame.

Year	Player, College
1994	Bobby Engram, Penn St.
1995	Terry Glenn, Ohio St.

Year	Player, College
1996	Marcus Harris, Wyoming
1997	Randy Moss, Marshall
1998	Troy Edwards, Louisiana Tech
1999	Troy Walters, Stanford

WALTER PAYTON PLAYER OF THE YEAR AWARD

First presented in 1987 to honor the top Division I-AA football player by the Sports Network and voted on by Division I-AA sports information directors. The award is named after Walter Payton, former Jackson State player and the National Football League's all-time leading rusher.

Year	Player, College, Position
1987	Kenny Gamble, Colgate, RB
1988	Dave Meggett, Towson, RB
1989	John Friesz, Idaho, QB
1990	Walter Dean, Grambling, RB
1991	Jamie Martin, Weber St., QB
1992	Michael Payton, Marshall, QB
1993	Doug Nussmeier, Idaho, QB
1994	Steve McNair, Alcorn St., QB
1995	Dave Dickenson, Montana, QB
1996	Archie Amerson, Northern Ariz., RB
1997	Brian Finneran, Villanova, WR
1998	Jerry Azumah, New Hampshire, RB
1999	Adrian Peterson, Ga. Southern, RB

ERNIE DAVIS AWARD

First presented in 1992 to honor a Division I-AA college football player who has overcome personal, athletic or academic adversity and performs in an exemplary manner. The annual award is presented by the American Sports Wire and is named after the late Ernie Davis, Syracuse halfback who won the Heisman Trophy in 1961.

Year	Player, College, Position
1992	Gilad Landau, Grambling, PK
1993	Jay Walker, Howard, QB
1994	Steve McNair, Alcorn St., QB
1995	Earl Holmes, Florida A&M, LB
1996	Jason DeCuir, Howard, PK
1997	DeMingo Graham, Hofstra, OL
1998	Chris Boden, Villanova, QB
1999	Matt Bushart, Southern U., P

HARLON HILL TROPHY

First presented in 1986 to honor the best Division II player by Division II sports information directors. The award is named after Harlon Hill, former receiver at North Alabama and the National Football League's most valuable player for the Chicago Bears in 1955.

Year	Player, College, Position
1986	Jeff Bentrim, North Dakota St., QB
1987	Johnny Bailey, Tex. A&M-Kingsville, RB
1988	Johnny Bailey, Tex. A&M-Kingsville, RB
1989	Johnny Bailey, Tex. A&M-Kingsville, RB
1990	Chris Simdorn, North Dakota St., QB
1991	Ronnie West, Pittsburg St., WR
1992	Ronald Moore, Pittsburg St., RB
1993	Roger Graham, New Haven, RB
1994	Chris Hatcher, Valdosta St., QB
1995	Ronald McKinnon, North Ala., LB
1996	Jarrett Anderson, Truman St., RB
1997	Irv Sigler, Bloomsburg, RB
1998	Brian Shay, Emporia St., RB
1999	Corte McGuffey, Northern Colo., QB

BRONKO NAGURSKI AWARD

First presented in 1993 to honor the nation's top collegiate defensive player. Presented by the Football Writers Association of America.

Year	Player, College, Position
1993	Rob Waldrop, Arizona, DL
1994	Warren Sapp, Miami (Fla.), DT
1995	Pat Fitzgerald, Northwestern, LB
1996	Pat Fitzgerald, Northwestern, LB
1997	Charles Woodson, Michigan, CB
1998	Champ Bailey, Georgia, DB
1999	Corey Moore, Virginia Tech, DE

GAGLIARDI TROPHY

First presented in 1993 to the nation's outstanding Division III player. Presented by the St. John's (Minn.) J-Club. The award is named after John Gagliardi, St. John's head coach for 43 seasons and one of only five coaches in college football history to win 300 games.

Year	Player, College, Position
1993	Jim Ballard, Mount Union, QB
1994	Carey Bender, Coe, RB
1995	Chris Palmer, St. John's (Minn.), WR
1996	Lon Erickson, Ill. Wesleyan, QB
1997	Bill Borchert, Mount Union, QB
1998	Scott Hvistendahl, Augsburg, WR/P
1999	Danny Ragsdale, Redlands, QB

MELBERGER AWARD

First presented in 1993 to the nation's outstanding Division III player by the Downtown Wilkes-Barre (Pa.) Touchdown Club.

Year	Player, College, Position
1993	Jim Ballard, Mount Union, QB
1994	Carey Bender, Coe, RB
1995	Craig Kusick, Wis.-La Crosse, QB
1996	Bill Borchert, Mount Union, QB
1997	Bill Borchert, Mount Union, QB
1998	Mike Burton, Trinity (Tex.), QB
1999	Scott Pingel, Westminster (Mo.), WR

BUCK BUCHANAN AWARD

First presented in 1995 to the nation's outstanding I-AA defensive player.

Year	Player, College, Position
1995	Dexter Coakley, LB, Appalachian St.
1996	Dexter Coakley, LB, Appalachian St.
1997	Chris McNeil, DE, N.C. A&T
1998	James Milton, LB, Western Ill.
1999	Al Lucas, DT, Troy St.

1999 COACHING AWARDS

EDDIE ROBINSON COACH OF THE YEAR (FWAA) — Frank Beamer, Virginia Tech (Presented by Home Depot and the Football Writers' Association of America)

WALTER CAMP/STREET & SMITH COACH OF THE YEAR – Frank Beamer, Virginia Tech (Presented by the Walter Camp Foundation and Street & Smith)

ASSOCIATED PRESS COACH OF THE YEAR – Frank Beamer, Virginia Tech (Presented by The Associated Press member newspapers, TV and radio stations)

BOBBY DODD COACH OF THE YEAR – Frank Beamer, Virginia Tech (Presented by the Bobby Dodd Coach of the Year Foundation, Atlanta, Georgia)

AFCA/GTE COACH OF THE YEAR (Division I-A) – Frank Beamer, Virginia Tech (Presented by the American Football Coaches Association)

AFCA/GTE COACH OF THE YEAR (Division I-AA) – Paul Johnson, Ga. Southern (Presented by the American Football Coaches Association)

AFCA/GTE COACH OF THE YEAR (NCAA Division II & NAIA Division I) – Mel Tjeerdsma, Northwest Mo. St. (Presented by the American Football Coaches Association)

AFCA/GTE COACH OF THE YEAR (NCAA Division III & NAIA Division II) — Frosty Westering, Pacific Lutheran (Presented by the American Football Coaches Association)

AFCA ASSISTANT COACH OF THE YEAR (Division I-A) – Jerry Sandusky, Penn St., Defensive Coordinator (Presented by the American Football Coaches Association)

AFCA ASSISTANT COACH OF THE YEAR (Division I-AA) – David Bailiff, Southwest Tex. St., Defensive Coordinator (Presented by the American Football Coaches Association)

AFCA ASSISTANT COACH OF THE YEAR (Division II) – Mike Moroski, UC Davis, Offensive Coordinator (Presented by the American Football Coaches Association)

AFCA ASSISTANT COACH OF THE YEAR (Division III) – Don Montgomery, Mount Union, Defensive Coordinator (Presented by the American Football Coaches Association)

GRANT TEAFF COACH OF THE YEAR AWARD – Ken Sparks, Carson-Newman (Div. II) (Presented by the Fellowship of Christian Athletes)

EDDIE ROBINSON I-AA COACH OF THE YEAR – Mickey Matthews, James Madison (Presented by The Sports Network)

2000 AMOS ALONZO STAGG AWARD – Tom Osborne, Nebraska (Presented by the American Football Coaches Association)

STREET & SMITH'S EDDIE ROBINSON COACH'S AWARD — L. C. Cole, Tennessee St. (Presented by Street & Smith magazine to the top coach in black college football)

COLLEGE FOOTBALL HALL OF FAME

Established: In 1947, by the National Football Foundation and College Hall of Fame, Inc. The first class of enshrinement of Division I or major-college players began in 1951. In 1996, the yearly classes elected were expanded to include other than Division I players. **Eligibility:** A nominated player must be out of college at least 10 years and a first-team all-America selection by a major selector during his career. For divisional (college-division) players, the player must have been a first-team selection on a recognized all-America team in Division I-AA, II and III and the NAIA. Coaches must be retired three years. The voting is done by a 12-member panel made up of athletics directors, conference and bowl officials, and media representatives.

Member players are listed with the final year they played in college, and member coaches are listed with the schools where they coached and the inclusive years of their career. ($) Indicates college-division member. (+) Indicates deceased members. (#) Indicates dual member of the Pro Football Hall of Fame.

Hall of Fame: Only two individuals are enshrined in the College Football Hall of Fame as both a player and a coach. Amos Alonzo Stagg was an all-American at Yale (1889) and was inducted as a coach in 1951. The other two-way inductee is Bobby Dodd, who played at Tennessee (1930) and was inducted as a coach in 1993.

PLAYERS

Player, College	Year
†Earl Abell, Colgate	1915
Alex Agase, Purdue/Illinois	1946
†Harry Agganis, Boston U.	1952
Frank Albert, Stanford	1941
†Ki Aldrich, TCU	1938
†Malcolm Aldrich, Yale	1921
†Joe Alexander, Syracuse	1920
Lance Alworth, Arkansas#	1961
†Alan Ameche, Wisconsin	1954
†Knowlton Ames, Princeton	1889
Warren Amling, Ohio St.	1946
Dick Anderson, Colorado	1967
Donny Anderson, Texas Tech	1965
†Hunk Anderson, Notre Dame	1921
Doug Atkins, Tennessee#	1952
Bob Babich, Miami (Ohio)	1968
†Everett Bacon, Wesleyan	1912
†Reds Bagnell, Pennsylvania	1950
†Hobey Baker, Princeton	1913
†John Baker, Southern California	1931
†Moon Baker, Northwestern	1926
Terry Baker, Oregon St.	1962
†Harold Ballin, Princeton	1914
†Bill Banker, Tulane	1929
Vince Banonis, Detroit	1941
†Stan Barnes, California	1921
†Charles Barrett, Cornell	1915
†Bert Baston, Minnesota	1916
†Cliff Battles, West Va. Wesleyan#	1931
Sammy Baugh, TCU#	1936
Maxie Baughan, Georgia Tech	1959
†James Bausch, Wichita St./Kansas	1930
Ron Beagle, Navy	1955
Gary Beban, UCLA	1967
Hub Bechtol, Texas Tech/Texas	1946
Ray Beck, Georgia Tech	1951
†John Beckett, Oregon	1916
Chuck Bednarik, Pennsylvania#	1948
Forrest Behm, Nebraska	1940
Bobby Bell, Minnesota#	1962
Joe Bellino, Navy	1960
†Marty Below, Wisconsin	1923
†Al Benbrook, Michigan	1910
Jeff Bentrim, North Dakota St. ($)	1986
†Charlie Berry, Lafayette	1924
Angelo Bertelli, Notre Dame	1943
Jay Berwanger, Chicago	1935
†Lawrence Bettencourt, St. Mary's (Cal.)	1927
Fred Biletnikoff, Florida St.#	1964
Doc Blanchard, Army	1946
†Al Blozis, Georgetown	1941
Ed Bock, Iowa St.	1938
†Lynn Bomar, Vanderbilt	1924
†Douglas Bomeisler, Yale	1912
†Albie Booth, Yale	1931
George Bork, Northern Ill. ($)	1963

SPECIAL AWARDS

AWARD WINNERS

Player, College	Year
†Fred Borries, Navy	1934
Bruce Bosley, West Virginia	1955
Don Bosseler, Miami (Fla.)	1956
Vic Bottari, California	1938
†Ben Boynton, Williams	1920
Terry Bradshaw, Louisiana Tech ($)	1969
†Charles Brewer, Harvard	1895
†Johnny Bright, Drake	1951
John Brodie, Stanford	1956
†George Brooke, Swarthmore/Pennsylvania	1895
Al Brosky, Illinois	1952
Bob Brown, Nebraska	1963
George Brown, Navy/San Diego St.	1947
†Gordon Brown, Yale	1900
Jim Brown, Syracuse#	1956
†John Brown Jr., Navy	1913
†Johnny Mack Brown, Alabama	1925
†Tay Brown, Southern California	1932
Ross Browner, Notre Dame	1977
Teel Bruner, Centre ($)	1985
†Buck Buchanan, Grambling ($)	1962
Brad Budde, Southern California	1979
†Paul Bunker, Army	1902
Chris Burford, Stanford	1959
Ron Burton, Northwestern	1959
Dick Butkus, Illinois#	1964
†Robert Butler, Wisconsin	1913
†George Cafego, Tennessee	1939
†Red Cagle, La.-Lafayette/Army	1929
†John Cain, Alabama	1932
Ed Cameron, Wash. & Lee	1924
†David Campbell, Harvard	1901
Earl Campbell, Texas	1977
†Jack Cannon, Notre Dame	1929
John Cappelletti, Penn St.	1973
†Frank Carideo, Notre Dame	1930
†Charles Carney, Illinois	1921
J. C. Caroline, Illinois	1954
Bill Carpenter, Army	1959
†Hunter Carpenter, Virginia Tech/North Carolina	1905
Charles Carroll, Washington	1928
Tommy Casanova, LSU	1971
†Edward Casey, Harvard	1919
Howard Cassady, Ohio St.	1955
†Guy Chamberlin, Neb. Wesleyan/Nebraska#	1915
Sam Chapman, California	1937
Bob Chappuis, Michigan	1947
†Paul Christman, Missouri	1940
Joe Cichy, North Dakota St. ($)	1970
†Dutch Clark, Colorado Col.#	1929
Paul Cleary, Southern California	1947
†Zora Clevenger, Indiana	1903
Jack Cloud, William & Mary	1949
†Gary Cochran, Princeton	1897
†Josh Cody, Vanderbilt	1919
Don Coleman, Michigan St.	1951
†Charlie Conerly, Mississippi	1947
George Connor, Holy Cross/Notre Dame#	1947
†William Corbin, Yale	1888
William Corbus, Stanford	1933
†Hector Cowan, Princeton	1889
†Edward Coy, Yale	1909
†Fred Crawford, Duke	1933
John David Crow, Texas A&M	1957
†Jim Crowley, Notre Dame	1924
Larry Csonka, Syracuse#	1967
Slade Cutter, Navy	1934
†Ziggie Czarobski, Notre Dame	1947
Carroll Dale, Virginia Tech	1959
†Gerald Dalrymple, Tulane	1931
†John Dalton, Navy	1911
†Charles Daly, Harvard/Army	1902
Averell Daniell, Pittsburgh	1936
†James Daniell, Ohio St.	1941
†Tom Davies, Pittsburgh	1921
†Ernie Davis, Syracuse	1961
Glenn Davis, Army	1946
Robert Davis, Georgia Tech	1947
Pete Dawkins, Army	1958
Tom Deery, Widener ($)	1981
†Joe Delaney, Northwestern St. ($)	1980
Steve DeLong, Tennessee	1964
Vern Den Herder, Central (Iowa) ($)	1970
Al DeRogatis, Duke	1948

Player, College	Year
†Paul DesJardien, Chicago	1914
Aubrey Devine, Iowa	1921
†John DeWitt, Princeton	1903
Buddy Dial, Rice	1958
Chuck Dicus, Arkansas	1970
Mike Ditka, Pittsburgh#	1960
Glenn Dobbs, Tulsa	1942
†Bobby Dodd, Tennessee	1930
Holland Donan, Princeton	1950
†Joseph Donchess, Pittsburgh	1929
Tony Dorsett, Pittsburgh#	1976
†Nathan Dougherty, Tennessee	1909
Nick Drahos, Cornell	1940
†Paddy Driscoll, Northwestern#	1916
†Morley Drury, Southern California	1927
Fred Dryer, San Diego St. ($)	1968
Joe Dudek, Plymouth St. ($)	1985
Bill Dudley, Virginia#	1941
Randy Duncan, Iowa	1958
Kenny Easley, UCLA	1980
†Walter Eckersall, Chicago	1906
†Turk Edwards, Washington St.#	1931
†William Edwards, Princeton	1899
†Ray Eichenlaub, Notre Dame	1914
Steve Eisenhauer, Navy	1953
Lawrence Elkins, Baylor	1964
Bump Elliott, Michigan/Purdue	1947
Pete Elliott, Michigan	1948
Dave Elmendorf, Texas A&M	1970
Ray Evans, Kansas	1947
†Albert Exendine, Carlisle	1907
†Nello Falaschi, Santa Clara	1936
Tom Fears, Santa Clara/UCLA#	1947
†Beattie Feathers, Tennessee	1933
Bob Fenimore, Oklahoma St.	1946
†Doc Fenton, LSU	1909
Bob Ferguson, Ohio St.	1961
John Ferraro, Southern California	1947
†Wes Fesler, Ohio St.	1930
†Bill Fincher, Davidson/Georgia Tech	1920
Bill Fischer, Notre Dame	1948
†Hamilton Fish, Harvard	1909
†Robert Fisher, Harvard	1911
†Allen Flowers, Davidson/Georgia Tech	1920
Charlie Flowers, Mississippi	1959
George Floyd, Eastern Ky. ($)	1981
†Danny Fortmann, Colgate#	1935
Bill Fralic, Pittsburgh	1984
Sam Francis, Nebraska	1936
†Ed Franco, Fordham	1937
†Clint Frank, Yale	1937
Rodney Franz, California	1949
Tucker Frederickson, Auburn	1964
†Benny Friedman, Michigan	1926
Roman Gabriel, North Carolina St.	1961
Bob Gain, Kentucky	1950
†Arnold Galiffa, Army	1949
Willie Galimore, Florida A&M ($)	1956
Hugh Gallarneau, Stanford	1940
†Edgar Garbisch, Wash. & Jeff./Army	1924
Mike Garrett, Southern California	1965
†Charles Gelbert, Pennsylvania	1896
†Forest Geyer, Oklahoma	1915
Jake Gibbs, Mississippi	1960
Paul Giel, Minnesota	1953
Frank Gifford, Southern California#	1951
Chris Gilbert, Texas	1968
†Walter Gilbert, Auburn	1936
Harry Gilmer, Alabama	1947
†George Gipp, Notre Dame	1920
†Chet Gladchuk, Boston College	1940
Bill Glass, Baylor	1956
Rich Glover, Nebraska	1972
Marshall Goldberg, Pittsburgh	1938
Gene Goodreault, Boston College	1940
†Walter Gordon, California	1918
†Paul Governali, Columbia	1942
Jim Grabowski, Illinois	1965
Randy Gradishar, Ohio St.	1973
Otto Graham, Northwestern#	1943
†Red Grange, Illinois#	1925
†Bobby Grayson, Stanford	1935
Hugh Green, Pittsburgh	1980
†Jack Green, Tulane/Army	1945

Player, College	Year
Joe Greene, North Texas#	1968
Bob Griese, Purdue#	1966
Archie Griffin, Ohio St.	1975
William Grinnell, Tufts ($)	1934
Jerry Groom, Notre Dame	1950
†Merle Gulick, Toledo/Hobart	1929
†Joe Guyon, Carlisle/Georgia Tech#	1918
John Hadl, Kansas	1961
†Edwin Hale, Mississippi Col.	1921
L. Parker Hall, Mississippi	1938
Jack Ham, Penn St.#	1970
Bob Hamilton, Stanford	1935
†Tom Hamilton, Navy	1926
John Hannah, Alabama	1972
†Vic Hanson, Syracuse	1926
†Pat Harder, Wisconsin	1942
†Tack Hardwick, Harvard	1914
†T. Truxton Hare, Pennsylvania	1900
†Chick Harley, Ohio St.	1919
Tom Harmon, Michigan	1940
Howard Harpster, Carnegie Mellon	1928
†Edward Hart, Princeton	1911
Leon Hart, Notre Dame	1949
Bill Hartman, Georgia	1937
Frank Hawkins, Nevada ($)	1980
†Homer Hazel, Rutgers	1924
Matt Hazeltine, California	1954
†Ed Healey, Holy Cross/Dartmouth#	1919
†Pudge Heffelfinger, Yale	1891
†Mel Hein, Washington St.#	1930
†Don Heinrich, Washington	1952
Ted Hendricks, Miami (Fla.)#	1968
†Wilbur Henry, Wash. & Jeff.#	1919
†Clarence Herschberger, Chicago	1898
†Robert Herwig, California	1937
†Willie Heston, San Jose St./Michigan	1904
†Herman Hickman, Tennessee	1931
†William Hickok, Yale	1894
†Dan Hill, Duke	1938
†Art Hillebrand, Princeton	1899
†Frank Hinkey, Yale	1894
†Carl Hinkle, Vanderbilt	1937
†Clarke Hinkle, Bucknell#	1931
Elroy Hirsch, Wisconsin/Michigan#	1943
†James Hitchcock, Auburn	1932
†Frank Hoffmann, Notre Dame	1931
†James J. Hogan, Yale	1904
†Brud Holland, Cornell	1938
†Don Holleder, Army	1955
†Bill Hollenback, Pennsylvania	1908
Mike Holovak, Boston College	1942
Pierce Holt, Angelo St. ($)	1987
E. J. Holub, Texas Tech	1960
Paul Hornung, Notre Dame#	1956
†Edwin Horrell, California	1924
†Les Horvath, Ohio St.	1944
Arthur Howe, Yale	1911
†Dixie Howell, Alabama	1934
†Cal Hubbard, Geneva/Centenary (La.)#	1926
John Hubbard, Amherst	1906
†Pooley Hubert, Alabama	1925
Sam Huff, West Virginia#	1955
Weldon Humble, La.-Lafayette/Rice	1946
Ricky Hunley, Arizona	1983
†Joel Hunt, Texas A&M	1927
†Ellery Huntington, Colgate	1913
†Don Hutson, Alabama#	1934
†Jonas Ingram, Navy	1906
†Cecil Isbell, Purdue	1937
†Harvey Jablonsky, Army/Washington (Mo.)	1933
Bo Jackson, Auburn	1985
†Vic Janowicz, Ohio St.	1951
†Darold Jenkins, Missouri	1941
Jackie Jensen, California	1948
†Herbert Joesting, Minnesota	1927
Billy Johnson, Widener ($)	1972
Bob Johnson, Tennessee	1967
Gary Johnson, Grambling ($)	1974
†Jimmie Johnson, Carlisle/Northwestern	1905
Ron Johnson, Michigan	1968
†Calvin Jones, Iowa	1955
†Gomer Jones, Ohio St.	1935
Lee Roy Jordan, Alabama	1962

Player, College	Year
†Frank Juhan, Sewanee	1910
Charlie Justice, North Carolina	1949
†Mort Kaer, Southern California	1926
Alex Karras, Iowa	1957
Ken Kavanaugh, LSU	1939
†Edgar Kaw, Cornell	1922
Dick Kazmaier, Princeton	1951
†Stan Keck, Princeton	1921
Larry Kelley, Yale	1936
†Wild Bill Kelly, Montana	1926
Doug Kenna, Army	1944
†George Kerr, Boston College	1940
†Henry Ketcham, Yale	1913
Leroy Keyes, Purdue	1968
†Glenn Killinger, Penn St.	1921
Billy Kilmer, UCLA	1960
†John Kilpatrick, Yale	1910
John Kimbrough, Texas A&M	1940
†Frank Kinard, Mississippi#	1937
Steve Kiner, Tennessee	1969
†Phillip King, Princeton	1893
†Nile Kinnick, Iowa	1939
†Harry Kipke, Michigan	1923
†John Kitzmiller, Oregon	1930
†Barton Koch, Baylor	1930
†Walt Koppisch, Columbia	1924
Ron Kramer, Michigan	1956
Alex Kroll, Yale/Rutgers	1961
Charlie Krueger, Texas A&M	1957
Malcolm Kutner, Texas	1941
Ted Kwalick, Penn St.	1968
†Steve Lach, Duke	1941
†Myles Lane, Dartmouth	1927
Johnny Lattner, Notre Dame	1953
Hank Lauricella, Tennessee	1951
†Lester Lautenschlaeger, Tulane	1925
†Elmer Layden, Notre Dame	1924
†Bobby Layne, Texas#	1947
†Langdon Lea, Princeton	1895
Eddie LeBaron, Pacific (Cal.)	1949
Jim LeClair, North Dakota ($)	1971
James Leech, VMI	1920
†Darrell Lester, TCU	1935
Bob Lilly, TCU#	1960
†Augie Lio, Georgetown	1940
Floyd Little, Syracuse	1966
†Gordon Locke, Iowa	1922
†Don Lourie, Princeton	1921
Neil Lomax, Portland St. ($)	1980
Chuck Long, Iowa	1985
Mel Long, Toledo	1971
†Frank Loria, Virginia Tech	1967
Richie Lucas, Penn St.	1959
Sid Luckman, Columbia#	1938
Johnny Lujack, Notre Dame	1947
†Pug Lund, Minnesota	1934
Jim Lynch, Notre Dame	1966
Ken MacAfee, Notre Dame	1977
Robert MacLeod, Dartmouth	1938
†Bart Macomber, Illinois	1916
Dicky Maegle, Rice	1954
†Ned Mahon, Harvard	1915
Johnny Majors, Tennessee	1956
†William Mallory, Yale	1923
Vaughn Mancha, Alabama	1947
†Gerald Mann, Southern Methodist	1927
Archie Manning, Mississippi	1970
Edgar Manske, Northwestern	1933
Ed Marinaro, Cornell	1971
†Vic Markov, Washington	1937
†Bobby Marshall, Minnesota	1906
Jim Martin, Notre Dame	1949
Ollie Matson, San Francisco#	1951
Ray Matthews, TCU	1927
†John Maulbetsch, Adrian/Michigan	1916
†Pete Mauthe, Penn St.	1912
†Robert Maxwell, Chicago/Swarthmore	1905
George McAfee, Duke#	1939
†Thomas McClung, Yale	1891
Bill McColl, Stanford	1951
†Jim McCormick, Princeton	1907
Tommy McDonald, Oklahoma	1956
†Jack McDowall, North Carolina St.	1927
Hugh McElhenny, Washington#	1951

Player, College	Year
†Gene McEver, Tennessee	1931
†John McEwan, Army	1916
Banks McFadden, Clemson	1939
Bud McFadin, Texas	1950
Mike McGee, Duke	1959
†Edward McGinley, Pennsylvania	1924
†John McGovern, Minnesota	1910
Thurman McGraw, Colorado St.	1949
Tyrone McGriff, Florida A&M ($)	1979
†Mike McKeever, Southern California	1960
†George McLaren, Pittsburgh	1918
Jim McMahon, Brigham Young	1981
†Dan McMillan, Southern California/California	1921
†Bo McMillin, Centre	1921
†Bob McWhorter, Georgia	1913
†Roy Mercer, Pennsylvania	1912
Don Meredith, Southern Methodist	1959
Frank Merritt, Army	1943
†Bert Metzger, Notre Dame	1930
†Wayne Meylan, Nebraska	1967
Lou Michaels, Kentucky	1957
John Michels, Tennessee	1952
Abe Mickal, LSU	1935
Creighton Miller, Notre Dame	1943
†Don Miller, Notre Dame	1924
†Eugene Miller, Penn St.	1913
†Fred Miller, Notre Dame	1928
†Rip Miller, Notre Dame	1924
†Wayne Millner, Notre Dame#	1935
†Century Milstead, Wabash/Yale	1923
†John Minds, Pennsylvania	1897
Skip Minisi, Pennsylvania/Navy	1947
Dick Modzelewski, Maryland	1952
†Alex Moffat, Princeton	1883
†Ed Molinski, Tennessee	1940
Cliff Montgomery, Columbia	1933
Wilbert Montgomery, Abilene Christian ($)	1976
Donn Moomaw, UCLA	1952
†William Morley, Columbia	1901
George Morris, Georgia Tech	1952
Larry Morris, Georgia Tech	1954
†Bill Morton, Dartmouth	1931
Craig Morton, California	1964
†Monk Moscrip, Stanford	1935
†Brick Muller, California	1922
†Bronko Nagurski, Minnesota#	1929
†Ernie Nevers, Stanford#	1925
†Marshall Newell, Harvard	1893
Harry Newman, Michigan	1932
Ozzie Newsome, Alabama	1977
Gifford Nielsen, Brigham Young	1977
Tommy Nobis, Texas	1965
Leo Nomellini, Minnesota#	1949
†Andrew Oberlander, Dartmouth	1925
†Davey O'Brien, TCU	1938
Ken O'Brien, UC Davis ($)	1982
†Pat O'Dea, Wisconsin	1899
Bob Odell, Pennsylvania	1943
†Jack O'Hearn, Cornell	1914
Robin Olds, Army	1942
†Elmer Oliphant, Army/Purdue	1917
Merlin Olsen, Utah St.#	1961
Dennis Onkotz, Penn St.	1969
†Bennie Oosterbaan, Michigan	1927
Charles O'Rourke, Boston College	1940
†John Orsi, Colgate	1931
†Win Osgood, Cornell/Pennsylvania	1894
Bill Osmanski, Holy Cross	1938
†George Owen, Harvard	1922
Jim Owens, Oklahoma	1949
Steve Owens, Oklahoma	1969
Alan Page, Notre Dame#	1966
Joe Palumbo, Virginia	1951
Jack Pardee, Texas A&M	1956
Babe Parilli, Kentucky	1951
Ace Parker, Duke#	1936
Jackie Parker, Mississippi St.	1953
Jim Parker, Ohio St.#	1956
Walter Payton, Jackson St. ($)	1974
†Vince Pazzetti, Wesleyan/Lehigh	1912
Chub Peabody, Harvard	1941
†Robert Peck, Pittsburgh	1916
Bob Pellegrini, Maryland	1955
†Stan Pennock, Harvard	1914

Player, College	Year
George Pfann, Cornell	1923
†H. D. Phillips, Sewanee	1905
Loyd Phillips, Arkansas	1966
Pete Pihos, Indiana#	1946
†Erny Pinckert, Southern California	1931
†John Pingel, Michigan St.	1938
Jim Plunkett, Stanford	1970
†Arthur Poe, Princeton	1899
†Fritz Pollard, Brown	1916
George Poole, Mississippi/North Carolina/Army	1948
Marvin Powell, Southern California	1976
Merv Pregulman, Michigan	1943
†Eddie Price, Tulane	1949
Greg Pruitt, Oklahoma	1972
Larry Pugh, Westminster (Pa.) ($)	1964
†Peter Pund, Georgia Tech	1928
Garrard Ramsey, William & Mary	1942
Gary Reasons, Northwestern St. ($)	1983
Rick Redman, Washington	1964
†Claude Reeds, Oklahoma	1913
Mike Reid, Penn St.	1969
Steve Reid, Northwestern	1936
†William Reid, Harvard	1899
Bob Reifsnyder, Navy	1958
Mel Renfro, Oregon	1963
†Pug Rentner, Northwestern	1932
†Bob Reynolds, Stanford	1935
†Bobby Reynolds, Nebraska	1952
Jerry Rhome, Southern Methodist/Tulsa	1964
Les Richter, California	1951
Pat Richter, Wisconsin	1962
†Jack Riley, Northwestern	1931
Dave Rimington, Nebraska	1982
†Charles Rinehart, Lafayette	1897
Jim Ritcher, North Carolina St.	1979
Richard Ritchie, Tex. A&M-Kingsville ($)	1976
J. D. Roberts, Oklahoma	1953
†Paul Robeson, Rutgers	1918
Dave Robinson, Penn St.	1962
Jerry Robinson, UCLA	1978
George Rogers, South Carolina	1980
†Ira Rodgers, West Virginia	1919
†Edward Rogers, Carlisle/Minnesota	1903
Johnny Roland, Missouri	1965
Joe Romig, Colorado	1961
†Aaron Rosenberg, Southern California	1933
Kyle Rote, Southern Methodist	1950
†Joe Routt, Texas A&M	1937
†Red Salmon, Notre Dame	1903
Alex Sarkisian, Northwestern	1948
†George Sauer, Nebraska	1933
George Savitsky, Pennsylvania	1947
James Saxton, Texas	1961
Gale Sayers, Kansas#	1964
Jack Scarbath, Maryland	1952
†Hunter Scarlett, Pennsylvania	1908
Bob Schloredt, Washington	1960
†Wear Schoonover, Arkansas	1929
†Dave Schreiner, Wisconsin	1942
†Germany Schultz, Michigan	1908
†Dutch Schwab, Lafayette	1922
†Marchy Schwartz, Notre Dame	1931
†Paul Schwegler, Washington	1931
Clyde Scott, Navy/Arkansas	1948
Richard Scott, Navy	1947
Tom Scott, Virginia	1952
†Henry Seibels, Sewanee	1900
Ron Sellers, Florida St.	1968
Lee Roy Selmon, Oklahoma#	1975
†Bill Shakespeare, Notre Dame	1935
Donnie Shell, South Carolina St. ($)	1973
†Murray Shelton, Cornell	1915
†Tom Shevlin, Yale	1905
†Bernie Shively, Illinois	1926
†Monk Simons, Tulane	1934
O. J. Simpson, Southern California#	1968
Billy Sims, Oklahoma	1979
Mike Singletary, Baylor	1980
Fred Sington, Alabama	1930
†Frank Sinkwich, Georgia	1942
Emil Sitko, Notre Dame	1949
†Joe Skladany, Pittsburgh	1933
†Duke Slater, Iowa	1921
†Bruce Smith, Minnesota	1941

SPECIAL AWARDS   257

Player, College	Year
Bubba Smith, Michigan St.	1966
†Clipper Smith, Notre Dame	1927
†Ernie Smith, Southern California	1932
Harry Smith, Southern California	1939
Jim Ray Smith, Baylor	1954
Riley Smith, Alabama	1935
†Vernon Smith, Georgia	1931
†Neil Snow, Michigan	1901
Al Sparlis, UCLA	1945
†Clarence Spears, Knox/Dartmouth	1915
†W. D. Spears, Vanderbilt	1927
†William Sprackling, Brown	1911
†Bud Sprague, Army/Texas	1928
Steve Spurrier, Florida	1966
Harrison Stafford, Texas	1932
†Amos Alonzo Stagg, Yale	1889
Bill Stanfill, Georgia	1968
†Max Starcevich, Washington	1936
Roger Staubach, Navy#	1964
†Walter Steffen, Chicago	1908
Joe Steffy, Tennessee/Army	1947
Herbert Stein, Pittsburgh	1921
Bob Steuber, DePauw/Missouri	1943
†Mal Stevens, Washburn/Yale	1923
Vincent Stevenson, Pennsylvania	1905
Jim Stillwagon, Ohio St.	1970
†Pete Stinchcomb, Ohio St.	1920
Brock Strom, Air Force	1958
†Ken Strong, New York U.#	1928
†George Strupper, Georgia Tech	1917
†Harry Stuhldreher, Notre Dame	1924
†Herb Sturhahn, Yale	1926
†Joe Stydahar, West Virginia#	1935
†Bob Suffridge, Tennessee	1940
Steve Suhey, Penn St.	1947
Pat Sullivan, Auburn	1971
†Frank Sundstrom, Cornell	1923
Lynn Swann, Southern California	1973
†Clarence Swanson, Nebraska	1921
†Bill Swiacki, Holy Cross/Columbia	1947
Jim Swink, TCU	1956
George Taliaferro, Indiana	1948
Fran Tarkenton, Georgia#	1960
John Tavener, Indiana	1944
Bruce Taylor, Boston U. ($)	1969
†Chuck Taylor, Stanford	1942
Aurelius Thomas, Ohio St.	1957
†Joe Thompson, Geneva/Pittsburgh	1906
Lynn Thomsen, Augustana (Ill.)$	1986
†Samuel Thorne, Yale	1895
†Jim Thorpe, Carlisle#	1912
†Ben Ticknor, Harvard	1930
†John Tigert, Vanderbilt	1903
Gaynell Tinsley, LSU	1936
Eric Tipton, Duke	1938
†Clayton Tonnemaker, Minnesota	1949
†Bob Torrey, Pennsylvania	1905
Randy Trautman, Boise St. ($)	1981
†Brick Travis, Tarkio/Missouri	1920
Charley Trippi, Georgia#	1946
†Edward Tryon, Colgate	1925
Jerry Tubbs, Oklahoma	1956
Bulldog Turner, Hardin-Simmons#	1939
Howard Twilley, Tulsa	1965
†Joe Utay, Texas A&M	1907
†Norm Van Brocklin, Oregon#	1948
†Dale Van Sickel, Florida	1929
†H. Van Surdam, Wesleyan	1905
†Dexter Very, Penn St.	1912
Billy Vessels, Oklahoma	1952
†Ernie Vick, Michigan	1921
†Hube Wagner, Pittsburgh	1913
†Doak Walker, Southern Methodist#	1949
Herschel Walker, Georgia	1982
†Bill Wallace, Rice	1935
†Adam Walsh, Notre Dame	1924
†Cotton Warburton, Southern California	1934
Bob Ward, Maryland	1951
†William Warner, Cornell	1902
†Kenny Washington, UCLA	1939
†Jim Weatherall, Oklahoma	1951
George Webster, Michigan St.	1966
Herman Wedemeyer, St. Mary's (Cal.)	1947
†Harold Weekes, Columbia	1902
Art Weiner, North Carolina	1949
†Ed Weir, Nebraska	1925
†Gus Welch, Carlisle	1914
†John Weller, Princeton	1935

Player, College	Year
†Percy Wendell, Harvard	1912
†Belford West, Colgate	1919
†Bob Westfall, Michigan	1941
†Babe Weyand, Army	1915
†Buck Wharton, Pennsylvania	1896
†Arthur Wheeler, Princeton	1894
Byron White, Colorado	1937
Charles White, Southern California	1979
Danny White, Arizona St.	1973
Ed White, California	1968
Randy White, Maryland#	1974
†Don Whitmire, Navy/Alabama	1944
†Frank Wickhorst, Navy	1926
Ed Widseth, Minnesota	1936
†Dick Wildung, Minnesota	1942
Bob Williams, Notre Dame	1950
Froggie Williams, Rice	1949
Bill Willis, Ohio St.#	1944
Bobby Wilson, Southern Methodist	1935
†George Wilson, Washington	1925
†Harry Wilson, Army/Penn St.	1927
Marc Wilson, Brigham Young	1979
Mike Wilson, Lafayette	1928
Albert Wistert, Michigan	1942
Alvin Wistert, Boston U./Michigan	1949
†Whitey Wistert, Michigan	1933
†Alex Wojciechowicz, Fordham#	1937
†Barry Wood, Harvard	1931
†Andy Wyant, Bucknell/Chicago	1894
†Bowden Wyatt, Tennessee	1938
†Clint Wyckoff, Cornell	1895
†Tommy Yarr, Notre Dame	1931
Ron Yary, Southern California	1967
†Lloyd Yoder, Carnegie Mellon	1926
†Buddy Young, Illinois	1946
†Harry Young, Wash. & Lee	1916
†Waddy Young, Oklahoma	1938
Jack Youngblood, Florida	1970
Jim Youngblood, Tennessee Tech ($)	1972
Gust Zarnas, Ohio St.	1937

COACHES

Coach	Year
†Joe Aillet	1989
†Bill Alexander	1951
†Ed Anderson	1971
†Ike Armstrong	1957
†Charlie Bachman	1978
Earl Banks	1992
†Harry Baujan	1990
†Matty Bell	1955
†Hugo Bezdek	1954
†Dana X. Bible	1951
†Bernie Bierman	1955
†Bob Blackman	1987
†Earl "Red" Blaik	1964
Frank Broyles	1983
†Paul "Bear" Bryant	1986
Harold Burry ($)	1996
Jim Butterfield ($)	1997
†Wally Butts	1997
Charlie Caldwell	1961
†Walter Camp	1951
Len Casanova	1977
†Frank Cavanaugh	1954
Jerry Claiborne	1999
†Dick Colman	1990
Don Coryell ($)	1999
†Fritz Crisler	1954
†Duffy Daugherty	1984
†Bob Devaney	1981
Dan Devine	1985
†Gil Dobie	1951
†Bobby Dodd	1993
†Michael Donahue	1951
Vince Dooley	1994
†Gus Dorais	1954
†Bill Edwards	1986
†Rip Engle	1973
†Don Faurot	1961
†Jake Gaither	1975
Sid Gillman#	1989
†Ernest Godfrey	1972
Ray Graves	1990
†Andy Gustafson	1985
†Edward Hall	1951
†Jack Hardin	1980
†Richard Harlow	1954

Coach	Year
†Harvey Harman	1981
†Jesse Harper	1971
†Percy Haughton	1951
†Woody Hayes	1983
†John W. Heisman	1954
†Robert Higgins	1954
†Paul Hoernemann ($)	1997
†Babe Hollingberry	1979
†Frank Howard	1989
†Bill Ingram	1973
Don James	1997
†Morley Jennings	1973
†Biff Jones	1954
†Howard Jones	1951
†Tad Jones	1958
†Lloyd Jordan	1978
†Ralph "Shug" Jordan	1982
†Andy Kerr	1951
Chuck Klausing ($)	1998
Frank Kush	1995
†Frank Leahy	1970
†George Little	1955
†Lou Little	1960
†Slip Madigan	1974
Dave Maurer	1991
Charlie McClendon	1986
Herb McCracken	1973
†Dan McGugin	1951
John McKay	1988
Allyn McKeen	1991
†Tuss McLaughry	1962
†John Merritt	1994
†Dutch Meyer	1956
†Jack Mollenkopf	1988
†Bernie Moore	1954
†Scrappy Moore	1980
†Ray Morrison	1954
†George Munger	1976
†Clarence "Biggie" Munn	1959
†Bill Murray	1974
†Frank Murray	1974
†Ed "Hook" Mylin	1974
†Earle "Greasy" Neale #	1967
†Jess Neely	1971
†David Nelson	1987
†Robert Neyland	1956
Billy Nicks ($)	1999
†Homer Norton	1971
†Frank "Buck" O'Neill	1951
Tom Osborne	1998
†Bennie Owen	1951
Ara Parseghian	1980
†Doyt Perry	1988
†Jimmy Phelan	1973
†Tommy Prothro	1991
John Ralston	1992
Bob Reade ($)	1998
†E. N. Robinson	1955
Eddie Robinson ($)	1997
†Knute Rockne	1951
†Dick Romney	1954
†Bill Roper	1951
Darrell Royal	1983
Adolph Rutschman ($)	1998
†Henry "Red" Sanders	1996
†George Sanford	1971
Glenn "Bo" Schembechler	1993
†Francis Schmidt	1971
†Ben Schwartzwalder	1982
†Clark Shaughnessy	1968
†Buck Shaw	1972
Edgar Sherman ($)	1996
†Andy Smith	1951
†Carl Snavely	1965
Jim Sochor ($)	1999
†Amos Alonzo Stagg	1951
†Gil Steinke ($)	1996
†Jock Sutherland	1951
†Jim Tatum	1984
†Frank Thomas	1951
†Lee Tressel ($)	1996
†Thad "Pie" Vann	1987
Johnny Vaught	1979
†Wallace Wade	1955
†Lynn "Pappy" Waldorf	1966
†Glenn "Pop" Warner	1951
Jim Young	1999
†E. E. "Tad" Wieman	1956

AWARD WINNERS

Coach	Year
†John Wilce	1954
†Bud Wilkinson	1969
†Henry Williams	1951
†George Woodruff	1963
†Warren Woodson	1989
†Bowden Wyatt	1997
†Fielding "Hurry Up" Yost	1951
Jim Young	1999
†Bob Zuppke	1951

†Deceased

DIVISION II NATIONAL HALL OF FAME
(at Florence, Alabama)

2000

Johnny Bailey, Tex. A&M-Kingsville, RB
Jeff Bentrim, North Dakota St., QB
Walter Payton, Jackson St., RB

First-Team All-Americans Below Division I-A

1999 Selectors (and division[s]): American Football Coaches Association (I-AA, II, III); Associated Press (I-AA, II, III); Football Gazette (I-AA, II, III); Sports Network (I-AA).

Selection of Associated Press Little All-America Teams began in 1934. Early AP selectors were not bound by NCAA membership classifications; therefore, several current Division I-A teams are included in this list.

The American Football Coaches Association began selecting all-America teams below Division I-A in 1967 for two College-Division classifications. Its College-Division I team includes NCAA Division II and National Association of Intercollegiate Athletics (NAIA) Division I players. The AFCA College-Division II team includes NCAA Division III and NAIA Division II players. The AFCA added a Division I-AA team in 1979; AP began selecting a Division I-AA team in 1982; the Sports Network added a Division I-AA team in 1994; and these players are included. In 1993, the College Sports Information Directors of America Division II team was added, selected by sports information directors from every NCAA Division II institution. In 1990, the Champion USA Division III team was added, selected by a panel of 25 sports information directors and replaced by the Hewlett-Packard Division III team in 1995. In 1993, Football Gazette's team was added for Divisions I-AA, II and III.

Nonmembers of the NCAA are included in this list, as are colleges that no longer play varsity football.

Players selected to a Division I-AA all-America team are indicated by (†). Current members of Division I-A are indicated by (*).

All-Americans are listed by college, year selected and position.

ABILENE CHRISTIAN (18)
48— V. T. Smith, B
51— Lester Wheeler, OT
52— Wallace Bullington, DB
65— Larry Cox, OT
69— Chip Bennett, LB
70— Jim Lindsey, QB
73— Wilbert Montgomery, RB
74— Chip Martin, DL
77— Chuck Sitton, DB
82— Grant Feasel, C
83— Mark Wilson, DB
84— Dan Remsberg, OT
87— Richard Van Druten, OT
89— John Layfield, OG
90— Dennis Brown, PK
91— Jay Jones, LB
97— Junior Filikitonga, DL
  Victor Burke, DB

ADAMS ST. (6)
79— Ronald Johnson, DB
84— Bill Stone, RB
87— Dave Humann, DB
95— Chris Perry, WR
97— Jason Van Dyke, P
98— Jason Van Dyke, P

AKRON* (9)
69— John Travis, OG
71— Michael Hatch, DB
76— Mark Van Horn, OG
  Steve Cockerham, LB
77— Steve Cockerham, LB
80— †Brad Reece, LB
81— †Brad Reece, LB
85— †Wayne Grant, DL
86— †Mike Clark, RB

UAB* (1)
94— †Derrick Ingram, WR

ALABAMA A&M (3)
87— Howard Ballard, OL
88— Fred Garner, DB
89— Barry Wagner, WR

ALABAMA ST. (3)
90— †Eddie Robinson, LB
91— †Patrick Johnson, OL
  †Eddie Robinson, LB

ALBANY (N.Y.) (3)
92— Scott Turrin, OL
94— Scott Turrin, OL
98— Matt Caliandro, DL

ALBANY ST. (GA.) (1)
72— Harold Little, DE

ALBION (15)
40— Walter Ptak, G
58— Tom Taylor, E
76— Steve Spencer, DL
86— Joe Felton, OG
  Mike Grant, DB
91— Hank Wineman, RB
93— Ron Dawson, OL
  Jeff Brooks, OL
94— Jeff Robinson, RB
  Martin Heyboer, C
  David Lefere, DB
95— David Lefere, DB
96— Jason Carriveau, OG
98— Pat Sloane, DL
  Jason Carriveau, OL

ALBRIGHT (7)
36— Richard Riffle, B
37— Richard Riffle, B
75— Chris Simcic, OL
95— Dennis Unger, PK
96— Ryan Ditze, WR
  Bob Maro, DB
98— Chris Morehouse, P

ALCORN ST. (14)
69— David Hadley, DB
70— Fred Carter, DT
71— Harry Gooden, LB
72— Alex Price, DT
73— Leonard Fairley, DB
74— Jerry Dismuke, OG
75— Lawrence Pillers, DE
76— Augusta Lee, RB
  Larry Warren, DT
79— †Leslie Frazier, DB
84— †Issiac Holt, DB
93— †Goree White, KR
94— †Steve McNair, QB
99— †Chad Slaughter, OL

ALFRED (7)
51— Ralph DiMicco, B
52— Ralph DiMicco, B
55— Charles Schultz, E
56— Charles Schultz, E
75— Joseph Van Cura, DE
82— Brian O'Neil, DB
92— Mark Obuszewski, DB

ALLEGHENY (21)
75— Charles Slater, OL
87— Mike Mates, OL
88— Mike Parker, DL
90— Jeff Filkovski, QB
  David LaCarte, DB
  John Marzca, C
91— Ron Bendekovic, OT
  Stanley Drayton, RB
  Tony Bifulco, DB
92— Ron Bendekovic, OT
  Stanley Drayton, RB
94— Matt Allison, OL
  Paul Bell, QB
  Marvin Farr, DB
95— Brian Adams, C
  Nick Reiser, DE
  Anson Park, OL
96— Chris Conrad, KR
  Nick Reiser, DL
  Bob Tatsch, DL
97— Jim Mormino, RB

AMERICAN INT'L (12)
71— Bruce Laird, RB
80— Ed Cebula, C
82— Paul Thompson, DT
85— Keith Barry, OL
86— Jon Provost, OL
87— Jon Provost, OL
88— Greg Doherty, OL
89— Lamont Cato, DB
90— George Patterson, DL
91— Gabe Mokwuah, DL
98— Ray Shuster, OL
99— Kavin Gailliard, RB

AMHERST (5)
42— Adrian Hasse, E
72— Richard Murphy, QB
73— Fred Scott, FL
96— Alex Bernstein, DL
97— Devin Moriarty, DL

ANDERSON (IND.) (1)
97— Justin Shively, P

ANGELO ST. (13)
75— James Cross, DB
78— Jerry Aldridge, RB
  Kelvin Smith, LB
81— Clay Weishuhn, LB
82— Mike Elarms, WR
83— Mike Thomas, K
85— Henry Jackson, LB
86— Pierce Holt, DL
87— Pierce Holt, DL
88— Henry Alsbrooks, LB

92— Jimmy Morris, P
93— Anthony Hooper, DB
95— Greg Stokes, LB

APPALACHIAN ST. (23)
48— John Caskey, E
63— Greg Van Orden, G
85— †Dino Hackett, LB
87— †Anthony Downs, DE
88— †Bjorn Nittmo, PK
89— †Derrick Graham, OL
  †Keith Collins, DB
91— †Harold Alexander, P
92— †Avery Hall, DL
  †Harold Alexander, P
94— †Chip Miller, DL
  †William Peebles, DL
  †Brad Ohrt, OL
  †Dexter Coakley, LB
  †Matt Stevens, DB
95— †Dexter Coakley, LB
  †Matt Stevens, DB
  †Chip Miller, DL
  †Scott Kadlub, C
96— †Scott Kadlub, C
  †Dexter Coakley, LB
97— †Jackie Avery, DL
99— †Corey Hall, DB

ARIZONA* (1)
41— Henry Stanton, E

ARKANSAS ST.* (17)
53— Richard Woit, B
64— Dan Summers, OG
65— Dan Summers, OG
68— Bill Bergey, LB
69— Dan Buckley, C
  Clovis Swinney, DT
70— Bill Phillips, OG
  Calvin Harrell, HB
71— Calvin Harrell, RB
  Dennis Meyer, DB
  Wayne Dorton, OG
73— Doug Lowrey, OG
84— †Carter Crawford, DL
85— †Carter Crawford, DL
86— †Randy Barnhill, OG
87— †Jim Wiseman, C
  †Charlie Fredrick, DT

ARKANSAS TECH (4)
58— Edward Meador, B
61— Powell McClellan, E
95— Piotr Styczen, PK
99— Todd Matthews, OG

ASHLAND (9)
70— Len Pettigrew, LB
78— Keith Dare, DL
85— Jeff Penko, OL
86— Vince Mazza, PK
89— Douglas Powell, DB
90— Morris Furman, LB
91— Ron Greer, LB
93— Bill Royce, DL
94— Sam Hohler, DE

AUGUSTANA (ILL.) (11)
72— Willie Van, DT
73— Robert Martin, OT
83— Kurt Kapischke, OL
84— Greg King, C
86— Lynn Thomsen, DL
87— Carlton Beasley, DL
88— John Bothe, OL
90— Barry Reade, PK
91— Mike Hesler, DL
92— George Annang, DL
95— Rusty Van Wetzinga, LB

AUGUSTANA (S.D.) (4)
60— John Simko, E
87— Tony Adkins, DL

FIRST-TEAM ALL-AMERICANS BELOW DIVISION I-A

88— Pete Jaros, DB
94— Bryan Schwartz, LB

AUGSBURG (2)
97— Scott Hvistendahl, WR
98— Scott Hvistendahl, WR

AURORA (1)
99— Jeramy Benson, DL

AUSTIN (10)
37— Wallace Johnson, C
79— Price Clifford, LB
80— Chris Luper, DB
81— Larry Shillings, QB
83— Ed Holt, DL
84— Jeff Timmons, PK
87— Otis Amy, WR
88— Otis Amy, WR
90— Jeff Cordell, DB
94— Brent Badger, P

AUSTIN PEAY (8)
65— Tim Chilcutt, DB
66— John Ogles, FB
70— Harold Roberts, OE
77— Bob Bible, LB
78— Mike Betts, DB
80— Brett Williams, DE
82— Charlie Tucker, OL
92— †Richard Darden, DL

AZUSA PACIFIC (2)
86— Christian Okoye, RB
95— Jake Wiersma, OL

BAKER (3)
83— Chris Brown, LB
85— Kevin Alewine, RB
90— John Campbell, OL

BALDWIN-WALLACE (12)
50— Norbert Hecker, E
68— Bob Quackenbush, DT
78— Jeff Jenkins, OL
80— Dan Delfino, DE
82— Pete Primeau, DL
83— Steve Varga, K
89— Doug Halbert, DL
91— John Koz, QB
      Jim Clardy, LB
94— Chris Kondik, PK
      Phil Sahley, DL
97— Fred Saylor, DL

BALL ST.* (4)
67— Oscar Lubke, OT
68— Amos Van Pelt, HB
72— Douglas Bell, C
73— Terry Schmidt, DB

BATES (1)
81— Larry DiGammarino, WR

BELOIT (1)
95— Maurice Redd, DB

BEMIDJI ST. (1)
83— Bruce Ecklund, TE

BENEDICTINE (ILL.) (3)
72— Mike Rogowski, LB
92— Bob McMillen, TE
93— Eric Green, KR

BENEDICTINE (KAN.) (1)
36— Leo Deutsch, E

BENTLEY (1)
99— Mark DeBrito, WR

BETHANY (W.VA.) (2)
77— Scott Lanz, P
93— Brian Darden, PK

BETHEL (KAN.) (1)
80— David Morford, C

BETHEL (MINN.) (1)
99— Chico Rowland, OL

BETHUNE-COOKMAN (3)
75— Willie Lee, DE
81— Booker Reese, DE
98— † James Souder, LB

BIRMINGHAM-SOUTHERN (1)
37— Walter Riddle, T

BISHOP (1)
81— Carlton Nelson, DL

BLOOMSBURG (12)
79— Mike Morucci, RB
82— Mike Blake, TE
83— Frank Sheptock, LB
84— Frank Sheptock, LB
85— Frank Sheptock, LB
      Tony Woods, DB
91— Eric Jonassen, OL
96— Ron Lelko, WR
      Sean Smith, KR
97— Irvin Sigler, RB
      Tim Baer, OL
98— Tim Baer, OG

BOISE ST. *(23)
72— Al Marshall, OE
73— Don Hutt, WR
74— Jim McMillan, QB
75— John Smith, FL
77— Chris Malmgren, DT
      Terry Hutt, WR
      Harold Cotton, OT
79— †Joe Aliotti, QB
      †Doug Scott, DT
80— †Randy Trautman, DT
81— †Randy Trautman, DT
      †Rick Woods, DB
82— †John Rade, DL
      †Carl Keever, LB
84— †Carl Keever, LB
85— †Marcus Koch, DL
87— †Tom DeWitz, OG
      †Pete Kwiatkowski, DT
90— †Erik Helgeson, DL
91— †Frank Robinson, DB
92— †Michael Dodd, PK
94— †Joe O'Brien, DL
      †Rashid Gayle, DB

BOSTON U. (19)
67— Dick Farley, DB
68— Bruce Taylor, DB
69— Bruce Taylor, DB
79— †Mal Najarian, RB
      †Tom Pierzga, DL
81— †Bob Speight, OT
      †Gregg Drew, RB
82— †Mike Mastrogiacomo, OG
83— †Paul Lewis, RB
84— Paul Lewis, RB
86— †Kevin Murphy, DT
87— †Mark Seals, DB
88— †Mark Seals, DB
89— †Daren Altieri, WR
93— †Chris Helon, DB
      †Andre Maksimov, C
94— †Andre Maksimov, C
96— †Brad Costello, P
97— †Brad Costello, P

BOWDOIN (1)
77— Steve McCabe, OL

BOWIE ST. (2)
80— Victor Jackson, CB
81— Marco Tongue, DB

BOWLING GREEN* (2)
59— Bob Zimpfer, T
82— †Andre Young, DL

BRADLEY (1)
38— Ted Panish, B

BRANDEIS (2)
54— William McKenna, E
56— James Stehlin, B

BRIDGEPORT (1)
72— Dennis Paldin, DB

BRI'WATER (MASS.) (1)
92— Erik Arthur, DL

BRIDGEWATER (VA.) (2)
75— C. J. DeWitt, SE
98— Mike Padgett, PK

BROCKPORT ST. (3)
90— Ed Smart, TE
93— Steve Milne, PK
97— Tom Massey, DB

BROWN (4)
96— Paul Choquette, TE
97— †Sean Morey, WR
      †Roderic Parson, DB
98— † Zach Burns, TE

BUCKNELL (10)
51— George Young, DT
60— Paul Terhes, B
64— Tom Mitchell, OE
65— Tom Mitchell, OE
74— Larry Schoenberger, LB
80— Mike McDonald, OT
90— †Mike Augsberger, DB
95— †Ed Burman, DL
96— † Brandon Little, LB
97— † Willie Hill, LB

BUENA VISTA (4)
72— Joe Kotval, OG
73— Joe Kotval, OG
76— Keith Kerkhoff, DL
87— Jim Higley, LB

BUFFALO* (4)
84— Gerry Quinlivan, LB
87— Steve Wojciechowski, LB
95— †Pete Conley, LB
96— †Michael Chichester, DB

BUFFALO ST. (3)
93— John Mattey, OL
98— Dan Lauta, OL
99— Jon Crumley, LB

BUTLER (2)
88— Steve Roberts, RB
94— † Arnold Mickens, RB

C. W. POST (5)
71— Gary Wichard, QB
77— John Mohring, DE
78— John Mohring, DE
81— Tom DeBona, WR
89— John Levelis, DL

UC DAVIS (17)
72— Bob Biggs, QB
      David Roberts, OT
76— Andrew Gagnon, OL
77— Chuck Fomasi, DT
78— Casey Merrill, DL
79— Jeffrey Allen, DB
82— Ken O'Brien, QB
83— Bo Eason, DB
84— Scott Barry, QB
85— Mike Wise, DL
94— Aaron Bennetts, TE
96— Josh Antstey, DE
97— Wes Terrell, TE
      Kevin Daft, QB
98— Wes Terrell, TE
99— Troy Larkin, OL
      Joe Caviglia, DB

UC RIVERSIDE (1)
75— Michael Johnson, SE

UC SANTA BARB. (3)
36— Douglas Oldershaw, G
37— Douglas Oldershaw, G
67— Paul Vallerga, DB

CALIF. (PA.) (1)
83— Perry Kemp, WR

CAL LUTHERAN (6)
72— Brian Kelley, LB
79— Mike Hagen, SE
95— Jeff Shea, P
96— Jeff Shea, P
97— Jeff Shea, P
99— Ryan Geisler, PK

CAL POLY (13)
53— Stan Sheriff, C
58— Charles Gonzales, G
66— David Edmondson, C
72— Mike Amos, DB
73— Fred Stewart, OG
78— Louis Jackson, RB
80— Louis Jackson, RB
      Robbie Martin, FL
81— Charles Daum, OL
84— Nick Frost, DB
89— Robert Morris, DL
90— Pat Moore, DL
91— Doug O'Neill, P

CAL ST. CHICO (1)
87— Chris Verhulst, TE

CAL ST. HAYWARD (4)
75— Greg Blankenship, LB

84— Ed Lively, DT
86— Fred Williams, OL
93— Jeff Williamson, TE

CAL ST. NORTHRIDGE (7)
75— Mel Wilson, DB
82— Pat Hauser, OT
83— Pat Hauser, OT
87— Kip Dukes, DB
91— Don Goodman, OL
94— †Joe Vaughn, DB
99— †Brennen Swanson, DE

CAL ST. SACRAMENTO (7)
64— William Fuller, OT
91— Troy Mills, RB
      Jim Crouch, DB
92— Jon Kirksey, DL
98— †Charles Roberts, RB
99— †Charles Roberts, RB
      †Jon Osterhout, OL

CANISIUS (3)
87— Tom Doctor, LB
88— Marty Hurley, DB
94— †Aaron Fix, PR

CAPITAL (3)
74— Greg Arnold, OG
80— John Phillips, DL
      Steve Wigton, C

CARLETON (1)
90— Jim Bradford, WR

CARNEGIE MELLON (4)
81— Ken Murawski, OL
85— Robert Butts, OL
91— Chuck Jackson, OT
93— Chad Wilson, LB

CARROLL (MONT.) (5)
76— Richard Dale, DB
79— Don Diggins, DL
87— Jeff Beaudry, DB
88— Paul Petrino, QB
89— Suitoa Keleti, OL

CARROLL (WIS.) (3)
74— Robert Helf, TE
90— Bill Nolan, P
93— Andy Ostrand, DB

CARSON-NEWMAN (16)
78— Tank Black, FL
80— Brad Payne, S
83— Dwight Wilson, OL
90— Robert Hardy, RB
92— Darryl Gooden, LB
93— Kendall James, KR
95— Steve Mellon, DL
      Anthony Davis, LB
96— Mike Clowney, DL
97— Cedric Killings, DL
      Jacques Rumph, RS
      Jon Jon Simmons, DB
98— Ques Rumph, RS
      Cedric Killings, DL
      Montrae Ford, DB
99— Cedric Killings, DL

CASE RESERVE (4)
41— Mike Yurcheshen, E
52— Al Feeny, DE
84— Fred Manley, DE
85— Mark Raiff, OL

CATAWBA (9)
34— Charles Garland, T
35— Charles Garland, T
45— Carroll Bowen, B
72— David Taylor, OT
74— Mike McDonald, LB
96— Greg Payne, PK
97— Maurice Miller, OL
98— Brian Hinson, OL
99— Brian Hinson, OL

CATHOLIC (7)
84— Chris McMahon, DB
94— Steve Wilkerson, WR
96— Matt Taylor, FB
      Jeff Clay, WR
97— Jeff Clay, WR
      Tony Faison, OL
99— Brian Hee, LB

CENTRAL (IOWA) (17)
70— Vernon Den Herder, DT

AWARD WINNERS

74— Al Dorenkamp, LB
77— Donald Taylor, RB
84— Scott Froehle, DB
85— Rich Thomas, DL
88— Mike Stumberg, DL
89— Mike Estes, DL
   Kris Reis, LB
92— Bill Maulder, LB
93— Jeff Helle, OL
94— Jeff Helle, OL
   Mark Kacmarynski, RB
   Rick Sanger, LB
95— Rick Sanger, LB
96— Mark Kacmarynski, RB
97— Matt Paulson, DB
98— Andrew Paulsen, DB

CENTRAL ARK. (6)
80— Otis Chandler, MG
84— David Burnette, DT
91— David Henson, DL
95— Bart Reynolds, DL
96— Don Struebing, C
99— Scott Stephens, P

CENTRAL CONN. ST. (4)
74— Mike Walton, C
84— Sal Cintorino, LB
88— Doug Magazu, DL
89— Doug Magazu, DL

UCF* (4)
87— Bernard Ford, WR
   Ed O'Brien, PK
93— †David Rhodes, WR
94— †Charlie Pierce, PK

CENTRAL MICH.* (4)
42— Warren Schmakel, G
59— Walter Beach, B
62— Ralph Soffredine, G
74— Rick Newsome, DL

CENTRAL MO. ST. (7)
68— Jim Urczyk, OT
85— Steve Huff, PK
88— Jeff Wright, DL
92— Bart Woods, DL
93— Bart Woods, DL
97— Shane Meyer, PK
99— Colston Weatherington, DL

CENTRAL OKLA. (11)
65— Jerome Bell, OE
78— Gary Smith, TE
94— Elton Rhoades, DB
   Joe Aska, RB
96— Johnny Luter, LB
97— Dustin McNeal, OL
98— Johnny Luter, LB
   John Fitzgerald, OG
   Reggie Donner, RB
   Brandon Carder, DB
99— Johnnie Jones, DB

CENTRAL ST. (OHIO) (9)
83— Mark Corbin, RB
84— Dave Dunham, OT
85— Mark Corbin, RB
86— Terry Morrow, RB
89— Kenneth Vines, OG
90— Eric Williams, OL
92— Marvin Coleman, DB
93— Marvin Coleman, DB
94— Hugh Douglas, DL

CENTRAL WASH. (4)
48— Robert Osgood, G
50— Jack Hawkins, G
88— Mike Estes, DL
91— Eric Lamphere, OL

CENTRE (7)
55— Gene Scott, B
84— Teel Bruner, DB
85— Teel Bruner, DB
86— Jeff Leonard, OL
88— John Gohmann, DL
89— Jeff Bezold, LB
97— Montas Allen, RS

CHADRON ST. (7)
74— Dennis Fitzgerald, DB
78— Rick Mastey, OL
90— David Jones, RB
94— Scott Doyle, PK
97— Kevin Homer, LB

99— Jess Clarke, TE
   Casey Beran, DL

CHAPMAN (1)
98— Keith Dykes, LB

CHATTANOOGA (22)
35— Robert Klein, E
38— Robert Sutton, G
39— Jack Gregory, T
45— Thomas Stewart, T
46— Gene Roberts, B
48— Ralph Hutchinson, T
49— Vincent Sarratore, G
51— Chester LaGod, DT
52— Chester LaGod, DT
54— Richard Young, B
57— Howard Clark, E
58— John Green, B
60— Charles Long, T
64— Jerry Harris, S
66— Harry Sorrell, OG
76— Tim Collins, LB
86— †Mike Makins, DL
89— †Pumpy Tudors, P
   †Junior Jackson, LB
90— †Troy Boeck, DL
   †Tony Hill, DL
   †Pumpy Tudors, P

CHICAGO (4)
91— Neal Cawi, DE
   Jeff Stolte, P
93— Frank Baker, FB
95— Derrick Brooms, KR

CITADEL (11)
82— Jim Ettari, DL
84— Jim Gabrish, OL
85— Jim Gabrish, OL
86— Scott Thompson, DT
88— †Carlos Avalos, OL
90— †DeRhon Robinson, OL
92— †Corey Cash, OL
   †Lester Smith, DB
94— †Levi Davis, OL
95— †Brad Keeney, DL
97— †Carlos Frank, KR

CLARION (11)
78— Jeff Langhans, OL
80— Steve Scillitani, MG
   Gary McCauley, TE
81— Gary McCauley, TE
83— Elton Brown, RB
85— Chuck Duffy, OL
87— Lou Weiers, DL
93— Tim Brown, TE
95— Kim Niedbala, DB
96— Chris Martin, OL
   Kim Niedbala, DB

CLARK ATLANTA (1)
79— Curtis Smith, OL

CLINCH VALLEY (1)
95— Shonn Bell, TE

COAST GUARD (3)
90— Ron Davies, DB
91— Ron Davies, DB
97— Ed Hernaez, LB

COE (8)
74— Dan Schmidt, OG
76— Paul Wagner, OT
85— Mike Matzen, P
90— Richard Matthews, DB
93— Carey Bender, RB
   Craig Chmelicek, OL
94— Carey Bender, RB
99— Zak Gordon, DB

COLGATE (11)
82— †Dave Wolf, LB
83— †Rich Erenberg, RB
84— Tom Stenglein, WR
85— Tom Stenglein, WR
86— †Kenny Gamble, RB
87— †Kenny Gamble, RB
   †Greg Manusky, LB
96— †Adam Sofran, LB
97— †Tim Girard, OL
98— †Corey Hill, WR
99— †Paul Clasby, OL

COL. OF EMPORIA (1)
51— William Chai, OG

COL. OF IDAHO (2)
53— Norman Hayes, T
54— R. C. Owens, E

COL. OF NEW JERSEY (6)
74— Eric Hamilton, C
83— John Aromando, WR
91— Chris Shaw, C
97— Jim Haines, OL
   Tom Ruggia, DL
98— Tom Ruggia, DL

COLORADO COL. (4)
72— Ed Smith, DE
73— Darryl Crawford, DB
82— Ray Bridges, DL
93— Todd Mays, DL

COLORADO MINES (6)
39— Lloyd Madden, B
41— Dick Moe, T
59— Vince Tesone, B
72— Roger Cirimotich, DB
86— Tim Baer, P
94— Pat Hogelin, P

CONCORD (2)
86— Kevin Johnson, LB
92— Chris Hairston, RB

CONCORDIA-M'HEAD (4)
77— Barry Bennett, DT
90— Mike Gindorff, DT
   Shayne Lindsay, NG
95— Tim Lowry, OL

CONNECTICUT (8)
45— Walter Trojanowski, B
73— Richard Foye, C
80— †Reggie Eccleston, WR
83— †John Dorsey, LB
88— †Glenn Antrum, WR
89— †Troy Ashley, LB
91— †Mark Didio, WR
97— †TaVarr Closs, OL

CORNELL (4)
82— †Dan Suren, TE
86— †Tom McHale, DE
93— †Chris Zingo, LB
96— †Chad Levitt, RB

CORNELL COLLEGE (2)
82— John Ward, WR
92— Brent Sands, DB

CORTLAND ST. (7)
67— Rodney Verkey, DE
89— Jim Cook, OL
90— Chris Lafferty, OG
   Vinny Swanda, LB
91— Vinny Swanda, LB
96— Pat Lalley, OL
97— Brian McAvan, OL

CUMBERLAND (KY.) (4)
87— David Carmichael, DB
89— Ralph McWilliams, OL
93— Doug Binkley, DB
94— Doug Binkley, LB

DAKOTA WESLEYAN (1)
45— Robert Kirkman, T

DARTMOUTH (4)
91— †Al Rosier, RB
92— †Dennis Durkin, PK
96— †Brian Larsen, OL
97— †Zach Walz, LB

DAVIDSON (2)
34— John Mackorell, B
99— †Ryan Crawford, DB

DAYTON (10)
36— Ralph Niehaus, T
78— Rick Chamberlin, LB
81— Chris Chaney, DB
84— David Kemp, LB
86— Gerry Meyer, OL
89— Mike Duvic, PK
90— Steve Harder, OL
91— Brian Olson, OL
92— Andy Pellegrino, LB
94— Tim Duvic, PK

DEFIANCE (1)
93— Sammy Williams, WR

DELAWARE (34)
42— Hugh Bogovich, G
46— Tony Stalloni, T
54— Don Miller, B
63— Mike Brown, C
66— Herb Slattery, OT
69— John Favero, LB
70— Conway Hayman, OG
71— Gardy Kahoe, RB
72— Joe Carbone, DE
   Dennis Johnson, DT
73— Jeff Cannon, DT
74— Ed Clark, LB
   Ray Sweeney, OG
75— Sam Miller, DE
76— Robert Pietuszka, DB
78— Jeff Komlo, QB
79— †Herb Beck, OG
   †Scott Brunner, QB
80— †Gary Kuhlman, OT
81— †Gary Kuhlman, OT
82— †George Schmitt, DB
85— †Jeff Rosen, OL
86— †Darrell Booker, LB
87— †James Anderson, WR
88— †Mike Renna, DL
89— †Mike Renna, DL
91— †Warren McIntire, DB
92— †Matt Morrill, DL
93— †Matt Morrill, DL
94— †Daryl Brown, RB
95— †Kenny Bailey, DB
96— †Kenny Bailey, DB
97— †Brian Smith, LB
98— †Eddie Conti, WR

DELAWARE ST. (4)
84— Gene Lake, RB
86— Joe Burton, DB
91— †Rod Milstead, OL
92— †LeRoy Thompson, DL

DELTA ST. (2)
67— Leland Hughes, OG
95— Jerome Williams, DB

DENISON (5)
47— William Hart, E
48— William Wehr, C
75— Dennis Thome, DL
79— Clay Sampson, RB
86— Dan Holland, DL

DePAUW (3)
63— Richard Dean, C
96— Scott Farnham, DB
   Jay Pettigrew, TE

DETROIT TECH (1)
39— Mike Kostiuk, T

DICKINSON (4)
91— Shaughn White, DB
92— Brian Ridgway, DL
94— Jason Fox, LB
98— Jason Shoff, DL

DICKINSON ST. (2)
81— Tony Moore, DL
92— Rory Farstveet, OL

DOANE (1)
66— Fred Davis, OT

DRAKE (5)
72— Mike Samples, DT
82— Pat Dunsmore, TE
   Craig Wederquist, OT
95— †Matt Garvis, LB
99— †Mike Foster, DL

DREXEL (2)
55— Vincent Vidas, T
56— Vincent Vidas, T

DUBUQUE (1)
96— Matt Plummer, WR

EAST CAROLINA* (1)
64— Bill Cline, HB

EAST CENTRAL (1)
84— Don Wilson, C

EAST STROUDSBURG (7)
65— Barry Roach, DB

FIRST-TEAM ALL-AMERICANS BELOW DIVISION I-A

75— William Stem, DB
79— Ronald Yakavonis, DL
83— Mike Reichenbach, LB
84— Andy Baranek, QB
91— Curtis Bunch, DB
94— Steve Hynes, OL

EAST TENN. ST. (9)
53— Hal Morrison, E
68— Ron Overbay, DB
70— William Casey, DB
85— George Cimadevilla, P
86— George Cimadevilla, P
94— †Jeff Johnson, WR
96— †James Russell, DL
97— †B. J. Adigun, WR
 †Mario Hankerson, LB

EASTERN ILL. (18)
72— Nate Anderson, RB
76— Ted Petersen, C
78— James Warring, WR
79— Chris Cobb, RB
 Pete Catan, DE
80— Pete Catan, DE
81— †Kevin Grey, DB
82— †Robert Williams, DB
 †Bob Norris, OG
83— †Robert Williams, DB
 †Chris Nicholson, DT
84— †Jerry Wright, WR
86— †Roy Banks, WR
88— †John Jurkovic, DL
89— †John Jurkovic, DL
90— †Tim Lance, DB
95— †Willie High, RB
 †Tim Carver, LB

EASTERN KY. (28)
69— Teddy Taylor, MG
74— Everett Talbert, RB
75— Junior Hardin, MG
76— Roosevelt Kelly, OL
79— †Bob McIntyre, LB
80— †George Floyd, DB
81— †George Floyd, DB
 †Kevin Greve, OG
82— †Steve Bird, WR
83— †Chris Sullivan, OL
84— †Chris Sullivan, C
85— †Joe Spadafino, OL
86— †Fred Harvey, LB
87— †Aaron Jones, DL
88— †Elroy Harris, RB
 †Jessie Small, DL
89— †Al Jacevicius, OL
90— †Kelly Blount, LB
 †Al Jacevicius, OL
91— †Carl Satterly, OL
 †Ernest Thompson, DL
92— †Markus Thomas, RB
93— †Chad Bratzke, DL
94— †James Hand, DL
95— †James Hand, OL
 †Marc Collins, P
96— †Tony McCombs, LB
98— †Tyrone Hopson, OL

EASTERN MICH.* (5)
68— John Schmidt, C
69— Robert Lints, MG
70— Dave Pureifory, DT
71— Dave Pureifory, DT
73— Jim Pietrzak, OT

EASTERN N.M. (9)
81— Brad Beck, RB
83— Kevin Kott, QB
87— Earl Jones, OL
89— Murray Garrett, DL
90— Anthony Pertile, DB
94— Conrad Hamilton, DB
95— Conrad Hamilton, DB
98— Michael Walton, LB
99— Michael Walton, LB

EASTERN ORE. (1)
96— Shea Little, OL

EASTERN WASH. (12)
57— Richard Huston, C
65— Mel Stanton, HB
73— Scott Garske, TE
81— John Tighe, OL
86— Ed Simmons, OT
87— †Eric Stein, P
91— †Kevin Sargent, OL
97— †Harry Leons, QB
 †Chris Scott, DL
 †Jim Buzzard, OL
98— †Bashir Levingston, RS
99— †Lance Knaevelsrud, OL

EDINBORO (5)
82— Rick Ruszkiewicz, K
89— Elbert Cole, RB
90— Ernest Priester, WR
93— Mike Kegarise, OL
95— Pat Schuster, DL

ELMHURST (1)
82— Lindsay Barich, OL

ELON (9)
50— Sal Gero, T
68— Richard McGeorge, OE
69— Richard McGeorge, OE
73— Glenn Ellis, DT
76— Ricky Locklear, DT
 Dan Bass, OL
77— Dan Bass, OL
80— Bobby Hedrick, RB
86— Ricky Sigmon, OL

EMORY & HENRY (17)
50— Robert Miller, B
51— Robert Miller, B
56— William Earp, C
68— Sonny Wade, B
85— Keith Furr, DB
 Rob McMillen, DL
86— Sandy Rogers, RB
87— Gary Collier, QB
88— Steve Bowman, DL
89— Doug Reavis, DB
90— Billy Salyers, OL
91— Jason Grooms, DL
92— Pat Buchanan, OL
 Scott Pruner, DL
97— Jamie Harless, DL
98— Mike Kassnove, DL
99— Charles Peterson, DB

EMPORIA ST. (9)
35— James Fraley, B
37— Harry Klein, E
68— Bruce Cerone, OE
69— Bruce Cerone, OE
91— Quincy Tillmon, RB
96— Brian Shay, RB
97— Brian Shay, RB
98— John Hesse, OL
 Brian Shay, RB

EUREKA (1)
95— Kurt Barth, WR

EVANSVILLE (3)
46— Robert Hawkins, T
93— †Hanz Hoag, TE
94— †Hanz Hoag, TE

FDU-MADISON (4)
84— Ira Epstein, DL
86— Eric Brey, DB
87— Frank Illidge, DL
93— Vic Moncato, P

FAIRMONT ST. (4)
67— Dave Williams, DT
84— Ed Coleman, WR
88— Lou Mabin, DB
99— Nathan White, P

FAYETTEVILLE ST. (1)
90— Terrence Smith, LB

FERRIS ST. (7)
76— Charles Evans, RB
92— Monty Brown, LB
93— Ed Phillion, DL
94— Tyree Dye, RB
95— Bill Love, QB
96— Kelly Chisholm, DL
99— Doc Proctor, PK

FERRUM (5)
87— Dave Harper, LB
88— Dave Harper, LB
89— Chris Warren, RB
90— Melvin Dillard, DB/KR
91— John Sheets, OG

FINDLAY (4)
65— Allen Smith, HB
80— Nelson Bolden, FB
85— Dana Wright, RB
90— Tim Russ, OL

FLORIDA A&M (20)
61— Curtis Miranda, C
62— Robert Paremore, B
67— Major Hazelton, DB
 John Eason, OE
73— Henry Lawrence, OT
75— Frank Poole, LB
77— Tyrone McGriff, OG
78— Tyrone McGriff, OG
79— Tyrone McGriff, OG
 †Kiser Lewis, C
80— †Gifford Ramsey, DB
83— †Ray Alexander, WR
95— Earl Holmes, LB
96— †Jamie Nails, OL
97— †Oteman Sampson, QB
 †Juan Toro, PK
98— †Patrick Bonner, QB
 †Jacquay Nunnally, WR
 †Juan Toro, PK
 †Olrick Johnson, LB

FLORIDA ST.* (1)
51— William Dawkins, OG

FORDHAM (1)
97— †Barry Cantrell, P

FORT HAYS ST. (2)
95— Lance Schwindt, TE
 Shawn Behr, QB

FORT LEWIS (3)
89— Eric Fadness, P
92— Johnny Cox, WR
93— Johnny Cox, AP

FORT VALLEY ST. (7)
74— Fred Harris, OT
80— Willie Canady, DB
81— Willie Canady, DB
83— Tugwan Taylor, LB
92— Joseph Best, DB
93— Joseph Best, DB
94— Tyrone Poole, DB

FRANKLIN (2)
82— Joe Chester, WR
95— Michael Brouwer, DB

FRANK. & MARSH. (9)
35— Woodrow Sponaugle, C
38— Sam Roeder, B
40— Alex Schibanoff, T
47— William Iannicelli, E
50— Charles Cope, C
81— Vin Carioscia, OL
82— Vin Carioscia, OL
89— Dale Amos, WR
95— Steve DeLuca, LB

FRESNO ST.* (5)
39— Jack Mulkey, E
40— Jack Mulkey, E
60— Douglas Brown, G
68— Tom McCall, LB
 Erv Hunt, DB

FROSTBURG ST. (11)
80— Terry Beamer, LB
82— Steve Forsythe, WR
83— Kevin Walsh, DL
85— Bill Bagley, WR
86— Marcus Wooley, LB
88— Ken Boyd, DB
89— Ken Boyd, DB
93— Russell Williams, DB
94— Joe Holland, DL
 Ariel Bell, KR
96— Ron Wallace, DB

FURMAN (14)
82— †Ernest Gibson, DB
83— †Ernest Gibson, DB
84— †Rock Hurst, LB
85— †Gene Reeder, C
88— †Jeff Blankenship, LB
89— †Kelly Fletcher, DL
90— †Steve Duggan, C
 †Kevin Kendrick, LB
91— †Eric Walter, OL
92— †Kota Suttle, LB
94— †Jim Richter, PK
97— †Bryan Dailer, DL
98— †Orlando Ruff, LB
99— †John Keith, DB

GALLAUDET (1)
87— Shannon Simon, OL

GARDNER-WEBB (4)
73— Richard Grissom, LB
87— Jeff Parker, PK
92— Rodney Robinson, WR
93— Gabe Wilkins, DL

GEORGETOWN (3)
73— Robert Morris, DE
74— Robert Morris, DE
91— Chris Murphy, DE

GEORGETOWN (KY.) (8)
74— Charles Pierson, OL
78— John Martinelli, OL
85— Rob McCrary, RB
87— Chris Reed, C
88— Chris Reed, C
89— Steve Blankenbaker, DL
91— Chris Hogan, DL
92— Chris Hogan, DL

GA. SOUTHERN (27)
85— †Vance Pike, OL
 †Tim Foley, PK
86— †Fred Stokes, OT
 †Tracy Ham, QB
87— †Flint Matthews, LB
 †Dennis Franklin, C
 †Tim Foley, PK
88— †Dennis Franklin, C
 †Darren Alford, DL
89— †Joe Ross, RB
 †Giff Smith, LB
90— †Giff Smith, DL
91— †Rodney Oglesby, DB
92— †Alex Mash, DL
93— †Alex Mash, DL
 †Franklin Stephens, OL
94— †Franklin Stephens, OL
96— †Edward Thomas, DL
97— †Roderick Russell, FB
98— †Matt Winslette, C
 †Adrian Peterson, RB
 †Mark Williams, OL
 †Voncellies Allen, DL
 †Arkee Thompson, DB
99— †Adrian Peterson, RB
 †Mark Williams, OL
 †Voncellies Allen, DL

GA. SOUTHWESTERN (2)
85— Roger Glover, LB
86— Roger Glover, LB

GETTYSBURG (7)
66— Joseph Egresitz, DE
83— Ray Condren, RB
84— Ray Condren, RB
85— Brian Barr, DB
94— Dwayne Marcus, FB
98— Paul Smith, RS
99— Paul Smith, RS

GLENVILLE ST. (7)
73— Scotty Hamilton, DB
83— Byron Brooks, RB
84— Mike Payne, DB
93— Chris George, WR
94— Chris George, WR
96— Carlos Ferralls, WR
97— Carlos Ferralls, WR

GONZAGA (2)
34— Ike Peterson, B
39— Tony Canadeo, B

GRAMBLING (28)
62— Junious Buchanan, T
64— Alphonse Dotson, OT
65— Willie Young, OG
 Frank Cornish, DT
69— Billy Manning, C
70— Richard Harris, DE
 Charles Roundtree, DT
71— Solomon Freelon, OG
 John Mendenhall, DE
72— Steve Dennis, DB
 Gary Johnson, DT

AWARD WINNERS

73— Gary Johnson, DT
   Willie Bryant, DB
74— Gary Johnson, DT
75— Sammie White, WR
   James Hunter, DB
79— †Joe Gordon, DT
   †Aldrich Allen, LB
   †Robert Salters, DB
80— †Trumaine Johnson, WR
   †Mike Barker, DT
81— †Andre Robinson, LB
82— †Trumaine Johnson, WR
83— †Robert Smith, DL
85— †James Harris, LB
90— †Walter Dean, RB
   †Jake Reed, WR
94— †Curtis Ceaser, WR

GRAND VALLEY ST. (6)
79— Ronald Essink, OL
89— Todd Tracey, DL
91— Chris Tiede, C
94— Mike Sheldon, OL
95— Diriki Mose, WR
96— Matt Potter, DE

GRINNELL (1)
99— Jeff Pedersen, TE

GROVE CITY (4)
87— Doug Hart, PK
97— Doug Steiner, FB
98— R. J. Bowers, FB
99— R. J. Bowers, FB

GUILFORD (3)
75— Steve Musulin, OT
91— Rodney Alexander, DE
94— Bryan Garland, OL

GUST. ADOLPHUS (8)
37— Wendell Butcher, B
50— Calvin Roberts, T
51— Haldo Norman, OE
52— Calvin Roberts, DT
54— Gene Nei, G
67— Richard Jaeger, LB
84— Kurt Ploeger, DL
97— Ryan Boutwell, PK

HAMILTON (2)
86— Joe Gilbert, OL
91— Eric Grey, RB

HAMLINE (4)
55— Dick Donlin, E
84— Kevin Graslewicz, WR
85— Ed Hitchcock, OL
89— Jon Voss, TE

HAMPDEN-SYDNEY (8)
48— Lynn Chewning, B
54— Stokeley Fulton, C
72— Michael Leidy, LB
74— Ed Kelley, DE
75— Ed Kelley, DE
77— Robert Wilson, OL
78— Tim Smith, DL
86— Jimmy Hondroulis, PK

HAMPTON (10)
84— Ike Readon, MG
85— Ike Readon, DL
93— Emerson Martin, OL
   Christopher Williams, DL
94— John Meredith, LB
95— †Hugh Hunter, DL
96— †Darrell Flythe, LB
97— †Cordell Taylor, DB
98— †Charles Preston, DL
99— †Deon Hunt, LB

HANOVER (6)
86— Jon Pinnick, QB
88— Mike Luker, WR
95— Ben Fox, WR
   Terry Peebles, QB
97— Kevin O'Donohue, LB
99— Anthony Weigleb, OL

HARDIN-SIMMONS (7)
37— Burns McKinney, B
39— Clyde Turner, C
40— Owen Goodnight, B
42— Rudy Mobley, B
46— Rudy Mobley, B
94— Colin McCormick, WR
99— Gary Gutierrez, OL

HARDING (3)
74— Barney Crawford, DL
91— Pat Gill, LB
94— Paul Simmons, LB

HARVARD (3)
82— †Mike Corbat, OL
84— † Roger Caron, OL
99— †Isaiah Kacyvenski, LB

HASTINGS (2)
84— Dennis Sullivan, OL
94— Jeff Drake, DL

HAWAII* (2)
41— Nolle Smith, B
68— Tim Buchanan, LB

HENDERSON ST. (3)
90— Todd Jones, OL
93— Chris Carter, P
96— Robert Thomas, LB

HILLSDALE (9)
49— William Young, B
55— Nate Clark, B
56— Nate Clark, B
75— Mark Law, OG
81— Mike Broome, OG
82— Ron Gladnick, DE
86— Al Huge, DL
87— Al Huge, DL
88— Rodney Patterson, LB

HOBART (6)
72— Don Aleksiewicz, RB
75— Rich Kowalski, RB
86— Brian Verdon, DB
93— Bill Palmer, DB
96— Nico Karagosian, TE
97— David Russell, DL

HOFSTRA (13)
83— Chuck Choinski, DL
86— Tom Salamone, P
88— Tom Salamone, P
90— George Tischler, LB
94— †Brian Clark, DB
95— †Dave Fiore, OL
   †Dave Ettinger, PK
   †Buck Buchanan, LB
96— †Eugene McAleer, LB
97— †Dave Ettinger, PK
   †Lance Schulters, DB
99— †Giovanni Carmazzi, QB
   †Jim Magda, DL

HOLY CROSS (14)
83— †Bruce Kozerski, OT
   † Steve Raquet, DL
84— †Bill McGovern, DB
   †Kevin Garvey, OG
85— †Gill Fenerty, RB
86— †Gordie Lockbaum, RB-DB
87— †Jeff Wiley, QB
   †Gordie Lockbaum, WR-SP
88— †Dennis Golden, OL
89— †Dave Murphy, DB
90— †Craig Callahan, RB
91— †Jerome Fuller, RB
93— †Rob Milanette, LB
95— †Tom Claro, OL

HOPE (2)
79— Craig Groendyk, OL
82— Kurt Brinks, C

HOWARD (4)
75— Ben Harris, DL
87— †Harvey Reed, RB
98— †Marques Douglas, DL
99— †Elijah Thurmon, WR

HOWARD PAYNE (8)
61— Ray Jacobs, T
72— Robert Woods, LB
73— Robert Woods, LB
92— Scott Lichner, QB
94— Steven Seale, OL
95— Sean Witherwax, DL
97— Sedrick Medlock, DB
98— Sedrick Medlock, DB

HUMBOLDT ST. (6)
61— Drew Roberts, E
62— Drew Roberts, E
76— Michael Gooing, OL
82— David Rush, MG

83— Dean Diaz, DB
95— Randy Matyshock, TE

HURON (1)
76— John Aldridge, OL

IDAHO *(14)
83— †Ken Hobart, QB
85— †Eric Yarber, WR
88— †John Friesz, QB
89— †John Friesz, QB
   †Lee Allen, WR
90— †Kasey Dunn, WR
91— †Kasey Dunn, WR
92— †Yo Murphy, WR
   †Jeff Robinson, DL
93— †Doug Nussmeier, QB
   †Mat Groshong, C
94— †Sherriden May, RB
   †Jim Mills, OL
95— †Ryan Phillips, DL

IDAHO ST. (7)
69— Ed Bell, OE
77— Ray Allred, MG
81— †Case de Bruijn, P
   †Mike Machurek, QB
83— †Jeff Kaiser, P
84— †Steve Anderson, DL
97— †Trevor Bell, DB

ILLINOIS COL. (1)
81— Joe Aiello, DL

ILLINOIS ST. (10)
68— Denny Nelson, OT
85— †Jim Meyer, OL
86— †Brian Gant, LB
88— †Mike McCabe, P
93— †Todd Kurz, PK
98— †Chad Pegues, DL
   †Galen Scott, LB
99— †Damien Gregory, DL
   †Mike Rodbro, OG
   †Sam Young, DB

ILL. WESLEYAN (8)
34— Tony Blazine, T
74— Caesar Douglas, OT
91— Chris Bisaillon, WR
92— Chris Bisaillon, WR
96— Adam Slotkus, C
   John Munch, LB
97— John Munch, LB
98— Kevin Fahey, DB

INDIANA (PA.) (21)
75— Lynn Hieber, QB
76— Jim Haslett, DE
77— Jim Haslett, DE
78— Jim Haslett, DE
79— Terrence Skelley, OE
80— Joe Cuigari, DT
84— Gregg Brenner, WR
86— Jim Angelo, OL
87— Troy Jackson, LB
88— Dean Cottrill, LB
90— Andrew Hill, WR
91— Tony Aliucci, QB
93— Matt Dalverny, OL
   Mike Geary, PK
   Michael Mann, RB
94— Jeff Turnage, DL
95— Jon Ruff, PK
   Jeff Turnage, DL
97— Barry Threats, DB
98— Barry Threats, DB
99— Leander Jordan, OL

INDIANA ST. (13)
69— Jeff Keller, DE
75— Chris Hicks, OL
   Vince Allen, RB
83— †Ed Martin, DE
84— †Wayne Davis, DB
85— †Vencie Glenn, DB
86— †Mike Simmonds, OL
93— †Shawn Moore, OL
94— †Dan Brandenburg, DL
95— †Dan Bradenburg, DL
   †Tom Allison, PK
98— †Troy Lefevra, DL
99— †DeJuan Alfonzo, DB/KR

INDIANAPOLIS (8)
83— Mark Bless, DL
84— Paul Loggan, DB

85— Tom Collins, DB
86— Dan Jester, TE
87— Thurman Montgomery, DL
91— Greg Matheis, DL
98— Ted Liette, LB
99— Josh Gentry, LB

IOWA WESLEYAN (1)
87— Mike Wiggins, P

ITHACA (14)
72— Robert Wojnar, OT
74— David Remick, RB
75— Larry Czarnecki, DT
79— John Laper, LB
80— Bob Ferrigno, HB
84— Bill Sheerin, DL
85— Tim Torrey, LB
90— Jeff Wittman, FB
91— Jeff Wittman, FB
92— Jeff Wittman, FB
   Dave Brumfield, OL
95— Scott Connolly, DL
98— Matt Buddenhagen, KR
   Mike Sansone, LB

JACKSON ST. (25)
62— Willie Richardson, E
69— Joe Stephens, OG
71— Jerome Barkum, OE
74— Walter Payton, RB
   Robert Brazile, LB
78— Robert Hardy, DT
80— †Larry Werts, DL
81— †Mike Fields, OT
85— †Jackie Walker, LB
86— †Kevin Dent, DB
87— †Kevin Dent, DB
88— †Lewis Tillman, RB
   †Kevin Dent, DB
89— †Darion Conner, LB
90— †Robert Turner, DB
91— †Deltrich Lockridge, OL
92— †Lester Holmes, OL
95— †Picasso Nelson, DB
96— †Sean Woodson, DB
   †Grailyn Pratt, QB
   †Otha Evans, LB
97— †Toby Myles, OL
98— †Sylvester Morris, WR
99— †Tommie Head, LB
   †Sylvester Morris, WR

JACKSONVILLE ST. (9)
52— Jodie Connell, OG
66— Ray Vinson, DB
70— Jimmy Champion, C
77— Jesse Baker, DT
78— Jesse Baker, DT
82— Ed Lett, QB
86— Joe Billingsley, OT
88— Joe Billingsley, OT
95— †Darron Edwards, DB

JAMES MADISON (14)
77— Woody Bergeria, DT
78— Rick Booth, OL
85— †Charles Haley, LB
86— †Carlo Bianchini, OG
89— †Steve Bates, DL
90— †Eupton Jackson, DB
93— †David McLeod, WR
94— †Dwight Robinson, DB
95— †John Coursey, PK
   †David Bailey, C
   †Ed Perry, TE
96— †Ed Perry, TE
97— †Tony Booth, DB
99— †Curtis Keaton, RB

JAMESTOWN (2)
76— Brent Tischer, OL
81— Ron Hausauer, OL

JOHN CARROLL (12)
50— Carl Taseff, B
74— Tim Barrett, RB
94— Jason Goldberg, PK
   Ryan Haley, P
95— Chris Anderson, LB
96— London Fletcher, LB
   Scott O'Donnell, DL
   Chris Anderson, LB
97— London Fletcher, LB
   David Ziegler, R

FIRST-TEAM ALL-AMERICANS BELOW DIVISION I-A

98— David Vitatoe, PK
99— Tom Rini, DB
JOHNS HOPKINS (3)
80— Bill Stromberg, WR
81— Bill Stromberg, WR
96— Jim Wilson, DL
JOHNSON SMITH (2)
82— Dan Beauford, DE
88— Ronald Capers, LB
JUNIATA (4)
54— Joe Veto, T
86— Steve Yerger, OL
87— Mark Dorner, DB
99— Matt Eisenberg, WR
KANSAS WESLEYAN (2)
35— Virgil Baker, G
56— Larry Houdek, B
KEAN (1)
87— Kevin McGuirl, TE
KENTUCKY ST. (3)
72— Wiley Epps, LB
98— Cletidus Hunt, DL
99— Ike Ihejeto, TE
KENYON (1)
74— Jim Myers, WR
KNOX (4)
86— Rich Schiele, TE
87— Chris Vogel, WR
96— Chris Warwick, PK
98— Josh Fourdyce, DL
KNOXVILLE (1)
77— Dwight Treadwell, OL
KUTZTOWN (3)
77— Steve Head, OG
95— John Mobley, LB
97— Denauld Brown, DL
LA SALLE (2)
38— George Somers, T
39— Frank Loughney, G
LA VERNE (3)
72— Dana Coleman, DT
91— Willie Reyna, QB
95— Anthony Jones, RB
LAFAYETTE (7)
79— †Rich Smith, TE
81— †Joe Skladany, LB
82— †Tony Green, DL
88— †Frank Baur, QB
92— †Edward Hudak, OL
96— †B. J. Galles, DB
97— †Dan Bengele, LB
LAKELAND (1)
89— Jeff Ogiego, P
LAMAR (5)
57— Dudley Meredith, T
61— Bobby Jancik, B
67— Spergon Wynn, OG
83— †Eugene Seale, LB
85— †Burton Murchison, RB
LAMBUTH (2)
93— Jo Jo Jones, RB
94— Jo Jo Jones, RB
LANE (1)
73— Edward Taylor, DT
LANGSTON (2)
73— Thomas Henderson, DE
94— Paul Reed, DB
LAWRENCE (11)
49— Claude Radtke, E
67— Charles McKee, QB
77— Frank Bouressa, C
78— Frank Bouressa, C
80— Scott Reppert, HB
81— Scott Reppert, HB
82— Scott Reppert, RB
83— Murray McDonough, DB
86— Dan Galante, DL
95— Brad Olson, RB
96— Brad Olson, FB
LEHIGH (22)
49— Robert Numbers, C
50— Dick Doyne, B

57— Dan Nolan, B
59— Walter Meincke, T
69— Thad Jamula, OT
71— John Hill, C
73— Kim McQuilken, QB
75— Joe Sterrett, QB
77— Steve Kreider, WR
   Mike Reiker, QB
79— †Dave Melone, OT
   †Jim McCormick, DL
80— †Bruce Rarig, LB
83— †John Shigo, LB
85— †Rennie Benn, WR
90— †Keith Petzold, OL
93— †Dave Cecchini, WR
95— †Brian Klingerman, WR
   †Rabih Abdullah, RB
96— †Ben Talbott, P
98— †Nick Martucci, DL
99— †Ian Eason, LB
LENOIR-RHYNE (5)
52— Steve Trudnak, B
62— Richard Kemp, B
67— Eddie Joyner, OT
92— Jason Monday, PK
94— Leonard Davis, RB
LEWIS & CLARK (2)
68— Bill Bailey, DT
91— Dan Ruhl, RB
LIBERTY (5)
82— John Sanders, LB
86— Mark Mathis, DB
95— †Andrew McFadden, KR
   †Tony Dews, TE
98— †Jesse Riley, LB
LINCOLN (MO.) (2)
53— Leo Lewis, B
54— Leo Lewis, B
LINFIELD (9)
57— Howard Morris, G
64— Norman Musser, C
72— Bernard Peterson, OE
75— Ken Cutcher, OL
78— Paul Dombroski, DB
80— Alan Schmidlin, QB
83— Steve Lopes, OL
84— Steve Boyea, OL
94— Darrin Causey, LB
LIVINGSTONE (2)
84— Jo Jo White, RB
98— Charles Cooley, OL
LOCK HAVEN (1)
45— Robert Eyer, E
LONG BEACH ST. (4)
68— Bill Parks, OE
69— Leon Burns, FB
70— Leon Burns, RB
71— Terry Metcalf, RB
LORAS (3)
47— Robert Hanlon, B
84— James Drew, P
97— Shane Davis, RB
LOS ANGELES ST. (1)
64— Walter Johnson, OG
LOUISIANA COLLEGE (1)
50— Bernard Calendar, E
LA.-LAFAYETTE* (1)
69— Glenn LaFleur, LB
LA.-MONROE* (19)
67— Vic Bender, C
70— Joe Profit, RB
72— Jimmy Edwards, RB
73— Glenn Fleming, MG
74— Glenn Fleming, MG
82— †Arthur Christophe, C
   †Bruce Daigle, DB
83— †Mike Grantham, OG
84— †Mike Grantham, OG
85— †Mike Turner, DL
87— †John Clement, OT
   †Claude Brumfield, DT
88— †Cyril Crutchfield, DB
89— †Jackie Harris, E
92— †Jeff Blackshear, OL
   †Vic Zordan, OL

   †Roosevelt Potts, RB
93— †Raymond Batiste, OL
   †James Folston, DL
LOUISIANA TECH* (15)
41— Garland Gregory, G
46— Mike Reed, G
68— Terry Bradshaw, QB
69— Terry Bradshaw, QB
72— Roger Carr, WR
73— Roger Carr, FL
74— Mike Barber, TE
   Fred Dean, DT
82— †Matt Dunigan, QB
84— †Doug Landry, LB
   †Walter Johnson, DE
85— †Doug Landry, LB
86— †Walter Johnson, LB-DE
87— †Glenell Sanders, LB
88— †Glenell Sanders, LB
LOUISVILLE* (1)
57— Leonard Lyles, B
LOYOLA (ILL.) (2)
35— Billy Roy, B
37— Clay Calhoun, B
LOYOLA MARYMOUNT (1)
42— Vince Pacewic, B
LUTHER (1)
57— Bruce Hartman, T
LYCOMING (10)
83— John Whalen, OL
85— Walt Zataveski, OL
89— Rick Bealer, RB
90— Rick Bealer, DB
91— Darrin Kenney, OT
   Don Kinney, DL
   Bill Small, LB
96— Michael Downey, OL
98— Jason Marraccini, QB
99— Cameron Coleman, DL
MacMURRAY (2)
97— Jamie Lee, RB
98— Jamie Lee, RB
MAINE (7)
65— John Huard, LB
66— John Huard, LB
80— †Lorenzo Bouier, RB
89— †Carl Smith, RB
   †Scott Hough, OL
90— †Claude Pettaway, DB
99— †Jojo Oliphant, DL
MAINE MARITIME (2)
92— Kirk Matthieu, RB
95— Rob Marchitello, RB
MARIETTA (1)
96— Dante Brown, RB
MARS HILL (3)
78— Alan Rice, OL
79— Steven Campbell, DB
87— Lee Marchman, LB
MARSHALL* (29)
37— William Smith, E
40— Jackie Hunt, B
41— Jackie Hunt, B
87— †Mike Barber, WR
   †Sean Doctor, TE
88— †Mike Barber, WR
   †Sean Doctor, TE
90— †Eric Ihnat, TE
91— †Phil Ratliff, OL
92— †Michael Payton, QB
   †Troy Brown, WR
   †Phil Ratliff, OL
93— †Chris Deaton, OL
   †William King, LB
   †Roger Johnson, DB
94— †Roger Johnson, DB
   †William Pannell, OL
   †Travis Colquitt, P
95— †Chris Parker, RB
   †William Pannell, OL
   †Billy Lyon, DL
   †Melvin Cunningham, DB
96— †Randy Moss, WR
   †Billy Lyon, DL
   †Aaron Ferguson, OL
   †B. J. Cohen, DL

   †Jermaine Swafford, LB
   †Eugene McAleer, LB
   †Melvin Cunningham, DB
MARTIN LUTHER (1)
97— John Feuersthaler, DB
MD.-EAST. SHORE (2)
64— John Smith, DT
68— Bill Thompson, DB
MARYVILLE (TENN.) (5)
67— Steve Dockery, LB
73— Earl McMahon, OG
77— Wayne Dunn, LB
92— Tom Smith, OL
93— Tom Smith, OL
MASSACHUSETTS (29)
52— Tony Chambers, OE
63— Paul Graham, T
64— Milt Morin, DE
67— Greg Landry, QB
71— William DeFlavio, MG
72— Steve Schubert, OE
73— Tim Berra, OE
75— Ned Deane, OL
76— Ron Harris, DB
77— Kevin Cummings, TE
   Bruce Kimball, OL
78— Bruce Kimball, OG
80— †Bob Manning, DB
81— †Garry Pearson, RB
82— †Garry Pearson, RB
85— †Mike Dwyer, DL
88— †John McKeown, LB
90— †Paul Mayberry, OL
92— †Don Caparotti, DB
93— †Bill Durkin, OL
94— †Breon Parker, DB
95— †Rene Ingoglia, RB
98— †Marcel Shipp, RB
   †Khari Samuel, LB
   †Kerry Taylor, LB
99— †Jeremy Robinson, DB
   †Kole Ayi, LB
   †Jerard White, DB
   †Sean Higgins, TE
MASS.-BOSTON (1)
92— Sean Munroe, WR
MASS.-DARTMOUTH (1)
98— Mike Cotton, DB
MASS. MARITIME (1)
95— Paul Diamantopoulos, DE
McMURRY (6)
49— Brad Rowland, B
50— Brad Rowland, B
58— Charles Davis, G
68— Telly Windham, DE
74— Randy Roemisch, OT
80— Rick Nolly, OL
McNEESE ST. (19)
52— Charles Kuehn, DE
69— Glenn Kidder, OG
72— James Moore, TE
74— James Files, OT
82— †Leonard Smith, DB
92— †Terry Irving, LB
93— †Jose Larios, PK
   †Terry Irving, LB
94— †Ronald Cherry, OL
95— †Kavika Pittman, DL
   †Marsh Buice, DL
   †Zack Bronson, DB
   †Vincent Landrum, LB
96— †Zack Bronson, DB
97— †Reggie Nelson, OL
   †Chris Fontenot, TE
   †Donnie Ashley, PR
98— †Reggie Nelson, OL
   †Charles Ayro, LB
MEMPHIS* (1)
54— Robert Patterson, G
MERCHANT MARINE (4)
52— Robert Wiechard, LB
69— Harvey Adams, DE
90— Harold Krebs, D
97— Anthony Jacobs, OL
MESA ST. (8)
82— Dean Haugum, DT

AWARD WINNERS

83— Dean Haugum, DL
84— Don Holmes, DB
85— Mike Berk, OL
86— Mike Berk, OL
88— Tracy Bennett, PK
89— Jeff Russell, OT
90— Brian Johnson, LB
METHODIST (1)
97— Trayfer Monroe, DB
MIAMI (FLA.)* (2)
45— Ed Cameron, G
 William Levitt, C
MIAMI (OHIO)* (1)
82— †Brian Pillman, MG
MICHIGAN TECH (1)
76— Jim VanWagner, RB
MIDDLE TENN. ST.* (12)
64— Jimbo Pearson, S
65— Keith Atchley, LB
83— †Robert Carroll, OL
84— Kelly Potter, PK
85— †Don Griffin, DB
88— †Don Thomas, LB
90— †Joe Campbell, RB
91— †Steve McAdoo, OL
 †Joe Campbell, RB
92— †Steve McAdoo, OL
93— †Pat Hicks, OL
95— †Nathaniel Claybrooks, DL
MIDDLEBURY (2)
36— George Anderson, G
83— Jonathan Good, DL
MIDLAND LUTHERAN (2)
76— Dave Marreel, DE
79— Scott Englehardt, OL
MILLERSVILLE (8)
76— Robert Parr, DB
80— Rob Riddick, RB
81— Mark Udovich, C
86— Jeff Hannis, DL
93— Scott Martin, DL
 Greg Faulkner, OL
95— Kevin Cannon, AP
98— Mike McFetridge, WR
MILLIKIN (2)
42— Virgil Wagner, B
92— Mike Hall, KR
MILLSAPS (12)
72— Rowan Torrey, DB
73— Michael Reams, LB
76— Rickie Haygood, QB
78— David Culpepper, LB
79— David Culpepper, LB
83— Edmond Donald, RB
85— Tommy Powell, LB
90— Sean Brewer, DL
91— Sean Brewer, DL
92— Sean Brewer, DL
93— Mitch Holloway, P
94— Kelvin Gladney, RB
MINN.-DULUTH (4)
74— Mark Johnson, DB
75— Terry Egerdahl, RB
76— Ted McKnight, RB
82— Gary Birkholz, OG
MINN. ST.-MANKATO (10)
73— Marty Kranz, DB
87— Duane Goldammer, OG
91— John Kelling, DB
93— Jamie Pass, QB
94— Josh Nelsen, WR
95— Mark Erickson, AP
96— Tywan Mitchell, WR
 Greg Janacek, PK
97— Tywan Mitchell, WR
98— Tywan Mitchell, WR
MISSISSIPPI COL. (11)
72— Ricky Herzog, FL
79— Calvin Howard, RB
80— Bert Lyles, DE
82— Major Everett, RB
83— Wayne Frazier, OL
85— Earl Conway, DL
88— Terry Fleming, DL
89— Terry Fleming, DL

90— Fred McAfee, RB
92— Johnny Poole, OL
93— Kelly Ray, C
MISSISSIPPI VAL. (8)
79— †Carl White, OG
83— †Jerry Rice, WR
84— †Jerry Rice, WR
 †Willie Totten, QB
87— †Vincent Brown, LB
91— †Ashley Ambrose, DB
97— †Terry Houzah, LB
98— †Terry Houzah, LB
MIT (1)
97— Duane Stevens, DB
MO.-ROLLA (5)
41— Ed Kromka, T
69— Frank Winfield, OG
74— Merle Dillow, TE
80— Bill Grantham, S
93— Elvind Listerud, PK
MO. SOUTHERN ST. (3)
93— Rod Smith, WR
 Ron Burton, LB
95— Yancy McKnight, OL
MISSOURI VALLEY (3)
47— James Nelson, G
48— James Nelson, G
49— Herbert McKinney, T
MONMOUTH (ILL.) (1)
75— Ron Baker, RB
MONTANA (24)
67— Bob Beers, LB
70— Ron Stein, DB
76— Greg Anderson, DB
79— †Jim Hard, FL
83— †Brian Salonen, TE
85— Mike Rice, P
87— †Larry Clarkson, OL
88— †Tim Hauck, DB
89— †Kirk Scafford, OL
 †Tim Hauck, DB
93— †Dave Dickenson, QB
 †Todd Ericson, OL
94— †Scott Gragg, OL
95— †Dave Dickenson, QB
 †Matt Wells, WR
 †Mike Agee, OL
 †Eric Simonson, OL
96— †Joe Douglass, WR
 †Mike Agee, OL
 †Brian Ah Yat, QB
 †Jason Crebo, LB
 †David Kempfert, OL
97— †Jason Crebo, LB
99— †Kelley Bryant, DL
MONTANA ST. (13)
66— Don Hass, HB
67— Don Hass, HB
70— Gary Gustafson, LB
73— Bill Kollar, DT
75— Steve Kracher, RB
76— Lester Leininger, DL
78— Jon Borchardt, OT
81— Larry Rubens, OL
84— †Mark Fellows, LB
 †Dirk Nelson, P
93— †Sean Hill, DB
97— †Neal Smith, DL
99— †Matthew Peot, P
MONTANA TECH (3)
73— James Persons, OT
80— Steve Hossler, HB
81— Craig Opatz, OL
MONTCLAIR ST. (14)
75— Barry Giblin, DB
77— Mario Benimeo, DT
79— Tom Morton, OL
80— Sam Mills, LB
81— Terrance Porter, WR
82— Mark Casale, QB
84— Jim Rennae, OL
85— Dan Zakashefski, DL
86— Dan Zakashefski, DL
89— Paul Cioffi, LB
90— Paul Cioffi, LB
93— Jeff Bargiel, DL
95— Jeff Bargiel, DL

96— Jeff Bargiel, DL
MOORHEAD ST. (2)
76— Rocky Gullickson, OG
84— Randy Sullivan, DB
MOREHEAD ST. (5)
38— John Horton, C
42— Vincent Zachem, C
69— Dave Haverdick, DT
82— †John Christopher, P
86— †Randy Poe, OG
MORGAN ST. (8)
65— Willie Lanier, LB
67— Jeff Queen, DE
70— Willie Germany, DB
72— Stan Cherry, LB
73— Eugene Simms, LB
78— Joe Fowlkes, DB
80— Mike Holston, WR
93— †Matthew Steeple, DL
MORNINGSIDE (2)
49— Connie Callahan, B
91— Jorge Diaz, PK
MOUNT UNION (24)
84— Troy Starr, LB
87— Russ Kring, RB
90— Ken Edelman, PK
 Dave Lasecki, LB
92— Mike Elder, OL
 Jim Ballard, QB
 Chris Dattilio, LB
93— Rob Atwood, TE
 Jim Ballard, QB
 Ed Bubonics, WR
 Mike Hallet, DL
94— Rob Rodgers, LB
95— Mike Wonderfer, OG
 Matt Liggett, DL
96— Bill Borchert, QB
 Joe Weimer, OL
 Josh Weber, OT
 Brian Wervey, LB
97— Bill Borchert, QB
 Joe Weimer, OL
 Vic Ricketts, G
98— Jason Hall, LB
 Kris Bugara, DB
99— Tom Bauer, OL
MUHLENBERG (4)
46— George Bibighaus, E
47— Harold Bell, B
93— Rob Lokerson, WR
99— Joshua Carter, KR
MURRAY ST. (7)
37— Elmer Cochran, G
73— Don Clayton, RB
79— †Terry Love, DB
86— †Charley Wiles, OL
95— †Derrick Cullors, RB
 †William Hampton, QB
96— †William Hampton, DB
MUSKINGUM (5)
40— Dave Evans, T
60— Bill Cooper, B
66— Mark DeVilling, DT
75— Jeff Heacock, DB
95— Connon Thompson, DB
NEB.-KEARNEY (4)
76— Dale Mitchell Johnson, DB
78— Doug Peterson, DB
95— Matt Bruggeman, DL
97— Mike Smith, RT
NEB.-OMAHA (11)
64— Gerald Allen, HB
68— Dan Klepper, OG
76— Dan Fulton, WR
77— Dan Fulton, OE
80— Tom Sutko, LB
82— John Walker, DT
83— Tim Carlson, LB
84— Ron Petersen, OT
86— Keith Coleman, LB
98— Chris Bober, OT
99— Chris Bober, OT
NEB. WESLEYAN (3)
90— Brad Bohn, DB
91— Darren Stohlmann, TE
92— Darren Stohlmann, TE

NEVADA* (23)
52— Neil Garrett, DB
74— Greg Grouwinkel, DB
78— James Curry, MG
 Frank Hawkins, RB
79— †Frank Hawkins, RB
 †Lee Fobbs, DB
80— †Frank Hawkins, RB
 †Bubba Puha, DL
81— †John Ramatici, LB
 †Tony Zendejas, K
82— †Tony Zendejas, K
 †Charles Mann, DT
83— †Tony Zendejas, K
 †Jim Werbeckes, OG
 †Tony Shaw, DB
85— †Greg Rea, DL
 †Marty Zendejas, PK
 †Pat Hunter, DB
86— †Henry Rolling, DE-LB
88— †Bernard Ellison, DB
90— †Bernard Ellison, DB
 †Treamelle Taylor, KR
91— †Matt Clafton, LB
UNLV* (3)
73— Mike Thomas, RB
74— Mike Thomas, RB
75— Joseph Ingersoll, DL
NEW HAMPSHIRE (14)
50— Ed Douglas, G
68— Al Whittman, DT
75— Kevin Martell, C
76— Bill Burnham, RB
77— Bill Burnham, RB
 Grady Vigneau, OT
85— †Paul Dufault, OL
87— †John Driscoll, OL
91— †Barry Bourassa, RB
 †Dwayne Sabb, LB
94— †Mike Foley, DL
97— †Jerry Azumah, RS/RB
98— †Jerry Azumah, RB
 †Walter Jones, OL
NEW HAVEN (14)
85— David Haubner, OL
87— Erik Lesinski, LB
88— Rob Thompson, OL
90— Jay McLucas, QB
92— Scott Emmert, OL
 Roger Graham, RB
93— Roger Graham, RB
 George Byrd, DB
 Tony Willis, WR
94— Roger Graham, RB
95— Scott Riggs, LB
96— Jesse Showerda, QB
97— Mario DiDino, OL
 Cazzie Kosciolek, QB
N.M. HIGHLANDS (8)
66— Carl Garrett, HB
67— Carl Garrett, HB
68— Carl Garrett, HB
81— Jay Lewis, DL
85— Neil Windham, LB
86— Tim Salz, PK
93— Rus Bailey, WR
96— Jamar Nailor, WR
NEWBERRY (3)
40— Dominic Collangelo, B
81— Stan Stanton, DL
97— Anthony Heatley, OL
NICHOLLS ST. (7)
76— Gerald Butler, OE
77— Rusty Rebowe, LB
81— †Dwight Walker, RB
82— †Clint Conque, LB
84— †Dewayne Harrison, TE
86— †Mark Carrier, WR
94— †Darryl Pounds, DB
NICHOLS (1)
81— Ed Zywien, LB
NORFOLK ST. (5)
79— Mike Ellis, DB
89— Arthur Jimmerson, LB
94— James Roe, WR
95— James Roe, WR
 Aaron Sparrow, QB

FIRST-TEAM ALL-AMERICANS BELOW DIVISION I-A

NORTH ALA. (20)
- 82— Don Smith, C
- 84— Daryl Smith, DB
- 85— Bruce Jones, DB
- 90— James Davis, LB
  - Mike Nord, OL
- 92— Harvey Summerhill, DB
- 93— Jeff Redcross, DL
  - Tyrone Rush, RB
  - Jeff Surbaugh, OL
  - Ronald McKinnon, LB
- 94— Jon Thompson, OL
  - Ronald McKinnon, LB
  - Marcus Keyes, DL
- 95— Jon Thompson, OL
  - Israel Raybon, DE
  - Ronald McKinnon, LB
  - Marcus Keyes, DL
- 96— Gerald Smith, DB
- 97— Reginald Ruffin, LB
  - Marcus Hill, DB

N.C. A&T (8)
- 69— Merl Code, DB
- 70— Melvin Holmes, OT
- 81— †Mike West, OL
- 86— †Ernest Riddick, NG
- 88— †Demetrius Harrison, LB
- 93— †Ronald Edwards, OL
- 95— †Jamain Stephens, OL
- 97— †Chris McNeil, DL

N.C. CENTRAL (5)
- 68— Doug Wilkerson, MG
- 69— Doug Wilkerson, OT
- 74— Charles Smith, DE
- 88— Earl Harvey, QB
- 96— Tommy Dorsey, LB

NORTH CENTRAL (1)
- 97— Jim Witte, OL

NORTH DAKOTA (26)
- 55— Steve Myhra, G
- 56— Steve Myhra, G
- 63— Neil Reuter, T
- 65— Dave Lince, DE
- 66— Roger Bonk, LB
- 71— Jim LeClair, LB
  - Dan Martinsen, DB
- 72— Mike Deutsch, RB
- 75— Bill Deutsch, RB
- 79— Paul Muckenhirn, TE
- 80— Todd Thomas, OT
- 81— Milson Jones, RB
- 89— Cory Solberg, PK
- 91— Shannon Burnell, RB
- 93— Shannon Burnell, RB
  - Kevin Robson, OL
- 94— Mike Mooney, LB
- 95— Dave Hillesheim, DE
- 96— Juan Gomez-Tagle, PK
  - Mark Callahan, DL
  - Tim Tibesar, LB
- 97— Phillip Moore, RB
  - Jim Kleinsasser, TE
- 98— Jim Kleinsasser, TE
  - Phillip Moore, RB
- 99— Kelly Howe, DB

NORTH DAKOTA ST. (30)
- 34— Melvin Hanson, B
- 46— Cliff Rothrock, C
- 66— Walt Odegaard, MG
- 67— Jim Ferge, LB
- 68— Jim Ferge, DT
  - Paul Hatchett, B
- 69— Paul Hatchett, HB
  - Joe Cichy, DB
- 70— Joe Cichy, DB
- 74— Jerry Dahl, DE
- 76— Rick Budde, LB
- 77— Lew Curry, OL
- 81— Wayne Schluchter, DB
- 82— Cliff Carmody, OG
  - Steve Garske, LB
- 83— Mike Whetstone, OG
- 84— Greg Hagfors, C
- 86— Jeff Bentrim, QB
  - Jim Dick, LB
- 87— Mike Favor, C
- 88— Matt Tracy, OL
  - Mike Favor, C
  - Yorrick Byers, LB

- 90— Phil Hansen, DL
  - Chris Simdorn, QB
- 93— Scott Fuchs, OL
  - T. R. McDonald, WR
- 95— Brad Servais, OL
- 97— Sean Fredricks, LB
- 99— Tim Strehlow, AP

NORTH PARK (2)
- 72— Greg Nugent, OE
- 90— John Love, QB

NORTH TEXAS* (6)
- 47— Frank Whitlow, T
- 51— Ray Renfro, DB
- 83— †Ronnie Hickman, DE
  - †Rayford Cooks, DL
- 88— †Rex Johnson, DL
- 90— †Mike Davis, DL

NORTHEASTERN (3)
- 72— Tom Rezzuti, DB
- 78— Dan Ross, TE
- 96— †Jerome Daniels, OL

NORTHEASTERN ST. (5)
- 69— Manuel Britto, HB
- 71— Roosevelt Manning, DT
- 74— Kevin Goodlet, DB
- 82— Cedric Mack, WR
- 94— Ricky Ceasar, DL

NORTHERN ARIZ. (19)
- 66— Rick Ries, LB
- 67— Bill Hanna, DE
- 68— Larry Small, OG
- 77— Larry Friedrichs, OL
  - Tom Jurich, K
- 78— Jerry Lumpkin, LB
- 79— †Ed Judie, LB
- 82— †Pete Mandley, WR
- 83— †Pete Mandley, WR
  - †James Gee, DT
- 86— †Goran Lingmerth, PK
- 89— †Darrell Jordan, LB
- 93— †Terry Belden, P
- 95— †Rayna Stewart, DB
  - †Kevin O'Leary, P
  - †Ben Petrucci, DL
- 96— †Archie Amerson, RB
  - †Ricky Pearsall, PR
- 97— †Dan Finn, OL

NORTHERN COLO. (20)
- 68— Jack O'Brien, DB
- 80— Todd Volkart, DT
- 81— Brad Wimmer, OL
- 82— Mark Mostek, OG
  - Kevin Jelden, PK
- 89— Vance Lechman, DB
- 90— Frank Wainwright, TE
- 92— David Oliver, OL
- 93— Jeff Pease, LB
- 94— Jeff Pease, LB
- 95— Tony Ramirez, OL
  - Tim Bowie, DB
- 96— Tony Ramirez, OL
  - Delano Washington, DB
- 97— Aaron Smith, DB
  - Dirk Johnson, DB
- 98— Aaron Smith, DL
  - Scott Zimmerman, LB
- 99— Corte McGuffey, QB
  - Jamie Heiner, LB

NORTHERN ILL.* (2)
- 62— George Bork, B
- 63— George Bork, B

NORTHERN IOWA (18)
- 52— Lou Bohnsack, C
- 60— George Asleson, G
- 61— Wendell Williams, G
- 64— Randy Schultz, FB
- 65— Randy Schultz, FB
- 67— Ray Pedersen, MG
- 75— Mike Timmermans, OT
- 85— Joe Fuller, DB
- 87— †Carl Boyd, RB
- 90— †Brian Mitchell, PK
- 91— †Brian Mitchell, PK
- 92— †Kenny Shedd, WR
  - †William Freeney, LB
- 94— †Andre Allen, LB
- 95— †Dedric Ward, WR
- 96— †Dedric Ward, WR

- 99— †Brad Meester, C
  - †Mike Furrey, WR

NORTHERN MICH. (7)
- 75— Daniel Stencil, OL
- 76— Maurice Mitchell, FL
- 77— Joseph Stemo, DB
- 82— George Works, RB
- 87— Jerry Woods, DB
- 88— Jerry Woods, DB
- 99— Ty Hartung, P

NORTHERN ST. (1)
- 76— Larry Kolbo, DL

NORTHWEST MO. ST. (13)
- 39— Marion Rogers, G
- 84— Steve Hansley, WR
- 89— Jason Agee, DB
- 96— Matt Uhde, DL
- 97— Chris Greisen, QB
- 98— Twan Young, DB
  - Aaron Crowe, LB
  - Chris Greisen, QB
  - Steve Coppinger, C
  - Aaron Becker, DL
- 99— Tony Miles, AP
  - David Purnell, PK
  - Chad Thompson, OG

N'WESTERN (IOWA) (1)
- 71— Kevin Korvor, DE

NORTHWESTERN ST. (15)
- 66— Al Dodd, DB
- 80— †Warren Griffith, C
  - †Joe Delaney, RB
- 81— †Gary Reasons, LB
- 82— †Gary Reasons, LB
- 83— †Gary Reasons, LB
- 84— †Arthur Berry, DT
- 87— †John Kulakowski, DE
- 91— †Andre Carron, LB
- 92— †Adrian Hardy, DB
  - †Marcus Spears, OL
- 93— †Marcus Spears, OL
- 97— †Tony Maranto, DB
- 98— †Jermaine Jones, DB
- 99— †Mike Green, DB

NORTHWOOD (3)
- 73— Bill Chandler, DT
- 74— Bill Chandler, DT
- 98— Tyrone Nelson, OL

NORWICH (3)
- 79— Milt Williams, RB
- 84— Beau Almodobar, WR
- 85— Mike Norman, OL

OBERLIN (1)
- 45— James Boswell, B

OCCIDENTAL (6)
- 76— Rick Fry, FL
- 77— Rick Fry, SE
- 82— Dan Osborn, P
- 83— Ron Scott, DB
- 89— David Hodges, LB
- 90— Peter Tucker, OL

OHIO* (2)
- 35— Art Lewis, T
- 60— Dick Grecni, C

OHIO NORTHERN (7)
- 95— LaVant King, WR
- 96— Jerry Adams, DB
- 98— Steve Vagedes, P
- 99— Jamal Robertson, RB
  - Kory Allen, OL
  - Jeremy Presar, DB
  - Steve Vagedes, P/WR

OHIO WESLEYAN (8)
- 34— John Turley, B
- 51— Dale Bruce, OE
- 71— Steve Dutton, DE
- 83— Eric DiMartino, LB
- 90— Jeff Court, OG
  - Neil Ringers, DL
- 91— Kevin Rucker, DL
- 96— Craig Anderson, LB

OKLA. PANHANDLE (2)
- 82— Tom Rollison, DB
- 83— Tom Rollison, DB

OTTERBEIN (3)
- 82— Jim Hoyle, K

- 90— Ron Severance, WR
- 91— Ron Severance, WR

OUACHITA BAPTIST (1)
- 79— Ezekiel Vaughn, LB

PACIFIC (CAL.) (4)
- 34— Cris Kjeldsen, G
- 47— Eddie LeBaron, B
- 48— Eddie LeBaron, B
- 49— Eddie LeBaron, B

PACIFIC LUTHERAN (9)
- 40— Marv Tommervik, B
- 41— Marv Tommervik, B
- 47— Dan D'Andrea, C
- 52— Ron Billings, DB
- 65— Marvin Peterson, C
- 78— John Zamberlin, LB
- 85— Mark Foege, PK
  - Tim Shannon, DB
- 88— Jon Kral, DL

PENNSYLVANIA (8)
- 86— †Marty Peterson, OL
- 88— †John Zinser, OL
- 90— †Joe Valerio, OL
- 93— †Miles Macik, WR
- 94— †Pat Goodwillie, LB
- 95— †Miles Macik, WR
  - †Tom McGarrity, DL
- 96— †Mitch Marrow, DL

PEPPERDINE (2)
- 47— Darwin Horn, B
- 55— Wixie Robinson, G

PERU ST. (4)
- 52— Robert Lade, OT
- 53— Robert Lade, T
- 81— Alvin Holder, RB
- 91— Tim Herman, DL

PILLSBURY (1)
- 85— Calvin Addison, RB

PITTSBURG ST. (20)
- 61— Gary Snadon, B
- 70— Mike Potchard, OT
- 78— Brian Byers, OL
- 88— Jesse Wall, OL
- 89— John Roderique, LB
- 90— Ron West, WR
- 91— Ron West, WR
- 92— Ronald Moore, RB
- 93— Doug Bullard, OL
- 94— Andy Sweet, LB
  - Chris Brown, DB
- 95— Phil Schepens, OT
  - B. J. McGivern, LB
  - Chris Brown, DB
- 96— Bob Goltra, OL
- 97— Sean McNamara, OL
  - Brian Moorman, P
- 98— Ben Peterson, DE
  - Brian Moorman, P
- 99— Andrew Poling, DB

PLYMOUTH ST. (8)
- 74— Robert Gibson, DB
- 82— Mark Barrows, LB
- 83— Joe Dudek, RB
- 84— Joe Dudek, RB
- 85— Joe Dudek, RB
- 91— Scott Allen, LB
- 94— Colby Compton, LB
- 95— Colby Compton, LB

POMONA-PITZER (1)
- 74— Larry Cenotto, QB

PORTLAND ST. (16)
- 76— June Jones, QB
- 77— Dave Stief, OE
- 79— †Stuart Gaussoin, SE
  - †Kurt Ijanoff, OT
- 80— †Neil Lomax, QB
- 84— Doug Mikolas, DL
- 88— Bary Naone, TE
  - Chris Crawford, QB
- 89— Darren Del'Andrae, QB
- 91— James Fuller, DB
- 92— John Charles, QB
- 93— Rick Cruz, LB
- 94— Sam Peoples, DB
  - Jesus Moreno, OT
- 95— Steve Papin, RB
- 98— †Bobby Singh, OL

AWARD WINNERS

265

PRAIRIE VIEW (2)
64— Otis Taylor, OE
70— Bivian Lee, DB

PRESBYTERIAN (8)
45— Andy Kavounis, G
46— Hank Caver, B
52— Joe Kirven, OE
68— Dan Eckstein, DB
71— Robert Norris, LB
78— Roy Walker, OL
79— Roy Walker, OL
83— Jimmie Turner, LB

PRINCETON (4)
87— †Dean Cain, DB
89— †Judd Garrett, RB
92— †Keith Elias, RB
93— †Keith Elias, RB

PRINCIPIA (1)
93— Matt Newton, WR

PUGET SOUND (9)
56— Robert Mitchell, G
63— Ralph Bauman, G
66— Joseph Peyton, OE
75— Bill Linnenkohl, LB
76— Dan Kuehl, DL
81— Bob Jackson, MG
82— Mike Bos, WR
83— Larry Smith, DB
87— Mike Oliphant, RB

RANDOLPH-MACON (9)
47— Albert Oley, G
57— Dave Young, G
79— Rick Eades, DL
80— Rick Eades, DL
84— Cody Dearing, QB
88— Aaron Boston, OL
96— Tim Armoska, LB
98— Chuck Davis, DL
99— Sean Eaton, WR

REDLANDS (2)
77— Randy Van Horn, OL
92— James Shields, DL

RENSSELAER (3)
96— Scott Catarelli, OL
98— Krishaun Gilmore, RB
99— Chris Swartz, DB

RHODE ISLAND (9)
55— Charles Gibbons, T
82— †Richard Pelzer, OL
83— †Tony DeLuca, DL
84— †Brian Forster, TE
85— †Brian Forster, TE
   †Tom Ehrhardt, QB
90— †Kevin Dent, DB
92— †Darren Rizzi, TE
96— †Frank Ferrara, DL

RHODES (5)
36— Henry Hammond, E
38— Gaylon Smith, B
76— Conrad Bradburn, DB
85— Jim Hever, PK
88— Larry Hayes, OL

RICHMOND (5)
84— †Eddie Martin, OL
97— †Shawn Barber, LB
   †Marc Megna, DL
98— †Marc Megna, DT
   †Eric King, OL

RIPON (6)
57— Peter Kasson, E
75— Dick Rehbein, C
76— Dick Rehbein, OL
79— Art Peters, TE
82— Bob Wallner, OL
95— Jim Wallace, DB

ROANOKE (1)
38— Kenneth Moore, E

ROCHESTER (7)
51— Jack Wilson, DE
52— Donald Bardell, DG
67— Dave Ragusa, LB
75— Ralph Gebhardt, DB
90— Craig Chodak, P
92— Brian Laudadio, DL
93— Geoff Long, DL

ROCKHURST (1)
41— Joe Kiernan, T

ROLLINS (1)
40— Charles Lingerfelt, E

ROSE-HULMAN (2)
77— Gary Ellis, DB
92— Todd Holthaus, PK

ROWAN (8)
78— Dino Hall, RB
93— Bill Fisher, DL
95— LeRoi Jones, LB
97— Terrick Grace, DB
98— Jarryn Avery, OL
99— John Gavlick, LB
   Jarryn Avery, OL
   Cornelius White, DL

SAGINAW VALLEY (7)
81— Eugene Marve, LB
84— Joe Rice, DL
90— David Cook, DB
92— Bill Schafer, TE
97— Paul Spicer, DL
   Kent Kraatz, OT
98— Lamar King, DL

ST. AMBROSE (5)
40— Nick Kerasiotis, G
51— Robert Flanagan, B
58— Robert Webb, B
87— Jerry Klosterman, DL
97— Craig Shepherd, OL

ST. BONAVENTURE (2)
46— Phil Colella, B
48— Frank LoVuola, E

ST. CLOUD ST. (4)
85— Mike Lambrecht, DL
95— Randy Martin, RB
96— Randy Martin, RB
97— Mike McKinney, WR

ST. JOHN'S (MINN.) (13)
65— Pat Whalin, DB
79— Ernie England, MG
82— Rick Bell, RB
83— Chris Biggins, TE
91— Pat Mayew, QB
93— Burt Chamberlin, OL
   Jim Wagner, DL
94— Jim Wagner, DL
95— Chris Palmer, WR
96— Jesse Redepenning, OL
98— Brandon Novak, LB
99— Brandon Novak, LB
   Phil Barry, P

ST. JOHN'S (N.Y.) (1)
83— Todd Jamison, QB

ST. LAWRENCE (2)
51— Ken Spencer, LB
77— Mitch Brown, DB

ST. MARY (KAN.) (1)
86— Joe Brinson, RB

ST. MARY'S (CAL.) (4)
79— Fran McDermott, DB
80— Fran McDermott, DB
88— Jon Braff, TE
92— Mike Estrella, PK

ST. MARY'S (TEX.) (1)
36— Douglas Locke, B

ST. NORBERT (2)
57— Norm Jarock, B
64— Dave Jauquet, DE

ST. OLAF (3)
53— John Gustafson, E
78— John Nahorniak, LB
80— Jon Anderson, DL

ST. THOMAS (MINN.) (10)
45— Theodore Molitor, E
48— Jack Salscheider, B
84— Neal Guggemos, DB
85— Neal Guggemos, DB
90— Gary Trettel, RB
91— Kevin DeVore, OL
94— Ryan Davis, TE
95— Ryan Davis, TE

96— Ryan Collins, TE
97— Ryan Collins, TE

SALISBURY ST. (5)
82— Mark Lagowski, LB
84— Joe Mammano, OL
85— Robb Disbennett, QB
86— Tom Kress, DL
95— Mark Hannah, LB

SAM HOUSTON ST. (3)
49— Charles Williams, E
52— Don Gottlob, B
91— †Michael Bankston, DL

SAMFORD (2)
36— Norman Cooper, C
94— †Anthony Jordan, AP

SAN DIEGO (3)
73— Bob Dulich, QB
81— Dan Herbert, DB
92— Robert Ray, P

SAN DIEGO ST.* (6)
35— John Butler, G
66— Don Horn, QB
67— Steve Duich, OT
   Haven Moses, OE
68— Fred Dryer, DE
   Lloyd Edwards, B

SAN FRANCISCO (1)
42— John Sanchez, T

SAN FRAN. ST. (7)
51— Robert Williamson, OT
60— Charles Fuller, B
67— Joe Koontz, OE
76— Forest Hancock, LB
78— Frank Duncan, DB
82— Poncho James, RB
84— Jim Jones, TE

SAN JOSE ST.* (2)
38— Lloyd Thomas, E
39— LeRoy Zimmerman, B

SANTA CLARA (8)
64— Lou Pastorini, LB
71— Ronald Sani, C
79— Jim Leonard, C
80— Brian Sullivan, K
82— Gary Hoffman, OT
83— Alex Vlahos, C
   Mike Rosselli, LB
85— Brent Jones, TE

SAVANNAH ST. (3)
79— Timothy Walker, DL
89— Shannon Sharpe, TE
96— Britt Henderson, DB

SEWANEE (9)
63— Martin Agnew, B
73— Mike Lumpkin, DE
77— Nino Austin, DB
79— John Hill, DB
80— Mallory Nimocs, TE
81— Greg Worsowicz, DB
86— Mark Kent, WR
90— Ray McGowan, DL
99— Antonio Crook, OL

SHEPHERD (3)
98— James Rooths, KR
99— Damian Beane, RB
   James Rooths, KR

SHIPPENSBURG (4)
53— Robert Adams, G
91— Jeff Fickes, DB
94— Doug Seidenstricker, DB
99— Jamie Ware, WR

SIENA (2)
95— †Reggie Greene, AP
97— †Reggie Greene, RB

SIMON FRASER (1)
90— Nick Mazzoli, WR

SIMPSON (6)
89— Ricky Gales, RB
96— Brent Parrott, DB
   Chris Whiney, OT
97— Jeremy Whalen, DL
98— Guy Leman, RB
   Clint Head, OL

SLIPPERY ROCK (8)
74— Ed O'Reilly, RB
75— Jerry Skocik, TE
76— Chris Thull, LB
77— Bob Schrantz, TE
78— Bob Schrantz, TE
85— Jeff Williams, P
97— Dave Sabolcik, OL
98— Matt Kinsinger, DL

SONOMA ST. (3)
86— Mike Henry, LB
92— Larry Allen, OL
93— Larry Allen, OL

SOUTH CAROLINA ST. (23)
67— Tyrone Caldwell, DE
71— James Evans, LB
72— Barney Chavous, DE
73— Donnie Shell, DB
75— Harry Carson, LB
76— Robert Sims, DL
77— Ricky Anderson, RB
79— †Phillip Murphy, DL
80— †Edwin Bailey, OG
81— †Anthony Reed, FB
   †Dwayne Jackson, DL
82— †Dwayne Jackson, DE
   †Anthony Reed, RB
   †Ralph Green, OT
   †John Courtney, DT
83— †Ralph Green, OT
89— †Eric Douglas, DE
91— †Robert Porcher, DL
93— †Anthony Cook, DE
94— †Anthony Cook, DL
96— †Raleigh Roundtree, OL
97— †Chartric Darby, DL
98— †Jermaine Derricott, DB

SOUTH DAKOTA (11)
68— John Kohler, OT
69— John Kohler, OT
71— Gene Macken, OG
72— Gary Kipling, OG
78— Bill Moats, DB
79— Benjamin Long, LB
83— Kurt Seibel, K
86— Jerry Glinsky, C
   Todd Salat, DB
88— Doug VanderEsch, LB
97— Brent Petersen, DL

SOUTH DAKOTA ST. (16)
67— Darwin Gonnerman, HB
68— Darwin Gonnerman, FB
74— Lynn Boden, OT
77— Bill Matthews, DE
79— Charles Loewen, OL
84— Rick Wegher, RB
85— Jeff Tiefenthaler, WR
86— Jeff Tiefenthaler, WR
91— Kevin Tetzlaff, OL
92— Doug Miller, LB
93— Adam Timmerman, DL
94— Jake Hines, TE
   Adam Vinatieri, P
   Adam Timmerman, OL
96— Tom O'Brien, C
99— Josh Ranek, RB

SOUTH DAKOTA TECH (1)
73— Charles Waite, DB

SOUTH FLA. (1)
98— †Bill Gramatica, PK

SOUTHEAST MO. ST. (4)
37— Wayne Goddard, T
94— †Doug Berg, DL
95— †Frank Russell, DB
97— †Angel Rubio, DL

SOUTHEASTERN LA. (3)
70— Ronnie Hornsby, LB
83— †Bret Wright, P
85— †Willie Shepherd, DL

SOUTHERN U. (7)
70— Isiah Robertson, LB
72— James Wright, OG
73— Godwin Turk, LB
79— †Ken Times, DL
87— †Gerald Perry, OT
93— †Sean Wallace, DB

FIRST-TEAM ALL-AMERICANS BELOW DIVISION I-A

95—†Kendell Shello, DL
SOUTHERN ARK. (4)
84— Greg Stuman, LB
85— Greg Stuman, LB
97— Fred Perry, LB
98— Jason Williams, PK
SOUTHERN CONN. ST. (9)
82— Mike Marshall, DB
83— Kevin Gray, OL
84— William Sixsmith, LB
86— Rick Atkinson, DB
91— Ron Lecointe, OL
92— Steve Lawrence, LB
94— Anthony Idone, DL
95—†Joe Andruzzi, OL
96—†Joe Andruzzi, OL
SOUTHERN ILL. (6)
70— Lionel Antoine, OE
71— Lionel Antoine, OE
83—†Donnell Daniel, DB
    †Terry Taylor, DB
96—†Mark Gagliano, P
99—†Cornell Craig, WR
SOUTHERN MISS.* (4)
53— Hugh Pepper, B
56— Don Owens, T
58— Robert Yencho, E
59— Hugh McInnis, E
SOUTHERN ORE. ST. (2)
75— Dennis Webber, LB
99— Griff Yates, RB
SOUTHERN UTAH (8)
79— Lane Martino, DL
87— Jeff McComb, P
89— Randy Bostic, C
90— Randy Bostic, C
95—†Micah Deckert, TE
97—†Jimmy Brimmer, LB
99—†John Uriarte, OL
    †Josh Roberts, DB
SOUTHWEST MO. ST. (11)
66— William Stringer, OG
87—†Matt Soraghan, LB
89—†Mark Christenson, OL
90—†DeAndre Smith, QB
91—†Bill Walter, DL
93—†Adrion Smith, DB
95—†DeLaun Fowler, LB
96—†Michael Cosey, RB
    †Wayne Boyer, PK
    †Mike Miano, DL
97—†Travis Brawner, PK
SOUTHWEST ST. (2)
87— James Ashley, WR
91— Wayne Hawkins, DE
SOUTHWEST TEX. ST. (12)
53— Pence Dacus, B
63— Jerry Cole, E
64— Jerry Cole, DB
72— Bob Daigle, C
75— Bobby Kotzur, DT
82— Tim Staskus, LB
83— Tim Staskus, LB
84—†Scott Forester, C
90—†Reggie Rivers, RB
91—†Ervin Thomas, C
94—†Don Wilkerson, RB
97—†Claude Mathis, RB
SOUTHWESTERN (KAN.) (2)
82— Tom Audley, DL
84— Jackie Jenson, RB
SOUTHWESTERN OKLA. (2)
77— Louis Blanton, DB
82— Richard Lockman, LB
SPRINGFIELD (14)
68— Dick Dobbert, C
70— John Curtis, OE
76— Roy Samuelsen, MG
78— Jack Quinn, DB
79— Jack Quinn, DB
80— Steve Foster, OT
81— Jon Richardson, LB
83— Wally Case, DT
    Ed Meachum, TE
85— Jim Anderson, LB

91— Fran Papasedero, DL
94— Matt Way, OL
96— Jamie McGourty, DL
98— John Cena, OL
STEPHEN F. AUSTIN (15)
51— James Terry, DE
79— Ronald Haynes, DL
85— James Noble, WR
86—†Darrell Harkless, DB
88—†Eric Lokey, LB
89—†David Whitmore, DB
93—†Cedric Walker, DB
95—†Joey Wylie, OL
    †Lee Kirk, OL
    †Damiyon Bell, DB
96—†Jeremiah Trotter, LB
97—†Mikhael Ricks, WR
    †Jeremiah Trotter, LB
98—†Chad Stanley, P
99—†Ka Ron Coleman, PR
STONY BROOK (2)
87— Chuck Downey, DB
88— David Lewis, P
SUL ROSS ST. (2)
65— Tom Nelson, DE
88— Francis Jones, DB
SUSQUEHANNA (5)
51— James Hazlett, C
90— Keith Henry, DL
92— Andy Watkins, LB
96— Jeremy Zieskoft, DB
99— Antonio Nash, DB
SWARTHMORE (1)
89— Marshall Happer, OL
TAMPA (5)
65— John Perry, DB
68— Ron Brown, MG
70— Leon McQuay, RB
71— Ron Mikolajczyk, OT
    Sammy Gellerstedt, MG
TENN.-MARTIN (3)
68— Julian Nunnamaker, OG
88— Emanuel McNeil, DL
91— Oscar Bunch, TE
TENNESSEE ST. (21)
67— Claude Humphrey, DT
68— Jim Marsalis, DB
69— Joe Jones, DE
70— Vernon Holland, OT
71— Cliff Brooks, DB
    Joe Gilliam, QB
72— Robert Woods, OT
    Waymond Bryant, LB
73— Waymond Bryant, LB
    Ed Jones, DE
74— Cleveland Elam, DE
81—†Mike Jones, WR
    †Malcolm Taylor, DT
82—†Walter Tate, OL
86—†Onzy Elam, LB
90—†Colin Godfrey, P
93—†Brent Alexander, DB
98—†Tyrone Butterfield, WR
99—†Lamar Carter, DL
    †Avion Black, RS
    †Michael Thompson, OL
TENNESSEE TECH (11)
52— Tom Fann, OT
59— Tom Hackler, E
60— Tom Hackler, E
61— David Baxter, T
69— Larry Schreiber, HB
71— Jim Youngblood, LB
72— Jim Youngblood, LB
74— Elois Grooms, DE
76— Ed Burns, OT
89— Ryan Weeks, PK
96—†Robert Taylor, DB
TENN. WESLEYAN (1)
92— Derrick Scott, PK
TEXAS-ARLINGTON (5)
66— Ken Ozee, DT
67— Robert Diem, OG
    Robert Willbanks, S
83—†Mark Cannon, C
84—†Bruce Collie, OL

TEX. A&M-COMMERCE (20)
38— Darrell Tully, B
53— Bruno Ashley, G
58— Sam McCord, B
59— Sam McCord, B
68— Chad Brown, OT
70— William Lewis, C
72— Curtis Wester, OG
73— Autry Beamon, DB
84— Alan Veingrad, OG
88— Kim Morton, DL
90— Terry Bagsby, DL
91— Eric Turner, DB
    Dwayne Phorne, OL
92— Eric Turner, DB
    Pat Williams, DB
93— Fred Woods, LB
    Billy Watkins, PK
95— Kevin Mathis, DB
96— Kevin Mathis, DB
99— Antonio Wilson, DL
TEX. A&M-KINGSVILLE (53)
40— Stuart Clarkson, C
41— Stuart Clarkson, C
59— Gerald Lambert, G
60— William Crafts, T
62— Douglas Harvey, C
63— Sid Blanks, B
65— Randy Johnson, QB
66— Dwayne Nix, OE
67— Dwayne Nix, OE
68— Dwayne Nix, OE
    Ray Hickl, OG
70— Dwight Harrison, DB
    Margarito Guerrero, MG
71— Eldridge Small, OE
    Levi Johnson, DB
72— Ernest Price, DE
74— Don Hardeman, RB
75— David Hill, TE
76— Richard Ritchie, QB
    Larry Grunewald, LB
77— Larry Collins, RB
    John Barefield, DE
78— Billy John, OT
79— Andy Hawkins, LB
80— Don Washington, CB
81— Durwood Roquemore, DB
82— Darrell Green, DB
83— Loyd Lewis, OG
84— Neal Lattue, PK
85— Charles Smith, C
86— Johnny Bailey, RB
    Moses Horn, OG
87— Johnny Bailey, RB
    Moses Horn, OG
88— Rod Mounts, OL
    Johnny Bailey, RB
    John Randle, DL
89— Johnny Bailey, RB
90— Keithen DeGrate, OL
91— Brian Nielsen, OL
92— Earl Dotson, OL
93— Anthony Phillips, DB
    Moke Simon, DL
94— Jeff Rodgers, DL
    Kevin Dogins, C
95— Jermane Mayberry, OT
    Jaime Martinez, OG
    Kevin Dogins, C
96— Todd Perkins, OT
97— Chris Hensley, LB
98— Cedric Johnson, DB
    Cliff Clemons, OL
99— Robert Garza, C
TEXAS LUTHERAN (3)
73— David Wehmeyer, RB
74— D. W. Rutledge, LB
75— Jerry Ellis, OL
TEXAS SOUTHERN (3)
70— Nathaniel Allen, DB
76— Freddie Dean, OL
92—†Michael Strahan, DL
TEXAS TECH* (2)
35— Herschel Ramsey, E
45— Walter Schlinkman, B
THOMAS MORE (4)
93— Mike Flesch, OL

96— Brent Moses, OL
97— Chris Wells, LB
98— Chris Wells, LB
TIFFIN (1)
93— Brian Diliberto, RB
TOLEDO* (1)
38— Dan Buckwick, G
TOWSON (12)
75— Dan Dullea, QB
76— Skip Chase, OE
77— Randy Bielski, DB
78— Ken Snoots, SE
82— Sean Landeta, P
83— Gary Rubeling, OG
84— Terry Brooks, OG
85— Stan Eisentooth, OL
86— David Haden, LB
93—†Tony Vinson, RB
94—†Mark Orlando, WR
99—†Jamal White, WR
TRINITY (CONN.) (8)
35— Mickey Kobrosky, B
36— Mickey Kobrosky, B
55— Charles Sticka, B
59— Roger LeClerc, B
70— David Kiarsis, HB
78— Pat McNamara, FL
93— Eric Mudry, DB
94— Greg Schramm, DB
TRINITY (TEX.) (12)
54— Alvin Beal, B
55— Hubert Cook, C
56— Milton Robichaux, E
67— Marvin Upshaw, DT
94— James Vallerie, LB
96— John Beckwith, LB
97— Paul Morris, PK
    Danny Palmer, G
98— David Coney, DL
99— David Coney, OL
    Ryan Deck, LB
    Mike Burton, QB
TROY ST. (22)
39— Sherrill Busby, E
73— Mark King, C
74— Mark King, C
76— Perry Griggs, OE
78— Tim Tucker, LB
80— Willie Tullis, QB
84— Mitch Geier, OG
86— Freddie Thomas, DB
87— Mike Turk, QB
    Freddie Thomas, DB
94—†Bob Hall, OL
95—†Bob Hall, OL
96—†Pratt Lyons, DL
    †Kerry Jenkins, OL
97—†Clifford Ivory, DB
    †Andy Swafford, KR
98—†Marcus Spriggs, DL
    †Cleve Roberts, OL
    †Al Lucas, DT
99—†Al Lucas, DT
    †Michael Moore, OT
    †Anthony Rabb, LB
TRUMAN (5)
60— Dale Mills, B
65— Richard Rhodes, OT
85— Chris Hegg, QB
93— Mike Roos, DL
96— Jarrett Anderson, RB
TUFTS (6)
34— William Grinnell, E
76— Tim Whelan, RB
78— Mark Buben, DL
79— Chris Connors, QB
80— Mike Brown, OL
86— Bob Patz, DL
TULSA* (1)
34— Rudy Prochaska, C
TUSCULUM (2)
94— Matt Schults, OL
95— Eric Claridy, RB
TUSKEGEE (2)
98— Che' Bryant, DB
99— Andre Dudley, DL

AWARD WINNERS

UNION (N.Y.) (10)
- 39— Sam Hammerstrom, B
- 82— Steve Bodmer, DL
- 83— Tim Howell, LB
- 84— Brian Cox, DE
- 85— Anthony Valente, DL
- 86— Rich Romer, DL
- 87— Rich Romer, DL
- 91— Greg Harrison, PK
- 93— Marco Lainez, LB
- 96— Roger Egbert, PK

UNION (TENN.) (2)
- 41— James Jones, B
- 42— James Jones, B

U.S. INT'L (2)
- 72— Jerry Robinson, DB
- 75— Steve Matson, FL

UPSALA (1)
- 64— Dick Giessuebel, LB

URSINUS (1)
- 96— Peter Hinckle, DB

VALDOSTA ST. (8)
- 82— Mark Catano, OL
- 86— Jessie Tuggle, LB
- 89— Randy Fisher, WR
- 90— Deon Searcy, DB
- 93— Chris Hatcher, QB
- 94— Chris Hatcher, QB
- 96— Lance Funderburk, QB
- 97— Richard Freeman, DL/DE

VALPARAISO (6)
- 51— Joe Pahr, B
- 71— Gary Puetz, OT
- 72— Gary Puetz, OT
- 76— John Belskis, DB
- 85— Mike Healey, WR
- 99— †Eric Kenesie, DB

VILLANOVA (9)
- 88— †Paul Berardelli, OL
- 89— †Bryan Russo, OL
- 91— †Curtis Eller, LB
- 92— †Curtis Eller, LB
- 94— †Tyrone Frazier, LB
- 96— †Brian Finneran, WR
- 97— †Brian Finneran, WR
  - †Chris Boden, QB
- 98— †Brian Westbrook, AP/WR

VMI (3)
- 88— †Mark Stock, WR
- 95— †Thomas Haskins, RB
- 96— †Thomas Haskins, RB

VIRGINIA ST. (5)
- 71— Larry Brooks, DT
- 84— John Greene, LB
- 85— James Ward, DL
- 98— Damon Thompson, AP
- 99— Damon Thompson, WR

VIRGINIA UNION (13)
- 73— Herb Scott, OG
- 74— Herb Scott, OG
- 75— Anthony Leonard, DB
- 77— Frank Dark, DB
- 79— Plummer Bullock, DE
- 80— William Dillon, DB
- 81— William Dillon, DB
- 82— William Dillon, DB
- 83— Larry Curtis, DT
- 88— Leroy Gause, LB
- 91— Paul DeBerry, DB
  - Kevin Williams, LB
- 99— Ronald Hardge, DB

WABASH (5)
- 76— Jimmy Parker, DB
- 77— David Harvey, QB
- 81— Pete Metzelaars, TE
- 88— Tim Pliske, PK
- 89— Mike Funk, WR

WAGNER (10)
- 67— John Gloistein, OT
- 80— Phil Theis, OL
- 81— Alonzo Patterson, RB
- 82— Alonzo Patterson, RB
- 83— Selwyn Davis, OT
- 86— Charles Stinson, DL
- 87— Rich Negrin, OT
- 88— Terry Underwood, RB
- 91— Walter Lopez, PK
- 99— †Rick Sarille, AP

WARTBURG (3)
- 94— Jamey Parker, OL
  - Vince Penningroth, DL
- 95— Vince Penningroth, DL

WASHBURN (2)
- 64— Robert Hardy, DB
- 88— Troy Slusser, WR

WASHINGTON (MO.) (8)
- 72— Shelby Jordan, LB
- 73— Stu Watkins, OE
- 74— Marion Stallings, DB
- 88— Paul Matthews, TE
- 94— Matt Gomric, LB
- 95— Chris Nalley, DB
- 96— Chris Nalley, DB
- 99— Tim Runnalls, DL

WASH. & JEFF. (14)
- 84— Ed Kusko, OL
- 87— A. J. Pagano, RB
- 91— Chris Babirad, RB
  - Gilbert Floyd, DB
- 92— Chris Babirad, RB
  - Todd Pivnick, OL
  - Kevin Pintar, OL
- 93— Jason Moore, OL
  - Shawn Prendergast, LB
- 94— Matt Szczypinski, DL
  - Mike Jones, OL
  - Mike Brooder, DL
- 95— Mike Jones, OL
- 96— Dan Primrose, DL

WASH. & LEE (5)
- 76— Tony Perry, OE
- 81— Mike Pressler, DL
- 83— Glenn Kirschner, OL
- 86— John Packett, OL
- 95— Robert Hall, DL

WAYNE ST. (NEB.) (3)
- 84— Herve Roussel, PK
- 85— Ruben Mendoza, OL
- 95— Brad Ottis, DL

WAYNESBURG (1)
- 41— Nick George, G

WEBER ST. (19)
- 66— Ronald McCall, DE
- 67— Lee White, FB
  - Jim Schmedding, OG
- 69— Carter Campbell, DE
- 70— Henry Reed, DE
- 71— David Taylor, OT
- 77— Dennis Duncanson, DB
- 78— Dennis Duncanson, DB
  - Randy Jordan, WR
- 80— †Mike Humiston, LB
- 89— †Peter Macon, WR
- 91— †Jamie Martin, QB
  - †Alfred Pupunu, WR
- 93— †Pat McNarney, TE
- 95— †Pokey Eckford, WR
- 96— †Scott Shields, DB
- 97— †Cameron Quayle, TE
  - †Scott Shields, DB/AP
- 98— †Scott Shields, DB

WESLEY (6)
- 91— Fran Naselli, KR
- 95— Brandon Steinheim, RB
- 96— Brandon Steinheim, RB
  - Demetrius Stevenson, DL
- 97— Nate Casella, LB
- 99— Sean McCullin, OL

WESLEYAN (CONN.) (7)
- 46— Bert VanderClute, G
- 48— Jack Geary, T
- 72— Robert Heller, C
- 73— Robert Heller, C
- 76— John McVicar, DL
- 77— John McVicar, DL
- 99— Matt Perceval, WR

WEST ALA. (5)
- 82— Charles Martin, DT
- 84— Andrew Fields, WR
- 87— Ronnie Glanton, OL
- 93— Matt Carman, WR
- 97— John Sedely, PK

WEST CHESTER (11)
- 52— Charles Weber, DG
- 58— Richard Emerich, T
- 61— Joe Iacone, B
- 62— Joe Iacone, B
- 72— Tim Pierantozzi, QB
- 76— William Blystone, RB
- 87— Ralph Tamm, OL
- 88— Bill Hess, WR
- 92— Lee Woodall, DL
- 98— Kevin Ingram, WR
- 99— Kevin Ingram, WR

WEST GA. (4)
- 96— Byron Slack, TE
- 97— Corey Jarrells, DB
  - Chris Williams, OT
- 98— Chris Williams, OL

WEST LIBERTY ST. (1)
- 97— Greg Dailer, WR

WEST TEX. A&M (5)
- 86— Stan Carraway, WR
- 90— Mark Bounds, P
- 94— Brad Bailey, WR
  - Brian Hurley, OL
- 95— Jon Mason, P

WEST VIRGINIA* (1)
- 34— Tod Goodwin, E

WEST VA. TECH (3)
- 82— Elliott Washington, DB
- 86— Calvin Wallace, OL
- 89— Phil Hudson, WR

WEST VA. WESLEYAN (2)
- 36— George Mike, T
- 82— Jerry Free, T

WESTERN CAROLINA (15)
- 49— Arthur Byrd, G
- 71— Steve Williams, DT
- 73— Mark Ferguson, OT
- 74— Jerry Gaines, SE
  - Steve Yates, LB
- 84— †Louis Cooper, DL
  - †Kirk Roach, PK
  - †Steve Kornegay, P
- 85— †Clyde Simmons, DL
- 86— †Alonzo Carmichael, TE
  - †Kirk Roach, PK
- 87— †Kirk Roach, PK
- 93— †Kerry Hayes, KR/WR
- 98— †Eric Johnson, DB
  - †Ken Hinsley, P

WESTERN CONN. ST. (1)
- 99— Greg Boucher, DL

WESTERN ILL. (22)
- 59— Bill Larson, B
- 61— Leroy Jackson, B
- 74— John Passananti, OT
- 76— Scott Levenhagen, TE
  - Greg Lee, DB
- 77— Craig Phalen, DT
- 78— Bill Huskisson, DL
- 80— Mike Maher, TE
  - Don Greco, OG
- 83— †Chris Gunderson, MG
- 84— †Chris Gunderson, T
- 86— †Frank Winters, C
  - †Todd Auer, DL
- 88— †Marlin Williams, DL
- 93— †Rodney Harrison, DB
- 94— †Ross Schulte, P
- 97— †Aaron Stecker, RB
  - †Jason Grott, OL
- 98— †David Watson, DE
  - †David Bowens, DL
  - †James Milton, LB
- 99— †Edgerton Hartwell, LB

WESTERN KY. (18)
- 64— Dale Lindsey, LB
- 70— Lawrence Brame, LB
- 73— Mike McKoy, DB
- 74— John Bushong, DL
  - Virgil Livers, DB
- 75— Rick Green, LB
- 77— Chip Carpenter, OL
- 80— †Pete Walters, OG
  - Tim Ford, DL
- 81— †Donnie Evans, DE
- 82— †Paul Gray, LB
- 83— †Paul Gray, LB
- 87— †James Edwards, DB
- 88— †Dean Tiebout, LB
  - †Joe Arnold, RB
- 95— †Brian Bixler, C
- 97— †Patrick Goodman, OL
- 98— †Patrick Goodman, C

WESTERN MD. (4)
- 51— Victor Makovitch, DG
- 78— Ricci Bonaccorsy, DL
- 79— Ricci Bonaccorsy, DL
- 98— Mat Mathias, OL

WESTERN MICH.* (1)
- 82— †Matt Meares, OL

WESTERN N.M. (4)
- 83— Jay Ogle, WR
- 88— Pat Maxwell, P
- 97— Anthony Gray, RB
- 98— Anthony Gray, RB

WESTERN ST. (9)
- 56— Bill Rhodes, B
- 78— Bill Campbell, DB
- 80— Justin Cross, OT
- 84— Jeff Guy, P
- 92— Reggie Alexander, WR
- 94— Derren Bryan, OL
- 96— Ben Kern, TE
  - Kurt Clay, DB
- 97— Shane Carwin, LB

WESTERN WASH. (3)
- 51— Norman Hash, DB
- 79— Patrick Locker, RB
- 95— Orlando Steinauer, DB

WESTMINSTER (MO.) (6)
- 97— Scott Pingel, WR
- 98— Scott Pingel, WR
  - Logan Stanley, TE
  - Justin Peery, QB
- 99— Scott Pingel, WR
  - Justin Peery, QB

WESTMINSTER (PA.) (10)
- 73— Robert Pontius, DB
- 77— Rex Macey, FL
- 82— Gary DeGruttola, LB
- 83— Scott Higgins, DB
- 86— Joe Keaney, LB
- 88— Kevin Myers, LB
- 89— Joe Micchia, QB
- 90— Brad Tokar, RB
- 91— Brian DeLorenzo, DL
- 92— Matt Raich, LB

WHEATON (ILL.) (11)
- 55— Dave Burnham, B
- 58— Robert Bakke, T
- 77— Larry Wagner, LB
- 78— Scott Hall, QB
- 83— Keith Bishop, QB
- 95— Doug Johnston, OL
  - Chip Parrish, LB
- 96— Chip Parrish, LB
  - Mark Loeffler, WR
- 97— Chris Brown, OL
- 99— Chris Baughman, PK

WHITTIER (3)
- 38— Myron Claxton, T
- 62— Richard Peter, T
- 77— Michael Ciacci, DB

WHITWORTH (4)
- 52— Pete Swanson, OG
- 54— Larry Paradis, T
- 85— Wayne Ralph, WR
- 86— Wayne Ralph, WR

WIDENER (15)
- 72— Billy Johnson, RB
- 73— Billy Johnson, RB
- 75— John Warrington, DB
- 76— Al Senni, OL
- 77— Chip Zawoiski, RB
- 79— Tom Deery, DB
- 80— Tom Deery, DB
- 81— Tom Deery, DB
- 82— Tony Stefanoni, DL
- 88— Dave Duffy, DL
- 94— O. J. McElroy, LB
  - Antoine Moore, DB
- 95— Blaise Coleman, LB

FIRST-TEAM ALL-AMERICANS BELOW DIVISION I-A

98— Bill Nourse, DL
99— Tom Eisenhower, LB

WILKES (3)
73— Jeff Grandinetti, DT
93— Jason Feese, DL
97— J. J. Fadden, DL

WILLAMETTE (14)
34— Loren Grannis, G
35— John Oravec, B
36— Richard Weisgerber, B
46— Marvin Goodman, E
58— William Long, C
59— Marvin Cisneros, G
64— Robert Burles, DT
65— Robert Burles, DT
69— Calvin Lee, LB
75— Gary Johnson, DL
82— Richard Milroy, DB
97— Kamell Eckroth-Bernard, DB
98— Brian Greer, OL

WILLIAM & MARY (10)
83— †Mario Shaffer, OL
86— †Michael Clemons, RB
89— †Steve Christie, P
90— †Pat Crowley, DL
93— †Craig Staub, DL
95— †Darren Sharper, DB
96— †Josh Beyer, OL
      †Darren Sharper, DB
97— †Ron Harrison, DB
99— †Brett Sterba, PK

WILLIAM JEWELL (4)
52— Al Conway, B
73— John Strada, OE
81— Guy Weber, DL
83— Mark Mundel, OL

WM. PATERSON (2)
92— Craig Paskas, DB
93— Craig Paskas, DB

WILLIAM PENN (1)
72— Bruce Polen, DB

WILLIAMS (7)
51— Charles Salmon, DG
69— Jack Maitland, HB
74— John Chandler, LB
78— Greg McAleenan, DB
90— George Rogers, DL
94— Bobby Walker, LB
95— Ethan Brooks, DL

WILMINGTON (OHIO) (2)
72— William Roll, OG
94— Jason Tincher, WR

WINGATE (1)
89— Jimmy Sutton, OT

WINONA ST. (3)
92— Dave Ludy, AP
94— Dave Ludy, AP
97— Jamey Hutchinson, DB

WINSTON-SALEM (7)
77— Cornelius Washington, DB
78— Tim Newsome, RB
84— Danny Moore, OG
87— Barry Turner, G
95— Richard Huntley, RB
96— LaTori Workman, RB
99— Thomas Washington, DL

WIS.-EAU CLAIRE (1)
81— Roger Vann, RB

WIS.-LA CROSSE (17)
52— Ted Levanhagen, LB
72— Bryon Buelow, DB
78— Joel Williams, LB
83— Jim Byrne, DL
85— Tom Newberry, OL
88— Ted Pretasky, RB
89— Terry Strouf, OL
91— Jon Lauscher, LB
92— Norris Thomas, DB
      Mike Breit, LB
93— Rick Schaaf, DL
95— Craig Kusick, QB
      Erik Halverson, OL
96— Erik Halverson, OL
      Mike Maslowski, LB
97— Ric Mathias, DB
99— Brock Ryan, DL

WIS.-MILWAUKEE (1)
70— Pete Papara, LB

WIS.-PLATTEVILLE (2)
73— William Vander Velden, DE
86— Mike Hintz, DB

WIS.-RIVER FALLS (5)
80— Gerald Sonsalla, OG
82— Roland Hall, LB
87— Greg Corning, RB
95— Brian Izdepski, OT
99— Joe Green, DL

WIS.-STEVENS POINT (8)
77— Reed Giordana, QB
81— Chuck Braun, WR
92— Randy Simpson, DB
93— Jimmy Henderson, RB
94— Randy Simpson, LB
97— Clint Kriewalt, LB

98— Clint Kriewalt, LB
99— Andy Palzkill, DB

WIS.-STOUT (1)
79— Joseph Bullis, DL

WIS.-SUPERIOR (3)
66— Mel Thake, DB
83— Larry Banks, MG
85— Phil Eiting, LB

WIS.-WHITEWATER (6)
75— William Barwick, OL
79— Jerry Young, WR
82— Daryl Schleim, DE
90— Reggie White, OL
96— Derrick LeVake, OL
97— Derrick LeVake, OL

WITTENBERG (28)
62— Donald Hunt, G
63— Bob Cherry, E
64— Chuck Green, QB
68— Jim Felts, DE
73— Steve Drongowski, OT
74— Arthur Thomas, LB
75— Robert Foster, LB
76— Dean Caven, DL
78— Dave Merritt, RB
79— Joe Govern, DL
80— Mike Dowds, DE
81— Bill Beach, DB
83— Bryant Lemon, DL
87— Eric Horstman, OL
88— Ken Bonner, OT
      Eric Horstman, OL
90— Jon Warga, RB
92— Taver Johnson, LB
93— Taver Johnson, LB
      Greg Brame, PK
95— Ron Cunningham, OT
      Jimmy Watts, PK
96— Xan Smith, OL
97— Jonathan Farley, C
      Kent Rafey, LB
      Russ Fedyk, KR
98— Ken Pope, DB
99— Casey Donaldson, RB

WOFFORD (12)
42— Aubrey Faust, E
47— Ken Dubard, T
49— Elbert Hammett, T
51— Jack Beeler, DB
57— Charles Bradshaw, B
61— Dan Lewis, G
70— Sterling Allen, OG
79— Keith Kinard, OL
90— David Wiley, OL

91— Tom Colter, OL
94— Brian Porzio, PK
97— †Dan Williams, OL/C

WOOSTER (2)
79— Blake Moore, C
99— Seth Duerr, LB

WORCESTER ST. (3)
92— Chris Butts, DB
93— Chris Butts, DB
94— Brian Fitzpatrick, DB

WORCESTER TECH (2)
97— Matt Surette, TE
98— Matt Surette, TE

XAVIER (OHIO) (1)
51— Tito Carinci, LB

YALE (1)
84— †John Zanieski, DL

YOUNGSTOWN ST. (25)
74— Don Calloway, DB
75— Don Calloway, DB
78— Ed McGlasson, OL
79— James Ferranti, OE
      Jeff Lear, OT
80— Jeff Gergel, LB
81— †Paris Wicks, RB
82— †Paris Wicks, RB
88— †Jim Zdelar, OL
89— †Paul Soltis, LB
90— †Tony Bowens, DL
91— †Pat Danko, DL
92— †Dave Roberts, DB
93— †Drew Garber, OL
      †Tamron Smith, RB
      †Jeff Wilkins, PK
94— †Randy Smith, KR
      †Leon Jones, LB
      †Lester Weaver, DB
      †Chris Sammarone, OL
95— † Leon Jones, LB
      †Jermaine Hopkins, DL
97— †Matt Hogg, OL
      †Harry Deligianis, DL
99— †Ian Dominelli, LB

NCAA Postgraduate Scholarship Winners

Following are football players who are NCAA postgraduate scholarship winners, whether or not they were able to accept the grant, plus all alternates (indicated by *) who accepted grants. The program began with the 1964 season. (Those who played in 1964 are listed as 1965 winners, those who played in 1965 as 1966 winners, etc.) To qualify, student-athletes must maintain a 3.000 grade-point average (on a 4.000 scale) during their collegiate careers and perform with distinction in varsity football.

ABILENE CHRISTIAN
71— James Lindsey
83— *Grant Feasel
85— Daniel Remsberg
86— *James Embry
      Craig Huff
90— William Clayton

ADAMS ST.
00— Ryan Hollingshead

ADRIAN
94— Jeffrey Toner

AIR FORCE
65— Edward Fausti
67— James Hogarty

68— Kenneth Zagzebski
69— *Richard Rivers Jr.
70— Charles Longnecker
      *Alfred Wurglitz
71— Ernest Jennings
      Robert Parker Jr.
72— Darryl Haas
73— Mark Prill
75— *Joseph Debes
84— Jeffrey Kubiak
86— Derek Brown
88— Chad Hennings
89— David Hlatky
90— Steven Wilson
91— Christopher Howard

92— Ronald James
93— Scott Hufford
95— Preston McConnell
96— Bret Cillessen
97— Carlton Hendrix
99— Charles Gilliam
00— Cale Bonds

UAB
97— John Rea
00— Lee Carter

ALABAMA
69— Donald Sutton
72— John Musso Jr.
75— Randy Hall
80— Steadman Shealy

ALABAMA ST.
92— Edward Robinson Jr.

ALBANY (N.Y.)
88— *Thomas Higgins

ALBION
81— Joel Manby
94— Michael Montico
95— Jeffrey Shooks
96— Timothy Schafer
97— Kyle Klein
98— Neil Johnson

ALBRIGHT
67— *Paul Chaiet

ALLEGHENY
65— David Wion
92— Darren Hadlock
97— Nicholas Reiser

ALMA
67— Keith Bird Jr.
79— Todd Friesner
99— Eric Brands
00— Dustin Armstrong

AMHERST
66— David Greenblatt
76— Geoffrey Miller
85— Raymond Nurme
96— Gregory Schneider

ANGELO ST.
99— Kyle Kirk

APPALACHIAN ST.
78— Gill Beck
93— D. J. Campbell

ARIZONA
69— William Michael Moody
78— Jon Abbott
80— Jeffrey Whitton
88— Charles Cecil
97— Wayne Wyatt

ARIZONA ST.
78— John Harris
90— Mark Tingstad

97— Devin Kendall
98— Patrick Tillman
ARKANSAS
70— Terry Stewart
71— William Burnett
79— William Bradford Shoup
85— *Mark Lee
ARKANSAS ST.
72— John Meyer
77— Thomas Humphreys
ARMY
66— Samuel Champi Jr.
68— Bohdan Neswiacheny
69— James McCall Jr.
   Thomas Wheelock
70— Theodore Shadid Jr.
78— Curtis Downs
81— *Stanley March
86— Donald Smith
   Douglas Black
88— William Conner
90— Michael Thorson
93— Michael McElrath
95— Eric Oliver
ASHLAND
78— Daniel Bogden
88— David Biondo
90— Douglas Powell
AUBURN
66— John Cochran
69— *Roger Giffin
85— Gregg Carr
90— James Lyle IV
AUGSBURG
90— Terry Mackenthun
98— Ted Schultz
AUGUSTANA (ILL.)
69— *Jeffrey Maurus
71— Kenneth Anderson
77— Joe Thompson
86— Steven Sanders
96— Thomas King
97— Ryan Carpenter
99— Chris Meskan
AUGUSTANA (S.D.)
72— Michael Olson
75— David Zelinsky
77— James Clemens
78— Dee Donlin
   Roger Goebel
90— *David Gubbrud
91— Scott Boyens
97— Mitchell Pruett
BALL ST.
67— *John Hostrawser
73— Gregory Mack
77— Arthur Yaroch
84— Richard Chitwood
88— Ronald Duncan
90— Theodore Ashburn
93— Troy Hoffer
BATES
79— Christopher Howard
BAYLOR
65— Michael Kennedy
66— Edward Whiddon
94— John Eric Joe
BENEDICTINE (ILL.)
70— David Cyr
71— Thomas Danaher
BOISE ST.
72— Brent McIver
76— *Glenn Sparks
79— Samuel Miller
82— Kip Bedard
92— Larry Stayner
93— David Tingstad
BOSTON COLLEGE
66— *Lawrence Marzetti
67— Michael O'Neill
69— Gary Andrachik
70— Robert Bouley
78— Richard Scudellari
87— Michael Degnan

BOSTON U.
69— Suren Donabedian Jr.
81— David Bengtson
BOWDOIN
65— Steven Ingram
67— Thomas Allen
BOWIE ST.
92— Mark Fitzgerald
BOWLING GREEN
77— Richard Preston
78— Mark Miller
91— Patrick Jackson
BRIDGEPORT
70— Terry Sparker
BRIGHAM YOUNG
67— Virgil Carter
76— Orrin Olsen
77— *Stephen Miller
78— Gifford Nielsen
80— Marc Wilson
82— Daniel Plater
83— Bart Oates
84— Steve Young
85— Marvin Allen
89— Charles Cutler
94— Eric Drage
97— Chad Lewis
BROWN
65— John Kelly Jr.
70— James Lukens
74— Douglas Jost
75— William Taylor
77— Scott Nelson
78— Louis Cole
79— Robert Forster
82— Travis Holcombe
95— Rene Abdalah
BUCKNELL
71— *Kenneth Donahue
74— John Dailey
75— Steve Leskinen
77— Lawrence Brunt
85— David Kucera
93— David Berardinelli
BUENA VISTA
77— Steven Trost
87— Michael Habben
94— Cary Murphy
BUFFALO ST.
87— James Dunbar
BUTLER
72— George Yearsich
78— William Ginn
85— Stephen Kollias
C. W. POST
79— John Luchsinger
CALIFORNIA
66— William Krum
67— John Schmidt
68— Robert Crittenden
70— James Calkins
71— Robert Richards
83— Harvey Salem
94— Douglas Brien
UC DAVIS
76— Daniel Carmazzi
   David Gellerman
77— Rolf Benirschke
79— Mark Markel
86— Robert Hagenau
90— *James Tomasin
92— Robert Kincade
   Michael Shepard
93— Brian Andersen
97— Mark Grieb
99— Wesley Terrell
UC RIVERSIDE
72— Tyrone Hooks
74— Gary Van Jandegian
CAL LUTHERAN
90— *Gregory Maw
CAL POLY
69— William Creighton

CAL TECH
67— William Mitchell
68— John Frazzini
74— Frank Hobbs Jr.
CANISIUS
84— Thomas Schott
CAPITAL
84— *Michael Linton
CARLETON
67— Robert Paarlberg
73— Mark Williams
83— Paul Vaaler
93— Arthur Gilliland
CARNEGIE MELLON
80— Gusty Sunseri
91— Robert O'Toole
99— Jason Funke
00— Mike Campie
CARROLL (WIS.)
77— Stephen Thompson
95— Christopher Klippel
CARTHAGE
70— William Radakovitz
CASE RESERVE
89— Christopher Nutter
91— James Meek
CENTRAL (IOWA)
71— Vernon Den Herder
87— Scott Lindell
89— Eric Perry
92— Richard Kacmarynski
96— Rick Sanger
CENTRAL ARK.
96— Brian Barnett
CENTRAL MICH.
77— John Wunderlich
80— *Michael Ball
85— Kevin Egnatuk
88— Robert Stebbins
92— Jeffrey Bender
CENTRAL MO. ST.
99— Shane Meyer
CENTRAL WASH.
70— Danny Collins
CENTRE
69— Glenn Shearer
86— Casteel "Teel" Bruner II
88— *Robert Clark
90— James Ellington
CHADRON ST.
96— Corey Campbell
CHATTANOOGA
67— Harvey Ouzts
72— *Frank Webb
74— John McBrayer
76— Russell Gardner
CHEYNEY
76— Steven Anderson
CHICAGO
86— *Bruce Montella
89— Paul Haar
94— Frank Baker
CINCINNATI
71— *Earl Willson
CITADEL
74— Thomas Leitner
79— Kenneth Caldwell
84— *William West IV
97— Derek Beres
CLAREMONT-M-S
68— Craig Dodel
70— *Gregory Long
71— Stephen Endemano
73— Christopher Stecher
74— Samuel Reece
CLEMSON
65— James Bell Jr.
68— James Addison
73— Benjamin Anderson
79— Stephen Fuller

COAST GUARD
73— Rodney Leis
74— Leonard Kelly
81— Bruce Hensel
89— *Ty Rinoski
   *Jeffery Peters
90— Richard Schachner
91— John Freda
COE
67— Lynn Harris
COLBY
71— Ronald Lupton
   Frank Apantaku
COLGATE
73— Kenneth Nelson
80— Angelo Colosimo
89— Donald Charney
COLORADO
93— James Hansen
COLORADO COL.
69— Steven Ehrhart
72— Randy Bobier
75— Bruce Kolbezen
84— Herman Motz III
97— Ryan Egeland
98— Christopher Smith
COLORADO MINES
66— Stuart Bennett
67— Michael Greensburg
   Charles Kirby
75— David Chambers
COLORADO ST.
65— Russel Mowrer
76— Mark Driscoll
87— Stephan Bartalo
88— Joseph Brookhart
93— Gregory Primus
96— Gregory Myers
99— Nathaniel Kvamme
COLUMBIA
72— John Sefcik
80— Mario Biaggi Jr.
CONNECTICUT
77— *Bernard Palmer
CORNELL
68— Ronald Kipicki
72— Thomas Albright
84— Derrick Harmon
CORNELL COLLEGE
65— Steven Miller
72— David Hilmers
73— Robert Ash
79— Brian Farrell
   Thomas Zinkula
81— *Timothy Garry
83— John Ward
93— Brent Sands
94— Matthew Miller
95— Mark McDermott
99— Matthew Weiss
DARTMOUTH
66— Anthony Yezer
68— Henry Paulson Jr.
69— Randolph Wallick
71— Willie Bogan
73— Frederick Radke
74— Thomas Csatari
   *Robert Funk
77— Patrick Sullivan
89— Paul Sorensen
95— O. Josh Bloom
98— Dominic Lanza
DAVIDSON
66— Stephen Smith
71— Rick Lyon
72— Robert Norris
86— *Louis Krempel
97— John Cowan Jr.
DAYTON
73— Timothy Quinn
76— Roy Gordon III
83— *Michael Pignatiello
91— Daniel Sharley

NCAA POSTGRADUATE SCHOLARSHIP WINNERS

DELAWARE
86— Brian Farrell

DELAWARE VALLEY
85— Daniel Glowatski

DELTA ST.
76— William Hood

DENISON
70— Richard Trumball
73— Steven Smiljanich
76— *Dennis Thome
78— David Holcombe
86— Brian Gearinger
88— Grant Jones
92— Jonathan Fortkamp
00— Jon Dunhan

DePAUW
68— Bruce Montgomerie
78— Mark Frazer
81— Jay True
85— Richard Bonaccorsi
86— Anthony deNicola
92— Thomas Beaulieu
00— Tyler Kelley

DICKINSON
66— Robert Averback
71— *John West
75— *Gerald Urich

DOANE
68— John Lothrop
70— Richard Held

DRAKE
73— Joseph Worobec

DREXEL
72— Blake Lynn Ferguson

DUBUQUE
82— Timothy Finn

DUKE
68— Robert Lasky
71— *Curt Rawley

EAST CARO.
92— Keith Arnold

EAST TENN. ST.
82— Jay Patterson

EASTERN KY.
78— Steven Frommeyer

EASTERN N.M.
66— Richard James

EASTERN WASH.
98— Steven Mattson

ELIZABETH CITY ST.
73— Darnell Johnson
80— David Nickelson

ELMHURST
80— Richard Green

EMORY & HENRY
82— Thomas Browder Jr.

EVANSVILLE
75— David Mattingly
76— Charles Uhde Jr.
79— *Neil Saunders

FERRIS ST.
79— Robert Williams
93— Monty Brown

FLORIDA
72— Carlos Alvarez
77— Darrell Carpenter
85— Garrison Rolle
87— Bret Wiechmann
90— *Cedric Smith
91— Huey Richardson
95— Michael Gilmore
97— Danny Wuerffel
99— Terrance Jackson

FLORIDA ST.
88— David Palmer
91— David Roberts
94— Kenneth Alexander
95— Derrick Brooks
98— Daryl Bush

FORDHAM
91— Eric Schweiker

FORT HAYS ST.
94— David Foster
99— Clinton Albers

FRANK. & MARSH.
69— Frank deGenova
83— *Robert Shepardson

FRESNO ST.
70— *Henry Corda
74— Dwayne Westphal
83— William Griever Jr.

FROSTBURG ST.
00— Marty Mood

FURMAN
77— Thomas Holcomb III
82— Charles Anderson
84— Ernest Gibson
86— *David Jager
87— Stephen Squire
90— Christopher Roper
92— Paul Siffri
    Eric Von Walter
96— William Phillip Jones

GANNON
97— Patrick Rodkey

GEORGETOWN
75— James Chesley Jr.
98— Stephen Iorio
00— Jim Gallagher

GEORGIA
68— Thomas Lawhorne Jr.
69— William Payne
71— Thomas Lyons
72— Thomas Nash Jr.
    Raleigh Mixon Robinson
78— Jeffrey Lewis
80— Jeffrey Pyburn
81— Christopher Welton
84— Terrell Hoage
88— Kim Stephens
89— Richard Tardits
99— Matthew Stinchcomb

GA. SOUTHERN
00— Voncellies Allen

GEORGIA TECH
68— William Eastman
75— James Robinson
81— Sheldon Fox
83— Ellis Gardner
86— John Ivemeyer

GETTYSBURG
70— *Herbert Ruby III
80— Richard Swartz

GRAMBLING
73— Stephen Dennis

GRINNELL
72— Edward Hirsch
80— *Derek Muehrcke
00— Troy Dougherty

GROVE CITY
95— Stephen Sems

GUST. ADOLPHUS
74— James Goodwin
81— *David Najarian

HAMLINE
85— Kyle Aug
91— Robert Hackney

HAMPDEN-SYDNEY
78— *Wilson Newell
80— Timothy Maxa

HARVARD
68— Alan Bersin
71— *Richard Frisbie
75— Patrick McInally
76— William Emper
81— Charles Durst
85— Brian Bergstrom
87— Scott Collins

HAWAII
68— James Roberts
73— *Don Satterlee

HIRAM
68— Sherman Riemenschneider
74— Donald Brunetti

HOLY CROSS
84— *Bruce Kozerski

HOPE
74— Ronald Posthuma
80— Craig Groendyk
83— Kurt Brinks
85— *Scott Jecmen
98— Brandon Graham

HOUSTON
86— Gary Schoppe
87— Robert Brezina
99— Peter deGroot

IDAHO
67— Michael Lavens
    Joseph McCollum Jr.
84— Boyce Bailey

IDAHO ST.
76— Richard Rodgers
92— Steven Boyenger

ILLINOIS
72— Robert Bucklin
73— Laurence McCarren Jr.
91— Curtis Lovelace
92— Michael Hopkins
93— John Wright

ILL. WESLEYAN
93— Christopher Bisaillon
97— Lon Erickson

INDIANA
73— Glenn Scolnik
79— David Abrams
81— Kevin Speer

INDIANA (PA.)
78— *John Mihota
84— Kenneth Moore

INDIANA ST.
86— Jeffrey Miller

INDIANAPOLIS
76— Rodney Pawlik

IONA
81— Neal Kurtti
82— *Paul Rupp

IOWA
69— Michael Miller
76— Robert Elliott
78— Rodney Sears
86— Larry Station Jr.
88— Michael Flagg
89— Charles Hartlieb
99— Matthew Reischl
    Derek Rose

IOWA ST.
70— William Bliss

JACKSON ST.
80— *Lester Walls

JACKSONVILLE ST.
79— Dewey Barker

JAMES MADISON
79— Warren Coleman
90— Mark Kiefer

JOHNS HOPKINS
73— Joseph Ouslander
74— Gunter Glocker
94— Steuart Markley
95— Michael House
99— Lawrence Gulotta

JUNIATA
72— Maurice Taylor
87— Robert Crossey

KANSAS
65— Ronald Oelschlager
69— David Morgan
72— Michael McCoy
73— John Schroll
78— Tom Fitch
87— Mark Henderson

KANSAS ST.
66— *Larry Anderson
83— James Gale
88— Matthew Garver

KENTUCKY
76— Thomas Ranieri

79— James Kovach
84— *Keith Martin
97— Michael Schellenberger

KENTUCKY ST.
68— James Jackson

KENYON
75— Patrick Clements

KNOX
88— Robert Monroe

LAFAYETTE
71— William Sprecher
76— Michael Kline
78— Victor Angeline III

LAMAR
73— *Richard Kubiak

LAWRENCE
68— Charles McKee
83— Christopher Matheus

LEBANON VALLEY
74— *Alan Shortell

LEHIGH
66— Robert Adelaar
68— Richard Miller
73— Thomas Benfield
75— James Addonizio
76— *Robert Liptak
77— *Michael Yaszemski
80— David Melone

LONG BEACH ST.
84— Joseph Donohue

LSU
79— Robert Dugas
83— James Britt
88— Ignazio Albergamo
91— Solomon Graves
94— Chad Loup
95— Michael Blanchard
98— Chad Kessler

LA.-LAFAYETTE
71— *George Coussa

LA.-MONROE
93— Darren Rimmer
94— Robert Cobb
    Michael Young

LUTHER
67— Thomas Altemeier
78— *Mark Larson
85— Larry Bonney

MARIETTA
98— Thomas Couhig

MARYLAND
78— Jonathan Claiborne

MARYVILLE (TENN.)
67— Frank Eggers II

MIT
91— Darcy Prather
92— Rodrigo Rubiano
93— Roderick Tranum
95— Corey Foster
99— Duane Stevens
00— Nik Kozy

McNEESE ST.
81— Daryl Burckel
86— Ross Leger

MEMPHIS
77— *James Mincey Jr.

MERCHANT MARINE
70— Robert Lavinia
76— *John Castagna

MIAMI (FLA.)
90— Robert Chudzinski
91— Michael Sullivan

MICHIGAN
67— David Fisher
74— David Gallagher
81— *John Wangler
82— Norm Betts
84— Stefan Humphries
    Thomas Dixon
86— Clayton Miller
87— Kenneth Higgins

AWARD WINNERS

93— Christopher Hutchinson
94— Marc Milia
98— Brian Griese
00— Rob Renes
MICHIGAN ST.
69— Allen Brenner
70— Donald Baird
94— Steven Wasylk
MICHIGAN TECH
72— Larry Ras
74— Bruce Trusock
75— Daniel Rhude
MIDDLE TENN. ST.
73— *Edwin Zaunbrecher
MIDDLEBURY
79— Franklin Kettle
MIDLAND LUTHERAN
76— Thomas Hale
MILLERSVILLE
92— Thomas Burns III
MILLIKIN
90— *Charles Martin
MILLSAPS
67— Edward Weller
73— *Russell Gill
92— David Harrison Jr.
99— Thomas Ingram
MINNESOTA
69— Robert Stein
71— Barry Mayer
73— Douglas Kingsriter
78— Robert Weber
99— Parc Williams
MINN. ST.-MANKATO
70— Bernard Maczuga
MISSISSIPPI
66— Stanley Hindman
69— Steve Hindman
81— Kenneth Toler Jr.
86— Richard Austin
87— Jeffrey Noblin
88— Daniel Hoskins
89— Charles Walls
91— Todd Sandroni
MISSISSIPPI COL.
80— Stephen Johnson
98— Joseph Fulcher
00— Michael Brown
MISSISSIPPI ST.
69— William Nelson
73— Frank Dowsing Jr.
75— James Webb
77— William Coltharp
93— Daniel Boyd
MISSOURI
66— Thomas Lynn
67— James Whitaker
69— *Charles Weber
71— John Weisenfels
79— Christopher Garlich
82— Van Darkow
99— Jacob Stueve
MO.-ROLLA
69— Robert Nicodemus
73— Kim Colter
81— Paul Janke
MONMOUTH (ILL.)
72— Dale Brooks
90— Brent Thurness
MONTANA
75— Rock Svennungsen
79— Steven Fisher
84— Brian Salonen
91— Michael McGowan
96— David Dickenson
97— Michael Bouchee
       Blaine McElmurry
98— Josh Branen
00— Dallas Neil
MONTANA ST.
65— Gene Carlson
68— Russell Dodge
71— Jay Groepper
77— Bert Markovich

79— Jon Borchardt
       James Mickelson
90— Derrick Isackson
92— Travis Annette
MOOREHEAD ST.
00— Erik Pederson
MORAVIAN
73— Daniel Joseph
94— Judson Frank
MOREHEAD ST.
92— James Appel
MORNINGSIDE
65— Larry White
MORRIS BROWN
83— Arthur Knight Jr.
MOUNT UNION
89— Paul Hrics
00— Tom Bauer
MUHLENBERG
73— Edward Salo
76— Eric Butler
78— Mark Stull
81— Arthur Scavone
91— Michael Hoffman
MURRAY ST.
71— Matthew Haug
78— Edward McFarland
81— *Kris Robbins
90— Eric Crigler
NAVY
65— William Donnelly
69— William Newton
70— Daniel Pike
75— *Timothy Harden
76— Chester Moeller II
81— Theodore Dumbauld
00— Terrence Anderson
NEBRASKA
70— Randall Reeves
71— *John Decker
72— Larry Jacobson
73— David Mason
74— Daniel Anderson
76— Thomas Heiser
77— Vince Ferragamo
78— Ted Harvey
79— James Pillen
80— Timothy Smith
81— Randy Schleusener
       Jeffrey Finn
82— Eric Lindquist
85— Scott Strasburger
88— Jeffrey Jamrog
89— Mark Blazek
90— Gerald Gdowski
       Jacob Young III
91— David Edeal
       Patrick Tyrance Jr.
92— Patrick Engelbert
93— Michael Stigge
94— Trev Alberts
95— Robert Zatechka
96— Aaron Graham
97— Jonathan Hesse
98— Grant Wistrom
99— Joel Makovicka
00— Tim DeBates
       Brian Shaw
NEB.-OMAHA
84— Kirk Hutton
       Clark Toner
99— Edward Thompson
NEB. WESLEYAN
97— Justin Rice
       Bren Chambers
98— Dusten Olds
       Chad Wemhoff
99— Ryan Shanesy
UNLV
95— Howard McGowan
NEW HAMPSHIRE
85— Richard Leclerc
NEW MEXICO
72— Roderick Long
76— Robert Berg
79— Robert Rumbaugh
83— George Parks

NEW MEXICO ST.
76— Ralph Jackson
77— *Joseph Fox
99— David Patterson
NORTH ALA.
82— *Warren Moore
NORTH CAROLINA
75— Christopher Kupec
81— William Donnalley
83— David Drechsler
91— Kevin Donnalley
N.C. CENTRAL
91— Anthony Cooley
NORTH CAROLINA ST.
75— Justus Everett
82— *Calvin Warren Jr.
NORTH DAKOTA
79— Dale Lian
81— Douglas Moen
82— Paul Franzmeier
85— Glen Kucera
88— Kurt Otto
89— Matthew Gulseth
93— Timothy Gelinske
97— Thomas Langer
       Timothy Tibesar
NORTH DAKOTA ST.
66— James Schindler
69— *Stephen Stephens
71— Joseph Cichy
75— Paul Cichy
84— Doug Hushka
89— Charles Stock
94— Arden Beachy
98— Sean Fredricks
NORTH TEXAS
68— Ruben Draper
77— Peter Morris
NORTHERN ARIZ.
78— Larry Friedrichs
00— Jake Crissup
NORTHERN COLO.
76— Robert Bliss
91— Thomas Langer
00— Corte McGuffey
NORTHERN IOWA
81— Owen Dockter
NORTHERN MICH.
73— Guy Falkenhagen
81— Phil Kessel
86— Keith Nelsen
NORTHWEST MO. ST.
82— Robert Gregory
97— Greg Teale
NORTHWESTERN
70— *Bruce Hubbard
74— Steven Craig
77— Randolph Dean
81— Charles Kern
96— Salvatore Valenzisi
       Ryan Padgett
99— Barry Gardner
NORTHWESTERN ST.
95— John Dippel
00— William Broussard
NORWICH
68— Richard Starbuck
74— Matthew Hincks
NOTRE DAME
67— Frederick Schnurr
68— James Smithberger
69— George Kunz
70— Michael Oriard
71— Lawrence DiNardo
72— Thomas Gatewood
73— Gregory Marx
74— David Casper
75— Peter Demmerle
       Reggie Barnett
79— Joseph Restic
81— Thomas Gibbons
82— John Krimm Jr.
86— Gregory Dingens
89— Reginald Ho
94— Timothy Ruddy
OCCIDENTAL
66— James Wanless

67— Richard Verry
69— John St. John
78— Richard Fry
80— *Timothy Bond
89— *Curtis Page
95— Davin Lundquist
OHIO
78— *Robert Weidaw
80— Mark Geisler
OHIO NORTHERN
79— Mark Palmer
82— Larry Egbert
OHIO ST.
65— Arnold Chonko
66— Donald Unverferth
67— Ray Pryor
69— David Foley
71— Rex Kern
74— Randolph Gradishar
76— Brian Baschnagel
77— William Lukens
80— James Laughlin
84— John Frank
85— David Crecelius
86— Michael Lanese
97— Greg Bellisari
OKLAHOMA
72— Larry Jack Mildren Jr.
73— Joe Wylie
81— Jay Jimerson
89— Anthony Phillips
91— Michael Sawatzky
OKLAHOMA ST.
83— *Doug Freeman
OLIVET
75— William Ziem
OREGON
79— *Willie Blasher Jr.
91— William Musgrave
OREGON ST.
69— William Enyart
69— *Jerry Belcher
PACIFIC (CAL.)
72— *Byron Cosgrove
78— Brian Peets
80— Bruce Filarsky
PENNSYLVANIA
68— Ben Mortensen
95— Michael Turner
98— John Bishop
99— David Rader
PENN ST.
66— Joseph Bellas
67— John Runnells III
71— Robert Holuba
72— David Joyner
73— Bruce Bannon
74— Mark Markovich
75— John Baiorunos
79— *Charles Correal
80— *Michael Guman
81— John Walsh
84— Harry Hamilton
85— Douglas Strange
87— Brian Silverling
90— Roger Thomas Duffy
94— Craig Fayak
95— Charles Pittman
00— Travis Forney
PITTSBURGH
79— Jeff Delaney
86— Robert Schilken
89— Mark Stepnoski
POMONA-PITZER
69— *Lee Piatek
77— Scott Borg
83— *Calvin Oishi
85— *Derek Watanabe
88— Edward Irick
93— Torin Cunningham
PORTLAND ST.
79— John Urness
PRINCETON
67— Charles Peters
69— Richard Sandler
70— Keith Mauney
76— Ronald Beible

NCAA POSTGRADUATE SCHOLARSHIP WINNERS

81— Mark Bailey
83— Brent Woods
86— James Petrucci
87— John Hammond
97— Marc Washington Jr.
99— Alexander Sierk

PUGET SOUND
68— Stephen Doolittle
79— *Patrick O'Loughlin
83— *Anthony Threlkeld

PURDUE
70— Michael Phipps
74— Robert Hoftiezer
75— Lawrence Burton

RANDOLPH-MACON
98— Joseph Seetoo

REDLANDS
65— Robert Jones
97— Morgan Bannister

RENSSELAER
67— Robert Darnall
69— John Contento

RHODES
71— John Churchill
79— *Philip Mischke
81— Jeffrey Lane
83— *Russell Ashford
85— *John Foropoulos
89— James Augustine

RICE
81— *Lamont Jefferson
91— Donald Hollas
96— James Lamy

RICHMOND
86— Leland Melvin

RIPON
65— Phillip Steans
69— Steven Thompson
80— Thomas Klofta

RUTGERS
90— Steven Tardy

ST. CLOUD ST.
90— Richard Rodgers

ST. FRANCIS (PA.)
87— Christopher Tantlinger
99— Matthew Farabaugh

ST. JOHN'S (MINN.)
92— Denis McDonough
96— Christopher Palmer

ST. JOSEPH'S (IND.)
80— Michael Bettinger

ST. NORBERT
66— Michael Ryan
88— Matthew Lang

ST. PAUL'S
80— Gerald Hicks

ST. THOMAS (MINN.)
75— Mark Dienhart
97— Christopher Esterley
00— Greg Kaiser

SAN DIEGO
96— Douglas Popovich
00— Michael Stadler

SAN DIEGO ST.
99— Scott Auerbach

SANTA CLARA
72— Ronald Sani
77— Mark Tiernan
81— *David Alfaro
85— Alexis Vlahos
87— Patrick Sende

SEWANEE
65— Frank Stubblefield
66— Douglas Paschall
69— James Beene
71— John Popham IV
77— Dudley West
82— Gregory Worsowicz
     Domenick Reina
83— Michael York
84— Michael Jordan
93— Jason Forrester
94— Frederick Cravens
96— Stephen Tudor

SHIPPENSBURG
77— Anthony Winter

SIMPSON
71— Richard Clogg
74— Hugh Lickiss
90— Roger Grover
94— Chad Earwood

SLIPPERY ROCK
98— David Sabolcik Jr.
00— Tim Kusniez

SOUTH CAROLINA
67— Steven Stanley Juk Jr.

SOUTH DAKOTA
79— Michael Schurrer
87— Todd Salat
93— Jason Seurer

SOUTH DAKOTA ST.
80— Charles Loewen
81— Paul Kippley
88— Daniel Sonnek
95— Jacob Hines

SOUTHEASTERN LA.
74— William Percy Jr.

SOUTHERN U.
70— Alden Roche

SOUTHERN CALIFORNIA
66— Charles Arrobio
69— Steven Sogge
70— Harry Khasigian
     Steve Lehmer
74— Monte Doris
75— Patrick Haden
76— Kevin Bruce
78— Gary Bethel
80— Brad Budde
     Paul McDonald
81— Gordon Adams
     *Jeffrey Fisher
85— Duane Bickett
86— Anthony Colorito
     *Matthew Koart
87— Jeffrey Bregel
90— John Jackson
96— Jeremy Hogue
97— Matthew Keneley

SOUTHERN COLO.
70— Gregory Smith
73— Collon Kennedy III

SOUTHERN METHODIST
83— *Brian O'Meara
85— *Monte Goen
87— David Adamson
93— Cary Brabham

SOUTHERN MISS.
83— Richard Thompson
84— Stephen Carmody

SOUTHERN UTAH
92— Stephen McDowell

SOUTHWEST MO. ST.
80— Richard Suchenski
     Mitchel Ware
85— Michael Armentrout
00— Travis Brawner

SOUTHWEST TEX. ST.
82— Michael Miller

STANFORD
65— *Joe Neal
66— *Terry DeSylvia
68— John Root
71— John Sande III
72— Jackie Brown
74— Randall Poltl
75— *Keith Rowen
76— Gerald Wilson
77— Duncan McColl
81— Milton McColl
84— John Bergren
85— Scott Carpenter
86— Matthew Soderlund
87— Brian Morris
88— Douglas Robison
95— Stephen Stenstrom
96— Eric Abrams
     David Walker
97— Marlon Evans

STONEHILL
93— Kevin Broderick

SUSQUEHANNA
77— Gerald Huesken
82— Daniel Distasio

SWARTHMORE
72— Christopher Leinberger
83— *John Walsh

SYRACUSE
78— *Robert Avery
86— Timothy Green
94— Patrick O'Neill
95— Eric Chenoweth

TEMPLE
74— Dwight Fulton

TENNESSEE
71— Donald Denbo
     Timothy Priest
77— Michael Mauck
81— Timothy Irwin
98— Peyton Manning

TEXAS
69— Corbin Robertson Jr.
71— Willie Zapalac Jr.
73— *Michael Bayer
74— Patrick Kelly
75— Wade Johnston
76— Robert Simmons
77— William Hamilton
97— Patrick Fitzgerald

TEXAS-ARLINGTON
69— Michael Baylor

UTEP
80— Eddie Forkerway
89— Patrick Hegarty
92— Robert Sesich

TEXAS A&M
69— Edward Hargett
71— David Elmendorf
72— Stephen Luebbehusen
88— Kip Corrington

TCU
67— John Richards
68— Eldon Gresham Jr.
73— Scott Walker
75— Terry Drennan
88— J. Clinton Hailey

TEXAS SOUTHERN
65— Leon Hardy

TEXAS TECH
65— James Ellis Jr.
68— John Scovell
75— Jeffrey Jobe
78— *Richard Arledge
85— *Bradford White
90— Thomas Mathiasmeier
00— Jesse Cockrum

THOMAS MORE
98— Michael Bramlage Jr.

TOLEDO
82— Tad Wampfler
89— Kenneth Moyer
95— Chadd Dehn
97— Craig Dues

TRINITY (CONN.)
67— *Howard Wrzosek
68— Keith Miles

TRINITY (TEX.)
84— *Peter Broderick
95— Martin Thompson
98— Mark Byarlay
     Jack Doran
00— Bo Edwards

TROY ST.
75— Mark King

TRUMAN
83— Roy Pettibone
99— Thomas Hernandez

TUFTS
65— Peter Smith
70— Robert Bass
79— *Don Leach
80— *James Ford
82— *Brian Gallagher
87— Robert Patz
92— Paulo Oliveira

TULSA
67— *Larry Williams
75— James Mack Lancaster II
98— Levi Gillen

TUSKEGEE
68— James Greene

UCLA
67— *Raymond Armstrong
     Dallas Grider
70— Gregory Jones
74— Steven Klosterman
76— John Sciarra
77— Jeffrey Dankworth
78— John Fowler Jr.
83— Cormac Carney
84— Richard Neuheisel
86— Michael Hartmeier
90— Richard Meyer
93— Carlton Gray
96— George Kase
99— Shawn Stuart
     Christian Sailer
00— Danny Farmer

UNION (N.Y.)
88— Richard Romer

UTAH
81— James Baldwin
93— Steven Young
95— Jason Jones

UTAH ST.
67— Ronnie Edwards
68— Garth Hall
70— Gary Anderson
76— Randall Stockham

VALDOSTA ST.
95— Christopher Hatcher

VALPARAISO
75— *Richard Seall

VANDERBILT
73— Barrett Sutton Jr.
75— Douglas Martin

VILLANOVA
77— David Graziano
89— Richard Spugnardi

VIRGINIA
67— Frederick Jones
83— Patrick Chester
94— Thomas Burns Jr.
96— Patrick Jeffers
98— Stephen Phelan Jr.

VMI
79— Robert Bookmiller
80— Richard Craig Jones

VIRGINIA TECH
73— Thomas Carpenito
97— Brandon Semones

WABASH
74— *Mark Nicolini
81— *Melvin Gore
83— David Broecker
87— James Herrmann
92— William Padgett

WAKE FOREST
70— Joseph Dobner
74— *Daniel Stroup
76— Thomas Fehring
78— *Michael McGlamry
83— Philip Denfeld
87— Toby Cole Jr.

WARTBURG
75— Conrad Mandsager
76— James Charles Peterson
82— *Rod Feddersen
94— Koby Kreinbring
96— Vincent Penningroth

WASHINGTON
65— William Douglas
67— Michael Ryan
72— *James Krieg
73— John Brady
77— Scott Phillips
78— Blair Bush
80— Bruce Harrell
82— Mark Jerue
83— Charles Nelson
     Mark Stewart

AWARD WINNERS

88— David Rill
92— Edward Cunningham
97— David Janoski
WASHINGTON (MO.)
94— Aaron Keen
98— Bradley Klein
WASH. & JEFF.
70— Edward Guna
82— Max Regula
91— David Conn
93— Raymond Cross Jr.
95— Michael Jones
WASH. & LEE
70— Michael Thornton
74— William Wallace Jr.
78— Jeffrey Slatcoff
79— Richard Wiles
80— *Scott Smith
81— Lonnie Nunley III
89— Michael Magoline
WASHINGTON ST.
67— Richard Sheron
68— A. Douglas Flansburg
83— Gregory Porter
84— Patrick Lynch Jr.
85— Daniel Lynch
WAYNE ST. (MICH.)
76— Edward Skowneski Jr.
81— Phillip Emery
WEBER ST.
68— Phillip Tuckett
74— *Douglas Smith
92— David Hall
94— Deric Gurley
98— Cameron Quayle

WESLEYAN (CONN.)
67— John Dwyer
69— Stuart Blackburn
71— James Lynch
78— John McVicar
00— Matt Perceval
WEST TEX. A&M
75— *Ben Bentley
82— Kevin Dennis
WEST VIRGINIA
74— Ade Dillion
    *Daniel Larcamp
82— Oliver Luck
WESTERN CARO.
94— Thomas Jackson III
WESTERN ILL.
89— Paul Singer
WESTERN KY.
72— Jimmy Barber
80— Charles DeLacey
WESTERN MD.
99— Thomas Lapato
WESTERN MICH.
68— Martin Barski
71— Jonathan Bull
WESTERN N.M.
68— Richard Mahoney
WESTERN ST.
98— Jason Eves
WESTMINSTER (PA.)
99— Brian Mihok
WHEATON (ILL.)
89— David Lauber
93— Bart Moseman

96— Pedro Arruza
99— Timothy Hardy
WHITTIER
76— John Getz
79— Mark Deven
87— *Timothy Younger
WILLAMETTE
87— *Gerry Preston
WILLIAM & MARY
78— G. Kenneth Smith
80— Clarence Gaines
85— Mark Kelso
WILLIAM JEWELL
66— Charles Scrogin
70— Thomas Dunn
    John Johnston
WILLIAMS
65— Jerry Jones
72— John Murray
95— Nathan Sleeper
96— Medley Gatewood
WINONA ST.
95— Nathan Gruber
WINSTON-SALEM
84— Eddie Sauls
WISCONSIN
66— David Fronek
80— Thomas Stauss
82— *David Mohapp
83— Mathew Vanden Boom
WIS.-LA CROSSE
97— Troy Harcey
WIS.-OSHKOSH
00— Craig Pierstorff

WIS.-PLATTEVILLE
87— Michael Hintz
WIS.-STEVENS POINT
98— Joel Hornby
00— Andy Palzkill
WIS.-WHITEWATER
96— Scott Hawig
WITTENBERG
82— William Beach
98— Kent Rafey
WOOSTER
80— Edward Blake Moore
00— Matt Mahaffey
WYOMING
74— Steven Cockreham
85— Bob Gustafson
89— Randall Welniak
96— Joseph Cummings
98— Jay Korth
    Cory Wedel
XAVIER (OHIO)
65— William Eastlake
YALE
66— *James Groninger
67— Howard Hilgendorf Jr.
69— Frederick Morris
71— Thomas Neville
72— David Bliss
75— John Burkus
77— *Stone Phillips
79— William Crowley
82— Richard Diana
91— Vincent Mooney
96— Matthew Siskosky
YOUNGSTOWN ST.
96— Mark Brungard

Academic All-America Hall of Fame

Since its inception in 1988, 36 former NCAA football players have been inducted into the GTE Academic All-America Hall of Fame. They were selected from among nominees by the College Sports Information Directors of America from past academic all-Americans of the 1950s, '60s, '70s and '80s. Following are the football selections by the year selected and each player's team, position and last year played:

1988
Pete Dawkins, Army, HB, 1958
Pat Haden, Southern California, QB, 1974
Rev. Donn Moomaw, UCLA, LB, 1953
Merlin Olsen, Utah St., T, 1961
1989
Carlos Alvarez, Florida, WR, 1971
Willie Bogan, Dartmouth, DB, 1970
Steve Bramwell, Washington, DB, 1965
Joe Romig, Colorado, G, 1961
Jim Swink, TCU, B, 1956
John Wilson, Michigan St., DB, 1952
1990
Joe Theismann, Notre Dame, QB, 1970
Howard Twilley, Tulsa, TE, 1965
1991
Terry Baker, Oregon St., QB, 1962
Joe Holland, Cornell, RB, 1978
David Joyner, Penn St., OT, 1971
Brock Strom, Air Force, T, 1958

1992
Alan Ameche, Wisconsin, RB, 1954
Stephen Eisenhauer, Navy, G, 1953
Randy Gradishar, Ohio St., LB, 1973
1993
Raymond Berry, Southern Methodist, E, 1954
Dave Casper, Notre Dame, E, 1973
Jim Grabowski, Illinois, FB, 1965
1994
Richard Mayo, Air Force, QB, 1961
Lee Roy Selmon, Oklahoma, DT, 1975
1995
Pat Richter, Wisconsin, E, 1962
1996
Wade Mitchell, Georgia Tech, QB, 1956
Bob Thomas, Notre Dame, K, 1973
Byron "Whizzer" White, Colorado, HB, 1937 (honorary selection)

1997
Todd Blackledge, Penn St., QB, 1983
Tim Foley, Purdue, DB, 1970
1998
Bernie Kosar, Miami (Fla.), QB, 1984
Jack Mildren, Oklahoma, QB, 1971
Marv Levy, Coe, RB, 1949 (honorary selection)
1999
John Fowler, UCLA, LB, 1978
Chad Hennings, Air Force, DL, 1988
2000
Oliver Luck, West Virginia, QB, 1981

Academic All-Americans by School

Since 1952, academic all-America teams have been selected by the College Sports Information Directors of America. To be eligible, student-athletes must be regular performers and have at least a 3.200 grade-point average (on a 4.000 scale) during their college careers. University division teams (I-A and I-AA) are complete in this list, but college division teams (II, III, NAIA) before 1970 are missing from CoSIDA archives, with few exceptions. Following are all known first-team selections:

ABILENE CHRISTIAN
63—Jack Griggs, LB
70—Jim Lindsey, QB
74—Greg Stirman, E
76—Bill Curbo, T
77—Bill Curbo, T
87—Bill Clayton, DL
88—Bill Clayton, DL
89—Bill Clayton, DL
90—Sean Grady, WR
ADRIAN
84—Steve Dembowski, QB
94—Jay Overmyer, DB

AIR FORCE
58—Brock Strom, T
59—Rich Mayo, B
60—Rich Mayo, B
70—Ernie Jennings, E
71—Darryl Haas, LB/K
72—Bob Homburg, DE
    Mark Prill, LB
73—Joe Debes, OT
74—Joe Debes, OT
78—Steve Hoog, WR
81—Mike France, LB
83—Jeff Kubiak, P
86—Chad Hennings, DL

ACADEMIC ALL-AMERICANS BY SCHOOL

87—Chad Hennings, DL
88—David Hlatky, OL
90—Chris Howard, RB
92—Grant Johnson, LB
AKRON
80—Andy Graham, PK
UAB
97—Johnny Rea, OL
ALABAMA
61—Tommy Brooker, E
Pat Trammell, B
64—Gaylon McCollough, C
65—Steve Sloan, QB
Dennis Homan, HB
67—Steve Davis, K
Bob Childs, LB
70—Johnny Musso, HB
71—Johnny Musso, HB
73—Randy Hall, DT
74—Randy Hall, DT
75—Danny Ridgeway, KS
79—Major Ogilvie, RB
ALABAMA A&M
89—Tracy Kendall, QB
90—Tracy Kendall, QB
ALBANY (N.Y.)
86—Thomas Higgins, OT
87—Thomas Higgins, OT
94—Andy Shein, WR
95—Rich Tallarico, OL
ALBION
82—Bruce Drogosch, LB
86—Michael Grant, DB
90—Scott Bissell, DB
93—Eric Baxmann, LB
Jeffrey Shooks, P
94—Jeffrey Shooks, P
95—David Lefere, DB
96—David Lefere, DB
ALFRED
89—Mark Szynkowski, OL
ALLEGHENY
81—Kevin Baird, P
91—Adam Lechman, OL
Darren Hadlock, LB
ALMA
86—Greg Luczak, TE
98—Rick Brands, PK
99—Dustin Armstrong, DB
AMERICAN INT'L
81—Todd Scyocurka, LB
99—Dan Grant, WR
ANGELO ST.
98—Kyle Kirk, LB
APPALACHIAN ST.
77—Gill Beck, C
92—D. J. Campbell, QB
ARIZONA
68—Mike Moody, OG
75—Jon Abbott, LB
76—Jon Abbott, T/LB
77—Jon Abbott, T/LB
79—Jeffrey Whitton, DL
87—Charles Cecil, DB
96—Wayne Wyatt, OL
ARIZONA ST.
66—Ken Dyer, OE
88—Mark Tingstad, LB
97—Patrick Tillman, LB
ARKANSAS
57—Gerald Nesbitt, FB
61—Lance Alworth, B
64—Ken Hatfield, B
65—Randy Stewart, C
Jim Lindsey, HB
Jack Brasuell, DB
68—Bob White, K
69—Bill Burnett, HB
Terry Stewart, DB
78—Brad Shoup, DB
ARK.-MONTICELLO
85—Ray Howard, OG
88—Sean Rochelle, QB

ARKANSAS ST.
59—Larry Zabrowski, OT
61—Jim McMurray, QB
ARKANSAS TECH
90—Karl Kuhn, TE
91—Karl Kuhn, TE
ARMY
55—Ralph Chesnauskas, E
57—James Kernan, C
Pete Dawkins, HB
58—Pete Dawkins, HB
59—Don Usry, E
65—Sam Champi, DE
67—Bud Neswiacheny, DE
69—Theodore Shadid, C
89—Michael Thorson, DB
92—Mike McElrath, DB
94—Eric Oliver, LB
ASHLAND
73—Mark Gulling, DB
74—Ron Brown, LB
76—Dan Bogden, E
77—Bruce Niehm, LB
81—Mark Braun, C
91—Thomas Shiban, RB
93—Jerry Spatny, DL
96—Chad DiFranco, DB
AUBURN
57—Jimmy Phillips, E
59—Jackie Burkett, C
60—Ed Dyas, B
65—Bill Cody, LB
69—Buddy McClinton, DB
74—Bobby Davis, LB
75—Chuck Fletcher, DT
76—Chris Vacarella, RB
84—Gregg Carr, LB
94—Matt Hawkins, PK
AUGSBURG
81—Paul Elliott, DL
97—Ted Schultz, TE
AUGUSTANA (ILL.)
75—George Wesbey, T
80—Bill Dannehl, WR
84—Steve Sanders, OT
85—Steve Sanders, OT
95—Ryan Carpenter, OL
96—Ryan Carpenter, OL
97—Chris Meskan, OL
98—Chris Meskan, OL
AUGUSTANA (S.D.)
72—Pat McNerney, T
73—Pat McNerney, T
74—Jim Clemens, G
75—Jim Clemens, C
77—Stan Biondi, K
86—David Gubbrud, DL
87—David Gubbrud, DL
88—David Gubbrud, LB
89—David Gubbrud, LB
96—Mitchell Pruett, TE
97—Thayne Munce, OL
AUSTIN
81—Gene Branum, PK
99—Joe Fox, OL
AUSTIN PEAY
74—Gregory Johnson, G
BAKER
61—John Jacobs, B
BALDWIN-WALLACE
70—Earl Stolberg, DB
72—John Yezerski, G
78—Roger Andrachik, RB
Greg Monda, LB
81—Chuck Krajacic, OG
88—Shawn Gorman, P
91—Tom Serdinak, P
93—Adrian Allison, DL
David Coverdale, DL
94—David Coverdale, DL
BALL ST.
83—Rich Chitwood, C
85—Ron Duncan, TE
86—Ron Duncan, TE
87—Ron Duncan, TE
88—Ted Ashburn, OL

Greg Shackelford, DL
89—Ted Ashburn, OL
David Haugh, DB
91—Troy Hoffer, DB
92—Troy Hoffer, DB
BATES
82—Neal Davidson, DB
BAYLOR
61—Ronnie Bull, RB
62—Don Trull, QB
63—Don Trull, QB
76—Cris Quinn, DE
89—Mike Welch, DB
90—Mike Welch, DB
96—Ty Atteberry, P
BELOIT
90—Shane Stadler, RB
BETHANY (KAN.)
86—Wade Gaeddert, DB
BLOOMSBURG
83—Dave Pepper, DL
BOISE ST.
71—Brent McIver, IL
73—Glenn Sparks, G
78—Sam Miller, DB
BOSTON COLLEGE
77—Richard Scudellari, LB
86—Michael Degnan, DL
BOSTON U.
83—Steve Shapiro, K
85—Brad Hokin, DB
93—Andre Maksimov, OL
94—Andre Maksimov, OL
BOWDOIN
84—Mike Siegel, P
93—Michael Turmelle, DB
BOWLING GREEN
75—John Boles, DE
89—Pat Jackson, LB
90—Pat Jackson, TE
BRIGHAM YOUNG
73—Steve Stratton, RB
80—Scott Phillips, RB
81—Dan Plater, WR
87—Chuck Cutler, WR
88—Chuck Cutler, WR
Tim Clark, DL
89—Fred Whittingham, RB
90—Andy Boyce, WR
93—Eric Drage, WR
BROCKPORT ST.
97—Tom Massey, DB
98—Tom Massey, DB
BROWN
81—Travis Holcombe, OG
82—Dave Folsom, DB
86—Marty Edwards, C
87—John Cuozzo, C
BUCKNELL
72—Douglas Nauman, T
John Ondrasik, DB
73—John Dailey, LB
74—Steve Leskinen, T
75—Larry Brunt, E
76—Larry Brunt, E
84—Rob Masonis, RB
Jim Reilly, TE
86—Mike Morrow, WR
91—David Berardinelli, WR
92—David Berardinelli, WR
BUENA VISTA
99—Ben Smith, RB
BUFFALO
63—Gerry Philbin, T
84—Gerry Quinlivan, LB
85—James Dunbar, C
86—James Dunbar, C
98—Dan Poulsen, DL
BUFFALO ST.
87—Clint Morano, OT
BUTLER
84—Steve Kollias, L
98—Nick Batalis, OL

Mike Goletz, DL
99—Mike Goletz, LB
C. W. POST
70—Art Canario, T
75—Frank Prochilo, RB
84—Bob Jahelka, DB
93—Jim Byrne, WR
CALIFORNIA
67—Bob Crittenden, DG
70—Robert Richards, OT
82—Harvey Salem, OT
UC DAVIS
72—Steve Algeo, LB
75—Dave Gellerman, LB
90—Mike Shepard, DL
98—Wes Terrell, TE
UC RIVERSIDE
71—Tyrone Hooks, HB
CAL LUTHERAN
81—John Walsh, OT
CANISIUS
82—Tom Schott, WR
83—Tom Schott, TE
86—Mike Panepinto, RB
CAPITAL
70—Ed Coy, E
83—Mike Linton, G
85—Kevin Sheets, WR
CARLETON
92—Scott Hanks, TE
CARNEGIE MELLON
76—Rick Lackner, LB
Dave Nackoul, E
84—Roger Roble, WR
87—Bryan Roessler, DL
Chris Haupt, LB
89—Robert O'Toole, LB
90—Frank Bellante, RB
Robert O'Toole, LB
94—Aaron Neal, TE
Merle Atkinson, DL
98—Jason Funke, DB
CARROLL (WIS.)
76—Stephen Thompson, QB
CARSON-NEWMAN
61—David Dale, E
93—Chris Horton, OL
94—Chris Horton, OL
CARTHAGE
61—Bob Halsey, B
77—Mark Phelps, QB
CASE RESERVE
75—John Kosko, T
82—Jim Donnelly, RB
83—Jim Donnelly, RB
84—Jim Donnelly, RB
88—Chris Hutter, TE
90—Michael Bissler, DB
95—Doug Finefrock, LB
96—Tom Mager, LB
Kenyon Meadows, DL
CENTRAL (IOWA)
79—Chris Adkins, LB
85—Scott Lindrell, LB
86—Scott Lindrell, LB
91—Rich Kacmarynski, RB
CENTRAL MICH.
70—Ralph Burde, DL
74—Mike Franckowiak, QB
John Wunderlich, T
79—Mike Ball, WR
84—John DeBoer, WR
91—Jeff Bender, QB
CENTRAL MO. ST.
97—Shane Meyer, PK
CENTRE
84—Teel Bruner, DB
85—Teel Bruner, DB
89—Bryan Ellington, DB
91—Eric Horstmyer, WR
CHADRON ST.
73—Jerry Sutton, LB
75—Bob Lacey, KS

AWARD WINNERS

79—Jerry Carder, TE
95—Corey Campbell, RB
99—Casey Beran, DL

CHAPMAN
96—Matt Hertzler, OL
97—Matt Hertzler, OL

CHEYNEY
75—Steve Anderson, G

CHICAGO
87—Paul Haar, OG
88—Paul Haar, OL
93—Frank Baker, RB

CINCINNATI
81—Kari Yli-Renko, OT
90—Kyle Stroh, DL
91—Kris Bjorson, TE
97—John Kobalka, DL

CITADEL
63—Vince Petno, E
76—Kenny Caldwell, LB
77—Kenny Caldwell, LB
78—Kenny Caldwell, LB
87—Thomas Frooman, RB
89—Thomas Frooman, RB

CLARION
96—Steve Witte, RB

CLEMSON
59—Lou Cordileone, T
78—Steve Fuller, QB
99—Kyle Young, OL

COAST GUARD
70—Charles Pike, LB
71—Bruce Melnick, DB
81—Mark Butt, DB

COE
93—Marcus Adkins, DL

COLGATE
78—Angelo Colosimo, RB
79—Angelo Colosimo, RB
85—Tom Stenglein, WR
89—Jeremy Garvey, TE

COLORADO
60—Joe Romig, G
61—Joe Romig, G
67—Kirk Tracy, OG
70—Jim Cooch, DB
73—Rick Stearns, LB
74—Rick Stearns, LB
75—Steve Young, DT
87—Eric McCarty, LB
90—Jim Hansen, OL
91—Jim Hansen, OL
92—Jim Hansen, OL
96—Ryan Olson, DL
97—Ryan Olson, DL

COLORADO COL.
96—Ryan Egeland, OL
    Ryan Haygood, DL

COLORADO MINES
72—Dave Chambers, RB
83—Charles Lane, T

COLORADO ST.
55—Gary Glick, B
69—Tom French, OT
86—Steve Bartalo, RB
95—Greg Myers, DB
98—Mike Newell, OL
    Nate Kvamme, LB

COLUMBIA
52—Mitch Price, B
53—John Gasella, T
56—Claude Benham, B
71—John Sefcik, HB

CORNELL
77—Joseph Holland, RB
78—Joseph Holland, RB
82—Derrick Harmon, RB
83—Derrick Harmon, RB
85—Dave Van Metre, DL

CORNELL COLLEGE
72—Rob Ash, QB
    Dewey Birkhofer, S
76—Joe Lauterbach, G
    Tom Zinkula, DT

77—Tom Zinkula, DT
78—Tom Zinkula, DL
82—John Ward, WR
91—Bruce Feldmann, QB
92—Brent Sands, DB
93—Mark McDermott, DB
94—Mark McDermott, DB
95—Mike Tressel, DB
97—Matt Weiss, DL
98—Matt Weiss, DL

CULVER-STOCKTON
95—Mason Kaiser, DB

DARTMOUTH
70—Willie Bogan, DB
83—Michael Patsis, DB
87—Paul Sorensen, LB
88—Paul Sorensen, LB
90—Brad Preble, DB
91—Mike Bobo, WR
    Tom Morrow, LB
92—Russ Torres, RB
94—David Shearer, WR
    Zach Lehman, DL
97—Dominic Lanza, OL

DAYTON
71—Tim Quinn, LB
72—Tim Quinn, DT
79—Scott Terry, QB
84—Greg French, K
    David Kemp, LB
    Jeff Slayback, L
85—Greg French, K
86—Gerry Meyer, OT
91—Brett Cuthbert, DB
    Dan Rosenbaum, DB
92—Steve Lochow, DL
    Dan Rosenbaum, DB
93—Steve Lochow, DL
    Brad Mager, DB
94—David Overhoiser, RB
96—Josh Lemmon, OL
98—Jacob Jones, RB
99—Jimmy Lee, RB

DEFIANCE
80—Jill Bailey, OT
    Mark Bockelman, TE

DELAWARE
70—Yancey Phillips, T
71—Robert Depew, DE
72—Robert Depew, DE

DELAWARE VALLEY
84—Dan Glowatski, WR

DELTA ST.
70—Hal Posey, RB
74—Billy Hood, E
    Ricky Lewis, LB
    Larry Miller, RB
75—Billy Hood, E
78—Terry Moody, DB
79—Charles Stavley, G

DENISON
75—Dennis Thome, LB
87—Grant Jones, DB
98—Jonathan Dunham, DB
99—Jonathan Dunham, DB

DePAUW
70—Jim Ceaser, LB
71—Jim Ceaser, LB
73—Neil Oslos, RB
80—Jay True, WR
85—Tony deNicola, QB
87—Michael Sherman, DB
90—Tom Beaulieu, DL
91—Tom Beaulieu, DL
    Matt Nelson, LB
94—Mike Callahan, LB

DICKINSON
74—Gerald Urich, RB
79—Scott Mumma, RB

DRAKE
74—Todd Gaffney, KS
83—Tom Holt, RB

DREXEL
70—Lynn Ferguson, S

DUBUQUE
80—Tim Finn, RB

DUKE
66—Roger Hayes, DE
67—Bob Lasky, DT
70—Curt Rawley, DT
86—Mike Diminick, DB
87—Mike Diminick, DB
88—Mike Diminick, DB
89—Doug Key, DL
93—Travis Pearson, LB

EAST STROUDSBURG
84—Ernie Siegrist, TE

EAST TENN. ST.
71—Ken Oster, DB

EASTERN ILL.
95—Tim Carver, LB

EASTERN KY.
77—Steve Frommeyer, S

EASTERN N.M.
80—Tom Sager, DL
81—Tom Sager, DL

EASTERN WASH.
97—Jeff Ogden, WR
    Steve Mattson, DL

ELON
73—John Rascoe, E
79—Bryan Burney, DB

EMORY & HENRY
71—Tom Wilson, LB

EMPORIA ST.
79—Tom Lingg, DL

EVANSVILLE
74—David Mattingly, S
76—Michael Pociask, C
87—Jeffery Willman, TE
97—Sean Bennett, RB

FERRIS ST.
81—Vic Trecha, OT
92—Monty Brown, LB

FINDLAY
97—Bo Hurley, QB

FLORIDA
65—Charles Casey, E
69—Carlos Alvarez, WR
71—Carlos Alvarez, WR
76—David Posey, KS
77—Wes Chandler, RB
80—Cris Collinsworth, WR
91—Brad Culpepper, DL
93—Michael Gilmore, DB
94—Terry Dean, QB
    Michael Gilmore, DB
95—Danny Wuerffel, QB
96—Danny Wuerffel, QB

FLORIDA A&M
90—Irvin Clark, DL

FLORIDA ST.
72—Gary Huff, QB
79—William Jones, DB
    Phil Williams, WR
80—William Jones, DB
81—Rohn Stark, P
94—Derrick Brooks, LB
96—Daryl Bush, LB
97—Daryl Bush, LB

FORDHAM
90—Eric Schweiker, OL

FORT HAYS ST.
75—Greg Custer, RB
82—Ron Johnson, P
85—Paul Nelson, DL
86—Paul Nelson, DL
89—Dean Gengler, OL

FORT LEWIS
72—Dee Tennison, E

FRANK. & MARSH.
77—Joe Fry, DB
78—Joe Fry, DB

FURMAN
76—Jeff Holcomb, T
85—Brian Jager, RB
88—Kelly Fletcher, DL
89—Kelly Fletcher, DL
    Chris Roper, LB

91—Eric Walter, OL
99—Stuart Rentz, RB

GEORGETOWN
71—Gerry O'Dowd, HB
86—Andrew Phelan, OG

GEORGETOWN (KY.)
89—Eric Chumbley, OL
92—Bobby Wasson, PK

GEORGIA
60—Francis Tarkenton, QB
65—Bob Etter, K
66—Bob Etter, K
    Lynn Hughes, DB
68—Bill Stanfill, DT
71—Tom Nash, OT
    Mixon Robinson, DE
77—Jeff Lewis, LB
82—Terry Hoage, DB
83—Terry Hoage, DB
92—Todd Peterson, PK
97—Matt Stinchcomb, OL
98—Matt Stinchcomb, OL

GA. SOUTHERN
95—Rob Stockton, DB
99—Voncellies Allen, DL

GA. SOUTHWESTERN
87—Gregory Slappery, RB

GEORGIA TECH
52—Ed Gossage, T
    Cecil Trainer, DE
    Larry Morris, LB
55—Wade Mitchell, B
56—Allen Ecker, G
66—Jim Breland, C
    W. J. Blaine, LB
    Bill Eastman, DB
67—Bill Eastman, DB
80—Sheldon Fox, LB
90—Stefen Scotton, RB
99—Dan Dyke, P

GETTYSBURG
79—Richard Swartz, LB

GRAMBLING
72—Floyd Harvey, RB
93—Gilad Landau, PK

GRAND VALLEY ST.
91—Mark Smith, OL
    Todd Wood, DB

GRINNELL
71—Edward Hirsch, E
81—David Smiley, TE
98—Richard Wemer, WR

GROVE CITY
74—Pat McCoy, LB
89—Travis Croll, P

GUST. ADOLPHUS
80—Dave Najarian, DL
81—Dave Najarian, LB
98—Dan Duncan, OL
99—Dan Duncan, OL

HAMLINE
73—Thomas Dufresne, E
89—Jon Voss, TE

HAMPDEN-SYDNEY
82—John Dickinson, OG
90—W. R. Jones, OL
91—David Brickhill, PK

HAMPTON
93—Tim Benson, WR

HARVARD
99—Ben Green, DB

HAWAII
97—Chris Shinnick, DB

HEIDELBERG
82—Jeff Kurtzman, DL
99—Joe Conduah, LB

HENDERSON ST.
98—Lee Daily, LB

HILLSDALE
61—James Richendollar, T
72—John Cervini, G
81—Mark Kellogg, LB
93—Jason Ahee, DB
96—Kyle Wojciechowski, OL

ACADEMIC ALL-AMERICANS BY SCHOOL

HOLY CROSS
83—Bruce Kozerski, T
85—Kevin Reilly, OT
87—Jeff Wiley, QB
91—Pete Dankert, DL

HOPE
73—Ronald Posthuma, T
79—Craig Groendyk, T
80—Greg Bekius, PK
82—Kurt Brinks, C
84—Scott Jecmen, DB
86—Timothy Chase, OG

HOUSTON
64—Horst Paul, E
76—Mark Mohr, DB
    Kevin Rollwage, OT
77—Kevin Rollwage, OT

IDAHO
70—Bruce Langmeade, T

IDAHO ST.
84—Brent Koetter, DB
91—Steve Boyenger, DB
96—Trevor Bell, DB

ILLINOIS
52—Bob Lenzini, DT
64—Jim Grabowski, FB
65—Jim Grabowski, FB
66—John Wright, E
70—Jim Rucks, DE
71—Bob Bucklin, DE
80—Dan Gregus, DL
81—Dan Gregus, DL
82—Dan Gregus, DL
91—Mike Hopkins, DB
92—John Wright Jr., WR
94—Brett Larsen, P
99—Josh Whitman, TE

ILLINOIS COL.
80—Jay Wessler, RB
94—Warren Dodson, OL

ILLINOIS ST.
76—Tony Barnes, C
80—Jeff Hembrough, DL
89—Dan Hackman, OL
95—Keith Goodnight, RB

ILL. WESLEYAN
71—Keith Ihlanfeldt, DE
80—Jim Eaton, DL
    Rick Hanna, DL
    Mike Watson, DB
81—Mike Watson, DB
91—Chris Bisaillon, WR
92—Chris Udovich, DL
95—Jason Richards, TE
96—Lon Erickson, QB

INDIANA
67—Harry Gonso, HB
72—Glenn Scolnik, RB
80—Kevin Speer, C
94—John Hammerstein, DL

INDIANA (PA.)
82—Kenny Moore, DB
83—Kenny Moore, DB

INDIANA ST.
71—Gary Brown, E
72—Michael Eads, E

INDIANAPOLIS
76—William Willan, E
95—Ted Munson, DL

IONA
80—Neal Kurtti, DL

IOWA
52—Bill Fenton, DE
53—Bill Fenton, DE
75—Bob Elliott, DB
85—Larry Station, LB

IOWA ST.
52—Max Burkett, DB
82—Mark Carlson, LB
99—Dave Brcka, LB

ITHACA
72—Dana Hallenbeck, LB
85—Brian Dougherty, DB
89—Peter Burns, OL

JACKSONVILLE ST.
77—Dewey Barker, E
78—Dewey Barker, TE

JAMES MADISON
78—Warren Coleman, OT

JOHN CARROLL
83—Nick D'Angelo, LB
    Jim Sferra, DL
85—Joe Burrello, LB
86—Joe Burrello, LB

JOHNS HOPKINS
77—Charles Hauck, DT
93—Michael House, DL
94—Michael House, DL
98—Chris Baugh, OL

JUNIATA
70—Ray Grabiak, DL
71—Ray Grabiak, DE
    Maurice Taylor, IL

KALAMAZOO
92—Sean Mullendore, LB

KANSAS
64—Fred Elder, T
67—Mike Sweatman, LB
68—Dave Morgan, LB
71—Mike McCoy, C
76—Tom Fitch, S
95—Darrin Simmons, P

KANSAS ST.
74—Don Lareau, LB
77—Floyd Dorsey, OG
81—Darren Gale, DB
82—Darren Gale, DB
    Mark Hundley, RB
85—Troy Faunce, P
95—Kevin Lockett, WR
96—Kevin Lockett, WR
    Jason Johnson, OL

KENT ST.
72—Mark Reihled, DB
91—Brad Smith, RB

KENTUCKY
74—Tom Ranieri, LB
78—Mark Keene, C
    Jim Kovach, LB
85—Ken Pietrowiak, C
98—Jeff Zurcher, DB

KENYON
77—Robert Jennings, RB
85—Dan Waldeck, TE

LA VERNE
82—Scott Shier, OT

LAFAYETTE
70—William Sprecher, T
74—Mike Kline, DB
79—Ed Rogusky, RB
80—Ed Rogusky, RB

LAWRENCE
81—Chris Matheus, DL
    Scott Reppert, RB
82—Chris Matheus, DL

LEHIGH
90—Shon Harker, DB

LEWIS & CLARK
61—Pat Clock, G
81—Dan Jones, WR

LIBERTY
98—Jarrol Everson, DL

LONG BEACH ST.
83—Joe Donohue, LB

LORAS
84—John Coyle, DL
    Pete Kovatsis, DB
85—John Coyle, DL
91—Mark Goedken, DL
93—Travis Michaels, LB

LA.-MONROE
70—Tom Miller, KS
74—Mike Bialas, T

LSU
59—Mickey Mangham, E
60—Charles Strange, C
61—Billy Booth, T
71—Jay Michaelson, KS
73—Tyler Lafauci, OG
    Joe Winkler, DB
74—Brad Davis, RB
77—Robert Dugas, OT
84—Juan Carlos Betanzos, PK
94—Michael Blanchard, OL
97—Chad Kessler, P

LUTHER
83—Larry Bonney, DL
84—Larry Bonney, DL
89—Larry Anderson, RB
90—Joel Nerem, DL
91—Joel Nerem, DL
95—Karl Borge, DL

LYCOMING
74—Thomas Vanaskie, DB
85—Mike Kern, DL

MACALESTER
82—Lee Schaefer, OG

MANSFIELD
83—John Delate, DB

MARIETTA
83—Matt Wurtzbacher, DL

MARS HILL
92—Brent Taylor, DL

MARSHALL
98—Chad Pennington, QB
99—Chad Pennington, QB

MARYLAND
53—Bernie Faloney, B
75—Kim Hoover, DE
78—Joe Muffler, DL

MARYVILLE (TENN.)
99—Kevin Hedrick, DL

MASSACHUSETTS
99—Mike Wynne, OL

MASS.-LOWELL
85—Don Williams, RB

MIT
89—Anthony Lapes, WR
90—Darcy Prather, LB
91—Rodrigo Rubiano, DL
92—Roderick Tranum, WR
93—Corey Foster, OL
94—Corey Foster, OL
95—Scott Vollrath, P
96—Duane Stevens, DB
    Brad Gray, DL
97—Duane Stevens, DB
    Mike Butville, LB
    Brad Gray, DL
99—Nik Kozy, DL
    Angus Huang, DB

McGILL
87—Bruno Pietrobon, WR

McNEESE ST.
78—Jim Downing, OT
79—Jim Downing, OT
90—David Easterling, DB

MEMPHIS
92—Pat Jansen, DL

MIAMI (FLA.)
59—Fran Curci, B
84—Bernie Kosar, QB

MIAMI (OHIO)
73—Andy Pederzolli, DB

MICHIGAN
52—Dick Balzhiser, B
55—Jim Orwig, T
57—Jim Orwig, T
64—Bob Timberlake, QB
66—Dave Fisher, FB
    Dick Vidmer, FB
69—Jim Mandich, OE
70—Phil Seymour, DE
71—Bruce Elliott, DB
72—Bill Hart, OG
74—Kirk Lewis, OG
75—Dan Jilek, DE
81—Norm Betts, TE
82—Stefan Humphries, OG
    Robert Thompson, LB
83—Stefan Humphries, OG
85—Clay Miller, OT
86—Kenneth Higgins, WR
99—Rob Renes, DL

MICHIGAN ST.
52—John Wilson, DB
53—Don Dohoney, E
55—Buck Nystrom, G
57—Blanche Martin, HB
65—Don Bierowicz, DT
    Don Japinga, DB
66—Pat Gallinagh, DT
68—Al Brenner, E/DB
69—Ron Saul, OG
    Rich Saul, DE
73—John Shinsky, DT
79—Alan Davis, DB
85—Dean Altobelli, DB
86—Dean Altobelli, DB
    Shane Bullough, LB
92—Steve Wasylk, DB
93—Steve Wasylk, DB

MICHIGAN TECH
71—Larry Ras, HB
73—Bruce Trusock, C
76—Jim Van Wagner, RB
92—Kurt Coduti, QB

MIDWESTERN ST.
95—Corby Walker, LB

MILLERSVILLE
91—Tom Burns, OL

MILLIKIN
61—Gerald Domesick, B
75—Frank Stone, G
78—Charlie Sammis, K
79—Eric Stevens, WR
83—Marc Knowles, WR
84—Tom Kreller, RB
85—Cary Bottorff, LB
    Tom Kreller, RB
90—Tim Eimermann, PK

MINNESOTA
56—Bob Hobert, T
60—Frank Brixius, T
68—Bob Stein, DE
70—Barry Mayer, RB
89—Brent Herbel, P
94—Justin Conzemius, DB

MINN ST.-MANKATO
74—Dan Miller, C

MISSISSIPPI
54—Harold Easterwood, C
59—Robert Khayat, T
    Charlie Flowers, B
61—Doug Elmore, B
65—Stan Hindman, G
68—Steve Hindman, HB
69—Julius Fagan, K
74—Greg Markow, DE
77—Robert Fabris, OE
    George Plasketes, DE
80—Ken Toler, WR
86—Danny Hoskins, OG
87—Danny Hoskins, OG
88—Wesley Walls, TE
89—Todd Sandroni, DB

MISSISSIPPI COL.
75—Anthony Saway, S
78—Steve Johnson, OT
79—Steve Johnson, OT
83—Wayne Frazier, C
97—Kyle Fulcher, LB

MISSISSIPPI ST.
53—Jackie Parker, B
56—Ron Bennett, E
72—Frank Dowsing, DB
73—Jimmy Webb, DE
76—Will Coltharp, DE
89—Stacy Russell, DB

MISSOURI
62—Tom Hertz, G
66—Dan Schuppan, DE
    Bill Powell, DT
68—Carl Garber, MG
70—John Weisenfels, LB
72—Greg Hill, KS
81—Van Darkow, LB

AWARD WINNERS

93—Matt Burgess, OL
98—Jake Stueve, TE

MO.-ROLLA
72—Kim Colter, DB
80—Paul Janke, OG
86—Tom Reed, RB
87—Jim Pfeiffer, OT
88—Jim Pfeiffer, OL
91—Don Huff, DB
92—Don Huff, DB
94—Brian Gilmore, LB
95—Brian Gilmore, LB
96—Brian Gilmore, LB

MO. SOUTHERN ST.
85—Mike Testman, DB
93—Chris Tedford, OL
94—Chris Tedford, OL

MONMOUTH (ILL.)
83—Robb Long, QB

MONTANA
77—Steve Fisher, DE
79—Ed Cerkovnik, DB
88—Michael McGowan, LB
89—Michael McGowan, LB
90—Michael McGowan, LB
93—Dave Dickenson, QB
95—Matt Wells, WR
96—Josh Branen, RB
    Blaine McElmurry, DB
98—Justin Olsen, WR
99—Vince Huntsberger, DB

MONTANA ST.
84—Dirk Nelson, P
88—Anders Larsson, PK
96—Devlan Geddes, DL

MONTCLAIR ST.
70—Bill Trimmer, DL
82—Daniel Deneher, KS

MOORHEAD ST.
88—Brad Shamla, DL
99—Adam Vossen, DL
    Eric Pederson, LB

MORAVIAN
87—Jeff Pollock, WR
96—Mike Paciulli, DB

MOREHEAD ST.
74—Don Russell, KS
90—James Appel, OL
91—James Appel, OL
96—Mike Appel, OL

MORGAN ST.
96—Willie Thompson, DL

MOUNT UNION
71—Dennis Montgomery, QB
84—Rick Marabito, L
86—Scott Gindlesberger, QB
87—Paul Hrics, C
98—Darin Kershner, WR

MUHLENBERG
70—Edward Salo, G
71—Edward Salo, IL
72—Edward Salo, C
75—Keith Ordemann, LB
80—Arthur Scavone, OT
89—Joe Zeszotarski, DL
90—Mike Hoffman, DB

MURRAY ST.
76—Eddie McFarland, DB

MUSKINGUM
78—Dan Radalia, DL
79—Dan Radalia, DL

NAVY
53—Steve Eisenhauer, G
57—Tom Forrestal, QB
58—Joe Tranchini, B
69—Dan Pike, RB
80—Ted Dumbauld, LB

NEBRASKA
62—James Huge, E
63—Dennis Calridge, B
66—Marv Mueller, OG
69—Randy Reeves, DB
71—Larry Jacobson, DT
    Jeff Kinney, HB

73—Frosty Anderson, E
75—Rik Bonness, C
    Tom Heiser, RB
76—Vince Ferragamo, QB
    Ted Harvey, DB
77—Ted Harvey, DB
78—George Andrews, DL
    James Pillen, DB
79—Rod Horn, DL
    Kelly Saalfeld, C
    Randy Schleusener, OG
80—Jeff Finn, TE
    Randy Schleusener, OG
81—Eric Lindquist, DB
    David Rimington, C
    Randy Theiss, OT
82—David Rimington, C
83—Scott Strasburger, DL
    Rob Stuckey, DL
84—Scott Strasburger, DL
    Rob Stuckey, DL
    Mark Traynowicz, C
86—Dale Klein, K
    Thomas Welter, OT
87—Jeffrey Jamrog, DL
    Mark Blazek, DB
88—Mark Blazek, DB
    John Kroeker, P
89—Gerry Gdowski, QB
    Jake Young, OL
90—David Edeal, OL
    Pat Tyrance, LB
    Jim Wanek, OL
91—Pat Engelbert, DL
    Mike Stigge, P
92—Mike Stigge, P
93—Rob Zatechka, OL
    Terry Connealy, DL
    Trev Alberts, LB
94—Matt Shaw, TE
    Rob Zatechka, OL
    Terry Connealy, DL
95—Aaron Graham, OL
96—Grant Wistrom, DL
97—Joel Mackovicka, RB
    Grant Wistrom, DL
98—Joel Makovicka, RB
    Chad Kelsay, DL
    William Lafleur, P
99—Kyle Vanden Bosch, DL
    Mike Brown, DB

NEB.-KEARNEY
70—John Makovicka, RB
75—Tim Brodahl, E
99—Volker Olbrich, PK

NEB.-OMAHA
82—Kirk Hutton, DB
    Clark Toner, LB
83—Kirk Hutton, DB
84—Jerry Kripal, QB

NEB. WESLEYAN
87—Pat Sweeney, DB
88—Pat Sweeney, DB
    Mike Surls, LB
89—Scott Shaffer, RB
    Scott Shipman, DB
95—Justin Rice, DL
96—Justin Rice, DL
97—Chad Wemhoff, WR
98—Ryan Shanesy, DL

NEVADA
82—David Heppe, P

NEW HAMPSHIRE
52—John Driscoll, T
84—Dave Morton, OL

NEW MEXICO
75—Bob Johnson, S
77—Robert Rumbaugh, DT
78—Robert Rumbaugh, DL
93—Justin Hall, OL
98—Chad Smith, DB

NEW MEXICO ST.
66—Jim Bohl, B
74—Ralph Jackson, OG
75—Ralph Jackson, OG
85—Andy Weiler, KS
92—Todd Cutler, TE
    Shane Hackney, OL
    Tim Mauck, LB
93—Tim Mauck, LB

96—David Patterson, WR
97—David Patterson, WR
98—David Patterson, WR
99—Corte McGuffey, QB

NICHOLS
89—David Kane, DB

NORTH CAROLINA
64—Ken Willard, QB
85—Kevin Anthony, QB

NORTH CAROLINA ST.
60—Roman Gabriel, QB
63—Joe Scarpati, B
67—Steve Warren, OT
71—Craig John, OG
73—Justus Everett, C
    Stan Fritts, RB
74—Justus Everett, C
80—Calvin Warren, P

NORTH DAKOTA
87—Kurt Otto, QB
88—Chuck Clairmont, OL
    Matt Gulseth, OG
92—Tim Gelinske, WR
    Mark Ewen, LB
96—Tim Tibesar, LB

NORTH DAKOTA ST.
71—Tomm Smail, DT
93—T. R. McDonald, WR

NORTH PARK
83—Mike Lilgegren, DB
85—Scott Love, WR
86—Todd Love, WR
87—Todd Love, WR

NORTH TEXAS
75—Pete Morris, LB
76—Pete Morris, LB

NORTHEASTERN
85—Shawn O'Malley, LB

NORTHERN ARIZ.
89—Chris Baniszewski, WR

NORTHERN COLO.
71—Charles Putnik, OG
81—Duane Hirsch, DL
    Ray Sperger, DB
82—Jim Bright, RB
89—Mike Yonkovich, DL
    Tom Langer, LB
90—Tom Langer, LB
98—Corte McGuffey, QB
99—Corte McGuffey, QB

NORTHERN IOWA
99—Brad Meester, OL

NORTHERN MICH.
83—Bob Stefanski, WR

NORTHWEST MO. ST.
81—Robert "Chip" Gregory, LB

NORTHWESTERN
56—Al Viola, G
58—Andy Cvercko, T
61—Larry Onesti, C
62—Paul Flatley, B
63—George Burman, E
70—Joe Zigulich, OG
76—Randolph Dean, E
80—Jim Ford, OT
86—Michael Baum, OT
    Bob Dirkes, DL
    Todd Krehbiel, DB
87—Mike Baum, OL
88—Mike Baum, OL
90—Ira Adler, PK
95—Sam Valenzisi, PK

N'WESTERN (IOWA)
83—Mark Muilenberg, RB
92—Joel Bundt, OL

N'WESTERN (OKLA.)
61—Stewart Arthurs, B

NORTHWESTERN ST.
92—Guy Hedrick, RB
94—John Dippel, OL

NORWICH
70—Gary Fry, RB

NOTRE DAME
52—Joe Heap, B

53—Joe Heap, B
54—Joe Heap, B
55—Don Schaefer, B
58—Bob Wetoska, E
63—Bob Lehmann, G
66—Tom Regner, OG
    Jim Lynch, LB
67—Jim Smithberger, DB
68—George Kunz, OT
69—Jim Reilly, OT
70—Tom Gatewood, E
    Larry DiNardo, OG
    Joe Theismann, QB
71—Greg Marx, DT
    Tom Gatewood, E
72—Michael Creaney, E
    Greg Marx, DT
73—David Casper, E
    Gary Potempa, LB
    Bob Thomas, K
74—Reggie Barnett, DB
    Pete Demmerle, E
77—Ken MacAfee, E
    Joe Restic, S
    Dave Vinson, OG
78—Joe Restic, DB
80—Bob Burger, OG
    Tom Gibbons, DB
81—John Krimm, DB
85—Greg Dingens, DL
87—Ted Gradel, PK
    Vince Phelan, P
92—Tim Ruddy, OL
93—Tim Ruddy, OL

OCCIDENTAL
88—Curtis Page, DL

OHIO
71—John Rousch, HB

OHIO NORTHERN
76—Jeff McFarlin, S
79—Robert Coll, WR
86—David Myers, DL
90—Chad Hummell, OL
97—Andy Roecker, OL

OHIO ST.
52—John Borton, B
54—Dick Hilinski, T
58—Bob White, B
61—Tom Perdue, E
65—Bill Ridder, MG
66—Dave Foley, OT
68—Dave Foley, OT
    Mark Stier, LB
69—Bill Urbanik, DT
71—Rick Simon, OG
73—Randy Gradishar, LB
74—Brian Baschnagel, RB
75—Brian Baschnagel, RB
76—Pete Johnson, RB
    Bill Lukens, OG
77—Jeff Logan, RB
80—Marcus Marek, LB
82—John Frank, TE
    Joseph Smith, OT
83—John Frank, TE
84—David Crecelius, DL
    Michael Lanese, WR
85—Michael Lanese, WR
89—Joseph Staysniak, OL
92—Leonard Hartman, OL
    Gregory Smith, DL
95—Greg Bellisari, LB
96—Greg Bellisari, LB
99—Ahmed Plummer, DB

OHIO WESLEYAN
70—Tony Heald, LB
    Tom Liller, E
81—Ric Kinnan, WR
85—Kevin Connell, OG
94—Craig Anderson, LB
95—Craig Anderson, LB
96—Craig Anderson, LB

OKLAHOMA
52—Tom Catlin, C
54—Carl Allison, E
56—Jerry Tubbs, C
57—Doyle Jenning, T
58—Ross Coyle, E

ACADEMIC ALL-AMERICANS BY SCHOOL

62—Wayne Lee, C
63—Newt Burton, G
64—Newt Burton, G
66—Ron Shotts, HB
67—Ron Shotts, HB
68—Eddie Hinton, DB
70—Joe Wylie, RB
71—Jack Mildren, QB
72—Joe Wylie, RB
74—Randy Hughes, S
75—Dewey Selmon, LB
Lee Roy Selmon, DT
80—Jay Jimerson, DB
86—Brian Bosworth, LB

OKLA. PANHANDLE
76—Larry Johnson, G

OKLAHOMA ST.
54—Dale Meinert, G
72—Tom Wolf, OT
73—Doug Tarrant, LB
74—Tom Wolf, OT
77—Joe Avanzini, DE

OREGON
62—Steve Barnett, T
65—Tim Casey, LB
86—Mike Preacher, P
90—Bill Musgrave, QB

OREGON ST.
62—Terry Baker, B
67—Bill Enyart, FB
68—Bill Enyart, FB
93—Chad Paulson, RB

OUACHITA BAPTIST
78—David Cowling, OG

PACIFIC (CAL.)
78—Bruce Filarsky, OG
79—Bruce Filarsky, DL

PACIFIC LUTHERAN
82—Curt Rodin, TE

PENNSYLVANIA
86—Rich Comizio, RB
99—Michael Germino, DL

PENN ST.
65—Joe Bellas, T
John Runnells, LB
66—John Runnells, LB
67—Rich Buzin, OT
69—Charlie Pittman, HB
Dennis Onkotz, LB
71—Dave Joyner, OT
72—Bruce Bannon, DE
73—Mark Markovich, OG
76—Chuck Benjamin, OT
78—Keith Dorney, OT
82—Todd Blackledge, QB
Harry Hamilton, DB
Scott Radicec, LB
83—Harry Hamilton, LB
84—Lance Hamilton, DB
Carmen Masciantonio, LB
85—Lance Hamilton, DB
86—John Shaffer, QB
94—Jeff Hartings, OL
Tony Pittman, DB
95—Jeff Hartings, OL
99—Travis Forney, PK

PITTSBURG ST.
72—Jay Sperry, RB
89—Brett Potts, DL
91—Mike Brockel, OL
92—Mike Brockel, OL
96—Brian Moorman, P
97—Brian Moorman, P
98—Ben Petersen, DL

PITTSBURGH
52—Dick Deitrick, DT
54—Lou Palatella, T
56—Joe Walton, E
58—Jon Guzik, G
76—Jeff Delaney, LB
80—Greg Meisner, DL
81—Rob Fada, OG
82—Rob Fada, OG
J. C. Pelusi, DL
88—Mark Stepnoski, OL

PORTLAND ST.
72—Bill Dials, T

77—John Urness, WR
78—John Urness, WR

PRINCETON
68—Dick Sandler, DT
76—Kevin Fox, OG
82—Kevin Guthrie, WR
83—Kevin Guthrie, WR
98—Alex Sierk, PK

PUGET SOUND
82—Buster Crook, DB

PURDUE
56—Len Dawson, QB
60—Jerry Beabout, T
65—Sal Ciampi, G
67—Jim Beirne, E
Lance Olssen, DT
68—Tim Foley, DB
69—Tim Foley, DB
Mike Phipps, QB
Bill Yanchar, DT
73—Bob Hoftiezer, DE
79—Ken Loushin, DL
80—Tim Seneff, DB
81—Tim Seneff, DB
89—Bruce Brineman, OL

RENSSELAER
95—Alic Scott, OL
96—Dan McGovern, RB
97—Chris Cochran, DL
98—Jason Kepler, OL
99—Jason Kepler, OL

RHODE ISLAND
76—Richard Moser, RB
77—Richard Moser, RB

RHODES
90—Robert Heck, DL

RICE
52—Richard Chapman, DG
53—Richard Chapman, DG
54—Dicky Maegle, B
69—Steve Bradshaw, DG
79—LaMont Jefferson, LB
83—Brian Patterson, DB
95—Jay Lamy, DB

ROCHESTER
82—Bob Cordaro, LB
92—Jeremy Hurd, RB
93—Jeremy Hurd, RB

ROSE-HULMAN
78—Rick Matovich, LB
79—Scott Lindner, DL
80—Scott Lindner, DL
Jim Novacek, P
83—Jack Grote, LB
84—Jack Grote, LB
88—Greg Kremer, LB
Shawn Ferron, PK
89—Shawn Ferron, PK
90—Ed Huonden, WR
92—Greg Hubbard, OL
93—Greg Hubbard, OL

SAGINAW VALLEY
93—Troy Hendrickson, PK

ST. CLOUD ST.
88—Rick Rodgers, DB
89—Rick Rodgers, DB

ST. FRANCIS (PA.)
93—Todd Eckenroad, WR
98—Matt Farabaugh, LB

ST. JOHN'S (MINN.)
72—Jim Kruzich, E
79—Terry Geraghty, DB
94—Chris Palmer, WR
Matthew Malmberg, RB
95—Chris Palmer, WR
97—Matt Emmerich, DB

ST. JOHN'S (N.Y.)
93—Anthony Russo, RB

ST. JOSEPH'S (IND.)
77—Mike Bettinger, DB
78—Mike Bettinger, DB
79—Mike Bettinger, DB
85—Ralph Laura, OT
88—Keith Woodason, OL
89—Jeff Fairchild, P

ST. NORBERT
86—Matthew Lang, LB
Karl Zacharias, P
87—Karl Zacharias, PK
Matthew Lang, LB
88—Mike Whitehouse, WR
89—Mike Whitehouse, WR
99—Mike Krueger, WR

ST. OLAF
61—Dave Hindermann, T

ST. THOMAS (MINN.)
73—Mark Dienhart, T
74—Mark Dienhart, T
77—Tom Kelly, OG
80—Doug Groebner, C
94—Curt Behrns, DB

SALVE REGINA
98—Mark DeBiasio, RB
99—Mark DeBiasio, RB

SAM HOUSTON ST.
72—Walter Anderson, KS
73—Walter Anderson, KS
93—Kevin Riley, DB

SAN DIEGO
87—Bryan Day, DB
88—Bryan Day, DB
94—Doug Popovich, DB
95—Doug Popovich, DB
96—Jeb Dougherty, DB

SAN DIEGO ST.
98—Scott Auerbach, DB

SAN JOSE ST.
75—Tim Toews, OG

SANTA CLARA
71—Ron Sani, IL
73—Alex Damascus, RB
74—Steve Lagorio, LB
75—Mark Tiernan, LB
76—Lou Marengo, KS
Mark Tiernan, LB
80—Dave Alfaro, QB

SHIPPENSBURG
76—Tony Winter, LB
82—Dave Butler, DL
94—Joel Yohn, PK
95—Joel Yohn, PK

SIMPSON
98—Guy Leman, RB

SOUTH CAROLINA
87—Mark Fryer, OL
88—Mark Fryer, OL
91—Joe Reeves, LB

SOUTH DAKOTA
78—Scott Pollock, QB
82—Jerus Campbell, DL
83—Jeff Sime, T
87—Dan Sonnek, RB

SOUTH DAKOTA ST.
74—Bob Gissler, E
75—Bill Matthews, T
77—Bill Matthews, DE
79—Tony Harris, PK
Paul Kippley, DB

SOUTHERN CALIFORNIA
52—Dick Nunis, DB
59—Mike McKeever, G
60—Mike McKeever, G
Marlin McKeever, E
65—Charles Arrobio, T
67—Steve Sogge, QB
68—Steve Sogge, QB
69—Harry Khasigian, OG
73—Pat Haden, QB
74—Pat Haden, QB
78—Rich Dimler, DL
79—Brad Budde, OG
Paul McDonald, QB
Keith Van Horne, T
84—Duane Bickett, LB
85—Matt Koart, DL
86—Jeffrey Bregel, OG
88—John Jackson, WR
89—John Jackson, WR
95—Jeremy Hogue, OL
Matt Keneley, DL
96—Matt Keneley, DL

SOUTHERN COLO.
83—Dan DeRose, LB

SOUTHERN CONN. ST.
84—Gerald Carbonaro, OL

SOUTHERN ILL.
70—Sam Finocchio, G
88—Charles Harmke, RB
91—Dwayne Summers, DL
Jon Manley, LB

SOUTHERN METHODIST
52—Dave Powell, E
53—Darrell Lafitte, G
54—Raymond Berry, E
55—David Hawk, G
57—Tom Koenig, G
58—Tom Koenig, G
62—Raymond Schoenke, T
66—John LaGrone, MG
Lynn Thornhill, OG
68—Jerry LeVias, OE
72—Cleve Whitener, LB
83—Brian O'Meara, T

SOUTHERN MISS.
92—James Singleton, DL
97—Jeremy Lindley, OL

SOUTHERN ORE.
97—Ian Reid, OL

SOUTHERN UTAH
88—Jim Andrus, RB
90—Steve McDowell, P

SOUTHWEST MO. ST.
73—Kent Stringer, QB
75—Kent Stringer, QB
78—Steve Newbold, WR

SOUTHWEST ST.
88—Bruce Saugstad, DB

SOUTHWEST TEX. ST.
72—Jimmy Jowers, LB
73—Jimmy Jowers, LB
78—Mike Ferris, OG
79—Mike Ferris, G
Allen Kiesling, DL
81—Mike Miller, QB

SPRINGFIELD
71—Bruce Rupert, LB
84—Sean Flanders, LB
85—Sean Flanders, DL

STANFORD
70—John Sande, C
Terry Ewing, DB
75—Don Stevenson, RB
76—Don Stevenson, RB
77—Guy Benjamin, QB
78—Vince Mulroy, WR
Jim Stephens, OG
79—Pat Bowe, TE
Milt McColl, LB
Joe St. Geme, DB
81—John Bergren, DL
Darrin Nelson, RB
82—John Bergren, DL
83—John Bergren, DL
85—Matt Soderlund, LB
87—Brad Muster, RB
90—Ed McCaffrey, WR
91—Tommy Vardell, RB
94—Justin Armour, WR
99—Troy Walters, WR

SUL ROSS ST.
73—Archie Nexon, RB

SUSQUEHANNA
75—Gerry Huesken, T
76—Gerry Huesken, T
80—Dan Distasio, LB
99—Dave Wonderlick, OL

SYRACUSE
60—Fred Mautino, E
71—Howard Goodman, LB
83—Tony Romano, LB
84—Tim Green, DL
85—Tim Green, DL
99—Mark Baniewicz, OL

AWARD WINNERS

ACADEMIC ALL-AMERICANS BY SCHOOL

TARLETON ST.
81—Ricky Bush, RB
90—Mike Loveless, OL

TENNESSEE
56—Charles Rader, T
57—Bill Johnson, G
65—Mack Gentry, DT
67—Bob Johnson, C
70—Tim Priest, DB
80—Timothy Irwin, OT
82—Mike Terry, DL
97—Peyton Manning, QB

TENN.-MARTIN
74—Randy West, E

TENNESSEE TECH
87—Andy Rittenhouse, DL
99—Wes Gallagher, OL

TEXAS
59—Maurice Doke, G
61—Johnny Treadwell, G
62—Johnny Treadwell, G
  Pat Culpepper, B
63—Duke Carlisle, B
66—Gene Bledsoe, OT
67—Mike Perrin, DE
  Corby Robertson, LB
68—Corby Robertson, LB
  Scott Henderson, LB
69—Scott Henderson, LB
  Bill Zapalac, DE
70—Scott Henderson, LB
  Bill Zapalac, LB
72—Mike Bayer, DB
  Tommy Keel, S
  Steve Oxley, T
73—Tommy Keel, S
83—Doug Dawson, G
88—Lee Brockman, DL
95—Pat Fitzgerald, TE
96—Pat Fitzgerald, TE
97—Dusty Renfro, LB

UTEP
88—Pat Hegarty, QB

TEXAS A&M
56—Jack Pardee, B
71—Steve Luebbehusen, LB
76—Kevin Monk, LB
77—Kevin Monk, LB
85—Kip Corrington, DB
86—Kip Corrington, DB
87—Kip Corrington, DB

TEX. A&M-COMMERCE
77—Mike Hall, OT

TEX. A&M-KINGSVILLE
72—Floyd Goodwin, T
73—Johnny Jackson, E
76—Wade Whitmer, DL
77—Joe Henke, LB
  Wade Whitmer, DL
78—Wade Whitmer, DL

TCU
52—Marshall Harris, T
55—Hugh Pitts, C
  Jim Swink, B
56—Jim Swink, B
57—John Nikkel, E
68—Jim Ray, G
72—Scott Walker, C
74—Terry Drennan, DB
80—John McClean, DL

TEXAS TECH
72—Jeff Jobe, E
79—Maury Buford, P
83—Chuck Alexander, DB
93—Robert King, P
99—Keith Cockrum, LB

THOMAS MORE
97—Mike Bramlage Jr., DB

TOLEDO
83—Michael Matz, DL
95—Craig Dues, LB

TRINITY (CONN.)
96—Joseph DeAngelis, OL

TRINITY (TEX.)
92—Jeff Bryan, OL
97—Mark Byarlay, RB

TRUMAN
73—Tom Roberts, T
78—Keith Driscoll, LB
79—Keith Driscoll, LB
92—K. C. Conaway, P

TUFTS
70—Bruce Zinsmeister, DL
81—Brian Gallagher, OG
83—Richard Guiunta, G
98—Eric Brum, DL

TULANE
71—David Hebert, DB

TULSA
64—Howard Twilley, E
65—Howard Twilley, E
74—Mack Lancaster, T
95—David Millwee, OL
96—Levi Gillen, DB
97—Levi Gillen, DB

UCLA
52—Ed Flynn, G
  Donn Moomaw, LB
53—Ira Pauly, C
54—Sam Boghosian, G
66—Ray Armstrong, E
75—John Sciarra, QB
77—John Fowler, LB
81—Cormac Carney, WR
  Tim Wrightman, TE
82—Cormac Carney, WR
85—Mike Hartmeier, OG
92—Carlton Gray, DB
95—George Kase, DL
98—Shawn Stuart, OL

UNION (N.Y.)
71—Tom Anacher, LB
73—Dave Ricks, DB
87—Richard Romer, DL
93—Greg Oswitt, OL
96—Roger Egbert, PK

URSINUS
86—Chuck Odgers, DB
87—Chuck Odgers, LB

UTAH
64—Mel Carpenter, T
71—Scott Robbins, DB
73—Steve Odom, RB
76—Dick Graham, E

UTAH ST.
61—Merlin Olsen, T
69—Gary Anderson, LB
74—Randy Stockham, DE
75—Randy Stockham, DE

VALDOSTA ST.
93—Chris Hatcher, QB
94—Chris Hatcher, QB

VANDERBILT
58—Don Donnell, C
68—Jim Burns, DB
74—Doug Martin, E
75—Damon Regen, LB
77—Greg Martin, K
83—Phil Roach, WR

VILLANOVA
86—Ron Sency, RB
88—Peter Lombardi, RB
92—Tim Matas, DL

VIRGINIA
72—Tom Kennedy, OG
75—Bob Meade, DT
92—Tom Burns, LB
93—Tom Burns, LB
95—Tiki Barber, RB
96—Tiki Barber, RB
97—Stephen Phelan, DB

VMI
78—Craig Jones, PK
79—Craig Jones, PK
84—David Twillie, OL
86—Dan Young, DL
88—Anthony McIntosh, DB

VIRGINIA TECH
67—Frank Loria, DB
72—Tommy Carpenito, LB

WABASH
70—Roscoe Fouts, DB
71—Kendrick Shelburne, DT
82—Dave Broecker, QB

WARTBURG
75—James Charles Peterson, DB
76—Randy Groth, DB
77—Neil Mandsager, LB
90—Jerrod Staack, OL
93—Koby Kreinbring, LB
94—Vince Penningroth, DL
95—Vince Penningroth, DL
99—Paul Seberger, TE

WASHINGTON
55—Jim Houston, E
63—Mike Briggs, T
64—Rick Redman, G
65—Steve Bramwell, DB
79—Bruce Harrell, LB
81—Mark Jerue, LB
  Chuck Nelson, PK
82—Chuck Nelson, PK
86—David Rill, LB
87—David Rill, LB
91—Ed Cunningham, OL

WASHINGTON (MO.)
97—Brad Klein, LB

WASH. & JEFF.
92—Raymond Cross, DL
93—Michael Jones, OL
94—Michael Jones, OL

WASH. & LEE
75—John Cocklereece, DB
78—George Ballantyne, LB
92—Evans Edwards, OL

WASHINGTON ST.
89—Jason Hanson, PK
90—Lee Tilleman, DL
  Jason Hanson, PK
91—Jason Hanson, PK

WAYNE ST. (MICH.)
71—Gary Schultz, DB
72—Walt Stasinski, DB

WAYNE ST. (NEB.)
99—Jeff Shabram, OL

WAYNESBURG
77—John Culp, RB
78—John Culp, RB
89—Andrew Barrish, OL
90—Andrew Barrish, OL
91—Karl Petrof, OL

WEBER ST.
97—Cameron Quayle, TE

WEST CHESTER
83—Eric Wentling, K
86—Gerald Desmond, K

WEST VIRGINIA
52—Paul Bischoff, E
54—Fred Wyant, B
55—Sam Huff, T
70—Kim West, K
80—Oliver Luck, QB
81—Oliver Luck, QB
83—Jeff Hostetler, QB
92—Mike Compton, OL
94—Matt Taffoni, OL
98—Eric de Groh, OL

WESTERN CARO.
75—Mike Wade, E
76—Mike Wade, LB
84—Eddie Maddox, RB

WESTERN ILL.
61—Jerry Blew, G
85—Jeff McKinney, RB
91—David Fierke, OL

WESTERN KY.
71—James Barber, LB
81—Tim Ford, DL
84—Mark Fatkin, OL
85—Mark Fatkin, OG
95—Brian Bixler, OL

WESTERN MD.
73—Chip Chaney, S
98—Tom Lapato, DB

WESTERN MICH.
70—Jon Bull, OT
94—Rich Kaiser, DL
95—Rich Kaiser, DL

WESTERN OREGON
61—Francis Tresler, C

WESTERN ST.
78—Bill Campbell, DB
88—Damon Lockhart, RB

WESTMINSTER (PA.)
73—Bob Clark, G
77—Scott McLuckey, LB
93—Brian Wilson, OL
98—Brian Mihok, DL

WHEATON (ILL.)
73—Bill Hyer, E
75—Eugene Campbell, RB
76—Eugene Campbell, RB
88—Paul Sternenberg, DL
92—Bart Moseman, DB
94—Pedro Arruza, RB
95—Jeff Brown, QB
  Pedro Arruzo, RB

WHITTIER
86—Brent Kane, DL

WIDENER
98—Brendon Richards, LB

WILKES
70—Al Kenney, C

WILLAMETTE
61—Stuart Hall

WILLIAM & MARY
74—John Gerdelman, RB
75—Ken Smith, DB
77—Ken Smith, DB
78—Robert Musculus, TE
84—Mark Kelso, DB
88—Chris Gessner, DB
90—Jeff Nielsen, LB
93—Craig Staub, DL

WM. PATERSON
92—John Trust, RB

WILMINGTON (OHIO)
99—Kevin Otte, L

WINONA ST.
93—Nathan Gruber, DB
94—Nathan Gruber, DB
97—Travis Walch, RB

WISCONSIN
52—Bob Kennedy, DG
53—Alan Ameche, B
54—Alan Ameche, B
58—Jon Hobbs, B
59—Dale Hackbart, B
62—Pat Richter, E
63—Ken Bowman, C
72—Rufus Ferguson, RB
82—Kyle Borland, LB
87—Don Davey, DL
88—Don Davey, DL
89—Don Davey, DL
90—Don Davey, DL

WIS.-EAU CLAIRE
74—Mark Anderson, RB
80—Mike Zeihen, DB

WIS.-LA CROSSE
95—Troy Harcey, WR
96—Troy Harcey, WR

WIS.-OSHKOSH
96—Rob Stoltz, WR
97—Ryan Hinske, WR
99—Craig Pierstoff, LB

WIS.-PLATTEVILLE
85—Mark Hintz, DB
  Mark Rae, P
86—Mike Hintz, QB
87—Mark Rae, P

WIS.-RIVER FALLS
91—Mike Olson, LB
95—Brian Izdepski, OT

WIS.-STEVENS POINT
97—Joel Hornby, DL

WIS.-WHITEWATER
95—Scott Hawig, OL

ACADEMIC ALL-AMERICANS BY SCHOOL

WITTENBERG
80— Bill Beach, DB
81— Bill Beach, DB
82— Tom Jones, OT
88— Paul Kungl, WR
90— Victor Terebuh, DB

WOOSTER
73— Dave Foy, LB
77— Blake Moore, C
78— Blake Moore, C

79— Blake Moore, C
80— Dale Fortner, DB
    John Weisensell, OG
99— Matt Mahaffey, P

WYOMING
65— Bob Dinges, DE
67— George Mills, OG
73— Mike Lopiccolo, OT
84— Bob Gustafson, OT
87— Patrick Arndt, OG

94— Ryan Christopherson, RB
95— Joe Cummings, DL
96— Jay Korth, OL
    Cory Wedel, PK
97— Jay Korth, OL
    Cory Wedel, PK
    Brian Lee, DB
98— Brian Brown, LB

YALE
68— Fred Morris, C

70— Tom Neville, DT
78— William Crowley, LB
81— Rich Diana, RB
    Frederick Leone, DL
89— Glover Lawrence, DL
91— Scott Wagner, DB
99— Eric Johnson, WR

YOUNGSTOWN ST.
93— John Quintana, TE
98— Anthony Pannunzio, DB

Bowl/All-Star Game Records

2000-01 Bowl Schedule	284
1999-00 Bowl Results	285
All-Time Bowl-Game Results	287
Team-by-Team Bowl Results	293
Major Bowl-Game Attendance	305
Individual Records	310
Team Records	311
Individual Record Lists	313
Team Record Lists	321
Longest Plays	332
Bowl Coaching Records	332
Conference Bowl Records	346
Award Winners in Bowl Games	348
Bowls and Polls	354
Bowl-Game Facts	359
Special Regular- and Postseason Games	360

2000-01 Bowl Schedule

(All starting times listed are Eastern Times)

AXA LIBERTY BOWL
Memphis, Tennessee, December 29, 2000, 1:30 p.m.
Steve Ehrhart, executive director
AXA Financial Group
3767 New Getwell Road
Memphis, Tennessee 38118
Phone: 901/795-7700 Fax: 901/795-7826
Televising Network: ESPN
Facility: Liberty Bowl Memorial Stadium
Capacity: 62,338
Title Sponsor: AXA Financial Group

CHICK-FIL-A PEACH BOWL
Atlanta, Georgia, December 29, 2000, 5 p.m.
Gary Stokan, president
Peach Bowl, Inc.
235 International Boulevard
Atlanta, Georgia 30303
Phone: 404/586-8500 Fax: 404/586-8508
Televising Network: ESPN
Facility: Georgia Dome
Capacity: 71,228
Title Sponsor: Chick-Fil-A

CRUCIAL.COM HUMANITARIAN BOWL
Boise, Idaho, December 28, 2000, 1 p.m.
Gene Bleymaier, interim director
Boise State University
Director of Athletics
1910 University Drive
Boise, Idaho 83725
Phone: 208/426-1981 Fax: 208/385-1178
Televising Network: ESPN2
Facility: Bronco Stadium
Capacity: 30,000
Title Sponsor: Crucial Technology

CULLIGAN HOLIDAY BOWL
San Diego, California, December 29, 2000, 8 p.m.
John K. Reid, executive director
San Diego Bowl Game Association
P.O. Box 601400
San Diego, California 92160
Phone: 619/283-5808 Fax: 619/281-7947
Televising Network: ESPN
Facility: Qualcomm Stadium
Capacity: 70,000
Title Sponsor: Culligan

EA SPORTS LAS VEGAS BOWL
Las Vegas, Nevada, December 21, 2000, 5 p.m.
Tina Kunzer-Murphy, managing director
Las Vegas Convention and Visitors Authority
3150 Paradise Road
Las Vegas, Nevada 89109-9096
Phone: 702/892-0711 Fax: 702/892-7515
Televising Network: ESPN2
Facility: Sam Boyd Stadium
Capacity: 40,000
Title Sponsors: EA Sports and the Las Vegas Convention and Visitors Authority

FEDEX ORANGE BOWL
Miami, Florida, January 3, 2001, 8:30 p.m.
Keith R. Tribble, executive director
Orange Bowl Committee
601 Brickell Key Drive, Suite 206
Miami, Florida 33131
Phone: 305/371-4600 Fax: 305/371-4318
Televising Network: ABC
Facility: Pro Player Stadium
Capacity: 75,014
Title Sponsor: Federal Express

GALLERYFURNITURE.COM BOWL
Houston, Texas, December 27, 2000, 8 p.m.
Jerry Ippoliti, president
galleryfurniture.com
603 Laguna Point
Toledo, Ohio 43528
Phone: 419/865-2544 Fax: 419/865-0768
Televising Network: ESPN
Facility: Astrodome
Capacity: 65,000
Title Sponsor: galleryfurniture.com

GMAC MOBILE ALABAMA BOWL
Mobile, Alabama, December 20, 2000, 7:30 p.m.
Allen Bud Ratliff, executive director
Mobile Alabama Bowl, Inc.
6159 Omni Park Drive, Suite B
Mobile, Alabama 36609
Phone: 334/635-0011 Fax: 334/666-0355
Televising Network: ESPN2
Facility: Ladd Peebles Stadium
Capacity: 40,048
Title Sponsors: GMAC Financial Services and the City of Mobile

HOMEPOINT.COM MUSIC CITY BOWL
Nashville, Tennessee, December 29, 2000, 1 p.m.
Scott Ramsey, executive director
Nashville Area Chamber of Commerce
401 Church Street, Suite 2700
Nashville, Tennessee 37219
Phone: 615/880-1900 Fax: 615/244-3540
Televising Network: ESPN
Facility: Adelphia Coliseum
Capacity: 67,000
Title Sponsor: homepoint.com

INSIGHT.COM BOWL
Tucson, Arizona, December 28, 2000, 6 p.m.
John Junker, executive director
Insight.com Bowl
3837 East Broadway Boulevard
Tucson, Arizona 85716-5407
Phone: 520/327-2695 Fax: 520/881-6860
Televising Network: ESPN
Facility: Arizona Stadium
Capacity: 54,884
Title Sponsor: Insight, Inc.

JEEP ALOHA CHRISTMAS FOOTBALL CLASSICS
Honolulu, Hawaii, December 24, 2000, 8:30 p.m.
and
December 25, 2000, 3:30 p.m.
Marcia J. Klompus, executive director
Aloha Sports, Inc.
1110 University Avenue, Suite 403
Honolulu, Hawaii 96826-1508
Phone: 808/947-4141 Fax: 808/941-9911
Televising Network: ABC/ESPN
Facility: Aloha Stadium
Capacity: 50,000
Title Sponsor: Jeep Division of Chrysler Corporation

MICRONPC.COM BOWL
Miami, December 28 or 30, 2000, 7:30 p.m.
Mitch Morrall, executive director
Sunshine Festival Football, Inc.
915 Middle River Drive, Suite 120
Fort Lauderdale, Florida 33304
Phone: 954/564-5000 Fax: 954/564-8902
Televising Network: Turner Sports (TBS)
Facility: Pro Player Stadium
Capacity: 75,014
Title Sponsor: Micron Electronics

MOTOR CITY BOWL
Pontiac, Michigan, December 27, 2000, 1:30, 2 or 2:30 p.m.
Ken Hoffman, executive director
Ford Division (Ford Motor Company)
1200 Featherstone Drive
Pontiac, Michigan 48342
Phone: 248/456-1694 Fax: 248/456-1691
Televising Network: ESPN
Facility: Pontiac Silverdome
Capacity: 80,000
Title Sponsor: Ford Division (Ford Motor Company)

NOKIA SUGAR BOWL
New Orleans, Louisiana, January 2, 2001, 8 p.m.
Paul J. Hoolahan, executive director
The Sugar Bowl Committee
1500 Sugar Bowl Drive
New Orleans, Louisiana 70112
Phone: 504/525-8573 Fax: 504/525-4867
Televising Network: ABC
Facility: Louisiana Superdome
Capacity: 71,023
Title Sponsor: Nokia Mobile Telephones

OURHOUSE.COM FLORIDA CITRUS BOWL
Orlando, Florida, January 1, 2001, 1 p.m.
Charles H. Rohe, executive director
Florida Citrus Sports Association, Inc.
One Citrus Bowl Place
Orlando, Florida 32805-2451
Phone: 407/423-2476 Fax: 407/425-8451
Televising Network: ABC
Facility: Florida Citrus Bowl
Capacity: 65,525
Title Sponsors: ourhouse.com and the Florida Department of Citrus

OUTBACK BOWL
Tampa, Florida, January 1, 2001, 11 a.m.
James P. McVay, executive director
Tampa Bay Bowl Association, Inc.
4511 North Himes Avenue, Suite 260
Tampa, Florida 33614
Phone: 813/874-2695 Fax: 813/873-1959
Televising Network: ESPN
Facility: Raymond James Stadium
Capacity: 65,933
Title Sponsor: Outback Steakhouse, Inc.

ROSE BOWL
Pasadena, California, January 1, 2001, 5 p.m.
John M. Dorger, president
Pasadena Tournament of Roses Association
391 South Orange Grove Boulevard
Pasadena, California 91184
Phone: 626/449-4100 Fax: 626/449-9786
Televising Network: ABC
Facility: Rose Bowl
Capacity: 89,905
Presenting Sponsor: AT&T

SANFORD INDEPENDENCE BOWL
Shreveport, Louisiana, December 31, 2000, 8:30 p.m.
Glen Krupica, executive director
Independence Bowl Foundation
P.O. Box 1723
Shreveport, Louisiana 71166
Phone: 318/221-0712 Fax: 318/221-7366
Televising Network: ESPN
Facility: Independence Stadium
Capacity: 50,459
Title Sponsor: Sanford

SBC COTTON BOWL CLASSIC
Dallas, Texas, January 1, 2001, 11 a.m.
Rick Baker, executive director
Cotton Bowl Athletic Association
P.O. Box 569420
Dallas, Texas 75356
Phone: 214/634-7525 Fax: 214/634-7764
Televising Network: Fox Sports Net/Fox Network
Facility: Cotton Bowl
Capacity: 68,252
Title Sponsor: SBC Communications

SILICON VALLEY CLASSIC
San Jose, California, December 31, 2000, 6:30 p.m.
Chuck Shelton, executive director
Silicon Valley Football Classic, Inc.
1393 South 7th Street
San Jose, California 95112
Phone: 408/924-1462 Fax: 408/924-1163
Televising Network: Fox Sports Net
Facility: Spartan Stadium, San Jose State University
Capacity: 30,578
Title Sponsor: TBD

SYLVANIA ALAMO BOWL
San Antonio, Texas, December 30, 2000, 7:30 p.m.
Derrick S. Fox, executive director
San Antonio Bowl Association, Inc.
100 Montana Street, Suite 3D01
San Antonio, Texas 78203-1031
Phone: 210/226-2695 Fax: 210/704-6399
Televising Network: ESPN
Facility: Alamodome
Capacity: 65,000
Title Sponsor: Sylvania

TOSTITOS FIESTA BOWL
Tempe, Arizona, January 1, 2001, 8 p.m.
John Junker, executive director
Arizona Sports Foundation
120 South Ash Avenue

2000-01 BOWL SCHEDULE

Tempe, Arizona 85281
Phone: 602/350-0900 Fax: 602/350-0915
Televising Network: ABC
Facility: Sun Devil Stadium
Capacity: 73,158
Title Sponsor: Tostitos

TOYOTA GATOR BOWL
Jacksonville, Florida, January 1, 2001, 12:30 p.m.
Richard M. Catlett, executive director
Toyota Motor Sales/Southeast Toyota
One Gator Bowl Boulevard

Jacksonville, Florida 32202
Phone: 904/798-1700 Fax: 904/632-2080
Televising Network: NBC
Facility: Alltel Stadium
Capacity: 76,940
Title Sponsor: Toyota Motor Sales, USA, Inc.

WELLS FARGO SUN BOWL
El Paso, Texas, December 29, 2000, 2:15 p.m.
Joyce E. Feinberg, executive director
Sun Bowl Association
4100 Rio Bravo, Suite 303

El Paso, Texas 79902-1049
Phone: 915/533-4416 Fax: 915/533-0661
Televising Network: CBS
Facility: Sun Bowl Stadium
Capacity: 51,171
Title Sponsor: Wells Fargo Corporation

1999-00 Bowl Results

Game-by-Game Summaries

LAS VEGAS BOWL
December 18, 1999
Sam Boyd Stadium
Las Vegas, Nevada

Fresno St. ....7 0 3 6 — 16
Utah ....7 0 7 3 — 17
Fresno St.—P. Williams 75 blocked field goal return (Hanna kick)
Utah—Anderson 34 run (Truhe kick)
Fresno St.—Hanna 27 field goal
Utah—Anderson 5 run (Truhe kick)
Fresno St.—Ward 2 run (kick failed)
Utah—Truhe 33 field goal

Game Statistics	Fresno St.	Utah
First Downs	16	25
Rushes-Yards	32-132	54-334
Passing Yards	147	214
Passes Comp-Att-Int	14-28-0	11-24-1
Punts-Avg.	5-37.2	4-39.0
Fumbles-Lost	0-0	2-0
Penalties-Yards	6-59	15-151
Time of Possession	24:06	35:54

Attendance: 28,227

MOBILE ALABAMA BOWL
December 22, 1999
Ladd-Peebles Stadium
Mobile, Alabama

TCU ....7 14 0 7 — 28
East Caro. ....7 0 7 0 — 14
East Caro.—Powell 58 pass from Garrard (Miller kick)
TCU—Tomlinson 2 run (Kaylakie kick)
TCU—Scarborough 21 pass from Printers (Kaylakie kick)
TCU—Tomlinson 3 run (Kaylakie kick)
East Caro.—J. Wilson 13 run (Miller kick)
TCU—Gary 32 interception return (Kaylakie kick)

Game Statistics	TCU	East Caro.
First Downs	16	12
Rushes-Yards	50-186	26-(-16)
Passing Yards	174	239
Passes Comp-Att-Int	13-19-1	20-37-1
Punts-Avg.	6-31.6	7-38.1
Fumbles-Lost	1-1	0-0
Penalties-Yards	8-80	3-15
Time of Possession	35:20	24:40

Attendance: 34,200

ALOHA CLASSIC
December 25, 1999
Aloha Stadium
Honolulu, Hawaii

Wake Forest ....3 0 10 10 — 23
Arizona St. ....0 3 0 0 — 3
Wake Forest—Burdick 22 field goal
Arizona St.—Barth 46 field goal
Wake Forest—Burdick 24 field goal
Wake Forest—Caldwell 56 pass from Sankey (Burdick kick)
Wake Forest—Kane 1 run (Burdick kick)
Wake Forest—Burdick 43 field goal

Game Statistics	Wake Forest	Arizona St.
First Downs	15	11
Rushes-Yards	48-162	36-94
Passing Yards	188	70
Passes Comp-Att-Int	13-22-1	15-26-0
Punts-Avg.	6-36.2	9-35.0
Fumbles-Lost	0-0	3-2
Penalties-Yards	1-15	3-21
Time of Possession	34:14	25:46

Attendance: 40,974

OAHU CLASSIC
December 25, 1999
Aloha Stadium
Honolulu, Hawaii

Hawaii ....0 10 10 3 — 23
Oregon St. ....7 3 0 7 — 17
Oregon St.—Simonton 1 run (Cesca kick)
Hawaii—Hannum 26 field goal
Hawaii—C. Harris 9 pass from Robinson (Hannum kick)
Oregon St.—Cesca 37 field goal
Hawaii—C. Harris 30 pass from Robinson (Hannum kick)
Hawaii—Hannum 22 field goal
Hawaii—Hannum 35 field goal
Oregon St.—Simonton 13 run (Cesca kick)

Game Statistics	Hawaii	Oregon St.
First Downs	21	14
Rushes-Yards	24-83	35-169
Passing Yards	266	269
Passes Comp-Att-Int	23-40-1	19-40-0
Punts-Avg.	4-40.8	6-36.0
Fumbles-Lost	3-1	3-1
Penalties-Yards	9-88	14-138
Time of Possession	28:51	31:09

Attendance: 40,974

MOTOR CITY BOWL
December 27, 1999
Pontiac Silverdome
Pontiac, Michigan

Brigham Young ......3 0 0 0 — 3
Marshall ....0 7 7 7 — 21
Brigham Young—Pochman 28 field goal
Marshall—Chapman 30 pass from Pennington (Malashevich kick)
Marshall—Chapman 87 run (Malashevich kick)
Marshall—Chapman 1 run (Malashevich kick)

Game Statistics	Brigham Young	Marshall
First Downs	12	14
Rushes-Yards	30-(-16)	31-147
Passing Yards	220	207
Passes Comp-Att-Int	16-29-2	17-28-1
Punts-Avg.	7-48.3	5-42.8
Fumbles-Lost	2-2	0-0
Penalties-Yards	8-81	11-84
Time of Possession	30:31	29:29

Attendance: 44,863

ALAMO BOWL
December 28, 1999
Alamodome
San Antonio, Texas

Penn St. ....7 7 0 10 — 24
Texas A&M ....0 0 0 0 — 0
Penn St.—Fox 34 interception return (Forney kick)
Penn St.—Drummond 45 pass from Casey (Forney kick)
Penn St.—Casey 4 run (Forney kick)
Penn St.—Forney 39 field goal

Game Statistics	Penn St.	Texas A&M
First Downs	17	16
Rushes-Yards	39-175	39-80
Passing Yards	146	122
Passes Comp-Att-Int	8-17-1	15-28-4
Punts-Avg.	4-45.5	3-52.0
Fumbles-Lost	0-0	2-1
Penalties-Yards	7-74	2-27
Time of Possession	29:23	30:37

Attendance: 65,380

MUSIC CITY BOWL
December 29, 1999
Adelphia Coliseum
Nashville, Tennessee

Syracuse ....0 7 0 13 — 20
Kentucky ....10 0 0 3 — 13
Kentucky—Shanklin 3 run (Samuel kick)
Kentucky—Samuel 22 field goal
Syracuse—K. Johnson 2 run (Trout kick)
Kentucky—Samuel 35 field goal
Syracuse—Mungro 32 run (Trout kick)
Syracuse—Mungro 24 run (run failed)

Game Statistics	Syracuse	Kentucky
First Downs	19	18
Rushes-Yards	47-276	23-57
Passing Yards	128	308
Passes Comp-Att-Int	11-15-0	30-45-1
Punts-Avg.	3-33.0	4-45.0
Fumbles-Lost	3-2	3-1
Penalties-Yards	3-20	4-20
Time of Possession	31:24	28:36

Attendance: 59,221

HOLIDAY BOWL
December 29, 1999
Qualcomm Stadium
San Diego, California

Washington ....6 7 7 0 — 20
Kansas St. ....7 3 7 7 — 24
Washington—J. Anderson 39 field goal
Kansas St.—Beasley 1 run (Rheem kick)
Washington—J. Anderson 47 field goal
Kansas St.—Rheem 41 field goal
Washington—Conniff 3 run (J. Anderson kick)
Kansas St.—Beasley 11 run (Rheem kick)
Washington—Shaw 5 run (J. Anderson kick)
Kansas St.—Beasley 1 run (Rheem kick)

Game Statistics	Washington	Kansas St.
First Downs	16	21
Rushes-Yards	29-75	43-138
Passing Yards	197	216
Passes Comp-Att-Int	18-27-1	15-31-1
Punts-Avg.	2-31.0	5-30.8
Fumbles-Lost	1-1	3-0
Penalties-Yards	7-49	11-75
Time of Possession	26:48	33:12

Attendance: 57,118

HUMANITARIAN BOWL
December 30, 1999
Bronco Stadium
Boise, Idaho

Louisville ....17 7 0 7 — 31
Boise St. ....14 7 6 7 — 34

Louisville—Hilbert 40 field goal
Boise St.—Hendricks 3 run (Calaycay kick)
Louisville—Jackson 54 pass from Redman (Hilbert kick)
Boise St.—Swan 4 pass from Hendricks (Calaycay kick)
Louisville—Parker 91 kickoff return (Hilbert kick)
Boise St.—Harts 80 interception return (Calaycay kick)
Louisville—Dorsey 8 pass from Redman (Hilbert kick)
Boise St.—Calaycay 26 field goal
Boise St.—Calaycay 46 field goal
Louisville—Moreau 3 run (Hilbert kick)
Boise St.—Malaythong 5 run (Calaycay kick)

Game Statistics	Louisville	Boise St.
First Downs	26	28
Rushes-Yards	32-89	42-198
Passing Yards	314	335
Passes Comp-Att-Int	26-47-3	20-39-0
Punts-Avg.	5-39.8	2-38.5
Fumbles-Lost	1-0	3-2
Penalties-Yards	14-120	5-61
Time of Possession	28:36	31:24

Attendance: 29,283

MICRONPC.COM BOWL
December 30, 1999
Pro Player Stadium
Miami, Florida

Illinois	14	28	7	14	— 63
Virginia	7	0	7	7	— 21

Illinois—Kittner 1 run (Rackers kick)
Virginia—Jones 7 run (Braverman kick)
Illinois—Harvey 47 run (Rackers kick)
Illinois—Kittner 30 pass from Lloyd (Rackers kick)
Illinois—Cook 61 pass from Kittner (Rackers kick)
Illinois—Havard 5 run (Rackers kick)
Illinois—Cook 1 pass from Kittner (Rackers kick)
Virginia—Coffey 5 pass from Ellis (Braverman kick)
Illinois—Havard 2 run (Rackers kick)
Illinois—Harvey 9 run (Rackers kick)
Illinois—Johnson 1 run (Rackers kick)
Virginia—Thompson 55 pass from Rivers (Braverman kick)

Game Statistics	Illinois	Virginia
First Downs	26	20
Rushes-Yards	48-325	36-172
Passing Yards	286	208
Passes Comp-Att-Int	16-26-1	17-35-1
Punts-Avg.	0-0.0	6-36.7
Fumbles-Lost	2-1	1-1
Penalties-Yards	5-39	5-25
Time of Possession	33:23	26:37

Attendance: 31,089

PEACH BOWL
December 30, 1999
Georgia Dome
Atlanta, Georgia

Clemson	0	0	0	7	— 7
Mississippi St.	0	0	3	14	— 17

Mississippi St.—Westerfield 39 field goal
Mississippi St.—Madkin 2 run (Westerfield kick)
Clemson—Streeter 1 run (Lazzara kick)
Mississippi St.—Walker 15 pass from Madkin (Westerfield kick)

Game Statistics	Clemson	Mississippi St.
First Downs	24	16
Rushes-Yards	34-85	33-89
Passing Yards	306	176
Passes Comp-Att-Int	25-56-5	17-38-0
Punts-Avg.	6-36.5	10-36.4
Fumbles-Lost	1-1	2-1
Penalties-Yards	8-82	21-188
Time of Possession	29:19	30:41

Attendance: 73,315

INSIGHT.COM BOWL
December 31, 1999
Arizona Stadium
Tucson, Arizona

Colorado	21	24	10	7	— 62
Boston College	0	7	7	14	— 28

Colorado—Johnson 10 run (Aldrich kick)
Colorado—Moschetti 2 run (Aldrich kick)
Colorado—Sykes 29 interception return (Aldrich kick)
Colorado—Barnes 21 interception return (Aldrich kick)
Colorado—Kelly 88 punt return (Aldrich kick)
Boston College—White 78 interception return (Matich kick)
Colorado—Johnson 2 run (Aldrich kick)
Colorado—Aldrich 26 field goal
Colorado—Aldrich 21 field goal
Boston College—Arndt fumble recovery in end zone (Matich kick)
Colorado—Hollowell 18 run (Aldrich kick)
Colorado—Colvin 4 run (Aldrich kick)
Boston College—Burke 2 pass from Hasselbeck (Matich kick)
Boston College—Bessette 9 blocked punt return (Matich kick)

Game Statistics	Colorado	Boston College
First Downs	29	12
Rushes-Yards	51-365	35-96
Passing Yards	158	159
Passes Comp-Att-Int	15-26-1	14-35-3
Punts-Avg.	3-28.0	6-41.0
Fumbles-Lost	1-0	2-1
Penalties-Yards	5-40	6-62
Time of Possession	33:12	28:48

Attendance: 35,762

SUN BOWL
December 31, 1999
Sun Bowl
El Paso, Texas

Minnesota	7	0	6	7	— 20
Oregon	0	7	10	7	— 24

Minnesota—Johnson 1 pass from Cockerham (Nystrom kick)
Oregon—Harrington 5 run (Villegas kick)
Minnesota—Bruce 38 pass from Cockerham (kick failed)
Oregon—Harrington 1 run (Villegas kick)
Oregon—Villegas 37 field goal
Minnesota—Johnson 7 pass from Cockerham (Nystrom kick)
Oregon—Howry 10 pass from Harrington (Villegas kick)

Game Statistics	Minnesota	Oregon
First Downs	19	22
Rushes-Yards	35-96	39-156
Passing Yards	257	232
Passes Comp-Att-Int	19-37-2	20-43-0
Punts-Avg.	7-46.1	8-40.6
Fumbles-Lost	1-1	2-1
Penalties-Yards	5-58	4-25
Time of Possession	24:35	35:25

Attendance: 48,757

LIBERTY BOWL
December 31, 1999
Liberty Bowl
Memphis, Tennessee

Colorado St.	3	14	0	0	— 17
Southern Miss.	13	7	3	0	— 23

Southern Miss.—William 5 fumble return (Hanna kick)
Colorado St.—Hurst 35 field goal
Southern Miss.—Francis blocked punt recovery in end zone (kick failed)
Colorado St.—Rice 2 run (Hurst kick)
Colorado St.—Woolstenhulme 38 pass from Newton (Hurst kick)
Southern Miss.—Nix 3 run (Hanna kick)
Southern Miss.—Hanna 25 field goal

Game Statistics	Colorado St.	Southern Miss.
First Downs	15	11
Rushes-Yards	32-82	34-90
Passing Yards	228	125
Passes Comp-Att-Int	20-46-1	13-30-1
Punts-Avg.	5-31.8	9-34.3
Fumbles-Lost	3-2	2-1
Penalties-Yards	8-71	11-59
Time of Possession	35:02	24:58

Attendance: 54,866

INDEPENDENCE BOWL
December 31, 1999
Independence Stadium
Shreveport, Louisiana

Mississippi	7	14	0	6	— 27
Oklahoma	3	0	15	7	— 25

Mississippi—McAllister 25 pass from Miller (Binkley kick)
Oklahoma—Duncan 34 field goal
Mississippi—Bettis 9 pass from Miller (Binkley kick)
Mississippi—McAllister 80 run (Binkley kick)
Oklahoma—Jackson 3 pass from Heupel (Duncan kick)
Oklahoma—Daniels 41 pass from Heupel (Hammons pass from Heupel)
Mississippi—Binkley 29 field goal
Oklahoma—Griffin 17 pass from Heupel (Duncan kick)
Mississippi—Binkley 39 field goal

Game Statistics	Mississippi	Oklahoma
First Downs	19	27
Rushes-Yards	33-159	23-91
Passing Yards	202	390
Passes Comp-Att-Int	18-29-2	39-54-1
Punts-Avg.	5-39.0	1-10.0
Fumbles-Lost	1-0	3-3
Penalties-Yards	3-13	4-35
Time of Possession	29:24	30:36

Attendance: 49,873

COTTON BOWL
January 1, 2000
Cotton Bowl
Dallas, Texas

Texas	0	3	3	0	— 6
Arkansas	3	0	7	17	— 27

Arkansas—Dodson 25 field goal
Texas—Stockton 35 field goal
Arkansas—Cobbs 30 pass from Stoerner (Dodson kick)
Texas—Stockton 22 field goal
Arkansas—Jenkins 42 run (Dodson kick)
Arkansas—Cobbs 37 run (Dodson kick)
Arkansas—Dodson 27 field goal

Game Statistics	Texas	Arkansas
First Downs	14	17
Rushes-Yards	25-(-27)	36-191
Passing Yards	212	194
Passes Comp-Att-Int	24-39-0	12-23-2
Punts-Avg.	9-39.7	4-39.0
Fumbles-Lost	0-0	0-0
Penalties-Yards	7-40	4-36
Time of Possession	31:30	28:30

Attendance: 72,723

OUTBACK BOWL
January 1, 2000
Raymond James Stadium
Tampa, Florida

Purdue	19	6	0	0	— 25
Georgia	0	10	8	3	— 28

Purdue—Daniels 3 pass from Brees (Dorsch kick)
Purdue—Daniels 11 pass from Brees (kick failed)
Purdue—Sutherland 21 pass from Brees (pass failed)
Purdue—James 32 pass from Brees (pass failed)
Georgia—Edwards 74 run (Hines kick)
Georgia—Hines 32 field goal
Georgia—Carter 8 run (Pass run)
Georgia—McMichael 8 pass from Carter (Hines kick)
Georgia—Hines 21 field goal

Game Statistics	Purdue	Georgia
First Downs	30	21
Rushes-Yards	29-150	34-154
Passing Yards	378	243
Passes Comp-Att-Int	36-60-1	20-33-0
Punts-Avg.	3-45.3	3-48.0
Fumbles-Lost	2-1	2-2
Penalties-Yards	14-153	10-55
Time of Possession	34:49	25:11

Attendance: 54,059

GATOR BOWL
January 1, 2000
Alltel Stadium
Jacksonville, Florida

Miami (Fla.)	7	14	0	7	— 28
Georgia Tech	0	7	6	0	— 13

Miami (Fla.)—Jackson 8 run (Crosland kick)
Miami (Fla.)—King 15 pass from Kelly (Crosland kick)
Georgia Tech—Hamilton 17 run (Manget kick)
Miami (Fla.)—Portis 73 run (Crosland kick)
Georgia Tech—Manget 25 field goal
Georgia Tech—Manget 36 field goal
Miami (Fla.)—Wayne 17 pass from Dorsey (Crosland kick)

Game Statistics	Miami (Fla.)	Georgia Tech
First Downs	22	29
Rushes-Yards	36-220	48-176
Passing Yards	208	245
Passes Comp-Att-Int	16-32-1	20-40-2
Punts-Avg.	5-42.6	6-26.2
Fumbles-Lost	0-0	0-0
Penalties-Yards	9-90	7-65
Time of Possession	27:40	32:20

Attendance: 43,416

GAME-BY-GAME SUMMARIES   287

FLORIDA CITRUS BOWL
January 1, 2000
Florida Citrus Bowl
Orlando, Florida

| Michigan St. | 3 | 17 | 6 | 11 | — | 37 |
| Florida | 7 | 14 | 6 | 7 | — | 34 |

Michigan St.—Edinger 46 field goal
Florida—Taylor 12 pass from Johnson (Chandler kick)
Michigan St.—Burress 37 pass from Burke (Edinger kick)
Michigan St.—Turner 24 fumble return (Edinger kick)
Florida—Taylor 8 pass from Johnson (Chandler kick)
Michigan St.—Edinger 20 field goal
Florida—Johnson 1 run (Chandler kick)
Michigan St.—Burress 21 pass from Burke (pass failed)
Florida—Taylor 39 pass from Johnson (run failed)
Florida—Gillespie fumble recovery in end zone (Chandler kick)
Michigan St.—Burress 30 pass from Burke (Scott pass from Burke)
Michigan St.—Edinger 39 field goal

Game Statistics	Michigan St.	Florida
First Downs	25	27
Rushes-Yards	40-143	30-67
Passing Yards	257	300
Passes Comp-Att-Int	21-35-2	25-51-0
Punts-Avg.	3-43.3	6-35.5
Fumbles-Lost	3-1	4-2
Penalties-Yards	7-80	10-100
Time of Possession	32:49	27:11

Attendance: 62,011

BOWL CHAMPIONSHIP SERIES BOWLS 1999-00:

ROSE BOWL
January 1, 2000
Rose Bowl
Pasadena, California

| Stanford | 0 | 9 | 0 | 0 | — | 9 |
| Wisconsin | 0 | 3 | 7 | 7 | — | 17 |

Stanford—Biselli 28 field goal
Wisconsin—Pisetsky 31 field goal
Stanford—Carter 1 run (run failed)
Wisconsin—Dayne 4 run (Pisetsky kick)
Wisconsin—Bollinger 1 run (Pisetsky kick)

Game Statistics	Stanford	Wisconsin
First Downs	14	16
Rushes-Yards	27-(-5)	53-226
Passing Yards	264	105
Passes Comp-Att-Int	18-35-0	7-14-0
Punts-Avg.	8-38.3	8-43.4
Fumbles-Lost	2-0	0-0
Penalties-Yards	7-50	8-72
Time of Possession	26:32	33:28

Attendance: 93,731

ORANGE BOWL
January 1, 2000
Pro Player Stadium
Miami, Florida

| Michigan | 0 | 7 | 21 | 0 | 7 | — | 35 |
| Alabama | 0 | 14 | 14 | 0 | 6 | — | 34 |

Alabama—Alexander 5 run (Pflugner kick)
Alabama—Alexander 6 run (Pflugner kick)
Michigan—Terrell 27 pass from Brady (Epstein kick)
Michigan—Terrell 57 pass from Brady (Epstein kick)
Alabama—Alexander 50 run (Pflugner kick)
Alabama—Milons 62 punt return (Pflugner kick)
Michigan—Terrell 20 pass from Brady (Epstein kick)
Michigan—Thomas 3 run (Epstein kick)
Michigan—Thompson 25 pass from Brady (Epstein kick)
Alabama—Carter 21 pass from Zow (kick failed)

Game Statistics	Michigan	Alabama
First Downs	18	12
Rushes-Yards	23-54	37-222
Passing Yards	369	121
Passes Comp-Att-Int	35-47-0	13-20-0
Punts-Avg.	8-43.4	9-34.4
Fumbles-Lost	2-1	1-0
Penalties-Yards	10-115	18-132
Time of Possession	32:08	27:52

Attendance: 70,461

FIESTA BOWL
January 2, 2000
Sun Devil Stadium
Tempe, Arizona

| Tennessee | 0 | 7 | 7 | 7 | — | 21 |
| Nebraska | 14 | 3 | 7 | 7 | — | 31 |

Nebraska—Alexander 7 run (Brown kick)
Nebraska—Newcombe 60 punt return (Brown kick)
Nebraska—Brown 31 field goal
Tennessee—Stallworth 9 pass from Martin (Walls kick)
Tennessee—Henry 4 run (Walls kick)
Nebraska—Golliday 13 pass from Crouch (Brown kick)
Nebraska—Buckhalter 2 run (Brown kick)
Tennessee—Stallworth 44 pass from Wilson (Walls kick)

Game Statistics	Tennessee	Nebraska
First Downs	17	23
Rushes-Yards	26-44	56-321
Passing Yards	267	148
Passes Comp-Att-Int	20-35-2	9-15-0
Punts-Avg.	7-43.1	6-39.5
Fumbles-Lost	1-0	1-1
Penalties-Yards	5-41	8-59
Time of Possession	26:05	33:55

Attendance: 71,526

SUGAR BOWL
January 4, 2000
Louisiana Superdome
New Orleans, Louisiana

| Virginia Tech | 7 | 7 | 15 | 0 | — | 29 |
| Florida St. | 14 | 14 | 0 | 18 | — | 46 |

Florida St.—Warrick 64 pass from Weinke (Janikowski kick)
Florida St.—Chaney 6 blocked punt return (Janikowski kick)
Virginia Tech—Davis 49 pass from Vick (Graham kick)
Florida St.—Dugans 63 pass from Weinke (Janikowski kick)
Florida St.—Warrick 59 punt return (Janikowski kick)
Virginia Tech—Vick 3 run (Graham kick)
Virginia Tech—Graham 23 field goal
Virginia Tech—Kendrick 29 run (pass failed)
Virginia Tech—Kendrick 6 run (pass failed)
Florida St.—Dugans 14 pass from Weinke (Warrick pass from Weinke)
Florida St.—Janikowski 32 field goal
Florida St.—Warrick 43 pass from Weinke (Janikowski kick)

Game Statistics	Virginia Tech	Florida St.
First Downs	24	15
Rushes-Yards	52-278	23-30
Passing Yards	225	329
Passes Comp-Att-Int	15-29-0	20-34-1
Punts-Avg.	6-29.3	7-44.3
Fumbles-Lost	3-3	2-0
Penalties-Yards	6-65	7-59
Time of Possession	36:25	23:35

Attendance: 79,280

All-Time Bowl-Game Results

Major Bowl Games

ROSE BOWL
Present Site: Pasadena, California
Stadium (Capacity): Rose Bowl (96,576)
Playing Surface: Grass
Playing Sites: Tournament Park, Pasadena (1902, 1916-22); Rose Bowl, Pasadena (1923-41); Duke Stadium, Durham, N.C. (1942); Rose Bowl (since 1943)

1-1-02—Michigan 49, Stanford 0
1-1-16—Washington St. 14, Brown 0
1-1-17—Oregon 14, Pennsylvania 0
1-1-18—Mare Island 19, Camp Lewis 7
1-1-19—Great Lakes 17, Mare Island 0
1-1-20—Harvard 7, Oregon 6
1-1-21—California 28, Ohio St. 0
1-2-22—California 0, Wash. & Jeff. 0
1-1-23—Southern California 14, Penn St. 3
1-1-24—Navy 14, Washington 14
1-1-25—Notre Dame 27, Stanford 10
1-1-26—Alabama 20, Washington 19
1-1-27—Alabama 7, Stanford 7
1-2-28—Stanford 7, Pittsburgh 6
1-1-29—Georgia Tech 8, California 7
1-1-30—Southern California 47, Pittsburgh 14
1-1-31—Alabama 24, Washington St. 0
1-1-32—Southern California 21, Tulane 12
1-2-33—Southern California 35, Pittsburgh 0
1-1-34—Columbia 7, Stanford 0
1-1-35—Alabama 29, Stanford 13
1-1-36—Stanford 7, Southern Methodist 0
1-1-37—Pittsburgh 21, Washington 0
1-1-38—California 13, Alabama 0
1-2-39—Southern California 7, Duke 3
1-1-40—Southern California 14, Tennessee 0
1-1-41—Stanford 21, Nebraska 13
1-1-42—Oregon St. 20, Duke 16 (at Durham)
1-1-43—Georgia 9, UCLA 0
1-1-44—Southern California 29, Washington 0
1-1-45—Southern California 25, Tennessee 0
1-1-46—Alabama 34, Southern California 14
1-1-47—Illinois 45, UCLA 14
1-1-48—Michigan 49, Southern California 0
1-1-49—Northwestern 20, California 14
1-2-50—Ohio St. 17, California 14
1-1-51—Michigan 14, California 6
1-1-52—Illinois 40, Stanford 7
1-1-53—Southern California 7, Wisconsin 0
1-1-54—Michigan St. 28, UCLA 20
1-1-55—Ohio St. 20, Southern California 7
1-2-56—Michigan 17, UCLA 14
1-1-57—Iowa 35, Oregon St. 19
1-1-58—Ohio St. 10, Oregon 7
1-1-59—Iowa 38, California 12
1-1-60—Washington 44, Wisconsin 8
1-2-61—Washington 17, Minnesota 7
1-1-62—Minnesota 21, UCLA 3
1-1-63—Southern California 42, Wisconsin 37
1-1-64—Illinois 17, Washington 7
1-1-65—Michigan 34, Oregon St. 7
1-1-66—UCLA 14, Michigan St. 12
1-2-67—Purdue 14, Southern California 13
1-1-68—Southern California 14, Indiana 3
1-1-69—Ohio St. 27, Southern California 16
1-1-70—Southern California 10, Michigan 3
1-1-71—Stanford 27, Ohio St. 17
1-1-72—Stanford 13, Michigan 12
1-1-73—Southern California 42, Ohio St. 17
1-1-74—Ohio St. 42, Southern California 21
1-1-75—Southern California 18, Ohio St. 17
1-1-76—UCLA 23, Ohio St. 10
1-1-77—Southern California 14, Michigan 6
1-2-78—Washington 27, Michigan 20
1-1-79—Southern California 17, Michigan 10
1-1-80—Southern California 17, Ohio St. 16
1-1-81—Michigan 23, Washington 6
1-1-82—Washington 28, Iowa 0
1-1-83—UCLA 24, Michigan 14

1-2-84—UCLA 45, Illinois 9
1-1-85—Southern California 20, Ohio St. 17
1-1-86—UCLA 45, Iowa 28
1-1-87—Arizona St. 22, Michigan 15
1-1-88—Michigan St. 20, Southern California 17
1-2-89—Michigan 22, Southern California 14
1-1-90—Southern California 17, Michigan 10
1-1-91—Washington 46, Iowa 34
1-1-92—Washington 34, Michigan 14
1-1-93—Michigan 38, Washington 31
1-1-94—Wisconsin 21, UCLA 16
1-2-95—Penn St. 38, Oregon 20
1-1-96—Southern California 41, Northwestern 32
1-1-97—Ohio St. 20, Arizona St. 17
1-1-98—Michigan 21, Washington St. 16
1-1-99—Wisconsin 38, UCLA 31
1-1-00—Wisconsin 17, Stanford 9

ORANGE BOWL

Present Site: Miami, Florida
Stadium (Capacity): Pro Player Stadium (75,014)
Playing Surface: Prescription Athletic Turf
Name Changes: Orange Bowl (1935-88); Federal Express Orange Bowl (since 1989)
Playing Sites: Miami Field Stadium (1935-37); Orange Bowl (1938-96); Joe Robbie Stadium, renamed Pro Player Stadium in 1996 (since 1997)

1-1-35—Bucknell 26, Miami (Fla.) 0
1-1-36—Catholic 20, Mississippi 19
1-1-37—Duquesne 13, Mississippi St. 12
1-1-38—Auburn 6, Michigan St. 0
1-2-39—Tennessee 17, Oklahoma 0
1-1-40—Georgia Tech 21, Missouri 7
1-1-41—Mississippi St. 14, Georgetown 7
1-1-42—Georgia 40, TCU 26
1-1-43—Alabama 37, Boston College 21
1-1-44—LSU 19, Texas A&M 14
1-1-45—Tulsa 26, Georgia Tech 12
1-1-46—Miami (Fla.) 13, Holy Cross 6
1-1-47—Rice 8, Tennessee 0
1-1-48—Georgia Tech 20, Kansas 14
1-1-49—Texas 41, Georgia 28
1-2-50—Santa Clara 21, Kentucky 13
1-1-51—Clemson 15, Miami (Fla.) 14
1-1-52—Georgia Tech 17, Baylor 14
1-1-53—Alabama 61, Syracuse 6
1-1-54—Oklahoma 7, Maryland 0
1-1-55—Duke 34, Nebraska 7
1-2-56—Oklahoma 20, Maryland 6
1-1-57—Colorado 27, Clemson 21
1-1-58—Oklahoma 48, Duke 21
1-1-59—Oklahoma 21, Syracuse 6
1-1-60—Georgia 14, Missouri 0
1-2-61—Missouri 21, Navy 14
1-1-62—LSU 25, Colorado 7
1-1-63—Alabama 17, Oklahoma 0
1-1-64—Nebraska 13, Auburn 7
1-1-65—Texas 21, Alabama 17
1-1-66—Alabama 39, Nebraska 28
1-2-67—Florida 27, Georgia Tech 12
1-1-68—Oklahoma 26, Tennessee 24
1-1-69—Penn St. 15, Kansas 14
1-1-70—Penn St. 10, Missouri 3
1-1-71—Nebraska 17, LSU 12
1-1-72—Nebraska 38, Alabama 6
1-1-73—Nebraska 40, Notre Dame 6
1-1-74—Penn St. 16, LSU 9
1-1-75—Notre Dame 13, Alabama 11
1-1-76—Oklahoma 14, Michigan 6
1-1-77—Ohio St. 27, Colorado 10
1-2-78—Arkansas 31, Oklahoma 6
1-1-79—Oklahoma 31, Nebraska 24
1-1-80—Oklahoma 24, Florida St. 7
1-1-81—Oklahoma 18, Florida St. 17
1-1-82—Clemson 22, Nebraska 15
1-1-83—Nebraska 21, LSU 20
1-2-84—Miami (Fla.) 31, Nebraska 30
1-1-85—Washington 28, Oklahoma 17
1-1-86—Oklahoma 25, Penn St. 10
1-1-87—Oklahoma 42, Arkansas 8
1-1-88—Miami 20, Oklahoma 14
1-2-89—Miami (Fla.) 23, Nebraska 3
1-1-90—Notre Dame 21, Colorado 6
1-1-91—Colorado 10, Notre Dame 9
1-1-92—Miami (Fla.) 22, Nebraska 0
1-1-93—Florida St. 27, Nebraska 14
1-1-94—Florida St. 18, Nebraska 16
1-1-95—Nebraska 24, Miami (Fla.) 17
1-1-96—Florida St. 31, Notre Dame 26
12-31-96—Nebraska 41, Virginia Tech 21
1-2-98—Nebraska 42, Tennessee 17
1-2-99—Florida 31, Syracuse 10
1-1-00—Michigan 35, Alabama 34 (ot)

SUGAR BOWL

Present Site: New Orleans, Louisiana
Stadium (Capacity): Louisiana Superdome (76,791)
Playing Surface: AstroTurf
Name Changes: Sugar Bowl (1935-87); USF&G Sugar Bowl (1988-95); Nokia Sugar Bowl (since 1996)
Playing Sites: Tulane Stadium, New Orleans (1935-74); Louisiana Superdome (since 1975)

1-1-35—Tulane 20, Temple 14
1-1-36—TCU 3, LSU 2
1-1-37—Santa Clara 21, LSU 14
1-1-38—Santa Clara 6, LSU 0
1-2-39—TCU 15, Carnegie Mellon 7
1-1-40—Texas A&M 14, Tulane 13
1-1-41—Boston College 19, Tennessee 13
1-1-42—Fordham 2, Missouri 0
1-1-43—Tennessee 14, Tulsa 7
1-1-44—Georgia Tech 20, Tulsa 18
1-1-45—Duke 29, Alabama 26
1-1-46—Oklahoma St. 33, St. Mary's (Cal.) 13
1-1-47—Georgia 20, North Carolina 10
1-1-48—Texas 27, Alabama 7
1-1-49—Oklahoma 14, North Carolina 6
1-2-50—Oklahoma 35, LSU 0
1-1-51—Kentucky 13, Oklahoma 7
1-1-52—Maryland 28, Tennessee 13
1-1-53—Georgia Tech 24, Mississippi 7
1-1-54—Georgia Tech 42, West Virginia 19
1-1-55—Navy 21, Mississippi 0
1-2-56—Georgia Tech 7, Pittsburgh 0
1-1-57—Baylor 13, Tennessee 7
1-1-58—Mississippi 39, Texas 7
1-1-59—LSU 7, Clemson 0
1-1-60—Mississippi 21, LSU 0
1-2-61—Mississippi 14, Rice 6
1-1-62—Alabama 10, Arkansas 3
1-1-63—Mississippi 17, Arkansas 13
1-1-64—Alabama 12, Mississippi 7
1-1-65—LSU 13, Syracuse 10
1-1-66—Missouri 20, Florida 18
1-2-67—Alabama 34, Nebraska 7
1-1-68—LSU 20, Wyoming 13
1-1-69—Arkansas 16, Georgia 2
1-1-70—Mississippi 27, Arkansas 22
1-1-71—Tennessee 34, Air Force 13
1-1-72—Oklahoma 40, Auburn 22
12-31-72—Oklahoma 14, Penn St. 0
12-31-73—Notre Dame 24, Alabama 23
12-31-74—Nebraska 13, Florida 10
12-31-75—Alabama 13, Penn St. 6
1-1-77—Pittsburgh 27, Georgia 3
1-2-78—Alabama 35, Ohio St. 6
1-1-79—Alabama 14, Penn St. 7
1-1-80—Alabama 24, Arkansas 9
1-1-81—Georgia 17, Notre Dame 10
1-1-82—Pittsburgh 24, Georgia 20
1-1-83—Penn St. 27, Georgia 23
1-2-84—Auburn 9, Michigan 7
1-1-85—Nebraska 28, LSU 10
1-1-86—Tennessee 35, Miami (Fla.) 7
1-1-87—Nebraska 30, LSU 15
1-1-88—Auburn 16, Syracuse 16
1-2-89—Florida St. 13, Auburn 7
1-1-90—Miami (Fla.) 33, Alabama 25
1-1-91—Tennessee 23, Virginia 22
1-1-92—Notre Dame 39, Florida 28
1-1-93—Alabama 34, Miami (Fla.) 13
1-1-94—Florida 41, West Virginia 7
1-2-95—Florida St. 23, Florida 17
12-31-95—Virginia Tech 28, Texas 10
1-2-97—Florida 52, Florida St. 20
1-1-98—Florida St. 31, Ohio St. 14
1-1-99—Ohio St. 24, Texas A&M 14
1-4-00—Florida St. 46, Virginia Tech 29

COTTON BOWL

Present Site: Dallas, Texas
Stadium (Capacity): Cotton Bowl (68,252)
Playing Surface: Grass
Name Changes: Cotton Bowl (1937-88, 1996); Mobil Cotton Bowl (1989-95); Southwestern Bell Cotton Bowl (1997-00); SBC Cotton Bowl Classic (since 2001)
Playing Sites: Fair Park Stadium, Dallas (1937); Cotton Bowl (since 1938)

1-1-37—TCU 16, Marquette 6
1-1-38—Rice 28, Colorado 14
1-2-39—St. Mary's (Cal.) 20, Texas Tech 13
1-1-40—Clemson 6, Boston College 3
1-1-41—Texas A&M 13, Fordham 12
1-1-42—Alabama 29, Texas A&M 21
1-1-43—Texas 14, Georgia Tech 7
1-1-44—Randolph Field 7, Texas 7
1-1-45—Oklahoma St. 34, TCU 0
1-1-46—Texas 40, Missouri 27
1-1-47—Arkansas 0, LSU 0
1-1-48—Penn St. 13, Southern Methodist 13
1-1-49—Southern Methodist 21, Oregon 13
1-2-50—Rice 27, North Carolina 13
1-1-51—Tennessee 20, Texas 14
1-1-52—Kentucky 20, TCU 7
1-1-53—Texas 16, Tennessee 0
1-1-54—Rice 28, Alabama 6
1-1-55—Georgia Tech 14, Arkansas 6
1-2-56—Mississippi 14, TCU 13
1-1-57—TCU 28, Syracuse 27
1-1-58—Navy 20, Rice 7
1-1-59—Air Force 0, TCU 0
1-1-60—Syracuse 23, Texas 14
1-2-61—Duke 7, Arkansas 6
1-1-62—Texas 12, Mississippi 7
1-1-63—LSU 13, Texas 0
1-1-64—Texas 28, Navy 6
1-1-65—Arkansas 10, Nebraska 7
1-1-66—LSU 14, Arkansas 7
12-31-66—Georgia 24, Southern Methodist 9
1-1-68—Texas A&M 20, Alabama 16
1-1-69—Texas 36, Tennessee 13
1-1-70—Texas 21, Notre Dame 17
1-1-71—Notre Dame 24, Texas 11
1-1-72—Penn St. 30, Texas 6
1-1-73—Texas 17, Alabama 13
1-1-74—Nebraska 19, Texas 3
1-1-75—Penn St. 41, Baylor 20
1-1-76—Arkansas 31, Georgia 10
1-1-77—Houston 30, Maryland 21
1-2-78—Notre Dame 38, Texas 10
1-1-79—Notre Dame 35, Houston 34
1-1-80—Houston 17, Nebraska 14
1-1-81—Alabama 30, Baylor 2
1-1-82—Texas 14, Alabama 12
1-1-83—Southern Methodist 7, Pittsburgh 3
1-2-84—Georgia 10, Texas 9
1-1-85—Boston College 45, Houston 28
1-1-86—Texas A&M 36, Auburn 16
1-1-87—Ohio St. 28, Texas A&M 12
1-1-88—Texas A&M 35, Notre Dame 10
1-2-89—UCLA 17, Arkansas 3
1-1-90—Tennessee 31, Arkansas 27
1-1-91—Miami (Fla.) 46, Texas 3
1-1-92—Florida St. 10, Texas A&M 2
1-1-93—Notre Dame 28, Texas A&M 3
1-1-94—Notre Dame 24, Texas A&M 21
1-2-95—Southern California 55, Texas Tech 14
1-1-96—Colorado 38, Oregon 6
1-1-97—Brigham Young 19, Kansas St. 15
1-1-98—UCLA 29, Texas A&M 23
1-1-99—Texas 38, Mississippi St. 11
1-1-00—Arkansas 27, Texas 6

SUN BOWL

Present Site: El Paso, Texas
Stadium (Capacity): Sun Bowl Stadium (51,270)
Playing Surface: AstroTurf
Name Changes: Sun Bowl (1936-86, 1994-95); John Hancock Sun Bowl (1987-88); John Hancock Bowl (1989-93); Norwest Bank Sun Bowl (1996); Norwest Sun Bowl (1997-99); Wells Fargo Sun Bowl (since 2000)
Playing Sites: Kidd Field, UTEP, El Paso (1936-62); Sun Bowl (since 1963)

ALL-TIME BOWL-GAME RESULTS

1-1-36—Hardin-Simmons 14, New Mexico St. 14
1-1-37—Hardin-Simmons 34, UTEP 6
1-1-38—West Virginia 7, Texas Tech 6
1-2-39—Utah 26, New Mexico 0
1-1-40—Arizona St. 0, Catholic 0
1-1-41—Case Reserve 26, Arizona St. 13
1-1-42—Tulsa 6, Texas Tech 0
1-1-43—Second Air Force 13, Hardin-Simmons 7
1-1-44—Southwestern (Tex.) 7, New Mexico 0
1-1-45—Southwestern (Tex.) 35, U. of Mexico 0
1-1-46—New Mexico 34, Denver 24
1-1-47—Cincinnati 18, Virginia Tech 6
1-1-48—Miami (Ohio) 13, Texas Tech 12
1-1-49—West Virginia 21, UTEP 12
1-2-50—UTEP 33, Georgetown 20
1-1-51—West Tex. A&M 14, Cincinnati 13
1-1-52—Texas Tech 25, Pacific (Cal.) 14
1-1-53—Pacific (Cal.) 26, Southern Miss. 7
1-1-54—UTEP 37, Southern Miss. 14
1-1-55—UTEP 47, Florida St. 20
1-2-56—Wyoming 21, Texas Tech 14
1-1-57—George Washington 13, UTEP 0
1-1-58—Louisville 34, Drake 0
12-31-58—Wyoming 14, Hardin-Simmons 6
12-31-59—New Mexico St. 28, North Texas 8
12-31-60—New Mexico St. 20, Utah St. 13
12-30-61—Villanova 17, Wichita St. 9
12-31-62—West Tex. A&M 15, Ohio 14
12-31-63—Oregon 21, Southern Methodist 14
12-26-64—Georgia 7, Texas Tech 0
12-31-65—UTEP 13, TCU 12
12-24-66—Wyoming 28, Florida St. 20
12-30-67—UTEP 14, Mississippi 7
12-28-68—Auburn 34, Arizona 10
12-20-69—Nebraska 45, Georgia 6
12-19-70—Georgia Tech 17, Texas Tech 9
12-18-71—LSU 33, Iowa St. 15
12-30-72—North Carolina 32, Texas Tech 28
12-29-73—Missouri 34, Auburn 17
12-28-74—Mississippi St. 26, North Carolina 24
12-26-75—Pittsburgh 33, Kansas 19
1-2-77—Texas A&M 37, Florida 14
12-31-77—Stanford 24, LSU 14
12-23-78—Texas 42, Maryland 0
12-22-79—Washington 14, Texas 7
12-27-80—Nebraska 31, Mississippi St. 17
12-26-81—Oklahoma 40, Houston 14
12-25-82—North Carolina 26, Texas 10
12-24-83—Alabama 28, Southern Methodist 7
12-22-84—Maryland 28, Tennessee 27
12-28-85—Arizona 13, Georgia 13
12-25-86—Alabama 28, Washington 6
12-25-87—Oklahoma St. 35, West Virginia 33
12-24-88—Alabama 29, Army 28
12-30-89—Pittsburgh 31, Texas A&M 28
12-31-90—Michigan St. 17, Southern California 16
12-31-91—UCLA 6, Illinois 3
12-31-92—Baylor 20, Arizona 15
12-24-93—Oklahoma 41, Texas Tech 10
12-30-94—Texas 35, North Carolina 31
12-29-95—Iowa 38, Washington 18
12-31-96—Stanford 38, Michigan St. 0
12-31-97—Arizona 20, Iowa 7
12-31-98—TCU 28, Southern California 19
12-31-99—Oregon 24, Minnesota 20

GATOR BOWL

Present Site: Jacksonville, Florida
Stadium (Capacity): Alltel Stadium (76,976)
Playing Surface: Grass
Name Changes: Gator Bowl (1946-85, 1991); Mazda Gator Bowl (1986-90); Outback Steakhouse Gator Bowl (1992-94); Toyota Gator Bowl (since 1995)
Playing Sites: Gator Bowl (1946-93); Florida Field, Gainesville, Fla. (1994); Jacksonville Municipal Stadium, renamed Alltel Stadium in 1997 (since 1995)

1-1-46—Wake Forest 26, South Carolina 14
1-1-47—Oklahoma 34, North Carolina St. 13
1-1-48—Georgia 20, Maryland 20
1-1-49—Clemson 24, Missouri 23
1-2-50—Maryland 20, Missouri 7
1-1-51—Wyoming 20, Wash. & Lee 7
1-1-52—Miami (Fla.) 14, Clemson 0
1-1-53—Florida 14, Tulsa 13
1-1-54—Texas Tech 35, Auburn 13
12-31-54—Auburn 33, Baylor 13
12-31-55—Vanderbilt 25, Auburn 13
12-29-56—Georgia Tech 21, Pittsburgh 14
12-28-57—Tennessee 3, Texas A&M 0
12-27-58—Mississippi 7, Florida 3
1-2-60—Arkansas 14, Georgia Tech 7
12-31-60—Florida 13, Baylor 12
12-30-61—Penn St. 30, Georgia Tech 15
12-29-62—Florida 17, Penn St. 7
12-28-63—North Carolina 35, Air Force 0
1-2-65—Florida St. 36, Oklahoma 19
12-31-65—Georgia Tech 31, Texas Tech 21
12-31-66—Tennessee 18, Syracuse 12
12-30-67—Florida St. 17, Penn St. 17
12-28-68—Missouri 35, Alabama 10
12-27-69—Florida 14, Tennessee 13
1-2-71—Auburn 35, Mississippi 28
12-31-71—Georgia 7, North Carolina 3
12-30-72—Auburn 24, Colorado 3
12-29-73—Texas Tech 28, Tennessee 19
12-30-74—Auburn 27, Texas 3
12-29-75—Maryland 13, Florida 0
12-27-76—Notre Dame 20, Penn St. 9
12-30-77—Pittsburgh 34, Clemson 3
12-29-78—Clemson 17, Ohio St. 15
12-28-79—North Carolina 17, Michigan 15
12-29-80—Pittsburgh 37, South Carolina 9
12-28-81—North Carolina 31, Arkansas 27
12-30-82—Florida St. 31, West Virginia 12
12-30-83—Florida 14, Iowa 6
12-28-84—Oklahoma St. 21, South Carolina 14
12-30-85—Florida St. 34, Oklahoma St. 23
12-27-86—Clemson 27, Stanford 21
12-31-87—LSU 30, South Carolina 13
1-1-89—Georgia 34, Michigan St. 27
12-30-89—Clemson 27, West Virginia 7
1-1-91—Michigan 35, Mississippi 3
12-29-91—Oklahoma 48, Virginia 14
12-31-92—Florida 27, North Carolina St. 10
12-31-93—Alabama 24, North Carolina 10
12-30-94—Tennessee 45, Virginia Tech 23
1-1-96—Syracuse 41, Clemson 0
1-1-97—North Carolina 20, West Virginia 13
1-1-98—North Carolina 42, Virginia Tech 3
1-1-99—Georgia Tech 35, Notre Dame 28
1-1-00—Miami (Fla.) 28, Georgia Tech 13

FLORIDA CITRUS BOWL

Present Site: Orlando, Florida
Stadium (Capacity): Florida Citrus Bowl (70,000)
Playing Surface: Grass
Name Changes: Tangerine Bowl (1947-82); Florida Citrus Bowl (1983-93); CompUSA Florida Citrus Bowl (1994-99); OurHouse.com Florida Citrus Bowl (since 2000)
Playing Sites: Tangerine Bowl, Orlando (1947-72); Florida Field, Gainesville (1973); Tangerine Bowl (now Florida Citrus Bowl) (1974-82); Orlando Stadium (now Florida Citrus Bowl) (1983-85); Florida Citrus Bowl (since 1986)

1-1-47—Catawba 31, Maryville (Tenn.) 6
1-1-48—Catawba 7, Marshall 0
1-1-49—Murray St. 21, Sul Ross St. 21
1-2-50—St. Vincent 7, Emory & Henry 6
1-1-51—Morris Harvey 35, Emory & Henry 14
1-1-52—Stetson 35, Arkansas St. 20
1-1-53—Tex. A&M-Commerce 33, Tennessee Tech 0
1-1-54—Arkansas St. 7, Tex. A&M-Commerce 7
1-1-55—Neb.-Omaha 7, Eastern Ky. 6
1-2-56—Juniata 6, Missouri Valley 6
1-1-57—West Tex. A&M 20, Southern Miss. 13
1-1-58—Tex. A&M-Commerce 10, Southern Miss. 9
12-27-58—Tex. A&M-Commerce 26, Missouri Valley 7
1-1-60—Middle Tenn. St. 21, Presbyterian 12
12-30-60—Citadel 27, Tennessee Tech 0
12-29-61—Lamar 21, Middle Tenn. St. 14
12-22-62—Houston 49, Miami (Ohio) 21
12-28-63—Western Ky. 27, Coast Guard 0
12-12-64—East Caro. 14, Massachusetts 13
12-11-65—East Caro. 31, Maine 0
12-10-66—Morgan St. 14, West Chester 6
12-16-67—Tenn.-Martin 25, West Chester 8
12-27-68—Richmond 49, Ohio 42
12-26-69—Toledo 56, Davidson 33
12-28-70—Toledo 40, William & Mary 12
12-28-71—Toledo 28, Richmond 3
12-29-72—Tampa 21, Kent 18
12-22-73—Miami (Ohio) 16, Florida 7
12-21-74—Miami (Ohio) 21, Georgia 10
12-20-75—Miami (Ohio) 20, South Carolina 7
12-18-76—Oklahoma St. 49, Brigham Young 21
12-23-77—Florida St. 40, Texas Tech 17
12-23-78—North Carolina St. 30, Pittsburgh 17
12-22-79—LSU 34, Wake Forest 10
12-20-80—Florida 35, Maryland 20
12-19-81—Missouri 19, Southern Miss. 17
12-18-82—Auburn 33, Boston College 26
12-17-83—Tennessee 30, Maryland 23
12-22-84—Florida St. 17, Georgia 17
12-28-85—Ohio St. 10, Brigham Young 7
1-1-87—Auburn 16, Southern California 7
1-1-88—Clemson 35, Penn St. 10
1-2-89—Clemson 13, Oklahoma 6
1-1-90—Illinois 31, Virginia 21
1-1-91—Georgia Tech 45, Nebraska 21
1-1-92—California 37, Clemson 13
1-1-93—Georgia 21, Ohio St. 14
1-1-94—Penn St. 31, Tennessee 13
1-2-95—Alabama 24, Ohio St. 17
1-1-96—Tennessee 20, Ohio St. 14
1-1-97—Tennessee 48, Northwestern 28
1-1-98—Florida 21, Penn St. 6
1-1-99—Michigan 45, Arkansas 31
1-1-00—Michigan St. 37, Florida 34

Note: No classified major teams participated in games from January 1, 1947, through January 1, 1960, or in 1961 and 1963 through 1967.

LIBERTY BOWL

Present Site: Memphis, Tennessee
Stadium (Capacity): Liberty Bowl Memorial Stadium (62,921)
Playing Surface: Prescription Athletic Turf
Name Changes: Liberty Bowl (1959-92); St. Jude Liberty Bowl (1993-96); AXA Equitable Liberty Bowl (since 1997)
Playing Sites: Municipal Stadium, Philadelphia (1959-63); Convention Hall, Atlantic City, N.J. (1964); Liberty Bowl Memorial Stadium (since 1965)

12-19-59—Penn St. 7, Alabama 0
12-17-60—Penn St. 41, Oregon 12
12-16-61—Syracuse 15, Miami (Fla.) 14
12-15-62—Oregon St. 6, Villanova 0
12-21-63—Mississippi St. 16, North Carolina St. 12
12-19-64—Utah 32, West Virginia 6
12-18-65—Mississippi 13, Auburn 7
12-10-66—Miami (Fla.) 14, Virginia Tech 7
12-16-67—North Carolina St. 14, Georgia 7
12-14-68—Mississippi 34, Virginia Tech 17
12-13-69—Colorado 47, Alabama 33
12-12-70—Tulane 17, Colorado 3
12-20-71—Tennessee 14, Arkansas 13
12-18-72—Georgia Tech 31, Iowa St. 30
12-17-73—North Carolina St. 31, Kansas 18
12-16-74—Tennessee 7, Maryland 3
12-22-75—Southern California 20, Texas A&M 0
12-20-76—Alabama 36, UCLA 6
12-19-77—Nebraska 21, North Carolina 17
12-23-78—Missouri 20, LSU 15
12-22-79—Penn St. 9, Tulane 6
12-27-80—Purdue 28, Missouri 25
12-30-81—Ohio St. 31, Navy 28
12-29-82—Alabama 21, Illinois 15
12-29-83—Notre Dame 19, Boston College 18
12-27-84—Auburn 21, Arkansas 15
12-27-85—Baylor 21, LSU 7
12-29-86—Tennessee 21, Minnesota 14
12-29-87—Georgia 20, Arkansas 17
12-28-88—Indiana 34, South Carolina 10
12-28-89—Mississippi 42, Air Force 29
12-27-90—Air Force 23, Ohio St. 11
12-29-91—Air Force 38, Mississippi St. 15
12-31-92—Mississippi 13, Air Force 0
12-28-93—Louisville 18, Michigan St. 7
12-31-94—Illinois 30, East Caro. 0
12-30-95—East Caro. 19, Stanford 13
12-27-96—Syracuse 30, Houston 17
12-31-97—Southern Miss. 41, Pittsburgh 7
12-31-98—Tulane 41, Brigham Young 27
12-31-99—Southern Miss. 23, Colorado St. 17

PEACH BOWL

Present Site: Atlanta, Georgia
Stadium (Capacity): Georgia Dome (71,228)
Name Changes: Peach Bowl (1968-96); Chick-Fil-A Peach Bowl (since 1997)
Playing Surface: AstroTurf
Playing Sites: Grant Field, Atlanta (1968-70); Atlanta/Fulton County (1971-92); Georgia Dome (since 1993)

12-30-68—LSU 31, Florida St. 27
12-30-69—West Virginia 14, South Carolina 3
12-30-70—Arizona St. 48, North Carolina 26
12-30-71—Mississippi 41, Georgia Tech 18
12-29-72—North Carolina St. 49, West Virginia 13
12-28-73—Georgia 17, Maryland 16
12-28-74—Texas Tech 6, Vanderbilt 6
12-31-75—West Virginia 13, North Carolina St. 10
12-31-76—Kentucky 21, North Carolina 0
12-31-77—North Carolina St. 24, Iowa St. 14
12-25-78—Purdue 41, Georgia Tech 21
12-31-79—Baylor 24, Clemson 18
1-2-81—Miami (Fla.) 20, Virginia Tech 10
12-31-81—West Virginia 26, Florida 6
12-31-82—Iowa 28, Tennessee 22
12-30-83—Florida St. 28, North Carolina 3
12-31-84—Virginia 27, Purdue 24
12-31-85—Army 31, Illinois 29
12-31-86—Virginia Tech 25, North Carolina St. 24
1-2-88—Tennessee 27, Indiana 22
12-31-88—North Carolina St. 28, Iowa 23
12-30-89—Syracuse 19, Georgia 18
12-29-90—Auburn 27, Indiana 23
1-1-92—East Caro. 37, North Carolina St. 34
1-2-93—North Carolina 21, Mississippi St. 17
12-31-93—Clemson 14, Kentucky 13
1-1-95—North Carolina 28, Mississippi St. 24
12-30-95—Virginia 34, Georgia 27
12-28-96—LSU 10, Clemson 7
1-2-98—Auburn 21, Clemson 17
12-31-98—Georgia 35, Virginia 33
12-30-99—Mississippi St. 17, Clemson 7

FIESTA BOWL

Present Site: Tempe, Arizona
Stadium (Capacity): Sun Devil Stadium (73,259)
Playing Surface: Grass
Name Changes: Fiesta Bowl (1971-85, 1991-92); Sunkist Fiesta Bowl (1986-90); IBM OS/2 Fiesta Bowl (1993-95); Tostitos Fiesta Bowl (since 1996)
Playing Sites: Sun Devil Stadium (since 1971)

12-27-71—Arizona St. 45, Florida St. 38
12-23-72—Arizona St. 49, Missouri 35
12-21-73—Arizona St. 28, Pittsburgh 7
12-28-74—Oklahoma St. 16, Brigham Young 6
12-26-75—Arizona St. 17, Nebraska 14
12-25-76—Oklahoma 41, Wyoming 7
12-25-77—Penn St. 42, Arizona St. 30
12-25-78—Arkansas 10, UCLA 10
12-25-79—Pittsburgh 16, Arizona 10
12-26-80—Penn St. 31, Ohio St. 19
1-1-82—Penn St. 26, Southern California 10
1-1-83—Arizona St. 32, Oklahoma 21
1-2-84—Ohio St. 28, Pittsburgh 23
1-1-85—UCLA 39, Miami (Fla.) 37
1-1-86—Michigan 27, Nebraska 23
1-2-87—Penn St. 14, Miami (Fla.) 10
1-1-88—Florida St. 31, Nebraska 28
1-2-89—Notre Dame 34, West Virginia 21
1-1-90—Florida St. 41, Nebraska 17
1-1-91—Louisville 34, Alabama 7
1-1-92—Penn St. 42, Tennessee 17
1-1-93—Syracuse 26, Colorado 22
1-1-94—Arizona 29, Miami (Fla.) 0
1-2-95—Colorado 41, Notre Dame 24
1-2-96—Nebraska 62, Florida 24
1-1-97—Penn St. 38, Texas 15
12-31-97—Kansas St. 35, Syracuse 18
1-4-99—Tennessee 23, Florida St. 16
1-2-00—Nebraska 31, Tennessee 21

INDEPENDENCE BOWL

Present Site: Shreveport, Louisiana
Stadium (Capacity): Independence Stadium (50,459)
Playing Surface: Grass
Name Changes: Independence Bowl (1976-89); Poulan Independence Bowl (1990); Poulan/Weed Eater Independence Bowl (1991-97); Sanford Independence Bowl (since 1998)
Playing Sites: Independence Stadium (since 1976)

12-13-76—McNeese St. 20, Tulsa 16
12-17-77—Louisiana Tech 24, Louisville 14
12-16-78—East Caro. 35, Louisiana Tech 13
12-15-79—Syracuse 31, McNeese St. 7
12-13-80—Southern Miss. 16, McNeese St. 14
12-12-81—Texas A&M 33, Oklahoma St. 16
12-11-82—Wisconsin 14, Kansas St. 3
12-10-83—Air Force 9, Mississippi 3
12-15-84—Air Force 23, Virginia Tech 7
12-21-85—Minnesota 20, Clemson 13
12-20-86—Mississippi 20, Texas Tech 17
12-19-87—Washington 24, Tulane 12
12-23-88—Southern Miss. 38, UTEP 18
12-16-89—Oregon 27, Tulsa 24
12-15-90—Louisiana Tech 34, Maryland 34
12-29-91—Georgia 24, Arkansas 15
12-31-92—Wake Forest 39, Oregon 35
12-31-93—Virginia Tech 45, Indiana 20
12-28-94—Virginia 20, TCU 10
12-29-95—LSU 45, Michigan St. 26
12-31-96—Auburn 32, Army 29
12-28-97—LSU 27, Notre Dame 9
12-31-98—Mississippi 35, Texas Tech 18
12-31-99—Mississippi 27, Oklahoma 25

HOLIDAY BOWL

Present Site: San Diego, California
Stadium (Capacity): Qualcomm Stadium (70,000)
Playing Surface: Grass
Name Changes: Holiday Bowl (1978-85); Sea World Holiday Bowl (1986-90); Thrifty Car Rental Holiday Bowl (1991-94); Plymouth Holiday Bowl (1995-97); Culligan Holiday Bowl (since 1998)
Playing Sites: San Diego Jack Murphy Stadium, renamed Qualcomm Stadium in 1997 (since 1978)

12-22-78—Navy 23, Brigham Young 16
12-21-79—Indiana 38, Brigham Young 37
12-19-80—Brigham Young 46, Southern Methodist 45
12-18-81—Brigham Young 38, Washington St. 36
12-17-82—Ohio St. 47, Brigham Young 17
12-23-83—Brigham Young 21, Missouri 17
12-21-84—Brigham Young 24, Michigan 17
12-22-85—Arkansas 18, Arizona St. 17
12-30-86—Iowa 39, San Diego St. 38
12-30-87—Iowa 20, Wyoming 19
12-30-88—Oklahoma St. 62, Wyoming 14
12-29-89—Penn St. 50, Brigham Young 39
12-29-90—Texas A&M 65, Brigham Young 14
12-30-91—Brigham Young 13, Iowa 13
12-30-92—Hawaii 27, Illinois 17
12-30-93—Ohio St. 28, Brigham Young 21
12-30-94—Michigan 24, Colorado St. 14
12-29-95—Kansas St. 54, Colorado St. 21
12-30-96—Colorado 33, Washington 21
12-29-97—Colorado St. 35, Missouri 24
12-30-98—Arizona 23, Nebraska 20
12-29-99—Kansas St. 24, Washington 20

ALOHA CLASSICS

Present Site: Honolulu, Hawaii
Stadium (Capacity): Aloha Stadium (50,000)
Playing Surface: AstroTurf
Name Changes: Aloha Bowl (1982-84); Eagle Aloha Bowl (1985-88); Jeep Eagle Aloha Bowl (1989-96); Eagle Aloha Bowl Football Classic (1997); Jeep Aloha Christmas Football Classics (since 1998)
Playing Sites: Aloha Stadium (since 1982)

12-25-82—Washington 21, Maryland 20
12-26-83—Penn St. 13, Washington 10
12-29-84—Southern Methodist 27, Notre Dame 20
12-28-85—Alabama 24, Southern California 3
12-27-86—Arizona 30, North Carolina 21
12-25-87—UCLA 20, Florida 16
12-25-88—Washington St. 24, Houston 22
12-25-89—Michigan St. 33, Hawaii 13
12-25-90—Syracuse 28, Arizona 0
12-25-91—Georgia Tech 18, Stanford 17
12-25-92—Kansas 23, Brigham Young 20
12-25-93—Colorado 41, Fresno St. 30
12-25-94—Boston College 12, Kansas St. 7
12-25-95—Kansas 51, UCLA 30
12-25-96—Navy 42, California 38
12-25-97—Washington 51, Michigan 23

Aloha Classic
12-25-98—Colorado 51, Oregon 43
12-25-99—Wake Forest 23, Arizona St. 3
Oahu Classic
12-25-98—Air Force 45, Washington 25
12-25-99—Hawaii 23, Oregon St. 17

OUTBACK BOWL

Present Site: Tampa, Florida
Stadium (Capacity): Raymond James Stadium (66,005)
Playing Surface: Grass
Name Changes: Hall of Fame Bowl (1986-95); Outback Bowl (since 1996)
Playing Sites: Tampa Stadium, renamed Houlihan's Stadium in 1997 (1986-97); Tampa Community Stadium (1998); Raymond James Stadium (since 1999)

12-23-86—Boston College 27, Georgia 24
1-2-88—Michigan 28, Alabama 24
1-2-89—Syracuse 23, LSU 10
1-1-90—Auburn 31, Ohio St. 14
1-1-91—Clemson 30, Illinois 0
1-1-92—Syracuse 24, Ohio St. 17
1-1-93—Tennessee 38, Boston College 23
1-1-94—Michigan 42, North Carolina St. 7
1-2-95—Wisconsin 34, Duke 20
1-1-96—Penn St. 43, Auburn 14
1-1-97—Alabama 17, Michigan 14
1-1-98—Georgia 33, Wisconsin 6
1-1-99—Penn St. 26, Kentucky 14
1-1-00—Georgia 28, Purdue 25 (ot)

INSIGHT.COM BOWL

Present Site: Tucson, Arizona
Stadium (Capacity): Arizona Stadium (55,883)
Playing Surface: Grass
Name Changes: Copper Bowl (1989, 1996); Domino's Pizza Copper Bowl (1990-91); Weiser Lock Copper Bowl (1992-95); Insight.com Bowl (since 1997)
Playing Sites: Arizona Stadium (since 1989)

12-31-89—Arizona 17, North Carolina St. 10
12-31-90—California 17, Wyoming 15
12-31-91—Indiana 24, Baylor 0
12-29-92—Washington St. 31, Utah 28
12-29-93—Kansas St. 52, Wyoming 17
12-29-94—Brigham Young 31, Oklahoma 6
12-27-95—Texas Tech 55, Air Force 41
12-27-96—Wisconsin 38, Utah 10
12-27-97—Arizona 20, New Mexico 14
12-26-98—Missouri 34, West Virginia 31
12-31-99—Colorado 62, Boston College 28

MICRONPC.COM BOWL

Present Site: Miami, Florida
Stadium (Capacity): Pro Player Stadium (75,014)
Playing Surface: Prescription Athletic Turf
Name Changes: Blockbuster Bowl (1990-93); Carquest Bowl (1994-97); MicronPC Bowl (1998); Micronpc.com Bowl (since 1999)
Playing Sites: Joe Robbie Stadium, renamed Pro Player Stadium in 1996 (since 1990)

12-28-90—Florida St. 24, Penn St. 17
12-28-91—Alabama 30, Colorado 25
1-1-93—Stanford 24, Penn St. 3
1-1-94—Boston College 31, Virginia 13
1-2-95—South Carolina 24, West Virginia 21
12-30-95—North Carolina 20, Arkansas 10
12-27-96—Miami (Fla.) 31, Virginia 21
12-29-97—Georgia Tech 35, West Virginia 30
12-29-98—Miami (Fla.) 46, North Carolina 23
12-30-99—Illinois 63, Virginia 21

LAS VEGAS BOWL

Present Site: Las Vegas, Nevada
Stadium (Capacity): Sam Boyd Stadium (40,000)
Playing Surface: Monsanto Turf (retractable)
Name Changes: Las Vegas Bowl (1992-98); EA Sports Las Vegas Bowl (since 1999)
Playing Sites: Sam Boyd Stadium (since 1992)

12-18-92—Bowling Green 35, Nevada 34
12-17-93—Utah St. 42, Ball St. 33
12-15-94—UNLV 52, Central Mich. 24
12-14-95—Toledo 40, Nevada 37 (ot)
12-19-96—Nevada 18, Ball St. 15
12-20-97—Oregon 41, Air Force 13
12-19-98—North Carolina 20, San Diego St. 13
12-18-99—Utah 17, Fresno St. 16

ALL-TIME BOWL-GAME RESULTS

ALAMO BOWL
Present Site: San Antonio, Texas
Stadium (Capacity): Alamodome (65,000)
Playing Surface: AstroTurf
Name Changes: Builders Square Alamo Bowl (1993-98); Sylvania Alamo Bowl (since 1999)
Playing Sites: Alamodome (since 1993)

12-31-93—California 37, Iowa 3
12-31-94—Washington St. 10, Baylor 3
12-28-95—Texas A&M 22, Michigan 20
12-29-96—Iowa 27, Texas Tech 0
12-30-97—Purdue 33, Oklahoma St. 20
12-29-98—Purdue 37, Kansas St. 34
12-28-99—Penn St. 24, Texas A&M 0

HUMANITARIAN BOWL
Present Site: Boise, Idaho
Stadium (Capacity): Bronco Stadium (30,000)
Playing Surface: Blue AstroTurf
Name Changes: Sports Humanitarian Bowl (1997); Humanitarian Bowl (1998); Crucial Humanitarian Bowl (since 1999)
Playing Sites: Bronco Stadium (since 1997)

12-29-97—Cincinnati 35, Utah St. 19
12-30-98—Idaho 42, Southern Miss. 35
12-30-99—Boise St. 34, Louisville 31

MOTOR CITY BOWL
Present Site: Pontiac, Michigan
Stadium (Capacity): Pontiac Silverdome (79,083)
Playing Surface: AstroTurf
Playing Sites: Pontiac Silverdome (since 1997)

12-26-97—Mississippi 34, Marshall 31
12-23-98—Marshall 48, Louisville 29
12-27-99—Marshall 21, Brigham Young 3

MUSIC CITY BOWL
Present Site: Nashville, Tennessee
Stadium (Capacity): Adelphia Coliseum (67,000)
Playing Surface: Grass
Name Changes: Music City Bowl (1998); HomePoint.com Music City Bowl (since 1999)
Playing Sites: Vanderbilt Stadium (1998); Adelphia Coliseum (since 1999)

12-29-98—Virginia Tech 38, Alabama 7
12-29-99—Syracuse 20, Kentucky 13

MOBILE ALABAMA BOWL
Present Site: Mobile, Alabama
Stadium (Capacity): Ladd-Peebles Stadium (40,646)
Playing Surface: Grass
Name Changes: Mobile Alabama Bowl (1999); GMAC Mobile Alabama Bowl (since 2000)
Playing Sites: Ladd-Peebles Stadium (since 1999)

12-22-99—TCU 28, East Caro. 14

Bowl-Game Title Sponsors

Bowl	Title Sponsor[s] (Year Began)	Bowl Name (Years)
Alamo	Builders Square (1993-98) Sylvania (since 1999)	Builders Square Alamo (1993-98) Sylvania Alamo (since 1999)
Aloha	Jeep Division of Chrysler (since 1985)	Aloha (1982-84) Eagle Aloha (1985-88) Jeep Eagle Aloha (1989-96) Eagle Aloha Bowl Football Classic (1997) Jeep Aloha Christmas Football Classics (since 1998)
Cotton	Mobil (1989-95) Southwestern Bell (1997) SBC Communications (since 2001)	Cotton (1937-88, 1996) Mobil Cotton (1989-95) Southwestern Bell (1997-00) SBC Cotton Bowl Classic (since 2001)
Fiesta	Sunkist (1986-90) IBM (1993-95) Tostitos (since 1996)	Fiesta (1971-85; 1991-92) Sunkist Fiesta (1986-90) IBM OS/2 Fiesta (1993-95) Tostitos Fiesta (since 1996)
Florida Citrus	Florida Department of Citrus (since 1983) Comp USA (1994-99) OurHouse.com (since 2000)	Tangerine (1947-82) Florida Citrus (1983-93) CompUSA Florida Citrus (since 1994) OurHouse.com Florida Citrus (since 2000)
Gator	Mazda (1986-91) Outback Steakhouse (1992-95) Toyota (since 1995)	Gator (1946-85) Mazda Gator (1986-91) Outback Steakhouse Gator (1992-94) Toyota Gator (since 1995)
Holiday	Sea World (1986-90) Thrifty Car Rental (1991-94) Plymouth (1995-97) Culligan (since 1998)	Holiday (1978-85) Sea World Holiday (1986-90) Thrifty Car Rental Holiday (1991-94) Plymouth Holiday (1995-97) Culligan Holiday (since 1998)
Humanitarian	Humanitarian Bowl Association (1997-1999) Crucial Technology (since 1999)	Sports Humanitarian (1997) Humanitarian (1998) Crucial Humanitarian (since 1999)
Independence	Poulan (1990-97) Sanford (since 1998)	Independence (1976-89) Poulan Independence (1990) Poulan/Weed Eater Independence (1991-97) Sanford Independence (since 1998)
Insight.com	Domino's Pizza (1990-91) Weiser Lock (1992-95) Insight.com (since 1997)	Copper (1989, 1996) Domino's Pizza Copper (1990-91) Weiser Lock Copper (1992-95) Insight.com (since 1997)
Las Vegas	None (1992-97) Las Vegas Convention & Visitor's Authority (since 1998) EA Sports (since 1999)	Las Vegas (1992-98) EA Sports Las Vegas (since 1999)
Liberty	St. Jude (1993-96) AXA/Equitable (since 1997)	Liberty (1959-92) St. Jude Liberty (1993-96) AXA/Equitable Liberty (since 1997)
Micronpc.com	Blockbuster (1990-93) Carquest Auto Parts (1994-97) Micron Electronics (since 1998)	Blockbuster (1990-93) Carquest (1994-97) Micron PC (since 1998) Micronpc.com (since 1999)
Mobile Alabama	Mobile Alabama, Inc. (1999) GMAC Financial Services and the City of Mobile (since 2000)	Mobile Alabama (1999) GMAC Mobile Alabama (since 2000)
Motor City	Motor City Bowl, Inc. (1997) Ford Division (Ford Motor Company) (since 1998)	Ford Motor City (1997) Motor City (since 1998)
Music City	American General (1998) HomePoint.com (since 1999)	Music City (1998) HomePoint.com Music City (since 1999)
Orange	Federal Express (since 1989)	Orange (1935-88) Federal Express Orange (since 1989)
Outback	None (1986-95) Outback Steakhouse (since 1996)	Hall of Fame (1986-95) Outback (since 1996)
Peach	None (1968-96) Chick-Fil-A (since 1997)	Peach (1968-96) Chick-Fil-A Peach (since 1997)
Rose	Pasadena Tournament of Roses Association (1902, 1916-98) AT&T (since 1999)	Rose (since 1902)
Sugar	USF&G Sugar (1988-95) Nokia Mobile Telephones (since 1996)	Sugar (1935-87) USF&G Sugar (1988-95) Nokia Sugar (since 1996)
Sun	John Hancock (1987-93) Norwest Corporation (1996-98) Wells Fargo (since 1999)	John Hancock Sun (1987-88) John Hancock (1989-93) Sun (1936-86, 1994-95) Norwest Bank Sun (1996) Norwest Sun (1997-98) Wells Fargo Sun (since 1999)

Bowl Financial Analysis, 1976-00

Year	No. Bowls	No. Teams	Total Payout	Per-Game Payout	Per-Team Payout
1976-77	11	22	$11,345,851	$515,714	$257,857
1977-78	12	24	13,323,638	1,110,303	555,152
1978-79	13	26	15,506,516	1,192,809	596,405
1979-80	13	26	17,219,624	1,324,586	662,293
1980-81	13	26	19,517,938	1,501,380	750,690
1981-82	14	28	21,791,222	1,556,516	778,258
1982-83	15	30	26,682,486	1,778,832	889,416
1983-84	15	30	32,535,788	2,169,052	1,084,526
1984-85	16	32	36,666,738	2,291,671	1,145,836
1985-86	16	32	36,995,864	2,312,242	1,156,121
1986-87	17	34	45,830,906	2,695,936	1,347,968
1987-88	17	34	48,251,516	2,838,324	1,419,162
1988-89	17	34	52,905,426	3,112,084	1,556,042
1989-90	18	36	58,208,058	3,233,781	1,616,891
1990-91	19	38	60,378,362	3,177,809	1,588,904
1991-92	18	36	63,494,554	3,527,475	1,763,738
1992-93	18	36	67,950,000	3,775,000	1,887,500
1993-94	19	38	71,006,000	3,737,158	1,868,579
1994-95	19	38	72,416,000	3,811,368	1,905,684
1995-96	18	36	101,390,000	5,632,778	2,816,389
1996-97	18	36	101,316,000	5,628,667	2,814,333
1997-98	20	40	108,750,000	5,437,500	2,718,750
1998-99	22	44	145,924,000	6,632,909	3,316,455
1999-00	23	46	146,000,000	6,373,913	3,186,957

27 Former Major Bowl Games

(Games in which at least one team was classified major that season)

ALAMO
(San Antonio, Texas)

1-4-47—Hardin-Simmons 20, Denver 0

ALL-AMERICAN
(Called Hall of Fame Classic, 1977-85)
(Birmingham, Ala.)

12-22-77—Maryland 17, Minnesota 7
12-20-78—Texas A&M 28, Iowa St. 12
12-29-79—Missouri 24, South Carolina 14
12-27-80—Arkansas 34, Tulane 15
12-31-81—Mississippi St. 10, Kansas 0
12-31-82—Air Force 36, Vanderbilt 28
12-22-83—West Virginia 20, Kentucky 16
12-29-84—Kentucky 20, Wisconsin 19
12-31-85—Georgia Tech 17, Michigan St. 14
12-31-86—Florida St. 27, Indiana 13
12-22-87—Virginia 22, Brigham Young 16
12-29-88—Florida 14, Illinois 10
12-28-89—Texas Tech 49, Duke 21
12-28-90—North Carolina St. 31, Southern Miss. 27

AVIATION
(Dayton, Ohio)

12-9-61—New Mexico 28, Western Mich. 12

BACARDI
(Cuban National Sports Festival at Havana)

1-1-37—Auburn 7, Villanova 7

BLUEBONNET
(Houston, Texas)

12-19-59—Clemson 23, TCU 7
12-17-60—Alabama 3, Texas 3
12-16-61—Kansas 33, Rice 7
12-22-62—Missouri 14, Georgia Tech 10
12-21-63—Baylor 14, LSU 7
12-19-64—Tulsa 14, Mississippi 7
12-18-65—Tennessee 27, Tulsa 6
12-17-66—Texas 19, Mississippi 0
12-23-67—Colorado 31, Miami (Fla.) 21
12-31-68—Southern Methodist 28, Oklahoma 27
12-31-69—Houston 36, Auburn 7
12-31-70—Alabama 24, Oklahoma 24
12-31-71—Colorado 29, Houston 17
12-30-72—Tennessee 24, LSU 17
12-29-73—Houston 47, Tulane 7
12-23-74—Houston 31, North Carolina St. 31
12-27-75—Texas 38, Colorado 21
12-31-76—Nebraska 27, Texas Tech 24
12-31-77—Southern California 47, Texas A&M 28
12-31-78—Stanford 25, Georgia 22
12-31-79—Purdue 27, Tennessee 22
12-31-80—North Carolina 16, Texas 7
12-31-81—Michigan 33, UCLA 14
12-31-82—Arkansas 28, Florida 24
12-31-83—Oklahoma St. 24, Baylor 14
12-31-84—West Virginia 31, TCU 14
12-31-85—Air Force 24, Texas 16
12-31-86—Baylor 21, Colorado 9
12-31-87—Texas 32, Pittsburgh 27

BLUEGRASS
(Louisville, Ky.)

12-13-58—Oklahoma St. 15, Florida St. 6

CALIFORNIA
(Fresno, Calif.)

12-19-81—Toledo 27, San Jose St. 25
12-18-82—Fresno St. 29, Bowling Green 28
12-17-83—Northern Ill. 20, Cal St. Fullerton 13
12-15-84—UNLV 30, *Toledo 13
12-14-85—Fresno St. 51, Bowling Green 7
12-13-86—San Jose St. 37, Miami (Ohio) 7
12-12-87—Eastern Mich. 30, San Jose St. 27
12-10-88—Fresno St. 35, Western Mich. 30
12-9-89—Fresno St. 27, Ball St. 6
12-8-90—San Jose St. 48, Central Mich. 24
12-14-91—Bowling Green 28, Fresno St. 21

*Won by forfeit.

CAMELLIA
(Lafayette, La.)

12-30-48—Hardin-Simmons 49, Wichita St. 12

CHERRY
(Pontiac, Mich.)

12-22-84—Army 10, Michigan St. 6
12-21-85—Maryland 35, Syracuse 18

DELTA
(Memphis, Tenn.)

1-1-48—Mississippi 13, TCU 9
1-1-49—William & Mary 20, Oklahoma St. 0

DIXIE BOWL
(Birmingham, Ala.)

1-1-48—Arkansas 21, William & Mary 19
1-1-49—Baylor 20, Wake Forest 7

DIXIE CLASSIC
(Dallas, Texas)

1-2-22—Texas A&M 22, Centre 14
1-1-25—West Va. Wesleyan 9, Southern Methodist 7
1-1-34—Arkansas 7, Centenary (La.) 7

FORT WORTH CLASSIC
(Fort Worth, Texas)

1-1-21—Centre 63, TCU 7

FREEDOM BOWL
(Anaheim, Calif.)

12-26-84—Iowa 55, Texas 17
12-30-85—Washington 20, Colorado 17
12-30-86—UCLA 31, Brigham Young 10
12-30-87—Arizona St. 33, Air Force 28
12-29-88—Brigham Young 20, Colorado 17
12-30-89—Washington 34, Florida 7
12-29-90—Colorado St. 32, Oregon 31
12-30-91—Tulsa 28, San Diego St. 17
12-29-92—Fresno St. 24, Southern California 7
12-30-93—Southern California 28, Utah 21
12-27-94—Utah 16, Arizona 13

GARDEN STATE
(East Rutherford, N.J.)

12-16-78—Arizona St. 34, Rutgers 18
12-15-79—Temple 28, California 17

12-14-80—Houston 35, Navy 0
12-13-81—Tennessee 28, Wisconsin 21

GOTHAM
(New York, N.Y.)

12-9-61—Baylor 24, Utah St. 9
12-15-62—Nebraska 36, Miami (Fla.) 34

GREAT LAKES
(Cleveland, Ohio)

12-6-47—Kentucky 24, Villanova 14

HARBOR
(San Diego, Calif.)

1-1-47—Montana St. 13, New Mexico 13
1-1-48—Hardin-Simmons 53, San Diego St. 0
1-1-49—Villanova 27, Nevada 7

LOS ANGELES CHRISTMAS FESTIVAL
(Los Angeles, Calif.)

12-25-24—Southern California 20, Missouri 7

MERCY
(Los Angeles, Calif.)

11-23-61—Fresno St. 36, Bowling Green 6

OIL
(Houston, Texas)

1-1-46—Georgia 20, Tulsa 6
1-1-47—Georgia Tech 41, St. Mary's (Cal.) 19

PASADENA
(Called Junior Rose in 1967)
(Pasadena, Calif.)

12-2-67—West Tex. A&M 35, Cal St. Northridge 13
12-6-69—San Diego St. 28, Boston U. 7
12-19-70—Long Beach St. 24, Louisville 24
12-18-71—Memphis 28, San Jose St. 9

PRESIDENTIAL CUP
(College Park, Md.)

12-9-50—Texas A&M 40, Georgia 20

RAISIN
(Fresno, Calif.)

1-1-46—Drake 13, Fresno St. 12
1-1-47—San Jose St. 20, Utah St. 0
1-1-48—Pacific (Cal.) 26, Wichita St. 14
1-1-49—Occidental 21, Colorado St. 20
12-31-49—San Jose St. 20, Texas Tech 13

SALAD
(Phoenix, Ariz.)

1-1-48—Nevada 13, North Texas 6
1-1-49—Drake 14, Arizona 13
1-1-50—Xavier (Ohio) 33, Arizona St. 21
1-1-51—Miami (Ohio) 34, Arizona St. 21
1-1-52—Houston 26, Dayton 21

SAN DIEGO EAST-WEST CHRISTMAS CLASSIC
(San Diego, Calif.)

12-26-21—Centre 38, Arizona 0
12-25-22—West Virginia 21, Gonzaga 13

SHRINE
(Little Rock, Ark.)

12-18-48—Hardin-Simmons 40, Ouachita Baptist 12

Other Major Postseason Games

There was a proliferation of postseason benefit games specially scheduled at the conclusion of the regular season during the Great Depression (principally in 1931) to raise money for relief of the unemployed in response to the President's Committee on Mobilization of Relief Resources and for other charitable causes.

The exact number of these games is unknown, but it is estimated that more than 100 college games were played nationwide during this period, often irrespective of the competing teams' records.

Most notable among these postseason games were the Tennessee-New York University game of 1931 and the Army-Navy contests of 1930 and 1931 (the two academies had severed athletics relations during 1928-31 and did not meet in regular-season play). All three games were played before huge crowds in New York City's Yankee Stadium.

Following is a list of the principal postseason benefit and charity games involving at least one major college. Not included (nor included in all-time team won-lost records) are several special feature, same-day double-header tournaments in 1931 in which four participating teams were paired to play halves or modified quarters.

Date	Site	Opposing Teams
12-6-30	New York	Colgate 7, New York U. 0
12-13-30	New York	Army 6, Navy 0
11-28-31	Kansas City	Temple 38, Missouri 6
11-28-31	Chicago	Purdue 7, Northwestern 0
11-28-31	Minneapolis	Minnesota 19, Ohio St. 7
11-28-31	Ann Arbor	Michigan 16, Wisconsin 0
11-28-31	Philadelphia	Penn St. 31, Lehigh 0
12-2-31	Chattanooga	Alabama 49, Chattanooga 0
12-3-31	Brooklyn	Manhattan 7, Rutgers 6

OTHER MAJOR POST-SEASON GAMES

Date	Site	Opposing Teams
12-5-31	Denver	Nebraska 20, Colorado St. 7
12-5-31	Pittsburgh	Carnegie Mellon 0, Duquesne 0
12-5-31	New York	Tennessee 13, New York U. 0
12-5-31	St. Louis	St. Louis 31, Missouri 6
12-5-31	Topeka	Kansas 6, Washburn 0
12-5-31	Wichita	Kansas St. 20, Wichita St. 6
12-5-31	Columbia	Centre 9, South Carolina 7
12-5-31	Norman	Oklahoma City 6, Oklahoma 0
12-12-31	New York	Army 17, Navy 7
12-12-31	Tulsa	Oklahoma 20, Tulsa 7
1-2-33	El Paso	Southern Methodist 26, UTEP 0
12-8-34	St. Louis	Southern Methodist 7, Washington (Mo.) 0

Team-by-Team Bowl Results

All-Time Bowl-Game Records

This list includes all bowls played by a current major team, providing its opponent was classified as a major that season or it was a major team then. The list excludes games in which a home team served as a predetermined, preseason host regardless of its record and/or games scheduled before the season, thus eliminating the old Pineapple, Glass and Palm Festival. Following is the alphabetical list showing the record of each current major team in all major bowls.

Team	W	L	T
Air Force	7	7	1
Alabama	28	19	3
Arizona	5	7	1
Arizona St.	10	7	1
Arkansas	10	17	3
Army	2	2	0
Auburn	14	10	2
Ball St.	0	3	0
Baylor	8	8	0
Boise St.	1	0	0
Boston College	5	6	0
Bowling Green	2	3	0
Brigham Young	7	14	0
California	5	7	1
Central Mich.	0	2	0
Cincinnati	2	1	0
Clemson	12	11	0
Colorado	11	12	0
Colorado St.	2	4	0
Duke	3	5	0
East Caro.	3	2	0
Eastern Mich.	1	0	0
Florida	13	14	0
Florida St.	17	8	2
Fresno St.	6	4	0
Georgia	18	14	3
Georgia Tech	19	9	0
Hawaii	2	1	0
Houston	7	6	1
Idaho	1	0	0
Illinois	6	7	0
Indiana	3	5	0
Iowa	8	7	1
Iowa St.	0	4	0
Kansas	3	5	0
Kansas St.	4	4	0
Kent	0	1	0
Kentucky	5	5	0
LSU	14	16	1
Louisiana Tech	1	1	1
Louisville	3	3	1
Marshall	2	1	0
Maryland	6	9	2
Memphis	1	0	0
Miami (Fla.)	13	11	0
Miami (Ohio)	5	2	0
Michigan	16	15	0
Michigan St.	6	9	0
Minnesota	2	4	0
Mississippi	17	11	0
Mississippi St.	5	6	0
Missouri	9	12	0
Navy	4	4	1

Team	W	L	T
Nebraska	19	19	0
Nevada	2	3	0
UNLV	#2	0	0
New Mexico	2	3	1
New Mexico St.	2	0	1
North Carolina	11	12	0
North Carolina St.	8	9	1
North Texas	0	2	0
Northern Ill.	1	0	0
Northwestern	1	2	0
Notre Dame	13	10	0
Ohio	0	2	0
Ohio St.	14	17	0
Oklahoma	20	12	1
Oklahoma St.	9	4	0
Oregon	5	9	0
Oregon St.	2	3	0
Penn St.	23	11	2
Pittsburgh	8	11	0
Purdue	6	2	0
Rice	4	3	0
Rutgers	0	1	0
San Diego St.	1	4	0
San Jose St.	4	3	0
South Carolina	1	8	0
Southern California	25	14	0
Southern Methodist	4	6	1
Southern Miss.	4	5	0
Stanford	9	9	1
Syracuse	11	8	1
Temple	1	1	0
Tennessee	22	18	0
Texas	18	19	2
UTEP	5	4	0
Texas A&M	12	13	0
TCU	6	10	1
Texas Tech	5	17	1
Toledo	5	1	0
Tulane	3	6	0
Tulsa	4	7	0
UCLA	11	10	1
Utah	4	3	0
Utah St.	2	3	0
Vanderbilt	1	1	1
Virginia	4	7	0
Virginia Tech	4	9	0
Wake Forest	3	2	0
Washington	13	12	1
Washington St.	4	3	0
West Virginia	8	12	0
Western Mich.	0	2	0
Wisconsin	6	6	0
Wyoming	4	6	0
TOTALS	**710**	**710**	**42**

#Later lost game by forfeit.
The following current Division I-A teams have not played in a major bowl game: Akron, UAB, Arkansas St., UCF, La.-Lafayette and La.-Monroe.

Major Bowl Records of Non-Division I-A Teams

Boston U. 0-1-0; Brown 0-1-0; Bucknell 1-0-0; Cal St. Fullerton 0-1-0; Cal St. Northridge 0-1-0; Carnegie Mellon 0-1-0; Case Reserve 1-0-0; Catholic 1-0-1; Centenary (La.) 0-0-1; Centre 2-1-0; Citadel 1-0-0; Columbia 1-0-0; Davidson 0-1-0; Dayton 0-1-0; Denver 0-2-0; Drake 2-1-0; Duquesne 0-0-1; Fordham 1-1-0; George Washington 0-1-0; Georgetown 0-2-0; Gonzaga 0-1-0; Hardin-Simmons 5-2-1; Harvard 1-0-0; Holy Cross 0-1-0; Long Beach St. 0-0-1; Marquette 0-1-0; McNeese St. 1-2-0; Montana St. 0-0-1; Occidental 1-0-0; Ouachita Baptist 0-1-0; Pacific (Cal.) 2-1-0; Pennsylvania 0-1-0; Randolph Field 0-0-1; Richmond 1-1-0; St. Mary's (Cal.) 1-2-0; Santa Clara 3-0-0; Second Air Force 1-0-0; Southwestern (Tex.) 2-0-0; Tampa 1-0-0; Tennessee Tech 0-1-0; U. of Mexico 0-1-0; Villanova 2-2-1; Wash. & Jeff. 0-0-1; Wash. & Lee 0-1-0; West Tex. A&M 3-0-0; West Va. Wesleyan 1-0-0; Wichita St. 0-3-0; William & Mary 1-2-0; Xavier (Ohio) 1-0-0. TOTALS: 39-37-8

All-Time Bowl Appearances

(Must be classified as a major bowl game where one team was considered a major college at the time.)

Team	Appearances
Alabama	50
Tennessee	40
Southern California	39
Texas	39
Nebraska	38
Penn St.	36
Georgia	35
Oklahoma	33
LSU	31
Michigan	31
Ohio St.	31
Arkansas	30
Florida St.	28
Georgia Tech	28
Mississippi	28
Florida	27
Auburn	26
Washington	26
Texas A&M	25

Team	Appearances
Miami (Fla.)	24
Clemson	23
Colorado	23
North Carolina	23
Notre Dame	23
Texas Tech	23
Brigham Young	22
UCLA	22
Missouri	21
Syracuse	20
West Virginia	20
Pittsburgh	19
Stanford	19
Arizona St.	18
North Carolina St.	18
Maryland	17
Baylor	16
Iowa	16

All-Time Bowl Victories

(Includes bowls where at least one team was classified a major college at the time.)

Team	Victories
Alabama	28
Southern California	25
Penn St.	23
Tennessee	22
Oklahoma	20
Georgia Tech	19
Nebraska	19
Georgia	18
Texas	18
Florida St.	17
Mississippi	17
Michigan	16
Auburn	14
LSU	14
Ohio St.	14

Team	Victories
Florida	13
Miami (Fla.)	13
Notre Dame	13
Washington	13
Clemson	12
Texas A&M	12
Colorado	11
North Carolina	11
Syracuse	11
UCLA	11
Arizona St.	10
Arkansas	10
Missouri	9
Oklahoma St.	9
Stanford	9

Team-by-Team Major Bowl Scores With Coach of Each Bowl Team

Listed below are the 106 I-A teams that have participated in history's 773 major bowl games (the term "major bowl" is defined above the alphabetical list of team bowl records). The teams are listed alphabetically, with each coach listed along with the bowl participated in, date played, opponent, score and team's all-time bowl-game record. Following the I-A list is a group of 49 teams that played in a major bowl game or games but are no longer classified as I-A.

School/Coach	Bowl/Date	Opponent/Score
AIR FORCE		
Ben Martin	Cotton 1-1-59	TCU 0-0
Ben Martin	Gator 12-28-63	North Carolina 0-35
Ben Martin	Sugar 1-1-71	Tennessee 13-34
Ken Hatfield	Hall of Fame 12-31-82	Vanderbilt 36-28
Ken Hatfield	Independence 12-10-83	Mississippi 9-3
Fisher DeBerry	Independence 12-15-84	Virginia Tech 23-7
Fisher DeBerry	Bluebonnet 12-31-85	Texas 24-16

School/Coach	Bowl/Date	Opponent/Score
Fisher DeBerry	Freedom 12-30-87	Arizona St. 28-33
Fisher DeBerry	Liberty 12-28-89	Mississippi 29-42
Fisher DeBerry	Liberty 12-27-90	Ohio St. 23-11
Fisher DeBerry	Liberty 12-29-91	Mississippi St. 38-15
Fisher DeBerry	Liberty 12-31-92	Mississippi 0-13
Fisher DeBerry	Copper 12-27-95	Texas Tech 41-55
Fisher DeBerry	Las Vegas 12-20-97	Oregon 13-41
Fisher DeBerry	Oahu Classic 12-25-98	Washington 45-25

All bowls 7-7-1

ALABAMA

Wallace Wade	Rose 1-1-26	Washington 20-19
Wallace Wade	Rose 1-1-27	Stanford 7-7
Wallace Wade	Rose 1-1-31	Washington St. 24-0
Frank Thomas	Rose 1-1-35	Stanford 29-13
Frank Thomas	Rose 1-1-38	California 0-13
Frank Thomas	Cotton 1-1-42	Texas A&M 29-21
Frank Thomas	Orange 1-1-43	Boston College 37-21
Frank Thomas	Sugar 1-1-45	Duke 26-29
Frank Thomas	Rose 1-1-46	Southern California 34-14
Harold "Red" Drew	Sugar 1-1-48	Texas 7-27
Harold "Red" Drew	Orange 1-1-53	Syracuse 61-6
Harold "Red" Drew	Cotton 1-1-54	Rice 6-28
Paul "Bear" Bryant	Liberty 12-19-59	Penn St. 0-7
Paul "Bear" Bryant	Bluebonnet 12-17-60	Texas 3-3
Paul "Bear" Bryant	Sugar 1-1-62	Arkansas 10-3
Paul "Bear" Bryant	Orange 1-1-63	Oklahoma 17-0
Paul "Bear" Bryant	Sugar 1-1-64	Mississippi 12-7
Paul "Bear" Bryant	Orange 1-1-65	Texas 17-21
Paul "Bear" Bryant	Orange 1-1-66	Nebraska 39-28
Paul "Bear" Bryant	Sugar 1-2-67	Nebraska 34-7
Paul "Bear" Bryant	Cotton 1-1-68	Texas A&M 16-20
Paul "Bear" Bryant	Gator 12-28-68	Missouri 10-35
Paul "Bear" Bryant	Liberty 12-13-69	Colorado 33-47
Paul "Bear" Bryant	Bluebonnet 12-31-70	Oklahoma 24-24
Paul "Bear" Bryant	Orange 1-1-72	Nebraska 6-38
Paul "Bear" Bryant	Cotton 1-1-73	Texas 13-17
Paul "Bear" Bryant	Sugar 12-31-73	Notre Dame 23-24
Paul "Bear" Bryant	Orange 1-1-75	Notre Dame 11-13
Paul "Bear" Bryant	Sugar 12-31-75	Penn St. 13-6
Paul "Bear" Bryant	Liberty 12-20-76	UCLA 36-6
Paul "Bear" Bryant	Sugar 1-2-78	Ohio St. 35-6
Paul "Bear" Bryant	Sugar 1-1-79	Penn St. 14-7
Paul "Bear" Bryant	Sugar 1-1-80	Arkansas 24-9
Paul "Bear" Bryant	Cotton 1-1-81	Baylor 30-2
Paul "Bear" Bryant	Cotton 1-1-82	Texas 12-14
Paul "Bear" Bryant	Liberty 12-29-82	Illinois 21-15
Ray Perkins	Sun 12-24-83	Southern Methodist 28-7
Ray Perkins	Aloha 12-28-85	Southern California 24-3
Ray Perkins	Sun 12-25-86	Washington 28-6
Bill Curry	Hall of Fame 1-2-88	Michigan 24-28
Bill Curry	Sun 12-24-88	Army 29-28
Bill Curry	Sugar 1-1-90	Miami (Fla.) 25-33
Gene Stallings	Fiesta 1-1-91	Louisville 7-34
Gene Stallings	Blockbuster 12-28-91	Colorado 30-25
Gene Stallings	Sugar 1-1-93	Miami (Fla.) 34-13
Gene Stallings	Gator 12-31-93	North Carolina 24-10
Gene Stallings	Florida Citrus 1-2-95	Ohio St. 24-17
Gene Stallings	Outback 1-1-97	Michigan 17-14
Mike DuBose	Music City 12-29-98	Virginia Tech 7-38
Mike DuBose	Orange 1-1-00	Michigan 34-35 (ot)

All bowls 28-19-3

ARIZONA

J. F. "Pop" McKale	San Diego East-West Christmas Classic 12-26-21	Centre 0-38
Miles Casteel	Salad 1-1-49	Drake 13-14
Darrell Mudra	Sun 12-28-68	Auburn 10-34
Tony Mason	Fiesta 12-25-79	Pittsburgh 10-16
Larry Smith	Sun 12-28-85	Georgia 13-13
Larry Smith	Aloha 12-27-86	North Carolina 30-21
Dick Tomey	Copper 12-31-89	North Carolina St. 17-10
Dick Tomey	Aloha 12-25-90	Syracuse 0-28
Dick Tomey	John Hancock 12-31-92	Baylor 15-20
Dick Tomey	Fiesta 1-1-94	Miami (Fla.) 29-0
Dick Tomey	Freedom 12-27-94	Utah 13-16
Dick Tomey	Insight.com 12-27-97	New Mexico 20-14
Dick Tomey	Holiday 12-30-98	Nebraska 23-20

All bowls 5-7-1

ARIZONA ST.

Millard "Dixie" Howell	Sun 1-1-40	Catholic 0-0
Millard "Dixie" Howell	Sun 1-1-41	Case Reserve 13-26
Ed Doherty	Salad 1-1-50	Xavier (Ohio) 21-33
Ed Doherty	Salad 1-1-51	Miami (Ohio) 21-34
Frank Kush	Peach 12-30-70	North Carolina 48-26
Frank Kush	Fiesta 12-27-71	Florida St. 45-38
Frank Kush	Fiesta 12-23-72	Missouri 49-35
Frank Kush	Fiesta 12-21-73	Pittsburgh 28-7
Frank Kush	Fiesta 12-26-75	Nebraska 17-14
Frank Kush	Fiesta 12-25-77	Penn St. 30-42
Frank Kush	Garden State 12-16-78	Rutgers 34-18
Darryl Rogers	Fiesta 1-1-83	Oklahoma 32-21
John Cooper	Holiday 12-22-85	Arkansas 17-18
John Cooper	Rose 1-1-87	Michigan 22-15
John Cooper	Freedom 12-30-87	Air Force 33-28
Bruce Snyder	Rose 1-1-97	Ohio St. 17-20
Bruce Snyder	Sun 12-31-97	Iowa 17-7
Bruce Snyder	Aloha Classic 12-25-99	Wake Forest 3-23

All bowls 10-7-1

ARKANSAS

Fred Thomsen	Dixie Classic 1-1-34	Centenary (La.) 7-7
John Barnhill	Cotton 1-1-47	LSU 0-0
John Barnhill	Dixie 1-1-48	William & Mary 21-19
Bowden Wyatt	Cotton 1-1-55	Georgia Tech 6-14
Frank Broyles	Gator 1-2-60	Georgia Tech 14-7
Frank Broyles	Cotton 1-2-61	Duke 6-7
Frank Broyles	Sugar 1-1-62	Alabama 3-10
Frank Broyles	Sugar 1-1-63	Mississippi 13-17
Frank Broyles	Cotton 1-1-65	Nebraska 10-7
Frank Broyles	Cotton 1-1-66	LSU 7-14
Frank Broyles	Sugar 1-1-69	Georgia 16-2
Frank Broyles	Sugar 1-1-70	Mississippi 22-27
Frank Broyles	Liberty 12-20-71	Tennessee 13-14
Frank Broyles	Cotton 1-1-76	Georgia 31-10
Frank Broyles	Orange 1-2-78	Oklahoma 31-6
Lou Holtz	Fiesta 12-25-78	UCLA 10-10
Lou Holtz	Sugar 1-1-80	Alabama 9-24
Lou Holtz	Hall of Fame 12-27-80	Tulane 34-15
Lou Holtz	Gator 12-28-81	North Carolina 27-31
Lou Holtz	Bluebonnet 12-31-82	Florida 28-24
Ken Hatfield	Liberty 12-27-84	Auburn 15-21
Ken Hatfield	Holiday 12-22-85	Arizona St. 18-17
Ken Hatfield	Orange 1-1-87	Oklahoma 8-42
Ken Hatfield	Liberty 12-29-87	Georgia 17-20
Ken Hatfield	Cotton 1-2-89	UCLA 3-17
Ken Hatfield	Cotton 1-1-90	Tennessee 27-31
Jack Crowe	Independence 12-29-91	Georgia 15-24
Danny Ford	Carquest 12-30-95	North Carolina 10-20
Houston Nutt	Florida Citrus 1-1-99	Michigan 31-45
Houston Nutt	Cotton 1-1-00	Texas 27-6

All bowls 10-17-3

ARMY

Jim Young	Cherry 12-22-84	Michigan St. 10-6
Jim Young	Peach 12-31-85	Illinois 31-29
Jim Young	Sun 12-24-88	Alabama 28-29
Bob Sutton	Independence 12-31-96	Auburn 29-32

All bowls 2-2-0

AUBURN

Jack Meagher	Bacardi, Cuba 1-1-37	Villanova 7-7
Jack Meagher	Orange 1-1-38	Michigan St. 6-0
Ralph "Shug" Jordan	Gator 1-1-54	Texas Tech 13-35
Ralph "Shug" Jordan	Gator 12-31-54	Baylor 33-13
Ralph "Shug" Jordan	Gator 12-31-55	Vanderbilt 13-25
Ralph "Shug" Jordan	Orange 1-1-64	Nebraska 7-13
Ralph "Shug" Jordan	Liberty 12-18-65	Mississippi 7-13
Ralph "Shug" Jordan	Sun 12-28-68	Arizona 34-10
Ralph "Shug" Jordan	Bluebonnet 12-31-69	Houston 7-36
Ralph "Shug" Jordan	Gator 1-2-71	Mississippi 35-28
Ralph "Shug" Jordan	Sugar 1-1-72	Oklahoma 22-40
Ralph "Shug" Jordan	Gator 12-30-72	Colorado 24-3
Ralph "Shug" Jordan	Sun 12-29-73	Missouri 17-34
Ralph "Shug" Jordan	Gator 12-30-74	Texas 27-3
Pat Dye	Tangerine 12-18-82	Boston College 33-26
Pat Dye	Sugar 1-2-84	Michigan 9-7
Pat Dye	Liberty 12-27-84	Arkansas 21-15
Pat Dye	Cotton 1-1-86	Texas A&M 16-36
Pat Dye	Florida Citrus 1-1-87	Southern California 16-7
Pat Dye	Sugar 1-1-88	Syracuse 16-16
Pat Dye	Sugar 1-2-89	Florida St. 7-13
Pat Dye	Hall of Fame 1-1-90	Ohio St. 31-24
Pat Dye	Peach 12-29-90	Indiana 27-23
Terry Bowden	Outback 1-1-96	Penn St. 14-43
Terry Bowden	Independence 12-31-96	Army 33-29
Terry Bowden	Peach 1-2-98	Clemson 21-17

All bowls 14-10-2

BALL ST.

Paul Schudel	California 12-9-89	Fresno St. 6-27
Paul Schudel	Las Vegas 12-17-93	Utah St. 33-42
Bill Lynch	Las Vegas 12-19-96	Nevada 15-18

All bowls 0-3-0

School/Coach	Bowl/Date	Opponent/Score
BAYLOR		
Bob Woodruff	Dixie 1-1-49	Wake Forest 20-7
George Sauer	Orange 1-1-52	Georgia Tech 14-17
George Sauer	Gator 12-31-54	Auburn 13-33
Sam Boyd	Sugar 1-1-57	Tennessee 13-7
John Bridgers	Gator 12-31-60	Florida 12-13
John Bridgers	Gotham 12-9-61	Utah St. 24-9
John Bridgers	Bluebonnet 12-21-63	LSU 14-7
Grant Teaff	Cotton 1-1-75	Penn St. 20-41
Grant Teaff	Peach 12-31-79	Clemson 24-18
Grant Teaff	Cotton 1-1-81	Alabama 2-30
Grant Teaff	Bluebonnet 12-31-83	Oklahoma St. 14-24
Grant Teaff	Liberty 12-27-85	LSU 21-7
Grant Teaff	Bluebonnet 12-31-86	Colorado 21-9
Grant Teaff	Copper 12-31-91	Indiana 0-24
Grant Teaff	John Hancock 12-31-92	Arizona 20-15
Chuck Reedy	Alamo 12-31-94	Washington St. 3-10

All bowls 8-8-0

BOISE ST.
Dirk Koetter	Humanitarian 12-30-99	Louisville 34-31

All bowls 1-1-0

BOSTON COLLEGE
Frank Leahy	Cotton 1-1-40	Clemson 3-6
Frank Leahy	Sugar 1-1-41	Tennessee 19-13
Denny Myers	Orange 1-1-43	Alabama 21-37
Jack Bicknell	Tangerine 12-18-82	Auburn 26-33
Jack Bicknell	Liberty 12-29-83	Notre Dame 18-19
Jack Bicknell	Cotton 1-1-85	Houston 45-28
Jack Bicknell	Hall of Fame 12-23-86	Georgia 27-24
Tom Coughlin	Hall of Fame 1-1-93	Tennessee 23-38
Tom Coughlin	Carquest 1-1-94	Virginia 31-13
Dan Henning	Aloha 12-25-94	Kansas St. 12-7
Tom O'Brien	Insight.com 12-31-99	Colorado 28-62

All bowls 5-6-0

BOWLING GREEN
Doyt Perry	Mercy 11-23-61	Fresno St. 6-36
Denny Stolz	California 12-18-82	Fresno St. 28-29
Denny Stolz	California 12-14-85	Fresno St. 7-51
Gary Blackney	California 12-14-91	Fresno St. 28-21
Gary Blackney	Las Vegas 12-18-92	Nevada 35-34

All bowls 2-3-0

BRIGHAM YOUNG
LaVell Edwards	Fiesta 12-28-74	Oklahoma St. 6-16
LaVell Edwards	Tangerine 12-18-76	Oklahoma St. 21-49
LaVell Edwards	Holiday 12-22-78	Navy 16-23
LaVell Edwards	Holiday 12-21-79	Indiana 37-38
LaVell Edwards	Holiday 12-19-80	Southern Methodist 46-45
LaVell Edwards	Holiday 12-18-81	Washington St. 38-36
LaVell Edwards	Holiday 12-17-82	Ohio St. 17-47
LaVell Edwards	Holiday 12-23-83	Missouri 21-17
LaVell Edwards	Holiday 12-21-84	Michigan 24-17
LaVell Edwards	Florida Citrus 12-28-85	Ohio St. 7-10
LaVell Edwards	Freedom 12-30-86	UCLA 10-31
LaVell Edwards	All-American 12-22-87	Virginia 16-22
LaVell Edwards	Freedom 12-29-88	Colorado 20-17
LaVell Edwards	Holiday 12-29-89	Penn St. 39-50
LaVell Edwards	Holiday 12-29-90	Texas A&M 14-65
LaVell Edwards	Holiday 12-30-91	Iowa 13-13
LaVell Edwards	Aloha 12-25-92	Kansas 20-23
LaVell Edwards	Holiday 12-30-93	Ohio St. 21-28
LaVell Edwards	Copper 12-29-94	Oklahoma 31-6
LaVell Edwards	Cotton 1-1-97	Kansas St. 19-15
LaVell Edwards	Liberty 12-31-98	Tulane 27-41
LaVell Edwards	Motor City 12-27-99	Marshall 3-21

All bowls 7-14-1

CALIFORNIA
Andy Smith	Rose 1-1-21	Ohio St. 28-0
Andy Smith	Rose 1-2-22	Wash. & Jeff. 0-0
Clarence "Nibs" Price	Rose 1-1-29	Georgia Tech 7-8
Leonard "Stub" Allison	Rose 1-1-38	Alabama 13-0
Lynn "Pappy" Waldorf	Rose 1-1-49	Northwestern 14-20
Lynn "Pappy" Waldorf	Rose 1-2-50	Ohio St. 14-17
Lynn "Pappy" Waldorf	Rose 1-1-51	Michigan 6-14
Pete Elliott	Rose 1-1-59	Iowa 12-38
Roger Theder	Garden State 12-15-79	Temple 17-28
Bruce Snyder	Copper 12-31-90	Wyoming 17-15
Bruce Snyder	Florida Citrus 1-1-92	Clemson 37-13
Keith Gilbertson	Alamo 12-31-93	Iowa 37-3
Steve Mariucci	Aloha 12-25-96	Navy 38-42

All bowls 5-7-1

School/Coach	Bowl/Date	Opponent/Score
CENTRAL MICH.		
Herb Deromedi	California 12-8-90	San Jose St. 24-48
Dick Flynn	Las Vegas 12-15-94	UNLV 24-52

All bowls 0-2-0

CINCINNATI
Ray Nolting	Sun 1-1-47	Virginia Tech 18-6
Sid Gillman	Sun 1-1-51	West Tex. A&M 13-14
Rick Minter	Humanitarian 12-29-97	Utah St. 35-19

All bowls 2-1-0

CLEMSON
Jess Neely	Cotton 1-1-40	Boston College 6-3
Frank Howard	Gator 1-1-49	Missouri 24-23
Frank Howard	Orange 1-1-51	Miami (Fla.) 15-14
Frank Howard	Gator 1-1-52	Miami (Fla.) 0-14
Frank Howard	Orange 1-1-57	Colorado 21-27
Frank Howard	Sugar 1-1-59	LSU 0-7
Frank Howard	Bluebonnet 12-19-59	TCU 23-7
Charley Pell	Gator 12-30-77	Pittsburgh 3-34
Danny Ford	Gator 12-29-78	Ohio St. 17-15
Danny Ford	Peach 12-31-79	Baylor 18-24
Danny Ford	Orange 1-1-82	Nebraska 22-15
Danny Ford	Independence 12-21-85	Minnesota 13-20
Danny Ford	Gator 12-27-86	Stanford 27-21
Danny Ford	Florida Citrus 1-1-88	Penn St. 35-10
Danny Ford	Florida Citrus 1-2-89	Oklahoma 23-6
Danny Ford	Gator 12-30-89	West Virginia 27-7
Ken Hatfield	Hall of Fame 1-1-91	Illinois 30-0
Ken Hatfield	Florida Citrus 1-1-92	California 13-37
Tommy West	Peach 12-31-93	Kentucky 14-13
Tommy West	Gator 1-1-96	Syracuse 0-41
Tommy West	Peach 12-28-96	LSU 7-10
Tommy West	Peach 1-2-98	Auburn 17-21
Tommy Bowden	Peach 12-30-99	Mississippi St. 7-17

All bowls 12-11-0

COLORADO
Bernard "Bunnie" Oaks	Cotton 1-1-38	Rice 14-28
Dallas Ward	Orange 1-1-57	Clemson 27-21
Sonny Grandelius	Orange 1-1-62	LSU 7-25
Eddie Crowder	Bluebonnet 12-23-67	Miami (Fla.) 31-21
Eddie Crowder	Liberty 12-13-69	Alabama 47-33
Eddie Crowder	Liberty 12-12-70	Tulane 3-17
Eddie Crowder	Bluebonnet 12-31-71	Houston 29-17
Eddie Crowder	Gator 12-30-72	Auburn 3-24
Bill Mallory	Bluebonnet 12-27-75	Texas 21-38
Bill Mallory	Orange 1-1-77	Ohio St. 10-27
Bill McCartney	Freedom 12-30-85	Washington 17-20
Bill McCartney	Bluebonnet 12-31-86	Baylor 9-21
Bill McCartney	Freedom 12-29-88	Brigham Young 17-20
Bill McCartney	Orange 1-1-90	Notre Dame 6-21
Bill McCartney	Orange 1-1-91	Notre Dame 10-9
Bill McCartney	Blockbuster 12-28-91	Alabama 25-30
Bill McCartney	Fiesta 1-1-93	Syracuse 22-26
Bill McCartney	Aloha 12-25-93	Fresno St. 41-30
Bill McCartney	Fiesta 1-2-95	Notre Dame 41-24
Rick Neuheisel	Cotton 1-1-96	Oregon 38-6
Rick Neuheisel	Holiday 12-30-96	Washington 33-21
Rick Neuheisel	Aloha Classic 12-25-98	Oregon 51-43
Gary Barnett	Insight.com 12-31-99	Boston College 62-28

All bowls 11-12-0

COLORADO ST.
Bob Davis	Raisin 1-1-49	Occidental 20-21
Earle Bruce	Freedom 12-24-90	Oregon 32-31
Sonny Lubick	Holiday 12-30-94	Michigan 14-24
Sonny Lubick	Holiday 12-29-95	Kansas St. 21-54
Sonny Lubick	Holiday 12-29-97	Missouri 35-24
Sonny Lubick	Liberty 12-31-99	Southern Miss. 17-23

All bowls 2-4-0

DUKE
Wallace Wade	Rose 1-2-39	Southern California 3-7
Wallace Wade	Rose 1-1-42	Oregon St. 16-20
Eddie Cameron	Sugar 1-1-45	Alabama 29-26
Bill Murray	Orange 1-1-55	Nebraska 34-7
Bill Murray	Orange 1-1-58	Oklahoma 21-48
Bill Murray	Cotton 1-2-61	Arkansas 7-6
Steve Spurrier	All-American 12-28-89	Texas Tech 21-49
Fred Goldsmith	Hall of Fame 1-2-95	Wisconsin 20-34

All bowls 3-5-0

EAST CARO.
Pat Dye	Independence 12-16-78	Louisiana Tech 35-13
Bill Lewis	Peach 1-1-92	North Carolina St. 37-34
Steve Logan	Liberty 12-31-94	Illinois 0-30

School/Coach	Bowl/Date	Opponent/Score
Steve Logan	Liberty 12-30-95	Stanford 19-13
Steve Logan	Mobile Alabama 12-22-99	TCU 14-28

All bowls 3-2-0

EASTERN MICH.
Jim Harkema	California 12-12-87	San Jose St. 30-27

All bowls 1-0-0

FLORIDA
Bob Woodruff	Gator 1-1-53	Tulsa 14-13
Bob Woodruff	Gator 12-27-58	Mississippi 3-7
Ray Graves	Gator 12-31-60	Baylor 13-12
Ray Graves	Gator 12-29-62	Penn St. 17-7
Ray Graves	Sugar 1-1-66	Missouri 18-20
Ray Graves	Orange 1-2-67	Georgia Tech 27-12
Ray Graves	Gator 12-27-69	Tennessee 14-13
Doug Dickey	Tangerine 12-22-73	Miami (Ohio) 7-16
Doug Dickey	Sugar 12-31-74	Nebraska 10-13
Doug Dickey	Gator 12-29-75	Maryland 0-13
Doug Dickey	Sun 1-2-77	Texas A&M 14-37
Charley Pell	Tangerine 12-20-80	Maryland 35-20
Charley Pell	Peach 12-31-81	West Virginia 6-26
Charley Pell	Bluebonnet 12-31-82	Arkansas 24-28
Charley Pell	Gator 12-30-83	Iowa 14-6
Galen Hall	Aloha 12-25-87	UCLA 16-20
Galen Hall	All-American 12-29-88	Illinois 14-10
Gary Darnell	Freedom 12-30-89	Washington 7-34
Steve Spurrier	Sugar 1-1-92	Notre Dame 28-39
Steve Spurrier	Gator 12-31-92	North Carolina St. 27-10
Steve Spurrier	Sugar 1-1-94	West Virginia 41-7
Steve Spurrier	Sugar 1-2-95	Florida St. 17-23
Steve Spurrier	Fiesta 1-2-96	Nebraska 24-62
Steve Spurrier	Sugar 1-2-97	Florida St. 52-20
Steve Spurrier	Florida Citrus 1-1-98	Penn St. 21-6
Steve Spurrier	Orange 1-2-99	Syracuse 31-10
Steve Spurrier	Florida Citrus 1-1-00	Michigan St. 34-37

All bowls 13-14-0

FLORIDA ST.
Tom Nugent	Sun 1-1-55	UTEP 20-47
Tom Nugent	Bluegrass 12-13-58	Oklahoma St. 6-15
Bill Peterson	Gator 1-2-65	Oklahoma 36-19
Bill Peterson	Sun 12-24-66	Wyoming 20-28
Bill Peterson	Gator 12-30-67	Penn St. 17-17
Bill Peterson	Peach 12-30-68	LSU 27-31
Larry Jones	Fiesta 12-27-71	Arizona St. 38-45
Bobby Bowden	Tangerine 12-23-77	Texas Tech 40-17
Bobby Bowden	Orange 1-1-80	Oklahoma 7-24
Bobby Bowden	Orange 1-1-81	Oklahoma 17-18
Bobby Bowden	Gator 12-30-82	West Virginia 31-12
Bobby Bowden	Peach 12-30-83	North Carolina 28-3
Bobby Bowden	Florida Citrus 12-22-84	Georgia 17-17
Bobby Bowden	Gator 12-30-85	Oklahoma St. 34-23
Bobby Bowden	All-American 12-31-86	Indiana 27-13
Bobby Bowden	Fiesta 1-1-88	Nebraska 31-28
Bobby Bowden	Sugar 1-2-89	Auburn 13-7
Bobby Bowden	Fiesta 1-1-90	Nebraska 41-17
Bobby Bowden	Blockbuster 12-28-90	Penn St. 24-17
Bobby Bowden	Cotton 1-1-92	Texas A&M 10-2
Bobby Bowden	Orange 1-1-93	Nebraska 27-14
Bobby Bowden	Orange 1-1-94	Nebraska 18-16
Bobby Bowden	Sugar 1-2-95	Florida 23-17
Bobby Bowden	Orange 1-1-96	Notre Dame 31-26
Bobby Bowden	Sugar 1-2-97	Florida 20-52
Bobby Bowden	Sugar 1-1-98	Ohio St. 31-14
Bobby Bowden	Fiesta 1-4-99	Tennessee 16-23
Bobby Bowden	Sugar 1-4-00	Virginia Tech 46-29

All bowls 17-9-2

FRESNO ST.
Alvin "Pix" Pierson	Raisin 1-1-46	Drake 12-13
Cecil Coleman	Mercy 11-23-61	Bowling Green 36-6
Jim Sweeney	California 12-18-82	Bowling Green 29-28
Jim Sweeney	California 12-14-85	Bowling Green 51-7
Jim Sweeney	California 12-10-88	Western Mich. 35-30
Jim Sweeney	California 12-9-89	Ball St. 27-6
Jim Sweeney	California 12-14-91	Bowling Green 21-28
Jim Sweeney	Freedom 12-29-92	Southern California 24-7
Jim Sweeney	Aloha 12-25-93	Colorado 30-41
Pat Hill	Las Vegas 12-18-99	Utah 16-17

All bowls 6-4-0

GEORGIA
Wally Butts	Orange 1-1-42	TCU 40-26
Wally Butts	Rose 1-1-43	UCLA 9-0
Wally Butts	Oil 1-1-46	Tulsa 20-6
Wally Butts	Sugar 1-1-47	North Carolina 20-10
Wally Butts	Gator 1-1-48	Maryland 20-20
Wally Butts	Orange 1-1-49	Texas 28-41
Wally Butts	Presidential 12-9-50	Texas A&M 20-40
Wally Butts	Orange 1-1-60	Missouri 14-0
Vince Dooley	Sun 12-26-64	Texas Tech 7-0
Vince Dooley	Cotton 12-31-66	Southern Methodist 24-9
Vince Dooley	Liberty 12-16-67	North Carolina St. 7-14
Vince Dooley	Sugar 1-1-69	Arkansas 2-16
Vince Dooley	Sun 12-20-69	Nebraska 6-45
Vince Dooley	Gator 12-31-71	North Carolina 7-3
Vince Dooley	Peach 12-28-73	Maryland 17-16
Vince Dooley	Tangerine 12-21-74	Miami (Ohio) 10-21
Vince Dooley	Cotton 1-1-76	Arkansas 10-31
Vince Dooley	Sugar 1-1-77	Pittsburgh 3-27
Vince Dooley	Bluebonnet 12-31-78	Stanford 22-25
Vince Dooley	Sugar 1-1-81	Notre Dame 17-10
Vince Dooley	Sugar 1-1-82	Pittsburgh 20-24
Vince Dooley	Sugar 1-1-83	Penn St. 23-27
Vince Dooley	Cotton 1-2-84	Texas 10-9
Vince Dooley	Florida Citrus 12-22-84	Florida St. 17-17
Vince Dooley	Sun 12-28-85	Arizona 13-13
Vince Dooley	Hall of Fame 12-23-86	Boston College 24-27
Vince Dooley	Liberty 12-29-87	Arkansas 20-17
Vince Dooley	Gator 1-1-89	Michigan St. 34-27
Ray Goff	Peach 12-30-89	Syracuse 18-19
Ray Goff	Independence 12-29-91	Arkansas 24-15
Ray Goff	Florida Citrus 1-1-93	Ohio St. 21-14
Ray Goff	Peach 12-30-95	Virginia 27-34
Jim Donnan	Outback 1-1-98	Wisconsin 33-6
Jim Donnan	Peach 12-31-98	Virginia 35-33
Jim Donnan	Outback 1-1-00	Purdue 28-25 (ot)

All bowls 18-14-3

GEORGIA TECH
Bill Alexander	Rose 1-1-29	California 8-7
Bill Alexander	Orange 1-1-40	Missouri 21-7
Bill Alexander	Cotton 1-1-43	Texas 7-14
Bill Alexander	Sugar 1-1-44	Tulsa 20-18
Bill Alexander	Orange 1-1-45	Tulsa 12-26
Bobby Dodd	Oil 1-1-47	St. Mary's (Cal.) 41-19
Bobby Dodd	Orange 1-1-48	Kansas 20-14
Bobby Dodd	Orange 1-1-52	Baylor 17-14
Bobby Dodd	Sugar 1-1-53	Mississippi 24-7
Bobby Dodd	Sugar 1-1-54	West Virginia 42-19
Bobby Dodd	Cotton 1-1-55	Arkansas 14-6
Bobby Dodd	Sugar 1-2-56	Pittsburgh 7-0
Bobby Dodd	Gator 12-29-56	Pittsburgh 21-14
Bobby Dodd	Gator 1-2-60	Arkansas 7-14
Bobby Dodd	Gator 12-30-61	Penn St. 15-30
Bobby Dodd	Bluebonnet 12-22-62	Missouri 10-14
Bobby Dodd	Gator 12-31-65	Texas Tech 31-21
Bobby Dodd	Orange 1-2-67	Florida 12-27
Bud Carson	Sun 12-19-70	Texas Tech 17-9
Bud Carson	Peach 12-30-71	Mississippi 18-41
Bill Fulcher	Liberty 12-18-72	Iowa St. 31-30
Pepper Rodgers	Peach 12-25-78	Purdue 21-41
Bill Curry	Hall of Fame 12-31-85	Michigan St. 17-14
Bobby Ross	Florida Citrus 1-1-91	Nebraska 45-21
Bobby Ross	Aloha 12-25-91	Stanford 18-17
George O'Leary	Carquest 12-29-97	West Virginia 35-30
George O'Leary	Gator 1-1-99	Notre Dame 35-28
George O'Leary	Gator 1-1-00	Miami (Fla.) 13-28

All bowls 19-9-0

HAWAII
Bob Wagner	Aloha 12-25-89	Michigan St. 13-33
Bob Wagner	Holiday 12-30-92	Illinois 27-17
June Jones	Oahu Classic 12-25-99	Oregon St. 23-17

All bowls 2-1-0

HOUSTON
Clyde Lee	Salad 1-1-52	Dayton 26-21
Bill Yeoman	Tangerine 12-22-62	Miami (Ohio) 49-21
Bill Yeoman	Bluebonnet 12-31-69	Auburn 36-7
Bill Yeoman	Bluebonnet 12-31-71	Colorado 17-29
Bill Yeoman	Bluebonnet 12-29-73	Tulane 47-7
Bill Yeoman	Bluebonnet 12-23-74	North Carolina St. 31-31
Bill Yeoman	Cotton 1-1-77	Maryland 30-21
Bill Yeoman	Cotton 1-1-79	Notre Dame 34-35
Bill Yeoman	Cotton 1-1-80	Nebraska 17-14
Bill Yeoman	Garden State 12-14-80	Navy 35-0
Bill Yeoman	Sun 12-26-81	Oklahoma 14-40
Bill Yeoman	Cotton 1-1-85	Boston College 28-45
Jack Pardee	Aloha 12-25-88	Washington St. 22-24
Kim Helton	Liberty 12-27-96	Syracuse 17-30

All bowls 7-6-1

TEAM-BY-TEAM BOWL RESULTS

School/Coach	Bowl/Date	Opponent/Score
IDAHO		
Chris Tormey	Humanitarian 12-30-98	Southern Miss. 42-35
All bowls 1-0-0		
ILLINOIS		
Ray Eliot	Rose 1-1-47	UCLA 45-14
Ray Eliot	Rose 1-1-52	Stanford 40-7
Pete Elliott	Rose 1-1-64	Washington 17-7
Mike White	Liberty 12-29-82	Alabama 15-21
Mike White	Rose 1-2-84	UCLA 9-45
Mike White	Peach 12-31-85	Army 29-31
John Mackovic	All-American 12-29-88	Florida 10-14
John Mackovic	Florida Citrus 1-1-90	Virginia 31-21
John Mackovic	Hall of Fame 1-1-91	Clemson 0-30
Lou Tepper	John Hancock 12-31-91	UCLA 3-6
Lou Tepper	Holiday 12-30-92	Hawaii 17-27
Lou Tepper	Liberty 12-31-94	East Caro. 30-0
Ron Turner	Micronpc.com 12-30-99	Virginia 63-21
All bowls 6-7-0		
INDIANA		
John Pont	Rose 1-1-68	Southern California 3-14
Lee Corso	Holiday 12-21-79	Brigham Young 38-37
Bill Mallory	All-American 12-31-86	Florida St. 13-27
Bill Mallory	Peach 1-2-88	Tennessee 22-27
Bill Mallory	Liberty 12-28-88	South Carolina 34-10
Bill Mallory	Peach 12-29-90	Auburn 23-27
Bill Mallory	Copper 12-31-91	Baylor 24-0
Bill Mallory	Independence 12-31-93	Virginia Tech 20-45
All bowls 3-5-0		
IOWA		
Forest Evashevski	Rose 1-1-57	Oregon St. 35-19
Forest Evashevski	Rose 1-1-59	California 38-12
Hayden Fry	Rose 1-1-82	Washington 0-28
Hayden Fry	Peach 12-31-82	Tennessee 28-22
Hayden Fry	Gator 12-30-83	Florida 6-14
Hayden Fry	Freedom 12-26-84	Texas 55-17
Hayden Fry	Rose 1-1-86	UCLA 28-45
Hayden Fry	Holiday 12-30-86	San Diego St. 39-38
Hayden Fry	Holiday 12-30-87	Wyoming 20-19
Hayden Fry	Peach 12-31-88	North Carolina St. 23-28
Hayden Fry	Rose 1-1-91	Washington 34-46
Hayden Fry	Holiday 12-30-91	Brigham Young 13-13
Hayden Fry	Alamo 12-31-93	California 3-37
Hayden Fry	Sun 12-29-95	Washington 38-18
Hayden Fry	Alamo 12-29-96	Texas Tech 27-0
Hayden Fry	Sun 12-31-97	Arizona St. 7-17
All bowls 8-7-1		
IOWA ST.		
Johnny Majors	Sun 12-18-71	LSU 15-33
Johnny Majors	Liberty 12-18-72	Georgia Tech 30-31
Earle Bruce	Peach 12-31-77	North Carolina St. 14-24
Earle Bruce	Hall of Fame 12-20-78	Texas A&M 12-28
All bowls 0-4-0		
KANSAS		
George Sauer	Orange 1-1-48	Georgia Tech 14-20
Jack Mitchell	Bluebonnet 12-16-61	Rice 33-7
Pepper Rodgers	Orange 1-1-69	Penn St. 14-15
Don Fambrough	Liberty 12-17-73	North Carolina St. 18-31
Bud Moore	Sun 12-26-75	Pittsburgh 19-33
Don Fambrough	Hall of Fame 12-31-81	Mississippi St. 0-10
Glen Mason	Aloha 12-25-92	Brigham Young 23-20
Glen Mason	Aloha 12-25-95	UCLA 51-30
All bowls 3-5-0		
KANSAS ST.		
Jim Dickey	Independence 12-11-82	Wisconsin 3-14
Bill Snyder	Copper 12-29-93	Wyoming 52-17
Bill Snyder	Aloha 12-25-94	Boston College 7-12
Bill Snyder	Holiday 12-29-95	Colorado St. 54-21
Bill Snyder	Cotton 1-1-97	Brigham Young 15-19
Bill Snyder	Fiesta 12-31-97	Syracuse 35-18
Bill Snyder	Alamo 12-29-98	Purdue 34-37
Bill Snyder	Holiday 12-29-99	Washington 24-20
All bowls 4-4-0		
KENT		
Don James	Tangerine 12-29-72	Tampa 18-21
All bowls 0-1-0		
KENTUCKY		
Paul "Bear" Bryant	Great Lakes 12-6-47	Villanova 24-14
Paul "Bear" Bryant	Orange 1-2-50	Santa Clara 13-21
Paul "Bear" Bryant	Sugar 1-1-51	Oklahoma 13-7
Paul "Bear" Bryant	Cotton 1-1-52	TCU 20-7
Fran Curci	Peach 12-31-76	North Carolina 21-0
Jerry Claiborne	Hall of Fame 12-22-83	West Virginia 16-20
Jerry Claiborne	Hall of Fame 12-29-84	Wisconsin 20-19
Bill Curry	Peach 12-31-93	Clemson 13-14
Hal Mumme	Outback 1-1-99	Penn St. 14-26
Hal Mumme	Music City 12-29-99	Syracuse 13-20
All bowls 5-5-0		
LSU		
Bernie Moore	Sugar 1-1-36	TCU 2-3
Bernie Moore	Sugar 1-1-37	Santa Clara 14-21
Bernie Moore	Sugar 1-1-38	Santa Clara 0-6
Bernie Moore	Orange 1-1-44	Texas A&M 19-14
Bernie Moore	Cotton 1-1-47	Arkansas 0-0
Gaynell Tinsley	Sugar 1-2-50	Oklahoma 0-35
Paul Dietzel	Sugar 1-1-59	Clemson 7-0
Paul Dietzel	Sugar 1-1-60	Mississippi 0-21
Paul Dietzel	Orange 1-1-62	Colorado 25-7
Charlie McClendon	Cotton 1-1-63	Texas 13-0
Charlie McClendon	Bluebonnet 12-21-63	Baylor 7-14
Charlie McClendon	Sugar 1-1-65	Syracuse 13-10
Charlie McClendon	Cotton 1-1-66	Arkansas 14-7
Charlie McClendon	Sugar 1-1-68	Wyoming 20-13
Charlie McClendon	Peach 12-30-68	Florida St. 31-27
Charlie McClendon	Orange 1-1-71	Nebraska 12-17
Charlie McClendon	Sun 12-18-71	Iowa St. 33-15
Charlie McClendon	Bluebonnet 12-30-72	Tennessee 17-24
Charlie McClendon	Orange 1-1-74	Penn St. 9-16
Charlie McClendon	Sun 12-31-77	Stanford 14-24
Charlie McClendon	Liberty 12-23-78	Missouri 15-20
Charlie McClendon	Tangerine 12-22-79	Wake Forest 34-10
Jerry Stovall	Orange 1-1-83	Nebraska 20-21
Bill Arnsparger	Sugar 1-1-85	Nebraska 10-28
Bill Arnsparger	Liberty 12-27-85	Baylor 7-21
Bill Arnsparger	Sugar 1-1-87	Nebraska 15-30
Mike Archer	Gator 12-31-87	South Carolina 30-13
Mike Archer	Hall of Fame 1-2-89	Syracuse 10-23
Gerry DiNardo	Independence 12-29-95	Michigan St. 45-26
Gerry DiNardo	Peach 12-28-96	Clemson 10-7
Gerry DiNardo	Independence 12-28-97	Notre Dame 27-9
All bowls 14-16-1		
LOUISIANA TECH		
Maxie Lambright	Independence 12-17-77	Louisville 24-14
Maxie Lambright	Independence 12-16-78	East Caro. 13-35
Joe Raymond Peace	Independence 12-15-90	Maryland 34-34
All bowls 1-1-1		
LOUISVILLE		
Frank Camp	Sun 1-1-58	Drake 34-20
Lee Corso	Pasadena 12-19-70	Long Beach St. 24-24
Vince Gibson	Independence 12-17-77	Louisiana Tech 14-24
Howard Schnellenberger	Fiesta 1-1-91	Alabama 34-7
Howard Schnellenberger	Liberty 12-28-93	Michigan St. 18-7
John L. Smith	Motor City 12-23-98	Marshall 29-48
John L. Smith	Humanitarian 12-30-99	Boise St. 31-34
All bowls 3-3-1		
MARSHALL		
Bob Pruett	Motor City 12-26-97	Mississippi 31-34
Bob Pruett	Motor City 12-23-98	Louisville 48-29
Bob Pruett	Motor City 12-27-99	Brigham Young 21-3
All bowls 2-1-0		
MARYLAND		
Jim Tatum	Gator 1-1-48	Georgia 20-20
Jim Tatum	Gator 1-2-50	Missouri 20-7
Jim Tatum	Sugar 1-1-52	Tennessee 28-13
Jim Tatum	Orange 1-1-54	Oklahoma 0-7
Jim Tatum	Orange 1-2-56	Oklahoma 6-20
Jerry Claiborne	Peach 12-28-73	Georgia 16-17
Jerry Claiborne	Liberty 12-16-74	Tennessee 3-7
Jerry Claiborne	Gator 12-29-75	Florida 13-0
Jerry Claiborne	Cotton 1-1-77	Houston 21-30
Jerry Claiborne	Hall of Fame 12-22-77	Minnesota 17-7
Jerry Claiborne	Sun 12-23-78	Texas 0-42
Jerry Claiborne	Tangerine 12-20-80	Florida 20-35
Bobby Ross	Aloha 12-25-82	Washington 20-21
Bobby Ross	Florida Citrus 12-17-83	Tennessee 23-30
Bobby Ross	Sun 12-22-84	Tennessee 28-27
Bobby Ross	Cherry 12-21-85	Syracuse 35-18
Joe Krivak	Independence 12-15-90	Louisiana Tech 34-34
All bowls 6-9-2		
MEMPHIS		
Billy Murphy	Pasadena 12-18-71	San Jose St. 28-9
All bowls 1-0-0		

TEAM-BY-TEAM BOWL RESULTS

School/Coach	Bowl/Date	Opponent/Score
MIAMI (FLA.)		
Tom McCann	Orange 1-1-35	Bucknell 0-26
Jack Harding	Orange 1-1-46	Holy Cross 13-6
Andy Gustafson	Orange 1-1-51	Clemson 14-15
Andy Gustafson	Gator 1-1-52	Clemson 14-0
Andy Gustafson	Liberty 12-16-61	Syracuse 14-15
Andy Gustafson	Gotham 12-15-62	Nebraska 34-36
Charlie Tate	Liberty 12-10-66	Virginia Tech 14-7
Charlie Tate	Bluebonnet 12-31-67	Colorado 21-31
Howard Schnellenberger	Peach 1-2-81	Virginia Tech 20-10
Howard Schnellenberger	Orange 1-2-84	Nebraska 31-30
Jimmy Johnson	Fiesta 1-1-85	UCLA 37-39
Jimmy Johnson	Sugar 1-1-86	Tennessee 7-35
Jimmy Johnson	Fiesta 1-2-87	Penn St. 10-14
Jimmy Johnson	Orange 1-1-88	Oklahoma 20-14
Jimmy Johnson	Orange 1-2-89	Nebraska 23-3
Dennis Erickson	Sugar 1-1-90	Alabama 33-25
Dennis Erickson	Cotton 1-1-91	Texas 46-3
Dennis Erickson	Orange 1-1-92	Nebraska 22-0
Dennis Erickson	Sugar 1-1-93	Alabama 13-34
Dennis Erickson	Fiesta 1-1-94	Arizona 0-29
Dennis Erickson	Orange 1-1-95	Nebraska 17-24
Butch Davis	Carquest 12-27-96	Virginia 31-21
Butch Davis	Micron PC 12-29-98	North Carolina St. 46-23
Butch Davis	Gator 1-1-00	Georgia Tech 28-13

All bowls 13-11-0

MIAMI (OHIO)		
Sid Gillman	Sun 1-1-48	Texas Tech 13-12
Woody Hayes	Salad 1-1-51	Arizona St. 34-21
John Pont	Tangerine 12-22-62	Houston 21-49
Bill Mallory	Tangerine 12-22-73	Florida 16-7
Dick Crum	Tangerine 12-21-74	Georgia 21-10
Dick Crum	Tangerine 12-20-75	South Carolina 20-7
Tim Rose	California 12-13-86	San Jose St. 7-37

All bowls 5-2-0

MICHIGAN		
Fielding "Hurry Up" Yost	Rose 1-1-02	Stanford 49-0
H. O. "Fritz" Crisler	Rose 1-1-48	Southern California 49-0
Bennie Oosterbaan	Rose 1-1-51	California 14-6
Chalmers "Bump" Elliott	Rose 1-1-65	Oregon St. 34-7
Glenn "Bo" Schembechler	Rose 1-1-70	Southern California 3-10
Glenn "Bo" Schembechler	Rose 1-1-72	Stanford 12-13
Glenn "Bo" Schembechler	Orange 1-1-76	Oklahoma 6-14
Glenn "Bo" Schembechler	Rose 1-1-77	Southern California 6-14
Glenn "Bo" Schembechler	Rose 1-2-78	Washington 20-27
Glenn "Bo" Schembechler	Rose 1-1-79	Southern California 10-17
Glenn "Bo" Schembechler	Gator 12-28-79	North Carolina 15-17
Glenn "Bo" Schembechler	Rose 1-1-81	Washington 23-6
Glenn "Bo" Schembechler	Bluebonnet 12-31-81	UCLA 33-14
Glenn "Bo" Schembechler	Rose 1-1-83	UCLA 14-24
Glenn "Bo" Schembechler	Sugar 1-2-84	Auburn 7-9
Glenn "Bo" Schembechler	Holiday 12-21-84	Brigham Young 17-24
Glenn "Bo" Schembechler	Fiesta 1-1-86	Nebraska 27-23
Glenn "Bo" Schembechler	Rose 1-1-87	Arizona St. 15-22
Glenn "Bo" Schembechler	Hall of Fame 1-2-88	Alabama 28-24
Glenn "Bo" Schembechler	Rose 1-2-89	Southern California 22-14
Glenn "Bo" Schembechler	Rose 1-1-90	Southern California 10-17
Gary Moeller	Gator 1-1-91	Mississippi 35-3
Gary Moeller	Rose 1-1-92	Washington 14-34
Gary Moeller	Rose 1-1-93	Washington 38-31
Gary Moeller	Hall of Fame 1-1-94	North Carolina St. 42-7
Gary Moeller	Holiday 12-30-94	Colorado St. 24-14
Lloyd Carr	Alamo 12-28-95	Texas A&M 20-22
Lloyd Carr	Outback 1-1-97	Alabama 14-17
Lloyd Carr	Rose 1-1-98	Washington St. 21-16
Lloyd Carr	Florida Citrus 1-1-99	Arkansas 45-31
Lloyd Carr	Orange 1-1-00	Alabama 35-34 (ot)

All bowls 16-15-0

MICHIGAN ST.		
Charlie Bachman	Orange 1-1-38	Auburn 0-6
Clarence "Biggie" Munn	Rose 1-1-54	UCLA 28-20
Duffy Daugherty	Rose 1-2-56	UCLA 17-14
Duffy Daugherty	Rose 1-1-66	UCLA 12-14
George Perles	Cherry 12-22-84	Army 6-10
George Perles	Hall of Fame 12-31-85	Georgia Tech 14-17
George Perles	Rose 1-1-88	Southern California 20-17
George Perles	Gator 1-1-89	Georgia 27-34
George Perles	Aloha 12-25-89	Hawaii 33-13
George Perles	John Hancock 12-31-90	Southern California 17-6
George Perles	Liberty 12-28-93	Louisville 7-18
Nick Saban	Independence 12-29-95	LSU 26-45
Nick Saban	Sun 12-31-96	Stanford 0-38
Nick Saban	Aloha 12-25-97	Washington 23-51

School/Coach	Bowl/Date	Opponent/Score
Bobby Williams	Florida Citrus 1-1-00	Florida 37-34

All bowls 6-9-0

MINNESOTA		
Murray Warmath	Rose 1-2-61	Washington 7-17
Murray Warmath	Rose 1-1-62	UCLA 21-3
Cal Stoll	Hall of Fame 12-22-77	Maryland 7-17
John Gutekunst	Independence 12-21-85	Clemson 20-13
John Gutekunst	Liberty 12-29-86	Tennessee 14-21
Glen Mason	Sun 12-31-99	Oregon 20-24

All bowls 2-4-0

MISSISSIPPI		
Ed Walker	Orange 1-1-36	Catholic 19-20
John Vaught	Delta 1-1-48	TCU 13-9
John Vaught	Sugar 1-1-53	Georgia Tech 7-24
John Vaught	Sugar 1-1-55	Navy 0-21
John Vaught	Cotton 1-2-56	TCU 14-13
John Vaught	Sugar 1-1-58	Texas 39-7
John Vaught	Gator 12-27-58	Florida 7-3
John Vaught	Sugar 1-1-60	LSU 21-0
John Vaught	Sugar 1-2-61	Rice 14-6
John Vaught	Cotton 1-1-62	Texas 7-12
John Vaught	Sugar 1-1-63	Arkansas 17-13
John Vaught	Sugar 1-1-64	Alabama 7-12
John Vaught	Bluebonnet 12-19-64	Tulsa 7-14
John Vaught	Liberty 12-18-65	Auburn 13-7
John Vaught	Bluebonnet 12-17-66	Texas 0-19
John Vaught	Sun 12-30-67	UTEP 7-14
John Vaught	Liberty 12-14-68	Virginia Tech 34-17
John Vaught	Sugar 1-1-70	Arkansas 27-22
John Vaught	Gator 1-2-71	Auburn 28-35
Billy Kinard	Peach 12-30-71	Georgia Tech 41-18
Billy Brewer	Independence 12-10-83	Air Force 3-9
Billy Brewer	Independence 12-20-86	Texas Tech 20-17
Billy Brewer	Liberty 12-28-89	Air Force 42-29
Billy Brewer	Gator 1-1-91	Michigan 3-35
Billy Brewer	Liberty 12-31-92	Air Force 13-0
Tommy Turberville	Motor City 12-26-97	Marshall 34-31
David Cutcliffe	Independence 12-31-98	Texas Tech 35-18
David Cutcliffe	Independence 12-31-99	Oklahoma 27-25

All bowls 17-11-0

MISSISSIPPI ST.		
Ralph Sasse	Orange 1-1-37	Duquesne 12-13
Allyn McKeen	Orange 1-1-41	Georgetown 14-7
Paul Davis	Liberty 12-21-63	North Carolina St. 16-12
Bob Tyler	Sun 12-28-74	North Carolina 26-24
Emory Bellard	Sun 12-27-80	Nebraska 17-31
Emory Bellard	Hall of Fame 12-31-81	Kansas 10-0
Jackie Sherrill	Liberty 12-29-91	Air Force 15-38
Jackie Sherrill	Peach 1-2-93	North Carolina 17-21
Jackie Sherrill	Peach 1-1-95	North Carolina St. 24-28
Jackie Sherrill	Cotton 1-1-99	Texas 11-38
Jackie Sherrill	Peach 12-30-99	Clemson 17-7

All bowls 5-6-0

MISSOURI		
Gwinn Henry	Los Angeles Christmas Festival 12-25-24	Southern California 7-20
Don Faurot	Orange 1-1-40	Georgia Tech 7-21
Don Faurot	Sugar 1-1-42	Fordham 0-2
Chauncey Simpson	Cotton 1-1-46	Texas 27-40
Don Faurot	Gator 1-1-49	Clemson 23-24
Don Faurot	Gator 1-2-50	Maryland 7-20
Dan Devine	Orange 1-1-60	Georgia 0-14
Dan Devine	Orange 1-2-61	Navy 21-14
Dan Devine	Bluebonnet 12-22-62	Georgia Tech 14-10
Dan Devine	Sugar 1-1-66	Florida 20-18
Dan Devine	Gator 12-28-68	Alabama 35-10
Dan Devine	Orange 1-1-70	Penn St. 3-10
Al Onofrio	Fiesta 12-23-72	Arizona St. 35-49
Al Onofrio	Sun 12-29-73	Auburn 34-17
Warren Powers	Liberty 12-23-78	LSU 20-15
Warren Powers	Hall of Fame 12-29-79	South Carolina 24-14
Warren Powers	Liberty 12-27-80	Purdue 25-28
Warren Powers	Tangerine 12-19-81	Southern Miss. 19-17
Warren Powers	Holiday 12-23-83	Brigham Young 17-21
Larry Smith	Holiday 12-29-97	Colorado St. 24-35
Larry Smith	Insight.com 12-26-98	West Virginia 34-31

All bowls 9-12-0

NAVY		
Bob Folwell	Rose 1-1-24	Washington 14-14
Eddie Erdelatz	Sugar 1-1-55	Mississippi 21-0
Eddie Erdelatz	Cotton 1-1-58	Rice 20-7

TEAM-BY-TEAM BOWL RESULTS

School/Coach	Bowl/Date	Opponent/Score
Wayne Hardin	Orange 1-1-61	Missouri 14-21
Wayne Hardin	Cotton 1-1-64	Texas 6-28
George Welsh	Holiday 12-22-78	Brigham Young 23-16
George Welsh	Garden State 12-14-80	Houston 0-35
George Welsh	Liberty 12-30-81	Ohio St. 28-31
Charlie Weatherbie	Aloha 12-25-96	California 42-38

All bowls 4-4-1

NEBRASKA

Coach	Bowl/Date	Opponent/Score
Lawrence McC. "Biff" Jones	Rose 1-1-41	Stanford 13-21
Bill Glassford	Orange 1-1-55	Duke 7-34
Bob Devaney	Gotham 12-15-62	Miami (Fla.) 36-34
Bob Devaney	Orange 1-1-64	Auburn 13-7
Bob Devaney	Cotton 1-1-65	Arkansas 7-10
Bob Devaney	Orange 1-1-66	Alabama 28-39
Bob Devaney	Sugar 1-2-67	Alabama 7-34
Bob Devaney	Sun 12-20-69	Georgia 45-6
Bob Devaney	Orange 1-1-71	LSU 17-12
Bob Devaney	Orange 1-1-72	Alabama 38-6
Bob Devaney	Orange 1-1-73	Notre Dame 40-6
Tom Osborne	Cotton 1-1-74	Texas 19-3
Tom Osborne	Sugar 12-31-74	Florida 13-10
Tom Osborne	Fiesta 12-26-75	Arizona St. 14-17
Tom Osborne	Bluebonnet 12-31-76	Texas Tech 27-24
Tom Osborne	Liberty 12-19-77	North Carolina 21-17
Tom Osborne	Orange 1-1-79	Oklahoma 24-31
Tom Osborne	Cotton 1-1-80	Houston 14-17
Tom Osborne	Sun 12-27-80	Mississippi St. 31-17
Tom Osborne	Orange 1-1-82	Clemson 15-22
Tom Osborne	Orange 1-1-83	LSU 21-20
Tom Osborne	Orange 1-2-84	Miami (Fla.) 30-31
Tom Osborne	Sugar 1-1-85	LSU 28-10
Tom Osborne	Fiesta 1-1-86	Michigan 23-27
Tom Osborne	Sugar 1-1-87	LSU 30-15
Tom Osborne	Fiesta 1-1-88	Florida St. 28-31
Tom Osborne	Orange 1-2-89	Miami (Fla.) 3-23
Tom Osborne	Fiesta 1-1-90	Florida St. 17-41
Tom Osborne	Florida Citrus 1-1-91	Georgia Tech 21-45
Tom Osborne	Orange 1-1-92	Miami (Fla.) 0-22
Tom Osborne	Orange 1-1-93	Florida St. 14-27
Tom Osborne	Orange 1-1-94	Florida St. 16-18
Tom Osborne	Orange 1-1-95	Miami (Fla.) 24-17
Tom Osborne	Fiesta 1-2-96	Florida 62-24
Tom Osborne	Orange 12-31-96	Virginia Tech 41-21
Tom Osborne	Orange 1-2-98	Tennessee 42-17
Frank Solich	Holiday 12-30-98	Arizona 20-23
Frank Solich	Fiesta 1-2-00	Tennessee 31-21

All bowls 19-19-0

NEVADA

Coach	Bowl/Date	Opponent/Score
Joe Sheeketski	Salad 1-1-48	North Texas 13-6
Joe Sheeketski	Harbor 1-1-49	Villanova 7-27
Chris Ault	Las Vegas 12-18-92	Bowling Green 34-35
Chris Ault	Las Vegas 12-14-95	Toledo 37-40 (ot)
Jeff Tisdel	Las Vegas 12-29-96	Ball St. 18-15

All bowls 2-3-0

UNLV

Coach	Bowl/Date	Opponent/Score
Harvey Hyde	California 12-15-84	Toledo 30-13
Jeff Horton	Las Vegas 12-15-94	Central Mich. 52-24

All bowls 2-0-0

NEW MEXICO

Coach	Bowl/Date	Opponent/Score
Ted Shipkey	Sun 1-2-39	Utah 0-26
Willis Barnes	Sun 1-1-44	Southwestern (Tex.) 0-7
Willis Barnes	Sun 1-1-46	Denver 34-24
Willis Barnes	Harbor 1-1-47	Montana St. 13-13
Bill Weeks	Aviation 12-9-61	Western Mich. 28-12
Dennis Franchione	Insight.com 12-27-97	Arizona 14-20

All bowls 2-3-1

NEW MEXICO ST.

Coach	Bowl/Date	Opponent/Score
Jerry Hines	Sun 1-1-36	Hardin-Simmons 14-14
Warren Woodson	Sun 12-31-59	North Texas 28-8
Warren Woodson	Sun 12-31-60	Utah St. 20-13

All bowls 2-0-1

NORTH CAROLINA

Coach	Bowl/Date	Opponent/Score
Carl Snavely	Sugar 1-1-47	Georgia 10-20
Carl Snavely	Sugar 1-1-49	Oklahoma 6-14
Carl Snavely	Cotton 1-2-50	Rice 13-27
Jim Hickey	Gator 12-28-63	Air Force 35-0
Bill Dooley	Peach 12-30-70	Arizona St. 26-48
Bill Dooley	Gator 12-31-71	Georgia 3-7
Bill Dooley	Sun 12-30-72	Texas Tech 32-28
Bill Dooley	Sun 12-28-74	Mississippi St. 24-26
Bill Dooley	Peach 12-31-76	Kentucky 0-21

School/Coach	Bowl/Date	Opponent/Score
Bill Dooley	Liberty 12-19-77	Nebraska 17-21
Dick Crum	Gator 12-28-79	Michigan 17-15
Dick Crum	Bluebonnet 12-31-80	Texas 16-7
Dick Crum	Gator 12-28-81	Arkansas 31-27
Dick Crum	Sun 12-25-82	Texas 26-10
Dick Crum	Peach 12-30-83	Florida St. 3-28
Dick Crum	Aloha 12-27-86	Arizona 21-30
Mack Brown	Peach 1-2-93	Mississippi St. 21-17
Mack Brown	Gator 12-31-93	Alabama 10-24
Mack Brown	Sun 12-30-94	Texas 31-35
Mack Brown	Carquest 12-30-95	Arkansas 20-10
Mack Brown	Gator 1-1-97	West Virginia 20-13
Carl Torbush	Gator 1-1-98	Virginia Tech 42-3
Carl Torbush	Las Vegas 12-19-98	San Diego St. 20-13

All bowls 11-12-0

NORTH CAROLINA ST.

Coach	Bowl/Date	Opponent/Score
Beattie Feathers	Gator 1-1-47	Oklahoma 13-34
Earle Edwards	Liberty 12-21-63	Mississippi St. 12-16
Earle Edwards	Liberty 12-16-67	Georgia 14-7
Lou Holtz	Peach 12-29-72	West Virginia 49-13
Lou Holtz	Liberty 12-17-73	Kansas 31-18
Lou Holtz	Bluebonnet 12-23-74	Houston 31-31
Lou Holtz	Peach 12-31-75	West Virginia 10-13
Bo Rein	Peach 12-31-77	Iowa St. 24-14
Bo Rein	Tangerine 12-23-78	Pittsburgh 30-17
Dick Sheridan	Peach 12-31-86	Virginia Tech 24-25
Dick Sheridan	Peach 12-31-88	Iowa 28-23
Dick Sheridan	Copper 12-31-89	Arizona 10-17
Dick Sheridan	All-American 12-28-90	Southern Miss. 31-27
Dick Sheridan	Peach 1-1-92	East Caro. 34-37
Dick Sheridan	Gator 12-31-92	Florida 10-27
Mike O'Cain	Hall of Fame 1-1-94	Michigan 7-42
Mike O'Cain	Peach 1-1-95	Mississippi St. 28-24
Mike O'Cain	Micron PC 12-29-98	Miami (Fla.) 23-46

All bowls 8-9-1

NORTH TEXAS

Coach	Bowl/Date	Opponent/Score
Odus Mitchell	Salad 1-1-48	Nevada 6-13
Odus Mitchell	Sun 12-31-59	New Mexico St. 8-28

All bowls 0-2-0

NORTHERN ILL.

Coach	Bowl/Date	Opponent/Score
Bill Mallory	California 12-17-83	Cal St. Fullerton 20-13

All bowls 1-0-0

NORTHWESTERN

Coach	Bowl/Date	Opponent/Score
Bob Voigts	Rose 1-1-49	California 20-14
Gary Barnett	Rose 1-1-96	Southern California 32-41
Gary Barnett	Florida Citrus 1-1-97	Tennessee 28-48

All bowls 1-2-0

NOTRE DAME

Coach	Bowl/Date	Opponent/Score
Knute Rockne	Rose 1-1-25	Stanford 27-10
Ara Parseghian	Cotton 1-1-70	Texas 17-21
Ara Parseghian	Cotton 1-1-71	Texas 24-11
Ara Parseghian	Orange 1-1-73	Nebraska 6-40
Ara Parseghian	Sugar 12-31-73	Alabama 24-23
Ara Parseghian	Orange 1-1-75	Alabama 13-11
Dan Devine	Gator 12-27-76	Penn St. 20-9
Dan Devine	Cotton 1-2-78	Texas 38-10
Dan Devine	Cotton 1-1-79	Houston 35-34
Dan Devine	Sugar 1-1-81	Georgia 10-17
Gerry Faust	Liberty 12-29-83	Boston College 19-18
Gerry Faust	Aloha 12-29-84	Southern Methodist 20-27
Lou Holtz	Cotton 1-1-88	Texas A&M 10-35
Lou Holtz	Fiesta 1-2-89	West Virginia 34-21
Lou Holtz	Orange 1-1-90	Colorado 21-6
Lou Holtz	Orange 1-1-91	Colorado 9-10
Lou Holtz	Sugar 1-1-92	Florida 39-28
Lou Holtz	Cotton 1-1-93	Texas A&M 28-3
Lou Holtz	Cotton 1-1-94	Texas A&M 24-21
Lou Holtz	Fiesta 1-2-95	Colorado 24-41
Lou Holtz	Orange 1-1-96	Florida St. 26-31
Bob Davie	Independence 12-28-97	LSU 9-27
Bob Davie	Gator 1-1-99	Georgia Tech 28-35

All bowls 13-10-0

OHIO

Coach	Bowl/Date	Opponent/Score
Bill Hess	Sun 12-31-62	West Tex. A&M 14-15
Bill Hess	Tangerine 12-27-68	Richmond 42-49

All bowls 0-2-0

OHIO ST.

Coach	Bowl/Date	Opponent/Score
John Wilce	Rose 1-1-21	California 0-28
Wes Fesler	Rose 1-2-50	California 17-14
Woody Hayes	Rose 1-1-55	Southern California 20-7

School/Coach	Bowl/Date	Opponent/Score
Woody Hayes	Rose 1-1-58	Oregon 10-7
Woody Hayes	Rose 1-1-69	Southern California 27-16
Woody Hayes	Rose 1-1-71	Stanford 17-27
Woody Hayes	Rose 1-1-73	Southern California 17-42
Woody Hayes	Rose 1-1-74	Southern California 42-21
Woody Hayes	Rose 1-1-75	Southern California 17-18
Woody Hayes	Rose 1-1-76	UCLA 10-23
Woody Hayes	Orange 1-1-77	Colorado 27-10
Woody Hayes	Sugar 1-2-78	Alabama 6-35
Woody Hayes	Gator 12-29-78	Clemson 15-17
Earle Bruce	Rose 1-1-80	Southern California 16-17
Earle Bruce	Fiesta 12-26-80	Penn St. 19-31
Earle Bruce	Liberty 12-30-81	Navy 31-28
Earle Bruce	Holiday 12-17-82	Brigham Young 47-17
Earle Bruce	Fiesta 1-2-84	Pittsburgh 28-23
Earle Bruce	Rose 1-1-85	Southern California 17-20
Earle Bruce	Florida Citrus 12-28-85	Brigham Young 10-7
Earle Bruce	Cotton 1-1-87	Texas A&M 28-12
John Cooper	Hall of Fame 1-1-90	Auburn 14-31
John Cooper	Liberty 12-27-90	Air Force 11-23
John Cooper	Hall of Fame 1-1-92	Syracuse 17-24
John Cooper	Florida Citrus 1-1-93	Georgia 14-21
John Cooper	Holiday 12-30-93	Brigham Young 28-21
John Cooper	Florida Citrus 1-2-95	Alabama 17-24
John Cooper	Florida Citrus 1-1-96	Tennessee 14-20
John Cooper	Rose 1-1-97	Arizona St. 20-17
John Cooper	Sugar 1-1-98	Florida St. 14-31
John Cooper	Sugar 1-1-99	Texas A&M 24-14

All bowls 14-17-0

OKLAHOMA

Tom Stidham	Orange 1-2-39	Tennessee 0-17
Jim Tatum	Gator 1-1-47	North Carolina St. 34-13
Bud Wilkinson	Sugar 1-1-49	North Carolina 14-6
Bud Wilkinson	Sugar 1-2-50	LSU 35-0
Bud Wilkinson	Sugar 1-1-51	Kentucky 7-13
Bud Wilkinson	Orange 1-1-54	Maryland 7-0
Bud Wilkinson	Orange 1-2-56	Maryland 20-6
Bud Wilkinson	Orange 1-1-58	Duke 48-21
Bud Wilkinson	Orange 1-1-59	Syracuse 21-6
Bud Wilkinson	Orange 1-1-63	Alabama 0-17
Gomer Jones	Gator 1-2-65	Florida St. 19-36
Chuck Fairbanks	Orange 1-1-68	Tennessee 26-24
Chuck Fairbanks	Bluebonnet 12-31-68	Southern Methodist 27-28
Chuck Fairbanks	Bluebonnet 12-31-70	Alabama 24-24
Chuck Fairbanks	Sugar 1-1-72	Auburn 40-22
Chuck Fairbanks	Sugar 12-31-72	Penn St. 14-0
Barry Switzer	Orange 1-1-76	Michigan 14-6
Barry Switzer	Fiesta 12-25-76	Wyoming 41-7
Barry Switzer	Orange 1-2-78	Arkansas 6-31
Barry Switzer	Orange 1-1-79	Nebraska 31-24
Barry Switzer	Orange 1-1-80	Florida St. 24-7
Barry Switzer	Orange 1-1-81	Florida St. 18-17
Barry Switzer	Sun 12-26-81	Houston 40-14
Barry Switzer	Fiesta 1-1-83	Arizona St. 21-32
Barry Switzer	Orange 1-1-85	Washington 17-28
Barry Switzer	Orange 1-1-86	Penn St. 25-10
Barry Switzer	Orange 1-1-87	Arkansas 42-8
Barry Switzer	Orange 1-1-88	Miami (Fla.) 14-20
Barry Switzer	Florida Citrus 1-2-89	Clemson 6-13
Gary Gibbs	Gator 12-29-91	Virginia 48-14
Gary Gibbs	John Hancock 12-24-93	Texas Tech 41-10
Gary Gibbs	Copper 12-29-94	Brigham Young 6-31
Bob Stoops	Independence 12-31-99	Mississippi 25-27

All bowls 20-12-1

OKLAHOMA ST.

Jim Lookabaugh	Cotton 1-1-45	TCU 34-0
Jim Lookabaugh	Sugar 1-1-46	St. Mary's (Cal.) 33-13
Jim Lookabaugh	Delta 1-1-49	William & Mary 0-20
Cliff Speegle	Bluegrass 12-13-58	Florida St. 15-6
Jim Stanley	Fiesta 12-28-74	Brigham Young 16-6
Jim Stanley	Tangerine 12-18-76	Brigham Young 49-12
Jimmy Johnson	Independence 12-12-81	Texas A&M 16-33
Jimmy Johnson	Bluebonnet 12-31-83	Baylor 24-14
Pat Jones	Gator 12-28-84	South Carolina 21-14
Pat Jones	Gator 12-30-85	Florida St. 23-34
Pat Jones	Sun 12-25-87	West Virginia 35-33
Pat Jones	Holiday 12-30-88	Wyoming 62-14
Bob Simmons	Alamo 12-30-97	Purdue 20-33

All bowls 9-4-0

OREGON

Hugo Bezdek	Rose 1-1-17	Pennsylvania 14-0
Charles "Shy" Huntington	Rose 1-1-20	Harvard 6-7

School/Coach	Bowl/Date	Opponent/Score
Jim Aiken	Cotton 1-1-49	Southern Methodist 13-21
Len Casanova	Rose 1-1-58	Ohio St. 7-10
Len Casanova	Liberty 12-17-60	Penn St. 12-41
Len Casanova	Sun 12-31-63	Southern Methodist 21-14
Rich Brooks	Independence 12-16-89	Tulsa 27-24
Rich Brooks	Freedom 12-29-90	Colorado St. 31-32
Rich Brooks	Independence 12-31-92	Wake Forest 35-39
Rich Brooks	Rose 1-2-95	Penn St. 20-38
Mike Bellotti	Cotton 1-1-96	Colorado 6-38
Mike Bellotti	Las Vegas 12-20-97	Air Force 41-13
Mike Bellotti	Aloha Classic 12-25-98	Colorado 43-51
Mike Bellotti	Sun 12-31-99	Minnesota 24-20

All bowls 5-9-0

OREGON ST.

Lon Stiner	Rose 1-1-42	Duke 20-16
Tommy Prothro	Rose 1-1-57	Iowa 19-35
Tommy Prothro	Liberty 12-15-62	Villanova 6-0
Tommy Prothro	Rose 1-1-65	Michigan 7-34
Dennis Erickson	Oahu Classic 12-25-99	Hawaii 17-23

All bowls 2-3-0

PENN ST.

Hugo Bezdek	Rose 1-1-23	Southern California 3-14
Bob Higgins	Cotton 1-1-48	Southern Methodist 13-13
Charles "Rip" Engle	Liberty 12-19-59	Alabama 7-0
Charles "Rip" Engle	Liberty 12-17-60	Oregon 41-12
Charles "Rip" Engle	Gator 12-30-61	Georgia Tech 30-15
Charles "Rip" Engle	Gator 12-29-62	Florida 7-17
Joe Paterno	Gator 12-30-67	Florida St. 17-17
Joe Paterno	Orange 1-1-69	Kansas 15-14
Joe Paterno	Orange 1-1-70	Missouri 10-3
Joe Paterno	Cotton 1-1-72	Texas 30-6
Joe Paterno	Sugar 12-31-72	Oklahoma 0-14
Joe Paterno	Orange 1-1-74	LSU 16-9
Joe Paterno	Cotton 1-1-75	Baylor 41-20
Joe Paterno	Sugar 12-31-75	Alabama 6-13
Joe Paterno	Gator 12-27-76	Notre Dame 9-20
Joe Paterno	Fiesta 12-25-77	Arizona St. 42-30
Joe Paterno	Sugar 1-1-79	Alabama 7-14
Joe Paterno	Liberty 12-22-79	Tulane 9-6
Joe Paterno	Fiesta 12-26-80	Ohio St. 31-19
Joe Paterno	Fiesta 1-1-82	Southern California 26-10
Joe Paterno	Sugar 1-1-83	Georgia 27-23
Joe Paterno	Aloha 12-26-83	Washington 13-10
Joe Paterno	Orange 1-1-86	Oklahoma 10-25
Joe Paterno	Fiesta 1-2-87	Miami (Fla.) 14-10
Joe Paterno	Florida Citrus 1-1-88	Clemson 10-35
Joe Paterno	Holiday 12-29-89	Brigham Young 50-39
Joe Paterno	Blockbuster 12-28-90	Florida St. 17-24
Joe Paterno	Fiesta 1-1-92	Tennessee 42-17
Joe Paterno	Blockbuster 1-1-93	Stanford 3-24
Joe Paterno	Florida Citrus 1-1-94	Tennessee 31-13
Joe Paterno	Rose 1-2-95	Oregon 38-20
Joe Paterno	Outback 1-1-96	Auburn 43-14
Joe Paterno	Fiesta 1-1-97	Texas 38-15
Joe Paterno	Flordia Citrus 1-1-98	Florida 6-21
Joe Paterno	Outback 1-1-99	Kentucky 26-14
Joe Paterno	Alamo 12-28-99	Texas A&M 24-0

All bowls 23-11-2

PITTSBURGH

Jock Sutherland	Rose 1-2-28	Stanford 6-7
Jock Sutherland	Rose 1-1-30	Southern California 14-47
Jock Sutherland	Rose 1-2-33	Southern California 0-35
Jock Sutherland	Rose 1-1-37	Washington 21-0
John Michelosen	Sugar 1-2-56	Georgia Tech 0-7
John Michelosen	Gator 12-29-56	Georgia Tech 14-21
Johnny Majors	Fiesta 12-21-73	Arizona St. 7-28
Johnny Majors	Sun 12-26-75	Kansas 33-19
Johnny Majors	Sugar 1-1-77	Georgia 27-3
Jackie Sherrill	Gator 12-30-77	Clemson 34-3
Jackie Sherrill	Tangerine 12-23-78	North Carolina St. 17-30
Jackie Sherrill	Fiesta 12-25-79	Arizona 16-10
Jackie Sherrill	Gator 12-29-80	South Carolina 37-9
Jackie Sherrill	Sugar 1-1-82	Georgia 24-20
Foge Fazio	Cotton 1-1-83	Southern Methodist 3-7
Foge Fazio	Fiesta 1-2-84	Ohio St. 23-28
Mike Gottfried	Bluebonnet 12-31-87	Texas 27-32
Paul Hackett	John Hancock 12-30-89	Texas A&M 31-28
Walt Harris	Liberty 12-31-97	Southern Miss. 7-41

All bowls 8-11-0

PURDUE

Jack Mollenkopf	Rose 1-2-67	Southern California 14-13
Jim Young	Peach 12-25-78	Georgia Tech 41-21

TEAM-BY-TEAM BOWL RESULTS

School/Coach	Bowl/Date	Opponent/Score
Jim Young	Bluebonnet 12-31-79	Tennessee 27-22
Jim Young	Liberty 12-27-80	Missouri 28-25
Leon Burtnett	Peach 12-31-84	Virginia 24-27
Joe Tiller	Alamo 12-30-97	Oklahoma St. 33-20
Joe Tiller	Alamo 12-29-98	Kansas St. 37-34
Joe Tiller	Outback 1-1-00	Georgia 25-28 (ot)

All bowls 6-2-0

RICE
Jimmy Kitts	Cotton 1-1-38	Colorado 28-14
Jess Neely	Orange 1-1-47	Tennessee 8-0
Jess Neely	Cotton 1-2-50	North Carolina 27-13
Jess Neely	Cotton 1-1-54	Alabama 28-6
Jess Neely	Cotton 1-1-58	Navy 7-20
Jess Neely	Sugar 1-2-61	Mississippi 6-14
Jess Neely	Bluebonnet 12-16-61	Kansas 7-33

All bowls 4-3-0

RUTGERS
Frank Burns	Garden State 12-16-78	Arizona St. 18-34

All bowls 0-1-0

SAN DIEGO ST.
Bill Schutte	Harbor 1-1-48	Hardin-Simmons 0-53
Don Coryell	Pasadena 12-6-69	Boston U. 28-7
Denny Stolz	Holiday 12-30-86	Iowa 38-39
Al Luginbill	Freedom 12-30-91	Tulsa 17-28
Ted Tollner	Las Vegas 12-19-98	North Carolina 13-20

All bowls 1-4-0

SAN JOSE ST.
Bill Hubbard	Raisin 1-1-47	Utah St. 20-0
Bill Hubbard	Raisin 12-31-49	Texas Tech 20-13
Dewey King	Pasadena 12-18-71	Memphis 9-28
Jack Elway	California 12-19-81	Toledo 25-27
Claude Gilbert	California 12-31-86	Miami (Ohio) 37-7
Claude Gilbert	California 12-12-87	Eastern Mich. 27-30
Terry Shea	California 12-8-90	Central Mich. 48-24

All bowls 4-3-0

SOUTH CAROLINA
Johnny McMillan	Gator 1-1-46	Wake Forest 14-26
Paul Dietzel	Peach 12-30-69	West Virginia 3-14
Jim Carlen	Tangerine 12-20-75	Miami (Ohio) 7-20
Jim Carlen	Hall of Fame 12-29-79	Missouri 14-24
Jim Carlen	Gator 12-29-80	Pittsburgh 9-37
Joe Morrison	Gator 12-28-84	Oklahoma St. 14-21
Joe Morrison	Gator 12-31-87	LSU 13-30
Joe Morrison	Liberty 12-28-88	Indiana 10-34
Brad Scott	Carquest 1-2-95	West Virginia 24-21

All bowls 1-8-0

SOUTHERN CALIFORNIA
Elmer "Gus" Henderson	Rose 1-1-23	Penn St. 14-3
Elmer "Gus" Henderson	Los Angeles Christmas Festival 12-25-24	Missouri 20-7
Howard Jones	Rose 1-1-30	Pittsburgh 47-14
Howard Jones	Rose 1-1-32	Tulane 21-12
Howard Jones	Rose 1-2-33	Pittsburgh 35-0
Howard Jones	Rose 1-2-39	Duke 7-3
Howard Jones	Rose 1-1-40	Tennessee 14-0
Jeff Cravath	Rose 1-1-44	Washington 29-0
Jeff Cravath	Rose 1-1-45	Tennessee 25-0
Jeff Cravath	Rose 1-1-46	Alabama 14-34
Jeff Cravath	Rose 1-1-48	Michigan 0-49
Jess Hill	Rose 1-1-53	Wisconsin 7-0
Jess Hill	Rose 1-1-55	Ohio St. 7-20
John McKay	Rose 1-1-63	Wisconsin 42-37
John McKay	Rose 1-2-67	Purdue 13-14
John McKay	Rose 1-1-68	Indiana 14-3
John McKay	Rose 1-1-69	Ohio St. 16-27
John McKay	Rose 1-1-70	Michigan 10-3
John McKay	Rose 1-1-73	Ohio St. 42-17
John McKay	Rose 1-1-74	Ohio St. 21-42
John McKay	Rose 1-1-75	Ohio St. 18-17
John McKay	Liberty 12-22-75	Texas A&M 20-0
John Robinson	Rose 1-1-77	Michigan 14-6
John Robinson	Bluebonnet 12-31-77	Texas A&M 47-28
John Robinson	Rose 1-1-79	Michigan 17-10
John Robinson	Rose 1-1-80	Ohio St. 17-16
John Robinson	Fiesta 1-1-82	Penn St. 10-26
Ted Tollner	Rose 1-1-85	Ohio St. 20-17
Ted Tollner	Aloha 12-28-85	Alabama 3-24
Ted Tollner	Florida Citrus 1-1-87	Auburn 7-16
Larry Smith	Rose 1-1-88	Michigan St. 17-20
Larry Smith	Rose 1-2-89	Michigan 14-22
Larry Smith	Rose 1-1-90	Michigan 17-10

School/Coach	Bowl/Date	Opponent/Score
Larry Smith	John Hancock 12-31-90	Michigan St. 16-17
Larry Smith	Freedom 12-29-92	Fresno St. 7-24
John Robinson	Freedom 12-30-93	Utah 28-21
John Robinson	Cotton 1-2-95	Texas Tech 55-14
John Robinson	Rose 1-1-96	Northwestern 41-32
Paul Hackett	Sun 12-31-98	TCU 19-28

All bowls 25-14-0

SOUTHERN METHODIST
Ray Morrison	Dixie Classic 1-1-25	West Va. Wesleyan 7-9
Matty Bell	Rose 1-1-36	Stanford 0-7
Matty Bell	Cotton 1-1-48	Penn St. 13-13
Matty Bell	Cotton 1-1-49	Oregon 21-13
Hayden Fry	Sun 12-31-63	Oregon 14-21
Hayden Fry	Cotton 12-31-66	Georgia 9-24
Hayden Fry	Bluebonnet 12-31-68	Oklahoma 28-27
Ron Meyer	Holiday 12-19-80	Brigham Young 45-46
Bobby Collins	Cotton 1-1-83	Pittsburgh 7-3
Bobby Collins	Sun 12-24-83	Alabama 7-28
Bobby Collins	Aloha 12-29-84	Notre Dame 27-20

All bowls 4-6-1

SOUTHERN MISS.
Thad "Pie" Vann	Sun 1-1-53	Pacific (Cal.) 7-26
Thad "Pie" Vann	Sun 1-1-54	UTEP 14-37
Bobby Collins	Independence 12-13-80	McNeese St. 16-14
Bobby Collins	Tangerine 12-19-81	Missouri 17-19
Curley Hallman	Independence 12-23-88	UTEP 38-18
Jeff Bower	All-American 12-28-90	North Carolina St. 27-31
Jeff Bower	Liberty 12-31-97	Pittsburgh 41-7
Jeff Bower	Humanitarian 12-30-98	Idaho 35-42
Jeff Bower	Liberty 12-31-99	Colorado St. 23-17

All bowls 4-5-0

STANFORD
Charlie Fickert	Rose 1-1-02	Michigan 0-49
Glenn "Pop" Warner	Rose 1-1-25	Notre Dame 10-27
Glenn "Pop" Warner	Rose 1-1-27	Alabama 7-7
Glenn "Pop" Warner	Rose 1-2-28	Pittsburgh 7-6
Claude "Tiny" Thornhill	Rose 1-1-34	Columbia 0-7
Claude "Tiny" Thornhill	Rose 1-1-35	Alabama 13-29
Claude "Tiny" Thornhill	Rose 1-1-36	Southern Methodist 7-0
Clark Shaughnessy	Rose 1-1-41	Nebraska 21-13
Chuck Taylor	Rose 1-1-52	Illinois 7-40
John Ralston	Rose 1-1-71	Ohio St. 27-17
John Ralston	Rose 1-1-72	Michigan 13-12
Bill Walsh	Sun 12-31-77	LSU 24-14
Bill Walsh	Bluebonnet 12-31-78	Georgia 25-22
Jack Elway	Gator 12-27-86	Clemson 21-27
Dennis Green	Aloha 12-25-91	Georgia Tech 17-18
Bill Walsh	Blockbuster 1-1-93	Penn St. 24-3
Tyrone Willingham	Liberty 12-30-95	East Caro. 13-19
Tyrone Willingham	Sun 12-31-96	Michigan St. 38-0
Tyrone Willingham	Rose 1-1-00	Wisconsin 9-17

All bowls 9-9-1

SYRACUSE
Ben Schwartzwalder	Orange 1-1-53	Alabama 6-61
Ben Schwartzwalder	Cotton 1-1-57	TCU 27-28
Ben Schwartzwalder	Orange 1-1-59	Oklahoma 6-21
Ben Schwartzwalder	Cotton 1-1-60	Texas 23-14
Ben Schwartzwalder	Liberty 12-16-61	Miami (Fla.) 15-14
Ben Schwartzwalder	Sugar 1-1-65	LSU 10-13
Ben Schwartzwalder	Gator 12-31-66	Tennessee 12-18
Frank Maloney	Independence 12-15-79	McNeese St. 31-7
Dick MacPherson	Cherry 12-21-85	Maryland 18-35
Dick MacPherson	Sugar 1-1-88	Auburn 16-16
Dick MacPherson	Hall of Fame 1-2-89	LSU 23-10
Dick MacPherson	Peach 12-30-89	Georgia 19-18
Dick MacPherson	Aloha 12-25-90	Arizona 28-0
Paul Pasqualoni	Hall of Fame 1-1-92	Ohio St. 24-17
Paul Pasqualoni	Fiesta 1-1-93	Colorado 26-22
Paul Pasqualoni	Gator 1-1-96	Clemson 41-0
Paul Pasqualoni	Liberty 12-27-96	Houston 30-17
Paul Pasqualoni	Fiesta 12-31-97	Kansas St. 18-35
Paul Pasqualoni	Orange 1-2-99	Florida 10-31
Paul Pasqualoni	Music City 12-29-99	Kentucky 20-13

All bowls 11-8-1

TEMPLE
Glenn "Pop" Warner	Sugar 1-1-35	Tulane 14-20
Wayne Hardin	Garden State 12-15-79	California 28-17

All bowls 1-1-0

TENNESSEE
Bob Neyland	Orange 1-2-39	Oklahoma 17-0

TEAM-BY-TEAM BOWL RESULTS

School/Coach	Bowl/Date	Opponent/Score
Bob Neyland	Rose 1-1-40	Southern California 0-14
Bob Neyland	Sugar 1-1-41	Boston College 13-19
John Barnhill	Sugar 1-1-43	Tulsa 14-7
John Barnhill	Rose 1-1-45	Southern California 0-25
Bob Neyland	Orange 1-1-47	Rice 0-8
Bob Neyland	Cotton 1-1-51	Texas 20-14
Bob Neyland	Sugar 1-1-52	Maryland 13-28
Bob Neyland	Cotton 1-1-53	Texas 0-16
Bowden Wyatt	Sugar 1-1-57	Baylor 7-13
Bowden Wyatt	Gator 12-28-57	Texas A&M 3-0
Doug Dickey	Bluebonnet 12-18-65	Tulsa 27-6
Doug Dickey	Gator 12-31-66	Syracuse 18-12
Doug Dickey	Orange 1-1-68	Oklahoma 24-26
Doug Dickey	Cotton 1-1-69	Texas 13-36
Doug Dickey	Gator 12-27-69	Florida 13-14
Bill Battle	Sugar 1-1-71	Air Force 34-13
Bill Battle	Liberty 12-20-71	Arkansas 14-13
Bill Battle	Bluebonnet 12-30-72	LSU 24-17
Bill Battle	Gator 12-29-73	Texas Tech 19-28
Bill Battle	Liberty 12-16-74	Maryland 7-3
Johnny Majors	Bluebonnet 12-31-79	Purdue 22-27
Johnny Majors	Garden State 12-13-81	Wisconsin 28-21
Johnny Majors	Peach 12-31-82	Iowa 22-28
Johnny Majors	Florida Citrus 12-17-83	Maryland 30-23
Johnny Majors	Sun 12-24-84	Maryland 27-28
Johnny Majors	Sugar 1-1-86	Miami (Fla.) 35-7
Johnny Majors	Liberty 12-29-86	Minnesota 21-14
Johnny Majors	Peach 1-2-88	Indiana 27-22
Johnny Majors	Cotton 1-1-90	Arkansas 31-27
Johnny Majors	Sugar 1-1-91	Virginia 23-22
Johnny Majors	Fiesta 1-1-92	Penn St. 17-42
Phillip Fulmer	Hall of Fame 1-1-93	Boston College 38-23
Phillip Fulmer	Florida Citrus 1-1-94	Penn St. 13-31
Phillip Fulmer	Gator 12-30-94	Virginia Tech 45-23
Phillip Fulmer	Florida Citrus 1-1-96	Ohio St. 20-14
Phillip Fulmer	Florida Citrus 1-1-97	Northwestern 48-28
Phillip Fulmer	Orange 1-2-98	Nebraska 17-42
Phillip Fulmer	Fiesta 1-4-99	Florida St. 23-16
Phillip Fulmer	Fiesta 1-2-00	Nebraska 21-31

All bowls 22-18-0

TEXAS

School/Coach	Bowl/Date	Opponent/Score
Dana Bible	Cotton 1-1-43	Georgia Tech 14-7
Dana Bible	Cotton 1-1-44	Randolph Field 7-7
Dana Bible	Cotton 1-1-46	Missouri 40-27
Blair Cherry	Sugar 1-1-48	Alabama 27-7
Blair Cherry	Orange 1-1-49	Georgia 41-28
Blair Cherry	Cotton 1-1-51	Tennessee 14-20
Ed Price	Cotton 1-1-53	Tennessee 16-0
Darrell Royal	Sugar 1-1-58	Mississippi 7-39
Darrell Royal	Cotton 1-1-60	Syracuse 14-23
Darrell Royal	Bluebonnet 12-17-60	Alabama 3-3
Darrell Royal	Cotton 1-1-62	Mississippi 12-7
Darrell Royal	Cotton 1-1-63	LSU 0-13
Darrell Royal	Cotton 1-1-64	Navy 28-6
Darrell Royal	Orange 1-1-65	Alabama 21-17
Darrell Royal	Bluebonnet 12-17-66	Mississippi 19-0
Darrell Royal	Cotton 1-1-69	Tennessee 36-13
Darrell Royal	Cotton 1-1-70	Notre Dame 21-17
Darrell Royal	Cotton 1-1-71	Notre Dame 11-24
Darrell Royal	Cotton 1-1-72	Penn St. 6-30
Darrell Royal	Cotton 1-1-73	Alabama 17-13
Darrell Royal	Cotton 1-1-74	Nebraska 3-19
Darrell Royal	Gator 12-30-74	Auburn 3-27
Darrell Royal	Bluebonnet 12-27-75	Colorado 38-21
Fred Akers	Cotton 1-2-78	Notre Dame 10-38
Fred Akers	Sun 12-23-78	Maryland 42-0
Fred Akers	Sun 12-22-79	Washington 7-14
Fred Akers	Bluebonnet 12-31-80	North Carolina 7-16
Fred Akers	Cotton 1-1-82	Alabama 14-12
Fred Akers	Sun 12-25-82	North Carolina 10-26
Fred Akers	Cotton 1-2-84	Georgia 9-10
Fred Akers	Freedom 12-26-84	Iowa 17-55
Fred Akers	Bluebonnet 12-31-85	Air Force 16-24
David McWilliams	Bluebonnet 12-31-87	Pittsburgh 32-27
David McWilliams	Cotton 1-1-91	Miami (Fla.) 3-46
John Mackovic	Sun 12-30-94	North Carolina 35-31
John Mackovic	Sugar 12-31-95	Virginia Tech 10-28
John Mackovic	Fiesta 1-1-97	Penn St. 15-38
Mack Brown	Cotton 1-1-99	Mississippi St. 38-11
Mack Brown	Cotton 1-1-00	Arkansas 6-27

All bowls 18-19-2

UTEP

School/Coach	Bowl/Date	Opponent/Score
Mack Saxon	Sun 1-1-37	Hardin-Simmons 6-34
Jack "Cactus Jack" Curtice	Sun 1-1-49	West Virginia 12-21
Jack "Cactus Jack" Curtice	Sun 1-2-50	Georgetown 33-20
Mike Brumbelow	Sun 1-1-54	Southern Miss. 37-14
Mike Brumbelow	Sun 1-1-55	Florida St. 47-20
Mike Brumbelow	Sun 1-1-57	George Washington 0-13
Bobby Dobbs	Sun 12-31-65	TCU 13-12
Bobby Dobbs	Sun 12-30-67	Mississippi 14-7
Bob Stull	Independence 12-23-88	Southern Miss. 18-38

All bowls 5-4-0

TEXAS A&M

School/Coach	Bowl/Date	Opponent/Score
Dana Bible	Dixie Classic 1-2-22	Centre 22-14
Homer Norton	Sugar 1-1-40	Tulane 14-13
Homer Norton	Cotton 1-1-41	Fordham 13-12
Homer Norton	Cotton 1-1-42	Alabama 21-29
Homer Norton	Orange 1-1-44	LSU 14-19
Harry Stiteler	Presidential 12-9-50	Georgia 40-20
Paul "Bear" Bryant	Gator 12-28-57	Tennessee 0-3
Gene Stallings	Cotton 1-1-68	Alabama 20-16
Emory Bellard	Liberty 12-22-75	Southern California 0-20
Emory Bellard	Sun 1-2-77	Florida 37-14
Emory Bellard	Bluebonnet 12-31-77	Southern California 28-47
Tom Wilson	Hall of Fame 12-20-78	Iowa St. 28-12
Tom Wilson	Independence 12-12-81	Oklahoma St. 33-16
Jackie Sherrill	Cotton 1-1-86	Auburn 36-16
Jackie Sherrill	Cotton 1-1-87	Ohio St. 12-28
Jackie Sherrill	Cotton 1-1-88	Notre Dame 35-10
R. C. Slocum	John Hancock 12-30-89	Pittsburgh 28-31
R. C. Slocum	Holiday 12-29-90	Brigham Young 65-14
R. C. Slocum	Cotton 1-1-92	Florida St. 2-10
R. C. Slocum	Cotton 1-1-93	Notre Dame 3-28
R. C. Slocum	Cotton 1-1-94	Notre Dame 21-24
R. C. Slocum	Alamo 12-28-95	Michigan 22-20
R. C. Slocum	Cotton 1-1-98	UCLA 23-29
R. C. Slocum	Sugar 1-1-99	Ohio St. 14-24
R. C. Slocum	Alamo 12-28-99	Penn St. 0-24

All bowls 12-13-0

TCU

School/Coach	Bowl/Date	Opponent/Score
Bill Driver	Fort Worth Classic 1-1-21	Centre 7-63
Leo "Dutch" Meyer	Sugar 1-1-36	LSU 3-2
Leo "Dutch" Meyer	Cotton 1-1-37	Marquette 16-6
Leo "Dutch" Meyer	Sugar 1-2-39	Carnegie Mellon 15-7
Leo "Dutch" Meyer	Orange 1-1-42	Georgia 26-40
Leo "Dutch" Meyer	Cotton 1-1-45	Oklahoma St. 0-34
Leo "Dutch" Meyer	Delta 1-1-48	Mississippi 9-13
Leo "Dutch" Meyer	Cotton 1-1-52	Kentucky 7-20
Abe Martin	Cotton 1-2-56	Mississippi 13-14
Abe Martin	Cotton 1-1-57	Syracuse 28-27
Abe Martin	Cotton 1-1-59	Air Force 0-0
Abe Martin	Bluebonnet 12-19-59	Clemson 7-23
Abe Martin	Sun 12-31-65	UTEP 12-13
Jim Wacker	Bluebonnet 12-31-84	West Virginia 14-31
Pat Sullivan	Independence 12-28-94	Virginia 10-20
Dennis Franchione	Sun 12-31-98	Southern California 28-19
Dennis Franchione	Mobile Alabama 12-22-99	East Caro. 28-14

All bowls 6-10-1

TEXAS TECH

School/Coach	Bowl/Date	Opponent/Score
Pete Cawthon	Sun 1-1-38	West Virginia 6-7
Pete Cawthon	Cotton 1-2-39	St. Mary's (Cal.) 13-20
Dell Morgan	Sun 1-1-42	Tulsa 0-6
Dell Morgan	Sun 1-1-48	Miami (Ohio) 12-13
Dell Morgan	Raisin 12-31-49	San Jose St. 13-20
DeWitt Weaver	Sun 1-1-52	Pacific (Cal.) 25-14
DeWitt Weaver	Gator 1-1-54	Auburn 35-13
DeWitt Weaver	Sun 1-2-56	Wyoming 14-21
J. T. King	Sun 12-26-64	Georgia 0-7
J. T. King	Gator 12-31-65	Georgia Tech 21-31
Jim Carlen	Sun 12-19-70	Georgia Tech 9-17
Jim Carlen	Sun 12-30-72	North Carolina 28-32
Jim Carlen	Gator 12-29-73	Tennessee 28-19
Jim Carlen	Peach 12-28-74	Vanderbilt 6-6
Steve Sloan	Bluebonnet 12-31-76	Nebraska 24-27
Steve Sloan	Tangerine 12-23-77	Florida St. 17-40
Spike Dykes	Independence 12-20-86	Mississippi 17-20
Spike Dykes	All-American 12-28-89	Duke 49-21
Spike Dykes	John Hancock 12-24-93	Oklahoma 10-41
Spike Dykes	Cotton 1-2-95	Southern California 14-55
Spike Dykes	Copper 12-27-95	Air Force 55-41
Spike Dykes	Alamo 12-29-96	Iowa 0-27
Spike Dykes	Independence 12-31-98	Mississippi 18-35

All bowls 5-17-1

TOLEDO

School/Coach	Bowl/Date	Opponent/Score
Frank Lauterbur	Tangerine 12-26-69	Davidson 56-33
Frank Lauterbur	Tangerine 12-28-70	William & Mary 40-12
Jack Murphy	Tangerine 12-28-71	Richmond 28-3

TEAM-BY-TEAM BOWL RESULTS

School/Coach	Bowl/Date	Opponent/Score
Chuck Stobart	California 12-19-81	San Jose St. 27-25
Dan Simrell	California 12-15-84	UNLV 13-30
Gary Pinkel	Las Vegas 12-14-95	Nevada 40-37 (ot)

All bowls 5-1-0

TULANE
Bernie Bierman	Rose 1-1-32	Southern California 12-21
Ted Cox	Sugar 1-1-35	Temple 20-14
Lowell "Red" Dawson	Sugar 1-1-40	Texas A&M 13-14
Jim Pittman	Liberty 12-12-70	Colorado 17-3
Bennie Ellender	Bluebonnet 12-29-73	Houston 7-47
Larry Smith	Liberty 12-22-79	Penn St. 6-9
Vince Gibson	Hall of Fame 12-27-80	Arkansas 15-34
Mack Brown	Independence 12-19-87	Washington 12-24
Tommy Bowden	Liberty 12-31-98	Brigham Young 41-27

All bowls 3-6-0

TULSA
Henry Frnka	Sun 1-1-42	Texas Tech 6-0
Henry Frnka	Sugar 1-1-43	Tennessee 7-14
Henry Frnka	Sugar 1-1-44	Georgia Tech 18-20
Henry Frnka	Orange 1-1-45	Georgia Tech 26-12
Henry Frnka	Oil 1-1-46	Georgia 6-20
J. O. "Buddy" Brothers	Gator 1-1-53	Florida 13-14
Glenn Dobbs	Bluebonnet 12-19-64	Mississippi 14-7
Glenn Dobbs	Bluebonnet 12-18-65	Tennessee 6-27
F. A. Dry	Independence 12-13-76	McNeese St. 16-20
Dave Rader	Independence 12-16-89	Oregon 24-27
Dave Rader	Freedom 12-30-91	San Diego St. 28-17

All bowls 4-7-0

UCLA
Edwin "Babe" Horrell	Rose 1-1-43	Georgia 0-9
Bert LaBrucherie	Rose 1-1-47	Illinois 14-45
Henry "Red" Sanders	Rose 1-1-54	Michigan St. 20-28
Henry "Red" Sanders	Rose 1-2-56	Michigan St. 14-17
Bill Barnes	Rose 1-1-62	Minnesota 3-21
Tommy Prothro	Rose 1-1-66	Michigan St. 14-12
Dick Vermeil	Rose 1-1-76	Ohio St. 23-10
Terry Donahue	Liberty 12-20-76	Alabama 6-36
Terry Donahue	Fiesta 12-25-78	Arkansas 10-10
Terry Donahue	Bluebonnet 12-31-81	Michigan 14-33
Terry Donahue	Rose 1-1-83	Michigan 24-14
Terry Donahue	Rose 1-2-84	Illinois 45-9
Terry Donahue	Fiesta 1-1-85	Miami (Fla.) 39-37
Terry Donahue	Rose 1-1-86	Iowa 45-28
Terry Donahue	Freedom 12-30-86	Brigham Young 31-10
Terry Donahue	Aloha 12-25-87	Florida 20-16
Terry Donahue	Cotton 1-1-89	Arkansas 17-3
Terry Donahue	John Hancock 12-31-91	Illinois 6-3
Terry Donahue	Rose 1-1-94	Wisconsin 16-21
Terry Donahue	Aloha 12-25-95	Kansas 30-51
Bob Toledo	Cotton 1-1-98	Texas A&M 29-23
Bob Toledo	Rose 1-1-99	Wisconsin 31-38

All bowls 11-10-1

UTAH
Ike Armstrong	Sun 1-2-39	New Mexico 26-0
Ray Nagel	Liberty 12-19-64	West Virginia 32-6
Ron McBride	Copper 12-29-92	Washington St. 28-31
Ron McBride	Freedom 12-30-93	Southern California 21-28
Ron McBride	Freedom 12-27-94	Arizona 16-13
Ron McBride	Copper 12-27-96	Wisconsin 10-38
Ron McBride	Las Vegas 12-18-99	Fresno St. 17-16

All bowls 4-3-0

UTAH ST.
E. L. "Dick" Romney	Raisin 1-1-47	San Jose St. 0-20
John Ralston	Sun 12-31-60	New Mexico St. 13-20
John Ralston	Gotham 12-9-61	Baylor 9-24
Charlie Weatherbie	Las Vegas 12-17-93	Ball St. 42-33
John L. Smith	Humanitarian 12-29-97	Cincinnati 19-35

All bowls 1-4-0

VANDERBILT
Art Guepe	Gator 12-31-55	Auburn 25-13
Steve Sloan	Peach 12-28-74	Texas Tech 6-6
George MacIntyre	Hall of Fame 12-31-82	Air Force 28-36

All bowls 1-1-1

VIRGINIA
George Welsh	Peach 12-31-84	Purdue 27-24
George Welsh	All-American 12-22-87	Brigham Young 22-16
George Welsh	Florida Citrus 1-1-90	Illinois 21-31
George Welsh	Sugar 1-1-91	Tennessee 22-23
George Welsh	Gator 12-29-91	Oklahoma 14-48
George Welsh	Carquest 1-1-94	Boston College 13-31
George Welsh	Independence 12-28-94	TCU 20-10
George Welsh	Peach 12-30-95	Georgia 34-27
George Welsh	Carquest 12-27-96	Miami (Fla.) 21-31
George Welsh	Peach 12-31-98	Georgia 33-35
George Welsh	Micronpc.com 12-30-99	Illinois 21-63

All bowls 4-7-0

VIRGINIA TECH
Jimmy Kitts	Sun 1-1-47	Cincinnati 6-18
Jerry Claiborne	Liberty 12-10-66	Miami (Fla.) 7-14
Jerry Claiborne	Liberty 12-14-68	Mississippi 17-34
Bill Dooley	Peach 1-2-81	Miami (Fla.) 10-20
Bill Dooley	Independence 12-15-84	Air Force 7-23
Bill Dooley	Peach 12-31-86	North Carolina St. 25-24
Frank Beamer	Independence 12-31-93	Indiana 45-20
Frank Beamer	Gator 12-30-94	Tennessee 23-45
Frank Beamer	Sugar 12-31-95	Texas 28-10
Frank Beamer	Orange 12-31-96	Nebraska 21-41
Frank Beamer	Gator 1-1-98	North Carolina 3-42
Frank Beamer	Music City 12-28-98	Alabama 38-7
Frank Beamer	Sugar 1-4-00	Florida St. 29-46

All bowls 4-9-0

WAKE FOREST
D. C. "Peahead" Walker	Gator 1-1-46	South Carolina 26-14
D. C. "Peahead" Walker	Dixie 1-1-49	Baylor 7-20
John Mackovic	Tangerine 12-22-79	LSU 10-34
Bill Dooley	Independence 12-31-92	Oregon 39-35
Jim Caldwell	Aloha Classic 12-25-99	Arizona St. 23-3

All bowls 3-2-0

WASHINGTON
Enoch Bagshaw	Rose 1-1-24	Navy 14-14
Enoch Bagshaw	Rose 1-1-26	Alabama 19-20
Jimmy Phelan	Rose 1-1-37	Pittsburgh 0-21
Ralph "Pest" Welch	Rose 1-1-44	Southern California 0-29
Jim Owens	Rose 1-1-60	Wisconsin 44-8
Jim Owens	Rose 1-2-61	Minnesota 17-7
Jim Owens	Rose 1-1-64	Illinois 7-17
Don James	Rose 1-2-78	Michigan 27-20
Don James	Sun 12-22-79	Texas 14-7
Don James	Rose 1-1-81	Michigan 6-23
Don James	Rose 1-1-82	Iowa 28-0
Don James	Aloha 12-25-82	Maryland 21-20
Don James	Aloha 12-26-83	Penn St. 10-13
Don James	Orange 1-1-85	Oklahoma 28-17
Don James	Freedom 12-30-85	Colorado 20-17
Don James	Sun 12-25-86	Alabama 6-28
Don James	Independence 12-19-87	Tulane 24-12
Don James	Freedom 12-30-89	Florida 34-7
Don James	Rose 1-1-91	Iowa 46-34
Don James	Rose 1-1-92	Michigan 34-14
Don James	Rose 1-1-93	Michigan 31-38
Jim Lambright	Sun 12-29-95	Iowa 18-38
Jim Lambright	Holiday 12-30-96	Colorado 21-33
Jim Lambright	Aloha 12-25-97	Michigan St. 51-23
Jim Lambright	Oahu Classic 12-25-98	Air Force 25-45
Rick Neuheisel	Holiday 12-29-99	Kansas St. 20-24

All bowls 13-12-1

WASHINGTON ST.
Bill "Lone Star" Dietz	Rose 1-1-16	Brown 14-0
Orin "Babe" Hollingbery	Rose 1-1-31	Alabama 0-24
Jim Walden	Holiday 12-18-81	Brigham Young 36-38
Dennis Erickson	Aloha 12-25-88	Houston 24-22
Mike Price	Copper 12-29-92	Utah 31-28
Mike Price	Alamo 12-31-94	Baylor 10-3
Mike Price	Rose 1-1-98	Michigan 16-21

All bowls 4-3-0

WEST VIRGINIA
Clarence "Doc" Spears	San Diego East-West Christmas Classic 12-25-22	Gonzaga 21-13
Marshall "Little Sleepy" Glenn	Sun 1-1-38	Texas Tech 7-6
Dud DeGroot	Sun 1-1-49	UTEP 21-12
Art Lewis	Sugar 1-1-54	Georgia Tech 19-42
Gene Corum	Liberty 12-19-64	Utah 6-32
Jim Carlen	Peach 12-30-69	South Carolina 14-3
Bobby Bowden	Peach 12-29-72	North Carolina St. 13-49
Bobby Bowden	Peach 12-31-75	North Carolina St. 13-10
Don Nehlen	Peach 12-31-81	Florida 26-6
Don Nehlen	Gator 12-30-82	Florida St. 12-31
Don Nehlen	Hall of Fame 12-22-83	Kentucky 20-16
Don Nehlen	Bluebonnet 12-31-84	TCU 31-14
Don Nehlen	Sun 12-25-87	Oklahoma St. 33-35

School/Coach	Bowl/Date	Opponent/Score
Don Nehlen	Fiesta 1-2-89	Notre Dame 21-34
Don Nehlen	Gator 12-30-89	Clemson 7-27
Don Nehlen	Sugar 1-1-94	Florida 7-41
Don Nehlen	Carquest 1-2-95	South Carolina 21-24
Don Nehlen	Gator 1-1-97	North Carolina 13-20
Don Nehlen	Carquest 12-29-97	Georgia Tech 30-35
Don Nehlen	Insight.com 12-26-98	Missouri 31-34
All bowls 8-12-0		

WESTERN MICH.
Merle Schlosser	Aviation 12-9-61	New Mexico 12-28
Al Molde	California 12-10-88	Fresno St. 30-35
All bowls 0-2-0		

WISCONSIN
Ivy Williamson	Rose 1-1-53	Southern California 0-7
Milt Bruhn	Rose 1-1-60	Washington 8-44
Milt Bruhn	Rose 1-2-63	Southern California 37-42
Dave McClain	Garden State 12-13-81	Tennessee 21-28
Dave McClain	Independence 12-11-82	Kansas St. 14-3
Dave McClain	Hall of Fame 12-29-84	Kentucky 19-20
Barry Alvarez	Rose 1-1-94	UCLA 21-16
Barry Alvarez	Hall of Fame 1-2-95	Duke 34-20
Barry Alvarez	Copper 12-27-96	Utah 38-10
Barry Alvarez	Outback 1-1-98	Georgia 6-33
Barry Alvarez	Rose 1-1-99	UCLA 38-31
Barry Alvarez	Rose 1-1-00	Stanford 17-9
All bowls 6-6-0		

WYOMING
Bowden Wyatt	Gator 1-1-51	Wash. & Lee 20-7
Phil Dickens	Sun 1-2-56	Texas Tech 21-14
Bob Devaney	Sun 12-31-58	Hardin-Simmons 14-6
Lloyd Eaton	Sun 12-24-66	Florida St. 28-20
loyd Eaton	Sugar 1-1-68	LSU 13-20
Fred Akers	Fiesta 12-25-76	Oklahoma 7-41
Paul Roach	Holiday 12-30-87	Iowa 19-20
Paul Roach	Holiday 12-30-88	Oklahoma St. 14-62
Paul Roach	Copper 12-31-90	California 15-17
Joe Tiller	Copper 12-29-93	Kansas St. 17-52
All bowls 4-6-0		

Played in Major Bowl—No Longer I-A

School/Coach	Bowl/Date	Opponent/Score
BOSTON U.		
Larry Naviaux	Pasadena 12-6-69	San Diego St. 7-28
All bowls 0-1-0		
BROWN		
Ed Robinson	Rose 1-1-16	Washington St. 0-14
All bowls 0-1-0		
BUCKNELL		
Edward "Hook" Mylin	Orange 1-1-35	Miami (Fla.) 26-0
All bowls 1-0-0		
CAL ST. FULLERTON		
Gene Murphy	California 12-17-83	Northern Ill. 13-20
All bowls 0-1-0		
CAL ST. NORTHRIDGE		
Sam Winningham	Pasadena 12-2-67	West Tex. A&M 13-35
All bowls 0-1-0		
CARNEGIE MELLON		
Bill Kern	Sugar 1-2-39	TCU 7-15
All bowls 0-1-0		
CASE RESERVE		
Bill Edwards	Sun 1-1-41	Arizona St. 26-13
All bowls 1-0-0		
CATHOLIC		
Arthur "Dutch" Bergman	Orange 1-1-36	Mississippi 20-19
Arthur "Dutch" Bergman	Sun 1-1-40	Arizona St. 0-0
All bowls 1-0-1		
CENTENARY (LA.)		
Homer Norton	Dixie Classic 1-1-34	Arkansas 7-7
All bowls 0-0-1		
CENTRE		
Charley Moran	Fort Worth Classic 1-1-21	TCU 63-7
Charley Moran	San Diego East-West Christmas Classic 12-26-21	Arizona 38-0
Charley Moran	Dixie Classic 1-2-22	Texas A&M 14-22
All bowls 2-1-0		

School/Coach	Bowl/Date	Opponent/Score
CITADEL		
Eddie Teague	Tangerine 12-30-60	Tennessee Tech 27-0
All bowls 1-0-0		
COLUMBIA		
Lou Little	Rose 1-1-34	Stanford 7-0
All bowls 1-0-0		
DAVIDSON		
Homer Smith	Tangerine 12-26-69	Toledo 33-56
All bowls 0-1-0		
DAYTON		
Joe Gavin	Salad 1-1-52	Houston 21-26
All bowls 0-1-0		
DENVER		
Clyde "Cac" Hubbard	Sun 1-1-46	New Mexico 24-34
Clyde "Cac" Hubbard	Alamo 1-4-47	Hardin-Simmons 0-20
All bowls 0-2-0		
DRAKE		
Vee Green	Raisin 1-1-46	Fresno St. 13-12
Al Kawal	Salad 1-1-49	Arizona 14-13
Warren Gaer	Sun 1-1-58	Louisville 20-34
All bowls 2-1-0		
DUQUESNE		
John "Little Clipper" Smith	Orange 1-1-37	Mississippi St. 13-12
All bowls 1-0-0		
FORDHAM		
Jim Crowley	Cotton 1-1-41	Texas A&M 12-13
Jim Crowley	Sugar 1-1-42	Missouri 2-0
All bowls 1-1-0		
GEO. WASHINGTON		
Eugene "Bo" Sherman	Sun 1-1-57	UTEP 13-0
All bowls 1-0-0		
GEORGETOWN		
Jack Hagerty	Orange 1-1-41	Mississippi St. 7-14
Bob Margarita	Sun 1-2-50	UTEP 20-33
All bowls 0-2-0		
GONZAGA		
Charles "Gus" Dorais	San Diego East-West Christmas Classic 12-15-22	West Virginia 13-21
All bowls 0-1-0		
HARDIN-SIMMONS		
Frank Kimbrough	Sun 1-1-36	New Mexico St. 14-14
Frank Kimbrough	Sun 1-1-37	UTEP 34-6
Warren Woodson	Sun 1-1-43	Second Air Force 7-13
Warren Woodson	Alamo 1-4-47	Denver 20-6
Warren Woodson	Harbor 1-1-48	San Diego St. 53-0
Warren Woodson	Shrine 12-18-48	Ouachita Baptist 40-12
Warren Woodson	Camellia 12-30-48	Wichita St. 29-12
Sammy Baugh	Sun 12-31-58	Wyoming 6-14
All bowls 5-2-1		
HARVARD		
Robert Fisher	Rose 1-1-20	Oregon 7-6
All bowls 1-0-0		
HOLY CROSS		
John "Ox" Da Grosa	Orange 1-1-46	Miami (Fla.) 6-13
All bowls 0-1-0		
LONG BEACH ST.		
Jim Stangeland	Pasadena 12-19-70	Louisville 24-24
All bowls 0-0-1		
MARQUETTE		
Frank Murray	Cotton 1-1-37	TCU 6-16
All bowls 0-1-0		
McNEESE ST.		
Jack Doland	Independence 12-13-76	Tulsa 20-16
Ernie Duplechin	Independence 12-15-79	Syracuse 7-31
Ernie Duplechin	Independence 12-13-80	Southern Miss. 14-16
All bowls 1-2-0		
MONTANA ST.		
Clyde Carpenter	Harbor 1-1-47	New Mexico 13-13
All bowls 0-0-1		
OCCIDENTAL		
Roy Dennis	Raisin 1-1-49	Colorado St. 21-20
All bowls 1-0-0		

PLAYED IN MAJOR BOWL—NO LONGER I-A

School/Coach	Bowl/Date	Opponent/Score
OUACHITA BAPTIST		
Wesley Bradshaw	Shrine 12-18-48	Hardin-Simmons 12-40
All bowls 0-1-0		
PACIFIC (CAL.)		
Larry Siemering	Raisin 1-1-48	Wichita St. 26-14
Ernie Jorge	Sun 1-1-52	Texas Tech 14-25
Ernie Jorge	Sun 1-1-53	Southern Miss. 26-7
All bowls 2-1-0		
PENNSYLVANIA		
Bob Folwell	Rose 1-1-17	Oregon 0-14
All bowls 0-1-0		
RANDOLPH FIELD		
Frank Tritico	Cotton 1-1-44	Texas 7-7
All bowls 0-0-1		
RICHMOND		
Frank Jones	Tangerine 12-27-68	Ohio 49-42
Frank Jones	Tangerine 12-28-71	Toledo 3-28
All bowls 1-1-0		
ST. MARY'S (CAL.)		
Edward "Slip" Madigan	Cotton 1-2-39	Texas Tech 20-13
Jimmy Phelan	Sugar 1-1-46	Oklahoma St. 13-33
Jimmy Phelan	Oil 1-1-47	Georgia Tech 19-41
All bowls 1-2-0		
SANTA CLARA		
Lawrence "Buck" Shaw	Sugar 1-1-37	LSU 21-14
Lawrence "Buck" Shaw	Sugar 1-1-38	LSU 6-0
Len Casanova	Orange 1-2-50	Kentucky 21-13
All bowls 3-0-0		
SECOND AIR FORCE		
Red Reese	Sun 1-1-43	Hardin-Simmons 13-7
All bowls 1-0-0		
SOUTHWESTERN (TEX.)		
Randolph R. M. Medley	Sun 1-1-44	New Mexico 7-0
Randolph R. M. Medley	Sun 1-1-45	U. of Mexico 35-0
All bowls 2-0-0		
TAMPA		
Earle Bruce	Tangerine 12-29-72	Kent 21-18
All bowls 1-0-0		

School/Coach	Bowl/Date	Opponent/Score
TENNESSEE TECH		
Wilburn Tucker	Tangerine 12-30-60	Citadel 0-27
All bowls 0-1-0		
U. OF MEXICO		
Bernard A. Hoban	Sun 1-1-45	Southwestern (Tex.) 0-35
All bowls 0-1-0		
VILLANOVA		
Maurice "Clipper" Smith	Bacardi, Cuba 1-1-37	Auburn 7-7
Jordan Olivar	Great Lakes 12-6-47	Kentucky 14-24
Jordan Olivar	Harbor 1-1-49	Nevada 27-7
Alex Bell	Sun 12-30-61	Wichita St. 17-9
Alex Bell	Liberty 12-15-62	Oregon St. 0-6
All bowls 2-2-1		
WASH. & JEFF.		
Earle "Greasy" Neale	Rose 1-2-22	California 0-0
All bowls 0-0-1		
WASH. & LEE		
George Barclay	Gator 1-1-51	Wyoming 7-20
All bowls 0-1-0		
WEST TEX. A&M		
Frank Kimbrough	Sun 1-1-51	Cincinnati 14-13
Joe Kerbel	Sun 12-31-62	Ohio 15-14
Joe Kerbel	Pasadena 12-2-67	Cal St. Northridge 35-13
All bowls 3-0-0		
WEST VA. WESLEYAN		
Bob Higgins	Dixie Classic 1-1-25	Southern Methodist 9-7
All bowls 1-0-0		
WICHITA ST.		
Ralph Graham	Raisin 1-1-48	Pacific (Cal.) 14-26
Jim Trimble	Camellia 12-30-48	Hardin-Simmons 12-49
Hank Foldberg	Sun 12-30-61	Villanova 9-17
All bowls 0-3-0		
WILLIAM & MARY		
Rube McCray	Dixie 1-1-48	Arkansas 19-21
Rube McCray	Delta 1-1-49	Oklahoma St. 20-0
Lou Holtz	Tangerine 12-28-70	Toledo 12-40
All bowls 1-2-0		
XAVIER (OHIO)		
Ed Kluska	Salad 1-1-50	Arizona St. 33-21
All bowls 1-0-0		

Major Bowl-Game Attendance

Total Yearly Attendance

Year	No. Bowls	Total Attendance	Per/Game Average
1902	1	8,000	8,000
1916	1	7,000	7,000
1917	1	26,000	26,000
1920	1	30,000	30,000
1921	2	51,000	25,500
1922	3	57,000	19,000
1923	2	48,000	24,000
1924	1	40,000	40,000
1925	3	107,000	35,667
1926	1	50,000	50,000
1927	1	57,417	57,417
1928	1	65,000	65,000
1929	1	66,604	66,604
1930	1	72,000	72,000
1931	1	60,000	60,000
1932	1	75,562	75,562
1933	1	78,874	78,874
1934	2	47,000	23,500
1935	3	111,634	37,211
1936	4	137,042	34,261
1937	6	176,396	29,399
1938	5	202,972	40,594
1939	5	224,643	44,929
1940	5	226,478	45,296
1941	5	253,735	50,747
1942	5	215,786	43,157
1943	5	240,166	48,033
1944	5	195,203	39,041
1945	5	236,279	47,256
1946	8	308,071	38,509
1947	10	304,316	30,432
1948	12	404,772	33,731
1949	13	442,531	34,041
1950	8	384,505	48,063
1951	8	392,548	49,069
1952	7	388,588	55,513
1953	6	366,299	61,050
1954	6	359,285	59,881
1955	6	357,871	59,645
1956	6	379,723	63,287
1957	6	369,162	61,527
1958	6	385,427	64,238
1959	7	392,394	56,056
1960	8	481,814	60,227
1961	9	490,113	54,457
1962	11	509,654	46,332
1963	10	481,722	48,172
1964	8	460,720	57,590
1965	8	448,541	56,068
1966	8	482,106	60,263
1967	8	521,427	65,178
1968	9	532,113	59,124
1969	10	585,621	58,562
1970	11	649,915	59,083
1971	11	623,072	56,643
1972	12	668,031	55,669
1973	11	668,461	60,769
1974	11	631,229	57,384
1975	11	597,079	54,280
1976	11	650,881	59,171
1977	12	660,429	55,036
1978	13	730,078	56,160
1979	15	726,064	48,404
1980	15	865,236	57,682
1981	15	856,730	57,115
1982	16	871,594	54,475
1983	16	919,193	57,450
1984	16	867,319	54,207
1985	18	977,374	54,299
1986	18	975,756	54,209
1987	18	958,933	53,274
1988	18	995,830	55,324
1989	17	937,323	55,137
1990	18	1,047,772	58,210
1991	19	1,048,306	55,174
1992	18	1,049,694	58,316
1993	18	973,570	54,087
1994	19	1,036,950	54,576
1995	19	1,064,640	56,034
1996	18	1,021,466	56,748
1997	18	985,292	54,738
1998	20	1,083,244	54,162
1999	22	1,224,414	55,655
2000	23	1,241,109	53,961

Bowl-by-Bowl Attendance

(Current site and stadium capacity in parentheses. For participating teams, refer to pages 287-291.)

ROSE BOWL

(Rose Bowl, Pasadena, Calif.; Capacity: 96,576)

Date	Attendance
1-1-02	8,000
1-1-16	7,000
1-1-17	26,000
1-1-20	30,000
1-1-21	42,000
1-2-22	40,000
1-1-23	43,000
1-1-24	40,000
1-1-25	53,000
1-1-26	50,000
1-1-27	57,417
1-2-28	65,000
1-1-29	66,604
1-1-30	72,000
1-1-31	60,000
1-1-32	75,562
1-2-33	78,874
1-1-34	35,000
1-1-35	84,474
1-1-36	84,474
1-1-37	87,196
1-1-38	90,000
1-2-39	89,452
1-1-40	92,200
1-1-41	91,500
1-1-42#	56,000
1-1-43	93,000
1-1-44	68,000
1-1-45	91,000
1-1-46	93,000
1-1-47	90,000
1-1-48	93,000
1-1-49	93,000
1-2-50	100,963
1-1-51	98,939
1-1-52	96,825
1-1-53	101,500
1-1-54	101,000
1-1-55	89,191
1-2-56	100,809
1-1-57	97,126
1-1-58	98,202
1-1-59	98,297
1-1-60	100,809
1-2-61	97,314
1-1-62	98,214
1-1-63	98,698
1-1-64	96,957
1-1-65	100,423
1-1-66	100,087
1-2-67	100,807
1-1-68	102,946
1-1-69	102,063
1-1-70	103,878
1-1-71	103,839
1-1-72	103,154
1-1-73	*106,869
1-1-74	105,267
1-1-75	106,721
1-1-76	105,464
1-1-77	106,182
1-2-78	105,312
1-1-79	105,629
1-1-80	105,526
1-1-81	104,863
1-1-82	105,611
1-1-83	104,991
1-2-84	103,217
1-1-85	102,594
1-1-86	103,292
1-1-87	103,168
1-1-88	103,847
1-2-89	101,688
1-1-90	103,450
1-1-91	101,273
1-1-92	103,566
1-1-93	94,236
1-1-94	101,237
1-2-95	102,247
1-1-96	100,102
1-1-97	100,635
1-1-98	101,219
1-1-99	93,872
1-1-00	93,731

*Record attendance. #Game held at Duke, Durham, N.C., due to war-time West Coast restrictions.

ORANGE BOWL

(Pro Player Stadium, Miami, Fla.; Capacity: 75,014)

Date	Attendance
1-1-35	5,134
1-1-36	6,568
1-1-37	9,210
1-1-38	18,972
1-2-39	32,191
1-1-40	29,278
1-1-41	29,554
1-1-42	35,786
1-1-43	25,166
1-1-44	25,203
1-1-45	23,279
1-1-46	35,709
1-1-47	36,152
1-1-48	59,578
1-1-49	60,523
1-2-50	64,816
1-1-51	65,181
1-1-52	65,839
1-1-53	66,280
1-1-54	68,640
1-1-55	68,750
1-2-56	76,561
1-1-57	73,280
1-1-58	76,561
1-1-59	75,281
1-1-60	72,186
1-2-61	72,212
1-1-62	68,150
1-1-63	72,880
1-1-64	72,647
1-1-65	72,647
1-1-66	72,214
1-2-67	72,426
1-1-68	77,993
1-1-69	77,719
1-1-70	77,282
1-1-71	80,699
1-1-72	78,151
1-1-73	80,010
1-1-74	60,477
1-1-75	71,801
1-1-76	76,799
1-1-77	65,537
1-2-78	60,987
1-1-79	66,365
1-1-80	66,714
1-1-81	71,043
1-1-82	72,748
1-1-83	68,713
1-2-84	72,549
1-1-85	56,294
1-1-86	74,178
1-1-87	52,717
1-1-88	74,760
1-2-89	79,480
1-1-90	81,190
1-1-91	77,062
1-1-92	77,747
1-1-93	57,324
1-1-94	81,536
1-1-95	*81,753
1-1-96	72,198
12-31-96	51,212
1-2-98	72,385
1-2-99	67,919
1-1-00	70,461

*Record attendance.

SUGAR BOWL

(Louisiana Superdome, New Orleans, La.; Capacity: 76,791)

Date	Attendance
1-1-35	22,026
1-1-36	35,000
1-1-37	41,000
1-1-38	45,000
1-2-39	50,000
1-1-40	73,000
1-1-41	73,181
1-1-42	72,000
1-1-43	70,000
1-1-44	69,000
1-1-45	72,000
1-1-46	75,000
1-1-47	73,300
1-1-48	72,000
1-1-49	82,000
1-2-50	82,470
1-1-51	82,000
1-1-52	82,000
1-1-53	82,000
1-1-54	76,000
1-1-55	82,000
1-2-56	80,175
1-1-57	81,000
1-1-58	82,000
1-1-59	82,000
1-1-60	83,000
1-2-61	82,851
1-1-62	82,910
1-1-63	82,900
1-1-64	80,785
1-1-65	65,000
1-1-66	67,421
1-2-67	82,000
1-1-68	78,963
1-1-69	82,113
1-1-70	82,500
1-1-71	78,655
1-1-72	84,031
12-31-72	80,123
12-31-73	*85,161
12-31-74	67,890
12-31-75	75,212
1-1-77	76,117
1-2-78	76,811
1-1-79	76,824
1-1-80	77,486
1-1-81	77,895
1-1-82	77,224
1-1-83	78,124
1-2-84	77,893
1-1-85	75,608
1-1-86	77,432
1-1-87	76,234
1-1-88	75,495
1-2-89	61,934
1-1-90	77,452
1-1-91	75,132
1-1-92	76,447
1-1-93	76,789
1-1-94	75,437
1-2-95	76,224
12-31-95	70,283
1-2-97	78,344
1-1-98	67,289
1-1-99	76,503
1-4-00	79,280

*Record attendance.

COTTON BOWL

(Cotton Bowl, Dallas, Texas; Capacity: 68,252)

Date	Attendance
1-1-37	17,000
1-1-38	37,000
1-2-39	40,000
1-1-40	20,000
1-1-41	45,500
1-1-42	38,000
1-1-43	36,000
1-1-44	15,000
1-1-45	37,000

MAJOR BOWL-GAME ATTENDANCE

Date	Attendance
1-1-46	45,000
1-1-47	38,000
1-1-48	43,000
1-1-49	69,000
1-2-50	75,347
1-1-51	75,349
1-1-52	75,347
1-1-53	75,504
1-1-54	75,504
1-1-55	75,504
1-2-56	75,504
1-1-57	68,000
1-1-58	75,504
1-1-59	75,504
1-1-60	75,504
1-2-61	74,000
1-1-62	75,504
1-1-63	75,504
1-1-64	75,504
1-1-65	75,504
1-1-66	76,200
12-31-66	75,400
1-1-68	75,504
1-1-69	72,000
1-1-70	73,000
1-1-71	72,000
1-1-72	72,000
1-1-73	72,000
1-1-74	67,500
1-1-75	67,500
1-1-76	74,500
1-1-77	54,500
1-2-78	*76,601
1-1-79	32,500
1-1-80	72,032
1-1-81	74,281
1-1-82	73,243
1-1-83	60,359
1-2-84	67,891
1-1-85	56,522
1-1-86	73,137
1-1-87	74,188
1-1-88	73,006
1-2-89	74,304
1-1-90	74,358
1-1-91	73,521
1-1-92	73,728
1-1-93	71,615
1-1-94	69,855
1-2-95	70,218
1-1-96	58,214
1-1-97	71,928
1-1-98	59,215
1-1-99	72,611
1-1-00	72,723

*Record attendance.

SUN BOWL#

(Sun Bowl, El Paso, Texas; Capacity: 51,270)

Date	Attendance
1-1-36	11,000
1-1-37	10,000
1-1-38	12,000
1-2-39	13,000
1-1-40	12,000
1-1-41	14,000
1-1-42	14,000
1-1-43	16,000
1-1-44	18,000
1-1-45	13,000
1-1-46	15,000
1-1-47	10,000
1-1-48	18,000
1-1-49	13,000
1-2-50	15,000
1-1-51	16,000
1-1-52	17,000
1-1-53	11,000
1-1-54	9,500
1-1-55	14,000
1-2-56	14,500
1-1-57	13,500
1-1-58	12,000
12-31-58	13,000
12-31-59	14,000
12-31-60	16,000
12-30-61	15,000
12-31-62	16,000
12-31-63	26,500
12-26-64	28,500
12-31-65	27,450
12-24-66	24,381
12-30-67	34,685
12-28-68	32,307
12-20-69	29,723
12-19-70	30,512
12-18-71	33,503
12-30-72	31,312
12-29-73	30,127
12-28-74	30,131
12-26-75	33,240
1-2-77	33,252
12-31-77	31,318
12-23-78	33,122
12-22-79	33,412
12-27-80	34,723
12-26-81	33,816
12-25-82	31,359
12-24-83	41,412
12-22-84	50,126
12-28-85	*52,203
12-25-86	48,722
12-25-87	43,240
12-24-88	48,719
12-30-89	44,887
12-31-90	50,562
12-31-91	42,821
12-31-92	41,622
12-24-93	43,848
12-30-94	50,612
12-29-95	49,116
12-31-96	42,721
12-31-97	49,104
12-31-98	46,612
12-31-99	48,757

*Record attendance. #Named John Hancock Bowl, 1989-93.

GATOR BOWL

(AllTel Stadium, Jacksonville, Fla.; Capacity: 76,976)

Date	Attendance
1-2-46	7,362
1-1-47	10,134
1-1-48	16,666
1-1-49	32,939
1-2-50	18,409
1-1-51	19,834
1-1-52	34,577
1-1-53	30,015
1-1-54	28,641
12-31-54	28,426
12-31-55	32,174
12-29-56	36,256
12-28-57	41,160
12-27-58	41,312
1-2-60	45,104
12-31-60	50,112
12-30-61	50,202
12-29-62	50,026
12-28-63	50,018
1-2-65	50,408
12-31-65	60,127
12-31-66	60,312
12-30-67	68,019
12-28-68	68,011
12-27-69	72,248
1-2-71	71,136
12-31-71	71,208
12-30-72	71,114
12-29-73	62,109
12-30-74	63,811
12-29-75	64,012
12-27-76	67,827
12-30-77	72,289
12-29-78	72,011
12-28-79	70,407
12-29-80	72,297
12-28-81	71,009
12-30-82	80,913
12-30-83	81,293
12-28-84	82,138
12-30-85	79,417
12-27-86	80,104
12-31-87	82,119
1-1-89	76,236
12-30-89	*82,911
1-1-91	68,927
12-29-91	62,003
12-31-92	71,233
12-31-93	67,205
12-30-94†	62,200
1-1-96	45,202
1-1-97	52,103
1-1-98	54,116
1-1-99	70,791
1-1-00	43,416

*Record attendance. †Played at Gainesville, Fla.

LIBERTY BOWL†

(Liberty Bowl Memorial Stadium, Memphis, Tenn.; Capacity: 62,921)

Date	Attendance
12-19-59	36,211
12-17-60	16,624
12-16-61	15,712
12-15-62	17,048
12-31-63	8,309
12-19-64	6,059
12-18-65	38,607
12-10-66	39,101
12-16-67	35,045
12-14-68	46,206
12-13-69	50,042
12-12-70	44,640
12-20-71	51,410
12-18-72	50,021
12-17-73	50,011
12-16-74	51,284
12-22-75	52,129
12-20-76	52,736
12-19-77	49,456
12-23-78	53,064
12-22-79	50,021
12-27-80	53,667
12-30-81	43,216
12-29-82	54,123
12-29-83	38,229
12-27-84	50,108
12-27-85	40,186
12-29-86	51,327
12-29-87	53,249
12-28-88	39,210
12-28-89	60,128
12-27-90	13,144
12-29-91	*61,497
12-31-92	32,107
12-28-93	21,097
12-31-94	33,280
12-30-95	47,398
12-27-96	49,163
12-31-97	50,209
12-31-98	52,192
12-31-99	54,866

*Record attendance. †Played at Philadelphia, 1959-63; Atlantic City, 1964; Memphis, from 1965.

FLORIDA CITRUS BOWL#

(Florida Citrus Bowl, Orlando, Fla.; Capacity: 70,000)

Date	Attendance
12-30-60	13,000
12-22-62	7,500
12-27-68	16,114
12-26-69	16,311
12-28-70	15,164
12-28-71	16,750
12-29-72	20,062
12-22-73@	37,234
12-21-74	20,246
12-20-75	20,247
12-18-76	37,812

Date	Attendance
12-23-77	44,502
12-23-78	31,356
12-22-79	38,666
12-20-80	52,541
12-19-81	50,045
12-18-82	51,296
12-17-83	50,183
12-22-84	51,821
12-28-85	50,920
1-1-87	51,113
1-1-88	53,152
1-2-89	53,571
1-1-90	60,016
1-1-91	72,328
1-1-92	64,192
1-1-93	65,861
1-1-94	72,456
1-2-95	71,195
1-1-96	70,797
1-1-97	63,467
1-1-98	*72,940
1-1-99	63,584
1-1-00	62,011

*Record attendance. #Named Tangerine Bowl before 1982. The first 14 games in the Tangerine Bowl, through 1-1-60, are not listed because no major teams were involved. The same is true for those games played in December 1961, 1963, 1964, 1965, 1966 and 1967. @ Played at Gainesville, Fla.

PEACH BOWL
(Georgia Dome, Atlanta, Ga.; Capacity: 71,228)

Date	Attendance
12-30-68	35,545
12-30-69	48,452
12-30-70	52,126
12-30-71	36,771
12-29-72	52,671
12-28-73	38,107
12-28-74	31,695
12-31-75	45,134
12-31-76	54,132
12-31-77	36,733
12-25-78	20,277
12-31-79	57,371
1-2-81	45,384
12-31-81	37,582
12-31-82	50,134
12-30-83	25,648
12-31-84	41,107
12-31-85	29,857
12-31-86	53,668
1-2-88	58,737
12-31-88	44,635
12-30-89	44,991
12-29-90	38,912
1-1-92	59,322
1-2-93	69,125
12-31-93	63,416
1-1-95	64,902
12-30-95	70,825
12-28-96	63,622
1-2-98	71,212
12-31-98	72,876
12-30-99	*73,315

*Record attendance.

FIESTA BOWL
(Sun Devil Stadium, Tempe, Ariz.; Capacity: 73,259)

Date	Attendance
12-27-71	51,089
12-23-72	51,318
12-21-73	50,878
12-28-74	50,878
12-26-75	51,396
12-25-76	48,174
12-25-77	57,727
12-25-78	55,227
12-25-79	55,347
12-26-80	66,738
1-1-82	71,053
1-1-83	70,533
1-2-84	66,484

Date	Attendance
1-1-85	60,310
1-1-86	72,454
1-2-87	73,098
1-1-88	72,112
1-2-89	74,911
1-1-90	73,953
1-1-91	69,098
1-1-92	71,133
1-1-93	70,224
1-1-94	72,260
1-1-95	73,968
1-2-96	79,864
1-1-97	65,106
12-31-97	69,367
1-4-99	*80,470
1-2-00	71,526

*Record attendance.

INDEPENDENCE BOWL
(Independence Stadium, Shreveport, La.; Capacity: 50,459)

Date	Attendance
12-13-76	15,542
12-17-77	18,500
12-16-78	18,200
12-15-79	27,234
12-13-80	45,000
12-12-81	47,300
12-11-82	49,503
12-10-83	41,274
12-15-84	41,000
12-21-85	42,800
12-20-86	46,369
12-19-87	41,683
12-23-88	20,242
12-16-89	30,333
12-15-90	48,325
12-29-91	46,932
12-31-92	31,337
12-31-93	33,819
12-28-94	27,242
12-29-95	48,835
12-31-96	41,366
12-28-97	*50,459
12-31-98	46,862
12-31-99	49,873

*Record attendance.

HOLIDAY BOWL
(Qualcomm Stadium, San Diego, Calif.; Capacity: 70,000)

Date	Attendance
12-28-78	52,500
12-21-79	52,200
12-19-80	50,214
12-18-81	52,419
12-17-82	52,533
12-23-83	51,480
12-21-84	61,243
12-22-85	42,324
12-30-86	59,473
12-30-87	61,892
12-30-88	60,718
12-29-89	61,113
12-29-90	61,441
12-30-91	60,646
12-30-92	44,457
12-30-93	52,108
12-30-94	59,453
12-29-95	51,051
12-30-96	54,749
12-29-97	50,761
12-30-98	*65,354
12-29-99	57,118

*Record attendance.

ALOHA & OAHU CLASSICS#
(Aloha Stadium, Honolulu, Hawaii; Capacity: 50,000)

Date	Attendance
12-25-82	30,055
12-26-83	37,212
12-29-84	41,777
12-28-85	35,183
12-27-86	26,743

Date	Attendance
12-25-87	24,839
12-25-88	35,132
12-25-89	*50,000
12-25-90	14,185
12-25-91	34,433
12-25-92	42,933
12-25-93	44,009
12-25-94	44,862
12-25-95	41,112
12-25-96	43,380
12-25-97	44,598
12-25-98 (Aloha)	46,451
12-25-98 (Oahu)	46,451
12-25-99 (Aloha)	40,974
12-25-99 (Oahu)	40,974

*Record attendance. #Named Aloha Bowl before 1998.

OUTBACK BOWL
(Formerly Hall of Fame)
(Raymond James Stadium, Tampa, Fla.; capacity: 66,005)

Date	Attendance
12-23-86	25,368
1-2-88	60,156
1-2-89	51,112
1-1-90	52,535
1-1-91	63,154
1-1-92	57,789
1-1-93	52,056
1-1-94	52,649
1-2-95	61,384
1-1-96	65,313
1-1-97	53,161
1-1-98	56,186
1-1-99	*66,005
1-1-00	54,059

*Record attendance.

INSIGHT.COM BOWL
(Arizona Stadium, Tucson, Ariz.; Capacity: 55,883)

Date	Attendance
12-31-89	37,237
12-31-90	36,340
12-31-91	35,752
12-29-92	40,876
12-29-93	49,075
12-29-94	45,122
12-27-95	41,004
12-27-96	42,122
12-27-97	*49,385
12-26-98	36,147
12-31-99	35,762

*Record attendance.

MICRONPC.COM BOWL#
(Pro Player Stadium, Miami, Fla.; Capacity: 75,014)

Date	Attendance
12-28-90	*74,021
12-28-91	52,644
1-1-93	45,554
1-1-94	38,516
1-2-95	50,833
12-30-95	34,428
12-27-96	46,418
12-29-97	28,262
12-29-98	44,387
12-30-99	31,089

*Record attendance. #Named Blockbuster Bowl before 1993 and named Carquest Bowl 1994-97.

LAS VEGAS BOWL
(Sam Boyd Stadium, Las Vegas, Nev.; Capacity: 40,000)

Date	Attendance
12-18-92	15,476
12-17-93	15,508
12-15-94	17,562
12-14-95	11,127
12-19-96	10,118
12-20-97	21,514
12-19-98	21,429
12-18-99	*28,227

*Record attendance.

MAJOR BOWL-GAME ATTENDANCE

ALAMO BOWL
(Alamodome, San Antonio, Texas; Capacity: 65,000)

Date	Attendance
12-31-93	45,716
12-31-94	44,106
12-28-95	64,597
12-29-96	55,677
12-30-97	55,552
12-29-98	60,780
12-28-99	*65,380

*Record attendance.

MOTOR CITY BOWL
(Pontiac Silverdome, Pontiac, Mich.; Capacity: 79,083)

Date	Attendance
12-26-97	43,340
12-23-98	32,206
12-27-99	*44,863

*Record attendance.

HUMANITARIAN BOWL
(Bronco Stadium, Boise, Idaho; Capacity: 30,000)

Date	Attendance
12-29-97	16,131
12-30-98	19,664
12-30-99	*29,283

*Record attendance.

MUSIC CITY BOWL
(Adelphia Coliseum, Nashville, Tenn.; Capacity: 67,000)

Date	Attendance
12-29-98	41,248
12-29-99	*59,221

*Record attendance.

MOBILE ALABAMA BOWL
(Ladd-Peebles Stadium, Mobile, Ala.; Capacity: 40,646)

Date	Attendance
12-22-99	34,200

Former Major Bowl Games
(For participating teams, refer to page 292.)

ALAMO
(San Antonio, Texas)

Date	Attendance
1-4-47	3,730

ALL-AMERICAN
(Birmingham, Ala.)

Date	Attendance
12-22-77	47,000
12-20-78	41,500
12-29-79	62,785
12-27-80	30,000
12-31-81	41,672
12-31-82	75,000
12-22-83	42,000
12-29-84	47,300
12-31-85	45,000
12-31-86	30,000
12-22-87	37,000
12-29-88	48,218
12-28-89	47,750
12-28-90	44,000

(Named Hall of Fame Classic until 1986 and then discontinued after 1990 game; played at Legion Field, capacity 75,952)

AVIATION
(Dayton, Ohio)

Date	Attendance
12-9-61	3,694

BACARDI
(Havana, Cuba)

Date	Attendance
1-1-37	12,000

BLUEBONNET
(Houston, Texas)

Date	Attendance
12-19-59	55,000
12-17-60	68,000
12-16-61	52,000
12-22-62	55,000
12-21-63	50,000
12-19-64	50,000
12-18-65	40,000
12-17-66	67,000
12-23-67	30,156
12-31-68	53,543
12-31-69	55,203
12-31-70	53,829
12-31-71	54,720
12-30-72	52,961
12-29-73	44,358
12-23-74	35,122
12-27-75	52,748
12-31-76	48,618
12-31-77	52,842
12-31-78	34,084
12-31-79	40,542
12-31-80	36,667
12-31-81	40,309
12-31-82	31,557
12-31-83	50,090
12-31-84	43,260
12-31-85	42,000
12-31-86	40,476
12-31-87	23,282

(Played at Rice Stadium 1959-67 and 1985, Astrodome 1968-84 and from 1986; Astrodome capacity 60,000)

BLUEGRASS
(Louisville, Ky.)

Date	Attendance
12-13-58	7,000

CALIFORNIA
(Fresno, Calif.)

Date	Attendance
12-19-81	15,565
12-18-82	30,000
12-17-83	20,464
12-15-84	21,741
12-14-85	32,554
12-13-86	10,743
12-12-87	24,000
12-10-88	31,272
12-9-89	31,610
12-8-90	25,431
12-14-91	34,825

CAMELLIA
(Lafayette, La.)

Date	Attendance
12-30-48	4,500

CHERRY
(Pontiac, Mich.)

Date	Attendance
12-22-84	70,332
12-21-85	51,858

DELTA
(Memphis, Tenn.)

Date	Attendance
1-1-48	28,120
1-1-49	15,069

DIXIE BOWL
(Birmingham, Ala.)

Date	Attendance
1-1-48	22,000
1-1-49	20,000

DIXIE CLASSIC
(Dallas, Texas)

Date	Attendance
1-2-22	12,000
1-1-25	7,000
1-1-34	12,000

FORT WORTH CLASSIC
(Fort Worth, Texas)

Date	Attendance
1-1-21	9,000

FREEDOM BOWL
(Anaheim, Calif.)

Date	Attendance
12-26-84	24,093
12-30-85	30,961
12-30-86	55,422
12-30-87	33,261
12-29-88	35,941
12-30-89	33,858
12-29-90	41,450
12-30-91	34,217
12-29-92	50,745
12-30-93	37,203
12-27-94	27,477

GARDEN STATE
(East Rutherford, N.J.)

Date	Attendance
12-16-78	33,402
12-15-79	55,493
12-14-80	41,417
12-13-81	38,782

GOTHAM
(New York, N.Y.)

Date	Attendance
12-9-61	15,123
12-15-62	6,166

GREAT LAKES
(Cleveland, Ohio)

Date	Attendance
12-6-47	14,908

HARBOR
(San Diego, Calif.)

Date	Attendance
1-1-47	7,000
1-1-48	12,000
1-1-49	20,000

LOS ANGELES CHRISTMAS FESTIVAL
(Los Angeles, Calif.)

Date	Attendance
12-25-24	47,000

MERCY
(Los Angeles, Calif.)

Date	Attendance
11-23-61	33,145

OIL
(Houston, Texas)

Date	Attendance
1-1-46	27,000
1-1-47	23,000

PASADENA
(Pasadena, Calif.)

Date	Attendance
12-2-67	28,802
12-6-69	41,276
12-19-70	20,472
12-18-71	15,244

PRESIDENTIAL CUP
(College Park, Md.)

Date	Attendance
12-9-50	12,245

RAISIN
(Fresno, Calif.)

Date	Attendance
1-1-46	10,000
1-1-47	13,000
1-1-48	13,000
1-1-49	10,000
12-31-49	9,000

SALAD
(Phoenix, Ariz.)

Date	Attendance
1-1-48	12,500
1-1-49	17,500
1-1-50	18,500
1-1-51	23,000
1-1-52	17,000

SAN DIEGO EAST-WEST CHRISTMAS CLASSIC
(San Diego, Calif.)

Date	Attendance
12-26-21	5,000
12-25-22	5,000

SHRINE
(Little Rock, Ark.)

Date	Attendance
12-18-48	5,000

Individual Records

Only official records after 1937 are included. Prior records are included if able to be substantiated. Each team's score is in parentheses after the team name. The year listed is the actual (calendar) year the game was played; the date is included if the bowl was played twice (i.e., January and December) during one calendar year. The list also includes discontinued bowls, marked with (D). Bowls are listed by the name of the bowl at the time it was played. All former bowl names and sites are listed with each present bowl history. The NCAA Statistics Service thanks former staff member Steve Boda for his valuable assistance in compiling these records.

Total Offense

MOST TOTAL PLAYS
74—(D) Tony Kimbrough, Western Mich. (30) vs. Fresno St. (35) (California, 1988) (431 yards)

MOST TOTAL YARDS
594—Ty Detmer, Brigham Young (39) vs. Penn St. (50) (Holiday, 1989) (18 rushing yards, 576 passing yards, 67 plays)

HIGHEST AVERAGE PER PLAY (Min. 10 Plays)
24.1—Dicky Maegle, Rice (28) vs. Alabama (6) (Cotton, 1954) (11 for 265)

MOST TOUCHDOWNS RESPONSIBLE FOR (TDs Scored & Passed For)
6—(D) Bobby Layne, Texas (40) vs. Missouri (27) (Cotton, 1946) (3 rush, 2 pass, 1 receiving); Chuck Long, Iowa (55) vs. Texas (17) (Freedom, 1984) (6 pass)

Rushing

MOST RUSHING ATTEMPTS
46—(D) Ron Jackson, Tulsa (28) vs. San Diego St. (17) (Freedom, 1991) (211 yards)

MOST NET RUSHING YARDS
280—(D) James Gray, Texas Tech (49) vs. Duke (21) (All-American, 1989) (33 carries)

MOST NET RUSHING YARDS BY A QUARTERBACK
199—Tommie Frazier, Nebraska (62) vs. Florida (24) (Fiesta, 1996) (16 carries)

HIGHEST AVERAGE PER RUSH (Min. 9 Carries)
24.1—Dicky Maegle, Rice (28) vs. Alabama (6) (Cotton, 1954) (11 for 265)

MOST NET RUSHING YARDS BY TWO RUSHERS, SAME TEAM, OVER 100 YARDS RUSHING EACH
373—Woody Green (202) & Brent McClanahan (171), Arizona St. (49) vs. Missouri (35) (Fiesta, 1972)

MOST RUSHING TOUCHDOWNS
5—Neil Snow, Michigan (49) vs. Stanford (0) (Rose, 1902) (touchdowns counted as five-point scores); Barry Sanders, Oklahoma St. (62) vs. Wyoming (14) (Holiday, 1988) (runs of 33, 2, 67, 1, 10 yards)

Passing

MOST PASS ATTEMPTS
63—Trent Dilfer, Fresno St. (30) vs. Colorado (41) (Aloha, 1993) (completed 37)

MOST PASS COMPLETIONS
43—(D) Steve Clarkson, San Jose St. (25) vs. Toledo (27) (California, 1981) (attempted 62)

MOST CONSECUTIVE PASS COMPLETIONS
19—Mike Bobo, Georgia (33) vs. Wisconsin (6) (Outback, 1998)

MOST NET PASSING YARDS
576—Ty Detmer, Brigham Young (39) vs. Penn St. (50) (Holiday, 1989) (42 of 59 with 2 interceptions)

MOST NET PASSING YARDS, ONE QUARTER
223—Browning Nagle, Louisville (34) vs. Alabama (7) (Fiesta, 1991) (1st quarter, 9 of 16)

MOST TOUCHDOWN PASSES THROWN
6—(D) Chuck Long, Iowa (55) vs. Texas (17) (Freedom, 1984) (29 of 39 with no interceptions) (touchdown passes of 6, 11, 33, 49, 4, 15 yards)

MOST PASSES HAD INTERCEPTED
6—Bruce Lee, Arizona (10) vs. Auburn (34) (Sun, 1968) (6 of 24)

HIGHEST COMPLETION PERCENTAGE (Min. 10 Attempts)
.929—Mike Bobo, Georgia (33) vs. Wisconsin (6) (Outback, 1998) (26 of 28 with no interceptions)

MOST YARDS PER PASS ATTEMPT (Min. 10 Attempts)
21.3—Chris McCoy, Navy (42) vs. California (38) (Aloha, 1996) (13 for 277)

MOST YARDS PER PASS COMPLETION (Min. 7 Completions)
30.8—Chris McCoy, Navy (42) vs. California (38) (Aloha, 1996) (9 for 277)

Receiving

MOST PASS RECEPTIONS
20—(D) Walker Gillette, Richmond (49) vs. Ohio (42) (Tangerine, 1968) (242 yards); Norman Jordan, Vanderbilt (28) vs. Air Force (36) (Hall of Fame, 1982) (173 yards)

MOST PASS RECEIVING YARDS
252—Andre Rison, Michigan St. (27) vs. Georgia (34) (Gator, Jan. 1, 1989) (9 catches)

HIGHEST AVERAGE PER CATCH (Min. 3 Receptions)
52.3—Phil Harris, Texas (28) vs. Navy (6) (Cotton, 1964) (3 for 157)

MOST TOUCHDOWNS RECEIVING
4—(D) Bob McChesney, Hardin-Simmons (49) vs. Wichita St. (12) (Camellia, 1948) (8 catches); Fred Biletnikoff, Florida St. (36) vs. Oklahoma (19) (Gator, Jan. 2, 1965) (13 catches)

Scoring

MOST POINTS SCORED
30—Barry Sanders, Oklahoma St. (62) vs. Wyoming (14) (Holiday, 1988) (5 touchdowns); (D) Sheldon Canley, San Jose St. (48) vs. Central Mich. (24) (California, 1990) (5 touchdowns)

MOST POINTS RESPONSIBLE FOR (TDs SCORED & PASSED FOR, EXTRA POINTS, AND FGs)
40—Bobby Layne, Texas (40) vs. Missouri (27) (Cotton, 1946) (18 rushing, 12 passing, 6 receiving and 4 PATs)

MOST TOUCHDOWNS SCORED
5—Neil Snow, Michigan (49) vs. Stanford (0) (Rose, 1902) (5 rushing five-point TDs); Barry Sanders, Oklahoma St. (62) vs. Wyoming (14) (Holiday, 1988) (5 rushing); (D) Sheldon Canley, San Jose St. (48) vs. Central Mich. (24) (California, 1990) (4 rushing, 1 receiving)

MOST TWO-POINT CONVERSIONS
2—Ernie Davis, Syracuse (23) vs. Texas (14) (Cotton, 1960) (2 receptions)

Kicking

MOST FIELD GOALS ATTEMPTED
6—Kyle Bryant, Texas A&M (22) vs. Michigan (20) (Alamo, 1995) (made 5)

MOST FIELD GOALS MADE
5—Jess Atkinson, Maryland (23) vs. Tennessee (30) (Florida Citrus, 1983) (18, 48, 31, 22, 26 yards); Arden Czyzewski, Florida (28) vs. Notre Dame (39) (Sugar, 1992) (26, 24, 36, 37, 24 yards); Tim Rogers, Mississippi St. (24) vs. North Carolina St. (28) (Peach, Jan. 1, 1995) (37, 21, 29, 36, 30 yards); Kyle Bryant, Texas A&M (22) vs. Michigan (20) (Alamo, 1995) (27, 49, 47, 31, 37 yards)

MOST EXTRA-POINT KICK ATTEMPTS
9—(D) James Weaver, Centre (63) vs. TCU (7) (Fort Worth Classic, 1921) (9 made); Bobby Luna, Alabama (61) vs. Syracuse (6) (Orange, 1953) (7 made); Layne Talbot, Texas A&M (65) vs. Brigham Young (14) (Holiday, 1990) (9 made)

MOST EXTRA-POINT KICKS MADE
9—(D) James Weaver, Centre (63) vs. TCU (7) (Fort Worth Classic, 1921) (9 attempts); Layne Talbot, Texas A&M (65) vs. Brigham Young (14) (Holiday, 1990) (9 attempts)

INDIVIDUAL RECORDS—KICKING

MOST POINTS BY A KICKER
16—Arden Czyzewski, Florida (28) vs. Notre Dame (39) (Sugar, 1992) (5 FGs, 1 PAT); Tim Rogers, Mississippi St. (24) vs. North Carolina St. (28) (Peach, Jan. 1, 1995) (5 FGs, 1 PAT); Kyle Bryant, Texas A&M (22) vs. Michigan (20) (Alamo, 1995) (5 FGs, 1 PAT)

Punting

MOST PUNTS
21—Everett Sweeney, Michigan (49) vs. Stanford (0) (Rose, 1902)

HIGHEST AVERAGE PER PUNT
(Min. 5 Punts)
52.7—Des Koch, Southern California (7) vs. Wisconsin (0) (Rose, 1953) (7 for 369)

Punt Returns

MOST PUNT RETURNS
9—Paddy Driscoll, Great Lakes (17) vs. Mare Island (0) (Rose, 1919) (115 yards); Buzy Rosenberg, Georgia (7) vs. North Carolina (3) (Gator, Dec. 31, 1971) (54 yards)

MOST PUNT RETURN YARDS
136—Johnny Rodgers, Nebraska (38) vs. Alabama (6) (Orange, 1972) (6 returns)

HIGHEST PUNT RETURN AVERAGE
(Min. 3 Returns)
40.7—George Fleming, Washington (44) vs. Wisconsin (8) (Rose, 1960) (3 for 122)

MOST TOUCHDOWNS ON PUNT RETURNS
2—James Henry, Southern Miss. (38) vs. UTEP (18) (Independence, 1988) (65 and 45 yards)

Kickoff Returns

MOST KICKOFF RETURNS
7—Homer Jones, Brigham Young (37) vs. Indiana (38) (Holiday, 1979) (126 yards); Jeff Sydner, Hawaii (13) vs. Michigan St. (33) (Aloha, 1989) (174 yards); Dale Carter, Tennessee (17) vs. Penn St. (42) (Fiesta, 1992) (132 yards)

MOST KICKOFF RETURN YARDS
220—Mike Rigell, Brigham Young (27) vs. Tulane (41) (Liberty, 1998) (6 returns)

HIGHEST KICKOFF RETURN AVERAGE
(Min. 2 Returns)
60.5—(D) Bob Smith, Texas A&M (40) vs. Georgia (20) (Presidential Cup, 1950) (2 for 121)

MOST TOUCHDOWNS ON KICKOFF RETURNS
1—Many players tied

Interceptions

MOST INTERCEPTIONS MADE
4—(D) Manuel Aja, Arizona St. (21) vs. Xavier (Ohio) (33) (Salad, 1950); Jim Dooley, Miami (Fla.) (14) vs. Clemson (0) (Gator, 1952)

MOST INTERCEPTION RETURN YARDAGE
148—Elmer Layden, Notre Dame (27) vs. Stanford (10) (Rose, 1925) (2 interceptions)

All-Purpose Yards

(Includes All Runs From Scrimmage, Pass Receptions and All Returns)

MOST ALL-PURPOSE PLAYS
(Must Have at Least One Reception or Return)
47—(D) Ron Jackson, Tulsa (28) vs. San Diego St. (17) (Freedom, 1991) (46 rushes, 1 reception)

MOST ALL-PURPOSE YARDS GAINED
(Must Have at Least One Reception or Return)
359—Sherman Williams, Alabama (24) vs. Ohio St. (17) (Florida Citrus, 1995) (166 rushing, 155 receiving, 38 kickoff returns)

Defensive Statistics

MOST TOTAL TACKLES MADE (Includes Assists)
31—Lee Roy Jordan, Alabama (17) vs. Oklahoma (0) (Orange, 1963)

MOST UNASSISTED TACKLES
18—Rod Smith, Notre Dame (39) vs. Florida (28) (Sugar, 1992)

MOST TACKLES MADE FOR LOSSES
5—Jimmy Walker, Arkansas (10) vs. UCLA (10) (Fiesta, 1978); (D) Michael Jones, Colorado (17) vs. Brigham Young (20) (Freedom, 1988) (20 yards)

MOST QUARTERBACK SACKS
6—Shay Muirbrook, Brigham Young (19) vs. Kansas St. (15) (Cotton, 1997)

MOST FUMBLE RECOVERIES
2—Rod Kirby, Pittsburgh (7) vs. Arizona St. (28) (Fiesta, 1973); (D) Michael Stewart, Fresno St. (51) vs. Bowling Green (7) (California, 1985); Randall Brown, Ohio St. (17) vs. Alabama (24) (Florida Citrus, 1995)

MOST BLOCKED KICKS
2—Carlton Williams, Pittsburgh (7) vs. Arizona St. (28) (Fiesta, 1973) (2 PATs); Bracey Walker, North Carolina (21) vs. Mississippi St. (17) (Peach, Jan. 2, 1993) (2 punts)

MOST BLOCKED PUNTS
2—Bracey Walker, North Carolina (21) vs. Mississippi St. (17) (Peach, Jan. 2, 1993)

MOST PASSES BROKEN UP
5—Dyshod Carter, Kansas St. (34) vs. Purdue (37) (Alamo, 1998)

Team Records

Totals for each team in both-team records are in brackets after the team's score.

Total Offense

MOST TOTAL PLAYS
96—North Carolina St. (10) vs. Arizona (17) (Copper, 1989) (310 yards)

MOST TOTAL PLAYS, BOTH TEAMS
175—Toledo (40) [95] & Nevada (37) [80] (ot) (Las Vegas, 1995) (974 yards)

MOST YARDS GAINED
718—Arizona St. (49) vs. Missouri (35) (Fiesta, 1972) (452 rushing, 266 passing)

MOST YARDS GAINED, BOTH TEAMS
1,143—(D) Southern California (47) [624] & Texas A&M (28) [519] (Bluebonnet, 1977) (148 plays)

HIGHEST AVERAGE GAINED PER PLAY
9.5—Louisville (34) vs. Alabama (7) (Fiesta, 1991) (60 for 571)

FEWEST PLAYS
35—Tennessee (0) vs. Texas (16) (Cotton, 1953) (29 rush, 6 pass)

FEWEST PLAYS, BOTH TEAMS
107—TCU (16) [54] & Marquette (6) [53] (Cotton, 1937)

FEWEST YARDS
Minus 21—U. of Mexico (0) vs. Southwestern (Tex.) (35) (Sun, 1945) (29 rushing, -50 passing)

FEWEST YARDS, BOTH TEAMS
260—Randolph Field (7) [150] & Texas (7) [110] (Cotton, 1944)

LOWEST AVERAGE GAINED PER PLAY
0.9—Tennessee (0) vs. Texas (16) (Cotton, 1953) (35 for 32)

Rushing

MOST RUSHING ATTEMPTS
87—Oklahoma (40) vs. Auburn (22) (Sugar, Jan. 1, 1972) (439 yards)

MOST RUSHING ATTEMPTS, BOTH TEAMS
122—Mississippi St. (26) [68] & North Carolina (24) [54] (Sun, 1974) (732 yards); (D) Southern California (47) [50] & Texas A&M (28) [72] (Bluebonnet, 1977) (864 yards)

MOST NET RUSHING YARDS
524—Nebraska (62) vs. Florida (24) (Fiesta, 1996) (68 attempts)

MOST NET RUSHING YARDS, BOTH TEAMS
864—(D) Southern California (47) [378] & Texas A&M (28) [486] (Bluebonnet, 1977) (122 attempts)

HIGHEST RUSHING AVERAGE
(Min. 30 Attempts)
9.3—Texas Tech (55) vs. Air Force (41) (Copper, 1995) (39 for 361)

FEWEST RUSHING ATTEMPTS
12—(D) Vanderbilt (28) vs. Air Force (36) (Hall of Fame, 1982) (35 yards)

FEWEST RUSHING ATTEMPTS, BOTH TEAMS
56—Mississippi (27) [33] & Oklahoma (25) [23] (Independence, 1999)

FEWEST RUSHING YARDS
Minus 61—Kansas St. (7) vs. Boston College (12) (Aloha, 1994) (23 attempts)

FEWEST RUSHING YARDS, BOTH TEAMS
51—(D) Utah (16) [6] & Arizona (13) [45] (Freedom, 1994)

LOWEST RUSHING AVERAGE
(Min. 20 Attempts)
Minus 2.7—Kansas St. (7) vs. Boston College (12) (Aloha, 1994) (23 for -61)

RUSHING DEFENSE, FEWEST YARDS ALLOWED
Minus 61—Boston College (12) vs. Kansas St. (7) (Aloha, 1994) (23 attempts)

Passing

MOST PASS ATTEMPTS
63—(D) San Jose St. (25) vs. Toledo (27) (California, 1981) (43 completions, 5 interceptions, 467 yards); Fresno St. (30) vs. Colorado (41) (Aloha, 1993) (37 completions, 1 interception, 523 yards)

MOST PASS ATTEMPTS, BOTH TEAMS
94—Mississippi St. (17) [38] & Clemson (7) [56] (Peach, 1999) (42 completions)

MOST PASS COMPLETIONS
43—(D) San Jose St. (25) vs. Toledo (27) (California, 1981) (63 attempts, 5 interceptions, 467 yards)

MOST PASS COMPLETIONS, BOTH TEAMS
61—Penn St. (38) [20] & Oregon (20) [41] (Rose, 1995) (92 attempts)

MOST PASSING YARDS
576—Brigham Young (39) vs. Penn St. (50) (Holiday, 1989) (42 completions, 59 attempts, 2 interceptions)

MOST PASSING YARDS, BOTH TEAMS
808—Washington St. (31) [492] & Utah (28) [316] (Copper, 1992) (88 attempts)

MOST PASSES HAD INTERCEPTED
8—Arizona (10) vs. Auburn (34) (Sun, 1968)

MOST PASSES HAD INTERCEPTED, BOTH TEAMS
12—Auburn (34) [4] & Arizona (10) [8] (Sun, 1968)

MOST PASSES ATTEMPTED WITHOUT AN INTERCEPTION
57—(D) Western Mich. (30) vs. Fresno St. (35) (California, 1988) (24 completions)

MOST PASSES ATTEMPTED BY BOTH TEAMS WITHOUT AN INTERCEPTION
93—Idaho (42) [41] & Southern Miss. (35) [52] (Humanitarian, 1998) (55 completions)

HIGHEST COMPLETION PERCENTAGE (Min. 10 Attempts)
.929—Texas (40) vs. Missouri (27) (Cotton, 1946) (13 of 14, no interceptions, 234 yards)

MOST YARDS PER ATTEMPT (Min. 10 Attempts)
21.7—Southern California (47) vs. Pittsburgh (14) (Rose, 1930) (13 for 282)

MOST YARDS PER COMPLETION (Min. 8 Completions)
35.2—Southern California (47) vs. Pittsburgh (14) (Rose, 1930) (8 for 282)

FEWEST PASS ATTEMPTS
2—West Virginia (14) vs. South Carolina (3) (Peach, 1969) (1 completion); (D) Army (10) vs. Michigan St. (6) (Cherry, 1984) (1 completion); Air Force (38) vs. Mississippi St. (15) (Liberty, 1991) (1 completion)

FEWEST PASS ATTEMPTS, BOTH TEAMS
9—Fordham (2) [4] & Missouri (0) [5] (Sugar, 1942)

FEWEST PASS COMPLETIONS
0—13 teams tied (see Team Record Lists)

FEWEST PASS COMPLETIONS, BOTH TEAMS
3—Arizona St. (0) [0] & Catholic (0) [3] (Sun, 1940)

FEWEST PASSING YARDS
Minus 50—U. of Mexico (0) vs. Southwestern (Tex.) (35) (Sun, 1945) (2 completions, 9 attempts, 3 interceptions)

FEWEST PASSING YARDS, BOTH TEAMS
15—Rice (8) [-17] & Tennessee (0) [32] (Orange, 1947)

LOWEST COMPLETION PERCENTAGE
.000—13 teams tied (see Team Record Lists)

FEWEST YARDS PER PASS ATTEMPT
Minus 5.6—U. of Mexico (0) vs. Southwestern (Tex.) (35) (Sun, 1945) (9 for -50)

FEWEST YARDS PER PASS COMPLETION (Min. 1 Completion)
Minus 25.0—U. of Mexico (0) vs. Southwestern (Tex.) (35) (Sun, 1945) (2 for -50)

Scoring

MOST TOUCHDOWNS
9—(D) Centre (63) vs. TCU (7) (Fort Worth Classic, 1921) (8 rush, 1 blocked punt recovery in end zone); Alabama (61) vs. Syracuse (6) (Orange, 1953) (4 rush, 3 pass, 1 punt return, 1 interception return); Texas A&M (65) vs. Brigham Young (14) (Holiday, 1990) (5 rush, 4 pass); Illinois (63) vs. Virginia (21) (Micronpc.com, 1999) (6 rush, 3 pass)

MOST TOUCHDOWNS, BOTH TEAMS
13—Richmond (49) [7] & Ohio (42) [6] (Tangerine, 1968); Texas Tech (55) [7] & Air Force (41) [6] (Copper, 1995)

MOST TOUCHDOWNS RUSHING
8—(D) Centre (63) vs. TCU (7) (Fort Worth Classic, 1921)

MOST TOUCHDOWNS RUSHING, BOTH TEAMS
12—Texas Tech (55) [6] & Air Force (41) [6] (Copper, 1995)

MOST TOUCHDOWNS PASSING
6—(D) Iowa (55) vs. Texas (17) (Freedom, 1984)

MOST TOUCHDOWNS PASSING, BOTH TEAMS
8—Richmond (49) [4] & Ohio (42) [4] (Tangerine, 1968); (D) Iowa (55) [6] & Texas (17) [2] (Freedom, 1984)

MOST FIELD GOALS MADE
5—Maryland (23) vs. Tennessee (30) (Florida Citrus, 1983) (18, 48, 31, 22, 26 yards); Florida (28) vs. Notre Dame (39) (Sugar, 1992) (26, 24, 36, 37, 24 yards); Mississippi St. (24) vs. North Carolina St. (28) (Peach, Jan. 1, 1995) (37, 21, 29, 36, 30 yards); Texas A&M (22) vs. Michigan (20) (Alamo, 1995) (27, 49, 47, 31, 37 yards)

MOST FIELD GOALS MADE, BOTH TEAMS
7—Texas A&M (22) [5] & Michigan (20) [2] (Alamo, 1995); North Carolina St. (28) [2] & Mississippi St. (24) [5] (Peach, Jan. 1, 1995)

MOST POINTS, WINNING TEAM
65—Texas A&M vs. Brigham Young (14) (Holiday, 1990)

MOST POINTS, LOSING TEAM
45—Southern Methodist vs. Brigham Young (46) (Holiday, 1980)

MOST POINTS, BOTH TEAMS
96—Texas Tech (55) & Air Force (41) (Copper, 1995)

LARGEST MARGIN OF VICTORY
55—Alabama (61) vs. Syracuse (6) (Orange, 1953)

FEWEST POINTS, WINNING TEAM
2—Fordham vs. Missouri (0) (Sugar, 1942)

FEWEST POINTS, LOSING TEAM
0—By many teams

FEWEST POINTS, BOTH TEAMS
0—California (0) & Wash. & Jeff. (0) (Rose, 1922); Arizona St. (0) & Catholic (0) (Sun, 1940); Arkansas (0) & LSU (0) (Cotton, 1947); Air Force (0) & TCU (0) (Cotton, 1959)

MOST POINTS SCORED IN FIRST HALF
45—Colorado (62) vs. Boston College (28) (Insight.com, 1999)

MOST POINTS SCORED IN SECOND HALF
45—Oklahoma St. (62) vs. Wyoming (14) (Holiday, 1988)

MOST POINTS SCORED IN FIRST HALF, BOTH TEAMS
63—Navy (42) [28] & California (38) [35] (Aloha, 1996)

MOST POINTS SCORED IN SECOND HALF, BOTH TEAMS
64—Penn St. (50) [38] & Brigham Young (39) [26] (Holiday, 1989); Kansas (51) [34] & UCLA (30) [30] (Aloha, 1995)

MOST POINTS SCORED EACH QUARTER
1st: 28—Southern California (55) vs. Texas Tech (14) (Cotton, 1995)
2nd: 29—Nebraska (62) vs. Florida (24) (Fiesta, 1996)
3rd: 31—(D) Iowa (55) vs. Texas (17) (Freedom, 1984)
4th: 30—Oklahoma (40) vs. Houston (14) (Sun, 1981)

MOST POINTS SCORED EACH QUARTER, BOTH TEAMS
1st: 28—Louisiana Tech (24) [21] & Louisville (14) [7] (Independence, 1977); Indiana (38) [14] & Brigham Young (37) [14] (Holiday, 1979); Texas Tech (55) [21] & Air Force (41) [7] (Copper, 1995); Southern California (55) [28] & Texas Tech (14) [0] (Cotton, 1995)
2nd: 43—Navy (42) [21] & California (38) [22] (Aloha, 1996)
3rd: 35—Oklahoma St. (62) [28] & Wyoming (14) [7] (Holiday, 1988); Kansas St. (54) [21] & Colorado St. (21) [14] (Holiday, 1995)
4th: 37—Oklahoma (40) [30] & Houston (14) [7] (Sun, 1981); Kansas (51) [14] & UCLA (30) [23] (Aloha, 1995)

First Downs

MOST FIRST DOWNS
36—Oklahoma (48) vs. Virginia (14) (Gator, Dec. 29, 1991) (16 rush, 18 pass, 2 penalty)

MOST FIRST DOWNS, BOTH TEAMS
61—Penn St. (50) [26] & Brigham Young (39) [35] (Holiday, 1989)

MOST FIRST DOWNS RUSHING
26—Oklahoma (40) vs. Auburn (22) (Sugar, Jan. 1, 1972)

MOST FIRST DOWNS RUSHING, BOTH TEAMS
36—Colorado (47) [24] & Alabama (33) [12] (Liberty, 1969); Miami (Fla.) (46) [16] & Texas (3) [20] (Cotton, 1991)

MOST FIRST DOWNS PASSING
27—Brigham Young (39) vs. Penn St. (50) (Holiday, 1989)

MOST FIRST DOWNS PASSING, BOTH TEAMS
38—Penn St. (50) [11] & Brigham Young (39) [27] (Holiday, 1989)

MOST FIRST DOWNS BY PENALTY
6—Texas (3) vs. Miami (Fla.) (46) (Cotton, 1991); Florida (52) vs. Florida St. (20) (Sugar, 1997)

MOST FIRST DOWNS BY PENALTY, BOTH TEAMS
8—Miami (Fla.) (46) [2] & Texas (3) [6] (Cotton, 1991); Texas A&M (22) [4] & Michigan (20) [4] (Alamo, 1995); Florida (52) [6] & Florida St. (20) [2] (Sugar, 1997)

FEWEST FIRST DOWNS
1—Arkansas (0) vs. LSU (0) (Cotton, 1947) (1 rush); Alabama (29) vs. Texas A&M (21) (Cotton, 1942) (1 pass)

FEWEST FIRST DOWNS, BOTH TEAMS
10—Randolph Field (7) [7] & Texas (7) [3] (Cotton, 1944)

FEWEST FIRST DOWNS RUSHING
0—Alabama (29) vs. Texas A&M (21) (Cotton, 1942); Navy (6) vs. Texas (28) (Cotton, 1964); Florida (18) vs. Missouri (20) (Sugar, 1966); Southern California (19) vs. TCU (28) (Sun, 1998)

FEWEST FIRST DOWNS RUSHING, BOTH TEAMS
3—Alabama (29) [0] & Texas A&M (21) [3] (Cotton, 1942)

FEWEST FIRST DOWNS PASSING
0—By 13 teams (see Team Record Lists)

FEWEST FIRST DOWNS PASSING, BOTH TEAMS
1—Alabama (10) [0] & Arkansas (3) [1] (Sugar, 1962)

Punting

MOST PUNTS
17—Duke (3) vs. Southern California (7) (Rose, 1939)

MOST PUNTS, BOTH TEAMS
28—Santa Clara (6) [14] & LSU (0) [14] (Sugar, 1938); Rice (8) [13] & Tennessee (0) [15] (Orange, 1947)

HIGHEST PUNTING AVERAGE (Min. 5 Punts)
53.9—Southern California (7) vs. Wisconsin (0) (Rose, 1953) (8 for 431)

FEWEST PUNTS
0—Oklahoma (41) vs. Wyoming (7) (Fiesta, 1976); Oklahoma St. (62) vs. Wyoming (14) (Holiday, 1988); Illinois (63) vs. Virginia (21) (Micronpc.com, 1999)

LOWEST PUNTING AVERAGE (Min. 3 Punts)
17.0—Nevada (34) vs. Bowling Green (35) (Las Vegas, 1992) (4 for 68); Kentucky (14) vs. Penn St. (26) (Outback, 1999) (3 for 51)

MOST PUNTS BLOCKED BY ONE TEAM
2—North Carolina St. (14) vs. Georgia (7) (Liberty, 1967); North Carolina (21) vs. Mississippi St. (17) (Peach, 1992)

TEAM RECORDS—PUNT RETURNS 313

Punt Returns

MOST PUNT RETURNS
9—Georgia (7) vs. North Carolina (3) (Gator, Dec. 31, 1971) (6.8 average)

MOST PUNT RETURN YARDS
136—Nebraska (38) vs. Alabama (6) (Orange, 1972) (6 returns)

HIGHEST PUNT RETURN AVERAGE
(Min. 3 Returns)
33.0—Kent (18) vs. Tampa (21) (Tangerine, 1972) (3 for 99)

Kickoff Returns

MOST KICKOFF RETURNS
10—Wyoming (14) vs. Oklahoma St. (62) (Holiday, 1988) (20.5 average); Florida (24) vs. Nebraska (62) (Fiesta, 1996) (26.8 average)

MOST KICKOFF RETURN YARDS
268—Florida (24) vs. Nebraska (62) (Fiesta, 1996) (10 returns)

HIGHEST KICKOFF RETURN AVERAGE
(Min. 3 Returns)
42.5—Tennessee (27) vs. Maryland (28) (Sun, 1984) (4 for 170)

Fumbles

MOST FUMBLES
11—Mississippi (7) vs. Alabama (12) (Sugar, 1964) (lost 6)

MOST FUMBLES, BOTH TEAMS
17—Alabama (12) [6] & Mississippi (7) [11] (Sugar, 1964) (lost 9)

MOST FUMBLES LOST
6—By five teams (see Team Record Lists)

MOST FUMBLES LOST, BOTH TEAMS
9—Alabama (12) [3] & Mississippi (7) [6] (Sugar, 1964) (17 fumbles)

Penalties

MOST PENALTIES
21—Mississippi St. (17) vs. Clemson (7) (Peach, 1999) (188 yards)

MOST PENALTIES, BOTH TEAMS
29—McNeese St. (20) [13] & Tulsa (16) [16] (Independence, 1976) (205 yards); Florida (52) [15] & Florida St. (20) [14] (Sugar, 1997) (217 yards); Mississippi St. (17) [21] & Clemson (7) [8] (Peach, 1999) (270 yards)

MOST YARDS PENALIZED
202—Miami (Fla.) (46) vs. Texas (3) (Cotton, 1991) (16 penalties)

MOST YARDS PENALIZED, BOTH TEAMS
270—Miami (Fla.) (46) [202] & Texas (3) [68] (Cotton, 1991); Mississippi St. (17) [188] & Clemson (7) [82] (Peach, 1999)

FEWEST PENALTIES
0—By eight teams (see Team Record Lists)

FEWEST PENALTIES, BOTH TEAMS
3—In five games (see Team Record Lists)

FEWEST YARDS PENALIZED
0—By eight teams (see Team Record Lists)

FEWEST YARDS PENALIZED, BOTH TEAMS
10—Duquesne (13) [5] & Mississippi St. (12) [5] (Orange, 1937)

Individual Record Lists

Only official records after 1937 are included. Prior records are included if able to be substantiated. Each team's score is in parentheses after the team name. The year listed is the actual (calendar) year the game was played; the date is included if the bowl was played twice (i.e., January and December) during one calendar year. The list also includes discontinued bowls, marked with (D). Bowls are listed by the name of the bowl at the time it was played: The Florida Citrus Bowl was the Tangerine Bowl in 1947-82; the first Hall of Fame Bowl (1977-85) was called the All-American Bowl in 1986-90; the second Hall of Fame Bowl (1986-95) is now called the Outback Bowl and is played in Tampa, Fla.; the Sun Bowl was called the John Hancock Bowl in 1989-93, the John Hancock Sun Bowl in 1987-88, and reverted to the Sun Bowl in 1994; the Blockbuster Bowl changed its name to the Carquest Bowl in 1993 and then to the Micronpc.com Bowl in 1998; and the Copper Bowl changed its name to the Insight.com Bowl in 1997.

Total Offense

MOST PLAYS
74—(D) Tony Kimbrough, Western Mich. (30) vs. Fresno St. (35) (California, 1988)
69—Drew Brees, Purdue (25) vs. Georgia (28) (ot) (Outback, 2000)
68—Hines Ward, Georgia (27) vs. Virginia (34) (Peach, Dec. 30, 1995)
67—Ty Detmer, Brigham Young (39) vs. Penn St. (50) (Holiday, 1989)
65—Shane Matthews, Florida (28) vs. Notre Dame (39) (Sugar, 1992)
65—Tony Eason, Illinois (15) vs. Alabama (21) (Liberty, 1982)
65—Buster O'Brien, Richmond (49) vs. Ohio (42) (Tangerine, 1968)
63—Drew Brees, Purdue (37) vs. Kansas St. (34) (Alamo, 1998)
63—(D) Steve Clarkson, San Jose St. (25) vs. Toledo (27) (California, 1981)
62—Mark Young, Mississippi (20) vs. Texas Tech (17) (Independence, 1986)
62—Jack Trudeau, Illinois (29) vs. Army (31) (Peach, 1985)
62—Dennis Sproul, Arizona St. (30) vs. Penn St. (42) (Fiesta, 1977)
61—Jeff Blake, East Caro. (37) vs. North Carolina St. (34) (Peach, 1992)
61—Shawn Halloran, Boston College (27) vs. Georgia (24) (Hall of Fame, 1986)
61—Kim Hammond, Florida St. (17) vs. Penn St. (17) (Gator, 1967)
60—Josh Heupel, Oklahoma (25) vs. Mississippi (27) (Independence, 1999)
59—Lee Roberts, Southern Miss. (35) vs. Idaho (42) (Humanitarian, 1998)
59—Vinny Testaverde, Miami (Fla.) (10) vs. Penn St. (14) (Fiesta, 1987)
59—Jim McMahon, Brigham Young (46) vs. Southern Methodist (45) (Holiday, 1980)
58—Tim Couch, Kentucky (14) vs. Penn St. (26) (Outback, 1999)
58—Terrence Jones, Tulane (12) vs. Washington (24) (Independence, 1987)
58—(D) Jerry Rhome, Tulsa (14) vs. Mississippi (7) (Bluebonnet, 1964)

MOST TOTAL YARDS
594—Ty Detmer, Brigham Young (39) vs. Penn St. (50) (Holiday, 1989) (576 pass)
486—Buster O'Brien, Richmond (49) vs. Ohio (42) (Tangerine, 1968) (447 pass)
481—(D) Chuck Long, Iowa (55) vs. Texas (17) (Freedom, 1984) (461 pass)
474—Trent Dilfer, Fresno St. (30) vs. Colorado (41) (Aloha, 1993) (523 pass)
469—Hines Ward, Georgia (27) vs. Virginia (34) (Peach, Dec. 30, 1995) (413 pass)
464—(D) Steve Clarkson, San Jose St. (25) vs. Toledo (27) (California, 1981) (467 pass)
457—Akili Smith, Oregon (43) vs. Colorado (51) (Aloha, 1998) (456 pass)
454—John Walsh, Brigham Young (31) vs. Oklahoma (6) (Copper, 1994) (454 pass)
446—Jim McMahon, Brigham Young (46) vs. Southern Methodist (45) (Holiday, 1980) (446 pass)
446—(D) Whit Taylor, Vanderbilt (28) vs. Air Force (36) (Hall of Fame, 1982) (452 pass)
445—Chad Pennington, Marshall (48) vs. Louisville (29) (Motor City, 1998) (411 pass)
431—(D) Tony Kimbrough, Western Mich. (30) vs. Fresno St. (35) (California, 1988) (366 pass)
431—Browning Nagle, Louisville (34) vs. Alabama (7) (Fiesta, 1991) (451 pass)
424—Marc Bulger, West Virginia (31) vs. Missouri (34) (Insight.com, 1998) 429 pass)
420—(D) Ralph Martini, San Jose St. (48) vs. Central Mich. (24) (California, 1990) (404 pass)
414—Peter Tom Willis, Florida St. (41) vs. Nebraska (17) (Fiesta, 1990) (422 pass)
413—Tony Eason, Illinois (15) vs. Alabama (21) (Liberty, 1982) (423 pass)
412—David Smith, Alabama (29) vs. Army (28) (John Hancock Sun, 1988) (412 pass)
410—Chuck Hartlieb, Iowa (23) vs. North Carolina St. (28) (Peach, Dec. 31, 1988) (428 pass)
408—Marc Wilson, Brigham Young (37) vs. Indiana (38) (Holiday, 1979) (380 pass)
407—Jack Trudeau, Illinois (29) vs. Army (31) (Peach, 1985) (401 pass)

HIGHEST AVERAGE PER PLAY
(Minimum 10 Plays)
24.1—Dicky Maegle, Rice (28) vs. Alabama (6) (Cotton, 1954) (11 for 265)
16.5—Chad Pennington, Marshall (48) vs. Louisville (29) (Motor City, 1998) (27 for 445)
14.1—Marcus Dupree, Oklahoma (21) vs. Arizona St. (32) (Fiesta, 1983) (17 for 239)
14.0—Bucky Richardson, Texas A&M (65) vs. Brigham Young (14) (Holiday, 1990) (23 for 322)
13.2—Kordell Stewart, Colorado (41) vs. Notre Dame (24) (Fiesta, 1995) (28 for 369)
12.2—Ger Schwedes, Syracuse (23) vs. Texas (14) (Cotton, 1960) (10 for 122)
12.0—Tony Rice, Notre Dame (34) vs. West Virginia (21) (Fiesta, 1989) (24 for 288)
11.3—Rob Johnson, Southern California (55) vs. Texas Tech (14) (Cotton, 1995) (24 for 271)
11.2—(D) Dwight Ford, Southern California (47) vs. Texas A&M (28) (Bluebonnet, 1977) (14 for 157)
11.1—Browning Nagle, Louisville (34) vs. Alabama (7) (Fiesta, 1991) (39 for 431)
10.8—Danny White, Arizona St. (49) vs. Missouri (35) (Fiesta, 1972) (27 for 291)
10.8—(D) Ralph Martini, San Jose St. (48) vs. Central Mich. (24) (California, 1990) (39 for 420)
10.8—Byron Hanspard, Texas Tech (55) vs. Air Force (41) (Copper, 1995) (24 for 260)
10.5—(D) Chuck Long, Iowa (55) vs. Texas (17) (Freedom, 1984) (46 for 481)
10.4—Frank Sinkwich, Georgia (40) vs. TCU (26) (Orange, 1942) (35 for 365)
10.3—Chuck Curtis, TCU (28) vs. Syracuse (27) (Cotton, 1957) (18 for 185)

MOST TOUCHDOWNS RESPONSIBLE FOR (TDS SCORED & PASSED FOR)
6—(D) Chuck Long, Iowa (55) vs. Texas (17) (Freedom, 1984) (6 pass)
6—Bobby Layne, Texas (40) vs. Missouri (27) (Cotton, 1946) (3 rush, 2 pass, 1 catch)
5—Michael Bishop, Kansas St. (35) vs. Syracuse (18) (Fiesta, 1997) (4 pass, 1 rush)
5—Jeff Blake, East Caro. (37) vs. North Carolina St. (34) (Peach, 1992) (4 pass, 1 rush)
5—Peter Tom Willis, Florida St. (41) vs. Nebraska (17) (Fiesta, 1990) (5 pass)
5—(D) Sheldon Canley, San Jose St. (48) vs. Central Mich. (24) (California, 1990) (4 rush, 1 pass)

5—Buster O'Brien, Richmond (49) vs. Ohio (42) (Tangerine, 1968) (4 pass, 1 rush)
5—Steve Tensi, Florida St. (36) vs. Oklahoma (19) (Gator, Jan. 2, 1965) (5 pass)
5—Neil Snow, Michigan (49) vs. Stanford (0) (Rose, 1902) (5 rush)

Rushing

MOST RUSHING ATTEMPTS
46—(D) Ron Jackson, Tulsa (28) vs. San Diego St. (17) (Freedom, 1991) (211 yards)
43—Fred Taylor, Florida (21) vs. Penn St. (6) (Florida Citrus, 1998) (234 yards)
41—Blake Ezor, Michigan (33) vs. Hawaii (13) (Aloha, 1989) (179 yards)
39—Terrell Fletcher, Wisconsin (34) vs. Duke (20) (Hall of Fame, 1995) (241 yards)
39—Raymont Harris, Ohio St. (28) vs. Brigham Young (21) (Holiday, 1993) (235 yards)
39—Errict Rhett, Florida (27) vs. North Carolina St. (10) (Gator, 1992) (182 yards)
39—Charlie Wysocki, Maryland (20) vs. Florida (35) (Tangerine, 1980) (159 yards)
39—Charles White, Southern California (17) vs. Ohio St. (16) (Rose, 1980) (247 yards)
37—(D) Charles Davis, Colorado (29) vs. Houston (17) (Bluebonnet, 1971) (202 yards)
36—LaDainian Tomlinson, TCU (28) vs. East Caro. (14) (Mobile Alabama, 1999) (124 yards)
36—Brent Moss, Wisconsin (21) vs. UCLA (16) (Rose, 1994) (158 yards)
36—Herschel Walker, Georgia (17) vs. Notre Dame (10) (Sugar, 1981) (150 yards)
36—Don McCauley, North Carolina (26) vs. Arizona St. (48) (Peach, 1970) (143 yards)
35—Blair Thomas, Penn St. (50) vs. Brigham Young (39) (Holiday, 1989) (186 yards)
35—Lorenzo White, Michigan St. (20) vs. Southern California (17) (Rose, 1988) (113 yards)
35—(D) Robert Newhouse, Houston (17) vs. Colorado (29) (Bluebonnet, 1971) (168 yards)
35—Ed Williams, West Virginia (14) vs. South Carolina (3) (Peach, 1969) (208 yards)
35—Bob Anderson, Colorado (47) vs. Alabama (33) (Liberty, 1969) (254 yards)
34—Ron Dayne, Wisconsin (17) vs. Stanford (9) (Rose, 2000) (200 yards)
34—Mike Anderson, Utah (17) vs. Fresno St. (16) (Las Vegas, 1999) (254 yards)
34—Rondell Mealey, LSU (27) vs. Notre Dame (9) (Independence, 1997) (222 yards)
34—(D) Curtis Dickey, Texas A&M (28) vs. Iowa St. (12) (Hall of Fame, 1978) (276 yards)
34—Vic Bottari, California (13) vs. Alabama (0) (Rose, 1938) (137 yards)
34—Ernie Nevers, Stanford (10) vs. Notre Dame (27) (Rose, 1925) (114 yards)

MOST NET RUSHING YARDS
280—(D) James Gray, Texas Tech (49) vs. Duke (21) (All-American, 1989) (33 carries)
276—(D) Curtis Dickey, Texas A&M (28) vs. Iowa St. (12) (Hall of Fame, 1978) (34 carries)
266—(D) Gaston Green, UCLA (31) vs. Brigham Young (10) (Freedom, 1986) (33 carries)
265—Dicky Maegle, Rice (28) vs. Alabama (6) (Cotton, 1954) (11 carries)
260—Byron Hanspard, Texas Tech (55) vs. Air Force (41) (Copper, 1995) (24 carries)
254—Bob Anderson, Colorado (47) vs. Alabama (33) (Liberty, 1969) (35 carries)
254—Mike Anderson, Utah (17) vs. Fresno St. (16) (Las Vegas, 1999) (34 carries)
250—Chuck Webb, Tennessee (31) vs. Arkansas (27) (Cotton, 1990) (26 carries)
247—Charles White, Southern California (17) vs. Ohio St. (16) (Rose, 1980) (39 carries)
246—Ron Dayne, Wisconsin (38) vs. Utah (10) (Copper, 1996) (30 carries)
246—Ron Dayne, Wisconsin (38) vs. UCLA (31) (Rose, 1999) (27 carries)
241—Terrell Fletcher, Wisconsin (34) vs. Duke (20) (Hall of Fame, 1995) (39 carries)
239—Marcus Dupree, Oklahoma (21) vs. Arizona St. (32) (Fiesta, 1983) (17 carries)
235—Tyrone Wheatley, Michigan (38) vs. Washington (31) (Rose, 1993) (15 carries)
235—Raymont Harris, Ohio St. (28) vs. Brigham Young (21) (Holiday, 1993) (39 carries)
234—Jamie Morris, Michigan (28) vs. Alabama (24) (Hall of Fame, 1988) (23 carries)
234—Kevin Faulk, LSU (45) vs. Michigan St. (26) (Independence, 1995) (25 carries)
234—Fred Taylor, Florida (21) vs. Penn St. (6) (Florida Citrus, 1998) (43 carries)
227—Eric Ball, UCLA (45) vs. Iowa (28) (Rose, 1986) (22 carries)
225—Craig James, Southern Methodist (45) vs. Brigham Young (46) (Holiday, 1980) (23 carries)
222—Barry Sanders, Oklahoma St. (62) vs. Wyoming (14) (Holiday, 1988) (29 carries)
222—Rondell Mealey, LSU (27) vs. Notre Dame (9) (Independence, 1997) (34 carries)
216—Floyd Little, Syracuse (12) vs. Tennessee (18) (Gator, 1966) (29 carries)
211—(D) Ron Jackson, Tulsa (28) vs. San Diego St. (17) (Freedom, 1991) (46 carries)
208—Ed Williams, West Virginia (14) vs. South Carolina (3) (Peach, 1969) (35 carries)
206—Ahman Green, Nebraska (42) vs. Tennessee (17) (Orange, 1998) (29 carries)
205—Roland Sales, Arkansas (31) vs. Oklahoma (6) (Orange, 1978) (22 carries)
205—(D) Sammie Smith, Florida St. (27) vs. Indiana (13) (All-American, 1986) (25 carries)
203—Ricky Williams, Texas (38) vs. Mississippi St. (11) (Cotton, 1999) (30 carries)
202—(D) Charles Davis, Colorado (29) vs. Houston (17) (Bluebonnet, 1971) (37 carries)
202—Woody Green, Arizona St. (49) vs. Missouri (35) (Fiesta, 1972) (25 carries)
202—Tony Dorsett, Pittsburgh (27) vs. Georgia (3) (Sugar, 1977) (32 carries)
201—Malcolm Thomas, Syracuse (30) vs. Houston (17) (Liberty, 1996) (24 carries)
201—Cortlen Johnson, Colorado (62) vs. Boston College (28), (Insight.com, 1999) (15 carries)
200—Ron Dayne, Wisconsin (17) vs. Stanford (9) (Rose, 2000) (34 carries)

MOST NET RUSHING YARDS BY A QUARTERBACK
199—Tommie Frazier, Nebraska (62) vs. Florida (24) (Fiesta, 1996) (16 carries)
180—(D) Mike Mosley, Texas A&M (28) vs. Southern California (47) (Bluebonnet, 1977) (20 carries)
164—Eddie Phillips, Texas (11) vs. Notre Dame (24) (Cotton, 1971) (23 carries)
149—Jack Mildren, Oklahoma (40) vs. Auburn (22) (Sugar, 1972) (30 carries)
143—Kordell Stewart, Colorado (41) vs. Notre Dame (24) (Fiesta, 1995) (7 carries)
136—(D) Nate Sassaman, Army (10) vs. Michigan St. (6) (Cherry, 1984) (28 carries)
133—(D) Eddie Wolgast, Arizona (13) vs. Drake (14) (Salad, 1949) (22 carries) (listed in newspaper accounts as halfback but also attempted 15 passes in game)
132—Corby Jones, Missouri (24) vs. Colorado St. (35) (Holiday, 1997) (20 carries)
129—Rex Kern, Ohio St. (17) vs. Stanford (27) (Rose, 1971) (20 carries)
129—Beau Morgan, Air Force (41) vs. Texas Tech (55) (Copper, 1995) (22 carries)
127—J. C. Watts, Oklahoma (24) vs. Florida St. (7) (Orange, 1980) (12 carries)
119—Bucky Richardson, Texas A&M (65) vs. Brigham Young (14) (Holiday, 1990) (12 carries)
113—Harry Gilmer, Alabama (34) vs. Southern California (14) (Rose, 1946)
109—Shaun King, Tulane (41) vs. Brigham Young (27) (Liberty, 1998) (16 carries)
107—Darrell Shepard, Oklahoma (40) vs. Houston (14) (Sun, 1981) (12 carries)
103—Major Harris, West Virginia (33) vs. Oklahoma St. (35) (John Hancock Sun, 1987)

HIGHEST AVERAGE PER RUSH
(Minimum 9 Carries)
24.1—Dicky Maegle, Rice (28) vs. Alabama (6) (Cotton, 1954) (11 for 265)
21.6—Bob Jeter, Iowa (38) vs. California (12) (Rose, 1959) (9 for 194)
15.7—Tyrone Wheatley, Michigan (38) vs. Washington (31) (Rose, 1993) (15 for 235)
14.2—(D) Gary Anderson, Arkansas (34) vs. Tulane (15) (Hall of Fame, 1980) (11 for 156)
14.1—Mike Holovak, Boston College (21) vs. Alabama (37) (Orange, 1943) (10 for 141)
14.1—Marcus Dupree, Oklahoma (21) vs. Arizona St. (32) (Fiesta, 1983) (17 for 239)
13.5—James Mungro, Syracuse (20) vs. Kentucky (13) (Music City, 1999) (12 for 162)
13.4—Cortlen Johnson, Colorado (62) vs. Boston College (28) (Insight.com, 1999) (15 for 201)
12.6—Ben Barnett, Army (28) vs. Alabama (29) (John Hancock Sun, 1988) (14 for 177)
12.6—Randy Baldwin, Mississippi (42) vs. Air Force (29) (Liberty, 1989) (14 for 177)
12.4—Tommie Frazier, Nebraska (62) vs. Florida (24) (Fiesta, 1996) (16 for 199)
12.3—George Smith, Texas Tech (28) vs. North Carolina (32) (Sun, 1972) (14 for 172)
11.2—Elliott Walker, Pittsburgh (33) vs. Kansas (19) (Sun, 1975) (11 for 123)
11.2—(D) Dwight Ford, Southern California (47) vs. Texas A&M (28) (Bluebonnet, 1977) (14 for 157)
10.9—Rodney Hampton, Georgia (34) vs. Michigan St. (27) (Gator, Jan. 1, 1989) (10 for 109)
10.8—Bobby Cavazos, Texas Tech (35) vs. Auburn (13) (Gator, Jan. 1, 1954) (13 for 141)
10.8—Byron Hanspard, Texas Tech (55) vs. Air Force (41) (Copper, 1995) (24 for 260)
10.6—J. C. Watts, Oklahoma (24) vs. Florida St. (7) (Orange, 1980) (12 for 127)
10.5—Ray Brown, Mississippi (39) vs. Texas (7) (Sugar, 1958) (15 for 157)
10.3—Eric Ball, UCLA (45) vs. Iowa (28) (Rose, 1986) (22 for 227)
10.2—(D) Bill Tobin, Missouri (14) vs. Georgia Tech (10) (Bluebonnet, 1962) (11 for 112)
10.2—Jamie Morris, Michigan (28) vs. Alabama (24) (Hall of Fame, 1988) (23 for 234)

THREE RUSHERS, SAME TEAM, GAINING MORE THAN 100 YARDS
366—Tony Dorsett (142), Elliott Walker (123) & Robert Haygood (QB) (101), Pittsburgh (33) vs. Kansas (19) (Sun, 1975)

TWO RUSHERS, SAME TEAM, GAINING MORE THAN 100 YARDS
373—Woody Green (202) & Brent McClanahan (171), Arizona St. (49) vs. Missouri (35) (Fiesta, 1972)
365—(D) George Woodard (185) & Mike Mosley (QB) (180), Texas A&M (28) vs. Southern California (47) (Bluebonnet, 1977)
365—Bob Anderson (254) & Jim Bratten (111), Colorado (47) vs. Alabama (33) (Liberty, 1969)
364—Tommie Frazier (QB) (199) & Lawrence Phillips (165), Nebraska (62) vs. Florida (24) (Fiesta, 1996)
347—Walter Packer (183) & Terry Vitrano (164), Mississippi St. (26) vs. North Carolina (24) (Sun, 1974)
343—(D) Charles White (186) & Dwight Ford (157), Southern California (47) vs. Texas A&M (28) (Bluebonnet, 1977)
330—Floyd Little (216) & Larry Csonka (114), Syracuse (12) vs. Tennessee (18) (Gator, 1966)
297—Monroe Eley (173) & Bob Thomas (124), Arizona St. (48) vs. North Carolina (26) (Peach, 1970)
292—Kelvin Bryant (148) & Ethan Horton (144), North Carolina (31) vs. Arkansas (27) (Gator, 1981)
291—Billy Sims (164) & J. C. Watts (QB) (127), Oklahoma (24) vs. Florida St. (7) (Orange, 1980)
288—Billy Sims (181) & Darrell Shepard (QB) (107), Oklahoma (40) vs. Houston (14) (Sun, 1981)
277—Danta Johnson (148) & Beau Morgan (QB) (129), Air Force (41) vs. Texas Tech (55) (Copper, 1995)
277—Willie Heston (170) & Neil Snow (107), Michigan (49) vs. Stanford (0) (Rose, 1902)
270—Anthony Brown (167) & Major Harris (QB) (103), West Virginia (33) vs. Oklahoma St. (35) (John Hancock Sun, 1987)

INDIVIDUAL RECORD LISTS—RUSHING   315

257—Sedrick Shaw (135) & Tavian Banks (122), Iowa (38) vs. Washington (18) (Sun, 1995)
253—Alois Blackwell (149) & Dyral Thomas (104), Houston (30) vs. Maryland (21) (Cotton, 1977)
246—T. Robert Hopkins (125) & Leonard Brown (121), Missouri (27) vs. Texas (40) (Cotton, 1946)
240—Jon Vaughn (128) & Ricky Powers (112), Michigan (35) vs. Mississippi (3) (Gator, Jan. 1, 1991)
237—James Rouse (134) & Barry Foster (103), Arkansas (27) vs. Tennessee (31) (Cotton, 1990)
237—Raymond Bybee (127) & Thomas Reamon (110), Missouri (34) vs. Auburn (17) (Sun, 1973)
236—Corby Jones (132) & Devin West (104), Missouri (24) vs. Colorado St. (35) (Holiday, 1997)
230—Rex Kern (QB) (129) & John Brockington (101), Ohio St. (17) vs. Stanford (27) (Rose, 1971)
224—Clinton Portis (117) & James Jackson (107), Miami (Fla.) (28) vs. Georgia Tech (13) (Gator, 2000)
223—Bucky Richardson (QB) (119) & Darren Lewis (104), Texas A&M (65) vs. Brigham Young (14) (Holiday, 1990)
222—(D) Marshall Johnson (114) & Donnie McGraw (108), Houston (47) vs. Tulane (7) (Bluebonnet, 1973)
218—Travis Sims (113) & Michael Carter (105), Hawaii (27) vs. Illinois (17) (Holiday, 1992)
218—Steve Giese (111) & Bob Torrey (107), Penn St. (42) vs. Arizona St. (30) (Fiesta, 1977)
215—Jeff Atkins (112) & Reggie Dupard (103), Southern Methodist (27) vs. Notre Dame (20) (Aloha, 1984)
215—Allen Pinkett (111) & Chris Smith (104), Notre Dame (19) vs. Boston College (18) (Liberty, 1983)
212—Toney Converse (103) & Shaun King (109), Tulane (41) vs. Brigham Young (27) (Liberty, 1998)
204—Johnny "Ham" Jones (104) & Johnny "Jam" Jones (100), Texas (42) vs. Maryland (0) (Sun, 1978)
201—Jerome Heavens (101) & Vagas Ferguson (100), Notre Dame (38) vs. Texas (10) (Cotton, 1978)

MOST RUSHING TOUCHDOWNS
5—Barry Sanders, Oklahoma St. (62) vs. Wyoming (14) (Holiday, 1988) (runs of 33, 2, 67, 1, 10)
5—Neil Snow, Michigan (49) vs. Stanford (0) (Rose, 1902) (five-point scores)
4—Ron Dayne, Wisconsin (38) vs. UCLA (31) (Rose, 1999) (runs of 54, 7, 10, 22)
4—Byron Hanspard, Texas Tech (55) vs. Air Force (41) (Copper, 1995) (runs of 2, 11, 2, 29)
4—Wasean Tait, Toledo (40) vs. Nevada (37) (ot) (Las Vegas, 1995) (runs of 18, 31, 26, 3)
4—(D) Ron Jackson, Tulsa (28) vs. San Diego St. (17) (Freedom, 1991) (runs of 10, 6, 3, 4)
4—(D) Sheldon Canley, San Jose St. (48) vs. Central Mich. (24) (California, 1990) (runs of 5, 22, 59, 5)
4—(D) James Gray, Texas Tech (49) vs. Duke (21) (All-American, 1989) (runs of 2, 54, 18, 32)
4—Thurman Thomas, Oklahoma St. (35) vs. West Virginia (33) (John Hancock Sun, 1987) (runs of 5, 9, 4, 4)
4—Eric Ball, UCLA (45) vs. Iowa (28) (Rose, 1986) (runs of 30, 40, 6, 32)
4—Terry Miller, Oklahoma St. (49) vs. Brigham Young (21) (Tangerine, 1976) (runs of 3, 78, 6, 1)
4—Sam Cunningham, Southern California (42) vs. Ohio St. (17) (Rose, 1973) (runs of 2, 1, 1, 1)
4—Woody Green, Arizona St. (49) vs. Missouri (35) (Fiesta, 1972) (runs of 2, 12, 17, 21)
4—Charles Cole, Toledo (56) vs. Davidson (33) (Tangerine, 1969) (runs of 1, 11, 16, 1)
4—(D) Gene Shannon, Houston (26) vs. Dayton (21) (Salad, 1952) (runs of 15, 19, 1, 10)

Passing

MOST PASS ATTEMPTS
63—Trent Dilfer, Fresno St. (30) vs. Colorado (41) (Aloha, 1993)
62—(D) Steve Clarkson, San Jose St. (25) vs. Toledo (27) (California, 1981)
61—Danny O'Neil, Oregon (20) vs. Penn St. (38) (Rose, 1995)
61—(D) Sean Covey, Brigham Young (16) vs. Virginia (22) (All-American, 1987)
60—Drew Brees, Purdue (25) vs. Georgia (28) (ot) (Outback, 2000)
59—Hines Ward, Georgia (27) vs. Virginia (34) (Peach, Dec. 30, 1995)
59—Ty Detmer, Brigham Young (39) vs. Penn St. (50) (Holiday, 1989)
58—Shane Matthews, Florida (28) vs. Notre Dame (39) (Sugar, 1992)
58—Buster O'Brien, Richmond (49) vs. Ohio (42) (Tangerine, 1968)
57—(D) Tony Kimbrough, Western Mich. (30) vs. Fresno St. (35) (California, 1988)
56—Gino Torretta, Miami (Fla.) (13) vs. Alabama (34) (Sugar, 1993)
55—Jack Trudeau, Illinois (29) vs. Army (31) (Peach, 1985)
55—Tony Eason, Illinois (15) vs. Alabama (21) (Liberty, 1982)
53—Josh Heupel, Oklahoma (25) vs. Mississippi (27) (Independence, 1999)
53—Drew Brees, Purdue (37) vs. Kansas St. (34) (Alamo, 1998)
53—Tim Cowan, Washington (21) vs. Maryland (20) (Aloha, 1982)
53—Kim Hammond, Florida St. (17) vs. Penn St. (17) (Gator, 1967)

52—David Smith, Alabama (29) vs. Army (28) (John Hancock Sun, 1988)
52—Shawn Halloran, Boston College (27) vs. Georgia (24) (Hall of Fame, 1986)
51—Lee Roberts, Southern Miss. (35) vs. Idaho (42) (Humanitarian, 1998)
51—Jeff Blake, East Caro. (37) vs. North Carolina St. (34) (Peach, 1992)
51—Danny McManus, Florida St. (31) vs. Nebraska (28) (Fiesta, 1988)
51—Chuck Hartlieb, Iowa (23) vs. North Carolina St. (28) (Peach, Dec. 31, 1988)
51—Craig Burnett, Wyoming (19) vs. Iowa (20) (Holiday, 1987)
51—(D) Whit Taylor, Vanderbilt (28) vs. Air Force (36) (Hall of Fame, 1982)

MOST PASS COMPLETIONS
43—(D) Steve Clarkson, San Jose St. (25) vs. Toledo (27) (California, 1981)
42—Ty Detmer, Brigham Young (39) vs. Penn St. (50) (Holiday, 1989)
41—Danny O'Neil, Oregon (20) vs. Penn St. (38) (Rose, 1995)
39—Josh Heupel, Oklahoma (25) vs. Mississippi (27) (Independence, 1999)
39—Buster O'Brien, Richmond (49) vs. Ohio (42) (Tangerine, 1968)
38—Jack Trudeau, Illinois (29) vs. Army (31) (Peach, 1985)
38—(D) Whit Taylor, Vanderbilt (28) vs. Air Force (36) (Hall of Fame, 1982)
37—Trent Dilfer, Fresno St. (30) vs. Colorado (41) (Aloha, 1993)
37—(D) Sean Covey, Brigham Young (16) vs. Virginia (22) (All-American, 1987)
37—Kim Hammond, Florida St. (17) vs. Penn St. (17) (Gator, 1967)
36—Drew Brees, Purdue (25) vs. Georgia (28) (ot) (Outback, 2000)
35—Tony Eason, Illinois (15) vs. Alabama (21) (Liberty, 1982)
34—Tom Brady, Michigan (35) vs. Alabama (34) (ot) (Orange, 2000)
34—Marc Bulger, West Virginia (31) vs. Missouri (34) (Insight.com, 1998)
33—David Smith, Alabama (29) vs. Army (28) (John Hancock Sun, 1988)
33—Tim Cowan, Washington (21) vs. Maryland (20) (Aloha, 1982)
33—Ron VanderKelen, Wisconsin (37) vs. Southern California (42) (Rose, 1963)
32—Jim McMahon, Brigham Young (46) vs. Southern Methodist (45) (Holiday, 1980)
31—Hines Ward, Georgia (27) vs. Virginia (34) (Peach, Dec. 30, 1995)
31—John Walsh, Brigham Young (31) vs. Oklahoma (6) (Copper, 1994)
31—Jeff Blake, East Caro. (37) vs. North Carolina St. (34) (Peach, 1992)
31—Stan White, Auburn (27) vs. Indiana (23) (Peach, 1990)
31—Shawn Halloran, Boston College (27) vs. Georgia (24) (Hall of Fame, 1986)
31—Mark Young, Mississippi (20) vs. Texas Tech (17) (Independence, 1986)
31—Bernie Kosar, Miami (Fla.) (37) vs. UCLA (39) (Fiesta, 1985)
31—John Congemi, Pittsburgh (23) vs. Ohio St. (28) (Fiesta, 1984)
31—(D) Jeff Tedford, Fresno St. (29) vs. Bowling Green (28) (California, 1982)

MOST CONSECUTIVE PASS COMPLETIONS
19—Mike Bobo, Georgia (33) vs. Wisconsin (6) (Outback, 1998)
10—Danny Wuerffel, Florida (17) vs. Florida St. (23) (Sugar, Jan. 2, 1995)
10—Rick Neuheisel, UCLA (45) vs. Illinois (9) (Rose, 1984)
9—(D) Rob Johnson, Southern California (28) vs. Utah (21) (Freedom, 1993)
9—Bill Montgomery, Arkansas (16) vs. Georgia (2) (Sugar, 1969)
9—Glenn Dobbs, Tulsa (7) vs. Tennessee (14) (Sugar, 1943)
8—Billy Roland, Houston (49) vs. Miami (Ohio) (21) (Tangerine, 1962)
8—Bobby Layne, Texas (40) vs. Missouri (27) (Cotton, 1946)
8—Harry Gilmer, Alabama (26) vs. Duke (29) (Sugar, 1945)
7—(D) Daniel Ford, Arizona St. (33) vs. Air Force (28) (Freedom, 1987)

MOST NET PASSING YARDS
(Followed by Comp.-Att.-Int.)
576—Ty Detmer, Brigham Young (39) vs. Penn St. (50) (Holiday, 1989) (42-59-2)
523—Trent Dilfer, Fresno St. (30) vs. Colorado (41) (Aloha, 1993) (37-63-1)
476—Drew Bledsoe, Washington St. (31) vs. Utah (28) (Copper, 1992) (30-46-1)
467—(D) Steve Clarkson, San Jose St. (25) vs. Toledo (27) (California, 1981) (43-62-5)
461—(D) Chuck Long, Iowa (55) vs. Texas (17) (Freedom, 1984) (29-39-0)
456—Danny O'Neil, Oregon (20) vs. Penn St. (38) (Rose, 1995) (41-61-2)
456—Akili Smith, Oregon (43) vs. Colorado (51) (Aloha, 1998) (24-46-2)
454—John Walsh, Brigham Young (31) vs. Oklahoma (6) (Copper, 1994) (31-45-0)
452—(D) Whit Taylor, Vanderbilt (28) vs. Air Force (36) (Hall of Fame, 1982) (38-51-3)
451—Browning Nagle, Louisville (34) vs. Alabama (7) (Fiesta, 1991) (20-33-1)
447—Buster O'Brien, Richmond (49) vs. Ohio (42) (Tangerine, 1968) (39-58-2)
446—Jim McMahon, Brigham Young (46) vs. Southern Methodist (45) (Holiday, 1980) (32-49-1)
429—Marc Bulger, West Virginia (31) vs. Missouri (34) (Insight.com, 1998) (34-50-1)
428—Chuck Hartlieb, Iowa (23) vs. North Carolina St. (28) (Peach, Dec. 31, 1988) (30-51-4)
423—Tony Eason, Illinois (15) vs. Alabama (21) (Liberty, 1982) (35-55-4)
422—Peter Tom Willis, Florida St. (41) vs. Nebraska (17) (Fiesta, 1990) (25-40-0)
413—Hines Ward, Georgia (27) vs. Virginia (34) (Peach, Dec. 30, 1995) (31-59-2)
412—David Smith, Alabama (29) vs. Army (28) (John Hancock Sun, 1988) (33-52-1)
411—Chad Pennington, Marshall (48) vs. Louisville (29) (Motor City, 1998) (18-24-0)
408—Peyton Manning, Tennessee (48) vs. Northwestern (28) (Florida Citrus, 1997) (27-39-0)
404—(D) Ralph Martini, San Jose St. (48) vs. Central Mich. (24) (California, 1990) (27-36-1)
401—Ron VanderKelen, Wisconsin (37) vs. Southern California (42) (Rose, 1963) (33-48-3)
401—Jack Trudeau, Illinois (29) vs. Army (31) (Peach, 1985) (38-55-2)

MOST NET PASSING YARDS, ONE QUARTER
223—Browning Nagle, Louisville (34) vs. Alabama (7) (Fiesta, 1991) (1st, 9 of 16)
202—(D) Bret Stafford, Texas (32) vs. Pittsburgh (27) (Bluebonnet, 1987) (1st)

MOST TOUCHDOWN PASSES THROWN
6—(D) Chuck Long, Iowa (55) vs. Texas (17) (Freedom, 1984) (29-39-0) (6, 11, 33, 49, 4, 15 yards)

BOWL/ALL-STAR RECORDS

5—Peter Tom Willis, Florida St. (41) vs. Nebraska (17) (Fiesta, 1990)
5—Steve Tensi, Florida St. (36) vs. Oklahoma (19) (Gator, Jan. 2, 1965)
4—John Walsh, Idaho (42) vs. Southern Miss. (35) (Humanitarian, 1998)
4—Chad Pennington, Marshall (48) vs. Louisville (29) (Motor City, 1998)
4—Marc Bulger, West Virginia (31) Missouri (34) (Insight.com, 1998)
4—Michael Bishop, Kansas St. (35) vs. Syracuse (18) (Fiesta, 1997)
4—Peyton Manning, Tennessee (48) vs. Northwestern (28) (Florida Citrus, 1997)
4—Danny Kanell, Florida St. (31) vs. Notre Dame (26) (Orange, 1996)
4—Wally Richardson, Penn St. (43) vs. Auburn (14) (Outback, 1996)
4—Brian Kavanagh, Kansas St. (54) vs. Colorado St. (21) (Holiday, 1995)
4—Johnny Johnson, Illinois (30) vs. East Caro. (0) (Liberty, 1994)
4—John Walsh, Brigham Young (31) vs. Oklahoma (6) (Copper, 1994)
4—Tony Sacca, Penn St. (42) vs. Tennessee (17) (Fiesta, 1992)
4—Jeff Blake, East Caro. (37) vs. North Carolina St. (34) (Peach, 1992)
4—Elvis Grbac, Michigan (35) vs. Mississippi (3) (Gator, Jan. 1, 1991)
4—Rick Neuheisel, UCLA (45) vs. Illinois (9) (Rose, 1984)
4—Jim McMahon, Brigham Young (46) vs. Southern Methodist (45) (Holiday, 1980)
4—Mark Herrmann, Purdue (28) vs. Missouri (25) (Liberty, 1980)
4—(D) Rob Hertel, Southern California (47) vs. Texas A&M (28) (Bluebonnet, 1977)
4—Matt Cavanaugh, Pittsburgh (34) vs. Clemson (3) (Gator, 1977)
4—Gordon Slade, Davidson (33) vs. Toledo (55) (Tangerine, 1969)
4—Buster O'Brien, Richmond (49) vs. Ohio (42) (Tangerine, 1968)
4—Cleve Bryant, Ohio (42) vs. Richmond (49) (Tangerine, 1968)
4—Pete Beathard, Southern California (42) vs. Wisconsin (37) (Rose, 1963)

MOST PASSES HAD INTERCEPTED
(Followed by Comp.-Att.-Int.)
6—Bruce Lee, Arizona (10) vs. Auburn (34) (Sun, 1968) (6-24-6)
5—Wade Hill, Arkansas (15) vs. Georgia (24) (Independence, 1991) (12-31-5)
5—Kevin Murray, Texas A&M (12) vs. Ohio St. (28) (Cotton, 1987) (12-31-5)
5—Vinny Testaverde, Miami (Fla.) (10) vs. Penn St. (14) (Fiesta, 1987) (26-50-5)
5—Jeff Wickersham, LSU (10) vs. Nebraska (28) (Sugar, 1985) (20-38-5)
5—(D) Steve Clarkson, San Jose St. (25) vs. Toledo (27) (California, 1981) (43-62-5)
5—Terry McMillan, Missouri (35) vs. Penn St. (10) (Orange, 1970) (6-28-5)
5—Paul Gilbert, Georgia (6) vs. Nebraska (45) (Sun, 1969) (10-30-5)

HIGHEST COMPLETION PERCENTAGE
(Minimum 10 Attempts) (Followed by Comp.-Att.-Int.)
.929—Mike Bobo, Georgia (33) vs. Wisconsin (6) (Outback, 1998) (26-28-0)
.917—Bobby Layne, Texas (40) vs. Missouri (27) (Cotton, 1946) (11-12-0)
.900—Ken Ploen, Iowa (35) vs. Oregon St. (19) (Rose, 1957) (9-10-0)
.846—Tom Sorley, Nebraska (21) vs. North Carolina (17) (Liberty, 1977) (11-13-0)
.833—Mike Gundy, Oklahoma St. (62) vs. Wyoming (14) (Holiday, 1988) (20-24-0)
.833—Richard Todd, Alabama (13) vs. Penn St. (6) (Sugar, 1975) (10-12-0)
.818—Bucky Richardson, Texas A&M (65) vs. Brigham Young (14) (Holiday, 1990) (9-11-0)
.806—Cale Gundy, Oklahoma (48) vs. Virginia (14) (Gator, Dec. 29, 1991) (25-31-0)
.800—Art Schlichter, Ohio St. (15) vs. Clemson (17) (Gator, 1978) (16-20-1)
.800—Jim Stevens, Georgia Tech (31) vs. Iowa St. (30) (Liberty, 1972) (12-15-0)
.800—Don Altman, Duke (7) vs. Arkansas (6) (Cotton, 1961) (12-15-0)
.800—Chuck Curtis, TCU (28) vs. Syracuse (27) (Cotton, 1957) (12-15-0)
.789—Charles Ortmann, Michigan (14) vs. California (6) (Rose, 1951) (15-19-0)
.786—Chad Hutchinson, Stanford (38) vs. Michigan St. (0) (Sun, 1996) (22-28-1)
.786—Mark Herrmann, Purdue (28) vs. Missouri (25) (Liberty, 1980) (22-28-0)

MOST YARDS PER PASS ATTEMPT
(Minimum 10 Attempts)
21.3—Chris McCoy, Navy (42) vs. California (38) (Aloha, 1996) (13 for 277)
19.4—Tony Rice, Notre Dame (34) vs. West Virginia (21) (Fiesta, 1989) (11 for 213)
18.7—Frank Sinkwich, Georgia (40) vs. TCU (26) (Orange, 1942) (13 for 243)
18.5—Bucky Richardson, Texas A&M (65) vs. Brigham Young (14) (Holiday, 1990) (11 for 203)
17.3—Don Rumley, New Mexico (34) vs. Denver (24) (Sun, 1946) (12 for 207)
17.1—Chad Pennington, Marshall (48) vs. Louisville (29) (Motor City, 1998) (24 for 411)
16.7—Blane Morgan, Air Force (45) vs. Washington (25) (Oahu, 1998) (16 for 267)
16.4—(D) Rob Hertel, Southern California (47) vs. Texas A&M (28) (Bluebonnet, 1977) (15 for 246)
15.4—James Street, Texas (36) vs. Tennessee (13) (Cotton, 1969) (13 for 200)
15.4—Tee Martin, Tennessee (23) vs. Florida St. (16) (Fiesta, 1999) (11 for 278)
14.2—Danny White, Arizona St. (28) vs. Pittsburgh (7) (Fiesta, 1973) (19 for 269)
13.8—Rob Johnson, Southern California (55) vs. Texas Tech (14) (Cotton, 1995) (21 for 289)
13.8—Michael Bishop, Kansas St. (35) vs. Syracuse (18) (Fiesta, 1997) (23 for 317)
13.7—Browning Nagle, Louisville (34) vs. Alabama (7) (Fiesta, 1991) (33 for 451)
13.6—Bob Churchich, Nebraska (28) vs. Alabama (39) (Orange, 1966) (17 for 232)
13.4—Donovan McNabb, Syracuse (41) vs. Clemson (0) (Gator, 1996) (23 for 309)
13.3—Scott Covington, Miami (Fla.) (46) vs. North Carolina St. (23) (Micron PC, 1998) (24 for 320)
13.2—Bobby Layne, Texas (40) vs. Missouri (27) (Cotton, 1946) (12 for 158)

MOST YARDS PER PASS COMPLETION
(Minimum 7 Completions)
30.8—Chris McCoy, Navy (42) vs. California (38) (Aloha, 1996) (9 for 277)
30.4—Duke Carlisle, Texas (28) vs. Navy (6) (Cotton, 1964) (7 for 213)
30.4—Tony Rice, Notre Dame (34) vs. West Virginia (21) (Fiesta, 1989) (7 for 213)
28.6—James Street, Texas (36) vs. Tennessee (13) (Cotton, 1969) (7 for 200)
27.0—Frank Sinkwich, Georgia (40) vs. TCU (26) (Orange, 1942) (9 for 243)

Receiving

MOST PASS RECEPTIONS
20—(D) Norman Jordan, Vanderbilt (28) vs. Air Force (36) (Hall of Fame, 1982) (173 yards)
20—Walker Gillette, Richmond (49) vs. Ohio (42) (Tangerine, 1968) (242 yards)
18—(D) Gerald Willhite, San Jose St. (25) vs. Toledo (27) (California, 1981) (124 yards)
15—(D) Stephone Paige, Fresno St. (29) vs. Bowling Green (28) (California, 1982) (246 yards)
14—Alex Van Dyke, Nevada (37) vs. Toledo (40) (ot) (Las Vegas, 1995) (176 yards)
14—J. J. Stokes, UCLA (16) vs. Wisconsin (21) (Rose, 1994) (176 yards)
14—Ron Sellers, Florida St. (17) vs. Penn St. (17) (Gator, 1967) (145 yards)
13—Plaxico Burress, Michigan St. (37) vs. Florida (34) (Florida Citrus, 2000) (185 yards)
13—Fred Biletnikoff, Florida St. (36) vs. Oklahoma (19) (Gator, Jan. 2, 1965) (192 yards)
12—Chris Daniels, Purdue (25) vs. Georgia (28) (ot) (Outback, 2000) (103 yards)
12—Sherrod Gideon, Southern Miss. (35) vs. Idaho (42) (Humanitarian, 1998) (117 yards)
12—Hines Ward, Georgia (33) vs. Wisconsin (6) (Outback, 1998) (122 yards)
12—Keyshawn Johnson, Southern California (41) vs. Northwestern (32) (Rose, 1996) (216 yards)
12—Luke Fisher, East Caro. (37) vs. North Carolina St. (34) (Peach, 1992) (144 yards)
12—Chuck Dicus, Arkansas (16) vs. Georgia (2) (Sugar, 1969) (169 yards)
12—Bill Moremen, Florida St. (17) vs. Penn St. (17) (Gator, 1967) (106 yards)
11—Travis Taylor, Florida (34) vs. Michigan St. (37) (Florida Citrus, 2000) (156 yards)
11—David Boston, Ohio St. (24) vs. Texas A&M (14) (Sugar, 1999) (105 yards)
11—Shawn Foreman, West Virginia (31) vs. Missouri (34) (Insight.com, 1998) (189 yards)
11—Isaac Jones, Purdue (37) vs. Kansas St. (34) (Alamo, 1998) (98 yards)
11—Josh Wilcox, Oregon (20) vs. Penn St. (38) (Rose, 1995) (135 yards)
11—Bill Khayat, Duke (20) vs. Wisconsin (34) (Hall of Fame, 1995) (109 yards)
11—(D) Mark Szlachcic, Bowling Green (28) vs. Fresno St. (21) (California, 1991) (189 yards)
11—Ronnie Harmon, Iowa (28) vs. UCLA (45) (Rose, 1986) (102 yards)
11—David Mills, Brigham Young (24) vs. Michigan (17) (Holiday, 1984) (103 yards)
11—(D) Chip Otten, Bowling Green (28) vs. Fresno St. (29) (California, 1982) (76 yards)
11—(D) Anthony Hancock, Tennessee (28) vs. Wisconsin (21) (Garden State, 1981) (196 yards)
11—Pat Richter, Wisconsin (37) vs. Southern California (42) (Rose, 1963) (163 yards)
11—(D) James Ingram, Baylor (14) vs. LSU (7) (Bluebonnet, 1963) (163 yards)
10—David Terrell, Michigan (35) vs. Alabama (34) (ot) (Orange, 2000) (150 yards)
10—Willie Gosha, Auburn (32) vs. Army (29) (Independence, 1996) (132 yards)
10—Damon Wilkins, Nevada (18) vs. Ball St. (15) (Las Vegas, 1996) (106 yards)
10—Larry Bowie, Georgia (27) vs. Virginia (34) (Peach, Dec. 30, 1995) (156 yards)
10—Johnnie Morton, Southern California (28) vs. Utah (21) (Freedom, 1993) (147 yards)
10—Mike Blair, Ball St. (33) vs. Utah St. (42) (Las Vegas, 1993) (66 yards)
10—Matt Bellini, Brigham Young (39) vs. Penn St. (50) (Holiday, 1989) (124 yards)
10—Hart Lee Dykes, Oklahoma St. (62) vs. Wyoming (14) (Holiday, 1988) (163 yards)
10—(D) David Miles, Brigham Young (16) vs. Virginia (22) (All-American, 1987) (188 yards)
10—Lakei Heimuli, Brigham Young (7) vs. Ohio St. (10) (Florida Citrus, 1985)
10—Bobby Joe Edmonds, Arkansas (15) vs. Auburn (21) (Liberty, 1984)
10—David Williams, Illinois (9) vs. UCLA (45) (Rose, 1984)
10—Kelly Smith, Brigham Young (24) vs. Michigan (17) (Holiday, 1984) (88 yards)
10—Paul Skansi, Washington (21) vs. Maryland (20) (Aloha, 1982) (87 yards)
10—(D) Tim Kearse, San Jose St. (25) vs. Toledo (27) (California, 1981) (104 yards)
10—Scott Phillips, Brigham Young (46) vs. Southern Methodist (45) (Holiday, 1980) (81 yards)
10—Gordon Jones, Pittsburgh (34) vs. Clemson (3) (Gator, 1977) (163 yards)
10—Bobby Crockett, Arkansas (7) vs. LSU (14) (Cotton, Jan. 1, 1966)
10—Ron Stover, Oregon (7) vs. Ohio St. (10) (Rose, 1958) (144 yards)

MOST PASS RECEIVING YARDS
252—Andre Rison, Michigan St. (27) vs. Georgia (34) (Gator, Jan. 1, 1989) (9 catches)
246—(D) Stephone Paige, Fresno St. (29) vs. Bowling Green (28) (California, 1982) (15 catches)
242—(D) Tony Jones, Texas (32) vs. Pittsburgh (27) (Bluebonnet, 1987) (8 catches)
242—Walker Gillette, Richmond (49) vs. Ohio (42) (Tangerine, 1968) (20 catches)
222—Keyshawn Johnson, Southern California (55) vs. Texas Tech (14) (Cotton, 1995) (8 catches)
216—Keyshawn Johnson, Southern California (41) vs. Northwestern (32) (Rose, 1996) (12 catches)
212—Phillip Bobo, Washington St. (31) vs. Utah (28) (Copper, 1992) (7 catches)
206—Darnell McDonald, Kansas St. (35) vs. Syracuse (18) (Fiesta, 1997) (7 catches)
201—(D) Bob McChesney, Hardin-Simmons (49) vs. Wichita St. (12) (Camellia, 1948) (8 catches)
199—Peerless Price, Tennessee (23) vs. Florida St. (16) (Fiesta, 1999) (4 catches)
196—(D) Anthony Hancock, Tennessee (28) vs. Wisconsin (21) (Garden State, 1981) (11 catches)
194—Cory Schemm, Navy (42) vs. California (38) (Aloha, 1996) (5 catches)
192—Fred Biletnikoff, Florida St. (36) vs. Oklahoma (19) (Gator, Jan. 2, 1965) (13 catches)
189—Shawn Foreman, West Virginia (31) vs. Missouri (34) (Insight.com, 1998) (11 catches)

INDIVIDUAL RECORD LISTS—RECEIVING 317

189—(D) Mark Szlachcic, Bowling Green (28) vs. Fresno St. (21) (California, 1991) (11 catches)
188—(D) David Miles, Brigham Young (16) vs. Virginia (22) (All-American, 1987) (10 catches)
186—Greg Hudson, Arizona St. (28) vs. Pittsburgh (7) (Fiesta, 1973) (8 catches)
185—Plaxico Burress, Michigan St. (37) vs. Florida (34) (Florida Citrus, 2000) (13 catches)
182—Rob Turner, Indiana (34) vs. South Carolina (10) (Liberty, 1988) (5 catches)
178—Ray Perkins, Alabama (34) vs. Nebraska (7) (Sugar, 1967) (7 catches)
177—Thomas Lewis, Indiana (20) vs. Virginia Tech (45) (Independence, 1993) (6 catches)
176—E. G. Green, Florida St. (31) vs. Ohio St. (14) (Sugar, 1998) (7 catches)
176—Alex Van Dyke, Nevada (37) vs. Toledo (40) (ot) (Las Vegas, 1995) (14 catches)
176—J. J. Stokes, UCLA (16) vs. Wisconsin (21) (Rose, 1994) (14 catches)
173—Marvin Harrison, Syracuse (41) vs. Clemson (0) (Gator, 1996) (7 catches)
173—(D) Norman Jordan, Vanderbilt (28) vs. Air Force (36) (Hall of Fame, 1982) (20 catches)
172—Cris Carter, Ohio St. (17) vs. Southern California (20) (Rose, 1985) (9 catches)

HIGHEST AVERAGE PER RECEPTION
(Minimum 3 Receptions)
52.3—Phil Harris, Texas (28) vs. Navy (6) (Cotton, 1964) (3 for 157)
49.8—Peerless Price, Tennessee (23) vs. Florida St. (16) (Fiesta, 1999) (4 for 199)
39.7—Ike Hilliard, Florida (17) vs. Florida St. (23) (Sugar, Jan. 2, 1995) (3 for 119)
38.8—Cory Schemm, Navy (42) vs. California (38) (Aloha, 1996) (5 for 194)
36.4—Rob Turner, Indiana (34) vs. South Carolina (10) (Liberty, 1988) (5 for 182)
36.3—Clarence Cannon, Boston College (31) vs. Virginia (13) (Carquest, 1994) (3 for 109)
35.5—Rodney Harris, Kansas (23) vs. Brigham Young (20) (Aloha, 1992) (4 for 142)
35.3—Anthony Carter, Michigan (15) vs. North Carolina (17) (Gator, 1979) (4 for 141)
34.3—(D) Andre Alexander, Fresno St. (35) vs. Western Mich. (30) (California, 1988) (3 for 103)
34.3—Ron Beverly, Arizona St. (49) vs. Missouri (35) (Fiesta, 1972) (3 for 103)
34.0—Durell Price, UCLA (31) vs. Wisconsin (38) (Rose, 1999) (3 for 102)
34.0—Jimmy Cefalo, Penn St. (41) vs. Baylor (20) (Cotton, 1975) (3 for 102)
33.7—Justin Shull, Colorado St. (14) vs. Michigan (24) (Holiday, 1994) (3 for 101)
33.7—J. D. Hill, Arizona St. (48) vs. North Carolina (26) (Peach, 1970) (3 for 101)
33.3—Tony Buford, Indiana (34) vs. South Carolina (10) (Liberty, 1988) (3 for 100)
33.2—Melvin Bonner, Baylor (20) vs. Arizona (15) (John Hancock, 1992) (5 for 166)
33.2—Todd Dixon, Wake Forest (39) vs. Oregon (35) (Independence, 1992) (5 for 166)
33.0—Ed Hervey, Southern California (55) vs. Texas Tech (14) (Cotton, 1995) (3 for 99)
32.3—Dez White, Georgia Tech (35) vs. Notre Dame (28) (Gator, 1999) (4 for 129)
32.2—Cotton Speyrer, Texas (36) vs. Tennessee (13) (Cotton, 1969) (5 for 161)
32.0—Darrin Chiaverini, Colorado (51) vs. Oregon (43) (Aloha, 1998) (3 for 96)
31.0—Olanda Truitt, Pittsburgh (31) vs. Texas A&M (28) (John Hancock, 1989) (4 for 124)
31.0—Clay Brown, Brigham Young (46) vs. Southern Methodist (45) (Holiday, 1980) (5 for 155)

MOST TOUCHDOWNS RECEIVING
4—Fred Biletnikoff, Florida St. (36) vs. Oklahoma (19) (Gator, Jan. 2, 1965) (13 catches)
4—(D) Bob McChesney, Hardin-Simmons (49) vs. Wichita St. (12) (Camellia, 1948) (8 catches)
3—Plaxico Burress, Michigan St. (37) vs. Florida (34) (Florida Citrus, 2000) (13 catches)
3—Travis Taylor, Florida (34) vs. Michigan St. (37) (Florida Citrus, 2000) (11 catches)
3—Darnell McDonald, Kansas St. (35) vs. Syracuse (18) (Fiesta, 1997) (7 catches)
3—Ike Hilliard, Florida (52) vs. Florida St. (20) (Sugar, 1997) (7 catches)
3—Keyshawn Johnson, Southern California (55) vs. Texas Tech (14) (Cotton, 1995) (8 catches)
3—(D) Ken Ealy, Central Mich. (24) vs. San Jose St. (48) (California, 1990) (7 catches)
3—Wendell Davis, LSU (30) vs. South Carolina (13) (Gator, 1987) (9 catches)
3—Anthony Allen, Washington (21) vs. Maryland (20) (Aloha, 1982) (8 catches)
3—(D) Norman Jordan, Vanderbilt (28) vs. Air Force (36) (Hall of Fame, 1982) (20 catches)
3—(D) Dwayne Dixon, Florida (24) vs. Arkansas (28) (Bluebonnet, 1982) (8 catches)
3—(D) Mervyn Fernandez, San Jose St. (25) vs. Toledo (27) (California, 1981) (9 catches)
3—Clay Brown, Brigham Young (46) vs. Southern Methodist (45) (Holiday, 1980) (5 catches)
3—Elliott Walker, Pittsburgh (34) vs. Clemson (3) (Gator, 1977) (6 catches)
3—Rhett Dawson, Florida St. (38) vs. Arizona St. (45) (Fiesta, 1971) (8 catches)
3—George Hannen, Davidson (33) vs. Toledo (56) (Tangerine, 1969)
3—Todd Snyder, Richmond (49) vs. Ohio (42) (Tangerine, 1968)

Scoring

MOST POINTS SCORED
30—(D) Sheldon Canley, San Jose St. (48) vs. Central Mich. (24) (California, 1990) (5 TDs)
30—Barry Sanders, Oklahoma St. (62) vs. Wyoming (14) (Holiday, 1988) (5 TDs)
28—Bobby Layne, Texas (40) vs. Missouri (27) (Cotton, 1946) (4 TDs, 4 PATs)
25—Neil Snow, Michigan (49) vs. Stanford (0) (Rose, 1902) (5 five-point TDs)
24—Ron Dayne, Wisconsin (38) vs. UCLA (31) (Rose, 1999) (4 TDs)
24—Byron Hanspard, Texas Tech (55) vs. Air Force (41) (Copper, 1995) (4 TDs)
24—Wasean Tait, Toledo (40) vs. Nevada (37) (ot) (Las Vegas, 1995) (4 TDs)
24—(D) Ron Jackson, Tulsa (28) vs. San Diego St. (17) (Freedom, 1991) (4 TDs)
24—(D) James Gray, Texas Tech (49) vs. Duke (21) (All-American, 1989) (4 TDs)
24—Thurman Thomas, Oklahoma St. (35) vs. West Virginia (33) (John Hancock Sun, 1987) (4 TDs)
24—Eric Ball, UCLA (45) vs. Iowa (28) (Rose, 1986) (4 TDs)
24—Terry Miller, Oklahoma St. (49) vs. Brigham Young (21) (Tangerine, 1976) (4 TDs)
24—Sam Cunningham, Southern California (42) vs. Ohio St. (17) (Rose, 1973) (4 TDs)
24—Johnny Rodgers, Nebraska (40) vs. Notre Dame (6) (Orange, 1973) (4 TDs)
24—Woody Green, Arizona St. (49) vs. Missouri (35) (Fiesta, 1972) (4 TDs)
24—Charles Cole, Toledo (56) vs. Davidson (33) (Tangerine, 1969) (4 TDs)
24—Fred Biletnikoff, Florida St. (36) vs. Oklahoma (19) (Gator, Jan. 2, 1965) (4 TDs)
24—Joe Lopasky, Houston (49) vs. Miami (Ohio) (21) (Tangerine, 1962) (4 TDs)
24—(D) Gene Shannon, Houston (26) vs. Dayton (21) (Salad, 1952) (4 TDs)
24—(D) Bob McChesney, Hardin-Simmons (49) vs. Wichita St. (12) (Camellia, 1948) (4 TDs)

MOST POINTS RESPONSIBLE FOR
(TDs Scored & Passed For, Extra Points, and FGs)
40—Bobby Layne, Texas (40) vs. Missouri (27) (Cotton, 1946) (18 rush, 12 pass, 6 receiving and 4 PATs)
36—(D) Chuck Long, Iowa (55) vs. Texas (17) (Freedom, 1984) (36 pass)
30—Michael Bishop, Kansas St., (35) vs. Syracuse (18) (Fiesta, 1997) (24 pass, 6 rush)
30—Jeff Blake, East Caro. (37) vs. North Carolina St. (34) (Peach, 1992) (24 pass, 6 rush)
30—(D) Sheldon Canley, San Jose St. (48) vs. Central Mich. (24) (California, 1990) (24 rush, 6 receiving)
30—Peter Tom Willis, Florida St. (41) vs. Nebraska (17) (Fiesta, 1990) (30 pass)
30—Barry Sanders, Oklahoma St. (62) vs. Wyoming (14) (Holiday, 1988) (30 rush)
30—Johnny Rodgers, Nebraska (40) vs. Notre Dame (6) (Orange, 1973) (18 rush, 6 pass, 6 receiving)
30—Steve Tensi, Florida St. (36) vs. Oklahoma (19) (Gator, Jan. 2, 1965) (30 pass)

MOST TOUCHDOWNS
5—(D) Sheldon Canley, San Jose St. (48) vs. Central Mich. (24) (California, 1990) (4 rush, 1 catch)
5—Barry Sanders, Oklahoma St. (62) vs. Wyoming (14) (Holiday, 1988) (5 rush)
5—Neil Snow, Michigan (49) vs. Stanford (0) (Rose, 1902) (5 rush five-point TDs)
4—Ron Dayne, Wisconsin (38) vs. UCLA (31) (Rose, 1999) (4 rush)
4—Byron Hanspard, Texas Tech (55) vs. Air Force (41) (Copper, 1995) (4 rush)
4—Wasean Tait, Toledo (40) vs. Nevada (37) (ot) (Las Vegas, 1995) (4 rush)
4—(D) Ron Jackson, Tulsa (28) vs. San Diego St. (17) (Freedom, 1991) (4 rush)
4—(D) James Gray, Texas Tech (49) vs. Duke (21) (All-American, 1989) (4 rush)
4—Thurman Thomas, Oklahoma St. (35) vs. West Virginia (33) (John Hancock Sun, 1987) (4 rush)
4—Eric Ball, UCLA (45) vs. Iowa (28) (Rose, 1986) (4 rush)
4—Terry Miller, Oklahoma St. (49) vs. Brigham Young (21) (Tangerine, 1976) (4 rush)
4—Sam Cunningham, Southern California (42) vs. Ohio St. (17) (Rose, 1973) (4 rush)
4—Johnny Rodgers, Nebraska (40) vs. Notre Dame (6) (Orange, 1973) (3 rush, 1 catch)
4—Woody Green, Arizona St. (49) vs. Missouri (35) (Fiesta, 1972) (4 rush)
4—Charles Cole, Toledo (56) vs. Davidson (33) (Tangerine, 1969) (4 rush)
4—Fred Biletnikoff, Florida St. (36) vs. Oklahoma (19) (Gator, Jan. 2, 1965) (4 catch)
4—Joe Lopasky, Houston (49) vs. Miami (Ohio) (21) (Tangerine, 1962) (2 rush, 1 catch, 1 punt return)
4—(D) Gene Shannon, Houston (26) vs. Dayton (21) (Salad, 1952) (4 rush)
4—(D) Bob McChesney, Hardin-Simmons (49) vs. Wichita St. (12) (Camellia, 1948) (4 catch)
4—Bobby Layne, Texas (40) vs. Missouri (27) (Cotton, 1946) (3 rush, 1 catch)
4—(D) Alvin McMillin, Centre (63) vs. TCU (7) (Fort Worth Classic, 1921) (4 rush)

MOST TWO-POINT CONVERSIONS
2—Ernie Davis, Syracuse (23) vs. Texas (14) (Cotton, 1960) (2 pass receptions)

Kicking

MOST FIELD GOALS ATTEMPTED
6—Kyle Bryant, Texas A&M (22) vs. Michigan (20) (Alamo, 1995) (5 made)
5—Travis Forney, Penn St. (26) vs. Kentucky (14) (Outback, 1999) (4 made)
5—Chad Holcomb, East Caro. (19) vs. Stanford (13) (Liberty, 1995) (4 made)
5—Dan Mowrey, Florida St. (23) vs. Florida (17) (Sugar, Jan. 2, 1995) (3 made)
5—Tim Rogers, Mississippi St. (24) vs. North Carolina St. (28) (Peach, Jan. 1, 1995) (5 made)
5—Scott Bentley, Florida St. (18) vs. Nebraska (16) (Orange, 1994) (4 made)
5—Arden Czyzewski, Florida (28) vs. Notre Dame (39) (Sugar, 1992) (5 made)
5—Jess Atkinson, Maryland (23) vs. Tennessee (30) (Florida Citrus, 1983) (5 made)
5—Bob White, Arkansas (16) vs. Georgia (2) (Sugar, 1969) (3 made)
5—Tim Davis, Alabama (12) vs. Mississippi (7) (Sugar, 1964) (4 made)
4—Brett Conway, Penn St. (43) vs. Auburn (14) (Outback, 1996) (3 made)
4—Kanon Parkman, Georgia (27) vs. Virginia (34) (Peach, Dec. 30, 1995) (4 made)
4—Carlos Huerta, Miami (Fla.) (22) vs. Nebraska (0) (Orange, 1992) (3 made)
4—Greg Worker, Wyoming (19) vs. Iowa (20) (Holiday, 1987) (2 made)
4—Tim Lashar, Oklahoma (25) vs. Penn St. (10) (Orange, 1986) (4 made)

BOWL/ALL-STAR RECORDS

4—Kent Bostrom, Arizona St. (17) vs. Arkansas (18) (Holiday, 1985) (3 made)
4—(D) Todd Gregoire, Wisconsin (19) vs. Kentucky (20) (Hall of Fame, 1984) (4 made)
4—Bill Capece, Florida St. (17) vs. Oklahoma (18) (Orange, 1981) (1 made)
4—David Hardy, Texas A&M (33) vs. Oklahoma St. (16) (Independence, 1981) (4 made)
4—Bob Lucchesi, Missouri (19) vs. Southern Miss. (17) (Tangerine, 1981) (4 made)
4—Paul Woodside, West Virginia (26) vs. Florida (6) (Peach, Dec. 31, 1981) (4 made)
4—(D) Fuad Reveiz, Tennessee (28) vs. Wisconsin (21) (Garden State, 1981) (2 made)
4—Dale Castro, Maryland (20) vs. Florida (35) (Tangerine, 1980) (4 made)
4—Brent Johnson, Brigham Young (37) vs. Indiana (38) (Holiday, 1979) (3 made)
4—Ricky Townsend, Tennessee (19) vs. Texas Tech (28) (Gator, 1973) (2 made)
4—Paul Rogers, Nebraska (45) vs. Georgia (6) (Sun, 1969) (4 made)

MOST FIELD GOALS MADE
5—Kyle Bryant, Texas A&M (22) vs. Michigan (20) (Alamo, 1995) (27, 49, 47, 31, 37 yards)
5—Tim Rogers, Mississippi St. (24) vs. North Carolina St. (28) (Peach, Jan. 1, 1995) (37, 21, 29, 36, 30 yards)
5—Arden Czyzewski, Florida (28) vs. Notre Dame (39) (Sugar, 1992) (26, 24, 36, 37, 24 yards)
5—Jess Atkinson, Maryland (23) vs. Tennessee (30) (Florida Citrus, 1983) (18, 48, 31, 22, 26 yards)
4—Travis Forney, Penn St. (26) vs. Kentucky (14) (Outback, 1999) (43, 26, 21, 25)
4—Chad Holcomb, East Caro. (19) vs. Stanford (13) (Liberty, 1995) (46, 26, 41, 34 yards)
4—Kanon Parkman, Georgia (27) vs. Virginia (34) (Peach, Dec. 30, 1995) (36, 37, 20, 42 yards)
4—Scott Bentley, Florida St. (18) vs. Nebraska (16) (Orange, 1994) (34, 25, 39, 22 yards)
4—Tim Lashar, Oklahoma (25) vs. Penn St. (10) (Orange, 1986) (26, 31, 21, 22 yards)
4—(D) Todd Gregoire, Wisconsin (19) vs. Kentucky (20) (Hall of Fame, 1984) (40, 27, 20, 40 yards)
4—David Hardy, Texas A&M (33) vs. Oklahoma St. (16) (Independence, 1981) (33, 32, 50, 18 yards)
4—Paul Woodside, West Virginia (26) vs. Florida (6) (Peach, Dec. 31, 1981) (35, 42, 49, 24 yards)
4—Bob Lucchesi, Missouri (19) vs. Southern Miss. (17) (Tangerine, 1981) (45, 41, 30, 28 yards)
4—Dale Castro, Maryland (20) vs. Florida (35) (Tangerine, 1980) (35, 27, 27, 43 yards)
4—Paul Rogers, Nebraska (45) vs. Georgia (6) (Sun, 1969) (50, 32, 42, 37 yards, all in 1st quarter)
4—Tim Davis, Alabama (12) vs. Mississippi (7) (Sugar, 1964) (31, 46, 22, 48 yards)

MOST EXTRA-POINT KICK ATTEMPTS
9—Neil Rackers, Illinois (63) vs. Virginia (21) (Micronpc.com, 1999) (9 made)
9—Layne Talbot, Texas A&M (65) vs. Brigham Young (14) (Holiday, 1990) (9 made)
9—Bobby Luna, Alabama (61) vs. Syracuse (6) (Orange, 1953) (7 made)
9—(D) James Weaver, Centre (63) vs. TCU (7) (Fort Worth Classic, 1921) (9 made)
8—Jeremy Aldrich, Colorado (62) vs. Boston College (28) (Insight.com, 1999) (8 made)
8—Cary Blanchard, Oklahoma St. (62) vs. Wyoming (14) (Holiday, 1988) (8 made)
8—Ken Crots, Toledo (56) vs. Davidson (33) (Tangerine, 1969) (8 made)
7—Martin Gramatica, Kansas St. (54) vs. Colorado St. (21) (Holiday, 1995) (6 made)
7—Tony Rogers, Texas Tech (55) vs. Air Force (41) (Copper, 1995) (7 made)
7—Cole Ford, Southern California (55) vs. Texas Tech (14) (Cotton, 1995) (7 made)
7—Scott Blanton, Oklahoma (48) vs. Virginia (14) (Gator, Dec. 29, 1991) (6 made)
7—(D) Barry Belli, Fresno St. (51) vs. Bowling Green (7) (California, 1985) (7 made)
7—(D) Tom Nichol, Iowa (55) vs. Texas (17) (Freedom, 1984) (7 made)
7—Juan Cruz, Arizona St. (49) vs. Missouri (35) (Fiesta, 1972) (7 made)
7—Ron Sewell, North Carolina St. (49) vs. West Virginia (13) (Peach, 1972) (7 made)
7—Don Ekstrand, Arizona St. (48) vs. North Carolina (26) (Peach, 1970) (6 made)
7—Bill McMillan, Houston (49) vs. Miami (Ohio) (21) (Tangerine, 1962) (7 made)
7—Jesse Whittenton, UTEP (47) vs. Florida St. (20) (Sun, 1955) (5 made)
7—Jim Brieske, Michigan (49) vs. UCLA (0) (Rose, 1948) (7 made)
7—(D) Pat Bailey, Hardin-Simmons (49) vs. Wichita St. (12) (Camellia, 1948) (7 made)

MOST EXTRA-POINT KICKS MADE
9—Neil Rackers, Illinois (63) vs. Virginia (21) (Micronpc.com, 1999) (9 attempts)
9—Layne Talbot, Texas A&M (65) vs. Brigham Young (14) (Holiday, 1990) (9 attempts)
9—(D) James Weaver, Centre (63) vs. TCU (7) (Fort Worth Classic, 1921) (9 attempts)
8—Jeremy Aldrich, Colorado (62) vs. Boston College (28) (Insight.com, 1999) (8 attempts)
8—Cary Blanchard, Oklahoma St. (62) vs. Wyoming (14) (Holiday, 1988) (8 attempts)
8—Ken Crots, Toledo (56) vs. Davidson (33) (Tangerine, 1969) (8 attempts)
7—Tony Rogers, Texas Tech (55) vs. Air Force (41) (Copper, 1995) (7 attempts)
7—Cole Ford, Southern California (55) vs. Texas Tech (14) (Cotton, 1995) (7 attempts)
7—(D) Barry Belli, Fresno St. (51) vs. Bowling Green (7) (California, 1985) (7 attempts)
7—(D) Tom Nichol, Iowa (55) vs. Texas (17) (Freedom, 1984) (7 attempts)
7—Juan Cruz, Arizona St. (49) vs. Missouri (35) (Fiesta, 1972) (7 attempts)
7—Ron Sewell, North Carolina St. (49) vs. West Virginia (13) (Peach, 1972) (7 attempts)
7—Bill McMillan, Houston (49) vs. Miami (Ohio) (21) (Tangerine, 1962) (7 attempts)
7—Bobby Luna, Alabama (61) vs. Syracuse (6) (Orange, 1953) (9 attempts)
7—Jim Brieske, Michigan (49) vs. UCLA (0) (Rose, 1948) (7 attempts)
7—(D) Pat Bailey, Hardin-Simmons (49) vs. Wichita St. (12) (Camellia, 1948) (7 attempts)

MOST POINTS BY A KICKER
16—Kyle Bryant, Texas A&M (22) vs. Michigan (20) (Alamo, 1995) (5 FGs, 1 PAT)
16—Tim Rogers, Mississippi St. (24) vs. North Carolina St. (28) (Peach, Jan. 1, 1995) (5 FGs, 1 PAT)
16—Arden Czyzewski, Florida (28) vs. Notre Dame (39) (Sugar, 1992) (5 FGs, 1 PAT)
15—Jeremy Aldrich, Colorado (51) vs. Oregon (43) (Aloha, 1998) (3 FGs, 6 PATs)
15—Jess Atkinson, Maryland (23) vs. Tennessee (30) (Florida Citrus, 1983) (5 FGs)
15—David Hardy, Texas A&M (33) vs. Oklahoma St. (16) (Independence, 1981) (4 FGs, 3 PATs)
15—Paul Rogers, Nebraska (45) vs. Georgia (6) (John Hancock, 1969) (4 FGs, 3 PATs)
14—Jeremy Aldrich, Colorado (62) vs. Boston College (28) (Insight.com, 1999) (2 FGs, 8 PATs)
14—Cary Blanchard, Oklahoma St. (62) vs. Wyoming (14) (Holiday, 1988) (2 FGs, 8 PATs)
14—Paul Woodside, West Virginia (26) vs. Florida (6) (Peach, Dec. 31, 1981) (4 FGs, 2 PATs)
13—Chad Holcomb, East Caro. (19) vs. Stanford (13) (Liberty, 1995) (4 FGs, 1 PAT)
13—Kanon Parkman, Georgia (27) vs. Virginia (34) (Peach, Dec. 30, 1995) (4 FGs, 1 PAT)
13—Tony Rogers, Texas Tech (55) vs. Air Force (41) (Copper, 1995) (2 FGs, 7 PATs)
13—Damon Shea, Nevada (37) vs. Toledo (40) (ot) (Las Vegas, 1995) (3 FGs, 4 PATs)
13—Cole Ford, Southern California (55) vs. Texas Tech (14) (Cotton, 1995) (2 FGs, 7 PATs)
13—Tim Lashar, Oklahoma (25) vs. Penn. St. (10) (Orange, 1986) (4 FGs, 1 PAT)
13—John Lee, UCLA (39) vs. Miami (Fla.) (37) (Fiesta, 1985) (3 FGs, 4 PATs)
13—(D) Tom Nichol, Iowa (55) vs. Texas (17) (Freedom, 1984) (2 FGs, 7 PATs)
13—(D) Todd Gregoire, Wisconsin (19) vs. Kentucky (20) (Hall of Fame, 1984) (4 FGs, 1 PAT)
13—Bob Lucchesi, Missouri (19) vs. Southern Miss. (17) (Tangerine, 1981) (4 FGs, 1 PAT)
13—Dave Johnson, Brigham Young (37) vs. Indiana (38) (Holiday, 1979) (3 FGs, 4 PATs)
12—Billy Malashevich, Marshall (48) vs. Louisville (29) (Motor City, 1998) (2 FGs, 6 PATs)
12—Scott Bentley, Florida St. (18) vs. Nebraska (16) (Orange, 1994) (4 FGs)
12—Chris Gardocki, Clemson (30) vs. Illinois (0) (Hall of Fame, 1991) (3 FGs, 3 PATs)
12—Ray Tarasi, Penn St. (50) vs. Brigham Young (39) (Holiday, 1989) (3 FGs, 3 PATs)
12—Luis Zendejas, Arizona St. (32) vs. Oklahoma (21) (Fiesta, 1983) (3 FGs, 3 PATs)
12—Dale Castro, Maryland (20) vs. Florida (35) (Tangerine, 1980) (4 FGs)
12—Nathan Ritter, North Carolina St. (30) vs. Pittsburgh (17) (Tangerine, 1978) (3 FGs, 3 PATs)
12—Buckey Berrey, Alabama (36) vs. UCLA (6) (Liberty, 1976) (3 FGs, 3 PATs)
12—Al Vitiello, Penn St. (30) vs. Texas (6) (Cotton, 1972) (3 FGs, 3 PATs)
12—Frank Fontes, Florida St. (38) vs. Arizona St. (45) (Fiesta, 1971) (3 FGs, 3 PATs)

Punting

MOST PUNTS
21—Everett Sweeney, Michigan (49) vs. Stanford (0) (Rose, 1902)
16—Lem Pratt, New Mexico St. (14) vs. Hardin-Simmons (14) (Sun, 1936) (38.4 average)
14—Sammy Baugh, TCU (3) vs. LSU (2) (Sugar, 1936)
13—Hugh Keeney, Rice (8) vs. Tennessee (0) (Orange, 1947)
13—N. A. Keithley, Tulsa (6) vs. Texas Tech (0) (Sun, 1942) (37.0 average)
13—Hugh McCullough, Oklahoma (0) vs. Tennessee (17) (Orange, 1939) (40.6 average)
13—Tyler, Hardin-Simmons (14) vs. New Mexico St. (14) (Sun, 1936) (45.2 average)
13—(D) Tom Murphy, Arkansas (7) vs. Centenary (La.) (7) (Dixie Classic, 1934) (44.0 average)
12—Mitch Berger, Colorado (25) vs. Alabama (30) (Blockbuster, 1991) (41.0 average)
12—Bob Parsons, Penn St. (10) vs. Missouri (3) (Orange, 1970) (42.6 average)
12—Jim Callahan, Texas Tech (0) vs. Tulsa (6) (Sun, 1942) (43.0 average)
12—Mike Palm, Penn St. (3) vs. Southern California (14) (Rose, 1923)

HIGHEST AVERAGE PER PUNT
(Minimum 5 Punts)
52.7—Des Koch, Southern California (7) vs. Wisconsin (0) (Rose, 1953) (7 for 369) (adjusted to current statistical rules)
52.4—Mike Sochko, Maryland (21) vs. Houston (30) (Cotton, 1977) (5 for 262)
52.0—Nick Gallery, Iowa (27) vs. Texas Tech (0) (Alamo, 1996) (5 for 260)
51.5—Nick Pietsch, Colorado (51) vs. Oregon (43) (Aloha, 1998) (6 for 309)
51.0—Chris Clauss, Penn St. (10) vs. Clemson (35) (Florida Citrus, 1988) (5 for 255)
50.0—Dana Moore, Mississippi St. (17) vs. Nebraska (31) (Sun, 1980) (5 for 250)
49.3—Chris McInally, Clemson (0) vs. Syracuse (41) (Gator, 1996) (6 for 296)
49.2—(D) Mark Simon, Air Force (24) vs. Texas (16) (Bluebonnet, 1985) (11 for 541)
49.2—Allen Meacham, Arkansas (3) vs. UCLA (17) (Cotton, 1989) (6 for 295)
49.0—Jim DiGuilio, Indiana (24) vs. Baylor (0) (Copper, 1991) (6 for 294)
49.0—(D) Dana Moore, Mississippi St. (10) vs. Kansas (0) (Hall of Fame, 1981) (9 for 441)
48.3—Jesse Sowards, Brigham Young (3) vs. Marshall (21) (Motor City, 1999) (7 for 338)
48.1—Robby Stevenson, Florida (52) vs. Florida St. (20) (Sugar, 1997) (7 for 337)
48.1—Brent Bartholomew, Ohio St. (14) vs. Tennessee (20) (Florida Citrus, 1996) (7 for 337)
48.0—Dan Eichloff, Kansas (23) vs. Brigham Young (20) (Aloha, 1992) (8 for 384)
47.9—Doug Helkowski, Penn St. (42) vs. Tennessee (17) (Fiesta, 1992) (9 for 431)
47.8—(D) Kevin Buenafe, UCLA (14) vs. Michigan (33) (Bluebonnet, 1981) (8 for 382)
47.6—Todd Thomsen, Oklahoma (42) vs. Arkansas (8) (Orange, 1987) (5 for 238)
47.5—Jerry Dowd, St. Mary's (Cal.) (20) vs. Texas Tech (13) (Cotton, 1939) (11 for 523)

INDIVIDUAL RECORD LISTS—PUNTING 319

47.4—Jason Bender, Georgia Tech (18) vs. Stanford (17) (Aloha, 1991) (7 for 332)
47.4—(D) Mike Mancini, Fresno St. (51) vs. Bowling Green (7) (California, 1985) (7 for 332)
47.4—(D) Jimmy Colquitt, Tennessee (28) vs. Wisconsin (21) (Garden State, 1981) (5 for 237)

Punt Returns

MOST PUNT RETURNS
9—Buzy Rosenberg, Georgia (7) vs. North Carolina (3) (Gator, Dec. 31, 1971) (54 yards)
9—Paddy Driscoll, Great Lakes (17) vs. Mare Island (0) (Rose, 1919) (115 yards)
8—Thomas Lewis, Indiana (20) vs. Virginia Tech (45) (Independence, 1993) (58 yards)
6—Dale Carter, Tennessee (17) vs. Penn St. (42) (Fiesta, 1992)
6—Joey Smith, Louisville (34) vs. Alabama (7) (Fiesta, 1991) (35 yards)
6—David Palmer, Alabama (30) vs. Colorado (25) (Blockbuster, 1991) (74 yards)
6—(D) Hesh Colar, San Jose St. (48) vs. Central Mich. (24) (California, 1990)
6—David Kintigh, Miami (Fla.) (10) vs. Penn St. (14) (Fiesta, 1987) (32 yards)
6—(D) Eric Metcalf, Texas (16) vs. Air Force (24) (Bluebonnet, 1985) (49 yards)
6—Vai Sikahema, Brigham Young (7) vs. Ohio St. (10) (Florida Citrus, 1985)
6—Ray Horton, Washington (21) vs. Maryland (20) (Aloha, 1982) (28 yards)
6—Bill Gribble, Washington St. (36) vs. Brigham Young (38) (Holiday, 1981) (39 yards)
6—Johnny Rodgers, Nebraska (38) vs. Alabama (6) (Orange, 1972) (136 yards)
6—Rick Sygar, Michigan (34) vs. Oregon St. (7) (Rose, 1965) (50 yards)
6—Billy Hair, Clemson (0) vs. Miami (Fla.) (14) (Gator, 1952) (73 yards)
6—Don Zimmerman, Tulane (12) vs. Southern California (21) (Rose, 1932)

MOST PUNT RETURN YARDS
136—Johnny Rodgers, Nebraska (38) vs. Alabama (6) (Orange, 1972) (6 returns)
122—George Fleming, Washington (44) vs. Wisconsin (8) (Rose, 1960) (3 returns)
122—Bobby Kellogg, Tulane (13) vs. Texas A&M (14) (Sugar, 1940) (5 returns)
115—Paddy Driscoll, Great Lakes (17) vs. Mare Island (0) (Rose, 1919) (9 returns)
110—James Henry, Southern Miss. (38) vs. UTEP (18) (Independence, 1988) (2 returns, touchdowns of 65 and 45 yards)
106—Kevin Baugh, Penn St. (27) vs. Georgia (23) (Sugar, 1983) (5 returns)
106—Steve Holden, Arizona St. (45) vs. Florida St. (38) (Fiesta, 1971) (3 returns)
104—Leo Daniels, Texas A&M (21) vs. Alabama (29) (Cotton, 1942) (5 returns)
103—Jon Staggers, Missouri (3) vs. Penn St. (10) (Orange, 1970)
89—Lawrence Williams, Texas Tech (28) vs. North Carolina (32) (Sun, 1972) (5 returns)
88—Ben Kelly, Colorado (62) vs. Boston College (28) (Insight.com, 1999) (1 return)
87—Vai Sikahema, Brigham Young (46) vs. Southern Methodist (45) (Holiday, 1980) (2 returns)
86—Bobby Majors, Tennessee (34) vs. Air Force (13) (Sugar, 1971) (4 returns)
86—Aramis Dandoy, Southern California (7) vs. Ohio St. (20) (Rose, 1955) (1 return)
82—Marcus Wall, North Carolina (31) vs. Texas (35) (Sun, 1994) (1 return)
82—Willie Drewrey, West Virginia (12) vs. Florida St. (31) (Gator, 1982) (1 return)
80—(D) Gary Anderson, Arkansas (34) vs. Tulane (15) (Hall of Fame, 1980) (2 returns)
80—Cecil Ingram, Alabama (61) vs. Syracuse (6) (Orange, 1953) (1 return)

HIGHEST PUNT RETURN AVERAGE
(Minimum 3 Returns)
40.7—George Fleming, Washington (44) vs. Wisconsin (8) (Rose, 1960) (3 for 122)
35.3—Steve Holden, Arizona St. (45) vs. Florida St. (38) (Fiesta, 1971) (3 for 106)
24.4—Bobby Kellogg, Tulane (13) vs. Texas A&M (14) (Sugar, 1940) (5 for 122)
24.0—Shayne Wasden, Auburn (31) vs. Ohio St. (14) (Hall of Fame, 1990) (3 for 72)
22.7—Johnny Rodgers, Nebraska (38) vs. Alabama (6) (Orange, 1972) (6 for 136)
21.5—Bobby Majors, Tennessee (34) vs. Air Force (13) (Sugar, 1971) (4 for 86)
21.0—Tiki Barber, Virginia (34) vs. Georgia (27) (Peach, Dec. 30, 1995) (3 for 63)
21.0—(D) Brian Williams, Kentucky (16) vs. West Virginia (20) (Hall of Fame, 1983) (3 for 63)
20.8—Leo Daniels, Texas A&M (21) vs. Alabama (29) (Cotton, 1942) (5 for 104)
19.5—(D) Zippy Morocco, Georgia (20) vs. Texas A&M (40) (Presidential Cup, 1950) (4 for 78)
19.3—Dave Liegi, Nebraska (14) vs. Houston (17) (Cotton, 1980) (3 for 58)
19.0—Gary Moss, Georgia (10) vs. Texas (9) (Cotton, 1984) (3 for 57)

Kickoff Returns

MOST KICKOFF RETURNS
7—Dale Carter, Tennessee (17) vs. Penn St. (42) (Fiesta, 1992) (132 yards)
7—Jeff Sydner, Hawaii (13) vs. Michigan St. (33) (Aloha, 1989) (174 yards)
7—Homer Jones, Brigham Young (37) vs. Indiana (38) (Holiday, 1979) (126 yards)
6—Mike Rigell, Brigham Young (27) vs. Tulane (41) (Liberty, 1998) (220 yards)
6—Deltha O'Neal, California (38) vs. Navy (42) (Aloha, 1996) (186 yards)
6—Dave Beazley, Northwestern (28) vs. Tennessee (48) (Florida Citrus, 1997) (137 yards)
6—Eugene Napoleon, West Virginia (21) vs. Notre Dame (34) (Fiesta, 1989) (107 yards)
6—Tim Brown, Notre Dame (10) vs. Texas A&M (35) (Cotton, 1988) (129 yards)
6—Leroy Thompson, Penn St. (10) vs. Clemson (35) (Florida Citrus, 1988)
6—(D) Anthony Roberson, Air Force (28) vs. Arizona St. (33) (Freedom, 1987) (109 yards)
6—Casey Tiumalu, Brigham Young (17) vs. Ohio St. (47) (Holiday, 1982) (116 yards)
6—Brian Nelson, Texas Tech (17) vs. Florida St. (40) (Tangerine, 1977) (143 yards)
6—Wally Henry, UCLA (6) vs. Alabama (36) (Liberty, 1976)
6—Steve Williams, Alabama (6) vs. Nebraska (38) (Orange, 1972)
6—Mike Fink, Missouri (35) vs. Arizona St. (49) (Fiesta, 1972) (203 yards)

MOST KICKOFF RETURN YARDS
220—Mike Rigell, Brigham Young (27) vs. Tulane (41) (Liberty, 1998) (6 returns)
203—Mike Fink, Missouri (35) vs. Arizona St. (49) (Fiesta, 1972) (6 returns)
186—Deltha O'Neal, California (38) vs. Navy (42) (Aloha, 1996) (6 returns)
178—Al Hoisch, UCLA (14) vs. Illinois (45) (Rose, 1947) (4 returns)
174—Jeff Sydner, Hawaii (13) vs. Michigan St. (33) (Aloha, 1989) (7 returns)
169—Jerome Thomas, Idaho (42) vs. Southern Miss. (35) (Humanitarian, 1998) (5 returns)
166—Willie Jones, Iowa St. (30) vs. Georgia Tech (31) (Liberty, 1972) (4 returns)
154—(D) Martin Mitchell, Tulane (7) vs. Houston (47) (Bluebonnet, 1973) (5 returns)
154—Dave Lowery, Brigham Young (21) vs. Oklahoma St. (49) (Tangerine, 1976) (4 returns)
148—Earl Allen, Houston (28) vs. Boston College (45) (Cotton, 1985) (4 returns)
147—Carlos Snow, Ohio St. (17) vs. Syracuse (24) (Hall of Fame, 1992) (4 returns)
144—Clint Johnson, Notre Dame (39) vs. Florida (28) (Sugar, 1992) (5 returns)
143—Barry Smith, Florida St. (38) vs. Arizona St. (45) (Fiesta, 1971) (5 returns)
143—Brian Nelson, Texas Tech (17) vs. Florida St. (40) (Tangerine, 1977) (6 returns)

HIGHEST KICKOFF RETURN AVERAGE
(Minimum 2 Returns)
60.5—(D) Bob Smith, Texas A&M (40) vs. Georgia (20) (Presidential Cup, 1950) (2 for 121)
60.0—Jerome Pathon, Washington (21) vs. Colorado (33) (Holiday, 1996) (2 for 120)
58.0—Eddie Kennison, LSU (45) vs. Michigan St. (26) (Independence, 1995) (2 for 116)
57.5—Pete Panuska, Tennessee (27) vs. Maryland (28) (Sun, 1984) (2 for 115)
55.5—Todd Snyder, Ohio (42) vs. Richmond (49) (Tangerine, 1968) (2 for 111)
46.7—(D) Cal Beck, Utah (16) vs. Arizona (13) (Freedom, 1994) (3 for 140)
44.5—Al Hoisch, UCLA (14) vs. Illinois (45) (Rose, 1947) (4 for 178)
43.7—Larry Key, Florida St. (40) vs. Texas Tech (17) (Tangerine, 1977) (3 for 131)
41.5—Willie Jones, Iowa St. (30) vs. Georgia Tech (31) (Liberty, 1972) (4 for 166)
41.0—Kevin Williams, Miami (Fla.) (46) vs. Texas (3) (Cotton, 1991) (2 for 82)
40.3—(D) Willie Gault, Tennessee (28) vs. Wisconsin (21) (Garden State, 1981) (3 for 121)
39.0—Damon Dunn, Stanford (13) vs. East Caro. (19) (Liberty, 1995) (3 for 117)
37.0—Earl Allen, Houston (28) vs. Boston College (45) (Cotton, 1985) (4 for 148)
36.8—Carlos Snow, Ohio St. (17) vs. Syracuse (24) (Hall of Fame, 1992) (4 for 147)
36.7—Mike Rigell, Brigham Young (27) vs. Tulane (41) (Liberty, 1998) (6 for 220)
33.8—Mike Fink, Missouri (35) vs. Arizona St. (49) (Fiesta, 1972) (6 for 203)
33.8—Demetrius Allen, Virginia (34) vs. Georgia (27) (Peach, Dec. 30, 1995) (4 for 135)
33.8—Jerome Thomas, Idaho (42) vs. Southern Miss. (35) (Humanitarian, 1998) (5 for 169)
33.2—Hudhaifa Ismaeli, Northwestern (32) vs. Southern California (41) (Rose, 1996) (5 for 166)
33.0—Derrick Mason, Michigan St. (26) vs. LSU (45) (Independence, 1995) (4 for 132)
32.6—Jim McElroy, UCLA (30) vs. Kansas (51) (Aloha, 1995) (5 for 163)
32.5—Reidel Anthony, Florida (24) vs. Nebraska (62) (Fiesta, 1996) (6 for 195)
32.0—Harry Jones, Kentucky (20) vs. TCU (7) (Cotton, 1952) (2 for 64)
32.0—Jim Brown, Syracuse (27) vs. TCU (28) (Cotton, 1957) (3 for 96)
32.0—(D) Eric Alozie, Washington (34) vs. Florida (7) (Freedom, 1989) (2 for 64)

Interceptions

MOST INTERCEPTIONS MADE
4—Jim Dooley, Miami (Fla.) (14) vs. Clemson (0) (Gator, 1952)
4—(D) Manuel Aja, Arizona St. (21) vs. Xavier (Ohio) (33) (Salad, 1950)
3—Michael Brooks, North Carolina St. (28) vs. Iowa (23) (Peach, Dec. 31, 1988)
3—Bud Hebert, Oklahoma (24) vs. Florida St. (7) (Orange, 1980)
3—Louis Campbell, Arkansas (13) vs. Tennessee (14) (Liberty, 1971)
3—Bud McClinton, Auburn (34) vs. Arizona (10) (Sun, 1968)
3—(D) Les Derrick, Texas (19) vs. Mississippi (0) (Bluebonnet, 1966)
3—(D) Tommy Luke, Mississippi (0) vs. Texas (19) (Bluebonnet, 1966)
3—Jerry Cook, Texas (12) vs. Mississippi (7) (Cotton, 1962)
3—Ray Brown, Mississippi (39) vs. Texas (7) (Sugar, 1958)
3—Bill Paulman, Stanford (7) vs. Southern Methodist (0) (Rose, 1936)
3—Shy Huntington, Oregon (14) vs. Pennsylvania (0) (Rose, 1917)

MOST INTERCEPTION RETURN YARDAGE
148—Elmer Layden, Notre Dame (27) vs. Stanford (10) (Rose, 1925) (2 interceptions)
95—Marcus Washington, Colorado (38) vs. Oregon (6) (Cotton, 1996) (1 interception)
94—David Baker, Oklahoma (48) vs. Duke (21) (Orange, 1958) (1 interception)
90—Norm Beal, Missouri (21) vs. Navy (14) (Orange, 1961) (1 interception)
90—Charlie Brembs, South Carolina (14) vs. Wake Forest (26) (Gator, 1946) (1 interception)
89—Al Hudson, Miami (Fla.) (13) vs. Holy Cross (6) (Orange, 1946) (1 interception)
88—Dwayne Rudd, Alabama (17) vs. Michigan (14) (Outback, 1997) (1 interception)
81—Gary Moss, Georgia (24) vs. Boston College (27) (Hall of Fame, 1986) (1 interception)
80—Russ Meredith, West Virginia (21) vs. Gonzaga (13) (San Diego East-West Christmas Classic, 1922) (1 interception)
79—Michael Jordan, Tulane (41) vs. Brigham Young (27) (Liberty, 1998) (1 interception)
77—George Halas, Great Lakes (17) vs. Mare Island (0) (Rose, 1919) (1 interception)
75—Hugh Morrow, Alabama (26) vs. Duke (29) (Sugar, 1945) (1 interception)

BOWL/ALL-STAR RECORDS

72—Alton Montgomery, Houston (22) vs. Washington St. (24) (Aloha, 1988) (1 interception)
70—Robert Bailey, Mississippi (34) vs. Virginia Tech (17) (Liberty, 1968) (1 interception)
70—(D) Mel McGaha, Arkansas (21) vs. William & Mary (19) (Dixie, 1948) (1 interception)
69—Chris Carter, Texas (35) vs. North Carolina (31) (Sun, 1994) (1 interception)
69—Howard Ehler, Florida St. (36) vs. Oklahoma (19) (Gator, Jan. 2, 1965) (1 interception)
67—John Matsock, Michigan St. (28) vs. UCLA (20) (Rose, 1954) (2 interceptions)

All-Purpose Yards

(Includes All Runs From Scrimmage, Pass Receptions and All Returns)

MOST ALL-PURPOSE PLAYS
(Must Have at Least One Reception or Return)

47—(D) Ron Jackson, Tulsa (28) vs. San Diego St. (17) (Freedom, 1991) (46 rush, 1 reception)
46—Errict Rhett, Florida (27) vs. North Carolina St. (10) (Gator, 1992) (39 rush, 7 receptions)
42—Blake Ezor, Michigan St. (33) vs. Hawaii (13) (Aloha, 1989) (41 rush, 1 reception)
41—Terrell Fletcher, Wisconsin (34) vs. Duke (20) (Hall of Fame, 1995) (39 rush, 1 reception, 1 kickoff return)
40—LaDainian Tomlinson, TCU (28) vs. East Caro. (14) (Mobile Alabama, 1999) (36 rush, 4 receptions)
39—(D) Marshall Faulk, San Diego St. (17) vs. Tulsa (28) (Freedom, 1991) (30 rush, 9 receptions)
37—Wasean Tait, Toledo (40) vs. Nevada (37) (ot) (Las Vegas, 1995) (31 rush, 6 receptions)
37—Sherman Williams, Alabama (24) vs. Ohio St. (17) (Florida Citrus, 1995) (27 rush, 8 receptions, 2 kickoff returns)
37—O. J. Simpson, Southern California (16) vs. Ohio St. (27) (Rose, 1969) (28 rush, 8 receptions, 1 kickoff return)
36—Rondell Mealey, LSU (27) vs. Notre Dame (9) (Independence, 1997) (34 rush, 2 kickoff returns)
36—Thurman Thomas, Oklahoma St. (35) vs. West Virginia (33) (John Hancock Sun, 1987) (33 rush, 6 receptions)
36—Bob Anderson, Colorado (47) vs. Alabama (33) (Liberty, 1969) (35 rush, 1 kickoff return)
35—Mike Anderson, Utah (17) vs. Fresno St. (16) (Las Vegas, 1999) (34 rush, 1 reception)
35—Ricky Williams, Texas (38) vs. Mississippi St. (11) (Cotton, 1999) (30 rush, 5 receptions)
35—Ricky Ervins, Southern California (17) vs. Michigan (10) (Rose, 1990) (30 rush, 5 receptions)
35—(D) Eric Bieniemy, Colorado (17) vs. Brigham Young (20) (Freedom, 1988) (33 rush, 2 receptions)
33—Leon Johnson, North Carolina (20) vs. West Virginia (13) (Gator, 1996) (25 rush, 3 receptions, 1 punt return, 4 kickoff returns)
33—Shaumbe Wright-Fair, Washington St. (31) vs. Utah (28) (Copper, 1992) (27 rush, 6 receptions)
33—(D) Greg Lewis, Washington (34) vs. Florida (7) (Freedom, 1989) (27 rush, 6 receptions)
33—Bo Jackson, Auburn (16) vs. Texas A&M (36) (Cotton, 1986) (31 rush, 2 receptions)

MOST ALL-PURPOSE YARDS GAINED
(Must Have at Least One Reception or Return)

359—Sherman Williams, Alabama (24) vs. Ohio St. (17) (Florida Citrus, 1995) (166 rush, 155 receptions, 38 kickoff returns)
303—(D) Bob Smith, Texas A&M (40) vs. Georgia (20) (Presidential Cup, 1950) (160 rush, 22 receptions, 121 kickoff returns)
283—Andre Coleman, Kansas St. (52) vs. Wyoming (17) (Copper, 1993) (7 rush, 144 receptions, 73 punt returns, 54 kickoff returns)
278—Byron Hanspard, Texas Tech (55) vs. Air Force (41) (Copper, 1995) (260 rush, 18 receptions)
277—Bob Anderson, Colorado (47) vs. Alabama (33) (Liberty, 1969) (254 rush, 23 kickoff returns)
276—O. J. Simpson, Southern California (16) vs. Ohio St. (27) (Rose, 1969) (171 rush, 85 receptions, 20 kickoff returns)
272—Pat Johnson, Oregon (41) vs. Air Force (13) (Las Vegas, 1997) (169 receptions, 49 punt returns, 54 kickoff returns)
269—Mike Anderson, Utah (17) vs. Fresno St. (16) (Las Vegas, 1999) (254 rush, 15 receptions)
256—Terrell Fletcher, Wisconsin (34) vs. Duke (20) (Hall of Fame, 1995) (241 rush, 8 receptions, 7 kickoff returns)
256—Rondell Mealey, LSU (27) vs. Notre Dame (9) (Independence, 1997) (222 rush, 34 kickoff returns)
248—Ricky Williams, Texas (38) vs. Mississippi St. (11) (Cotton, 1999) (203 rush, 45 receptions)
247—(D) Wilford White, Arizona St. (21) vs. Miami (Ohio) (34) (Salad, 1951) (106 rush, 87 receptions, 54 kickoff returns)
246—Ernie Jones, Indiana (22) vs. Tennessee (27) (Peach, 1987) (15 rush, 150 receptions, 81 kickoff returns)
246—Demetrius Allen, Virginia (34) vs. Georgia (27) (Peach, Dec. 30, 1995) (111 receiving, 135 kickoff returns)

242—Errict Rhett, Florida (27) vs. North Carolina St. (10) (Gator, 1992) (182 rush, 60 receptions)
239—Tyrone Wheatley, Michigan (38) vs. Washington (31) (Rose, 1993) (235 rush, 4 receptions)
238—Wasean Tait, Toledo (40) vs. Nevada (37) (ot) (Las Vegas, 1995) (185 rush, 53 receptions)
237—Ahman Green, Nebraska (42) vs. Tennessee (17) (Orange, 1998) (206 rush, 31 receptions)
236—(D) Gary Anderson, Arkansas (34) vs. Tulane (15) (Hall of Fame, 1980) (156 rush, 80 punt returns)
230—Jamie Morris, Michigan (28) vs. Alabama (24) (Hall of Fame, 1987) (234 rush, -4 receptions)
228—Phillip Bobo, Washington St. (31) vs. Utah (28) (Copper, 1992) (16 rush, 212 receptions)
227—Marcus Wall, North Carolina (31) vs. Texas (35) (Sun, 1994) (30 rush, 82 receptions, 82 punt returns, 33 kickoff returns)
225—(D) Ron Jackson, Tulsa (28) vs. San Diego St. (17) (Freedom, 1991) (211 rush, 14 receptions)
223—Donny Anderson, Texas Tech (21) vs. Georgia Tech (31) (Gator, 1966) (85 rush, 138 receptions)
212—Troy Stradford, Boston College (45) vs. Houston (28) (Cotton, 1985) (196 rush, 16 receptions)
211—(D) Charles White, Southern California (47) vs. Texas A&M (28) (Bluebonnet, 1977) (186 rush, 25 receptions)
208—(D) Sheldon Canley, San Jose St. (48) vs. Central Mich. (24) (California, 1990) (164 rush, 44 receptions)

Defensive Statistics

MOST TOTAL TACKLES MADE
(Includes Assists)

31—Lee Roy Jordan, Alabama (17) vs. Oklahoma (0) (Orange, 1963)
22—Bubba Brown, Clemson (17) vs. Ohio St. (15) (Gator, 1978)
22—Gordy Ceresino, Stanford (24) vs. LSU (14) (Sun, Dec. 31, 1977)
20—Vada Murray, Michigan (10) vs. Southern California (17) (Rose, 1990)
20—(D) Gordy Ceresino, Stanford (25) vs. Georgia (22) (Bluebonnet, 1978)
18—Allen Stansberry, LSU (45) vs. Michigan St. (26) (Independence, 1995)
18—Ted Johnson, Colorado (41) vs. Notre Dame (24) (Fiesta, 1995)
18—Rod Smith, Notre Dame (39) vs. Florida (28) (Sugar, 1992)
18—Erick Anderson, Michigan (10) vs. Southern California (17) (Rose, 1990)
18—(D) Yepi Pauu, San Jose St. (27) vs. Eastern Mich. (30) (California, 1987)
18—Garland Rivers, Michigan (17) vs. Brigham Young (24) (Holiday, 1984)
18—(D) Terry Hubbard, Cal St. Fullerton (13) vs. Northern Ill. (20) (California, 1983)
18—(D) Don Turner, Fresno St. (29) vs. Bowling Green (28) (California, 1982)
18—Matt Millen, Penn St. (42) vs. Arizona St. (30) (Fiesta, 1977)

MOST UNASSISTED TACKLES

18—Rod Smith, Notre Dame (39) vs. Florida (28) (Sugar, 1992)
17—Garland Rivers, Michigan (17) vs. Brigham Young (24) (Holiday, 1984)
15—Lynn Evans, Missouri (35) vs. Arizona St. (49) (Fiesta, 1972)
15—(D) Ken Norton Jr., UCLA (31) vs. Brigham Young (10) (Freedom, 1986)
15—Randy Neal, Virginia (13) vs. Boston College (31) (Carquest, 1994)

MOST TACKLES MADE FOR LOSSES

5—(D) Michael Jones, Colorado (17) vs. Brigham Young (20) (Freedom, 1988) (20 yards)
5—Jimmy Walker, Arkansas (10) vs. UCLA (10) (Fiesta, 1978)
4—Courtney Brown, Penn St. (26) vs. Kentucky (14) (Outback, 1999)
4—Sedrick Hodge, North Carolina (20) vs. San Diego St. (13) (Las Vegas, 1998)
4—Mike Pringley, North Carolina (20) vs. San Diego St. (13) (Las Vegas, 1998)
4—Chike Okeafor, Purdue (37) vs. Kansas St. (34) (Alamo, 1998)
4—Corey Terry, Tennessee (48) vs. Northwestern (17) (Florida Citrus, 1997)
4—Clint Bruce, Navy (42) vs. California (38) (Aloha, 1996)
4—Montae Reagor, Texas Tech (0) vs. Iowa (27) (Alamo, 1996)
4—Reggie Garnett, Michigan St. (0) vs. Stanford (38) (Sun, 1996)
4—Matt Finkes, Ohio St. (14) vs. Tennessee (20) (Florida Citrus, 1996)
4—(D) Ken Norton Jr., UCLA (31) vs. Brigham Young (10) (Freedom, 1986)
3—Dat Nguyen, Texas A&M (14) vs. Ohio St. (24) (Sugar, 1999)
3—Cornelius Anthony, Texas A&M (14) vs. Ohio St. (24) (Sugar, 1999)
3—Eric Westmoreland, Tennessee (23) vs. Florida St. (16) (Fiesta, 1999)
3—Marc Matock, Southern California (19) vs. TCU (28) (Sun, 1998)
3—Kenny Smith, Alabama (7) vs. Virginia Tech (38) (Music City, 1998)
3—Chris Hoke, Brigham Young (27) vs. Tulane (41) (Liberty, 1998)
3—Raymone Lacey, TCU (28) vs. Southern California (19) (Sun, 1998)
3—James Hamilton, North Carolina (20) vs. West Virginia (13) (Gator, 1996)
3—Mike Vrabel, Ohio St. (14) vs. Tennessee (20) (Florida Citrus, 1996)
3—Nate Hemsley, Syracuse (41) vs. Clemson (0) (Gator, 1996)
3—Marcus Jones, North Carolina (20) vs. Arkansas (10) (Carquest, Dec. 30, 1995)
3—(D) Guy Boliaux, Wisconsin (21) vs. Tennessee (28) (Garden State, 1981)

MOST QUARTERBACK SACKS

6—Shay Muirbrook, Brigham Young (19) vs. Kansas St. (15) (Cotton, 1997)
4—Rusty Medearis, Miami (Fla.) (22) vs. Nebraska (0) (Orange, 1992)
4—Bobby Bell, Missouri (17) vs. Brigham Young (21) (Holiday, 1983)
3—Chike Okeafor, Purdue (37) vs. Kansas St. (34) (Alamo, 1998)
3—Andy Katzenmoyer, Ohio St. (20) vs. Arizona St. (17) (Rose, 1997)

INDIVIDUAL RECORD LISTS—DEFENSIVE STATISTICS 321

3—Travis Ochs, Kansas St. (15) vs. Brigham Young (19) (Cotton, 1997)
3—Trevor Pryce, Clemson (7) vs. LSU (10) (Peach, 1996)
3—Jamie Sharper, Virginia (21) vs. Miami (Fla.) (31) (Carquest, 1996)
3—Mike Crawford, Nevada (18) vs. Ball St. (15) (Las Vegas, 1996)
3—Gabe Northern, LSU (45) vs. Michigan St. (26) (Independence, 1995)
3—James Gillyard, LSU (45) vs. Michigan St. (26) (Independence, 1995)
3—Dewayne Harris, Miami (24) vs. Miami (Fla.) (17) (Orange, 1995)
3—Trev Alberts, Nebraska (16) vs. Florida St. (18) (Orange, 1994)
3—(D) Alfred Williams, Colorado (17) vs. Brigham Young (20) (Freedom, 1988)
3—(D) Jim Wahler, UCLA (31) vs. Brigham Young (10) (Freedom, 1986)
3—James Mosley, Texas Tech (17) vs. Mississippi (20) (Independence, 1986)
3—(D) Ernie Barnes, Mississippi St. (10) vs. Kansas (0) (Hall of Fame, 1981)

FUMBLE RECOVERIES
2—Rod Kirby, Pittsburgh (7) vs. Arizona St. (28) (Fiesta, 1973)
2—(D) Michael Stewart, Fresno St. (51) vs. Bowling Green (7) (California, 1985)
2—Randall Brown, Ohio St. (17) vs. Alabama (24) (Florida Citrus, 1995)

BLOCKED KICKS
2—Carlton Williams, Pittsburgh (7) vs. Arizona St. (28) (Fiesta, 1973)

2—Bracey Walker, North Carolina (21) vs. Mississippi St. (17) (Peach, Jan. 2, 1993)

PASSES BROKEN UP
5—Dyshod Carter, Kansas St. (34) Purdue (37) (Alamo, 1998)
4—Chris Cummings, LSU (27) vs. Notre Dame (9) (Independence, 1997)
3—Sedrick Curry, Texas A&M (14) vs. Ohio St. (24) (Sugar, 1999)
3—Ahmed Plummer, Ohio St. (24) vs. Texas A&M (14) (Sugar, 1999)
3—Damen Wheeler, Colorado (51) vs. Oregon (43) (Aloha, 1998)
3—Damion McIntosh, Kansas St. (34) vs. Purdue (37) (Alamo, 1998)
3—Kevin Hill, Idaho (42) vs. Southern Miss. (35) (Humanitarian, 1998)
3—Robert Williams, North Carolina (20) vs. West Virginia (13) (Gator, 1996)
3—Mark Tate, Penn St. (43) vs. Auburn (14) (Outback, 1996)
3—Kwame Ellis, Stanford (13) vs. East Caro. (19) (Liberty, 1995)
3—Mickey Dalton, Air Force (41) vs. Texas Tech (55) (Copper, 1995)
3—Barron Miles, Nebraska (24) vs. Miami (Fla.) (17) (Orange, 1995)
3—Sam McKiver, Virginia (20) vs. TCU (10) (Independence, 1994)
3—Percy Ellsworth, Virginia (20) vs. TCU (10) (Independence, 1994)
3—Tyrone Williams, Nebraska (16) vs. Florida St. (18) (Orange, 1994)
3—(D) John Herpin, Southern California (28) vs. Utah (21) (Freedom, 1993)
3—Demouy Williams, Washington (24) vs. Tulane (12) (Independence, 1987)

Team Record Lists

Only official records after 1937 are included. Prior records are included if able to be substantiated. Each team's score is in parentheses after the team name. Totals for each team in both-team records are in brackets after the team's score. The year listed is the actual (calendar) year the game was played; the date is included if the bowl was played twice (i.e., January and December) during one calendar year. The list also includes discontinued bowls, marked with (D). Bowls are listed by the name of the bowl at the time it was played: The Florida Citrus Bowl was the Tangerine Bowl in 1947-82; the first Hall of Fame Bowl (1977-85) was called the All-American Bowl in 1986-90; the second Hall of Fame Bowl (1986-95) is now called the Outback Bowl and is played in Tampa, Fla.; the Sun Bowl was called the John Hancock Bowl in 1989-93, the John Hancock Sun Bowl in 1987-88, and reverted to the Sun Bowl in 1994; the Blockbuster Bowl changed its name to the Carquest Bowl in 1993 and then to the Micronpc.com Bowl in 1998; and the Copper Bowl changed its name to the Insight.com Bowl in 1997.

Total Offense

MOST TOTAL PLAYS
96—North Carolina St. (10) vs. Arizona (17) (Copper, 1989) (310 yards)
95—Georgia (27) vs. Virginia (34) (Peach, Dec. 30, 1995) (525 yards)
95—Toledo (40) vs. Nevada (37) (ot) (Las Vegas, 1995) (561 yards)
95—North Carolina St. (28) vs. Iowa (23) (Peach, Dec. 31, 1988) (431 yards)
94—Arkansas (27) vs. Tennessee (31) (Cotton, 1990) (568 yards)
93—Miami (Fla.) (10) vs. Penn St. (14) (Fiesta, 1987) (445 yards)
92—Southern Miss. (35) vs. Idaho (42) (Humanitarian, 1998) (479 yards)
92—Oregon (20) vs. Penn St. (38) (Rose, 1995) (501 yards)
92—Washington St. (24) vs. Houston (22) (Aloha, 1988) (460 yards)
92—(D) Western Mich. (30) vs. Fresno St. (35) (California, 1988) (503 yards)
92—(D) Purdue (27) vs. Tennessee (22) (Bluebonnet, 1979) (483 yards)
92—Arizona St. (30) vs. Penn St. (42) (Fiesta, 1977) (426 yards)
91—Florida (28) vs. Notre Dame (39) (Sugar, 1992) (511 yards)
91—Baylor (21) vs. LSU (7) (Liberty, 1985) (489 yards)
90—Clemson (7) vs. Mississippi St. (17) (Peach, 1999) (391 yards)
90—Virginia Tech (25) vs. North Carolina St. (24) (Peach, 1986) (487 yards)
90—Maryland (0) vs. Texas (42) (Sun, 1978) (248 yards)
90—Nebraska (40) vs. Notre Dame (6) (Orange, 1973) (560 yards)
90—(D) Oklahoma (27) vs. Southern Methodist (28) (Bluebonnet, 1968)
90—Richmond (49) vs. Ohio (42) (Tangerine, 1968) (556 yards)

MOST TOTAL PLAYS, BOTH TEAMS
175—Toledo (40) [95] & Nevada (37) [80] (ot) (Las Vegas, 1995) (974 yards)
171—Auburn (34) [82] & Arizona (10) [89] (Sun, 1968) (537 yards)
167—Idaho (42) [75] & Southern Miss. (35) [92] (Humanitarian, 1998) (900 yards)
167—(D) Fresno St. (35) [75] & Western Mich. (30) [92] (California, 1988) (943 yards)
167—Arizona St. (45) [86] & Florida St. (38) [81] (Fiesta, 1971) (863 yards)
166—Colorado (47) [86] & Alabama (33) [80] (Liberty, 1969) (930 yards)
165—North Carolina St. (28) [95] & Iowa (23) [70] (Peach, Dec. 31, 1988)
165—East Caro. (35) [80] & Louisiana Tech (13) [85] (Independence, 1978) (607 yards)
165—Penn St. (42) [73] & Arizona St. (30) [92] (Fiesta, 1977) (777 yards)
163—Nebraska (45) [88] & Georgia (6) [75] (Sun, 1969) (540 yards)
162—Penn St. (38) [70] & Oregon (20) [92] (Rose, 1995) (931 yards)
161—Mississippi St. (17) [71] & Clemson (7) [90] (Peach, 1999) (656 yards)
161—Ohio St. (28) [78] & Pittsburgh (23) [83] (Fiesta, 1984) (897 yards)
161—Auburn (35) [84] & Mississippi (28) [77] (Gator, Jan. 2, 1971) (1,024 yards)

160—Boise St. (34) [81] & Louisville (31) [79] (Humanitarian, 1999) (936 yards)
160—Texas (35) [76] & North Carolina (31) [84] (Sun, 1994) (903 yards)
160—Texas Tech (55) [80] & Air Force (41) [80] (Copper, 1995) (1,120 yards)
160—Mississippi (42) [78] & Air Force (29) [82] (Liberty, 1989) (1,047 yards)
159—Notre Dame (39) [68] & Florida (28) [91] (Sugar, 1992) (944 yards)
159—Notre Dame (38) [85] & Texas (10) [74] (Cotton, 1978) (690 yards)
159—Texas (42) [69] & Maryland (0) [90] (Sun, 1978) (517 yards)

MOST YARDS GAINED
718—Arizona St. (49) vs. Missouri (35) (Fiesta, 1972) (452 rush, 266 pass)
715—Michigan (35) vs. Mississippi (3) (Gator, Jan. 1, 1991) (324 rush, 391 pass)
698—Oklahoma St. (62) vs. Wyoming (14) (Holiday, 1988) (320 rush, 378 pass)
680—Texas A&M (65) vs. Brigham Young (14) (Holiday, 1989) (356 rush, 324 pass)
655—(D) Houston (47) vs. Tulane (7) (Bluebonnet, 1973) (402 rush, 253 pass)
651—Brigham Young (39) vs. Penn St. (50) (Holiday, 1989) (75 rush, 576 pass)
646—Navy (42) vs. California (38) (Aloha, 1996) (251 rush, 395 pass)
642—(D) San Jose St. (48) vs. Central Mich. (24) (California, 1990) (200 rush, 442 pass)
629—Nebraska (62) vs. Florida (24) (Fiesta, 1996) (524 rush, 105 pass)
624—(D) Southern California (47) vs. Texas A&M (28) (Bluebonnet, 1977) (378 rush, 246 pass)
618—Oklahoma (48) vs. Virginia (14) (Gator, Dec. 29, 1991) (261 rush, 357 pass)
613—Marshall (48) vs. Louisville (29) (Motor City, 1998) (202 rush, 411 pass)
611—Illinois (63) vs. Virginia (21) (Micronpc.com, 1999) (325 rush, 286 pass)
606—Texas Tech (55) vs. Air Force (41) (Copper, 1995) (361 rush, 245 pass)
596—Alabama (61) vs. Syracuse (6) (Orange, 1953) (296 rush, 300 pass)
594—Miami (Fla.) (46) vs. North Carolina St. (23) (Micron PC, 1998) (269 rush, 325 pass)
589—UNLV (52) vs. Central Mich. (24) (Las Vegas, 1994) (301 rush, 288 pass)
583—Oregon (41) vs. Air Force (13) (Las Vegas, 1997) (266 rush, 317 pass)
578—Southern California (55) vs. Texas Tech (14) (Cotton, 1995) (143 rush, 435 pass)
575—Indiana (34) vs. South Carolina (10) (Liberty, 1988) (185 rush, 390 pass)
571—Louisville (34) vs. Alabama (7) (Fiesta, 1991) (113 rush, 458 pass)
569—Florida St. (34) vs. Oklahoma St. (23) (Gator, 1985) (231 rush, 338 pass)
568—Arkansas (27) vs. Tennessee (31) (Cotton, 1990) (361 rush, 207 pass)
566—Pittsburgh (34) vs. Clemson (3) (Gator, 1977) (179 rush, 387 pass)

MOST YARDS GAINED, BOTH TEAMS
1,143—(D) Southern California (47) [624] & Texas A&M (28) [519] (Bluebonnet, 1977) (148 plays)
1,129—Arizona St. (49) [718] & Missouri (35) [411] (Fiesta, 1972) (134 plays)
1,120—Texas Tech (55) [606] & Air Force (41) [514] (Copper, 1995) (160 plays)
1,115—Penn St. (50) [464] & Brigham Young (39) [651] (Holiday, 1989) (157 plays)
1,092—Miami (Fla.) (46) [594] & North Carolina St. (23) [498] (Micron PC, 1998) (149 plays)
1,080—Navy (42) [646] & California (38) [434] (Aloha, 1996) (147 plays)
1,048—Michigan (35) [715] & Mississippi (3) [333] (Gator, Jan. 1, 1991) (153 plays)
1,047—Mississippi (42) [533] & Air Force (29) [514] (Liberty, 1989) (160 plays)
1,045—Marshall (48) [611] & Louisville (29) [432] (Motor City, 1998) (144 plays)
1,038—Tennessee (31) [470] & Arkansas (27) [568] (Cotton, 1990) (155 plays)
1,035—Wisconsin (38) [497] & UCLA (31) [538] (Rose, 1999) (139 plays)
1,024—Auburn (35) [559] & Mississippi (28) [465] (Gator, Jan. 2, 1971) (161 plays)
1,018—Mississippi (34) [511] & Marshall (31) [507] (Motor City, 1997) (155 plays)
1,007—(D) Toledo (27) [486] & San Jose St. (25) [521] (California, 1981) (158 plays)
991—Illinois (63) [611] & Virginia (21) [380] (Micronpc.com, 1999) (145 plays)
978—Pittsburgh (31) [530] & Texas A&M (28) [448] (John Hancock, 1989) (158 plays)
974—Toledo (40) [561] & Nevada (37) [413] (ot) (Las Vegas, 1995) (175 plays)
965—UNLV (52) [589] & Central Mich. (24) [376] (Las Vegas, 1994) (145 plays)
954—Mississippi (27) [427] & Arkansas (22) [527] (Sugar, 1970)
950—Texas (40) [436] & Missouri (27) [514] (Cotton, 1946)
944—Notre Dame (39) [433] & Florida (28) [511] (Sugar, 1992) (159 plays)

BOWL/ALL-STAR RECORDS

HIGHEST AVERAGE GAINED PER PLAY
9.5—Louisville (34) vs. Alabama (7) (Fiesta, 1991) (60 for 571)
9.1—Miami (Fla.) (46) vs. North Carolina St. (23) (Micron PC, 1998) (65 for 594)
9.1—Navy (42) vs. California (38) (Aloha, 1996) (71 for 646)
8.9—Marshall (48) vs. Louisville (29) (Motor City, 1998) (69 for 613)
8.7—Oklahoma St. (62) vs. Wyoming (14) (Holiday, 1988) (80 for 698)
8.4—Michigan (35) vs. Mississippi (3) (Gator, Jan. 1, 1991) (85 for 715)
8.3—Texas A&M (65) vs. Brigham Young (14) (Holiday, 1990) (82 for 680)
8.3—Illinois (63) vs. Virginia (21) (Micronpc.com, 1999) (74 for 611)
8.1—Arizona St. (49) vs. Missouri (35) (Fiesta, 1972) (89 for 718)
8.0—Oregon (41) vs. Air Force (13) (Las Vegas, 1997) (73 for 583)
7.9—Brigham Young (39) vs. Penn St. (50) (Holiday, 1989) (82 for 651)
7.7—Alabama (61) vs. Syracuse (6) (Orange, 1953) (77 for 596)
7.7—(D) Vanderbilt (28) vs. Air Force (36) (Hall of Fame, 1982) (63 for 487)
7.7—Tennessee (31) vs. Arkansas (27) (Cotton, 1990) (61 for 470)
7.7—Kansas (51) vs. UCLA (30) (Aloha, 1995) (71 for 548)
7.6—Florida St. (41) vs. Nebraska (17) (Fiesta, 1990) (65 for 494)
7.6—Texas Tech (55) vs. Air Force (41) (Copper, 1995) (80 for 606)
7.6—Nebraska (62) vs. Florida (24) (Fiesta, 1996) (83 for 629)
7.5—Kansas St. (52) vs. Wyoming (17) (Copper, 1993) (71 for 536)
7.5—(D) Houston (47) vs. Tulane (7) (Bluebonnet, 1973) (87 for 655)
7.5—Iowa (38) vs. California (12) (Rose, 1959) (69 for 516)
7.5—Marshall (31) vs. Mississippi (34) (Motor City, 1997) (68 for 507)
7.4—(D) UCLA (31) vs. Brigham Young (10) (Freedom, 1986) (70 for 518)
7.3—(D) UNLV (30) vs. Toledo (13) (California, 1984) (56 for 409)
7.3—(D) San Jose St. (48) vs. Central Mich. (24) (California, 1990) (88 for 642)
7.3—UCLA (31) vs. Wisconsin (38) (Rose, 1999) (74 for 538)

FEWEST PLAYS
35—Tennessee (0) vs. Texas (16) (Cotton, 1953) (29 rush, 6 pass)
36—Arkansas (3) vs. UCLA (17) (Cotton, 1989) (22 rush, 14 pass)
37—TCU (0) vs. Oklahoma St. (34) (Cotton, 1945) (27 rush, 10 pass)
38—Iowa (3) vs. California (37) (Alamo, 1993) (21 rush, 17 pass)

FEWEST PLAYS, BOTH TEAMS
107—TCU (16) [54] & Marquette (6) [53] (Cotton, 1937)

FEWEST YARDS
-21—U. of Mexico (0) vs. Southwestern (Tex.) (35) (Sun, 1945) (29 rush, -50 pass)
23—Alabama (10) vs. Missouri (35) (Gator, 1968) (-45 rush, 68 pass)
32—Tennessee (0) vs. Texas (16) (Cotton, 1953) (-14 rush, 46 pass)
38—Miami (Fla.) (0) vs. Bucknell (26) (Orange, 1935) (20 rush, 18 pass)
41—Southern California (14) vs. Alabama (34) (Rose, 1946) (6 rush, 35 pass)
42—Arkansas (3) vs. UCLA (17) (Cotton, 1989) (21 rush, 21 pass)
48—New Mexico (0) vs. Southwestern (Tex.) (7) (Sun, 1944) (38 rush, 10 pass)
54—Arkansas (0) vs. LSU (0) (Cotton, 1947) (54 rush, 0 pass)
57—Michigan St. (0) vs. Auburn (6) (Orange, 1938) (32 rush, 25 pass)

FEWEST YARDS, BOTH TEAMS
260—Randolph Field (7) [150] & Texas (7) [110] (Cotton, 1944)
263—LSU (19) [92] & Texas A&M (14) [171] (Orange, 1944)

Rushing

MOST RUSHING ATTEMPTS
87—Oklahoma (40) vs. Auburn (22) (Sugar, Jan. 1, 1972) (439 yards)
82—Missouri (35) vs. Alabama (10) (Gator, 1968) (402 yards)
79—West Virginia (14) vs. South Carolina (3) (Peach, 1969) (356 yards)
79—Georgia Tech (31) vs. Texas Tech (21) (Gator, Dec. 31, 1965) (364 yards)
78—(D) Houston (35) vs. Navy (0) (Garden State, 1980) (405 yards)
78—Texas (16) vs. Tennessee (0) (Cotton, 1953) (296 yards)
76—Oklahoma (14) vs. Penn St. (0) (Sugar, Dec. 31, 1972) (278 yards)
74—Oklahoma (41) vs. Wyoming (7) (Fiesta, 1976) (415 yards)
74—Michigan (12) vs. Stanford (13) (Rose, 1972) (264 yards)
74—Ohio St. (20) vs. Southern California (7) (Rose, 1955) (305 yards)
73—Syracuse (31) vs. McNeese St. (7) (Independence, 1979) (276 yards)
73—Penn St. (41) vs. Oregon (12) (Liberty, 1960) (301 yards)
72—Arkansas (27) vs. Tennessee (31) (Cotton, 1990) (361 yards)
72—North Carolina St. (28) vs. Iowa (23) (Peach, Dec. 31, 1988) (236 yards)
72—Texas A&M (28) vs. Southern California (47) (Bluebonnet, 1977) (486 yards)

MOST RUSHING ATTEMPTS, BOTH TEAMS
122—(D) Southern California (47) [50] & Texas A&M (28) [72] (Bluebonnet, 1977) (864 yards)
122—Mississippi St. (26) [68] & North Carolina (24) [54] (Sun, 1974) (732 yards)
120—Pittsburgh (33) [53] & Kansas (19) [67] (Sun, 1975) (714 yards)
117—Oklahoma (14) [65] & Michigan (6) [52] (Orange, 1976) (451 yards)
117—West Virginia (14) [79] & South Carolina (3) [38] (Peach, 1969) (420 yards)
116—Oklahoma (41) [74] & Wyoming (7) [42] (Fiesta, 1976) (568 yards)
116—Colorado (47) [70] & Alabama (33) [46] (Liberty, 1969) (628 yards)
115—Southern California (7) [47] & Wisconsin (0) [68] (Rose, 1953) (259 yards)
113—Oklahoma (40) [54] & Houston (14) [59] (Sun, 1981) (566 yards)
113—(D) Houston (35) [78] & Navy (0) [35] (Garden State, 1980) (540 yards)
113—Missouri (34) [71] & Auburn (17) [42] (Sun, 1973) (408 yards)
112—Arkansas (31) [65] & Georgia (10) [47] (Cotton, 1976) (426 yards)
112—(D) Colorado (29) [62] & Houston (17) [50] (Bluebonnet, 1971) (552 yards)

MOST NET RUSHING YARDS
524—Nebraska (62) vs. Florida (24) (Fiesta, 1996) (68 attempts)
486—(D) Texas A&M (28) vs. Southern California (47) (Bluebonnet, 1977) (72 attempts)
473—Colorado (47) vs. Alabama (33) (Liberty, 1969) (70 attempts)
455—Mississippi St. (26) vs. North Carolina (24) (Sun, 1974) (68 attempts)
452—Arizona St. (49) vs. Missouri (35) (Fiesta, 1972) (65 attempts)
439—Oklahoma (40) vs. Auburn (22) (Sugar, Jan. 1, 1972) (87 attempts)
434—Oklahoma (41) vs. Wyoming (7) (Fiesta, 1976) (74 attempts)
431—Air Force (41) vs. Texas Tech (55) (Copper, 1995) (67 attempts)
429—Iowa (38) vs. California (12) (Rose, 1959) (55 attempts)
423—Auburn (33) vs. Baylor (13) (Gator, Dec. 31, 1954) (48 attempts)
423—(D) UCLA (31) vs. Brigham Young (10) (Freedom, 1986) (49 attempts)
417—Oklahoma (21) vs. Arizona St. (32) (Fiesta, 1983) (63 attempts)
411—Oklahoma (24) vs. Florida St. (7) (Orange, 1980) (62 attempts)
409—Oklahoma (40) vs. Houston (14) (Sun, 1981) (54 attempts)
409—Nebraska (42) vs. Tennessee (17) (Orange, 1998) (68 attempts)
408—Missouri (27) vs. Texas (40) (Cotton, 1946)
405—(D) Houston (35) vs. Navy (0) (Garden State, 1980) (78 attempts)
402—Houston (47) vs. Tulane (7) (Bluebonnet, 1973) (58 attempts)

MOST NET RUSHING YARDS, BOTH TEAMS
864—(D) Southern California (47) [378] & Texas A&M (28) [486] (Bluebonnet, 1977) (122 attempts)
792—Texas Tech (55) [361] & Air Force (41) [431] (Copper, 1995) (107 attempts)
732—Mississippi St. (26) [455] & North Carolina (24) [277] (Sun, 1974) (122 attempts)
714—Pittsburgh (33) [372] & Kansas (19) [342] (Sun, 1975) (120 attempts)
701—Arizona St. (49) [453] & Missouri (35) [248] (Fiesta, 1972) (109 attempts)
681—Tennessee (31) [320] & Arkansas (27) [361] (Cotton, 1990) (110 attempts)
643—Iowa (38) [429] & California (12) [214] (Rose, 1959) (108 attempts)
628—Colorado (47) [473] & Alabama (33) [155] (Liberty, 1969) (116 attempts)
616—Oklahoma (41) [434] & Wyoming (7) [182] (Fiesta, 1976) (116 attempts)
610—Texas (40) [202] & Missouri (27) [408] (Cotton, 1946)

HIGHEST RUSHING AVERAGE
(Minimum 30 Attempts)
9.3—Texas Tech (55) vs. Air Force (41) (Copper, 1995) (39 for 361)
8.6—(D) UCLA (31) vs. Brigham Young (10) (Freedom, 1986) (49 for 423)
8.6—Michigan (38) vs. Washington (31) (Rose, 1993) (36 for 308)
8.4—Tennessee (31) vs. Arkansas (27) (Cotton, 1990) (38 for 320)
8.0—Toledo (56) vs. Davidson (33) (Tangerine, 1969) (42 for 334)
7.8—Iowa (38) vs. California (12) (Rose, 1959) (55 for 429)
7.7—Texas Tech (28) vs. North Carolina (32) (Sun, 1972) (38 for 293)
7.7—Nebraska (62) vs. Florida (24) (Fiesta, 1996) (68 for 524)
7.6—Oklahoma (42) vs. Arkansas (8) (Orange, 1987) (48 for 366)
7.6—Oklahoma (40) vs. Houston (14) (Sun, 1981) (54 for 409)
7.6—(D) Southern California (47) vs. Texas A&M (28) (Bluebonnet, 1977) (50 for 378)
7.4—Michigan (35) vs. Mississippi (3) (Gator, Jan. 1, 1991) (53 for 391)
7.2—Boston College (28) vs. Colorado (62) (Insight.com, 1999) (51 for 365)
7.1—Wisconsin (38) vs. UCLA (31) (Rose, 1999) (48 for 343)
7.1—Boston College (45) vs. Houston (28) (Cotton, 1985) (50 for 353)
7.0—Pittsburgh (33) vs. Kansas (19) (Sun, 1975) (53 for 372)
7.0—Arizona St. (49) vs. Missouri (35) (Fiesta, 1972) (65 for 453)

FEWEST RUSHING ATTEMPTS
12—(D) Vanderbilt (28) vs. Air Force (36) (Hall of Fame, 1982) (35 yards)
16—Florida (18) vs. Missouri (20) (Sugar, 1966) (-2 yards)
16—Colorado (7) vs. LSU (25) (Orange, 1962) (24 yards)
17—(D) Duke (21) vs. Texas Tech (49) (All-American, 1989) (67 yards)
17—Illinois (9) vs. UCLA (45) (Rose, 1984) (0 yards)
18—Brigham Young (46) vs. Southern Methodist (45) (Holiday, 1980) (-2 yards)
19—Iowa (23) vs. North Carolina St. (28) (Peach, Dec. 31, 1988) (46 yards)
19—Baylor (13) vs. Auburn (33) (Gator, Dec. 31, 1954) (108 yards)
20—Utah St. (19) vs. Cincinnati (35) (Humanitarian, 1997) (76 yards)
20—(D) San Jose St. (27) vs. Eastern Mich. (30) (California, 1987) (81 yards)
20—Tulane (6) vs. Penn St. (9) (Liberty, 1979) (-8 yards)
21—Tennessee (17) vs. Nebraska (42) (Orange, 1998) (128 yards)
21—Florida (24) vs. Nebraska (62) (Fiesta, 1996) (-28 yards)
21—Iowa (3) vs. California (37) (Alamo, 1993) (20 yards)
21—Brigham Young (14) vs. Texas A&M (65) (Holiday, 1990) (-12 yards)
21—Houston (22) vs. Washington (24) (Aloha, 1988) (68 yards)
21—Wyoming (19) vs. Iowa (20) (Holiday, 1987) (43 yards)
21—(D) San Jose St. (25) vs. Toledo (27) (California, 1981) (54 yards)

FEWEST RUSHING ATTEMPTS, BOTH TEAMS
56—Mississippi (27) [33] & Oklahoma (25) [23] (Independence, 1999)
57—Iowa (20) [36] & Wyoming (19) [21] (Holiday, 1987)
59—Hawaii (23) [24] & Oregon St. (17) [35] (Oahu Classic, 1999)
60—Michigan (35) [23] & Alabama (34) [37] (ot) (Orange, 2000)
61—Marshall (21) [31] & Brigham Young (3) [30] (Motor City, 1999)
61—Arkansas (27) [36] & Texas (6) [25] (Cotton, 2000)
62—Mississippi (34) [39] & Marshall (31) [23] (Motor City, 1997)
63—Georgia (28) [34] & Purdue (25) [29] (ot) (Outback, 2000)
63—Auburn (21) [36] & Clemson (17) [27] (Peach, 1998)
63—(D) Southern California (28) [38] & Utah (21) [25] (Freedom, 1993)
65—Purdue (33) [28] & Oklahoma St. (20) [37] (Alamo, 1997)
66—Southern Miss. (23) [34] & Colorado St. (17) [32] (Liberty, 1999)
66—Southern California (41) [27] & Northwestern (32) [39] (Rose, 1996)
66—Brigham Young (13) [33] & Iowa (13) [33] (Holiday, 1991)

TEAM RECORD LISTS—RUSHING 323

66—Miami (Fla.) (23) [28] & Nebraska (3) [38] (Orange, 1989)
66—TCU (16) [34] & Marquette (6) [32] (Cotton, 1937)
67—Mississippi St. (17) [33] & Clemson (7) [34] (Peach, 1999)
67—UCLA (6) [41] & Illinois (3) [26] (John Hancock, 1991)
67—Southern California (7) [39] & Duke (3) [28] (Rose, 1939)
68—Tennessee (20) [32] & Ohio St. (14) [36] (Florida Citrus, 1996)
68—(D) Fresno St. (29) [24] & Bowling Green (28) [44] (California, 1982)
69—Michigan (21) [41] & Washington St. (16) [28] (Rose, 1998)
69—(D) Utah (16) [32] & Arizona (13) [37] (Freedom, 1994)

FEWEST RUSHING YARDS
-61—Kansas St. (7) vs. Boston College (12) (Aloha, 1994) (23 attempts)
-45—Alabama (10) vs. Missouri (35) (Gator, 1968) (29 attempts)
-30—Florida (6) vs. West Virginia (26) (Peach, Dec. 31, 1981) (34 attempts)
-28—Florida (24) vs. Nebraska (62) (Fiesta, 1996) (21 attempts)
-27—Texas (6) vs. Arkansas (27) (Cotton, 2000) (25 attempts)
-23—Southern California (19) vs. TCU (28) (Sun, 1998) (21 attempts)
-21—Florida St. (20) vs. Wyoming (28) (Sun, 1966) (31 attempts)
-16—Brigham Young (3) vs. Marshall (21) (Motor City, 1999) (30 attempts)
-15—LSU (0) vs. Mississippi (20) (Sugar, 1960)
-14—Navy (6) vs. Texas (28) (Cotton, 1964) (29 attempts)
-14—Tennessee (0) vs. Texas (16) (Cotton, 1953) (29 attempts)
-12—Brigham Young (14) vs. Texas A&M (65) (Holiday, 1990) (21 attempts)
-12—Air Force (13) vs. Tennessee (34) (Sugar, 1971)
-11—Colorado (25) vs. Alabama (30) (Blockbuster, 1991) (30 attempts)
-8—Tulane (6) vs. Penn St. (9) (Liberty, 1979) (20 attempts)
-8—Navy (14) vs. Missouri (21) (Orange, 1961) (24 attempts)
-5—Stanford (9) vs. Wisconsin (17) (Rose, 2000) (27 attempts)
-2—Brigham Young (46) vs. Southern Methodist (45) (Holiday, 1980) (24 attempts)
-2—Florida (18) vs. Missouri (20) (Sugar, 1966) (16 attempts)

FEWEST RUSHING YARDS, BOTH TEAMS
51—(D) Utah (16) [6] & Arizona (13) [45] (Freedom, 1994)
74—Tennessee (34) [86] & Air Force (13) [-12] (Sugar, 1971)
81—Washington St. (10) [7] & Baylor (3) [74] (Alamo, 1994)
81—Florida St. (23) [76] & Florida (17) [5] (Sugar, Jan. 2, 1995)
88—Boston College (12) [149] & Kansas St. (7) [-61] (Aloha, 1994)
131—Purdue (37) [5] & Kansas St. (34) [126] (Alamo, 1998)
131—Marshall (21) [147] & Brigham Young (3) [-16] (Motor City, 1999)
137—Iowa (20) [94] & Wyoming (19) [43] (Holiday, 1987)
143—Brigham Young (31) [71] & Oklahoma (6) [72] (Copper, 1994)
145—Arkansas (10) [45] & Nebraska (7) [100] (Cotton, 1965)
147—(D) San Jose St. (37) [123] & Miami (Ohio) (7) [24] (California, 1986)

LOWEST RUSHING AVERAGE
(Minimum 20 Attempts)
-2.7—Kansas St. (7) vs. Boston College (12) (Aloha, 1994) (23 for -61)
-1.6—Alabama (10) vs. Missouri (35) (Gator, 1968) (29 for -45)
-1.3—Florida (24) vs. Nebraska (62) (Fiesta, 1996) (21 for -28)
-1.1—Texas (6) vs. Arkansas (27) (Cotton, 2000) (25 for -27)
-1.1—Southern California (19) vs. TCU (28) (Sun, 1998) (21 for -23)
-0.9—Florida (6) vs. West Virginia (26) (Peach, Dec. 31, 1981) (32 for -30)
-0.7—Florida St. (20) vs. Wyoming (28) (Sun, 1966) (31 for -21)
-0.6—Brigham Young (14) vs. Texas A&M (65) (Holiday, 1990) (21 for -12)
-0.5—Brigham Young (3) vs. Marshall (21) (Motor City, 1999) (30 for -16)
-0.5—Navy (6) vs. Texas (28) (Cotton, 1964) (29 for -14)
-0.5—Tennessee (0) vs. Texas (16) (Cotton, 1953) (29 for -14)
-0.4—Colorado (25) vs. Alabama (30) (Blockbuster, 1991) (30 for -11)
-0.3—Navy (14) vs. Missouri (21) (Orange, 1961) (24 for -8)

RUSHING DEFENSE, FEWEST YARDS ALLOWED
-61—Boston College (12) vs. Kansas St. (7) (Aloha, 1994) (23 attempts)
-45—Missouri (35) vs. Alabama (10) (Gator, 1968) (29 attempts)
-30—West Virginia (26) vs. Florida (6) (Peach, Dec. 31, 1981) (32 attempts)
-28—Nebraska (62) vs. Florida (24) (Fiesta, 1996) (21 attempts)
-27—Texas (6) vs. Arkansas (27) (Cotton, 2000) (25 attempts)
-23—TCU (28) vs. Southern California (19) (Sun, 1998) (21 attempts)
-21—Wyoming (28) vs. Florida St. (20) (Sun, 1966) (31 attempts)
-16—Brigham Young (3) vs. Marshall (21) (Motor City, 1999) (30 attempts)
-15—Mississippi (20) vs. LSU (0) (Sugar, 1960)
-14—Texas (28) vs. Navy (6) (Cotton, 1964) (29 attempts)
-14—Texas (16) vs. Tennessee (0) (Cotton, 1953) (29 attempts)
-12—Texas A&M (65) vs. Brigham Young (14) (Holiday, 1990) (21 attempts)
-12—Tennessee (34) vs. Air Force (13) (Sugar, 1971)
-11—Alabama (30) vs. Colorado (25) (Blockbuster, 1991) (30 attempts)
-8—Penn St. (9) vs. Tulane (6) (Liberty, 1979) (20 attempts)
-8—Missouri (21) vs. Navy (14) (Orange, 1961) (24 attempts)
-5—Stanford (9) vs. Wisconsin (17) (Rose, 2000) (27 attempts)
-2—Southern Methodist (45) vs. Brigham Young (46) (Holiday, 1980) (24 attempts)
-2—Missouri (20) vs. Florida (18) (Sugar, 1966) (16 attempts)

Passing

MOST PASS ATTEMPTS
(Followed by Comp.-Att.-Int. and Yardage)
63—Fresno St. (30) vs. Colorado (41) (Aloha, 1993) (37-63-1, 523 yards)
63—(D) San Jose St. (25) vs. Toledo (27) (California, 1981) (43-63-5, 467 yards)
61—Oregon (20) vs. Penn St. (38) (Rose, 1995) (41-61-2, 456 yards)
61—(D) Brigham Young (16) vs. Virginia (22) (All-American, 1987) (37-61-1, 394 yards)

60—Purdue (25) vs. Georgia (28) (ot) (Outback, 2000) (36-60-1, 378 yards)
59—Georgia (27) vs. Virginia (34) (Peach, Dec. 30, 1995) (31-59-2, 413 yards)
59—Brigham Young (39) vs. Penn St. (50) (Holiday, 1989) (42-59-2, 576 yards)
58—Florida (28) vs. Notre Dame (39) (Sugar, 1992) (28-58-2, 370 yards)
58—Illinois (15) vs. Alabama (21) (Liberty, 1982) (35-58-7, 423 yards)
58—Richmond (49) vs. Ohio (42) (Tangerine, 1968) (39-58-2, 447 yards)
57—(D) Western Mich. (30) vs. Fresno St. (35) (California, 1988) (24-57-0, 366 yards)
56—Clemson (7) vs. Mississippi St. (17) (Peach, 1999) (25-56-5, 306 yards)
56—Miami (Fla.) (13) vs. Alabama (34) (Sugar, 1993) (24-56-3, 278 yards)
56—Washington (21) vs. Maryland (20) (Aloha, 1982) (35-56-0, 369 yards)
55—Illinois (29) vs. Army (31) (Peach, 1985) (38-55-2, 401 yards)
55—Florida St. (17) vs. Penn St. (17) (Gator, 1967) (38-55-4, 363 yards)
54—Oklahoma (25) vs. Mississippi (27) (Independence, 1999) (39-54-1, 390 yards)
54—Louisville (29) vs. Marshall (48) (Motor City, 1998) (35-54-1, 336 yards)
53—Purdue (37) vs. Kansas St. (34) (Alamo, 1998) (25-53-2, 230 yards)
52—Southern Miss. (35) vs. Idaho (42) (Humanitarian, 1998) (31-52-0, 312 yards)
52—Alabama (29) vs. Army (28) (John Hancock Sun, 1988) (33-52-1, 412 yards)
52—Louisiana Tech (13) vs. East Caro. (35) (Independence, 1978) (18-52-3, 263 yards)

MOST PASS ATTEMPTS, BOTH TEAMS
94—Mississippi St. (17) [38] & Clemson (7) [56] (Peach, 1999) (42 completed)
93—Georgia (28) [33] & Purdue (25) [60] (ot) (Outback, 2000) (56 completed)
93—Idaho (42) [41] & Southern Miss. (35) [52] (Humanitarian, 1998) (55 completed)
93—Mississippi (34) [48] & Marshall (31) [45] (Motor City, 1997) (52 completed)
92—Toledo (40) [41] & Nevada (37) [51] (ot) (Las Vegas, 1995) (50 completed)
92—Penn St. (38) [31] & Oregon (20) [61] (Rose, 1995) (61 completed)
92—Tennessee (34) [46] & Air Force (13) [46] (Sugar, 1971) (47 completed)
91—Richmond (49) [58] & Ohio (42) [33] (Tangerine, 1968) (56 completed)
90—Bowling Green (35) [41] & Nevada (34) [49] (Las Vegas, 1992) (54 completed)
90—Mississippi (20) [50] & Texas Tech (17) [40] (Independence, 1986) (48 completed)
88—Washington St. (31) [48] & Utah (28) [40] (Copper, 1992) (53 completed)
88—Washington (21) [56] & Maryland (20) [32] (Aloha, 1982) (54 completed)
86—Michigan St. (37) [35] & Florida (34) [51] (Florida Citrus, 2000) (46 completed)
86—Boise St. (34) [39] & Louisville (31) [47] (Humanitarian, 1999) (46 completed)
86—(D) Fresno St. (35) [29] & Western Mich. (30) [57] (California, 1988) (39 completed)
86—Iowa (20) [35] & Wyoming (19) [51] (Holiday, 1987) (49 completed)
85—Ohio St. (10) [35] & Brigham Young (7) [50] (Florida Citrus, 1985) (45 completed)
85—(D) Toledo (27) [22] & San Jose St. (25) [63] (California, 1981) (54 completed)
84—Florida St. (23) [41] & Florida (17) [43] (Sugar, Jan. 2, 1995) (54 completed)
84—(D) Southern California (28) [44] & Utah (21) [40] (Freedom, 1993) (53 completed)
83—Mississippi (27) [29] & Oklahoma (25) [54] (Independence, 1999) (47 completed)
83—Southern California (41) [44] & Northwestern (32) [39] (Rose, 1996) (52 completed)
83—Auburn (35) [44] & Mississippi (28) [39] (Gator, Jan. 2, 1971) (50 completed)
82—Tulane (41) [38] & Brigham Young (27) [44] (Liberty, 1998) (50 completed)
82—(D) Fresno St. (29) [50] & Bowling Green (28) [32] (California, 1982) (53 completed)

MOST PASS COMPLETIONS
(Followed by Comp.-Att.-Int. and Yardage)
43—(D) San Jose St. (25) vs. Toledo (27) (California, 1981) (43-63-5, 467 yards)
42—Brigham Young (39) vs. Penn St. (50) (Holiday, 1989) (42-59-2, 576 yards)
41—Oregon (20) vs. Penn St. (38) (Rose, 1995) (41-61-2, 456 yards)
39—Oklahoma (25) vs. Mississippi (27) (Independence, 1999) (39-54-1, 390 yards)
39—Richmond (49) vs. Ohio (42) (Tangerine, 1968) (39-58-2, 447 yards)
38—Illinois (29) vs. Army (31) (Peach, 1985) (38-55-2, 401 yards)
38—(D) Vanderbilt (28) vs. Air Force (36) (Hall of Fame, 1982) (38-51-3, 452 yards)
38—Florida St. (17) vs. Penn St. (17) (Gator, 1967) (38-55-4, 363 yards)
37—Fresno St. (30) vs. Colorado (41) (Aloha, 1993) (37-63-1, 523 yards)
37—(D) Brigham Young (16) vs. Virginia (22) (All-American, 1987) (37-61-1, 394 yards)
36—Purdue (25) vs. Georgia (28) (ot) (Outback, 2000) (36-60-1, 378 yards)
35—Michigan (35) vs. Alabama (34) (ot) (Orange, 2000) (35-47-0, 369 yards)
35—Louisville (29) vs. Marshall (48) (Motor City, 1998) (35-54-1, 336 yards)
35—West Virginia (31) vs. Missouri (34) (Insight.com, 1998) (35-51-2, 452 yards)
35—Brigham Young (24) vs. Michigan (17) (Holiday, 1984) (35-49-3, 371 yards)
35—Illinois (15) vs. Alabama (21) (Liberty, 1982) (35-58-7, 423 yards)
35—Washington (21) vs. Maryland (20) (Aloha, 1982) (35-56-0, 369 yards)
34—Wisconsin (37) vs. Southern California (42) (Rose, 1963) (34-49-3, 419 yards)
33—Alabama (29) vs. Army (28) (John Hancock Sun, 1988) (33-52-1, 412 yards)

MOST PASS COMPLETIONS, BOTH TEAMS
61—Penn St. (38) [20] & Oregon (20) [41] (Rose, 1995) (92 attempted)
56—Georgia (28) [20] & Purdue (25) [36] (ot) (Outback, 2000) (93 attempted)
56—Richmond (49) [39] & Ohio (42) [17] (Tangerine, 1968) (91 attempted)
55—Idaho (42) [24] & Southern Miss. (35) [31] (Humanitarian, 1998) (93 attempted)
54—Florida St. (23) [24] & Florida (17) [30] (Sugar, Jan. 2, 1995) (84 attempted)
54—Bowling Green (35) [25] & Nevada (34) [29] (Las Vegas, 1992) (90 attempted)
54—Washington (21) [35] & Maryland (20) [19] (Aloha, 1982) (88 attempted)
54—(D) Toledo (27) [11] & San Jose St. (25) [43] (California, 1981) (85 attempted)
53—Louisville (29) [35] & Marshall (48) [18] (Motor City, 1998) (78 attempted)
53—(D) Southern California (28) [30] & Utah (21) [23] (Freedom, 1993) (84 attempted)

BOWL/ALL-STAR RECORDS

53—Washington St. (31) [32] & Utah (28) [21] (Copper, 1992) (88 attempted)
53—Penn St. (50) [11] & Brigham Young (39) [42] (Holiday, 1989) (80 attempted)
53—(D) Fresno St. (29) [31] & Bowling Green (28) [22] (California, 1982) (82 attempted)
52—Mississippi (34) [29] & Marshall (31) [23] (Motor City, 1997) (93 attempted)
52—Southern California (41) [29] & Northwestern (32) [23] (Rose, 1996) (83 attempted)
50—Tulane (41) [23] & Brigham Young (27) [27] (Liberty, 1998) (82 attempted)
50—Toledo (40) [23] & Nevada (37) [27] (ot) (Las Vegas, 1995) (92 attempted)
50—Kansas St. (52) [19] & Wyoming (17) [31] (Copper, 1993) (79 attempted)
50—Auburn (35) [27] & Mississippi (28) [23] (Gator, Jan. 2, 1971) (83 attempted)
49—Iowa (20) [21] & Wyoming (19) [28] (Holiday, 1987) (86 attempted)
49—UCLA (39) [18] & Miami (Fla.) (37) [31] (Fiesta, 1985) (71 attempted)
49—(D) Air Force (36) [11] & Vanderbilt (28) [38] (Hall of Fame, 1982) (68 attempted)
48—Michigan (35) [35] & Alabama (34) [13] (ot) (Orange, 2000) (67 attempted)
48—Brigham Young (13) [29] & Iowa (13) [19] (Holiday, 1991) (72 attempted)
48—LSU (30) [20] & South Carolina (13) [28] (Gator, 1987) (79 attempted)
48—Mississippi (20) [31] & Texas Tech (17) [17] (Independence, 1986) (90 attempted)

MOST PASSING YARDS
(Followed by Comp.-Att.-Int.)
576—Brigham Young (39) vs. Penn St. (50) (Holiday, 1989) (42-59-2)
523—Fresno St. (30) vs. Colorado (41) (Aloha, 1993) (37-63-1)
492—Washington St. (31) vs. Utah (28) (Copper, 1992) (32-48-1)
485—Brigham Young (31) vs. Oklahoma (6) (Copper, 1994) (23-46-0)
469—(D) Iowa (55) vs. Texas (17) (Freedom, 1984) (30-40-0)
467—(D) San Jose St. (25) vs. Toledo (27) (California, 1981) (43-63-5)
458—Louisville (34) vs. Alabama (7) (Fiesta, 1991) (21-39-3)
456—Oregon (20) vs. Penn St. (38) (Rose, 1995) (41-61-2)
456—Oregon (43) vs. Colorado (51) (Aloha, 1998) (24-46-2)
455—Florida St. (40) vs. Texas Tech (17) (Tangerine, 1977) (25-35-0)
452—(D) Vanderbilt (28) vs. Air Force (36) (Hall of Fame, 1982) (38-51-3)
452—West Virginia (31) vs. Missouri (34) (Insight.com, 1998) (35-51-2)
449—Florida (17) vs. Florida St. (23) (Sugar, Jan. 2, 1995) (30-43-1)
447—Richmond (49) vs. Ohio (42) (Tangerine, 1968) (39-58-2)
446—Brigham Young (46) vs. Southern Methodist (45) (Holiday, 1980) (32-49-1)
442—(D) San Jose St. (48) vs. Central Mich. (24) (California, 1990) (32-43-1)
435—Southern California (55) vs. Texas Tech (14) (Cotton, 1995) (24-35-0)
428—Iowa (23) vs. North Carolina St. (28) (Peach, Dec. 31, 1988) (30-51-4)
423—Illinois (15) vs. Alabama (21) (Liberty, 1982) (35-58-7)
422—Florida St. (41) vs. Nebraska (17) (Fiesta, 1990) (25-41-0)
419—Wisconsin (37) vs. Southern California (42) (Rose, 1963) (34-49-3)
418—UCLA (31) vs. Wisconsin (38) (Rose, 1999) (21-36-1)
413—Georgia (27) vs. Virginia (34) (Peach, Dec. 30, 1995) (31-59-2)
412—Alabama (29) vs. Army (28) (John Hancock Sun, 1988) (33-52-1)

MOST PASSING YARDS, BOTH TEAMS
808—Washington St. (31) [492] & Utah (28) [316] (Copper, 1992) (88 attempted)
791—Penn St. (50) [215] & Brigham Young (39) [576] (Holiday, 1989) (80 attempted)
774—Florida St. (23) [325] & Florida (17) [449] (Sugar, Jan. 2, 1995) (84 attempted)
747—Marshall (48) [411] & Louisville (29) [336] (Motor City, 1998) (78 attempted)
734—Florida St. (40) [455] & Texas Tech (17) [279] (Tangerine, 1977) (63 attempted)
732—(D) Toledo (27) [265] & San Jose St. (25) [467] (California, 1981) (85 attempted)
727—Southern California (41) [391] & Northwestern (32) [336] (Rose, 1996) (83 attempted)
708—Navy (42) [395] & California (38) [313] (Aloha, 1996) (59 attempted)
677—Colorado (51) [221] & Oregon (43) [456] (Aloha, 1998) (70 attempted)
672—Southern California (42) [253] & Wisconsin (37) [419] (Rose, 1963) (69 attempted)
669—Mississippi (34) [332] & Marshall (31) [337] (Motor City, 1997) (93 attempted)
662—(D) San Jose St. (48) [442] & Central Mich. (24) [220] (California, 1990) (68 attempted)
658—Penn St. (38) [202] & Oregon (20) [456] (Rose, 1995) (92 attempted)
654—(D) Iowa (55) [469] & Texas (17) [185] (Freedom, 1984) (74 attempted)
653—Idaho (42) [291] & Southern Miss. (35) [362] (Humanitarian, 1998) (93 attempted)
649—Boise St. (34) [335] & Louisville (31) [314] (Humanitarian, 1999) (86 attempted)
648—Brigham Young (31) [485] & Oklahoma (6) [163] (Copper, 1994) (76 attempted)
647—Colorado (41) [124] & Fresno St. (30) [523] (Aloha, 1993) (78 attempted)
640—Southern California (55) [435] & Texas Tech (14) [205] (Cotton, 1995) (72 attempted)
631—(D) Southern California (28) [345] & Utah (21) [286] (Freedom, 1993) (84 attempted)
629—Florida St. (41) [422] & Nebraska (17) [207] (Fiesta, 1990) (67 attempted)
627—Georgia Tech (35) [274] & West Virginia (30) [353] (Carquest, 1997) (76 attempted)
623—North Carolina St. (28) [195] & Iowa (23) [428] (Peach, Dec. 31, 1988) (74 attempted)

MOST PASSES HAD INTERCEPTED
8—Arizona (10) vs. Auburn (34) (Sun, 1968)
7—Illinois (15) vs. Alabama (21) (Liberty, 1982)
7—Missouri (3) vs. Penn St. (10) (Orange, 1970)
7—Texas A&M (21) vs. Alabama (29) (Cotton, 1942)
6—Georgia (6) vs. Nebraska (45) (Sun, 1969)
6—TCU (26) vs. Georgia (40) (Orange, 1942)
6—Southern Methodist (0) vs. Stanford (7) (Rose, 1936)

MOST PASSES HAD INTERCEPTED, BOTH TEAMS
12—Auburn (34) [4] & Arizona (10) [8] (Sun, 1968)

10—Georgia (40) [6] & TCU (26) [4] (Orange, 1942)
9—Alabama (21) [2] & Illinois (15) [7] (Liberty, 1982)
8—Ohio St. (28) [3] & Texas A&M (12) [5] (Cotton, 1987)
8—Nebraska (28) [3] & LSU (10) [5] (Sugar, 1985)
8—Penn St. (10) [1] & Missouri (3) [7] (Orange, 1970)
8—Nebraska (45) [2] & Georgia (6) [6] (Sun, 1969)
8—Texas (12) [3] & Mississippi (7) [5] (Cotton, 1962)

MOST PASSES ATTEMPTED WITHOUT AN INTERCEPTION
(Followed by Comp.-Att.-Int. and Yardage)
57—(D) Western Mich. (30) vs. Fresno St. (35) (California, 1988) (24-57-0, 366 yards)
52—Southern Miss. (35) vs. Idaho (42) (Humanitarian, 1998) (31-52-0, 362 yards)
51—Nevada (37) vs. Toledo (40) (ot) (Las Vegas, 1995) (27-51-0, 330 yards)
51—Florida (34) vs. Michigan St. (37) (Florida Citrus, 2000) (25-51-0, 300 yards)

MOST PASSES ATTEMPTED BY BOTH TEAMS WITHOUT AN INTERCEPTION
(Followed by Comp.-Att.-Int. and Yardage)
93—Idaho (42) [41] & Southern Miss. (35) [52] (Humanitarian, 1998) (55-93-0, 653 yards)
90—Bowling Green (35) [49] & Nevada (34) [41] (Las Vegas, 1992) (54-90-0, 597 yards)

HIGHEST COMPLETION PERCENTAGE
(Minimum 10 Attempts) (Followed by Comp.-Att.-Int. and Yardage)
.929—Texas (40) vs. Missouri (27) (Cotton, 1946) (13-14-0, 234 yards)
.900—Mississippi (13) vs. Air Force (0) (Liberty, 1992) (9-10-0, 163 yards)
.897—Georgia (33) vs. Wisconsin (6) (Outback, 1998) (26-29-0, 267 yards)
.889—Texas A&M (65) vs. Brigham Young (14) (Holiday, 1990) (16-18-0, 324 yards)
.833—Alabama (13) vs. Penn St. (6) (Sugar, 1975) (10-12-0, 210 yards)
.828—Oklahoma St. (62) vs. Wyoming (14) (Holiday, 1988) (24-29-0, 378 yards)
.824—Nebraska (21) vs. North Carolina (17) (Liberty, 1977) (14-17-2, 161 yards)
.813—TCU (28) vs. Syracuse (27) (Cotton, 1957) (13-16-0, 202 yards)
.800—Ohio St. (15) vs. Clemson (17) (Gator, 1978) (16-20-1, 205 yards)
.800—Georgia Tech (31) vs. Iowa St. (30) (Liberty, 1972) (12-15-1, 157 yards)
.778—Tennessee (27) vs. Indiana (22) (Peach, 1987) (14-18-0, 279 yards)
.771—Washington St. (10) vs. Baylor (3) (Alamo, 1994) (27-35-0, 286 yards)
.765—Illinois (17) vs. Hawaii (27) (Holiday, 1992) (26-34-1, 248 yards)
.765—Duke (7) vs. Arkansas (6) (Cotton, 1961) (13-17-1, 93 yards)
.763—Iowa (28) vs. UCLA (45) (Rose, 1986) (29-38-1, 319 yards)
.750—Colorado St. (35) vs. Missouri (24) (Holiday, 1997) (18-24-0, 206 yards)
.750—Kansas St. (54) vs. Colorado St. (21) (Holiday, 1995) (24-32-1, 324 yards)
.750—Oklahoma (48) vs. Virginia (14) (Gator, Dec. 29, 1991) (27-36-0, 357 yards)
.750—(D) Iowa (55) vs. Texas (17) (Freedom, 1984) (30-40-0, 469 yards)

MOST YARDS PER ATTEMPT
(Minimum 10 Attempts)
21.7—Southern California (47) vs. Pittsburgh (14) (Rose, 1930) (13 for 282)
18.8—Navy (42) vs. California (38) (Aloha, 1996) (21 for 295)
18.0—Texas A&M (65) vs. Brigham Young (14) (Holiday, 1990) (18 for 324)
17.5—Alabama (13) vs. Penn St. (6) (Sugar, 1975) (12 for 210)
17.1—Marshall (48) vs. Louisville (29) (Motor City, 1998) (24 for 411)
16.7—Texas (40) vs. Missouri (27) (Cotton, 1946) (14 for 234)
16.7—Texas (36) vs. Tennessee (13) (Cotton, 1969) (14 for 234)
16.7—Air Force (45) vs. Washington (25) (Oahu Classic, 1998) (16 for 267)
13.8—Kansas St. (35) vs. Syracuse (18) (Fiesta, 1997) (23 for 317)

MOST YARDS PER COMPLETION
(Minimum 8 Completions)
35.2—Southern California (47) vs. Pittsburgh (14) (Rose, 1930) (8 for 282)
29.3—Texas (28) vs. Navy (6) (Cotton, 1964) (8 for 234)
29.3—Texas (36) vs. Tennessee (13) (Cotton, 1969) (8 for 234)

FEWEST PASS ATTEMPTS
2—Air Force (38) vs. Mississippi St. (15) (Liberty, 1991) (completed 1)
2—(D) Army (10) vs. Michigan St. (6) (Cherry, 1984) (completed 1)
2—West Virginia (14) vs. South Carolina (3) (Peach, 1969) (completed 1)
3—Air Force (23) vs. Ohio St. (11) (Liberty, 1990) (completed 1)
3—Oklahoma (31) vs. Nebraska (24) (Orange, 1979) (completed 2)
3—Georgia Tech (21) vs. Pittsburgh (14) (Gator, 1956) (completed 3)
3—Georgia Tech (7) vs. Pittsburgh (0) (Sugar, 1956) (completed 0)
3—Miami (Fla.) (14) vs. Clemson (0) (Gator, 1952) (completed 2)
3—Hardin-Simmons (7) vs. Second Air Force (13) (Sun, 1943) (completed 1)
3—Catholic (20) vs. Mississippi (19) (Orange, 1936) (completed 1)

FEWEST PASS ATTEMPTS, BOTH TEAMS
9—Fordham (2) [4] & Missouri (0) [5] (Sugar, 1942)
13—Colorado (27) [9] & Clemson (21) [4] (Orange, 1957)
14—Texas (16) [8] & Tennessee (0) [6] (Cotton, 1953)
15—Utah (26) [4] & New Mexico (0) [11] (Sun, 1939)
15—LSU (7) [11] & Clemson (0) [4] (Sugar, 1959)

FEWEST PASS COMPLETIONS
(Followed by Comp.-Att.-Int.)
0—Army (28) vs. Alabama (29) (John Hancock Sun, 1988) (0-6-1)
0—Missouri (35) vs. Alabama (10) (Gator, 1968) (0-6-2)
0—(D) Missouri (14) vs. Georgia Tech (10) (Bluebonnet, 1962) (0-7-2)
0—(D) New Mexico (28) vs. Western Mich. (12) (Aviation, 1961) (0-4-0)
0—Utah St. (13) vs. New Mexico St. (20) (Sun, 1960) (0-4-0)
0—Georgia Tech (7) vs. Pittsburgh (0) (Sugar, 1956) (0-3-1)
0—Arkansas (0) vs. LSU (0) (Cotton, 1947) (0-4-0)

TEAM RECORD LISTS—PASSING 325

0—Rice (8) vs. Tennessee (0) (Orange, 1947) (0-6-2)
0—Miami (Fla.) (13) vs. Holy Cross (6) (Orange, 1946) (0-10-3)
0—Fordham (2) vs. Missouri (0) (Sugar, 1942) (0-4-0)
0—Arizona St. (0) vs. Catholic (0) (Sun, 1940) (0-7-2)
0—Tulane (13) vs. Texas A&M (14) (Sugar, 1940) (0-4-0)
0—West Virginia (7) vs. Texas Tech (6) (Sun, 1938) (0-7-0)

FEWEST PASS COMPLETIONS, BOTH TEAMS
3—Arizona St. (0) [0] & Catholic (0) [3] (Sun, 1940)
4—Penn St. (7) [2] & Alabama (0) [2] (Liberty, 1959)
5—Oklahoma (14) [3] & Michigan (6) [2] (Orange, 1976)
5—Kentucky (21) [2] & North Carolina (0) [3] (Peach, 1976)
5—Texas (16) [2] & Tennessee (0) [3] (Cotton, 1953)
5—Arkansas (0) [0] & LSU (0) [5] (Cotton, 1947)
5—Wake Forest (26) [1] & South Carolina (14) [4] (Gator, 1946)
5—Utah (26) [1] & New Mexico (0) [4] (Sun, 1939)

FEWEST PASSING YARDS
(Followed by Comp.-Att.-Int.)
-50—U. of Mexico (0) vs. Southwestern (Tex.) (35) (Sun, 1945) (2-9-3)
-17—Rice (8) vs. Tennessee (0) (Orange, 1947) (0-6-2)
-2—Oklahoma (40) vs. Houston (14) (Sun, 1981) (1-5-1)
0—Army (28) vs. Alabama (29) (John Hancock Sun, 1988) (0-6-1)
0—Missouri (35) vs. Alabama (10) (Gator, 1968) (0-6-2)
0—(D) Missouri (14) vs. Georgia Tech (10) (Bluebonnet, 1962) (0-7-2)
0—(D) New Mexico (28) vs. Western Mich. (12) (Aviation, 1961) (0-4-0)
0—Utah St. (13) vs. New Mexico St. (20) (Sun, 1960) (0-4-0)
0—Georgia Tech (7) vs. Pittsburgh (0) (Sugar, 1956) (0-3-1)
0—Arkansas (0) vs. LSU (0) (Cotton, 1947) (0-4-1)
0—Rice (8) vs. Tennessee (0) (Orange, 1947) (0-6-2)
0—Miami (Fla.) (13) vs. Holy Cross (6) (Orange, 1946) (0-10-3)
0—Fordham (2) vs. Missouri (0) (Sugar, 1942) (0-4-0)
0—Tulane (13) vs. Texas A&M (14) (Sugar, 1940) (0-4-0)
0—Arizona St. (0) vs. Catholic (0) (Sun, 1940) (0-7-2)
0—West Virginia (7) vs. Texas Tech (6) (Sun, 1938) (0-7-0)
0—California (0) vs. Wash. & Jeff. (0) (Rose, 1922)
0—Oregon (6) vs. Harvard (7) (Rose, 1920)

FEWEST PASSING YARDS, BOTH TEAMS
15—Rice (8) [-17] & Tennessee (0) [32] (Orange, 1947)
16—Arkansas (0) [0] & LSU (0) [16] (Cotton, 1947)
16—Arizona St. (0) [0] & Catholic (0) [16] (Sun, 1940)
21—Fordham (2) [0] & Missouri (0) [21] (Sugar, 1942)
40—Kentucky (21) [16] & North Carolina (0) [24] (Peach, 1976)
52—Colorado (27) [25] & Clemson (21) [27] (Orange, 1957)
59—Miami (Fla.) (13) [0] & Holy Cross (6) [59] (Orange, 1946)
60—North Carolina (26) [10] & Texas (10) [50] (Sun, 1982)
68—Penn St. (7) [41] & Alabama (0) [27] (Liberty, 1959)
68—Missouri (35) [0] & Alabama (10) [68] (Gator, 1968)
74—Oklahoma (41) [23] & Wyoming (7) [51] (Fiesta, 1976)
75—Southwestern (Tex.) (7) [65] & New Mexico (0) [10] (Sun, 1944)
77—Utah (26) [18] & New Mexico (0) [59] (Sun, 1939)
78—Texas (16) [32] & Tennessee (0) [46] (Cotton, 1953)

LOWEST COMPLETION PERCENTAGE
(Followed by Comp.-Att.-Int.)
.000—Army (28) vs. Alabama (29) (John Hancock Sun, 1988) (0-6-1)
.000—Missouri (35) vs. Alabama (10) (Gator, 1968) (0-6-2)
.000—(D) Missouri (14) vs. Georgia Tech (10) (Bluebonnet, 1962) (0-7-2)
.000—(D) New Mexico (28) vs. Western Mich. (12) (Aviation, 1961) (0-4-0)
.000—Utah St. (13) vs. New Mexico St. (20) (Sun, 1960) (0-4-0)
.000—Georgia Tech (7) vs. Pittsburgh (0) (Sugar, 1956) (0-3-1)
.000—Arkansas (0) vs. LSU (0) (Cotton, 1947) (0-4-1)
.000—Rice (8) vs. Tennessee (0) (Orange, 1947) (0-6-2)
.000—Miami (Fla.) (13) vs. Holy Cross (6) (Orange, 1946) (0-10-3)
.000—Fordham (2) vs. Missouri (0) (Sugar, 1942) (0-4-0)
.000—Arizona St. (0) vs. Catholic (0) (Sun, 1940) (0-7-2)
.000—Tulane (13) vs. Texas A&M (14) (Sugar, 1940) (0-4-0)
.000—West Virginia (7) vs. Texas Tech (6) (Sun, 1938) (0-7-0)

FEWEST YARDS PER PASS ATTEMPT
-5.6—U. of Mexico (0) vs. Southwestern (Tex.) (35) (Sun, 1945) (9 for -50)
-2.8—Rice (8) vs. Tennessee (0) (Orange, 1947) (6 for -17)
-0.4—Oklahoma (40) vs. Houston (14) (Sun, 1981) (5 for -2)
0.0—Army (28) vs. Alabama (29) (John Hancock Sun, 1988) (6 for 0)
0.0—Missouri (35) vs. Alabama (10) (Gator, 1968) (6 for 0)
0.0—(D) Missouri (14) vs. Georgia Tech (10) (Bluebonnet, 1962) (7 for 0)
0.0—(D) New Mexico (28) vs. Western Mich. (12) (Aviation, 1961) (4 for 0)
0.0—Utah St. (13) vs. New Mexico St. (20) (Sun, 1960) (4 for 0)
0.0—Georgia Tech (7) vs. Pittsburgh (0) (Sugar, 1956) (3 for 0)
0.0—Arkansas (0) vs. LSU (0) (Cotton, 1947) (4 for 0)
0.0—Rice (8) vs. Tennessee (0) (Orange, 1947) (6 for 0)
0.0—Miami (Fla.) (13) vs. Holy Cross (6) (Orange, 1946) (10 for 0)
0.0—Fordham (2) vs. Missouri (0) (Sugar, 1942) (4 for 0)
0.0—Arizona St. (0) vs. Catholic (0) (Sun, 1940) (7 for 0)
0.0—Tulane (13) vs. Texas A&M (14) (Sugar, 1940) (4 for 0)
0.0—West Virginia (7) vs. Texas Tech (6) (Sun, 1938) (7 for 0)

FEWEST YARDS PER PASS COMPLETION
(Minimum 1 completion)
-25.0—U. of Mexico (0) vs. Southwestern (Tex.) (35) (Sun, 1945) (2 for -50)
-2.0—Oklahoma (40) vs. Houston (14) (Sun, 1981) (1 for -2)

3.0—West Virginia (14) vs. South Carolina (3) (Peach, 1969) (1 for 3)
3.2—LSU (0) vs. Arkansas (0) (Cotton, 1947) (5 for 16)
3.3—New Mexico (0) vs. Southwestern (Tex.) (7) (Sun, 1944) (3 for 10)
3.3—North Carolina (26) vs. Texas (10) (Sun, 1982) (3 for 10)
4.5—Alabama (34) vs. Miami (Fla.) (13) (Sugar, 1993) (4 for 18)
4.6—Texas (14) vs. Georgia Tech (7) (Cotton, 1943) (5 for 23)
4.8—UTEP (33) vs. Georgetown (20) (Sun, 1950) (5 for 24)
5.3—Case Reserve (26) vs. Arizona St. (13) (Sun, 1941) (3 for 16)
5.3—Arkansas (3) vs. UCLA (17) (Cotton, 1989) (4 for 21)

Scoring

MOST TOUCHDOWNS
9—Illinois (63) vs. Virginia (21) (Micronpc.com, 1999) (6 rush, 3 pass)
9—Texas A&M (65) vs. Brigham Young (14) (Holiday, 1990) (5 rush, 4 pass)
9—Alabama (61) vs. Syracuse (6) (Orange, 1953) (4 rush, 3 pass, 1 punt return, 1 interception return)
9—(D) Centre (63) vs. TCU (7) (Fort Worth Classic, 1921) (8 rush, 1 blocked punt recovery in end zone)
8—Colorado (62) vs. Boston College (28) (Insight.com, 1999) (5 rush, 2 interception return, 1 punt return)
8—Nebraska (62) vs. Florida (24) (Fiesta, 1996) (6 rush, 1 pass, 1 interception return)
8—Kansas St. (54) vs. Colorado St. (21) (Holiday, 1995) (4 rush, 4 pass)
8—Oklahoma St. (62) vs. Wyoming (14) (Holiday, 1988) (6 rush, 2 pass)
8—Toledo (56) vs. Davidson (33) (Tangerine, 1969) (4 rush, 3 pass, 1 fumble return)
7—Washington (51) vs. Michigan St. (23) (Aloha, 1997) (3 rush, 2 pass, 2 interception returns)
7—Texas Tech (55) vs. Air Force (41) (Copper, 1995) (6 rush, 1 pass)
7—Southern California (55) vs. Texas Tech (14) (Cotton, 1995) (1 rush, 5 pass, 1 interception retrun)
7—UNLV (52) vs. Central Mich. (24) (Las Vegas, 1994) (3 rush, 3 pass, 1 fumble return)
7—Kansas St. (52) vs. Wyoming (17) (Copper, 1993) (3 rush, 2 pass, 1 punt return, 1 interception return)
7—Oklahoma (48) vs. Virginia (14) (Gator, Dec. 29, 1991) (4 rush, 2 pass, 1 blocked punt return)
7—(D) Texas Tech (49) vs. Duke (21) (All-American, 1989) (6 rush, 1 pass)
7—(D) Fresno St. (51) vs. Bowling Green (7) (California, 1985) (4 rush, 3 pass)
7—(D) Iowa (55) vs. Texas (17) (Freedom, 1984) (1 rush, 6 pass)
7—(D) Houston (47) vs. Tulane (7) (Bluebonnet, 1973) (7 rush)
7—Arizona St. (49) vs. Missouri (35) (Fiesta, 1972) (5 rush, 2 pass)
7—North Carolina St. (49) vs. West Virginia (13) (Peach, 1972) (4 rush, 3 pass)
7—Arizona St. (48) vs. North Carolina (26) (Peach, 1970) (6 rush, 1 pass)
7—Houston (49) vs. Miami (Ohio) (21) (Tangerine, 1962) (4 rush, 2 pass, 1 punt return)
7—Oklahoma (48) vs. Duke (21) (Orange, 1958) (3 rush, 2 pass, 1 pass interception return, 1 intercepted lateral return)
7—UTEP (47) vs. Florida St. (20) (Sun, 1955) (4 rush, 3 pass)
7—Michigan (49) vs. Southern California (0) (Rose, 1948) (3 rush, 4 pass)
7—Illinois (45) vs. UCLA (14) (Rose, 1947) (5 rush, 2 pass interception returns)

MOST TOUCHDOWNS, BOTH TEAMS
13—Texas Tech (55) [7] & Air Force (41) [6] (Copper, 1995)
13—Richmond (49) [7] & Ohio (42) [6] (Tangerine, 1968)
12—Colorado (62) [8] & Boston College (28) [4] (Insight.com, 1999)
12—Illinois (63) [9] & Virginia (21) [3] (Micronpc.com, 1999)
12—Colorado (51) [6] & Oregon (43) [6] (Aloha, 1998)
11—Idaho (42) [6] & Southern Miss. (35) [5] (Humanitarian, 1998)
11—Navy (42) [6] & California (38) [5] (Aloha, 1996)
11—Nebraska (62) [8] & Florida (24) [3] (Fiesta, 1996)
11—Kansas St. (54) [8] & Colorado St. (21) [3] (Holiday, 1995)
11—Washington (46) [6] & Iowa (34) [5] (Rose, 1991)
11—Texas A&M (65) [9] & Brigham Young (14) [2] (Holiday, 1990)
11—Penn St. (50) [6] & Brigham Young (39) [5] (Holiday, 1989)
11—Arizona St. (49) [7] & Missouri (35) [4] (Fiesta, 1971)
11—Arizona St. (48) [7] & North Carolina (26) [4] (Peach, 1970)
11—Southern California (42) [6] & Wisconsin (37) [5] (Rose, 1963)
10—Marshall (48) [6] & Louisville (29) [4] (Motor City, 1998)
10—Washington (51) [7] & Michigan St. (23) [3] (Aloha, 1997)
10—UNLV (52) [7] & Central Mich. (24) [3] (Las Vegas, 1994)
10—Utah St. (42) [6] & Ball St. (33) [4] (Las Vegas, 1993)
10—East Caro. (37) [5] & North Carolina St. (34) [5] (Peach, 1992)
10—(D) Texas Tech (49) [7] & Duke (21) [3] (All-American, 1989)
10—Mississippi (42) [6] & Air Force (29) [4] (Liberty, 1989)
10—Oklahoma St. (62) [8] & Wyoming (14) [2] (Holiday, 1988)
10—Boston College (45) [6] & Houston (28) [4] (Cotton, 1985)
10—Colorado (47) [6] & Alabama (33) [4] (Liberty, 1969)
10—(D) Nebraska (36) [5] & Miami (Fla.) (34) [5] (Gotham, 1962)
10—UTEP (47) [7] & Florida St. (20) [3] (Sun, 1955)
10—Alabama (61) [9] & Syracuse (6) [1] (Orange, 1953)

MOST TOUCHDOWNS RUSHING
8—(D) Centre (63) vs. TCU (7) (Fort Worth Classic, 1921)
7—(D) Houston (47) vs. Tulane (7) (Bluebonnet, 1973)
6—Illinois (63) vs. Virginia (21) (Micronpc.com, 1999)
6—Nebraska (42) vs. Tennessee (17) (Orange, 1998)

BOWL/ALL-STAR RECORDS

6—Navy (42) vs. California (38) (Aloha, 1996)
6—Nebraska (62) vs. Florida (24) (Fiesta, 1996)
6—Texas Tech (55) vs. Air Force (41) (Copper, 1995)
6—Air Force (41) vs. Texas Tech (55) (Copper, 1995)
6—(D) Texas Tech (49) vs. Duke (21) (All-American, 1989)
6—Oklahoma St. (62) vs. Wyoming (14) (Holiday, 1988)
6—Oklahoma (42) vs. Arkansas (8) (Orange, 1987)
6—Ohio St. (47) vs. Brigham Young (17) (Holiday, 1982)
6—Oklahoma St. (49) vs. Brigham Young (21) (Tangerine, 1976)
6—Arizona St. (48) vs. North Carolina (26) (Peach, 1970)
6—Michigan (49) vs. Stanford (0) (Rose, 1902)

MOST TOUCHDOWNS RUSHING, BOTH TEAMS
12—Texas Tech (55) [6] & Air Force (41) [6] (Copper, 1995)
9—Arizona St. (48) [6] & North Carolina (26) [3] (Peach, 1970)
8—Oklahoma St. (62) [6] & Wyoming (14) [2] (Holiday, 1988)
8—Colorado (47) [5] & Alabama (33) [3] (Liberty, 1969)
7—Illinois (63) [6] & Virginia (21) [1] (Micronpc.com, 1999)
7—Navy (42) [6] & California (38) [1] (Aloha, 1996)
7—Nebraska (62) [6] & Florida (24) [1] (Fiesta, 1996)
7—Kansas St. (54) [4] & Colorado St. (21) [3] (Holiday, 1995)
7—Oklahoma (42) [6] & Arkansas (8) [1] (Orange, 1987)
7—Oklahoma St. (35) [4] & West Virginia (33) [3] (John Hancock Sun, 1987)
7—UCLA (45) [5] & Iowa (28) [2] (Rose, 1986)
7—Oklahoma St. (49) [6] & Brigham Young (21) [1] (Tangerine, 1976)
7—Arizona St. (49) [5] & Missouri (35) [2] (Fiesta, 1972)
7—Penn St. (41) [5] & Oregon (12) [2] (Liberty, 1960)

MOST TOUCHDOWNS PASSING
6—(D) Iowa (55) vs. Texas (17) (Freedom, 1984)
5—Southern California (55) vs. Texas Tech (14) (Cotton, 1995)
5—Florida St. (41) vs. Nebraska (17) (Fiesta, 1990)
5—Florida St. (36) vs. Oklahoma (19) (Gator, Jan. 2, 1965)
4—Purdue (25) vs. Georgia (28) (ot) (Outback, 2000)
4—Michigan (35) vs. Alabama (34) (ot) (Orange, 2000)
4—Florida St. (46) vs. Virginia Tech (29) (Sugar, 2000)
4—Marshall (48) vs. Louisville (29) (Motor City, 1998)
4—West Virginia (31) vs. Missouri (34) (Insight.com, 1998)
4—Colorado (51) vs. Oregon (43) (Aloha, 1998)
4—Kansas St. (35) vs. Syracuse (18) (Fiesta, 1997)
4—Florida St. (31) vs. Notre Dame (26) (Orange, 1996)
4—Penn St. (43) vs. Auburn (14) (Outback, 1996)
4—Kansas St. (54) vs. Colorado St. (21) (Holiday, 1995)
4—East Caro. (37) vs. North Carolina St. (34) (Peach, 1992)
4—Miami (Fla.) (46) vs. Texas (3) (Cotton, 1991)
4—Michigan (35) vs. Mississippi (3) (Gator, Jan. 1, 1991)
4—Texas A&M (65) vs. Brigham Young (14) (Holiday, 1990)
4—UCLA (45) vs. Illinois (9) (Rose, 1984)
4—Purdue (28) vs. Missouri (25) (Liberty, 1980)
4—Pittsburgh (34) vs. Clemson (3) (Gator, 1977)
4—Florida St. (40) vs. Texas Tech (17) (Tangerine, 1977)
4—Davidson (33) vs. Toledo (56) (Tangerine, 1969)
4—Richmond (49) vs. Ohio (42) (Tangerine, 1968)
4—Ohio (42) vs. Richmond (49) (Tangerine, 1968)
4—Southern California (42) vs. Wisconsin (37) (Rose, 1963)
4—Michigan (49) vs. Southern California (0) (Rose, 1948)
4—Georgia (40) vs. TCU (26) (Orange, 1942)
4—Southern California (47) vs. Pittsburgh (14) (Rose, 1930)

MOST TOUCHDOWNS PASSING, BOTH TEAMS
8—(D) Iowa (55) [6] & Texas (17) [2] (Freedom, 1984)
8—Richmond (49) [4] & Ohio (42) [4] (Tangerine, 1968)
7—Florida St. (31) [4] & Notre Dame (26) [3] (Orange, 1996)
7—East Caro. (37) [4] & North Carolina St. (34) [3] (Peach, 1992)
7—Toledo (56) [3] & Davidson (33) [4] (Tangerine, 1969)
7—Georgia (40) [4] & TCU (26) [3] (Orange, 1942)
6—Michigan St. (37) [3] & Florida (34) [3] (Florida Citrus, 2000)
6—Purdue (37) [3] & Kansas St. (34) [3] (Alamo, 1998)
6—Mississippi (34) [3] & Marshall (31) [3] (Motor City, 1997)
6—Southern California (55) [5] & Texas Tech (14) [1] (Cotton, 1995)
6—Kansas (51) [3] & UCLA (30) [3] (Aloha, 1995)
6—Utah St. (42) [3] & Ball St. (33) [3] (Las Vegas, 1993)
6—Miami (Fla.) (33) [3] & Alabama (25) [3] (Sugar, 1990)
6—Florida St. (41) [5] & Nebraska (17) [1] (Fiesta, 1990)
6—Texas A&M (65) [4] & Brigham Young (14) [2] (Holiday, 1990)
6—Florida St. (36) [5] & Oklahoma (19) [1] (Gator, Jan. 2, 1965)
6—Southern California (42) [4] & Wisconsin (37) [2] (Rose, 1963)

MOST FIELD GOALS MADE
5—Texas A&M (22) vs. Michigan (20) (Alamo, 1995) (27, 49, 47, 31, 37 yards)
5—Mississippi St. (24) vs. North Carolina St. (28) (Peach, Jan. 1, 1995) (37, 21, 29, 36, 30 yards)
5—Florida (28) vs. Notre Dame (39) (Sugar, 1992) (26, 24, 36, 37, 24 yards)
5—Maryland (23) vs. Tennessee (30) (Florida Citrus, 1983) (18, 48, 31, 22, 26 yards)
4—East Caro. (19) vs. Stanford (13) (Liberty, 1995) (46, 26, 41, 34 yards)
4—Oklahoma (25) vs. Penn St. (10) (Orange, 1986) (31, 31, 21, 22 yards)
4—North Carolina (26) vs. Texas (10) (Sun, 1982) (53, 47, 24, 42 yards)
4—Texas A&M (33) vs. Oklahoma St. (16) (Independence, 1981) (33, 32, 50, 18 yards)
4—West Virginia (26) vs. Florida (6) (Peach, Dec. 31, 1981) (35, 42, 49, 24 yards)
4—Missouri (19) vs. Southern Miss. (17) (Tangerine, 1981) (45, 41, 30, 28 yards)
4—Nebraska (45) vs. Georgia (6) (Sun, 1969) (50, 32, 42, 37 yards)
4—Alabama (12) vs. Mississippi (7) (Sugar, 1964) (46, 31, 34, 48 yards)

MOST FIELD GOALS MADE, BOTH TEAMS
7—Texas A&M (22) [5] & Michigan (20) [2] (Alamo, 1995)
7—North Carolina St. (28) [2] & Mississippi St. (24) [5] (Peach, Jan. 1, 1995)
6—Notre Dame (39) [1] & Florida (28) [5] (Sugar, 1992)
6—Syracuse (16) [3] & Auburn (16) [3] (Sugar, 1988)
6—Tennessee (30) [1] & Maryland (23) [5] (Florida Citrus, 1983)
5—LSU (27) [2] & Notre Dame (9) [3] (Independence, 1997)
5—Penn St. (50) [3] & Brigham Young (39) [2] (Holiday, 1989)
5—Oklahoma (25) [4] & Penn St. (10) [1] (Orange, 1986)
5—North Carolina (26) [4] & Texas (10) [1] (Sun, 1982)
5—Texas A&M (33) [4] & Oklahoma St. (16) [1] (Independence, 1981)
5—Missouri (19) [4] & Southern Miss. (17) [1] (Tangerine, 1981)
5—Penn St. (9) [3] & Tulane (6) [2] (Liberty, 1979)
5—Penn St. (30) [3] & Texas (6) [2] (Cotton, 1972)

MOST POINTS, WINNING TEAM
65—Texas A&M vs. Brigham Young (14) (Holiday, 1990)
63—Illinois vs. Virginia (21) (Micronpc.com, 1999)
62—Colorado vs. Boston College (28) (Insight.com, 1999)
62—Nebraska vs. Florida (24) (Fiesta, 1996)
62—Oklahoma St. vs. Wyoming (14) (Holiday, 1988)
61—Alabama vs. Syracuse (6) (Orange, 1953)
56—Toledo vs. Davidson (33) (Tangerine, 1969)
55—Texas Tech vs. Air Force (41) (Copper, 1995)
55—Southern California vs. Texas Tech (14) (Cotton, 1995)
55—(D) Iowa vs. Texas (17) (Freedom, 1984)
54—Kansas St. vs. Colorado St. (21) (Holiday, 1995)
52—Florida vs. Florida St. (20) (Sugar, 1997)
52—UNLV vs. Central Mich. (24) (Las Vegas, 1994)
52—Kansas St. vs. Wyoming (17) (Copper, 1993)
51—Colorado vs. Oregon (43) (Aloha, 1998)
51—Washington vs. Michigan St. (23) (Aloha, 1997)
51—Kansas vs. UCLA (30) (Aloha, 1995)
51—(D) Fresno St. vs. Bowling Green (7) (California, 1985)
50—Penn St. vs. Brigham Young (39) (Holiday, 1989)
49—(D) Texas Tech vs. Duke (21) (All-American, 1989)
49—Oklahoma St. vs. Brigham Young (21) (Tangerine, 1976)
49—North Carolina St. vs. West Virginia (13) (Peach, 1972)
49—Arizona St. vs. Missouri (35) (Fiesta, 1972)
49—Richmond vs. Ohio (42) (Tangerine, 1968)
49—Michigan vs. Southern California (0) (Rose, 1948)

MOST POINTS, LOSING TEAM
45—Southern Methodist vs. Brigham Young (46) (Holiday, 1980)
43—Oregon vs. Colorado (51) (Aloha, 1998)
42—Ohio vs. Richmond (49) (Tangerine, 1968)
41—Air Force vs. Texas Tech (55) (Copper, 1995)
39—Brigham Young vs. Penn St. (50) (Holiday, 1989)
38—California vs. Navy (42) (Aloha, 1996)
38—San Diego St. vs. Iowa (39) (Holiday, 1986)
38—Florida St. vs. Arizona St. (45) (Fiesta, 1971)
37—Nevada vs. Toledo (40) (ot) (Las Vegas, 1995)
37—Miami (Fla.) vs. UCLA (39) (Fiesta, 1985)
37—Brigham Young vs. Indiana (38) (Holiday, 1979)
37—Wisconsin vs. Southern California (42) (Rose, 1963)
36—Washington St. vs. Brigham Young (38) (Holiday, 1981)
35—Southern Miss. vs. Idaho (42) (Humanitarian, 1998)
35—Oregon vs. Wake Forest (39) (Independence, 1992)
35—Missouri vs. Arizona St. (49) (Fiesta, 1972)
34—Alabama vs. Michigan (35) (ot) (Orange, 2000)
34—Florida vs. Michigan St. (37) (Florida Citrus, 2000)
34—Kansas St. vs. Purdue (37) (Alamo, 1998)
34—Nevada vs. Bowling Green (35) (Las Vegas, 1992)
34—North Carolina St. vs. East Caro. (37) (Peach, 1992)
34—Iowa vs. Washington (46) (Rose, 1991)
34—Houston vs. Notre Dame (35) (Cotton, 1979)
34—(D) Miami (Fla.) vs. Nebraska (36) (Gotham, 1962)

MOST POINTS, BOTH TEAMS
96—Texas Tech (55) & Air Force (41) (Copper, 1995)
94—Colorado (51) & Oregon (43) (Aloha, 1998)
91—Brigham Young (46) & Southern Methodist (45) (Holiday, 1980)
91—Richmond (49) & Ohio (42) (Tangerine, 1968)
90—Colorado (62) & Boston College (28) (Insight.com, 1999)
89—Penn St. (50) & Brigham Young (39) (Holiday, 1989)
89—Toledo (56) & Davidson (33) (Tangerine, 1969)
86—Nebraska (62) & Florida (24) (Fiesta, 1996)
84—Illinois (63) & Virginia (21) (Micronpc.com, 1999)
84—Arizona St. (49) & Missouri (35) (Fiesta, 1972)
83—Arizona St. (45) & Florida St. (38) (Fiesta, 1971)
81—Kansas (51) & UCLA (30) (Aloha, 1995)
80—Navy (42) & California (38) (Aloha, 1996)
80—Washington (46) & Iowa (34) (Rose, 1991)
80—Colorado (47) & Alabama (33) (Liberty, 1969)

TEAM RECORD LISTS—SCORING

79—Texas A&M (65) & Brigham Young (14) (Holiday, 1990)
79—Southern California (42) & Wisconsin (37) (Rose, 1963)
77—Marshall (48) & Louisville (29) (Motor City, 1998)
77—Idaho (42) & Southern Miss. (35) (Humanitarian, 1998)
77—Toledo (40) & Nevada (37) (ot) (Las Vegas, 1995)
77—Iowa (39) & San Diego St. (38) (Holiday, 1986)
76—Michigan (45) & Arkansas (31) (Florida Citrus, 1999)
76—Tennessee (48) & Northwestern (28) (Florida Citrus, 1997)
76—UNLV (52) & Central Mich. (24) (Las Vegas, 1994)
76—Oklahoma St. (62) & Wyoming (14) (Holiday, 1988)
76—UCLA (39) & Miami (Fla.) (37) (Fiesta, 1985)
75—Florida St. (46) & Virginia Tech (29) (Sugar, 2000)
75—Kansas St. (54) & Colorado St. (21) (Holiday, 1995)
75—Utah St. (42) & Ball St. (33) (Las Vegas, 1993)
75—Indiana (38) & Brigham Young (37) (Holiday, 1979)
75—Houston (47) & Miami (Ohio) (28) (Tangerine, 1962)

LARGEST MARGIN OF VICTORY
55—Alabama (61) vs. Syracuse (6) (Orange, 1953)
51—Texas A&M (65) vs. Brigham Young (14) (Holiday, 1990)
48—Oklahoma St. (62) vs. Wyoming (14) (Holiday, 1988)
44—(D) Fresno St. (51) vs. Bowling Green (7) (California, 1985)
43—Miami (Fla.) (46) vs. Texas (3) (Cotton, 1991)
42—Illinois (63) vs. Virginia (21) (Micronpc.com, 1999)
42—Texas (42) vs. Maryland (0) (Sun, 1978)
41—Syracuse (41) vs. Clemson (0) (Gator, 1996)
41—Southern California (55) vs. Texas Tech (14) (Cotton, 1995)
40—(D) Houston (47) vs. Tulane (7) (Bluebonnet, 1973)
39—North Carolina (42) vs. Virginia Tech (3) (Gator, 1998)
39—Nebraska (45) vs. Georgia (6) (Sun, 1969)
38—Stanford (38) vs. Michigan St. (0) (Sun, 1996)
38—Nebraska (62) vs. Florida (24) (Fiesta, 1996)
38—(D) Iowa (55) vs. Texas (17) (Freedom, 1984)
36—North Carolina St. (49) vs. West Virginia (13) (Peach, 1972)
35—Michigan (42) vs. North Carolina St. (7) (Hall of Fame, 1994)
35—Kansas St. (52) vs. Wyoming (17) (Copper, 1993)
35—(D) Houston (35) vs. Navy (0) (Garden State, 1980)
35—North Carolina (35) vs. Air Force (0) (Gator, 1963)
35—Oklahoma (35) vs. LSU (0) (Sugar, 1950)
35—Southwestern (Tex.) (35) vs. U. of Mexico (0) (Sun, 1945)

FEWEST POINTS, WINNING TEAM
2—Fordham vs. Missouri (0) (Sugar, 1942)
3—Tennessee vs. Texas A&M (0) (Gator, 1957)
3—TCU vs. LSU (2) (Sugar, 1936)
6—UCLA vs. Illinois (3) (John Hancock, 1991)
6—Oregon St. vs. Villanova (0) (Liberty, 1962)
6—Tulsa vs. Texas Tech (0) (Sun, 1942)
6—Clemson vs. Boston College (3) (Cotton, 1940)
6—Auburn vs. Michigan St. (0) (Orange, 1938)
6—Santa Clara vs. LSU (0) (Sugar, 1938)

FEWEST POINTS, LOSING TEAM
0—By many teams

FEWEST POINTS, BOTH TEAMS
0—Air Force (0) & TCU (0) (Cotton, 1959)
0—Arkansas (0) & LSU (0) (Cotton, 1947)
0—Arizona St. (0) & Catholic (0) (Sun, 1940)
0—California (0) & Wash. & Jeff. (0) (Rose, 1922)

MOST POINTS SCORED IN ONE HALF
45—Colorado (62) vs. Boston College (28) (Insight.com, 1999) (1st half)
45—Oklahoma St. (62) vs. Wyoming (14) (Holiday, 1988) (2nd half)
42—Illinois (63) vs. Virginia (21) (Micronpc.com, 1999) (1st half)
42—Toledo (56) vs. Davidson (33) (Tangerine, 1969) (1st half)
40—Alabama (61) vs. Syracuse (6) (Orange, 1953) (2nd half)
38—Penn St. (50) vs. Brigham Young (39) (Holiday, 1989) (2nd half)
38—Penn St. (41) vs. Baylor (20) (Cotton, 1975) (2nd half)
38—Mississippi (41) vs. Georgia Tech (18) (Peach, 1971) (1st half)
37—Colorado (51) vs. Oregon (43) (Aloha, 1998) (1st half)
37—Texas A&M (65) vs. Brigham Young (14) (Holiday, 1990) (1st half)
35—California (38) vs. Navy (42) (Aloha, 1996) (1st half)
35—Nebraska (62) vs. Florida (24) (Fiesta, 1996) (1st half)
35—Tennessee (45) vs. Virginia Tech (23) (Gator, 1994) (1st half)
35—Penn St. (42) vs. Tennessee (17) (Fiesta, 1992) (2nd half)
35—Southern California (42) vs. Ohio St. (17) (Rose, 1973) (2nd half)
35—North Carolina St. (49) vs. West Virginia (13) (Peach, 1972) (2nd half)
35—Houston (49) vs. Miami (Ohio) (21) (Tangerine, 1962) (1st half)
34—Kansas (51) vs. UCLA (30) (Aloha, 1995) (2nd half)
34—Southern California (55) vs. Texas Tech (14) (Cotton, 1995) (2nd half)
34—Oklahoma (48) vs. Virginia (14) (Gator, Dec. 29, 1991) (1st half)
34—Purdue (41) vs. Georgia Tech (21) (Peach, 1978) (1st half)
34—Oklahoma (48) vs. Duke (21) (Orange, 1958) (2nd half)
34—UTEP (47) vs. Florida St. (20) (Sun, 1955) (1st half)

MOST POINTS SCORED IN ONE HALF, BOTH TEAMS
64—Kansas (51) [34] & UCLA (30) [30] (Aloha, 1995) (2nd half)
64—Penn St. (50) [38] & Brigham Young (39) [26] (Holiday, 1989) (2nd half)
63—Navy (42) [28] & California (38) [35] (Aloha, 1996) (1st half)
54—Utah St. (42) [21] & Ball St. (33) [33] (Las Vegas, 1993) (2nd half)
52—Colorado (62) [45] & Boston College (28) [7] (Insight.com, 1999) (1st half)
52—Tennessee (48) [31] & Northwestern (28) [21] (Florida Citrus, 1997) (1st half)
52—Texas Tech (55) [24] & Air Force (41) [28] (Copper, 1995) (2nd half)
52—Oklahoma St. (62) [45] & Wyoming (14) [7] (Holiday, 1988) (2nd half)
51—Colorado (51) [37] & Oregon (43) [14] (Aloha, 1998) (1st half)
51—Penn St. (41) [38] & Baylor (20) [13] (Cotton, 1975) (2nd half)
49—Illinois (63) [42] & Virginia (21) [7] (Micronpc.com, 1999) (1st half)
49—Idaho (42) [28] & Southern Miss. (35) [21] (Humanitarian, 1998) (1st half)
49—Brigham Young (46) [33] & Southern Methodist (45) [16] (Holiday, 1980) (2nd half)
49—(D) Houston (31) [28] & North Carolina St. (31) [21] (Bluebonnet, 1974) (2nd half)
49—Arizona St. (49) [21] & Missouri (35) [28] (Fiesta, 1972) (2nd half)
49—Arizona St. (45) [21] & Florida St. (38) [28] (Fiesta, 1971) (1st half)
49—Toledo (56) [42] & Davidson (33) [7] (Tangerine, 1969) (1st half)
49—Richmond (49) [28] & Ohio (42) [21] (Tangerine, 1968) (1st half)
48—Oklahoma (48) [34] & Duke (21) [14] (Orange, 1958) (2nd half)
47—Arizona St. (48) [21] & North Carolina (26) [26] (Peach, 1970) (1st half)
45—Boise St. (34) [21] & Louisville (31) [24] (Humanitarian, 1999) (1st half)
45—Wisconsin (38) [24] & UCLA (31) [21] (Rose, 1999) (1st half)
45—Colorado (33) [24] & Washington (21) [21] (Holiday, 1996) (1st half)
45—LSU (45) [21] & Michigan St. (26) [24] (Independence, 1995) (1st half)
45—Tennessee (45) [35] & Virginia Tech (23) [10] (Gator, 1994) (1st half)
45—Boston College (45) [31] & Houston (28) [14] (Cotton, 1985) (1st half)
45—Southern California (42) [35] & Ohio St. (17) [10] (Rose, 1973) (2nd half)

MOST POINTS SCORED IN ONE QUARTER
31—(D) Iowa (55) vs. Texas (17) (Freedom, 1984) (3rd quarter)
30—Oklahoma (40) vs. Houston (14) (Sun, 1981) (4th quarter)
29—Nebraska (62) vs. Florida (24) (Fiesta, 1996) (2nd quarter)
28—Illinois (63) vs. Virginia (21) (Micronpc.com, 1999) (2nd quarter)
28—Southern California (55) vs. Texas Tech (14) (Cotton, 1995) (1st quarter)
28—Oklahoma St. (62) vs. Wyoming (14) (Holiday, 1988) (3rd quarter)
28—Missouri (34) vs. Auburn (17) (Sun, 1973) (2nd quarter)
28—Mississippi (41) vs. Georgia Tech (18) (Peach, 1971) (2nd quarter)
28—Toledo (56) vs. Davidson (33) (Tangerine, 1969) (2nd quarter)
28—Houston (49) vs. Miami (Ohio) (21) (Tangerine, 1962) (2nd quarter)
27—Penn St. (43) vs. Auburn (14) (Outback, 1996) (3rd quarter)
27—Oklahoma (48) vs. Virginia (14) (Gator, Dec. 29, 1991) (2nd quarter)
27—Brigham Young (46) vs. Southern Methodist (45) (Holiday, 1980) (4th quarter)
27—Oklahoma (48) vs. Duke (21) (Orange, 1958) (4th quarter)
27—UTEP (47) vs. Florida St. (20) (Sun, 1955) (2nd quarter)
27—Illinois (40) vs. Stanford (7) (Rose, 1952) (4th quarter)
26—North Carolina (26) vs. Arizona St. (48) (Peach, 1970) (2nd quarter)
25—Louisville (34) vs. Alabama (7) (Fiesta, 1991) (1st quarter)

MOST POINTS SCORED IN ONE QUARTER, BOTH TEAMS
43—Navy (42) [21] & California (38) [22] (Aloha, 1996) (2nd quarter)
40—Arizona St. (48) [14] & North Carolina (26) [26] (Peach, 1970) (2nd quarter)
38—Missouri (34) [28] & Auburn (17) [10] (Sun, 1973) (2nd quarter)
37—Kansas (51) [14] & UCLA (30) [23] (Aloha, 1995) (4th quarter)
37—Oklahoma (40) [30] & Houston (14) [7] (Sun, 1981) (4th quarter)
35—Michigan (35) [21] & Alabama (34) [14] (Orange, 2000) (3rd quarter)
35—Marshall (48) [14] & Louisville (29) [21] (Motor City, 1998) (2nd quarter)
35—Kansas St. (54) [21] & Colorado St. (21) [14] (Holiday, 1995) (3rd quarter)
35—Oklahoma St. (62) [28] & Wyoming (14) [7] (Holiday, 1988) (3rd quarter)
35—Oklahoma St. (49) [21] & Brigham Young (21) [14] (Tangerine, 1976) (2nd quarter)
35—(D) Houston (31) [21] & North Carolina St. (31) [14] (Bluebonnet, 1974) (4th quarter)
35—Arizona St. (49) [21] & Missouri (35) [14] (Fiesta, 1972) (4th quarter)
35—Richmond (49) [21] & Ohio (42) [14] (Tangerine, 1968) (2nd quarter)
34—Colorado (51) [20] & Oregon (43) [14] (Aloha, 1998) (2nd quarter)
34—Oklahoma (48) [27] & Virginia (14) [7] (Gator, Dec. 29, 1991) (2nd quarter)
34—Penn St. (50) [21] & Brigham Young (39) [13] (Holiday, 1989) (4th quarter)
34—Brigham Young (46) [27] & Southern Methodist (45) [7] (Holiday, 1980) (4th quarter)
34—Penn St. (42) [18] & Arizona St. (30) [16] (Fiesta, 1977) (4th quarter)
34—Mississippi (41) [28] & Georgia Tech (18) [6] (Peach, 1971) (2nd quarter)
34—Oklahoma (48) [27] & Duke (21) [7] (Orange, 1958) (4th quarter)

First Downs

MOST FIRST DOWNS
36—Oklahoma (48) vs. Virginia (14) (Gator, Dec. 29, 1991) (16 rush, 18 pass, 2 penalty)
35—Michigan (35) vs. Mississippi (3) (Gator, Jan. 1, 1991) (20 rush, 14 pass, 1 penalty)
35—Brigham Young (39) vs. Penn St. (50) (Holiday, 1989) (8 rush, 27 pass, 0 penalty)
34—Fresno St. (30) vs. Colorado (41) (Aloha, 1993) (4 rush, 25 pass, 5 penalty)
34—Oklahoma St. (62) vs. Wyoming (14) (Holiday, 1988) (15 rush, 17 pass, 2 penalty)
34—(D) Miami (Fla.) (34) vs. Nebraska (36) (Gotham, 1962)
33—Toledo (40) vs. Nevada (37) (ot) (Las Vegas, 1995) (19 rush, 12 pass, 2 penalty)
33—Arizona St. (49) vs. Missouri (35) (Fiesta, 1972) (22 rush, 11 pass, 0 penalty)
32—Brigham Young (24) vs. Michigan (17) (Holiday, 1984)
32—Richmond (49) vs. Ohio (42) (Tangerine, 1968) (8 rush, 24 pass, 0 penalty)
32—Wisconsin (37) vs. Southern California (42) (Rose, 1963) (7 rush, 23 pass, 2 penalty)

31—North Carolina St. (23) vs. Miami (Fla.) (46) (Micron PC, 1998) (18 rush, 10 pass, 3 penalty)
31—UCLA (16) vs. Wisconsin (21) (Rose, 1994)
31—Arkansas (27) vs. Tennessee (31) (Cotton, 1990) (21 rush, 10 pass, 0 penalty)
31—Florida St. (34) vs. Oklahoma St. (23) (Gator, 1985) (10 rush, 21 pass, 0 penalty)
31—Brigham Young (37) vs. Indiana (38) (Holiday, 1979) (9 rush, 21 pass, 1 penalty)
31—(D) Purdue (27) vs. Tennessee (22) (Bluebonnet, 1979)
31—(D) Houston (26) vs. Dayton (21) (Salad, 1952) (25 rush, 6 pass, 0 penalty)

MOST FIRST DOWNS, BOTH TEAMS
61—Penn St. (50) [26] & Brigham Young (39) [35] (Holiday, 1989)
58—Miami (Fla.) (46) [27] & North Carolina St. (23) [31] (Micron PC, 1998)
56—Toledo (40) [33] & Nevada (37) [23] (ot) (Las Vegas, 1995)
56—Mississippi (42) [30] & Air Force (29) [26] (Liberty, 1989)
55—Michigan (35) [35] & Mississippi (3) [20] (Gator, Jan. 1, 1991)
54—Boise St. (34) [28] & Louisville (31) [26] (Humanitarian, 1999)
54—UCLA (45) [29] & Iowa (28) [25] (Rose, 1986)
54—Florida St. (34) [31] & Oklahoma St. (23) [23] (Gator, 1985)
53—Marshall (48) [27] & Louisville (29) [26] (Motor City, 1998)
53—Texas Tech (55) [28] & Air Force (41) [25] (Copper, 1995)
53—Colorado (41) [19] & Fresno St. (30) [34] (Aloha, 1993)
53—Tennessee (23) [28] & Virginia (22) [25] (Sugar, 1991)
53—Colorado (47) [29] & Alabama (33) [24] (Liberty, 1969)
52—Michigan St. (37) [25] & Florida (34) [27] (Florida Citrus, 2000)
52—Mississippi (34) [29] & Marshall (31) [23] (Motor City, 1997)
52—Georgia Tech (35) [28] & West Virginia (30) [24] (Carquest, 1997)
52—Wisconsin (21) [21] & UCLA (16) [31] (Rose, 1994)
52—Notre Dame (39) [23] & Florida (28) [29] (Sugar, 1992)
52—Indiana (38) [21] & Brigham Young (37) [31] (Holiday, 1979)
51—Georgia (28) [21] & Purdue (25) [30] (ot) (Outback, 2000)
51—Miami (Fla.) (28) [22] & Georgia Tech (13) [29] (Gator, 2000)
51—Idaho (42) [26] & Southern Miss. (35) [25] (Humanitarian, 1998)
51—Tennessee (48) [29] & Northwestern (28) [22] (Florida Citrus, 1997)
51—Texas (35) & North Carolina (31) (Sun, 1994)
51—(D) Arkansas (28) [28] & Florida (24) [23] (Bluebonnet, 1982)
50—(D) Toledo (27) [21] & San Jose St. (25) [29] (California, 1981)
50—Texas (21) [25] & Notre Dame (17) [25] (Cotton, 1970)

MOST FIRST DOWNS RUSHING
26—Oklahoma (40) vs. Auburn (22) (Sugar, Jan. 1, 1972)
25—(D) Houston (26) vs. Dayton (21) (Salad, 1952)
24—Colorado (47) vs. Alabama (33) (Liberty, 1969)
23—Georgia Tech (31) vs. Texas Tech (21) (Gator, Dec. 31, 1965)
22—Syracuse (30) vs. Houston (17) (Liberty, 1996)
22—(D) Arkansas (28) vs. Florida (24) (Bluebonnet, 1982)
22—Oklahoma (41) vs. Wyoming (7) (Fiesta, 1976)
22—Arizona St. (49) vs. Missouri (35) (Fiesta, 1972)
21—Nebraska (62) vs. Florida (24) (Fiesta, 1996)
21—Arkansas (27) vs. Tennessee (31) (Cotton, 1990)
21—Florida St. (7) vs. Oklahoma (24) (Orange, 1980)
21—(D) Houston (35) vs. Navy (0) (Garden State, 1980)
21—Mississippi St. (26) vs. North Carolina (24) (Sun, 1974)
21—Missouri (35) vs. Alabama (10) (Gator, 1968)

MOST FIRST DOWNS RUSHING, BOTH TEAMS
36—Miami (Fla.) (46) [16] & Texas (3) [20] (Cotton, 1991)
36—Colorado (47) [24] & Alabama (33) [12] (Liberty, 1969)
32—Miami (Fla.) (46) [14] & North Carolina St. (23) [18] (Micron PC, 1998)
32—Texas Tech (55) [15] & Air Force (41) [17] (Copper, 1995)
32—Tennessee (31) [11] & Arkansas (27) [21] (Cotton, 1990)
32—Oklahoma (41) [22] & Wyoming (7) [10] (Fiesta, 1976)
32—Arizona St. (49) [22] & Missouri (35) [10] (Fiesta, 1972)
32—Texas (21) [19] & Notre Dame (17) [13] (Cotton, 1970)
31—Air Force (38) [18] & Mississippi St. (15) [13] (Liberty, 1991)

MOST FIRST DOWNS PASSING
27—Brigham Young (39) vs. Penn St. (50) (Holiday, 1989)
25—Fresno St. (30) vs. Colorado (41) (Aloha, 1993)
24—West Virginia (31) vs. Missouri (34) (Insight.com, 1998)
24—Richmond (49) vs. Ohio (42) (Tangerine, 1968)
23—Tennessee (48) vs. Northwestern (28) (Florida Citrus, 1997)
23—(D) San Jose St. (25) vs. Toledo (27) (California, 1981)
23—Wisconsin (37) vs. Southern California (42) (Rose, 1963)
21—Southern California (41) vs. Northwestern (32) (Rose, 1996)
21—(D) Fresno St. (29) vs. Bowling Green (28) (California, 1982)
21—Brigham Young (46) vs. Southern Methodist (45) (Holiday, 1980)
21—Brigham Young (37) vs. Indiana (38) (Holiday, 1979)
20—Nevada (18) vs. Ball St. (15) (Las Vegas, 1996)
20—Mississippi (20) vs. Texas Tech (17) (Independence, 1986)
20—Brigham Young (24) vs. Michigan (17) (Holiday, 1984)
20—(D) Vanderbilt (28) vs. Air Force (36) (Hall of Fame, 1982)
19—Brigham Young (21) vs. Ohio St. (28) (Holiday, 1993)
19—(D) Oregon (31) vs. Colorado St. (32) (Freedom, 1990)
19—Florida St. (31) vs. Nebraska (28) (Fiesta, 1988)
19—Florida St. (34) vs. Oklahoma (23) (Gator, 1985)
19—Illinois (29) vs. Army (31) (Peach, 1985)

MOST FIRST DOWNS PASSING, BOTH TEAMS
38—Penn St. (50) [11] & Brigham Young (39) [27] (Holiday, 1989)

36—Tennessee (48) [23] & Northwestern (28) [13] (Florida Citrus, 1997)
32—Southern California (41) [21] & Northwestern (32) [11] (Rose, 1996)
31—Missouri (34) [7] & West Virginia (31) [24] (Insight.com, 1998)
30—Idaho (42) [15] & Southern Miss. (35) [15] (Humanitarian, 1998)
30—Georgia Tech (35) [15] & West Virginia (30) [15] (Carquest, 1997)
30—Colorado (41) [5] & Fresno St. (30) [25] (Aloha, 1993)
30—(D) Fresno St. (29) [21] & Bowling Green (28) [9] (California, 1982)
30—Richmond (49) [24] & Ohio (42) [6] (Tangerine, 1968)
29—Navy (42) [12] & California (38) [17] (Aloha, 1996)
29—Mississippi (42) [17] & Air Force (29) [12] (Liberty, 1989)
29—Indiana (38) [8] & Brigham Young (37) [21] (Holiday, 1979)
28—Ohio St. (28) [12] & Pittsburgh (23) [16] (Fiesta, 1984)
27—Florida St. (23) [12] & Florida (17) [15] (Sugar, Jan. 2, 1995)
27—Brigham Young (31) [18] & Oklahoma (6) [9] (Copper, 1994)
27—Arizona St. (45) [13] & Florida St. (38) [14] (Fiesta, 1971)
26—Boston College (31) [16] & Virginia (13) [10] (Carquest, 1994)
26—(D) Southern California (28) [15] & Utah (21) [11] (Freedom, 1993)
26—Brigham Young (24) [20] & Michigan (17) [6] (Holiday, 1984)
26—Washington (21) [15] & Maryland (20) [11] (Aloha, 1982)
26—(D) Air Force (36) [6] & Vanderbilt (28) [20] (Hall of Fame, 1982)
25—Nevada (18) [20] & Ball St. (15) [5] (Las Vegas, 1996)
25—Wisconsin (34) [8] & Duke (20) [17] (Hall of Fame, 1995)
25—Texas (35) [9] & North Carolina (31) [16] (Sun, 1994)
25—Oklahoma St. (62) [17] & Wyoming (14) [8] (Holiday, 1988)
25—Florida St. (31) [19] & Nebraska (28) [6] (Fiesta, 1988)
25—Miami (Fla.) (31) [15] & Nebraska (30) [10] (Orange, 1984)
25—Brigham Young (46) [21] & Southern Methodist (45) [4] (Holiday, 1980)

MOST FIRST DOWNS BY PENALTY
6—Florida (52) vs. Florida St. (20) (Sugar, 1997)
6—Texas (3) vs. Miami (Fla.) (46) (Cotton, 1991)
5—Iowa (27) vs. Texas Tech (0) (Alamo, 1996)
5—(D) Arizona (13) vs. Utah (16) (Freedom, 1994)
5—Fresno St. (30) vs. Colorado (41) (Aloha, 1993)
5—West Virginia (21) vs. Notre Dame (34) (Fiesta, 1989)
5—(D) Washington (34) vs. Florida (7) (Freedom, 1989)
5—(D) Western Mich. (30) vs. Fresno St. (35) (California, 1988)
5—Miami (Fla.) (7) vs. Tennessee (35) (Sugar, 1986)
5—(D) Miami (Ohio) (7) vs. San Jose St. (37) (California, 1986)
4—Purdue (37) vs. Kansas St. (34) (Alamo, 1998)
4—Oregon (43) vs. Colorado (51) (Aloha, 1998)
4—Syracuse (18) vs. Kansas St. (35) (Fiesta, 1997)
4—Northwestern (28) vs. Tennessee (48) (Florida Citrus, 1997)
4—Texas A&M (22) vs. Michigan (20) (Alamo, 1995)
4—Michigan (20) vs. Texas A&M (22) (Alamo, 1995)
4—Texas (35) vs. North Carolina (31) (Sun, 1994)
4—Alabama (25) vs. Miami (Fla.) (33) (Sugar, 1990)
4—Brigham Young (14) vs. Texas A&M (65) (Holiday, 1990)
4—Georgia (10) vs. Texas (9) (Cotton, 1984)
4—(D) Iowa (55) vs. Texas (17) (Freedom, 1984)
4—(D) Vanderbilt (28) vs. Air Force (36) (Hall of Fame, 1982)
4—Maryland (20) vs. Florida (35) (Tangerine, 1980)
4—Baylor (20) vs. Penn St. (41) (Cotton, 1975)
4—Arkansas (13) vs. Tennessee (14) (Liberty, 1971)
4—Arizona St. (45) vs. Florida St. (38) (Fiesta, 1971)
4—Alabama (33) vs. Colorado (47) (Liberty, 1969)
4—Texas A&M (21) vs. Alabama (29) (Cotton, 1942)

MOST FIRST DOWNS BY PENALTY, BOTH TEAMS
8—Florida (52) [6] & Florida St. (20) [2] (Sugar, 1997)
8—Texas A&M (22) [4] & Michigan (20) [4] (Alamo, 1995)
8—Miami (Fla.) (46) [2] & Texas (3) [6] (Cotton, 1991)
7—Iowa (27) [5] & Texas Tech (0) [2] (Alamo, 1996)
7—(D) Washington (34) [5] & Florida (7) [2] (Freedom, 1989)
7—Tennessee (35) [2] & Miami (Fla.) (7) [5] (Sugar, 1986)
6—Tennessee (48) [2] & Northwestern (28) [4] (Florida Citrus, 1997)
6—Colorado (41) [1] & Fresno St. (30) [5] (Aloha, 1993)
6—Miami (Fla.) (33) [2] & Alabama (25) [4] (Sugar, 1990)
5—Texas A&M (14) [3] & Ohio St. (24) [2] (Sugar, 1999)
5—Idaho (42) [3] & Southern Miss. (35) [2] (Humanitarian, 1998)
5—Colorado (51) [1] & Oregon (43) [4] (Aloha, 1998)
5—North Carolina (20) [3] & West Virginia (13) [2] (Gator, 1996)
5—Texas (35) [4] & North Carolina (31) [1] (Sun, 1994)
5—(D) Utah (16) [0] & Arizona (13) [5] (Freedom, 1994)
5—Florida (41) [3] & West Virginia (7) [2] (Sugar, 1994)
5—Texas A&M (65) [1] & Brigham Young (14) [4] (Holiday, 1990)
5—Notre Dame (34) [0] & West Virginia (21) [5] (Fiesta, 1989)
5—Georgia (10) [4] & Texas (9) [1] (Cotton, 1984)
5—Southern Methodist (7) [3] & Pittsburgh (3) [2] (Cotton, 1983)
5—Pittsburgh (16) [3] & Arizona (10) [2] (Fiesta, 1979)
5—Penn St. (41) [1] & Baylor (20) [4] (Cotton, 1975)

FEWEST FIRST DOWNS
1—Alabama (29) vs. Texas A&M (21) (Cotton, 1942) (passing)
1—Arkansas (0) vs. LSU (0) (Cotton, 1947) (rushing)
2—Michigan St. (0) vs. Auburn (6) (Orange, 1938) (1 rushing, 1 passing)

TEAM RECORD LISTS—FIRST DOWNS

FEWEST FIRST DOWNS, BOTH TEAMS
- 10—Texas (7) [3] & Randolph Field (7) [7] (Cotton, 1944)
- 12—LSU (19) [4] & Texas A&M (14) [8] (Orange, 1944)

FEWEST FIRST DOWNS RUSHING
- 0—Southern California (19) vs. TCU (28) (Sun, 1998)
- 0—Florida (18) vs. Missouri (20) (Sugar, 1966)
- 0—Navy (6) vs. Texas (28) (Cotton, 1964)
- 0—Alabama (29) vs. Texas A&M (21) (Cotton, 1942)

FEWEST FIRST DOWNS RUSHING, BOTH TEAMS
- 3—Alabama (29) [0] & Texas A&M (21) [3] (Cotton, 1942)
- 8—(D) Southern California (28) [4] & Utah (21) [4] (Freedom, 1993)
- 9—Texas (28) [9] & Navy (6) [0] (Cotton, 1964)
- 9—Florida St. (41) [2] & Nebraska (17) [7] (Fiesta, 1990)

FEWEST FIRST DOWNS PASSING
- 0—Army (28) vs. Alabama (29) (John Hancock Sun, 1988)
- 0—Oklahoma (40) vs. Houston (10) (Sun, 1981)
- 0—West Virginia (14) vs. South Carolina (3) (Peach, 1969)
- 0—Missouri (35) vs. Alabama (10) (Gator, 1968)
- 0—Virginia Tech (7) vs. Miami (Fla.) (14) (Liberty, 1966)
- 0—Auburn (7) vs. Mississippi (13) (Liberty, 1965)
- 0—Alabama (10) vs. Arkansas (3) (Sugar, 1962)
- 0—(D) Missouri (14) vs. Georgia Tech (10) (Bluebonnet, 1962)
- 0—Utah St. (13) vs. New Mexico St. (20) (Sun, 1960)
- 0—Arkansas (0) vs. LSU (0) (Cotton, 1947)
- 0—Fordham (2) vs. Missouri (0) (Sugar, 1942)
- 0—Arizona St. (0) vs. Catholic (0) (Sun, 1940)
- 0—West Virginia (7) vs. Texas Tech (6) (Sun, 1938)

FEWEST FIRST DOWNS PASSING, BOTH TEAMS
- 1—Alabama (10) [0] & Arkansas (3) [1] (Sugar, 1962)
- 4—Rice (28) [3] & Colorado (14) [1] (Cotton, 1938)
- 4—Texas (16) [2] & Tennessee (0) [2] (Cotton, 1953)
- 4—Oklahoma (41) [1] & Wyoming (7) [3] (Fiesta, 1976)

Punting

MOST PUNTS
- 17—Duke (3) vs. Southern California (7) (Rose, 1939)
- 16—Alabama (29) vs. Texas A&M (21) (Cotton, 1942)
- 16—New Mexico St. (14) vs. Hardin-Simmons (14) (Sun, 1936)
- 15—Tennessee (0) vs. Rice (8) (Orange, 1947)
- 14—Tulsa (7) vs. Tennessee (14) (Sugar, 1943)
- 14—Santa Clara (6) vs. LSU (0) (Sugar, 1938)
- 14—LSU (0) vs. Santa Clara (6) (Sugar, 1938)
- 14—TCU (3) vs. LSU (2) (Sugar, 1936)
- 13—Rice (8) vs. Tennessee (0) (Orange, 1947)
- 13—Tennessee (0) vs. Southern California (25) (Rose, 1945)
- 13—Oklahoma (0) vs. Tennessee (17) (Orange, 1939)
- 13—Catholic (20) vs. Mississippi (19) (Orange, 1936)
- 13—LSU (2) vs. TCU (3) (Sugar, 1936)
- 13—Miami (Fla.) (0) vs. Bucknell (26) (Orange, 1935)

MOST PUNTS, BOTH TEAMS
- 28—Santa Clara (6) [14] & LSU (0) [14] (Sugar, 1938)
- 28—Rice (8) [13] & Tennessee (0) [15] (Orange, 1947)
- 27—TCU (3) [14] & LSU (2) [13] (Sugar, 1936)
- 25—Tennessee (17) [12] & Oklahoma (0) [13] (Orange, 1939)
- 24—Catholic (20) [13] & Mississippi (19) [11] (Orange, 1936)
- 23—UTEP (14) [12] & Mississippi (7) [11] (Sun, 1967)
- 22—Auburn (6) [10] & Michigan St. (0) [12] (Orange, 1938)

HIGHEST PUNTING AVERAGE
(Minimum 5 Punts)
- 53.9—Southern California (7) vs. Wisconsin (0) (Rose, 1953) (8 for 431)
- 52.3—Tennessee (17) vs. Nebraska (42) (Orange, 1998) (6 for 314)
- 52.0—Iowa (27) vs. Texas Tech (0) (Alamo, 1996) (5 for 260)
- 51.5—Colorado (51) vs. Oregon (43) (Aloha, 1998) (6 for 309)
- 51.0—Penn St. (10) vs. Clemson (35) (Florida Citrus, 1988) (5 for 255)
- 50.0—Nevada (37) vs. Toledo (40) (ot) (Las Vegas, 1995) (5 for 250)
- 50.0—Mississippi St. (17) vs. Nebraska (31) (Sun, 1980) (5 for 250)
- 49.3—Clemson (0) vs. Syracuse (41) (Gator, 1996) (6 for 296)
- 49.2—(D) Air Force (24) vs. Texas (16) (Bluebonnet, 1985) (11 for 541)
- 49.2—Arkansas (3) vs. UCLA (17) (Cotton, 1989) (6 for 295)
- 49.0—Iowa (3) vs. Arizona St. (17) (Sun, 1997) (8 for 392)
- 49.0—Indiana (24) vs. Baylor (0) (Copper, 1991) (6 for 294)
- 49.0—(D) Mississippi St. (10) vs. Kansas (0) (Hall of Fame, 1981) (9 for 441)
- 48.3—Brigham Young (3) vs. Marshall (21) (Motor City, 1999) (7 for 338)
- 48.1—Florida (52) vs. Florida St. (20) (Sugar, 1997) (7 for 337)
- 48.1—Ohio St. (14) vs. Tennessee (20) (Florida Citrus, 1996) (7 for 337)
- 48.0—Oklahoma (41) vs. Texas Tech (10) (John Hancock, 1993) (7 for 336)
- 48.0—Kansas (23) vs. Brigham Young (20) (Aloha, 1992) (8 for 384)
- 47.9—Penn St. (42) vs. Tennessee (17) (Fiesta, 1992) (9 for 431)
- 47.9—Oregon St. (20) vs. Duke (16) (Rose, 1942) (7 for 335)
- 47.6—Oklahoma (42) vs. Arkansas (8) (Orange, 1987) (5 for 238)
- 47.5—St. Mary's (Cal.) (20) vs. Texas Tech (13) (Cotton, 1939) (11 for 523)
- 47.4—Georgia Tech (18) vs. Stanford (17) (Aloha, 1991) (7 for 332)
- 47.4—(D) Fresno St. (51) vs. Bowling Green (7) (California, 1985) (7 for 332)
- 47.4—(D) Tennessee (28) vs. Wisconsin (21) (Garden State, 1981) (5 for 237)

FEWEST PUNTS
- 0—Illinois (63) vs. Virginia (21) (Micronpc.com, 1999)
- 0—Oklahoma St. (62) vs. Wyoming (14) (Holiday, 1988)
- 0—Oklahoma (41) vs. Wyoming (7) (Fiesta, 1976)
- 1—Oklahoma (25) vs. Mississippi (27) (Independence, 1999)
- 1—Nebraska (62) vs. Florida (24) (Fiesta, 1996)
- 1—Brigham Young (39) vs. Penn St. (50) (Holiday, 1989)
- 1—Nebraska (21) vs. LSU (20) (Orange, 1983)
- 1—North Carolina St. (31) vs. Kansas (18) (Liberty, 1973)
- 1—Utah (32) vs. West Virginia (6) (Liberty, 1964)
- 1—(D) Miami (Fla.) (34) vs. Nebraska (36) (Gotham, 1962)
- 1—Georgia Tech (42) vs. West Virginia (19) (Sugar, 1954)
- 1—West Virginia (19) vs. Georgia Tech (42) (Sugar, 1954)
- 1—Missouri (23) vs. Clemson (24) (Gator, 1949)

LOWEST PUNTING AVERAGE
(Minimum 3 Punts)
- 17.0—Nevada (34) vs. Bowling Green (35) (Las Vegas, 1992) (4 for 68)
- 17.0—Kentucky (14) vs. Penn St. (26) (Outback, 1999) (3 for 51)
- 19.0—Cincinnati (18) vs. Virginia Tech (6) (Sun, 1947) (6 for 114)
- 22.0—Mississippi St. (16) vs. North Carolina St. (12) (Liberty, 1963) (3 for 66)
- 23.0—Bowling Green (35) vs. Nevada (34) (Las Vegas, 1992) (5 for 115)
- 25.5—Houston (34) vs. Notre Dame (35) (Cotton, 1979) (10 for 255)
- 26.1—Michigan (14) vs. Alabama (17) (Outback, 1997) (7 for 183)
- 26.3—Oklahoma St. (34) vs. TCU (0) (Cotton, 1945) (6 for 158)
- 26.3—Rice (28) vs. Alabama (6) (Cotton, 1954) (8 for 210)
- 26.3—Notre Dame (35) vs. Houston (34) (Cotton, 1979) (7 for 184)

MOST PUNTS BLOCKED BY ONE TEAM
- 2—LSU (25) vs. Colorado (7) (Orange, 1962)
- 2—North Carolina St. (14) vs. Georgia (7) (Liberty, 1967)
- 2—North Carolina (21) vs. Mississippi St. (17) (Peach, Jan. 2, 1993)

Punt Returns

MOST PUNT RETURNS
- 9—Georgia (7) vs. North Carolina (3) (Gator, Dec. 31, 1971) (6.8 average)
- 8—Indiana (20) vs. Virginia Tech (45) (Independence, 1993) (7.3 average)
- 8—Tennessee (34) vs. Air Force (13) (Sugar, 1971) (10.8 average)
- 8—Mississippi (7) vs. UTEP (14) (Sun, 1967) (9.4 average)
- 8—Michigan (34) vs. Oregon St. (7) (Rose, 1965) (10.6 average)
- 7—Stanford (38) vs. Michigan St. (0) (Sun, 1996) (13.4 average)
- 7—Louisville (34) vs. Alabama (7) (Fiesta, 1991) (7.3 average)
- 6—UCLA (29) vs. Texas A&M (23) (Cotton, 1998) (11.0 average)
- 6—Florida (52) vs. Florida St. (20) (Sugar, 1997) (11.5 average)
- 6—Ohio St. (14) vs. Tennessee (20) (Florida Citrus, 1996) (5.0 average)
- 6—Tennessee (17) vs. Penn St. (42) (Fiesta, 1992) (8.2 average)
- 6—Clemson (30) vs. Illinois (0) (Hall of Fame, 1991)
- 6—(D) San Jose St. (48) vs. Central Mich. (24) (California, 1990)
- 6—Brigham Young (7) vs. Ohio St. (10) (Florida Citrus, 1985)
- 6—Texas (9) vs. Georgia (10) (Cotton, 1984) (2.5 average)
- 6—Washington (21) vs. Maryland (20) (Aloha, 1982) (4.7 average)
- 6—(D) Vanderbilt (28) vs. Air Force (36) (Hall of Fame, 1982)
- 6—Washington St. (36) vs. Brigham Young (38) (Holiday, 1981)
- 6—Nebraska (38) vs. Alabama (6) (Orange, 1972) (22.7 average)
- 6—Miami (Fla.) (14) vs. Syracuse (15) (Liberty, 1961) (13.0 average)
- 6—Air Force (0) vs. TCU (0) (Cotton, 1959) (5.8 average)
- 6—Tulane (13) vs. Texas A&M (14) (Sugar, 1940) (21.0 average)
- 6—Tulane (20) vs. Temple (14) (Sugar, 1935)
- 6—Tulane (12) vs. Southern California (21) (Rose, 1932)

MOST PUNT RETURN YARDS
- 136—Nebraska (38) vs. Alabama (6) (Orange, 1972) (6 returns)
- 128—Oklahoma (20) vs. Duke (21) (Orange, 1958)
- 126—Tulane (13) vs. Texas A&M (14) (Sugar, 1940) (6 returns)
- 124—Washington (44) vs. Wisconsin (8) (Rose, 1960) (4 returns)
- 124—California (37) vs. Clemson (13) (Florida Citrus, 1992) (5 returns)
- 108—Southern Miss. (38) vs. UTEP (18) (Independence, 1988) (2 returns)
- 107—Arizona St. (45) vs. Florida (38) (Fiesta, 1971) (5 returns)
- 104—Texas A&M (21) vs. Alabama (29) (Cotton, 1942) (5 returns)
- 100—Virginia (34) vs. Georgia (27) (Peach, Dec. 30, 1995) (4 returns)
- 99—Kent (18) vs. Tampa (21) (Tangerine, 1972) (3 returns)
- 98—Brigham Young (46) vs. Southern Methodist (45) (Holiday, 1980) (3 returns)
- 94—Denver (24) vs. New Mexico (34) (Sun, 1946)
- 94—Stanford (38) vs. Michigan St. (0) (Sun, 1996) (7 returns)
- 93—Auburn (35) vs. Mississippi (28) (Gator, Jan. 2, 1971) (4 returns)
- 92—Southern California (7) vs. Ohio St. (20) (Rose, 1955) (2 returns)
- 89—Nebraska (28) vs. Florida St. (31) (Fiesta, 1988) (3 returns)
- 88—Penn St. (42) vs. Arizona St. (30) (Fiesta, 1977) (2 returns)

HIGHEST PUNT RETURN AVERAGE
(Minimum 3 Returns)
- 33.0—Kent (18) vs. Tampa (21) (Tangerine, 1972) (3 for 99)
- 32.7—Brigham Young (46) vs. Southern Methodist (45) (Holiday, 1980) (3 for 98)
- 31.0—Washington (44) vs. Wisconsin (8) (Rose, 1960) (4 for 124)

30.7—Michigan (42) vs. North Carolina St. (7) (Hall of Fame, 1994) (3 for 92)
29.7—Nebraska (28) vs. Florida St. (31) (Fiesta, 1988) (3 for 89)
27.6—Kansas St. (52) vs. Wyoming (17) (Copper, 1993) (3 for 83)
25.0—Virginia (34) vs. Georgia (27) (Peach, Dec. 30, 1995) (4 for 100)
24.8—California (37) vs. Clemson (13) (Florida Citrus, 1992) (5 for 124)
24.0—Auburn (31) vs. Ohio St. (14) (Hall of Fame, 1990) (3 for 72)
23.3—Auburn (35) vs. Mississippi (28) (Gator, Jan. 2, 1971) (4 for 93)
22.7—Nebraska (38) vs. Alabama (6) (Orange, 1972) (6 for 136)
21.4—Arizona St. (45) vs. Florida St. (38) (Fiesta, 1971) (5 for 107)
21.0—Tulane (13) vs. Texas A&M (14) (Sugar, 1940) (6 for 126)
21.0—Arkansas (6) vs. Duke (7) (Cotton, 1961) (3 for 63)
20.8—Texas A&M (21) vs. Alabama (29) (Cotton, 1942) (5 for 104)
19.5—(D) Georgia (20) vs. Texas A&M (40) (Presidential Cup, 1950) (4 for 78)
19.3—Nebraska (14) vs. Houston (17) (Cotton, 1980) (3 for 58)

Kickoff Returns

MOST KICKOFF RETURNS
10—Florida (24) vs. Nebraska (62) (Fiesta, 1996) (26.8 average)
10—Wyoming (14) vs. Oklahoma St. (62) (Holiday, 1988) (20.5 average)
9—Brigham Young (14) vs. Texas A&M (65) (Holiday, 1990) (18.2 average)
8—Brigham Young (27) vs. Tulane (41) (Liberty, 1998) (31.0 average)
8—North Carolina St. (23) vs. Miami (Fla.) (46) (Micron PC, 1998) (18.3 average)
8—Virginia Tech (3) vs. North Carolina (42) (Gator, 1998) (19.4 average)
8—Florida St. (20) vs. Florida (52) (Sugar, 1997) (19.0 average)
8—Northwestern (32) vs. Southern California (41) (Rose, 1996) (28.1 average)
8—Nebraska (21) vs. Georgia Tech (45) (Florida Citrus, 1991) (23.6 average)
8—Notre Dame (10) vs. Texas A&M (35) (Cotton, 1988) (18.9 average)
8—Texas Tech (17) vs. Florida St. (40) (Tangerine, 1977)
8—UCLA (6) vs. Alabama (36) (Liberty, 1976) (17.6 average)
8—Brigham Young (21) vs. Oklahoma St. (49) (Tangerine, 1976)
8—(D) Tulane (7) vs. Houston (47) (Bluebonnet, 1973) (28.1 average)
8—Missouri (35) vs. Arizona St. (49) (Fiesta, 1972) (32.3 average)
8—Arizona St. (45) vs. Florida St. (38) (Fiesta, 1971) (16.4 average)
8—Florida (38) vs. Arizona St. (45) (Fiesta, 1971) (23.0 average)
8—Colorado (47) vs. Alabama (33) (Liberty, 1969) (27.8 average)
8—Ohio (42) vs. Richmond (49) (Tangerine, 1968)
8—Florida St. (20) vs. UTEP (47) (Sun, 1955)
8—UCLA (14) vs. Illinois (45) (Rose, 1947) (32.4 average)

MOST KICKOFF RETURN YARDS
268—Florida (24) vs. Nebraska (62) (Fiesta, 1996) (10 returns)
259—UCLA (14) vs. Illinois (45) (Rose, 1947) (8 returns)
258—Missouri (35) vs. Arizona St. (49) (Fiesta, 1972) (8 returns)
248—Brigham Young (27) vs. Tulane (41) (Liberty, 1998) (8 returns)
225—(D) Tulane (7) vs. Houston (47) (Bluebonnet, 1973) (8 returns)
225—Northwestern (32) vs. Southern California (41) (Rose, 1996) (8 returns)
222—Colorado (47) vs. Alabama (33) (Liberty, 1969) (8 returns)
207—California (38) vs. Navy (42) (Aloha, 1996) (7 returns)
205—Wyoming (14) vs. Oklahoma (62) (Holiday, 1988) (10 returns)
204—Brigham Young (21) vs. Oklahoma St. (49) (Tangerine, 1976) (8 returns)
191—Houston (22) vs. Washington St. (24) (Aloha, 1988) (5 returns)
189—Nebraska (21) vs. Georgia Tech (45) (Florida Citrus, 1991) (8 returns)
188—Stanford (13) vs. East Caro. (19) (Liberty, 1995) (6 returns)
187—Houston (28) vs. Boston College (45) (Cotton, 1985) (7 returns)
187—Idaho (42) vs. Southern Miss. (35) (Humanitarian, 1998) (6 returns)
184—Florida St. (38) vs. Arizona St. (45) (Fiesta, 1971) (8 returns)
179—Washington (21) vs. Colorado (33) (Holiday, 1996) (5 returns)
176—Missouri (34) vs. West Virginia (31) (Insight.com, 1998) (6 returns)
174—Hawaii (13) vs. Michigan St. (33) (Aloha, 1989) (7 returns)
170—Tennessee (27) vs. Maryland (28) (John Hancock, 1984) (4 returns)
169—Oregon St. (19) vs. Iowa (35) (Rose, 1957) (5 returns)
164—Brigham Young (14) vs. Texas A&M (65) (Holiday, 1990) (9 returns)

HIGHEST KICKOFF RETURN AVERAGE
(Minimum 3 Returns)
42.5—Tennessee (27) vs. Maryland (28) (John Hancock, 1984) (4 for 170)
38.3—Fresno St. (30) vs. Colorado (41) (Aloha, 1993) (3 for 115)
38.3—Ohio St. (28) vs. Pittsburgh (23) (Fiesta, 1984) (4 for 153)
38.2—Houston (22) vs. Washington St. (24) (Aloha, 1988) (5 for 191)
37.5—LSU (45) vs. Michigan St. (26) (Independence, 1995) (4 for 150)
37.5—Notre Dame (24) vs. Alabama (23) (Sugar, 1973) (4 for 150)
36.8—Ohio St. (17) vs. Syracuse (24) (Hall of Fame, 1992) (4 for 147)
36.7—Indiana (20) vs. Virginia Tech (45) (Independence, 1993) (3 for 110)
35.8—Washington (21) vs. Colorado (33) (Holiday, 1996) (5 for 179)
33.8—Oregon St. (19) vs. Iowa (35) (Rose, 1957) (5 for 169)
32.8—Florida St. (40) vs. Texas Tech (17) (Tangerine, 1977) (4 for 131)
32.6—UCLA (30) vs. Kansas (51) (Aloha, 1995) (5 for 163)
32.4—UCLA (14) vs. Illinois (45) (Rose, 1947) (8 for 259)
32.3—Missouri (35) vs. Arizona St. (49) (Fiesta, 1972) (8 for 258)
31.7—Penn St. (41) vs. Baylor (20) (Cotton, 1975) (3 for 95)
31.6—Virginia Tech (21) vs. Nebraska (41) (Orange, 1996) (3 for 95)
31.5—Kentucky (14) vs. Penn St. (26) (Outback, 1999) (4 for 126)
31.3—Penn St. (38) vs. Texas (15) (Fiesta, 1997) (4 for 125)
31.3—Stanford (13) vs. East Caro. (19) (Liberty, 1995) (6 for 188)
31.2—Idaho (42) vs. Southern Miss. (35) (Humanitarian, 1998) (6 for 187)
31.0—Brigham Young (27) vs. Tulane (41) (Liberty, 1998) (8 for 248)
29.5—California (38) vs. Navy (42) (Aloha, 1996) (7 for 207)
29.4—Virginia (34) vs. Georgia (27) (Peach, Dec. 30, 1995) (5 for 147)
29.3—Missouri (34) vs. West Virginia (31) (Insight.com, 1998) (6 for 176)
29.0—Mississippi St. (17) vs. Nebraska (31) (Sun, 1980) (4 for 116)
28.1—Northwestern (32) vs. Southern California (41) (Rose, 1996) (8 for 225)
27.8—Brigham Young (21) vs. Ohio St. (28) (Holiday, 1993) (5 for 139)
27.6—Houston (17) vs. Syracuse (30) (Liberty, 1996) (5 for 138)
27.2—West Virginia (30) vs. Georgia Tech (35) (Carquest, 1997) (6 for 163)
27.0—Arizona St. (17) vs. Arkansas (18) (Holiday, 1985) (3 for 81)
26.8—Florida (24) vs. Nebraska (62) (Fiesta, 1996) (10 for 268)
26.7—Houston (28) vs. Boston College (45) (Cotton, 1985) (7 for 187)

Fumbles

MOST FUMBLES
11—Mississippi (7) vs. Alabama (12) (Sugar, 1964) (lost 6)
9—Texas (11) vs. Notre Dame (24) (Cotton, 1971) (lost 5)
8—North Carolina St. (28) vs. Iowa (23) (Peach, Dec. 31, 1988) (lost 5)
8—(D) Houston (35) vs. Navy (0) (Garden State, 1980) (lost 3)
8—Louisville (14) vs. Louisiana Tech (24) (Independence, 1977) (lost 3)
8—North Texas (8) vs. New Mexico St. (28) (Sun, 1959) (lost 6)
8—TCU (0) vs. Air Force (0) (Cotton, 1959) (lost 3)
8—Colorado (27) vs. Clemson (21) (Orange, 1957) (lost 3)
7—(D) Florida (7) vs. Washington (34) (Freedom, 1989) (lost 3)
7—Hawaii (13) vs. Michigan St. (33) (Aloha, 1989) (lost 4)
7—(D) Toledo (27) vs. San Jose St. (25) (California, 1981) (lost 2)
7—(D) Texas A&M (28) vs. Southern California (47) (Bluebonnet, 1977) (lost 5)
7—Auburn (27) vs. Texas (3) (Gator, 1974) (lost 5)
7—Tennessee (34) vs. Air Force (13) (Sugar, 1971) (lost 4)
7—Air Force (13) vs. Tennessee (34) (Sugar, 1971) (lost 3)
7—Georgia (2) vs. Arkansas (16) (Sugar, 1969) (lost 5)
7—Alabama (0) vs. Penn St. (7) (Liberty, 1959) (lost 4)
7—Southern California (7) vs. Ohio St. (20) (Rose, 1955) (lost 3)
7—Wash. & Lee (7) vs. Wyoming (20) (Gator, 1951) (lost 2)
7—Missouri (7) vs. Maryland (20) (Gator, 1950)
7—(D) Georgia (20) vs. Texas A&M (40) (Presidential Cup, 1950)
7—(D) Arizona St. (21) vs. Xavier (Ohio) (33) (Salad, 1950) (lost 6)

MOST FUMBLES, BOTH TEAMS
17—Alabama (12) [6] & Mississippi (7) [11] (Sugar, 1964) (lost 9)
14—Louisiana Tech (24) [6] & Louisville (14) [8] (Independence, 1977) (lost 6)
14—Tennessee (34) [7] & Air Force (13) [7] (Sugar, 1971) (lost 7)
13—TCU (0) [8] & Air Force (0) [5] (Cotton, 1959) (lost 6)
12—North Carolina St. (28) [8] & Iowa (23) [4] (Peach, Dec. 31, 1988) (lost 8)
12—(D) Houston (35) [8] & Navy (0) [4] (Garden State, 1980) (lost 6)
12—New Mexico St. (28) [4] & North Texas (8) [8] (Sun, 1959) (lost 8)
11—(D) Toledo (27) [7] & San Jose St. (25) [4] (California, 1981) (lost 3)
11—Oklahoma (41) [6] & Wyoming (7) [5] (Fiesta, 1976)
10—Alabama (30) [5] & Baylor (2) [5] (Cotton, 1981) (lost 5)
10—(D) Houston (31) [5] & North Carolina St. (31) [5] (Bluebonnet, 1974) (lost 4)
10—Notre Dame (24) [1] & Texas (11) [9] (Cotton, 1971) (lost 6)
10—Illinois (17) [5] & Washington (7) [5] (Rose, 1964) (lost 6)
10—Navy (20) [5] & Rice (7) [5] (Cotton, 1958) (lost 8)
10—Mississippi (7) [5] & Florida (3) [5] (Gator, 1958) (lost 5)
10—Texas (16) [5] & Tennessee (0) [5] (Cotton, 1953) (lost 6)

MOST FUMBLES LOST
6—Texas A&M (2) vs. Florida St. (10) (Cotton, 1992) (6 fumbles)
6—East Caro. (31) vs. Maine (0) (Tangerine, 1965) (6 fumbles)
6—Mississippi (7) vs. Alabama (12) (Sugar, 1964) (11 fumbles)
6—North Texas (8) vs. New Mexico St. (28) (Sun, 1959) (8 fumbles)
6—(D) Arizona St. (21) vs. Xavier (Ohio) (33) (Salad, 1950) (7 fumbles)
5—Southern Miss. (35) vs. Idaho (42) (Humanitarian, 1998) (6 fumbles)
5—UCLA (16) vs. Wisconsin (21) (Rose, 1994) (5 fumbles)
5—North Carolina St. (28) vs. Iowa (23) (Peach, Dec. 31, 1988) (8 fumbles)
5—North Carolina (21) vs. Arizona (30) (Aloha, 1986) (5 fumbles)
5—(D) Bowling Green (7) vs. Fresno St. (51) (California, 1985) (6 fumbles)
5—(D) Georgia (22) vs. Stanford (25) (Bluebonnet, 1978) (6 fumbles)
5—(D) Texas A&M (28) vs. Southern California (47) (Bluebonnet, 1977) (7 fumbles)
5—Auburn (27) vs. Texas (3) (Gator, 1974) (7 fumbles)
5—Texas (11) vs. Notre Dame (24) (Cotton, 1971) (9 fumbles)
5—Georgia (2) vs. Arkansas (16) (Sugar, 1969) (7 fumbles)
5—(D) Utah St. (9) vs. Baylor (24) (Gotham, 1961) (5 fumbles)
5—Rice (7) vs. Navy (20) (Cotton, 1958) (5 fumbles)
5—Auburn (13) vs. Vanderbilt (25) (Gator, 1955) (5 fumbles)
5—Oklahoma (7) vs. Kentucky (13) (Sugar, 1951)
5—Missouri (7) vs. Maryland (20) (Gator, 1950) (7 fumbles)
5—Texas A&M (21) vs. Alabama (29) (Cotton, 1942) (6 fumbles)

MOST FUMBLES LOST, BOTH TEAMS
9—Alabama (12) [3] & Mississippi (7) [6] (Sugar, 1964) (17 fumbles)
8—Idaho (42) [3] & Southern Miss. (35) [5] (Humanitarian, 1998) (9 fumbles)
8—North Carolina St. (28) [5] & Iowa (23) [3] (Peach, Dec. 31, 1988) (12 fumbles)
8—New Mexico St. (28) [2] & North Texas (8) [6] (Sun, 1959) (12 fumbles)
8—Navy (20) [3] & Rice (7) [5] (Cotton, 1958) (10 fumbles)

TEAM RECORD LISTS—FUMBLES 331

7—Florida St. (10) [1] & Texas A&M (2) [6] (Cotton, 1992) (7 fumbles)
7—Texas A&M (37) [3] & Florida (14) [4] (Sun, Jan. 2, 1977) (8 fumbles)
7—Arizona St. (28) [3] & Pittsburgh (7) [4] (Fiesta, 1973) (9 fumbles)
7—Tennessee (34) [4] & Air Force (13) [3] (Sugar, 1971) (14 fumbles)
7—Michigan St. (28) [4] & UCLA (20) [3] (Rose, 1954) (8 fumbles)

Penalties

MOST PENALTIES
21—Mississippi St. (17) vs. Clemson (7) (Peach, 1999) (188 yards)
20—(D) Fresno St. (35) vs. Western Mich. (30) (California, 1988) (166 yards)
19—Oregon (41) vs. Air Force (13) (Las Vegas, 1997) (166 yards)
18—Alabama (34) vs. Michigan (35) (ot) (Orange, 2000) (132 yards)
18—Washington St. (31) vs. Utah (28) (Copper, 1992) (136 yards)
17—Tennessee (17) vs. Oklahoma (0) (Orange, 1939) (157 yards)
16—Miami (Fla.) (46) vs. Texas (3) (Cotton, 1991) (202 yards)
16—Tulsa (16) vs. McNeese St. (20) (Independence, 1976) (100 yards)
15—Utah (17) vs. Fresno St. (16) (Las Vegas, 1999) (151 yards)
15—Florida (52) vs. Florida St. (20) (Sugar, 1997) (102 yards)
15—Washington St. (10) vs. Baylor (3) (Alamo, 1994) (110 yards)
15—Illinois (30) vs. East Caro. (0) (Liberty, 1994) (164 yards)
15—Utah St. (42) vs. Ball St. (33) (Las Vegas, 1993) (150 yards)
15—Miami (Fla.) (7) vs. Tennessee (35) (Sugar, 1986) (120 yards)
15—(D) Michigan (33) vs. UCLA (14) (Bluebonnet, 1981) (148 yards)
14—Oregon St. (17) vs. Hawaii (23) (Oahu Classic, 1999) (138 yards)
14—Louisville (31) vs. Boise St. (34) (Humanitarian, 1999) (120 yards)
14—Purdue (25) vs. Georgia (28) (ot) (Outback, 2000) (153 yards)
14—Kentucky (14) vs. Penn St. (26) (Outback, 1999) (103 yards)
14—Marshall (48) vs. Louisville (29) (Motor City, 1998) (123 yards)
14—Kansas St. (34) vs. Purdue (37) (Alamo, 1998) (125 yards)
14—Florida St. (20) vs. Florida (52) (Sugar, 1997) (115 yards)
14—(D) San Jose St. (37) vs. Miami (Ohio) (7) (California, 1986) (163 yards)

MOST PENALTIES, BOTH TEAMS
29—Mississippi St. (17) [21] & Clemson (7) [8] (Peach, 1999) (270 yards)
29—Florida (52) [15] & Florida St. (20) [14] (Sugar, 1997) (217 yards)
29—McNeese St. (20) [13] & Tulsa (16) [16] (Independence, 1976) (205 yards)
28—Michigan (35) [10] & Alabama (34) [18] (ot) (Orange, 2000) (247 yards)
28—(D) Fresno St. (35) [20] & Western Mich. (30) [8] (California, 1988) (231 yards)
27—Marshall (48) [14] & Louisville (29) [13] (Motor City, 1998) (232 yards)
26—Oregon (41) [19] & Air Force (13) [7] (Las Vegas, 1997) (223 yards)
26—Tennessee (35) [11] & Miami (Fla.) [7] [15] (Sugar, 1986) (245 yards)
26—Tennessee (17) [17] & Oklahoma (0) [9] (Orange, 1939) (221 yards)
25—Washington St. (31) [18] & Utah (28) [7] (Copper, 1992) (191 yards)
24—Georgia (28) [10] & Purdue (25) [14] (ot) (Outback, 2000) (208 yards)
24—Miami (Fla.) (46) [16] & Texas (3) [8] (Cotton, 1991) (270 yards)
24—(D) San Jose St. (37) [14] & Miami (Ohio) (7) [10] (California, 1986) (264 yards)
24—(D) Michigan (33) [15] & UCLA (14) [9] (Bluebonnet, 1981) (242 yards)
23—Hawaii (23) [9] & Oregon St. (17) [14] (Oahu Classic, 1999) (226 yards)
23—Kansas St. (54) [12] & Colorado St. (21) [11] (Holiday, 1995) (219 yards)
23—(D) Fresno St. (51) [12] & Bowling Green (7) [11] (California, 1985) (183 yards)
22—Penn St. (26) [8] & Kentucky (14) [14] (Outback, 1999) (161 yards)
22—(D) Eastern Mich. (30) [9] & San Jose St. (27) [13] (California, 1987) (162 yards)
21—Utah (17) [15] & Fresno St. (16) [6] (Las Vegas, 1999) (210 yards)
21—Florida St. (16) [12] & Tennessee (23) [9] (Fiesta, 1999) (165 yards)
21—Purdue (37) [7] & Kansas St. (34) [14] (Alamo, 1998) (160 yards)
21—Illinois (30) [15] & East Caro. (0) [6] (Liberty, 1994) (204 yards)
21—Florida St. (18) [10] & Nebraska (16) [11] (Orange, 1994) (184 yards)
21—Ohio St. (47) [12] & Brigham Young (17) [9] (Holiday, 1982) (184 yards)
21—Oklahoma St. (16) [12] & Brigham Young (6) [9] (Fiesta, 1974) (150 yards)

MOST YARDS PENALIZED
202—Miami (Fla.) (46) vs. Texas (3) (Cotton, 1991) (16 penalties)
188—Mississippi St. (17) vs. Clemson (7) (Peach, 1999) (21 penalties)
166—Oregon (41) vs. Air Force (13) (Las Vegas, 1997) (19 penalties)
166—(D) Fresno St. (35) vs. Western Mich. (30) (California, 1988) (20 penalties)
164—Illinois (30) vs. East Caro. (0) (Liberty, 1994) (15 penalties)
163—(D) San Jose St. (37) vs. Miami (Ohio) (7) (California, 1986) (14 penalties)
153—Purdue (25) vs. Georgia (28) (ot) (Outback, 2000) (14 penalties)
151—Utah (17) vs. Fresno St. (16) (Las Vegas, 1999) (15 penalties)
150—Utah St. (42) vs. Ball St. (33) (Las Vegas, 1993) (15 penalties)
150—Oklahoma (48) vs. Duke (21) (Orange, 1958) (12 penalties)
148—(D) Michigan (33) vs. UCLA (14) (Bluebonnet, 1981) (15 penalties)
143—Miami (Fla.) (22) vs. Nebraska (0) (Orange, 1992) (12 penalties)
140—Lamar (21) vs. Middle Tenn. St. (19) (Tangerine, 1961) (13 penalties)
138—Oregon St. (17) vs. Hawaii (23) (Oahu Classic, 1999) (14 penalties)
136—Washington St. (31) vs. Utah (28) (Copper, 1992) (18 penalties)
135—Florida St. (41) vs. Nebraska (17) (Fiesta, 1990) (13 penalties)
132—Alabama (34) vs. Michigan (35) (ot) (Orange, 2000) (18 penalties)
130—LSU (15) vs. Nebraska (30) (Sugar, 1987) (12 penalties)
130—Tennessee (17) vs. Oklahoma (0) (Orange, 1939)

MOST YARDS PENALIZED, BOTH TEAMS
270—Miami (Fla.) (46) [202] & Texas (3) [68] (Cotton, 1991)
270—Mississippi St. (17) [188] & Clemson (7) [82] (Peach, 1999)
264—(D) San Jose St. (37) [163] & Miami (Ohio) (7) [101] (California, 1986)
247—Michigan (35) [115] & Alabama (34) [132] (ot) (Orange, 2000)
245—Tennessee (35) [125] & Miami (Fla.) (7) [120] (Sugar, 1986)
242—(D) Michigan (33) [148] & UCLA (14) [94] (Bluebonnet, 1981)
232—Marshall (48) [123] & Louisville (29) [109] (Motor City, 1998)
231—(D) Fresno St. (35) [166] & Western Mich. (30) [65] (California, 1988)
226—Hawaii (23) [88] & Oregon St. (17) [138] (Oahu Classic, 1999)
223—Oregon (41) [166] & Air Force (13) [57] (Las Vegas, 1997)
221—Tennessee (17) [130] & Oklahoma (0) [91] (Orange, 1939)
219—Kansas St. (54) [124] & Colorado St. (21) [95] (Holiday, 1995)
217—Florida (52) [102] & Florida St. (20) [115] (Sugar, 1997)
210—Utah (17) [151] & Fresno St. (16) [59] (Las Vegas, 1999)
208—Georgia (28) [55] & Purdue (25) [153] (ot) (Outback, 2000)
205—McNeese St. (20) [105] & Tulsa (16) [100] (Independence, 1976)
204—Illinois (30) [164] & East Caro. (0) [40] (Liberty, 1994)

FEWEST PENALTIES
0—Southern Methodist (7) vs. Alabama (28) (Sun, 1983)
0—Louisiana Tech (13) vs. East Caro. (35) (Independence, 1978)
0—Texas (17) vs. Alabama (13) (Cotton, 1973)
0—(D) Rice (7) vs. Kansas (33) (Bluebonnet, 1961)
0—Pittsburgh (14) vs. Georgia Tech (21) (Gator, 1956)
0—Clemson (0) vs. Miami (Fla.) (14) (Gator, 1952)
0—Texas (7) vs. Randolph Field (7) (Cotton, 1944)
0—Alabama (20) vs. Washington (19) (Rose, 1926)

FEWEST PENALTIES, BOTH TEAMS
3—Alabama (28) [3] & Southern Methodist (7) [0] (Sun, 1983)
3—Penn St. (30) [2] & Texas (6) [1] (Cotton, 1972)
3—Texas (21) [1] & Notre Dame (17) [2] (Cotton, 1970)
3—Penn St. (15) [1] & Kansas (14) [2] (Orange, 1969)
3—(D) Kansas (33) [3] & Rice (7) [0] (Bluebonnet, 1961)

FEWEST YARDS PENALIZED
0—Southern Methodist (7) vs. Alabama (28) (Sun, 1983)
0—Louisiana Tech (13) vs. East Caro. (35) (Independence, 1978)
0—Texas (17) vs. Alabama (13) (Cotton, 1973)
0—(D) Rice (7) vs. Kansas (33) (Bluebonnet, 1961)
0—Pittsburgh (14) vs. Georgia Tech (21) (Gator, 1956)
0—Clemson (0) vs. Miami (Fla.) (14) (Gator, 1952)
0—Texas (7) vs. Randolph Field (7) (Cotton, 1944)
0—Alabama (20) vs. Washington (19) (Rose, 1926)

FEWEST YARDS PENALIZED, BOTH TEAMS
10—Duquesne (13) [5] & Mississippi St. (12) [5] (Orange, 1937)
15—(D) Kansas (33) [15] vs. Rice (7) [0] (Bluebonnet, 1961)
15—Texas (21) [5] & Notre Dame (17) [10] (Cotton, 1970)

Miscellaneous Records

SCORELESS TIES#
1959—Air Force 0, TCU 0 (Cotton)
1947—Arkansas 0, LSU 0 (Cotton)
1940—Arizona St. 0, Catholic 0 (Sun)
1922—California 0, Wash. & Jeff. 0 (Rose)

TIE GAMES#
(Not Scoreless)
1991—Brigham Young 13, Iowa 13 (Holiday)
1990—Louisiana Tech 34, Maryland 34 (Independence)
1988—Auburn 16, Syracuse 16 (Sugar)
1985—Arizona 13, Georgia 13 (Sun)
1984—Florida St. 17, Georgia 17 (Florida Citrus)
1978—Arkansas 10, UCLA 10 (Fiesta)
1977—(D) Maryland 17, Minnesota 17 (Hall of Fame)
1974—Texas Tech 6, Vanderbilt 6 (Peach)
1974—(D) Houston 31, North Carolina St. 31 (Bluebonnet)
1970—(D) Alabama 24, Oklahoma 24 (Bluebonnet)
1970—(D) Long Beach St. 24, Louisville 24 (Pasadena)
1967—Florida St. 17, Penn St. 17 (Gator)
1960—(D) Alabama 3, Texas 3 (Bluebonnet)
1948—Georgia 20, Maryland 20 (Gator)
1948—Penn St. 13, Southern Methodist 13 (Cotton)
1947—(D) Montana St. 13, New Mexico 13 (Harbor)
1944—Randolph Field 7, Texas 7 (Cotton)
1937—(D) Auburn 7, Villanova 7 (Bacardi)
1936—Hardin-Simmons 14, New Mexico St. 14 (Sun)
1934—(D) Arkansas 7, Centenary (La.) 7 (Dixie Classic)
1927—Alabama 7, Stanford 7 (Rose)
1924—Navy 14, Washington 14 (Rose)

LARGEST DEFICIT OVERCOME TO WIN
25—Georgia (28) vs. Purdue (25) (ot) (Outback, 2000) (trailed 25-0 in 2nd quarter)
22—Brigham Young (46) vs. Southern Methodist (45) (Holiday, 1980) (trailed 35-13 in 3rd quarter and then trailed 45-25 with four minutes remaining in the game)
22—Notre Dame (35) vs. Houston (34) (Cotton, 1979) (trailed 34-12 in 4th quarter)
21—(D) Fresno St. (29) vs. Bowling Green (28) (California, 1982) (trailed 21-0 in 2nd quarter)
19—Wake Forest (39) vs. Oregon (35) (Independence, 1992) (trailed 29-10 in 3rd quarter)

BOWL/ALL-STAR RECORDS

14—Colorado (33) vs. Washington (21) (Holiday, 1996) (trailed 14-0 with 3:10 remaining in first quarter)
14—Rice (28) vs. Colorado (14) (Cotton, 1938) (trailed 14-0 in 2nd quarter)
13—Mississippi (14) vs. TCU (13) (Cotton, 1956) (trailed 13-0 in 2nd quarter)
11—Michigan (27) vs. Nebraska (23) (Fiesta, 1986) (trailed 14-3 in 3rd quarter)

OVERTIME GAMES#
1995—Toledo (40) vs. Nevada (37) (Las Vegas) (1 ot)
2000—Georgia (28) vs. Purdue (25) (Outback) (1 ot); Michigan (35) vs. Alabama (34) (Orange) (1 ot)

#Beginning in 1995-96, tied bowl games were allowed to use a tiebreaker system.

Longest Plays

(D) Denotes discontinued bowl. Year listed is actual year bowl was played.

LONGEST RUNS FROM SCRIMMAGE

Yds.	Player, Team (Score) vs. Opponent (Score)	Bowl, Year
99*	Terry Baker (QB), Oregon St. (6) vs. Villanova (0)	Liberty, 1962
95*#	Dicky Maegle, Rice (28) vs. Alabama (6)	Cotton, 1954
94*(D)	Dwight Ford, Southern California (47) vs. Texas A&M (28)	Bluebonnet, 1977
94*	Larry Smith, Florida (27) vs. Georgia Tech (12)	Orange, 1967
94*	Hascall Henshaw, Arizona St. (13) vs. Case Reserve (26)	Sun, 1941

#Famous bench-tackle play; Maegle tackled on Alabama 40-yard line by Tommy Lewis, awarded touchdown. *Scored touchdown on play.

LONGEST PASS PLAYS

Yds.	Player, Team (Score) vs. Opponent (Score)	Bowl, Year
95*	Ronnie Fletcher to Ben Hart, Oklahoma (19) vs. Florida St. (36)	Gator, Jan. 2, 1965
93*(D)	Stan Heath to Tommy Kalminir, Nevada (13) vs. North Texas (6)	Salad, 1948
91*(D)	Mark Barsotti to Stephen Shelley, Fresno St. (27) vs. Ball St. (6)	California, 1989
89*	Pete Gonzalez to Jake Hoffart, Pittsburgh (7) vs. Southern Miss. (41)	Liberty, 1997
88*	Michael Bishop to Darnell McDonald, Kansas St. (34) vs. Purdue (37)	Alamo, 1998
88*	Dave Schnell to Rob Turner, Indiana (34) vs. South Carolina (10)	Liberty, 1988
87*	Mike Thomas to L. C. Stevens, North Carolina (20) vs. Arkansas (10)	Carquest, Dec. 30, 1995
87*	Drew Bledsoe to Phillip Bobo, Washington St. (31) vs. Utah (28)	Copper, 1992
87*	Randy Wright to Tim Stracka, Wisconsin (14) vs. Kansas St. (3)	Independence, 1982
87*	Ger Schwedes to Ernie Davis, Syracuse (23) vs. Texas (14)	Cotton, 1960
86*	Brad Otton to Keyshawn Johnson, Southern California (55) vs. Texas Tech (14)	Cotton, 1995

*Scored touchdown on play.

LONGEST FIELD GOALS

Yds.	Player, Team (Score) vs. Opponent (Score)	Bowl, Year
62	Tony Franklin, Texas A&M (37) vs. Florida (14)	Sun, Jan. 2, 1977
56	Greg Cox, Miami (Fla.) (20) vs. Oklahoma (14)	Orange, 1988
55(D)	Russell Erxleben, Texas (38) vs. Colorado (21)	Bluebonnet, 1975
54	Carlos Huerta, Miami (22) vs. Nebraska (0)	Orange, 1992
54	Quin Rodriguez, Southern California (16) vs. Michigan St. (17)	John Hancock, 1990
54	Luis Zendejas, Arizona St. (32) vs. Oklahoma (21)	Fiesta, 1983

LONGEST PUNTS

Yds.	Player, Team (Score) vs. Opponent (Score)	Bowl, Year
84$	Kyle Rote, Southern Methodist (21) vs. Oregon (13)	Cotton, 1949
82	Ike Pickle, Mississippi St. (12) vs. Duquesne (13)	Orange, 1937
80	Elmer Layden, Notre Dame (27) vs. Stanford (10)	Rose, 1925
79$	Doak Walker, Southern Methodist (21) vs. Oregon (13)	Cotton, 1949
77	Mike Sochko, Maryland (21) vs. Houston (30)	Cotton, 1977
73	Sean Reali, Syracuse (41) vs. Clemson (0)	Gator, 1996

$Quick kick.

LONGEST PUNT RETURNS

Yds.	Player, Team (Score) vs. Opponent (Score)	Bowl, Year
88*	Ben Kelly, Colorado (62) vs. Boston College (28)	Insight.com, 1999
86*	Aramis Dandoy, Southern California (7) vs. Ohio St. (20)	Rose, 1955
85*	Darran Hall, Colorado St. (35) vs. Missouri (24)	Holiday, 1997
83*	Vai Sikahema, Brigham Young (46) vs. Southern Methodist (45)	Holiday, 1980
82*	Marcus Wall, North Carolina (31) vs. Texas (35)	Sun, 1994
82	Willie Drewrey, West Virginia (12) vs. Florida St. (31)	Gator, 1982
80*(D)	Gary Anderson, Arkansas (34) vs. Tulane (15)	Hall of Fame, 1980

Yds.	Player, Team (Score) vs. Opponent (Score)	Bowl, Year
80*	Cecil Ingram, Alabama (61) vs. Syracuse (6)	Orange, 1953

*Scored touchdown on play.

LONGEST KICKOFF RETURNS

Yds.	Player, Team (Score) vs. Opponent (Score)	Bowl, Year
100*	Deltha O'Neal, California (38) vs. Navy (42)	Aloha, 1996
100*	Derrick Mason, Michigan St. (26) vs. LSU (45)	Independence, 1995
100*	Kirby Dar Dar, Syracuse (26) vs. Colorado (22)	Fiesta, 1993
100*	Pete Panuska, Tennessee (27) vs. Maryland (28)	Sun, 1984
100*	Dave Lowery, Brigham Young (21) vs. Oklahoma St. (49)	Tangerine, 1976
100*	Mike Fink, Missouri (35) vs. Arizona St. (49)	Fiesta, 1972
100*(D)	Bob Smith, Texas A&M (40) vs. Georgia (20)	Presidential Cup, 1950
100*!	Al Hoisch, UCLA (14) vs. Illinois (45)	Rose, 1947

*Scored touchdown on play. !Rose Bowl records carry as 103-yard return.

LONGEST INTERCEPTION RETURNS

Yds.	Player, Team (Score) vs. Opponent (Score)	Bowl, Year
95*	Marcus Washington, Colorado (38) vs. Oregon (6)	Cotton, 1996
94*	David Baker, Oklahoma (48) vs. Duke (21)	Orange, 1958
91*	Don Hoover, Ohio (14) vs. West Tex. A&M (15)	Sun, 1962
90*	Norm Beal, Missouri (21) vs. Navy (14)	Orange, 1961
90*	Charlie Brembs, South Carolina (14) vs. Wake Forest (26)	Gator, 1946
90*(D)	G. P. Jackson, TCU (7) vs. Centre (63)	Fort Worth Classic, 1921

*Scored touchdown on play.

LONGEST MISCELLANEOUS RETURNS

Yds.	Player, Team (Score) vs. Opponent (Score)	Bowl, Year
98	Greg Mather, Navy (14) vs. Missouri (21) (Int. Lat.)	Orange, 1961
80	Antonio Banks, Virginia Tech (45) vs. Indiana (20) (Blocked field goal return)	Independence, 1993
79	Tremain Mack, Miami (Fla.) (31) vs. Virginia (21) (Live Fum.)	Carquest, 1996
75	Payton Williams, Fresno St. (16) vs. Utah (17) (Blocked field goal return)	Las Vegas, 1999
73	Dick Carpenter, Oklahoma (48) vs. Duke (21) (Int. Lat.)	Orange, 1958
70	Carlos Posey, Missouri (34) vs. West Virginia (31) (Blocked punt return)	Insight.com, 1998
65	Steve Manstedt, Nebraska (19) vs. Texas (3) (Live Fum.)	Cotton, 1974

Bowl Coaching Records

All-Time Bowl Appearances

(Ranked by Most Bowl Games Coached)

Coach (Teams Taken to Bowl)	G	W-L-T	Pct.
*Joe Paterno, Penn St.	30	20-9-1	.683
Bear Bryant, Alabama, Texas A&M, Kentucky	29	15-12-2	.552
Tom Osborne, Nebraska	25	12-13-0	.480
*Bobby Bowden, West Virginia, Florida St.	23	17-5-1	.761
*LaVell Edwards, Brigham Young	22	7-14-1	.341
*Lou Holtz, William & Mary, North Carolina St., Arkansas, Notre Dame	20	10-8-2	.550
Vince Dooley, Georgia	20	8-10-2	.450
John Vaught, Mississippi	18	10-8-0	.556
Hayden Fry, Southern Methodist, Iowa	17	7-9-1	.441
Bo Schembechler, Michigan	17	5-12-0	.294
Johnny Majors, Iowa St., Pittsburgh, Tennessee	16	9-7-0	.563
Darrell Royal, Texas	16	8-7-1	.531
Don James, Kent, Washington	15	10-5-0	.667
*George Welsh, Navy, Virginia	14	5-9-0	.357
Bobby Dodd, Georgia Tech	13	9-4-0	.692
Terry Donahue, UCLA	13	8-4-1	.654
Barry Switzer, Oklahoma	13	8-5-0	.615
Charlie McClendon, LSU	13	7-6-0	.538
Earle Bruce, Ohio St., Colorado St.	12	7-5-0	.583
Woody Hayes, Miami (Ohio), Ohio St.	12	6-6-0	.500
Shug Jordan, Auburn	12	5-7-0	.417

*Active coach. Ties computed as half won and half lost.

All-Time Bowl Victories

Coach	Wins	Record	Coach	Wins	Record
*Joe Paterno	20	20-9-1	Darrell Royal	8	8-7-1
*Bobby Bowden	17	17-5-1	Vince Dooley	8	8-10-2
Paul "Bear" Bryant	15	15-12-2	*John Robinson	7	7-1-0
Tom Osborne	12	12-13-0	Pat Dye	7	7-2-1
Don James	10	10-5-0	Bob Devaney	7	7-3-0
John Vaught	10	10-8-0	Dan Devine	7	7-3-0
*Lou Holtz	10	10-8-2	Earle Bruce	7	7-5-0
Bobby Dodd	9	9-4-0	Charlie McClendon	7	7-6-0
Johnny Majors	9	9-7-0	Hayden Fry	7	7-9-1
Terry Donahue	8	8-4-1	*LaVell Edwards	7	7-14-1
Barry Switzer	8	8-5-0			

*Active coach.

All-Time Bowl Winning Percentage

(Minimum 11 Games)

Coach, Last Team Coached	G	W-L-T	Pct.
*Bobby Bowden, Florida St.	23	17-5-1	.761
Bobby Dodd, Georgia Tech	13	9-4-0	.692
*Joe Paterno, Penn St.	30	20-9-1	.683
Don James, Washington	15	10-5-0	.667
Terry Donahue, UCLA	13	8-4-1	.654
Barry Switzer, Oklahoma	13	8-5-0	.615
Bill Yeoman, Houston	11	6-4-1	.591
Earle Bruce, Colorado St.	12	7-5-0	.583
Johnny Majors, Pittsburgh	16	9-7-0	.563
John Vaught, Mississippi	18	10-8-0	.556
Paul "Bear" Bryant, Alabama	29	15-12-2	.552
*Lou Holtz, South Carolina	20	10-8-2	.550
Charlie McClendon, LSU	13	7-6-0	.538
Darrell Royal, Texas	16	8-7-1	.531
Woody Hayes, Ohio St.	12	6-6-0	.500
Tom Osborne, Nebraska	25	12-13-0	.480
Vince Dooley, Georgia	20	8-10-2	.450
Hayden Fry, Iowa	17	7-9-1	.441
Shug Jordan, Auburn	12	5-7-0	.417
*George Welsh, Virginia	14	5-9-0	.357
*LaVell Edwards, Brigham Young	22	7-14-1	.341
Glenn "Bo" Schembechler, Michigan	17	5-12-0	.294
Jerry Claiborne, Kentucky	11	3-8-0	.273

*Active coach. Ties computed as half won and half lost.

All-Time Bowl Coaching History

A total of 457 coaches have head-coached in history's 773 major bowl games (the term "major bowl" is defined above the alphabetical list of team bowl records). Below is an alphabetical list of all 457 bowl coaches, with their alma mater and year, their birth date, and their game-by-game bowl records, with name and date of each bowl, opponent, final score (own score first) and opposing coach (in parentheses). A handful coached service teams or colleges never in the major category but are included because they coached against a major team in a major bowl.

Coach/School — Bowl/Date — Opponent/Score (Coach)

JIM AIKEN, 0-1-0 (Wash. & Jeff. '22) Born 5-26-1899
Oregon — Cotton 1-1-49 — Southern Methodist 12-21 (Matty Bell)

FRED AKERS, 2-8-0 (Arkansas '60) Born 3-17-38
Wyoming — Fiesta 12-19-76 — Oklahoma 7-41 (Barry Switzer)
Texas — Cotton 1-2-78 — Notre Dame 10-38 (Dan Devine)
Texas — Sun 12-23-78 — Maryland 42-0 (Jerry Claiborne)
Texas — Sun 12-22-79 — Washington 7-14 (Don James)
Texas — Bluebonnet 12-31-80 — North Carolina 7-16 (Dick Crum)
Texas — Cotton 1-1-82 — Alabama 14-12 (Paul "Bear" Bryant)
Texas — Sun 12-25-82 — North Carolina 10-26 (Dick Crum)
Texas — Cotton 1-2-84 — Georgia 9-10 (Vince Dooley)
Texas — Freedom 12-26-84 — Iowa 17-55 (Hayden Fry)
Texas — Bluebonnet 12-31-85 — Air Force 16-24 (Fisher DeBerry)

BILL ALEXANDER, 3-2-0 (Georgia Tech '12) Born 6-6-1889
Georgia Tech — Rose 1-1-29 — California 8-7 (Clarence "Nibs" Price)
Georgia Tech — Orange 1-1-40 — Missouri 21-7 (Don Faurot)
Georgia Tech — Cotton 1-1-43 — Texas 7-14 (Dana Bible)
Georgia Tech — Sugar 1-1-44 — Tulsa 20-18 (Henry Frnka)
Georgia Tech — Orange 1-1-45 — Tulsa 12-26 (Henry Frnka)

LEONARD "STUB" ALLISON, 1-0-0 (Carleton '17) Born 1892
California — Rose 1-1-38 — Alabama 13-0 (Frank Thomas)

BARRY ALVAREZ, 5-1-0 (Nebraska '69) Born 12-30-46
Wisconsin — Rose 1-1-94 — UCLA 21-16 (Terry Donahue)
Wisconsin — Hall of Fame 1-2-95 — Duke 34-20 (Fred Goldsmith)
Wisconsin — Copper 12-27-96 — Utah 38-10 (Ron McBride)
Wisconsin — Outback 1-1-98 — Georgia 6-33 (Jim Donnan)
Wisconsin — Rose 1-1-99 — UCLA 38-31 (Bob Toledo)
Wisconsin — Rose 1-1-00 — Stanford 17-9 (Tyrone Willingham)

MIKE ARCHER, 1-1-0 (Miami [Fla.] '75) Born 7-26-53
LSU — Gator 12-31-87 — South Carolina 30-13 (Joe Morrison)
LSU — Hall of Fame 1-2-89 — Syracuse 10-23 (Dick MacPherson)

IKE ARMSTRONG, 1-0-0 (Drake '23) Born 6-8-1895
Utah — Sun 1-2-39 — New Mexico 16-0 (Ted Shipkey)

BILL ARNSPARGER, 0-3-0 (Miami [Ohio] '50) Born 12-16-26
LSU — Sugar 1-1-85 — Nebraska 10-28 (Tom Osborne)
LSU — Liberty 12-27-85 — Baylor 7-21 (Grant Teaff)
LSU — Sugar 1-1-87 — Nebraska 15-30 (Tom Osborne)

CHRIS AULT, 0-2-0 (Nevada '68) Born 11-8-47
Nevada — Las Vegas 12-18-92 — Bowling Green 34-35 (Gary Blackney)
Nevada — Las Vegas 12-14-95 — Toledo 37-40 (ot) (Gary Pinkel)

CHARLEY BACHMAN, 0-1-0 (Notre Dame '17) Born 12-1-92
Michigan St. — Orange 1-1-38 — Auburn 0-6 (Jack Meagher)

ENOCH BAGSHAW, 0-1-1 (Washington '08) Born 1884
Washington — Rose 1-1-24 — Navy 14-14 (Bob Folwell)
Washington — Rose 1-1-26 — Alabama 19-20 (Wallace Wade)

GEORGE BARCLAY, 1-0-0 (North Carolina '35) Born 5-14-11
Wash. & Lee — Gator 1-1-51 — Wyoming 7-20 (Bowden Wyatt)

BILL BARNES, 0-1-0 (Tennessee '41) Born 10-20-17
UCLA — Rose 1-1-62 — Minnesota 3-21 (Murray Warmath)

WILLIS BARNES, 1-1-1 (Nebraska) Born 10-22-1900
New Mexico — Sun 1-1-44 — Southwestern (Tex.) 0-7 (R. M. Medley)
New Mexico — Sun 1-1-46 — Denver 34-24 (Clyde "Cac" Hubbard)
New Mexico — Harbor 1-1-47 — Montana St. 13-13 (Clyde Carpenter)

GARY BARNETT, 1-2-0 (Missouri '69) Born 5-23-46
Northwestern — Rose 1-1-96 — Southern California 32-41 (John Robinson)
Northwestern — Fla. Citrus 1-1-97 — Tennessee 28-48 (Phillip Fulmer)
Colorado — Insight.com 12-31-99 — Boston College 62-28 (Tom O'Brien)

JOHN BARNHILL, 2-1-1 (Tennessee '28) Born 2-21-03
Tennessee — Sugar 1-1-43 — Tulsa 14-7 (Henry Frnka)
Tennessee — Rose 1-1-45 — Southern California 0-25 (Jeff Cravath)
Arkansas — Cotton 1-1-47 — LSU 0-0 (Bernie Moore)
Arkansas — Dixie 1-1-48 — William & Mary 21-19 (Rube McCray)

BILL BATTLE, 4-1-0 (Alabama '63) Born 12-8-41
Tennessee — Sugar 1-1-71 — Air Force 34-13 (Ben Martin)
Tennessee — Liberty 12-20-71 — Arkansas 14-13 (Frank Broyles)
Tennessee — Bluebonnet 12-30-72 — LSU 24-17 (Charlie McClendon)
Tennessee — Gator 12-29-73 — Texas Tech 19-28 (Jim Carlen)
Tennessee — Liberty 12-16-74 — Maryland 7-3 (Jerry Claiborne)

SAMMY BAUGH, 0-1-0 (TCU '37) Born 3-17-14
Hardin-Simmons — Sun 12-31-58 — Wyoming 6-14 (Bob Devaney)

FRANK BEAMER, 3-4-0 (Virginia Tech '69) Born 10-18-46
Virginia Tech — Independence 12-31-93 — Indiana 45-20 (Bill Mallory)
Virginia Tech — Gator 12-30-94 — Tennessee 23-45 (Phillip Fulmer)
Virginia Tech — Sugar 12-31-95 — Texas 28-10 (John Mackovic)
Virginia Tech — Orange 12-31-96 — Nebraska 21-41 (Tom Osborne)
Virginia Tech — Gator 1-1-98 — North Carolina 3-42 (Carl Torbush)
Virginia Tech — Music City 12-29-98 — Alabama 38-7 (Mike DuBose)
Virginia Tech — Sugar 1-4-00 — Florida St. 29-46 (Bobby Bowden)

ALEX BELL, 1-1-0 (Villanova '38) Born 8-12-15
Villanova — Sun 12-20-61 — Wichita St. 17-9 (Hank Foldberg)
Villanova — Liberty 12-15-62 — Oregon St. 0-6 (Tommy Prothro)

MATTY BELL, 1-1-1 (Centre '20) Born 2-22-1899
Southern Methodist — Rose 1-1-36 — Stanford 0-7 (Claude "Tiny" Thornhill)
Southern Methodist — Cotton 1-1-48 — Penn St. 13-13 (Bob Higgins)
Southern Methodist — Cotton 1-1-49 — Oregon 21-13 (Jim Aiken)

EMORY BELLARD, 2-3-0 (Southwest Tex. St. '49) Born 12-17-27
Texas A&M — Liberty 12-22-75 — Southern California 0-20 (John McKay)
Texas A&M — Sun 1-2-77 — Florida 37-14 (Doug Dickey)
Texas A&M — Bluebonnet 12-31-77 — Southern California 28-47 (John Robinson)
Mississippi St. — Sun 12-27-80 — Nebraska 17-31 (Tom Osborne)
Mississippi St. — Hall of Fame 12-31-81 — Kansas 10-0 (Don Fambrough)

MIKE BELLOTTI, 2-2-0 (UC Davis '73) Born 12-21-50
Oregon — Cotton 1-1-96 — Colorado 6-38 (Rick Neuheisel)
Oregon — Las Vegas 12-20-97 — Air Force 41-13 (Fisher DeBerry)
Oregon — Aloha Classic 12-25-98 — Colorado 43-51 (Rick Neuheisel)
Oregon — Sun 12-31-99 — Minnesota 24-20 (Glen Mason)

ARTHUR "DUTCH" BERGMAN, 1-0-1 (Notre Dame '20) Born 2-23-1895
Catholic — Orange 1-1-36 — Mississippi 20-19 (Ed Walker)
Catholic — Sun 1-1-40 — Arizona St. 0-0 (Millard "Dixie" Howell)

HUGO BEZDEK, 1-1-0 (Chicago '06) Born 4-1-1884
Oregon — Rose 1-1-17 — Pennsylvania 14-0 (Bob Folwell)
Penn St. — Rose 1-1-23 — Southern California 3-14 (Elmer "Gus" Henderson)

DANA BIBLE, 3-0-1 (Carson-Newman '12) Born 10-8-1891
Texas A&M — Dixie Classic 1-2-22 — Centre 22-14 (Charley Moran)

Coach/School	Bowl/Date	Opponent/Score (Coach)
Texas	Cotton 1-1-43	Georgia Tech 14-7 (Bill Alexander)
Texas	Cotton 1-1-44	Randolph Field 7-7 (Frank Tritico)
Texas	Cotton 1-1-46	Missouri 40-27 (Chauncey Simpson)

JACK BICKNELL, 2-2-0 (Montclair St. '60) Born 2-20-38

Boston College	Tangerine 12-18-82	Auburn 26-33 (Pat Dye)
Boston College	Liberty 12-29-83	Notre Dame 18-19 (Gerry Faust)
Boston College	Cotton 1-1-85	Houston 45-28 (Bill Yeoman)
Boston College	Hall of Fame 12-23-86	Georgia 27-24 (Vince Dooley)

BERNIE BIERMAN, 0-1-0 (Minnesota '16) Born 3-11-1894

Tulane	Rose 1-1-32	Southern California 12-21 (Howard Jones)

GARY BLACKNEY, 2-0-0 (Connecticut '67) Born 12-10-55

Bowling Green	California 12-14-91	Fresno St. 28-21 (Jim Sweeney)
Bowling Green	Las Vegas 12-18-92	Nevada 35-34 (Chris Ault)

BOBBY BOWDEN, 17-5-1 (Samford '53) Born 11-8-29

West Virginia	Peach 12-29-72	North Carolina St. 13-49 (Lou Holtz)
West Virginia	Peach 12-31-75	North Carolina St. 13-10 (Lou Holtz)
Florida St.	Tangerine 12-23-77	Texas Tech 40-17 (Steve Sloan)
Florida St.	Orange 1-1-80	Oklahoma 7-24 (Barry Switzer)
Florida St.	Orange 1-1-81	Oklahoma 17-18 (Barry Switzer)
Florida St.	Gator 12-30-82	West Virginia 31-12 (Don Nehlen)
Florida St.	Peach 12-30-83	North Carolina 28-3 (Dick Crum)
Florida St.	Fla. Citrus 12-22-84	Georgia 17-17 (Vince Dooley)
Florida St.	Gator 12-30-85	Oklahoma St. 34-23 (Pat Jones)
Florida St.	All-American 12-31-86	Indiana 27-13 (Bill Mallory)
Florida St.	Fiesta 1-1-88	Nebraska 31-28 (Tom Osborne)
Florida St.	Sugar 1-2-89	Auburn 13-7 (Pat Dye)
Florida St.	Fiesta 1-1-90	Nebraska 41-17 (Tom Osborne)
Florida St.	Blockbuster 12-28-90	Penn St. 24-17 (Joe Paterno)
Florida St.	Cotton 1-1-92	Texas A&M 10-2 (R. C. Slocum)
Florida St.	Orange 1-1-93	Nebraska 27-14 (Tom Osborne)
Florida St.	Orange 1-1-94	Nebraska 18-16 (Tom Osborne)
Florida St.	Sugar 1-2-95	Florida 23-17 (Steve Spurrier)
Florida St.	Orange 1-1-96	Notre Dame 31-26 (Lou Holtz)
Florida St.	Sugar 1-2-97	Florida 20-52 (Steve Spurrier)
Florida St.	Sugar 1-1-98	Ohio St. 31-14 (John Cooper)
Florida St.	Fiesta 1-4-99	Tennessee 16-23 (Phillip Fulmer)
Florida St.	Sugar 1-4-00	Virginia Tech 46-29 (Frank Beamer)

TERRY BOWDEN, 2-1-0 (West Virginia '78) Born 2-24-56

Auburn	Outback 1-1-96	Penn St. 14-43 (Joe Paterno)
Auburn	Independence 12-31-96	Army 32-29 (Bob Sutton)
Auburn	Peach 1-2-98	Clemson 21-17 (Tommy West)

TOMMY BOWDEN, 1-0-0 (West Virginia '77) Born 7-10-54

Clemson	Peach 12-30-99	Mississippi St. 7-17 (Jackie Sherrill)

JEFF BOWER, 2-2-0 (Southern Miss. '76) Born 5-28-53

Southern Miss.	All-American 12-28-90	North Carolina St. 27-31 (Dick Sheridan)
Southern Miss.	Liberty 12-31-97	Pittsburgh 41-7 (Walt Harris)
Southern Miss.	Humanitarian 12-30-98	Idaho 35-42 (Chris Tormey)
Southern Miss.	Liberty 12-31-99	Colorado St. 23-17 (Sonny Lubick)

SAM BOYD, 1-0-0 (Baylor '38) Born 8-12-15

Baylor	Sugar 1-1-57	Tennessee 13-7 (Bowden Wyatt)

WESLEY BRADSHAW, 0-1-0 (Baylor '23) Born 11-26-1898

Ouachita Baptist	Shrine 12-18-48	Hardin-Simmons 12-40 (Warren Woodson)

BILLY BREWER, 3-2-0 (Mississippi '61) Born 10-8-35

Mississippi	Independence 12-10-83	Air Force 3-9 (Ken Hatfield)
Mississippi	Independence 12-20-86	Texas Tech 20-17 (Spike Dykes)
Mississippi	All-American 12-29-89	Air Force 42-29 (Fisher DeBerry)
Mississippi	Gator 1-1-91	Michigan 3-35 (Gary Moeller)
Mississippi	Liberty 12-31-92	Air Force 13-0 (Fisher DeBerry)

JOHN BRIDGERS, 2-1-0 (Auburn '47) Born 1-13-22

Baylor	Gator 12-31-60	Florida 12-13 (Ray Graves)
Baylor	Gotham 12-9-61	Utah St. 24-9 (John Ralston)
Baylor	Bluebonnet 12-21-63	LSU 14-7 (Charlie McClendon)

RICH BROOKS, 1-3-0 (Oregon St. '63) Born 8-20-41

Oregon	Independence 12-16-89	Tulsa 27-24 (Dave Rader)
Oregon	Freedom 12-29-90	Colorado St. 31-32 (Earle Bruce)
Oregon	Independence 12-31-92	Wake Forest 35-39 (Bill Dooley)
Oregon	Rose 1-2-95	Penn St. 20-38 (Joe Paterno)

J. O. "BUDDY" BROTHERS, 0-1-0 (Texas Tech '31) Born 5-29-09

Tulsa	Gator 1-1-53	Florida 13-14 (Bob Woodruff)

MACK BROWN, 4-4-0 (Florida St. '74) Born 8-27-51

Tulane	Independence 12-19-87	Washington 12-24 (Don James)
North Carolina	Peach 1-2-93	Mississippi St. 21-17 (Jackie Sherrill)
North Carolina	Gator 12-31-93	Alabama 10-24 (Gene Stallings)
North Carolina	Sun 12-30-94	Texas 31-35 (John Mackovic)
North Carolina	Carquest 12-30-95	Arkansas 20-10 (Danny Ford)
North Carolina	Gator 1-1-97	West Virginia 20-13 (Don Nehlen)
Texas	Cotton 1-1-99	Mississippi St. 38-11 (Jackie Sherrill)
Texas	Cotton 1-1-00	Arkansas 6-27 (Houston Nutt)

FRANK BROYLES, 4-6-0 (Georgia Tech '47) Born 12-26-24

Arkansas	Gator 1-2-60	Georgia Tech 14-7 (Bobby Dodd)
Arkansas	Cotton 1-2-61	Duke 6-7 (Bill Murray)
Arkansas	Sugar 1-1-62	Alabama 3-10 (Paul "Bear" Bryant)
Arkansas	Sugar 1-1-63	Mississippi 13-17 (John Vaught)
Arkansas	Cotton 1-1-65	Nebraska 10-7 (Bob Devaney)
Arkansas	Cotton 1-1-66	LSU 7-14 (Charlie McClendon)
Arkansas	Sugar 1-1-69	Georgia 16-2 (Vince Dooley)
Arkansas	Sugar 1-1-70	Mississippi 22-27 (John Vaught)
Arkansas	Liberty 12-20-71	Tennessee 13-14 (Bill Battle)
Arkansas	Cotton 1-1-76	Georgia 31-10 (Vince Dooley)

EARLE BRUCE, 7-5-0 (Ohio St. '53) Born 3-8-31

Tampa	Tangerine 12-29-72	Kent 21-18 (Don James)
Iowa St.	Peach 12-31-77	North Carolina St. 14-24 (Bo Rein)
Iowa St.	Hall of Fame 12-20-78	Texas A&M 12-28 (Tom Wilson)
Ohio St.	Rose 1-1-80	Southern California 16-17 (John Robinson)
Ohio St.	Fiesta 12-26-80	Penn St. 19-31 (Joe Paterno)
Ohio St.	Liberty 12-30-81	Navy 31-28 (George Welsh)
Ohio St.	Holiday 12-17-82	Brigham Young 47-17 (LaVell Edwards)
Ohio St.	Fiesta 1-2-84	Pittsburgh 28-23 (Foge Fazio)
Ohio St.	Rose 1-1-85	Southern California 17-20 (Ted Tollner)
Ohio St.	Fla. Citrus 12-28-85	Brigham Young 10-7 (LaVell Edwards)
Ohio St.	Cotton 1-1-87	Texas A&M 28-12 (Jackie Sherrill)
Colorado St.	Freedom 12-29-90	Oregon 32-31 (Rich Brooks)

MILT BRUHN, 0-2-0 (Minnesota '35) Born 7-28-12

Wisconsin	Rose 1-1-60	Washington 8-44 (Jim Owens)
Wisconsin	Rose 1-2-63	Southern California 37-42 (John McKay)

MIKE BRUMBELOW, 2-1-0 (TCU '30) Born 7-13-06

UTEP	Sun 1-1-54	Southern Miss. 37-14 (Thad "Pie" Vann)
UTEP	Sun 1-1-55	Florida St. 47-20 (Tom Nugent)
UTEP	Sun 1-1-57	George Washington 0-13 (Eugene "Bo" Sherman)

PAUL "BEAR" BRYANT, 15-12-2 (Alabama '36) Born 9-11-13

Kentucky	Great Lakes 12-6-47	Villanova 24-14 (Jordan Oliver)
Kentucky	Orange 1-2-50	Santa Clara 13-21 (Len Casanova)
Kentucky	Sugar 1-1-51	Oklahoma 13-7 (Bud Wilkinson)
Kentucky	Cotton 1-1-52	TCU 20-7 (Leo "Dutch" Meyer)
Texas A&M	Gator 12-28-57	Tennessee 0-3 (Bowden Wyatt)
Alabama	Liberty 12-19-59	Penn St. 0-7 (Charles "Rip" Engle)
Alabama	Bluebonnet 12-17-60	Texas 3-3 (Darrell Royal)
Alabama	Sugar 1-1-62	Arkansas 10-3 (Frank Broyles)
Alabama	Orange 1-1-63	Oklahoma 17-0 (Bud Wilkinson)
Alabama	Sugar 1-1-64	Mississippi 12-7 (John Vaught)
Alabama	Orange 1-1-65	Texas 17-21 (Darrell Royal)
Alabama	Orange 1-1-66	Nebraska 39-28 (Bob Devaney)
Alabama	Sugar 1-2-67	Nebraska 34-7 (Bob Devaney)
Alabama	Cotton 1-1-68	Texas A&M 16-20 (Gene Stallings)
Alabama	Gator 12-28-68	Missouri 10-35 (Dan Devine)
Alabama	Liberty 12-13-69	Colorado 33-47 (Eddie Crowder)
Alabama	Bluebonnet 12-31-70	Oklahoma 24-24 (Chuck Fairbanks)
Alabama	Orange 1-1-72	Nebraska 6-38 (Bob Devaney)
Alabama	Cotton 1-1-73	Texas 13-17 (Darrell Royal)
Alabama	Sugar 12-31-73	Notre Dame 23-24 (Ara Parseghian)
Alabama	Orange 1-1-75	Notre Dame 11-13 (Ara Parseghian)
Alabama	Sugar 12-31-75	Penn St. 13-6 (Joe Paterno)
Alabama	Liberty 12-20-76	UCLA 36-6 (Terry Donahue)
Alabama	Sugar 1-2-78	Ohio St. 35-6 (Woody Hayes)
Alabama	Sugar 1-1-79	Penn St. 14-7 (Joe Paterno)
Alabama	Sugar 1-1-80	Arkansas 24-9 (Lou Holtz)
Alabama	Cotton 1-1-81	Baylor 30-2 (Grant Teaff)
Alabama	Cotton 1-1-82	Texas 12-14 (Fred Akers)
Alabama	Liberty 12-29-82	Illinois 21-15 (Mike White)

FRANK BURNS, 0-1-0 (Rutgers '49) Born 3-16-28

Rutgers	Garden State 12-16-78	Arizona St. 18-34 (Frank Kush)

LEON BURTNETT, 0-1-0 (Southwestern [Kan.] '65) Born 5-30-43

Purdue	Peach 12-31-84	Virginia 24-27 (George Welsh)

WALLY BUTTS, 5-2-1 (Mercer '28) Born 2-7-05

Georgia	Orange 1-1-42	TCU 40-26 (Leo "Dutch" Meyer)
Georgia	Rose 1-1-43	UCLA 9-0 (Edwin "Babe" Horrell)
Georgia	Oil 1-1-46	Tulsa 20-6 (Henry Frnka)
Georgia	Sugar 1-1-47	North Carolina 20-10 (Carl Snavely)
Georgia	Gator 1-1-48	Maryland 20-20 (Jim Tatum)
Georgia	Orange 1-1-49	Texas 28-41 (Blair Cherry)
Georgia	Presidential Cup 12-9-50	Texas A&M 20-40 (Harry Stiteler)
Georgia	Orange 1-1-60	Missouri 14-0 (Dan Devine)

JIM CALDWELL, 1-0-0 (Iowa '77) Born 1-16-55

Wake Forest	Aloha Classic 12-25-99	Arizona St. 23-3 (Bruce Snyder)

EDDIE CAMERON, 1-0-0 (Wash. & Lee '24) Born 4-22-02

Duke	Sugar 1-1-45	Alabama 29-26 (Frank Thomas)

FRANK CAMP, 1-0-0 (Transylvania '30) Born 12-23-05

Louisville	Sun 1-1-58	Drake 34-20 (Warren Gaer)

JIM CARLEN, 2-5-1 (Georgia Tech '55) Born 7-11-33

West Virginia	Peach 12-30-69	South Carolina 14-3 (Paul Dietzel)
Texas Tech	Sun 12-19-70	Georgia Tech 9-17 (Bud Carson)
Texas Tech	Sun 12-30-72	North Carolina 28-32 (Bill Dooley)
Texas Tech	Gator 12-29-73	Tennessee 28-19 (Bill Battle)
Texas Tech	Peach 12-28-74	Vanderbilt 6-6 (Steve Sloan)

Coach/School	Bowl/Date	Opponent/Score (Coach)
South Carolina	Tangerine 12-20-75	Miami (Ohio) 7-20 (Dick Crum)
South Carolina	Hall of Fame 12-29-79	Missouri 14-24 (Warren Powers)
South Carolina	Gator 12-29-80	Pittsburgh 8-37 (Jackie Sherrill)

CLYDE CARPENTER, 0-0-1 (Montana '32) Born 4-17-08
| Montana St. | Harbor 1-1-47 | New Mexico 13-13 (Willis Barnes) |

LLOYD CARR, 3-2-0 (Northern Mich. '68) Born 7-30-45
Michigan	Alamo 12-28-95	Texas A&M 20-22 (R. C. Slocum)
Michigan	Outback 1-1-97	Alabama 14-17 (Gene Stallings)
Michigan	Rose 1-1-98	Washington St. 21-16 (Mike Price)
Michigan	Florida Citrus 1-1-99	Arkansas 45-31 (Houston Nutt)
Michigan	Orange 1-1-00	Alabama 35-34 (ot) (Mike DuBose)

BUD CARSON, 1-1-0 (North Carolina '52) Born 4-28-30
| Georgia Tech | Sun 12-19-70 | Texas Tech 17-9 (Jim Carlen) |
| Georgia Tech | Peach 12-30-71 | Mississippi 18-41 (Billy Kinard) |

LEN CASANOVA, 2-2-0 (Santa Clara '27) Born 6-12-05
Santa Clara	Orange 1-2-50	Kentucky 21-13 (Paul "Bear" Bryant)
Oregon	Rose 1-1-58	Ohio St. 7-10 (Woody Hayes)
Oregon	Liberty 12-17-60	Penn St. 12-41 (Charles "Rip" Engle)
Oregon	Sun 12-31-63	Southern Methodist 21-14 (Hayden Fry)

MILES CASTEEL, 0-1-0 (Kalamazoo '25) Born 12-30-1896
| Arizona | Salad 1-1-49 | Drake 13-14 (Al Kawal) |

PETE CAWTHON, 0-2-0 (Southwestern [Tex.] '20) Born 8-24-1898
| Texas Tech | Sun 1-1-38 | West Virginia 6-7 (Marshall "Little Sleepy" Glenn) |
| Texas Tech | Cotton 1-2-39 | St. Mary's (Cal.) 13-20 (Edward "Slip" Madigan) |

BLAIR CHERRY, 2-1-0 (TCU '24) Born 9-7-01
Texas	Sugar 1-1-48	Alabama 27-7 (Harold "Red" Drew)
Texas	Orange 1-1-49	Georgia 41-28 (Wally Butts)
Texas	Cotton 1-1-51	Tennessee 14-20 (Bob Neyland)

JERRY CLAIBORNE, 3-8-0 (Kentucky '50) Born 8-26-28
Virginia Tech	Liberty 12-10-66	Miami (Fla.) 7-14 (Charlie Tate)
Virginia Tech	Liberty 12-14-68	Mississippi 17-34 (John Vaught)
Maryland	Peach 12-28-73	Georgia 16-17 (Vince Dooley)
Maryland	Liberty 12-16-74	Tennessee 3-7 (Bill Battle)
Maryland	Gator 12-29-75	Florida 13-0 (Doug Dickey)
Maryland	Cotton 1-1-77	Houston 21-30 (Bill Yeoman)
Maryland	Hall of Fame 12-22-77	Minnesota 17-7 (Cal Stoll)
Maryland	Sun 12-23-78	Texas 0-42 (Fred Akers)
Maryland	Tangerine 12-20-80	Florida 20-35 (Charley Pell)
Kentucky	Hall of Fame 12-22-83	West Virginia 16-20 (Don Nehlen)
Kentucky	Hall of Fame 12-29-84	Wisconsin 20-19 (Dave McClain)

CECIL COLEMAN, 1-0-0 (Arizona St. '50) Born 4-12-26
| Fresno St. | Mercy 11-23-61 | Bowling Green 36-6 (Doyt Perry) |

BOBBY COLLINS, 3-2-0 (Mississippi St. '55) Born 10-25-33
Southern Miss.	Independence 12-13-70	McNeese St. 16-14 (Ernie Duplechin)
Southern Miss.	Tangerine 12-19-81	Missouri 17-19 (Warren Powers)
Southern Methodist	Cotton 1-1-83	Pittsburgh 7-3 (Foge Fazio)
Southern Methodist	Sun 12-24-83	Alabama 7-28 (Ray Perkins)
Southern Methodist	Aloha 12-29-84	Notre Dame 27-20 (Gerry Faust)

JOHN COOPER, 5-8-0 (Iowa St. '62) Born 7-2-37
Arizona St.	Holiday 12-22-85	Arkansas 17-18 (Ken Hatfield)
Arizona St.	Rose 1-1-87	Michigan 22-15 (Glenn "Bo" Schembechler)
Arizona St.	Freedom 12-30-87	Air Force 33-30 (Fisher DeBerry)
Ohio St.	Hall of Fame 1-1-90	Auburn 14-31 (Pat Dye)
Ohio St.	Liberty 12-27-90	Air Force 11-23 (Fisher DeBerry)
Ohio St.	Hall of Fame 1-1-92	Syracuse 17-24 (Paul Pasqualoni)
Ohio St.	Fla. Citrus 1-1-93	Georgia 14-21 (Ray Goff)
Ohio St.	Holiday 12-30-93	Brigham Young 28-21 (LaVell Edwards)
Ohio St.	Fla. Citrus 1-2-95	Alabama 17-24 (Gene Stallings)
Ohio St.	Fla. Citrus 1-1-96	Tennessee 14-20 (Phillip Fulmer)
Ohio St.	Rose 1-1-97	Arizona St. 20-17 (Bruce Snyder)
Ohio St.	Sugar 1-1-98	Florida St. 14-31 (Bobby Bowden)
Ohio St.	Sugar 1-1-99	Texas A&M 24-14 (R.C. Slocum)

LEE CORSO, 1-0-1 (Florida St. '57) Born 8-7-35
| Louisville | Pasadena 12-19-70 | Long Beach St. 24-24 (Jim Stangeland) |
| Indiana | Holiday 12-21-79 | Brigham Young 38-37 (LaVell Edwards) |

GENE CORUM, 0-1-0 (West Virginia '48) Born 5-29-21
| West Virginia | Liberty 12-19-64 | Utah 6-32 (Ray Nagel) |

DON CORYELL, 1-0-0 (Washington '50) Born 10-17-24
| San Diego St. | Pasadena 12-6-69 | Boston U. 28-7 (Larry Naviaux) |

TOM COUGHLIN, 1-1-0 (Syracuse '68) Born 8-31-46
| Boston College | Hall of Fame 1-1-93 | Tennessee 23-38 (Phillip Fulmer) |
| Boston College | Carquest 1-1-94 | Virginia 31-13 (George Welsh) |

TED COX, 1-0-0 (Minnesota '26) Born 6-30-03
| Tulane | Sugar 1-1-35 | Temple 20-14 (Glenn "Pop" Warner) |

JEFF CRAVATH, 2-2-0 (Southern California '27) Born 2-5-05
Southern California	Rose 1-1-44	Washington 29-0 (Ralph "Pest" Welch)
Southern California	Rose 1-1-45	Tennessee 25-0 (John Barnhill)
Southern California	Rose 1-1-46	Alabama 14-34 (Frank Thomas)
Southern California	Rose 1-1-48	Michigan 0-49 (H. O. "Fritz" Crisler)

H. O. "FRITZ" CRISLER, 1-0-0 (Chicago '22) Born 1-2-1899
| Michigan | Rose 1-1-48 | Southern California 49-0 (Jeff Cravath) |

EDDIE CROWDER, 3-2-0 (Oklahoma '55) Born 8-26-31
Colorado	Bluebonnet 12-23-67	Miami (Fla.) 31-21 (Charlie Tate)
Colorado	Liberty 12-13-69	Alabama 47-33 (Paul "Bear" Bryant)
Colorado	Liberty 12-12-70	Tulane 3-17 (Jim Pittman)
Colorado	Bluebonnet 12-31-71	Houston 29-17 (Bill Yeoman)
Colorado	Gator 12-20-72	Auburn 3-24 (Ralph "Shug" Jordan)

JACK CROWE, 0-1-0 (UAB '70) Born 4-6-48
| Arkansas | Independence 12-29-91 | Georgia 15-24 (Ray Goff) |

JIM CROWLEY, 1-1-0 (Notre Dame '25) Born 9-10-02
| Fordham | Cotton 1-1-41 | Texas A&M 12-13 (Homer Norton) |
| Fordham | Sugar 1-1-42 | Missouri 2-0 (Don Faurot) |

DICK CRUM, 6-2-0 (Mount Union '57) Born 4-29-34
Miami (Ohio)	Tangerine 12-21-74	Georgia 21-10 (Vince Dooley)
Miami (Ohio)	Tangerine 12-20-75	South Carolina 20-7 (Jim Carlen)
North Carolina	Gator 12-28-79	Michigan 17-15 (Glenn "Bo" Schembechler)
North Carolina	Bluebonnet 12-31-80	Texas 16-7 (Fred Akers)
North Carolina	Gator 12-28-81	Arkansas 31-27 (Lou Holtz)
North Carolina	Sun 12-25-82	Texas 26-10 (Fred Akers)
North Carolina	Peach 12-30-83	Florida St. 3-28 (Bobby Bowden)
North Carolina	Aloha 12-27-86	Arizona 21-30 (Larry Smith)

FRAN CURCI, 1-0-0 (Miami [Fla.] '60) Born 6-11-38
| Kentucky | Peach 12-31-76 | North Carolina 21-0 (Bill Dooley) |

BILL CURRY, 2-3-0 (Georgia Tech '65) Born 10-21-42
Georgia Tech	Hall of Fame 12-31-85	Michigan St. 17-14 (George Perles)
Alabama	Hall of Fame 1-2-88	Michigan 24-28 (Glenn "Bo" Schembechler)
Alabama	Sun 12-24-88	Army 29-28 (Jim Young)
Alabama	Sugar 1-1-90	Miami (Fla.) 25-33 (Dennis Erickson)
Kentucky	Peach 12-31-93	Clemson 13-14 (Tommy West)

JACK "CACTUS JACK" CURTICE, 1-1-0 (Transylvania '30) Born 5-24-07
| UTEP | Sun 1-1-49 | West Virginia 12-21 (Dud DeGroot) |
| UTEP | Sun 1-2-50 | Georgetown 33-20 (Bob Margarita) |

DAVID CUTCLIFFE, 2-0-0 (Alabama '76) Born 9-16-54
| Mississippi | Independence 12-31-98 | Texas Tech 35-18 (Spike Dykes) |
| Mississippi | Independence 12-31-99 | Oklahoma 27-25 (Bob Stoops) |

JOHN "OX" Da GROSA, 0-1-0 (Colgate '26) Born 2-17-02
| Holy Cross | Orange 1-1-46 | Miami (Fla.) 6-13 (Jack Harding) |

GARY DARNELL, 0-1-0 (Oklahoma St. '71) Born 10-15-48
| Florida | Freedom 12-29-89 | Washington 7-34 (Don James) |

DUFFY DAUGHERTY, 1-1-0 (Syracuse '40) Born 9-8-15
| Michigan St. | Rose 1-2-56 | UCLA 17-14 (Henry "Red" Sanders) |
| Michigan St. | Rose 1-1-66 | UCLA 12-14 (Tommy Prothro) |

BOB DAVIE, 0-2-0 (Youngstown St. '76) Born 9-30-54
| Notre Dame | Independence 12-28-97 | LSU 9-27 (Gerry DiNardo) |
| Notre Dame | Gator 1-1-99 | Georgia Tech 28-35 (George O'Leary) |

BOB DAVIS, 0-1-0 (Utah '30) Born 2-13-08
| Colorado St. | Raisin 1-1-49 | Occidental 20-21 (Roy Dennis) |

BUTCH DAVIS, 3-0-0 (Arkansas '74) Born 11-17-51
Miami (Fla.)	Carquest 12-27-96	Virginia 31-21 (Geroge Welsh)
Miami (Fla.)	Micron PC 12-29-98	North Carolina St. 46-23 (Mike O'Cain)
Miami (Fla.)	Gator 1-1-00	Georgia Tech 28-13 (George O'Leary)

PAUL DAVIS, 1-0-0 (Mississippi '47) Born 2-3-22
| Mississippi St. | Liberty 12-21-63 | North Carolina St. 16-12 (Earle Edwards) |

LOWELL "RED" DAWSON, 0-1-0 (Tulane '30) Born 12-26-06
| Tulane | Sugar 1-1-40 | Texas A&M 13-14 (Homer Norton) |

FISHER DeBERRY, 5-5-0 (Wofford '60) Born 9-9-38
Air Force	Independence 12-15-84	Virginia Tech 23-7 (Bill Dooley)
Air Force	Bluebonnet 12-31-85	Texas 24-16 (Fred Akers)
Air Force	Freedom 12-30-87	Arizona St. 28-33 (John Cooper)
Air Force	Liberty 12-29-89	Mississippi 29-42 (Billy Brewer)
Air Force	Liberty 12-27-90	Ohio St. 23-11 (John Cooper)
Air Force	Liberty 12-29-91	Mississippi St. 38-15 (Jackie Sherrill)
Air Force	Liberty 12-31-92	Mississippi 0-13 (Billy Brewer)
Air Force	Copper 12-27-95	Texas Tech 41-55 (Spike Dykes)
Air Force	Las Vegas 12-20-97	Oregon 13-41 (Mike Bellotti)
Air Force	Oahu Classic 12-25-98	Washington 45-25 (Jim Lambright)

DUD DeGROOT, 1-0-0 (Stanford '24) Born 11-20-1895
| West Virginia | Sun 1-1-49 | UTEP 21-12 (Jack "Cactus Jack" Curtice) |

ROY DENNIS, 1-0-0 (Occidental '33) Born 5-13-05
| Occidental | Raisin 1-1-49 | Colorado St. 21-20 (Bob Davis) |

HERB DEROMEDI, 0-1-0 (Michigan '60) Born 5-26-39
| Central Mich. | California 12-8-90 | San Jose St. 24-48 (Terry Shea) |

BOB DEVANEY, 7-3-0 (Alma '39) Born 4-2-15
| Wyoming | Sun 12-31-58 | Hardin-Simmons 14-6 (Sammy Baugh) |
| Nebraska | Gotham 12-15-62 | Miami (Fla.) 36-34 (Andy Gustafson) |

Coach/School	Bowl/Date	Opponent/Score (Coach)
Nebraska	Orange 1-1-64	Auburn 13-7 (Ralph "Shug" Jordan)
Nebraska	Cotton 1-1-65	Arkansas 7-10 (Frank Broyles)
Nebraska	Orange 1-1-66	Alabama 28-39 (Paul "Bear" Bryant)
Nebraska	Sugar 1-2-67	Alabama 7-34 (Paul "Bear" Bryant)
Nebraska	Sun 12-20-69	Georgia 45-6 (Vince Dooley)
Nebraska	Orange 1-1-71	LSU 17-12 (Charlie McClendon)
Nebraska	Orange 1-1-72	Alabama 38-6 (Paul "Bear" Bryant)
Nebraska	Orange 1-1-73	Notre Dame 40-6 (Ara Parseghian)

DAN DEVINE, 7-3-0 (Minn.-Duluth '48) Born 12-23-24
Missouri	Orange 1-1-60	Georgia 0-14 (Wally Butts)
Missouri	Orange 1-2-61	Navy 21-14 (Wayne Hardin)
Missouri	Bluebonnet 12-22-62	Georgia Tech 14-10 (Bobby Dodd)
Missouri	Sugar 1-1-66	Florida 20-18 (Ray Graves)
Missouri	Gator 12-28-68	Alabama 35-10 (Paul "Bear" Bryant)
Missouri	Orange 1-1-70	Penn St. 3-10 (Joe Paterno)
Notre Dame	Gator 12-27-76	Penn St. 20-9 (Joe Paterno)
Notre Dame	Cotton 1-2-78	Texas 38-10 (Fred Akers)
Notre Dame	Cotton 1-1-79	Houston 35-34 (Bill Yeoman)
Notre Dame	Sugar 1-1-81	Georgia 10-17 (Vince Dooley)

PHIL DICKENS, 1-0-0 (Tennessee '37) Born 6-29-14
| Wyoming | Sun 1-2-56 | Texas Tech 21-14 (DeWitt Weaver) |

DOUG DICKEY, 2-7-0 (Florida '54) Born 6-24-32
Tennessee	Bluebonnet 12-18-65	Tulsa 27-6 (Glenn Dobbs)
Tennessee	Gator 12-31-66	Syracuse 18-12 (Ben Schwartzwalder)
Tennessee	Orange 1-1-68	Oklahoma 24-26 (Chuck Fairbanks)
Tennessee	Cotton 1-1-69	Texas 13-35 (Darrell Royal)
Tennessee	Gator 12-27-69	Florida 13-14 (Ray Graves)
Florida	Tangerine 12-22-73	Miami (Ohio) 7-16 (Bill Mallory)
Florida	Sugar 12-31-74	Nebraska 10-13 (Tom Osborne)
Florida	Gator 12-29-75	Maryland 0-13 (Jerry Claiborne)
Florida	Sun 1-2-77	Texas A&M 14-37 (Emory Bellard)

JIM DICKEY, 0-1-0 (Houston '56) Born 3-22-34
| Kansas St. | Independence 12-11-82 | Wisconsin 3-14 (Dave McClain) |

BILL "LONE STAR" DIETZ, 1-0-0 (Carlisle '12) Born 8-15-1885
| Washington St. | Rose 1-1-16 | Brown 14-0 (Ed Robinson) |

PAUL DIETZEL, 2-2-0 (Miami [Ohio] '48) Born 9-5-24
LSU	Sugar 1-1-59	Clemson 7-0 (Frank Howard)
LSU	Sugar 1-1-60	Mississippi 0-21 (John Vaught)
LSU	Orange 1-1-62	Colorado 25-7 (Sonny Grandelius)
South Carolina	Peach 12-20-69	West Virginia 3-14 (Jim Carlen)

GERRY DiNARDO, 3-0-0 (Notre Dame '75) Born 11-10-52
LSU	Independence 12-29-95	Michigan St. 45-26 (Nick Saban)
LSU	Peach 12-28-96	Clemson 10-7 (Tommy West)
LSU	Independence 12-28-97	Notre Dame 27-9 (Bob Davie)

BOBBY DOBBS, 2-0-0 (Army '46) Born 10-13-22
| UTEP | Sun 12-31-65 | TCU 13-12 (Abe Martin) |
| UTEP | Sun 12-30-67 | Mississippi 14-7 (John Vaught) |

GLENN DOBBS, 1-1-0 (Tulsa '43) Born 7-12-20
| Tulsa | Bluebonnet 12-19-64 | Mississippi 14-7 (John Vaught) |
| Tulsa | Bluebonnet 12-18-65 | Tennessee 6-27 (Doug Dickey) |

BOBBY DODD, 9-4-0 (Tennessee '31) Born 11-11-08
Georgia Tech	Oil 1-1-47	St. Mary's (Cal.) 41-19 (Jimmy Phelan)
Georgia Tech	Orange 1-1-48	Kansas 20-14 (George Sauer)
Georgia Tech	Orange 1-1-52	Baylor 17-14 (George Sauer)
Georgia Tech	Sugar 1-1-53	Mississippi 24-7 (John Vaught)
Georgia Tech	Sugar 1-1-54	West Virginia 42-19 (Art Lewis)
Georgia Tech	Cotton 1-1-55	Arkansas 14-6 (Bowden Wyatt)
Georgia Tech	Sugar 1-2-56	Pittsburgh 7-0 (John Michelosen)
Georgia Tech	Gator 12-29-56	Pittsburgh 21-14 (John Michelosen)
Georgia Tech	Gator 1-2-60	Arkansas 7-14 (Frank Broyles)
Georgia Tech	Gator 12-30-61	Penn St. 15-30 (Charles "Rip" Engle)
Georgia Tech	Bluebonnet 12-22-62	Missouri 10-14 (Dan Devine)
Georgia Tech	Gator 12-31-65	Texas Tech 31-21 (J. T. King)
Georgia Tech	Orange 1-2-67	Florida 12-27 (Ray Graves)

ED DOHERTY, 0-2-0 (Boston College '44) Born 7-25-18
| Arizona St. | Salad 1-1-50 | Xavier (Ohio) 21-33 (Ed Kluska) |
| Arizona St. | Salad 1-1-51 | Miami (Ohio) 21-34 (Woody Hayes) |

JACK DOLAND, 1-0-0 (Tulane '50) Born 3-3-28
| McNeese St. | Independence 12-13-76 | Tulsa 20-16 (F. A. Dry) |

TERRY DONAHUE, 8-4-1 (UCLA '67) Born 6-24-44
UCLA	Liberty 12-30-76	Alabama 6-36 (Paul "Bear" Bryant)
UCLA	Fiesta 12-25-78	Arkansas 10-10 (Lou Holtz)
UCLA	Bluebonnet 12-31-81	Michigan 14-33 (Glenn "Bo" Schembechler)
UCLA	Rose 1-1-83	Michigan 24-14 (Glenn "Bo" Schembechler)
UCLA	Rose 1-2-84	Illinois 45-9 (Mike White)
UCLA	Fiesta 1-1-85	Miami (Fla.) 39-37 (Jimmy Johnson)
UCLA	Rose 1-1-86	Iowa 45-28 (Hayden Fry)
UCLA	Freedom 12-30-86	Brigham Young 31-10 (LaVell Edwards)
UCLA	Aloha 12-25-87	Florida 20-16 (Galen Hall)
UCLA	Cotton 1-2-89	Arkansas 17-3 (Ken Hatfield)
UCLA	John Hancock 12-31-91	Illinois 6-3 (Lou Tepper)
UCLA	Rose 1-1-94	Wisconsin 16-21 (Barry Alvarez)
UCLA	Aloha 12-25-95	Kansas 30-51 (Glen Mason)

JIM DONNAN, 3-0-0 (North Carolina St. '68) Born 1-29-45
Georgia	Outback 1-1-98	Wisconsin 33-6 (Barry Alvarez)
Georgia	Peach 12-31-98	Virginia 35-33 (George Welsh)
Georgia	Outback 1-1-00	Purdue 28-25 (ot) (Joe Tiller)

BILL DOOLEY, 3-7-0 (Mississippi St. '56) Born 5-19-34
North Carolina	Peach 12-30-70	Arizona St. 26-48 (Frank Kush)
North Carolina	Gator 12-31-71	Georgia 3-7 (Vince Dooley)
North Carolina	Sun 12-30-72	Texas Tech 32-28 (Jim Carlen)
North Carolina	Sun 12-28-74	Mississippi St. 24-26 (Bob Tyler)
North Carolina	Peach 12-31-76	Kentucky 0-21 (Fran Curci)
North Carolina	Liberty 12-19-77	Nebraska 17-21 (Tom Osborne)
Virginia Tech	Peach 1-2-81	Miami (Fla.) 10-20 (Howard Schnellenberger)
Virginia Tech	Independence 12-15-84	Air Force 7-23 (Fisher DeBerry)
Virginia Tech	Peach 12-31-86	North Carolina St. 25-24 (Dick Sheridan)
Wake Forest	Independence 12-31-92	Oregon 39-35 (Rich Brooks)

VINCE DOOLEY, 8-10-2 (Auburn '54) Born 9-4-32
Georgia	Sun 12-26-64	Texas Tech 7-0 (J. T. King)
Georgia	Cotton 12-31-66	Southern Methodist 24-9 (Hayden Fry)
Georgia	Liberty 12-16-67	North Carolina St. 7-14 (Earle Edwards)
Georgia	Sugar 1-1-69	Arkansas 2-16 (Frank Broyles)
Georgia	Sun 12-20-69	Nebraska 6-45 (Bob Devaney)
Georgia	Gator 12-31-71	North Carolina 7-3 (Bill Dooley)
Georgia	Peach 12-28-73	Maryland 17-16 (Jerry Claiborne)
Georgia	Tangerine 12-21-74	Miami (Ohio) 10-21 (Dick Crum)
Georgia	Cotton 1-1-76	Arkansas 10-31 (Frank Broyles)
Georgia	Sugar 1-1-77	Pittsburgh 3-27 (Johnny Majors)
Georgia	Bluebonnet 12-31-78	Stanford 22-25 (Bill Walsh)
Georgia	Sugar 1-1-81	Notre Dame 17-10 (Dan Devine)
Georgia	Sugar 1-1-82	Pittsburgh 20-24 (Jackie Sherrill)
Georgia	Sugar 1-1-83	Penn St. 23-27 (Joe Paterno)
Georgia	Cotton 1-2-84	Texas 10-9 (Fred Akers)
Georgia	Fla. Citrus 12-22-84	Florida St. 17-17 (Bobby Bowden)
Georgia	Sun 1-1-85	Arizona 13-13 (Larry Smith)
Georgia	Hall of Fame 12-23-86	Boston College 24-27 (Jack Bicknell)
Georgia	Liberty 12-29-87	Arkansas 20-17 (Ken Hatfield)
Georgia	Gator 1-1-89	Michigan St. 34-27 (George Perles)

CHARLES "GUS" DORAIS, 0-1-0 (Notre Dame '14) Born 7-21-1891
| Gonzaga | San Diego East-West Christmas Classic 12-25-22 | West Virginia 13-21 (Clarence "Doc" Spears) |

HAROLD "RED" DREW, 1-2-0 (Bates '16) Born 11-9-1894
Alabama	Sugar 1-1-48	Texas 7-27 (Blair Cherry)
Alabama	Orange 1-1-53	Syracuse 61-6 (Ben Schwartzwalder)
Alabama	Cotton 1-1-54	Rice 6-28 (Jess Neely)

BILL DRIVER, 0-1-0 (Missouri '09) Born 11-7-1883
| TCU | Fort Worth Classic 1-1-21 | Centre 7-63 (Charley Moran) |

F. A. DRY, 0-1-0 (Oklahoma St. '53) Born 9-2-31
| Tulsa | Independence 12-13-76 | McNeese St. 16-20 (Jack Doland) |

MIKE DuBOSE, 0-2-0 (Alabama '74) Born 1-5-53
| Alabama | Music City 12-29-98 | Virginia Tech 7-38 (Frank Beamer) |
| Alabama | Orange 1-1-00 | Michigan 34-35 (ot) (Lloyd Carr) |

ERNIE DUPLECHIN, 0-2-0 (Louisiana Col. '55) Born 7-19-32
| McNeese St. | Independence 12-15-79 | Syracuse 7-31 (Frank Maloney) |
| McNeese St. | Independence 12-13-80 | Southern Miss. 14-16 (Bobby Collins) |

PAT DYE, 7-2-1 (Georgia '62) Born 11-6-39
East Caro.	Independence 12-16-78	Louisiana Tech 35-13 (Maxie Lambright)
Auburn	Tangerine 12-18-82	Boston College 33-26 (Jack Bicknell)
Auburn	Sugar 1-2-84	Michigan 9-7 (Glenn "Bo" Schembechler)
Auburn	Liberty 12-27-84	Arkansas 21-15 (Ken Hatfield)
Auburn	Cotton 1-1-86	Texas A&M 16-36 (Jackie Sherrill)
Auburn	Fla. Citrus 1-1-87	Southern California 16-7 (Ted Tollner)
Auburn	Sugar 1-1-88	Syracuse 16-16 (Dick MacPherson)
Auburn	Sugar 1-2-89	Florida St. 7-13 (Bobby Bowden)
Auburn	Hall of Fame 1-1-90	Ohio St. 31-14 (John Cooper)
Auburn	Peach 12-29-90	Indiana 27-23 (Bill Mallory)

SPIKE DYKES, 2-5-0 (Stephen F. Austin '59) Born 4-15-38
Texas Tech	Independence 12-20-86	Mississippi 17-20 (Billy Brewer)
Texas Tech	All-American 12-28-89	Duke 49-21 (Steve Spurrier)
Texas Tech	John Hancock 12-24-93	Oklahoma 10-41 (Gary Gibbs)
Texas Tech	Cotton 1-2-95	Southern California 14-55 (John Robinson)
Texas Tech	Copper 12-27-95	Air Force 55-41 (Fisher DeBerry)
Texas Tech	Alamo 12-29-96	Iowa 0-27 (Hayden Fry)
Texas Tech	Independence 12-31-98	Mississippi 18-35 (David Cutcliffe)

LLOYD EATON, 1-1-0 (Black Hills St. '40) Born 3-23-18
| Wyoming | Sun 12-24-66 | Florida St. 28-20 (Bill Peterson) |
| Wyoming | Sugar 1-1-68 | LSU 13-20 (Charlie McClendon) |

BILL EDWARDS, 1-0-0 (Wittenberg '31) Born 6-21-05
| Case Reserve | Sun 1-1-41 | Arizona St. 26-13 (Millard "Dixie" Howell) |

EARLE EDWARDS, 1-1-0 (Penn St. '31) Born 11-10-08
| North Carolina St. | Liberty 12-21-63 | Mississippi 12-16 (Paul Davis) |
| North Carolina St. | Liberty 12-16-67 | Georgia 14-7 (Vince Dooley) |

BOWL COACHING RECORDS

Coach/School	Bowl/Date	Opponent/Score (Coach)
LaVELL EDWARDS, 7-14-1	(Utah St. '52)	Born 10-11-30
Brigham Young	Fiesta 12-28-74	Oklahoma St. 6-16 (Jim Stanley)
Brigham Young	Tangerine 12-18-76	Oklahoma St. 21-49 (Jim Stanley)
Brigham Young	Holiday 12-22-78	Navy 16-23 (George Welsh)
Brigham Young	Holiday 12-21-79	Indiana 37-38 (Lee Corso)
Brigham Young	Holiday 12-19-80	Southern Methodist 46-45 (Ron Meyer)
Brigham Young	Holiday 12-18-81	Washington St. 38-36 (Jim Walden)
Brigham Young	Holiday 12-17-82	Ohio St. 17-47 (Earle Bruce)
Brigham Young	Holiday 12-23-83	Missouri 21-17 (Warren Powers)
Brigham Young	Holiday 12-21-84	Michigan 24-17 (Glenn "Bo" Schembechler)
Brigham Young	Fla. Citrus 12-28-85	Ohio St. 7-10 (Earle Bruce)
Brigham Young	Freedom 12-30-86	UCLA 10-31 (Terry Donahue)
Brigham Young	All-American 12-22-87	Virginia 16-22 (George Welsh)
Brigham Young	Freedom 12-29-88	Colorado 20-17 (Bill McCartney)
Brigham Young	Holiday 12-29-89	Penn St. 39-50 (Joe Paterno)
Brigham Young	Holiday 12-29-90	Texas A&M 14-65 (R. C. Slocum)
Brigham Young	Holiday 12-30-91	Iowa 13-13 (Hayden Fry)
Brigham Young	Aloha 12-25-92	Kansas 20-23 (Glen Mason)
Brigham Young	Holiday 12-30-93	Ohio St. 21-28 (John Cooper)
Brigham Young	Copper 12-29-94	Oklahoma 31-6 (Gary Gibbs)
Brigham Young	Cotton 1-1-97	Kansas St. 19-15 (Bill Snyder)
Brigham Young	Liberty 12-31-98	Tulane 27-14 (Chris Scelfo)
Brigham Young	Motor City 12-27-99	Marshall 3-21 (Bob Pruett)
RAY ELIOT, 2-0-0	(Illinois '32)	Born 6-13-05
Illinois	Rose 1-1-47	UCLA 45-14 (Bert LaBrucherie)
Illinois	Rose 1-1-52	Stanford 40-7 (Chuck Taylor)
BENNIE ELLENDER, 0-1-0	(Tulane '48)	Born 3-2-25
Tulane	Bluebonnet 12-29-73	Houston 7-47 (Bill Yeoman)
CHALMERS "BUMP" ELLIOTT, 1-0-0	(Michigan '48)	Born 1-30-25
Michigan	Rose 1-1-65	Oregon St. 34-7 (Tommy Prothro)
PETE ELLIOTT, 1-1-0	(Michigan '49)	Born 9-29-26
California	Rose 1-1-59	Iowa 12-38 (Forest Evashevski)
Illinois	Rose 1-1-64	Washington 17-7 (Jim Owens)
JACK ELWAY, 0-2-0	(Washington St. '53)	Born 5-30-31
San Jose St.	California 12-19-81	Toledo 25-27 (Chuck Stobart)
Stanford	Gator 12-27-86	Clemson 21-27 (Danny Ford)
CHARLES "RIP" ENGLE, 3-1-0	(Western Md. '30)	Born 3-26-06
Penn St.	Liberty 12-19-53	Alabama 7-0 (Paul "Bear" Bryant)
Penn St.	Liberty 12-17-60	Oregon 41-12 (Len Casanova)
Penn St.	Gator 12-30-61	Georgia Tech 30-15 (Bobby Dodd)
Penn St.	Gator 12-29-62	Florida 7-17 (Ray Graves)
EDDIE ERDELATZ, 2-0-0	(St. Mary's [Cal.] '36)	Born 4-21-13
Navy	Sugar 1-1-55	Mississippi 21-0 (John Vaught)
Navy	Cotton 1-1-58	Rice 20-7 (Jess Neely)
DENNIS ERICKSON, 4-4-0	(Montana St. '70)	Born 3-24-47
Washington St.	Aloha 12-25-88	Houston 24-22 (Jack Pardee)
Miami (Fla.)	Sugar 1-1-90	Alabama 33-25 (Bill Curry)
Miami (Fla.)	Cotton 1-1-91	Texas 46-3 (David McWilliams)
Miami (Fla.)	Orange 1-1-92	Nebraska 22-0 (Tom Osborne)
Miami (Fla.)	Sugar 1-1-93	Alabama 13-34 (Gene Stallings)
Miami (Fla.)	Fiesta 1-1-94	Arizona 0-24 (Dick Tomey)
Miami (Fla.)	Orange 1-1-95	Nebraska 17-24 (Tom Osborne)
Oregon St.	Oahu Classic 12-25-99	Hawaii 17-23 (June Jones)
FOREST EVASHEVSKI, 2-0-0	(Michigan '41)	Born 2-19-18
Iowa	Rose 1-1-57	Oregon St. 35-19 (Tommy Prothro)
Iowa	Rose 1-1-59	California 38-12 (Pete Elliott)
CHUCK FAIRBANKS, 3-1-1	(Michigan St. '55)	Born 6-10-33
Oklahoma	Orange 1-1-68	Tennessee 26-24 (Doug Dickey)
Oklahoma	Bluebonnet 12-31-68	Southern Methodist 27-28 (Hayden Fry)
Oklahoma	Bluebonnet 12-31-70	Alabama 24-24 (Paul "Bear" Bryant)
Oklahoma	Sugar 1-1-72	Auburn 40-22 (Ralph "Shug" Jordan)
Oklahoma	Sugar 12-31-72	Penn St. 14-0 (Joe Paterno)
DON FAMBROUGH, 0-2-0	(Kansas '48)	Born 10-19-22
Kansas	Liberty 12-17-73	North Carolina St. 18-31 (Lou Holtz)
Kansas	Hall of Fame 12-31-81	Mississippi St. 0-10 (Emory Bellard)
DON FAUROT, 0-4-0	(Missouri '25)	Born 6-23-02
Missouri	Orange 1-1-40	Georgia Tech 7-21 (Bill Alexander)
Missouri	Sugar 1-1-42	Fordham 0-2 (Jim Crowley)
Missouri	Gator 1-1-49	Clemson 23-24 (Frank Howard)
Missouri	Gator 1-2-50	Maryland 7-21 (Jim Tatum)
GERRY FAUST, 1-1-0	(Dayton '58)	Born 5-21-35
Notre Dame	Liberty 12-29-83	Boston College 19-18 (Jack Bicknell)
Notre Dame	Aloha 12-29-84	Southern Methodist 20-27 (Bobby Collins)
FOGE FAZIO, 0-2-0	(Pittsburgh '60)	Born 2-28-39
Pittsburgh	Cotton 1-1-83	Southern Methodist 3-7 (Bobby Collins)
Pittsburgh	Fiesta 1-2-84	Ohio St. 23-28 (Earle Bruce)
BEATTIE FEATHERS, 0-1-0	(Tennessee '34)	Born 6-1-12
North Carolina St.	Gator 1-1-47	Oklahoma 13-34 (Jim Tatum)
WES FESLER, 1-0-0	(Ohio St. '32)	Born 6-29-08
Ohio St.	Rose 1-2-50	California 17-14 (Lynn "Pappy" Waldorf)

Coach/School	Bowl/Date	Opponent/Score (Coach)
CHARLIE FICKERT, 0-1-0	(Stanford '98)	Born 2-23-1873
Stanford	Rose 1-1-02	Michigan 0-49 (Fielding "Hurry Up" Yost)
ROBERT FISHER, 1-0-0	(Harvard '12)	Born 12-3-1888
Harvard	Rose 1-1-20	Oregon 7-6 (Charles "Shy" Huntington)
DICK FLYNN, 0-1-0	(Michigan St. '65)	Born 7-17-43
Central Mich.	Las Vegas 12-15-94	UNLV 24-52 (Jeff Horton)
HANK FOLDBERG, 0-1-0	(Army '48)	Born 3-12-23
Wichita St.	Sun 12-30-61	Villanova 9-17 (Alex Bell)
BOB FOLWELL, 0-1-1	(Pennsylvania '08)	Born 1885
Pennsylvania	Rose 1-1-17	Oregon 0-14 (Hugo Bezdek)
Navy	Rose 1-1-24	Washington 14-14 (Enoch Bagshaw)
DANNY FORD, 6-3-0	(Alabama '70)	Born 4-2-48
Clemson	Gator 12-29-78	Ohio St. 17-15 (Woody Hayes)
Clemson	Peach 12-31-79	Baylor 18-24 (Grant Teaff)
Clemson	Orange 1-1-82	Nebraska 22-15 (Tom Osborne)
Clemson	Independence 12-21-85	Minnesota 13-20 (John Gutekunst)
Clemson	Gator 12-27-86	Stanford 27-21 (Jack Elway)
Clemson	Fla. Citrus 1-1-88	Penn St. 35-10 (Joe Paterno)
Clemson	Fla. Citrus 1-2-89	Oklahoma 23-6 (Barry Switzer)
Clemson	Gator 12-30-89	West Virginia 27-7 (Don Nehlen)
Arkansas	Carquest 12-30-95	North Carolina 10-20 (Mack Brown)
DENNIS FRANCHIONE, 1-2-0	(Pittsburg St. '73)	Born 3-28-51
New Mexico	Insight.com 12-27-97	Arizona 14-20 (Dick Tomey)
TCU	Sun 12-31-98	Southern California 28-19 (Paul Hackett)
TCU	Mobile Alabama 12-22-99	East Caro. 28-14 (Steve Logan)
HENRY FRNKA, 2-3-0	(Austin '26)	Born 3-16-03
Tulsa	Sun 1-1-42	Texas Tech 6-0 (Dell Morgan)
Tulsa	Sugar 1-1-43	Tennessee 7-14 (John Barnhill)
Tulsa	Sugar 1-1-44	Georgia Tech 18-20 (Bill Alexander)
Tulsa	Orange 1-1-45	Georgia Tech 26-12 (Bill Alexander)
Tulsa	Oil 1-1-46	Georgia 6-20 (Wally Butts)
HAYDEN FRY, 7-9-1	(Baylor '51)	Born 2-28-29
Southern Methodist	Sun 12-31-63	Oregon 13-21 (Len Casanova)
Southern Methodist	Cotton 12-31-66	Georgia 9-24 (Vince Dooley)
Southern Methodist	Bluebonnet 12-31-68	Oklahoma 28-27 (Chuck Fairbanks)
Iowa	Rose 1-1-82	Washington 0-28 (Don James)
Iowa	Peach 12-31-82	Tennessee 28-22 (Johnny Majors)
Iowa	Gator 12-30-83	Florida 6-14 (Charley Pell)
Iowa	Freedom 12-26-84	Texas 55-17 (Fred Akers)
Iowa	Rose 1-1-86	UCLA 28-45 (Terry Donahue)
Iowa	Holiday 12-30-86	San Diego St. 39-38 (Denny Stolz)
Iowa	Holiday 12-30-87	Wyoming 20-19 (Paul Roach)
Iowa	Peach 12-31-88	North Carolina St. 23-29 (Dick Sheridan)
Iowa	Rose 1-1-91	Washington 34-46 (Don James)
Iowa	Holiday 12-30-91	Brigham Young 13-13 (LaVell Edwards)
Iowa	Alamo 12-31-93	California 3-37 (Keith Gilbertson)
Iowa	Sun 12-29-95	Washington 38-18 (Jim Lambright)
Iowa	Alamo 12-29-96	Texas Tech 27-0 (Spike Dykes)
Iowa	Sun 12-29-97	Arizona St. 7-17 (Bruce Snyder)
BILL FULCHER, 1-0-0	(Georgia Tech '57)	Born 2-9-34
Georgia Tech	Liberty 12-18-72	Iowa St. 31-30 (Johnny Majors)
PHILLIP FULMER, 5-3-0	(Tennessee '72)	Born 9-1-50
Tennessee	Hall of Fame 1-1-93	Boston College 38-23 (Tom Coughlin)
Tennessee	Fla. Citrus 1-1-94	Penn St. 13-31 (Joe Paterno)
Tennessee	Gator 12-30-94	Virginia Tech 45-23 (Frank Beamer)
Tennessee	Fla. Citrus 1-1-96	Ohio St. 20-14 (John Cooper)
Tennessee	Fla. Citrus 1-1-97	Northwestern 48-28 (Gary Barnett)
Tennessee	Orange 1-2-98	Nebraska 17-42 (Tom Osborne)
Tennessee	Fiesta 1-4-99	Florida St. 23-16 (Bobby Bowden)
Tennessee	Fiesta 1-2-00	Nebraska 21-31 (Frank Solich)
WARREN GAER, 0-1-0	(Drake '35)	Born 2-7-12
Drake	Sun 1-1-58	Louisville 20-34 (Frank Camp)
JOE GAVIN, 0-1-0	(Notre Dame '31)	Born 3-20-08
Dayton	Salad 1-1-52	Houston 21-26 (Clyde Lee)
GARY GIBBS, 2-1-0	(Oklahoma '75)	Born 8-13-52
Oklahoma	Gator 12-29-91	Virginia 48-14 (George Welsh)
Oklahoma	John Hancock 12-24-93	Texas Tech 41-10 (Spike Dykes)
Oklahoma	Copper 12-29-94	Brigham Young 6-31 (LaVell Edwards)
VINCE GIBSON, 0-2-0	(Florida St. '55)	Born 3-27-33
Louisville	Independence 12-17-77	Louisiana Tech 14-24 (Maxie Lambright)
Tulane	Hall of Fame 12-27-80	Arkansas 15-34 (Lou Holtz)
CLAUDE GILBERT, 1-1-0	(San Jose St. '59)	Born 7-10-32
San Jose St.	California 12-13-86	Miami (Ohio) 37-7 (Tim Rose)
San Jose St.	California 12-12-87	Eastern Mich. 27-30 (Jim Harkema)
KEITH GILBERTSON, 1-0-0	(Central Wash. '71)	Born 5-15-48
California	Alamo 12-31-93	Iowa 37-3 (Hayden Fry)
SID GILLMAN, 1-1-0	(Ohio St. '34)	Born 10-26-11
Miami (Ohio)	Sun 1-1-48	Texas Tech 13-12 (Dell Morgan)
Cincinnati	Sun 1-1-51	West Tex. A&M 13-14 (Frank Kimbrough)
BILL GLASSFORD, 0-1-0	(Pittsburgh '37)	Born 3-8-14
Nebraska	Orange 1-1-55	Duke 7-34 (Bill Murray)

Coach/School	Bowl/Date	Opponent/Score (Coach)
MARSHALL "LITTLE SLEEPY" GLENN, 1-0-0	(West Virginia '31)	Born 4-22-08
West Virginia	Sun 1-1-38	Texas Tech 7-6 (Pete Cawthon)
RAY GOFF, 2-2-0	(Georgia '78)	Born 7-10-55
Georgia	Peach 12-30-89	Syracuse 18-19 (Dick MacPherson)
Georgia	Independence 12-29-91	Arkansas 24-15 (Jack Crowe)
Georgia	Fla. Citrus 1-1-93	Ohio St. 21-14 (John Cooper)
Georgia	Peach 12-30-95	Virginia 27-34 (George Welsh)
FRED GOLDSMITH, 0-1-0	(Florida '67)	Born 3-3-44
Duke	Hall of Fame 1-2-95	Wisconsin 20-34 (Barry Alvarez)
MIKE GOTTFRIED, 0-1-0	(Morehead St. '66)	Born 12-17-44
Pittsburgh	Bluebonnet 12-31-87	Texas 27-32 (David McWilliams)
RALPH GRAHAM, 0-1-0	(Kansas St. '34)	Born 8-16-10
Wichita St.	Raisin 1-1-48	Pacific (Cal.) 14-26 (Larry Siemering)
SONNY GRANDELIUS, 0-1-0	(Michigan St. '51)	Born 4-16-29
Colorado	Orange 1-1-62	LSU 7-25 (Paul Dietzel)
RAY GRAVES, 4-1-0	(Tennessee '43)	Born 12-31-18
Florida	Gator 12-31-60	Baylor 13-12 (John Bridgers)
Florida	Gator 12-29-62	Penn St. 17-7 (Charles "Rip" Engle)
Florida	Sugar 1-1-66	Missouri 18-20 (Dan Devine)
Florida	Orange 1-2-67	Georgia Tech 27-12 (Bobby Dodd)
Florida	Gator 12-27-69	Tennessee 14-13 (Doug Dickey)
DENNIS GREEN, 0-1-0	(Iowa '71)	Born 2-17-49
Stanford	Aloha 12-25-91	Georgia Tech 17-18 (Bobby Ross)
VEE GREEN, 1-0-0	(Illinois '24)	Born 10-9-1900
Drake	Raisin 1-1-46	Fresno St. 13-12 (Alvin "Pix" Pierson)
ART GUEPE, 1-0-0	(Marquette '37)	Born 1-28-15
Vanderbilt	Gator 12-31-55	Auburn 25-13 (Ralph "Shug" Jordan)
ANDY GUSTAFSON, 1-3-0	(Pittsburgh '26)	Born 4-3-03
Miami (Fla.)	Orange 1-1-51	Clemson 14-15 (Frank Howard)
Miami (Fla.)	Gator 1-1-52	Clemson 14-0 (Frank Howard)
Miami (Fla.)	Liberty 12-16-61	Syracuse 14-15 (Ben Schwartzwalder)
Miami (Fla.)	Gotham 12-15-62	Nebraska 34-36 (Bob Devaney)
JOHN GUTEKUNST, 1-1-0	(Duke '66)	Born 4-13-44
Minnesota	Independence 12-21-85	Clemson 20-13 (Danny Ford)
Minnesota	Liberty 12-29-86	Tennessee 14-21 (Johnny Majors)
PAUL HACKETT, 1-1-0	(UC Davis '69)	Born 6-5-47
Pittsburgh	John Hancock 12-30-89	Texas A&M 31-28 (R. C. Slocum)
Southern California	Sun 12-31-98	TCU 19-28 (Dennis Franchione)
JACK HAGERTY, 0-1-0	(Georgetown '26)	Born 7-3-03
Georgetown	Orange 1-1-41	Mississippi St. 7-14 (Alvin McKeen)
GALEN HALL, 1-1-0	(Penn St. '62)	Born 8-14-40
Florida	Aloha 12-25-87	UCLA 16-20 (Terry Donahue)
Florida	All-American 12-29-88	Illinois 14-10 (John Mackovic)
CURLEY HALLMAN, 1-0-0	(Texas A&M '70)	Born 9-3-47
Southern Miss.	Independence 12-23-88	UTEP 38-18 (Bob Stull)
WAYNE HARDIN, 1-2-0	(Pacific [Cal.] '50)	Born 3-23-27
Navy	Orange 1-2-61	Missouri 14-21 (Dan Devine)
Navy	Cotton 1-1-64	Texas 6-28 (Darrell Royal)
Temple	Garden State 12-15-79	California 28-17 (Roger Theder)
JACK HARDING, 1-0-0	(Pittsburgh '26)	Born 1-5-1898
Miami (Fla.)	Orange 1-1-48	Holy Cross 13-6 (John "Ox" Da Grosa)
JIM HARKEMA, 1-0-0	(Kalamazoo '64)	Born 6-25-42
Eastern Mich.	California 12-12-87	San Jose St. 30-27 (Claude Gilbert)
WALT HARRIS, 0-1-0	(Pacific [Cal.] '68)	Born 11-9-46
Pittsburgh	Liberty 12-31-97	Southern Miss. 7-41 (Jeff Bower)
KEN HATFIELD, 4-6-0	(Arkansas '65)	Born 6-8-43
Air Force	Hall of Fame 12-31-82	Vanderbilt 36-28 (George MacIntyre)
Air Force	Independence 12-10-83	Mississippi 9-3 (Billy Brewer)
Arkansas	Liberty 12-27-84	Auburn 15-21 (Pat Dye)
Arkansas	Holiday 12-22-85	Arizona St. 18-17 (John Cooper)
Arkansas	Orange 1-1-87	Oklahoma 8-42 (Barry Switzer)
Arkansas	Liberty 12-29-87	Georgia 17-20 (Vince Dooley)
Arkansas	Cotton 1-2-89	UCLA 3-17 (Terry Donahue)
Arkansas	Cotton 1-1-90	Tennessee 27-31 (Johnny Majors)
Clemson	Hall of Fame 1-1-91	Illinois 30-0 (John Mackovic)
Clemson	Fla. Citrus 1-1-92	California 13-37 (Bruce Snyder)
WOODY HAYES, 6-6-0	(Denison '35)	Born 2-14-13
Miami (Ohio)	Salad 1-1-51	Arizona St. 34-21 (Ed Doherty)
Ohio St.	Rose 1-1-55	Southern California 20-7 (Jess Hill)
Ohio St.	Rose 1-1-58	Oregon 10-7 (Len Casanova)
Ohio St.	Rose 1-1-69	Southern California 27-16 (John McKay)
Ohio St.	Rose 1-1-71	Stanford 17-27 (John Ralston)
Ohio St.	Rose 1-1-73	Southern California 17-42 (John McKay)
Ohio St.	Rose 1-1-74	Southern California 42-21 (John McKay)
Ohio St.	Rose 1-1-75	Southern California 17-18 (John McKay)
Ohio St.	Rose 1-1-76	UCLA 10-23 (Dick Vermeil)
Ohio St.	Orange 1-1-77	Colorado 27-10 (Bill Mallory)
Ohio St.	Sugar 1-2-78	Alabama 6-35 (Paul "Bear" Bryant)
Ohio St.	Gator 12-29-78	Clemson 15-17 (Danny Ford)
KIM HELTON, 0-1-0	(Florida '70)	Born 7-28-48
Houston	Liberty 12-27-96	Syracuse 17-30 (Paul Pasqualoni)

Coach/School	Bowl/Date	Opponent/Score (Coach)
ELMER "GUS" HENDERSON, 2-0-0	(Oberlin '12)	Born 3-10-1889
Southern California	Rose 1-1-23	Penn St. 14-3 (Hugo Bezdek)
Southern California	L.A. Christmas Festival 12-25-24	Missouri 20-7 (Gwinn Henry)
DAN HENNING, 1-0-0	(William & Mary '64)	Born 7-21-42
Boston College	Aloha 12-25-94	Kansas St. 12-7 (Bill Snyder)
GWINN HENRY, 0-1-0	(Howard Payne '17)	Born 8-5-1887
Missouri	L.A. Christmas Festival 12-25-24	Southern California 7-20 (Elmer "Gus" Henderson)
BILL HESS, 0-2-0	(Ohio '47)	Born 2-5-23
Ohio	Sun 12-31-62	West Tex. A&M 14-15 (Joe Kerbel)
Ohio	Tangerine 12-27-68	Richmond 42-49 (Frank Jones)
JIM HICKEY, 1-0-0	(William & Mary '42)	Born 1-22-20
North Carolina	Gator 12-28-63	Air Force 35-0 (Ben Martin)
BOB HIGGINS, 1-0-1	(Penn St. '20)	Born 12-24-1893
West Va. Wesleyan	Dixie Classic 1-1-25	Southern Methodist 9-7 (Ray Morrison)
Penn St.	Cotton 1-1-48	Southern Methodist 13-13 (Matty Bell)
JESS HILL, 1-1-0	(Southern California '30)	Born 1-20-07
Southern California	Rose 1-1-53	Wisconsin 7-0 (Ivy Williamson)
Southern California	Rose 1-1-55	Ohio St. 7-20 (Woody Hayes)
PAT HILL, 0-1-0	(UC Riverside '73)	Born 12-17-51
Fresno St.	Las Vegas 12-18-99	Utah 16-17 (Ron McBride)
JERRY HINES, 0-0-1	(New Mexico St. '26)	Born 10-11-03
New Mexico St.	Sun 1-1-36	Hardin-Simmons 14-14 (Frank Kimbrough)
BERNARD A. HOBAN, 0-1-0	(Dartmouth '12)	Born 4-21-1890
U. of Mexico	Sun 1-1-45	Southwestern (Tex.) 0-35 (Randolph R. M. Medley)
ORIN "BABE" HOLLINGBERY, 0-1-0	(No college)	Born 7-15-1893
Washington St.	Rose 1-1-31	Alabama 0-24 (Wallace Wade)
LOU HOLTZ, 10-8-2	(Kent St. '59)	Born 1-6-37
William & Mary	Tangerine 12-28-70	Toledo 12-40 (Frank Lauterbur)
North Carolina St.	Peach 12-29-72	West Virginia 49-13 (Bobby Bowden)
North Carolina St.	Liberty 12-17-73	Kansas 31-18 (Don Fambrough)
North Carolina St.	Bluebonnet 12-23-74	Houston 31-31 (Bill Yeoman)
North Carolina St.	Peach 12-31-75	West Virginia 10-13 (Bobby Bowden)
Arkansas	Orange 1-2-78	Oklahoma 31-6 (Barry Switzer)
Arkansas	Fiesta 12-25-78	UCLA 10-10 (Terry Donahue)
Arkansas	Sugar 1-1-80	Alabama 9-24 (Paul "Bear" Bryant)
Arkansas	Hall of Fame 12-27-80	Tulane 34-15 (Vince Gibson)
Arkansas	Gator 12-28-81	North Carolina 27-31 (Dick Crum)
Arkansas	Bluebonnet 12-31-82	Florida 28-24 (Charley Pell)
Notre Dame	Cotton 1-1-88	Texas A&M 10-35 (Jackie Sherrill)
Notre Dame	Fiesta 1-2-89	West Virginia 34-21 (Don Nehlen)
Notre Dame	Orange 1-1-90	Colorado 21-6 (Bill McCartney)
Notre Dame	Orange 1-1-91	Colorado 9-10 (Bill McCartney)
Notre Dame	Sugar 1-1-92	Florida 39-28 (Steve Spurrier)
Notre Dame	Cotton 1-1-93	Texas A&M 28-3 (R. C. Slocum)
Notre Dame	Cotton 1-1-94	Texas A&M 24-21 (R. C. Slocum)
Notre Dame	Fiesta 1-2-95	Colorado 24-41 (Bill McCartney)
Notre Dame	Orange 1-1-96	Florida St. 26-31 (Bobby Bowden)
EDWIN "BABE" HORRELL, 0-1-0	(California '26)	Born 9-29-02
UCLA	Rose 1-1-43	Georgia 0-9 (Wally Butts)
JEFF HORTON, 1-0-0	(Nevada '81)	Born 7-13-57
UNLV	Las Vegas 12-15-94	Central Mich. 52-24 (Dick Flynn)
FRANK HOWARD, 3-3-0	(Alabama '31)	Born 3-25-09
Clemson	Gator 1-1-49	Missouri 24-23 (Don Faurot)
Clemson	Orange 1-1-51	Miami (Fla.) 15-14 (Andy Gustafson)
Clemson	Gator 1-1-52	Miami (Fla.) 0-14 (Andy Gustafson)
Clemson	Orange 1-1-57	Colorado 21-27 (Dallas Ward)
Clemson	Sugar 1-1-59	LSU 0-7 (Paul Dietzel)
Clemson	Bluebonnet 12-19-59	TCU 23-7 (Abe Martin)
MILLARD "DIXIE" HOWELL, 0-1-1	(Alabama '35)	Born 11-24-12
Arizona St.	Sun 1-1-40	Catholic 0-0 (Arthur "Dutch" Bergman)
Arizona St.	Sun 1-1-41	Case Reserve 13-26 (Bill Edwards)
BILL HUBBARD, 2-0-0	(Stanford '30)	Born 2-5-07
San Jose St.	Raisin 1-1-47	Utah St. 20-0 (E. L. "Dick" Romney)
San Jose St.	Raisin 12-31-49	Texas Tech 20-13 (Dell Morgan)
CLYDE "CAC" HUBBARD, 0-2-0	(Oregon St. '21)	Born 9-13-1897
Denver	Sun 1-1-46	New Mexico 24-34 (Willis Barnes)
Denver	Alamo 1-4-47	Hardin-Simmons 0-20 (Warren Woodson)
CHARLES "SHY" HUNTINGTON, 0-1-0	(Oregon)	Born 7-7-1891
Oregon	Rose 1-1-20	Harvard 6-7 (Robert Fisher)
HARVEY HYDE, 1-0-0	(Redlands '62)	Born 7-13-39
UNLV	California 12-15-84	Toledo 30-13 (Dan Simrell)
DON JAMES, 10-5-0	(Miami [Fla.] '54)	Born 12-31-32
Kent	Tangerine 12-29-72	Tampa 18-21 (Earle Bruce)
Washington	Rose 1-2-78	Michigan 27-20 (Glenn "Bo" Schembechler)

Coach/School	Bowl/Date	Opponent/Score (Coach)
Washington	Sun 12-22-79	Texas 14-7 (Fred Akers)
Washington	Rose 1-1-81	Michigan 6-23 (Glenn "Bo" Schembechler)
Washington	Rose 1-1-82	Iowa 28-0 (Hayden Fry)
Washington	Aloha 12-25-82	Maryland 21-20 (Bobby Ross)
Washington	Aloha 12-26-83	Penn St. 10-13 (Joe Paterno)
Washington	Orange 1-1-85	Oklahoma 28-17 (Barry Switzer)
Washington	Freedom 12-30-85	Colorado 20-17 (Bill McCartney)
Washington	Sun 12-25-86	Alabama 6-28 (Ray Perkins)
Washington	Independence 12-18-87	Tulane 24-12 (Mack Brown)
Washington	Freedom 12-29-89	Florida 34-7 (Gary Darnell)
Washington	Rose 1-1-91	Iowa 46-34 (Hayden Fry)
Washington	Rose 1-1-92	Michigan 34-14 (Gary Moeller)
Washington	Rose 1-1-93	Michigan 31-38 (Gary Moeller)

JIMMY JOHNSON, 3-4-0 (Arkansas '65) Born 7-16-43
Oklahoma St.	Independence 12-12-81	Texas A&M 16-33 (Tom Wilson)
Oklahoma St.	Bluebonnet 12-31-83	Baylor 24-14 (Grant Teaff)
Miami (Fla.)	Fiesta 1-1-85	UCLA 37-39 (Terry Donahue)
Miami (Fla.)	Sugar 1-1-86	Tennessee 7-35 (Johnny Majors)
Miami (Fla.)	Fiesta 1-2-87	Penn St. 10-14 (Joe Paterno)
Miami (Fla.)	Orange 1-1-88	Oklahoma 20-14 (Barry Switzer)
Miami (Fla.)	Orange 1-2-89	Nebraska 23-3 (Tom Osborne)

FRANK JONES, 1-1-0 (North Carolina '48) Born 8-30-21
| Richmond | Tangerine 12-27-68 | Ohio 49-42 (Bill Hess) |
| Richmond | Tangerine 12-28-71 | Toledo 3-28 (John Murphy) |

GOMER JONES, 0-1-0 (Ohio St. '36) Born 2-26-14
| Oklahoma | Gator 1-2-65 | Florida St. 19-36 (Bill Peterson) |

HOWARD JONES, 5-0-0 (Yale '08) Born 8-23-1885
Southern California	Rose 1-1-30	Pittsburgh 47-14 (Jock Sutherland)
Southern California	Rose 1-1-32	Tulane 21-12 (Bernie Bierman)
Southern California	Rose 1-2-33	Pittsburgh 35-0 (Jock Sutherland)
Southern California	Rose 1-2-39	Duke 7-3 (Wallace Wade)
Southern California	Rose 1-1-40	Tennessee 14-0 (Bob Neyland)

JUNE JONES, 1-0-0 (Portland St. '77) Born 2-14-53
| Hawaii | Oahu Classic 12-25-99 | Oregon St. 23-17 (Dennis Erickson) |

LARRY JONES, 0-1-0 (LSU '54) Born 12-18-33
| Florida St. | Fiesta 12-27-71 | Arizona St. 38-45 (Frank Kush) |

LAWRENCE McC. "BIFF" JONES, 0-1-0 (Army '17) Born 10-8-95
| Nebraska | Rose 1-1-41 | Stanford 13-21 (Clark Shaughnessy) |

PAT JONES, 3-1-0 (Arkansas '69) Born 11-4-47
Oklahoma St.	Gator 12-28-84	South Carolina 21-14 (Joe Morrison)
Oklahoma St.	Gator 12-30-85	Florida St. 23-34 (Bobby Bowden)
Oklahoma St.	Sun 12-25-87	West Virginia 35-33 (Don Nehlen)
Oklahoma St.	Holiday 12-30-88	Wyoming 62-14 (Paul Roach)

RALPH "SHUG" JORDAN, 5-7-0 (Auburn '32) Born 9-25-10
Auburn	Gator 1-1-54	Texas Tech 13-35 (DeWitt Weaver)
Auburn	Gator 12-31-54	Baylor 33-13 (George Sauer)
Auburn	Gator 12-31-55	Vanderbilt 13-25 (Art Gueppe)
Auburn	Orange 1-1-64	Nebraska 7-13 (Bob Devaney)
Auburn	Liberty 12-18-65	Mississippi 7-13 (John Vaught)
Auburn	Sun 12-28-68	Arizona 34-10 (Darrell Mudra)
Auburn	Bluebonnet 12-31-69	Houston 7-36 (Bill Yeoman)
Auburn	Gator 1-2-71	Mississippi 35-28 (John Vaught)
Auburn	Sugar 1-1-72	Oklahoma 22-40 (Chuck Fairbanks)
Auburn	Gator 12-30-72	Colorado 24-3 (Eddie Crowder)
Auburn	Sun 12-29-73	Missouri 17-34 (Al Onofrio)
Auburn	Gator 12-30-74	Texas 27-3 (Darrell Royal)

ERNIE JORGE, 1-1-0 (St. Mary's [Cal.] '36) Born 10-7-14
| Pacific (Cal.) | Sun 1-1-52 | Texas Tech 14-25 (DeWitt Weaver) |
| Pacific (Cal.) | Sun 1-1-53 | Southern Miss. 26-7 (Thad "Pie" Vann) |

AL KAWAL, 1-0-0 (Northwestern '35) Born 7-4-12
| Drake | Salad 1-1-49 | Arizona 14-13 (Miles Casteel) |

JOE KERBEL, 2-0-0 (Oklahoma '47) Born 5-3-21
| West Tex. A&M | Sun 12-21-62 | Ohio 15-14 (Bill Hess) |
| West Tex. A&M | Pasadena 12-2-67 | Cal St. Northridge 35-13 (Sam Winningham) |

BILL KERN, 0-1-0 (Pittsburgh '28) Born 9-2-06
| Carnegie Mellon | Sugar 1-2-39 | TCU 7-15 (Leo "Dutch" Meyer) |

FRANK KIMBROUGH, 2-0-1 (Hardin-Simmons '26) Born 6-24-04
Hardin-Simmons	Sun 1-1-36	New Mexico St. 14-14 (Jerry Hines)
Hardin-Simmons	Sun 1-1-37	UTEP 34-6 (Max Saxon)
West Tex. A&M	Sun 1-1-51	Cincinnati 14-13 (Sid Gillman)

BILLY KINARD, 1-0-0 (Mississippi '56) Born 12-16-33
| Mississippi | Peach 12-30-71 | Georgia Tech 41-18 (Bud Carson) |

DEWEY KING, 0-1-0 (North Dakota '50) Born 10-1-25
| San Jose St. | Pasadena 12-18-71 | Memphis 9-28 (Billy Murphy) |

J. T. KING, 0-2-0 (Texas '38) Born 10-22-12
| Texas Tech | Sun 12-26-64 | Georgia 0-7 (Vince Dooley) |
| Texas Tech | Gator 12-31-65 | Georgia Tech 21-31 (Bobby Dodd) |

JIMMY KITTS, 1-1-0 (Southern Methodist) Born 6-14-1900
| Rice | Cotton 1-1-38 | Colorado 28-14 (Bernard "Bunnie" Oakes) |

Coach/School	Bowl/Date	Opponent/Score (Coach)
Virginia Tech	Sun 1-1-47	Cincinnati 6-18 (Ray Nolting)

ED KLUSKA, 1-0-0 (Xavier, Ohio '40) Born 5-21-18
| Xavier (Ohio) | Salad 1-1-50 | Arizona St. 33-21 (Ed Doherty) |

DIRK KOETTER, 1-0-0 (Idaho St. '81) Born 2-5-59
| Boise St. | Humanitarian 12-30-99 | Louisville 34-31 (John L. Smith) |

JOE KRIVAK, 0-0-1 (Syracuse '57) Born 3-20-35
| Maryland | Independence 12-15-90 | Louisiana Tech 34-34 (Joe Raymond Peace) |

FRANK KUSH, 6-1-0 (Michigan St. '53) Born 1-20-29
Arizona St.	Peach 12-30-70	North Carolina 48-26 (Bill Dooley)
Arizona St.	Fiesta 12-27-71	Florida St. 45-38 (Larry Jones)
Arizona St.	Fiesta 12-23-72	Missouri 49-35 (Al Onofrio)
Arizona St.	Fiesta 12-21-73	Pittsburgh 28-7 (Johnny Majors)
Arizona St.	Fiesta 12-26-75	Nebraska 17-14 (Tom Osborne)
Arizona St.	Fiesta 12-25-77	Penn St. 30-42 (Joe Paterno)
Arizona St.	Garden State 12-16-78	Rutgers 34-18 (Frank Burns)

BERT LaBRUCHERIE, 0-1-0 (UCLA '29) Born 1-19-05
| UCLA | Rose 1-1-47 | Illinois 14-45 (Ray Eliot) |

JIM LAMBRIGHT, 1-3-0 (Washington '65) Born 4-26-42
Washington	Sun 12-29-95	Iowa 18-38 (Hayden Fry)
Washington	Holiday 12-30-96	Colorado 21-33 (Rick Neuheisel)
Washington	Aloha 12-25-97	Michigan St. 51-23 (Nick Saban)
Washington	Oahu Classic 12-25-98	Air Force 25-45 (Fisher DeBerry)

MAXIE LAMBRIGHT, 1-1-0 (Southern Miss. '49) Born 6-3-24
| Louisiana Tech | Independence 12-17-77 | Louisville 24-14 (Vince Gibson) |
| Louisiana Tech | Independence 12-16-78 | East Caro. 13-35 (Pat Dye) |

FRANK LAUTERBUR, 2-0-0 (Mount Union '49) Born 8-8-25
| Toledo | Tangerine 12-26-69 | Davidson 56-33 (Homer Smith) |
| Toledo | Tangerine 12-28-70 | William & Mary 40-12 (Lou Holtz) |

FRANK LEAHY, 1-1-0 (Notre Dame '31) Born 8-27-08
| Boston College | Cotton 1-1-40 | Clemson 3-6 (Jess Neely) |
| Boston College | Sugar 1-1-41 | Tennessee 19-13 (Bob Neyland) |

CLYDE LEE, 1-0-0 (Centenary [La.] '32) Born 2-11-08
| Houston | Salad 1-1-52 | Dayton 26-21 (Joe Gavin) |

ART LEWIS, 0-1-0 (Ohio '36) Born 2-18-11
| West Virginia | Sugar 1-1-54 | Georgia Tech 19-42 (Bobby Dodd) |

BILL LEWIS, 1-0-0 (East Stroudsburg '63) Born 8-5-41
| East Caro. | Peach 1-1-92 | North Carolina St. 37-34 (Dick Sheridan) |

LOU LITTLE, 1-0-0 (Pennsylvania '20) Born 12-6-1893
| Columbia | Rose 1-1-34 | Stanford 7-0 (Claude "Tiny" Thornhill) |

STEVE LOGAN, 1-2-0 (Tulsa '75) Born 2-3-53
East Caro.	Liberty 12-31-94	Illinois 0-30 (Lou Tepper)
East Caro.	Liberty 12-30-95	Stanford 19-13 (Tyrone Willingham)
East Caro.	Mobile Alabama 12-22-99	TCU 14-28 (Dennis Franchione)

JIM LOOKABAUGH, 2-1-0 (Oklahoma St. '25) Born 6-15-02
Oklahoma St.	Cotton 1-1-45	TCU 34-0 (Leo "Dutch" Meyer)
Oklahoma St.	Sugar 1-1-46	St. Mary's (Cal.) 33-13 (Jimmy Phelan)
Oklahoma St.	Delta 1-1-49	William & Mary 0-20 (Rube McCray)

SONNY LUBICK, 1-3-0 (Western Mont. '60) Born 3-12-37
Colorado St.	Holiday 12-30-94	Michigan 14-24 (Gary Moeller)
Colorado St.	Holiday 12-29-95	Kansas St. 21-54 (Bill Snyder)
Colorado St.	Holiday 12-29-97	Missouri 35-24 (Larry Smith)
Colorado St.	Liberty 12-31-99	Southern Miss. 17-23 (Jeff Bower)

AL LUGINBILL, 0-1-0 (Cal Poly Pomona '67) Born 11-3-46
| San Diego St. | Freedom 12-30-91 | Tulsa 17-28 (Dave Rader) |

BILL LYNCH, 0-1-0 (Butler '77) Born 6-12-54
| Ball St. | Las Vegas 12-19-96 | Nevada 15-18 (Jeff Tisdel) |

GEORGE MacINTYRE, 0-1-0 (Miami [Fla.] '61) Born 4-30-39
| Vanderbilt | Hall of Fame 12-31-82 | Air Force 28-36 (Ken Hatfield) |

JOHN MACKOVIC, 2-5-0 (Wake Forest '65) Born 10-1-43
Wake Forest	Tangerine 12-22-79	LSU 10-34 (Charlie McClendon)
Illinois	All-American 12-29-88	Florida 10-14 (Galen Hall)
Illinois	Fla. Citrus 1-1-90	Virginia 31-21 (George Welsh)
Illinois	Hall of Fame 1-1-91	Clemson 0-30 (Ken Hatfield)
Texas	Sun 12-30-94	North Carolina 35-31 (Mack Brown)
Texas	Sugar 12-31-95	Virginia Tech 10-28 (Frank Beamer)
Texas	Fiesta 1-1-97	Penn St. 15-38 (Joe Paterno)

DICK MacPHERSON, 3-1-1 (Springfield '58) Born 11-4-30
Syracuse	Cherry 12-21-85	Maryland 18-35 (Bobby Ross)
Syracuse	Sugar 1-1-88	Auburn 16-16 (Pat Dye)
Syracuse	Hall of Fame 1-2-89	LSU 23-10 (Mike Archer)
Syracuse	Peach 12-30-89	Georgia 19-18 (Ray Goff)
Syracuse	Aloha 12-25-90	Arizona 28-0 (Dick Tomey)

EDWARD "SLIP" MADIGAN, 1-0-0 (Notre Dame '20) Born 11-18-1895
| St. Mary's (Cal.) | Cotton 1-2-39 | Texas Tech 20-13 (Pete Cawthon) |

JOHNNY MAJORS, 9-7-0 (Tennessee '57) Born 5-21-35
Iowa St.	Sun 12-18-71	LSU 15-33 (Charlie McClendon)
Iowa St.	Liberty 12-18-72	Georgia Tech 30-31 (Bill Fulcher)
Pittsburgh	Fiesta 12-21-73	Arizona St. 7-28 (Frank Kush)

Coach/School	Bowl/Date	Opponent/Score (Coach)
Pittsburgh	Sun 12-26-75	Kansas 33-19 (Bud Moore)
Pittsburgh	Sugar 1-1-77	Georgia 27-3 (Vince Dooley)
Tennessee	Bluebonnet 12-31-79	Purdue 22-27 (Jim Young)
Tennessee	Garden State 12-13-81	Wisconsin 28-21 (Dave McClain)
Tennessee	Peach 12-31-82	Iowa 22-28 (Hayden Fry)
Tennessee	Fla. Citrus 12-17-83	Maryland 30-23 (Bobby Ross)
Tennessee	Sun 12-24-84	Maryland 27-28 (Bobby Ross)
Tennessee	Sugar 1-1-86	Miami (Fla.) 35-7 (Jimmy Johnson)
Tennessee	Liberty 12-29-86	Minnesota 21-14 (John Gutekunst)
Tennessee	Peach 1-2-88	Indiana 27-22 (Bill Mallory)
Tennessee	Cotton 1-1-90	Arkansas 31-27 (Ken Hatfield)
Tennessee	Sugar 1-1-91	Virginia 23-22 (George Welsh)
Tennessee	Fiesta 1-1-92	Penn St. 17-42 (Joe Paterno)

BILL MALLORY, 4-6-0 (Miami (Ohio) '57) Born 5-30-35
Miami (Ohio)	Tangerine 12-22-73	Florida 16-7 (Doug Dickey)
Colorado	Bluebonnet 12-27-75	Texas 21-38 (Darrell Royal)
Colorado	Orange 1-1-77	Ohio St. 10-27 (Woody Hayes)
Northern Ill.	California 12-17-83	Cal St. Fullerton 20-13 (Gene Murphy)
Indiana	All-American 12-31-86	Florida St. 13-27 (Bobby Bowden)
Indiana	Peach 1-2-88	Tennessee 22-27 (Johnny Majors)
Indiana	Liberty 12-28-88	South Carolina 34-10 (Joe Morrison)
Indiana	Peach 12-29-90	Auburn 23-27 (Pat Dye)
Indiana	Copper 12-31-91	Baylor 24-0 (Grant Teaff)
Indiana	Independence 12-31-93	Virginia Tech 20-45 (Frank Beamer)

FRANK MALONEY, 1-0-0 (Michigan '62) Born 9-26-40
Syracuse	Independence 12-15-79	McNeese St. 31-7 (Ernie Duplechin)

BOB MARGARITA, 0-1-0 (Brown '44) Born 11-3-20
Georgetown	Sun 1-2-50	UTEP 20-33 (Jack "Cactus Jack" Curtice)

STEVE MARIUCCI, 0-1-0 (Northern Mich. '77) Born 11-4-55
California	Aloha 12-25-96	Navy 38-42 (Charlie Weatherbie)

ABE MARTIN, 1-3-1 (TCU '32) Born 10-8-08
TCU	Cotton 1-2-56	Mississippi 13-14 (John Vaught)
TCU	Cotton 1-1-57	Syracuse 28-27 (Ben Schwartzwalder)
TCU	Cotton 1-1-59	Air Force 0-0 (Ben Martin)
TCU	Bluebonnet 12-19-59	Clemson 7-23 (Frank Howard)
TCU	Sun 12-31-65	UTEP 12-13 (Bobby Dobbs)

BEN MARTIN, 0-2-1 (Navy '46) Born 6-28-21
Air Force	Cotton 1-1-59	TCU 0-0 (Abe Martin)
Air Force	Gator 12-28-63	North Carolina 0-35 (Jim Hickey)
Air Force	Sugar 1-1-71	Tennessee 13-34 (Bill Battle)

GLEN MASON, 2-1-0 (Ohio St. '72) Born 4-9-50
Kansas	Aloha 12-25-92	Brigham Young 23-20 (LaVell Edwards)
Kansas	Aloha 12-25-95	UCLA 51-30 (Terry Donahue)
Minnesota	Sun 12-31-99	Oregon 20-24 (Mike Bellotti)

TONY MASON, 0-1-0 (Clarion '50) Born 3-2-30
Arizona	Fiesta 12-25-79	Pittsburgh 10-16 (Jackie Sherrill)

RON McBRIDE, 2-3-0 (San Jose St. '63) Born 10-14-39
Utah	Copper 12-29-92	Washington 28-31 (Mike Price)
Utah	Freedom 12-30-93	Southern California 21-28 (John Robinson)
Utah	Freedom 12-27-94	Arizona 16-13 (Dick Tomey)
Utah	Copper 12-27-96	Wisconsin 10-38 (Barry Alvarez)
Utah	Las Vegas 12-18-99	Fresno St. 17-16 (Pat Hill)

TOM McCANN, 0-1-0 (Illinois '24) Born 11-7-1898
Miami (Fla.)	Orange 1-1-35	Bucknell 0-26 (Edward "Hook" Mylin)

BILL McCARTNEY, 3-6-0 (Missouri '62) Born 8-22-40
Colorado	Freedom 12-30-85	Washington 17-20 (Don James)
Colorado	Bluebonnet 12-31-86	Baylor 9-21 (Grant Teaff)
Colorado	Freedom 12-29-88	Brigham Young 17-20 (LaVell Edwards)
Colorado	Orange 1-1-90	Notre Dame 6-21 (Lou Holtz)
Colorado	Orange 1-1-91	Notre Dame 10-9 (Lou Holtz)
Colorado	Blockbuster 12-28-91	Alabama 25-30 (Gene Stallings)
Colorado	Fiesta 1-1-93	Syracuse 22-26 (Paul Pasqualoni)
Colorado	Aloha 12-25-93	Fresno St. 41-30 (Jim Sweeney)
Colorado	Fiesta 1-2-95	Notre Dame 41-24 (Lou Holtz)

DAVE McCLAIN, 1-2-0 (Bowling Green '60) Born 1-28-38
Wisconsin	Garden State 12-13-81	Tennessee 21-28 (Johnny Majors)
Wisconsin	Independence 12-11-82	Kansas St. 14-3 (Jim Dickey)
Wisconsin	Hall of Fame 12-29-84	Kentucky 19-20 (Jerry Claiborne)

CHARLIE McCLENDON, 7-6-0 (Kentucky '50) Born 10-17-22
LSU	Cotton 1-1-63	Texas 13-0 (Darrell Royal)
LSU	Bluebonnet 12-21-63	Baylor 7-14 (John Bridgers)
LSU	Sugar 1-1-65	Syracuse 13-10 (Ben Schwartzwalder)
LSU	Cotton 1-1-66	Arkansas 14-7 (Frank Broyles)
LSU	Sugar 1-1-68	Wyoming 20-13 (Lloyd Eaton)
LSU	Peach 12-30-68	Florida St. 31-27 (Bill Peterson)
LSU	Orange 1-1-71	Nebraska 12-17 (Bob Devaney)
LSU	Sun 12-18-71	Iowa St. 33-15 (Johnny Majors)
LSU	Bluebonnet 12-30-72	Tennessee 17-24 (Bill Battle)
LSU	Orange 1-1-74	Penn St. 9-16 (Joe Paterno)
LSU	Sun 12-31-77	Stanford 14-24 (Bill Walsh)
LSU	Liberty 12-23-78	Missouri 15-20 (Warren Powers)
LSU	Tangerine 12-22-79	Wake Forest 34-10 (John Mackovic)

RUBE McCRAY, 1-1-0 (Ky. Wesleyan '30) Born 6-13-05
William & Mary	Dixie 1-1-48	Arkansas 19-21 (John Barnhill)
William & Mary	Delta 1-1-49	Oklahoma St. 20-0 (Jim Lookabaugh)

J. F. "POP" McKALE, 0-1-0 (Albion '10) Born 6-12-1887
Arizona	San Diego East-West Christmas Classic 12-26-21	Centre 0-38 (Charley Moran)

JOHN McKAY, 6-3-0 (Oregon St. '50) Born 7-5-23
Southern California	Rose 1-2-63	Wisconsin 42-37 (Milt Bruhn)
Southern California	Rose 1-2-67	Purdue 13-14 (Jack Mollenkopf)
Southern California	Rose 1-1-68	Indiana 14-3 (John Pont)
Southern California	Rose 1-1-69	Ohio St. 16-27 (Woody Hayes)
Southern California	Rose 1-1-70	Michigan 10-3 (Glenn "Bo" Schembechler)
Southern California	Rose 1-1-73	Ohio St. 42-17 (Woody Hayes)
Southern California	Rose 1-1-74	Ohio St. 21-42 (Woody Hayes)
Southern California	Rose 1-1-75	Ohio St. 18-17 (Woody Hayes)
Southern California	Liberty 12-22-75	Texas A&M 20-0 (Emory Bellard)

ALLYN McKEEN, 1-0-0 (Tennessee '29) Born 1-26-05
Mississippi St.	Orange 1-1-41	Georgetown 14-7 (Jack Hagerty)

JOHNNIE McMILLAN, 0-1-0 (South Carolina '41) Born 1-27-19
South Carolina	Gator 1-1-46	Wake Forest 14-26 (D. C. "Peahead" Walker)

DAVID McWILLIAMS, 1-1-0 (Texas '64) Born 4-18-42
Texas	Bluebonnet 12-31-87	Pittsburgh 32-27 (Mike Gottfried)
Texas	Cotton 1-1-91	Miami (Fla.) 3-46 (Dennis Erickson)

JACK MEAGHER, 1-0-1 (Notre Dame '17) Born 7-4-1894
Auburn	Bacardi, Cuba 1-1-37	Villanova 7-7 (Maurice "Clipper" Smith)
Auburn	Orange 1-1-38	Michigan St. 6-0 (Charlie Bachman)

RANDOLPH R. M. MEDLEY, 2-0-0 (Mo. Wesleyan '21) Born 9-22-1898
Southwestern (Tex.)	Sun 1-1-44	New Mexico 7-0 (Willis Barnes)
Southwestern (Tex.)	Sun 1-1-45	U. of Mexico 35-0 (Bernard A. Hoban)

LEO "DUTCH" MEYER, 3-4-0 (TCU '22) Born 1-15-1898
TCU	Sugar 1-1-36	LSU 3-2 (Bernie Moore)
TCU	Cotton 1-1-37	Marquette 16-6 (Frank Murray)
TCU	Sugar 1-2-39	Carnegie Mellon 15-7 (Bill Kern)
TCU	Orange 1-1-42	Georgia 26-40 (Wally Butts)
TCU	Cotton 1-1-45	Oklahoma 0-34 (Jim Lookabaugh)
TCU	Delta 1-1-48	Mississippi 9-13 (John Vaught)
TCU	Cotton 1-1-52	Kentucky 7-20 (Paul "Bear" Bryant)

RON MEYER, 0-1-0 (Purdue '63) Born 2-17-41
Southern Methodist	Holiday 12-19-80	Brigham Young 45-46 (LaVell Edwards)

RICK MINTER, 1-0-0 (Henderson St. '77) Born 10-4-54
Cincinnati	Humanitarian 12-29-97	Utah St. 35-19 (John L. Smith)

JOHN MICHELOSEN, 0-2-0 (Pittsburgh '38) Born 2-13-16
Pittsburgh	Sugar 1-2-56	Georgia Tech 0-7 (Bobby Dodd)
Pittsburgh	Gator 12-29-56	Georgia Tech 14-21 (Bobby Dodd)

JACK MITCHELL, 1-0-0 (Oklahoma '49) Born 12-3-24
Kansas	Bluebonnet 12-16-61	Rice 33-7 (Jess Neely)

ODUS MITCHELL, 0-2-0 (West Tex. A&M '25) Born 6-29-1899
North Texas	Salad 1-1-48	Nevada 6-13 (Joe Sheeketski)
North Texas	Sun 12-31-59	New Mexico St. 8-28 (Warren Woodson)

GARY MOELLER, 4-1-0 (Ohio St. '63) Born 1-26-41
Michigan	Gator 1-1-91	Mississippi 35-3 (Billy Brewer)
Michigan	Rose 1-1-92	Washington 14-34 (Don James)
Michigan	Rose 1-1-93	Washington 38-31 (Don James)
Michigan	Hall of Fame 1-1-94	North Carolina St. 42-7 (Mike O'Cain)
Michigan	Holiday 12-30-94	Colorado St. 24-14 (Sonny Lubick)

AL MOLDE, 0-1-0 (Gust. Adolphus '66) Born 11-15-43
Western Mich.	California 12-10-88	Fresno St. 30-35 (Jim Sweeney)

JACK MOLLENKOPF, 1-0-0 (Bowling Green '31) Born 11-24-05
Purdue	Rose 1-2-67	Southern California 14-13 (John McKay)

BERNIE MOORE, 1-3-1 (Carson-Newman '17) Born 4-30-1895
LSU	Sugar 1-1-36	TCU 2-3 (Leo "Dutch" Meyer)
LSU	Sugar 1-1-37	Santa Clara 14-21 (Lawrence "Buck" Shaw)
LSU	Sugar 1-1-38	Santa Clara 0-6 (Lawrence "Buck" Shaw)
LSU	Orange 1-1-44	Texas A&M 19-14 (Homer Norton)
LSU	Cotton 1-1-47	Arkansas 0-0 (John Barnhill)

BUD MOORE, 0-1-0 (Alabama '61) Born 10-16-39
Kansas	Sun 12-26-75	Pittsburgh 19-33 (Johnny Majors)

CHARLEY MORAN, 2-1-0 (Tennessee '98) Born 2-22-1878
Centre	Fort Worth Classic 1-1-21	TCU 63-7 (Bill Driver)
Centre	San Diego East-West Christmas Classic 12-26-21	Arizona 38-0 (J. F. "Pop" McKale)
Centre	Dixie Classic 1-2-22	Texas A&M 14-22 (Dana Bible)

DELL MORGAN, 0-3-0 (Austin '25) Born 2-14-02
Texas Tech.............. Sun 1-1-42 Tulsa 0-6 (Henry Frnka)
Texas Tech.............. Sun 1-1-48 Miami (Ohio) 12-13 (Sid Gillman)
Texas Tech.............. Raisin 12-31-49 San Jose St. 13-20 (Bill Hubbard)

JOE MORRISON, 0-3-0 (Cincinnati '59) Born 8-21-37
South Carolina........ Gator 12-28-84 Oklahoma St. 14-21 (Pat Jones)
South Carolina........ Gator 12-31-87 LSU 13-30 (Mike Archer)
South Carolina........ Liberty 12-28-88 Indiana 10-34 (Bill Mallory)

RAY MORRISON, 0-1-0 (Vanderbilt '12) Born 2-28-1885
Southern Methodist.. Dixie Classic 1-1-25 West Va. Wesleyan 7-9 (Bob Higgins)

DARRELL MUDRA, 0-1-0 (Peru St. '51) Born 1-4-29
Arizona .... Sun 12-28-68 Auburn 10-34 (Ralph "Shug" Jordan)

HAL MUMME, 0-2-0 (Tarleton St. '75) Born 3-29-52
Kentucky.................. Outback 1-1-99 Penn St. 14-26 (Joe Paterno)
Kentucky.................. Music City 12-29-99 Syracuse 13-20 (Paul Pasqualoni)

CLARENCE "BIGGIE" MUNN, 1-0-0 (Minnesota '32) Born 9-11-08
Michigan St. .... Rose 1-1-54 UCLA 28-20 (Henry "Red" Sanders)

BILLY MURPHY, 1-0-0 (Mississippi St. '47) Born 1-13-21
Memphis .... Pasadena 12-18-71 San Jose St. 28-9 (Dewey King)

GENE MURPHY, 0-1-0 (North Dakota '62) Born 8-6-39
Cal St. Fullerton........ California 12-17-83 Northern Ill. 13-20 (Bill Mallory)

JACK MURPHY, 1-0-0 (Heidelberg '54) Born 8-6-32
Toledo .... Tangerine 12-28-71 Richmond 28-3 (Frank Jones)

BILL MURRAY, 2-1-0 (Duke '31) Born 9-9-08
Duke .... Orange 1-1-55 Nebraska 34-7 (Bill Glassford)
Duke .... Orange 1-1-58 Oklahoma 21-48 (Bud Wilkinson)
Duke .... Cotton 1-2-61 Arkansas 7-6 (Frank Broyles)

FRANK MURRAY, 0-1-0 (Tufts '08) Born 2-12-85
Marquette................ Cotton 1-1-37 TCU 6-16 (Leo "Dutch" Meyer)

DENNY MYERS, 0-1-0 (Iowa '30) Born 11-10-05
Boston College......... Orange 1-1-43 Alabama 21-37 (Frank Thomas)

EDWARD "HOOK" MYLIN, 1-0-0 (Frank. & Marsh.) Born 10-23-1897
Bucknell................... Orange 1-1-35 Miami (Fla.) 26-0 (Tom McCann)

RAY NAGEL, 1-0-0 (UCLA '50) Born 5-18-27
Utah......................... Liberty 12-19-64 West Virginia 32-6 (Gene Corum)

LARRY NAVIAUX, 0-1-0 (Nebraska '59) Born 12-17-36
Boston U.................. Pasadena 12-6-69 San Diego St. 7-28 (Don Coryell)

EARLE "GREASY" NEALE, 0-0-1 (West Va. Wesleyan '14) Born 11-5-1891
Wash. & Jeff........... Rose 1-2-22 California 0-0 (Andy Smith)

JESS NEELY, 4-3-0 (Vanderbilt '23) Born 1-4-1898
Clemson .... Cotton 1-1-40 Boston College 6-3 (Frank Leahy)
Rice.......................... Orange 1-1-47 Tennessee 8-0 (Bob Neyland)
Rice.......................... Cotton 1-2-50 North Carolina 27-13 (Carl Snavely)
Rice.......................... Cotton 1-1-54 Alabama 28-6 (Harold "Red" Drew)
Rice.......................... Cotton 1-1-58 Navy 7-20 (Eddie Erdelatz)
Rice.......................... Sugar 1-2-61 Mississippi 6-14 (John Vaught)
Rice.......................... Bluebonnet 12-16-61 Kansas 7-33 (Jack Mitchell)

DON NEHLEN, 3-9-0 (Bowling Green '58) Born 1-1-36
West Virginia .... Peach 12-31-81 Florida 26-6 (Charley Pell)
West Virginia .... Gator 12-30-82 Florida St. 12-31 (Bobby Bowden)
West Virginia .... Hall of Fame 12-22-83 Kentucky 20-16 (Jerry Claiborne)
West Virginia .... Bluebonnet 12-31-84 TCU 31-14 (Jim Wacker)
West Virginia .... Sun 12-25-87 Oklahoma St. 33-35 (Pat Jones)
West Virginia .... Fiesta 1-2-89 Notre Dame 21-34 (Lou Holtz)
West Virginia .... Gator 12-30-89 Clemson 7-27 (Danny Ford)
West Virginia .... Sugar 1-1-94 Florida 7-41 (Steve Spurrier)
West Virginia .... Carquest 1-2-95 South Carolina 21-24 (Brad Scott)
West Virginia .... Gator 1-1-97 North Carolina 13-20 (Mack Brown)
West Virginia .... Carquest 12-29-97 Georgia Tech 30-35 (George O'Leary)
West Virginia .... Insight.com 12-26-98 Missouri 31-34 (Larry Smith)

RICK NEUHEISEL, 3-1-0 (UCLA '84) Born 2-7-61
Colorado .... Cotton 1-1-96 Oregon 38-6 (Mike Bellotti)
Colorado .... Holiday 12-30-96 Washington 33-21 (Jim Lambright)
Colorado .... Aloha Classic 12-25-98 Oregon 51-43 (Mike Bellotti)
Washington .... Holiday 12-29-99 Kansas St. 20-24 (Bill Snyder)

BOB NEYLAND, 2-5-0 (Army '16) Born 2-17-1892
Tennessee............... Orange 1-2-39 Oklahoma 17-0 (Tom Stidham)
Tennessee............... Rose 1-1-40 Southern California 0-14 (Howard Jones)
Tennessee............... Sugar 1-1-41 Boston College 13-19 (Frank Leahy)
Tennessee............... Orange 1-1-47 Rice 0-8 (Jess Neely)
Tennessee............... Cotton 1-1-51 Texas 20-14 (Blair Cherry)
Tennessee............... Sugar 1-1-52 Maryland 13-28 (Jim Tatum)
Tennessee............... Cotton 1-1-53 Texas 0-16 (Ed Price)

RAY NOLTING, 1-0-0 (Cincinnati '36) Born 11-8-13
Cincinnati................ Sun 1-1-47 Virginia Tech 18-6 (Jimmy Kitts)

HOMER NORTON, 2-2-1 (Birmingham Southern '16) Born 12-30-1896
Centenary (La.)........ Dixie Classic 1-1-34 Arkansas 7-7 (Fred Thomsen)
Texas A&M............. Sugar 1-1-40 Tulane 14-13 (Lowell "Red" Dawson)
Texas A&M............. Cotton 1-1-41 Fordham 13-12 (Jim Crowley)
Texas A&M............. Cotton 1-1-42 Alabama 21-29 (Frank Thomas)
Texas A&M............. Orange 1-1-44 LSU 14-19 (Bernie Moore)

TOM NUGENT, 0-2-0 (Ithaca '36) Born 2-24-16
Florida St................. Sun 1-1-55 UTEP 20-47 (Mike Brumbelow)
Florida St................. Bluegrass 12-13-58 Oklahoma St. 6-15 (Cliff Speegle)

HOUSTON NUTT, 1-1-0 (Oklahoma St. '81) Born 10-14-57
Arkansas .... Fla. Citrus 1-1-99 Michigan 31-45 (Lloyd Carr)
Arkansas .... Cotton 1-1-00 Texas 27-6 (Mack Brown)

TOM O'BRIEN, 0-1-0 (Navy '71) Born 10-5-48
Boston College......... Insight.com 12-31-99 Colorado 28-62 (Gary Barnett)

MIKE O'CAIN, 1-2-0 (Clemson '77) Born 7-20-54
North Carolina St. ... Hall of Fame 1-1-94 Michigan 7-42 (Gary Moeller)
North Carolina St. ... Peach 1-1-95 Mississippi St. 28-24 (Jackie Sherrill)
North Carolina St. ... Micron PC 12-29-98 Miami (Fla.) 23-46 (Butch Davis)

GEORGE O'LEARY, 2-1-0 (New Hampshire '68) Born 8-17-46
Georgia Tech........... Carquest 12-29-97 West Virginia 35-30 (Don Nehlen)
Georgia Tech........... Gator 1-1-99 Notre Dame 35-28 (Bob Davie)
Georgia Tech........... Gator 1-1-00 Miami (Fla.) 13-28 (Butch Davis)

BERNARD "BUNNIE" OAKES, 0-1-0 (Illinois '24) Born 9-15-1898
Colorado .... Cotton 1-1-38 Rice 14-28 (Jimmy Kitts)

JORDAN OLIVAR, 1-1-0 (Villanova '38) Born 1-30-15
Villanova .... Great Lakes 12-6-47 Kentucky 14-24 (Paul "Bear" Bryant)
Villanova .... Harbor 1-1-49 Nevada 27-7 (Joe Sheeketski)

AL ONOFRIO, 1-1-0 (Arizona St. '43) Born 3-15-21
Missouri................... Fiesta 12-23-72 Arizona St. 35-49 (Frank Kush)
Missouri................... Sun 12-29-73 Auburn 34-17 (Ralph "Shug" Jordan)

BENNIE OOSTERBAAN, 1-0-0 (Michigan '28) Born 2-24-06
Michigan .... Rose 1-1-51 California 14-6 (Lynn "Pappy" Waldorf)

TOM OSBORNE, 12-13-0 (Hastings '59) Born 2-23-37
Nebraska .... Cotton 1-1-74 Texas 19-3 (Darrell Royal)
Nebraska .... Sugar 12-31-74 Florida 13-10 (Doug Dickey)
Nebraska .... Fiesta 12-26-75 Arizona St. 14-17 (Frank Kush)
Nebraska .... Bluebonnet 12-31-76 Texas Tech 27-24 (Steve Sloan)
Nebraska .... Liberty 12-19-77 North Carolina 21-17 (Bill Dooley)
Nebraska .... Orange 1-1-79 Oklahoma 24-31 (Barry Switzer)
Nebraska .... Cotton 1-1-80 Houston 14-17 (Bill Yeoman)
Nebraska .... Sun 12-27-80 Mississippi St. 31-17 (Emory Bellard)
Nebraska .... Orange 1-1-82 Clemson 15-22 (Danny Ford)
Nebraska .... Orange 1-1-83 LSU 21-20 (Jerry Stovall)
Nebraska .... Orange 1-2-84 Miami (Fla.) 30-31 (Howard Schnellenberger)
Nebraska .... Sugar 1-1-85 LSU 28-10 (Bill Arnsparger)
Nebraska .... Fiesta 1-1-86 Michigan 23-27 (Glenn "Bo" Schembechler)
Nebraska .... Sugar 1-1-87 LSU 30-15 (Bill Arnsparger)
Nebraska .... Fiesta 1-1-88 Florida St. 28-31 (Bobby Bowden)
Nebraska .... Orange 1-2-89 Miami (Fla.) 3-23 (Jimmy Johnson)
Nebraska .... Fiesta 1-1-90 Florida St. 17-41 (Bobby Bowden)
Nebraska .... Fla. Citrus 1-1-91 Georgia Tech 21-45 (Bobby Ross)
Nebraska .... Orange 1-1-92 Miami (Fla.) 0-22 (Dennis Erickson)
Nebraska .... Orange 1-1-93 Florida St. 14-27 (Bobby Bowden)
Nebraska .... Orange 1-1-94 Florida St. 16-18 (Bobby Bowden)
Nebraska .... Orange 1-1-95 Miami (Fla.) 24-17 (Dennis Erickson)
Nebraska .... Fiesta 1-2-96 Florida 62-24 (Steve Spurrier)
Nebraska .... Orange 12-31-96 Virginia Tech 41-21 (Frank Beamer)
Nebraska .... Orange 1-2-98 Tennessee 42-17 (Phillip Fulmer)

JIM OWENS, 2-1-0 (Oklahoma '50) Born 3-6-27
Washington .... Rose 1-1-60 Wisconsin 44-8 (Milt Bruhn)
Washington .... Rose 1-2-61 Minnesota 17-7 (Murray Warmath)
Washington .... Rose 1-1-64 Illinois 7-17 (Pete Elliott)

JACK PARDEE, 0-1-0 (Texas A&M '57) Born 4-9-36
Houston .... Aloha 12-25-88 Washington St. 22-24 (Dennis Erickson)

ARA PARSEGHIAN, 3-2-0 (Miami, Ohio '49) Born 5-21-23
Notre Dame .... Cotton 1-1-70 Texas 17-21 (Darrell Royal)
Notre Dame .... Cotton 1-1-71 Texas 24-11 (Darrell Royal)
Notre Dame .... Orange 1-1-73 Nebraska 6-40 (Bob Devaney)
Notre Dame .... Sugar 12-31-73 Alabama 24-23 (Paul "Bear" Bryant)
Notre Dame .... Orange 1-1-75 Alabama 13-11 (Paul "Bear" Bryant)

PAUL PASQUALONI, 5-2-0 (Penn St. '72) Born 8-16-49
Syracuse.................. Hall of Fame 1-1-92 Ohio St. 24-17 (John Cooper)
Syracuse.................. Fiesta 1-1-93 Colorado 26-22 (Bill McCartney)
Syracuse.................. Gator 1-1-96 Clemson 41-0 (Tommy West)
Syracuse.................. Liberty 12-27-96 Houston 30-17 (Kim Helton)
Syracuse.................. Fiesta 12-31-97 Kansas St. 18-35 (Bill Snyder)
Syracuse.................. Orange 1-2-99 Florida 10-31 (Steve Spurrier)
Syracuse.................. Music City 12-29-99 Kentucky 20-13 (Hal Mumme)

JOE PATERNO, 20-9-1 (Brown '50) Born 12-21-26
Penn St. .... Gator 12-30-67 Florida St. 17-17 (Bill Peterson)
Penn St. .... Orange 1-1-69 Kansas 15-14 (Pepper Rodgers)
Penn St. .... Orange 1-1-70 Missouri 10-3 (Dan Devine)
Penn St. .... Cotton 1-1-72 Texas 30-6 (Darrell Royal)
Penn St. .... Sugar 12-31-72 Oklahoma 0-14 (Chuck Fairbanks)
Penn St. .... Orange 1-1-74 LSU 16-9 (Charlie McClendon)
Penn St. .... Cotton 1-1-75 Baylor 41-20 (Grant Teaff)
Penn St. .... Sugar 12-31-75 Alabama 6-13 (Paul "Bear" Bryant)

Coach/School	Bowl/Date	Opponent/Score (Coach)
Penn St.	Gator 12-27-76	Notre Dame 9-20 (Dan Devine)
Penn St.	Fiesta 12-25-77	Arizona St. 42-30 (Frank Kush)
Penn St.	Sugar 1-1-79	Alabama 7-14 (Paul "Bear" Bryant)
Penn St.	Liberty 12-22-79	Tulane 9-6 (Larry Smith)
Penn St.	Fiesta 12-26-80	Ohio St. 31-19 (Earle Bruce)
Penn St.	Fiesta 1-1-82	Southern California 26-10 (John Robinson)
Penn St.	Sugar 1-1-83	Georgia 27-23 (Vince Dooley)
Penn St.	Aloha 12-26-83	Washington 13-10 (Don James)
Penn St.	Orange 1-1-86	Oklahoma 10-25 (Barry Switzer)
Penn St.	Fiesta 1-1-87	Miami (Fla.) 14-10 (Jimmy Johnson)
Penn St.	Fla. Citrus 1-1-88	Clemson 10-35 (Danny Ford)
Penn St.	Holiday 12-29-89	Brigham Young 50-39 (LaVell Edwards)
Penn St.	Blockbuster 12-28-90	Florida St. 17-24 (Bobby Bowden)
Penn St.	Fiesta 1-1-92	Tennessee 42-17 (Johnny Majors)
Penn St.	Blockbuster 1-1-93	Stanford 3-24 (Bill Walsh)
Penn St.	Fla. Citrus 1-1-94	Tennessee 31-13 (Phillip Fulmer)
Penn St.	Rose 1-2-95	Oregon 38-20 (Rich Brooks)
Penn St.	Outback 1-1-96	Auburn 43-14 (Terry Bowden)
Penn St.	Fiesta 1-1-97	Texas 38-15 (John Mackovic)
Penn St.	Alamo 12-28-99	Texas A&M 24-0 (R.C. Slocum)
Penn St.	Fla. Citrus 1-1-98	Florida 6-21 (Steve Spurrier)
Penn St.	Outback 1-1-99	Kentucky 26–14 (Hal Mumme)
Penn St.	Alamo 12-28-99	Texas A&M 24-0 (R. C. Slocum)

JOE RAYMOND PEACE, 0-0-1 (Louisiana Tech '68) Born 6-5-45
Louisiana Tech ... Independence 12-15-90 Maryland 34-34 (Joe Krivak)

CHARLEY PELL, 2-3-0 (Alabama '64) Born 2-27-41
Clemson	Gator 12-30-77	Pittsburgh 3-34 (Jackie Sherrill)
Florida	Tangerine 12-20-80	Maryland 35-20 (Jerry Claiborne)
Florida	Peach 12-31-81	West Virginia 6-26 (Don Nehlen)
Florida	Bluebonnet 12-31-82	Arkansas 24-28 (Lou Holtz)
Florida	Gator 12-30-83	Iowa 14-6 (Hayden Fry)

RAY PERKINS, 3-0-0 (Alabama '67) Born 11-6-41
Alabama	Sun 12-24-83	Southern Methodist 28-7 (Bobby Collins)
Alabama	Aloha 12-28-85	Southern California 24-3 (Ted Tollner)
Alabama	Sun 12-26-86	Washington 28-6 (Don James)

GEORGE PERLES, 3-4-0 (Michigan St. '60) Born 7-16-34
Michigan St.	Cherry 12-22-84	Army 6-10 (Jim Young)
Michigan St.	Hall of Fame 12-31-85	Georgia Tech 14-17 (Bill Curry)
Michigan St.	Rose 1-1-88	Southern California 20-17 (Larry Smith)
Michigan St.	Gator 1-1-89	Georgia 27-34 (Vince Dooley)
Michigan St.	Aloha 12-25-89	Hawaii 33-13 (Bob Wagner)
Michigan St.	John Hancock 12-31-90	Southern California 17-16 (Larry Smith)
Michigan St.	Liberty 12-28-93	Louisville 7-18 (Howard Schnellenberger)

DOYT PERRY, 0-1-0 (Bowling Green '32) Born 1-6-10
Bowling Green ... Mercy 11-23-61 Fresno St. 6-36 (Cecil Coleman)

BILL PETERSON, 1-2-1 (Ohio Northern '46) Born 5-14-20
Florida St.	Gator 1-2-65	Oklahoma 36-19 (Gomer Jones)
Florida St.	Sun 12-24-66	Wyoming 20-28 (Lloyd Eaton)
Florida St.	Gator 12-30-67	Penn St. 17-17 (Joe Paterno)
Florida St.	Peach 12-30-68	LSU 27-31 (Charlie McClendon)

JIMMY PHELAN, 0-3-0 (Notre Dame '19) Born 12-5-1892
Washington	Rose 1-1-37	Pittsburgh 0-21 (Jock Sutherland)
St. Mary's (Cal.)	Sugar 1-1-46	Oklahoma St. 12-33 (Jim Lookabaugh)
St. Mary's (Cal.)	Oil 1-1-47	Georgia Tech 19-41 (Bobby Dodd)

ALVIN "PIX" PIERSON, 0-1-0 (Nevada '22) Born 7-25-1898
Fresno St. ... Raisin 1-1-46 Drake 12-13 (Vee Green)

GARY PINKEL, 1-0-0 (Kent St. '75) Born 4-27-52
Toledo ... Las Vegas 12-14-95 Nevada 40-37 (ot) (Chris Ault)

JIM PITTMAN, 1-0-0 (Mississippi St. '50) Born 8-28-25
Tulane ... Liberty 12-12-70 Colorado 17-3 (Eddie Crowder)

JOHN PONT, 0-2-0 (Miami, Ohio '52) Born 11-13-27
| Miami (Ohio) | Tangerine 12-22-52 | Houston 21-49 (Bill Yeoman) |
| Indiana | Rose 1-1-68 | Southern California 3-14 (John McKay) |

WARREN POWERS, 3-2-0 (Nebraska '63) Born 2-19-41
Missouri	Liberty 12-23-78	LSU 20-15 (Charlie McClendon)
Missouri	Hall of Fame 12-29-79	South Carolina 24-14 (Jim Carlen)
Missouri	Liberty 12-27-80	Purdue 25-28 (Jim Young)
Missouri	Tangerine 12-19-81	Southern Miss. 19-17 (Bobby Collins)
Missouri	Holiday 12-23-83	Brigham Young 17-21 (LaVell Edwards)

CLARENCE "NIBS" PRICE, 0-1-0 (California '14) Born 1889
California ... Rose 1-1-29 Georgia Tech 7-8 (Bill Alexander)

ED PRICE, 1-0-0 (Texas '33) Born 1-12-09
Texas ... Cotton 1-1-53 Tennessee 16-0 (Bob Neyland)

MIKE PRICE, 2-1-0 (Puget Sound '69) Born 4-6-46
Washington St.	Copper 12-29-92	Utah 31-28 (Ron McBride)
Washington St.	Alamo 12-31-94	Baylor 10-3 (Chuck Reedy)
Washington St.	Rose 1-1-98	Michigan 16-21 (Lloyd Carr)

TOMMY PROTHRO, 2-2-0 (Duke '42) Born 7-20-20
Oregon St.	Rose 1-1-57	Iowa 19-35 (Forest Evashevski)
Oregon St.	Liberty 12-15-62	Villanova 6-0 (Alex Bell)
Oregon St.	Rose 1-1-65	Michigan 7-34 (Chalmers "Bump" Elliott)
UCLA	Rose 1-1-66	Michigan St. 14-12 (Duffy Daugherty)

BOB PRUETT, 2-1-0 (Marshall '65) Born 6-30-43
Marshall ... Motor City 12-26-97 Mississippi 31-34 (Tommy Tuberville)

Coach/School	Bowl/Date	Opponent/Score (Coach)
Marshall	Motor City 12-23-98	Louisville 48-29 (John L. Smith)
Marshall	Motor City 12-27-99	Brigham Young 21-3 (LaVell Edwards)

DAVE RADER, 1-1-0 (Tulsa '80) Born 3-9-57
| Tulsa | Independence 12-16-89 | Oregon 24-27 (Rich Brooks) |
| Tulsa | Freedom 12-30-91 | San Diego St. 28-17 (Al Luginbill) |

JOHN RALSTON, 2-2-0 (California '54) Born 4-25-27
Utah St.	Sun 12-31-60	New Mexico St. 13-20 (Warren Woodson)
Utah St.	Gotham 12-9-61	Baylor 9-24 (John Bridgers)
Stanford	Rose 1-1-71	Ohio St. 27-17 (Woody Hayes)
Stanford	Rose 1-1-72	Michigan 13-12 (Glenn "Bo" Schembechler)

CHUCK REEDY, 0-1-0 (Appalachian St. '71) Born 5-31-49
Baylor ... Alamo 12-31-94 Washington St. 3-10 (Mike Price)

RED REESE, 1-0-0 (Washington St. '25) Born 3-2-1899
Second Air Force ... Sun 1-1-43 Hardin-Simmons 13-7 (Warren Woodson)

BO REIN, 2-0-0 (Ohio St. '68) Born 7-20-45
| North Carolina St. | Peach 12-31-77 | Iowa St. 24-14 (Earle Bruce) |
| North Carolina St. | Tangerine 12-23-78 | Pittsburgh 30-17 (Jackie Sherrill) |

PAUL ROACH, 0-3-0 (Black Hills St. '52) Born 10-24-27
Wyoming	Holiday 12-30-87	Iowa 19-20 (Hayden Fry)
Wyoming	Holiday 12-30-88	Oklahoma St. 14-62 (Pat Jones)
Wyoming	Copper 12-31-90	California 15-17 (Bruce Snyder)

ED ROBINSON, 0-1-0 (Brown '96) Born 10-15-73
Brown ... Rose 1-1-16 Washington St. 0-14 (Bill "Lone Star" Dietz)

JOHN ROBINSON, 7-1-0 (Oregon '58) Born 7-25-35
Southern California	Rose 1-1-77	Michigan 14-6 (Glenn "Bo" Schembechler)
Southern California	Bluebonnet 12-31-77	Texas A&M 47-28 (Emory Bellard)
Southern California	Rose 1-1-79	Michigan 17-10 (Glenn "Bo" Schembechler)
Southern California	Rose 1-1-80	Ohio St. 17-16 (Earle Bruce)
Southern California	Fiesta 1-1-82	Penn St. 10-26 (Joe Paterno)
Southern California	Freedom 12-30-93	Utah 28-21 (Ron McBride)
Southern California	Cotton 1-2-95	Texas Tech 55-14 (Spike Dykes)
Southern California	Rose 1-1-96	Northwestern 41-32 (Gary Barnett)

KNUTE ROCKNE, 1-0-0 (Notre Dame '14) Born 3-4-1888
Notre Dame ... Rose 1-1-25 Stanford 27-10 (Glenn "Pop" Warner)

PEPPER RODGERS, 0-2-0 (Georgia Tech '55) Born 10-8-31
| Kansas | Orange 1-1-69 | Penn St. 14-15 (Joe Paterno) |
| Georgia Tech | Peach 12-25-78 | Purdue 21-41 (Jim Young) |

DARRYL ROGERS, 1-0-0 (Fresno St. '57) Born 5-28-34
Arizona St. ... Fiesta 1-1-83 Oklahoma 32-21 (Barry Switzer)

E. L. "DICK" ROMNEY, 0-1-0 (Utah '17) Born 2-12-1895
Utah St. ... Raisin 1-1-47 San Jose St. 0-20 (Bill Hubbard)

TIM ROSE, 0-1-0 (Xavier [Ohio] '62) Born 10-14-41
Miami (Ohio) ... California 12-13-86 San Jose St. 7-37 (Claude Gilbert)

BOBBY ROSS, 4-2-0 (VMI '59) Born 12-23-36
Maryland	Aloha 12-25-82	Washington 20-21 (Don James)
Maryland	Fla. Citrus 12-17-83	Tennessee 23-30 (Johnny Majors)
Maryland	Sun 12-22-84	Tennessee 28-27 (Johnny Majors)
Maryland	Cherry 12-21-85	Syracuse 35-18 (Dick MacPherson)
Georgia Tech	Fla. Citrus 1-1-91	Nebraska 45-21 (Tom Osborne)
Georgia Tech	Aloha 12-25-91	Stanford 18-17 (Dennis Green)

DARRELL ROYAL, 8-7-1 (Oklahoma '50) Born 7-6-24
Texas	Sugar 1-1-58	Mississippi 7-39 (John Vaught)
Texas	Cotton 1-1-60	Syracuse 14-23 (Ben Schwartzwalder)
Texas	Bluebonnet 12-17-60	Alabama 3-3 (Paul "Bear" Bryant)
Texas	Cotton 1-1-62	Mississippi 12-7 (John Vaught)
Texas	Cotton 1-1-63	LSU 0-13 (Charlie McClendon)
Texas	Cotton 1-1-64	Navy 28-6 (Wayne Hardin)
Texas	Orange 1-1-65	Alabama 21-17 (Paul "Bear" Bryant)
Texas	Bluebonnet 12-17-66	Mississippi 19-0 (John Vaught)
Texas	Cotton 1-1-69	Tennessee 36-13 (Doug Dickey)
Texas	Cotton 1-1-70	Notre Dame 21-17 (Ara Parseghian)
Texas	Cotton 1-1-71	Notre Dame 11-24 (Ara Parseghian)
Texas	Cotton 1-1-72	Penn St. 6-30 (Joe Paterno)
Texas	Cotton 1-1-73	Alabama 17-13 (Paul "Bear" Bryant)
Texas	Cotton 1-1-74	Nebraska 3-19 (Tom Osborne)
Texas	Gator 12-30-74	Auburn 3-27 (Ralph "Shug" Jordan)
Texas	Bluebonnet 12-27-75	Colorado 38-21 (Bill Mallory)

NICK SABAN, 0-3-0 (Kent '73) Born 10-31-51
Michigan St.	Independence 12-29-95	LSU 26-45 (Gerry DiNardo)
Michigan St.	Sun 12-31-96	Stanford 0-38 (Tyrone Willingham)
Michigan St.	Aloha 12-25-97	Washington 23-51 (Jim Lambright)

HENRY "RED" SANDERS, 0-2-0 (Vanderbilt '27) Born 3-7-05
| UCLA | Rose 1-1-54 | Michigan St. 20-28 (Clarence "Biggie" Munn) |
| UCLA | Rose 1-2-56 | Michigan St. 14-17 (Duffy Daugherty) |

BOWL COACHING RECORDS

Coach/School	Bowl/Date	Opponent/Score (Coach)
RALPH SASSE, 0-1-0 (Army '10) Born 7-19-89		
Mississippi St.	Orange 1-1-37	Duquesne 12-13 (John Smith)
GEORGE SAUER, 0-3-0 (Nebraska '34) Born 12-11-10		
Kansas	Orange 1-1-48	Georgia Tech 14-20 (Bobby Dodd)
Baylor	Orange 1-1-52	Georgia Tech 14-17 (Bobby Dodd)
Baylor	Gator 12-31-54	Auburn 13-33 (Ralph "Shug" Jordan)
MACK SAXON, 0-1-0 (Texas) Born 1901		
UTEP	Sun 1-1-37	Hardin-Simmons 6-34 (Frank Kimbrough)
CHRIS SCELFO, 1-0-0 (La.-Monroe '85)		
Tulane	Liberty 12-31-98	Brigham Young 41-27 (LaVell Edwards)
GLENN "BO" SCHEMBECHLER, 5-12-0 (Miami [Ohio] '51) Born 4-1-29		
Michigan	Rose 1-1-70	Southern California 3-10 (John McKay)
Michigan	Rose 1-1-72	Stanford 12-13 (John Ralston)
Michigan	Orange 1-1-76	Oklahoma 6-14 (Barry Switzer)
Michigan	Rose 1-1-77	Southern California 6-14 (John Robinson)
Michigan	Rose 1-2-78	Washington 20-27 (Don James)
Michigan	Rose 1-1-79	Southern California 10-17 (John Robinson)
Michigan	Gator 12-28-79	North Carolina 15-17 (Dick Crum)
Michigan	Rose 1-1-81	Washington 23-6 (Don James)
Michigan	Bluebonnet 12-31-81	UCLA 33-14 (Terry Donahue)
Michigan	Rose 1-1-83	UCLA 14-24 (Terry Donahue)
Michigan	Sugar 1-2-84	Auburn 7-9 (Pat Dye)
Michigan	Holiday 12-21-84	Brigham Young 17-24 (LaVell Edwards)
Michigan	Fiesta 1-1-86	Nebraska 27-23 (Tom Osborne)
Michigan	Rose 1-1-87	Arizona St. 15-22 (John Cooper)
Michigan	Hall of Fame 1-2-88	Alabama 28-24 (Bill Curry)
Michigan	Rose 1-2-89	Southern California 22-14 (Larry Smith)
Michigan	Rose 1-1-90	Southern California 10-17 (Larry Smith)
MERLE SCHLOSSER, 0-1-0 (Illinois '50) Born 10-14-27		
Western Mich.	Aviation 12-9-61	New Mexico 12-28 (Bill Weeks)
HOWARD SCHNELLENBERGER, 4-0-0 (Kentucky '56) Born 3-16-34		
Miami (Fla.)	Peach 1-2-81	Virginia Tech 20-10 (Bill Dooley)
Miami (Fla.)	Orange 1-2-84	Nebraska 31-30 (Tom Osborne)
Louisville	Fiesta 1-1-91	Alabama 34-7 (Gene Stallings)
Louisville	Liberty 12-28-93	Michigan St. 18-7 (George Perles)
PAUL SCHUDEL, 0-2-0 (Miami [Ohio] '66) Born 7-2-44		
Ball St.	California 12-9-89	Fresno St. 6-27 (Jim Sweeney)
Ball St.	Las Vegas 12-17-93	Utah St. 33-42 (Charlie Weatherbie)
BILL SCHUTTE, 0-1-0 (Idaho '33) Born 5-7-10		
San Diego St.	Harbor 1-1-48	Hardin-Simmons 0-53 (Warren Woodson)
BEN SCHWARTZWALDER, 2-5-0 (West Virginia '35) Born 6-2-09		
Syracuse	Orange 1-1-53	Alabama 6-61 (Harold "Red" Drew)
Syracuse	Cotton 1-1-57	TCU 27-28 (Abe Martin)
Syracuse	Orange 1-1-59	Oklahoma 6-21 (Bud Wilkinson)
Syracuse	Cotton 1-1-60	Texas 23-14 (Darrell Royal)
Syracuse	Liberty 12-16-61	Miami (Fla.) 15-14 (Andy Gustafson)
Syracuse	Sugar 1-1-65	LSU 10-13 (Charlie McClendon)
Syracuse	Gator 12-31-66	Tennessee 12-18 (Doug Dickey)
BRAD SCOTT, 1-0-0 (Mo.-Rolla '76) Born 9-30-54		
South Carolina	Carquest 1-2-95	West Virginia 24-21 (Don Nehlen)
CLARK SHAUGHNESSY, 1-0-0 (Minnesota '14) Born 3-6-1892		
Stanford	Rose 1-1-41	Nebraska 21-13 (Lawrence McC. "Biff" Jones)
LAWRENCE "BUCK" SHAW, 2-0-0 (Notre Dame '22) Born 3-28-99		
Santa Clara	Sugar 1-1-37	LSU 21-14 (Bernie Moore)
Santa Clara	Sugar 1-1-38	LSU 6-0 (Bernie Moore)
TERRY SHEA, 1-0-0 (Oregon '68) Born 6-12-46		
San Jose St.	California 12-8-90	Central Mich. 48-24 (Herb Deromedi)
JOE SHEEKETSKI, 1-1-0 (Notre Dame '33) Born 4-15-09		
Nevada	Salad 1-1-48	North Texas 13-6 (Odus Mitchell)
Nevada	Harbor 1-1-49	Villanova 7-27 (Jordan Olivar)
DICK SHERIDAN, 2-4-0 (South Carolina '64) Born 8-9-41		
North Carolina St.	Peach 12-31-86	Virginia Tech 24-25 (Bill Dooley)
North Carolina St.	Peach 12-31-88	Iowa 28-23 (Hayden Fry)
North Carolina St.	Copper 12-31-89	Arizona 10-17 (Dick Tomey)
North Carolina St.	All-American 12-28-90	Southern Miss. 31-27 (Jeff Bower)
North Carolina St.	Peach 1-1-92	East Caro. 34-37 (Bill Lewis)
North Carolina St.	Gator 12-31-92	Florida 10-27 (Steve Spurrier)
EUGENE "BO" SHERMAN, 1-0-0 (Henderson St. '30) Born 7-5-08		
Geo. Washington	Sun 1-1-57	UTEP 13-0 (Mike Brumbelow)
JACKIE SHERRILL, 7-6-0 (Alabama '66) Born 11-28-43		
Pittsburgh	Gator 12-30-77	Clemson 34-3 (Charley Pell)
Pittsburgh	Tangerine 12-23-78	North Carolina St. 30-17 (Bo Rein)
Pittsburgh	Fiesta 12-25-79	Arizona 16-10 (Tony Mason)
Pittsburgh	Gator 12-29-80	South Carolina 37-9 (Jim Carlen)
Pittsburgh	Sugar 1-1-82	Georgia 24-20 (Vince Dooley)
Texas A&M	Cotton 1-1-86	Auburn 36-16 (Pat Dye)
Texas A&M	Cotton 1-1-87	Ohio St. 12-28 (Earle Bruce)
Texas A&M	Cotton 1-1-88	Notre Dame 35-10 (Lou Holtz)
Mississippi St.	Liberty 12-29-91	Air Force 15-38 (Fisher DeBerry)
Mississippi St.	Peach 1-2-93	North Carolina 17-21 (Mack Brown)
Mississippi St.	Peach 1-1-95	North Carolina St. 24-28 (Mike O'Cain)
Mississippi St.	Cotton 1-1-99	Texas 11-38 (Mack Brown)
Mississippi St.	Peach 12-30-99	Clemson 17-7 (Tommy Bowden)
TED SHIPKEY, 0-1-0 (Stanford '27) Born 9-28-04		
New Mexico	Sun 1-2-39	Utah 0-28 (Ike Armstrong)
LARRY SIEMERING, 1-0-0 (San Francisco '35) Born 11-24-10		
Pacific (Cal.)	Raisin 1-1-48	Wichita St. 26-14 (Ralph Graham)
BOB SIMMONS, 0-1-0 (Bowling Green '71) Born 6-13-48		
Oklahoma St.	Alamo 12-30-97	Purdue 20-33 (Joe Tiller)
CHAUNCEY SIMPSON, 0-1-0 (Missouri '25) Born 12-21-02		
Missouri	Cotton 1-1-46	Texas 27-40 (Dana Bible)
DAN SIMRELL, 0-1-0 (Toledo '65) Born 4-9-43		
Toledo	California 12-15-84	UNLV 13-30 (Harvey Hyde)
STEVE SLOAN, 0-2-1 (Alabama '66) Born 8-19-44		
Vanderbilt	Peach 12-28-74	Texas Tech 6-6 (Jim Carlen)
Texas Tech	Bluebonnet 12-31-76	Nebraska 24-27 (Tom Osborne)
Texas Tech	Tangerine 12-23-77	Florida St. 17-40 (Bobby Bowden)
R. C. SLOCUM, 2-7-0 (McNeese St. '67) Born 11-7-44		
Texas A&M	John Hancock 12-30-89	Pittsburgh 28-31 (Paul Hackett)
Texas A&M	Holiday 12-29-90	Brigham Young 65-14 (LaVell Edwards)
Texas A&M	Cotton 1-1-92	Florida St. 2-10 (Bobby Bowden)
Texas A&M	Cotton 1-1-93	Notre Dame 3-28 (Lou Holtz)
Texas A&M	Cotton 1-1-94	Notre Dame 21-24 (Lou Holtz)
Texas A&M	Alamo 12-28-95	Michigan 22-20 (Lloyd Carr)
Texas A&M	Cotton 1-1-98	UCLA 23-29 (Bob Toledo)
Texas A&M	Sugar 1-1-99	Ohio St. 14-24 (John Cooper)
Texas A&M	Alamo 12-28-99	Penn St. 0-24 (Joe Paterno)
ANDY SMITH, 1-0-1 (Pennsylvania '06) Born 9-10-1883		
California	Rose 1-1-21	Ohio St. 28-0 (John Wilce)
California	Rose 1-2-22	Wash. & Jeff. 0-0 (Earle "Greasy" Neale)
HOMER SMITH, 0-1-0 (Princeton '54) Born 10-9-31		
Davidson	Tangerine 12-26-69	Toledo 33-56 (Frank Lauterbur)
JOHN L. SMITH, 0-3-0 (Weber St. '71) Born 11-5-48		
Utah St.	Humanitarian 12-29-97	Cincinnati 19-35 (Rick Minter)
Louisville	Motor City 12-23-98	Marshall 29-48 (Bob Pruett)
Louisville	Humanitarian 12-30-99	Boise St. 31-34 (Dirk Koetter)
JOHN "LITTLE CLIPPER" SMITH, 1-0-0 (Notre Dame '29) Born 12-12-04		
Duquesne	Orange 1-1-37	Mississippi St. 13-12 (Ralph Sasse)
LARRY SMITH, 3-6-1 (Bowling Green '62) Born 9-12-39		
Tulane	Liberty 12-22-79	Penn St. 6-9 (Joe Paterno)
Arizona	Sun 12-28-85	Georgia 13-13 (Vince Dooley)
Arizona	Aloha 12-27-86	North Carolina 30-21 (Dick Crum)
Southern California	Rose 1-1-88	Michigan St. 17-20 (George Perles)
Southern California	Rose 1-2-89	Michigan 14-22 (Glenn "Bo" Schembechler)
Southern California	Rose 1-1-90	Michigan 17-10 (Glenn "Bo" Schembechler)
Southern California	John Hancock 12-31-90	Michigan St. 16-17 (George Perles)
Southern California	Freedom 12-29-92	Fresno St. 7-24 (Jim Sweeney)
Missouri	Holiday 12-29-97	Colorado St. 24-35 (Sonny Lubick)
Missouri	Insight.com 12-26-98	West Virginia 34-31 (Don Nehlen)
MAURICE "CLIPPER" SMITH, 0-0-1 (Notre Dame '21) Born 10-15-1898		
Villanova	Bacardi, Cuba 1-1-37	Auburn 7-7 (Jack Meagher)
CARL SNAVELY, 0-3-0 (Lebanon Valley '15) Born 7-30-1894		
North Carolina	Sugar 1-1-47	Georgia 10-20 (Wally Butts)
North Carolina	Sugar 1-1-49	Oklahoma 6-14 (Bud Wilkinson)
North Carolina	Cotton 1-2-50	Rice 13-27 (Jess Neely)
BILL SNYDER, 4-3-0 (William Jewell '63) Born 10-7-41		
Kansas St.	Copper 12-29-93	Wyoming 52-17 (Joe Tiller)
Kansas St.	Aloha 12-25-94	Boston College 7-12 (Dan Henning)
Kansas St.	Holiday 12-29-95	Colorado St. 54-21 (Sonny Lubick)
Kansas St.	Cotton 1-1-97	Brigham Young 15-19 (LaVell Edwards)
Kansas St.	Fiesta 12-31-97	Syracuse 35-18 (Paul Pasqualoni)
Kansas St.	Alamo 12-29-98	Purdue 34-37 (Joe Tiller)
Kansas St.	Holiday 12-29-99	Washington 24-20 (Rick Neuheisel)
BRUCE SNYDER, 3-2-0 (Oregon '62) Born 3-14-40		
California	Copper 12-31-90	Wyoming 17-15 (Paul Roach)
California	Fla. Citrus 1-1-92	Clemson 37-13 (Ken Hatfield)
Arizona St.	Rose 1-1-97	Ohio St. 17-20 (John Cooper)
Arizona St.	Sun 12-31-97	Iowa 17-7 (Hayden Fry)
Arizona St.	Aloha Classic 12-25-99	Wake Forest 3-23 (Jim Caldwell)
FRANK SOLICH, 1-1-0 (Nebraska '66) Born 9-8-44		
Nebraska	Holiday 12-30-98	Arizona 20-23 (Dick Tomey)
Nebraska	Fiesta 1-2-00	Tennessee 31-21 (Phillip Fulmer)
CLARENCE "DOC" SPEARS, 1-0-0 (Dartmouth '16) Born 7-24-1894		
West Virginia	San Diego East-West Christmas Classic 12-25-22	Gonzaga 21-13 (Charles "Gus" Dorais)
CLIFF SPEEGLE, 1-0-0 (Oklahoma '41) Born 11-4-17		
Oklahoma St.	Bluegrass 12-13-58	Florida St. 15-6 (Tom Nugent)

Coach/School	Bowl/Date	Opponent/Score (Coach)
STEVE SPURRIER, 5-5-0	(Florida '67)	Born 4-20-45
Duke	All-American 12-28-89	Texas Tech 21-49 (Spike Dykes)
Florida	Sugar 1-1-92	Notre Dame 28-39 (Lou Holtz)
Florida	Gator 12-31-92	North Carolina St. 27-10 (Dick Sheridan)
Florida	Sugar 1-1-94	West Virginia 41-7 (Don Nehlen)
Florida	Sugar 1-2-95	Florida St. 17-23 (Bobby Bowden)
Florida	Fiesta 1-2-96	Nebraska 24-62 (Tom Osborne)
Florida	Sugar 1-2-97	Florida St. 52-20 (Bobby Bowden)
Florida	Fla. Citrus 1-1-98	Penn St. 21-6 (Joe Paterno)
Florida	Orange 1-2-99	Syracuse 31-10 (Paul Pasqualoni)
Florida	Fla. Citrus 1-1-00	Michigan St. 34-37 (Bobby Williams)
GENE STALLINGS, 6-1-0	(Texas A&M '57)	Born 3-2-35
Texas A&M	Cotton 1-1-68	Alabama 20-16 (Paul "Bear" Bryant)
Alabama	Fiesta 1-1-91	Louisville 7-34 (Howard Schnellenberger)
Alabama	Blockbuster 12-28-91	Colorado 30-25 (Bill McCartney)
Alabama	Sugar 1-1-93	Miami (Fla.) 34-13 (Dennis Erickson)
Alabama	Gator 12-31-93	North Carolina 24-10 (Mack Brown)
Alabama	Fla. Citrus 1-2-95	Ohio St. 24-17 (John Cooper)
Alabama	Outback 1-1-97	Michigan 17-14 (Lloyd Carr)
JIM STANGELAND, 0-0-1	(Arizona St. '48)	Born 12-21-21
Long Beach St.	Pasadena 12-19-70	Louisville 24-24 (Lee Corso)
JIM STANLEY, 2-0-0	(Texas A&M '59)	Born 5-22-35
Oklahoma St.	Fiesta 12-28-74	Brigham Young 16-6 (LaVell Edwards)
Oklahoma St.	Tangerine 12-18-76	Brigham Young 49-12 (LaVell Edwards)
TOM STIDHAM, 0-1-0	(Haskell '27)	Born 3-27-04
Oklahoma	Orange 1-2-39	Tennessee 0-17 (Bob Neyland)
LON STINER, 1-0-0	(Nebraska '27)	Born 6-20-03
Oregon St.	Rose 1-1-42	Duke 20-16 (Wallace Wade)
HARRY STITELER, 1-0-0	(Texas A&M '31)	Born 9-17-09
Texas A&M	Presidential Cup 12-9-50	Georgia 40-20 (Wally Butts)
CHUCK STOBART, 1-0-0	(Ohio '59)	Born 10-27-34
Toledo	California 12-19-81	San Jose St. 27-25 (Jack Elway)
CAL STOLL, 0-1-0	(Minnesota '50)	Born 12-12-23
Minnesota	Hall of Fame 12-22-77	Maryland 7-17 (Jerry Claiborne)
DENNY STOLZ, 0-3-0	(Alma '55)	Born 9-12-34
Bowling Green	California 12-18-82	Fresno St. 28-29 (Jim Sweeney)
Bowling Green	California 12-14-85	Fresno St. 7-51 (Jim Sweeney)
San Diego St.	Holiday 12-30-86	Iowa 38-39 (Hayden Fry)
BOB STOOPS, 0-1-0	(Iowa '83)	Born 9-6-60
Oklahoma	Independence 12-31-99	Mississippi 25-27 (David Cutcliffe)
JERRY STOVALL, 0-1-0	(LSU '63)	Born 4-30-41
LSU	Orange 1-1-83	Nebraska 20-21 (Tom Osborne)
BOB STULL, 0-1-0	(Kansas St. '68)	Born 11-21-45
UTEP	Independence 12-23-88	Southern Miss. 18-38 (Curley Hallman)
PAT SULLIVAN, 0-1-0	(Auburn '72)	Born 1-18-50
TCU	Independence 12-28-94	Virginia 10-20 (George Welsh)
JOCK SUTHERLAND, 1-3-0	(Pittsburgh '18)	Born 3-21-1889
Pittsburgh	Rose 1-1-28	Stanford 6-7 (Glenn "Pop" Warner)
Pittsburgh	Rose 1-1-30	Southern California 14-47 (Howard Jones)
Pittsburgh	Rose 1-2-33	Southern California 0-35 (Howard Jones)
Pittsburgh	Rose 1-1-37	Washington 21-0 (Jimmy Phelan)
BOB SUTTON, 0-1-0	(Eastern Mich. '74)	Born 1-28-51
Army	Independence 12-31-96	Auburn 29-32 (Terry Bowden)
JIM SWEENEY, 5-2-0	(Portland '51)	Born 9-1-29
Fresno St.	California 12-18-82	Bowling Green 29-28 (Denny Stolz)
Fresno St.	California 12-14-85	Bowling Green 51-7 (Denny Stolz)
Fresno St.	California 12-10-88	Western Mich. 35-30 (Al Molde)
Fresno St.	California 12-9-89	Ball St. 27-8 (Paul Schudel)
Fresno St.	California 12-13-91	Bowling Green 21-28 (Gary Blackney)
Fresno St.	Freedom 12-29-92	Southern California 24-7 (Larry Smith)
Fresno St.	Aloha 12-25-93	Colorado 30-41 (Bill McCartney)
BARRY SWITZER, 8-5-0	(Arkansas '60)	Born 10-5-37
Oklahoma	Orange 1-1-76	Michigan 14-6 (Glenn "Bo" Schembechler)
Oklahoma	Fiesta 12-25-76	Wyoming 41-7 (Fred Akers)
Oklahoma	Orange 1-2-78	Arkansas 6-31 (Lou Holtz)
Oklahoma	Orange 1-1-79	Nebraska 31-24 (Tom Osborne)
Oklahoma	Orange 1-1-80	Florida St. 24-7 (Bobby Bowden)
Oklahoma	Orange 1-1-81	Florida St. 18-17 (Bobby Bowden)
Oklahoma	Sun 12-26-81	Houston 40-14 (Bill Yeoman)
Oklahoma	Fiesta 1-1-83	Arizona St. 21-32 (Darryl Rogers)
Oklahoma	Orange 1-1-85	Washington 17-28 (Don James)
Oklahoma	Orange 1-1-86	Penn St. 25-10 (Joe Paterno)
Oklahoma	Orange 1-1-87	Arkansas 42-8 (Ken Hatfield)
Oklahoma	Orange 1-1-88	Miami (Fla.) 14-20 (Jimmy Johnson)
Oklahoma	Fla. Citrus 1-2-89	Clemson 6-13 (Danny Ford)
CHARLIE TATE, 1-1-0	(Florida '42)	Born 2-20-21
Miami (Fla.)	Liberty 12-10-66	Virginia Tech 14-7 (Jerry Claiborne)
Miami (Fla.)	Bluebonnet 12-23-67	Colorado 21-31 (Eddie Crowder)

Coach/School	Bowl/Date	Opponent/Score (Coach)
JIM TATUM, 3-2-1	(North Carolina '35)	Born 7-22-13
Oklahoma	Gator 1-1-47	North Carolina St. 34-13 (Beattie Feathers)
Maryland	Gator 1-1-48	Georgia 20-20 (Wally Butts)
Maryland	Gator 1-2-50	Missouri 20-7 (Don Faurot)
Maryland	Sugar 1-1-52	Tennessee 28-13 (Bob Neyland)
Maryland	Orange 1-1-54	Oklahoma 0-7 (Bud Wilkinson)
Maryland	Orange 1-2-56	Oklahoma 6-20 (Bud Wilkinson)
CHUCK TAYLOR, 0-1-0	(Stanford '43)	Born 1-24-20
Stanford	Rose 1-1-52	Illinois 7-40 (Ray Eliot)
GRANT TEAFF, 4-4-0	(McMurry '56)	Born 11-12-33
Baylor	Cotton 1-1-75	Penn St. 20-41 (Joe Paterno)
Baylor	Peach 12-31-79	Clemson 24-18 (Danny Ford)
Baylor	Cotton 1-1-81	Alabama 2-30 (Paul "Bear" Bryant)
Baylor	Bluebonnet 12-31-83	Oklahoma St. 14-24 (Jimmy Johnson)
Baylor	Liberty 12-27-85	LSU 21-7 (Bill Arnsparger)
Baylor	Bluebonnet 12-31-86	Colorado 21-9 (Bill McCartney)
Baylor	Copper 12-31-91	Indiana 0-24 (Bill Mallory)
Baylor	John Hancock 12-31-92	Arizona 20-15 (Dick Tomey)
EDDIE TEAGUE, 1-0-0	(North Carolina '44)	Born 12-14-21
Citadel	Tangerine 12-30-60	Tennessee Tech 27-0 (Wilburn Tucker)
LOU TEPPER, 1-2-0	(Rutgers '67)	Born 7-21-45
Illinois	John Hancock 12-31-91	UCLA 3-6 (Terry Donahue)
Illinois	Holiday 12-30-92	Hawaii 17-27 (Bob Wagner)
Illinois	Liberty 12-31-94	East Caro. 30-0 (Steve Logan)
ROBERT THEDER, 0-1-0	(Western Mich. '63)	Born 9-22-39
California	Garden State 12-15-79	Temple 17-28 (Wayne Hardin)
FRANK THOMAS, 4-2-0	(Notre Dame '23)	Born 11-14-1898
Alabama	Rose 1-1-35	Stanford 29-13 (Claude "Tiny" Thornhill)
Alabama	Rose 1-1-38	California 0-13 (Leonard "Stub" Allison)
Alabama	Cotton 1-1-42	Texas A&M 29-21 (Homer Norton)
Alabama	Orange 1-1-43	Boston College 37-21 (Denny Myers)
Alabama	Sugar 1-1-45	Duke 26-29 (Eddie Cameron)
Alabama	Rose 1-1-46	Southern California 34-14 (Jeff Cravath)
FRED THOMSEN, 0-0-1	(Nebraska '25)	Born 4-25-1897
Arkansas	Dixie Classic 1-1-34	Centenary (La.) 7-7 (Homer Norton)
CLAUDE "TINY" THORNHILL, 1-2-0	(Pittsburgh '17)	Born 4-14-1893
Stanford	Rose 1-1-34	Columbia 0-7 (Lou Little)
Stanford	Rose 1-1-35	Alabama 13-29 (Frank Thomas)
Stanford	Rose 1-1-36	Southern Methodist 7-0 (Matty Bell)
JOE TILLER, 2-2-0	(Montana St. '64)	Born 12-7-42
Wyoming	Copper 12-29-93	Kansas St. 17-52 (Bill Snyder)
Purdue	Alamo 12-30-97	Oklahoma St. 33-20 (Bob Simmons)
Purdue	Alamo 12-29-98	Kansas St. 37-34 (Bill Snyder)
Purdue	Outback 1-1-00	Georgia 25-28 (ot) (Jim Donnan)
GAYNELL TINSLEY, 0-1-0	(LSU '37)	Born 2-1-15
LSU	Sugar 1-2-50	Oklahoma 0-35 (Bud Wilkinson)
JEFF TISDEL, 1-0-0	(Nevada '77)	Born 1-10-56
Nevada	Las Vegas 12-19-96	Ball St. 18-15 (Bill Lynch)
BOB TOLEDO, 1-1-0	(San Francisco St. '68)	Born 3-4-46
UCLA	Cotton 1-1-98	Texas A&M 29-23 (R. C. Slocum)
UCLA	Rose 1-1-99	Wisconsin 31-38 (Barry Alvarez)
TED TOLLNER, 1-3-0	(Cal Poly '62)	Born 5-29-40
Southern California	Rose 1-1-85	Ohio St. 20-17 (Earle Bruce)
Southern California	Aloha 12-28-85	Alabama 3-24 (Ray Perkins)
Southern California	Fla. Citrus 1-1-87	Auburn 7-16 (Pat Dye)
San Diego St.	Las Vegas 12-19-98	North Carolina 13-20 (Carl Torbush)
DICK TOMEY, 4-3-0	(DePauw '61)	Born 6-20-38
Arizona	Copper 12-30-89	North Carolina St. 17-10 (Dick Sheridan)
Arizona	Aloha 12-28-90	Syracuse 0-28 (Dick MacPherson)
Arizona	John Hancock 12-31-92	Baylor 15-20 (Grant Teaff)
Arizona	Fiesta 1-1-94	Miami (Fla.) 29-0 (Dennis Erickson)
Arizona	Freedom 12-27-94	Utah 13-16 (Ron McBride)
Arizona	Insight.com 12-27-97	New Mexico 20-14 (Dennis Franchione)
Arizona	Holiday 12-30-98	Nebraska 23-20 (Frank Solich)
CARL TORBUSH, 2-0-0	(Carson-Newman '74)	Born 10-11-51
North Carolina	Gator 1-1-98	Virginia Tech 42-3 (Frank Beamer)
North Carolina	Las Vegas 12-19-98	San Diego St. 20-13 (Ted Tollner)
CHRIS TORMEY, 1-0-0	(Idaho '78)	Born 5-1-55
Idaho	Humanitarian 12-30-98	Southern Miss. 42-35 (Jeff Bower)
JIM TRIMBLE, 0-1-0	(Indiana '42)	Born 5-29-18
Wichita St.	Camellia 12-30-48	Hardin-Simmons 12-49 (Warren Woodson)
FRANK TRITICO, 0-0-1	(La.-Lafayette '34)	Born 3-25-09
Randolph Field	Cotton 1-1-44	Texas 7-7 (Dana Bible)
TOMMY TUBERVILLE, 2-0-0	(Southern Ark. '76)	Born 9-18-54
Mississippi	Motor City 12-26-97	Marshall 34-31 (Bob Pruett)
Mississippi	Independence 12-31-98	Texas Tech 35-18 (Spike Dykes)
WILBURN TUCKER, 0-1-0	(Tennessee Tech '43)	Born 8-11-20
Tennessee Tech	Tangerine 12-30-60	Citadel 0-27 (Eddie Teague)
RON TURNER, 1-0-0	(Pacific [Cal.] '77)	Born 12-5-53
Illinois	Micronpc.com 12-30-99	Virginia 63-21 (George Welsh)

BOWL COACHING RECORDS 345

Coach/School	Bowl/Date	Opponent/Score (Coach)
BOB TYLER, 1-0-0	(Mississippi '58)	Born 7-4-32
Mississippi St.	Sun 12-28-74	North Carolina 26-24 (Bill Dooley)
THAD "PIE" VANN, 0-2-0	(Mississippi '28)	Born 9-22-07
Southern Miss.	Sun 1-1-53	Pacific (Cal.) 7-26 (Ernie Jorge)
Southern Miss.	Sun 1-1-54	UTEP 14-37 (Mike Brumbelow)
JOHN VAUGHT, 10-8-0	(TCU '33) Born 5-6-08	
Mississippi	Delta 1-1-48	TCU 13-9 (Leo "Dutch" Meyer)
Mississippi	Sugar 1-1-53	Georgia Tech 7-24 (Bobby Dodd)
Mississippi	Sugar 1-1-55	Navy 0-21 (Eddie Erdelatz)
Mississippi	Cotton 1-2-56	TCU 14-13 (Abe Martin)
Mississippi	Sugar 1-1-58	Texas 39-7 (Darrell Royal)
Mississippi	Gator 12-27-58	Florida 7-3 (Bob Woodruff)
Mississippi	Sugar 1-1-60	LSU 21-0 (Paul Dietzel)
Mississippi	Sugar 1-2-61	Rice 14-6 (Jess Neely)
Mississippi	Cotton 1-1-62	Texas 7-12 (Darrell Royal)
Mississippi	Sugar 1-1-63	Arkansas 17-13 (Frank Broyles)
Mississippi	Sugar 1-1-64	Alabama 7-12 (Paul "Bear" Bryant)
Mississippi	Bluebonnet 12-19-64	Tulsa 7-14 (Glenn Dobbs)
Mississippi	Liberty 12-18-65	Auburn 13-7 (Ralph "Shug" Jordan)
Mississippi	Bluebonnet 12-17-66	Texas 0-19 (Darrell Royal)
Mississippi	Sun 12-30-67	UTEP 7-14 (Bobby Dobbs)
Mississippi	Liberty 12-14-68	Virginia Tech 34-17 (Jerry Claiborne)
Mississippi	Sugar 1-1-70	Arkansas 27-22 (Frank Broyles)
Mississippi	Gator 1-2-71	Auburn 28-35 (Ralph "Shug" Jordan)
DICK VERMEIL, 1-0-0	(San Jose St. '58)	Born 10-30-36
UCLA	Rose 1-1-76	Ohio St. 23-10 (Woody Hayes)
BOB VOIGTS, 1-0-0	(Northwestern '39)	Born 3-29-16
Northwestern	Rose 1-1-49	California 20-14 (Lynn "Pappy" Waldorf)
JIM WACKER, 0-1-0	(Valparaiso '60)	Born 4-28-37
TCU	Bluebonnet 12-31-84	West Virginia 14-31 (Don Nehlen)
WALLACE WADE, 2-2-1	(Brown '17) Born 6-15-1892	
Alabama	Rose 1-1-26	Washington 20-19 (Enoch Bagshaw)
Alabama	Rose 1-1-27	Stanford 7-7 (Glenn "Pop" Warner)
Alabama	Rose 1-1-31	Washington St. 24-0 (Orin "Babe" Hollingbery)
Duke	Rose 1-2-39	Southern California 3-7 (Howard Jones)
Duke	Rose 1-1-42	Oregon St. 16-20 (Lon Stiner)
BOB WAGNER, 1-1-0	(Wittenberg '69)	Born 5-16-47
Hawaii	Aloha 12-25-89	Michigan St. 13-33 (George Perles)
Hawaii	Holiday 12-30-92	Illinois 27-17 (Lou Tepper)
JIM WALDEN, 0-1-0	(Wyoming '60)	Born 4-10-38
Washington St.	Holiday 12-18-81	Brigham Young 36-38 (LaVell Edwards)
LYNN "PAPPY" WALDORF, 0-3-0	(Syracuse '25)	Born 10-3-02
California	Rose 1-1-49	Northwestern 14-20 (Bob Voigts)
California	Rose 1-2-50	Ohio St. 14-17 (Wes Fesler)
California	Rose 1-1-51	Michigan 6-14 (Bennie Oosterbaan)
D. C. "PEAHEAD" WALKER, 1-1-0	(Samford '22)	Born 2-17-1900
Wake Forest	Gator 1-1-46	South Carolina 26-14 (Johnnie McMillan)
Wake Forest	Dixie 1-1-49	Baylor 7-20 (Bob Woodruff)
ED WALKER, 0-1-0	(Stanford '27)	Born 3-25-01
Mississippi	Orange 1-1-36	Catholic 19-20 (Arthur "Dutch" Bergman)
BILL WALSH, 3-0-0	(San Jose St. '54)	Born 11-30-31
Stanford	Sun 12-31-77	LSU 24-14 (Charlie McClendon)
Stanford	Bluebonnet 12-31-78	Georgia 25-22 (Vince Dooley)
Stanford	Blockbuster 1-1-93	Penn St. 24-3 (Joe Paterno)
DALLAS WARD, 1-0-0	(Oregon St. '27)	Born 8-11-06
Colorado	Orange 1-1-57	Clemson 27-21 (Frank Howard)
MURRAY WARMATH, 1-1-0	(Tennessee '35)	Born 12-26-13
Minnesota	Rose 1-2-61	Washington 7-17 (Jim Owens)
Minnesota	Rose 1-1-62	UCLA 21-3 (Bill Barnes)
GLENN "POP" WARNER, 1-2-1	(Cornell '95)	Born 4-5-1871
Stanford	Rose 1-1-25	Notre Dame 10-27 (Knute Rockne)
Stanford	Rose 1-1-27	Alabama 7-7 (Wallace Wade)
Stanford	Rose 1-2-28	Pittsburgh 7-6 (Jock Sutherland)
Temple	Sugar 1-1-35	Tulane 14-20 (Ted Cox)
CHARLIE WEATHERBIE, 2-0-0	(Oklahoma St. '77)	Born 1-17-55
Utah St.	Las Vegas 12-17-93	Ball St. 42-33 (Paul Schudel)
Navy	Aloha 12-25-96	California 42-38 (Steve Mariucci)
DeWITT WEAVER, 2-1-0	(Tennessee '37)	Born 5-11-12
Texas Tech	Sun 1-1-52	Pacific (Cal.) 25-14 (Ernie Jorge)
Texas Tech	Gator 1-1-54	Auburn 35-13 (Ralph "Shug" Jordan)
Texas Tech	Sun 1-2-56	Wyoming 14-21 (Phil Dickens)
BILL WEEKS, 1-0-0	(Iowa St. '51)	Born 10-20-29
New Mexico	Aviation 12-9-61	Western Mich. 28-12 (Merle Schlosser)
RALPH "PEST" WELCH, 0-1-0	(Purdue '30)	Born 8-11-07
Washington	Rose 1-1-44	Southern California 0-29 (Jeff Cravath)
GEORGE WELSH, 5-9-0	(Navy '56)	Born 8-26-33
Navy	Holiday 12-22-78	Brigham Young 23-16 (LaVell Edwards)
Navy	Garden State 12-14-80	Houston 0-35 (Bill Yeoman)
Navy	Liberty 12-30-81	Ohio St. 28-31 (Earle Bruce)
Virginia	Peach 12-31-84	Purdue 27-24 (Leon Burtnett)
Virginia	All-American 12-22-87	Brigham Young 22-16 (LaVell Edwards)
Virginia	Fla. Citrus 1-1-90	Illinois 21-31 (John Mackovic)
Virginia	Sugar 1-1-91	Tennessee 22-23 (Johnny Majors)
Virginia	Gator 12-29-91	Oklahoma 14-48 (Gary Gibbs)
Virginia	Carquest 1-1-94	Boston College 13-31 (Tom Coughlin)
Virginia	Independence 12-28-94	TCU 20-10 (Pat Sullivan)
Virginia	Peach 12-30-95	Georgia 34-27 (Ray Goff)
Virginia	Carquest 12-27-96	Miami (Fla.) 21-31 (Butch Davis)
Virginia	Peach 12-31-98	Georgia 33-35 (Jim Donnan)
Virginia	Micronpc.com 12-30-99	Illinois 21-63 (Ron Turner)
TOMMY WEST, 1-3-0	(Tennessee '75)	Born 7-31-54
Clemson	Peach 12-31-93	Kentucky 14-13 (Bill Curry)
Clemson	Gator 1-1-96	Syracuse 0-41 (Paul Pasqualoni)
Clemson	Peach 12-28-96	LSU 7-10 (Gerry DiNardo)
Clemson	Peach 1-2-98	Auburn 17-21 (Terry Bowden)
MIKE WHITE, 0-3-0	(California '58)	Born 1-3-36
Illinois	Liberty 12-29-82	Alabama 15-21 (Paul "Bear" Bryant)
Illinois	Rose 1-2-84	UCLA 9-45 (Terry Donahue)
Illinois	Peach 12-31-85	Army 29-31 (Jim Young)
JOHN WILCE, 0-1-0	(Wisconsin '10)	Born 5-12-88
Ohio St.	Rose 1-1-21	California 0-28 (Andy Smith)
BUD WILKINSON, 6-2-0	(Minnesota '37)	Born 4-12-16
Oklahoma	Sugar 1-1-49	North Carolina 14-6 (Carl Snavely)
Oklahoma	Sugar 1-2-50	LSU 35-0 (Gaynell Tinsley)
Oklahoma	Sugar 1-1-51	Kentucky 7-13 (Paul "Bear" Bryant)
Oklahoma	Orange 1-1-54	Maryland 7-0 (Jim Tatum)
Oklahoma	Orange 1-2-56	Maryland 20-6 (Jim Tatum)
Oklahoma	Orange 1-1-58	Duke 48-21 (Bill Murray)
Oklahoma	Orange 1-1-59	Syracuse 21-6 (Ben Schwartzwalder)
Oklahoma	Orange 1-1-63	Alabama 0-17 (Paul "Bear" Bryant)
BOBBY WILLIAMS, 1-0-0	(Purdue '82)	Born 11-21-58
Michigan St.	Fla. Citrus 1-1-00	Florida 37-34 (Steve Spurrier)
IVY WILLIAMSON, 0-1-0	(Michigan '33)	Born 2-4-11
Wisconsin	Rose 1-1-53	Southern California 0-7 (Jess Hill)
TYRONE WILLINGHAM, 1-2-0	(Michigan St. '77)	Born 12-30-53
Stanford	Liberty 12-30-95	East Caro. 13-19 (Steve Logan)
Stanford	Sun 12-31-96	Michigan St. 38-0 (Nick Saban)
Stanford	Rose 1-1-00	Wisconsin 9-17 (Barry Alvarez)
TOM WILSON, 2-0-0	(Texas Tech '66)	Born 2-24-44
Texas A&M	Hall of Fame 12-20-78	Iowa St. 28-12 (Earle Bruce)
Texas A&M	Independence 12-12-81	Oklahoma St. 33-16 (Jimmy Johnson)
SAM WINNINGHAM, 0-1-0	(Colorado '50)	Born 10-11-26
Cal St. Northridge	Pasadena 12-2-67	West Tex. A&M 13-35 (Joe Kerbel)
BOB WOODRUFF, 2-1-0	(Tennessee '39)	Born 3-14-16
Baylor	Dixie 1-1-49	Wake Forest 20-7 (D. C. "Peahead" Walker)
Florida	Gator 1-1-53	Tulsa 14-13 (J. O. "Buddy" Brothers)
Florida	Gator 12-27-58	Mississippi 3-7 (John Vaught)
WARREN WOODSON, 6-1-0	(Baylor '24)	Born 2-24-03
Hardin-Simmons	Sun 1-1-43	Second Air Force 7-13 (Red Reese)
Hardin-Simmons	Alamo 1-4-47	Denver 20-6 (Clyde "Cac" Hubbard)
Hardin-Simmons	Harbor 1-1-48	San Diego St. 53-0 (Bill Schutte)
Hardin-Simmons	Shrine 12-18-48	Ouachita Baptist 40-12 (Wesley Bradshaw)
Hardin-Simmons	Camellia 12-30-48	Wichita St. 49-12 (Jim Trimble)
New Mexico St.	Sun 12-31-59	North Texas 28-8 (Odus Mitchell)
New Mexico St.	Sun 12-31-60	Utah St. 20-13 (John Ralston)
BOWDEN WYATT, 2-2-0	(Tennessee '39)	Born 11-3-17
Wyoming	Gator 1-1-51	Wash. & Lee 20-7 (George Barclay)
Arkansas	Cotton 1-1-55	Georgia Tech 6-14 (Bobby Dodd)
Tennessee	Sugar 1-1-57	Baylor 7-13 (Sam Boyd)
Tennessee	Gator 12-26-57	Texas A&M 3-0 (Paul "Bear" Bryant)
BILL YEOMAN, 6-4-1	(Army '50)	Born 12-26-27
Houston	Tangerine 12-22-62	Miami (Ohio) 49-21 (John Pont)
Houston	Bluebonnet 12-31-69	Auburn 36-7 (Ralph "Shug" Jordan)
Houston	Bluebonnet 12-31-71	Colorado 17-29 (Eddie Crowder)
Houston	Bluebonnet 12-29-73	Tulane 47-7 (Bennie Ellender)
Houston	Bluebonnet 12-23-74	North Carolina St. 31-31 (Lou Holtz)
Houston	Cotton 1-1-77	Maryland 30-21 (Jerry Claiborne)
Houston	Cotton 1-1-79	Notre Dame 34-35 (Dan Devine)
Houston	Cotton 1-1-80	Nebraska 17-14 (Tom Osborne)
Houston	Garden State 12-14-80	Navy 35-0 (George Welsh)
Houston	Sun 12-26-81	Oklahoma 14-40 (Barry Switzer)
Houston	Cotton 1-1-85	Boston College 28-45 (Jack Bicknell)
FIELDING "HURRY UP" YOST, 1-0-0	(Lafayette '97)	Born 4-30-1871
Michigan	Rose 1-1-02	Stanford 49-0 (Charlie Fickert)
JIM YOUNG, 5-1-0	(Bowling Green '57)	Born 4-21-35
Purdue	Peach 12-25-78	Georgia Tech 41-21 (Pepper Rodgers)
Purdue	Bluebonnet 12-31-79	Tennessee 27-22 (Johnny Majors)
Purdue	Liberty 12-27-80	Missouri 28-25 (Warren Powers)
Army	Cherry 12-22-84	Michigan St. 10-6 (George Perles)
Army	Peach 12-31-85	Illinois 31-29 (Mike White)
Army	Sun 12-24-88	Alabama 28-29 (Bill Curry)

BOWL/ALL-STAR RECORDS

Coaches Who Have Taken More Than One Team to a Bowl Game

FOUR TEAMS (4)
Earle Bruce: Tampa, Iowa St., Ohio St. & Colorado St.
* Lou Holtz: William & Mary, North Carolina St., Arkansas & Notre Dame
Bill Mallory: Miami (Ohio), Colorado, Northern Ill. & Indiana
* Larry Smith: Tulane, Arizona, Southern California & Missouri

THREE TEAMS (12)
* Mack Brown: Tulane, North Carolina & Texas
Bear Bryant: Kentucky, Texas A&M & Alabama
Jim Carlen: West Virginia, Texas Tech & South Carolina
Jerry Claiborne: Virginia Tech, Maryland & Kentucky
Bill Curry: Georgia Tech, Alabama & Kentucky
Bill Dooley: North Carolina, Virginia Tech & Wake Forest
*Dennis Erickson: Washington St., Miami (Fla.) & Oregon St.
* Ken Hatfield: Air Force, Arkansas & Clemson
John Mackovic: Wake Forest, Illinois & Texas
Johnny Majors: Iowa St., Pittsburgh & Tennessee
* Jackie Sherrill: Pittsburgh, Texas A&M & Mississippi St.
Bowden Wyatt: Wyoming, Arkansas & Tennessee

TWO TEAMS (62)
Fred Akers: Wyoming & Texas
*Gary Barnett: Northwestern & Colorado
John Barnhill: Tennessee & Arkansas
Emory Bellard: Texas A&M & Mississippi St.
Hugo Bezdek: Oregon & Penn St.
Dana X. Bible: Texas A&M & Texas
* Bobby Bowden: West Virginia & Florida St.
Len Casanova: Santa Clara & Oregon
Bobby Collins: Southern Miss. & Southern Methodist
* John Cooper: Arizona St. & Ohio St.
Lee Corso: Louisville & Indiana
Dick Crum: Miami (Ohio) & North Carolina
Bob Devaney: Wyoming & Nebraska
Dan Devine: Missouri & Notre Dame
Doug Dickey: Tennessee & Florida
Paul Dietzel: LSU & South Carolina
Pat Dye: East Caro. & Auburn
Pete Elliott: California & Illinois
Jack Elway: San Jose St. & Stanford
Bob Folwell: Pennsylvania & Navy
Danny Ford: Clemson & Arkansas
* Dennis Franchione: New Mexico & TCU
Hayden Fry: Southern Methodist & Iowa
Vince Gibson: Louisville & Tulane
Sid Gillman: Miami (Ohio) & Cincinnati
Paul Hackett: Pittsburgh & Southern California
Wayne Hardin: Navy & Temple
Woody Hayes: Miami (Ohio) & Ohio St.
Bob Higgins: West Va. Wesleyan & Penn St.
Don James: Kent & Washington
Jimmy Johnson: Oklahoma St. & Miami (Fla.)
Frank Kimbrough: Hardin-Simmons & West Tex. A&M
Jimmy Kitts: Rice & Virginia Tech
* Glen Mason: Kansas & Minnesota
Jess Neely: Clemson & Rice
* Rick Neuheisel: Colorado & Washington
Homer Norton: Centenary (La.) & Texas A&M
Charley Pell: Clemson & Florida
Jimmy Phelan: Washington & St. Mary's (Cal.)
John Pont: Miami (Ohio) & Indiana
Tommy Prothro: Oregon St. & UCLA
John Ralston: Utah St. & Stanford
Pepper Rodgers: Kansas & Georgia Tech
Bobby Ross: Maryland & Georgia Tech
George Sauer: Kansas & Baylor
Howard Schnellenberger: Miami (Fla.) & Louisville
Steve Sloan: Vanderbilt & Texas Tech
* John L. Smith: Utah St. & Louisville
* Bruce Snyder: California & Arizona St.
* Steve Spurrier: Duke & Florida
Gene Stallings: Texas A&M & Alabama
Denny Stolz: Bowling Green & San Diego St.
Jim Tatum: Oklahoma & Maryland
* Joe Tiller: Wyoming & Purdue
* Ted Tollner: Southern California & San Diego St.
Wallace Wade: Alabama & Duke
Pop Warner: Stanford & Temple
* Charlie Weatherbie: Utah St. & Navy
* George Welsh: Navy & Virginia
Bob Woodruff: Baylor & Florida
Warren Woodson: Hardin-Simmons & New Mexico St.
Jim Young: Purdue & Army

*Active coach.

Coaches With the Most Years Taking One College to a Bowl Game

Coach, Team Taken	Bowls	Consecutive Years
* Joe Paterno, Penn St.	30	13 (1971-83)
Tom Osborne, Nebraska	25	25 (1973-97)
Bear Bryant, Alabama	24	24 (1959-82)
* LaVell Edwards, Brigham Young	22	17 (1978-94)
* Bobby Bowden, Florida St.	20	19 (1982-00)
Vince Dooley, Georgia	20	9 (1980-88)
John Vaught, Mississippi	18	14 (1957-70)
Bo Schembechler, Michigan	17	15 (1975-89)
Darrell Royal, Texas	16	8 (1968-75)
Don James, Washington	14	9 (1979-87)
Hayden Fry, Iowa	14	8 (1981-88)
Bobby Dodd, Georgia Tech	13	6 (1951-56)
Terry Donahue, UCLA	13	8 (1981-88)
Charlie McClendon, LSU	13	4 (1970-73)
Barry Switzer, Oklahoma	13	8 (1975-82)
Ralph Jordan, Auburn	12	7 (1968-74)
Woody Hayes, Ohio St.	11	7 (1972-78)
Johnny Majors, Tennessee	11	7 (1981-87)
* Don Nehlen, West Virginia	11	4 (1981-84)
Bill Yeoman, Houston	11	4 (1978-81)
Frank Broyles, Arkansas	10	4 (1959-62)
* John Cooper, Ohio St.	10	10 (1990-99)
* Fisher DeBerry, Air Force	10	4 (1989-92)
* George Welsh, Virginia	10	4 (1993-96)
Fred Akers, Texas	9	9 (1977-85)
Bob Devaney, Nebraska	9	5 (1962-66)
Pat Dye, Auburn	9	9 (1982-90)
* Lou Holtz, Notre Dame	9	9 (1987-95)
Bill McCartney, Colorado	9	7 (1988-94)
John McKay, Southern California	9	4 (1966-69; 1972-75)
* R. C. Slocum, Texas A&M	9	5 (1989-94)
* Steve Spurrier, Florida	9	9 (1992-00)
Earle Bruce, Ohio St.	8	8 (1979-86)
Wally Butts, Georgia	8	4 (1945-48)
Danny Ford, Clemson	8	5 (1985-89)
* John Robinson, Southern California	8	4 (1976-79)
Grant Teaff, Baylor	8	2 (1979-80; 1985-86; 1991-92)
Bud Wilkinson, Oklahoma	8	3 (1948-50)

*Active coach.

Coaches Who Have Coached in a Bowl Game and Also Coached a Team in the NCAA Basketball Tournament

Coach, School	Bowl	NCAA Tournament
Clarence "Nibs" Price, California	Rose 1-1-29	NCAA 1946
E. L. "Dick" Romney, Utah St.	Raisin 1-1-47	NCAA 1939

Conference Bowl Records

1999-00 Bowl Records by Conference

Conference (Teams in Bowls)	W-L-T	Pct.
Big West (1)	1-0-0	1.000
Mid-American (1)	1-0-0	1.000
Big Ten (7)	5-2-0	.714
Western Athletic (3)	2-1-0	.667
Big East (4)	2-2-0	.500
Big 12 (6)	3-3-0	.500
Southeastern (8)	4-4-0	.500
Atlantic Coast (5)	2-3-0	.400
Conference USA (3)	1-2-0	.333
Mountain West (3)	1-2-0	.333
Pacific-10 (5)	1-4-0	.200

All-Time Conference Bowl Records

(Through 1999-00 Bowls, Using Present Conference Alignments)

ATLANTIC COAST CONFERENCE

School	Bowls	W-L-T	Pct.	Last Appearance
Clemson	23	12-11-0	.522	1999 Peach
Duke	8	3-5-0	.375	1995 Hall of Fame
Florida St.	28	17-9-2	.643	2000 Sugar
Georgia Tech	28	19-9-0	.679	2000 Gator

ALL-TIME CONFERENCE BOWL RECORDS

School	Bowls	W-L-T	Pct.	Last Appearance
Maryland	17	6-9-2	.412	1990 Independence
North Carolina	23	11-12-0	.455	1998 Las Vegas
North Carolina St.	18	8-9-1	.472	1998 Micronpc.com
Virginia	11	4-7-0	.364	1999 Micronpc.com
Wake Forest	5	3-2-0	.600	1999 Aloha Classic
Current Members	**161**	**83-73-5**	**.525**	

BIG EAST CONFERENCE

School	Bowls	W-L-T	Pct.	Last Appearance
Boston College	11	5-6-0	.455	1999 Insight.com
Miami (Fla.)	24	13-11-0	.542	2000 Gator
Pittsburgh	19	8-11-0	.421	1989 John Hancock
Rutgers	1	0-1-0	.000	1978 Garden State
Syracuse	20	11-8-1	.575	1999 Music City
Temple	2	1-1-0	.500	1979 Garden State
Virginia Tech	13	4-9-0	.308	2000 Sugar
West Virginia	20	8-12-0	.400	1998 Insight.com
Current Members	**110**	**50-59-1**	**.459**	

BIG 12 CONFERENCE

School	Bowls	W-L-T	Pct.	Last Appearance
North				
Colorado	23	11-12-0	.478	1999 Insight.com
Iowa St.	4	0-4-0	.000	1978 Hall of Fame
Kansas	8	3-5-0	.375	1995 Aloha
Kansas St.	8	4-4-0	.500	1999 Holiday
Missouri	20	9-11-0	.450	1998 Insight.com
Nebraska	38	19-19-0	.500	2000 Fiesta
South				
Baylor	16	8-8-0	.500	1994 Alamo
Oklahoma	33	20-12-1	.621	1999 Independence
Oklahoma St.	13	9-4-0	.692	1997 Alamo
Texas	39	18-19-2	.487	2000 Cotton
Texas A&M	25	12-13-0	.480	1999 Alamo
Texas Tech	23	5-17-1	.239	1998 Independence
Current Members	**250**	**118-128-4**	**.480**	

BIG TEN CONFERENCE

School	Bowls	W-L-T	Pct.	Last Appearance
Illinois	13	6-7-0	.462	1999 Micronpc.com
Indiana	8	3-5-0	.375	1993 Independence
Iowa	16	8-7-1	.531	1997 Sun
Michigan	31	16-15-0	.516	2000 Orange
Michigan St.	15	6-9-0	.400	2000 Florida Citrus
Minnesota	6	2-4-0	.333	1999 Sun
Northwestern	3	1-2-0	.333	1997 Florida Citrus
Ohio St.	31	14-17-0	.452	1999 Sugar
Penn St.	36	23-11-2	.667	1999 Alamo
Purdue	8	6-2-0	.750	2000 Outback
Wisconsin	12	6-6-0	.500	2000 Rose
Current Members	**179**	**91-85-3**	**.517**	

BIG WEST CONFERENCE

School	Bowls	W-L-T	Pct.	Last Appearance
Arkansas St.	0	0-0-0		Has never appeared
Boise St.	1	1-0-0	1.000	1999 Humanitarian
Idaho	1	1-0-0	1.000	1998 Humanitarian
Nevada	5	2-3-0	.400	1996 Las Vegas
New Mexico St.	3	2-0-1	.833	1960 Sun
North Texas	2	0-2-0	.000	1959 Sun
Utah St.	5	1-4-0	.200	1997 Humanitarian
Current Members	**17**	**7-9-1**	**.441**	

CONFERENCE USA

School	Bowls	W-L-T	Pct.	Last Appearance
UAB	0	0-0-0	.000	Has never appeared
Army	4	2-2-0	.500	1996 Independence
Cincinnati	3	2-1-0	.667	1997 Humanitarian
East Caro.	5	3-2-0	.600	1999 Mobile Alabama
Houston	14	7-6-1	.536	1996 Liberty
Louisville	7	3-3-1	.500	1999 Humanitarian
Memphis	1	1-0-0	1.000	1971 Pasadena
Southern Miss.	9	4-5-0	.444	1999 Liberty
Tulane	9	3-6-0	.333	1998 Liberty
Current Members	**52**	**25-25-2**	**.500**	

MID-AMERICAN CONFERENCE

School	Bowls	W-L-T	Pct.	Last Appearance
East				
Akron	0	0-0-0	.000	Has never appeared
Bowling Green	5	2-3-0	.400	1992 Las Vegas
Buffalo	0	0-0-0	.000	Has never appeared
Kent St.	1	0-1-0	.000	1972 Tangerine
Marshall	3	2-1-0	.667	1999 Motor City
Miami (Ohio)	7	5-2-0	.714	1986 California
Ohio	2	0-2-0	.000	1968 Tangerine
West				
Ball St.	3	0-3-0	.000	1996 Las Vegas
Central Mich.	2	0-2-0	.000	1994 Las Vegas
Eastern Mich.	1	1-0-0	1.000	1987 California
Northern Ill.	1	1-0-0	1.000	1983 California
Toledo	6	5-1-0	.833	1995 Las Vegas
Western Mich.	2	0-2-0	.000	1988 California
Current Members	**33**	**16-17-0**	**.485**	

MOUNTAIN WEST CONFERENCE

School	Bowls	W-L-T	Pct.	Last Appearance
Air Force	15	7-7-1	.500	1998 Oahu Classic
Brigham Young	22	7-14-1	.341	1999 Motor City
Colorado St.	6	2-4-0	.333	1999 Liberty
UNLV	2	2-0-0	1.000	1994 Las Vegas
New Mexico	6	2-3-1	.417	1997 Insight.com
San Diego St.	5	1-4-0	.200	1998 Las Vegas
Utah	7	4-3-0	.571	1999 Las Vegas
Wyoming	10	4-6-0	.400	1993 Copper
Current Members	**73**	**29-41-3**	**.418**	

PACIFIC-10 CONFERENCE

School	Bowls	W-L-T	Pct.	Last Appearance
Arizona	13	5-7-1	.423	1998 Holiday
Arizona St.	18	10-7-1	.583	1999 Aloha Classic
California	13	5-7-1	.423	1996 Aloha
Oregon	14	5-9-0	.357	1999 Sun
Oregon St.	5	2-3-0	.400	1999 Oahu Classic
Southern California	39	25-14-0	.641	1998 Sun
Stanford	19	9-9-1	.500	2000 Rose
UCLA	22	11-10-1	.523	1999 Rose
Washington	26	13-12-1	.519	1999 Holiday
Washington St.	7	4-3-0	.571	1998 Rose
Current Members	**176**	**89-81-6**	**.523**	

SOUTHEASTERN CONFERENCE

School	Bowls	W-L-T	Pct.	Last Appearance
Eastern				
Florida	27	13-14-0	.481	2000 Florida Citrus
Georgia	35	18-14-3	.557	2000 Outback
Kentucky	10	5-5-0	.500	1999 Music City
South Carolina	9	1-8-0	.111	1995 Carquest
Tennessee	40	22-18-0	.550	2000 Fiesta
Vanderbilt	3	1-1-1	.500	1982 Hall of Fame
Western				
Alabama	50	28-19-3	.590	2000 Orange
Arkansas	30	10-17-3	.383	2000 Cotton
Auburn	26	14-10-2	.577	1998 Peach
LSU	31	14-16-1	.468	1997 Independence
Mississippi	28	17-11-0	.607	1999 Independence
Mississippi St.	11	5-6-0	.455	1999 Peach
Current Members	**300**	**148-139-13**	**.515**	

WESTERN ATHLETIC CONFERENCE

School	Bowls	W-L-T	Pct.	Last Appearance
Fresno St.	10	6-4-0	.600	1999 Las Vegas
Hawaii	3	2-1-0	.667	1999 Oahu Classic
Rice	7	4-3-0	.571	1961 Bluebonnet
San Jose St.	7	4-3-0	.571	1990 California
Southern Methodist	11	4-6-1	.409	1984 Aloha
TCU	17	6-10-1	.382	1999 Mobile Alabama
UTEP	9	5-4-0	.556	1988 Independence
Tulsa	11	4-7-0	.364	1991 Freedom
Current Members	**75**	**35-38-2**	**.480**	

INDEPENDENTS

School	Bowls	W-L-T	Pct.	Last Appearance
UCF	0	0-0-0	.000	Has never appeared
Connecticut	0	0-0-0	.000	Has never appeared
La.-Lafayette	0	0-0-0	.000	Has never appeared
La.-Monroe	0	0-0-0	.000	Has never appeared
Louisiana Tech	3	1-1-1	.500	1990 Independence
Middle Tenn. St.	0	0-0-0	.000	Has never appeared
Navy	9	4-4-1	.500	1996 Aloha
Notre Dame	23	13-10-0	.565	1999 Gator
Current Members	**35**	**18-15-2**	**.543**	

Award Winners in Bowl Games

Most Valuable Players in Major Bowls

Bowls that are played twice in the same calendar year (i.e., January and December) are listed in chronological order.

ALAMO BOWL

Year	Player, Team, Position
1993	Dave Barr, California, quarterback (offense)
	Jerrott Willard, California, linebacker (defense)
	Larry Blue, Iowa, defensive tackle (sportsmanship award)
1994	Chad Davis, Washington St., quarterback (offense)
	Ron Childs, Washington St., linebacker (defense)
	Adrian Robinson, Baylor, defensive back (sportsmanship award)
1995	Kyle Bryant, Texas A&M, kicker (offense)
	Keith Mitchell, Texas A&M, linebacker (defense)
	Jarrett Irons, Michigan, linebacker (sportsmanship award)
1996	Sedrick Shaw, Iowa, running back (offense)
	James DeVries, Iowa, defensive lineman (defense)
	Shane Dunn, Texas Tech (sportsmanship award)
1997	Billy Dicken, Purdue, quarterback (offense)
	Adrian Beasley, Purdue, safety (defense)
	Kevin Williams, Oklahoma St., cornerback (sportsmanship award)
1998	Drew Brees, Purdue, quarterback (offense)
	Rosevelt Colvin, Purdue, defensive end (defense)
	Jarrod Cooper, Kansas St., free safety (sportsmanship award)
1999	Rashard Casey, Penn St., quarterback (offense)
	LaVar Arrington, Penn St., linebacker (defense)

ALOHA BOWL

Year	Player, Team, Position
1982	Offense—Tim Cowan, Washington, quarterback
	Defense—Tony Caldwell, Washington, linebacker
1983	Offense—Danny Greene, Washington, wide receiver
	Defense—George Reynolds, Penn St., punter
1984	Offense—Jeff Atkins, Southern Methodist, running back
	Defense—Jerry Ball, Southern Methodist, nose guard
1985	Offense—Gene Jelks, Alabama, running back
	Defense—Cornelius Bennett, Alabama, linebacker
1986	Offense—Alfred Jenkins, Arizona, quarterback
	Defense—Chuck Cecil, Arizona, safety
1987*	Troy Aikman, UCLA, quarterback
	Emmitt Smith, Florida, running back
1988	David Dacus, Houston, quarterback
	Victor Wood, Washington St., wide receiver
1989	Blake Ezor, Michigan St., tailback
	Chris Roscoe, Hawaii, wide receiver
1990	Todd Burden, Arizona, cornerback
	Marvin Graves, Syracuse, quarterback
1991	Tommy Vardell, Stanford, running back
	Shawn Jones, Georgia Tech, quarterback
1992	Tom Young, Brigham Young, quarterback
	Dana Stubblefield, Kansas, defensive tackle
1993	Rashaan Salaam, Colorado, tailback
	Trent Dilfer, Fresno St., quarterback
1994	David Green, Boston College, running back (offense)
	Mike Mamula, Boston College, defensive end (defense)
	Joe Gordon, Kansas St., cornerback
1995	Mark Williams, Kansas, quarterback
	Karim Abdul-Jabbar, UCLA, running back
1996	Chris McCoy, Navy, quarterback
	Pat Barnes, California, quarterback
1997	Rashaan Shehee, Washington, running back
	Aloha Classic
1998	Mike Moschetti, Colorado, quarterback
	Akili Smith, Oregon, quarterback
1999	Ben Sankey, Wake Forest, quarterback
	Oahu Classic
1998	Blane Morgan, Air Force, quarterback
1999	Avion Weaver, Hawaii, running back

*Began selecting one MVP for each team.

COTTON BOWL

Year	Player, Team, Position
1937	Ki Aldrich, TCU, center
	Sammy Baugh, TCU, quarterback
	L. D. Meyer, TCU, end
1938	Ernie Lain, Rice, back
	Byron "Whizzer" White, Colorado, quarterback
1939	Jerry Dowd, St. Mary's (Tex.), center
	Elmer Tarbox, Texas Tech, back
1940	Banks McFadden, Clemson, back
1941	Charles Henke, Texas A&M, guard
	John Kimbrough, Texas A&M, fullback
	Chip Routt, Texas A&M, tackle
	Lou De Filippo, Fordham, center
	Joe Ungerer, Fordham, tackle
1942	Martin Ruby, Texas A&M, tackle
	Jimmy Nelson, Alabama, halfback
	Holt Rast, Alabama, end
	Don Whitmire, Alabama, tackle
1943	Jack Freeman, Texas, guard
	Roy McKay, Texas, fullback
	Stanley Mauldin, Texas, tackle
	Harvey Hardy, Georgia Tech, guard
	Jack Marshall, Georgia Tech, end
1944	Joe Parker, Texas, end
	Martin Ruby, Randolph Field, tackle
	Glenn Dobbs, Randolph Field, quarterback
1945	Neil Armstrong, Oklahoma St., end
	Bob Fenimore, Oklahoma St., back
	Ralph Foster, Oklahoma St., tackle
1946	Hub Bechtol, Texas, end
	Bobby Layne, Texas, back
	Jim Kekeris, Missouri, tackle
1947	Alton Baldwin, Arkansas, end
	Y. A. Tittle, LSU, quarterback
1948	Doak Walker, Southern Methodist, back
	Steve Suhey, Penn St., guard
1949	Kyle Rote, Southern Methodist, back
	Doak Walker, Southern Methodist, back
	Brad Ecklund, Oregon, center
	Norm Van Brocklin, Oregon, quarterback
1950	Billy Burkhalter, Rice, halfback
	Joe Watson, Rice, center
	James "Froggie" Williams, Rice, end
1951	Bud McFadin, Texas, guard
	Andy Kozar, Tennessee, fullback
	Hank Lauricella, Tennessee, halfback
	Horace "Bud" Sherrod, Tennessee, defensive end
1952	Keith Flowers, TCU, fullback
	Emery Clark, Kentucky, halfback
	Ray Correll, Kentucky, guard
	Vito "Babe" Parilli, Kentucky, quarterback
1953	Richard Ochoa, Texas, fullback
	Harley Sewell, Texas, guard
	Bob Griesbach, Tennessee, linebacker
1954	Richard Chapman, Rice, tackle
	Dan Hart, Rice, end
	Dicky Maegle, Rice, halfback
1955	Bud Brooks, Arkansas, guard
	George Humphreys, Georgia Tech, fullback
1956	Buddy Alliston, Mississippi, guard
	Eagle Day, Mississippi, quarterback
1957	Norman Hamilton, TCU, tackle
	Jim Brown, Syracuse, halfback
1958	Tom Forrestal, Navy, quarterback
	Tony Stremic, Navy, guard
1959	Jack Spikes, TCU, fullback
	Dave Phillips, Air Force, tackle
1960	Maurice Doke, Texas, guard
	Ernie Davis, Syracuse, halfback
1961	Lance Alworth, Arkansas, halfback
	Dwight Bumgarner, Duke, tackle
1962	Mike Cotten, Texas, quarterback
	Bob Moser, Texas, end
1963	Johnny Treadwell, Texas, guard
	Lynn Amedee, LSU, quarterback
1964	Scott Appleton, Texas, tackle
	Duke Carlisle, Texas, quarterback
1965	Ronnie Caveness, Arkansas, linebacker
	Fred Marshall, Arkansas, quarterback
1966	Joe Labruzzo, LSU, tailback
	David McCormick, LSU, tackle
1966	Kent Lawrence, Georgia, tailback
	George Patton, Georgia, tackle

Year	Player, Team, Position
1968	Grady Allen, Texas A&M, defensive end
	Edd Hargett, Texas A&M, quarterback
	Bill Hobbs, Texas A&M, linebacker
1969	Tom Campbell, Texas, linebacker
	Charles "Cotton" Speyrer, Texas, wide receiver
	James Street, Texas, quarterback
1970	Steve Worster, Texas, fullback
	Bob Olson, Notre Dame, linebacker
1971	Eddie Phillips, Texas, quarterback
	Clarence Ellis, Notre Dame, cornerback
1972	Bruce Bannon, Penn St., defensive end
	Lydell Mitchell, Penn St., running back
1973	Randy Braband, Texas, linebacker
	Alan Lowry, Texas, quarterback
1974	Wade Johnston, Texas, running back
	Tony Davis, Nebraska, tailback
1975	Ken Quesenberry, Baylor, safety
	Tom Shuman, Penn St., quarterback
1976	Ike Forte, Arkansas, running back
	Hal McAfee, Arkansas, linebacker
1977	Alois Blackwell, Houston, running back
	Mark Mohr, Houston, cornerback
1978	Vagas Ferguson, Notre Dame, running back
	Bob Golic, Notre Dame, linebacker
1979	David Hodge, Houston, linebacker
	Joe Montana, Notre Dame, quarterback
1980	Terry Elston, Houston, quarterback
	David Hodge, Houston, linebacker
1981	Warren Lyles, Alabama, nose guard
	Major Ogilvie, Alabama, running back
1982	Robert Brewer, Texas, quarterback
	Robbie Jones, Alabama, linebacker
1983	Wes Hopkins, Southern Methodist, strong safety
	Lance McIlhenny, Southern Methodist, quarterback
1984	Jeff Leiding, Texas, linebacker
	John Lastinger, Georgia, quarterback
1985	Bill Romanowski, Boston College, linebacker
	Steve Strachan, Boston College, fullback
1986	Domingo Bryant, Texas A&M, strong safety
	Bo Jackson, Auburn, tailback
1987	Chris Spielman, Ohio St., linebacker
	Roger Vick, Texas A&M, fullback
1988	Adam Bob, Texas A&M, linebacker
	Bucky Richardson, Texas A&M, quarterback
1989	LaSalle Harper, Arkansas, linebacker
	Troy Aikman, UCLA, quarterback
1990	Carl Pickens, Tennessee, free safety
	Chuck Webb, Tennessee, tailback
1991	Craig Erickson, Miami (Fla.), quarterback
	Russell Maryland, Miami (Fla.), defensive lineman
1992	Sean Jackson, Florida St., running back
	Chris Crooms, Texas A&M, safety
1993	Rick Mirer, Notre Dame, quarterback
	Devon McDonald, Notre Dame, defensive end
1994	Lee Becton, Notre Dame, running back
	Antonio Shorter, Texas A&M, linebacker
1995	Keyshawn Johnson, Southern California, wide receiver
	John Herpin, Southern California, cornerback
1996	Herchell Troutman, Colorado, running back
	Marcus Washington, Colorado, defensive back
1997	Steve Sarkisian, Brigham Young, quarterback
	Kevin Lockett, Kansas St., wide receiver
	Shay Muirbrook, Brigham Young, linebacker
1998	Cade McNown, UCLA, quarterback
	Dat Nguyen, Texas A&M, linebacker
1999	Ricky Williams, Texas, running back
	Aaron Babino, Texas, linebacker
2000	Cedric Cobbs, Arkansas, running back
	D. J. Cooper, Arkansas, linebacker

FIESTA BOWL

Year	Player, Team, Position
1971	Gary Huff, Florida St., quarterback
	Junior Ah You, Arizona St., defensive end
1972	Woody Green, Arizona St., halfback
	Mike Fink, Missouri, defensive back
1973	Greg Hudson, Arizona St., split end
	Mike Haynes, Arizona St., cornerback

AWARD WINNERS IN BOWL GAMES

Year	Player, Team, Position
1974	Kenny Walker, Oklahoma St., running back
	Phillip Dokes, Oklahoma St., defensive tackle
1975	John Jefferson, Arizona St., split end
	Larry Gordon, Arizona St., linebacker
1976	Thomas Lott, Oklahoma, quarterback
	Terry Peters, Oklahoma, cornerback
1977	Matt Millen, Penn St., linebacker
	Dennis Sproul, Arizona St., quarterback (sportsmanship award)
1978	James Owens, UCLA, running back
	Jimmy Walker, Arkansas, defensive tackle
	Kenny Easley, UCLA, safety (sportsmanship award)
1979	Mark Schubert, Pittsburgh, kicker
	Dave Liggins, Arizona, safety
	Dan Fidler, Pittsburgh, offensive guard (sportsmanship award)
1980	Curt Warner, Penn St., running back
	Frank Case, Penn St., defensive end (sportsmanship award)
1982	Curt Warner, Penn St., running back
	Leo Wisniewski, Penn St., nose tackle
	George Achica, Southern California, nose guard (sportsmanship award)
1983	Marcus Dupree, Oklahoma, running back
	Jim Jeffcoat, Arizona St., defensive lineman
	Paul Ferrer, Oklahoma, center (sportsmanship award)
1984	John Congemi, Pittsburgh, quarterback
	Rowland Tatum, Ohio St., linebacker (sportsmanship award)
1985	Gaston Green, UCLA, tailback
	James Washington, UCLA, defensive back
	Bruce Fleming, Miami (Fla.), linebacker (sportsmanship award)
1986	Jamie Morris, Michigan, running back
	Mark Messner, Michigan, defensive tackle
	Mike Mallory, Michigan, linebacker (sportsmanship award)
1987	D. J. Dozier, Penn St., running back
	Shane Conlan, Penn St., linebacker
	Paul O'Connor, Miami (Fla.), offensive guard (sportsmanship award)
1988	Danny McManus, Florida St., quarterback
	Neil Smith, Nebraska, defensive lineman
	Steve Forch, Nebraska, linebacker (sportsmanship award)
1989	Tony Rice, Notre Dame, quarterback
	Frank Stams, Notre Dame, defensive end
	Chris Parker, West Virginia, defensive lineman (sportsmanship award)
1990	Peter Tom Willis, Florida St., quarterback
	Odell Haggins, Florida St., nose guard
	Jake Young, Nebraska, center (sportsmanship award)
1991	Browning Nagle, Louisville, quarterback
	Ray Buchanan, Louisville, free safety
1992	O. J. McDuffie, Penn St., wide receiver
	Reggie Givens, Penn St., outside linebacker
1993	Marvin Graves, Syracuse, quarterback
	Kevin Mitchell, Syracuse, nose guard
1994	Chuck Levy, Arizona, running back
	Tedy Bruschi, Arizona, defensive end
	Paul White, Miami (Fla.), cornerback (sportsmanship award)
1995	Kordell Stewart, Colorado, quarterback
	Shannon Clavelle, Colorado, defensive tackle
	Oliver Gibson, Notre Dame, nose guard (sportsmanship award)
1996	Tommie Frazier, Nebraska, quarterback
	Michael Booker, Nebraska, cornerback
	Danny Wuerffel, Florida, quarterback (sportsmanship award)
1997	Curtis Enis, Penn St., tailback
	Brandon Noble, Penn St., defensive tackle
	Ryan Fiebiger, Texas, center (sportsmanship award)
1998	Michael Bishop, Kansas St., quarterback
	Travis Ochs, Kansas St., linebacker
	Jason Walters, Syracuse, end (sportsmanship)
1999	Peerless Price, Tennessee, wide receiver
	Dwayne Goodrich, Tennessee, cornerback
	Ross Brannon, Florida St., offensive tackle (sportsmanship)
2000	Eric Crouch, Nebraska, quarterback
	Mike Brown, Nebraska, defensive back (defense)

FLORIDA CITRUS BOWL
(Named Tangerine Bowl, 1947-82)

Players of the Game (Pre-1977)

Year	Player, Team, Position
1949	Dale McDaniels, Murray St.
	Ted Scown, Sul Ross St.
1950	Don Henigan, St. Vincent
	Chick Davis, Emory & Henry
1951	Pete Anania, Morris Harvey
	Charles Hubbard, Morris Harvey
1952	Bill Johnson, Stetson
	Dave Laude, Stetson
1953	Marvin Brown, Tex. A&M-Commerce
1954	Billy Ray Norris, Tex. A&M-Commerce
	Bobby Spann, Arkansas St.
1955	Bill Englehardt, Neb.-Omaha
1956	Pat Tarquinio, Juniata
1957	Ron Mills, West Tex. A&M
1958	Garry Berry, Tex. A&M-Commerce
	Neal Hinson, Tex. A&M-Commerce
1958	Sam McCord, Tex. A&M-Commerce
1960	Bucky Pitts, Middle Tenn. St.
	Bob Waters, Presbyterian
1960	Jerry Nettles, Citadel
1961	Win Herbert, Lamar
1962	Joe Lopasky, Houston
	Billy Roland, Houston
1963	Sharon Miller, Western Ky.
1964	Bill Cline, East Caro.
	Jerry Whelchel, Massachusetts
1965	Dave Alexander, East Caro.
1966	Willie Lanier, Morgan St.
1967	Errol Hook, Tenn.-Martin
	Gordon Lambert, Tenn.-Martin
1968	Buster O'Brien, Richmond, back
	Walker Gillette, Richmond, lineman
1969	Chuck Ealy, Toledo, back
	Dan Crockett, Toledo, lineman
1970	Chuck Ealy, Toledo, back
	Vince Hubler, William & Mary, lineman
1971	Chuck Ealy, Toledo, back
	Mel Long, Toledo, lineman
1972	Freddie Solomon, Tampa, back
	Jack Lambert, Kent, lineman
1973	Chuck Varner, Miami (Ohio), back
	Brad Cousino, Miami (Ohio), lineman
1974	Sherman Smith, Miami (Ohio), back
	Brad Cousino, Miami (Ohio), lineman (tie)
	John Roudebush, Miami (Ohio), lineman (tie)
1975	Rob Carpenter, Miami (Ohio), back
	Jeff Kelly, Miami (Ohio), lineman
1976	Terry Miller, Oklahoma St., back
	Phillip Dokes, Oklahoma St., lineman

Most Valuable Player (1977-Present)

Year	Player, Team, Position
1977	Jimmy Jordan, Florida St., quarterback
1978	Ted Brown, North Carolina St., running back
1979	David Woodley, LSU, quarterback
1980	Cris Collinsworth, Florida, wide receiver
1981	Jeff Gaylord, Missouri, linebacker
1982	Randy Campbell, Auburn, quarterback
1983	Johnnie Jones, Tennessee, running back
1984	James Jackson, Georgia, quarterback
1985	Larry Kolic, Ohio St., middle guard
1987	Aundray Bruce, Auburn, linebacker
1988	Rodney Williams, Clemson, quarterback
1989	Terry Allen, Clemson, tailback
1990	Jeff George, Illinois, quarterback
1991	Shawn Jones, Georgia Tech, quarterback
1992	Mike Pawlawski, California, quarterback
1993	Garrison Hearst, Georgia, running back
1994	Bobby Engram, Penn St., wide receiver (overall)
	Charlie Garner, Tennessee, tailback (offense)
	Lee Rubin, Penn St., free safety (defense)
	Raymond Austin, Tennessee, strong safety (defense)
1995	Sherman Williams, Alabama, running back (overall)
	Joey Galloway, Ohio St., wide receiver (offense)
	Dameian Jeffries, Alabama, defensive end (defense)
	Matt Finkes, Ohio St., defensive end (defense)
1996	Jay Graham, Tennessee, running back (overall)
	Rickey Dudley, Ohio St., tight end (offense)
	Leonard Little, Tennessee, defensive end (defense)
	Matt Finkes, Ohio St., defensive end (defense)
1997	Peyton Manning, Tennessee, quarterback (overall)
	Brian Musso, Northwestern, wide receiver (offense)
	Tyrone Hines, Tennessee, linebacker (defense)
	Mike Nelson, Northwestern, linebacker (defense)
1998	Fred Taylor, Florida, tailback (overall)
	Fred Weary, Florida, cornerback (defense)
	Chris Eberly, Penn St., tailback (offense)
	Brandon Short, Penn St., linebacker (defense)
1999	Anthony Thomas, Michigan, running back
	Sam Sword, Michigan, linebacker (defense)
2000	Plaxico Burress, Michigan St., wide receiver (overall)
	Travis Taylor, Florida, wide receiver (offense)
	Julien Peterson, Michigan St. (defense)
	Andra Davis, Florida (defense)

GATOR BOWL

Year	Player, Team
1946	Nick Sacrinty, Wake Forest
1947	Joe Golding, Oklahoma
1948	Lu Gambino, Maryland
1949	Bobby Gage, Clemson
1950	Bob Ward, Maryland
1951	Eddie Talboom, Wyoming
1952	Jim Dooley, Miami (Fla.)
1953	Marv Matuszak, Tulsa
	John Hall, Florida
1954	Vince Dooley, Auburn
	Bobby Cavazos, Texas Tech
1954	Billy Hooper, Baylor
	Joe Childress, Auburn
1955	Joe Childress, Auburn
	Don Orr, Vanderbilt
1956	Corny Salvaterra, Pittsburgh
	Wade Mitchell, Georgia Tech
1957	John David Crow, Texas A&M
	Bobby Gordon, Tennessee
1958	Dave Hudson, Florida
	Bobby Franklin, Mississippi
1960	Maxie Baughan, Georgia Tech
	Jim Mooty, Arkansas
1960	Bobby Ply, Baylor
	Larry Libertore, Florida
1961	Joe Auer, Georgia Tech
	Galen Hall, Penn St.
1962	Dave Robinson, Penn St.
	Tom Shannon, Florida
1963	David Sicks, Air Force
	Ken Willard, North Carolina
1965	Carl McAdams, Oklahoma
	Fred Biletnikoff, Florida St.
	Steve Tensi, Florida
1965	Donny Anderson, Texas Tech
	Lenny Snow, Georgia Tech
1966	Floyd Little, Syracuse
	Dewey Warren, Tennessee
1967	Tom Sherman, Penn St.
	Kim Hammond, Florida St.
1968	Mike Hall, Alabama
	Terry McMillan, Missouri
1969	Curt Watson, Tennessee
	Mike Kelley, Florida
1971	Archie Manning, Mississippi
	Pat Sullivan, Auburn
1971	James Webster, North Carolina
	Jimmy Poulos, Georgia
1972	Mark Cooney, Colorado
	Wade Whatley, Auburn
1973	Haskell Stanback, Tennessee
	Joe Barnes, Texas Tech
1974	Earl Campbell, Texas
	Phil Gargis, Auburn
1975	Sammy Green, Florida
	Steve Atkins, Maryland
1976	Jim Cefalo, Penn St.
	Al Hunter, Notre Dame
1977	Jerry Butler, Clemson
	Matt Cavanaugh, Pittsburgh
1978	Art Schlichter, Ohio St.
	Steve Fuller, Clemson
1979	John Wangler, Michigan
	Anthony Carter, Michigan
	Matt Kupec, North Carolina
	Amos Lawrence, North Carolina
1980	George Rogers, South Carolina
	Rick Trocano, Pittsburgh
1981	Gary Anderson, Arkansas
	Kelvin Bryant, North Carolina
	Ethan Horton, North Carolina
1982	Paul Woodside, West Virginia
	Greg Allen, Florida St.
1983	Owen Gill, Iowa
	Tony Lilly, Florida
1984	Mike Hold, South Carolina
	Thurman Thomas, Oklahoma St.
1985	Thurman Thomas, Oklahoma St.
	Chip Ferguson, Florida St.
1986	Brad Muster, Stanford
	Rodney Williams, Clemson

Year	Player, Team
1987	Harold Green, South Carolina
	Wendell Davis, LSU
1989	Andre Rison, Michigan St.
	Wayne Johnson, Georgia
1989	Mike Fox, West Virginia
	Levon Kirkland, Clemson
1991	Tyrone Ashley, Mississippi
	Michigan offensive line: Tom Dohring, Matt Elliott, Steve Everitt, Dean Dingman, Greg Skrepenak
1991	Cale Gundy, Oklahoma
	Tyrone Lewis, Virginia
1992	Errict Rhett, Florida
	Reggie Lawrence, North Carolina St.
1993	Brian Burgdorf, Alabama
	Corey Holliday, North Carolina
1994	James Stewart, Tennessee
	Dwayne Thomas, Virginia Tech
1996	Donovan McNabb, Syracuse, quarterback
	Peter Ford, Clemson, cornerback
1997	Oscar Davenport, North Carolina, quarterback
	David Saunders, West Virginia, wide receiver
1998	Chris Keldorf, North Carolina, quarterback
	Al Clark, Virginia Tech, quarterback
1999	Dez White, Georgia Tech, wide receiver
	Joe Hamilton, Georgia Tech, running back
	Autry Denson, Notre Dame, running back
2000	Nate Webster, Miami (Fla.), linebacker

HOLIDAY BOWL

Year	Player, Team, Position
1978	Phil McConkey, Navy, wide receiver
1979	Marc Wilson, Brigham Young, quarterback
	Tim Wilbur, Indiana, cornerback
1980	Jim McMahon, Brigham Young, quarterback
	Craig James, Southern Methodist, running back
1981	Jim McMahon, Brigham Young, quarterback
	Kyle Whittingham, Brigham Young, linebacker
1982	Tim Spencer, Ohio St., running back
	Garcia Lane, Ohio St., cornerback
1983	Steve Young, Brigham Young, quarterback
	Bobby Bell, Missouri, defensive end
1984	Robbie Bosco, Brigham Young, quarterback
	Leon White, Brigham Young, linebacker
1985	Bobby Joe Edmonds, Arkansas, running back
	Greg Battle, Arizona St., linebacker
1986	Todd Santos, San Diego St., quarterback (co-offensive)
	Mark Vlasic, Iowa, quarterback (co-offensive)
	Richard Brown, San Diego St., linebacker
1987	Craig Burnett, Wyoming, quarterback
	Anthony Wright, Iowa, cornerback
1988	Barry Sanders, Oklahoma St., running back
	Sim Drain, Oklahoma St., linebacker
1989	Blair Thomas, Penn St., running back
	Ty Detmer, Brigham Young, quarterback
1990	Bucky Richardson, Texas A&M, quarterback
	William Thomas, Texas A&M, linebacker
1991	Ty Detmer, Brigham Young, quarterback
	Josh Arnold, Brigham Young, defensive back (co-defensive)
	Carlos James, Iowa, defensive back (co-defensive)
1992	Michael Carter, Hawaii, quarterback
	Junior Tagoai, Hawaii, defensive tackle
1993	John Walsh, Brigham Young, quarterback (co-offensive)
	Raymont Harris, Ohio St., running back (co-offensive)
	Lorenzo Styles, Ohio St., linebacker
1994	Todd Collins, Michigan, quarterback (co-offensive)
	Anthoney Hill, Colorado St., quarterback (co-offensive)
	Matt Dyson, Michigan, linebacker
1995	Brian Kavanagh, Kansas St., quarterback (offense)
	Mario Smith, Kansas St., defensive back (defense)
1996	Koy Detmer, Colorado, quarterback (offense)
	Nick Ziegler, Colorado, defensive end (defense)
1997	Moses Moreno, Colorado St., quarterback
	Darran Hall, Colorado St., wide receiver
1998	Keith Smith, Arizona, quarterback
	Chris McAlister, Arizona, cornerback
1999	Jonathan Beasley, Kansas St., quarterback
	Darren Howard, Kansas St., linebacker

HUMANITARIAN BOWL

Year	Player, Team, Position
1997	Steve Smith, Utah St., wide receiver
	Chad Plummer, Cincinnati, linebacker
1998	Lee Roberts, Southern Miss., quarterback
	John Walsh, Idaho, quarterback

Year	Player, Team, Position
1999	Brock Forsey, Boise St., running back
	Chris Redman, Louisville, quarterback

INDEPENDENCE BOWL

Year	Player, Team, Position
1976	Terry McFarland, McNeese St., quarterback
	Terry Clark, Tulsa, cornerback
1977	Keith Thibodeaux, Louisiana Tech, quarterback
	Otis Wilson, Louisville, linebacker
1978	Theodore Sutton, East Caro., fullback
	Zack Valentine, East Caro., defensive end
1979	Joe Morris, Syracuse, running back
	Clay Carroll, McNeese St., defensive tackle
1980	Stephan Starring, McNeese St., quarterback
	Jerald Baylis, Southern Miss., nose guard
1981	Gary Kubiak, Texas A&M, quarterback
	Mike Green, Oklahoma St., linebacker
1982	Randy Wright, Wisconsin, quarterback
	Tim Krumrie, Wisconsin, nose guard
1983	Marty Louthan, Air Force, quarterback
	Andre Townsend, Mississippi, defensive tackle
1984	Bart Weiss, Air Force, quarterback
	Scott Thomas, Air Force, safety
1985	Rickey Foggie, Minnesota, quarterback
	Bruce Holmes, Minnesota, linebacker
1986	Mark Young, Mississippi, quarterback
	James Mosley, Texas Tech, defensive end
1987	Chris Chandler, Washington, quarterback
	David Rill, Washington, linebacker
1988	James Henry, Southern Miss., punt returner/cornerback
1989	Bill Musgrave, Oregon, quarterback
	Chris Oldham, Oregon, defensive back
1990	Mike Richardson, Louisiana Tech, running back
	Lorenzo Baker, Louisiana Tech, linebacker
1991	Andre Hastings, Georgia, flanker
	Torrey Evans, Georgia, linebacker
1992	Todd Dixon, Wake Forest, split end
1993	Maurice DeShazo, Virginia Tech, quarterback
	Antonio Banks, Virginia Tech, safety
1994	Mike Groh, Virginia, quarterback
	Mike Frederick, Virginia, defensive end
1995	Kevin Faulk, LSU, running back
	Gabe Northern, LSU, defensive end
1996	Dameyune Craig, Auburn, quarterback
	Takeo Spikes, Auburn, linebacker
	Ben Kotwica, Army, linebacker
1997	Rondell Mealey, LSU, running back
	Arnold Miller, LSU, defensive end
1998	Romaro Miller, Mississippi, quarterback
1999	Tim Strickland, Mississippi, cornerback

INSIGHT.COM BOWL
(Named Copper Bowl, 1989-96)

Year	Player, Team, Position
1989	Shane Montgomery, North Carolina St., quarterback
	Scott Geyer, Arizona, defensive back
1990	Mike Pawlawski, California, quarterback
	Robert Midgett, Wyoming, linebacker
1991	Vaughn Dunbar, Indiana, tailback
	Mark Hagen, Indiana, linebacker
1992	Drew Bledsoe, Washington St., quarterback (overall)
	Phillip Bobo, Washington St., wide receiver (offense)
	Kareem Leary, Utah, defensive back (defense)
1993	Andre Coleman, Kansas St., wide receiver (offense)
	Kenny McEntyre, Kansas St., cornerback (defense)
1994	John Walsh, Brigham Young, quarterback (overall)
	Jamal Willis, Brigham Young, running back (offense)
	Broderick Simpson, Oklahoma, linebacker (defense)
1995	Byron Hanspard, Texas Tech, running back (overall)
	Zebbie Lethridge, Texas Tech, quarterback (offense)
	Mickey Dalton, Air Force, cornerback (defense)
1996	Ron Dayne, Wisconsin, running back
1997	Kelvin Eafon, Arizona, running back
1998	Julian Jones, Missouri, free safety
1999	Cortlen Johnson, Colorado, running back

LAS VEGAS BOWL

Year	Player, Team, Position
1992	Chris Vargas, Nevada, quarterback
1993	Anthony Calvillo, Utah St., quarterback
	Mike Neu, Ball St., quarterback
1994	Henry Bailey, UNLV, running back

Year	Player, Team, Position
1995	Wasean Tait, Toledo, running back
	Alex Van Dyke, Nevada, wide receiver
1996	Brad Maynard, Ball St., punter
	Mike Crawford, Nevada, linebacker
1997	Pat Johnson, Oregon, wide receiver
	Bryce Fisher, Air Force, defensive tackle
1998	Joe Tuipala, San Diego St., linebacker
	Ronald Curry, North Carolina, quarterback
1999	Mike Anderson, Utah, running back

LIBERTY BOWL

Year	Player, Team
1959	Jay Huffman, Penn St.
1960	Dick Hoak, Penn St.
1961	Ernie Davis, Syracuse
1962	Terry Baker, Oregon St.
1963	Ode Burrell, Mississippi St.
1964	Ernest Adler, Utah
1965	Tom Bryan, Auburn
1966	Jimmy Cox, Miami (Fla.)
1967	Jim Donnan, North Carolina St.
1968	Steve Hindman, Mississippi
1969	Bob Anderson, Colorado
1970	Dave Abercrombie, Tulane
1971	Joe Ferguson, Arkansas
1972	Jim Stevens, Georgia Tech
1973	Stan Fritts, North Carolina St.
1974	Randy White, Maryland
1975	Ricky Bell, Southern California
1976	Barry Krauss, Alabama
1977	Matt Kupec, North Carolina
1978	James Wilder, Missouri
1979	Roch Hontas, Tulane
1980	Mark Herrmann, Purdue
1981	Eddie Meyers, Navy
1982	Jeremiah Castille, Alabama
1983	Doug Flutie, Boston College
1984	Bo Jackson, Auburn
1985	Cody Carlson, Baylor
1986	Jeff Francis, Tennessee
1987	Greg Thomas, Arkansas
1988	Dave Schnell, Indiana
1989	Randy Baldwin, Mississippi
1990	Rob Perez, Air Force
1991	Rob Perez, Air Force
1992	Cassius Ware, Mississippi
1993	Jeff Brohm, Louisville
1994	Johnny Johnson, Illinois
1995	Kwame Ellis, Stanford, cornerback
1996	Malcolm Thomas, Syracuse, running back
1997	Sherrod Gideon, Southern Miss., wide receiver
1998	Shaun King, Tulane, quarterback
1999	Adalius Thomas, Southern Miss., defensive end

MICRONPC.COM BOWL
(Named Blockbuster Bowl, 1990-92; Carquest Bowl, 1993-97)

Brian Piccolo Most Valuable Player Award

Year	Player, Team, Position
1990	Amp Lee, Florida St., running back
1991	David Palmer, Alabama, wide receiver
1992	Darrien Gordon, Stanford, cornerback
1993	Glenn Foley, Boston College, quarterback
1995	Steve Taneyhill, South Carolina, quarterback
1995	Leon Johnson, North Carolina, running back
1996	Tremain Mack, Miami (Fla.), strong safety
1997	Joe Hamilton, Georgia Tech, quarterback
1998	Scott Covington, Miami (Fla.), quarterback
1999	Kurt Kittner, Illinois, quarterback

MOBILE ALABAMA BOWL

Year	Player, Team, Position
1999	Casey Printers, TCU, quarterback

MOTOR CITY BOWL

Year	Player, Team, Position
1997	Deuce McCallister, Mississippi, running back
	B. J. Cohen, Marshall, defensive end
1998	Chad Pennington, Marshall, quarterback
1999	Doug Chapman, Marshall, running back

MUSIC CITY BOWL

Year	Player, Team, Position
1998	Corey Moore, Virginia Tech, defensive end
1999	James Mungro, Syracuse, running back

AWARD WINNERS IN BOWL GAMES

ORANGE BOWL

Year	Player, Team, Position
1965	Joe Namath, Alabama, quarterback
1966	Steve Sloan, Alabama, quarterback
1967	Larry Smith, Florida, tailback
1968	Bob Warmack, Oklahoma, quarterback
1969	Donnie Shanklin, Kansas, halfback
1970	Chuck Burkhart, Penn St., quarterback
	Mike Reid, Penn St., defensive tackle
1971	Jerry Tagge, Nebraska, quarterback
	Willie Harper, Nebraska, defensive end
1972	Jerry Tagge, Nebraska, quarterback
	Rich Glover, Nebraska, defensive guard
1973	Johnny Rodgers, Nebraska, wingback
	Rich Glover, Nebraska, defensive guard
1974	Tom Shuman, Penn St., quarterback
	Randy Crowder, Penn St., defensive tackle
1975	Wayne Bullock, Notre Dame, fullback
	Leroy Cook, Alabama, defensive end
1976	Steve Davis, Oklahoma, quarterback
	Lee Roy Selmon, Oklahoma, defensive tackle
1977	Rod Gerald, Ohio St., quarterback
	Tom Cousineau, Ohio St., linebacker
1978	Roland Sales, Arkansas, running back
	Reggie Freeman, Arkansas, nose guard
1979	Billy Sims, Oklahoma, running back
	Reggie Kinlaw, Oklahoma, nose guard
1980	J. C. Watts, Oklahoma, quarterback
	Bud Hebert, Oklahoma, free safety
1981	J. C. Watts, Oklahoma, quarterback
	Jarvis Coursey, Florida St., defensive end
1982	Homer Jordan, Clemson, quarterback
	Jeff Davis, Clemson, linebacker
1983	Turner Gill, Nebraska, quarterback
	Dave Rimington, Nebraska, center
1984	Bernie Kosar, Miami (Fla.), quarterback
	Jack Fernandez, Miami (Fla.), linebacker
1985	Jacque Robinson, Washington, tailback
	Ron Holmes, Washington, defensive tackle
1986	Sonny Brown, Oklahoma, defensive back
	Tim Lashar, Oklahoma, kicker
1987	Dante Jones, Oklahoma, linebacker
	Spencer Tillman, Oklahoma, halfback
1988	Bernard Clark, Miami (Fla.), linebacker
	Darrell Reed, Oklahoma, defensive end
1989	Steve Walsh, Miami (Fla.), quarterback
	Charles Fryar, Nebraska, cornerback
1990	Raghib Ismail, Notre Dame, tailback/wide receiver
	Darian Hagan, Colorado, quarterback
1991	Charles Johnson, Colorado, quarterback
	Chris Zorich, Notre Dame, nose guard
1992	Larry Jones, Miami (Fla.), running back
	Tyrone Leggett, Nebraska, cornerback
1993	Charlie Ward, Florida St., quarterback
	Corey Dixon, Nebraska, split end
1994	Tommie Frazier, Nebraska, quarterback
	Charlie Ward, Florida St., quarterback
1995	Tommie Frazier, Nebraska, quarterback
	Chris T. Jones, Miami (Fla.), wide receiver
1996	Andre Cooper, Florida St., wide receiver
	Derrick Mayes, Notre Dame, wide receiver
1997	Damon Benning, Nebraska, running back
	Ken Oxendine, Virginia Tech, running back
1998	Ahman Green, Nebraska, running back
1999	Travis Taylor, Florida, wide receiver
2000	David Terrell, Michigan, wide receiver

OUTBACK BOWL
(Named Hall of Fame Bowl, 1986-95)

Year	Player, Team, Position
1986	Shawn Halloran, Boston College, quarterback
	James Jackson, Georgia, quarterback
1988	Jamie Morris, Michigan, tailback
	Bobby Humphrey, Alabama, tailback
1989	Robert Drummond, Syracuse, running back
1990	Reggie Slack, Auburn, quarterback
	Derek Isaman, Ohio St., linebacker
1991	DeChane Cameron, Clemson, quarterback
1992	Marvin Graves, Syracuse, quarterback
1993	Heath Shuler, Tennessee, quarterback
1994	Tyrone Wheatley, Michigan, running back
1995	Terrell Fletcher, Wisconsin, running back
1996	Bobby Engram, Penn St., wide receiver
1997	Dwayne Rudd, Alabama, linebacker
1998	Mike Bobo, Georgia, quarterback
1999	Courtney Brown, Penn St., defensive end
2000	Drew Brees, Purdue, quarterback

PEACH BOWL

Year	Player, Team, Position
1968	Mike Hillman, LSU (offense)
	Buddy Millican, Florida St. (defense)
1969	Ed Williams, West Virginia (offense)
	Carl Crennel, West Virginia (defense)
1970	Monroe Eley, Arizona St. (offense)
	Junior Ah You, Arizona St. (defense)
1971	Norris Weese, Mississippi (offense)
	Crowell Armstrong, Mississippi (defense)
1972	Dave Buckey, North Carolina St. (offense)
	George Bell, North Carolina St. (defense)
1973	Louis Carter, Maryland (offense)
	Sylvester Boler, Georgia (defense)
1974	Larry Isaac, Texas Tech (offense)
	Dennis Harrison, Vanderbilt (defense)
1975	Dan Kendra, West Virginia (offense)
	Ray Marshall, West Virginia (defense)
1976	Rod Stewart, Kentucky (offense)
	Mike Martin, Kentucky (defense)
1977	Johnny Evans, North Carolina St. (offense)
	Richard Carter, North Carolina St. (defense)
1978	Mark Herrmann, Purdue (offense)
	Calvin Clark, Purdue (defense)
1979	Mike Brannan, Baylor (offense)
	Andrew Melontree, Baylor (defense)
1980	Jim Kelly, Miami (Fla.) (offense)
	Jim Burt, Miami (Fla.) (defense)
1981	Mickey Walczak, West Virginia (offense)
	Don Stemple, West Virginia (defense)
1982	Chuck Long, Iowa (offense)
	Clay Uhlenhake, Iowa (defense)
1983	Eric Thomas, Florida St. (offense)
	Alphonso Carreker, Florida St. (defense)
1984	Howard Petty, Virginia (offense)
	Ray Daly, Virginia (defense)
1985	Rob Healy, Army (offense)
	Peel Chronister, Army (defense)
1986	Erik Kramer, North Carolina St. (offense)
	Derrick Taylor, North Carolina St. (defense)
1987	Reggie Cobb, Tennessee (offense)
	Van Waiters, Indiana (defense)
1988	Shane Montgomery, North Carolina St. (offense)
	Michael Brooks, North Carolina St. (defense)
1989	Michael Owens, Syracuse (offense)
	Rodney Hampton, Georgia (offense)
	Terry Wooden, Syracuse (defense)
	Morris Lewis, Georgia (defense)
1990	Stan White, Auburn (offense)
	Vaughn Dunbar, Indiana (offense)
	Darrel Crawford, Auburn (defense)
	Mike Dumas, Indiana (defense)
1991	Jeff Blake, East Caro. (offense)
	Terry Jordan, North Carolina St. (offense)
	Robert Jones, East Caro. (defense)
	Billy Ray Haynes, North Carolina St. (defense)
1993	Natrone Means, North Carolina, running back (offense)
	Greg Plump, Mississippi St., quarterback (offense)
	Bracey Walker, North Carolina, strong safety (defense)
	Marc Woodard, Mississippi St., linebacker (defense)
1993	Emory Smith, Clemson, fullback (offense)
	Pookie Jones, Kentucky, quarterback (offense)
	Brentson Buckner, Clemson, tackle (defense)
	Zane Beehn, Kentucky, end (defense)
1995	Treymayne Stephens, North Carolina St., running back
1995	Tiki Barber, Virginia, running back (offense)
	Hines Ward, Georgia, quarterback (offense)
	Skeet Jones, Virginia, linebacker (defense)
	Whit Marshall, Georgia, linebacker (defense)
1996	Herb Tyler, LSU, quarterback (offense)
	Raymond Priester, Clemson, running back (offense)
	Anthony McFarland, LSU, defensive lineman (defense)
	Trevor Pryce, Clemson, defensive lineman (defense)
1998	Dameyune Craig, Auburn, quarterback
	Takeo Spikes, Auburn, linebacker
	Raymond Priester, Clemson, running back
	Rahim Abdullah, Clemson, linebacker
1999	Brian Wofford, Clemson, wide receiver
	Chad Carson, Clemson, linebacker
	Robert Bean, Mississippi St., cornerback

ROSE BOWL

Year	Player, Team, Position
1902	Neil Snow, Michigan, fullback
1916	Carl Dietz, Washington St., fullback
1917	John Beckett, Oregon, tackle
1918	Hollis Huntington, Mare Island, fullback
1919	George Halas, Great Lakes, end
1920	Edward Casey, Harvard, halfback
1921	Harold "Brick" Muller, California, end
1922	Russell Stein, Wash. & Jeff., tackle
1923	Leo Calland, Southern California, guard
1924	Ira McKee, Navy, quarterback
1925	Elmer Layden, Notre Dame, fullback
	Ernie Nevers, Stanford, fullback
1926	Johnny Mack Brown, Alabama, halfback
	George Wilson, Washington, halfback
1927	Fred Pickhard, Alabama, tackle
1928	Clifford Hoffman, Stanford, fullback
1929	Benjamin Lom, California, halfback
1930	Russell Saunders, Southern California, quarterback
1931	John "Monk" Campbell, Alabama, quarterback
1932	Ernie Pinckert, Southern California, halfback
1933	Homer Griffith, Southern California, quarterback
1934	Cliff Montgomery, Columbia, quarterback
1935	Millard "Dixie" Howell, Alabama, halfback
1936	James "Monk" Moscrip, Stanford, end
	Keith Topping, Stanford, end
1937	William Daddio, Pittsburgh, end
1938	Victor Bottari, California, halfback
1939	Doyle Nave, Southern California, quarterback
	Alvin Krueger, Southern California, end
1940	Ambrose Schindler, Southern California, quarterback
1941	Peter Kmetovic, Stanford, halfback
1942	Donald Durdan, Oregon St., halfback
1943	Charles Trippi, Georgia, halfback
1944	Norman Verry, Southern California, guard
1945	James Hardy, Southern California, quarterback
1946	Harry Gilmer, Alabama, halfback
1947	Claude "Buddy" Young, Illinois, halfback
	Julius Rykovich, Illinois, halfback
1948	Robert Chappius, Michigan, halfback
1949	Frank Aschenbrenner, Northwestern, halfback
1950	Fred Morrison, Ohio St., fullback
1951	Donald Dufek, Michigan, fullback
1952	William Tate, Illinois, halfback
1953	Rudy Bukich, Southern California, quarterback
1954	Billy Wells, Michigan St., halfback
1955	Dave Leggett, Ohio St., quarterback
1956	Walter Kowalczyk, Michigan St., halfback
1957	Kenneth Ploen, Iowa, quarterback
1958	Jack Crabtree, Oregon, quarterback
1959	Bob Jeter, Iowa, halfback
1960	Bob Schloredt, Washington, quarterback
	George Fleming, Washington, halfback
1961	Bob Schloredt, Washington, quarterback
1962	Sandy Stephens, Minnesota, quarterback
1963	Pete Beathard, Southern California, quarterback
	Ron VanderKelen, Wisconsin, quarterback
1964	Jim Grabowski, Illinois, fullback
1965	Mel Anthony, Michigan, fullback
1966	Bob Stiles, UCLA, defensive back
1967	John Charles, Purdue, halfback
1968	O. J. Simpson, Southern California, tailback
1969	Rex Kern, Ohio St., quarterback
1970	Bob Chandler, Southern California, flanker
1971	Jim Plunkett, Stanford, quarterback
1972	Don Bunce, Stanford, quarterback
1973	Sam Cunningham, Southern California, fullback
1974	Cornelius Greene, Ohio St., quarterback
1975	Pat Haden, Southern California, quarterback
	John McKay Jr., Southern California, split end
1976	John Sciarra, UCLA, quarterback
1977	Vince Evans, Southern California, quarterback
1978	Warren Moon, Washington, quarterback
1979	Charles White, Southern California, tailback
	Rick Leach, Michigan, quarterback
1980	Charles White, Southern California, tailback
1981	Butch Woolfolk, Michigan, running back
1982	Jacque Robinson, Washington, quarterback
1983	Don Rogers, UCLA, free safety
	Tom Ramsey, UCLA, quarterback
1984	Rick Neuheisel, UCLA, quarterback
1985	Tim Green, Southern California, quarterback
	Jack Del Rio, Southern California, linebacker
1986	Eric Ball, UCLA, tailback
1987	Jeff Van Raaphorst, Arizona St., quarterback
1988	Percy Snow, Michigan St., linebacker
1989	Leroy Hoard, Michigan, fullback

Year	Player, Team, Position
1990	Ricky Ervins, Southern California, tailback
1991	Mark Brunell, Washington, quarterback
1992	Steve Emtman, Washington, defensive tackle
	Billy Joe Hobert, Washington, quarterback
1993	Tyrone Wheatley, Michigan, running back
1994	Brent Moss, Wisconsin, tailback
1995	Danny O'Neil, Oregon, quarterback
	Ki-Jana Carter, Penn St., running back
1996	Keyshawn Johnson, Southern California, wide receiver
1997	Joe Germaine, Ohio St., quarterback
1998	Brian Griese, Michigan, quarterback
1999	Ron Dayne, Wisconsin, running back
2000	Ron Dayne, Wisconsin, running back

SUGAR BOWL

Miller-Digby Memorial Trophy

Year	Player, Team, Position
1948	Bobby Layne, Texas, quarterback
1949	Jack Mitchell, Oklahoma, quarterback
1950	Leon Heath, Oklahoma, fullback
1951	Walt Yowarsky, Kentucky, tackle
1952	Ed Modzelewski, Maryland, fullback
1953	Leon Hardemann, Georgia Tech, halfback
1954	"Pepper" Rodgers, Georgia Tech, quarterback
1955	Joe Gattuso, Navy, halfback
1956	Franklin Brooks, Georgia Tech, guard
1957	Del Shofner, Baylor, halfback
1958	Raymond Brown, Mississippi, halfback
1959	Billy Cannon, LSU, halfback
1960	Bobby Franklin, Mississippi, quarterback
1961	Jake Gibbs, Mississippi, quarterback
1962	Mike Fracchia, Alabama, fullback
1963	Glynn Griffing, Mississippi, quarterback
1964	Tim Davis, Alabama, kicker
1965	Doug Moreau, LSU, flanker
1966	Steve Spurrier, Florida, quarterback
1967	Kenny Stabler, Alabama, quarterback
1968	Glenn Smith, LSU, halfback
1969	Chuck Dicus, Arkansas, flanker
1970	Archie Manning, Mississippi, quarterback
1971	Bobby Scott, Tennessee, quarterback
1972	Jack Mildren, Oklahoma, quarterback
1972	Tinker Owens, Oklahoma, flanker
1973	Tom Clements, Notre Dame, quarterback
1974	Tony Davis, Nebraska, fullback
1975	Richard Todd, Alabama, quarterback
1977	Matt Cavanaugh, Pittsburgh, quarterback
1978	Jeff Rutledge, Alabama, quarterback
1979	Barry Krauss, Alabama, linebacker
1980	Major Ogilvie, Alabama, running back
1981	Herschel Walker, Georgia, running back
1982	Dan Marino, Pittsburgh, quarterback
1983	Todd Blackledge, Penn St., quarterback
1984	Bo Jackson, Auburn, running back
1985	Craig Sundberg, Nebraska, quarterback
1986	Daryl Dickey, Tennessee, quarterback
1987	Steve Taylor, Nebraska, quarterback
1988	Don McPherson, Syracuse, quarterback
1989	Sammie Smith, Florida St., running back
1990	Craig Erickson, Miami (Fla.), quarterback
1991	Andy Kelly, Tennessee, quarterback
1992	Jerome Bettis, Notre Dame, fullback
1993	Derrick Lassic, Alabama, running back
1994	Errict Rhett, Florida, running back
1995	Warrick Dunn, Florida St., running back
1995	Bryan Still, Virginia Tech, wide receiver
1997	Danny Wuerffel, Florida, quarterback
1998	E. G. Green, Florida St., wide receiver
1999	David Boston, Ohio St., wide receiver
2000	Peter Warrick, Florida St., wide receiver

SUN BOWL

(Named John Hancock Bowl, 1989-93)
C. M. Hendricks Most Valuable Player Trophy (1954-Present)
Jimmy Rogers Jr. Most Valuable Lineman Trophy (1961-Present)
John Folmer Most Valuable Special Teams Trophy (1994)

Year	Player, Team, Position
1950	Harvey Gabriel, UTEP, halfback
1951	Bill Cross, West Tex. A&M, end
1952	Junior Arteburn, Texas Tech, quarterback
1953	Tom McCormick, Pacific (Cal.), halfback
1954	Dick Shinaut, UTEP, quarterback
1955	Jesse Whittenton, UTEP, quarterback
1956	Jim Crawford, Wyoming, halfback
1957	Claude Austin, George Washington
1958	Leonard Kucewski, Wyoming, guard
1959	Charley Johnson, New Mexico St., quarterback
1960	Charley Johnson, New Mexico St., quarterback

Year	Player, Team, Position
1961	Billy Joe, Villanova, fullback
	Richie Ross, Villanova, guard
1962	Jerry Logan, West Tex. A&M, halfback
	Don Hoovler, Ohio, guard
1963	Bob Berry, Oregon, quarterback
	John Hughes, Southern Methodist, guard
1964	Preston Ridlehuber, Georgia, quarterback
	Jim Wilson, Georgia, tackle
1965	Billy Stevens, UTEP, quarterback
	Ronny Nixon, TCU, tackle
1966	Jim Kiick, Wyoming, tailback
	Jerry Durling, Wyoming, middle guard
1967	Billy Stevens, UTEP, quarterback
	Fred Carr, UTEP, linebacker
1968	Buddy McClintock, Auburn, defensive back
	David Campbell, Auburn, tackle
1969	Paul Rogers, Nebraska, halfback
	Jerry Murtaugh, Nebraska, linebacker
1970	Rock Perdoni, Georgia Tech, defensive tackle
	Bill Flowers, Georgia Tech, linebacker
1971	Bert Jones, LSU, quarterback
	Matt Blair, Iowa St., linebacker
1972	George Smith, Texas Tech, halfback
	Ecomet Burley, Texas Tech, defensive tackle
1973	Ray Bybee, Missouri, fullback
	John Kelsey, Missouri, tight end
1974	Terry Vitrano, Mississippi St., fullback
	Jimmy Webb, Mississippi St., defensive tackle
1975	Robert Haygood, Pittsburgh, quarterback
	Al Romano, Pittsburgh, middle guard
1977	Tony Franklin, Texas A&M, kicker
	Edgar Fields, Texas A&M, defensive tackle
1977	Charles Alexander, LSU, tailback
	Gordy Ceresino, Stanford, linebacker
1978	Johnny "Ham" Jones, Texas, running back
	Dwight Jefferson, Texas, defensive end
1979	Paul Skansi, Washington, flanker
	Doug Martin, Washington, defensive tackle
1980	Jeff Quinn, Nebraska, quarterback
	Jimmy Williams, Nebraska, defensive end
1981	Darrell Shepard, Oklahoma, quarterback
	Rick Bryan, Oklahoma, defensive tackle
1982	Ethan Horton, North Carolina, tailback
	Ronnie Mullins, Texas, defensive end
1983	Walter Lewis, Alabama, quarterback
	Wes Neighbors, Alabama, center
1984	Rick Badanjek, Maryland, fullback
	Carl Zander, Tennessee, linebacker
1985	Max Zendejas, Arizona, kicker
	Peter Anderson, Georgia, center
1986	Cornelius Bennett, Alabama, defensive end
	Steve Alvord, Washington, middle guard
1987	Thurman Thomas, Oklahoma St., running back
	Darnell Warren, West Virginia, linebacker
1988	David Smith, Alabama, quarterback
	Derrick Thomas, Alabama, linebacker
1989	Alex Van Pelt, Pittsburgh, quarterback
	Anthony Williams, Texas A&M, linebacker
1990	Courtney Hawkins, Michigan St., wide receiver
	Craig Hartsuyker, Southern California, linebacker
1991	Arnold Ale, UCLA, inside linebacker
	Jimmy Rogers Jr., Illinois, lineman
1992	Melvin Bonner, Baylor, flanker
1993	Jerald Moore, Oklahoma, running back
1994	Priest Holmes, Texas, running back
	Blake Brockermeyer, Texas, offensive lineman
	Marcus Wall, North Carolina, wide receiver
1995	Sedrick Shaw, Iowa, running back
	Jared DeVries, Iowa, defensive tackle
	Brion Hurley, Iowa, kicker
1996	Troy Walters, Stanford, flanker
	Kailee Wong, Stanford, defensive end
	Chad Hutchinson, Stanford, quarterback
1997	Mike Martin, Arizona St., running back
1998	Basil Mitchell, TCU, tailback
	London Dunlap, TCU, defensive end
	Adam Abrams, Southern California, placekicker
1999	Billy Cockerham, Minnesota, quarterback
	Dyron Russ, Minnesota, tackle
	Ryan Rindels, Minnesota, punter

Most Valuable Players in Former Major Bowls

ALL-AMERICAN BOWL
(Birmingham, Ala.; Known as Hall of Fame Classic, 1977-85)

Year	Player, Team, Position
1977	Chuck White, Maryland, split end
	Charles Johnson, Maryland, defensive tackle

Year	Player, Team, Position
1978	Curtis Dickey, Texas A&M, running back
1979	Phil Bradley, Missouri, quarterback
1980	Gary Anderson, Arkansas, running back
	Billy Ray Smith, Arkansas, linebacker
1981	John Bond, Mississippi St., quarterback
	Johnie Cooks, Mississippi St., linebacker
1982	Whit Taylor, Vanderbilt, quarterback
	Carl Dieudonne, Air Force, defensive end
1983	Jeff Hostetler, West Virginia, quarterback
1984	Mark Logan, Kentucky, running back
	Todd Gregoire, Wisconsin, placekicker
1985	Mark Ingram, Michigan St., wide receiver
1986	Sammie Smith, Florida St., running back
1987	Scott Secules, Virginia, quarterback
1988	Emmitt Smith, Florida, running back
1989	Jerry Gray, Texas Tech, running back
1990	Brett Favre, Southern Miss., quarterback

AVIATION BOWL
(Dayton, Ohio)

Year	Player, Team, Position
1961	Bobby Santiago, New Mexico, running back
	Chuck Cummings, New Mexico, guard

BLUEBONNET BOWL
(Houston, Texas)

Year	Player, Team
1959	Lowndes Shingles, Clemson
	Bob Lilly, TCU
1960	James Saxton, Texas
	Lee Roy Jordan, Alabama
1961	Ken Coleman, Kansas
	Elvin Basham, Kansas
1962	Bill Tobin, Missouri
	Conrad Hitchler, Missouri
1963	Don Trull, Baylor
	James Ingram, Baylor
1964	Jerry Rhome, Tulsa
	Willy Townes, Tulsa
1965	Dewey Warren, Tennessee
	Frank Emanuel, Tennessee
1966	Chris Gilbert, Texas
	Fred Edwards, Texas
1967	Bob Anderson, Colorado
	Ted Hendricks, Miami (Fla.)
1968	Joe Pearce, Oklahoma
	Rufus Cormier, Southern Methodist
1969	Jim Strong, Houston
	Jerry Drones, Houston
1970	Greg Pruitt, Oklahoma
	Jeff Rouzie, Alabama
1971	Charlie Davis, Colorado
	Butch Brezina, Houston
1972	Condredge Holloway, Tennessee
	Carl Johnson, Tennessee
1973	D. C. Nobles, Houston
	Deryl McGallion, Houston
1974	John Housmann, Houston
	Mack Mitchell, Houston
1975	Earl Campbell, Texas
	Tim Campbell, Texas
1976	Chuck Malito, Nebraska
	Rodney Allison, Texas Tech
1977	Rob Hertel, Southern California
	Walt Underwood, Southern California
1978	Steve Dils, Stanford
	Gordy Ceresino, Stanford
1979	Mark Herrmann, Purdue
	Roland James, Tennessee
1980	Amos Lawrence, North Carolina
	Steve Streater, North Carolina
1981	Butch Woolfolk, Michigan
	Ben Needham, Michigan
1982	Gary Anderson, Arkansas
	Dwayne Dixon, Florida
1983	Rusty Hilger, Oklahoma St.
	Alfred Anderson, Baylor
1984	Willie Drewrey, West Virginia
1985	Pat Evans, Air Force
	James McKinney, Texas
1986	Ray Berry, Baylor
	Mark Hatcher, Colorado
1987	Tony Jones, Texas
	Zeke Gadson, Pittsburgh

BLUEGRASS BOWL
(Louisville, Ky.)

Year	Player, Team
1958	Forrest Campbell, Oklahoma St.

CALIFORNIA RAISIN BOWL
(Beginning in 1992, Mid-American Conference and Big West Conference winners met in Las Vegas Bowl)

Year	Player, Team, Position
1981	Arnold Smiley, Toledo, running back
	Marlin Russell, Toledo, linebacker
1982	Chip Otten, Bowling Green, tailback
	Jac Tomasello, Bowling Green, defensive back
1983	Lou Wicks, Northern Ill., fullback
	James Pruitt, Cal St. Fullerton, wide receiver
1984	Randall Cunningham, UNLV, quarterback
	Steve Morgan, Toledo, tailback
1985	Mike Mancini, Fresno St., punter
	Greg Meehan, Bowling Green, flanker
1986	Mike Perez, San Jose St., quarterback
	Andrew Marlatt, Miami (Ohio), defensive tackle
1987	Gary Patton, Eastern Mich., tailback
	Mike Perez, San Jose St., quarterback
1988	Darrell Rosette, Fresno St., running back
	Tony Kimbrough, Western Mich., quarterback
1989	Ron Cox, Fresno St., linebacker
	Sean Jones, Ball St., wide receiver
1990	Sheldon Canley, San Jose St., tailback
	Ken Ealy, Central Mich., wide receiver
1991	Mark Szlachcic, Bowling Green, wide receiver
	Mark Barsotti, Fresno St., quarterback

CHERRY BOWL
(Pontiac, Mich.)

Year	Player, Team
1984	Nate Sassaman, Army
1985	Stan Gelbaugh, Maryland
	Scott Shankweiler, Maryland

DELTA BOWL
(Memphis, Tenn.)

Year	Player, Team
1948	Charlie Conerly, Mississippi

FREEDOM BOWL
(Anaheim, Calif.)

Year	Player, Team, Position
1984	Chuck Long, Iowa, quarterback
	William Harris, Texas, tight end
1985	Chris Chandler, Washington, quarterback
	Barry Helton, Colorado, punter
1986	Gaston Green, UCLA, tailback
	Shane Shumway, Brigham Young, defensive back
1987	Daniel Ford, Arizona St., quarterback
	Chad Hennings, Air Force, defensive tackle
1988	Ty Detmer, Brigham Young, quarterback
	Eric Bieniemy, Colorado, halfback
1989	Cary Conklin, Washington, quarterback
	Huey Richardson, Florida, linebacker
1990	Todd Yert, Colorado St., running back
	Bill Musgrave, Oregon, quarterback
1991	Marshall Faulk, San Diego St., running back
	Ron Jackson, Tulsa, running back
1992	Lorenzo Neal, Fresno St., fullback

Year	Player, Team, Position
	Estrus Crayton, Southern California, tailback
1993	Johnnie Morton, Southern California, wide receiver
	Henry Lusk, Utah, wide receiver
1994	Tedy Bruschi, Arizona, defensive end
	Cal Beck, Utah, kick returner

GARDEN STATE BOWL
(East Rutherford, N.J.)

Year	Player, Team
1978	John Mistler, Arizona St.
1979	Mark Bright, Temple
1980	Terald Clark, Houston
1981	Steve Alatorre, Tennessee
	Anthony Hancock, Tennessee
	Randy Wright, Wisconsin

GOTHAM BOWL
(New York, N.Y.)

Year	Player, Team
1961	Don Trull, Baylor
1962	Willie Ross, Nebraska
	George Mira, Miami (Fla.)

HARBOR BOWL
(San Diego, Calif.)

Year	Player, Team
1947	Bryan Brock, New Mexico
	Bill Nelson, Montana St.

MERCY BOWL
(Los Angeles, Calif.)

Year	Player, Team
1961	Beau Carter, Fresno St.

PASADENA BOWL
(Pasadena, Calif.; called Junior Rose Bowl in 1967)

Year	Player, Team
1967	Eugene "Mercury" Morris, West Tex. A&M
	Albie Owens, West Tex. A&M
1969	John Featherstone, San Diego St.
1970	Leon Burns, Long Beach St.
	Paul Mattingly, Louisville
1971	Tom Carlsen, Memphis
	Dornell Harris, Memphis

PRESIDENTIAL CUP
(College Park, Md.)

Year	Player, Team
1950	Bob Smith, Texas A&M
	Zippy Morocco, Georgia

SALAD BOWL
(Phoenix, Ariz.)

Year	Player, Team
1950	Bob McQuade, Xavier
	Wilford White, Arizona St.
1951	Jim Bailey, Miami (Ohio)
1952	Gene Shannon, Houston

Heisman Trophy Winners in Bowl Games

YEAR-BY-YEAR BOWL RESULTS FOR HEISMAN WINNERS

(Includes bowl games immediately after award of Heisman Trophy)

Of the 64 winners of the 65 Heisman Trophies (Archie Griffin won twice), 40 played in bowl games after they received their prize. Of those 40 players, only 20 were on the winning team in the bowl.

Houston's Andre Ware is the only Heisman recipient to miss a bowl date since 1969. The Cougars were on probation during the 1989 season and were ineligible for selection to a bowl. Before that lapse, Oklahoma's Steve Owens in 1969 was the last Heisman awardee not to participate in a bowl game.

Only three of the first 22 Heisman Trophy winners played in bowl games after receiving the award—TCU's Davey O'Brien in 1938, Georgia's Frank Sinkwich in 1942 and Southern Methodist's Doak Walker in 1948.

Year	Heisman Winner, Team, Position	Bowl (Opponent, Result)
1935	Jay Berwanger, Chicago, HB	Did not play in bowl
1936	Larry Kelley, Yale, E	Did not play in bowl
1937	Clint Frank, Yale, HB	Did not play in bowl
1938	Davey O'Brien, TCU, QB	Sugar (Carnegie Mellon, W 15-7)
1939	Nile Kinnick, Iowa, HB	Did not play in bowl
1940	Tom Harmon, Michigan, HB	Did not play in bowl
1941	Bruce Smith, Minnesota, HB	Did not play in bowl
1942	Frank Sinkwich, Georgia, HB	Rose (UCLA, W 9-0)
1943	Angelo Bertelli, Notre Dame, QB	Did not play in bowl
1944	Les Horvath, Ohio St., QB	Did not play in bowl
1945	Doc Blanchard, Army, FB	Did not play in bowl
1946	Glenn Davis, Army, HB	Did not play in bowl
1947	Johnny Lujack, Notre Dame, QB	Did not play in bowl
1948	Doak Walker, Southern Methodist, HB	Cotton (Oregon, W 21-13)
1949	Leon Hart, Notre Dame, E	Did not play in bowl
1950	Vic Janowicz, Ohio St., HB	Did not play in bowl
1951	Dick Kazmeier, Princeton, HB	Did not play in bowl
1952	Billy Vessels, Oklahoma, HB	Did not play in bowl
1953	John Lattner, Notre Dame, HB	Did not play in bowl
1954	Alan Ameche, Wisconsin, FB	Did not play in bowl
1955	Howard Cassady, Ohio St., HB	Did not play in bowl
1956	Paul Hornung, Notre Dame, QB	Did not play in bowl
1957	John David Crow, Texas A&M, HB	Gator (Tennessee, L 3-0)
1958	Pete Dawkins, Army, HB	Did not play in bowl
1959	Billy Cannon, LSU, HB	Sugar (Mississippi, L 21-0)
1960	Joe Bellino, Navy, HB	Orange (Missouri, L 21-14)
1961	Ernie Davis, Syracuse, HB	Liberty (Miami, Fla., W 15-14)
1962	Terry Baker, Oregon St., QB	Liberty (Villanova, W 6-0)
1963	Roger Staubach, Navy, QB	Cotton (Texas, L 28-6)
1964	John Huarte, Notre Dame, QB	Did not play in bowl
1965	Mike Garrett, Southern California, HB	Did not play in bowl
1966	Steve Spurrier, Florida, QB	Orange (Georgia Tech, W 27-12)
1967	Gary Beban, UCLA, QB	Did not play in bowl
1968	O. J. Simpson, Southern California, HB	Rose (Ohio St., L 27-16)
1969	Steve Owens, Oklahoma, HB	Did not play in bowl
1970	Jim Plunkett, Stanford, QB	Rose (Ohio St., W 27-17)
1971	Pat Sullivan, Auburn, QB	Sugar (Oklahoma, L 40-22)
1972	Johnny Rodgers, Nebraska, FL	Orange (Notre Dame, W 40-6)
1973	John Cappelletti, Penn St., HB	Orange (LSU, W 16-9)
1974	Archie Griffin, Ohio St., HB	Rose (Southern California, L 18-17)
1975	Archie Griffin, Ohio St., HB	Rose (UCLA, L 23-10)
1976	Tony Dorsett, Pittsburgh, HB	Sugar (Georgia, W 27-3)
1977	Earl Campbell, Texas, HB	Cotton (Notre Dame, L 38-10)
1978	Billy Sims, Oklahoma, HB	Orange (Nebraska, W 31-24)
1979	Charles White, Southern California, HB	Rose (Ohio St., W 17-16)
1980	George Rogers, South Carolina, HB	Gator (Pittsburgh, L 37-9)
1981	Marcus Allen, Southern California, HB	Fiesta (Penn St., L 26-10)
1982	Herschel Walker, Georgia, HB	Sugar (Penn St., L 27-23)
1983	Mike Rozier, Nebraska, HB	Orange (Miami, Fla., L 31-30)
1984	Doug Flutie, Boston College, QB	Cotton (Houston, W 45-28)
1985	Bo Jackson, Auburn, HB	Cotton (Texas A&M, L 36-16)
1986	Vinny Testaverde, Miami (Fla.), QB	Fiesta (Penn St., L 14-10)
1987	Tim Brown, Notre Dame, WR	Cotton (Texas A&M, L 35-10)
1988	Barry Sanders, Oklahoma St., RB	Holiday (Wyoming, W 62-14)
1989	Andre Ware, Houston, QB	Did not play in bowl
1990	Ty Detmer, Brigham Young, QB	Holiday (Texas A&M, L 65-14)
1991	Desmond Howard, Michigan, WR	Rose (Washington, L 34-14)
1992	Gino Torretta, Miami (Fla.), QB	Sugar (Alabama, L 34-13)
1993	Charlie Ward, Florida St., QB	Orange (Nebraska, W 18-16)
1994	Rashaan Salaam, Colorado, RB	Fiesta (Notre Dame, W 41-24)
1995	Eddie George, Ohio St., RB	Fla. Citrus (Tennessee, L 20-14)
1996	Danny Wuerffel, Florida, QB	Sugar (Florida St., W 52-20)
1997	Charles Woodson, Michigan, CB	Rose (Washington St., W 21-16)
1998	Ricky Williams, Texas, RB	Cotton (Mississippi St., W 38-11)
1999	Ron Dayne, Wisconsin, RB	Rose (Stanford, W 17-9)

BOWLS FOR HEISMAN WINNERS

Bowl	Heisman Winner Year	Heisman Winners
Rose	1942, 1968, 1970, 1974, 1975, 1979, 1991, 1997, 1999	9
Orange	1960, 1966, 1972, 1973, 1978, 1983, 1993	7
Sugar	1938, 1959, 1971, 1976, 1982, 1992, 1996	7
Cotton	1948, 1963, 1977, 1984, 1985, 1987, 1998	7
Fiesta	1981, 1986, 1994	3
Gator	1957, 1980	2
Holiday	1988, 1990	2
Liberty	1961, 1962	2
Fla. Citrus	1995	1

HEISMAN TROPHY WINNERS WHO WERE BOWL-GAME MVPs

Heisman Winner, Team (Year Won)	Bowl, Year Played
Doak Walker, Southern Methodist (1948)	Cotton, 1948
Doak Walker, Southern Methodist (1948)	Cotton, 1949
John David Crow, Texas A&M (1957)	Gator, 1957
Billy Cannon, LSU (1959)	Sugar, 1959
Ernie Davis, Syracuse (1961)	Cotton, 1960
Ernie Davis, Syracuse (1961)	Liberty, 1961
Terry Baker, Oregon St. (1962)	Liberty, 1962
Steve Spurrier, Florida (1966)	Sugar, 1966
O. J. Simpson, Southern California (1968)	Rose, 1968
Jim Plunkett, Stanford (1970)	Rose, 1971
Pat Sullivan, Auburn (1971)	Gator, 1971
Johnny Rodgers, Nebraska (1972)	Orange, 1973
Earl Campbell, Texas (1977)	Gator, 1974
Earl Campbell, Texas (1977)	Bluebonnet, 1975*
Billy Sims, Oklahoma (1978)	Orange, 1979
Charles White, Southern California (1979)	Rose, 1979
Charles White, Southern California (1979)	Rose, 1980
George Rogers, South Carolina (1980)	Gator, 1980
Herschel Walker, Georgia (1982)	Sugar, 1981
Doug Flutie, Boston College (1984)	Liberty, 1983
Bo Jackson, Auburn (1985)	Sugar, 1984
Bo Jackson, Auburn (1985)	Liberty, 1984
Bo Jackson, Auburn (1985)	Cotton, 1986
Barry Sanders, Oklahoma St. (1988)	Holiday, 1988
Ty Detmer, Brigham Young (1990)	Freedom, 1988*
Ty Detmer, Brigham Young (1990)	Holiday, 1989
Ty Detmer, Brigham Young (1990)	Holiday, 1991
Charlie Ward, Florida St. (1993)	Orange, 1994
Danny Wuerffel, Florida (1996)	Sugar, 1997
Ricky Williams, Texas (1998)	Cotton, 1999
Ron Dayne, Wisconsin (1999)	Rose, 1999
Ron Dayne, Wisconsin (1999)	Rose, 2000

*Discontinued bowl.

Bowls and Polls

Associated Press No. 1 Teams Defeated in Bowl Games

Date	Bowl	Teams Involved	Score	New No. 1
1-1-51	Sugar	No. 7 Kentucky beat No. 1 Oklahoma	13-7	Same
1-1-52	Sugar	No. 3 Maryland beat No. 1 Tennessee	28-13	Same
1-1-54	Orange	No. 4 Oklahoma beat No. 1 Maryland	7-0	Same
1-1-61	Rose	No. 6 Washington beat No. 1 Minnesota	17-7	Same
1-1-65	Orange	No. 5 Texas beat No. 1 Alabama	21-17	Same
1-1-71	Cotton	No. 6 Notre Dame beat No. 1 Texas	24-11	Nebraska
12-31-73	Sugar	No. 3 Notre Dame beat No. 1 Alabama	24-23	Notre Dame
1-1-76	Rose	No. 11 UCLA beat No. 1 Ohio St.	23-10	Oklahoma
1-2-78	Cotton	No. 5 Notre Dame beat No. 1 Texas	38-10	Notre Dame
1-1-79	Sugar	No. 2 Alabama beat No. 1 Penn St.	14-7	Alabama
1-1-83	Sugar	No. 2 Penn St. beat No. 1 Georgia	27-23	Penn St.
1-2-84	Orange	No. 5 Miami (Fla.) beat No. 1 Nebraska	31-30	Miami (Fla.)
1-1-86	Orange	No. 3 Oklahoma beat No. 1 Penn St.	25-10	Oklahoma
1-2-87	Fiesta	No. 2 Penn St. beat No. 1 Miami (Fla.)	14-10	Penn St.
1-1-88	Orange	No. 2 Miami (Fla.) beat No. 1 Oklahoma	20-14	Miami (Fla.)
1-1-90	Orange	No. 4 Notre Dame beat No. 1 Colorado	21-6	Miami (Fla.)
1-1-93	Sugar	No. 2 Alabama beat No. 1 Miami (Fla.)	34-13	Alabama
1-2-97	Sugar	No. 3 Florida beat No. 1 Florida St.	52-20	Florida

Associated Press No. 1 Vs. No. 2 in Bowl Games

Date	Bowl	Teams, Score
1-1-63	Rose	No. 1 Southern California 42, No. 2 Wisconsin 37
1-1-64	Cotton	No. 1 Texas 28, No. 2 Navy 6
1-1-69	Rose	No. 1 Ohio St. 27, No. 2 Southern California 16
1-1-72	Orange	No. 1 Nebraska 38, No. 2 Alabama 6
1-1-79	Sugar	No. 2 Alabama 14, No. 1 Penn St. 7
1-1-83	Sugar	No. 2 Penn St. 27, No. 1 Georgia 23
1-2-87	Fiesta	No. 2 Penn St. 14, No. 1 Miami (Fla.) 10
1-1-88	Orange	No. 2 Miami (Fla.) 20, No. 1 Oklahoma 14
1-1-93	Sugar*	No. 2 Alabama 34, No. 1 Miami (Fla.) 13
1-1-94	Orange*	No. 1 Florida St. 18, No. 2 Nebraska 16
1-2-96	Fiesta*	No. 1 Nebraska 62, No. 2 Florida 24
1-4-99	Fiesta#	No. 1 Tennessee 23, No. 2 Florida St. 16
1-4-00	Sugar#	No. 1 Florida St. 46, No. 2 Virginia Tech 29

*Bowl alliance matched the No. 1 and No. 2 teams. #Bowl Championship Series matched the No. 1 and No. 2 teams.

Bowl Games and the National Championship

(How the bowl games determined the national champion from 1965 to present. Year listed is the football season before the bowl games.)
Note: The national champion was selected before the bowl games as follows: Associated Press (1936-64 and 1966-67); United Press International (1950-73); Football Writers Association of America (1954), and National Football Foundation and Hall of Fame (1959-70).

1965 The Associated Press (AP) selected Alabama as national champion after it defeated Nebraska, 39-28, in the Orange Bowl on January 1, 1966.

1968 AP selected Ohio State as national champion after it defeated Southern Californiaifornia, 27-16, in the Rose Bowl on January 1, 1969.

1969 AP selected Texas as national champion after it defeated Notre Dame, 21-17, in the Cotton Bowl on January 1, 1970.

1970 AP selected Nebraska as national champion after it defeated LSU, 17-12, in the Orange Bowl on January 1, 1971.

1971 AP selected Nebraska as national champion after it defeated Alabama, 38-6, in the Orange Bowl on January 1, 1972.

1972 AP selected Southern Californiaifornia as national champion after it defeated Ohio State, 42-17, in the Rose Bowl on January 1, 1973.

1973 AP selected Notre Dame as national champion after it defeated Alabama, 24-23, in the Sugar Bowl on December 31, 1973.

Beginning in 1974, all four of the national polls waited until after the bowl-game results before selecting a national champion. The following list shows how the bowl games figured in the final national championship polls for AP and UPI:

1974 First year of the agreement between the American Football Coaches Association (AFCA) and the UPI Board of Coaches to declare any teams on NCAA probation ineligible for the poll. AP—Oklahoma (11-0-0) did not participate in a bowl game because of NCAA probation. UPI—Southern Californiaifornia (10-1-1) defeated Ohio State, 18-17, in the Rose Bowl on January 1, 1975.

1975 AP and UPI both selected Oklahoma (11-1-0). Coach Barry Switzer's Sooners defeated Michigan, 14-6, in the Orange Bowl on January 1, 1976. Ohio State had led the AP poll for nine consecutive weeks until a 23-10 loss to UCLA in the Rose Bowl on January 1, 1976. Oklahoma had led the AP poll for the first four weeks of the year.

1976 AP and UPI both selected Tony Dorsett-led Pittsburgh (12-0-0). Pittsburgh whipped Georgia, 27-3, in the Sugar Bowl on January 1, 1977. Pittsburgh took over the No. 1 position from Michigan in the ninth week of the season en route to an undefeated year.

1977 AP and UPI were in agreement again, picking Notre Dame as national titlist. The Irish crushed previously undefeated and top-ranked Texas, 38-10, in the Cotton Bowl on January 2, 1978. Notre Dame was the sixth team to be ranked No. 1 during the 1977 season in the AP poll.

1978 This was the last time until the 1991 season that the two polls split on a national champion, with AP selecting Alabama (11-1-0) and UPI going for Southern Californiaifornia (12-1-0). Alabama, ranked No. 2 in the AP poll, upset No. 1 Penn State, 14-7, in the Sugar Bowl on January 1, 1979. Alabama had been ranked No. 1 in the first two weeks of the season until a 24-14 loss to Southern Californiaifornia.

1979 Unbeaten Alabama (12-0-0) was the unanimous choice of both polls. Bear Bryant's Tide whipped Arkansas easily, 24-9, in the Sugar Bowl on January 1, 1980, to claim the title.

1980 Georgia made it three No. 1's in a row for the Southeastern Conference with an undefeated season (12-0-0) to take the top spot in both polls. Vince Dooley's Bulldogs downed Notre Dame, 17-10, behind freshman phenom Herschel Walker in the Sugar Bowl on January 1, 1981.

1981 Both polls selected unbeaten Clemson (12-0-0). The Tigers gave coach Danny Ford the first Clemson national football championship with a 22-15 victory over Nebraska in the Orange Bowl on January 1, 1982. Clemson did not take over the AP No. 1 slot until the next-to-last poll of the year.

1982 AP and UPI both selected Penn State (11-1-0). The Nittany Lions were No. 2 in the AP poll but knocked off No. 1 Georgia, 27-23, in the Sugar Bowl on January 1, 1983. Georgia had led the AP poll for the final five weeks of the season.

1983 AP and UPI had no choice but to select Miami (Florida) as the unanimous champion after the No. 2 Hurricanes downed No. 1 Nebraska, 31-30, in the Orange Bowl on January 2, 1984. Many observers felt this may have been the most exciting Orange Bowl ever played as the Cornhuskers failed on a two-point conversion attempt with 48 seconds remaining. Nebraska had led the AP poll since the first week of the season.

1984 Unknown and a victim of the Mountain time zone, Brigham Young (13-0-0) overcame many obstacles to ascend to No. 1 in both polls. Coach LaVell Edwards' Cougars downed Michigan, 24-17, in the Holiday Bowl on December 21, 1984. BYU took over the top spot in the AP poll with three weeks left in the season after four other teams came and went as the top-rated team.

1985 Oklahoma (11-1-0) returned as the unanimous choice of both polls. Barry Switzer's Sooners knocked off top-rated Penn State, 25-10, in the Orange Bowl on January 1, 1986, to claim the national title.

1986 Penn State (12-0-0) had to battle top-rated Miami (Florida) in the Fiesta Bowl to take the top slot in both polls. Joe Paterno's No. 2 Nittany Lions upset the Hurricanes, 14-10, on January 2, 1987, to claim the championship. Miami (Florida) had been ranked No. 1 for the final 10 weeks of the season.

1987 Miami (Florida) (12-0-0) bounced back to a similar scenario as Jimmy Johnson's Hurricanes played underdog and finished ranked first in both polls. The No. 2 Hurricanes beat No. 1-ranked Oklahoma, 20-14, in the Orange Bowl on January 1, 1988. The Sooners had been the top-rated AP team for 13 of the season's 15 polls.

1988 Notre Dame (12-0-0) finished as the top team in both polls and gave the Fiesta Bowl its second national title game in three seasons. Lou Holtz's Irish whipped West Virginia, 34-21, on January 2, 1989, to claim their eighth AP title. Notre Dame took over the top spot in the poll from UCLA in the ninth week of the season.

1989 Miami (Florida) (11-1-0) claimed its second national title in three years in both polls. The Hurricanes downed Alabama, 33-25, in the Sugar Bowl on January 1, 1990, while No. 1-ranked Colorado lost to Notre Dame, 21-6, in the Orange Bowl to clear the way. Notre Dame led the AP poll for 12 of the 15 weeks.

1990 Colorado (11-1-0) and Georgia Tech (11-0-1) split the polls for the first time since 1978 with the Buffs taking the AP vote and the Jackets the UPI. Colorado bounced back from a disappointing 1989 title march to edge Notre Dame, 10-9, in the Orange Bowl on January 1, 1991. Georgia Tech had little trouble with Nebraska, 45-21, in the Florida Citrus Bowl on January 1, 1991, to finish as Division I-A's only undefeated team.

1991 Miami (Florida) (12-0-0) and Washington (12-0-0) kept Division I-A playoff talk alive with a split in the national polls for the second consecutive year. The Hurricanes took the AP vote, while the Huskies took both the USA Today/CNN and UPI polls. If either had stumbled in a bowl, then the other would have been a unanimous selection. However, Washington drubbed Michigan, 34-14, in the Rose Bowl, and Miami (Florida) had little trouble shutting out Nebraska, 22-0, in the Orange Bowl later that evening.

1992 No. 2 Alabama (13-0-0) turned in a magnificent performance in the Sugar Bowl by upsetting No. 1 Miami (Florida), 34-13, in a game dominated by the Crimson Tide. It marked the first year of the bowl coalition, and the bowlmeisters managed to match the top two teams for the national championship. It also marked the 17th time that a No. 1 team in the AP poll was knocked off in a bowl game since 1951. Alabama was named No. 1 in all polls after the January 1, 1993, matchup.

1993 No. 1 Florida State downed No. 2 Nebraska, 18-16, in the Orange Bowl to become a unanimous national champion. Notre Dame, winner over Texas A&M (24-21) in the Cotton Bowl, wanted to claim the title after beating the Seminoles in the regular season. But a late-season loss to Boston College cost the Irish in the polls. Florida State was No. 1 in all polls after the bowls.

1994 No. 1 Nebraska halted a seven-game bowl losing streak by posting a come-from-behind victory, 24-17, over Miami (Florida) in the Orange Bowl to cap a perfect 13-0 season with the national title. No. 2 Penn State, also undefeated at 12-0, downed Oregon, 38-20, in the Rose Bowl but had to settle for second place in the polls. Nebraska was No. 1 in all polls after the bowls.

1995 Another unanimous year for undefeated and No. 1 Nebraska. The Cornhuskers posted back-to-back national titles with a convincing 62-24 victory over No. 2 Florida in the bowl alliance's Fiesta Bowl matchup.

1996 No. 3 Florida took the national crown in all polls after meeting and beating No. 1 Florida State, 52-20, in the bowl alliance matchup in the Sugar Bowl. Just a month earlier, the Seminoles had knocked off No. 1 Florida and the Gators returned the favor. No. 2 Arizona State was defeated, 20-17, by Ohio State in the non-alliance Rose Bowl and dropped out of national championship consideration.

1997 In the last year before the bowl alliance would include the Rose Bowl, the two top-ranked teams—Michigan and Nebraska—never met for the title. Michigan, the final No. 1 in the Associated Press media poll defeated Washington State, 21-16, in the Rose Bowl while Nebraska, No. 1 in the final USA Today/ESPN coaches' poll, rolled over Tennessee, 42-17, in the Orange Bowl. Both teams were rewarded with a piece of the national title. It was the fourth time in the 1990s that the national champion was either shared or unclear.

1998 In the first year of the Bowl Championship Series (BCS), the No. 1 and No. 2 teams (Tennessee and Florida State, respectively) met for the title in the Fiesta. The BCS rankings were a compilation of the Associated Press, USA Today/ESPN, Seattle Times, New York Times, Sagarin polls and schedule strength to arrive at the top two teams. Tennessee defeated Florida State, 23-16, and was a unanimous No. 1 in all polls.

1999 In the second year of the BCS, No. 1 Florida State met No. 2 Virginia Tech in the Sugar Bowl. Florida State downed the Hokies, 46-29, to capture the title. The Seminoles, ranked No. 1 all year, went wire-to-wire in most polls for its second national prize in the 1990s.

Bowl Results of Teams Ranked in The Associated Press Poll

The bowls and national polls have been perpetually linked since 1936, when The Associated Press introduced its weekly college football poll. The final AP poll was released at the end of the regular season until 1965, when bowl results were included for one year, dropped for two more and then added again in 1968 until the present. This is a list of the key bowl games as they related to the AP poll since 1936 (with pertinent references made to other polls where applicable).

(Key to polls: AP, Associated Press; UPI, United Press International; FW, Football Writers; NFF, National Football Foundation and Hall of Fame; USA/CNN, USA Today/Cable News Network; USA/NFF, USA Today/National Football Foundation and Hall of Fame; UPI/NFF, United Press International/National Football Foundation and Hall of Fame.)

1936 SUGAR—No. 6 Santa Clara beat No. 2 LSU, 21-14; ROSE—No. 3 Pittsburgh beat No. 5 Washington, 21-0; ORANGE—No. 14 Duquesne beat unranked Mississippi St., 13-12; COTTON—No. 16 TCU beat No. 20 Marquette, 16-6. (Minnesota selected No. 1 but did not play in a bowl)

1937 ROSE—No. 2 California beat No. 4 Alabama, 13-0; SUGAR—No. 9 Santa Clara beat No. 8 LSU, 6-0; COTTON—No. 18 Rice beat No. 17 Colorado, 28-14. (Pittsburgh selected No. 1 but did not play in a bowl)

1938 SUGAR—No. 1 TCU beat No. 6 Carnegie Mellon, 15-7; ORANGE—No. 2 Tennessee beat No. 4 Oklahoma, 17-0; ROSE—No. 7 Southern California beat No. 3 Duke, 7-3; COTTON—Unranked St. Mary's (Cal.) beat No. 11 Texas Tech, 20-13. (TCU selected No. 1)

1939 SUGAR—No. 1 Texas A&M beat No. 5 Tulane, 14-13; ROSE—No. 3 Southern California beat No. 2 Tennessee, 14-0; ORANGE—No. 16 Georgia Tech beat No. 6 Missouri, 21-7; COTTON—No. 12 Clemson beat No. 11 Boston College, 6-3. (Texas A&M selected No. 1)

1940 ROSE—No. 2 Stanford beat No. 7 Nebraska, 21-13; SUGAR—No. 5 Boston College beat No. 4 Tennessee, 19-13; COTTON—No. 6 Texas A&M beat No. 12 Fordham, 13-12; ORANGE—No. 9 Mississippi St. beat No. 13 Georgetown, 14-7. (Minnesota selected No. 1 but did not play in a bowl)

1941 ROSE—No. 12 Oregon St. beat No. 2 Duke, 20-16 (played at Durham, N.C., because of World War II); SUGAR—No. 2 Fordham beat No. 7 Missouri, 2-0; COTTON—No. 20 Alabama beat No. 9 Texas A&M, 29-21; ORANGE—No. 14 Georgia beat unranked TCU, 40-26. (Minnesota selected No. 1 but did not play in a bowl)

1942 ROSE—No. 2 Georgia beat No. 13 UCLA, 9-0; SUGAR—No. 7 Tennessee beat No. 4 Tulsa, 14-7; COTTON—No. 11 Texas beat No. 5 Georgia Tech, 14-7; ORANGE—No. 10 Alabama beat No. 8 Boston College, 37-21. (Ohio St. selected No. 1 but did not play in a bowl)

1943 ROSE—Unranked Southern California beat No. 12 Washington, 29-0; COTTON—No. 14 Texas tied unranked Randolph Field, 7-7; SUGAR—No. 13 Georgia Tech beat No. 15 Tulsa, 20-18. (Notre Dame selected No. 1 but did not play in a bowl)

1944 ROSE—No. 7 Southern California beat No. 12 Tennessee, 25-0; ORANGE—Unranked Tulsa beat No. 13 Georgia Tech, 26-12; No. 3 Randolph Field beat No. 20 Second Air Force, 13-6, in a battle of military powers. (Army selected No. 1 but did not play in a bowl)

1945 ROSE—No. 2 Alabama beat No. 11 Southern California, 34-14; COTTON—No. 10 Texas beat unranked Missouri, 40-27; ORANGE—Unranked Miami (Fla.) beat No. 16 Holy Cross, 13-6; SUGAR—No. 5 Oklahoma St. beat No. 7 St. Mary's (Cal.), 33-13. (Army selected No. 1 but did not play in a bowl)

1946 COTTON—No. 8 LSU tied No. 16 Arkansas, 0-0; ROSE—No. 5 Illinois beat No. 4 UCLA, 45-14; SUGAR—No. 3 Georgia beat No. 9 North Carolina, 20-10; ORANGE—No. 10 Rice beat No. 7 Tennessee, 8-0. (Notre Dame selected No. 1 but did not play in a bowl)

1947 ORANGE—No. 10 Georgia Tech beat No. 12 Kansas, 20-14; ROSE—No. 2 Michigan beat No. 8 Southern California, 49-0; SUGAR—No. 5 Texas beat No. 6 Alabama, 27-7; COTTON—No. 3 Southern Methodist tied No. 4 Penn St., 13-13. (Notre Dame selected No. 1 but did not play in a bowl; Michigan also declared champion in vote after Rose Bowl victory but AP kept Notre Dame as vote of record)

1948 ROSE—No. 7 Northwestern beat No. 4 California, 20-14; COTTON—No. 10 Southern Methodist beat No. 9 Oregon, 21-13; SUGAR—No. 5 Oklahoma beat No. 3 North Carolina, 14-6; ORANGE—Unranked Texas beat No. 8 Georgia, 41-28. (Michigan selected No. 1 but did not play in a bowl)

1949 ORANGE—No. 15 Santa Clara beat No. 11 Kentucky, 21-13; COTTON—No. 5 Rice beat No. 16 North Carolina, 27-13; ROSE—No. 6 Ohio St. beat No. 3 California, 17-14; SUGAR—No. 2 Oklahoma beat No. 9 LSU, 35-0. (Notre Dame selected No. 1 but did not play in a bowl)

1950 ROSE—No. 9 Michigan beat No. 5 California, 14-6; SUGAR—No. 7 Kentucky beat No. 1 Oklahoma, 13-7; ORANGE—No. 10 Clemson beat No. 15 Miami (Fla.), 15-14; COTTON—No. 4 Tennessee beat No. 3 Texas, 20-14. (Oklahoma selected No. 1 in vote before losing in Sugar Bowl)

1951 COTTON—No. 15 Kentucky beat No. 11 TCU, 20-7; ORANGE—No. 5 Georgia Tech beat No. 9 Baylor, 17-14; ROSE—No. 4 Illinois beat No. 7 Stanford, 40-7; SUGAR—No. 3 Maryland beat No. 1 Tennessee, 28-13. (Tennessee selected No. 1 in vote before losing in Sugar Bowl)

1952 ROSE—No. 5 Southern California beat No. 11 Wisconsin, 7-0; SUGAR—No. 2 Georgia Tech beat No. 7 Mississippi, 24-7; ORANGE—No. 9 Alabama beat No. 14 Syracuse, 61-6; COTTON—No. 10 Texas beat No. 8 Tennessee, 16-0. (Michigan St. selected No. 1 but did not play in a bowl)

1953 SUGAR—No. 8 Georgia Tech beat No. 10 West Virginia, 42-19; ORANGE—No. 4 Oklahoma beat No. 1 Maryland, 7-0; COTTON—No. 5 Rice beat No. 13 Alabama, 28-6; ROSE—No. 3 Michigan St. beat No. 5 UCLA, 28-20. (Maryland selected No. 1 before losing in Orange Bowl)

1954 ROSE—No. 1 Ohio St. beat No. 17 Southern California, 20-7; ORANGE—No. 14 Duke beat unranked Nebraska, 34-7; SUGAR—No. 5 Navy beat No. 6 Mississippi, 21-0; COTTON—Unranked Georgia Tech beat No. 10 Arkansas, 14-6. (Ohio St. remained No. 1 but UCLA named in UPI and FW polls)

1955 GATOR—Unranked Vanderbilt beat No. 8 Auburn, 25-13; ROSE—No. 2 Michigan St. beat No. 4 UCLA, 17-14; ORANGE—No. 1 Oklahoma beat No. 3 Maryland, 20-6; COTTON—No. 10 Mississippi beat No. 6 TCU, 14-13; SUGAR—No. 7 Georgia Tech beat No. 11 Pittsburgh, 7-0. (Oklahoma remained No. 1)

1956 SUGAR—No. 11 Baylor beat No. 2 Tennessee, 13-7; ORANGE—No. 20 Colorado beat No. 19 Clemson, 27-21; GATOR—No. 4 Georgia Tech beat No. 13 Pittsburgh, 21-14; ROSE—No. 3 Iowa beat No. 10 Oregon St., 35-19; COTTON—No. 14 TCU beat No. 8 Syracuse, 28-27. (Oklahoma selected No. 1 but did not play in a bowl)

1957 GATOR—No. 13 Tennessee beat No. 9 Texas A&M, 3-0; ROSE—No. 2 Ohio St. beat unranked Oregon, 10-7; COTTON—No. 5 Navy beat No. 8 Rice, 20-7; ORANGE—No. 4 Oklahoma beat No. 16 Duke, 48-21; SUGAR—No. 7 Mississippi beat No. 11 Texas, 39-7. (Auburn selected No. 1 but did not play in a bowl; Ohio St. selected No. 1 in both FW and FW polls)

1958 SUGAR—No. 1 LSU beat No. 12 Clemson, 7-0; COTTON—No. 6 Air Force tied No. 10 TCU, 0-0; ROSE—No. 2 Iowa beat No. 16 California, 38-12; ORANGE—No. 5 Oklahoma beat No. 9 Syracuse, 21-6. (LSU remained No. 1 in AP and UPI but Iowa selected in FW poll)

1959 COTTON—No. 1 Syracuse beat No. 4 Texas, 23-14; ROSE—No. 8 Washington beat No. 6 Wisconsin, 44-8; ORANGE—No. 5 Georgia beat No. 18 Missouri, 14-0; SUGAR—No. 2 Mississippi beat No. 3 LSU, 21-0; BLUEBONNET—No. 11 Clemson beat No. 7 TCU, 23-7; LIBERTY—No. 12 Penn St. beat No. 10 Alabama, 7-0; GATOR—No. 9 Arkansas beat unranked Georgia Tech, 14-7. (Syracuse selected No. 1 by all four polls)

1960 ROSE—No. 6 Washington beat No. 1 Minnesota, 17-7; COTTON—No. 10 Duke beat No. 7 Arkansas, 7-6; SUGAR—No. 2 Mississippi beat unranked Rice, 14-6; ORANGE—No. 5 Missouri beat No. 4 Navy, 21-14; BLUEBONNET—No. 9 Alabama tied unranked Texas, 3-3. (Minnesota selected No. 1 by AP, UPI and NFF before losing in Rose Bowl; Mississippi named No. 1 in FW poll)

1961 COTTON—No. 3 Texas beat No. 5 Mississippi, 12-7; SUGAR—No. 1 Alabama beat No. 9 Arkansas, 10-3; ORANGE—No. 4 LSU beat No. 7 Colorado, 25-7; GOTHAM—Unranked Baylor beat No. 10 Utah St., 24-9; ROSE—No. 6 Minnesota beat No. 16 UCLA, 21-3. (Alabama selected No. 1 in AP, UPI and NFF, but Ohio St. picked by FW poll)

1962 ROSE—No. 1 Southern California beat No. 2 Wisconsin, 42-37; SUGAR—No. 3 Mississippi beat No. 6 Arkansas, 17-13; COTTON—No. 5 LSU beat No. 4 Texas, 13-0; GATOR—Unranked Florida beat No. 9 Penn St., 17-7; ORANGE—No. 5 Alabama beat No. 8 Oklahoma, 17-0. (Southern California selected No. 1 by all four polls)

1963 COTTON—No. 1 Texas beat No. 2 Navy, 28-6; ORANGE—No. 6 Nebraska beat No. 5 Auburn, 13-7; ROSE—No. 3 Illinois beat unranked Washington, 17-7; SUGAR—No. 8 Alabama beat No. 7 Mississippi, 12-7. (Texas selected No. 1 by all four polls)

1964 ORANGE—No. 5 Texas beat No. 1 Alabama, 21-17; ROSE—No. 4 Michigan beat No. 8 Oregon St., 34-7; COTTON—No. 2 Arkansas beat No. 6 Nebraska, 10-7; SUGAR—No. 7 LSU beat unranked Syracuse, 13-10. (Alabama selected No. 1 by AP and UPI before losing in the Orange Bowl, while Arkansas No. 1 in FW poll and Notre Dame No. 1 in NFF poll)

1965 *(First year final poll taken after bowl games)* ROSE—No. 5 UCLA beat No. 1 Michigan St., 14-12; COTTON—Unranked LSU beat No. 2 Arkansas, 14-7; SUGAR—No. 6 Missouri beat unranked Florida, 20-18; ORANGE—No. 4 Alabama beat No. 3 Nebraska, 39-28; BLUEBONNET—No. 7 Tennessee beat unranked Tulsa, 27-6; GATOR—Unranked Georgia Tech beat No. 10 Texas Tech, 31-21. (Alabama selected No. 1 in final poll but Michigan St. named by UPI and NFF polls and they tied in FW poll)

1966 *(Returned to final poll taken before bowls)* SUGAR—No. 3 Alabama beat No. 6 Nebraska, 34-7; ROSE—No. 7 Purdue beat unranked Southern California, 14-13; COTTON—No. 4 Georgia beat No. 10 Southern Methodist, 24-9; ORANGE—Unranked Florida beat No. 8 Georgia Tech, 27-12; LIBERTY—No. 9 Miami (Fla.) beat unranked Virginia Tech, 14-7. (Notre Dame selected No. 1 by AP, UPI and FW polls and tied with Michigan St. in NFF poll; neither team played in a bowl game and they tied in a regular-season game)

1967 ROSE—No. 1 Southern California beat No. 4 Indiana, 14-3; SUGAR—Unranked LSU beat No. 9 Wyoming, 20-13; ORANGE—No. 3 Oklahoma beat No. 2 Tennessee, 26-24; COTTON—Unranked Texas A&M beat No. 8 Alabama, 20-16; GATOR—No. 10 Penn St. tied unranked Florida St., 17-17. (Southern California selected No. 1 in all four polls)

1968 *(Returned to final poll taken after bowl games)* ROSE—No. 1 Ohio St. beat No. 2 Southern California, 27-16; SUGAR—No. 9 Arkansas beat No. 4 Georgia, 16-2; ORANGE—No. 3 Penn St. beat No. 6 Kansas, 15-14; COTTON—No. 5 Texas beat No. 8 Tennessee, 36-13; BLUEBONNET—No. 20 Southern Methodist beat No. 10 Oklahoma, 28-27; GATOR—No. 16 Missouri beat No. 12 Alabama, 35-10. (Ohio St. remained No. 1)

1969 COTTON—No. 1 Texas beat No. 9 Notre Dame, 21-17; SUGAR—No. 13 Mississippi beat No. 3 Arkansas, 27-22; ORANGE—No. 2 Penn St. beat No. 6 Missouri, 10-3; ROSE—No. 5 Southern California beat No. 7 Michigan, 10-3. (Texas remained No. 1)

1970 COTTON—No. 6 Notre Dame beat No. 1 Texas, 24-11; ROSE—No. 12 Stanford beat No. 2 Ohio St., 27-17; SUGAR—No. 5 Tennessee beat No. 11 Air Force, 34-13; ORANGE—No. 3 Nebraska beat No. 8 LSU, 17-12; PEACH—No. 9 Arizona St. beat unranked North Carolina, 48-26. (Nebraska selected No. 1 in AP and FW polls while Texas was No. 1 in UPI and tied with Ohio St. in NFF poll)

1971 ORANGE—No. 1 Nebraska beat No. 2 Alabama, 38-6; SUGAR—No. 3 Oklahoma beat No. 5 Auburn, 40-22; ROSE—No. 16 Stanford beat No. 4 Michigan, 13-12; GATOR—No. 6 Georgia beat North Carolina, 7-3; COTTON—No. 10 Penn St. beat No. 12 Texas, 30-6; FIESTA—No. 8 Arizona St. beat unranked Florida St., 45-38; BLUEBONNET—No. 7 Colorado beat No. 15 Houston, 29-17. (Nebraska remained No. 1 in all four polls)

1972 ROSE—No. 1 Southern California beat No. 3 Ohio St., 42-17; COTTON—No. 7 Texas beat No. 4 Alabama, 17-13; SUGAR—No. 2 Oklahoma beat No. 5 Penn St., 14-0; ORANGE—No. 9 Nebraska beat No. 12 Notre Dame, 40-6; GATOR—No. 6

Auburn beat No. 13 Colorado, 24-3; BLUEBONNET—No. 11 Tennessee beat No. 10 LSU, 24-17. (Southern California remained No. 1 in all four polls)

1973 SUGAR—No. 3 Notre Dame beat No. 1 Alabama, 24-23; ROSE—No. 4 Ohio St. beat No. 7 Southern California, 42-21; ORANGE—No. 6 Penn St. beat No. 13 LSU, 16-9; COTTON—No. 12 Nebraska beat No. 8 Texas, 19-3; FIESTA—No. 10 Arizona St. beat unranked Pittsburgh, 28-7; BLUEBONNET—No. 14 Houston beat No. 17 Tulane, 47-7. (Notre Dame selected No. 1 in AP, FW and NFF polls, Alabama named No. 1 by UPI but No. 2 Oklahoma was on probation and could not go to a bowl game)

1974 ROSE—No. 5 Southern California beat No. 3 Ohio St., 18-17; ORANGE—No. 9 Notre Dame beat No. 2 Alabama, 13-11; GATOR—No. 6 Auburn beat No. 11 Texas, 27-3; COTTON—No. 7 Penn St. beat No. 12 Baylor, 41-20; SUGAR—No. 8 Nebraska beat No. 18 Florida, 13-10; LIBERTY—Unranked Tennessee beat No. 10 Maryland, 7-3. (Oklahoma selected No. 1 in AP poll despite being on probation and not able to participate in bowl game; Southern California named No. 1 by UPI, FW and NFF polls)

1975 ROSE—No. 11 UCLA beat No. 1 Ohio St., 23-10; ORANGE—No. 3 Oklahoma beat No. 5 Michigan, 14-6; LIBERTY—No. 17 Southern California beat No. 2 Texas A&M, 20-0; SUGAR—No. 4 Alabama beat No. 8 Penn St., 13-6; FIESTA—No. 7 Arizona St. beat No. 6 Nebraska, 17-14; COTTON—No. 18 Arkansas beat No. 12 Georgia, 31-10; BLUEBONNET—No. 9 Texas beat No. 10 Colorado, 38-21. (Oklahoma selected No. 1 in all four polls)

1976 SUGAR—No. 1 Pittsburgh beat No. 5 Georgia, 27-3; ROSE—No. 3 Southern California beat No. 2 Michigan, 14-6; COTTON—No. 6 Houston beat No. 4 Maryland, 30-21; LIBERTY—No. 16 Alabama beat No. 7 UCLA, 36-6; ORANGE—No. 11 Ohio St. beat No. 12 Colorado, 27-10; FIESTA—No. 8 Oklahoma beat unranked Wyoming, 41-7; SUN—No. 10 Texas A&M beat unranked Florida, 37-14; BLUEBONNET—No. 13 Nebraska beat No. 9 Texas Tech, 27-24. (Pittsburgh remained No. 1 in all four polls)

1977 COTTON—No. 5 Notre Dame beat No. 1 Texas, 38-10; ORANGE—No. 6 Arkansas beat No. 2 Oklahoma, 31-6; SUGAR—No. 3 Alabama beat No. 9 Ohio St., 35-6; ROSE—No. 13 Washington beat No. 4 Michigan, 27-20; FIESTA—No. 8 Penn St. beat No. 15 Arizona St., 42-30; GATOR—No. 10 Pittsburgh beat No. 11 Clemson, 34-3. (Notre Dame selected No. 1 in all four polls)

1978 SUGAR—No. 2 Alabama beat No. 1 Penn St., 14-7; ROSE—No. 3 Southern California beat No. 5 Michigan, 17-10; ORANGE—No. 4 Oklahoma beat No. 6 Nebraska, 31-24; COTTON—No. 10 Notre Dame beat No. 9 Houston, 35-34; GATOR—No. 7 Clemson beat No. 20 Ohio St., 17-15; FIESTA—No. 8 Arkansas tied No. 15 UCLA, 10-10. (Alabama selected No. 1 in AP, FW and NFF polls, while Southern California named in UPI)

1979 ROSE—No. 3 Southern California beat No. 1 Ohio St., 17-16; SUGAR—No. 2 Alabama beat No. 6 Arkansas, 24-9; ORANGE—No. 5 Oklahoma beat No. 4 Florida St., 24-7; COTTON—No. 8 Houston beat No. 7 Nebraska, 17-14; SUN—No. 13 Washington beat No. 11 Texas, 14-7; FIESTA—No. 10 Pittsburgh beat unranked Arizona, 16-10. (Alabama selected No. 1 in all four polls)

1980 SUGAR—No. 1 Georgia beat No. 7 Notre Dame, 17-10; ORANGE—No. 4 Oklahoma beat No. 2 Florida St., 18-17; ROSE—No. 5 Michigan beat No. 16 Washington, 23-6; COTTON—No. 9 Alabama beat No. 6 Baylor, 30-2; GATOR—No. 3 Pittsburgh beat No. 18 South Carolina, 37-9; SUN—No. 8 Nebraska beat No. 17 Mississippi St., 31-17; FIESTA—No. 10 Penn St. beat No. 11 Ohio St., 31-19; BLUEBONNET—No. 13 North Carolina beat unranked Texas, 16-7. (Georgia remained No. 1 in all four polls)

1981 ORANGE—No. 1 Clemson beat No. 4 Nebraska, 22-15; SUGAR—No. 10 Pittsburgh beat No. 2 Georgia, 24-20; COTTON—No. 6 Texas beat No. 3 Alabama, 14-12; GATOR—No. 11 North Carolina beat unranked Arkansas, 31-27; ROSE—No. 12 Washington beat No. 13 Iowa, 28-0; FIESTA—No. 7 Penn St. beat No. 8 Southern California, 26-10. (Clemson remained No. 1 in all four polls)

1982 SUGAR—No. 2 Penn St. beat No. 1 Georgia, 27-23; ORANGE—No. 5 Nebraska beat No. 13 LSU, 21-20; COTTON—No. 4 Southern Methodist beat No. 6 Pittsburgh, 7-3; ROSE—No. 5 UCLA beat No. 19 Michigan, 24-14; ALOHA—No. 9 Washington beat No. 16 Maryland, 21-20; FIESTA—No. 11 Arizona St. beat No. 12 Oklahoma, 32-21; BLUEBONNET—No. 14 Arkansas beat unranked Florida, 28-24. (Penn St. selected No. 1 in all four polls)

1983 ORANGE—No. 5 Miami (Fla.) beat No. 1 Nebraska, 31-30; COTTON—No. 7 Georgia beat No. 2 Texas, 10-9; SUGAR—No. 3 Auburn beat No. 8 Michigan, 9-7; ROSE—Unranked UCLA beat No. 4 Illinois, 45-9; HOLIDAY—No. 9 Brigham Young beat unranked Missouri, 21-17; GATOR—No. 11 Florida beat No. 10 Iowa, 14-6; FIESTA—No. 14 Ohio St. beat No. 15 Pittsburgh, 28-23. (Miami [Fla.], selected No. 1 in all four polls)

1984 HOLIDAY—No. 1 Brigham Young beat unranked Michigan, 24-17; ORANGE—No. 4 Washington beat No. 2 Oklahoma, 28-17; SUGAR—No. 5 Nebraska beat No. 11 LSU, 28-10; ROSE—No. 18 Southern California beat No. 6 Ohio St., 20-17; COTTON—No. 8 Boston College beat unranked Houston, 45-28; GATOR—No. 9 Oklahoma St. beat No. 7 South Carolina, 21-14; ALOHA—No. 10 Southern Methodist beat No. 17 Notre Dame, 27-20. (Brigham Young remained No. 1 in all four polls)

1985 ORANGE—No. 3 Oklahoma beat No. 1 Penn St., 25-10; SUGAR—No. 8 Tennessee beat No. 2 Miami (Fla.), 35-7; ROSE—No. 13 UCLA beat No. 4 Iowa, 45-28; COTTON—No. 11 Texas A&M beat No. 16 Auburn, 36-16; FIESTA—No. 5 Michigan beat No. 7 Nebraska, 27-23; BLUEBONNET—No. 10 Air Force beat unranked Texas, 24-16. (Oklahoma selected No. 1 in all four polls)

1986 FIESTA—No. 2 Penn St. beat No. 1 Miami (Fla.), 14-10; ORANGE—No. 3 Oklahoma beat No. 9 Arkansas, 42-8; ROSE—No. 7 Arizona St. beat No. 4 Michigan, 22-15; SUGAR—No. 6 Nebraska beat No. 5 LSU, 30-15; COTTON—No. 11 Ohio St. beat No. 8 Texas A&M, 28-12; CITRUS—No. 10 Auburn beat unranked Southern California, 16-7; SUN—No. 13 Alabama beat No. 12 Washington, 28-6. (Penn St. selected No. 1 in all four polls)

1987 ORANGE—No. 2 Miami (Fla.) beat No. 1 Oklahoma, 20-14; FIESTA—No. 3 Florida St. beat No. 5 Nebraska, 31-28; SUGAR—No. 4 Syracuse tied No. 6 Auburn, 16-16; ROSE—No. 8 Michigan St. beat No. 16 Southern California, 20-17; COTTON—No. 13 Texas A&M beat No. 12 Notre Dame, 35-10; GATOR—No. 7 LSU beat No. 9 South Carolina, 30-13; ALOHA—No. 10 UCLA beat unranked Florida, 20-16. (Miami [Fla.], selected No. 1 in all four polls)

1988 FIESTA—No. 1 Notre Dame beat No. 3 West Virginia, 34-21; ORANGE—No. 2 Miami (Fla.) beat No. 6 Nebraska, 23-3; SUGAR—No. 4 Florida St. beat No. 7 Auburn, 13-7; ROSE—No. 11 Michigan beat No. 5 Southern California, 22-14; COTTON—No. 9 UCLA beat No. 8 Arkansas, 17-3; CITRUS—No. 13 Clemson beat No. 10 Oklahoma, 13-6. (Notre Dame selected No. 1 in all four polls)

1989 ORANGE—No. 4 Notre Dame beat No. 1 Colorado, 21-6; SUGAR—No. 2 Miami (Fla.) beat No. 7 Alabama, 33-25; ROSE—No. 12 Southern California beat No. 3 Michigan, 17-10; COTTON—No. 8 Tennessee beat No. 10 Arkansas, 31-27; FIESTA—No. 5 Florida St. beat No. 6 Nebraska, 41-17; HALL OF FAME—No. 9 Auburn beat No. 21 Ohio St., 31-14; CITRUS—No. 11 Illinois beat No. 15 Virginia, 31-21. (Miami [Fla.], selected No. 1 in all four polls)

1990 ORANGE—No. 1 Colorado beat No. 5 Notre Dame, 10-9; CITRUS—No. 2 Georgia Tech beat No. 19 Nebraska, 45-21; COTTON—No. 4 Miami (Fla.) beat No. 3 Texas, 46-3; BLOCKBUSTER—No. 6 Florida St. beat No. 7 Penn St., 24-17; ROSE—No. 8 Washington beat No. 17 Iowa, 46-34; GATOR—No. 12 Michigan beat No. 23 Mississippi, 35-3; SUGAR—No. 10 Tennessee beat unranked Virginia, 23-22. (Colorado selected No. 1 in AP, FW and NFF polls, but Georgia Tech picked in UPI poll)

1991 ORANGE—No. 1 Miami (Fla.) beat No. 11 Nebraska, 22-0; ROSE—No. 2 Washington beat No. 4 Michigan, 34-14; COTTON—No. 5 Florida St. beat No. 9 Texas A&M, 10-3; BLOCKBUSTER—No. 8 Alabama beat No. 15 Colorado, 30-25; SUGAR—No. 18 Notre Dame beat No. 3 Florida, 39-28; FIESTA—No. 6 Penn St. beat No. 10 Tennessee, 42-17; CITRUS—No. 14 California beat No. 13 Clemson, 37-13; PEACH—No. 12 East Caro. beat No. 21 North Carolina St., 37-34; HOLIDAY—No. 7 Iowa tied unranked Brigham Young, 13-13. (Miami [Fla.], selected No. 1 in AP poll, while Washington named in USA/CNN, NFF and FW polls)

1992 SUGAR—No. 2 Alabama beat No. 1 Miami (Fla.), 34-13; GATOR—No. 14 Florida beat No. 12 North Carolina St., 27-10; COTTON—No. 5 Notre Dame beat No. 4 Texas A&M, 28-3; HALL OF FAME—No. 7 Tennessee beat No. 16 Boston College, 38-23; CITRUS—No. 8 Georgia beat No. 15 Ohio St., 21-14; ROSE—No. 7 Michigan beat No. 9 Washington, 38-31; ORANGE—No. 3 Florida St. beat No. 11 Nebraska, 27-14; FIESTA—No. 6 Syracuse beat No. 10 Colorado, 26-22; BLOCKBUSTER—No. 13 Stanford beat No. 18 Penn St., 24-3; PEACH—No. 19 North Carolina beat No. 24 Mississippi St., 21-17; COPPER—No. 18 Washington St. beat unranked Utah, 31-28. (Alabama selected No. 1 in all four polls)

1993 ORANGE—No. 1 Florida St. beat No. 2 Nebraska, 18-16; SUGAR—No. 8 Florida beat No. 3 West Virginia, 41-7; ROSE—No. 9 Wisconsin beat No. 14 UCLA, 21-16; COTTON—No. 4 Notre Dame beat No. 7 Texas A&M, 24-21; CARQUEST—No. 15 Boston College beat unranked Virginia, 31-13; FIESTA—No. 16 Arizona beat No. 10 Miami (Fla.), 29-0; FLORIDA CITRUS—No. 13 Penn St. beat No. 6 Tennessee, 31-13; HALL OF FAME—No. 23 Michigan beat unranked North Carolina St., 42-7; GATOR—No. 18 Alabama beat No. 12 North Carolina, 24-10; PEACH—No. 24 Clemson beat unranked Kentucky, 14-13; INDEPENDENCE—No. 22 Virginia Tech beat unranked Indiana, 45-20; HOLIDAY—No. 11 Ohio St. beat unranked Brigham Young, 28-21; COPPER—No. 20 Kansas St. beat unranked Wyoming, 52-17; LIBERTY—No. 25 Louisville beat unranked Michigan St., 18-7; ALOHA—No. 17 Colorado beat No. 25 Fresno St., 41-30; JOHN HANCOCK—No. 19 Oklahoma beat unranked Texas Tech, 41-10. (Florida St. selected in all four major polls—AP, FW, USA/CNN and USA/NFF)

1994 ORANGE—No. 1 Nebraska beat No. 3 Miami (Fla.), 24-17; ROSE—No. 2 Penn St. beat No. 12 Oregon, 38-20; FIESTA—No. 4 Colorado beat unranked Notre Dame, 41-24; SUGAR—No. 7 Florida St. beat No. 5 Florida, 23-17; FLORIDA CITRUS—No. 6 Alabama beat No. 13 Ohio St., 24-17; FREEDOM—No. 14 Utah beat No. 15 Arizona, 16-13; ALOHA—Unranked Boston College beat No. 11 Kansas St., 12-7; HOLIDAY—No. 20 Michigan beat No. 10 Colorado St., 24-14; PEACH—No. 23 North Carolina St. beat No. 16 Mississippi St., 28-24; INDEPENDENCE—No. 18 Virginia beat unranked TCU, 20-10; SUN—Unranked Texas beat No. 19 North Carolina, 35-31; GATOR—Unranked Tennessee beat No. 17 Virginia Tech, 45-23. (Nebraska selected in all four major polls—AP, UPI, USA/CNN and FW)

1995 FIESTA—No. 1 Nebraska beat No. 2 Florida, 62-24; ROSE—No. 17 Southern California beat No. 3 Northwestern, 41-32; FLORIDA CITRUS—No. 4 Tennessee beat No. 4 Ohio St., 20-14; ORANGE—No. 8 Florida St. beat No. 6 Notre Dame, 31-26; COTTON—No. 7 Colorado beat No. 22 Oregon, 38-6; SUGAR—No. 13 Virginia Tech beat No. 9 Texas, 28-10; HOLIDAY—No. 10 Kansas St. beat unranked Colorado St., 54-21; ALOHA—No. 11 Kansas beat unranked UCLA, 51-30; ALAMO—No. 19 Texas A&M beat No. 14 Michigan, 22-20; OUTBACK—No. 15 Penn St. beat No. 16 Auburn, 43-14; PEACH—No. 18 Virginia beat unranked Georgia, 34-27. (Nebraska selected in all four major polls—AP, UPI, USA/CNN and FW)

1996 SUGAR—No. 3 Florida beat No. 1 Florida St., 52-20; FIESTA—No. 7 Penn St. beat No. 20 Texas, 38-15; ROSE—No. 4 Ohio St. beat No. 2 Arizona St., 20-17; COTTON—No. 5 Brigham Young beat No. 14 Kansas St., 19-15; FLORIDA CITRUS—No. 9 Tennessee beat No. 11 Northwestern, 48-28; GATOR—No. 12 North Carolina beat No. 25 West Virginia, 20-13; OUTBACK—No. 16 Alabama beat No. 15 Michigan, 17-14; ORANGE—No. 6 Nebraska beat No. 10 Virginia Tech, 41-21; INDEPENDENCE—Unranked Auburn beat No. 24 Army, 32-29; SUN—Unranked Stanford beat unranked Michigan St., 38-0; HOLIDAY—No. 8 Colorado beat No. 13 Washington, 33-21; ALAMO—No. 21 Iowa beat unranked Texas Tech, 27-0; PEACH—No. 17 LSU beat unranked Clemson, 10-7; COPPER—Unranked Wisconsin beat unranked Utah, 38-10; CARQUEST—No. 19 Miami (Fla.) beat unranked Virginia, 31-21; LIBERTY—No. 23 Syracuse beat unranked Houston, 30-17; ALOHA—Unranked Navy beat unranked California, 42-38; LAS VEGAS—Unranked Nevada beat unranked Ball St., 18-15. (Florida selected in all four major polls—AP, USA/CNN, FW and NFF/HOF)

1997 ROSE—No. 1 Michigan beat No. 9 Washington St., 21-16; ORANGE—No. 2 Nebraska beat No. 7 Tennessee, 42-17; SUGAR—No. 3 Florida beat No. 12 Ohio St., 31-14; FIESTA—No. 8 Kansas St. beat No. 21 Syracuse, 35-18; COTTON—No. 5

UCLA beat No. 20 Texas A&M, 29-23; FLORIDA CITRUS—No. 4 Florida beat No. 16 Penn St., 21-6; ALAMO—No. 15 Purdue beat No. 24 Oklahoma St., 33-20; GATOR—No. 6 North Carolina beat unranked Virginia Tech, 42-3; HOLIDAY—No. 17 Colorado St. beat No. 23 Missouri, 35-24; PEACH—No. 11 Auburn beat unranked Clemson, 21-17; LAS VEGAS—Unranked Oregon beat unranked Air Force, 41-13; ALOHA—No. 18 Washington beat unranked Michigan St., 51-23; MOTOR CITY—No. 22 Mississippi beat unranked Marshall, 34-31; INSIGHT.COM—Unranked Arizona beat unranked New Mexico, 20-14; INDEPENDENCE—No. 13 LSU beat unranked Notre Dame, 27-9; CARQUEST—No. 25 Georgia Tech beat unranked West Virginia, 35-30; HUMANITARIAN—Unranked Cincinnati beat unranked Utah St., 35-19; SUN—No. 14 Arizona St. beat unranked Iowa, 17-7; LIBERTY—No. 19 Southern Miss. beat unranked Pittsburgh, 41-7; OUTBACK—No. 10 Georgia beat unranked Wisconsin, 33-6. (Michigan selected by AP [media], FW and NFF/HOF while Nebraska was picked by the USA/ESPN [coaches])

1998 FIESTA—No. 1 Tennessee beat No. 2 Florida St., 23-16; SUGAR—No. 3 Ohio St. beat No. 8 Texas A&M, 24-14; ROSE—No. 9 Wisconsin beat No. 6 UCLA, 38-31; ORANGE—No. 7 Florida beat No. 18 Syracuse, 31-10; HOLIDAY—No. 5 Arizona beat No. 14 Nebraska, 23-20; FLORIDA CITRUS—No. 15 Michigan beat No. 11 Arkansas, 45-31; GATOR—No. 12 Georgia Tech beat No. 17 Notre Dame, 35-28; COTTON—No. 20 Texas beat No. 25 Mississippi St., 38-11; PEACH—No. 19 Georgia beat No. 13 Virginia, 35-33; LIBERTY—No. 10 Tulane beat unranked Brigham Young, 41-27; OUTBACK—No. 22 Penn St. beat unranked Kentucky, 26-14; MICRON PC—No. 24 Miami (Fla.) beat unranked North Carolina St., 46-23; OAHU CLASSIC—No. 16 Air Force beat unranked Washington, 45-25; ALOHA CLASSIC—Unranked Colorado beat No. 21 Oregon, 51-43; INSIGHT.COM—No. 23 Missouri beat unranked West Virginia, 34-31; LAS VEGAS—Unranked North Carolina beat unranked San Diego St., 20-13; MOTOR CITY—Unranked Marshall beat unranked Louisville, 48-29; MUSIC CITY—Unranked Virginia Tech beat unranked Alabama, 38-7; HUMANITARIAN—Unranked Idaho beat unranked Southern Miss., 42-35; SUN—Unranked TCU beat unranked Southern California, 28-19; INDEPENDENCE—Unranked Mississippi beat unranked Texas Tech, 35-18. (Tennessee, No. 1 in the BCS poll, defeated No. 2 Florida St., 23-16, in the Fiesta Bowl and was named champion in all four major polls—AP [media], USA/ESPN [coaches], FW and NFF/HOF)

1999 SUGAR—No. 1 Florida St. beat No. 2 Virginia Tech, 46-29; FIESTA—No. 3 Nebraska beat No. 6 Tennessee, 31-21; ROSE—No. 4 Wisconsin beat No. 22 Stanford, 17-9; ORANGE—No. 8 Michigan beat No. 5 Alabama, 35-34 in overtime; HOLIDAY—No. 7 Kansas St. beat unranked Washington, 24-20; FLORIDA CITRUS—No. 9 Michigan St. beat No. 10 Florida, 37-34; MOTOR CITY—No. 11 Marshall beat unranked Brigham Young, 21-3; SUN—Unranked Oregon beat No. 12 Minnesota, 24-20; ALAMO—No. 13 Penn St. beat No. 18 Texas A&M, 24-0; COTTON—No. 24 Arkansas beat No. 14 Texas, 27-6; PEACH—No. 15 Mississippi St. beat unranked Clemson, 17-7; LIBERTY—No. 16 Southern Miss. beat unranked Colorado St., 23-17; GATOR—No. 23 Miami (Fla.) beat No. 17 Georgia Tech, 28-13; OUTBACK—No. 21 Georgia beat No. 19 Purdue, 28-25 in overtime; INSIGHT.COM—Unranked Colorado beat No. 25 Boston College, 62-28; LAS VEGAS—Unranked Utah beat unranked Fresno St., 17-16; MOBILE ALABAMA—Unranked TCU beat unranked East Caro., 28-14; ALOHA CLASSIC—Unranked Wake Forest beat unranked Arizona St., 23-3; OAHU CLASSIC—Unranked Hawaii beat unranked Oregon St., 23-17; MUSIC CITY—Unranked Syracuse beat unranked Kentucky, 20-13; HUMANITARIAN—Unranked Boise St. beat unranked Louisville, 34-31; MICRONPC.COM—Unranked Illinois beat unranked Virginia, 63-21; INDEPENDENCE—Unranked Mississippi beat unranked Oklahoma, 27-25. (BCS No. 1 Florida St. beat BCS No. 2 Virginia Tech, 46-29, in the Sugar Bowl and was selected champion in all four major polls—AP [media], USA/ESPN [coaches], FW and NFF/HOF)

Most Consecutive Bowl-Game Victories

(Bowls do not have to be in consecutive years; year listed is calendar year in which bowl was played)

College	Victories (Years)
Florida St.	11 (1985-86-88-89-90-90-92-93-94-95-96)
Southern California	9 (1923-24-30-32-33-39-40-44-45)
UCLA	8 (1983-84-85-86-86-87-89-91)
Georgia Tech	8 (1947-48-52-53-54-55-56-56)
Syracuse	7 (1989-89-90-92-93-96-97)
Colorado	6 (1993-95-96-97-98-99)
Penn St.	6 (1994-95-96-97-98-99)
Alabama	6 (1975-76-78-79-80-81)
Nebraska	6 (1969-71-72-73-74-74)
Arizona St.	5 (1970-71-72-73-75)

College	Victories (Years)
Alabama	5 (1991-93-93-95-97)
Notre Dame	5 (1973-75-76-78-79)
Tennessee	5 (1986-86-88-90-91)
Penn St.	5 (1979-80-81-82-83)
Air Force	4 (1982-83-84-85)
Alabama	4 (1982-83-85-86)
North Carolina	4 (1979-80-81-82)
Michigan	4 (1902-48-51-65)
Southern California	3 (1993-95-96)
California	3 (1990-92-93)
Notre Dame	3 (1992-93-94)

Most Consecutive Seasons With Bowl-Game Victories

11 Florida St.—85 Gator, Oklahoma St. 34-23; 86 All-American, Indiana 27-13; 87 Fiesta, Nebraska 31-28; 88 Sugar, Auburn 13-7; 89 Fiesta, Nebraska 41-17; 90 Blockbuster, Penn St. 24-17; 92 Cotton, Texas A&M 10-2; 93 Orange, Nebraska 27-14; 94 Orange, Nebraska 18-16; 95 Sugar, Florida 23-17; 96 Orange, Notre Dame 31-26. Coach: Bobby Bowden.
7 UCLA—83 Rose, Michigan 24-14; 84 Rose, Illinois 45-9; 85 Fiesta, Miami (Fla.) 39-37; 86 Rose, Iowa 45-28; 86 Freedom, Brigham Young 31-10; 87 Aloha, Florida 20-16; 89 Cotton, Arkansas, 17-3. Coach: Terry Donahue.
6 Georgia Tech—52 Orange, Baylor 17-14; 53 Sugar, Mississippi 24-7; 54 Sugar, West Virginia 42-19; 55 Cotton, Arkansas 14-6; 56 Sugar, Pittsburgh 7-0; 56 Gator, Pittsburgh 21-14. Coach: Bobby Dodd.
6 Nebraska—71 Orange, LSU 17-12; 72 Orange, Alabama 38-6; 73 Orange, Notre Dame 40-6; 74 Cotton, Texas 19-3; 69 Sun, Georgia 45-6; 74 Sugar, Florida 13-10; Coaches: Bob Devaney first 4 games, Tom Osborne last 2.
6 Alabama—75 Sugar, Penn St. 13-6; 76 Liberty, UCLA 36-6; 78 Sugar, Ohio St. 35-6; 79 Sugar, Penn St. 14-7; 80 Sugar, Arkansas 24-9; 81 Cotton, Baylor 30-2. Coach: Paul "Bear" Bryant.

Active Consecutive Appearances in Bowl Games

(Must have appeared in 1999-00 bowls)

Team	Appearances	Team	Appearances
Nebraska	31	Penn St.	11
Michigan	25	Tennessee	11
Florida St.	18		

Most Bowl Teams Faced in 1999

(Teams that faced the most 1999-00 bowl teams during their 1999 regular-season schedule)

Team	No. Faced	Team	No. Faced
South Carolina	9	Duke	6
Notre Dame	8	Florida	6
Ohio St.	8	Florida St.	6
Alabama	7	Iowa	6
California	7	Kentucky	6
Indiana	7	Miami (Fla.)	6
LSU	7	Michigan	6
North Carolina St.	7	Michigan St.	6
Northwestern	7	Nebraska	6
UCLA	7	Oklahoma St.	6
Vanderbilt	7	Penn St.	6
Washington St.	7	Rutgers	6
Arizona	6	Temple	6
Auburn	6	Texas	6
Baylor	6	Virginia	6
Clemson	6	Washington	6

Undefeated, Untied Team Matchups in Bowl Games

Bowl	Date	Winner (Record Going In, Coach)	Loser (Record Going In, Coach)
Rose	1-1-21	California 28 (8-0, Andy Smith)	Ohio St. 0 (7-0, John Wilce)
Rose	1-2-22	0-0 tie: California (9-0, Andy Smith); Wash. & Jeff. (10-0, Earle "Greasy" Neale)	
Rose	1-1-27	7-7 tie: Alabama (9-0, Wallace Wade); Stanford (10-0, Glenn "Pop" Warner)	
Rose	1-1-31	Alabama 24 (9-0, Wallace Wade)	Washington St. 0 (9-0, Orin "Babe" Hollingbery)
Orange	1-2-39	Tennessee 17 (10-0, Bob Neyland)	Oklahoma 0 (10-0, Tom Stidham)
Sugar	1-1-41	Boston College 19 (10-0, Frank Leahy)	Tennessee 13 (10-0, Bob Neyland)
Sugar	1-1-52	Maryland 28 (9-0, Jim Tatum)	Tennessee 13 (10-0, Bob Neyland)
Orange	1-2-56	Oklahoma 20 (10-0, Bud Wilkinson)	Maryland 6 (10-0, Jim Tatum)
Orange	1-1-72	Nebraska 38 (12-0, Bob Devaney)	Alabama 6 (11-0, Paul "Bear" Bryant)
Sugar	12-31-73	Notre Dame 24 (10-0, Ara Parseghian)	Alabama 23 (11-0, Paul "Bear" Bryant)

Bowl	Date	Winner (Record Going In, Coach)	Loser (Record Going In, Coach)
Fiesta	1-2-87	Penn St. 14 (11-0, Joe Paterno)	Miami (Fla.) 10 (11-0, Jimmy Johnson)
Orange	1-1-88	Miami (Fla.) 20 (11-0, Jimmy Johnson)	Oklahoma 14 (11-0, Barry Switzer)
Fiesta	1-2-89	Notre Dame 34 (11-0, Lou Holtz)	West Virginia 21 (11-0, Don Nehlen)
Sugar	1-1-93	Alabama 34 (12-0, Gene Stallings)	Miami (Fla.) 13 (11-0, Dennis Erickson)
Fiesta	1-2-96	Nebraska 62 (11-0, Tom Osborne)	Florida 24 (12-0, Steve Spurrier)
Sugar	1-4-00	Florida St. 46 (11-0, Bobby Bowden)	Virginia Tech 29 (11-0, Frank Beamer)

Undefeated Team Matchups in Bowl Games

(Both teams were undefeated but one or both was tied one or more times)

Bowl	Date	Winner (Record Going In, Coach)	Loser (Record Going In, Coach)
Rose	1-1-25	Notre Dame 27 (9-0, Knute Rockne)	Stanford 10 (7-0-1, Glenn "Pop" Warner)
Rose	1-1-26	Alabama 20 (9-0, Wallace Wade)	Washington 19 (10-0-1, Enoch Bagshaw)
Rose	1-2-33	Southern California 35 (9-0, Howard Jones)	Pittsburgh 0 (8-0-2, Jock Sutherland)
Rose	1-1-35	Alabama 29 (9-0, Frank Thomas)	Stanford 13 (9-0-1, Claude "Tiny" Thornhill)
Rose	1-1-38	California 13 (9-0-1, Leonard "Stub" Allison)	Alabama 0 (9-0, Frank Thomas)
Rose	1-1-40	Southern California 14 (7-0-2, Howard Jones)	Tennessee 0 (10-0, Bob Neyland)
Sugar	1-1-40	Texas A&M 14 (10-0, Homer Norton)	Tulane 13 (8-0-1, Lowell "Red" Dawson)
Rose	1-1-45	Southern California 25 (7-0-2, Jeff Cravath)	Tennessee 0 (7-0-1, John Barnhill)
Cotton	1-1-48	13-13 tie: Penn St. (9-0, Bob Higgins); Southern Methodist (9-0-1, Matty Bell)	
Orange	1-1-51	Clemson 15 (8-0-1, Frank Howard)	Miami (Fla.) 14 (9-0-1, Andy Gustafson)
Sugar	1-1-53	Georgia Tech 24 (11-0, Bobby Dodd)	Mississippi 7 (8-0-2, John Vaught)
Rose	1-1-69	Ohio St. 27 (9-0, Woody Hayes)	Southern California 16 (9-0-1, John McKay)
Rose	1-1-80	Southern California 17 (10-0-1, John Robinson)	Ohio St. 16 (11-0, Earle Bruce)
California	12-14-85	Fresno St. 51 (10-0-1, Jim Sweeney)	Bowling Green 7 (11-0, Denny Stolz)

Bowl Rematches of Regular-Season Opponents

Date	Regular Season	Date	Bowl-Game Rematch
10-9-43	Texas A&M 28, LSU 13	1-1-44	(Orange) LSU 19, Texas A&M 14
11-22-45	South Carolina 13, Wake Forest 13	1-1-46	(Gator) Wake Forest 26, South Carolina 14
10-6-56	Iowa 14, Oregon St. 13	1-1-57	(Rose) Iowa 35, Oregon St. 19
10-31-59	LSU 7, Mississippi 3	1-1-60	(Sugar) Mississippi 21, LSU 0
9-18-65	Michigan St. 13, UCLA 3	1-1-66	(Rose) UCLA 14, Michigan St. 12
10-4-75	Ohio St. 41, UCLA 20	1-1-76	(Rose) UCLA 23, Ohio St. 10
11-11-78	Nebraska 17, Oklahoma 14	1-1-79	(Orange) Oklahoma 31, Nebraska 24
9-25-82	UCLA 31, Michigan 27	1-1-83	(Rose) UCLA 24, Michigan 14
9-7-87	Michigan St. 27, Southern California 13	1-1-88	(Rose) Michigan St. 20, Southern California 17
11-26-94	Florida 31, Florida St. 31	1-2-95	(Sugar) Florida St. 23, Florida 17
9-23-95	Toledo 49, Nevada 35	12-14-95	(Las Vegas) Toledo 40, Nevada 37 (ot)
11-30-96	Florida St. 24, Florida 21	1-2-97	(Sugar) Florida 52, Florida St. 20
11-15-97	Notre Dame 24, LSU 6	12-28-97	(Independence) LSU 27, Notre Dame 9

Bowl-Game Facts

The Bowl/Basketball Connection

Ten times in history, a football bowl winner also won the NCAA men's basketball championship during the same academic year. They are as follows:

Year	School	Bowl	Date of Bowl
1999-00	Michigan St.	Florida Citrus	1-1-00
1992-93	North Carolina	Peach	1-2-93
1988-89	Michigan	Rose	1-2-89
1981-82	North Carolina	Gator	12-28-81
1973-74	North Carolina St.	Liberty	12-17-73
1965-66	UTEP	Sun	12-31-65
1950-51	Kentucky	Sugar	1-1-51
1947-48	Kentucky	Great Lakes	12-6-47
1945-46	Oklahoma St.	Sugar	1-1-46
1944-45	Oklahoma St.	Cotton	1-1-45

One-Time Wonders

Eight major-college teams have played in only one bowl game in their football history, and five of those have posted victories. The one-time bowlers (listed alphabetically) are as follows:

School	Date	Bowl	Opponent (Score)
Boise St.	12-30-99	Humanitarian	Louisville (34-31)
Eastern Mich.	12-12-87	California	San Jose St. (30-27)
Idaho	12-30-98	Humanitarian	Southern Miss. (42-35)
Kent St.	12-29-72	Tangerine	Tampa (18-21)
Long Beach St.	12-19-70	Pasadena	Louisville (24-24)
Memphis	12-18-71	Pasadena	San Jose St. (28-9)
Northern Ill.	12-17-83	California	Cal St. Fullerton (20-13)
Rutgers	12-16-78	Garden State	Arizona St. (18-34)

Year-by-Year Bowl Facts

(A note about bowl-game dates: Traditionally, bowl games have been played on January 1, but as more bowl games joined the holiday lineup, schedule adjustments were made whereby some bowl games are now played as early as mid-December. In the interest of avoiding confusion, all years referred to in bowl records are the actual calendar year in which the bowl game was played.)

1917 Coach Hugo Bezdek led the first of three teams to the Rose Bowl from 1917 to 1923. His Oregon team beat Pennsylvania, 14-0, in 1917; his Mare Island squad defeated Camp Lewis, 19-7, in 1918; and his Penn State team lost to Southern California, 14-3, in 1923. In his 1923 trip with the Nittany Lions, Bezdek almost came to blows with Southern California coach Elmer "Gloomy Gus" Henderson because Penn State did not arrive for the game until an hour after the scheduled kickoff time. Henderson accused Bezdek of not taking the field until the hot California sun had gone down to give his winterized Easterners an advantage.

1919 George Halas (yes, "Papa Bear") was the player of the game for Great Lakes Naval Training Station in Chicago as the Sailors shut out Mare Island, 17-0, in another of the wartime Rose Bowls.

1923 The first Rose Bowl game actually played in the stadium in Pasadena saw Southern California defeat Penn State, 14-3.

1926 Johnny Mack Brown, one of Hollywood's most famous movie cowboys, also was one of college football's most exciting players at Alabama. He was selected player of the game for the Rose Bowl in the Crimson Tide's 20-19 victory over Washington.

1927 The Rose Bowl becomes the first coast-to-coast radio broadcast of a sporting event.

1929 The Rose Bowl game became one of the most famous in bowl history because of California player Roy Riegels' now-legendary wrong-way run. Early in the second quarter, with each team just changing possessions, Georgia Tech was on its own 20. Tech halfback Stumpy Thompson broke for a seven-yard run, fumbled, and Riegels picked up the ball, momentarily headed for the Tech goal, then reversed his field and started running the wrong way. Teammate Benny Lom tried to stop him and finally did on the California one-yard line, where the dazed Riegels was pounced on by a group of Tech

1938 The first Orange Bowl played in Miami's new stadium, which seated 22,000 at the time, saw Auburn edge Michigan State, 6-0. Also, in the second annual Cotton Bowl, Colorado's do-it-all standout Byron "Whizzer" White, the Rhodes Scholar and future U.S. Supreme Court justice, passed for one score and returned a pass interception for another, but the Buffs lost to Rice, 28-14.

tacklers. Lom went back to punt on the next play and the kick was blocked out of the end zone for a safety, which decided the contest, eventually won by Georgia Tech, 8-7.

1941 On December 6, 1941, Hawaii defeated Willamette, 20-6, but a second Rainbows' postseason game, scheduled with San Jose State for the next week, was cancelled after the attack on Pearl Harbor.

1942 You would think a team making only one first down and gaining only 75 yards to its opponent's 309 yards could not come out of a game a 29-21 victor, but it happened in the Cotton Bowl as Alabama downed Texas A&M. The Tide intercepted seven of A&M's 42 passes and recovered five Aggie fumbles. Also, the Rose Bowl was moved for one year to Durham, N.C., because of wartime considerations that precluded large gatherings on the West Coast, and Oregon State downed Duke, 20-16.

1946 The first and only bowl game decided after time expired was the Orange Bowl when Miami (Florida) downed Holy Cross, 13-6. Time expired as Miami halfback Al Hudson returned an 89-yard intercepted pass for the deciding score.

1949 A Pacific Coast team had never been allowed to play in a major bowl other than the Rose Bowl, but the conference leadership let Oregon play in the Cotton Bowl against Southern Methodist. Doak Walker and Kyle Rote led Southern Methodist to a 20-13 victory over the Ducks and quarterback Norm Van Brocklin. John McKay, later the head coach at Southern California, also was on the Oregon roster.

1953 The Rose, Cotton, Sugar and Orange Bowls were televised nationally for the first time.

1954 Dicky Maegle of Rice may be the best-remembered bowl player, not because of his 265 yards rushing and three touchdowns vs. Alabama in 1954, but because of what happened on a 95-yard scoring run. Alabama's Tommy Lewis became infamous by coming off the bench to tackle Maegle in the Cotton Bowl, won by Rice, 28-6.

1960 In one of those pupil-vs.-teacher battles, former Georgia Tech player and assistant coach Frank Broyles led his Arkansas Razorbacks to a 14-7 Gator Bowl victory over his former coach, Bobby Dodd, and the Yellow Jackets.

1962 Oregon State quarterback Terry Baker turned in the longest run in bowl history with a 99-yard scamper to down Villanova, 6-0, in the Liberty Bowl. Baker, an outstanding athlete, became the only Heisman Trophy winner to play in an NCAA Final Four basketball game later that academic year (1963).

1964 Utah and West Virginia became the first teams to play a major bowl game indoors when they met in the Atlantic City Convention Hall. Utah won the Liberty Bowl, 32-6, beneath the bright indoor lights.

1965 The first Orange Bowl played under the lights in Miami saw Texas stun national champion Alabama and quarterback Joe Namath, 21-17.

1968 It was the student beating the teacher in the Cotton Bowl as Texas A&M head coach Gene Stallings saw his Aggies hold on for a 20-16 victory over Alabama and legendary head coach Paul "Bear" Bryant. Stallings had played (at Texas A&M) and coached (at Alabama) under Bryant. The "Bear" met Stallings at midfield after the contest and lifted the 6-foot-3 Aggie coach up in admiration. Also, the Astro-Bluebonnet Bowl (also known as the Bluebonnet Bowl) became the first bowl game to be played in a domed stadium as the Astrodome served as the site of the December 31, 1968, game between Southern Methodist (28) and Oklahoma (27).

1970 Three of the four legendary Four Horsemen of Notre Dame came to Dallas to watch the Fighting Irish drop a 21-17 Cotton Bowl game to Texas. The only other time Notre Dame had played in a bowl game was the 1925 Rose Bowl, when the Four Horsemen led the Irish to a 27-10 victory over Stanford.

1971 Notre Dame snapped the second-longest winning streak going into a bowl game by halting Texas' 30-game string, 24-11, in the Cotton Bowl. In 1951, Kentucky had stopped Oklahoma's 31-game streak in the Sugar Bowl, 13-7.

1976 Archie Griffin started his fourth straight Rose Bowl for Ohio State (1973-76), totaling 412 yards on 79 carries in the four games. The Buckeyes, under legendary head coach Woody Hayes, won only the 1974 contest, but Griffin is the only player to win two Heisman Trophies (1974-75).

1989 Texas Tech's James Gray set a college bowl record with 280 yards rushing in the All-American Bowl against Duke. Brigham Young's Ty Detmer set the bowl passing mark with 576 yards versus Penn State in the Holiday Bowl.

Special Regular- and Postseason Games

Postseason Games

UNSANCTIONED OR OTHER BOWLS

The following bowl and/or postseason games were unsanctioned by the NCAA or otherwise had no team classified as major college at the time of the bowl. Most are postseason games; in many cases, complete dates and/or statistics are not available and the scores are listed only to provide a historical reference. Attendance of the game, if known, is listed in parentheses after the score.

ALL-SPORTS BOWL
(Oklahoma City, Okla.)
12-9-61—Okla. Panhandle 28, Langston 14 (8,000)
12-8-62—Neb.-Omaha 34, East Central 21 (2,500)
12-7-63—Northeastern St. 59, Slippery Rock 12
12-5-64—Sul Ross St. 21, East Central 13

ALUMINUM BOWL (NAIA Title Game)
(Little Rock, Ark.)
12-22-56—Montana St. 0, St. Joseph's (Ind.) 0

ANGEL BOWL
(Los Angeles, Calif.)
12-28-46—Florida A&M 6, Wiley 6 (12,000)

AZALEA BOWL
(Orlando, Fla.)
1-1-46—Knoxville 18, Florida Normal 0 (4,000)

AZALEA CLASSIC
(Mobile, Ala.)
12-4-71—Jackson St. 40, Alabama A&M 21
12-7-74—Bethune-Cookman 19, Langston 3 (1,000)

AZTEC BOWL
(Mexico City, Mexico)
12-50—Whittier 27, Mexico All-Stars 14
12-53—Mexico City 45, Eastern N.M. 26

BEAN BOWL
(Scottsbluff, Neb.)
11-24-49—Idaho St. 20, Chadron St. 2
11-23-50—Doane 14, Northern Colo. 6

BEAVER BOWL
(Corry, Pa.)
11-15-58—Slippery Rock 6, Edinboro 0 (3,000)

BICENTENNIAL BOWL
(Little Rock, Ark.)
11-29-75—Henderson St. 27, East Central 14 (2,000)

BICENTENNIAL BOWL
(Richmond, Va.)
12-11-76—South Carolina St. 26, Norfolk St. 10 (7,500)

BOOT HILL BOWL
(Dodge City, Kan.)
12-70—Cameron 13, N.M. Highlands 12
12-4-71—Dakota St. 23, Northwestern Okla. 20 (2,000)
12-2-72—William Penn 17, Emporia St. 14 (2,000)
12-1-73—Millikin 51, Bethany (Kan.) 7 (1,600)
11-30-74—Washburn 21, Millikin 7 (2,500)
11-22-75—Buena Vista 24, St. Mary's (Kan.) 21 (2,700)
11-20-76—Benedictine 29, Washburn 14 (3,000)
11-19-77—Mo. Western St. 35, Benedictine 30 (1,000)
11-18-78—Chadron St. 30, Baker (Kan.) 19 (3,000)
11-17-79—Pittsburg St. 43, Peru St. 14 (2,800)
11-21-80—Cameron 34, Adams St. 16

BOTANY BOWL
11-24-55—Neb.-Kearney 34, Northern St. 13

BOY'S RANCH BOWL
(Abilene, Texas)
12-13-47—Missouri Valley 20, McMurry 13 (2,500)

BURLEY BOWL
(Johnson City, Tenn.)
1-1-46—High Point 7, Milligan 7 (3,500)
11-28-46—Southeastern La. 21, Milligan 13 (7,500)
11-27-47—West Chester 20, Carson-Newman 6 (10,000)
11-25-48—West Chester 7, Appalachian St. 2 (12,000)
11-24-49—Emory & Henry 32, Hanover 0 (12,000)
11-23-50—Emory & Henry 26, Appalachian St. 6 (12,000)
11-22-51—Morris Harvey (now Charleston) 27, Lebanon Valley 20 (9,000)
11-27-52—East Tenn. St. 34, Emory & Henry 16
11-26-53—East Tenn. St. 48, Emory & Henry 12
11-25-54—Appalachian St. 28, East Tenn. St. 13
11-24-55—East Tenn. St. 7, Appalachian St. 0
11-22-56—Memphis 32, East Tenn. St. 12

CAJUN BOWL
12-47—McNeese St. 0, Southern Ark. 0

CATTLE BOWL
(Fort Worth, Texas)
1-1-47—Ark.-Pine Bluff 7, Lane 0 (1,000)
1-1-48—Samuel Huston 7, Philander Smith 0 (800)

CEMENT BOWL
(Allentown, Pa.)
12-8-62—West Chester 46, Hofstra 12

CHARITY BOWL
(Los Angeles, Calif.)
12-25-37—Fresno St. 27, Central Ark. 26 (5,000)

CHRISTMAS BOWL
(Natchitoches, La.)
12-6-58—Northwestern St. 18, Sam Houston St. 11
12-5-59—Delta St. 19, East Central 0

CIGAR BOWL
(Tampa, Fla.)
1-1-47—Delaware 21, Rollins 7 (9,500)
1-1-48—Missouri Valley 26, West Chester 7 (10,000)
1-1-49—Missouri Valley 13, St. Thomas (Minn.) 13 (11,000)
1-2-50—Florida St. 19, Wofford 6 (14,000)
1-1-51—Wis.-La Crosse 47, Valparaiso 14 (12,000)
12-29-51—Brooke Army Medical 20, Camp LeJeune Marines 0 (7,500) (see Cigar Bowl in Service Games)
12-13-52—Tampa 21, Lenoir-Rhyne 12 (7,500)
1-1-54—Missouri Valley 12, Wis.-La Crosse 12 (5,000)
12-17-56—Tampa 21, Morris Harvey (now Charleston) 0

CITRACADO BOWL
(see Citracado Bowl in Service Games)

COCONUT BOWL
(Miami, Fla.)
1-1-42—Florida Normal 0, Miami All-Stars 0 (9,000)
1-1-46—Bethune-Cookman 32, Albany St. (Ga.) 0 (5,000)
1-1-47—Bethune-Cookman 13, Columbia (S.C.) Sporting Club 0 (5,000)

CORN BOWL
(Bloomington, Ill.)
11-27-47—Southern Ill. 21, North Central 0 (5,500)
11-25-48—Ill. Wesleyan 6, Eastern Ill. 0 (8,500)
11-24-49—Western Ill. 13, Wheaton (Ill.) 0 (4,567)
11-23-50—Mo.-Rolla 7, Illinois St. 6 (2,500)
11-22-51—Lewis 21, William Jewell 12 (2,000)
11-26-53—Western Ill. 32, Iowa Wesleyan 0

SPECIAL POSTSEASON GAMES

11-24-55—Luther 24, Western Ill. 20 (3,100)

COSMOPOLITAN BOWL
(Alexandria, La.)
12-51—McNeese St. 13, Louisiana Col. 6

COTTON-TOBACCO BOWL
(Greensboro, N.C.)
1-1-46—Johnson Smith 18, Allen 6
1-1-47—Norfolk St. 0, Richmond 0 (10,000)

COWBOY BOWL
(Lawton, Okla.)
12-11-71—Howard Payne 16, Cameron 13
12-9-72—Harding 30, Langston 27

DIXIE CLASSIC
(Dallas, Texas)
1-1-34—Arkansas 7, Centenary 7 (12,000)

DOLL AND TOY CHARITY GAME
(Gulfport, Miss.)
12-3-37—Southern Miss. 7, Appalachian St. 0 (2,000)

EASTERN BOWL
(Allentown, Pa.)
12-14-63—East Caro. 27, Northeastern 6 (2,700)

ELKS BOWL
1-2-54—Morris Harvey (now Charleston) 12, East Caro. 0 (4,500) (at Greenville, N.C.)
12-11-54—Newberry 20, Appalachian St. 13 (at Raleigh, N.C.)

FISH BOWL
(Corpus Christi, Texas)
11-48—Southwestern (Tex.) 7, Corpus Christi 0

FISH BOWL
(Norfolk, Va.)
12-4-48—Hampton 20, Central St. 19

FLOWER BOWL
(Jacksonville, Fla.)
1-1-42—Johnson Smith 13, Lane 0 (4,500)
1-1-43—N.C. A&T 14, Southern U. 6 (2,000)
1-1-44—Allen 33, Winston-Salem 0 (2,000)
1-1-45—Texas College 18, N.C. A&T 0 (5,000)
1-1-46—Grambling 19, Lane 6 (6,000)
1-1-47—Delaware St. 7, Florida Normal 6 (3,000)
1-1-48—Bethune-Cookman 6, Lane 0 (3,000)

FRUIT BOWL
(San Francisco, Calif.)
12-14-47—Central St. 26, Prairie View 0 (9,000)
12-5-48—Southern U. 30, San Fran. St. 0 (5,000)

GATE CITY BOWL
(Atlanta, Ga.)
12-21-74—Tuskegee 15, Norfolk St. 14 (6,252)

GLASS BOWL
(Toledo, Ohio)
12-7-46—Toledo 21, Bates 12 (12,000)
12-6-47—Toledo 20, New Hampshire 14 (13,500)
12-4-48—Toledo 27, Oklahoma City 14 (8,500)
12-3-49—Cincinnati 33, Toledo 13

GOLD BOWL
(Richmond, Va.)
12-3-77—South Carolina St. 10, Winston-Salem 7 (14,000)
12-2-78—Virginia Union 21, N.C. A&T 6 (7,500)
12-1-79—South Carolina St. 39, Norfolk St. 7 (8,000)
12-6-80—N.C. A&T 37, N.C. Central 0 (3,374)

GOLDEN ISLES BOWL
(Brunswick, Ga.)
12-1-62—McNeese St. 21, Samford 14

GRAPE BOWL
(Lodi, Calif.)
12-13-47—Pacific (Cal.) 35, Utah St. 21 (12,000)
12-11-48—Hardin-Simmons 35, Pacific (Cal.) 35 (10,000)

GREAT LAKES BOWL
(Cleveland, Ohio)
12-5-48—John Carroll 14, Canisius 13 (18,000)

GREAT SOUTHWEST BOWL
(Grand Prairie, Texas)
12-31-60—Tex. A&M-Kingsville 45, Arkansas Tech 14 (3,900)

HOLIDAY BOWL
(St. Petersburg, Fla.)
12-21-57—Pittsburg St. 27, Hillsdale 26
12-20-58—Northeastern St. 19, Northern Ariz. 13
12-19-59—Tex. A&M-Kingsville 20, Lenoir-Rhyne 7 (9,500)
12-10-60—Lenoir-Rhyne 15, Humboldt St. 14 (also served as NAIA national title game)

HOOSIER BOWL
(See Turkey Bowl)

INTERNATIONAL BOWL
12-52—Tex. A&M-Kingsville 49, Hereico Colegio Military 0

IODINE BOWL
(Charleston, S.C.)
12-3-49—Johnson Smith 20, Allen 12
12-9-50—Allen 20, Bethune-Cookman 0 (1,000)
12-1-51—Allen 33, Morris College 14 (3,000)
12-5-53—Allen 33, Paul Quinn 6

KICKAPOO BOWL
(Wichita Falls, Texas)
12-5-47—Midwestern St. 39, Central Ark. 20 (5,000)

LIONS BOWL
(Ruston, La.)
12-46—Grambling 69, Miss. Industrial 12
12-5-47—Grambling 47, Bethune-Cookman 6
12-49—Grambling 21, Texas College 18
12-2-50—Bishop 35, Grambling 0
12-1-51—Grambling 52, Bishop 0 (at Shreveport, La.)
12-6-52—Grambling 27, Alcorn St. 13 (at Monroe, La.)

LIONS BOWL
(Salisbury, N.C.)
12-13-52—Clarion 13, East Caro. 6 (3,000)

MERCY BOWL II
(Anaheim, Calif.)
12-11-71—Cal St. Fullerton 17, Fresno St. 14 (16,854)

MINERAL WATER BOWL
(Excelsior Springs, Mo.)
11-25-54—Hastings 20, Col. of Emporia 14 (4,000)
11-24-55—Missouri Valley 31, Hastings 7
11-22-56—St. Benedict's 14, Northeastern St. 13 (2,000)
11-30-57—William Jewell 33, Hastings 14 (2,000)
11-22-58—Lincoln (Mo.) 21, Emporia St. 0 (2,500)
11-28-59—Col. of Emporia 21, Austin (Tex.) 20 (3,000)
11-26-60—Hillsdale 17, Northern Iowa 6 (6,000)
11-25-61—Truman 22, Parsons 8 (8,000)
11-24-62—Adams St. 23, Northern Ill. 20
11-30-63—Northern Ill. 21, Southwest Mo. St. 14
11-28-64—North Dakota St. 14, Western St. 13 (4,500)
11-27-65—North Dakota 37, Northern Ill. 20
11-26-66—Adams St. 14, Southwest Mo. St. 8 (5,500)
11-25-67—Doane 14, William Jewell 14 (6,500)
11-30-68—Doane 10, Central Mo. St. 0 (6,000)
11-29-69—St. John's (Minn.) 21, Simpson 0 (5,000)
11-28-70—Franklin 40, Wayne St. (Neb.) 12 (2,500)
12-4-71—Bethany (Kan.) 17, Missouri Valley 14 (2,500)
11-18-72—Ottawa 27, Friends 20 (4,500)
11-73—William Jewell 20, St. Mary's (Kan.) 9
11-23-74—Midland 32, Friends 6 (1,500)
11-22-75—Mo. Western St. 44, Graceland (Ia.) 0 (3,300)

MIRZA SHRINE BOWL
(Pittsburg, Kan.)
12-1-50—Central Mo. St. 32, Pittsburg St. 21

MISSOURI-KANSAS BOWL
(Kansas City, Mo.)
12-4-48—Emporia St. 34, Southwest Mo. St. 20

MOILA SHRINE CLASSIC
(St. Joseph, Mo.)
11-24-79—Mo. Western St. 72, William Jewell 44 (1,600)
11-22-80—Truman 17, Pittsburg St. 14 (500)

NATIONAL CLASSIC
(Greensboro, N.C.)
12-4-54—N.C. Central 19, Tennessee St. 6

NEW YEAR'S CLASSIC
(Honolulu, Hawaii)
1-1-34—Santa Clara 26, Hawaii 7
1-1-35—Hawaii 14, California 0 (later called Poi Bowl)

OIL BOWL
(Houston, Texas)
1-1-44—La.-Lafayette 24, Ark.-Monticello 7 (12,000)

OLEANDER BOWL
(Galveston, Texas)
1-2-50—McMurry 19, Missouri Valley 13 (7,500)

OLYMPIAN BOWL
(see Pythian Bowl)

OPTIMIST BOWL
(Houston, Texas)
12-21-46—North Texas 14, Pacific (Cal.) 13 (5,000)

ORANGE BLOSSOM CLASSIC
(Miami, Fla.)
12-2-33—Florida A&M 9, Howard 6
12-13-34—Florida A&M 13, Virginia St. 12
12-12-35—Kentucky St. 19, Florida A&M 10
12-5-36—Prairie View 25, Florida A&M 0
12-9-37—Florida A&M 25, Hampton 20
12-8-38—Florida A&M 9, Kentucky St. 7
12-9-39—Florida A&M 42, Wiley 0
12-7-40—Central St. 0, Florida A&M 0
12-6-41—Florida A&M 15, Tuskegee 7
12-12-42—Florida A&M 12, Texas College 6
12-4-43—Hampton 39, Florida A&M 0
12-9-44—Virginia St. 19, Florida A&M 6
12-8-45—Wiley 32, Florida A&M 6
12-7-46—Lincoln (Pa.) 20, Florida A&M 0 (at Tampa)
12-6-47—Florida A&M 7, Hampton 0
12-4-48—Virginia Union 10, Florida A&M 6 (16,000)
12-10-49—N.C. A&T 20, Florida A&M 14
12-2-50—Central St. 13, Florida A&M 6
12-1-51—Florida A&M 67, N.C. Central 6
12-6-52—Florida A&M 29, Virginia St. 7
12-5-53—Prairie View 33, Florida A&M 27
12-4-54—Florida A&M 67, Md.-East. Shore 19
12-3-55—Grambling 28, Florida A&M 21
12-1-56—Tennessee St. 41, Florida A&M 39
12-14-57—Florida A&M 27, Md.-East. Shore 21
12-13-58—Prairie View 26, Florida A&M 8
12-5-59—Florida A&M 28, Prairie View 7
12-10-60—Florida A&M 40, Langston 26
12-9-61—Florida A&M 14, Jackson St. 8 (47,791)
12-8-62—Jackson St. 22, Florida A&M 6
12-14-63—Morgan St. 30, Florida A&M 7
12-5-64—Florida A&M 42, Grambling 15
12-4-65—Morgan St. 36, Florida A&M 7
12-3-66—Florida A&M 43, Alabama A&M 26
12-2-67—Grambling 28, Florida A&M 25
12-7-68—Alcorn St. 36, Florida A&M 9 (37,398)
12-6-69—Florida A&M 23, Grambling 19 (36,784) (at Tallahassee, Fla.)
12-12-70—Jacksonville St. 21, Florida A&M 7 (31,184)
12-11-71—Florida A&M 27, Kentucky St. 9 (26,161)
12-2-72—Florida A&M 41, Md.-East. Shore 21 (21,606)
12-8-73—Florida A&M 23, South Carolina St. 12 (18,996)
12-7-74—Florida A&M 17, Howard 13 (20,166)
12-6-75—Florida A&M 40, Kentucky St. 13 (27,875)
12-4-76—Florida A&M 26, Central St. 21 (18,000)
12-3-77—Florida A&M 37, Delaware St. 15 (29,493)
12-2-78—Florida A&M 31, Grambling 7

ORCHID BOWL
(Mexico City, Mexico)
1-1-45—Louisiana Col. 10, U. of Mexico 0 (8,000)
12-28-46—Mississippi Col. 43, U. of Mexico 7 (7,500)

PALM FESTIVAL
(Miami, Fla.)
1-2-33—Miami (Fla.) 7, Manhattan 0 (6,000)
1-1-34—Duquesne 33, Miami (Fla.) 7 (3,500) (forerunner to Orange Bowl)

PALMETTO SHRINE
(Columbia, S.C.)
12-10-55—Lenoir-Rhyne 14, Newberry 13 (6,000)

PAPER BOWL
(Pensacola, Fla.)
12-18-48—Jacksonville St. 19, Troy St. 0
12-16-49—Jacksonville St. 12, West Ala. 7 (3,000)
12-2-50—Pensacola Alumni Cardinals 7, Jacksonville St. 6 (3,600)

PEACH BLOSSOM CLASSIC
(Atlanta, Ga.)
12-9-39—Morris Brown 13, Virginia St. 7
12-6-40—Morris Brown 28, Kentucky St. 6 (1,500)
12-6-41—Morris Brown 7, N.C. Central 6 (6,000) (at Columbus, Ga.)
12-4-42—Morris Brown 20, Lane 0 (3,000) (at Columbus, Ga.)

PEACH BOWL
(Macon, Ga.)
12-13-46—Tenn. Wesleyan 14, Ga. Military 13 (5,000)
12-6-47—Virginia St. 48, Morris Brown 0
12-3-49—Morris Brown 33, Texas College 28 (at Atlanta, Ga.)

PEANUT BOWL
(Dothan, Ala.)
12-21-68—Ouachita Baptist 39, West Ala. 6

PEAR BOWL
(Medford, Ore.)
11-28-46—Southern Ore. St. 13, Central Wash. 8 (3,000) (at Ashland, Ore.)

11-27-47—Pacific Lutheran 27, Southern Ore. St. 21
11-25-48—Col. of Idaho 27, Southern Ore. St. 20 (2,500)
11-24-49—Pacific (Ore.) 33, UC Davis 15 (4,000)
11-23-50—Lewis & Clark 61, San Fran. St. 7 (4,000)
11-24-51—Pacific (Ore.) 25, UC Davis 7 (4,000)

PECAN BOWL
(Orangeburg, S.C.)
12-7-46—South Carolina St. 13, Johnson Smith 6
12-13-47—South Carolina St. 7, Allen 0 (3,000)

PELICAN BOWL
(New Orleans, La.)
12-2-72—Grambling 56, N.C. Central 6 (22,500) (at Durham, N.C.)
12-7-74—Grambling 28, South Carolina St. 7 (30,120)
12-27-75—Southern U. 15, South Carolina St. 12 (6,748)

PENINSULA BOWL
(Charleston, S.C.)
12-2-50—Allen 47, South Carolina St. 13 (7,500)

PHILLIPS FIELD BOWL
(Tampa, Fla.)
12-8-51—Tampa 7, Brandeis 0

PIEDMONT TOBACCO BOWL
(Fayetteville, N.C.)
12-7-46—Allen 40, Fayetteville St. 6 (900)

PINEAPPLE BOWL
(Honolulu, Hawaii)
1-1-40—Oregon St. 39, Hawaii 6 (formerly called Poi Bowl)
1-1-41—Fresno St. 3, Hawaii 0
1-1-47—Hawaii 19, Utah 16 (25,000)
1-1-48—Hawaii 33, Redlands 32 (12,000)
1-1-49—Oregon St. 47, Hawaii 27 (15,000)
1-2-50—Stanford 74, Hawaii 20
1-1-51—Hawaii 28, Denver 27
1-1-52—San Diego St. 34, Hawaii 13

PITTSBURGH CHARITY GAME
(Pittsburgh, Pa.)
12-5-31—Carnegie Mellon 0, Duquesne 0 (42,539) (see Other Postseason Games)

POI BOWL
(Honolulu, Hawaii)
1-1-36—Southern California 38, Hawaii 6
1-2-37—Hawaii 18, Honolulu All-Stars 12
1-1-38—Washington 53, Hawaii 13 (13,500)
1-2-39—UCLA 32, Hawaii 7 (later called Pineapple Bowl)

POULTRY BOWL
(Gainesville, Ga.)
12-8-73—Stephen F. Austin 31, Gardner-Webb 10 (2,500)
12-7-74—Guilford 7, William Penn 7 (1,000) (at Greensboro, N.C.) (Guilford awarded win on 10-8 edge in first downs)

PRAIRIE VIEW BOWL
(Also called Bayou City Bowl)
(Houston, Texas)
1-1-29—Atlanta 7, Prairie View 0
1-1-30—Fisk 20, Prairie View 0
1-1-31—Tuskegee 19, Prairie View 7
1-1-32—Prairie View 27, Alabama St. 2
1-1-33—Prairie View 14, Tuskegee 0
1-1-34—Prairie View 20, Langston 0
1-1-35—Tuskegee 15, Prairie View 6
1-1-36—Wiley 7, Prairie View 6
1-1-37—Tuskegee 6, Prairie View 0 (3,000)
1-1-38—Prairie View 27, Florida A&M 14
1-2-39—Prairie View 34, Tuskegee 0
1-1-40—Prairie View 7, Xavier (La.) 6
1-1-41—Prairie View 7, Alabama St. 6
1-1-42—Kentucky St. 19, Prairie View 13
1-1-43—Langston 18, Prairie View 13
1-1-44—Prairie View 6, Wiley 0 (5,000)
1-1-45—Wiley 26, Prairie View 0 (4,000)
1-1-46—Prairie View 14, Tuskegee 0 (10,000)
1-1-47—Prairie View 14, Lincoln (Mo.) 0 (1,500) (called Houston Bowl)
1-1-48—Texas Southern 13, Prairie View 0
1-1-49—Central St. 6, Prairie View 0 (9,000)
1-2-50—Prairie View 27, Fisk 6 (4,718)
1-1-51—Prairie View 6, Bishop 0
1-1-52—Prairie View 27, Ark.-Pine Bluff 26
1-1-53—Texas Southern 13, Prairie View 12 (13,000)
1-1-54—Prairie View 33, Texas Southern 8
1-1-55—Prairie View 14, Texas Southern 12 (10,000)
1-2-56—Prairie View 59, Fisk 0 (7,500)
1-1-57—Prairie View 27, Texas Southern 6
1-1-58—Prairie View 6, Texas Southern 6 (3,500)
1-1-59—Prairie View 34, Langston 8
1-1-60—Prairie View 47, Wiley 10 (1,200)

12-31-60—Prairie View 19, Ark.-Pine Bluff 8 (1,400)
12-1-62—Prairie View 37, Central St. 16

PRETZEL BOWL
(Reading, Pa.)
11-24-51—West Chester 32, Albright 9 (7,500)

PYTHIAN BOWL
(Salisbury, N.C.)
11-26-49—Appalachian St. 21, Catawba 7
12-9-50—West Liberty St. 28, Appalachian St. 26
12-8-51—Lenoir-Rhyne 13, Calif. (Pa.) 7 (4,500)

REFRIGERATOR BOWL
(Evansville Ind.)
12-4-48—Evansville 13, Missouri Valley 7 (7,500)
12-3-49—Evansville 22, Hillsdale 7
12-2-50—Abilene Christian 13, Gust. Adolphus 7 (8,000)
12-2-51—Arkansas St. 46, Camp Breckinridge 12 (10,000)
12-7-52—Western Ky. 34, Arkansas St. 19 (9,500)
12-6-53—Sam Houston St. 14, Col. of Idaho 12 (7,500)
12-5-54—Delaware 19, Kent 7 (4,500)
12-4-55—Jacksonville St. 12, Rhode Island 10 (7,000)
12-1-56—Sam Houston St. 27, Middle Tenn. St. 13 (3,000)

RICE BOWL
(Stuggart, Ark.)
12-57—Arkansas Tech 19, Ark.-Monticello 7
12-58—Louisiana Col. 39, Arkansas Tech 12
12-2-60—East Central 25, Henderson St. 7

ROCKET BOWL
(Huntsville, Ala.)
11-19-60—Maryville (Tenn.) 19, Millsaps 0

SAN JACINTO SHRINE BOWL
(Pasadena, Texas)
12-4-76—Abilene Christian 22, Harding 12 (8,000)

SHARE BOWL
(Knoxville, Tenn.)
12-11-71—Carson-Newman 54, Fairmont St. 3 (1,200)

SHRIMP BOWL
(Galveston, Texas)
12-27-52—Sam Houston St. 41, Northeastern St. 20 (3,500)

SHRINE BOWL
(Ardmore, Okla.)
12-9-72—Southwestern Okla. 28, Angelo St. 6

SILVER BOWL
(Mexico City, Mexico)
12-20-47—Mexico All-Stars 24, Randolph Field 19
12-11-48—Pacific Fleet 33, Mexico All-Stars 26
12-17-49—Trinity (Tex.) 52, Mexico 6

SMOKY MOUNTAIN BOWL
(Bristol, Tenn.)
11-24-49—West Liberty St. 20, Western Caro. 0 (1,000)

SPACE CITY BOWL
(Huntsville, Ala.)
11-24-66—Jacksonville St. 41, Ark.-Monticello 30
12-9-67—Samford 20, Ark.-Monticello 7

STEEL BOWL
(Birmingham, Ala.)
1-1-41—Morris Brown 19, Central St. 3 (8,000)
1-1-42—Southern College All-Stars 26, Nashville Pros 13
1-1-52—Bethune-Cookman 27, Texas College 13 (1,500) (see Vulcan Bowl)

SUGAR CUP CLASSIC
(New Orleans, La.)
11-28-64—Grambling 42, Bishop 6

TANGERINE BOWL#
(Orlando, Fla.)
1-1-47—Catawba 31, Maryville (Tenn.) 6
1-1-48—Catawba 7, Marshall 0
1-1-49—Murray 21, Sul Ross St. 21
1-2-50—St. Vincent (Pa.) 7, Emory & Henry 6
1-1-51—Morris Harvey (now Charleston) 35, Emory & Henry 14
1-1-52—Stetson 35, Arkansas St. 20 (12,500)
1-1-53—Tex. A&M-Commerce 33, Tennessee Tech 0 (12,340)
1-1-54—Arkansas St. 7, Tex. A&M-Commerce 7
1-1-55—Neb.-Omaha 7, Eastern Ky. 6
1-2-56—Juniata 6, Missouri Valley 0 (10,000)
1-1-57—West Tex. A&M 20, Southern Miss. 13 (11,000)
1-1-58—Tex. A&M-Commerce 10, Southern Miss. 9
12-27-58—Tex. A&M-Commerce St. 26, Missouri Valley 7 (4,000)
1-1-60—Middle Tenn. St. 21, Presbyterian 12 (12,500)
12-29-61—Lamar 21, Middle Tenn. St. 14

12-28-63—Western Ky. 27, Coast Guard 0 (7,500)
12-12-64—East Caro. 14, Massachusetts 13
12-11-65—East Caro. 31, Maine 0 (8,350)
12-10-66—Morgan St. 14, West Chester 6
12-16-67—Tenn.-Martin 25, West Chester 8

TEXHOMA BOWL
(Denison, Texas)
12-10-48—Ouachita Baptist 7, Southeastern Okla. 0
11-25-49—Austin (Tex.) 27, East Central 6

TEXTILE BOWL
(Spartanburg, S.C.)
11-30-74—Wofford 20, South Carolina St. 0 (3,000)

TOBACCO BOWL
(Lexington, Ky.)
12-14-46—Muhlenberg 26, St. Bonaventure 25 (3,000)

TROPICAL BOWL
12-18-51—Morris Brown 21, Alcorn St. 0
12-13-52—Bethune-Cookman 54, Albany St. (Ga.) 0
12-12-53—Virginia Union 13, Bethune-Cookman 0

TURKEY BOWL
11-28-46—Evansville 19, Northern Ill. 7 (12,000) (also called Hoosier Bowl)

VULCAN BOWL
(Birmingham, Ala.)
1-1-42—Langston 13, Morris Brown 0 (7,000)
1-1-43—Texas College 13, Tuskegee 10 (6,000)
1-1-44—Tuskegee 12, Clark (Ga.) 7 (6,000)
1-1-45—Tennessee St. 13, Tuskegee 0 (5,000)
1-1-46—Tennessee St. 33, Texas College 9 (9,000)
1-1-47—Tennessee St. 32, Louisville Municipal 0 (4,000)
1-2-48—Central St. 27, Grambling 21 (8,000)
1-1-49—Kentucky St. 23, N.C. A&T 13 (5,000)
1-1-52—Bethune-Cookman 27, Texas College 13 (1,500) (see Steel Bowl)

WILL ROGERS BOWL
(Oklahoma City, Okla.)
1-1-47—Pepperdine 38, Neb. Wesleyan 13 (800)

YAM BOWL
(Dallas, Texas)
12-25-46—Texas Southern 64, Tuskegee 7 (5,000)
12-25-47—Southern U. 46, Fort Valley St. 0 (1,200)

#Became Florida Citrus Bowl (no classified major teams participated in games from January 1, 1947, through January 1, 1960, or in 1961 and 1963 through 1967.

SERVICE GAMES

AIRBORNE BOWL
12-15-57—101st Airborne 20, 82nd Airborne 14
12-5-59—Fort Campbell 26, Fort Bragg 7

ARAB BOWL
(Oran, Africa)
1-1-44—Army 10, Navy 7 (15,000)

ARMY ALL-STAR GAMES
8-30-42—Washington Redskins 26, Western Army All-Stars 7 (at Los Angeles, Calif.)
9-6-42—Western Army All-Stars 16, Chicago Cardinals 10 (at Denver, Colo.)
9-9-42—Western Army All-Stars 12, Detroit Lions 0 (at Detroit, Mich.)
9-12-42—Eastern Army All-Stars 16, New York Giants 0 (at New York, N.Y.)
9-13-42—Green Bay Packers 36, Western Army All-Stars 21 (at Milwaukee, Wis.)
9-16-42—Eastern Army All-Stars 13, Brooklyn Dodgers 7 (at Baltimore, Md.)
9-19-42—New York Giants 10, Western Army All-Stars 7 (at New York, N.Y.)
9-20-42—Chicago Bears 14, Eastern Army All-Stars 7 (at Boston, Mass.)

ARMY PACIFIC OLYMPICS
(Osaka, Japan)
1-13-46—11th Airborne Angels 27, Clark Field 6
1-27-46—11th Airborne Angels 18, Honolulu All-Stars 0

ARMY-NAVY BENEFIT BOWL
(Tallahassee, Fla.)
12-20-52—Parris Island 49, Fort Benning 0

ATOM BOWL
(Nagasaki, Japan)
12-45—Nishahaya Tigers 14, Bertelli's Bears 13 (2,000)

BAMBINO BOWL
(Bari, Italy)
11-23-44—Technical School 13, Playboys 0 (5,000)

SPECIAL POSTSEASON GAMES

BAMBOO BOWL
(Manila, Philippines)
1-1-46—Clark Field Acpacs 14, Leyte Base 12 (40,000)
1-1-47—Manila Raiders 13, Scofield Barracks 6 (12,000)
12-47—Ryukgus Command Sea Horses 21, Hawaiian Mid-Pacific Commandos 0
1-1-50—All-Navy Guam 19, Clark Air Force Base 7

BLUEBONNET BOWL
(Houston, Texas)
12-25-46—Texas Southern 49, Camp Hood 0

CHERRY BOWL
(Yokohama, Japan)
1-1-52—Camp Drake 26, Yoksuka Naval Base 12

CHIGGER BOWL
(Dutch Guiana)
1-1-45—Army Air Base Bonecrushers 6, Army Airway Rams 0 (1,200)

CHINA BOWL
(Shanghai)
1-27-46—Navy All-Stars 12, Army All-Stars 0
1-1-47—11th Airborne 12, Army-Navy All-Stars 6
1-1-48—Marines (Guam) 45, China All-Stars 0

CIGAR BOWL
12-29-51—Brooke Army Medical 20, Camp LeJeune 0 (7,500)

CITRICADO BOWL
12-56—San Diego Marines 25, UC Santa Barb. 14

COCONUT BOWL
(New Guinea)
1-6-45—Bulldogs 18, Crimson Tide 7 (3,000)

COFFEE BOWL
(London, England)
3-19-44—United States 18, Canada 0

CONCH BOWL
(Key West, Fla.)
11-24-57—Keesler Air Force Base 27, Maxwell Air Force 7
11-28-58—Keesler Air Force Base 14, Maxwell Air Force 8

COSMOPOLITAN BOWL
(Alexandria, La.)
12-50—Camp Polk 26, Louisiana Col. 7
12-52—Louisiana Col. 14, Alexander Air Base 0

ELECTRONICS BOWL
(Biloxi, Miss.)
12-9-51—Keesler Air Force Base 13, Camp LeJeune 0
12-53—Eglin Air Force Base 19, Keesler Air Force Base 8
12-54—Shaw Air Force Base 20, Keesler Air Force Base 19

EUROPEAN "ORANGE BOWL"
(Heidelberg, Germany)
12-7-46—1st Division Artillery 27, 60th Infantry 13

EUROPEAN "ROSE BOWL"
(Augsburg, Germany)
12-7-46—9th Division 20, 16th Infantry 7 (3,000)

EUROPEAN "SUGAR BOWL"
(Nuremberg, Germany)
12-7-46—Grafenwohr Military 0, 39th Infantry 0

G. I. BOWL
(London, England)
11-12-44—Army G.I.'s 20, Navy Bluejackets 0 (60,000)

ICE BOWL
(Fairbanks, Alaska)
1-1-49—Ladd Air Force Base 0, University of Alaska 0 (500)
1-2-50—University of Alaska 3, Ladd Air Force Base 0
1-1-51—University of Alaska 0, Ladd Air Force Base 0
12-30-52—Ladd Air Force Base 47, University of Alaska 0

IRANIAN BOWL
(Teheran, Iran)
12-12-44—Camp Amirabad 20, Camp Khorramsahr 0 (9,000)

JUNGLE BOWL
(Southwest Pacific)
1-1-45—American All-Stars 49, Marines 0 (6,400)

LILY BOWL
(Hamilton, Bermuda)
1-3-43—Army 19, Navy 18
1-1-44—Navy 19, Army 0
1-7-45—Navy 39, Army 6 (11,000)
1-5-47—Army 7, Navy 7 (9,000)

1-1-48—Air Force 12, Navy 12
1-1-49—Navy All-Stars 25, Kindley Fliers 6

MARINE BOWL
(Pritchard Field, Southwest Pacific)
12-24-44—4th Marines 0, 29th Marines 0 (7,000)

MISSILE BOWL
(Orlando, Fla.)
12-3-60—Quantico Marines 36, Pensacola Air Force Base 6
12-9-61—Fort Eustis 25, Quantico Marines 24
12-15-62—Fort Campbell 14, Lackland Air Force Base 10
12-14-63—Quantico Marines 13, San Diego Marines 10
12-5-64—Fort Benning 9, Fort Eustis 3

PALMETTO SHRINE
(Charleston, S.C.)
1-1-55—Fort Jackson 26, Shaw Air Force Base 21

PARC DES PRINCES BOWL
(Paris, France)
12-19-44—9th Air Force 6, 1st General Hospital 0 (20,000)

POI BOWL
(Honolulu, Hawaii)
(Pacific Ocean Areas Service Championship)
1-8-45—Navy 14, Army Air Force 0 (29,000)

POINSETTIA BOWL
(San Diego, Calif.)
12-20-52—Bolling Air Force Base 35, San Diego NTC 14
12-19-53—Fort Ord 55, Quantico Marines 19
12-19-54—Fort Sill 27, Bolling Air Force Base 6
12-17-55—Fort Ord 35, Pensacola NAS 13

POTATO BOWL
(Belfast, Ireland)
1-1-44—Galloping Gaels 0, Wolverines 0

RICE BOWL
(Tokyo, Japan)
1-1-46—11th Airborne Angels 25, 41st Division 12 (15,000)
12-46—Yokota Air Base 13, 1st AD 8 (7,000)
1-1-48—Korea All-Stars 19, Japan All-Stars 13
1-1-49—Army Ground Forces 13, Air Force 7 (20,000)
1-1-50—Air Force All-Stars 18, Army All-Stars 14
1-1-53—Camp Drake 25, Yokosuka Naval Base 6
1-1-54—Camp Fisher 19, Nagoya Air Base 13
1-1-55—Air Force 21, Marines 14
12-31-55—Air Force 33, Army 14 (40,000)
12-30-56—Army 21, Air Force 6
12-7-57—Johnson Air Base Vanguards 6, Marine Corps Sukiran Streaks 0
12-20-58—Air Force 20, Army 0

RIVIERA BOWL
(Marseille, France)
1-1-45—Railway Shop Battalion Unit 37, Army All-Stars 0 (18,000)

SALAD BOWL
(Phoenix, Ariz.)
1-1-53—San Diego Navy 81, 101st Airborne 20
1-1-54—Fort Ord 67, Great Lakes 12

SATELLITE BOWL
(Cocoa, Fla.)
12-29-57—Fort Carson 12, Fort Dix 6

SHRIMP BOWL
(Galveston, Texas)
1-1-55—Fort Ord 36, Fort Hood 0
12-18-55—Fort Hood 33, Little Creek 13
12-8-56—Bolling Air Force Base 29, Fort Hood 14
12-15-57—Bolling Air Force Base 28, San Diego Marines 7
12-14-58—Eglin Air Force Base 15, Brooke Medics 7
12-13-59—Quantico Marines 90, McClellan Air Force Base 0

SHURI BOWL
12-58—Air Force 60, Marine Corps 0

SPAGHETTI BOWL
(Florence, Italy)
1-1-45—5th Army 20, 12th Air Force 0 (20,000)
1-1-53—Salzburg Army 12, Wiesbaden AFC 7 (at Leghorn, Italy)

SUKIYAKI BOWL
12-56—Air Force 29, Marines 7

TEA BOWL
(London, England)
2-13-44—Canada 16, United States 6 (30,000)

12-31-44—Air Service Command Warriors 13, 8th Air Force Shuttle Raiders 0 (12,000)

TREASURY BOWL
(New York, N.Y.)
12-16-44—Randolph Field 13, 2nd Air Force 6 (8,356)

TYPHOON BOWL
12-56—Army 13, Marines 0

VALOR BOWL
(Chattanooga, Tenn.)
12-7-57—Hamilton Air Force Base 12, Quantico Marines 6

POSTSEASON BOWL INVOLVING NON-I-A TEAMS

HERITAGE BOWL
Site: Atlanta, Ga.
Stadium (Capacity): Georgia Dome (71,228)
Name Changes: Alamo Heritage Bowl (1991); Heritage Bowl (1993-94, 96-99); Jim Walters Heritage Bowl (1995)
Playing Surface: AstroTurf
Playing Sites: Joe Robbie Stadium, Miami (1991); Bragg Memorial Stadium, Tallahassee (1993); Georgia Dome, Atlanta (since 1994)

Date	Score (Attendance)
12-21-91	Alabama St. 36, N.C. A&T 13 (7,724)
1-2-93	Grambling 45, Florida A&M 15 (11,273)
1-1-94	Southern U. 11, South Carolina St. 0 (36,128)
12-30-94	South Carolina St. 31, Grambling 27 (22,179)
12-29-95	Southern U. 30, Florida A&M 25 (25,164)
12-31-96	Howard 27, Southern U. 24 (18,126)
12-27-97	Southern U. 34, South Carolina St. 28 (32,629)
12-26-98	Southern U. 28, Bethune-Cookman 2 (32,955)
12-18-99	Hampton 24, Southern U. 3 (29,561)

NCAA-CERTIFIED ALL-STAR GAMES

EAST-WEST SHRINE CLASSIC
Present Site: Palo Alto, Calif.
Stadium (Capacity): Stanford (85,500)
Playing Surface: Grass
Playing Sites: Ewing Field, San Francisco (1925); Kezar Stadium, San Francisco (1927-41); Sugar Bowl, New Orleans (1942); Kezar Stadium, San Francisco (1943-66); Candlestick Park, San Francisco (1967-68); Stanford Stadium, Palo Alto (1969); Oakland Coliseum (1971); Candlestick Park, San Francisco (1971-73); Stanford Stadium, Palo Alto (since 1974)

Date	Score (Attendance)
12-26-25	West 7-0 (20,000)
1-1-27	West 7-3 (15,000)
12-26-27	West 16-6 (27,500)
12-29-28	East 20-0 (55,000)
1-1-30	East 19-7 (58,000)
12-27-30	West 3-0 (40,000)
1-1-32	East 6-0 (45,000)
1-2-33	West 21-13 (45,000)
1-1-34	West 12-0 (35,000)
1-1-35	West 19-13 (52,000)
1-1-36	East 19-3 (55,000)
1-1-37	East 3-0 (38,000)
1-1-38	Tie 0-0 (55,000)
1-2-39	West 14-0 (60,000)
1-1-40	West 28-11 (50,000)
1-1-41	West 20-14 (60,000)
1-3-42	Tie 6-6 (35,000)
1-1-43	East 13-12 (57,000)
1-1-44	Tie 13-13 (55,000)
1-1-45	West 13-7 (60,000)
1-1-46	Tie 7-7 (60,000)
1-1-47	West 13-9 (60,000)
1-1-48	East 40-9 (60,000)
1-1-49	East 14-12 (59,000)
12-31-49	East 28-6 (60,000)
12-30-50	West 16-7 (60,000)
12-29-51	East 15-14 (60,000)
12-27-52	East 21-20 (60,000)
1-2-54	West 31-7 (60,000)
1-1-55	East 13-12 (60,000)
12-31-55	East 29-6 (60,000)
12-29-56	West 7-6 (60,000)
12-28-57	West 27-13 (60,000)
12-27-58	East 26-14 (60,000)
1-2-60	West 21-14 (60,000)

Date	Score (Attendance)
12-31-60	East 7-0 (60,000)
12-30-61	West 21-8 (60,000)
12-29-62	East 25-19 (60,000)
12-28-63	Tie 6-6 (60,000)
1-2-65	West 11-7 (60,000)
12-31-65	West 22-7 (47,000)
12-31-66	East 45-22 (46,000)
12-30-67	East 16-14 (29,000)
12-28-68	West 18-7 (29,000)
12-27-69	West 15-0 (70,000)
1-2-71	West 17-13 (50,000)
12-31-71	West 17-13 (35,000)
12-30-72	East 9-3 (37,000)
12-29-73	East 35-7 (30,000)
12-28-74	East 16-14 (35,000)
1-3-76	West 21-14 (75,000)
1-2-77	West 30-14 (45,000)
12-31-77	West 23-3 (65,000)
1-6-79	East 56-17 (72,000)
1-5-80	West 20-10 (75,000)
1-10-81	East 21-3 (76,000)
1-9-82	West 20-13 (75,000)
1-15-83	East 26-25 (72,999)
1-7-84	East 27-19 (77,000)
1-5-85	West 21-10 (72,000)
1-11-86	East 18-7 (77,000)
1-10-87	West 24-21 (74,000)
1-16-88	West 16-13 (62,000)
1-15-89	East 24-6 (76,000)
1-21-90	West 22-21 (78,000)
1-26-91	West 24-21 (72,000)
1-19-92	West 14-6 (83,000)
1-24-93	East 31-17 (84,000)
1-15-94	West 29-28 (60,000)
1-14-95	West 30-28 (35,079)
1-13-96	West 34-18 (68,500)
1-11-97	East 17-13 (62,500)
1-10-98	West 24-7 (32,500)
1-16-99	East 20-10 (50,000)
1-15-00	East 35-21 (65,246)

Series record: West won 39, East 31, 5 ties.

BLUE-GRAY ALL-STAR CLASSIC
Present Site: Montgomery, Ala.
Stadium (Capacity): Cramton Bowl (24,600)
Playing Surface: Grass
Playing Sites: Cramton Bowl, Montgomery (since 1939)

Date	Score (Attendance)
1-2-39	Blue 7-0 (8,000)
12-30-39	Gray 33-20 (10,000)
12-28-40	Blue 14-12 (14,000)
12-27-41	Gray 16-0 (15,571)
12-26-42	Gray 24-0 (16,000)
1943	No Game
12-30-44	Gray 24-7 (16,000)
12-29-45	Blue 26-0 (20,000)
12-28-46	Gray 20-13 (22,500)
12-27-47	Gray 33-6 (22,500)
12-25-48	Blue 19-13 (15,000)
12-31-49	Gray 27-13 (21,500)
12-30-50	Gray 31-6 (21,000)
12-29-51	Gray 20-14 (21,000)
12-27-52	Gray 28-7 (22,000)
12-26-53	Gray 40-20 (18,500)
12-25-54	Blue 14-7 (18,000)
12-31-55	Gray 20-19 (19,000)
12-29-56	Blue 14-0 (21,000)
12-28-57	Gray 21-20 (16,000)
12-27-58	Blue 16-0 (16,000)
12-26-59	Blue 20-8 (20,000)
12-31-60	Blue 35-7 (18,000)
12-30-61	Gray 9-7 (18,000)
12-29-62	Blue 10-6 (20,000)
12-28-63	Gray 21-14 (20,000)
12-26-64	Blue 10-6 (16,000)
12-25-65	Gray 23-19 (18,000)
12-24-66	Blue 14-9 (18,000)
12-30-67	Blue 22-16 (23,350)
12-28-68	Gray 28-7 (18,000)
12-27-69	Tie 6-6 (21,500)
12-28-70	Gray 38-7 (23,000)
12-28-71	Gray 9-0 (24,000)
12-27-72	Gray 27-15 (20,000)
12-18-73	Blue 20-14 (21,000)
12-17-74	Blue 29-24 (12,000)
12-19-75	Blue 14-13 (10,000)
12-24-76	Gray 31-10 (16,000)
12-30-77	Blue 20-16 (5,000)
12-29-78	Gray 28-24 (18,380)
12-25-79	Blue 22-13 (18,312)
12-25-80	Blue 24-23 (25,000)
12-25-81	Blue 21-9 (19,000)
12-25-82	Gray 20-10 (21,000)
12-25-83	Gray 17-13 (2,000)
12-25-84	Gray 33-6 (24,080)
12-25-85	Blue 27-20 (18,500)
12-25-86	Blue 31-7 (18,500)
12-25-87	Gray 12-10 (20,300)
12-25-88	Blue 22-21 (20,000)
12-25-89	Gray 28-10 (16,000)
12-25-90	Blue 17-14 (17,500)
12-25-91	Gray 20-12 (21,000)
12-25-92	Gray 27-17 (20,500)
12-25-93	Gray 17-10 (18,500)
12-25-94	Blue 38-27 (23,500)
12-25-95	Blue 26-7 (18,500)
12-25-96	Blue 44-34 (17,000)
12-25-97	Gray 31-24 (25,214)
12-25-98	Gray 31-24 (17,500)
12-25-99	Tie 22-22 (15,531)

Series record: Gray won 32, Blue 27, 2 ties.

HULA BOWL
Present Site: Maui, Hawaii
Stadium (Capacity): War Memorial (24,000)
Playing Surface: Grass
Format: From 1947 through 1950, the College All-Stars played the Hawaii All-Stars. Beginning in 1951, the Hawaiian team was augmented by players from the National Football League. This format, however, was changed to an all-collegiate contest—first between the East and West, then between North and South (in 1963), and then back to East and West in 1974 and 1995-96. In 1994, the format went to a collection of collegiate all-stars versus a collection of Hawaiian former collegiate players. In 1997, it reverted back to North-South. Teams are broken down into players from the northern United States (team named Kai, Hawaiian for ocean) against southern United States (team named Alna, Hawaiian for land)
Playing Sites: Honolulu Stadium (1960-74); Aloha Stadium (1975-98); War Memorial (since 1999)

Date	Score (Attendance)
1-10-60	East 34-8 (23,000)
1-8-61	East 14-7 (17,017)
1-7-62	Tie 7-7 (20,598)
1-6-63	North 20-13 (20,000)
1-4-64	North 20-13 (18,177)
1-9-65	South 16-14 (22,100)
1-8-66	North 27-26 (25,000)
1-7-67	North 28-27 (23,500)
1-6-68	North 50-6 (21,000)
1-4-69	North 13-7 (23,000)
1-10-70	South 35-13 (25,000)
1-9-71	North 42-32 (23,500)
1-8-72	North 24-7 (23,000)
1-6-73	South 17-3 (23,000)
1-5-74	East 24-14 (23,000)
1-4-75	East 34-25 (22,000)
1-10-76	East 16-0 (45,458)
1-8-77	West 20-17 (45,579)
1-7-78	West 42-22 (48,197)
1-6-79	East 29-24 (49,132)
1-5-80	East 17-10 (47,096)
1-10-81	West 24-17 (39,010)
1-9-82	West 26-23 (43,002)
1-15-83	East 30-14 (39,456)
1-7-84	West 21-16 (34,216)
1-5-85	East 34-14 (30,767)
1-11-86	West 23-10 (29,564)
1-10-87	West 16-14 (17,775)
1-16-88	West 20-18 (26,737)
1-7-89	East 21-10 (25,000)
1-13-90	West 21-13 (28,742)
1-19-91	East 23-10 (21,926)
1-11-92	West 27-20 (23,112)
1-16-93	West 13-10 (25,479)
1-22-94	College All-Stars 28-15 (33,947)
1-22-95	East 20-9 (19,074)
1-21-96	East 17-10 (25,112)
1-19-97	South 26, North 13 (24,725)
1-18-98	South 20, North 19 (20,079)
1-24-99	South 34, North 14 (23,719)
12-22-99	Tie 28-28 (23,719)

Series records: North-South (1963-73, 97-99)—North won 8, South 6, 1 tie; East-West (1960-62, 1974-93 and 1995-96)—East won 13, West 11, 1 tie; College All-Stars vs. Hawaiian All-Stars (1994)—College All-Stars won 1, Hawaiian All-Stars 0.

SENIOR BOWL
Played at Ladd-Peebles Stadium in Mobile, Ala., since 1951 under the auspices of the National Football League. North and South teams are composed of senior players who have used all of their collegiate eligibility. In 1991, the teams switched from North and South to AFC and NFC; in 1994, the teams switched back to North and South.

Date	Score (Attendance)
1-7-50	South 22, North 13 (at Jacksonville, Fla.)
1-6-51	South 19, North 18
1-5-52	North 20, South 6
1-3-53	North 28, South 13
1-9-54	North 20, South 14
1-8-55	South 12, North 6
1-7-56	South 12, North 2
1-5-57	South 21, North 7
1-11-58	North 15, South 13
1-3-59	South 21, North 12
1-9-60	North 26, South 7 (40,119)
1-7-61	South 33, North 26
1-6-62	South 42, North 7
1-5-63	South 33, North 27
1-4-64	South 28, North 21 (37,094)
1-9-65	Tie 7-7 (40,605)
1-8-66	South 27, North 18
1-7-67	North 35, South 13
1-6-68	South 34, North 21
1-11-69	North 27, South 16
1-10-70	Tie 37-37
1-9-71	North 31, South 13 (40,646)
1-8-72	North 26, South 21 (40,646)
1-6-73	South 33, North 30 (40,646)
1-12-74	North 16, South 13 (40,646)
1-11-75	Tie 17-17 (40,646)
1-10-76	North 42, South 35 (40,646)
1-9-77	North 27, South 24 (40,646)
1-7-78	Tie 17-17 (40,646)
1-13-79	South 41, North 21 (40,100)
1-12-80	North 57, South 3 (40,646)
1-17-81	North 23, South 10 (40,102)
1-16-82	South 27, North 10 (39,410)
1-22-83	North 14, South 6 (37,511)
1-14-84	South 21, North 20 (38,254)
1-12-85	South 23, North 7 (33,500)
1-18-86	North 31, South 17 (40,646)
1-17-87	South 42, North 38
1-23-88	North 21, South 7
1-21-89	South 13, North 12 (39,742)
1-20-90	North 41, South 0 (42,400)
1-19-91	AFC 38, NFC 28 (37,500)
1-18-92	AFC 13, NFC 10 (37,100)
1-16-93	NFC 21, AFC 6 (37,124)
1-22-94	South 35, North 32 (39,200)
1-21-95	South 14, North 7 (40,007)
1-20-96	North 25, South 10 (40,700)
1-18-97	North 35, South 14 (40,646)
1-17-98	South 31, North 8 (40,820)
1-23-99	South 31, North 21 (41,000)
1-22-00	North 24, South 21 (40,646)

Series records: North-South (1950-90 and 1994 to present)—South won 23, North 21, 4 ties; AFC-NFC (1991-93)—AFC won 2, NFC 1.

ALL-STAR GRIDIRON CLASSIC
Present Site: Orlando, Fla.
Stadium (Capacity): Florida Citrus Bowl (70,000)
Playing Surface: Grass

Date	Score (Attendance)
1-16-99	Team Florida 17, Team USA 9 (29,725)
1-15-00	Team USA 21, Team Florida 14 (21,298)

DISCONTINUED ALL-STAR FOOTBALL GAMES
Many of these games were identified without complete information such as scores, teams, sites or dates. Please send any updates or additional information to: NCAA Statistics Service, P.O. Box 6222, Indianapolis, Indiana 46206-6222.

SPECIAL POSTSEASON GAMES

ALL-AMERICAN BOWL (1969-77)
(Tampa, Fla.)

Date	Score (Attendance)
1-4-69	North 21, South 15 (16,380)
1-3-70	South 24, North 23 (17,642)
1-10-71	North 39, South 2 (12,000)
1-9-72	North 27, South 8 (20,137)
1-7-73	North 10, South 6 (23,416)
1-6-74	North 28, South 7 (24,536)
1-5-75	South 28, North 22 (19,246)
1-10-76	North 21, South 14 (15,321)
1-2-77	North 21, South 20 (14,207)

AMERICAN COLLEGE ALL-STAR GAME (1948)
(Los Angeles, Calif.)

Date	Score
12-18-48	American All-Stars 43, Canadian All-Stars 0
12-26-48	American All-Stars 14, Hawaiian All-Stars 0

BLACK COLLEGE ALL-STAR BOWL (1979-82)

Date	Score (Location, Attendance)
1-7-79	East 25, West 20 (at New Orleans, La.)
1-5-80	West 27, East 21 (ot) (at New Orleans, La.)
1-17-81	West 19, East 10 (at Jackson, Miss.) (7,500)
1-16-82	West 7, East 0 (at Jackson, Miss.)

CAMP FOOTBALL FOUNDATION BOWL (1974)

CANADIAN-AMERICAN BOWL (1978-79)
(Tampa, Fla.)

Date	Score (Attendance)
1-8-78	U.S. All-Stars 22, Canadian All-Stars 7 (11,328)
1-6-79	U.S. All-Stars 34, Canadian All-Stars 14 (11,033)

CHALLENGE BOWL (1978-79)
(Seattle, Wash.)

Date	Score (Attendance)
1-14-78	Pacific-8 27, Big Ten 20 (20,578)
1-13-79	Pacific-10 36, Big Eight 23 (23,961)

CHICAGO COLLEGE ALL-STAR FOOTBALL GAME (1934-76)

An all-star team composed of the top senior collegiate players met the National Football League champions (1933-66) or the Super Bowl champions (1967-75) from the previous season, beginning in 1934. The only time the all-stars did not play the league champions was in 1935. All games except 1943 and 1944 were played at Soldier Field, Chicago, Ill. The 1943 and 1944 games were played at Dyche Stadium, Evanston, Ill.

Date	Score (Attendance)
8-31-34	(Tie) Chicago Bears 0-0 (79,432)
8-29-35	Chicago Bears 5, All-Stars 0 (77,450)
9-2-36	(Tie) Detroit 7-7 (76,000)
9-1-37	All-Stars 6, Green Bay 0 (84,560)
8-31-38	All-Stars 28, Washington 16 (74,250)
8-30-39	New York Giants 9, All-Stars 0 (81,456)
8-29-40	Green Bay 45, All-Stars 28 (84,567)
8-28-41	Chicago Bears 37, All-Stars 13 (98,203)
8-28-42	Chicago Bears 21, All-Stars 0 (101,100)
8-25-43	All-Stars 27, Washington 7 (48,471)
8-30-44	Chicago Bears 24, All-Stars 21 (48,769)
8-30-45	Green Bay 19, All-Stars 7 (92,753)
8-23-46	All-Stars 16, Los Angeles 0 (97,380)
8-22-47	All-Stars 16, Chicago Bears 0 (105,840)
8-20-48	Chicago Cardinals 28, All-Stars 0 (101,220)
8-12-49	Philadelphia 38, All-Stars 0 (93,780)
8-11-50	All-Stars 17, Philadelphia 7 (88,885)
8-17-51	Cleveland 33, All-Stars 0 (92,180)
8-15-52	Los Angeles 10, All-Stars 7 (88,316)
8-14-53	Detroit 24, All-Stars 10 (93,818)
8-13-54	Detroit 31, All-Stars 6 (93,470)
8-12-55	All-Stars 30, Cleveland 27 (75,000)
8-10-56	Cleveland 26, All-Stars 0 (75,000)
8-9-57	New York Giants 22, All-Stars 12 (75,000)
8-15-58	All-Stars 35, Detroit 19 (70,000)
8-14-59	Baltimore 29, All-Stars 0 (70,000)
8-12-60	Baltimore 32, All-Stars 7 (70,000)
8-4-61	Philadelphia 28, All-Stars 14 (66,000)
8-3-62	Green Bay 42, All-Stars 20 (65,000)
8-2-63	All-Stars 20, Green Bay 17 (65,000)
8-7-64	Chicago Bears 28, All-Stars 17 (65,000)

Date	Score (Attendance)
8-6-65	Cleveland 24, All-Stars 16 (68,000)
8-5-66	Green Bay 38, All-Stars 0 (72,000)
8-4-67	Green Bay 27, All-Stars 0 (70,934)
8-2-68	Green Bay 34, All-Stars 17 (69,917)
8-1-69	New York Jets 26, All-Stars 24 (74,208)
7-31-70	Kansas City 24, All-Stars 3 (69,940)
7-30-71	Baltimore 24, All-Stars 17 (52,289)
7-28-72	Dallas 20, All-Stars 7 (54,162)
7-27-73	Miami 14, All-Stars 3 (54,103)
1974	No game played
8-1-75	Pittsburgh 21, All-Stars 14 (54,103)
7-23-76	*Pittsburgh 24, All-Stars 0 (52,895)

*Game was not completed due to thunderstorms.

CHRISTIAN BOWL (1955)
(Murfreesboro, Tenn.)

Date	Score (Attendance)
12-26-55	East 21, West 10 (4,000)

COACHES ALL-AMERICAN GAME (1961-76)

Date	Score (Attendance)

at Buffalo, N.Y.

6-23-61	West 30, East 20 (12,913)
6-29-62	East 13, West 8 (22,759)
6-29-63	West 22, East 21 (20,840)
6-27-64	East 18, West 15 (21,112)
6-26-65	East 34, West 14 (25,501)

at Atlanta, Ga.

7-9-66	West 24, East 7 (38,236)
7-9-67	East 12, West 9 (29,145)
6-28-68	West 34, East 20 (21,120)
6-28-69	West 14, East 10 (17,008)

at Lubbock, Texas

6-28-70	East 34, West 27 (42,150)
6-26-71	West 33, East 28 (43,320)
6-24-72	East 42, West 20 (42,314)
6-23-73	West 20, East 6 (43,272)
6-22-74	West 36, East 6 (42,368)
6-21-75	East 23, West 21 (36,108)
6-19-76	West 35, East 17 (36,504)

COPPER BOWL (1958-60)
(Tempe, Ariz.)

Date	Score (Attendance)
12-20-58	Southwest All-Stars 22, National All-Stars 13 (12,000)
12-26-59	National All-Stars 21, Southwest All-Stars 6 (16,000)
12-31-60	National All-Stars 27, Southwest All-Stars 8 (8,000)

CRUSADE BOWL (1963)
(Baltimore, Md.)

Date	Score (Attendance)
1-6-63	East 38, West 10 (2,400)

DALLAS ALL-STAR GAME (1936-39)
(Dallas, Texas)

Date	Score
9-7-36	Southwest All-Stars 7, Chicago Bears 6
9-6-37	Southwest All-Stars 6, Chicago Bears 0
9-5-38	Southwest All-Stars 13, Washington Redskins 7
9-4-39	Green Bay Packers 31, Southwest All-Stars 20

DIXIE CLASSIC (1928-31)
(Dallas, Texas)

Date	Score (Attendance)
12-29-28	Southwest Conference 14, Small Texas Schools 6
1-1-29	Big Six Conference 14, Southwest Conference 6 (10,000)
1-1-30	Midwest 25, Southwest Conference 12 (15,000)
1-1-31	Southwest Conference 18, Midwest 0 (14,000)

EAST-WEST BLACK ALL-STAR GAME (1971)
(Houston, Texas)

Date	Score (Attendance)
12-11-71	East 19, West 10 (5,156)

EAST-WEST COLLEGE ALL-STAR GAME (1932)
(Demonstrated at Tenth Olympiad, Los Angeles, Calif.; East team composed of players from Harvard, Princeton and Yale, West team composed of players from California, Southern California and Stanford)

Date	Score (Attendance)
8-8-32	West 7, East 6 (50,000)

FREEDOM BOWL ALL-STAR CLASSIC (1984-86)
(Atlanta, Ga.)
Southwestern Athletic Conference vs. Mid-Eastern Athletic Conference.

Date	Score (Attendance)
1-14-84	SWAC 36, MEAC 22 (16,097)
1-12-85	SWAC 14, MEAC 0 (18,352)
1-11-86	SWAC 16, MEAC 14 (10,200)

FREEDOM BOWL ALL-STAR CLASSIC (1990)
(Houston, Texas)

Date	Score
1-13-90	North 14, South 13

FREEDOM CLASSIC (1976)

Year	Score (Attendance)
1976	West 12, East 9 (6,654)

JAPAN BOWL
(Yokohama, Japan)

Date	Score (Attendance)
1-18-76	West 27-18 (68,000)
1-16-77	West 21-10 (58,000)
1-15-78	East 26-10 (32,500)
1-14-79	East 33-14 (55,000)
1-13-80	West 28-17 (27,000)
1-17-81	West 25-13 (30,000)
1-16-82	West 28-17 (28,000)
1-23-83	West 30-21 (30,000)
1-15-84	West 26-21 (26,000)
1-13-85	West 28-14 (30,000)
1-11-86	East 31-14 (30,000)
1-11-87	West 24-17 (30,000)
1-10-88	West 17-3 (30,000)
1-15-89	East 30-7 (29,000)
1-13-90	East 24-10 (27,000)
1-12-91	West 20-14 (30,000)
1-11-92	East 14-13 (50,000)
1-9-93	East 27-13 (46,000)

LOS ANGELES ALL-STAR GAME (1948)
(Los Angeles, Calif.)

Date	Score
1-18-48	West 34, East 20

MARTIN LUTHER KING ALL-AMERICA CLASSIC (1990-91)
(Division I-A vs. all other divisions)

Date	Score (Attendance)
1-15-90	All Div. All-Stars 35, I-A All-Stars 24 (350) (at San Jose, Calif.)
1-14-91	I-A All-Stars 21, All Div. All-Stars 14 (6,272) (at St. Petersburg, Fla.)

NORTH-SOUTH ALL-STAR SHRINE GAME (1930-34, 1948-73, 1976)

Date	Score (Attendance)
1-1-30	North 21, South 12 (20,000) (at Atlanta, Ga.) (Southern Conference All-Star Game)
12-28-30	South 7, North 0 (2,000) (at New York, N.Y.)
12-10-32	South 7, North 6 (500) (at Baltimore, Md.)
12-24-33	North 3, South 0 (5,000) (at New York, N.Y.)
1-1-34	North 7, South 0 (12,000) (at Knoxville, Tenn.) (Southeastern Conference All-Star Game)

at Miami, Fla.

12-25-48	South 24, North 14 (33,056)
12-25-49	North 20, South 14 (37,378)
12-25-50	South 14, North 9 (39,132)
12-25-51	South 35, North 7 (39,995)
12-25-52	North 21, South 21 (42,866)
12-25-53	South 20, North 0 (44,715)
12-25-54	South 20, North 17 (37,847)
12-25-55	South 20, North 7 (42,179)
12-26-56	North 17, South 7 (39,181)
12-25-57	North 23, South 20 (28,303)
12-27-58	South 49, North 20 (35,519)
12-26-59	North 27, South 17 (35,185)
12-26-60	North 41, South 14 (26,146)
12-25-61	South 35, North 16 (18,892)
12-22-62	South 15, North 14 (16,952)
12-21-63	South 23, North 14 (19,120)
12-25-64	North 37, South 30 (29,124)
12-25-65	South 21, North 14 (25,640)
12-26-66	North 27, South 14 (28,569)
12-25-67	North 24, South 0 (17,400)
12-25-68	North 3, South 0 (18,063)
12-25-69	North 31, South 10 (23,527)
12-25-70	North 28, South 7 (15,402)
12-27-71	South 7, North 6 (18,640)
12-25-72	North 17, South 10 (18,013)
12-25-73	South 27, North 6 (10,672)

at Pontiac, Mich.
Date	Score
12-17-76	South 24, North 0 (41,627)

OHIO SHRINE BOWL (1972-76)
(Columbus, Ohio)
Date	Score
12-9-72	East 20, West 7
12-1-73	East 8, West 6
12-7-74	East 27, West 6
1975	West 17, East 7
12-4-76	East 24, West 8 (played elsewhere)

OLYMPIA GOLD BOWL (1982)
(San Diego, Calif.)
Date	Score (Attendance)
1-16-82	National All-Stars 30, American All-Stars 21 (22,316)

OLYMPIC GAME (1933)
(Chicago, Ill.)
Date	Score (Attendance)
8-24-33	East 13, West 7 (50,000)

OPTIMIST ALL-AMERICA BOWL (1958-62)
(Tucson, Ariz.)
Date	Score (Attendance)
1-4-58	College All-Stars 56, Tucson Cowboys 28
1-3-59	Major-College 14, Small-College 12 (10,000)
1-2-60	Major College 53, Small-College 0 (14,500)
12-26-60	Major-College 25, Small-College 12
12-30-61	Major-College 31, Small-College 0 (14,000)
12-29-62	Small-College 14, Major-College 13

POTATO BOWL (1967)
(Bakersfield, Calif.)
Date	Score (Attendance)
12-23-67	North 23, South 7 (5,600)

ROCKY MOUNTAIN CONFERENCE-NORTH CENTRAL CONFERENCE GAME (1930)
(Elks Charity Bowl)
(Denver, Colo.)
Date	Score
1-1-30	North Central 13, Rocky Mountain 6

SALAD BOWL ALL-STAR GAME (1955)
(Phoenix, Ariz.)
Date	Score (Attendance)
1-1-55	Skyline Conference 20, Border Conference 13 (8,000)
12-31-55	Border Conference 13, Skyline Conference 10

SHERIDAN BLACK ALL-STAR GAME (1979-82)
(See Black College All-Star Bowl)

SMOKE BOWL (1941)
(Richmond, Va.)
Date	Score (Attendance)
1-1-41	Norfolk All-Stars 16, Richmond All-Stars 2 (5,000)

SOUTHWEST CHALLENGE BOWL (1963-64)
(Corpus Christi, Texas)
Date	Score (Attendance)
1-5-63	National 33, Southwest 13

Date	Score (Attendance)
1-4-64	National 66, Southwest 14 (10,200)

U.S. BOWL (1962)
(Washington, D.C.)
(Teams were composed of players selected in the recent NFL draft)
Date	Score
1-7-62	West 33, East 19

Special Regular-Season Games

REGULAR-SEASON GAMES PLAYED IN USA

EDDIE ROBINSON CLASSIC
Present Site: South Bend, Ind.
Stadium (Capacity): Notre Dame (80,225)
Playing Surface: Grass
Playing Sites: Memorial Stadium, Lincoln, Neb. (1998); Notre Dame Stadium, South Bend, Ind. (1999)

Date	Teams
8-29-98	Nebraska 56, Louisiana Tech 27 (76,021)
8-28-99	Notre Dame 48, Kansas 13 (80,012)

BCA CLASSIC
Present Site: Blacksburg, Va.
Stadium (Capacity): Lane (50,000)
Playing Surface: Grass
Sponsor: Black Coaches' Association
Playing Sites: Spartan Stadium (1998); Royal-Memorial Stadium (1999); Lane Stadium (2000)

Date	Teams
8-29-98	Colorado St. 23, Michigan St. 16 (68,624)
8-28-99	North Carolina St. 23, Texas 20 (82,252)
8-27-00	Georgia Tech at Virginia Tech

KICKOFF CLASSIC
Present Site: East Rutherford, N.J.
Stadium (Capacity): Giants Stadium (76,000)
Playing Surface: AstroTurf
Sponsor: National Association of Collegiate Directors of Athletics (NACDA). It is a permitted 12th regular-season game.
Playing Site: Giants Stadium (since 1983)

Date	Teams, Score (Attendance)
8-29-83	Nebraska 44, Penn St. 6 (71,123)
8-27-84	Miami (Fla.) 20, Auburn 18 (51,131)
8-29-85	Brigham Young 28, Boston College 14 (51,227)
8-27-86	Alabama 16, Ohio St. 10 (68,296)
8-30-87	Tennessee 23, Iowa 22 (54,681)
8-27-88	Nebraska 23, Texas A&M 14 (58,172)
8-31-89	Notre Dame 36, Virginia 13 (77,323)
8-31-90	Southern California 34, Syracuse 16 (57,293)
8-28-91	Penn St. 34, Georgia Tech 22 (77,409)
8-29-92	North Carolina St. 24, Iowa 14 (46,251)
8-28-93	Florida St. 42, Kansas 0 (51,734)
8-28-94	Nebraska 31, West Virginia 0 (58,233)
8-27-95	Ohio St. 38, Boston College 6 (62,711)
8-25-96	Penn St. 24, Southern California 7 (77,716)
8-24-97	Syracuse 34, Wisconsin 0 (51,185)
8-31-98	Florida St. 23, Texas A&M 14 (59,232)
8-29-99	Miami (Fla.) 23, Ohio St. 12 (73,037)
8-27-00	Penn St. vs. Southern California

PIGSKIN CLASSIC
Present Site: Jacksonville, Fla.
Stadium (Capacity): Alltel (76,976)
Playing Surface: Grass
Sponsor: None. It is a permitted 12th regular-season game.
Playing Sites: Anaheim Stadium (1990-94); Michigan Stadium (1995); Cougar Stadium (1996); Soldier Field (1997); L.A. Memorial Coliseum (1998); Beaver Stadium (1999); Alltel Stadium (2000)

Date	Teams, Score (Attendance)
8-26-90	Colorado 31, Tennessee 31 (33,458)
8-29-91	Florida St. 44, Brigham Young 28 (38,363)
8-26-92	Texas A&M 10, Stanford 7 (35,240)
8-29-93	North Carolina 31, Southern California 9 (49,309)
8-29-94	Ohio St. 34, Fresno St. 10 (28,513)
8-26-95	Michigan 18, Virginia 17 (101,444)
8-24-96	Brigham Young 41, Texas A&M 37 (55,229)
8-23-97	Northwestern 24, Oklahoma 0 (36,804)
8-30-98	Southern California 27, Purdue 17 (56,623)
8-28-99	Penn St. 41, Arizona 7 (97,168)
8-26-00	Florida St. vs. Brigham Young

BIG 12 CONFERENCE CHAMPIONSHIP
Present Site: San Antonio, Tex.
Stadium (Capacity): Alamodome (65,000)
Playing Surface: AstroTurf
Playing Sites: Trans World Dome, St. Louis, Mo. (1996; 1998); Alamodome, San Antonio, Tex. (1997; 1999)

Date	Teams, Score (Attendance)
12-7-96	Texas (South Div.) 37, Nebraska (North Div.) 27 (63,109)
12-6-97	Nebraska (North Div.) 54, Texas A&M (South Div.) 15 (64,824)
12-5-98	Texas A&M (South Div.) 36, Kansas St. (North Div.) 33 (60,789)
12-4-99	Nebraska (North Div.) 22, Texas (South Div.) 6 (65,035)

MID-AMERICAN CONFERENCE CHAMPIONSHIP
Present Site: Huntington, W.Va.
Stadium (Capacity): Marshall University (30,000)
Playing Surface: Poly Turf
Playing Site: Marshall University Stadium (since 1997)

Date	Teams Score (Attendance)
12-5-97	Marshall (East Div.) 34, Toledo (West Div.) 14 (28,021)
12-4-98	Marshall (East Div.) 23, Toledo (West Div.) 14 (28,085)
12-3-99	Marshall (East Div.) 34, Western Mich. (West Div.) 30 (28,069)

SOUTHEASTERN CONFERENCE CHAMPIONSHIP
Present Site: Atlanta, Ga.
Stadium (Capacity): Georgia Dome (71,228)
Playing Surface: AstroTurf
Playing Sites: Legion Field (1992-93); Georgia Dome (since 1994)

Date	Teams, Score (Attendance)
12-5-92	Alabama (Western Div.) 28, Florida (Eastern Div.) 21 (83,091) (at Birmingham, Ala.)
12-4-93	Florida (Eastern Div.) 28, Alabama (Western Div.) 13 (76,345) (at Birmingham, Ala.)
12-3-94	Florida (Eastern Div.) 24, Alabama (Western Div.) 23 (74,751)
12-2-95	Florida (Eastern Div.) 34, Arkansas (Western Div.) 3 (71,325)
12-7-96	Florida (Eastern Div.) 45, Alabama (Western Div.) 30 (74,132)
12-6-97	Tennessee (Eastern Div.) 30, Auburn (Western Div.) 29 (74,896)
12-5-98	Tennessee (Eastern Div.) 24, Mississippi St. (Western Div.) 14 (74,795)
12-4-99	Alabama (Western Div.) 34, Florida (Eastern Div.) 7 (74,309)

WESTERN ATHLETIC CONFERENCE CHAMPIONSHIP
Site: Las Vegas, Nev.
Stadium (Capacity): Sam Boyd (32,000)
Playing Surface: Monsanto Turf
Playing Site: Sam Boyd Stadium (1996-98)

Date	Teams, Score (Attendance)
12-7-96	Brigham Young (Mountain Div.) 28, Wyoming (Pacific Div.) 25 (41,238)
12-6-97	Colorado St. (Pacific Div.) 41, New Mexico (Mountain Div.) 13 (12,706)
12-5-98	Air Force (Pacific Div.) 20, Brigham Young (Mountain Div.) 13 (32,745)

REGULAR-SEASON GAMES PLAYED IN FOREIGN COUNTRIES

TOKYO, JAPAN
(Called Mirage Bowl 1976-85, Coca-Cola Classic from 1986. Played at Tokyo Olympic Memorial Stadium 1976-87, Tokyo Dome from 1988-93.)

Date	Teams, Score (Attendance)
9-4-76	Grambling 42, Morgan St. 16 (50,000)
12-11-77	Grambling 35, Temple 32 (50,000)
12-10-78	Temple 28, Boston College 24 (55,000)
11-24-79	Notre Dame 40, Miami (Fla.) 15 (62,574)
11-30-80	UCLA 34, Oregon St. 3 (86,000)
11-28-81	Air Force 21, San Diego St. 16 (80,000)
11-27-82	Clemson 21, Wake Forest 17 (64,700)
11-26-83	Southern Methodist 34, Houston 12 (70,000)
11-17-84	Army 45, Montana 31 (60,000)
11-30-85	Southern California 20, Oregon 6 (65,000)
11-30-86	Stanford 29, Arizona 24 (55,000)
11-28-87	California 17, Washington St. 17 (45,000)
12-3-88	Oklahoma St. 45, Texas Tech 42 (56,000)
12-4-89	Syracuse 24, Louisville 13 (50,000)
12-2-90	Houston 62, Arizona St. 45 (50,000)
11-30-91	Clemson 33, Duke 21 (50,000)
12-6-92	Nebraska 38, Kansas St. 24 (50,000)
12-5-92	Wisconsin 41, Michigan St. 20 (51,500)

MELBOURNE, AUSTRALIA

Date	Teams, Score (Attendance)
12-6-85*	Wyoming 24, UTEP 21 (22,000)
12-4-87†	Brigham Young 30, Colorado St. 26 (76,652)

*Played at V.F.L. Park. †Played at Princes Park.

YOKOHAMA, JAPAN

Date	Teams, Score (Attendance)
12-2-78	Brigham Young 28, UNLV 24 (27,500)

OSAKA, JAPAN

Date	Teams, Score (Attendance)
9-3-78	Utah St. 10, Idaho St. 0 (15,000)

HAVANA, CUBA
(Played at Almandares Park)

SPECIAL REGULAR-SEASON GAMES

Date **Teams, Score (Attendance)**
12-25-07 LSU 56, Havana University 0 (10,000)

DUBLIN, IRELAND
#Called Emerald Isle Classic. Played at Lansdowne Road Stadium. ¢Played at Croke Park.

Date **Teams, Score (Attendance)**
11-19-88 Boston College 38, Army 24 (45,525)#
12-2-89 Pittsburgh 46, Rutgers 29 (19,800)#
11-2-96 Notre Dame 54, Navy 27 (38,651)¢

LONDON, ENGLAND

Date **Teams, Score (Attendance)**
10-16-88 Richmond 20, Boston U. 17 (6,000)

MILAN, ITALY
(Played at The Arena.)

Date **Teams, Score (Attendance)**
10-28-89 Villanova 28, Rhode Island 25 (5,000)

LIMERICK, IRELAND
(Wild Geese Classic. Played at Limerick Gaelic Grounds.)

Date **Teams, Score (Attendance)**
11-16-91 Holy Cross 24, Fordham 19 (17,411)

FRANKFURT, GERMANY
(Played at Wald Stadium.)

Date **Teams, Score (Attendance)**
9-19-92 Heidelberg 7, Otterbein 7 (4,351)

GALWAY, IRELAND
(Called Christopher Columbus Classic.)

Date **Teams, Score (Attendance)**
11-29-92 Bowdoin 7, Tufts 6 (2,500)

HAMILTON, BERMUDA
(Played at Bermuda National Soccer Stadium.)

Date **Teams, Score (Attendance)**
11-20-93 Georgetown 17, Wash. & Lee 14 (3,218)
11-19-94 Davidson 28, Sewanee 14 (2,000)
10-28-95 Fordham 17, Holy Cross 10 (2,436)

EXHIBITION GAMES
(Games involving an active NCAA member versus an exhibition opponent played in the United States. Not counted as a regular-season game.)

ORLANDO, FLORIDA
(Played at Citrus Bowl)

Date **Teams, Score (Attendance)**
10-3-92 UCF 42, Moscow Bears 6 (5,412)

EXHIBITION GAMES PLAYED IN FOREIGN COUNTRIES
(Games involving an active NCAA member versus a team from another country. Not counted as a regular-season game.)

KYOTO, JAPAN
(Played at Nishi Kyogoku Stadium)

Date **Teams, Score (Attendance)**
3-29-97 Harvard 42, Kyoto 35 (16,000)

COLLEGE FOOTBALL TROPHY GAMES
Following is a list of the current college football trophy games. The games are listed alphabetically by the trophy-object name. The date refers to the season the trophy was first exchanged and is not necessarily the start of competition between the participants. A game involving interdivision teams is listed in the higher-division classification.

DIVISION I-A

Trophy	Date	Colleges
Anniversary Award	1985	Bowling Green-Kent
Apple Cup	1962	Washington-Washington St.
Axe	1933	California-Stanford
Band Drum	1935	Kansas-Missouri
Battle for the Bell	1997	Marshall-Ohio
Bayou Bucket	1974	Houston-Rice
Beehive Boot	1971	Brigham Young, Utah, Utah St., Southern Utah, Weber St.
Bell	1927	Missouri-Nebraska
Bell Clapper	1931	Oklahoma-Oklahoma St.
Big Game	1979	Arizona-Arizona St.
Black Diamond Trophy	1997	Virginia Tech-West Virginia
Blue Key Victory Bell	1940	Ball St.-Indiana St.
Brass Spittoon	1950	Indiana-Michigan St.
Brass Spittoon	1981	New Mexico St.-UTEP
Bronze Boot	1968	Colorado St.-Wyoming
Cannon	1943	Illinois-Purdue
Commander in Chief's	1972	Air Force, Army, Navy
Commonwealth Cup	1996	Virginia-Virginia Tech
Cy-Hawk	1977	Iowa-Iowa St.
Floyd of Rosedale	1935	Iowa-Minnesota
Foy-O.D.K.	1948	Alabama-Auburn
Fremont Cannon	1970	Nevada-UNLV
Golden Boot	1996	LSU-Arkansas
Golden Egg	1927	Mississippi-Mississippi St.
Golden Hat	1941	Oklahoma-Texas
Governor's Cup	1969	Kansas-Kansas St.
Governor's Cup	1958	Florida-Florida St.
Governor's Cup	1983	Colorado-Colorado St.
Governor's Cup	1994	Louisville-Kentucky
Govenor's Cup	1995	Georgia-Georgia Tech
Governor's Flag*	1953	Arizona-Arizona St.
Governor's Victory Bell	1993	Minnesota-Penn St.
Illibuck	1925	Illinois-Ohio St.
Iron Bowl	1983	Alabama-Auburn
Jefferson-Epps Trophy	1995	Florida St.-Virginia
Keg of Nails	1950	Cincinnati-Louisville
Kit Carson Rifle	1938	Arizona-New Mexico
Land Grant Trophy	1993	Michigan St.-Penn St.
Little Brown Jug	1909	Michigan-Minnesota
Mayors' Cup	1998	Rice-Southern Methodist
Megaphone	1949	Michigan St.-Notre Dame
Old Oaken Bucket	1925	Indiana-Purdue
Old Wagon Wheel	1948	Brigham Young-Utah St.
Paniolo Trophy	1979	Hawaii-Wyoming
Paul Bunyan Axe	1948	Minnesota-Wisconsin
Paul Bunyan-Governor of Michigan	1953	Michigan-Michigan St.
Peace Pipe	1929	Missouri-Oklahoma
Peace Pipe	1955	Miami (Ohio)-Western Mich.
Peace Pipe	1980	Bowling Green-Toledo
Ram-Falcon	1980	Air Force-Colorado St.
Sabine Shoe	1937	Lamar-La.-Lafayette
Schwartzwalder Trophy	1993	Syracuse-West Virginia
Shillelagh	1952	Notre Dame-Southern California
Shillelagh	1958	Notre Dame-Purdue
Silver Spade/Brass Spittoon	1955	New Mexico St.-UTEP
Steel Tire	1976	Akron-Youngstown St.
Telephone	1960	Iowa St.-Missouri
Textile Bowl	1981	Clemson-North Carolina St.
Tomahawk	1945	Illinois-Northwestern
Victory Bell	1942	Southern California-UCLA
Victory Bell	1948	Cincinnati-Miami (Ohio)
Victory Bell	1948	Duke-North Carolina
Wagon Wheel	1946	Akron-Kent St.
Williams Trophy	1998	Rice-Tulsa

*Changed to Big Game Trophy in 1979.

DIVISION I-AA

Trophy	Date	Colleges
Battle for the Paddle	1998	Nicholls St.-Southwest Texas St.
Bill Knight	1986	Massachusetts-New Hampshire
Brice-Colwell Musket	1946	Maine-New Hampshire
Chief Caddo	1962	Northwestern St.-Stephen F. Austin
Field Cup	1983	Evansville-Ky. Wesleyan
Gem State	1978	Boise St., Idaho, Idaho St.
Governor's	1979	Central Conn. St.-Southern Conn. St.
Governor's Cup	1972	Brown-Rhode Island
Governor's Cup	1975	Dartmouth-Princeton
Governor's Cup	1984	Eastern Wash.-Idaho
Grizzly-Bobcat Painting	1984	Montana-Montana St.
Harvey—Shin-A-Ninny Totem Pole	1961	Middle Tenn. St.-Tennessee Tech
Little Brown Stein	1938	Idaho-Montana
Mare's	1987	Murray St.–Tenn.-Martin
Ol' Mountain Jug	1976	Appalachian St.-Western Caro.
Ol' School Bell	1988	Jacksonville St.-Troy St.
Ram—Crusader Cup	1951	Fordham-Holy Cross
Red Belt	1978	Murray St.-Western Ky.
Ron Rogerson Memorial	1988	Maine-Rhode Island
Silver Shako	1976	Citadel-VMI
Team of Game's MVP	1960	Lafayette-Lehigh
Top Dog	1971	Butler-Indianapolis
Victory Carriage	1960	UC Davis-Cal St. Sacramento

NON-NCAA MEMBERS

Trophy	Date	Colleges
Home Stake-Gold Mine	1950	Black Hills St.-South Dak. Tech
Paint Bucket	1961	Jamestown-Valley City St.

Coaching Records

All-Division Coaching Records 370
Division I-A Coaching Records 371
Division I-AA Coaching Records 391
Division II Coaching Records 395
Division III Coaching Records 398
Coaching Honors..402

All-Division Coaching Records

Coaches With Career Winning Percentage of .800 or Better

This list includes all coaches in history with a winning percentage of at least .800 over a career of at least 10 seasons at four-year colleges (regardless of division or association). Bowl and playoff games included.

Coach (Alma Mater) (Colleges Coached, Tenure)	Years	Won	Lost	Tied	Pct.
#Larry Kehres (Mount Union '71) (Mount Union 1986—)	†14	150	17	3	.891
Knute Rockne (Notre Dame '14) (Notre Dame 1918-30)	13	105	12	5	.881
Frank Leahy (Notre Dame '31) (Boston College 1939-40; Notre Dame 1941-43, 1946-53)	13	107	13	9	.864
Bob Reade (Cornell College '54) (Augustana [Ill.] 1979-94)	†16	146	23	1	.862
#Dick Farley (Boston U. '68) (Williams 1987—)	†13	88	13	3	.861
Doyt Perry (Bowling Green '32) (Bowling Green 1955-64)	†10	77	11	5	.855
George Woodruff (Yale '89) (Pennsylvania 1892-1901; Illinois 1903; Carlisle 1905)	12	142	25	2	.846
#Chuck Broyles (Pittsburg St. '70) (Pittsburg St. 1990—)	†10	103	18	2	.846
Jake Gaither (Knoxville '27) (Florida A&M 1945-69)	†25	203	36	4	.844
Dave Maurer (Denison '54) (Wittenberg 1969-83)	†15	129	23	3	.842
Paul Hoerneman (Heidelberg '38) (Heidelberg 1946-59)	†14	102	18	4	.839
Barry Switzer (Arkansas '60) (Oklahoma 1973-88)	16	157	29	4	.837
Tom Osborne (Hastings '59) (Nebraska 1973-97)	25	255	49	3	.836
Don Coryell (Washington '50) (Whittier 1957-59; San Diego St. 1961-72)	†15	127	24	3	.834
Percy Haughton (Harvard '99) (Cornell 1899-1900; Harvard 1908-16; Columbia 1923-24)	13	96	17	6	.832
#Mike Kelly (Manchester '70) (Dayton 1981—)	†19	177	36	1	.829
Bob Neyland (Army '16) (Tennessee 1926-34, 1936-40, 1946-52)	21	173	31	12	.829
Fielding Yost (Lafayette '97) (Ohio Wesleyan 1897; Nebraska 1898; Kansas 1899; Stanford 1900; Michigan 1901-23, 1925-26)	29	196	36	12	.828
Bud Wilkinson (Minnesota '37) (Oklahoma 1947-63)	17	145	29	4	.826
Chuck Klausing (Slippery Rock '48) (Indiana [Pa.] 1964-69; Carnegie Mellon 1976-85)	†16	123	26	2	.821
Vernon McCain (Langston '31) (Md.-East. Shore 1948-63)	†16	102	21	5	.816
Jock Sutherland (Pittsburgh '18) (Lafayette 1919-23; Pittsburgh 1924-38)	20	144	28	14	.812
#Ken Sparks (Carson-Newman '68) (Carson-Newman 1980—)	†20	197	46	2	.808
Ron Schipper (Hope '52) (Central [Iowa] 1961-96)	†36	287	67	3	.808
Bob Devaney (Alma '39) (Wyoming 1957-61; Nebraska 1962-72)	16	136	30	7	.806
Biggie Munn (Minnesota '32) (Albright 1935-36; Syracuse 1946; Michigan St. 1947-53)	10	71	16	3	.805
Sid Gillman (Ohio St. '34) (Miami [Ohio] 1944-47; Cincinnati 1949-54)	†10	81	19	2	.804

†Zero to nine years in Division I-A. #Active coach.

Coaches With 200 or More Career Victories

This list includes all coaches who have won at least 200 games at four-year colleges (regardless of classification or association). Bowl and playoff games included.

Coach (Alma Mater) (Colleges Coached, Tenure)	Years	Won	Lost	Tied	Pct.
Eddie Robinson (Leland '41) (Grambling 1941-42, 1945-97)	†55	408	165	15	.707
#John Gagliardi (Colorado Col. '49) (Carroll [Mont.] 1949-52; St. John's [Minn.] 1953—)	†51	364	107	11	.767
Bear Bryant (Alabama '36) (Maryland 1945; Kentucky 1946-53; Texas A&M 1954-57; Alabama 1958-82)	38	323	85	17	.780
Pop Warner (Cornell '95) (Georgia 1895-96; Cornell 1897-98; Carlisle 1899-1903; Cornell 1904-06; Carlisle 1907-14; Pittsburgh 1915-23; Stanford 1924-32; Temple 1933-38)	44	319	106	32	.733
#Joe Paterno (Brown '50) (Penn St. 1966—)	34	317	83	3	.790
Amos Alonzo Stagg (Yale '88) (Springfield 1890-91; Chicago 1892-1932; Pacific [Cal.] 1933-46)	57	314	199	35	.605
#Bobby Bowden (Samford '53) (Samford 1959-62; West Virginia 1970-75; Florida St. 1976—)	34	304	85	4	.779
Ron Schipper (Hope '52) (Central [Iowa] 1961-96)	†36	287	67	3	.808
#Roy Kidd (Eastern Ky. '54) (Eastern Ky. 1964—)	†36	293	112	8	.719
#Tubby Raymond (Michigan '50) (Delaware 1966—)	†34	284	111	3	.717
#Frosty Westering (Neb.-Omaha '52) (Pacific Lutheran 1965—)	†35	277	84	7	.762
Roger Harring (Wis.-La Crosse '58) (Wis.-La Crosse 1969-99)	†31	261	75	7	.771
Tom Osborne (Hastings '59) (Nebraska 1973-97)	25	255	49	3	.836
Jim Malosky (Minnesota '51) (Minn.-Duluth 1958-97)	†40	255	125	13	.665
#LaVell Edwards (Utah St. '52) (Brigham Young 1972—)	28	251	95	3	.724
Woody Hayes (Denison '35) (Denison 1946-48; Miami [Ohio] 1949-50; Ohio St. 1951-78)	33	238	72	10	.759
Bo Schembechler (Miami [Ohio] '51) (Miami [Ohio] 1963-68; Michigan 1969-89)	27	234	65	8	.775
Arnett Mumford (Wilberforce '24) (Jarvis 1924-26; Bishop 1927-29; Texas College 1931-35; Southern U. 1936-42, 1944-61)	†36	233	85	23	.717
††John Merritt (Kentucky St. '50) (Jackson St. 1953-62; Tennessee St. 1963-83)	†31	232	65	11	.771
Hayden Fry (Baylor '51) (Southern Methodist 1962-72; North Texas 1973-78; Iowa 1979-98)	37	232	178	10	.564
Fred Long (Millikin '18) (Paul Quinn 1921-22; Wiley 1923-47; Prairie View 1948; Texas College 1949-55; Wiley 1956-65)	†45	227	151	31	.593
Ron Harms (Valparaiso '59) (Concordia, Neb. 1964-69; Adams St. 1970-73; Tex. A&M-Kingsville 1979-99)	†31	219	112	4	.660
Fred Martinelli (Otterbein '51) (Ashland 1959-93)	†35	217	119	12	.641
#Lou Holtz (Kent St. '59) (William & Mary 1969-71; North Carolina St. 1972-75; Arkansas 1977-83; Minnesota 1984-85; Notre Dame 1986-96; South Carolina 1999—)	28	216	106	7	.667
#Gene Carpenter (Huron '63) (Adams St. 1968; Millersville 1970—)	†31	214	86	6	.709
#Jim Christopherson (Concordia-M'head '60) (Concordia-M'head 1969—)	†31	213	96	7	.685
#Frank Girardi (West Chester '61) (Lycoming 1972—)	†28	211	66	5	.757
Jess Neely (Vanderbilt '24) (Southwestern [Tenn.] 1924-27; Clemson 1931-39; Rice 1940-66)	40	207	176	19	.539
Jim Butterfield (Maine '53) (Ithaca 1967-93)	†27	206	71	1	.743
#Billy Joe (Villanova '63) (Cheyney 1972-78; Central St. [Ohio] 1981-93; Florida A&M 1994—)	†26	205	82	4	.711
Jake Gaither (Knoxville '27) (Florida A&M 1945-69)	†25	203	36	4	.844
Warren Woodson (Baylor '24) (Conway St. 1935-40; Hardin-Simmons 1941-42, 1946-51; Arizona 1952-56; New Mexico St. 1958-67; Trinity [Tex.] 1972-73)	31	203	95	14	.673
Vince Dooley (Auburn '54) (Georgia 1964-88)	25	201	77	10	.715
Eddie Anderson (Notre Dame '22) (Loras 1922-24; DePaul 1925-31; Holy Cross 1933-38; Iowa 1939-42, 1946-49; Holy Cross 1950-64)	39	201	128	15	.606
Darrell Mudra (Peru St. '51) (Adams St. 1959-62; North Dakota St. 1963-65; Arizona 1967-68; Western Ill. 1969-73; Florida St. 1974-75; Eastern Ill. 1978-82; Northern Iowa 1983-87)	†26	200	81	4	.709
Jim Sweeney (Portland '51) (Montana St. 1963-67; Washington St. 1968-75; Fresno St. 1976-96)	32	200	154	4	.564

†Zero to nine years in Division I-A. ††Tennessee State's participation in 1981 and 1982 Division I-AA championships (1-2 record) vacated by action of the NCAA Committee on Infractions. #Active coach.

MATCHUPS OF COACHES EACH WITH 200 VICTORIES

Matchups of Coaches Each With 200 Victories

Date	Coaches, Teams (Victories Going In)	Winner (Score)
11-11-61	Arnett Mumford, Southern U. (232) Fred Long, Wiley (215)	Wiley (21-19)
1-1-78 Sugar Bowl	Bear Bryant, Alabama (272) Woody Hayes, Ohio St. (231)	Alabama (35-6)
10-11-80	Eddie Robinson, Grambling (284) John Merritt, Tennessee St. (200)	Grambling (52-27)
10-10-81	Eddie Robinson, Grambling (294) John Merritt, Tennessee St. (209)	Tennessee St. (14-10)
10-9-82	Eddie Robinson, Grambling (301) John Merritt, Tennessee St. (218)	Tennessee St. (22-8)
10-8-83	Eddie Robinson, Grambling (308) John Merritt, Tennessee St. (228)	Tie (7-7)
11-28-87	John Gagliardi, St. John's (Minn.) (251) Ron Schipper, Central (Iowa) (202)	Central (Iowa) (13-3)
11-25-89	John Gagliardi, St. John's (Minn.) (268) Ron Schipper, Central (Iowa) (224)	St. John's (Minn.) (27-24)
12-28-90 Blockbuster Bowl	Joe Paterno, Penn St. (229) Bobby Bowden, Florida St. (204)	Florida St. (24-17)
11-27-93	John Gagliardi, St. John's (Minn.) (305) Roger Harring, Wis.-La Crosse (210)	St. John's (Minn.) (47-25)
1-1-94 Orange Bowl	Bobby Bowden, Florida St. (238) Tom Osborne, Nebraska (206)	Florida St. (18-16)
9-17-94	Joe Paterno, Penn St. (258) Hayden Fry, Iowa (202)	Penn St. (61-21)
10-21-95	Joe Paterno, Penn St. (273) Hayden Fry, Iowa (210)	Penn St. (41-27)
1-1-96 Orange Bowl	Bobby Bowden, Florida St. (258) Lou Holtz, Notre Dame (208)	Florida St. (31-26)
10-19-96	Joe Paterno, Penn St. (284) Hayden Fry, Iowa (217)	Iowa (21-20)
11-17-96	Jim Malosky, Minn.-Duluth (250) Roger Harring, Wis.-La Crosse (241)	Minn.-Duluth (17-3)
11-30-96	John Gagliardi, St. John's (Minn.) (336) Roger Harring, Wis.-La Crosse (242)	Wis.-La Crosse (37-30)
12-4-99	John Gagliardi, St. John's (Minn.) (364) Frosty Westering, Pacific Lutheran (274)	Pacific Lutheran (19-9)

Coaches With 200 or More Victories at One College

(Bowl and Playoff Games Included)

Coach (College, Tenure)	Years	Won	Lost	Tied	Pct.
Eddie Robinson, Grambling (1941-42, 45-97)	†55	408	165	15	.707
#John Gagliardi, St. John's (Minn.) (1953–)	†47	339	101	10	.764
#Joe Paterno, Penn St. (1966–)	34	317	83	3	.790
#Roy Kidd, Eastern Ky. (1964–)	†36	293	112	8	.719
Ron Schipper, Central (Iowa) (1961-96)	†36	287	67	3	.808
#Tubby Raymond, Delaware (1966–)	†34	284	111	3	.717
#Frosty Westering, Pacific Lutheran (1965–)	†35	277	84	7	.762
Roger Harring, Wis.-La Crosse (1969-99)	†31	261	75	7	.771
Tom Osborne, Nebraska (1973-97)	25	255	49	3	.836
Jim Malosky, Minn.-Duluth (1958–)	†40	255	125	13	.665
#LaVell Edwards, Brigham Young (1972–)	28	251	95	3	.723
Amos Alonzo Stagg, Chicago (1892-32)	41	244	111	27	.674
Bear Bryant, Alabama (1958-82)	25	232	46	9	.824
#Bobby Bowden, Florida St. (1976–)	24	231	53	4	.809
Fred Martinelli, Ashland (1959-93)	†35	217	119	12	.641
#Frank Girardi, Lycoming (1972–)	†28	211	66	5	.757
Jim Butterfield, Ithaca (1967-93)	†27	206	71	1	.743
Woody Hayes, Ohio St. (1951-78)	28	205	61	10	.761
Jake Gaither, Florida A&M (1945-69)	†25	203	36	4	.844
Vince Dooley, Georgia (1964-88)	25	201	77	10	.715

†Zero to nine years in Division I-A. #Active coach.

Division I-A Coaching Records

Winningest Active Division I-A Coaches

(Minimum five years as Division I-A head coach; record at four-year colleges only.)

BY PERCENTAGE

Coach, College	Years	Won	Lost	Tied	†Pct.	Bowls W-L-T
Phillip Fulmer, Tennessee	8	76	14	0	.84444	5-3-0
Lloyd Carr, Michigan	5	49	13	0	.79032	3-2-0
Joe Paterno, Penn St.	34	317	83	3	.79032	20-9-1

Coach, College	Years	Won	Lost	Tied	†Pct.	W-L-T
JBobby Bowden, Florida St.	34	304	85	4	.77863	17-5-1
Steve Spurrier, Florida	13	122	35	2	.77358	5-5-0
R. C. Slocum, Texas A&M	11	102	32	2	.75735	2-7-0
Dennis Erickson, Oregon St.	14	120	45	1	.72590	4-4-0
LaVell Edwards, Brigham Young	28	251	95	3	.72350	7-14-1
John Robinson, UNLV	13	107	43	4	.70779	7-1-0
Paul Pasqualoni, Syracuse	14	109	48	1	.69304	5-2-0
John Cooper, Ohio St.	23	184	80	6	.69259	5-8-0
Bill Snyder, Kansas St.	11	88	40	1	.68605	4-3-0
Butch Davis, Miami (Fla.)	5	40	19	0	.67797	3-0-0
Rick Neuheisel, Washington	5	40	19	0	.67797	3-1-0
Lou Holtz, South Carolina	28	216	106	7	.66717	10-8-2
Dennis Franchione, TCU	17	128	64	2	.66495	2-1-0
Jackie Sherrill, Mississippi St.	22	164	89	4	.64591	7-6-0
Fisher DeBerry, Air Force	16	126	69	1	.64541	5-5-0
Gary Pinkel, Toledo	9	63	36	3	.63235	1-0-0
Sonny Lubick, Colorado St.	11	78	46	0	.62903	1-3-0
John L. Smith, Louisville	11	83	49	0	.62879	0-3-0
Nick Saban, LSU	6	43	26	1	.62143	0-3-0
Don Nehlen, West Virginia	29	195	123	8	.61043	3-9-0
Barry Alvarez, Wisconsin	10	70	44	4	.61017	5-1-0
Frank Beamer, Virginia Tech	19	130	83	4	.60829	3-4-0
Ron McBride, Utah	10	71	46	0	.60684	2-3-0
Joe Tiller, Purdue	9	64	42	1	.60280	2-2-0
Ken Hatfield, Rice	21	144	96	4	.59836	4-6-0
Dick Tomey, Arizona	23	153	104	7	.59280	4-3-0
George Welsh, Virginia	27	183	126	4	.59105	5-9-0
George O'Leary, Georgia Tech	6	36	25	0	.59016	2-1-0
Randy Walker, Northwestern	10	62	43	5	.58636	0-0-0
Gary Blackney, Bowling Green	9	58	41	2	.58416	2-0-0
Jeff Bower, Southern Miss.	10	59	43	1	.57767	2-2-0
Mike Bellotti, Oregon	10	60	45	2	.57009	2-2-0
Steve Logan, East Caro.	8	51	40	0	.56044	1-2-0
Mack Brown, Texas	16	104	82	1	.55882	4-4-0
Ted Tollner, San Diego St.	10	63	52	1	.54741	1-3-0
Bill Lynch, Ball St.	10	57	47	3	.54673	0-1-0
Tommy Tuberville, Auburn	5	31	26	0	.54386	2-0-0
Larry Smith, Missouri	23	140	118	7	.54151	3-6-1
Bruce Snyder, Arizona St.	20	118	101	6	.53778	3-2-0
Tyrone Willingham, Stanford	5	30	27	1	.52586	1-2-0
Bob Toledo, UCLA	10	58	53	0	.52252	1-1-0
Mike Price, Washington St.	19	105	110	0	.48837	2-1-0
Charlie Weatherbie, Navy	8	44	47	0	.48352	2-0-0
Glen Mason, Minnesota	14	75	83	1	.47484	2-1-0
Bob Simmons, Oklahoma St.	5	27	30	0	.47368	0-1-0
Jim Grobe, Ohio	5	26	29	1	.47321	0-0-0
Paul Hackett, Southern California	6	27	31	1	.46610	1-1-0
Gary Barnett, Colorado	10	51	60	2	.46018	2-1-0
Rip Scherer, Memphis	9	47	56	1	.45631	0-0-0
Rick Minter, Cincinnati	6	27	39	1	.41045	1-0-0
Terry Shea, Rutgers	6	23	42	2	.35821	1-0-0
Walt Harris, Pittsburgh	6	24	45	0	.34783	0-1-0
Lee Owens, Akron	5	19	36	0	.34545	0-0-0
Watson Brown, UAB	15	56	108	0	.34242	0-0-0
Jim Caldwell, Wake Forest	7	24	54	0	.30769	1-0-0
Woody Widenhofer, Vanderbilt	7	22	54	1	.29221	0-0-0
Dan McCarney, Iowa St.	5	13	42	0	.23636	0-0-0

Less than five years in Division I-A (school followed by years in I-A, includes record at all four-year colleges):

Coach, College	Years	Won	Lost	Tied	†Pct.	W-L-T
Jim Donnan, Georgia (4)	10	96	36	0	.72727	3-0-0
Bobby Keasler, La.-Monroe (1)	10	83	40	2	.67200	0-0-0
Mick Dennehy, Utah St. (0)	6	49	25	0	.66216	0-0-0
Terry Allen, Kansas (3)	11	89	46	0	.65926	0-0-0
Hal Mumme, Kentucky (3)	11	83	44	1	.65234	0-2-0
Houston Nutt, Arkansas (3)	7	52	30	0	.63415	1-1-0
Bobby Wallace, Temple (2)	12	86	54	1	.61348	0-0-0
Chris Tormey, Nevada (4)	5	33	23	0	.58929	1-0-0
Mike Cavan, Southern Meth. (3)	14	82	67	2	.54967	0-0-0
Gary Darnell, Western Mich. (4)	7	28	45	0	.38356	0-1-0
Dave Baldwin, San Jose St. (3)	5	20	34	0	.37037	0-0-0
Craig Cirbus, Buffalo (1)	5	17	38	0	.30909	0-0-0

+Ties computed as half won and half lost. Overall record includes bowl and playoff games. *Includes record in NCAA and/or NAIA championships.

BY VICTORIES

(Minimum 100 Victories)

Coach, College, Win Pct.	Won
Joe Paterno, Penn St.	317
Bobby Bowden, Florida St.	304
LaVell Edwards, Brigham Young	251
Lou Holtz, South Carolina	216
Don Nehlen, West Virginia	195

Coach, College, Win Pct.	Won
John Cooper, Ohio St.	184
George Welsh, Virginia	183
Jackie Sherrill, Mississippi St	164
Dick Tomey, Arizona	153
Ken Hatfield, Rice	144

Coach, College, Win Pct.	Won
Larry Smith, Missouri	140
Frank Beamer, Virginia Tech	130
Dennis Franchione, TCU	128
Fisher DeBerry, Air Force	126
Steve Spurrier, Florida	122
Dennis Erickson, Oregon St.	120

Coach, College, Win Pct.	Won
Bruce Snyder, Arizona St.	118
Paul Pasqualoni, Syracuse	109
John Robinson, UNLV	107
Mike Price, Washington St.	105
Mack Brown, Texas	104
R. C. Slocum, Texas A&M	102

Winningest All-Time Division I-A Coaches

Minimum 10 years as head coach at Division I institutions; record at four-year colleges only; bowl games included; ties computed as half won, half lost. Active coaches indicated by (*). College Football Hall of Fame members indicated by (†).

BY PERCENTAGE

Coach (Alma Mater) (Colleges Coached, Tenure)	Years	Won	Lost	Tied	Pct.
Knute Rockne (Notre Dame '14)† (Notre Dame 1918-30)	13	105	12	5	.881
Frank Leahy (Notre Dame '31)† (Boston College 1939-40; Notre Dame 1941-43, 1946-53)	13	107	13	9	.864
George Woodruff (Yale 1889)† (Pennsylvania 1892-01; Illinois 1903; Carlisle 1905)	12	142	25	2	.846
Barry Switzer (Arkansas '60) (Oklahoma 1973-88)	16	157	29	4	.837
Tom Osborne (Hastings '59)† (Nebraska 1973-97)	25	255	49	3	.836
Percy Haughton (Harvard 1899)† (Cornell 1899-00; Harvard 1908-16; Columbia 1923-24)	13	96	17	6	.832
Bob Neyland (Army '16)† (Tennessee 1926-34, 1936-40, 1946-52)	21	173	31	12	.829
Fielding Yost (West Virginia 1895)† (Ohio Wesleyan 1897; Nebraska 1898; Kansas 1899; Stanford 1900; Michigan 1901-23, 1925-26)	29	196	36	12	.828
Bud Wilkinson (Minnesota '37)† (Oklahoma 1947-63)	17	145	29	4	.826
Jock Sutherland (Pittsburgh '18)† (Lafayette 1919-23; Pittsburgh 1924-38)	20	144	28	14	.812
Bob Devaney (Alma '39)† (Wyoming 1957-61; Nebraska 1962-72)	16	136	30	7	.806
Frank Thomas (Notre Dame '23)† (Chattanooga 1925-28; Alabama 1931-42, 1944-46)	19	141	33	9	.795
*Joe Paterno (Brown '50) (Penn St. 1966—)	34	317	83	3	.790
Henry Williams (Yale 1891)† (Army 1891; Minnesota 1900-21)	23	141	34	12	.786
Gil Dobie (Minnesota '02)† (North Dakota St. 1906-07; Washington 1908-16; Navy 1917-19; Cornell 1920-35; Boston College 1936-38)	33	180	45	15	.781
Bear Bryant (Alabama '36)† (Maryland 1945; Kentucky 1946-53; Texas A&M 1954-57; Alabama 1958-82)	38	323	85	17	.780
*Bobby Bowden (Samford '53)√ (Samford 1959-62; West Virginia 1970-75; Florida St.1976—)	34	304	85	4	.779
Fred Folsom (Dartmouth 1895) (Colorado 1895-99, 1901-02; Dartmouth 1903-06; Colorado 1908-15)	19	106	28	6	.779
Bo Schembechler (Miami, Ohio '51)† (Miami [Ohio] 1963-68; Michigan 1969-89)	27	234	65	8	.775
*Steve Spurrier (Florida '67) (Duke 1987-89; Florida 1990—)	13	122	35	2	.774
Fritz Crisler (Chicago '22)† (Minnesota 1930-31; Princeton 1932-37; Michigan 1938-47)	18	116	32	9	.768
Charley Moran (Tennessee 1898) (Texas A&M 1909-14; Centre 1919-23; Bucknell 1924-26; Catawba 1930-33)	18	122	33	12	.766
Wallace Wade (Brown '17)† (Alabama 1923-30; Duke 1931-41, 1946-50)	24	171	49	10	.765
Frank Kush (Michigan St. '53)† (Arizona St. 1958-79)	22	176	54	1	.764
Dan McGugin (Michigan '04)† (Vanderbilt 1904-17, 1919-34)	30	197	55	19	.762
Jimmy Crowley (Notre Dame '25)# (Michigan St. 1929-32; Fordham 1933-41)	13	78	21	10	.761
Andy Smith (Penn St., Pennsylvania '05)† (Pennsylvania 1909-12; Purdue 1913-15; California 1916-25)	17	116	32	13	.761
Woody Hayes (Denison '35)† (Denison 1946-48; Miami [Ohio] 1949-50; Ohio St. 1951-78)	33	238	72	10	.759
Red Blaik (Miami, Ohio '18; Army '20)† (Dartmouth 1934-40; Army 1941-58)	25	166	48	14	.759

Coach (Alma Mater) (Colleges Coached, Tenure)	Years	Won	Lost	Tied	Pct.
*R. C. Slocum (McNeese St. '67) (Texas A&M 1989—)	11	102	32	2	.757
Darrell Royal (Oklahoma '50)† (Mississippi St. 1954-55; Washington 1956; Texas 1957-76)	23	184	60	5	.749
John McKay (Oregon '50)† (Southern California 1960-75)	16	127	40	8	.749
John Vaught (TCU '33)† (Mississippi 1947-70, 1973)	25	190	61	12	.745
Dan Devine (Minn.-Duluth '48)† (Arizona St. 1955-57; Missouri 1958-70; Notre Dame 1975-80)	22	172	57	9	.742
Gus Henderson (Oberlin '12) (Southern California 1919-24; Tulsa 1925-35; Occidental 1940-42)	20	126	42	7	.740
Ara Parseghian (Miami [Ohio] '49)† (Miami [Ohio] 1951-55; Northwestern 1956-63; Notre Dame 1964-74)	24	170	58	6	.739
Elmer Layden (Notre Dame '25)# (Loras 1925-26; Duquesne 1927-33; Notre Dame 1934-40)	16	103	34	11	.733
Pop Warner (Cornell 1895)† (Georgia 1895-96; Cornell 1897-98; Carlisle 1899-03; Cornell 1904-06; Carlisle 1907-14; Pittsburgh 1915-23; Stanford 1924-32; Temple 1933-38)	44	319	106	32	.733
Howard Jones (Yale '08)† (Syracuse 1908; Yale 1909; Ohio St. 1910; Yale 1913; Iowa 1916-23; Duke 1924; Southern California 1925-40)	29	194	64	21	.733
Frank Cavanaugh (Dartmouth 1897)† (Cincinnati 1898; Holy Cross 1903-05; Dartmouth 1911-16; Boston College 1919-26; Fordham 1927-32)	24	145	48	17	.731
Jim Tatum (North Carolina '35)† (North Carolina 1942; Oklahoma 1946; Maryland 1947-55; North Carolina 1956-58)	14	100	35	7	.729
*Dennis Erickson (Montana St. '69) (Idaho 1982-85; Wyoming 1986; Washington St. 1987-88; Miami [Fla.] 1989-94; Oregon St. 1999—)	14	120	45	1	.726
*LaVell Edwards (Utah St. '52) (Brigham Young 1972—)	28	251	95	3	.724
Francis Schmidt (Nebraska '14)† (Tulsa 1919-21; Arkansas 1922-28; TCU 1929-33; Ohio St. 1934-40; Idaho 1941-42)	24	158	57	11	.723
Bill Roper (Princeton '03)† (VMI 1903-04; Princeton 1906-08; Missouri 1909; Princeton 1910-11; Swarthmore 1915-16; Princeton 1919-30)	22	112	37	19	.723
Doc Kennedy (Kansas & Pennsylvania '03) (Kansas 1904-10; Haskell 1911-16)	13	85	31	7	.720
Tad Jones (Yale '08)† (Syracuse 1909-10; Yale 1916, 1920-27)	11	66	24	6	.719
Vince Dooley (Auburn '54)† (Georgia 1964-88)	25	201	77	10	.715
Dana Bible (Carson-Newman '12)† (Mississippi Col. 1913-15; LSU 1916; Texas A&M 1917, 1919-28; Nebraska 1929-36; Texas 1937-46)	33	198	72	23	.715
Bobby Dodd (Tennessee '31)†# (Georgia Tech 1945-66)	22	165	64	8	.713
John Heisman (Brown 1890, Pennsylvania 1892)† (Oberlin 1892; Akron 1893; Oberlin 1894; Auburn 1895-99; Clemson 1900-03; Georgia Tech 1904-19; Pennsylvania 1920-22; Wash. & Jeff. 1923; Rice 1924-27)	36	185	70	17	.711
Jumbo Stiehm (Wisconsin '09) (Ripon 1910; Nebraska 1911-15; Indiana 1916-21)	12	59	23	4	.709
Red Sanders (Vanderbilt '27)† (Vanderbilt 1940-42, 1946-48; UCLA 1949-57)	15	102	41	3	.709
*John Robinson (Oregon '58) (Southern California 1976-82, 1993-97; UNLV 1999—)	13	107	43	4	.708
Pat Dye (Georgia '62) (East Carolina 1974-79; Wyoming 1980; Auburn 1981-92)	19	153	62	5	.707
Chick Meehan (Syracuse '18) (Syracuse 1920-24; New York U. 1925-31; Manhattan 1932-37)	18	115	44	14	.705

WINNINGEST ACTIVE DIVISION I-A COACHES—BY PERCENTAGE

Coach (Alma Mater)
(Colleges Coached, Tenure)	Years	Won	Lost	Tied	Pct.
John McEwan (Army '17)	10	59	23	6	.705
(Army 1923-25; Oregon 1926-29; Holy Cross 1930-32)				
Bennie Owen (Kansas '00)†	27	155	60	19	.703
(Washburn 1900; Bethany [Kan.] 1901-04; Oklahoma 1905-26)				
Ike Armstrong (Drake '23)†	25	140	55	15	.702
(Utah 1925-49)				
Frank Broyles (Georgia Tech '47)†	20	149	62	6	.700
(Missouri 1957; Arkansas 1958-76)				
Biff Jones (Army '17)†	14	87	33	15	.700
(Army 1926-29; LSU 1932-34; Oklahoma 1935-36; Nebraska 1937-41)				

#Member of College Football Hall of Fame as a player. ‡Last game of 1978 season counted as full season. √Includes games forfeited, team and/or individual statistics abrogated, and coaching records changed by action of the NCAA Committee on Infractions.

All-Time Division I-A Coaching Victories

Minimum 10 years as head coach at Division I institutions; record at four-year colleges only; bowl games included. After each coach's name is his alma mater, year graduated, total years coached, won-lost record and percentage, tenure at each college coached, and won-lost record there. Active coaches are denoted by an asterisk (*).

(Minimum 155 Victories)

323 Bear Bryant (Born 9-11-13 Moro Bottoms, Ark.; Died 1-26-83)
   Alabama 1936 (38: 323-85-17 .780)
   Maryland 1945 (6-2-1); Kentucky 1946-53 (60-23-5); Texas A&M 1954-57 (25-14-2); Alabama 1958-82 (232-46-9)

319 Pop Warner (Born 4-5-1871 Springville, N.Y.; Died 9-7-54)
   Cornell 1895 (44: 319-106-32 .733)
   Georgia 1895-96 (7-4-0); Cornell 1897-98, 1904-06 (36-13-3); Carlisle 1899-1903, 1907-14 (114-42-8); Pittsburgh 1915-23 (60-12-4); Stanford 1924-32 (71-17-8); Temple 1933-38 (31-18-9)

317 *Joe Paterno (Born 12-21-26 Brooklyn, N.Y.)
   Brown 1951 (34: 317-83-3 .790)
   Penn St. 1966-99 (317-83-3)

314 Amos Alonzo Stagg (Born 8-16-1862 West Orange, N.J.; Died 3-17-65)
   Yale 1888 (57: 314-199-35 .605)
   Springfield 1890-91 (10-11-1); Chicago 1892-1932 (244-111-27); Pacific (Cal.) 1933-46 (60-77-7)

304 *Bobby Bowden (Born 11-8-29 Birmingham, Ala.)
   Samford 1953 (√34: 304-85-4 .779)
   Samford 1959-62 (31-6-0); West Virginia 1970-75 (√42-26-0); Florida St. 1976-99 (231-53-4)

255 Tom Osborne (Born 2-23-37 Hastings, Neb.)
   Hastings 1959 (25: 255-49-3 .836)
   Nebraska 1973-97 (255-49-3)

251 *LaVell Edwards (Born 10-11-30 Provo, Utah)
   Utah St. 1952 (28: 251-95-3 .724)
   Brigham Young 1972-99 (251-95-3)

238 Woody Hayes (Born 2-13-14 Clifton, Ohio; Died 3-12-87)
   Denison 1935 (33: 238-72-10 .759)
   Denison 1946-48 (19-6-0); Miami (Ohio) 1949-50 (14-5-0); Ohio St. 1951-78 (205-61-10)

234 Bo Schembechler (Born 9-1-29 Barberton, Ohio)
   Miami (Ohio) 1951 (27: 234-65-8 .775)
   Miami (Ohio) 1963-68 (40-17-3); Michigan 1969-89 (194-48-5)

232 Hayden Fry (Born 2-28-29 Odessa, Texas)
   Baylor 1951 (√37: 232-178-10 .564)
   Southern Methodist 1962-72 (49-66-1); North Texas 1973-78 (√40-23-3); Iowa 1979-98 (142-89-6)

216 *Lou Holtz (Born 1-6-37 Follansbee, W.Va.)
   Kent St. 1959 (28: 216-106-7 .667)
   William & Mary 1969-71 (13-20-0); North Carolina St. 1972-75 (33-12-3); Arkansas 1977-83 (60-21-2); Minnesota 1984-85 (10-12-0); Notre Dame 1986-96 (100-30-2); South Carolina 1999 (0-11-0)

207 Jess Neely (Born 1-4-1898 Smyrna, Tenn.; Died 4-9-83)
   Vanderbilt 1924 (40: 207-176-19 .539)
   Rhodes 1924-27 (20-17-2); Clemson 1931-39 (43-35-7); Rice 1940-66 (144-124-10)

203 Warren Woodson (Born 2-24-03 Fort Worth, Texas; Died 2-22-98)
   Baylor 1924 (31: 203-95-14 .673)
   Central Ark. 1935-39 (40-8-3); Hardin-Simmons 1941-42, 1946-51 (58-24-6); Arizona 1952-56 (26-22-2); New Mexico St. 1958-67 (63-36-3); Trinity (Tex.) 1972-73 (16-5-0)

201 Vince Dooley (Born 9-4-32 Mobile, Ala.)
   Auburn 1954 (25: 201-77-10 .715)
   Georgia 1964-88 (201-77-10)

201 Eddie Anderson (Born 11-13-1900 Mason City, Iowa; Died 4-26-74)
   Notre Dame 1922 (39: 201-128-15 .606)
   Loras 1922-24 (16-6-2); DePaul 1925-31 (21-22-3); Holy Cross 1933-38, 1950-64 (129-67-8); Iowa 1939-42, 1946-49 (35-33-2)

200 Jim Sweeney (Born 9-1-29 Butte, Mont.)
   Portland 1951 (32: 200-154-4 .564)
   Montana St. 1963-67 (31-20-0); Washington St. 1968-75 (26-59-1); Fresno St. 1976-77, 1980-96 (143-75-3)

198 Dana X. Bible (Born 10-8-1891 Jefferson City, Tenn.; Died 1-19-80)
   Carson-Newman 1912 (33: 198-72-23 .715)
   Mississippi Col. 1913-15 (12-7-2); LSU 1916 (1-0-2); Texas A&M 1917, 1919-28 (72-19-9); Nebraska 1929-36 (50-15-7); Texas 1937-46 (63-31-3)

197 Dan McGugin (Born 7-29-1879 Tingley, Iowa; Died 1-19-36)
   Michigan 1904 (30: 197-55-19 .762)
   Vanderbilt 1904-17, 1919-34 (197-55-19)

196 Fielding Yost (Born 4-30-1871 Fairview, W.Va.; Died 8-20-46)
   West Virginia '95 (29: 196-36-12 .828)
   Ohio Wesleyan 1897 (7-1-1); Nebraska 1898 (7-4-0); Kansas 1899 (10-0-0); Stanford 1900 (7-2-1); Michigan 1901-23, 1925-26 (165-29-10)

195 *Don Nehlen (Born 1-1-36 Canton, Ohio)
   Bowling Green 1958 (29: 195-123-8 .610)
   Bowling Green 1968-76 (53-35-4); West Virginia 1980-99 (142-88-4)

194 Howard Jones (Born 8-23-1885 Excello, Ohio; Died 7-27-41)
   Yale 1908 (29: 194-64-21 .733)
   Syracuse 1908 (6-3-1); Yale 1909, 1913 (15-2-3); Ohio St. 1910 (6-1-3); Iowa 1916-23 (42-17-1); Duke 1924 (4-5-0); Southern California 1925-40 (121-36-13)

190 John Vaught (Born 5-6-08 Olney, Texas)
   TCU 1933 (25: 190-61-12 .745)
   Mississippi 1947-70, 1973 (190-61-12)

185 John Heisman (Born 10-23-1869 Cleveland, Ohio; Died 10-3-36)
   Brown 1890 (36: 185-70-17 .711)
   Oberlin 1892, 1894 (11-3-1); Akron 1893 (5-2-0); Auburn 1895-99 (12-4-2); Clemson 1900-03 (19-3-2); Georgia Tech 1904-19 (102-29-6); Pennsylvania 1920-22 (16-10-2); Wash. & Jeff. 1923 (6-1-1); Rice 1924-27 (14-18-3)

185 Johnny Majors (Born 5-21-35 Lynchburg, Tenn.)
   Tennessee 1957 (29: 185-137-10 .572)
   Iowa St. 1968-72 (24-30-1); Pittsburgh 1973-76, 1993-96 (45-45-1); Tennessee 1977-92 (116-62-8)

184 Darrell Royal (Born 7-6-24 Hollis, Okla.)
   Oklahoma 1950 (23: 184-60-5 .749)
   Mississippi St. 1954-55 (12-8-0); Washington 1956 (5-5-0); Texas 1957-76 (167-47-5)

184 *John Cooper (Born 7-2-37 Powell, Tenn.)
   Iowa St. 1962 (23: 184-80-6 .693)
   Tulsa 1977-84 (56-32-0); Arizona St. 1985-87 (25-9-2); Ohio St. 1988-99 (104-39-4)

183 *George Welsh (Born 8-26-33 Coaldale, Pa.)
   Navy 1960 (27: 183-126-4 .591)
   Navy 1973-81 (55-46-1); Virginia 1982-99 (128-81-3)

180 Gil Dobie (Born 1-31-1879 Hastings, Minn.; Died 12-24-48)
   Minnesota 1902 (33: 180-45-15 .781)
   North Dakota St. 1906-07 (7-0-0); Washington 1908-16 (58-0-3); Navy 1917-19 (17-3-0); Cornell 1920-35 (82-36-7); Boston College 1936-38 (16-6-5)

180 Carl Snavely (Born 7-30-1894 Omaha, Neb.; Died 7-12-75)
   Lebanon Valley 1915 (32: 180-96-16 .644)
   Bucknell 1927-33 (42-16-8); North Carolina 1934-35, 1945-52 (59-35-5); Cornell 1936-44 (46-26-3); Washington (Mo.) 1953-58 (33-19-0)

179 Jerry Claiborne (Born 8-26-28 Hopkinsville, Ky.)
   Kentucky 1950 (28: 179-122-8 .592)
   Virginia Tech 1961-70 (61-39-2); Maryland 1972-81 (77-37-3); Kentucky 1982-89 (41-46-3)

178 Ben Schwartzwalder (Born 6-2-09 Point Pleasant, W.Va.; Died 4-28-93)
   West Virginia 1933 (28: 178-96-3 .648)
   Muhlenberg 1946-48 (25-5-0); Syracuse 1949-73 (153-91-3)

176 Frank Kush (Born 1-20-29 Windber, Pa.)
   Michigan St. 1953 (22: 176-54-1 .764)
   Arizona St. 1958-79 (176-54-1)

176 Don James (Born 12-31-32 Massillon, Ohio)
   Miami (Fla.) 1954 (22: 176-78-3 .691)
   Kent 1971-74 (25-19-1); Washington 1975-92 (151-59-2)

176 Ralph Jordan (Born 9-25-10 Selma, Ala.; Died 7-17-80)
   Auburn 1932 (√25: 176-83-6 .675)
   Auburn 1951-75 (√176-83-6)

174 Pappy Waldorf (Born 10-3-02 Clifton Springs, N.Y.; Died 8-15-81)
   Syracuse 1925 (31: 174-100-22 .625)
   Oklahoma City 1925-27 (17-11-3); Oklahoma St. 1929-33 (34-10-7); Kansas St. 1934 (7-2-1); Northwestern 1935-46 (49-45-7); California 1947-56 (67-32-4)

173 Bob Neyland (Born 2-17-92 Greenville, Texas; Died 3-28-62)
   Army 1916 (21: 173-31-12 .829)
   Tennessee 1926-34, 1936-40, 1946-52 (173-31-12)

172 Dan Devine (Born 12-23-24 Augusta, Wis.)
   Minn.-Duluth 1948 (22: 172-57-9 .742)
   Arizona St. 1955-57 (27-3-1); Missouri 1958-70 (92-38-7); Notre Dame 1975-80 (53-16-1)

171 Wallace Wade (Born 6-15-1892 Trenton, Tenn.; Died 10-7-86)
   Brown 1917 (24: 171-49-10 .765)
   Alabama 1923-30 (61-13-3); Duke 1931-41, 1946-50 (110-36-7)

170 Ara Parseghian (Born 5-21-23 Akron, Ohio)
   Miami (Ohio) 1949 (24: 170-58-6 .739)
   Miami (Ohio) 1951-55 (39-6-1); Northwestern 1956-63 (36-35-1); Notre Dame 1964-74 (95-17-4)

170 Grant Teaff (Born 11-12-33 Hermleigh, Texas)
   McMurry 1956 (30: 170-151-8 .529)
   McMurry 1960-65 (23-35-2); Angelo St. 1969-71 (19-11-0); Baylor 1972-92 (128-105-6)

168 Al Molde (Born 11-15-43 Montevideo, Minn.)
   Gust. Adolphus 1966 (26: 168-104-8 .614)
   Sioux Falls 1971-72 (5-12-1); Minn.-Morris 1973-79 (52-21-1); Central Mo. St. 1980-82 (17-9-4); Eastern Ill. 1983-86 (32-15-0); Western Mich. 1987-96 (62-47-2)
168 Bob Blackman (Born 7-7-18 De Soto, Iowa)
   Southern California 1941 (30: 168-112-7 .598)
   Denver 1953-54 (12-6-2); Dartmouth 1955-70 (104-37-3); Illinois 1971-76 (29-36-1); Cornell 1977-82 (23-33-1)
167 Bill Mallory (Born 5-30-35 Sandusky, Ohio)
   Miami (Ohio) 1957 (27:167-130-4 .561)
   Miami (Ohio) 1969-73 (39-12-0); Colorado 1974-78 (35-21-1); Northern Ill. 1980-83 (25-19-0); Indiana 1984-96 (68-78-3)
166 Red Blaik (Born 2-17-1897 Detroit, Mich.; Died 5-6-89)
   Miami (Ohio) 1918; Army 1920 (25: 166-48-14 .759)
   Dartmouth 1934-40 (45-15-4); Army 1941-58 (121-33-10)
165 Bobby Dodd (Born 11-11-08 Galax, Va.; Died 6-21-88)
   Tennessee 1931 (22: 165-64-8 .713)
   Georgia Tech 1945-66 (165-64-8)
165 Frank Howard (Born 3-25-09 Barlow Bend, Ala.; Died 1-25-96)
   Alabama 1931 (30: 165-118-12 .580)
   Clemson 1940-69 (165-118-12)
164 *Jackie Sherrill (Born 11-28-43 Duncan, Okla.)
   Alabama 1966 (22: 146-89-4 .646)
   Washington St. 1976 (3-8-0); Pittsburgh 1977-81 (50-9-1); Texas A&M 1982-88 (52-28-1); Mississippi St. 1991-99 (59-44-2)
163 Don Faurot (Born 6-23-02 Mountain Grove, Mo.; Died 10-18-95)
   Missouri 1925 (28: 163-93-13 .630)
   Truman 1926-34 (63-13-3); Missouri 1935-42, 1946-56 (100-80-10)
162 Ossie Solem (Born 12-13-1891 Minneapolis, Minn.; Died 10-26-70)
   Minnesota 1915 (37: 162-117-20 .575)
   Luther 1920 (5-1-1); Drake 1921-31 (54-35-2); Iowa 1932-36 (15-21-4); Syracuse 1937-45 (30-27-6); Springfield 1946-57 (58-33-7)
161 Bill Dooley (Born 5-19-34 Mobile, Ala.)
   Mississippi St. 1956 (26: 161-127-5 .558)
   North Carolina 1967-77 (69-53-2); Virginia Tech 1978-86 (64-37-1); Wake Forest 1987-92 (29-36-2)
160 Bill Yeoman (Born 12-26-27 Elnora, Ind.)
   Army 1949 (25: 160-108-8 .595)
   Houston 1962-86 (160-108-8)
160 Jim Wacker (Born 4-28-37 Detroit, Mich.)
   Valparaiso 1960 (26: 160-130-3 .551)
   Texas Lutheran 1971-75 (38-16-0); North Dakota St. 1976-78 (24-9-1); Southwest Tex. St. 1979-82 (42-8-0); TCU 1983-91 (40-58-2); Minnesota 1992-96 (16-39-0)
158 Francis Schmidt (Born 12-3-1885 Downs, Kan.; Died 9-19-44)
   Nebraska 1914 (24: 158-57-11 .723)
   Tulsa 1919-21 (24-3-2); Arkansas 1922-28 (42-20-3); TCU 1929-33 (46-6-5); Ohio St. 1934-40 (39-16-1); Idaho 1941-42 (7-12-0)
157 Barry Switzer (Born 10-5-37 Crossett, Ark.)
   Arkansas 1960 (16: 157-29-4 .837)
   Oklahoma 1973-88 (157-29-4)
157 Edward Robinson (Born 10-15-1873 Lynn, Miss.; Died 3-10-45)
   Brown 1896 (27: 157-88-13 .632)
   Nebraska 1896-97 (11-4-1); Brown 1898-1901, 1904-07, 1910-1925 (140-82-12); Maine 1902 (6-2-0)
155 Bennie Owen (Born 7-24-1875 Chicago, Ill.; Died 2-9-70)
   Kansas 1900 (27: 155-60-19 .703)
   Washburn 1900 (6-2-0); Bethany (Kan.) 1901-04 (27-4-3); Oklahoma 1905-26 (122-54-16)
155 Ray Morrison (Born 2-28-1885 Switzerland Co., Ind.; Died 11-19-82)
   Vanderbilt 1912 (34: 155-130-33 .539)
   Southern Methodist 1915-16, 1922-34 (84-44-22); Vanderbilt 1918, 1935-39 (29-22-2); Temple 1940-48 (31-38-9); Austin 1949-52 (11-26-0)

√Includes games forfeited, team and/or individual statistics abrogated, and coaching records changed by action of the NCAA Committee on Infractions.

Division I-A Best Career Starts by Wins

(Head coaches with at least half their seasons at major college at the time and minimum five years coached)

1 SEASON

Coach, Team	Season	W	L	T	Pct.
George Woodruff, Pennsylvania	1892	15	1	0	.938
Walter Camp, Yale	1888	13	0	0	1.000
Bill Battle, Tennessee	1970	11	1	0	.917
*Gary Blackney, Bowling Green	1991	11	1	0	.917
*John Robinson, Southern California	1976	11	1	0	.917
Dick Crum, Miami (Ohio)	1974	10	0	1	.955
Barry Switzer, Oklahoma	1973	10	0	1	.955
Chuck Fairbanks, Oklahoma	1967	10	1	0	.909
Larry Siemering, Pacific (Cal.)	1947	10	1	0	.909
Dwight Wallace, Ball St.	1978	10	1	0	.909
Mike Archer, LSU	1987	10	1	1	.875

2 SEASONS

Coach, Team	Seasons	W	L	T	Pct.
Walter Camp, Yale	1888-89	28	1	0	.966
George Woodruff, Pennsylvania	1892-93	27	4	0	.871
Barry Switzer, Oklahoma	1973-74	21	0	1	.977
Dick Crum, Miami (Ohio)	1974-75	21	1	1	.935
Bill Battle, Tennessee	1970-71	21	3	0	.875
*Gary Blackney, Bowling Green	1991-92	21	3	0	.875
Frank Leahy, Boston College	1939-40	20	2	0	.909
Ron Meyer, UNLV	1973-74	20	4	0	.833
*Fisher DeBerry, Air Force	1984-85	20	5	0	.800
Dutch Meyer, TCU	1934-35	20	5	0	.800
Herb Deromedi, Central Mich.	1978-79	19	2	1	.886
*John Robinson, Southern California	1976-77	19	5	0	.792

3 SEASONS

Coach, Team(s)	Seasons	W	L	T	Pct.
Walter Camp, Yale	1888-90	41	2	0	.953
George Woodruff, Pennsylvania	1892-94	39	4	0	.907
Barry Switzer, Oklahoma	1973-75	32	1	1	.956
Bill Battle, Tennessee	1970-72	31	5	0	.861
*John Robinson, Southern California	1976-78	31	6	0	.838
Dutch Meyer, TCU	1934-36	29	7	2	.789
Frank Leahy, Boston College, Notre Dame	1939-41	28	2	1	.919
Larry Siemering, Pacific (Cal.)	1947-49	28	2	2	.906
Bud Wilkinson, Oklahoma	1947-49	28	3	1	.891
Herb Deromedi, Central Mich.	1978-80	28	4	1	.864
Tom Osborne, Nebraska	1973-75	28	7	1	.792

4 SEASONS

Coach, Team(s)	Seasons	W	L	T	Pct.
Walter Camp, Yale	1888-91	54	2	0	.964
George Woodruff, Pennsylvania	1892-95	53	4	0	.930
*John Robinson, Southern California	1976-79	42	6	1	.867
Barry Switzer, Oklahoma	1973-76	41	3	2	.935
Bill Battle, Tennessee	1970-73	39	9	0	.813
*R. C. Slocum, Texas A&M	1989-92	39	10	1	.790
Bud Wilkinson, Oklahoma	1947-50	38	4	1	.895
Tom Osborne, Nebraska	1973-76	37	10	2	.776
*Gary Blackney, Bowling Green	1991-94	36	8	2	.804
Frank Leahy, Boston College, Notre Dame	1939-42	35	4	3	.869
Larry Siemering, Pacific (Cal.)	1947-50	35	5	3	.849
*Joe Paterno, Penn St.	1966-69	35	7	1	.826
Claude Gilbert, San Diego St.	1973-76	35	7	2	.818
Herb Deromedi, Central Mich.	1978-81	35	8	1	.807
*Fisher DeBerry, Air Force	1984-87	35	14	0	.714

5 SEASONS

Coach, Team(s)	Seasons	W	L	T	Pct.
Walter Camp, Yale, Stanford	1888-92	69	2	2	.959
George Woodruff, Pennsylvania	1892-96	67	5	0	.931
Barry Switzer, Oklahoma	1973-77	51	5	2	.896
*John Robinson, Southern California	1976-80	50	8	2	.850
*R. C. Slocum, Texas A&M	1989-93	49	12	1	.798
*Lloyd Carr, Michigan	1995-99	49	13	0	.790
Henry Williams, Army, Minnesota	1891, 1900-03	47	4	6	.877
Bud Wilkinson, Oklahoma	1947-51	46	6	1	.877
Bill Battle, Tennessee	1970-74	46	12	2	.783
Tom Osborne, Nebraska	1973-77	46	13	2	.770
Claude Gilbert, San Diego St.	1973-77	45	8	2	.836

6 SEASONS

Coach, Team(s)	Seasons	W	L	T	Pct.
George Woodruff, Pennsylvania	1892-97	82	5	0	.943
Walter Camp, Yale, Stanford	1888-92, 94	75	5	2	.927
Barry Switzer, Oklahoma	1973-78	62	6	2	.900
Henry Williams, Army, Minnesota	1891, 1900-04	60	4	6	.900
*John Robinson, Southern California	1976-81	59	11	2	.833
*R. C. Slocum, Texas A&M	1989-94	59	12	2	.822
Tom Osborne, Nebraska	1973-78	55	16	2	.767
*Phillip Fulmer, Tennessee	1992-97	54	11	0	.841
Bud Wilkinson, Oklahoma	1947-52	54	7	2	.873
Fielding Yost, Ohio Wesleyan, Nebraska, Kansas, Stanford, Michigan	1897-1902	53	7	2	.871
*Joe Paterno, Penn St.	1966-71	53	11	1	.823
*Jackie Sherrill, Washington St., Pittsburgh	1976-81	53	17	1	.754
Bill Battle, Tennessee	1970-75	53	17	2	.750

7 SEASONS

Coach, Team(s)	Seasons	W	L	T	Pct.
George Woodruff, Pennsylvania	1892-98	94	6	0	.940
Walter Camp, Yale, Stanford	1888-92, 94-95	79	5	3	.925
Barry Switzer, Oklahoma	1973-79	73	7	2	.902
Henry Williams, Army, Minnesota	1891, 1900-05	70	5	6	.901
*R. C. Slocum, Texas A&M	1989-95	68	15	2	.812
*Phillip Fulmer, Tennessee	1992-98	67	11	0	.859
*John Robinson, Southern California	1976-82	67	14	2	.819

DIVISION I-A BEST CAREER STARTS BY WINS

Coach, Team(s)	Seasons	W	L	T	Pct.
Tom Osborne, Nebraska	1973-79	65	18	2	.776
Fielding Yost, Ohio Wesleyan, Nebraska, Kansas, Stanford, Michigan	1897-1903	64	7	3	.897
Bud Wilkinson, Oklahoma	1947-53	63	8	3	.872
*Joe Paterno, Penn St.	1966-72	63	13	1	.825
Amos Alonzo Stagg, Springfield, Chicago	1890-96	63	31	7	.658

8 SEASONS

Coach, Team(s)	Seasons	W	L	T	Pct.
George Woodruff, Pennsylvania	1892-99	102	9	2	.912
Barry Switzer, Oklahoma	1973-80	83	9	2	.894
*Phillip Fulmer, Tennessee	1992-99	76	14	0	.844
*Joe Paterno, Penn St.	1966-73	75	13	1	.848
*John Robinson, Southern California	1976-82, 93	75	19	2	.792
Tom Osborne, Nebraska	1973-80	75	20	2	.784
Fielding Yost, Ohio Wesleyan, Nebraska, Kansas, Stanford, Michigan	1897-1904	74	7	3	.898
Henry Williams, Army, Minnesota	1891, 1900-06	74	6	6	.895
*R. C. Slocum, Texas A&M	1989-96	74	21	2	.773
Amos Alonzo Stagg, Springfield, Chicago	1890-97	74	32	7	.686
Bud Wilkinson, Oklahoma	1947-54	73	8	3	.887
Frank Leahy, Boston College, Notre Dame	1939-43, 46-48	70	5	5	.882

9 SEASONS

Coach, Team(s)	Seasons	W	L	T	Pct.
George Woodruff, Pennsylvania	1892-1900	114	10	2	.913
Barry Switzer, Oklahoma	1973-81	90	13	3	.863
Fielding Yost, Ohio Wesleyan, Nebraska, Kansas, Stanford, Michigan	1897-1905	86	8	3	.902
*Joe Paterno, Penn St.	1966-74	85	15	1	.847
Bud Wilkinson, Oklahoma	1947-55	84	8	3	.900
Tom Osborne, Nebraska	1973-81	84	23	2	.780
*R. C. Slocum, Texas A&M	1989-97	83	25	2	.764
*John Robinson, Southern California	1976-82, 93-94	83	22	3	.782
Amos Alonzo Stagg, Springfield, Chicago	1890-98	83	34	7	.698
*Steve Spurrier, Duke, Florida	1987-95	81	26	2	.752
Frank Leahy, Boston College, Notre Dame	1939-43, 46-49	80	5	5	.917
Bob Neyland, Tennessee	1926-34	76	7	5	.892
Henry Williams, Army, Minnesota	1891, 1900-07	76	8	7	.874
Dick Crum, Miami (Ohio), North Carolina	1974-82	76	26	2	.740
Fred Akers, Wyoming, Texas	1975-83	76	30	1	.715

10 SEASONS

Coach, Team(s)	Seasons	W	L	T	Pct.
George Woodruff, Pennsylvania	1892-1901	124	15	2	.887
Barry Switzer, Oklahoma	1973-82	98	17	3	.843
Tom Osborne, Nebraska	1973-82	96	24	2	.795
Amos Alonzo Stagg, Springfield, Chicago	1890-99	95	34	9	.721
*R. C. Slocum, Texas A&M	1989-98	94	28	2	.766
Bud Wilkinson, Oklahoma	1947-56	94	8	3	.910
*Joe Paterno, Penn St.	1966-75	94	18	1	.836
*Steve Spurrier, Duke, Florida	1987-96	93	27	2	.770
*John Robinson, Southern California	1976-82, 93-95	92	24	4	.783
Fielding Yost, Ohio Wesleyan, Nebraska, Kansas, Stanford, Michigan	1897-1906	90	9	3	.897
Frank Leahy, Boston College, Notre Dame	1939-43, 46-50	84	9	6	.879
Dick Crum, Miami (Ohio), North Carolina	1974-83	84	30	2	.733
*Dennis Erickson, Idaho, Wyoming, Washington St., Miami (Fla.)	1982-91	83	34	1	.708
Fred Akers, Wyoming, Texas	1975-84	83	34	2	.706

11 SEASONS

Coach, Team(s)	Seasons	W	L	T	Pct.
George Woodruff, Pennsylvania, Illinois	1892-1901, 03	132	21	2	.858
Tom Osborne, Nebraska	1973-83	108	25	2	.807
Barry Switzer, Oklahoma	1973-83	106	21	3	.827
Bud Wilkinson, Oklahoma	1947-57	104	9	3	.909
*Steve Spurrier, Duke, Florida	1987-97	103	29	2	.776
*R. C. Slocum, Texas A&M	1989-99	102	32	2	.757
Amos Alonzo Stagg, Springfield, Chicago	1890-1900	102	39	10	.709
*Joe Paterno, Penn St.	1966-76	101	23	1	.812
*John Robinson, Southern California	1976-82, 93-96	98	30	4	.758
Fielding Yost, Ohio Wesleyan, Nebraska, Kansas, Stanford, Michigan	1897-1907	95	10	3	.894
*Dennis Erickson, Idaho, Wyoming, Washington St., Miami (Fla.)	1982-92	94	35	1	.727
Frank Leahy, Boston College, Notre Dame	1939-43, 46-51	91	11	7	.867
Bobby Dodd, Georgia Tech	1945-55	91	27	3	.764
Fred Akers, Wyoming, Texas	1975-85	91	38	2	.702

12 SEASONS

Coach, Team(s)	Seasons	W	L	T	Pct.
George Woodruff, Pennsylvania, Illinois, Carlisle	1892-1901, 03, 05	142	25	2	.846
Tom Osborne, Nebraska	1973-84	118	27	2	.810
Barry Switzer, Oklahoma	1973-84	115	23	4	.824
Bud Wilkinson, Oklahoma	1947-58	114	10	3	.909
*Steve Spurrier, Duke, Florida	1987-98	113	31	2	.781
*Joe Paterno, Penn St.	1966-77	112	24	1	.821
Amos Alonzo Stagg, Springfield, Chicago	1890-1901	107	44	12	.693
*John Robinson, Southern California	1976-82, 93-97	104	35	4	.741
Dennis Erickson, Idaho, Wyoming, Washington St., Miami (Fla.)	1982-93	103	38	1	.729
Bobby Dodd, Georgia Tech	1945-56	101	28	3	.777
Fielding Yost, Ohio Wesleyan, Nebraska, Kansas, Stanford, Michigan	1897-1908	100	12	4	.879
Bob Neyland, Tennessee	1926-34, 36-38	99	12	8	.866

13 SEASONS

Coach, Team(s)	Seasons	W	L	T	Pct.
Tom Osborne, Nebraska	1973-85	127	30	2	.805
Barry Switzer, Oklahoma	1973-85	126	24	4	.831
*Joe Paterno, Penn St.	1966-78	123	25	1	.829
*Steve Spurrier, Duke, Florida	1987-99	122	35	2	.774
Bud Wilkinson, Oklahoma	1947-59	121	13	3	.894
*LaVell Edwards, Brigham Young	1972-84	118	37	1	.760
Amos Alonzo Stagg, Springfield, Chicago	1890-1902	118	45	12	.709
*Dennis Erickson, Idaho, Wyoming, Washington St., Miami (Fla.)	1982-94	113	40	1	.737
Bob Neyland, Tennessee	1926-34, 36-39	109	13	8	.869
Terry Donahue, UCLA	1976-88	108	38	7	.729
*John Robinson, Southern California, UNLV	1976-82, 93-97, 99	107	43	4	.708
Frank Leahy, Boston College, Notre Dame	1939-43, 46-53	107	13	9	.864

14 SEASONS

Coach, Team(s)	Seasons	W	L	T	Pct.
Barry Switzer, Oklahoma	1973-86	137	25	4	.837
Tom Osborne, Nebraska	1973-86	137	32	2	.807
*Joe Paterno, Penn St.	1966-79	131	29	1	.817
*LaVell Edwards, Brigham Young	1972-85	129	40	1	.762
Amos Alonzo Stagg, Springfield, Chicago	1890-1903	128	47	13	.715
Bud Wilkinson, Oklahoma	1947-60	124	19	4	.857
*Dennis Erickson, Idaho, Wyoming, Washington St., Miami (Fla.), Oregon St.	1982-94, 99	120	45	1	.726
Bob Neyland, Tennessee	1926-34, 36-40	119	14	8	.872
Bo Schembechler, Miami (Ohio), Michigan	1963-76	116	28	6	.793
Pat Dye, East Caro., Wyoming, Auburn	1974-87	115	44	3	.719
Bob Devaney, Wyoming, Nebraska	1957-70	114	28	6	.791

15 SEASONS

Coach, Team(s)	Seasons	W	L	T	Pct.
Barry Switzer, Oklahoma	1973-87	148	26	4	.843
Tom Osborne, Nebraska	1973-87	147	34	2	.809
*Joe Paterno, Penn St.	1966-80	141	31	1	.818
*LaVell Edwards, Brigham Young	1972-86	137	45	1	.751
Amos Alonzo Stagg, Springfield, Chicago	1890-1904	136	48	14	.722
Bud Wilkinson, Oklahoma	1947-61	129	24	4	.834
Bob Neyland, Tennessee	1926-34, 36-40, 46	128	16	8	.868
Bob Devaney, Wyoming, Nebraska	1957-71	127	28	6	.807
Bo Schembechler, Miami (Ohio), Michigan	1963-77	126	30	6	.796
Pat Dye, East Caro., Wyoming, Auburn	1974-88	125	46	3	.727

16 SEASONS

Coach, Team(s)	Seasons	W	L	T	Pct.
Tom Osborne, Nebraska	1973-88	158	36	2	.811
Barry Switzer, Oklahoma	1973-88	157	29	4	.837
*Joe Paterno, Penn St.	1966-81	151	33	1	.819
*LaVell Edwards, Brigham Young	1972-87	146	49	1	.747
Amos Alonzo Stagg, Springfield, Chicago	1890-1905	146	48	14	.736
Bud Wilkinson, Oklahoma	1947-62	137	27	4	.827
Bob Devaney, Wyoming, Nebraska	1957-72	136	30	7	.806
Bo Schembechler, Miami (Ohio), Michigan	1963-78	136	32	6	.799
Pat Dye, East Caro., Wyoming, Auburn	1974-89	135	48	3	.734
Bob Neyland, Tennessee	1926-34, 36-40, 46-47	133	21	8	.846

17 SEASONS

Coach, Team(s)	Seasons	W	L	T	Pct.
Tom Osborne, Nebraska	1973-89	168	38	2	.813
*Joe Paterno, Penn St.	1966-82	162	34	1	.825
*LaVell Edwards, Brigham Young	1972-88	155	53	1	.744
Amos Alonzo Stagg, Springfield, Chicago	1890-1906	150	49	15	.736
Bud Wilkinson, Oklahoma	1947-63	145	29	4	.826
Bo Schembechler, Miami (Ohio), Michigan	1963-79	144	36	6	.790
Pat Dye, East Caro., Wyoming, Auburn	1974-90	143	51	4	.732
Frank Kush, Arizona St.	1958-74	139	39	1	.779

DIVISION I-A BEST CAREER STARTS BY WINS

Coach, Team(s)	Seasons	W	L	T	Pct.
Bob Neyland, Tennessee	1926-34, 36-40, 46-48	137	25	10	.826
Johnny Vaught, Mississippi	1947-63	137	32	9	.795
Tony Knap, Utah St., Boise St., UNLV	1963-66, 68-80	137	47	4	.739

18 SEASONS

Coach, Team(s)	Seasons	W	L	T	Pct.
Tom Osborne, Nebraska	1973-90	177	41	2	.809
*Joe Paterno, Penn St.	1966-83	170	38	2	.814
*LaVell Edwards, Brigham Young	1972-89	165	56	1	.745
Bo Schembechler, Miami (Ohio), Michigan	1963-80	154	38	6	.793
Amos Alonzo Stagg, Springfield, Chicago	1890-1907	154	50	15	.737
Frank Kush, Arizona St.	1958-75	151	39	1	.793
Pat Dye, East Caro., Wyoming, Auburn	1974-91	148	57	4	.718
Bob Neyland, Tennessee	1926-34, 36-40, 46-49	144	27	11	.821
Darrell Royal, Mississippi St., Washington, Texas	1954-71	143	45	4	.755
Tony Knap, Utah St., Boise St., UNLV	1963-66, 68-81	143	53	4	.725

19 SEASONS

Coach, Team(s)	Seasons	W	L	T	Pct.
Tom Osborne, Nebraska	1973-91	186	43	3	.808
*Joe Paterno, Penn St.	1966-84	176	43	2	.801
*LaVell Edwards, Brigham Young	1972-90	175	59	1	.747
Bo Schembechler, Miami (Ohio), Michigan	1963-81	163	41	6	.790
Amos Alonzo Stagg, Springfield, Chicago	1890-1908	159	50	16	.742
Bob Neyland, Tennessee	1926-34, 36-40, 46-50	155	28	11	.827
Frank Kush, Arizona St.	1958-76	155	46	1	.770
Darrell Royal, Mississippi St., Washington, Texas	1954-72	153	46	4	.764
Pat Dye, East Caro., Wyoming, Auburn	1974-92	153	62	5	.707
Pop Warner, Georgia, Cornell, Carlisle	1895-1913	152	50	10	.741

20 SEASONS

Coach, Team(s)	Seasons	W	L	T	Pct.
Tom Osborne, Nebraska	1973-92	195	46	3	.805
*Joe Paterno, Penn St.	1966-85	187	44	2	.807
*LaVell Edwards, Brigham Young	1972-91	183	62	1	.744
Bo Schembechler, Miami (Ohio), Michigan	1963-82	171	45	6	.784
Bob Neyland, Tennessee	1926-34, 36-40, 46-51	165	29	11	.832
Frank Kush, Arizona St.	1958-77	164	49	1	.769
Amos Alonzo Stagg, Springfield, Chicago	1890-1909	163	51	18	.741
Darrell Royal, Mississippi St., Washington, Texas	1954-73	161	49	4	.762
Vince Dooley, Georgia	1964-83	161	60	7	.721
Johnny Vaught, Mississippi	1947-66	157	44	10	.768
Pop Warner, Georgia, Cornell, Carlisle	1895-1914	157	59	11	.716
*John Cooper, Tulsa, Arizona St., Ohio St.	1977-96	157	70	6	.687

21 SEASONS

Coach, Team(s)	Seasons	W	L	T	Pct.
Tom Osborne, Nebraska	1973-93	206	47	3	.811
*Joe Paterno, Penn St.	1966-86	199	44	2	.816
*LaVell Edwards, Brigham Young	1972-92	191	67	3	.738
Bo Schembechler, Miami (Ohio), Michigan	1963-83	180	48	6	.782
Bob Neyland, Tennessee	1926-34, 36-40, 46-52	173	31	12	.829
Frank Kush, Arizona St.	1958-78	173	52	1	.768
Darrell Royal, Mississippi St., Washington, Texas	1954-74	169	53	4	.757
Vince Dooley, Georgia	1964-84	168	64	8	.717
*John Cooper, Tulsa, Arizona St., Ohio St.	1977-97	167	73	6	.691
Don James, Kent, Washington	1971-91	167	75	3	.688
Amos Alonzo Stagg, Springfield, Chicago	1890-1910	165	56	18	.728
Pop Warner, Georgia, Cornell, Carlisle, Pittsburgh	1895-1915	165	59	11	.726

22 SEASONS

Coach, Team(s)	Seasons	W	L	T	Pct.
Tom Osborne, Nebraska	1973-94	219	47	3	.820
*Joe Paterno, Penn St.	1966-87	207	48	2	.809
*LaVell Edwards, Brigham Young	1972-93	197	73	3	.727
Bo Schembechler, Miami (Ohio), Michigan	1963-84	186	54	6	.768
Darrell Royal, Mississippi St., Washington, Texas	1954-75	179	55	4	.761
*John Cooper, Tulsa, Arizona St., Ohio St.	1977-98	178	74	6	.702
Frank Kush, Arizona St.	1958-79	176	54	1	.764
Don James, Kent, Washington	1971-92	176	78	3	.691
Vince Dooley, Georgia	1964-85	175	67	10	.714
*Bobby Bowden, Samford, West Virginia, Florida St.	1959-62, 70-87	174	69	3	.713

Coach, Team(s)	Seasons	W	L	T	Pct.
Pop Warner, Georgia, Cornell, Carlisle, Pittsburgh	1895-1916	173	59	11	.735

23 SEASONS

Coach, Team(s)	Seasons	W	L	T	Pct.
Tom Osborne, Nebraska	1973-95	231	47	3	.827
*Joe Paterno, Penn St.	1966-88	212	54	2	.795
*LaVell Edwards, Brigham Young	1972-94	207	76	3	.729
Bo Schembechler, Miami (Ohio), Michigan	1963-85	196	55	7	.773
*Bobby Bowden, Samford, West Virginia, Florida St.	1959-62, 70-88	185	70	3	.723
*John Cooper, Tulsa, Arizona St., Ohio St.	1977-99	184	80	6	.693
Darrell Royal, Mississippi St., Washington, Texas	1954-76	184	60	5	.749
Pop Warner, Georgia, Cornell, Carlisle, Pittsburgh	1895-1917	183	59	11	.745
Vince Dooley, Georgia	1964-86	183	71	10	.712
*Lou Holtz, William & Mary, North Carolina St., Arkansas, Minnesota, Notre Dame	1969-92	182	83	6	.683
Bear Bryant, Maryland, Kentucky, Texas A&M, Alabama	1945-67	179	53	15	.755
Johnny Vaught, Mississippi	1947-69	178	54	12	.754

24 SEASONS

Coach, Team(s)	Seasons	W	L	T	Pct.
Tom Osborne, Nebraska	1973-96	242	49	3	.828
*Joe Paterno, Penn St.	1966-89	220	57	2	.791
*LaVell Edwards, Brigham Young	1972-95	214	80	3	.726
Bo Schembechler, Miami (Ohio), Michigan	1963-86	207	57	7	.777
*Bobby Bowden, Samford, West Virginia, Florida St.	1959-62, 70-89	195	72	3	.728
*Lou Holtz, William & Mary, North Carolina St., Arkansas, Minnesota, Notre Dame	1969-93	193	84	6	.693
Vince Dooley, Georgia	1964-87	192	74	10	.714
Bear Bryant, Maryland, Kentucky, Texas A&M, Alabama	1945-68	187	56	15	.754
Pop Warner, Georgia, Cornell, Carlisle, Pittsburgh	1895-1918	187	60	11	.746
Johnny Vaught, Mississippi	1947-70	185	58	12	.749
Amos Alonzo Stagg, Springfield, Chicago	1890-1913	184	58	18	.742

25 SEASONS

Coach, Team(s)	Seasons	W	L	T	Pct.
Tom Osborne, Nebraska	1973-97	255	49	3	.836
*Joe Paterno, Penn St.	1966-90	229	60	3	.789
*LaVell Edwards, Brigham Young	1972-96	228	81	3	.736
Bo Schembechler, Miami (Ohio), Michigan	1963-87	215	61	7	.772
*Bobby Bowden, Samford, West Virginia, Florida St.	1959-62, 70-90	205	74	3	.732
Vince Dooley, Georgia	1964-88	201	77	10	.715
*Lou Holtz, William & Mary, North Carolina St., Arkansas, Minnesota, Notre Dame	1969-94	199	89	7	.686
Bear Bryant, Maryland, Kentucky, Texas A&M, Alabama	1945-69	193	61	15	.745
Pop Warner, Georgia, Cornell, Carlisle, Pittsburgh	1895-1919	193	62	12	.745
Johnny Vaught, Mississippi	1947-70, 73	190	61	12	.745
Amos Alonzo Stagg, Springfield, Chicago	1890-1914	188	60	19	.740

26 SEASONS

Coach, Team(s)	Seasons	W	L	T	Pct.
*Joe Paterno, Penn St.	1966-91	240	62	3	.792
*LaVell Edwards, Brigham Young	1972-97	234	86	3	.729
Bo Schembechler, Miami (Ohio), Michigan	1963-88	224	63	8	.773
*Bobby Bowden, Samford, West Virginia, Florida St.	1959-62, 70-91	216	76	3	.737
*Lou Holtz, William & Mary, North Carolina St., Arkansas, Minnesota, Notre Dame	1969-95	208	92	7	.689
Pop Warner, Georgia, Cornell, Carlisle, Pittsburgh	1895-1920	199	62	14	.749
Bear Bryant, Maryland, Kentucky, Texas A&M, Alabama	1945-70	199	66	16	.737
Amos Alonzo Stagg, Springfield, Chicago	1890-1915	193	62	19	.739

27 SEASONS

Coach, Team(s)	Seasons	W	L	T	Pct.
*Joe Paterno, Penn St.	1966-92	247	67	3	.784
*LaVell Edwards, Brigham Young	1972-98	243	91	3	.726
Bo Schembechler, Miami (Ohio), Michigan	1963-89	234	65	8	.775
*Bobby Bowden, Samford, West Virginia, Florida St.	1959-62, 70-92	227	77	3	.744
*Lou Holtz, William & Mary, North Carolina St., Arkansas, Minnesota, Notre Dame	1969-96	216	95	7	.690
Bear Bryant, Maryland, Kentucky, Texas A&M, Alabama	1945-71	210	67	16	.744

DIVISION I-A BEST CAREER STARTS BY WINS

Coach, Team(s)	Seasons	W	L	T	Pct.
Pop Warner, Georgia, Cornell, Carlisle, Pittsburgh	1895-1921	204	65	15	.745
Amos Alonzo Stagg, Springfield, Chicago	1890-1916	196	66	19	.731

28 SEASONS

Coach, Team(s)	Seasons	W	L	T	Pct.
*Joe Paterno, Penn St.	1966-93	257	69	3	.786
*LaVell Edwards, Brigham Young	1972-99	251	95	3	.724
*Bobby Bowden, Samford, West Virginia, Florida St.	1959-62, 70-93	239	78	3	.752
Bear Bryant, Maryland, Kentucky, Texas A&M, Alabama	1945-72	220	69	16	.748
*Lou Holtz, William & Mary, North Carolina St., Arkansas, Minnesota, Notre Dame, South Carolina	1969-96, 99	216	106	7	.667
Pop Warner, Georgia, Cornell, Carlisle, Pittsburgh	1895-1922	212	67	15	.747
Amos Alonzo Stagg, Springfield, Chicago	1890-1917	199	68	20	.728
Woody Hayes, Denison, Miami (Ohio), Ohio St.	1946-73	192	60	8	.754
*Don Nehlen, Bowling Green, West Virginia	1968-76, 80-98	191	116	8	.619
Howard Jones, Syracuse, Yale, Ohio St., Iowa, Duke, Southern California	1908-10, 13, 16-39	191	60	19	.743

29 SEASONS

Coach, Team(s)	Seasons	W	L	T	Pct.
*Joe Paterno, Penn St.	1966-94	269	69	3	.793
*Bobby Bowden, Samford, West Virginia, Florida St.	1959-62, 70-94	249	79	4	.756
Bear Bryant, Maryland, Kentucky, Texas A&M, Alabama	1945-73	231	70	16	.754
Pop Warner, Georgia, Cornell, Carlisle, Pittsburgh	1895-1923	217	71	15	.741
Woody Hayes, Denison, Miami (Ohio), Ohio St.	1946-74	202	62	8	.757
Amos Alonzo Stagg, Springfield, Chicago	1890-1918	199	74	20	.713
Fielding Yost, Ohio Wesleyan, Nebraska, Kansas, Stanford, Michigan	1897-1923, 25-26	196	36	12	.828
*Don Nehlen, Bowling Green, West Virginia	1968-76, 80-99	195	123	8	.610
Howard Jones, Syracuse, Yale, Ohio St., Iowa, Duke, Southern California	1908-10, 13, 16-40	194	64	21	.733
Dan McGugin, Vanderbilt	1904-17, 19-33	191	52	19	.765

30 SEASONS

Coach, Team(s)	Seasons	W	L	T	Pct.
*Joe Paterno, Penn St.	1966-95	278	72	3	.792
*Bobby Bowden, Samford, West Virginia, Florida St.	1959-62, 70-95	259	81	4	.759
Bear Bryant, Maryland, Kentucky, Texas A&M, Alabama	1945-74	242	71	16	.760
Pop Warner, Georgia, Cornell, Carlisle, Pittsburgh, Stanford	1895-1924	224	72	16	.744
Woody Hayes, Denison, Miami (Ohio), Ohio St.	1946-75	213	63	8	.764
Amos Alonzo Stagg, Springfield, Chicago	1890-1919	204	76	20	.713

31 SEASONS

Coach, Team(s)	Seasons	W	L	T	Pct.
*Joe Paterno, Penn St.	1966-96	289	74	3	.794
*Bobby Bowden, Samford, West Virginia, Florida St.	1959-62, 70-96	270	82	4	.764
Bear Bryant, Maryland, Kentucky, Texas A&M, Alabama	1945-75	253	72	16	.765
Pop Warner, Georgia, Cornell, Carlisle, Pittsburgh, Stanford	1895-1925	231	74	16	.745
Woody Hayes, Denison, Miami (Ohio), Ohio St.	1946-76	222	65	9	.765
Amos Alonzo Stagg, Springfield, Chicago	1890-1920	207	80	20	.707
Warren Woodson, Central Ark., Hardin-Simmons, Arizona, New Mexico St., Trinity (Tex.)	1935-42, 46-56, 58-67, 72-73	203	95	14	.673
Dana X. Bible, Mississippi Col., LSU, Texas A&M, Nebraska, Texas	1913-17, 19-44	180	69	23	.704

32 SEASONS

Coach, Team(s)	Seasons	W	L	T	Pct.
*Joe Paterno, Penn St.	1966-97	298	77	3	.792
*Bobby Bowden, Samford, West Virginia, Florida St.	1959-62, 70-97	281	83	4	.769
Bear Bryant, Maryland, Kentucky, Texas A&M, Alabama	1945-76	262	75	16	.765
Pop Warner, Georgia, Cornell, Carlisle, Pittsburgh, Stanford	1895-1926	241	74	17	.752
Woody Hayes, Denison, Miami (Ohio), Ohio St.	1946-77	231	68	9	.765
Amos Alonzo Stagg, Springfield, Chicago	1890-1921	213	81	20	.710
*Hayden Fry, Southern Methodist, North Texas, Iowa	1962-93	200	153	9	.565
Dana X. Bible, Mississippi Col., LSU, Texas A&M, Nebraska, Texas	1913-17, 19-45	190	70	23	.712

33 SEASONS

Coach, Team(s)	Seasons	W	L	T	Pct.
*Joe Paterno, Penn St.	1966-98	307	80	3	.791
*Bobby Bowden, Samford, West Virginia, Florida St.	1959-62, 70-98	292	85	4	.772
Bear Bryant, Maryland, Kentucky, Texas A&M, Alabama	1945-77	273	76	16	.770
Pop Warner, Georgia, Cornell, Carlisle, Pittsburgh, Stanford	1895-1927	249	76	18	.752
Woody Hayes, Denison, Miami (Ohio), Ohio St.	1946-78	238	72	10	.759
Amos Alonzo Stagg, Springfield, Chicago	1890-1922	219	82	20	.713
*Hayden Fry, Southern Methodist, North Texas, Iowa	1962-94	205	158	10	.563
Dana X. Bible, Mississippi Col., LSU, Texas A&M, Nebraska, Texas	1913-17, 19-46	198	72	23	.715

34 SEASONS

Coach, Team(s)	Seasons	W	L	T	Pct.
*Joe Paterno, Penn St.	1966-99	317	83	3	.790
*Bobby Bowden, Samford, West Virginia, Florida St.	1959-62, 70-99	304	85	4	.779
Bear Bryant, Maryland, Kentucky, Texas A&M, Alabama	1945-78	284	77	16	.775
Pop Warner, Georgia, Cornell, Carlisle, Pittsburgh, Stanford	1895-1928	257	79	19	.751
Amos Alonzo Stagg, Springfield, Chicago	1890-1923	226	83	20	.717
*Hayden Fry, Southern Methodist, North Texas, Iowa	1962-95	213	162	10	.566

35 SEASONS

Coach, Team(s)	Seasons	W	L	T	Pct.
Bear Bryant, Maryland, Kentucky, Texas A&M, Alabama	1945-79	296	77	16	.781
Pop Warner, Georgia, Cornell, Carlisle, Pittsburgh, Stanford	1895-1929	266	81	19	.753
Amos Alonzo Stagg, Springfield, Chicago	1890-1924	230	84	23	.717
*Hayden Fry, Southern Methodist, North Texas, Iowa	1962-96	222	165	10	.572

36 SEASONS

Coach, Team(s)	Seasons	W	L	T	Pct.
Bear Bryant, Maryland, Kentucky, Texas A&M, Alabama	1945-80	306	79	16	.783
Pop Warner, Georgia, Cornell, Carlisle, Pittsburgh, Stanford	1895-1930	275	82	20	.756
Amos Alonzo Stagg, Springfield, Chicago	1890-1925	233	88	24	.710
*Hayden Fry, Southern Methodist, North Texas, Iowa	1962-97	229	170	10	.572

37 SEASONS

Coach, Team(s)	Seasons	W	L	T	Pct.
Bear Bryant, Maryland, Kentucky, Texas A&M, Alabama	1945-81	315	81	17	.783
Pop Warner, Georgia, Cornell, Carlisle, Pittsburgh, Stanford	1895-1931	282	84	22	.755
Amos Alonzo Stagg, Springfield, Chicago	1890-1926	235	94	24	.700

38 SEASONS

Coach, Team(s)	Seasons	W	L	T	Pct.
Bear Bryant, Maryland, Kentucky, Texas A&M, Alabama	1945-82	323	85	17	.780
Pop Warner, Georgia, Cornell, Carlisle, Pittsburgh, Stanford	1895-1932	288	88	23	.751
Amos Alonzo Stagg, Springfield, Chicago	1890-1927	239	98	24	.695
Jess Neely, Rhodes, Clemson, Rice	1924-27, 31-64	203	160	19	.556

39 SEASONS

Coach, Team(s)	Seasons	W	L	T	Pct.
Pop Warner, Georgia, Cornell, Carlisle, Pittsburgh, Stanford, Temple	1895-1933	293	91	23	.748
Amos Alonzo Stagg, Springfield, Chicago	1890-1928	241	105	24	.684
Jess Neely, Rhodes, Clemson, Rice	1924-27, 31-65	205	168	19	.539
Eddie Anderson, Loras, DePaul, Holy Cross, Iowa	1922-42, 46-64	201	128	15	.606

40 SEASONS

Coach, Team(s)	Seasons	W	L	T	Pct.
Pop Warner, Georgia, Cornell, Carlisle, Pittsburgh, Stanford, Temple	1895-1934	300	92	25	.749
Amos Alonzo Stagg, Springfield, Chicago	1890-1929	248	108	24	.684
Jess Neely, Rhodes, Clemson, Rice	1924-27, 31-66	207	176	19	.539

41 SEASONS

Coach, Team(s)	Seasons	W	L	T	Pct.
Pop Warner, Georgia, Cornell, Carlisle, Pittsburgh, Stanford, Temple	1895-1935	307	95	25	.748
Amos Alonzo Stagg, Springfield, Chicago	1890-1930	249	113	26	.675

42 SEASONS

Coach, Team(s)	Seasons	W	L	T	Pct.
Pop Warner, Georgia, Cornell, Carlisle, Pittsburgh, Stanford, Temple	1895-1936	313	98	27	.745
Amos Alonzo Stagg, Springfield, Chicago	1890-1931	251	118	27	.668

43 SEASONS

Coach, Team(s)	Seasons	W	L	T	Pct.
Pop Warner, Georgia, Cornell, Carlisle, Pittsburgh, Stanford, Temple	1895-1937	316	100	31	.742
Amos Alonzo Stagg, Springfield, Chicago	1890-1932	254	122	28	.663

44 SEASONS

Coach, Team(s)	Seasons	W	L	T	Pct.
Pop Warner, Georgia, Cornell, Carlisle, Pittsburgh, Stanford, Temple	1895-1938	319	106	32	.733
Amos Alonzo Stagg, Springfield, Chicago, Pacific (Cal.)	1890-1933	259	127	28	.659

*Active coach.

Division I-A Best Career Starts by Percentage

(Head coaches with at least half their seasons at major college at the time and minimum five years coached)

1 SEASON

Coach, Team	Season	W	L	T	Pct.
Walter Camp, Yale	1888	13	0	0	1.000
Dan McGugin, Vanderbilt	1904	9	0	0	1.000
Bennie Oosterbaan, Michigan	1948	9	0	0	1.000
Carroll Widdoes, Ohio St.	1944	9	0	0	1.000
Galen Hall, Florida	1984	8	0	0	1.000
William Dietz, Washington St.	1915	7	0	0	1.000
John Heisman, Oberlin	1892	7	0	0	1.000
Dick Crum, Miami (Ohio)	1974	10	0	1	.955
Barry Switzer, Oklahoma	1973	10	0	1	.955
Aldo Donelli, Duquesne	1939	8	0	1	.944
Francis Schmidt, Tulsa	1919	8	0	1	.944

2 SEASONS

Coach, Team	Seasons	W	L	T	Pct.
Barry Switzer, Oklahoma	1973-74	21	0	1	.977
Walter Camp, Yale	1888-89	28	1	0	.966
Francis Schmidt, Tulsa	1919-20	18	0	2	.950
John Bateman, Rutgers	1960-61	17	1	0	.944
Dan McGugin, Vanderbilt	1904-05	16	1	0	.941
Dick Crum, Miami (Ohio)	1974-75	21	1	1	.935
Galen Hall, Florida	1984-85	17	1	1	.921
Bob Neyland, Tennessee	1926-27	16	1	1	.917
Aldo Donelli, Duquesne	1939-40	15	1	1	.912
Charley Moran, Texas A&M	1909-10	15	1	1	.912

3 SEASONS

Coach, Team	Seasons	W	L	T	Pct.
Barry Switzer, Oklahoma	1973-75	32	1	1	.956
Walter Camp, Yale	1888-90	41	2	0	.953
Aldo Donelli, Duquesne	1939-41	23	1	1	.940
Bob Neyland, Tennessee	1926-28	25	1	2	.929
Dan McGugin, Vanderbilt	1904-06	24	2	0	.923
Frank Leahy, Boston College, Notre Dame	1939-41	28	2	1	.919
Knute Rockne, Notre Dame	1918-20	21	1	2	.917
Elmer Henderson, Southern California	1919-21	20	2	0	.909
George Woodruff, Pennsylvania	1892-94	39	4	0	.907
Larry Siemering, Pacific (Cal.)	1947-49	28	2	2	.906

4 SEASONS

Coach, Team(s)	Seasons	W	L	T	Pct.
Gil Dobie, North Dakota St., Washington	1906-09	20	0	1	.976
Walter Camp, Yale	1888-91	54	2	0	.964
Barry Switzer, Oklahoma	1973-76	41	3	2	.935
Bob Neyland, Tennessee	1926-29	34	1	3	.934
George Woodruff, Pennsylvania	1892-95	53	4	0	.930
Knute Rockne, Notre Dame	1918-21	31	2	2	.914
Elmer Henderson, Southern California	1919-22	30	3	0	.909
Wallace Wade, Alabama	1923-26	34	3	2	.897
William Murray, Delaware	1940-42, 46	30	3	1	.897
Bud Wilkinson, Oklahoma	1947-50	38	4	1	.895

5 SEASONS

Coach, Team(s)	Seasons	W	L	T	Pct.
Gil Dobie, North Dakota St., Washington	1906-10	26	0	1	.981
Walter Camp, Yale, Stanford	1888-92	69	2	2	.959
George Woodruff, Pennsylvania	1892-96	67	5	0	.931
Bob Neyland, Tennessee	1926-30	43	2	3	.927
Knute Rockne, Notre Dame	1918-22	39	3	3	.900
Barry Switzer, Oklahoma	1973-77	51	5	2	.896
Elmer Henderson, Southern California	1919-23	36	5	0	.878
Bud Wilkinson, Oklahoma	1947-51	46	6	1	.877
Henry Williams, Army, Minnesota	1891, 1900-03	47	4	6	.877
Frank Leahy, Boston College, Notre Dame	1939-43	44	5	3	.875

6 SEASONS

Coach, Team(s)	Seasons	W	L	T	Pct.
Gil Dobie, North Dakota St., Washington	1906-11	33	0	1	.985
George Woodruff, Pennsylvania	1892-97	82	5	0	.943
Bob Neyland, Tennessee	1926-31	52	2	4	.931
Walter Camp, Yale, Stanford	1888-92, 94	75	5	2	.927
Knute Rockne, Notre Dame	1918-23	48	4	3	.900
Barry Switzer, Oklahoma	1973-78	62	6	2	.900
Henry Williams, Army, Minnesota	1891, 1900-04	60	4	6	.900
Frank Leahy, Boston College, Notre Dame	1939-43, 46	52	5	4	.885
Bud Wilkinson, Oklahoma	1947-52	54	7	2	.873
Fielding Yost, Ohio Wesleyan, Nebraska, Kansas, Stanford, Michigan	1897-1902	53	7	2	.871

7 SEASONS

Coach, Team(s)	Seasons	W	L	T	Pct.
Gil Dobie, North Dakota St., Washington	1906-12	39	0	1	.988
George Woodruff, Pennsylvania	1892-98	94	6	0	.940
Bob Neyland, Tennessee	1926-32	61	2	5	.934
Walter Camp, Yale, Stanford	1888-92, 94-95	79	5	3	.925
Knute Rockne, Notre Dame	1918-24	58	4	3	.915
Barry Switzer, Oklahoma	1973-79	73	7	2	.902
Henry Williams, Army, Minnesota	1891, 1900-05	70	5	6	.901
Frank Leahy, Boston College, Notre Dame	1939-43, 46-47	61	5	4	.900
Fielding Yost, Ohio Wesleyan, Nebraska, Kansas, Stanford, Michigan	1897-1903	64	7	3	.897
Bud Wilkinson, Oklahoma	1947-53	63	8	3	.872

8 SEASONS

Coach, Team(s)	Seasons	W	L	T	Pct.
Gil Dobie, North Dakota St., Washington	1906-13	46	0	1	.989
George Woodruff, Pennsylvania	1892-99	102	9	2	.912
Bob Neyland, Tennessee	1926-33	68	5	5	.904
Fielding Yost, Ohio Wesleyan, Nebraska, Kansas, Stanford, Michigan	1897-1904	74	7	3	.898
Henry Williams, Army, Minnesota	1891, 1900-06	74	6	6	.895
Barry Switzer, Oklahoma	1973-80	83	9	2	.894
Knute Rockne, Notre Dame	1918-25	65	6	4	.893
Bud Wilkinson, Oklahoma	1947-54	73	8	3	.887
Frank Leahy, Boston College, Notre Dame	1939-43, 46-48	70	5	5	.882
Percy Haughton, Cornell, Harvard	1899-1900, 08-13	66	8	3	.877

9 SEASONS

Coach, Team(s)	Seasons	W	L	T	Pct.
Gil Dobie, North Dakota St., Washington	1906-14	52	0	2	.981
Frank Leahy, Boston College, Notre Dame	1939-43, 46-49	80	5	5	.917
George Woodruff, Pennsylvania	1892-1900	114	10	2	.913
Fielding Yost, Ohio Wesleyan, Nebraska, Kansas, Stanford, Michigan	1897-1905	86	8	3	.902
Bud Wilkinson, Oklahoma	1947-55	84	8	3	.900
Knute Rockne, Notre Dame	1918-26	74	7	4	.894
Bob Neyland, Tennessee	1926-34	76	7	5	.892
Percy Haughton, Cornell, Harvard	1899-1900, 08-14	73	8	5	.878
Henry Williams, Army, Minnesota	1891, 1900-07	76	8	7	.874
Barry Switzer, Oklahoma	1973-81	90	13	3	.863

10 SEASONS

Coach, Team(s)	Seasons	W	L	T	Pct.
Gil Dobie, North Dakota St., Washington	1906-15	59	0	2	.984
Bud Wilkinson, Oklahoma	1947-56	94	8	3	.910
Fielding Yost, Ohio Wesleyan, Nebraska, Kansas, Stanford, Michigan	1897-1906	90	9	3	.897
Knute Rockne, Notre Dame	1918-27	81	8	5	.888
George Woodruff, Pennsylvania	1892-1901	124	15	2	.887
Percy Haughton, Cornell, Harvard	1899-1900, 08-15	81	9	5	.879
Frank Leahy, Boston College, Notre Dame	1939-43, 46-50	84	9	6	.879
Bob Neyland, Tennessee	1926-34, 36	82	9	7	.872
Henry Williams, Army, Minnesota	1891, 1900-08	79	10	8	.856
Barry Switzer, Oklahoma	1973-82	98	17	3	.843

DIVISION I-A BEST CAREER STARTS BY PERCENTAGE

11 SEASONS

Coach, Team(s)	Seasons	W	L	T	Pct.
Gil Dobie, North Dakota St., Washington	1906-16	65	0	3	.978
Bud Wilkinson, Oklahoma	1947-57	104	9	3	.909
Fielding Yost, Ohio Wesleyan, Nebraska, Kansas, Stanford, Michigan	1897-1907	95	10	3	.894
Frank Leahy, Boston College, Notre Dame	1939-43, 46-51	91	11	7	.867
Percy Haughton, Cornell, Harvard	1899-1900, 08-16	88	12	5	.862
Knute Rockne, Notre Dame	1918-28	86	12	5	.859
George Woodruff, Pennsylvania, Illinois	1892-1901, 03	132	21	2	.858
Henry Williams, Army, Minnesota	1891, 1900-09	85	11	8	.856
Bob Neyland, Tennessee	1926-34, 36-37	88	12	8	.852
Charley Moran, Texas A&M, Centre	1909-14, 19-23	80	14	5	.833

12 SEASONS

Coach, Team(s)	Seasons	W	L	T	Pct.
Gil Dobie, North Dakota St., Washington, Navy	1906-17	72	1	3	.967
Bud Wilkinson, Oklahoma	1947-58	114	10	3	.909
Fielding Yost, Ohio Wesleyan, Nebraska, Kansas, Stanford, Michigan	1897-1908	100	12	4	.879
Knute Rockne, Notre Dame	1918-29	95	12	5	.871
Bob Neyland, Tennessee	1926-34, 36-38	99	12	8	.866
Frank Leahy, Boston College, Notre Dame	1939-43, 46-52	98	13	8	.857
Henry Williams, Army, Minnesota	1891, 1900-10	91	12	8	.856
George Woodruff, Pennsylvania, Illinois, Carlisle	1892-1901, 03, 05	142	25	2	.846
Percy Haughton, Cornell, Harvard, Columbia	1899-1900, 08-16, 23	92	16	6	.833
Charley Moran, Texas A&M, Centre, Bucknell	1909-14, 19-24	88	16	5	.830

13 SEASONS

Coach, Team(s)	Seasons	W	L	T	Pct.
Gil Dobie, North Dakota St., Washington, Navy	1906-18	76	2	3	.957
Bud Wilkinson, Oklahoma	1947-59	121	13	3	.894
Knute Rockne, Notre Dame	1918-30	105	12	5	.881
Fielding Yost, Ohio Wesleyan, Nebraska, Kansas, Stanford, Michigan	1897-1909	106	13	4	.878
Bob Neyland, Tennessee	1926-34, 36-39	109	13	8	.869
Frank Leahy, Boston College, Notre Dame	1939-43, 46-53	107	13	9	.864
Henry Williams, Army, Minnesota	1891, 1900-11	97	12	9	.860
Percy Haughton, Cornell, Harvard, Columbia	1899-1900, 08-16, 23-24	96	17	6	.832
Barry Switzer, Oklahoma	1973-85	126	24	4	.831
*Joe Paterno, Penn St.	1966-78	123	25	1	.829

14 SEASONS

Coach, Team(s)	Seasons	W	L	T	Pct.
Gil Dobie, North Dakota St., Washington, Navy	1906-19	82	3	3	.949
Bob Neyland, Tennessee	1926-34, 36-40	119	14	8	.872
Fielding Yost, Ohio Wesleyan, Nebraska, Kansas, Stanford, Michigan	1897-1910	109	13	7	.872
Bud Wilkinson, Oklahoma	1947-60	124	19	4	.857
Henry Williams, Army, Minnesota	1891, 1900-12	101	15	9	.844
Barry Switzer, Oklahoma	1973-86	137	25	4	.837
*Joe Paterno, Penn St.	1966-79	131	29	1	.817
Fred Folsom, Colorado, Dartmouth	1895-99, 1901-06, 08-10	83	17	5	.814
Elmer Henderson, Southern California, Tulsa	1919-32	101	23	3	.807
Tom Osborne, Nebraska	1973-86	137	32	2	.807

15 SEASONS

Coach, Team(s)	Seasons	W	L	T	Pct.
Gil Dobie, North Dakota St., Washington, Navy, Cornell	1906-20	88	5	3	.932
Bob Neyland, Tennessee	1926-34, 36-40, 46	128	16	8	.868
Fielding Yost, Ohio Wesleyan, Nebraska, Kansas, Stanford, Michigan	1897-1911	114	14	9	.858
Barry Switzer, Oklahoma	1973-87	148	26	4	.843
Henry Williams, Army, Minnesota	1891, 1900-13	106	17	9	.837
Bud Wilkinson, Oklahoma	1947-61	129	24	4	.834
Fred Folsom, Colorado, Dartmouth	1895-99, 1901-06, 08-11	89	17	5	.824
*Joe Paterno, Penn St.	1966-80	141	31	1	.818
Elmer Henderson, Southern California, Tulsa	1919-33	107	24	3	.810
Tom Osborne, Nebraska	1973-87	147	34	2	.809

16 SEASONS

Coach, Team(s)	Seasons	W	L	T	Pct.
Gil Dobie, North Dakota St., Washington, Navy, Cornell	1906-21	96	5	3	.938
Fielding Yost, Ohio Wesleyan, Nebraska, Kansas, Stanford, Michigan	1897-1912	119	16	9	.858
Bob Neyland, Tennessee	1926-34, 36-40, 46-47	133	21	8	.846
Henry Williams, Army, Minnesota	1891, 1900-14	112	18	9	.838
Barry Switzer, Oklahoma	1973-88	157	29	4	.837
Bud Wilkinson, Oklahoma	1947-62	137	27	4	.827
*Joe Paterno, Penn St.	1966-81	151	33	1	.819
Fred Folsom, Colorado, Dartmouth	1895-99, 1901-06, 08-12	95	20	5	.813
Tom Osborne, Nebraska	1973-88	158	36	2	.811
Bob Devaney, Wyoming, Nebraska	1957-72	136	30	7	.806

17 SEASONS

Coach, Team(s)	Seasons	W	L	T	Pct.
Gil Dobie, North Dakota St., Washington, Navy, Cornell	1906-22	104	5	3	.942
Fielding Yost, Ohio Wesleyan, Nebraska, Kansas, Stanford, Michigan	1897-1913	125	17	9	.858
Henry Williams, Army, Minnesota	1891, 1900-15	118	18	10	.842
Bud Wilkinson, Oklahoma	1947-63	145	29	4	.826
Bob Neyland, Tennessee	1926-34, 36-40, 46-48	137	25	10	.826
*Joe Paterno, Penn St.	1966-82	162	34	1	.825
Tom Osborne, Nebraska	1973-89	168	38	2	.813
Fred Folsom, Colorado, Dartmouth	1895-99, 1901-06, 08-13	100	21	6	.811
Wallace Wade, Alabama, Duke	1923-39	130	29	6	.806
Red Blaik, Dartmouth, Army	1934-50	120	26	10	.801
Jock Sutherland, Lafayette, Pittsburgh	1919-35	119	25	12	.801

18 SEASONS

Coach, Team(s)	Seasons	W	L	T	Pct.
Gil Dobie, North Dakota St., Washington, Navy, Cornell	1906-23	112	5	3	.946
Fielding Yost, Ohio Wesleyan, Nebraska, Kansas, Stanford, Michigan	1897-1914	131	20	9	.847
Henry Williams, Army, Minnesota	1891, 1900-16	124	19	10	.843
Bob Neyland, Tennessee	1926-34, 36-40, 46-49	144	27	11	.821
*Joe Paterno, Penn St.	1966-83	170	38	2	.814
Fred Folsom, Colorado, Dartmouth	1895-99, 1901-06, 08-14	105	22	6	.812
Tom Osborne, Nebraska	1973-90	177	41	2	.809
Frank Thomas, Chattanooga, Alabama	1925-28, 31-42, 44-45	134	29	9	.805
Wallace Wade, Alabama, Duke	1923-40	137	31	6	.805
Jock Sutherland, Lafayette, Pittsburgh	1919-36	127	26	13	.804

19 SEASONS

Coach, Team(s)	Seasons	W	L	T	Pct.
Gil Dobie, North Dakota St., Washington, Navy, Cornell	1906-24	116	9	3	.918
Henry Williams, Army, Minnesota	1891, 1900-17	128	20	10	.842
Fielding Yost, Ohio Wesleyan, Nebraska, Kansas, Stanford, Michigan	1897-1915	135	23	10	.833
Bob Neyland, Tennessee	1926-34, 36-40, 46-50	155	28	11	.827
Jock Sutherland, Lafayette, Pittsburgh	1919-37	136	26	14	.813
Wallace Wade, Alabama, Duke	1923-41	146	32	6	.810
Tom Osborne, Nebraska	1973-91	186	43	3	.808
*Joe Paterno, Penn St.	1966-84	176	43	2	.801
Frank Thomas, Chattanooga, Alabama	1925-28, 31-42, 44-46	141	33	9	.795
Bo Schembechler, Miami (Ohio), Michigan	1963-81	163	41	6	.790

20 SEASONS

Coach, Team(s)	Seasons	W	L	T	Pct.
Gil Dobie, North Dakota St., Washington, Navy, Cornell	1906-25	122	11	3	.908
Henry Williams, Army, Minnesota	1891, 1900-18	133	22	11	.834
Bob Neyland, Tennessee	1926-34, 36-40, 46-51	165	29	11	.832
Fielding Yost, Ohio Wesleyan, Nebraska, Kansas, Stanford, Michigan	1897-1916	142	25	10	.831
Jock Sutherland, Lafayette, Pittsburgh	1919-38	144	28	14	.812
*Joe Paterno, Penn St.	1966-85	187	44	2	.807
Tom Osborne, Nebraska	1973-92	195	46	3	.805
Wallace Wade, Alabama, Duke	1923-41, 46	150	37	6	.793
Bo Schembechler, Miami (Ohio), Michigan	1963-82	171	45	6	.784
Dan McGugin, Vanderbilt	1904-17, 19-24	131	33	12	.778

21 SEASONS

Coach, Team(s)	Seasons	W	L	T	Pct.
Gil Dobie, North Dakota St., Washington, Navy, Cornell	1906-26	128	12	4	.903
Fielding Yost, Ohio Wesleyan, Nebraska, Kansas, Stanford, Michigan	1897-1917	150	27	10	.829

Coach, Team(s)	Seasons	W	L	T	Pct.
Bob Neyland, Tennessee	1926-34, 36-40, 46-52	173	31	12	.829
Henry Williams, Army, Minnesota	1891, 1900-19	137	24	12	.827
*Joe Paterno, Penn St.	1966-86	199	44	2	.816
Tom Osborne, Nebraska	1973-93	206	47	3	.811
Wallace Wade, Alabama, Duke	1923-41, 46-47	154	40	8	.782
Bo Schembechler, Miami (Ohio), Michigan	1963-83	180	48	6	.782
Howard Jones, Syracuse, Yale, Ohio St., Iowa, Duke, Southern California	1908-10, 13, 16-32	147	38	10	.779
Dan McGugin, Vanderbilt	1904-17, 19-25	137	36	12	.773

22 SEASONS

Coach, Team(s)	Seasons	W	L	T	Pct.
Gil Dobie, North Dakota St., Washington, Navy, Cornell	1906-27	131	15	6	.882
Fielding Yost, Ohio Wesleyan, Nebraska, Kansas, Stanford, Michigan	1897-1918	155	27	10	.833
Tom Osborne, Nebraska	1973-94	219	47	3	.820
*Joe Paterno, Penn St.	1966-87	207	48	2	.809
Henry Williams, Army, Minnesota	1891, 1900-20	138	30	12	.800
Howard Jones, Syracuse, Yale, Ohio St., Iowa, Duke, Southern California	1908-10, 13, 16-33	157	39	11	.785
Dan McGugin, Vanderbilt	1904-17, 19-26	145	37	12	.778
Wallace Wade, Alabama, Duke	1923-41, 46-48	158	43	10	.773
Bo Schembechler, Miami (Ohio), Michigan	1963-84	186	54	6	.768
Bear Bryant, Maryland, Kentucky, Texas A&M, Alabama	1945-66	171	51	14	.767

23 SEASONS

Coach, Team(s)	Seasons	W	L	T	Pct.
Gil Dobie, North Dakota St., Washington, Navy, Cornell	1906-28	134	18	8	.863
Tom Osborne, Nebraska	1973-95	231	47	3	.827
Fielding Yost, Ohio Wesleyan, Nebraska, Kansas, Stanford, Michigan	1897-1919	158	31	10	.819
*Joe Paterno, Penn St.	1966-88	212	54	2	.795
Henry Williams, Army, Minnesota	1891, 1900-21	141	34	12	.786
Dan McGugin, Vanderbilt	1904-17, 19-27	153	38	14	.780
Bo Schembechler, Miami (Ohio), Michigan	1963-85	196	55	7	.773
Wallace Wade, Alabama, Duke	1923-41, 46-49	164	46	10	.768
Howard Jones, Syracuse, Yale, Ohio St., Iowa, Duke, Southern California	1908-10, 13, 16-34	161	45	12	.766
Bear Bryant, Maryland, Kentucky, Texas A&M, Alabama	1945-67	179	53	15	.755
Johnny Vaught, Mississippi	1947-69	178	54	12	.754

24 SEASONS

Coach, Team(s)	Seasons	W	L	T	Pct.
Gil Dobie, North Dakota St., Washington, Navy, Cornell	1906-29	140	20	8	.857
Tom Osborne, Nebraska	1973-96	242	49	3	.828
Fielding Yost, Ohio Wesleyan, Nebraska, Kansas, Stanford, Michigan	1897-1920	163	33	10	.816
*Joe Paterno, Penn St.	1966-89	220	57	3	.791
Dan McGugin, Vanderbilt	1904-17, 19-28	161	40	14	.781
Bo Schembechler, Miami (Ohio), Michigan	1963-86	207	57	7	.777
Wallace Wade, Alabama, Duke	1923-41, 46-50	171	49	10	.765
Bear Bryant, Maryland, Kentucky, Texas A&M, Alabama	1945-68	187	56	15	.754
Red Blaik, Dartmouth, Army	1934-57	158	48	13	.751
Johnny Vaught, Mississippi	1947-70	185	58	12	.749
Howard Jones, Syracuse, Yale, Ohio St., Iowa, Duke, Southern California	1908-10, 13, 16-35	166	52	12	.748

25 SEASONS

Coach, Team(s)	Seasons	W	L	T	Pct.
Gil Dobie, North Dakota St., Washington, Navy, Cornell	1906-30	146	22	8	.852
Tom Osborne, Nebraska	1973-97	255	49	3	.836
Fielding Yost, Ohio Wesleyan, Nebraska, Kansas, Stanford, Michigan	1897-1921	168	34	11	.815
*Joe Paterno, Penn St.	1966-90	229	60	3	.789
Dan McGugin, Vanderbilt	1904-17, 19-29	168	42	14	.781
Bo Schembechler, Miami (Ohio), Michigan	1963-87	215	61	7	.772
Red Blaik, Dartmouth, Army	1934-58	166	48	14	.759
John Heisman, Oberlin, Akron, Auburn, Clemson, Georgia Tech	1892-1916	127	37	11	.757
Howard Jones, Syracuse, Yale, Ohio St., Iowa, Duke, Southern California	1908-10, 13, 16-36	170	54	15	.755
Woody Hayes, Denison, Miami (Ohio), Ohio St.	1946-70	167	54	7	.748
Bear Bryant, Maryland, Kentucky, Texas A&M, Alabama	1945-69	193	61	15	.745

26 SEASONS

Coach, Team(s)	Seasons	W	L	T	Pct.
Gil Dobie, North Dakota St., Washington, Navy, Cornell	1906-31	153	23	8	.853
Fielding Yost, Ohio Wesleyan, Nebraska, Kansas, Stanford, Michigan	1897-1922	174	34	12	.818
*Joe Paterno, Penn St.	1966-91	240	62	3	.792
Dan McGugin, Vanderbilt	1904-17, 19-30	176	44	14	.782
Bo Schembechler, Miami (Ohio), Michigan	1963-88	224	63	8	.773
John Heisman, Oberlin, Akron, Auburn, Clemson, Georgia Tech	1892-1917	136	37	11	.769
Pop Warner, Georgia, Cornell, Carlisle, Pittsburgh	1895-1920	199	62	14	.749
Woody Hayes, Denison, Miami (Ohio), Ohio St.	1946-71	173	58	7	.742
Amos Alonzo Stagg, Springfield, Chicago	1890-1915	193	62	19	.739
*Bobby Bowden, Samford, West Virginia, Florida St.	1959-62, 70-91	216	76	3	.737

27 SEASONS

Coach, Team(s)	Seasons	W	L	T	Pct.
Gil Dobie, North Dakota St., Washington, Navy, Cornell	1906-32	158	25	9	.846
Fielding Yost, Ohio Wesleyan, Nebraska, Kansas, Stanford, Michigan	1897-1923	182	34	12	.825
*Joe Paterno, Penn St.	1966-92	247	67	3	.784
Bo Schembechler, Miami (Ohio), Michigan	1963-89	234	65	8	.775
Dan McGugin, Vanderbilt	1904-17, 19-31	181	48	14	.774
John Heisman, Oberlin, Akron, Auburn, Clemson, Georgia Tech	1892-1918	142	38	11	.772
Woody Hayes, Denison, Miami (Ohio), Ohio St.	1946-72	182	60	7	.745
Pop Warner, Georgia, Cornell, Carlisle, Pittsburgh	1895-1921	204	65	15	.745
*Bobby Bowden, Samford, West Virginia, Florida St.	1959-62, 70-92	227	77	3	.744
Bear Bryant, Maryland, Kentucky, Texas A&M, Alabama	1945-71	210	67	16	.744

28 SEASONS

Coach, Team(s)	Seasons	W	L	T	Pct.
Gil Dobie, North Dakota St., Washington, Navy, Cornell	1906-33	162	28	9	.837
Fielding Yost, Ohio Wesleyan, Nebraska, Kansas, Stanford, Michigan	1897-1923, 25	189	35	12	.826
*Joe Paterno, Penn St.	1966-93	257	69	3	.786
Dan McGugin, Vanderbilt	1904-17, 19-32	187	49	16	.774
John Heisman, Oberlin, Akron, Auburn, Clemson, Georgia Tech	1892-1919	149	41	11	.769
Woody Hayes, Denison, Miami (Ohio), Ohio St.	1946-73	192	60	8	.754
*Bobby Bowden, Samford, West Virginia, Florida St.	1959-62, 70-93	239	78	3	.752
Bear Bryant, Maryland, Kentucky, Texas A&M, Alabama	1945-72	220	69	16	.748
Pop Warner, Georgia, Cornell, Carlisle, Pittsburgh	1895-1922	212	67	15	.747
Howard Jones, Syracuse, Yale, Ohio St., Iowa, Duke, Southern California	1908-10, 13, 16-39	191	60	19	.743

29 SEASONS

Coach, Team(s)	Seasons	W	L	T	Pct.
Fielding Yost, Ohio Wesleyan, Nebraska, Kansas, Stanford, Michigan	1897-1923, 25-26	196	36	12	.828
Gil Dobie, North Dakota St., Washington, Navy, Cornell	1906-34	164	33	9	.818
*Joe Paterno, Penn St.	1966-94	269	69	3	.793
Dan McGugin, Vanderbilt	1904-17, 19-33	191	52	19	.765
John Heisman, Oberlin, Akron, Auburn, Clemson, Georgia Tech, Pennsylvania	1892-1920	155	45	11	.761
Woody Hayes, Denison, Miami (Ohio), Ohio St.	1946-74	202	62	8	.757
*Bobby Bowden, Samford, West Virginia, Florida St.	1959-62, 70-94	249	79	4	.756
Bear Bryant, Maryland, Kentucky, Texas A&M, Alabama	1945-73	231	70	16	.754
Pop Warner, Georgia, Cornell, Carlisle, Pittsburgh	1895-1923	217	71	15	.741
Howard Jones, Syracuse, Yale, Ohio St., Iowa, Duke, Southern California	1908-10, 13, 16-40	194	64	21	.733

30 SEASONS

Coach, Team(s)	Seasons	W	L	T	Pct.
Gil Dobie, North Dakota St., Washington, Navy, Cornell	1906-35	164	39	10	.793
*Joe Paterno, Penn St.	1966-95	278	72	3	.792

DIVISION I-A BEST CAREER STARTS BY PERCENTAGE

Coach, Team(s)	Seasons	W	L	T	Pct.
Woody Hayes, Denison, Miami (Ohio), Ohio St.	1946-75	213	63	8	.764
Dan McGugin, Vanderbilt	1904-17, 19-34	197	55	19	.762
Bear Bryant, Maryland, Kentucky, Texas A&M, Alabama	1945-74	242	71	16	.760
*Bobby Bowden, Samford, West Virginia, Florida St.	1959-62, 70-95	259	81	4	.759
John Heisman, Oberlin, Akron, Auburn, Clemson, Georgia Tech, Pennsylvania	1892-1921	159	48	13	.752
Pop Warner, Georgia, Cornell, Carlisle, Pittsburgh, Stanford	1895-1924	224	72	16	.744
Amos Alonzo Stagg, Springfield, Chicago	1890-1919	204	76	20	.713
Dana X. Bible, Mississippi Col., LSU, Texas A&M, Nebraska, Texas	1913-17, 19-43	175	67	23	.704

31 SEASONS

Coach, Team(s)	Seasons	W	L	T	Pct.
*Joe Paterno, Penn St.	1966-96	289	74	3	.794
Gil Dobie, North Dakota St., Washington, Navy, Cornell, Boston College	1906-36	170	40	12	.793
Bear Bryant, Maryland, Kentucky, Texas A&M, Alabama	1945-75	253	72	16	.765
Woody Hayes, Denison, Miami (Ohio), Ohio St.	1946-76	222	65	9	.765
*Bobby Bowden, Samford, West Virginia, Florida St.	1959-62, 70-96	270	82	4	.764
John Heisman, Oberlin, Akron, Auburn, Clemson, Georgia Tech, Pennsylvania	1892-1922	165	51	13	.749
Pop Warner, Georgia, Cornell, Carlisle, Pittsburgh, Stanford	1895-1925	231	74	16	.745
Amos Alonzo Stagg, Springfield, Chicago	1890-1920	207	80	20	.707
Dana X. Bible, Mississippi Col., LSU, Texas A&M, Nebraska, Texas	1913-17, 19-44	180	69	23	.704

32 SEASONS

Coach, Team(s)	Seasons	W	L	T	Pct.
*Joe Paterno, Penn St.	1966-97	298	77	3	.792
Gil Dobie, North Dakota St., Washington, Navy, Cornell, Boston College	1906-37	174	44	13	.781
*Bobby Bowden, Stamford, West Virginia, Florida St.	1959-62, 70-97	281	83	4	.769
Bear Bryant, Maryland, Kentucky, Texas A&M, Alabama	1945-76	262	75	16	.765
Woody Hayes, Denison, Miami (Ohio), Ohio St.	1946-77	231	68	9	.765
Pop Warner, Georgia, Cornell, Carlisle, Pittsburgh, Stanford	1895-1926	241	74	17	.752
John Heisman, Oberlin, Akron, Auburn, Clemson, Georgia Tech, Pennsylvania, Wash. & Jeff.	1892-1923	171	52	14	.751
Dana X. Bible, Mississippi Col., LSU, Texas A&M, Nebraska, Texas	1913-17, 19-45	190	70	23	.712
Amos Alonzo Stagg, Springfield, Chicago	1890-1921	213	81	20	.710

33 SEASONS

Coach, Team(s)	Seasons	W	L	T	Pct.
*Joe Paterno, Penn St.	1966-98	307	80	3	.791
Gil Dobie, North Dakota St., Washington, Navy, Cornell, Boston College	1906-38	180	45	15	.781
*Bobby Bowden, Samford, West Virginia	1959-62, 70-98	292	85	4	.772
Bear Bryant, Maryland, Kentucky, Texas A&M, Alabama	1945-77	273	76	16	.770
Woody Hayes, Denison, Miami (Ohio), Ohio St.	1946-78	238	72	10	.759
Pop Warner, Georgia, Cornell, Carlisle, Pittsburgh, Stanford	1895-1927	249	76	18	.752
John Heisman, Oberlin, Akron, Auburn, Clemson, Georgia Tech, Pennsylvania, Wash. & Jeff., Rice	1892-1924	175	56	14	.743
Dana X. Bible, Mississippi Col., LSU, Texas A&M, Nebraska, Texas	1913-17, 19-46	198	72	23	.715
Amos Alonzo Stagg, Springfield, Chicago	1890-1922	219	82	20	.713

34 SEASONS

Coach, Team(s)	Seasons	W	L	T	Pct.
*Joe Paterno, Penn St.	1996-99	317	83	3	.790
*Bobby Bowden, Samford, West Virginia, Florida St.	1959-62, 70-99	304	85	4	.779
Bear Bryant, Maryland, Kentucky, Texas A&M, Alabama	1945-78	284	77	16	.775
Pop Warner, Georgia, Cornell, Carlisle, Pittsburgh, Stanford	1895-1928	257	79	19	.751
John Heisman, Oberlin, Akron, Auburn, Clemson, Georgia Tech, Pennsylvania, Wash. & Jeff., Rice	1892-1925	179	60	15	.734
Amos Alonzo Stagg, Springfield, Chicago	1890-1923	226	83	20	.717

35 SEASONS

Coach, Team(s)	Seasons	W	L	T	Pct.
Bear Bryant, Maryland, Kentucky, Texas A&M, Alabama	1945-79	296	77	16	.781
Pop Warner, Georgia, Cornell, Carlisle, Pittsburgh, Stanford	1895-1929	266	81	19	.753
John Heisman, Oberlin, Akron, Auburn, Clemson, Georgia Tech, Pennsylvania, Wash. & Jeff., Rice	1892-1926	183	64	16	.726
Amos Alonzo Stagg, Springfield, Chicago	1890-1924	230	84	23	.717

36 SEASONS

Coach, Team(s)	Seasons	W	L	T	Pct.
Bear Bryant, Maryland, Kentucky, Texas A&M, Alabama	1945-80	306	79	16	.783
Pop Warner, Georgia, Cornell, Carlisle, Pittsburgh, Stanford	1895-1930	275	82	20	.756
John Heisman, Oberlin, Akron, Auburn, Clemson, Georgia Tech, Pennsylvania, Wash. & Jeff., Rice	1892-1927	185	70	17	.711
Amos Alonzo Stagg, Springfield, Chicago	1890-1925	233	88	24	.710

37 SEASONS

Coach, Team(s)	Seasons	W	L	T	Pct.
Bear Bryant, Maryland, Kentucky, Texas A&M, Alabama	1945-81	315	81	17	.783
Pop Warner, Georgia, Cornell, Carlisle, Pittsburgh, Stanford	1895-1931	282	84	22	.755
Amos Alonzo Stagg, Springfield, Chicago	1890-1926	235	94	24	.700
Eddie Anderson, Loras, DePaul, Holy Cross, Iowa	1922-31, 33-42, 46-62	194	117	14	.618

38 SEASONS

Coach, Team(s)	Seasons	W	L	T	Pct.
Bear Bryant, Maryland, Kentucky, Texas A&M, Alabama	1945-82	323	85	17	.780
Pop Warner, Georgia, Cornell, Carlisle, Pittsburgh, Stanford	1895-1932	288	88	23	.751
Amos Alonzo Stagg, Springfield, Chicago	1890-1927	239	98	24	.695
Eddie Anderson, Loras, DePaul, Holy Cross, Iowa	1922-31, 33-42, 46-63	196	123	15	.609

39 SEASONS

Coach, Team(s)	Seasons	W	L	T	Pct.
Pop Warner, Georgia, Cornell, Carlisle, Pittsburgh, Stanford, Temple	1895-1933	293	91	23	.748
Amos Alonzo Stagg, Springfield, Chicago	1890-1928	241	105	24	.684
Eddie Anderson, Loras, DePaul, Holy Cross, Iowa	1922-31, 33-42, 46-64	201	128	15	.606

40 SEASONS

Coach, Team(s)	Seasons	W	L	T	Pct.
Pop Warner, Georgia, Cornell, Carlisle, Pittsburgh, Stanford, Temple	1895-1934	300	92	25	.749
Amos Alonzo Stagg, Springfield, Chicago	1890-1929	248	108	24	.684

41 SEASONS

Coach, Team(s)	Seasons	W	L	T	Pct.
Pop Warner, Georgia, Cornell, Carlisle, Pittsburgh, Stanford, Temple	1895-1935	307	95	25	.748
Amos Alonzo Stagg, Springfield, Chicago	1890-1930	249	113	26	.675

42 SEASONS

Coach, Team(s)	Seasons	W	L	T	Pct.
Pop Warner, Georgia, Cornell, Carlisle, Pittsburgh, Stanford, Temple	1895-1936	313	98	27	.745
Amos Alonzo Stagg, Springfield, Chicago	1890-1931	251	118	27	.668

43 SEASONS

Coach, Team(s)	Seasons	W	L	T	Pct.
Pop Warner, Georgia, Cornell, Carlisle, Pittsburgh, Stanford, Temple	1895-1937	316	100	31	.742
Amos Alonzo Stagg, Springfield, Chicago	1890-1932	254	122	28	.663

44 SEASONS

Coach, Team(s)	Seasons	W	L	T	Pct.
Pop Warner, Georgia, Cornell, Carlisle, Pittsburgh, Stanford, Temple	1895-1938	319	106	32	.733
Amos Alonzo Stagg, Springfield, Chicago, Pacific (Cal.)	1890-1933	259	127	28	.659

*Active coach.

Coaches to Reach 100, 200 and 300 Victories

(Must have five years or 50 victories at a school that was classified as a major college at the time)

100 VICTORIES

Coach (Date Reached Milestone) (Schools Coached and Years)	Age in Yrs.-Days	WHEN MILESTONE REACHED Career Game (Record)	Career Yr.-Game
FRED AKERS (9-17-88) (Wyoming 1975-76, Texas 1977-86, Purdue 1987-90)	50-184	155th (100-52-3)	14-2
WILLIAM ALEXANDER (11-18-39) (Georgia Tech 1920-44)	49-233	189th (100-74-15)	20-7
EDDIE ANDERSON (10-12-46) (Loras 1922-24, DePaul 1925-31, Holy Cross 1933-38, Iowa 1939-42, 1946-49, Holy Cross 1950-64)	45-333	160th (100-50-10)	21-4
IKE ARMSTRONG (10-17-42) (Utah 1925-49)	47-131	141st (100-30-11)	18-4
#FRANK BEAMER (11-9-96) (Murray St. 1981-86, Virginia Tech 1987—)	50-22	177th (100-73-4)	16-8
MATTY BELL (11-5-38) (Haskell 1920-21, Carroll [Wis.] 1922, TCU 1923-28, Texas A&M 1929-34, Southern Methodist 1935-41, 1945-49)	39-256	169th (100-60-9)	18-6
HUGO BEZDEK (11-22-24) (Oregon 1906, Arkansas 1908-12, Oregon 1913-17, Penn St. 1918-29, Delaware Valley 1949)	40-120	147th (100-34-13)	18-9
DANA X. BIBLE (11-21-31) (Mississippi Col. 1913-15, LSU 1916, Texas A&M 1917, 1919-28, Nebraska 1929-36, Texas 1937-46)	40-44	149th (100-31-18)	18-8
BERNIE BIERMAN (11-11-39) (Montana St. 1919-21, Mississippi St. 1925-26, Tulane 1927-31, Minnesota 1932-41, 1945-50)	45-245	149th (100-38-11)	18-6
BOB BLACKMAN (9-27-69) (Denver 1953-54, Dartmouth 1955-70, Illinois 1971-76, Cornell 1977-82)	51-82	147th (100-42-5)	17-1
RED BLAIK (10-23-48) (Dartmouth 1934-40, Army 1941-58)	51-249	134th (100-25-9)	15-5
#BOBBY BOWDEN (10-7-78) (Samford 1959-62, West Virginia 1970-75, Florida St. 1976—)	48-333	144th (100-44-0)	14-5
TERRY BOWDEN (12-31-96) (Salem-Teikyo 1983-85, Samford 1987-92, Auburn 1993-98)	40-280	147th (100-45-2)	13-12
BILLY BREWER (10-6-90) (Southeast La. 1974-79, Louisiana Tech 1980-82, Mississippi 1983-93)	54-363	184th (100-78-6)	17-5
#MACK BROWN (10-9-99) (Appalachian St. 1983, Tulane 1985-87, North Carolina 1988-97, Texas 1998—)	48-43	180th (100-79-1)	16-7
FRANK BROYLES (11-27-69) (Missouri 1957, Arkansas 1958-76)	44-336	138th (100-36-2)	13-9
EARLE BRUCE (11-3-84) (Tampa 1972, Iowa St. 1973-78, Ohio St. 1979-87, Northern Iowa 1988, Colorado St. 1989-92)	53-240	149th (100-49-0)	13-9
BEAR BRYANT (11-7-59) (Maryland 1945, Kentucky 1946-53, Texas A&M 1954-57, Alabama 1958-82)	46-57	154th (100-44-10)	15-7
WALLY BUTTS (11-15-52) (Georgia 1939-60)	47-281	151st (100-44-7)	14-9
CHARLIE CALDWELL (10-21-50) (Williams 1928-42, Princeton 1945-56)	48-80	163rd (100-55-8)	21-4
FRANK CAMP (10-23-65) (Louisville 1946-68)	60-39	182nd (100-80-2)	20-6
JIM CARLEN (11-8-80) (West Virginia 1966-69, Texas Tech 1970-74, South Carolina 1975-81)	47-120	167th (100-61-6)	15-9
LEN CASANOVA (10-2-65) (Santa Clara 1946-49, Pittsburgh 1950, Oregon 1951-66)	59-263	192nd (100-82-10)	20-3
FRANK CAVANAUGH (10-3-25) (Cincinnati 1898, Holy Cross 1903-05, Dartmouth 1911-16, Boston College 1919-26, Fordham 1927-32)	49-158	143rd (100-32-11)	17-1
JERRY CLAIBORNE (11-6-76) (Virginia Tech 1961-70, Maryland 1972-81, Kentucky 1982-89)	48-72	158th (100-54-4)	15-9
#JOHN COOPER (11-17-90) (Tulsa 1977-84, Arizona St. 1985-87, Ohio St. 1988—)	53-137	162nd (100-57-5)	14-10
CARMEN COZZA (10-4-80) (Yale 1965-96)	50-116	138th (100-35-3)	16-3
FRITZ CRISLER (11-24-45) (Minnesota 1930-31, Princeton 1932-37, Michigan 1938-47)	46-316	138th (100-30-8)	16-10
DICK CRUM (11-15-86) (Miami [Ohio] 1974-77, North Carolina 1978-87, Kent St. 1988-90)	52-200	148th (100-44-4)	13-10
JACK CURTICE (10-3-64) (West Tex. A&M 1940-41, UTEP 1946-49, Utah 1950-57, Stanford 1958-61, UC Santa Barb. 1962-69)	56-118	202nd (100-95-7)	21-1
DUFFY DAUGHERTY (9-25-71) (Michigan St. 1954-72)	56-17	164th (100-60-4)	18-3
#FISHER DeBERRY (9-6-97) (Air Force 1984—)	59-89	161st (100-60-1)	14-2
DUDLEY DeGROOT (9-17-49) (UC Santa Barb. 1926-28, San Jose St. 1932-39, Rochester 1940-43, West Virginia 1948-49, New Mexico 1950-52)	49-302	152nd (100-44-8)	17-1
HERB DEROMEDI (11-16-91) (Central Mich. 1978-93)	52-171	153rd (100-43-10)	14-11
BOB DEVANEY (11-8-69) (Wyoming 1957-61, Nebraska 1962-72)	54-209	133rd (100-28-5)	13-8

DIVISION I-A COACHES TO REACH 100 VICTORIES

Coach (Date Reached Milestone) (Schools Coached and Years)	Age in Yrs.-Days	Career Game (Record)	Career Yr.-Game
DAN DEVINE (10-12-68) (Arizona St. 1955-57, Missouri 1958-70, Notre Dame 1975-80)	43-293	139th (100-31-8)	14-4
DOUG DICKEY (11-27-77) (Tennessee 1964-69, Florida 1970-78)	45-202	156th (100-50-6)	14-10
PAUL DIETZEL (10-6-73) (LSU 1955-61, Army 1962-65, South Carolina 1966-74)	47-188	191st (100-86-5)	19-4
GIL DOBIE (10-20-22) (North Dakota St. 1906-07, Washington 1908-16, Navy 1917-19, Cornell 1920-35, Boston College 1936-38)	43-262	108th (100-5-3)	17-4
BOBBY DODD (12-1-56) (Georgia Tech 1945-66)	48-20	131st (100-28-3)	12-10
MIKE DONAHUE (9-29-23) (Auburn 1904-06, 1908-22, LSU 1923-27)	42-111	140th (100-35-5)	19-1
TERRY DONAHUE (9-10-88) (UCLA 1976-95)	44-78	143rd (100-36-7)	13-2
ALDO DONELLI (10-16-65) (Duquesne 1939-42, Boston U. 1947-56, Columbia 1957-67)	58-86	197th (100-89-8)	23-4
BILL DOOLEY (11-27-82) (North Carolina 1967-77, Virginia Tech 1978-86, Wake Forest 1987-92)	48-192	180th (100-78-2)	16-11
VINCE DOOLEY (9-24-77) (Georgia 1964-88)	45-20	149th (100-44-5)	14-3
FRED DUNLAP (10-29-83) (Lehigh 1965-75, Colgate 1976-87)	55-194	195th (100-91-4)	19-8
PAT DYE (10-4-86) (East Caro. 1974-79, Wyoming 1980, Auburn 1981-92)	46-332	142nd (100-41-1)	13-4
LLOYD EATON (10-4-69) (Alma 1949-55, Northern Mich. 1956, Wyoming 1962-70)	51-101	145th (100-40-5)	16-3
#LAVELL EDWARDS (10-22-83) (Brigham Young 1972—)	53-11	138th (100-37-1)	12-7
RAY ELIOT (10-10-59) (Illinois Col. 1933-36, Illinois 1942-59)	54-119	191st (100-79-12)	22-3
RIP ENGLE (10-21-61) (Brown 1944-49, Penn St. 1950-65)	55-209	161st (100-53-8)	18-5
#DENNIS ERICKSON (10-30-93) (Idaho 1982-85, Wyoming 1986, Washington St. 1987-88, Miami [Fla.] 1989-94, Oregon St. 1999—)	46-334	137th (100-36-1)	12-7
DON FAUROT (11-1-41) (Truman 1926-34, Missouri 1935-42, 1946-56)	39-131	171st (100-63-8)	16-6
FRED FOLSOM (11-1-13) (Colorado 1895-1902, Dartmouth 1903-06, Colorado 1908-15)	41-357	126th (100-20-6)	17-6
DANNY FORD (11-13-93) (Clemson 1978-89, Arkansas 1993-97)	45-225	139th (100-34-5)	13-9
#DENNIS FRANCHIONE (9-7-96) (Southwestern [Kan.] 1981-82, Pittsburg St. 1985-89; Southwest Tex. St. 1990-91, New Mexico 1992-97, TCU 1998—)	45-163	148th (100-46-2)	14-2
HAYDEN FRY (9-26-81) (Southern Methodist 1962-72, North Texas 1973-78, Iowa 1979-97)	52-185	207th (100-103-4)	20-3
ANDY GUSTAFSON (9-29-61) (Virginia Tech 1926-29, Miami [Fla.] 1948-63)	58-179	168th (100-64-4)	18-3
WAYNE HARDIN (10-13-79) (Navy 1959-64, Temple 1970-82)	52-204	159th (100-54-5)	16-6
JIM HARKEMA (9-16-89) (Grand Valley St. 1973-82, Eastern Mich. 1983-92)	47-83	167th (100-63-4)	17-3
DICK HARLOW (11-3-34) (Penn St. 1915-17, Colgate 1922-25, Western Md. 1926-34, Harvard 1935-42, 1945-47)	44-67	142nd (100-31-11)	16-5
HARVEY HARMAN (10-4-47) (Haverford 1922-29, Sewanee 1930, Pennsylvania 1931-37, Rutgers 1938-55)	46-334	177th (100-70-7)	22-2
#KEN HATFIELD (11-20-91) (Air Force 1979-83, Arkansas 1984-89, Clemson 1990-93, Rice 1994—)	48-174	155th (100-52-3)	13-11
WOODY HAYES (10-21-61) (Denison 1946-48, Miami [Ohio] 1949-50, Ohio St. 1951-78)	48-249	140th (100-34-6)	16-4
JOHN HEISMAN (9-27-13) (Oberlin 1892, Akron 1893, Oberlin 1894, Auburn 1895-99, Clemson 1900-03, Georgia Tech 1904-19, Pennsylvania 1920-22, Wash. & Jeff. 1923, Rice 1924-27)	43-339	142nd (100-33-9)	22-1
GUS HENDERSON (11-24-32) (Southern California 1919-24, Tulsa 1925-35, Occidental 1940-42)	43-259	126th (100-23-3)	14-8
BILL HESS (9-4-76) (Ohio 1958-77)	51-106	182nd (100-78-4)	19-1
JIM HESS (9-5-87) (Angelo St. 1974-81, Stephen F. Austin 1982-88, New Mexico St. 1990-96)	50-278	147th (100-43-4)	14-1
#LOU HOLTZ (12-31-82) (William & Mary 1969-71, North Carolina St. 1972-75, Arkansas 1977-83, Minnesota 1984-85, Notre Dame 1986-96, South Carolina 1999—)	45-359	153rd (100-48-5)	13-12
FRANK HOWARD (9-27-58) (Clemson 1940-69)	49-186	175th (100-65-10)	19-2
DON JAMES (9-15-84) (Kent 1971-74, Washington 1975-92)	51-258	153rd (100-52-1)	14-2
MORLEY JENNINGS (10-3-31) (Ouachita Baptist 1912-25, Baylor 1926-40)	46-253	136th (100-33-3)	20-1
HOWARD JONES (12-3-27) (Syracuse 1908, Yale 1909, Ohio St. 1910, Yale 1913, Iowa 1916-23, Duke 1924, Southern California 1925-40)	42-102	142nd (100-33-9)	16-10

Vince Dooley spent his entire coaching career with Georgia, guiding the Bulldogs to a 201-77-10 record from 1964-88.

Coach (Date Reached Milestone) (Schools Coached and Years)	Age in Yrs.-Days	Career Game (Record)	Career Yr.-Game
LLOYD JORDAN (10-27-56) (Amherst 1932-49, Harvard 1950-56)	55-317	172nd (100-65-7)	22-4
SHUG JORDAN (10-9-65) (Auburn 1951-75)	55-14	148th (100-43-5)	15-4
FRANK KIMBROUGH (9-29-56) (Hardin-Simmons 1935-40, Baylor 1941-42, 1945-46, West Tex. A&M 1947-57)	52-97	181st (100-73-8)	20-3
TONY KNAP (10-2-76) (Utah St. 1963-66, Boise St. 1968-75, UNLV 1976-81)	61-298	135th (100-33-2)	13-4
FRANK KUSH (12-30-70) (Arizona St. 1958-79)	41-344	131st (100-30-1)	13-11
ELMER LAYDEN (10-26-40) (Loras 1925-26, Duquesne 1927-33, Notre Dame 1934-40)	37-175	143rd (100-32-11)	16-4
FRANK LEAHY (10-3-53) (Boston College 1939-40, Notre Dame 1941-53)	45-37	121st (100-13-8)	13-2
LOU LITTLE (9-26-42) (Georgetown 1924-29, Columbia 1930-56)	48-294	161st (100-49-12)	19-1
DICK MacPHERSON (10-28-89) (Massachusetts 1971-77, Syracuse 1981-90)	58-358	171st (100-68-3)	16-7
JOHNNY MAJORS (11-19-83) (Iowa St. 1968-72, Pittsburgh 1973-76, Tennessee 1977-92, Pittsburgh 1993-96)	48-181	185th (100-81-4)	16-10
BILL MALLORY (9-14-85) (Miami [Ohio] 1969-73, Colorado 1974-78, Northern Ill. 1980-83, Indiana 1984-96)	50-107	164th (100-63-1)	16-1
BEN MARTIN (11-20-76) (Virginia 1956-57, Air Force 1958-77)	55-145	217th (100-108-9)	21-11
CHARLIE McCLENDON (11-2-74) (LSU 1962-79)	46-222	141st (100-35-6)	13-7
DAN McGUGIN (11-15-19) (Vanderbilt 1904-34)	40-78	132nd (100-25-7)	15-7
JOHN McKAY (1-1-73) (Southern California 1960-75)	49-209	139th (100-33-6)	13-12
TUSS McLAUGHRY (10-25-41) (Westminster [Pa.] 1916-18, 1921, Amherst 1922-25, Brown 1926-40, Dartmouth 1941-42, 1945-54)	48-109	196th (100-86-10)	23-5
CHICK MEEHAN (9-28-35) (Syracuse 1920-24, New York U. 1925-31, Manhattan 1932-37)	42-23	146th (100-34-12)	16-2
DUTCH MEYER (9-29-51) (TCU 1934-52)	53-204	182nd (100-71-11)	18-2
CHUCK MILLS (9-15-84) (Pomona-Pitzer 1959-61, Indiana [Pa.] 1962-63, Merchant Marine 1964, Utah St. 1967-72, Wake Forest 1973-77, Southern Ore. St. 1980-88, Coast Guard 1997)	55-287	213th (100-109-4)	22-2
ODUS MITCHELL (11-25-61) (North Texas 1946-66)	59-116	167th (100-59-8)	16-10
AL MOLDE (10-11-86) (Sioux Falls 1971-72, Minn.-Morris 1973-79, Central Mo. St. 1980-82, Eastern Ill. 1983-86, Western Mich. 1987-96)	42-330	162nd (100-56-6)	16-6
CHARLEY MORAN (9-27-30) (Texas A&M 1909-14, Centre 1919-23, Bucknell 1924-26, Catawba 1930-33)	52-217	131st (100-24-7)	15-1
JOE MORRISON (10-29-88) (Chattanooga 1973-79, New Mexico 1980-82, South Carolina 1983-88)	51-69	176th (100-69-7)	16-8
RAY MORRISON (10-2-37) (Southern Methodist 1915-16, Vanderbilt 1918, Southern Methodist 1922-34, Vanderbilt 1935-39, Temple 1940-48, Austin College 1949-52)	52-216	177th (100-54-23)	19-2
BILL MURRAY (11-22-58) (Delaware 1940-42, 1946-50, Duke 1951-65)	50-74	149th (100-40-9)	16-10
JESS NEELY (10-19-46) (Rhodes 1924-27, Clemson 1931-39, Rice 1940-66)	48-288	190th (100-79-11)	20-4
#DON NEHLEN (11-16-85) (Bowling Green 1968-76, West Virginia 1980—)	48-319	162nd (100-57-5)	15-10
BOB NEYLAND (9-29-39) (Tennessee 1926-34, 1936-40, 1946-52)	47-224	120th (100-12-8)	13-1
BOB ODELL (9-24-77) (Bucknell 1958-64, Pennsylvania 1965-70, Williams 1971-86)	55-203	166th (100-64-2)	20-1
JORDAN OLIVAR (10-15-60) (Villanova 1943-48, Loyola Marymount 1949-51, Yale 1952-60)	45-258	159th (100-53-6)	18-4
TOM OSBORNE (9-24-83) (Nebraska 1973-97)	46-211	126th (100-24-2)	11-4
BENNIE OWEN (10-4-15) (Washburn 1900, Bethany [Kan.] 1901-04, Oklahoma 1905-26)	40-72	136th (100-28-8)	16-5
ARA PARSEGHIAN (11-26-66) (Miami [Ohio] 1951-55, Northwestern 1956-63, Notre Dame 1964-74)	43-189	147th (100-43-4)	16-10
#PAUL PASQUALONI (11-14-98) (Western Conn. St. 1982-86, Syracuse 1991—)	49-92	143rd (100-42-1)	13-9
#JOE PATERNO (11-6-76) (Penn St. 1966—)	49-320	122nd (100-21-1)	11-9
#MIKE PRICE (9-5-98) (Weber St. 1981-88, Washington St. 1989—)	52-152	193rd (100-93-0)	18-1
TOMMY PROTHRO (9-19-70) (Oregon St. 1955-64, UCLA 1965-70)	50-38	155th (100-50-5)	16-2

DIVISION I-A COACHES TO REACH 100 VICTORIES

	WHEN MILESTONE REACHED		
Coach (Date Reached Milestone) **(Schools Coached and Years)**	**Age in Yrs.-Days**	**Career Game (Record)**	**Career Yr.-Game**
EDWARD ROBINSON (11-6-15) (Nebraska 1896-97, Brown 1898-1901, Maine 1902, Brown 1904-07, 1910-25)	41-344	165th (100-56-9)	17-7
#JOHN ROBINSON (10-4-97) (Southern California 1976-82, 93-97, UNLV 1999—)	62-71	136th (100-32-4)	12-4
KNUTE ROCKNE (11-1-30) (Notre Dame 1918-30)	42-242	117th (100-12-5)	13-5
DARRYL ROGERS (9-12-81) (Cal St. Hayward 1965, Fresno St. 1966-72, San Jose St. 1973-75, Michigan St. 1976-79, Arizona St. 1980-84)	47-106	176th (100-70-6)	17-1
BILL ROPER (10-8-27) (VMI 1903-04, Princeton 1906-08, Missouri 1909, Princeton 1910-11, Swarthmore 1915-16, Princeton 1919-30)	47-47	141st (100-26-15)	19-2
DARRELL ROYAL (10-7-67) (Mississippi St. 1954-55, Washington 1956, Texas 1957-76)	43-93	141st (100-38-3)	14-3
RED SANDERS (11-9-57) (Vanderbilt 1940-48, UCLA 1949-57)	52-216	144th (100-41-3)	15-8
PHILIP SARBOE (12-1-60) (Central Wash. 1941-42, Washington St. 1945-49, Humboldt St. 1951-65, Hawaii 1966)	48-233	160th (100-53-7)	17-11
BO SCHEMBECHLER (10-4-75) (Miami [Ohio] 1963-68, Michigan 1969-89)	46-33	130th (100-24-6)	13-4
FRANCIS SCHMIDT (11-5-32) (Tulsa 1919-21, Arkansas 1922-28, TCU 1929-33, Ohio St. 1934-40, Idaho 1941-42)	46-336	136th (100-27-9)	14-8
HOWARD SCHNELLENBERGER (10-28-95) (Miami [Fla.] 1979-83, Louisville 1985-94, Oklahoma 1995)	61-226	177th (100-74-3)	16-8
BEN SCHWARTZWALDER (9-30-65) (Muhlenberg 1946-48, Syracuse 1949-73)	52-120	143rd (100-41-2)	16-2
CLARK SHAUGHNESSY (10-20-34) (Tulane 1915-20, 1922-26, Loyola [Ill.] 1927-32, Chicago 1933-39, Stanford 1940-41, Maryland 1942, Pittsburgh 1943-45, Maryland 1946, Hawaii 1965)	42-228	164th (100-50-14)	19-3
DICK SHERIDAN (10-6-90) (Furman 1978-85, North Carolina St. 1986-92)	49-58	147th (100-43-4)	13-6
#JACKIE SHERRILL (10-8-88) (Washington St. 1976, Pittsburgh 1977-81, Texas A&M 1982-88, Mississippi St. 1991—)	44-314	145th (100-43-2)	13-5
#R. C. SLOCUM (10-30-99) (Texas A&M 1989—)	54-357	132nd (100-30-2)	11-8
ANDY SMITH (11-10-23) (Pennsylvania 1909-12, Purdue 1913-15, California 1916-25)	40-71	140th (100-29-11)	15-8
CLIPPER SMITH (11-6-42) (Gonzaga 1925-28, Santa Clara 1929-35, Villanova 1936-42, San Francisco 1946, Lafayette 1949-51)	44-81	159th (100-47-12)	18-5
#LARRY SMITH (11-10-90) (Tulane 1976-79, Arizona 1980-86, Southern California 1987-92, Missouri 1994—)	51-59	170th (100-65-5)	15-10
CARL SNAVELY (9-30-44) (Bucknell 1927-33, North Carolina 1934-35, Cornell 1936-44, North Carolina 1945-52, Washington [Mo.] 1953-58)	50-60	152nd (100-40-12)	18-2
#BRUCE SNYDER (9-13-97) (Utah St. 1976-82, California 1987-91, Arizona St. 1992—)	57-183	192nd (100-86-6)	18-2
OSSIE SOLEM (10-24-42) (Luther 1920, Drake 1921-31, Iowa 1932-36, Syracuse 1937-45, Springfield 1946-57)	50-315	183rd (100-71-12)	23-5
#STEVE SPURRIER (11-8-97) (Duke 1987-89, Florida 1990—)	52-202	131st (100-29-2)	11-9
AMOS ALONZO STAGG (10-6-1900) (Springfield 1890-91, Chicago 1892-1932, Pacific [Cal.] 1933-46)	38-51	143rd (100-34-9)	11-6
DENNY STOLZ (9-14-85) (Alma 1965-70, Michigan St. 1973-75, Bowling Green 1977-85, San Diego St. 1986-88)	51-2	175th (100-73-2)	18-2
ABE STUBER (10-16-48) (Westminster [Mo.] 1929-31, Southeast Mo. St. 1932-44, 1946, Iowa St. 1947-52)	43-338	162nd (100-54-8)	19-5
JOCK SUTHERLAND (10-14-33) (Lafayette 1919-23, Pittsburgh 1924-38)	44-207	132nd (100-22-10)	15-4
JIM SWEENEY (9-8-84) (Montana St. 1963-67, Washington St. 1968-75, Fresno St. 1976-77, 1980-96)	55-7	206th (100-105-1)	20-2
BARRY SWITZER (9-24-83) (Oklahoma 1973-88)	45-353	122nd (100-18-4)	11-3
JIM TATUM (11-8-58) (North Carolina 1942, Oklahoma 1946, Maryland 1947-55, North Carolina 1956-58)	45-78	140th (100-33-7)	14-8
GRANT TEAFF (9-25-82) (McMurry 1960-65, Angelo St. 1969-71, Baylor 1972-92)	48-317	206th (100-101-5)	20-3
FRANK THOMAS (11-9-40) (Chattanooga 1925-28, Alabama 1931-42, 1944-46)	41-359	128th (100-21-7)	14-6
#DICK TOMEY (9-4-93) (Hawaii 1977-86, Arizona 1987—)	55-76	182nd (100-75-7)	17-1
PIE VANN (10-6-62) (Southern Miss. 1949-68)	55-14	137th (100-36-1)	14-4
JOHNNY VAUGHT (11-28-59) (Mississippi 1947-73)	51-206	135th (100-29-6)	13-10

DIVISION I-A COACHES TO REACH 100 VICTORIES

Coach (Date Reached Milestone) (Schools Coached and Years)	Age in Yrs.-Days	Career Game (Record)	Career Yr.-Game
JIM WACKER (11-14-81) (Texas Lutheran 1971-75, North Dakota St. 1976-78, Southwest Tex. St. 1979-82, TCU 1983-91, Minnesota 1992-96)	44-200	134th (100-33-1)	12-10
WALLACE WADE (10-3-36) (Alabama 1923-30, Duke 1931-41, 1946-50)	44-110	129th (100-24-5)	14-3
PAPPY WALDORF (10-27-45) (Oklahoma City 1925-27, Oklahoma St. 1929-33, Kansas St. 1934, Northwestern 1935-46, California 1947-56)	43-24	173rd (100-56-17)	20-5
POP WARNER (11-26-08) (Georgia 1895-96, Cornell 1897-98, Carlisle 1899-1903, Cornell 1904-06, Carlisle 1907-14, Pittsburgh 1915-23, Stanford 1924-32, Temple 1933-38)	37-235	145th (100-38-7)	14-11
#GEORGE WELSH (10-14-89) (Navy 1973-81, Virginia 1982—)	56-49	188th (100-85-3)	17-7
BUD WILKINSON (11-2-57) (Oklahoma 1947-63)	41-193	111th (100-8-3)	11-6
HENRY WILLIAMS (10-2-12) (Army 1891, Minnesota 1900-21)	43-98	122nd (100-13-9)	14-4
GEORGE WOODRUFF (11-11-1898) (Pennsylvania 1892-1901, Illinois 1903, Carlisle 1905)	35-261	109th (100-9-0)	8-11
WARREN WOODSON (9-27-52) (Conway 1935-40, Hardin-Simmons 1941-51, Arizona St. 1952-56, New Mexico St. 1958-67, Trinity [Tex.] 1972-73)	49-215	141st (100-32-9)	15-2
BILL YEOMAN (9-12-77) (Houston 1962-86)	49-260	161st (100-56-5)	16-1
FIELDING YOST (11-7-08) (Ohio Wesleyan 1897, Nebraska 1898, Kansas 1899, Stanford 1900, Michigan 1901-23, 1925-26)	37-191	114th (100-10-4)	12-6
JIM YOUNG (9-10-88) (Arizona 1973-76, Purdue 1977-81, Army 1983-90)	53-142	160th (100-58-2)	15-1
JOHN YOVICSIN (11-16-68) (Gettysburg 1952-56, Harvard 1957-70)	50-131	150th (100-45-5)	17-8
JOSEPH YUKICA (11-20-82) (New Hampshire 1966-67, Boston College 1968-77, Dartmouth 1978-86)	51-177	169th (100-68-1)	17-10
ROBERT ZUPPKE (11-12-32) (Illinois 1913-41)	53-102	152nd (100-44-8)	20-9

#Active coach.

200 VICTORIES

Coach (Date Reached Milestone)	Age in Yrs.-Days	Career Game (Record)	Career Yr.-Game
Eddie Anderson (11-14-64)	64-1	342nd (200-127-15)	39-8
#Bobby Bowden (10-27-90)	60-353	279th (200-76-3)	25-7
Bear Bryant (9-10-71)	57-364	282nd (200-66-16)	27-1
Vince Dooley (11-26-88)	56-84	286th (200-76-10)	25-11
#LaVell Edwards (9-23-94)	64-348	277th (200-74-3)	23-4
Hayden Fry (11-20-93)	64-265	361st (200-152-9)	32-11
Woody Hayes (11-2-74)	61-261	268th (200-60-8)	29-8
#Lou Holtz (9-9-95)	58-243	297th (200-90-7)	26-2
Jess Neely (9-26-64)	66-265	373rd (200-155-18)	38-1
Tom Osborne (10-7-93)	56-224	249th (200-46-3)	21-5
#Joe Paterno (9-5-87)	60-258	246th (200-44-2)	22-1
Bo Schembechler (10-4-86)	57-33	262nd (200-55-7)	24-4
Jim Sweeney (11-2-96)	67-62	326th (200-158-4)	32-8
Amos Alonzo Stagg (10-11-19)	57-56	294th (200-74-20)	30-1
Pop Warner (9-24-21)	50-172	276th (200-62-14)	28-1
Warren Woodson (10-13-73)	70-231	307th (200-93-14)	31-6

#Active coach.

EDDIE ROBINSON
A Coach For The Ages

Because Grambling is not a Division I-A member, most football historians agree that Grambling's Eddie Robinson not be listed in the major college coaches' section. But there is no denying that the Tigers' former head coach belongs in any mention of great collegiate coaches.

Robinson, who retired following the 1997 season, compiled one of the most impressive coaching legacies in collegiate history. He is the only college football coach with more than 400 victories (408) and he has coached in more games (588) than any other coach in the 131 years of college football.

Only the legendary Amos Alonzo Stagg had more years as a college head coach (57) than Robinson's 55 seasons at Grambling (he coached two war years at Grambling High School). Robinson began his career in 1941, at the start of World War II and continued through more than half a century of change.

Here is a breakdown of the milestone victories in his career:

Victory No.	(Date Reached Milestone)	Age in Yrs.-Days	Career Game (Record)	Career Yr.-Game
100th	(11-9-57)	38-270	146th (100-39-7)	15-6
200th	(10-16-71)	52-246	285th (200-74-11)	29-6
300th	(9-25-82)	63-225	411th (300-98-13)	40-3
400th	(10-7-95)	76-237	560th (400-145-15)	53-5

300 VICTORIES

		WHEN MILESTONE REACHED	
Coach (Date Reached Milestone)	Age in Yrs.-Days	Career Game (Record)	Career Yr.-Game
#Joe Paterno (9-12-98)	71-266	380th (300-77-3)	32-2
#Bobby Bowden (10-23-99)	69-349	389th (300-85-4)	34-8
Bear Bryant (10-3-80)	67-22	393rd (300-77-16)	36-4
Amos Alonzo Stagg (11-6-43)	81-82	507th (300-173-34)	54-7
Pop Warner (11-24-34)	63-233	415th (300-91-24)	41-8

#Active coach.

Other Coaching Milestones

(Must have five years or 50 victories at a school that was classified as a major college at the time)

YOUNGEST COACHES TO REACH 100 VICTORIES

Coach	Age in Yrs.-Days
George Woodruff	35-261
Elmer Layden	37-175
Fielding Yost	37-191
Pop Warner	37-235
Amos Alonzo Stagg	38-51
Don Faurot	39-131
Matty Bell	39-256
Dana X. Bible	40-44
Andy Smith	40-71
Bennie Owen	40-72
Dan McGugin	40-78
Hugo Bezdek	40-120
Terry Bowden	40-280

YOUNGEST COACHES TO REACH 200 VICTORIES

Coach	Age in Yrs.-Days
Pop Warner	50-172
Vince Dooley	56-84
Tom Osborne	56-224
Bo Schembechler	57-33
Amos Alonzo Stagg	57-56
Bear Bryant	57-364
*Lou Holtz	58-243

YOUNGEST COACHES TO REACH 300 VICTORIES

Coach	Age in Yrs.-Days
Pop Warner	63-233
Bear Bryant	67-22
*Bobby Bowden	69-349
*Joe Paterno	71-266
Amos Alonzo Stagg	81-82

FEWEST GAMES TO REACH 100 VICTORIES

Coach	Career Game (Record at Time)
Gil Dobie	108 (100-5-3)
George Woodruff	109 (100-9-0)
Bud Wilkinson	111 (100-8-3)
Fielding Yost	114 (100-10-4)
Knute Rockne	117 (100-12-5)
Bob Neyland	120 (100-12-8)
Frank Leahy	121 (100-13-8)
*Joe Paterno	122 (100-21-1)
Barry Switzer	122 (100-18-4)
Henry Williams	122 (100-13-9)
Fred Folsom	126 (100-20-6)
Gus Henderson	126 (100-23-3)
Tom Osborne	126 (100-24-2)
Frank Thomas	128 (100-21-7)
Wallace Wade	129 (100-24-5)
Bo Schembechler	130 (100-24-6)
Bobby Dodd	131 (100-28-3)
*Steve Spurrier	131 (100-29-2)
Frank Kush	131 (100-30-1)
Charley Moran	131 (100-24-7)
Dan McGugin	132 (100-25-7)
*R. C. Slocum	132 (100-30-2)
Jock Sutherland	132 (100-22-10)
Bob Devaney	133 (100-28-5)
Red Blaik	134 (100-25-9)
Jim Wacker	134 (100-33-1)

Coach	Career Game (Record at Time)
Tony Knap	135 (100-33-2)
Johnny Vaught	135 (100-29-6)
Morley Jennings	136 (100-33-3)
Bennie Owen	136 (100-28-8)
*John Robinson	136 (100-32-4)
Francis Schmidt	136 (100-27-9)
*Dennis Erickson	137 (100-36-1)
Pie Vann	137 (100-36-1)
Frank Broyles	138 (100-36-2)
Carmen Cozza	138 (100-35-3)
Fritz Crisler	138 (100-30-8)
*LaVell Edwards	138 (100-37-1)
Dan Devine	139 (100-31-8)
Danny Ford	139 (100-34-5)
John McKay	139 (100-33-6)

*Active coach.

FEWEST GAMES TO REACH 200 VICTORIES

Coach	Career Game (Record at Time)
*Joe Paterno	246 (200-44-2)
Tom Osborne	249 (200-46-3)
Bo Schembechler	262 (200-55-7)
Woody Hayes	268 (200-60-8)
Pop Warner	276 (200-62-14)
*LaVell Edwards	277 (200-74-3)
*Bobby Bowden	279 (200-76-3)
Bear Bryant	282 (200-66-16)
Vince Dooley	286 (200-76-10)
Amos Alonzo Stagg	294 (200-74-20)

*Active coach.

FEWEST GAMES TO REACH 300 VICTORIES

Coach	Career Game (Record at Time)
*Joe Paterno	380 (300-77-3)
*Bobby Bowden	389 (300-85-4)
Bear Bryant	393 (300-77-16)
Pop Warner	415 (300-91-24)
Amos Alonzo Stagg	507 (300-173-34)

*Active coach.

All-Time Division I Coaching Longevity Records

(Minimum 10 Head-Coaching Seasons in Division I; Bowl Games Included)

MOST GAMES

Games	Coach, School(s) and Years
548	Amos Alonzo Stagg, Springfield 1890-91, Chicago 1892-1932, Pacific (Cal.) 1933-46
457	Pop Warner, Georgia 1895-96, Cornell 1897-98 and 1904-06, Carlisle 1899-1903 and 1907-14, Pittsburgh 1915-23, Stanford 1924-32, Temple 1933-38
425	Bear Bryant, Maryland 1945, Kentucky 1946-53, Texas A&M 1954-57, Alabama 1958-82
420	Hayden Fry, Southern Methodist 1962-72, North Texas 1973-78, Iowa 1979-98
403	*Joe Paterno, Penn St. 1966-99
402	Jess Neely, Rhodes 1924-27, Clemson 1931-39, Rice 1940-66
393	*Bobby Bowden, Samford 1959-62, West Virginia 1970-75, Florida St. 1976-99
368	Jim Sweeney, Montana St. 1963-67, Washington St. 1968-75, Fresno St. 1976-77 and 1980-96
349	*LaVell Edwards, Brigham Young 1972-99
344	Eddie Anderson, Loras 1922-24, DePaul 1925-31, Holy Cross 1933-38 and 1950-64, Iowa 1939-42 and 1946-49
332	Johnny Majors, Iowa St. 1968-72, Pittsburgh 1973-76 and 1993-96, Tennessee 1977-92
329	Grant Teaff, McMurry 1960-65, Angelo St. 1969-71, Baylor 1972-92

Games	Coach, School(s) and Years
329	*Lou Holtz, William & Mary 1969-71, North Carolina St. 1972-75, Arkansas 1977-83, Minnesota 1984-85, Notre Dame 1986-96, South Carolina 1999
326	*Don Nehlen, Bowling Green 1968-76, West Virginia 1980-99
320	Woody Hayes, Denison 1946-48, Miami (Ohio) 1949-50, Ohio St. 1951-78
318	Ray Morrison, Southern Methodist 1915-16 and 1922-34, Vanderbilt 1918 and 1935-39, Temple 1940-48, Austin 1949-52
313	*George Welsh, Navy 1973-81, Virginia 1982-99
312	Warren Woodson, Central Ark. 1935-39, Hardin-Simmons 1941-42 and 1946-51, Arizona 1952-56, New Mexico St. 1958-67, Trinity (Tex.) 1972-73
309	Jerry Claiborne, Virginia Tech 1961-70, Maryland 1972-81, Kentucky 1982-89
307	Bo Schembechler, Miami (Ohio) 1963-68, Michigan 1969-89
307	Tom Osborne, Nebraska 1973-97
301	Bill Mallory, Miami (Ohio) 1969-73, Colorado 1974-78, Northern Ill. 1980-83, Indiana 1984-96
299	Ossie Solem, Luther 1920, Drake 1921-31, Iowa 1932-36, Syracuse 1937-42 and 1944-45, Springfield 1946-57
296	Tuss McLaughry, Westminster 1916, 1918 and 1921, Amherst 1922-25, Brown 1926-40, Dartmouth 1941-54
296	Pappy Waldorf, Oklahoma City 1925-27, Oklahoma St. 1929-33, Kansas St. 1934, Northwestern 1935-46, California 1947-56
295	Frank Howard, Clemson 1940-69
293	Dana X. Bible, Mississippi Col. 1913-15, LSU 1916, Texas A&M 1917 and 1919-28, Nebraska 1929-36, Texas 1937-46
293	Bill Dooley, North Carolina 1967-77, Virginia Tech 1978-86, Wake Forest 1987-92
293	Jim Wacker, Texas Lutheran 1971-75, North Dakota St. 1976-78, Southwest Tex. St. 1979-82, TCU 1983-91, Minnesota 1992-95
292	Lou Little, Georgetown 1924-29, Columbia 1930-56
292	Carl Snavely, Bucknell 1927-33, North Carolina 1934-35 and 1945-52, Cornell 1936-44, Washington (Mo.) 1953-58
288	Vince Dooley, Georgia 1964-88
287	Bob Blackman, Denver 1953-54, Dartmouth 1955-70, Illinois 1971-76, Cornell 1977-82
282	Clark Shaughnessy, Tulane 1915-20 and 1922-26, Loyola (Ill.) 1927-32, Chicago 1933-39, Stanford 1940-41, Maryland 1942 and 1946, Pittsburgh 1943-45, Hawaii 1965
279	Howard Jones, Syracuse 1908, Yale 1909 and 1913, Ohio St. 1910, Iowa 1916-23, Duke 1924, Southern California 1925-40
277	Ben Schwartzwalder, Muhlenberg 1946-48, Syracuse 1949-73
276	Bill Yeoman, Houston 1962-86
272	John Heisman, Oberlin 1892 and 1894, Akron 1893, Auburn 1895-99, Clemson 1900-03, Georgia Tech 1904-19, Pennsylvania 1920-22, Wash. & Jeff. 1923, Rice 1924-27
271	Dan McGugin, Vanderbilt 1904-17 and 1919-34
271	Chuck Mills, Pomona-Pitzer 1959-61, Indiana (Pa.) 1962-63, Merchant Marine 1964, Utah St. 1967-72, Wake Forest 1973-77, Southern Ore. St. 1980-88, Coast Guard 1997
270	*John Cooper, Tulsa 1977-84, Arizona St. 1985-87, Ohio St. 1988-99
269	Don Faurot, Truman 1926-34, Missouri 1935-42 and 1946-56
265	Shug Jordan, Auburn 1951-75
265	*Larry Smith, Tulane 1976-79, Arizona 1980-86, Southern California 1987-92, Missouri 1994-99
264	*Dick Tomey, Hawaii 1977-86, Arizona 1986-99
263	John Vaught, Mississippi 1947-70 and 1973
260	Jack Curtice, West Tex. A&M 1940-41, UTEP 1946-49, Utah 1950-57, Stanford 1958-61, UC Santa Barb. 1962-69
260	Frank Dobson, Georgia 1909, Clemson 1910-12, Richmond 1913-17 and 1919-33, South Carolina 1918, Maryland 1935-39
258	Edward Robinson, Nebraska 1896-97, Brown 1898-1901, 1904-07 and 1910-25
257	Don James, Kent 1971-74, Washington 1975-92
257	*Jackie Sherrill, Washington St. 1976, Pittsburgh 1977-81, Texas A&M 1982-88, Mississippi St. 1991-99
256	Matty Bell, Haskell 1920-21, Carroll (Wis.) 1922, TCU 1923-28, Texas A&M 1929-33, Southern Methodist 1935-41 and 1945-49
252	Harvey Harman, Haverford 1922-29, Sewanee 1930, Pennsylvania 1931-37, Rutgers 1938-55

*Active.

MOST YEARS

Years	Coach, School(s) and Years
57	Amos Alonzo Stagg, Springfield 1890-91, Chicago 1892-1932, Pacific (Cal.) 1933-46
44	Pop Warner, Georgia 1895-96, Cornell 1897-98 and 1904-06, Carlisle 1899-1903 and 1907-14, Pittsburgh 1915-23, Stanford 1924-32, Temple 1933-38
40	Jess Neely, Rhodes 1924-27, Clemson 1931-39, Rice 1940-66
39	Eddie Anderson, Loras 1922-24, DePaul 1925-31, Holy Cross 1933-38 and 1950-54, Iowa 1939-42 and 1946-49
38	Bear Bryant, Maryland 1945, Kentucky 1946-53, Texas A&M 1954-57, Alabama 1958-82
37	Ossie Solem, Luther 1920, Drake 1921-31, Iowa 1932-36, Syracuse 1937-45, Springfield 1946-57
37	Hayden Fry, Southern Methodist 1962-72, North Texas 1973-78, Iowa 1979-98

Years	Coach, School(s) and Years
36	John Heisman, Oberlin 1892 and 1894, Akron 1893, Auburn 1895-99, Clemson 1900-03, Georgia Tech 1904-19, Pennsylvania 1920-22, Wash. & Jeff. 1923, Rice 1924-27
34	Tuss McLaughry, Westminster 1916, 1918 and 1921, Amherst 1922-25, Brown 1926-40, Dartmouth 1941-54
34	Ray Morrison, Southern Methodist 1915-16 and 1922-34, Vanderbilt 1918 and 1935-39, Temple 1940-48, Austin 1949-52
34	*Bobby Bowden, Samford 1959-62, West Virginia 1970-75, Florida St. 1976-99
34	*Joe Paterno, Penn St. 1966-99
33	Dana X. Bible, Mississippi Col. 1913-15, LSU 1916, Texas A&M 1917 and 1919-28, Nebraska 1929-36, Texas 1937-46
33	Gil Dobie, North Dakota St. 1906-07, Washington 1908-16, Navy 1917-19, Cornell 1920-35, Boston College 1936-38
33	Woody Hayes, Denison 1946-48, Miami (Ohio) 1949-50, Ohio St. 1951-78
33	Lou Little, Georgetown 1924-29, Columbia 1930-56
32	Clark Shaughnessy, Tulane 1915-20 and 1922-26, Loyola (Ill.) 1927-32, Chicago 1933-39, Stanford 1940-41, Maryland 1942 and 1946, Pittsburgh 1943-45, Hawaii 1965
32	Carl Snavely, Bucknell 1927-33, North Carolina 1934-35 and 1945-52, Cornell 1936-44, Washington (Mo.) 1953-58
32	William Spaulding, Western Mich. 1907-21, Minnesota 1922-24, UCLA 1925-38
32	Jim Sweeney, Montana St. 1963-67, Washington St. 1968-75, Fresno St. 1976-77 and 1980-96
31	Pappy Waldorf, Oklahoma City 1925-27, Oklahoma St. 1929-33, Kansas St. 1934, Northwestern 1935-46, California 1947-56
31	Warren Woodson, Central Ark. 1935-39, Hardin-Simmons 1941-42 and 1946-51, Arizona 1952-56, New Mexico St. 1958-67, Trinity (Tex.) 1972-73
30	Bob Blackman, Denver 1953-54, Dartmouth 1955-70, Illinois 1971-76, Cornell 1977-82
30	Frank Dobson, Georgia 1909, Clemson 1910-12, Richmond 1913-17 and 1919-33, South Carolina 1918, Maryland 1935-39
30	Harvey Harman, Haverford 1922-29, Sewanee 1930, Pennsylvania 1931-37, Rutgers 1938-55
30	Frank Howard, Clemson 1940-69
30	Dan McGugin, Vanderbilt 1904-17 and 1919-34
30	Grant Teaff, McMurry 1960-65, Angelo St. 1969-71, Baylor 1972-92

*Active.

MOST SCHOOLS

(Must Have Coached at Least One Division I or Major-College Team)

Schools	Coach, Schools and Years
8	John Heisman, Oberlin 1892 and 1894, Akron 1893, Auburn 1895-99, Clemson 1900-03, Georgia Tech 1904-19, Pennsylvania 1920-22, Wash. & Jeff. 1923, Rice 1924-27
7	Darrell Mudra, Adams St. 1959-62, North Dakota St. 1963-65, Arizona 1967-68, Western Ill. 1969-73, Florida St. 1974-75, Eastern Ill. 1978-82, Northern Iowa 1983-87
7	Lou Saban, Case Reserve 1950-52, Northwestern 1955, Western Ill. 1957-59, Maryland 1966, Miami (Fla.) 1977-78, Army 1979, UCF 1983-84
7	Clark Shaughnessy, Tulane 1915-20 and 1922-26, Loyola (Ill.) 1927-32, Chicago 1933-39, Stanford 1940-41, Maryland 1942 and 1946, Pittsburgh 1943-45, Hawaii 1965
7	Clarence Spears, Dartmouth 1917-20, West Virginia 1921-24, Minnesota 1925-29, Oregon 1930-31, Wisconsin 1932-35, Toledo 1936-42, Maryland 1943-44
7	Chuck Mills, Pomona-Pitzer 1959-61, Indiana (Pa.) 1962-63, Merchant Marine 1964, Utah St. 1967-72, Wake Forest 1973-77, Southern Ore. St. 1980-88, Coast Guard 1997
6	*Lou Holtz, William & Mary 1969-71, North Carolina St. 1972-75, Arkansas 1977-83, Minnesota 1984-85, Notre Dame 1986-96, South Carolina 1999
6	Howard Jones, Syracuse 1908, Yale 1909 and 1913, Ohio St. 1910, Iowa 1916-23, Duke 1924, Southern California 1925-40
6	Pop Warner, Georgia 1895-96, Cornell 1897-98 and 1904-06, Carlisle 1899-1903 and 1907-14, Pittsburgh 1915-23, Stanford 1924-32, Temple 1933-38
5	Matty Bell, Haskell 1920-21, Carroll (Wis.) 1922, TCU 1923-28, Texas A&M 1929-33, Southern Methodist 1935-41 and 1945-49
5	Dana X. Bible, Mississippi Col. 1913-15, LSU 1916, Texas A&M 1917 and 1919-28, Nebraska 1929-36, Texas 1937-46
5	*Watson Brown, Austin Peay 1979-80, Cincinnati 1983, Rice 1984-85, Vanderbilt 1986-90, UAB 1995-99
5	Earle Bruce, Tampa 1972, Iowa St. 1973-78, Ohio St. 1979-87, Northern Iowa 1988, Colorado St. 1989-92
5	Frank Cavanaugh, Cincinnati 1898, Holy Cross 1903-05, Dartmouth 1911-16, Boston College 1919-26, Fordham 1927-32
5	Jack Curtice, West Tex. A&M 1940-41, UTEP 1946-49, Utah 1950-57, Stanford 1958-61, UC Santa Barb. 1962-69
5	Dudley DeGroot, UC Santa Barb. 1926-28, San Jose St. 1932-39, Rochester 1940-43, West Virginia 1948-49, New Mexico 1950-52
5	Gil Dobie, North Dakota St. 1906-07, Washington 1908-16, Navy 1917-19, Cornell 1920-35, Boston College 1936-38
5	Frank Dobson, Georgia 1909, Clemson 1910-12, Richmond 1913-17 and 1919-33, South Carolina 1918, Maryland 1935-39

DIVISION I-A COACHING LONGEVITY RECORDS—MOST SCHOOLS

Schools	Coach, Schools and Years
5	Ed Doherty, Arizona St. 1947-50, Rhode Island 1951, Arizona 1957-58, Xavier (Ohio) 1959-61, Holy Cross 1971-75
5	Red Drew, Trinity (Conn.) 1921-23, Birmingham So. 1924-27, Chattanooga 1929-30, Mississippi 1946, Alabama 1947-54
5	*Dennis Franchione, Southwestern (Kan.) 1981-82, Pittsburg St. 1985-89, Southwest Tex. St. 1990-91, New Mexico 1992-97, TCU 1998-99
5	Stuart Holcomb, Findlay 1932-35, Muskingum 1936-40, Wash. & Jeff. 1941, Miami (Ohio) 1942-43, Purdue 1947-55
5	Al Molde, Sioux Falls 1971-72, Minn.-Morris 1973-79, Central Mo. St. 1980-82, Eastern Ill. 1983-86, Western Mich. 1987-96
5	*Dennis Erickson, Idaho 1982-85, Wyoming 1986, Washington St. 1987-88, Miami (Fla.) 1989-94, Oregon St. 1999
5	Darryl Rogers, Cal St. Hayward 1965, Fresno St. 1966-72, San Jose St. 1973-75, Michigan St. 1976-79, Arizona St. 1980-84
5	John Rowland, Henderson St. 1925-30, Ouachita Baptist 1931, Citadel 1940-42, Oklahoma City 1946-47, Geo. Washington 1948-51
5	Francis Schmidt, Tulsa 1919-21, Arkansas 1922-28, TCU 1929-33, Ohio St. 1934-40, Idaho 1941-42
5	Clipper Smith, Gonzaga 1925-28, Santa Clara 1929-35, Villanova 1936-42, San Francisco 1946, Lafayette 1949-51
5	Ossie Solem, Luther 1920, Drake 1921-31, Iowa 1932-36, Syracuse 1937-45, Springfield 1946-57
5	Skip Stahley, Delaware 1934, Brown 1941-43, Geo. Washington 1946-47, Toledo 1948-49, Idaho 1954-60
5	Jim Wacker, Texas Lutheran 1971-75, North Dakota St. 1976-78, Southwest Tex. St. 1979-82, TCU 1983-91, Minnesota 1992-96
5	Pappy Waldorf, Oklahoma City 1925-27, Oklahoma St. 1929-33, Kansas St. 1934, Northwestern 1935-46, California 1947-56
5	Warren Woodson, Central Ark. 1935-39, Hardin-Simmons 1941-42, Arizona 1952-56, New Mexico St. 1958-67, Trinity (Tex.) 1972-73
5	Fielding Yost, Ohio Wesleyan 1897, Nebraska 1898, Kansas 1899, Stanford 1900, Michigan 1901-23 and 1925-26
4	Eddie Anderson, Loras 1922-24, DePaul 1925-31, Holy Cross 1933-38 and 1950-64, Iowa 1939-42 and 1946-49
4	Charles Bachman, Northwestern 1919, Kansas St. 1920-27, Florida 1928-32, Michigan St. 1933-42 and 1944-46
4	Jerry Berndt, DePauw 1979-80, Pennsylvania 1981-85, Rice 1986-88, Temple 1989-92
4	Bob Blackman, Denver 1953-54, Dartmouth 1955-70, Illinois 1971-76, Cornell 1977-82
4	*Mack Brown, Appalachian St. 1983, Tulane 1985-87, North Carolina 1988-97, Texas 1998-99
4	Bear Bryant, Maryland 1945, Kentucky 1946-53, Texas A&M 1954-57, Alabama 1958-82
4	Pete Elliott, Nebraska 1956, California 1957-59, Illinois 1960-66, Miami (Fla.) 1973-74
4	Wesley Fesler, Wesleyan (Conn.) 1941-42, Pittsburgh 1946, Ohio St. 1947-50, Minnesota 1951-53
4	Mike Gottfried, Murray St. 1978-80, Cincinnati 1981-82, Kansas 1983-85, Pittsburgh 1986-89
4	Harvey Harman, Haverford 1922-29, Sewanee 1930, Pennsylvania 1931-37, Rutgers 1938-55
4	*Ken Hatfield, Air Force 1979-83, Arkansas 1984-89, Clemson 1990-93, Rice 1994-99
4	Bill Mallory, Miami (Ohio) 1969-73, Colorado 1974-78, Northern Ill. 1980-83, Indiana 1984-96
4	Tuss McLaughry, Westminster 1916, 1918 and 1921, Amherst 1922-25, Brown 1926-40, Dartmouth 1941-54
4	Joe McMullen, Stetson 1950-51, Wash. & Jeff. 1952-53, Akron 1954-60, San Jose St. 1969-70
4	Bill Meek, Kansas St. 1951-54, Houston 1955-56, Southern Methodist 1957-61, Utah 1968-73
4	Charley Moran, Texas A&M 1909-14, Centre 1919-23, Bucknell 1924-26, Catawba 1930-31
4	Ray Morrison, Southern Methodist 1915-16 and 1922-34, Vanderbilt 1918 and 1935-39, Temple 1940-48, Austin 1949-52
4	Frank Navarro, Williams 1963-67, Columbia 1968-73, Wabash 1974-77, Princeton 1978-84
4	John Pont, Miami (Ohio) 1956-62, Yale 1963-64, Indiana 1965-72, Northwestern 1973-77
4	Bill Roper, VMI 1903-04, Princeton 1906-08, 1910-11 and 1919-30, Missouri 1909, Swarthmore 1915-16
4	Philip Sarboe, Central Wash. 1941-42, Washington St. 1945-49, Humboldt St. 1951-65, Hawaii 1966
4	George Sauer, New Hampshire 1937-41, Kansas 1946-47, Navy 1948-49, Baylor 1950-55
4	*Jackie Sherrill, Washington St. 1976, Pittsburgh 1977-81, Texas A&M 1982-88, Mississippi St. 1991-99
4	Steve Sloan, Vanderbilt 1973-74, Texas Tech 1975-77, Mississippi 1978-82, Duke 1983-86
4	*Larry Smith, Tulane 1976-79, Arizona 1980-86, Southern California 1987-92, Missouri 1994-99
4	Carl Snavely, Bucknell 1927-33, North Carolina 1934-35 and 1945-52, Cornell 1936-44, Washington (Mo.) 1953-58
4	Denny Stolz, Alma 1965-70, Michigan St. 1973-75, Bowling Green 1977-85, San Diego St. 1986-88

*Active.

MOST YEARS COACHED AT ONE COLLEGE
(Minimum 15 Years)

Coach, College (Years)	Years	School W-L-T	Overall W-L-T
Amos Alonzo Stagg, Chicago (1892-1932)	41	244-111-27	314-199-35
*Joe Paterno, Penn St. (1966-99)	34 #	317-83-3	317-83-3
Frank Howard, Clemson (1940-69)	30 #	165-118-12	165-118-12
Dan McGugin, Vanderbilt (1904-17, 1919-34)	30	197-55-19	197-55-19
Robert Zuppke, Illinois (1913-41)	29 #	131-81-13	131-81-13
Woody Hayes, Ohio St. (1951-78)	28	205-61-10	238-72-10
Lou Little, Columbia (1930-56)	27	110-116-10	151-128-13
Jess Neely, Rice (1940-66)	27	144-124-10	207-176-19
*LaVell Edwards, Brigham Young (1972-99)	28 #	251-95-3	251-95-3
William Alexander, Georgia Tech (1920-44)	25 #	134-95-15	134-95-15
Ike Armstrong, Utah (1925-49)	25 #	140-55-15	140-55-15
Bear Bryant, Alabama (1958-82)	25	232-46-9	323-85-17
Vince Dooley, Georgia (1964-88)	25 #	201-77-10	201-77-10
Ralph Jordan, Auburn (1951-75)	25 #	176-83-6	176-83-6
Ben Schwartzwalder, Syracuse (1949-73)	25	153-91-3	178-96-3
John Vaught, Mississippi (1947-70, 1973)	25 #	190-61-12	190-61-12
Bill Yeoman, Houston (1962-86)	25 #	160-108-8	160-108-8
Fielding Yost, Michigan (1901-23, 1925-26)	25	165-29-10	196-36-12
Tom Osborne, Nebraska (1973-97)	25 #	255-49-3	255-49-3
Edward Robinson, Brown (1898-1901, 1904-07, 1910-25)	24	140-82-12	157-88-13
Frank Camp, Louisville (1946-68)	23 #	118-96-2	118-96-2
*Bobby Bowden, Florida St. (1976-99)	24	231-53-4	304-85-4
Wally Butts, Georgia (1939-60)	22 #	140-86-9	140-86-9
Bobby Dodd, Georgia Tech (1945-66)	22	165-64-8	165-64-8
Frank Kush, Arizona St. (1958-79)	22 #	176-54-1	176-54-1
Bennie Owen, Oklahoma (1905-26)	22	122-54-16	155-60-19
Henry Williams, Minnesota (1900-21)	22	140-33-11	141-34-12
Eddie Anderson, Holy Cross (1933-38, 1950-64)	21	129-67-8	201-128-15
Bob Neyland, Tennessee (1926-34, 1936-40, 1946-52)	21 #	173-31-12	173-31-12
Bo Schembechler, Michigan (1969-89)	21	194-48-5	234-65-8
Grant Teaff, Baylor (1972-92)	21	128-105-6	170-151-8
Terry Donahue, UCLA (1976-95)	20 #	151-74-8	151-74-8
Bill Hess, Ohio (1958-77)	20 #	107-92-4	107-92-4
Ben Martin, Air Force (1958-77)	20	96-103-9	102-116-10
Darrell Royal, Texas (1957-76)	20	167-47-5	184-60-5
Pie Vann, Southern Miss. (1949-68)	20 #	139-59-2	139-59-2
Chris Ault, Nevada (1976-92, 1994-95)	19 #	163-63-1	163-63-1
Frank Broyles, Arkansas (1958-76)	19	144-58-5	149-62-6
Robert Higgins, Penn St. (1930-48)	19	91-57-10	123-79-18
Hayden Fry, Iowa (1979-98)	20	143-89-6	232-178-10
Jim Sweeney, Fresno St. (1976-77, 1980-96)	19	143-75-3	200-154-4
*Don Nehlen, West Virginia (1980-99)	20	142-88-4	195-123-8
Red Blaik, Army (1941-58)	18	121-33-10	166-48-14
Rich Brooks, Oregon (1977-94)	18 #	91-109-4	91-109-4
Ray Eliot, Illinois (1942-59)	18	83-73-11	102-82-13
Don James, Washington (1975-92)	18	151-59-2	176-78-3
Charlie McClendon, LSU (1962-79)	18 #	137-59-7	137-59-7
Jim Owens, Washington (1957-74)	18	99-82-6	99-82-6
Murray Warmath, Minnesota (1954-71)	18	87-78-7	97-84-10
*George Welsh, Virginia (1982-99)	18	128-80-3	183-126-4
Johnny Majors, Tennessee (1977-92)	17	120-69-8	185-137-10
Earle Edwards, North Carolina St. (1954-70)	17 #	77-88-8	77-88-8
Bud Wilkinson, Oklahoma (1947-63)	17 #	145-29-4	145-29-4
*Fisher DeBerry, Air Force (1984-99)	16 #	126-69-1	126-69-1
Bob Blackman, Dartmouth (1955-70)	16	104-37-3	168-112-7
Len Casanova, Oregon (1951-66)	16	82-73-8	104-94-11
Herb Deromedi, Central Mich. (1978-93)	16 #	110-55-10	110-55-10
Gil Dobie, Cornell (1920-35)	16	82-36-7	180-45-15
Rip Engle, Penn St. (1950-65)	16	104-48-4	132-68-8
Andy Gustafson, Miami (Fla.) (1948-63)	16	93-65-3	115-78-4
John Heisman, Georgia Tech (1904-19)	16	102-29-6	185-70-17
Howard Jones, Southern California (1925-40)	16	121-36-13	194-64-21
John McKay, Southern California (1960-75)	16 #	127-40-8	127-40-8
Barry Switzer, Oklahoma (1973-88)	16 #	157-29-4	157-29-4
Wallace Wade, Duke (1931-41, 1946-50)	16	110-36-7	171-49-10
Rex Enright, South Carolina (1938-42, 1946-55)	15 #	64-69-7	64-69-7
Morley Jennings, Baylor (1926-40)	15	83-60-6	153-75-18
Ray Morrison, Southern Methodist (1915-16, 1922-34)	15	84-44-22	155-130-33
Bill Murray, Duke (1951-65)	15	83-51-9	142-67-11
Jock Sutherland, Pittsburgh (1924-38)	15	111-20-12	144-28-14
Frank Thomas, Alabama (1931-42, 1944-46)	15	115-24-7	141-33-9

*Active coach. #Never coached at any other college.

Active Coaching Longevity Records

(Minimum Five Years as a Division I-A Head Coach; Includes Bowl Games)

MOST GAMES

Games	Coach, School(s) and Years
403	Joe Paterno, Penn St., 1966-99
393	Bobby Bowden, Samford 1959-62, West Virginia 1970-75, Florida St. 1976-99
349	LaVell Edwards, Brigham Young 1972-99
329	Lou Holtz, William & Mary 1969-71, North Carolina St. 1972-75, Arkansas 1977-83, Minnesota 1984-85, Notre Dame 1986-96, South Carolina 1999
326	Don Nehlen, Bowling Green 1968-76, West Virginia 1980-99
313	George Welsh, Navy 1973-81, Virginia 1982-99
270	John Cooper, Tulsa 1977-84, Arizona St. 1985-87, Ohio St. 1988-99
265	Larry Smith, Tulane 1976-79, Arizona 1980-86, Southern California 1987-92, Missouri 1994-99
264	Dick Tomey, Hawaii 1977-86, Arizona 1987-99
257	Jackie Sherrill, Washington St. 1976, Pittsburgh 1977-81, Texas A&M 1982-88, Mississippi St. 1991-99
244	Ken Hatfield, Air Force 1979-83, Arkansas 1984-89, Clemson 1990-93, Rice 1994-99
225	Bruce Snyder, Utah St. 1976-82, California 1987-91, Arizona St. 1992-99
217	Frank Beamer, Murray St. 1981-86, Virginia Tech 1987-99
215	Mike Price, Weber St. 1981-88, Washington St. 1989-99

MOST YEARS

Years	Coach, School(s) and Years
34	Bobby Bowden, Samford 1959-62, West Virginia 1970-75, Florida St. 1976-99
34	Joe Paterno, Penn St. 1966-99
29	Don Nehlen, Bowling Green 1968-76, West Virginia 1980-99
28	LaVell Edwards, Brigham Young 1972-99
28	Lou Holtz, William & Mary 1969-71, North Carolina St. 1972-75, Arkansas 1977-83, Minnesota 1984-85, Notre Dame 1986-96, South Carolina 1999
27	George Welsh, Navy 1973-81, Virginia 1982-99
23	John Cooper, Tulsa 1977-84, Arizona 1985-87, Ohio St. 1988-99
23	Larry Smith, Tulane 1976-79, Arizona 1980-86, Southern California 1987-92, Missouri 1994-99
23	Dick Tomey, Hawaii 1977-86, Arizona 1987-99
22	Jackie Sherrill, Washington St. 1976, Pittsburgh 1977-81, Texas A&M 1982-88, Mississippi St. 1991-99
21	Ken Hatfield, Air Force 1979-83, Arkansas 1984-89, Clemson 1990-93, Rice 1994-99
20	Bruce Snyder, Utah St. 1976-82, California 1987-91, Arizona St. 1992-99
19	Frank Beamer, Murray St. 1981-86, Virginia Tech 1987-99
19	Mike Price, Weber St. 1981-88, Washington St. 1989-99

MOST YEARS AT CURRENT SCHOOL

Years	Coach, School and Years
34	Joe Paterno, Penn St. 1966-99
28	LaVell Edwards, Brigham Young 1972-99
24	Bobby Bowden, Florida St. 1976-99
20	Don Nehlen, West Virginia 1980-99
18	George Welsh, Virginia 1982-99
16	Fisher DeBerry, Air Force 1984-99

MOST SCHOOLS

Schools	Coach, Schools and Years
6	Lou Holtz, William & Mary 1969-71, North Carolina St. 1972-75, Arkansas 1977-83, Minnesota 1984-85, Notre Dame 1986-96, South Carolina 1999
5	Dennis Erickson, Idaho 1982-85, Wyoming 1986, Washington St. 1987-88, Miami (Fla.) 1989-94, Oregon St. 1999
5	Watson Brown, Austin Peay 1979-80, Cincinnati 1983, Rice 1984-85, Vanderbilt 1986-90, UAB 1995-99
5	Dennis Franchione, Southwestern (Kan.) 1981-82, Pittsburg St. 1985-89, Southwest Tex. St. 1990-91, New Mexico 1992-97, TCU 1998-99
4	Ken Hatfield, Air Force 1979-83, Arkansas 1984-89, Clemson 1990-93, Rice 1994-99
4	Jackie Sherrill, Washington St. 1976, Pittsburgh 1977-81, Texas A&M 1982-88, Mississippi St. 1991-99
4	Larry Smith, Tulane 1976-79, Arizona 1980-86, Southern California 1987-92, Missouri 1994-99
4	Mack Brown, Appalachian St. 1983, Tulane 1985-87, North Carolina 1988-97, Texas 1998-99
3	Bobby Bowden, Samford 1959-62, West Virginia 1970-75, Florida St. 1976-99

Major-College Brother vs. Brother Coaching Matchups

(Thanks to Tex Noel of Bedford, Indiana)
(Each brother's victories in parentheses)

Mack Brown, Tulane (2), vs. Watson, Vanderbilt (0), 1986-87
Vince Dooley, Georgia (1), vs. Bill, North Carolina (0), 1971 Gator Bowl
Bump Elliott, Michigan (6), vs. Pete, Illinois (1), 1960-66
Howard Jones, Yale 1909 and Iowa 1922 (2), vs. Tad, Syracuse 1909 and Yale 1922 (0)
Pop Warner, Cornell (0) vs. Bill, Colgate (0) (tie), 1906

Annual Division I-A Head-Coaching Changes

Year	Changes	Teams	Pct.
1947	27	125	.216
1948	24	121	.198
1949	22	114	.193
1950	23	119	.193
1951	23	115	.200
1952	15	113	.133
1953	18	111	.162
1954	14	103	.136
1955	23	103	.223
1956	19	105	.181
1957	22	108	.204
1958	18	109	.165
1959	18	110	.164
1960	18	114	.158
1961	11	112	.098
1962	20	119	.168
1963	12	118	.102
1964	14	116	.121
1965	16	114	.140
1966	16	116	.138
1967	21	114	.184
1968	14	114	.123
1969	22	118	.186
1970	13	118	.110
1971	27	119	.227
1972	17	121	.140
1973	36	126	†.286
1974	28	128	.219
1975	18	134	.134
1976	23	137	.168
1977	27	144	.188
1978	27	139	.194
1979	26	139	.187
1980	27	139	.194
1981	17	137	.123
1982	17	97	.175
1983	22	105	.210
1984	16	105	.152
1985	15	105	.143
1986	22	105	.210
1987	24	104	.231
1988	9	104	.087
1989	19	106	.179
1990	20	106	.189
1991	16	106	.151
1992	16	107	.150
1993	15	106	.142
1994	15	107	.140
1995	21	108	.194
1996	9	111	*.081
1997	24	112	.214
1998	14	112	.125
1999	20	114	.175
2000	14	114	.123

*Record low. †Record high.

Records of Division I-A First-Year Head Coaches

(Coaches with no previous head-coaching experience at a four-year college.)

Year	No.	Won	Lost	Tied	Pct.	Bowl Record	Won	Lost	Tied	Pct.	Bowl Record
1948	14	56	68	7	.454	0-1	76	52	8	.588	2-1
1949	8	26	49	3	.353	0-1	35	41	4	.463	0-0
1950	10	37	56	4	.402	0-0	49	42	6	.536	2-0
1951	13	60	67	4	.473	1-2	39	88	7	.317	1-1
1952	8	31	42	3	.428	0-0	38	40	0	.487	0-0
1953	8	29	45	5	.399	0-0	48	28	7	.620	1-2
1954	8	31	43	4	.423	0-0	40	33	7	.543	1-0
1955	9	36	50	4	.422	0-1	36	52	1	.410	0-0
1956	14	47	80	11	.380	1-0	61	68	6	.474	0-1
1957	9	32	50	6	.398	0-0	44	42	2	.511	0-0
1958	7	26	44	0	.371	0-0	37	31	2	.543	0-0
1959	8	34	43	2	.443	0-0	41	35	2	.538	0-1
1960	14	54	80	5	.406	1-0	57	78	2	.423	0-0
1961	8	26	50	0	.342	0-0	38	38	2	.500	0-0
1962	12	40	74	4	.356	2-0	52	66	2	.442	1-1
1963	8	23	49	6	.333	0-0	32	46	1	.411	0-1
1964	12	45	67	7	.408	1-1	42	71	4	.376	0-0
1965	8	28	47	2	.377	0-0	36	42	1	.462	0-0
1966	10	46	50	3	.480	0-0	38	56	5	.409	0-0
1967	18	58	114	5	.342	1-0	60	116	4	.344	0-1
1968	6	19	40	1	.325	0-0	20	38	2	.350	0-0
1969	15	49	90	1	.353	0-0	62	85	3	.423	0-1
1970	10	45	61	1	.425	1-0	46	54	0	.460	0-2
1971	12	57	72	0	.442	1-1	64	61	0	.512	0-1
1972	11	57	64	1	.471	1-0	53	64	2	.454	1-0
1973	14	84	63	8	.568	1-0	83	71	2	.538	3-0
1974	17	63	116	5	.356	1-0	78	105	1	.427	1-0
1975	10	38	72	0	.345	0-1	43	67	0	.391	0-0
1976	15	57	109	2	.345	3-1	72	91	5	.443	3-1
1977	14	55	94	5	.373	1-0	66	88	3	.430	0-2
1978	16	68	104	3	.397	0-0	77	96	3	.446	0-1
1979	11	53	66	3	.447	0-0	66	57	1	.536	2-2
1980	12	54	75	2	.420	0-0	60	68	3	.469	1-0
1981	6	25	40	0	.385	0-0	31	35	1	.470	0-1
1982	10	51	59	1	.464	0-1	58	57	2	.504	2-2
1983	12	51	82	2	.385	1-0	60	73	1	.451	1-1
1984	7	47	28	1	*.625	2-1	45	35	1	.562	3-0
1985	5	19	37	0	.339	0-0	20	32	4	.393	0-0
1986	12	53	81	0	.396	0-1	56	76	3	.426	1-1
1987	9	51	49	3	.510	1-1	52	50	1	.510	0-2
1988	4	25	20	0	.556	1-0	22	23	1	.489	1-1
1989	7	32	49	1	.396	0-2	39	43	0	.476	1-2
1990	9	46	42	2	.522	1-1	41	48	0	.461	0-1
1991	10	38	72	1	.347	1-0	46	64	2	.420	0-2
1992	4	15	20	1	.431	0-0	32	14	0	.696	1-1
1993	8	29	58	2	.337	0-1	41	51	1	.446	2-2
1994	7	30	40	2	.431	2-1	40	39	0	.506	1-0
1995	10	57	56	2	.504	1-2	45	65	3	.412	2-1
1996	6	27	42	0	.391	1-1	29	38	1	.434	0-1
1997	11	47	79	0	.373	0-1	56	70	0	.444	1-1
1998	9	44	59	0	.427	0-2	52	52	0	.500	1-2
1999	8	40	51	0	.440	1-1	34	55	0	.382	0-0

*Record percentage for first-year coaches. 1984 coaches and their records, with bowl game indicated by an asterisk (*): Pat Jones, Oklahoma St. (*10-2-0); Galen Hall, Florida (8-0-0, took over from Charley Pell after three games); Bill Arnsparger, LSU (8-*3-1); Fisher DeBerry, Air Force (*8-4-0); Dick Anderson, Rutgers (7-3-0); Mike Sheppard, Long Beach St. (4-7-0); Ron Chismar, Wichita St. (2-9-0).

Most Victories by First-Year Head Coaches

Coach, College, Year	W	L	T
Gary Blackney, Bowling Green, 1991	*11	1	0
John Robinson, Southern California, 1976	*11	1	0
Bill Battle, Tennessee, 1970	*11	1	0
Dick Crum, Miami (Ohio), 1974	*10	0	1
Barry Switzer, Oklahoma, 1973	10	0	1
John Jenkins, Houston, 1990	10	1	0
Dwight Wallace, Ball St., 1978	10	1	0
Chuck Fairbanks, Oklahoma, 1967	*10	1	0
Mike Archer, LSU, 1987	*10	1	1
Rick Neuheisel, Colorado, 1995	*10	2	0
Curley Hallman, Southern Miss., 1988	*10	2	0
Pat Jones, Oklahoma St., 1984	*10	2	0
Earle Bruce, Tampa, 1972	*10	2	0
Billy Kinard, Mississippi, 1971	*10	2	0

*Bowl game victory included.
Only first-year coach to win a national championship: Bennie Oosterbaan, Michigan, 1948 (9-0-0).

Division I-AA Coaching Records

Winningest Active Division I-AA Coaches

(Minimum five years as Division I-A and/or Division I-AA head coach; record at four-year colleges only.)

BY PERCENTAGE

Coach, College	Years	Won	Lost	Tied	†Pct.	Playoffs# W-L-T
Mike Kelly, Dayton	19	177	36	1	.82944	13-8-0
Al Bagnoli, Pennsylvania	18	143	41	0	.77717	7-6-0
Pete Richardson, Southern U.	12	107	32	1	.76786	0-3-0
Larry Blakeney, Troy St.	9	82	27	1	.75000	5-6-0
Joe Gardi, Hofstra	10	81	29	2	.73214	3-4-0
Roy Kidd, Eastern Ky.	36	293	112	8	.71913	17-16-0
Tubby Raymond, Delaware	34	284	111	3	.71734	20-14-0
Joe Taylor, Hampton	17	132	51	4	.71658	1-7-0
Greg Gattuso, Duquesne	7	53	21	0	.71622	0-0-0
Walt Hameline, Wagner	19	141	56	2	.71357	4-2-0
Billy Joe, Florida A&M	26	205	82	4	.71134	3-4-0
Jim Tressel, Youngstown St.	14	126	54	2	.69780	23-5-0
Joe Walton, Robert Morris	6	42	18	1	.69672	0-0-0
Mark Whipple, Massachusetts	12	92	41	0	.69173	8-3-0
Tim Stowers, Rhode Island	6	51	23	0	.68919	6-2-0
Bob Benson, Georgetown	7	48	22	0	.68571	0-0-0
Bill Hayes, N. C. A&T	24	175	90	2	.65918	2-5-0
Tom Gadd, Bucknell	5	36	19	0	.65455	0-0-0
Kevin Higgins, Lehigh	6	44	24	1	.64493	1-2-0
Rob Ash, Drake	20	128	70	5	.64286	0-0-0
Bob Ricca, St. John's (N.Y.)	22	140	85	1	.62168	0-0-0
Andy Talley, Villanova	20	128	78	2	.62019	2-6-0
L. C. Cole, Alabama St.	5	28	18	0	.60870	0-2-0
John Lyons, Dartmouth	8	48	31	0	.60625	0-0-0
Jimmye Laycock, William & Mary	20	135	90	2	.59912	2-5-0
Jim Parady, Marist	8	48	32	1	.59877	0-0-0
Randy Ball, Southwest Mo. St.	10	69	47	1	.59402	3-4-0
Steve Wilson, Howard	11	73	50	0	.59350	0-1-0
Willie Jeffries, South Carolina St.	27	170	119	6	.58644	2-3-0
Gordy Combs, Towson	8	48	34	0	.58537	0-0-0
Kevin Callahan, Monmouth	6	33	25	0	.56897	0-0-0
Pete Hurt, Samford	6	37	28	1	.56818	0-0-0
Bobby Johnson, Furman	6	39	30	0	.56522	1-2-0
Ron Randleman, Sam Houston St.	31	184	141	6	.56495	0-2-0
Jerry Moore, Appalachian St.	18	115	91	2	.55769	3-7-0
Jim Reid, Richmond	11	65	55	3	.54065	0-3-0
Bill Thomas, Texas Southern	11	64	55	3	.53689	1-1-0
Mike Kramer, Montana St.	6	37	32	0	.53623	2-1-0
Matt Ballard, Morehead St.	12	63	58	1	.52049	0-0-0
Bob Spoo, Eastern Ill.	13	76	71	1	.51689	1-3-0
Jack Harbaugh, Western Ky.	16	85	86	3	.49713	1-1-0
Mike Ayers, Wofford	15	81	82	2	.49697	0-2-0
Ken LaRose, Butler	8	39	41	0	.48750	0-0-0
Tim Murphy, Harvard	13	60	77	1	.43841	0-1-0
Ron Cooper, Alabama A&M	7	33	44	0	.42857	0-0-0
Tom Horne, Valparaiso	14	60	82	2	.42361	0-0-0
Dan Allen, Holy Cross	10	46	67	0	.40708	1-2-0
Jack Cosgrove, Maine	7	31	46	0	.40260	0-0-0
Maurice Forte, Norfolk St.	7	27	48	1	.36184	0-1-0
Ray Tellier, Columbia	16	55	100	3	.35759	0-1-0
Sal Cintorino, Central Conn. St.	8	28	51	0	.35443	0-0-0
Chuck Williams, Canisius	5	16	34	0	.32000	0-0-0
John Volek, Cal St. Sacramento	5	17	37	1	.31818	0-0-0
David Dowd, Charleston So.	9	19	73	0	.20652	0-0-0

Less than five years as Division I-A and/or Division I-AA head coach (school followed by years in I-A or I-AA, includes record at all four-year colleges):

Mike Dunbar, Northern Iowa (3)	9	76	20	1	.78866	0-0-0
Joe Glenn, Montana (0)	15	118	54	1	.68497	10-5-0
Jack Siedlecki, Yale (3)	12	72	35	2	.66972	0-1-0
Bill Manlove, La Salle (3)	30	199	102	1	.66060	9-5-0
Lee Hardman, Ark.-Pine Bluff (2)	7	47	30	0	.61039	0-0-0

WINNINGEST ACTIVE DIVISION I-AA COACHES BY PERCENTAGE

Coach, College	Years	Won	Lost	Tied	†Pct.	Playoffs# W-L-T
Tim Walsh, Portland St. (2)	11	72	49	0	.59504	2-3-0
Kevin Kiesel, Fairfield (4)	7	41	29	1	.58451	0-0-0
Robert Ford, Albany (N.Y.) (1)	31	174	124	1	.58361	1-1-0
Sam Kornhauser, Stony Brook (1)	16	75	78	2	.49032	0-0-0
Steve Gilbert, Jacksonville (2)	11	48	59	0	.44860	0-1-0
Bill Schmitz, Austin Peay (3)	7	27	44	0	.38028	0-1-0
Jack Crowe, Jacksonville St. (3)	5	14	30	0	.31818	0-0-0

+Ties computed as half won and half lost. Overall record includes bowl and playoff games. #Playoffs include all divisional championships as well as bowl games, conference playoff games and NAIA playoffs.

BY VICTORIES
(Minimum 100 Victories)

Coach, College, Win Pct.	Won
Roy Kidd, Eastern Ky.	293
Tubby Raymond, Delaware	284
Billy Joe, Florida A&M	205
Ron Randleman, Sam Houston St.	184
Mike Kelly, Dayton	177
Bill Hayes, N.C. A&T	175
Willie Jeffries, South Carolina St.	170
Al Bagnoli, Pennsylvania	143
Walt Hameline, Wagner	141
Bob Ricca, St. John's (N.Y.)	140
Jimmye Laycock, William & Mary	135
Joe Taylor, Hampton	132
Rob Ash, Drake	128
Andy Talley, Villanova	128
Jim Tressel, Youngstown St.	126
Jerry Moore, Appalachian St.	115
Pete Richardson, Southern U.	

Less than five years in Division I-A and/or I-AA:

Bill Manlove, La Salle	199
Bob Ford, Albany (N.Y.)	174
Joe Glenn, Montana	118

Annual Division I-AA Head-Coaching Changes

(From the 1982 reorganization of the division for parallel comparisons)

Year	Changes	Teams	Pct.
1982	7	92	.076
1983	17	84	.202
1984	14	87	.161
1985	11	87	.126
1986	18	86	.209
1987	13	87	.149
1988	12	88	.136
1989	21	89	†.236
1990	16	89	.180
1991	6	87	*.069
1992	14	89	.157
1993	13	#115	.113
1994	17	116	.147
1995	11	119	.092
1996	11	116	.095
1997	20	118	.169
1998	14	119	.118
1999	17	122	.139
2000	24	122	.197

*Record low. †Record high. #Twenty-seven teams switched from Divisions II & III to I-AA.

Division I-AA Championship Coaches

All coaches who have coached teams in the Division I-AA championship playoffs since 1978 are listed here with their playoff record, alma mater and year graduated, team, year coached, opponent, and score.

Dan Allen (1-2) (Hanover '78)
Boston U. .... 93 Northern Iowa 27-21 (2 ot)
Boston U. .... 93 Idaho 14-21
Boston U. .... 94 Eastern Ky. 23-30

Pokey Allen (3-1) (Utah '65)
Boise St. .... 94 North Texas 42-20
Boise St. .... 94 Appalachian St. 17-14
Boise St. .... 94 Marshall 28-24
Boise St. .... 94 Youngstown St. 14-28

Terry Allen (6-7) (Northern Iowa '79)
Northern Iowa .... 90 Boise St. 3-20
Northern Iowa .... 91 Weber St. 38-21
Northern Iowa .... 91 Marshall 13-41
Northern Iowa .... 92 Eastern Wash. 17-14
Northern Iowa .... 92 McNeese St. 29-7
Northern Iowa .... 92 Youngstown St. 7-19
Northern Iowa .... 93 Boston U. 21-27 (2 ot)
Northern Iowa .... 94 Montana 20-23
Northern Iowa .... 95 Murray St. 35-34
Northern Iowa .... 95 Marshall 24-41
Northern Iowa .... 96 Eastern Ill. 21-14
Northern Iowa .... 96 William & Mary 38-35
Northern Iowa .... 96 Marshall 14-31

Dave Arnold (3-0) (Drake '67)
Montana St. .... 84 Arkansas St. 31-24
Montana St. .... 84 Rhode Island 32-20
Montana St. .... 84* Louisiana Tech 19-6

Dave Arslanian (0-1) (Weber St. '72)
Weber St. .... 91 Northern Iowa 21-38

Chris Ault (9-7) (Nevada '68)
Nevada .... 78 Massachusetts 21-44
Nevada .... 79 Eastern Ky. 30-33
Nevada .... 83 Idaho St. 27-20
Nevada .... 83 North Texas 20-17 (ot)
Nevada .... 83 Southern Ill. 7-23
Nevada .... 85 Arkansas St. 24-23
Nevada .... 85 Furman 12-35
Nevada .... 86 Idaho 27-7
Nevada .... 86 Tennessee St. 33-6
Nevada .... 86 Ga. Southern 38-48
Nevada .... 90 La.-Monroe 27-14
Nevada .... 90 Furman 42-35 (3 ot)
Nevada .... 90 Boise St. 59-52 (3 ot)
Nevada .... 90 Southern Ill. 13-36
Nevada .... 91 McNeese St. 22-16
Nevada .... 91 Youngstown St. 28-30

Stephen Axman (0-1) (C. W. Post '69)
Northern Ariz. .... 96 Furman 31-42

Randy Ball (3-4) (Truman '73)
Western Ill. .... 91 Marshall 17-20 (ot)
Western Ill. .... 96 Murray St. 6-34
Western Ill. .... 97 Jackson St. 31-24
Western Ill. .... 97 McNeese St. 12-14
Western Ill. .... 98 Montana 52-9
Western Ill. .... 98 Florida A&M 24-21
Western Ill. .... 98 Ga. Southern 14-42

Darren Barbier (0-1) (Nicholls St. '82)
Nicholls St. .... 96 Montana 3-48

Frank Beamer (0-1) (Virginia Tech '69)
Murray St. .... 86 Eastern Ill. 21-28

Todd Berry (2-2) (Tulsa '83)
Illinois St. .... 98 Northwestern St. 28-48
Illinois St. .... 99 Colgate 56-13
Illinois St. .... 99 Hofstra 37-20
Illinois St. .... 99 Ga. Southern 17-28

Dick Biddle (0-3) (Duke '71)
Colgate .... 97 Villanova 28-49
Colgate .... 98 Ga. Southern 28-49
Colgate .... 99 Illinois St. 13-56

Larry Blakeney (5-6) (Auburn '70)
Troy St. .... 93 Stephen F. Austin 42-20
Troy St. .... 93 McNeese St. 35-28
Troy St. .... 93 Marshall 21-24
Troy St. .... 94 James Madison 26-45
Troy St. .... 95 Ga. Southern 21-24
Troy St. .... 96 Florida A&M 29-25
Troy St. .... 96 Murray St. 31-3
Troy St. .... 96 Montana 7-70
Troy St. .... 98 Florida A&M 17-27
Troy St. .... 99 James Madison 27-7
Troy St. .... 99 Florida A&M 10-17

Terry Bowden (2-2) (West Virginia '78)
Samford .... 91 New Hampshire 29-13
Samford .... 91 James Madison 24-21
Samford .... 91 Youngstown St. 0-10
Samford .... 92 Delaware 21-56

Bill Bowes (0-2) (Penn St. '65)
New Hampshire .... 91 Samford 13-29
New Hampshire .... 94 Appalachian St. 10-17 (ot)

Jesse Branch (1-2) (Arkansas '64)
Southwest Mo. St. .. 89 Maine 38-35
Southwest Mo. St. .. 89 Stephen F. Austin 25-55
Southwest Mo. St. .. 90 Idaho 35-41

Billy Brewer (1-1) (Mississippi '61)
Louisiana Tech .... 82 South Carolina St. 38-3
Louisiana Tech .... 82 Delaware 0-17

James Carson (0-3) (Jackson St. '63)
Jackson St. .... 95 Marshall 8-38
Jackson St. .... 96 William & Mary 6-45
Jackson St. .... 97 Western Ill. 24-31

Rick Carter (0-1) (Earlham '65)
Holy Cross .... 83 Western Carolina 21-28

Marino Casem (0-1) (Xavier [La.] '56)
Alcorn St. .... 84 Louisiana Tech 21-44

Mike Cavan (1-1) (Georgia '72)
East Tenn. St. .... 96 Villanova 35-29
East Tenn. St. .... 96 Montana 14-44

George Chaump (4-2) (Bloomsburg '58)
Marshall .... 87 James Madison 41-12
Marshall .... 87 Weber St. 51-23
Marshall .... 87 Appalachian St. 24-10
Marshall .... 87 La.-Monroe 42-43
Marshall .... 88 North Texas 7-0
Marshall .... 88 Furman 9-13

L. C. Cole (0-2) (Nebraska '80)
Tennessee St. .... 98 Appalachian St. 31-45
Tennessee St. .... 99 N.C. A&T 10-24

Pat Collins (4-0) (Louisiana Tech '63)
La.-Monroe .... 87 North Texas 30-9
La.-Monroe .... 87 Eastern Ky. 33-32
La.-Monroe .... 87 Northern Iowa 44-41 (ot)
La.-Monroe .... 87* Marshall 43-42

Archie Cooley Jr. (0-1) (Jackson St. '62)
Mississippi Val. ...... 84 Louisiana Tech 19-66

Bruce Craddock (0-1) (Truman '66)
Western Ill. .... 88 Western Ky. 32-35

Jim Criner (3-1) (Cal Poly Pomona '61)
Boise St. .... 80 Grambling 14-9
Boise St. .... 80* Eastern Ky. 31-29
Boise St. .... 81 Jackson St. 19-7
Boise St. .... 81 Eastern Ky. 17-23

Bill Davis (2-2) (Johnson Smith '65)
South Carolina St. .. 81 Tennessee St. 26-25
South Carolina St. .. 81 Idaho St. 12-41
South Carolina St. .. 82 Furman 17-0
South Carolina St. .. 82 Louisiana Tech 3-38

Rey Dempsey (3-0) (Geneva '58)
Southern Ill. .... 83 Indiana St. 23-7
Southern Ill. .... 83 Nevada 23-7
Southern Ill. .... 83* Western Carolina 43-7

Mick Dennehy (3-4) (Montana '73)
Montana .... 96 Nicholls St. 48-3
Montana .... 96 East Tenn. St. 44-14
Montana .... 96 Troy St. 70-7
Montana .... 96 Marshall 29-49
Montana .... 97 McNeese St. 14-19
Montana .... 98 Western Ill. 9-52
Montana .... 99 Youngstown St. 27-30

Jim Dennison (0-1) (Wooster '60)
Akron .... 85 Rhode Island 27-35

Jim Donnan (15-4) (North Carolina St. '67)
Marshall .... 91 Western Ill. 20-17 (ot)
Marshall .... 91 Northern Iowa 41-13
Marshall .... 91 Eastern Ky. 14-7
Marshall .... 91 Youngstown St. 17-25
Marshall .... 92 Eastern Ky. 44-0
Marshall .... 92 Middle Tenn. St. 35-21
Marshall .... 92 Delaware 28-7

DIVISION I-AA COACHING RECORDS—CHAMPIONSHIP COACHES

Marshall............ 92* Youngstown St. 31-28
Marshall............ 93 Howard 28-14
Marshall............ 93 Delaware 34-31
Marshall............ 93 Troy St. 24-21
Marshall............ 93 Youngstown St. 5-17
Marshall............ 94 Middle Tenn. St. 49-14
Marshall............ 94 James Madison 28-21 (ot)
Marshall............ 94 Boise St. 24-28
Marshall............ 95 Jackson St. 38-8
Marshall............ 95 Northern Iowa 41-24
Marshall............ 95 McNeese St. 25-13
Marshall............ 95 Montana 20-22

Boots Donnelly (6-7) (Middle Tenn. St. '65)
Middle Tenn. St. ....84 Eastern Ky. 27-10
Middle Tenn. St. ....84 Indiana St. 42-41 (3 ot)
Middle Tenn. St. ....84 Louisiana Tech 13-21
Middle Tenn. St. ....85 Ga. Southern 21-28
Middle Tenn. St. ....89 Appalachian St. 24-21
Middle Tenn. St. ....89 Ga. Southern 3-45
Middle Tenn. St. ....90 Jackson St. 28-7
Middle Tenn. St. ....90 Boise St. 13-20
Middle Tenn. St. ....91 Sam Houston St. 20-19 (ot)
Middle Tenn. St. ....91 Eastern Ky. 13-23
Middle Tenn. St. ....92 Appalachian St. 35-10
Middle Tenn. St. ....92 Marshall 21-35
Middle Tenn. St. ....94 Marshall 14-49

Larry Donovan (0-1) (Nebraska '64)
Montana............ 82 Idaho 7-21

Fred Dunlap (1-2) (Colgate '50)
Colgate............. 82 Boston U. 21-7
Colgate............. 82 Delaware 13-20
Colgate............. 83 Western Carolina 23-24

Dennis Erickson (1-2) (Montana St. '70)
Idaho............... 82 Montana 21-7
Idaho............... 82 Eastern Ky. 30-38
Idaho............... 85 Eastern Wash. 38-42

Mo Forte (0-1) (Minnesota '71)
N.C. A&T............ 86 Ga. Southern 21-52

Joe Gardi (1-3) (Maryland '60)
Hofstra.............. 95 Delaware 17-38
Hofstra.............. 97 Delaware 14-24
Hofstra.............. 99 Lehigh 27-15
Hofstra.............. 99 Illinois St. 20-37

Keith Gilbertson (2-3) (Central Wash. '71)
Idaho............... 86 Nevada 7-27
Idaho............... 87 Weber St. 30-59
Idaho............... 88 Montana 38-19
Idaho............... 88 Northwestern St. 38-30
Idaho............... 88 Furman 7-38

Sam Goodwin (3-3) (Henderson St. '66)
Northwestern St. ....88 Boise St. 22-13
Northwestern St. ....88 Idaho 30-38
Northwestern St. ....97 Eastern Wash. 10-40
Northwestern St. ....98 Illinois St. 48-28
Northwestern St. ....98 Appalachian St. 31-20
Northwestern St. ....98 Massachusetts 31-41

W. C. Gorden (0-9) (Tennessee St. '52)
Jackson St. ....78 Florida A&M 10-15
Jackson St. ....81 Boise St. 7-19
Jackson St. ....82 Eastern Ill. 13-16 (ot)
Jackson St. ....85 Ga. Southern 0-27
Jackson St. ....86 Tennessee St. 23-32
Jackson St. ....87 Arkansas St. 32-35
Jackson St. ....88 Stephen F. Austin 0-24
Jackson St. ....89 Montana 7-48
Jackson St. ....90 Middle Tenn. St. 7-28

Mike Gottfried (0-1) (Morehead St. '66)
Murray St. ....79 Lehigh 9-28

Lynn Graves (%3-1) (Stephen F. Austin '65)
Stephen F. Austin ....89% Grambling 59-56
Stephen F. Austin ....89% Southwest Mo. St. 55-25
Stephen F. Austin ....89% Furman 21-19
Stephen F. Austin ....89% Ga. Southern 34-37

Bob Griffin (2-3) (Southern Conn. St. '63)
Rhode Island ....81 Idaho St. 0-51
Rhode Island ....84 Richmond 23-17
Rhode Island ....84 Montana St. 20-32
Rhode Island ....85 Akron 35-27
Rhode Island ....85 Furman 15-59

Skip Hall (2-2) (Concordia-M'head '66)
Boise St. ....88 Northwestern St. 13-22
Boise St. ....90 Northern Iowa 20-3
Boise St. ....90 Middle Tenn. St. 20-13
Boise St. ....90 Nevada 52-59 (3 ot)

Jack Harbaugh (1-1) (Bowling Green '61)
Western Ky. ....97 Eastern Ky. 42-14

Western Ky. ....97 Eastern Wash. 21-38

Bill Hayes (1-2) (N.C. Central '64)
N.C. A&T............ 92 Citadel 0-44
N.C. A&T............ 99 Tennessee St. 24-10
N.C. A&T............ 99 Youngstown St. 3-41

Jim Hess (1-1) (Southeastern Okla. '59)
Stephen F. Austin ....88 Jackson St. 24-0
Stephen F. Austin ....88 Ga. Southern 6-27

Kevin Higgins (1-2) (West Chester '79)
Lehigh.............. 98 Richmond 24-33
Lehigh.............. 98 Massachusetts 21-27
Lehigh.............. 99 Hofstra 15-27

Skip Holtz (1-1) (Notre Dame '86)
Connecticut .... 98 Hampton 42-34
Connecticut .... 98 Ga. Southern 30-52

Rudy Hubbard (2-0) (Ohio St. '68)
Florida A&M .... 78 Jackson St. 15-10
Florida A&M .... 78* Massachusetts 35-28

Sonny Jackson (1-1) (Nicholls St. '63)
Nicholls St. .... 86 Appalachian St. 28-26
Nicholls St. .... 86 Ga. Southern 31-55

Billy Joe (3-4) (Villanova '63)
Florida A&M .... 96 Troy St. 25-29
Florida A&M .... 97 Ga. Southern 37-52
Florida A&M .... 98 Troy St. 27-17
Florida A&M .... 98 Western Ill. 21-24
Florida A&M .... 99 Appalachian St. 44-29
Florida A&M .... 99 Troy St. 17-10
Florida A&M .... 99 Youngstown St. 24-27

Bobby Johnson (1-2) (Clemson '73)
Furman .... 96 Northern Ariz. 42-31
Furman .... 96 Marshall 0-54
Furman .... 99 Massachusetts 23-30 (ot)

Paul Johnson (8-2) (Western Carolina '79)
Ga. Southern .... 97 Florida A&M 52-37
Ga. Southern .... 97 Delaware 7-16
Ga. Southern .... 98 Colgate 49-28
Ga. Southern .... 98 Connecticut 52-30
Ga. Southern .... 98 Western Ill. 42-14
Ga. Southern .... 98 Massachusetts 43-55
Ga. Southern .... 99 Northern Ariz. 72-29
Ga. Southern .... 99 Massachusetts 38-21
Ga. Southern .... 99 Illinois St. 28-17
Ga. Southern .... 99* Youngstown St. 59-24

Cardell Jones (0-2) (Alcorn St. '65)
Alcorn St. .... 92 La.-Monroe 27-78
Alcorn St. .... 94 Youngstown St. 20-63

Bobby Keasler (8-7) (La.-Monroe '70)
McNeese St. .... 91 Nevada 16-22
McNeese St. .... 92 Idaho 23-20
McNeese St. .... 92 Northern Iowa 7-29
McNeese St. .... 93 William & Mary 34-28
McNeese St. .... 93 Troy St. 28-35
McNeese St. .... 94 Idaho 38-21
McNeese St. .... 94 Montana 28-30
McNeese St. .... 95 Idaho 33-3
McNeese St. .... 95 Delaware 52-18
McNeese St. .... 95 Marshall 13-25
McNeese St. .... 97 Montana 19-14
McNeese St. .... 97 Western Ill. 14-12
McNeese St. .... 97 Delaware 23-21
McNeese St. .... 97 Youngstown St. 9-10
McNeese St. .... 98 Massachusetts 19-21

Roy Kidd (16-15) (Eastern Ky. '54)
Eastern Ky. .... 79 Nevada 33-30
Eastern Ky. .... 79* Lehigh 30-7
Eastern Ky. .... 80 Lehigh 23-20
Eastern Ky. .... 80 Boise St. 29-31
Eastern Ky. .... 81 Delaware 35-28
Eastern Ky. .... 81 Boise St. 23-17
Eastern Ky. .... 81 Idaho St. 23-34
Eastern Ky. .... 82 Idaho St. 38-30
Eastern Ky. .... 82 Tennessee St. 13-7
Eastern Ky. .... 82* Delaware 17-14
Eastern Ky. .... 83 Boston U. 20-24
Eastern Ky. .... 84 Middle Tenn. St. 10-27
Eastern Ky. .... 86 Furman 23-10
Eastern Ky. .... 86 Eastern Ill. 24-22
Eastern Ky. .... 86 Arkansas St. 10-24
Eastern Ky. .... 87 Western Ky. 40-17
Eastern Ky. .... 88 Massachusetts 28-17
Eastern Ky. .... 88 Western Ky. 41-24
Eastern Ky. .... 88 Ga. Southern 17-21
Eastern Ky. .... 89 Youngstown St. 24-28

Eastern Ky. .... 90 Furman 17-45
Eastern Ky. .... 91 Appalachian St. 14-3
Eastern Ky. .... 91 Middle Tenn. St. 23-13
Eastern Ky. .... 91 Marshall 7-14
Eastern Ky. .... 92 Marshall 0-44
Eastern Ky. .... 93 Ga. Southern 12-14
Eastern Ky. .... 94 Boston U. 30-23
Eastern Ky. .... 94 Youngstown St. 15-18
Eastern Ky. .... 95 Montana 0-48
Eastern Ky. .... 97 Western Ky. 14-42

Jim Koetter (0-1) (Idaho St. '61)
Idaho St. .... 83 Nevada 20-27

Dave Kragthorpe (3-0) (Utah St. '55)
Idaho St. .... 81 Rhode Island 51-0
Idaho St. .... 81 South Carolina St. 41-12
Idaho St. .... 81* Eastern Ky. 34-23

Mike Kramer (2-1) (Idaho '77)
Eastern Wash. ..... 97 Northwestern St. 40-10
Eastern Wash. ..... 97 Western Ky. 38-21
Eastern Wash. ..... 97 Youngstown St. 14-25

Larry Lacewell (6-4) (Ark.-Monticello '59)
Arkansas St. .... 84 Chattanooga 37-10
Arkansas St. .... 84 Montana St. 14-31
Arkansas St. .... 85 Grambling 10-7
Arkansas St. .... 85 Nevada 23-24
Arkansas St. .... 86 Sam Houston St. 48-7
Arkansas St. .... 86 Delaware 55-14
Arkansas St. .... 86 Eastern Ky. 24-10
Arkansas St. .... 86 Ga. Southern 21-48
Arkansas St. .... 87 Jackson St. 35-32
Arkansas St. .... 87 Northern Iowa 28-49

Jimmye Laycock (2-5) (William & Mary '70)
William & Mary..... 86 Delaware 17-51
William & Mary..... 89 Furman 10-24
William & Mary..... 90 Massachusetts 38-0
William & Mary..... 90 UCF 38-52
William & Mary..... 93 McNeese St. 28-34
William & Mary..... 96 Jackson St. 45-6
William & Mary..... 96 Northern Iowa 35-38

Tom Lichtenberg (0-1) (Louisville '62)
Maine............... 89 Southwest Mo. St. 35-38

Mickey Matthews (0-1) (West Tex. A&M '86)
James Madison...... 99 Troy St. 7-27

Gene McDowell (2-2) (Florida St. '63)
UCF................. 90 Youngstown St. 20-17
UCF................. 90 William & Mary 52-38
UCF................. 90 Ga. Southern 7-44
UCF................. 93 Youngstown St. 30-56

John Merritt (†1-2) (Kentucky St. '50)
Tennessee St. ...... 81† South Carolina St. 25-26 (ot)
Tennessee St. ...... 82† Eastern Ill. 20-19
Tennessee St. ...... 82† Eastern Ky. 7-13

Al Molde (1-2) (Gust. Adolphus '66)
Eastern Ill. .... 83 Indiana St. 13-16 (2 ot)
Eastern Ill. .... 86 Murray St. 38-21
Eastern Ill. .... 86 Eastern Ky. 22-24

Jerry Moore (3-7) (Baylor '61)
Appalachian St. .... 89 Middle Tenn. St. 21-24
Appalachian St. .... 91 Eastern Ky. 3-14
Appalachian St. .... 92 Middle Tenn. St. 10-35
Appalachian St. .... 94 New Hampshire 17-10 (ot)
Appalachian St. .... 94 Boise St. 14-17
Appalachian St. .... 95 James Madison 31-24
Appalachian St. .... 95 Stephen F. Austin 17-27
Appalachian St. .... 98 Tennessee St. 45-31
Appalachian St. .... 98 Northwestern St. 20-31
Appalachian St. .... 99 Florida A&M 29-44

Darrell Mudra (4-3) (Peru St. '51)
Eastern Ill. .... 82 Jackson St. 16-13 (ot)
Eastern Ill. .... 82 Tennessee St. 19-20
Northern Iowa ..... 85 Eastern Wash. 17-14
Northern Iowa ..... 85 Ga. Southern 33-40
Northern Iowa ..... 87 Youngstown St. 31-24
Northern Iowa ..... 87 Arkansas St. 49-28
Northern Iowa ..... 87 La.-Monroe 41-44 (ot)

Tim Murphy (0-1) (Springfield '78)
Maine............... 87 Ga. Southern 28-31 (ot)

Corky Nelson (0-3) (Southwest Tex. St. '64)
North Texas .... 83 Nevada 17-20
North Texas .... 87 La.-Monroe 9-30
North Texas .... 88 Marshall 0-7

Buddy Nix (0-1) (West Ala. '61)
Chattanooga .... 84 Arkansas St. 10-37

Houston Nutt (1-2) (Oklahoma St. '81)
Murray St. .... 95 Northern Iowa 34-35
Murray St. .... 96 Western Ill. 34-6
Murray St. .... 96 Troy St. 3-31

John Pearce (2-2) (Tex. A&M-Commerce '70)
Stephen F. Austin .... 93 Troy St. 20-42
Stephen F. Austin .... 95 Eastern Ill. 34-29
Stephen F. Austin .... 95 Appalachian St. 27-17
Stephen F. Austin .... 95 Montana 14-70

Bob Pickett (1-1) (Maine '59)
Massachusetts......... 78 Nevada 44-21
Massachusetts......... 78 Florida A&M 28-35

Mike Price (1-1) (Puget Sound '69)
Weber St. .... 87 Idaho 59-30
Weber St. .... 87 Marshall 23-51

Bob Pruett (4-0) (Marshall '65)
Marshall................ 96 Delaware 59-14
Marshall................ 96 Furman 54-0
Marshall................ 96 Northern Iowa 31-14
Marshall................ 96* Montana 49-29

Joe Purzycki (0-1) (Delaware '71)
James Madison........ 87 Marshall 12-41

Dennis Raetz (1-2) (Nebraska '68)
Indiana St. .... 83 Eastern Ill. 16-13 (2 ot)
Indiana St. .... 83 Southern Ill. 7-23
Indiana St. .... 84 Middle Tenn. St. 41-42 (3 ot)

Ron Randleman (0-2) (William Penn '64)
Sam Houston St. ..... 86 Arkansas St. 7-48
Sam Houston St. .... 91 Middle Tenn. St. 19-20 (ot)

Tubby Raymond (9-10) (Michigan '50)
Delaware .... 81 Eastern Ky. 28-35
Delaware .... 82 Colgate 20-13
Delaware .... 82 Louisiana Tech 17-0
Delaware .... 82 Eastern Ky. 14-17
Delaware .... 86 William & Mary 51-17
Delaware .... 86 Arkansas St. 14-55
Delaware .... 88 Furman 7-21
Delaware .... 91 James Madison 35-42 (2 ot)
Delaware .... 92 Samford 56-21
Delaware .... 92 La.-Monroe 41-18
Delaware .... 92 Marshall 7-28
Delaware .... 93 Montana 49-48
Delaware .... 93 Marshall 31-34
Delaware .... 93 Hofstra 38-17
Delaware .... 95 McNeese St. 18-52
Delaware .... 96 Marshall 14-59
Delaware .... 97 Hofstra 24-14
Delaware .... 97 Ga. Southern 16-7
Delaware .... 97 McNeese St. 21-23

Don Read (8-4) (Cal St. Sacramento '59)
Montana .... 88 Idaho 19-38
Montana .... 89 Jackson St. 48-7
Montana .... 89 Eastern Ill. 25-19
Montana .... 89 Ga. Southern 15-45
Montana .... 93 Delaware 48-49
Montana .... 94 Northern Iowa 23-20
Montana .... 94 McNeese St. 30-28
Montana .... 94 Youngstown St. 9-28
Montana .... 95 Eastern Ky. 48-0
Montana .... 95 Ga. Southern 45-0
Montana .... 95 Stephen F. Austin 70-14
Montana .... 95* Marshall 22-20

Jim Reid (0-3) (Maine '73)
Massachusetts......... 88 Eastern Ky. 17-28
Massachusetts......... 90 William & Mary 0-38
Richmond .... 98 Lehigh 23-24

Dave Roberts (2-5) (Western Carolina '68)
Western Ky. .... 87 Eastern Ky. 17-40
Western Ky. .... 88 Western Ill. 35-32
Western Ky. .... 88 Eastern Ky. 24-41
La.-Monroe .... 90 Nevada 14-27
La.-Monroe .... 92 Alcorn St. 78-27
La.-Monroe .... 92 Delaware 18-41
La.-Monroe .... 93 Idaho 31-34

Eddie Robinson (0-3) (Leland '41)
Grambling.............. 80 Boise St. 9-14
Grambling.............. 85 Arkansas St. 7-10
Grambling.............. 89 Stephen F. Austin 56-59

Erk Russell (16-2) (Auburn '49)
Ga. Southern.......... 85 Jackson St. 27-0
Ga. Southern.......... 85 Middle Tenn. St. 28-21
Ga. Southern.......... 85 Northern Iowa 40-33
Ga. Southern.......... 85* Furman 44-42
Ga. Southern.......... 86 N.C. A&T 52-21
Ga. Southern.......... 86 Nicholls St. 55-31
Ga. Southern.......... 86 Nevada 48-38
Ga. Southern.......... 86* Arkansas St. 48-21
Ga. Southern.......... 87 Maine 31-28 (ot)
Ga. Southern.......... 87 Appalachian St. 0-19
Ga. Southern.......... 88 Citadel 38-20
Ga. Southern.......... 88 Stephen F. Austin 27-6
Ga. Southern.......... 88 Eastern Ky. 21-17
Ga. Southern.......... 88 Furman 12-17
Ga. Southern.......... 89 Villanova 52-36
Ga. Southern.......... 89 Middle Tenn. St. 45-3
Ga. Southern.......... 89 Montana 45-15
Ga. Southern.......... 89* Stephen F. Austin 37-34

Jimmy Satterfield (7-3) (South Carolina '62)
Furman .... 86 Eastern Ky. 10-23
Furman .... 88 Delaware 21-7
Furman .... 88 Marshall 13-9
Furman .... 88 Idaho 38-7
Furman .... 88* Ga. Southern 17-12
Furman .... 89 William & Mary 24-10
Furman .... 89 Youngstown St. 42-23
Furman .... 89 Stephen F. Austin 19-21
Furman .... 90 Eastern Ky. 45-17
Furman .... 90 Nevada 35-42 (3 ot)

Rip Scherer (2-2) (William & Mary '74)
James Madison....... 91 Delaware 42-35 (2 ot)
James Madison....... 91 Samford 21-24
James Madison....... 94 Troy St. 45-26
James Madison....... 94 Marshall 21-28 (ot)

Dal Shealy (1-2) (Carson-Newman '60)
Richmond .... 84 Boston U. 35-33
Richmond .... 84 Rhode Island 17-23
Richmond .... 87 Appalachian St. 3-20

Dick Sheridan (3-3) (South Carolina '64)
Furman .... 82 South Carolina St. 0-17
Furman .... 83 Boston U. 35-16
Furman .... 83 Western Carolina 7-14
Furman .... 85 Rhode Island 59-15
Furman .... 85 Nevada 55-12
Furman .... 85 Ga. Southern 42-44

Matt Simon (0-1) (Eastern N.M. '76)
North Texas............ 94 Boise St. 20-24

John L. Smith (3-5) (Weber St. '71)
Idaho .... 89 Eastern Ill. 21-38
Idaho .... 90 Southwest Mo. St. 41-35
Idaho .... 90 Ga. Southern 27-28
Idaho .... 92 McNeese St. 20-23
Idaho .... 93 La.-Monroe 34-31
Idaho .... 93 Boston U. 21-14
Idaho .... 93 Youngstown St. 16-35
Idaho .... 94 McNeese St. 21-38

Jerome Souers (0-1) (Oregon '83)
Northern Ariz. .... 99 Ga. Southern 29-72

Bob Spoo (1-3) (Purdue '60)
Eastern Ill. .... 89 Idaho 38-21
Eastern Ill. .... 89 Montana 19-25
Eastern Ill. .... 95 Stephen F. Austin 29-34
Eastern Ill. .... 96 Northern Iowa 14-21

Tim Stowers (6-2) (Auburn '79)
Ga. Southern.......... 90 Citadel 31-0
Ga. Southern.......... 90 Middle Tenn. St. 28-27
Ga. Southern.......... 90 UCF 44-7
Ga. Southern.......... 90* Nevada 36-13
Ga. Southern.......... 93 Eastern Ky. 14-12
Ga. Southern.......... 93 Youngstown St. 14-34
Ga. Southern.......... 95 Troy St. 24-21
Ga. Southern.......... 95 Montana 0-45

Charlie Taaffe (1-3) (Siena '73)
Citadel.................. 88 Ga. Southern 20-38
Citadel.................. 90 Ga. Southern 0-31
Citadel.................. 92 N.C. A&T 44-0
Citadel.................. 92 Youngstown St. 17-42

Andy Talley (1-5) (Southern Conn. St. '67)
Villanova................ 89 Ga. Southern 36-52
Villanova................ 91 Youngstown St. 16-17
Villanova................ 92 Youngstown St. 20-23
Villanova................ 96 East Tenn. St. 29-35
Villanova................ 97 Colgate 49-28
Villanova................ 97 Youngstown St. 34-37

Joe Taylor (0-2) (Western Ill. '72)
Hampton................ 97 Youngstown St. 13-28
Hampton................ 98 Connecticut 34-42

Rick Taylor (1-3) (Gettysburg '64)
Boston U. .... 82 Colgate 7-21
Boston U. .... 83 Eastern Ky. 24-20
Boston U. .... 83 Furman 16-35
Boston U. .... 84 Richmond 33-35

Bill Thomas (1-1) (Tennessee St. '71)
Tennessee St. .... 86 Jackson St. 32-23
Tennessee St. .... 86 Nevada 6-33

Chris Tormey (0-1) (Idaho '78)
Idaho .... 95 McNeese St. 3-33

Jim Tressel (23-5) (Baldwin-Wallace '75)
Youngstown St. ...... 87 Northern Iowa 28-31
Youngstown St. ...... 89 Eastern Ky. 28-24
Youngstown St. ...... 89 Furman 23-42
Youngstown St. ...... 90 UCF 17-20
Youngstown St. ...... 91 Villanova 17-16
Youngstown St. ...... 91 Nevada 30-28
Youngstown St. ...... 91 Samford 10-0
Youngstown St. ...... 91* Marshall 25-17
Youngstown St. ...... 92 Villanova 23-20
Youngstown St. ...... 92 Citadel 42-17
Youngstown St. ...... 92 Northern Iowa 19-7
Youngstown St. ...... 92 Marshall 28-31
Youngstown St. ...... 93 UCF 56-30
Youngstown St. ...... 93 Ga. Southern 34-14
Youngstown St. ...... 93 Idaho 35-16
Youngstown St. ...... 93* Marshall 17-5
Youngstown St. ...... 94 Alcorn St. 63-20
Youngstown St. ...... 94 Eastern Ky. 18-15
Youngstown St. ...... 94 Montana 28-9
Youngstown St. ...... 94* Boise St. 28-14
Youngstown St. ...... 97 Hampton 28-13
Youngstown St. ...... 97 Villanova 37-34
Youngstown St. ...... 97 Eastern Wash. 25-14
Youngstown St. ...... 97* McNeese St. 10-9
Youngstown St. ...... 99 Montana 30-27
Youngstown St. ...... 99 N.C. A&T 41-3
Youngstown St. ...... 99 Florida A&M 27-24
Youngstown St. ...... 99 Ga. Southern 24-59

Bob Waters (3-1) (Presbyterian '60)
Western Carolina ... 83 Colgate 24-23
Western Carolina ... 83 Holy Cross 28-21
Western Carolina ... 83 Furman 14-7
Western Carolina ... 83 Southern Ill. 7-43

Mark Whipple (5-1) (Brown '79)
Massachusetts......... 98 McNeese St. 21-19
Massachusetts......... 98 Lehigh 27-21
Massachusetts......... 98 Northwestern St. 41-31
Massachusetts......... 98* Ga. Southern 55-43
Massachusetts......... 99 Furman 30-23 (ot)
Massachusetts......... 99 Ga. Southern 21-38

John Whitehead (1-2) (East Stroudsburg '50)
Lehigh .... 79 Murray St. 28-9
Lehigh .... 79 Eastern Ky. 7-30
Lehigh .... 80 Eastern Ky. 20-23

A. L. Williams (3-1) (Louisiana Tech '57)
Louisiana Tech........ 84 Mississippi Val. 66-19
Louisiana Tech........ 84 Alcorn St. 44-21
Louisiana Tech........ 84 Middle Tenn. St. 21-13
Louisiana Tech........ 84 Montana St. 6-19

Steve Wilson (0-1) (Howard '79)
Howard .... 93 Marshall 14-28

Alex Wood (0-1) (Iowa '79)
James Madison....... 95 Appalachian St. 24-31

Sparky Woods (2-2) (Carson-Newman '76)
Appalachian St. ..... 86 Nicholls St. 26-28
Appalachian St. ..... 87 Richmond 20-3
Appalachian St. ..... 87 Ga. Southern 19-0
Appalachian St. ..... 87 Marshall 10-24

Dick Zornes (1-2) (Eastern Wash. '68)
Eastern Wash. .... 85 Idaho 42-38
Eastern Wash. .... 85 Northern Iowa 14-17
Eastern Wash. .... 85 Northern Iowa 14-17

*National championship. †Tennessee State's participation vacated by action of the NCAA Committee on Infractions. %Stephen F. Austin's participation vacated by action of the NCAA Committee on Infractions.

Division II Coaching Records

Winningest Active Division II Coaches

(Minimum five years as college head coach; record at four-year colleges only.)

BY PERCENTAGE

Coach, College	Years	Won	Lost	Tied	†Pct.	Playoffs# W-L-T
Chuck Broyles, Pittsburg St.	10	103	18	2	.84553	12-8-0
Ken Sparks, Carson-Newman	20	197	46	2	.80816	12-7-0
David Bennett, Catawba	5	41	14	0	.74545	1-1-0
Peter Yetten, Bentley	12	84	30	1	.73478	0-0-0
Kay Dalton, Northern Colo.	5	33	12	0	.73333	0-0-0
Jim Miceli, Bryant	5	33	13	0	.71739	0-0-0
Bob Biggs, UC Davis	7	59	23	1	.71687	6-5-0
Danny Hale, Bloomsburg	12	92	37	1	.71154	0-2-0
Gene Carpenter, Millersville	31	214	86	6	.70915	2-5-0
Frank Cignetti, Indiana (Pa.)	18	149	62	1	.70519	14-10-0
Brian Kelly, Grand Valley St.	9	70	29	2	.70297	0-3-0
Jerry Kill, Emporia St.	6	43	20	0	.68254	0-0-0
Rudy Abrams, N.C. Central	6	40	20	1	.66393	0-0-0
Brad Smith, Chadron St.	13	91	46	1	.66304	0-2-0
George Mihalik, Slippery Rock	12	86	43	4	.66165	3-3-0
Mel Tjeerdsma, Northwest Mo. St.	16	117	59	4	.66111	10-2-0
Jeff Pierce, Ferris St.	5	37	19	0	.66071	3-2-0
Carl Iverson, Western St.	16	106	54	3	.65951	0-3-0
Willard Bailey, Virginia Union	27	183	97	7	.64983	0-6-0
Eric Holm, Northern Mich.	10	70	38	0	.64815	0-3-0
Jerry Vandergriff, Angelo St.	18	124	67	2	.64767	2-2-0
Bob Nielson, Minn.-Duluth	11	73	41	1	.63913	3-3-0
Hampton Smith, Albany St. (Ga.)	24	157	90	4	.63347	1-5-0
Rick Daniels, West Chester	11	74	44	1	.62605	0-3-0
Gary Howard, Central Okla.	23	147	88	6	.62241	2-3-0
Lou Anderson, Virginia St.	9	56	36	0	.60870	0-0-0
Stan McGarvey, West Tex. A&M	15	97	62	4	.60736	0-0-0
Monte Cater, Shepherd	19	115	74	2	.60733	1-2-0
Randy Hedberg, St. Cloud St.	9	48	31	2	.60494	0-0-0
Tom Eckert, Northeastern St.	13	85	55	3	.60490	2-1-0
Steve Patton, Gardner-Webb	8	51	35	1	.59195	0-0-0
Morris Sloan, Southeastern Okla.	11	64	44	4	.58929	0-0-0
Steve Roberts, Southern Ark.	6	34	25	1	.57500	0-1-0
Dan Simrell, Findlay	8	50	37	2	.57303	0-0-0
Rocky Rees, Shippensburg	15	92	69	2	.57055	2-2-0
Dennis Douds, East Stroudsburg	26	149	112	3	.57008	0-1-0
Pat Behrns, Neb.-Omaha	12	74	56	0	.56923	0-2-0
Gary Keller, Ashland	6	35	27	0	.56452	0-1-0
Art Wilkins, American Int'l	6	36	28	0	.56250	0-0-0
Rick Comegy, Tuskegee	8	48	39	0	.55172	0-0-0
Tony DeMeo, Washburn	17	86	71	4	.54658	0-0-0
Malen Luke, Clarion	12	67	56	0	.54472	2-1-0
Randy Tribble, Harding	6	32	28	1	.53279	0-0-0
John Ware, Truman	5	29	25	0	.53704	0-0-0
Dennis Roland, Southwest Baptist	13	73	66	0	.52518	0-0-0
Randy Awrey, Saginaw Valley	10	52	47	1	.52500	0-0-0
Bud Elliott, Eastern N.M.	32	173	158	9	.52206	0-1-0
Joe Kimball, Mercyhurst	7	35	32	1	.52206	0-0-0
George Small, Kentucky St.	5	29	27	0	.51786	0-0-0
Kermit Blount, Winston-Salem	7	31	29	3	.51587	0-0-0
Richard Cavanaugh, Southern Conn. St.	15	77	74	1	.50987	0-0-0
Joe Polizzi, Indianapolis	6	32	31	1	.50781	0-0-0
Bill Cooke, Mo. Southern St.	5	23	23	1	.50000	0-0-0
Paul Sharp, Southwestern Okla.	14	70	70	1	.50000	0-0-0
Greg Lusardi, Pace	6	30	30	0	.50000	0-0-0
Doug Sams, Fairmont St.	9	45	46	0	.49451	0-0-0
Joseph Crosby, Morris Brown	6	31	32	1	.49231	0-0-0
Fred Whitmire, Humboldt St.	9	44	47	2	.48387	0-0-0
Dan Runkle, Minn. St.-Mankato	19	101	109	2	.48113	2-3-0
Tim Clifton, Mars Hill	7	35	38	0	.47945	0-0-0
Bob Eaton, West Liberty St.	10	46	53	1	.46500	0-0-0
Bob Brush, Wingate	5	23	27	0	.46000	0-0-0
John Johnson, Ky. Wesleyan	6	28	33	0	.45902	0-0-0
Bill Struble, West Va. Wesleyan	17	77	92	0	.45562	0-0-0
Bernie Anderson, Michigan Tech	13	58	70	0	.45313	0-0-0
Lou Tepper, Edinboro	5	25	31	2	.44828	0-0-0
Pat Riepma, Northwood	7	31	39	2	.44444	0-0-0
Todd Knight, Ouachita Baptist	7	31	39	2	.44444	0-1-0
Mike Taylor, Newberry	8	38	49	0	.43678	0-0-0
Ralph Micheli, Moorhead St.	17	70	92	2	.43293	0-1-0
Jim Heinitz, Augustana (S. D.)	12	56	74	1	.43130	0-2-0
Cecil Leonard, Miles	6	23	35	1	.39831	0-0-0
Dennis Darnell, East Central	6	22	41	1	.35156	0-0-0
Mike Slovick, St. Francis (Ill.)	6	14	51	0	.21538	0-0-0

#Record in NCAA Division II championship. +Ties computed as half won and half lost.

BY VICTORIES

(Minimum 100 Victories)

Coach, College	Won
Gene Carpenter, Millersville	214
Ken Sparks, Carson-Newman	197
Willard Bailey, Virginia Union	183
Bud Elliott, Eastern N.M.	173
Hampton Smith, Albany St. (Ga.)	157
Frank Cignetti, Indiana (Pa.)	149
Dennis Douds, East Stroudsburg	149
Gary Howard, Central Okla.	147
Jerry Vandergriff, Angelo St.	124
Mel Tjeerdsma, Northwest Mo. St.	117
Monte Cater, Shepherd	115
Carl Iverson, Western St.	106
Chuck Broyles, Pittsburg St.	103
Dan Runkle, Minn. St.-Mankato	101

Division II Championship Coaches

All coaches who have coached teams in the Division II championship playoffs since 1973 are listed here with their playoff record, alma mater and year graduated, team, year coached, opponent, and score.

Phil Albert (1-3) (Arizona '66)
Towson 83   North Dakota St. 17-24
Towson 84   Norfolk St. 31-21
Towson 84   Troy St. 3-45
Towson 86   Central St. 0-31

Pokey Allen (10-5) (Utah '65)
Portland St. 87   Minn. St.-Mankato 27-21
Portland St. 87   Northern Mich. 13-7
Portland St. 87   Troy St. 17-31
Portland St. 88   Bowie St. 34-17
Portland St. 88   Jacksonville St. 20-13
Portland St. 88   Tex. A&M-Kingsville 35-27
Portland St. 88   North Dakota St. 21-35
Portland St. 89   West Chester 56-50 (3 ot)
Portland St. 89   Indiana (Pa.) 0-17
Portland St. 91   Northern Colo. 28-24
Portland St. 91   Minn. St.-Mankato 37-27
Portland St. 91   Pittsburg St. 21-53
Portland St. 92   UC Davis 42-28
Portland St. 92   Tex. A&M-Kingsville 35-30
Portland St. 92   Pittsburg St. 38-41

Mike Ayers (0-2) (Georgetown [Ky.] '74)
Wofford 90   Mississippi Col. 19-70
Wofford 91   Mississippi Col. 15-28

Bob Babich (0-1) (Tulsa '84)
North Dakota St. 97   Northwest Mo. St. 28-39

Willard Bailey (0-6) (Norfolk St. '62)
Virginia Union 79   Delaware 28-58
Virginia Union 80   North Ala. 8-17
Virginia Union 81   Shippensburg 27-40
Virginia Union 82   North Dakota St. 20-21
Virginia Union 83   North Ala. 14-16
Norfolk St. 84   Towson 21-31

Bob Bartolomeo (0-1) (Butler '77)
Butler 91   Pittsburg St. 16-26

Tom Beck (0-2) (Northern Ill. '61)
Grand Valley St. 89   Indiana (Pa.) 24-34
Grand Valley St. 90   Tex. A&M-Commerce 14-20

Pat Behrns (0-2) (Dakota St. '72)
Neb.-Omaha 96   Northwest Mo. St. 21-22
Neb.-Omaha 98   Northwest Mo. St. 14-28

David Bennett (1-1) (Presbyterian '84)
Catawba 99   Fort Valley St. 48-17
Catawba 99   Carson-Newman 25-28

Bob Biggs (6-5) (UC Davis '73)
UC Davis 93   Fort Hays St. 37-34
UC Davis 93   Tex. A&M-Kingsville 28-51
UC Davis 96   Tex. A&M-Kingsville 17-14
UC Davis 96   Central Okla. 26-6
UC Davis 96   Carson-Newman 26-29
UC Davis 97   Tex. A&M-Kingsville 37-34
UC Davis 97   Angelo St. 50-33
UC Davis 97   New Haven 25-27
UC Davis 98   Tex. A&M-Kingsville 21-54
UC Davis 99   Central Okla. 33-17
UC Davis 99   Northeastern St. 14-19

Bob Blasi (0-1) (Colorado St. '53)
Northern Colo. 80   Eastern Ill. 14-21

Bill Bowes (1-2) (Penn St. '65)
New Hampshire 75   Lehigh 35-21
New Hampshire 75   Western Ky. 3-14
New Hampshire 76   Montana St. 16-17

Chuck Broyles (12-8) (Pittsburg St. '70)
Pittsburg St. 90   Truman 59-3
Pittsburg St. 90   Tex. A&M-Commerce 60-28
Pittsburg St. 90   North Dakota St. 29-39
Pittsburg St. 91   Butler 26-16
Pittsburg St. 91   Tex. A&M-Commerce 38-28
Pittsburg St. 91   Portland St. 53-21
Pittsburg St. .... 91*   Jacksonville St. 23-6
Pittsburg St. 92   North Dakota St. 26-21
Pittsburg St. 92   North Dakota St. 38-37 (ot)
Pittsburg St. 92   Portland St. 41-38
Pittsburg St. 92   Jacksonville St. 13-17
Pittsburg St. 93   North Dakota 14-17
Pittsburg St. 94   North Dakota St. 12-18 (3 ot)
Pittsburg St. 95   Northern Colo. 36-17
Pittsburg St. 95   North Dakota St. 9-7
Pittsburg St. 95   Tex. A&M-Kingsville 28-25 (ot)
Pittsburg St. 95   North Ala. 7-27
Pittsburg St. 96   Northern Colo. 21-24
Pittsburg St. 97   Northern Colo. 16-24

Pittsburg St. .... 99 Northern Colo. 31-34
Sandy Buda (1-2) (Kansas '67)
Neb.-Omaha .... 78 Youngstown St. 14-21
Neb.-Omaha .... 84 Northwest Mo. St. 28-15
Neb.-Omaha .... 84 North Dakota St. 14-25
Bill Burgess (12-4) (Auburn '63)
Jacksonville St. .... 88 West Chester 63-24
Jacksonville St. .... 88 Portland St. 13-20
Jacksonville St. .... 89 Alabama A&M 33-9
Jacksonville St. .... 89 North Dakota St. 21-17
Jacksonville St. .... 89 Angelo St. 34-16
Jacksonville St. .... 89 Mississippi Col. 0-3
Jacksonville St. .... 90 North Ala. 38-14
Jacksonville St. .... 90 Mississippi Col. 7-14
Jacksonville St. .... 91 Winston-Salem 49-24
Jacksonville St. .... 91 Mississippi Col. 35-7
Jacksonville St. .... 91 Indiana (Pa.) 27-20
Jacksonville St. .... 91 Pittsburg St. 6-23
Jacksonville St. .... 92 Savannah St. 41-16
Jacksonville St. .... 92 North Ala. 14-12
Jacksonville St. .... 92 New Haven 46-35
Jacksonville St. .... 92* Pittsburg St. 17-13
Bob Burt (0-1) (Cal St. Los Angeles '62)
Cal St. Northridge .. 90 Cal Poly 7-14
Gene Carpenter (2-3) (Huron '63)
Millersville .... 88 Indiana (Pa.) 27-24
Millersville .... 88 North Dakota St. 26-36
Millersville .... 95 Ferris St. 26-36
Millersville .... 99 Shepherd 21-14
Millersville .... 99 Indiana (Pa.) 21-26
Marino Casem (0-1) (Xavier [La.] '56)
Alcorn St. .... 74 UNLV 22-35
Monte Cater (1-2) (Millikin '71)
Shepherd .... 98 Indiana (Pa.) 9-6
Shepherd .... 98 Slippery Rock 20-31
Shepherd .... 99 Millersville 14-21
Frank Cignetti (14-10) (Indiana [Pa.] '60)
Indiana (Pa.) .... 87 UCF 10-12
Indiana (Pa.) .... 88 Millersville 24-27
Indiana (Pa.) .... 89 Grand Valley St. 34-24
Indiana (Pa.) .... 89 Portland St. 17-0
Indiana (Pa.) .... 89 Mississippi Col. 14-26
Indiana (Pa.) .... 90 Winston-Salem 48-0
Indiana (Pa.) .... 90 Edinboro 14-7
Indiana (Pa.) .... 90 Mississippi Col. 27-8
Indiana (Pa.) .... 90 North Dakota St. 11-51
Indiana (Pa.) .... 91 Virginia Union 56-7
Indiana (Pa.) .... 91 Shippensburg 52-7
Indiana (Pa.) .... 91 Jacksonville St. 20-27
Indiana (Pa.) .... 93 Ferris St. 28-21
Indiana (Pa.) .... 93 New Haven 38-35
Indiana (Pa.) .... 93 North Dakota 21-6
Indiana (Pa.) .... 93 North Ala. 34-41
Indiana (Pa.) .... 94 Grand Valley St. 35-27
Indiana (Pa.) .... 94 Ferris St. 21-17
Indiana (Pa.) .... 94 Tex. A&M-Kingsville 20-46
Indiana (Pa.) .... 96 Ferris St. 23-24
Indiana (Pa.) .... 98 Shepherd 6-9
Indiana (Pa.) .... 99 Slippery Rock 27-20 (ot)
Indiana (Pa.) .... 99 Millersville 26-21
Indiana (Pa.) .... 99 Northwest Mo. St. 12-20
Bob Cortese (0-2) (Colorado '67)
Fort Hays St. .... 93 UC Davis 34-37
Fort Hays St. .... 95 Tex. A&M-Kingsville 28-59
Bruce Craddock (0-1) (Truman '66)
Truman .... 82 Jacksonville St. 21-34
Rick Daniels (0-3) (West Chester '75)
West Chester .... 89 Portland St. 50-56 (3 ot)
West Chester .... 92 New Haven 26-38
West Chester .... 94 Ferris St. 40-43
Bill Davis (0-1) (Johnson Smith '65)
Savannah St. .... 92 Jacksonville St. 16-41
Rey Dempsey (0-1) (Geneva '58)
Youngstown St. .... 74 Delaware 14-35
Jim Dennison (2-1) (Wooster '60)
Akron .... 76 UNLV 26-6
Akron .... 76 Northern Mich. 29-26
Akron .... 76 Montana St. 13-24
Dennis Douds (0-1) (Slippery Rock '63)
East Stroudsburg ..... 91 Shippensburg 33-34
Fred Dunlap (0-2) (Colgate '50)
Lehigh .... 73 Western Ky. 16-25
Lehigh .... 75 New Hampshire 21-35
Tom Eckert (2-1) (Northeastern St. '66)
Northeastern St. ...... 99 Western Wash. 27-24 (ot)
Northeastern St. ...... 99 UC Davis 19-14
Northeastern St. ...... 99 Carson-Newman 7-42
Bud Elliott (0-1) (Baker '53)
Northwest Mo. St. ... 89 Pittsburg St. 7-28
Jimmy Feix (4-2) (Western Ky. '53)
Western Ky. .... 73 Lehigh 25-16
Western Ky. .... 73 Grambling 28-20
Western Ky. .... 73 Louisiana Tech 0-34
Western Ky. .... 75 Northern Iowa 14-12
Western Ky. .... 75 New Hampshire 14-3
Western Ky. .... 75 Northern Mich. 14-16
Charlie Fisher (0-2) (Springfield '81)
West Ga. .... 95 Carson-Newman 26-37
West Ga. .... 96 Carson-Newman 7-41
Bob Foster (0-2) (UC Davis '62)
UC Davis .... 89 Angelo St. 23-28
UC Davis .... 92 Portland St. 28-42
Dennis Franchione (1-1) (Pittsburg St. '73)
Pittsburg St. .... 89 Northwest Mo. St. 28-7
Pittsburg St. .... 89 Angelo St. 21-24
Fred Freeman (0-1) (Mississippi Val. '66)
Hampton .... 85 Bloomsburg 28-38
Jim Fuller (3-5) (Alabama '67)
Jacksonville St. .... 77 Northern Ariz. 35-0
Jacksonville St. .... 77 North Dakota St. 31-7
Jacksonville St. .... 77 Lehigh 0-33
Jacksonville St. .... 78 Delaware 27-42
Jacksonville St. .... 80 Cal Poly 0-15
Jacksonville St. .... 81 Southwest Tex. St. 22-38
Jacksonville St. .... 82 Truman 34-21
Jacksonville St. .... 82 Southwest Tex. St. 14-19
Chan Gailey (3-0) (Florida '74)
Troy St. .... 84 Central St. 31-21
Troy St. .... 84 Towson 45-3
Troy St. .... 84* North Dakota St. 18-17
Joe Glenn (10-5) (South Dakota '71)
Northern Colo. .... 90 North Dakota St. 7-17
Northern Colo. .... 91 Portland St. 24-28
Northern Colo. .... 95 Pittsburg St. 17-36
Northern Colo. .... 96 Pittsburg St. 24-21
Northern Colo. .... 96 Northwest Mo. St. 27-26
Northern Colo. .... 96 Clarion 19-18
Northern Colo. .... 96* Carson-Newman 23-14
Northern Colo. .... 97 Pittsburg St. 24-16
Northern Colo. .... 97 Northwest Mo. St. 35-19
Northern Colo. .... 97 Carson-Newman 30-29
Northern Colo. .... 97* New Haven 51-0
Northern Colo. .... 98 North Dakota 52-24
Northern Colo. .... 98 Northwest Mo. St. 17-42
Northern Colo. .... 99 Pittsburg St. 34-31
Northern Colo. .... 99 Northwest Mo. St. 35-41
Ray Greene (1-1) (Akron '63)
Alabama A&M .... 79 Morgan St. 27-7
Alabama A&M .... 79 Youngstown St. 0-52
John Gregory (0-1) (Northern Iowa '61)
South Dakota St. .... 79 Youngstown St. 7-50
Herb Grenke (1-1) (Wis.-Milwaukee '63)
Northern Mich. ...... 87 Angelo St. 23-20 (ot)
Northern Mich. ...... 87 Portland St. 7-13
Wayne Grubb (4-3) (Tennessee '61)
North Ala. .... 80 Virginia Union 17-8
North Ala. .... 80 Eastern Ill. 31-56
North Ala. .... 83 Virginia Union 16-14
North Ala. .... 83 Central St. 24-27
North Ala. .... 85 Fort Valley St. 14-7
North Ala. .... 85 Bloomsburg 34-0
North Ala. .... 85 North Dakota St. 7-35
Rocky Hager (12-5) (Minot St. '74)
North Dakota St. .... 88 Augustana (S.D.) 49-7
North Dakota St. .... 88 Millersville 36-26
North Dakota St. .... 88 Cal St. Sacramento 42-20
North Dakota St. .... 88* Portland St. 35-21
North Dakota St. .... 89 Edinboro 45-32
North Dakota St. .... 89 Jacksonville St. 17-21
North Dakota St. .... 89 Northern Colo. 17-7
North Dakota St. .... 90 Cal Poly 47-0
North Dakota St. .... 90 Pittsburg St. 39-29
North Dakota St. .... 90* Indiana (Pa.) 51-11
North Dakota St. .... 91 Minn. St.-Mankato 7-27
North Dakota St. .... 92 Truman 42-7
North Dakota St. .... 92 Pittsburg St. 37-38 (ot)
North Dakota St. .... 94 Pittsburg St. 18-12 (3 ot)
North Dakota St. .... 94 North Dakota 7-14
North Dakota St. .... 95 North Dakota 41-10
North Dakota St. .... 95 Pittsburg St. 7-9
Danny Hale (0-2) (West Chester '68)
West Chester .... 88 Jacksonville St. 24-63
Bloomsburg .... 96 Clarion 29-42
Ron Harms (12-9) (Valparaiso '59)
Tex. A&M-Kingsville .. 88 Mississippi Col. 39-15
Tex. A&M-Kingsville .. 88 Tenn.-Martin 34-0
Tex. A&M-Kingsville .. 88 Portland St. 27-35
Tex. A&M-Kingsville .. 89 Mississippi Col. 19-34
Tex. A&M-Kingsville .. 89 Western St. 22-13
Tex. A&M-Kingsville .. 92 Portland St. 30-35
Tex. A&M-Kingsville .. 93 Portland St. 50-15
Tex. A&M-Kingsville .. 93 UC Davis 51-28
Tex. A&M-Kingsville .. 93 North Ala. 25-27
Tex. A&M-Kingsville .. 94 Western St. 43-7
Tex. A&M-Kingsville .. 94 Portland St. 21-16
Tex. A&M-Kingsville .. 94 Indiana (Pa.) 46-20
Tex. A&M-Kingsville .. 94 North Ala. 10-16
Tex. A&M-Kingsville .. 95 Fort Hays St. 59-28
Tex. A&M-Kingsville .. 95 Portland St. 30-3
Tex. A&M-Kingsville .. 95 Pittsburg St. 25-28 (ot)
Tex. A&M-Kingsville .. 96 UC Davis 14-17
Tex. A&M-Kingsville .. 97 UC Davis 34-37
Tex. A&M-Kingsville .. 98 UC Davis 54-21
Tex. A&M-Kingsville .. 98 Central Okla. 24-21 (ot)
Tex. A&M-Kingsville .. 98 Northwest Mo. St. 34-49
Joe Harper (3-1) (UCLA '59)
Cal Poly .... 78 Winston-Salem 0-17
Cal Poly .... 80 Jacksonville St. 15-0
Cal Poly .... 80 Santa Clara 38-14
Cal Poly .... 80* Eastern Ill. 21-13
Bill Hayes (1-2) (N.C. Central '64)
Winston-Salem .... 78 Cal Poly 17-0
Winston-Salem .... 78 Delaware 0-41
Winston-Salem .... 87 Troy St. 14-45
Jim Heinitz (0-2) (South Dakota St. '72)
Augustana (S.D.) ..... 88 North Dakota St. 7-49
Augustana (S.D.) ..... 89 St. Cloud St. 20-27
Andy Hinson (0-1) (Bethune-Cookman '53)
Bethune-Cookman ... 77 UC Davis 16-34
Sonny Holland (3-0) (Montana St. '60)
Montana St. .... 76 New Hampshire 17-16
Montana St. .... 76 North Dakota St. 10-3
Montana St. .... 76* Akron 24-13
Tom Hollman (1-5) (Ohio Northern '68)
Edinboro .... 89 North Dakota St. 32-45
Edinboro .... 90 Virginia Union 38-14

Joe Glenn, now the head coach at Montana, won back-to-back Division II championships with Northern Colorado in 1996 and 1997.

DIVISION II COACHING RECORDS—CHAMPIONSHIP COACHES   397

Edinboro 90   Indiana (Pa.) 7-14
Edinboro 92   Ferris St. 15-19
Edinboro 93   New Haven 28-48
Edinboro 95   New Haven 12-27
Eric Holm (0-3) (Truman '81)
Truman 90   Pittsburg St. 3-59
Truman 92   North Dakota St. 7-42
Truman 94   North Dakota 6-18
Gary Howard (2-3) (Arkansas '64)
Central Okla. 96   Chadron St. 23-21
Central Okla. 96   UC Davis 6-26
Central Okla. 98   Chadron St. 21-19
Central Okla. 98   Tex. A&M-Kingsville 21-24 (ot)
Central Okla. 99   UC Davis 17-33
Carl Iverson (0-3) (Whitman '62)
Western St. 92   Tex. A&M-Kingsville 13-22
Western St. 94   Tex. A&M-Kingsville 7-43
Western St. 97   Angelo St. 12-46
Billy Joe (3-4) (Villanova '63)
Central St. 83   Southwest Tex. St. 24-16
Central St. 83   North Ala. 27-24
Central St. 83   North Dakota St. 21-41
Central St. 84   Troy St. 21-31
Central St. 85   South Dakota 10-13 (2 ot)
Central St. 86   Towson 31-0
Central St. 86   North Dakota St. 12-35
Gary Keller (0-1) (Bluffton '73)
Ashland 97   Slippery Rock 20-30
Brian Kelly (0-3) (Assumption '83)
Grand Valley St. 91   Tex. A&M-Commerce 15-36
Grand Valley St. 94   Indiana (Pa.) 27-35
Grand Valley St. 98   Slippery Rock 21-37
Roy Kidd (0-1) (Eastern Ky. '54)
Eastern Ky. 76   North Dakota St. 7-10
Jim King (1-1)
West Ala. 75   North Dakota 34-14
West Ala. 75   Northern Mich. 26-28
Tony Knap (1-4) (Idaho '39)
Boise St. 73   South Dakota 53-10
Boise St. 73   Louisiana Tech 34-38
Boise St. 74   Central Mich. 6-20
Boise St. 75   Northern Mich. 21-24
UNLV 76   Akron 6-26
Todd Knight (0-1) (Ouachita Baptist '86)
Delta St. 98   Fort Valley St. 14-21
Roy Kramer (3-0) (Maryville [Tenn.] '53)
Central Mich. 74   Boise St. 20-6
Central Mich. 74   Louisiana Tech 35-14
Central Mich. .... 74*   Delaware 54-14
Gil Krueger (4-2) (Marquette '52)
Northern Mich. 75   Boise St. 24-21
Northern Mich. 75   West Ala. 28-26
Northern Mich. ..... 75*   Western Ky. 16-14
Northern Mich. 76   Delaware 28-17
Northern Mich. 76   Akron 26-29
Northern Mich. 77   North Dakota St. 6-20
Maxie Lambright (4-1) (Southern Miss. '49)
Louisiana Tech 73   Western Ill. 18-13
Louisiana Tech 73   Boise St. 38-34
Louisiana Tech ...... 73*   Western Ky. 34-0
Louisiana Tech 74   Western Carolina 10-7
Louisiana Tech 74   Central Mich. 14-35
George Landis (1-1) (Penn St. '71)
Bloomsburg 85   Hampton 38-28
Bloomsburg 85   North Ala. 0-34
Jon Lantz (0-1) (Okla. Panhandle '74)
Mo. Southern St. ... 93   Minn St.-Mankato 13-34
Henry Lattimore (1-1) (Jackson St. '57)
N.C. Central 88   Winston-Salem 31-16
N.C. Central 88   Cal St. Sacramento 7-56
Dale Lennon (0-1) (North Dakota '85)
North Dakota 99   Northwest Mo. St. 13-20 (ot)
Malen Luke (2-1) (Westminster [Pa.] '76)
Clarion 96   Bloomsburg 42-29
Clarion 96   Ferris St. 23-21
Clarion 96   Northern Colo. 18-19
Bill Lynch (0-1) (Butler '77)
Butler 88   Tenn.-Martin 6-23
Dick MacPherson (0-1) (Springfield '58)
Massachusetts 77   Lehigh 23-30
George Mahalik (3-3) (Slippery Rock '74)
Slippery Rock 97   Ashland 30-20
Slippery Rock 97   New Haven 21-49
Slippery Rock 98   Grand Valley St. 37-21
Slippery Rock 98   Shepherd 31-20

Slippery Rock 98   Carson-Newman 21-47
Slippery Rock 99   Indiana (Pa.) 20-27 (ot)
Pat Malley (1-1) (Santa Clara '53)
Santa Clara............ 80   Northern Mich. 27-26
Santa Clara............ 80   Cal Poly 14-38
Noel Martin (1-1) (Nebraska '63)
St. Cloud St. 89   Augustana (S.D.) 27-20
St. Cloud St. 89   Mississippi Col. 24-55
Fred Martinelli (0-1) (Otterbein '51)
Ashland 86   North Dakota St. 0-50
Bob Mattos (2-1) (Cal St. Sacramento '64)
Cal St. Sacramento.. 88   UC Davis 35-14
Cal St. Sacramento.. 88   N.C. Central 56-7
Cal St. Sacramento.. 88   North Dakota St. 20-42
Gene McDowell (1-1) (Florida St. '65)
UCF....................... 87   Indiana (Pa.) 12-10
UCF....................... 87   Troy St. 10-31
Don McLeary (1-1) (Tennessee '70)
Tenn.-Martin 88   Butler 23-6
Tenn.-Martin 88   Tex. A&M-Kingsville 0-34
Terry McMillan (1-1) (Southern Miss. '69)
Mississippi Col. 91   Wofford 28-15
Mississippi Col. 91   Jacksonville St. 7-35
Ron Meyer (1-1) (Purdue '63)
UNLV 74   Alcorn St. 35-22
UNLV 74   Delaware 11-49
Don Morton (8-3) (Augustana [Ill.] '69)
North Dakota St. 81   Puget Sound 24-10
North Dakota St. 81   Shippensburg 18-6
North Dakota St. 81   Southwest Tex. St. 13-42
North Dakota St. 82   Virginia Union 21-20
North Dakota St. 82   UC Davis 14-19
North Dakota St. 83   Towson 24-17
North Dakota St. 83   UC Davis 26-17
North Dakota St. .... 83*   Central St. 41-21
North Dakota St. 84   UC Davis 31-23
North Dakota St. 84   Neb.-Omaha 25-14
North Dakota St. 84   Troy St. 17-18
Darrell Mudra (5-2) (Peru St. '51)
Western Ill. 73   Louisiana Tech 13-18
Eastern Ill. 78   UC Davis 35-31
Eastern Ill. 78   Youngstown St. 26-22
Eastern Ill. .... 78*   Delaware 10-9
Eastern Ill. 80   Northern Colo. 21-14
Eastern Ill. 80   North Ala. 56-31
Eastern Ill. 80   Cal Poly 13-21
Steve Mullins (0-1) (Ark-Monticello '80)
Arkansas Tech 99   Carson-Newman 28-40
Hal Mumme (2-2) (Tarleton St. '75)
Valdosta St. 94   Albany St. (Ga.) 14-7
Valdosta St. 94   North Ala. 24-27 (2 ot)
Valdosta St. 96   Albany St. (Ga.) 38-28
Valdosta St. 96   Carson-Newman 19-24
Gene Murphy (0-1) (North Dakota '62)
North Dakota 79   Mississippi Col. 15-35
Bill Narduzzi (3-2) (Miami [Ohio] '59)
Youngstown St. 78   Neb.-Omaha 21-14
Youngstown St. 78   Eastern Ill. 22-26
Youngstown St. 79   South Dakota St. 50-7
Youngstown St. 79   Alabama A&M 52-0
Youngstown St. 79   Delaware 21-38
John O'Hara (0-1) (Okla. Panhandle '67)
Southwest Tex. St. .. 83   Central St. 16-24
Jerry Olson (0-1) (Valley City St. '55)
North Dakota 75   West Ala. 14-34
Keith Otterbein (3-2) (Ferris St. '79)
Ferris St. 92   Edinboro 19-15
Ferris St. 92   New Haven 13-35
Ferris St. 93   Indiana (Pa.) 21-28
Ferris St. 94   West Chester 43-40
Ferris St. 94   Indiana (Pa.) 17-21
Jeff Pierce (3-2) (Ferris St. '79)
Ferris St. 95   Millersville 36-26
Ferris St. 95   New Haven 17-9
Ferris St. 95   North Ala. 7-45
Ferris St. 96   Indiana (Pa.) 24-23
Ferris St. 96   Clarion 21-23
Doug Porter (0-1) (Xavier [La.] '52)
Fort Valley St. 82   Southwest Tex. St. 6-27
George Pugh (0-1) (Alabama '76)
Alabama A&M....... 89   Jacksonville St. 9-33
Bill Rademacher (1-3) (Northern Mich. '63)
Northern Mich. 80   Santa Clara 6-27
Northern Mich. 81   Elizabeth City St. 55-6

Northern Mich. 81   Southwest Tex. St. 0-62
Northern Mich. 82   UC Davis 21-42
Vito Ragazzo (1-1) (William & Mary '51)
Shippensburg 81   Virginia Union 40-27
Shippensburg 81   North Dakota St. 6-18
Tubby Raymond (7-4) (Michigan '50)
Delaware 73   Grambling 8-17
Delaware 74   Youngstown St. 35-14
Delaware 74   UNLV 49-11
Delaware 74   Central Mich. 14-54
Delaware 76   Northern Mich. 17-28
Delaware 78   Jacksonville St. 42-27
Delaware 78   Winston-Salem 41-0
Delaware 78   Eastern Ill. 9-10
Delaware 79   Virginia Union 58-28
Delaware 79   Mississippi Col. 60-10
Delaware .... 79*   Youngstown St. 38-21
Rocky Rees (1-1) (West Chester '71)
Shippensburg 91   East Stroudsburg 34-33
Shippensburg 91   Indiana (Pa.) 7-52
Rick Rhodes (4-1)
Troy St. 86   Virginia Union 31-7
Troy St. 86   South Dakota 28-42
Troy St. 87   Winston-Salem 45-14
Troy St. 87   Central Fla. 31-10
Troy St. .... 87*   Portland St. 31-17
Pete Richardson (0-3) (Dayton '68)
Winston-Salem 88   N.C. Central 16-31
Winston-Salem 90   Indiana (Pa.) 0-48
Winston-Salem 91   Jacksonville St. 24-49
Steve Roberts (0-1) (Ouachita Baptist '87)
Southern Ark. 97   Albany St. (Ga.) 6-10
Eddie Robinson (1-1) (Leland '41)
Grambling.............. 73   Delaware 17-8
Grambling.............. 73   Western Ky. 20-28
Warren Ruggerio (0-1) (Delaware '88)
Glenville St. 97   New Haven 7-47
Dan Runkle (2-3) (Illinois Col. '68)
Minn. St.-Mankato .. 87   Portland St. 21-27
Minn. St.-Mankato .. 91   North Dakota St. 27-7
Minn. St.-Mankato .. 91   Portland St. 27-37
Minn. St.-Mankato .. 93   Mo. Southern St. 34-13
Minn. St.-Mankato .. 93   North Dakota 21-54
Joe Salem (0-2) (Minnesota '61)
South Dakota......... 73   Boise St. 10-53
Northern Ariz. 77   Jacksonville St. 0-35
Kent Schoolfield (1-2) (Florida A&M '70)
Fort Valley St. 98   Delta St. 21-14
Fort Valley St. 98   Carson-Newman 31-38 (ot)
Fort Valley St. 99   Catawba 17-48
Lyle Setencich (1-1) (Fresno St. '68)
Cal Poly 90   Cal St. Northridge 14-7
Cal Poly 90   North Dakota 0-47
Stan Sheriff (0-1) (Cal Poly '54)
Northern Iowa 75   Western Ky. 12-14
Sanders Shiver (0-1) (Carson-Newman '76)
Bowie St. 88   Portland St. 17-34
Ron Simonson (0-1) (Portland St. '65)
Puget Sound 81   North Dakota St. 10-24
Brad Smith (0-2) (Western Ill. '72)
Chadron St. 96   Central Okla. 21-23
Chadron St. 98   Central Okla. 19-21
Hampton Smith (1-5) (Mississippi Val. '57)
Albany St. (Ga.) 93   Hampton 7-33
Albany St. (Ga.) 94   Valdosta St. 7-14
Albany St. (Ga.) 95   North Ala. 28-38
Albany St. (Ga.) 96   Valdosta St. 28-38
Albany St. (Ga.) 97   Southern Ark. 10-6
Albany St. (Ga.) 97   Carson-Newman 22-23
Rob Smith (0-1) (Washington '81)
Western Wash. 99   Northeastern St. 24-27 (ot)
Jim Sochor (4-8) (San Fran. St. '60)
UC Davis 77   Bethune-Cookman 34-16
UC Davis 77   Lehigh 30-39
UC Davis 78   Eastern Ill. 31-35
UC Davis 82   Northern Mich. 42-21
UC Davis 82   North Dakota St. 19-14
UC Davis 82   Southwest Tex. St. 9-34
UC Davis 83   Butler 25-6
UC Davis 83   North Dakota St. 17-26
UC Davis 84   North Dakota St. 23-31
UC Davis 85   North Dakota St. 12-31
UC Davis 86   South Dakota 23-26
UC Davis 88   Cal St. Sacramento 14-35

Earle Solomonson (6-0) (Augsburg '69)
North Dakota St.	85	UC Davis 31-12
North Dakota St.	85	South Dakota 16-7
North Dakota St.	85*	North Ala. 35-7
North Dakota St.	86	Ashland 50-0
North Dakota St.	86	Central St. 35-1 2
North Dakota St.	86*	South Dakota 27-7

Tony Sparano (4-2) (New Haven '82)
New Haven	95	Edinboro 27-12
New Haven	95	Ferris St. 9-17
New Haven	97	Glenville St. 47-7
New Haven	97	Slippery Rock 49-21
New Haven	97	UC Davis 27-25
New Haven	97	Northern Colo. 0-51

Ken Sparks (12-7) (Carson-Newman '68)
Carson-Newman	93	North Ala. 28-38
Carson-Newman	94	North Ala. 13-17
Carson-Newman	95	West Ga. 37-26
Carson-Newman	95	North Ala. 7-28
Carson-Newman	96	West Ga. 41-7
Carson-Newman	96	Valdosta St. 24-19
Carson-Newman	96	UC Davis 29-26
Carson-Newman	96	Northern Colo. 14-23
Carson-Newman	97	North Ala. 21-7
Carson-Newman	97	Albany St. (Ga.) 23-22
Carson-Newman	97	Northern Colo. 29-30
Carson-Newman	98	West Ga. 30-20
Carson-Newman	98	Fort Valley St. 38-31 (ot)
Carson-Newman	98	Slippery Rock 47-21
Carson-Newman	98	Northwest Mo. St. 6-24
Carson-Newman	99	Arkansas Tech 40-28
Carson-Newman	99	Catawba 28-25
Carson-Newman	99	Northeastern St. 42-7
Carson-Newman	99*	Northwest Mo. St. 52-58 (4 ot)

Glenn Spencer (0-1) (Georgia Tech '86)
West Ga.	98	Carson-Newman 20-30

Bill Sylvester (0-1) (Butler '50)
Butler	83	UC Davis 6-25

Joe Taylor (1-5) (Western Ill. '72)
Virginia Union	86	Troy St. 7-31
Virginia Union	90	Edinboro 14-38
Virginia Union	91	Indiana (Pa.) 7-56
Hampton	92	North Ala. 21-33
Hampton	93	Albany St. (Ga.) 33-7
Hampton	93	North Ala. 20-45

Clarence Thomas (0-1)
Morgan St.	79	Alabama A&M 7-27

Roger Thomas (4-5) (Augustana [Ill.] '69)
North Dakota	92	Pittsburg St. 21-26
North Dakota	93	Pittsburg St. 17-14
North Dakota	93	Minn. St.-Mankato 54-21
North Dakota	93	Indiana (Pa.) 6-21
North Dakota	94	Truman 18-6
North Dakota	94	North Dakota St. 14-7
North Dakota	94	North Ala. 7-35
North Dakota	95	North Dakota St. 10-41
North Dakota	98	Northern Colo. 24-52

Vern Thomsen (0-1) (Peru St. '61)
Northwest Mo. St.	84	Neb.-Omaha 15-28

Mel Tjeerdsma (10-2) (Southern St. '67)
Northwest Mo. St.	96	Neb.-Omaha 22-21
Northwest Mo. St.	96	Northern Colo. 26-27
Northwest Mo. St.	97	North Dakota St. 39-28
Northwest Mo. St.	97	Northern Colo. 19-35
Northwest Mo. St.	98	Neb.-Omaha 28-14
Northwest Mo. St.	98	Northern Colo. 42-17
Northwest Mo. St.	98	Tex. A&M-Kingsville 49-34
Northwest Mo. St.	98*	Carson-Newman 24-6
Northwest Mo. St.	99	North Dakota 20-13 (ot)
Northwest Mo. St.	99	Northern Colo. 41-35
Northwest Mo. St.	99	Indiana (Pa.) 20-12
Northwest Mo. St.	99*	Carson-Newman 58-52 (4 ot)

Dave Triplett (3-2) (Iowa '72)
South Dakota	85	Central St. 13-10 (2 ot)
South Dakota	85	North Dakota St. 7-16
South Dakota	86	UC Davis 26-23
South Dakota	86	Troy St. 42-28
South Dakota	86	North Dakota St. 7-27

Jerry Vandergriff (3-4) (Corpus Christi '65)
Angelo St.	87	Northern Mich. 20-23 (ot)
Angelo St.	89	UC Davis 28-23
Angelo St.	89	Pittsburg St. 24-21
Angelo St.	89	Jacksonville St. 16-34
Angelo St.	94	Portland St. 0-29
Angelo St.	97	Western St. 46-12
Angelo St.	97	UC Davis 33-50

Eddie Vowell (2-3) (Southwestern Okla. '69)
Tex. A&M-Commerce	90	Grand Valley St. 20-14
Tex. A&M-Commerce	90	Pittsburg St. 28-60
Tex. A&M-Commerce	91	Grand Valley St. 36-15
Tex. A&M-Commerce	91	Pittsburg St. 28-38
Tex. A&M-Commerce	95	Portland St. 35-56

Jim Wacker (8-2) (Valparaiso '60)
North Dakota St.	76	Eastern Ky. 10-7
North Dakota St.	76	Montana St. 3-10
North Dakota St.	77	Northern Mich. 20-6
North Dakota St.	77	Jacksonville St. 7-31
Southwest Tex. St.	81	Jacksonville St. 38-22
Southwest Tex. St.	81	Northern Mich. 62-0
Southwest Tex. St.	81*	North Dakota 42-13
Southwest Tex. St.	82	Fort Valley St. 27-6
Southwest Tex. St.	82	Jacksonville St. 19-14
Southwest Tex. St.	82*	UC Davis 34-9

Gerald Walker (0-1) (Lincoln [Mo.] '62)
Fort Valley St.	85	North Ala. 7-14

Bobby Wallace (13-3) (Mississippi St. '76)
North Ala.	90	Jacksonville St. 14-38
North Ala.	92	Hampton 33-21
North Ala.	92	Jacksonville St. 12-14
North Ala.	93	Carson-Newman 38-28
North Ala.	93	Hampton 45-20
North Ala.	93	Tex. A&M-Kingsville 27-25
North Ala.	93*	Indiana (Pa.) 41-34
North Ala.	94	Carson-Newman 17-13
North Ala.	94	Valdosta St. 27-24 (2 ot)
North Ala.	94	North Dakota 35-7
North Ala.	94*	Tex. A&M-Kingsville 16-10
North Ala.	95	Albany St. (Ga.) 38-28
North Ala.	95	Carson-Newman 28-7
North Ala.	95	Ferris St. 45-7
North Ala.	95*	Pittsburg St. 27-7
North Ala.	97	Carson-Newman 7-21

Tim Walsh (2-3) (UC Riverside '77)
Portland St.	93	Tex. A&M-Kingsville 15-50
Portland St.	94	Angelo St. 29-0
Portland St.	94	Tex. A&M-Kingsville 16-21
Portland St.	95	Tex. A&M-Commerce 56-35
Portland St.	95	Tex. A&M-Kingsville 3-30

Johnnie Walton (0-1) (Elizabeth City St. '69)
Elizabeth City St.	81	Northern Mich. 6-55

Bob Waters (0-1) (Presbyterian '60)
Western Carolina	74	Louisiana Tech 7-10

Mark Whipple (3-2) (Brown '79)
New Haven	92	West Chester 38-26
New Haven	92	Ferris St. 35-13
New Haven	92	Jacksonville St. 35-46
New Haven	93	Edinboro 48-28
New Haven	93	Indiana (Pa.) 35-38

John Whitehead (3-0) (East Stroudsburg '50)
Lehigh	77	Massachusetts 30-23
Lehigh	77	UC Davis 39-30
Lehigh	77*	Jacksonville St. 33-0

John Williams (†7-3) (Mississippi Col. '57)
Mississippi Col.	79	North Dakota 35-15
Mississippi Col.	79	Delaware 10-60
Mississippi Col.	88	Tex. A&M-Kingsville 15-39
Mississippi Col.	89†	Tex. A&M-Kingsville 34-19
Mississippi Col.	89†	St. Cloud St. 55-24
Mississippi Col.	89†	Indiana (Pa.) 26-14
Mississippi Col.	89†*	Jacksonville St. 3-0
Mississippi Col.	90†	Wofford 70-19
Mississippi Col.	90†	Jacksonville St. 14-7
Mississippi Col.	90†	Indiana (Pa.) 8-27

*National championship. †Mississippi College's participation vacated by action of the NCAA Committee on Infractions.

Division III Coaching Records

Winningest Active Division III Coaches

(Minimum five years as college head coach; record at four-year colleges only.)

BY PERCENTAGE

Coach, College	Years	Won	Lost	Tied	+Pct.	Playoffs# W-L-T
Larry Kehres, Mount Union	14	150	17	3	.89118	24-6-0
Dick Farley, Williams	13	88	13	3	.86058	0-0-0
Tom Clark, Catholic	6	50	10	1	.82787	0-3-0
K. C. Keeler, Rowan	7	70	17	1	.80114	18-6-0
John Gagliardi, St. John's (Minn.)	51	364	107	11	.76660	16-11-0
Frosty Westering, Pacific Lutheran	35	277	84	7	.76223	5-1-0
Frank Girardi, Lycoming	28	211	66	5	.75709	12-10-0
Bob Packard, Baldwin-Wallace	19	144	46	2	.75521	0-2-0
Wayne Perry, Hanover	8	62	21	4	.74699	0-3-0
Rich Lackner, Carnegie Mellon	14	102	35	2	.74101	0-1-0
Jim Barnes, Augustana (Ill.)	5	37	13	0	.74000	1-1-0
Jimmie Keeling, Hardin-Simmons	10	81	29	0	.73636	2-1-0
Lou Wacker, Emory & Henry	18	138	51	0	.73016	3-4-0
Joe King, Rensselaer	11	73	28	2	.71845	0-1-0
John Audino, Union (N.Y.)	10	71	28	0	.71717	1-1-0
Jim Williams, Simpson	13	96	38	1	.71481	2-5-0
Mike Welch, Ithaca	6	45	18	0	.71429	2-1-0
Mike Drass, Wesley	7	50	20	1	.71127	0-0-0
Vance Gibson, Howard Payne	5	35	15	0	.70000	0-0-0
John Miech, Wis.-Stevens Point	12	83	35	0	.70000	0-1-0
Darwin Breaux, Dickinson	7	50	22	1	.69178	0-1-0
Norm Eash, Ill. Wesleyan	13	83	37	1	.69008	2-2-0
Mike Maynard, Redlands	12	75	34	1	.68636	0-2-0
Jim Christopherson, Concordia-M'head	31	213	96	7	.68513	7-4-1
Doug Neibhur, Millikin	11	72	33	1	.68396	0-2-0
Rick Giancola, Montclair St.	17	118	56	2	.67614	5-4-0
Steve Briggs, Susquehanna	10	68	34	0	.66667	2-1-0
Greg Carlson, Wabash	17	106	53	2	.66460	0-0-0
Bob Berezowitz, Wis.-Whitewater	15	101	50	4	.66452	1-3-0
Bob Frey, MacMurray	5	33	17	0	.66000	0-0-0
Mike Hollway, Ohio Wesleyan	13	85	44	1	.65769	0-0-0
John O'Grady, Wis.-River Falls	11	71	38	3	.64732	1-2-0
Ron Ernst, Ripon	9	55	30	0	.64706	0-0-0
Steve Johnson, Bethel (Minn.)	10	64	35	0	.64646	0-0-0
Steven Mohr, Trinity (Tex.)	10	69	38	0	.64486	5-4-0
Don Morel, La Verne	5	29	16	0	.64444	0-0-0
Roger Caron, Pomona-Pitzer	6	32	18	0	.64000	0-0-0
Tom Gilburg, Frank. & Marsh.	25	155	87	0	.63934	0-0-0

WINNINGEST ACTIVE DIVISION III COACHES BY PERCENTAGE

Coach, College	Years	Won	Lost	Tied	+Pct.	Playoffs# W-L-T
Tom Shea, William Penn	15	97	55	3	.63548	0-0-0
Eric Hamilton, Col. Of New Jersey	23	143	84	6	.62661	3-4-0
Tim Keating, Western Md.	12	74	44	3	.62397	1-3-0
Scot Dapp, Moravian	13	82	50	1	.62030	1-2-0
Nick Mourouzis, DePauw	19	115	70	4	.61905	0-0-0
Charlie Pravata, Merchant Marine	9	52	33	2	.60920	2-1-0
Dick Maloney, Chicago	6	34	22	0	.60714	0-0-0
Ed Sweeney, Frostburg St.	15	92	59	4	.60645	0-2-0
Jim Scott, Aurora	14	72	50	3	.58800	0-1-0
Craig Rundle, Albion	14	77	54	1	.58712	0-1-0
Jerry Boyes, Buffalo St.	14	82	58	0	.58571	2-7-0
Larry Kindbom, Washington (Mo.)	17	98	70	1	.58284	0-1-0
Bill Kavanaugh, Mass.-Dartmouth	10	56	41	0	.57732	0-0-0
Steve Miller, Cornell College	21	111	82	3	.57398	0-1-0
Don Ruggeri, Mass. Maritime	27	139	106	1	.56707	0-0-0
Bob Bierie, Loras	14	80	61	1	.56690	0-0-0
Brien Cullen, Worcester St.	15	81	62	1	.56643	0-0-0
Jim Margraff, Johns Hopkins	10	55	42	3	.56500	0-0-0
Dale Widolff, Occidental	18	93	72	2	.56287	1-3-0
Frank Hauser, Wesleyan (Conn.)	8	36	28	0	.56250	0-0-0
Dick Tressel, Hamline	22	121	94	3	.56221	0-0-0
Peter Mazzaferro, Bri'water (Mass.)	36	180	139	11	.56212	0-1-0
Jum Cole, Alma	9	46	36	0	.56098	0-1-0
Mickey Heinecken, Middlebury	27	119	95	2	.55556	0-0-0
Nick Fletcher, Denison	5	27	22	0	.55102	0-0-0
Mike Cragg, Hobart	5	26	22	0	.54167	0-0-0
Barry Streeter, Gettysburg	22	118	100	5	.54036	2-1-0
Mike Hodgson, Maine Maritime	6	31	27	0	.53448	0-0-0
Dave Murray, Alfred	10	55	48	1	.53365	0-1-0
Ed DeGeorge, Beloit	23	111	100	4	.52594	0-0-0
Mike DeLong, Springfield	18	91	82	2	.52571	0-1-0
Ken Visser, Chapman	9	42	38	1	.52469	0-0-0
Rocco Salomone, Brockport St.	5	25	23	1	.52041	0-0-0
Bill Samko, Tufts	13	56	54	1	.50901	0-0-0
Merle Masonholder, Carroll (Wis.)	18	83	81	0	.50610	0-0-0
Jack Osberg, Augsburg	9	46	45	0	.50549	1-1-0
Tom Kaczkowski, Ohio Northern	14	70	69	2	.50355	1-1-0
Terry Price, Maranatha Baptist	22	102	103	1	.49757	0-0-0
Dean Kreps, Hope	5	22	23	0	.48889	0-0-0
Bob Sullivan, Carleton	21	100	105	0	.48780	0-1-0
Jim Sypult, Methodist	8	39	41	0	.48750	0-0-0
Jeff Heacock, Muskingum	19	89	94	4	.48663	0-0-0
Jay Schoenebeck, Gust. Adolphus	6	29	31	0	.48333	0-0-0
Phil Wilks, Maryville (Tenn.)	12	57	61	0	.48305	0-0-0
Dan Baranik, Waynesburg	6	26	28	0	.48148	0-0-0
Steve Stetson, Hartwick	14	62	67	4	.48120	0-0-0
Frank Miriello, Wash. & Lee	5	23	25	1	.47959	0-0-0
Paul Rudolph, Upper Iowa	9	43	47	0	.47778	0-0-0
Mike Ketchum, Guilford	9	42	46	0	.47727	0-0-0
Gene Epley, Marietta	8	37	41	2	.47500	0-0-0
Dave Davis, Ferrum	6	27	31	0	.46552	0-0-0
Steve Marino, Westfield St.	10	45	52	1	.46429	0-0-0
Larry Terry, Wis.-La Crosse	5	25	29	1	.46364	0-0-0
John Tully, Whitworth	10	45	54	1	.45500	0-0-0
Steve Campos, Bethany (W.Va.)	7	31	38	1	.45000	0-0-0
Jim Lyall, Adrian	10	39	50	1	.43889	0-0-0
Chris Smith, Grove City	16	63	85	2	.42667	0-0-0
Rick Candaele, Claremont-M-S	8	31	42	0	.42466	0-0-0
Roy Miller, New Jersey City	15	62	84	0	.42466	0-0-0
Tom Austin, Colby	14	47	64	1	.42411	0-0-0
Theophilus Danzy, Stillman	11	44	61	3	.42130	0-0-0
Mike Wallace, Wilmington (Ohio)	9	36	51	1	.41477	0-0-0
Dennis Gorsline, Martin Luther	29	103	153	1	.40272	0-0-0
Dwight Smith, MIT	12	39	59	1	.39899	0-0-0
Carlin Carpenter, Bluffton	10	38	58	0	.39583	0-0-0
Regis Scafe, John Carroll	6	23	37	1	.38333	0-0-0
Greg Wallace, Grinnell	12	41	68	1	.37727	0-0-0
Larry Shank, Heidelberg	10	36	61	3	.37500	0-0-0
Ed Meierkort, Wis.-Stout	7	26	44	0	.37143	0-0-0
Bill Unsworth, Franklin	10	35	61	1	.36598	0-0-0
Sherman Wood, Salisbury St.	7	25	44	1	.36429	0-0-0
Dave Harms, Manchester	5	18	32	0	.36000	0-0-0
A. Wallace Hood, Otterbein	5	18	32	0	.36000	0-0-0
Tim Rucks, Carthage	10	30	56	4	.35556	0-0-0
Gerry Martin, Western New Eng.	9	25	53	1	.32278	0-0-0
William T. Kirlen, FDU-Madison	23	64	136	1	.32090	0-0-0
Vince Arduini, Kenyon	5	15	34	1	.31000	0-0-0
Bob Tyler, Millsaps	7	23	53	2	.30769	1-0-0
Greg Polnasek, Colorado Col.	7	19	47	0	.28788	0-0-0
Paul Vosburgh, St. John Fisher	12	32	80	1	.28761	0-0-0
Randy Moore, Lake Forest	5	13	34	0	.27660	0-0-0
Frank Carr, Earlham	15	37	108	1	.25517	0-0-0
Rich Mannello, King's (Pa.)	7	17	51	1	.25362	0-0-0
Michael Clark, Bridgewater (Va.)	5	12	37	1	.25000	0-0-0
Dallas Hilliar, Olivet	7	15	48	0	.23810	0-0-0
Paul Krohn, Elmhurst	7	14	48	1	.23016	0-0-0
Bob Thomas, Hiram	8	16	64	0	.20000	0-0-0
Gordon Elliott, Puget Sound	6	11	44	0	.20000	0-0-0
Mike Strachan, Framingham St.	6	10	46	1	.18421	0-0-0
Mike Liljegren, North Park	5	6	39	0	.13333	0-0-0

#Record in Division III Championship and/or bowl games. +Ties computed as half won and half lost.

BY VICTORIES
(Minimum 100 Victories)

Coach, College, Win Pct.	Won
John Gagliardi, St. John's (Minn.)	364
Frosty Westering, Pacific Lutheran	277
Jim Christopherson, Concordia-M'head	213
Frank Girardi, Lycoming	211
Peter Mazzaferro, Bri'water (Mass.)	180
Tom Gilburg, Frank. & Marsh.	155
Larry Kehres, Mount Union	150
Bob Packard, Baldwin-Wallace	144
Eric Hamilton, Col. Of New Jersey	143
Don Ruggeri, Mass. Maritime	139
Lou Wacker, Emory & Henry	138
Dick Tressel, Hamline	121
Mickey Heinecken, Middlebury	119
Rick Giancola, Montclair St.	118
Barry Streeter, Gettysburg	118
Nick Mourouzis, DePauw	115
Steve Miller, Cornell College	111
Ed DeGeorge, Beloit	111
Greg Carlson, Wabash	106
Dennis Gorsline, Martin Luther	103
Rich Lackner, Carnegie Mellon	102
Terry Price, Maranatha Baptist	102
Bob Berezowitz, Wis.-Whitewater	101
Bob Sullivan, Carleton	100

Division III Championship Coaches

All coaches who have coached teams in the Division III championship playoffs since 1973 are listed here with their playoff record, alma mater and year graduated, team, year coached, opponent, and score.

Phil Albert (2-1) (Arizona '66)
Towson .... 76 LIU-C. W. Post 14-10
Towson .... 76 St. Lawrence 38-36
Towson .... 76 St. John's (Minn.) 28-31

Dom Anile (0-1) (C. W. Post '59)
C. W. Post .... 76 Towson 10-14

John Audino (1-2) (Notre Dame '75)
Union (N.Y.) .... 93 Wm. Paterson 7-17
Union (N.Y.) .... 95 Plymouth St. 24-7
Union (N.Y.) .... 95 Rowan 7-38

Don Ault (0-1) (West Liberty St. '52)
Bethany (W.Va.) ..... 80 Widener 12-43

Al Bagnoli (7-6) (Central Conn. St. '74)
Union (N.Y.) .... 83 Hofstra 51-19
Union (N.Y.) .... 83 Salisbury St. 23-21
Union (N.Y.) .... 83 Augustana (Ill.) 17-21
Union (N.Y.) .... 84 Plymouth St. 26-14
Union (N.Y.) .... 84 Augustana (Ill.) 6-23
Union (N.Y.) .... 85 Ithaca 12-13
Union (N.Y.) .... 86 Ithaca 17-24 (ot)
Union (N.Y.) .... 89 Cortland St. 42-14
Union (N.Y.) .... 89 Montclair St. 45-6
Union (N.Y.) .... 89 Ferrum 37-21
Union (N.Y.) .... 89 Dayton 7-17
Union (N.Y.) .... 91 Mass.-Lowell 55-16
Union (N.Y.) .... 91 Ithaca 23-35

John Banaszak (1-1) (Eastern Mich. '75)
Wash. & Jeff. .... 99 Lycoming 14-7
Wash. & Jeff. .... 99 Hardin-Simmons 3-51

Bob Berezowitz (1-3) (Wis.-Whitewater '67)
Wis.-Whitewater..... 88 Simpson 29-27
Wis.-Whitewater..... 88 Central (Iowa) 13-16
Wis.-Whitewater..... 90 St. Thomas (Minn.) 23-24
Wis.-Whitewater..... 97 Simpson 31-34

Don Birmingham (0-2) (Westmar '62)
Dubuque .... 79 Ithaca 7-27
Dubuque .... 80 Minn.-Morris 35-41

J. R. Bishop (1-1) (Franklin '61)
Wheaton (Ill.) .... 95 Wittenberg 63-41
Wheaton (Ill.) .... 95 Mount Union 14-40

Jim Blackburn (0-1) (Virginia '71)
Randolph-Macon..... 84 Wash. & Jeff. 21-22

Bill Bless (0-1) (Indianapolis '63)
Indianapolis............ 75 Wittenberg 13-17

Jerry Boyes (2-7) (Ithaca '76)
Buffalo St. .... 92 Ithaca 28-26
Buffalo St. .... 92 Rowan 19-28
Buffalo St. .... 93 Rowan 6-29
Buffalo St. .... 94 Ithaca 7-10 (2 ot)
Buffalo St. .... 95 Rowan 7-46
Buffalo St. .... 96 Rowan 20-21
Buffalo St. .... 98 Springfield 38-35
Buffalo St. .... 98 Rowan 17-19
Buffalo St. .... 99 Montclair St. 34-37

Darwin Breaux (0-1) (West Chester '77)
Dickinson .... 94 Widener 0-14

Steve Briggs (2-1) (Springfield '84)
Susquehanna .... 91 Dickinson 21-20
Susquehanna .... 91 Lycoming 31-24
Susquehanna .... 91 Ithaca 13-49

Don Brown (1-2) (Norwich '77)
Plymouth St. .... 94 Merchant Marine 19-18
Plymouth St. .... 94 Ithaca 7-22
Plymouth St. .... 95 Union (N.Y.) 7-24

John Bunting (2-2) (North Carolina '72)
Rowan .... 91 Ithaca 10-31
Rowan .... 92 Worcester Tech 41-14
Rowan .... 92 Buffalo St. 28-19
Rowan .... 92 Wash. & Jeff. 13-18

Jim Butterfield (21-8) (Maine '53)
Ithaca .... 74 Slippery Rock 27-14
Ithaca .... 74 Central (Iowa) 8-10
Ithaca .... 75 Fort Valley St. 41-12
Ithaca .... 75 Widener 23-14
Ithaca .... 75 Wittenberg 0-28
Ithaca .... 78 Wittenberg 3-6
Ithaca .... 79 Dubuque 27-7
Ithaca .... 79 Carnegie Mellon 15-6
Ithaca .... 79* Wittenberg 14-10
Ithaca .... 80 Wagner 41-13
Ithaca .... 80 Minn.-Morris 36-0
Ithaca .... 80 Dayton 0-63
Ithaca .... 85 Union (N.Y.) 13-12
Ithaca .... 85 Montclair St. 50-28
Ithaca .... 85 Gettysburg 34-0
Ithaca .... 85 Augustana (Ill.) 7-20
Ithaca .... 86 Union (N.Y.) 24-17 (ot)
Ithaca .... 86 Montclair St. 29-15
Ithaca .... 86 Salisbury St. 40-44
Ithaca .... 88 Wagner 34-31 (ot)
Ithaca .... 88 Cortland St. 24-17
Ithaca .... 88 Ferrum 62-28
Ithaca .... 88* Central (Iowa) 39-24
Ithaca .... 90 Col. of New Jersey 14-24
Ithaca .... 91 Rowan 31-10
Ithaca .... 91 Union (N.Y.) 35-23
Ithaca .... 91 Susquehanna 49-13
Ithaca .... 91* Dayton 34-20
Ithaca .... 92 Buffalo St. 26-28

Jim Byers (0-1) (Michigan '59)
Evansville .... 74 Central (Iowa) 16-17

Don Canfield (0-1)
Wartburg .... 82 Bishop 7-32

Jerry Carle (0-1) (Northwestern '48)
Colorado Col. ...... 75 Millsaps 21-28

Gene Carpenter (0-1) (Huron '63)
Millersville .... 79 Wittenberg 14-21

Rick Carter (3-1) (Earlham '65)
Dayton .... 78 Carnegie Mellon 21-24
Dayton .... 80 Baldwin-Wallace 34-0
Dayton .... 80 Widener 28-24
Dayton .... 80* Ithaca 63-0

John Cervino (0-1) (West Va. Wesleyan '82)
Western Conn. St. . 99 Montclair St. 24-32

Don Charlton (0-1) (Lock Haven '65)
Hiram .... 87 Augustana (Ill.) 0-53

Jim Christopherson (2-4) (Concordia-M'head '60)
Concordia-M'head .. 86 Wis.-Stevens Point 24-15
Concordia-M'head .. 86 Central (Iowa) 17-14
Concordia-M'head .. 86 Augustana (Ill.) 7-41
Concordia-M'head .. 88 Central (Iowa) 0-7
Concordia-M'head .. 95 Wis.-La Crosse 7-45
Concordia-M'head .. 97 Augsburg 22-34

Tom Clark (0-3) (Maryland '86)
Catholic .... 97 Trinity (Tex.) 33-44
Catholic .... 98 Lycoming 14-49
Catholic .... 99 Western Md. 16-20

Vic Clark (0-1) (Indiana St. '71)
Thomas More .... 92 Emory & Henry 0-17

Mike Clary (0-1) (Rhodes '77)
Rhodes .... 88 Ferrum 10-35

Jim Cole (0-1) (Alma '74)
Alma .... 99 Wittenberg 19-42

Jay Cottone (0-1) (Norwich '71)
Plymouth St. .... 84 Union (N.Y.) 14-26

Bill Cubit (1-2) (Delaware '75)
Widener .... 94 Dickinson 14-0
Widener .... 94 Wash. & Jeff. 21-37
Widener .... 95 Lycoming 27-31

Scot Dapp (1-2) (West Chester '73)
Moravian .... 88 Widener 17-7
Moravian .... 88 Ferrum 28-49
Moravian .... 93 Wash. & Jeff. 7-27

Harper Davis (1-1) (Mississippi St. '49)
Millsaps .... 75 Colorado Col. 28-21
Millsaps .... 75 Wittenberg 22-55

Tony DeCarlo (1-2) (Kent '62)
John Carroll .... 89 Dayton 10-35
John Carroll .... 97 Hanover 30-20
John Carroll .... 97 Mount Union 7-59

Mike DeLong (0-1) (Springfield '74)
Springfield .... 98 Buffalo St. 35-38

Joe DeMelfi (0-1) (Delta St. '66)
Wilkes .... 93 Frostburg St. 25-26

Bob Di Spirito (0-1) (Rhode Island '53)
Slippery Rock .... 74 Ithaca 14-27

Norm Eash (2-2) (Ill. Wesleyan '75)
Ill. Wesleyan .... 92 Aurora 21-12
Ill. Wesleyan .... 92 Mount Union 27-49
Ill. Wesleyan .... 96 Albion 23-20
Ill. Wesleyan .... 96 Mount Union 14-49

Ed Farrell (0-1) (Rutgers '56)
Bridgeport .... 73 Juniata 14-35

Joe Fincham (2-2) (Ohio '88)
Wittenberg .... 98 Millikin 13-10
Wittenberg .... 98 Mount Union 19-21
Wittenberg .... 99 Alma 42-19
Wittenberg .... 99 Ohio Northern 24-58

Bob Ford (1-1) (Springfield '59)
Albany (N.Y.) .... 77 Hampden-Sydney 51-45
Albany (N.Y.) .... 77 Widener 15-33

Stokeley Fulton (0-1) (Hampden-Sydney '55)
Hampden-Sydney .... 77 Albany (N.Y.) 45-51

John Gagliardi (16-10) (Colorado Col. '49)
St. John's (Minn.) ... 76 Augustana (Ill.) 46-7
St. John's (Minn.) ... 76 Buena Vista 61-0
St. John's (Minn.) ... 76* Towson 31-28
St. John's (Minn.) ... 77 Wabash 9-20
St. John's (Minn.) ... 85 Occidental 10-28
St. John's (Minn.) ... 87 Gust. Adolphus 7-3
St. John's (Minn.) ... 87 Central (Iowa) 3-13
St. John's (Minn.) ... 89 Simpson 42-35
St. John's (Minn.) ... 89 Central (Iowa) 27-24
St. John's (Minn.) ... 89 Dayton 0-28
St. John's (Minn.) ... 91 Coe 75-2
St. John's (Minn.) ... 91 Wis.-La Crosse 29-10
St. John's (Minn.) ... 91 Dayton 7-19
St. John's (Minn.) ... 93 Coe 32-14
St. John's (Minn.) ... 93 Wis.-La Crosse 47-25
St. John's (Minn.) ... 93 Mount Union 8-56
St. John's (Minn.) ... 94 La Verne 51-12
St. John's (Minn.) ... 94 Wartburg 42-14
St. John's (Minn.) ... 94 Albion 16-19
St. John's (Minn.) ... 96 Simpson 21-18
St. John's (Minn.) ... 96 Wis.-La Crosse 30-37
St. John's (Minn.) ... 98 Pacific Lutheran 33-20
St. John's (Minn.) ... 98 Wis.-Eau Claire 7-10
St. John's (Minn.) ... 99 Wis.-Stevens Point 23-10
St. John's (Minn.) ... 99 Central (Iowa) 10-9
St. John's (Minn.) ... 99 Pacific Lutheran 9-19

Gerry Gallagher (1-1) (Wm. Paterson '74)
Wm. Paterson .... 93 Union (N.Y.) 17-7
Wm. Paterson .... 93 Rowan 0-37

Joe Gardi (2-1) (Maryland '60)
Hofstra .... 90 Cortland St. 35-9
Hofstra .... 90 Col. of New Jersey 38-3
Hofstra .... 90 Lycoming 10-20

Rick Giancola (5-4) (Rowan '68)
Montclair St. .... 85 Western Conn. St. 28-0
Montclair St. .... 85 Ithaca 28-50
Montclair St. .... 86 Hofstra 24-21
Montclair St. .... 86 Ithaca 15-29
Montclair St. .... 89 Hofstra 23-6
Montclair St. .... 89 Union (N.Y.) 6-45
Montclair St. .... 99 Buffalo St. 37-34
Montclair St. .... 99 Western Conn. St. 32-24
Montclair St. .... 99 Rowan 13-42

Steve Gilbert (0-1) (West Chester '79)
Ursinus .... 96 Lycoming 24-31

Frank Girardi (12-10) (West Chester '61)
Lycoming .... 85 Gettysburg 10-14
Lycoming .... 89 Dickinson 21-0
Lycoming .... 89 Ferrum 24-49
Lycoming .... 90 Carnegie Mellon 17-7
Lycoming .... 90 Wash. & Jeff. 24-0
Lycoming .... 90 Hofstra 20-10
Lycoming .... 90 Allegheny 14-21 (ot)
Lycoming .... 91 Wash. & Jeff. 18-16
Lycoming .... 91 Susquehanna 24-31
Lycoming .... 92 Wash. & Jeff. 0-33
Lycoming .... 95 Widener 31-27
Lycoming .... 95 Wash. & Jeff. 0-48
Lycoming .... 96 Ursinus 31-24
Lycoming .... 96 Albright 31-13
Lycoming .... 96 Rowan 14-33
Lycoming .... 97 Western Md. 27-13
Lycoming .... 97 Trinity (Tex.) 46-26
Lycoming .... 97 Rowan 28-20
Lycoming .... 97* Mount Union 12-61
Lycoming .... 98 Catholic 49-14
Lycoming .... 98 Trinity (Tex.) 21-37
Lycoming .... 99 Wash. & Jeff. 7-14

Larry Glueck (1-1) (Villanova '63)
Fordham .... 87 Hofstra 41-6
Fordham .... 87 Wagner 0-21

Paul Guenther (1-1) (Ursinus '94)
Ursinus .... 99 Bri'water (Mass.) 43-38
Ursinus .... 99 Rowan 0-55

Walt Hameline (4-2) (Brockport St. '75)
Wagner .... 82 St. Lawrence 34-43
Wagner .... 87 Rochester 38-14
Wagner .... 87 Fordham 21-0
Wagner .... 87 Emory & Henry 20-15
Wagner .... 87* Dayton 19-3
Wagner .... 88 Ithaca 31-34 (ot)

Eric Hamilton (3-4) (Col. of New Jersey '75)
Col. of New Jersey .. 90 Ithaca 24-14
Col. of New Jersey .. 90 Hofstra 3-38
Col. of New Jersey .. 96 Coast Guard 17-16
Col. of New Jersey .. 96 Rowan 3-7
Col. of New Jersey .. 97 Cortland St. 34-30
Col. of New Jersey .. 97 Rowan 7-13
Col. of New Jersey .. 98 Rowan 2-26

Roger Harring (13-5) (Wis.-La Crosse '58)
Wis.-La Crosse ...... 83 Occidental 43-42
Wis.-La Crosse ...... 83 Augustana (Ill.) 15-21
Wis.-La Crosse ...... 91 Simpson 28-13
Wis.-La Crosse ...... 91 St. John's (Minn.) 10-29
Wis.-La Crosse ...... 92 Redlands 47-26
Wis.-La Crosse ...... 92 Central (Iowa) 34-9
Wis.-La Crosse ...... 92 Mount Union 29-24
Wis.-La Crosse ...... 92* Wash. & Jeff. 16-12
Wis.-La Crosse ...... 93 Wartburg 55-26
Wis.-La Crosse ...... 93 St. John's (Minn.) 25-47
Wis.-La Crosse ...... 95 Concordia-M'head 45-7
Wis.-La Crosse ...... 95 Wis.-River Falls 28-14
Wis.-La Crosse ...... 95 Mount Union 20-17
Wis.-La Crosse ...... 95* Rowan 36-7
Wis.-La Crosse ...... 96 Wis.-River Falls 44-0
Wis.-La Crosse ...... 96 St. John's (Minn.) 37-30
Wis.-La Crosse ...... 96 Mount Union 21-39
Wis.-La Crosse ...... 99 Central (Iowa) 17-38

Jim Hershberger (1-2) (Northern Iowa '57)
Buena Vista .... 76 Carroll (Wis.) 20-14 (ot)
Buena Vista .... 76 St. John's (Minn.) 0-61
Buena Vista .... 86 Central (Iowa) 0-37

Fred Hill (1-1) (Upsala '57)
Montclair St. .... 81 Alfred 13-12
Montclair St. .... 81 Widener 12-23

Rex Huigens (0-1) (La Verne '70)
La Verne .... 94 St. John's (Minn.) 12-51

James Jones (1-1) (Bishop '49)
Bishop .... 82 Wartburg 32-7
Bishop .... 82 West Ga. 6-27

Frank Joranko (0-1) (Albion '52)
Albion .... 77 Minn.-Morris 10-13

Rich Kacmarynski (1-2) (Central [Iowa] '92)
Central (Iowa) ...... 98 Wis.-Eau Claire 21-28
Central (Iowa) ...... 99 Wis.-La Crosse 38-17
Central (Iowa) ...... 99 St. John's (Minn.) 9-10

Tom Kaczkowski (2-1) (Illinois '78)
Ohio Northern ...... 99 Hanover 56-14
Ohio Northern ...... 99 Wittenberg 58-24
Ohio Northern ...... 99 Mount Union 31-56

Dennis Kayser (1-2) (Ithaca '69)
Cortland St. .... 88 Hofstra 32-27
Cortland St. .... 88 Ithaca 17-24
Cortland St. .... 89 Union (N.Y.) 14-42

Tim Keating (1-3) (Bethany [W.Va.] '75)
Western Md. .... 97 Lycoming 13-27
Western Md. .... 98 Trinity (Tex.) 20-30
Western Md. .... 99 Catholic 20-16
Western Md. .... 99 Trinity (Tex.) 16-20

DIVISION III COACHING RECORDS—CHAMPIONSHIP COACHES

K. C. Keeler (18-6) (Delaware '81)
Rowan	93	Buffalo St. 29-6
Rowan	93	Wm. Paterson 37-0
Rowan	93	Wash. & Jeff. 23-16
Rowan	93	Mount Union 24-34
Rowan	95	Buffalo St. 46-7
Rowan	95	Union (N.Y.) 38-7
Rowan	95	Wash. & Jeff. 28-15
Rowan	95	Wis.-La Crosse 7-36
Rowan	96	Buffalo St. 21-20
Rowan	96	Col. of New Jersey 7-3
Rowan	96	Lycoming 33-14
Rowan	96	Mount Union 24-56
Rowan	97	Coast Guard 43-0
Rowan	97	Col. of New Jersey 13-7
Rowan	97	Lycoming 20-28
Rowan	98	Col. of New Jersey 26-2
Rowan	98	Buffalo St. 19-17
Rowan	98	Wis.-Eau Claire 22-19
Rowan	98	Mount Union 24-44
Rowan	99	Rensselaer 29-10
Rowan	99	Ursinus 55-0
Rowan	99	Montclair St. 42-13
Rowan	99	Mount Union 24-17 (ot)
Rowan	99*	Pacific Lutheran 13-42

Jimmie Keeling (2-1) (Howard Payne '58)
Hardin-Simmons	99	Washington (Mo.) 28-21
Hardin-Simmons	99	Wash. & Jeff. 51-3
Hardin-Simmons	99	Trinity (Tex.) 33-40

Larry Kehres (24-6) (Mount Union '71)
Mount Union	86	Dayton 42-36
Mount Union	86	Augustana (Ill.) 7-16
Mount Union	90	Allegheny 15-26
Mount Union	92	Dayton 27-10
Mount Union	92	Ill. Wesleyan 49-27
Mount Union	92	Wis.-La Crosse 24-29
Mount Union	93	Allegheny 40-7
Mount Union	93	Albion 30-16
Mount Union	93	St. John's (Minn.) 56-8
Mount Union	93*	Rowan 34-24
Mount Union	94	Allegheny 28-19
Mount Union	94	Albion 33-34
Mount Union	95	Hanover 52-18
Mount Union	95	Wheaton (Ill.) 40-14
Mount Union	95	Wis.-La Crosse 17-20
Mount Union	96	Allegheny 31-26
Mount Union	96	Ill. Wesleyan 49-14
Mount Union	96	Wis.-La Crosse 39-21
Mount Union	96*	Rowan 56-24
Mount Union	97	Allegheny 34-30
Mount Union	97	John Carroll 59-7
Mount Union	97	Simpson 54-7
Mount Union	97*	Lycoming 61-12
Mount Union	98	Albion 21-19
Mount Union	98	Wittenberg 21-19
Mount Union	98	Trinity (Tex.) 34-29
Mount Union	98*	Rowan 44-24
Mount Union	99	Augustana (Ill.) 42-33
Mount Union	99	Ohio Northern 56-31
Mount Union	99	Rowan 17-24 (ot)

Mike Kelly (13-8) (Manchester '70)
Dayton	81	Augustana (Ill.) 19-7
Dayton	81	Lawrence 38-0
Dayton	81	Widener 10-17
Dayton	84	Augustana (Ill.) 13-14
Dayton	86	Mount Union 36-42
Dayton	87	Capital 52-28
Dayton	87	Augustana (Ill.) 38-36
Dayton	87	Central (Iowa) 34-0
Dayton	87	Wagner 3-19
Dayton	88	Wittenberg 28-35 (2 ot)
Dayton	89	John Carroll 35-10
Dayton	89	Millikin 28-16
Dayton	89	St. John's (Minn.) 28-0
Dayton	89*	Union (N.Y.) 17-7
Dayton	90	Augustana (Ill.) 24-14
Dayton	90	Allegheny 23-31
Dayton	91	Baldwin-Wallace 27-10
Dayton	91	Allegheny 28-25 (ot)
Dayton	91	St. John's (Minn.) 19-7
Dayton	91	Ithaca 20-34
Dayton	92	Mount Union 10-27

Larry Kindbom (0-1) (Kalamazoo '74)
Washington (Mo.)	99	Hardin-Simmons 21-28

Joe King (0-1) (Siena '70)
Rensselaer	99	Rowan 10-29

Chuck Klausing (2-4) (Slippery Rock '48)
Carnegie Mellon	78	Dayton 24-21
Carnegie Mellon	78	Baldwin-Wallace 6-31
Carnegie Mellon	79	Minn.-Morris 31-25
Carnegie Mellon	79	Ithaca 6-15
Carnegie Mellon	83	Salisbury St. 14-16
Carnegie Mellon	85	Salisbury St. 22-35

Mickey Kwiatkowski (0-5) (Delaware '70)
Hofstra	83	Union (N.Y.) 19-51
Hofstra	86	Montclair St. 21-24
Hofstra	87	Fordham 6-41
Hofstra	88	Cortland St. 27-32
Hofstra	89	Montclair St. 6-23

Ron Labadie (0-2) (Adrian '71)
Adrian	83	Augustana (Ill.) 21-22
Adrian	88	Augustana (Ill.) 7-25

Rich Lackner (0-1) (Carnegie Mellon '79)
Carnegie Mellon	90	Lycoming 7-17

Don LaViolette (0-1) (St. Norbert '54)
St. Norbert	89	Central (Iowa) 7-55

D. J. LeRoy (0-3) (Wis.-Eau Claire '79)
Wis.-Stevens Point	86	Concordia-M'head 15-24
Coe	91	St. John's (Minn.) 2-75
Coe	93	St. John's (Minn.) 14-32

Leon Lomax (0-1) (Fort Valley St. '43)
Fort Valley St.	75	Ithaca 12-41

John Luckhardt (13-11) (Purdue '67)
Wash. & Jeff.	84	Randolph-Macon 22-21
Wash. & Jeff.	84	Central (Iowa) 0-20
Wash. & Jeff.	86	Susquehanna 20-28
Wash. & Jeff.	87	Allegheny 23-17 (ot)
Wash. & Jeff.	87	Emory & Henry 16-23
Wash. & Jeff.	89	Ferrum 7-41
Wash. & Jeff.	90	Ferrum 10-7
Wash. & Jeff.	90	Lycoming 0-24
Wash. & Jeff.	91	Lycoming 16-18
Wash. & Jeff.	92	Lycoming 33-0
Wash. & Jeff.	92	Emory & Henry 51-15
Wash. & Jeff.	92	Rowan 18-13
Wash. & Jeff.	92	Wis.-La Crosse 12-16
Wash. & Jeff.	93	Moravian 27-7
Wash. & Jeff.	93	Frostburg St. 28-7
Wash. & Jeff.	93	Rowan 16-23
Wash. & Jeff.	94	Trinity (Tex.) 28-0
Wash. & Jeff.	94	Widener 37-21
Wash. & Jeff.	94	Ithaca 23-19
Wash. & Jeff.	94	Albion 15-38
Wash. & Jeff.	95	Emory & Henry 35-16
Wash. & Jeff.	95	Lycoming 48-0
Wash. & Jeff.	95	Rowan 15-28
Wash. & Jeff.	96	Albright 17-31

Dan MacNeil (0-1) (Cortland St. '79)
Cortland St.	97	Col. of New Jersey 30-34

Ron Maier (1-1) (Bentley '86)
Albright	96	Wash. & Jeff. 31-17
Albright	96	Lycoming 13-31

Mike Manley (0-1) (Anderson [Ind.] '73)
Anderson (Ind.)	93	Albion 21-41

Bill Manlove (9-5) (Temple '58)
Widener	75	Albright 14-6
Widener	75	Ithaca 14-23
Widener	77	Central (Iowa) 19-0
Widener	77	Albany (N.Y.) 33-15
Widener	77*	Wabash 39-36
Widener	79	Baldwin-Wallace 29-8
Widener	79	Wittenberg 14-17
Widener	80	Bethany (W.Va.) 43-12
Widener	80	Dayton 24-28
Widener	81	West Ga. 10-3
Widener	81	Montclair St. 23-12
Widener	81*	Dayton 17-10
Widener	82	West Ga. 24-31 (3 ot)
Widener	88	Moravian 7-17

Dave Maurer (9-2) (Denison '54)
Wittenberg	73	San Diego 21-14
Wittenberg	73*	Juniata 41-0
Wittenberg	75	Indianapolis 17-13
Wittenberg	75	Millsaps 55-22
Wittenberg	75*	Ithaca 28-0
Wittenberg	78	Ithaca 6-3
Wittenberg	78	Minn.-Morris 35-14
Wittenberg	78	Baldwin-Wallace 10-24
Wittenberg	79	Millersville 21-14
Wittenberg	79	Widener 17-14
Wittenberg	79	Ithaca 10-14

Mike Maynard (0-2) (Ill. Wesleyan '80)
Redlands	90	Central (Iowa) 14-24
Redlands	92	Wis.-La Crosse 26-47

Peter Mazzaferro (0-1) (Centre '54)
Bri'water (Mass.)	99	Ursinus 38-43

Mike McGlinchey (6-4) (Delaware '67)
Salisbury St.	83	Carnegie Mellon 16-14
Salisbury St.	83	Union (N.Y.) 21-23
Salisbury St.	85	Carnegie Mellon 35-22
Salisbury St.	85	Gettysburg 6-22
Salisbury St.	86	Emory & Henry 34-20
Salisbury St.	86	Susquehanna 31-17
Salisbury St.	86	Ithaca 44-40
Salisbury St.	86	Augustana (Ill.) 3-31
Frostburg St.	93	Wilkes 26-25
Frostburg St.	93	Wash. & Jeff. 7-28

John Miech (0-1) (Wis.-Stevens Point '75)
Wis.-Stevens Point	99	St. John's (Minn.) 17-38

Steve Miller (0-1) (Cornell College '65)
Carroll (Wis.)	76	Buena Vista 14-20 (ot)

Chuck Mills (0-1) (Illinois St. '50)
Coast Guard	97	Rowan 0-43

Steve Mohr (5-4) (Denison '76)
Trinity (Tex.)	94	Wash. & Jeff. 0-28
Trinity (Tex.)	97	Catholic 44-33
Trinity (Tex.)	97	Lycoming 26-46
Trinity (Tex.)	98	Western Md. 30-20
Trinity (Tex.)	98	Lycoming 37-21
Trinity (Tex.)	98	Mount Union 29-34
Trinity (Tex.)	99	Western Md. 20-16
Trinity (Tex.)	99	Hardin-Simmons 40-33
Trinity (Tex.)	99	Pacific Lutheran 28-49

Al Molde (2-3) (Gust. Adolphus '66)
Minn.-Morris	77	Albion 13-10
Minn.-Morris	77	Wabash 21-37
Minn.-Morris	78	St. Olaf 23-10
Minn.-Morris	78	Wittenberg 14-35
Minn.-Morris	79	Carnegie Mellon 25-31

Ron Murphy (1-1) (Wittenberg '60)
Wittenberg	88	Dayton 35-28 (2 ot)
Wittenberg	88	Augustana (Ill.) 14-28

Dave Murray (0-1) (Springfield '81)
Cortland St.	90	Hofstra 9-35

Walt Nadzak (1-1) (Denison '57)
Juniata	73	Bridgeport 35-14
Juniata	73	Wittenberg 0-41

Frank Navarro (2-1) (Maryland '53)
Wabash	77	St. John's (Minn.) 20-9
Wabash	77	Minn.-Morris 37-21
Wabash	77	Widener 36-39

Doug Neibuhr (0-2) (Millikin '75)
Wittenberg	95	Wheaton (Ill.) 41-63
Millikin	97	Wittenberg 10-13

Ben Newcomb (0-1) (Augustana [S.D.] '57)
Augustana (Ill.)	76	St. John's (Minn.) 7-46

Bob Nielson (3-3) (Wartburg '81)
Wartburg	93	Wis.-La Crosse 26-55
Wartburg	94	Central (Iowa) 22-21
Wartburg	94	St. John's (Minn.) 14-42
Wis.-Eau Claire	98	Central (Iowa) 28-21
Wis.-Eau Claire	98	St. John's (Minn.) 10-7
Wis.-Eau Claire	98	Rowan 19-22

Hank Norton (4-4) (Lynchburg '51)
Ferrum	87	Emory & Henry 7-49
Ferrum	88	Rhodes 35-10
Ferrum	88	Moravian 49-28
Ferrum	88	Ithaca 28-62
Ferrum	89	Wash. & Jeff. 41-7
Ferrum	89	Lycoming 49-24
Ferrum	89	Union (N.Y.) 21-37
Ferrum	89	Wash. & Jeff. 7-10

John O'Grady (1-2) (Wis.-River Falls '79)
Wis.-River Falls	95	Central (Iowa) 10-7
Wis.-River Falls	95	Wis.-La Crosse 14-28
Wis.-River Falls	96	Wis.-La Crosse 0-44

Ken O'Keefe (5-5) (John Carroll '75)
Allegheny	90	Mount Union 26-15
Allegheny	90	Dayton 31-23
Allegheny	90	Central (Iowa) 24-7
Allegheny	90*	Lycoming 21-14 (ot)

Allegheny	91	Albion 24-21 (ot)	
Allegheny	91	Dayton 25-28 (ot)	
Allegheny	93	Mount Union 7-40	
Allegheny	94	Mount Union 19-28	
Allegheny	96	Mount Union 26-31	
Allegheny	97	Mount Union 30-34	

Jack Osberg (1-1) (Ausburg '62)
Augsburg	97	Concordia-M'head 34-22	
Augsburg	97	Simpson 21-61	

Bob Packard (0-2) (Baldwin-Wallace '65)
Baldwin-Wallace	82	Augustana (Ill.) 22-28	
Baldwin-Wallace	91	Dayton 10-27	

Paul Pasqualoni (0-1) (Penn St. '72)
Western Conn. St.	85	Montclair St. 0-28	

Bobby Pate (3-1) (Georgia '63)
West Ga.	81	Widener 3-10	
West Ga.	82	Widener 31-24 (3 ot)	
West Ga.	82	Bishop 27-6	
West Ga.	82*	Augustana (Ill.) 14-0	

C. Wayne Perry (0-3) (DePauw '72)
Hanover	95	Mount Union 18-52	
Hanover	97	John Carroll 20-30	
Hanover	99	Ohio Northern 14-56	

Keith Piper (0-1) (Baldwin-Wallace '48)
Denison	85	Mount Union 3-35	

Carl Poelker (1-1) (Millikin '68)
Millikin	89	Augustana (Ill.) 21-12	
Millikin	89	Dayton 16-28	

Tom Porter (0-1) (St. Olaf '51)
St. Olaf	78	Minn.-Morris 10-23	

John Potsklan (0-2) (Penn St. '49)
Albright	75	Widener 6-14	
Albright	76	St. Lawrence 7-26	

Charlie Pravata (0-1) (Adelphi '72)
Merchant Marine	94	Plymouth St. 18-19	

Jim Purtill (0-1) (Miami [Ohio] '78)
St. Norbert	99	Augustana (Ill.) 32-39	

Steve Raarup (0-1) (Gust. Adolphus '53)
Gust. Adolphus	87	St. John's (Minn.) 3-7	

Bob Reade (19-7) (Cornell College '54)
Augustana (Ill.)	81	Dayton 7-19	
Augustana (Ill.)	82	Baldwin-Wallace 28-22	
Augustana (Ill.)	82	St. Lawrence 14-0	
Augustana (Ill.)	82	West Ga. 0-14	
Augustana (Ill.)	83	Adrian 22-21	
Augustana (Ill.)	83	Wis.-La Crosse 21-15	
Augustana (Ill.)	83*	Union (N.Y.) 21-17	
Augustana (Ill.)	84	Dayton 14-13	
Augustana (Ill.)	84	Union (N.Y.) 23-6	
Augustana (Ill.)	84*	Central (Iowa) 21-12	
Augustana (Ill.)	85	Albion 26-10	
Augustana (Ill.)	85	Mount Union 21-14	
Augustana (Ill.)	85	Central (Iowa) 14-7	
Augustana (Ill.)	85*	Ithaca 20-7	
Augustana (Ill.)	86	Hope 34-10	
Augustana (Ill.)	86	Mount Union 16-7	
Augustana (Ill.)	86	Concordia-M'head 41-7	
Augustana (Ill.)	86*	Salisbury St. 31-3	
Augustana (Ill.)	87	Hiram 53-0	
Augustana (Ill.)	87	Dayton 36-38	
Augustana (Ill.)	88	Adrian 25-7	
Augustana (Ill.)	88	Wittenberg 28-14	
Augustana (Ill.)	88	Central (Iowa) 17-23 (2 ot)	
Augustana (Ill.)	89	Millikin 12-21	
Augustana (Ill.)	90	Dayton 14-24	
Augustana (Ill.)	94	Albion 21-28	

Rocky Rees (1-1) (West Chester '71)
Susquehanna	86	Wash. & Jeff. 28-20	
Susquehanna	86	Salisbury St. 17-31	

Ron Roberts (1-1) (Wisconsin '54)
Lawrence	81	Minn.-Morris 21-14 (ot)	
Lawrence	81	Dayton 0-38	

Craig Rundle (0-1) (Albion '74)
Albion	98	Mount Union 19-21	

Bill Russo (0-1)
Wagner	80	Ithaca 13-41	

Sam Sanders (0-1) (Buffalo '60)
Alfred	81	Montclair St. 12-13	

Dennis Scannell (0-1) (Villanova '74)
Mass.-Lowell	91	Union (N.Y.) 16-55	

Ron Schipper (16-11) (Hope '52)
Central (Iowa)	74	Evansville 17-16	
Central (Iowa)	74*	Ithaca 10-8	
Central (Iowa)	77	Widener 0-19	
Central (Iowa)	84	Occidental 23-22	
Central (Iowa)	84	Wash. & Jeff. 20-0	
Central (Iowa)	84	Augustana (Ill.) 12-21	
Central (Iowa)	85	Coe 27-7	
Central (Iowa)	85	Occidental 71-0	
Central (Iowa)	85	Augustana (Ill.) 7-14	
Central (Iowa)	86	Buena Vista 37-0	
Central (Iowa)	86	Concordia-M'head 14-17	
Central (Iowa)	87	Menlo 17-0	
Central (Iowa)	87	St. John's (Minn.) 13-3	
Central (Iowa)	87	Dayton 0-34	
Central (Iowa)	88	Concordia-M'head 7-0	
Central (Iowa)	88	Wis.-Whitewater 16-13	
Central (Iowa)	88	Augustana (Ill.) 23-17 (2 ot)	
Central (Iowa)	88	Ithaca 24-39	
Central (Iowa)	89	St. Norbert 55-7	
Central (Iowa)	89	St. John's (Minn.) 24-27	
Central (Iowa)	90	Redlands 24-14	
Central (Iowa)	90	St. Thomas (Minn.) 33-32	
Central (Iowa)	90	Allegheny 7-24	
Central (Iowa)	92	Carleton 20-8	
Central (Iowa)	92	Wis.-La Crosse 9-34	
Central (Iowa)	94	Wartburg 21-22	
Central (Iowa)	95	Wis.-River Falls 7-10	

Pete Schmidt (5-4) (Alma '70)
Albion	85	Augustana (Ill.) 10-26	
Albion	91	Allegheny 21-24 (ot)	
Albion	93	Anderson (Ind.) 41-21	
Albion	93	Mount Union 16-30	
Albion	94	Augustana (Ill.) 28-21	
Albion	94	Mount Union 34-33	
Albion	94	St. John's (Minn.) 19-16	
Albion	94*	Wash. & Jeff. 38-15	
Albion	96	Ill. Wesleyan 20-23	

Bill Schmitz (0-1) (Coast Guard '76)
Coast Guard	96	Col. of New Jersey 16-17	

Tom Schmulbach (1-1) (Western Ill. '69)
Augustana (Ill.)	99	St. Norbert 39-32	
Augustana (Ill.)	99	Mount Union 33-42	

Jim Scott (0-1) (Luther '61)
Aurora	92	Ill. Wesleyan 12-21	

Jack Siedlecki (0-1) (Union [N.Y.] '73)
Worcester Tech	92	Rowan 14-41	

Dick Smith (1-2) (Coe '68)
Minn.-Morris	80	Dubuque 41-35	
Minn.-Morris	80	Ithaca 0-36	
Minn.-Morris	81	Lawrence 14-21 (OT)	

Ray Smith (0-1) (UCLA '61)
Hope	86	Augustana (Ill.) 10-34	

Ray Solari (0-1) (California '51)
Menlo	87	Central (Iowa) 0-17	

Mark Speckman (0-1) (Azusa Pacific '77)
Willamette	99	Pacific Lutheran 24-28	

Ted Stratford (1-2) (St. Lawrence '57)
St. Lawrence	76	Albright 26-7	
St. Lawrence	76	Towson 36-38	
St. Lawrence	78	Baldwin-Wallace 7-71	

Barry Streeter (2-1) (Lebanon Valley '71)
Gettysburg	85	Lycoming 14-10	
Gettysburg	85	Salisbury St. 22-6	
Gettysburg	85	Ithaca 0-34	

Bob Sullivan (0-1) (St. John's [Minn.] '59)
Carleton	92	Central (Iowa) 8-20	

Ed Sweeney (0-2) (C. W. Post '71)
Dickinson	89	Lycoming 0-21	
Dickinson	91	Susquehanna 20-21	

Andy Talley (1-1) (Southern Conn. St. '67)
St. Lawrence	82	Wagner 43-34	
St. Lawrence	82	Augustana (Ill.) 0-14	

Ray Tellier (0-1) (Connecticut '73)
Rochester	87	Wagner 14-38	

Bob Thurness (0-1) (Coe '62)
Coe	85	Central (Iowa) 7-27	

Lee Tressel (3-2) (Baldwin-Wallace '48)
Baldwin-Wallace	78	St. Lawrence 71-7	
Baldwin-Wallace	78	Carnegie Mellon 31-6	
Baldwin-Wallace	78*	Wittenberg 24-10	
Baldwin-Wallace	79	Widener 8-29	
Baldwin-Wallace	80	Dayton 0-34	

Peter Vaas (0-1) (Holy Cross '74)
Allegheny	87	Wash. & Jeff. 17-23 (ot)	

Andy Vinci (0-1) (Cal St. Los Angeles '63)
San Diego	73	Wittenberg 14-21	

Ken Wable (1-1) (Muskingum '52)
Mount Union	85	Denison 35-3	
Mount Union	85	Augustana (Ill.) 14-21	

Lou Wacker (3-4) (Richmond '56)
Emory & Henry	86	Salisbury St. 20-34	
Emory & Henry	87	Ferrum 49-7	
Emory & Henry	87	Wash. & Jeff. 23-16	
Emory & Henry	87	Wagner 15-20	
Emory & Henry	92	Thomas More 17-0	
Emory & Henry	92	Wash. & Jeff. 15-51	
Emory & Henry	95	Wash. & Jeff. 16-35	

Vic Wallace (1-1) (Cornell College '65)
St. Thomas (Minn.)	90	Wis.-Whitewater 24-23	
St. Thomas (Minn.)	90	Central (Iowa) 32-33	

Michael Welch (2-1) (Ithaca '73)
Ithaca	94	Buffalo St. 10-7 (2 OT)	
Ithaca	94	Plymouth St. 22-7	
Ithaca	94	Wash. & Jeff. 19-23	

Roger Welsh (0-1) (Muskingum '64)
Capital	87	Dayton 28-52	

Frosty Westering (5-1) (Neb.-Omaha '52)
Pacific Lutheran	98	St. John's (Minn.) 20-33	
Pacific Lutheran	99	Willamette 28-24	
Pacific Lutheran	99	Wartburg 49-14	
Pacific Lutheran	99	St. John's (Minn.) 19-9	
Pacific Lutheran	99	Trinity (Tex.) 49-28	
Pacific Lutheran	99*	Rowan 42-13	

Dale Widolff (1-3) (Indiana Central '75)
Occidental	83	Wis.-La Crosse 42-43	
Occidental	84	Central (Iowa) 22-23	
Occidental	85	St. John's (Minn.) 28-10	
Occidental	85	Central (Iowa) 0-71	

Jim Williams (2-5) (Northern Iowa '60)
Simpson	88	Wis.-Whitewater 27-29	
Simpson	89	St. John's (Minn.) 35-42	
Simpson	91	Wis.-La Crosse 13-28	
Simpson	96	St. John's (Minn.) 18-21	
Simpson	97	Wis.-Whitewater 34-31	
Simpson	97	Augsburg 61-21	
Simpson	97	Mount Union 7-54	

Rick Willis (0-1) (Cornell '88)
Wartburg	99	Pacific Lutheran 14-49	

*National championship.

Coaching Honors

Division I-A Coach-of-the-Year Award

(Selected by the American Football Coaches Association and the Football Writers Association of America)

AFCA

1935	Lynn Waldorf, Northwestern
1936	Dick Harlow, Harvard
1937	Edward Mylin, Lafayette
1938	Bill Kern, Carnegie Mellon
1939	Eddie Anderson, Iowa
1940	Clark Shaughnessy, Stanford
1941	Frank Leahy, Notre Dame
1942	Bill Alexander, Georgia Tech
1943	Amos Alonzo Stagg, Pacific (Cal.)
1944	Carroll Widdoes, Ohio St.
1945	Bo McMillin, Indiana

COACHING HONORS

1946	Red Blaik, Army
1947	Fritz Crisler, Michigan
1948	Bennie Oosterbaan, Michigan
1949	Bud Wilkinson, Oklahoma
1950	Charlie Caldwell, Princeton
1951	Chuck Taylor, Stanford
1952	Biggie Munn, Michigan St.
1953	Jim Tatum, Maryland
1954	Red Sanders, UCLA
1955	Duffy Daugherty, Michigan St.
1956	Bowden Wyatt, Tennessee
1957	Woody Hayes, Ohio St.
1958	Paul Dietzel, LSU
1959	Ben Schwartzwalder, Syracuse
1960	Murray Warmath, Minnesota
1961	Bear Bryant, Alabama
1962	John McKay, Southern California
1963	Darrell Royal, Texas
1964	Frank Broyles, Arkansas, and Ara Parseghian, Notre Dame
1965	Tommy Prothro, UCLA
1966	Tom Cahill, Army
1967	John Pont, Indiana
1968	Joe Paterno, Penn St.
1969	Bo Schembechler, Michigan
1970	Charlie McClendon, LSU, and Darrell Royal, Texas
1971	Bear Bryant, Alabama
1972	John McKay, Southern California
1973	Bear Bryant, Alabama
1974	Grant Teaff, Baylor
1975	Frank Kush, Arizona St.
1976	Johnny Majors, Pittsburgh
1977	Don James, Washington
1978	Joe Paterno, Penn St.
1979	Earle Bruce, Ohio St.
1980	Vince Dooley, Georgia
1981	Danny Ford, Clemson
1982	Joe Paterno, Penn St.
1983	Ken Hatfield, Air Force
1984	LaVell Edwards, Brigham Young
1985	Fisher DeBerry, Air Force
1986	Joe Paterno, Penn St.
1987	Dick MacPherson, Syracuse
1988	Don Nehlen, West Virginia
1989	Bill McCartney, Colorado
1990	Bobby Ross, Georgia Tech
1991	Bill Lewis, East Carolina
1992	Gene Stallings, Alabama
1993	Barry Alvarez, Wisconsin
1994	Tom Osborne, Nebraska
1995	Gary Barnett, Northwestern
1996	Bruce Snyder, Arizona St.
1997	Lloyd Carr, Michigan
1998	Phillip Fulmer, Tennessee
1999	Frank Beamer, Virginia Tech

FWAA

1957	Woody Hayes, Ohio St.
1958	Paul Dietzel, LSU
1959	Ben Schwartzwalder, Syracuse
1960	Murray Warmath, Minnesota
1961	Darrell Royal, Texas
1962	John McKay, Southern California
1963	Darrell Royal, Texas
1964	Ara Parseghian, Notre Dame
1965	Duffy Daugherty, Michigan St.
1966	Tom Cahill, Army
1967	John Pont, Indiana
1968	Woody Hayes, Ohio St.
1969	Bo Schembechler, Michigan
1970	Alex Agase, Northwestern
1971	Bob Devaney, Nebraska
1972	John McKay, Southern California
1973	Johnny Majors, Pittsburgh
1974	Grant Teaff, Baylor
1975	Woody Hayes, Ohio St.
1976	Johnny Majors, Pittsburgh
1977	Lou Holtz, Arkansas
1978	Joe Paterno, Penn St.
1979	Earle Bruce, Ohio St.
1980	Vince Dooley, Georgia
1981	Danny Ford, Clemson
1982	Joe Paterno, Penn St.
1983	Howard Schnellenberger, Miami (Fla.)
1984	LaVell Edwards, Brigham Young
1985	Fisher DeBerry, Air Force
1986	Joe Paterno, Penn St.
1987	Dick MacPherson, Syracuse
1988	Lou Holtz, Notre Dame
1989	Bill McCartney, Colorado
1990	Bobby Ross, Georgia Tech
1991	Don James, Washington
1992	Gene Stallings, Alabama
1993	Terry Bowden, Auburn
1994	Rich Brooks, Oregon
1995	Gary Barnett, Northwestern
1996	Bruce Snyder, Arizona St.
1997	Mike Price, Washington St.
1998	Phillip Fulmer, Tennessee
1999	Frank Beamer, Virginia Tech

Division I-AA Coach-of-the-Year Award

(Selected by the American Football Coaches Association)

1983	Rey Dempsey, Southern Ill.
1984	Dave Arnold, Montana St.
1985	Dick Sheridan, Furman
1986	Erk Russell, Ga. Southern
1987	Mark Duffner, Holy Cross
1988	Jimmy Satterfield, Furman
1989	Erk Russell, Ga. Southern
1990	Tim Stowers, Ga. Southern
1991	Mark Duffner, Holy Cross
1992	Charlie Taafe, Citadel
1993	Dan Allen, Boston U.
1994	Jim Tressel, Youngstown St.
1995	Don Read, Montana
1996	Ray Tellier, Columbia
1997	Andy Talley, Villanova
1998	Mark Whipple, Massachusetts
1999	Paul Johnson, Ga. Southern

Small College Coach-of-the-Year Awards

(Selected by the American Football Coaches Association)

COLLEGE DIVISION

1960	Warren Woodson, New Mexico St.
1961	Jake Gaither, Florida A&M
1962	Bill Edwards, Wittenberg
1963	Bill Edwards, Wittenberg
1964	Clarence Stasavich, East Carolina
1965	Jack Curtice, UC Santa Barb.
1966	Dan Jessee, Trinity (Conn.)
1967	Scrappy Moore, Chattanooga
1968	Jim Root, New Hampshire
1969	Larry Naviaux, Boston U.
1970	Bennie Ellender, Arkansas St.
1971	Tubby Raymond, Delaware
1972	Tubby Raymond, Delaware
1973	Dave Maurer, Wittenberg
1974	Roy Kramer, Central Mich.
1975	Dave Maurer, Wittenberg
1976	Jim Dennison, Akron
1977	Bill Manlove, Widener
1978	Lee Tressel, Baldwin-Wallace
1979	Bill Narduzzi, Youngstown St.
1980	Rick Carter, Dayton
1981	Vito Ragazzo, Shippensburg
1982	Jim Wacker, Southwest Tex. St.

COLLEGE DIVISION I

(NCAA Division II and NAIA Division I)

1983	Don Morton, North Dakota St.
1984	Chan Gailey, Troy St.
1985	George Landis, Bloomsburg
1986	Earle Solomonson, North Dakota St.
1987	Rick Rhoades, Troy St.
1988	Rocky Hager, North Dakota St.
1989	John Williams, Mississippi Col.
1990	Rocky Hager, North Dakota St.
1991	Frank Cignetti, Indiana (Pa.)
1992	Bill Burgess, Jacksonville St.
1993	Bobby Wallace, North Ala.
1994	Bobby Wallace, North Ala.
1995	Bobby Wallace, North Ala.
1996	Joe Glenn, Northern Colo.
1997	Joe Glenn, Northern Colo.
1998	Mel Tjeerdsma, Northwest Mo. St.
1999	Mel Tjeerdsma, Northwest Mo. St.

COLLEGE DIVISION II

(NCAA Division III and NAIA Division II)

1983	Bob Reade, Augustana (Ill.)
1984	Bob Reade, Augustana (Ill.)
1985	Bob Reade, Augustana (Ill.)
1986	Bob Reade, Augustana (Ill.)
1987	Walt Hameline, Wagner
1988	Jim Butterfield, Ithaca
1989	Mike Kelly, Dayton
1990	Ken O'Keefe, Allegheny
1991	Mike Kelly, Dayton
1992	John Luckhardt, Wash. & Jeff.
1993	Larry Kehres, Mount Union
1994	Pete Schmidt, Albion
1995	Roger Harring, Wis.-La Crosse
1996	Larry Kehres, Mount Union
1997	Larry Kehres, Mount Union
1998	Larry Kehres, Mount Union
1999	Frosty Westering, Pacific Lutheran

Northwest Missouri State's Mel Tjeerdsma won his second consecutive College Division I Coach-of-the-Year award in 1999 after the Bearcats successfully defended their NCAA Division II title.

Added and Discontinued Programs

Nationally Prominent Teams That Permanently
  Dropped Football 406
Added or Resumed Programs Since 1968 406
Discontinued Programs Since 1950 407

Nationally Prominent Teams That Permanently Dropped Football

Listed alphabetically at right are the all-time records of teams formerly classified as major college that permanently discontinued football. Also included are those teams that, retroactively, are considered to have been major college (before the advent of official classification in 1937) by virtue of their schedules (i.e., at least half of their games versus other major-college opponents). All schools listed were considered to have been major college or classified in either Division I-A or I-AA for a minimum of 10 consecutive seasons.

Team	Inclusive Seasons	Years	Won	Lost	Tied	Pct.†
Cal St. Fullerton	1970-1992	23	107	150	3	.417
Carlisle Indian School	1893-1917	25	167	88	13	.647
Centenary (La.)	1894-1947	36	148	100	21	.589
Creighton	1900-1942	43	183	139	27	.563
Denver	1885-1960	73	273	262	40	.510
Detroit	1896-1964	64	305	200	25	.599
George Washington	1890-1966	58	209	240	34	.468
Gonzaga	1892-1941	39	130	99	20	.562
Haskell Institute	1896-1938	43	199	166	18	.543
Lamar	1951-1989	39	171	225	9	.433
Long Beach St.	1955-1991	37	199	183	4	.521
Manhattan	1923-1942	20	77	75	11	.506
Marquette	1892-1960	68	273	220	38	.550
New York U.	1873-1952	66	201	231	32	.468
Pacific (Cal.)	1919-1995	77	346	397	23	.467
St. Louis	1899-1949	49	235	179	33	.563
San Francisco	*1924-1951; 1959-1971	38	133	169	20	.444
Texas-Arlington	1959-1985	27	129	150	2	.463
Wichita St.	1897-1986	89	375	402	47	.484
Xavier (Ohio)	1900-1973	61	302	223	21	.572

†Ties computed as half won and half lost. *Discontinued football during 1952 after having been classified major college. Resumed at the Division II level during 1959-71, when it was discontinued again.

Added or Resumed Programs Since 1968

NCAA Member Colleges

1968 (4)
Boise St.; *Chicago; New Jersey City; UNLV.

1969 (2)
*Adelphi (dropped 1972); Towson

1970 (6)
Cal St. Fullerton (dropped 1993); *Fordham; *Georgetown; Plattsburgh St. (dropped 1979); Plymouth St.; *St. Mary's (Cal.).

1971 (6)
Boston St. (dropped 1982); Dist. Columbia (dropped 1974); Federal City (dropped 1975); *New England Col. (dropped 1973); Rochester Tech (dropped 1978); St. Peter's (suspended after one game 1984, resumed 1985, dropped 1988, resumed 1989).

1972 (6)
Kean; *Lake Forest; Nicholls St.; Salisbury St.; *San Diego; Wm. Paterson.

1973 (7)
Albany St. (N.Y.); *Benedictine; Bowie St.; James Madison; New Haven; New York Tech (dropped 1984); Seton Hall (dropped 1982).

1974 (2)
FDU-Madison; Framingham St.

1975 (2)
*Brooklyn (dropped 1991); *Canisius.

1976 (1)
Oswego St. (dropped 1977).

1977 (2)
*Catholic; *Minn. St.-Mankato

1978 (7)
*Buffalo; Dist. Columbia; Iona; Marist; Pace; *St. Francis (Pa.); *St. John's (N.Y.).

1979 (2)
UCF; *Duquesne.

1980 (5)
*Loras; Mass.-Lowell; *Miles (dropped 1989, resumed 1990); Ramapo (dropped 1993); *Sonoma St. (dropped 1997)

1981 (4)
Buffalo St.; Mercyhurst; *West Ga.; Western New Eng.

1982 (2)
Valdosta St.; Westfield St.

1983 (2)
*Ky. Wesleyan; Stony Brook.

1984 (3)
Fitchburg St.; *Ga. Southern; *Samford.

1985 (6)
Ferrum; MacMurray; N.Y. Maritime (dropped 1986, resumed 1987, dropped 1989); *St. Peter's (dropped 1988, resumed 1989); *Villanova; Worcester St.

1986 (4)
*UC Santa Barb.; Menlo; *Quincy; Wesley.

1987 (5)
*Aurora; *Drake; Gallaudet; *N.Y. Maritime (dropped 1989); St. John Fisher.

1988 (7)
Assumption; Bentley; Mass.-Boston; Mass.-Dartmouth; *MIT (last team was in 1901); Siena; Stonehill.

1989 (4)
*Gannon; Methodist; *St. Peter's; *Southern Methodist.

1990 (3)
*Hardin-Simmons; *Miles; Thomas More.

1991 (3)
UAB; Charleston So.; Sacred Heart.

1992 (1)
*West Tex. A&M.

1993 (3)
*King's (Pa.); Monmouth; Salve Regina.

1994 (2)
Chapman; Robert Morris.

1996 (3)
Fairfield; Merrimack; Westminster (Mo.)

1997 (2)
*La Salle; South Fla.

1998 (1)
Jacksonville

1999 (2)
Bryant; St. Anselm

*Previously dropped football.

Non-NCAA Senior Colleges

1968 (2)
#Mo. Southern St.; #Southwest St.

1970 (1)
#Mo. Western St.

1971 (3)
Concordia (St. Paul); #Gardner-Webb; #Grand Valley St.

1972 (5)
#Dr. Martin Luther; #Mars Hill; N'western (Minn.); Pillsbury; #Western Conn. St.

1973 (2)
#Liberty; #Mass. Maritime.

1974 (3)
#*N.M. Highlands; #Northeastern Ill. (dropped 1988); #Saginaw Valley.

1976 (2)
#Maranatha Baptist; #Mesa St.

1977 (2)
Evangel; Olivet Nazarene.

1978 (3)
*Baptist Christian (dropped 1983); *St. Ambrose; *Yankton (dropped 1984).

1979 (2)
Fort Lauderdale (dropped 1982); Lubbock Christian (dropped 1983).

1980 (1)
Mid-America Nazarene.

1983 (2)
Ga. Southwestern (dropped 1989); #Loras.

1984 (3)
St. Paul Bible; #Southwest Baptist; *Union (Ky.).

1985 (4)
*Cumberland (Ky.); *Lambuth; *Tenn. Wesleyan; Tiffin.

1986 (4)
*#St. Francis (Ill.); Trinity Bible (N.D.); Urbana; #Wingate.

ADDED OR RESUMED PROGRAMS SINCE 1968—NON-NCAA SENIOR COLLEGES 407

1987 (1)
#Greenville.

1988 (5)
Campbellsville; Mary; #Midwestern St.; Trinity (Ill.); *Western Mont.

1990 (3)
*Cumberland; Lindenwood; #Mt. St. Joseph (Ohio).

1991 (3)
#Clinch Valley; #Lees-McRae (dropped 1994); #*Tusculum.

1993 (6)
#Ark.-Pine Bluff; *Bethel (Tenn.); #Chowan; Malone; St. Xavier (Ill.); Sue Bennett.

1996 (1)
*McKendree

1998 (1)
#*Texas Lutheran

2000 (1)
Paul Quinn (dropped 1961)

*Previously dropped football. #Now NCAA member.

Discontinued Programs Since 1950

(Includes NCAA member colleges and non-member colleges; also colleges that closed or merged with other institutions.)

1950 (9)
Alliance; Canisius (resumed 1975); Huntington; Oklahoma City; *Portland; Rio Grande; Rollins; *Saint Louis; Steubenville.

1951 (38)
Arkansas Col.; Atlantic Christian; Canterbury; Catholic (resumed 1977); CCNY; Corpus Christi (resumed 1954, dropped 1967); Daniel Baker; Detroit Tech; *Duquesne (resumed 1979); East Tex. Baptist; Gannon (resumed 1989); *Georgetown (resumed 1970); Glassboro St. (resumed 1964—name changed to Rowan in 1992); Hartwick; High Point; LeMoyne-Owen; Lowell Textile; Lycoming (resumed 1954); McKendree (resumed 1996); Milligan; Mt. St. Mary's (Md.); Nevada (resumed 1952); New Bedford Textile; New England Col. (resumed 1971, dropped 1973); Niagara; Northern Idaho; Panzer; St. Mary's (Cal.) (resumed 1970); St. Michael's (N.M.); Shurtleff (resumed 1953, dropped 1954); Southern Idaho; Southwestern (Tenn.) (resumed 1952—name changed to Rhodes in 1986); Southwestern (Tex.); Tillotson; Tusculum (resumed 1991); Washington (Md.); West Va. Wesleyan (resumed 1953); William Penn (resumed 1953).

1952 (13)
Aquinas; Clarkson; Erskine; Louisville Municipal; *Loyola Marymount; Nebraska Central; Rider; Samuel Huston; *San Francisco (resumed 1959, dropped 1972); Shaw (resumed 1953, dropped 1979); St. Bonaventure; St. Martin's; Teikyo Westmar (resumed 1953).

1953 (10)
Arnold; Aurora; Bethel (Tenn.) (resumed 1993); Cedarville; Champlain; Davis & Elkins (resumed 1955, dropped 1962); Georgetown (Ky.) (resumed 1955); *New York U.; *Santa Clara (resumed 1959, dropped 1993); Union (Tenn.).

1954 (8)
Adelphi (resumed 1969, dropped 1972); Case Tech (resumed 1955); Quincy (resumed 1986); St. Francis (Pa.) (resumed 1978); St. Michael's (Vt.); Shurtleff; *Wash. & Lee (resumed 1955); York (Neb.).

1955 (2)
*Fordham (resumed 1970); St. Mary's (Minn.).

1956 (4)
Brooklyn (resumed 1975, dropped 1991); Hendrix (resumed 1957, dropped 1961); William Carey; Wisconsin Extension.

1957 (4)
Lewis; Midwestern (Iowa) (resumed 1966); Morris Harvey; Stetson.

1959 (2)
Florida N&I; West Ga. (resumed 1981).

1960 (5)
Brandeis; Leland; Loras (resumed 1980); St. Ambrose (resumed 1978); Xavier (La.).

1961 (9)
*Denver; Hawaii (resumed 1962); Hendrix; Lincoln (Pa.); *Marquette; Paul Quinn; Scranton; Texas College; Tougaloo.

1962 (5)
Azusa Pacific (resumed 1965); Davis & Elkins; San Diego (resumed 1972); Southern Cal Col.; Westminster (Utah) (resumed 1965, dropped 1979).

1963 (3)
Benedictine (resumed 1973); *Hardin-Simmons (resumed 1990); St. Vincent (Pa.).

1964 (2)
King's (Pa.) (resumed 1993); Paine.

1965 (7)
Claflin; *Detroit; Dillard; Miss. Industrial; Morris; Philander Smith; Rust.

1966 (1)
St. Augustine's.

1967 (6)
Benedict; Corpus Christi; *George Washington; Jarvis Christian; Ozarks; South Caro. Trade.

1968 (2)
Edward Waters; Frederick.

1969 (6)
Allen; Case Tech and Western Reserve merged to form Case Reserve; George Fox; Louisiana Col.; UC San Diego; Wiley.

1971 (5)
Bradley; *Buffalo (resumed 1978); Hiram Scott; Lake Forest (resumed 1972); Parsons.

1972 (8)
Adelphi; UC Santa Barb. (resumed 1986); Haverford; North Dak.-Ellendale; Northern Mont.; Northwood (Tex.); San Francisco; Sonoma St. (resumed 1980).

1973 (2)
New England Col.; N.M. Highlands (resumed 1974).

1974 (6)
Col. of Emporia; Dist. Columbia; Drexel; Ill.-Chicago; Samford (resumed 1984); *Xavier (Ohio).

1975 (6)
Baptist Christian (resumed 1978, dropped 1983); Bridgeport; Federal City; *Tampa; Vermont; Wis.-Milwaukee.

1976 (3)
UC Riverside; Minn. St.-Mankato (resumed 1977); Northland.

1977 (4)
Cal Tech; Oswego St.; Whitman; Yankton (resumed 1978, dropped 1984).

1978 (3)
Cal St. Los Angeles; Col. of Idaho; Rochester Tech.

1979 (5)
Miles (resumed 1980, dropped 1989, resumed 1990); Mont. St.-Billings; Plattsburgh St.; Shaw; Westminster (Utah).

1980 (3)
†Gallaudet; Md.-East. Shore; U.S. Int'l.

1981 (2)
Bluefield St.; *Villanova (resumed 1985).

1982 (4)
Boston St.; Fort Lauderdale; Milton; Seton Hall.

1983 (3)
Baptist Christian; Cal Poly Pomona; Lubbock Christian.

1984 (5)
Fisk; New York Tech; St. Peter's (suspended after one game, resumed 1985, dropped 1988, resumed 1989); So. Dak.-Springfield; Yankton.

1985 (1)
Southern Colo.

1986 (4)
Drake (resumed 1987); N.Y. Maritime (resumed 1987, dropped 1989); Southeastern La.; *Texas-Arlington.

1987 (4)
Bishop; *Southern Methodist (resumed 1989); Western Mont. (resumed 1988); *Wichita St.

1988 (4)
Northeastern Ill.; St. Paul's; St. Peter's (resumed 1989); Texas Lutheran (resumed 1998).

1989 (3)
Ga. Southwestern; Miles (resumed 1990); N.Y. Maritime.

1990 (2)
*Lamar; Lincoln (Mo.).

1991 (3)
Brooklyn; Tarkio; West Tex. A&M (resumed 1992).

1992 (3)
*Long Beach St.; Pacific (Ore.); St. Mary of the Plains.

1993 (5)
*Cal St. Fullerton; Cameron; Ramapo; Santa Clara; Wis.-Superior.

1994 (4)
Cal St. Hayward; Lees-McRae; Oregon Tech; Upsala.

1995 (1)
San Fran. St.

1996 (1)
*Pacific (Cal.).

1997 (2)
Cal St. Chico; Sonoma St.

1998 (2)
Boston U.; Evansville

*Classified major college previous year. †Did not play a 7-game varsity schedule, 1980-86, and returned to club status in 1995.

Championship Results

Division I-AA Championship 410
Division II Championship 419
Division III Championship 427

Georgia Southern quarterback Greg Hill gained 111 of the Eagles' Division I-AA championship record 638 rushing yards in the 1999 title game against Youngstown State.

Division I-AA Championship

1999 Title Game Summary

FINLEY STADIUM/DAVENPORT FIELD, CHATTANOOGA, TENNESSEE; DECEMBER 18

	Ga. Southern	Youngstown St.
First Downs	24	17
Rushing Yardage	638	163
Passing Yardage	17	175
Passes (Comp.-Att.-Int.)	1-4-0	11-20-1
Punts (Number-Average)	1-25.0	7-36.0
Fumbles (Number-Lost)	1-0	1-0
Penalties (Number-Yards)	9-82	3-11
Ga. Southern	10 28 7 14—59	
Youngstown St.	7 7 3 7—24	

FIRST QUARTER
Ga. Southern—Chris Chambers 25 field goal (44 yards in 9 plays, 10:20 left)
Youngstown St.—Adrian Brown 2 run (Mark Griffith kick) (76 yards in 11 plays, 4:51 left)
Ga. Southern—Greg Hill 42 run (Chambers kick) (72 yards in 5 plays, 2:51 left)

SECOND QUARTER
Youngstown St.—Jeff Ryan 3 run (Griffith kick) (73 yards in 8 plays, 14:34 left)
Ga. Southern—Adrian Peterson 3 run (Chambers kick) (78 yards in 11 plays, 10:25 left)
Ga. Southern—Bennie Cunningham 57 run (Chambers kick) (57 yards in 1 play, 9:05 left)
Ga. Southern—Peterson 22 run (Chambers kick) (72 yards in 2 plays, 5:27 left)
Ga. Southern—Anthony Williams 72 punt return (Chambers kick) (2:09 left)

THIRD QUARTER
Youngstown St.—Griffith 30 field goal (41 yards in 5 plays, 4:47 left)
Ga. Southern—Peterson 1 run (Chambers kick) (66 yards in 5 plays, 3:05 left)

FOURTH QUARTER
Ga. Southern—Mark Myers 5 run (Chambers kick) (90 yards in 10 plays, 9:57 left)
Ga. Southern—J. R. Revere 66 run (Chambers kick) (71 yards in 2 plays, 7:13 left)
Youngstown St.—Brown 1 run (Griffith kick) (71 yards in 8 plays, 3:48 left)

INDIVIDUAL LEADERS
Rushing—Ga. Southern: Peterson, 247 yards on 25 carries; Youngstown St.: Brown, 160 yards on 22 carries.
Passing—Ga. Southern: Hill, 1 of 4 for 17 yards; Youngstown St.: Ryan, 11 of 20 for 175 yards.
Receiving—Ga. Southern: Dedric Parham, 1 catch for 17 yards; Youngstown St.: Renauld Ray, 4 catches for 90 yards, and Elliott Giles, 2 catches for 46 yards.

NCAA I-AA Football Championship History

1978 At the 72nd NCAA Convention (January 1978) in Atlanta, Ga., the membership voted to establish the Division I-AA Football Championship and a statistics program for the division. The format for the first I-AA championship, held in Wichita Falls, Texas, was a single-elimination, four-team tournament. Florida A&M defeated Massachusetts, 35-28, in the title game. The game was televised by ABC.

1981 The championship expanded to include eight teams in a single-elimination tournament.

1982 The championship expanded to include 12 teams. Eight teams played first-round games at campus sites, and the top four teams, seeded by the Division I-AA Football Committee, received byes.

1986 The championship field expanded to its current format of 16 teams with each team playing a first-round game.

1987 Northeast Louisiana defeated Marshall, 43-42, in the closest game in championship history.

1989 A then-record 25,725 fans watched Georgia Southern down Stephen F. Austin, 37-34, in the championship game at Allen E. Paulson Stadium in Statesboro, Ga.

1990 Georgia Southern won its fourth I-AA championship, adding to its titles in 1985, 1986 and 1989.

1991 Youngstown State won its first national championship with a 25-17 victory over Marshall. Penguin head coach Jim Tressel joined his father, Lee, as the only father-son combination to win NCAA football titles. Lee Tressel won the 1978 Division III championship at Baldwin-Wallace.

1992 A then-record crowd of 31,304 in Huntington, W.Va., saw Marshall return the favor with a 31-28 win over Youngstown State for its first I-AA title.

1993 The I-AA championship provided for a maximum field of 16 teams. Six member conferences (Big Sky, Gateway, Ohio Valley, Southern, Southland and Yankee) were granted automatic qualification for their respective winners. Youngstown State won its second I-AA title with a 17-5 victory over Marshall before a crowd of 29,218 in Huntington, W. Va.

1994 Youngstown State won its third national title in four years with a 28-14 victory over Boise State.

1995 Montana won its first Division I-AA title before a championship record crowd of 32,106 in Huntington, W.Va.

1996 Marshall, making its fifth visit to the championship game since 1991, won its second Division I-AA title with a 49-29 victory over defending champion Montana before 30,052 in Huntington, W. Va.

1997 Youngstown State won its fourth national title in the 1990s with a 10-9 victory over McNeese State in Chattanooga, Tennessee.

1999 Georgia Southern closed out the century with another national title, posting a 59-24 victory over Youngstown State. The Eagles won their fifth title, surpassing Youngstown State's four championships and taking over the division lead in crowns.

DIVISION I-AA CHAMPIONSHIP—ALL-TIME CHAMPIONSHIP RESULTS

Division I-AA All-Time Championship Results

Year	Champion	Coach	Score	Runner-Up	Site	Attendance
1978	Florida A&M	Rudy Hubbard	35-28	Massachusetts	Wichita Falls, Texas	13,604
1979	Eastern Ky.	Roy Kidd	30-7	Lehigh	Orlando, Fla.	5,500
1980	Boise St.	Jim Criner	31-29	Eastern Ky.	Sacramento, Calif.	8,157
1981	Idaho St.	Dave Kragthorpe	34-23	Eastern Ky.	Wichita Falls, Texas	11,003
1982	Eastern Ky.	Roy Kidd	17-14	Delaware	Wichita Falls, Texas	11,257
1983	Southern Ill.	Rey Dempsey	43-7	Western Caro.	Charleston, S.C.	15,950
1984	Montana St.	Dave Arnold	19-6	Louisiana Tech	Charleston, S.C.	9,125
1985	Ga. Southern	Erk Russell	44-42	Furman	Tacoma, Wash.	5,306
1986	Ga. Southern	Erk Russell	48-21	Arkansas St.	Tacoma, Wash.	4,419
1987	La.-Monroe	Pat Collins	43-42	Marshall	Pocatello, Idaho	11,513
1988	Furman	Jimmy Satterfield	17-12	Ga. Southern	Pocatello, Idaho	11,500
1989	Ga. Southern	Erk Russell	37-34	*Stephen F. Austin	Statesboro, Ga.	25,725
1990	Ga. Southern	Tim Stowers	36-13	Nevada	Statesboro, Ga.	23,204
1991	Youngstown St.	Jim Tressel	25-17	Marshall	Statesboro, Ga.	12,667
1992	Marshall	Jim Donnan	31-28	Youngstown St.	Huntington, W.Va.	31,304
1993	Youngstown St.	Jim Tressel	17-5	Marshall	Huntington, W.Va.	29,218
1994	Youngstown St.	Jim Tressel	28-14	Boise St.	Huntington, W.Va.	27,674
1995	Montana	Don Read	22-20	Marshall	Huntington, W.Va.	32,106
1996	Marshall	Bob Pruett	49-29	Montana	Huntington, W.Va.	30,052
1997	Youngstown St.	Jim Tressel	10-9	McNeese St.	Chattanooga, Tenn.	14,771
1998	Massachusetts	Mark Whipple	55-43	Ga. Southern	Chattanooga, Tenn.	17,501
1999	Ga. Southern	Paul Johnson	59-24	Youngstown St.	Chattanooga, Tenn.	20,052

*Stephen F. Austin's participation in 1989 Division I-AA championship vacated.

1999 Division I-AA Championship Results

FIRST ROUND
N.C. A&T 24, Tennessee St. 10
Youngstown St. 30, Montana 27
Troy St. 27, James Madison 7
Florida A&M 44, Appalachian St. 29
Hofstra 27, Lehigh 15
Illinois St. 56, Colgate 13
Massachusetts 30, Furman 23 (ot)
Ga. Southern 72, Northern Ariz. 29

QUARTERFINALS
Youngstown St. 41, N.C. A&T 3
Florida A&M 17, Troy St. 10
Illinois St. 37, Hofstra 20
Ga. Southern 38, Massachusetts 21

SEMIFINALS
Youngstown St. 27, Florida A&M 24
Ga. Southern 28, Illinois St. 17

CHAMPIONSHIP
Ga. Southern 59, Youngstown St. 24

Individual Records

GAME

NET YARDS RUSHING
333—Adrian Peterson, Ga. Southern (38) vs. Massachusetts (21), 12-4-99.

RUSHES ATTEMPTED
46—Tamron Smith, Youngstown St. (10) vs. Samford (0), 12-14-91.

TOUCHDOWNS BY RUSHING
6—Sean Sanders, Weber St. (59) vs. Idaho (30), 11-28-87.

NET YARDS PASSING
517—Todd Hammel, Stephen F. Austin (59) vs. Grambling (56), 11-25-89.

PASSES ATTEMPTED
82—Steve McNair, Alcorn St. (20) vs. Youngstown St. (63), 11-25-94.

PASSES COMPLETED
52—Steve McNair, Alcorn St. (20) vs. Youngstown St. (63), 11-25-94.

PASSES INTERCEPTED
7—Jeff Gilbert, Western Caro. (7) vs. Southern Ill. (43), 12-17-83.

TOUCHDOWN PASSES
6—Mike Smith, Northern Iowa (41) vs. La.-Monroe (44), 12-12-87; Clemente Gordon, Grambling (56) vs. Stephen F. Austin (59), 11-25-89.

COMPLETION PERCENTAGE (Min. 15 Attempts)
.882—Jeff Ryan, Youngstown St. (41) vs. N.C. A&T (3), 12-4-99 (15 of 17).

NET YARDS RUSHING AND PASSING
539—Todd Hammel, Stephen F. Austin (59) vs. Grambling (56), 11-25-89 (22 rushing, 517 passing).

RUSHING AND PASSING PLAYS
91—Steve McNair, Alcorn St. (20) vs. Youngstown St. (63), 11-25-94 (9 rushing, 82 passing).

PUNTING AVERAGE (Min. 3 Punts)
51.8—Jeff Baker, Western Ill. (24) vs. Florida A&M (21), 12-5-98 (8 for 414).

PUNTS
14—Fred McRae, Jackson St. (0) vs. Stephen F. Austin (24), 11-26-88.

RECEPTIONS
18—Brian Forster, Rhode Island (23) vs. Richmond (17), 12-1-84.

NET YARDS RECEIVING
288—Randy Moss, Marshall (59) vs. Delaware (14), 11-30-96 (8 catches).

TOUCHDOWN RECEPTIONS
4—Tony DiMaggio, Rhode Island (35) vs. Akron (27), 11-30-85; Randy Moss, Marshall (49) vs. Montana (29), 12-21-96.

INTERCEPTIONS
4—Greg Shipp, Southern Ill. (43) vs. Western Caro. (7), 12-17-83.

YARDS GAINED ON INTERCEPTION RETURNS
117—Kevin Sullivan, Massachusetts (44) vs. Nevada (21), 12-9-78.

YARDS GAINED ON PUNT RETURNS
121—Darren Sharper, William & Mary (45) vs. Jackson St. (6), 11-30-96.

YARDS GAINED ON KICKOFF RETURNS
232—Mike Cadore, Eastern Ky. (32) vs. La.-Monroe (33), 12-5-87, 6 returns, 1 for 99-yard TD.

POINTS
36—Sean Sanders, Weber St. (59) vs. Idaho (30), 11-28-87.

TOUCHDOWNS
6—Sean Sanders, Weber St. (59) vs. Idaho (30), 11-28-87.

EXTRA POINTS
10—Andy Larson, Montana (70) vs. Stephen F. Austin (14), 12-9-95.

FIELD GOALS
4—Jeff Wilkins, Youngstown St. (19) vs. Northern Iowa (7), 12-12-92; Jose Larios, McNeese St. (33) vs. Idaho (3), 11-25-95; Shonz LaFrenz, McNeese St. (19) vs. Massachusetts (21), 11-28-98.

TOURNAMENT

NET YARDS RUSHING
897—Adrian Peterson, Ga. Southern, 1999 (134 vs. Northern Ariz., 333 vs. Massachusetts, 183 vs. Illinois St., 247 vs. Youngstown St.)

RUSHES ATTEMPTED
123—Ray Whalen, Nevada, 1990 (21 vs. La.-Monroe, 34 vs. Furman, 44 vs. Boise St., 24 vs. Ga. Southern).

NET YARDS PASSING
1,500—Dave Dickenson, Montana, 1995 (441 vs. Eastern Ky., 408 vs. Ga. Southern, 370 vs. Stephen F. Austin, 281 vs. Marshall).

PASSES ATTEMPTED
177—Jeff Gilbert, Western Caro., 1983 (47 vs. Colgate, 52 vs. Holy Cross, 45 vs. Furman, 33 vs. Southern Ill.); Brian Ah Yat, Montana, 1996 (48 vs. Nicholls St., 34 vs. East Tenn. St., 40 vs. Troy St., 55 vs. Marshall).

PASSES COMPLETED
122—Dave Dickenson, Montana, 1995 (31 vs. Eastern Ky., 37 vs. Ga. Southern, 25 vs. Stephen F. Austin, 29 vs. Marshall).

PASSES INTERCEPTED
11—Todd Hammel, Stephen F. Austin, 1989 (0 vs. Grambling, 4 vs. Southwest Mo. St., 2 vs. Furman, 5 vs. Ga. Southern).

TOUCHDOWN PASSES
14—Todd Hammel, Stephen F. Austin, 1989 (5 vs. Grambling, 4 vs. Southwest Mo. St., 2 vs. Furman, 3 vs. Ga. Southern).

COMPLETION PERCENTAGE (Min. 40 Completions)
.769—Giovanni Carmazzi, Hofstra, 1999, 50 of 65 (22-30 vs. Lehigh, 28-35 vs. Illinois St.)

RECEPTIONS
41—Joe Douglass, Montana, 1996 (10 vs. Nicholls St., 10 vs. East Tenn. St., 8 vs. Troy St., 13 vs. Marshall).

NET YARDS RECEIVING
636—Randy Moss, Marshall, 1996 (288 vs. Delaware, 82 vs. Furman, 46 vs. Northern Iowa, 220 vs. Montana).

TOUCHDOWN RECEPTIONS
10—Randy Moss, Marshall, 1996 (3 vs. Delaware, 2 vs. Furman, 1 vs. Northern Iowa, 4 vs. Montana).

POINTS
74—Adrian Peterson, Ga. Southern, 1999 (6 vs. Northern Ariz., 32 vs. Massachusetts, 18 vs. Illinois St., 18 vs. Youngstown St.).

TOUCHDOWNS
12—Adrian Peterson, Ga. Southern, 1999 (1 vs. Northern Ariz., 5 vs. Massachusetts, 3 vs. Illinois St., 3 vs. Youngstown St.).

LONGEST PLAYS

RUSH
90—Henry Fields, McNeese St. (38) vs. Idaho (21), 11-26-94, TD.

PASS (Including Run)
90—Paul Singer 22 pass to Derek Swanson and 68 fumble recovery advancement by Steve Williams, Western Ill. (32) vs. Western Ky. (35), 11-26-88.

FIELD GOAL
56—Tony Zendejas, Nevada (27) vs. Idaho St. (20), 11-26-83.

PUNT
88—Mike Cassidy, Rhode Island (20) vs. Montana St. (32), 12-8-84.

PUNT RETURN
84—Rob Friese, Eastern Wash. (14) vs. Northern Iowa (17), 12-7-85, TD.

KICKOFF RETURN
100—Chris Fontenette, McNeese St. (7) vs. Northern Iowa (29), 12-5-92, TD.

INTERCEPTION RETURN
100—Melvin Cunningham, Marshall (28) vs. James Madison (21) (ot), 12-3-94, TD; Paul Williams, Delaware (38) vs. Hofstra (17), 11-25-95, TD.

FUMBLE RETURN
95—Randy Smith, Youngstown St. (63) vs. Alcorn St. (20), 11-25-94, TD.

Team Records

GAME

FIRST DOWNS
41—Montana (45) vs. Ga. Southern (0), 12-2-95.

FIRST DOWNS BY RUSHING
26—La.-Monroe (78) vs. Alcorn St. (27), 11-28-92.

FIRST DOWNS BY PASSING
29—Alcorn St. (20) vs. Youngstown St. (63), 11-25-94.

NET YARDS RUSHING
638—Ga. Southern (59) vs. Youngstown St. (24), 12-18-99.

RUSHES ATTEMPTED
81—Youngstown St. (10) vs. Samford (0), 12-14-91.

NET YARDS PASSING
537—Montana (30) vs. McNeese St. (28), 12-3-94.

PASSES ATTEMPTED
90—Rhode Island (15) vs. Furman (59), 12-7-85.

PASSES COMPLETED
52—Alcorn St. (20) vs. Youngstown St. (63), 11-25-94.

PASSES INTERCEPTED
7—Western Caro. (7) vs. Southern Ill. (43), 12-17-83; Rhode Island (15) vs. Furman (59), 12-7-85; Weber St. (23) vs. Marshall (51), 12-5-87.

COMPLETION PERCENTAGE (Min. 20 Attempts)
.850—Illinois St. (37) vs. Hofstra (20), 12-4-99 (34 of 40).

NET YARDS RUSHING AND PASSING
742—La.-Monroe (78) vs. Alcorn St. (27), 11-28-92 (502 rushing, 240 passing).

RUSHING AND PASSING PLAYS
114—Nevada (42) vs. Furman (35) (3 ot), 12-1-90 (47 rushing, 67 passing).

PUNTING AVERAGE (Min. 4 punts)
51.8—Western Ill. (24) vs. Florida A&M (21), 12-5-98 (8 for 414).

PUNTS
14—Jackson St. (0) vs. Stephen F. Austin (24), 11-26-88.

PUNTS BLOCKED
2—Florida A&M (35) vs. Massachusetts (28), 12-16-78; Boise St. (14) vs. Grambling (9), 12-13-80.

YARDS GAINED ON PUNT RETURNS
128—William & Mary (45) vs. Jackson St. (6), 11-30-96.

YARDS GAINED ON KICKOFF RETURNS
232—Eastern Ky. (32) vs. La.-Monroe (33), 12-5-87.

YARDS GAINED ON INTERCEPTION RETURNS
164—Marshall (51) vs. Weber St. (23), 12-5-87.

YARDS PENALIZED
172—Tennessee St. (32) vs. Jackson St. (23), 11-29-86.

FUMBLES LOST
7—Jackson St. (8) vs. Marshall (38), 11-25-95.

POINTS
78—La.-Monroe vs. Alcorn St. (27), 11-28-92.

TOURNAMENT

FIRST DOWNS
125—Montana, 1995 (25 vs. Eastern Ky., 41 vs. Ga. Southern, 38 vs. Stephen F. Austin, 21 vs. Marshall).

NET YARDS RUSHING
2,030—Ga. Southern, 1999 (559 vs. Northern Ariz., 470 vs. Massachusetts, 363 vs. Illinois St., 638 vs. Youngstown St.).

NET YARDS PASSING
1,703—Montana, 1996 (447 vs. Nicholls St., 467 vs. East Tenn. St., 454 vs. Troy St., 335 vs. Marshall).

NET YARDS RUSHING AND PASSING
2,253—Ga. Southern, 1999 (659 vs. Northern Ariz., 500 vs. Massachusetts, 439 vs. Illinois St., 655 vs. Youngstown St.).

PASSES ATTEMPTED
197—Montana, 1996 (53 vs. Nicholls St., 44 vs. East Tenn. St., 45 vs. Troy St., 55 vs. Marshall).

PASSES COMPLETED
137—Montana, 1995 (35 vs. Eastern Ky., 42 vs. Ga. Southern, 31 vs. Stephen F. Austin, 29 vs. Marshall).

PASSES INTERCEPTED
11—Stephen F. Austin, 1989 (0 vs. Grambling, 4 vs. Southwest Mo. St., 2 vs. Furman, 5 vs. Ga. Southern).

PUNTS
29—Northern Iowa, 1992 (11 vs. Eastern Wash., 10 vs. McNeese St., 8 vs. Youngstown St.).

YARDS PENALIZED
350—Ga. Southern, 1986 (106 vs. N.C. A&T, 104 vs. Nicholls St., 75 vs. Nevada, 65 vs. Arkansas St.).

FUMBLES LOST
9—Nevada, 1983 (3 vs. Idaho St., 4 vs. North Texas, 2 vs. Southern Ill.); Youngstown St., 1991 (3 vs. Villanova, 1 vs. Nevada, 4 vs. Samford, 1 vs. Marshall); Ga. Southern, 1998 (1 vs. Colgate, 2 vs. Connecticut, 0 vs. Western Ill., 6 vs. Massachusetts).

POINTS
203—Ga. Southern, 1986 (52 vs. N.C. A&T, 55 vs. Nicholls St., 48 vs. Nevada, 48 vs. Arkansas St.).

Championship Game Records

INDIVIDUAL

NET YARDS RUSHING
247—Adrian Peterson, Ga. Southern (59) vs. Youngstown St. (24), 1999 (25 carries).

RUSHES ATTEMPTED
35—Marcel Shipp, Massachusetts (55) vs. Ga. Southern (43), 1998 (244 yards).

TOUCHDOWNS BY RUSHING
4—John Bagwell, Furman (42) vs. Ga. Southern (44), 1985.

NET YARDS PASSING
474—Tony Peterson, Marshall (42) vs. La.-Monroe (43), 1987 (28 of 54).

PASSES ATTEMPTED
57—Kelly Bradley, Montana St. (19) vs. Louisiana Tech (6), 1984 (32 completions).

PASSES COMPLETED
36—Brian Ah Yat, Montana (29) vs. Marshall (49), 1996 (55 attempts).

PASSES HAD INTERCEPTED
7—Jeff Gilbert, Western Caro. (7) vs. Southern Ill. (43), 1983.

TOUCHDOWN PASSES COMPLETED
4— Tracy Ham, Ga. Southern (44) vs. Furman (42), 1985; Tony Peterson, Marshall (42) vs. La.-Monroe (43), 1987; Eric Kresser, Marshall (49) vs. Montana (29), 1996.

COMPLETION PERCENTAGE (Min. 8 Attempts)
.875—Mark Brungard, Youngstown St. (17) vs. Marshall (5), 1993 (7 of 8).

NET YARDS RUSHING AND PASSING
509—Tracy Ham, Ga. Southern (44) vs. Furman (42), 1985 (90 rushing, 419 passing; 56 plays).

NUMBER OF RUSHING AND PASSING PLAYS
67—Brian Ah Yat, Montana (29) vs. Marshall (49), 1996 (12 rush, 55 pass; 301 yards).

PUNTING AVERAGE (Min. 3 Punts)
51.0—Andrew Maclay, Massachusetts (55) vs. Ga. Southern (43), 1998 (4 for 204).

NUMBER OF PUNTS
10—Rick Titus, Delaware (14) vs. Eastern Ky. (17), 1982 (41.6 average).

PASSES CAUGHT
13—Joe Douglass, Montana (29) vs. Marshall (49), 1996 (117 yards).

NET YARDS RECEIVING
220—Randy Moss, Marshall (49) vs. Montana (29), 1996 (9 catches).

TOUCHDOWN PASSES CAUGHT
4—Randy Moss, Marshall (49) vs. Montana (29), 1996 (9 catches for 220 yards).

PASSES INTERCEPTED
4—Greg Shipp, Southern Ill. (43) vs. Western Caro. (7), 1983.

YARDS GAINED ON INTERCEPTION RETURNS
58—Chris Cook, Boise St. (14) vs. Youngstown St. (28), 1994 (1 interception).

YARDS GAINED ON PUNT RETURNS
99—Anthony Williams, Ga. Southern (59) vs. Youngstown St. (24), 1999 (6 returns).

YARDS GAINED ON KICKOFF RETURNS
213—Andre Coleman, Youngstown St. (24) vs. Ga. Southern (59), 1999 (9 returns).

POINTS
24—John Bagwell, Furman (42) vs. Ga. Southern (44), 1985; Randy Moss, Marshall (49) vs. Montana (29), 1996.

TOUCHDOWNS
4—John Bagwell, Furman (42) vs. Ga. Southern (44), 1985; Randy Moss, Marshall (49) vs. Montana (29), 1996.

EXTRA POINTS
8—Chris Chambers, Ga. Southern (59) vs. Youngstown St. (24), 1999.

FIELD GOALS
4—Tim Foley, Ga. Southern (48) vs. Arkansas St. (21), 1986.

LONGEST RUSH
66—J. R. Revere, Ga. Southern (59) vs Youngstown St. (24), 1999.

LONGEST PASS COMPLETION
79—Tracy Ham to Ricky Harris, Ga. Southern (48) vs. Arkansas St. (21), 1986.

LONGEST FIELD GOAL
55—David Cool, Ga. Southern (12) vs. Furman (17), 1988.

LONGEST PUNT
72—Rick Titus, Delaware (14) vs. Eastern Ky. (17), 1982.

TEAM

FIRST DOWNS
31—Montana (29) vs. Marshall (49), 1996 (11 rush, 17 pass, 3 penalty).

FIRST DOWNS BY RUSHING
23—Ga. Southern (59) vs. Youngstown St. (24), 1999.

FIRST DOWNS BY PASSING
19—Marshall (42) vs. La.-Monroe (43), 1987.

FIRST DOWNS BY PENALTY
3— Eastern Ky. (23) vs. Idaho St. (34), 1981; Furman (42) vs. Ga. Southern (44), 1985; La.-Monroe (43) vs. Marshall (42), 1987; Montana (29) vs. Marshall (49), 1996.

NET YARDS RUSHING
638—Ga. Southern (59) vs. Youngstown St. (24), 1999 (59 attempts).

RUSHES ATTEMPTED
76—Florida A&M (35) vs. Massachusetts (28), 1978 (470 yards).

NET YARDS PASSING
474—Marshall (42) vs. La.-Monroe (43), 1987 (28 of 54).

PASSES ATTEMPTED
57—Montana St. (19) vs. Louisiana Tech (6), 1984 (32 completions).

PASSES COMPLETED
36—Montana (29) vs. Marshall (49), 1996 (55 attempts).

COMPLETION PERCENTAGE
(Min. 10 Attempts)
.760—Southern Ill. (43) vs. Western Caro. (7), 1983 (19 of 25).

PASSES HAD INTERCEPTED
7—Western Caro. (7) vs. Southern Ill. (43), 1983.

NET YARDS RUSHING AND PASSING
655—Ga. Southern (59) vs. Youngstown St. (24), 1999 (638 rushing, 17 passing; 63 plays).

RUSHING AND PASSING PLAYS
90—Montana (29) vs. Marshall (49), 1996 (35 rushing, 55 passing; 430 yards).

PUNTING AVERAGE
(Min. 3 Punts)
51.0—Massachusetts (55) vs. Ga. Southern (43), 1998 (4 for 204).

NUMBER OF PUNTS
10—Delaware (14) vs. Eastern Ky. (17), 1982 (41.6 average).

YARDS GAINED ON PUNT RETURNS
99—Ga. Southern (59) vs. Youngstown St. (24), 1999 (7 returns).

YARDS GAINED ON KICKOFF RETURNS
229—Western Caro. (7) vs. Southern Ill. (43), 1983 (8 returns).

YARDS GAINED ON INTERCEPTION RETURNS
70—Marshall (31) vs. Youngstown St. (28), 1992 (2 interceptions).

YARDS PENALIZED
162—Idaho St. (34) vs. Eastern Ky. (23), 1981 (12 penalties).

FUMBLES
6—Ga. Southern (43) vs. Massachusetts (55), 1998 (6 lost).

FUMBLES LOST
6—Ga. Southern (43) vs. Massachusetts (55), 1998 (6 fumbles).

POINTS
59—Ga. Southern vs. Youngstown St. (24), 1999.

ATTENDANCE
32,106—Marshall University Stadium, Huntington, W.Va., 1995.

Year-by-Year Division I-AA Championship Results

Year (Number of Teams)	Coach	Record	Result
1978 (4)			
Florida A&M	Rudy Hubbard	2-0	Champion
Massachusetts	Bob Pickett	1-1	Second
Jackson St.	W. C. Gorden	0-1	Lost 1st Round
Nevada	Chris Ault	0-1	Lost 1st Round
1979 (4)			
Eastern Ky.	Roy Kidd	2-0	Champion
Lehigh	John Whitehead	1-1	Second
Murray St.	Mike Gottfried	0-1	Lost 1st Round
Nevada	Chris Ault	0-1	Lost 1st Round
1980 (4)			
Boise St.	Jim Criner	2-0	Champion
Eastern Ky.	Roy Kidd	1-1	Second
Grambling	Eddie Robinson	0-1	Lost 1st Round
Lehigh	John Whitehead	0-1	Lost 1st Round
1981 (8)			
Idaho St.	Dave Kragthorpe	3-0	Champion
Eastern Ky.	Roy Kidd	2-1	Second
Boise St.	Jim Criner	1-1	Semifinalist
South Carolina St.	Bill Davis	1-1	Semifinalist
Delaware	Tubby Raymond	0-1	Lost 1st Round
Jackson St.	W. C. Gorden	0-1	Lost 1st Round
Rhode Island	Bob Griffin	0-1	Lost 1st Round
*Tennessee St.	John Merritt	0-1	Vacated
1982 (12)			
Eastern Ky.	Roy Kidd	3-0	Champion
Delaware	Tubby Raymond	2-1	Second
Louisiana Tech	Billy Brewer	1-1	Semifinalist
*Tennessee St.	John Merritt	1-1	Vacated
Colgate	Fred Dunlap	1-1	Quarterfinalist
Eastern Ill.	Darrell Mudra	1-1	Quarterfinalist
Idaho	Dennis Erickson	1-1	Quarterfinalist
South Carolina St.	Bill Davis	1-1	Quarterfinalist
Boston U.	Rick Taylor	0-1	Lost 1st Round
Furman	Dick Sheridan	0-1	Lost 1st Round
Jackson St.	W. C. Gorden	0-1	Lost 1st Round
Montana	Larry Donovan	0-1	Lost 1st Round
1983 (12)			
Southern Ill.	Rey Dempsey	3-0	Champion
Western Caro.	Bob Waters	3-1	Second
Furman	Dick Sheridan	1-1	Semifinalist
Nevada	Chris Ault	2-1	Semifinalist
Boston U.	Rick Taylor	1-1	Quarterfinalist
Holy Cross	Rick Carter	0-1	Quarterfinalist
Indiana St.	Dennis Raetz	1-1	Quarterfinalist
North Texas	Corky Nelson	0-1	Quarterfinalist
Colgate	Fred Dunlap	0-1	Lost 1st Round
Eastern Ill.	Al Molde	0-1	Lost 1st Round
Eastern Ky.	Roy Kidd	0-1	Lost 1st Round
Idaho St.	Jim Koetter	0-1	Lost 1st Round
1984 (12)			
Montana St.	Dave Arnold	3-0	Champion
Louisiana Tech	A. L. Williams	3-1	Second
Middle Tenn. St.	James Donnelly	2-1	Semifinalist
Rhode Island	Bob Griffin	1-1	Semifinalist
Alcorn St.	Marino Casem	0-1	Quarterfinalist
Arkansas St.	Larry Lacewell	1-1	Quarterfinalist
Indiana St.	Dennis Raetz	0-1	Quarterfinalist
Richmond	Dal Shealy	1-1	Quarterfinalist
Boston U.	Rick Taylor	0-1	Lost 1st Round
Eastern Ky.	Roy Kidd	0-1	Lost 1st Round
Mississippi Val.	Archie Cooley Jr.	0-1	Lost 1st Round
Chattanooga	Buddy Nix	0-1	Lost 1st Round
1985 (12)			
Ga. Southern	Erk Russell	4-0	Champion
Furman	Dick Sheridan	2-1	Second
Nevada	Chris Ault	1-1	Semifinalist
Northern Iowa	Darrell Mudra	1-1	Semifinalist
Arkansas St.	Larry Lacewell	1-1	Quarterfinalist
Eastern Wash.	Dick Zornes	1-1	Quarterfinalist
Middle Tenn. St.	James Donnelly	0-1	Quarterfinalist
Rhode Island	Bob Griffin	1-1	Quarterfinalist
Akron	Jim Dennison	0-1	Lost 1st Round
Grambling	Eddie Robinson	0-1	Lost 1st Round
Idaho	Dennis Erickson	0-1	Lost 1st Round
Jackson St.	W. C. Gorden	0-1	Lost 1st Round
1986 (16)			
Ga. Southern	Erk Russell	4-0	Champion
Arkansas St.	Larry Lacewell	3-1	Second
Eastern Ky.	Roy Kidd	2-1	Semifinalist
Nevada	Chris Ault	2-1	Semifinalist

Year (Number of Teams)	Coach	Record	Result
Delaware	Tubby Raymond	1-1	Quarterfinalist
Eastern Ill.	Al Molde	1-1	Quarterfinalist
Nicholls St.	Sonny Jackson	1-1	Quarterfinalist
Tennessee St.	William Thomas	1-1	Quarterfinalist
Appalachian St.	Sparky Woods	0-1	Lost 1st Round
Furman	Jimmy Satterfield	0-1	Lost 1st Round
Idaho	Keith Gilbertson	0-1	Lost 1st Round
Jackson St.	W. C. Gorden	0-1	Lost 1st Round
Murray St.	Frank Beamer	0-1	Lost 1st Round
N.C. A&T	Maurice Forte	0-1	Lost 1st Round
Sam Houston St.	Ron Randleman	0-1	Lost 1st Round
William & Mary	Jimmye Laycock	0-1	Lost 1st Round

1987 (16)

La.-Monroe	Pat Collins	4-0	Champion
Marshall	George Chaump	3-1	Second
Appalachian St.	Sparky Woods	2-1	Semifinalist
Northern Iowa	Darrell Mudra	2-1	Semifinalist
Arkansas St.	Larry Lacewell	1-1	Quarterfinalist
Eastern Ky.	Roy Kidd	1-1	Quarterfinalist
Ga. Southern	Erk Russell	1-1	Quarterfinalist
Weber St.	Mike Price	1-1	Quarterfinalist
Idaho	Keith Gilbertson	0-1	Lost 1st Round
Jackson St.	W. C. Gorden	0-1	Lost 1st Round
James Madison	Joe Purzycki	0-1	Lost 1st Round
Maine	Tim Murphy	0-1	Lost 1st Round
North Texas	Corky Nelson	0-1	Lost 1st Round
Richmond	Dal Shealy	0-1	Lost 1st Round
Western Ky.	Dave Roberts	0-1	Lost 1st Round
Youngstown St.	Jim Tressel	0-1	Lost 1st Round

1988 (16)

Furman	Jimmy Satterfield	4-0	Champion
Ga. Southern	Erk Russell	3-1	Second
Eastern Ky.	Roy Kidd	2-1	Semifinalist
Idaho	Keith Gilbertson	2-1	Semifinalist
Marshall	George Chaump	1-1	Quarterfinalist
Northwestern St.	Sam Goodwin	1-1	Quarterfinalist
Stephen F. Austin	Jim Hess	1-1	Quarterfinalist
Western Ky.	Dave Roberts	1-1	Quarterfinalist
Boise St.	Skip Hall	0-1	Lost 1st Round
Citadel	Charlie Taaffe	0-1	Lost 1st Round
Delaware	Tubby Raymond	0-1	Lost 1st Round
Jackson St.	W. C. Gorden	0-1	Lost 1st Round
Massachusetts	Jim Reid	0-1	Lost 1st Round
Montana	Don Read	0-1	Lost 1st Round
North Texas	Corky Nelson	0-1	Lost 1st Round
Western Ill.	Bruce Craddock	0-1	Lost 1st Round

1989 (16)

Ga. Southern	Erk Russell	4-0	Champion
*Stephen F. Austin	Lynn Graves	3-1	Vacated
Furman	Jimmy Satterfield	2-1	Semifinalist
Montana	Don Read	2-1	Semifinalist
Eastern Ill.	Bob Spoo	1-1	Quarterfinalist
Middle Tenn. St.	James Donnelly	1-1	Quarterfinalist
Southwest Mo. St.	Jesse Branch	1-1	Quarterfinalist
Youngstown St.	Jim Tressel	1-1	Quarterfinalist
Appalachian St.	Jerry Moore	0-1	Lost 1st Round
Eastern Ky.	Roy Kidd	0-1	Lost 1st Round
Grambling	Eddie Robinson	0-1	Lost 1st Round
Idaho	John L. Smith	0-1	Lost 1st Round
Jackson St.	W. C. Gorden	0-1	Lost 1st Round
Maine	Tom Lichtenberg	0-1	Lost 1st Round
Villanova	Andy Talley	0-1	Lost 1st Round
William & Mary	Jimmye Laycock	0-1	Lost 1st Round

1990 (16)

Ga. Southern	Tim Stowers	4-0	Champion
Nevada	Chris Ault	3-1	Second
Boise St.	Skip Hall	2-1	Semifinalist
UCF	Gene McDowell	2-1	Semifinalist
Furman	Jimmy Satterfield	1-1	Quarterfinalist
Idaho	John L. Smith	1-1	Quarterfinalist
Middle Tenn. St.	James Donnelly	1-1	Quarterfinalist
William & Mary	Jimmye Laycock	1-1	Quarterfinalist
Citadel	Charlie Taaffe	0-1	Lost 1st Round
Eastern Ky.	Roy Kidd	0-1	Lost 1st Round
Jackson St.	W. C. Gorden	0-1	Lost 1st Round
La.-Monroe	Dave Roberts	0-1	Lost 1st Round
Massachusetts	Jim Reid	0-1	Lost 1st Round
Northern Iowa	Terry Allen	0-1	Lost 1st Round
Southwest Mo. St.	Jesse Branch	0-1	Lost 1st Round
Youngstown St.	Jim Tressel	0-1	Lost 1st Round

1991 (16)

Youngstown St.	Jim Tressel	4-0	Champion
Marshall	Jim Donnan	3-1	Second
Eastern Ky.	Roy Kidd	2-1	Semifinalist
Samford	Terry Bowden	2-1	Semifinalist
James Madison	Rip Scherer	1-1	Quarterfinalist
Middle Tenn. St.	James Donnelly	1-1	Quarterfinalist
Nevada	Chris Ault	1-1	Quarterfinalist
Northern Iowa	Terry Allen	1-1	Quarterfinalist
Appalachian St.	Jerry Moore	0-1	Lost 1st Round
Delaware	Tubby Raymond	0-1	Lost 1st Round
McNeese St.	Bobby Keasler	0-1	Lost 1st Round
New Hampshire	Bill Bowes	0-1	Lost 1st Round
Sam Houston St.	Ron Randleman	0-1	Lost 1st Round
Villanova	Andy Talley	0-1	Lost 1st Round
Weber St.	Dave Arslanian	0-1	Lost 1st Round
Western Ill.	Randy Ball	0-1	Lost 1st Round

1992 (16)

Marshall	Jim Donnan	4-0	Champion
Youngstown St.	Jim Tressel	3-1	Second
Delaware	Tubby Raymond	2-1	Semifinalist
Northern Iowa	Terry Allen	2-1	Semifinalist
Citadel	Charlie Taaffe	1-1	Quarterfinalist
La.-Monroe	Dave Roberts	1-1	Quarterfinalist
McNeese St.	Bobby Keasler	1-1	Quarterfinalist
Middle Tenn. St.	James Donnelly	1-1	Quarterfinalist
Alcorn St.	Cardell Jones	0-1	Lost 1st Round
Appalachian St.	Jerry Moore	0-1	Lost 1st Round
Eastern Ky.	Roy Kidd	0-1	Lost 1st Round
Eastern Wash.	Dick Zornes	0-1	Lost 1st Round
Idaho	John L. Smith	0-1	Lost 1st Round
N.C. A&T	Bill Hayes	0-1	Lost 1st Round
Samford	Terry Bowden	0-1	Lost 1st Round
Villanova	Andy Talley	0-1	Lost 1st Round

1993 (16)

Youngstown St.	Jim Tressel	4-0	Champion
Marshall	Jim Donnan	3-1	Second
Idaho	John L. Smith	2-1	Semifinalist
Troy St.	Larry Blakeney	2-1	Semifinalist
Boston U.	Dan Allen	1-1	Quarterfinalist
Delaware	Tubby Raymond	1-1	Quarterfinalist
Ga. Southern	Tim Stowers	1-1	Quarterfinalist
McNeese St.	Bobby Keasler	1-1	Quarterfinalist
UCF	Gene McDowell	0-1	Lost 1st Round
Eastern Ky.	Roy Kidd	0-1	Lost 1st Round
Howard	Steve Wilson	0-1	Lost 1st Round
La.-Monroe	Dave Roberts	0-1	Lost 1st Round
Montana	Don Read	0-1	Lost 1st Round
Northern Iowa	Terry Allen	0-1	Lost 1st Round
Stephen F. Austin	John Pearce	0-1	Lost 1st Round
William & Mary	Jimmye Laycock	0-1	Lost 1st Round

1994 (16)

Youngstown St.	Jim Tressel	4-0	Champion
Boise St.	Pokey Allen	3-1	Second
Marshall	Jim Donnan	2-1	Semifinalist
Montana	Don Read	2-1	Semifinalist
Appalachian St.	Jerry Moore	1-1	Quarterfinalist
Eastern Ky.	Roy Kidd	1-1	Quarterfinalist
James Madison	Rip Scherer	1-1	Quarterfinalist
McNeese St.	Bobby Keasler	1-1	Quarterfinalist
Alcorn St.	Cardell Jones	0-1	Lost 1st Round
Boston U.	Dan Allen	0-1	Lost 1st Round
Idaho	John L. Smith	0-1	Lost 1st Round
Middle Tenn. St.	James Donnelly	0-1	Lost 1st Round
New Hampshire	Bill Bowes	0-1	Lost 1st Round
North Texas	Matt Simon	0-1	Lost 1st Round
Northern Iowa	Terry Allen	0-1	Lost 1st Round
Troy St.	Larry Blakeney	0-1	Lost 1st Round

1995 (16)

Montana	Don Read	4-0	Champion
Marshall	Jim Donnan	3-1	Second
McNeese St.	Bobby Keasler	2-1	Semifinalist
Stephen F. Austin	John Pearce	2-1	Semifinalist
Appalachian St.	Jerry Moore	1-1	Quarterfinalist
Delaware	Tubby Raymond	1-1	Quarterfinalist
Ga. Southern	Tim Stowers	1-1	Quarterfinalist
Northern Iowa	Terry Allen	1-1	Quarterfinalist
Eastern Ill.	Bob Spoo	0-1	Lost 1st Round
Eastern Ky.	Roy Kidd	0-1	Lost 1st Round
Hofstra	Joe Gardi	0-1	Lost 1st Round
Idaho	Chris Tormey	0-1	Lost 1st Round
Jackson St.	James Carson	0-1	Lost 1st Round
James Madison	Alex Wood	0-1	Lost 1st Round

DIVISION I-AA CHAMPIONSHIP—YEAR-BY-YEAR RESULTS   415

Year (Number of Teams)	Coach	Record	Result
Murray St.	Houston Nutt	0-1	Lost 1st Round
Troy St.	Larry Blakeney	0-1	Lost 1st Round

1996 (16)

Marshall	Bob Pruett	4-0	Champion
Montana	Mick Dennehy	3-1	Second
Northern Iowa	Terry Allen	2-1	Semifinalist
Troy St.	Larry Blakeney	2-1	Semifinalist
East Tenn. St.	Mike Cavan	1-1	Quarterfinalist
Furman	Bobby Johnson	1-1	Quarterfinalist
Murray St.	Houston Nutt	1-1	Quarterfinalist
William & Mary	Jimmye Laycock	1-1	Quarterfinalist
Delaware	Tubby Raymond	0-1	Lost 1st Round
Eastern Ill.	Bob Spoo	0-1	Lost 1st Round
Florida A&M	Billy Joe	0-1	Lost 1st Round
Jackson St.	James Carson	0-1	Lost 1st Round
Nicholls St.	Darren Barbier	0-1	Lost 1st Round
Northern Ariz.	Stephen Axman	0-1	Lost 1st Round
Villanova	Andy Talley	0-1	Lost 1st Round
Western Ill.	Randy Ball	0-1	Lost 1st Round

1997 (16)

Youngstown St.	Jim Tressel	4-0	Champion
McNeese St.	Bobby Keasler	3-1	Second
Delaware	Tubby Raymond	2-1	Semifinalist
Eastern Wash.	Mike Kramer	2-1	Semifinalist
Ga. Southern	Paul Johnson	1-1	Quarterfinalist
Villanova	Andy Talley	1-1	Quarterfinalist
Western Ill.	Randy Ball	1-1	Quarterfinalist
Western Ky.	Jack Harbaugh	1-1	Quarterfinalist
Colgate	Dick Biddle	0-1	Lost 1st Round
Eastern Ky.	Roy Kidd	0-1	Lost 1st Round
Florida A&M	Billy Joe	0-1	Lost 1st Round
Hampton	Joe Taylor	0-1	Lost 1st Round
Hofstra	Joe Gardi	0-1	Lost 1st Round
Jackson St.	James Carson	0-1	Lost 1st Round
Montana	Mick Dennehy	0-1	Lost 1st Round
Northwestern St.	Sam Goodwin	0-1	Lost 1st Round

1998 (16)

Massachusetts	Mark Whipple	4-0	Champion
Ga. Southern	Paul Johnson	3-1	Second
Northwestern St.	Sam Goodwin	2-1	Semifinalist
Western Ill.	Randy Ball	2-1	Semifinalist
Appalachian St.	Jerry Moore	1-1	Quarterfinalist
Connecticut	Skip Holtz	1-1	Quarterfinalist
Florida A&M	Billy Joe	1-1	Quarterfinalist
Lehigh	Kevin Higgins	1-1	Quarterfinalist
Colgate	Dick Biddle	0-1	Lost 1st Round
Hampton	Joe Taylor	0-1	Lost 1st Round
Illinois St.	Todd Berry	0-1	Lost 1st Round
McNeese St.	Bobby Keasler	0-1	Lost 1st Round
Montana	Mick Dennehy	0-1	Lost 1st Round
Richmond	Jim Reid	0-1	Lost 1st Round
Tennessee St.	L. C. Cole	0-1	Lost 1st Round
Troy St.	Larry Blakeney	0-1	Lost 1st Round

1999 (16)

Ga. Southern	Paul Johnson	4-0	Champion
Youngstown St.	Jim Tressel	3-1	Second
Florida A&M	Billy Joe	2-1	Semifinalist
Illinois St.	Todd Berry	2-1	Semifinalist
Hofstra	Joe Gardi	1-1	Quarterfinalist
Massachusetts	Mark Whipple	1-1	Quarterfinalist
N.C. A&T	Bill Hayes	1-1	Quarterfinalist
Troy St.	Larry Blakeney	1-1	Quarterfinalist
Appalachian St.	Jerry Moore	0-1	Lost 1st Round
Colgate	Dick Biddle	0-1	Lost 1st Round
Furman	Bobby Johnson	0-1	Lost 1st Round
James Madison	Mickey Matthews	0-1	Lost 1st Round
Lehigh	Kevin Higgins	0-1	Lost 1st Round
Montana	Mick Dennehy	0-1	Lost 1st Round
Northern Ariz.	Jerome Souers	0-1	Lost 1st Round
Tennessee St.	L. C. Cole	0-1	Lost 1st Round

*Competition in championship vacated by action of the NCAA Committee on Infractions.

Division I-AA Championship Record of Each College by Coach

(69 Colleges; 1978-99)

	Yrs	Won	Lost	CH	2D
AKRON					
Jim Dennison (Wooster '60) 85	1	0	1	0	0
ALCORN ST.					
Marino Casem (Xavier [La.] '56) 84	1	0	1	0	0
Cardell Jones (Alcorn St. '65) 92, 94	2	0	2	0	0
TOTAL	3	0	3	0	0
APPALACHIAN ST.					
Sparky Woods (Carson-Newman '76) 86, 87	2	2	2	0	0
Jerry Moore (Baylor '61) 89, 91, 92, 94, 95, 98,99	7	3	7	0	0
TOTAL	9	5	9	0	0
ARKANSAS ST.					
Larry Lacewell (Ark.-Monticello '59) 84, 85, 86-2D, 87	4	6	4	0	1
BOISE ST.					
Jim Criner (Cal Poly Pomona '61) 80-CH, 81	2	3	1	1	0
Skip Hall (Concordia-M'head '66) 88, 90	2	2	2	0	0
Pokey Allen (Utah '65) 94-2D	1	3	1	0	1
TOTAL	5	8	4	1	1
BOSTON U.					
Rick Taylor (Gettysburg '64) 82, 83, 84	3	1	3	0	0
Dan Allen (Hanover '78) 93, 94	2	1	2	0	0
TOTAL	5	2	5	0	0
UCF					
Gene McDowell (Florida St. '63) 90, 93	2	2	2	0	0
CHATTANOOGA					
Buddy Nix (West Ala. '61) 84	1	0	1	0	0
CITADEL					
Charlie Taaffe (Siena '73) 88, 90, 92	3	1	3	0	0
COLGATE					
Fred Dunlap (Colgate '50) 82, 83	2	1	2	0	0
Dick Biddle (Duke '71) 97, 98, 99	3	0	3	0	0
TOTAL	5	1	5	0	0
DELAWARE					
Harold "Tubby" Raymond (Michigan '50) 81, 82-2D, 86, 88, 91, 92, 93, 95, 96, 97	10	9	10	0	1
EAST TENN. ST.					
Mike Cavan (Georgia '72) 96	1	1	1	0	0
EASTERN ILL.					
Darrell Mudra (Peru St. '51) 82	1	1	1	0	0
Al Molde (Gust. Adolphus '66) 83, 86	2	1	2	0	0
Bob Spoo (Purdue '60) 89, 95, 96	3	1	3	0	0
TOTAL	6	3	6	0	0
EASTERN KY.					
Roy Kidd (Eastern Ky. '54) 79-CH, 80-2D, 81-2D, 82-CH, 83, 84, 86, 87, 88, 89, 90, 91, 92, 93, 94, 95, 97	17	16	15	2	2
EASTERN WASH.					
Dick Zornes (Eastern Wash. '68) 85, 92	2	1	2	0	0
Mike Kramer (Idaho '77) 97	1	2	1	0	0
TOTAL	3	3	3	0	0
FLORIDA A&M					
Rudy Hubbard (Ohio St. '68) 78-CH	1	2	0	1	0
Billy Joe (Villanova '63) 96, 97, 98, 99	4	3	4	0	0
TOTAL	5	5	4	1	0
FURMAN					
Dick Sheridan (South Carolina '64) 82, 83, 85-2D	3	3	3	0	1
Jimmy Satterfield (South Carolina '62) 86, 88-CH, 89, 90	4	7	3	1	0
Bobby Johnson (Clemson '73) 96, 99	2	1	2	0	0
TOTAL	9	11	8	1	1
GA. SOUTHERN					
Erk Russell (Auburn '49) 85-CH, 86-CH, 87, 88-2D, 89-CH	5	16	2	3	1
Tim Stowers (Auburn '79) 90-CH, 93, 95	3	6	2	1	0
Paul Johnson (Western Caro. '74) 97, 98-2D, 99-CH	3	8	2	1	1
TOTAL	11	30	6	5	2
GRAMBLING					
Eddie Robinson (Leland '41) 80, 85, 89	3	0	3	0	0
HOFSTRA					
Joe Gardi (Maryland '60) 95, 97, 99	3	1	3	0	0
HOLY CROSS					
Rick Carter (Earlham '65) 83	1	0	1	0	0
HOWARD					
Steve Wilson (Howard '79) 93	1	0	1	0	0
IDAHO					
Dennis Erickson (Montana St. '70) 82, 85	2	1	2	0	0

CHAMPIONSHIP RESULTS

	Yrs	Won	Lost	CH	2D
Keith Gilbertson (Central Wash. '71) 86, 87, 88	3	2	3	0	0
John L. Smith (Weber St. '71) 89, 90, 92, 93, 94	5	3	5	0	0
Chris Tormey (Idaho '78) 95	1	0	1	0	0
TOTAL	11	6	11	0	0
IDAHO ST.					
Dave Kragthorpe (Utah St. '55) 81-CH	1	3	0	1	0
Jim Koetter (Idaho St. '61) 83	1	0	1	0	0
TOTAL	2	3	1	1	0
ILLINOIS ST.					
Todd Berry (Tulsa '83) 99	1	2	1	0	0
INDIANA ST.					
Dennis Raetz (Nebraska '68) 83, 84	2	1	2	0	0
JACKSON ST.					
W. C. Gorden (Tennessee St. '52) 78, 81, 82, 85, 86, 87, 88, 89, 90	9	0	9	0	0
James Carson (Jackson St. '63) 95, 96, 97	3	0	3	0	0
TOTAL	12	0	12	0	0
JAMES MADISON					
Joe Purzycki (Delaware '71) 87	1	0	1	0	0
Rip Scherer (William & Mary '74) 91, 94	2	2	2	0	0
Alex Wood (Iowa '79) 95	1	0	1	0	0
Mickey Matthews (West Tex. A&M '76) 99	1	0	1	0	0
TOTAL	5	2	5	0	0
LEHIGH					
John Whitehead (East Stroudsburg '50) 79-2D, 80	2	1	2	0	1
Kevin Higgins (West Chester '77) 98, 99	2	1	2	0	0
TOTAL	4	2	4	0	1
LA.-MONROE					
Pat Collins (Louisiana Tech '63) 87-CH	1	4	0	1	0
Dave Roberts (Western Caro. '68) 90, 92, 93	3	1	3	0	0
TOTAL	4	5	3	1	0
LOUISIANA TECH					
Billy Brewer (Mississippi '61) 82	1	1	1	0	0
A. L. Williams (Louisiana Tech '57) 84-2D	1	3	1	0	1
TOTAL	2	4	2	0	1
MAINE					
Tim Murphy (Springfield '78) 87	1	0	1	0	0
Tom Lichtenberg (Louisville '62) 89	1	0	1	0	0
TOTAL	2	0	2	0	0
MARSHALL					
George Chaump (Bloomsburg '58) 87-2D, 88	2	4	2	0	1
Jim Donnan (North Carolina St. '67) 91-2D, 92-CH, 93-2D, 94, 95-2D	5	15	4	1	3
Bob Pruett (Marshall '65) 96-CH	1	4	0	1	0
TOTAL	8	23	6	2	4
MASSACHUSETTS					
Bob Pickett (Maine '59) 78-2D	1	1	1	0	1
Jim Reid (Maine '73) 88, 90	2	0	2	0	0
Mark Whipple (Brown '79) 98-CH, 99	2	5	1	1	0
TOTAL	5	6	4	1	1
McNEESE ST.					
Bobby Keasler (La.-Monroe '70) 91, 92, 93, 94, 95, 97-2D, 98	7	8	7	0	1
MIDDLE TENN. ST.					
James "Boots" Donnelly (Middle Tenn. St. '65) 84, 85, 89, 90, 91, 92, 94	7	6	7	0	0
MISSISSIPPI VAL.					
Archie Cooley Jr. (Jackson St. '62) 84	1	0	1	0	0
MONTANA					
Larry Donovan (Nebraska '64) 82	1	0	1	0	0
Don Read (Cal St. Sacramento '59) 88, 89, 93, 94, 95-CH	5	8	4	1	0
Mick Dennehy (Montana '73) 96-2D, 97, 98, 99	4	3	4	0	1
TOTAL	10	11	9	1	1
MONTANA ST.					
Dave Arnold (Drake '67) 84-CH	1	3	0	1	0
MURRAY ST.					
Mike Gottfried (Morehead St. '66) 79	1	0	1	0	0
Frank Beamer (Virginia Tech '69) 86	1	0	1	0	0
Houston Nutt (Oklahoma St. '81) 95, 96	2	1	2	0	0
TOTAL	4	1	4	0	0
NEVADA					
Chris Ault (Nevada '68) 78, 79, 83, 85, 86, 90-2D, 91	7	9	7	0	1

	Yrs	Won	Lost	CH	2D
NEW HAMPSHIRE					
Bill Bowes (Penn St. '65) 91, 94	2	0	2	0	0
NICHOLLS ST.					
Sonny Jackson (Nicholls St. '63) 86	1	1	1	0	0
Darren Barbier (Nicholls St. '82) 96	1	0	1	0	0
TOTAL	2	1	2	0	0
N.C. A&T					
Maurice "Mo" Forte (Minnesota '71) 86	1	0	1	0	0
Bill Hayes (N.C. Central '64) 92, 99	2	1	2	0	0
TOTAL	3	1	3	0	0
NORTH TEXAS					
Corky Nelson (Southwest Tex. St. '64) 83, 87, 88	3	0	3	0	0
Matt Simon (Eastern N.M. '76) 94	1	0	1	0	0
TOTAL	4	0	4	0	0
NORTHERN ARIZ.					
Stephen Axman (C. W. Post '69) 96	1	0	1	0	0
Jerome Souers (Oregon '83) 99	1	0	1	0	0
TOTAL	2	0	2	0	0
NORTHERN IOWA					
Darrell Mudra (Peru St. '51) 85, 87	2	3	2	0	0
Terry Allen (Northern Iowa '79) 90, 91, 92, 93, 94, 95, 96	7	6	7	0	0
TOTAL	9	9	9	0	0
NORTHWESTERN ST.					
Sam Goodwin (Henderson St. '66) 88, 97, 98	3	3	3	0	0
RHODE ISLAND					
Bob Griffin (Southern Conn. St. '63) 81, 84, 85	3	2	3	0	0
RICHMOND					
Dal Shealy (Carson-Newman '60) 84, 87	2	1	2	0	0
Jim Reid (Maine '73) 98	1	0	1	0	0
TOTAL	3	1	3	0	0
SAM HOUSTON ST.					
Ron Randleman (William Penn '64) 86, 91	2	0	2	0	0
SAMFORD					
Terry Bowden (West Virginia '78) 91, 92	2	2	2	0	0
SOUTH CAROLINA ST.					
Bill Davis (Johnson Smith '65) 81, 82	2	2	2	0	0
SOUTHERN ILL.					
Rey Dempsey (Geneva '58) 83-CH	1	3	0	1	0
SOUTHWEST MO. ST.					
Jesse Branch (Arkansas '64) 89, 90	2	1	2	0	0
STEPHEN F. AUSTIN¢					
Jim Hess (Southeastern Okla. '59) 88	1	1	1	0	0
Lynn Graves (Stephen F. Austin '65) 89-2D	1	3	1	0	1
John Pearce (Tex. A&M-Kingsville '70) 93, 95	2	2	2	0	0
TOTAL	4	6	4	0	1
TENNESSEE ST.*					
John Merritt (Kentucky St. '50) 81, 82	2	1	2	0	0
Bill Thomas (Tennessee St. '71) 86	1	1	1	0	0
L. C. Cole (Nebraska '80) 98, 99	2	0	2	0	0
TOTAL	5	2	5	0	0
TROY ST.					
Larry Blakeney (Auburn '70) 93, 94, 95, 96, 98, 99	6	5	6	0	0
VILLANOVA					
Andy Talley (Southern Conn. St. '67) 89, 91, 92, 96, 97	5	1	5	0	0
WEBER ST.					
Mike Price (Puget Sound '69) 87	1	1	1	0	0
Dave Arslanian (Weber St. '72) 91	1	0	1	0	0
TOTAL	2	1	2	0	0
WESTERN CARO.					
Bob Waters (Presbyterian '60) 83-2D	1	3	1	0	1
WESTERN ILL.					
Bruce Craddock (Truman '66) 88	1	0	1	0	0
Randy Ball (Truman '73) 91, 96, 97, 98	4	3	4	0	0
TOTAL	5	3	5	0	0
WESTERN KY.					
Dave Roberts (Western Caro. '68) 87, 88	2	1	2	0	0
Jack Harbaugh (Bowling Green '61) 97	1	1	1	0	0
TOTAL	3	2	3	0	0
WILLIAM & MARY					
Jimmye Laycock (William & Mary '70) 86, 89, 90, 93, 96	5	2	5	0	0

DIVISION I-AA CHAMPIONSHIP—SCHOOL RECORDS

YOUNGSTOWN ST.

	Yrs	Won	Lost	CH	2D
Jim Tressel (Baldwin-Wallace '75) 87, 89, 90, 91-CH, 92-2D, 93-CH, 94-CH, 97-CH, 99-2D	9	23	5	4	2

*Tennessee State's competition in the 1981 and 1982 Division I-AA championships was vacated by action of the NCAA Committee on Infractions (official record is 1-1).
¢Stephen F. Austin's competition in the 1989 Division I-AA championship was vacated by action of the NCAA Committee on Infractions (official record is 1-2).

Division I-AA Championship Attendance History

Year	Teams	G	Total Attend.	Avg. PG
1978	4	3	34,630	11,543
1979	4	3	20,300	6,767
1980	4	3	36,957	12,319
1981	8	7	81,455	11,636
1982	12	11	106,801	9,709
1983	12	11	103,631	9,421
1984	12	11	122,142	11,104
1985	12	11	86,996	7,909
1986	16	15	153,832	10,255
1987	16	15	133,956	8,930
1988	16	15	146,782	9,785
1989	16	15	145,198	9,680
1990	16	15	180,027	12,002
1991	16	15	169,605	11,307
1992	16	15	199,450	13,297
1993	16	15	178,884	11,926
1994	16	15	209,761	13,984
1995	16	15	209,367	13,958
1996	16	15	178,768	11,918
1997	16	15	152,219	10,418
1998	16	15	146,084	9,739
1999	16	15	178,742	11,916

1978
First Round (12/9):

	Site	Attendance
Florida A&M 15, Jackson St. 10	Jackson, Miss.	7,000
Massachusetts 44, Nevada 21	Reno, Nev.	14,026

Championship (12/16):
Florida A&M 35, Massachusetts 28	Wichita Falls, Tex.	13,604

1979
First Round (12/8):

	Site	Attendance
Lehigh 28, Murray St. 9	Murray, Ky.	10,000
Eastern Ky. 33, Nevada 30 (2 ot)	Richmond, Ky.	5,100

Championship (12/15):
Eastern Ky. 30, Lehigh 7	Orlando, Fla.	5,200

1980
First Round (12/13):

	Site	Attendance
Eastern Ky. 23, Lehigh 20	Bethlehem, Pa.	11,500
Boise St. 14, Grambling 9	Boise, Id.	17,300

Championship (12/20):
Boise St. 31, Eastern Ky. 29	Sacramento, Cal.	8,157

1981
First Round (12/5):

	Site	Attendance
Eastern Ky. 35, Delaware 28	Richmond, Ky.	8,100
Boise St. 19, Jackson St. 7	Jackson, Miss.	11,500
Idaho St. 51, Rhode Island 0	Pocatello, Id.	12,153
South Carolina St. 26, Tennessee St. 25 (ot)	Orangeburg, S.C.	6,224

Semifinals (12/12):
Eastern Ky. 23, Boise St. 17	Boise, Id.	20,176
Idaho St. 41, South Carolina St. 12	Pocatello, Id.	12,300

Championship (12/19):
Idaho St. 34, Eastern Ky. 23	Wichita Falls, Tex.	11,002

1982
First Round (11/27):

	Site	Attendance
Idaho 21, Montana 7	Moscow, Id.	8,000
Eastern Ill. 16, Jackson St. 13 (ot)	Charleston, Ill.	5,000
South Carolina St. 17, Furman 0	Greenville, S.C.	13,865
Colgate 21, Boston U. 7	Hamilton, N.Y.	5,000

Quarterfinals (12/4):
Eastern Ky. 38, Idaho 30	Richmond, Ky.	10,893
Tennessee St. 20, Eastern Ill. 19	Nashville, Tenn.	8,000
Louisiana Tech 38, South Carolina St. 3	Ruston, La.	13,000
Delaware 20, Colgate 13	Newark, Del.	11,448

Semifinals (12/11):
Eastern Ky. 13, Tennessee St. 7	Richmond, Ky.	7,338
Delaware 17, Louisiana Tech 0	Ruston, La.	13,000

Championship (12/18):
Eastern Ky. 17, Delaware 14	Wichita Falls, Tex.	11,257

1983
First Round (11/27):

	Site	Attendance
Indiana St. 16, Eastern Ill. 13 (2 ot)	Terre Haute, Ind.	6,222
Nevada 27, Idaho St. 20	Pocatello, Id.	10,333
Western Caro. 24, Colgate 23	Cullowhee, N.C.	6,500
Boston U. 24, Eastern Ky. 20	Richmond, Ky.	4,800

Quarterfinals (12/3):
Southern Ill. 23, Indiana St. 7	Carbondale, Ill.	8,000
Nevada 20, North Texas 17 (ot)	Reno, Nev.	7,878
Western Caro. 28, Holy Cross 21	Worcester, Mass.	10,814
Furman 35, Boston U. 16	Greenville, S.C.	7,600

Semifinals (12/10):
Southern Ill. 23, Nevada 7	Carbondale, Ill.	12,500
Western Caro. 14, Furman 7	Greenville, S.C.	13,034

Championship (12/17):
Southern Ill. 43, Western Caro. 7	Charleston, S.C.	15,950

1984
First Round (11/24):

	Site	Attendance
Louisiana Tech 66, Mississippi Val. 19	Ruston, La.	17,500
Middle Tenn. St. 27, Eastern Ky. 10	Richmond, Ky.	4,800
Richmond 35, Boston U. 33	Richmond, Va.	11,236
Arkansas St. 37, Chattanooga 10	Jonesboro, Ark.	10,872

Quarterfinals (12/1):
Louisiana Tech 44, Alcorn St. 21	Jackson, Miss.	16,204
Middle Tenn. St. 42, Indiana St. 41 (3 ot)	Terre Haute, Ind.	6,225
Rhode Island 23, Richmond 17	Kingston, R.I.	10,446
Montana St. 31, Arkansas St. 14	Bozeman, Mont.	12,037

Semifinals (12/8):
Louisiana Tech 21, Middle Tenn. St. 13	Murfreesboro, Tenn.	11,000
Montana St. 32, Rhode Island 20	Bozeman, Mont.	12,697

Championship (12/15):
Montana St. 19, Louisiana Tech 6	Charleston, S.C.	9,125

1985
First Round (11/30):

	Site	Attendance
Ga. Southern 27, Jackson St. 0	Statesboro, Ga.	4,128
Eastern Wash. 42, Idaho 38	Moscow, Id.	6,500
Rhode Island 35, Akron 27	Kingston, R.I.	7,317
Arkansas St. 10, Grambling 7	Jonesboro, Ark.	5,730

Quarterfinals (12/7):
Ga. Southern 28, Middle Tenn. St. 21	Murfreesboro, Tenn.	9,500
Northern Iowa 17, Eastern Wash. 14	Cedar Falls, Ia.	6,220
Furman 59, Rhode Island 15	Greenville, S.C.	9,454
Nevada 24, Arkansas St. 23	Reno, Nev.	10,241

Semifinals (12/14):
Ga. Southern 40, Northern Iowa 33	Cedar Falls, Ia.	12,300
Furman 35, Nevada 12	Greenville, S.C.	10,300

Championship (12/21):
Ga. Southern 44, Furman 42	Tacoma, Wash.	5,306

1986
First Round (11/29):

	Site	Attendance
Nevada 27, Idaho 7	Reno, Nev.	13,715
Tennessee St. 32, Jackson St. 23	Jackson, Miss.	24,000
Ga. Southern 52, N.C. A&T 21	Statesboro, Ga.	7,767
Nicholls St. 28, Appalachian St. 26	Boone, N.C.	6,250
Arkansas St. 48, Sam Houston St. 7	Jonesboro, Ark.	4,500
Delaware 51, William & Mary 17	Williamsburg, Va.	6,340
Eastern Ill. 28, Murray St. 21	Charleston, Ill.	9,500
Eastern Ky. 23, Furman 10	Greenville, S.C.	8,000

Quarterfinals (12/6):
Nevada 33, Tennessee St. 6	Reno, Nev.	13,102
Ga. Southern 55, Nicholls St. 31	Statesboro, Ga.	9,121
Arkansas St. 55, Delaware 14	Newark, Del.	12,018
Eastern Ky. 24, Eastern Ill. 22	Charleston, Ill.	9,500

Semifinals (12/13):
Ga. Southern 48, Nevada 38	Reno, Nev.	15,100
Arkansas St. 24, Eastern Ky. 10	Jonesboro, Ark.	10,500

Championship (12/20):
Ga. Southern 48, Arkansas St. 21	Tacoma, Wash.	4,419

1987
First Round (11/28):

	Site	Attendance
Appalachian St. 20, Richmond 3	Boone, N.C.	4,138
Ga. Southern 31, Maine 28 (ot)	Statesboro, Ga.	9,440
Weber St. 59, Idaho 30	Moscow, Id.	4,900
Marshall 41, James Madison 12	Huntington, W.Va.	15,584
La.-Monroe 30, North Texas 9	Monroe, La.	9,500
Eastern Ky. 40, Western Ky. 17	Richmond, Ky.	4,050
Northern Iowa 31, Youngstown St. 28	Cedar Falls, Ia.	3,887
Arkansas St. 35, Jackson St. 32	Jackson, Miss.	7,500

Quarterfinals (12/5):
Appalachian St. 19, Ga. Southern 0	Boone, N.C.	9,229
Marshall 51, Weber St. 23	Huntington, W.Va.	13,197
La.-Monroe 33, Eastern Ky. 32	Monroe, La.	10,475
Northern Iowa 49, Arkansas St. 28	Cedar Falls, Ia.	6,100

Semifinals (12/12):
Marshall 24, Appalachian St. 10	Boone, N.C.	10,000
La.-Monroe 44, Northern Iowa 41 (2ot)	Monroe, La.	14,443

Championship (12/19):
La.-Monroe 43, Marshall 42	Pocatello, Id.	11,513

1988
First Round (11/26):

	Site	Attendance
Idaho 38, Montana 19	Moscow, Id.	5,500
Northwestern St. 22, Boise St. 13	Boise, Id.	10,537
Furman 21, Delaware 7	Greenville, S.C.	7,487

First Round (11/26):
	Site	Attendance
Marshall 7, North Texas 0	Huntington, W.Va.	15,086
Ga. Southern 38, Citadel 20	Statesboro, Ga.	11,011
Stephen F. Austin 24, Jackson St. 0	Nacogdoches, Tex.	5,384
Western Ky. 35, Western Ill. 32	Macomb, Ill.	6,000
Eastern Ky. 28, Massachusetts 17	Richmond, Ky.	4,600

Quarterfinals (12/3):
Idaho 38, Northwestern St. 30	Moscow, Id.	6,800
Furman 13, Marshall 9	Huntington, W.Va.	16,820
Ga. Southern 27, Stephen F. Austin 6	Statesboro, Ga.	12,289
Eastern Ky. 41, Western Ky. 24	Richmnond, Ky.	8,100

Semifinals (12/10):
Furman 38, Idaho 7	Greenville, S.C.	11,645
Ga. Southern 21, Eastern Ky. 17	Statesboro, Ga.	14,023

Championship (12/17):
Furman 17, Ga. Southern 12	Pocatello, Id.	11,500

1989
First Round (11/25):
	Site	Attendance
Ga. Southern 52, Villanova 36	Statesboro, Ga.	10,161
Middle Tenn. St. 24, Appalachian St. 21	Murfreesboro, Tenn.	5,000
Eastern Ill. 38, Idaho 21	Moscow, Id.	6,025
Montana 48, Jackson St. 7	Missoula, Mont.	11,854
Furman 24, William & Mary 10	Greenville, S.C.	8,642
Youngstown St. 28, Eastern Ky. 24	Richmond, Ky.	3,898
Stephen F. Austin 59, Grambling 56	Nacogdoches, Tex.	7,106
Southwest Mo. St. 38, Maine 35	Springfield, Mo.	7,270

Quarterfinals (12/2):
Ga. Southern 45, Middle Tenn. St. 3	Statesboro, Ga.	11,272
Montana 25, Eastern Ill. 19	Missoula, Mont.	12,285
Furman 42, Youngstown St. 23	Greenville, S.C.	8,033
Stephen F. Austin 55, Southwest Mo. St. 25	Nacogdoches, Tex.	10,491

Semifinals (12/9):
Ga. Southern 45, Montana 15	Statesboro, Ga.	10,421
Stephen F. Austin 21, Furman 19	Greenville, S.C.	7,015

Championship (12/16):
Ga. Southern 37, Stephen F. Austin 34	Statesboro, Ga.	25,725

1990
First Round (11/24):
	Site	Attendance
Middle Tenn. St. 28, Jackson St. 7	Murfreesboro, Tenn.	7,000
Boise St. 20, Northern Iowa 3	Boise, Id.	11,691
Nevada 27, La.-Monroe 14	Reno, Nev.	11,008
Furman 45, Eastern Ky. 17	Richmond, Ky.	4,528
UCF 20, Youngstown St. 17	Youngstown, Ohio	5,000
William & Mary 38, Massachusetts 0	Williamsburg, Va.	5,000
Ga. Southern 31, Citadel 0	Statesboro, Ga.	11,881
Idaho 41, Southwest Mo. St. 35	Springfield, Mo.	8,750

Quarterfinals (12/1):
Boise St. 20, Middle Tenn. St. 13	Boise, Id.	15,849
Nevada 42, Furman 35 (3 ot)	Reno, Nev.	11,519
UCF 52, William & Mary 38	Orlando, Fla.	20,067
Ga. Southern 28, Idaho 27	Statesboro, Ga.	11,571

Semifinals (12/8):
Nevada 59, Boise St. 52 (3 ot)	Reno, Nev.	19,776
Ga. Southern 44, UCF 7	Statesboro, Ga.	13,183

Championship (12/15):
Ga. Southern 36, Nevada 13	Statesboro, Ga.	23,204

1991
First Round (11/30):
	Site	Attendance
Nevada 22, McNeese St. 16	Reno, Nev.	15,000
Youngstown St. 17, Villanova 16	Youngstown, Ohio	9,556
James Madison 42, Delaware 35 (2 ot)	Newark, Del.	14,905
Samford 29, New Hampshire 13	Durham, N.H.	6,034
Eastern Ky. 14, Appalachian St. 3	Richmond, Ky.	2,750
Middle Tenn. St. 20, Sam Houston St. 19 (ot)	Murfreesboro, Tenn.	2,000
Northern Iowa 38, Weber St. 21	Cedar Falls, Ia.	8,723
Marshall 20, Western Ill. 17 (ot)	Huntington, W.Va.	16,840

Quarterfinals (12/7):
Youngstown St. 30, Nevada 28	Reno, Nev.	13,476
Samford 24, James Madison 21	Harrisonburg, Va.	9,028
Eastern Ky. 23, Middle Tenn. St. 13	Richmond, Ky.	3,650
Marshall 41, Northern Iowa 13	Huntington, W.Va.	16,889

Semifinals (12/14):
Youngstown St. 10, Samford 0	Youngstown, Ohio	17,003
Marshall 14, Eastern Ky. 7	Huntington, W.Va.	21,084

Championship (12/21):
Youngstown St. 25, Marshall 17	Statesboro, Ga.	12,667

1992
First Round (11/28):
	Site	Attendance
La.-Monroe 78, Alcorn St. 27	Monroe, La.	14,416
Delaware 56, Samford 21	Newark, Del.	11,364
Middle Tenn. St. 35, Appalachian St. 10	Murfreesboro, Tenn.	4,000
Marshall 44, Eastern Ky. 0	Huntington, W.Va.	16,598
Citadel 44, N.C. A&T 0	Charleston, S.C.	12,300
Youngstown St. 23, Villanova 20	Youngstown, Ohio	9,465
Northern Iowa 17, Eastern Wash. 14	Cedar Falls, Ia.	13,149
McNeese St. 23, Idaho 20	Moscow, Id.	6,000

Quarterfinals (12/5):
Delaware 41, La.-Monroe 18	Monroe, La.	10,172
Marshall 35, Middle Tenn. St. 21	Huntington, W.Va.	14,011
Youngstown St. 42, Citadel 17	Charleston, S.C.	12,300
Northern Iowa 29, McNeese St. 7	Cedar Falls, Ia.	13,375

Semifinals (12/12):
Marshall 28, Delaware 7	Huntington, W.Va.	16,323
Youngstown St. 19, Northern Iowa 7	Cedar Falls, Ia.	14,682

Championship (12/19):
Marshall 31, Youngstown St. 28	Huntington, W.Va.	31,304

1993
First Round (11/27):
	Site	Attendance
Ga. Southern 14, Eastern Ky. 12	Statesboro, Ga.	7,278
Youngstown St. 56, UCF 30	Youngstown, Ohio	7,408
Boston U. 27, Northern Iowa 21 (2 ot)	Boston, Mass.	6,882
Idaho 34, La.-Monroe 31	Monroe, La.	5,500
Delaware 49, Montana 48	Missoula, Mont.	11,271
Marshall 28, Howard 14	Huntington, W.Va.	13,554
McNeese St. 34, William & Mary 28	Lake Charles, La.	17,167
Troy St. 42, Stephen F. Austin 20	Troy, Ala.	4,500

Quarterfinals (12/4):
Youngstown St. 34, Ga. Southern 14	Youngstown, Ohio	9,503
Idaho 21, Boston U. 14	Moscow, Id.	8,800
Marshall 34, Delaware 31	Huntington, W.Va.	13,687
Troy St. 35, McNeese St. 28	Lake Charles, La.	20,000

Semifinals (12/11):
Youngstown St. 35, Idaho 16	Youngstown, Ohio	9,644
Marshall 24, Troy St. 21	Huntington, W.Va.	14,472

Championship (12/18):
Youngstown St. 17, Marshall 5	Huntington, W.Va.	29,218

1994
First Round (11/26):
	Site	Attendance
Youngstown St. 63, Alcorn St. 20	Youngstown, Ohio	17,795
Eastern Ky. 30, Boston U. 23	Richmond, Ky.	4,111
McNeese St. 38, Idaho 21	Lake Charles, La.	16,000
Montana 23, Northern Iowa 20	Missoula, Mont.	7,958
Marshall 49, Middle Tenn. St. 14	Huntington, W.Va.	17,349
James Madison 45, Troy St. 26	Harrisonburg, Va.	5,200
Boise St. 24, North Texas 20	Boise, Id.	14,706
Appalachian St. 17, New Hampshire 10 (ot)	Durham, N.H.	7,329

Quarterfinals (12/3):
Youngstown St. 18, Eastern Ky. 15	Youngstown, Ohio	16,023
Montana 30, McNeese St. 28	Missoula, Mont.	8,419
Marshall 28, James Madison 21 (ot)	Huntington, W.Va.	16,494
Boise St. 17, Appalachian St. 14	Boise, Id.	15,302

Semifinals (12/10):
Youngstown St. 28, Montana 9	Youngstown, Ohio	15,333
Boise St. 28, Marshall 24	Boise, Id.	20,068

Championship (12/17):
Youngstown St. 28, Boise St. 14	Huntington, W.Va.	27,674

1995
First Round (11/25):
	Site	Attendance
McNeese St. 33, Idaho 3	Lake Charles, La.	15,736
Delaware 38, Hofstra 17	Newark, Del.	13,295
Northern Iowa 35, Murray St. 34	Murray, Ky.	7,635
Marshall 38, Jackson St. 8	Huntington, W.Va.	13,035
Appalachian St. 31, James Madison 24	Boone, N.C.	9,467
Stephen F. Austin 34, Eastern Ill. 29	Nacogdoches, Tex.	3,552
Ga. Southern 24, Troy St. 21	Troy, Ala.	6,000
Montana 48, Eastern Ky. 0	Missoula, Mont.	13,830

Quarterfinals (12/2):
McNeese St. 52, Delaware 18	Lake Charles, La.	17,239
Marshall 41, Northern Iowa 24	Huntington, W.Va.	14,472
Stephen F. Austin 27, Appalachian St. 17	Boone, N.C.	8,941
Montana 45, Ga. Southern 0	Missoula, Mont.	18,518

Semifinals (12/9):
Marshall 25, McNeese St. 13	Lake Charles, La.	18,018
Montana 70, Stephen F. Austin 14	Missoula, Mont.	18,523

Championship (12/16):
Montana 22, Marshall 20	Huntington, W.Va.	32,106

1996
First Round (11/30):
	Site	Attendance
Montana 48, Nicholls St. 3	Missoula, Mont.	13,438
East Tenn. St. 35, Villanova 29	Johnson City, Tenn.	4,939
Troy St. 29, Florida A&M 25	Troy, Ala.	10,200
Murray St. 34, Western Ill. 6	Murray, Ky.	2,753
Marshall 59, Delaware 14	Huntington, W.Va.	15,429
Furman 42, Northern Ariz. 31	Flagstaff, Ariz.	8,700
Northern Iowa 21, Eastern Ill. 14	Cedar Falls, Ia.	10,402
William & Mary 45, Jackson St. 6	Williamsburg, Va.	4,057

Quarterfinals (12/7):
Montana 44, East Tenn. St. 14	Missoula, Mont.	15,025
Troy St. 31, Murray St. 3	Troy, Ala.	6,100
Marshall 54, Furman 0	Huntington, W.Va.	14,096
Northern Iowa 38, William & Mary 35	Cedar Falls, Ia.	10,796

Semifinals (12/14):
Montana 70, Troy St. 7	Missoula, Mont.	18,367
Marshall 31, Northern Iowa 14	Huntington, W.Va.	14,414

DIVISION I-AA CHAMPIONSHIP—ATTENDANCE HISTORY

Championship (12/21):
Marshall 49, Montana 29 — Huntington, W.Va. — 30,052

1997

First Round (11/29):

	Site	Attendance
Villanova 49, Colgate 28	Villanova, Pa.	8,875
Youngstown St. 28, Hampton 13	Youngstown, Ohio	12,431
Western Ky. 42, Eastern Ky. 14	Bowling Green, Ky.	9,000
Eastern Wash. 40, Northwestern St. 10	Cheney, Wash.	6,384
Delaware 24, Hofstra 14	Newark, Del.	14,075
Ga. Southern 52, Florida A&M 37	Statesboro, Ga.	10,409
McNeese St. 19, Montana 14	Lake Charles, La.	13,681
Western Ill. 31, Jackson St. 24	Macomb, Ill.	8,980

Quarterfinals (12/6):

Youngstown St. 37, Villanova 34	Villanova, Pa.	7,591
Eastern Wash. 38, Western Ky. 21	Cheney, Wash.	6,829
Delaware 16, Ga. Southern 7	Newark, Del.	11,203
McNeese St. 14, Western Ill. 12	Macomb, Ill.	5,000

Semifinals (12/13):

Youngstown St. 25, Eastern Wash. 14	Cheney, Wash.	8,529
McNeese St. 23, Delaware 21	Newark, Del.	14,461

Championship (12/20):
Youngstown St. 10, McNeese St. 9 — Chattanooga, Tenn. — 14,771

1998

First Round (11/28):

	Site	Attendance
Ga. Southern 49, Colgate 28	Statesboro, Ga.	7,676
Connecticut 42, Hampton 34	Storrs, Conn.	6,193
Florida A&M 27, Troy St. 17	Tallahassee, Fla.	16,509
Western Ill. 52, Montana 9	Macomb, Ill.	3,614
Lehigh 24, Richmond 23	Richmond, Va.	10,254
Massachusetts 21, McNeese St. 19	Lake Charles, La.	11,349
Appalachian St. 45, Tennessee St. 31	Boone, N.C.	3,885

First Round (11/28):

	Site	Attendance
Northwestern St. 48, Illinois St. 28	Natchitoches, La.	8,118

Quarterfinals (12/5):

Ga. Southern 52, Connecticut 30	Statesboro, Ga.	9,096
Western Ill. 24, Florida A&M 21 (12/4)	Macomb, Ill.	7,400
Massachusetts 27, Lehigh 21	Amherst, Mass.	12,108
Northwestern St. 31, Appalachian St. 20	Natchitoches, La.	10,817

Semifinals (12/12):

Ga. Southern 42, Western Ill. 14	Statesboro, Ga.	11,140
Massachusetts 41, Northwestern St. 31	Natchitoches, La.	10,424

Championship (12/19):
Massachusetts 55, Ga. Southern 43 — Chattanooga, Tenn. — 17,501

1999

First Round (11/27):

	Site	Attendance
N.C. A&T 24, Tennessee St. 10	Nashville, Tenn.	10,736
Youngstown St. 30, Montana 27	Missoula, Mont.	17,261
Troy St. 27, James Madison 7	Troy, Ala.	17,102
Florida A&M 44, Appalachian St. 29	Boone, N.C.	6,837
Hofstra 27, Lehigh 15	Hempstead, N.Y.	6,770
Illinois St. 56, Colgate 13	Normal, Ill.	7,133
Massachusetts 30, Furman 23 (ot)	Greenville, S.C.	7,215
Ga. Southern 72, Northern Ariz. 29	Statesboro, Ga.	7,140

Quarterfinals (12/4):

Youngstown St. 41, N.C. A&T 3	Youngstown, Ohio	16,955
Illinois St. 37, Hofstra 20	Hempstead, N.Y.	5,586
Florida A&M 17, Troy St. 10	Troy, Ala.	12,689
Ga. Southern 38, Massachusetts 21	Statesboro, Ga.	13,121

Semifinals (12/11):

Youngstown St. 27, Florida A&M 24	Youngstown, Ohio	17,846
Ga. Southern 28, Illinois St. 17	Statesboro, Ga.	12,299

Championship (12/20):
Ga. Southern 59, Youngstown St. 24 — Chattanooga, Tenn. — 20,052

Division II Championship

1999 Title Game Summary

BRALY MUNICIPAL STADIUM, FLORENCE, ALABAMA; DECEMBER 11

	Northwest Mo. St.	Carson-Newman
First Downs	26	30
Rushing Yardage	137	419
Passing Yardage	298	108
Passes (Comp.-Att.-Int.)	24-45-3	7-22-1
Punts (Number-Average)	4-41.5	3-37.3
Fumbles (Number-Lost)	0-0	2-2
Penalties (Number-Yards)	13-93	12-87
Northwest Mo. St.	7 0 7 30 0 0 8 6	—58
Carson-Newman	10 14 6 14 0 0 8 0	—52

FIRST QUARTER
Northwest Mo. St.—David Jansen 18 run (David Purnell kick) (67 yards in 10 plays, 9:21 left)
Carson-Newman—Ryan Fleming 38 field goal (53 yards in 11 plays, 5:28 left)
Carson-Newman—Ques Rumph 86 punt return (Fleming kick) (3:39 left)

SECOND QUARTER
Carson-Newman—Melvin Oates 1 run (Fleming kick) (55 yards in 12 plays, 8:27 left)
Carson-Newman—Myron Refoure 20 run (Fleming kick) (67 yards in 8 plays, 3:32 left)

THIRD QUARTER
Northwest Mo. St.—Seneca Holmes 20 pass from Travis Miles (Purnell kick) (79 yards in 8 plays, 11:54 left)
Carson-Newman—Melvin Oates 1 run (kick failed) (53 yards in 6 plays, 4:54 left)

FOURTH QUARTER
Northwest Mo. St.—Tony Miles 7 pass from Travis Miles (Steve Comer pass from Travis Miles) (35 yards in 9 plays, 12:44 left)
Carson-Newman—Leonard Guyton 10 run (Fleming kick) (54 yards in 9 plays, 7:39 left)
Northwest Mo. St.—Tony Miles 81 kickoff return (Purnell kick) (7:25 left)
Carson-Newman—Antwon Oliver 12 run (Fleming kick) (76 yards in 8 plays, 3:34 left)
Northwest Mo. St.—J. R. Hill 7 pass from Travis Miles (Purnell kick) (74 yards in 6 plays, 2:41 left)
Northwest Mo. St.—Hill 34 pass from Travis Miles (Ryan George pass from Travis Miles) (74 yards in 7 plays, 0:10 left)

THIRD OVERTIME
Carson-Newman—Oliver 1 run (Guyton run) (25 yards in 8 plays)
Northwest Mo. St.—Tony Miles 15 run (Comer pass from Travis Miles) (25 yards in 3 plays)

FOURTH OVERTIME
Northwest Mo. St.—Hill 13 pass from Travis Miles (run failed) (25 yards in 3 plays)

INDIVIDUAL LEADERS
Rushing—Carson-Newman: Oliver, 194 yards on 30 carries; Northwest Mo. St.: Jansen, 54 yards on 18 carries.

Tony Miles hauls in a touchdown pass during Northwest Missouri State's fourth-quarter comeback against Carson-Newman in the 1999 championship game. The Bearcats exploded for 30 points to send the contest into overtime, and successfully defended their 1998 title by winning 58-52 in the fourth extra period.

Passing—Carson-Newman: Guyton, 7 of 22 for 108 yards; Northwest Mo. St.: Travis Miles, 24 of 45 for 298 yards.
Receiving—Carson-Newman: Rumph, 3 catches for 36 yards, and Jarvonni Jackson, 2 catches for 20 yards; Northwest Mo. St.: Hill, 7 catches for 120 yards, and Tony Miles, 6 catches for 65 yards.

Division II All-Time Championship Results

Year	Champion	Coach	Score	Runner-Up	Site
1973	Louisiana Tech	Maxie Lambright	34-0	Western Ky.	Sacramento, Calif.
1974	Central Mich.	Roy Kramer	54-14	Delaware	Sacramento, Calif.
1975	Northern Mich.	Gil Krueger	16-14	Western Ky.	Sacramento, Calif.
1976	Montana St.	Sonny Holland	24-13	Akron	Wichita Falls, Texas
1977	Lehigh	John Whitehead	33-0	Jacksonville St.	Wichita Falls, Texas
1978	Eastern Ill.	Darrell Mudra	10-9	Delaware	Longview, Texas
1979	Delaware	Tubby Raymond	38-21	Youngstown St.	Albuquerque, N.M.
1980	Cal Poly	Joe Harper	21-13	Eastern Ill.	Albuquerque, N.M.
1981	Southwest Tex. St.	Jim Wacker	42-13	North Dakota St.	McAllen, Texas
1982	Southwest Tex. St.	Jim Wacker	34-9	UC Davis	McAllen, Texas
1983	North Dakota St.	Don Morton	41-21	Central St.	McAllen, Texas
1984	Troy St.	Chan Gailey	18-17	North Dakota St.	McAllen, Texas
1985	North Dakota St.	Earle Solomonson	35-7	North Ala.	McAllen, Texas
1986	North Dakota St.	Earle Solomonson	27-7	South Dakota	Florence, Ala.
1987	Troy St.	Rick Rhoades	31-17	Portland St.	Florence, Ala.
1988	North Dakota St.	Rocky Hager	35-21	Portland St.	Florence, Ala.
1989	*Mississippi Col.	John Williams	3-0	Jacksonville St.	Florence, Ala.
1990	North Dakota St.	Rocky Hager	51-11	Indiana (Pa.)	Florence, Ala.
1991	Pittsburg St.	Chuck Broyles	23-6	Jacksonville St.	Florence, Ala.
1992	Jacksonville St.	Bill Burgess	17-13	Pittsburg St.	Florence, Ala.
1993	North Ala.	Bobby Wallace	41-34	Indiana (Pa.)	Florence, Ala.
1994	North Ala.	Bobby Wallace	16-10	Tex. A&M-Kingsville	Florence, Ala.
1995	North Ala.	Bobby Wallace	27-7	Pittsburg St.	Florence, Ala.
1996	Northern Colo.	Joe Glenn	23-14	Carson-Newman	Florence, Ala.
1997	Northern Colo.	Joe Glenn	51-0	New Haven	Florence, Ala.
1998	Northwest Mo. St.	Mel Tjeerdsma	24-6	Carson-Newman	Florence, Ala.
1999	Northwest Mo. St.	Mel Tjeerdsma	58-52 (4 ot)	Carson-Newman	Florence, Ala.

*Mississippi College's participation in the 1989 Division II championship vacated by the NCAA Committee on Infractions.

Regional Championship Results

Before 1973, there was no Division II Football Championship. Instead, four regional bowl games were played in order to provide postseason action for what then were called NCAA College Division member institutions. Following are the results of those bowl games:

Year	Champion	Coach	Score	Runner-Up	Site
EAST (TANGERINE BOWL)					
1964	East Caro.	Clarence Stasavich	14-13	Massachusetts	Orlando, Fla.
1965	East Caro.	Clarence Stasavich	31-0	Maine	Orlando, Fla.
1966	Morgan St.	Earl Banks	14-6	West Chester	Orlando, Fla.
1967	Tenn.-Martin	Robert Carroll	25-8	West Chester	Orlando, Fla.
EAST (BOARDWALK BOWL)					
1968	Delaware	Tubby Raymond	31-24	Indiana (Pa.)	Atlantic City, N.J.
1969	Delaware	Tubby Raymond	31-13	N.C. Central	Atlantic City, N.J.
1970	Delaware	Tubby Raymond	38-23	Morgan St.	Atlantic City, N.J.
1971	Delaware	Tubby Raymond	72-22	C. W. Post	Atlantic City, N.J.
1972	Massachusetts	Dick MacPherson	35-14	UC Davis	Atlantic City, N.J.
MIDEAST (GRANTLAND RICE BOWL)					
1964	Middle Tenn. St.	Charles Murphy	20-0	Muskingum	Murfreesboro, Tenn.
1965	Ball St.	Ray Louthen	14-14	—	Murfreesboro, Tenn.
	Tennessee St.	John Merritt			
1966	Tennessee St.	John Merritt	34-7	Muskingum	Murfreesboro, Tenn.
1967	Eastern Ky.	Roy Kidd	27-13	Ball St.	Murfreesboro, Tenn.
1968	Louisiana Tech	Maxie Lambright	33-13	Akron	Murfreesboro, Tenn.
1969	East Tenn. St.	John Bell	34-14	Louisiana Tech	Baton Rouge, La.
1970	Tennessee St.	John Merritt	26-25	La.-Lafayette	Baton Rouge, La.
1971	Tennessee St.	John Merritt	26-23	McNeese St.	Baton Rouge, La.
1972	Louisiana Tech	Maxie Lambright	35-0	Tennessee Tech	Baton Rouge, La.
MIDWEST (PECAN BOWL)					
1964	Northern Iowa	Stan Sheriff	19-17	Lamar	Abilene, Texas
1965	North Dakota St.	Darrell Mudra	20-7	Grambling	Abilene, Texas
1966	North Dakota	Marv Helling	42-24	Parsons	Abilene, Texas
1967	Texas-Arlington	Burley Bearden	13-0	North Dakota St.	Abilene, Texas
1968	North Dakota St.	Ron Erhardt	23-14	Arkansas St.	Arlington, Texas
1969	Arkansas St.	Bennie Ellender	29-21	Drake	Arlington, Texas
1970	Arkansas St.	Bennie Ellender	38-21	Central Mo. St.	Arlington, Texas
MIDWEST (PIONEER BOWL)					
1971	Louisiana Tech	Maxie Lambright	14-3	Eastern Mich.	Wichita Falls, Texas
1972	Tennessee St.	John Merritt	29-7	Drake	Wichita Falls, Texas
WEST (CAMELLIA BOWL)					
1964	Montana St.	Jim Sweeney	28-7	Cal St. Sacramento	Sacramento, Calif.
1965	Cal St. Los Angeles	Homer Beatty	18-10	UC Santa Barb.	Sacramento, Calif.

DIVISION II CHAMPIONSHIP—REGIONAL CHAMPIONSHIP RESULTS

Year	Champion	Coach	Score	Runner-Up	Site
1966	San Diego St.	Don Coryell	28-7	Montana St.	Sacramento, Calif.
1967	San Diego St.	Don Coryell	27-6	San Fran. St.	Sacramento, Calif.
1968	Humboldt St.	Frank VanDeren	29-14	Fresno St.	Sacramento, Calif.
1969	North Dakota St.	Ron Erhardt	30-3	Montana	Sacramento, Calif.
1970	North Dakota St.	Ron Erhardt	31-16	Montana	Sacramento, Calif.
1971	Boise St.	Tony Knap	32-28	Cal St. Chico	Sacramento, Calif.
1972	North Dakota	Jerry Olson	38-21	Cal Poly	Sacramento, Calif.

1999 Division II Championship Results

FIRST ROUND
Carson-Newman 40, Arkansas Tech 28
Catawba 48, Fort Valley St. 17
UC Davis 33, Central Okla. 17
Northeastern St. 27, Western Wash. 24 (ot)
Indiana (Pa.) 27, Slippery Rock 20 (ot)
Millersville 21, Shepherd 14
Northern Colo. 34, Pittsburg St. 31
Northwest Mo. St. 20, North Dakota 13 (ot)

QUARTERFINALS
Carson-Newman 28, Catawba 25
Northeastern St. 19, UC Davis 14
Indiana (Pa.) 26, Millersville 21
Northwest Mo. St. 41, Northern Colo. 35

SEMIFINALS
Carson-Newman 42, Northeastern St. 7
Northwest Mo. St. 20, Indiana (Pa.) 12

CHAMPIONSHIP
Northwest Mo. St. 58, Carson-Newman 52 (4 ot)

Individual Records

GAME

NET YARDS RUSHING
379—Ronald Moore, Pittsburg St. (41) vs. Portland St. (38), 12-5-92.

RUSHES ATTEMPTED
51—Terry Morrow, Central St. (31) vs. Towson (0), 11-28-86.

TOUCHDOWNS BY RUSHING
5—Ronald Moore, Pittsburg St. (38) vs. North Dakota St. (37) (ot), 11-28-92; Ronald Moore, Pittsburg St. (41) vs. Portland St. (38), 12-5-92.

NET YARDS PASSING
482—Kevin Daft, UC Davis (25) vs. New Haven (27), 12-6-97.

PASSES ATTEMPTED
64—Kevin Daft, UC Davis (25) vs. New Haven (27), 12-6-97.

PASSES COMPLETED
43—Kevin Daft, UC Davis (25) vs. New Haven (27), 12-6-97.

PASSES INTERCEPTED
6—Dennis Tomek, Western Ky. (28) vs. Grambling (20), 12-8-73.

TOUCHDOWN PASSES
6—Darren Del'Andrae, Portland St. (56) vs. West Chester (50) (3 ot), 11-18-89.

COMPLETION PERCENTAGE (Min. 10 Attempts)
.909—Kevin Feeney, North Dakota St. (41) vs. North Dakota (10), 11-18-95 (10 of 11).

NET YARDS RUSHING AND PASSING
505—Kevin Daft, UC Davis (25) vs. New Haven (27), 12-6-97 (23 rushing, 482 passing).

RUSHING AND PASSING PLAYS
69—Kevin Daft, UC Davis (25) vs. New Haven (27), 12-6-97 (5 rushing, 64 passing).

PUNTING AVERAGE (Min. 3 Punts)
53.7—Chris Humes, UC Davis (23) vs. Angelo St. (28), 11-18-89 (7 for 376).

PUNTS
11—Charlie Johnson, Western Ky. (28) vs. Grambling (20), 12-8-73; Billy Becher, Northeastern St. (19) vs. UC Davis (14), 11-27-99.

RECEPTIONS
14—Don Hutt, Boise St. (34) vs. Louisiana Tech (38), 12-8-73.

NET YARDS RECEIVING
220—Steve Hansley, Northwest Mo. St. (15) vs. Neb.-Omaha (28), 11-24-84.

TOUCHDOWN RECEPTIONS
4—Steve Kreider, Lehigh (30) vs. Massachusetts (23), 11-26-77; Scott Asman, West Chester (50) vs. Portland St. (56) (3 ot), 11-18-89; Brian Penecale, West Chester (40) vs. Ferris St. (43), 11-19-94.

INTERCEPTIONS
4—Vince Buck, Central St. (31) vs. Towson (0), 11-28-86.

YARDS GAINED ON INTERCEPTION RETURNS
113—Darren Ryals, Millersville (27) vs. Indiana (Pa.) (24), 2 returns for 53- and 60-yard TDs, 11-19-88.

YARDS GAINED ON PUNT RETURNS
138—Rick Caswell, Western Ky. (14) vs. New Hampshire (3), 12-6-75.

YARDS GAINED ON KICKOFF RETURNS
215—Sean Smith, Bloomsburg (29) vs. Clarion (42), 11-23-96.

POINTS
32—Ronald Moore, Pittsburg St. (38) vs. North Dakota St. (37) (ot), 11-28-92; Ronald Moore, Pittsburg St. (41) vs. Portland St. (38), 12-5-92.

TOUCHDOWNS
5—Ronald Moore, Pittsburg St. (38) vs. North Dakota St. (37) (ot), 11-28-92; Ronald Moore, Pittsburg St. (41) vs. Portland St. (38), 12-5-92; Dexter Deese, Tex. A&M-Kingsville (43) vs. Western St. (7), 11-19-94.

EXTRA POINTS
9—Ashley Kay, Jacksonville St. (63) vs. West Chester (24), 11-19-88.

FIELD GOALS
4—Mario Ferretti, Northern Mich. (55) vs. Elizabeth City St. (6), 11-28-81; Ken Kubisz, North Dakota St. (26) vs. UC Davis (17), 12-3-83.

TOURNAMENT

NET YARDS RUSHING
721—Ronald Moore, Pittsburg St., 1992 (108 vs. North Dakota, 151 vs. North Dakota St., 379 vs. Portland St., 83 vs. Jacksonville St.).

RUSHES ATTEMPTED
117—Ronald Moore, Pittsburg St., 1992 (29 vs. North Dakota, 31 vs. North Dakota St., 37 vs. Portland St., 20 vs. Jacksonville St.).

NET YARDS PASSING
1,226—Chris Crawford, Portland St., 1988 (248 vs. Bowie St., 375 vs. Jacksonville St., 270 vs. Tex. A&M-Kingsville, 333 vs. North Dakota St.).

PASSES ATTEMPTED
153—Travis Miles, Northwest Mo. St., 1999 (42 vs. North Dakota, 36 vs. Northern Colo., 30 vs. Indiana [Pa.], 45 vs. Carson-Newman).

PASSES COMPLETED
94—Chris Crawford, Portland St., 1988 (20 vs. Bowie St., 27 vs. Jacksonville St., 25 vs. Tex. A&M-Kingsville, 22 vs. North Dakota St.).

PASSES INTERCEPTED
9—Dennis Tomek, Western Ky., 1973 (0 vs. Lehigh, 6 vs. Grambling, 3 vs. Louisiana Tech).

TOUCHDOWN PASSES
13—Chris Greisen, Northwest Mo. St., 1998 (3 vs. Neb.-Omaha, 3 vs. Northern Colo., 5 vs. Tex. A&M-Kingsville, 2 vs. Carson-Newman).

COMPLETION PERCENTAGE (Min. 2 Games)
.824—Mike Turk, Troy St., 1984, 14 of 17 (4-5 vs. Central St., 5-5 vs. Towson, 5-7 vs. North Dakota St.).

RECEPTIONS
29—Tony Miles, Northwest Mo. St., 1999 (11 vs. North Dakota, 7 vs. Northern Colo., 5 vs. Indiana [Pa.], 6 vs. Carson-Newman).

NET YARDS RECEIVING
452—Henry Newson, Portland St., 1991 (94 vs. Northern Colo., 209 vs. Minn. St.-Mankato, 149 vs. Pittsburg St.).

TOUCHDOWN RECEPTIONS
7—Steve Kreider, Lehigh, 1977 (4 vs. Massachusetts, 1 vs. UC Davis, 2 vs. Jacksonville St.).

POINTS
88—Ronald Moore, Pittsburg St., 1992 (18 vs. North Dakota, 32 vs. North Dakota St., 32 vs. Portland St., 6 vs. Jacksonville St.).

TOUCHDOWNS
14—Ronald Moore, Pittsburg St., 1992 (3 vs. North Dakota, 5 vs. North Dakota St., 5 vs. Portland St., 1 vs. Jacksonville St.).

LONGEST PLAYS

RUSH
98—Wesley Whiten, Tex. A&M-Kingsville (59) vs. Fort Hays St. (28), 11-18-95, TD.

PASS (INCLUDING RUN)
99—Ken Suhl to Tony Willis, New Haven (35) vs. Ferris St. (13), 11-28-92, TD.

FIELD GOAL
50—Ted Clem, Troy St. (18) vs. North Dakota St. (17), 12-8-84.

PUNT
76—Chris Humes, UC Davis (23) vs. Angelo St. (28), 11-18-89.

PUNT RETURN
87—Rick Caswell, Western Ky. (14) vs. New Hampshire (3), 12-6-75, TD.

KICKOFF RETURN
100—Ken Bowles, UNLV (6) vs. Akron (26), 11-26-76, TD.

INTERCEPTION RETURN
100—Charles Harris, Jacksonville St. (34) vs. Truman (21), 11-27-82, TD.

FUMBLE RETURN
77—Jeffrey Rodgers, Tex. A&M-Kingsville (30) vs. Portland St. (35), 11-28-92, TD.

Team Records

GAME

FIRST DOWNS
34—Delaware (60) vs. Mississippi Col. (10), 12-1-79; Cal St. Sacramento (56) vs. N.C. Central (7), 11-26-88.

DIVISION II CHAMPIONSHIP—TEAM RECORDS

FIRST DOWNS BY RUSHING
26—Carson-Newman (40) vs. Arkansas Tech (28), 11-20-99.

FIRST DOWNS BY PASSING
25—UC Davis (25) vs. New Haven (27), 12-6-97.

NET YARDS RUSHING
566—Jacksonville St. (63) vs. West Chester (24), 11-19-88.

RUSHES ATTEMPTED
84—Southwest Tex. St. (34) vs. UC Davis (9), 12-11-82.

NET YARDS PASSING
482—UC Davis (25) vs. New Haven (27), 12-6-97.

PASSES ATTEMPTED
64—UC Davis (25) vs. New Haven (27), 12-6-97.

PASSES COMPLETED
43—UC Davis (25) vs. New Haven (27), 12-6-97.

PASSES INTERCEPTED
7—Towson (0) vs. Central St. (31), 11-28-86.

COMPLETION PERCENTAGE (Min. 10 Attempts)
.909—North Dakota St. (41) vs. North Dakota (10), 11-18-95 (10 of 11).

NET YARDS RUSHING AND PASSING
695—Northern Mich. (55) vs. Elizabeth City St. (6), 11-28-81 (231 rushing, 464 passing).

RUSHING AND PASSING PLAYS
99—Carson-Newman (52) vs. Northwest Mo. St. (58) (4 ot), 12-11-99 (77 rushing, 22 passing).

PUNTING AVERAGE (Min. 3 Punts)
53.7—UC Davis (23) vs. Angelo St. (28), 11-18-89 (7 for 376).

PUNTS
12—Delaware (8) vs. Grambling (17), 12-1-73; Western Ky. (0) vs. Louisiana Tech (34), 12-15-73.

PUNTS BLOCKED
2—Truman (21) vs. Jacksonville St. (34), 11-27-82.

YARDS GAINED ON PUNT RETURNS
140—Southwest Tex. St. (62) vs. Northern Mich. (0), 12-5-81.

YARDS GAINED ON KICKOFF RETURNS
215—Bloomsburg (29) vs. Clarion (42), 11-23-96.

YARDS GAINED ON INTERCEPTION RETURNS
131—Millersville (27) vs. Indiana (Pa.) (24), 11-19-88.

YARDS PENALIZED
185—Tex. A&M-Kingsville (30) vs. Portland St. (3), 11-25-95.

PENALTIES
18—Portland St. (16) vs. Tex. A&M-Kingsville (21), 11-26-94.

FUMBLES
10—Winston-Salem (0) vs. Delaware (41), 12-2-78.

FUMBLES LOST
7—Louisiana Tech (10) vs. Western Caro. (7), 11-30-74.

POINTS
*63—Jacksonville St. vs. West Chester (24), 11-19-88.

*Mississippi Col. defeated Wofford, 70-19, on 11-17-90, but its participation in the championship was vacated.

TOURNAMENT

FIRST DOWNS
103—Carson-Newman, 1999 (33 vs. Arkansas Tech, 14 vs. Catawba, 26 vs. Northeastern St., 30 vs. Northwest Mo. St.).

NET YARDS RUSHING
1,660—North Dakota St., 1988 (474 vs. Augustana [S.D.], 434 vs. Millersville, 413 vs. Cal St. Sacramento, 339 vs. Portland St.).

NET YARDS PASSING
1,226—Portland St., 1988 (248 vs. Bowie St., 375 vs. Jacksonville St., 270 vs. Tex. A&M-Kingsville, 333 vs. North Dakota St.).

NET YARDS RUSHING AND PASSING
2,032—North Ala., 1993 (455 vs. Carson-Newman, 570 vs. Hampton, 470 vs. Tex. A&M-Kingsville, 537 vs. Indiana [Pa.]).

PASSES ATTEMPTED
156—Northwest Mo. St., 1999 (43 vs. North Dakota, 37 vs. Northern Colo., 31 vs. Indiana [Pa.], 45 vs. Carson-Newman).

PASSES COMPLETED
94—Portland St., 1988 (20 vs. Bowie St., 27 vs. Jacksonville St., 25 vs. Tex. A&M-Kingsville, 22 vs. North Dakota St.).

PASSES INTERCEPTED
10—Western Ky., 1973 (0 vs. Lehigh, 6 vs. Grambling, 4 vs. Louisiana Tech).

NUMBER OF PUNTS
29—Western Ky., 1973 (6 vs. Lehigh, 11 vs. Grambling, 12 vs. Louisiana Tech).

YARDS PENALIZED
362—Carson-Newman, 1999 (102 vs. Arkansas Tech, 79 vs. Catawba, 94 vs. Northeastern St., 87 vs. Northwest Mo. St.).

FUMBLES
16—Delaware, 1978 (8 vs. Jacksonville St., 2 vs. Winston-Salem, 6 vs. Eastern Ill.).

FUMBLES LOST
12—Delaware, 1978 (6 vs. Jacksonville St., 2 vs. Winston-Salem, 4 vs. Eastern Ill.).

POINTS
162—North Dakota St., 1988 (49 vs. Augustana [S.D.], 36 vs. Millersville, 42 vs. Cal St. Sacramento, 35 vs. Portland St.); Carson-Newman, 1999 (40 vs. Arkansas Tech, 28 vs. Catawba, 42 vs. Northeastern St., 52 vs. Northwest Mo. St.).

Year-by-Year Division II Championship Results

Year (Number of Teams)	Coach	Record	Result
1973 (8)			
Louisiana Tech	Maxie Lambright	3-0	Champion
Western Ky.	Jimmy Feix	2-1	Second
Boise St.	Tony Knap	1-1	Semifinalist
Grambling	Eddie Robinson	1-1	Semifinalist
Delaware	Tubby Raymond	0-1	Lost 1st Round
Lehigh	Fred Dunlap	0-1	Lost 1st Round
South Dakota	Joe Salem	0-1	Lost 1st Round
Western Ill.	Darrell Mudra	0-1	Lost 1st Round
1974 (8)			
Central Mich.	Roy Kramer	3-0	Champion
Delaware	Tubby Raymond	2-1	Second
Louisiana Tech	Maxie Lambright	1-1	Semifinalist
UNLV	Ron Meyer	1-1	Semifinalist
Alcorn St.	Marino Casem	0-1	Lost 1st Round
Boise St.	Tony Knap	0-1	Lost 1st Round
Western Caro.	Bob Waters	0-1	Lost 1st Round
Youngstown St.	Rey Dempsey	0-1	Lost 1st Round
1975 (8)			
Northern Mich.	Gil Krueger	3-0	Champion
Western Ky.	Jimmy Feix	2-1	Second
New Hampshire	Bill Bowes	1-1	Semifinalist
West Ala.	Jim King	1-1	Semifinalist
Boise St.	Tony Knap	0-1	Lost 1st Round
Lehigh	Fred Dunlap	0-1	Lost 1st Round
North Dakota	Jerry Olson	0-1	Lost 1st Round
Northern Iowa	Stan Sheriff	0-1	Lost 1st Round
1976 (8)			
Montana St.	Sonny Holland	3-0	Champion
Akron	Jim Dennison	2-1	Second
North Dakota St.	Jim Wacker	1-1	Semifinalist
Northern Mich.	Gil Krueger	1-1	Semifinalist
Delaware	Tubby Raymond	0-1	Lost 1st Round
Eastern Ky.	Roy Kidd	0-1	Lost 1st Round
UNLV	Tony Knap	0-1	Lost 1st Round
New Hampshire	Bill Bowes	0-1	Lost 1st Round
1977 (8)			
Lehigh	John Whitehead	3-0	Champion
Jacksonville St.	Jim Fuller	2-1	Second
UC Davis	Jim Sochor	1-1	Semifinalist
North Dakota St.	Jim Wacker	1-1	Semifinalist
Bethune-Cookman	Andy Hinson	0-1	Lost 1st Round
Massachusetts	Dick MacPherson	0-1	Lost 1st Round
Northern Ariz.	Joe Salem	0-1	Lost 1st Round
Northern Mich.	Gil Krueger	0-1	Lost 1st Round
1978 (8)			
Eastern Ill.	Darrell Mudra	3-0	Champion
Delaware	Tubby Raymond	2-1	Second
Winston-Salem	Bill Hayes	1-1	Semifinalist
Youngstown St.	Bill Narduzzi	1-1	Semifinalist
UC Davis	Jim Sochor	0-1	Lost 1st Round
Cal Poly	Joe Harper	0-1	Lost 1st Round
Jacksonville St.	Jim Fuller	0-1	Lost 1st Round
Neb.-Omaha	Sandy Buda	0-1	Lost 1st Round
1979 (8)			
Delaware	Tubby Raymond	3-0	Champion
Youngstown St.	Bill Narduzzi	2-1	Second
Alabama A&M	Ray Greene	1-1	Semifinalist
Mississippi Col.	John Williams	1-1	Semifinalist
Morgan St.	Clarence Thomas	0-1	Lost 1st Round
North Dakota	Gene Murphy	0-1	Lost 1st Round
South Dakota St.	John Gregory	0-1	Lost 1st Round
Virginia Union	Willard Bailey	0-1	Lost 1st Round
1980 (8)			
Cal Poly	Joe Harper	3-0	Champion
Eastern Ill.	Darrell Mudra	2-1	Second
North Ala.	Wayne Grubb	1-1	Semifinalist
Santa Clara	Pat Malley	1-1	Semifinalist

DIVISION II CHAMPIONSHIP—YEAR-BY-YEAR RESULTS

Year (Number of Teams)	Coach	Record	Result
Jacksonville St.	Jim Fuller	0-1	Lost 1st Round
Northern Colo.	Bob Blasi	0-1	Lost 1st Round
Northern Mich.	Bill Rademacher	0-1	Lost 1st Round
Virginia Union	Willard Bailey	0-1	Lost 1st Round

1981 (8)

Southwest Tex. St.	Jim Wacker	3-0	Champion
North Dakota St.	Don Morton	2-1	Second
Northern Mich.	Bill Rademacher	1-1	Semifinalist
Shippensburg	Vito Ragazzo	1-1	Semifinalist
Elizabeth City St.	Johnnie Walton	0-1	Lost 1st Round
Jacksonville St.	Jim Fuller	0-1	Lost 1st Round
Puget Sound	Ron Simonson	0-1	Lost 1st Round
Virginia Union	Willard Bailey	0-1	Lost 1st Round

1982 (8)

Southwest Tex. St.	Jim Wacker	3-0	Champion
UC Davis	Jim Sochor	2-1	Second
Jacksonville St.	Jim Fuller	1-1	Semifinalist
North Dakota St.	Don Morton	1-1	Semifinalist
Fort Valley St.	Doug Porter	0-1	Lost 1st Round
Northern Mich.	Bill Rademacher	0-1	Lost 1st Round
Truman	Bruce Craddock	0-1	Lost 1st Round
Virginia Union	Willard Bailey	0-1	Lost 1st Round

1983 (8)

North Dakota St.	Don Morton	3-0	Champion
Central St.	Billy Joe	2-1	Second
UC Davis	Jim Sochor	1-1	Semifinalist
North Ala.	Wayne Grubb	1-1	Semifinalist
Butler	Bill Sylvester	0-1	Lost 1st Round
Southwest Tex. St.	John O'Hara	0-1	Lost 1st Round
Towson	Phil Albert	0-1	Lost 1st Round
Virginia Union	Willard Bailey	0-1	Lost 1st Round

1984 (8)

Troy St.	Chan Gailey	3-0	Champion
North Dakota St.	Don Morton	2-1	Second
Neb.-Omaha	Sandy Buda	1-1	Semifinalist
Towson	Phil Albert	1-1	Semifinalist
UC Davis	Jim Sochor	0-1	Lost 1st Round
Central St.	Billy Joe	0-1	Lost 1st Round
Norfolk St.	Willard Bailey	0-1	Lost 1st Round
Northwest Mo. St.	Vern Thomsen	0-1	Lost 1st Round

1985 (8)

North Dakota St.	Earle Solomonson	3-0	Champion
North Ala.	Wayne Grubb	2-1	Second
Bloomsburg	George Landis	1-1	Semifinalist
South Dakota	Dave Triplett	1-1	Semifinalist
UC Davis	Jim Sochor	0-1	Lost 1st Round
Central St.	Billy Joe	0-1	Lost 1st Round
Fort Valley St.	Gerald Walker	0-1	Lost 1st Round
Hampton	Fred Freeman	0-1	Lost 1st Round

1986 (8)

North Dakota St.	Earle Solomonson	3-0	Champion
South Dakota	Dave Triplett	2-1	Second
Central St.	Billy Joe	1-1	Semifinalist
Troy St.	Rick Rhodes	1-1	Semifinalist
Ashland	Fred Martinelli	0-1	Lost 1st Round
UC Davis	Jim Sochor	0-1	Lost 1st Round
Towson	Phil Albert	0-1	Lost 1st Round
Virginia Union	Joe Taylor	0-1	Lost 1st Round

1987 (8)

Troy St.	Rick Rhodes	3-0	Champion
Portland St.	Pokey Allen	2-1	Second
UCF	Gene McDowell	1-1	Semifinalist
Northern Mich.	Herb Grenke	1-1	Semifinalist
Angelo St.	Jerry Vandergriff	0-1	Lost 1st Round
Indiana (Pa.)	Frank Cignetti	0-1	Lost 1st Round
Minn. St.-Mankato	Dan Runkle	0-1	Lost 1st Round
Winston-Salem	Bill Hayes	0-1	Lost 1st Round

1988 (16)

North Dakota St.	Rocky Hager	4-0	Champion
Portland St.	Pokey Allen	3-1	Second
Cal St. Sacramento	Bob Mattos	2-1	Semifinalist
Tex. A&M-Kingsville	Ron Harms	2-1	Semifinalist
Jacksonville St.	Bill Burgess	1-1	Quarterfinalist
Millersville	Gene Carpenter	1-1	Quarterfinalist
N.C. Central	Henry Lattimore	1-1	Quarterfinalist
Tenn.-Martin	Don McLeary	1-1	Quarterfinalist
Augustana (S.D.)	Jim Heinitz	0-1	Lost 1st Round
Bowie St.	Sanders Shiver	0-1	Lost 1st Round
Butler	Bill Lynch	0-1	Lost 1st Round
UC Davis	Jim Sochor	0-1	Lost 1st Round
Indiana (Pa.)	Frank Cignetti	0-1	Lost 1st Round
Mississippi Col.	John Williams	0-1	Lost 1st Round
West Chester	Danny Hale	0-1	Lost 1st Round
Winston-Salem	Pete Richardson	0-1	Lost 1st Round

1989 (16)

*Mississippi Col.	John Williams	4-0	Champion
Jacksonville St.	Bill Burgess	3-1	Second
Angelo St.	Jerry Vandergriff	2-1	Semifinalist
Indiana (Pa.)	Frank Cignetti	2-1	Semifinalist
North Dakota St.	Rocky Hager	1-1	Quarterfinalist
Pittsburg St.	Dennis Franchione	1-1	Quarterfinalist
Portland St.	Pokey Allen	1-1	Quarterfinalist
St. Cloud St.	Noel Martin	1-1	Quarterfinalist
Alabama A&M	George Pugh	0-1	Lost 1st Round
Augustana (S.D.)	Jim Heinitz	0-1	Lost 1st Round
UC Davis	Bob Foster	0-1	Lost 1st Round
Edinboro	Tom Hollman	0-1	Lost 1st Round
Grand Valley St.	Tom Beck	0-1	Lost 1st Round
Northwest Mo. St.	Bud Elliott	0-1	Lost 1st Round
Tex. A&M-Kingsville	Ron Harms	0-1	Lost 1st Round
West Chester	Rick Daniels	0-1	Lost 1st Round

1990 (16)

North Dakota St.	Rocky Hager	4-0	Champion
Indiana (Pa.)	Frank Cignetti	3-1	Second
*Mississippi Col.	John Williams	2-1	Semifinalist
Pittsburg St.	Chuck Broyles	2-1	Semifinalist
Cal Poly	Lyle Setencich	1-1	Quarterfinalist
Edinboro	Tom Hollman	1-1	Quarterfinalist
Jacksonville St.	Bill Burgess	1-1	Quarterfinalist
Tex. A&M-Commerce	Eddie Vowell	1-1	Quarterfinalist
Cal St. Northridge	Bob Burt	0-1	Lost 1st Round
Grand Valley St.	Tom Beck	0-1	Lost 1st Round
North Ala.	Bobby Wallace	0-1	Lost 1st Round
Northern Colo.	Joe Glenn	0-1	Lost 1st Round
Truman	Eric Holm	0-1	Lost 1st Round
Virginia Union	Joe Taylor	0-1	Lost 1st Round
Winston-Salem	Pete Richardson	0-1	Lost 1st Round
Wofford	Mike Ayers	0-1	Lost 1st Round

1991 (16)

Pittsburg St.	Chuck Broyles	4-0	Champion
Jacksonville St.	Bill Burgess	3-1	Second
Indiana (Pa.)	Frank Cignetti	2-1	Semifinalist
Portland St.	Pokey Allen	2-1	Semifinalist
Minn. St.-Mankato	Dan Runkle	1-1	Quarterfinalist
Mississippi Col.	Terry McMillan	1-1	Quarterfinalist
Shippensburg	Rocky Rees	1-1	Quarterfinalist
Tex. A&M-Commerce	Eddie Vowell	1-1	Quarterfinalist
Butler	Bob Bartolomeo	0-1	Lost 1st Round
East Stroudsburg	Dennis Douds	0-1	Lost 1st Round
Grand Valley St.	Brian Kelly	0-1	Lost 1st Round
North Dakota St.	Rocky Hager	0-1	Lost 1st Round
Northern Colo.	Joe Glenn	0-1	Lost 1st Round
Virginia Union	Joe Taylor	0-1	Lost 1st Round
Winston-Salem	Pete Richardson	0-1	Lost 1st Round
Wofford	Mike Ayers	0-1	Lost 1st Round

1992 (16)

Jacksonville St.	Bill Burgess	4-0	Champion
Pittsburg St.	Chuck Broyles	3-1	Second
New Haven	Mark Whipple	2-1	Semifinalist
Portland St.	Pokey Allen	2-1	Semifinalist
Ferris St.	Keith Otterbein	1-1	Quarterfinalist
North Ala.	Bobby Wallace	1-1	Quarterfinalist
North Dakota St.	Rocky Hager	1-1	Quarterfinalist
Tex. A&M-Kingsville	Ron Harms	1-1	Quarterfinalist
UC Davis	Bob Foster	0-1	Lost 1st Round
Edinboro	Tom Hollman	0-1	Lost 1st Round
Hampton	Joe Taylor	0-1	Lost 1st Round
North Dakota	Roger Thomas	0-1	Lost 1st Round
Savannah St.	Bill Davis	0-1	Lost 1st Round
Truman	Eric Holm	0-1	Lost 1st Round
West Chester	Rick Daniels	0-1	Lost 1st Round
Western St.	Carl Iverson	0-1	Lost 1st Round

1993 (16)

North Ala.	Bobby Wallace	4-0	Champion
Indiana (Pa.)	Frank Cignetti	3-1	Second
North Dakota	Roger Thomas	2-1	Semifinalist
Tex. A&M-Kingsville	Ron Harms	2-1	Semifinalist
UC Davis	Bob Biggs	1-1	Quarterfinalist
Hampton	Joe Taylor	1-1	Quarterfinalist
Minn. St.-Mankato	Dan Runkle	1-1	Quarterfinalist
New Haven	Mark Whipple	1-1	Quarterfinalist
Albany St. (Ga.)	Hampton Smith	0-1	Lost 1st Round
Carson-Newman	Ken Sparks	0-1	Lost 1st Round

Year (Number of Teams)	Coach	Record	Result
Edinboro	Tom Hollman	0-1	Lost 1st Round
Ferris St.	Keith Otterbein	0-1	Lost 1st Round
Fort Hays St.	Bob Cortese	0-1	Lost 1st Round
Mo. Southern St.	Jon Lantz	0-1	Lost 1st Round
Pittsburg St.	Chuck Broyles	0-1	Lost 1st Round
Portland St.	Tim Walsh	0-1	Lost 1st Round

1994 (16)

North Ala.	Bobby Wallace	4-0	Champion
Tex. A&M-Kingsville	Ron Harms	3-1	Second
Indiana (Pa.)	Frank Cignetti	2-1	Semifinalist
North Dakota	Roger Thomas	2-1	Semifinalist
Ferris St.	Keith Otterbein	1-1	Quarterfinalist
North Dakota St.	Rocky Hager	1-1	Quarterfinalist
Portland St.	Tim Walsh	1-1	Quarterfinalist
Valdosta St.	Hal Mumme	1-1	Quarterfinalist
Albany St. (Ga.)	Hampton Smith	0-1	Lost 1st Round
Angelo St.	Jerry Vandergriff	0-1	Lost 1st Round
Carson-Newman	Ken Sparks	0-1	Lost 1st Round
Grand Valley St.	Brian Kelly	0-1	Lost 1st Round
Pittsburg St.	Chuck Broyles	0-1	Lost 1st Round
Truman	Eric Holm	0-1	Lost 1st Round
West Chester	Rick Daniels	0-1	Lost 1st Round
Western St.	Carl Iverson	0-1	Lost 1st Round

1995 (16)

North Ala.	Bobby Wallace	4-0	Champion
Pittsburg St.	Chuck Broyles	3-1	Second
Ferris St.	Jeff Pierce	2-1	Semifinalist
Tex. A&M-Kingsville	Ron Harms	2-1	Semifinalist
Carson-Newman	Ken Sparks	1-1	Quarterfinalist
New Haven	Tony Sparano	1-1	Quarterfinalist
North Dakota St.	Rocky Hager	1-1	Quarterfinalist
Portland St.	Tim Walsh	1-1	Quarterfinalist
Albany St. (Ga.)	Hampton Smith	0-1	Lost 1st Round
Edinboro	Tom Hollman	0-1	Lost 1st Round
Fort Hays St.	Bob Cortese	0-1	Lost 1st Round
Millersville	Gene Carpenter	0-1	Lost 1st Round
North Dakota	Roger Thomas	0-1	Lost 1st Round
Northern Colo.	Joe Glenn	0-1	Lost 1st Round
Tex. A&M-Commerce	Eddie Vowell	0-1	Lost 1st Round
West Ga.	Charlie Fisher	0-1	Lost 1st Round

1996 (16)

Northern Colo.	Joe Glenn	4-0	Champion
Carson-Newman	Ken Sparks	3-1	Second
UC Davis	Bob Biggs	2-1	Semifinalist
Clarion	Malen Luke	2-1	Semifinalist
Central Okla.	Gary Howard	1-1	Quarterfinalist
Ferris St.	Jeff Pierce	1-1	Quarterfinalist
Northwest Mo. St.	Mel Tjeerdsma	1-1	Quarterfinalist
Valdosta St.	Hal Mumme	1-1	Quarterfinalist
Bloomsburg	Danny Hale	0-1	Lost 1st Round
Indiana (Pa.)	Frank Cignetti	0-1	Lost 1st Round
Pittsburg St.	Chuck Broyles	0-1	Lost 1st Round
Neb.-Omaha	Pat Behrns	0-1	Lost 1st Round
Albany St. (Ga.)	Hampton Smith	0-1	Lost 1st Round
West Ga.	Charlie Fisher	0-1	Lost 1st Round
Chadron St.	Brad Smith	0-1	Lost 1st Round
Tex. A&M-Kingsville	Ron Harms	0-1	Lost 1st Round

1997 (16)

Northern Colo.	Joe Glenn	4-0	Champion
New Haven	Tony Sparano	3-1	Second
UC Davis	Bob Biggs	2-1	Semifinalist
Carson-Newman	Ken Sparks	2-1	Semifinalist
Angelo St.	Jerry Vandergriff	1-1	Quarterfinalist
Slippery Rock	George Mahalik	1-1	Quarterfinalist
Northwest Mo. St.	Mel Tjeerdsma	1-1	Quarterfinalist
Albany St. (Ga.)	Hampton Smith	1-1	Quarterfinalist
Tex. A&M-Kingsville	Ron Harms	0-1	Lost 1st Round
Western St.	Carl Iverson	0-1	Lost 1st Round
Glenville St.	Warren Ruggerio	0-1	Lost 1st Round
Ashland	Gary Keller	0-1	Lost 1st Round
North Dakota St.	Bob Babich	0-1	Lost 1st Round
Pittsburg St.	Chuck Broyles	0-1	Lost 1st Round
North Ala.	Bobby Wallace	0-1	Lost 1st Round
Southern Ark.	Steve Roberts	0-1	Lost 1st Round

1998 (16)

Northwest Mo. St.	Mel Tjeerdsma	4-0	Champion
Carson-Newman	Ken Sparks	3-1	Second
Slippery Rock	George Mahalik	2-1	Semifinalist
Tex. A&M-Kingsville	Ron Harms	2-1	Semifinalist
Central Okla.	Gary Howard	1-1	Quarterfinalist
Fort Valley St.	Kent Schoolfield	1-1	Quarterfinalist
Northern Colo.	Joe Glen	1-1	Quarterfinalist
Shepherd	Monte Cater	1-1	Quarterfinalist
UC Davis	Bob Biggs	0-1	Lost 1st Round
Chadron St.	Brad Smith	0-1	Lost 1st Round
Delta St.	Todd Knight	0-1	Lost 1st Round
Grand Valley St.	Brian Kelly	0-1	Lost 1st Round
Indiana (Pa.)	Frank Cignetti	0-1	Lost 1st Round
Neb.-Omaha	Pat Behrns	0-1	Lost 1st Round
North Dakota	Roger Thomas	0-1	Lost 1st Round
West Ga.	Glenn Spencer	0-1	Lost 1st Round

1999 (16)

Northwest Mo. St.	Mel Tjeerdsma	4-0	Champion
Carson-Newman	Ken Sparks	3-1	Second
Indiana (Pa.)	Frank Cignetti	2-1	Semifinalist
Northeastern St.	Tom Eckert	2-1	Semifinalist
UC Davis	Bob Biggs	1-1	Quarterfinalist
Catawba	David Bennett	1-1	Quarterfinalist
Millersville	Gene Carpenter	1-1	Quarterfinalist
Northern Colo.	Joe Glenn	1-1	Quarterfinalist
Arkansas Tech	Steve Mullins	0-1	Lost 1st Round
Central Okla.	Gary Howard	0-1	Lost 1st Round
Fort Valley St.	Kent Schoolfield	0-1	Lost 1st Round
North Dakota	Dale Lennon	0-1	Lost 1st Round
Pittsburg St.	Chuck Broyles	0-1	Lost 1st Round
Shepherd	Monte Cater	0-1	Lost 1st Round
Slippery Rock	George Mihalik	0-1	Lost 1st Round
Western Wash.	Rob Smith	0-1	Lost 1st Round

*Competition in championship vacated by action of the NCAA Committee on Infractions.

Division II Championship Record of Each College by Coach

(97 Colleges; 1973-99)

	Yrs	Won	Lost	CH	2D
AKRON					
Jim Dennison (Wooster '60) 76-2D	1	2	1	0	1
ALABAMA A&M					
Ray Green (Akron '63) 79	1	1	1	0	0
George Pugh (Alabama '76) 89	1	0	1	0	0
TOTAL	2	1	2	0	0
ALBANY ST. (GA.)					
Hampton Smith (Mississippi Val. '57) 93, 94, 95, 96, 97	5	1	5	0	0
ALCORN ST.					
Marino Casem (Xavier [La.] '56) 74	1	0	1	0	0
ANGELO ST.					
Jerry Vandergriff (Tex. A&M-Corp. Chris. '65) 87, 89, 94, 97	4	3	4	0	0
ARKANSAS TECH					
Steve Mullins (Ark.-Monticello '80) 99	1	0	1	0	0
ASHLAND					
Fred Martinelli (Otterbein '51) 86	1	0	1	0	0
Gary Keller (Bluffton '73) 97	1	0	1	0	0
TOTAL	2	0	2	0	0
AUGUSTANA (S.D.)					
Jim Heinitz (South Dakota St. '72) 88, 89	2	0	2	0	0
BETHUNE-COOKMAN					
Andy Hinson (Bethune-Cookman '53) 77	1	0	1	0	0
BLOOMSBURG					
George Landis (Penn St. '71) 85	1	1	1	0	0
Danny Hale (West Chester '68) 96	1	0	1	0	0
TOTAL	2	1	2	0	0
BOISE ST.					
Tony Knap (Idaho '39) 73, 74, 75	3	1	3	0	0
BOWIE ST.					
Sanders Shiver (Carson-Newman '76) 88	1	0	1	0	0
BUTLER					
Bill Sylvester (Butler '50) 83	1	0	1	0	0
Bill Lynch (Butler '77) 88	1	0	1	0	0
Bob Bartolomeo (Butler '77) 91	1	0	1	0	0
TOTAL	3	0	3	0	0
UC DAVIS					
Jim Sochor (San Fran. St. '60) 77, 78, 82-2D, 83, 84, 85, 86, 88	8	4	8	0	1

de
DIVISION II CHAMPIONSHIP—SCHOOL RECORDS

	Yrs	Won	Lost	CH	2D
Bob Foster (UC Davis '62) 89, 92	2	0	2	0	0
Bob Biggs (UC Davis '73) 93, 96, 97, 98, 99	5	6	5	0	0
TOTAL	15	10	15	0	1
CAL POLY					
Joe Harper (UCLA '59) 78, 80-CH	2	3	1	1	0
Lyle Setencich (Fresno St. '68) 90	1	1	1	0	0
TOTAL	3	4	2	1	0
CAL ST. NORTHRIDGE					
Bob Burt (Cal St. Los Angeles '62) 90	1	0	1	0	0
CAL ST. SACRAMENTO					
Bob Mattos (Cal St. Sacramento '64) 88	1	2	1	0	0
CARSON-NEWMAN					
Ken Sparks (Carson-Newman '68) 93, 94, 95, 96-2D, 97, 98-2D, 99-2D	7	12	7	0	3
CATAWBA					
David Bennett (Presbyterian '84) 99	1	1	1	0	0
UCF					
Gene McDowell (Florida St. '65) 87	1	1	1	0	0
CENTRAL MICH.					
Roy Kramer (Maryville [Tenn.] '53) 74-CH	1	3	0	1	0
CENTRAL OKLA.					
Gary Howard (Arkansas '64) 96, 98, 99	3	2	3	0	0
CENTRAL ST.					
Billy Joe (Villanova '63) 83-2D, 84, 85, 86	4	3	4	0	1
CHADRON ST.					
Brad Smith (Western Ill. '72) 96, 98	2	0	2	0	0
CLARION					
Malen Luke (Westminster [Pa.] '76) 96	1	2	1	0	0
DELAWARE					
Harold "Tubby" Raymond (Michigan '50) 73, 74-2D, 76, 78-2D, 79-CH	5	7	4	1	2
DELTA ST.					
Todd Knight (Ouachita Baptist '86) 98	1	0	1	0	0
EAST STROUDSBURG					
Dennis Douds (Slippery Rock '63) 91	1	0	1	0	0
EASTERN ILL.					
Darrell Mudra (Peru St. '51) 78-CH, 80-2D	2	5	1	1	1
EASTERN KY.					
Roy Kidd (Eastern Ky. '54) 76	1	0	1	0	0
EDINBORO					
Tom Hollman (Ohio Northern '68) 89, 90, 92, 93, 95	5	1	5	0	0
ELIZABETH CITY ST.					
Johnnie Walton (Elizabeth City St. '69) 81	1	0	1	0	0
FERRIS ST.					
Keith Otterbein (Ferris St. '79) 92, 93, 94	3	2	3	0	0
Jeff Pierce (Ferris St. '79) 95, 96	2	3	2	0	0
TOTAL	5	5	5	0	0
FORT HAYS ST.					
Bob Cortese (Colorado '67) 93, 95	2	0	2	0	0
FORT VALLEY ST.					
Doug Porter (Xavier [La.] '52) 82	1	0	1	0	0
Gerald Walker (Lincoln [Mo.] '62) 85	1	0	1	0	0
Kent Schoolfield (Florida A&M '70) 98, 99	2	1	2	0	0
TOTAL	4	1	4	0	0
GLENVILLE ST.					
Warren Ruggerio (Delaware '88) 97	1	0	1	0	0
GRAMBLING					
Eddie Robinson (Leland '41) 73	1	1	1	0	0
GRAND VALLEY ST.					
Tom Beck (Northern Ill. '61) 89, 90	2	0	2	0	0
Brian Kelly (Assumption '83) 91, 94, 98	3	0	3	0	0
TOTAL	5	0	5	0	0
HAMPTON					
Fred Freeman (Mississippi Val. '66) 85	1	0	1	0	0
Joe Taylor (Western Ill. '72) 92, 93	2	1	2	0	0
TOTAL	3	1	3	0	0
INDIANA (PA.)					
Frank Cignetti (Indiana [Pa.] '60) 87, 88, 89, 90-2D, 91, 93-2D, 94, 96, 98, 99	10	14	10	0	2
JACKSONVILLE ST.					
Jim Fuller (Alabama '67) 77-2D, 78, 80, 81, 82	5	3	5	0	1
Bill Burgess (Auburn '63) 88, 89-2D, 90, 91-2D, 92-CH	5	12	4	1	2
TOTAL	10	15	9	1	3
LEHIGH					
Fred Dunlap (Colgate '50) 73, 75	2	0	2	0	0

	Yrs	Won	Lost	CH	2D
John Whitehead (East Stroudsburg '50) 77-CH	1	3	0	1	0
TOTAL	3	3	2	1	0
LOUISIANA TECH					
Maxie Lambright (Southern Miss. '49) 73-CH, 74	2	4	1	1	0
MASSACHUSETTS					
Dick MacPherson (Springfield '58) 77	1	0	1	0	0
MILLERSVILLE					
Gene Carpenter (Huron '63) 88, 95, 99	3	2	3	0	0
MINN. ST.-MANKATO					
Dan Runkle (Illinois Col. '68) 87, 91, 93	3	2	3	0	0
MISSISSIPPI COL.*					
John Williams (Mississippi Col. '57) 79, 88, 89-CH, 90	4	7	3	1	0
Terry McMillan (Southern Miss. '69) 91	1	1	1	0	0
TOTAL	5	8	4	1	0
MO. SOUTHERN ST.					
Jon Lantz (Okla. Panhandle '74) 93	1	0	1	0	0
MONTANA ST.					
Sonny Holland (Montana St. '60) 76-CH	1	3	0	1	0
MORGAN ST.					
Clarence Thomas 79	1	0	1	0	0
NEB.-OMAHA					
Sandy Buda (Kansas '67) 78, 84	2	1	2	0	0
Pat Behrns (Dakota St. '72) 96, 98	2	0	2	0	0
TOTAL	4	1	4	0	0
UNLV					
Ron Meyer (Purdue '63) 74	1	1	1	0	0
Tony Knap (Idaho '39) 76	1	0	1	0	0
TOTAL	2	1	2	0	0
NEW HAMPSHIRE					
Bill Bowes (Penn St. '65) 75, 76	2	1	2	0	0
NEW HAVEN					
Mark Whipple (Brown '79) 92, 93	2	3	2	0	0
Tony Sparano (New Haven '82) 95, 97-2D	2	4	2	0	1
TOTAL	4	7	4	0	1
NORFOLK ST.					
Willard Bailey (Norfolk St. '62) 84	1	0	1	0	0
NORTH ALA.					
Wayne Grubb (Tennessee '61) 80, 83, 85-2D	3	4	3	0	1
Bobby Wallace (Mississippi St. '76) 90, 92, 93-CH, 94-CH, 95-CH, 97	6	13	3	3	0
TOTAL	9	17	6	3	1
N.C. CENTRAL					
Henry Lattimore (Jackson St. '57) 88	1	1	1	0	0
NORTH DAKOTA					
Jerry Olson (Valley City St. '55) 75	1	0	1	0	0
Gene Murphy (North Dakota '62) 79	1	0	1	0	0
Roger Thomas (Augustana [Ill.] '69) 92, 93, 94, 95, 98	5	4	5	0	0
Dale Lennon (North Dakota '85) 99	1	0	1	0	0
TOTAL	8	4	8	0	0
NORTH DAKOTA ST.					
Jim Wacker (Valparaiso '60) 76, 77	2	2	2	0	0
Don Morton (Augustana [Ill.] '69) 81-2D, 82, 83-CH, 84-2D	4	8	3	1	2
Earle Solomonson (Augsburg '69) 85-CH, 86-CH	2	6	0	2	0
Rocky Hager (Minot St. '74) 88-CH, 89, 90-CH, 91, 92, 94, 95	7	12	5	2	0
Bob Babich (Tulsa '84) 97	1	0	1	0	0
TOTAL	16	28	11	5	2
NORTHEASTERN ST.					
Tom Eckert (Northeastern St. '66) 99	1	2	1	0	0
NORTHERN ARIZ.					
Joe Salem (Minnesota '61) 77	1	0	1	0	0
NORTHERN COLO.					
Bob Blasi (Colorado St. '53) 80	1	0	1	0	0
Joe Glenn (South Dakota '71) 90, 91, 95, 96-CH, 97-CH, 98, 99	7	10	5	2	0
TOTAL	8	10	7	2	0
NORTHERN IOWA					
Stan Sheriff (Cal Poly '54) 75	1	0	1	0	0
NORTHERN MICH.					
Gil Krueger (Marquette '52) 75-CH, 76, 77	3	4	2	1	0
Bill Rademacher (Northern Mich. '63) 80, 81, 82	3	1	3	0	0

CHAMPIONSHIP RESULTS

425

	Yrs	Won	Lost	CH	2D
Herb Grenke (Wis.-Milwaukee '63) 87	1	1	1	0	0
TOTAL	7	6	6	1	0

NORTHWEST MO. ST.
	Yrs	Won	Lost	CH	2D
Vern Thomsen (Peru St. '61) 84	1	0	1	0	0
Bud Elliott (Baker '53) 89	1	0	1	0	0
Mel Tjeerdsma (Southern St. [S.D.] '67) 96, 97, 98-CH, 99-CH	4	10	2	2	0
TOTAL	6	10	4	2	0

PITTSBURG ST.
	Yrs	Won	Lost	CH	2D
Dennis Franchione (Pittsburg St. '73) 89	1	1	1	0	0
Chuck Broyles (Pittsburg St. '70) 90, 91-CH, 92-2D, 93, 94, 95-2D, 96, 97, 99	9	12	8	1	2
TOTAL	10	13	9	1	2

PORTLAND ST.
	Yrs	Won	Lost	CH	2D
Pokey Allen (Utah '65) 87-2D, 88-2D, 89, 91, 92	5	10	5	0	2
Tim Walsh (UC Riverside '77) 93, 94, 95	3	2	3	0	0
TOTAL	8	12	8	0	2

PUGET SOUND
	Yrs	Won	Lost	CH	2D
Ron Simonson (Portland St. '65) 81	1	0	1	0	0

ST. CLOUD ST.
	Yrs	Won	Lost	CH	2D
Noel Martin (Nebraska '63) 89	1	1	1	0	0

SANTA CLARA
	Yrs	Won	Lost	CH	2D
Pat Malley (Santa Clara '53) 80	1	1	1	0	0

SAVANNAH ST.
	Yrs	Won	Lost	CH	2D
Bill Davis (Johnson Smith '65) 92	1	0	1	0	0

SHEPHERD
	Yrs	Won	Lost	CH	2D
Monte Cater (Millikin '71) 98, 99	2	1	2	0	0

SHIPPENSBURG
	Yrs	Won	Lost	CH	2D
Vito Ragazzo (William & Mary '51) 81	1	1	1	0	0
Rocky Rees (West Chester '71) 91	1	1	1	0	0
TOTAL	2	2	2	0	0

SLIPPERY ROCK
	Yrs	Won	Lost	CH	2D
George Mahalik (Slippery Rock '74) 97, 98, 99	3	3	3	0	0

SOUTH DAKOTA
	Yrs	Won	Lost	CH	2D
Joe Salem (Minnesota '61) 73	1	0	1	0	0
Dave Triplett (Iowa '72) 85, 86-2D	2	3	2	0	1
TOTAL	3	3	3	0	1

SOUTH DAKOTA ST.
	Yrs	Won	Lost	CH	2D
John Gregory (Northern Iowa '61) 79	1	0	1	0	0

SOUTHERN ARK.
	Yrs	Won	Lost	CH	2D
Steve Roberts (Ouachita Baptist '87) 97	1	0	1	0	0

SOUTHWEST TEX. ST.
	Yrs	Won	Lost	CH	2D
Jim Wacker (Valparaiso '60) 81-CH, 82-CH	2	6	0	2	0
John O'Hara (Okla. Panhandle '67) 83	1	0	1	0	0
TOTAL	3	6	1	2	0

TENN.-MARTIN
	Yrs	Won	Lost	CH	2D
Don McLeary (Tennessee '70) 88	1	1	1	0	0

TEX. A&M-COMMERCE
	Yrs	Won	Lost	CH	2D
Eddie Vowell (Southwestern Okla. '69) 90, 91, 95	3	2	3	0	0

TEX. A&M-KINGSVILLE
	Yrs	Won	Lost	CH	2D
Ron Harms (Valparaiso '59) 88, 89, 92, 93, 94-2D, 95, 96, 97, 98	9	12	9	0	1

TOWSON
	Yrs	Won	Lost	CH	2D
Phil Albert (Arizona '66) 83, 84, 86	3	1	3	0	0

TROY ST.
	Yrs	Won	Lost	CH	2D
Chan Gailey (Florida '74) 84-CH	1	3	0	1	0
Rick Rhoades 86, 87-CH	2	4	1	1	0
TOTAL	3	7	1	2	0

TRUMAN
	Yrs	Won	Lost	CH	2D
Bruce Craddock (Truman '66) 82	1	0	1	0	0
Eric Holm (Truman '81) 90, 92, 94	3	0	3	0	0
TOTAL	4	0	4	0	0

VALDOSTA ST.
	Yrs	Won	Lost	CH	2D
Hal Mumme (Tarleton St. '75) 94, 96	2	2	2	0	0

VIRGINIA UNION
	Yrs	Won	Lost	CH	2D
Willard Bailey (Norfolk St. '62) 79, 80, 81, 82, 83	5	0	5	0	0
Joe Taylor (Western Ill. '72) 86, 90, 91	3	0	3	0	0
TOTAL	8	0	8	0	0

WEST ALA.
	Yrs	Won	Lost	CH	2D
Jim King 75	1	1	1	0	0

WEST CHESTER
	Yrs	Won	Lost	CH	2D
Danny Hale (West Chester '68) 88	1	0	1	0	0
Rick Daniels (West Chester '75) 89, 92, 94	3	0	3	0	0
TOTAL	4	0	4	0	0

WEST GA.
	Yrs	Won	Lost	CH	2D
Charlie Fisher (Springfield '81) 95, 96	2	0	2	0	0
Glenn Spencer (Georgia Tech '86) 98	1	0	1	0	0
TOTAL	3	0	3	0	0

WESTERN CARO.
	Yrs	Won	Lost	CH	2D
Bob Waters (Presbyterian '60) 74	1	0	1	0	0

WESTERN ILL.
	Yrs	Won	Lost	CH	2D
Darrell Mudra (Peru St. '51) 73	1	0	1	0	0

WESTERN KY.
	Yrs	Won	Lost	CH	2D
Jimmy Feix (Western Ky. '53) 73-2D, 75-2D	2	4	2	0	2

WESTERN ST.
	Yrs	Won	Lost	CH	2D
Carl Iverson (Whitman '62) 92, 94, 97	3	0	3	0	0

WESTERN WASH.
	Yrs	Won	Lost	CH	2D
Rob Smith (Washington '81) 99	1	0	1	0	0

WINSTON-SALEM
	Yrs	Won	Lost	CH	2D
Bill Hayes (N.C. Central '64) 78, 87	2	1	2	0	0
Pete Richardson (Dayton '68) 88, 90, 91	3	0	3	0	0
TOTAL	5	1	5	0	0

WOFFORD
	Yrs	Won	Lost	CH	2D
Mike Ayers (Georgetown [Ky.] '74) 90, 91	2	0	2	0	0

YOUNGSTOWN ST.
	Yrs	Won	Lost	CH	2D
Rey Dempsey (Geneva '58) 74	1	0	1	0	0
Bill Narduzzi (Miami [Ohio] '59) 78, 79-2D	2	3	2	0	1
TOTAL	3	3	3	0	1

*Mississippi College's competition in the 1989 and 1990 Division II championships was vacated by action of the NCAA Committee on Infractions (official record is 2-3).

All-Time Results

1973 First Round: Grambling 17, Delaware 8; Western Ky. 25, Lehigh 16; Louisiana Tech 18, Western Ill. 13; Boise St. 53, South Dakota 10. **Semifinals:** Western Ky. 28, Grambling 20; Louisiana Tech 38, Boise St. 34. **Championship:** Louisiana Tech 34, Western Ky. 0.

1974 First Round: Central Mich. 20, Boise St. 6; Louisiana Tech 10, Western Caro. 7; UNLV 35, Alcorn St. 22; Delaware 49, Youngstown St. 14. **Semifinals:** Central Mich. 35, Louisiana Tech 14; Delaware 49, UNLV 11. **Championship:** Central Mich. 54, Delaware 14.

1975 First Round: Northern Mich. 24, Boise St. 21; West Ala. 34, North Dakota 14; Western Ky. 14, Northern Iowa 12; New Hampshire 35, Lehigh 21. **Semifinals:** Northern Mich. 28, West Ala. 26; Western Ky. 14, New Hampshire 3. **Championship:** Northern Mich. 16, Western Ky. 14.

1976 First Round: Akron 26, UNLV 6; Northern Mich. 28, Delaware 17; North Dakota St. 10, Eastern Ky. 7; Montana St. 17, New Hampshire 16. **Semifinals:** Akron 29, Northern Mich. 26; Montana St. 10, North Dakota St. 3. **Championship:** Montana St. 24, Akron 13.

1977 First Round: UC Davis 34, Bethune-Cookman 16; Lehigh 30, Massachusetts 23; North Dakota St. 20, Northern Mich. 6; Jacksonville St. 35, Northern Ariz. 0. **Semifinals:** Lehigh 39, UC Davis 30; Jacksonville St. 31, North Dakota St. 7. **Championship:** Lehigh 33, Jacksonville St. 0.

1978 First Round: Winston-Salem 17, Cal Poly 0; Delaware 42, Jacksonville St. 27; Youngstown St. 21, Neb.-Omaha 14; Eastern Ill. 35, UC Davis 31. **Semifinals:** Delaware 41, Winston-Salem 0; Eastern Ill. 26, Youngstown St. 22. **Championship:** Eastern Ill. 10, Delaware 9.

1979 First Round: Delaware 58, Virginia Union 28; Mississippi Col. 35, North Dakota 15; Youngstown St. 50, South Dakota St. 7; Alabama A&M 27, Morgan St. 7. **Semifinals:** Delaware 60, Mississippi Col. 10; Youngstown St. 52, Alabama A&M 0. **Championship:** Delaware 38, Youngstown St. 21.

1980 First Round: Eastern Ill. 21, Northern Colo. 14; North Ala. 17, Virginia Union 8; Santa Clara 27, Northern Mich. 26; Cal Poly 15, Jacksonville St. 7. **Semifinals:** Eastern Ill. 56, North Ala. 31; Cal Poly 38, Santa Clara 14. **Championship:** Cal Poly 21, Eastern Ill. 13.

1981 First Round: Northern Mich. 55, Elizabeth City St. 6; Southwest Tex. 38, Jacksonville St. 22; North Dakota St. 24, Puget Sound 10; Shippensburg 40, Virginia Union 27. **Semifinals:** Southwest Tex. St. 62, Northern Mich. 0; North Dakota St. 18, Shippensburg 6. **Championship:** Southwest Tex. St. 42, North Dakota St. 13.

1982 First Round: Southwest Tex. St. 27, Fort Valley St. 6; Jacksonville St. 34, Truman 21; North Dakota St. 21, Virginia Union 20; UC Davis 42, Northern Mich. 21. **Semifinals:** Southwest Tex. St. 19, Jacksonville St. 14; UC Davis 19, North Dakota St. 14. **Championship:** Southwest Tex. St. 34, UC Davis 9.

1983 First Round: UC Davis 25, Butler 6; North Dakota St. 24, Towson 17; North Ala. 16, Virginia Union 14; Central St. 24, Southwest Tex. St. 16. **Semifinals:** North Dakota St. 26, UC Davis 17; Central St. 27, North Ala. 24. **Championship:** North Dakota St. 41, Central St. 21.

1984 First Round: North Dakota St. 31, UC Davis 23; Neb.-Omaha 28, Northwest Mo. St. 15; Troy St. 31, Central St. 21; Towson 31, Shippensburg 6. **Semifinals:** North Dakota St. 25, Neb.-Omaha 14; Troy St. 45, Towson 3. **Championship:** Troy St. 18, North Dakota St. 17.

1985 First Round: North Dakota St. 31, UC Davis 12;

DIVISION II CHAMPIONSHIP—ALL-TIME RESULTS

South Dakota 13, Central St. 10 (2 ot); Bloomsburg 38, Hampton 28; North Ala. 14, Fort Valley St. 7. **Semifinals:** North Dakota St. 16, South Dakota 7; North Ala. 34, Bloomsburg 0. **Championship:** North Dakota St. 35, North Ala. 7.

1986 First Round: North Dakota St. 50, Ashland 0; Central St. 31, Towson 0; Troy St. 31, Virginia Union 7; South Dakota 26, UC Davis 23. **Semifinals:** North Dakota St. 35, Central St. 12; South Dakota 42, Troy St. 28. **Championship:** North Dakota St. 27, South Dakota 7.

1987 First Round: Portland St. 27, Minn. St.-Mankato 21; Northern Mich. 23, Angelo St. 20 (ot); UCF 12, Indiana (Pa.) 10; Troy St. 45, Winston-Salem 14. **Semifinals:** Portland St. 13, Northern Mich. 7; Troy St. 31, Central Fla. 10. **Championship:** Troy St. 31, Portland St. 17.

1988 First Round: North Dakota St. 49, Augustana (S.D.) 7; Millersville 27, Indiana (Pa.) 24; Cal St. Sacramento 35, UC Davis 14; N.C. Central 31, Winston-Salem 16; Tex. A&M-Kingsville 39, Mississippi Col. 15; Tenn.-Martin 23, Butler 6; Portland St. 34, Bowie St. 17; Jacksonville St. 63, West Chester 24. **Quarterfinals:** North Dakota St. 36, Millersville 26; Cal St. Sacramento 56, N.C. Central 7; Tex. A&M-Kingsville 34, Tenn.-Martin 0; Portland St. 20, Jacksonville St. 13. **Semifinals:** North Dakota St. 42, Cal St. Sacramento 20; Portland St. 35, Tex. A&M-Kingsville 27. **Championship:** North Dakota St. 35, Portland St. 21.

1989 First Round: *Mississippi Col. 34, Tex. A&M-Kingsville 19; St. Cloud St. 27, Augustana (S.D.) 20; Portland St. 56, West Chester 50 (3 ot); Indiana (Pa.) 34, Grand Valley St. 24; Pittsburg St. 28, Northwest Mo. St. 7; Angelo St. 28, UC Davis 23; North Dakota St. 45, Edinboro 32; Jacksonville St. 33, Alabama A&M 9. **Quarterfinals:** *Mississippi Col. 55, St. Cloud St. 24; Indiana (Pa.) 17, Portland St. 0; Angelo St. 24, Pittsburg St. 21; Jacksonville St. 21, North Dakota St. 17. **Semifinals:** *Mississippi Col. 26, Indiana (Pa.) 14; Jacksonville St. 34, Angelo St. 16. **Championship:** *Mississippi Col. 3, Jacksonville St. 0.

*Mississippi College's participation in 1989 playoff vacated.

1990 First Round: *Mississippi Col. 70, Wofford 19; Jacksonville St. 38, North Ala. 14; Indiana (Pa.) 48, Winston-Salem 0; Edinboro 38, Virginia Union 14; North Dakota St. 17, Northern Colo. 7; Cal Poly 14, Cal St. Northridge 7; Pittsburg St. 59, Truman 7; Tex. A&M-Commerce 20, Grand Valley St. 14. **Quarterfinals:** *Mississippi Col. 14, Jacksonville St. 7; Indiana (Pa.) 14, Edinboro 7; North Dakota St. 47, Cal Poly 0; Pittsburg St. 60, Tex. A&M-Commerce 28. **Semifinals:** Indiana (Pa.) 27, *Mississippi Col. 8; North Dakota St. 39, Pittsburg St. 29. **Championship:** North Dakota St. 51, Indiana (Pa.) 11.

*Mississippi College's participation in 1990 playoff vacated.

1991 First Round: Pittsburg St. 26, Butler 16; Tex. A&M-Commerce 36, Grand Valley St. 15; Portland St. 28, Northern Colo. 24; Minn. St.-Mankato 27, North Dakota St. 7; Jacksonville St. 49, Winston-Salem 24; Mississippi Col. 28, Wofford 15; Indiana (Pa.) 56, Virginia Union 7; Shippensburg 34, East Stroudsburg 33 (ot). **Quarterfinals:** Pittsburg St. 38, Tex. A&M-Commerce 28; Portland St. 37, Minn. St.-Mankato 27; Jacksonville St. 35, Mississippi Col. 7; Indiana (Pa.) 52, Shippensburg 7. **Semifinals:** Pittsburg St. 53, Portland St. 21; Jacksonville St. 41, Indiana (Pa.) 20. **Championship:** Pittsburg St. 23, Jacksonville St. 6.

1992 First Round: Ferris St. 19, Edinboro 15; New Haven 38, West Chester 26; Jacksonville St. 41, Savannah St. 16; North Ala. 33, Hampton 21; Tex. A&M-Kingsville 22, Western St. 13; Portland St. 42, UC Davis 28; Pittsburg St. 26, North Dakota 21; North Dakota St. 42, Truman 7. **Quarterfinals:** New Haven 25, Ferris St. 13; Jacksonville St. 14, North Ala. 12; Portland St. 35, Tex. A&M-Kingsville 30; Pittsburg St. 38, North Dakota St. 37 (ot). **Semifinals:** Jacksonville St. 46, New Haven 35; Pittsburg St. 41, Portland St. 38. **Championship:** Jacksonville St. 17, Pittsburg St. 13.

1993 First Round: North Ala. 38, Carson-Newman 28; Hampton 33, Albany St. (Ga.) 7; Tex. A&M-Kingsville 50, Portland St. 15; UC Davis 37, Fort Hays St. 34; Minn. St.-Mankato 34, Mo. Southern St. 13; North Dakota 17, Pittsburg St. 14; New Haven 48, Edinboro 28; Indiana (Pa.) 28, Ferris St. 21. **Quarterfinals:** North Ala. 45, Hampton 20; Tex. A&M-Kingsville 51, UC Davis 28; North Dakota 54, Minn. St.-Mankato 21; Indiana (Pa.) 38, New Haven 35. **Semifinals:** North Ala. 27, Tex. A&M-Kingsville 25; Indiana (Pa.) 21, North Dakota 6. **Championship:** North Ala. 41, Indiana (Pa.) 34.

1994 First Round: Ferris St. 43, West Chester 40; Indiana (Pa.) 35, Grand Valley St. 27; Tex. A&M-Kingsville 43, Western St. 7; Portland St. 29, Angelo St. 0; North Dakota St. 18, Pittsburg St. 12 (3 ot); North Dakota 18, Truman 6; North Ala. 17, Carson-Newman 13; Valdosta St. 14, Albany St. (Ga.) 7. **Quarterfinals:** Indiana (Pa.) 21, Ferris St. 17; Tex. A&M-Kingsville 21, Portland St. 16; North Dakota 14, North Dakota St. 7; North Ala. 27, Valdosta St. 24 (2 ot). **Semifinals:** Tex. A&M-Kingsville 46, Indiana (Pa.) 20; North Ala. 35, North Dakota 7. **Championship:** North Ala. 16, Tex. A&M-Kingsville 10.

1995 First Round: Ferris St. 36, Millersville 26; New Haven 27, Edinboro 12; North Ala. 38, Albany St. (Ga.) 28; Carson-Newman 37, West Ga. 26; Pittsburg St. 36, Northern Colo. 17; North Dakota St. 41, North Dakota 10; Tex. A&M-Kingsville 59, Fort Hays St. 28; Portland St. 56, Tex. A&M-Commerce 35. **Quarterfinals:** Ferris St. 17, New Haven 9; North Ala. 28, Carson-Newman 7; Pittsburg St. 9, North Dakota St. 7; Tex. A&M-Kingsville 30, Portland St. 3. **Semifinals:** North Ala. 45, Ferris St. 7; Pittsburg St. 28, Tex. A&M-Kingsville 25 (ot).

Championship: North Ala. 27, Pittsburg St. 7.

1996 First Round: Clarion 42, Bloomsburg 29; Ferris St. 24, Indiana (Pa.) 23; Northern Colo. 24, Pittsburg St. 21; Northwest Mo. St. 22, Neb.-Omaha 21; Valdosta St. 38, Albany St. (Ga.) 28; Carson-Newman 41, West Ga. 7; Central Okla. 23, Chadron St. 21; UC Davis 17, Tex. A&M-Kingsville 14. **Quarterfinals:** Clarion 23, Ferris St. 21; Northern Colo. 27, Northwest Mo. St. 26; Carson-Newman 24, Valdosta St. 19; UC Davis 26, Central Okla. 7. **Semifinals:** Northern Colo. 19, Clarion 18; Carson-Newman 29, UC Davis 26. **Championship:** Northern Colo. 23, Carson-Newman 14.

1997 First Round: UC Davis 37, Tex. A&M-Kingsville 34; Angelo St. 46, Western St. 12; New Haven 47, Glenville St. 7; Slippery Rock 30, Ashland 20; Northwest Mo. St. 39, North Dakota St. 28; Northern Colo. 24, Pittsburg St. 16; Carson-Newman 21, North Ala. 7; Albany St. (Ga.) 10, Southern Ark. 6. **Quarterfinals:** UC Davis 50, Angelo St. 33; New Haven 49, Slippery Rock 21; Northern Colo. 35, Northwest Mo. St. 19; Carson-Newman 23, Albany St. (Ga.) 22. **Semifinals:** New Haven 27, UC Davis 25; Northern Colo. 30, Carson-Newman 29. **Championship:** Northern Colo. 51, New Haven 0.

1998 First Round: Carson-Newman 30, West Ga. 20; Fort Valley St. 21, Delta St. 12; Slippery Rock 37, Grand Valley St. 14; Shepherd 9, Indiana (Pa.) 6; Northwest Mo. St. 28, Neb.-Omaha 14; Northern Colo. 52, North Dakota 24; Central Okla. 23, Chadron St. 19; Tex. A&M-Kingsville 54, UC Davis 21. **Quarterfinals:** Carson-Newman 38, Fort Valley St. 31 (ot); Slippery Rock 31, Shepherd 20; Northwest Mo. St. 42, Northern Colo. 17; Tex. A&M-Kingsville 24, Central Okla. 21 (ot). **Semifinals:** Carson-Newman 47, Slippery Rock 21; Northwest Mo. St. 49, Tex. A&M-Kingsville 34. **Championship:** Northwest Mo. St. 24, Carson-Newman 6.

1999 First Round: Carson-Newman 40, Arkansas Tech 28; Catawba 48, Fort Valley St. 17; UC Davis 33, Central Okla. 17; Northeastern St. 27, Western Wash. 24 (ot); Indiana (Pa.) 27, Slippery Rock 20 (ot); Millersville 21, Shepherd 14; Northern Colo. 34, Pittsburg St. 31; Northwest Mo. St. 20, North Dakota 13 (ot). **Quarterfinals:** Carson-Newman 28, Catawba 25; Northeastern St. 19, UC Davis 14; Indiana (Pa.) 26, Millersville 21; Northwest Mo. St. 41, Northern Colo. 35. **Semifinals:** Carson-Newman 42, Northeastern St. 7; Northwest Mo. St. 20, Indiana (Pa.) 12. **Championship:** Northwest Mo. St. 58, Carson-Newman 52 (4 ot).

Division III Championship

1999 Title Game Summary

**SALEM STADIUM, SALEM, VA.;
DECEMBER 18, 1999**

	Rowan	Pacific Lutheran
First Downs	15	20
Rushing Yardage	-63	120
Passing Yardage	264	276
Passes (Comp.-Att.-Int.)	26-46-2	18-28-0
Punts (Number-Average)	6-31.0	5-32.2
Fumbles (Number-Lost)	3-2	3-1
Penalties (Number-Yards)	9-70	4-35
Rowan	7 0 6 0—13	
Pacific Lutheran	14 13 8 7—42	

FIRST QUARTER
Pacific Lutheran—Todd McDevitt 31 pass from Chad Johnson (Scott Sarrenson kick) (31 yards in 1 play, 12:53 left)
Rowan—Mike Warker 1 run (Nick Frade kick) (78 yards in 9 plays, 2:10 left)
Pacific Lutheran—Anthony Hicks 1 run (Sarrenson kick) (75 yards in 5 plays, 0:26 left)

SECOND QUARTER
Pacific Lutheran—Kevin Lint 5 run (Sarrenson kick) (59 yards in 10 plays, 10:12 left)
Pacific Lutheran—Johnson 1 run (kick blocked) (41 yards in 3 plays, 1:05 left)

Pacific Lutheran's Anthony Hicks (26) set tournament records for touchdowns (11) and points (66) in 1999, as the Lutes posted five victories on their way to the championship.

THIRD QUARTER
Pacific Lutheran—McDevitt 13 pass from Johnson (Jess Nelson pass from Johnson) (13 yards in 3 plays, 14:27 left)
Rowan—Taman Bryant 26 pass from Warker (kick blocked) (47 yards in 8 plays, 10:32 left)

FOURTH QUARTER
Pacific Lutheran—Hicks 20 run (Sarrenson kick) (39 yards in 6 plays, 2:18 left)

INDIVIDUAL LEADERS
Rushing—Rowan: Antwine Simmons, 3 yards on 1 carry; Pacific Lutheran: Hicks, 73 yards on 22 carries.
Passing—Rowan: Warker, 26 of 46 for 264 yards; Pacific Lutheran: Johnson, 18 of 28 for 276 yards.
Receiving—Rowan: Bryant, 13 catches for 141 yards, and Scott Lipford, 8 catches for 94 yards; Pacific Lutheran: Hicks, 4 catches for 78 yards, and McDevitt, 4 catches for 63 yards.

Division III All-Time Championship Results

Year	Champion	Coach	Score	Runner-Up	Site
1973	Wittenberg	Dave Maurer	41-0	Juniata	Phenix City, Ala.
1974	Central (Iowa)	Ron Schipper	10-8	Ithaca	Phenix City, Ala.
1975	Wittenberg	Dave Maurer	28-0	Ithaca	Phenix City, Ala.
1976	St. John's (Minn.)	John Gagliardi	31-28	Towson	Phenix City, Ala.
1977	Widener	Bill Manlove	39-36	Wabash	Phenix City, Ala.
1978	Baldwin-Wallace	Lee Tressel	24-10	Wittenberg	Phenix City, Ala.
1979	Ithaca	Jim Butterfield	14-10	Wittenberg	Phenix City, Ala.
1980	Dayton	Rick Carter	63-0	Ithaca	Phenix City, Ala.
1981	Widener	Bill Manlove	17-10	Dayton	Phenix City, Ala.
1982	West Ga.	Bobby Pate	14-0	Augustana (Ill.)	Phenix City, Ala.
1983	Augustana (Ill.)	Bob Reade	21-17	Union (N.Y.)	Kings Island, Ohio
1984	Augustana (Ill.)	Bob Reade	21-12	Central (Iowa)	Kings Island, Ohio
1985	Augustana (Ill.)	Bob Reade	20-7	Ithaca	Phenix City, Ala.
1986	Augustana (Ill.)	Bob Reade	31-3	Salisbury St.	Phenix City, Ala.
1987	Wagner	Walt Hameline	19-3	Dayton	Phenix City, Ala.
1988	Ithaca	Jim Butterfield	39-24	Central (Iowa)	Phenix City, Ala.
1989	Dayton	Mike Kelly	17-7	Union (N.Y.)	Phenix City, Ala.
1990	Allegheny	Ken O'Keefe	21-14 (OT)	Lycoming	Bradenton, Fla.
1991	Ithaca	Jim Butterfield	34-20	Dayton	Bradenton, Fla.
1992	Wis.-La Crosse	Roger Harring	16-12	Wash. & Jeff.	Bradenton, Fla.
1993	Mount Union	Larry Kehres	34-24	Rowan	Salem, Va.
1994	Albion	Pete Schmidt	38-15	Wash. & Jeff.	Salem, Va.
1995	Wis.-La Crosse	Roger Harring	36-7	Rowan	Salem, Va.
1996	Mount Union	Larry Kehres	56-24	Rowan	Salem, Va.
1997	Mount Union	Larry Kehres	61-12	Lycoming	Salem, Va.
1998	Mount Union	Larry Kehres	44-24	Rowan	Salem, Va.
1999	Pacific Lutheran	Frosty Westering	42-13	Rowan	Salem, Va.

Regional Championship Results
(Before Division III Championship)

Year	Champion	Coach	Score	Runner-Up	Site

EAST (KNUTE ROCKNE BOWL)
1969	Randolph-Macon	Ted Keller	47-28	Bridgeport	Bridgeport, Conn.
1970	Montclair St.	Clary Anderson	7-6	Hampden-Sydney	Atlantic City, N.J.
1971	Bridgeport	Ed Farrell	17-12	Hampden-Sydney	Atlantic City, N.J.
1972	Bridgeport	Ed Farrell	27-22	Slippery Rock	Atlantic City, N.J.

WEST (AMOS ALONZO STAGG BOWL)
1969	Wittenberg	Dave Maurer	27-21	William Jewell	Springfield, Ohio
1970	Capital	Gene Slaughter	34-21	Luther	Columbus, Ohio
1971	Samford*		20-10	Ohio Wesleyan	Phenix City, Ala.
1972	Heidelberg	Pete Riesen	28-16	Fort Valley St.	Phenix City, Ala.

*Samford's participation in the Amos Alonzo Stagg Bowl vacated by the NCAA Committee in Infractions.

1999 Division III Championship Results

FIRST ROUND
Augustana (Ill.) 39, St. Norbert 32
Ohio Northern 56, Hanover 14
Wittenberg 42, Alma 19
Montclair St. 37, Buffalo St. 34
Rowan 29, Rensselaer 10
Ursinus 43, Bri'water (Mass.) 38
Pacific Lutheran 28, Willamette 24
Central (Iowa) 38, Wis.-La Crosse 17
St. John's (Minn.) 23, Wis.-Stevens Point 10
Western Md. 20, Catholic 16
Hardin-Simmons 28, Washington (Mo.) 21
Wash. & Jeff. 14, Lycoming 7

SECOND ROUND
Mount Union 42, Augustana (Ill.) 33
Ohio Northern 58, Wittenberg 24
Montclair St. 32, Western Conn. St. 24
Rowan 55, Ursinus 0
Pacific Lutheran 49, Wartburg 14
St. John's (Minn.) 10, Central (Iowa) 9
Trinity (Tex.) 20, Western Md. 16
Hardin-Simmons 51, Wash. & Jeff. 3

QUARTERFINALS
Mount Union 56, Ohio Northern 31
Rowan 42, Montclair St. 13
Pacific Lutheran 19, St. John's (Minn.) 9
Trinity (Tex.) 40, Hardin-Simmons 33

SEMIFINALS
Rowan 24, Mount Union 17 (ot)
Pacific Lutheran 49, Trinity (Tex.) 28

CHAMPIONSHIP
Pacific Lutheran 42, Rowan 13

Individual Records

GAME

NET YARDS RUSHING
389—Ricky Gales, Simpson (35) vs. St. John's (Minn.) (42), 11-18-89.

RUSHES ATTEMPTED
51—Ricky Gales, Simpson (35) vs. St. John's (Minn.) (42), 11-18-89.

TOUCHDOWNS BY RUSHING
5—Jeff Norman, St. John's (Minn.) (46) vs. Augustana

DIVISION III CHAMPIONSHIP—INDIVIDUAL RECORDS

(Ill.) (7), 11-20-76; Mike Coppa, Salisbury St. (44) vs. Ithaca (40), 12-6-86; Paul Parker, Ithaca (62) vs. Ferrum (28), 12-3-88; Kevin Hofacre, Dayton (35) vs. John Carroll (10), 11-18-89.

NET YARDS PASSING
584—Bill Borchert, Mount Union (52) vs. Hanover (18), 11-18-95.

PASSES ATTEMPTED
67—Vic Ameye, Widener (27) vs. Lycoming (31), 11-18-95; Terry Peebles, Hanover (18) vs. Mount Union (52), 11-18-95.

PASSES COMPLETED
39—Michael Burton, Trinity (Tex.) (28) vs. Pacific Lutheran (49), 12-11-99.

PASSES INTERCEPTED
7—Rick Steil, Dubuque (7) vs. Ithaca (27), 11-17-79.

TOUCHDOWN PASSES
8—Jim Ballard, Mount Union (56) vs. St. John's (Minn.) (8), 12-4-93.

COMPLETION PERCENTAGE (Min. 10 Attempts)
.900—Robb Disbennett, Salisbury St. (16) vs. Carnegie Mellon (14), 11-19-83 (18 of 20).

NET YARDS RUSHING AND PASSING
595—Bill Borchert, Mount Union (52) vs. Hanover (18), 11-18-95 (11 rushing, 584 passing).

RUSHING AND PASSING PLAYS
77—Terry Peebles, Hanover (18) vs. Mount Union (52), 11-18-95 (10 rushing, 67 passing).

PUNTING AVERAGE (Min. 3 Punts)
48.6—Phil Macken, Minn.-Morris (25) vs. Carnegie Mellon (31), 11-17-79 (7 for 340).

PUNTS
14—Tim Flynn, Gettysburg (14) vs. Lycoming (10), 11-23-85.

RECEPTIONS
17—Jeff Clay, Catholic (33) vs. Trinity (Tex.) (44), 11-22-97.

NET YARDS RECEIVING
265—Todd Zufra, Mount Union (52) vs. Hanover (18), 11-18-95 (16 catches).

TOUCHDOWN RECEPTIONS
4—Kirk Liesimer, Ill. Wesleyan (27) vs. Mount Union (49), 11-28-92; Rob Atwood, Mount Union (56) vs. St. John's (Minn.) (8), 12-4-93.

INTERCEPTIONS
3—John Bertino, Ithaca (27) vs. Dubuque (7), 11-17-79; Troy Westerman, Augustana (Ill.) (23) vs. Union (N.Y.) (6), 11-24-84; Mike Gray, Augustana (Ill.) (23) vs. Union (N.Y.) (6), 11-24-84; Rich Samuelson, Union (N.Y.) (17) vs. Ithaca (24) (ot), 11-22-86; Mike Gray, Augustana (Ill.) (31) vs. Salisbury St. (3), 12-13-86; Tom Knapp, Ithaca (39) vs. Central (Iowa) (24), 12-10-88; Bill Luette, Rowan (37) vs. Wm. Paterson (0), 11-27-93; David Lefere, Albion (19) vs. St. John's (Minn.) (16), 12-3-94; Arnell Palmer, Rowan (28) vs. Wash. & Jeff. (15), 12-2-95; Logan Ramirez, Trinity (Tex.) (40) vs. Hardin-Simmons (33), 12-4-99.

YARDS GAINED ON INTERCEPTION RETURNS
158—Beau LaBore, St. John's (Minn.) (23) vs. Wis.-Stevens Point (10), 11-20-99 (2 interceptions).

YARDS GAINED ON PUNT RETURNS
140—David Ziegler, John Carroll (30) vs. Hanover (20), 11-22-97.

YARDS GAINED ON KICKOFF RETURNS
197—Jeremy Unertl, Wis.-La Crosse (17) vs. Central (Iowa) (38), 11-20-99.

POINTS
36—Mike Coppa, Salisbury St. (44) vs. Ithaca (40), 12-6-86.

TOUCHDOWNS
6—Mike Coppa, Salisbury St. (44) vs. Ithaca (40), 12-6-86.

EXTRA POINTS
9—Tim Robinson, Baldwin-Wallace (71) vs. St. Lawrence (7), 11-18-78.

TOURNAMENT

NET YARDS RUSHING
882—Chris Babirad, Wash. & Jeff., 1992 (285 vs. Lycoming, 286 vs. Emory & Henry, 207 vs. Rowan, 104 vs. Wis.-La Crosse).

RUSHES ATTEMPTED
129—Chris Babirad, Wash. & Jeff., 1992 (37 vs. Lycoming, 31 vs. Emory & Henry, 36 vs. Rowan, 25 vs. Wis.-La Crosse).

NET YARDS PASSING
1,402—Bill Borchert, Mount Union, 1997 (317 vs. Allegheny, 278 vs. John Carroll, 396 vs. Simpson, 411 vs. Lycoming).

PASSES ATTEMPTED
152—Gary Smeck, Mount Union, 1998 (39 vs. Albion, 43 vs. Wittenberg, 36 vs. Trinity [Tex.], 34 vs. Rowan).

PASSES COMPLETED
99—Gary Smeck, Mount Union, 1998 (30 vs. Albion, 29 vs. Wittenberg, 21 vs. Trinity [Tex.], 19 vs. Rowan).

PASSES INTERCEPTED
9—Rollie Wiebers, Buena Vista, 1976 (4 vs. Carroll [Wis.], 5 vs. St. John's [Minn.]).

TOUCHDOWN PASSES
17—Jim Ballard, Mount Union, 1993 (5 vs. Allegheny, 1 vs. Albion, 8 vs. St. John's [Minn.], 3 vs. Rowan); Bill Borchert, Mount Union, 1996 (4 vs. Allegheny, 3 vs. Ill. Wesleyan, 3 vs. Wis.-La Crosse, 7 vs. Rowan).

COMPLETION PERCENTAGE (Min. 2 Games)
.676—Bill Borchert, Mount Union, 1994, 46 of 68 (23-34 vs. Allegheny, 23-34 vs. Albion).

RECEPTIONS
39—Nick Ismailoff, Ithaca, 1991 (12 vs. Rowan, 6 vs. Union [N.Y.], 11 vs. Susquehanna, 10 vs. Dayton).

NET YARDS RECEIVING
599—Nick Ismailoff, Ithaca, 1991 (179 vs. Rowan, 122 vs. Union [N.Y.], 105 vs. Susquehanna, 193 vs. Dayton).

TOUCHDOWN RECEPTIONS
6—Rob Atwood, Mount Union, 1993 (0 vs. Allegheny, 0 vs. Albion, 4 vs. St. John's [Minn.], 2 vs. Rowan); Chris Begley, Wash. & Jeff., 1995 (3 vs. Emory & Henry, 2 vs. Lycoming, 1 vs. Rowan); Adam Marino, Mount Union, 1998 (1 vs. Albion, 2 vs. Wittenberg, 3 vs. Trinity [Tex.], 0 vs. Rowan); Kirk Rogers, Hardin-Simmons, 1999 (2 vs. Washington [Mo.], 3 vs. Wash. & Jeff., 1 vs. Trinity [Tex.]).

POINTS
66—Anthony Hicks, Pacific Lutheran, 1999 (24 vs. Wartburg, 6 vs. St. John's [Minn.], 24 vs. Trinity [Tex.], 12 vs. Rowan).

TOUCHDOWNS
11—Anthony Hicks, Pacific Lutheran, 1999 (4 vs. Wartburg, 1 vs. St. John's [Minn.], 4 vs. Trinity [Tex.], 2 vs. Rowan).

LONGEST PLAYS

RUSH
93—Rick Papke, Augustana (Ill.) (17) vs. Central (Iowa) (23), 12-3-88, TD.

PASS (Including Run)
96—Mark Blom to Tom McDonald, Central (Iowa) (37) vs. Buena Vista (0), 11-22-86, TD.

FIELD GOAL
52—Rod Vesling, St. Lawrence (43) vs. Wagner (34), 11-20-82.

PUNT
79—Tom Hansen, Ithaca (3) vs. Wittenberg (6), 11-18-78.

PUNT RETURN
84—David Ziegler, John Carroll (30) vs. Hanover (20), 11-22-97, TD.

KICKOFF RETURN
100—Tom Deery, Widener (23) vs. Montclair St. (12), 11-30-81, TD.

INTERCEPTION RETURN
100—Jay Zunic, Ithaca (31) vs. Rowan (10), 11-23-91, TD.

FUMBLE RETURN
95—Clinton Tabb, Rowan (42) vs. Montclair St. (13), 12-4-99, TD.

Team Records

GAME

FIRST DOWNS
40—Mount Union (52) vs. Hanover (18), 11-18-95.

FIRST DOWNS BY RUSHING
30—Central (Iowa) (71) vs. Occidental (0), 12-7-85.

FIRST DOWNS BY PASSING
34—Mount Union (52) vs. Hanover (18), 11-18-95.

NET YARDS RUSHING
530—St. John's (Minn.) (46) vs. Augustana (Ill.) (7), 11-20-76.

RUSHES ATTEMPTED
83—Baldwin-Wallace (31) vs. Carnegie Mellon (6), 11-25-78; Augustana (Ill.) (33) vs. Mount Union (42), 11-27-99.

NET YARDS PASSING
614—Mount Union (52) vs. Hanover (18), 11-18-95.

PASSES ATTEMPTED
67—Hanover (18) vs. Mount Union (52), 11-18-95; Widener (27) vs. Lycoming (31), 11-18-95.

PASSES COMPLETED
39—Mount Union (52) vs. Hanover (18), 11-18-95; Trinity (Tex.) (28) vs. Pacific Lutheran (49), 12-11-99.

PASSES INTERCEPTED
9—Dubuque (7) vs. Ithaca (27), 11-17-79.

COMPLETION PERCENTAGE (Min. 10 Attempts)
.857—Salisbury St. (16) vs. Carnegie Mellon (14), 11-19-83 (18 of 21).

NET YARDS RUSHING AND PASSING
773—Mount Union (52) vs. Hanover (18), 11-18-95 (159 rushing, 614 passing).

RUSHING AND PASSING PLAYS
101—Union (N.Y.) (45) vs. Montclair St. (6), 11-25-89 (63 rushing, 38 passing).

PUNTING AVERAGE
48.6—Minn.-Morris (25) vs. Carnegie Mellon (31), 11-17-79 (7 for 340).

PUNTS
14—Gettysburg (14) vs. Lycoming (10), 11-23-85.

YARDS GAINED ON INTERCEPTION RETURNS
176—Augustana (Ill.) (14) vs. St. Lawrence (0), 11-27-82.

YARDS GAINED ON PUNT RETURNS
140—John Carroll (30) vs. Hanover (20), 11-22-97.

YARDS GAINED ON KICKOFF RETURNS
234—Ithaca (40) vs. Salisbury St. (44), 12-6-86.

YARDS PENALIZED
166—Ferrum (49) vs. Moravian (28), 11-26-88.

FUMBLES LOST
6—Albright (7) vs. St. Lawrence (26), 11-20-76; St. John's (Minn.) (7) vs. Dayton (19), 12-7-91.

POINTS
75—St. John's (Minn.) vs. Coe (2), 11-23-91.

TOURNAMENT

FIRST DOWNS
112—Mount Union, 1997 (24 vs. Allegheny, 32 vs. John Carroll, 23 vs. Simpson, 33 vs. Lycoming).

NET YARDS RUSHING
1,377—Ithaca, 1988 (251 vs. Wagner, 293 vs. Cortland St., 425 vs. Ferrum, 408 vs. Central [Iowa]).

NET YARDS PASSING
1,441—Mount Union, 1997 (317 vs. Allegheny, 289 vs. John Carroll, 396 vs. Simpson, 439 vs. Lycoming).

NET YARDS RUSHING AND PASSING
2,470—Mount Union, 1997 (528 vs. Allegheny, 601 vs. John Carroll, 644 vs. Simpson, 697 vs. Lycoming).

PASSES ATTEMPTED
152—Mount Union, 1998 (39 vs. Albion, 43 vs. Wittenberg, 36 vs. Trinity [Tex.], 34 vs. Rowan).

PASSES COMPLETED
99—Mount Union, 1998 (30 vs. Albion, 29 vs. Wittenberg, 21 vs. Trinity [Tex.], 19 vs. Rowan).

PASSES INTERCEPTED
11—Hofstra, 1990 (5 vs. Cortland St., 3 vs. Col. of New Jersey, 3 vs. Lycoming).

PUNTS
30—Central (Iowa), 1988 (12 vs. Concordia-M'head, 8 vs. Wis.-Whitewater, 5 vs. Augustana [Ill.], 5 vs. Ithaca).

YARDS PENALIZED
331—Wagner, 1987 (61 vs. Rochester, 80 vs. Fordham, 87 vs. Emory & Henry, 103 vs. Dayton).

FUMBLES LOST
10—Wittenberg, 1978 (4 vs. Ithaca, 2 vs. Minn.-Morris, 4 vs. Baldwin-Wallace); Rowan, 1995 (2 vs. Buffalo St., 4 vs. Union [N.Y.], 2 vs. Wash. & Jeff., 2 vs. Wis.-La Crosse).

POINTS
208—Mount Union, 1997 (34 vs. Allegheny, 59 vs. John Carroll, 54 vs. Simpson, 61 vs. Lycoming).

Year-by-Year Division III Championship Results

Year (Number of Teams)	Coach	Record	Result
1973 (4)			
Wittenberg	Dave Maurer	2-0	Champion
Juniata	Walt Nadzak	1-1	Second
Bridgeport	Ed Farrell	0-1	Semifinalist
San Diego	Andy Vinci	0-1	Semifinalist
1974 (4)			
Central (Iowa)	Ron Schipper	2-0	Champion
Ithaca	Jim Butterfield	1-1	Second
Evansville	Jim Byers	0-1	Semifinalist
Slippery Rock	Bob Di Spirito	0-1	Semifinalist
1975 (8)			
Wittenberg	Dave Maurer	3-0	Champion
Ithaca	Jim Butterfield	2-1	Second
Millsaps	Harper Davis	1-1	Semifinalist
Widener	Bill Manlove	1-1	Semifinalist
Albright	John Potsklan	0-1	Lost 1st Round
Colorado Col.	Jerry Carle	0-1	Lost 1st Round
Fort Valley St.	Leon Lomax	0-1	Lost 1st Round
Indianapolis	Bill Bless	0-1	Lost 1st Round
1976 (8)			
St. John's (Minn.)	John Gagliardi	3-0	Champion
Towson	Phil Albert	2-1	Second
Buena Vista	Jim Hershberger	1-1	Semifinalist
St. Lawrence	Ted Stratford	1-1	Semifinalist
Albright	John Potsklan	0-1	Lost 1st Round
Augustana (Ill.)	Ben Newcomb	0-1	Lost 1st Round
C. W. Post	Dom Anile	0-1	Lost 1st Round
Carroll (Wis.)	Steve Miller	0-1	Lost 1st Round
1977 (8)			
Widener	Bill Manlove	3-0	Champion
Wabash	Frank Navarro	2-1	Second
Albany (N.Y.)	Bob Ford	1-1	Semifinalist
Minn.-Morris	Al Molde	1-1	Semifinalist
Albion	Frank Joranko	0-1	Lost 1st Round
Central (Iowa)	Ron Schipper	0-1	Lost 1st Round
Hampden-Sydney	Stokeley Fulton	0-1	Lost 1st Round
St. John's (Minn.)	John Gagliardi	0-1	Lost 1st Round
1978 (8)			
Baldwin-Wallace	Lee Tressel	3-0	Champion
Wittenberg	Dave Maurer	2-1	Second
Carnegie Mellon	Chuck Klausing	1-1	Semifinalist
Minn.-Morris	Al Molde	1-1	Semifinalist
Dayton	Rick Carter	0-1	Lost 1st Round
Ithaca	Jim Butterfield	0-1	Lost 1st Round
St. Lawrence	Ted Stratford	0-1	Lost 1st Round
St. Olaf	Tom Porter	0-1	Lost 1st Round
1979 (8)			
Ithaca	Jim Butterfield	3-0	Champion
Wittenberg	Dave Maurer	2-1	Second
Carnegie Mellon	Chuck Klausing	1-1	Semifinalist
Widener	Bill Manlove	1-1	Semifinalist
Baldwin-Wallace	Lee Tressel	0-1	Lost 1st Round
Dubuque	Don Birmingham	0-1	Lost 1st Round
Millersville	Gene Carpenter	0-1	Lost 1st Round
Minn.-Morris	Al Molde	0-1	Lost 1st Round
1980 (8)			
Dayton	Rick Carter	3-0	Champion
Ithaca	Jim Butterfield	2-1	Second
Minn.-Morris	Dick Smith	1-1	Semifinalist
Widener	Bill Manlove	1-1	Semifinalist
Baldwin-Wallace	Lee Tressel	0-1	Lost 1st Round
Bethany (W.Va.)	Don Ault	0-1	Lost 1st Round
Dubuque	Don Birmingham	0-1	Lost 1st Round
Wagner	Bill Russo	0-1	Lost 1st Round
1981 (8)			
Widener	Bill Manlove	3-0	Champion
Dayton	Mike Kelly	2-1	Second
Lawrence	Ron Roberts	1-1	Semifinalist
Montclair St.	Fred Hill	1-1	Semifinalist
Alfred	Sam Sanders	0-1	Lost 1st Round
Augustana (Ill.)	Bob Reade	0-1	Lost 1st Round
Minn.-Morris	Dick Smith	0-1	Lost 1st Round
West Ga.	Bobby Pate	0-1	Lost 1st Round
1982 (8)			
West Ga.	Bobby Pate	3-0	Champion
Augustana (Ill.)	Bob Reade	2-1	Second
Bishop	James Jones	1-1	Semifinalist
St. Lawrence	Andy Talley	1-1	Semifinalist
Baldwin-Wallace	Bob Packard	0-1	Lost 1st Round
Wagner	Walt Hameline	0-1	Lost 1st Round
Wartburg	Don Canfield	0-1	Lost 1st Round
Widener	Bill Manlove	0-1	Lost 1st Round
1983 (8)			
Augustana (Ill.)	Bob Reade	3-0	Champion
Union (N.Y.)	Al Bagnoli	2-1	Second
Salisbury St.	Mike McGlinchey	1-1	Semifinalist
Wis.-La Crosse	Roger Harring	1-1	Semifinalist
Adrian	Ron Labadie	0-1	Lost 1st Round
Carnegie Mellon	Chuck Klausing	0-1	Lost 1st Round
Hofstra	Mickey Kwiatkowski	0-1	Lost 1st Round
Occidental	Dale Widolff	0-1	Lost 1st Round
1984 (8)			
Augustana (Ill.)	Bob Reade	3-0	Champion
Central (Iowa)	Ron Schipper	2-1	Second
Union (N.Y.)	Al Bagnoli	1-1	Semifinalist
Wash. & Jeff.	John Luckhardt	1-1	Semifinalist
Dayton	Mike Kelly	0-1	Lost 1st Round
Occidental	Dale Widolff	0-1	Lost 1st Round
Plymouth St.	Jay Cottone	0-1	Lost 1st Round
Randolph-Macon	Jim Blackburn	0-1	Lost 1st Round
1985 (16)			
Augustana (Ill.)	Bob Reade	4-0	Champion
Ithaca	Jim Butterfield	3-1	Second
Central (Iowa)	Ron Schipper	2-1	Semifinalist
Gettysburg	Barry Streeter	2-1	Semifinalist
Montclair St.	Rick Giancola	1-1	Quarterfinalist
Mount Union	Ken Wable	1-1	Quarterfinalist
Occidental	Dale Widolff	1-1	Quarterfinalist
Salisbury St.	Mike McGlinchey	1-1	Quarterfinalist
Albion	Pete Schmidt	0-1	Lost 1st Round
Carnegie Mellon	Chuck Klausing	0-1	Lost 1st Round
Coe	Bob Thurness	0-1	Lost 1st Round
Denison	Keith Piper	0-1	Lost 1st Round
Lycoming	Frank Girardi	0-1	Lost 1st Round
St. John's (Minn.)	John Gagliardi	0-1	Lost 1st Round
Union (N.Y.)	Al Bagnoli	0-1	Lost 1st Round
Western Conn. St.	Paul Pasqualoni	0-1	Lost 1st Round
1986 (16)			
Augustana (Ill.)	Bob Reade	4-0	Champion
Salisbury St.	Mike McGlinchey	3-1	Second
Concordia-M'head	Jim Christopherson	2-1	Semifinalist
Ithaca	Jim Butterfield	2-1	Semifinalist
Central (Iowa)	Ron Schipper	1-1	Quarterfinalist
Montclair St.	Rick Giancola	1-1	Quarterfinalist
Mount Union	Larry Kehres	1-1	Quarterfinalist
Susquehanna	Rocky Rees	1-1	Quarterfinalist
Buena Vista	Jim Hershberger	0-1	Lost 1st Round

DIVISION III CHAMPIONSHIP—YEAR-BY-YEAR RESULTS

Year (Number of Teams)	Coach	Record	Result
Dayton	Mike Kelly	0-1	Lost 1st Round
Emory & Henry	Lou Wacker	0-1	Lost 1st Round
Hofstra	Mickey Kwiatkowski	0-1	Lost 1st Round
Hope	Ray Smith	0-1	Lost 1st Round
Union (N.Y.)	Al Bagnoli	0-1	Lost 1st Round
Wash. & Jeff.	John Luckhardt	0-1	Lost 1st Round
Wis.-Stevens Point	D. J. LeRoy	0-1	Lost 1st Round

1987 (16)

Wagner	Walt Hameline	4-0	Champion
Dayton	Mike Kelly	3-1	Second
Central (Iowa)	Ron Schipper	2-1	Semifinalist
Emory & Henry	Lou Wacker	2-1	Semifinalist
Augustana (Ill.)	Bob Reade	1-1	Quarterfinalist
Fordham	Larry Glueck	1-1	Quarterfinalist
St. John's (Minn.)	John Gagliardi	1-1	Quarterfinalist
Wash. & Jeff.	John Luckhardt	1-1	Quarterfinalist
Allegheny	Peter Vaas	0-1	Lost 1st Round
Capital	Roger Welsh	0-1	Lost 1st Round
Ferrum	Hank Norton	0-1	Lost 1st Round
Gust. Adolphus	Steve Raarup	0-1	Lost 1st Round
Hiram	Don Charlton	0-1	Lost 1st Round
Hofstra	Mickey Kwiatkowski	0-1	Lost 1st Round
Menlo	Ray Solari	0-1	Lost 1st Round
Rochester	Ray Tellier	0-1	Lost 1st Round

1988 (16)

Ithaca	Jim Butterfield	4-0	Champion
Central (Iowa)	Ron Schipper	3-1	Second
Augustana (Ill.)	Bob Reade	2-1	Semifinalist
Ferrum	Hank Norton	2-1	Semifinalist
Cortland St.	Dennis Kayser	1-1	Quarterfinalist
Moravian	Scot Dapp	1-1	Quarterfinalist
Wis.-Whitewater	Bob Berezowitz	1-1	Quarterfinalist
Wittenberg	Ron Murphy	1-1	Quarterfinalist
Adrian	Ron Labadie	0-1	Lost Regionals
Concordia-M'head	Jim Christopherson	0-1	Lost Regionals
Dayton	Mike Kelly	0-1	Lost Regionals
Hofstra	Mickey Kwiatkowski	0-1	Lost Regionals
Rhodes	Mike Clary	0-1	Lost Regionals
Simpson	Jim Williams	0-1	Lost Regionals
Wagner	Walt Hameline	0-1	Lost Regionals
Widener	Bill Manlove	0-1	Lost Regionals

1989 (16)

Dayton	Mike Kelly	4-0	Champion
Union (N.Y.)	Al Bagnoli	3-1	Second
Ferrum	Hank Norton	2-1	Semifinalist
St. John's (Minn.)	John Gagliardi	2-1	Semifinalist
Central (Iowa)	Ron Schipper	1-1	Quarterfinalist
Lycoming	Frank Girardi	1-1	Quarterfinalist
Millikin	Carl Poelker	1-1	Quarterfinalist
Montclair St.	Rick Giancola	1-1	Quarterfinalist
Augustana (Ill.)	Bob Reade	0-1	Lost Regionals
Cortland St.	Dennis Kayser	0-1	Lost Regionals
Dickinson	Ed Sweeney	0-1	Lost Regionals
Hofstra	Mickey Kwiatkowski	0-1	Lost Regionals
John Carroll	Tony DeCarlo	0-1	Lost Regionals
St. Norbert	Don LaViolette	0-1	Lost Regionals
Simpson	Jim Williams	0-1	Lost Regionals
Wash. & Jeff.	John Luckhardt	0-1	Lost Regionals

1990 (16)

Allegheny	Ken O'Keefe	4-0	Champion
Lycoming	Frank Girardi	3-1	Second
Central (Iowa)	Ron Schipper	2-1	Semifinalist
Hofstra	Joe Gardi	2-1	Semifinalist
Dayton	Mike Kelly	1-1	Quarterfinalist
Col. of New Jersey	Eric Hamilton	1-1	Quarterfinalist
St. Thomas (Minn.)	Vic Wallace	1-1	Quarterfinalist
Wash. & Jeff.	John Luckhardt	1-1	Quarterfinalist
Augustana (Ill.)	Bob Reade	0-1	Lost Regionals
Carnegie Mellon	Rich Lackner	0-1	Lost Regionals
Cortland St.	Dave Murray	0-1	Lost Regionals
Ferrum	Hank Norton	0-1	Lost Regionals
Ithaca	Jim Butterfield	0-1	Lost Regionals
Mount Union	Larry Kehres	0-1	Lost Regionals
Redlands	Mike Maynard	0-1	Lost Regionals
Wis.-Whitewater	Bob Berezowitz	0-1	Lost Regionals

1991 (16)

Ithaca	Jim Butterfield	4-0	Champion
Dayton	Mike Kelly	3-1	Second
St. John's (Minn.)	John Gagliardi	2-1	Semifinalist
Susquehanna	Steve Briggs	2-1	Semifinalist
Allegheny	Ken O'Keefe	1-1	Quarterfinalist
Lycoming	Frank Girardi	1-1	Quarterfinalist
Union (N.Y.)	Al Bagnoli	1-1	Quarterfinalist
Wis.-La Crosse	Roger Harring	1-1	Quarterfinalist
Albion	Pete Schmidt	0-1	Lost Regionals
Baldwin-Wallace	Bob Packard	0-1	Lost Regionals
Coe	D. J. LeRoy	0-1	Lost Regionals
Dickinson	Ed Sweeney	0-1	Lost Regionals
Mass.-Lowell	Dennis Scannell	0-1	Lost Regionals
Rowan	John Bunting	0-1	Lost Regionals
Simpson	Jim Williams	0-1	Lost Regionals
Wash. & Jeff.	John Luckhardt	0-1	Lost Regionals

1992 (16)

Wis.-La Crosse	Roger Harring	4-0	Champion
Wash. & Jeff.	John Luckhardt	3-1	Second
Mount Union	Larry Kehres	2-1	Semifinalist
Rowan	John Bunting	2-1	Semifinalist
Buffalo St.	Jerry Boyes	1-1	Quarterfinalist
Central (Iowa)	Ron Schipper	1-1	Quarterfinalist
Emory & Henry	Lou Wacker	1-1	Quarterfinalist
Ill. Wesleyan	Norm Eash	1-1	Quarterfinalist
Aurora	Jim Scott	0-1	Lost Regionals
Carleton	Bob Sullivan	0-1	Lost Regionals
Dayton	Mike Kelly	0-1	Lost Regionals
Ithaca	Jim Butterfield	0-1	Lost Regionals
Lycoming	Frank Girardi	0-1	Lost Regionals
Redlands	Mike Maynard	0-1	Lost Regionals
Thomas More	Vic Clark	0-1	Lost Regionals
Worcester Tech	Jack Siedlecki	0-1	Lost Regionals

1993 (16)

Mount Union	Larry Kehres	4-0	Champion
Rowan	K. C. Keeler	3-1	Second
St. John's (Minn.)	John Gagliardi	2-1	Semifinalist
Wash. & Jeff.	John Luckhardt	2-1	Semifinalist
Albion	Pete Schmidt	1-1	Quarterfinalist
Frostburg St.	Mike McGlinchey	1-1	Quarterfinalist
Wm. Paterson	Gerry Gallagher	1-1	Quarterfinalist
Wis.-La Crosse	Roger Harring	1-1	Quarterfinalist
Allegheny	Ken O'Keefe	0-1	Lost Regionals
Anderson (Ind.)	Mike Manley	0-1	Lost Regionals
Buffalo St.	Jerry Boyes	0-1	Lost Regionals
Coe	D. J. LeRoy	0-1	Lost Regionals
Moravian	Scot Dapp	0-1	Lost Regionals
Union (N.Y.)	John Audino	0-1	Lost Regionals
Wartburg	Bob Nielson	0-1	Lost Regionals
Wilkes	Joe DeMelfi	0-1	Lost Regionals

1994 (16)

Albion	Pete Schmidt	4-0	Champion
Wash. & Jeff.	John Luckhardt	3-1	Second
Ithaca	Michael Welch	2-1	Semifinalist
St. John's (Minn.)	John Gagliardi	2-1	Semifinalist
Mount Union	Larry Kehres	1-1	Quarterfinalist
Plymouth St.	Don Brown	1-1	Quarterfinalist
Wartburg	Bob Nielson	1-1	Quarterfinalist
Widener	Bill Cubit	1-1	Quarterfinalist
Allegheny	Ken O'Keefe	0-1	Lost Regionals
Augustana (Ill.)	Bob Reade	0-1	Lost Regionals
Buffalo St.	Jerry Boyes	0-1	Lost Regionals
Central (Iowa)	Ron Schipper	0-1	Lost Regionals
Dickinson	Darwin Breaux	0-1	Lost Regionals
La Verne	Rex Huigens	0-1	Lost Regionals
Merchant Marine	Charlie Pravata	0-1	Lost Regionals
Trinity (Tex.)	Steven Mohr	0-1	Lost Regionals

1995 (16)

Wis.-La Crosse	Roger Harring	4-0	Champion
Rowan	K. C. Keeler	3-1	Second
Mount Union	Larry Kehres	2-1	Semifinalist
Wash. & Jeff.	John Luckhardt	2-1	Semifinalist
Lycoming	Frank Girardi	1-1	Quarterfinalist
Union (N.Y.)	John Audino	1-1	Quarterfinalist
Wheaton (Ill.)	J. R. Bishop	1-1	Quarterfinalist
Wis.-River Falls	John O'Grady	1-1	Quarterfinalist
Buffalo St.	Jerry Boyes	0-1	Lost Regionals
Central (Iowa)	Ron Schipper	0-1	Lost Regionals
Concordia-M'head	Jim Christopherson	0-1	Lost Regionals
Emory & Henry	Lou Wacker	0-1	Lost Regionals
Hanover	C. Wayne Perry	0-1	Lost Regionals
Plymouth St.	Don Brown	0-1	Lost Regionals
Widener	Bill Cubit	0-1	Lost Regionals
Wittenberg	Doug Neibuhr	0-1	Lost Regionals

1996 (16)

Mount Union	Larry Kehres	4-0	Champion

CHAMPIONSHIP RESULTS

431

Year (Number of Teams)	Coach	Record	Result
Rowan	K. C. Keeler	3-1	Second
Wis.-La Crosse	Roger Harring	2-1	Semifinalist
Lycoming	Frank Girardi	2-1	Semifinalist
Ill. Wesleyan	Norm Eash	1-1	Quarterfinalist
St. John's (Minn.)	John Gagliardi	1-1	Quarterfinalist
Albright	Ron Maier	1-1	Quarterfinalist
Col. of New Jersey	Eric Hamilton	1-1	Quarterfinalist
Allegheny	Ken O'Keefe	0-1	Lost Regionals
Albion	Pete Schmidt	0-1	Lost Regionals
Wis.-River Falls	John O'Grady	0-1	Lost Regionals
Simpson	Jim Williams	0-1	Lost Regionals
Ursinus	Steve Gilbert	0-1	Lost Regionals
Wash. & Jeff.	John Luckhardt	0-1	Lost Regionals
Buffalo St.	Jerry Boyes	0-1	Lost Regionals
Coast Guard	Bill Schmitz	0-1	Lost Regionals

1997 (16)

Mount Union	Larry Kehres	4-0	Champion
Lycoming	Frank Girardi	3-1	Second
Simpson	Jim Williams	2-1	Semifinalist
Rowan	K. C. Keeler	2-1	Semifinalist
John Carroll	Tony DeCarlo	1-1	Quarterfinalist
Augsburg	Jack Osberg	1-1	Quarterfinalist
Trinity (Tex.)	Steven Mohr	1-1	Quarterfinalist
Col. of New Jersey	Eric Hamilton	1-1	Quarterfinalist
Allegheny	Ken O'Keefe	0-1	Lost 1st Round
Hanover	C. Wayne Perry	0-1	Lost 1st Round
Wis.-Whitewater	Bob Berezowitz	0-1	Lost 1st Round
Concordia-M'head	Jim Christopherson	0-1	Lost 1st Round
Western Md.	Tim Keating	0-1	Lost 1st Round
Catholic	Tom Clark	0-1	Lost 1st Round
Coast Guard	Chuck Mills	0-1	Lost 1st Round
Cortland St.	Dan MacNeil	0-1	Lost 1st Round

1998 (16)

Mount Union	Larry Kehres	4-0	Champion
Rowan	K. C. Keeler	3-1	Second
Trinity (Tex.)	Steven Mohr	2-1	Semifinalist
Wis.-Eau Claire	Bob Nielson	2-1	Semifinalist
Wittenberg	Joe Fincham	1-1	Quarterfinalist
Lycoming	Frank Girardi	1-1	Quarterfinalist
St. John's (Minn.)	John Gagliardi	1-1	Quarterfinalist
Buffalo St.	Jerry Boyes	1-1	Quarterfinalist
Albion	Craig Rundle	0-1	Lost 1st Round
Millikin	Doug Neibuhr	0-1	Lost 1st Round
Catholic	Tom Clark	0-1	Lost 1st Round
Western Md.	Tim Keating	0-1	Lost 1st Round
Central (Iowa)	Rich Kacmarynski	0-1	Lost 1st Round
Pacific Lutheran	Frosty Westering	0-1	Lost 1st Round
Springfield	Mike DeLong	0-1	Lost 1st Round
Col. of New Jersey	Eric Hamilton	0-1	Lost 1st Round

1999 (28)

Pacific Lutheran	Frosty Westering	5-0	Champion
Rowan	K. C. Keeler	3-1	Second
Mount Union	Larry Kehres	2-1	Semifinalist
Trinity (Tex.)	Steven Mohr	2-1	Semifinalist
Hardin-Simmons	Jimmie Keeling	2-1	Quarterfinalist
Montclair St.	Rick Giancola	2-1	Quarterfinalist
Ohio Northern	Tom Kaczkowski	2-1	Quarterfinalist
St. John's (Minn.)	John Gagliardi	2-1	Quarterfinalist
Augustana (Ill.)	Tom Schmulbach	1-1	Lost 2nd Round
Central (Iowa)	Rich Kacmarynski	1-1	Lost 2nd Round
Ursinus	Paul Guenther	1-1	Lost 2nd Round
Wartburg	Rick Willis	0-1	Lost 2nd Round
Wash. & Jeff.	John Banaszak	1-1	Lost 2nd Round
Western Conn. St.	John Cervino	0-1	Lost 2nd Round
Western Md.	Tim Keating	1-1	Lost 2nd Round
Wittenberg	Joe Fincham	1-1	Lost 2nd Round
Alma	Jim Cole	0-1	Lost 1st Round
Bri'water (Mass.)	Peter Mazzaferro	0-1	Lost 1st Round
Buffalo St.	Jerry Boyes	0-1	Lost 1st Round
Catholic	Tom Clark	0-1	Lost 1st Round
Hanover	Wayne Perry	0-1	Lost 1st Round
Lycoming	Frank Girardi	0-1	Lost 1st Round
Rensselaer	Joe King	0-1	Lost 1st Round
St. Norbert	Jim Purtill	0-1	Lost 1st Round
Washington (Mo.)	Larry Kindbom	0-1	Lost 1st Round
Willamette	Mark Speckman	0-1	Lost 1st Round
Wis.-La Crosse	Roger Harring	0-1	Lost 1st Round
Wis.-Stevens Point	John Miech	0-1	Lost 1st Round

Division III Championship Record of Each College by Coach

(103 Colleges; 1973-99)

	Yrs	Won	Lost	CH	2D
ADRIAN					
Ron Labadie (Adrian '71) 83, 88	2	0	2	0	0
ALBANY (N.Y.)					
Bob Ford (Springfield '59) 77	1	1	1	0	0
ALBION					
Frank Joranko (Albion '52) 77	1	0	1	0	0
Pete Schmidt (Alma '70) 85, 91, 93, 94-CH, 96	5	5	4	1	0
Craig Rundle (Albion '74) 98	1	0	1	0	0
TOTAL	7	5	6	1	0
ALBRIGHT					
John Potsklan (Penn St. '49) 75, 76	2	0	2	0	0
Ron Maier (Bentley '86) 96	1	1	1	0	0
TOTAL	3	1	3	0	0
ALFRED					
Sam Sanders (Buffalo '60) 81	1	0	1	0	0
ALLEGHENY					
Peter Vaas (Holy Cross '74) 87	1	0	1	0	0
Ken O'Keefe (John Carroll '75) 90-CH, 91, 93, 94, 96, 97	6	5	5	1	0
TOTAL	7	5	6	1	0
ALMA					
Jim Cole (Alma '74) 99	1	0	1	0	0
ANDERSON (IND.)					
Mike Manley (Anderson [Ind.] '73) 93	1	0	1	0	0
AUGSBURG					
Jack Osberg (Augsburg '62) 97	1	1	1	0	0
AUGUSTANA (ILL.)					
Ben Newcomb 76	1	0	1	0	0
Bob Reade (Cornell College '54) 81, 82-2D, 83-CH, 84-CH, 85-CH, 86-CH, 87, 88, 89, 90, 94	11	19	7	4	1
Tom Schmulbach (Western Ill. '69) 99	1	1	1	0	0
TOTAL	13	20	9	4	1
AURORA					
Jim Scott (Luther '61) 92	1	0	1	0	0
BALDWIN-WALLACE					
Lee Tressel (Baldwin-Wallace '48) 78-CH, 79, 80	3	3	2	1	0
Bob Packard (Baldwin-Wallace '65) 82, 91	2	0	2	0	0
TOTAL	5	3	4	1	0
BETHANY (W.VA.)					
Don Ault (West Liberty St. '52) 80	1	0	1	0	0
BISHOP					
James Jones (Bishop '49) 82	1	1	1	0	0
BRIDGEPORT					
Ed Farrell (Rutgers '56) 73	1	0	1	0	0
BRI'WATER (MASS.)					
Peter Mazzaferro (Centre '54) 99	1	0	1	0	0
BUENA VISTA					
Jim Hershberger (Northern Iowa '57) 76, 86	2	1	2	0	0
BUFFALO ST.					
Jerry Boyes (Ithaca '76) 92, 93, 94, 95, 96, 98, 99	7	2	7	0	0
C. W. POST					
Dom Anile (C. W. Post '59) 76	1	0	1	0	0
CAPITAL					
Roger Welsh (Muskingum '64) 87	1	0	1	0	0
CARLETON					
Bob Sullivan (St. John's [Minn.] '59) 92	1	0	1	0	0
CARNEGIE MELLON					
Chuck Klausing (Slippery Rock '48) 78, 79, 83, 85	4	2	4	0	0
Rich Lackner (Carnegie Mellon '79) 90	1	0	1	0	0
TOTAL	5	2	5	0	0
CARROLL (WIS.)					
Steve Miller (Cornell College '65) 76	1	0	1	0	0
CATHOLIC					
Tom Clark (Maryland '86) 97, 98, 99	3	0	3	0	0

DIVISION III CHAMPIONSHIP—SCHOOL RECORDS

	Yrs	Won	Lost	CH	2D
CENTRAL (IOWA)					
Ron Schipper (Hope '52) 74-CH, 77, 84-2D, 85, 86, 87, 88-2D, 89, 90, 92, 94, 95	12	16	11	1	2
Rich Kacmarynski (Central [Iowa] '92) 98, 99	2	1	2	0	0
TOTAL	14	17	13	1	2
COAST GUARD					
Bill Schmitz (Coast Guard '76) 96	1	0	1	0	0
Chuck Mills 97	1	0	1	0	0
TOTAL	2	0	2	0	0
COE					
Bob Thurness (Coe '62) 85	1	0	1	0	0
D. J. LeRoy (Wis.-Eau Claire '79) 91, 93	2	0	2	0	0
TOTAL	3	0	3	0	0
COLORADO COL.					
Jerry Carle (Northwestern '48) 75	1	0	1	0	0
CONCORDIA-M'HEAD					
Jim Christopherson (Concordia-M'head '60) 86, 88, 95, 97	4	2	4	0	0
CORTLAND ST.					
Dennis Kayser (Ithaca '74) 88, 89	2	1	2	0	0
Dave Murray (Springfield '81) 90	1	0	1	0	0
Dan MacNeil (Cortland St. '79) 97	1	0	1	0	0
TOTAL	4	1	4	0	0
DAYTON					
Rick Carter (Earlham '65) 78, 80-CH	2	3	1	1	0
Mike Kelly (Manchester '70) 81-2D, 84, 86, 87-2D, 88, 89-CH, 90, 91-2D, 92	9	13	8	1	3
TOTAL	11	16	9	2	3
DENISON					
Keith Piper (Baldwin-Wallace '48) 85	1	0	1	0	0
DICKINSON					
Ed Sweeney (C. W. Post '71) 89, 91	2	0	2	0	0
Darwin Breaux (West Chester '77) 94	1	0	1	0	0
TOTAL	3	0	3	0	0
DUBUQUE					
Don Birmingham (Westmar '62) 79, 80	2	0	2	0	0
EMORY & HENRY					
Lou Wacker (Richmond '56) 86, 87, 92, 95	4	3	4	0	0
EVANSVILLE					
Jim Byers (Michigan '59) 74	1	0	1	0	0
FERRUM					
Hank Norton (Lynchburg '51) 87, 88, 89, 90	4	4	4	0	0
FORDHAM					
Larry Glueck (Villanova '63) 87	1	1	1	0	0
FORT VALLEY ST.					
Leon Lomax (Fort Valley St. '43) 75	1	0	1	0	0
FROSTBURG ST.					
Mike McGlinchey (Delaware '67) 93	1	1	1	0	0
GETTYSBURG					
Barry Streeter (Lebanon Valley '71) 85	1	2	1	0	0
GUST. ADOLPHUS					
Steve Raarup (Gust. Adolphus '53) 87	1	0	1	0	0
HAMPDEN-SYDNEY					
Stokeley Fulton (Hampden-Sydney '55) 77	1	0	1	0	0
HANOVER					
C. Wayne Perry (DePauw '72) 95, 97, 99	3	0	3	0	0
HARDIN-SIMMONS					
Jimmie Keeling (Howard Payne '58) 99	1	0	1	0	0
HIRAM					
Don Charlton (Lock Haven '65) 87	1	0	1	0	0
HOFSTRA					
Mickey Kwiatkowski (Delaware '70) 83, 86, 87, 88, 89	5	0	5	0	0
Joe Gardi (Maryland '60) 90	1	2	1	0	0
TOTAL	6	2	6	0	0
HOPE					
Ray Smith (UCLA '61) 86	1	0	1	0	0
ILL. WESLEYAN					
Norm Eash (Ill. Wesleyan '75) 92, 96	2	2	2	0	0
INDIANAPOLIS					
Bill Bless (Indianapolis '63) 75	1	0	1	0	0
ITHACA					
Jim Butterfield (Maine '53) 74-2D, 75-2D, 78, 79-CH, 80-2D, 85-2D, 86, 88-CH, 90, 91-CH, 92	11	21	8	3	4
Michael Welch (Ithaca '73) 94	1	2	1	0	0
TOTAL	12	23	9	3	4

	Yrs	Won	Lost	CH	2D
JOHN CARROLL					
Tony DeCarlo (Kent '62) 89, 97	2	1	2	0	0
JUNIATA					
Walt Nadzak (Denison '57) 73-2D	1	1	1	0	1
LA VERNE					
Rex Huigens (La Verne '70) 94	1	0	1	0	0
LAWRENCE					
Ron Roberts (Wisconsin '54) 81	1	1	1	0	0
LYCOMING					
Frank Girardi (West Chester '61) 85, 89, 90-2D, 91, 92, 95, 96, 97-2D, 98, 99	10	12	10	0	1
MASS.-LOWELL					
Dennis Scannell (Villanova '74) 91	1	0	1	0	0
MENLO					
Ray Solari (California '51) 87	1	0	1	0	0
MERCHANT MARINE					
Charlie Pravata (Adelphi '72) 94	1	0	1	0	0
MILLERSVILLE					
Gene Carpenter (Huron '63) 79	1	0	1	0	0
MILLIKIN					
Carl Poelker (Millikin '68) 89	1	1	1	0	0
Doug Neibuhr (Millikin '75) 98	1	0	1	0	0
TOTAL	2	1	2	0	0
MILLSAPS					
Harper Davis (Mississippi St. '49) 75	1	1	1	0	0
MINN.-MORRIS					
Al Molde (Gust. Adolphus '66) 77, 78, 79	3	2	3	0	0
Dick Smith (Coe '68) 80, 81	2	1	2	0	0
TOTAL	5	3	5	0	0
MONTCLAIR ST.					
Fred Hill (Upsala '57) 81	1	1	1	0	0
Rick Giancola (Rowan '68) 85, 86, 89, 99	4	5	4	0	0
TOTAL	5	6	5	0	0
MORAVIAN					
Scot Dapp (West Chester '73) 88, 93	2	1	2	0	0
MOUNT UNION					
Ken Wable (Muskingum '52) 85	1	1	1	0	0
Larry Kehres (Mount Union '71) 86, 90, 92, 93-CH, 94, 95, 96-CH, 97-CH, 98-CH, 99	10	24	6	3	0
TOTAL	11	25	7	3	0
COL. OF NEW JERSEY					
Eric Hamilton (Col. of New Jersey '75) 90, 96, 97, 98	4	3	4	0	0
OCCIDENTAL					
Dale Widolff (Indiana Central '75) 83, 84, 85	3	1	3	0	0
OHIO NORTHERN					
Tom Kaczkowski (Illinois '78) 99	1	2	1	0	0
PACIFIC LUTHERAN					
Frosty Westering (Neb.-Omaha '52) 98, 99-CH	2	5	1	1	0
PLYMOUTH ST.					
Jay Cottone (Norwich '71) 84	1	0	1	0	0
Don Brown (Norwich '77) 94, 95	2	1	2	0	0
TOTAL	3	1	3	0	0
RANDOLPH-MACON					
Jim Blackburn (Virginia '71) 84	1	0	1	0	0
REDLANDS					
Mike Maynard (Ill. Wesleyan '80) 90, 92	2	0	2	0	0
RENSSELAER					
Joe King (Siena '70) 99	1	0	1	0	0
RHODES					
Mike Clary (Rhodes '77) 88	1	0	1	0	0
ROCHESTER					
Ray Tellier (Connecticut '73) 87	1	0	1	0	0
ROWAN					
John Bunting (North Carolina '72) 91, 92	2	2	2	0	0
K. C. Keeler (Delaware '81) 93-2D, 95-2D, 96-2D, 97, 98-2D, 99-2D	6	17	6	0	5
TOTAL	8	19	8	0	5
ST. JOHN'S (MINN.)					
John Gagliardi (Colorado Col. '49) 76-CH, 77, 85, 87, 89, 91, 93, 94, 96, 98, 99	11	16	10	1	0
ST. LAWRENCE					
Ted Stratford (St. Lawrence '57) 76, 78	2	1	2	0	0
Andy Talley (Southern Conn. St. '67) 82	1	1	1	0	0
TOTAL	3	2	3	0	0

DIVISION III CHAMPIONSHIP—SCHOOL RECORDS

	Yrs	Won	Lost	CH	2D
ST. NORBERT					
Don LaViolette (St. Norbert '54) 89	1	0	1	0	0
Jim Purtill (Miami [Ohio] '78) 99	1	0	1	0	0
TOTAL	2	0	2	0	0
ST. OLAF					
Tom Porter (St. Olaf '51) 78	1	0	1	0	0
ST. THOMAS (MINN.)					
Vic Wallace (Cornell College '65) 90	1	1	1	0	0
SALISBURY ST.					
Mike McGlinchey (Delaware '67) 83, 85, 86-2D	3	5	3	0	1
SAN DIEGO					
Andy Vinci (Cal St. Los Angeles '63) 73	1	0	1	0	0
SIMPSON					
Jim Williams (Northern Iowa '60) 88, 89, 91, 96, 97	5	2	5	0	0
SLIPPERY ROCK					
Bob Di Spirito (Rhode Island '53) 74	1	0	1	0	0
SPRINGFIELD					
Mike DeLong (Springfield '74) 98	1	0	1	0	0
SUSQUEHANNA					
Rocky Rees (West Chester '71) 86	1	1	1	0	0
Steve Briggs (Springfield '84) 91	1	2	1	0	0
TOTAL	2	3	2	0	0
THOMAS MORE					
Vic Clark (Indiana St. '71) 92	1	0	1	0	0
TOWSON					
Phil Albert (Arizona '66) 76-2D	1	2	1	0	1
TRINITY (TEX.)					
Steven Mohr (Denison '76) 94, 97, 98, 99	4	5	4	0	0
UNION (N.Y.)					
Al Bagnoli (Central Conn. St. '74) 83-2D, 84, 85, 86, 89-2D, 91	6	7	6	0	2
John Audino (Notre Dame '75) 93, 95	2	1	2	0	0
TOTAL	8	8	8	0	2
URSINUS					
Steve Gilbert (West Chester '79) 96	1	0	1	0	0
Paul Guenther (Ursinus '94) 99	1	1	1	0	0
TOTAL	2	1	2	0	0
WABASH					
Frank Navarro (Maryland '53) 77-2D	1	2	1	0	1
WAGNER					
Bill Russo 80	1	0	1	0	0
Walt Hameline (Brockport St. '75) 82, 87-CH, 88	3	4	2	1	0
TOTAL	4	4	3	1	0
WARTBURG					
Don Canfield 82	1	0	1	0	0
Bob Nielson (Wartburg '81) 93, 94	2	1	2	0	0
Rick Willis (Cornell College '88) 99	1	0	1	0	0
TOTAL	4	1	4	0	0

	Yrs	Won	Lost	CH	2D
WASHINGTON (MO.)					
Larry Kindbom (Kalamazoo '74) 99	1	0	1	0	0
WASH. & JEFF.					
John Luckhardt (Purdue '67) 84, 86, 87, 89, 90, 91 92-2D, 93, 94-2D, 95, 96	11	13	11	0	2
John Banaszak (Eastern Mich. '75) 99	1	1	1	0	0
TOTAL	12	14	12	0	2
WEST GA.					
Bobby Pate (Georgia '63) 81, 82-CH	2	3	1	1	0
WESTERN CONN. ST.					
Paul Pasqualoni (Penn St. '72) 85	1	0	1	0	0
John Cervino (West Va. Wesleyan '82) 99	1	0	1	0	0
TOTAL	2	0	2	0	0
WESTERN MD.					
Tim Keating (Bethany [W.Va.] '75) 97, 98, 99	3	1	3	0	0
WHEATON (ILL.)					
J. R. Bishop (Franklin '61) 95	1	1	1	0	0
WIDENER					
Bill Manlove (Temple '58) 75, 77-CH, 79, 80, 81-CH, 82, 88	7	9	5	2	0
Bill Cubit (Delaware '75) 94, 95	2	1	2	0	0
TOTAL	9	10	7	2	0
WILKES					
Joe DeMelfi (Delta St. '66) 93	1	0	1	0	0
WILLAMETTE					
Mark Speckman (Azusa Pacific '77) 99	1	0	1	0	0
WM. PATERSON					
Gerry Gallagher (Wm. Paterson '74) 93	1	1	1	0	0
WIS-EAU CLAIRE					
Bob Nielson (Wartburg '82) 98	1	2	1	0	0
WIS.-LA CROSSE					
Roger Harring (Wis.-La Crosse '58) 83, 91, 92-CH, 93, 95-CH, 96, 99	7	13	5	2	0
WIS.-RIVER FALLS					
John O'Grady (Wis.-River Falls '79) 95, 96	2	1	2	0	0
WIS.-STEVENS POINT					
D. J. LeRoy (Wis.-Eau Claire '79) 86	1	0	1	0	0
John Miech (Wis.-Stevens Point '75) 99	1	0	1	0	0
TOTAL	2	0	2	0	0
WIS.-WHITEWATER					
Bob Berezowitz (Wis.-Whitewater '67) 88, 90, 97	3	1	3	0	0
WITTENBERG					
Dave Maurer (Denison '54) 73-CH, 75-CH, 78-2D, 79-2D	4	9	2	2	2
Ron Murphy 88	1	1	1	0	0
Doug Neibuhr (Millikin '75) 95	1	0	1	0	0
Joe Fincham (Ohio '88) 98, 99	2	2	2	0	0
TOTAL	8	12	6	2	2
WORCESTER TECH					
Jack Siedlecki (Union [N.Y.] '73) 92	1	0	1	0	0

All-Time Results

1973 Semifinals: Juniata 35, Bridgeport 14; Wittenberg 21, San Diego 14. **Championship:** Wittenberg 41, Juniata 0.

1974 Semifinals: Central (Iowa) 17, Evansville 16; Ithaca 27, Slippery Rock 14. **Championship:** Central (Iowa) 10, Ithaca 8.

1975 First Round: Widener 14, Albright 6; Ithaca 41, Fort Valley St. 12; Wittenberg 17, Indianapolis 13; Millsaps 28, Colorado Col. 21. **Semifinals:** Ithaca 23, Widener 14; Wittenberg 55, Millsaps 22. **Championship:** Wittenberg 28, Ithaca 0.

1976 First Round: St. John's (Minn.) 46, Augustana (Ill.) 7; Buena Vista 20, Carroll (Wis.) 14 (ot); St. Lawrence 26, Albright 7; Towson 14, C. W. Post 10. **Semifinals:** St. John's (Minn.) 61, Buena Vista 0; Towson 38, St. Lawrence 36. **Championship:** St. John's (Minn.) 31, Towson 28.

1977 First Round: Minn.-Morris 13, Albion 10; Wabash 20, St. John's (Minn.) 9; Widener 19, Central (Iowa) 0; Albany (N.Y.) 51, Hampden-Sydney 45. **Semifinals:** Wabash 37, Minn.-Morris 21; Widener 33, Albany (N.Y.) 15. **Championship:** Widener 39, Wabash 36.

1978 First Round: Minn.-Morris 23, St. Olaf 10; Wittenberg 6, Ithaca 3; Carnegie Mellon 24, Dayton 21; Baldwin-Wallace 71, St. Lawrence 7. **Semifinals:** Wittenberg 35, Minn.-Morris 14; Baldwin-Wallace 31, Carnegie Mellon 6. **Championship:** Baldwin-Wallace 24, Wittenberg 10.

1979 First Round: Wittenberg 21, Millersville 14; Widener 29, Baldwin-Wallace 8; Carnegie Mellon 31, Minn.-Morris 25; Ithaca 27, Dubuque 7. **Semifinals:** Wittenberg 17, Widener 14; Ithaca 15, Carnegie Mellon 6. **Championship:** Ithaca 14, Wittenberg 10.

1980 First Round: Ithaca 41, Wagner 13; Minn.-Morris 41, Dubuque 35; Dayton 34, Baldwin-Wallace 0; Widener 43, Bethany (W.Va.) 12. **Semifinals:** Ithaca 36, Minn.-Morris 0; Dayton 28, Widener 24. **Championship:** Dayton 63, Ithaca 0.

1981 First Round: Dayton 19, Augustana (Ill.) 7; Lawrence 21, Minn.-Morris 14 (ot); Montclair St. 13, Alfred 12; Widener 10, West Ga. 3. **Semifinals:** Dayton 38, Lawrence 21; Widener 23, Montclair St. 12. **Championship:** Widener 17, Dayton 14.

1982 First Round: Augustana (Ill.) 28, Baldwin-Wallace 22; St. Lawrence 43, Wagner 34; Bishop 32, Wartburg 7; West Ga. 31, Widener 24 (3 ot). **Semifinals:** Augustana (Ill.) 14, St. Lawrence 0; West Ga. 27, Bishop 6. **Championship:** West Ga. 14, Augustana (Ill.) 0.

1983 First Round: Union (N.Y.) 51, Hofstra 19; Salisbury St. 16, Carnegie Mellon 14; Augustana (Ill.) 22, Adrian 21; Wis.-La Crosse 43, Occidental 42. **Semifinals:** Union (N.Y.) 23, Salisbury St. 21; Augustana (Ill.) 21, Wis.-La Crosse 15. **Championship:** Augustana (Ill.) 21, Union (N.Y.) 17.

1984 First Round: Union (N.Y.) 26, Plymouth St. 14; Augustana (Ill.) 14, Dayton 13; Wash. & Jeff. 22, Randolph-Macon 21; Central (Iowa) 23, Occidental 22. **Semifinals:** Augustana (Ill.) 23, Union (N.Y.) 6; Central (Iowa) 20, Wash. & Jeff. 0. **Championship:** Augustana (Ill.) 21, Central (Iowa) 12.

1985 First Round: Ithaca 13, Union (N.Y.) 12; Montclair St. 28, Western Conn. St. 0; Salisbury St. 35, Carnegie Mellon 22; Gettysburg 14, Lycoming 10; Augustana (Ill.) 26, Albion 10; Mount Union 35, Denison 3; Central (Iowa) 27, Coe 7; Occidental 28, St. John's (Minn.) 10. **Quarterfinals:** Ithaca 50, Montclair St. 28; Gettysburg 22, Salisbury St. 6; Augustana (Ill.) 21, Mount Union 14; Central (Iowa) 71, Occidental 0. **Semifinals:** Ithaca 34, Gettysburg 0; Augustana (Ill.) 14, Central (Iowa) 7. **Championship:** Augustana (Ill.) 20, Ithaca 17.

1986 First Round: Ithaca 24, Union (N.Y.) 17 (ot); Montclair St. 24, Hofstra 21; Susquehanna 28, Wash. & Jeff. 20; Salisbury St. 34, Emory & Henry 20; Mount Union 42, Dayton 36; Augustana (Ill.) 34, Hope 10;

DIVISION III CHAMPIONSHIP—ALL-TIME RESULTS

Central (Iowa) 37, Buena Vista 0; Concordia-M'head 24, Wis.-Stevens Point 15. **Quarterfinals:** Ithaca 29, Montclair St. 15; Salisbury St. 31, Susquehanna 17; Augustana (Ill.) 16, Mount Union 7; Concordia-M'head 17, Central (Iowa) 14. **Semifinals:** Salisbury St. 44, Ithaca 40; Augustana (Ill.) 41, Concordia-M'head 7. **Championship:** Augustana (Ill.) 31, Salisbury St. 3.

1987 First Round: Wagner 38, Rochester 14; Fordham 41, Hofstra 6; Wash. & Jeff. 23, Allegheny 17 (ot); Emory & Henry 49, Ferrum 7; Dayton 52, Capital 28; Augustana (Ill.) 53, Hiram 0; St. John's (Minn.) 7, Gust. Adolphus 3; Central (Iowa) 17, Menlo 0. **Quarterfinals:** Wagner 21, Fordham 0; Emory & Henry 23, Wash. & Jeff. 16; Dayton 38, Augustana (Ill.) 36; Central (Iowa) 13, St. John's (Minn.) 3. **Semifinals:** Wagner 20, Emory & Henry 15; Dayton 34, Central (Iowa) 0. **Championship:** Wagner 19, Dayton 3.

1988 Regionals: Cortland St. 32, Hofstra 27; Ithaca 34, Wagner 31 (ot); Ferrum 34, Rhodes 10; Moravian 17, Widener 7; Wittenberg 35, Dayton 28 (ot); Augustana (Ill.) 25, Adrian 7; Central (Iowa) 7, Concordia-M'head 0; Wis.-Whitewater 29, Simpson 27. **Quarterfinals:** Ithaca 24, Cortland St. 17; Ferrum 49, Moravian 28; Augustana (Ill.) 28, Wittenberg 14; Central (Iowa) 16, Wis.-Whitewater 13. **Semifinals:** Ithaca 62, Ferrum 28; Central (Iowa) 23, Augustana (Ill.) 17 (2 ot). **Championship:** Ithaca 39, Central (Iowa) 24.

1989 Regionals: Union (N.Y.) 42, Cortland St. 14; Montclair St. 23, Hofstra 6; Lycoming 21, Dickinson 0; Ferrum 41, Wash. & Jeff. 7; Dayton 35, John Carroll 10; Millikin 21, Augustana (Ill.) 12; Central (Iowa) 55, St. Norbert 7; St. John's (Minn.) 42, Simpson 35. **Quarterfinals:** Union (N.Y.) 45, Montclair St. 6; Ferrum 49, Lycoming 24; Dayton 28, Millikin 16; St. John's (Minn.) 27, Central (Iowa) 24. **Semifinals:** Union (N.Y.) 37, Ferrum 21; Dayton 28, St. John's (Minn.) 0. **Championship:** Dayton 17, Union (N.Y.) 7.

1990 Regionals: Hofstra 35, Cortland St. 9; Col. of New Jersey 24, Ithaca 14; Wash. & Jeff. 10, Ferrum 7; Lycoming 17, Carnegie Mellon 7; Dayton 24, Augustana (Ill.) 14; Allegheny 26, Mount Union 15; St. Thomas (Minn.) 24, Wis.-Whitewater 23; Central (Iowa) 24, Redlands 14. **Quarterfinals:** Hofstra 38, Col. of New Jersey 3; Lycoming 24, Wash. & Jeff. 0; Allegheny 31, Dayton 23; Central (Iowa) 33, St. Thomas (Minn.) 32. **Semifinals:** Lycoming 20, Hofstra 10; Allegheny 24, Central (Iowa) 7. **Championship:** Allegheny 21, Lycoming 14 (ot).

1991 Regionals: St. John's (Minn.) 75, Coe 2; Wis.-La Crosse 28, Simpson 13; Allegheny 24, Albion 21 (ot); Dayton 27, Baldwin-Wallace 10; Ithaca 31, Rowan 10; Union (N.Y.) 55, Mass.-Lowell 16; Lycoming 18, Wash. & Jeff. 16; Susquehanna 21, Dickinson 20. **Quarterfinals:** St. John's (Minn.) 29, Wis.-La Crosse 10; Dayton 28, Allegheny 25 (ot); Ithaca 35, Union (N.Y.) 23; Susquehanna 31, Lycoming 24. **Semifinals:** Dayton 19, St. John's (Minn.) 7; Ithaca 49, Susquehanna 13. **Championship:** Ithaca 34, Dayton 20.

1992 Regionals: Mount Union 27, Dayton 10; Ill. Wesleyan 21, Aurora 12; Central (Iowa) 20, Carleton 8; Wis.-La Crosse 47, Redlands 26; Emory & Henry 17, Thomas More 0; Wash. & Jeff. 33, Lycoming 0; Rowan 41, Worcester Tech 14; Buffalo St. 28, Ithaca 26. **Quarterfinals:** Mount Union 49, Ill. Wesleyan 27; Wis.-La Crosse 34, Central (Iowa) 9; Wash. & Jeff. 51, Emory & Henry 15; Rowan 28, Buffalo St. 19. **Semifinals:** Wis.-La Crosse 29, Mount Union 24; Wash. & Jeff. 18, Rowan 13. **Championship:** Wis.-La Crosse 16, Wash. & Jeff. 12.

1993 Regionals: Mount Union 40, Allegheny 7; Albion 41, Anderson (Ind.) 21; Wis.-La Crosse 55, Wartburg 26; St. John's (Minn.) 32, Coe 14; Wash. & Jeff. 27, Moravian 7; Frostburg St. 26, Wilkes 25; Rowan 29, Buffalo St. 6; Wm. Paterson 17, Union (N.Y.) 7. **Quarterfinals:** Mount Union 30, Albion 16; St. John's (Minn.) 47, Wis.-La Crosse 25; Wash. & Jeff. 28, Frostburg St. 7; Rowan 37, Wm. Paterson 0. **Semifinals:** Mount Union 56, St. John's (Minn.) 8; Rowan 23, Wash. & Jeff. 16. **Championship:** Mount Union 34, Rowan 24.

1994 Regionals: Mount Union 28, Allegheny 19; Albion 28, Augustana (Ill.) 21; Wartburg 22, Central (Iowa) 21; St. John's (Minn.) 51, La Verne 12; Widener 14, Dickinson 0; Wash. & Jeff. 28, Trinity (Tex.) 0; Plymouth St. 19, Merchant Marine 18; Ithaca 10, Buffalo St. 7 (2 ot). **Quarterfinals:** Albion 34, Mount Union 33; St. John's (Minn.) 42, Wartburg 14; Wash. & Jeff. 37, Widener 21; Ithaca 22, Plymouth St. 7. **Semifinals:** Albion 19, St. John's (Minn.) 16; Wash. & Jeff. 23, Ithaca 19. **Championship:** Albion 38, Wash. & Jeff. 15.

1995 Regionals: Mount Union 52, Hanover 18; Wheaton (Ill.) 63, Wittenberg 41; Wis.-La Crosse 45, Concordia-M'head 7; Wis.-River Falls 10, Central (Iowa) 7; Wash. & Jeff. 35, Emory & Henry 16; Lycoming 31, Widener 27; Rowan 46, Buffalo St. 7; Union (N.Y.) 24, Plymouth St. 7. **Quarterfinals:** Mount Union 40, Wheaton (Ill.) 14; Wis.-La Crosse 28, Wis.-River Falls 14; Wash. & Jeff. 48, Lycoming 0; Rowan 38, Union (N.Y.) 7. **Semifinals:** Wis.-La Crosse 20, Mount Union 17; Rowan 28, Wash. & Jeff. 15. **Championship:** Wis.-La Crosse 36, Rowan 7.

1996 Regionals: Mount Union 31, Allegheny 26; Ill. Wesleyan 23, Albion 20; Wis.-La Crosse 44, Wis.-River Falls 0; St John's (Minn.) 21, Simpson 18; Lycoming 31, Ursinus 24; Albright 31, Wash. & Jeff. 17; Rowan 21, Buffalo St. 20; Col. of New Jersey 17, Coast Guard 16. **Quarterfinals:** Mount Union 49, Ill. Wesleyan 14; Wis.-La Crosse 37, St. John's (Minn.) 30; Lycoming 31, Albright 13; Rowan 7, Col. of New Jersey 3. **Semifinals:** Mount Union 39, Wis.-La Crosse 21; Rowan 33, Lycoming 14. **Championship:** Mount Union 56, Rowan 24.

1997 First Round: Mount Union 34, Allegheny 30; John Carroll 30, Hanover 20; Simpson 34, Wis.-Whitewater 31; Augsburg 34, Concordia-M'head 22; Lycoming 27, Western Md. 13; Trinity (Tex.) 44, Catholic 33; Rowan 43, Coast Guard 0; Col. of New Jersey 34, Cortland St. 30. **Quarterfinals:** Mount Union 59, John Carroll 7; Simpson 61, Augsburg 21; Lycoming 46, Trinity (Tex.) 26; Rowan 13, Col. of New Jersey 7. **Semifinals:** Mount Union 54, Simpson 7; Lycoming 28, Rowan 20. **Championship:** Mount Union 61, Lycoming 12.

1998 First Round: Mount Union 21, Albion 19; Wittenberg 13, Millikin 10; Lycoming 49, Catholic 14; Trinity (Tex.) 30, Western Md. 20; Wis.-Eau Claire 28, Central (Iowa) 21; St. John's (Minn.) 33, Pacific Lutheran 20; Buffalo St. 38, Springfield 35; Rowan 26, Col. of New Jersey 2. **Quarterfinals:** Mount Union 21, Wittenberg 19; Trinity (Tex.) 37, Lycoming 21; Wis.-Eau Claire 10, St. John's (Minn.) 7; Rowan 19, Buffalo St. 17. **Semifinals:** Mount Union 34, Trinity (Tex.) 29; Rowan 22, Wis.-Eau Claire 19. **Championship:** Mount Union 44, Rowan 24.

1999 First Round: Augustana (Ill.) 39, St. Norbert 32; Ohio Northern 56, Hanover 14; Wittenberg 42, Alma 19; Montclair St. 37, Buffalo St. 34; Rowan 29, Rensselaer 10; Ursinus 43, Bri'water (Mass.) 38; Pacific Lutheran 28, Willamette 7; Central (Iowa) 38, Wis.-La Crosse 17; St. John's (Minn.) 23, Wis.-Stevens Point 10; Western Md. 20, Catholic 16; Hardin-Simmons 28, Washington (Mo.) 21; Wash. & Jeff. 14, Lycoming 7. **Second Round:** Mount Union 42, Augustana (Ill.) 33; Ohio Northern 58, Wittenberg 24; Montclair St. 32, Western Conn. St. 24; Rowan 55, Ursinus 0; Pacific Lutheran 49, Wartburg 14; St. John's (Minn.) 10, Central (Iowa) 9; Trinity (Tex.) 20, Western Md. 16; Hardin-Simmons 51, Wash. & Jeff. 3. **Quarterfinals:** Mount Union 56, Ohio Northern 31; Rowan 42, Montclair St. 13; Pacific Lutheran 19, St. John's (Minn.) 9; Trinity (Tex.) 40, Hardin-Simmons 33. **Semifinals:** Rowan 24, Mount Union 17 (ot); Pacific Lutheran 49, Trinity (Tex.) 28. **Championship:** Pacific Lutheran 42, Rowan 13.

Attendance Records

All-Time College Football Attendance 438
All-Time NCAA Attendance 438
Annual Conference Attendance Leaders 439
Largest Regular-Season Crowds 443
1999 Attendance 444
Annual Team Attendance Leaders 447

All-Time College Football Attendance

(Includes all divisions and non-NCAA teams)

Year	No. Teams	G	Total Attendance	P/G Avg.	Yearly Change Total	Percent
1948	685	—	19,134,159	—	—	—
1949	682	—	19,651,995	—	Up 517,836	+2.71
1950	674	—	18,961,688	—	Dn 690,307	-3.51
1951	635	—	17,480,533	—	Dn 1,481,155	-7.81
1952	625	—	17,288,062	—	Dn 192,471	-1.10
1953	618	—	16,681,731	—	Dn 606,331	-3.51
1954	614	—	17,048,603	—	Up 366,872	+2.20
1955	621	—	17,266,556	—	Up 217,953	+1.28
1956	618	—	18,031,805	—	Up 765,249	+4.43
1957	618	2,586	18,290,724	7,073	Up 258,919	+1.44
1958	618	2,673	19,280,709	7,213	Up 989,985	+5.41
1959	623	2,695	19,615,344	7,278	Up 334,635	+1.74
1960	620	2,711	20,403,409	7,526	Up 788,065	+4.02
1961	616	2,697	20,677,604	7,667	Up 274,195	+1.34
1962	610	2,679	21,227,162	7,924	Up 549,558	+2.66
1963	616	2,686	22,237,094	8,279	Up 1,009,932	+4.76
1964	622	2,745	23,354,477	8,508	Up 1,117,383	+5.02
1965	616	2,749	24,682,572	8,979	Up 1,328,095	+5.69
1966	616	2,768	25,275,899	9,131	Up 593,327	+2.40
1967	610	2,764	26,430,639	9,562	Up 1,154,740	+4.57
1968	612	2,786	27,025,846	9,701	Up 595,207	+2.25
1969	615	2,820	27,626,160	9,797	Up 600,314	+2.22
1970	617	2,895	29,465,604	10,178	Up 1,839,444	+6.66
1971	618	2,955	30,455,442	10,306	Up 989,838	+3.36
1972	620	2,997	30,828,802	10,287	Up 373,360	+1.23
1973	630	3,062	31,282,540	10,216	Up 453,738	+1.47
1974	634	3,101	31,234,855	10,073	Dn 47,685	-0.15
1975	634	3,089	31,687,847	10,258	Up 452,992	+1.45
1976	637	3,108	32,012,008	10,299	Up 324,161	+1.02
1977	638	3,145	32,905,178	10,463	Up 893,170	+2.79

Beginning in 1978, attendance includes NCAA teams only.

All-Time NCAA Attendance

Annual Total NCAA Attendance

(Includes Only NCAA Teams, All Divisions)

Year	No. Teams	G	Total Attendance	P/G Avg.	Yearly Change Total	Percent
1978	484	2,422	32,369,730	13,365	—	—
1979	478	2,381	32,874,755	13,807	Up 505,025	+1.56
1980	485	2,451	33,707,772	13,753	Up 833,017	+2.53
1981	497	2,505	34,230,471	13,665	Up 522,699	+1.55
1982	510	2,569	35,176,195	13,693	Up 945,724	+2.76
1983	505	2,557	34,817,264	13,616	Dn 358,931	-1.02
1984	501	2,542	35,211,076	*13,852	Up 393,812	+1.13
1985	509	2,599	34,951,548	13,448	Dn 259,528	-0.74
1986	510	2,605	35,030,902	13,448	Up 79,354	+2.27
1987	507	2,589	35,007,541	13,522	Dn 23,361	-0.07
1988	524	2,644	34,323,842	12,982	Dn 683,699	-1.95
1989	524	2,630	35,116,188	13,352	Up 792,346	-2.31
1990	533	2,704	35,329,946	13,066	Up 213,758	+0.61
1991	548	2,776	35,528,220	12,798	Up 198,274	+0.56
1992	552	2,824	35,225,431	12,474	Dn 302,789	-0.65
1993	560	2,888	34,870,634	12,074	Dn 354,797	-1.01
1994	568	2,907	36,459,896	12,542	Up 1,591,352	+4.56
1995	565	2,923	35,637,784	12,192	Dn 822,112	-2.25
1996	566	2,925	36,083,053	12,336	Up 445,269	+1.25
1997	581	2,998	36,857,849	12,294	Up 774,796	+2.15
1998	595	3,044	37,491,078	12,316	Up 633,229	+1.72
1999	*601	*3,137	*39,482,657	12,586	*Up 1,991,477	*+5.31

*Record.

Annual Division I-A Attendance

Year	Teams	G	Attendance	Avg.
1976	137	796	23,917,522	30,047
1977	144	799	24,613,285	30,805
1978	139	772	25,017,915	32,407
1979	139	774	25,862,801	33,414
1980	139	776	26,499,022	34,148
1981	137	768	26,588,688	34,621
1982	97	567	24,771,855	*43,689
1983	105	602	25,381,761	42,162
1984	105	606	25,783,807	42,548
1985	105	605	25,434,412	42,040
1986	105	611	25,692,095	42,049
1987	104	607	25,471,744	41,963
1988	104	605	25,079,490	41,454
1989	106	603	25,307,915	41,970
1990	106	615	25,513,098	41,485
1991	106	610	25,646,067	42,043
1992	107	617	25,402,046	41,170
1993	106	613	25,305,438	41,281
1994	107	614	25,590,190	41,678
1995	108	623	25,836,469	41,471
1996	111	644	26,620,942	41,337
1997	112	655	27,565,959	42,085
1998	112	651	27,674,217	42,510
1999	114	666	*29,032,973	43,593

*Record.

Annual Division I-AA Attendance

Year	Teams	G	Attendance	Avg.
1978	38	201	2,032,766	10,113
1979	39	211	2,073,890	9,829
1980	46	251	2,617,932	10,430
1981	50	270	2,950,156	10,927
1982	92	483	5,655,519	*11,709
1983	84	450	4,879,709	10,844
1984	87	465	5,061,480	10,885
1985	87	471	5,143,077	10,919
1986	86	456	5,044,992	11,064
1987	87	460	5,129,250	11,151
1988	88	465	4,801,637	10,326
1989	89	471	5,278,520	11,020
1990	87	473	5,328,477	11,265
1991	89	490	5,386,425	10,993
1992	88	485	5,057,955	10,429
1993	115	623	5,356,873	8,599
1994	117	643	*6,193,989	9,633
1995	119	647	5,660,329	8,749
1996	116	629	5,255,033	8,355
1997	118	642	5,212,048	8,118
1998	119	631	5,555,862	8,805
1999	122	661	5,949,345	9,001

*Record.

Annual Division II Attendance

Year	Teams	G	Attendance	Avg.
1978	103	518	*2,871,683	*5,544
1979	105	526	2,775,569	5,277
1980	111	546	2,584,765	4,734
1981	121	589	2,726,537	4,629
1982	126	618	2,745,964	4,443
1983	122	611	2,705,892	4,429
1984	114	568	2,413,947	4,250
1985	114	569	2,475,325	4,350
1986	111	551	2,404,852	4,365
1987	107	541	2,424,041	4,481
1988	117	580	2,570,964	4,493
1989	116	579	2,572,496	4,428
1990	120	580	2,472,811	4,263
1991	128	622	2,490,929	4,005
1992	129	643	2,733,094	4,251
1993	142	718	2,572,053	3,582
1994	142	704	2,791,074	3,965
1995	138	705	2,459,792	3,489
1996	139	701	2,514,241	3,587
1997	142	710	2,349,442	3,309
1998	149	747	2,443,660	3,271
1999	147	749	2,504,118	3,343

*Record.

Annual Division III Attendance

Year	Teams	G	Attendance	Avg.
1978	204	931	*2,447,366	*2,629
1979	195	870	2,162,495	2,486
1980	189	878	2,006,053	2,285

ALL-TIME NCAA ATTENDANCE—ANNUAL DIVISION III ATTENDANCE

Year	Teams	G	Attendance	Avg.
1981	189	878	1,965,090	2,238
1982	195	901	2,002,857	2,223
1983	194	894	1,849,902	2,069
1984	195	903	1,951,842	2,162
1985	203	954	1,898,734	1,990
1986	208	987	1,888,963	1,914
1987	209	981	1,982,506	2,021
1988	215	994	1,871,751	1,883
1989	213	977	1,957,257	1,948
1990	220	1,036	2,015,560	1,946
1991	225	1,054	2,004,799	1,902
1992	228	1,079	2,032,336	1,884
1993	197	934	1,636,270	1,752
1994	202	946	1,884,643	1,992
1995	200	948	1,681,194	1,773
1996	200	951	1,692,837	1,780
1997	209	991	1,730,400	1,746
1998	215	1,015	1,817,339	1,790
1999	218	1,061	1,996,221	1,881

*Record.

Annual Conference Attendance Leaders

(Based on per-game average; minimum 20 games)

Division I-A

Year	Conference	Teams	Attendance	P/G Avg.
1978	Big Ten	10	3,668,926	61,149
1979	Big Ten	10	3,865,170	63,363
1980	Big Ten	10	3,781,232	64,089
1981	Big Ten	10	3,818,728	63,645
1982	Big Ten	10	3,935,722	66,707
1983	Big Ten	10	3,710,931	67,471
1984	Big Ten	10	3,943,802	67,997
1985	Big Ten	10	4,015,693	66,928
1986	Big Ten	10	4,006,845	65,686
1987	Big Ten	10	3,990,524	65,418
1988	Southeastern	10	3,912,241	63,101
1989	Southeastern	10	4,123,005	65,445
1990	Southeastern	10	4,215,400	63,870
1991	Southeastern	10	4,063,190	66,610
1992	Southeastern	12	4,844,014	63,737
1993	Big Ten	11	4,320,397	63,535
1994	Big Ten	11	4,452,839	66,460
1995	Big Ten	11	4,592,499	67,537
1996	Big Ten	11	4,321,276	67,520
1997	Big Ten	11	4,744,211	67,774
1998	Southeastern	12	5,059,534	69,309
1999	Southeastern	12	*5,500,664	*70,521

*Record.

Division I-AA

Year	Conference	Teams	Attendance	P/G Avg.
1978	Southwestern Athletic	5	483,159	17,895
1979	Southwestern Athletic	6	513,768	16,055
1980	Southwestern Athletic	7	611,234	16,085
1981	Southwestern Athletic	7	662,221	18,921
1982	Southwestern Athletic	7	634,505	18,129
1983	Southwestern Athletic	8	709,160	16,117
1984	Southwestern Athletic	8	702,186	17,555
1985	Southwestern Athletic	8	790,296	17,961
1986	Southwestern Athletic	8	621,584	16,357
1987	Southwestern Athletic	8	697,534	16,608
1988	Southwestern Athletic	8	541,127	14,240
1989	Southwestern Athletic	8	796,844	18,110
1990	Southwestern Athletic	7	828,169	20,704
1991	Southwestern Athletic	8	856,491	18,223
1992	Southwestern Athletic	8	873,772	20,804
1993	Southwestern Athletic	8	772,714	18,398
1994	Southwestern Athletic	8	*958,508	*23,378
1995	Southwestern Athletic	8	628,702	16,545
1996	Southwestern Athletic	8	600,798	15,405
1997	Southwestern Athletic	8	567,929	15,776
1998	Southwestern Athletic	9	516,042	13,580
1999	Southwestern Athletic	10	781,226	15,318

*Record.

Division II

Year	Conference	Teams	Attendance	P/G Avg.
1978	Mid-Continent	6	237,458	9,133
1979	Mid-Continent	6	313,790	9,509
1980	Southern Intercollegiate	12	356,744	7,280
1981	Lone Star	8	340,876	7,575
1982	Lone Star	8	348,780	8,507
1983	Lone Star	8	296,350	7,228
1984	Central Intercollegiate	12	418,075	6,743
1985	Central Intercollegiate	12	378,160	6,099
1986	Central Intercollegiate	12	380,172	6,670
1987	Lone Star	6	208,709	6,325
1988	Central Intercollegiate	12	343,070	6,473
1989	Lone Star	8	249,570	5,942
1990	Southern Intercollegiate	9	264,741	6,967
1991	Central Intercollegiate	11	349,962	6,603
1992	Southern Intercollegiate	9	344,504	7,489
1993	Southern Intercollegiate	9	342,446	8,352
1994	Southern Intercollegiate	9	*456,289	*10,140
1995	Southern Intercollegiate	10	321,751	6,846
1996	Southern Intercollegiate	10	310,491	6,750
1997	Southern Intercollegiate	10	314,975	6,562
1998	Southern Intercollegiate	11	399,277	7,005
1999	Southern Intercollegiate	10	305,640	6,946

*Record.

Division III

Year	Conference	Teams	Attendance	P/G Avg.
1979	Great Lakes	6	90,531	3,482
1980	Great Lakes	7	113,307	3,333
1981	Ohio Athletic	14	*196,640	2,979
1982	New Jersey State	7	98,502	2,985
1983	Heartland	7	121,825	3,384
1984	Heartland	7	107,500	2,986
1985	Ohio Athletic	9	125,074	2,719
1986	Heartland	7	91,793	2,550
1987	Heartland	6	84,815	3,029
1988	Heartland	5	82,966	2,963
1989	Old Dominion	5	70,676	2,945
1990	Old Dominion	6	86,238	2,974
1991	Old Dominion	6	101,774	3,283
1992	Old Dominion	6	100,132	3,338
1993	Old Dominion	6	96,526	3,218
1994	Old Dominion	6	111,334	*3,976
1995	Old Dominion	6	105,819	3,527
1996	Old Dominion	6	90,277	3,113
1997	Old Dominion	6	92,810	3,094
1998	Old Dominion	6	112,329	3,744
1999	Old Dominion	7	103,435	2,955

*Record. Note: 1978 figures not available.

Annual Division I-A Conference Attendance

(Since 1978)

ATLANTIC COAST CONFERENCE

Season	Teams	Games	Attendance	P/G	Change in Pct.	Avg.
1978	7	39	1,475,410	37,831	Up	3.88
1979	7	40	1,620,776	40,519	Up	7.11
1980	7	41	1,590,495	38,793	Dn	4.26
1981	7	40	1,589,152	39,729	Up	2.41
1982	7	41	1,706,451	41,621	Up	4.76
1983	8	49	2,087,800	42,608	Up	3.71
1984	8	46	1,998,274	43,441	Up	1.96
1985	8	48	2,029,574	42,283	Dn	2.67
1986	8	45	1,848,949	41,088	Dn	2.83
1987	8	47	1,970,198	41,919	Up	2.02
1988	8	47	1,911,949	40,680	Dn	2.96
1989	8	49	2,010,317	41,027	Up	0.85
1990	8	47	1,988,781	42,314	Up	3.14
1991	8	51	2,257,413	44,263	Up	4.61
1992	9	53	2,332,674	44,013	Dn	4.62
1993	9	54	2,379,045	44,056	Up	0.10
1994	9	51	2,248,700	44,092	Up	0.08

Season	Teams	Games	Attendance	P/G	Pct.	Change in Avg.
1995	9	51	2,329,868	45,684	Up	3.61
1996	9	50	2,203,849	44,077	Dn	3.52
1997	9	52	2,333,784	44,880	Up	1.82
1998	9	51	2,330,879	45,704	Up	1.84
1999	9	51	2,298,711	45,073	Dn	1.38

BIG EAST CONFERENCE

Season	Teams	Games	Attendance	P/G	Pct.	Change in Avg.
1991	8	47	1,788,611	38,056	Dn	7.00
1992	8	48	1,847,269	38,485	Up	1.13
1993	8	47	1,787,843	38,039	Dn	1.16
1994	8	46	1,902,096	41,350	Up	8.70
1995	8	44	1,679,043	38,160	Dn	7.71
1996	8	47	1,825,870	38,848	Up	1.80
1997	8	46	1,657,056	36,023	Dn	7.27
1998	8	48	1,914,957	39,895	Up	10.75
1999	8	46	1,837,478	39,945	Up	0.13

BIG TEN CONFERENCE

Season	Teams	Games	Attendance	P/G	Pct.	Change in Avg.
1978	10	60	3,668,926	61,149	Up	2.87
1979	10	61	3,865,170	63,363	Up	3.62
1980	10	59	3,781,232	64,089	Up	1.15
1981	10	60	3,818,728	63,645	Dn	0.69
1982	10	59	3,935,722	66,707	Up	4.81
1983	10	55	3,710,931	67,471	Up	1.15
1984	10	58	3,943,802	67,997	Up	0.78
1985	10	60	4,015,693	66,928	Dn	1.57
1986	10	61	4,006,845	65,686	Dn	1.86
1987	10	61	3,990,524	65,418	Dn	0.41
1988	10	59	3,714,231	62,953	Dn	3.77
1989	10	59	3,492,647	59,197	Dn	5.97
1990	10	60	3,533,504	58,892	Dn	0.52
1991	10	61	3,674,654	60,240	Up	2.29
1992	10	60	3,600,410	60,007	Dn	0.39
1993	11	68	4,320,397	63,535	Up	0.60
1994	11	67	4,452,839	66,460	Up	4.60
1995	11	68	4,592,499	67,537	Up	1.62
1996	11	64	4,321,276	67,520	Dn	0.03
1997	11	70	4,744,211	67,774	Up	0.04
1998	11	65	4,354,383	66,991	Dn	1.16
1999	11	70	4,701,095	67,159	Up	0.25

BIG 12 CONFERENCE

Season	Teams	Games	Attendance	P/G	Pct.	Change in Avg.
1996	12	69	3,549,474	51,442	Up	3.39
1997	12	71	3,640,692	51,277	Dn	0.03
1998	12	71	3,661,740	51,574	Up	0.58
1999	12	72	3,904,491	54,229	Up	5.15

BIG WEST CONFERENCE

Season	Teams	Games	Attendance	P/G	Pct.	Change in Avg.
1988	8	38	570,533	15,014	Up	2.58
1989	8	37	528,921	14,295	Dn	4.79
1990	8	41	650,800	15,873	Up	11.04
1991	8	37	570,332	15,414	Dn	2.89
1992	7	36	515,291	14,314	Up	4.44
1993	10	48	778,224	16,213	Up	6.49
1994	10	49	705,539	14,399	Dn	11.19
1995	10	51	793,452	15,558	Up	8.05
1996	6	34	554,684	16,314	Dn	14.87
1997	6	32	584,020	18,251	Up	11.87
1998	7	37	631,791	17,075	Dn	3.81
1999	7	35	669,254	19,122	Up	11.99

CONFERENCE USA

Season	Teams	Games	Attendance	P/G	Pct.	Change in Avg.
1996	6	33	825,899	25,027	Up	12.87
1997	7	38	963,239	25,348	Dn	0.09
1998	8	44	1,239,052	28,160	Up	27.97
1999	9	52	1,476,223	28,389	Up	5.07

MID-AMERICAN CONFERENCE

Season	Teams	Games	Attendance	P/G	Pct.	Change in Avg.
1978	10	51	722,026	14,157	Up	14.36
1979	10	52	696,784	13,400	Dn	5.35
1980	10	51	714,415	14,008	Up	4.54
1981	10	53	804,158	15,173	Up	8.32
1982@	10	51	980,087	19,217	Up	26.65
1983	10	51	884,888	17,351	Dn	9.71
1984	10	53	918,133	17,323	Dn	0.16
1985	10	49	719,024	14,674	Dn	15.29
1986	9	47	679,866	14,465	Up	2.18
1987	9	45	652,285	14,495	Up	0.21
1988	9	46	765,563	16,643	Up	14.82
1989	9	44	689,698	15,675	Dn	5.82
1990	9	45	744,368	16,542	Up	5.53
1991	9	45	608,485	13,522	Dn	18.26
1992	10	49	704,233	14,372	Up	5.97
1993	10	51	726,847	14,252	Dn	0.83
1994	10	51	754,296	14,790	Up	3.77
1995	10	50	748,138	14,963	Up	1.17
1996	10	50	787,035	15,741	Up	5.18
1997	12	63	1,130,939	17,951	Up	13.44
1998	12	61	1,022,567	16,763	Dn	6.62
1999	13	67	1,195,463	17,843	Up	5.32

@Mid-American and Missouri Valley divided between I-A and I-AA.

MOUNTAIN WEST CONFERENCE
(Members came from Western Athletic Conference)

Season	Teams	Games	Attendance	P/G	Pct.	Change in Avg.
1999	8	43	1,489,527	34,640	Up	3.12

PACIFIC-10 CONFERENCE

Season	Teams	Games	Attendance	P/G	Pct.	Change in Avg.
1978	10	57	2,632,755	46,189	Up	5.56
1979	10	59	2,741,656	46,469	Up	0.61
1980	10	58	2,777,146	47,882	Up	3.04
1981	10	59	2,772,237	46,987	Dn	1.87
1982	10	59	2,745,676	46,537	Dn	0.96
1983	10	58	2,740,406	47,248	Up	1.53
1984	10	63	2,976,655	47,248	No Change	
1985	10	56	2,665,356	47,596	Up	0.74
1986	10	59	2,856,910	48,422	Up	1.74
1987	10	57	2,866,723	50,293	Up	3.86
1988	10	60	3,058,637	50,977	Up	1.36
1989	10	60	3,006,176	50,103	Dn	1.71
1990	10	58	2,872,173	49,520	Dn	1.16
1991	10	59	2,851,991	48,339	Dn	2.38
1992	10	60	2,825,401	47,090	Dn	2.58
1993	10	57	2,731,361	47,919	Up	1.76
1994	10	59	2,785,373	47,210	Dn	1.48
1995	10	57	2,680,510	47,026	Dn	0.39
1996	10	58	2,761,006	47,604	Up	1.23
1997	10	60	2,891,522	48,192	Up	1.24
1998	10	60	3,024,262	50,404	Up	4.59
1999	10	59	2,857,994	48,441	Dn	3.89

SOUTHEASTERN CONFERENCE

Season	Teams	Games	Attendance	P/G	Pct.	Change in Avg.
1978	10	61	3,464,112	56,789	Up	2.62
1979	10	59	3,376,833	57,234	Up	0.78
1980	10	66	3,951,104	59,865	Up	4.60
1981	10	61	3,846,492	63,057	Up	5.33
1982	10	66	4,206,507	63,735	Up	1.08
1983	10	65	4,214,702	64,842	Up	1.74
1984	10	63	4,007,351	63,609	Dn	1.90
1985	10	63	4,017,104	63,764	Up	0.24
1986	10	69	4,351,832	63,070	Dn	1.09
1987	10	64	4,117,046	64,329	Up	2.00
1988	10	62	3,912,241	63,101	Dn	1.91
1989	10	63	4,123,005	65,445	Up	3.71
1990	10	66	4,215,400	63,870	Dn	2.41
1991	10	61	4,063,190	66,610	Up	4.29
1992	12	76	4,844,014	63,737	Dn	1.26
1993	12	78	4,897,564	62,789	Dn	1.49
1994	12	77	4,891,615	63,527	Up	1.18
1995	12	76	4,827,834	63,524	Dn	0.01
1996	12	76	4,932,802	64,905	Up	2.17
1997	12	76	5,005,126	65,857	Up	1.47
1998	12	73	5,059,534	69,309	Up	5.24
1999	12	78	5,500,664	70,521	Up	1.75

WESTERN ATHLETIC CONFERENCE

Season	Teams	Games	Attendance	P/G	Pct.	Change in Avg.
1978	7	37	906,518	24,500	Dn	1.84
1979	8	47	1,349,156	28,705	Up	7.02
1980	9	51	1,354,492	26,559	Dn	5.41
1981	9	51	1,443,515	28,304	Up	6.57

ANNUAL DIVISION I-A CONFERENCE ATTENDANCE

Season	Teams	Games	Attendance	P/G	Change in Pct.	Avg.
1982	9	53	1,605,684	30,296	Up	7.04
1983	9	52	1,567,062	30,136	Dn	0.53
1984	9	55	1,741,793	31,669	Up	5.09
1985	9	55	1,744,123	31,711	Up	0.13
1986	9	51	1,748,857	34,291	Up	8.14
1987	9	54	1,927,572	35,696	Up	4.10
1988	9	54	1,795,735	33,254	Dn	6.84
1989	9	55	1,844,999	33,545	Up	0.88
1990	9	55	1,784,807	32,451	Dn	3.26
1991	9	55	1,883,861	34,252	Up	5.55
1992	10	60	2,111,587	35,193	Up	2.85
1993	10	61	2,109,441	34,581	Dn	1.74
1994	10	61	2,090,620	34,272	Dn	0.89
1995	10	63	1,987,860	31,553	Dn	7.93
1996	16	91	2,615,219	28,739	Up	2.38
1997	16	92	2,758,817	29,987	Up	4.34
1998	16	91	2,594,194	28,508	Dn	4.93
1999	8	45	1,207,602	26,836	Up	11.57

ALL-TIME ATTENDANCE OTHER CONFERENCES
(Conferences that either discontinued or changed names)

BIG EIGHT CONFERENCE
(All members went into Big 12 Conference after 1995 season)

Season	Teams	Games	Attendance	P/G	Change in Pct.	Avg.
1978	8	48	2,549,553	53,116	Dn	1.45
1979	8	46	2,457,633	53,427	Up	0.59
1980	8	49	2,629,195	53,657	Up	0.43
1981	8	50	2,559,480	51,190	Dn	4.60
1982	8	48	2,377,389	49,529	Dn	3.24
1983	8	49	2,398,184	48,943	Dn	1.18
1984	8	45	2,247,010	49,934	Up	2.02
1985	8	54	2,504,509	46,380	Dn	7.12
1986	8	49	2,242,082	45,757	Dn	1.34
1987	8	49	2,182,199	44,535	Dn	2.67
1988	8	49	2,184,333	44,578	Up	0.10
1989	8	49	2,362,465	48,214	Up	8.16
1990	8	49	2,257,825	46,078	Dn	4.43
1991	8	49	2,308,238	47,107	Up	2.23
1992	8	47	2,247,907	47,828	Up	1.53
1993	8	48	2,126,247	44,297	Dn	7.38
1994	8	46	2,194,545	47,708	Up	7.70
1995	8	50	2,414,804	48,296	Up	1.23

IVY GROUP
(Went into Division I-AA after 1981 season)

Season	Teams	Games	Attendance	P/G	Change in Pct.	Avg.
1978	8	40	547,395	13,685	Up	4.87
1979	8	40	534,597	13,365	Dn	2.34
1980	8	43	514,433	11,964	Dn	10.48
1981	8	41	564,059	13,758	Up	14.99

MISSOURI VALLEY CONFERENCE
(Conference discontinued after 1985 season)

Season	Teams	Games	Attendance	P/G	Change in Pct.	Avg.
1978	7	39	523,565	13,425	Up	5.83
1979	7	37	481,706	13,019	Dn	3.02
1980	7	35	473,462	13,527	Up	3.90
1981	8	43	575,174	13,376	Dn	3.34
1982	8	40	594,515	14,863	Up	11.12
1983	7	37	412,412	11,146	Dn	23.63
1984	7	37	427,112	11,544	Up	3.57
1985	5	26	308,137	11,851	Dn	8.32

PACIFIC COAST CONFERENCE
(Became Big West Conference after 1987 season)

Season	Teams	Games	Attendance	P/G	Change in Pct.	Avg.
1978	6	29	279,772	9,647	Dn	3.81
1979	6	25	322,305	12,892	Up	33.64
1980	6	28	353,022	12,608	Dn	2.20
1981	6	27	360,005	13,334	Up	5.76
1982	7	34	487,638	14,342	Dn	6.98
1983	7	35	500,380	14,297	Dn	0.31
1984	8	39	597,420	15,318	Up	5.52
1985	8	40	654,045	16,351	Up	6.74
1986	8	42	753,466	17,940	Up	9.72
1987	8	41	600,129	14,637	Dn	18.41

SOUTHERN CONFERENCE
(Went into Division I-AA after 1981 season)

Season	Teams	Games	Attendance	P/G	Change in Pct.	Avg.
1978	7	34	372,009	10,941	Up	11.20
1979	8	47	478,107	10,172	Up	0.64
1980	8	40	484,727	12,118	Up	19.13
1981	8	42	459,576	10,942	Dn	9.70

SOUTHLAND CONFERENCE
(Went into Division I-AA after 1981 season)

Season	Teams	Games	Attendance	P/G	Change in Pct.	Avg.
1978	6	37	467,915	12,646	Dn	13.67
1979	6	31	491,917	15,868	Up	25.48
1980	6	32	452,311	14,135	Dn	10.92
1981	6	30	427,106	14,237	Up	0.72

SOUTHWEST CONFERENCE
(Discontinued after 1995 season; teams went to Big 12 and Western Athletic Conferences)

Season	Teams	Games	Attendance	P/G	Change in Pct.	Avg.
1978	9	45	2,033,212	45,182	Up	15.46
1979	9	52	2,301,148	44,253	Dn	2.06
1980	9	54	2,263,881	41,924	Dn	5.26
1981	9	54	2,232,757	41,347	Dn	1.38
1982	9	52	2,226,009	42,808	Up	3.53
1983	9	56	2,292,540	40,938	Dn	4.37
1984	9	53	2,177,507	41,085	Up	0.36
1985	9	51	2,077,717	40,740	Dn	0.84
1986	9	53	2,006,663	37,862	Dn	7.06
1987	8	48	1,859,454	38,739	Up	2.32
1988	8	46	1,774,120	38,568	Dn	0.44
1989	9	51	1,914,608	37,541	Dn	2.66
1990	9	53	2,087,248	39,382	Up	4.90
1991	9	50	2,062,309	41,246	Up	4.73
1992	8	47	1,697,152	36,110	Dn	10.52
1993	8	45	1,587,652	35,281	Dn	2.30
1994	8	43	1,588,955	36,952	Up	4.74
1995	8	43	1,653,888	38,463	Up	4.09

Annual Division I-AA Conference Attendance
(Since 1978)

ATLANTIC 10 CONFERENCE
(Formerly Yankee Conference)

Season	Teams	Games	Attendance	P/G	Change in Pct.	Avg.
1978	6	32	207,502	6,484	Dn	9.81
1979	6	29	197,293	6,803	Up	4.92
1980	6	32	211,822	6,619	Dn	2.70
1981	6	29	233,680	8,058	Up	21.74
1982	6	32	254,789	7,962	Dn	1.19
1983	6	30	218,186	7,273	Dn	8.65
1984	6	31	284,709	9,184	Up	26.28
1985	6	36	257,170	7,144	Dn	22.21
1986	8	44	486,299	11,052	Up	13.48
1987	8	43	408,170	9,492	Dn	14.12
1988	9	47	447,641	9,524	Dn	0.27
1989	9	48	460,683	9,598	Up	0.78
1990	9	49	423,459	8,642	Dn	9.96
1991	9	48	431,522	8,990	Up	4.03
1992	9	53	461,366	8,705	Dn	3.17
1993	12	67	550,245	8,213	Dn	7.09
1994	12	67	630,847	9,416	Up	14.65
1995	12	66	578,742	8,769	Dn	6.87
1996	12	64	526,442	8,226	Dn	6.19
1997	12	65	486,798	7,489	Dn	8.96
1998	11	59	533,945	9,050	Up	14.85
1999	11	61	563,885	9,244	Up	2.14

BIG SKY CONFERENCE

Season	Teams	Games	Attendance	P/G	Change in Pct.	Avg.
1978	7	36	393,274	10,924	Up	4.16
1979	8	47	463,920	9,871	Dn	7.70
1980	8	45	520,250	11,561	Up	17.12
1981	8	47	538,920	11,466	Dn	0.82
1982	8	43	463,393	10,777	Dn	6.01

Season	Teams	Games	Attendance	P/G	Pct.	Change in Avg.
1983	8	44	474,167	10,777	No change	
1984	8	47	475,645	10,120	Dn	6.10
1985	8	48	481,015	10,021	Up	0.98
1986	8	46	469,368	10,204	Up	1.83
1987	9	52	537,300	10,333	Up	7.37
1988	9	50	513,467	10,269	Dn	0.62
1989	9	52	550,975	10,596	Up	3.18
1990	9	50	531,060	10,621	Up	0.24
1991	9	56	623,326	11,131	Up	4.80
1992	8	46	437,592	9,513	Dn	1.13
1993	8	48	460,613	9,596	Up	0.87
1994	8	47	530,089	11,278	Up	17.53
1995	8	46	530,022	11,522	Up	2.16
1996	8	44	360,082	8,184	Up	4.63
1997	8	47	385,728	8,207	Up	0.03
1998	9	49	398,690	8,137	Dn	1.12
1999	9	50	492,618	9,852	Up	21.08

GATEWAY FOOTBALL CONFERENCE

Season	Teams	Games	Attendance	P/G	Pct.	Change in Avg.
1985	6	35	281,632	8,047	Up	8.01
1986	7	37	351,972	9,513	Up	16.03
1987	7	36	315,318	8,759	Dn	7.93
1988	7	36	332,800	9,244	Up	5.54
1989	7	40	315,633	7,891	Dn	14.64
1990	7	36	313,409	8,706	Up	10.33
1991	7	38	332,482	8,750	Up	0.51
1992	7	40	345,823	8,646	Dn	1.19
1993	7	36	285,921	7,942	Dn	8.14
1994	7	40	293,437	7,336	Dn	7.63
1995	7	41	317,344	7,740	Up	5.51
1996	6	33	294,724	8,931	Up	11.37
1997	7	41	399,221	9,737	Up	6.24
1998	7	39	366,029	9,385	Dn	3.62
1999	7	39	392,203	10,056	Up	7.15

IVY GROUP

Season	Teams	Games	Attendance	P/G	Pct.	Change in Avg.
1982	8	44	602,857	13,701	Dn	0.41
1983	8	43	653,263	15,192	Up	10.88
1984	8	39	591,562	15,168	Dn	0.16
1985	8	41	562,184	13,712	Dn	9.60
1986	8	43	543,983	12,651	Dn	7.74
1987	8	42	602,480	14,345	Up	13.39
1988	8	42	513,674	12,230	Dn	14.74
1989	8	43	557,872	12,974	Up	6.08
1990	8	41	471,245	11,494	Dn	11.41
1991	8	39	466,928	11,973	Up	4.17
1992	8	40	401,980	10,050	Dn	16.06
1993	8	42	420,915	10,022	Dn	0.28
1994	8	42	445,900	10,617	Up	5.94
1995	8	42	396,539	9,441	Dn	11.08
1996	8	40	413,112	10,328	Up	9.40
1997	8	39	284,650	7,299	Dn	29.33
1998	8	40	445,801	11,145	Up	52.69
1999	8	44	516,589	11,741	Up	5.35

METRO ATLANTIC ATHLETIC CONFERENCE

Season	Teams	Games	Attendance	P/G	Pct.	Change in Avg.
1993	6	29	34,483	1,189	Up	13.02
1994	7	35	41,364	1,182	Dn	2.72
1995	8	37	51,549	1,393	Up	4.74
1996	9	41	57,742	1,408	Up	1.08
1997	9	46	69,249	1,505	Up	6.89
1998	9	44	75,134	1,708	Up	13.49
1999	9	46	96,105	2,089	Up	22.31

MID-EASTERN ATHLETIC CONFERENCE

Season	Teams	Games	Attendance	P/G	Pct.	Change in Avg.
1978	4	19	141,234	7,433	Dn	2.96
1979	4	24	131,942	5,498	Dn	26.03
1980	6	29	308,530	10,639	Up	10.20
1981	6	35	357,982	10,228	Dn	3.86
1982	6	35	358,315	10,238	Up	0.10
1983	6	34	335,664	9,872	Dn	3.57
1984	5	27	209,612	7,763	Dn	8.30
1985	5	23	263,687	11,465	Up	47.69
1986	6	32	270,405	8,450	Dn	22.56
1987	6	30	354,899	11,830	Up	40.00
1988	7	39	466,030	11,948	Dn	2.34
1989	7	41	521,529	12,720	Up	6.45
1990	7	36	475,909	13,220	Up	3.93

Season	Teams	Games	Attendance	P/G	Pct.	Change in Avg.
1991	7	40	578,412	14,460	Up	9.38
1992	7	38	450,962	11,867	Dn	17.93
1993	7	40	440,012	11,000	Dn	7.31
1994	7	40	556,159	13,904	Up	26.40
1995	8	37	350,770	9,480	Dn	21.02
1996	8	41	445,672	10,870	Up	20.00
1997	9	42	427,794	10,186	Up	10.22
1998	9	41	466,929	11,389	Up	11.81
1999	9	41	479,754	11,701	Up	2.74

NORTHEAST CONFERENCE

Season	Teams	Games	Attendance	P/G	Pct.	Change in Avg.
1996	5	27	40,800	1,511	Dn	10.70
1997	5	24	37,014	1,542	Up	2.05
1998	5	24	36,189	1,508	Dn	2.20
1999	8	37	70,411	1,903	Up	26.19

OHIO VALLEY CONFERENCE

Season	Teams	Games	Attendance	P/G	Pct.	Change in Avg.
1978	7	37	355,893	9,619	Dn	8.47
1979	7	36	349,165	9,699	Up	0.83
1980	8	45	470,001	10,444	Up	0.59
1981	9	47	428,182	9,110	Dn	7.99
1982	8	43	367,591	8,549	Dn	2.48
1983	8	44	356,124	8,094	Dn	5.32
1984	8	45	377,991	8,400	Up	3.78
1985	8	44	420,016	9,546	Up	13.64
1986	8	44	379,014	8,614	Dn	9.76
1987	7	35	277,978	7,942	Up	7.95
1988	7	38	302,609	7,963	Dn	23.00
1989	7	34	296,739	8,728	Up	9.61
1990	7	40	465,183	11,630	Up	33.25
1991	8	42	316,755	7,542	Dn	30.54
1992	9	49	395,264	8,067	Up	8.83
1993	9	49	294,714	6,015	Dn	25.44
1994	9	49	354,903	7,243	Up	20.42
1995	9	50	373,967	7,479	Up	3.26
1996	9	49	363,960	7,426	Dn	4.64
1997	8	42	265,345	6,318	Dn	23.99
1998	8	42	365,046	8,692	Up	37.58
1999	8	42	346,085	8,240	Dn	5.20

PATRIOT LEAGUE

Season	Teams	Games	Attendance	P/G	Pct.	Change in Avg.
1990	6	30	223,893	7,463	Up	3.15
1991	6	32	231,155	7,224	Dn	3.20
1992	6	31	202,187	6,522	Dn	9.72
1993	6	29	165,581	5,710	Dn	12.45
1994	6	32	198,274	6,196	Up	8.51
1995	6	29	157,625	5,435	Dn	12.28
1996	6	32	185,275	5,790	Up	6.53
1997	7	38	175,992	4,631	Dn	13.94
1998	7	40	239,275	5,982	Up	29.17
1999	7	39	194,058	4,976	Dn	16.82

PIONEER FOOTBALL LEAGUE

Season	Teams	Games	Attendance	P/G	Pct.	Change in Avg.
1993	6	32	94,995	2,969	Dn	16.15
1994	6	32	129,678	4,052	Up	36.48
1995	6	32	115,148	3,598	Up	11.20
1996	6	31	117,406	3,787	Up	5.25
1997	6	30	109,234	3,641	Dn	3.86
1998	5	27	103,882	3,847	Dn	6.65
1999	5	28	116,840	4,173	Up	8.47

SOUTHERN CONFERENCE

Season	Teams	Games	Attendance	P/G	Pct.	Change in Avg.
1982	8	42	451,214	10,743	Dn	1.82
1983	9	47	442,328	9,411	Dn	3.63
1984	9	49	497,040	10,144	Up	7.79
1985	9	49	501,420	10,233	Up	0.88
1986	9	47	484,589	10,310	Up	0.75
1987	8	47	516,773	10,995	Dn	1.29
1988	8	43	479,649	11,155	Up	1.46
1989	8	44	495,918	11,271	Up	1.04
1990	8	44	504,248	11,415	Up	1.28
1991	8	46	574,059	12,480	Up	9.33
1992	9	55	700,613	12,738	Dn	1.25
1993	9	51	617,620	12,110	Dn	4.93
1994	9	53	667,283	12,590	Up	3.96

Season	Teams	Games	Attendance	P/G	Change in Pct.	Avg.
1995	9	47	532,530	11,330	Dn	10.01
1996	9	51	578,350	11,340	Up	0.09
1997	9	52	491,680	9,455	Dn	1.44
1998	9	50	483,003	9,660	Up	2.17
1999	9	49	514,800	10,506	Up	8.76

SOUTHLAND FOOTBALL LEAGUE
(Formerly Southland Conference)

Season	Teams	Games	Attendance	P/G	Change in Pct.	Avg.
1982	6	31	438,147	14,134	Up	0.63
1983	7	35	469,010	13,400	Dn	1.60
1984	7	38	458,259	12,059	Dn	10.01
1985	7	35	408,960	11,685	Dn	3.10
1986	6	30	395,515	13,184	Up	3.82
1987	7	35	412,898	11,797	Up	3.67
1988	7	40	441,301	11,033	Up	6.48
1989	7	38	423,772	11,152	Up	1.08
1990	7	38	436,110	11,477	Up	2.91
1991	8	41	392,513	9,573	Dn	9.65
1992	8	45	429,971	9,555	Dn	0.19
1993	8	43	403,508	9,384	Dn	1.79
1994	7	43	435,078	10,118	Up	19.87
1995	6	33	316,426	9,589	Up	5.53
1996	8	46	411,357	8,943	Dn	10.29
1997	8	46	388,593	8,448	Dn	5.54
1998	8	44	460,335	10,462	Up	23.84
1999	8	44	406,336	9,235	Dn	11.73

SOUTHWESTERN ATHLETIC CONFERENCE

Season	Teams	Games	Attendance	P/G	Change in Pct.	Avg.
1978	5	27	483,159	17,895	Dn	5.30
1979	6	32	513,768	16,055	Up	1.02
1980	7	38	611,234	16,085	Up	4.58
1981	7	35	662,221	18,921	Up	17.63
1982	7	35	634,505	18,129	Dn	4.19
1983	8	44	709,160	16,117	Dn	5.11
1984	8	40	702,186	17,555	Up	8.92
1985	8	44	790,296	17,961	Up	2.31
1986	8	38	621,584	16,357	Dn	8.93
1987	8	42	697,534	16,608	Up	1.53
1988	8	38	541,127	14,240	Dn	14.26
1989	8	44	796,844	18,110	Up	27.18
1990	7	40	828,169	20,704	Up	10.85
1991	8	47	856,491	18,223	Dn	11.98
1992	8	42	873,772	20,804	Up	14.16
1993	8	42	772,714	18,398	Dn	11.57
1994	8	41	958,508	23,378	Up	27.04
1995	8	38	628,702	16,545	Dn	29.23
1996	8	39	600,798	15,405	Dn	6.35
1997	8	36	567,929	15,776	Up	2.41
1998	9	38	516,042	13,580	Dn	11.66
1999	10	51	781,226	15,318	Up	16.90

ALL-TIME ATTENDANCE OTHER CONFERENCES
(Conferences that either discontinued or changed names)

AMERICAN WEST CONFERENCE

Season	Teams	Games	Attendance	P/G	Change in Pct.	Avg.
1994	4	20	82,986	4,149	Dn	8.77
1995	4	23	97,798	4,252	Up	2.48

COLONIAL ATHLETIC ASSOCIATION

Season	Teams	Games	Attendance	P/G	Change in Pct.	Avg.
1986	5	24	241,192	10,050	Up	23.97
1987	6	29	241,831	8,339	Dn	5.39
1988	6	31	195,686	6,312	Dn	24.31
1989	5	26	196,767	7,568	Up	3.25

GULF STAR CONFERENCE
(Teams went to Southland Conference)

Season	Teams	Games	Attendance	P/G	Change in Pct.	Avg.
1984	4	20	149,516	7,476	Dn	9.23
1985	4	22	166,046	7,548	Up	0.96
1986	5	25	211,094	8,444	Up	17.72

MID-CONTINENT CONFERENCE
(Discontinued after 1984 season; Four members went to Gateway)

Season	Teams	Games	Attendance	P/G	Change in Pct.	Avg.
1981	3	17	140,506	8,265	Up	4.74
1982	4	23	191,975	8,347	Up	7.73
1983	4	21	167,219	7,963	Dn	4.60
1984	4	24	175,181	7,299	Dn	8.34

Largest Regular-Season Crowds

Largest Regular-Season Crowds*

Attendance	Date	Home	Visitor
111,794	11-6-99	MIchigan 37,	Northwestern 3
111,575	11-20-99	Michigan 24,	Ohio St. 17
111,523	9-4-99	Michigan 26,	Notre Dame 22
111,238	9-26-98	Michigan 29,	Michigan St. 17
111,217	11-14-98	Michigan 27,	Wisconsin 10
111,019	11-7-98	Michigan 27,	Penn St. 0
111,012	9-12-98	Michigan 28,	Syracuse 38
110,863	10-24-98	Michigan 21,	Indiana 10
110,501	9-11-99	Michigan 37,	Rice 3
110,468	10-2-99	Michigan 38,	Purdue 12
110,438	9-19-98	Michigan 59,	Eastern Mich. 20
110,188	10-23-99	Michigan 29,	Illinois 35
107,653	9-19-98	Tennessee 20,	Florida 17
107,619	11-6-99	Tennessee 38,	Notre Dame 14
107,597	9-4-99	Tennessee 42,	Wyoming 17
107,289	10-24-98	Tennessee 35,	Alabama 18
107,261	9-25-99	Tennessee 17,	Memphis 16
107,252	11-21-98	Tennessee 59,	Kentucky 21
107,247	10-9-99	Tennessee 37,	Georgia 20
106,508	11-7-98	Tennessee 37,	UAB 13
107,608	9-21-96	Tennessee 29,	Florida 35
107,073	11-8-97	Tennessee 44,	Southern Miss. 20
106,986	11-22-97	Michigan 20,	Ohio St. 14
106,867	11-20-93	Michigan 28,	Ohio St. 0
106,851	9-11-93	Michigan 23,	Notre Dame 27
106,832	10-15-94	Michigan 24,	Penn St. 31
106,788	10-10-92	Michigan 35,	Michigan St. 10
106,700	10-26-96	Tennessee 20,	Alabama 13
106,683	11-29-97	Tennessee 17,	Vanderbilt 10
106,656	10-11-97	Tennessee 38,	Georgia 13

*In the 52 seasons official national attendance records have been maintained.

WEEKS WITH LARGEST TOTAL ATTENDANCE FOR THE TOP-10 ATTENDED GAMES

Total	Date
886,688	10-2-99
879,063	9-4-99
865,498	9-11-99
863,215	11-6-99
862,941	9-4-93
862,016	9-19-98
857,115	10-10-92
855,722	11-22-97
854,835	9-30-95
853,640	9-21-96
852,246	9-12-98
851,257	11-21-98
848,356	9-7-96
847,327	11-18-97
843,076	11-11-97
842,802	11-7-98
842,483	9-25-99
842,043	11-2-96
839,206	9-26-98
836,427	11-20-99
836,424	11-14-98
834,370	10-8-94
833,285	10-22-83
832,196	11-13-99
831,666	9-13-97
829,425	11-1-97

1999 Top Ten Regular-Season Crowds

Attendance	Home	Visitor	Date	Site
111,794*	Michigan 37,	Northwestern 3	11-6	Ann Arbor, Mich.
111,575	Michigan 24,	Ohio St. 17	11-20	Ann Arbor, Mich.
111,523	Michigan 26,	Notre Dame 22	9-4	Ann Arbor, Mich.
110,501	Michigan 37,	Rice 3	9-11	Ann Arbor, Mich.
110,468	Michigan 38,	Purdue 12	10-2	Ann Arbor, Mich.
110,188	Michigan 29,	Illinois 35	10-23	Ann Arbor, Mich.
107,619	Tennessee 38,	Notre Dame 14	11-6	Knoxville, Tenn.
107,597	Tennessee 42,	Wyoming 17	9-4	Knoxville, Tenn.
107,261	Tennessee 17,	Memphis 16	9-25	Knoxville, Tenn.
107,247	Tennessee 37,	Georgia 20	10-9	Knoxville, Tenn.

*Largest All-Time Regular-Season Crowd since 1948.

Pre-1948 Regular-Season Crowds in Excess of 100,000

Attendance	Date	Site	Opponents, Score
120,000*	11-26-27	Soldier Field, Chicago	Notre Dame 7, Southern California 6
120,000*	10-13-28	Soldier Field, Chicago	Notre Dame 7, Navy 0
112,912	11-16-29	Soldier Field, Chicago	Notre Dame 13, Southern California 12
110,000*	11-27-26	Soldier Field, Chicago	Army 21, Navy 21
110,000*	11-29-30	Soldier Field, Chicago	Notre Dame 7, Army 6
104,953	12-6-47	Los Angeles	Notre Dame 38, Southern California 7

Estimated attendance; others are audited figures.

Additional Records

Highest Average Attendance Per Home Game: 111,175, Michigan, 1999 (667,049 in 6)

Highest Total Home Attendance: 745,139, Michigan, 1997 (7 games)

Highest Total Attendance, Home and Away: 1,044,370, Michigan, 1997 (11 games)

Highest Bowl Game Attendance: 106,869, 1973 Rose Bowl (Southern California 42, Ohio St. 17)

Most Consecutive Home Sellout Crowds: 233, Nebraska (current, from Nov. 3, 1962)

Most Consecutive 100,000-Plus Crowds: 154, Michigan (current, from Nov. 8, 1975)

1999 Attendance

Division I-A

		Games	Attendance	Average	Change in Avg.
1.	Michigan	6	667,049	111,175	210
2.	Tennessee	7	747,870	106,839	-75
3.	Penn St.	7	675,503	96,500	-31
4.	Ohio St.	7	654,192	93,456	-46
5.	Georgia	6	516,702	86,117	499
6.	Florida	6	512,960	85,493	195
7.	Texas	6	496,036	82,673	5,232
8.	Auburn	7	566,333	80,905	-206
9.	Notre Dame	7	560,084	80,012	0
10.	Florida St.	6	472,350	78,725	-1,765
11.	LSU	7	550,409	78,630	-1,660
12.	Clemson	5	391,510	78,302	9,373
13.	South Carolina	6	469,635	78,273	3,529
14.	Wisconsin	6	468,487	78,081	653
15.	Nebraska	6	466,375	77,729	1,543
16.	Alabama	7	536,328	76,618	-6,052
17.	Oklahoma	5	373,320	74,664	3,887
18.	Michigan St.	6	444,886	74,148	4,006
19.	Texas A&M	6	438,755	73,126	14,833
20.	Washington	6	430,738	71,790	434
21.	Kentucky	6	406,536	67,756	10,019
22.	Brigham Young	6	391,111	65,185	2,484
23.	Purdue	6	380,826	63,471	10,405
24.	Iowa	6	380,786	63,464	-4,866
25.	Missouri	6	350,242	58,374	1,039
26.	Southern California	6	345,091	57,515	-3,384
27.	Arizona St.	6	343,227	57,205	-4,185
28.	Arkansas	6	321,840	53,640	1,041
29.	Virginia Tech	6	315,111	52,519	3,474
30.	Colorado	6	312,751	52,125	5,622
31.	Arizona	6	299,686	49,948	2,032
32.	UCLA	6	298,951	49,825	-23,884
33.	Stanford	6	298,430	49,738	14,962
34.	Kansas St.	7	334,959	47,851	5,632
35.	Mississippi	6	280,973	46,829	737
36.	Syracuse	6	280,274	46,712	-1,185
37.	Virginia	6	277,900	46,317	2,557
38.	Air Force	5	229,907	45,981	327
39.	Texas Tech	5	229,472	45,894	2,638
40.	Georgia Tech	6	274,624	45,771	5,300
41.	West Virginia	6	273,371	45,562	-8,574
42.	Minnesota	7	318,086	45,441	5,598
43.	Illinois	6	271,745	45,291	5,701
44.	North Carolina St.	5	225,240	45,048	5,107
45.	Oregon	6	263,622	43,937	-232
46.	North Carolina	6	262,000	43,667	-12,003
47.	Oklahoma St.	6	258,490	43,082	1,426
48.	California	5	214,700	42,940	-5,810
49.	East Carolina	7	294,255	42,036	10,293
50.	Boston College	5	206,734	41,347	147
51.	Vanderbilt	7	280,094	40,013	8,283
52.	Miami (Fla.)	6	235,578	39,263	-3,939
53.	Utah	5	195,853	39,171	357
54.	Iowa St.	6	233,578	38,930	3,749
55.	Hawaii	9	347,712	38,635	9,282
56.	Louisville	7	268,729	38,390	-1,289
57.	Mississippi St.	7	264,749	37,821	436
58.	Fresno St.	6	223,384	37,231	128
59.	Indiana	7	247,617	35,374	-1,079
60.	UTEP	5	171,671	34,334	14,190
61.	Navy	5	170,234	34,047	830
62.	Kansas	7	235,500	33,643	1,276
63.	Army	6	198,297	33,050	-3,879
64.	Pittsburgh	7	229,201	32,743	-8,208
65.	Oregon St.	6	195,101	32,517	3,969
66.	Maryland	6	193,275	32,213	3,865
67.	Northwestern	6	185,070	30,845	-10,062
68.	Baylor	6	175,013	29,169	-4,528
69.	Marshall	7	200,715	28,674	3,886
70.	San Diego St.	5	141,138	28,228	3,748
71.	Colorado St.	5	137,884	27,577	-3,715
72.	Memphis	6	161,597	26,933	3,454
73.	Western Mich.	5	134,368	26,874	5,007
74.	UNLV	5	131,543	26,309	8,308
75.	TCU	6	157,738	26,290	-892
76.	Rutgers	6	155,188	25,865	2,568
77.	Southern Miss.	5	129,168	25,834	1,272
78.	Louisiana Tech	4	101,633	25,408	8,661
79.	Rice	4	101,200	25,300	3,185
80.	Idaho	4	100,805	25,201	11,912
81.	Washington St.	6	146,191	24,365	-10,302
82.	New Mexico	6	142,879	23,813	-2,659
83.	Boise St.	7	160,853	22,979	-666
84.	UCF	6	131,530	21,922	-729
85.	Nevada	6	128,841	21,474	380
86.	Toledo	7	149,968	21,424	-2,387
87.	Temple	4	83,084	20,771	5,644
88.	Tulane	5	103,217	20,643	-7,300
89.	UAB	5	102,244	20,449	2,284
90.	Houston	5	100,014	20,003	3,707
91.	Wyoming	6	119,212	19,869	1,943
92.	Cincinnati	6	118,702	19,784	-4,351
93.	Southern Methodist	5	98,127	19,625	1,408
94.	Wake Forest	6	116,509	19,418	-1,515
95.	Central Mich.	5	96,316	19,263	-1,336
96.	Ohio	5	95,224	19,045	627
97.	Ball St.	4	73,541	18,385	-2,036
98.	Duke	5	88,303	17,661	-6,036
99.	North Texas	4	69,793	17,448	7,222
100.	Utah St.	5	87,199	17,440	3,193
101.	Miami (Ohio)	5	86,813	17,363	2,233
102.	Buffalo	5	84,196	16,839	-2,996
103.	La.-Lafayette	5	79,507	15,901	6,353
104.	Northern Ill.	5	76,760	15,352	2,834
105.	New Mexico St.	4	59,264	14,816	-5,526
106.	Tulsa	6	83,850	13,975	-5,369
107.	Arkansas St.	5	68,801	13,760	501
108.	La.-Monroe	4	54,204	13,551	-1,688
109.	Middle Tenn. St.	5	62,359	12,472	-8,842
110.	Bowling Green	5	57,186	11,437	160
111.	Kent St.	5	51,708	10,342	2,639
112.	Akron	5	41,378	8,276	-137
113.	Eastern Mich.	4	27,326	6,832	-5,171
114.	San Jose St.	4	23,920	5,980	-6,552

Division I-AA

		Games	Attendance	Average	Change in Avg.
1.	Jackson St.	6	173,600	28,933	14,656
2.	Yale	5	137,592	27,518	14,112
3.	Southern U.	5	128,671	25,734	3,021
4.	South Fla.	7	175,371	25,053	-2,090
5.	N.C. A&T	6	131,726	21,954	5,986
6.	Portland St.	5	103,603	20,721	14,062
7.	Delaware	6	122,229	20,372	1,215
8.	Tennessee St.	5	97,588	19,518	2,435
9.	Montana	6	112,378	18,730	385
10.	Florida A&M	4	73,654	18,414	1,061
11.	Appalachian St.	5	91,777	18,355	3,440
12.	Ga. Southern	5	84,200	16,840	3,686

1999 ATTENDANCE—DIVISION I-AA

	Games	Attendance	Average	Change in Avg.
13. Alabama St.	6	99,754	16,626	5,111
14. Princeton	6	97,505	16,251	-5,971
15. Texas Southern	6	96,867	16,145	7,777
16. Youngstown St.	6	96,034	16,006	-297
17. South Carolina St.	4	62,223	15,556	2,923
18. Massachusetts	5	73,420	14,684	1,733
19. Troy St.	5	73,125	14,625	-2,366
20. Citadel	6	87,258	14,543	1,252
21. McNeese St.	6	80,190	13,365	-3,414
22. Howard	5	62,089	12,418	663
23. Lehigh	5	61,276	12,255	2,174
24. Southwest Mo. St.	6	72,590	12,098	2,453
25. James Madison	5	59,400	11,880	1,463
26. Alcorn St.	5	58,162	11,632	-9,395
27. Furman	5	58,105	11,621	2,081
28. Grambling	4	46,243	11,561	1,259
29. Richmond	6	67,523	11,254	-3,219
30. Pennsylvania	7	78,544	11,221	-781
31. Mississippi Val.	5	55,990	11,198	5,103
32. Cal St. Sacramento	6	66,470	11,078	5,592
33. Alabama A&M	5	53,602	10,720	1,228
34. Northern Iowa	6	63,246	10,541	-108
35. Eastern Ky.	5	52,480	10,496	579
36. Villanova	5	51,196	10,239	1,833
37. Cornell	5	50,980	10,196	941
38. Connecticut	6	57,770	9,628	335
39. Brown	6	56,309	9,385	2,991
40. Northwestern St.	5	46,778	9,356	-1,776
41. Ark.-Pine Bluff	5	46,527	9,305	-2,908
42. Jacksonville St.	6	54,539	9,090	-2,826
43. Bethune-Cookman	6	54,413	9,069	999
44. Western Ky.	5	45,050	9,010	1,453
45. Montana St.	6	53,522	8,920	642
46. Harvard	5	43,520	8,704	-1,651
47. Western Caro.	6	51,262	8,544	-1,099
48. Stephen F. Austin	6	49,763	8,294	-26
49. Sam Houston St.	5	41,000	8,200	-539
50. Hampton	4	32,726	8,182	-2,205
51. Morgan St.	1	8,115	8,115	-184
52. Southwest Tex. St.	6	47,484	7,914	1,582
53. Northern Ariz.	4	31,427	7,857	-515
54. Liberty	5	38,801	7,760	-2,492
55. Western Ill.	6	46,558	7,760	-1,860
56. William & Mary	5	36,951	7,390	-635
57. Southern Ill.	5	36,100	7,220	400
58. Weber St.	6	42,966	7,161	-1,565
59. Wofford	5	35,702	7,140	-113
60. Chattanooga	5	35,372	7,074	-234
61. Illinois St.	5	34,966	6,993	-289
62. Norfolk St.	6	40,451	6,742	-7,569
63. Dartmouth	5	33,690	6,738	-779
64. Southeast Mo. St.	6	39,629	6,605	-190
65. Dayton	6	38,136	6,356	-79
66. Eastern Ill.	5	31,263	6,253	245
67. Morehead St.	5	30,963	6,193	832
68. Tennessee Tech	4	24,712	6,178	1,968
69. East Tenn. St.	6	37,016	6,169	209
70. Hofstra	5	30,542	6,108	1,232
71. Cal Poly	5	30,125	6,025	-195
72. Elon	6	34,906	5,818	1,017
73. VMI	6	34,108	5,685	-68
74. Holy Cross	6	33,916	5,653	-727
75. Maine	6	33,416	5,569	-223
76. Prairie View	4	21,810	5,453	-4,362
77. Eastern Wash.	6	31,962	5,327	36
78. Drake	5	26,191	5,238	1,105
79. Southern Utah	4	20,362	5,091	1,506
80. Idaho St.	6	30,225	5,038	-317
81. Samford	6	29,409	4,902	900
82. Murray St.	6	29,329	4,888	-4,282
83. New Hampshire	5	21,886	4,377	967
84. Tenn.-Martin	6	26,034	4,339	956
85. Indiana St.	5	21,539	4,308	198
86. Cal St. Northridge	5	20,065	4,013	-469
87. Lafayette	6	23,300	3,883	-3,363
88. Fordham	6	22,439	3,740	21
89. Columbia	5	18,449	3,690	-2,917
90. Duquesne	5	18,344	3,669	-138
91. Robert Morris	5	18,236	3,647	2,986
92. Marist	6	20,764	3,461	1,832
93. Bucknell	6	20,624	3,437	-2,539
94. Rhode Island	6	20,163	3,361	-814
95. Colgate	5	16,747	3,349	-1,878
96. Northeastern	6	19,931	3,322	-1,536
97. San Diego	7	22,275	3,182	-55
98. Towson	5	15,756	3,151	-176
99. Valparaiso	5	15,525	3,105	543
100. Austin Peay	5	15,290	3,058	-252
101. Albany (N.Y.)	4	11,876	2,969	-16
102. Butler	5	14,713	2,943	-307
103. Delaware St.	5	14,357	2,871	-98
104. La Salle	5	13,935	2,787	1,650
105. Davidson	5	13,795	2,759	585
106. Nicholls St.	5	13,457	2,691	-499
107. Monmouth	4	10,586	2,647	-313
108. Charleston So.	5	13,105	2,621	480
109. Georgetown	6	13,419	2,237	684
110. Fairfield	6	11,495	1,916	-738
111. St. Mary's (Cal.)	6	10,700	1,783	-536
112. Wagner	4	6,828	1,707	-188
113. Iona	5	7,796	1,559	-7
114. Jacksonville	5	7,415	1,483	-1,293
115. Sacred Heart	5	7,325	1,465	-435
116. Stony Brook	5	6,621	1,324	435
117. St. John's (N.Y.)	5	6,072	1,214	-118
118. Central Conn. St.	5	4,895	979	-29
119. Siena	5	4,519	904	38
120. St. Francis (Pa.)	5	4,044	809	-107
121. St. Peter's	4	3,219	805	244
122. Canisius	4	2,614	654	-136

Division II

	Games	Attendance	Average
1. Tuskegee	4	53,342	13,336
2. Morehouse	4	47,532	11,883
3. Presbyterian	5	3,983	11,752
4. North Dakota St.	6	68,457	11,410
5. Winston-Salem	7	67,355	9,622
6. Albany St. (Ga.)	3	25,348	8,449
7. Neb.-Omaha	5	40,500	8,100
8. North Dakota	6	46,880	7,813
9. Northwest Mo. St.	6	44,950	7,492
10. Pittsburg St.	5	36,860	7,372
11. Fort Valley St.	6	43,459	7,243
12. Savannah St.	5	36,061	7,212
13. Ashland	5	35,800	7,160
14. Angelo St.	6	41,500	6,917
15. UC Davis	5	34,436	6,887
16. Northern Colo.	5	34,381	6,876
17. Tex. A&M-Kingsville	5	33,700	6,740
18. Bowie St.	4	26,100	6,525
19. South Dakota St.	5	30,694	6,139
20. Mo. Southern St.	5	30,350	6,070
21. Morris Brown	5	30,115	6,023
22. Indiana (Pa.)	5	29,002	5,800
23. West Chester	4	21,901	5,475
24. Kentucky St.	4	21,700	5,425
25. Slippery Rock	6	31,955	5,326

Division III

	Games	Attendance	Average
1. Mount Union	5	28,717	5,743
2. St. John's (Minn.)	5	28,075	5,615
3. Emory & Henry	5	27,090	5,418
4. Mississippi Col.	6	30,058	5,010
5. Baldwin-Wallace	4	17,730	4,433
6. Rowan	4	16,700	4,175
7. Williams	4	16,523	4,131
8. Ithaca	5	20,458	4,092
9. Trinity (Conn.)	4	16,028	4,007
10. Wash. & Jeff.	5	19,300	3,860
11. Wash. & Lee	5	19,200	3,840
12. McMurry	4	14,575	3,644
13. St. Thomas (Minn.)	5	18,200	3,640
14. North Central	5	18,108	3,622
15. Grove City	6	21,690	3,615
16. Simpson	5	17,423	3,485
17. Wesleyan (Conn.)	4	13,900	3,475
18. Lycoming	4	13,795	3,449
19. Hampden-Sydney	5	16,600	3,320
20. Bethel (Minn.)	5	16,517	3,303
21. Heidelberg	5	16,502	3,300
22. Wartburg	6	19,400	3,233
23. Tufts	4	12,600	3,150
24. Gust. Adolphus	4	12,487	3,122
25. Muhlenberg	5	15,551	3,110

ATTENDANCE RECORDS

Divisions I-A and I-AA Conferences and Independent Groups

	Total Teams	Games	1999 Attend.	Avg. PG	Change† In Avg.	Change† In Total
1. Southeastern (I-A)	12	78	*5,500,664	*70,521	Up 1,212	Up 441,130
2. Big Ten (I-A)	11	70	4,701,095	67,159	Up 168	Up 346,712
3. Big 12 (I-A)	12	72	*3,904,491	*54,229	Up 2,655	Up 242,751
4. Pacific-10 (I-A)	10	59	2,857,994	48,441	Dn 1,963	Dn 166,268
5. Atlantic Coast (I-A)	9	51	2,298,711	45,073	Dn 631	Dn 32,168
6. Big East (I-A)	8	46	1,837,478	39,945	Up 50	Dn 77,479
7. Mountain West (I-A)@	8	43	*1,489,527	*34,640	Up 1,082	Dn 21,923
8. Div. I-A Indep.#	7	36	1,159,551	32,210	Up 1,898	Up 68,309
9. Conference USA (I-A)#	9	52	*1,476,223	*28,389	Up 1,428	Up 128,180
10. Western Ath. (I-A)#	8	45	1,207,602	26,836	Up 3,298	Up 124,858
11. Big West (I-A)	7	35	669,254	*19,122	Up 2,047	Up 37,463
12. Mid-American (I-A)#	13	67	*1,195,463	17,843	Up 891	Up 93,555
13. SW Athletic (I-AA)#	10	51	781,226	15,318	Up 2,295	Up 208,232
14. Ivy (I-AA)	8	44	516,589	11,741	Up 596	Up 70,788
15. Mid-East. Ath. (I-AA)	9	41	479,754	11,701	Up 312	Up 12,825
16. Southern (I-AA)	9	49	514,800	10,506	Up 846	Up 31,797
17. Gateway FB (I-AA)	7	39	392,203	*10,056	Up 671	Up 26,174
18. Big Sky (I-AA)	9	50	492,618	9,852	Up 1,715	Up 93,928
19. Atlantic 10 FB (I-AA)	11	61	563,885	9,244	Up 194	Up 29,940
20. Southland FB (I-AA)	8	44	406,336	9,235	Dn 1,227	Dn 53,999
21. Ohio Valley (I-AA)#	8	42	346,085	8,240	Up 847	Up 13,394
22. Div. I-AA Indep.#	14	74	456,856	6,174	Dn 61	Dn 10,780
23. Patriot (I-AA)	7	39	194,067	4,976	Dn 1,006	Dn 45,217
24. Pioneer FB (I-AA)	5	28	116,840	*4,173	Up 326	Up 12,958
25. Metro Atlantic (I-AA)#	9	46	*96,105	*2,089	Up 377	Up 24,221
26. Northeast (I-AA)#	8	37	*70,411	*1,903	Up 395	Up 6,813
I-A Neutral Sites		12	734,920	61,243	—	—
I-AA Neutral Sites		16	521,579	32,599	—	—
Division I-A#	114	666	*29,032,973	43,593	Up 1,083	Up 1,358,756
Division I-AA#	122	661	5,949,345	9,001	Up 196	Up 393,381
I-A & I-AA Combined	236	1,327	34,982,318	26,362	Up 442	Up 1,752,137
II Neutral Sites		8	18,498	2,312	—	—
III Neutral Sites		12	64,481	5,373	—	—
Division II#	147	749	2,504,118	3,343	Up 72	Up 60,458
Division III#	218	1,061	1,996,221	1,881	Up 91	Up 178,882
ALL NCAA TEAMS	*601	*3,137	*39,482,657	12,586	Up 270	Up 1,991,477

By Percentage of Capacity: Div. I-A: 80.4 percent—Southeastern 100.4; Big 12 93.8; Big Ten 90.9; Atlantic Coast 85.7; Mountain West 79.7; Pacific-10 73.4; Big East 71.6; I-A Independents 66.4; Conference USA 61.0; Mid-American 58.9; Western Athletic 57.2; Big West 57.1. **Div. I-AA:** 54.5 percent—Mid-Eastern 68.8; Southern 68.8; Atlantic 10 68.7; Metro Atlantic 63.0; Big Sky 62.6; Southwestern Ath. 61.4; Gateway 58.4; Southland 58.2; I-AA Independents 45.8; Patriot 41.2; Ohio Valley 39.4; Pioneer FB 38.4; Ivy 36.2; Northeast 34.2.

#Did not have same lineup in 1999 as in 1998. @New conference. *Record high for this conference. †The 1999 figures used for comparison reflect changes in conference and division lineups to provide parallel, valid comparisons.

Conferences and Independent Groups Below Division I-AA

	Total Teams	Games	1999 Attend.	Avg. PG	Change† In Avg	Change In Total
1. Southern Intercoll. (II)#	10	44	305,640	6,946	Dn 323	Dn 50,535
2. North Central (II)	10	54	286,107	5,298	Up 63	Up 7,070
3. Central Intercoll. (II)	9	43	216,928	5,045	Up 1,584	Up 74,968
4. Mid-America Intercoll. (II)	10	55	231,291	4,205	Up 658	Up 36,189
5. Lone Star (II)	15	76	291,080	3,830	Dn 150	Dn 23,357
6. Gulf South (II)	10	51	194,725	3,818	Up 147	Up 3,824
7. Pennsylvania (II)	14	75	244,579	3,261	Up 204	Up 18,398
8. Old Dominion (III)#	7	35	103,435	2,955	Dn 690	Dn 27,800
9. Great Lakes Intercoll. (II)#	11	62	178,819	2,884	Dn 469	Up 1,116
10. American Southwest (III)	6	28	79,988	2,857	Up 72	Dn 3,556
11. Ohio Athletic (III)	10	48	124,202	2,588	Up 241	Up 4,485
12. Columbia Football (II)	3	13	33,512	2,578	Up 96	Up 1,241
13. Minnesota Intercoll. (III)	10	48	120,704	2,515	Dn 295	Dn 132
14. New Eng. Small Coll. (III)	10	40	104,943	2,624	Up 23	Up 914
15. South Atlantic (II)#	9	48	113,417	2,363	Dn 125	Up 1,451
16. Presidents' Athletic (III)#	5	26	60,861	2,341	Up 928	Up 31,182
17. Division II Indep.#	10	44	101,906	2,316	Up 662	Up 17,569
18. Wisconsin Intercoll. (III)	8	34	77,460	2,278	Dn 118	Dn 15,966
19. Middle Atlantic (III)	11	53	116,852	2,205	Up 171	Up 7,035
20. Illinois & Wisconsin (III)	8	37	79,958	2,161	Up 566	Up 24,133
21. Rocky Mountain (II)	9	46	97,537	2,120	Up 484	Up 27,188
22. Michigan Intercoll. (III)	6	29	60,410	2,083	Dn 225	Up 414
23. Southern Colleg. (III)#	7	34	66,995	1,970	Up 139	Up 1,090
24. New Jersey Ath. (III)	6	27	51,921	1,923	Up 269	Up 650
25. Northwest (III)#	6	30	57,350	1,912	Up 396	Up 17,937
26. Centennial FB (III)	8	40	74,261	1,857	Up 141	Up 5,612

1999 ATTENDANCE—CONFERENCES AND INDEPENDENT GROUPS BELOW DIVISION I-AA

	Total Teams	Games	1999 Attend.	Avg. PG	Change† In Avg		Change In Total	
27. Heartland Coll. (III)#	8	40	71,675	1,792	Dn	48	Dn	3,777
28. Iowa Intercoll. (III)#	11	56	100,249	1,790	Up	20	Up	1,097
29. Northern Sun (II)	7	34	58,636	1,725	Up	3	Up	6,988
30. Upstate Colleg. (III)#	4	21	35,355	1,684	Up	247	Up	12,363
31. University Ath. (III)	5	25	41,063	1,643	Up	34	Up	2,456
32. North Coast (III)#	8	42	68,719	1,636	Dn	108	Dn	1,036
33. Freedom FB (III)	7	38	61,395	1,616	Up	166	Up	13,546
34. Atlantic Central FB (III)	6	30	47,719	1,591	Dn	7	Up	1,378
35. West Virginia (II)	8	40	60,399	1,510	Dn	286	Dn	4,266
36. Division III Indep.#	21	92	122,166	1,328	Up	119	Up	3,677
37. Southern Calif. (III)	6	27	35,526	1,316	Dn	157	Dn	4,235
38. Eastern Football (II)	11	56	71,044	1,269	Up	76	Up	4,260
39. Midwest (III)	10	51	56,091	1,100	Up	93	Up	6,727
40. Illini-Badger (III)	5	24	23,715	988	Up	123	Up	1,230
41. New England FB (III)	14	67	57,729	862	Up	13	Up	1,707
42. St. Louis (III)#	4	22	17,548	798	Up	77	Up	3,845

@New conference. #Did not have the same lineup in 1999 as in 1998. $Rochester is a member of both the University Athletic Association and the Upstate Collegiate Athletic Conference. Case Reserve is a member of both the University Athletic Association and the North Coast Athletic Conference. Their attendance figures are included in each conference figure but counted only once for division totals. +The figures used for comparison reflect changes in conference and division lineups to provide parallel, valid comparisons.

Annual Team Attendance Leaders

Annual Leading Division I-A Teams in Per-Game Home Attendance

Year/Teams	G	Attendance	Avg.
1949			
Michigan	6	563,363	93,894
Ohio St.	5	382,146	76,429
Southern Methodist	8	484,000	60,500
1950			
Michigan	6	493,924	82,321
Ohio St.	5	368,021	73,604
Southern Methodist	5	309,000	61,800
1951			
Ohio St.	6	455,737	75,956
Michigan	6	445,635	74,273
Illinois	4	237,035	59,259
1952			
Ohio St.	6	453,911	75,652
Michigan	6	395,907	65,985
Texas	#5	311,160	62,232
1953			
Ohio St.	5	397,998	79,600
Southern California	6	413,617	68,936
Michigan	6	353,860	58,977
1954			
Ohio St.	6	479,840	79,973
Michigan	6	409,454	68,242
UCLA	5	318,371	63,674
1955			
Michigan	7	544,838	77,834
Ohio St.	7	493,178	70,454
Southern California	7	467,085	66,726
1956			
Ohio St.	6	494,575	82,429
Michigan	7	566,145	80,878
Minnesota	6	375,407	62,568
1957			
Michigan	6	504,954	84,159
Ohio St.	6	484,118	80,686
Minnesota	5	319,942	63,988
1958			
Ohio St.	6	499,352	82,225
Michigan	6	405,115	67,519
LSU	5	296,576	59,315
1959			
Ohio St.	6	495,536	82,589
Michigan	6	456,385	76,064
LSU	7	408,727	58,390
1960			
Ohio St.	5	413,583	82,717
Michigan St.	4	274,367	68,592
Michigan	6	374,682	62,447

Year/Teams	G	Attendance	Avg.
1961			
Ohio St.	5	414,712	82,942
Michigan	7	514,924	73,561
LSU	6	381,409	63,651
1962			
Ohio St.	6	497,644	82,941
Michigan St.	4	272,568	68,142
LSU	6	397,701	66,284
1963			
Ohio St.	5	416,023	83,205
LSU	6	396,846	66,141
Michigan St.	5	326,597	65,319
1964			
Ohio St.	7	583,740	83,391
Michigan St.	4	284,933	71,233
Michigan	6	388,829	64,805
1965			
Ohio St.	5	416,282	83,256
Michigan	6	480,487	80,081
Michigan St.	5	346,296	69,259
1966			
Ohio St.	6	488,399	81,400
Michigan St.	6	426,750	71,125
Michigan	6	413,599	68,933
1967			
Ohio St.	5	383,502	76,700
Michigan	6	447,289	74,548
Michigan St.	6	411,916	68,653
1968			
Ohio St.	6	482,564	80,427
Southern California	5	354,945	70,989
Michigan St.	6	414,177	69,030
1969			
Ohio St.	5	431,175	86,235
Michigan	6	428,780	71,463
Michigan St.	5	352,123	70,425
1970			
Ohio St.	5	432,451	86,490
Michigan	6	476,164	79,361
Purdue	5	340,090	68,018
1971			
Ohio St.	6	506,699	84,450
Michigan	7	564,376	80,625
Wisconsin	6	408,885	68,148
1972			
Michigan	6	513,398	85,566
Ohio St.	6	509,420	84,903
Nebraska	6	456,859	76,143
1973			
Ohio St.	6	523,369	87,228
Michigan	7	595,171	85,024
Nebraska	6	456,726	76,121

Year/Teams	G	Attendance	Avg.
1974			
Michigan	6	562,105	93,684
Ohio St.	6	525,314	87,552
Nebraska	7	534,388	76,341
1975			
Michigan	7	689,146	98,449
Ohio St.	6	527,141	87,856
Nebraska	7	533,368	76,195
1976			
Michigan	7	722,113	103,159
Ohio St.	6	526,216	87,702
Tennessee	7	564,922	80,703
1977			
Michigan	7	729,418	104,203
Ohio St.	6	525,535	87,589
Tennessee	7	582,979	83,283
1978			
Michigan	6	629,690	104,948
Ohio St.	7	614,881	87,840
Tennessee	†8	627,381	78,422
1979			
Michigan	7	730,315	104,331
Ohio St.	7	611,794	87,399
Tennessee	6	512,139	85,357
1980			
Michigan	6	625,750	104,292
Tennessee	†8	709,193	88,649
Ohio St.	7	615,476	87,925
1981			
Michigan	6	632,990	105,498
Tennessee	6	558,996	93,166
Ohio St.	6	521,760	86,960
1982			
Michigan	6	631,743	105,291
Tennessee	6	561,102	93,517
Ohio St.	7	623,152	89,022
1983			
Michigan	6	626,916	104,486
Ohio St.	6	534,110	89,018
Tennessee	†8	679,420	84,928
1984			
Michigan	7	726,734	103,819
Tennessee	7	654,602	93,515
Ohio St.	6	536,691	89,449
1985			
Michigan	6	633,530	105,588
Tennessee	7	658,690	94,099
Ohio St.	6	535,284	89,214
1986			
Michigan	6	631,261	105,210
Tennessee	7	643,317	91,902

Year/Teams	G	Attendance	Avg.
Ohio St.	6	536,210	89,368
1987			
Michigan	7	731,281	104,469
Tennessee	‡8	705,434	88,179
Ohio St.	6	511,772	85,295
1988			
Michigan	6	628,807	104,801
Tennessee	6	551,677	91,946
Ohio St.	6	516,972	86,162
1989			
Michigan	6	632,136	105,356
Tennessee	6	563,502	93,917
Ohio St.	6	511,812	85,302
1990			
Michigan	6	627,046	104,508
Tennessee	7	666,540	95,220
Ohio St.	6	536,297	89,383
1991			
Michigan	6	632,024	105,337
Tennessee	6	578,389	96,398
Penn St.	6	575,077	95,846
1992			
Michigan	6	635,201	105,867
Tennessee	6	575,544	95,924
Penn St.	6	569,195	94,866
1993			
Michigan	7	739,620	105,660
Tennessee	7	667,280	95,326
Penn St.	6	564,190	94,032
1994			
Michigan	6	637,300	106,217
Penn St.	6	577,731	96,289
Tennessee	6	573,821	95,637
1995			
Michigan	7	726,368	103,767
Tennessee	7	662,857	94,694
Penn St.	6	561,546	93,591
1996			
Michigan	6	635,589	105,932
Tennessee	6	632,509	105,418
Penn St.	6	577,001	96,167
1997			
Tennessee	6	639,227	106,538
Michigan	7	745,139	106,448
Penn St.	6	582,517	97,086
1998			
Michigan	6	665,787	110,965
Tennessee	6	641,484	106,914
Penn St.	6	579,190	96,532
1999			
Michigan	6	667,049	*111,175
Tennessee	7	*747,870	106,839
Penn St.	7	675,503	96,500

*Record. #Includes neutral-site game (Oklahoma) at Dallas counted as a home game (75,500). †Includes neutral-site game at Memphis counted as a home game. Attendance: 1978 (40,879), 1980 (50,003), 1983 (20,135). ‡Includes neutral-site game at East Rutherford (54,681).

Annual Leading Division I-AA Teams in Per-Game Home Attendance

Year	Team	Avg.
1978	Southern U.	28,333
1979	Grambling	29,900
1980	Southern U.	29,708
1981	Grambling	30,835
1982	Southern U.	32,265
1983	Jackson St.	29,117
1984	Jackson St.	29,215
1985	Yale	29,347
1986	Jackson St.	25,177
1987	Jackson St.	32,734
1988	Jackson St.	26,500
1989	Jackson St.	32,269
1990	Grambling	30,152
1991	Grambling	27,181
1992	Southern U.	28,906
1993	Jackson St.	28,917
1994	Alcorn St.	26,203
1995	Jackson St.	34,849
1996	Alcorn St.	21,536
1997	Jackson St.	*38,873
1998	South Florida	27,143
1999	Jackson St.	28,933

*Record.

Annual Leading Division II Teams in Per-Game Home Attendance

Year	Team	Avg.
1958	Southern Miss.	11,998
1959	Southern Miss.	13,964
1960	Florida A&M	12,083
1961	Akron	12,988
1962	Mississippi Col.	13,125
1963	San Diego St.	14,200
1964	Southern U.	12,633
1965	San Diego St.	15,227
1966	San Diego St.	15,972
1967	San Diego St.	*41,030
1968	San Diego St.	36,969
1969	Grambling	27,680
1970	Tampa	24,204
1971	Grambling	29,341
1972	Grambling	22,663
1973	Morgan St.	22,371
1974	Southern U.	33,563
1975	Texas Southern	22,800
1976	Southern U.	25,864
1977	Florida A&M	21,376
1978	Delaware	18,981
1979	Delaware	19,644
1980	Alabama A&M	15,820
1981	Norfolk St.	19,750
1982	Norfolk St.	16,183
1983	Norfolk St.	15,417
1984	Norfolk St.	18,500
1985	Norfolk St.	18,430
1986	Norfolk St.	13,836
1987	North Dakota St.	14,120
1988	UCF	21,905
1989	North Dakota St.	16,833
1990	Norfolk St.	14,904
1991	Norfolk St.	16,779
1992	Norfolk St.	14,196
1993	Norfolk St.	15,346
1994	Clark Atlanta	20,223
1995	Norfolk St.	16,593
1996	Norfolk St.	15,676
1997	North Dakota St.	12,512
1998	Tuskegee	13,269
1999	Tuskegee	13,336

*Record.

Annual Leading Division III Teams in Per-Game Home Attendance

Year	Team	Avg.
1974	Albany St. (Ga.)	9,380
1975	Wittenberg	7,000
1976	Morehouse	11,600
1977	Dayton	10,315
1978	Dayton	9,827
1979	UCF	11,240
1980	UCF	10,450
1981	Dayton	10,025
1982	Dayton	7,906
1983	Dayton	6,542
1984	Dayton	8,332
1985	Villanova	11,740
1986	Villanova	*11,883
1987	Trinity (Conn.)	6,254
1988	St. John's (Minn.)	5,788
1989	Dayton	5,962
1990	Dayton	6,185
1991	Dayton	7,657
1992	Dayton	6,098
1993	St. John's (Minn.)	6,655
1994	Hampden-Sydney	6,614
1995	St. John's (Minn.)	6,574
1996	St. John's (Minn.)	6,834
1997	Emory & Henry	5,853
1998	St. John's (Minn.)	6,562
1999	Mount Union	5,743

*Record.

1999 Statistical Leaders

1999 Division I-A Individual Leaders.....................450
1999 Division I-A Team Leaders..........................452
Longest Division I-A Plays of 1999 454
1999 Division I-AA Individual Leaders 455
1999 Division I-AA Team Leaders 457
Longest Division I-AA Plays of 1999.....................459
1999 Division II Individual Leaders 459
1999 Division II Team Leaders..............................462
Longest Division II Plays of 1999...........................463
1999 Division III Individual Leaders......................464
1999 Division III Team Leaders.............................466
Longest Division III Plays of 1999 468

1999 Division I-A Individual Leaders

Rushing

	1999 Class	G	Car.	Yards	Avg.	TD	Yds.PG
LaDainian Tomlinson, TCU	Jr.	11	268	1850	6.9	18	168.18
Ron Dayne, Wisconsin	Sr.	11	303	1834	6.1	19	166.73
Thomas Jones, Virginia	Sr.	11	334	1798	5.4	16	163.45
Travis Prentice, Miami (Ohio)	Sr.	11	354	1659	4.7	17	150.82
Lamont Jordan, Maryland	Jr.	11	266	1632	6.1	16	148.36
Demario Brown, Utah St.	Sr.	11	279	1536	5.5	14	139.64
Trung Canidate, Arizona	Sr.	12	253	1602	6.3	11	133.50
Frank Moreau, Louisville	Sr.	10	233	1289	5.5	17	128.90
Darren Davis, Iowa St.	Sr.	11	287	1388	4.8	14	126.18
Shaun Alexander, Alabama	Sr.	11	302	1383	4.6	19	125.73
Robert Cooper, Cincinnati	Sr.	10	248	1245	5.0	7	124.50
Thomas Hamner, Minnesota	Sr.	11	288	1362	4.7	10	123.82
Ken Simonton, Oregon St.	So.	11	276	1329	4.8	17	120.82
Kevin McDougal, Colorado St.	Sr.	10	207	1164	5.6	8	116.40
Anthony Thomas, Michigan	Jr.	11	283	1257	4.4	16	114.27
Avon Cobourne, West Virginia	Fr.	10	224	1139	5.1	10	113.90
Reuben Droughns, Oregon	Sr.	10	256	1139	4.4	9	113.90
Ketric Sanford, Houston	Sr.	11	224	1199	5.4	12	109.00
J. R. Redmond, Arizona St.	Sr.	10	224	1085	4.8	12	108.50
Chester Taylor, Toledo	Jr.	11	182	1176	6.5	12	106.91

Passing Efficiency

(Min. 15 att. per game)	1999 Class	G	Att.	Cmp.	Cmp. Pct.	Int.	Int. Pct.	Yards	Yds./Att.	TD	TD Pct.	Rating Points
Michael Vick, Virginia Tech	So.	10	152	90	59.21	5	3.29	1,840	12.11	12	7.89	180.4
Joe Hamilton, Georgia Tech	Sr.	11	305	203	66.56	11	3.61	3,060	10.03	29	9.51	175.0
Chad Pennington, Marshall	Sr.	12	405	275	67.90	11	2.72	3,799	9.38	37	9.14	171.4
Billy Volek, Fresno St.	Sr.	12	355	235	66.20	3	.85	2,559	7.21	30	8.45	152.9
Tim Rattay, Louisiana Tech	Sr.	10	516	342	66.28	12	2.33	3,922	7.60	35	6.78	147.9
Jay Stuckey, UTEP	Sr.	12	225	145	64.44	13	5.78	1,918	8.52	15	6.67	146.5
Chris Weinke, Florida St.	Jr.	11	377	232	61.54	14	3.71	3,103	8.23	25	6.63	145.1
Dan Ellis, Virginia	Jr.	10	258	156	60.47	10	3.88	2,050	7.95	20	7.75	145.0
Jeff Kelly, Southern Miss.	So.	11	260	153	58.85	11	4.23	2,062	7.93	21	8.08	143.7
Tim Lester, Western Mich.	Sr.	12	470	282	60.00	13	2.77	3,639	7.74	34	7.23	143.4
Todd Husak, Stanford	Sr.	10	308	176	57.14	11	3.57	2,688	8.73	18	5.84	142.6
Chris Redman, Louisville	Sr.	11	489	317	64.83	13	2.66	3,647	7.46	29	5.93	141.7
Mike Moschetti, Colorado	Sr.	10	331	204	61.63	12	3.63	2,693	8.14	18	5.44	140.7
Jarious Jackson, Notre Dame	Sr.	12	316	184	58.23	14	4.43	2,753	8.71	17	5.38	140.3

Total Offense

	RUSHING Car.	Gain	Loss	Net	PASSING Att.	Yards	Plays	TOTAL OFFENSE Yards	Avg.	TDR*	Yds.PG
Tim Rattay, Louisiana Tech	46	67	179	-112	516	3,922	562	3,810	6.78	35	381.00
Joe Hamilton, Georgia Tech	154	861	127	734	305	3,060	459	3,794	8.27	35	344.91
Drew Brees, Purdue	70	315	134	181	494	3,531	564	3,712	6.58	25	337.45
David Neill, Nevada	100	505	296	209	423	3,402	523	3,611	6.90	25	328.27
Chad Pennington, Marshall	55	204	99	105	405	3,799	460	3,904	8.49	39	325.33
Chris Redman, Louisville	43	68	178	-110	489	3,647	532	3,537	6.65	30	321.55
Kevin Feterik, Brigham Young	88	256	333	-77	452	3,554	540	3,477	6.44	26	316.09
Dan Robinson, Hawaii	60	105	196	-91	556	3,853	616	3,762	6.11	32	313.50
Josh Heupel, Oklahoma	47	98	196	-98	500	3,460	547	3,362	6.15	35	305.64
Patrick Ramsey, Tulane	64	99	160	-61	513	3,410	577	3,349	5.80	26	304.45
Tim Lester, Western Mich.	55	154	189	-35	470	3,639	525	3,604	6.86	35	300.33
Vic Penn, UCF	100	481	313	168	455	3,078	555	3,246	5.85	20	295.09
Dusty Bonner, Kentucky	111	281	422	-141	465	3,266	576	3,125	5.43	29	284.09
Mike Moschetti, Colorado	85	305	180	125	331	2,693	416	2,818	6.77	23	281.80
Antwaan Randle El, Indiana	224	991	203	788	279	2,277	503	3,065	6.09	30	278.64
Chris Weinke, Florida St.	31	40	149	-109	377	3,103	408	2,994	7.34	25	272.18

*Touchdowns responsible for are players' TDs scored and passed for.

Joe Hamilton of Georgia Tech placed second in Division I-A in both passing efficiency (175.0) and total offense (344.91 yards per game) in 1999.

Receptions Per Game

	1999 Class	G	Rec.	Yards	TD	Rec.PG
Trevor Insley, Nevada	Sr.	11	134	2,060	13	12.18
Chris Daniels, Purdue	Sr.	11	109	1,133	5	9.91
Jajuan Dawson, Tulane	Sr.	10	96	1,051	8	9.60
Arnold Jackson, Louisville	Sr.	11	101	1,209	9	9.18
James Whalen, Kentucky	Sr.	11	90	1,019	10	8.18
Charles Lee, UCF	Sr.	11	87	1,133	5	7.91
Peter Warrick, Florida St.	Sr.	9	71	934	8	7.89
Drew Haddad, Buffalo	Sr.	11	85	1,158	6	7.73
Kwame Cavil, Texas	Jr.	13	100	1,188	6	7.69
James Jordan, Louisiana Tech	So.	11	81	824	11	7.36
Dennis Northcutt, Arizona	Sr.	12	88	1,422	8	7.33
Adrian Burnette, Tulane	Jr.	11	79	1,095	7	7.18
John Simon, Louisiana Tech	So.	11	79	757	2	7.18
Delwyn Daigre, Louisiana Tech	So.	11	77	1,084	9	7.00
Latef Grim, Pittsburgh	Jr.	11	75	1,106	4	6.82

Receiving Yards Per Game

	1999 Class	G	Rec.	Yards	TD	Yds.PG
Trevor Insley, Nevada	Sr.	11	134	2,060	13	187.27
Troy Walters, Stanford	Sr.	11	74	1,456	10	132.36
Dennis Northcutt, Arizona	Sr.	12	88	1,422	8	118.50
Arnold Jackson, Louisville	Sr.	11	101	1,209	9	109.91
Drew Haddad, Buffalo	Sr.	11	85	1,158	6	105.27
Jajuan Dawson, Tulane	Sr.	10	96	1,051	8	105.10
Dwight Carter, Hawaii	Sr.	12	77	1,253	9	104.42
Peter Warrick, Florida St.	Sr.	9	71	934	8	103.78
Chris Daniels, Purdue	Sr.	11	109	1,133	5	103.00
Charles Lee, UCF	Sr.	11	87	1,133	5	103.00
Latef Grim, Pittsburgh	Jr.	11	75	1,106	4	100.55
Kelly Campbell, Georgia Tech	So.	11	69	1,105	10	100.45
Adrian Burnette, Tulane	Jr.	11	79	1,095	7	99.55
Jammarl O'Neal, Central Mich.	Fr.	11	59	1,085	6	98.64
Delwyn Daigre, Louisiana Tech	So.	11	77	1,084	9	98.55

Interceptions

	1999 Class	G	Int.	Yards	TD	Int.PG
Deltha O'Neal, California	Sr.	11	9	280	4	.82
Deon Grant, Tennessee	Jr.	11	9	167	1	.82
Rodregis Brooks, UAB	Jr.	11	9	152	1	.82
Erik Olson, Colorado St.	Sr.	9	6	93	1	.67
Jamar Fletcher, Wisconsin	So.	11	7	135	2	.64
Mike James, Houston	Sr.	11	7	57	1	.64
Anthony Vontoure, Washington	So.	10	6	99	2	.60
Kevin Harvey, Temple	Sr.	10	6	55	1	.60
Quincy Lejay, Hawaii	Sr.	12	7	151	3	.58
Tim Smith, Stanford	Sr.	11	6	86	0	.55
Robert Carswell, Clemson	Jr.	11	6	72	0	.55

Scoring

	1999 Class	G	TD	XP	FG	Pts.	Pts.PG
Shaun Alexander, Alabama	Sr.	11	24	0	0	144	13.09
Travis Prentice, Miami (Ohio)	Sr.	11	21	0	0	126	11.45
Sebastian Janikowski, Florida St.	Jr.	11	0	47	23	116	10.55
Ron Dayne, Wisconsin	Sr.	11	19	0	0	114	10.36
Frank Moreau, Louisville	Sr.	10	17	0	0	102	10.20
LaDainian Tomlinson, TCU	Jr.	11	18	0	0	108	9.82
Shayne Graham, Virginia Tech	Sr.	11	0	56	17	107	9.73
Ken Simonton, Oregon St.	So.	11	17	4	0	106	9.64
Travis Zachery, Clemson	So.	10	16	0	0	96	9.60
Jamie Rheem, Kansas St.	Jr.	10	0	41	18	95	9.50
Thomas Jones, Virginia	Sr.	11	17	0	0	102	9.27
Lamont Jordan, Maryland	Jr.	11	17	0	0	102	9.27
Neil Rackers, Illinois	Sr.	11	1	35	20	101	9.18
Travis Forney, Penn St.	Sr.	12	0	44	21	107	8.92

All-Purpose Yards

	1999 Class	G	Rush	Rec.	PR	KOR	Total Yards	Yds.PG
Trevor Insley, Nevada	Sr.	11	5	2,060	111	0	2,176	197.82
Dennis Northcutt, Arizona	Sr.	12	200	1,422	436	191	2,249	187.42
Thomas Jones, Virginia	Sr.	11	1,798	239	17	0	2,054	186.73
LaDainian Tomlinson, TCU	Jr.	11	1,850	55	0	69	1,974	179.45
Travis Prentice, Miami (Ohio)	Sr.	11	1,659	270	0	0	1,929	175.36
Troy Walters, Stanford	Sr.	11	6	1,456	131	284	1,877	170.64
Deuce McAllister, Mississippi	Jr.	10	809	201	30	652	1,692	169.20
Ron Dayne, Wisconsin	Sr.	11	1,834	9	0	0	1,843	167.55
Lamont Jordan, Maryland	Jr.	11	1,632	208	0	0	1,840	167.27
Demario Brown, Utah St.	Sr.	11	1,536	282	0	0	1,818	165.27
Shaun Alexander, Alabama	Sr.	11	1,383	323	0	90	1,796	163.27
Frank Moreau, Louisville	Sr.	10	1,289	285	0	0	1,574	157.40
Trung Canidate, Arizona	Sr.	12	1,602	253	0	0	1,855	154.58
Thomas Hamner, Minnesota	Sr.	11	1,362	298	0	0	1,660	150.91
Anthony Thomas, Michigan	Jr.	11	1,257	166	0	216	1,639	149.00
Dez White, Georgia Tech	Jr.	11	67	860	0	689	1,616	146.91
Deonce Whitaker, San Jose St.	Jr.	9	769	138	0	396	1,303	144.78
Darren Davis, Iowa St.	Sr.	11	1,388	160	0	43	1,591	144.64
Ketric Sanford, Houston	Sr.	11	1,199	113	0	277	1,589	144.45
Robert Cooper, Cincinnati	Sr.	10	1,245	180	0	0	1,425	142.50

California's Deltha O'Neal tied for the Division I-A lead in interceptions in 1999, grabbing nine in 11 games, and was fourth in kickoff returns (29.21 yards per return). He returned four of his interceptions for touchdowns to set a new division record.

Dennis Northcutt of Arizona made an impact in several different ways in 1999. The Wildcat led Division I-A in punt returns (18.96 yards per return), came in second in all-purpose yards (187.42 yards per game) and wound up third in receiving yards per game (118.50).

Punt Returns

(Min. 1.2 per game)	1999 Class	No.	Yds.	TD	Avg.
Dennis Northcutt, Arizona	Sr.	23	436	2	18.96
Bobby Newcombe, Nebraska	Jr.	16	294	1	18.38
Vinny Sutherland, Purdue	Jr.	17	295	2	17.35
Rodregis Brooks, UAB	Jr.	19	325	0	17.11
Stevonne Smith, Utah	Jr.	29	495	3	17.07

Kickoff Returns

(Min. 1.2 per game)	1999 Class	No.	Yds.	TD	Avg.
James Williams, Marshall	Sr.	15	493	1	32.87
Brandon Daniels, Oklahoma	Sr.	16	508	1	31.75
John Stone, Wake Forest	So.	13	389	1	29.92
Deltha O'Neal, California	Sr.	19	555	1	29.21
Ben Kelly, Colorado	Jr.	19	547	2	28.79

Punting

(Min. 3.6 per game)	1999 Class	No.	Avg.
Andrew Bayes, East Caro.	Sr.	47	48.06
Brian Schmitz, North Carolina	Sr.	74	47.81
Shane Lechler, Texas A&M	Sr.	60	46.45
Ray Cheetany, UNLV	Jr.	65	45.38
Dan Hadenfeldt, Nebraska	Sr.	65	44.98

Field Goals

	1999 Class	G	FGA	FG	Pct.	FGPG
Sebastian Janikowski, Florida St.	Jr.	11	30	23	.767	2.09
Neil Rackers, Illinois	Sr.	11	25	20	.800	1.82
Jamie Rheem, Kansas St.	Jr.	10	21	18	.857	1.80
Jeff Chandler, Florida	Jr.	12	24	21	.875	1.75
Travis Forney, Penn St.	Sr.	12	26	21	.808	1.75

1999 Division I-A Team Leaders

Total Offense

	G	Plays	Yds.	Avg.	TD*	Yds.PG
Georgia Tech	11	822	5,599	6.8	58	509.00
Nevada	11	843	5,192	6.2	39	472.00
Arizona	12	870	5,663	6.5	42	471.92
Louisiana Tech	11	822	5,181	6.3	50	471.00
Stanford	11	793	5,138	6.5	47	467.09
Louisville	11	851	5,136	6.0	48	466.91
Marshall	12	841	5,584	6.6	57	465.33
Purdue	11	859	5,016	5.8	38	456.00
Virginia Tech	11	758	4,970	6.6	49	451.82
Oregon St.	11	857	4,774	5.6	41	434.00
Oklahoma	11	808	4,699	5.8	49	427.18
Florida St.	11	820	4,683	5.7	44	425.73
Brigham Young	11	833	4,682	5.6	38	425.64
Colorado	11	843	4,674	5.5	37	424.91
Wisconsin	11	788	4,671	5.9	44	424.64
Cincinnati	11	870	4,668	5.4	36	424.36
Oregon	11	819	4,657	5.7	41	423.36

*Touchdowns scored by rushing/passing only.

Total Defense

	G	Plays	Yds.	Avg.	TD*	Yds.PG
Mississippi St.	11	734	2,448	3.3	14	222.5
Kansas St.	11	693	2,585	3.7	18	235.0
Virginia Tech	11	732	2,720	3.7	15	247.3
Nebraska	12	815	3,022	3.7	17	251.8
TCU	11	729	3,129	4.3	24	284.5
Texas	13	876	3,727	4.3	28	286.7
Marshall	12	882	3,516	4.0	11	293.0
Southern Miss.	11	754	3,235	4.3	14	294.1
Alabama	12	749	3,568	4.8	26	297.3
Oklahoma St.	11	683	3,273	4.8	30	297.5
Tennessee	11	708	3,275	4.6	18	297.7
Michigan St.	11	764	3,289	4.3	23	299.0
Texas A&M	11	766	3,310	4.3	24	300.9
Syracuse	11	738	3,313	4.5	22	301.2

*Touchdowns allowed by rushing or passing only.

Rushing Offense

	G	Car.	Yds.	Avg.	TD	Yds.PG
Navy	12	680	3,506	5.2	30	292.2
Air Force	11	635	3,140	4.9	25	285.5
Wisconsin	11	583	3,075	5.3	34	279.5
Nebraska	12	633	3,191	5.0	37	265.9
Army	11	636	2,915	4.6	24	265.0
Ohio	11	624	2,883	4.6	26	262.1
Rice	11	655	2,835	4.3	22	257.7
Virginia Tech	11	559	2,793	5.0	35	253.9
TCU	11	518	2,640	5.1	26	240.0
Toledo	11	492	2,631	5.3	21	239.2
Minnesota	11	517	2,630	5.1	25	239.1
Maryland	11	492	2,545	5.2	22	231.4
Georgia Tech	11	503	2,482	4.9	29	225.6
New Mexico St.	11	576	2,450	4.3	22	222.7
Arizona	12	504	2,626	5.2	23	218.8
Houston	11	465	2,306	5.0	22	209.6

Rushing Defense

	G	Car.	Yds.	Avg.	TD	Yds.PG
Mississippi St.	11	403	736	1.8	7	66.9
Alabama	12	335	904	2.7	6	75.3
Virginia Tech	11	388	835	2.2	5	75.9
Mississippi	11	369	846	2.3	10	76.9
Michigan St.	11	376	847	2.3	7	77.0
Nebraska	12	427	928	2.2	6	77.3
Tennessee	11	364	986	2.7	3	89.6
Southern Miss.	11	403	1,006	2.5	6	91.5
Florida	12	416	1,099	2.6	15	91.6
Florida St.	11	387	1,087	2.8	6	98.8
Marshall	12	450	1,208	2.7	3	100.7
Arkansas	11	392	1,109	2.8	14	100.8
TCU	11	408	1,110	2.7	11	100.9
Brigham Young	11	389	1,132	2.9	9	102.9
Auburn	11	358	1,133	3.2	11	103.0
Georgia	11	356	1,150	3.2	14	104.5

Scoring Offense

	G	Pts.	Avg.
Virginia Tech	11	455	41.4
Georgia Tech	11	448	40.7
Kansas St.	11	433	39.4
Louisville	11	412	37.5

1999 DIVISION I-A TEAM LEADERS

	G	Pts.	Avg.
Florida St.	11	412	37.5
Stanford	11	409	37.2
Marshall	12	442	36.8
Oklahoma	11	405	36.8
Wisconsin	11	392	35.6
Louisiana Tech	11	389	35.4
Oregon	11	386	35.1
Nebraska	12	411	34.3
Texas	13	444	34.2
Miami (Fla.)	12	404	33.7
Fresno St.	12	397	33.1
Boise St.	12	396	33.0
Utah	11	363	33.0
Penn St.	12	393	32.8
Purdue	11	359	32.6

Scoring Defense

	G	Pts.	Avg.
Virginia Tech	11	116	10.5
Marshall	12	134	11.2
Nebraska	12	150	12.5
Kansas St.	11	144	13.1
Wisconsin	11	145	13.2
Mississippi St.	11	149	13.5
Tennessee	11	163	14.8
Southern Miss.	11	172	15.6
Minnesota	11	172	15.6
Florida St.	11	174	15.8
Memphis	11	182	16.5
Miami (Fla.)	12	207	17.3

Pass Efficiency Defense

	G	Att.	Cmp.	Cmp. Pct.	Int.	Int. Pct.	Yards	Yds./ Att.	TD	TD Pct.	Rating Points
Kansas St.	11	315	118	37.46	21	6.67	1,364	4.33	5	1.59	65.74
Nebraska	12	388	165	42.53	18	4.64	2,094	5.40	11	2.84	87.94
Marshall	12	432	226	52.31	24	5.56	2,308	5.34	8	1.85	92.19
Mississippi St.	11	331	172	51.96	15	4.53	1,712	5.17	7	2.11	93.33
Wisconsin	11	351	176	50.14	16	4.56	1,994	5.68	8	2.28	96.27
Utah	11	359	179	49.86	16	4.46	2,113	5.89	7	1.95	96.82
Virginia Tech	11	344	166	48.26	10	2.91	1,885	5.48	10	2.91	98.06
Minnesota	11	340	159	46.76	8	2.35	1,921	5.65	9	2.65	98.25
Oregon St.	11	355	174	49.01	13	3.66	2,104	5.93	8	2.25	98.91
East Caro.	11	389	200	51.41	17	4.37	2,305	5.93	10	2.57	100.93
Miami (Fla.)	12	396	214	54.04	17	4.29	2,307	5.83	8	2.02	101.06
Texas	13	374	166	44.39	10	2.67	2,353	6.29	11	2.94	101.59
New Mexico St.	11	344	156	45.35	16	4.65	2,147	6.24	17	4.94	104.78
Texas A&M	11	363	203	55.92	17	4.68	2,053	5.66	12	3.31	104.97

Net Punting

	Punts	Avg.	No. Ret.	Yds. Ret.	Net Avg.
Texas A&M	60	46.5	25	227	42.7
Florida St.	46	42.7	16	107	40.3
Michigan St.	60	42.8	26	155	40.2
Kentucky	49	41.0	13	53	39.9
New Mexico St.	63	42.0	23	136	39.9
San Jose St.	58	43.3	35	198	39.9
Oklahoma	55	42.1	18	123	39.9
Tennessee	57	42.6	28	159	39.8
California	87	43.6	42	341	39.7
North Carolina	81	47.7	45	654	39.6
Georgia Tech	31	42.8	13	102	39.5
Nebraska	67	43.6	33	281	39.4
Cincinnati	55	42.2	14	154	39.4
Wisconsin	42	40.9	15	64	39.3
North Texas	84	42.4	42	266	39.2
Pittsburgh	63	40.5	21	88	39.1

Punt Returns

	G	No.	Yds.	TD	Avg.
UAB	11	23	440	2	19.1
Arizona	12	29	509	2	17.6
Colorado St.	11	34	567	2	16.7
Utah	11	41	654	3	16.0
Oklahoma St.	11	45	679	2	15.1

	G	Pts.	Avg.
Utah	11	194	17.6
East Caro.	11	197	17.9
TCU	11	199	18.1
Oklahoma	11	202	18.4
Mississippi	11	203	18.5
Wake Forest	11	206	18.7
Texas A&M	11	208	18.9
Arkansas	11	208	18.9

Passing Offense

	G	Att.	Cmp.	Int.	Pct.	Yards	Yds./ Att.	TD	Yds.PG
Louisiana Tech	11	566	372	12	65.7	4,434	7.8	38	403.1
Louisville	11	501	322	13	64.3	3,687	7.4	29	335.2
Hawaii	12	577	297	19	51.5	3,944	6.8	28	328.7
Purdue	11	508	306	12	60.2	3,608	7.1	23	328.0
Tulane	11	556	326	25	58.6	3,600	6.5	25	327.3
Nevada	11	457	263	9	57.5	3,590	7.9	20	326.4
Marshall	12	427	286	11	67.0	3,901	9.1	37	325.1
Brigham Young	11	458	280	16	61.1	3,567	7.8	25	324.3
Oklahoma	11	512	319	15	62.3	3,539	6.9	31	321.7
Stanford	11	385	219	12	56.9	3,448	9.0	25	313.5
Western Mich.	12	477	286	13	60.0	3,742	7.8	34	311.8
Florida St.	11	423	250	17	59.1	3,332	7.9	27	302.9
Kentucky	11	468	304	13	65.0	3,289	7.0	26	299.0
Oregon St.	11	432	211	9	48.8	3,160	7.3	18	287.3
UCF	11	472	268	11	56.8	3,159	6.7	16	287.2
Georgia Tech	11	319	208	12	65.2	3,117	9.8	29	283.4
Texas	13	504	290	10	57.5	3,572	7.1	23	274.8

	G	No.	Yds.	TD	Avg.
Purdue	11	21	313	2	14.9
Pittsburgh	11	25	354	1	14.2
East Caro.	11	30	424	1	14.1
Kentucky	11	18	248	1	13.8
Minnesota	11	44	605	2	13.8
Miami (Fla.)	12	40	528	2	13.2
Southern Miss.	11	27	345	0	12.8
Utah St.	11	33	420	1	12.7
Michigan St.	11	46	584	2	12.7
Oklahoma	11	38	482	2	12.7
San Jose St.	10	22	277	1	12.6
Notre Dame	12	21	263	1	12.5
Wisconsin	11	24	298	1	12.4
Florida St.	11	37	459	1	12.4
Virginia Tech	11	42	518	1	12.3

Kickoff Returns

	G	No.	Yds.	TD	Avg.
TCU	11	27	742	1	27.5
Maryland	11	28	740	1	26.4
UNLV	11	39	993	1	25.5
Oregon	11	45	1,120	1	24.9
Wyoming	11	27	670	1	24.8
Oklahoma	11	30	743	1	24.8
Wisconsin	11	19	470	2	24.7
Marshall	12	28	691	1	24.7
Virginia Tech	11	22	539	0	24.5
Kansas St.	11	30	728	0	24.3

Turnover Margin

	TURNOVERS GAINED			TURNOVERS LOST			Margin/
	Fum.	Int.	Total	Fum.	Int.	Total	Game
Kansas St.	17	21	38	12	9	21	1.55
Illinois	11	14	25	7	5	12	1.18
Southern California	18	21	39	11	14	25	1.17
Marshall	6	24	30	6	11	17	1.08
Wisconsin	6	16	22	8	3	11	1.00
Stanford	13	17	30	8	12	20	.91
Southern Miss.	15	15	30	6	14	20	.91
Michigan	12	10	22	4	8	12	.91
Texas	23	10	33	12	10	22	.85
Boise St.	15	14	29	5	14	19	.83

Longest Division I-A Plays of 1999

Rushing

Player, Team (Opponent)	Yards
Deonce Whitaker, San Jose St. (LSU)	80
Dennis Northcutt, Arizona (Oregon)	80
Dan Alexander, Nebraska (Colorado)	80
LaDainian Tomlinson, TCU (Arkansas St.)	79
Raheem Lambert, Navy (Rice)	79
William Andrews, Northern Ill. (Ball St.)	79
Trung Canidate, Arizona (Washington)	74
Deon Burnett, Washington St. (La.-Lafayette)	73
Arland Bruce, Minnesota (Iowa)	73
Chester Taylor, Toledo (Bowling Green)	72

Passing

Passer-Receiver, Team (Opponent)	Yards
Drew Brees-Vinny Sutherland, Purdue (Northwestern)	99
Randy McCown-Chris Taylor, Texas A&M (Tulsa)	96
Chris Finlen-Darrell Hill, Northern Ill. (Eastern Mich.)	96
Billy Cockerham-Antoine Henderson, Minnesota (Ohio)	89
Jonathan Beasley-Quincy Morgan, Kansas St. (Kansas)	88
Mike Moschetti-Javon Green, Colorado (Oklahoma)	88
Jack Hawley-Derrick Lewis, San Diego St. (UNLV)	87
Ben Leard-Ronney Daniels, Auburn (LSU)	84
Dan Ellis-Thomas Jones, Virginia (Buffalo)	84
Neil Suber-Ken Coutain, Memphis (Tennessee)	82

Interception Returns

Player, Team (Opponent)	Yards
Deltha O'Neal, California (Oregon)	100
Adrian Singleton, UAB (Cincinnati)	96
T. J. Turner, Michigan St. (Purdue)	88
Antwon Black, North Carolina (Virginia)	82
Ja'quay Wilburn, North Texas (Texas Tech)	81
Aric Morris, Michigan St. (Purdue)	76
Michael Brown, Louisville (Chattanooga)	74

Player, Team (Opponent)	Yards
Lamar Chapman, Kansas St. (UTEP)	69
Jerry Porter, West Virginia (Miami [Ohio])	68
Benji Peacock, Northern Ill. (Kent)	67

Punt Returns

Player, Team (Opponent)	Yards
Bruce Branch, Penn St. (Indiana)	90
Dallas Davis, Colorado St. (Utah)	89
Bobby Newcombe, Nebraska (Kansas)	86
Antonio Brown, West Virginia (Rutgers)	80
Bruce Branch, Penn St. (Michigan)	79
Peter Warrick, Florida St. (North Carolina)	75
Robert Kilow, Arkansas St. (Idaho)	75
Luke Leverson, Minnesota (Illinois)	74
Henri Cholds, Kansas (Cal St. Northridge)	71
Eric Parker, Tennessee (Memphis)	69
Hank Poteat, Pittsburgh (Temple)	69

Kickoff Returns

Player, Team (Opponent)	Yards
Leonard Scott, Tennessee (Georgia)	100
Bo Carroll, Florida (LSU)	100
Ben Kelly, Colorado (Missouri)	100
Lincoln Dupree, Eastern Mich. (Northern Ill.)	100
Deltha O'Neal, California (Stanford)	100
Rashad McDade, Western Mich. (Youngstown St.)	99
Zek Parker, Louisville (Chattanooga)	97
Carl Nesmith, Kansas (Colorado)	*97
Len Ware, UNLV (Utah)	97
William Andrews, Northern Ill. (Buffalo)	95

*Did not score.

Field Goals

Player, Team (Opponent)	Yards
Terence Kitchens, Texas A&M (Southern Miss.)	62
Jamie Rheem, Kansas St. (Utah St.)	57
Hayden Epstein, Michigan (Michigan St.)	56
Aaron Elling, Wyoming (Colorado St.)	56
John Anderson, Washington (UCLA)	56
Brad Bohn, Utah St. (Brigham Young)	55
Aaron Elling, Wyoming (Weber St.)	55
Paul Edinger, Michigan St. (Wisconsin)	55
Kevin Kerr, Ohio (Miami [Ohio])	55

Punts

Player, Team (Opponent)	Yards
Mark Fazzolari, West Virginia (Virginia Tech)	78
Jeff Ferguson, Oklahoma (Colorado)	73
Brian Schmitz, North Carolina (Houston)	72
Pat Fleming, Bowling Green (Central Mich.)	68
Dan Hadenfeldt, Nebraska (Colorado)	67
Brad Kroft, Ball St. (Akron)	65
Dan Hadenfeldt, Nebraska (Colorado)	64
Kent Baker, Northern Ill. (Western Mich.)	63
Jeremy Aldrich, Colorado (Missouri)	63
Brian Schmitz, North Carolina (Duke)	62

1999 Division I-AA Individual Leaders

Rushing

	1999 Class	G	Car.	Yards	Avg.	TD	Yds.PG
Charles Roberts, Cal St. Sacramento	Jr.	11	303	2,082	6.9	22	189.27
Adrian Peterson, Ga. Southern	So.	11	248	1,807	7.3	28	164.27
Randall Joseph, Colgate	Jr.	9	193	1,446	7.5	15	160.67
Corey Holmes, Mississippi Val.	Jr.	11	331	1,692	5.1	11	153.82
Curtis Keaton, James Madison	Sr.	11	290	1,659	5.7	19	150.82
Marcel Shipp, Massachusetts	Jr.	11	327	1,572	4.8	20	142.91
Ralph Saldiveri, Iona	Jr.	10	255	1,400	5.5	16	140.00
Rick Sarille, Wagner	Sr.	10	274	1,373	5.0	15	137.30
Derek O'Neal, South Carolina St.	Sr.	10	297	1,352	4.6	15	135.20
Charles Dunn, Portland St.	Jr.	11	279	1,478	5.3	16	134.36
Jimmy Lee, Dayton	Sr.	8	172	1,052	6.1	10	131.50
Tony Taylor, Northwestern St.	So.	11	263	1,441	5.5	16	131.00
Jovan Griffith, Eastern Wash.	So.	10	210	1,275	6.1	14	127.50
Craig Young, Cal Poly	Sr.	11	275	1,380	5.0	8	125.45
Louis Ivory, Furman	So.	11	230	1,376	6.0	14	125.09
Ronald Jean, Lehigh	Sr.	11	264	1,358	5.1	23	123.45
Destry Wright, Jackson St.	Sr.	14	322	1,703	5.3	12	121.64
Kris Ryan, Pennsylvania	So.	10	214	1,197	5.6	10	119.70
Charles Tharp, Western Ill.	Jr.	11	282	1,311	4.6	12	119.18
Matt Cannon, Southern Utah	Jr.	11	203	1,310	6.5	23	119.09

Passing Efficiency

(Min. 15 att. per game)

	1999 Class	G	Att.	Cmp.	Cmp. Pct.	Int.	Int. Pct.	Yards	Yds./Att.	TD	TD Pct.	Rating Points
Drew Miller, Montana	Jr.	10	368	240	65.22	8	2.17	3,461	9.40	32	8.70	168.6
Mark Washington, Jackson St.	Sr.	12	287	147	51.22	10	3.48	2,788	9.71	29	10.10	159.2
Jimmy Blanchard, Portland St.	Jr.	11	355	212	59.72	3	.85	3,098	8.73	29	8.17	158.3
Phil Stambaugh, Lehigh	Sr.	11	347	236	68.01	13	3.75	2,995	8.63	26	7.49	157.7
JaJuan Seider, Florida A&M	Sr.	11	253	150	59.29	2	.79	2,086	8.25	23	9.09	157.0
Chris Chaloupka, Sam Houston St.	Sr.	10	271	168	61.99	13	4.80	2,503	9.24	21	7.75	155.6
Ryan Helming, Northern Iowa	Jr.	11	403	253	62.78	14	3.47	3,469	8.61	31	7.69	153.5
Justin Fuente, Murray St.	Sr.	11	400	240	60.00	9	2.25	3,497	8.74	27	6.75	151.2
Jay Rodgers, Southwest Mo. St.	Sr.	11	326	206	63.19	13	3.99	2,741	8.41	24	7.36	150.1
Ricky Ray, Cal St. Sacramento	Jr.	10	291	182	62.54	8	2.75	2,422	8.32	20	6.87	149.6
Brock Nutter, Troy St.	So.	11	218	125	57.34	7	3.21	1,994	9.15	13	5.96	147.4
Jim Lopusznick, Fairfield	Sr.	10	298	160	53.69	7	2.35	2,281	7.65	27	9.06	143.2
Lionel Hayes, Grambling	Sr.	11	366	188	51.37	6	1.64	2,935	8.02	30	8.20	142.5
Sherard Poteete, Southern Ill.	Jr.	11	348	203	58.33	10	2.87	2,777	7.98	24	6.90	142.4
Chris Perkins, Tennessee St.	Sr.	10	176	103	58.52	6	3.41	1,385	7.87	13	7.39	142.2
Ryan Vena, Colgate	Sr.	11	229	134	58.52	12	5.24	1,917	8.37	16	6.99	141.4
David Corley, William & Mary	Fr.	11	221	123	55.66	9	4.07	1,760	7.96	18	8.14	141.3
Giovanni Carmazzi, Hofstra	Sr.	11	346	216	62.43	10	2.89	2,651	7.66	21	6.07	141.0
Travis Brown, Northern Ariz.	Sr.	11	420	246	58.57	7	1.67	3,057	7.28	31	7.38	140.7
Tony Bellamy, Alabama A&M	Jr.	10	164	88	53.66	5	3.05	1,342	8.18	12	7.32	140.4

Total Offense

	RUSHING Car.	Gain	Loss	Net	PASSING Att.	Yards	TOTAL OFFENSE Plays	Yards	Avg.	TDR*	Yds.PG
Joe Lee, Towson	31	13	150	-137	577	4,168	608	4,031	6.63	22	366.45
Drew Miller, Montana	26	16	162	-146	368	3,461	394	3,315	8.41	32	331.50
James Perry, Brown	25	40	112	-72	467	3,255	492	3,183	6.47	27	318.30
Chris Sanders, Chattanooga	34	47	95	-48	490	3,539	524	3,491	6.66	28	317.36
Ryan Helming, Northern Iowa	46	121	121	0	403	3,469	449	3,469	7.73	34	315.36
David Dinkins, Morehead St.	200	1,424	286	1,138	265	2,011	465	3,149	6.77	40	314.90
Marcus Brady, Cal St. Northridge	92	390	297	93	483	3,326	575	3,419	5.95	25	310.82
Justin Fuente, Murray St.	36	42	132	-90	400	3,497	436	3,407	7.81	28	309.73
Sherard Poteete, Southern Ill.	128	746	219	527	348	2,777	476	3,304	6.94	35	300.36
Joe Walland, Yale	99	493	130	363	302	2,207	401	2,570	6.41	21	285.56
Jimmy Blanchard, Portland St.	38	114	111	3	355	3,098	393	3,101	7.89	29	281.91
Kevin McCarthy, Idaho St.	110	331	308	23	414	3,032	524	3,055	5.83	24	277.73
Travis Brown, Northern Ariz.	37	86	104	-18	420	3,057	457	3,039	6.65	34	276.27
Chris Boden, Villanova	52	109	130	-21	474	3,058	526	3,037	5.77	24	276.09
Giovanni Carmazzi, Hofstra	103	538	166	372	346	2,651	449	3,023	6.73	32	274.82
Jim Lopusznick, Fairfield	111	593	160	433	298	2,281	409	2,714	6.64	29	271.40
Ricky Rahne, Cornell	44	111	177	-66	389	2,762	433	2,696	6.23	25	269.60
Phil Stambaugh, Lehigh	37	68	166	-98	347	2,995	384	2,897	7.54	26	263.36

*Touchdowns responsible for are players' TDs scored and passed for.

Montana's Drew Miller completed over 65 percent of his passing attempts and threw for 32 touchdowns in 1999 to top Division I-AA in passing efficiency (168.6) and finish second in total offense (331.50 yards per game).

Receptions Per Game

	1999 Class	G	Rec.	Yards	TD	Rec.PG
Murle Sango, Villanova	So.	11	98	1,064	10	8.91
Stephen Campbell, Brown	Jr.	10	89	1,107	11	8.90
Elijah Thurmon, Howard	Sr.	11	84	1,366	9	7.64
Jamal White, Towson	So.	11	82	1,322	8	7.45
Phil Wendler, Princeton	Sr.	10	74	822	4	7.40
Joe Splendorio, Cornell	Jr.	9	65	944	10	7.22
Jason Corle, Towson	Sr.	10	72	864	8	7.20
Cornell Craig, Southern Ill.	Sr.	11	77	1,419	15	7.00
Gerry McDermott, Fordham	Sr.	11	77	911	7	7.00
Cos Dematteo, Chattanooga	So.	11	76	977	11	6.91
Mike Furrey, Northern Iowa	Sr.	11	74	1,179	10	6.73
Francis St. Paul, Northern Ariz.	Jr.	10	67	987	13	6.70
Eric Johnson, Yale	Jr.	10	67	858	9	6.70

Receiving Yards Per Game

	1999 Class	G	Rec.	Yards	TD	Yds.PG
Cornell Craig, Southern Ill.	Sr.	11	77	1,419	15	129.00
Elijah Thurmon, Howard	Sr.	11	84	1,366	9	124.18
Gerald Foster, Duquesne	Sr.	11	72	1,340	10	121.82
Jamal White, Towson	So.	11	82	1,322	8	120.18
Stephen Campbell, Brown	Jr.	10	89	1,107	11	110.70
Mike Furrey, Northern Iowa	Sr.	11	74	1,179	10	107.18
Sylvester Morris, Jackson St.	Sr.	12	69	1,286	13	107.17
Terry Charles, Portland St.	So.	11	62	1,171	10	106.45
Scotty Anderson, Grambling	Jr.	11	65	1,168	15	106.18
Matt Dominguez, Sam Houston St.	Jr.	11	67	1,155	13	105.00
Joe Splendorio, Cornell	Jr.	9	65	944	10	104.89
Francis St. Paul, Northern Ariz.	Jr.	10	67	987	13	98.70
Gharun Hester, Georgetown	Jr.	11	48	1,073	13	97.55
Murle Sango, Villanova	So.	11	98	1,064	10	96.73

Ronald Jean cracked the top five in Division I-AA in two categories last year. The Lehigh standout was second in scoring (14.18 points per game) and fourth in all-purpose yards (180.91 yards per game).

Interceptions

	1999 Class	G	Int.	Yards	TD	Int.PG
Ryan Crawford, Davidson	Jr.	11	8	63	0	.73
Jim Gallagher, Georgetown	Sr.	11	7	84	1	.64
Dan Mulhern, Delaware	Fr.	11	7	65	0	.64
Lance Small, Rhode Island	So.	11	7	60	0	.64
Eric Kenesie, Valparaiso	Sr.	11	7	35	0	.64
Harry Sutton, Iona	So.	10	6	187	1	.60
Todd Tomich, Yale	Jr.	10	6	103	1	.60
Melvin Coleman, Morgan St.	Jr.	10	6	32	0	.60
Patrick Shelley, Stony Brook	Sr.	10	6	31	0	.60
Ricky Crestwell, Towson	Jr.	9	5	169	2	.56

Scoring

	1999 Class	G	TD	XP	FG	Pts.	Pts.PG
Adrian Peterson, Ga. Southern	So.	11	29	0	0	174	15.82
Ronald Jean, Lehigh	Sr.	11	26	0	0	156	14.18
Charles Roberts, Cal St. Sacramento	Jr.	11	22	6	0	138	12.55
Matt Cannon, Southern Utah	Jr.	11	23	0	0	138	12.55
David Dinkins, Morehead St.	Jr.	10	20	2	0	122	12.20
Marcel Shipp, Massachusetts	Jr.	11	21	0	0	126	11.45
Jermaine Hutchinson, Howard	Jr.	11	20	0	0	120	10.91
Curtis Keaton, James Madison	Sr.	11	20	0	0	120	10.91
Charles Dunn, Portland St.	Jr.	11	19	0	0	114	10.36
Jason Corle, Towson	Sr.	10	17	0	0	102	10.20
Rick Sarille, Wagner	Sr.	10	17	0	0	102	10.20
Randall Joseph, Colgate	Jr.	9	15	0	0	90	10.00
Rob Belli, Georgetown	Sr.	11	18	0	0	108	9.82
Ralph Saldiveri, Iona	Jr.	10	16	2	0	98	9.80
Ka Ron Coleman, Stephen F. Austin	Sr.	10	16	2	0	98	9.80
Ronney Jenkins, Northern Ariz.	Jr.	11	17	2	0	104	9.45
Jason Marrow, Bucknell	Jr.	11	17	0	0	102	9.27
Derek O'Neal, South Carolina St.	Sr.	10	15	2	0	92	9.20
David George, Dayton	Jr.	10	15	0	0	90	9.00
Jovan Griffith, Eastern Wash.	So.	10	15	0	0	90	9.00

All-Purpose Yards

	1999 Class	G	Rush	Rec.	PR	KOR	Total Yards	Yds.PG
Rick Sarille, Wagner	Sr.	10	1,373	226	0	475	2,074	207.40
Charles Roberts, Cal St. Sacramento	Jr.	11	2,082	108	12	0	2,202	200.18
Cornell Craig, Southern Ill.	Sr.	11	1	1,419	190	394	2,004	182.18
Ronald Jean, Lehigh	Sr.	11	1,358	163	0	469	1,990	180.91
Adrian Peterson, Ga. Southern	So.	11	1,807	163	0	0	1,970	179.09
Murle Sango, Villanova	So.	11	145	1,064	159	550	1,918	174.36
Curtis Keaton, James Madison	Sr.	11	1,659	63	0	195	1,917	174.27
Corey Holmes, Mississippi Val.	Jr.	11	1,692	215	0	0	1,907	173.36
Donte Small, Duquesne	So.	11	1,309	109	0	477	1,895	172.27
Nick Whitworth, Idaho St.	Jr.	11	1,093	472	0	309	1,874	170.36
Marcel Shipp, Massachusetts	Jr.	11	1,572	253	0	0	1,825	165.91
Ka Ron Coleman, Stephen F. Austin	Sr.	10	929	219	348	152	1,648	164.80
Destry Wright, Jackson St.	Sr.	12	1,643	198	121	0	1,962	163.50
Avion Black, Tennessee St.	Jr.	11	-7	893	105	786	1,777	161.55
Komlan Lonergan, William & Mary	So.	10	582	53	234	743	1,612	161.20
Jason Corle, Towson	Sr.	10	719	864	26	0	1,609	160.90
Randall Joseph, Colgate	Jr.	9	1,446	0	0	0	1,446	160.67
Ronney Jenkins, Northern Ariz.	Jr.	11	1,051	716	0	0	1,767	160.64
Donald Dorsey, Robert Morris	Sr.	9	1,070	205	2	168	1,445	160.56
Jimmy Lee, Dayton	Sr.	8	1,052	94	0	130	1,276	159.50
Tony Taylor, Northwestern St.	So.	11	1,441	77	0	231	1,749	159.00

1999 DIVISION I-AA INDIVIDUAL LEADERS

Punt Returns

(Min. 1.2 per game)	1999 Class	No.	Yds.	TD	Avg.
Ka Ron, Coleman, Stephen F. Austin	Sr.	17	348	1	20.47
Jordan Younger, Connecticut	Sr.	15	238	2	15.87
Dejuan Alfonzo, Indiana St.	Sr.	22	332	1	15.09
Lennard Byrd, Maine	So.	27	405	1	15.00
Aaron Overton, Drake	Fr.	19	278	1	14.63

Kickoff Returns

(Min. 1.2 per game)	1999 Class	No.	Yds.	TD	Avg.
Cordell Roane, Richmond	Fr.	13	470	1	36.15
Avion Black, Tennessee St.	Jr.	23	786	3	34.17
Lamont Brightful, Eastern Wash.	Jr.	26	882	2	33.92
Tulsa Payette, Austin Peay	So.	15	435	0	29.00
Rashad Brewer, Samford	Jr.	16	450	0	28.13

Punting

(Min. 3.6 per game)	1999 Class	No.	Avg.
Matthew Peot, Montana St.	Jr.	48	45.73
Brian Bivens, Murray St.	Fr.	43	44.79
Ethan Beck, Cal St. Northridge	Jr.	41	43.44
Rick Barrow, Southwest Tex. St.	Jr.	66	42.53
Brian Reilly, Appalachian St.	Sr.	41	42.41

Field Goals

	1999 Class	G	FGA	FG	Pct.	FGPG
Brett Sterba, William & Mary	Jr.	11	23	18	.783	1.64
David Collett, Tennessee Tech	So.	10	24	16	.667	1.60
Jason Feinberg, Pennsylvania	Jr.	10	21	15	.714	1.50
Mike Minnoch, Weber St.	Jr.	10	17	13	.765	1.30
Pete Garces, Idaho St.	Sr.	10	19	13	.684	1.30
Mike Murawczyk, Yale	Jr.	10	19	13	.684	1.30
Ted Woodard, Stephen F. Austin	Sr.	11	19	14	.737	1.27
Mike Glover, James Madison	So.	11	19	14	.737	1.27
Dan Frantz, Portland St.	Jr	11	19	14	.737	1.27
Scott Brown, Cal St. Sacramento	Sr.	11	21	14	.667	1.27
Justin Mattingly, Southern U.	So.	12	20	15	.750	1.25
Chris Mandell, Monmouth	Jr.	10	16	12	.750	1.20
Jeff Carlo, Robert Morris	So.	10	21	12	.571	1.20

1999 Division I-AA Team Leaders

Total Offense

	G	Plays	Yds.	Avg.	TD*	Yds.PG
Ga. Southern	11	795	6,069	7.6	71	551.73
Montana	11	810	5,691	7.0	66	517.36
Jackson St.	12	885	5,866	6.6	58	488.83
Morehead St.	10	756	4,822	6.4	51	482.20
Towson	11	927	5,258	5.7	37	478.00
Southern Utah	11	801	5,251	6.6	54	477.36
Northern Iowa	11	823	5,235	6.4	50	475.91
Wofford	11	834	5,212	6.2	47	473.82
Murray St.	11	789	5,175	6.6	49	470.45
Cal St. Sacramento	11	793	5,174	6.5	51	470.36
Florida A&M	11	806	5,096	6.3	61	463.27
Lehigh	11	806	5,084	6.3	58	462.18
Portland St.	11	796	5,063	6.4	48	460.27
Brown	10	789	4,593	5.8	41	459.30
Colgate	11	835	5,043	6.0	53	458.45
New Hampshire	11	879	5,030	5.7	41	457.27

*Touchdowns scored by rushing or passing only.

Total Defense

	G	Plays	Yds.	Avg.	TD*	Yds.PG
St. John's (N.Y.)	11	677	2,197	3.2	18	199.7
Fairfield	11	681	2,610	3.8	20	237.3
N.C. A&T	11	763	2,853	3.7	20	259.4
Wagner	10	608	2,619	4.3	24	261.9
Drake	11	733	2,893	3.9	21	263.0
Southwest Tex. St.	11	697	3,012	4.3	24	273.8
Elon	11	670	3,037	4.5	21	276.1
Tennessee Tech	10	635	2,783	4.4	21	278.3
Robert Morris	10	633	2,795	4.4	21	279.5
Siena	10	685	2,797	4.1	27	279.7
Georgetown	11	789	3,100	3.9	22	281.8
Troy St.	11	715	3,146	4.4	25	286.0
Valparaiso	11	722	3,152	4.4	27	286.5
Colgate	11	745	3,175	4.3	26	288.6
Northwestern St.	11	718	3,181	4.4	23	289.2
Duquesne	11	728	3,206	4.4	28	291.5
Ga. Southern	11	728	3,208	4.4	20	291.6

*Touchdowns allowed by rushing or passing only.

Rushing Offense

	G	Car.	Yds.	Avg.	TD	Yds.PG
Ga. Southern	11	654	4,609	7.0	61	419.0
Wofford	11	691	3,867	5.6	38	351.5
Southern Utah	11	640	3,739	5.8	47	339.9
Samford	11	627	3,439	5.5	41	312.6
Elon	11	694	3,278	4.7	31	298.0
Furman	11	548	3,170	5.8	42	288.2
Western Ky.	11	614	3,115	5.1	25	283.2
Morehead St.	10	488	2,811	5.8	31	281.1
Colgate	11	592	3,053	5.2	37	277.5
Indiana St.	11	595	2,985	5.0	27	271.4
Appalachian St.	11	469	2,733	5.8	29	248.5
Dayton	10	509	2,395	4.7	36	239.5
Cal St. Sacramento	11	479	2,584	5.4	30	234.9
Delaware	11	557	2,539	4.6	30	230.8
Stephen F. Austin	11	448	2,532	5.7	30	230.2
South Carolina St.	10	499	2,185	4.4	26	218.5
Hampton	11	560	2,383	4.3	28	216.6
New Hampshire	11	509	2,369	4.7	23	215.4

Rushing Defense

	G	Car.	Yds.	Avg.	TD	Yds.PG
Jackson St.	12	393	813	2.1	9	67.8
Wagner	10	363	680	1.9	6	68.0
Colgate	11	348	765	2.2	13	69.5
St. John's (N.Y.)	11	414	832	2.0	10	75.6
Fairfield	11	368	854	2.3	6	77.6
Harvard	10	308	802	2.6	9	80.2
Pennsylvania	10	344	842	2.4	5	84.2
Yale	10	335	906	2.7	4	90.6
Brown	10	326	971	3.0	18	97.1
Troy St.	11	360	1,070	3.0	11	97.3
Valparaiso	11	398	1,089	2.7	10	99.0
Georgetown	11	439	1,108	2.5	13	100.7
Davidson	11	406	1,111	2.7	11	101.0
Southern U.	12	430	1,251	2.9	10	104.3
Siena	10	408	1,050	2.6	11	105.0
Montana	11	370	1,163	3.1	9	105.7

Scoring Offense

	G	Pts.	Avg.
Ga. Southern	11	550	50.0
Montana	11	510	46.4
Florida A&M	11	498	45.3
Lehigh	11	463	42.1
Southern Ill.	11	424	38.5
Colgate	11	417	37.9
Tennessee St.	11	416	37.8
Murray St.	11	415	37.7
Cal St. Sacramento	11	414	37.6
Jackson St.	12	448	37.3
Furman	11	409	37.2
Fairfield	11	408	37.1
Albany (N.Y.)	9	333	37.0
Northern Iowa	11	400	36.4
Southern Utah	11	399	36.3
Portland St.	11	399	36.3
Morehead St.	10	359	35.9
Duquesne	11	393	35.7

Scoring Defense

	G	Pts.	Avg.
St. John's (N.Y.)	11	142	12.9
Fairfield	11	147	13.4
N.C. A&T	11	151	13.7
Georgetown	11	166	15.1
Ga. Southern	11	171	15.5
Robert Morris	10	156	15.6
Hofstra	11	172	15.6
Drake	11	173	15.7
Appalachian St.	11	175	15.9
Yale	10	160	16.0
Massachusetts	11	183	16.6
Furman	11	190	17.3
Albany (N.Y.)	9	156	17.3
Lehigh	11	193	17.5
Elon	11	193	17.5
Tennessee Tech	10	177	17.7
Colgate	11	197	17.9
Valparaiso	11	199	18.1
Troy St.	11	200	18.2

Passing Offense

	G	Att.	Cmp.	Int.	Pct.	Yards	Yds./Att.	TD	Yds.PG
Towson	11	584	325	13	55.7	4,193	7.2	23	381.2
Montana	11	438	282	10	64.4	4,070	9.3	40	370.0
Northern Iowa	11	439	279	14	63.6	3,717	8.5	33	337.9
Chattanooga	11	496	300	14	60.5	3,591	7.2	28	326.5
Brown	10	469	310	16	66.1	3,262	7.0	27	326.2
Florida A&M	11	452	241	9	53.3	3,580	7.9	38	325.5
Murray St.	11	405	241	9	59.5	3,506	8.7	27	318.7
Cal St. Northridge	11	499	305	18	61.1	3,445	6.9	24	313.2
Idaho St.	11	473	258	11	54.5	3,387	7.2	29	307.9
Tennessee St.	11	397	234	9	58.9	3,377	8.5	31	307.0
Northern Ariz.	11	464	268	8	57.8	3,351	7.2	32	304.6
Portland St.	11	383	228	3	59.5	3,274	8.5	30	297.6
Sam Houston St.	11	374	232	16	62.0	3,260	8.7	27	296.4
Cornell	10	401	233	13	58.1	2,861	7.1	26	286.1
Southern Ill.	11	394	223	10	56.6	3,102	7.9	27	282.0

Pass Efficiency Defense

	G	Att.	Cmp.	Cmp. Pct.	Int.	Int. Pct.	Yards	Yds./Att.	TD	TD Pct.	Rating Points
Robert Morris	10	232	90	38.79	20	8.62	1,322	5.70	8	3.45	80.80
Massachusetts	11	352	167	47.44	26	7.39	1,879	5.34	9	2.56	85.95
St. John's (N.Y.)	11	263	115	43.73	14	5.32	1,365	5.19	8	3.04	86.71
Fairfield	11	313	125	39.94	23	7.35	1,756	5.61	14	4.47	87.13
San Diego	10	259	116	44.79	17	6.56	1,529	5.90	5	1.93	87.62
Drake	11	301	139	46.18	14	4.65	1,520	5.05	9	2.99	89.16
Georgetown	11	350	165	47.14	23	6.57	1,992	5.69	9	2.57	90.29
N.C. A&T	11	289	133	46.02	13	4.50	1,576	5.45	7	2.42	90.82
Florida A&M	11	340	140	41.18	17	5.00	1,767	5.20	17	5.00	91.33
Southern U.	12	446	196	43.95	24	5.38	2,634	5.91	16	3.59	94.63
Texas Southern	11	346	144	41.62	13	3.76	2,002	5.79	13	3.76	95.11
Ga. Southern	11	292	137	46.92	15	5.14	1,764	6.04	7	2.40	95.30
Duquesne	11	302	149	49.34	23	7.62	1,763	5.84	13	4.30	97.35
Hofstra	11	335	172	51.34	16	4.78	1,794	5.36	11	3.28	97.61
William & Mary	11	333	166	49.85	14	4.20	1,988	5.97	7	2.10	98.53

Net Punting

	Punts	Avg.	No. Ret.	Yds. Ret.	Net Avg.
Southwest Mo. St.	40	41.1	10	46	40.0
Montana St.	55	42.5	24	198	38.9
Ga. Southern	23	41.1	9	55	38.7
Tennessee St.	45	39.9	11	69	38.4
Western Caro.	65	41.9	29	249	38.1
Appalachian St.	42	41.4	16	148	37.9
Eastern Ky.	58	39.2	19	80	37.8
South Fla.	76	40.3	23	204	37.6
Montana	36	39.1	10	67	37.3
Connecticut	67	40.4	35	231	37.0
Western Ill.	56	39.4	16	139	36.9
McNeese St.	57	41.3	25	252	36.9
Lehigh	36	39.2	19	85	36.8

Punt Returns

	G	No.	Yds.	TD	Avg.
Stephen F. Austin	11	28	536	1	19.1
Indiana St.	11	25	393	2	15.7
Connecticut	11	19	298	3	15.7
Citadel	11	18	272	1	15.1
Southwest Mo. St.	11	27	400	2	14.8
Maine	11	28	411	1	14.7
Jacksonville St.	11	27	381	0	14.1
Morgan St.	10	14	194	0	13.9
Texas Southern	11	47	641	2	13.6
James Madison	11	30	406	1	13.5
Western Ill.	11	33	437	2	13.2
McNeese St.	11	38	495	2	13.0
Ark.-Pine Bluff	11	23	295	3	12.8
New Hampshire	11	19	241	1	12.7
Eastern Ill.	12	23	290	1	12.6
Northern Iowa	11	37	453	2	12.2
Drake	11	27	330	1	12.2

Kickoff Returns

	G	No.	Yds.	TD	Avg.
Tennessee St.	11	45	1,256	3	27.9
Eastern Wash.	11	42	1,103	2	26.3
Portland St.	11	48	1,164	0	24.3
Montana St.	11	38	906	1	23.8
Alabama A&M	11	43	982	1	22.8
Ga. Southern	11	36	818	1	22.7
Bucknell	11	38	859	0	22.6
Appalachian St.	11	25	562	0	22.5

1999 DIVISION I-AA TEAM LEADERS

	G	No.	Yds.	TD	Avg.
Troy St.	11	34	762	0	22.4
Southwest Mo. St.	11	37	828	0	22.4
South Fla.	11	40	890	0	22.3
Furman	11	35	776	3	22.2
Northeastern	11	55	1,219	0	22.2
Samford	11	40	872	0	21.8
N.C. A&T	11	26	565	2	21.7
Southeast Mo. St.	11	48	1,042	0	21.7
Alabama St.	11	59	1,279	2	21.7
Lafayette	11	46	996	0	21.7

Turnover Margin

	TURNOVERS GAINED Fum.	Int.	Total	TURNOVERS LOST Fum.	Int.	Total	Margin/Game
Valparaiso	17	22	39	10	13	23	1.45
Grambling	13	19	32	10	6	16	1.45
Fairfield	12	23	35	11	9	20	1.36
Western Ill.	10	22	32	9	8	17	1.36
Yale	7	14	21	1	8	9	1.20
Northern Ariz.	11	16	27	6	8	14	1.18
Stephen F. Austin	12	14	26	5	8	13	1.18
Albany (N.Y.)	11	15	26	9	7	16	1.11
Robert Morris	12	20	32	13	8	21	1.10

Longest Division I-AA Plays of 1999

Rushing

Player, Team (Opponent)	Yards
Rod Smart, Western Ky. (Eastern Ky.)	89
Oscar Arzu, San Diego (Butler)	85
Maurice Smith, N.C. A&T (Elon)	80
Curtis Keaton, James Madison (South Fla.)	80
Ronney Jenkins, Northern Ariz. (Southwest Tex. St.)	78
Cory Jessup, Western Ky. (Cumberland)	75
Broderick Benson, Southeast Mo. St. (Eastern Ill.)	75
Derick Logan, Eastern Ky. (Western Ky.)	73
Derrick O'Neal, South Carolina St. (Benedict)	72
Tyrone Browning, Eastern Ky. (Western Ky.)	72
Shane Ricketts, Western Ky. (Tennessee St.)	72

Passing

Passer-Receiver, Team (Opponent)	Yards
Jimmy Blanchard-Terry Charles, Portland St. (Eastern Wash.)	99
Brad Smith-Sullivan Beard, Nicholls St. (Jacksonville St.)	97
Steve Tryon-J. T. Kirk, Robert Morris (Sacred Heart)	94

Passer-Receiver, Team (Opponent)	Yards
Keith Toolan-Anthony Liquore, Central Conn. St. (Sacred Heart)	89
Chris Samms-Joe Levens, Eastern Wash. (Idaho St.)	88
Ryan Vana-Joe Parks, Colgate (Dartmouth)	80
Brock Nutter-Mareno Philyaw, Troy St. (South Fla.)	80
Andy Huegli-John Schulte, Valparaiso (Butler)	80
J. J. Mont-Gharun Hester, Georgetown (St. John's [N.Y.])	75
Ricky Ray-Scott Towne, Cal St. Sacramento (Eastern Wash.)	75

Interception Returns

Player, Team (Opponent)	Yards
Ryan Hadden, Ga. Southern (Chattanooga)	98
Nick Ober, Butler (Lindenwood)	84
Ricky Crestwell, Towson (Lafayette)	76
Kevin Strange, Davidson (Randolph-Macon)	76
Jimmy McClain, Troy St. (South Fla.)	71

Punt Returns

Player, Team (Opponent)	Yards
Frank Cutolo, Eastern Ill. (UCF)	80
Vincent Bates, Cornell (Harvard)	73
Cornell Roane, Richmond (Rhode Island)	68
Jordan Younger, Connecticut (Villanova)	68
Nick Towns, Eastern Ky. (Southeast Mo. St.)	61

Kickoff Returns

Player, Team (Opponent)	Yards
Lamont Brightful, Eastern Wash. (Central Wash.)	100
Joey Hamilton, Jacksonville St. (Samford)	100
Lamont Brightful, Eastern Wash. (Idaho St.)	93
Arie Grey, Montana St. (Portland St.)	92
Gary Johnson, Villanova (Youngstown St.)	92
Ryan Zimpleman, Butler (Morehead St.)	91

Field Goals

Player, Team (Opponent)	Yards
Chris Chambers, Ga. Southern (Oregon St.)	57
Pete Garces, Idaho St. (Portland St.)	55
Pete Garces, Idaho St. (Eastern Wash.)	55
Kyle Leisher, Nicholls St. (Western Ill.)	55
Pete Garces, Idaho St. (Montana)	54
William Cundiff, Drake (Wis.-Stevens Point)	54
Pete Garces, Idaho St. (Montana St.)	54

Punts

Player, Team (Opponent)	Yards
Ashley Johnson, Tennessee St. (Western Ky.)	78
Jay Holmes, Tenn.-Martin (Southeast Mo. St.)	70
Mike Scifres, Western Ill. (Northern Ill.)	68
Mike Glover, James Madison (South Fla.)	66
Mike Kraft, Sacred Heart (Albany [N.Y.])	66

1999 Division II Individual Leaders

Rushing

	1999 Class	G	Car.	Yards	TD	Yds.PG
Kavin Gailliard, American Int'l	Sr.	12	320	2,653	32	221.1
Josh Ranek, South Dakota St.	So.	11	329	2,055	25	186.8
Wesley Cates, Calif. (Pa.)	So.	11	298	1,935	23	175.9
Mo Harris, Ferris St.	Sr.	10	212	1,653	11	165.3
Jamel White, South Dakota	Sr.	11	316	1,807	19	164.3
Damian Beane, Shepherd	Sr.	10	289	1,623	13	162.3
Calvin Bryant, Merrimack	Sr.	10	253	1,554	17	155.4
Tyrone Morgan, Northern St.	Jr.	11	288	1,684	17	153.1
Rashaan Dumas, Southern Conn. St.	Sr.	9	244	1,311	17	145.7
Lee Brannon, Mansfield	Sr.	10	307	1,411	6	141.1
Carlton Booe, Northeastern St.	Sr.	10	241	1,370	17	137.0
Elroy Brown, Wayne St. (Neb.)	Jr.	10	231	1,360	18	136.0
Lamar Gordon, North Dakota St.	So.	11	259	1,495	22	135.9

American International's Kavin Gailliard set Division II season records in rushing yards (2,653), rushing touchdowns (32), total touchdowns (34), points scored (206) and all-purpose yards (3,064) in 1999.

Josh Ranek of South Dakota State finished second in rushing (186.8 yards per game) and scoring (15.5 points per game) in Division II in 1999.

	1999 Class	G	Car.	Yards	TD	Yds.PG
Austin Martin, Bryant	Fr.	9	245	1,216	5	135.1
Jason Graham, Central Mo. St.	Jr.	11	263	1,442	15	131.1
Kevin Clive, Assumption	Fr.	10	253	1,268	13	126.8
Greg Briley, Central Okla.	So.	10	208	1,242	15	124.2
Michael Scott, Tuskegee	Sr.	11	246	1,346	13	122.4
Alvon Brown, Kentucky St.	So.	11	237	1,344	13	122.2
Marlion Jackson, Saginaw Valley	So.	10	233	1,197	14	119.7
T. J. Schraufnagel, Minn. St.-Mankato	So.	11	302	1,241	15	112.8
Kwanzi Watts, Neb.-Omaha	Jr.	10	162	1,119	14	111.9
Johnny McHenry, Southeastern Okla.	Jr.	9	167	1,006	12	111.8
Aamir Dew, Indiana (Pa.)	So.	9	140	1,002	9	111.3
Robert Davidson, Fairmont St.	Sr.	9	212	1,001	13	111.2

Passing Efficiency

(Min. 15 att. per game)	1999 Class	G	Att.	Cmp.	Pct.	Int.	Yards	TD	Rating Points
Rick Hebert, American Int'l	Sr.	12	234	166	70.9	4	2,351	25	187.2
Corte McGuffey, Northern Colo.	Sr.	11	296	189	63.8	11	2,893	31	173.0
Eric Miller, Bloomsburg	Jr.	10	270	171	63.3	6	2,571	25	169.4
Justin Coleman, Neb.-Kearney	Jr.	10	311	179	57.5	7	3,167	28	168.3
Chris Gicking, Shippensburg	Jr.	11	294	164	55.7	5	2,832	25	161.3
Drew Folmar, Millersville	Jr.	10	316	199	62.9	4	2,700	26	159.3
J.T. O'Sullivan, UC Davis	So.	10	280	176	62.8	11	2,618	21	158.3
Ryan Johnson, North Dakota St.	Jr.	11	224	127	56.7	8	2,153	18	156.8
Todd Cunningham, Presbyterian	So.	11	314	205	65.2	7	2,602	25	156.7
Richard Fuentes, N.M. Highlands	Sr.	11	299	171	57.1	7	2,780	20	152.7
Scott Mitchell, Western Wash.	So.	10	269	169	62.8	4	2,101	20	150.0
Mike Mitros, West Chester	Sr.	10	361	228	63.1	12	2,862	29	149.6
Matt McCarthy, Ferris St.	Sr.	10	357	210	58.8	7	2,721	31	147.6
Kevin Nawracaj, Central Ark.	Sr.	10	263	143	54.3	12	2,422	19	146.4
Joe Jacobs, Emporia St.	Sr.	11	253	151	57.4	12	2,071	25	145.8

Total Offense

	1999 Class	G	Plays	Yards	Yds.PG
Ted Larkin, Bentley	Jr.	11	545	3,490	317.3
Matt Kissell, Mercyhurst	Sr.	10	599	3,070	307.0
Justin Coleman, Neb.-Kearney	Jr.	10	370	2,966	296.6
Mike Mitros, West Chester	Sr.	10	423	2,928	292.8
Corte McGuffey, Northern Colo.	Sr.	11	366	3,031	275.5
Drew Folmar, Millersville	Jr.	10	372	2,730	273.0
Brian Baughman, Wingate	Sr.	11	567	3,002	272.9
Kevin Dickinson, Southern Conn. St.	Jr.	10	378	2,713	271.3
Matt McCarthy, Ferris St.	Sr.	10	373	2,688	268.8
Eric Howe, Truman	So.	11	472	2,937	267.0
Zach Witt, Minn. St.-Mankato	Sr.	11	436	2,888	262.5
Luke Cullins, Harding	Sr.	10	416	2,618	261.8

Receptions Per Game

	1999 Class	G	Rec.	Yards	TD	Rec.PG
Mark DeBrito, Bentley	Sr.	11	101	1,637	19	9.2
Kevin Ingram, West Chester	Sr.	9	82	1,050	16	9.1
Damon Thompson, Virginia St.	Jr.	10	90	1,517	10	9.0
Sean Scott, Millersville	Jr.	8	67	1,030	6	8.4
Mike Juhasz, North Dakota	Sr.	10	79	895	9	7.9
Lester McCoy, Emporia St.	Jr.	11	84	1,277	16	7.6
Clarence Coleman, Ferris St.	So.	10	72	1,124	10	7.2
Ed Bailey, Mercyhurst	Jr.	10	72	955	9	7.2
Damien Hoffman, Minn.-Morris	Jr.	11	76	980	5	6.9
Neal Mozdzierz, Ferris St.	Sr.	10	69	942	14	6.9
Brian Dolph, Saginaw Valley	Jr.	8	55	878	9	6.9
Mike Lelko, Bloomsburg	Jr.	11	75	980	10	6.8
Raheem Duncan, Southern Conn. St.	Sr.	10	68	992	6	6.8
Terry Robertson, Kutztown	Jr.	10	68	742	5	6.8
Jamie Ware, Shippensburg	Sr.	11	74	1,334	10	6.7
Tom Chisholm, Pace	So.	10	67	981	7	6.7
Rollie Casas, Texas Lutheran	So.	9	60	700	7	6.7
Brad Bolemon, Presbyterian	Sr.	11	72	683	7	6.5
Andrew Blakley, Truman	Fr.	11	71	805	7	6.5
Matt Holmlund, Augustana (S.D.)	So.	11	71	739	4	6.5

Receiving Yards Per Game

	1999 Class	G	Rec.	Yards	TD	Yds.PG
Damon Thompson, Virginia St.	Jr.	10	90	1,517	10	151.7
Mark DeBrito, Bentley	Sr.	11	101	1,637	19	148.8
Sean Scott, Millersville	Jr.	8	67	1,030	6	128.8
Matt Wilson, Bloomsburg	Sr.	11	64	1,345	16	122.3
Jamie Ware, Shippensburg	Sr.	11	74	1,334	10	121.3
Kevin Ingram, West Chester	Sr.	9	82	1,050	16	116.7
Lester McCoy, Emporia St.	Jr.	11	84	1,277	16	116.1
Clarence Coleman, Ferris St.	So.	10	72	1,124	10	112.4
Ben Clampitt, Western Wash.	Sr.	10	61	1114	13	111.4
Brian Dolph, Saginaw Valley	Jr.	8	55	878	9	109.8
Elvert Eden, New Haven	Jr.	10	62	1,006	7	100.6
Raheem Duncan, Southern Conn. St.	Sr.	10	68	992	6	99.2
Tom Chisholm, Pace	So.	10	67	981	7	98.1

1999 DIVISION II INDIVIDUAL LEADERS

All-Purpose Yards

	1999 Class	G	Rush	Rec.	PR	KOR	Int.	Total Yards	Yds.PG
Kavin Gailliard, American Int'l	Sr.	12	2,653	289	0	122	0	3,064	255.33
Damon Thompson, Virginia St.	Jr.	10	88	1,517	410	465	0	2,480	248.00
Jamel White, South Dakota	Sr.	11	1,807	640	0	0	0	2,447	222.45
Josh Ranek, South Dakota St.	So.	11	2,055	258	0	0	0	2,313	210.27
Steve Eichert, Bloomsburg	Jr.	10	943	68	129	809	0	1,949	194.90
Mo Harris, Ferris St.	Sr.	10	1,653	130	0	141	0	1,924	192.40
Calvin Bryant, Merrimack	Sr.	10	1,554	15	0	319	0	1,888	188.80
Wesley Cates, Calif. (Pa.)	So.	11	1,935	58	3	77	0	2,073	188.45
Tyrone Morgan, Northern St.	Jr.	11	1,684	0	0	370	0	2,054	186.73
Clarence Coleman, Ferris St.	So.	10	1,124	374	0	364	0	1,862	186.20
Rashaan Dumas, Southern Conn. St.	Sr.	9	1,311	106	1	91	0	1,509	167.67
Damian Beane, Shepherd	Sr.	10	1,623	29	0	0	0	1,652	165.20
Carson Walch, Winona St.	Sr.	11	852	155	295	513	0	1,815	165.00
Michael Scott, Tuskegee	Sr.	11	1,346	151	0	307	0	1,804	164.00
Anthonio Newton, Ky. Wesleyan	So.	11	730	495	179	338	0	1,742	158.36
Marlion Jackson, Saginaw Valley	So.	10	1,197	296	0	61	0	1,554	155.40
Ketric Barnes, New Haven	Jr.	10	3	801	225	525	0	1,554	155.40
Aamir Dew, Indiana (Pa.)	So.	9	1,002	6	0	376	0	1,384	153.78
Kevin Clive, Assumption	Fr.	10	1,268	265	0	0	0	1,533	153.30
Brent Lesniak, Grand Valley St.	Fr.	9	908	60	0	397	0	1,365	151.67
Mark DeBrito, Bentley	Sr.	11	2	1,637	0	0	0	1,639	149.00
Lee Brannon, Mansfield	Sr.	10	1,411	75	0	0	0	1,486	148.60
Elroy Brown, Wayne St. (Neb.)	Jr.	10	1,360	118	0	0	0	1,478	147.80
Tony Miles, Northwest Mo. St.	Jr.	11	78	713	405	417	0	1,613	146.64
Lamar Gordon, North Dakota St.	So.	11	1,495	114	0	0	0	1,609	146.27

South Dakota's Jamel White scored 144 points and gained 2,447 all-purpose yards in 1999 to place third in both categories in Division II.

Interceptions

	1999 Class	G	No.	Yards	Int.PG
Tommie Dawson, Virginia Union	Jr.	8	8	79	1.0
Jerico Washington, Clark Atlanta	So.	8	6	117	.8
Brent Burnside, Mo. Western St.	Sr.	11	8	117	.7
Craig Neuhaus, Neb.-Kearney	So.	10	7	65	.7
Jon Johnson, Mansfield	Jr.	10	7	0	.7
Claudio Pesce, C. W. Post	Sr.	9	6	101	.7
Bob Parker, American Int'l	Jr.	12	8	67	.7
Jamaal Garman, Fort Valley St.	Sr.	11	7	139	.6
Brian Polk, Slippery Rock	Sr.	11	7	149	.6
Toy Williams, Mars Hill	Jr.	11	7	96	.6
Mike Slomczewski, Winona St.	Jr.	11	7	23	.6

Scoring

	1999 Class	G	TD	XP	FG	Pts.	Pts.PG
Kavin Gailliard, American Int'l	Sr.	12	34	2	0	206	17.2
Josh Ranek, South Dakota St.	So.	11	28	2	0	170	15.5
Jamel White, South Dakota	Sr.	11	24	0	0	144	13.1
Wesley Cates, Calif. (Pa.)	So.	11	23	0	0	138	12.5
Lamar Gordon, North Dakota St.	So.	11	22	0	0	132	12.0
Rashaan Dumas, Southern Conn. St.	Sr.	9	17	0	0	102	11.3
Kevin Ingram, West Chester	Sr.	9	16	4	0	100	11.1
Elroy Brown, Wayne St. (Neb.)	Jr.	10	18	2	0	110	11.0
David Jansen, Northwest Mo. St.	Jr.	11	20	0	0	120	10.9
Troy Hambrick, Savannah St.	Sr.	11	19	2	0	116	10.5
Mark DeBrito, Bentley	Sr.	11	19	0	0	114	10.4
Carlton Booe, Northeastern St.	Sr.	10	17	0	0	102	10.2
Sleepie Tollie, Northwood	So.	10	17	0	0	102	10.2
Calvin Bryant, Merrimack	Sr.	10	17	0	0	102	10.2
Robert Davidson, Fairmont St.	Sr.	9	15	0	0	90	10.0
Tyrone Morgan, Northern St.	Jr.	11	18	0	0	108	9.8
Marlion Jackson, Saginaw Valley	So.	10	15	4	0	94	9.4
Lester McCoy, Emporia St.	Jr.	11	16	4	0	100	9.1
Anthonio Newton, Ky. Wesleyan	So.	11	16	4	0	100	9.1
Neal Mozdzierz, Ferris St.	Sr.	10	14	6	0	90	9.0
Greg Briley, Central Okla.	So.	10	15	0	0	90	9.0
Kevin Clive, Assumption	Fr.	10	15	0	0	90	9.0
Andre Braxton, Virginia Union	Jr.	9	12	8	0	80	8.9
T. J. Schraufnagel, Minn. St.-Mankato	So.	11	16	0	0	96	8.7
Matt Wilson, Bloomsburg	Sr.	11	16	0	0	96	8.7
John Flamish, Millersville	Jr.	10	14	2	0	86	8.6

Punt Returns

(Min. 1.2 per game)	1999 Class	No.	Yds.	Avg.
James Rooths, Shepherd	Jr.	15	366	24.4
Tony Miles, Northwest Mo. St.	Jr.	19	405	21.3
Eddie Jackson, Tusculum	Jr.	14	231	16.5
Antonio Murphy, Albany St. (Ga.)	Fr.	12	198	16.5
Jamone Mims, Northern Mich.	Jr.	13	207	15.9
Nate Lehman, St. Cloud St.	So.	15	235	15.7
Shock Davis, Angelo St.	Sr.	18	278	15.4
Johnnie Jones, Central Okla.	Sr.	33	501	15.2
Vonnie Armistad, West Ala.	So.	19	277	14.6
Stuart Cash, Arkansas Tech	Sr.	26	377	14.5
Chris Pointer, Kentucky St.	Sr.	17	241	14.2
Eric Doggett, Valdosta St.	Sr.	32	452	14.1
Clarence Coleman, Ferris St.	So.	27	374	13.9

Kickoff Returns

(Min. 1.2 per game)	1999 Class	No.	Yds.	Avg.
Brian Polk, Slippery Rock	Sr.	15	513	34.2
Ryan Bedlan, Neb.-Kearney	Jr.	13	427	32.8
Travis Smith, Presbyterian	Jr.	20	643	32.2
Carson Walch, Winona St.	Sr.	16	513	32.1
Marcus Long, Northeastern St.	Jr.	17	539	31.7
Jason Patterson, Central Wash.	So.	13	395	30.4
Michael Lloyd, Savannah St.	Fr.	12	361	30.1
Alton Lusk, Central Okla.	Sr.	17	505	29.7
John Noble, Kutztown	Fr.	13	386	29.7
Matt Jackson, Northwood	So.	19	542	28.5
Tim Strehlow, North Dakota St.	Sr.	14	395	28.2
Clarence Coleman, Ferris St.	So.	13	364	28.0
Shannon Poppinga, Augustana (S.D.)	Sr.	15	417	27.8

Punting

(Min. 3.6 per game)	1999 Class	No.	Avg.
Nathan White, Fairmont St.	So.	43	44.9
Ryan Schneider, Winona St.	Sr.	38	44.6
Jeff Works, Ouachita Baptist	Sr.	55	43.7
Andrew Patton, Harding	Sr.	52	43.4
Ryan Corn, Western St.	Jr.	51	43.0
Brian Johnson, Wayne St. (Neb.)	Sr.	52	42.4

Field Goals

(Min. 3.6 per game)	1999 Class	No.	Avg.
Adam Ryan, Fort Hays St.	Jr.	75	42.4
Ryan Dutton, Minn. St.-Mankato	Jr.	41	42.0
Jonathan Thomas, Clark Atlanta	Sr.	63	41.9
Chris Enloe, Southeastern Okla.	Sr.	48	41.9
Mike Borrall, Morningside	Jr.	65	41.7

Field Goals

	1999 Class	G	FGA	FG	Pct.	FGPG
Milan Smado, Southeastern Okla.	So.	11	19	17	89.5	1.55
Aaron Turner, Chadron St.	Jr.	10	20	15	75.0	1.50
Jeremy Thompson, Harding	Sr.	10	21	14	66.7	1.40
Volker Olbrich, Neb.-Kearney	Sr.	10	19	14	73.7	1.40
Jason Williams, Southern Ark.	Jr.	10	26	14	53.8	1.40
Paul Peletz, Arkansas Tech	Jr.	11	20	15	75.0	1.36
Kevin Craft, Ark.-Monticello	Jr.	11	22	15	68.2	1.36
Rusty Evans, Fort Lewis	Sr.	11	20	15	75.0	1.36
Cameron Peterka, North Dakota	So.	10	15	12	80.0	1.20
Dominic Lombardi, Mesa St.	Fr.	10	15	12	80.0	1.20
Matt Mapes, Lock Haven	Jr.	11	15	13	86.7	1.18
Aaron Pederson, North Dakota St.	So.	11	17	13	76.5	1.18
Troy Severson, Neb.-Omaha	Fr.	11	18	13	72.2	1.18
Shawn Thomas, Winston-Salem	Sr.	10	19	11	57.9	1.10

1999 Division II Team Leaders

Total Offense

	G	Plays	Yds.	Yds.PG
Ferris St.	10	745	5,345	534.5
American Int'l	12	789	5,943	495.3
Southern Conn. St.	10	768	4,887	488.7
Bloomsburg	11	810	5,159	469.0
Neb.-Omaha	11	776	5,109	464.5
Carson-Newman	10	651	4,615	461.5
Neb.-Kearney	10	691	4,611	461.1
West Chester	10	720	4,580	458.0
Shepherd	10	687	4,533	453.3
Shippensburg	11	783	4,951	450.1
North Dakota St.	11	774	4,826	438.7
Grand Valley St.	10	757	4,279	427.9
Northwest Mo. St.	11	768	4,652	422.9
South Dakota St.	11	735	4,649	422.6
Northern Colo.	11	729	4,629	420.8
Wayne St. (Neb.)	11	848	4,618	419.8
Pittsburg St.	11	779	4,590	417.3

Total Defense

	G	Plays	Yds.	Yds.PG
Northeastern St.	11	628	1,987	180.6
Albany St. (Ga.)	10	562	2,058	205.8
Virginia Union	10	604	2,226	222.6
Catawba	11	694	2,518	228.9
Winston-Salem	10	603	2,317	231.7
Shepherd	10	649	2,367	236.7
Southwestern Okla.	10	597	2,484	248.4
Kentucky St.	11	594	2,733	248.5
Tex. A&M-Kingsville	11	630	2,769	251.7
Pittsburg St.	11	720	2,822	256.5
Southwest St.	11	717	2,831	257.4
Northern St.	11	673	2,837	257.9
Central Mo. St.	11	744	2,883	262.1
Indiana (Pa.)	10	662	2,652	265.2
Western Wash.	10	683	2,706	270.6
Slippery Rock	11	721	2,982	271.1
Central Wash.	9	578	2,451	272.3
Midwestern St.	11	720	3,020	274.5

Rushing Offense

	G	Car.	Yds.	Yds.PG
Neb.-Omaha	11	604	3,687	335.2
Carson-Newman	10	515	3,317	331.7
Pittsburg St.	11	666	3,636	330.5
American Int'l	12	545	3,524	293.7
Calif. (Pa.)	11	583	3,178	288.9
Southern Ark.	10	550	2,852	285.2
Mesa St.	11	573	3,132	284.7
Shepherd	10	470	2,774	277.4
Northern St.	11	556	2,929	266.3
N.C. Central	10	537	2,661	266.1
Northwood	10	537	2,644	264.4
Northeastern St.	11	607	2,901	263.7
C. W. Post	10	490	2,611	261.1
Virginia Union	10	484	2,573	257.3
Southeastern Okla.	11	519	2,763	251.2
Merrimack	10	500	2,504	250.4
Eastern N.M.	11	531	2,675	243.2

Rushing Defense

	G	Car.	Yds.	Yds.PG
Catawba	11	367	587	53.4
Western Wash.	10	346	599	59.9
Southwest St.	11	382	693	63.0
Shepherd	10	329	647	64.7
Virginia Union	10	326	686	68.6
Chadron St.	10	350	788	78.8
Albany St. (Ga.)	10	331	863	86.3
UC Davis	10	356	911	91.1
Tex. A&M-Kingsville	11	396	1,044	94.9
Carson-Newman	10	340	971	97.1
Winston-Salem	10	340	972	97.2
Miles	10	358	988	98.8
Indianapolis	11	437	1,119	101.7
Northern St.	11	356	1,144	104.0
North Dakota St.	11	368	1,156	105.1
Northeastern St.	11	431	1,161	105.5

Scoring Offense

	G	TD	XP	2XP	DXP	FG	SAF	Pts.	Avg.
Ferris St.	10	65	52	7	00	5	1	473	47.3
Carson-Newman	10	61	56	2	00	3	0	435	43.5
American Int'l	12	72	50	3	01	3	1	501	41.8
Neb.-Kearney	10	52	47	0	00	15	0	404	40.4
Shepherd	10	56	44	2	00	6	0	402	40.2
North Dakota St.	11	57	53	1	01	13	0	438	39.8
Northern Colo.	11	58	52	2	00	10	0	434	39.5
Northwest Mo. St.	11	56	56	0	00	12	0	428	38.9
Slippery Rock	11	57	47	2	00	11	1	428	38.9
West Chester	10	55	39	4	00	3	1	388	38.8
Bloomsburg	11	56	37	3	00	7	0	400	36.4
Shippensburg	11	53	43	2	01	9	2	398	36.2
Presbyterian	11	54	44	2	01	5	3	395	35.9
Northern St.	11	51	43	3	00	10	1	387	35.2
Neb.-Omaha	11	51	40	1	00	13	0	387	35.2
Millersville	10	48	40	2	01	5	1	351	35.1
Pittsburg St.	11	52	47	1	00	8	0	385	35.0

Scoring Defense

	G	TD	XP	2XP	DXP	FG	SAF	Pts.	Avg.
Pittsburg St.	11	11	10	1	0	8	1	104	9.5
Winston-Salem	10	13	8	0	0	3	0	95	9.5
Catawba	11	16	14	0	0	2	0	116	10.5
North Dakota	10	14	12	0	0	5	0	111	11.1
Northeastern St.	11	15	15	0	0	6	2	127	11.5
Virginia Union	10	18	7	0	0	3	0	124	12.4
Shepherd	10	16	14	0	0	5	0	125	12.5
Indiana (Pa.)	10	17	15	0	1	7	0	140	14.0
Albany St. (Ga.)	0	21	11	2	0	1	0	144	14.4
Indianapolis	11	21	17	0	0	8	1	169	15.4
Southwestern Okla.	0	22	13	1	1	4	0	161	16.1
N.C. Central	10	19	16	0	0	10	1	162	16.2
Carson-Newman	0	22	15	1	0	4	0	163	16.3
Merrimack	10	22	15	3	0	3	2	166	16.6
Eastern N.M.	11	23	18	2	0	7	1	183	16.6
North Dakota St.	11	26	20	1	0	2	0	184	16.7

1999 DIVISION II TEAM LEADERS

Passing Offense

	G	Att.	Cmp.	Pct.	Int.	Yards	Yds.PG
Neb.-Kearney	10	337	198	58.8	7	3,386	338.6
Bentley	11	491	271	55.2	15	3,390	308.2
Mercyhurst	10	467	239	51.2	15	3,057	305.7
Ferris St.	10	396	236	59.6	8	3,051	305.1
Wingate	11	489	284	58.1	17	3,345	304.1
West Chester	10	376	237	63.0	13	2,944	294.4
Truman	11	438	231	52.7	17	3,138	285.3
New Haven	10	385	185	48.1	16	2,835	283.5
N.M. Highlands	11	342	191	55.8	10	3,089	280.8
Shippensburg	11	323	181	56.0	7	3,071	279.2
Northern Colo.	11	309	195	63.1	11	3,020	274.5
Millersville	10	321	203	63.2	4	2,741	274.1
UC Davis	10	303	189	62.4	11	2,737	273.7
Presbyterian	11	349	228	65.3	9	2,955	268.6
Harding	10	360	196	54.4	11	2,678	267.8
Bloomsburg	11	320	194	60.6	10	2,945	267.7
Chadron St.	10	357	185	51.8	15	2,664	266.4
Southern Conn. St.	10	336	206	61.3	10	2,654	265.4
Virginia St.	10	316	168	53.2	17	2,615	261.5

Pass Efficiency Defense

	G	Att.	Cmp.	Pct.	Int.	Yards	TD	Rating Points
Northeastern St.	11	197	72	36.5	14	826	1	59.2
Southwestern Okla.	10	203	72	35.4	12	720	6	63.2
Winston-Salem	10	263	100	38.0	21	1,345	4	70.0
Virginia Union	10	278	103	37.0	27	1,540	10	76.0
Pittsburg St.	11	252	109	43.2	17	1,272	5	78.7
Clark Atlanta	10	180	80	44.4	18	915	7	80.0
Albany St. (Ga.)	10	231	96	41.5	14	1,195	7	82.9
Shepherd	10	320	132	41.2	19	1,720	9	83.8
Eastern N.M.	11	240	83	34.5	10	1,408	7	85.2
Livingstone	11	252	101	40.0	18	1,397	10	85.5
Indiana (Pa.)	10	298	136	45.6	11	1,584	4	87.3
Southern Ark.	10	233	98	42.0	14	1,393	58	7.3
Northern St.	11	317	137	43.2	17	1,693	14	91.9
Fort Valley St.	11	315	150	47.6	11	1,775	4	92.2
Tuskegee	11	350	148	42.2	19	1,997	15	93.5
Fairmont St.	10	267	118	44.1	13	1,637	7	94.6
North Dakota	10	271	125	46.1	10	1,518	8	95.5

Net Punting

	Punts	Yds.	Avg.	No. Ret.	Yds. Ret.	Net Avg.
Fairmont St.	44	1930	43.86	18	165	40.11
Harding	52	2255	43.36	26	211	39.30
North Dakota St.	37	1558	42.10	19	123	38.78
UC Davis	49	1957	39.93	22	95	38.00
North Dakota	50	2038	40.76	23	141	37.94
Morningside	66	2727	41.31	34	226	37.89
Fort Hays St.	75	3179	42.38	41	360	37.58
Clark Atlanta	63	2637	41.85	31	276	37.47
Chadron St.	49	1959	39.97	22	125	37.42
East Stroudsburg	66	2584	39.15	29	150	36.87
Southern Conn. St.	28	1078	38.50	4	46	36.85
Ouachita Baptist	55	2401	43.65	37	379	36.76
Neb.-Kearney	49	1937	39.53	22	143	36.61
Northern Mich.	58	2419	41.70	29	306	36.43
Western St.	57	2351	41.24	29	278	36.36

Punt Returns

	G	No.	Yds.	TD	Avg.
Northwest Mo. St.	11	29	521	2	17.96
Shepherd	10	23	405	3	17.60
Mo. Western St.	11	16	259	1	16.18
Arkansas Tech	11	38	607	1	15.97
Central Okla.	10	39	561	3	14.38
Minn.-Morris	11	11	158	0	14.36
Chadron St.	10	50	714	2	14.28
Ferris St.	10	29	407	2	14.03
Valdosta St.	11	37	498	1	13.45
Virginia St.	10	31	416	1	13.41
Slippery Rock	11	35	457	4	13.05
Fairmont St.	10	25	319	2	12.76
Winston-Salem	10	28	357	2	12.75
Angelo St.	11	25	311	1	12.44
West Ala.	11	30	373	2	12.43

	G	No.	Yds.	TD	Avg.
Harding	10	30	372	1	12.40
Winona St.	11	24	295	0	12.29

Kickoff Returns

	G	No.	Yds.	TD	Avg.
Northeastern St.	11	29	824	1	28.41
Neb.-Kearney	10	24	681	2	28.37
Slippery Rock	11	35	893	2	25.51
Northwood	10	27	682	0	25.25
Northern St.	11	42	1,051	2	25.02
Western St.	11	31	764	1	24.64
Kutztown	10	42	1,027	1	24.45
Central Wash.	9	33	797	1	24.15
Fort Hays St.	11	34	821	1	24.14
Central Okla.	10	26	626	0	24.07
Edinboro	11	54	1,270	1	23.51
Fairmont St.	10	41	954	0	23.26
Presbyterian	11	42	977	1	23.26
Winona St.	11	44	1,012	3	23.00
Indianapolis	11	35	805	0	23.00
Fort Valley St.	11	35	796	2	22.74
East Stroudsburg	11	59	1,341	0	22.72
Savannah St.	11	44	996	1	22.63

Turnover Margin

	G	TURNOVERS GAINED Fum.	Int.	Total	TURNOVERS LOST Fum.	Int.	Total	Margin/Game
American Int'l	12	17	28	45	7	5	12	2.75
Winston-Salem	10	17	21	38	11	1	12	2.60
Pittsburg St.	11	22	17	39	16	6	22	1.54
Catawba	11	20	13	33	10	7	17	1.45
South Dakota St.	11	21	5	27	5	7	12	1.36
Arkansas Tech	11	23	15	38	10	13	23	1.36
Presbyterian	11	17	14	31	7	9	16	1.36
Virginia Union	10	9	27	36	16	7	23	1.30
Shepherd	10	12	19	31	10	8	18	1.30
Central Okla.	10	16	13	29	10	6	16	1.30
North Dakota St.	11	14	17	31	9	8	17	1.27
Neb.-Kearney	10	14	14	28	10	7	17	1.10
Southern Ark.	10	17	14	31	15	5	20	1.10
East Stroudsburg	11	12	19	31	5	14	19	1.09

Longest Division II Plays of 1999

Rushing

Player, Team (Opponent)	Yards
Ronaie Maye, Carson-Newman (Lenoir-Rhyne)	99
Antwon Oliver, Carson-Newman (Presbyterian)	95
Lateef Walker, Pittsburg St. (North Ala.)	95
Vic Gilmore, Newberry (Wingate)	93
Josh Ingram, Mesa St. (Colorado Mines)	93
Dalevon Smith, Shepherd (Fairmont St.)	92
Justin Matthews, Central Okla. (East Central)	91
Larry Piediscalzo, Pace (St. Anselm)	90
Ian Smart, C. W. Post (Stonehill)	90
Jamel White, South Dakota (Truman)	89
Anthonio Newton, Ky. Wesleyan (Gannon)	87
Kent Schoolfield, Fort Valley St. (Lane)	86
Dorrian Glenn, Slippery Rock (Shippensburg)	85
Antoine Lacy, Eastern N.M. (Western N.M.)	85

Passing

Passer-Receiver, Team (Opponent)	Yards
Brian Eyerman-Greg Dorsey, Indiana (Pa.) (Shippensburg)	98
Justin Coleman-Ryan Bedlan, Neb.-Kearney (N.M. Highlands)	95
John Paul McMurry-Greg Lawson, Ark.-Monticello (Central Ark.)	95
Kevin Nawracaj-Tony Lockhart, Central Ark. (West Ga.)	95
Ricky Fritz-Jeff Wenngatz, Minn.-Duluth (Bemidji St.)	93
Drew Folmar-Sean Scott, Millersville (Bloomsburg)	91
Lateef Walker-Mike Brown, Pittsburg St. (North Ala.)	91
Justin Coleman-Ryan Bedlan, Neb.-Kearney (Western St.)	90

1999 Division II Longest Plays

Passer-Receiver, Team (Opponent)	Yards
Bryan Harman-Jason Trent, Fairmont St. (Campbellsville)	90
Eric Miller-Matt Wilson, Bloomsburg (Edinboro)	90
George Harp-Greg Washington, Arkansas Tech (Northwest Mo. St.)	89
Jeff Leopold-Jarrod Pruiett, Ashland (Wayne St. [Mich.])	89
Garrett Small-Brian Dolph, Saginaw Valley (Wayne St. [Mich.])	89
Brad Bolemon-Kevie Smith, Presbyterian (West Ga.)	86
Andy Rennerfeldt-Brock Beran, South Dakota St. (Morningside)	86

Interception Returns

Player, Team (Opponent)	Yards
Tonmar Johnson, Eastern N.M. (Midwestern St.)	100
Bershard Tillman, Harding (Northeastern St.)	100
Antonio Printup, Fort Valley St. (Clark Atlanta)	97
Matt Walsh, Stonehill (Assumption)	97
Chris Haglund, Moorhead St. (Wis.-Oshkosh)	89
Chad Geiger, Neb.-Omaha (Minn. St.-Mankato)	87
Bryan Rosser, N.M. Highlands (Colorado Mines)	83
Jordan Sweet, Mesa St. (Colorado Mines)	80
Edgar Carson, Savannah St. (Morris Brown)	77
Jesse Liggins, South Dakota St. (Grand Valley St.)	77
Tony Donald, Western St. (Fort Lewis)	75
Jamaal Garman, Fort Valley St. (Valdosta St.)	75
Brian Polk, Slippery Rock (Lock Haven)	75
Dan Culliver, Fairmont St. (Glenville St.)	71
Quincy Tisdale, Indiana (Pa.) (Bloomsburg)	71

Punt Returns

Player, Team (Opponent)	Yards
Nate Lehman, St. Cloud St. (Wis.-River Falls)	95
Vonnie Armistad, West Ala. (North Ala.)	90
Clarence Coleman, Ferris St. (Findlay)	90
Vonnie Armistad, West Ala. (Valdosta St.)	85
Dondre Gilliam, Millersville (Edinboro)	85
Carlton Jones, Livingstone (Albany St. [Ga.])	85
James Rooths, Shepherd (Concord)	85
Stuart Cash, Arkansas Tech (West Ala.)	84
Johnnie Jones, Central Okla. (Ouachita Baptist)	84
Johnnie Jones, Central Okla. (Midwestern St.)	83
Paul Fatigate, West Va. Wesleyan (Calif. [Pa.])	82
Chris Pointer, Kentucky St. (Albany St. [Ga.])	82
Tony Miles, Northwest Mo. St. (Central Mo. St.)	80
Brandon Sicilia, Western St. (Colorado Mines)	79
Tony Miles, Northwest Mo. St. (Truman)	78

Kickoff Returns

Player, Team (Opponent)	Yards
Ryan Bedlan, Neb.-Kearney (N.M. Highlands)	100
Kerry Byers, Mo. Southern St. (Truman)	100

Player, Team (Opponent)	Yards
Derrick Foster, Tex. A&M-Kingsville (Angelo St.)	100
Jimmy Evans, Western St. (N.M. Highlands)	99
Jason Patterson, Central Wash. (Humboldt St.)	99
Demetrius Dixon, Quincy (St. Francis [Ill.])	96
Ketric Barnes, New Haven (Jackson St.)	95
Ketric Barnes, New Haven (South Fla.)	95
Carson Walch, Winona St. (Minn.-Crookston)	95
Clarence Coleman, Ferris St. (North Dakota St.)	94
Jim Kennedy, C. W. Post (Stony Brook)	94
Ryan Bedlan, Neb.-Kearney (Neb.-Omaha)	93
Michael Scott, Tuskegee (Savannah St.)	93

Field Goals

Player, Team (Opponent)	Yards
Doc Proctor, Ferris St. (Michigan Tech)	62
Erich Hitzeman, St. Joseph's (Ind.) (Wayne St. [Mich.])	57
Erich Hitzeman, St. Joseph's (Ind.) (Valparaiso)	54
Pat Brougham, Western St. (Weber St.)	52
Erich Hitzeman, St. Joseph's (Ind.) (Wayne St. [Mich.])	52
Jeff Klee, Truman (Pittsburg St.)	52
Mike Carter, Tusculum (Livingstone)	51
Rusty Evans, Fort Lewis (Adams St.)	51
Jeff Klee, Truman (Mo.-Rolla)	51
Troy Severson, Neb.-Omaha (Augustana [S.D.])	51
Jason Lee, Tuskegee (Benedict)	50
Volker Olbrich, Neb.-Kearney (Adams St.)	50
Marc Powers, Western N.M. (Southeastern Okla.)	49
Jose Rua, Kentucky St. (Lane)	49
Jason Williams, Southern Ark. (Southeastern Okla.)	49

Punts

Player, Team (Opponent)	Yards
Steve Beller, Concord (West Va. Tech)	83
Andrew Patton, Harding (Southwestern Okla.)	82
Kenny Zordani, Fort Lewis (Adams St.)	82
Mike Borrall, Morningside (North Dakota)	81
Jeff Griffis, Saginaw Valley (Northern Mich.)	81
Jose Rua, Kentucky St. (Clark Atlanta)	80
Jon McCartney, Westminster (Pa.) (Mercyhurst)	76
Jonathan Thomas, Clark Atlanta (Kentucky St.)	76
Josh Hodsdon, Colorado Mines (Adams St.)	71
Ryan McLane, Stonehill (Assumption)	71
Dennis Nisbet, Indianapolis (New Haven)	70
Kenny Zordani, Fort Lewis (Western St.)	70

1999 Division III Individual Leaders

Rushing

	1999 Class	G	Car.	Yards	TD	Yds.PG
R. J. Bowers, Grove City	Jr.	10	344	2,098	25	209.8
Kenneth Sasu, Marietta	Jr.	9	332	1,770	15	196.7
D'Andra Freeman, Fitchburg St.	Sr.	10	365	1,871	14	187.1
Steve Tardif, Maine Maritime	Sr.	9	271	1,567	14	174.1
Ben Smith, Buena Vista	Sr.	10	254	1,583	16	158.3
Paul Smith, Gettysburg	Sr.	10	237	1,546	15	154.6
Jamal Robertson, Ohio Northern	Jr.	10	237	1,544	19	154.4
Jason Votzakis, Westfield St.	Sr.	10	267	1,469	12	146.9
Anthony Togliatti, Kenyon	Sr.	10	290	1,466	12	146.6
Casey Donaldson, Wittenberg	Jr.	9	236	1,308	15	145.3
Ron Lewis, Montclair St.	Sr.	8	195	1,138	16	142.3
Kris Brown, Olivet	Jr.	9	265	1,265	6	140.6
Kevin Cahill, Springfield	Jr.	10	243	1,345	18	134.5
Patrick Bowman, Illinois Col.	So.	10	281	1,330	10	133.0
Drew Sherman, Knox	Sr.	10	284	1,318	13	131.8
Eric Hamilton, Concordia (Wis.)	So.	9	153	1,186	9	131.8
David Burrill, Mass. Maritime	So.	10	288	1,313	11	131.3
Richard Green, Howard Payne	Jr.	10	246	1,307	9	130.7
Damian Putney, Whitworth	Jr.	10	266	1,293	12	129.3
Anthony Hicks, Pacific Lutheran	Sr.	9	144	1,155	13	128.3

With 209.8 rushing yards and 15.4 points per game, R. J. Bowers of Grove City topped Division III in two departments.

1999 DIVISION III INDIVIDUAL LEADERS

	1999 Class	G	Car.	Yards	TD	Yds.PG
Andrew Notarfrancesco, Catholic	Sr.	10	233	1,271	19	127.1
Frank Peters, Case Reserve	Sr.	10	300	1,256	9	125.6
Matt Fox, Nichols	Jr.	9	250	1,130	13	125.6
Jeff Brock, Heidelberg	Sr.	10	300	1,255	9	125.5
Seto Berry, Bri'water (Mass.)	Jr.	10	181	1,219	16	121.9

Passing Efficiency

(Min. 15 att. per game)	1999 Class	G	Att.	Cmp.	Pct.	Int.	Yards	TD	Rating Points
Gary Smeck, Mount Union	Jr.	10	199	131	65.8	3	2,274	30	208.6
Matt LeFever, Western Conn. St.	Jr.	10	158	95	60.1	7	1,874	25	203.1
Danny Ragsdale, Redlands	Sr.	9	380	247	65.0	7	3,639	33	170.4
Jesse Lowry, Thomas More	Fr.	9	159	98	61.6	4	1,540	14	167.1
Dan Mauer, Bri'water (Mass.)	Sr.	10	168	86	51.1	12	1,672	23	165.7
Dan Blahy, La Verne	Sr.	9	266	157	59.0	4	2,556	23	165.3
Justin Peery, Westminster (Mo.)	Sr.	10	498	329	66.0	15	4,092	54	164.9
Brad Boyd, Hardin-Simmons	Jr.	10	315	192	60.9	17	3,134	27	162.0
Adam Ryan, Wilmington (Ohio)	So.	10	372	212	56.9	10	3,343	34	157.3
Matt Wheeler, Wartburg	Sr.	10	274	159	58.0	10	2,372	28	157.2
Michael McCabe, Muhlenberg	Jr.	10	297	179	60.2	8	2,560	26	156.2
Joel Parrett, Bluffton	Sr.	10	267	179	67.0	10	2,354	18	155.9
Matt D'Orazio, Otterbein	Sr.	10	338	189	55.9	9	2,798	36	155.3
Bryan Banta, Claremont-M-S	Sr.	9	164	86	52.4	2	1,456	15	154.8

Total Offense

	1999 Class	G	Plays	Yards	Yds.PG
Justin Peery, Westminster (Mo.)	Sr.	10	599	4,419	441.9
Danny Ragsdale, Redlands	Sr.	9	464	3,855	428.3
Adam Ryan, Wilmington (Ohio)	So.	10	280	3,478	347.8
Brian Partlow, Randolph-Macon	Sr.	10	566	3,400	340.0
Josh Wakefield, Alma	Sr.	9	476	2,990	332.2
Eric Bruns, Hanover	Sr.	10	488	3,252	325.2
Brad Boyd, Hardin-Simmons	Jr.	10	381	3,236	323.6
Dan Blahy, La Verne	Sr.	9	369	2,905	322.8
Travis McMahen, Franklin	Sr.	10	536	3,220	322.0
Matt D'Orazio, Otterbein	Sr.	10	423	3,073	307.3

Receptions Per Game

	1999 Class	G	Rec.	Yards	TD	Rec.PG
Scott Pingel, Westminster (Mo.)	Sr.	10	136	1,648	24	13.6
Sean Eaton, Randolph-Macon	Sr.	10	95	1,289	15	9.5
Mike Groll, Defiance	Sr.	9	84	1,010	11	9.3
Tarrik Wilson, Hanover	Sr.	9	83	974	7	9.2
Darryl DeShields, Greenville	Fr.	10	92	1,515	12	9.2
Matt Perceval, Wesleyan (Conn.)	Sr.	8	73	1,137	13	9.1
Jon Troy, Tufts	Sr.	8	70	855	5	8.8
Vince Annel, Knox	Sr.	10	87	1,062	6	8.7
Jeff Pederson, Grinnell	So.	10	84	918	14	8.4
Chad Hustead, Redlands	Jr.	9	72	1,150	18	8.0
Jason Coulie, Bates	Sr.	8	63	852	5	7.9
Aaron Paulin, Concordia (Wis.)	Jr.	10	77	1,032	13	7.7
Michael Becker, Randolph-Macon	Jr.	10	77	1,015	5	7.7
Matt Eisenberg, Juniata	Jr.	10	76	1,547	19	7.6
Kurt Casper, Wabash	So.	10	75	902	6	7.5
Mark Jacobson, Martin Luther	Sr.	8	59	826	13	7.4
Jeff Halstead, Puget Sound	Sr.	9	66	956	8	7.3
Adam Marino, Mount Union	Jr.	10	73	1,456	19	7.3
Mike Hunter, Catholic	Sr.	10	73	1,014	8	7.3

Receiving Yards Per Game

	1999 Class	G	Rec.	Yards	TD	Yds.PG
Scott Pingel, Westminster (Mo.)	Sr.	10	136	1,648	24	164.8
Matt Eisenberg, Juniata	Jr.	10	76	1,547	19	154.7
Darryl DeShields, Greenville	Fr.	10	92	1,515	12	151.5
Adam Marino, Mount Union	Jr.	10	73	1,456	19	145.6
Matt Perceval, Wesleyan (Conn.)	Sr.	8	73	1,137	13	142.1
Stacy Seidl, Lawrence	Sr.	10	60	1,343	12	134.3
Sean Eaton, Randolph-Macon	Sr.	10	95	1,289	15	128.9

	1999 Class	G	Rec.	Yards	TD	Yds.PG
Chad Hustead, Redlands	Jr.	9	72	1,150	18	127.8
Derek Baker, Buffalo St.	Jr.	9	51	1,091	9	121.2
Ben Streby, Otterbein	Sr.	10	69	1,203	19	120.3
Joe Rettler, Ripon	Sr.	10	61	1,186	11	118.6
Jonathan Cain, Wilmington (Ohio)	So.	10	69	1,155	14	115.5

Interceptions

	1999 Class	G	No.	Yards	Int.PG
Steven Cella, Trinity (Conn.)	Jr.	8	9	106	1.1
Eric Newsome, Hobart	Jr.	8	9	148	1.1
Chris Swartz, Rensselaer	Jr.	9	10	118	1.1
Jeremy Presar, Ohio Northern	Jr.	10	10	40	1.0
Charles Verdone, Benedictine (Ill.)	Jr.	10	10	101	1.0
Antonio Nash, Susquehanna	Fr.	10	10	90	1.0
Jason Fosdick, Augustana (Ill.)	Sr.	9	9	165	1.0
Andy Palzkill, Wis.-Stevens Point	Sr.	10	9	130	.9
Brian Portilla, Wis.-La Crosse	So.	10	9	114	.9
Seth Mastrine, Wooster	Jr.	10	9	111	.9
Bobby Hill, Lakeland	So.	9	8	163	.9

Scoring

	1999 Class	G	TD	XP	FG	Pts.	Pts.PG
R. J. Bowers, Grove City	Jr.	10	25	4	0	154	15.4
Scott Pingel, Westminster (Mo.)	Sr.	10	24	4	0	148	14.8
Andrew Notarfrancesco, Catholic	Sr.	10	23	0	0	138	13.8
Chuck Moore, Mount Union	Jr.	10	22	0	0	132	13.2
Ron Lewis, Montclair St.	Sr.	8	16	0	0	96	12.0
Jamal Robertson, Ohio Northern	Jr.	10	20	0	0	120	12.0
Matt Eisenberg, Juniata	Jr.	10	19	6	0	120	12.0
Chad Hustead, Redlands	Jr.	9	18	0	0	108	12.0
Kevin Cahill, Springfield	Jr.	10	18	10	0	118	11.8
Adam Marino, Mount Union	Jr.	10	19	2	0	116	11.6
Ben Streby, Otterbein	Sr.	10	19	2	0	116	11.6
Paul Smith, Gettysburg	Sr.	10	19	0	0	114	11.4
Daryl Gholson, Greensboro	Jr.	9	16	0	0	96	10.7
Anthony Hicks, Pacific Lutheran	Sr.	9	16	0	0	96	10.7
Kenneth Sasu, Marietta	Jr.	9	16	0	0	96	10.7
Tyson Goings, Bluffton	Jr.	10	17	4	0	106	10.6
Steve Tardif, Maine Maritime	Sr.	9	15	2	0	92	10.2
Darrell Souhrada, Wis.-Eau Claire	Jr.	10	17	0	0	102	10.2
Travis Prunty, Gust. Adolphus	Sr.	10	17	0	0	102	10.2
Brandon Ford, Redlands	Jr.	9	15	0	0	90	10.0
Casey Donaldson, Wittenberg	Jr.	9	15	0	0	90	10.0

STATISTICAL LEADERS

All-Purpose Yards

	1999 Class	G	Rush	Rec.	PR	KOR	Int.	Total Yards	Yds.PG
Paul Smith, Gettysburg	Sr.	10	1,546	301	255	615	0	2,717	271.70
Kenneth Sasu, Marietta	Jr.	9	1,770	82	0	374	0	2,226	247.33
Steve Tardif, Maine Maritime	Sr.	9	1,567	149	0	479	8	2,203	244.78
R. J. Bowers, Grove City	Jr.	10	2,098	34	0	240	0	2,372	237.20
Matt Eisenberg, Juniata	Jr.	10	16	1,547	205	345	0	2,113	211.30
Joshua Carter, Muhlenberg	So.	10	67	698	337	981	0	2,083	208.30
D'Andra Freeman, Fitchburg St.	Sr.	10	1,871	91	0	29	0	1,991	199.10
Mike Groll, Defiance	Sr.	9	18	1,010	149	527	0	1,704	189.33
Jim Larkin, Franklin	Sr.	10	126	1,026	94	627	0	1,873	187.30
Matt Perceval, Wesleyan (Conn.)	Sr.	8	4	1,137	63	261	0	1,465	183.13
Shannon King, Wis.-Oshkosh	Sr.	10	72	939	262	525	0	1,798	179.80
Ben Smith, Buena Vista	Sr.	10	1,583	51	0	109	0	1,743	174.30
Drew Sherman, Knox	Sr.	10	1,318	259	8	154	0	1,739	173.90
Jamal Robertson, Ohio Northern	Jr.	10	1,544	187	0	0	0	1,731	173.10
Jeff Halstead, Puget Sound	Sr.	9	0	956	0	601	0	1,557	173.00
Marvin Qualls, Chapman	Jr.	9	32	1,025	244	244	0	1,545	171.67
Mike McKenzie, Millsaps	Sr.	8	768	190	0	384	0	1,342	167.75
Eric Hamilton, Concordia (Wis.)	So.	9	1,186	322	0	0	0	1,508	167.56
Michael Becker, Randolph-Macon	Jr.	10	0	1,015	163	491	0	1,669	166.90
Brent Bardellini, Western Conn. St.	Sr.	10	27	981	447	213	0	1,668	166.80
Chuck Moore, Mount Union	Jr.	10	1,114	190	150	209	0	1,663	166.30
Scott Pingel, Westminster (Mo.)	Sr.	10	0	1,648	0	0	0	1,648	164.80
Marvin Langley, Western New Eng.	So.	10	1,050	75	85	430	0	1,640	164.00
Anthony Hicks, Pacific Lutheran	Sr.	9	1,155	307	0	0	0	1,462	162.44
Brian Girardi, Cortland St.	Sr.	10	30	916	52	608	0	1,606	160.60

Marietta's Kenneth Sasu averaged 247.33 all-purpose yards in 1999 to finish second in Division III.

Punt Returns

(Min. 1.2 per game)	1999 Class	No.	Yds.	Avg.
Jake Wolter, Wis.-Whitewater	Jr.	12	230	19.2
Rodney McNeil, Westminster (Mo.)	Jr.	16	304	19.0
Spencer Ingram, Salve Regina	Fr.	22	413	18.8
Mike Benson, Coast Guard	Jr.	17	315	18.5
James Parker, Catholic	So.	17	282	16.6
Keidric Dixon, McMurry	Jr.	11	180	16.4
Bobby Kraft, John Carroll	Sr.	13	21	116.2
Jared Arn, Wis.-La Crosse	Sr.	19	300	15.8
Jeff Brennan, Buena Vista	Sr.	22	345	15.7
Brian Britt, Centre	Jr.	29	440	15.2

Kickoff Returns

(Min. 1.2 per game)	1999 Class	No.	Yds.	Avg.
David Ziegler, John Carroll	Sr.	11	393	35.7
Joshua Carter, Muhlenberg	So.	28	981	35.0
Elliot Turner, Greenville	So.	26	869	33.4
Gary Stone, Bethel (Minn.)	Sr.	22	721	32.8
Edwin Short, Wilmington (Ohio)	So.	13	404	31.1
Josh Snook, Maranatha Baptist	So.	15	455	30.3
Chad Valentyne, Wis.-Stevens Point	Fr.	18	530	29.4
Seth Haskins, Salisbury St.	Jr.	11	322	29.3
Cory Snyder, Washington (Mo.)	Jr.	15	433	28.9
Andre Summers, Wesley	Jr.	15	430	28.7
Kevin Gniadek, Worcester St.	Jr.	18	512	28.4

Punting

(Min. 3.6 per game)	1999 Class	No.	Avg.
Steve Vagedes, Ohio Northern	Sr.	37	46.2
Phil Barry, St. John's (Minn.)	Sr.	49	44.4
Wilson Hillman, Mississippi Col.	Jr.	61	42.0
Keith Scranton, Brockport St.	Sr.	69	41.5
Richard Harr, Ferrum	Sr.	51	40.9
Mark Kevern, Cal Lutheran	Sr.	36	40.8
Mark Olschefskie, Wesleyan (Conn.)	Sr.	40	40.7
John Shaffer, Lycoming	Jr.	39	40.7
Matt Mahaffey, Wooster	Sr.	49	40.5
Brett Dorsett, Otterbein	Jr.	41	40.5
Ryan Jordan, North Central	So.	74	40.5
Ryan Fournier, Worcester Tech	Sr.	47	40.4

Field Goals

	1999 Class	G	FGA	FG	Pct.	FGPG
Ryan Geisler, Cal Lutheran	Jr.	9	18	14	77.8	1.56
Haakon Nelson, St. Olaf	Sr.	10	20	15	75.0	1.50
Chris Baughman, Wheaton (Ill.)	Jr.	9	13	12	92.3	1.33
Keith Debbaudt, Albion	Jr.	9	16	11	68.8	1.22
Roman Natoli, Chicago	So.	9	20	11	55.0	1.22
Andy English, Rhodes	Fr.	9	14	10	71.4	1.11
George Merrill, Albright	So.	10	17	11	64.7	1.10
Wade Obermeyer, Maryville (Tenn.)	Sr.	10	16	11	68.8	1.10
Rich Dwyer, FDU-Madison	Sr.	10	13	11	84.6	1.10
Adam Kennett, Western Conn. St.	Sr.	10	16	11	68.8	1.10
Christian White, Gust. Adolphus	Jr.	10	16	10	62.5	1.00
Kevin Cherwa, Randolph-Macon	Jr.	10	16	10	62.5	1.00
Seth Olson, Bethel (Minn.)	Jr.	10	18	10	55.6	1.00
David Gaulke, Wis.-Oshkosh	So.	10	15	10	66.7	1.00
Brent Grablachoff, Montclair St.	Fr.	8	10	8	80.0	1.00

1999 Division III Team Leaders

Total Offense

	G	Plays	Yds.	Yds.PG
Mount Union	10	731	5,595	559.5
Westminster (Mo.)	10	757	5,270	527.0
Redlands	9	639	4,580	508.9
McMurry	9	638	4,462	495.8
Wilmington (Ohio)	10	761	4,948	494.8
Alma	9	735	4,362	484.7
Catholic	10	742	4,815	481.5
Hardin-Simmons	10	694	4,778	477.8
Ohio Northern	10	746	4,710	471.0
Pacific Lutheran	9	594	4,183	464.8

Total Defense

	G	Plays	Yds.	Yds.PG
Washington (Mo.)	10	606	1,921	192.1
Union (N.Y.)	10	638	1,945	194.5
Trinity (Tex.)	10	643	2,002	200.2

1999 Division III Team Leaders

	G	Plays	Yds.	Yds.PG
Salve Regina	10	578	2,109	210.9
Montclair St.	8	500	1,796	224.5
Amherst	8	502	1,807	225.9
Rowan	9	598	2,079	231.0
Western Md.	10	634	2,320	232.0
Ohio Wesleyan	10	681	2,349	234.9
Chicago	9	631	2,117	235.2

Rushing Offense

	G	Car.	Yds.	Yds.PG
Springfield	10	597	3,753	375.3
Augustana (Ill.)	9	566	2,963	329.2
Wis.-River Falls	10	610	3,206	320.6
Willamette	10	528	3,183	318.3
Grove City	10	564	2,987	298.7
Ferrum	10	592	2,777	277.7
Bri'water (Mass.)	10	467	2,751	275.1
Buena Vista	10	529	2,744	274.4
Mount Union	10	486	2,715	271.5
Allegheny	10	563	2,636	263.6
Salve Regina	10	521	2,585	258.5
Sewanee	10	506	2,579	257.9
Beloit	10	560	2,535	253.5
Pacific Lutheran	9	372	2,261	251.2
Wittenberg	10	531	2,489	248.9

Rushing Defense

	G	Car.	Yds.	Yds.PG
Rowan	9	249	323	35.9
Washington (Mo.)	10	317	498	49.8
La Verne	9	280	514	57.1
Aurora	10	292	635	63.5
FDU-Madison	10	335	637	63.7
Union (N.Y.)	10	353	644	64.4
Trinity (Tex.)	10	316	679	67.9
Rensselaer	9	298	646	71.8
Pomona-Pitzer	8	267	622	77.8
St. John's (Minn.)	10	373	795	79.5
Wilmington (Ohio)	10	337	797	79.7
Wilkes	0	349	805	80.5
Trinity (Conn.)	8	293	645	80.6
Willamette	10	343	826	82.6
Williams	8	279	664	83.0

Scoring Offense

	G	TD	XP	2XP	DXP	FG	SAF	Pts.	Avg.
Mount Union	10	73	67	10	0	9	0	534	53.4
Westminster (Mo.)	10	71	47	70	1	1	0	492	49.2
Redlands	9	55	51	10	0	6	0	401	44.6
Bri'water (Mass.)	10	61	52	20	0	2	1	430	43.0
McMurry	9	52	40	50	0	4	1	376	41.8
Pacific Lutheran	9	54	44	20	0	0	0	372	41.3
Catholic	10	54	46	30	1	7	1	401	40.1
Trinity (Tex.)	10	53	49	10	0	8	0	393	39.3
Wilmington (Ohio)	10	56	36	30	0	5	0	393	39.3
Western Conn. St.	10	52	41	10	0	11	2	392	39.2

Scoring Defense

	G	TD	XP	2XP	DXP	FG	SAF	Pts.	Avg.
Lycoming	9	6	4	0	0	4	1	54	6.0
Western Md.	10	11	9	1	0	0	0	77	7.7
Rensselaer	9	10	7	0	0	2	0	73	8.1
Trinity (Tex.)	10	11	6	1	0	3	2	87	8.7
Ohio Wesleyan	10	13	9	3	0	2	11	01	10.1
Ferrum	10	12	10	0	0	7	0	103	10.3
Millikin	9	14	7	0	0	1	0	94	10.4
Williams	8	12	9	0	0	1	0	84	10.5
Union (N.Y.)	10	14	13	1	0	2	11	07	10.7
Wittenberg	0	14	8	3	0	4	0	110	11.0

Passing Offense

	G	Att.	Cmp.	Pct.	Int.	Yards	Yds.PG
Redlands	9	406	260	64.0	93	796	421.8
Westminster (Mo.)	10	512	335	65.4	174	171	417.1
Greenville	10	485	286	59.0	183	776	377.6
Franklin	10	524	279	53.2	193	707	370.7

	G	Att.	Cmp.	Pct.	Int.	Yards	Yds.PG
Randolph-Macon	0	525	279	53.1	203	549	354.9
Wilmington (Ohio)	10	330	217	65.8	103	405	340.5
Hardin-Simmons	10	325	198	60.9	173	209	320.9
Juniata	10	383	207	54.0	113	163	316.3
Alma	9	403	214	53.1	162	834	314.9
Hanover	10	409	262	64.1	143	105	310.5

Pass Efficiency Defense

	G	Att.	Cmp.	Pct.	Int.	Yards	TD	Rating Points
Union (N.Y.)	10	285	111	38.9	19	1,301	5	69.7
Chicago	9	270	108	40.0	24	1,323	7	71.9
Ferrum	10	247	107	43.3	16	1,030	5	72.1
Central (Iowa)	10	263	95	36.1	21	1,292	10	74.0
Allegheny	10	313	143	45.6	19	1,295	8	76.7
Rensselaer	9	285	117	41.0	25	1,625	5	77.2
Hobart	9	261	108	41.3	25	1,429	8	78.3
Lycoming	9	263	112	42.5	20	1,385	6	79.1
Trinity (Tex.)	0	327	150	45.8	10	1,323	6	79.8
Washington (Mo.)	0	289	123	42.5	19	1,423	9	81.0

Net Punting

	Punts	Yds.	Avg.	No. Ret.	Yds. Ret.	Net Avg.
Ohio Northern	43	1,950	45.34	17	175	41.27
St. John's (Minn.)	50	2,176	43.52	16	146	40.60
Baldwin-Wallace	57	2,273	39.87	19	51	38.98
Lycoming	39	1,586	40.66	7	93	38.28
Brockport St.	69	2,862	41.47	39	253	37.81
Albion	55	2,167	39.40	22	101	37.56
Wooster	51	2,059	40.37	20	146	37.50
North Central	74	2,995	40.47	41	236	37.28
Allegheny	51	1,996	39.13	20	97	37.23
Wesleyan (Conn.)	40	1,628	40.70	19	140	37.20

Punt Returns

	G	No.	Yds.	TD	Avg.
Westminster (Mo.)	10	20	401	1	20.05
Wis.-Eau Claire	10	17	313	1	18.41
Mount Union	10	22	389	2	17.68
Loras	10	20	350	2	17.50
Manchester	10	12	209	2	17.41
Salve Regina	10	32	526	2	16.43
Maine Maritime	9	15	238	1	15.86
Buffalo St.	9	14	219	1	15.64
MacMurray	10	32	485	3	15.15
Coast Guard	10	21	315	1	15.00

Kickoff Returns

	G	No.	Yds.	TD	Avg.
Muhlenberg	10	39	1,119	3	28.69
Greenville	10	44	1,208	2	27.45
Bethel (Minn.)	10	34	921	3	27.08
Baldwin-Wallace	10	29	748	1	25.79
Kalamazoo	9	37	940	1	25.40
Washington (Mo.)	10	26	659	1	25.34
John Carroll	10	35	877	4	25.05
Upper Iowa	10	31	766	3	24.70
Trinity (Tex.)	10	20	491	0	24.55
Worcester St.	10	37	882	0	23.83

Turnover Margin

	G	TURNOVERS GAINED Fum.	Int.	Total	TURNOVERS LOST Fum.	Int.	Total	Margin/Game
Rensselaer	9	15	25	40	6	12	18	2.44
Western Md.	10	11	18	29	2	4	6	2.30
Wis.-Stevens Point	10	14	24	38	10	7	17	2.10
Bethel (Minn.)	10	13	23	36	6	10	16	2.00
Central (Iowa)	10	18	21	39	8	12	20	1.90
Claremont-M-S	9	8	18	26	7	2	9	1.88
Millikin	9	13	17	30	9	4	13	1.88
Rowan	9	9	22	31	7	8	15	1.77
Chicago	9	9	24	33	10	8	18	1.66
Bluffton	10	13	19	32	6	10	16	1.60
Mount Union	10	11	17	28	10	3	13	1.50

		TURNOVERS GAINED			TURNOVERS LOST			Margin/
	G	Fum.	Int.	Total	Fum.	Int.	Total	Game
Union (N.Y.)	0	18	19	37	8	14	22	1.50
Buena Vista	10	15	21	36	11	10	21	1.50
Frostburg St.	10	13	17	30	8	7	15	1.50
Wartburg	10	7	22	29	5	10	15	1.40
St. Thomas (Minn.)	10	16	16	32	7	11	18	1.40

Longest Division III Plays of 1999

Rushing

Player, Team (Opponent)	Yards
Eric Carlson, Bethel (Minn.) (St. Olaf)	97
Chris Sullivan, Wash. & Lee (Swarthmore)	94
Drew Onkst, Juniata (Wilkes)	92
Chris Rodgers, McMurry (Austin)	90
Dan Boyle, Catholic (Emory & Henry)	87
Ben Smith, Buena Vista (Dubuque)	87
Richard Green, Howard Payne (McMurry)	85
Patrick Baca, Hardin-Simmons (Wis.-Whitewater)	85
Mike Hankins, Wilkes (Susquehanna)	85
Lamont Boone, Chowan (Methodist)	83
Ben Smith, Buena Vista (Loras)	83
Jared Arn, Wis.-La Crosse (Washburn)	83

Passing

Passer-Receiver, Team (Opponent)	Yards
Dan Pincelli-John Nowak, Hartwick (Union [N.Y.])	99
Reid Geibel-James Denegall, Heidelberg (Marietta)	98
Joe Montrella-Matt Eisenberg, Juniata (Wilkes)	95
Mike Kornblau-Darryl Deshields, Greenville (Maranatha Baptist)	95
Sean Keenan-Matt Student, Williams (Trinity [Conn.])	95
Tom Pierantozzi-Jim Demaise, King's (Pa.) (Susquehanna)	91
Alan Beversdorf-Shannon King, Wis.-Oshkosh (Wis.-La Crosse)	91
Corey Stanger-Ben Sieben, St. John's (Minn.) (Wis.-Eau Claire)	91
Josh Boraas-Nick Wagner, Wis.-La Crosse (Wis.-Whitewater)	90
Jason Lutz-Marcus Richardson, Bridgewater (Va.) (Guilford)	89
Jesse Lowry-Phil Beverly, Thomas More (Defiance)	89

Interception Returns

Player, Team (Opponent)	Yards
Jeremy Jones, Mississippi Col. (Austin)	100
Eric Heyman, Centre (Kenyon)	99
Kevin Myers, Dickinson (Hobart)	98
Brian Davis, Buena Vista (William Penn)	95
Benny Graham, Millikin (North Central)	90
Mark Anderson, Aurora (MacMurray)	90
Mark Anderson, Aurora (Eureka)	90
Ben Jarvis, Salve Regina (Worcester St.)	90

Punt Returns

Player, Team (Opponent)	Yards
Kirk Midthun, Bethel (Minn.) (St. Thomas [Minn.])	88
Antonio Nash, Susquehanna (Dickinson)	85

Player, Team (Opponent)	Yards
Tony Scruggs, Ohio Northern (Capital)	83
Darren Reed, Manchester (Olivet)	82
Jared Arn, Wis.-La Crosse (Wis.-Eau Claire)	82
Chris Crutchley, Wis.-Eau Claire (Wis.-River Falls)	82
Gary Bolden, MacMurray (Lakeland)	80

Kickoff Returns

Player, Team (Opponent)	Yards
Greg Ortberg, Dubuque (Upper Iowa)	100
Paul Sage, Colorado Col. (Pomona-Pitzer)	100
Michael Kirtman, Pomona-Pitzer (Colorado Col.)	100
Jared Owens, Albion (Hope)	99
John Beasley, Sewanee (Trinity [Tex.])	99
Marcus Canady, Coast Guard (Worcester Tech)	97
Lamar Wilson, Buffalo St. (Wash. & Jeff.)	97
Harrison Bernstein, Johns Hopkins (Merchant Marine)	95
David Ziegler, John Carroll (Ohio Northern)	95
Steve Grove, Claremont-M-S (La Verne)	95
Jerome Robinson, Widener (Western Md.)	95
Cory Snyder, Washington (Mo.) (Wabash)	95
Rex Gray, Simpson (Luther)	95

Field Goals

Player, Team (Opponent)	Yards
Joel Aromi, Concordia (Ill.) (Eureka)	53
David Gottschalk, Concordia (Ill.) (MacMurray)	49
Tom Hillemeier, Kalamazoo (Olivet)	48
B. J. Black, Hanover (Wilmington [Ohio])	48
Rob Johnston, Wis.-Whitewater (Wis.-River Falls)	48
Skip Sullivan, Trinity (Conn.) (Wesleyan [Conn.])	48
Brett Majors, Simpson (Buena Vista)	48
Adam Kennett, Western Conn. St. (Norwich)	47
Bill Lovendale, Curry (Salve Regina)	46
Jeremy Skura, Franklin (Hanover)	45
Jason Pritchard, Central (Iowa) (Luther)	45
Chad Turner, Austin (Mississippi Col.)	45
Rob Johnston, Wis.-Whitewater (Lambuth)	45
David Gaulke, Wis.-Oshkosh (Wis.-Eau Claire)	45
Jim English, Thomas More (Methodist)	45

Punts

Player, Team (Opponent)	Yards
Steve Vagedes, Ohio Northern (Capital)	88
Tim Tackett, Linfield (Lewis & Clark)	79
Phil Barry, St. John's (Minn.) (Concordia-M'head)	79
Matt Gallatin, Wittenberg (Ohio Wesleyan)	77
Ryan Jordan, North Central (North Park)	75
Terry Wood, Grinnell (Knox)	74
Gary Stone, Bethel (Minn.) (St. John's [Minn.])	74
Scot Amrozowics, Rochester (Carnegie Mellon)	74
Tom Pierantozzi, King's (Pa.) (Albright)	73
Seef Grauer, Eureka (Greenville)	72
Phil Barry, St. John's (Minn.) (Augsburg)	72

Conference Standings and Champions

1999 Conference Standings.................................470
Major-College Alignment History........................471
All-Time Conference Champions..........................476
Discontinued Conferences 483

1999 Conference Standings

(Full-season records do not include postseason play; ties in standings broken by full-season records unless otherwise noted.)

Division I-A

ATLANTIC COAST CONFERENCE

Team	Conference W	L	Pct.	Full Season W	L	Pct.
Florida St.	8	0	1.000	11	0	1.000
Georgia Tech	5	3	.625	8	3	.727
Virginia	5	3	.625	7	4	.636
Clemson	5	3	.625	6	5	.545
Wake Forest	3	5	.375	6	5	.545
North Carolina St.	3	5	.375	6	6	.500
Duke	3	5	.375	3	8	.273
Maryland	2	6	.250	5	6	.455
North Carolina	2	6	.250	3	8	.273

Bowl Games (2-3): Wake Forest (1-0, beat Arizona St., 23-3, in Aloha); Virginia (0-1, lost to Illinois, 63-21, in Micronpc.com); Clemson (0-1, lost to Mississippi St., 17-7, in Peach); Georgia Tech (0-1, lost to Miami [Fla.], 28-13, in Gator); Florida St. (1-0, beat Virginia Tech, 46-29, in Sugar).

BIG EAST CONFERENCE

Team	Conference W	L	Pct.	Full Season W	L	Pct.
Virginia Tech	7	0	1.000	11	0	1.000
Miami (Fla.)	6	1	.857	8	4	.667
Boston College	4	3	.571	8	3	.727
Syracuse	3	4	.429	6	5	.545
West Virginia	3	4	.429	4	7	.364
Pittsburgh	2	5	.286	5	6	.455
Temple	2	5	.286	2	9	.182
Rutgers	1	6	.143	1	10	.091

Bowl Games (2-2): Syracuse (1-0, beat Kentucky, 20-13, in Music City); Miami (Fla.) (1-0, beat Georgia Tech, 28-13, in Gator); Boston College (0-1, lost to Colorado, 62-28, in Insight.com); Virginia Tech (0-1, lost to Florida St., 46-29, in Sugar).

BIG TEN CONFERENCE

Team	Conference W	L	Pct.	Full Season W	L	Pct.
Wisconsin	7	1	.875	9	2	.818
Michigan	6	2	.750	9	2	.818
Michigan St.	6	2	.750	9	2	.818
Penn St.	5	3	.625	9	3	.750
Minnesota	5	3	.625	8	3	.727
Illinois	4	4	.500	7	4	.636
Purdue	4	4	.500	7	4	.636
Ohio St.	3	5	.375	6	6	.500
Indiana	3	5	.375	4	7	.364
Northwestern	1	7	.125	3	8	.273
Iowa	0	8	.000	1	10	.091

Bowl Games (5-2): Penn St. (1-0, beat Texas A&M, 24-0, in Alamo); Illinois (1-0, beat Virginia, 63-21, in Micronpc.com); Minnesota (0-1, lost to Oregon, 24-20, in Sun); Purdue (0-1, lost to Georgia, 28-25 [ot], in Outback); Michigan St. (1-0, beat Florida, 37-34, in Florida Citrus); Wisconsin (1-0, beat Stanford, 17-9, in Rose); Michigan (1-0, beat Alabama, 35-34 [ot], in Orange).

BIG 12 CONFERENCE

Team	Conference W	L	Pct.	Full Season W	L	Pct.
North						
Nebraska#	7	1	.875	11	1	.917
Kansas St.	7	1	.875	10	1	.909
Colorado	5	3	.625	6	5	.545
Kansas	3	5	.375	5	7	.417
Iowa St.	1	7	.125	4	7	.364
Missouri	1	7	.125	4	7	.364
South						
Texas#	6	2	.750	9	4	.692
Texas Tech	5	3	.625	6	5	.545
Oklahoma	5	3	.625	7	4	.636
Texas A&M	5	3	.571	8	3	.727
Oklahoma St.	3	5	.375	5	6	.455
Baylor	0	8	.000	1	10	.091

Bowl Games: Colorado (1-0, defeated Oregon, 51-43, in Aloha); Missouri (1-0, defeated West Virginia, 34-31, in Insight.com); Kansas St. (0-1, lost to Purdue, 37-34, in Alamo); Nebraska (0-1, lost to Arizona, 23-20, in Holiday); Texas Tech (0-1, lost to Mississippi, 35-18, in Independence); Texas (1-0, defeated Mississippi St., 38-11, in Cotton); Texas A&M (0-1, lost to Ohio St., 24-14, in Sugar).

Bowl Games (3-3): Texas A&M (0-1, lost to Penn St., 24-0, in Alamo); Kansas St. (1-0, beat Washington, 24-20, in Holiday); Colorado (1-0, beat Boston College, 62-28, in Insight.com); Oklahoma (0-1, lost to Mississippi, 27-25, in Independence); Texas (0-1, lost to Arkansas, 27-6, in Cotton); Nebraska (1-0, beat Tennessee, 31-21, in Fiesta).

#Overall record includes Big 12 championship game on December 4, in which Nebraska defeated Texas, 22-6, in San Antonio, Texas.

BIG WEST CONFERENCE

Team	Conference W	L	Pct.	Full Season W	L	Pct.
Boise St.	5	1	.833	9	3	.750
Idaho	4	2	.667	7	4	.636
New Mexico St.	3	3	.500	6	5	.545
Arkansas St.	3	3	.500	4	7	.364
Utah St.	3	3	.500	4	7	.364
Nevada	2	4	.333	3	8	.273
North Texas	1	5	.167	2	9	.182

Bowl Game (1-0): Boise St. (1-0, beat Louisville, 34-31, in Humanitarian).

CONFERENCE USA

Team	Conference W	L	Pct.	Full Season W	L	Pct.
Southern Miss.	6	0	1.000	8	3	.727
East Carolina	4	2	.667	9	2	.818
Louisville	4	2	.667	7	4	.636
UAB	4	2	.667	5	6	.455
Memphis	4	2	.667	5	6	.455
Houston	3	3	.500	4	6	.636
Army	1	5	.167	3	8	.273
Tulane	1	5	.167	3	8	.273
Cincinnati	0	6	.000	3	8	.273

Bowl Games (1-2): East Carolina (0-1, lost to TCU, 28-14, in Mobile Alabama); Louisville (0-1, lost to Boise St., 34-31, in Humanitarian); Southern Miss. (1-0, beat Colorado St., 23-17, in Liberty).

MID-AMERICAN CONFERENCE

Team	Conference W	L	Pct.	Full Season W	L	Pct.
East						
Marshall#	8	0	1.000	12	0	1.000
Miami (Ohio)	6	2	.750	7	4	.636
Akron	5	3	.625	7	4	.636
Ohio	5	3	.625	5	6	.455
Bowling Green	3	5	.375	5	6	.455
Kent	2	6	.250	2	9	.182
Buffalo	0	8	.000	0	11	.000
West						
Western Mich.#	6	2	.750	7	5	.583
Toledo	5	3	.625	6	5	.545
Northern Ill.	5	3	.625	5	6	.455
Eastern Mich.	4	4	.500	4	7	.364
Central Mich.	3	5	.375	4	7	.364
Ball St.	0	8	.000	0	11	.000

Bowl Game (1-0): Marshall (1-0, beat Brigham Young, 21-3, in Motor City).

#Overall record includes MAC championship game on December 3, in which Marshall defeated Western Michigan, 34-30, in Huntington, West Virginia.

MOUNTAIN WEST CONFERENCE

Team	Conference W	L	Pct.	Full Season W	L	Pct.
Brigham Young	5	2	.714	8	3	.727
Colorado St.	5	2	.714	8	3	.727
Utah	5	2	.714	8	3	.727
Wyoming	4	3	.571	7	4	.636
San Diego St.	3	4	.429	5	6	.455
New Mexico	3	4	.429	4	7	.364
Air Force	2	5	.286	6	5	.545
UNLV	1	6	.143	3	8	.273

Bowl Games (1-2): Utah (1-0, beat Fresno St., 17-16, in Las Vegas); Brigham Young (0-1, lost to Marshall, 21-3, in Motor City); Colorado St. (0-1, lost to Southern Miss., 23-17, in Liberty).

PACIFIC-10 CONFERENCE

Team	Conference W	L	Pct.	Full Season W	L	Pct.
Stanford	7	1	.875	8	3	.727
Oregon	6	2	.750	8	3	.727
Washington	6	2	.750	7	4	.636
Arizona St.	5	3	.625	6	5	.545
Oregon St.	4	4	.500	7	4	.636
Arizona	3	5	.375	6	6	.500
Southern California	3	5	.375	6	6	.600
California	3	5	.375	4	7	.364
UCLA	2	6	.250	4	7	.364
Washington St.	1	7	.125	3	9	.250

Bowl Games (1-4): Arizona St. (0-1, lost to Wake Forest, 23-3, in Aloha); Oregon St. (0-1, lost to Hawaii, 23-17, in Oahu); Washington (0-1, lost to Kansas St., 24-20, in Holiday); Oregon (1-0, beat Minnesota, 24-20, in Sun); Stanford (0-1, lost to Wisconsin, 17-9, in Rose).

SOUTHEASTERN CONFERENCE

Team	Conference W	L	Pct.	Full Season W	L	Pct.
East						
Florida#	7	1	.875	9	3	.750
Tennessee	6	2	.750	9	2	.818
Georgia	5	3	.625	7	4	.636
Kentucky	4	4	.500	6	5	.545
Vanderbilt	2	6	.250	5	6	.455
South Carolina	0	8	.000	0	11	.000
West						
Alabama#	7	1	.875	10	2	.833
Mississippi St.	6	2	.750	9	2	.818
Mississippi	4	4	.500	7	4	.636
Arkansas	4	4	.500	7	4	.636
Auburn	2	6	.250	5	6	.455
LSU	1	7	.125	3	8	.273

Bowl Games (4-4): Kentucky (0-1, lost to Syracuse, 20-13, in Music City); Mississippi St. (1-0, beat Clemson, 17-7, in Peach); Mississippi (1-0, beat Oklahoma, 27-25, in Independence); Arkansas (1-0, beat Texas, 27-6, in Cotton); Georgia (1-0, beat Purdue, 28-25 [ot], in Outback); Florida (0-1, lost to Michigan St., 37-34, in Florida Citrus); Alabama (0-1, lost to Michigan, 35-34 [ot], in Orange); Tennessee (0-1, lost to Nebraska, 31-21, in Fiesta).

#Overall record includes SEC championship game on December 4, in which Alabama defeated Florida, 34-7, in Atlanta, Georgia.

WESTERN ATHLETIC CONFERENCE

Team	Conference W	L	Pct.	Full Season W	L	Pct.
Fresno St.	5	2	.714	8	4	.667
Hawaii	5	2	.714	8	4	.667
TCU	5	2	.714	7	4	.636
Rice	4	3	.571	5	6	.455
Southern Methodist	3	3	.500	4	6	.400
UTEP	3	4	.429	5	7	.417
San Jose St.	1	5	.167	3	7	.300
Tulsa	1	6	.143	2	9	.182

Bowl Games (2-1): Fresno St. (0-1, lost to Utah, 17-16, in Las Vegas); TCU (1-0, beat East Carolina, 28-14, in Mobile Alabama); Hawaii (1-0, beat Oregon St., 23-17, in Oahu).

I-A INDEPENDENTS

Team	Full Season W	L	Pct.
Louisiana Tech	8	3	.727
La.-Monroe	5	6	.455
Navy	5	7	.417
Notre Dame	5	7	.417
UCF	4	7	.364
Middle Tenn. St.	3	8	.273
La.-Lafayette	2	9	.182

Major-College Alignment History

(Originally called major-college, now Division I-A)

Team	Years Major
Air Force	1957-present
Akron	1987-present
Alabama	1937-present
UAB	1996-present
Alcorn St.	1977
Appalachian St.	1974-81
Arizona	1939-40, 46-present
Arizona St.	1946-48, 50-54, 56-present
Arkansas	1937-40, 46-present
Arkansas St.	1975-81, 92-present
Army	1937-40, 46-present
Auburn	1937-40, 46-present
Ball St.	1975-81, 83-present
Baylor	1937-40, 46-present
Boise St.	1996-present
Boston College	1939-40, 46-present
Boston U.	1939-40, 47-65
Bowling Green	1961-81, 83-present
Brigham Young	1938-40, 46-present
Brown	1937-40, 46-81
Bucknell	1938-40, 46-47
Buffalo	1962-70, 99-present
California	1937-40, 46-present
Cal St. Fullerton	1976-92
Carnegie Tech	1937-40
Case Reserve	1948
Centenary	1938-47
UCF	1996-present
Central Mich.	1975-present
Chattanooga	1946-48, 50, 77-81
Chicago	1937-39
Cincinnati	1946, 48-81, 83-present
Citadel	1939, 46-52, 59-81
Clemson	1937-40, 46-present
Colgate	1937-40, 46-81
Colorado	1937-40, 46-present
Colorado Col.	1946-47
Colorado St.	1940, 46-present
Columbia	1938-40, 46-81
Cornell	1937-40, 46-81
Creighton	1939-42
Dartmouth	1937-40, 46-81
Davidson	1937-40, 46-53, 67-76
Dayton	1956-76
Denver	1940-60
Detroit	1939-64
Drake	1939-40, 46-58, 73-80
Duke	1937-40, 46-present
Duquesne	1937-40, 47-50
East Caro.	1966-present
East Tenn. St.	1978-81
Eastern Mich.	1976-81, 83-present
Florida	1937-40, 46-present
Florida St.	1955-present
Fordham	1937-40, 46-54
Fresno St.	1973-present
Furman	1946-53, 55-57, 65, 73-81
Georgetown	1937-40, 46-50
George Washington	1939-66
Georgia	1937-40, 46-present
Georgia Tech	1937-40, 46-present
Gonzaga	1938-41
Grambling	1977
Hardin-Simmons	1946-48, 50-62
Harvard	1937-40, 46-81
Haskell	1937-38
Hawaii	1974-present
Holy Cross	1938-40, 46-81
Houston	1949-present
Idaho	1938-40, 46-67, 69-77, 97-present
Illinois	1937-40, 46-present
Illinois St.	1976-81
Indiana	1937-40, 46-present
Indiana St.	1976-81
Iowa	1937-40, 46-present
Iowa St.	1937-40, 46-present
Jackson St.	1977
Kansas	1937-40, 46-present
Kansas St.	1937-40, 46-present
Kent St.	1962-81, 83-present
Kentucky	1937, 40-present
Lafayette	1938-40, 46-50
Lamar	1974-81
Lehigh	1938-40, 46-47
Long Beach St.	1973-91
La.-Lafayette	1974-present
La.-Monroe	1975-81, 94-present
LSU	1937-40, 46-present
Louisiana Tech	1975-81, 89-present
Louisville	1951, 62-present
Loyola Marymount	1950-51
Loyola (Ill.)	1940
Manhattan	1937-42
Marquette	1937-60
Marshall	1962-81, 98-present
Maryland	1937, 40, 46-present
McNeese St.	1975-81
Memphis	1960-present
Merchant Marine	1946-47
Miami (Fla.)	1946-present
Miami (Ohio)	1948-49, 61-81, 83-present
Michigan	1937-40, 46-present
Michigan St.	1937-40, 46-present
Middle Tenn. St.	1999-present
Minnesota	1937-40, 46-present
Mississippi	1937-40, 46-present
Mississippi St.	1937-40, 46-present
Missouri	1937-40, 46-present
Montana	1939-40, 46-62
Montana St.	1946-48
Navy	1937-40, 46-present
Nebraska	1937-40, 46-present
UNLV	1978-present
Nevada	1946-50, 92-present
New Hampshire	1940
New Mexico	1940, 46-present
New Mexico St.	1946-47, 52-53, 59-present
New York U.	1937-48, 51-52
North Carolina	1937-40, 46-present
North Carolina St.	1940, 46-present
North Texas	1957-81, 95-present
Northern Ariz.	1946-47
Northern Colo.	1946-47
Northern Ill.	1969-81, 83-present
Northwestern	1937-40, 46-present
Northwestern St.	1976-77
Notre Dame	1937-40, 46-present
Ohio	1948, 61-81, 83-present
Ohio St.	1937-40, 46-present
Oklahoma	1937-40, 46-present
Oklahoma St.	1939-40, 46-present
Oregon	1937-40, 46-present
Oregon St.	1937-40, 46-present
Pacific (Cal.)	1950-60, 62-63, 66, 69-95
Pennsylvania	1937-40, 46-81
Penn St.	1938-40, 46-present
Pittsburgh	1937-40, 46-present
Portland	1946-48
Princeton	1937-40, 46-81
Purdue	1937-40, 46-present
Rice	1937-40, 46-present
Richmond	1940, 46-81
Rutgers	1946-present
St. Louis	1940-49
St. Mary's (Cal.)	1937-40, 46-50
San Diego St.	1969-present
San Francisco	1940-51
San Jose St.	1939-40, 50-present
Santa Clara	1937-42, 46-52
Sewanee	1937
South Carolina	1939-40, 46-present
Southern California	1937-40, 46-present
Southern Ill.	1973-81
Southern Methodist	1937-40, 46-86, 89-present
Southern Miss.	1960, 63-present
Southern U.	1977
Stanford	1937-40, 46-present
Syracuse	1937-40, 46-present
Tampa	1973-74
Temple	1938-40, 46-53, 71-present
Tennessee	1937-40, 46-present
Tennessee St.	1977-80
Texas	1937-40, 46-present
Texas-Arlington	1972-81
Texas A&M	1937-40, 46-present
TCU	1937-40, 46-present
UTEP	1940, 46-present
Texas Southern	1977
Texas Tech	1937-40, 46-present
Toledo	1962-present
Trinity (Tex.)	1960
Tulane	1937-40, 46-present
Tulsa	1937-40, 46-present
UCLA	1937-40, 46-present
Utah	1938-40, 46-present
Utah St.	1939-40, 46-present
Vanderbilt	1937-40, 46-present
Villanova	1939-40, 46-80
Virginia	1940, 46-present
VMI	1939-40, 46-81
Virginia Tech	1940, 46-present
Wake Forest	1939-40, 46-present
Washington	1937-40, 46-present
Wash. & Lee	1940, 46-53
Washington (Mo.)	1937-40
Washington St.	1937-40, 46-present
West Tex. A&M	1946-47, 51-53, 58-80
West Virginia	1939-40, 46-present
Western Caro.	1977-81
Western Mich.	1962-present
Wichita St.	1946-86
William & Mary	1940, 46-81
Wisconsin	1937-40, 46-present
Wyoming	1940, 46-present
Xavier (Ohio)	1960-73
Yale	1937-40, 46-81

Division I-AA

ATLANTIC 10 CONFERENCE

Team	Conference W	L	Pct.	Full Season W	L	Pct.
James Madison	7	1	.875	8	3	.727
Massachusetts	7	1	.889	8	3	.727
Villanova	6	2	.750	7	4	.636
Delaware	5	3	.625	7	4	.636
William & Mary	5	3	.625	6	5	.545
Connecticut	3	5	.375	4	7	.364
Maine	3	5	.375	4	7	.364
New Hampshire	3	5	.375	5	6	.455
Richmond	3	6	.333	5	6	.455
Northeastern	1	7	.125	2	9	.182
Rhode Island	1	7	.125	1	10	.091

NCAA Division I-AA Playoffs (1-2): Massachusetts (1-1, beat Furman, 30-23 [ot], in first round; lost to Ga. Southern, 38-21, in quarterfinals); James Madison (0-1, lost to Troy St., 27-7, in first round)

BIG SKY CONFERENCE

Team	Conference W	L	Pct.	Full Season W	L	Pct.
Montana	7	1	.875	9	2	.818
Portland St.	6	2	.750	8	3	.727
Northern Ariz.	6	2	.750	8	3	.727
Eastern Wash.	6	2	.750	7	4	.636
Cal St. Northridge	4	4	.500	5	6	.455
Cal St. Sacramento	3	5	.375	6	5	.545
Weber St.	2	6	.250	3	8	.273
Idaho St.	1	7	.125	3	8	.273
Montana St.	1	7	.125	3	8	.273

NCAA Division I-AA Playoffs (0-2): Montana (0-1, lost to Youngstown St., 30-27, in first round); Northern Ariz. (0-1, lost to Ga. Southern, 72-29, in first round)

GATEWAY ATHLETIC CONFERENCE

Team	Conference W	L	Pct.	Full Season W	L	Pct.
Illinois St.	6	1	1.000	9	2	.818
Youngstown St.	5	1	.833	9	2	.818
Northern Iowa	3	3	.500	8	3	.727
Western Ill.	2	4	.333	7	4	.636
Southwest Mo. St.	2	4	.333	5	6	.455
Indiana St.	2	4	.333	3	8	.273
Southern Ill.	1	5	.167	5	6	.455

NCAA Division I-AA Playoffs (5-2): Illinois St. (2-1, beat Colgate, 56-13, in first round; beat Hofstra, 37-20, in quarterfinals; lost to Ga. Southern, 28-17, in semifinals); Youngstown St. (3-1, beat Montana, 30-27, in first round; beat N.C. A&T, 41-3, in quarterfinals; beat Florida A&M, 27-24, in semifinals; lost to Ga. Southern, 59-24, in championship game)

IVY GROUP

Team	Conference W	L	Pct.	Full Season W	L	Pct.
Brown	6	1	.857	9	1	.900
Yale	6	1	.857	9	1	.900
Cornell	5	2	.714	7	3	.700
Pennsylvania	4	3	.571	5	5	.500
Harvard	3	4	.429	5	5	.500
Dartmouth	2	5	.286	2	8	.200
Columbia	1	6	.143	3	7	.300
Princeton	1	6	.143	3	7	.300

METRO ATLANTIC ATHLETIC CONFERENCE

Team	Conference W	L	Pct.	Full Season W	L	Pct.
Fairfield#	7	1	.875	9	2	.818
Georgetown	7	1	.875	9	2	.818
Duquesne	6	2	.750	8	3	.727
Marist	5	3	.625	6	5	.545
Iona	4	4	.500	5	5	.500
La Salle	3	5	.375	4	6	.400
Siena	3	5	.375	3	7	.300
St. Peter's	1	7	.125	1	10	.091
Canisius	0	8	.000	1	10	.091

#Fairfield did not compete for the MAAC championship.

MID-EASTERN ATHLETIC CONFERENCE

Team	Conference W	L	Pct.	Full Season W	L	Pct.
N.C. A&T	8	0	1.000	10	1	.909
Florida A&M	7	1	.875	8	3	.727
Hampton	5	3	.625	7	4	.636
Bethune-Cookman	4	4	.500	7	4	.636
Howard	4	4	.500	5	6	.455
Delaware St.	4	4	.500	4	7	.364
South Carolina St.	2	5	.286	4	6	.400
Norfolk St.	1	7	.125	2	9	.182
Morgan St.	0	7	.000	2	8	.200

NCAA Division I-AA Playoffs (3-2): N.C. A&T (1-1, beat Tennessee St., 24-10, in first round; lost to Youngstown St., 41-3, in quarterfinals); Florida A&M (2-1, beat Appalachian St., 44-29, in first round; beat Troy St., 17-10, in quarterfinals; lost to Youngstown St., 27-24, in semifinals)

Heritage Bowl: Hampton (1-0, beat Southern U., 24-3, on December 18, in Atlanta, Georgia)

NORTHEAST CONFERENCE

Team	Conference W	L	Pct.	Full Season W	L	Pct.
Robert Morris	7	0	1.000	8	2	.800
Albany (N.Y.)	6	1	.857	7	2	.778
Wagner	5	2	.714	5	5	.500
Stony Brook	4	3	.571	5	5	.500
Central Conn. St.	3	4	.429	4	6	.400
Monmouth	2	5	.286	2	8	.200
St. Francis (Pa.)	1	6	.143	2	9	.182
Sacred Heart	0	7	.000	2	9	.182

OHIO VALLEY CONFERENCE

Team	Conference W	L	Pct.	Full Season W	L	Pct.
Tennessee St.	7	0	1.000	11	0	1.000
Murray St.	5	2	.714	7	4	.636
Eastern Ky.	4	3	.571	7	4	.636
Western Ky.	4	3	.571	6	5	.545
Tennessee Tech	4	3	.571	5	5	.500
Southeast Mo. St.	2	5	.286	3	8	.273
Eastern Ill.	2	5	.286	2	10	.167
Tenn.-Martin	0	7	.000	1	10	.091

NCAA Division I-AA Playoffs (0-1): Tennessee St. (0-1, lost to N.C. A&T, 24-10, in first round)

PATRIOT LEAGUE

Team	Conference W	L	Pct.	Full Season W	L	Pct.
Colgate	5	1	.833	10	1	.909
Lehigh	5	1	.833	10	1	.909
Towson	4	2	.667	7	4	.636
Bucknell	3	3	.500	7	4	.636
Lafayette	2	4	.333	4	7	.364
Holy Cross	2	4	.333	3	8	.273
Fordham	0	6	.000	0	11	.000

NCAA Division I-AA Playoffs (0-2): Colgate (0-1, lost to Illinois St., 56-13, in first round); Lehigh (0-1, lost to Hofstra, 27-15, in first round)

PIONEER FOOTBALL LEAGUE

Team	Conference W	L	Pct.	Full Season W	L	Pct.
Dayton	4	0	1.000	6	4	.600
Valparaiso	3	1	.750	9	2	.818
Drake	2	2	.500	7	4	.636
San Diego	1	3	.250	5	5	.500
Butler	0	4	.000	5	5	.500

SOUTHERN CONFERENCE

Team	Conference W	L	Pct.	Full Season W	L	Pct.
Ga. Southern#	7	1	.875	9	2	.818
Appalachian St.#	7	1	.875	9	2	.818
Furman#	7	1	.875	9	2	.818
Wofford	5	3	.625	6	5	.545
East Tenn. St.	4	4	.500	6	5	.545
Chattanooga	3	5	.375	5	6	.455
Western Carolina	2	6	.250	3	8	.273
Citadel	1	7	.125	2	9	.182
VMI	0	8	.000	1	10	.091

#Tri-champions. Furman received the automatic berth in the I-AA playoffs following a blind draw by the commissioner.

NCAA Division I-AA Playoffs (4-2): Ga. Southern (4-0, beat Northern Ariz., 72-29, in first round; beat Massachusetts, 38-21, in quarterfinals; beat Illinois St., 28-17, in semifinals; beat Youngstown St., 59-24, in championship game); Appalachian St. (0-1, lost to Florida A&M, 44-29, in first round); Furman (0-1, lost to Massachusetts, 30-23 [ot], in first round)

SOUTHLAND FOOTBALL LEAGUE

Team	Conference W	L	Pct.	Full Season W	L	Pct.
Troy St.	6	1	.857	10	1	.909
Stephen F. Austin	6	1	.857	8	3	.727
McNeese St.	5	2	.714	6	5	.545
Sam Houston St.	4	3	.571	6	5	.545
Northwestern St.	3	4	.429	4	7	.364
Southwest Tex. St.	2	5	.286	3	8	.273
Jacksonville St.	1	6	.143	2	9	.182
Nicholls St.	1	6	.143	1	10	.091

NCAA Division I-AA Playoffs (1-1): Troy St. (1-1, beat James Madison, 27-7, in first round; lost to Florida A&M, 17-10, in quarterfinals)

SOUTHWESTERN ATHLETIC CONFERENCE

Team	Conference W	L	Pct.	Full Season W	L	Pct.
Eastern						
Jackson St.#	7	2	.778	9	3	.750
Alabama A&M	4	4	.500	6	5	.545
Mississippi Val.	3	5	.375	3	8	.273
Alabama St.	2	6	.250	2	9	.182
Alcorn St.	2	7	.222	3	7	.300
Western						
Southern U.#	9	0	1.000	11	1	.917
Grambling	6	3	.667	7	4	.636
Texas Southern	4	3	.571	6	5	.545
Ark.-Pine Bluff	5	4	.556	5	5	.500
Prairie View	0	8	.000	2	8	.200

#Overall record includes SWAC championship game on December 11, in which Southern U. defeated Jackson St., 31-30, in Birmingham, Alabama.

Heritage Bowl: Southern U. (0-1, lost to Hampton, 24-3, on December 18, in Atlanta, Georgia)

I-AA INDEPENDENTS

Team	Full Season W	L	Pct.
Hofstra	10	1	.909
Elon	9	2	.818
Davidson	8	3	.727
Southern Utah	8	3	.727
Samford	7	4	.636
South Fla.	7	4	.636
St. John's (N.Y.)	7	4	.636
Morehead St.	5	5	.500
Charleston So.	4	6	.400
Liberty	4	7	.364
Jacksonville	3	6	.333
Austin Peay	3	8	.273
Cal Poly	3	8	.273
St. Mary's (Cal.)	2	9	.182

NCAA Division I-AA Playoffs (1-1): Hofstra (1-1, beat Lehigh, 27-15, in first round; lost to Illinois St., 37-20, in quarterfinals)

… CONFERENCE STANDINGS—DIVISION II

Division II

CENTRAL INTERCOLLEGIATE ATHLETIC ASSOCIATION*

Team	Conference W	L	Pct.	Full Season W	L	Pct.
Winston-Salem#	7	0	1.000	8	3	.727
Virginia Union	5	1	.833	8	2	.800
Virginia St.	5	2	.714	6	4	.600
Bowie St.	4	3	.571	5	4	.556
N. C. Central	4	3	.571	5	5	.500
Johnson Smith	2	6	.250	2	9	.182
Livingstone	2	5	.286	4	7	.364
Fayetteville St.	1	6	.143	1	10	.091
Elizabeth City St.	1	6	.143	1	10	.091

*Plays designated games.

#Overall record includes Pioneer Bowl on December 18, in which Winston-Salem defeated Tuskegee, 23-7, in Atlanta, Georgia.

COLUMBIA FOOTBALL ASSOCIATION

Team	Conference W	L	Pct.	Full Season W	L	Pct.
Western Wash.	4	0	1.000	8	2	.800
Western Ore.	3	1	.750	5	5	.500
Central Wash.	2	2	.500	4	5	.444
Simon Fraser	1	3	.250	4	6	.400
Humboldt St.	0	4	.000	3	7	.300

NCAA Division II Playoffs (0-1): Western Wash. (0-1, lost to Northeastern St, 27-24 [ot], in first round)

EASTERN FOOTBALL CONFERENCE

Team	Conference W	L	Pct.	Full Season W	L	Pct.
Atlantic						
C. W. Post#	7	1	.875	9	2	.818
Southern Conn. St.	6	2	.750	7	3	.700
Merrimack	6	3	.667	7	3	.700
St. Anselm	4	4	.500	4	5	.444
Mass.-Lowell	3	6	.333	3	7	.300
Central						
American Int'l#	8	1	.889	10	2	.833
Pace	5	3	.625	6	4	.600
Bryant	4	4	.500	5	4	.556
Bentley	3	6	.333	4	7	.364
Assumption	1	7	.125	3	7	.300
Stonehill	0	10	.000	0	10	.000

#Overall record includes EFC championship game on November 20, in which American Int'l defeated C. W. Post, 41-20.

GREAT LAKES INTERCOLLEGIATE CONFERENCE

Team	Conference W	L	Pct.	Full Season W	L	Pct.
Northwood	7	2	.778	8	2	.800
Ferris St.	7	2	.778	7	3	.700
Ashland	7	3	.700	7	3	.700
Hillsdale	6	3	.667	8	3	.727
Northern Mich.	6	3	.667	6	4	.600
Michigan Tech	6	4	.600	6	4	.600
Indianapolis	5	4	.556	7	4	.636
Grand Valley	5	4	.556	5	5	.500
Mercyhurst	4	5	.444	5	5	.500
Saginaw Valley	4	5	.444	4	6	.400
Westminster (Pa.)	2	8	.200	3	8	.273
Findlay	2	8	.200	2	8	.200
Wayne St. (Mich.)	0	10	.000	0	11	.000

GULF SOUTH CONFERENCE

Team	Conference W	L	Pct.	Full Season W	L	Pct.
Arkansas Tech	8	1	.889	9	2	.818
Southern Ark.	7	2	.778	8	2	.800
West Georgia	7	2	.778	8	3	.727
Delta St.	6	3	.667	6	4	.600
North Ala.	5	4	.556	5	6	.455
Central Ark.	3	6	.333	4	6	.400
Ark.-Monticello	3	6	.333	4	7	.364
Valdosta St.	3	6	.333	4	7	.364
Henderson St.	2	7	.222	2	9	.182
West Ala.	1	8	.111	1	10	.091

NCAA Division II Playoffs (0-1): Arkansas Tech (0-1, lost to Carson-Newman, 40-28, in first round)

LONE STAR CONFERENCE

Team	Conference W	L	Pct.	Full Season W	L	Pct.
North						
Northeastern St.	7	2	.778	8	3	.727
Southeastern St.	7	2	.778	7	4	.636
Central Okla.	6	2	.750	8	2	.800
Southwestern Okla.	4	5	.444	5	5	.500
Harding	3	5	.375	5	5	.500
East Central	3	5	.375	3	7	.300
Ouachita Baptist	1	7	.125	3	7	.300
South						
Eastern N.M.	6	3	.667	8	3	.727
Angelo St.	6	3	.667	7	4	.636
Tarleton St.	5	4	.556	5	6	.455

Team	Conference W	L	Pct.	Full Season W	L	Pct.
Tex. A&M-Kingsville	5	4	.556	5	6	.455
Abilene Christian	4	4	.444	4	6	.400
Tex. A&M-Commerce	4	5	.444	4	7	.364
Midwestern St.	3	6	.333	4	7	.364
West Tex. A&M	2	7	.222	2	8	.273

NCAA Division II Playoffs (2-2): Central Okla. (0-1, lost to UC Davis, 33-17, in first round); Northeastern St. (2-1, beat Western Wash., 27-24 [ot], in first round; beat UC Davis, 19-14, in quarterfinals; lost to Carson-Newman, 42-7, in semifinals)

MID-AMERICAN INTERCOLLEGIATE ATHLETICS ASSOCIATION

Team	Conference W	L	Pct.	Full Season W	L	Pct.
Northwest Mo. St.	9	0	1.000	10	1	.909
Pittsburg St.	8	1	.889	10	1	.909
Mo. Western St.	6	3	.667	7	4	.636
Central Mo. St.	5	4	.556	7	4	.636
Washburn	4	5	.444	6	5	.545
Emporia St.	4	5	.444	5	6	.455
Truman St.	4	5	.444	4	7	.364
Mo. Southern St.	3	6	.333	5	6	.455
Southwest Baptist	2	7	.222	2	9	.182
Mo.-Rolla	0	9	.000	0	11	.000

NCAA Division II Playoffs (4-1): Northwest Mo. St. (4-0, beat North Dakota, 20-13 [ot], in first round; beat Northern Colo., 41-35, in quarterfinals; beat Indiana (Pa.), 20-12, in semifinals; beat Carson-Newman, 58-52 [4 ot], in championship game); Pittsburg St. (0-1, lost to Northern Colo., 34-31, in first round)

NORTH CENTRAL INTERCOLLEGIATE ATHLETIC CONFERENCE

Team	Conference W	L	Pct.	Full Season W	L	Pct.
Northern Colo.	8	1	.889	10	1	.909
North Dakota	8	1	.889	9	1	.900
North Dakota St.	7	2	.778	9	2	.818
South Dakota St.	6	3	.667	8	3	.727
Neb.-Omaha	5	4	.556	7	4	.636
Augustana (S.D.)	3	6	.333	5	6	.455
South Dakota	3	6	.333	4	7	.364
Minn. St.-Mankato	2	7	.222	4	7	.364
Morningside	2	7	.222	3	8	.273
St. Cloud St.	1	8	.111	3	8	.273

NCAA Division II Playoffs (1-2): Northern Colo. (1-1, beat Pittsburg St., 34-31, in first round; lost to Northwest Mo. St., 41-35, in quarterfinals); North Dakota (0-1, lost to Northwest Mo. St., 20-13 [ot], in first round)

NORTHERN SUN INTERCOLLEGIATE ATHLETIC CONFERENCE

Team	Conference W	L	Pct.	Full Season W	L	Pct.
Northern St.	8	0	1.000	9	2	.818
Bemidji St.	6	2	.750	8	3	.727
Winona St.	6	2	.750	7	4	.636
Moorhead St.	5	3	.625	7	4	.636
Southwest St.	5	3	.625	6	5	.545
Minn.-Duluth	3	5	.375	3	8	.273
Wayne St. (Neb.)#	3	5	.375	3	8	.273
Minn.-Crookston	2	6	.250	3	7	.300
Concordia-St. Paul	2	6	.250	2	7	.222
Minn.-Morris	0	8	.000	0	11	.000

#Not eligible for NSIC championship.

PENNSYLVANIA STATE ATHLETIC CONFERENCE

Team	Conference W	L	Pct.	Full Season W	L	Pct.
Eastern Division						
West Chester	6	0	1.000	7	3	.700
Millersville	5	1	.833	8	2	.800
Bloomsburg	4	2	.667	7	4	.636
Kutztown	3	3	.500	4	6	.400
East Stroudsburg	2	4	.333	4	7	.364
Mansfield	1	5	.167	1	9	.100
Cheyney	0	6	.000	1	10	.091
Western Division						
Slippery Rock	6	0	1.000	10	1	.909
Indiana (Pa.)	5	1	.833	7	3	.700
Shippensburg	4	2	.667	8	3	.727
Calif. (Pa.)	2	4	.333	5	6	.455
Clarion	2	4	.333	3	7	.300
Edinboro	2	4	.333	3	8	.273
Lock Haven	0	6	.000	2	9	.182

NCAA Division II Playoffs (3-3): Slippery Rock (0-1, lost to Indiana [Pa.], 27-20 [ot], in first round); Indiana (Pa.) (2-1, beat Slippery Rock, 27-20 [ot], in first round; beat Millersville, 26-21, in quarterfinals; lost to Northwest Mo. St., 20-12, in semifinals); Millersville (1-1, beat Shepherd, 21-14, in first round; lost to Indiana [Pa.], 26-21, in quarterfinals)

ROCKY MOUNTAIN ATHLETIC CONFERENCE

Team	Conference W	L	Pct.	Full Season W	L	Pct.
Chadron St.	7	1	.875	7	3	.700
N.M. Highlands	7	1	.875	7	4	.636
Neb.-Kearney	6	2	.750	7	3	.700
Mesa St.	4	4	.500	6	5	.545
Western St.	4	4	.500	5	6	.455
Adams St.	4	4	.500	4	6	.400
Fort Hays St.	2	6	.250	2	9	.182
Fort Lewis	2	6	.250	2	9	.182
Colorado Mines	0	8	.000	1	9	.100

SOUTH ATLANTIC CONFERENCE

Team	Conference W	L	Pct.	Full Season W	L	Pct.
Carson-Newman	8	0	1.000	10	0	1.000
Catawba	7	1	.875	10	1	.909
Mars Hill	5	3	.625	7	4	.636
Gardner-Webb	4	4	.500	7	4	.636
Presbyterian	4	4	.500	7	4	.636
Lenoir-Rhyne	3	5	.375	5	6	.455
Newberry	3	5	.375	5	6	.455
Wingate	2	6	.250	3	8	.273
Tusculum	0	8	.000	2	9	.182

NCAA Division II Playoffs (4-2): Carson-Newman (3-1, beat Arkansas Tech, 40-28, in first round; beat Catawba, 28-25, in quarterfinals; beat Northeastern St., 42-7, in semifinals; lost to Northwest Mo. St., 58-52 [4 ot], in championship game); Catawba (1-1, beat Fort Valley St., 48-17, in first round; lost to Carson-Newman, 28-25, in quarterfinals)

SOUTHERN INTERCOLLEGIATE ATHLETIC CONFERENCE*

Team	Conference W	L	Pct.	Full Season W	L	Pct.
Fort Valley St.	5	1	.833	10	1	.909
Tuskegee#	5	1	.833	9	3	.750
Albany St. (Ga.)	4	2	.667	7	3	.700
Kentucky St.	4	2	.667	5	6	.455
Miles	2	4	.333	3	7	.300
Lane	2	4	.333	2	8	.200
Clark Atlanta	1	5	.167	3	7	.300
Morehouse	1	5	.167	2	8	.200
Morris Brown$	—	—	.000	6	5	.545
Savannah St.$	—	—	.000	5	6	.455

*Plays designated games.

#Overall record includes Pioneer Bowl on December 18, in which Winston-Salem defeated Tuskegee, 23-7, in Atlanta, Georgia. $Not eligible for SIAC championship.

NCAA Division II Playoffs (0-1): Fort Valley St. (0-1, lost to Catawba, 48-17, in first round)

WEST VIRGINIA INTERCOLLEGIATE ATHLETIC CONFERENCE

Team	Conference W	L	Pct.	Full Season W	L	Pct.
Shepherd	6	0	1.000	9	1	.900
Fairmont St.	5	1	.833	8	2	.800
West Liberty St.	4	2	.667	6	4	.600
West Virginia St.	2	4	.333	5	5	.500
Glenville St.	2	4	.333	5	6	.455
West Va. Wesleyan	2	4	.333	2	8	.200
Concord	1	5	.167	3	8	.273
West Va. Tech	1	6	.143	1	10	.091

NCAA Division II Playoffs (0-1): Shepherd (0-1, lost to Millersville, 21-14, in first round)

DIVISION II INDEPENDENTS

Team	Full Season W	L	Pct.
UC Davis	9	1	.900
New Haven	5	5	.500
Western N.M.	4	5	.444
St. Joseph's (Ind.)	4	7	.364
Texas Lutheran	3	7	.300
Quincy	3	8	.273
Okla. Panhandle	1	9	.100

NCAA Division II Playoffs (1-1): UC Davis (1-1, beat Central Okla., 33-17, in first round; lost to Northeastern St., 19-14, in quarterfinals)

Division III

AMERICAN SOUTHWEST CONFERENCE

Team	Conference W	L	Pct.	Full Season W	L	Pct.
Hardin-Simmons	7	0	1.000	10	0	1.000
McMurry	6	1	.857	7	2	.778
Howard Payne	4	3	.571	5	5	.500
Mississippi Col.	3	4	.429	6	4	.600
Mary-Hardin Baylor	3	4	.429	4	6	.400
Austin	2	5	.286	3	7	.300
Texas Lutheran	2	5	.286	3	7	.300
Sul Ross St.	1	6	.143	2	8	.200

NCAA Division III Playoffs (2-1): Hardin-Simmons (2-1, beat Washington [Mo.], 28-21, in first round; beat Wash. & Jeff., 51-3, in second round; lost to Trinity [Tex.], 40-33, in quarterfinals)

ATLANTIC CENTRAL FOOTBALL CONFERENCE

Team	Conference W	L	Pct.	Full Season W	L	Pct.
Frostburg St.*	5	1	.833	8	2	.800
Wesley	4	2	.667	6	4	.600
Ferrum	4	2	.667	6	4	.600
Chowan	2	4	.333	5	4	.556
Greensboro	2	4	.333	3	6	.333
Methodist	2	4	.333	3	7	.300
Salisbury St.	2	4	.333	2	7	.222

*Record does not include loss to Carnegie Mellon, 28-10, in ECAC Southwest championship game on November 20.

CENTENNIAL CONFERENCE

Team	Conference W	L	Pct.	Full Season W	L	Pct.
Western Md.	7	0	1.000	10	0	1.000
Ursinus	6	1	.857	9	1	.900
Muhlenberg	4	3	.571	6	4	.600
Dickinson	4	3	.571	6	4	.600
Johns Hopkins	3	4	.429	4	6	.400
Gettysburg	2	5	.286	3	7	.300
Frank. & Marsh.	1	6	.143	2	8	.200
Swarthmore	0	7	.000	1	8	.111

NCAA Division III Playoffs (2-2): Western Md. (1-1, beat Catholic, 20-16, in first round; lost to Trinity [Tex.], 20-16, in second round); Ursinus (1-1, beat Bri'water [Mass.], 43-38, in first round; lost to Rowan, 55-0, in second round)

FREEDOM FOOTBALL CONFERENCE

Team	Conference W	L	Pct.	Full Season W	L	Pct.
Western Conn. St.	6	0	1.000	10	0	1.000
Worcester Tech	3	3	.500	5	4	.556
Plymouth St.*	4	2	.667	7	3	.700
Springfield	4	2	.667	4	6	.400
Coast Guard	1	5	.167	1	9	.100
Norwich	1	5	.167	4	6	.400
Merchant Marine	2	4	.333	3	7	.300

*Record does not include victory over Salve Regina, 13-7, in the ECAC Northeast championship game on November 20.

NCAA Division III Playoffs (0-1): Western Conn. St. (0-1, lost to Montclair St., 32-24, in second round)

HEARTLAND COLLEGIATE ATHLETIC CONFERENCE

Team	Conference W	L	Pct.	Full Season W	L	Pct.
Hanover	7	0	1.000	10	0	1.000
Wabash	5	2	.714	5	5	.500
Wilmington (Ohio)	6	1	.857	9	1	.900
Bluffton	4	3	.571	7	3	.300
Franklin	2	5	.286	4	6	.400
Anderson	2	5	.286	2	8	.200
Mt. St. Joseph	2	5	.286	3	7	.300
Manchester	0	7	.000	2	8	.200

NCAA Division III Playoffs (0-1): Hanover (0-1, lost to Ohio Northern, 56-14, in first round)

ILLINI-BADGER CONFERENCE

Team	Conference W	L	Pct.	Full Season W	L	Pct.
Aurora	7	0	1.000	8	2	.800
MacMurray#	4	3	.571	6	4	.600
Lakeland	4	3	.571	5	5	.500
Concordia (Wis.)	4	3	.571	5	5	.500
Benedictine (Ill.)	3	4	.429	6	4	.600
Greenville (Ill.)#	3	4	.429	5	5	.500
Eureka	3	4	.429	4	6	.400
Concordia (Ill.)	0	7	.000	2	8	.200

#Also member of the St. Louis Intercollegiate Conference.

COLLEGE CONFERENCE OF ILLINOIS AND WISCONSIN

Team	Conference W	L	Pct.	Full Season W	L	Pct.
Augustana (Ill.)	6	1	.857	8	1	.889
Wheaton (Ill.)	5	2	.714	7	2	.778
Millikin	5	2	.714	7	2	.778
Ill. Wesleyan	4	3	.571	6	3	.667
Carthage	4	3	.571	5	4	.556
North Central	2	5	.286	2	7	.222
North Park	1	6	.143	2	7	.222
Elmhurst	1	6	.143	2	7	.222

NCAA Division III Playoffs (1-1): Augustana (Ill.) (1-1, beat St. Norbert, 39-32, in first round; lost to Mount Union, 42-33, in second round)

IOWA INTERCOLLEGIATE ATHLETIC CONFERENCE

Team	Conference W	L	Pct.	Full Season W	L	Pct.
Wartburg	10	0	1.000	10	0	1.000
Central (Iowa)	9	1	.900	9	1	.900
Buena Vista	7	3	.700	7	3	.700
Upper Iowa	6	4	.600	6	4	.600
Simpson	6	4	.600	6	4	.600
Coe	4	6	.400	4	6	.400
Loras	4	6	.400	4	6	.400
William Penn	3	7	.300	3	7	.300
Cornell College	3	7	.300	3	7	.300
Luther	2	8	.200	2	8	.200
Dubuque	1	9	.100	1	9	.100

NCAA Division III Playoffs (1-2): Wartburg (0-1, lost to Pacific Lutheran, 49-14, in second round); Central (Iowa) (1-1, beat Wis.-La Crosse, 38-17, in first round; lost to St. John's [Minn.], 10-9, in second round)

MICHIGAN INTERCOLLEGIATE ATHLETIC CONFERENCE

Team	Conference W	L	Pct.	Full Season W	L	Pct.
Alma	5	1	.833	8	1	.889
Albion	5	1	.833	6	3	.667
Hope	5	1	.833	5	4	.556
Defiance	3	3	.500	4	5	.444
Kalamazoo	2	4	.333	3	6	.333
Adrian	1	5	.167	2	7	.222
Olivet	0	6	.000	0	9	.000

NCAA Division III Playoffs (0-1): Alma (0-1, lost to Wittenberg, 42-19, in first round)

MIDDLE ATLANTIC STATES COLLEGIATE ATHLETIC CONFERENCE

Team	Conference W	L	Pct.	Full Season W	L	Pct.
Commonwealth League						
Susquehanna	4	1	.800	7	3	.700
Widener	3	2	.600	6	4	.600
Juniata	3	2	.600	6	4	.600
Albright	2	3	.400	3	7	.300
Lebanon Valley	2	3	.400	2	8	.200
Moravian	1	4	.200	2	8	.200
Freedom League						
Lycoming	4	0	1.000	9	0	1.000
Wilkes*	3	1	.750	6	4	.600
FDU-Madison^	2	2	.500	5	5	.500
King's (Pa.)	1	3	.250	5	5	.500
Delaware Valley	0	4	.000	2	8	.200

*Record does not include victory over FDU-Madison, 27-6, in ECAC Southeast championship game on November 20. ^Record does not include loss to Wilkes, 27-6, in ECAC Southeast championship game on November 20.

NCAA Division III Playoffs (0-1): Lycoming (0-1, lost to Wash. & Jeff., 14-7, in first round)

MIDWEST COLLEGIATE ATHLETIC CONFERENCE

Team	Conference W	L	Pct.	Full Season W	L	Pct.
St. Norbert	9	0	1.000	9	1	.900
Grinnell	7	2	.778	7	3	.700
Beloit	6	3	.667	7	3	.700
Ripon	6	3	.667	6	4	.600
Lake Forest	4	5	.444	5	5	.500
Carroll (Wis.)	4	5	.444	5	5	.500
Lawrence	3	6	.333	3	7	.300
Knox	2	7	.222	3	7	.300
Illinois Col.	2	7	.222	2	8	.200
Monmouth (Ill.)	2	7	.222	2	8	.200

NCAA Division III Playoffs (0-1): St. Norbert (0-1, lost to Augustana [Ill.], 39-32, in first round)

MINNESOTA INTERCOLLEGIATE ATHLETIC CONFERENCE

Team	Conference W	L	Pct.	Full Season W	L	Pct.
St. John's (Minn.)	8	1	.889	9	1	.900
Bethel (Minn.)	7	2	.778	8	2	.800
St. Thomas (Minn.)	7	2	.778	7	3	.700
Gust. Adolphus	6	3	.667	7	3	.700
Concordia-M'head	6	3	.667	6	4	.600
Augsburg	5	4	.556	6	4	.600
St. Olaf	3	6	.333	3	7	.300
Carleton	1	8	.111	2	8	.200
Hamline	1	8	.111	2	8	.200
Macalester	1	8	.111	2	8	.200

NCAA Division III Playoffs (2-1): St. John's (Minn.) (2-1, beat Wis.-Stevens Point, 23-10, in first round; beat Central [Iowa], 10-9, in second round; lost to Pacific Lutheran, 19-9, in quarterfinals)

NEW ENGLAND FOOTBALL CONFERENCE

Team	Conference W	L	Pct.	Full Season W	L	Pct.
Blue Division						
Salve Regina*	8	0	1.000	8	2	.800

CONFERENCE STANDINGS—DIVISION III

Team	Conference W	L	Pct.	Full Season W	L	Pct.
Curry	6	2	.750	7	3	.700
Nichols	5	3	.625	6	3	.667
MIT	5	3	.625	6	4	.600
Mass.-Dartmouth	2	6	.250	3	7	.300
Western New Eng.	2	6	.333	3	7	.300
Mass.-Boston	0	8	.000	0	10	.000

Red Division

Team	W	L	Pct.	W	L	Pct.
Bri'water (Mass.)	8	0	1.000	10	0	1.000
Mass. Maritime	6	2	.750	8	2	.800
Fitchburg St.	4	4	.500	6	4	.600
Westfield St.	4	4	.500	4	6	.400
Maine Maritime	3	5	.375	3	6	.333
Framingham St.	1	7	.125	2	8	.200
Worcester St.	1	7	.125	1	9	.100

*Record does not include loss to Plymouth St., 13-7, in the ECAC Northeast championship game on November 20.

NCAA Division III Playoffs (0-1): Bri'water (Mass.) (0-1, lost to Ursinus, 43-38, in first round).

NEW ENGLAND SMALL COLLEGE ATHLETIC FOOTBALL CONFERENCE#

Team	Full Season W	L	Pct.
Williams	7	1	.875
Middlebury	6	2	.750
Trinity (Conn.)	5	3	.625
Amherst	5	3	.625
Wesleyan (Conn.)	5	3	.625
Bates	4	4	.500
Tufts	4	4	.500
Colby	3	5	.375
Bowdoin	1	7	.125
Hamilton	0	8	.000

#The NESCAC does not keep conference standings.

NEW JERSEY ATHLETIC CONFERENCE

Team	Conference W	L	Pct.	Full Season W	L	Pct.
Montclair St.	5	0	1.000	7	1	.875
Rowan	4	1	.800	8	1	.889
Col. of New Jersey	3	2	.600	4	5	.444
New Jersey City	2	3	.400	3	7	.300
Wm. Paterson	1	4	.200	2	8	.200
Kean	0	5	.000	0	8	.000

NCAA Division III Playoffs (6-2): Rowan (4-1, beat Rensselaer, 29-10, in first round; beat Ursinus, 55-0, in second round; beat Montclair St., 42-13, in quarterfinals; beat Mount Union, 24-17 [ot], in semifinals; lost to Pacific Lutheran, 42-13, in championship game); Montclair St. (2-1, beat Buffalo St., 37-34, in first round; beat Western Conn. St., 32-24, in second round; lost to Rowan, 42-13, in quarterfinals)

NORTH COAST ATHLETIC CONFERENCE

Team	Conference W	L	Pct.	Full Season W	L	Pct.
Wittenberg	6	0	1.000	10	0	1.000
Ohio Wesleyan	4	2	.667	8	2	.800
Wooster	4	2	.667	8	2	.800
Allegheny	4	2	.667	6	4	.600
Denison	2	4	.333	4	6	.400
Earlham	1	5	.167	2	8	.200
Kenyon	1	5	.167	2	8	.200
Oberlin	0	6	.000	0	10	.000

NCAA Division III Playoffs (1-1): Wittenberg (1-1, beat Alma, 42-19, in first round; lost to Ohio Northern, 58-24, in second round)

NORTHWEST CONFERENCE OF INDEPENDENT COLLEGES

Team	Conference W	L	Pct.	Full Season W	L	Pct.
Willamette	5	0	1.000	7	3	.700
Pacific Lutheran	4	1	.800	8	1	.889
Linfield	3	2	.600	6	3	.667
Whitworth	2	3	.400	5	5	.500
Puget Sound	1	4	.200	1	8	.111
Lewis & Clark	0	5	.000	0	9	.000

NCAA Division III Playoffs (5-1): Pacific Lutheran (5-0, beat Willamette, 28-24, in first round; beat Wartburg, 49-14, in second round; beat St. John's [Minn.], 19-9, in quarterfinals; beat Trinity [Tex.], 49-28, in semifinals; beat Rowan, 42-13, in championship game); Willamette (0-1, lost to Pacific Lutheran, 28-24, in first round)

OHIO ATHLETIC CONFERENCE

Team	Conference W	L	Pct.	Full Season W	L	Pct.
Mount Union	9	0	1.000	10	0	1.00
Ohio Northern	8	1	.889	9	1	.900
John Carroll	6	3	.667	7	3	.700
Otterbein	6	3	.667	7	3	.700
Baldwin-Wallace	6	3	.667	6	4	.600
Heidelberg	4	5	.444	4	6	.400
Muskingum	2	7	.222	3	7	.300
Capital	2	7	.222	2	8	.200
Marietta	2	7	.222	2	8	.200
Hiram	0	9	.000	0	10	.000

NCAA Division III Playoffs (4-2): Mount Union (2-1, beat Augustana [Ill.], 42-33, in second round; beat Ohio Northern, 56-31, in quarterfinals; lost to Rowan, 24-17 [ot], in semifinals); Ohio Northern (2-1, beat Hanover, 56-14, in first round; beat Wittenberg, 58-24, in second round; lost to Mount Union, 56-31, in quarterfinals)

OLD DOMINION ATHLETIC CONFERENCE

Team	Conference W	L	Pct.	Full Season W	L	Pct.
Catholic	6	0	1.000	9	1	.900
Emory & Henry	4	2	.667	6	4	.600
Randolph-Macon	4	2	.667	5	5	.500
Bridgewater (Va.)	3	3	.500	5	5	.500
Wash. & Lee	3	3	.500	5	5	.500
Guilford	2	4	.333	4	6	.400
Hampden-Sydney	0	6	.000	1	9	.100

Designated league games: Catholic 34, Salisbury St. 2; Wash. & Lee 23, Centre (Ky.) 17.

NCAA Division III Playoffs (0-1): Catholic (0-1, lost to Western Md., 20-16, in first round)

PRESIDENTS' ATHLETIC CONFERENCE

Team	Conference W	L	Pct.	Full Season W	L	Pct.
Wash. & Jeff.	4	0	1.000	8	2	.800
Grove City	3	1	.750	6	4	.600
Waynesburg	2	2	.500	5	4	.556
Bethany (W.Va.)	1	3	.250	4	6	.400
Thiel	0	4	.000	3	7	.300

NCAA Division III Playoffs (1-1): Wash. & Jeff. (1-1, beat Lycoming, 14-7, in first round; lost to Hardin-Simmons, 51-3, in second round)

ST. LOUIS INTERCOLLEGIATE ATHLETIC CONFERENCE

Team	Conference W	L	Pct.	Full Season W	L	Pct.
Westminster (Mo.)	2	1	.667	8	2	.800
MacMurray#	2	1	.667	6	4	.600
Greenville#	2	1	.667	5	5	.500
Blackburn	0	3	.000	2	8	.200

#Also a member of the Illini-Badger Football Conference.

SOUTHERN COLLEGIATE ATHLETIC CONFERENCE

Team	Conference W	L	Pct.	Full Season W	L	Pct.
Trinity (Tex.)	6	0	1.000	10	0	1.000
Rhodes	4	2	.667	6	3	.667
Sewanee	4	2	.667	6	4	.600
Centre	3	3	.500	5	5	.500
DePauw	3	3	.500	5	5	.500
Millsaps	1	5	.167	2	8	.200
Rose-Hulman	1	5	.167	2	8	.200

NCAA Division III Playoffs (2-1): Trinity (Tex.) (2-1, beat Western Md., 20-16, in first round; beat Hardin-Simmons, 40-33, in quarterfinals; lost to Pacific Lutheran, 49-28, in semifinals)

SOUTHERN CALIFORNIA INTERCOLLEGIATE ATHLETIC CONFERENCE

Team	Conference W	L	Pct.	Full Season W	L	Pct.
Redlands	5	0	1.000	7	2	.778
La Verne	4	1	.800	7	2	.778
Cal Lutheran	3	2	.600	3	6	.333
Claremont-M-S	2	3	.400	5	4	.556
Occidental	1	4	.200	2	7	.222
Whittier	0	5	.000	0	9	.000

UNIVERSITY ATHLETIC ASSOCIATION

Team	Conference W	L	Pct.	Full Season W	L	Pct.
Washington (Mo.)	4	0	1.000	8	2	.800
Carnegie Mellon*	3	1	.750	7	3	.700
Rochester#	2	2	.500	3	6	.333
Chicago	1	3	.250	5	4	.556
Case Reserve	0	4	.000	2	8	.200

*Record does not include victory over Frostburg St., 28-10, in ECAC Southwest championship game on November 20. #Also a member of the Upstate Collegiate Athletic Association.

NCAA Division III Playoffs (0-1): Washington (Mo.) (0-1, lost to Hardin-Simmons, 28-21, in first round)

UPSTATE COLLEGIATE ATHLETIC CONFERENCE

Team	Conference W	L	Pct.	Full Season W	L	Pct.
Rensselaer	4	0	1.000	9	0	1.000
Union (N.Y.)*	3	1	.750	8	2	.800
Hobart	2	2	.500	5	4	.556
Rochester#	1	3	.250	3	6	.333
St. Lawrence	0	4	.000	0	10	.000

*Record does not include victory over Ithaca, 31-7, in ECAC Northwest championship game on November 20. #Also a member of the University Athletic Association.

NCAA Division III Playoffs (0-1): Rensselaer (0-1, lost to Rowan, 29-10, in first round)

WISCONSIN INTERCOLLEGIATE ATHLETIC CONFERENCE

Team	Conference W	L	Pct.	Full Season W	L	Pct.
Wis.-Stevens Point	6	1	.857	9	1	.900
Wis.-La Crosse	6	1	.857	7	3	.700
Wis.-Platteville	3	4	.429	5	5	.500
Wis.-River Falls	5	2	.714	6	4	.600
Wis.-Eau Claire	2	5	.286	2	8	.200
Wis.-Whitewater	3	4	.429	3	7	.300
Wis.-Oshkosh	2	5	.286	3	7	.300
Wis.-Stout	1	6	.143	1	9	.100

NCAA Division III Playoffs (0-2): Wis.-Stevens Point (0-1, lost to St. John's [Minn.], 23-10, in first round); Wis.-La Crosse (0-1, lost to Central [Iowa], 38-17, in first round)

DIVISION III INDEPENDENTS

Team	Full Season W	L	Pct.
Pomona-Pitzer	7	1	.875
Buffalo St.	7	2	.778
Ithaca*	7	3	.700
Maryville (Tenn.)	7	3	.700
Thomas More	7	3	.700
Martin Luther	5	3	.625
Alfred	6	4	.600
Brockport St.	6	4	.600
Hartwick	6	4	.600
Chapman	5	4	.556
Menlo	5	4	.556
Cortland St.	5	5	.500
Eastern Ore.	5	5	.500
Neb. Wesleyan	4	6	.400
Principia	3	5	.375
Maranatha Baptist	3	6	.333
Stillman	3	6	.333
Colorado Col.	2	7	.222
St. John Fisher	1	8	.111

*Record does not include loss to Union (N.Y.), 31-7, in ECAC Northwest championship game on November 20.

NCAA Division III Playoffs (0-1): Buffalo St. (0-1, lost to Montclair St., 37-34, in first round)

All-Time Conference Champions

Division I-A

ATLANTIC COAST CONFERENCE

Founded: In 1953 when charter members all left the Southern Conference to form the ACC. **Charter members** (7): Clemson, Duke, Maryland, North Carolina, North Carolina St., South Carolina and Wake Forest. **Admitted later** (3): Virginia (1953), Georgia Tech (1978) and Florida St. (1992). **Withdrew later** (1): South Carolina (1971). **Current members** (9): Clemson, Duke, Florida St., Georgia Tech, Maryland, North Carolina, North Carolina St., Virginia and Wake Forest.

Year	Champion (Record)
1953	Duke (4-0) & Maryland (3-0)
1954	Duke (4-0)
1955	Maryland (4-0) & Duke (4-0)
1956	Clemson (4-0-1)
1957	North Carolina St. (5-0-1)
1958	Clemson (5-1)
1959	Clemson (6-1)
1960	Duke (5-1)
1961	Duke (5-1)
1962	Duke (6-0)
1963	North Carolina (6-1) & North Carolina St. (6-1)
1964	North Carolina St. (5-2)
1965	Clemson (5-2) & North Carolina St. (5-2)
1966	Clemson (6-1)
1967	Clemson (6-0)
1968	North Carolina St. (6-1)
1969	South Carolina (6-0)
1970	Wake Forest (5-1)
1971	North Carolina (6-0)
1972	North Carolina (6-0)
1973	North Carolina St. (6-0)
1974	Maryland (6-0)
1975	Maryland (5-0)
1976	Maryland (5-0)
1977	North Carolina (5-0-1)
1978	Clemson (6-0)
1979	North Carolina St. (5-1)
1980	North Carolina (6-0)
1981	Clemson (6-0)
1982	Clemson (6-0)
1983	Maryland (5-0)
1984	Maryland (5-0)
1985	Maryland (6-0)
1986	Clemson (5-1-1)
1987	Clemson (6-1)
1988	Clemson (6-1)
1989	Virginia (6-1) & Duke (6-1)
1990	Georgia Tech (6-0-1)
1991	Clemson (6-0-1)
1992	Florida St. (8-0)
1993	Florida St. (8-0)
1994	Florida St. (8-0)
1995	Virginia (7-1) & Florida St. (7-1)
1996	Florida St. (8-0)
1997	Florida St. (8-0)
1998	Florida St. (7-1) & Georgia Tech (7-1)
1999	Florida St. (8-0)

BIG EAST CONFERENCE

Founded: In 1991 when eight charter members all went from independent status to form the Big East. **Charter members** (8): Boston College, Miami (Fla.), Pittsburgh, Rutgers (football only), Syracuse, Temple (football only), Virginia Tech (football only) and West Virginia (football only). **Current members** (8): Boston College, Miami (Fla.), Pittsburgh, Rutgers, Syracuse, Temple, Virginia Tech and West Virginia. **Note:** In 1991 and 1992, the team ranked highest in the USA Today/CNN coaches poll was declared champion. Beginning in 1993, the champion was decided by a seven-game round-robin schedule.

Year	Champion (Record)
1991	Miami (Fla.) (2-0, No. 1) & Syracuse (5-0, No. 16)
1992	Miami (Fla.) (4-0, No. 1)
1993	West Virginia (7-0)
1994	Miami (Fla.) (7-0)
1995	Virginia Tech (6-1) & Miami (Fla.) (6-1)
1996	Virginia Tech (6-1), Miami (Fla.) (6-1) & Syracuse (6-1)
1997	Syracuse (6-1)
1998	Syracuse (6-1)
1999	Virginia Tech (7-0)

BIG TEN CONFERENCE

Founded: In 1895 as the Intercollegiate Conference of Faculty Representatives, better known as the Western Conference. **Charter members** (7): Chicago, Illinois, Michigan, Minnesota, Northwestern, Purdue and Wisconsin. **Admitted later** (5): Indiana (1899), Iowa (1899), Ohio St. (1912), Michigan St. (1950) and Penn St. (1993). **Withdrew later** (2): Michigan (1907, rejoined in 1917) and Chicago (1940). **Note:** Iowa belonged to both the Missouri Valley and Western Conferences from 1907 to 1910. Unofficially called the Big Ten from 1912 until after 1939, then Big Nine from 1940 until Michigan St. began conference play in 1953. Formally renamed **Big Ten** in 1984. **Current members** (11): Illinois, Indiana, Iowa, Michigan, Michigan St., Minnesota, Northwestern, Ohio St., Penn St., Purdue and Wisconsin.

Year	Champion (Record)
1896	Wisconsin (2-0-1)
1897	Wisconsin (3-0)
1898	Michigan (3-0)
1899	Chicago (4-0)
1900	Iowa (3-0-1) & Minnesota (3-0-1)
1901	Michigan (4-0) & Wisconsin (2-0)
1902	Michigan (5-0)
1903	Michigan (3-0-1), Minnesota (3-0-1) & Northwestern (1-0-2)
1904	Minnesota (3-0) & Michigan (2-0)
1905	Chicago (7-0)
1906	Wisconsin (3-0), Minnesota (2-0) & Michigan (1-0)
1907	Chicago (4-0)
1908	Chicago (5-0)
1909	Minnesota (3-0)
1910	Illinois (4-0) & Minnesota (2-0)
1911	Minnesota (3-0-1)
1912	Wisconsin (6-0)
1913	Chicago (7-0)
1914	Illinois (6-0)
1915	Minnesota (3-0-1) & Illinois (3-0-2)
1916	Ohio St. (4-0)
1917	Ohio St. (4-0)
1918	Illinois (4-0), Michigan (2-0) & Purdue (1-0)
1919	Illinois (6-1)
1920	Ohio St. (5-0)
1921	Iowa (5-0)
1922	Iowa (5-0) & Michigan (4-0)
1923	Illinois (5-0) & Michigan (4-0)
1924	Chicago (3-0-3)
1925	Michigan (5-1)
1926	Michigan (5-0) & Northwestern (5-0)
1927	Illinois (5-0)
1928	Illinois (4-1)
1929	Purdue (5-0)
1930	Michigan (5-0) & Northwestern (5-0)
1931	Purdue (5-1), Michigan (5-1) & Northwestern (5-1)
1932	Michigan (6-0)
1933	Michigan (5-0-1)
1934	Minnesota (5-0)
1935	Minnesota (5-0) & Ohio St. (5-0)
1936	Northwestern (6-0)
1937	Minnesota (5-0)
1938	Minnesota (4-1)
1939	Ohio St. (5-1)
1940	Minnesota (6-0)
1941	Minnesota (5-0)
1942	Ohio St. (5-1)
1943	Purdue (6-0) & Michigan (6-0)
1944	Ohio St. (6-0)
1945	Indiana (5-0-1)
1946	Illinois (6-1)
1947	Michigan (6-0)
1948	Michigan (6-0)
1949	Ohio St. (4-1-1) & Michigan (4-1-1)
1950	Michigan (4-1-1)
1951	Illinois (5-0-1)
1952	Wisconsin (4-1-1) & Purdue (4-1-1)
1953	Michigan St. (5-1) & Illinois (5-1)
1954	Ohio St. (7-0)
1955	Ohio St. (6-0)
1956	Iowa (5-1)
1957	Ohio St. (7-0)
1958	Iowa (5-1)
1959	Wisconsin (5-2)
1960	Minnesota (5-1) & Iowa (5-1)
1961	Ohio St. (6-0)
1962	Wisconsin (6-1)
1963	Illinois (5-1-1)
1964	Michigan (6-1)
1965	Michigan St. (7-0)
1966	Michigan St. (7-0)
1967	Indiana (6-1), Purdue (6-1) & Minnesota (6-1)
1968	Ohio St. (7-0)
1969	Ohio St. (6-1) & Michigan (6-1)
1970	Ohio St. (7-0)
1971	Michigan (8-0)
1972	Ohio St. (8-0) & Michigan (7-1)
1973	Ohio St. (7-0-1) & Michigan (7-0-1)
1974	Ohio St. (7-1) & Michigan (7-1)
1975	Ohio St. (8-0)
1976	Michigan (7-1) & Ohio St. (7-1)
1977	Michigan (7-1) & Ohio St. (7-1)
1978	Michigan (7-1) & Michigan St. (7-1)
1979	Ohio St. (8-0)
1980	Michigan (8-0)
1981	Iowa (6-2) & Ohio St. (6-2)
1982	Michigan (8-1)
1983	Illinois (9-0)
1984	Ohio St. (7-2)
1985	Iowa (7-1)
1986	Michigan (7-1) & Ohio St. (7-1)
1987	Michigan St. (7-0-1)
1988	Michigan (7-0-1)
1989	Michigan (8-0)
1990	Iowa (6-2), Michigan (6-2), Michigan St. (6-2) & Illinois (6-2)
1991	Michigan (8-0)
1992	Michigan (6-0-2)
1993	Ohio St. (6-1-1) & Wisconsin (6-1-1)
1994	Penn St. (8-0)
1995	Northwestern (8-0)
1996	Ohio St. (7-1) & Northwestern (7-1)
1997	Michigan (8-0)
1998	Ohio St. (7-1), Wisconsin (7-1) & Michigan (7-1)
1999	Wisconsin (7-1)

BIG 12 CONFERENCE

Founded: In 1996 when 12 charter members combined eight members of Big Eight Conference with four former Southwest Conference members. **Charter members** (12): Baylor, Colorado, Iowa St., Kansas, Kansas St., Missouri, Nebraska, Oklahoma, Oklahoma St., Texas, Texas A&M and Texas Tech. **Current members** (12): Baylor, Colorado, Iowa St., Kansas, Kansas St., Missouri, Nebraska, Oklahoma, Oklahoma St., Texas, Texas A&M and Texas Tech.

Year	Champion (Record)
1996	Texas (6-2)
1997	Nebraska (8-0)
1998	Texas A&M (7-1)
1999	Nebraska (7-1)

In 1996, the Big 12 began a championship game to determine the league's representative in the BCS bowls. Following are the results of the North Division Champion (N) vs. the South Division Champion (S):

1996	Texas (S) 37, Nebraska (N) 27
1997	Nebraska (N) 54, Texas A&M (S) 15
1998	Texas A&M (S) 36, Kansas St. (N) 33 (2 ot)
1999	Nebraska (N) 22, Texas (S) 6

BIG WEST CONFERENCE

Founded: In 1969 as the Pacific Coast Athletic Association (PCAA). **Charter members** (7): UC Santa Barb., Cal St. Los Angeles, Fresno St., Long Beach St., Pacific (Cal.), San Diego St. and San Jose St. **Admitted later** (12): Cal St. Fullerton (1974), Utah St. (1977), UNLV (1982), New Mexico St. (1983), Nevada (1992), Arkansas St. (1993), La.-Lafayette (1993), Boise St. (1996), Louisiana Tech (1993), Northern Ill. (1993), Idaho (1996), North Texas (1996) and Arkansas St. (1998). **Withdrew later** (13): UC Santa Barb. (1972), Cal St. Los Angeles (1974), San Diego St. (1976), Fresno St. (1991), Long Beach St. (1991, dropped football), Cal St. Fullerton (1992, dropped football), Arkansas St. (1996), La.-Lafayette (1996), Louisiana Tech (1996), UNLV (1996), Northern Ill. (1996), Pacific (Cal.) (1996, dropped football) and San Jose St. (1996). Renamed **Big West** in 1988. **Current members** (7): Arkansas St., Boise St., Idaho, Nevada, New Mexico St., North Texas and Utah St.

ALL-TIME CONFERENCE CHAMPIONS—DIVISION I-A

Year	Champion (Record)
1969	San Diego St. (6-0)
1970	Long Beach St. (5-1) & San Diego St. (5-1)
1971	Long Beach St. (5-1)
1972	San Diego St. (4-0)
1973	San Diego St. (3-0-1)
1974	San Diego St. (4-0)
1975	San Jose St. (5-0)
1976	San Jose St. (4-0)
1977	Fresno St. (4-0)
1978	San Jose St. (4-1) & Utah St. (4-1)
1979	Utah St. (5-0)
1980	Long Beach St. (5-0)
1981	San Jose St. (5-0)
1982	Fresno St. (6-0)
1983	Cal St. Fullerton (5-1)
1984	Cal St. Fullerton (6-1)#
1985	Fresno St. (7-0)
1986	San Jose St. (7-0)
1987	San Jose St. (7-0)
1988	Fresno St. (7-0)
1989	Fresno St. (7-0)
1990	San Jose St. (7-0)
1991	Fresno St. (6-1) & San Jose St. (6-1)
1992	Nevada (5-1)
1993	La.-Lafayette (5-1) & Utah St. (5-1)
1994	La.-Lafayette (5-1), Nevada (5-1) & UNLV (5-1)
1995	Nevada (6-0)
1996	Nevada (4-1) & Utah St. (4-1)
1997	Utah St. (4-1) & Nevada (4-1)
1998	Idaho (4-1)
1999	Boise St. (5-1)

#UNLV forfeited title.

CONFERENCE USA

Founded: In 1996 when five charter members went from independent status and one former Southwest Conference member combined to form Conference USA. **Charter members** (6): Cincinnati, Houston, Louisville, Memphis, Southern Miss. and Tulane. **Admitted later** (3): East Caro. (1997), Army (1998) and UAB (1999). **Current members** (9): UAB, Army, Cincinnati, East Caro., Houston, Louisville, Memphis, Southern Miss. and Tulane.

Year	Champion (Record)
1996	Houston (4-1) & Southern Miss. (4-1)
1997	Southern Miss. (6-0)
1998	Tulane (6-0)
1999	Southern Miss. (6-0)

MID-AMERICAN ATHLETIC CONFERENCE

Founded: In 1946. **Charter members** (6): Butler, Cincinnati, Miami (Ohio), Ohio, Western Mich. and Western Reserve (now Case Reserve). **Admitted later** (11): Kent St. (now Kent) (1951), Toledo (1951), Bowling Green (1952), Marshall (1954 and 1997), Central Mich. (1972), Eastern Mich. (1972), Ball St. (1973), Northern Ill. (1973 and 1997), Akron (1992) and Buffalo (1999). **Withdrew later** (5): Butler (1950), Cincinnati (1953), Case Reserve (1955), Marshall (1969) and Northern Ill. (1986). **Current members** (13): Akron, Ball St., Bowling Green, Buffalo, Central Mich., Eastern Mich., Kent, Marshall, Miami (Ohio), Northern Ill., Ohio, Toledo and Western Mich.

Year	Champion (Record)
1947	Cincinnati (3-1)
1948	Miami (Ohio) (4-0)
1949	Cincinnati (4-0)
1950	Miami (Ohio) (4-0)
1951	Cincinnati (3-0)
1952	Cincinnati (3-0)
1953	Ohio (5-0-1)
1954	Miami (Ohio) (4-0)
1955	Miami (Ohio) (5-0)
1956	Bowling Green (5-0-1)
1957	Miami (Ohio) (5-0)
1958	Miami (Ohio) (5-0)
1959	Bowling Green (6-0)
1960	Ohio (6-0)
1961	Bowling Green (5-1)
1962	Bowling Green (5-0-1)
1963	Ohio (5-1)
1964	Bowling Green (5-1)
1965	Bowling Green (5-1) & Miami (Ohio) (5-1)
1966	Miami (Ohio) (5-1) & Western Mich. (5-1)
1967	Toledo (5-1) & Ohio (5-1)
1968	Ohio (6-0)
1969	Toledo (5-0)
1970	Toledo (5-0)
1971	Toledo (5-0)

Year	Champion (Record)
1972	Kent (4-1)
1973	Miami (Ohio) (5-0)
1974	Miami (Ohio) (5-0)
1975	Miami (Ohio) (6-0)
1976	Ball St. (4-1)
1977	Miami (Ohio) (5-0)
1978	Ball St. (8-0)
1979	Central Mich. (8-0-1)
1980	Central Mich. (7-2)
1981	Toledo (8-1)
1982	Bowling Green (7-2)
1983	Northern Ill. (8-1)
1984	Toledo (7-1-1)
1985	Bowling Green (9-0)
1986	Miami (Ohio) (6-2)
1987	Eastern Mich. (7-1)
1988	Western Mich. (7-1)
1989	Ball St. (6-1-1)
1990	Central Mich. (7-1)
1991	Bowling Green (8-0)
1992	Bowling Green (8-0)
1993	Ball St. (7-0-1)
1994	Central Mich. (8-1)
1995	Toledo (7-0-1)
1996	Ball St. (7-1)
1997	Marshall (7-1)
1998	Marshall (7-1)
1999	Marshall (8-0)

Since 1997, the MAC has conducted a championship game between the East and West division champion to determine a league champion. Following are the results of the East Division champion (E) vs. the West Division champion (W):

1997	Marshall (E) 34, Toledo (W) 14
1998	Marshall (E) 23, Toledo (W) 17
1999	Marshall (E) 34, Western Mich. (W) 30

MOUNTAIN WEST CONFERENCE

Founded: In 1999. **Charter members (8):** Air Force, Brigham Young, Colorado St., UNLV, New Mexico, San Diego St., Utah and Wyoming. All left the Western Athletic Conference after two years of 16-team league. **Current Members (8):** Air Force, Brigham Young, Colorado St., UNLV, New Mexico, San Diego St., Utah and Wyoming.

Year	Champion (Record)
1999	Brigham Young (5-2), Colorado St. (5-2) & Utah (5-2)

PACIFIC-10 CONFERENCE

Founded: In 1915 as the **Pacific Coast Conference** by group of four charter members. **Charter members** (4): California, Oregon, Oregon St. and Washington. **Admitted later** (6): Washington St. (1917), Stanford (1918), Idaho (1922), Southern California (1922), Montana (1924) and UCLA (1928). **Withdrew later** (2): Montana (1950) and Idaho (1958).

The Pacific Coast Conference dissolved in 1959 and the Athletic Association of Western Universities was founded with five charter members. **Charter members** (5): California, Southern California, Stanford, UCLA and Washington. **Admitted later** (5): Washington St. (1962), Oregon (1964), Oregon St. (1964), Arizona (1978) and Arizona St. (1978). Conference renamed **Pacific-8** in 1968 and **Pacific-10** in 1978. **Current members** (10): Arizona, Arizona St., California, Oregon, Oregon St., Southern California, Stanford, UCLA, Washington and Washington St.

Year	Champion (Record)
1916	Washington (3-0-1)
1917	Washington (3-0)
1918	California (3-0)
1919	Oregon (2-1) & Washington (2-1)
1920	California (3-0)
1921	California (5-0)
1922	California (3-0)
1923	California (5-0)
1924	Stanford (3-0-1)
1925	Washington (5-0)
1926	Stanford (4-0)
1927	Southern California (4-0-1) & Stanford (4-0-1)
1928	Southern California (4-0-1)
1929	Southern California (6-1)
1930	Washington St. (6-0)
1931	Southern California (7-0)
1932	Southern California (6-0)
1933	Oregon (4-1) & Stanford (4-1)
1934	Stanford (5-0)
1935	California (4-1), Stanford (4-1) & UCLA (4-1)
1936	Washington (6-0-1)

Year	Champion (Record)
1937	California (6-0-1)
1938	Southern California (6-1) & California (6-1)
1939	Southern California (5-0-2) & UCLA (5-0-3)
1940	Stanford (7-0)
1941	Oregon St. (7-2)
1942	UCLA (6-1)
1943	Southern California (4-0)
1944	Southern California (3-0-2)
1945	Southern California (6-0)
1946	UCLA (7-0)
1947	Southern California (6-0)
1948	California (6-0) & Oregon (6-0)
1949	California (7-0)
1950	California (5-0-1)
1951	Stanford (6-1)
1952	Southern California (6-0)
1953	UCLA (6-1)
1954	UCLA (6-0)
1955	UCLA (6-0)
1956	Oregon St. (6-1-1)
1957	Oregon (6-2) & Oregon St. (6-2)
1958	California (6-1)
1959	Washington (3-1), Southern California (3-1) & UCLA (3-1)
1960	Washington (4-0)
1961	UCLA (3-1)
1962	Southern California (4-0)
1963	Washington (4-1)
1964	Oregon St. (3-1) & Southern California (3-1)
1965	UCLA (4-0)
1966	Southern California (4-1)
1967	Southern California (6-1)
1968	Southern California (6-0)
1969	Southern California (6-0)
1970	Stanford (6-1)
1971	Stanford (6-1)
1972	Southern California (7-0)
1973	Southern California (7-0)
1974	Southern California (6-0-1)
1975	UCLA (6-1) & California (6-1)
1976	Southern California (7-0)
1977	Washington (6-1)
1978	Southern California (6-1)
1979	Southern California (6-0-1)
1980	Washington (6-1)
1981	Washington (6-2)
1982	UCLA (5-1-1)
1983	UCLA (6-1-1)
1984	Southern California (7-1)
1985	UCLA (6-2)
1986	Arizona St. (5-1-1)
1987	Southern California (7-1) & UCLA (7-1)
1988	Southern California (8-0)
1989	Southern California (6-0-1)
1990	Washington (7-1)
1991	Washington (8-0)
1992	Stanford (6-2) & Washington (6-2)
1993	UCLA (6-2), Arizona (6-2) & Southern California (6-2)
1994	Oregon (7-1)
1995	Southern California (6-1-1) & Washington (6-1-1)
1996	Arizona St. (8-0)
1997	Washington St. (7-1) & UCLA (7-1)
1998	UCLA (8-0)
1999	Stanford (7-1)

SOUTHEASTERN CONFERENCE

Founded: In 1933 when charter members all left the **Southern Conference** to become the SEC. **Charter members** (13): Alabama, Auburn, Florida, Georgia, Georgia Tech, Kentucky, LSU, Mississippi, Mississippi St., Sewanee, Tennessee, Tulane and Vanderbilt. **Admitted later** (2): Arkansas (1992) and South Carolina (1992). **Withdrew later** (3): Sewanee (1940), Georgia Tech (1964) and Tulane (1966). **Current members** (12): Alabama, Arkansas, Auburn, Florida, Georgia, Kentucky, LSU, Mississippi, Mississippi St., South Carolina, Tennessee and Vanderbilt.

Year	Champion (Record)
1933	Alabama (5-0-1)
1934	Tulane (8-0) & Alabama (7-0)
1935	LSU (5-0)
1936	LSU (6-0)
1937	Alabama (6-0)
1938	Tennessee (7-0)
1939	Tennessee (6-0), Georgia Tech (6-0) & Tulane (5-0)
1940	Tennessee (5-0)
1941	Mississippi St. (4-0-1)
1942	Georgia (6-1)

Year	Champion (Record)
1943	Georgia Tech (4-0)
1944	Georgia Tech (4-0)
1945	Alabama (6-0)
1946	Georgia (5-0) & Tennessee (5-0)
1947	Mississippi (6-1)
1948	Georgia (6-0)
1949	Tulane (5-1)
1950	Kentucky (5-1)
1951	Georgia Tech (7-0) & Tennessee (5-0)
1952	Georgia (6-0)
1953	Alabama (4-0-3)
1954	Mississippi (5-1)
1955	Mississippi (5-1)
1956	Tennessee (6-0)
1957	Auburn (7-0)
1958	LSU (6-0)
1959	Georgia (7-0)
1960	Mississippi (5-0-1)
1961	Alabama (7-0) & LSU (6-0)
1962	Mississippi (6-0)
1963	Mississippi (5-0-1)
1964	Alabama (8-0)
1965	Alabama (6-1-1)
1966	Alabama (6-0) & Georgia (6-0)
1967	Tennessee (6-0)
1968	Georgia (5-0-1)
1969	Tennessee (5-1)
1970	LSU (5-0)
1971	Alabama (7-0)
1972	Alabama (7-1)
1973	Alabama (8-0)
1974	Alabama (6-0)
1975	Alabama (6-0)
1976	Georgia (5-1) & Kentucky (5-1)
1977	Alabama (7-0) & Kentucky (6-0)
1978	Alabama (6-0)
1979	Alabama (6-0)
1980	Georgia (6-0)
1981	Georgia (6-0) & Alabama (6-0)
1982	Georgia (6-0)
1983	Auburn (6-0)
1984	Florida (5-0-1)#
1985	Tennessee (5-1)*
1986	LSU (5-1)
1987	Auburn (5-0-1)
1988	Auburn (6-1) & LSU (6-1)
1989	Alabama (6-1), Tennessee (6-1) & Auburn (6-1)
1990	Tennessee (5-1-1)*
1991	Florida (7-0)
1992	Alabama (8-0)
1993	Florida (7-1)*
1994	Florida (7-1)
1995	Florida (8-0)
1996	Florida (8-0)
1997	Tennessee (7-1)
1998	Tennessee (8-0)
1999	Florida (7-1) & Alabama (7-1)

#Title vacated. *Ineligible for title (probation): Florida (5-1) in 1985, Florida (6-1) in 1990 and Auburn (8-0) in 1993.

Since 1992, the SEC has conducted a championship game to determine the league's representative in the BCS bowls. Following are the results year-by-year of the Western Division champion (W) vs. the Eastern Division champion (E):

1992	Alabama (W) 28, Florida (E) 21
1993	Florida (E) 28, Alabama (W) 13
1994	Florida (E) 24, Alabama (W) 23
1995	Florida (E) 34, Arkansas (W) 3
1996	Florida (E) 45, Alabama (W) 30
1997	Tennessee (E) 30, Auburn (W) 29
1998	Tennessee (E) 24, Mississippi St. (W) 14
1999	Alabama (W) 34, Florida (E) 7

WESTERN ATHLETIC CONFERENCE

Founded: In 1962 when charter members left the Skyline and Border Conferences to form the WAC. In 1996, three former Southwest Conference members joined two former Big West members and one former independent team to form a 16-team league, the largest conference alignment ever in Division I-A. The league was divided into Mountain and Pacific divisions. In 1999, eight members split off to form the Mountain West Conference. **Charter members** (6): Arizona (from Border), Arizona St. (from Border), Brigham Young (from Skyline), New Mexico (from Skyline), Utah (from Skyline) and Wyoming (from Skyline). **Admitted later** (12): Colorado St. (1968), UTEP (1968), San Diego St. (1978), Hawaii (1979), Air Force (1980), Fresno St. (1992), UNLV (1996), Rice (1996), San Jose St. (1996), Southern Methodist (1996), TCU (1996) and Tulsa (1996). **Withdrew later** (10): Arizona (1978), Arizona St. (1978), Air Force (1999), Brigham Young (1999), Colorado St. (1999), UNLV (1999), New Mexico (1999), San Diego St. (1999), Utah (1999) and Wyoming (1999). **Current members** (8): Fresno St., Hawaii, Rice, San Jose St., Southern Methodist, UTEP, TCU and Tulsa.

Year	Champion (Record)
1962	New Mexico (2-1-1)
1963	New Mexico (3-1)
1964	Arizona (3-1), Utah (3-1) & New Mexico (3-1)
1965	Brigham Young (4-1)
1966	Wyoming (5-0)
1967	Wyoming (5-0)
1968	Wyoming (6-1)
1969	Arizona St. (6-1)
1970	Arizona St. (7-0)
1971	Arizona St. (7-0)
1972	Arizona St. (5-1)
1973	Arizona (6-1) & Arizona St. (6-1)
1974	Brigham Young (6-0-1)
1975	Arizona St. (7-0)
1976	Brigham Young (6-1) & Wyoming (6-1)
1977	Arizona St. (6-1) & Brigham Young (6-1)
1978	Brigham Young (5-1)
1979	Brigham Young (7-0)
1980	Brigham Young (6-1)
1981	Brigham Young (7-1)
1982	Brigham Young (7-1)
1983	Brigham Young (7-0)
1984	Brigham Young (8-0)
1985	Air Force (7-1) & Brigham Young (7-1)
1986	San Diego St. (7-1)
1987	Wyoming (8-0)
1988	Wyoming (8-0)
1989	Brigham Young (7-1)
1990	Brigham Young (7-1)
1991	Brigham Young (7-0-1)
1992	Hawaii (6-2), Fresno St. (6-2) & Brigham Young (6-2)
1993	Wyoming (6-2), Fresno St. (6-2) & Brigham Young (6-2)
1994	Colorado St. (7-1)
1995	Colorado St. (6-2), Air Force (6-2), Utah (6-2) & Brigham Young (6-2)
1996	Brigham Young (8-0)
1997	Colorado St. (7-1)
1998	Air Force (7-1)
1999	Fresno St. (5-2), Hawaii (5-2) & TCU (5-2)

From 1996-98, the WAC conducted a championship game to determine the league's representative in the BCS bowls. Following are the results of the Mountain Division Champion (M) vs. the Pacific Division Champion (P):

1996	Brigham Young (M) 28, Wyoming (P) 25
1997	Colorado St. (P) 41, New Mexico (M) 13
1998	Air Force (M) 20, Brigham Young (P) 13

Division I-AA

ATLANTIC 10 FOOTBALL CONFERENCE

Founded: In 1947 as the Yankee Conference by six institutions from the old New England College Conference. **Charter members** (6): Connecticut, Maine, Massachusetts, New Hampshire, Rhode Island and Vermont. **Admitted later** (8): Boston U. (1971), Holy Cross (1971), Delaware (1983), Richmond (1984), Villanova (1985), James Madison (1993), Northeastern (1993) and William & Mary (1993). **Withdrew later** (4): Holy Cross (1972), Vermont (1974, dropped football), Boston U. (1997, dropped football) and Connecticut (2000). **Current members** (10): Delaware, James Madison, Maine, Massachusetts, New Hampshire, Northeastern, Rhode Island, Richmond, Villanova and William & Mary. **Note:** The league officially changed its name to Atlantic 10 Football Conference in 1997 and is divided into the New England and Mid-Atlantic Divisions.

Year	Champion (Record)
1947	New Hampshire (4-0)
1948	New Hampshire (3-1)
1949	Connecticut (2-0-1) & Maine (2-0-1)
1950	New Hampshire (4-0)
1951	Maine (3-0-1)
1952	Connecticut (3-1), Maine (3-1) & Rhode Island (3-1)
1953	New Hampshire (3-1) & Rhode Island (3-1)
1954	New Hampshire (4-0)
1955	Rhode Island (4-0-1)
1956	Connecticut (3-0-1)
1957	Connecticut (3-0-1) & Rhode Island (3-0-1)
1958	Connecticut (4-0)
1959	Connecticut (4-0)
1960	Connecticut (3-1)
1961	Maine (5-0)
1962	New Hampshire (4-0-1)
1963	Massachusetts (5-0)
1964	Massachusetts (5-0)
1965	Maine (5-0)
1966	Massachusetts (5-0)
1967	Massachusetts (5-0)
1968	Connecticut (4-1) & New Hampshire (4-1)
1969	Massachusetts (5-0)
1970	Connecticut (4-0-1)
1971	Connecticut (3-1-1) & Massachusetts (3-1-1)
1972	Massachusetts (5-0)
1973	Connecticut (5-0-1)
1974	Maine (4-2) & Massachusetts (4-2)
1975	New Hampshire (5-0)
1976	New Hampshire (4-1)
1977	Massachusetts (5-0)
1978	Massachusetts (5-0)*
1979	Massachusetts (4-1)
1980	Boston U. (5-0)
1981	Rhode Island (4-1) & Massachusetts (4-1)
1982	Boston U. (3-2)*, Connecticut (3-2), Maine (3-2) and Massachusetts (3-2)
1983	Boston U. (4-1)* & Connecticut (4-1)
1984	Boston U. (4-1)* & Rhode Island (4-1)*
1985	Rhode Island (5-0)*
1986	Connecticut (5-2), Delaware (5-2)* & Massachusetts (5-2)
1987	Maine (6-1)* & Richmond (6-1)*
1988	Delaware (6-2)* & Massachusetts (6-2)*
1989	Connecticut (6-2), Maine (6-2)* & Villanova (6-2)*
1990	Massachusetts (7-1)*
1991	Delaware (7-1)* & Villanova (7-1)*
1992	Delaware (7-1)*
1993	Boston U. (9-0)*
1994	New Hampshire (8-0)*
1995	Delaware (8-0)*
1996	William & Mary (7-1)*
1997	Villanova (8-0)*
1998	Richmond (7-1)*
1999	James Madison (7-1)* & Massachusetts (7-1)*

*Participated in NCAA Division I-AA Championship.

BIG SKY CONFERENCE

Founded: In 1963 when six charter members—Gonzaga, Idaho, Idaho St., Montana, Montana St. and Weber St.—banded together to form the Big Sky. **Admitted later** (7): Boise St. (1970), Northern Ariz. (1970), Nevada (1979, replacing charter member Gonzaga), Eastern Wash. (1987), Cal St. Northridge (1996), Cal St. Sacramento (1996) and Portland St. (1996). **Withdrew later** (4): Gonzaga (1979), Nevada (1992), Boise St. (1996) and Idaho (1996). **Current members** (9): Cal St. Northridge, Cal St. Sacramento, Eastern Wash., Idaho St., Montana, Montana St., Northern Ariz., Portland St. and Weber St.

Year	Champion (Record)
1963	Idaho St. (3-1)
1964	Montana St. (3-0)
1965	Weber St. (3-1) & Idaho (3-1)
1966	Montana St. (4-0)
1967	Montana St. (4-0)
1968	Weber St. (3-1), Montana St. (3-1) & Idaho (3-1)
1969	Montana (4-0)#
1970	Montana (5-0)
1971	Idaho (4-1)
1972	Montana St. (5-1)
1973	Boise St. (6-0)#
1974	Boise St. (6-0)#
1975	Boise St. (5-0-1)#
1976	Montana St. (6-0)#
1977	Boise St. (6-0)
1978	Northern Ariz. (6-0)
1979	Montana St. (6-1)
1980	Boise St. (6-1)
1981	Idaho St. (6-1)*
1982	Montana (5-2)*
1983	Nevada (6-1)*
1984	Montana St. (6-1)*
1985	Idaho (6-1)*
1986	Nevada (7-0)*
1987	Idaho (7-1)*

ALL-TIME CONFERENCE CHAMPIONS—DIVISION I-AA

Year	Champion (Record)
1988	Idaho (7-1)*
1989	Idaho (8-0)*
1990	Nevada (7-1)*
1991	Nevada (8-0)*
1992	Idaho (6-1)* & Eastern Wash. (6-1)*
1993	Montana (7-0)*
1994	Boise St. (6-1)*
1995	Montana (6-1)*
1996	Montana (7-0)*
1997	Eastern Wash. (7-1)*
1998	Montana (6-2)*
1999	Montana (7-1)*

#Participated in NCAA Division II Championship.
*Participated in NCAA Division I-AA Championship.

GATEWAY FOOTBALL CONFERENCE

Founded: In 1982 as a women's athletics organization by 10 Midwestern universities. Six members started as a football conference in 1985. **Charter members** (6): (Football) Eastern Ill., Illinois St., Northern Iowa, Southern Ill., Southwest Mo. St. and Western Ill. Four members—Eastern Ill., Northern Iowa, Southwest Mo. St. and Western Ill.—were members of the Mid-Continent Conference for football. **Admitted later** (2): Indiana St. (1986) and Youngstown St. (1997). **Withdrew later** (1): Eastern Ill. (1996). **Current members** (7): Illinois St., Indiana St., Northern Iowa, Southern Ill., Southwest Mo. St., Western Ill. and Youngstown St.

Year	Champion (Record)
1985	Northern Iowa (5-0)*
1986	Eastern Ill. (5-1)*
1987	Northern Iowa (6-0)*
1988	Western Ill. (6-0)*
1989	Southwest Mo. St. (5-1)*
1990	Northern Iowa (5-1)*
1991	Northern Iowa (5-1)*
1992	Northern Iowa (5-1)*
1993	Northern Iowa (5-1)*
1994	Northern Iowa (6-0)*
1995	Northern Iowa (5-1)* & Eastern Ill. (5-1)*#
1996	Northern Iowa (5-0)*
1997	Western Ill. (6-0)*
1998	Western Ill. (5-1)*
1999	Illinois St. (6-0)*

*Participated in NCAA Division I-AA Championship.
#Northern Iowa defeated Eastern Ill., 17-7, on October 7.

IVY GROUP

Founded: In 1956 by a group of eight charter members. **Charter members** (8): Brown, Columbia, Cornell, Dartmouth, Harvard, Pennsylvania, Princeton and Yale. **Current members** (8): Brown, Columbia, Cornell, Dartmouth, Harvard, Pennsylvania, Princeton and Yale.

Year	Champion (Record)
1956	Yale (7-0)
1957	Princeton (6-1)
1958	Dartmouth (6-1)
1959	Pennsylvania (6-1)
1960	Yale (7-0)
1961	Columbia (6-1) & Harvard (6-1)
1962	Dartmouth (7-0)
1963	Dartmouth (5-2) & Princeton (5-2)
1964	Princeton (7-0)
1965	Dartmouth (7-0)
1966	Dartmouth (6-1), Harvard (6-1) & Princeton (6-1)
1967	Yale (7-0)
1968	Harvard (6-0-1) & Yale (6-0-1)
1969	Dartmouth (6-1), Yale (6-1) & Princeton (6-1)
1970	Dartmouth (7-0)
1971	Cornell (6-1) & Dartmouth (6-1)
1972	Dartmouth (5-1-1)
1973	Dartmouth (6-1)
1974	Harvard (6-1) & Yale (6-1)
1975	Harvard (6-1)
1976	Brown (6-1) & Yale (6-1)
1977	Yale (6-1)
1978	Dartmouth (6-1)
1979	Yale (6-1)
1980	Yale (6-1)
1981	Yale (6-1) & Dartmouth (6-1)
1982	Harvard (5-2), Pennsylvania (5-2) & Dartmouth (5-2)
1983	Harvard (5-1-1) & Pennsylvania (5-1-1)
1984	Pennsylvania (7-0)
1985	Pennsylvania (6-1)
1986	Pennsylvania (7-0)
1987	Harvard (6-1)
1988	Pennsylvania (6-1) & Cornell (6-1)
1989	Princeton (6-1) & Yale (6-1)
1990	Cornell (6-1) & Dartmouth (6-1)
1991	Dartmouth (6-0-1)
1992	Dartmouth (6-1) & Princeton (6-1)
1993	Pennsylvania (7-0)
1994	Pennsylvania (7-0)
1995	Princeton (5-1-1)
1996	Dartmouth (7-0)
1997	Harvard (7-0)
1998	Pennsylvania (6-1)
1999	Brown (6-1) & Yale (6-1)

METRO ATLANTIC ATHLETIC CONFERENCE

Founded: Began in Division I-AA in 1993 with Canisius, Georgetown, Iona, St. John's (N.Y.), St. Peter's and Siena as charter members. **Admitted later** (3): Duquesne (1994), Marist (1994) and Fairfield (1996). **Withdrew later** (0): None. **Current members** (9): Canisius, Duquesne, Fairfield, Georgetown, Iona, Marist, St. John's (N.Y.), St. Peter's and Siena.

Year	Champion (Record)
1993	Iona (5-0)
1994	Marist (6-1) & St. John's (N.Y.) (6-1)
1995	Duquesne (7-0)
1996	Duquesne (8-0)
1997	Georgetown (7-0)
1998	Fairfield (6-1) & Georgetown (6-1)
1999	Georgetown (7-1)

MID-EASTERN ATHLETIC CONFERENCE

Founded: In 1970 with first playing season in 1971 by six charter members. **Charter members** (6): Delaware St., Howard, Morgan St., N.C. A&T, N.C. Central and South Carolina St. **Admitted later** (4): Bethune-Cookman (1979), Florida A&M (1979), Hampton (1996) and Norfolk St. (1997). **Withdrew later** (3): Morgan St. (1979), N.C. Central (1979) and Florida A&M (1984). **Readmitted** (2): Morgan St. (1984) and Florida A&M (1986). **Current members** (9): Bethune-Cookman, Delaware St., Florida A&M, Hampton, Howard, Morgan St., Norfolk St., N.C. A&T and South Carolina St.

Year	Champion (Record)
1971	Morgan St. (5-0-1)
1972	N.C. Central (5-1)
1973	N.C. Central (5-1)
1974	South Carolina St. (5-1)
1975	South Carolina St. (5-1)
1976	South Carolina St. (5-1)
1977	South Carolina St. (6-0)
1978	South Carolina St. (5-0-1)
1979	Morgan St. (5-0)#
1980	South Carolina St. (5-0)
1981	South Carolina St. (5-0)*
1982	South Carolina St. (4-1)*
1983	South Carolina St. (4-0)
1984	Bethune-Cookman (4-0)
1985	Delaware St. (4-0)
1986	N.C. A&T (4-1)*
1987	Howard (5-0)
1988	Bethune-Cookman (4-2), Florida A&M (4-2) & Delaware St. (4-2)
1989	Delaware St. (5-1)
1990	Florida A&M (6-0)
1991	N.C. A&T (5-1)√
1992	N.C. A&T (5-1)*
1993	Howard (6-0)
1994	South Carolina St. (6-0)√
1995	Florida A&M (6-0)√
1996	Florida A&M (7-0)*
1997	Hampton (7-0)*
1998	Florida A&M (7-1)* & Hampton (7-1)*
1999	N.C. A&T (8-0)*

#Participated in NCAA Division II Championship.
*Participated in NCAA Division I-AA Championship.
√Participated in Division I-AA Heritage Bowl.

NORTHEAST CONFERENCE

Founded: In 1996 when five charter members all went from independent status to form the Northeast Conference. **Charter members** (5): Central Conn. St., Monmouth, Robert Morris, St. Francis (Pa.) and Wagner. **Admitted later** (3): Sacred Heart (1998), Albany (N.Y.) (1999) and Stony Brook (1999). **Current members** (8): Albany (N.Y.), Central Conn. St., Monmouth, Robert Morris, Sacred Heart, St. Francis (Pa.), Stony Brook and Wagner.

Year	Champion (Record)
1996	Robert Morris (3-1) & Monmouth (3-1)
1997	Robert Morris (4-0)
1998	Monmouth (4-1) & Robert Morris (4-1)
1999	Robert Morris (7-0)

OHIO VALLEY CONFERENCE

Founded: In 1948 by six charter members, five of which withdrew from the Kentucky Intercollegiate Athletic Conference (Eastern Ky., Louisville, Morehead St., Murray St. and Western Ky.), plus Evansville. **Charter members** (6): Eastern Ky., Evansville, Louisville, Morehead St., Murray St. and Western Ky. **Admitted later** (12): Marshall (1949), Tennessee Tech (1949), Middle Tenn. St. (1952), East Tenn. St. (1957), Austin Peay (1962), Akron (1979), Youngstown St. (1980), Tennessee St. (1988), Southeast Mo. St. (1991), Tenn.-Martin (1992), Eastern Ill. (1996) and Western Ky. (1999). **Withdrew later** (8): Louisville (1949), Evansville (1952), Marshall (1952), East Tenn. St. (1979), Western Ky. (1982), Akron (1987), Youngstown St. (1988), Morehead St. (1996) and Western Ky. (1999), Austin Peay (1997) and Middle Tenn. St. (1998). **Current members** (8): Eastern Ill., Eastern Ky., Murray St., Southeast Mo. St., Tennessee St., Tennessee Tech and Western Ky.

Team	Champion (Record)
1948	Murray St. (3-1)
1949	Evansville (3-1)
1950	Murray St. (5-0-1)
1951	Murray St. (5-1)
1952	Tennessee St. (4-1) & Western Ky. (4-1)
1953	Tennessee Tech (5-0)
1954	Eastern Ky. (5-0)
1955	Tennessee Tech (5-0)
1956	Middle Tenn. St. (5-0)
1957	Middle Tenn. St. (5-0)
1958	Middle Tenn. St. (5-1) & Tennessee Tech (5-1)
1959	Middle Tenn. St. (5-0-1) & Tennessee Tech (5-0-1)
1960	Tennessee Tech (6-0)
1961	Tennessee Tech (6-0)
1962	East Tenn. St. (4-2)
1963	Western Ky. (7-0)
1964	Middle Tenn. St. (6-1)
1965	Middle Tenn. St. (7-0)
1966	Morehead St. (6-1)
1967	Eastern Ky. (5-0-2)#
1968	Eastern Ky. (5-0)
1969	East Tenn. St. (6-0-1)#
1970	Western Ky. (5-1-1)
1971	Western Ky. (5-2)
1972	Tennessee Tech (7-0)#
1973	Western Ky. (7-0)#
1974	Eastern Ky. (6-1)
1975	Tennessee Tech (6-1) & Western Ky. (6-1)#
1976	Eastern Ky. (6-1)#
1977	Austin Peay (6-1)
1978	Western Ky. (6-0)
1979	Murray St. (6-0)*
1980	Western Ky. (6-1)
1981	Eastern Ky. (8-0)*
1982	Eastern Ky. (7-0)*
1983	Eastern Ky. (6-1)*
1984	Eastern Ky. (6-1)*
1985	Middle Tenn. St. (7-0)*
1986	Murray St. (5-2)
1987	Eastern Ky. (5-1)* & Youngstown St. (5-1)
1988	Eastern Ky. (6-0)*
1989	Middle Tenn. St. (6-0)*
1990	Middle Tenn. St. (5-1)* & Eastern Ky. (5-1)*
1991	Eastern Ky. (7-0)*
1992	Middle Tenn. St. (8-0)*
1993	Eastern Ky. (8-0)*
1994	Eastern Ky. (8-0)*
1995	Murray St. (8-0)*
1996	Murray St. (8-0)*
1997	Eastern Ky. (7-0)*
1998	Tennessee St. (6-1)*
1999	Tennessee St. (7-0)*

#Participated in NCAA Division II Championship.
*Participated in NCAA Division I-AA Championship.

PATRIOT LEAGUE

Founded: In 1984 originally as the Colonial League with six charter members. **Charter members** (6): Bucknell, Colgate, Davidson, Holy Cross, Lafayette and Lehigh. **Admitted later** (2): Fordham (1990) and Towson (1997). **Withdrew later** (1): Davidson (1989). **Current**

members (7): Bucknell, Colgate, Fordham, Holy Cross, Lafayette, Lehigh and Towson.

Year	Champion (Record)
1986	Holy Cross (4-0)
1987	Holy Cross (4-0)
1988	Lafayette (5-0)
1989	Holy Cross (4-0)
1990	Holy Cross (5-0)
1991	Holy Cross (5-0)
1992	Lafayette (5-0)
1993	Lehigh (4-1)
1994	Lafayette (5-0)
1995	Lehigh (5-0)
1996	Bucknell (4-1)
1997	Colgate (6-0)*
1998	Lehigh (6-0)*
1999	Colgate (5-1)* & Lehigh (5-1)*

*Participated in NCAA Division I-AA Championship.

PIONEER FOOTBALL LEAGUE

Founded: Started in 1993 with Division I-AA charter members Butler, Dayton, Drake, Evansville, San Diego and Valparaiso. **Admitted later** (0): None. **Withdrew later** (1): Evansville (1997, dropped football). **Current members** (5): Butler, Dayton, Drake, San Diego and Valparaiso.

Year	Champion (Record)
1993	Dayton (5-0)
1994	Dayton (4-1) & Butler (4-1)
1995	Drake (5-0)
1996	Dayton (5-0)
1997	Dayton (5-0)
1998	Drake (4-0)
1999	Dayton (4-0)

SOUTHERN CONFERENCE

Founded: In 1921 by 14 institutions to form the Southern Intercollegiate Conference. Roots for the conference can actually be traced back to 1894 when several football-playing schools formed a confederation known as the Southeastern Intercollegiate Athletic Association. **Charter members** (14): Alabama, Auburn, Clemson, Georgia, Georgia Tech, Kentucky, Maryland, Mississippi St., North Carolina, North Carolina St., Tennessee, Virginia, Virginia Tech and Wash. & Lee. **Admitted later** (17): Florida (1922), LSU (1922), Mississippi (1922), South Carolina (1922), Tulane (1922), Vanderbilt (1922), VMI (1924), Citadel (1936), Furman (1936), West Virginia (1951), Appalachian St. (1971), Marshall (1976), Chattanooga (1976), Western Caro. (1976), East Tenn. St. (1978), Ga. Southern (1992) and Wofford (1997). **Withdrew later:** Since 1922, membership has changed drastically, with a total of 39 schools having been affiliated with the league, including 11 of the 12 schools currently comprising the Southeastern Conference and eight of the nine schools currently comprising the Atlantic Coast Conference. **Current members** (9): Appalachian St., Chattanooga, Citadel, East Tenn. St., Furman, Ga. Southern, VMI, Western Caro. and Wofford.

Year	Champion (Record)√
1922	Georgia Tech
1923	Vanderbilt
1924	Alabama
1925	Alabama
1926	Alabama
1927	Georgia Tech
1928	Georgia Tech
1929	Tulane
1930	Alabama & Tulane
1931	Tulane
1932	Tennessee & Auburn
1933	Duke (4-0)
1934	Wash. & Lee (4-0)
1935	Duke (5-0)
1936	Duke (7-0)
1937	Maryland (2-0)
1938	Duke (5-0)
1939	Clemson (4-0)
1940	Clemson (4-0)
1941	Duke (5-0)
1942	William & Mary (4-0)
1943	Duke (4-0)
1944	Duke (4-0)
1945	Duke (4-0)
1946	North Carolina (4-0-1)
1947	William & Mary (7-1)
1948	Clemson (5-0)

Year	Champion (Record)√
1949	North Carolina (5-0)
1950	Wash. & Lee (6-0)
1951	Maryland (5-0) & VMI (5-0)
1952	Duke (5-0)
1953	West Virginia (4-0)
1954	West Virginia (3-0)
1955	West Virginia (4-0)
1956	West Virginia (5-0)
1957	VMI (6-0)
1958	West Virginia (4-0)
1959	VMI (6-0-1)
1960	VMI (4-1)
1961	Citadel (5-1)
1962	VMI (6-0)
1963	Virginia Tech (5-0)
1964	West Virginia (5-0)
1965	West Virginia (4-0)
1966	East Caro. (4-1-1) & William & Mary (4-1-1)
1967	West Virginia (4-0-1)
1968	Richmond (6-0)
1969	Davidson (5-1) & Richmond (5-1)
1970	William & Mary (3-1)
1971	Richmond (5-1)
1972	East Caro. (7-0)
1973	East Caro. (7-0)
1974	VMI (5-1)
1975	Richmond (5-0)
1976	East Caro. (4-1)
1977	Chattanooga (4-1) & VMI (4-1)
1978	Furman (4-1) & Chattanooga (4-1)
1979	Chattanooga (5-1)
1980	Furman (7-0)
1981	Furman (5-2)
1982	Furman (6-1)*
1983	Furman (6-0-1)*
1984	Chattanooga (5-1)*
1985	Furman (6-0)*
1986	Appalachian St. (6-0-1)*
1987	Appalachian St. (7-0)*
1988	Furman (6-1)* & Marshall (6-1)*
1989	Furman (7-0)*
1990	Furman (6-1)*
1991	Appalachian St. (6-1)*
1992	Citadel (6-1)*
1993	Ga. Southern (7-1)*
1994	Marshall (7-1)*
1995	Appalachian St. (8-0)*
1996	Marshall (8-0)*
1997	Ga. Southern (7-1)*
1998	Ga. Southern (8-0)*
1999	Appalachian St. (7-1)*, Furman (7-1)* & Ga. Southern (7-1)*

*Participated in NCAA Division I-AA Championship. √No records available until 1933.

SOUTHLAND FOOTBALL LEAGUE

Founded: In 1963 by a group of five institutions. **Charter members** (5): Abilene Christian, Arkansas St., Lamar, Texas-Arlington and Trinity (Tex.). **Admitted later** (12): La.-Lafayette (1971), Louisiana Tech (1971), La.-Monroe (1972), McNeese St. (1972), North Texas (1982), Northwestern St. (1987), Sam Houston St. (1987), Southwest Tex. St. (1987), Stephen F. Austin (1987), Nicholls St. (1992), Jacksonville St. (1996) and Troy St. (1996). **Withdrew later** (9): Trinity (Tex.) (1972), Abilene Christian (1973), La.-Lafayette (1982), Texas-Arlington (1986, dropped football), Arkansas St. (1987), Lamar (1987), Louisiana Tech (1987), North Texas (1995) and La.-Monroe (1996). **Current members** (8): Jacksonville St., McNeese St., Nicholls St., Northwestern St., Sam Houston St., Southwest Tex. St., Stephen F. Austin and Troy St.

Year	Champion (Record)
1964	Lamar (3-0-1)
1965	Lamar (3-1)
1966	Texas-Arlington (3-1)
1967	Texas-Arlington (4-0)
1968	Arkansas St. (3-0-1)
1969	Arkansas St. (4-0)
1970	Arkansas St. (4-0)
1971	Louisiana Tech (4-1)
1972	Louisiana Tech (5-0)
1973	Louisiana Tech (5-0)
1974	Louisiana Tech (5-0)
1975	Arkansas St. (5-0)
1976	La.-Lafayette (4-1) & McNeese St. (4-1)
1977	Louisiana Tech (5-0)
1978	Louisiana Tech (4-1)
1979	McNeese St. (5-0)
1980	McNeese St. (5-0)
1981	Texas-Arlington (4-1)

Year	Champion (Record)
1982	Louisiana Tech (5-0)*
1983	La.-Monroe (5-1) & North Texas (5-1)*
1984	Louisiana Tech (5-1)*
1985	Arkansas St. (5-1)*
1986	Arkansas St. (5-0)*
1987	La.-Monroe (6-0)*
1988	Northwestern St. (6-0)*
1989	Stephen F. Austin (5-0-1)*
1990	La.-Monroe (5-1)*
1991	McNeese St. (4-1-2)*
1992	La.-Monroe (7-0)*
1993	McNeese St. (7-0)*
1994	North Texas (5-0-1)*
1995	McNeese St. (5-0)*
1996	Troy St. (5-1)*
1997	McNeese St. (6-1)* & Northwestern St. (6-1)*
1998	Northwestern St. (6-1)*
1999	Troy St. (6-1)* & Stephen F. Austin (6-1)*

*Participated in NCAA Division I-AA Championship.

SOUTHWESTERN ATHLETIC CONFERENCE

Founded: In 1920 by a group of six institutions. **Charter members** (6): Bishop, Paul Quinn, Prairie View, Sam Houston College, Texas College and Wiley. **Admitted later** (10): Langston (1931), Southern U. (1934), Arkansas AM&N (1936), Texas Southern (1954), Grambling (1958), Jackson St. (1958), Alcorn St. (1962), Mississippi Val. (1968), Alabama St. (1982), Ark.-Pine Bluff (1998) and Alabama A&M (1999). **Withdrew later** (8): Paul Quinn (1929), Bishop (1956), Langston (1957), Sam Houston College (1959), Texas College (1961), Wiley (1968), Arkansas AM&N (1970) and Prairie View (1990, dropped program, readmitted 1991). **Current members** (10): Alabama A&M, Alabama St., Alcorn St., Ark.-Pine Bluff, Grambling, Jackson St., Mississippi Val., Prairie View, Southern U. and Texas Southern.

Year	Champion (Record)√
1921	Wiley
1922	Paul Quinn
1923	Wiley
1924	Paul Quinn
1925	Bishop
1926	Sam Houston College
1927	Wiley
1928	Wiley
1929	Wiley
1930	Wiley
1931	Prairie View
1932	Wiley
1933	Langston & Prairie View
1934	Texas College
1935	Texas College
1936	Texas College & Langston
1937	Southern U. & Langston
1938	Southern U. & Langston
1939	Langston
1940	Southern U. & Langston
1941	No champion
1942	Texas College
1943	No champion
1944	Wiley (5-1), Texas College (5-1) & Langston (5-1)
1945	Wiley (6-0)
1946	Southern U. (5-1)
1947	Southern U. (7-0)
1948	Southern U. (7-0)
1949	Southern U. (6-0-1) & Langston (6-0-1)
1950	Southern U. (7-0)
1951	Prairie View (6-1)
1952	Prairie View (6-0)
1953	Prairie View (6-0)
1954	Prairie View (6-0)
1955	Southern U. (6-1)
1956	Texas Southern (5-1) & Langston (5-1)
1957	Wiley (6-0)
1958	Prairie View (5-0)
1959	Southern U. (7-0)
1960	Southern U. (6-1), Prairie View (6-1) & Grambling (6-1)
1961	Jackson St. (6-1)
1962	Jackson St. (6-1)
1963	Prairie View (7-0)
1964	Prairie View (7-0)
1965	Grambling (6-1)
1966	Southern U. (4-2-1), Grambling (4-2-1), Texas Southern (4-2-1) & Arkansas AM&N (4-2-1)
1967	Grambling (6-1)
1968	Alcorn St. (6-1), Grambling (6-1) & Texas Southern (6-1)
1969	Alcorn St. (6-0-1)

ALL-TIME CONFERENCE CHAMPIONS—DIVISION I-AA

Year	Champion (Record√)
1970	Alcorn St. (6-0)
1971	Grambling (5-1)
1972	Grambling (5-1) & Jackson St. (5-1)
1973	Grambling (5-1) & Jackson St. (5-1)
1974	Alcorn St. (5-1) & Grambling (5-1)
1975	Grambling (4-2) & Southern U. (4-2)
1976	Alcorn St. (5-1)
1977	Grambling (6-0)
1978	Grambling (5-0-1)
1979	Grambling (5-1) & Alcorn St. (5-1)
1980	Grambling (5-1)* & Jackson St. (5-1)
1981	Jackson St. (5-1)*
1982	Jackson St. (6-0)*
1983	Grambling (6-0-1)
1984	Alcorn St. (7-0)*
1985	Jackson St. (6-1)* & Grambling (6-1)*
1986	Jackson St. (7-0)*
1987	Jackson St. (7-0)*
1988	Jackson St. (7-0)*
1989	Jackson St. (7-0)*
1990	Jackson St. (5-1)*
1991	Alabama St. (6-0-1)#
1992	Alcorn St. (7-0)*
1993	Southern U. (7-0)#
1994	Grambling (6-1)# & Alcorn St. (6-1)*
1995	Jackson St. (7-0)*
1996	Jackson St. (6-1)*
1997	Southern U. (8-0)#
1998	Southern U. (8-0)#
1999	Southern U. (9-0)#

√No records available until 1944. *Participated in NCAA Division I-AA Championship. #Participated in Division I-AA Heritage Bowl.

Division II

(Information prior to 1997 researched and submitted by Jeff Hodges, SID, University of North Alabama.)

CENTRAL INTERCOLLEGIATE ATHLETIC ASSOCIATION

Year	Champion
1970	Virginia St.
1971	Elizabeth City St.
1972	Virginia St.
1973	Virginia Union
1974	Norfolk St.
1975	Norfolk St.
1976	Norfolk St.
1977	Winston-Salem
1978	Winston-Salem
1979	Virginia Union
1980	N.C. Central
1981	Virginia Union
1982	Virginia Union
1983	Virginia Union
1984	Norfolk St.
1985	Hampton
1986	Virginia Union
1987	Winston-Salem
1988	Winston-Salem
1989	Bowie St.
1990	Winston-Salem
1991	Winston-Salem
1992	Hampton
1993	Hampton
1994	Hampton
1995	Virginia St.
1996	Virginia St.
1997	Livingstone, Virginia St. & Virginia Union
1998	Livingstone & Winston-Salem
1999	Winston-Salem

EASTERN COLLEGIATE FOOTBALL CONFERENCE

Year	Champion
1993	Bentley
1994	Bentley
1995	Stonehill
1996	Salve Regina
1997	Albany (N.Y.)
1998	Albany (N.Y.)
1999	American Int'l

GULF SOUTH CONFERENCE

Year	Champion
1972	Northwestern St.
1973	Troy St.
1974	Jacksonville St.
1975	Nicholls St.
1976	Troy St.
1977	Jacksonville St.
1978	Jacksonville St.
1979	Mississippi Col.
1980	North Ala.
1981	Jacksonville St.
1982	Jacksonville St.
1983	North Ala.
1984	Troy St.
1985	North Ala.
1986	Troy St.
1987	Troy St.
1988	Tenn.-Martin, Jacksonville St. & Mississippi Col.
1989	Jacksonville St.
1990	Mississippi Col.
1991	Jacksonville St.
1992	Jacksonville St.
1993	North Ala.
1994	North Ala.
1995	North Ala.
1996	Valdosta St.
1997	Southern Ark. & West Ga.
1998	Delta St. & West Ga.
1999	Arkansas Tech

LONE STAR CONFERENCE

Year	Champion
1933	Tex. A&M-Commerce
1934	Tex. A&M-Commerce
1935	Tex. A&M-Commerce, North Texas & Stephen F. Austin
1937	Tex. A&M-Commerce
1938	Tex. A&M-Commerce
1939	North Texas
1940	North Texas
1941	North Texas
1942	Tex. A&M-Commerce
1943-45	None
1946	North Texas
1947	North Texas
1948	Southwest Tex. St.
1949	Tex. A&M-Commerce
1950	Sul Ross St.
1951	Tex. A&M-Commerce
1952	Tex. A&M-Commerce
1953	Tex. A&M-Commerce
1954	Tex. A&M-Commerce & Southwest Tex. St.
1955	Tex. A&M-Commerce, Sam Houston St. & Southwest Tex. St.
1956	Sam Houston St.
1957	Tex. A&M-Commerce & Lamar
1958	Tex. A&M-Commerce
1959	Tex. A&M-Kingsville
1960	Tex. A&M-Kingsville
1961	Sam Houston St.
1962	Tex. A&M-Kingsville
1963	Southwest Tex. St.
1964	Sam Houston St.
1965	Sul Ross St.
1966	Tex. A&M-Commerce
1967	Tex. A&M-Kingsville
1968	Tex. A&M-Kingsville
1969	Tex. A&M-Kingsville & Tex. A&M-Commerce
1970	Tex. A&M-Kingsville
1971	Howard Payne
1972	Tex. A&M-Commerce
1973	Abilene Christian
1974	Tex. A&M-Kingsville
1975	Tex. A&M-Kingsville
1976	Tex. A&M-Kingsville
1977	Tex. A&M-Kingsville & Abilene Christian
1978	Angelo St.
1979	Tex. A&M-Kingsville
1980	Southwest Tex. St.
1981	Southwest Tex. St.
1982	Southwest Tex. St.
1983	Tex. A&M-Commerce & Southwest Tex. St.
1984	Angelo St.
1985	Tex. A&M-Kingsville
1986	West Tex. A&M
1987	Tex. A&M-Kingsville & Angelo St.
1988	Tex. A&M-Kingsville
1989	Tex. A&M-Kingsville
1990	Tex. A&M-Commerce
1991	Eastern N.M.
1992	Tex. A&M-Kingsville
1993	Tex. A&M-Kingsville
1994	Tex. A&M-Kingsville
1995	Tex. A&M-Kingsville
1996	Tex. A&M-Kingsville
1997	Tex. A&M-Kingsville
1998	Central Okla.
1999	Central Okla., Northeastern St. & Southeastern St.

MID-AMERICA INTERCOLLEGIATE ATHLETICS ASSOCIATION

(Formerly Missouri Intercollegiate Athletic Association)

Year	Champion
1924	Truman
1925	Northwest Mo. St.
1926	Central Mo. St.
1927	Truman
1928	Truman & Southwest Mo. St.
1929	Truman
1930	Truman
1931	Northwest Mo. St.
1932	Truman
1933	Truman
1934	Truman
1935	Truman
1936	Truman
1937	Southeast Mo. St.
1938	Northwest Mo. St.
1939	Northwest Mo. St.
1940	Southwest Mo. St.
1941	Northwest Mo. St. & Mo.-Rolla
1942	Northwest Mo. St. & Southeast Mo. St.
1943-45	None
1946	Southeast Mo. St.
1947	Mo.-Rolla
1948	Northwest Mo. St. Southwest Mo. St.
1949	Mo.-Rolla
1950	Mo.-Rolla
1951	Truman Southwest Mo. St.
1952	Northwest Mo. St. Truman
1953	Truman
1954	Truman
1955	Southeast Mo. St.
1956	Central Mo. St. Mo.-Rolla
1957	Southeast Mo. St.
1958	Southeast Mo. St.
1959	Southeast Mo. St.
1960	Truman
1961	Truman
1962	Southeast Mo. St.
1963	Southwest Mo. St.
1964	Truman
1965	Truman
1966	Southwest Mo. St.
1967	Southeast Mo. St.
1968	Southeast Mo. St.
1969	Truman & Southeast Mo. St.
1970	Central Mo. St. & Truman
1971	Truman
1972	Lincoln (Mo.) & Truman
1973	Southeast Mo. St.
1974	Northwest Mo. St.
1975	Southeast Mo. St.
1976	Truman & Southeast Mo. St.
1977	Mo.-Rolla & Southeast Mo. St.
1978	Southwest Mo. St.
1979	Northwest Mo. St.
1980	Mo.-Rolla
1981	Truman
1982	Truman
1983	Central Mo. St. & Mo.-Rolla
1984	Northwest Mo. St.
1985	Truman
1986	Central Mo. St.
1987	Central Mo. St. & Southeast Mo. St.
1988	Central Mo. St., Truman & Southeast Mo. St.
1989	Pittsburg St.
1990	Pittsburg St.
1991	Pittsburg St.
1992	Pittsburg St.
1993	Mo. Southern St.
1994	Pittsburg St.
1995	Pittsburg St.

Year	Champion
1996	Northwest Mo. St. & Pittsburg St.
1997	Northwest Mo. St.
1998	Northwest Mo. St.
1999	Northwest Mo. St.

MIDWEST INTERCOLLEGIATE FOOTBALL CONFERENCE

(Great Lakes Intercollegiate Athletic Conference from 1973-89)

Year	Champion
1973	Northwood
1974	Ferris St. & Northwood
1975	Wayne St. (Mich.)
1976	Northwood
1977	Grand Valley St.
1978	Grand Valley St.
1979	Saginaw Valley
1980	Hillsdale
1981	Grand Valley St.
1982	Hillsdale
1983	Saginaw Valley St.
1984	Saginaw Valley St.
1985	Hillsdale
1986	Hillsdale
1987	Northern Mich.
1988	Hillsdale
1989	Grand Valley St.
1990	Grand Valley St.
1991	Butler
1992	Ferris St., Butler, Grand Valley St. & Hillsdale
1993	Ferris St.
1994	Ferris St.
1995	Ferris St.
1996	Ferris St.
1997	Grand Valley St. & Ashland
1998	Grand Valley St.
1999	Northwood & Ferris St.

NORTH CENTRAL CONFERENCE

Year	Champion
1922	South Dakota St.
1923	Morningside
1924	South Dakota St.
1925	North Dakota St. & Creighton
1926	South Dakota St.
1927	South Dakota & Creighton
1928	North Dakota
1929	North Dakota
1930	North Dakota
1931	North Dakota
1932	North Dakota St.
1933	South Dakota St.
1934	North Dakota
1935	North Dakota St.
1936	North Dakota
1937	North Dakota
1938	South Dakota
1939	North Dakota, South Dakota St. & South Dakota
1940	Northern Iowa
1941	Northern Iowa
1942	Northern Iowa & Augustana (S.D.)
1943-45	None
1946	Northern Iowa
1947	Northern Iowa & South Dakota
1948	Northern Iowa
1949	Northern Iowa & South Dakota St.
1950	South Dakota St.
1951	South Dakota
1952	Northern Iowa
1953	South Dakota St.
1954	Morningside & South Dakota St.
1955	South Dakota St.
1956	Morningside
1957	South Dakota St.
1958	North Dakota
1959	Augustana (S.D.)
1960	Northern Iowa
1961	Northern Iowa & South Dakota St.
1962	Northern Iowa & South Dakota St.
1963	South Dakota St.
1964	North Dakota St., Northern Iowa & North Dakota
1965	North Dakota St.
1966	North Dakota St. & North Dakota
1967	North Dakota St.
1968	North Dakota St.
1969	North Dakota St.
1970	North Dakota St.

Year	Champion
1971	North Dakota
1972	North Dakota St., North Dakota & South Dakota
1973	North Dakota St. & South Dakota
1974	North Dakota St., North Dakota & South Dakota
1975	North Dakota
1976	North Dakota St.
1977	North Dakota St.
1978	South Dakota
1979	North Dakota
1980	Northern Colo.
1981	North Dakota St.
1982	North Dakota St.
1983	North Dakota St. & Neb.-Omaha
1984	North Dakota St. & Neb.-Omaha
1985	North Dakota St.
1986	North Dakota St.
1987	Minn. St.-Mankato
1988	North Dakota St.
1989	St. Cloud St.
1990	North Dakota St.
1991	North Dakota St.
1992	North Dakota St.
1993	North Dakota & Minn. St.-Mankato
1994	North Dakota St. & North Dakota
1995	North Dakota
1996	Neb.-Omaha
1997	Northern Colo.
1998	Neb.-Omaha & Northern Colo.
1999	Northern Colo. & North Dakota

NORTHERN SUN INTERCOLLEGIATE ATHLETIC CONFERENCE

(Northern Intercollegiate Athletic Conference from 1932-92)

Year	Champion
1932	Minn. St.-Mankato, Moorhead St., St. Cloud St. & Minn.-Duluth
1933	St. Cloud St.
1934	Minn.-Duluth
1935	Minn. St.-Mankato & Moorhead St.
1936	St. Cloud St.
1937	Minn.-Duluth
1938	Minn. St.-Mankato & Minn.-Duluth
1939	Winona St.
1940	St. Cloud St.
1941	St. Cloud St.
1942	Minn. St.-Mankato & St. Cloud St.
1943-45	None
1946	Minn. St.-Mankato & Minn.-Duluth
1947	Bemidji St. & Winona St.
1948	Minn. St.-Mankato, St. Cloud St & Minn.-Duluth
1949	Minn. St.-Mankato
1950	Bemidji St. & Minn. St.-Mankato
1951	St. Cloud St.
1952	Moorhead St. & St. Cloud St.
1953	St. Cloud St.
1954	St. Cloud St.
1955	St. Cloud St.
1956	Winona St.
1957	Bemidji St. & Winona St.
1958	Minn. St.-Mankato
1959	Bemidji St., Minn. St.-Mankato & Michigan Tech
1960	Minn. St.-Mankato
1961	Minn. St.-Mankato
1962	Winona St.
1963	Michigan Tech
1964	Winona St.
1965	Michigan Tech
1966	Moorhead St.
1967	St. Cloud St.
1968	Minn. St.-Mankato & Winona St.
1969	Michigan Tech
1970	Michigan Tech, St. Cloud St & Minn.-Morris
1971	Moorhead St.
1972	Michigan Tech
1973	Moorhead St.
1974	Michigan Tech
1975	Minn.-Morris
1976	Minn.-Morris
1977	Minn.-Morris
1978	Minn.-Morris
1979	Moorhead St. & Minn.-Duluth
1980	Minn.-Duluth
1981	Moorhead St.
1982	Moorhead St.
1983	Winona St.
1984	Moorhead St. & Minn.-Morris
1985	Minn.-Duluth
1986	Minn.-Morris

Year	Champion
1987	Minn.-Morris
1988	Moorhead St.
1989	Moorhead St.
1990	Minn.-Duluth, Southwest St. & Northern St.
1991	Moorhead St.
1992	Northern St.
1993	Winona St.
1994	Winona St.
1995	Minn.-Duluth & Moorhead St.
1996	Minn.-Duluth
1997	Winona St.
1998	Winona St.
1999	Northern St.

PENNSYLVANIA STATE ATHLETIC CONFERENCE

Year	Champion
1934	Indiana (Pa.)
1935	Shippensburg
1936	Lock Haven
1937	Lock Haven
1938	Mansfield
1939	Slippery Rock
1940	Indiana (Pa.) & Millersville
1941	Millersville
1942	East Stroudsburg
1943-45	None
1946	Calif. (Pa.)
1947	Mansfield
1948	Bloomsburg
1949	Bloomsburg
1950	West Chester
1951	Bloomsburg
1952	West Chester
1953	West Chester
1954	East Stroudsburg, Bloomsburg & West Chester
1955	Bloomsburg
1956	West Chester
1957	Lock Haven
1958	Calif. (Pa.)
1959	West Chester
1960	West Chester
1961	West Chester
1962	Slippery Rock
1963	West Chester
1964	East Stroudsburg
1965	East Stroudsburg
1966	Clarion
1967	West Chester
1968	East Stroudsburg
1969	West Chester
1970	Edinboro
1971	West Chester
1972	Slippery Rock
1973	Slippery Rock
1974	Slippery Rock
1975	East Stroudsburg
1976	East Stroudsburg
1977	Clarion
1978	East Stroudsburg
1979	Lock Haven
1980	Clarion
1981	Shippensburg
1982	East Stroudsburg
1983	Clarion
1984	Calif. (Pa.)
1985	Bloomsburg
1986	Indiana (Pa.)
1987	Indiana (Pa.)
1988	Millersville (East)
	Shippensburg (West)
1989	West Chester & Millersville (East)
	Edinboro (West)
1990	Millersville (East)
	Indiana (Pa.) (West)
1991	East Stroudsburg (East)
	Indiana (Pa.) (West)
1992	West Chester (East)
	Indiana (Pa.) (West)
1993	Millersville (East)
	Indiana (Pa.) (West)
1994	Bloomsburg & West Chester (East)
	Indiana (Pa.) (West)
1995	Millersville & Bloomsburg (East)
	Edinboro (West)
1996	Bloomsburg (East)
	Clarion (West)
1997	Bloomsburg (East)
	Slippery Rock (West)

ALL-TIME CONFERENCE CHAMPIONS—DIVISION II

Year	Champion
1998	Millersville (East)
	Slippery Rock (West)
1999	West Chester (East)
	Slippery Rock (West)

ROCKY MOUNTAIN ATHLETIC CONFERENCE

Year	Champion
1972	Adams St.
1973	Western St.
1974	Western St.
1975	Western St.
1976	Western St.
1977	Western St.
1978	Western St.
1979	Western St.
1980	Southern Colo. & Adams St.
1981	N.M. Highlands
1982	Mesa St.
1983	Mesa St.
1984	Fort Lewis
1985	Mesa St.
1986	Mesa St.
1987	Mesa St.
1988	Mesa St.
1989	Adams St.
1990	Mesa St.
1991	Western St.
1992	Western St.
1993	Fort Hays St.
1994	Western St.
1995	Fort Hays St. & Western St.
1996	Chadron St.
1997	Western St.
1998	Chadron St. & Western St.
1999	Chadron St. & N.M. Highlands

SOUTH ATLANTIC CONFERENCE

Year	Champion
1975	Lenoir-Rhyne
1976	Elon
1977	Elon
1978	Elon & Presbyterian
1979	Presbyterian
1980	Elon & Mars Hill
1981	Elon
1982	Carson-Newman
1983	Carson-Newman
1984	Carson-Newman
1985	Mars Hill
1986	Carson-Newman
1987	Gardner-Webb
1988	Carson-Newman, Catawba & Lenoir-Rhyne
1989	Carson-Newman
1990	Carson-Newman
1991	Carson-Newman
1992	Gardner-Webb
1993	Carson-Newman
1994	Carson-Newman & Lenoir-Rhyne
1995	Carson-Newman
1996	Carson-Newman & Catawba

Year	Champion
1997	Carson-Newman
1998	Carson-Newman
1999	Carson-Newman

SOUTHERN INTERCOLLEGIATE ATHLETIC CONFERENCE

(SIAC was split into Divisions A and B from 1966-69, reorganized into Divisions II and III from 1970-77 and became a Division II-only conference in 1978)

Year	Champion
1913	Fisk
1914	Talladega
1915	Fisk
1916	Morehouse
1917	Tuskegee
1918	Talladega
1919	Fisk
1920	Morehouse
1921	Morehouse
1922	Morehouse
1923	Fisk & Morehouse
1924	Tuskegee
1925	Tuskegee
1926	Tuskegee
1927	Tuskegee
1928	Clark Atlanta & Tuskegee
1929	Tuskegee
1930	Tuskegee
1931	Tuskegee
1932	Tuskegee
1933	Tuskegee
1934	Morris Brown
1935	Alabama St.
1936	Tuskegee
1937	Florida A&M
1938	Florida A&M
1939	Alabama St.
1940	Morris Brown
1941	Morris Brown
1942	Florida A&M
1943	Florida A&M
1944	Tuskegee
1945	Florida A&M
1946	Florida A&M
1947	Florida A&M
1948	Florida A&M
1949	Florida A&M
1950	Florida A&M
1951	Morris Brown
1952	Florida A&M
1953	Florida A&M
1954	Florida A&M
1955	Florida A&M
1956	Florida A&M
1957	Florida A&M
1958	Florida A&M
1959	Florida A&M
1960	Florida A&M
1961	Florida A&M
1962	Alabama A&M
1963	Florida A&M

Year	Champion
1964	Florida A&M
1965	Florida A&M
1966	Alabama A&M (A)
	Alabama St. (B)
1967	Florida A&M (A)
	Tuskegee (B)
1968	Florida A&M (A)
	Tuskegee (B)
1969	Florida A&M (A)
	Tuskegee (B)
1970	Tuskegee (II)
	Fort Valley St. (III)
1971	Alabama A&M (II)
	Fort Valley St. (III)
1972	Alabama A&M (II)
	Fort Valley St. (III)
1973	Bethune-Cookman (II)
	Fisk (III)
1974	Tuskegee (II)
	Clark Atlanta (III)
1975	Bethune-Cookman (II)
	Fisk (III)
1976	Bethune-Cookman (II)
	Fort Valley St. (III)
1977	Florida A&M (II)
	Clark Atlanta & Miles (III)
1978	Florida A&M
1979	Alabama A&M
1980	Alabama A&M
1981	Alabama A&M
1982	Fort Valley St.
1983	Fort Valley St.
1984	Albany St. (Ga.)
1985	Albany St. (Ga.) & Fort Valley St.
1986	Albany St. (Ga.)
1987	Alabama A&M & Tuskegee
1988	Albany St. (Ga.)
1989	Alabama A&M
1990	Alabama A&M
1991	Alabama A&M, Clark Atlanta, Morehouse, Fort Valley St. & Tuskegee
1992	Fort Valley St.
1993	Albany St. (Ga.)
1994	Albany St. (Ga.)
1995	Albany St. (Ga.)
1996	Albany St. (Ga.)
1997	Albany St. (Ga.)
1998	Tuskegee
1999	Fort Valley St. & Tuskegee

WEST VIRGINIA INTERCOLLEGIATE ATHLETIC CONFERENCE

Year	Champion
1993	Glenville St.
1994	Glenville St. & Shepherd
1995	West Va. Wesleyan & Glenville St.
1996	Glenville St. & Fairmont St.
1997	Shepherd & Glenville St.
1998	Shepherd
1999	Shepherd

Discontinued Conferences

Division I-A

BIG EIGHT CONFERENCE

Founded: Originally founded in 1907 as the Missouri Valley Intercollegiate Athletic Association. Charter members were Iowa, Kansas, Missouri, Nebraska and Washington (Mo.). Six schools were admitted later: Drake (1908), Iowa St. (1908), Kansas St. (1913), Grinnell (1919), Oklahoma (1920) and Oklahoma St. (1925). Iowa withdrew in 1911. The Big Six Conference was founded in 1928 when charter members left the MVIAA. Iowa St., Kansas, Kansas St., Missouri, Nebraska and Oklahoma were joined by Colorado (1948) (known as Big Seven) and Oklahoma St. (1958) (known as Big Eight until 1996). All eight members of Big Eight joined four former Southwest Conference members (Baylor, Texas, Texas A&M and Texas Tech) to form Big 12 Conference in 1996.

Year	Champion (Record)
1907	Iowa (1-0) & Nebraska (1-0)
1908	Kansas (4-0)
1909	Missouri (4-0-1)
1910	Nebraska (2-0)
1911	Iowa St. (2-0-1) & Nebraska (2-0-1)
1912	Iowa St. (2-0) & Nebraska (2-0)
1913	Missouri (4-0) & Nebraska (3-0)
1914	Nebraska (3-0)
1915	Nebraska (4-0)
1916	Nebraska (3-1)
1917	Nebraska (2-0)
1918	No Champion—War
1919	Missouri (4-0-1)

Year	Champion (Record)
1920	Oklahoma (4-0-1)
1921	Nebraska (3-0)
1922	Nebraska (5-0)
1923	Nebraska (3-0-2)
1924	Missouri (5-1)
1925	Missouri (5-1)
1926	Oklahoma St. (3-0-1)
1927	Missouri (5-1)
1928	Nebraska (4-0)
1929	Nebraska (3-0-2)
1930	Kansas (4-1)
1931	Nebraska (5-0)
1932	Nebraska (5-0)
1933	Nebraska (5-0)
1934	Kansas St. (5-0)
1935	Nebraska (4-0-1)
1936	Nebraska (5-0)

Year	Champion (Record)
1937	Nebraska (3-0-2)
1938	Oklahoma (5-0)
1939	Missouri (5-0)
1940	Nebraska (5-0)
1941	Missouri (5-0)
1942	Missouri (4-0-1)
1943	Oklahoma (5-0)
1944	Oklahoma (4-0-1)
1945	Missouri (5-0)
1946	Oklahoma (4-1) & Kansas (4-1)
1947	Kansas (4-0-1) & Oklahoma (4-0-1)
1948	Oklahoma (5-0)
1949	Oklahoma (5-0)
1950	Oklahoma (6-0)
1951	Oklahoma (6-0)
1952	Oklahoma (5-0-1)
1953	Oklahoma (6-0)
1954	Oklahoma (6-0)
1955	Oklahoma (6-0)
1956	Oklahoma (6-0)
1957	Oklahoma (6-0)
1958	Oklahoma (6-0)
1959	Oklahoma (5-1)
1960	Missouri (7-0)
1961	Colorado (7-0)
1962	Oklahoma (7-0)
1963	Nebraska (7-0)
1964	Nebraska (6-1)
1965	Nebraska (7-0)
1966	Nebraska (6-1)
1967	Oklahoma (7-0)
1968	Kansas (6-1) & Oklahoma (6-1)
1969	Missouri (6-1) & Nebraska (6-1)
1970	Nebraska (7-0)
1971	Nebraska (7-0)
1972	Nebraska (5-1-1)*
1973	Oklahoma (7-0)
1974	Oklahoma (7-0)
1975	Nebraska (6-1) & Oklahoma (6-1)
1976	Colorado (5-2), Oklahoma (5-2) & Oklahoma St. (5-2)
1977	Oklahoma (7-0)
1978	Nebraska (6-1) & Oklahoma (6-1)
1979	Oklahoma (7-0)
1980	Oklahoma (7-0)
1981	Nebraska (7-0)
1982	Nebraska (7-0)
1983	Nebraska (7-0)
1984	Oklahoma (6-1) & Nebraska (6-1)
1985	Oklahoma (7-0)
1986	Oklahoma (7-0)
1987	Oklahoma (7-0)
1988	Nebraska (7-0)
1989	Colorado (7-0)
1990	Colorado (7-0)
1991	Colorado (6-0-1) & Nebraska (6-0-1)
1992	Nebraska (6-1)
1993	Nebraska (7-0)
1994	Nebraska (7-0)
1995	Nebraska (7-0)

*Oklahoma (5-1-1) forfeited title.

BORDER INTERCOLLEGIATE ATHLETIC ASSOCIATION

Founded: In 1931 as Border Intercollegiate Athletic Association. Charters members were Arizona, Arizona St. Teachers' (Flagstaff) (now Northern Ariz.), Arizona St. Teachers' (Tempe) (now Arizona St.), New Mexico and New Mexico A&M (now New Mexico St.). Texas Tech admitted in 1932, Texas Mines (now UTEP) admitted in 1935, and Hardin-Simmons and West Texas St. Teachers' (now West Tex. A&M) in 1941.

Year	Champion (Record)
1931	Arizona St. (3-1)
1932	Texas Tech (2-0)*
1933	Texas Tech (1-0)*
1934	Texas Tech (1-0)*
1935	Arizona (4-0)
1936	Arizona (3-0-1)
1937	Texas Tech (3-0)
1938	New Mexico St. (4-1)**
	New Mexico (4-2)**
1939	Arizona St. (4-0)
1940	Arizona St. (3-0-1)
1941	Arizona (5-0)
1942	Hardin-Simmons (3-0-1)
	Texas Tech (3-0-1)
1943	No full conference program
1944	Texas Tech (2-0)
1945	Arizona (1-0)
1946	Hardin-Simmons (6-0)
1947	Texas Tech (4-0)

*Texas Tech has been listed by some as conference champion for the years 1932, 1933 and 1934, but conference rules forbade an official conference championship. This was due to the fact that the conference covered such a large area that games between all members were not practical.

**Texas Tech won its two conference games in 1938 but did not win the official championship since it did not meet the conference three-game requirement. Its victory over New Mexico did not count toward the championship, permitting New Mexico to share championship honors with New Mexico St.

MISSOURI VALLEY CONFERENCE

Founded: Originally founded as the Missouri Valley Intercollegiate Athletic Association. Several charter members left in 1928 to form the Big Six Conference, which became the Big Eight later. But Drake, Grinnell, Oklahoma A&M (now Oklahoma St.) and Washington (Mo.) continued the MVIAA. Creighton joined in 1928, Butler in 1932, Tulsa and Washburn in 1935, St. Louis in 1937, Wichita St. in 1947, Bradley and Detroit in 1949, Houston in 1951, Cincinnati and North Texas in 1957, Louisville in 1964, Memphis in 1968, and West Tex. A&M in 1972.

Year	Champion
1928	Drake
1929	Drake
1930	Drake & Oklahoma St.
1931	Drake
1932	Oklahoma St.
1933	Drake & Oklahoma St.
1934	Washington (Mo.)
1935	Washington (Mo.) & Tulsa
1936	Tulsa & Creighton
1937	Tulsa
1938	Tulsa
1939	Washington (Mo.)
1940	Tulsa
1941	Tulsa
1942	Tulsa
1943	Tulsa
1944	Oklahoma St.
1945	Oklahoma St.
1946	Tulsa
1947	Tulsa
1948	Oklahoma St.
1949	Detroit
1950	Tulsa
1951	Tulsa
1952	Houston
1953	Oklahoma St. & Detroit
1954	Wichita St.
1955	Wichita St. & Detroit
1956	Houston
1957	Houston
1958	North Texas
1959	North Texas & Houston
1960	Wichita St.
1961	Wichita St.
1962	Tulsa
1963	Cincinnati & Wichita St.
1964	Cincinnati
1965	Tulsa
1966	North Texas & Tulsa
1967	North Texas
1968	Memphis
1969	Memphis
1970	Louisville
1971	Memphis
1972	Louisville, West Tex. A&M & Drake
1973	North Texas
1974	Tulsa
1975	Tulsa
1976	Tulsa & New Mexico St.
1977	West Tex. A&M
1978	New Mexico St.
1979	West Tex. A&M
1980	Tulsa
1981	Drake & Tulsa
1982	Tulsa
1983	Tulsa
1984	Tulsa
1985	Tulsa

OLD ROCKY MOUNTAIN CONFERENCE
(Mountain States Athletic Conference and Big Seven Conference)

Founded: This conference predates every conference except the Big Ten and consisted of Brigham Young (1922), Colorado (1900), Colorado Agricultural College (now Colorado St.) (1900), Colorado St. College (1900), Denver (1900), Utah (1902), Utah St. (1902) and Wyoming (1905). Before 1938, these schools were part of the Rocky Mountain Conference, other members of which, at that time, were Colorado College, Colorado Mines, Greeley St. Teachers' (now Northern Colo.), Montana St. (1917) and Western St. Teachers' (now Western St.) (1925). A split took place in 1938, when the Mountain States Athletic Conference or "Big Seven" was formed. The name Rocky Mountain Conference was retained by the last six schools after 1938. Some members went into the Western Athletic Conference when the RMC was dissolved in 1962.

Year	Champion
1900	Colorado College
1901	Colorado
1902	Colorado
1903	Colorado
1904	Colorado Mines
1905	Colorado Mines
1906	Colorado Mines
1907	Colorado Mines
1908	Denver
1909	Denver
1910	Colorado
1911	Colorado
1912	Colorado Mines
1913	Colorado
1914	Colorado Mines
1915	Colorado Aggies
1916	Colorado Aggies
1917	Denver
1918	Colorado Mines
1919	Colorado Aggies
1920	Colorado Aggies
1921	Utah St.
1922	Utah
1923	Colorado
1924	Colorado
1925	Colorado Aggies
1926	Utah
1927	Colorado Aggies
1928	Utah
1929	Utah
1930	Utah
1931	Utah
1932	Utah
1933	Utah, Denver* & Colorado St.*
1934	Colorado, Northern Colo. & Colorado St.*
1935	Colorado & Utah St.*
1936	Utah St.
1937	Colorado
1938	Utah (4-0-2)
1939	Colorado (5-1-0)
1940	Utah (5-1-0)
1941	Utah (4-0-2)
1942	Colorado & Utah (5-1-0)
1943	Colorado (2-0-0)
1944	Colorado (2-0-0)
1945	Denver (4-1-0)
1946	Utah St. & Denver (4-1-1)
1947	Utah (6-0-0)
1948	Utah
1949	Wyoming
1950	Wyoming
1951	Utah
1952	Utah
1953	Utah
1954	Denver
1955	Colorado St.
1956	Wyoming
1957	Utah
1958	Wyoming
1959	Wyoming
1960	Wyoming & Utah St.
1961	Wyoming & Utah St.

*In final ratings, according to conference rules, tie games were not counted in awarding championships. Thus, teams marked with * shared the championship because one or more ties were not counted in their conference records.

DISCONTINUED CONFERENCES—DIVISION I-A

SOUTHLAND CONFERENCE
(I-A only 1975-79, now I-AA conference)

SOUTHWEST CONFERENCE

Founded: In 1914 as the Southwest Athletic Conference with charter members Arkansas, Baylor, Oklahoma, Oklahoma St., Rice, Southwestern (Tex.), Texas and Texas A&M. Five teams were added: Southern Methodist (1918), Phillips (1920), TCU (1923), Texas Tech (1960) and Houston (1976). Five withdrew: Southwestern (Texas) (1917), Oklahoma (1920), Phillips (1921), Oklahoma St. (1925) and Arkansas (1992). Of the eight members in the final (1995) season, four (Baylor, Texas, Texas A&M and Texas Tech) joined with eight members of the Big Eight Conference to form the Big 12 Conference in 1996. The other members in 1996: Houston (to Conference USA), Rice (to Western Athletic Conference), Southern Methodist (to Western Athletic Conference) and TCU (to Western Athletic Conference).

Year	Champion (Record)
1914	No champion
1915	Oklahoma (3-0)*
1916	No champion
1917	Texas A&M (2-0)
1918	No champion
1919	Texas A&M (4-0)
1920	Texas (5-0)
1921	Texas A&M (3-0-2)
1922	Baylor (5-0)
1923	Southern Methodist (5-0)
1924	Baylor (4-0-1)
1925	Texas A&M (4-1)
1926	Southern Methodist (5-0)
1927	Texas A&M (4-0-1)
1928	Texas (5-1)
1929	TCU (4-0-1)
1930	Texas (4-1)
1931	Southern Methodist (5-0-1)
1932	TCU (6-0)
1933	No champion*
1934	Rice (5-1)
1935	Southern Methodist (6-0)
1936	Arkansas (5-1)
1937	Rice (4-1-1)
1938	TCU (6-0)
1939	Texas A&M (6-0)
1940	Texas A&M (5-1)
1941	Texas A&M (5-1)
1942	Texas (5-0)
1943	Texas (5-0)
1944	TCU (3-1-1)
1945	Texas (5-1)
1946	Rice (5-1) & Arkansas (5-1)
1947	Southern Methodist (5-0-1)
1948	Southern Methodist (5-0-1)
1949	Rice (6-0)
1950	Texas (6-0)
1951	TCU (5-1)
1952	Texas (6-0)
1953	Rice (5-1) & Texas (5-1)
1954	Arkansas (5-1)
1955	TCU (5-1)
1956	Texas A&M (6-0)
1957	Rice (5-1)
1958	TCU (5-1)
1959	Texas (5-1), TCU (5-1) & Arkansas (5-1)
1960	Arkansas (6-1)
1961	Texas (6-1) & Arkansas (6-1)
1962	Texas (6-0-1)
1963	Texas (7-0)
1964	Arkansas (7-0)
1965	Arkansas (7-0)
1966	Southern Methodist (6-1)
1967	Texas A&M (6-1)
1968	Texas (6-1) & Arkansas (6-1)
1969	Texas (7-0)
1970	Texas (7-0)
1971	Texas (6-1)
1972	Texas (7-0)
1973	Texas (7-0)
1974	Baylor (6-1)
1975	Arkansas (6-1), Texas A&M (6-1) & Texas (6-1)
1976	Houston (7-1) & Texas Tech (7-1)
1977	Texas (8-0)
1978	Houston (7-1)
1979	Houston (7-1) & Arkansas (7-1)
1980	Baylor (8-0)
1981	Southern Methodist (7-1)¢
1982	Southern Methodist (7-0-1)
1983	Texas (8-0)
1984	Southern Methodist (6-2) & Houston (6-2)
1985	Texas A&M (7-1)
1986	Texas A&M (7-1)
1987	Texas A&M (6-1)
1988	Arkansas (7-0)
1989	Arkansas (7-1)
1990	Texas (8-0)
1991	Texas A&M (8-0)
1992	Texas A&M (7-0)
1993	Texas A&M (7-0)
1994	Baylor (4-3), Rice (4-3), Texas (4-3), TCU (4-3) & Texas Tech (4-3)*
1995	Texas (7-0)

*Forfeited title: Baylor (3-0) in 1915, Arkansas (4-1) in 1933 and Texas A&M (6-0-1) in 1994 on probation.
¢Southern Methodist on probation; did not forfeit championship.

Division I-AA

AMERICAN WEST CONFERENCE

Founded: Started Division I-AA play in 1993 with charter members Cal St. Northridge, Cal St. Sacramento and Southern Utah. Other members were UC Davis and Cal Poly (both Division II members at the time). Cal Poly became a Division I-AA member in 1994, and UC Davis withdrew in 1994. Last-year members were Cal Poly (became independent), Cal St. Northridge (to Big Sky Conference), Cal St. Sacramento (to Big Sky Conference) and Southern Utah (became independent).

Year	Champion (Record)
1993	Southern Utah (3-1) & UC Davis (3-1)#
1994	Cal Poly (3-0)
1995	Cal St. Sacramento (3-0)

#Participated in NCAA Division II Championship.

Division II

NORTHERN CALIFORNIA ATHLETIC CONFERENCE
(Far Western Football Conference from 1929-81)

Year	Champion (Record)
1925	St. Mary's (Cal.)
1926	St. Mary's (Cal.)
1927	St. Mary's (Cal.)
1928	St. Mary's (Cal.)
1929	UC Davis
1930	Fresno St.
1931	None
1932	Nevada & San Jose St.
1933	Nevada
1934	Fresno St. & San Jose St.
1935	Fresno St.
1936	Pacific (Cal.)
1937	Fresno St.
1938	Pacific (Cal.)
1939	Nevada
1940	Pacific (Cal.)
1941	Pacific (Cal.)
1942	Pacific (Cal.)
1943-46	None
1947	UC Davis Southern Ore.
1948	Cal St. Chico & Southern Ore.
1949	UC Davis
1950	San Fran. St.
1951	UC Davis
1952	Humboldt St.
1953	Cal St. Chico
1954	San Fran. St.
1955	Cal St. Chico
1956	UC Davis, Humboldt St. & San Fran. St.
1957	San Fran. St.
1958	San Fran. St.
1959	San Fran. St.
1960	Humboldt St.
1961	Humboldt St. & San Fran. St.
1962	San Fran. St.
1963	UC Davis, San Fran. St. & Humboldt St.
1964	Cal St. Sacramento
1965	San Fran. St.
1966	Cal St. Sacramento
1967	San Fran. St.
1968	Humboldt St.
1969	Cal St. Hayward
1970	Cal St. Chico
1971	UC Davis & Cal St. Chico
1972	UC Davis
1973	UC Davis & Cal St. Chico
1974	UC Davis
1975	UC Davis
1976	UC Davis
1977	UC Davis
1978	UC Davis
1979	UC Davis
1980	UC Davis
1981	UC Davis & Cal St. Hayward
1982	UC Davis
1983	UC Davis
1984	UC Davis
1985	UC Davis
1986	UC Davis
1987	UC Davis
1988	UC Davis
1989	UC Davis
1990	UC Davis
1991	Sonoma St.
1992	UC Davis
1993	Cal St. Chico
1994	Humboldt St. & Cal St. Chico
1995	Humboldt St.
1996	Cal St. Chico

2000 Schedules/ 1999 Results

2000 Schedules and 1999 Results for
   All Divisions 488
2000 Divisions I-A and I-AA Schedules
   by Date 581

2000 Schedules and 1999 Results for All Divisions

Listed alphabetically in this section are 2000 schedules and 1999 results for all football-playing NCAA member institutions. The division designation for each school is indicated to the right of the school location.

Coaching records (below head coaches' names) are for all seasons as the head coach at any four-year collegiate institution.

Game dates and starting times are subject to change.
■ **Designates home games.**
* **Designates night games. Neutral sites are listed in brackets.**

ABILENE CHRISTIAN
Abilene, TX 79699 II

Coach: Gary Gaines, Angelo St. 1971
(First year as head coach)

2000 SCHEDULE
Northeastern St.	*Sept. 16
East Central ■	*Sept. 23
Eastern N.M.	Sept. 30
Southeastern Okla. ■	*Oct. 7
Angelo St. ■	Oct. 14
Tarleton St.	Oct. 21
Tex. A&M-Commerce ■	*Oct. 28
Texas A&M-Kingsville	*Nov. 4
West Tex. A&M ■	*Nov. 11

1999 RESULTS (4-6-0)
34	Stephen F. Austin	51
30	Southeastern Okla.	43
28	Southwestern Okla.	18
31	Eastern N.M.	28
26	Midwestern St.	16
6	Angelo St.	28
9	Tarleton St.	14
21	Tex. A&M-Commerce	17
14	Texas A&M-Kingsville	40
9	West Tex. A&M	21
208		**276**

Nickname: Wildcats.
Stadium: Shotwell (1959), 15,000 capacity. Natural turf.
Colors: Purple & White.
Conference: Lone Star.
SID: Lance Fleming, 915-674-2693.
AD: Stan D. Lambert.

ADAMS ST.
Alamosa, CO 81102 II

Coach: Wayne McGinn, Adams St. 1982
Record: 1 Year, 6-5-0

2000 SCHEDULE
Southwestern Okla. ■	Sept. 2
Angelo St.	*Sept. 9
Fort Hays St. ■	Sept. 16
Neb.-Kearney ■	Sept. 23
N.M. Highlands	Sept. 30
Mesa St.	*Oct. 7
Western St. (Colo.) ■	Oct. 21
Colorado Mines ■	Oct. 28
Chadron St.	Nov. 4
Fort Lewis	Nov. 11

1999 RESULTS (4-6-0)
13	Southwestern Okla.	17
7	Angelo St.	53
21	Neb.-Kearney	51
24	N.M. Highlands	27
21	Mesa St.	49
21	Western St. (Colo.)	24
44	Colorado Mines	7
38	Chadron St.	23
28	Fort Lewis	25
31	Fort Hays St.	13
248		**289**

Nickname: Grizzlies.
Stadium: Rex Field (1949), 2,800 capacity. Natural turf.
Colors: Green & White.
Conference: Rocky Mountain Athletic.
SID: Jeff Storm, 719-589-7825.
AD: Larry Mortensen

ADRIAN
Adrian, MI 49221 III

Coach: Jim Lyall, Michigan 1974
Record: 10 Years, 39-50-1

2000 SCHEDULE
Baldwin-Wallace	*Sept. 9
Defiance ■	Sept. 16
Carthage	Sept. 23
Thomas More	Sept. 30
Wis. Lutheran ■	Oct. 7
Olivet ■	Oct. 14
Albion	Oct. 21
Hope ■	Oct. 28
Alma	Nov. 4
Kalamazoo ■	Nov. 11

1999 RESULTS (2-7-0)
28	Defiance	35
22	Heidelberg	15
27	Buffalo St.	42
21	Wilmington (Ohio)	47
6	Albion	33
35	Olivet	28
15	Hope	38
6	Alma	31
20	Kalamazoo	23
180		**292**

Nickname: Bulldogs.
Stadium: Maple (1960), 5,000 capacity. Natural turf.
Colors: Gold & Black.
Conference: Michigan Intercollegiate Athletic Assn.
SID: Darcy Gifford, 517-264-3176.
AD: Henry Mensing.

AIR FORCE
USAF Academy, CO 80840 ....I-A

Coach: Fisher DeBerry, Wofford 1960
Record: 16 Years, 126-69-1

2000 SCHEDULE
Cal St. Northridge ■	Sept. 2
Brigham Young ■	Sept. 9
Utah	Sept. 23
UNLV	*Sept. 30
Navy ■	Oct. 7
Wyoming	Oct. 14
New Mexico ■	Oct. 21
Notre Dame	Oct. 28
Army	Nov. 4
Colorado St. ■	Nov. 11
San Diego St. ■	Nov. 18

1999 RESULTS (6-5-0)
37	Villanova	13
31	Washington	21
7	Wyoming	10
23	San Diego St.	22
19	Navy	14
15	Utah	21
20	Brigham Young	27
28	Army	0
35	UNLV	16
21	Colorado St.	41
28	New Mexico	33
264		**218**

Nickname: Falcons.
Stadium: Falcon (1962), 52,480 capacity. Natural turf.
Colors: Blue & Silver.
Conference: Mountain West.
SID: Dave Kellogg, 719-472-2313.
AD: Randall W. Spetman.

AKRON
Akron, OH 44325 ....I-A

Coach: Lee Owens, Bluffton 1977
Record: 5 Years, 19-36-0

2000 SCHEDULE
Virginia Tech	Sept. 2
Central Mich.	Sept. 9
UCF ■	*Sept. 16
Ohio	Sept. 23
Miami (Ohio) ■	*Sept. 30
Bowling Green	Oct. 7
Northern Ill. ■	*Oct. 14
Connecticut ■	*Oct. 21
Marshall ■	*Oct. 28
Buffalo ■	*Nov. 11
Kent St.	Nov. 18

1999 RESULTS (7-4-0)
24	Penn St.	70
17	Buffalo	10
25	Temple	15
17	Eastern Mich.	38
31	Ball St.	9
41	Ohio	28
55	Bowling Green	25
35	Navy	29
10	Western Mich.	24
23	Miami (Ohio)	32
37	Kent St.	34
315		**314**

Nickname: Zips.
Stadium: Rubber Bowl (1940), 35,202 capacity. Artificial turf.
Colors: Blue & Gold.
Conference: Mid-American.
SID: Jeff Brewer, 330-972-7468.
AD: Dennis E. Helsel.

ALABAMA
Tuscaloosa, AL 35487 ....I-A

Coach: Mike DuBose, Alabama 1975
Record: 3 Years, 21-15-0

2000 SCHEDULE
UCLA	Sept. 2
Vanderbilt ■	Sept. 9
Southern Miss. ■	Sept. 16
Arkansas	*Sept. 23
South Carolina ■	Sept. 30
Mississippi ■	Oct. 14
Tennessee	Oct. 21
UCF ■	Oct. 28
LSU	Nov. 4
Mississippi St.	Nov. 11
Auburn ■	Nov. 18

1999 RESULTS (10-2-0)
28	Vanderbilt	17
37	Houston	10
28	Louisiana Tech	29
35	Arkansas	28
40	Florida	39
30	Mississippi	24
7	Tennessee	21
35	Southern Miss.	14
23	LSU	17
19	Mississippi St.	7
28	Auburn	17
34	Florida	7
344		**230**

ORANGE BOWL
34	Michigan	35

Nickname: Crimson Tide.
Stadium: Bryant-Denny (1929), 83,818 capacity. Natural turf.
Colors: Crimson & White.
Conference: Southeastern.
SID: Larry White, 205-348-6084.
AD: Mal Moore.

ALABAMA A&M
Normal, AL 35762 .... I-AA

Coach: Ron Cooper, Jacksonville St. 1982
Record: 7 Years, 33-44-0

2000 SCHEDULE
Troy St. ■	*Sept. 2
Henderson St. ■	*Sept. 9
Grambling ■	*Sept. 16
Prairie View ■	*Sept. 23
Mississippi Val. ■	Sept. 30
Southern U. ■	*Oct. 7
Morris Brown	Oct. 14
Alabama St. [Birmingham, AL]	Oct. 28
Jackson St.	Nov. 4
Alcorn St. ■	Nov. 11
Ark.-Pine Bluff	Nov. 18

1999 RESULTS (6-5-0)
37	Jacksonville St.	20
31	Grambling	36
26	Mississippi Val.	19
27	Prairie View	3
15	Tennessee St.	36
12	Southern U.	29
54	Tuskegee	0
18	Jackson St.	28
15	Alabama St.	10
35	Alcorn St.	26
17	Ark.-Pine Bluff	23
287		**230**

Nickname: Bulldogs.
Stadium: Bulldog (N/A), 20,000 capacity. Natural turf.
Colors: Maroon & White.
Conference: Southwestern Athletic.
SID: Ashley Balch, 205-851-5368.
AD: James A. Martin Sr.

ALABAMA ST.
Montgomery, AL 36101 .... I-AA

Coach: L. C. Cole, Nebraska 1980
Record: 4 Years, 28-18-0

2000 SCHEDULE
Tennessee St.	*Sept. 2
Alcorn St.	*Sept. 9
Troy St.	Sept. 16
Ark.-Pine Bluff ■	*Sept. 23
Southern U.	*Sept. 30
Jackson St. [Mobile, AL]	Oct. 7
Prairie View	Oct. 14
Alabama A&M [Birmingham, AL]	Oct. 28
Grambling	Nov. 4
Mississippi Val. ■	Nov. 11
Tuskegee ■	Nov. 23

1999 RESULTS (2-9-0)
8	Tennessee St.	41
27	Alcorn St.	38
20	Troy St.	27
13	Southern U.	36
35	Mississippi Val.	27
17	Jackson St.	44
21	Ark.-Pine Bluff	35
10	Alabama A&M	15
13	Grambling	36
42	Prairie View	27
34	Tuskegee	37
240		**363**

Nickname: Hornets.
Stadium: Cramton (1922), 24,600 capacity. Natural turf.
Colors: Black & Gold.
Conference: Southwestern Athletic.
SID: Kevin J. Manns, 205-293-4511.
AD: W. Curtis Williams.

UAB
Birmingham, AL 35294 .... I-A

Coach: Watson Brown, Vanderbilt 1973
Record: 15 Years, 56-108-1

2000 SCHEDULE
Chattanooga ■	*Sept. 7
Kansas	*Sept. 16
LSU	*Sept. 23
La.-Lafayette ■	Sept. 30
Louisville ■	Oct. 7
Memphis ■	Oct. 14
Middle Tenn. St. ■	Oct. 21
East Caro.	Oct. 28
Cincinnati	Nov. 4
Southern Miss. ■	Nov. 11
Army	Nov. 18

1999 RESULTS (5-6-0)
28	Missouri	31
10	Virginia Tech	31
29	Houston	10
47	La.-Monroe	0
14	Memphis	38
24	Cincinnati	21
3	Wake Forest	47
14	Louisville	23
36	East Caro.	17
20	Louisiana Tech	41
23	Tulane	20
248		**279**

Nickname: Blazers.
Stadium: Legion Field (1927), 80,391 capacity. Natural turf.
Colors: Forest Green & Old Gold.
Conference: Conference USA.
SID: Grant Shingleton, 205-934-0722.
AD: B. Gene Bartow

ALBANY ST. (GA.)
Albany, GA 31705 II

Coach: Hampton Smith, Mississippi Val. 1956
Record: 24 Years, 157-90-4

2000 SCHEDULE
Valdosta St. ■	*Aug. 26
Miles ■	*Sept. 3
Lane ■	Sept. 23
Tuskegee	Oct. 7
Savannah St. ■	Oct. 7
Kentucky St.	Oct. 14
Clark Atlanta ■	Oct. 21
Morehouse	Nov. 4
Fort Valley St. [Columbus, GA]	Nov. 11

1999 RESULTS (7-3-0)
6	Valdosta St.	18
25	Miles	27
38	Kentucky St.	33
35	Morehouse	3
17	Savannah St.	14
46	Mississippi Val.	8
42	Clark Atlanta	0
3	Morris Brown	7
34	Livingstone	13
24	Fort Valley St.	21
270		**144**

Nickname: Golden Rams.
Stadium: Mills Memorial (1957), 11,000 capacity. Natural turf.
Colors: Blue & Gold.
Conference: Southern Intercollegiate Athletic.
SID: Edythe Y. Bradley, 912-430-4672.
AD: Dan Land.

ALBANY (N.Y.)
Albany, NY 12222 .... I-AA

Coach: Robert Ford, Springfield 1959
Record: 31 Years, 174-124-1

2000 SCHEDULE
Northeastern	Sept. 9
Rowan	Sept. 16
Wagner ■	*Sept. 23
Stony Brook	Sept. 30
St. Francis (Pa.)	Oct. 7
St. John's (N.Y.)	*Oct. 13
Sacred Heart	Oct. 21
Central Conn. St. ■	Oct. 28
Monmouth ■	Nov. 4
Robert Morris	Nov. 11
Hofstra	Nov. 18

1999 RESULTS (7-2-0)
35	Central Conn. St.	13
24	Monmouth	16
37	Rowan	38
44	Stony Brook	21
37	Wagner	21
40	Mass.-Lowell	0
55	St. Francis (Pa.)	17
20	Robert Morris	30
41	Sacred Heart	0
333		**156**

Nickname: Great Danes.
Stadium: University Field (1967), 10,000 capacity. Natural turf.
Colors: Purple & Gold.
Conference: Northeast.
SID: Brian DePasquale, 518-442-3072.
AD: Gail Cummings-Danson.

ALBION
Albion, MI 49224 III

Coach: Craig Rundle, Albion 1974
Record: 14 Years, 77-54-1

2000 SCHEDULE
MacMurray	Sept. 2
Tri-State	Sept. 9
Buffalo St. ■	Sept. 16
Washington (Mo.) ■	Sept. 23
Butler ■	Oct. 7
Alma	Oct. 14
Adrian ■	Oct. 21
Olivet ■	Oct. 28
Kalamazoo	Nov. 4
Hope	Nov. 11

1999 RESULTS (6-3-0)
20	Butler	27
0	Mount Union	38
49	Manchester	23
35	Defiance	21
33	Adrian	6
16	Kalamazoo	14
42	Olivet	14
20	Hope	14
17	Alma	20
232		**177**

Nickname: Britons.
Stadium: Sprankle-Sprandel (1976), 4,244 capacity. Natural turf.
Colors: Purple & Gold.
Conference: Michigan Intercollegiate Athletic Assn.
SID: Robin Hartman, 517-629-0434.
AD: Jim Conway.

ALBRIGHT
Reading, PA 19612 III

Coach: E. J. Sandusky, Penn St. 1993
Record: 3 Years, 16-14-0

2000 SCHEDULE
Wilkes ■	*Sept. 9
Moravian	Sept. 16
FDU-Madison ■	*Sept. 23
Juniata	Sept. 30
Widener	Oct. 7
Lebanon Valley ■	*Oct. 14
Lycoming	Oct. 21
King's (Pa.) ■	Oct. 28
Delaware Valley ■	Nov. 4
Susquehanna	Nov. 11

1999 RESULTS (3-7-0)
15	Wilkes	36
21	Moravian	8
3	FDU-Madison	24
24	Juniata	45
27	Widener	35
21	Lebanon Valley	7
9	Lycoming	43
33	King's (Pa.)	37
37	Delaware Valley	13

20 Susquehanna	27
210	**275**

Nickname: Lions.
Stadium: Eugene L. Shirk (1925), 7,000 capacity. Natural turf.
Colors: Red & White.
Conference: Middle Atlantic.
SID: Mark Lukens, 610-921-7833.
AD: Sally Ann Stetler.

ALCORN ST.
Lorman, MS 39096...I-AA

Coach: Johnny Thomas, Alcorn St. 1978
Record: 2 Years, 8-13-0

2000 SCHEDULE
Grambling	*Sept. 2
Alabama St. ■	*Sept. 9
Fort Valley St. ■	*Sept. 16
McNeese St. ■	*Sept. 23
Ark.-Pine Bluff [St. Louis, MO]	Sept. 30
Prairie View ■	*Oct. 7
Texas Southern ■	Oct. 14
Southern U. ■	Oct. 21
Mississippi Val.	Nov. 4
Alabama A&M	Nov. 11
Jackson St.	Nov. 18

1999 RESULTS (3-7-0)
25	Grambling	41
38	Alabama St.	27
17	Ark.-Pine Bluff	33
41	Morehouse	27
61	Prairie View	0
21	Texas Southern	23
6	Southern U.	28
26	Mississippi Val.	30
26	Alabama A&M	35
6	Jackson St.	58
267		**302**

Nickname: Braves.
Stadium: Jack Spinks (1992), 25,000 capacity. Natural turf.
Colors: Purple & Gold.
Conference: Southwestern Athletic.
SID: Peter Forest, 601-877-6466.
AD: Lloyd N. Hill.

ALFRED
Alfred, NY 14802..III

Coach: David Murray, Springfield 1981
Record: 10 Years, 55-48-1

2000 SCHEDULE
St. John Fisher ■	*Sept. 2
Ithaca ■	Sept. 9
St. Lawrence	Sept. 16
Carnegie Mellon ■	Sept. 23
Union (N.Y.)	Sept. 30
Hartwick	Oct. 14
Hobart	Oct. 21
Wm. Paterson ■	Oct. 28
Canisius ■	Nov. 4
Grove City	Nov. 11

1999 RESULTS (6-4-0)
20	Salisbury St.	13
39	St. Lawrence	23
7	Carnegie Mellon	31
20	St. John Fisher	14
31	Hartwick	17
23	Canisius	16
20	Hobart	29
14	Grove City	28
7	Bethany (W.Va.)	21
55	Oberlin	16
236		**208**

Nickname: Saxons.
Stadium: Merrill Field (1926), 5,000 capacity. Artificial turf.
Colors: Purple & Gold.
Conference: Division III Independent.
SID: Mark Whitehouse, 607-871-2103.
AD: James M. Moretti.

ALLEGHENY
Meadville, PA 16335..III

Coach: Blair Hrovat, Edinboro 1985
Record: 2 Years, 14-6-0

2000 SCHEDULE
Mount Union ■	Sept. 2
Wash. & Jeff. ■	Sept. 9
Frostburg St. ■	Sept. 16
Denison	Sept. 23
Wittenberg ■	Sept. 30
Hiram	Oct. 7
Kenyon ■	Oct. 14
Wabash	Oct. 28
Wooster	Nov. 4
Ohio Wesleyan ■	Nov. 11

1999 RESULTS (6-4-0)
0	Malone	7
13	Wash. & Jeff.	19
30	Denison	13
17	Ohio Wesleyan	3
10	Wooster	13
17	Wittenberg	20
67	Earlham	0
42	Kenyon	0
48	Buffalo St.	8
61	St. Francis (Ill.)	55
305		**138**

Nickname: Gators.
Stadium: Robertson Field (1948), 5,000 capacity. Natural turf.
Colors: Blue & Gold.
Conference: North Coast Athletic.
SID: Jeff Schaefer, 814-332-6755.
AD: Richard A. Creehan.

ALMA
Alma, MI 48801...III

Coach: Jim Cole, Alma 1974
Record: 9 Years, 46-36-0

2000 SCHEDULE
Wilmington (Ohio) ■	Sept. 9
Wittenberg	Sept. 16
Franklin ■	Sept. 23
Hanover	Sept. 30
Gannon ■	Oct. 7
Albion ■	Oct. 14
Hope	Oct. 21
Kalamazoo	Oct. 28
Adrian ■	Nov. 4
Olivet	Nov. 11

1999 RESULTS (8-1-0)
46	Defiance	21
46	Olivet Nazarene	29
46	Franklin	38
35	Thomas More	7
48	Olivet	28
7	Hope	62
12	Kalamazoo	7
31	Adrian	6
20	Albion	17
291		**215**

DIVISION III CHAMPIONSHIP
19	Wittenberg	42

Nickname: Scots.
Stadium: Bahlke Field (1986), 4,000 capacity. Artificial turf.
Colors: Maroon & Cream.
Conference: Michigan Intercollegiate Athletic Assn.
SID: Eric Sieger, 517-463-7323.
AD: Denny Griffin.

AMERICAN INT'L
Springfield, MA 01109..II

Coach: Art Wilkins, Bucknell 1972
Record: 6 Years, 36-28-0

2000 SCHEDULE
Northeastern	Sept. 2
C. W. Post ■	Sept. 9
Stonehill	Sept. 16
Bentley ■	Sept. 23
Merrimack	Sept. 30
Assumption	Oct. 7
Southern Conn. St.	*Oct. 13
Massachusetts	Oct. 21
Pace ■	Oct. 28
Bryant	Nov. 4
Mass.-Lowell ■	Nov. 11

1999 RESULTS (9-2-0)
7	Northeastern	44
34	C. W. Post	0
62	Stonehill	7
44	Bentley	26
28	Merrimack	31
56	Assumption	14
36	Southern Conn. St.	24
34	Ithaca	17
48	Pace	21
60	Bryant	20
51	Mass.-Lowell	21
460		**225**

EASTERN FOOTBALL CONF. CHAMPIONSHIP
41	C. W. Post	20

Nickname: Yellow Jackets.
Stadium: J. H. Miller Field (1964), 5,000 capacity. Natural turf.
Colors: Gold, White & Black.
Conference: Eastern Football.
SID: Doug Monson, 413-747-6544.
AD: Robert E. Burke.

AMHERST
Amherst, MA 01002..III

Coach: E. J. Mills, Dayton 1988
Record: 3 Years, 17-7-0

2000 SCHEDULE
Hamilton ■	Sept. 23
Bowdoin	Sept. 30
Middlebury	Oct. 7
Colby ■	Oct. 14
Wesleyan (Conn.)	Oct. 21
Tufts ■	Oct. 28
Trinity (Conn.)	Nov. 4
Williams■	Nov. 11

1999 RESULTS (5-3-0)
7	Bates	19
10	Bowdoin	7
13	Middlebury	14
24	Colby	17
28	Wesleyan (Conn.)	14
10	Tufts	7
27	Trinity (Conn.)	0
7	Williams	10
126		**88**

Nickname: Lord Jeffs.
Stadium: Pratt Field (1891), 8,000 capacity. Natural turf.
Colors: Purple & White.
Conference: NESCAC.
SID: To be named, 413-542-2390.
AD: Peter J. Gooding.

ANDERSON (IND.)
Anderson, IN 46012..III

Coach: Steve Barrows, Ohio 1986
Record: 1 Year, 2-8-0

2000 SCHEDULE
Thomas More	Sept. 2
Taylor (Ind.) ■	Sept. 9
Olivet ■	Sept. 23
Bluffton	Sept. 30
Franklin ■	Oct. 7
Mt. St. Joseph ■	Oct. 14
Rockford	Oct. 21
Hanover	Oct. 28
Defiance ■	Nov. 4
Manchester	Nov. 11

1999 RESULTS (2-8-0)
18	Thomas More	32
6	Taylor (Ind.)	33
3	Wheaton (Ill.)	42
13	Wabash	31
14	Mt. St. Joseph	11
17	Bluffton	48
6	Franklin	34
12	Hanover	31
23	Wilmington (Ohio)	40
27	Manchester	25
139		**327**

Nickname: Ravens.
Stadium: Macholtz (0000), 4,200 capacity. Natural turf.
Colors: Orange & Black.
Conference: Heartland Collegiate Athletic.
SID: Dave Wilson, 317-641-4479.
AD: A. Barrett Bates.

ANGELO ST.
San Angelo, TX 76909 II

Coach: Jerry Vandergriff, Corpus Christi 1964
Record: 18 Years, 124-67-2

2000 SCHEDULE
Northern Colo.	Sept. 2
Adams St. ■	*Sept. 9
East Central	*Sept. 16
West Tex. A&M	*Sept. 30
Eastern N.M. ■	*Oct. 7
Abilene Christian	Oct. 14
Northeastern St.	Oct. 21
Tarleton St. ■	*Oct. 28
Tex. A&M-Commerce	Nov. 4
Texas A&M-Kingsville ■	Nov. 11

1999 RESULTS (7-4-0)
14	Northern Colo.	51
53	Adams St.	7
34	Central Okla.	37
31	Harding	28
28	West Tex. A&M	7
24	Eastern N.M.	19
28	Abilene Christian	6
21	Midwestern St.	19
27	Tarleton St.	17
10	Tex. A&M-Commerce	14
38	Texas A&M-Kingsville	42
308		**247**

Nickname: Rams.
Stadium: San Angelo (1962), 17,500 capacity. Natural turf.
Colors: Blue & Gold.
Conference: Lone Star.
SID: M. L. Stark Hinkle, 915-942-2248.
AD: Jerry Vandergriff.

APPALACHIAN ST.
Boone, NC 28608..................................I-AA

Coach: Jerry Moore, Baylor 1961
Record: 18 Years, 115-91-2

2000 SCHEDULE
Wake Forest	*Aug. 31
Troy St. ■	*Sept. 9
Citadel ■	Sept. 23
East Tenn. St.	*Sept. 30
Furman ■	Oct. 7
Ga. Southern	Oct. 14
Wofford ■	Oct. 21
Chattanooga	Oct. 28
VMI ■	Nov. 4
Western Caro.	Nov. 11
Liberty ■	Nov. 18

1999 RESULTS (9-2-0)
15	Auburn	22
34	Eastern Ky.	20
51	Citadel	0
23	East Tenn. St.	19
21	Furman	35
17	Ga. Southern	16
21	Wofford	20
62	Chattanooga	14
34	VMI	7
34	Western Caro.	10
28	Liberty	12
340		**175**

DIVISION I-AA CHAMPIONSHIP
29	Florida A&M	44

Nickname: Mountaineers.
Stadium: Kidd Brewer (1962), 16,650 capacity. Artificial turf.
Colors: Black & Gold.
Conference: Southern.
SID: Bill Dyer, 704-262-3080.
AD: Roachel Laney.

ARIZONA
Tucson, AZ 85721 ....I-A

Coach: Dick Tomey, DePauw 1961
Record: 23 Years, 153-104-7

2000 SCHEDULE
Utah	*Sept. 2
Ohio St. ■	*Sept. 9
San Diego St. ■	*Sept. 16
Stanford	Sept. 30
Southern California	Oct. 7
Washington St. ■	*Oct. 14
Oregon	*Oct. 21
UCLA ■	Oct. 28
Washington	Nov. 4
Oregon St. ■	*Nov. 11
Arizona St. ■	Nov. 24

1999 RESULTS (6-6-0)
7	Penn St.	41
35	TCU	31
34	Middle Tenn. St.	19
22	Stanford	50
30	Washington St.	24
31	Southern California	24
34	UTEP	21
41	Oregon	44
33	UCLA	7
25	Washington	33
20	Oregon St.	28
27	Arizona St.	42
339		**364**

Nickname: Wildcats.
Stadium: Arizona (1928), 56,500 capacity. Natural turf.
Colors: Cardinal & Navy.
Conference: Pacific-10.
SID: Tom Duddleston Jr., 602-621-4163.
AD: Jim Livengood.

ARIZONA ST.
Tempe, AZ 85287......................................I-A

Coach: Bruce Snyder, Oregon 1963
Record: 20 Years, 118-101-6

2000 SCHEDULE
San Diego St.	*Aug. 31
Colorado St. ■	*Sept. 16
Utah St. ■	*Sept. 23
UCLA	*Sept. 30
California ■	*Oct. 7
Washington ■	*Oct. 14
Washington St.	Oct. 21
Oregon ■	*Oct. 28
Southern California ■	*Nov. 4
Stanford	Nov. 11
Arizona	Nov. 24

1999 RESULTS (6-5-0)
31	Texas Tech	13
7	New Mexico St.	35
23	California	24
28	UCLA	27
17	Notre Dame	48
28	Washington	7
33	Washington St.	21
17	Oregon	20
26	Southern California	16
30	Stanford	50
42	Arizona	27
282		**288**

ALOHA BOWL
3	Wake Forest	23

Nickname: Sun Devils.
Stadium: Sun Devil (1959), 73,656 capacity. Natural turf.
Colors: Maroon & Gold.
Conference: Pacific-10.
SID: Mark Brand, 602-965-6592.
AD: To be named.

ARKANSAS
Fayetteville, AR 72701...............................I-A

Coach: Houston Nutt, Oklahoma 1981
Record: 7 Years, 52-30-0

2000 SCHEDULE
Southwest Mo. St. [Little Rock, AR]	*Sept. 2
Boise St. [Little Rock, AR]	*Sept. 16
Alabama ■	*Sept. 23
Georgia ■	*Sept. 30
La.-Monroe ■	*Oct. 7
South Carolina	Oct. 14
Auburn	Oct. 28
Mississippi ■	Nov. 4
Tennessee	Nov. 11
Mississippi St.	Nov. 18
LSU [Little Rock, AR]	Nov. 24

1999 RESULTS (7-4-0)
26	Southern Methodist	0
44	La.-Monroe	6
28	Alabama	35
20	Kentucky	31
58	Middle Tenn. St.	6
48	South Carolina	14
34	Auburn	10
16	Mississippi	38
28	Tennessee	24
14	Mississippi St.	9
10	LSU	35
326		**208**

COTTON BOWL
27	Texas	6

Nickname: Razorbacks.
Stadium: Razorback (1938), 50,018 capacity. Natural turf.
Colors: Cardinal & White.
Conference: Southeastern.
SID: To be named, 501-575-2751.
AD: J. Frank Broyles.

ARKANSAS ST.
State University, AR 72467 ....I-A

Coach: Joe Hollis, Auburn 1969
Record: 4 Years, 10-22-1

2000 SCHEDULE
North Carolina St.	*Sept. 2
Oklahoma	*Sept. 9
Memphis ■	*Sept. 16
TCU	*Sept. 23
Richmond ■	*Sept. 30
Mississippi	Oct. 7
Idaho	*Oct. 14
New Mexico St. ■	Oct. 21
Utah St.	Oct. 28
Boise St. ■	Nov. 4
North Texas ■	Nov. 11

1999 RESULTS (4-7-0)
3	Illinois	41
14	Mississippi	38
26	Memphis	31
21	TCU	24
45	Sam Houston St.	20
14	Utah St.	20
24	Idaho	30
14	North Texas	10
31	La.-Lafayette	27

10	Boise St.	63
44	Nevada	28
246		**332**

Nickname: Indians.
Stadium: Indian (1974), 33,410 capacity. Natural turf.
Colors: Scarlet & Black.
Conference: Big West.
SID: Gina Bowman, 501-972-2541.
AD: D. Barry Dowd.

ARKANSAS TECH
Russellville, AR 72801..................................II

Coach: Steve Mullins, Ark.-Monticello 1980
Record: 3 Years, 18-15-0

2000 SCHEDULE
Carson-Newman [Rome, GA] ....*Sept. 2
Harding ■ ....*Sept. 16
West Ga. ....*Sept. 23
Ouachita Baptist ....Sept. 30
West Ala. ■ ....Oct. 7
Ark.-Monticello ....Oct. 14
Southern Ark. ■ ....Oct. 21
Henderson St. ....Oct. 28
Delta St. ■ ....Nov. 4
Central Ark. ■ ....Nov. 11

1999 RESULTS (9-2-0)
14	Northwest Mo. St.	31
33	Southwest Baptist	0
10	Delta St.	17
32	West Ala.	17
21	Valdosta St.	14
31	Henderson St.	14
54	Central Ark.	27
46	Ark.-Monticello	27
24	North Ala.	21
41	West Ga.	23
20	Southern Ark.	17
326		**208**

DIVISION II CHAMPIONSHIP
| 28 | Carson-Newman | 40 |

Nickname: Wonder Boys.
Stadium: Buerkle Field (1970), 6,000 capacity. Natural turf.
Colors: Green & Gold.
Conference: Gulf South.
SID: Larry Smith, 501-968-0645.
AD: Earle Doman.

ARK.-MONTICELLO
Monticello, AR 71656.............................II

Coach: Clarence Holley, Arkansas Tech 1985
Record: 1 Year, 4-7-0

2000 SCHEDULE
Tusculum ....Sept. 2
North Ala. ....*Sept. 9
Okla. Panhandle ■ ....Sept. 16
West Ala. ■ ....*Sept. 23
West Ga. ■ ....Sept. 30
Ouachita Baptist ....Oct. 7
Arkansas Tech ■ ....Oct. 14
Central Ark. ....Oct. 21
Southern Ark. ■ ....Oct. 28
Henderson St. ■ ....Nov. 4
Delta St. ....*Nov. 9

1999 RESULTS (4-7-0)
14	Mo. Southern St.	35
30	Stillman	7
10	West Ga.	20
23	Southern Ark.	20
13	North Ala.	16
48	Central Ark.	54
24	Henderson St.	37
27	Arkansas Tech	46
35	Valdosta St.	31
23	West Ala.	17
8	Delta St.	40
255		**323**

Nickname: Boll Weevils.
Stadium: Cotton Boll (0000), 6,500 capacity. Natural turf.
Colors: Kelly Green & White.
Conference: Gulf South.
SID: Tim Munn, 870-460-1074.
AD: Alvy Early.

ARK.-PINE BLUFF
Pine Bluff, AR 71611..........................I-AA

Coach: Lee Hardman, Ark.-Pine Bluff 1971
Record: 7 Years, 47-30-0

2000 SCHEDULE
Mississippi Val. ....*Sept. 2
Southern U. ■ ....*Sept. 9
Alabama St. ....*Sept. 23
Alcorn St. [St. Louis, MO] ....Sept. 30
Texas Southern ....*Oct. 7
Grambling [Shreveport, LA] ....Oct. 14
Kentucky St. ■ ....*Oct. 21
Jackson St. ■ ....*Oct. 28
Prairie View ■ ....Nov. 4
Lane ....Nov. 11
Alabama A&M ■ ....Nov. 18

1999 RESULTS (6-5-0)
13	Mississippi Val.	9
9	Southern U.	17
13	Hampton	26
33	Alcorn St.	17
7	Texas Southern	20
35	Alabama St.	21
19	Grambling	24
0	Jackson St.	41
30	Prairie View	6
44	Lane	28
23	Alabama A&M	17
226		**226**

Nickname: Golden Lions.
Stadium: Pumphrey (1951), 6,000 capacity. Natural turf.
Colors: Black & Gold.
Conference: Southwestern Athletic.
SID: Carl Wimper, 501-543-8675.
AD: H. O. Clemmons.

ARMY
West Point, NY 10996..........................I-A

Coach: Todd Terry, Tulsa 1983
Record: 4 Years, 24-24-0

2000 SCHEDULE
Cincinnati ....*Sept. 4
Boston College ■ ....Sept. 9
Houston ....*Sept. 16
Memphis ■ ....Sept. 23
New Mexico St. ....*Oct. 7
East Caro. ....Oct. 14
Tulane ■ ....Oct. 21
Air Force ■ ....Nov. 4
Louisville ....Nov. 11
UAB ■ ....Nov. 18
Navy [Baltimore, MD] ....Dec. 2

1999 RESULTS (3-8-0)
15	Wake Forest	34
28	Tulane	48
41	Ball St.	21
14	East Caro.	33
59	Louisville	52
0	Southern Miss.	24
35	New Mexico St.	18
0	Air Force	28
10	Memphis	14
14	Houston	26
9	Navy	19
225		**317**

Nickname: Cadets/Black Knights.
Stadium: Michie (1924), 39,929 capacity. Artificial turf.
Colors: Black, Gold & Gray.
Conference: Conference USA.
SID: Bob Beretta, 914-938-3303.
AD: Richard I. Greenspan.

ASHLAND
Ashland, OH 44805..................................II

Coach: Gary Keller, Bluffton 1973
Record: 6 Years, 35-27-0

2000 SCHEDULE
Edinboro ....Sept. 2
Wayne St. (Mich.) ....Sept. 9
Findlay ■ ....*Sept. 16
Grand Valley St. ....Sept. 23
Saginaw Valley ■ ....Sept. 30
Hillsdale ....*Oct. 7
Michigan Tech ■ ....Oct. 14
Northern Mich. ....Oct. 21
Northwood ■ ....Oct. 28
Indianapolis ■ ....Nov. 4
Mercyhurst ....Nov. 11

1999 RESULTS (7-3-0)
17	Hillsdale	29
14	Northern Mich.	10
46	Wayne St. (Mich.)	7
24	Westminster (Pa.)	10
39	Michigan Tech	14
26	Ferris St.	22
32	Mercyhurst	7
26	Grand Valley St.	44
10	Indianapolis	30
46	Findlay	14
280		**187**

Nickname: Eagles.
Stadium: Community (1963), 5,700 capacity. Natural turf.
Colors: Purple & Gold.
Conference: Great Lakes Intercollegiate Athletic.
SID: Al King, 419-289-5442.
AD: Bill Goldring.

ASSUMPTION
Worcester, MA 01615..............................II

Coach: Sean Mahoney, Worcester St. 1985
Record: 2 Years, 6-15-0

2000 SCHEDULE
Sacred Heart ....*Sept. 2
Framingham St. ....Sept. 9
Merrimack ■ ....Sept. 16
Bryant ....Sept. 23
St. Anselm ■ ....Sept. 30
American Int'l ■ ....Oct. 7
Stonehill ....Oct. 14
Pace ....Oct. 21
Bentley ....Oct. 28
Mass.-Lowell ■ ....Nov. 4
Mount Ida ■ ....Nov. 11

1999 RESULTS (3-7-0)
32	Sacred Heart	14
13	Bryant	20
21	Merrimack	49
29	St. Anselm	37
14	American Int'l	56
39	Stonehill	28
7	Pace	10
14	Bentley	54
27	Mass.-Lowell	34
20	Mount Ida	18
216		**320**

Nickname: Greyhounds.
Stadium: Rocheleau Field (1961), 1,200 capacity. Natural turf.
Colors: Royal Blue & White.
Conference: Eastern Football.
SID: Steve Morris, 508-767-7240.
AD: Rita M. Castagna.

AUBURN
Auburn Univ., AL 36849........................I-A

2000 SCHEDULES AND 1999 RESULTS

Coach: Tommy Tuberville, Southern Ark. 1976
Record: 5 Years, 30-26-0

2000 SCHEDULE

Wyoming ■	*Aug. 31
Mississippi	*Sept. 9
LSU ■	*Sept. 16
Northern Ill. ■	*Sept. 23
Vanderbilt ■	Sept. 30
Mississippi St.	Oct. 7
Florida	Oct. 14
Louisiana Tech ■	Oct. 21
Arkansas ■	Oct. 28
Georgia ■	Nov. 11
Alabama	Nov. 18

1999 RESULTS (5-6-0)

22	Appalachian St.	15
30	Idaho	23
41	LSU	7
17	Mississippi	24
0	Tennessee	24
16	Mississippi St.	18
14	Florida	32
10	Arkansas	34
28	UCF	10
38	Georgia	21
17	Alabama	28
233		**236**

Nickname: Tigers.
Stadium: Jordan-Hare (1939), 85,214 capacity. Natural turf.
Colors: Orange & Blue.
Conference: Southeastern.
SID: To be named, 334-844-9800.
AD: David E. Housel.

AUGSBURG
Minneapolis, MN 55454 III

Coach: Jack Osberg, Augsburg 1962
Record: 9 Years, 46-45-0

2000 SCHEDULE

Wis.-Eau Claire ■	*Sept. 9
Carleton ■	*Sept. 16
St. John's (Minn.)	Sept. 23
St. Olaf	Sept. 30
St. Thomas (Minn.) ■	Oct. 7
Macalester	Oct. 14
Gust. Adolphus ■	Oct. 21
Hamline	Oct. 28
Concordia-M'head [Minneapolis, MN]	Nov. 4
Bethel (Minn.) ■	Nov. 11

1999 RESULTS (6-4-0)

29	Mayville St.	27
15	Hamline	10
30	St. Olaf	27
0	St. John's (Minn.)	55
12	Gust. Adolphus	38
27	Macalester	7
20	St. Thomas (Minn.)	30
52	Carleton	7
14	Bethel (Minn.)	31
7	Concordia-M'head	5
206		**237**

Nickname: Auggies.
Stadium: Anderson-Nelson Field (1984), 2,000 capacity. Artificial turf.
Colors: Maroon & Gray.
Conference: Minnesota Intercollegiate Athletic.
SID: Don Stoner, 612-330-1677.
AD: Paul Grauer.

AUGUSTANA (ILL.)
Rock Island, IL 61201 III

Coach: Jim Barnes, Augustana (Ill.) 1981
Record: 5 Years, 37-13-0

2000 SCHEDULE

Eureka ■	Sept. 9
Wis.-Platteville	*Sept. 16
Wis. Lutheran ■	Sept. 23
Elmhurst	Sept. 30
Ill. Wesleyan ■	Oct. 7
North Park	Oct. 14
Millikin ■	Oct. 21
North Central ■	Oct. 28
Carthage	Nov. 4
Wheaton (Ill.) ■	Nov. 11

1999 RESULTS (8-1-0)

34	Hope	33
31	Wis.-Platteville	6
7	Millikin	20
41	Ill. Wesleyan	0
40	Elmhurst	6
40	North Central	14
30	North Park	13
31	Carthage	9
31	Wheaton (Ill.)	19
285		**120**

DIVISION III CHAMPIONSHIP

39	St. Norbert	32
33	Mount Union	42

Nickname: Vikings.
Stadium: Ericson Field (1938), 3,200 capacity. Natural turf.
Colors: Gold & Blue.
Conference: College Conf. of Illinois & Wisconsin.
SID: Dave Wrath, 309-794-7265.
AD: Gregory D. Wallace.

AUGUSTANA (S.D.)
Sioux Falls, SD 57197 II

Coach: Jim Heinitz, South Dakota St. 1972
Record: 12 Years, 56-74-1

2000 SCHEDULE

Northern St.	*Sept. 2
Southwest St.	*Sept. 9
South Dakota St. ■	Sept. 16
St. Cloud St. ■	Sept. 23
South Dakota	*Sept. 30
North Dakota St. ■	Oct. 7
Morningside	Oct. 14
Minn. St.-Mankato ■	Oct. 21
North Dakota	Oct. 28
Neb.-Omaha	Nov. 4
Northern Colo. ■	Nov. 11

1999 RESULTS (5-6-0)

56	Northern St.	25
21	Wis.-River Falls	7
31	South Dakota St.	38
10	St. Cloud St.	13
35	South Dakota	21
14	North Dakota St.	30
14	Morningside	20
38	Minn. St.-Mankato	21
0	North Dakota	27
31	Neb.-Omaha	24
32	Northern Colo.	48
282		**274**

Nickname: Vikings.
Stadium: Howard Wood (1957), 10,000 capacity. Natural turf.
Colors: Navy & Yellow.
Conference: North Central Intercollegiate Athletic.
SID: Karen Madsen, 605-336-4335.
AD: Billl Gross.

AURORA
Aurora, IL 60506 III

Coach: Jim Scott, Luther 1961
Record: 14 Years, 72-50-3

2000 SCHEDULE

Bethel (Minn.)	Sept. 9
Ill. Wesleyan ■	Sept. 16
Benedictine (Ill.) ■	Sept. 23
Concordia (Ill.)	Sept. 30
Eureka ■	Oct. 7
Lakeland ■	Oct. 14
MacMurray	Oct. 21
Greenville	Oct. 28
Concordia (Wis.) ■	Nov. 4
Valparaiso	Nov. 11

1999 RESULTS (8-2-0)

20	Urbana	6
12	Millikin	14
20	MacMurray	13
18	Eureka	15
34	Benedictine (Ill.)	3
40	Concordia (Ill.)	0
33	Concordia (Wis.)	21
59	Greenville	14
49	Lakeland	32
0	Valparaiso	31
285		**149**

Nickname: Spartans.
Stadium: Aurora Field (N/A), 1,500 capacity. Natural turf.
Colors: Royal Blue & White.
Conference: Illini-Badger.
SID: Al Benson, 708-844-5479.
AD: Mark Walsh.

AUSTIN
Sherman, TX 75090 III

Coach: David Norman, Austin 1983
Record: 6 Years, 22-37-0

2000 SCHEDULE

Millsaps ■	*Sept. 9
Hardin-Simmons ■	Sept. 16
Mary Hardin-Baylor	Sept. 23
McMurry ■	Sept. 30
East Tex. Baptist	Oct. 7
Texas Lutheran	Oct. 14
Louisiana Col. ■	Oct. 21
Mississippi Col.	Oct. 28
Howard Payne ■	Nov. 4
Sul Ross St.	Nov. 11

1999 RESULTS (3-7-0)

20	Millsaps	27
20	Neb. Wesleyan	19
7	Trinity (Tex.)	48
31	Texas Lutheran	34
21	Howard Payne	28
14	Hardin-Simmons	50
34	Mary Hardin-Baylor	21
41	McMurry	62
31	Sul Ross St.	2
24	Mississippi Col.	50
243		**341**

Nickname: Kangaroos.
Stadium: Jerry Apple (2000), 2,500 capacity. Natural turf.
Colors: Crimson & Gold.
Conference: American Southwest.
SID: Chuck Sadowski, 214-892-9101.
AD: Timothy P. MIllerick.

AUSTIN PEAY
Clarksville, TN 37044 ....I-AA

Coach: Bill Schmitz, Coast Guard 1976
Record: 7 Years, 27-44-0

2000 SCHEDULE

Cumberland (Tenn.)	Aug. 31
Catawba ■	*Sept. 9
Valparaiso	Sept. 23
Jacksonville	Sept. 30
Dayton ■	*Oct. 7
Charleston So. ■	Oct. 14
Ky. Wesleyan	*Oct. 21
Morehead St. ■	Oct. 28
Virginia-Wise ■	Nov. 4
Davidson ■	Nov. 11
South Fla.	Nov. 18

1999 RESULTS (3-8-0)

27	Cumberland (Tenn.)	22
0	Samford	51
21	Dayton	49
36	Campbellsville	35
21	Jacksonville	28
17	Charleston So.	39
38	Ky. Wesleyan	28
7	Morehead St.	47

SCHEDULES/RESULTS

28	Virginia-Wise	34
22	Davidson	38
23	Valparaiso	52
240		**423**

Nickname: Governors.
Stadium: Governors (1946), 10,000 capacity. Artificial turf.
Colors: Red & White.
Conference: Division I-AA Independent.
SID: Brad Kirtley, 615-648-7561.
AD: Dave Loos.

BALDWIN-WALLACE
Berea, OH 44017 III

Coach: Bob Packard, Baldwin-Wallace 1965
Record: 19 Years, 144-46-2

2000 SCHEDULE
Adrian ■	*Sept. 9
Wilmington (Ohio)	Sept. 16
Ohio Northern ■	Sept. 23
Capital	Sept. 30
Heidelberg	Oct. 7
Otterbein ■	Oct. 14
Muskingum ■	Oct. 21
Marietta	Oct. 28
Mount Union ■	Nov. 4
John Carroll	Nov. 11

1999 RESULTS (6-4-0)
21	Wittenberg	26
12	Otterbein	32
44	Marietta	7
36	Hiram	21
3	Ohio Northern	21
29	John Carroll	20
46	Capital	28
28	Muskingum	0
34	Heidelberg	6
7	Mount Union	26
260		**187**

Nickname: Yellow Jackets.
Stadium: George Finnie (1971), 8,100 capacity. Artificial turf.
Colors: Brown & Gold.
Conference: Ohio Athletic.
SID: Kevin Ruple, 216-826-2327.
AD: Stephen Bankson.

BALL ST.
Muncie, IN 47306 ....I-A

Coach: Bill Lynch, Butler 1977
Record: 10 Years, 57-47-3

2000 SCHEDULE
Florida	*Sept. 2
Western Ill. ■	Sept. 9
Kansas St.	*Sept. 16
Northern Ill. ■	Sept. 30
Miami (Ohio)	Oct. 7
Eastern Mich. ■	Oct. 14
Buffalo	Oct. 21
Central Mich.	Oct. 28
Western Mich. ■	Nov. 4
Toledo	Nov. 11
Connecticut ■	Nov. 18

1999 RESULTS (0-11-0)
9	Indiana	21
10	Wisconsin	50
10	Toledo	23
21	Army	41
9	Akron	31
17	Northern Ill.	37
0	Western Mich.	28
25	Ohio	37
21	Eastern Mich.	31
14	Bowling Green	35
21	Central Mich.	27
157		**361**

Nickname: Cardinals.
Stadium: Ball State (1967), 21,581 capacity. Natural turf.
Colors: Cardinal & White.
Conference: Mid-American.
SID: Joe Hernandez, 317-285-8242.
AD: Andrea Seger.

BATES
Lewiston, ME 04240 III

Coach: Mark Harriman, Springfield 1980
Record: 2 Years, 5-11-0

2000 SCHEDULE
Trinity (Conn.)	Sept. 23
Tufts	Oct. 1
Williams ■	Oct. 7
Wesleyan (Conn.) ■	Oct. 14
Middlebury	Oct. 21
Colby ■	Oct. 28
Bowdoin	Nov. 4
Hamilton ■	Nov. 11

1999 RESULTS (4-4-0)
19	Amherst	7
10	Tufts	13
10	Williams	34
29	Wesleyan (Conn.)	36
9	Middlebury	12
20	Colby	17
38	Bowdoin	7
28	Hamilton	0
163		**126**

Nickname: Bobcats.
Stadium: Garcelon Field (1900), 3,000 capacity. Natural turf.
Colors: Garnet.
Conference: NESCAC.
SID: Adam Levin, 207-786-6411.
AD: Suzanne R. Coffey.

BAYLOR
Waco, TX 76798 ....I-A

Coach: Kevin Steele, Tennessee 1981
Record: 1 Year, 1-10-0

2000 SCHEDULE
North Texas	*Aug. 31
Minnesota ■	Sept. 16
South Fla. ■	*Sept. 23
Iowa St. ■	*Sept. 30
Texas Tech	*Oct. 7
Texas A&M ■	Oct. 14
Nebraska	Oct. 21
Texas	Oct. 28
Oklahoma ■	Nov. 4
Missouri ■	Nov. 11
Oklahoma St.	Nov. 18

1999 RESULTS (1-10-0)
29	Boston College	30
24	UNLV	27
10	Oklahoma	41
0	Texas	62
23	North Texas	10
13	Texas A&M	45
7	Texas Tech	35
7	Kansas St.	48
10	Kansas	45
0	Colorado	37
14	Oklahoma St.	34
137		**414**

Nickname: Bears.
Stadium: Floyd Casey (1950), 50,000 capacity. Natural turf.
Colors: Green & Gold.
Conference: Big 12.
SID: Brian McCallum, 817-755-2743.
AD: Thomas I. Stanton.

BELOIT
Beloit, WI 53511 III

Coach: Ed DeGeorge, Colorado Col. 1964
Record: 23 Years, 111-100-1

2000 SCHEDULE
Concordia (Wis.)	Sept. 9
Grinnell	Sept. 16
Monmouth (Ill.) ■	Sept. 23
Lake Forest	Sept. 30
Lawrence	Oct. 7
Illinois Col.	Oct. 14
Knox ■	Oct. 21
Carroll (Wis.) ■	Oct. 28
St. Norbert	Nov. 4
Ripon ■	Nov. 11

1999 RESULTS (7-3-0)
20	Concordia (Wis.)	16
20	Grinnell	28
47	Monmouth (Ill.)	13
38	Lake Forest	14
31	Lawrence	14
30	Illinois Col.	20
20	Knox	14
26	Carroll (Wis.)	34
10	St. Norbert	35
23	Ripon	22
265		**210**

Nickname: Buccaneers.
Stadium: Strong (1934), 3,500 capacity. Natural turf.
Colors: Navy Blue & Gold.
Conference: Midwest Collegiate Athletic.
SID: Nate Llewellyn, 608-363-2229.
AD: Edward J. DeGeorge.

BEMIDJI ST.
Bemidji, MN 56601 II

Coach: Jeff Tesch, Moorhead St. 1978
Record: 4 Years, 18-23-0

2000 SCHEDULE
Minot St.	*Sept. 2
St. Thomas (Minn.) ■	Sept. 9
Wayne St. (Neb.)	Sept. 16
Northern St. ■	Sept. 23
Concordia-St. Paul	Sept. 30
Southwest St. ■	Oct. 7
Moorhead St.	Oct. 14
Minn.-Duluth	Oct. 21
Minn.-Morris ■	Oct. 28
Minn.-Crookston ■	Nov. 4
Wis.-River Falls [Minneapolis, MN]	*Nov. 10

1999 RESULTS (8-3-0)
28	Minot St.	7
24	St. Thomas (Minn.)	14
52	Wayne St. (Neb.)	38
17	Northern St.	45
54	Concordia-St. Paul	7
13	Southwest St.	10
25	Moorhead St.	32
35	Minn.-Duluth	26
53	Minn.-Morris	20
38	Minn.-Crookston	31
23	Wis.-Stevens Point	35
362		**265**

Nickname: Beavers.
Stadium: BSU (1937), 4,000 capacity. Natural turf.
Colors: Kelly Green & White.
Conference: Northern Sun Intercollegiate Athletic.
SID: Ron Christian, 218-755-2763.
AD: Robert H. Peters.

BENEDICTINE (ILL.)
Lisle, IL 60532 III

Coach: Jeff Hand, Clarion 1992
Record: 1 Year, 6-4-0

2000 SCHEDULE
North Central ■	Sept. 9
Elmhurst	Sept. 16
Aurora	Sept. 23
Eureka ■	Sept. 30
MacMurray	Oct. 7
Concordia (Wis.)	Oct. 14
Concordia (Ill.) ■	Oct. 21
Lakeland	Oct. 28

Greenville ■...Nov. 4
Chicago ■..Nov. 11

1999 RESULTS (6-4-0)
23	Blackburn	13
16	North Central	10
28	Elmhurst	21
0	Eureka	12
27	Concordia (Ill.)	20
3	Aurora	34
3	Concordia (Wis.)	45
30	Greenville	14
31	Lakeland	28
17	MacMurray	35
178		232

Nickname: Eagles.
Stadium: Alumni Memorial (1910), 2,500 capacity. Natural turf.
Colors: Cardinal & White.
Conference: Illini-Badger.
SID: Renee Kanak, 708-960-1500.
AD: John J. Stachniak.

BENTLEY
Waltham, MA 02154...II

Coach: Peter Yetten, Boston U. 1971
Record: 12 Years, 84-30-1

2000 SCHEDULE
Gannon ■...*Sept. 1
Merrimack..Sept. 9
Southern Conn. St. ■..*Sept. 15
American Int'l..Sept. 23
Mass.-Lowell...Sept. 29
Bryant ■...*Oct. 5
Pace ■..Oct. 14
Plymouth St..Oct. 21
Assumption ■..Oct. 28
C. W. Post..Nov. 4
Stonehill ■...Nov. 11

1999 RESULTS (4-7-0)
30	Gannon	14
9	Merrimack	14
0	Southern Conn. St.	38
26	American Int'l	44
27	Mass.-Lowell	14
39	Bryant	44
27	Pace	34
12	Plymouth St.	17
54	Assumption	14
21	C. W. Post	28
48	Stonehill	27
293		288

Nickname: Falcons.
Stadium: Bentley College (1990), 3,200 capacity. Natural turf.
Colors: Royal Blue & Gold.
Conference: Eastern Football.
SID: Dick Lipe, 617-891-2334.
SD: Robert De Felice.

BETHANY (W.VA.)
Bethany, WV 26032...III

Coach: Steve Campos, Indiana (Pa.) 1982
Record: 6 Years, 23-33-1

2000 SCHEDULE
Shenandoah ■...Sept. 2
Apprentice...Sept. 9
Carnegie Mellon..*Sept. 16
Gallaudet..Sept. 23
Waynesburg..Sept. 30
Westminster (Pa.)..Oct. 7
Wash. & Jeff. ■..Oct. 14
Thiel ■...Oct. 21
Grove City ■..Oct. 28
Chicago..Nov. 4

1999 RESULTS (4-6-0)
14	Bluffton	35
30	Apprentice	0
10	Carnegie Mellon	17
3	Grove City	24
21	Waynesburg	26
0	Chicago	12
13	Wash. & Jeff.	42
9	Thiel	6
21	Maryville (Tenn.)	9
21	Alfred	7
142		178

Nickname: Bison.
Stadium: Bethany Field (1938), 1,000 capacity. Natural turf.
Colors: Green & White.
Conference: Presidents' Athletic.
SID: Brian Rose, 304-829-7292.
AD: Wallace B. Neel.

BETHEL (MINN.)
St. Paul, MN 55112..III

Coach: Steve Johnson, Bethel (Minn.) 1980
Record: 11 Years, 67-41-1

2000 SCHEDULE
Aurora ■..Sept. 9
Macalester..*Sept. 16
Gust. Adolphus ■..Sept. 23
Hamline..Sept. 30
St. Olaf ■...Oct. 7
Concordia-M'head ■...Oct. 14
Carleton..Oct. 21
St. John's (Minn.) ■...Oct. 28
St. Thomas (Minn.) [Minneapolis, MN]..................*Nov. 3
Augsburg..Nov. 11

1999 RESULTS (8-2-0)
59	Trinity (Ill.)	21
15	Concordia-M'head	17
41	Hamline	14
39	St. Olaf	13
24	St. John's (Minn.)	20
20	Gust. Adolphus	26
74	Macalester	0
22	St. Thomas (Minn.)	20
31	Augsburg	14
47	Carleton	26
372		171

Nickname: Royals.
Stadium: Armstrong (1996), 3,500 capacity. Natural turf.
Colors: Blue & Gold.
Conference: Minnesota Intercollegiate Athletic.
SID: Greg Peterson, 612-638-6394.
AD: David A. Klostreich.

BETHUNE-COOKMAN
Daytona Beach, FL 32114..I-AA

Coach: Alvin Wyatt Sr., Bethune-Cookman 1970
Record: 3 Years, 19-14-0

2000 SCHEDULE
Savannah St. [Jacksonville, FL]..............................Sept. 2
Norfolk St. ■...Sept. 9
Johnson Smith ■...Sept. 16
Morris Brown..*Sept. 23
Morgan St...Sept. 30
Delaware St. ■..Oct. 7
South Carolina St. ■...*Oct. 14
N.C. A&T..Oct. 28
Hampton...Nov. 4
Howard...*Nov. 11
Florida A&M [Orlando, FL].....................................Nov. 18

1999 RESULTS (7-4-0)
17	Savannah St.	14
28	Morgan St.	25
27	Howard	31
28	Morris Brown	16
29	Delaware St.	43
26	Johnson Smith	6
30	South Carolina St.	27
18	N.C. A&T	19
34	Hampton	27
26	Norfolk St.	6
14	Florida A&M	63
277		277

Nickname: Wildcats.
Stadium: Municipal (0000), 10,000 capacity. Natural turf.
Colors: Maroon & Gold.
Conference: Mid-Eastern Athletic.
SID: Charles D. Jackson, 904-255-1401.
AD: Lynn W. Thompson.

BLACKBURN
Carlinville, IL 62626...III

Coach: Jim Chinn
1 Year, 2-8-0

2000 SCHEDULE
Illinois Col...Sept. 2
MacMurray ■..Sept. 9
Northwestern (Minn.)..Sept. 16
Millikin...Sept. 23
Westminster (Mo.) ■...Sept. 30
Rockford ■..Oct. 7
DePauw ■..Oct. 14
Maryville (Tenn.) ■..Oct. 28
Bethel (Tenn.)...Nov. 4
Greenville ■...Nov. 11

1999 RESULTS (2-8-0)
13	Benedictine (Ill.)	23
7	MacMurray	34
18	Franklin	45
6	Millikin	63
21	Martin Luther	28
44	Greenville	46
9	Westminster (Mo.)	63
35	Principia	7
17	Northwestern (Minn.)	20
17	Maranatha Baptist	14
187		343

Nickname: Battlin' Beavers.
Stadium: Blackburn College (1989), 1,500 capacity. Natural turf.
Colors: Scarlet & Black.
Conference: St. Louis Intercollegiate Athletic.
SID: To be named, 217-854-3231.
AD: Joe Ramsey.

BLOOMSBURG
Bloomsburg, PA 17815..II

Coach: Danny Hale, West Chester 1968
Record: 12 Years, 92-37-1

2000 SCHEDULE
Carson-Newman [Sevierville, TN]..........................*Aug. 26
Shippensburg..Sept. 9
Lock Haven ■..Sept. 16
Cheyney ■...Sept. 23
West Chester..*Sept. 30
Indiana (Pa.) ■..Oct. 7
East Stroudsburg ■...Oct. 14
Mansfield..Oct. 21
Millersville ■..Oct. 28
Kutztown..Nov. 4
Slippery Rock...Nov. 11

1999 RESULTS (7-4-0)
37	New Haven	47
36	Shippensburg	28
44	Lock Haven	24
10	Indiana (Pa.)	35
42	Kutztown	33
21	Millersville	31
17	West Chester	35
48	Cheyney	6
27	East Stroudsburg	21
53	Mansfield	21
65	Edinboro	16
400		297

Nickname: Huskies.
Stadium: Redman (1974), 5,000 capacity. Natural turf.
Colors: Maroon & Gold.
Conference: Pennsylvania State Athletic.
SID: Tom McGuire, 717-389-4413.
AD: Mary Gardner.

BLUFFTON
Bluffton, OH 45817 III

Coach: Carlin Carpenter, Defiance 1964
Record: 21 Years, 88-110-1

2000 SCHEDULE
Malone ■	Sept. 2
Hiram ■	Sept. 9
Thiel	Sept. 16
Anderson (Ind.) ■	Sept. 30
Mt. St. Joseph ■	Oct. 7
Hanover	Oct. 14
Manchester ■	Oct. 21
Franklin	Oct. 28
Thomas More ■	Nov. 4
Defiance	Nov. 11

1999 RESULTS (7-3-0)
35	Bethany (W.Va.)	14
47	Hiram	26
30	Grove City	22
38	Hanover	41
7	Wabash	27
48	Anderson (Ind.)	17
26	Manchester	10
27	Mt. St. Joseph	26
28	Franklin	7
28	Wilmington (Ohio)	31
314		**221**

Nickname: Beavers.
Stadium: Salzman (1993), 3,000 capacity. Natural turf.
Colors: Royal Purple & White.
Conference: Heartland Collegiate Athletic.
SID: Tim Stried, 419-358-3241.
AD: Carlin B. Carpenter.

BOISE ST.
Boise, ID 83725 ....I-A

Coach: Dirk Koetter, Idaho St. 1981
Record: 2 Years, 16-8-0

2000 SCHEDULE
New Mexico	*Sept. 2
Northern Iowa ■	*Sept. 9
Arkansas [Little Rock, AR]	*Sept. 16
Central Mich.	Sept. 23
Washington St.	Oct. 7
Eastern Wash.	Oct. 14
North Texas ■	Oct. 21
New Mexico St.	*Oct. 28
Arkansas St.	Nov. 4
Utah St. ■	Nov. 11
Idaho ■	Nov. 18

1999 RESULTS (9-3-0)
7	UCLA	38
35	Southern Utah	27
19	Hawaii	34
20	New Mexico	9
26	Utah	20
41	Eastern Wash.	7
10	North Texas	17
52	Nevada	17
33	Utah St.	27
63	Arkansas St.	10
45	New Mexico St.	26
45	Idaho	14
396		**246**

HUMANITARIAN BOWL
34	Louisville	31

Nickname: Broncos.
Stadium: Bronco (1970), 30,000 capacity. Artificial turf.
Colors: Orange & Blue.
Conference: Big West.
SID: Max Corbet, 208-385-1515.
AD: Gene Bleymaier.

BOSTON COLLEGE
Chestnut Hill, MA 02467 ....I-A

Coach: Tom O'Brien, Navy 1971
Record: 3 Years, 16-18-0

2000 SCHEDULE
West Virginia	Sept. 2
Army	Sept. 9
Navy ■	Sept. 23
Virginia Tech	Sept. 30
Connecticut ■	Oct. 7
Syracuse ■	Oct. 14
Pittsburgh	Oct. 21
Rutgers ■	Oct. 28
Temple ■	Nov. 4
Notre Dame	Nov. 11
Miami (Fla.)	Nov. 25

1999 RESULTS (8-3-0)
30	Baylor	29
14	Navy	10
27	Rutgers	7
33	Northeastern	22
14	Temple	24
20	Pittsburgh	16
28	Miami (Fla.)	31
24	Syracuse	23
34	West Virginia	17
31	Notre Dame	29
14	Virginia Tech	38
269		**246**

INSIGHT.COM BOWL
28	Colorado	62

Nickname: Eagles.
Stadium: Alumni (1957), 44,500 capacity. Artificial turf.
Colors: Maroon & Gold.
Conference: Big East.
SID: Chris Cameron, 617-552-3004.
AD: Gene De Filippo.

BOWDOIN
Brunswick, ME 04011 III

Coach: Dave Caputi, Middlebury 1981
(First year as head coach)

2000 SCHEDULE
Middlebury	Sept. 23
Amherst ■	Sept. 30
Tufts ■	Oct. 7
Hamilton	Oct. 14
Trinity (Conn.) ■	Oct. 21
Wesleyan (Conn.)	Oct. 28
Bates ■	Nov. 4
Colby	Nov. 11

1999 RESULTS (1-7-0)
0	Williams	42
7	Amherst	10
13	Tufts	38
22	Hamilton	12
0	Trinity (Conn.)	26
14	Wesleyan (Conn.)	35
7	Bates	38
0	Colby	20
63		**221**

Nickname: Polar Bears.
Stadium: Whittier Field (1896), 6,000 capacity. Natural turf.
Colors: White.
Conference: NESCAC.
SID: Jac Coyne, 207-725-3254.
AD: Jeffrey H. Ward.

BOWIE ST.
Bowie, MD 20715 II

Coach: Henry Frazier III, Bowie St. 1993
Record: 1 Year, 5-4-0

2000 SCHEDULE
Johnson Smith ■	Sept. 2
Winston-Salem	*Sept. 9
Cheyney	Sept. 16
West Virginia St.	Sept. 23
Virginia Union ■	Sept. 30
Morehouse	Oct. 7
Elizabeth City St. ■	Oct. 14
Morehead St.	Oct. 21
Fayetteville St.	Oct. 28
Virginia St. ■	Nov. 4

1999 RESULTS (5-4-0)
20	Cheyney	6
0	Millersville	41
23	Johnson Smith	19
14	Livingstone	42
6	Virginia Union	39
20	Elizabeth City St.	6
26	N.C. Central	25
40	Fayetteville St.	21
32	Virginia St.	56
181		**255**

Nickname: Bulldogs.
Stadium: Bulldog (1992), 6,000 capacity. Natural turf.
Colors: Black & Gold.
Conference: Central Intercollegiate Athletic.
SID: Scott Rouch, 301-464-7710.
AD: David Y. Thomas.

BOWLING GREEN
Bowling Green, OH 43403 ....I-A

Coach: Gary Blackney, Connecticut 1967
Record: 9 Years, 58-41-2

2000 SCHEDULE
Michigan	Sept. 2
Pittsburgh ■	Sept. 9
Temple	*Sept. 16
Buffalo	*Sept. 23
Kent St.	*Sept. 30
Akron	Oct. 7
Miami (Ohio)	Oct. 14
Eastern Mich. ■	*Oct. 21
Marshall ■	Nov. 4
Ohio ■	Nov. 11
Toledo	*Nov. 22

1999 RESULTS (5-6-0)
10	Pittsburgh	30
40	Tennessee Tech	15
16	Marshall	35
27	Kent St.	41
34	Toledo	23
31	Miami (Ohio)	45
25	Akron	55
14	Ohio	17
31	Central Mich.	7
35	Ball St.	14
33	UCF	30
296		**312**

Nickname: Falcons.
Stadium: Doyt Perry (1966), 30,599 capacity. Natural turf.
Colors: Orange & Brown.
Conference: Mid-American.
SID: Steve Barr, 419-372-7075.
AD: Paul Krebs.

BRI'WATER (MASS.)
Bridgewater, MA 02325 III

Coach: Peter Mazzaferro, Centre 1954
Record: 36 Years, 180-139-11

2000 SCHEDULE
Nichols	Sept. 9
Worcester St.	*Sept. 15
Framingham St. ■	Sept. 23
Maine Maritime	Sept. 30
MIT ■	Oct. 7
Westfield St.	Oct. 14
Mass.-Dartmouth ■	Oct. 21
Fitchburg St.	Oct. 28
Mass. Maritime ■	Nov. 4

1999 RESULTS (10-0-0)
36	Springfield	29
39	Salve Regina	28
41	Worcester St.	17
49	Framingham St.	12
48	Maine Maritime	16
54	MIT	21
49	Westfield St.	19

31	Mass.-Dartmouth	24
42	Fitchburg St.	14
41	Mass. Maritime	23
430		**203**

DIVISION III CHAMPIONSHIP
| 38 | Ursinus | 43 |

Nickname: Bears.
Stadium: College (1974), 3,000 capacity. Natural turf.
Colors: Crimson & White.
Conference: New England Football.
SID: Michael Storey, 617-697-1352.
AD: John C. Harper.

BRIDGEWATER (VA.)
Bridgewater, VA 22812 III

Coach: Michael Clark, Cincinnati 1979
Record: 5 Years, 12-37-1

2000 SCHEDULE
Western Md.	Sept. 2
Shenandoah	Sept. 9
Emory & Henry	Sept. 16
Hampden-Sydney ■	Sept. 30
Maryville (Tenn.) ■	Oct. 7
Guilford	Oct. 14
Johns Hopkins ■	Oct. 21
Wash. & Lee ■	Oct. 28
Randolph-Macon	Nov. 4
Catholic	Nov. 11

1999 RESULTS (5-5-0)
0	Western Md.	24
21	Emory & Henry	24
14	Ferrum	7
40	Hampden-Sydney	7
20	Maryville (Tenn.)	21
41	Guilford	14
37	Johns Hopkins	24
38	Wash. & Lee	44
42	Randolph-Macon	14
14	Catholic	35
267		**214**

Nickname: Eagles.
Stadium: Jopson Field (1971), 3,000 capacity. Natural turf.
Colors: Crimson & Gold.
Conference: Old Dominion Athletic.
SID: Scott Garbarini, 703-828-5360.
AD: Thomas M. Kinder.

BRIGHAM YOUNG
Provo, UT 84602 ....I-A

Coach: LaVell Edwards, Utah St. 1952
Record: 28 Years, 251-95-3

2000 SCHEDULE
Florida St. [Jacksonville, FL]	*Aug. 26
Virginia	Sept. 2
Air Force	Sept. 9
Mississippi St. ■	*Sept. 14
UNLV ■	Sept. 23
Syracuse	*Sept. 30
Utah St. ■	*Oct. 6
San Diego St. ■	Oct. 21
Wyoming	*Oct. 26
Colorado St.	*Nov. 2
New Mexico ■	Nov. 18
Utah	Nov. 24

1999 RESULTS (8-3-0)
35	Washington	28
34	Colorado St.	13
40	Virginia	45
34	Utah St.	31
38	California	28
31	New Mexico	7
29	UNLV	0
27	Air Force	20
30	San Diego St.	7
17	Wyoming	31
17	Utah	20
332		**230**

MOTOR CITY BOWL
| 3 | Marshall | 21 |

Nickname: Cougars.
Stadium: Cougar (1964), 65,000 capacity. Natural turf.
Colors: Blue & White.
Conference: Mountain West.
SID: Jeff Reynolds, 801-378-4911.
AD: Q. Val Hale.

BROCKPORT ST.
Brockport, NY 14420 III

Coach: Rocco Salomone, Brockport St. 1988
Record: 5 Years, 25-23-1

2000 SCHEDULE
Cortland St.	Sept. 2
New Jersey City	Sept. 9
Plymouth St.	Sept. 16
Buffalo St. ■	Sept. 30
Ithaca ■	Oct. 7
Frostburg St.	Oct. 14
St. John Fisher ■	Oct. 21
Mount Ida ■	Oct. 28
Col. of New Jersey ■	Nov. 4

1999 RESULTS (6-4-0)
48	New Jersey City	21
13	Plymouth St.	10
15	Montclair St.	30
12	Buffalo St.	14
0	Ithaca	10
18	Frostburg St.	35
7	St. John Fisher	0
33	Thiel	21
12	Col. of New Jersey	7
28	Cortland St.	24
186		**172**

Nickname: Golden Eagles.
Stadium: Special Olympics (1979), 10,000 capacity. Natural turf.
Colors: Green & Gold.
Conference: Division III Independent.
SID: Mike Andriatch, 716-395-2218.
AD: Linda J. Case.

BROWN
Providence, RI 02912 ....I-AA

Coach: Phil Estes, New Hampshire 1981
Record: 2 Years, 16-4-0

2000 SCHEDULE
San Diego ■	Sept. 16
Harvard ■	Sept. 23
Rhode Island	Sept. 30
Fordham	Oct. 7
Princeton	Oct. 14
Cornell ■	Oct. 21
Pennsylvania	Oct. 28
Yale ■	Nov. 4
Dartmouth	Nov. 11
Columbia ■	Nov. 18

1999 RESULTS (9-1-0)
25	Yale	24
35	Lafayette	28
28	Cornell	33
53	Princeton	30
27	Rhode Island	25
44	Pennsylvania	37
37	Fordham	18
17	Harvard	10
35	Dartmouth	28
23	Columbia	6
324		**239**

Nickname: Bears.
Stadium: Brown (1925), 20,000 capacity. Natural turf.
Colors: Seal Brown, Cardinal & White.
Conference: Ivy.
SID: Christopher Humm, 401-863-2219.
AD: David T. Roach.

BRYANT
Smithfield, RI 02917 II

Coach Jim Miceli, Southern Conn. St. 1979
Record: 5 Years, 33-13-0

2000 SCHEDULE
Sacred Heart	Sept. 9
Pace ■	Sept. 16
Assumption ■	Sept. 23
Mount Ida	Sept. 30
Bentley	*Oct. 5
St. Anselm ■	Oct. 14
Mass.-Lowell	Oct. 21
Stonehill	Oct. 28
American Int'l ■	Nov. 4
Merrimack	Nov. 11

1999 RESULTS (5-4-0)
20	Assumption	13
7	Pace	13
31	Mount Ida	20
44	Bentley	39
27	St. Anselm	7
3	Mass.-Lowell	13
24	Stonehill	7
20	American Int'l	60
10	Merrimack	20
186		**192**

Nickname: Bulldogs.
Stadium: Bulldog (N/A), 3,000 capacity, natural turf.
Colors: Black & Gold.
Conference: Eastern Football.
SID: Chuck Sullivan, 401-232-6072.
AD: Dan Gavitt.

BUCKNELL
Lewisburg, PA 17837 ....I-AA

Coach: Tom Gadd, UC Riverside 1970
Record: 5 Years, 36-19-0

2000 SCHEDULE
Richmond	*Sept. 2
Cornell ■	Sept. 16
Columbia ■	Sept. 23
Duquesne ■	Sept. 30
Georgetown	Oct. 7
Lafayette ■	Oct. 14
Lehigh	Oct. 21
Fordham ■	Oct. 28
Holy Cross	Nov. 4
Towson	Nov. 11
Colgate ■	Nov. 18

1999 RESULTS (7-4-0)
37	Morgan St.	10
21	Colgate	16
20	Towson	27
38	Delaware St.	28
23	Pennsylvania	16
7	Columbia	10
49	Duquesne	20
21	Lafayette	22
32	Holy Cross	21
27	Lehigh	48
45	Fordham	15
320		**233**

Nickname: Bison.
Stadium: Christy Mathewson (1924), 13,100 capacity. Natural turf.
Colors: Orange & Blue.
Conference: Patriot.
SID: Todd Newcomb, 717-524-1227.
AD: John P. Hardt.

BUENA VISTA
Storm Lake, IA 50588 III

Coach: Steve Osterberger, Drake 1991
(First year as head coach)

2000 SCHEDULE
Luther ■	Sept. 2
Upper Iowa	Sept. 16
Central (Iowa) ■	Sept. 23
William Penn ■	Sept. 30
Wartburg	Oct. 7
Simpson	Oct. 14
Dubuque ■	Oct. 21

Loras	Oct. 28
Coe ■	Nov. 4
Cornell College ■	Nov. 11

1999 RESULTS (7-3-0)
17	Upper Iowa	7
38	William Penn	14
27	Wartburg	49
59	Cornell College	7
20	Loras	16
20	Simpson	3
29	Luther	7
55	Dubuque	13
31	Coe	34
13	Central (Iowa)	14
309		**164**

Nickname: Beavers.
Stadium: J. Leslie Rollins (1980), 3,500 capacity. Natural turf.
Colors: Blue & Gold.
Conference: Iowa Intercollegiate Athletic.
SID: Paul Misner, 712-749-2633.
AD: To be announced

BUFFALO
Buffalo, NY 14260 ....I-A

Coach: Craig Cirbus, Buffalo 1980
Record: 5 Years, 17-38-0

2000 SCHEDULE
Syracuse	*Sept. 2
Rutgers	*Sept. 9
Connecticut ■	*Sept. 16
Bowling Green ■	*Sept. 23
Marshall	*Sept. 30
Ohio	*Oct. 7
Ball St. ■	Oct. 21
Northern Ill.	Oct. 28
Kent ■	Nov. 4
Akron	*Nov. 11
Miami (Ohio) ■	Nov. 18

1999 RESULTS (0-11-0)
10	Akron	17
0	Connecticut	23
6	Ohio	45
21	Northern Ill.	45
19	Central Mich.	38
17	Western Mich.	45
3	Marshall	59
20	Kent St.	41
13	Hofstra	20
21	Virginia	50
0	Miami (Ohio)	43
130		**426**

Nickname: Bulls.
Stadium: UB Stadium (1993), 31,000 capacity. Natural turf.
Colors: Royal Blue & White.
Conference: Mid-American.
SID: Paul Vecchio, 716-645-6311.
AD: Robert J. Arkeilpane.

BUFFALO ST.
Buffalo, NY 14222 III

Coach: Jerry Boyes, Ithaca 1976
Record: 14 Years, 82-58-0

2000 SCHEDULE
Robert Morris	Sept. 2
Mansfield ■	Sept. 9
Albion	Sept. 16
Cortland St. ■	Sept. 23
Brockport St.	Sept. 30
Rowan ■	Oct. 7
St. John Fisher	*Oct. 14
Montclair St. ■	Oct. 21
Ithaca	Nov. 4
Wash. & Jeff. ■	Nov. 11

1999 RESULTS (7-2-0)
32	Robert Morris	20
42	Adrian	27
20	Cortland St.	17

14	Brockport St.	12
7	Rowan	43
32	St. John Fisher	3
40	Wash. & Jeff.	21
8	Allegheny	48
42	Ithaca	35
237		**226**

DIVISION III CHAMPIONSHIP
| 34 | Montclair St. | 37 |

Nickname: Bengals.
Stadium: Coyer Field (1964), 3,000 capacity. Natural turf.
Colors: Orange & Black.
Conference: Division III Independent.
SID: Paul Martello, 716-878-6030.
AD: Jerry S. Boyes.

BUTLER
Indianapolis, IN 46208 ....I-AA

Coach: Ken LaRose, Butler 1980
Record: 8 Years, 39-41-0

2000 SCHEDULE
St. Francis (Ind.) ■	Sept. 2
Morehead St.	*Sept. 9
St. Francis (Pa.) ■	Sept. 16
Georgetown	Sept. 23
Dayton ■	Sept. 30
Albion	Oct. 7
Valparaiso	Oct. 14
San Diego ■	Oct. 21
Drake	Oct. 28
Quincy	Nov. 4

1999 RESULTS (5-5-0)
27	Albion	20
34	Morehead St.	56
21	St. Francis (Pa.)	7
34	Wesley	19
7	Dayton	42
20	Valparaiso	38
14	San Diego	42
6	Drake	53
27	Quincy	12
27	Lindenwood	16
217		**305**

Nickname: Bulldogs.
Stadium: Butler Bowl (1927), 19,000 capacity. Natural turf.
Colors: Blue & White.
Conference: Pioneer Football.
SID: Jim McGrath, 317-940-9671.
AD: John C. Parry.

C. W. POST
Brookville, NY 11548 II

Coach: Bryan Collins, St. John's (N.Y.) 1987
Record: 2 Years, 16-5-0

2000 SCHEDULE
American Int'l	Sept. 9
Mass.-Lowell ■	Sept. 16
St. Anselm	Sept. 23
Stonehill ■	Sept. 30
Monmouth	Oct. 7
Merrimack	Oct. 14
Southern Conn. St. ■	Oct. 28
Bentley ■	Nov. 4
Pace	Nov. 11

1999 RESULTS (9-1-0)
0	American Int'l	34
28	Mass.-Lowell	7
50	St. Anselm	7
38	Stonehill	21
30	Monmouth	26
35	Merrimack	0
44	Stony Brook	20
36	Southern Conn. St.	27
28	Bentley	21
30	Pace	17
319		**180**

EASTERN FOOTBALL CONF. CHAMPIONSHIP
| 20 | American Int'l | 41 |

Nickname: Pioneers.
Stadium: Hickox Field (1966), 5,000 capacity. Natural turf.
Colors: Green & Gold.
Conference: Eastern Football.
SID: Brad Sullivan, 516-299-4156.
AD: Vincent Salamone.

CALIFORNIA
Berkeley, CA 94720 ....I-A

Coach: Tom Holmoe, Brigham Young 1983
Record: 3 Years, 12-21-0

2000 SCHEDULE
Utah ■	Sept. 9
Illinois	Sept. 16
Fresno St.	Sept. 23
Washington St. ■	Sept. 30
Arizona St.	*Oct. 7
UCLA ■	Oct. 14
Washington	Oct. 21
Southern California	Oct. 28
Oregon St. ■	Nov. 4
Oregon	Nov. 11
Stanford ■	Nov. 18

1999 RESULTS (4-7-0)
21	Rutgers	7
0	Nebraska	45
24	Arizona St.	23
7	Washington St.	31
28	Brigham Young	38
17	UCLA	0
27	Washington	31
17	Southern California	7
7	Oregon St.	17
19	Oregon	24
13	Stanford	31
180		**254**

Nickname: Golden Bears.
Stadium: Memorial (1923), 75,082 capacity. Natural turf.
Colors: Blue & Gold.
Conference: Pacific-10.
SID: Kevin Reneau, 510-642-5363.
AD: John V. Kasser.

UC DAVIS
Davis, CA 95616 II

Coach: Bob Biggs, UC Davis 1973
Record: 7 Years, 59-23-1

2000 SCHEDULE
N.M. Highlands ■	*Sept. 2
Eastern Ore. ■	*Sept. 9
West Chester	Sept. 16
St. Mary's (Cal.) ■	*Sept. 30
Western Ore.	Oct. 7
Southern Utah ■	Oct. 14
Cal Poly	*Oct. 21
Cal St. Sacramento ■	Oct. 28
Central Wash.	Nov. 4
Western Wash.	Nov. 11

1999 RESULTS (9-1-0)
36	Tex. A&M-Commerce	0
40	Western Ore.	33
27	Cal St. Sacramento	48
42	New Haven	16
43	Humboldt St.	16
24	Southern Utah	9
28	St. Mary's (Cal.)	14
31	Cal Poly	24
20	Central Wash.	13
55	Western Wash.	24
346		**197**

DIVISION II CHAMPIONSHIP
| 33 | Central Okla. | 17 |
| 14 | Northeastern St. | 19 |

Nickname: Aggies.
Stadium: Toomey Field (1949), 10,111 capacity. Natural turf.

2000 SCHEDULES AND 1999 RESULTS

499

Colors: Yale Blue & Gold.
Conference: Division II Independent.
SID: Doug Dull, 916-752-3505.
AD: Greg Warzecka.

CAL LUTHERAN
Thousand Oaks, CA 91360 III

Coach: Scott Squires, Pacific Lutheran 1988
Record: 4 Years, 16-20-0

2000 SCHEDULE
Pacific Lutheran ....Sept. 9
Redlands ....*Sept. 23
Chapman ■ ....Sept. 30
Menlo ■ ....Oct. 7
Azusa Pacific ■ ....Oct. 14
La Verne ■ ....Oct. 21
Whittier ....Oct. 28
Occidental ■ ....Nov. 4
Claremont-M-S ....Nov. 11

1999 RESULTS (3-6-0)
26	Pacific Lutheran	28
14	San Diego	30
3	Whitworth	28
48	Whittier	12
31	Claremont-M-S	21
23	Occidental	16
32	La Verne	35
38	Menlo	41
20	Redlands	51
235		**262**

Nickname: Kingsmen.
Stadium: Mt. Clef (1962), 2,000 capacity. Natural turf.
Colors: Purple & Gold.
Conference: Southern California Intercollegiate Athletic.
SID: John Czimbal, 805-493-3153.
AD: Bruce D. Bryde.

CAL POLY
San Luis Obispo, CA 93407 ....I-AA

Coach: Larry Welsh, Northern Ariz. 1966
Record: 3 Years, 16-17-0

2000 SCHEDULE
Cal St. Sacramento ....*Sept. 9
Montana ....Sept. 16
Montana St. ....Sept. 23
Southern Utah ....*Sept. 30
St. Mary's (Cal.) ■ ....*Oct. 7
Western N.M. ■ ....*Oct. 14
UC Davis ■ ....*Oct. 21
Hofstra ■ ....Oct. 28
Northern Iowa ■ ....Nov. 4
Cal St. Northridge ....Nov. 11
Youngstown St. ■ ....Nov. 18

1999 RESULTS (3-8-0)
21	Northern Ariz.	55
40	Montana St.	37
3	Hofstra	38
38	Southern Utah	10
21	Northern Iowa	42
7	Youngstown St.	10
24	UC Davis	31
28	Portland St.	42
14	Montana	28
24	St. Mary's (Cal.)	21
26	Cal St. Sacramento	31
246		**345**

Nickname: Mustangs.
Stadium: Mustang (1935), 8,500 capacity. Natural turf.
Colors: Green & Gold.
Conference: Division I-AA Independent.
SID: Jason Sullivan, 805-756-6531.
AD: John F. McCutcheon.

CAL ST. NORTHRIDGE
Northridge, CA 91330 ....I-AA

Coach: Jeff Kearin, Loyola Marymount 1983
Record: 1 Year, 5-6-0

2000 SCHEDULE
Air Force ....Sept. 2
Southwest Tex. St. ....*Sept. 9
Northern Ariz. ■ ....Sept. 16
Idaho St. ■ ....Sept. 30
Weber St. ....*Oct. 5
Montana ....Oct. 14
Montana St. ....Oct. 21
Eastern Wash. ■ ....Oct. 28
Cal St. Sacramento ....*Nov. 4
Cal Poly ■ ....Nov. 11
Portland St. ....Nov. 18

1999 RESULTS (5-6-0)
38	Western Ore.	19
14	Kansas	71
41	Eastern Wash.	48
41	Idaho St.	27
27	Montana	48
36	Cal St. Sacramento	14
24	Montana St.	21
30	Weber St.	28
21	Portland St.	34
16	Southern Methodist	58
10	Northern Ariz.	30
298		**398**

Nickname: Matadors.
Stadium: North Campus (1971), 6,500 capacity. Natural turf.
Colors: Red, White & Black.
Conference: Big Sky.
SID: Ryan Finney, 818-677-3243.
AD: Richard Dull.

CAL ST. SACRAMENTO
Sacramento, CA 95819 ....I-AA

Coach: John Volek, UC Riverside 1968
Record: 5 Years, 17-37-1

2000 SCHEDULE
St. Mary's (Cal.) ....Sept. 2
Cal Poly ■ ....*Sept. 9
Portland St. ■ ....*Sept. 16
Idaho St. ....*Sept. 23
Weber St. ■ ....*Sept. 30
Montana ....Oct. 7
Montana St. ■ ....*Oct. 14
Eastern Wash. ....Oct. 21
UC Davis ....Oct. 28
Cal St. Northridge ■ ....*Nov. 4
Northern Ariz. ....Nov. 11

1999 RESULTS (6-5-0)
41	St. Mary's (Cal.)	7
38	Montana	41
48	UC Davis	27
41	Montana St.	10
49	Weber St.	52
41	Portland St.	14
14	Cal St. Northridge	36
49	Northern Ariz.	51
21	Eastern Wash.	26
41	Idaho St.	20
31	Cal Poly	26
414		**310**

Nickname: Hornets.
Stadium: Hornet Field (1964), 21,418 capacity. Natural turf.
Colors: Green & Gold.
Conference: Big Sky.
SID: Bill Macriss, 916-278-6896.
AD: Debby Colberg.

CALIF. (PA.)
California, PA 15419 II

Coach: Mike Kolakowski, Ohio Northern 1979
Record: 3 Years, 11-21-0

2000 SCHEDULE
Geneva ....*Aug. 31
Fairmont St. ....*Sept. 9
West Va. Wesleyan ■ ....*Sept. 16
Mansfield ....Sept. 23
Edinboro ....Sept. 30
Clarion ■ ....*Oct. 7
Slippery Rock ....Oct. 14
Lock Haven ■ ....Oct. 21
Shippensburg ....Oct. 28
Indiana (Pa.) ■ ....Nov. 4
Cheyney ....Nov. 11

1999 RESULTS (5-6-0)
28	Glenville St.	35
49	Fairmont St.	51
42	West Va. Wesleyan	8
44	Mansfield	11
48	Cheyney	14
33	Lock Haven	12
21	Slippery Rock	31
40	Edinboro	35
14	Indiana (Pa.)	42
0	Shippensburg	30
14	Clarion	28
333		**297**

Nickname: Vulcans.
Stadium: Adamson (1970), 5,000 capacity. Natural turf.
Colors: Red & Black.
Conference: Pennsylvania State Athletic.
SID: David W. Smith, 412-938-4552.
AD: Thomas G. Pucci.

CANISIUS
Buffalo, NY 14208 ....I-AA

Coach: Ed Argast, Colgate 1978
(First year as head coach)

2000 SCHEDULE
Iona ....Sept. 9
St. Peter's ■ ....Sept. 16
Gannon ....Sept. 23
La Salle ■ ....Oct. 7
Rochester ....Oct. 14
Siena ■ ....Oct. 21
Marist ....Oct. 28
Alfred ....Nov. 4
Fairfield ....Nov. 11
Duquesne ■ ....Nov. 18

1999 RESULTS (1-10-0)
26	Rochester	14
22	St. Peter's	33
20	Fairfield	59
7	Marist	49
6	La Salle	19
16	Alfred	23
6	Siena	38
12	Iona	34
0	St. John's (N.Y.)	45
6	Georgetown	49
12	Duquesne	68
133		**431**

Nickname: Golden Griffins.
Stadium: Demske Sports Complex (1989), 1,000 capacity. Artificial turf.
Colors: Blue & Gold.
Conference: Metro Atlantic Athletic.
SID: R. J. Hydorn, 716-888-2977.
AD: Timothy J. Dillion.

CAPITAL
Columbus, OH 43209 III

Coach: Jim Collins, Wittenberg 1988
Record: 3 Years, 6-24-0

2000 SCHEDULE
Thiel ■ ....Sept. 2
Heidelberg ....Sept. 16
Otterbein ....*Sept. 23
Baldwin-Wallace ....Sept. 30
Muskingum ■ ....Oct. 7
Marietta ....Oct. 14
Mount Union ■ ....*Oct. 21
John Carroll ....Oct. 28
Ohio Northern ■ ....Nov. 4
Wilmington (Ohio) ....Nov. 11

1999 RESULTS (2-8-0)
| 0 | Thiel | 19 |
| 12 | John Carroll | 51 |

SCHEDULES/RESULTS

21	Muskingum	42
9	Heidelberg	33
24	Otterbein	49
41	Hiram	27
28	Baldwin-Wallace	46
19	Mount Union	73
49	Marietta	21
28	Ohio Northern	61
231		**422**

Nickname: Crusaders.
Stadium: Bernlohr (1928), 2,000 capacity. Natural turf.
Colors: Purple & White.
Conference: Ohio Athletic.
SID: Chris Rollman, 614-236-6174.
AD: Roger Welsh.

CARLETON
Northfield, MN 55057 III

Coach: Bob Sullivan, St. John's (Minn.) '59
Record: 21 Years, 100-105-0

2000 SCHEDULE
Northwestern (Minn.)	Sept. 9
Augsburg	*Sept. 16
St. Thomas (Minn.) ■	Sept. 23
Macalester	Sept. 30
Gust. Adolphus ■	Oct. 7
Hamline	Oct. 14
Bethel (Minn.) ■	Oct. 21
Concordia-M'head	Oct. 28
St. John's (Minn.) [Minneapolis, MN]	Nov. 4
St. Olaf ■	Nov. 11

1999 RESULTS (2-8-0)
21	Northwestern (Minn.)	14
0	Gust. Adolphus	38
6	Concordia-M'head	35
26	Macalester	27
16	Hamline	13
6	St. Thomas (Minn.)	27
19	St. Olaf	27
7	Augsburg	52
6	St. John's (Minn.)	41
26	Bethel (Minn.)	47
133		**321**

Nickname: Knights.
Stadium: Laird (1926), 7,500 capacity. Natural turf.
Colors: Maize & Blue.
Conference: Minnesota Intercollegiate Athletic.
SID: Rob Lewis, 507-663-4045.
AD: Leon Lunder.

CARNEGIE MELLON
Pittsburgh, PA 15213 III

Coach: Rich Lackner, Carnegie Mellon 1979
Record: 14 Years, 102-35-2

2000 SCHEDULE
Denison	Sept. 2
Case Reserve	Sept. 9
Bethany (W.Va.) ■	*Sept. 16
Alfred	Sept. 23
Frank. & Marsh. ■	Sept. 30
Washington (Mo.)	*Oct. 14
Chicago ■	Oct. 21
Rochester ■	Oct. 28
Grove City	Nov. 4
Gannon ■	Nov. 11

1999 RESULTS (7-3-0)
31	Denison	13
42	Case Reserve	0
17	Bethany (W.Va.)	10
31	Alfred	7
3	Dickinson	7
13	Chicago	10
7	Washington (Mo.)	24
33	Rochester	15
30	Juniata	7
7	Thomas More	23
214		**116**

ECAC PLAYOFF
28	Frostburg St.	10

Nickname: Tartans.

Stadium: Gesling (1990), 3,500 capacity. Artificial turf.
Colors: Cardinal, White & Grey.
Conference: University Athletic Association.
SID: Jon Surmacz, 412-268-3087.
AD: John H. Harvey.

CARROLL (WIS.)
Waukesha, WI 53186 III

Coach: Merle Masonholder, Northern Iowa 1966
Record: 18 Years, 83-81-0

2000 SCHEDULE
North Park	Sept. 9
St. Norbert	Sept. 16
Ripon ■	Sept. 23
Grinnell	Sept. 30
Monmouth (Ill.) ■	Oct. 7
Knox	Oct. 14
Lawrence ■	Oct. 21
Beloit	Oct. 28
Illinois Col. ■	Nov. 4
Lake Forest ■	Nov. 11

1999 RESULTS (5-5-0)
34	North Park	28
3	St. Norbert	28
7	Ripon	36
14	Grinnell	17
42	Monmouth (Ill.)	19
35	Knox	14
14	Lawrence	45
34	Beloit	26
27	Illinois Col.	20
14	Lake Forest	21
224		**254**

Nickname: Pioneers.
Stadium: Van Male Field (1976), 4,200 capacity. Natural turf.
Colors: Orange & White.
Conference: Midwest Collegiate Athletic.
SID: Shawn Ama, 414-524-7376.
AD: Jane F. Hopp.

CARSON-NEWMAN
Jefferson City, TN 37760 II

Coach: Ken Sparks, Carson-Newman 1968
Record: 20 Years, 197-46-2

2000 SCHEDULE
Bloomsburg [Sevierville, TN]	*Aug. 26
Arkansas Tech [Rome, GA]	*Sept. 2
Western Ore.	Sept. 16
Lenoir-Rhyne	*Sept. 23
Mars Hill ■	Sept. 30
Presbyterian	Oct. 7
Tusculum ■	Oct. 14
Newberry ■	Oct. 21
Catawba	Oct. 28
Wingate ■	Nov. 4

1999 RESULTS (10-0-0)
41	Geneva	7
41	Saginaw Valley	7
43	Presbyterian	40
49	Tusculum	12
28	Catawba	17
64	Wingate	15
41	Mars Hill	14
28	Gardner-Webb	6
55	Lenoir-Rhyne	14
45	Newberry	31
435		**163**

DIVISION II CHAMPIONSHIP
40	Arkansas Tech	28
28	Catawba	25
42	Northeastern St.	7
52	Northwest Mo. St.	58

Nickname: Eagles.
Stadium: Burke-Tarr (1966), 5,000 capacity. Natural turf.
Colors: Orange & Blue.
Conference: South Atlantic.
SID: Marlin Curnutt, 423-471-3477.
AD: David W. Barger.

CARTHAGE
Kenosha, WI 53140 III

Coach: Tim Rucks, Carthage 1983
Record: 10 Years, 30-56-4

2000 SCHEDULE
Lakeland	Sept. 9
Martin Luther	Sept. 16
Adrian	Sept. 23
Millikin ■	Sept. 30
North Central	*Oct. 7
Wheaton (Ill.)	Oct. 14
Elmhurst ■	Oct. 21
Ill. Wesleyan	Oct. 28
Augustana (Ill.) ■	Nov. 4
North Park	Nov. 11

1999 RESULTS (5-4-0)
21	St. Olaf	14
7	Lakeland	26
28	North Park	0
14	Wheaton (Ill.)	30
27	Ill. Wesleyan	44
7	Millikin	6
33	Elmhurst	9
9	Augustana (Ill.)	31
27	North Central	18
173		**178**

Nickname: Redmen.
Stadium: Art Keller Field (1965), 3,100 capacity. Natural turf.
Colors: Red, White & Black.
Conference: College Conf. of Illinois & Wisconsin.
SID: Steve Marovich, 414-551-5740.
AD: Robert R. Bonn.

CASE RESERVE
Cleveland, OH 44106 III

Coach: Peter Germano, Ohio Wesleyan 1982
1 Year, 2-8-0

2000 SCHEDULE
Carnegie Mellon ■	Sept. 9
Washington (Mo.)	Sept. 16
Oberlin	Sept. 23
Chicago ■	Sept. 30
Kenyon	Oct. 7
Merchant Marine	Oct. 14
Rose-Hulman ■	Oct. 21
Denison	Oct. 28
Hiram ■	Nov. 4
Rochester	Nov. 11

1999 RESULTS (2-8-0)
0	Carnegie Mellon	42
14	Rochester	21
7	Washington (Mo.)	42
7	Ohio Wesleyan	27
16	Earlham	0
14	Denison	21
21	Wittenberg	49
42	Oberlin	6
27	Wooster	31
21	Chicago	41
169		**280**

Nickname: Spartans.
Stadium: E.L. Finnigan Field (1968), 3,000 capacity. Natural turf.
Colors: Blue, Gray & White.
Conference: University Athletic Association.
SID: Creg Jantz, 216-368-6517.
AD: David M. Hutter.

CATAWBA
Salisbury, NC 28144 II

Coach: David Bennett, Presbyterian 1984
Record: 5 Years, 41-14-0

2000 SCHEDULE
Livingstone ■	Sept. 2
Austin Peay	*Sept. 9
Wingate ■	Sept. 16

2000 SCHEDULES AND 1999 RESULTS   501

Presbyterian ■...Sept. 23
Newberry ....*Sept. 30
Tusculum ....Oct. 7
North Greenville ■..Oct. 21
Carson-Newman ■..Oct. 28
Mars Hill..Nov. 4
Lenoir-Rhyne..Nov. 11

1999 RESULTS (10-1-0)
17	Winston-Salem	14
36	Tusculum	21
34	Mars Hill	7
36	West Va. Wesleyan	0
17	Carson-Newman	28
24	Presbyterian	10
34	Gardner-Webb	7
20	Miles	6
34	Newberry	3
54	Wingate	13
24	Lenoir-Rhyne	7
330		**116**

DIVISION II CHAMPIONSHIP
48	Fort Valley St.	17
25	Carson-Newman	28

Nickname: Indians.
Stadium: Shuford Field (1926), 4,000 capacity. Natural turf.
Colors: Blue & White.
Conference: South Atlantic.
SID: Jim Lewis, 704-637-4720.
AD: Dennis Davidson.

CATHOLIC
Washington, DC 20064..............................III

Coach: Tom Clark, Maryland 1986
Record: 6 Years, 50-10-1

2000 SCHEDULE
John Carroll..Sept. 2
Frank. & Marsh..Sept. 9
Randolph-Macon ....Sept. 23
La Salle ■...Sept. 30
Wash. & Lee ■...Oct. 7
Methodist..Oct. 14
Hampden-Sydney...Oct. 21
Emory & Henry..Oct. 28
Guilford ■..Nov. 4
Bridgewater (Va.) ■..Nov. 11

1999 RESULTS (9-1-0)
21	John Carroll	26
46	Frank. & Marsh.	12
63	Newport News	7
34	Salisbury St.	2
35	Randolph-Macon	26
49	Methodist	21
45	Hampden-Sydney	7
42	Emory & Henry	19
31	Guilford	13
35	Bridgewater (Va.)	14
401		**147**

DIVISION III CHAMPIONSHIP
16	Western Md.	20

Nickname: Cardinals.
Stadium: Dufour Field (1985), 3,500 capacity. Natural turf.
Colors: Cardinal Red & Black.
Conference: Old Dominion Athletic.
SID: Chris McManes, 202-319-5610.
AD: Robert J. Talbot.

CENTRAL (IOWA)
Pella, IA 50219 III

Coach: Rich Kacmarynski, Central (Iowa) 1992
Record: 3 Years, 28-5-0

2000 SCHEDULE
Upper Iowa...Sept. 2
Luther..Sept. 9
Cornell College ■...Sept. 16
Buena Vista ■..Sept. 23
Loras ■...Sept. 30
Simpson ■...Oct. 7

William Penn...Oct. 21
Coe ■...Oct. 28
Wartburg ■..Nov. 4
Dubuque...Nov. 11

1999 RESULTS (9-1-0)
44	Cornell College	0
32	Loras	13
29	Simpson	13
43	Luther	7
39	Dubuque	14
28	Coe	21
14	Upper Iowa	0
38	William Penn	7
23	Wartburg	40
14	Buena Vista	13
304		**128**

DIVISION III CHAMPIONSHIP
38	Wis.-La Crosse	17
9	St. John's (Minn.)	10

Nickname: Flying Dutchmen.
Stadium: Kuyper (1977), 5,000 capacity. Natural turf.
Colors: Red & White.
Conference: Iowa Intercollegiate Athletic.
SID: Larry Happel, 515-628-5278.
AD: Al Dorenkamp.

CENTRAL ARK.
Conway, AR 72035 II

Coach: Clint Conque, Nicholls St. 1983
(First year as head coach)

2000 SCHEDULE
Nicholls St..*Aug. 31
Southwest Baptist ■...*Sept. 9
Ouachita Baptist..*Sept. 16
Valdosta St...*Sept. 23
North Ala. ■..*Sept. 30
Harding ....*Oct. 7
Henderson St. ....*Oct. 14
Ark.-Monticello ■...Oct. 21
Delta St..Oct. 28
Southern Ark...Nov. 4
Arkansas Tech ....Nov. 11

1999 RESULTS (4-6-0)
27	West Tex. A&M	20
14	West Ga.	38
17	North Ala.	24
20	Southern Ark.	29
54	Ark.-Monticello	48
27	Arkansas Tech	54
20	Valdosta St.	33
26	West Ala.	10
31	Delta St.	14
21	Henderson St.	24
257		**294**

Nickname: Bears.
Stadium: Estes (1939), 8,500 capacity. Natural turf.
Colors: Purple & Gray.
Conference: Gulf South.
SID: Steve East, 501-450-5743.
AD: Arch Jones.

CENTRAL CONN. ST.
New Britain, CT 06050 ....I-AA

Coach: Sal Cintorio, Central Conn. St. 1986
Record: 8 Years, 28-51-0

2000 SCHEDULE
Frostburg St. ■..Sept. 9
Sacred Heart ....Sept. 16
Monmouth ....Sept. 23
St. John's (N.Y.) ■...Sept. 30
San Diego...Oct. 7
Wagner ■..Oct. 14
Robert Morris ....Oct. 21
Albany (N.Y.) ■..Oct. 28
St. Francis (Pa.) ■...Nov. 4
Stony Brook ■...Nov. 11

1999 RESULTS (4-6-0)
13	Albany (N.Y.)	35
16	Frostburg St.	22

24	Robert Morris	27
14	Fairfield	41
35	St. Francis (Pa.)	13
16	Wagner	35
37	Sacred Heart	12
14	Stony Brook	27
30	Southern Conn. St.	23
28	Monmouth	21
227		**256**

Nickname: Blue Devils.
Stadium: Willow Brook Park (1969), 12,000 capacity. Natural turf.
Colors: Blue & White.
Conference: Northeast.
SID: Kathy Pulek, 203-832-3089.
AD: Charles Jones Jr.

UCF
Orlando, FL 32816 ....I-A

Coach: Mike Kruczek, Boston College 1976
Record: 2 Years, 13-9-0

2000 SCHEDULE
Georgia Tech...*Sept. 2
Northwestern St. ■..*Sept. 9
Akron ....*Sept. 16
William & Mary ■...*Sept. 23
Eastern Mich. ....Sept. 30
Northern Ill. ....Oct. 7
Eastern Ky. ■..*Oct. 14
La.-Monroe ■..Oct. 21
Alabama...Oct. 28
Louisiana Tech..*Nov. 4
Virginia Tech ■..*Nov. 11

1999 RESULTS (4-7-0)
13	Purdue	47
27	Florida	58
10	Georgia Tech	41
23	Georgia	24
31	Eastern Ill.	21
28	Nicholls St.	0
35	Louisiana Tech	46
31	Eastern Mich.	6
10	Auburn	28
39	Middle Tenn. St.	14
30	Bowling Green	33
277		**318**

Nickname: Golden Knights.
Stadium: Florida Citrus (1936), 70,188 capacity. Natural turf.
Colors: Black & Gold.
Conference: Division I-A Independent.
SID: John Marini, 407-823-2729.
AD: Steve Sloan.

CENTRAL MICH.
Mount Pleasant, MI 48859........................I-A

Coach: Mike DeBord, Manchester 1978
(First year as head coach)

2000 SCHEDULE
Purdue...Sept. 2
Akron ■..Sept. 9
Wyoming..Sept. 16
Boise St. ■...Sept. 23
Toledo..*Sept. 30
Kent St. ■..Oct. 7
Ohio...Oct. 21
Ball St. ■...Oct. 28
Eastern Mich. ....Nov. 4
Western Mich. ■...Nov. 11
Northern Ill. ....Nov. 18

1999 RESULTS (4-7-0)
33	Eastern Ill.	17
7	Syracuse	47
16	Purdue	58
16	Miami (Ohio)	24
16	Western Mich.	38
38	Buffalo	19
27	Northern Ill.	31
7	Bowling Green	31

13	Toledo	32
29	Eastern Mich.	26
27	Ball St.	21
229		**344**

Nickname: Chippewas.
Stadium: Kelly-Shorts (1972), 30,199 capacity. Artificial turf.
Colors: Maroon & Gold.
Conference: Mid-American.
SID: Fred Stabley Jr., 517-774-3277.
AD: Herb Deromedi.

CENTRAL MO. ST.
Warrensburg, MO 64093 II

Coach: Willie Fritz, Pittsburg St. 1983
Record: 3 Years, 20-13-0

2000 SCHEDULE
Winona St. ■	*Aug. 31
Quincy ■	*Sept. 9
Emporia St. ■	*Sept. 16
Pittsburg St.	*Sept. 23
Washburn ■	Sept. 30
Truman	Oct. 7
Mo.-Rolla	Oct. 14
Mo. Western St. ■	Oct. 21
Southwest Baptist ■	Oct. 28
Mo. Southern St.	Nov. 4
Northwest Mo. St. ■	Nov. 11

1999 RESULTS (7-4-0)
60	Quincy	13
30	Winona St.	24
12	Emporia St.	41
7	Pittsburg St.	14
32	Washburn	18
13	Truman	24
41	Mo.-Rolla	0
35	Mo. Western St.	28
49	Southwest Baptist	3
47	Mo. Southern St.	7
14	Northwest Mo. St.	41
340		**213**

Nickname: Mules.
Stadium: Audrey J. Walton (1995), 10,000 capacity. Natural turf.
Colors: Cardinal & Black.
Conference: Mid-America Intercollegiate Athletic.
SID: Bill Turnage, 816-543-4312.
AD: Jerry M. Hughes.

CENTRAL OKLA.
Edmond, OK 73034 II

Coach: Gary Howard, Arkansas 1964
Record: 23 Years, 147-88-6

2000 SCHEDULE
Stephen F. Austin	*Aug. 31
Tex. A&M-Commerce ■	Sept. 16
Eastern N.M.	*Sept. 23
Midwestern St. ■	Sept. 30
Southwestern Okla.	Oct. 7
Texas A&M-Kingsville	*Oct. 14
East Central ■	Oct. 21
Southeastern Okla. ■	Nov. 4
Northeastern St.	Nov. 11

1999 RESULTS (8-2-0)
28	Emporia St.	25
37	Angelo St.	34
42	Midwestern St.	14
44	Langston	6
31	East Central	7
42	Harding	30
41	Ouachita Baptist	20
18	Southwestern Okla.	16
14	Southeastern Okla.	20
7	Northeastern St.	12
304		**184**

DIVISION II CHAMPIONSHIP
17	UC Davis	33

Nickname: Bronchos.
Stadium: Wantland (1965), 10,000 capacity. Natural turf.
Colors: Bronze & Blue.
Conference: Lone Star.
SID: Mike Kirk, 405-341-2980.
AD: John E. Wagnon.

CENTRAL WASH.
Ellensburg, WA 98926 II

Coach: John Zamberlin, Pacific Lutheran 1979
Record: 3 Years, 16-13-0

2000 SCHEDULE
North Dakota	Sept. 2
Carroll (Mont.) ■	Sept. 9
Western Mont.	Sept. 16
St. Mary's (Cal.)	Sept. 23
Western Wash.	Sept. 30
New Haven	Oct. 7
Humboldt St. ■	Oct. 21
Western Ore. ■	Oct. 28
UC Davis ■	Nov. 4
Simon Fraser	Nov. 11

1999 RESULTS (4-5-0)
14	Eastern Wash.	44
7	Northern Iowa	44
52	Carroll (Mont.)	7
27	St. Mary's (Cal.)	7
43	Humboldt St.	7
7	Western Wash.	27
19	Western Ore.	30
13	UC Davis	20
43	Simon Fraser	14
225		**200**

Nickname: Wildcats.
Stadium: Tomlinson (NA), 4,000 capacity. Natural turf.
Colors: Crimson & Black.
Conference: Division II Independent.
SID: Bob Guptill, 509-963-1485.
AD: Gary C. Frederick.

CENTRE
Danville, KY 40422 III

Coach: Andy Frye, Muskingum 1981
Record: 2 Years, 8-12-0

2000 SCHEDULE
Earlham	*Sept. 9
Rhodes	Sept. 16
Wash. & Lee ■	Sept. 23
Sewanee ■	Sept. 30
Millsaps	Oct. 7
Maryville (Tenn.)	Oct. 14
Trinity (Tex.) ■	Oct. 21
DePauw ■	Oct. 28
Davidson	Nov. 4
Rose-Hulman	Nov. 11

1999 RESULTS (5-5-0)
34	Kenyon	14
21	Rhodes	14
17	Wash. & Lee	23
17	Sewanee	31
24	Millsaps	22
30	Maryville (Tenn.)	23
0	Trinity (Tex.)	38
23	DePauw	26
14	Davidson	24
36	Rose-Hulman	14
216		**229**

Nickname: Colonels.
Stadium: Farris (1925), 2,500 capacity. Natural turf.
Colors: Gold & White.
Conference: Southern Collegiate Athletic.
SID: Glenn Osborne, 606-238-8746.
AD: Joe McDaniel.

CHADRON ST.
Chadron, NE 69337 II

Coach: Brad Smith, Western Ill. 1972
Record: 13 Years, 91-46-1

2000 SCHEDULE
Wis.-River Falls ■	Sept. 2
Northern Ariz.	Sept. 9
Colorado Mines	Sept. 16
Fort Lewis ■	Sept. 23
Mesa St.	Sept. 30
Neb.-Kearney ■	Oct. 7
Western St. (Colo.) ■	Oct. 14
N.M. Highlands	Oct. 21
Adams St. ■	Nov. 4
Fort Hays St.	Nov. 11

1999 RESULTS (7-3-0)
10	Montana St.	20
24	Fort Lewis	7
42	Mesa St.	19
24	Neb.-Kearney	18
10	Western St. (Colo.)	6
56	N.M. Highlands	42
14	Western Wash.	26
23	Adams St.	38
31	Fort Hays St.	3
55	Colorado Mines	3
289		**182**

Nickname: Eagles.
Stadium: Elliott Field (1930), 2,500 capacity. Natural turf.
Colors: Cardinal & White.
Conference: Rocky Mountain Athletic.
SID: Con Marshall, 308-432-6212.
AD: Bradley Roy Smith.

CHAPMAN
Orange, CA 92866 III

Coach: Ken Visser, Occidental 1968
Record: 9 Years, 42-38-1

2000 SCHEDULE
Willamette ■	*Sept. 9
Whitworth	Sept. 16
Whittier ■	*Sept. 23
Cal Lutheran	Sept. 30
Redlands	*Oct. 7
Occidental ■	*Oct. 14
La Verne ■	*Oct. 28
Azusa Pacific	Nov. 4
Menlo	Nov. 11

1999 RESULTS (5-4-0)
37	Millsaps	3
13	Willamette	42
29	Howard Payne	20
45	Redlands	48
33	La Verne	35
44	Menlo	33
44	Whittier	7
62	Occidental	17
21	Azusa Pacific	42
328		**247**

Nickname: Panthers.
Stadium: Chapman (0000), 3,000 capacity. Natural turf.
Colors: Cardinal & Gray.
Conference: Division III Independent.
SID: Doug Aiken, 714-997-6900.
AD: David Currey.

CHARLESTON SO.
Charleston, SC 29423 ....I-AA

Coach: David Dowd, Guilford 1976
Record: 9 Years, 19-73-0

2000 SCHEDULE
Guilford ■	Sept. 2
Presbyterian	Sept. 9
West Virginia St. ■	Sept. 16
Wofford	Sept. 23
Jacksonville ■	Oct. 7
Austin Peay	Oct. 14
VMI	Oct. 21
Elon	Oct. 28
Samford	Nov. 4
Liberty	Nov. 11
East Tenn. St.	*Nov. 18

1999 RESULTS (4-6-0)

14	South Carolina St.	20
14	Presbyterian	40
13	Wofford	35
14	Lenoir-Rhyne	7
26	Newberry	27
39	Austin Peay	17
14	Liberty	34
13	Elon	38
35	Tusculum	21
37	Jacksonville	17
219		256

Nickname: Buccaneers.
Stadium: CSU (1970), 3,000 capacity. Natural turf.
Colors: Blue & Gold.
Conference: Division I-AA Independent.
SID: Ken Gerlinger, 803-863-7688.
AD: W. Howard Bagwell.

CHATTANOOGA
Chattanooga, TN 37403..........................I-AA

Coach: Donnie Kirkpatrick, Lenoir-Rhyne 1982
(First year as head coach)

2000 SCHEDULE

Samford ■	*Aug. 31
UAB	*Sept. 7
Mississippi Val. ■	Sept. 16
Ga. Southern ■	*Sept. 23
Wofford	Sept. 30
VMI ■	*Oct. 14
Western Caro.	Oct. 21
Appalachian St. ■	Oct. 28
Citadel	Nov. 4
East Tenn. St. ■	Nov. 11
Furman	Nov. 18

1999 RESULTS (5-6-0)

29	Samford	27
30	Louisville	58
49	Savannah St.	0
10	Ga. Southern	49
34	Wofford	41
27	VMI	0
56	Western Caro.	28
14	Appalachian St.	62
30	Citadel	27
14	East Tenn. St.	28
35	Furman	40
328		360

Nickname: Mocs.
Stadium: Finley (1997), 20,000 capacity. Natural turf.
Colors: Navy Blue & Gold.
Conference: Southern.
SID: Jeff Romero, 423-755-4618.
AD: L. Oval Jaynes.

CHEYNEY
Cheyney, PA 19319..........................II

Coach: John Parker, Mo. Valley 1986
Record: 4 Years, 7-35-0

2000 SCHEDULE

Glenville St.	Sept. 9
Bowie St. ■	Sept. 16
Bloomsburg	Sept. 23
Mansfield ■	Sept. 30
Millersville	Oct. 7
Lock Haven ■	Oct. 14
Kutztown	Oct. 21
East Stroudsburg ■	Oct. 28
West Chester ■	Nov. 4
Calif. (Pa.)	Nov. 11

1999 RESULTS (1-10-0)

6	Bowie St.	20
12	Virginia Union	41
12	Elizabeth City St.	7
26	Lock Haven	53
14	Calif. (Pa.)	48
6	Kutztown	27
22	East Stroudsburg	55
6	Bloomsburg	48
12	Mansfield	35
23	West Chester	56
18	Millersville	48
157		438

Nickname: Wolves.
Stadium: O'Shield-Stevenson (0000), 3,500 capacity. Natural turf.
Colors: Blue & White.
Conference: Pennsylvania State Athletic.
SID: Len Margolis, 610-399-2287.
AD: Gregory K. P. Smith.

CHICAGO
Chicago, IL 60637..........................III

Coach: Dick Maloney, Mass.-Boston 1974
Record: 6 Years, 34-22-0

2000 SCHEDULE

Lake Forest	Sept. 9
Rose-Hulman ■	Sept. 16
North Central	*Sept. 23
Case Reserve	Sept. 30
Rochester ■	Oct. 7
Carnegie Mellon	Oct. 21
Washington (Mo.) ■	Oct. 28
Bethany (W.Va.) ■	Nov. 4
Benedictine (Ill.)	Nov. 11

1999 RESULTS (5-4-0)

14	Lake Forest	16
22	Rose-Hulman	20
7	North Central	0
9	DePauw	6
12	Bethany (W.Va.)	0
10	Carnegie Mellon	13
3	Rochester	6
3	Washington (Mo.)	20
41	Case Reserve	21
121		102

Nickname: Maroons.
Stadium: Stagg Field (1969), 1,500 capacity. Natural turf.
Colors: White & Maroon.
Conference: University Athletic Association.
SID: Dave Hilbert, 312-702-4638.
AD: Thomas Weingartner.

CHOWAN
Murfreesboro, NC 27855..........................III

Coach: Steve Lee, Lock Haven 1978
Record: 2 Years, 10-9-0

2000 SCHEDULE

Methodist ■	Sept. 2
Greensboro	*Sept. 9
Newport News	Sept. 23
Frostburg St. ■	Sept. 30
Salisbury St.	Oct. 7
Ferrum	Oct. 14
Averett ■	Oct. 21
Stillman	Oct. 28
Wesley ■	Nov. 4

1999 RESULTS (5-4-0)

25	Methodist	14
35	Greensboro	28
21	Newport News	20
25	Frostburg St.	30
27	Salisbury St.	31
7	Ferrum	17
25	Stillman	12
14	Wesley	40
27	New Jersey City	20
206		212

Nickname: Braves.
Stadium: James G. Garrison (NA), 3,500 capacity. Natural turf.
Colors: Columbia Blue & White.
Conference: Atlantic Central Football.
SID: Bill Stiles, 252-398-6286.
AD: Steven D. Lee.

CINCINNATI
Cincinnati, OH 45221..........................I-A

Coach: Rick Minter, Henderson St. 1977
Record: 6 Years, 27-39-1

2000 SCHEDULE

Army ■	*Sept. 4
Syracuse ■	Sept. 9
Wisconsin	Sept. 16
Indiana	Sept. 23
Tulane	Sept. 30
Houston	Oct. 7
Louisville	Oct. 14
Miami (Ohio) ■	Oct. 28
UAB ■	Nov. 4
Memphis	Nov. 11
Southern Miss. ■	Nov. 18

1999 RESULTS (3-8-0)

41	Kent St.	3
24	Troy St.	31
17	Wisconsin	12
20	Ohio St.	34
20	Houston	23
21	UAB	24
20	Southern Miss.	28
52	Miami (Ohio)	42
13	Louisville	23
34	East Caro.	48
13	Memphis	21
275		289

Nickname: Bearcats.
Stadium: Nippert (1916), 35,000 capacity. Artificial turf.
Colors: Red & Black.
Conference: Conference USA.
SID: Tom Hathaway, 513-556-5191.
AD: Robert G. Goin.

CITADEL
Charleston, SC 29409..........................I-AA

Coach: Don Powers, Western Caro. 1966
Record: 4 Years, 17-27-0

2000 SCHEDULE

Clemson	*Sept. 2
Delaware	*Sept. 9
Western Caro. ■	*Sept. 16
Appalachian St.	Sept. 23
South Carolina St. ■	Sept. 30
East Tenn. St. ■	Oct. 7
Furman	Oct. 14
Ga. Southern ■	Oct. 21
Wofford	Oct. 28
Chattanooga ■	Nov. 4
VMI	Nov. 11

1999 RESULTS (2-9-0)

10	East Tenn. St.	28
16	Delaware	26
0	Appalachian St.	51
20	South Carolina St.	14
0	Vanderbilt	58
17	Furman	31
17	Ga. Southern	34
16	Wofford	47
27	Chattanooga	30
7	VMI	6
17	Western Caro.	24
147		349

Nickname: Bulldogs.
Stadium: Johnson Hagood (1948), 21,000 capacity. Natural turf.
Colors: Blue & White.
Conference: Southern.
SID: Art Chase, 803-953-5120.
AD: Walt Nadzak.

CLAREMONT-M-S
Claremont, CA 91711..........................III

Coach: Rick Candaele, Coll. of Idaho 1969
Record: 8 Years, 31-42-0

2000 SCHEDULE

Grinnell	Sept. 9
Puget Sound ■	*Sept. 16
La Verne ■	*Sept. 23

Lewis & Clark .... Sept. 30
Occidental ....*Oct. 7
Whittier ■ ....*Oct. 14
Redlands ....*Oct. 28
Pomona-Pitzer ....Nov. 4
Cal Lutheran ■ ....Nov. 11

1999 RESULTS (5-4-0)
35	Grinnell	29
31	Colorado Col.	13
23	Occidental	14
28	La Verne	31
41	Lewis & Clark	10
21	Cal Lutheran	31
15	Whittier	13
10	Redlands	63
21	Pomona-Pitzer	24
225		**228**

Nickname: Stags.
Stadium: Zinda Field (1955), 3,000 capacity. Natural turf.
Colors: Maroon, Gold & White.
Conference: Southern California Intercollegiate Athletic.
SID: Kelly Beck, 909-607-3138.
AD: David Wells.

CLARION
Clarion, PA 16214 II

Coach: Malen Luke, Westminster (Pa.) 1976
Record: 12 Years, 67-56-0

2000 SCHEDULE
East Stroudsburg ■ ....Sept. 2
New Haven ....Sept. 9
Tiffin ....*Sept. 16
Shippensburg ■ ....Sept. 23
Kutztown ....Sept. 30
Calif. (Pa.) ....*Oct. 7
Edinboro ■ ....Oct. 14
Slippery Rock ....Oct. 21
Indiana (Pa.) ....Oct. 28
Lock Haven ....Nov. 4
West Chester ■ ....Nov. 11

1999 RESULTS (3-7-0)
21	New Haven	28
0	Shepherd	7
31	Kutztown	21
7	Slippery Rock	45
29	Edinboro	30
26	Shippensburg	32
0	Indiana (Pa.)	26
20	West Chester	62
44	Lock Haven	41
28	Calif. (Pa.)	14
206		**306**

Nickname: Golden Eagles.
Stadium: Memorial Field (1965), 5,000 capacity. Natural turf.
Colors: Blue & Gold.
Conference: Pennsylvania State Athletic.
SID: Rich Herman, 814-226-2334.
AD: Robert Carlson.

CLARK ATLANTA
Atlanta, GA 30314 II

Coach: Curtis Crockett, Clark 1964
Record: 1 Year, 3-7-0

2000 SCHEDULE
Morehouse [Atlanta, GA] ....Sept. 4
Kentucky St. ....Sept. 9
Morris Brown ■ ....*Sept. 16
Miles ■ ....Sept. 23
Lane [Memphis, TN] ....*Sept. 30
Lincoln (Mo.) ■ ....Oct. 7
Fort Valley St. [Griffin, GA] ....*Oct. 14
Albany St. (Ga.) ....Oct. 21
Tuskegee [La Grange, GA] ....Oct. 28
Stillman ....Nov. 11

1999 RESULTS (3-7-0)
16	Morris Brown	19
7	Savannah St.	34
7	Kentucky St.	38
10	Miles	21
7	Lane	3
31	Lincoln (Mo.)	0
7	Fort Valley St.	34
0	Albany St. (Ga.)	42
16	Tuskegee	27
28	Morehouse	7
129		**225**

Nickname: Panthers.
Stadium: Panther's (0000), 6,000 capacity. Artificial turf.
Colors: Red, Black & Grey.
Conference: Southern Intercollegiate Athletic.
SID: Cecil B. McKay, 404-880-8029.
AD: Richard Cosby.

CLEMSON
Clemson, SC 29634 .... I-A

Coach: Tommy Bowden, West Virginia 1977
Record: 3 Years, 24-10-0

2000 SCHEDULE
Citadel ■ ....*Sept. 2
Missouri ■ ....Sept. 9
Wake Forest ■ ....Sept. 16
Virginia ....Sept. 23
Duke ....Sept. 30
North Carolina St. ■ ....Oct. 7
Maryland ....Oct. 14
North Carolina ....Oct. 21
Georgia Tech ■ ....*Oct. 28
Florida St. ....*Nov. 4
South Carolina ■ ....Nov. 18

1999 RESULTS (6-5-0)
10	Marshall	13
33	Virginia	14
11	Virginia Tech	31
31	North Carolina	20
31	North Carolina St.	35
42	Maryland	30
14	Florida St.	17
12	Wake Forest	3
58	Duke	7
42	Georgia Tech	45
31	South Carolina	21
315		**236**

PEACH BOWL
7	Mississippi St.	17

Nickname: Tigers.
Stadium: Memorial (1942), 81,473 capacity. Natural turf.
Colors: Purple & Orange.
Conference: Atlantic Coast.
SID: Tim Bourret, 803-656-2114.
AD: Robert W. Robinson

COAST GUARD
New London, CT 06320 III

Coach: Bill George, Ithaca 1980
1 Year, 1-9-0

2000 SCHEDULE
Salve Regina ■ ....Sept. 9
Rensselaer ■ ....Sept. 16
Springfield ....Sept. 23
Norwich ....Sept. 30
Mount Ida ....Oct. 7
Western Conn. St. ■ ....Oct. 14
Union (N.Y.) ....Oct. 21
Plymouth St. ■ ....Oct. 28
Worcester Tech ....Nov. 4
Merchant Marine ....Nov. 11

1999 RESULTS (1-9-0)
7	Mass. Maritime	19
3	Rensselaer	42
31	Springfield	20
10	Norwich	30
7	Mount Ida	40
14	Western Conn. St.	65
14	Union (N.Y.)	24
0	Plymouth St.	42
23	Worcester Tech	27
21	Merchant Marine	24
130		**333**

Nickname: Bears.
Stadium: Cadet Memorial Field (1932), 4,500 capacity. Natural turf.
Colors: Blue, White & Orange.
Conference: Freedom Football.
SID: Jason Southard, 860-437-6800.
AD: Raymond Cieplik.

COE
Cedar Rapids, IA 52402 III

Coach: Erik Raeburn, Mount Union 1994
(First year as head coach)

2000 SCHEDULE
William Penn ....Sept. 2
Dubuque ■ ....Sept. 9
Loras ■ ....Sept. 16
Cornell College ....Sept. 23
Simpson ■ ....Sept. 30
Luther ....Oct. 7
Upper Iowa ....Oct. 14
Wartburg ■ ....Oct. 21
Central (Iowa) ....Oct. 28
Buena Vista ■ ....Nov. 4

1999 RESULTS (4-6-0)
34	Loras	20
9	Simpson	10
35	Luther	7
63	Dubuque	27
21	Central (Iowa)	28
31	Upper Iowa	32
21	William Penn	35
13	Wartburg	33
34	Buena Vista	31
23	Cornell College	32
284		**255**

Nickname: Kohawks.
Stadium: Clark (1989), 2,000 capacity. Natural turf.
Colors: Crimson & Gold.
Conference: Iowa Intercollegiate Athletic.
SID: Michael Levin, 319-399-8570.
AD: J. Barron Bremner.

COLBY
Waterville, ME 04901 III

Coach: Tom Austin, Maine 1963
Record: 14 Years, 47-64-1

2000 SCHEDULE
Williams ....Sept. 23
Middlebury ■ ....Sept. 30
Wesleyan (Conn.) ■ ....Oct. 7
Amherst ....Oct. 14
Hamilton ■ ....Oct. 21
Bates ....Oct. 28
Tufts ....Nov. 4
Bowdoin ■ ....Nov. 11

1999 RESULTS (3-5-0)
3	Trinity (Conn.)	35
19	Middlebury	41
13	Wesleyan (Conn.)	7
17	Amherst	24
48	Hamilton	14
17	Bates	20
26	Tufts	27
20	Bowdoin	0
163		**168**

Nickname: White Mules.
Stadium: Seaverns (1948), 5,000 capacity. Natural turf.
Colors: Blue & Gray.
Conference: NESCAC.
SID: To be named, 207-872-3227.
AD: Richard L. Whitmore Jr.

COLGATE
Hamilton, NY 13346 .... I-AA

Coach: Dick Biddle, Duke 1971
Record: 4 Years, 31-16-0

2000 SCHEDULE
Connecticut	*Sept. 9
Dartmouth	Sept. 16
Fordham ■	Sept. 23
Towson	Sept. 30
Princeton ■	Oct. 7
Cornell	Oct. 14
St. Mary's (Cal.) ■	Oct. 21
Lafayette ■	Oct. 28
Lehigh	Nov. 4
Holy Cross ■	Nov. 11
Bucknell	Nov. 18

1999 RESULTS (10-1-0)
28	Maine	21
16	Bucknell	21
49	Fordham	24
35	Dartmouth	3
24	Harvard	21
56	Lafayette	14
55	Cornell	16
43	St. Mary's (Cal.)	13
28	Lehigh	24
38	Towson	14
45	Holy Cross	26
417		**197**

DIVISION I-AA CHAMPIONSHIP
13	Illinois St.	56

Nickname: Red Raiders.
Stadium: Andy Kerr (1937), 10,221 capacity. Natural turf.
Colors: Maroon, Gray & White.
Conference: Patriot.
SID: Bob Cornell, 315-824-7616.
AD: Mark H. Murphy.

COLORADO
Boulder, CO 80309 ....I-A

Coach: Gary Barnett, Missouri 1969
Record: 10 Years, 51-60-2

2000 SCHEDULE
Colorado St. [Denver, CO]	Sept. 2
Southern California	Sept. 9
Washington ■	Sept. 16
Kansas St. ■	Sept. 30
Texas A&M	Oct. 7
Texas ■	Oct. 14
Kansas	Oct. 21
Oklahoma St. ■	Oct. 28
Missouri	Nov. 4
Iowa St. ■	Nov. 11
Nebraska	Nov. 24

1999 RESULTS (6-5-0)
14	Colorado St.	41
63	San Jose St.	35
51	Kansas	17
24	Washington	31
46	Missouri	39
10	Texas Tech	31
16	Iowa St.	12
38	Oklahoma	24
14	Kansas St.	20
37	Baylor	0
30	Nebraska	33
343		**283**

INSIGHT.COM BOWL
62	Boston College	28

Nickname: Golden Buffaloes.
Stadium: Folsom (1924), 51,655 capacity. Natural turf.
Colors: Silver, Gold & Black.
Conference: Big 12.
SID: David Plati, 303-492-5626.
AD: Richard A. Tharp.

COLORADO COL.
Colorado Springs, CO 80903 III

Coach: Greg Polnasek, Wis.-Eau Claire 1979
Record: 7 Years, 19-47-0

2000 SCHEDULE
Tabor ■	Sept. 9
Pomona-Pitzer ■	Sept. 16
Occidental	Sept. 23
Principia	Sept. 30
Kalamazoo ■	Oct. 7
Westminster (Mo.) ■	Oct. 14
Rhodes	Oct. 21
Lewis & Clark ■	Oct. 28
Washington (Mo.)	Nov. 4

1999 RESULTS (2-7-0)
14	Pomona-Pitzer	42
6	Willamette	51
13	Claremont-M-S	31
40	Millsaps	37
31	Trinity Bible (N.D.)	22
10	Occidental	13
28	Rhodes	38
26	Westminster (Mo.)	63
0	Washington (Mo.)	23
168		**320**

Nickname: Tigers.
Stadium: Washburn Field (1898), 2,000 capacity. Natural turf.
Colors: Black & Gold.
Conference: Division III Independent.
SID: Dave Moross, 719-389-6755.
AD: V. Martin Scarano.

COLORADO MINES
Golden, CO 80401 II

Coach: Bob Stitt, Doane 1986
(First year as head coach)

2000 SCHEDULE
Mid-America Naz.	Sept. 2
Okla. Panhandle	Sept. 9
Chadron St. ■	Sept. 16
Fort Hays St. ■	Sept. 23
Neb.-Kearney	Sept. 30
Fort Lewis	Oct. 7
N.M. Highlands ■	Oct. 14
Mesa St. ■	Oct. 21
Adams St.	Oct. 28
Western St. (Colo.)	Nov. 4

1999 RESULTS (1-9-0)
46	South Dakota Tech	29
6	Montana Tech	36
15	Fort Hays St.	54
0	Neb.-Kearney	70
0	Fort Lewis	33
6	N.M. Highlands	48
0	Mesa St.	47
7	Adams St.	44
17	Western St. (Colo.)	31
3	Chadron St.	55
100		**447**

Nickname: Orediggers.
Stadium: Brooks Field (1922), 5,000 capacity. Natural turf.
Colors: Silver & Blue.
Conference: Rocky Mountain Athletic.
SID: Jeff Duggan, 303-273-3300.
AD: Marvin L. Kay.

COLORADO ST.
Fort Collins, CO 80523 ....I-A

Coach: Sonny Lubick, Western Mont. 1960
Record: 11 Years, 78-46-0

2000 SCHEDULE
Colorado [Denver, CO]	Sept. 2
East Tenn. St. ■	Sept. 9
Arizona St.	*Sept. 16
Nevada	Sept. 30
New Mexico ■	Oct. 7
UNLV ■	Oct. 14
Utah	Oct. 21
San Diego St.	Oct. 28
Brigham Young ■	*Nov. 2
Air Force	Nov. 11
Wyoming ■	*Nov. 16

1999 RESULTS (8-3-0)
41	Colorado	14
38	Nevada	33
13	Brigham Young	34
46	New Mexico St.	7
13	Fresno St.	44
10	San Diego St.	17
24	Wyoming	13
31	Utah	24
36	New Mexico	22
41	Air Force	21
35	UNLV	17
328		**246**

LIBERTY BOWL
17	Southern Miss.	23

Nickname: Rams.
Stadium: Hughes (1968), 30,000 capacity. Natural turf.
Colors: Green & Gold.
Conference: Mountain West.
SID: Gary Ozzello, 303-491-5067.
AD: Tim L. Weiser.

COLUMBIA
New York, NY 10027 ....I-AA

Coach: Ray Tellier, Connecticut 1973
Record: 16 Years, 55-100-3

2000 SCHEDULE
Fordham ■	*Sept. 16
Bucknell	Sept. 23
Princeton ■	Sept. 30
Lafayette	Oct. 7
Pennsylvania	Oct. 14
Dartmouth ■	Oct. 21
Yale	Oct. 28
Harvard	Nov. 4
Cornell ■	Nov. 11
Brown	Nov. 18

1999 RESULTS (3-7-0)
7	Harvard	24
28	Towson	13
13	Lehigh	63
10	Bucknell	7
17	Pennsylvania	41
29	Yale	41
15	Princeton	44
21	Dartmouth	14
29	Cornell	31
6	Brown	23
175		**301**

Nickname: Lions.
Stadium: Lawrence A. Wien (1984), 17,000 capacity. Artificial turf.
Colors: Columbia Blue & White.
Conference: Ivy.
SID: Brian Bodine, 212-854-2534.
AD: John A. Reeves.

CONCORD
Athens, WV 24712 II

Coach: Ollie Pottmeyer, Glenville St. 1964
Record: 1 Year, 3-8-0

2000 SCHEDULE
Lenoir-Rhyne	*Aug. 26
Wingate ■	Sept. 2
Gardner-Webb	*Sept. 9
Virginia-Wise ■	Sept. 23
Shepherd	Sept. 30
West Liberty St. ■	Oct. 7
Glenville St. ■	Oct. 14
West Va. Wesleyan	Oct. 21
West Virginia St.	Oct. 28
Fairmont St. ■	Nov. 4
West Va. Tech	Nov. 11

1999 RESULTS (3-8-0)
12	Lenoir-Rhyne	21
14	VMI	15
30	Cumberland (Tenn.)	17
10	Virginia-Wise	35
20	Shepherd	43
13	West Liberty St.	17

7	Glenville St.	6
20	West Va. Wesleyan	7
14	West Virginia St.	42
13	Fairmont St.	34
21	West Va. Tech	26
174		**263**

Nickname: Mountain Lions.
Stadium: Callahan (N/A), 5,000 capacity. Natural turf.
Colors: Maroon & Gray.
Conference: West Virginia Intercollegiate.
SID: Don Christie, 304-384-5347.
AD: Ronals Macosko.

CONCORDIA (ILL.)
River Forest, IL 60305 III

Coach: Brian Baker-Watson, Benedictine (Ill.) 1990
(First year as head coach)

2000 SCHEDULE
Crown	Sept. 2
North Park ■	Sept. 16
Concordia (Wis.)	Sept. 23
Aurora ■	Sept. 30
Lakeland ■	Oct. 7
Greenville	Oct. 14
Benedictine (Ill.)	Oct. 21
Eureka ■	Oct. 28
MacMurray	Nov. 4

1999 RESULTS (2-8-0)
29	Crown	26
27	Principia	20
0	North Park	30
20	Benedictine (Ill.)	27
20	Lakeland	41
0	Aurora	40
3	MacMurray	48
24	Concordia (Wis.)	83
20	Eureka	53
35	Greenville	42
178		**410**

Nickname: Cougars.
Stadium: Concordia (2000), 1,500 capacity. Artificial turf.
Colors: Maroon & Gold.
Conference: Illini-Badger.
SID: Jim Egan, 708-209-3116.
AD: Janet L. Fisher.

CONCORDIA (WIS.)
Mequon, WI 53097 III

Coach: Jeffrey Gabrielsen, Ripon 1980
Record: 10 Years, 58-35-0

2000 SCHEDULE
Beloit ■	Sept. 9
Wis. Lutheran	*Sept. 16
Concordia (Ill.) ■	Sept. 23
Lakeland	Sept. 30
Greenville ■	Oct. 7
Benedictine (Ill.) ■	Oct. 14
Eureka	Oct. 21
MacMurray ■	Oct. 28
Aurora	Nov. 4
Concordia (Neb.)	Nov. 11

1999 RESULTS (5-5-0)
14	Mt. Senario	49
16	Beloit	20
38	Concordia (Neb.)	31
16	Lakeland	30
21	MacMurray	14
34	Eureka	18
45	Benedictine (Ill.)	3
21	Aurora	33
83	Concordia (Ill.)	24
31	Greenville	40
319		**262**

Nickname: Falcons.
Stadium: Century (NA), 2,500 capacity. Natural turf.
Colors: Royal Blue & White.
Conference: Illini-Badger.
SID: Kenneth L. Witte, 414-243-4404.
AD: Kenneth L. Witte.

CONCORDIA-M'HEAD
Moorhead, MN 56562 III

Coach: Jim Christopherson, Concordia-M'head 1960
Record: 31 Years, 213-96-7

2000 SCHEDULE
Moorhead St.	Sept. 2
St. Thomas (Minn.)	Sept. 16
Macalester ■	Sept. 23
Gust. Adolphus	Sept. 30
Hamline ■	Oct. 7
Bethel (Minn.)	Oct. 14
St. Olaf ■	Oct. 21
Carleton	Oct. 28
Augsburg [Minneapolis, MN]	Nov. 4
St. John's (Minn.)	Nov. 11

1999 RESULTS (6-4-0)
7	Moorhead St.	44
17	Bethel (Minn.)	15
35	Carleton	6
14	Hamline	6
17	St. Olaf	10
3	St. John's (Minn.)	7
44	Gust. Adolphus	10
40	Macalester	0
7	St. Thomas (Minn.)	22
5	Augsburg	7
189		**127**

Nickname: Cobbers.
Stadium: Jake Christiansen (N/A), 7,500 capacity. Natural turf.
Colors: Maroon & Gold.
Conference: Minnesota Intercollegiate Athletic.
SID: Jerry Pyle, 218-299-3194.
AD: Armin Pipho.

CONNECTICUT
Storrs, CT 06269 ....I-AA

Coach: Randy Edsall, Syracuse 1980
1 Year, 4-7-0

2000 SCHEDULE
Eastern Mich.	*Sept. 2
Colgate ■	*Sept. 9
Buffalo	*Sept. 16
Northeastern ■	Sept. 23
Louisville	Sept. 30
Boston College	Oct. 7
Akron	*Oct. 21
South Fla. ■	Oct. 28
Middle Tenn. St. ■	Nov. 4
Rhode Island	Nov. 11
Ball St.	Nov. 18

1999 RESULTS (4-7-0)
17	Hofstra	56
14	Kentucky	45
23	Buffalo	0
34	Maine	20
20	Rhode Island	9
45	Villanova	48
14	James Madison	48
21	Richmond	28
29	Northeastern	24
18	New Hampshire	43
20	Massachusetts	62
255		**383**

Nickname: Huskies.
Stadium: Memorial (1953), 16,200 capacity. Natural turf.
Colors: Blue & White.
Conference: Division I-AA Independent.
SID: Kyle Muncy, 203-486-3531.
AD: Lewis Perkins.

CORNELL
Ithaca, NY 14853 ....I-AA

Coach: Pete Mangurian, LSU 1978
Record: 2 Years, 11-9-0

2000 SCHEDULE
Bucknell	Sept. 16
Yale ■	Sept. 23
Lehigh	Sept. 30
Harvard	Oct. 7
Colgate ■	Oct. 14
Brown	Oct. 21
Princeton ■	Oct. 28
Dartmouth ■	Nov. 4
Columbia	Nov. 11
Pennsylvania ■	Nov. 18

1999 RESULTS (7-3-0)
20	Princeton	3
42	Fordham	14
33	Brown	28
24	Harvard	23
16	Colgate	55
17	Dartmouth	20
31	Wagner	14
20	Yale	37
31	Columbia	29
20	Pennsylvania	12
254		**235**

Nickname: Big Red.
Stadium: Schoellkopf (1915), 25,597 capacity. Artificial turf.
Colors: Carnelian & White.
Conference: Ivy.
SID: Patrick Gillespie, 607-255-3753.
AD: Andy Noel.

CORNELL COLLEGE
Mt. Vernon, IA 52314 III

Coach: Steve Miller, Cornell College 1965
Record: 21 Years, 111-84-2

2000 SCHEDULE
Simpson ■	Sept. 2
Wartburg	Sept. 9
Central (Iowa)	Sept. 16
Coe ■	Sept. 23
Upper Iowa ■	Sept. 30
William Penn	Oct. 7
Loras ■	Oct. 14
Luther	Oct. 21
Dubuque ■	Nov. 4
Buena Vista	Nov. 11

1999 RESULTS (3-7-0)
0	Central (Iowa)	44
13	Upper Iowa	68
32	William Penn	28
13	Wartburg	56
7	Buena Vista	59
19	Loras	22
8	Simpson	50
41	Luther	35
27	Dubuque	28
32	Coe	23
192		**413**

Nickname: Rams.
Stadium: Ash Park Field (1922), 2,500 capacity. Natural turf.
Colors: Purple & White.
Conference: Iowa Intercollegiate Athletic.
SID: Darren Miller, 319-895-4483.
AD: Stephen Miller.

CORTLAND ST.
Cortland, NY 13045 III

Coach: Dan MacNeill, Cortland St. 1979
Record: 3 Years, 17-14-0

2000 SCHEDULE
Brockport St. ■	Sept. 2
Col. of New Jersey ■	Sept. 9
Kean ■	Sept. 16
Buffalo St.	Sept. 23
Montclair St.	Sept. 30

New Jersey City ....Oct. 7
Rowan ....Oct. 14
Wm. Paterson ■ ....Oct. 21
Springfield ....Oct. 28
Ithaca ■ ....Nov. 11

1999 RESULTS (5-5-0)
16	Montclair St.	41
26	Kean	13
17	Buffalo St.	20
28	Wash. & Jeff.	33
73	New Jersey City	7
9	Rowan	30
45	Wm. Paterson	7
21	Springfield	18
26	Ithaca	21
24	Brockport St.	28
285		**218**

Nickname: Red Dragons.
Stadium: Davis Field (1959), 5,000 capacity. Natural turf.
Colors: Red & White.
Conference: New Jersey Athletic.
SID: Fran Elia, 607-753-5673.
AD: Lee Roberts.

CURRY
Milton, MA 02186 III

Coach: Steve Nelson, North Dakota St. 1974
Record: 2 Years, 13-7-0

2000 SCHEDULE
Norwich ....Sept. 2
Maine Maritime ■ ....Sept. 9
Framingham St. ....Sept. 16
MIT ■ ....Sept. 23
Nichols ....Sept. 30
Western New Eng. ....Oct. 7
Salve Regina ■ ....Oct. 14
Fitchburg St. ....Oct. 21
Mass.-Boston ....Oct. 28
Mass.-Dartmouth ■ ....Nov. 4

1999 RESULTS (7-3-0)
7	Norwich	27
21	Maine Maritime	15
16	Framingham St.	20
17	MIT	14
15	Nichols	14
30	Western New Eng.	22
3	Salve Regina	14
28	Fitchburg St.	21
33	Mass.-Boston	0
21	Mass.-Dartmouth	17
191		**164**

Nickname: Colonels.
Stadium: D. Forbes Will Field (NA), 1,500 capacity. Natural turf.
Colors: Purple & White.
Conference: New England Football.
SID: Ken Golner, 617-333-2324.
AD: Steve Nelson.

DARTMOUTH
Hanover, NH 03755 ....I-AA

Coach: John Lyons, Pennsylvania 1974
Record: 8 Years, 48-31-1

2000 SCHEDULE
Colgate ■ ....Sept. 16
New Hampshire ....Sept. 23
Pennsylvania ....Sept. 30
Yale ■ ....Oct. 7
Holy Cross ■ ....Oct. 14
Columbia ....Oct. 21
Harvard ■ ....Oct. 28
Cornell ....Nov. 4
Brown ■ ....Nov. 11
Princeton ....Nov. 18

1999 RESULTS (2-8-0)
6	Pennsylvania	17
3	Colgate	35
10	Lafayette	20
14	Lehigh	30
3	Yale	44
20	Cornell	17
21	Harvard	63
14	Columbia	21
28	Brown	35
19	Princeton	18
138		**300**

Nickname: Big Green.
Stadium: Memorial Field (1923), 20,416 capacity. Natural turf.
Colors: Green & White.
Conference: Ivy.
SID: Kathy Slattery, 603-646-2468.
AD: Richard Jaeger.

DAVIDSON
Davidson, NC 28036 ....I-AA

Coach: Joe Susan, Delaware 1977
(First year as head coach)

2000 SCHEDULE
Jacksonville ■ ....Sept. 9
Sewanee ....Sept. 16
Emory & Henry ■ ....Sept. 23
Morehead St. ■ ....Oct. 7
San Diego ....*Oct. 14
Randolph-Macon ■ ....Oct. 21
Hampden-Sydney ....Oct. 28
Centre ■ ....Nov. 4
Austin Peay ....Nov. 11
Georgetown ■ ....Nov. 18

1999 RESULTS (8-3-0)
0	Morehead St.	40
15	Jacksonville	20
21	Sewanee	0
13	Emory & Henry	17
28	Guilford	21
35	Wash. & Lee	28
28	Georgetown	27
24	Randolph-Macon	16
31	Hampden-Sydney	12
24	Centre	14
38	Austin Peay	22
257		**217**

Nickname: Wildcats.
Stadium: Richardson Field (1924), 5,200 capacity. Natural turf.
Colors: Red & Black.
Conference: Division I-AA Independent.
SID: Rick Bender, 704-892-2374.
AD: James E. Murphy III.

DAYTON
Dayton, OH 45469 ....I-AA

Coach: Mike Kelly, Manchester 1970
Record: 19 Years, 177-36-1

2000 SCHEDULE
Tiffin ■ ....*Aug. 31
Ohio Northern ■ ....*Sept. 9
Yale ....Sept. 16
Morehead St. ■ ....*Sept. 23
Butler ....Sept. 30
Austin Peay ....*Oct. 7
Robert Morris ■ ....Oct. 14
Drake ....Oct. 21
St. Joseph's (Ind.) ■ ....Oct. 28
Valparaiso ....Nov. 4
San Diego ....*Nov. 11

1999 RESULTS (6-4-0)
31	McKendree	38
7	Robert Morris	34
49	Austin Peay	21
39	Morehead St.	50
42	Butler	7
41	San Diego	0
20	Drake	14
35	St. Joseph's (Ind.)	6
34	Valparaiso	10
27	Towson	30
325		**210**

Nickname: Flyers.
Stadium: Welcome (1949), 11,000 capacity. Artificial turf.
Colors: Red & Blue.
Conference: Pioneer Football.
SID: Doug Hauschild, 513-229-4460.
AD: Ted Kissell.

DEPAUW
Greencastle, IN 46135 III

Coach: Nick Mourouzis, Miami (Ohio) 1959
Record: 19 Years, 115-70-4

2000 SCHEDULE
Rhodes ....Sept. 2
Hanover ■ ....Sept. 9
Hope ....Sept. 16
Trinity (Tex.) ■ ....Sept. 23
Sewanee ■ ....Oct. 7
Blackburn ....Oct. 14
Millsaps ....*Oct. 21
Centre ....Oct. 28
Rose-Hulman ■ ....Nov. 4
Wabash ....Nov. 11

1999 RESULTS (5-5-0)
14	Rhodes	33
20	Ill. Wesleyan	28
27	Hope	21
0	Trinity (Tex.)	44
6	Chicago	9
14	Sewanee	33
41	Millsaps	10
26	Centre	23
33	Rose-Hulman	0
21	Wabash	7
202		**208**

Nickname: Tigers.
Stadium: Blackstock (1941), 4,000 capacity. Natural turf.
Colors: Old Gold & Black.
Conference: Southern Collegiate Athletic.
SID: Bill Wagner, 317-658-4630.
AD: Page Cotton Jr.

DEFIANCE
Defiance, OH 43512 III

Coach: Greg Pscodna, Adrian 1986
Record: 4 Years, 11-25-0

2000 SCHEDULE
Olivet ■ ....Sept. 2
Adrian ....Sept. 16
Rockford ....Sept. 23
Mt. St. Joseph ....Sept. 30
Hanover ■ ....Oct. 7
Manchester ....Oct. 14
Franklin ■ ....Oct. 21
Thomas More ■ ....Oct. 28
Anderson (Ind.) ....Nov. 4
Bluffton ■ ....Nov. 11

1999 RESULTS (4-5-0)
35	Adrian	28
21	Alma	46
10	Kalamazoo	0
42	Olivet	24
21	Albion	35
7	Hope	40
15	Ohio Wesleyan	36
30	Thomas More	45
20	Thiel	13
201		**267**

Nickname: Yellow Jackets.
Stadium: Justin F. Coressel (1994), 4,176 capacity. Natural turf.
Colors: Purple & Gold.
Conference: Heartland Collegiate Athletic.
SID: Bryan Albright, 419-783-2346.
AD: Richard A. Kaiser.

DELAWARE ST.
Dover, DE 19901 ....I-AA

Coach: Ben Blacknall, N.C. A&T 1973
(First year as head coach)

2000 SCHEDULE
Florida A&M ■	....	Sept. 2
Elon	....	*Sept. 9
Fayetteville St. ■	....	Sept. 16
Liberty ■	....	Sept. 23
Hampton ■	....	Sept. 30
Bethune-Cookman	....	Oct. 7
Morgan St.	....	Oct. 21
South Carolina St. ■	....	Oct. 28
N.C. A&T ■	....	Nov. 4
Norfolk St.	....	Nov. 11
Howard	....	Nov. 18

1999 RESULTS (4-7-0)
0	Hampton	21
28	Elon	51
26	Norfolk St.	6
28	Bucknell	38
43	Bethune-Cookman	29
14	Hofstra	58
34	Morgan St.	20
19	Florida A&M	48
13	N.C. A&T	24
14	South Carolina St.	34
42	Howard	25
261		**354**

Nickname: Hornets.
Stadium: Alumni Field (1957), 5,000 capacity. Natural turf.
Colors: Red & Columbia Blue.
Conference: Mid-Eastern Athletic.
SID: Dennis Jones, 302-739-4926.
AD: William Collick.

DELAWARE VALLEY
Doylestown, PA 18901 III

Coach: Matt DiBernardo, Tampa 1990
(First year as head coach)

2000 SCHEDULE
Moravian ■	....	Sept. 9
Montclair St. ■	....	Sept. 16
Widener ■	....	Sept. 23
FDU-Madison	....	Sept. 30
Wilkes	....	Oct. 7
King's (Pa.) ■	....	Oct. 14
Juniata	....	Oct. 21
Lycoming ■	....	Oct. 28
Albright	....	Nov. 4
Lebanon Valley	....	Nov. 11

1999 RESULTS (2-8-0)
33	Wm. Paterson	38
26	Moravian	20
27	Widener	40
19	FDU-Madison	38
0	Wilkes	54
0	King's (Pa.)	21
6	Juniata	42
0	Lycoming	34
13	Albright	37
10	Lebanon Valley	3
134		**327**

Nickname: Aggies.
Stadium: James Work (1978), 4,500 capacity. Natural turf.
Colors: Green & Gold.
Conference: Middle Atlantic.
SID: Matthew Levy, 215-489-2937.
AD: Frank Wolfgang.

DELAWARE
Newark, DE 19716 ....I-AA

Coach: Tubby Raymond, Michigan 1950
Record: 34 Years, 284-111-3

2000 SCHEDULE
Rhode Island	....	Sept. 2
Citadel ■	....	*Sept. 9
Hofstra	....	*Sept. 16
West Chester ■	....	*Sept. 23
Northeastern ■	....	Sept. 30
Richmond	....	Oct. 7
William & Mary	....	Oct. 14
James Madison	....	Oct. 28
New Hampshire ■	....	Nov. 4
Massachusetts	....	Nov. 11
Villanova ■	....	Nov. 18

1999 RESULTS (7-4-0)
34	William & Mary	27
26	Citadel	16
29	West Chester	10
7	James Madison	21
41	Richmond	33
35	Lehigh	42
19	Massachusetts	26
37	Northeastern	34
14	New Hampshire	10
35	Rhode Island	0
45	Villanova	51
322		**270**

Nickname: Fightin' Blue Hens.
Stadium: Delaware (1952), 22,000 capacity. Natural turf.
Colors: Blue & Gold.
Conference: Atlantic 10.
SID: Scott Selheimer, 302-831-2186.
AD: Edgar N. Johnson.

DELTA ST.
Cleveland, MS 38733 II

Coach: Steve Campbell, Troy St. 1987
1 Year, 6-4-0

2000 SCHEDULE
Belhaven (Jackson, MS)	....	Sept. 2
Mississippi Val.	....	*Sept. 9
West Ala.	....	Sept. 16
North Ala. ■	....	Sept. 23
Harding ■	....	Sept. 30
Valdosta St.	....	Oct. 7
Southern Ark.	....	Oct. 14
Henderson St. ■	....	Oct. 21
Central Ark.	....	Oct. 28
Arkansas Tech	....	Nov. 4
Ark.-Monticello ■	....	*Nov. 9

1999 RESULTS (6-4-0)
31	Sam Houston St.	38
17	Arkansas Tech	10
9	Valdosta St.	6
27	West Ala.	20
35	Henderson St.	3
33	North Ala.	7
31	West Ga.	42
0	Southern Ark.	28
14	Central Ark.	31
40	Ark.-Monticello	8
237		**193**

Nickname: Statesmen.
Stadium: Travis E. Parker Field (1970), 8,000 capacity. Natural turf.
Colors: Green & White.
Conference: Gulf South.
SID: Fred Sington, 601-846-4677.
AD: James H. Jordan.

DENISON
Granville, OH 43023 III

Coach: Nick Fletcher, Johns Hopkins 1976
Record: 5 Years, 27-22-0

2000 SCHEDULE
Carnegie Mellon ■	....	Sept. 2
Waynesburg	....	Sept. 9
Allegheny ■	....	Sept. 23
Kenyon	....	Sept. 30
Wittenberg	....	Oct. 7
Ohio Wesleyan ■	....	Oct. 14
Earlham	....	Oct. 21
Case Reserve ■	....	Oct. 28
Wabash	....	Nov. 4
Oberlin ■	....	Nov. 11

1999 RESULTS (4-6-0)
13	Carnegie Mellon	31
0	Muskingum	33
13	Allegheny	30
63	Oberlin	7
7	Wittenberg	42
21	Case Reserve	14
21	Ohio Wesleyan	34
0	Wooster	45
38	Earllham	0
24	Kenyon	17
200		**253**

Nickname: Big Red.
Stadium: Deeds Field (1922), 5,000 capacity. Natural turf.
Colors: Red & White.
Conference: North Coast Athletic.
SID: Jack Hire, 614-587-6546.
AD: Larry Scheiderer.

DICKINSON
Carlisle, PA 17013 III

Coach: Darwin Breaux, West Chester 1977
Record: 7 Years, 50-22-1

2000 SCHEDULE
Hobart ■	....	Sept. 11
Muhlenberg	....	Sept. 18
Susquehanna ■	....	Sept. 25
Carnegie Mellon	....	Oct. 2
Frank. & Marsh.	....	Oct. 9
Western Md. ■	....	Oct. 16
Swarthmore	....	Oct. 23
Johns Hopkins ■	....	Oct. 30
Gettysburg	....	Nov. 6
Ursinus ■	....	Nov. 13

1999 RESULTS (6-4-0)
32	Hobart	20
13	Muhlenberg	30
6	Susquehanna	42
7	Carnegie Mellon	3
31	Frank. & Marsh.	26
0	Western Md.	42
24	Swarthmore	14
37	Johns Hopkins	21
35	Gettysburg	14
30	Ursinus	32
215		**244**

Nickname: Red Devils.
Stadium: Biddle Field (1909), 2,577 capacity. Natural turf.
Colors: Red & White.
Conference: Centennial.
SID: Charles McGuire, 717-245-1652.
AD: Leslie J. Poolman.

DRAKE
Des Moines, IA 50311 ....I-AA

Coach: Rob Ash, Cornell College 1973
Record: 20 Years, 128-70-5

2000 SCHEDULE
McKendree ■	....	Sept. 2
St. Ambrose	....	*Sept. 9
Wis.-Stevens Point	....	Sept. 16
San Diego	....	Sept. 30
Valparaiso ■	....	Oct. 7
Southern Ill.	....	Oct. 14
Dayton	....	Oct. 21
Butler ■	....	Oct. 28
Jacksonville ■	....	Nov. 4
St. Mary's (Cal.)	....	Nov. 11
Towson	....	Nov. 18

1999 RESULTS (7-4-0)
21	Morningside	17

47	St. Ambrose	3
17	Wis.-Stevens Point	28
48	Quincy	7
17	Valparaiso	27
38	St. Mary's (Cal.)	7
14	Dayton	20
53	Butler	6
41	San Diego	20
34	Jacksonville	14
0	Western Ill.	24
330		**173**

Nickname: Bulldogs.
Stadium: Drake (1925), 18,000 capacity. Natural turf.
Colors: Blue & White.
Conference: Pioneer Football.
SID: Mike Mahon, 515-271-3012.
AD: Dave Blank.

DUBUQUE
Dubuque, IA 52001..................................III

Coach: Mike Murray, Ill. Wesleyan 1984
Record: 3 Years, 4-26-0

2000 SCHEDULE
Wartburg ■	Sept. 2
Coe	Sept. 9
Simpson ■	Sept. 16
Loras	Sept. 23
Luther	Sept. 30
William Penn ■	Oct. 14
Buena Vista	Oct. 21
Upper Iowa ■	Oct. 28
Cornell College	Nov. 4
Central (Iowa) ■	Nov. 11

1999 RESULTS (1-9-0)
6	Simpson	31
17	Luther	38
14	Central (Iowa)	39
27	Coe	63
25	Upper Iowa	55
23	William Penn	30
0	Wartburg	28
13	Buena Vista	55
25	Loras	35
28	Cornell College	27
178		**401**

Nickname: Spartans.
Stadium: Chalmers Field (1942), 2,800 capacity. Natural turf.
Colors: Blue and White.
Conference: Iowa Intercollegiate Athletic.
SID: Greg Yoko, 319-589-3225.
AD: Michael Elbe.

DUKE
Durham, NC 27708..................................I-A

Coach: Carl Franks, Duke 1983
1 Year, 3-8-0

2000 SCHEDULE
East Caro. ■	Sept. 2
Northwestern	Sept. 9
Virginia ■	Sept. 16
Vanderbilt	Sept. 23
Clemson ■	Sept. 30
Florida St.	*Oct. 14
Georgia Tech	Oct. 21
Maryland ■	Oct. 28
Wake Forest	Nov. 4
North Carolina St.	Nov. 11
North Carolina ■	Nov. 18

1999 RESULTS (3-8-0)
9	East Caro.	27
12	Northwestern	15
14	Vanderbilt	31
23	Florida St.	51
14	Virginia	17
31	Georgia Tech	38
24	North Carolina St.	31
25	Maryland	22
7	Clemson	58

48	Wake Forest	35
0	North Carolina	38
217		**363**

Nickname: Blue Devils.
Stadium: Wallace Wade (1929), 33,941 capacity. Natural turf.
Colors: Royal Blue & White.
Conference: Atlantic Coast.
SID: Mike Cragg, 919-684-2633.
AD: Joe Alleva.

DUQUESNE
Pittsburgh, PA 15282..................................I-AA

Coach: Greg Gattuso, Penn St. 1983
Record: 7 Years, 53-21-0

2000 SCHEDULE
VMI	Sept. 2
La Salle	Sept. 9
Fairfield ■	Sept. 16
Marist ■	Sept. 23
Bucknell	Sept. 30
Georgetown ■	Oct. 14
Iona ■	Oct. 21
St. Peter's	Oct. 28
Siena	Nov. 4
Lafayette ■	Nov. 11
Canisius	Nov. 18

1999 RESULTS (8-3-0)
32	La Salle	3
21	Fairfield	34
31	Marist	0
51	St. Peter's	6
10	St. John's (N.Y.)	3
20	Bucknell	49
50	Iona	62
49	Siena	17
33	Georgetown	21
28	Lafayette	17
68	Canisius	12
347		**186**

Nickname: Dukes.
Stadium: Arthur J. Rooney Field (1993), 4,500 capacity. Artificial turf.
Colors: Red & Blue.
Conference: Atlantic 10.
SID: Dave Saba, 412-396-5861.
AD: Brian Colleary.

EARLHAM
Richmond, IN 47374..................................III

Coach: Frank Carr, Albion 1978
Record: 15 Years, 37-108-0

2000 SCHEDULE
Rose-Hulman	*Sept. 2
Centre ■	*Sept. 9
Oberlin	Sept. 16
Manchester	Sept. 23
Hiram ■	Sept. 30
Ohio Wesleyan	Oct. 7
Wabash ■	Oct. 14
Denison ■	Oct. 21
Wittenberg	Nov. 4
Kenyon ■	Nov. 11

1999 RESULTS (2-8-0)
7	Franklin	48
29	Oberlin	27
6	Wittenberg	62
14	Kenyon	6
0	Case Reserve	16
6	Wooster	46
0	Allegheny	67
12	Rose-Hulman	26
0	Denison	38
0	Ohio Wesleyan	36
74		**372**

Nickname: Quakers.
Stadium: M. O. Ross Field (1975), 1,500 capacity. Natural turf.
Colors: Maroon & White.

Conference: North Coast Athletic.
SID: David Knight, 317-983-1416.
AD: Porter Miller.

EAST CARO.
Greenville, NC 27858..................................I-A

Coach: Steve Logan, Tulsa 1975
Record: 8 Years, 51-40-0

2000 SCHEDULE
Duke	Sept. 2
Virginia Tech ■	*Sept. 7
Tulane ■	Sept. 16
Syracuse ■	Sept. 23
Memphis	*Oct. 7
Army ■	Oct. 14
Louisville	*Oct. 19
UAB ■	Oct. 28
Houston	Nov. 11
West Virginia	Nov. 18
Southern Miss.	Nov. 25

1999 RESULTS (9-2-0)
30	West Virginia	23
27	Duke	9
21	South Carolina	3
27	Miami (Fla.)	23
33	Army	14
22	Southern Miss.	39
52	Tulane	7
19	Houston	3
17	UAB	36
48	Cincinnati	34
23	North Carolina St.	6
319		**197**

MOBILE ALABAMA BOWL
| 14 | TCU | 28 |

Nickname: Pirates.
Stadium: Dowdy-Ficklen (1963), 43,000 capacity. Natural turf.
Colors: Purple & Gold.
Conference: Conference USA.
SID: Norm Reilly, 919-328-4522.
AD: Mike Hamrick.

EAST CENTRAL
Ada, OK 74820..................................II

Coach: Dennis Darnell, Southwest Mo. St. 1969
Record: 6 Years, 22-41-1

2000 SCHEDULE
Northwestern Okla.	*Sept. 2
Emporia St. ■	*Sept. 9
Angelo St. ■	*Sept. 16
Abilene Christian	*Sept. 23
Northeastern St. ■	*Sept. 30
Midwestern St.	*Oct. 7
Southwestern Okla. ■	Oct. 14
Central Okla.	Oct. 21
West Tex. A&M ■	Oct. 28
Okla. Panhandle	Nov. 4
Southeastern Okla.	Nov. 11

1999 RESULTS (3-7-0)
0	Northwestern Okla.	25
5	Midwestern St.	36
14	Texas A&M-Kingsville	20
31	Tarleton St.	33
3	Northeastern St.	40
7	Central Okla.	31
7	Harding	30
14	Ouachita Baptist	7
17	Southwestern Okla.	7
14	Southeastern Okla.	13
112		**242**

Nickname: Tigers.
Stadium: Norris Field (NA), 5,000 capacity. Natural turf.
Colors: Orange & Black.
Conference: Lone Star.
SID: Steve McGaughey, 580-310-5258.
AD: Tim Green.

EAST STROUDSBURG
East Stroudsburg, PA 18301 II

Coach: Dennis Douds, Slippery Rock 1963
Record: 26 Years, 149-112-3

2000 SCHEDULE
Clarion	Sept. 2
West Chester	*Sept. 9
Glenville St.	Sept. 16
Shepherd ■	Sept. 23
Millersville ■	Sept. 30
Kutztown ■	Oct. 7
Bloomsburg	Oct. 14
Shippensburg ■	Oct. 21
Cheyney	Oct. 28
Mansfield ■	Nov. 4
Edinboro	Nov. 11

1999 RESULTS (4-7-0)
28	Lock Haven	24
27	Shepherd	33
38	Glenville St.	34
10	Slippery Rock	47
3	West Chester	49
0	Shippensburg	37
55	Cheyney	22
10	Kutztown	24
21	Bloomsburg	27
29	Millersville	54
41	Mansfield	20
262		**371**

Nickname: Warriors.
Stadium: Eiler-Martin (1969), 6,000 capacity. Natural turf.
Colors: Red & Black.
Conference: Pennsylvania State Athletic.
SID: Peter Nevins, 570-422-3312.
AD: Joy M. Richman.

EAST TENN. ST.
Johnson City, TN 37614 ....I-AA

Coach: Paul Hamilton, Appalachian St. 1981
Record: 3 Years, 17-16-0

2000 SCHEDULE
Liberty	*Sept. 2
Colorado St.	Sept. 9
VMI ■	Sept. 16
Western Caro.	*Sept. 23
Appalachian St. ■	*Sept. 30
Citadel	Oct. 7
Furman ■	*Oct. 21
Ga. Southern	Oct. 28
Wofford ■	Nov. 4
Chattanooga	Nov. 11
Charleston So. ■	*Nov. 18

1999 RESULTS (6-5-0)
28	Citadel	10
61	West Va. Tech	0
26	VMI	17
38	Western Caro.	10
19	Appalachian St.	23
24	Liberty	12
21	Furman	48
6	Ga. Southern	55
14	Wofford	38
28	Chattanooga	14
7	Middle Tenn. St.	24
271		**251**

Nickname: Buccaneers.
Stadium: Memorial (1977), 12,000 capacity. Artificial turf.
Colors: Blue & Gold.
Conference: Southern.
SID: David Lang, 615-929-4220.
AD: Frank S. Pergolizzi.

EASTERN ILL.
Charleston, IL 61920 ....I-AA

Coach: Bob Spoo, Purdue 1960
Record: 13 Years, 76-71-1

2000 SCHEDULE
Indiana St.	*Aug. 31
Ky. Wesleyan ■	*Sept. 9
Toledo	*Sept. 16
Tenn.-Martin	Sept. 23
Tennessee St. ■	Oct. 7
Murray St. ■	Oct. 14
Tennessee Tech	Oct. 21
Western Ky.	Oct. 28
Southeast Mo. St. ■	Nov. 4
Illinois St.	Nov. 11
Eastern Ky. ■	Nov. 18

1999 RESULTS (2-10-0)
17	Central Mich.	33
27	Hawaii	31
6	Southern Ill.	34
42	Tenn.-Martin	21
21	UCF	31
25	Tennessee St.	43
32	Murray St.	37
7	Tennessee Tech	14
15	Western Ky.	38
38	Southeast Mo. St.	45
17	Illinois St.	24
20	Eastern Ky.	14
267		**365**

Nickname: Panthers.
Stadium: O'Brien (1970), 10,000 capacity. Natural turf.
Colors: Blue & Gray.
Conference: Ohio Valley.
SID: Dave Kidwell, 217-581-6408.
AD: Richard A. McDuffie.

EASTERN KY.
Richmond, KY 40475 ....I-AA

Coach: Roy Kidd, Eastern Ky. 1954
Record: 36 Years, 293-112-8

2000 SCHEDULE
Glenville St. ■	*Aug. 31
Indiana St.	*Sept. 9
Tennessee Tech ■	*Sept. 23
Southeast Mo. St. ■	*Sept. 30
Western Ky.	Oct. 7
UCF	*Oct. 14
Tenn.-Martin	Oct. 21
Tennessee St. ■	*Oct. 26
Murray St. ■	Nov. 4
Kentucky St. ■	Nov. 11
Eastern Ill.	Nov. 18

1999 RESULTS (7-4-0)
27	Kentucky St.	21
20	Appalachian St.	34
31	Indiana St.	24
17	Samford	16
37	Southeast Mo. St.	28
30	Western Ky.	10
54	Tenn.-Martin	7
28	Tennessee St.	33
30	Murray St.	45
23	Tennessee Tech	20
14	Eastern Ill.	20
311		**258**

Nickname: Colonels.
Stadium: Roy Kidd (1969), 20,000 capacity. Natural turf.
Colors: Maroon & White.
Conference: Ohio Valley.
SID: Karl Park, 606-622-1253.
AD: Jeffrey P. Long.

EASTERN MICH.
Ypsilanti, MI 48197 ....I-A

Coach: Jeff Woodruff, Kent St. 1979
(First year as head coach)

2000 SCHEDULE
Connecticut ■	*Sept. 2
Miami (Ohio) ■	*Sept. 9
South Carolina	*Sept. 16
Temple	*Sept. 23
UCF ■	Sept. 30
Toledo ■	Oct. 7
Ball St.	Oct. 14
Bowling Green	*Oct. 21
Central Mich. ■	Nov. 4
Northern Ill. ■	Nov. 11
Western Mich.	Nov. 18

1999 RESULTS (4-7-0)
7	Michigan St.	51
14	Miami (Ohio)	35
38	Akron	17
10	Louisville	45
37	Western Mich.	40
27	Ohio	26
20	Toledo	13
6	UCF	31
31	Ball St.	21
26	Central Mich.	29
23	Northern Ill.	30
239		**338**

Nickname: Eagles.
Stadium: Rynearson (1969), 30,200 capacity. Artificial turf.
Colors: Green & White.
Conference: Mid-American.
SID: Jim Streeter, 313-487-0317.
AD: David L. Diles.

EASTERN N.M.
Portales, NM 88130 II

Coach: Bud Elliott, Baker (Kan.) 1953
Record: 32 Years, 173-158-9

2000 SCHEDULE
Western N.M. ■	*Sept. 2
N.M. Highlands	*Sept. 9
Midwestern St. ■	*Sept. 16
Central Okla. ■	*Sept. 23
Abilene Christian ■	Sept. 30
Angelo St.	*Oct. 7
Tarleton St. ■	*Oct. 14
Tex. A&M-Commerce	Oct. 21
Texas A&M-Kingsville ■	Oct. 28
West Tex. A&M	Nov. 4

1999 RESULTS (8-3-0)
33	Western N.M.	13
54	N.M. Highlands	7
23	Ouachita Baptist	0
20	Northeastern St.	14
28	Abilene Christian	31
19	Angelo St.	24
27	Tarleton St.	13
21	Tex. A&M-Commerce	10
7	Texas A&M-Kingsville	42
24	West Tex. A&M	16
38	Midwestern St.	13
294		**183**

Nickname: Greyhounds.
Stadium: Greyhound (1969), 6,500 capacity. Natural turf.
Colors: Green & Silver.
Conference: Lone Star.
SID: Robert McKinney, 505-562-4309.
AD: Rosemarie Stallman.

EASTERN ORE.
La Grande, OR 97850 III

Coach: Rob Cushman, Puget Sound 1978
Record: 3 Years, 13-17-0

2000 SCHEDULE
UC Davis	*Sept. 9
Carroll (Mont.)	Sept. 16
Simon Fraser ■	Sept. 23
Montana Tech ■	Sept. 30
Pacific Lutheran	Oct. 7
Linfield ■	Oct. 14
Willamette	Oct. 21
Whitworth	Oct. 28
Puget Sound ■	Nov. 4
Southern Ore.	Nov. 11

1999 RESULTS (5-5-0)

28	Idaho St.	54
2	Southern Ore.	34
28	Carroll (Mont.)	21
35	Western Ore.	34
35	Pacific Lutheran	41
41	Puget Sound	14
28	Willamette	7
29	Linfield	36
69	Lewis & Clark	3
28	Whitworth	31

Nickname: Mountaineers.
Stadium: Community (NA), 3,000 capacity. Natural turf.
Colors: Blue & Gold.
Conference: Division III Independent.
SID: Dave Girrard, 541-962-3732.
AD: Peggy Anderson.

EASTERN WASH.
Cheney, WA 99004 .... I-AA

Coach: Paul Wulff, Washington St. 1990
(First year as head coach)

2000 SCHEDULE

Oregon St.	Sept. 2
Western Ore. ■	*Sept. 9
Idaho St. ■	*Sept. 16
Weber St.	*Sept. 23
Montana [Spokane, WA]	*Sept. 30
Montana St.	Oct. 7
Boise St.	Oct. 14
Cal St. Sacramento ■	Oct. 21
Cal St. Northridge	Oct. 28
Northern Ariz. ■	Nov. 4
Portland St.	Nov. 11

1999 RESULTS (7-4-0)

21	Idaho	48
44	Central Wash.	14
39	Portland St.	48
48	Cal St. Northridge	41
14	Northern Ariz.	10
7	Boise St.	41
45	Idaho St.	38
7	Montana	25
26	Cal St. Sacramento	21
45	Montana St.	23
30	Weber St.	27
326		**336**

Nickname: Eagles.
Stadium: Woodward (1967), 6,000 capacity. Natural turf.
Colors: Red & White.
Conference: Big Sky.
SID: Dave Cook, 509-359-6334.
AD: Scott Barnes.

EDINBORO
Edinboro, PA 16444 II

Coach: Lou Tepper, Rutgers 1967
Record: 5 Years, 25-31-2

2000 SCHEDULE

Ashland ■	Sept. 2
Youngstown St.	*Sept. 9
Mercyhurst ■	Sept. 16
Slippery Rock	Sept. 23
Calif. (Pa.) ■	Sept. 30
Lock Haven	*Oct. 7
Clarion	Oct. 14
Indiana (Pa.) ■	Oct. 21
West Chester	Oct. 28
Shippensburg ■	Nov. 4
East Stroudsburg ■	Nov. 11

1999 RESULTS (3-8-0)

10	Hillsdale	28
29	Glenville St.	20
20	Mercyhurst	34
10	Millersville	20
10	Shippensburg	52
30	Clarion	29
38	Lock Haven	7
35	Calif. (Pa.)	40
17	Slippery Rock	34
7	Indiana (Pa.)	18
16	Bloomsburg	65
222		**347**

Nickname: Fighting Scots.
Stadium: Sox Harrison (1965), 5,000 capacity. Natural turf.
Colors: Red & White.
Conference: Pennsylvania State Athletic.
SID: Bob Shreve, 814-732-2811.
AD: Bruce R. Baumgartner.

ELIZABETH CITY ST.
Elizabeth City, NC 27909 II

Coach: John Wright, Virginia Union 1971
(First year as head coach)

2000 SCHEDULE

Virginia Union ■	*Sept. 2
Fayetteville St. [Rocky Mount, NC]	Sept. 9
Morehouse	Sept. 16
N.C. Central	Sept. 23
Johnson Smith	*Sept. 30
Virginia St.	Oct. 7
Bowie St.	Oct. 14
Livingstone	*Oct. 21
Benedict ■	Oct. 28
Winston-Salem ■	Nov. 4

1999 RESULTS (1-10-0)

12	Savannah St.	50
6	Fayetteville St.	13
7	Cheyney	12
6	Johnson Smith	27
6	N.C. Central	35
6	Virginia Union	40
6	Bowie St.	20
34	Livingstone	33
12	Benedict	31
6	Winston-Salem	21
17	Virginia St.	45
118		**327**

Nickname: Vikings.
Stadium: Roebuck (NA), 6,500 capacity. Natural turf.
Colors: Royal Blue & White.
Conference: Central Intercollegiate Athletic.
SID: Kirt Campbell, 919-335-3278.
AD: Edward McLean.

ELMHURST
Elmhurst, IL 60126 III

Coach: Paul Krohn, Minn. St.-Mankato 1976
Record: 7 Years, 14-48-1

2000 SCHEDULE

Ripon	Sept. 9
Benedictine (Ill.) ■	Sept. 16
Ohio Wesleyan	Sept. 23
Augustana (Ill.) ■	Sept. 30
North Park ■	Oct. 7
Ill. Wesleyan	Oct. 14
Carthage	Oct. 21
Wheaton (Ill.) ■	Oct. 28
Millikin ■	Nov. 4
North Central	Nov. 11

1999 RESULTS (2-7-0)

18	Ripon	6
21	Benedictine (Ill.)	28
26	Ill. Wesleyan	31
10	North Central	14
6	Augustana (Ill.)	40
19	North Park	26
9	Carthage	33
22	Wheaton (Ill.)	16
0	Millikin	35
131		**229**

Nickname: Bluejays.
Stadium: Langhorst (1920), 2,500 capacity. Natural turf.
Colors: Blue & White.
Conference: College Conf. of Illinois & Wisconsin.
SID: Charley Henderson, 708-617-3380.
AD: Christopher Ragsdale.

ELON
Elon College, NC 27244 .... I-AA

Coach: Al Seagraves, Shippensburg 1975
Record: 4 Years, 25-19-0

2000 SCHEDULE

Furman	*Sept. 2
Delaware St. ■	*Sept. 9
Western Ky. ■	Sept. 16
N.C. A&T	*Sept. 23
New Haven ■	Sept. 30
Gardner-Webb ■	Oct. 7
Samford	Oct. 14
Hofstra	Oct. 21
Charleston So.	Oct. 28
Liberty ■	Nov. 4
Ga. Southern	Nov. 11

1999 RESULTS (9-2-0)

24	Furman	22
51	Delaware St.	28
35	North Ala.	15
40	N.C. A&T	7
20	New Haven	16
14	Western Ill.	20
34	Samford	31
9	Hofstra	21
38	Charleston So.	13
38	Liberty	14
41	Morehead St.	6
344		**193**

Nickname: Phoenix
Stadium: Burlington Memorial (1949), 10,000 capacity. Natural turf.
Colors: Maroon & Gold.
Conference: Division I-AA Independent.
SID: David Hibbard, 910-584-2316.
AD: Alan J. White.

EMORY & HENRY
Emory, VA 24327 III

Coach: Lou Wacker, Richmond 1956
Record: 18 Years, 138-51-0

2000 SCHEDULE

Ferrum	Sept. 9
Bridgewater (Va.) ■	Sept. 16
Davidson	Sept. 23
Averett ■	Sept. 30
Hampden-Sydney	Oct. 7
Randolph-Macon ■	Oct. 14
Guilford	Oct. 21
Catholic ■	Oct. 28
Wash. & Lee	Nov. 4
Maryville (Tenn.) ■	Nov. 11

1999 RESULTS (6-4-0)

17	Wash. & Jeff.	24
12	Ferrum	7
24	Bridgewater (Va.)	21
17	Davidson	13
36	Hampden-Sydney	7
23	Randolph-Macon	36
24	Guilford	7
19	Catholic	42
23	Wash. & Lee	21
10	Maryville (Tenn.)	21
205		**199**

Nickname: Wasps.
Stadium: Fullerton Field (0000), 5,500 capacity. Natural turf.
Colors: Blue & Gold.
Conference: Old Dominion Athletic.
SID: Nathan Graybeal, 540-944-6830.
AD: J. Thomas Fowlkes.

EMPORIA ST.
Emporia, KS 66801 II

Coach: Jerry Kill, Southwestern 1983
Record: 6 Years, 43-20-0

2000 SCHEDULE
Fort Hays St. ■		*Aug. 31
East Central		*Sept. 9
Central Mo. St.		*Sept. 16
Mo. Southern St. ■		*Sept. 23
Mo.-Rolla ■		Sept. 30
Southwest Baptist		Oct. 7
Pittsburg St. ■		Oct. 14
Northwest Mo. St.		Oct. 21
Truman ■		Oct. 28
Mo. Western St.		Nov. 4
Washburn		Nov. 11

1999 RESULTS (5-6-0)
31	Fort Hays St.	14
25	Central Okla.	28
41	Central Mo. St.	12
12	Mo. Southern St.	29
48	Mo.-Rolla	6
31	Southwest Baptist	0
7	Pittsburg St.	21
28	Northwest Mo. St.	59
24	Truman	31
7	Mo. Western St.	27
45	Washburn	20
299		**247**

Nickname: Hornets.
Stadium: Welch (1937), 7,000 capacity. Natural turf.
Colors: Black & Gold.
Conference: Mid-America Intercollegiate Athletic.
SID: J. D. Campbell, 316-341-5454.
AD: Kent Weiser.

EUREKA
Eureka, IL 61530 III

Coach: Darrell Crouch

2000 SCHEDULE
Monmouth (Ill.) ■		Sept. 2
Augustana (Ill.)		Sept. 9
Millikin		Sept. 16
Greenville ■		Sept. 23
Benedictine (Ill.) ■		Sept. 30
Aurora		Oct. 7
MacMurray ■		Oct. 14
Concordia (Wis.) ■		Oct. 21
Concordia (Ill.)		Oct. 28
Lakeland ■		Nov. 4

1999 RESULTS (4-6-0)
14	Ky. Wesleyan	20
42	Monmouth (Ill.)	28
17	Hanover	35
12	Benedictine (Ill.)	0
15	Aurora	18
18	Concordia (Wis.)	34
41	Greenville	13
7	Lakeland	52
7	MacMurray	13
53	Concordia (Ill.)	20
226		**233**

Nickname: Red Devils.
Stadium: McKinzie (1913), 3,000 capacity. Natural turf.
Colors: Maroon & Gold.
Conference: Illini-Badger.
SID: Mike Mason, 309-467-6370.
AD: Joe Barth.

FAIRFIELD
Fairfield, CT 06430 .... I-AA

Coach: Kevin Kiesel, Gettysburg 1981
Record: 7 Years, 41-30-1

2000 SCHEDULE
Fordham		Sept. 9
Duquesne		Sept. 16
Iona ■		Sept. 30
Siena		Oct. 7
St. Peter's ■		Oct. 14
Georgetown ■		Oct. 28
Marist		Nov. 4
Canisius ■		Nov. 11
La Salle		Nov. 18

Jacksonville [Orlando, FL] ....*Nov. 24

1999 RESULTS (9-2-0)
42	Iona	6
34	Duquesne	21
59	Canisius	20
41	Central Conn. St.	14
27	Siena	0
23	Holy Cross	24
24	St. John's (N.Y.)	16
14	Georgetown	21
57	Marist	7
42	La Salle	0
45	St. Peter's	18
408		**147**

Nickname: Stags.
Stadium: Alumni (0000), 3,000 capacity. Natural turf.
Colors: Red & White.
Conference: Metro Atlantic Athletic.
SID: Jack Jones, 203-254-4000.
AD: Eugene Doris.

FDU-MADISON
Madison, NJ 07940 III

Coach: William Klika Jr., Colgate 1967
Record: 23 Years, 64-136-1

2000 SCHEDULE
Susquehanna ■		Sept. 2
Widener		Sept. 9
Wilkes ■		*Sept. 15
Albright		*Sept. 23
Delaware Valley ■		Sept. 30
Wm. Paterson ■		Oct. 6
Moravian		Oct. 21
Juniata		Oct. 28
King's (Pa.) ■		Nov. 4
Lycoming		Nov. 11

1999 RESULTS (5-5-0)
3	Susquehanna	20
23	Widener	25
19	Wilkes	32
24	Albright	3
38	Delaware Valley	19
17	Wm. Paterson	7
13	Moravian	10
18	Juniata	45
26	King's (Pa.)	20
3	Lycoming	27
184		**208**

ECAC PLAYOFFS
36	Wilkes	27

Nickname: Devils.
Stadium: Devils (1973), 4,000 capacity. Natural turf.
Colors: Black, FDU Blue & White.
Conference: Middle Atlantic.
SID: W. Scott Giglio, 201-443-8965.
AD: William T. Klika Jr.

FAIRMONT ST.
Fairmont, WV 26554 II

Coach: Doug Sams, Oregon St. 1978
Record: 9 Years, 45-46-0

2000 SCHEDULE
Campbellsville		Sept. 2
Calif. (Pa.) ■		*Sept. 9
Slippery Rock		Sept. 16
West Va. Tech ■		Sept. 30
Glenville St.		Oct. 7
Shepherd		Oct. 14
West Liberty St. ■		Oct. 21
West Va. Wesleyan ■		Oct. 28
Concord		Nov. 4
West Virginia St. ■		Nov. 11

1999 RESULTS (8-2-0)
43	Campbellsville	7
51	Calif. (Pa.)	49
10	Slippery Rock	34
37	West Va. Tech	24
49	Glenville St.	19
7	Shepherd	42
29	West Liberty St.	19
55	West Va. Wesleyan	26
34	Concord	13
31	West Virginia St.	20
346		**253**

Nickname: Falcons.
Stadium: Rosier Field (1929), 6,000 capacity. Natural turf.
Colors: Maroon & White.
Conference: West Virginia Intercollegiate Athletic.
SID: Jim Brinkman, 304-367-4264.
AD: David W. Cooper.

FAYETTEVILLE ST.
Fayetteville, NC 28301 II

Coach: Kenny Phillips, N.C. A&T
(First year as head coach)

2000 SCHEDULE
Benedict [Columbia, SC]		Aug. 26
Elizabeth City St. [Rocky Mount, NC]		Sept. 9
Delaware St.		Sept. 16
Livingstone ■		*Sept. 23
Winston-Salem ■		*Sept. 30
N.C. Central ■		*Oct. 7
Virginia St. ■		*Oct. 14
Johnson Smith		Oct. 21
Bowie St. ■		Oct. 28
Virginia Union		Nov. 4

1999 RESULTS (1-10-0)
14	Benedict	34
0	Ga. Southern	76
13	Elizabeth City St.	6
14	Liberty	48
7	N.C. Central	32
7	Virginia St.	50
0	Winston-Salem	44
20	Johnson Smith	31
21	Bowie St.	40
14	Virginia Union	49
7	Livingstone	34
117		**444**

Nickname: Broncos.
Stadium: Jeralds Ath. Complex (1993), 6,100 capacity. Natural turf.
Colors: White & Royal Blue.
Conference: Central Intercollegiate Athletic Association.
SID: Marion Crowe Jr., 910-486-1349.
AD: Horace T. Small.

FERRIS ST.
Big Rapids, MI 49307 II

Coach: Jeff Pierce, Ferris St. 1979
Record: 5 Years, 37-19-0

2000 SCHEDULE
Indiana (Pa.)		*Sept. 2
Findlay		*Sept. 9
Saginaw Valley ■		*Sept. 16
Wayne St. (Mich.) ■		Sept. 23
Northwood		Sept. 30
Grand Valley St.		Oct. 7
Mercyhurst		Oct. 14
Michigan Tech		Oct. 21
Northern Mich. ■		Oct. 28
Hillsdale ■		Nov. 4
Indianapolis		Nov. 11

1999 RESULTS (7-3-0)
35	North Dakota St.	55
56	Saginaw Valley	14
56	Findlay	14
46	Northwood	36
45	Northern Mich.	27
62	Wayne St. (Mich.)	20
22	Ashland	26
66	Michigan Tech	7
37	Hillsdale	40
48	Grand Valley St.	23
473		**262**

Nickname: Bulldogs.

Stadium: Top Taggart Field (1957), 9,100 capacity. Artificial turf.
Colors: Crimson & Gold.
Conference: Great Lakes Intercollegiate Athletic.
SID: Joe Gorby, 616-592-2336.
AD: Tom Kirinovic.

FERRUM
Ferrum, VA 24088...III

Coach: Dave Davis, Elon 1971
Record: 6 Years, 27-31-0

2000 SCHEDULE
Averett ■	Sept. 2
Emory & Henry ■	Sept. 9
Greensboro ■	Sept. 16
Shenandoah	Sept. 23
Methodist	Sept. 30
Chowan ■	Oct. 14
Frostburg St. ■	Oct. 21
Guilford	Oct. 28
Salisbury St. ■	Nov. 4
Wesley	Nov. 11

1999 RESULTS (6-4-0)
22	Apprentice	0
7	Emory & Henry	12
7	Greensboro	13
7	Bridgewater (Va.)	14
14	Methodist	16
17	Guilford	14
17	Chowan	7
20	Frostburg St.	17
37	Salisbury St.	3
9	Wesley	7
157		103

Nickname: Panthers.
Stadium: Adams (1970), 5,500 capacity. Natural turf.
Colors: Black & Gold.
Conference: Atlantic Central Football.
SID: Gary Holden, 540-365-4306.
AD: T. Michael Kinder.

FINDLAY
Findlay, OH 45840....................................II

Coach: Dan Simrell, Toledo 1966
Record: 8 Years, 50-37-2

2000 SCHEDULE
Ferris St. ■	*Sept. 9
Ashland	*Sept. 16
Hillsdale ■	*Sept. 23
Wayne St. (Mich.)	Sept. 30
Indianapolis ■	Oct. 7
Northern Mich. ■	*Oct. 14
Northwood	Oct. 21
Saginaw Valley	Oct. 28
Mercyhurst ■	Nov. 4
Michigan Tech	Nov. 11

1999 RESULTS (2-8-0)
39	Wayne St. (Mich.)	15
14	Ferris St.	56
9	Grand Valley St.	37
14	Indianapolis	7
7	Northern Mich.	32
14	Hillsdale	17
19	Westminster (Pa.)	22
14	Northwood	33
14	Mercyhurst	28
14	Ashland	46
158		293

Nickname: Oilers.
Stadium: Donnell (0000), 7,500 capacity. Natural turf.
Colors: Orange & Black.
Conference: Great Lakes Intercollegiate Athletic.
SID: Dave Faiella, 419-424-4727.
AD: Steven Rackley.

FITCHBURG ST.
Fitchburg, MA 01420..III

Coach: Dave Flynn, Union (N.Y.) 1993
Record: 2 Years, 9-11-0

2000 SCHEDULE
Mass.-Boston	Sept. 9
Westfield St.	Sept. 16
Worcester St. ■	Sept. 23
Mass. Maritime ■	Sept. 30
Framingham St.	Oct. 7
Maine Maritime	Oct. 14
Curry ■	Oct. 21
Bri'water (Mass.) ■	Oct. 28
Western New Eng.	Nov. 4

1999 RESULTS (6-4-0)
41	Mass.-Boston	8
9	Nichols	21
34	Westfield St.	20
25	Worcester St.	16
23	Mass. Maritime	44
21	Framingham St.	13
26	Maine Maritime	20
21	Curry	28
14	Bri'water (Mass.)	42
43	Western New Eng.	28
257		240

Nickname: Falcons.
Stadium: Robert Elliot (1984), 1,200 capacity. Natural turf.
Colors: Green, Gold & White.
Conference: New England Football.
SID: Jonathan Harper, 508-665-3343.
AD: Sue E. Lauder.

FLORIDA
Gainesville, FL 32611..I-A

Coach: Steve Spurrier, Florida 1967
Record: 13 Years, 122-35-2

2000 SCHEDULE
Ball St. ■	*Sept. 2
Middle Tenn. St. ■	*Sept. 9
Tennessee	Sept. 16
Kentucky ■	Sept. 23
Mississippi St.	Sept. 30
LSU ■	Oct. 7
Auburn ■	Oct. 14
Georgia [Jacksonville, FL]	Oct. 28
Vanderbilt	Nov. 4
South Carolina ■	Nov. 11
Florida St.	Nov. 18

1999 RESULTS (9-3-0)
55	Western Mich.	26
58	UCF	27
23	Tennessee	21
38	Kentucky	10
39	Alabama	40
31	LSU	10
32	Auburn	14
30	Georgia	14
13	Vanderbilt	6
20	South Carolina	3
23	Florida St.	30
7	Alabama	34
369		235

FLORIDA CITRUS BOWL
34	Syracuse	37

Nickname: Gators.
Stadium: Florida Field (1929), 83,000 capacity. Natural turf.
Colors: Orange & Blue.
Conference: Southeastern.
SID: John Humenik, 352-375-4683.
AD: Jeremy Foley.

FLORIDA A&M
Tallahassee, FL 32307.....................................I-AA

Coach: Billy Joe, Villanova 1963
26 Years, 205-82-4

2000 SCHEDULE
Delaware St.	Sept. 2
Morgan St. ■	*Sept. 9
South Carolina St. [Jacksonville, FL]	Sept. 16
Tennessee St. [Atlanta, GA]	Sept. 23
Howard ■	*Sept. 30
Grambling [Indianapolis, IN]	Oct. 7
N.C. A&T ■	Oct. 14
Norfolk St.	Oct. 21
Hampton	Oct. 28
Southern U.	*Nov. 4
Bethune-Cookman [Orlando, FL]	Nov. 18

1999 RESULTS (8-3-0)
3	Miami (Fla.)	57
56	Norfolk St.	7
25	Tennessee St.	42
76	South Carolina St.	17
66	Morgan St.	10
40	Howard	34
41	Hampton	6
48	Delaware St.	19
65	Southern U.	18
15	N.C. A&T	30
63	Bethune-Cookman	14
498		254

DIVISION I-AA CHAMPIONSHIP
44	Appalachian St.	29
17	Troy St.	10
24	Youngstown St.	27

Nickname: Rattlers.
Stadium: Bragg Memorial (1957), 25,500 capacity. Natural turf.
Colors: Orange & Green.
Conference: Mid-Eastern Athletic.
SID: Alvin Hollins, 904-599-3200.
AD: Kenneth Riley.

FLORIDA ST.
Tallahassee, FL 32306..............................I-A

Coach: Bobby Bowden, Samford 1953
Record: 34 Years, 304-85-4

2000 SCHEDULE
Brigham Young [Jacksonville, FL]	*Aug. 26
Georgia Tech	*Sept. 9
North Carolina ■	Sept. 16
Louisville ■	*Sept. 23
Maryland	*Sept. 28
Miami (Fla.)	Oct. 7
Duke ■	*Oct. 14
Virginia	Oct. 21
North Carolina St.	*Oct. 28
Clemson ■	*Nov. 4
Wake Forest	Nov. 11
Florida ■	Nov. 18

1999 RESULTS (11-0-0)
41	Louisiana Tech	7
41	Georgia Tech	35
42	North Carolina St.	11
42	North Carolina	10
51	Duke	23
31	Miami (Fla.)	21
33	Wake Forest	10
17	Clemson	14
35	Virginia	10
49	Maryland	10
30	Florida	23
412		174

SUGAR BOWL
46	Virginia Tech	29

Nickname: Seminoles.
Stadium: Doak S. Campbell (1950), 80,000 capacity. Natural turf.
Colors: Garnet & Gold.
Conference: Atlantic Coast.
SID: Rob Wilson, 904-644-1403.
AD: David R. Hart Jr.

FORDHAM
Bronx, NY 10458....................................I-AA

Coach: Dave Clawson, Williams 1989
Record: 1 Year, 0-11-0

2000 SCHEDULE
Towson ■	Sept. 2
Fairfield ■	Sept. 9
Columbia	*Sept. 16
Colgate	Sept. 23

Georgetown...Sept. 30
Brown ■..Oct. 7
Yale ■...Oct. 14
Bucknell...Oct. 28
Lafayette ■..Nov. 4
Lehigh...Nov. 11
Holy Cross...Nov. 18

1999 RESULTS (0-11-0)
7	Lehigh	49
24	Colgate	49
14	Cornell	42
0	Princeton	27
18	Pennsylvania	35
30	Harvard	37
23	Towson	25
18	Brown	37
7	Lafayette	27
14	Holy Cross	37
15	Bucknell	45
170		**410**

Nickname: Rams.
Stadium: Jack Coffey Field (1930), 7,000 capacity. Natural turf.
Colors: Maroon & White.
Conference: Pioneer Football.
SID: Joe DiBari, 718-817-4240.
AD: Francis X. Mc Laughlin.

FORT HAYS ST.
Hays, KS 67601 II

Coach: Jeff Leiker, Washburn 1985
Record: 2 Years, 8-14-0

2000 SCHEDULE
Emporia St. ....*Aug. 31
Mo. Western St. ■ ....*Sept. 9
Adams St. ....Sept. 16
Colorado Mines ....Sept. 23
Fort Lewis ■ ....Sept. 30
Mesa St. ■ ....Oct. 14
Neb.-Kearney ....*Oct. 21
Western St. (Colo.) ....Oct. 28
N.M. Highlands ■ ....Nov. 4
Chadron St. ■ ....Nov. 11

1999 RESULTS (2-9-0)
14	Emporia St.	31
14	Washburn	17
54	Colorado Mines	15
6	Fort Lewis	26
7	Northwestern Okla.	35
14	Mesa St.	26
12	Neb.-Kearney	13
23	Western St. (Colo.)	3
19	N.M. Highlands	45
3	Chadron St.	31
13	Adams St.	31
179		**273**

Nickname: Tigers.
Stadium: Lewis Field (1936), 6,362 capacity. Artificial turf.
Colors: Black & Gold.
Conference: Rocky Mountain Athletic.
SID: Jack Kuestermeyer, 913-628-5903.
AD: Thomas E. Spicer.

FORT LEWIS
Durango, CO 81301 II

Coach: Todd Throckmorton, Mo. Western St. 1987
(First year as head coach)

2000 SCHEDULE
Carroll (Mont.) ■ ....*Aug. 26
Southern Utah ....*Sept. 2
Western St. (Colo.) ■ ....Sept. 16
Chadron St. ....Sept. 23
Fort Hays St. ....Sept. 30
Colorado Mines ■ ....Oct. 7
Neb.-Kearney ■ ....Oct. 14
Western N.M. ....Oct. 21
N.M. Highlands ....Oct. 28
Mesa St. ....Nov. 4
Adams St. ■ ....Nov. 11

1999 RESULTS (2-9-0)
20	Western N.M.	27
7	Southern Utah	50
3	Idaho St.	42
7	Chadron St.	24
26	Fort Hays St.	6
33	Colorado Mines	0
13	Neb.-Kearney	79
10	N.M. Highlands	31
19	Mesa St.	21
25	Adams St.	28
10	Western St. (Colo.)	35
173		**343**

Nickname: Skyhawks.
Stadium: Ray Dennison Memorial (1958), 4,000 capacity. Natural turf.
Colors: Navy & Gold.
Conference: Rocky Mountain Athletic.
SID: Chris Aaland, 970-247-7441.
AD: Joel R. Smith Jr.

FORT VALLEY ST.
Fort Valley, GA 31030 II

Coach: Kent Schoolfield, Florida A&M 1970
Record: 3 Years, 26-10-0

2000 SCHEDULE
Morehouse ■ ....*Aug. 26
Valdosta St. ....*Sept. 2
Lane ....*Sept. 9
Alcorn St. ....*Sept. 16
Kentucky St. ■ ....*Sept. 23
Benedict ■ ....*Sept. 30
Miles ....Oct. 7
Clark Atlanta [Griffin, GA] ....*Oct. 14
Tuskegee ....Oct. 21
Savannah St. ....Oct. 28
Albany St. (Ga.) [Columbus, GA] ....Nov. 11

1999 RESULTS (10-1-0)
14	Morehouse	6
24	Valdosta St.	13
44	Lane	17
28	Morris Brown	21
27	Kentucky St.	20
17	Miles	7
34	Clark Atlanta	7
31	Tuskegee	28
35	Savannah St.	25
24	Benedict	17
21	Albany St. (Ga.)	24
299		**185**

DIVISION II CHAMPIONSHIP
17	Catawba	48

Nickname: Wildcats.
Stadium: Wildcat (1957), 7,500 capacity. Natural turf.
Colors: Old Gold & Blue.
Conference: Southern Intercollegiate Athletic.
SID: Russell Boone Jr., 912-825-6437.
AD: Edmond Wyche.

FRAMINGHAM ST.
Framingham, MA 01701 III

Coach: Michael Strachan, Swedish Sports 1990
Record: 6 Years, 10-46-1

2000 SCHEDULE
Mass.-Boston ■ ....Sept. 2
Assumption ■ ....Sept. 9
Curry ■ ....Sept. 16
Bri'water (Mass.) ....Sept. 23
Westfield St. ....Sept. 30
Fitchburg St. ■ ....Oct. 7
Worcester St. ....Oct. 14
Western New Eng. ■ ....Oct. 21
Mass. Maritime ....Oct. 28
Maine Maritime ■ ....Nov. 4

1999 RESULTS (2-8-0)
12	MIT	20
20	Mass.-Boston	6
20	Curry	16
12	Bri'water (Mass.)	49
13	Westfield St.	31
13	Fitchburg St.	21
26	Worcester St.	27
14	Western New Eng.	20
20	Mass. Maritime	22
27	Maine Maritime	46
177		**258**

Nickname: Rams.
Stadium: Maple Street Field (N/A), 1,500 capacity. Natural turf.
Colors: Black & Gold.
Conference: New England Football.
SID: David Rourke, 508-626-4612.
AD: Thomas M. Kelley.

FRANKLIN
Franklin, IN 46131 III

Coach: Bill Unsworth, Franklin 1971
Record: 10 Years, 35-61-1

2000 SCHEDULE
Wis.-Stout ■ ....Sept. 9
North Central ■ ....Sept. 16
Alma ....Sept. 23
Manchester ■ ....Sept. 30
Anderson (Ind.) ....Oct. 7
Thomas More ....Oct. 14
Defiance ....Oct. 21
Bluffton ■ ....Oct. 28
Mt. St. Joseph ....Nov. 4
Hanover ....Nov. 11

1999 RESULTS (4-6-0)
48	Earlham	7
45	Blackburn	18
38	Alma	46
22	Manchester	6
6	Wilmington (Ohio)	55
29	Mt. St. Joseph	46
34	Anderson (Ind.)	6
21	Wabash	31
7	Bluffton	28
10	Hanover	27
260		**270**

Nickname: Grizzlies.
Stadium: Faught (1998), 2,000 capacity. Natural turf.
Colors: Navy Blue & Old Gold.
Conference: Heartland Collegiate Athletic.
SID: Kevin Elixman, 317-738-8184.
AD: Kerry N. Prather.

FRANK. & MARSH.
Lancaster, PA 17604 III

Coach: Tom Gilburg, Syracuse 1961
Record: 25 Years, 155-87-2

2000 SCHEDULE
Catholic ■ ....Sept. 9
Ursinus ■ ....Sept. 16
Muhlenberg ....Sept. 23
Carnegie Mellon ■ ....Sept. 30
Dickinson ....Oct. 7
Hobart ■ ....Oct. 14
Western Md. ■ ....Oct. 21
Swarthmore ....Oct. 28
Johns Hopkins ■ ....Nov. 4
Gettysburg ....Nov. 11

1999 RESULTS (2-8-0)
12	Catholic	46
20	Ursinus	27
13	Muhlenberg	42
0	Union (N.Y.)	17
26	Dickinson	31
7	Hobart	35
0	Western Md.	19
17	Swarthmore	15
33	Johns Hopkins	35
22	Gettysburg	12
150		**279**

Nickname: Diplomats.
Stadium: Sponaugle-Williamson (1920), 4,000 capacity. Natural turf.

Colors: Blue & White.
Conference: Centennial.
SID: To be named, 717-291-3838.
AD: Robert D. Bunnell.

FRESNO ST.
Fresno, CA 93740 ....I-A

Coach: Pat Hill, UC Riverside 1973
Record: 3 Years, 19-17-0

2000 SCHEDULE
Ohio St.	Sept. 2
UCLA	Sept. 9
California ■	Sept. 23
Rice	*Oct. 5
Nevada ■	Oct. 14
UTEP	*Oct. 21
Tulsa ■	*Oct. 28
Hawaii ■	Nov. 4
TCU	Nov. 11
Southern Methodist ■	Nov. 18
San Jose St.	Nov. 25

1999 RESULTS (8-4-0)
34	Portland St.	6
23	Oregon St.	46
21	UCLA	35
49	Nevada	24
26	TCU	19
44	Colorado St.	13
14	Southern Methodist	24
24	UTEP	23
28	Tulsa	14
47	Rice	18
24	Hawaii	31
63	San Jose St.	12
397		265

LAS VEGAS BOWL
16	Utah	17

Nickname: Bulldogs.
Stadium: Bulldog (1980), 41,031 capacity. Natural turf.
Colors: Bulldog Red & Blue.
Conference: Western Athletic.
SID: Steve Weakland, 209-278-2509.
AD: Allen R. Bohl.

FROSTBURG ST.
Frostburg, MD 21532 III

Coach: Rubin Stevenson
(First year as head coach)

2000 SCHEDULE
Central Conn. St.	Sept. 9
Allegheny	Sept. 16
Methodist ■	Sept. 23
Chowan	Sept. 30
Wesley ■	Oct. 7
Brockport St. ■	Oct. 14
Ferrum	Oct. 21
New Jersey City ■	Oct. 28
Greensboro	Nov. 4
Salisbury St. [Washington, DC]	Nov. 11

1999 RESULTS (8-2-0)
22	Central Conn. St.	16
38	West Va. Tech	21
24	Methodist	10
30	Chowan	25
42	Wesley	17
35	Brockport St.	18
17	Ferrum	20
31	Ky. Wesleyan	43
32	Greensboro	7
23	Salisbury St.	22
294		199

ECAC PLAYOFF
10	Carnegie Mellon	28

Nickname: Bobcats.
Stadium: Bobcat (1974), 4,000 capacity. Natural turf.
Colors: Red, White & Black.
Conference: Atlantic Central Football.
SID: To be named, 301-687-4371.
AD: Diane M. Morea.

FURMAN
Greenville, SC 29613 ....I-AA

Coach: Bobby Johnson, Clemson 1973
Record: 6 Years, 39-30-0

2000 SCHEDULE
Elon ■	*Sept. 2
Newberry ■	*Sept. 9
William & Mary ■	*Sept. 16
VMI	Sept. 23
Western Caro. ■	Sept. 30
Appalachian St.	Oct. 7
Citadel ■	Oct. 14
East Tenn. St.	*Oct. 21
Ga. Southern ■	Nov. 4
Wofford	Nov. 11
Chattanooga ■	Nov. 18

1999 RESULTS (9-2-0)
22	Elon	24
52	William & Mary	6
58	VMI	0
27	Western Caro.	19
35	Appalachian St.	21
31	Citadel	17
48	East Tenn. St.	21
28	North Carolina	3
38	Ga. Southern	41
30	Wofford	3
40	Chattanooga	35
409		190

DIVISION I-AA CHAMPIONSHIP
23	Massachusetts	30

Nickname: Paladins.
Stadium: Paladin (1981), 16,000 capacity. Natural turf.
Colors: Purple & White.
Conference: Southern.
SID: Hunter Reid, 864-294-2061.
AD: John M. Block.

GANNON
Erie, PA 16541 II

Coach: Bill Elias, Massachusetts 1977
Record: 1 Year, 1-9-0

2000 SCHEDULE
Bentley	*Sept. 1
Tiffin	Sept. 9
West Va. Tech ■	Sept. 16
Canisius ■	Sept. 23
Ky. Wesleyan ■	Sept. 30
Alma	Oct. 7
Walsh ■	Oct. 14
Westminster (Pa.)	Oct. 28
Merrimack ■	Nov. 4
Carnegie Mellon	Nov. 11

1999 RESULTS (1-9-0)
14	Bentley	30
0	Southern Conn. St.	27
43	Waynesburg	50
21	Pace	43
7	Ky. Wesleyan	34
7	Hillsdale	41
0	Northwood	49
21	St. Francis (Ill.)	17
0	Westminster (Pa.)	52
20	Merrimack	31
133		374

Nickname: Golden Knights.
Stadium: Erie Veterans Mem. (1958), 10,500 capacity. Artificial turf.
Colors: Maroon & Gold.
Conference: Division II Independent.
SID: Dan Teliski, 814-871-7418.
AD: Mike Corbett.

GARDNER-WEBB
Boiling Springs, NC 28017 II

Coach: Steve Patton, Furman 1977
Record: 8 Years, 51-35-1

2000 SCHEDULE
Morris Brown	*Sept. 2
Concord ■	*Sept. 9
Liberty	*Sept. 16
Mars Hill ■	Sept. 23
Northwestern St.	*Sept. 30
Elon	Oct. 7
Virginia Union ■	Oct. 14
Samford	Oct. 21
New Hampshire	Nov. 11
Savannah St. ■	Nov. 18

1999 RESULTS (7-4-0)
51	Johnson Smith	0
16	N.C. Central	0
48	North Greenville	0
31	Newberry	34
35	Wingate	25
27	Lenoir-Rhyne	14
7	Catawba	34
6	Carson-Newman	28
24	Tusculum	21
31	Presbyterian	20
14	Mars Hill	20
290		196

Nickname: Runnin' Bulldogs.
Stadium: Spangler (1969), 5,000 capacity. Natural turf.
Colors: Scarlet, White & Black.
Conference: South Atlantic.
SID: Marc Rabb, 704-434-4355.
AD: Chuck Burch.

GEORGETOWN
Washington, DC 20057 ....I-AA

Coach: Bob Benson, Vermont 1986
Record: 7 Years, 48-22-0

2000 SCHEDULE
Holy Cross ■	Sept. 9
Wagner	Sept. 16
Butler	Sept. 23
Fordham ■	Sept. 30
Bucknell ■	Oct. 7
Duquesne	Oct. 14
Marist	Oct. 21
Fairfield	Oct. 28
Iona ■	Nov. 4
St. Peter's ■	Nov. 11
Davidson	Nov. 18

1999 RESULTS (9-2-0)
34	Holy Cross	16
47	Siena	12
30	St. John's (N.Y.)	7
28	Iona	0
41	Marist	40
27	Davidson	28
14	St. Peter's	3
21	Fairfield	14
21	Duquesne	33
49	Canisius	6
52	La Salle	7
364		166

Nickname: Hoyas.
Stadium: Kehoe Field (1979), 2,400 capacity. Artificial turf.
Colors: Blue & Gray.
Conference: Metro Atlantic Athletic.
SID: Mike Tuberosa, 202-687-2492.
AD: Joseph C. Lang.

GEORGIA
Athens, GA 30602 ....I-A

Coach: Jim Donnan, North Carolina St. 1968
Record: 10 Years, 96-36-0

2000 SCHEDULE
Ga. Southern ■	*Sept. 2
South Carolina	*Sept. 9
New Mexico St. ■	Sept. 23
Arkansas	*Sept. 30
Tennessee ■	Oct. 7
Vanderbilt ■	Oct. 14
Kentucky	*Oct. 21

Florida [Jacksonville, FL] .... Oct. 28
Auburn .... Nov. 11
Mississippi ■ .... Nov. 18
Georgia Tech ■ .... Nov. 25

1999 RESULTS (7-4-0)
38	Utah St.	7
24	South Carolina	9
24	UCF	23
23	LSU	22
20	Tennessee	37
27	Vanderbilt	17
49	Kentucky	34
14	Florida	30
21	Auburn	38
20	Mississippi	17
48	Georgia Tech	51
308		285

OUTBACK BOWL
28	Purdue	25

Nickname: Bulldogs.
Stadium: Sanford (1929), 86,117 capacity. Natural turf.
Colors: Red & Black.
Conference: Southeastern.
SID: Claude Felton, 706-542-1621.
AD: Vincent J. Dooley.

GA. SOUTHERN
Statesboro, GA 30460 .... I-AA

Coach: Paul Johnson, Western Caro. 1979
Record: 3 Years, 37-6-0

2000 SCHEDULE
Georgia .... *Sept. 2
Johnson Smith ■ .... *Sept. 9
Wofford ■ .... Sept. 16
Chattanooga .... *Sept. 23
VMI ■ .... Sept. 30
Western Caro. .... *Oct. 7
Appalachian St. ■ .... Oct. 14
Citadel .... Oct. 21
East Tenn. St. ■ .... Oct. 28
Furman .... Nov. 4
Elon ■ .... Nov. 11

1999 RESULTS (9-2-0)
76	Fayetteville St.	0
55	Wofford	14
41	Oregon St.	48
49	Chattanooga	10
62	VMI	0
70	Western Caro.	7
16	Appalachian St.	17
34	Citadel	17
55	East Tenn. St.	6
41	Furman	38
51	Jacksonville St.	14
550		171

I-AA CHAMPIONSHIP
72	Northern Ariz.	29
38	Massachusetts	21
28	Illinois St.	17
59	Youngstown St.	24

Nickname: Eagles.
Stadium: Paulson (1984), 18,000 capacity. Natural turf.
Colors: Blue & White.
Conference: Southern.
SID: Tom McClellan, 912-681-5239.
AD: Samuel Q. Baker.

GEORGIA TECH
Atlanta, GA 30332 .... I-A

Coach: George O'Leary, New Hampshire 1968
Record: 6 Years, 36-25-0

2000 SCHEDULE
Virginia Tech .... *Aug. 27
UCF ■ .... *Sept. 2
Florida St. ■ .... *Sept. 9
Navy ■ .... Sept. 16
North Carolina St. .... *Sept. 21
North Carolina .... Sept. 30
Wake Forest ■ .... Oct. 14

Duke ■ .... Oct. 21
Clemson .... Oct. 28
Virginia ■ .... *Nov. 9
Maryland .... Nov. 18
Georgia .... Nov. 25

1999 RESULTS (8-3-0)
49	Navy	14
35	Florida St.	41
41	UCF	10
49	Maryland	31
31	North Carolina	24
38	Duke	31
48	North Carolina St.	21
38	Virginia	45
45	Clemson	42
23	Wake Forest	26
51	Georgia	48
448		333

GATOR BOWL
13	Miami (Fla.)	28

Nickname: Yellow Jackets.
Stadium: Bobby Dodd/Grant Field (1913), 46,000 capacity. Natural turf.
Colors: Old Gold & White.
Conference: Atlantic Coast.
SID: Mike Stamus, 404-894-5445.
AD: David T. Braine.

GETTYSBURG
Gettysburg, PA 17325 III

Coach: Barry Streeter, Lebanon Valley 1971
Record: 22 Years, 118-100-5

2000 SCHEDULE
Randolph-Macon .... Sept. 2
Hampden-Sydney ■ .... Sept. 9
Western Md. .... Sept. 16
Swarthmore .... Sept. 23
Johns Hopkins .... *Sept. 29
Ursinus ■ .... Oct. 14
Muhlenberg .... Oct. 21
St. Lawrence ■ .... Oct. 28
Dickinson .... Nov. 4
Frank. & Marsh. ■ .... Nov. 11

1999 RESULTS (3-7-0)
20	Randolph-Macon	54
14	Hampden-Sydney	28
0	Western Md.	44
55	Swarthmore	8
13	Johns Hopkins	37
35	Ursinus	55
42	Muhlenberg	28
59	St. Lawrence	28
14	Dickinson	35
12	Frank. & Marsh.	22
264		339

Nickname: Bullets.
Stadium: Musselman (1965), 6,176 capacity. Natural turf.
Colors: Orange & Blue.
Conference: Centennial.
SID: Matt Daskivich, 717-337-6527.
AD: Charles W. Winters.

GLENVILLE ST.
Glenville, WV 26351 II

Coach: Paul Shaffner, Ithaca 1982
(First year as head coach)

2000 SCHEDULE
Eastern Ky. .... *Aug. 31
Cheyney ■ .... Sept. 9
East Stroudsburg ■ .... Sept. 16
St. Joseph's (Ind.) .... Sept. 23
West Va. Wesleyan .... Sept. 30
Fairmont St. ■ .... Oct. 7
Concord .... Oct. 14
West Va. Tech ■ .... Oct. 21
Shepherd .... Oct. 28
West Virginia St. ■ .... Nov. 4
West Liberty St. .... Nov. 11

1999 RESULTS (5-6-0)
35	Calif. (Pa.)	28
20	Edinboro	29
7	St. Joseph's (Ind.)	3
34	East Stroudsburg	38
17	West Va. Wesleyan	7
19	Fairmont St.	49
6	Concord	7
46	West Va. Tech	17
17	Shepherd	22
24	West Virginia St.	32
44	West Liberty St.	34
269		266

Nickname: Pioneers.
Stadium: Pioneer (1977), 5,000 capacity. Natural turf.
Colors: Royal Blue & White.
Conference: West Virginia Intercollegiate Athletic.
SID: Aaron Rose, 304-462-4102.
AD: Steven Harold.

GRAMBLING
Grambling, LA 71245 .... I-AA

Coach: Doug Williams, Grambling 1978
Record: 3 Years, 15-18-0

2000 SCHEDULE
Alcorn St. ■ .... *Sept. 2
Louisville .... *Sept. 9
Alabama A&M .... *Sept. 16
Mississippi Val. .... *Sept. 23
Prairie View [Dallas, TX] .... *Sept. 30
Florida A&M [Indianapolis, IN] .... Oct. 7
Ark.-Pine Bluff [Shreveport, LA] .... Oct. 14
Jackson St. ■ .... Oct. 21
Texas Southern .... *Oct. 28
Alabama St. ■ .... Nov. 4
Southern U. [New Orleans, LA] .... *Nov. 25

1999 RESULTS (7-4-0)
41	Alcorn St.	25
36	Alabama A&M	31
6	Jackson St.	31
7	Hampton	27
47	Prairie View	19
42	Mississippi Val.	19
24	Ark.-Pine Bluff	19
20	Texas Southern	21
36	Alabama St.	13
25	Winston-Salem	23
31	Southern U.	37
315		265

Nickname: Tigers.
Stadium: Robinson (1983), 19,600 capacity. Natural turf.
Colors: Black & Gold.
Conference: Southwestern Athletic.
SID: Stanley O. Lewis, 318-274-2479.
AD: Albert Dennis.

GRAND VALLEY ST.
Allendale, MI 49401 II

Coach: Brian Kelly, Assumption 1983
Record: 9 Years, 70-29-2

2000 SCHEDULE
South Dakota St. .... Sept. 2
Saginaw Valley .... Sept. 9
Northwood ■ .... *Sept. 16
Ashland .... Sept. 23
Northern Mich. .... Sept. 30
Ferris St. ■ .... Oct. 7
Indianapolis ■ .... Oct. 14
Mercyhurst .... Oct. 21
Michigan Tech ■ .... Oct. 28
Wayne St. (Mich.) .... Nov. 4
Hillsdale .... *Nov. 11

1999 RESULTS (5-5-0)
20	South Dakota St.	35
30	Northwood	41
14	Indianapolis	30
37	Findlay	9
26	Mercyhurst	19
31	Saginaw Valley	7

13	Northern Mich.	51
44	Ashland	26
21	Michigan Tech	7
23	Ferris St.	48
259		**273**

Nickname: Lakers.
Stadium: Arend D. Lubbers (1979), 4,146 capacity. Natural turf.
Colors: Blue, Black & White.
Conference: Great Lakes Intercollegiate Athletic.
SID: Tim Nott, 616-895-3275.
AD: Tim W. Selgo.

GREENSBORO
Greensboro, NC 27401 III

Coach: Marion Kirby, Lenoir-Rhyne 1964
Record: 3 Years, 6-22-0

2000 SCHEDULE
Chowan ■ ....*Sept. 9
Ferrum ....Sept. 16
Salisbury St. ....Sept. 23
Wesley ■ ....Sept. 30
Shenandoah ■ ....Oct. 7
Averett ....Oct. 14
Apprentice ....Oct. 21
Methodist ■ ....*Oct. 28
Frostburg St. ■ ....Nov. 4
Guilford ....Nov. 11

1999 RESULTS (3-6-0)
13	Ferrum	7
28	Chowan	35
42	Salisbury St.	13
21	Wesley	35
41	Jacksonville	48
35	Apprentice	16
29	Methodist	32
7	Frostburg St.	32
14	Guilford	15
230		**233**

Nickname: The Pride.
Stadium: Jamieson (NA), 10,000 capacity. Natural turf.
Colors: Green & White.
Conference: Atlantic Central Football.
SID: Bob Lowe, 336-272-7102.
AD: Kim A. Strable.

GREENVILLE
Greenville, IL 62246 III

Coach: Rob Harley
Record: 2 Years, 7-13-0

2000 SCHEDULE
Maranatha Baptist ....Sept. 9
Westminster (Mo.) ■ ....Sept. 16
Eureka ....Sept. 23
MacMurray ■ ....*Sept. 30
Concordia (Wis.) ....Oct. 7
Concordia (Ill.) ■ ....Oct. 14
Lakeland ....Oct. 21
Aurora ■ ....Oct. 28
Benedictine (Ill.) ....Nov. 4
Blackburn ....Nov. 11

1999 RESULTS (5-5-0)
60	MacMurray	53
40	Maranatha Baptist	21
27	Westminster (Mo.)	55
33	Lakeland	53
46	Blackburn	44
13	Eureka	41
14	Benedictine (Ill.)	30
14	Aurora	59
40	Concordia (Wis.)	31
42	Concordia (Ill.)	35
329		**422**

Nickname: Panthers.
Stadium: Francis Field (NA), 2,000 capacity.
Colors: Orange & Black.
Conference: Illini-Badger.
SID: Sharon Alger, 618-664-1840.
AD: Doug Faulkner.

GRINNELL
Grinnell, IA 50112 III

Coach: Greg Wallace, Mo. Valley 1970
Record: 12 Years, 41-68-1

2000 SCHEDULE
Claremont-M-S ■ ....Sept. 9
Beloit ....Sept. 16
Lake Forest ....Sept. 23
Carroll (Wis.) ■ ....Sept. 30
Illinois Col. ....Oct. 7
Ripon ....Oct. 14
St. Norbert ....Oct. 21
Knox ■ ....Oct. 28
Monmouth (Ill.) ....Nov. 4
Lawrence ....Nov. 11

1999 RESULTS (7-3-0)
29	Claremont-M-S	35
28	Beloit	20
24	Lake Forest	21
17	Carroll (Wis.)	14
53	Illinois Col.	35
20	Ripon	63
40	St. Norbert	43
48	Knox	25
29	Monmouth (Ill.)	28
51	Lawrence	14
339		**298**

Nickname: Pioneers.
Stadium: Rosenbloom (1911), 1,750 capacity. Natural turf.
Colors: Scarlet & Black.
Conference: Midwest Collegiate Athletic.
SID: Andy Hamilton, 515-269-3832.
AD: Diane Fairchild.

GROVE CITY
Grove City, PA 16127 III

Coach: Chris Smith, Grove City 1972
Record: 16 Years, 63-85-2

2000 SCHEDULE
Dickinson ....Sept. 2
Kenyon ■ ....Sept. 9
Wooster ....Sept. 16
Thiel ■ ....Sept. 30
Wash. & Jeff. ....Oct. 7
Waynesburg ....Oct. 14
Westminster (Pa.) ■ ....Oct. 21
Bethany (W.Va.) ....Oct. 28
Carnegie Mellon ■ ....Nov. 4
Alfred ■ ....Nov. 11

1999 RESULTS (6-4-0)
28	Wooster	31
9	Ohio Wesleyan	14
22	Bluffton	30
24	Bethany (W.Va.)	3
56	Thiel	0
10	Wash. & Jeff.	33
28	Waynesburg	24
45	Kenyon	26
28	Alfred	14
31	Muhlenberg	24
281		**199**

Nickname: Wolverines.
Stadium: Thorn Field (1981), 3,500 capacity. Natural turf.
Colors: Crimson & White.
Conference: Presidents' Athletic.
SID: Joe Klimchak, 412-458-3365.
AD: Christopher Smith.

GUILFORD
Greensboro, NC 27410 III

Coach: Mike Ketchum, Guilford 1978
Record: 9 Years, 42-46-0

2000 SCHEDULE
Charleston So. ....Sept. 2
Methodist ....Sept. 9
Wash. & Lee ■ ....Sept. 16
Hampden-Sydney ....Sept. 23
Randolph-Macon ....Oct. 7
Bridgewater (Va.) ■ ....Oct. 14
Emory & Henry ■ ....Oct. 21
Ferrum ■ ....Oct. 28
Catholic ....Nov. 4
Greensboro ■ ....Nov. 11

1999 RESULTS (4-6-0)
21	Methodist	16
22	Wash. & Lee	20
17	Hampden-Sydney	15
21	Davidson	28
14	Ferrum	17
14	Bridgewater (Va.)	41
7	Emory & Henry	24
0	Randolph-Macon	27
13	Catholic	31
15	Greensboro	14
144		**233**

Nickname: Quakers.
Stadium: Armfield Athletic (1960), 3,500 capacity. Natural turf.
Colors: Crimson & Gray.
Conference: Old Dominion Athletic.
SID: Dave Walters, 910-316-2107.
AD: Michael R. Ketchum.

GUST. ADOLPHUS
St. Peter, MN 56082 III

Coach: Jay Schoenebeck, Gust. Adolphus 1980
Record: 6 Years, 29-31-0

2000 SCHEDULE
Trinity (Tex.) ....*Sept. 9
Hamline ■ ....Sept. 16
Bethel (Minn.) ....Sept. 23
Concordia-M'head ■ ....Sept. 30
Carleton ....Oct. 7
St. John's (Minn.) ■ ....Oct. 14
Augsburg ....Oct. 21
St. Thomas (Minn.) ■ ....Oct. 28
St. Olaf [Minneapolis, MN] ....*Nov. 4
Macalester ....Nov. 11

1999 RESULTS (7-3-0)
38	Martin Luther	14
38	Carleton	0
49	Macalester	6
17	St. Thomas (Minn.)	18
38	Augsburg	12
26	Bethel (Minn.)	20
10	Concordia-M'head	44
19	Hamline	7
36	St. Olaf	17
16	St. John's (Minn.)	31
287		**169**

Nickname: Golden Gusties.
Stadium: Hollingsworth Field (1929), 5,500 capacity. Natural turf.
Colors: Black & Gold.
Conference: Minnesota Intercollegiate Athletic.
SID: Tim Kennedy, 507-933-7647.
AD: Alan Molde.

HAMILTON
Clinton, NY 13323 III

Coach: Tim Pendergast, Cortland St. 1980
(First year as head coach)

2000 SCHEDULE
Amherst ....Sept. 23
Wesleyan (Conn.) ....Sept. 30
Trinity (Conn.) ■ ....Oct. 7
Bowdoin ■ ....Oct. 14
Colby ....Oct. 21
Williams ■ ....Oct. 28
Middlebury ■ ....Nov. 4
Bates ....Nov. 11

1999 RESULTS (0-8-0)
| 25 | Tufts | 28 |
| 6 | Wesleyan (Conn.) | 34 |

17	Trinity (Conn.)	31
12	Bowdoin	22
14	Colby	48
13	Williams	42
23	Middlebury	27
0	Bates	28
110		**260**

Nickname: Continentals.
Stadium: Steuben Field (N/A), 2,500 capacity. Natural turf.
Colors: Buff & Blue.
Conference: NESCAC.
SID: Stephen Jaynes, 315-859-4685.
AD: Thomas E. Murphy.

HAMLINE
St. Paul, MN 55104 III

Coach: Dick Tressel, Baldwin-Wallace 1970
Record: 22 Years, 121-94-2

2000 SCHEDULE
St. Norbert ■	Sept. 9
Gust. Adolphus	Sept. 16
St. Olaf ■	Sept. 23
Bethel (Minn.) ■	Sept. 30
Concordia-M'head	Oct. 7
Carleton	Oct. 14
St. John's (Minn.)	Oct. 21
Augsburg ■	Oct. 28
Macalester [Minneapolis, MN]	*Nov. 3
St. Thomas (Minn.)	Nov. 11

1999 RESULTS (2-8-0)
30	Jamestown	9
10	Augsburg	15
14	Bethel (Minn.)	41
6	Concordia-M'head	14
13	Carleton	16
20	St. Olaf	25
3	St. John's (Minn.)	20
7	Gust. Adolphus	19
45	Macalester	14
3	St. Thomas (Minn.)	13
151		**186**

Nickname: Pipers.
Stadium: Norton (1921), 2,000 capacity. Natural turf.
Colors: Red & Grey.
Conference: Minnesota Intercollegiate Athletic.
SID: Tom Gilles, 612-641-2242.
AD: Richard Tressel.

HAMPDEN-SYDNEY
Hampden-Sydney, VA 23943 III

Coach: Marty Favret, Catholic 1984
(First year as head coach)

2000 SCHEDULE
Sewanee	Sept. 2
Gettysburg	Sept. 9
Guilford ■	Sept. 23
Bridgewater (Va.)	Sept. 30
Emory & Henry ■	Oct. 7
Wash. & Lee	Oct. 14
Catholic ■	Oct. 21
Davidson ■	Oct. 28
Maryville (Tenn.)	Nov. 4
Randolph-Macon ■	Nov. 11

1999 RESULTS (1-9-0)
0	Sewanee	14
28	Gettysburg	14
15	Guilford	17
7	Bridgewater (Va.)	40
7	Emory & Henry	36
12	Wash. & Lee	24
7	Catholic	45
12	Davidson	31
3	Maryville (Tenn.)	13
7	Randolph-Macon	33
98		**267**

Nickname: Tigers.
Stadium: Hundley (1964), 2,400 capacity. Natural turf.
Colors: Garnet & Gray.
Conference: Old Dominion Athletic.
SID: Dan McCormick, 804-223-6156.
AD: Joseph E. Bush.

HAMPTON
Hampton, VA 23668 ....I-AA

Coach: Joe Taylor, Western Ill. 1972
Record: 17 Years, 132-51-4

2000 SCHEDULE
New Hampshire ■	Sept. 2
Howard	Sept. 9
Winston-Salem ■	Sept. 16
Delaware St.	Sept. 30
Norfolk St.	Oct. 14
South Carolina St.	Oct. 21
Florida A&M	Oct. 28
Bethune-Cookman ■	Nov. 4
N.C. A&T ■	Nov. 11
Morgan St.	Nov. 18

1999 RESULTS (7-4-0)
21	Delaware St.	0
28	Howard	27
26	Ark.-Pine Bluff	13
27	Grambling	7
6	Southern U.	21
24	N.C. A&T	41
28	Norfolk St.	27
6	Florida A&M	41
39	South Carolina St.	27
27	Bethune-Cookman	34
34	Morgan St.	14
266		**252**

HERITAGE BOWL
24	Southern U.	3

Nickname: Pirates.
Stadium: Armstrong Field (1928), 11,000 capacity. Natural turf.
Colors: Royal Blue & White.
Conference: Mid-Eastern Athletic.
SID: LeCounte Conaway, 804-727-5757.
AD: Dennis E. Thomas.

HANOVER
Hanover, IN 47243 III

Coach: C. Wayne Perry, DePauw 1972
Record: 18 Years, 127-52-2

2000 SCHEDULE
DePauw	Sept. 9
Thomas More	Sept. 16
Wash. & Jeff. ■	Sept. 23
Alma ■	Sept. 30
Defiance	Oct. 7
Bluffton	Oct. 14
Mt. St. Joseph	Oct. 21
Anderson (Ind.) ■	Oct. 28
Manchester ■	Nov. 4
Franklin	Nov. 11

1999 RESULTS (10-0-0)
45	Thomas More	19
35	Eureka	17
30	Wash. & Jeff.	13
41	Bluffton	38
45	Manchester	14
30	Wilmington (Ohio)	15
29	Mt. St. Joseph	25
31	Anderson (Ind.)	12
28	Wabash	18
27	Franklin	10
341		**181**

DIVISION III CHAMPIONSHIP
14	Ohio Northern	56

Nickname: Panthers.
Stadium: L. S. Ayers Field (1973), 4,000 capacity. Natural turf.
Colors: Red & Blue.
Conference: Heartland Collegiate Athletic.
SID: Carter Cloyd, 812-866-7010.
AD: Lynn Hall.

HARDIN-SIMMONS
Abilene, TX 79698 III

Coach: Jimmie Keeling, Howard Payne 1958
Record: 10 Years, 81-29-0

2000 SCHEDULE
Wis.-Whitewater ■	Sept. 9
Austin	Sept. 16
Texas Lutheran ■	Sept. 23
Louisiana Col.	Sept. 30
Mississippi Col. ■	Oct. 7
Howard Payne	Oct. 14
Sul Ross St. ■	Oct. 21
East Tex. Baptist	Oct. 28
Mary Hardin-Baylor	Nov. 4
McMurry ■	Nov. 11

1999 RESULTS (10-0-0)
25	Wis.-Whitewater	7
38	Okla. Panhandle	31
35	Southwestern (Kan.)	9
28	Sul Ross St.	23
35	Mississippi Col.	23
50	Austin	14
38	Howard Payne	34
35	Texas Lutheran	26
28	Mary Hardin-Baylor	21
63	McMurry	28
375		**216**

DIVISION III CHAMPIONSHIP
28	Washington (Mo.)	21
51	Wash. & Jeff.	3
33	Trinity (Tex.)	40

Nickname: Cowboys.
Stadium: Shelton (1993), 4,000 capacity. Natural turf.
Colors: Purple & Gold.
Conference: American Southwest.
SID: Kevin Carmody, 915-670-1273.
AD: John Neese.

HARDING
Searcy, AR 72149 II

Coach: Randy Tribble, Harding 1977
Record: 6 Years, 32-28-1

2000 SCHEDULE
Tarleton St. ■	*Sept. 2
Tennessee Tech	*Sept. 9
Arkansas Tech	*Sept. 16
Henderson St. ■	*Sept. 23
Delta St.	Sept. 30
Central Ark.	*Oct. 7
Valdosta St. ■	*Oct. 14
North Ala. ■	Oct. 21
West Ga.	Oct. 28
West Ala.	Nov. 4
Ouachita Baptist ■	Nov. 11

1999 RESULTS (5-5-0)
44	Tarleton St.	16
21	West Ala.	19
38	Midwestern St.	35
28	Angelo St.	31
27	Southeastern Okla.	41
28	Northeastern St.	34
30	Central Okla.	42
30	East Central	7
41	Ouachita Baptist	7
22	Southwestern Okla.	31
309		**263**

Nickname: Bisons.
Stadium: Alumni (1959), 4,500 capacity. Natural turf.
Colors: Black & Gold.
Conference: Lone Star.
SID: Scott Goode, 501-279-4760.
AD: Greg Harnden.

HARTWICK
Oneonta, NY 13820 III

Coach: Steve Stetson, Dartmouth 1973
Record: 14 Years, 62-67-4

2000 SCHEDULES AND 1999 RESULTS

2000 SCHEDULE
King's (Pa.) ■	*Sept. 2
Siena	*Sept. 9
St. Anselm ■	Sept. 16
Mount Ida	Sept. 23
St. John Fisher	*Sept. 30
Alfred ■	Oct. 14
Rensselaer	Oct. 21
Union (N.Y.) ■	Oct. 28
Muhlenberg	Nov. 4
St. Lawrence ■	Nov. 11

1999 RESULTS (6-4-0)
18	King's (Pa.)	28
27	Westfield St.	15
21	St. Anselm	10
38	St. John Fisher	2
17	Alfred	31
25	Norwich	22
3	Rensselaer	48
14	Union (N.Y.)	34
56	Mount Ida	16
38	St. Lawrence	28
257		**234**

Nickname: Hawks.
Stadium: AstroTurf Field (1985), 1,200 capacity. Artificial turf.
Colors: Royal Blue & White.
Conference: Division III Independent.
SID: Bill Sodoma, 607-431-4703.
AD: Kenneth Kutler.

HARVARD
Boston, MA 02163 ....I-AA

Coach: Tim Murphy, Springfield 1978
Record: 13 Years, 60-77-1

2000 SCHEDULE
Holy Cross ■	Sept. 16
Brown	Sept. 23
Lafayette	Sept. 30
Cornell ■	Oct. 7
Lehigh ■	Oct. 14
Princeton	Oct. 21
Dartmouth	Oct. 28
Columbia ■	Nov. 4
Pennsylvania	Nov. 11
Yale ■	Nov. 18

1999 RESULTS (5-5-0)
24	Columbia	7
25	Holy Cross	17
21	Colgate	24
23	Cornell	24
37	Fordham	30
13	Princeton	6
63	Dartmouth	21
10	Brown	17
17	Pennsylvania	21
21	Yale	24
254		**191**

Nickname: Crimson.
Stadium: Harvard (1903), 30,898 capacity. Natural turf.
Colors: Crimson, Black & White.
Conference: Ivy.
SID: John Veneziano, 617-495-2206.
AD: William J. Cleary Jr.

HAWAII
Honolulu, HI 96822 ....I-A

Coach: June Jones, Portland St. 1977
Record: 1 Year, 9-4-0

2000 SCHEDULE
Portland St. ■	*Sept. 9
UTEP	*Sept. 23
Tulsa ■	*Sept. 30
TCU	*Oct. 7
Southern Methodist ■	*Oct. 14
Rice	Oct. 21
San Jose St. ■	*Oct. 28
Fresno St.	Nov. 4
Nevada ■	*Nov. 11
Louisiana Tech ■	*Nov. 18
Wisconsin ■	*Nov. 25
UNLV ■	*Dec. 2

1999 RESULTS (8-4-0)
7	Southern California	62
31	Eastern Ill.	27
34	Boise St.	19
20	Southern Methodist	0
33	UTEP	3
19	Rice	38
35	Tulsa	21
14	TCU	34
62	San Jose St.	41
31	Fresno St.	24
48	Navy	41
14	Washington St.	22
348		**332**

OAHU CLASSIC
23	Oregon St.	17

Nickname: Rainbows.
Stadium: Aloha (1975), 50,000 capacity. Artificial turf.
Colors: Green & White.
Conference: Western Athletic.
SID: Lois Manin, 808-956-7523.
AD: Hugh Yoshida.

HEIDELBERG
Tiffin, OH 44883 III

Coach: Larry Shank, Shepherd
Record: 10 Years, 36-61-3

2000 SCHEDULE
Wittenberg ■	*Sept. 9
Capital ■	Sept. 16
Marietta	*Sept. 23
John Carroll	Sept. 30
Baldwin-Wallace ■	Oct. 7
Ohio Northern ■	Oct. 14
Wilmington (Ohio)	Oct. 21
Otterbein	Oct. 28
Muskingum	Nov. 4
Mount Union	Nov. 11

1999 RESULTS (4-6-0)
15	Adrian	22
0	Ohio Northern	35
50	Hiram	6
33	Capital	9
0	Mount Union	66
33	Marietta	27
3	Otterbein	30
10	John Carroll	21
6	Baldwin-Wallace	34
31	Muskingum	22
181		**272**

Nickname: Berg.
Stadium: Frost-Kalnow (1941), 7,500 capacity. Artificial turf.
Colors: Red, Orange & Black.
Conference: Ohio Athletic.
SID: Toby Boyce, 419-448-2140.
AD: John D. Hill.

HENDERSON ST.
Arkadelphia, AR 72000 II

Coach: Patrick Nix, Auburn 1995
Record: 1 Year, 2-9-0

2000 SCHEDULE
Ouachita Baptist ■	*Sept. 2
Alabama A&M	*Sept. 9
West Ga.	*Sept. 16
Harding	*Sept. 23
Valdosta St.	Sept. 30
North Ala.	Oct. 7
Central Ark. ■	*Oct. 14
Delta St.	Oct. 21
Arkansas Tech	Oct. 28
Ark.-Monticello	Nov. 4
Southern Ark. ■	Nov. 11

1999 RESULTS (2-9-0)
14	Ouachita Baptist	34
3	Valdosta St.	39
3	Southwest Mo. St.	50
7	West Ala.	28
14	Arkansas Tech	31
3	Delta St.	35
37	Ark.-Monticello	24
14	North Ala.	21
13	West Ga.	33
3	Southern Ark.	31
24	Central Ark.	21
135		**347**

Nickname: Reddies.
Stadium: Carpenter-Haygood (1968), 9,600 capacity. Natural turf.
Colors: Red & Gray.
Conference: Gulf South.
SID: David Worlock, 501-230-5197.
AD: Kenneth J. Turner.

HILLSDALE
Hillsdale, MI 49242 II

Coach: Dave Dye, Baldwin-Wallace 1967
Record: 3 Years, 15-18-0

2000 SCHEDULE
Saginaw Valley ■	*Aug. 31
Northwood	*Sept. 9
Northern Mich. ■	*Sept. 16
Findlay	*Sept. 23
Michigan Tech	Sept. 30
Ashland ■	*Oct. 7
Wayne St. (Mich.) ■	*Oct. 14
Indianapolis	Oct. 21
Mercyhurst ■	Oct. 28
Ferris St.	Nov. 4
Grand Valley St. ■	*Nov. 11

1999 RESULTS (8-3-0)
28	Edinboro	10
29	Ashland	17
7	Michigan Tech	31
30	Westminster (Pa.)	17
42	Mercyhurst	40
41	Gannon	7
17	Findlay	14
24	Wayne St. (Mich.)	9
40	Ferris St.	37
33	Saginaw Valley	38
9	Indianapolis	34
300		**254**

Nickname: Chargers.
Stadium: Frank Waters (1982), 8,500 capacity. Natural turf.
Colors: Royal Blue & White.
Conference: Great Lakes Intercollegiate Athletic.
SID: Greg Younger, 517-437-7364.
AD: Michael J. Kovalchik.

HIRAM
Hiram, OH 44234 III

Coach: Bobby Thomas, Hiram 1979
Record: 8 Years, 16-64-0

2000 SCHEDULE
Bluffton	Sept. 9
Kenyon ■	Sept. 16
Mt. St. Joseph	Sept. 23
Earlham	Sept. 30
Allegheny ■	Oct. 7
Oberlin	Oct. 14
Wabash ■	Oct. 21
Wittenberg	Oct. 28
Case Reserve	Nov. 4
Wooster	Nov. 11

1999 RESULTS (0-10-0)
26	Bluffton	47
0	Mount Union	59
6	Heidelberg	50
21	Baldwin-Wallace	36
20	Muskingum	56
27	Capital	41

0	Ohio Northern	54
14	Marietta	38
9	Otterbein	60
13	John Carroll	50
136		**491**

Nickname: Terriers.
Stadium: Charles Henry Field (1963), 3,500 capacity. Natural turf.
Colors: Red & Blue.
Conference: North Coast Athletic.
SID: Tom Cammett, 216-569-5495.
AD: Bobby Thomas.

HOBART
Geneva, NY 14456..III

Coach: Mike Cragg, Slippery Rock 1981
Record: 5 Years, 26-22-0

2000 SCHEDULE
Dickinson ■	Sept. 9
Rochester	Sept. 16
Union (N.Y.)	Sept. 23
St. Lawrence ■	Sept. 30
Frank. & Marsh.	Oct. 14
Alfred ■	Oct. 21
Ithaca ■	Oct. 28
St. John Fisher	Nov. 4
Rensselaer ■	Nov. 11

1999 RESULTS (5-4-0)
20	Dickinson	32
14	Union (N.Y.)	20
28	St. Lawrence	10
48	Rochester	21
35	Frank. & Marsh.	7
29	Alfred	20
13	Ithaca	44
16	St. John Fisher	0
6	Rensselaer	17
209		**171**

Nickname: Statesmen.
Stadium: Boswell (1975), 4,500 capacity. Natural turf.
Colors: Forest Green & White.
Conference: Upstate Collegiate Athl Assn.
SID: Kenneth DeBolt, 315-781-3538.
AD: Michael J. Hanna.

HOFSTRA
Hempstead, NY 11549........................I-AA

Coach: Joe Gardi, Maryland 1960
Record: 10 Years, 81-29-2

2000 SCHEDULE
Montana	Sept. 2
Maine	*Sept. 9
Delaware ■	*Sept. 16
Rhode Island ■	*Sept. 23
Massachusetts	Sept. 30
Portland St.	Oct. 7
Liberty ■	*Oct. 13
Elon ■	Oct. 21
Cal Poly	Oct. 28
Youngstown St.	Nov. 4
Albany (N.Y.) ■	Nov. 18

1999 RESULTS (10-1-0)
56	Connecticut	17
27	Maine	19
28	Rhode Island	13
38	Cal Poly	3
27	Massachusetts	14
58	Delaware St.	14
21	Richmond	31
21	Elon	9
20	Buffalo	13
42	South Fla.	23
34	James Madison	16
372		**172**

DIVISION I-AA CHAMPIONSHIP
27	Lehigh	15
20	Illinois St.	37

Nickname: Flying Dutchmen.

Stadium: Hofstra (1963), 15,000 capacity. Artificial turf.
Colors: Blue, White & Gold.
Conference: Division I-AA Independent.
SID: Jim Sheehan, 516-463-6764.
AD: Harry H. Royle.

HOLY CROSS
Worcester, MA 01610........................I-AA

Coach: Dan Allen, Hanover 1978
Record: 10 Years, 46-67-0

2000 SCHEDULE
Georgetown	Sept. 9
Harvard	Sept. 16
Towson ■	Sept. 23
Yale	Sept. 30
Pennsylvania ■	Oct. 7
Dartmouth	Oct. 14
Lafayette	Oct. 21
Lehigh ■	Oct. 28
Bucknell ■	Nov. 4
Colgate	Nov. 11
Fordham ■	Nov. 18

1999 RESULTS (3-8-0)
16	Georgetown	34
30	Lafayette	12
17	Harvard	25
0	Towson	14
14	Yale	34
24	Fairfield	23
8	Lehigh	62
26	St. Mary's (Cal.)	28
21	Bucknell	32
37	Fordham	14
26	Colgate	45
219		**323**

Nickname: Crusaders.
Stadium: Fitton Field (1924), 23,500 capacity. Natural turf.
Colors: Royal Purple.
Conference: Patriot.
SID: Frank Mastrandrea, 203-870-4750.
AD: Richard M. Regan Jr.

HOPE
Holland, MI 49422..............................III

Coach: Dean Kreps, Monmouth 1983
Record: 5 Years, 22-23-0

2000 SCHEDULE
Valparaiso ■	*Sept. 9
DePauw	Sept. 16
Wheaton (Ill.) ■	Sept. 23
Wis. Lutheran	Sept. 30
Kalamazoo	Oct. 14
Alma ■	Oct. 21
Adrian	Oct. 28
Olivet	Nov. 4
Albion ■	Nov. 11

1999 RESULTS (5-4-0)
33	Augustana (Ill.)	34
21	DePauw	27
11	Ill. Wesleyan	19
40	Defiance	7
62	Alma	7
38	Adrian	15
14	Albion	20
30	Olivet	6
44	Kalamazoo	28
293		**163**

Nickname: Flying Dutchmen.
Stadium: Holland Municipal (1979), 5,322 capacity. Natural turf.
Colors: Blue & Orange.
Conference: Michigan Intercollegiate Athletic Association.
SID: Tom Renner, 616-395-7860.
AD: Raymond E. Smith.

HOUSTON
Houston, TX 77204.............................I-A

Coach: Dana Dimel, Kansas St. 1986
Record: 3 Years, 22-13-0

2000 SCHEDULE
Rice	*Sept. 2
LSU	*Sept. 9
Army ■	*Sept. 16
Texas	Sept. 23
Southern Methodist ■	*Sept. 30
Cincinnati	Oct. 7
Memphis	*Oct. 21
Southern Miss. ■	Oct. 28
Tulane	Nov. 4
East Caro.	Nov. 11
Louisville ■	Nov. 18

1999 RESULTS (7-4-0)
28	Rice	3
10	Alabama	37
45	La.-Lafayette	0
10	UAB	29
23	Cincinnati	20
20	North Carolina	12
33	Louisville	39
3	East Caro.	19
36	Tulane	31
20	LSU	7
26	Army	14
254		**317**

Nickname: Cougars.
Stadium: John O'Quinn/Robertson (1942), 32,000 capacity. Natural turf.
Colors: Scarlet & White.
Conference: Conference USA.
SID: Chris Burkhalter, 713-743-9404.
AD: Chester S. Gladchuk.

HOWARD
Washington, DC 20059......................I-AA

Coach: Steve Wilson, Howard 1979
Record: 11 Years, 73-50-0

2000 SCHEDULE
Jackson St. [Chicago, IL]	Sept. 2
Hampton	Sept. 9
Maine	*Sept. 16
Morgan St. ■	Sept. 23
Florida A&M	*Sept. 30
Towson	Oct. 14
N.C. A&T ■	Oct. 21
Norfolk St. ■	Oct. 28
South Carolina St.	Nov. 4
Bethune-Cookman ■	*Nov. 11
Delaware St. ■	Nov. 18

1999 RESULTS (5-6-0)
21	Jackson St.	35
27	Hampton	28
31	Bethune-Cookman	27
32	Texas Southern	20
34	Florida A&M	40
33	Towson	49
0	N.C. A&T	51
29	Norfolk St.	23
49	South Carolina St.	42
42	Morgan St.	38
25	Delaware St.	42
323		**395**

Nickname: Bison.
Stadium: Greene (1986), 7,500 capacity. Artificial turf.
Colors: Blue, White & Red.
Conference: Mid-Eastern Athletic.
SID: Edward Hill, 202-806-9200.
AD: Hank Ford.

HOWARD PAYNE
Brownwood, TX 76801......................III

Coach: Vance Gibson, Austin 1975
Record: 8 Years, 53-28-0

2000 SCHEDULE
Wis.-Whitewater	Sept. 2
Louisiana Col.	Sept. 16
Mississippi Col. ■	Sept. 23

East Tex. Baptist ■ ....Sept. 30
Sul Ross St. ....Oct. 7
Hardin-Simmons ■ ....Oct. 14
Mary Hardin-Baylor ....Oct. 21
McMurry ■ ....Oct. 28
Austin ....Nov. 4
Texas Lutheran ■ ....Nov. 11

1999 RESULTS (5-5-0)
17	Midland Lutheran	13
7	Prairie View	21
20	Chapman	29
21	Mississippi Col.	14
28	Austin	21
42	Texas Lutheran	7
34	Hardin-Simmons	38
9	Mary Hardin-Baylor	12
31	McMurry	41
50	Sul Ross St.	20
259		**216**

Nickname: Yellow Jackets.
Stadium: Gordon Wood (0000), 7,600 capacity. Natural turf.
Colors: Gold & Blue.
Conference: American Southwest.
SID: Nadir Dalleh, 915-649-8034.
AD: Phil Fuller.

HUMBOLDT ST.
Arcata, CA 95521 II

Coach: Doug Adkins
(First year as head coach)
2000 SCHEDULE
Montana Tech ....Sept. 2
Montana St. ....Sept. 9
St. Mary's (Cal.) ■ ....*Sept. 16
Rocky Mountain ■ ....Sept. 23
Southern Ore. ■ ....*Sept. 30
Azusa Pacific ....Oct. 7
Simon Fraser ■ ....Oct. 14
Central Wash. ....Oct. 21
Lenoir-Rhyne ■ ....Oct. 28
Western Wash. ....Nov. 4
Western Ore. ....Nov. 11

1999 RESULTS (3-7-0)
28	Montana Tech	14
3	St. Mary's (Cal.)	40
38	Azusa Pacific	34
9	Willamette	3
16	UC Davis	43
7	Central Wash.	43
32	Western Ore.	41
20	Simon Fraser	24
0	Western Wash.	58
14	Southern Ore.	20
167		**320**

Nickname: Lumberjacks.
Stadium: Redwood Bowl (1946), 7,000 capacity. Natural turf.
Colors: Green & Gold.
Conference: Division II Independent.
SID: Dan Pambianco, 707-826-3631.
AD: Michael S. Swan.

IDAHO
Moscow, ID 83843 ....I-A

Coach: Tom Cable, Idaho 1986
(First year as head coach)
2000 SCHEDULE
Washington ....Sept. 2
Montana ■ ....Sept. 9
Oregon ....Sept. 16
Washington St. ....Sept. 23
Montana St. ■ ....*Sept. 30
West Virginia ....Oct. 7
Arkansas St. ■ ....*Oct. 14
Utah St. ....Oct. 21
North Texas ....Nov. 4
New Mexico St. ■ ....*Nov. 11
Boise St. ....Nov. 18

1999 RESULTS (7-4-0)
48	Eastern Wash.	21
23	Auburn	30
28	Washington St.	17
13	Wyoming	28
28	North Texas	10
30	Arkansas St.	24
31	Utah St.	3
14	New Mexico St.	42
42	Nevada	33
33	Montana	30
14	Boise St.	45
304		**283**

Nickname: Vandals.
Stadium: Kibbie Dome (1975), 16,000 capacity. Artificial turf.
Colors: Silver & Gold.
Conference: Big West.
SID: Becky Paull, 208-885-0211.
AD: Mike R. Bohn.

IDAHO ST.
Pocatello, ID 83209 ....I-AA

Coach: Larry Lewis, Boise St. 1981
Record: 1 Year, 3-8-0
2000 SCHEDULE
Montana Tech ■ ....*Sept. 9
Eastern Wash. ....*Sept. 16
Cal St. Sacramento ■ ....*Sept. 23
Cal St. Northridge ....Sept. 30
Northern Ariz. ■ ....*Oct. 7
Portland St. ....Oct. 14
Southern Utah ■ ....Oct. 21
Weber St. ....*Oct. 28
Montana ....Nov. 4
Montana St. ■ ....*Nov. 11
Utah St. ....Nov. 18

1999 RESULTS (3-8-0)
54	Eastern Ore.	28
42	Fort Lewis	3
24	Weber St.	27
13	Portland St.	52
27	Cal St. Northridge	41
28	Northern Ariz.	43
38	Eastern Wash.	45
47	Southern Utah	63
23	Montana	73
20	Cal St. Sacramento	41
29	Montana St.	13
345		**429**

Nickname: Bengals.
Stadium: Holt Arena (1970), 12,000 capacity. Artificial turf.
Colors: Orange & Black.
Conference: Big Sky.
SID: Frank Mercogliano, 208-236-3651.
AD: Howard L. Gauthier.

ILLINOIS
Champaign, IL 61820 ....I-A

Coach: Ron Turner, Pacific (Cal.) 1977
Record: 4 Years, 18-27-0
2000 SCHEDULE
Middle Tenn. St. ■ ....Sept. 2
San Diego St. ....*Sept. 9
California ■ ....Sept. 16
Michigan ■ ....*Sept. 23
Minnesota ....Sept. 30
Iowa ....Oct. 14
Penn St. ....Oct. 21
Michigan St. ....Oct. 28
Indiana ■ ....Nov. 4
Ohio St. ....Nov. 11
Northwestern ....Nov. 18

1999 RESULTS (7-4-0)
41	Arkansas St.	3
38	San Diego St.	10
41	Louisville	36
10	Michigan St.	27
31	Indiana	34
7	Minnesota	37
35	Michigan	29
7	Penn St.	27
40	Iowa	24
46	Ohio St.	20
29	Northwestern	7
325		**254**

MICRONPC.COM BOWL
63	Virginia	21

Nickname: Fighting Illini.
Stadium: Memorial (1923), 70,904 capacity. Artificial turf.
Colors: Orange & Blue.
Conference: Big Ten.
SID: Kent Brown, 217-333-1391.
AD: Ronald E. Guenther.

ILLINOIS COL.
Jacksonville, IL 62650 III

Coach: Tom Rowland, Illinois Col. 1968
Record: 2 Years, 2-17-0
2000 SCHEDULE
Blackburn ■ ....Sept. 2
Lawrence ■ ....Sept. 16
Knox ....Sept. 23
Monmouth (Ill.) ....Sept. 30
Grinnell ....Oct. 7
Beloit ■ ....Oct. 14
Lake Forest ....Oct. 21
Ripon ■ ....Oct. 28
Carroll (Wis.) ....Nov. 4
St. Norbert ....Nov. 11

1999 RESULTS (2-8-0)
36	Westminster (Mo.)	56
21	Lawrence	16
35	Knox	34
28	Monmouth (Ill.)	42
35	Grinnell	53
20	Beloit	30
7	Lake Forest	27
28	Ripon	65
20	Carroll (Wis.)	27
31	St. Norbert	40
261		**390**

Nickname: Blueboys.
Stadium: England Field (1960), 2,500 capacity. Natural turf.
Colors: Blue & White.
Conference: Midwest Collegiate Athletic.
SID: James T. Murphy, 217-245-3048.
AD: William D. Merris.

ILLINOIS ST.
Normal, IL 61761 ....I-AA

Coach: Denver Johnson, Tulsa 1981
Record: 3 Years, 21-12-0
2000 SCHEDULE
West Va. Tech ■ ....*Aug. 31
Northern Ill. ....*Sept. 9
Southeast Mo. St. ....*Sept. 16
Northern Iowa ....Sept. 30
Youngstown St. ■ ....Oct. 7
Indiana St. ....Oct. 14
Prairie View ■ ....Oct. 21
Southern Ill. ■ ....Oct. 28
Western Ill. ....Nov. 4
Eastern Ill. ■ ....Nov. 11
Southwest Mo. St. ■ ....Nov. 18

1999 RESULTS (9-2-0)
41	Truman	9
55	Southeast Mo. St.	7
7	Minnesota	55
46	Southwest Mo. St.	42
47	Northern Iowa	28
20	Indiana St.	17
13	South Fla.	14
55	Southern Ill.	48
31	Youngstown St.	28
38	Western Ill.	30
24	Eastern Ill.	17
377		**295**

DIVISION I-AA CHAMPIONSHIP
56	Colgate	13
37	Hofstra	20
17	Ga. Southern	28

Nickname: Redbirds.
Stadium: Hancock (1967), 15,000 capacity. Artificial turf.
Colors: Red & White.
Conference: Gateway Football.
SID: Kenny Mossman, 309-438-3825.
AD: Perk Weisenburger.

ILL. WESLEYAN
Bloomington, IL 61702..................................III

Coach: Norm Eash, Ill. Wesleyan 1975
Record: 13 Years, 83-37-1

2000 SCHEDULE
Washington (Mo.) ■	Sept. 9
Aurora	Sept. 16
Taylor (Ind.)	Sept. 23
North Park ■	Sept. 30
Augustana (Ill.)	Oct. 7
Elmhurst ■	Oct. 14
Wheaton (Ill.)	Oct. 21
Carthage ■	Oct. 28
North Central	Nov. 4
Millikin ■	Nov. 11

1999 RESULTS (6-3-0)
28	DePauw	20
19	Hope	11
31	Elmhurst	26
0	Augustana (Ill.)	41
44	Carthage	27
20	Wheaton (Ill.)	22
14	North Central	6
20	Millikin	42
7	North Park	6
183		**201**

Nickname: Titans.
Stadium: Wesleyan (1893), 3,500 capacity. Natural turf.
Colors: Green & White.
Conference: College Conf. of Illinois & Wisconsin.
SID: Stew Salowitz, 309-556-3206.
AD: Dennis Bridges.

INDIANA
Bloomington, IN 47405..................................I-A

Coach: Cam Cameron, Indiana 1983
Record: 3 Years, 10-23-0

2000 SCHEDULE
North Carolina St. ■	Sept. 9
Kentucky	Sept. 16
Cincinnati ■	Sept. 23
Iowa ■	Sept. 30
Northwestern	Oct. 7
Michigan	Oct. 14
Minnesota ■	Oct. 21
Penn St. [Indianapolis, IN]	*Oct. 28
Illinois	Nov. 4
Wisconsin ■	Nov. 11
Purdue	Nov. 18

1999 RESULTS (4-7-0)
21	Ball St.	9
30	North Carolina	42
35	Kentucky	44
24	Penn St.	45
34	Illinois	31
34	Northwestern	17
0	Wisconsin	59
38	Iowa	31
31	Michigan	34
20	Minnesota	44
24	Purdue	30
245		**305**

Nickname: Hoosiers.
Stadium: Memorial (1960), 52,354 capacity. Natural turf.
Colors: Cream & Crimson.
Conference: Big Ten.
SID: Todd Starowitz, 812-855-9610.
AD: Clarence Doninger.

INDIANA (PA.)
Indiana, PA 15705.....................................II

Coach: Frank Cignetti, Indiana (Pa.) 1960
Record: 18 Years, 149-62-1

2000 SCHEDULE
Ferris St. ■	*Sept. 2
New Haven ■	*Sept. 16
Lock Haven	Sept. 23
Slippery Rock ■	*Sept. 30
Bloomsburg	Oct. 7
Shippensburg ■	Oct. 14
Edinboro	Oct. 21
Clarion ■	Oct. 28
Calif. (Pa.)	Nov. 4
Millersville ■	Nov. 11

1999 RESULTS (7-3-0)
12	West Chester	9
7	Youngstown St.	13
35	Bloomsburg	10
27	Lock Haven	9
14	Slippery Rock	52
9	Millersville	10
26	Clarion	0
42	Calif. (Pa.)	14
18	Edinboro	7
43	Shippensburg	16
233		**140**

DIVISION II CHAMPIONSHIP
27	Slippery Rock	20
26	Millersville	21
12	Northwest Mo. St.	20

Nickname: Indians.
Stadium: Miller (1962), 6,500 capacity. Artificial turf.
Colors: Crimson & Gray.
Conference: Pennsylvania State Athletic.
SID: Mike Hoffman, 412-357-2747.
AD: Frank J. Condino.

INDIANA ST.
Terre Haute, IN 47809.............................I-AA

Coach: Tim McGuire, Nebraska 1975
Record: 4 Years, 15-29-0

2000 SCHEDULE
Eastern Ill. ■	*Aug. 31
Eastern Ky. ■	*Sept. 9
Western Mich.	*Sept. 16
Murray St.	*Sept. 23
Western Ill.	Sept. 30
Southwest Mo. St. ■	Oct. 7
Illinois St.	Oct. 14
Northern Iowa ■	Oct. 21
Youngstown St.	Oct. 28
Southern Ill.	Nov. 4
Western Ky.	Nov. 11

1999 RESULTS (3-8-0)
7	Iowa St.	33
0	Oklahoma	49
24	Eastern Ky.	31
28	Youngstown St.	31
17	Illinois St.	20
34	Southeast Mo. St.	13
39	Western Ill.	36
21	Northern Iowa	44
66	Southern Ill.	45
34	Western Ky.	40
14	Southwest Mo. St.	31
284		**373**

Nickname: Sycamores.
Stadium: Memorial (1970), 12,764 capacity. Artificial turf.
Colors: Blue & White.
Conference: Gateway Football.
SID: Kent Johnson, 812-237-4160.
AD: Andrea Myers.

INDIANAPOLIS
Indianapolis, IN 46227.................................II

Coach: Joe Polizzi, Hillsdale 1976
Record: 6 Years, 32-31-1

2000 SCHEDULE
St. Joseph's (Ind.) ■	Sept. 2
Northern Mich.	*Sept. 9
Michigan Tech ■	Sept. 16
Saginaw Valley	Sept. 23
Mercyhurst ■	Sept. 30
Findlay	Oct. 7
Grand Valley St.	Oct. 14
Hillsdale ■	Oct. 21
Wayne St. (Mich.) ■	Oct. 28
Ashland	Nov. 4
Ferris St. ■	Nov. 11

1999 RESULTS (7-4-0)
19	St. Joseph's (Ind.)	10
9	Westminster (Pa.)	6
30	Grand Valley St.	14
20	Mercyhurst	27
7	Findlay	14
8	Northwood	17
26	Wayne St. (Mich.)	19
30	New Haven	24
7	Northern Mich.	19
30	Ashland	10
34	Hillsdale	9
220		**169**

Nickname: Greyhounds.
Stadium: Key (1971), 5,500 capacity. Natural turf.
Colors: Crimson & Grey.
Conference: Great Lakes Intercollegiate Athletic.
SID: Joe Gentry, 317-788-3494.
AD: David J. Huffman.

IONA
New Rochelle, NY 10801........................I-AA

Coach: Jim Pisegna
(First year as head coach)

2000 SCHEDULE
Canisius ■	Sept. 9
La Salle ■	Sept. 16
Montclair St. ■	Sept. 23
Fairfield	Sept. 30
St. Peter's ■	Oct. 7
Marist	Oct. 14
Duquesne	Oct. 21
Sacred Heart	Oct. 28
Georgetown	Nov. 4
Siena	Nov. 11
St. John's (N.Y.) ■	Nov. 18

1999 RESULTS (5-5-0)
6	Fairfield	42
31	La Salle	23
24	Sacred Heart	0
0	Georgetown	28
20	St. Peter's	15
0	Siena	14
62	Duquesne	50
34	Canisius	12
29	Marist	40
33	St. John's (N.Y.)	47
239		**271**

Nickname: Gaels.
Stadium: Mazzella Field (1989), 1,200 capacity. Artificial turf.
Colors: Maroon & Gold.
Conference: Metro Atlantic Athletic.
SID: Dave Cagianello, 914-633-2334.
AD: Rich Petriccione.

IOWA
Iowa City, IA 52242..................................I-A

Coach: Kirk Ferentz, Connecticut 1978
Record: 4 Years, 13-31-0

2000 SCHEDULES AND 1999 RESULTS

2000 SCHEDULE
Kansas St. [Kansas City, MO]	Aug. 26
Western Mich. ■	Sept. 9
Iowa St. ■	Sept. 16
Nebraska	Sept. 23
Indiana	Sept. 30
Michigan St. ■	Oct. 7
Illinois	Oct. 14
Ohio St. ■	Oct. 21
Wisconsin ■	Oct. 28
Penn St.	Nov. 4
Northwestern ■	Nov. 11
Minnesota	Nov. 18

1999 RESULTS (1-10-0)
7	Nebraska	42
10	Iowa St.	17
24	Northern Ill.	0
3	Michigan St.	49
7	Penn St.	31
21	Northwestern	23
31	Indiana	38
11	Ohio St.	41
24	Illinois	40
3	Wisconsin	41
21	Minnesota	25
162		**347**

Nickname: Hawkeyes.
Stadium: Kinnick (1929), 70,397 capacity. Natural turf.
Colors: Old Gold & Black.
Conference: Big Ten.
SID: Phil Haddy, 319-335-9411.
AD: Robert A. Bowlsby.

IOWA ST.
Ames, IA 50011 .... I-A

Coach: Dan McCarney, Iowa 1975
Record: 5 Years, 13-42-0

2000 SCHEDULE
Ohio ■	Sept. 2
UNLV ■	Sept. 9
Iowa	Sept. 16
Baylor	*Sept. 30
Nebraska ■	Oct. 7
Oklahoma St.	Oct. 14
Texas A&M ■	Oct. 21
Missouri ■	Oct. 28
Kansas St.	Nov. 4
Colorado	Nov. 11
Kansas ■	Nov. 18

1999 RESULTS (4-7-0)
33	Indiana St.	7
17	Iowa	10
24	UNLV	0
28	Kansas St.	35
14	Nebraska	49
24	Missouri	21
12	Colorado	16
41	Texas	44
16	Texas Tech	28
10	Oklahoma	31
28	Kansas	31
247		**272**

Nickname: Cyclones.
Stadium: Jack Trice (1975), 43,000 capacity. Natural turf.
Colors: Cardinal & Gold.
Conference: Big 12.
SID: Tom Kroeschell, 515-294-3372.
AD: Eugene D. Smith.

ITHACA
Ithaca, NY 14850 III

Coach: Michael Welch, Ithaca 1973
Record: 6 Years, 45-18-0

2000 SCHEDULE
Alfred	Sept. 9
Mansfield ■	Sept. 16
St. John Fisher	Sept. 23
Springfield ■	Sept. 30
Brockport St.	Oct. 7
St. Lawrence ■	Oct. 14
Wilkes ■	Oct. 21
Hobart	Oct. 28
Buffalo St. ■	Nov. 4
Cortland St.	Nov. 11

1999 RESULTS (7-3-0)
44	St. John Fisher	0
21	Mansfield	7
21	Col. of New Jersey	14
45	Springfield	42
10	Brockport St.	0
43	St. Lawrence	14
17	American Int'l	34
44	Hobart	13
21	Cortland St.	26
35	Buffalo St.	42
301		**192**

ECAC PLAYOFF
7	Union (N.Y.)	31

Nickname: Bombers.
Stadium: Butterfield (1958), 5,000 capacity. Natural turf.
Colors: Blue & Gold.
Conference: Division III Independent.
SID: Mike Warwick, 607-274-3825.
AD: Kristen M. Ford.

JACKSON ST.
Jackson, MS 39217 .... I-AA

Coach: Robert Hughes, Jackson St. 1967
Record: 1 Year, 9-3-0

2000 SCHEDULE
Howard [Chicago, IL]	Sept. 2
Texas Southern ■	*Sept. 9
Tennessee St. [Memphis, TN]	*Sept. 16
Southern U.	Sept. 23
Alabama St. [Mobile, AL]	Oct. 7
Mississippi Val. ■	*Oct. 14
Grambling	Oct. 21
Ark.-Pine Bluff ■	*Oct. 28
Alabama A&M ■	Nov. 4
New Haven ■	Nov. 11
Alcorn St. ■	Nov. 18

1999 RESULTS (9-3-0)
35	Howard	21
33	Tennessee St.	48
31	Grambling	6
63	Mississippi Val.	0
44	Alabama St.	17
14	Southern U.	26
28	Alabama A&M	18
41	Ark.-Pine Bluff	0
41	Texas Southern	24
30	New Haven	23
58	Alcorn St.	6
30	Southern U.	31
448		**220**

Nickname: Tigers.
Stadium: Mississippi Memorial (1949), 62,512 capacity. Natural turf.
Colors: Blue & White.
Conference: Southwestern Athletic.
SID: Samuel Jefferson, 601-968-2273.
AD: Robert L Braddy Sr.

JACKSONVILLE
Jacksonville, FL 32211 .... I-AA

Coach: Steve Gilbert, West Chester 1979
Record: 11 Years, 48-59-0

2000 SCHEDULE
Lenoir-Rhyne ■	Sept. 2
Davidson	Sept. 9
Tusculum	Sept. 16
Austin Peay ■	Sept. 30
Charleston So.	Oct. 7
Virginia-Wise	Oct. 21
Stony Brook ■	Oct. 28
Drake	Nov. 4
Wagner ■	Nov. 11
Monmouth ■	Nov. 18
Fairfield [Orlando, FL]	*Nov. 24

1999 RESULTS (3-6-0)
13	Lenoir-Rhyne	28
20	Davidson	15
13	Mississippi Col.	16
28	Austin Peay	21
48	Greensboro	41
12	Virginia-Wise	17
14	Drake	34
36	Tusculum	42
17	Charleston So.	37
201		**251**

Nickname: Dolphins.
Stadium: Milne Field (NA), 5,000 capacity. Natural turf.
Colors: Green & White.
Conference: Division I-AA Independent.
SID: Ramsey Baker, 904-745-7402.
AD: To be named.

JACKSONVILLE ST.
Jacksonville, AL 36265 .... I-AA

Coach: Jack Crowe, UAB 1970
Record: 5 Years, 14-30-0

2000 SCHEDULE
South Fla.	Sept. 2
Nicholls St.	*Sept. 9
Samford ■	*Sept. 21
Sam Houston St. ■	Oct. 7
McNeese St.	*Oct. 14
Southwest Tex. St.	Oct. 21
Stephen F. Austin ■	Oct. 28
Northwestern St. ■	Nov. 4
La.-Lafayette	Nov. 11
Troy St. ■	Nov. 18

1999 RESULTS (2-9-0)
20	Alabama A&M	37
68	Union (Ky.)	13
42	Nicholls St.	45
18	Samford	34
17	Sam Houston St.	51
36	McNeese St.	39
17	Southwest Tex. St.	10
16	Stephen F. Austin	33
7	Northwestern St.	35
14	Ga. Southern	51
16	Troy St.	35
271		**383**

Nickname: Gamecocks.
Stadium: Paul Snow (1947), 15,000 capacity. Natural turf.
Colors: Red & White.
Conference: Southland Football.
SID: Greg Seitz, 205-782-5377.
AD: Joe Davidson.

JAMES MADISON
Harrisonburg, VA 22807 .... I-AA

Coach: Mickey Matthews, West Tex. A&M 1976
Record: 1 Year, 8-4-0

2000 SCHEDULE
Lock Haven ■	*Sept. 2
Liberty ■	*Sept. 9
South Fla.	Sept. 16
New Hampshire ■	Sept. 30
Villanova ■	Oct. 7
Rhode Island	Oct. 14
William & Mary ■	Oct. 21
Delaware	Oct. 28
Maine ■	Nov. 4
Richmond	Nov. 11
Northeastern	Nov. 18

1999 RESULTS (8-3-0)
0	Virginia Tech	47
29	Northeastern	21
35	New Hampshire	28
21	Delaware	7
23	Villanova	20
30	William & Mary	20

48	Connecticut	14
13	South Fla.	3
20	Maine	26
31	Richmond	13
16	Hofstra	34
266		**233**

DIVISION I-AA CHAMPIONSHIP
| 7 | Troy St. | 27 |

Nickname: Dukes.
Stadium: Bridgeforth (1974), 12,500 capacity. Artificial turf.
Colors: Purple & Gold.
Conference: Atlantic 10.
SID: Gary Michael, 540-568-6154.
AD: Jeffrey T. Bourne.

JOHN CARROLL
University Hgts., OH 44118 III

Coach: Regis Scafe, Case Reserve 1971
Record: 6 Years, 23-37-0

2000 SCHEDULE
Catholic ■	Sept. 2
Marietta ■	Sept. 16
Mount Union	Sept. 23
Heidelberg ■	Sept. 30
Wilmington (Ohio) ■	Oct. 7
Muskingum	Oct. 14
Ohio Northern	Oct. 21
Capital ■	Oct. 28
Otterbein	*Nov. 4
Baldwin-Wallace ■	Nov. 11

1999 RESULTS (7-3-0)
26	Catholic	21
51	Capital	12
27	Otterbein	24
51	Mount Union	57
10	Marietta	0
20	Baldwin-Wallace	29
45	Muskingum	7
21	Heidelberg	10
23	Ohio Northern	36
50	Hiram	13
324		**209**

Nickname: Blue Streaks.
Stadium: Wasmer Field (1968), 3,500 capacity. Artificial turf.
Colors: Blue & Gold.
Conference: Ohio Athletic.
SID: Chris Wenzler, 216-397-4676.
AD: Anthony J. De Carlo.

JOHNS HOPKINS
Baltimore, MD 21218 III

Coach: Jim Margraff, Johns Hopkins 1982
Record: 10 Years, 55-42-3

2000 SCHEDULE
Wash. & Lee	Sept. 9
Swarthmore	Sept. 16
Merchant Marine ■	Sept. 23
Gettysburg ■	*Sept. 29
Ursinus	Oct. 7
Muhlenberg ■	Oct. 14
Bridgewater (Va.)	Oct. 21
Dickinson ■	Oct. 28
Frank. & Marsh.	Nov. 4
Western Md. ■	Nov. 11

1999 RESULTS (4-6-0)
31	Wash. & Lee	14
37	Swarthmore	3
20	Merchant Marine	24
37	Gettysburg	13
18	Ursinus	20
18	Muhlenberg	42
24	Bridgewater (Va.)	37
21	Dickinson	37
35	Frank. & Marsh.	33
7	Western Md.	37
248		**260**

Nickname: Blue Jays.
Stadium: Homewood Field (1906), 10,000 capacity. Artificial turf.
Colors: Blue & Black.
Conference: Centennial.
SID: Ernie Larossa, 410-889-4636.
AD: Thomas P. Calder.

JOHNSON SMITH
Charlotte, NC 28216 II

Coach: Timothy Harkness, Johnson Smith 1977
Record: 1 Year, 2-9-0

2000 SCHEDULE
Bowie St.	Sept. 2
Ga. Southern	*Sept. 9
Bethune-Cookman	Sept. 16
Tuskegee	Sept. 23
Elizabeth City St. ■	*Sept. 30
Virginia Union	Oct. 7
Livingstone	*Oct. 14
Fayetteville St. ■	Oct. 21
Winston-Salem ■	Oct. 28
N.C. Central	Nov. 4

1999 RESULTS (2-9-0)
0	Gardner-Webb	51
6	Virginia St.	27
19	Bowie St.	23
27	Elizabeth City St.	6
2	Liberty	38
6	Bethune-Cookman	26
8	Livingstone	30
31	Fayetteville St.	20
6	Winston-Salem	25
7	N.C. Central	35
6	Virginia Union	50
118		**331**

Nickname: Golden Bulls.
Stadium: Memorial (1990), 26,000 capacity. Natural turf.
Colors: Blue & Gold.
Conference: Central Intercollegiate Athletic Association.
SID: Patricia Harvey, 704-378-1205.
AD: Catherine Wright.

JUNIATA
Huntingdon, PA 16652 III

Coach: Kevin Burke, Gettysburg 1990
Record: 2 Years, 11-9-0

2000 SCHEDULE
Lycoming	Sept. 9
Lebanon Valley ■	Sept. 16
Wilkes	Sept. 23
Albright ■	Sept. 30
Susquehanna	Oct. 7
Moravian	Oct. 14
Delaware Valley ■	Oct. 21
FDU-Madison	Oct. 28
Waynesburg ■	Nov. 4
Widener ■	Nov. 11

1999 RESULTS (6-4-0)
13	Lycoming	19
36	Lebanon Valley	3
38	Wilkes	21
45	Albright	24
7	Susquehanna	27
37	Moravian	38
42	Delaware Valley	6
45	FDU-Madison	18
7	Carnegie Mellon	30
59	Widener	45
329		**231**

Nickname: Eagles.
Stadium: Chuck Knox (1988), 3,000 capacity. Natural turf.
Colors: Yale Blue & Old Gold.
Conference: Middle Atlantic.
SID: Bub Parker, 814-643-4310.
AD: Lawrence R. Bock.

KALAMAZOO
Kalamazoo, MI 49006 III

Coach: Tim Rogers, Beloit 1988
Record: 2 Years, 7-11-0

2000 SCHEDULE
Wooster ■	Sept. 9
Mt. St. Joseph ■	Sept. 16
Rose-Hulman	Sept. 23
Colorado Col.	Oct. 7
Hope ■	Oct. 14
Olivet	Oct. 21
Alma ■	Oct. 28
Albion	Nov. 4
Adrian	Nov. 11

1999 RESULTS (3-6-0)
0	Wooster	23
0	Defiance	10
15	Rose-Hulman	20
25	MacMurray	20
14	Albion	16
7	Alma	12
24	Olivet	3
23	Adrian	20
28	Hope	44
136		**168**

Nickname: Hornets.
Stadium: Angell Field (1946), 3,000 capacity. Natural turf.
Colors: Orange & Black.
Conference: Michigan Intercollegiate Athletic Association.
SID: Steve Wideen, 616-337-7287.
AD: Robert L. Kent.

KANSAS
Lawrence, KS 66045 ....I-A

Coach: Terry Allen, Northern Iowa 1979
Record: 11 Years, 89-46-0

2000 SCHEDULE
Southern Methodist	*Sept. 2
UAB ■	*Sept. 16
Southern Ill. ■	*Sept. 23
Oklahoma	Sept. 30
Kansas St. ■	Oct. 7
Missouri	Oct. 14
Colorado ■	Oct. 21
Texas Tech ■	Oct. 28
Nebraska	Nov. 4
Texas ■	Nov. 11
Iowa St.	Nov. 18

1999 RESULTS (5-7-0)
13	Notre Dame	48
71	Cal St. Northridge	14
17	Colorado	51
13	San Diego St.	41
27	Southern Methodist	9
9	Kansas St.	50
17	Texas A&M	34
21	Missouri	0
17	Nebraska	24
45	Baylor	10
13	Oklahoma St.	45
31	Iowa St.	28
294		**354**

Nickname: Jayhawks.
Stadium: Memorial (1921), 50,250 capacity. Artificial turf.
Colors: Crimson & Blue.
Conference: Big 12.
SID: Doug Vance, 913-864-3417.
AD: Robert E. Frederick.

KANSAS ST.
Manhattan, KS 66506 ....I-A

Coach: Bill Snyder, William Jewell 1963
Record: 11 Years, 88-40-1

2000 SCHEDULES AND 1999 RESULTS

2000 SCHEDULE
Iowa [Kansas City, MO]		Aug. 26
Louisiana Tech ■		*Sept. 2
Ball St. ■		*Sept. 16
North Texas ■		Sept. 23
Colorado		Sept. 30
Kansas		Oct. 7
Oklahoma ■		Oct. 14
Texas Tech ■		Oct. 21
Texas A&M		Oct. 28
Iowa St. ■		Nov. 4
Nebraska ■		Nov. 11
Missouri		Nov. 18

1999 RESULTS (10-1-0)
40	Temple	0
40	UTEP	7
35	Iowa St.	28
35	Texas	17
50	Kansas	9
40	Utah St.	0
44	Oklahoma St.	21
48	Baylor	7
20	Colorado	14
15	Nebraska	41
66	Missouri	0
433		**144**

HOLIDAY BOWL
24	Washington	20

Nickname: Wildcats.
Stadium: K S U (1968), 50,000 capacity. Artificial turf.
Colors: Purple & White.
Conference: Big 12.
SID: Doug Dull, 913-532-6735.
AD: Max F. Urick.

KEAN
Union, NJ 07083.................................III

Coach: Joe Loth, Otterbein 1990
(First year as head coach)

2000 SCHEDULE
Thiel ■		Sept. 9
Cortland St.		Sept. 16
Wesley ■		Sept. 23
Wm. Paterson		Sept. 30
Montclair St. ■		Oct. 6
New Jersey City		Oct. 14
Mount Ida ■		Oct. 21
Rowan ■		*Oct. 27
Ursinus		Nov. 4
Col. of New Jersey		Nov. 11

1999 RESULTS (0-9-0)
7	Rensselaer	55
13	Cortland St.	26
12	Wm. Paterson	29
7	Montclair St.	63
0	New Jersey City	41
12	Mount Ida	26
0	Rowan	44
0	Plymouth St.	40
20	Col. of New Jersey	38
71		**362**

Nickname: Cougars.
Stadium: Kean Alumni (1999), 2,750 capacity. Artificial turf.
Colors: Royal Blue & Silver.
Conference: New Jersey Athletic.
SID: Eric M. Nutt, 908-527-2939.
AD: Glenn Hedden.

KENT ST.
Kent, OH 44242.................................I-A

Coach: Dean Pees, Bowling Green 1971
Record: 2 Years, 2-20-0

2000 SCHEDULE
Pittsburgh		Sept. 2
Purdue		Sept. 9
Youngstown St. ■		*Sept. 16
Miami (Ohio)		Sept. 23
Bowling Green ■		*Sept. 30
Central Mich.		Oct. 7
Ohio ■		Oct. 14
Marshall		Oct. 21
Western Mich. ■		Oct. 28
Buffalo		Nov. 4
Akron		Nov. 18

1999 RESULTS (2-9-0)
3	Cincinnati	41
28	Navy	48
23	Pittsburgh	30
41	Bowling Green	27
3	Ohio	31
7	Toledo	47
10	Miami (Ohio)	17
7	Northern Ill.	50
41	Buffalo	20
16	Marshall	28
34	Akron	37
213		**376**

Nickname: Golden Flashes.
Stadium: Dix (1969), 30,520 capacity. Artificial turf.
Colors: Navy Blue & Gold.
Conference: Mid-American.
SID: Will Roleson, 330-672-2110.
AD: Laing E. Kennedy.

KENTUCKY
Lexington, KY 40506.................................I-A

Coach: Hal Mumme, Tarleton St. 1975
Record: 11 Years, 83-44-1

2000 SCHEDULE
Louisville		*Sept. 2
South Fla. ■		Sept. 9
Indiana ■		Sept. 16
Florida		Sept. 23
Mississippi		*Sept. 30
South Carolina ■		*Oct. 7
LSU		*Oct. 14
Georgia ■		*Oct. 21
Mississippi St. ■		Nov. 4
Vanderbilt ■		Nov. 11
Tennessee		Nov. 18

1999 RESULTS (6-5-0)
28	Louisville	56
45	Connecticut	14
44	Indiana	35
10	Florida	38
31	Arkansas	20
30	South Carolina	10
31	LSU	5
34	Georgia	49
22	Mississippi St.	23
19	Vanderbilt	17
21	Tennessee	56
315		**323**

MUSIC CITY BOWL
13	Syracuse	20

Nickname: Wildcats.
Stadium: Commonwealth (1973), 68,000 capacity. Natural turf.
Colors: Blue & White.
Conference: Southeastern.
SID: Tony Neely, 606-257-3838.
AD: C. M. Newton.

KENTUCKY ST.
Frankfort, KY 40601.................................II

Coach: George Small, N.C. A&T 1979
Record: 5 Years, 29-27-0

2000 SCHEDULE
Miles		Aug. 26
West Virginia St. ■		Sept. 2
Clark Atlanta ■		Sept. 9
Ky. Wesleyan		Sept. 16
Fort Valley St.		*Sept. 23
Tuskegee		Sept. 30
Lane ■		Oct. 7
Albany St. (Ga.)		Oct. 14
Ark.-Pine Bluff		*Oct. 21
Morehouse		Oct. 28
Eastern Ky.		Nov. 11

1999 RESULTS (5-6-0)
33	Miles	12
21	Eastern Ky.	27
33	Albany St. (Ga.)	38
38	Clark Atlanta	7
20	Fort Valley St.	27
17	Tuskegee	30
16	Lane	36
24	Savannah St.	23
17	Morehouse	12
47	Morris Brown	24
14	Benedict	21
280		**257**

Nickname: Thorobreds.
Stadium: Alumni Field (1978), 6,000 capacity. Natural turf.
Colors: Green & Gold.
Conference: Southern Intercollegiate Athletic.
SID: Ron Braden, 502-227-6011.
AD: Derrick K. Ramsey.

KY. WESLEYAN
Owensboro, KY 42301.................................II

Coach: John Johnson, Northern Mich. 1984
Record: 6 Years, 28-33-0

2000 SCHEDULE
Mo.-Rolla		Sept. 2
Eastern Ill.		*Sept. 9
Kentucky St. ■		Sept. 16
Westminster (Mo.) ■		Sept. 23
Gannon		Sept. 30
Campbellsville		Oct. 14
Austin Peay ■		*Oct. 21
Quincy ■		Oct. 28
Morehead St.		Nov. 4
Cumberland (Tenn.)		Nov. 11

1999 RESULTS (7-4-0)
20	Eureka	14
48	Bethel (Tenn.)	15
30	Thomas More	24
51	Westminster (Mo.)	35
34	Gannon	7
17	St. Joseph's (Ind.)	25
41	Quincy	14
28	Austin Peay	38
43	Frostburg St.	31
21	Morehead St.	56
0	Murray St.	53
333		**312**

Nickname: Panthers.
Stadium: Apollo (1989), 3,000 capacity. Natural turf.
Colors: Purple & White.
Conference: Division II Independent.
SID: Roy Pickerill, 502-926-3111.
AD: Larry E. Moore.

KENYON
Gambier, OH 43022.................................III

Coach: Vince Arduini, Norwich 1977
Record: 5 Years, 15-34-1

2000 SCHEDULE
Grove City		Sept. 9
Hiram		Sept. 16
Wooster ■		Sept. 23
Denison ■		Sept. 30
Case Reserve		Oct. 7
Allegheny		Oct. 14
Oberlin		Oct. 21
Ohio Wesleyan ■		Oct. 28
Thiel ■		Nov. 4
Earlham		Nov. 11

1999 RESULTS (1-9-0)
14	Centre	34
7	Thiel	21
8	Wooster	45
6	Earlham	14
7	Ohio Wesleyan	21
49	Oberlin	7
26	Grove City	45
0	Allegheny	42

SCHEDULES/RESULTS

3	Wittenberg	48
17	Denison	24
137		**301**

Nickname: Lords.
Stadium: McBride Field (1962), 2,500 capacity. Natural turf.
Colors: Purple & White.
Conference: North Coast Athletic.
SID: Joe Wasiluk, 614-427-5471.
AD: To be named.

KING'S (PA.)
Wilkes-Barre, PA 18711................................III

Coach: Richard Mannello, Springfield 1983
Record: 7 Years, 17-51-1

2000 SCHEDULE
Hartwick	*Sept. 2
Susquehanna ■	Sept. 16
Lycoming ■	Sept. 23
Lebanon Valley	Sept. 30
Moravian ■	Oct. 7
Delaware Valley	Oct. 14
Widener ■	Oct. 21
Albright	Oct. 28
FDU-Madison	Nov. 4
Wilkes ■	Nov. 11

1999 RESULTS (5-5-0)
28	Hartwick	18
26	Susquehanna	27
0	Lycoming	41
24	Lebanon Valley	5
21	Moravian	19
21	Delaware Valley	0
14	Widener	45
37	Albright	33
20	FDU-Madison	26
6	Wilkes	30
197		**244**

Nickname: Monarchs.
Stadium: Monarch Fields (N/A), 3,000 capacity. Natural turf.
Colors: Red & Gold.
Conference: Middle Atlantic.
SID: Bob Ziadie, 717-826-5934.
AD: John J. Dorish.

KNOX
Galesburg, IL 61401................................III

Coach: Andy Gibbons, Culver Stockton 1990
Record: 4 Years, 20-18-0

2000 SCHEDULE
Millikin ■	Sept. 9
Ripon	Sept. 16
Illinois Col. ■	Sept. 23
Lawrence	Sept. 30
St. Norbert ■	Oct. 7
Carroll (Wis.) ■	Oct. 14
Beloit	Oct. 21
Grinnell	Oct. 28
Lake Forest ■	Nov. 4
Monmouth (Ill.)	Nov. 11

1999 RESULTS (3-7-0)
42	Northwestern (Minn.)	35
14	Ripon	33
34	Illinois Col.	35
15	Lawrence	14
17	St. Norbert	38
14	Carroll (Wis.)	35
14	Beloit	20
25	Grinnell	48
28	Lake Forest	13
26	Monmouth (Ill.)	27
229		**298**

Nickname: Prairie Fire.
Stadium: Knox Bowl (1968), 6,000 capacity. Natural turf.
Colors: Purple & Gold.
Conference: Midwest Intercollegiate Athletic.
SID: Bill Spilman, 309-341-7379.
AD: Dan Calandro.

KUTZTOWN
Kutztown, PA 19530................................II

Coach: David Keeny, Kutztown 1983
Record: 2 Years, 9-11-0

2000 SCHEDULE
Maine [Portland, ME]	*Aug. 31
Lock Haven	*Sept. 9
Siena	Sept. 16
Millersville	*Sept. 23
Clarion ■	Sept. 30
East Stroudsburg	Oct. 7
West Chester	Oct. 14
Cheyney	Oct. 21
Mansfield	Oct. 28
Bloomsburg ■	Nov. 4
Shippensburg	Nov. 11

1999 RESULTS (4-6-0)
37	Lock Haven	7
12	Shippensburg	42
21	Clarion	31
33	Bloomsburg	42
27	Cheyney	6
51	Mansfield	14
24	East Stroudsburg	10
28	Millersville	35
38	Slippery Rock	68
30	West Chester	55
301		**310**

Nickname: Golden Bears.
Stadium: University Field (1987), 5,600 capacity. Natural turf.
Colors: Maroon & Gold.
Conference: Pennsylvania State Athletic.
SID: Josh Leiboff, 610-683-4182.
AD: Clark Yeager.

LA SALLE
Philadelphia, PA 19141................................I-AA

Coach: Bill Manlove, Temple 1958
Record: 30 Years, 199-102-1

2000 SCHEDULE
St. Francis (Pa.)	Sept. 2
Duquesne ■	Sept. 9
Iona	Sept. 16
Siena ■	Sept. 23
Catholic	Sept. 30
Canisius	Oct. 7
Shenandoah ■	Oct. 21
St. John's (N.Y.)	Oct. 28
St. Peter's	*Nov. 4
Marist ■	Nov. 11
Fairfield	Nov. 18

1999 RESULTS (4-6-0)
44	St. Francis (Pa.)	7
3	Duquesne	32
23	Iona	31
17	Siena	7
19	Canisius	6
23	Marist	41
10	St. John's (N.Y.)	21
35	St. Peter's	13
0	Fairfield	42
7	Georgetown	52
181		**252**

Nickname: Explorers.
Stadium: McCarthy (0000), 7,500 capacity. Natural turf.
Colors: Blue & Gold.
Conference: Metro Atlantic Athletic.
SID: Kevin Currie, 215-951-1605.
AD: Thomas M. Brennan.

LA VERNE
La Verne, CA 91750................................III

Coach: Don Morel, La Verne 1987
Record: 5 Years, 29-16-0

2000 SCHEDULE
Azusa Pacific	*Sept. 16
Claremont-M-S	*Sept. 23
Occidental ■	Sept. 30
Pomona-Pitzer ■	Oct. 7
Redlands	Oct. 14
Cal Lutheran	Oct. 21
Chapman	*Oct. 28
Menlo ■	Nov. 4
Whittier	*Nov. 11

1999 RESULTS (7-2-0)
35	Occidental	3
45	Whittier	0
31	Claremont-M-S	28
15	Pomona-Pitzer	14
35	Chapman	33
21	Redlands	22
35	Cal Lutheran	32
45	Azusa Pacific	47
47	Menlo	41
309		**220**

Nickname: Leopards, Leos.
Stadium: Ortmayer (1991), 1,500 capacity. Natural turf.
Colors: Orange & Green.
Conference: Southern California Intercollegiate Athletic.
SID: Daniel Mulville, 909-593-3511.
AD: Jimmy M. Paschal.

LAFAYETTE
Easton, PA 18042................................I-AA

Coach: Frank Tavani, Lebanon Valley 1975
(First year as head coach)

2000 SCHEDULE
Towson ■	Sept. 9
Princeton ■	Sept. 16
Pennsylvania	Sept. 23
Harvard ■	Sept. 30
Columbia	Oct. 7
Bucknell	Oct. 14
Holy Cross ■	Oct. 21
Colgate	Oct. 28
Fordham	Nov. 4
Duquesne ■	Nov. 11
Lehigh ■	Nov. 18

1999 RESULTS (4-7-0)
7	Towson	35
12	Holy Cross	30
28	Brown	35
20	Dartmouth	10
14	Colgate	56
10	Princeton	22
22	Bucknell	21
38	Marist	13
27	Fordham	7
17	Duquesne	28
12	Lehigh	14
207		**271**

Nickname: Leopards.
Stadium: Fisher Field (1926), 13,750 capacity. Natural turf.
Colors: Maroon & White.
Conference: Patriot.
SID: Scott D. Morse, 610-250-5122.
AD: Eve Atkinson.

LAKE FOREST
Lake Forest, IL 60045................................III

Coach: Randy Moore, Iowa 1984
Record: 5 Years, 13-34-0

2000 SCHEDULE
Chicago ■	Sept. 9
Monmouth (Ill.)	Sept. 16
Grinnell ■	Sept. 23
Beloit ■	Sept. 30
Ripon	Oct. 7
Lawrence	Oct. 14
Illinois Col. ■	Oct. 21
St. Norbert ■	Oct. 28
Knox	Nov. 4
Carroll (Wis.)	Nov. 11

1999 RESULTS (5-5-0)

16	Chicago	14
42	Monmouth (Ill.)	14
21	Grinnell	24
14	Beloit	38
36	Ripon	43
56	Lawrence	32
27	Illinois Col.	7
21	St. Norbert	41
13	Knox	28
21	Carroll (Wis.)	14
250		**211**

Nickname: Foresters.
Stadium: Farwell Field (N/A), 2,000 capacity. Natural turf.
Colors: Red & Black.
Conference: Midwest Intercollegiate Athletic.
SID: Scott Rucker, 708-735-6011.
AD: Jackie A. Slaats.

LAKELAND
Sheboygan, WI 53082 III

Coach: Jeff Hynes, Concordia (Wis.) 1992
Record: 1 Year, 5-5-0

2000 SCHEDULE

Wis.-Stout ■	Sept. 2
Carthage ■	Sept. 9
MacMurray	Sept. 23
Concordia (Wis.) ■	Sept. 30
Concordia (Ill.)	Oct. 7
Aurora	Oct. 14
Greenville ■	Oct. 21
Benedictine (Ill.) ■	Oct. 28
Eureka	Nov. 4
Mt. Senario	Nov. 11

1999 RESULTS (5-5-0)

17	Wis.-Platteville	20
26	Carthage	7
30	Concordia (Wis.)	16
53	Greenville	33
41	Concordia (Ill.)	20
21	MacMurray	35
52	Eureka	7
28	Benedictine (Ill.)	31
32	Aurora	49
21	Mt. Senario	44
321		**262**

Nickname: Muskies.
Stadium: Taylor Field (1958), 1,500 capacity. Natural turf.
Colors: Navy & Gold.
Conference: Illini-Badger.
SID: John Weber, 414-565-1411.
AD: Jane Bouche.

LANE
Jackson, TN 38301 II

Coach: Eric Carter, South Carolina St. 1985
(First year as head coach)

2000 SCHEDULE

Lincoln (Mo.) ■	Sept. 2
Fort Valley St. ■	*Sept. 9
Texas Southern	*Sept. 16
Albany St. (Ga.)	Sept. 23
Clark Atlanta [Memphis, TN]	*Sept. 30
Kentucky St.	Oct. 7
Benedict ■	*Oct. 14
Morehouse	Oct. 21
Miles ■	Oct. 28
Tuskegee	Nov. 4
Ark.-Pine Bluff	Nov. 11

1999 RESULTS (2-8-0)

17	Morris Brown	19
17	Fort Valley St.	44
15	Texas Southern	38
10	Morehouse	40
3	Clark Atlanta	7
36	Kentucky St.	16
30	Miles	25
12	Benedict	43
28	Tuskegee	36
28	Ark.-Pine Bluff	44
196		**312**

Nickname: Dragons.
Stadium: Rothrock (1930), 3,500 capacity. Natural turf.
Colors: Blue & Red.
Conference: Southern Intercollegiate Athletic.
SID: Kimberly Walker, 901-426-7651.
AD: J. L. Perry.

LAWRENCE
Appleton, WI 54912 III

Coach: David Brown, Coe
Record: 1 Year, 3-7-0

2000 SCHEDULE

Macalester	*Sept. 9
Illinois Col.	Sept. 16
St. Norbert ■	*Sept. 23
Knox ■	Sept. 30
Beloit	Oct. 7
Lake Forest	Oct. 14
Carroll (Wis.)	Oct. 21
Monmouth (Ill.) ■	Oct. 28
Ripon	Nov. 4
Grinnell ■	Nov. 11

1999 RESULTS (3-7-0)

8	Pomona-Pitzer	23
16	Illinois Col.	21
14	St. Norbert	43
14	Knox	15
14	Beloit	31
32	Lake Forest	56
45	Carroll (Wis.)	14
19	Monmouth (Ill.)	13
25	Ripon	22
14	Grinnell	51
201		**289**

Nickname: Vikings.
Stadium: Banta Bowl (1965), 5,255 capacity. Natural turf.
Colors: Navy & White.
Conference: Midwest Intercollegiate Athletic.
SID: Joe Vanden Acker, 920-832-7346.
AD: David Brown.

LEBANON VALLEY
Annville, PA 17003 III

Coach: Mike Silecchia, Mansfield 1978
Record: 2 Years, 3-17-0

2000 SCHEDULE

Ursinus	Sept. 9
Juniata	Sept. 16
Moravian	Sept. 23
King's (Pa.) ■	Sept. 30
Lycoming ■	Oct. 7
Albright	*Oct. 14
Susquehanna ■	Oct. 21
Wilkes	Oct. 28
Widener	Nov. 4
Delaware Valley ■	Nov. 11

1999 RESULTS (2-8-0)

7	Ursinus	25
3	Juniata	36
24	Moravian	13
5	King's (Pa.)	24
7	Lycoming	41
7	Albright	21
17	Susquehanna	14
25	Wilkes	27
0	Widener	32
3	Delaware Valley	10
98		**243**

Nickname: Flying Dutchmen.
Stadium: Arnold Field (1969), 2,500 capacity. Natural turf.
Colors: Royal Blue, White & Red.
Conference: Middle Atlantic.
SID: Gregg Matalas, 717-867-6033.
AD: Louis A. Sorrentino.

LEHIGH
Bethlehem, PA 18015 .... I-AA

Coach: Kevin Higgins, West Chester 1977
Record: 6 Years, 44-24-1

2000 SCHEDULE

Wofford	*Sept. 9
Pennsylvania ■	Sept. 16
Princeton	*Sept. 23
Cornell ■	Sept. 30
Towson	Oct. 7
Harvard	Oct. 14
Bucknell ■	Oct. 21
Holy Cross	Oct. 28
Colgate ■	Nov. 4
Fordham ■	Nov. 11
Lafayette	Nov. 18

1999 RESULTS (10-1-0)

49	Fordham	7
56	Monmouth	10
31	Princeton	0
63	Columbia	13
30	Dartmouth	14
42	Delaware	35
62	Holy Cross	8
44	Towson	39
24	Colgate	28
48	Bucknell	27
14	Lafayette	12
463		**193**

DIVISION I-AA CHAMPIONSHIP

15	Hofstra	27

Nickname: Mountain Hawks.
Stadium: Goodman (1988), 16,000 capacity. Natural turf.
Colors: Brown & White.
Conference: Patriot.
SID: Glenn Hofmann, 610-758-3174.
AD: Joseph D. Sterrett.

LENOIR-RHYNE
Hickory, NC 28603 II

Coach: Bill Hart, Rowan 1973
Record: 3 Years, 7-25-0

2000 SCHEDULE

Concord ■	*Aug. 26
Jacksonville	Sept. 2
Western Caro.	*Sept. 9
Presbyterian	Sept. 16
Carson-Newman ■	*Sept. 23
Tusculum	Sept. 30
Wingate	Oct. 7
Mars Hill ■	Oct. 21
Humboldt St.	Oct. 28
Newberry ■	*Nov. 4
Catawba ■	Nov. 11

1999 RESULTS (5-6-0)

21	Concord	12
28	Jacksonville	13
21	Tusculum	14
24	Presbyterian	21
7	Charleston So.	14
14	Gardner-Webb	27
28	Wingate	21
21	Newberry	24
14	Carson-Newman	55
7	Mars Hill	33
7	Catawba	24
192		**258**

Nickname: Bears.
Stadium: Moretz (1923), 8,500 capacity. Natural turf.
Colors: Red & Black.
Conference: South Atlantic.
SID: Michael MacEachern, 704-328-7174.
AD: Jane Jenkins.

LEWIS & CLARK
Portland, OR 97219 III

Coach: Mike Fanger, Lewis & Clark 1990
Record: 1 Year, 0-9-0

2000 SCHEDULE

Redlands ■	Sept. 16
Pomona-Pitzer	Sept. 23
Claremont-M-S ■	Sept. 30
Puget Sound	Oct. 7
Pacific Lutheran ■	Oct. 14
Linfield ■	Oct. 21
Colorado Col.	Oct. 28
Willamette	Nov. 4
Whitworth ■	Nov. 11

1999 RESULTS (0-9-0)

0	Redlands	49
7	Simon Fraser	26
10	Linfield	65
10	Claremont-M-S	41
20	Puget Sound	26
10	Pacific Lutheran	63
3	Eastern Ore.	69
6	Willamette	42
0	Whitworth	52
66		**433**

Nickname: Pioneers.
Stadium: Griswold (NA), 3,700 capacity. Artificial turf.
Colors: Orange & Black.
Conference: Northwest.
SID: Patrick Stewart, 503-768-7067.
AD: Steve Wallo.

LIBERTY
Lynchburg, VA 24502 ....I-AA

Coach: Ken Karcher, Tulane 1986
(First year as head coach)

2000 SCHEDULE

East Tenn. St. ■	*Sept. 2
James Madison	*Sept. 9
Gardner-Webb ■	*Sept. 16
Delaware St.	Sept. 23
Wingate ■	*Sept. 30
Hofstra	*Oct. 13
South Fla.	*Oct. 21
Samford ■	Oct. 28
Elon	Nov. 4
Charleston So. ■	Nov. 11
Appalachian St.	Nov. 18

1999 RESULTS (4-7-0)

21	Virginia Union	12
3	Marshall	63
15	Tennessee Tech	18
48	Fayetteville St.	14
38	Johnson Smith	2
0	South Fla.	28
12	East Tenn. St.	24
34	Charleston So.	14
28	Samford	34
14	Elon	38
12	Appalachian St.	28
225		**275**

Nickname: Flames.
Stadium: Williams (1989), 12,000 capacity. Artificial turf.
Colors: Red, White & Blue.
Conference: Division I-AA Independent.
SID: Todd Wetmore, 804-582-2292.
AD: Kim Graham.

LINFIELD
McMinnville, OR 97128 III

Coach: Jay Locey, Oregon St. 1976
Record: 4 Years, 24-12-0

2000 SCHEDULE

Menlo ■	Sept. 9
Southern Ore. ■	Sept. 16
Pacific Lutheran	Sept. 30
Whittier	*Oct. 7
Eastern Ore.	Oct. 14
Lewis & Clark	Oct. 21
Puget Sound ■	Oct. 28
Whitworth	Nov. 4

Willamette ■	Nov. 11

1999 RESULTS (6-3-0)

48	Redlands	0
10	Southern Ore.	40
28	Menlo	19
65	Lewis & Clark	10
31	Whitworth	7
36	Eastern Ore. U.	29
23	Pacific Lutheran	56
42	Puget Sound	0
7	Willamette	28
290		**189**

Nickname: Wildcats.
Stadium: Maxwell Field (0000), 2,250 capacity. Natural turf.
Colors: Purple & Red.
Conference: Northwest.
SID: Kelly Bird, 503-434-2439.
AD: Scott Carnahan.

LIVINGSTONE
Salisbury, NC 28144 II

Coach: Gregory Richardson, N.C. Central 1974
Record: 1 Year, 4-7-0

2000 SCHEDULE

Catawba	Sept. 2
Tusculum ■	*Sept. 9
Virginia Union [Roanoke, VA]	Sept. 16
Fayetteville St.	*Sept. 23
Virginia St.	Sept. 30
Winston-Salem	Oct. 7
Johnson Smith ■	*Oct. 14
Elizabeth City St. ■	*Oct. 21
N.C. Central ■	Oct. 28
Benedict	Nov. 4

1999 RESULTS (4-7-0)

9	Tusculum	11
37	Newberry	34
6	Virginia Union	24
42	Bowie St.	14
0	Virginia St.	17
0	Winston-Salem	34
30	Johnson Smith	8
33	Elizabeth City St.	34
6	N.C. Central	12
13	Albany St. (Ga.)	34
34	Fayetteville St.	7
210		**229**

Nickname: Blue Bears.
Stadium: Alumni (NA), 4,000 capacity. Natural turf.
Colors: Columbia Blue & Black.
Conference: Central Intercollegiate Athletic Association.
SID: Leonard L. Haynes IV, 704-638-5586.
AD: Clifton Huff.

LOCK HAVEN
Lock Haven, PA 17745 II

Coach: Mark Luther, Penn St. 1992
(First year as head coach)

2000 SCHEDULE

James Madison	*Sept. 2
Kutztown ■	*Sept. 9
Bloomsburg	Sept. 16
Indiana (Pa.) ■	Sept. 23
Shippensburg	Sept. 30
Edinboro ■	*Oct. 7
Cheyney	Oct. 14
Calif. (Pa.)	Oct. 21
Slippery Rock ■	Oct. 28
Clarion	Nov. 4
Mansfield ■	Nov. 11

1999 RESULTS (2-9-0)

24	East Stroudsburg	28
7	Kutztown	37
24	Bloomsburg	44
53	Cheyney	26
9	Indiana (Pa.)	27
12	Calif. (Pa.)	33
7	Edinboro	38
31	Mansfield	0

7	Shippensburg	68
41	Clarion	44
17	Slippery Rock	38
232		**383**

Nickname: Bald Eagles.
Stadium: Hubert Jack (N/A), 3,000 capacity. Artificial turf.
Colors: Crimson & White.
Conference: Pennsylvania State Athletic.
SID: Danielle Barney, 570-893-2350.
AD: Sharon E. Taylor.

LORAS
Dubuque, IA 52004 III

Coach: Bob Bierie, Loras 1965
Record: 14 Years, 80-61-1

2000 SCHEDULE

William Penn ■	Sept. 9
Coe	Sept. 16
Dubuque ■	Sept. 23
Central (Iowa)	Sept. 30
Upper Iowa ■	Oct. 7
Cornell College	Oct. 14
Simpson	Oct. 21
Buena Vista ■	Oct. 28
Luther	Nov. 4
Wartburg	Nov. 11

1999 RESULTS (4-6-0)

20	Coe	34
13	Central (Iowa)	32
18	Upper Iowa	15
32	William Penn	20
19	Wartburg	30
16	Buena Vista	20
22	Cornell College	19
28	Simpson	29
28	Luther	31
35	Dubuque	25
231		**255**

Nickname: Duhawks.
Stadium: Rock Bowl (1945), 3,000 capacity. Natural turf.
Colors: Purple & Gold.
Conference: Iowa Intercollegiate Athletic.
SID: Dave Beyer, 319-588-7407.
AD: Greg Capell.

LA.-LAFAYETTE
Lafayette, LA 70504 ....I-A

Coach: Jerry Baldwin, Mississippi Val. 1975
Record: 1 Year, 2-9-0

2000 SCHEDULE

Sam Houston St. ■	*Sept. 2
Texas	Sept. 9
Texas Tech	*Sept. 16
Northwestern St. ■	*Sept. 23
UAB	Sept. 30
Tulane ■	Oct. 7
Louisiana Tech	*Oct. 14
North Texas ■	*Oct. 28
La.-Monroe	*Nov. 4
Middle Tenn. St.	Nov. 18

1999 RESULTS (2-9-0)

7	Oklahoma St.	24
17	Texas Tech	38
0	Houston	45
45	Middle Tenn. St.	31
31	Louisiana Tech	41
0	Washington St.	44
32	Tulane	48
7	La.-Monroe	31
27	Arkansas St.	31
0	Southern Miss.	48
37	Wofford	34
203		**415**

Nickname: Ragin' Cajuns.
Stadium: Cajun Field (1971), 31,000 capacity. Natural turf.

Colors: Vermilion & White.
Conference: Division I-A Independent.
SID: Jeff Conrad, 318-482-6331.
AD: Nelson Schexnayder Jr.

LA.-MONROE
Monroe, LA 71209 ....I-A

Coach: Bobby Keasler, La.-Monroe 1970
Record: 10 Years, 83-40-2

2000 SCHEDULE
Minnesota	Sept. 2
Memphis	*Sept. 9
Nicholls St. ■	*Sept. 16
Tennessee	Sept. 23
Southwest Tex. St. ■	*Sept. 30
Arkansas	*Oct. 7
Middle Tenn. St.	*Oct. 14
UCF	Oct. 21
La.-Lafayette ■	*Nov. 4
Louisiana Tech ■	*Nov. 11
Wofford ■	Nov. 18

1999 RESULTS (5-6-0)
27	Nicholls St.	10
0	Minnesota	35
6	Arkansas	44
38	Northwestern St.	7
0	UAB	47
0	Utah	42
20	Wyoming	38
31	La.-Lafayette	7
10	Middle Tenn. St.	0
17	Louisiana Tech	58
37	Tulsa	34
186		**322**

Nickname: Indians.
Stadium: Malone (1978), 30,427 capacity. Natural turf.
Colors: Maroon & Gold.
Conference: Division I-A Independent.
SID: Cory Rogers, 318-342-5460.
AD: Warner Alford.

LSU
Baton Rouge, LA 70803 ....I-A

Coach: Nick Saban, Kent St. 1973
Record: 6 Years, 43-26-1

2000 SCHEDULE
Western Caro. ■	*Sept. 2
Houston ■	*Sept. 9
Auburn	*Sept. 16
UAB ■	*Sept. 23
Tennessee ■	*Sept. 30
Florida	Oct. 7
Kentucky ■	*Oct. 14
Mississippi St. ■	*Oct. 21
Alabama	Nov. 4
Mississippi	Nov. 11
Arkansas [Little Rock, AR]	Nov. 24

1999 RESULTS (3-8-0)
29	San Jose St.	21
52	North Texas	0
7	Auburn	41
22	Georgia	23
10	Florida	31
5	Kentucky	31
16	Mississippi St.	17
23	Mississippi	42
17	Alabama	23
7	Houston	20
35	Arkansas	10
223		**259**

Nickname: Fighting Tigers.
Stadium: Tiger (1924), 91,600 capacity. Natural turf.
Colors: Purple & Gold.
Conference: Southeastern.
SID: Herb Vincent, 504-388-8226.
AD: Joe Dean.

LOUISIANA TECH
Ruston, LA 71272 ....I-A

Coach: Jack Bicknell III, Boston College 1984
Record: 1 Year, 8-3-0

2000 SCHEDULE
Mississippi Val. ■	*Aug. 26
Kansas St.	*Sept. 2
Penn St.	Sept. 9
Stephen F. Austin ■	*Sept. 16
Tulsa	*Sept. 23
Middle Tenn. St.	*Oct. 7
La.-Lafayette ■	*Oct. 14
Auburn	Oct. 21
Miami (Fla.)	Oct. 28
UCF ■	*Nov. 4
La.-Monroe	*Nov. 11
Hawaii	*Nov. 18

1999 RESULTS (8-3-0)
7	Florida St.	41
17	Texas A&M	37
55	Sam Houston St.	17
29	Alabama	28
41	La.-Lafayette	31
42	Middle Tenn. St.	18
46	UCF	35
34	Toledo	17
58	La.-Monroe	17
41	UAB	20
19	Southern California	45
389		**306**

Nickname: Bulldogs.
Stadium: Joe Aillet (1968), 30,600 capacity. Natural turf.
Colors: Red & Blue.
Conference: Division I-A Independent.
SID: Brian Millen, 318-257-3144.
AD: Jim M. Oakes.

LOUISVILLE
Louisville, KY 40292 ....I-A

Coach: John L. Smith, Weber St. 1971
Record: 11 Years, 83-49-0

2000 SCHEDULE
Kentucky ■	*Sept. 2
Grambling ■	*Sept. 9
Florida St.	*Sept. 23
Connecticut ■	Sept. 30
UAB	Oct. 7
Cincinnati ■	Oct. 14
East Caro. ■	*Oct. 19
Tulane ■	Oct. 28
Southern Miss.	Nov. 4
Army ■	Nov. 11
Houston	Nov. 18

1999 RESULTS (7-4-0)
56	Kentucky	28
58	Chattanooga	30
36	Illinois	41
21	Oklahoma	42
45	Eastern Mich.	10
52	Army	59
32	Memphis	31
39	Houston	33
23	UAB	14
23	Cincinnati	13
27	Southern Miss.	30
412		**331**

HUMANITARIAN BOWL
31	Boise St.	34

Nickname: Cardinals.
Stadium: Papa John's Cardinal (19989), 42,000 capacity. Natural turf.
Colors: Red, Black & White.
Conference: Conference USA.
SID: Kenny Klein, 502-852-6581.
AD: Thomas M. Jurich.

LUTHER
Decorah, IA 52101 III

Coach: Brad Pole, Rocky Mountain 1979
Record: 4 Years, 12-28-0

2000 SCHEDULE
Buena Vista	Sept. 2
Central (Iowa) ■	Sept. 9
Simpson	Sept. 23
Dubuque ■	Sept. 30
Coe ■	Oct. 7
Wartburg	Oct. 14
Cornell College ■	Oct. 21
William Penn ■	Oct. 28
Loras	Nov. 4
Upper Iowa	Nov. 11

1999 RESULTS (2-8-0)
38	Dubuque	17
7	Coe	35
7	Central (Iowa)	43
14	Upper Iowa	31
22	William Penn	28
17	Wartburg	20
7	Buena Vista	29
35	Cornell College	41
31	Loras	28
0	Simpson	41
178		**313**

Nickname: Norse.
Stadium: Carlson (1966), 5,000 capacity. Natural turf.
Colors: Blue & White.
Conference: Iowa Intercollegiate Athletic.
SID: Dave Blanchard, 319-387-1586.
AD: Joe Thompson.

LYCOMING
Williamsport, PA 17701 III

Coach: Frank Girardi, West Chester 1961
Record: 28 Years, 211-66-5

2000 SCHEDULE
Juniata ■	Sept. 9
Widener	Sept. 16
King's (Pa.) ■	Sept. 23
Lebanon Valley	Oct. 7
Wilkes ■	Oct. 14
Albright ■	Oct. 21
Delaware Valley	Oct. 28
Susquehanna ■	Nov. 4
FDU-Madison ■	Nov. 11

1999 RESULTS (9-0-0)
19	Juniata	13
30	Widener	0
41	King's (Pa.)	0
41	Lebanon Valley	7
20	Wilkes	15
43	Albright	9
34	Delaware Valley	0
36	Susquehanna	7
27	FDU-Madison	3
291		**54**

DIVISION III CHAMPIONSHIP
7	Wash. & Jeff.	14

Nickname: Warriors.
Stadium: Person Field (1962), 2,500 capacity. Natural turf.
Colors: Blue & Gold.
Conference: Middle Atlantic.
SID: Jeff Michaels, 570-321-4028.
AD: Frank L. Girardi.

MACALESTER
St. Paul, MN 55105 III

Coach: Dennis Czech, Macalester 1983
Record: 2 Years, 4-16-0

2000 SCHEDULE
Lawrence ■	*Sept. 9
Bethel (Minn.) ■	*Sept. 16
Concordia-M'head	Sept. 23
Carleton	Sept. 30
St. John's (Minn.)	Oct. 7
Augsburg ■	Oct. 14
St. Thomas (Minn.)	Oct. 21
St. Olaf	Oct. 28
Hamline [Minneapolis, MN]	*Nov. 3
Gust. Adolphus ■	Nov. 11

1999 RESULTS (2-8-0)

35	Crown	22
7	St. John's (Minn.)	42
6	Gust. Adolphus	49
27	Carleton	26
14	St. Thomas (Minn.)	60
7	Augsburg	27
0	Bethel (Minn.)	74
0	Concordia-M'head	40
14	Hamline	45
17	St. Olaf	47
127		**432**

Nickname: Scots.
Stadium: Macalester (1965), 4,000 capacity. Natural turf.
Colors: Orange & Blue.
Conference: Minnesota Intercollegiate Athletic.
SID: Andy Johnson, 612-696-6533.
AD: Irv Cross.

MACMURRAY
Jacksonville, IL 62650 III

Coach: Bob Frey, Mount Union 1985
Record: 5 Years, 33-17-0

2000 SCHEDULE

Albion ■	Sept. 2
Blackburn	Sept. 9
Lakeland ■	Sept. 23
Greenville	*Sept. 30
Benedictine (Ill.) ■	Oct. 7
Eureka	Oct. 14
Aurora ■	Oct. 21
Concordia (Wis.)	Oct. 28
Concordia (Ill.) ■	Nov. 4
Westminster (Mo.)	Nov. 11

1999 RESULTS (6-4-0)

53	Greenville	60
34	Blackburn	7
13	Aurora	20
14	Concordia (Wis.)	21
20	Kalamazoo	25
35	Lakeland	21
48	Concordia (Ill.)	3
13	Eureka	7
35	Benedictine (Ill.)	17
56	Westminster (Mo.)	49
321		**230**

Nickname: Highlanders.
Stadium: Highlander (1984), 5,000 capacity. Natural turf.
Colors: Scarlet & Navy.
Conference: St. Louis Intercollegiate Athletic.
SID: Kris Doorey, 217-479-7143.
AD: Robert E. Gay.

MAINE
Orono, ME 04469 .... I-AA

Coach: Jack Cosgrove, Maine 1978
Record: 7 Years, 31-46-0

2000 SCHEDULE

Kutztown [Portland, ME]	*Aug. 31
Hofstra ■	*Sept. 9
Howard ■	*Sept. 16
Villanova	Sept. 23
William & Mary ■	*Sept. 30
Massachusetts	Oct. 14
Richmond	Oct. 21
Rhode Island ■	Oct. 28
James Madison	Nov. 4
Northeastern ■	Nov. 11
New Hampshire	Nov. 18

1999 RESULTS (4-7-0)

21	Colgate	28
19	Hofstra	27
21	Richmond	14
20	Connecticut	34
35	McNeese St.	7
17	Massachusetts	38
14	Rhode Island	23
13	William & Mary	37
26	James Madison	20
20	Northeastern	14
20	New Hampshire	31
226		**273**

Nickname: Black Bears.
Stadium: Alumni (1942), 10,000 capacity. Artificial turf.
Colors: Blue & White.
Conference: Atlantic 10.
SID: Joe Roberts, 207-581-1086.
AD: Suzanne J. Tyler.

MAINE MARITIME
Castine, ME 04421 III

Coach: Mike Hodgson, Maine 1979
Record: 6 Years, 31-27-0

2000 SCHEDULE

Curry	Sept. 9
Mass. Maritime ■	Sept. 16
Mass.-Dartmouth	Sept. 23
Bri'water (Mass.) ■	Sept. 30
Westfield St.	Oct. 7
Fitchburg St. ■	Oct. 14
Salve Regina	Oct. 21
Worcester St. ■	Oct. 28
Framingham St.	Nov. 4

1999 RESULTS (3-6-0)

15	Curry	21
22	Mass. Maritime	28
20	Mass.-Dartmouth	3
16	Bri'water (Mass.)	48
13	Westfield St.	14
20	Fitchburg St.	26
20	Salve Regina	22
30	Worcester St.	27
46	Framingham St.	27
202		**216**

Nickname: Mariners.
Stadium: Ritchie (1965), 3,500 capacity. Artificial turf.
Colors: Royal Blue & Gold.
Conference: New England Football.
SID: To be named, 207-326-2259.
AD: William J. Mottola.

MANCHESTER
North Manchester, IN 46962 III

Coach: Dave Harms, Drake 1980
Record: 5 Years, 18-32-0

2000 SCHEDULE

Wabash ■	Sept. 9
Olivet	Sept. 16
Earlham ■	Sept. 23
Franklin	Sept. 30
Thomas More	Oct. 7
Defiance ■	Oct. 14
Bluffton	Oct. 21
Mt. St. Joseph ■	Oct. 28
Hanover	Nov. 4
Anderson (Ind.) ■	Nov. 11

1999 RESULTS (2-8-0)

39	Waynesburg	37
37	Olivet	21
23	Albion	49
6	Franklin	22
14	Hanover	45
3	Wabash	23
10	Bluffton	26
0	Wilmington (Ohio)	39
21	Mt. St. Joseph	28
25	Anderson (Ind.)	27
178		**317**

Nickname: Spartans.
Stadium: Burt Memorial (NA), 4,500 capacity. Natural turf.
Colors: Black & Gold.
Conference: Heartland Collegiate Athletic.
SID: Doug Shoemaker, 219-982-5035.
AD: Tom Jarman.

MANSFIELD
Mansfield, PA 16933 II

Coach: Joe Gilbert, Hamilton 1987
(First year as head coach)

2000 SCHEDULE

Buffalo St.	Sept. 9
Ithaca	Sept. 16
Calif. (Pa.) ■	Sept. 23
Cheyney	Sept. 30
West Chester ■	Oct. 7
Millersville	Oct. 14
Bloomsburg ■	Oct. 21
Kutztown ■	Oct. 28
East Stroudsburg	Nov. 4
Lock Haven	Nov. 11

1999 RESULTS (1-9-0)

15	West Liberty St.	36
7	Ithaca	21
11	Calif. (Pa.)	44
25	Millersville	42
6	West Chester	42
14	Kutztown	51
0	Lock Haven	31
35	Cheyney	12
21	Bloomsburg	53
20	East Stroudsburg	41
154		**373**

Nickname: Mountaineers.
Stadium: Van Norman Field (1964), 4,000 capacity. Natural turf.
Colors: Red & Black.
Conference: Pennsylvania State Athletic.
SID: Steve McCloskey, 570-662-4845.
AD: Roger N. Maisner.

MARANATHA BAPTIST
Watertown, WI 53094 III

Coach: Terry Price, Pillsbury 1971
Record: 22 Years, 102-103-1

2000 SCHEDULE

Greenville ■	Sept. 9
Rockford ■	Sept. 16
Crown	Sept. 23
Northwestern (Minn.) ■	Sept. 30
Trinity Bible (N.D.)	Oct. 7
Mt. Senario	Oct. 14
Martin Luther ■	Oct. 21
Wis. Lutheran	Nov. 4

1999 RESULTS (2-6-0)

21	Greenville	40
43	Crown	42
28	Northwestern (Minn.)	27
28	Trinity Bible (N.D.)	29
22	Westminster (Mo.)	47
13	Martin Luther	45
6	Mt. Senario	49
14	Blackburn	17
175		**296**

Nickname: Crusaders.
Stadium: Maranatha (NA), 3,000 capacity. Natural turf.
Colors: Navy Blue & Gold.
Conference: Division III Independent.
SID: Greg Wright, 920-206-2376.
AD: Greg Weniger.

MARIETTA
Marietta, OH 45750 III

Coach: Gene Epley, Indiana (Pa.) 1965
Record: 13 Years, 55-73-3

2000 SCHEDULE

Waynesburg	Sept. 2
John Carroll	Sept. 16
Heidelberg ■	*Sept. 23
Muskingum	*Sept. 30
Mount Union	Oct. 7
Capital ■	Oct. 14
Otterbein	Oct. 21

Baldwin-Wallace ■ .... Oct. 28
Wilmington (Ohio) ■ .... Nov. 4
Ohio Northern .... Nov. 11

1999 RESULTS (2-8-0)
23	Waynesburg	28
35	Muskingum	19
7	Baldwin-Wallace	44
10	Ohio Northern	32
0	John Carroll	10
27	Heidelberg	33
21	Mount Union	56
38	Hiram	14
21	Capital	49
14	Otterbein	37
196		**322**

Nickname: Pioneers.
Stadium: Don Drumm Field (1935), 7,000 capacity. Natural turf.
Colors: Navy Blue & White.
Conference: Ohio Athletic.
SID: Brian Deitz, 614-376-4891.
AD: Debora Lazorik.

MARIST
Poughkeepsie, NY 12601 .... I-AA

Coach: Jim Parady, Maine 1984
Record: 8 Years, 48-32-1

2000 SCHEDULE
Western Conn. St. ■ .... Sept. 2
St. Peter's .... *Sept. 7
Duquesne .... Sept. 23
Wagner .... Sept. 30
Iona ■ .... Oct. 14
Georgetown ■ .... Oct. 21
Canisius .... Oct. 28
Fairfield ■ .... Nov. 4
La Salle .... Nov. 11
Siena .... Nov. 18

1999 RESULTS (6-5-0)
20	St. Peter's	0
0	St. John's (N.Y.)	16
0	Duquesne	31
49	Canisius	7
40	Georgetown	41
41	La Salle	23
20	Wagner	17
13	Lafayette	38
7	Fairfield	57
40	Iona	29
29	Siena	7
259		**266**

Nickname: Red Foxes.
Stadium: Leonidoff Field (1972), 2,500 capacity. Natural turf.
Colors: Red & White.
Conference: Metro Atlantic Athletic.
SID: Jill Skotarczak, 914-575-3000.
AD: Timothy S. Murray.

MARS HILL
Mars Hill, NC 28754 II

Coach: Tim Clifton, Mercer 1976
Record: 7 Years, 35-38-0

2000 SCHEDULE
Newberry .... *Sept. 16
Gardner-Webb .... *Sept. 23
Carson-Newman .... Sept. 30
Virginia-Wise .... Oct. 7
Presbyterian ■ .... Oct. 14
Lenoir-Rhyne .... Oct. 21
Wingate .... Oct. 28
Catawba ■ .... Nov. 4
Tusculum ■ .... Nov. 11

1999 RESULTS (7-4-0)
0	Western Caro.	59
53	North Greenville	0
7	Catawba	34
37	Wingate	7
51	Newberry	14
34	Tusculum	7
14	Carson-Newman	41
14	Presbyterian	35
17	Virginia-Wise	14
33	Lenoir-Rhyne	7
20	Gardner-Webb	14
280		**232**

Nickname: Lions.
Stadium: Meares (1965), 5,000 capacity. Natural turf.
Colors: Blue & Gold.
Conference: South Atlantic.
SID: Rick Baker, 704-689-1373.
AD: David Riggins.

MARSHALL
Huntington, WV 25755 .... I-A

Coach: Bob Pruett, Marshall 1965
Record: 4 Years, 50-4-0

2000 SCHEDULE
Southeast Mo. St. ■ .... *Aug. 31
Michigan St. .... Sept. 9
North Carolina .... Sept. 23
Buffalo ■ .... *Sept. 30
Western Mich. ■ .... *Oct. 5
Toledo .... *Oct. 14
Kent St. ■ .... Oct. 21
Akron .... *Oct. 28
Bowling Green .... Nov. 4
Miami (Ohio) ■ .... *Nov. 11
Ohio .... Nov. 18

1999 RESULTS (12-0-0)
13	Clemson	10
63	Liberty	3
35	Bowling Green	16
34	Temple	0
32	Miami (Ohio)	14
38	Toledo	13
59	Buffalo	3
41	Northern Ill.	9
28	Kent St.	16
31	Western Mich.	17
34	Ohio	3
34	Western Mich.	30
442		**134**

MOTOR CITY BOWL
21	Brigham Young	3

Nickname: Thundering Herd.
Stadium: Marshall University (1991), 40,000 capacity. Artificial turf.
Colors: Green & White.
Conference: Mid-American.
SID: Ricky Hazel, 304-696-5275.
AD: Lance West.

MARTIN LUTHER
New Ulm, MN 56073 III

Coach: Dennis Gorsline, Northern Mich. 1965
Record: 29 Years, 103-153-1

2000 SCHEDULE
St. Olaf ■ .... Sept. 9
Carthage ■ .... Sept. 16
Mt. Senario .... Sept. 23
Crown ■ .... Sept. 30
Northwestern (Minn.) ■ .... Oct. 7
Trinity Bible (N.D.) ■ .... Oct. 14
Maranatha Baptist .... Oct. 21

1999 RESULTS (5-3-0)
28	Trinity Bible (N.D.)	12
14	Gust. Adolphus	38
0	Dakota St.	28
28	Blackburn	21
17	Northwestern (Minn.)	14
39	Mt. Senario	47
45	Maranatha Baptist	13
52	Crown	38
223		**211**

Nickname: Knights.
Stadium: MLC Bowl (N/A), 1,500 capacity. Natural turf.
Colors: Black, Red & White.
Conference: Division III Independent.
SID: Nick Guillaume, 507-354-8221.
AD: James M. Unke.

MARY HARDIN-BAYLOR
Belton, TX 76513 III

Coach: Pete Fredenburg, Southwest Tex. 1970
Record: 2 Years, 7-13-0

2000 SCHEDULE
Belhaven ■ .... *Sept. 9
McMurry .... *Sept. 16
Austin ■ .... Sept. 23
Texas Lutheran .... *Sept. 30
Louisiana Col. ■ .... Oct. 7
Mississippi Col. .... *Oct. 14
Howard Payne ■ .... Oct. 21
Sul Ross St. .... *Oct. 28
Hardin-Simmons ■ .... Nov. 4
East Tex. Baptist .... Nov. 11

1999 RESULTS (4-6-0)
13	Trinity (Tex.)	28
16	Belhaven	19
48	Southwestern Assemblies of God	0
7	McMurry	21
16	Sul Ross St.	15
30	Mississippi Col.	27
21	Austin	34
12	Howard Payne	9
21	Hardin-Simmons	28
24	Texas Lutheran	34
208		**215**

Nickname: Crusaders.
Stadium: Tiger Field (1996), 7,000 capacity. Natural turf.
Colors: Purple, Gold & White.
Conference: American Southwest.
SID: Jon Wallin, 254-939-4611.
AD: Ben Shipp.

MARYLAND
College Park, MD 20740 .... I-A

Coach: Ron Vanderlinden, Albion 1978
Record: 3 Years, 10-23-0

2000 SCHEDULE
Temple ■ .... *Sept. 9
West Virginia .... Sept. 16
Middle Tenn. St. ■ .... *Sept. 23
Florida St. ■ .... *Sept. 28
Virginia .... Oct. 7
Clemson .... Oct. 14
Wake Forest ■ .... Oct. 21
Duke .... Oct. 28
North Carolina St. ■ .... Nov. 4
North Carolina .... Nov. 11
Georgia Tech ■ .... Nov. 18

1999 RESULTS (5-6-0)
6	Temple	0
51	Western Caro.	10
33	West Virginia	0
31	Georgia Tech	49
17	Wake Forest	14
30	Clemson	42
45	North Carolina	7
22	Duke	25
17	North Carolina St.	30
10	Florida St.	49
30	Virginia	34
292		**260**

Nickname: Terps.
Stadium: Byrd (1950), 48,000 capacity. Natural turf.
Colors: Red, White, Black & Gold.
Conference: Atlantic Coast.
SID: Dave Haglund, 301-314-7064.
AD: Deborah A. Yow.

MARYVILLE (TENN.)
Maryville, TN 37804 III

Coach: Phil Wilks, Marshall 1970
Record: 12 Years, 56-63-0

2000 SCHEDULE

Cumberland (Ky.) ■	Sept. 2
Rhodes ■	Sept. 9
Stillman	Sept. 16
Millsaps ■	Sept. 30
Bridgewater (Va.)	Oct. 7
Centre ■	Oct. 14
Bethel (Tenn.)	Oct. 21
Blackburn	Oct. 28
Hampden-Sydney ■	Nov. 4
Emory & Henry	Nov. 11

1999 RESULTS (7-3-0)

19	Rhodes	30
27	Stillman	6
24	Cumberland (Ky.)	21
30	Millsaps	10
21	Bridgewater (Va.)	20
23	Centre	30
28	Bethel (Tenn.)	0
9	Bethany (W.Va.)	21
13	Hampden-Sydney	3
21	Emory & Henry	10
215		**151**

Nickname: Scots.
Stadium: Lloyd Thorton (1993), 2,500 capacity. Natural turf.
Colors: Orange & Garnet.
Conference: Division III Independent.
SID: Eric Etchison & Karen Bea, 615-981-8283.
AD: Randall D. Lambert.

MASSACHUSETTS
Amherst, MA 01003 .... I-AA

Coach: Mark Whipple, Brown 1979
Record: 12 Years, 92-41-0

2000 SCHEDULE

William & Mary ■	*Aug. 31
Richmond	Sept. 16
New Haven ■	Sept. 23
Hofstra ■	Sept. 30
Northeastern	Oct. 7
Maine ■	Oct. 14
American Int'l ■	Oct. 21
New Hampshire	Oct. 28
Villanova	Nov. 4
Delaware ■	Nov. 11
Rhode Island	Nov. 18

1999 RESULTS (8-3-0)

34	New Hampshire	19
21	Villanova	26
3	Toledo	24
14	Hofstra	27
77	Northeastern	0
38	Maine	17
26	Delaware	19
31	Rhode Island	9
33	Richmond	6
25	William & Mary	16
62	Connecticut	20
364		**183**

DIVISION I-AA CHAMPIONSHIP

30	Furman	23
21	Ga. Southern	38

Nickname: Minutemen.
Stadium: Warren McGuirk (1965), 17,000 capacity. Natural turf.
Colors: Maroon & White.
Conference: Atlantic 10.
SID: Charles Bare, 413-545-2439.
AD: Robert K. Marcum.

MASS.-BOSTON
Boston, MA 02125 III

Coach: Paul Castonia, Trinity (Conn.) 1986
Record: 2 Years, 0-20-0

2000 SCHEDULE

Framingham St.	Sept. 2
Fitchburg St. ■	Sept. 9
Mass.-Dartmouth ■	Sept. 16
Nichols	Sept. 23
Western New Eng. ■	Sept. 30
Salve Regina	Oct. 7
Mass. Maritime	Oct. 14
Westfield St. ■	Oct. 21
Curry	Oct. 28
MIT	Nov. 4

1999 RESULTS (0-10-0)

8	Fitchburg St.	41
6	Framingham St.	20
6	Mass.-Dartmouth	58
0	Nichols	28
15	Western New Eng.	31
0	Salve Regina	41
7	Mass. Maritime	35
14	Westfield St.	52
0	Curry	33
0	MIT	13
56		**352**

Nickname: Beacons.
Stadium: Clark Field (1981), 750 capacity. Natural turf.
Colors: Blue & White.
Conference: New England Football.
SID: Jim Reddish, 617-287-7815.
AD: Charlie Titus.

MASS.-DARTMOUTH
North Dartmouth, MA 02747 III

Coach: Bill Kavanaugh, Stonehill 1972
Record: 10 Years, 56-41-0

2000 SCHEDULE

Springfield	*Sept. 8
Mass.-Boston	Sept. 16
Maine Maritime ■	Sept. 23
MIT	Sept. 30
Nichols ■	Oct. 7
Western New Eng. ■	Oct. 14
Bri'water (Mass.)	Oct. 21
Salve Regina ■	Oct. 28
Curry	Nov. 4

1999 RESULTS (3-7-0)

18	Western Conn. St.	50
10	Worcester St.	3
58	Mass.-Boston	6
3	Maine Maritime	20
29	MIT	30
3	Nichols	15
34	Western New Eng.	6
24	Bri'water (Mass.)	31
14	Salve Regina	40
17	Curry	21
291		**108**

Nickname: Corsairs.
Stadium: Corsair (0000), 1,850 capacity. Natural turf.
Colors: Blue, White & Gold.
Conference: New England Football.
SID: Bill Gathright, 508-999-8727.
AD: Robert W. Mullen.

MIT
Cambridge, MA 02139 III

Coach: Dwight Smith, Bates 1975
Record: 12 Years, 39-59-1

2000 SCHEDULE

Mass. Maritime ■	Sept. 9
Salve Regina ■	Sept. 16
Curry	Sept. 23
Mass.-Dartmouth ■	Sept. 30
Bri'water (Mass.)	Oct. 7
Nichols	Oct. 14
Worcester St. ■	Oct. 21
Western New Eng.	Oct. 28
Mass.-Boston ■	Nov. 4

1999 RESULTS (6-4-0)

20	Framingham St.	12
2	Mass. Maritime	20
14	Salve Regina	53
14	Curry	17
30	Mass.-Dartmouth	29
21	Bri'water (Mass.)	54
18	Nichols	14
27	Worcester St.	7
34	Western New Eng.	9
13	Mass.-Boston	0
193		**215**

Nickname: Engineers.
Stadium: Steinbrenner (1980), 1,600 capacity. Natural turf.
Colors: Cardinal & Gray.
Conference: New England Football.
SID: Roger F. Crosley, 617-253-7946.
AD: Richard A. Hill.

MASS.-LOWELL
Lowell, MA 01854 II

Coach: Sandy Ruggles, Northeastern 1973
Record: 4 Years, 13-27-0

2000 SCHEDULE

Worcester Tech	*Sept. 1
St. Anselm ■	*Sept. 8
C. W. Post	Sept. 16
Southern Conn. St.	*Sept. 22
Bentley	Sept. 29
Stonehill ■	*Oct. 5
Bryant ■	Oct. 21
Merrimack ■	Oct. 28
Assumption	Nov. 4
American Int'l	Nov. 11

1999 RESULTS (3-7-0)

18	St. Anselm	46
7	C. W. Post	28
0	Southern Conn. St.	20
14	Bentley	27
26	Stonehill	21
0	Albany (N.Y.)	40
13	Bryant	3
7	Merrimack	28
34	Assumption	27
21	American Int'l	51
140		**291**

Nickname: River Hawks.
Stadium: New Stadium (2000), 7,000 capacity. Natural turf.
Colors: Red, White & Blue.
Conference: Eastern Football.
SID: Chris O'Donnell, 978-934-2306.
AD: Dana K. Skinner.

MASS. MARITIME
Buzzards Bay, MA 02532 III

Coach: Don Ruggeri, Springfield 1962
Record: 27 Years, 139-106-1

2000 SCHEDULE

MIT ■	Sept. 9
Maine Maritime	Sept. 16
Westfield St. ■	Sept. 23
Fitchburg St.	Sept. 30
Worcester St. ■	Oct. 7
Mass.-Boston ■	Oct. 14
Nichols	Oct. 21
Framingham St. ■	Oct. 28
Bri'water (Mass.) ■	Nov. 4

1999 RESULTS (8-2-0)

19	Coast Guard	7
20	MIT	2
28	Maine Maritime	22
14	Westfield St.	9
44	Fitchburg St.	23
27	Worcester St.	26
35	Mass.-Boston	7
27	Nichols	28
22	Framingham St.	20
23	Bri'water (Mass.)	41
259		**185**

Nickname: Buccaneers.
Stadium: Commander Ellis (1972), 3,000 capacity. Natural turf.
Colors: Blue & Gold.

2000 SCHEDULES AND 1999 RESULTS 533

Conference: New England Football.
SID: Leroy Thompson, 508-830-5054.
AD: Robert Corradi.

McMURRY
Abilene, TX 79697 III

Coach: Steve Keenum, McMurry 1980
Record: 8 Years, 27-49-0

2000 SCHEDULE
William Jewell		Sept. 9
Mary Hardin-Baylor ■		*Sept. 16
East Tex. Baptist		Sept. 23
Austin		Sept. 30
Texas Lutheran ■		*Oct. 7
Louisiana Col.		Oct. 14
Mississippi Col. ■		Oct. 21
Howard Payne		Oct. 28
Sul Ross St. ■		Nov. 4
Hardin-Simmons		Nov. 11

1999 RESULTS (7-2-0)
50	Sul Ross St.	25
19	Trinity (Tex.)	27
21	Mary Hardin-Baylor	7
68	Texas Lutheran	21
59	Sul Ross St.	16
28	Mississippi Col.	27
62	Austin	41
41	Howard Payne	31
28	Hardin-Simmons	63
376		**258**

Nickname: Indians.
Stadium: Indian (N/A), 4,500 capacity. Natural turf.
Colors: Maroon & White.
Conference: American Southwest.
SID: Chris Myers, 915-793-4605.
AD: Marvin Stringfellow.

McNEESE ST.
Lake Charles, LA 70609 ....I-AA

Coach: Tommy Tate, McNeese St. 1979
(First year as head coach)

2000 SCHEDULE
Miami (Fla.)		*Aug. 31
Prairie View [Houston, TX]		*Sept. 9
Southwest Mo. St. ■		*Sept. 16
Alcorn St.		*Sept. 23
Stephen F. Austin ■		*Oct. 7
Jacksonville St. ■		*Oct. 14
Northwestern St.		Oct. 21
Sam Houston St.		Oct. 28
Southwest Tex. St. ■		*Nov. 4
Troy St.		Nov. 11
Nicholls St. ■		*Nov. 18

1999 RESULTS (6-5-0)
17	Northern Iowa	41
24	Texas A&M-Kingsville	10
24	Southern Utah	31
7	Maine	35
14	Stephen F. Austin	40
39	Jacksonville St.	36
20	Northwestern St.	17
3	Sam Houston St.	20
10	Southwest Tex. St.	7
24	Troy St.	7
38	Nicholls St.	0
220		**244**

Nickname: Cowboys.
Stadium: Cowboy (1965), 17,500 capacity. Natural turf.
Colors: Blue & Gold.
Conference: Southland Football.
SID: Louis Bonnette, 318-475-5207.
AD: Sonny Watkins.

MEMPHIS
Memphis, TN 38152 ....I-A

Coach: Rip Scherer, William & Mary 1974
Record: 9 Years, 47-56-0

2000 SCHEDULE
Mississippi St. ■		Sept. 2
La.-Monroe ■		*Sept. 9
Arkansas St.		*Sept. 16
Army		Sept. 23
Southern Miss.		*Sept. 30
East Caro. ■		*Oct. 7
UAB		Oct. 14
Houston ■		*Oct. 21
Tennessee ■		Nov. 4
Cincinnati ■		Nov. 11
Tulane		Nov. 18

1999 RESULTS (5-6-0)
0	Mississippi	3
10	Mississippi St.	13
31	Arkansas St.	26
16	Tennessee	17
17	Missouri	27
38	UAB	14
31	Louisville	32
49	Tulane	7
5	Southern Miss.	20
14	Army	10
21	Cincinnati	13
232		**182**

Nickname: Tigers.
Stadium: Liberty Bowl (1965), 62,380 capacity. Natural turf.
Colors: Blue & Gray.
Conference: Conference USA.
SID: Bob Winn, 901-678-2337.
AD: R. C. Johnson.

MENLO
Atherton, CA 94027 III

Coach: Doug Cosbie, Santa Clara 1987
Record: 1 Year, 5-4-0

2000 SCHEDULE
Linfield		Sept. 9
Occidental ■		Sept. 16
San Diego		*Sept. 23
Whittier ■		Sept. 30
Cal Lutheran		Oct. 7
St. Mary's (Cal.)		Oct. 14
Pomona-Pitzer ■		Oct. 21
La Verne		Nov. 4
Chapman ■		Nov. 11

1999 RESULTS (5-4-0)
24	Whitworth	21
19	Linfield	28
45	Whittier	32
0	Southern Ore.	34
19	Merchant Marine	14
33	Chapman	44
42	Occidental	27
41	Cal Lutheran	38
41	La Verne	47
264		**285**

Nickname: Oaks.
Stadium: Connor Field (1972), 1,000 capacity. Natural turf.
Colors: Navy Blue & White.
Conference: Division III Independent.
SID: Matt Monroe, 415-688-3780.
AD: Keith Larsen.

MERCHANT MARINE
Kings Point, NY 11024 III

Coach: Charlie Pravata, Adelphi 1972
Record: 9 Years, 52-33-2

2000 SCHEDULE
Muhlenberg		Sept. 2
Norwich		Sept. 9
Springfield ■		Sept. 16
Johns Hopkins		Sept. 23
Worcester Tech		Sept. 30
Plymouth St. ■		Oct. 7
Case Reserve ■		Oct. 14
Western Conn. St.		Nov. 4
Coast Guard ■		Nov. 11

1999 RESULTS (3-7-0)
24	Muhlenberg	42
21	Norwich	20
35	Springfield	41
24	Johns Hopkins	20
28	Worcester Tech	49
27	Plymouth St.	49
14	Menlo	19
0	Thomas More	28
21	Western Conn. St.	45
24	Coast Guard	21
218		**334**

Nickname: Mariners.
Stadium: Capt. Tomb Field (1945), 5,840 capacity. Natural turf.
Colors: Blue & Gray.
Conference: Freedom Football.
SID: Kim Robinson, 516-773-5455.
AD: Susan Petersen-Lubow.

MERCYHURST
Erie, PA 16546 II

Coach: Joe Kimball, Syracuse 1975
Record: 7 Years, 35-32-1

2000 SCHEDULE
Wayne St. (Mich.) ■		Sept. 2
Michigan Tech		Sept. 9
Edinboro		Sept. 16
Northwood ■		Sept. 23
Indianapolis		Sept. 30
Saginaw Valley ■		Oct. 7
Ferris St.		Oct. 14
Grand Valley St. ■		Oct. 21
Hillsdale		Oct. 28
Findlay		Nov. 4
Ashland ■		Nov. 11

1999 RESULTS (5-5-0)
49	Wayne St. (Mich.)	35
26	Michigan Tech	41
34	Edinboro	20
27	Indianapolis	20
40	Hillsdale	42
19	Grand Valley St.	26
17	Westminster (Pa.)	7
7	Ashland	32
33	Saginaw Valley	40
28	Findlay	14
280		**277**

Nickname: Lakers.
Stadium: Louis J. Tullio Field (1996), 2,300 capacity. Artificial turf.
Colors: Blue & Green.
Conference: Great Lakes Intercollegiate Athletic.
SID: John Leisering, 814-824-2525.
AD: Peter J. Russo.

MERRIMACK
North Andover, MA 01845 II

Coach: Thomas Caito, Boston U. 1960
Record: 4 Years, 18-19-0

2000 SCHEDULE
Bentley ■		Sept. 9
Assumption		Sept. 16
Stonehill		Sept. 23
American Int'l ■		Sept. 30
Southern Conn. St.		*Oct. 6
LIU-C.W. Post ■		Oct. 14
St. Anselm		Oct. 21
Mass.-Lowell		Oct. 28
Gannon		Nov. 4
Bryant ■		Nov. 11

1999 RESULTS (7-3-0)
14	Bentley	9
49	Assumption	21
25	Stonehill	0
31	American Int'l	28
17	Southern Conn. St.	29
0	C. W. Post	35
5	St. Anselm	7
28	Mass.-Lowell	7

31	Gannon	20
20	Bryant	10
220		**166**

Nickname: Warriors.
Stadium: Merrimack (NA), 2,000 capacity. Natural turf.
Colors: Navy Blue & Gold.
Conference: Eastern Football.
SID: Larry Napolitano, 508-837-5341.
AD: Robert M. De Gregorio Jr.

MESA ST.
Grand Junction, CO 81501 II

Coach: Joe Ramunno, Wyoming 1984
Record: 2 Years, 11-11-0

2000 SCHEDULE
Western Ore. ■	Sept. 2
Pittsburg St. [Wichita, KS]	Sept. 9
Western N.M.	Sept. 16
Western St. (Colo.)	Sept. 23
Chadron St. ■	Sept. 30
Adams St.	*Oct. 7
Fort Hays St.	Oct. 14
Colorado Mines	Oct. 21
Neb.-Kearney ■	Oct. 28
Fort Lewis ■	Nov. 4
N.M. Highlands	Nov. 11

1999 RESULTS (6-5-0)
52	Okla. Panhandle	7
33	Western Mont.	19
10	Western St. (Colo.)	45
19	Chadron St.	42
49	Adams St.	21
26	Fort Hays St.	14
47	Colorado Mines	0
20	Neb.-Kearney	44
21	Fort Lewis	19
36	N.M. Highlands	44
14	Western N.M.	21
327		**276**

Nickname: Mavericks.
Stadium: Stocker (1949), 8,000 capacity. Natural turf.
Colors: Gold, White & Maroon.
Conference: Rocky Mountain Athletic.
SID: Tish Elliott, 970-248-1143.
AD: Doug Schakel.

METHODIST
Fayetteville, NC 28311 III

Coach: Jim Sypult, West Virginia 1967
Record: 8 Years, 39-41-0

2000 SCHEDULE
Chowan	Sept. 2
Guilford ■	Sept. 9
Salisbury St. ■	Sept. 16
Frostburg St.	Sept. 23
Ferrum ■	Sept. 30
Catholic ■	Oct. 14
Wesley	Oct. 21
Greensboro	*Oct. 28
Averett ■	Nov. 4
Apprentice	Nov. 11

1999 RESULTS (3-7-0)
14	Chowan	25
16	Guilford	21
6	Salisbury St.	21
10	Frostburg St.	24
16	Ferrum	14
21	Catholic	49
20	Wesley	34
32	Greensboro	29
13	Thomas More	24
38	Apprentice	37
186		**278**

Nickname: Monarchs.
Stadium: Monarch Field (1989), 1,500 capacity. Natural turf.
Colors: Green & Gold.
Conference: Atlantic Central Football.
SID: Lee Glenn, 910-630-7172.
AD: Robert McEvoy.

MIAMI (FLA.)
Coral Gables, FL 33146 ....I-A

Coach: Butch Davis, Arkansas 1974
Record: 5 Years, 40-19-0

2000 SCHEDULE
McNeese St. ■	*Aug. 31
Washington	Sept. 9
West Virginia	Sept. 23
Rutgers	*Sept. 30
Florida St. ■	Oct. 7
Temple	Oct. 21
Louisiana Tech ■	Oct. 28
Virginia Tech ■	Nov. 4
Pittsburgh ■	Nov. 11
Syracuse	Nov. 18
Boston College ■	Nov. 25

1999 RESULTS (8-4-0)
23	Ohio St.	12
57	Florida A&M	3
23	Penn St.	27
23	East Caro.	27
21	Florida St.	31
31	Boston College	28
28	West Virginia	20
33	Pittsburgh	3
10	Virginia Tech	43
55	Rutgers	0
45	Syracuse	13
55	Temple	0
404		**207**

GATOR BOWL
| 28 | Georgia Tech | 13 |

Nickname: Hurricanes.
Stadium: Orange Bowl (1935), 74,476 capacity. Natural turf.
Colors: Orange, Green & White.
Conference: Big East.
SID: Bob Burda, 305-284-3244.
AD: Paul T. Dee.

MIAMI (OHIO)
Oxford, OH 45056 ....I-A

Coach: Terry Hoeppner, Franklin 1969
Record: 1 Year, 7-4-0

2000 SCHEDULE
Vanderbilt	*Sept. 2
Eastern Mich.	Sept. 9
Ohio St.	Sept. 16
Kent St. ■	Sept. 23
Akron	*Sept. 30
Ball St. ■	Oct. 7
Bowling Green ■	Oct. 14
Cincinnati	Oct. 28
Ohio ■	Nov. 4
Marshall	*Nov. 11
Buffalo	Nov. 18

1999 RESULTS (7-4-0)
28	Northwestern	3
27	West Virginia	43
35	Eastern Mich.	14
24	Central Mich.	16
14	Marshall	32
45	Bowling Green	31
17	Kent St.	10
42	Cincinnati	52
32	Akron	23
28	Ohio	40
43	Buffalo	0
335		**264**

Nickname: RedHawks.
Stadium: Fred C. Yager (1983), 30,000 capacity. Natural turf.
Colors: Red & White.
Conference: Mid-American.
SID: Mike Wolf, 513-529-4327.
AD: Joel Maturi.

MICHIGAN
Ann Arbor, MI 48109 ....I-A

Coach: Lloyd Carr, Northern Mich. 1968
Record: 5 Years, 49-13-0

2000 SCHEDULE
Bowling Green ■	Sept. 2
Rice ■	Sept. 9
UCLA	Sept. 16
Illinois	*Sept. 23
Wisconsin ■	Sept. 30
Purdue	Oct. 7
Indiana ■	Oct. 14
Michigan St. ■	Oct. 21
Northwestern	Nov. 4
Penn St. ■	Nov. 11
Ohio St.	Nov. 18

1999 RESULTS (9-2-0)
26	Notre Dame	22
37	Rice	3
18	Syracuse	13
21	Wisconsin	16
38	Purdue	12
31	Michigan St.	34
29	Illinois	35
34	Indiana	31
37	Northwestern	3
31	Penn St.	27
24	Ohio St.	17
326		**213**

ORANGE BOWL
| 35 | Alabama | 34 |

Nickname: Wolverines.
Stadium: Michigan (1927), 107,501 capacity. Natural turf.
Colors: Maize & Blue.
Conference: Big Ten.
SID: Bruce Madej, 313-763-4423.
AD: William C. Martin.

MICHIGAN ST.
East Lansing, MI 48824 ....I-A

Coach: Bobby Williams, Purdue 1982
Record: 1 Year, 1-0-0

2000 SCHEDULE
Marshall ■	Sept. 9
Missouri	Sept. 16
Notre Dame ■	Sept. 23
Northwestern ■	Sept. 30
Iowa	Oct. 7
Wisconsin ■	Oct. 14
Michigan	Oct. 21
Illinois ■	Oct. 28
Ohio St.	Nov. 4
Purdue ■	Nov. 11
Penn St.	Nov. 18

1999 RESULTS (9-2-0)
27	Oregon	20
51	Eastern Mich.	7
23	Notre Dame	13
27	Illinois	10
49	Iowa	3
34	Michigan	31
28	Purdue	52
10	Wisconsin	40
23	Ohio St.	7
34	Northwestern	0
35	Penn St.	28
341		**211**

FLORIDA CITRUS BOWL
| 37 | Florida | 34 |

Nickname: Spartans.
Stadium: Spartan (1957), 72,027 capacity. Artificial turf.
Colors: Green & White.
Conference: Big Ten.
SID: John Lewandowski, 517-355-2271.
AD: Clarence Underwood Jr.

MICHIGAN TECH
Houghton, MI 49931.................................II

Coach: Bernie Anderson, Northern Mich. 1978
Record: 13 Years, 58-70-0

2000 SCHEDULE
Mercyhurst ■		Sept. 9
Indianapolis		Sept. 16
Northern Mich.		Sept. 23
Hillsdale ■		Sept. 30
Northwood ■		Oct. 7
Ashland		Oct. 14
Ferris St. ■		Oct. 21
Grand Valley St.		Oct. 28
Saginaw Valley		Nov. 4
Findlay ■		Nov. 11

1999 RESULTS (6-4-0)
10	Westminster (Pa.)	0
41	Mercyhurst	26
31	Hillsdale	7
35	Saginaw Valley	33
14	Ashland	39
7	Northern Mich.	31
7	Ferris St.	66
22	Wayne St. (Mich.)	10
7	Grand Valley St.	21
23	Northwood	14
197		**247**

Nickname: Huskies.
Stadium: Sherman Field (1954), 3,000 capacity. Natural turf.
Colors: Silver, Gold & Black.
Conference: Great Lakes Intercollegiate Athletic.
SID: Dave Fischer, 906-487-2350.
AD: J. Richard Yeo.

MIDDLE TENN. ST.
Murfreesboro, TN 37132..............................I-A

Coach: Andy McCollum, Austin Peay 1981
Record: 1 Year, 3-8-0

2000 SCHEDULE
Illinois		Sept. 2
Florida		*Sept. 9
Murray St. ■		*Sept. 16
Maryland		*Sept. 23
Louisiana Tech ■		*Oct. 7
La.-Monroe ■		*Oct. 14
UAB		Oct. 21
Mississippi St.		Oct. 28
Connecticut		Nov. 4
South Fla. ■		Nov. 11
La.-Lafayette ■		Nov. 18

1999 RESULTS (3-8-0)
7	Mississippi St.	40
19	Arizona	34
52	Wofford	42
31	La.-Lafayette	45
31	Troy St.	48
6	Arkansas	58
18	Louisiana Tech	42
0	La.-Monroe	10
70	Tenn.-Martin	14
14	UCF	39
24	East Tenn. St.	7
272		**379**

Nickname: Blue Raiders.
Stadium: Johnny Floyd (1933), 30,788 capacity. Artificial turf.
Colors: Royal Blue, White & Silver.
Conference: Division I-A Independent.
SID: Mark Owens, 615-898-2450.
AD: Lee G. Fowler.

MIDDLEBURY
Middlebury, VT 05753..............................III

Coach: Mickey Heinecken, Delaware 1961
Record: 27 Years, 119-95-2

2000 SCHEDULE
Bowdoin ■		Sept. 23
Colby		Sept. 30
Amherst ■		Oct. 7
Williams		Oct. 14
Bates ■		Oct. 21
Trinity (Conn.)		Oct. 28
Hamilton		Nov. 4
Tufts ■		Nov. 11

1999 RESULTS (6-2-0)
21	Wesleyan (Conn.)	28
41	Colby	19
14	Amherst	13
0	Williams	25
12	Bates	9
14	Trinity (Conn.)	10
27	Hamilton	23
22	Tufts	10
151		**137**

Nickname: Panthers.
Stadium: Alumni (1991), 3,500 capacity. Natural turf.
Colors: Blue & White.
Conference: NESCAC.
SID: Brad Nadeau, 802-443-5193.
AD: Russell Reilly.

MIDWESTERN ST.
Wichita Falls, TX 76308..............................II

Coach: Linwood Ferguson, East Caro. 1973
Record: 1 Year, 4-7-0

2000 SCHEDULE
Southwest Tex. St.		*Aug. 31
West Tex. A&M ■		*Sept. 9
Eastern N.M.		*Sept. 16
Tex. A&M-Commerce		*Sept. 23
Central Okla.		Sept. 30
East Central ■		*Oct. 7
Okla. Panhandle ■		*Oct. 14
Southeastern Okla.		Oct. 21
Northeastern St.		Oct. 28
Tarleton St.		*Nov. 4
Southwestern Okla. ■		Nov. 11

1999 RESULTS (4-7-0)
3	Southwest Tex. St.	45
36	East Central	5
35	Harding	38
14	Central Okla.	42
7	Tex. A&M-Commerce	10
16	Abilene Christian	26
10	Texas A&M-Kingsville	7
19	Angelo St.	21
24	West Tex. A&M	0
21	Tarleton St.	3
13	Eastern N.M.	38
198		**235**

Nickname: Indians.
Stadium: Memorial (N/A), 14,000 capacity. Artificial turf.
Colors: Maroon & Gold.
Conference: Lone Star.
SID: Stan Wagnon, 940-397-4769.
AD: Robert D. McBee.

MILES
Birmingham, AL 35208..............................II

Coach: Cecil Leonard, Tuskegee 1969
Record: 6 Years, 23-35-1

2000 SCHEDULE
Kentucky St. ■		Aug. 26
Albany St. (Ga.)		*Sept. 3
West Ala. ■		Sept. 9
Tuskegee		Sept. 16
Clark Atlanta		Sept. 23
Fort Valley St. ■		Oct. 7
Benedict ■		Oct. 21
Lane		Oct. 28
Morehouse ■		Nov. 11

1999 RESULTS (3-7-0)
12	Kentucky St.	33
27	Albany St. (Ga.)	25
14	Morehouse	6
7	Tuskegee	13
21	Clark Atlanta	10
7	Morris Brown	13
7	Fort Valley St.	17
25	Lane	30
6	Catawba	20
12	Savannah St.	49
138		**216**

Nickname: Golden Bears.
Stadium: Alumni (N/A), 3,400 capacity. Natural turf.
Colors: Purple & Gold.
Conference: Southern Intercollegiate Athletic.
SID: Willie K. Patterson Jr., 205-923-8323.
AD: Augustus James.

MILLERSVILLE
Millersville, PA 17551..............................II

Coach: Gene Carpenter, Huron 1963
Record: 31 Years, 214-86-6

2000 SCHEDULE
Villanova		Sept. 9
Shippensburg ■		*Sept. 16
Kutztown ■		*Sept. 23
East Stroudsburg		Sept. 30
Cheyney ■		Oct. 7
Mansfield ■		Oct. 14
West Chester		*Oct. 21
Bloomsburg		Oct. 28
Slippery Rock ■		Nov. 4
Indiana (Pa.)		Nov. 11

1999 RESULTS (8-2-0)
41	Bowie St.	0
35	New Haven	38
20	Edinboro	10
42	Mansfield	25
31	Bloomsburg	21
10	Indiana (Pa.)	9
35	West Chester	40
35	Kutztown	28
54	East Stroudsburg	29
48	Cheyney	18
351		**218**

DIVISION II CHAMPIONSHIP
21	Shepherd	14
21	Indiana (Pa.)	26

Nickname: Marauders.
Stadium: Biemesderfer (1970), 6,500 capacity. Natural turf.
Colors: Black & Gold.
Conference: Pennsylvania State Athletic.
SID: Greg Wright, 717-872-3100.
AD: Daniel N. Audette.

MILLIKIN
Decatur, IL 62522..............................III

Coach: Doug Neibuhr, Millikin 1975
Record: 11 Years, 72-33-1

2000 SCHEDULE
Knox		Sept. 9
Eureka ■		Sept. 16
Blackburn ■		Sept. 23
Carthage		Sept. 30
Wheaton (Ill.) ■		Oct. 7
North Central		Oct. 14
Augustana (Ill.) ■		Oct. 21
North Park ■		Oct. 28
Elmhurst		Nov. 4
Ill. Wesleyan		Nov. 11

1999 RESULTS (7-2-0)
14	Aurora	12
63	Blackburn	6
20	Augustana (Ill.)	7
36	North Park	6
45	North Central	13
6	Carthage	7
14	Wheaton (Ill.)	23
42	Ill. Wesleyan	20
35	Elmhurst	0
275		**94**

Nickname: Big Blue.
Stadium: Frank M. Lindsay Field (1987), 4,000 capacity. Natural turf.
Colors: Royal Blue & White.
Conference: College Conf. of Illinois & Wisconsin.
SID: David Johnson, 217-424-6350.
AD: Lori Kerans.

MILLSAPS
Jackson, MS 39210 III

Coach: Bob Tyler, Mississippi 1958
Record: 7 Years, 23-53-2

2000 SCHEDULE
Mississippi Col. [Jackson, MS]	*Sept. 2
Austin	*Sept. 9
Bethel (Tenn.) ■	*Sept. 23
Maryville (Tenn.)	Sept. 30
Centre ■	Oct. 7
Rose-Hulman	Oct. 14
DePauw ■	*Oct. 21
Sewanee	Oct. 28
Rhodes	Nov. 4
Trinity (Tex.) ■	Nov. 11

1999 RESULTS (2-8-0)
27	Austin	20
3	Chapman	37
37	Colorado Col.	40
10	Maryville (Tenn.)	30
22	Centre	24
35	Rose-Hulman	28
10	DePauw	41
12	Sewanee	35
25	Rhodes	32
7	Trinity (Tex.)	49
188		336

Nickname: Majors.
Stadium: Alumni Field (1920), 4,000 capacity. Natural turf.
Colors: Purple & White.
Conference: Southern Collegiate Athletic.
SID: Cara Lynn Rasmussen, 601-974-1195.
AD: Ron Jurney.

MINNESOTA
Minneapolis, MN 55455 ....I-A

Coach: Glen Mason, Ohio St. 1972
Record: 14 Years, 75-83-1

2000 SCHEDULE
La.-Monroe ■	Sept. 2
Ohio ■	Sept. 9
Baylor	Sept. 16
Purdue	Sept. 23
Illinois ■	Sept. 30
Penn St. ■	Oct. 7
Ohio St.	Oct. 14
Indiana	Oct. 21
Northwestern ■	Oct. 28
Wisconsin	Nov. 4
Iowa ■	Nov. 18

1999 RESULTS (8-3-0)
33	Ohio	7
35	La.-Monroe	0
55	Illinois St.	7
33	Northwestern	14
17	Wisconsin	20
37	Illinois	7
17	Ohio St.	20
28	Purdue	33
24	Penn St.	23
44	Indiana	20
25	Iowa	21
348		172

SUN BOWL
20	Oregon	24

Nickname: Golden Gophers.
Stadium: Metrodome (1982), 63,669 capacity. Artificial turf.
Colors: Maroon & Gold.
Conference: Big Ten.
SID: To be named, 612-625-4090.
AD: To be named.

MINN. ST.-MANKATO
Mankato, MN 56002 II

Coach: Dan Runkle, Illinois Col. 1968
Record: 19 Years, 101-109-2

2000 SCHEDULE
Minn.-Duluth	*Sept. 2
Northwest Mo. St. ■	Sept. 9
Neb.-Omaha ■	Sept. 16
North Dakota	Sept. 23
Northern Colo.	Sept. 30
South Dakota St.	Oct. 7
St. Cloud St. ■	Oct. 14
Augustana (S.D.)	Oct. 21
North Dakota St. ■	Oct. 28
Morningside	Nov. 4
South Dakota	Nov. 11

1999 RESULTS (4-7-0)
37	Minn.-Duluth	15
55	Mo. Western St.	41
31	Neb.-Omaha	62
28	North Dakota	35
23	Northern Colo.	26
28	South Dakota St.	34
28	St. Cloud St.	20
21	Augustana (S.D.)	38
14	North Dakota St.	56
24	Morningside	13
29	South Dakota	35
318		375

Nickname: Mavericks.
Stadium: Blakeslee Field (1962), 7,500 capacity. Natural turf.
Colors: Purple & Gold.
Conference: North Central Intercollegiate Athletic.
SID: Paul Allan, 507-389-2625.
AD: Don Amiot.

MINN.-DULUTH
Duluth, MN 55812 II

Coach: Bob Nielson, Wartburg 1982
Record: 11 Years, 73-41-1

2000 SCHEDULE
Minn. St.-Mankato ■	*Sept. 2
St. Cloud St. ■	*Sept. 9
Minn.-Crookston ■	*Sept. 16
Southwest St.	Sept. 23
Moorhead St.	Sept. 30
Concordia-St. Paul ■	Oct. 7
Northern St.	Oct. 14
Bemidji St. ■	Oct. 21
Wayne St. (Neb.) ■	Oct. 28
Winona St.	Nov. 4
Wis.-Stout [Minneapolis, MN]	*Nov. 11

1999 RESULTS (3-8-0)
15	Minn. St.-Mankato	37
0	St. Cloud St.	49
27	Minn.-Crookston	24
9	Southwest St.	14
14	Moorhead St.	20
27	Concordia-St. Paul	35
7	Northern St.	16
26	Bemidji St.	35
31	Wayne St. (Neb.)	19
21	Winona St.	17
21	Wis.-La Crosse	22
198		288

Nickname: Bulldogs.
Stadium: Griggs Field (1966), 4,000 capacity. Artificial turf.
Colors: Maroon & Gold.
Conference: Northern Sun Intercollegiate Athletic.
SID: Bob Nygaard, 218-726-8191.
AD: Robert Corran.

MINN.-MORRIS
Morris, MN 56267 II

Coach: Ken Crandall, Fort Hays St. 1990
Record: 2 Years, 1-20-0

2000 SCHEDULE
Valley City St.	Sept. 2
Morningside	*Sept. 9
Southwest St.	Sept. 16
Concordia-St. Paul	Sept. 23
Winona St. ■	Sept. 30
Northern St. ■	Oct. 7
Minn.-Crookston	Oct. 14
Moorhead St. ■	Oct. 21
Bemidji St.	Oct. 28
Wayne St. (Neb.)	Nov. 4
Wis.-Oshkosh (Minneapolis, MN)	*Nov. 10

1999 RESULTS (0-11-0)
13	Valley City St.	23
27	Wis.-Stout	48
6	Southwest St.	53
21	Concordia-St. Paul	43
6	Winona St.	46
7	Northern St.	48
7	Minn.-Crookston	24
12	Moorhead St.	41
20	Bemidji St.	53
21	Wayne St. (Neb.)	70
15	Wis.-Platteville	46
155		495

Nickname: Cougars.
Stadium: UMM Field (0000), 5,000 capacity. Natural turf.
Colors: Maroon & Gold.
Conference: Northern Sun Intercollegiate Athletic.
SID: John Griffin, 612-589-6423.
AD: Mark Fohl.

MISSISSIPPI
University, MS 38677 ....I-A

Coach: David Cutcliffe, Alabama 1976
Record: 2 Years, 9-4-0

2000 SCHEDULE
Tulane ■	Sept. 2
Auburn ■	*Sept. 9
Vanderbilt	Sept. 16
Kentucky ■	*Sept. 30
Arkansas St. ■	Oct. 7
Alabama	Oct. 14
UNLV ■	Oct. 28
Arkansas	Nov. 4
LSU ■	Nov. 11
Georgia	Nov. 18
Mississippi St. ■	*Nov. 23

1999 RESULTS (7-4-0)
3	Memphis	0
38	Arkansas St.	14
34	Vanderbilt	37
24	Auburn	17
36	South Carolina	10
20	Tulane	13
24	Alabama	30
42	LSU	23
38	Arkansas	16
17	Georgia	20
20	Mississippi St.	23
296		203

INDEPENDENCE BOWL
27	Oklahoma	25

Nickname: Rebels.
Stadium: Vaught-Hemingway (1941), 50,577 capacity. Natural turf.
Colors: Red & Blue.
Conference: Southeastern.
SID: Langston Rogers, 601-232-7522.
AD: John W. Shafer.

MISSISSIPPI COL.
Clinton, MS 39058 III

Coach: Johnny Mills, Mississippi Col. 1973
(First year as head coach)

2000 SCHEDULE

Millsaps [Jackson, MS]	*Sept. 2
East Tex. Baptist ■	Sept. 16
Howard Payne	Sept. 23
Sul Ross St. ■	Sept. 30
Hardin-Simmons	Oct. 7
Mary Hardin-Baylor ■	*Oct. 14
McMurry	Oct. 21
Austin ■	Oct. 28
Texas Lutheran	Nov. 4
Louisiana Col. ■	Nov. 11

1999 RESULTS (6-4-0)

10	Stillman		7
38	Belhaven		21
16	Jacksonville		13
14	Howard Payne		21
23	Hardin-Simmons		35
27	Mary Hardin-Baylor		30
27	McMurry		28
36	Sul Ross St.		20
28	Texas Lutheran		6
50	Austin		24
269			**205**

Nickname: Choctaws.
Stadium: Robinson-Hale (1985), 8,500 capacity. Natural turf.
Colors: Blue & Gold.
Conference: American Southwest.
SID: Will Chandler, 601-925-3255.
AD: To be named.

MISSISSIPPI ST.
Miss. State, MS 39762 .... I-A

Coach: Jackie Sherrill, Alabama 1966
Record: 22 Years, 164-89-4

2000 SCHEDULE

Memphis	Sept. 2
Brigham Young	*Sept. 14
South Carolina	Sept. 23
Florida ■	Sept. 30
Auburn ■	Oct. 7
LSU	*Oct. 21
Middle Tenn. St. ■	Oct. 28
Kentucky	Nov. 4
Alabama ■	Nov. 11
Arkansas ■	Nov. 18
Mississippi	*Nov. 23

1999 RESULTS (9-2-0)

40	Middle Tenn. St.		7
13	Memphis		10
29	Oklahoma St.		11
17	South Carolina		0
42	Vanderbilt		14
18	Auburn		16
17	LSU		16
23	Kentucky		22
7	Alabama		19
9	Arkansas		14
23	Mississippi		20
238			**149**

PEACH BOWL
17	Clemson		7

Nickname: Bulldogs.
Stadium: Scott Field (1935), 40,656 capacity. Natural turf.
Colors: Maroon & White.
Conference: Southeastern.
SID: Mike Nemeth, 601-325-2703.
AD: Larry Templeton.

MISSISSIPPI VAL.
Itta Bena, MS 38941 .... I-AA

Coach: LaTraia Jones, New Mexico St. 1978
Record: 1 Year, 3-8-0

2000 SCHEDULE

Louisiana Tech	*Aug. 26
Ark.-Pine Bluff ■	*Sept. 2
Delta St. ■	*Sept. 9
Chattanooga	Sept. 16
Grambling ■	*Sept. 23
Alabama A&M	Sept. 30
Jackson St.	*Oct. 14
Texas Southern	*Oct. 21
Prairie View	Oct. 28
Alcorn St. ■	Nov. 4
Alabama St.	Nov. 11

1999 RESULTS (3-8-0)

9	Ark.-Pine Bluff		13
7	Western Ill.		77
19	Alabama A&M		26
0	Jackson St.		63
27	Alabama St.		35
19	Grambling		42
8	Albany St. (Ga.)		46
18	Texas Southern		13
14	Prairie View		12
30	Alcorn St.		26
19	Morris Brown		20
170			**373**

Nickname: Delta Devils.
Stadium: Magnolia (1958), 10,500 capacity. Natural turf.
Colors: Green & White.
Conference: Southwestern Athletic.
SID: Chuck Prophet, 601-254-3551.
AD: Charles Prophet.

MISSOURI
Columbia, MO 65211 .... I-A

Coach: Larry Smith, Bowling Green 1962
Record: 23 Years, 140-118-7

2000 SCHEDULE

Western Ill. ■	*Sept. 2
Clemson	Sept. 9
Michigan St. ■	Sept. 16
Nebraska	Sept. 30
Oklahoma St. ■	Oct. 7
Kansas ■	Oct. 14
Texas	Oct. 21
Iowa St.	Oct. 28
Colorado ■	Nov. 4
Baylor	Nov. 11
Kansas St. ■	Nov. 18

1999 RESULTS (4-7-0)

31	UAB		28
48	Western Mich.		34
10	Nebraska		40
27	Memphis		17
39	Colorado		46
21	Iowa St.		24
0	Kansas		21
34	Texas Tech		7
0	Oklahoma		37
14	Texas A&M		51
0	Kansas St.		66
224			**371**

Nickname: Tigers.
Stadium: Memorial/Faurot Field (1926), 62,000 capacity. Natural turf.
Colors: Old Gold & Black.
Conference: Big 12.
SID: Bob Brendel, 573-882-0712.
AD: Michael F. Alden.

MO.-ROLLA
Rolla, MO 65401 II

Coach: Kirby Cannon, Southwest Mo. St. 1981
Record: 1 Year, 0-11-0

2000 SCHEDULE

Ky. Wesleyan ■	Sept. 2
Missouri Valley	Sept. 9
Mo. Western St. ■	*Sept. 16
Truman ■	Sept. 23
Emporia St.	Sept. 30
Washburn ■	Oct. 7
Central Mo. St. ■	Oct. 14
Southwest Baptist	Oct. 21
Pittsburg St. ■	Oct. 28
Northwest Mo. St.	Nov. 4
Mo. Southern St. ■	Nov. 11

1999 RESULTS (0-11-0)

16	Quincy		23
20	Missouri Valley		28
10	Mo. Western St.		56
0	Truman		15
6	Emporia St.		48
18	Washburn		53
0	Central Mo. St.		41
7	Southwest Baptist		14
0	Pittsburg St.		62
3	Northwest Mo. St.		34
0	Mo. Southern St.		37
80			**411**

Nickname: Miners.
Stadium: Jackling Field (1967), 8,000 capacity. Natural turf.
Colors: Silver & Gold.
Conference: Mid-America Intercollegiate Athletic.
SID: John Kean, 314-341-4140.
AD: Mark Mullin.

MO. SOUTHERN ST.
Joplin, MO 64801 II

Coach: Bill Cooke, Fort Lewis 1973
Record: 5 Years, 23-23-1

2000 SCHEDULE

Northeastern St.	*Sept. 2
Southwest Mo. St.	*Sept. 9
Washburn ■	*Sept. 16
Emporia St.	*Sept. 23
Southwest Baptist ■	Sept. 30
Pittsburg St.	*Oct. 7
Northwest Mo. St. ■	*Oct. 14
Truman	Oct. 21
Mo. Western St. ■	*Oct. 28
Central Mo. St. ■	Nov. 4
Mo.-Rolla	Nov. 11

1999 RESULTS (5-6-0)

35	Ark.-Monticello		14
28	Northeastern St.		7
28	Washburn		35
29	Emporia St.		12
39	Southwest Baptist		0
8	Pittsburg St.		36
13	Northwest Mo. St.		52
40	Truman		45
6	Mo. Western St.		13
7	Central Mo. St.		47
37	Mo.-Rolla		0
270			**261**

Nickname: Lions.
Stadium: Fred G. Hughes (1975), 7,000 capacity. Artificial turf.
Colors: Green & Gold.
Conference: Mid-America Intercollegiate Athletic.
SID: Joe Moore, 417-625-9359.
AD: Jim Frazier.

MO. WESTERN ST.
St. Joseph, MO 64507 II

Coach: Jerry Partridge, Mo. Western St. 1985
Record: 3 Years, 17-16-0

2000 SCHEDULE

South Dakota ■	*Aug. 31
Fort Hays St.	*Sept. 9
Mo.-Rolla ■	*Sept. 16
Washburn	*Sept. 23
Pittsburg St. ■	Sept. 30
Northwest Mo. St.	Oct. 7
Truman ■	Oct. 14
Central Mo. St.	Oct. 21
Mo. Southern St.	*Oct. 28
Emporia St. ■	Nov. 4
Southwest Baptist	Nov. 11

1999 RESULTS (7-4-0)

40	Southeastern Okla.		21
41	Minn. St.-Mankato		55

56	Mo.-Rolla	10
42	Washburn	10
6	Pittsburg St.	31
34	Northwest Mo. St.	38
28	Truman	19
28	Central Mo. St.	35
13	Mo. Southern St.	6
27	Emporia St.	7
55	Southwest Baptist	7
370		**239**

Nickname: Griffons.
Stadium: Spratt (1979), 6,000 capacity. Natural turf.
Colors: Black & Gold.
Conference: Mid-America Intercollegiate Athletic.
SID: To be named, 816-271-4257.
AD: Peter Chapman.

MONMOUTH (ILL.)
Monmouth, IL 61462 III

Coach: Steve Bell, Bemidji St. 1991
(First year as head coach)

2000 SCHEDULE
Eureka	Sept. 2
Lake Forest ■	Sept. 16
Beloit	Sept. 23
Illinois Col. ■	Sept. 30
Carroll (Wis.)	Oct. 7
St. Norbert ■	Oct. 14
Ripon	Oct. 21
Lawrence	Oct. 28
Grinnell ■	Nov. 4
Knox ■	Nov. 11

1999 RESULTS (2-8-0)
28	Eureka	42
14	Lake Forest	42
13	Beloit	47
42	Illinois Col.	28
19	Carroll (Wis.)	42
28	St. Norbert	41
22	Ripon	25
13	Lawrence	19
28	Grinnell	29
27	Knox	26
234		**341**

Nickname: Fighting Scots.
Stadium: Bobby Woll Field (1981), 3,000 capacity. Natural turf.
Colors: Crimson & White.
Conference: Midwest Intercollegiate Athletic.
SID: Barry McNamara/Dan Nolan, 309-457-2173.
AD: Terry L. Glasgow.

MONMOUTH
West Long Branch, NJ 07764 ....I-AA

Coach: Kevin Callahan, Rochester 1977
Record: 6 Years, 33-25-0

2000 SCHEDULE
Wagner	Sept. 9
Robert Morris	Sept. 16
Central Conn. St. ■	Sept. 23
Sacred Heart ■	Sept. 30
C. W. Post	Oct. 7
St. Francis (Pa.) ■	Oct. 14
Stony Brook ■	Oct. 21
Towson ■	Oct. 28
Albany (N.Y.)	Nov. 4
St. John's (N.Y.)	*Nov. 10
Jacksonville	Nov. 18

1999 RESULTS (2-8-0)
7	Towson	34
16	Albany (N.Y.)	24
10	Lehigh	56
3	Stony Brook	7
26	C. W. Post	30
20	St. Francis (Pa.)	9
16	Robert Morris	34
37	Sacred Heart	17
3	Wagner	35
21	Central Conn. St.	28
159		**274**

Nickname: Hawks.
Stadium: Kessler Field (1993), 4,600 capacity. Natural turf.
Colors: Royal Blue & White.
Conference: Northeast.
SID: To be named, 908-728-7103.
AD: Marilyn A. McNeil.

MONTANA
Missoula, MT 59812 ....I-AA

Coach: Joe Glenn, South Dakota 1971
Record: 15 Years, 118-54-1

2000 SCHEDULE
Hofstra ■	Sept. 2
Idaho	Sept. 9
Cal Poly ■	Sept. 16
Eastern Wash. [Spokane, WA]	*Sept. 30
Cal St. Sacramento	Oct. 7
Cal St. Northridge	Oct. 14
Northern Ariz. ■	Oct. 21
Portland St.	Oct. 28
Idaho St. ■	Nov. 4
Weber St.	Nov. 11
Montana St.	Nov. 18

1999 RESULTS (9-2-0)
45	South Dakota	13
41	Cal St. Sacramento	38
81	Weber St.	22
48	Portland St.	51
48	Cal St. Northridge	27
42	Northern Ariz.	23
25	Eastern Wash.	7
73	Idaho St.	23
28	Cal Poly	14
30	Idaho	33
49	Montana St.	3
510		**254**

DIVISION I-AA CHAMPIONSHIP
| 27 | Youngstown St. | 30 |

Nickname: Grizzlies.
Stadium: Washington-Grizzly (1986), 18,845 capacity. Natural turf.
Colors: Copper, Silver & Gold.
Conference: Big Sky.
SID: Dave Guffey, 406-243-6899.
AD: Wayne Hogan.

MONTANA ST.
Bozeman, MT 59717 ....I-AA

Coach: Mike Kramer, Idaho 1977
Record: 6 Years, 37-32-0

2000 SCHEDULE
Humboldt St. ■	Sept. 9
Weber St. ■	Sept. 16
Cal Poly ■	Sept. 23
Idaho	*Sept. 30
Eastern Wash. ■	Oct. 7
Cal St. Sacramento	*Oct. 14
Cal St. Northridge ■	Oct. 21
Northern Ariz.	Oct. 28
Portland St. ■	Nov. 4
Idaho St.	*Nov. 11
Montana	Nov. 18

1999 RESULTS (3-8-0)
20	Chadron St.	10
65	Western N.M.	8
37	Cal Poly	40
10	Cal St. Sacramento	41
29	Weber St.	6
28	Portland St.	49
21	Cal St. Northridge	24
20	Northern Ariz.	49
23	Eastern Wash.	45
13	Idaho St.	29
3	Montana	49
269		**350**

Nickname: Bobcats.
Stadium: Reno H. Sales (1973), 15,197 capacity. Natural turf.
Colors: Blue & Gold.
Conference: Big Sky.
SID: Bill Lamberty, 406-994-5133.
AD: Chuck Lindemenn.

MONTCLAIR ST.
Upper Montclair, NJ 07043 III

Coach: Rick Giancola, Rowan 1968
Record: 17 Years, 118-56-2

2000 SCHEDULE
Delaware Valley	Sept. 16
Iona	Sept. 23
Cortland St.	Sept. 30
Kean	Oct. 6
Wm. Paterson ■	*Oct. 14
Buffalo St.	Oct. 21
Col. of New Jersey ■	*Oct. 28
New Jersey City	Nov. 4
Rowan ■	Nov. 11

1999 RESULTS (7-1-0)
41	Cortland St.	16
30	Brockport St.	15
63	Kean	7
41	Wm. Paterson	21
13	Western Conn. St.	27
19	Col. of New Jersey	13
38	New Jersey City	17
28	Rowan	24
273		**140**

DIVISION III CHAMPIONSHIP
37	Buffalo St.	34
32	Western Conn. St.	24
13	Rowan	42

Nickname: Red Hawks.
Stadium: Sprague (1934), 6,000 capacity. Artificial turf.
Colors: Scarlet & White.
Conference: New Jersey Athletic.
SID: Mike Scala, 973-655-5249.
AD: Holly P. Gera.

MOORHEAD ST.
Moorhead, MN 56563 II

Coach: Ralph Micheli, Macalester 1970
Record: 17 Years, 70-92-2

2000 SCHEDULE
Concordia-M'head ■	Sept. 2
North Dakota St.	*Sept. 9
Winona St.	Sept. 16
Minn.-Crookston ■	Sept. 23
Minn.-Duluth ■	Sept. 30
Wayne St. (Neb.)	Oct. 7
Bemidji St. ■	Oct. 14
Minn.-Morris	Oct. 21
Southwest St.	Oct. 28
Northern St. ■	Nov. 4
Wis.-Eau Claire [Minneapolis, MN]	*Nov. 11

1999 RESULTS (7-4-0)
44	Concordia-M'head	7
20	North Dakota St.	71
17	Winona St.	21
29	Minn.-Crookston	17
20	Minn.-Duluth	14
31	Wayne St. (Neb.)	25
32	Bemidji St.	25
41	Minn.-Morris	12
6	Southwest St.	7
24	Northern St.	56
56	Wis.-Oshkosh	7
320		**262**

Nickname: Dragons.
Stadium: Alex Nemzek (1960), 5,000 capacity. Natural turf.
Colors: Scarlet & White.
Conference: Northern Sun Intercollegiate Athletic.
SID: Larry Scott, 218-236-2113.
AD: Katy Wilson.

MORAVIAN
Bethlehem, PA 18018 III

Coach: Scot Dapp, West Chester 1973
Record: 13 Years, 82-50-1

2000 SCHEDULE
Delaware Valley		Sept. 9
Albright ■		Sept. 16
Lebanon Valley		Sept. 23
Widener ■		Sept. 30
King's (Pa.)		Oct. 7
Juniata ■		Oct. 14
FDU-Madison ■		Oct. 21
Susquehanna		Oct. 28
Wilkes		Nov. 4
Muhlenberg ■		Nov. 11

1999 RESULTS (2-8-0)
20	Delaware Valley	26
8	Albright	21
13	Lebanon Valley	24
14	Widener	40
19	King's (Pa.)	21
38	Juniata	37
10	FDU-Madison	13
24	Susquehanna	27
28	Wilkes	22
26	Muhlenberg	52
200		**283**

Nickname: Greyhounds.
Stadium: Steel Field (1932), 2,200 capacity. Natural turf.
Colors: Blue & Grey.
Conference: Middle Atlantic.
SID: Mark Fleming, 610-861-1472.
AD: James R. Walker.

MOREHEAD ST.
Morehead, KY 40351 ....I-AA

Coach: Matt Ballard, Gardner-Webb 1979
Record: 12 Years, 63-58-1

2000 SCHEDULE
Butler ■		*Sept. 9
Dayton		*Sept. 23
Valparaiso		Sept. 30
Davidson		Oct. 7
Bowie St. ■		Oct. 21
Austin Peay		Oct. 28
Ky. Wesleyan ■		Nov. 4
Southern Utah		Nov. 11

1999 RESULTS (5-5-0)
40	Davidson	0
56	Butler	34
50	Dayton	39
28	West Ga.	34
22	New Haven	52
21	Valparaiso	31
47	Austin Peay	7
56	Ky. Wesleyan	21
6	Elon	41
33	Southern Utah	51
359		**310**

Nickname: Eagles.
Stadium: Jayne (1964), 10,000 capacity. Artificial turf.
Colors: Blue & Gold.
Conference: Division I-AA Independent.
SID: Randy Stacy, 606-783-2500.
AD: Michael Mincey.

MOREHOUSE
Atlanta, GA 30314 II

Coach: Anthony Jones, Wichita St. 1984
Record: 1 Year, 2-8-0

2000 SCHEDULE
Fort Valley St.		*Aug. 26
Clark Atlanta [Atlanta, GA]		Sept. 4
Virginia Union		Sept. 9
Elizabeth City St. ■		Sept. 16
Benedict		Sept. 23
Bowie St. ■		Oct. 7
Tuskegee [Columbus, GA]		*Oct. 14
Lane ■		Oct. 21
Kentucky St.		Oct. 28
Albany St. (Ga.) ■		Nov. 4
Miles		Nov. 11

1999 RESULTS (2-8-0)
6	Fort Valley St.	14
6	Miles	14
3	Albany St. (Ga.)	35
40	Lane	10
27	Alcorn St.	41
6	Tuskegee	9
33	Benedict	32
9	Morris Brown	27
12	Kentucky St.	17
7	Clark Atlanta	28
149		**227**

Nickname: Tigers.
Stadium: B. T. Harvey (1983), 9,850 capacity. Natural turf.
Colors: Maroon & White.
Conference: Southern Intercollegiate Athletic.
SID: James E. Nix, 404-681-2800.
AD: Arthur J. McAfee Jr.

MORGAN ST.
Baltimore, MD 21251 ....I-AA

Coach: Stanley Mitchell, Morgan St. 1976
Record: 1 Year, 2-8-0

2000 SCHEDULE
Florida A&M		*Sept. 9
Towson		Sept. 16
Howard		Sept. 23
Bethune-Cookman ■		Sept. 30
N.C. A&T		Oct. 7
Savannah St.		Oct. 14
Delaware St.		Oct. 21
Western Ill.		Oct. 28
Norfolk St.		Nov. 4
South Carolina St.		Nov. 11
Hampton ■		Nov. 18

1999 RESULTS (2-8-0)
10	Bucknell	37
25	Bethune-Cookman	28
24	Rhode Island	21
10	Florida A&M	66
28	Towson	22
6	N.C. A&T	30
20	Delaware St.	34
16	Norfolk St.	20
38	Howard	42
14	Hampton	34
191		**334**

Nickname: Bears.
Stadium: Hughes (1934), 10,000 capacity. Natural turf.
Colors: Blue & Orange.
Conference: Mid-Eastern Athletic.
SID: Joe McIver, 410-319-3831.
AD: To be named.

MORNINGSIDE
Sioux City, IA 51106 II

Coach: Dave Elliott, Michigan 1975
Record: 4 Years, 6-38-0

2000 SCHEDULE
Northern Iowa		*Aug. 31
Minn.-Morris ■		*Sept. 9
Northern Colo.		Sept. 16
Neb.-Omaha ■		Sept. 23
South Dakota St.		Sept. 30
North Dakota		Oct. 7
Augustana (S.D.) ■		Oct. 14
St. Cloud St.		Oct. 21
South Dakota ■		Oct. 28
Minn. St.-Mankato ■		Nov. 4
North Dakota St.		*Nov. 11

1999 RESULTS (3-8-0)
17	Drake	21
21	Minn.-Crookston	14
7	Northern Colo.	52
30	Neb.-Omaha	42
30	South Dakota St.	34
6	North Dakota	31
20	Augustana (S.D.)	14
30	St. Cloud St.	24
0	South Dakota	21
13	Minn. St.-Mankato	24
6	North Dakota St.	38
180		**315**

Nickname: Mustangs.
Stadium: Roberts (1939), 9,000 capacity. Natural turf.
Colors: Maroon & White.
Conference: North Central Intercollegiate Athletic.
SID: Dave Rebstock, 712-274-5127.
AD: Beth Sibenaller.

MORRIS BROWN
Atlanta, GA 30314 II

Coach: Joseph C. Crosby Jr., N.C. A&T 1977
Record: 6 Years, 31-32-2

2000 SCHEDULE
Gardner-Webb ■		*Sept. 2
Tuskegee		Sept. 9
Clark Atlanta		*Sept. 16
Bethune-Cookman ■		*Sept. 23
N.C. Central [Philadelphia, PA]		Sept. 30
Alabama A&M		Oct. 14
Savannah St. [Augusta, GA]		Oct. 21
Southern U.		*Oct. 28
Texas Southern ■		Nov. 4

1999 RESULTS (6-5-0)
19	Lane	17
19	Clark Atlanta	16
7	Tuskegee	14
21	Fort Valley St.	28
16	Bethune-Cookman	28
13	Miles	7
35	Savannah St.	43
27	Morehouse	9
7	Albany St. (Ga.)	3
24	Kentucky St.	47
20	Mississippi Val.	19
208		**231**

Nickname: Wolverines.
Stadium: A.F. Herndon (1996), 18,000 capacity. Artificial turf.
Colors: Purple & Black.
Conference: Southern Intercollegiate Athletic.
SID: Charles E. Mooney, 404-220-3628.
AD: Gene Bright.

MT. ST. JOSEPH
Cincinnati, OH 45233 III

Coach: Rod Huber, Cincinnati 1988
(First year as head coach)

2000 SCHEDULE
Muskingum		Sept. 2
Otterbein ■		Sept. 9
Kalamazoo		Sept. 16
Hiram ■		Sept. 23
Defiance ■		Sept. 30
Bluffton		Oct. 7
Anderson (Ind.)		Oct. 14
Hanover		Oct. 21
Manchester		Oct. 28
Franklin ■		Nov. 4

1999 RESULTS (3-7-0)
35	Olivet	13
15	Otterbein	30
10	Urbana	13
21	Wabash	34
8	Wilmington (Ohio)	45
11	Anderson (Ind.)	14
46	Franklin	29
25	Hanover	29
26	Bluffton	27
28	Manchester	21
225		**255**

Nickname: Lions.
Stadium: Elder High School (N/A), 4,000 capacity. Natural turf.
Colors: Blue & Gold.
Conference: Heartland Collegiate Athletic.
SID: Steven F. Radcliffe, 513-244-4927.
AD: Steven F. Radcliffe.

MOUNT UNION
Alliance, OH 44601 III

Coach: Larry Kehres, Mount Union 1971
Record: 14 Years, 150-17-3

2000 SCHEDULE
Allegheny	Sept. 2
Otterbein	*Sept. 16
John Carroll ■	Sept. 23
Ohio Northern	Sept. 30
Marietta ■	Oct. 7
Wilmington (Ohio) ■	Oct. 14
Capital	*Oct. 21
Muskingum ■	Oct. 28
Baldwin-Wallace	Nov. 4
Heidelberg ■	Nov. 11

1999 RESULTS (10-0-0)
38	Albion	0
59	Hiram	0
56	Ohio Northern	24
57	John Carroll	51
66	Heidelberg	0
44	Otterbein	20
56	Marietta	21
73	Capital	19
59	Muskingum	21
26	Baldwin-Wallace	7
534		**163**

DIVISION III CHAMPIONSHIP
42	Augustana (Ill.)	33
56	Ohio Northern	31
17	Rowan	24

Nickname: Purple Raiders.
Stadium: Mt. Union (1915), 5,800 capacity. Natural turf.
Colors: Purple & White.
Conference: Ohio Athletic.
SID: Michael De Matteis, 216-823-6093.
AD: Larry Kehres.

MUHLENBERG
Allentown, PA 18104 III

Coach: Mike Donnelly, Ithaca 1975
Record: 3 Years, 12-18-0

2000 SCHEDULE
Merchant Marine ■	Sept. 2
Dickinson	Sept. 16
Frank. & Marsh. ■	Sept. 23
Western Md.	Sept. 30
Swarthmore ■	Oct. 7
Johns Hopkins	Oct. 14
Gettysburg ■	Oct. 21
Ursinus	Oct. 28
Hartwick ■	Nov. 4
Moravian	Nov. 11

1999 RESULTS (6-4-0)
42	Merchant Marine	24
30	Dickinson	13
42	Frank. & Marsh.	13
14	Western Md.	21
35	Swarthmore	0
42	Johns Hopkins	18
28	Gettysburg	42
23	Ursinus	35
24	Grove City	31
52	Moravian	26
332		**223**

Nickname: Mules.
Stadium: Scotty Wood (1998), 3,000 capacity. Artificial turf.
Colors: Cardinal & Grey.
Conference: Centennial.

SID: Mike Falk, 610-821-3232.
AD: Stephen P. Erber.

MURRAY ST.
Murray, KY 42071 ....I-AA

Coach: Joe Pannunzio, Southern Colo. 1982
(First year as head coach)

2000 SCHEDULE
Southern Ill. ■	*Aug. 31
Samford	*Sept. 7
Middle Tenn. St. ■	*Sept. 16
Indiana St. ■	*Sept. 23
Western Ky. ■	*Sept. 30
Tenn.-Martin	Oct. 7
Eastern Ill.	Oct. 14
Southeast Mo. St.	Oct. 21
Tennessee Tech ■	Oct. 28
Eastern Ky.	Nov. 4
Tennessee St. ■	Nov. 11

1999 RESULTS (7-4-0)
10	Wisconsin	49
51	Southern Ill.	58
45	Southeast Mo. St.	18
15	Western Ky.	21
62	Tenn.-Martin	14
37	Eastern Ill.	32
34	Samford	27
22	Tennessee Tech	11
45	Eastern Ky.	30
41	Tennessee St.	42
53	Ky. Wesleyan	0
415		**302**

Nickname: Racers.
Stadium: Stewart (1973), 16,800 capacity. Artificial turf.
Colors: Blue & Gold.
Conference: Ohio Valley.
SID: Steve Parker, 502-762-4271.
AD: E. W. Dennison.

MUSKINGUM
New Concord, OH 43762 III

Coach: Jeff Heacock, Muskingum 1976
Record: 19 Years, 89-94-4

2000 SCHEDULE
Mt. St. Joseph ■	Sept. 2
Ohio Northern	Sept. 16
Wilmington (Ohio) ■	*Sept. 23
Marietta ■	*Sept. 30
Capital	Oct. 7
John Carroll ■	Oct. 14
Baldwin-Wallace	Oct. 21
Mount Union	Oct. 28
Heidelberg ■	Nov. 4
Otterbein	Nov. 11

1999 RESULTS (3-7-0)
33	Denison	0
19	Marietta	35
42	Capital	21
22	Otterbein	48
56	Hiram	20
28	Ohio Northern	32
7	John Carroll	45
0	Baldwin-Wallace	28
21	Mount Union	59
22	Heidelberg	31
250		**319**

Nickname: Fighting Muskies.
Stadium: McConagha (1925), 5,000 capacity. Natural turf.
Colors: Black & Magenta.
Conference: Ohio Athletic.
SID: Bobby Lee, 614-826-8022.
AD: Jeffrey W. Heacock.

NAVY
Annapolis, MD 21402 ....I-A

Coach: Charlie Weatherbie, Oklahoma St. 1977
Record: 8 Years, 44-47-0

2000 SCHEDULE
Temple ■	*Sept. 2
Georgia Tech	Sept. 16
Boston College	Sept. 23
TCU ■	Sept. 30
Air Force	Oct. 7
Notre Dame [Orlando, FL]	Oct. 14
Rutgers ■	Oct. 21
Toledo ■	Oct. 28
Tulane	Nov. 11
Wake Forest ■	Nov. 18
Army [Baltimore, MD]	Dec. 2

1999 RESULTS (5-7-0)
14	Georgia Tech	49
48	Kent St.	28
10	Boston College	14
17	Rice	20
31	West Virginia	28
14	Air Force	19
29	Akron	35
24	Notre Dame	28
34	Rutgers	7
45	Tulane	21
41	Hawaii	48
19	Army	9
326		**306**

Nickname: Midshipmen.
Stadium: Navy-Marine Corps Mem. (1959), 30,000 capacity. Natural turf.
Colors: Navy Blue & Gold.
Conference: Division I-A Independent.
SID: Scott Strasemeier, 410-268-6226.
AD: Jack Lengyel.

NEBRASKA
Lincoln, NE 68588 ....I-A

Coach: Frank Solich, Nebraska 1966
Record: 2 Years, 21-5-0

2000 SCHEDULE
San Jose St. ■	Sept. 2
Notre Dame	Sept. 9
Iowa ■	Sept. 23
Missouri ■	Sept. 30
Iowa St.	Oct. 7
Texas Tech	*Oct. 14
Baylor	Oct. 21
Oklahoma	Oct. 28
Kansas ■	Nov. 4
Kansas St.	Nov. 11
Colorado ■	Nov. 24

1999 RESULTS (11-1-0)
42	Iowa	7
45	California	0
20	Southern Miss.	13
40	Missouri	10
38	Oklahoma St.	14
49	Iowa St.	14
20	Texas	24
24	Kansas	17
37	Texas A&M	0
41	Kansas St.	15
33	Colorado	30
22	Texas	6
411		**150**

FIESTA BOWL
31	Tennessee	21

Nickname: Cornhuskers.
Stadium: Memorial (1923), 74,031 capacity. Artificial turf.
Colors: Scarlet & Cream.
Conference: Big 12.
SID: Chris Anderson, 402-472-2263.
AD: C. William Byrne Jr.

NEB.-KEARNEY
Kearney, NE 68849 II

Coach: Darrell Morris, Northwest Mo. St. 1983

(First year as head coach)

2000 SCHEDULE

Wayne St. (Neb.) ■		*Aug. 31
Neb.-Omaha		*Sept. 9
N.M. Highlands ■		Sept. 16
Adams St.		Sept. 23
Colorado Mines ■		Sept. 30
Chadron St.		Oct. 7
Fort Lewis		Oct. 14
Fort Hays St. ■		*Oct. 21
Mesa St.		Oct. 28
Western St. (Colo.) ■		Nov. 11

1999 RESULTS (7-3-0)

59	Wayne St. (Neb.)	17
26	Neb.-Omaha	29
51	Adams St.	21
70	Colorado Mines	0
18	Chadron St.	24
79	Fort Lewis	13
13	Fort Hays St.	12
44	Mesa St.	20
23	Western St. (Colo.)	17
21	N.M. Highlands	37
404		**190**

Nickname: Antelopes, Lopers.
Stadium: Foster Field (1929), 6,500 capacity. Natural turf.
Colors: Royal Blue & Light Old Gold.
Conference: Rocky Mountain Athletic.
SID: Peter Yazvac, 308-865-8334.
AD: Michael L. Sumpter.

NEB.-OMAHA
Omaha, NE 68182.................................II

Coach: Pat Behrns, Dakota St. 1972
Record: 12 Years, 74-56-0

2000 SCHEDULE

Northwest Mo. St.		Sept. 2
Neb.-Kearney ■		*Sept. 9
Minn. St.-Mankato		Sept. 16
Morningside		Sept. 23
St. Cloud St. ■		Sept. 30
Northern Colo. ■		Oct. 7
South Dakota		*Oct. 14
North Dakota St. ■		Oct. 21
South Dakota St.		Oct. 28
Augustana (S.D.) ■		Nov. 4
North Dakota ■		Nov. 11

1999 RESULTS (7-4-0)

40	Northwest Mo. St.	17
29	Neb.-Kearney	26
62	Minn. St.-Mankato	31
42	Morningside	30
30	St. Cloud St.	20
39	Northern Colo.	43
54	South Dakota	23
14	North Dakota St.	31
40	South Dakota St.	34
24	Augustana (S.D.)	31
13	North Dakota	31
387		**317**

Nickname: Mavericks.
Stadium: Al F. Caniglia Field (1949), 9,500 capacity. Artificial turf.
Colors: Black & Crimson.
Conference: North Central Intercollegiate Athletic.
SID: Gary Anderson, 402-554-2305.
AD: Robert Danenhauer.

NEB. WESLEYAN
Lincoln, NE 68504.................................III

Coach: Brian Keller, Neb. Wesleyan 1983
Record: 4 Years, 17-23-0

2000 SCHEDULE

Iowa Wesleyan ■		Sept. 2
Dana		Sept. 9
Northwestern (Iowa) ■		Sept. 16
Dak. Wesleyan		Sept. 23
Doane ■		Oct. 7
Hastings		Oct. 14
Concordia (Neb.) ■		Oct. 21
Sioux Falls		Oct. 28
Midland Lutheran ■		Nov. 4
Peru St.		Nov. 11

1999 RESULTS (4-6-0)

19	Austin	20
35	Iowa Wesleyan	7
12	Doane	33
14	Midland Lutheran	17
14	Concordia (Neb.)	24
24	Northwestern (Iowa)	3
24	Hastings	41
14	Dana	21
10	Sioux Falls	6
41	Peru St.	27
207		**199**

Nickname: Plainsmen.
Stadium: Abel (1986), 2,000 capacity. Natural turf.
Colors: Yellow & Brown.
Conference: Division III Independent.
SID: Karl Skinner, 402-465-2151.
AD: Ira Zeff.

NEVADA
Reno, NV 89557.................................I-A

Coach: Chris Tormey, Idaho 1978
Record: 5 Years, 33-23-0

2000 SCHEDULE

Oregon		Sept. 2
TCU ■		Sept. 9
Wyoming		Sept. 23
Colorado St. ■		Sept. 30
UNLV		*Oct. 7
Fresno St.		Oct. 14
San Jose St. ■		Oct. 21
Southern Methodist		*Oct. 28
UTEP ■		Nov. 4
Hawaii		*Nov. 11
Rice ■		Nov. 18
Tulsa		Nov. 25

1999 RESULTS (3-8-0)

13	Oregon St.	28
33	Colorado St.	38
10	Oregon	72
24	Fresno St.	49
26	UNLV	12
23	New Mexico St.	16
17	Boise St.	52
41	North Texas	28
33	Idaho	42
28	Arkansas St.	44
35	Utah St.	37
283		**418**

Nickname: Wolf Pack.
Stadium: Mackay (1967), 31,545 capacity. Natural turf.
Colors: Silver & Blue.
Conference: Western Athletic.
SID: Jamie Klund, 702-784-4600.
AD: Chris Ault.

UNLV
Las Vegas, NV 89154.................................I-A

Coach: John Robinson, Oregon 1958
Record: 13 Years, 107-43-4

2000 SCHEDULE

Iowa St.		Sept. 9
North Texas ■		*Sept. 16
Brigham Young		Sept. 23
Air Force ■		*Sept. 30
Nevada		*Oct. 7
Colorado St.		Oct. 14
Wyoming ■		Oct. 21
Mississippi		Oct. 28
Utah		Nov. 4
New Mexico		Nov. 11
San Diego St.		Nov. 25
Hawaii		*Dec. 2

1999 RESULTS (3-8-0)

26	North Texas	3
27	Baylor	24
0	Iowa St.	24
14	Utah	52
12	Nevada	26
35	Wyoming	32
0	Brigham Young	29
6	New Mexico	27
16	Air Force	35
7	San Diego St.	37
17	Colorado St.	35
160		**324**

Nickname: Rebels.
Stadium: Sam Boyd (1971), 36,800 capacity. Natural turf.
Colors: Scarlet & Gray.
Conference: Mountain West.
SID: Mark Wallington, 702-895-4472.
AD: Charles W. Cavagnaro.

NEW HAMPSHIRE
Durham, NH 03824.................................I-AA

Coach: Sean McDonnell, New Hampshire 1978
Record: 1 Year, 5-6-0

2000 SCHEDULE

Hampton		Sept. 2
Rhode Island ■		Sept. 9
Northeastern ■		Sept. 16
Dartmouth ■		Sept. 23
James Madison		Sept. 30
Richmond ■		Oct. 14
Villanova		Oct. 21
Massachusetts ■		Oct. 28
Delaware		Nov. 4
Gardner-Webb ■		Nov. 11
Maine		Nov. 18

1999 RESULTS (5-6-0)

37	Rhode Island	14
19	Massachusetts	34
28	James Madison	35
17	Richmond	27
38	Stephen F. Austin	28
33	Northeastern	31
41	South Fla.	42
28	Villanova	31
10	Delaware	14
43	Connecticut	18
31	Maine	20
325		**294**

Nickname: Wildcats.
Stadium: Cowell (1936), 9,571 capacity. Natural turf.
Colors: Blue & White.
Conference: Atlantic 10.
SID: Scott Stapin, 603-862-2585.
AD: Judith L. Ray.

NEW HAVEN
West Haven, CT 06516.................................II

Coach: Darren Rizzi, Rhode Island 1992
Record: 1 Year, 5-5-0

2000 SCHEDULE

West Chester		*Aug. 31
Clarion ■		Sept. 9
Indiana (Pa.)		*Sept. 16
Massachusetts		Sept. 23
Elon		Sept. 30
Central Wash.		Oct. 7
St. Joseph's (Ind.) ■		Oct. 14
Southern Conn. St.		*Nov. 3
Jackson St.		Nov. 11

1999 RESULTS (5-5-0)

47	Bloomsburg	37
28	Clarion	21
38	Millersville	35
16	UC Davis	42
16	Elon	20
52	Morehead St.	22
24	Indianapolis	30
42	St. Joseph's (Ind.)	21

27	South Fla.	41
23	Jackson St.	30
313		**299**

Nickname: Chargers.
Stadium: Robert B. Dodds (NA), 3,500 capacity. Natural turf.
Colors: Blue & Gold.
Conference: Division II Independent.
SID: Tom Pincince, 203-932-7025.
AD: Deborah Chin.

COL. OF NEW JERSEY
Ewing, NJ 08628 III

Coach: Eric Hamilton, Col. of New Jersey 1975
Record: 23 Years, 143-84-6

2000 SCHEDULE
Cortland St.	Sept. 9
Wm. Paterson ■	*Sept. 15
Rowan ■	*Sept. 29
Union (N.Y.) ■	Oct. 7
Salisbury St.	Oct. 14
New Jersey City ■	Oct. 21
Montclair St.	*Oct. 28
Brockport St.	Nov. 4
Kean ■	Nov. 11

1999 RESULTS (4-5-0)
28	Wm. Paterson	0
14	Ithaca	21
3	Rowan	40
3	Union (N.Y.)	20
35	Salisbury St.	14
49	New Jersey City	7
13	Montclair St.	19
7	Brockport St.	12
38	Kean	20
190		**153**

Nickname: Lions.
Stadium: Lions (1984), 5,000 capacity. Artificial turf.
Colors: Blue & Gold.
Conference: New Jersey Athletic.
SID: Ann Bready, 609-771-2517.
AD: Kevin A. Mc Hugh.

NEW JERSEY CITY
Jersey City, NJ 07305 III

Coach: Roy Miller, New Jersey City 1969
Record: 15 Years, 62-84-0

2000 SCHEDULE
Pace	Sept. 2
Brockport St. ■	Sept. 9
Western Conn. St.	Sept. 16
Rowan	*Sept. 22
Cortland St. ■	Oct. 7
Kean ■	Oct. 14
Col. of New Jersey	Oct. 21
Frostburg St.	Oct. 28
Montclair St. ■	Nov. 4
Wm. Paterson	Nov. 11

1999 RESULTS (3-7-0)
29	Pace	17
21	Brockport St.	48
7	Western Conn. St.	28
21	Rowan	49
7	Cortland St.	73
41	Kean	0
7	Col. of New Jersey	49
33	Wm. Paterson	21
17	Montclair St.	38
20	Chowan	27
203		**350**

Nickname: Gothic Knights.
Stadium: Thomas Gerrity Ath. Complex (1986), 3,000 capacity. Natural turf.
Colors: Green & Gold.
Conference: New Jersey Athletic.
SID: Tracy King, 201-200-3301.
AD: Lawrence R. Schiner.

NEW MEXICO
Albuquerque, NM 87131 ....I-A

Coach: Rocky Long, New Mexico 1974
Record: 2 Years, 7-16-0

2000 SCHEDULE
Texas Tech	*Aug. 26
Boise St. ■	*Sept. 2
Oregon St. ■	*Sept. 9
New Mexico St.	*Sept. 16
Northern Ariz. ■	*Sept. 23
Wyoming ■	*Sept. 30
Colorado St.	Oct. 7
Air Force	Oct. 21
Utah ■	Oct. 28
San Diego St. ■	Nov. 4
UNLV	Nov. 11
Brigham Young	Nov. 18

1999 RESULTS (4-7-0)
10	UTEP	13
28	New Mexico St.	35
45	Northern Ariz.	14
9	Boise St.	20
24	San Diego St.	21
7	Brigham Young	31
27	UNLV	6
22	Colorado St.	36
7	Utah	52
28	Wyoming	42
33	Air Force	28
240		**298**

Nickname: Lobos.
Stadium: University (1960), 31,218 capacity. Natural turf.
Colors: Cherry & Silver.
Conference: Mountain West.
SID: Greg Remington, 505-277-2026.
AD: Rudy Davalos.

N.M. HIGHLANDS
Las Vegas, NM 87701 II

Coach: Ed Rifilato, Idaho 1985
Record: 1 Year, 7-4-0

2000 SCHEDULE
UC Davis	*Sept. 2
Eastern N.M. ■	*Sept. 9
Neb.-Kearney	Sept. 16
Western N.M.	Sept. 23
Adams St. ■	Sept. 30
Western St. (Colo.)	Oct. 7
Colorado Mines	Oct. 14
Chadron St. ■	Oct. 21
Fort Lewis ■	Oct. 28
Fort Hays St.	Nov. 4
Mesa St. ■	Nov. 11

1999 RESULTS (7-4-0)
7	New Mexico St.	73
7	Eastern N.M.	54
7	Western N.M.	14
27	Adams St.	24
45	Western St. (Colo.)	38
48	Colorado Mines	6
42	Chadron St.	56
31	Fort Lewis	10
45	Fort Hays St.	19
44	Mesa St.	36
37	Neb.-Kearney	21
340		**351**

Nickname: Cowboys.
Stadium: Perkins (NA), 5,000 capacity. Natural turf.
Colors: Purple & White.
Conference: Rocky Mountain Athletic.
SID: Jesse Gallegos, 505-454-3387.
AD: Joe L. Singleton.

NEW MEXICO ST.
Las Cruces, NM 88003 ....I-A

Coach: Tony Samuel, Nebraska 1979
Record: 3 Years, 11-22-0

2000 SCHEDULE
South Carolina	*Sept. 2
New Mexico ■	*Sept. 16
Georgia	Sept. 23
UTEP	*Sept. 30
Army ■	*Oct. 7
Tulsa ■	*Oct. 14
Arkansas St.	Oct. 21
Boise St. ■	*Oct. 28
Utah St. ■	*Nov. 4
Idaho	*Nov. 11
North Texas	Nov. 18

1999 RESULTS (6-5-0)
73	N.M. Highlands	7
35	New Mexico	28
35	Arizona St.	7
23	UTEP	54
7	Colorado St.	46
16	Nevada	23
18	Army	35
42	Idaho	14
14	Utah St.	6
26	Boise St.	45
22	North Texas	9
311		**274**

Nickname: Aggies.
Stadium: Aggie Memorial (1978), 30,343 capacity. Natural turf.
Colors: Crimson & White.
Conference: Big West.
SID: Heath Nielsen, 505-646-3929.
AD: Brian Faison.

NEWBERRY
Newberry, SC 29108 II

Coach: Mike Taylor, Newberry 1976
Record: 8 Years, 38-49-0

2000 SCHEDULE
North Greenville	Sept. 2
Furman	*Sept. 9
Mars Hill ■	*Sept. 16
West Va. Wesleyan	Sept. 23
Catawba ■	*Sept. 30
Benedict	Oct. 7
Wingate ■	Oct. 14
Carson-Newman	Oct. 21
Tusculum	*Oct. 28
Lenoir-Rhyne	*Nov. 4
Presbyterian	Nov. 11

1999 RESULTS (5-6-0)
34	Livingstone	37
16	West Virginia St.	14
39	Wingate	42
34	Gardner-Webb	31
14	Mars Hill	51
27	Charleston So.	26
35	Tusculum	20
24	Lenoir-Rhyne	21
3	Catawba	34
31	Carson-Newman	45
35	Presbyterian	45
292		**366**

Nickname: Indians.
Stadium: Setzler Field (1930), 4,000 capacity. Natural turf.
Colors: Scarlet & Gray.
Conference: South Atlantic.
SID: Darrell Orand, 803-321-5667.
AD: Wm. Grafton Young.

NICHOLLS ST.
Thibodaux, LA 70310 ....I-AA

Coach: Daryl Daye, LSU 1986
Record: 1 Year, 1-10-0

2000 SCHEDULE
Central Ark. ■	*Aug. 31
Jacksonville St. ■	*Sept. 9
La.-Monroe	*Sept. 16
Western Ill.	Sept. 23
Samford	*Sept. 30

Southwest Tex. St. .... Oct. 7
Northwestern St. ■ .... Oct. 14
Stephen F. Austin ■ ....*Oct. 21
Troy St. .... Oct. 28
Sam Houston St. ■ ....*Nov. 4
McNeese St. ....*Nov. 18

1999 RESULTS (1-10-0)
10	La.-Monroe	27
13	Western Ill.	14
45	Jacksonville St.	42
17	Northwestern St.	42
0	Southwest Tex. St.	16
0	UCF	28
7	Stephen F. Austin	38
0	Troy St.	20
0	McNeese St.	38
17	Sam Houston St.	69
24	Samford	28
133		**362**

Nickname: Colonels.
Stadium: John L. Guidry (1972), 12,800 capacity. Natural turf.
Colors: Red & Gray.
Conference: Southland Football.
SID: Jack Duggan, 504-448-4282.
AD: Stan Williamson.

NICHOLS
Dudley, MA 01571 III

Coach: Bill Carven, Nichols 1994
Record: 1 Year, 6-3-0

2000 SCHEDULE
Bri'water (Mass.) ■ .... Sept. 9
Western New Eng. .... Sept. 16
Mass.-Boston ■ .... Sept. 23
Curry ■ .... Sept. 30
Mass.-Dartmouth .... Oct. 7
MIT ■ .... Oct. 14
Mass. Maritime ■ .... Oct. 21
Westfield St. .... Oct. 28
Salve Regina .... Nov. 4

1999 RESULTS (6-3-0)
21	Fitchburg St.	9
19	Western New Eng.	7
28	Mass.-Boston	0
14	Curry	15
15	Mass.-Dartmouth	3
14	MIT	18
28	Mass. Maritime	27
35	Westfield St.	13
21	Salve Regina	34
195		**126**

Nickname: Bison.
Stadium: Bison Bowl (1961), 3,000 capacity. Natural turf.
Colors: Black & Green.
Conference: New England Football.
SID: Mike Serijan, 508-943-1560.
AD: To be named.

NORFOLK ST.
Norfolk, VA 23504 .... I-AA

Coach: Maurice Forte, Minnesota 1970
Record: 7 Years, 27-48-1

2000 SCHEDULE
Virginia St. ■ ....*Sept. 2
Bethune-Cookman .... Sept. 9
Villanova .... Sept. 16
N.C. A&T ....*Sept. 30
South Carolina St. ■ .... Oct. 7
Hampton .... Oct. 14
Florida A&M ■ .... Oct. 21
Howard .... Oct. 28
Morgan St. ■ .... Nov. 4
Delaware St. ■ .... Nov. 11
Texas Southern [San Diego, CA] .... Nov. 18

1999 RESULTS (2-9-0)
19	Virginia St.	7
7	Florida A&M	56
6	Delaware St.	26
14	N.C. A&T	28
23	South Carolina St.	27
27	Hampton	28
9	Virginia Union	21
23	Howard	29
20	Morgan St.	16
6	Bethune-Cookman	26
6	Texas Southern	22
160		**286**

Nickname: Spartans.
Stadium: Price (1997), 27,700 capacity. Natural turf.
Colors: Green & Gold.
Conference: Mid-Eastern Athletic.
SID: Glen Mason, 804-683-8444.
AD: Orby Moss Jr.

NORTH ALA.
Florence, AL 35632 II

Coach: Bill Hyde, Samford 1962
Record: 2 Years, 13-8-0

2000 SCHEDULE
Pittsburg St. ....*Sept. 2
Ark.-Monticello ■ ....*Sept. 9
Delta St. .... Sept. 23
Central Ark. ....*Sept. 30
Henderson St. ■ .... Oct. 7
Ouachita Baptist ■ .... Oct. 14
Harding .... Oct. 21
Valdosta St. ■ .... Oct. 28
West Ga. ■ .... Nov. 4
West Ala. .... Nov. 11

1999 RESULTS (5-6-0)
21	Pittsburg St.	28
14	Southern Ark.	24
15	Elon	35
24	Central Ark.	17
16	Ark.-Monticello	13
7	West Ga.	21
7	Delta St.	33
21	Henderson St.	14
21	Arkansas Tech	24
31	Valdosta St.	28
51	West Ala.	33
228		**270**

Nickname: Lions.
Stadium: Braly (1940), 14,215 capacity. Natural turf.
Colors: Purple & Gold.
Conference: Gulf South.
SID: Jeff Hodges, 205-760-4595.
AD: K. Dan Summy.

NORTH CAROLINA
Chapel Hill, NC 27514 .... I-A

Coach: Carl Torbush, Carson-Newman 1974
Record: 4 Years, 14-21-0

2000 SCHEDULE
Tulsa ■ .... Sept. 2
Wake Forest ....*Sept. 9
Florida St. .... Sept. 16
Marshall ■ .... Sept. 23
Georgia Tech .... Sept. 30
North Carolina St. ■ .... Oct. 14
Clemson ■ .... Oct. 21
Virginia .... Oct. 28
Pittsburgh .... Nov. 4
Maryland ■ .... Nov. 11
Duke .... Nov. 18

1999 RESULTS (3-8-0)
17	Virginia	20
42	Indiana	30
10	Florida St.	42
20	Clemson	31
24	Georgia Tech	31
12	Houston	20
7	Maryland	45
3	Furman	28
3	Wake Forest	19
10	North Carolina St.	6
38	Duke	0
186		**272**

Nickname: Tar Heels.
Stadium: Kenan (1927), 60,000 capacity. Natural turf.
Colors: Carolina Blue & White.
Conference: Atlantic Coast.
SID: Steve Kirschner, 919-962-2123.
AD: Richard A. Baddour.

N.C. A&T
Greensboro, NC 27411 .... I-AA

Coach: Bill Hayes, N.C. Central 1965
Record: 24 Years, 175-90-2

2000 SCHEDULE
N.C. Central [Raleigh, NC] ....*Sept. 3
Tennessee St. [Cincinnati, OH] .... Sept. 9
Elon ■ ....*Sept. 23
Norfolk St. ■ ....*Sept. 30
Morgan St. ■ .... Oct. 7
Florida A&M .... Oct. 14
Howard .... Oct. 21
Bethune-Cookman ■ .... Oct. 28
Delaware St. .... Nov. 4
Hampton .... Nov. 11
South Carolina St. [Charlotte, NC] .... Nov. 18

1999 RESULTS (10-1-0)
20	N.C. Central	7
20	Winston-Salem	7
7	Elon	40
28	Norfolk St.	14
41	Hampton	24
30	Morgan St.	6
51	Howard	0
19	Bethune-Cookman	18
24	Delaware St.	13
30	Florida A&M	15
27	South Carolina St.	7
297		**151**

DIVISION I-AA CHAMPIONSHIP
24	Tennessee St.	10
3	Youngstown St.	41

Nickname: Aggies.
Stadium: Aggie (1981), 21,000 capacity. Natural turf.
Colors: Blue & Gold.
Conference: Mid-Eastern Athletic.
SID: Donal O. Ware, 919-334-7141.
AD: Alfonso Scandrett Jr.

N.C. CENTRAL
Durham, NC 27707 II

Coach: Rudy Abrams, Livingstone 1964
Record: 6 Years, 40-20-1

2000 SCHEDULE
N.C. A&T [Raleigh, NC] ....*Sept. 3
Benedict .... Sept. 9
Virginia St. ■ .... Sept. 16
Elizabeth City St. ■ .... Sept. 23
Morris Brown [Philadelphia, PA] .... Sept. 30
Fayetteville St. ....*Oct. 7
Winston-Salem ■ .... Oct. 14
Virginia Union ■ .... Oct. 21
Livingstone .... Oct. 28
Johnson Smith ■ .... Nov. 4

1999 RESULTS (5-5-0)
7	N.C. A&T	20
0	Gardner-Webb	16
28	Virginia St.	35
28	Benedict	19
35	Elizabeth City St.	6
32	Fayetteville St.	7
7	Winston-Salem	20
25	Bowie St.	26
12	Livingstone	6
35	Johnson Smith	7
209		**162**

Nickname: Eagles.
Stadium: O'Kelly-Riddick (1975), 11,500 capacity. Natural turf.

NORTH CAROLINA ST.
Raleigh, NC 27695 ....I-A

Coach: Chuck Amato, North Carolina St. 1969
(First year as head coach)

2000 SCHEDULE
Arkansas St. ■	*Sept. 2
Indiana	Sept. 9
Southern Methodist ■	*Sept. 16
Georgia Tech ■	*Sept. 21
Clemson	Oct. 7
North Carolina	Oct. 14
Florida St. ■	*Oct. 28
Maryland	Nov. 4
Duke ■	Nov. 11
Virginia	Nov. 18
Wake Forest ■	Nov. 25

1999 RESULTS (6-6-0)
23	Texas	20
10	South Carolina	0
38	William & Mary	9
11	Florida St.	42
7	Wake Forest	31
35	Clemson	31
26	Virginia	47
31	Duke	24
21	Georgia Tech	48
30	Maryland	17
6	North Carolina	10
6	East Caro.	23
244		**302**

Nickname: Wolfpack.
Stadium: Carter-Finley (1966), 51,500 capacity. Natural turf.
Colors: Red & White.
Conference: Atlantic Coast.
SID: Annabelle Vaughan, 919-515-2102.
AD: Leslie G. Robinson.

NORTH CENTRAL
Naperville, IL 60566 III

Coach: Joe DeGeorge, Beloit 1988
Record: 2 Years, 5-13-0

2000 SCHEDULE
Benedictine (Ill.)	Sept. 9
Franklin	Sept. 16
Chicago ■	*Sept. 23
Wheaton (Ill.)	Sept. 30
Carthage ■	*Oct. 7
Millikin ■	Oct. 14
North Park	Oct. 21
Augustana (Ill.)	Oct. 28
Ill. Wesleyan ■	Nov. 4
Elmhurst	Nov. 11

1999 RESULTS (2-7-0)
10	Benedictine (Ill.)	16
0	Chicago	7
13	Wheaton (Ill.)	49
14	Elmhurst	10
13	Millikin	45
14	Augustana (Ill.)	40
6	Ill. Wesleyan	14
14	North Park	10
18	Carthage	27
102		**218**

Nickname: Cardinals.
Stadium: Cardinal (NA), 5,000 capacity. Natural turf.
Colors: Cardinal & White.
Conference: College Conf. of Illinois & Wisconsin.
SID: Joe Dennis, 708-637-5302.
AD: Walter J. Johnson.

NORTH DAKOTA
Grand Forks, ND 58202 II

Coach: Dale Lennon, North Dakota 1985
Record: 3 Years, 21-11-0

2000 SCHEDULE
Central Wash.	Sept. 2
Minn.-Crookston ■	Sept. 9
South Dakota ■	Sept. 16
Minn. St.-Mankato	Sept. 23
North Dakota St.	Sept. 30
Morningside ■	Oct. 7
Northern Colo.	Oct. 14
South Dakota St. ■	Oct. 21
Augustana (S.D.) ■	Oct. 28
St. Cloud St.	Nov. 4
Neb.-Omaha	Nov. 11

1999 RESULTS (9-1-0)
29	Northern Mich.	0
17	South Dakota	10
35	Minn. St.-Mankato	28
13	North Dakota St.	10
31	Morningside	6
24	Northern Colo.	16
7	South Dakota St.	21
27	Augustana (S.D.)	0
45	St. Cloud St.	7
31	Neb.-Omaha	13
259		**111**

DIVISION II CHAMPIONSHIP
13	Northwest Mo. St.	20

Nickname: Fighting Sioux.
Stadium: Memorial (1927), 10,000 capacity. Artificial turf.
Colors: Green & White.
Conference: North Central Intercollegiate Athletic.
SID: To be named, 701-777-2985.
AD: Roger Thomas.

NORTH DAKOTA ST.
Fargo, ND 58105 II

Coach: Bob Babich, Tulsa 1984
Record: 3 Years, 25-9-0

2000 SCHEDULE
Texas A&M-Kingsville ■	*Aug. 31
Moorhead St. ■	*Sept. 9
St. Cloud St.	Sept. 16
South Dakota ■	*Sept. 23
North Dakota	Sept. 30
Augustana (S.D.)	Oct. 7
South Dakota St. ■	Oct. 14
Neb.-Omaha	Oct. 21
Minn. St.-Mankato	Oct. 28
Northern Colo. ■	Nov. 4
Morningside ■	*Nov. 11

1999 RESULTS (9-2-0)
55	Ferris St.	35
71	Moorhead St.	20
35	St. Cloud St.	6
45	South Dakota	14
10	North Dakota	13
30	Augustana (S.D.)	14
28	South Dakota St.	7
31	Neb.-Omaha	14
56	Minn. St.-Mankato	14
39	Northern Colo.	41
38	Morningside	6
438		**184**

Nickname: Bison.
Stadium: FargoDome (1992), 18,700 capacity. Artificial turf.
Colors: Yellow & Green.
Conference: North Central Intercollegiate Athletic.
SID: George Ellis, 701-231-8331.
AD: Robert Entzion.

NORTH PARK
Chicago, IL 60625 III

Coach: Mike Liljegren, North Park 1985
Record: 5 Years, 6-39-0

2000 SCHEDULE
Northwestern (Minn.) ■	Sept. 2
Carroll (Wis.) ■	Sept. 9
Concordia (Ill.)	Sept. 16
Ill. Wesleyan ■	Sept. 30
Elmhurst	Oct. 7
Augustana (Ill.) ■	Oct. 14
North Central ■	Oct. 21
Millikin	Oct. 28
Wheaton (Ill.) ■	Nov. 4
Carthage ■	Nov. 11

1999 RESULTS (2-7-0)
28	Carroll (Wis.)	34
30	Concordia (Ill.)	0
0	Carthage	28
6	Millikin	36
15	Wheaton (Ill.)	36
26	Elmhurst	19
13	Augustana (Ill.)	30
10	North Central	14
6	Ill. Wesleyan	7
134		**204**

Nickname: Vikings.
Stadium: Hedstrand Field (1955), 2,500 capacity. Natural turf.
Colors: Blue & Gold.
Conference: College Conf. of Illinois & Wisconsin.
SID: Chris Nelson, 312-244-5675.
AD: Jack Surridge.

NORTH TEXAS
Denton, TX 76203 ....I-A

Coach: Darrell Dickey, Kansas St. 1984
Record: 2 Years, 5-17-0

2000 SCHEDULE
Baylor ■	*Aug. 31
Texas Tech	*Sept. 9
UNLV	*Sept. 16
Kansas St.	Sept. 23
Samford ■	*Oct. 5
Utah St.	Oct. 14
Boise St.	Oct. 21
La.-Lafayette	*Oct. 28
Idaho ■	Nov. 4
Arkansas St.	Nov. 11
New Mexico St. ■	Nov. 18

1999 RESULTS (2-9-0)
3	UNLV	26
0	LSU	52
21	Texas Tech	14
10	Baylor	23
10	Idaho	28
17	Boise St.	10
10	Arkansas St.	14
28	Nevada	41
3	TCU	27
9	New Mexico St.	22
7	Utah St.	34
118		**291**

Nickname: Mean Green Eagles.
Stadium: Fouts Field (1952), 30,500 capacity. Artificial turf.
Colors: Green & White.
Conference: Big West.
SID: Sean Johnson, 817-565-2476.
AD: Craig P. Helwig.

NORTHEASTERN
Boston, MA 02115 ....I-AA

Coach: Don Brown, Norwich 1977
(First year as head coach)

2000 SCHEDULE
American Int'l ■	Sept. 2
Albany (N.Y.) ■	Sept. 9
New Hampshire	Sept. 16
Connecticut	Sept. 23
Delaware	Sept. 30
Massachusetts ■	Oct. 7
Villanova ■	Oct. 14
Rhode Island ■	Oct. 21
William & Mary	Oct. 28
Maine	Nov. 11

(Colors: Maroon & Gray. Conference: Central Intercollegiate Athletic Association. SID: Kyle Serba, 919-560-5427. AD: William E. Lide.)

James Madison ■..Nov. 18

1999 RESULTS (2-9-0)
44	American Int'l	7
21	James Madison	29
30	William & Mary	42
22	Boston College	33
0	Massachusetts	77
31	New Hampshire	33
16	Villanova	45
34	Delaware	37
24	Connecticut	29
14	Maine	20
20	Rhode Island	10
256		**362**

Nickname: Huskies.
Stadium: E.S. Parsons (1933), 7,000 capacity. Artificial turf.
Colors: Red & Black.
Conference: Atlantic 10.
SID: Jack Grinold, 617-373-2691.
AD: Ian McCaw.

NORTHEASTERN ST.
Tahlequah, OK 74464..............................II

Coach: Tom Eckert, NE Okla. St. 1966
Record: 13 Years, 85-55-3

2000 SCHEDULE
Mo. Southern St. ■	*Sept. 2
Abilene Christian ■	*Sept. 16
West Tex. A&M	*Sept. 23
East Central	*Sept. 30
Okla. Panhandle ■	Oct. 7
Southeastern Okla.	Oct. 14
Angelo St. ■	Oct. 21
Midwestern St.	Oct. 28
Southwestern Okla.	Nov. 4
Central Okla. ■	Nov. 11

1999 RESULTS (8-3-0)
9	Texas A&M-Kingsville	2
7	Mo. Southern St.	28
19	Tex. A&M-Commerce	14
14	Eastern N.M.	20
40	East Central	3
34	Harding	28
57	Ouachita Baptist	0
12	Southwestern Okla.	15
30	Southeastern Okla.	3
64	Okla. Panhandle	7
12	Central Okla.	7
298		**127**

DIVISION II CHAMPIONSHIP
27	Western Wash.	24
19	UC Davis	14
7	Carson-Newman	42

Nickname: Redmen.
Stadium: Gable Field (0000), 12,000 capacity. Natural turf.
Colors: Green & White.
Conference: Lone Star.
SID: Scott Pettus, 918-458-2071.
AD: Gil Cloud.

NORTHERN ARIZ.
Flagstaff, AZ 86011..............................I-AA

Coach: Jerome Souers, Oregon 1983
Record: 2 Years, 14-9-0

2000 SCHEDULE
Chadron St. ■	Sept. 9
Cal St. Northridge	Sept. 16
New Mexico	*Sept. 23
Portland St. ■	Sept. 30
Idaho St.	*Oct. 7
Weber St. ■	Oct. 14
Montana	Oct. 21
Montana St. ■	Oct. 28
Eastern Wash.	Nov. 4
Cal St. Sacramento ■	Nov. 11
Southern Utah ■	Nov. 18

1999 RESULTS (8-3-0)
55	Cal Poly	21
14	New Mexico	45
29	Southwest Tex. St.	26
10	Eastern Wash.	14
43	Idaho St.	28
23	Montana	42
51	Cal St. Sacramento	49
49	Montana St.	20
36	Weber St.	19
40	Portland St.	24
30	Cal St. Northridge	10
380		**298**

DIVISION I-AA CHAMPIONSHIP
29	Ga. Southern	72

Nickname: Lumberjacks.
Stadium: Walkup Skydome (1977), 15,300 capacity. Artificial turf.
Colors: Blue & Gold.
Conference: Big Sky.
SID: Kevin Klintworth, 520-523-6792.
AD: Steven P. Holton.

NORTHERN COLO.
Greeley, CO 80639..............................II

Coach: Kay Dalton, Colorado St. 1954
Record: 5 Years, 33-12-0

2000 SCHEDULE
Angelo St. ■	Sept. 2
Western St. (Colo.) ■	Sept. 9
Morningside	Sept. 16
South Dakota St.	Sept. 23
Minn. St.-Mankato ■	Sept. 30
Neb.-Omaha	Oct. 7
North Dakota ■	Oct. 14
South Dakota	*Oct. 21
St. Cloud St.	Oct. 28
North Dakota St.	Nov. 4
Augustana (S.D.)	Nov. 11

1999 RESULTS (10-1-0)
51	Angelo St.	14
38	Western St. (Colo.)	31
52	Morningside	7
45	South Dakota St.	18
26	Minn. St.-Mankato	23
43	Neb.-Omaha	39
16	North Dakota	24
35	South Dakota	27
39	St. Cloud St.	3
41	North Dakota St.	39
48	Augustana (S.D.)	32
434		**257**

DIVISION II CHAMPIONSHIP
34	Pittsburg St.	31
35	Northwest Mo. St.	41

Nickname: Bears.
Stadium: Nottingham Field (1995), 7,000 capacity. Natural turf.
Colors: Blue & Gold.
Conference: North Central Intercollegiate Athletic.
SID: Dave Moll, 303-351-2150.
AD: James E. Fallis.

NORTHERN ILL.
De Kalb, IL 60115..............................I-A

Coach: Joe Novak, Miami (Ohio) 1967
Record: 4 Years, 8-36-0

2000 SCHEDULE
Northwestern	*Aug. 31
Illinois St. ■	*Sept. 9
Auburn	*Sept. 23
Ball St.	Sept. 30
UCF ■	Oct. 7
Akron	*Oct. 14
Western Mich.	Oct. 21
Buffalo ■	Oct. 28
Toledo ■	Nov. 4
Eastern Mich.	Nov. 11
Central Mich. ■	Nov. 18

1999 RESULTS (5-6-0)
21	Western Ill.	27
31	Vanderbilt	34
0	Iowa	24
21	Western Mich.	24
45	Buffalo	21
37	Ball St.	17
31	Central Mich.	27
50	Kent St.	7
9	Marshall	41
14	Toledo	44
30	Eastern Mich.	23
289		**289**

Nickname: Huskies.
Stadium: Huskie (1965), 31,000 capacity. Artificial turf.
Colors: Cardinal & Black.
Conference: Mid-American.
SID: Mike Korcek, 815-753-1706.
AD: Cary Groth.

NORTHERN IOWA
Cedar Falls, IA 50614..............................I-AA

Coach: Mike Dunbar, Washington 1972
Record: 9 Years, 76-20-1

2000 SCHEDULE
Morningside ■	*Aug. 31
Boise St.	*Sept. 9
Southern Ill.	Sept. 16
Stephen F. Austin	Sept. 23
Illinois St.	Sept. 30
Youngstown St.	Oct. 14
Indiana St.	Oct. 21
Southwest Mo. St. ■	*Oct. 28
Cal Poly	Nov. 4
Prairie View ■	*Nov. 11
Western Ill. ■	*Nov. 18

1999 RESULTS (8-3-0)
41	McNeese St.	17
36	Ohio	21
44	Central Wash.	7
34	Southern Ill.	14
28	Illinois St.	47
42	Cal Poly	21
29	Southwest Mo. St.	17
20	Youngstown St.	29
44	Indiana St.	21
27	Western Ill.	46
55	Southwest St.	14
400		**254**

Nickname: Panthers.
Stadium: U.N.I.-Dome (1976), 16,324 capacity. Artificial turf.
Colors: Purple & Old Gold.
Conference: Gateway Football.
SID: Nancy Justis, 319-273-6354.
AD: Rick R. Hartzell.

NORTHERN MICH.
Marquette, MI 49855..............................II

Coach: Eric Holm, Truman 1981
Record: 10 Years, 70-38-0

2000 SCHEDULE
Truman	Sept. 2
Indianapolis ■	*Sept. 9
Hillsdale	*Sept. 16
Michigan Tech ■	Sept. 23
Grand Valley St. ■	Sept. 30
Wayne St. (Mich.)	Oct. 7
Findlay	*Oct. 14
Ashland ■	Oct. 21
Ferris St.	Oct. 28
Northwood	Nov. 4
Saginaw Valley	*Nov. 11

1999 RESULTS (6-4-0)
0	North Dakota	29
10	Ashland	14
42	Saginaw Valley	28
27	Ferris St.	45

32	Findlay	7
31	Michigan Tech	7
51	Grand Valley St.	13
19	Indianapolis	7
30	Northwood	41
33	Westminster (Pa.)	27
275		**218**

Nickname: Wildcats.
Stadium: Superior Dome (1991), 8,000 capacity. Artificial turf.
Colors: Old Gold & Olive Green.
Conference: Great Lakes Intercollegiate Athletic.
SID: Jim Pinar, 906-227-2720.
AD: Richard Comley.

NORTHERN ST.
Aberdeen, SD 57401 II

Coach: Ken Heupel, Northern St. 1983
Record: 2 Years, 17-5-0

2000 SCHEDULE
Augustana (S.D.) ■	*Sept. 2
Wis.-Stevens Point	*Sept. 9
Concordia-St. Paul ■	Sept. 16
Bemidji St.	Sept. 23
Southwest St. ■	Sept. 30
Minn.-Morris	Oct. 7
Minn.-Duluth ■	Oct. 14
Minn.-Crookston	Oct. 21
Winona St. ■	Oct. 28
Moorhead St.	Nov. 4
Wis.-La Crosse [Minneapolis, MN]	*Nov. 11

1999 RESULTS (9-2-0)
25	Augustana (S.D.)	56
26	Wis.-Stevens Point	28
42	Concordia-St. Paul	17
45	Bemidji St.	17
20	Southwest St.	6
48	Minn.-Morris	7
16	Minn.-Duluth	7
45	Minn.-Crookston	17
37	Winona St.	34
56	Moorhead St.	24
27	Wis.-Eau Claire	20
387		**233**

Nickname: Wolves.
Stadium: Swisher (1975), 6,000 capacity. Natural turf.
Colors: Maroon & Gold.
Conference: Northern Sun Intercollegiate Athletic.
SID: Bruce Bachmeier, 605-626-7748.
AD: Robert A. Olson.

NORTHWEST MO. ST.
Maryville, MO 64468 II

Coach: Mel Tjeerdsma, Southern St. (S.D.)
Record: 16 Years, 117-59-4

2000 SCHEDULE
Neb.-Omaha ■	Sept. 2
Minn. St.-Mankato	Sept. 9
Pittsburg St. ■	Sept. 16
Southwest Baptist	Sept. 23
Truman	Sept. 30
Mo. Western St. ■	Oct. 7
Mo. Southern St.	*Oct. 14
Emporia St. ■	Oct. 21
Washburn	Oct. 28
Mo.-Rolla ■	Nov. 4
Central Mo. St.	Nov. 11

1999 RESULTS (10-1-0)
31	Arkansas Tech	14
17	Neb.-Omaha	40
27	Pittsburg St.	21
52	Southwest Baptist	0
42	Truman	32
38	Mo. Western St.	34
52	Mo. Southern St.	13
59	Emporia St.	28
35	Washburn	10
34	Mo.-Rolla	3
41	Central Mo. St.	14
428		**209**

DIVISION II CHAMPIONSHIP
20	North Dakota	13
41	Northern Colo.	35
20	Indiana (Pa.)	12
58	Carson-Newman	52

Nickname: Bearcats.
Stadium: Rickenbrode (1917), 7,500 capacity. Natural turf.
Colors: Green & White.
Conference: Mid-America Intercollegiate Athletic.
SID: Andy Seeley, 816-562-1118.
AD: James C. Redd.

NORTHWESTERN
Evanston, IL 60208 ....I-A

Coach: Randy Walker, Miami (Ohio) 1976
Record: 10 Years, 62-43-5

2000 SCHEDULE
Northern Ill. ■	*Aug. 31
Duke ■	Sept. 9
TCU	*Sept. 16
Wisconsin	Sept. 23
Michigan St.	Sept. 30
Indiana ■	Oct. 7
Purdue ■	Oct. 14
Minnesota	Oct. 28
Michigan ■	Nov. 4
Iowa	Nov. 11
Illinois ■	Nov. 18

1999 RESULTS (3-8-0)
3	Miami (Ohio)	28
17	TCU	7
15	Duke	12
23	Purdue	31
14	Minnesota	33
17	Indiana	34
23	Iowa	21
19	Wisconsin	35
3	Michigan	37
0	Michigan St.	34
7	Illinois	29
141		**301**

Nickname: Wildcats.
Stadium: Ryan Field (1997), 47,129 capacity. Natural turf.
Colors: Purple & White.
Conference: Big Ten.
SID: Brad Hurlbut, 847-491-7503.
AD: Rick Taylor.

NORTHWESTERN ST.
Natchitoches, LA 71497 ....I-AA

Coach: Steve Roberts, Ouachita Baptist 1987
Record: 6 Years, 34-25-1

2000 SCHEDULE
Southern U. ■	*Sept. 2
UCF	*Sept. 9
La.-Lafayette	*Sept. 23
Gardner-Webb ■	*Sept. 30
Troy St. ■	*Oct. 7
Nicholls St.	Oct. 14
McNeese St. ■	Oct. 21
Southwest Tex. St.	Oct. 28
Jacksonville St.	Nov. 4
Sam Houston St. ■	Nov. 11
Stephen F. Austin	Nov. 18

1999 RESULTS (4-7-0)
13	Southern U.	20
6	Southern Miss.	40
52	Tarleton St.	6
7	La.-Monroe	38
42	Nicholls St.	17
21	Troy St.	24
17	McNeese St.	20
36	Southwest Tex. St.	21
35	Jacksonville St.	7
0	Sam Houston St.	21
14	Stephen F. Austin	29
243		**243**

Nickname: Demons.

Stadium: Turpin (1976), 15,971 capacity. Artificial turf.
Colors: Purple, White & Orange.
Conference: Southland Football.
SID: Doug Ireland, 318-357-6467.
AD: Gregory S. Burke.

NORTHWOOD
Midland, MI 48640 II

Coach: Pat Riepma, Hillsdale 1983
Record: 7 Years, 31-39-2

2000 SCHEDULE
Hillsdale ■	*Sept. 9
Grand Valley St.	*Sept. 16
Mercyhurst	Sept. 23
Ferris St. ■	Sept. 30
Michigan Tech	Oct. 7
Saginaw Valley	Oct. 14
Findlay ■	Oct. 21
Ashland	Oct. 28
Northern Mich. ■	Nov. 4
Wayne St. (Mich.) ■	Nov. 11

1999 RESULTS (8-2-0)
41	Grand Valley St.	30
45	Westminster (Pa.)	14
36	Ferris St.	46
27	Wayne St. (Mich.)	24
17	Indianapolis	8
49	Gannon	0
28	Saginaw Valley	24
33	Findlay	14
41	Northern Mich.	30
14	Michigan Tech	23
331		**213**

Nickname: Timberwolves.
Stadium: Louis Juillerat (1964), 2,500 capacity. Natural turf.
Colors: Columbia Blue & White.
Conference: Great Lakes Intercollegiate Athletic.
SID: David Marsh, 517-837-4239.
AD: David W. Coffey.

NORWICH
Northfield, VT 05663 III

Coach: Mike Yesalonia, Norwich 1982
Record: 3 Years, 10-20-0

2000 SCHEDULE
Curry ■	Sept. 2
Merchant Marine ■	Sept. 9
St. John Fisher	Sept. 16
Plymouth St.	Sept. 23
Coast Guard ■	Sept. 30
Worcester Tech ■	Oct. 7
Mount Ida	Oct. 14
St. Lawrence	Oct. 21
Springfield ■	Nov. 4
Western Conn. St.	Nov. 11

1999 RESULTS (4-6-0)
27	Curry	7
20	Merchant Marine	21
23	St. John Fisher	3
7	Plymouth St.	17
30	Coast Guard	10
25	Worcester Tech	28
22	Hartwick	25
16	St. Lawrence	13
7	Springfield	28
17	Western Conn. St.	27
194		**179**

Nickname: Cadets.
Stadium: Sabine Field (1921), 5,000 capacity. Natural turf.
Colors: Maroon & Gold.
Conference: Freedom Football.
SID: Todd Bamford, 802-485-2160.
AD: Anthony A. Mariano.

NOTRE DAME
Notre Dame, IN 46556 ....I-A

Coach: Bob Davie, Youngstown St. 1976
Record: 3 Years, 21-16-0

2000 SCHEDULE

Texas A&M	Sept. 2
Nebraska ■	Sept. 9
Purdue ■	Sept. 16
Michigan St.	Sept. 23
Stanford ■	Oct. 7
Navy [Orlando, FL]	Oct. 14
West Virginia	Oct. 21
Air Force ■	Oct. 28
Boston College ■	Nov. 11
Rutgers	Nov. 18
Southern California	Nov. 25

1999 RESULTS (5-7-0)

48	Kansas	13
22	Michigan	26
23	Purdue	28
13	Michigan St.	23
34	Oklahoma	30
48	Arizona St.	17
25	Southern California	24
28	Navy	24
14	Tennessee	38
27	Pittsburgh	37
29	Boston College	31
37	Stanford	40
348		**331**

Nickname: Fighting Irish.
Stadium: Notre Dame (1930), 80,012 capacity. Natural turf.
Colors: Blue & Gold.
Conference: Division I-A Independent.
SID: John Heisler, 219-631-7516.
AD: Kevin M. White.

OBERLIN
Oberlin, OH 44074 III

Coach: Jeff Ramsey, UC Davis 1983
Record: 1 Year, 0-10-0

2000 SCHEDULE

Swarthmore ■	Sept. 2
Pomona-Pitzer	Sept. 9
Earlham ■	Sept. 16
Case Reserve ■	Sept. 23
Wabash	Sept. 30
Hiram ■	Oct. 14
Kenyon	Oct. 21
Wooster ■	Oct. 28
Ohio Wesleyan	Nov. 4
Denison	Nov. 11

1999 RESULTS (0-10-0)

6	Swarthmore	42
12	Thiel	63
27	Earlham	29
0	Pomona-Pitzer	65
7	Denison	63
0	Wooster	71
7	Kenyon	49
6	Case Reserve	42
0	Ohio Wesleyan	47
16	Alfred	55
81		**526**

Nickname: Yeomen.
Stadium: Dill Field (1925), 3,500 capacity. Natural turf.
Colors: Crimson & Gold.
Conference: North Coast Athletic.
SID: Jeff Miller, 216-775-8503.
AD: Michael S. Muska.

OCCIDENTAL
Los Angeles, CA 90041 III

Coach: Dale Widolff, Indiana Central 1975
Record: 18 Years, 93-72-2

2000 SCHEDULE

Menlo	Sept. 16
Colorado Col. ■	Sept. 23
La Verne	Sept. 30
Claremont-M-S ■	*Oct. 7
Chapman	*Oct. 14
Whittier ■	Oct. 21
Pomona-Pitzer ■	*Oct. 28
Cal Lutheran	Nov. 4
Redlands	*Nov. 11

1999 RESULTS (2-7-0)

3	La Verne	35
0	Pomona-Pitzer	28
14	Claremont-M-S	23
14	Redlands	43
13	Colorado Col.	10
16	Cal Lutheran	23
27	Menlo	42
17	Chapman	62
17	Whittier	7
121		**273**

Nickname: Tigers.
Stadium: Patterson Field (1900), 3,000 capacity. Natural turf.
Colors: Orange & Black.
Conference: Southern California Intercollegiate Athletic.
SID: Jenna Panatier, 213-259-2699.
AD: James Kerman.

OHIO
Athens, OH 45701 .... I-A

Coach: Jim Grobe, Virginia 1975
Record: 5 Years, 26-29-1

2000 SCHEDULE

Iowa St.	Sept. 2
Minnesota	Sept. 9
Tennessee Tech ■	Sept. 16
Akron ■	Sept. 23
Western Mich.	Sept. 30
Buffalo ■	*Oct. 7
Kent St.	Oct. 14
Central Mich. ■	Oct. 21
Miami (Ohio)	Nov. 4
Bowling Green	Nov. 11
Marshall ■	Nov. 18

1999 RESULTS (5-6-0)

7	Minnesota	33
21	Northern Iowa	36
16	Ohio St.	40
45	Buffalo	6
31	Kent St.	3
28	Akron	41
26	Eastern Mich.	27
17	Bowling Green	14
37	Ball St.	25
40	Miami (Ohio)	28
3	Marshall	34
271		**287**

Nickname: Bobcats.
Stadium: Peden (1929), 20,000 capacity. Natural turf.
Colors: Hunter Green & White.
Conference: Mid-American.
SID: Heather Czeczok, 614-593-1299.
AD: Thomas C. Boeh.

OHIO NORTHERN
Ada, OH 45810 III

Coach: Tom Kaczkowski, Illinois 1978
Record: 14 Years, 71-69-2

2000 SCHEDULE

Dayton	*Sept. 9
Muskingum ■	Sept. 16
Baldwin-Wallace	Sept. 23
Mount Union ■	Sept. 30
Otterbein	*Oct. 7
Heidelberg	Oct. 14
John Carroll ■	Oct. 21
Wilmington (Ohio)	Oct. 28
Capital	Nov. 4
Marietta ■	Nov. 11

1999 RESULTS (9-1-0)

38	Wabash	6
35	Heidelberg	0
24	Mount Union	56
32	Marietta	10
21	Baldwin-Wallace	3
32	Muskingum	28
54	Hiram	0
37	Otterbein	0
36	John Carroll	23
61	Capital	28
370		**154**

DIVISION III CHAMPIONSHIP

56	Hanover	14
58	Wittenberg	24
31	Mount Union	56

Nickname: Polar Bears.
Stadium: Ada Memorial (1948), 4,000 capacity. Natural turf.
Colors: Orange & Black.
Conference: Ohio Athletic.
SID: Tim Glon, 419-772-2046.
AD: Thomas E. Simmons.

OHIO ST.
Columbus, OH 43210 .... I-A

Coach: John Cooper, Iowa St. 1962
Record: 23 Years, 184-80-6

2000 SCHEDULE

Fresno St. ■	Sept. 2
Arizona	*Sept. 9
Miami (Ohio) ■	Sept. 16
Penn St. ■	Sept. 23
Wisconsin	Oct. 7
Minnesota ■	Oct. 14
Iowa	Oct. 21
Purdue	Oct. 28
Michigan St. ■	Nov. 4
Illinois	Nov. 11
Michigan ■	Nov. 18

1999 RESULTS (6-6-0)

12	Miami (Fla.)	23
42	UCLA	20
40	Ohio	16
34	Cincinnati	20
17	Wisconsin	42
25	Purdue	22
10	Penn St.	23
20	Minnesota	17
41	Iowa	11
7	Michigan St.	23
20	Illinois	46
17	Michigan	24
285		**287**

Nickname: Buckeyes.
Stadium: Ohio (1922), 91,470 capacity. Natural turf.
Colors: Scarlet & Gray.
Conference: Big Ten.
SID: Steve Snapp, 614-292-6861.
AD: Ferdinand A. Geiger.

OHIO WESLEYAN
Delaware, OH 43015 III

Coach: Mike Hollway, Michigan 1974
Record: 13 Years, 85-44-1

2000 SCHEDULE

Olivet	Sept. 9
Waynesburg ■	Sept. 16
Elmhurst ■	Sept. 23
Wooster	Sept. 30
Earlham ■	Oct. 7
Denison	Oct. 14
Wittenberg ■	Oct. 21
Kenyon	Oct. 28
Oberlin ■	Nov. 4
Allegheny	Nov. 11

1999 RESULTS (8-2-0)

14	Grove City	9
14	Wooster	11
3	Allegheny	17
27	Case Reserve	7
21	Kenyon	5
36	Defiance	15
34	Denison	21
0	Wittenberg	14
47	Oberlin	0

36	Earlham	0
232		**101**

Nickname: Battling Bishops.
Stadium: Selby (1929), 9,600 capacity. Natural turf.
Colors: Red & Black.
Conference: North Coast Athletic.
SID: Mark Beckenbach, 614-368-3340.
AD: John A. Martin.

OKLAHOMA
Norman, OK 73019 .... I-A

Coach: Bob Stoops, Iowa 1983
Record: 1 Year, 7-5-0

2000 SCHEDULE
UTEP ■	*Sept. 2
Arkansas St. ■	*Sept. 9
Rice ■	Sept. 23
Kansas ■	Sept. 30
Texas [Dallas, TX]	Oct. 7
Kansas St.	Oct. 14
Nebraska ■	Oct. 28
Baylor	Nov. 4
Texas A&M	Nov. 11
Texas Tech	Nov. 18
Oklahoma St.	Nov. 25

1999 RESULTS (7-4-0)
49	Indiana St.	0
41	Baylor	10
42	Louisville	21
30	Notre Dame	34
28	Texas	38
51	Texas A&M	6
24	Colorado	38
37	Missouri	0
31	Iowa St.	10
28	Texas Tech	38
44	Oklahoma St.	7
405		**202**

INDEPENDENCE BOWL
| 25 | Mississippi | 27 |

Nickname: Sooners.
Stadium: Memorial (1923), 72,765 capacity. Natural turf.
Colors: Crimson & Cream.
Conference: Big 12.
SID: Mike Prusinski, 405-325-8228.
AD: Joseph R. Castiglione.

OKLA. PANHANDLE
Goodwell, OK 73939 II

Coach: Ralph Young,
Record: 11 Years, 42-58-0

2000 SCHEDULE
Northwestern Okla.	*Aug. 26
Dana ■	*Sept. 2
Colorado Mines ■	Sept. 9
Ark.-Monticello	Sept. 16
Peru St. ■	Sept. 23
Western St. (Colo.)	Sept. 30
Northeastern St.	Oct. 7
Midwestern St.	*Oct. 14
Southwestern Okla.	Oct. 21
Western N.M.	Oct. 28
East Central ■	Nov. 4

1999 RESULTS (1-9-0)
20	West Tex. A&M	30
7	Mesa St.	52
6	Northwestern Okla.	21
31	Hardin-Simmons	38
0	Western St. (Colo.)	43
14	Peru St.	49
7	Langston	38
20	Prairie View	21
20	Western N.M.	17
7	Northeastern St.	64

Nickname: Aggies.
Stadium: Carl Wooten (N/A), 5,000 capacity. Natural turf.
Colors: Royal Blue & Red.
Conference: Division II Independent.
SID: Karen Lang, 580-349-2611.
AD: Kevin Emerick.

OKLAHOMA ST.
Stillwater, OK 74078 .... I-A

Coach: Bob Simmons, Bowling Green 1971
Record: 5 Years, 27-30-0

2000 SCHEDULE
Tulsa	*Sept. 9
Southwest Tex. St. ■	*Sept. 16
Southern Miss. ■	*Sept. 23
Texas	Sept. 30
Missouri	Oct. 7
Iowa St. ■	Oct. 14
Colorado	Oct. 28
Texas A&M ■	Nov. 4
Texas Tech	Nov. 11
Baylor ■	Nov. 18
Oklahoma	Nov. 25

1999 RESULTS (5-6-0)
24	La.-Lafayette	7
46	Tulsa	9
11	Mississippi St.	29
14	Nebraska	38
41	Texas Tech	21
21	Kansas St.	44
3	Texas A&M	21
21	Texas	34
45	Kansas	13
34	Baylor	14
7	Oklahoma	44
267		**274**

Nickname: Cowboys.
Stadium: Lewis (1920), 50,614 capacity. Artificial turf.
Colors: Orange & Black.
Conference: Big 12.
SID: Steve Buzzard, 405-744-5749.
AD: Terry Don Phillips.

OLIVET
Olivet, MI 49076 III

Coach: Dallas Hilliar, Central Mich. 1968
Record: 7 Years, 15-48-0

2000 SCHEDULE
Defiance	Sept. 2
Ohio Wesleyan ■	Sept. 9
Manchester ■	Sept. 16
Anderson (Ind.)	Sept. 23
Rockford	Sept. 30
Adrian	Oct. 14
Kalamazoo ■	Oct. 21
Albion	Oct. 28
Hope ■	Nov. 4
Alma	Nov. 11

1999 RESULTS (0-9-0)
13	Mt. St. Joseph	35
10	Wilmington (Ohio)	41
21	Manchester	37
24	Defiance	42
28	Alma	48
28	Adrian	35
14	Albion	42
3	Kalamazoo	24
6	Hope	30
147		**334**

Nickname: Comets.
Stadium: Griswold Field (1972), 3,500 capacity. Natural turf.
Colors: Crimson & White.
Conference: Michigan Intercollegiate Athletic.
SID: Scott Hirko, 616-749-7156.
AD: Charlie Wilson.

OREGON
Eugene, OR 97401 .... I-A

Coach: Mike Bellotti, UC Davis 1973
Record: 10 Years, 60-45-2

2000 SCHEDULE
Nevada ■	Sept. 2
Wisconsin	Sept. 9
Idaho ■	Sept. 16
UCLA ■	Sept. 23
Washington ■	Sept. 30
Southern California	Oct. 14
Arizona ■	*Oct. 21
Arizona St.	*Oct. 28
Washington St.	Nov. 4
California ■	Nov. 11
Oregon St.	Nov. 18

1999 RESULTS (8-3-0)
20	Michigan St.	27
47	UTEP	28
72	Nevada	10
33	Southern California	30
20	Washington	34
29	UCLA	34
44	Arizona	41
20	Arizona St.	17
52	Washington St.	10
24	California	19
25	Oregon St.	14
386		**264**

SUN BOWL
| 24 | Minnesota | 20 |

Nickname: Ducks.
Stadium: Autzen (1967), 41,698 capacity. Artificial turf.
Colors: Green & Yellow.
Conference: Pacific-10.
SID: David Williford, 503-346-5488.
AD: William Moos.

OREGON ST.
Corvallis, OR 97331 .... I-A

Coach: Dennis Erickson, Montana St. 1969
Record: 14 Years, 120-45-1

2000 SCHEDULE
Eastern Wash. ■	Sept. 2
New Mexico ■	*Sept. 9
San Diego St. ■	Sept. 23
Southern California ■	Sept. 30
Washington	*Oct. 7
Stanford ■	Oct. 14
UCLA	Oct. 21
Washington St. ■	Oct. 28
California	Nov. 4
Arizona	*Nov. 11
Oregon ■	Nov. 18

1999 RESULTS (7-4-0)
28	Nevada	13
46	Fresno St.	23
48	Ga. Southern	41
29	Southern California	37
21	Washington	47
17	Stanford	21
55	UCLA	7
27	Washington St.	13
17	California	7
28	Arizona	20
14	Oregon	25
330		**254**

OAHU CLASSIC
| 17 | Hawaii | 23 |

Nickname: Beavers.
Stadium: Reser (1953), 35,362 capacity. Artificial turf.
Colors: Orange & Black.
Conference: Pacific-10.
SID: Hal Cowan, 503-737-3720.
AD: Mitch S. Barnhart.

OTTERBEIN
Westerville, OH 43081 III

Coach: A. Wallace Hood, Ohio Wesleyan 1957
Record: 23 Years, 108-106-8

2000 SCHEDULE
Mt. St. Joseph	Sept. 9
Mount Union ■	*Sept. 16

2000 SCHEDULES AND 1999 RESULTS 549

Capital	*Sept. 23
Wilmington (Ohio)	Sept. 30
Ohio Northern	*Oct. 7
Baldwin-Wallace	Oct. 14
Marietta ■	Oct. 21
Heidelberg	Oct. 28
John Carroll ■	*Nov. 4
Muskingum ■	Nov. 11

1999 RESULTS (7-3-0)

30	Mt. St. Joseph	15
32	Baldwin-Wallace	12
24	John Carroll	27
48	Muskingum	22
49	Capital	24
20	Mount Union	44
30	Heidelberg	3
0	Ohio Northern	37
60	Hiram	9
37	Marietta	14
300		**207**

Nickname: Cardinals.
Stadium: Memorial (1946), 4,000 capacity. Natural turf.
Colors: Tan & Cardinal.
Conference: Ohio Athletic.
SID: Ed Syguda, 614-823-1600.
AD: Richard E. Reynolds.

OUACHITA BAPTIST
Arkadelphia, AR 71999..................................II

Coach: Todd Knight, Ouachita Baptist 1986
Record: 7 Years, 31-39-2

2000 SCHEDULE

Henderson St.	*Sept. 2
Central Ark. ■	*Sept. 16
Southern Ark.	*Sept. 23
Arkansas Tech ■	Sept. 30
Ark.-Monticello ■	Oct. 7
North Ala.	Oct. 14
West Ga. ■	Oct. 21
West Ala. ■	Oct. 28
Valdosta St.	Nov. 4
Harding	Nov. 11

1999 RESULTS (3-7-0)

34	Henderson St.	14
28	Southwest Baptist	21
0	Eastern N.M.	23
22	Tex. A&M-Commerce	21
3	Southwestern Okla.	14
19	Southeastern Okla.	49
0	Northeastern St.	57
20	Central Okla.	41
7	East Central	14
7	Harding	41
140		**295**

Nickname: Tigers.
Stadium: A. U. Williams Field (N/A), 5,200 capacity. Natural turf.
Colors: Purple & Gold.
Conference: Lone Star.
SID: Mac Sisson, 870-245-5208.
AD: David R. Sharp.

PACE
Pleasantville, NY 10570..................................II

Coach: Gregory Lusardi, Slippery Rock 1975
Record: 6 Years, 30-30-0

2000 SCHEDULE

New Jersey City ■	Sept. 2
Stonehill ■	Sept. 9
Bryant	Sept. 16
St. Peter's	*Sept. 22
Southern Conn. St. ■	Sept. 30
St. Anselm	Oct. 7
Bentley	Oct. 14
Assumption ■	Oct. 21
American Int'l	Oct. 28
C. W. Post ■	Nov. 11

1999 RESULTS (6-4-0)

17	New Jersey City	29
26	Stonehill	13
13	Bryant	7
43	Gannon	21
14	Southern Conn. St.	42
34	St. Anselm	15
34	Bentley	27
10	Assumption	7
21	American Int'l	48
17	C. W. Post	30
229		**239**

Nickname: Setters.
Stadium: Finnerty Field (1969), 1,500 capacity. Natural turf.
Colors: Blue & Gold.
Conference: Eastern Football.
SID: Nick Renda, 914-773-3411.
AD: Joseph F. O'Donnell.

PACIFIC LUTHERAN
Tacoma, WA 98447..................................III

Coach: Frosty Westering, Neb.-Omaha 1952
Record: 35 Years, 277-84-7

2000 SCHEDULE

Cal Lutheran ■	Sept. 9
Simon Fraser ■	Sept. 16
Whitworth	Sept. 23
Linfield ■	Sept. 30
Eastern Ore. ■	Oct. 7
Lewis & Clark	Oct. 14
Willamette ■	Oct. 28
Southern Ore.	Nov. 4
Puget Sound	Nov. 11

1999 RESULTS (8-1-0)

28	Cal Lutheran	26
47	Southern Ore.	23
41	Eastern Ore.	35
20	Willamette	29
33	Whitworth	7
63	Lewis & Clark	10
56	Linfield	23
35	Simon Fraser	13
49	Puget Sound	13
253		**164**

DIVISION III CHAMPIONSHIP

28	Willamette	24
49	Wartburg	14
19	St. John's (Minn.)	9
49	Trinity (Tex.)	28
42	Rowan	13

Nickname: Lutes.
Stadium: Sparks (N/A), 4,500 capacity. Artificial turf.
Colors: Black & Gold.
Conference: Northwest.
SID: Nick Dawson, 253-535-7356.
AD: Paul Hoseth.

PENNSYLVANIA
Philadelphia, PA 19104..................................I-AA

Coach: Al Bagnoli, Central Conn. St. 1975
Record: 18 Years, 143-41-0

2000 SCHEDULE

Lehigh	Sept. 16
Lafayette ■	Sept. 23
Dartmouth ■	Sept. 30
Holy Cross	Oct. 7
Columbia ■	Oct. 14
Yale	Oct. 21
Brown ■	Oct. 28
Princeton	Nov. 4
Harvard ■	Nov. 11
Cornell	Nov. 18

1999 RESULTS (5-5-0)

17	Dartmouth	6
6	Villanova	34
16	Bucknell	23
35	Fordham	18
41	Columbia	17
37	Brown	44
19	Yale	23
41	Princeton	13
21	Harvard	17
12	Cornell	20
245		**215**

Nickname: Quakers.
Stadium: Franklin Field (1895), 53,000 capacity. Artificial turf.
Colors: Red & Blue.
Conference: Ivy.
SID: Shaun May, 215-898-6128.
AD: Steve Bilsky.

PENN ST.
University Park, PA 16802..................................I-A

Coach: Joe Paterno, Brown 1950
Record: 34 Years, 317-83-3

2000 SCHEDULE

Southern California [East Rutherford, NJ]	Aug. 27
Toledo ■	Sept. 2
Louisiana Tech ■	Sept. 9
Pittsburgh	Sept. 16
Ohio St.	Sept. 23
Purdue ■	Sept. 30
Minnesota	Oct. 7
Illinois ■	Oct. 21
Indiana [Indianapolis, IN]	*Oct. 28
Iowa	Nov. 4
Michigan	Nov. 11
Michigan St. ■	Nov. 18

1999 RESULTS (9-3-0)

41	Arizona	7
70	Akron	24
20	Pittsburgh	17
27	Miami (Fla.)	23
45	Indiana	24
31	Iowa	7
23	Ohio St.	10
31	Purdue	25
27	Illinois	7
23	Minnesota	24
27	Michigan	31
28	Michigan St.	35
393		**234**

ALAMO BOWL

24	Texas A&M	0

Nickname: Nittany Lions.
Stadium: Beaver (1960), 93,967 capacity. Natural turf.
Colors: Blue & White.
Conference: Big Ten.
SID: Jeff Nelson, 814-865-1757.
AD: Timothy M. Curley.

PITTSBURG ST.
Pittsburg, KS 66762..................................II

Coach: Chuck Broyles, Pittsburg St. 1970
Record: 9 Years, 93-16-2

2000 SCHEDULE

North Ala. ■	*Sept. 2
Mesa St. ■	*Sept. 9
Northwest Mo. St.	Sept. 16
Central Mo. St. ■	*Sept. 23
Mo. Western St.	*Sept. 30
Mo. Southern St. ■	*Oct. 7
Emporia St.	Oct. 14
Washburn ■	Oct. 21
Mo.-Rolla	Oct. 28
Southwest Baptist ■	Nov. 4
Truman ■	Nov. 11

1999 RESULTS (10-1-0)

28	North Ala.	21
51	Tex. A&M-Commerce	3
21	Northwest Mo. St.	27
14	Central Mo. St.	7
31	Mo. Western St.	6
36	Mo. Southern St.	8
21	Emporia St.	7
27	Washburn	8
62	Mo.-Rolla	0
65	Southwest Baptist	0
29	Truman	17
385		**104**

SCHEDULES/RESULTS

DIVISION II CHAMPIONSHIP
31 Northern Colo. 34
Nickname: Gorillas.
Stadium: Carnie Smith (1924), 5,600 capacity. Natural turf.
Colors: Crimson & Gold.
Conference: Mid-America Intercollegiate Athletic.
SID: Dan Wilkes, 316/235-4188.
AD: Chuck Broyles.

PITTSBURGH
Pittsburgh, PA 15260..................................I-A

Coach: Walt Harris, Pacific (Cal.) 1968
Record: 6 Years, 24-45-0

2000 SCHEDULE
Kent St. ■	Sept. 2
Bowling Green	Sept. 9
Penn St. ■	Sept. 16
Rutgers	Sept. 23
Syracuse	Oct. 7
Boston College ■	Oct. 21
Virginia Tech	Oct. 28
North Carolina ■	Nov. 4
Miami (Fla.)	Nov. 11
Temple	Nov. 18
West Virginia ■	Nov. 24

1999 RESULTS (5-6-0)
30	Bowling Green	10
17	Penn St.	20
30	Kent St.	23
55	Temple	24
17	Syracuse	24
16	Boston College	20
38	Rutgers	15
17	Virginia Tech	30
3	Miami (Fla.)	33
37	Notre Dame	27
21	West Virginia	52
281		**278**

Nickname: Panthers.
Stadium: Three Rivers (1970), 59,600 capacity. Artificial turf.
Colors: Gold & Blue.
Conference: Big East.
SID: E. J. Borghetti, 412-648-8240.
AD: Steven C. Pederson.

PLYMOUTH ST.
Plymouth, NH 03264..................................III

Coach: Chris Rorke, Dartmouth 1989
Record: 1 Year, 8-3-0

2000 SCHEDULE
Rensselaer	Sept. 9
Brockport St. ■	Sept. 16
Norwich ■	Sept. 23
Western Conn. St.	Sept. 30
Merchant Marine	Oct. 7
Springfield	Oct. 14
Bentley ■	Oct. 21
Coast Guard	Oct. 28
Mount Ida ■	Nov. 4
Worcester Tech	Nov. 11

1999 RESULTS (7-3-0)
16	Salve Regina	7
10	Brockport St.	13
17	Norwich	7
9	Western Conn. St.	12
49	Merchant Marine	27
33	Springfield	51
17	Bentley	12
42	Coast Guard	0
40	Kean	0
21	Worcester Tech	0
254		**129**

ECAC PLAYOFF
13 Salve Regina 7
Nickname: Panthers.
Stadium: Currier Memorial Field (1970), 1,000 capacity. Natural turf.
Colors: Green & White.
Conference: Freedom Football.
SID: Kent Cherrington, 603-535-2477.
AD: Stephen R. Bamford.

POMONA-PITZER
Claremont, CA 91711..................................III

Coach: Roger Caron, Harvard 1985
Record: 6 Years, 32-18-0

2000 SCHEDULE
Oberlin ■	Sept. 9
Colorado Col.	Sept. 16
Lewis & Clark ■	Sept. 23
La Verne	Oct. 7
Puget Sound	Oct. 14
Menlo	Oct. 21
Occidental	*Oct. 28
Claremont-M-S ■	Nov. 4

1999 RESULTS (7-1-0)
42	Colorado Col.	14
23	Lawrence	8
28	Occidental	0
65	Oberlin	0
14	La Verne	15
33	Whittier	12
57	Puget Sound	43
24	Claremont-M-S	21
286		**113**

Nickname: Sagehens.
Stadium: Merritt Field (1991), 2,000 capacity. Natural turf.
Colors: Blue, Orange & White.
Conference: Division III Independent.
SID: Kirk Reynolds, 909-621-8429.
AD: Daniel Bridges.

PORTLAND ST.
Portland, OR 97207..................................I-AA

Coach: Tim Walsh, UC Riverside 1977
Record: 11 Years, 72-49-0

2000 SCHEDULE
Western Wash. ■	Sept. 2
Hawaii	*Sept. 9
Cal St. Sacramento	*Sept. 16
Northern Ariz.	Sept. 30
Hofstra	Oct. 7
Idaho St. ■	Oct. 14
Weber St.	Oct. 21
Montana ■	Oct. 28
Montana St.	Nov. 4
Eastern Wash. ■	Nov. 11
Cal St. Northridge ■	Nov. 18

1999 RESULTS (8-3-0)
6	Fresno St.	34
48	Western Wash.	28
48	Eastern Wash.	39
52	Idaho St.	13
51	Montana	48
14	Cal St. Sacramento	41
49	Montana St.	28
31	Weber St.	14
42	Cal Poly	28
34	Cal St. Northridge	21
24	Northern Ariz.	40
399		**334**

Nickname: Vikings.
Stadium: Civic (1928), 30,000 capacity. Artificial turf.
Colors: Forest Green & White.
Conference: Big Sky.
SID: Mike Lund, 503-725-2525.
AD: James M. Sterk.

PRAIRIE VIEW
Prairie View, TX 77446..................................I-AA

Coach: To be named

2000 SCHEDULE
Texas Southern [Houston, TX]	*Sept. 2
McNeese St. [Houston, TX]	*Sept. 9
Southern U. [Houston, TX]	*Sept. 16
Alabama A&M ■	*Sept. 23
Grambling [Dallas, TX]	*Sept. 30
Alcorn St. ■	*Oct. 7
Alabama St. ■	Oct. 14
Illinois St.	Oct. 21
Mississippi Val.	Oct. 28
Ark.-Pine Bluff	Nov. 4
Northern Iowa	*Nov. 11

1999 RESULTS (2-8-0)
0	Texas Southern	34
21	Howard Payne	7
0	Southern U.	42
3	Alabama A&M	27
19	Grambling	47
0	Alcorn St.	61
21	Okla. Panhandle	20
12	Mississippi Val.	14
6	Ark.-Pine Bluff	30
27	Alabama St.	42
109		**324**

Nickname: Panthers.
Stadium: Blackshear (1960), 6,000 capacity. Natural turf.
Colors: Purple & Gold.
Conference: Southwestern Athletic.
SID: Harlan S. Robinson, 409-857-2114.
AD: Walter W. Redd.

PRESBYTERIAN
Clinton, SC 29325..................................II

Coach: Daryl Dickey, Tennessee 1986
Record: 3 Years, 20-13-0

2000 SCHEDULE
West Ga.	*Sept. 2
Charleston So. ■	Sept. 9
Lenoir-Rhyne ■	Sept. 16
Catawba	Sept. 23
Carson-Newman	Oct. 7
Mars Hill	Oct. 14
Wingate	Oct. 21
Virginia-Wise	Oct. 28
Tusculum	Nov. 4
Newberry ■	Nov. 11

1999 RESULTS (7-4-0)
41	West Ga.	40
40	Charleston So.	14
40	Carson-Newman	43
21	Lenoir-Rhyne	24
51	Tusculum	21
10	Catawba	24
49	Virginia-Wise	34
35	Mars Hill	14
43	Wingate	35
20	Gardner-Webb	31
45	Newberry	35
395		**315**

Nickname: Blue Hose.
Stadium: Bailey Memorial (N/A), 5,000 capacity. Natural turf.
Colors: Garnet & Blue.
Conference: South Atlantic.
SID: Al Ansley, 803-833-8252.
AD: J. Allen Morris.

PRINCETON
Princeton, NJ 08544..................................I-AA

Coach: Roger Hughes, Doane 1982
(First year as head coach)

2000 SCHEDULE
Lafayette	Sept. 16
Lehigh ■	*Sept. 23
Columbia	Sept. 30
Colgate	Oct. 7
Brown ■	Oct. 14
Harvard ■	Oct. 21
Cornell	Oct. 28
Pennsylvania ■	Nov. 4
Yale	Nov. 11
Dartmouth ■	Nov. 18

1999 RESULTS (3-7-0)

3	Cornell	20
0	Lehigh	31
27	Fordham	0
30	Brown	53
22	Lafayette	10
6	Harvard	13
44	Columbia	15
13	Pennsylvania	41
21	Yale	23
18	Dartmouth	19
184		**225**

Nickname: Tigers.
Stadium: Princeton (1998), 27,800 capacity. Natural turf.
Colors: Orange & Black.
Conference: Ivy.
SID: Jerry Price, 609-258-3568.
AD: Gary D. Walters.

PRINCIPIA
Elsah, IL 62028 III

Coach: Rod Humenuik, Southern California 1959
Record: 2 Years, 2-12-0

2000 SCHEDULE
Trinity (Ill.) ■	Sept. 2
Trinity Bible (N.D.) ■	Sept. 9
Crown	*Sept. 16
Haskell	*Sept. 23
Colorado Col. ■	Sept. 30
Averett ■	Oct. 7
Rockford ■	Oct. 14
Wis. Lutheran ■	Oct. 21
Shenandoah	*Nov. 4

1999 RESULTS (2-4-0)
38	Southwestern Assemblies of God	8
20	Concordia (Ill.)	27
14	Bethel (Tenn.)	35
46	Crown	42
7	Blackburn	35
27	Trinity Bible (N.D.)	29
152		**176**

Nickname: Panthers.
Stadium: Clark Field (1937), 1,000 capacity. Natural turf.
Colors: Navy Blue & Gold.
Conference: Division III Independent.
SID: Mary Ann Sprague, 618-374-5372.
AD: To Be named.

PUGET SOUND
Tacoma, WA 98416 III

Coach: Gordon Elliott, Puget Sound 1976
Record: 6 Years, 11-44-0

2000 SCHEDULE
Simon Fraser ■	Sept. 9
Claremont-M-S	*Sept. 16
Willamette	Sept. 23
Lewis & Clark ■	Oct. 7
Pomona-Pitzer ■	Oct. 14
Whitworth ■	Oct. 21
Linfield	Oct. 28
Eastern Ore.	Nov. 4
Pacific Lutheran ■	Nov. 11

1999 RESULTS (1-8-0)
0	Simon Fraser	31
12	Western Ore.	44
12	Whitworth	45
14	Eastern Ore.	41
26	Lewis & Clark	20
14	Willamette	41
43	Pomona-Pitzer	57
0	Linfield	42
13	Pacific Lutheran	49
134		**370**

Nickname: Loggers.
Stadium: Baker (1964), 6,000 capacity. Natural turf.
Colors: Maroon & White.
Conference: Northwest.
SID: Robin Hamilton, 206-756-3140.
AD: Richard P. Ulrich.

PURDUE
West Lafayette, IN 47907 ....I-A

Coach: Joe Tiller, Montana St. 1965
Record: 9 Years, 64-42-1

2000 SCHEDULE
Central Mich. ■	Sept. 2
Kent ■	Sept. 9
Notre Dame	Sept. 16
Minnesota	Sept. 23
Penn St.	Sept. 30
Michigan ■	Oct. 7
Northwestern	Oct. 14
Wisconsin	Oct. 21
Ohio St. ■	Oct. 28
Michigan St.	Nov. 11
Indiana ■	Nov. 18

1999 RESULTS (7-4-0)
47	UCF	13
28	Notre Dame	23
58	Central Mich.	16
31	Northwestern	23
12	Michigan	38
22	Ohio St.	25
52	Michigan St.	28
25	Penn St.	31
33	Minnesota	28
21	Wisconsin	28
30	Indiana	24
359		**277**

OUTBACK BOWL
25	Georgia	28

Nickname: Boilermakers.
Stadium: Ross-Ade (1924), 67,332 capacity. Natural turf.
Colors: Old Gold & Black.
Conference: Big Ten.
SID: Tom Schott, 317-494-3202.
AD: Morgan J. Burke.

QUINCY
Quincy, IL 62301 II

Coach: Brian Cox, Western Ill. 1989
Record: 3 Years, 7-24-0

2000 SCHEDULE
Southwest Baptist	*Sept. 2
Central Mo. St.	*Sept. 9
St. Francis (Ill.)	*Sept. 16
West Va. Tech ■	Sept. 23
Belhaven ■	Sept. 30
St. Joseph's (Ind.)	Oct. 7
Northwestern Okla. ■	Oct. 21
Ky. Wesleyan	Oct. 28
Butler ■	Nov. 4
Culver-Stockton ■	Nov. 11

1999 RESULTS (3-8-0)
13	Central Mo. St.	60
23	Mo.-Rolla	16
12	McKendree	38
14	St. Xavier	21
7	Drake	48
7	St. Joseph's (Ind.)	41
46	St. Francis (Ill.)	34
14	Ky. Wesleyan	41
21	Ottawa	42
12	Butler	27
24	Culver-Stockton	20
193		**388**

Nickname: Hawks.
Stadium: QU (1938), 2,500 capacity. Natural turf.
Colors: Brown, White & Gold.
Conference: Division II Independent.
SID: J. D. Hamilton, 217-228-5277.
AD: James Naumovich.

RANDOLPH-MACON
Ashland, VA 23005 III

Coach: Scott Boone, Wabash 1981
Record: 3 Years, 20-10-0

2000 SCHEDULE
Gettysburg ■	Sept. 2
Western Md. ■	Sept. 9
Wash. & Jeff.	Sept. 16
Catholic ■	Sept. 23
Wash. & Lee	Sept. 30
Guilford ■	Oct. 7
Emory & Henry	Oct. 14
Davidson	Oct. 21
Bridgewater (Va.) ■	Nov. 4
Hampden-Sydney	Nov. 11

1999 RESULTS (5-5-0)
54	Gettysburg	20
7	Western Md.	28
28	Wash. & Jeff.	55
30	Wash. & Lee	23
26	Catholic	35
36	Emory & Henry	23
16	Davidson	24
27	Guilford	0
14	Bridgewater (Va.)	42
33	Hampden-Sydney	7
271		**257**

Nickname: Yellow Jackets.
Stadium: Day Field (1953), 5,000 capacity. Natural turf.
Colors: Lemon & Black.
Conference: Old Dominion Athletic.
SID: To be named, 804-798-8372.
AD: Gregg Waters.

REDLANDS
Redlands, CA 92373 III

Coach: Mike Maynard, Ill. Wesleyan 1980
Record: 12 Years, 75-34-1

2000 SCHEDULE
Whitworth ■	*Sept. 9
Lewis & Clark	Sept. 16
Cal Lutheran ■	*Sept. 23
Azusa Pacific	*Sept. 30
Chapman ■	*Oct. 7
La Verne	Oct. 14
Claremont-M-S ■	*Oct. 28
Whittier	*Nov. 4
Occidental ■	*Nov. 11

1999 RESULTS (7-2-0)
0	Linfield	48
49	Lewis & Clark	0
52	Azusa Pacific	59
43	Occidental	14
48	Chapman	45
22	La Verne	21
63	Claremont-M-S	10
73	Whittier	3
51	Cal Lutheran	20
401		**220**

Nickname: Bulldogs.
Stadium: Ted Runner (1968), 7,000 capacity. Natural turf.
Colors: Maroon & Gray.
Conference: Southern California Intercollegiate Athletic.
SID: To be named, 909-335-4031.
AD: Carl R. Clapp.

RENSSELAER
Troy, NY 12180 III

Coach: Joe King, Siena 1970
Record: 11 Years, 74-28-2

2000 SCHEDULE
Plymouth St. ■	Sept. 9
Coast Guard	Sept. 16
Worcester Tech ■	Sept. 23

Rochester		Sept. 30
Union (N.Y.)		Oct. 14
Hartwick ■		Oct. 21
St. John Fisher ■		Oct. 28
St. Lawrence ■		Nov. 4
Hobart		Nov. 11

1999 RESULTS (9-0-0)

55	Kean	7
42	Coast Guard	3
42	Worcester Tech	27
34	Rochester	6
16	Union (N.Y.)	7
48	Hartwick	3
38	St. John Fisher	7
32	St. Lawrence	7
17	Hobart	6
324		**73**

DIVISION III CHAMPIONSHIP

10	Rowan	29

Nickname: Engineers.
Stadium: '86 Field (1912), 3,000 capacity. Natural turf.
Colors: Cherry & White.
Conference: Upstate Collegiate Athletic Association.
SID: Kevin Beattie, 518-276-2187.
AD: Robert F. Ducatte.

RHODE ISLAND
Kingston, RI 02881 .... I-AA

Coach: Tim Stowers, Auburn 1980
Record: 6 Years, 51-23-0

2000 SCHEDULE

Delaware ■	Sept. 2
New Hampshire	Sept. 9
Hofstra	*Sept. 23
Brown ■	Sept. 30
William & Mary	Oct. 7
James Madison ■	Oct. 14
Northeastern	Oct. 21
Maine	Oct. 28
Richmond ■	Nov. 4
Connecticut	Nov. 11
Massachusetts ■	Nov. 18

1999 RESULTS (1-10-0)

14	New Hampshire	37
13	Hofstra	28
21	Morgan St.	24
9	Connecticut	20
38	Richmond	41
25	Brown	27
23	Maine	14
9	Massachusetts	31
6	William & Mary	24
0	Delaware	35
10	Northeastern	20
168		**301**

Nickname: Rams.
Stadium: Meade Stadium (1928), 6,470 capacity. Natural turf.
Colors: Light & Dark Blue & White.
Conference: Atlantic 10.
SID: Mike Ballweg, 401-874-2401.
AD: Ronald J. Petro.

RHODES
Memphis, TN 38112 III

Coach: Joe White, Springfield 1984
Record: 3 Years, 13-15-0

2000 SCHEDULE

DePauw ■	Sept. 2
Maryville (Tenn.)	Sept. 9
Centre ■	Sept. 16
Washington (Mo.) ■	Sept. 30
Rose-Hulman	Oct. 7
Sewanee	Oct. 14
Colorado Col. ■	Oct. 21
Trinity (Tex.)	Oct. 28
Millsaps ■	Nov. 4

1999 RESULTS (6-3-0)

33	DePauw	14
30	Maryville (Tenn.)	19
14	Centre	21
7	Washington (Mo.)	12
51	Rose-Hulman	14
23	Sewanee	21
38	Colorado Col.	28
17	Trinity (Tex.)	45
32	Millsaps	25
245		**199**

Nickname: Lynx.
Stadium: Fargason Field (NA), 3,300 capacity. Natural turf.
Colors: Red, Black & White.
Conference: Southern Collegiate Athletic.
SID: To be named, 901-726-3940.
AD: Mike Clary.

RICE
Houston, TX 77005 .... I-A

Coach: Ken Hatfield, Arkansas 1965
Record: 21 Years, 144-96-4

2000 SCHEDULE

Houston ■	*Sept. 2
Michigan	Sept. 9
Tulsa ■	*Sept. 16
Oklahoma	Sept. 23
San Jose St.	Sept. 30
Fresno St. ■	*Oct. 5
Hawaii ■	Oct. 21
TCU	Oct. 28
Southern Methodist ■	Nov. 4
UTEP	*Nov. 11
Nevada	Nov. 18

1999 RESULTS (5-6-0)

3	Houston	28
3	Michigan	37
13	Texas	18
20	Navy	17
20	Tulsa	10
38	Hawaii	19
49	San Jose St.	7
42	TCU	21
2	Southern Methodist	27
18	Fresno St.	47
29	UTEP	30
237		**261**

Nickname: Owls.
Stadium: Rice (1950), 70,000 capacity. Artificial turf.
Colors: Blue & Gray.
Conference: Western Athletic.
SID: Bill Cousins, 713-527-4034.
AD: John R. May.

RICHMOND
Richmond, VA 23173 .... I-AA

Coach: Jim Reid, Maine 1973
Record: 11 Years, 65-55-3

2000 SCHEDULE

Bucknell ■	*Sept. 2
Virginia	Sept. 9
Massachusetts ■	Sept. 16
Arkansas St.	*Sept. 30
Delaware ■	Oct. 7
New Hampshire	Oct. 14
Maine ■	Oct. 21
Villanova	Oct. 28
Rhode Island	Nov. 4
James Madison ■	Nov. 11
William & Mary	Nov. 18

1999 RESULTS (5-6-0)

42	VMI	6
30	Villanova	35
14	Maine	21
27	New Hampshire	17
33	Delaware	41
41	Rhode Island	38
31	Hofstra	21
28	Connecticut	21
6	Massachusetts	33
13	James Madison	31
14	William & Mary	31
279		**295**

Nickname: Spiders.
Stadium: Richmond (1929), 21,319 capacity. Natural turf.
Colors: Red & Blue.
Conference: Atlantic 10.
SID: Phil Stanton, 804-289-8320.
AD: Jim Miller.

RIPON
Ripon, WI 54971 III

Coach: Ron Ernst, Neb. Wesleyan 1980
Record: 9 Years, 55-30-0

2000 SCHEDULE

Elmhurst ■	Sept. 9
Knox ■	Sept. 16
Carroll (Wis.)	Sept. 23
St. Norbert	Sept. 30
Lake Forest ■	Oct. 7
Grinnell	Oct. 14
Monmouth (Ill.) ■	Oct. 21
Illinois Col.	Oct. 28
Lawrence ■	Nov. 4
Beloit	Nov. 11

1999 RESULTS (6-4-0)

6	Elmhurst	18
33	Knox	14
36	Carroll (Wis.)	7
17	St. Norbert	35
43	Lake Forest	36
63	Grinnell	20
25	Monmouth (Ill.)	22
65	Illinois Col.	28
22	Lawrence	25
22	Beloit	23
332		**228**

Nickname: Red Hawks.
Stadium: Ingalls Field (1888), 2,500 capacity. Natural turf.
Colors: Red & White.
Conference: Midwest Collegiate Athletic.
SID: Chris Graham, 414-748-8133.
AD: Robert G. Gillespie.

ROBERT MORRIS
Moon Township, PA 15108 .... I-AA

Coach: Joe Walton, Pittsburgh 1957
Record: 6 Years, 42-18-1

2000 SCHEDULE

Buffalo St. ■	Sept. 2
Monmouth ■	Sept. 16
St. Francis (Pa.)	Sept. 30
St. John's (N.Y.) ■	Oct. 7
Dayton	Oct. 14
Central Conn. St. ■	Oct. 21
Wagner	Oct. 28
Sacred Heart	Nov. 4
Albany (N.Y.) ■	Nov. 11
Stony Brook	Nov. 18

1999 RESULTS (8-2-0)

20	Buffalo St.	32
34	Dayton	7
13	Valparaiso	17
27	Central Conn. St.	24
23	Wagner	21
48	Sacred Heart	0
34	Monmouth	16
30	Albany (N.Y.)	20
49	St. Francis (Pa.)	0
50	Stony Brook	19
328		**156**

Nickname: Colonials.
Stadium: Moon (1950), 7,000 capacity. Natural turf.
Colors: Blue & White.
Conference: Northeast.
SID: Marty Galosi, 412-262-8314.
AD: Susan K. Hofacre.

ROCHESTER
Rochester, NY 14627 III

Coach: Mark Kreydt, Rochester 1988
Record: 2 Years, 4-14-0

2000 SCHEDULE
St. John Fisher ....*Sept. 9
Hobart ■ ....Sept. 16
St. Lawrence ....Sept. 23
Rensselaer ■ ....Sept. 30
Chicago ....Oct. 7
Canisius ■ ....Oct. 14
Washington (Mo.) ■ ....*Oct. 21
Carnegie Mellon ....Oct. 28
Union (N.Y.) ■ ....Nov. 4
Case Reserve ■ ....Nov. 11

1999 RESULTS (3-6-0)
14	Canisius	26
21	Case Reserve	14
28	St. Lawrence	17
6	Rensselaer	34
21	Hobart	48
7	Washington (Mo.)	41
6	Chicago	3
15	Carnegie Mellon	33
0	Union (N.Y.)	52
118		**268**

Nickname: Yellowjackets.
Stadium: Fauver (1930), 5,000 capacity. Artificial turf.
Colors: Yellow & Blue.
Conference: University Athletic Assoc.
SID: Dennis O'Donnell, 716-275-5955.
AD: George Vander Zwaag.

ROCKFORD
Rockford, IL 61108 III

Coach: Vic Clark
Record: 9 Years, 61-29-0

2000 SCHEDULE
Wis. Lutheran ■ ....Sept. 2
Crown ■ ....*Sept. 9
Maranatha Baptist ....Sept. 16
Defiance ■ ....Sept. 23
Olivet ■ ....Sept. 30
Blackburn ....Oct. 7
Principia ....Oct. 14
Anderson (Ind.) ■ ....Oct. 21
Wis. Lutheran ....Oct. 28
Trinity Bible (N.D.) ....Nov. 4

1999 RESULTS (3-6-0)
(None, first varsity season in 2000)

Nickname: Regents.
Colors: Purple & White.
Conference: Division III Independent.
SID: Bill Lavery, 815-394-5063.
AD: Bill Langston.

ROSE-HULMAN
Terre Haute, IN 47803 III

Coach: Russ Mollet, Southwest Mo. St. 1975
Record: 1 Year, 2-8-0

2000 SCHEDULE
Earlham ■ ....*Sept. 2
Sewanee ....Sept. 9
Chicago ....Sept. 16
Kalamazoo ■ ....Sept. 23
Trinity (Tex.) ■ ....*Sept. 30
Rhodes ■ ....Oct. 7
Millsaps ■ ....Oct. 14
Case Reserve ....Oct. 21
DePauw ....Nov. 4
Centre ■ ....Nov. 11

1999 RESULTS (2-8-0)
13	Washington (Mo.)	25
15	Sewanee	44
20	Chicago	22
20	Kalamazoo	15
0	Trinity (Tex.)	51
14	Rhodes	51
28	Millsaps	35
26	Earlham	12
0	DePauw	33
14	Centre	36
150		**324**

Nickname: Fightin' Engineers.
Stadium: Phil Brown Field (NA), 2,500 capacity. Natural turf.
Colors: Old Rose & White.
Conference: Southern Collegiate Athletic.
SID: Kevin Lanke, 812-877-8180.
AD: Gregory K. Ruark.

ROWAN
Glassboro, NJ 08028 III

Coach: K. C. Keeler, Delaware 1981
Record: 7 Years, 70-17-1

2000 SCHEDULE
Wesley ■ ....Sept. 9
Albany (N.Y.) ■ ....Sept. 16
New Jersey City ■ ....*Sept. 22
Col. of New Jersey ....*Sept. 29
Buffalo St. ....Oct. 7
Cortland St. ■ ....Oct. 14
Kean ....*Oct. 27
Wm. Paterson ■ ....Nov. 4
Montclair St. ....Nov. 11

1999 RESULTS (8-1-0)
29	Wesley	6
38	Albany (N.Y.)	37
49	New Jersey City	21
40	Col. of New Jersey	3
43	Buffalo St.	7
30	Cortland St.	9
44	Kean	0
41	Wm. Paterson	0
24	Montclair St.	28
338		**111**

DIVISION III CHAMPIONSHIP
29	Rensselaer	10
55	Ursinus	0
42	Montclair St.	13
24	Mount Union	17
13	Pacific Lutheran	42

Nickname: Profs.
Stadium: John Page Field (NA), 5,000 capacity. Natural turf.
Colors: Brown & Gold.
Conference: New Jersey Athletic.
SID: Sheila Stevenson, 856-256-4252.
AD: Joy L. Reighn.

RUTGERS
New Brunswick, NJ 08903 ....I-A

Coach: Terry Shea, Oregon 1968
Record: 6 Years, 23-42-2

2000 SCHEDULE
Villanova ■ ....*Sept. 2
Buffalo ■ ....*Sept. 9
Virginia Tech ....Sept. 16
Pittsburgh ....Sept. 23
Miami (Fla.) ■ ....*Sept. 30
Temple ■ ....Oct. 14
Navy ....Oct. 21
Boston College ....Oct. 28
West Virginia ■ ....Nov. 11
Notre Dame ■ ....Nov. 18
Syracuse ....Nov. 25

1999 RESULTS (1-10-0)
7	California	21
21	Texas	38
7	Boston College	27
10	Wake Forest	17
20	Virginia Tech	58
16	West Virginia	62
15	Pittsburgh	38
28	Temple	56
7	Navy	34
24	Syracuse	21
0	Miami (Fla.)	55
155		**427**

Nickname: Scarlet Knights.
Stadium: Rutgers (1994), 41,500 capacity. Natural turf.
Colors: Scarlet.
Conference: Big East.
SID: John Wooding, 908-445-4200.
AD: Robert E. Mulcahy.

SACRED HEART
Fairfield, CT 06432 ....I-AA

Coach: Jim Fleming, Sewanee 1982
(First year as head coach)

2000 SCHEDULE
Assumption ■ ....*Sept. 2
Bryant ■ ....Sept. 9
Central Conn. St. ■ ....Sept. 16
St. John's (N.Y.) ....*Sept. 22
Monmouth ....Sept. 30
Stony Brook ....Oct. 14
Albany (N.Y.) ■ ....Oct. 21
Iona ■ ....Oct. 28
Robert Morris ....Nov. 4
St. Francis (Pa.) ....Nov. 11
Wagner ■ ....Nov. 18

1999 RESULTS (2-9-0)
14	Assumption	32
9	Siena	7
0	Wagner	33
0	Iona	24
23	St. Francis (Pa.)	24
21	Stony Brook	48
0	Robert Morris	48
12	Central Conn. St.	37
17	Monmouth	37
0	Albany (N.Y.)	41
37	St. Peter's	18
133		**349**

Nickname: Pioneers.
Stadium: Campus Field (1993), 3,500 capacity. Artificial turf.
Colors: Scarlet & White.
Conference: Northeast.
SID: Matthew Bucci, 203-371-7885.
AD: C. Donald Cook.

SAGINAW VALLEY
University Center, MI 48710 II

Coach: Randy Avery, Northern Mich. 1978
Record: 10 Years, 52-47-1

2000 SCHEDULE
Hillsdale ....*Aug. 31
Grand Valley St. ■ ....Sept. 9
Ferris St. ....*Sept. 16
Indianapolis ■ ....Sept. 23
Ashland ....Sept. 30
Mercyhurst ....Oct. 7
Northwood ■ ....Oct. 14
Wayne St. (Mich.) ....Oct. 21
Findlay ■ ....Oct. 28
Michigan Tech ■ ....Nov. 4
Northern Mich. ....*Nov. 11

1999 RESULTS (4-6-0)
7	Carson-Newman	41
14	Ferris St.	56
45	Wayne St. (Mich.)	33
28	Northern Mich.	42
33	Michigan Tech	35
36	Westminster (Pa.)	30
7	Grand Valley St.	31
24	Northwood	28
40	Mercyhurst	33
38	Hillsdale	33
272		**362**

Nickname: Cardinals.
Stadium: Harvey R. Wickes (1975), 4,028 capacity. Natural turf.

ST. ANSELM
Manchester, NH 03102.................................II

Coach: Geoff Harlan, Middlebury 1986
Record: 1 Year, 4-5-0

2000 SCHEDULE
Mass.-Lowell	*Sept. 8
Hartwick	Sept. 16
C. W. Post ■	Sept. 23
Assumption	Sept. 30
Pace ■	Oct. 7
Bryant	Oct. 14
Merrimack ■	Oct. 21
Siena ■	Oct. 28
Stonehill	Nov. 4
Southern Conn. St. ■	Nov. 11

1999 RESULTS (4-5-0)
46	Mass.-Lowell	18
10	Hartwick	21
7	C. W. Post	50
37	Assumption	29
15	Pace	34
7	Bryant	27
7	Merrimack	5
33	Stonehill	27
42	Southern Conn. St.	66
204		**277**

Nickname: Hawks.
Stadium: Grappone (1999), 2,500 capacity. Natural turf.
Colors: Blue & White.
Conference: Eastern Football.
SID: Ken Belbin, 603-641-7810.
AD: Edward Cannon.

ST. CLOUD ST.
St. Cloud, MN 56301.................................II

Coach: Randy Hedberg, Minot St. 1977
Record: 9 Years, 48-31-2

2000 SCHEDULE
Minn.-Duluth	*Sept. 9
North Dakota St. ■	Sept. 16
Augustana (S.D.)	Sept. 23
Neb.-Omaha	Sept. 30
South Dakota ■	Oct. 7
Minn. St.-Mankato	Oct. 14
Morningside ■	Oct. 21
Northern Colo.	Oct. 28
North Dakota	Nov. 4
South Dakota St. ■	Nov. 11

1999 RESULTS (3-8-0)
22	Wis.-River Falls	17
49	Minn.-Duluth	0
6	North Dakota St.	35
13	Augustana (S.D.)	10
20	Neb.-Omaha	30
22	South Dakota	43
20	Minn. St.-Mankato	28
24	Morningside	30
3	Northern Colo.	39
7	North Dakota	45
19	South Dakota St.	28
205		**305**

Nickname: Huskies.
Stadium: Selke Field (1937), 4,000 capacity. Natural turf.
Colors: Red & Black.
Conference: North Central Intercollegiate Athletic.
SID: Anne Abicht, 320-255-2141.
AD: Morris Kurtz.

ST. FRANCIS (PA.)
Loretto, PA 15940.................................I-AA

Coach: David Jaumotte, Purdue 1984
Record: 1 Year, 2-9-0

2000 SCHEDULE
La Salle ■	Sept. 2
St. John's (N.Y.) ■	Sept. 9
Butler	Sept. 16
Stony Brook ■	Sept. 23
Robert Morris ■	Sept. 30
Albany (N.Y.)	Oct. 7
Monmouth	Oct. 14
Wagner ■	Oct. 21
Central Conn. St.	Nov. 4
Sacred Heart ■	Nov. 11
St. Peter's	*Nov. 18

1999 RESULTS (2-9-0)
7	La Salle	44
0	St. John's (N.Y.)	35
7	Butler	21
13	Wagner	45
24	Sacred Heart	23
13	Central Conn. St.	35
9	Monmouth	20
17	Albany (N.Y.)	55
21	St. Peter's	8
0	Robert Morris	49
6	Stony Brook	24
117		**359**

Nickname: Red Flash.
Stadium: Pine Bowl (1979), 1,500 capacity. Natural turf.
Colors: Red & White.
Conference: Northeast.
SID: Pat Farabaugh, 814-472-3128.
AD: Jeffrey M. Eisen.

ST. JOHN FISHER
Rochester, NY 14618.................................III

Coach: Paul Vosburgh, William Penn 1975
Record: 12 Years, 32-80-1

2000 SCHEDULE
Alfred	*Sept. 2
Rochester ■	*Sept. 9
Norwich ■	Sept. 16
Ithaca	Sept. 23
Hartwick ■	*Sept. 30
St. Lawrence	Oct. 7
Buffalo St. ■	*Oct. 14
Brockport St.	Oct. 21
Rensselaer	Oct. 28
Hobart ■	Nov. 4

1999 RESULTS (1-8-0)
0	Ithaca	44
3	Norwich	23
2	Hartwick	38
14	Alfred	20
52	St. Lawrence	31
3	Buffalo St.	32
0	Brockport St.	7
7	Rensselaer	38
0	Hobart	16
81		**249**

Nickname: Cardinals.
Stadium: Growney (NA), 2,100 capacity. Artificial turf.
Colors: Cardinal Red & Gold.
Conference: Division III Independent.
SID: Norm Kieffer, 716-385-8309.
AD: Robert A. Ward.

ST. JOHN'S (N.Y.)
Jamaica, NY 11439.................................I-AA

Coach: Bob Ricca, C. W. Post 1969
Record: 22 Years, 140-85-1

2000 SCHEDULE
St. Francis (Pa.)	Sept. 9
Stony Brook	Sept. 16
Sacred Heart ■	*Sept. 22
Central Conn. St.	Sept. 30
Robert Morris	Oct. 7
Albany (N.Y.) ■	*Oct. 13
St. Peter's	*Oct. 21
La Salle ■	Oct. 28
Wagner	Nov. 4
Monmouth ■	*Nov. 10
Iona	Nov. 18

1999 RESULTS (7-4-0)
35	St. Francis (Pa.)	0
16	Marist	0
7	Georgetown	30
3	Duquesne	10
31	St. Peter's	0
16	Fairfield	24
21	La Salle	10
45	Canisius	0
20	Siena	7
47	Iona	33
6	Stony Brook	28
247		**142**

Nickname: Red Storm.
Stadium: Memorial Field (1961), 3,000 capacity. Artificial turf.
Colors: Red & White.
Conference: Division I-AA Independent.
SID: Dominic Scianna, 718-990-6367.
AD: Edward J. Manetta Jr.

ST. JOHN'S (MINN.)
Collegeville, MN 56321.................................III

Coach: John Gagliardi, Colorado Col. 1949
Record: 51 Years, 364-107-11

2000 SCHEDULE
Wis.-Eau Claire	*Sept. 2
St. Olaf	Sept. 16
Augsburg ■	Sept. 23
St. Thomas (Minn.)	Sept. 30
Macalester ■	Oct. 7
Gust. Adolphus	Oct. 14
Hamline ■	Oct. 21
Bethel (Minn.)	Oct. 28
Carleton [Minneapolis, MN]	Nov. 4
Concordia-M'head ■	Nov. 11

1999 RESULTS (9-1-0)
40	Wis.-Eau Claire	28
42	Macalester	7
34	St. Thomas (Minn.)	18
55	Augsburg	0
20	Bethel (Minn.)	24
7	Concordia-M'head	3
20	Hamline	3
21	St. Olaf	14
41	Carleton	6
31	Gust. Adolphus	16
311		**119**

DIVISION III CHAMPIONSHIP
23	Wis.-Stevens Point	10
10	Central (Iowa)	9
9	Pacific Lutheran	19

Nickname: Johnnies.
Stadium: Clemens (1908), 5,500 capacity. Natural turf.
Colors: Cardinal & Blue.
Conference: Minnesota Intercollegiate Athletic.
SID: Michael Hemmesch, 320-363-2595.
AD: Jim E. Smith.

ST. JOSEPH'S (IND.)
Rensselaer, IN 47978.................................II

Coach: Tom Riva, Albion 1990
Record: 3 Years, 16-17-0

2000 SCHEDULE
Indianapolis	Sept. 2
St. Francis (Ill.) ■	Sept. 9
Shepherd	Sept. 16
Glenville St. ■	Sept. 23
Tri-State ■	Sept. 30
Quincy ■	Oct. 7
New Haven	Oct. 14
Valparaiso ■	Oct. 21
Dayton	Oct. 28
Georgetown (Ky.)	Nov. 11

Colors: Red, White & Blue.
Conference: Great Lakes Intercollegiate Athletic.
SID: Tom Waske, 517-790-4053.
AD: Richard P. Thompson.

1999 RESULTS (4-7-0)

10	Indianapolis	19
21	Georgetown (Ky.)	33
12	Malone	6
3	Glenville St.	7
41	Quincy	7
25	Ky. Wesleyan	17
24	St. Francis (Ill.)	27
6	Dayton	35
21	New Haven	42
10	Valparaiso	33
23	Wayne St. (Mich.)	15
196		**241**

Nickname: Pumas.
Stadium: Alumni Field (1947), 4,000 capacity. Natural turf.
Colors: Cardinal & Purple.
Conference: Division II Independent.
SID: Joe Danahey, 219-866-6141.
AD: Bill Massoels.

ST. LAWRENCE
Canton, NY 13617 III

Coach: Greg Burton, Cortland St. 1986
Record: 2 Years, 1-18-0

2000 SCHEDULE

Union (N.Y.)	Sept. 9
Alfred ■	Sept. 16
Rochester ■	Sept. 23
Hobart	Sept. 30
St. John Fisher ■	Oct. 7
Ithaca	Oct. 14
Norwich ■	Oct. 21
Gettysburg	Oct. 28
Rensselaer	Nov. 4
Hartwick	Nov. 11

1999 RESULTS (0-10-0)

17	Union (N.Y.)	45
23	Alfred	39
17	Rochester	28
10	Hobart	28
31	St. John Fisher	52
14	Ithaca	43
13	Norwich	16
28	Gettysburg	59
7	Rensselaer	32
28	Hartwick	38
188		**380**

Nickname: Saints.
Stadium: Weeks Field (1999), 3,000 capacity. Natural turf.
Colors: Scarlet & Brown.
Conference: Upstate Collegiate Athletic Assn.
SID: Wally Johnson, 315-379-5588.
AD: Margaret F. Strait.

ST. MARY'S (CAL.)
Moraga, CA 94556 ....I-AA

Coach: Mike Landis, Randolph-Macon 1986
Record: 7 Years, 35-36-1

2000 SCHEDULE

Cal St. Sacramento ■	Sept. 2
Western Wash. ■	Sept. 9
Humboldt St.	*Sept. 16
Central Wash. ■	Sept. 23
UC Davis	*Sept. 30
Cal Poly	*Oct. 7
Menlo ■	Oct. 14
Colgate	Oct. 21
Southern Utah	Oct. 28
Towson ■	Nov. 4
Drake ■	Nov. 11

1999 RESULTS (2-9-0)

7	Cal St. Sacramento	41
40	Humboldt St.	3
3	San Jose St.	38
7	Western Wash.	20
7	Central Wash.	27
7	Drake	38
14	UC Davis	28
13	Colgate	43
28	Holy Cross	26
22	Southern Utah	57
21	Cal Poly	24
169		**345**

Nickname: Gaels.
Stadium: St. Mary's (1972), 8,000 capacity. Natural turf.
Colors: Red & Blue.
Conference: Division I-AA Independent.
SID: To be named, 510-631-4402.
AD: Richard J. Mazzuto.

ST. NORBERT
De Pere, WI 54115 III

Coach: Jim Purtill, Miami (Ohio) 1978
Record: 1 Year, 9-2-0

2000 SCHEDULE

Hamline	Sept. 9
Carroll (Wis.) ■	Sept. 16
Lawrence	*Sept. 23
Ripon ■	Sept. 30
Knox	Oct. 7
Monmouth (Ill.)	Oct. 14
Grinnell ■	Oct. 21
Lake Forest	Oct. 28
Beloit ■	Nov. 4
Illinois Col. ■	Nov. 11

1999 RESULTS (9-1-0)

14	Wis.-Oshkosh	24
28	Carroll (Wis.)	3
43	Lawrence	14
35	Ripon	17
38	Knox	17
41	Monmouth (Ill.)	28
43	Grinnell	40
41	Lake Forest	21
35	Beloit	10
40	Illinois Col.	31
358		**205**

DIVISION III CHAMPIONSHIP

32	Augustana (Ill.)	39

Nickname: Green Knights.
Stadium: Minahan (1937), 3,100 capacity. Natural turf.
Colors: Green & Gold.
Conference: Midwest Collegiate Athletic.
SID: Dan Lukes, 414-337-4077.
AD: Donald Maslinski.

ST. OLAF
Northfield, MN 55057 III

Coach: Paul Miller, Minn.-Morris 1973
Record: 3 Years, 7-23-0

2000 SCHEDULE

Martin Luther	Sept. 9
St. John's (Minn.) ■	Sept. 16
Hamline	Sept. 23
Augsburg ■	Sept. 30
Bethel (Minn.)	Oct. 7
St. Thomas (Minn.) ■	Oct. 14
Concordia-M'head	Oct. 21
Macalester ■	Oct. 28
Gust. Adolphus [Minneapolis, MN]	*Nov. 4
Carleton	Nov. 11

1999 RESULTS (3-7-0)

14	Carthage	21
3	St. Thomas (Minn.)	33
27	Augsburg	30
13	Bethel (Minn.)	39
10	Concordia-M'head	17
25	Hamline	20
27	Carleton	19
14	St. John's (Minn.)	21
17	Gust. Adolphus	36
47	Macalester	17
197		**253**

Nickname: Oles.

Stadium: Manitou Field (1930), 5,000 capacity. Natural turf.
Colors: Black & Old Gold.
Conference: Minnesota Intercollegiate Athletic.
SID: Chris Blissett, 507-646-3834.
AD: Cynthia Book.

ST. PETER'S
Jersey City, NJ 07306 ....I-AA

Coach: Rob Stern
Record: 1 Year, 1-10-0

2000 SCHEDULE

Marist ■	*Sept. 7
Canisius	Sept. 16
Pace ■	*Sept. 22
Siena ■	*Sept. 30
Iona	Oct. 7
Fairfield	Oct. 14
St. John's (N.Y.) ■	*Oct. 21
Duquesne ■	Oct. 28
La Salle ■	*Nov. 4
Georgetown	Nov. 11
St. Francis (Pa.) ■	*Nov. 18

1999 RESULTS (1-10-0)

0	Marist	20
33	Canisius	22
11	Siena	26
6	Duquesne	51
15	Iona	20
0	St. John's (N.Y.)	31
3	Georgetown	14
8	St. Francis (Pa.)	21
13	La Salle	35
18	Sacred Heart	37
18	Fairfield	45
125		**322**

Nickname: Peacocks.
Stadium: Cochrane (1990), 4,000 capacity. Artificial turf.
Colors: Blue & White.
Conference: Metro Atlantic Athletic.
SID: Tim Camp, 201-915-9101.
AD: William A. Stein.

ST. THOMAS (MINN.)
St. Paul, MN 55105 III

Coach: Don Roney, St. Thomas 1983
Record: 2 Years, 14-6-0

2000 SCHEDULE

Bemidji St.	Sept. 9
Concordia-M'head ■	Sept. 16
Carleton	Sept. 23
St. John's (Minn.) ■	Sept. 30
Augsburg	Oct. 7
St. Olaf	Oct. 14
Macalester ■	Oct. 21
Gust. Adolphus	Oct. 28
Bethel (Minn.) [Minneapolis, MN]	*Nov. 3
Hamline ■	Nov. 11

1999 RESULTS (7-3-0)

14	Bemidji St.	24
33	St. Olaf	3
18	St. John's (Minn.)	34
18	Gust. Adolphus	17
60	Macalester	14
27	Carleton	6
30	Augsburg	20
20	Bethel (Minn.)	22
22	Concordia-M'head	7
13	Hamline	3
255		**150**

Nickname: Tommies.
Stadium: O'Shaughnessy (1948), 5,025 capacity. Natural turf.
Colors: Purple & Grey.
Conference: Minnesota Intercollegiate Athletic.
SID: Gene McGivern, 612-962-5903.
AD: Stephen J. Fritz.

SALISBURY ST.
Salisbury, MD 21801 III

Coach: Sherman Wood, Salisbury St. 1984
Record: 7 Years, 25-44-1

2000 SCHEDULE
Newport News..Sept. 2
Wm. Paterson ■...Sept. 9
Methodist...Sept. 16
Greensboro ■...Sept. 23
Shenandoah ....Sept. 30
Chowan ■..Oct. 7
Col. of New Jersey ■....................................Oct. 14
Wesley..Oct. 28
Ferrum..Nov. 4
Frostburg St. [Washington, DC] ....Nov. 11

1999 RESULTS (2-7-0)
13	Alfred..................................	20
21	Methodist.............................	6
13	Greensboro...........................	42
2	Catholic...............................	34
31	Chowan................................	27
14	Col. of New Jersey................	35
7	Wesley..................................	14
3	Ferrum..................................	37
22	Frostburg St.	23
126		**238**

Nickname: Sea Gulls.
Stadium: Sea Gull (1980), 2,500 capacity. Natural turf.
Colors: Maroon & Gold.
Conference: Atlantic Central Football.
SID: G. Paul Ohanian, 410-543-6016.
AD: Michael Vienna.

SALVE REGINA
Newport, RI 02840......................................III

Coach: Art Bell, Rhode Island
(First year as head coach)

2000 SCHEDULE
Coast Guard ....Sept. 9
MIT..Sept. 16
Western New Eng. ■...................................Sept. 23
Worcester St. ....Sept. 30
Mass.-Boston ■...Oct. 7
Curry..Oct. 14
Maine Maritime ■.......................................Oct. 21
Mass.-Dartmouth ....Oct. 28
Nichols ■...Nov. 4

1999 RESULTS (8-2-0)
7	Plymouth St.	16
28	Bri'water (Mass.)..................	39
53	MIT.......................................	14
26	Western New Eng.	9
35	Worcester St.	7
41	Mass.-Boston.......................	0
14	Curry.....................................	3
22	Maine Maritime....................	20
40	Mass.-Dartmouth	14
34	Nichols.................................	21
300		**143**

ECAC PLAYOFF
7	Plymouth St.	13

Nickname: Seahawks.
Stadium: Toppa Field (1996), 1,500 capacity. Natural turf.
Colors: Blue, Green & White.
Conference: New England Football.
SID: Ed Habershaw, 401-847-6650.
AD: Del Malloy.

SAM HOUSTON ST.
Huntsville, TX 77340 ....I-AA

Coach: Ron Randleman, William Penn 1964
Record: 31 Years, 184-141-6

2000 SCHEDULE
La.-Lafayette ....*Sept. 2
Southeastern Okla. ■.................................*Sept. 7
Western Ill. ....Sept. 16
Texas A&M-Kingsville ■.............................*Sept. 23
Jacksonville St. ....Oct. 7
Stephen F. Austin ....Oct. 14
Troy St. ■..*Oct. 21
McNeese St. ■...Oct. 28
Nicholls St. ....*Nov. 4
Northwestern St. ....Nov. 11
Southwest Tex. St. ■...................................Nov. 18

1999 RESULTS (6-5-0)
38	Delta St.	31
17	Louisiana Tech.....................	55
34	Texas A&M-Kingsville...........	24
20	Arkansas St.	45
51	Jacksonville St.	17
31	Stephen F. Austin.................	45
16	Troy St.	41
20	McNeese St.	3
69	Nicholls St.	17
21	Northwestern St.	0
14	Southwest Tex. St.	20
311		**298**

Nickname: Bearkats.
Stadium: Elliott T. Bowers (1986), 14,000 capacity. Artificial turf.
Colors: Orange & White.
Conference: Southland Football.
SID: Paul Ridings Jr., 409-294-1764.
AD: Bobby Williams.

SAMFORD
Birmingham, AL 35229 ....I-AA

Coach: Pete Hurt, Mississippi Col. 1978
Record: 6 Years, 37-28-1

2000 SCHEDULE
Chattanooga ....*Aug. 31
Murray St. ■...*Sept. 7
Tenn.-Martin ■...*Sept. 14
Jacksonville St. ....*Sept. 21
Nicholls St. ■..*Sept. 30
North Texas ....*Oct. 5
Elon...Oct. 14
Gardner-Webb ■...Oct. 21
Liberty...Oct. 28
Charleston So. ■...Nov. 4
Tennessee Tech..*Nov. 9

1999 RESULTS (7-4-0)
27	Chattanooga........................	29
51	Austin Peay..........................	0
32	Tenn.-Martin	7
16	Eastern Ky.	17
34	Jacksonville St.	18
31	Elon	34
27	Murray St.	34
34	Liberty..................................	28
35	Western Caro.	32
28	Nicholls St.	24
19	Tennessee Tech....................	15
334		**238**

Nickname: Bulldogs.
Stadium: Seibert (1960), 6,700 capacity. Natural turf.
Colors: Red & Blue.
Conference: Division I-AA Independent.
SID: Matt Sullivan, 205-870-2799.
AD: Bob Roller.

SAN DIEGO
San Diego, CA 92110 ....I-AA

Coach: Kevin McGarry, San Diego 1979
Record: 4 Years, 19-22-0

2000 SCHEDULE
Azusa Pacific ....*Sept. 2
Whittier ....*Sept. 9
Brown ....Sept. 16
Menlo ■...*Sept. 23
Drake...Sept. 30
Central Conn. St. ■.....................................Oct. 7
Davidson ■..*Oct. 14
Butler ....Oct. 21
Valparaiso ■..*Oct. 28
Dayton ■...*Nov. 11

1999 RESULTS (5-5-0)
19	Azusa Pacific.......................	26
40	Whittier................................	13
30	Cal Lutheran	14
6	Yale......................................	17
0	Dayton	41
42	Butler	14
7	Valparaiso	14
20	Drake	41
20	Stony Brook.........................	9
31	Wagner	12
215		**201**

Nickname: Toreros.
Stadium: USD Torero (1955), 4,000 capacity. Natural turf.
Colors: Columbia Blue, Navy & White.
Conference: Pioneer Football.
SID: Ted Gosen, 619-260-4745.
AD: Thomas Iannacone.

SAN DIEGO ST.
San Diego, CA 92182 ....I-A

Coach: Ted Tollner, Cal Poly 1962
Record: 10 Years, 63-52-1

2000 SCHEDULE
Arizona St. ■...*Aug. 31
Illinois ■..*Sept. 9
Arizona ....*Sept. 16
Oregon St. ....Sept. 23
Wyoming...Oct. 7
Utah ■...*Oct. 14
Brigham Young ....Oct. 21
Colorado St. ....Oct. 28
New Mexico ....Nov. 4
Air Force..Nov. 18
UNLV ■...Nov. 25

1999 RESULTS (5-6-0)
41	South Fla.	12
10	Illinois..................................	38
21	Southern California.............	24
41	Kansas.................................	13
22	Air Force	23
21	New Mexico	24
17	Colorado St.	10
16	Utah.....................................	38
7	Brigham Young....................	30
37	UNLV....................................	7
39	Wyoming..............................	7
272		**226**

Nickname: Aztecs.
Stadium: Qualcomm (1967), 71,300 capacity. Natural turf.
Colors: Scarlet & Black.
Conference: Mountain West.
SID: John Rosenthal, 619-594-5547.
AD: Richard M. Bay.

SAN JOSE ST.
San Jose, CA 95192 ....I-A

Coach: Dave Baldwin, Cal St. Northridge 1978
Record: 5 Years, 20-34-0

2000 SCHEDULE
Nebraska...Sept. 2
Stanford...*Sept. 9
Southern Utah ■...*Sept. 16
Southern California....................................Sept. 23
Rice ■..Sept. 30
Southern Methodist ....*Oct. 7
UTEP..*Oct. 14
Nevada..Oct. 21
Hawaii...*Oct. 28
TCU ■..Nov. 4
Tulsa ....Nov. 18
Fresno St. ■..Nov. 25

1999 RESULTS (3-7-0)
21	LSU......................................	29
35	Colorado..............................	63

38	St. Mary's (Cal.)	3
34	Tulsa	10
44	Stanford	39
0	TCU	42
7	Rice	49
26	UTEP	42
41	Hawaii	62
12	Fresno St.	63
258		**402**

Nickname: Spartans.
Stadium: Spartan (1933), 30,456 capacity. Natural turf.
Colors: Gold, White & Blue.
Conference: Western Athletic.
SID: Lawrence Fan, 408-924-1217.
AD: Charles Bell.

SAVANNAH ST.
Savannah, GA 31404 II

Coach: Steven Wilks,
Record: 1 Year, 5-6-0

2000 SCHEDULE
Bethune-Cookman [Jacksonville, FL]	Sept. 2
South Carolina St.	Sept. 9
Virginia St.	*Sept. 23
Albany St. (Ga.)	Oct. 7
Morgan St. ■	Oct. 14
Morris Brown [Augusta, GA]	Oct. 21
Fort Valley St. ■	Oct. 28
Tuskegee ■	Nov. 11
Gardner-Webb	Nov. 18

1999 RESULTS (5-6-0)
50	Elizabeth City St.	12
14	Bethune-Cookman	17
34	Clark Atlanta	7
0	Chattanooga	49
31	Virginia St.	21
14	Albany St. (Ga.)	17
43	Morris Brown	35
23	Kentucky St.	24
25	Fort Valley St.	35
49	Miles	12
36	Tuskegee	51
319		**280**

Nickname: Tigers.
Stadium: Ted Wright (1967), 7,500 capacity. Natural turf.
Colors: Blue & Orange.
Conference: Southern Intercollegiate Athletic.
SID: Lee Grant Pearson, 912-356-2446.
AD: Charles J. Elmore.

SEWANEE
Sewanee, TN 37383 III

Coach: John Windham, Vanderbilt 1986
Record: 4 Years, 17-19-0

2000 SCHEDULE
Hampden-Sydney ■	Sept. 2
Rose-Hulman ■	Sept. 9
Davidson ■	Sept. 16
Stillman ■	Sept. 23
Centre	Sept. 30
DePauw	Oct. 7
Rhodes ■	Oct. 14
Wash. & Lee	Oct. 21
Millsaps ■	Oct. 28
Trinity (Tex.)	Nov. 4

1999 RESULTS (6-4-0)
14	Hampden-Sydney	0
44	Rose-Hulman	15
0	Davidson	21
31	Centre	17
33	DePauw	14
21	Rhodes	23
28	Wash. & Lee	31
35	Millsaps	12
9	Trinity (Tex.)	41
30	Stillman	18
245		**192**

Nickname: Tigers.

Stadium: McGee Field (1935), 1,500 capacity. Natural turf.
Colors: Purple & White.
Conference: Southern Collegiate Athletic.
SID: Larry Dagenhart, 615-598-1136.
AD: Mark Webb.

SHEPHERD
Shepherdstown, WV 25443 II

Coach: Monte Cater, Millikin 1971
Record: 19 Years, 115-74-2

2000 SCHEDULE
Shippensburg	Sept. 2
St. Joseph's (Ind.) ■	Sept. 16
East Stroudsburg	Sept. 23
Concord ■	Sept. 30
West Va. Tech	Oct. 7
Fairmont St. ■	Oct. 14
West Virginia St.	Oct. 21
Glenville St. ■	Oct. 28
West Liberty St.	Nov. 4
West Va. Wesleyan ■	Nov. 11

1999 RESULTS (9-1-0)
21	Shippensburg	24
33	East Stroudsburg	27
7	Clarion	0
43	Concord	20
60	West Va. Tech	6
42	Fairmont St.	7
63	West Virginia St.	14
22	Glenville St.	17
56	West Liberty St.	7
55	West Va. Wesleyan	3
402		**125**

DIVISION II CHAMPIONSHIP
| 14 | Millersville | 21 |

Nickname: Rams.
Stadium: Ram (1959), 3,000 capacity. Natural turf.
Colors: Blue & Gold.
Conference: West Virginia Intercollegiate Athletic.
SID: Chip Ransom, 304-876-5228.
AD: Monte Cater.

SHIPPENSBURG
Shippensburg, PA 17257 II

Coach: Rocky Rees, West Chester 1971
Record: 10 Years, 56-54-1

1999 SCHEDULE
Shepherd ■	Sept. 2
Bloomsburg ■	Sept. 9
Millersville	*Sept. 16
Clarion	Sept. 23
Lock Haven ■	Sept. 30
Slippery Rock ■	Oct. 7
Indiana (Pa.)	Oct. 14
East Stroudsburg	Oct. 21
Calif. (Pa.) ■	Oct. 28
Edinboro	Nov. 4
Kutztown ■	Nov. 11

1999 RESULTS (8-3-0)
24	Shepherd	21
28	Bloomsburg	36
42	Kutztown	12
48	West Chester	30
52	Edinboro	10
37	East Stroudsburg	0
32	Clarion	26
21	Slippery Rock	27
68	Lock Haven	7
30	Calif. (Pa.)	0
16	Indiana (Pa.)	43
398		**212**

Nickname: Red Raiders.
Stadium: Grove (1972), 7,700 capacity. Natural turf.
Colors: Red & Blue.
Conference: Pennsylvania State Athletic.
SID: John R. Alosi, 717-532-9121.
AD: James G. Pribula.

SIENA
Loudonville, NY 12211 .... I-AA

Coach: Jay Bateman, Randolph-Macon 1995
(First year as head coach)

2000 SCHEDULE
Hartwick ■	*Sept. 9
Kutztown	Sept. 16
La Salle	Sept. 23
St. Peter's	*Sept. 30
Fairfield ■	Oct. 7
Canisius	Oct. 21
St. Anselm	Oct. 28
Duquesne ■	Nov. 4
Iona	Nov. 11
Marist ■	Nov. 18

1999 RESULTS (3-7-0)
7	Sacred Heart	9
12	Georgetown	47
26	St. Peter's	11
7	La Salle	17
0	Fairfield	27
14	Iona	0
38	Canisius	6
17	Duquesne	49
7	St. John's (N.Y.)	20
7	Marist	29
135		**215**

Nickname: Saints.
Stadium: Heritage Park (NA), 5,500 capacity. Natural turf.
Colors: Green & Gold.
Conference: Metro Atlantic Athletic.
SID: Jason Rich, 518-783-2411.
AD: John M. D'Argenio.

SIMPSON
Indianola, IA 50125 III

Coach: Jim Williams, Northern Iowa 1956
Record: 13 Years, 96-38-1

2000 SCHEDULE
Cornell College	Sept. 2
Upper Iowa ■	Sept. 9
Dubuque	Sept. 16
Luther ■	Sept. 23
Coe	Sept. 30
Central (Iowa)	Oct. 7
Buena Vista ■	Oct. 14
Loras	Oct. 21
Wartburg	Oct. 28
William Penn ■	Nov. 11

1999 RESULTS (6-4-0)
31	Dubuque	6
10	Coe	9
13	Central (Iowa)	29
7	Upper Iowa	21
30	William Penn	21
10	Wartburg	42
3	Buena Vista	20
50	Cornell College	8
29	Loras	28
41	Luther	0
224		**184**

Nickname: Storm.
Stadium: Bill Buxton (1990), 5,000 capacity. Natural turf.
Colors: Red & Gold.
Conference: Iowa Intercollegiate Athletic.
SID: Matthew F. Turk, 515-961-1577.
AD: John Sirianni.

SLIPPERY ROCK
Slippery Rock, PA 16057 II

Coach: George Mihalik, Slippery Rock 1974
Record: 12 Years, 86-43-4

2000 SCHEDULE
| Youngstown St. | *Aug. 31 |
| West Va. Wesleyan | Sept. 9 |

Fairmont St. ■..Sept. 16
Edinboro ■..Sept. 23
Indiana (Pa.) ■...*Sept. 30
Shippensburg..Oct. 7
Calif. (Pa.) ■..Oct. 14
Clarion ■..Oct. 21
Lock Haven..Oct. 28
Millersville...Nov. 4
Bloomsburg ■...Nov. 11

1999 RESULTS (10-1-0)

14	Youngstown St.	44
38	West Va. Wesleyan	3
34	Fairmont St.	10
47	East Stroudsburg	10
45	Clarion	7
52	Indiana (Pa.)	14
31	Calif. (Pa.)	21
27	Shippensburg	21
34	Edinboro	17
68	Kutztown	38
38	Lock Haven	17
428		**202**

DIVISION II CHAMPIONSHIP
20 Indiana (Pa.)..27

Nickname: Rockets, The Rock.
Stadium: N. Kerr Thompson (1974), 10,000 capacity.
 Natural turf.
Colors: Green & White.
Conference: Pennsylvania State Athletic.
SID: To be named, 412-738-2777.
AD: Paul A. Lueken.

SOUTH CAROLINA
Columbia, SC 29208 ....I-A

Coach: Lou Holtz, Kent St. 1959
Record: 28 Years, 216-106-7

2000 SCHEDULE
New Mexico St. ■.....................................*Sept. 2
Georgia ■...*Sept. 9
Eastern Mich. ■.......................................*Sept. 16
Mississippi St..Sept. 23
Alabama..Sept. 30
Kentucky...*Oct. 7
Arkansas ■...Oct. 14
Vanderbilt...Oct. 21
Tennessee ■...Oct. 28
Florida..Nov. 11
Clemson..Nov. 18

1999 RESULTS (0-11-0)

0	North Carolina St.	10
9	Georgia	24
3	East Caro.	21
0	Mississippi St.	17
10	Mississippi	36
10	Kentucky	30
14	Arkansas	48
10	Vanderbilt	11
7	Tennessee	30
3	Florida	20
21	Clemson	31
87		**278**

Nickname: Fighting Gamecocks.
Stadium: Williams-Brice (1934), 80,250 capacity.
 Natural turf.
Colors: Garnet & Black.
Conference: Southeastern.
SID: Kerry Tharp, 803-777-5204.
AD: Michael B. Mc Gee.

SOUTH CAROLINA ST.
Orangeburg, SC 29117 ....I-AA

Coach: Willie E. Jeffries, South Carolina St. 1960
Record: 27 Years, 170-119-6

2000 SCHEDULE
Winston-Salem ■......................................*Sept. 2
Savannah St. ■..Sept. 9
Florida A&M [Jacksonville, FL]...................Sept. 16
Citadel...Sept. 30
Norfolk St...Oct. 7
Bethune-Cookman...................................*Oct. 14
Hampton ■..Oct. 21
Delaware St..Oct. 28
Howard ■...Nov. 4
Morgan St. ■..Nov. 11
N.C. A&T [Charlotte, NC]..........................Nov. 18

1999 RESULTS (4-6-0)

20	Charleston So.	14
26	Benedict	23
17	Florida A&M	76
14	Citadel	20
27	Norfolk St.	23
27	Bethune-Cookman	30
27	Hampton	39
42	Howard	49
34	Delaware St.	14
7	N.C. A&T	27
241		**315**

Nickname: Bulldogs.
Stadium: Dawson Bulldog (1955), 22,000 capacity.
 Natural turf.
Colors: Garnet & Blue.
Conference: Mid-Eastern Athletic.
SID: Bill Hamilton, 803-536-7060.
AD: Timothy J. Autry Jr.

SOUTH DAKOTA
Vermillion, SD 57069 II

Coach: John Austin, South Dakota 1980
Record: 1 Year, 4-7-0

2000 SCHEDULE
Mo. Western St..*Aug. 31
Truman ■...*Sept. 9
North Dakota...Sept. 16
North Dakota St......................................*Sept. 23
Augustana (S.D.) ■..................................*Sept. 30
St. Cloud St...Oct. 7
Neb.-Omaha ■..*Oct. 14
Northern Colo. ■.....................................*Oct. 21
Morningside..Oct. 28
South Dakota St......................................Nov. 4
Minn. St.-Mankato ■................................Nov. 11

1999 RESULTS (4-7-0)

13	Montana	45
38	Truman	21
10	North Dakota	17
14	North Dakota St.	45
21	Augustana (S.D.)	35
43	St. Cloud St.	22
23	Neb.-Omaha	54
27	Northern Colo.	35
21	Morningside	0
30	South Dakota St.	43
35	Minn. St.-Mankato	29
275		**346**

Nickname: Coyotes.
Stadium: DakotaDome (1979), 10,000 capacity.
 Artificial turf.
Colors: Vermillion & White.
Conference: North Central Intercollegiate Athletic.
SID: Kyle Johnson, 605-677-5927.
AD: Kelly J. Higgins.

SOUTH DAKOTA ST.
Brookings, SD 57007 II

Coach: John Stiegelmeier, South Dakota St. 1979
Record: 3 Years, 18-14-0

2000 SCHEDULE
Grand Valley St. ■....................................Sept. 2
Wayne St. (Neb.) ■..................................Sept. 9
Augustana (S.D.).....................................Sept. 16
Northern Colo..Sept. 23
Morningside..Sept. 30
Minn. St.-Mankato ■................................Oct. 7
North Dakota St.......................................Oct. 14
North Dakota...Oct. 21
Neb.-Omaha ■..Oct. 28
South Dakota ■.......................................Nov. 4
St. Cloud St...Nov. 11

1999 RESULTS (8-3-0)

35	Grand Valley St.	20
59	Wayne St. (Neb.)	31
38	Augustana (S.D.)	31
18	Northern Colo.	45
34	Morningside	30
34	Minn. St.-Mankato	28
7	North Dakota St.	28
21	North Dakota	7
34	Neb.-Omaha	40
43	South Dakota	30
28	St. Cloud St.	19
351		**309**

Nickname: Jackrabbits.
Stadium: Coughlin-Alumni (1962), 16,000 capacity.
 Natural turf.
Colors: Yellow & Blue.
Conference: North Central Intercollegiate Athletic.
SID: Ron Lenz, 605-688-4623.
AD: Fred M. Oien.

SOUTH FLA.
Tampa, FL 33620 ....I-AA

Coach: Jim Leavitt, Missouri 1978
Record: 3 Years, 20-13-0

1999 SCHEDULE
Jacksonville St. ■......................................Sept. 2
Kentucky...Sept. 9
James Madison ■....................................Sept. 16
Baylor..*Sept. 23
Troy St. ■...Sept. 30
Southern Miss..*Oct. 7
Liberty...*Oct. 21
Connecticut...Oct. 28
Western Ky. ■..*Nov. 4
Middle Tenn. St.......................................Nov. 11
Austin Peay ■..Nov. 18

1999 RESULTS (7-4-0)

12	San Diego St.	41
17	Southwest Tex. St.	10
21	Western Ky.	6
24	Troy St.	41
21	Southern Ill.	14
28	Liberty	0
14	Illinois St.	13
42	New Hampshire	41
3	James Madison	13
41	New Haven	27
23	Hofstra	42
246		**248**

Nickname: Bulls.
Stadium: Raymond James (1998), 65,000 capacity.
 Natural turf.
Colors: Green & Gold.
Conference: Division I-AA Independent.
SID: John Gerdes, 813-974-4086.
AD: Paul S. Griffin.

SOUTHEAST MO. ST.
Cape Girardeau, MO 63701 ....I-AA

Coach: Tim Billings, Southeastern Okla. 1980
(First year as head coach)

2000 SCHEDULE
Marshall...*Aug. 31
Southern Ill..Sept. 9
Illinois St. ■..*Sept. 16
Western Ky. ■..*Sept. 23
Eastern Ky. ■...*Sept. 30
Tennessee Tech.......................................Oct. 14
Murray St...Oct. 21
Tenn.-Martin ■...*Oct. 28
Eastern Ill...Nov. 4
Southwest Mo. St....................................Nov. 11
Tennessee St...Nov. 18

1999 RESULTS (3-8-0)

25	Southern Ill.	43
7	Illinois St.	55
18	Murray St.	45
10	Western Ky.	21

28	Eastern Ky.	37
7	Tennessee Tech	21
13	Indiana St.	34
28	Southwest Mo. St.	23
36	Tenn.-Martin	7
45	Eastern Ill.	38
28	Tennessee St.	35
245		**359**

Nickname: Indians.
Stadium: Houck (1930), 10,000 capacity. Artificial turf.
Colors: Red & Black.
Conference: Ohio Valley.
SID: Ron Hines, 573-651-2294.
AD: Don Kaverman.

SOUTHEASTERN OKLA.
Durant, OK 74701 II

Coach: Morris Sloan, Southeastern Okla. 1973
Record: 11 Years, 64-44-4
2000 SCHEDULE
Southern Ark. ■	*Sept. 2
Sam Houston St.	*Sept. 7
Texas A&M-Kingsville ■	*Sept. 16
Tarleton St.	*Sept. 23
Abilene Christian	*Oct. 7
Northeastern St. ■	Oct. 14
Midwestern St.	Oct. 21
Southwestern Okla. ■	Oct. 28
Central Okla.	Nov. 4
East Central ■	Nov. 11

1999 RESULTS (7-4-0)
21	Mo. Western St.	40
27	Southern Ark.	34
43	Abilene Christian	30
31	West Tex. A&M	24
41	Harding	27
49	Ouachita Baptist	19
21	Southwestern Okla.	16
46	Western N.M.	36
3	Northeastern St.	30
20	Central Okla.	14
13	East Central	14
315		**284**

Nickname: Savages.
Stadium: Paul Laird Field (NA), 4,000 capacity. Natural turf.
Colors: Blue & Gold.
Conference: Lone Star.
SID: Harold Harmon, 580-924-4388.
AD: Donald A. Parham.

SOUTHERN ARK.
Magnolia, AR 71753 II

Coach: John Bland, Arkansas 1989
(First year as head coach)
2000 SCHEDULE
Southeastern Okla.	*Sept. 2
Valdosta St. ■	*Sept. 16
Ouachita Baptist ■	*Sept. 23
West Ala.	Sept. 30
West Ga.	*Oct. 7
Delta St. ■	Oct. 14
Arkansas Tech	Oct. 21
Ark.-Monticello ■	Oct. 28
Central Ark. ■	Nov. 4
Henderson St.	Nov. 11

1999 RESULTS (8-2-0)
34	Southeastern Okla.	27
24	North Ala.	14
20	Ark.-Monticello	23
29	West Ga.	24
29	Central Ark.	20
28	Valdosta St.	14
30	West Ala.	24
28	Delta St.	0
31	Henderson St.	3
17	Arkansas Tech	20
270		**169**

Nickname: Muleriders.
Stadium: Wilkins (1949), 6,000 capacity. Natural turf.
Colors: Royal Blue & Old Gold.
Conference: Gulf South.
SID: Harold Jameson, 870-235-4104.
AD: Jay Adcox.

SOUTHERN CALIFORNIA
Los Angeles, CA 90089 .... I-A

Coach: Paul Hackett, UC Davis 1969
Record: 5 Years, 27-31-1
2000 SCHEDULE
Penn St. [East Rutherford, NJ]	Aug. 27
Colorado ■	Sept. 9
San Jose St. ■	Sept. 23
Oregon St.	Sept. 30
Arizona ■	Oct. 7
Oregon ■	Oct. 14
Stanford	Oct. 21
California ■	Oct. 28
Arizona St.	*Nov. 4
Washington St. ■	Nov. 11
UCLA	Nov. 18
Notre Dame ■	Nov. 25

1999 RESULTS (6-6-0)
62	Hawaii	7
24	San Diego St.	21
30	Oregon	33
37	Oregon St.	29
24	Arizona	31
24	Notre Dame	25
31	Stanford	35
7	California	17
16	Arizona St.	26
31	Washington St.	28
17	UCLA	7
45	Louisiana Tech	19
348		**278**

Nickname: Trojans.
Stadium: L.A. Coliseum (1923), 92,000 capacity. Natural turf.
Colors: Cardinal & Gold.
Conference: Pacific-10.
SID: Tim Tessalone, 213-740-8480.
AD: Michael Garrett.

SOUTHERN CONN. ST.
New Haven, CT 06515 II

Coach: Richard Cavanaugh, American Int'l 1976
Record: 15 Years, 77-74-1
2000 SCHEDULE
Stony Brook	Sept. 9
Bentley	*Sept. 15
Mass.-Lowell ■	*Sept. 22
Pace	Sept. 30
Merrimack ■	*Oct. 6
American Int'l ■	*Oct. 13
Stonehill	Oct. 21
C. W. Post	Oct. 28
New Haven ■	*Nov. 3
St. Anselm	Nov. 11

1999 RESULTS (7-3-0)
27	Gannon	0
38	Bentley	0
20	Mass.-Lowell	0
42	Pace	14
29	Merrimack	17
24	American Int'l	36
49	Stonehill	0
27	C. W. Post	36
23	Central Conn. St.	30
66	St. Anselm	42
345		**175**

Nickname: Owls.
Stadium: Jess Dow Field (1988), 6,000 capacity. Artificial turf.
Colors: Blue & White.
Conference: Eastern Football.
SID: Richard Leddy, 203-392-6005.
AD: Darryl D. Rogers.

SOUTHERN ILL.
Carbondale, IL 62901 .... I-AA

Coach: Jan Quarless, Northern Mich. 1973
Record: 4 Years, 12-28-0
2000 SCHEDULE
Murray St.	*Aug. 31
Southeast Mo. St. ■	Sept. 9
Northern Iowa ■	Sept. 16
Kansas	*Sept. 23
Western Ill. ■	Oct. 7
Drake	Oct. 14
Southwest Mo. St.	Oct. 21
Illinois St.	Oct. 28
Indiana St. ■	Nov. 4
Youngstown St.	Nov. 11
Western Ky.	Nov. 18

1999 RESULTS (5-6-0)
43	Southeast Mo. St.	25
58	Murray St.	51
34	Eastern Ill.	6
14	Northern Iowa	34
14	South Fla.	21
37	Youngstown St.	43
27	Western Ill.	68
48	Illinois St.	55
52	Southwest Mo. St.	49
45	Indiana St.	66
52	Western Ky.	14
424		**432**

Nickname: Salukis.
Stadium: McAndrew (1975), 17,324 capacity. Artificial turf.
Colors: Maroon & White.
Conference: Gateway Football.
SID: Fred Huff, 618-453-7235.
AD: Paul Kowaczyk.

SOUTHERN METHODIST
Dallas, TX 75275 .... I-A

Coach: Mike Cavan, Georgia 1972
Record: 14 Years, 82-67-2
2000 SCHEDULE
Kansas ■	*Sept. 2
UTEP	*Sept. 9
North Carolina St.	*Sept. 16
Tulane ■	*Sept. 23
Houston	*Sept. 30
San Jose St. ■	*Oct. 7
Hawaii	*Oct. 14
Nevada ■	*Oct. 28
Rice	Nov. 4
Tulsa ■	*Nov. 11
Fresno St.	Nov. 18
TCU ■	Nov. 25

1999 RESULTS (4-6-0)
0	Arkansas	26
19	Tulane	53
0	Hawaii	20
9	Kansas	27
28	UTEP	42
24	Fresno St.	14
27	Rice	2
58	Cal St. Northridge	16
28	Tulsa	14
0	TCU	21
193		**235**

Nickname: Mustangs.
Stadium: Gerald J. Ford (2000), 32,000 capacity. Natural turf.
Colors: Red & Blue.
Conference: Western Athletic.
SID: To be named, 214-768-2883.
AD: W. James Copeland Jr.

SOUTHERN MISS.
Hattiesburg, MS 39402 .... I-A

Coach: Jeff Bower, Southern Miss. 1976
Record: 9 Years, 59-43-1

2000 SCHEDULE

Tennessee		*Sept. 2
Alabama		Sept. 16
Oklahoma St.		*Sept. 23
Memphis ■		*Sept. 30
South Fla. ■		*Oct. 7
Tulane		Oct. 14
Houston		Oct. 28
Louisville ■		Nov. 4
UAB		Nov. 11
Cincinnati		Nov. 18
East Caro. ■		Nov. 25

1999 RESULTS (8-3-0)

48	Tulane	14
40	Northwestern St.	6
13	Nebraska	20
6	Texas A&M	23
39	East Caro.	22
24	Army	0
28	Cincinnati	20
14	Alabama	35
20	Memphis	5
48	La.-Lafayette	0
30	Louisville	27
310		172

LIBERTY BOWL

23	Colorado St.	17

Nickname: Golden Eagles.
Stadium: Roberts (1976), 33,000 capacity. Natural turf.
Colors: Black & Gold.
Conference: Conference USA.
SID: M.R. Napier, 601-266-4503.
AD: Richard C. Giannini.

SOUTHERN U.
Baton Rouge, LA 70813 .... I-AA

Coach: Pete Richardson, Dayton 1968
Record: 12 Years, 107-32-1

2000 SCHEDULE

Northwestern St.		*Sept. 2
Ark.-Pine Bluff		*Sept. 9
Prairie View [Houston, TX]		*Sept. 16
Jackson St. ■		Sept. 23
Alabama St. ■		*Sept. 30
Alabama A&M		*Oct. 7
Alcorn St.		Oct. 21
Morris Brown ■		*Oct. 28
Florida A&M ■		*Nov. 4
Texas Southern ■		*Nov. 11
Grambling [New Orleans, LA]		*Nov. 25

1999 RESULTS (11-1-0)

20	Northwestern St.	13
17	Ark.-Pine Bluff	9
42	Prairie View	0
36	Alabama St.	13
21	Hampton	6
29	Alabama A&M	12
26	Jackson St.	14
28	Alcorn St.	6
18	Florida A&M	65
23	Texas Southern	14
37	Grambling	31
31	Jackson St.	30
328		213

HERITAGE BOWL

3	Hampton	24

Nickname: Jaguars.
Stadium: A.W. Mumford (1928), 24,000 capacity. Natural turf.
Colors: Blue & Gold.
Conference: Southwestern Athletic.
SID: Michael Jones, 504-771-4142.
AD: Brenda L. Edmond.

SOUTHERN UTAH
Cedar City, UT 84720 .... I-AA

Coach: C. Ray Gregory, Emory & Henry 1986
Record: 3 Years, 18-15-0

2000 SCHEDULE

Fort Lewis ■		*Sept. 2
Utah St.		*Sept. 9
San Jose St.		*Sept. 16
Cal Poly ■		*Sept. 30
UC Davis		Oct. 14
Idaho St.		Oct. 21
St. Mary's (Cal.) ■		Oct. 28
Rocky Mountain ■		Nov. 4
Morehead St. ■		Nov. 11
Northern Ariz.		Nov. 18

1999 RESULTS (8-3-0)

50	Fort Lewis	7
27	Boise St.	35
31	McNeese St.	24
30	Montana Tech	12
10	Cal Poly	38
9	UC Davis	24
39	Weber St.	7
63	Idaho St.	47
57	St. Mary's (Cal.)	22
32	Southwest Tex. St.	28
51	Morehead St.	33
399		277

Nickname: Thunderbirds.
Stadium: Eccles Coliseum (1967), 9,500 capacity. Natural turf.
Colors: Scarlett & White.
Conference: Division I-AA Independent.
SID: Neil Gardner, 801-586-7753.
AD: Jack Bishop.

SOUTHWEST BAPTIST
Bolivar, MO 65613 II

Coach: Dennis Roland, Boston U. 1978
Record: 13 Years, 73-66-0

2000 SCHEDULE

Quincy ■		*Sept. 2
Central Ark.		*Sept. 9
Truman		Sept. 16
Northwest Mo. St. ■		Sept. 23
Mo. Southern St.		Sept. 30
Emporia St. ■		Oct. 7
Washburn		Oct. 14
Mo.-Rolla ■		Oct. 21
Central Mo. St.		Oct. 28
Pittsburg St.		Nov. 4
Mo. Western St. ■		Nov. 11

1999 RESULTS (2-9-0)

0	Arkansas Tech	33
21	Ouachita Baptist	28
18	Truman	16
0	Northwest Mo. St.	52
0	Mo. Southern St.	39
0	Emporia St.	31
0	Washburn	36
14	Mo.-Rolla	7
3	Central Mo. St.	49
0	Pittsburg St.	65
7	Mo. Western St.	55
63		411

Nickname: Bearcats.
Stadium: Plaster (1986), 2,500 capacity. Natural turf.
Colors: Purple & White.
Conference: Mid-America Intercollegiate Athletic.
SID: Steve Schwepker, 417-326-1799.
AD: Dennis F. Roland.

SOUTHWEST MO. ST.
Springfield, MO 65804 .... I-AA

Coach: Randy Ball, Truman 1973
Record: 10 Years, 69-47-1

2000 SCHEDULE

Arkansas [Little Rock, AR]		*Sept. 2
Mo. Southern St. ■		*Sept. 9
McNeese St.		*Sept. 16
Youngstown St. ■		*Sept. 30
Indiana St.		Oct. 7
Western Ill. ■		Oct. 14

Southern Ill. ■		Oct. 21
Northern Iowa		Oct. 28
Tenn.-Martin ■		Nov. 4
Southeast Mo. St. ■		Nov. 11
Illinois St.		Nov. 18

1999 RESULTS (5-6-0)

21	Tulsa	45
37	Texas Southern	7
50	Henderson St.	3
42	Illinois St.	46
27	Western Ill.	17
17	Northern Iowa	29
23	Southeast Mo. St.	28
49	Southern Ill.	52
14	Youngstown St.	17
62	Tenn.-Martin	7
31	Indiana St.	14
373		265

Nickname: Bears.
Stadium: Plaster Field (1941), 16,300 capacity. Artificial turf.
Colors: Maroon & White.
Conference: Gateway Football.
SID: Mark Stillwell, 417-836-5402.
AD: Bill Rowe Jr.

SOUTHWEST ST.
Marshall, MN 56258 II

Coach: Curt Strasheim, Minn. St.-Mankato 1984
(First year as head coach)

2000 SCHEDULE

Wis.-Oshkosh ■		*Sept. 1
Augustana (S.D.) ■		*Sept. 9
Minn.-Morris ■		Sept. 16
Minn.-Duluth ■		Sept. 23
Northern St.		Sept. 30
Bemidji St.		Oct. 7
Winona St.		Oct. 14
Wayne St. (Neb.)		Oct. 21
Moorhead St. ■		Oct. 28
Concordia-St. Paul		Nov. 4
Wis.-Platteville [Minneapolis, MN]		*Nov. 11

1999 RESULTS (6-5-0)

7	Mary	28
53	Minn.-Morris	6
14	Minn.-Duluth	9
6	Northern St.	20
10	Bemidji St.	13
9	Winona St.	13
44	Wayne St. (Neb.)	16
7	Moorhead St.	6
44	Concordia-St. Paul	0
43	Wis.-Stout	23
14	Northern Iowa	55
251		189

Nickname: Mustangs.
Stadium: Mattke Field (1971), 5,000 capacity. Natural turf.
Colors: Brown & Gold.
Conference: Northern Sun Intercollegiate Athletic.
SID: Kelly Loft, 507-537-7177.
AD: Lloyd "Butch" Raymond.

SOUTHWEST TEX. ST.
San Marcos, TX 78666 .... I-AA

Coach: Bob DeBesse, Southwest Tex. St. 1981
Record: 3 Years, 12-21-0

2000 SCHEDULE

Midwestern St. ■		*Aug. 31
Cal St. Northridge ■		*Sept. 9
Oklahoma St.		*Sept. 16
La.-Monroe		*Sept. 30
Nicholls St. ■		Oct. 7
Troy St.		*Oct. 14
Jacksonville St. ■		Oct. 21
Northwestern St. ■		Oct. 28
McNeese St.		*Nov. 4
Stephen F. Austin ■		Nov. 11
Sam Houston St.		Nov. 18

1999 RESULTS (3-8-0)
45	Midwestern St.	3
10	South Fla.	17
17	Stephen F. Austin	28
26	Northern Ariz.	29
16	Nicholls St.	0
17	Troy St.	24
10	Jacksonville St.	17
21	Northwestern St.	36
7	McNeese St.	10
28	Southern Utah	32
20	Sam Houston St.	14
217		**210**

Nickname: Bobcats.
Stadium: Bobcat (1981), 14,104 capacity. Natural turf.
Colors: Maroon & Gold.
Conference: Southland Football.
SID: Tony Brubaker, 512-245-2966.
AD: James Wacker.

SOUTHWESTERN OKLA.
Weatherford, OK 73096 II

Coach: Paul Sharp, Ouachita Baptist 1974
Record: 14 Years, 70-70-1

2000 SCHEDULE
Adams St.	Sept. 2
Texas A&M-Kingsville	*Sept. 9
Tarleton St. ■	*Sept. 16
Tex. A&M-Commerce ■	*Sept. 30
Central Okla. ■	Oct. 7
East Central	Oct. 14
Okla. Panhandle ■	Oct. 21
Southeastern Okla.	Oct. 28
Northeastern St. ■	Nov. 4
Midwestern St.	Nov. 11

1999 RESULTS (5-5-0)
17	Adams St.	13
3	Tarleton St.	7
25	West Tex. A&M	20
18	Abilene Christian	28
14	Ouachita Baptist	3
16	Southeastern Okla.	21
15	Northeastern St.	12
16	Central Okla.	18
7	East Central	17
31	Harding	22
162		**161**

Nickname: Bulldogs.
Stadium: Milam (NA), 9,000 capacity. Natural turf.
Colors: Navy Blue & White.
Conference: Lone Star.
SID: Chris Doyle, 580-774-7122.
AD: Cecil Perkins.

SPRINGFIELD
Springfield, MA 01109 III

Coach: Mike DeLong, Springfield 1974
Record: 18 Years, 91-82-2

2000 SCHEDULE
Mass.-Dartmouth ■	*Sept. 8
Merchant Marine	Sept. 16
Coast Guard ■	Sept. 23
Ithaca	Sept. 30
Western Conn. St. ■	*Oct. 6
Plymouth St. ■	Oct. 14
Worcester Tech	*Oct. 21
Cortland St. ■	Oct. 28
Norwich	Nov. 4
Union (N.Y.) ■	Nov. 11

1999 RESULTS (4-6-0)
29	Bri'water (Mass.)	36
41	Merchant Marine	35
20	Coast Guard	31
42	Ithaca	45
48	Western Conn. St.	56
51	Plymouth St.	33
52	Worcester Tech	17
18	Cortland St.	21
28	Norwich	7
22	Union (N.Y.)	37
351		**318**

Nickname: The Pride.
Stadium: Benedum Field (1971), 2,500 capacity. Artificial turf.
Colors: Maroon & White.
Conference: Freedom Football.
SID: Ken Cerino, 413-748-3341.
AD: Cathie A. Schweitzer.

STANFORD
Stanford, CA 94305 ....I-A

Coach: Tyrone Willingham, Michigan St. 1977
Record: 5 Years, 30-27-1

2000 SCHEDULE
Washington St.	*Sept. 2
San Jose St. ■	*Sept. 9
Texas ■	*Sept. 16
Arizona ■	Sept. 30
Notre Dame	Oct. 7
Oregon St.	Oct. 14
Southern California ■	Oct. 21
Washington ■	Oct. 28
UCLA	Nov. 4
Arizona St. ■	Nov. 11
California	Nov. 18

1999 RESULTS (8-3-0)
17	Texas	69
54	Washington St.	17
50	Arizona	22
42	UCLA	32
39	San Jose St.	44
21	Oregon St.	17
35	Southern California	31
30	Washington	35
50	Arizona St.	30
31	California	13
40	Notre Dame	37
409		**347**

ROSE BOWL
9	Wisconsin	17

Nickname: Cardinal.
Stadium: Stanford (1921), 85,500 capacity. Natural turf.
Colors: Cardinal & White.
Conference: Pacific-10.
SID: Gary Migdol, 415-723-4418.
AD: Edward Leland.

STEPHEN F. AUSTIN
Nacogdoches, TX 75962 ....I-AA

Coach: Mike Santiago, Southern Utah 1977
Record: 1 Year, 8-3-0

2000 SCHEDULE
Central Okla. ■	*Aug. 31
Tex. A&M-Commerce ■	*Sept. 9
Louisiana Tech	*Sept. 16
Northern Iowa	Sept. 23
McNeese St.	*Oct. 7
Sam Houston St. ■	Oct. 14
Nicholls St.	*Oct. 21
Jacksonville St.	Oct. 28
Troy St. ■	Nov. 4
Southwest Tex. St.	Nov. 11
Northwestern St. ■	Nov. 18

1999 RESULTS (8-3-0)
51	Abilene Christian	34
17	Utah St.	51
28	Southwest Tex. St.	17
28	New Hampshire	38
40	McNeese St.	14
45	Sam Houston St.	31
38	Nicholls St.	7
33	Jacksonville St.	16
7	Troy St.	27
73	Wingate	11
29	Northwestern St.	14
389		**260**

Nickname: Lumberjacks.
Stadium: Homer Bryce (1973), 14,575 capacity. Artificial turf.
Colors: Purple & White.
Conference: Southland Football.
SID: Rob Meyers, 409-468-2606.
AD: Steve McCarty.

STILLMAN
Tuscaloosa, AL 35403 III

Coach: Theophilus Danzy, Tennessee St. 1953
Record: 11 Years, 44-61-3

2000 SCHEDULE
West Ala. ■	Sept. 2
Union (Ky.)	Sept. 9
Maryville (Tenn.) ■	Sept. 16
Sewanee	Sept. 23
Bethel (Tenn.) ■	Sept. 30
Newport News ■	Oct. 7
Lincoln (Mo.)	Oct. 14
Chowan ■	Oct. 28
Clark Atlanta ■	Nov. 11

1999 RESULTS (3-5-0)
7	Ark.-Monticello	30
7	Mississippi Col.	10
6	Maryville (Tenn.)	27
13	Union (Ky.)	10
28	Bethel (Tenn.)	16
29	Newport News	12
12	Chowan	25
18	Sewanee	30
120		**160**

Nickname: Tigers.
Stadium: Stillman (1999), 5,000 capacity. Natural turf.
Colors: Old Gold & Royal Blue.
Conference: Division III Independent.
AD: To be named.

STONEHILL
North Easton, MA 02357 II

Coach: Rich Beal, Wesleyan 1985
Record: 1 Year, 0-10-0

2000 SCHEDULE
Pace	Sept. 9
American Int'l ■	Sept. 16
Merrimack ■	Sept. 23
C. W. Post	Sept. 30
Mass.-Lowell	*Oct. 5
Assumption ■	Oct. 14
Southern Conn. St.	Oct. 21
Bryant ■	Oct. 28
St. Anselm ■	Nov. 4
Bentley	Nov. 11

1999 RESULTS (0-10-0)
13	Pace	26
7	American Int'l	62
0	Merrimack	25
21	C. W. Post	38
21	Mass.-Lowell	26
28	Assumption	39
0	Southern Conn. St.	49
7	Bryant	24
27	St. Anselm	33
27	Bentley	48
151		**370**

Nickname: Chieftains.
Stadium: Chieftain (1980), 2,000 capacity. Natural turf.
Colors: Purple & White.
Conference: Eastern Football.
SID: Jim Seavey, 508-230-1352.
AD: Paula Sullivan.

STONY BROOK
Stony Brook, NY 11794 ....I-AA

Coach: Sam Kornhauser, Missouri Valley 1971
Record: 16 Years, 75-78-2

2000 SCHEDULE
Southern Conn. St. ■ ....Sept. 9
St. John's (N.Y.) ■ ....Sept. 16
St. Francis (Pa.) ....Sept. 23
Albany (N.Y.) ■ ....Sept. 30
Wagner ....Oct. 7
Sacred Heart ■ ....Oct. 14
Monmouth ....Oct. 21
Jacksonville ....Oct. 28
Central Conn. St. ....Nov. 11
Robert Morris ■ ....Nov. 18

1999 RESULTS (5-5-0)
12	Wagner	24
7	Monmouth	3
21	Albany (N.Y.)	44
48	Sacred Heart	21
20	C. W. Post	44
27	Central Conn. St.	14
9	San Diego	20
24	St. Francis (Pa.)	6
19	Robert Morris	50
28	St. John's (N.Y.)	6
215		**232**

Nickname: Seawolves.
Stadium: Seawolves (1978), 2,000 capacity. Natural turf.
Colors: Scarlet & Gray.
Conference: Northeast.
SID: Rob Emmerich, 516-632-6312.
AD: Sandra R. Weeden.

SUL ROSS ST.
Alpine, TX 79832 III

Coach: Jack Waggoner, Sul Ross St. 1962
Record: 1 Year, 2-8-0

2000 SCHEDULE
Texas Lutheran ■ ....Sept. 16
Louisiana Col. ■ ....*Sept. 23
Mississippi Col. ....Sept. 30
Howard Payne ■ ....Oct. 7
East Tex. Baptist ....Oct. 14
Hardin-Simmons ....Oct. 21
Mary Hardin-Baylor ■ ....*Oct. 28
McMurry ....Nov. 4
Austin ■ ....Nov. 11

1999 RESULTS (2-8-0)
25	McMurry	50
20	Langston	18
12	Western N.M.	47
23	Hardin-Simmons	28
15	Mary Hardin-Baylor	16
16	McMurry	59
44	Texas Lutheran	40
20	Mississippi Col.	36
2	Austin	31
20	Howard Payne	50
197		**375**

Nickname: Lobos.
Stadium: Jackson Field (0000), 2,500 capacity. Natural turf.
Colors: Scarlet & Gray.
Conference: American Southwest.
SID: Steve Lang, 915-837-8061.
AD: Kay Whitley.

SUSQUEHANNA
Selinsgrove, PA 17870 III

Coach: Steve Briggs, Springfield 1984
Record: 10 Years, 68-34-0

2000 SCHEDULE
FDU-Madison ....Sept. 2
King's (Pa.) ....Sept. 16
Dickinson ■ ....Sept. 23
Wilkes ■ ....Sept. 30
Juniata ■ ....Oct. 7
Widener ....Oct. 14
Lebanon Valley ....Oct. 21
Moravian ■ ....Oct. 28
Lycoming ....Nov. 4
Albright ....Nov. 11

1999 RESULTS (7-3-0)
20	FDU-Madison	3
27	King's (Pa.)	26
42	Dickinson	6
0	Wilkes	26
27	Juniata	7
28	Widener	7
14	Lebanon Valley	17
27	Moravian	24
7	Lycoming	36
27	Albright	20
219		**172**

Nickname: Crusaders.
Stadium: Lopardo/Stagg Field (2000), 3,500 capacity. Natural turf.
Colors: Orange & Maroon.
Conference: Middle Atlantic.
SID: Jim Miller, 570-372-4119.
AD: Donald Harnum.

SWARTHMORE
Swarthmore, PA 19081 III

Coach: Peter Alvanos, Drexel 1988
Record: 2 Years, 1-16-0

2000 SCHEDULE
Oberlin ....Sept. 2
Johns Hopkins ■ ....Sept. 16
Gettysburg ....Sept. 23
Ursinus ■ ....Sept. 30
Muhlenberg ....Oct. 7
Dickinson ....Oct. 21
Frank. & Marsh. ■ ....Oct. 28
Western Md. ....Nov. 4
Wash. & Lee ....Nov. 11

1999 RESULTS (1-8-0)
42	Oberlin	6
3	Johns Hopkins	37
8	Gettysburg	55
0	Ursinus	59
0	Muhlenberg	35
14	Dickinson	24
15	Frank. & Marsh.	17
14	Western Md.	41
13	Wash. & Lee	40
109		**314**

Nickname: Garnet Tide.
Stadium: Clothier (1950), 2,000 capacity. Natural turf.
Colors: Garnet & White.
Conference: Centennial.
SID: Mark Duzenski, 610-328-8206.
AD: Robert E. Williams.

SYRACUSE
Syracuse, NY 13244 ....I-A

Coach: Paul Pasqualoni, Penn St. 1972
Record: 14 Years, 109-48-1

2000 SCHEDULE
Buffalo ■ ....*Sept. 2
Cincinnati ....Sept. 9
East Caro. ....Sept. 23
Brigham Young ■ ....*Sept. 30
Pittsburgh ....Oct. 7
Boston College ....Oct. 14
Virginia Tech ■ ....Oct. 21
West Virginia ....Nov. 4
Temple ....Nov. 11
Miami (Fla.) ■ ....Nov. 18
Rutgers ■ ....Nov. 25

1999 RESULTS (6-5-0)
35	Toledo	12
47	Central Mich.	7
13	Michigan	18
30	West Virginia	7
47	Tulane	17
24	Pittsburgh	17
0	Virginia Tech	62
23	Boston College	24
27	Temple	10
21	Rutgers	24
13	Miami (Fla.)	45
280		**243**

MUSIC CITY BOWL
20 Kentucky 13

Nickname: Orangemen.
Stadium: Carrier Dome (1980), 49,550 capacity. Artificial turf.
Colors: Orange.
Conference: Big East.
SID: Sue Cornelius Edson, 315-443-2608.
AD: John J. Crouthamel.

TARLETON ST.
Stephenville, TX 76402 II

Coach: Todd Whitten, Stephen F. Austin 1987
Record: 1 Year, 5-5-0

2000 SCHEDULE
Harding ....*Sept. 2
Western N.M. ■ ....*Sept. 9
Southwestern Okla. ....*Sept. 16
Southeastern Okla. ....*Sept. 23
Texas A&M-Kingsville ....*Sept. 30
West Tex. A&M ■ ....*Oct. 7
Eastern N.M. ....*Oct. 14
Abilene Christian ■ ....Oct. 21
Angelo St. ....*Oct. 28
Midwestern St. ■ ....*Nov. 4
Tex. A&M-Commerce ■ ....*Nov. 11

1999 RESULTS (5-6-0)
16	Harding	44
7	Southwestern Okla.	3
6	Northwestern St.	52
33	East Central	31
23	Texas A&M-Kingsville	7
6	West Tex. A&M	7
13	Eastern N.M.	27
14	Abilene Christian	9
17	Angelo St.	27
3	Midwestern St.	21
27	Tex. A&M-Commerce	23
165		**251**

Nickname: Texans.
Stadium: Memorial (1976), 7,000 capacity. Natural turf.
Colors: Purple & White.
Conference: Lone Star.
SID: To be named, 817-968-9077.
AD: Lonn Reisman.

TEMPLE
Philadelphia, PA 19122 ....I-A

Coach: Bobby Wallace, Mississippi St. 1976
Record: 12 Years, 86-54-1

2000 SCHEDULE
Navy ....*Sept. 2
Maryland ....*Sept. 9
Bowling Green ■ ....*Sept. 16
Eastern Mich. ■ ....*Sept. 23
West Virginia ■ ....*Sept. 28
Virginia Tech ....Oct. 7
Rutgers ....Oct. 14
Miami (Fla.) ■ ....Oct. 21
Boston College ....Nov. 4
Syracuse ■ ....Nov. 11
Pittsburgh ■ ....Nov. 18

1999 RESULTS (2-9-0)
0	Maryland	6
0	Kansas St.	40
15	Akron	25
0	Marshall	34
24	Pittsburgh	55
24	Boston College	14
17	West Virginia	20
56	Rutgers	28
10	Syracuse	27
7	Virginia Tech	62
0	Miami (Fla.)	55
153		**366**

Nickname: Owls.
Stadium: Veterans (1971), 66,592 capacity. Artificial turf.
Colors: Cherry & White.
Conference: Big East.

TENNESSEE
Knoxville, TN 37996 .... I-A

Coach: Phillip Fulmer, Tennessee 1972
Record: 8 Years, 76-14-0

2000 SCHEDULE
Southern Miss. ■	*Sept. 2
Florida ■	Sept. 16
La.-Monroe ■	Sept. 23
LSU	*Sept. 30
Georgia	Oct. 7
Alabama ■	Oct. 21
South Carolina	Oct. 28
Memphis	Nov. 4
Arkansas ■	Nov. 11
Kentucky ■	Nov. 18
Vanderbilt	Nov. 25

1999 RESULTS (9-2-0)
42	Wyoming	17
21	Florida	23
17	Memphis	16
24	Auburn	0
37	Georgia	20
21	Alabama	7
30	South Carolina	7
38	Notre Dame	14
24	Arkansas	28
56	Kentucky	21
38	Vanderbilt	10
348		**163**

FIESTA BOWL
21	Nebraska	31

Nickname: Volunteers.
Stadium: Neyland (1921), 104,000 capacity. Natural turf.
Colors: Orange & White.
Conference: Southeastern.
SID: Bud Ford, 423-974-1212.
AD: Douglas A. Dickey.

TENNESSEE ST.
Nashville, TN 37209 .... I-AA

Coach: James Reese, Tennessee St. 1991
(First year as head coach)

2000 SCHEDULE
Alabama St. ■	*Sept. 2
N.C. A&T [Cincinnati, OH]	Sept. 9
Jackson St. [Memphis, TN]	*Sept. 16
Florida A&M [Atlanta, GA]	Sept. 23
Eastern Ill.	Oct. 7
Tenn.-Martin ■	*Oct. 14
Western Ky. ■	Oct. 21
Eastern Ky.	*Oct. 26
Tennessee Tech	Nov. 4
Murray St.	Nov. 11
Southeast Mo. St. ■	Nov. 18

1999 RESULTS (11-0-0)
41	Alabama St.	8
48	Jackson St.	33
42	Florida A&M	25
36	Alabama A&M	15
43	Eastern Ill.	25
43	Tenn.-Martin	7
28	Western Ky.	21
33	Eastern Ky.	28
25	Tennessee Tech	19
42	Murray St.	41
35	Southeast Mo. St.	28
416		**250**

DIVISION I-AA CHAMPIONSHIP
10	N.C. A&T	24

Nickname: Tigers.
Stadium: Adelphia Coliseum (1999), 67,000 capacity. Natural turf.
Colors: Blue & White.
Conference: Ohio Valley.
SID: Johnny Franks, 615-963-5851.
AD: James Smith.

SID: Brian Kirschner, 215-204-7445.
AD: David P. O'Brien.

TENNESSEE TECH
Cookeville, TN 38505 .... I-AA

Coach: Mike Hennigan, Tennessee Tech 1973
Record: 4 Years, 20-23-0

2000 SCHEDULE
Harding ■	*Sept. 9
Ohio	Sept. 16
Eastern Ky. ■	*Sept. 23
Tenn.-Martin ■	Sept. 30
Southeast Mo. St. ■	Oct. 7
Western Ky.	Oct. 14
Eastern Ill. ■	Oct. 21
Murray St.	Oct. 28
Tennessee St. ■	Nov. 4
Samford ■	*Nov. 9
Western Caro.	Nov. 18

1999 RESULTS (5-5-0)
15	Bowling Green	40
18	Liberty	15
45	Tenn.-Martin	9
21	Southeast Mo. St.	7
23	Western Ky.	10
14	Eastern Ill.	7
11	Murray St.	22
19	Tennessee St.	25
20	Eastern Ky.	23
15	Samford	19
201		**177**

Nickname: Golden Eagles.
Stadium: Tucker (1966), 16,500 capacity. Artificial turf.
Colors: Purple & Gold.
Conference: Ohio Valley.
SID: Rob Schabert, 615-372-3088.
AD: David Larimore.

TENN.-MARTIN
Martin, TN 38238 .... I-AA

Coach: Sam McCorkle, West Ala. 1973
(First year as head coach)

2000 SCHEDULE
Lambuth ■	*Aug. 31
Western Ky.	Sept. 9
Samford	*Sept. 14
Eastern Ill. ■	Sept. 23
Tennessee Tech	Sept. 30
Murray St. ■	Oct. 7
Tennessee St.	*Oct. 14
Eastern Ky. ■	Oct. 21
Southeast Mo. St.	*Oct. 28
Southwest Mo. St.	Nov. 4
Wingate ■	Nov. 11

1999 RESULTS (1-10-0)
10	Western Ky.	34
25	Lambuth	19
7	Samford	32
21	Eastern Ill.	42
9	Tennessee Tech	45
14	Murray St.	62
7	Tennessee St.	43
7	Eastern Ky.	54
7	Southeast Mo. St.	36
14	Middle Tenn. St.	70
7	Southwest Mo. St.	62
128		**499**

Nickname: Skyhawks.
Stadium: UT Martin (1964), 7,500 capacity. Natural turf.
Colors: Orange, White & Royal Blue.
Conference: Ohio Valley.
SID: Lee Wilmot, 901-587-7630.
AD: Benny Hollis.

TEXAS
Austin, TX 78712 .... I-A

Coach: Mack Brown, Florida St. 1974
Record: 16 Years, 104-82-1

2000 SCHEDULE
La.-Lafayette ■	Sept. 9
Stanford	*Sept. 16
Houston ■	Sept. 23
Oklahoma St. ■	Sept. 30
Oklahoma [Dallas, TX]	Oct. 7
Colorado	Oct. 14
Missouri ■	Oct. 21
Baylor ■	Oct. 28
Texas Tech	Nov. 4
Kansas	Nov. 11
Texas A&M ■	Nov. 24

1999 RESULTS (9-4-0)
20	North Carolina St.	23
69	Stanford	17
38	Rutgers	21
18	Rice	13
62	Baylor	0
17	Kansas St.	35
38	Oklahoma	28
24	Nebraska	20
44	Iowa St.	41
34	Oklahoma St.	21
58	Texas Tech	7
16	Texas A&M	20
6	Nebraska	22
444		**268**

COTTON BOWL
6	Arkansas	27

Nickname: Longhorns.
Stadium: Royal-Memorial (1924), 80,082 capacity. Natural turf.
Colors: Burnt Orange & White.
Conference: Big 12.
SID: John Bianco, 512-471-7437.
AD: DeLoss Dodds.

TEXAS A&M
College Station, TX 77843 .... I-A

Coach: R. C. Slocum, McNeese St. 1967
Record: 11 Years, 102-32-2

2000 SCHEDULE
Notre Dame	Sept. 2
Wyoming ■	*Sept. 9
UTEP ■	*Sept. 16
Texas Tech ■	Sept. 30
Colorado ■	Oct. 7
Baylor	Oct. 14
Iowa St.	Oct. 21
Kansas St. ■	Oct. 28
Oklahoma St.	Nov. 4
Oklahoma ■	Nov. 11
Texas	Nov. 24

1999 RESULTS (8-3-0)
37	Louisiana Tech	17
62	Tulsa	13
23	Southern Miss.	6
19	Texas Tech	21
45	Baylor	13
34	Kansas	17
6	Oklahoma	51
21	Oklahoma St.	3
0	Nebraska	37
51	Missouri	14
20	Texas	16
318		**208**

ALAMO BOWL
0	Penn St.	24

Nickname: Aggies.
Stadium: Kyle Field (1925), 70,210 capacity. Natural turf.
Colors: Maroon & White.
Conference: Big 12.
SID: Alan Cannon, 409-845-5725.
AD: Wally W. Groff.

TEX. A&M-COMMERCE
Commerce, TX 75429 II

Coach: Eddie Brister, Austin College 1972
Record: 1 Year, 4-7-0

2000 SCHEDULE

Abilene Christian [North Richland Hills, TX]	*Sept. 2
Stephen F. Austin	*Sept. 9
Central Okla.	Sept. 16
Midwestern St. ■	*Sept. 23
Southwestern Okla.	*Sept. 30
Texas A&M-Kingsville ■	Oct. 7
West Tex. A&M	*Oct. 14
Eastern N.M. ■	Oct. 21
Abilene Christian	*Oct. 28
Angelo St. ■	Nov. 4
Tarleton St.	*Nov. 11

1999 RESULTS (4-7-0)

0	UC Davis	36
3	Pittsburg St.	51
14	Northeastern St.	19
21	Ouachita Baptist	22
10	Midwestern St.	7
14	Texas A&M-Kingsville	10
9	West Tex. A&M	3
10	Eastern N.M.	21
17	Abilene Christian	21
14	Angelo St.	10
23	Tarleton St.	27
135		227

Nickname: Lions.
Stadium: Memorial (1950), 10,000 capacity. Natural turf.
Colors: Blue & Gold.
Conference: Lone Star.
SID: Bill Powers, 903-886-5131.
AD: Paul D. Peak.

TEXAS A&M-KINGSVILLE
Kingsville, TX 78363 II

Coach: Richard Cundiff, Lincoln Mem. 1973
(First year as head coach)

2000 SCHEDULE

North Dakota St. ■	*Aug. 31
Southwestern Okla. ■	*Sept. 9
Southeastern Okla.	*Sept. 16
Sam Houston St.	*Sept. 23
Tarleton St. ■	*Sept. 30
Tex. A&M-Commerce	Oct. 7
Central Okla. ■	*Oct. 14
West Tex. A&M ■	*Oct. 21
Eastern N.M.	Oct. 28
Abilene Christian ■	*Nov. 4
Angelo St.	Nov. 11

1999 RESULTS (5-6-0)

2	Northeastern St.	9
10	McNeese St.	24
20	East Central	14
24	Sam Houston St.	34
7	Tarleton St.	23
10	Tex. A&M-Commerce	14
7	Midwestern St.	10
35	West Tex. A&M	14
42	Eastern N.M.	7
40	Abilene Christian	14
42	Angelo St.	38
239		201

Nickname: Javelinas.
Stadium: Javelina (1950), 15,000 capacity. Natural turf.
Colors: Blue & Gold.
Conference: Lone Star.
SID: Fred Nuesch, 512-593-3908.
AD: Ron Harms.

TCU
Fort Worth, TX 76129 .... I-A

Coach: Dennis Franchione, Pittsburg St. 1973
Record: 17 Years, 128-64-2

2000 SCHEDULE

Nevada	Sept. 9
Northwestern ■	*Sept. 16
Arkansas St. ■	*Sept. 23
Navy	Sept. 30
Hawaii ■	*Oct. 7
Tulsa	*Oct. 21
Rice ■	Oct. 28
San Jose St.	Nov. 4
Fresno St. ■	Nov. 11
UTEP	Nov. 18
Southern Methodist	Nov. 25

1999 RESULTS (7-4-0)

31	Arizona	35
7	Northwestern	17
24	Arkansas St.	21
19	Fresno St.	26
42	San Jose St.	0
56	Tulsa	17
21	Rice	42
34	Hawaii	14
27	North Texas	3
52	UTEP	24
21	Southern Methodist	0
334		199

MOBILE ALABAMA BOWL

28	East Caro.	14

Nickname: Horned Frogs.
Stadium: Amon G. Carter (1929), 46,000 capacity. Natural turf.
Colors: Purple & White.
Conference: Western Athletic.
SID: Rick Covington, 817-921-7969.
AD: Eric C. Hyman.

UTEP
El Paso, TX 79968 .... I-A

Coach: Gary Nord, Louisville 1979
(First year as head coach)

2000 SCHEDULE

Oklahoma	*Sept. 2
Southern Methodist ■	*Sept. 9
Texas A&M	*Sept. 16
Hawaii ■	*Sept. 23
New Mexico St. ■	*Sept. 30
Tulsa	*Oct. 7
San Jose St.	*Oct. 14
Fresno St. ■	*Oct. 21
Nevada	Nov. 4
Rice ■	*Nov. 11
TCU	Nov. 18

1999 RESULTS (5-7-0)

13	New Mexico	10
28	Oregon	47
7	Kansas St.	40
54	New Mexico St.	23
3	Hawaii	33
42	Southern Methodist	28
21	Arizona	34
23	Fresno St.	24
42	San Jose St.	26
19	Tulsa	43
30	Rice	29
24	TCU	52
306		389

Nickname: Miners.
Stadium: Sun Bowl (1963), 52,000 capacity. Artificial turf.
Colors: Orange, White & Blue.
Conference: Western Athletic.
SID: Jeff Darby, 915-747-5330.
AD: Bob Stull.

TEXAS LUTHERAN
Seguin, TX 78155 II

Coach: Bryan Marmion, Linfield 1989
Record: 2 Years, 7-13-0

2000 SCHEDULE

Trinity (Tex.) ■	*Sept. 2
Sul Ross St.	Sept. 16
Hardin-Simmons	Sept. 23
Mary Hardin-Baylor ■	*Sept. 30
McMurry	*Oct. 7
Austin ■	Oct. 14
East Tex. Baptist ■	Oct. 21
Louisiana Col.	Oct. 28
Mississippi Col. ■	Nov. 4
Howard Payne	Nov. 11

1999 RESULTS (3-7-0)

7	Langston	31
13	McPherson	34
53	Southwestern Assemblies of God	16
34	Austin	31
21	McMurry	68
7	Howard Payne	42
40	Sul Ross St.	44
26	Hardin-Simmons	35
6	Mississippi Col.	28
34	Mary Hardin-Baylor	24
241		353

Nickname: Bulldogs.
Stadium: Matador (1959), 9,500 capacity. Natural turf.
Colors: Black & Gold.
Conference: American Southwest.
SID: Tim Clark, 830-372-6877.
AD: Bill Miller.

TEXAS SOUTHERN
Houston, TX 77004 .... I-AA

Coach: Bill Thomas, Tennessee St. 1970
Record: 11 Years, 65-54-3

2000 SCHEDULE

Prairie View [Houston, TX]	*Sept. 2
Jackson St.	*Sept. 9
Lane ■	*Sept. 16
Langston ■	*Sept. 30
Ark.-Pine Bluff ■	*Oct. 7
Alcorn St.	Oct. 14
Mississippi Val. ■	*Oct. 21
Grambling ■	*Oct. 28
Morris Brown	Nov. 4
Southern U.	*Nov. 11
Norfolk St. [San Diego, CA]	Nov. 18

1999 RESULTS (6-5-0)

34	Prairie View	0
7	Southwest Mo. St.	37
38	Lane	15
20	Howard	32
20	Ark.-Pine Bluff	7
23	Alcorn St.	21
13	Mississippi Val.	18
21	Grambling	20
24	Jackson St.	41
14	Southern U.	23
22	Norfolk St.	6
236		220

Nickname: Tigers.
Stadium: Robertson (1965), 33,000 capacity. Natural turf.
Colors: Maroon & Gray.
Conference: Southwestern Athletic.
SID: LaTanya Dunn, 713-527-7270.
AD: William A. Thomas.

TEXAS TECH
Lubbock, TX 79409 .... I-A

Coach: Mike Leach, Brigham Young 1983
(First year as head coach)

2000 SCHEDULE

New Mexico ■	*Aug. 26
Utah St. ■	*Sept. 2
North Texas ■	*Sept. 9
La.-Lafayette ■	*Sept. 16
Texas A&M	Sept. 30
Baylor	*Oct. 7
Nebraska ■	*Oct. 14
Kansas St.	Oct. 21
Kansas ■	Oct. 28
Texas	Nov. 4
Oklahoma St. ■	Nov. 11
Oklahoma	Nov. 18

1999 RESULTS (6-5-0)
13	Arizona St.	31
38	La.-Lafayette	17
14	North Texas	21
21	Texas A&M	19
21	Oklahoma St.	41
31	Colorado	10
35	Baylor	7
7	Missouri	34
28	Iowa St.	16
7	Texas	58
38	Oklahoma	28
253		**282**

Nickname: Red Raiders.
Stadium: Jones (1947), 50,500 capacity. Artificial turf.
Colors: Scarlet & Black.
Conference: Big 12.
SID: Kent Partridge, 806-742-2770.
AD: Gerald L. Myers.

THIEL
Greenville, PA 16125 III

Coach: David Armstrong, Mercyhurst 1986
Record: 4 Years, 6-34-0

2000 SCHEDULE
Capital	Sept. 2
Kean	Sept. 9
Bluffton ■	Sept. 16
Thomas More ■	Sept. 23
Grove City	Sept. 30
Waynesburg ■	Oct. 7
Westminster (Pa.) ■	Oct. 14
Bethany (W.Va.) ■	Oct. 21
Wash. & Jeff. ■	Oct. 28
Kenyon	Nov. 4

1999 RESULTS (3-7-0)
19	Capital	0
63	Oberlin	12
21	Kenyon	7
6	Thomas More	14
0	Grove City	56
7	Waynesburg	40
6	Bethany (W.Va.)	9
21	Brockport St.	33
13	Defiance	20
6	Wash. & Jeff.	51
162		**242**

Nickname: Tomcats.
Stadium: Stewart Field (1954), 5,000 capacity. Natural turf.
Colors: Navy Blue & Old Gold.
Conference: Presidents' Athletic.
SID: Robb Dietrich, 412-589-2187.
AD: David A. Armstrong.

THOMAS MORE
Crestview Hills, KY 41017 III

Coach: Dean Paul, Mount Union 1990
Record: 1 Year, 7-3-0

2000 SCHEDULE
Anderson (Ind.) ■	Sept. 2
Urbana	Sept. 9
Hanover ■	Sept. 16
Thiel	Sept. 23
Adrian ■	Sept. 30
Manchester ■	Oct. 7
Franklin ■	Oct. 14
Westminster (Mo.)	Oct. 21
Defiance	Oct. 28
Bluffton	Nov. 4

1999 RESULTS (7-3-0)
32	Anderson (Ind.)	18
19	Hanover	45
24	Ky. Wesleyan	30
14	Thiel	6
7	Alma	35
42	Bethel (Tenn.)	0
28	Merchant Marine	0
45	Defiance	30
24	Methodist	13
23	Carnegie Mellon	7
258		**184**

Nickname: Saints.
Stadium: Thomas More (1945), 2,000 capacity. Natural turf.
Colors: Royal Blue, White & Silver.
Conference: Division III Independent.
SID: James Neyhouse, 606-344-3673.
AD: Todd Asalon.

TOLEDO
Toledo, OH 43606 .... I-A

Coach: Gary Pinkel, Kent St. 1975
Record: 9 Years, 63-36-3

2000 SCHEDULE
Penn St.	Sept. 2
Weber St. ■	*Sept. 9
Eastern Ill. ■	*Sept. 16
Western Mich.	*Sept. 23
Central Mich. ■	*Sept. 30
Eastern Mich.	Oct. 7
Marshall ■	*Oct. 14
Navy	Oct. 28
Northern Ill.	Nov. 4
Ball St. ■	Nov. 11
Bowling Green ■	*Nov. 22

1999 RESULTS (6-5-0)
12	Syracuse	35
23	Ball St.	10
24	Massachusetts	3
23	Bowling Green	34
47	Kent St.	7
13	Marshall	38
13	Eastern Mich.	20
17	Louisiana Tech	34
32	Central Mich.	13
44	Northern Ill.	14
45	Western Mich.	21
293		**229**

Nickname: Rockets.
Stadium: Glass Bowl (1937), 26,248 capacity. Artificial turf.
Colors: Blue & Gold.
Conference: Mid-American.
SID: Paul Helgren, 419-530-3790.
AD: Peter A. Liske.

TOWSON
Towson, MD 21252 .... I-AA

Coach: Gordy Combs, Towson 1972
Record: 8 Years, 48-34-0

2000 SCHEDULE
Fordham	Sept. 2
Lafayette	Sept. 9
Morgan St. ■	Sept. 16
Holy Cross	Sept. 23
Colgate ■	Sept. 30
Lehigh ■	Oct. 7
Howard ■	Oct. 14
Monmouth	Oct. 28
St. Mary's (Cal.)	Nov. 4
Bucknell ■	Nov. 11
Drake	Nov. 18

1999 RESULTS (7-4-0)
34	Monmouth	7
35	Lafayette	7
27	Bucknell	20
13	Columbia	28
14	Holy Cross	0
22	Morgan St.	28
49	Howard	33
25	Fordham	23
39	Lehigh	44
30	Dayton	27
14	Colgate	38
302		**255**

Nickname: Tigers.
Stadium: Minnegan Stadium (1978), 5,000 capacity. Artificial turf.
Colors: Gold, White & Black.
Conference: Patriot.
SID: Peter Schlehr, 410-830-2232.
AD: Wayne Edwards.

TRINITY (CONN.)
Hartford, CT 06106 III

Coach: Charles Priore, Albany (N.Y.) 1982
(First year as head coach)

2000 SCHEDULE
Bates ■	Sept. 23
Williams	Sept. 30
Hamilton	Oct. 7
Tufts ■	Oct. 14
Bowdoin	Oct. 21
Middlebury ■	Oct. 28
Amherst ■	Nov. 4
Wesleyan (Conn.)	Nov. 11

1999 RESULTS (5-3-0)
35	Colby	3
0	Williams	17
31	Hamilton	17
13	Tufts	7
26	Bowdoin	0
10	Middlebury	14
0	Amherst	27
26	Wesleyan (Conn.)	12
141		**97**

Nickname: Bantams.
Stadium: Jessee Field (1900), 6,500 capacity. Natural turf.
Colors: Blue & Gold.
Conference: NESCAC.
SID: Dave Kingsley, 203-297-2137.
AD: Richard J. Hazelton.

TRINITY (TEX.)
San Antonio, TX 78212 III

Coach: Steven Mohr, Denison 1976
Record: 10 Years, 69-38-0

2000 SCHEDULE
Texas Lutheran	*Sept. 2
Gust. Adolphus ■	*Sept. 9
Willamette ■	*Sept. 16
DePauw	Sept. 23
Rose-Hulman ■	*Sept. 30
Washington (Mo.)	Oct. 7
Centre ■	Oct. 21
Rhodes ■	Oct. 28
Sewanee ■	Nov. 4
Millsaps	Nov. 11

1999 RESULTS (10-0-0)
28	Mary Hardin-Baylor	13
27	McMurry	19
48	Austin	7
44	DePauw	0
51	Rose-Hulman	0
25	Washington (Mo.)	15
38	Centre	0
45	Rhodes	17
41	Sewanee	9
49	Millsaps	7
396		**87**

DIVISION III CHAMPIONSHIP
20	Western Md.	16
40	Hardin-Simmons	33
28	Pacific Lutheran	49

Nickname: Tigers.
Stadium: E. M. Stevens (1972), 3,500 capacity. Natural turf.
Colors: Maroon & White.
Conference: Southern Collegiate Athletic.
SID: Granger Huntress, 210-736-8447.
AD: Robert C. King.

TROY ST.
Troy, AL 36082 .... I-AA

Coach: Larry Blakeney, Auburn 1970
Record: 9 Years, 82-27-1

2000 SCHEDULE

Alabama A&M	*Sept. 2
Appalachian St.	*Sept. 9
Alabama St. ■	Sept. 16
South Fla.	Sept. 30
Northwestern St.	*Oct. 7
Southwest Tex. ■	*Oct. 14
Sam Houston St.	*Oct. 21
Nicholls St. ■	Oct. 28
Stephen F. Austin	Nov. 4
McNeese St. ■	Nov. 11
Jacksonville St.	Nov. 18

1999 RESULTS (10-1-0)

31	Cincinnati	24
27	Alabama St.	20
41	South Fla.	24
48	Middle Tenn. St.	31
24	Northwestern St.	21
24	Southwest Tex. St.	17
41	Sam Houston St.	16
20	Nicholls St.	0
27	Stephen F. Austin	7
7	McNeese St.	24
35	Jacksonville St.	16
325		200

DIVISION I-AA CHAMPIONSHIP

27	James Madison	7
10	Florida A&M	17

Nickname: Trojans.
Stadium: Memorial (1950), 17,500 capacity. Natural turf.
Colors: Cardinal, Silver & Black.
Conference: Southland Football.
SID: Jim Horten, 205-670-3480.
AD: Johnny Williams.

TRUMAN

Kirksville, MO 63501 II

Coach: John Ware, Drake 1981
Record: 5 Years, 29-25-0

2000 SCHEDULE

Northern Mich. ■	Sept. 2
South Dakota	*Sept. 9
Southwest Baptist ■	Sept. 16
Mo.-Rolla	Sept. 23
Northwest Mo. St. ■	Sept. 30
Central Mo. St.	Oct. 7
Mo. Western St.	Oct. 14
Mo. Southern St. ■	Oct. 21
Emporia St.	Oct. 28
Washburn ■	Nov. 4
Pittsburg St.	Nov. 11

1999 RESULTS (4-7-0)

9	Illinois St.	41
21	South Dakota	38
16	Southwest Baptist	18
15	Mo.-Rolla	0
32	Northwest Mo. St.	42
24	Central Mo. St.	13
19	Mo. Western St.	28
45	Mo. Southern St.	40
31	Emporia St.	24
18	Washburn	52
17	Pittsburg St.	29
247		325

Nickname: Bulldogs.
Stadium: Stokes (1962), 4,000 capacity. Natural turf.
Colors: Purple & White.
Conference: Mid-America Intercollegiate Athletic.
SID: Melissa Ware, 816-785-4127.
AD: Jerry Wollmering.

TUFTS

Medford, MA 02155 III

Coach: Bill Samko, Connecticut 1973
Record: 13 Years, 56-54-1

2000 SCHEDULE

Wesleyan (Conn.) ■	Sept. 23
Bates	Oct. 1
Bowdoin	Oct. 7
Trinity (Conn.)	Oct. 14
Williams ■	Oct. 21
Amherst	Oct. 28
Colby	Nov. 4
Middlebury	Nov. 11

1999 RESULTS (4-4-0)

28	Hamilton	25
13	Bates	10
38	Bowdoin	13
7	Trinity (Conn.)	13
21	Williams	28
7	Amherst	10
27	Colby	26
10	Middlebury	22
151		147

Nickname: Jumbos.
Stadium: Ellis Oval (1923), 6,000 capacity. Natural turf.
Colors: Brown & Blue.
Conference: NESCAC.
SID: Paul Sweeney, 617-627-3586.
AD: Bill Gehling.

TULANE

New Orleans, LA 70118 .... I-A

Coach: Chris Scelfo, La.-Monroe 1985
Record: 2 Years, 4-8-0

2000 SCHEDULE

Mississippi	Sept. 2
East Caro.	Sept. 16
Southern Methodist	*Sept. 23
Cincinnati	Sept. 30
La.-Lafayette	Oct. 7
Southern Miss. ■	Oct. 14
Army	Oct. 21
Louisville	Oct. 28
Houston ■	Nov. 4
Navy ■	Nov. 11
Memphis ■	Nov. 18

1999 RESULTS (3-8-0)

14	Southern Miss.	48
53	Southern Methodist	19
48	Army	28
17	Syracuse	47
13	Mississippi	20
48	La.-Lafayette	32
7	East Caro.	52
7	Memphis	49
31	Houston	36
21	Navy	45
20	UAB	23
279		299

Nickname: Green Wave.
Stadium: Superdome (1975), 69,767 capacity. Artificial turf.
Colors: Olive Green & Sky Blue.
Conference: Conference USA.
SID: Richard Paige, 504-865-5506.
AD: Rick Dickson.

TULSA

Tulsa, OK 74104 .... I-A

Coach: Keith Burns, Arkansas 1984
(First year as head coach)

1999 SCHEDULE

North Carolina	Sept. 2
Oklahoma St. ■	*Sept. 9
Rice	*Sept. 16
Louisiana Tech ■	*Sept. 23
Hawaii	*Sept. 30
UTEP ■	*Oct. 7
New Mexico St.	*Oct. 14
TCU	*Oct. 21
Fresno St.	*Oct. 28
Southern Methodist	*Nov. 11
San Jose St. ■	Nov. 18
Nevada ■	Nov. 25

1999 RESULTS (2-9-0)

45	Southwest Mo. St.	21
9	Oklahoma St.	46
13	Texas A&M	62
10	San Jose St.	34
10	Rice	20
17	TCU	56
21	Hawaii	35
14	Fresno St.	28
43	UTEP	19
34	La.-Monroe	37
14	Southern Methodist	28
230		386

Nickname: Golden Hurricane.
Stadium: Skelly (1930), 40,385 capacity. Artificial turf.
Colors: Blue, Red & Gold.
Conference: Western Athletic.
SID: Don Tomkalski, 918-631-2395.
AD: Judy Mac Leod.

TUSCULUM

Greeneville, TN 37743 II

Coach: Frankie DeBusk, Furman 1991
Record: 2 Years, 7-15-0

2000 SCHEDULE

West Va. Tech ■	Aug. 26
Ark.-Monticello ■	Sept. 2
Livingstone	*Sept. 9
Jacksonville	Sept. 16
Wingate	Sept. 23
Lenoir-Rhyne ■	Sept. 30
Catawba ■	Oct. 7
Carson-Newman	Oct. 14
Newberry	*Oct. 28
Presbyterian ■	Nov. 4
Mars Hill	Nov. 11

1999 RESULTS (2-9-0)

11	Livingstone	9
21	Catawba	36
14	Lenoir-Rhyne	21
12	Carson-Newman	49
21	Presbyterian	51
7	Mars Hill	34
20	Newberry	35
14	Wingate	38
21	Gardner-Webb	24
21	Charleston So.	35
42	Jacksonville	36
204		368

Nickname: Pioneers.
Stadium: Pioneer Field (1991), 4,000 capacity. Natural turf.
Colors: Black & Orange.
Conference: South Atlantic.
SID: Dom Donnelly, 423-636-7326.
AD: Ed Hoffmeyer.

TUSKEGEE

Tuskegee, AL 36088 II

Coach: Rick Comegy, Millersville 1976
Record: 8 Years, 48-39-0

2000 SCHEDULE

Morris Brown ■	Sept. 9
Miles ■	Sept. 16
Johnson Smith ■	Sept. 23
Kentucky St. ■	Sept. 30
Albany St. (Ga.) ■	Oct. 7
Morehouse [Columbus, GA]	*Oct. 14
Fort Valley St.	Oct. 21
Clark Atlanta [La Grange, GA]	Oct. 28
Lane	Nov. 4
Savannah St.	Nov. 11
Alabama St.	Nov. 23

1999 RESULTS (9-3-0)

25	Benedict	13
14	Morris Brown	7
13	Miles	7
30	Kentucky St.	17
9	Morehouse	6
0	Alabama A&M	54

28	Fort Valley St.	31
27	Clark Atlanta	16
36	Lane	28
51	Savannah St.	36
37	Alabama St.	34
7	Winston-Salem	23
277		**272**

Nickname: Golden Tigers.
Stadium: Alumni Bowl (1925), 10,000 capacity. Natural turf.
Colors: Crimson & Gold.
Conference: Southern Intercollegiate Athletic.
SID: Arnold Houston, 334-727-8150.
AD: Rick Comegy.

UCLA
Los Angeles, CA 90095 .... I-A

Coach: Bob Toledo, San Fran. St. 1968
Record: 10 Years, 58-53-0

2000 SCHEDULE
Alabama ■	Sept. 2
Fresno St. ■	Sept. 9
Michigan ■	Sept. 16
Oregon	Sept. 23
Arizona St. ■	*Sept. 30
California	Oct. 14
Oregon St. ■	Oct. 21
Arizona	Oct. 28
Stanford ■	Nov. 4
Washington	Nov. 11
Southern California ■	Nov. 18

1999 RESULTS (4-7-0)
38	Boise St.	7
20	Ohio St.	42
35	Fresno St.	21
32	Stanford	42
27	Arizona St.	28
34	Oregon	29
0	California	17
7	Oregon St.	55
7	Arizona	33
23	Washington	20
7	Southern California	17
230		**311**

Nickname: Bruins.
Stadium: Rose Bowl (1922), 95,000 capacity. Natural turf.
Colors: Navy Blue & Gold.
Conference: Pacific-10.
SID: Marc Dellins, 310-206-6831.
AD: Peter T. Dalis.

UNION (N.Y.)
Schenectady, NY 12308 III

Coach: John Audino, Notre Dame 1975
Record: 10 Years, 71-28-0

2000 SCHEDULE
St. Lawrence ■	Sept. 9
Worcester Tech	Sept. 16
Hobart ■	Sept. 23
Alfred ■	Sept. 30
Col. of New Jersey	Oct. 7
Rensselaer ■	Oct. 14
Coast Guard ■	Oct. 21
Hartwick	Oct. 28
Rochester	Nov. 4
Springfield	Nov. 11

1999 RESULTS (8-2-0)
45	St. Lawrence	17
3	Worcester Tech	7
20	Hobart	14
17	Frank. & Marsh.	0
20	Col. of New Jersey	3
7	Rensselaer	16
24	Coast Guard	14
34	Hartwick	14
52	Rochester	0
37	Springfield	22
259		**105**

ECAC PLAYOFFS
| 31 | Ithaca | 7 |

Nickname: Dutchmen.
Stadium: Frank Bailey Field (1981), 2,000 capacity. Artificial turf.
Colors: Garnet.
Conference: Upstate Collegiate Athletic Assn.
SID: George Cuttita, 518-388-6170.
AD: Richard S. Sakala.

UPPER IOWA
Fayette, IA 52142 III

Coach: Craig Johnston, Coe 1989
(First year as head coach)

2000 SCHEDULE
Central (Iowa) ■	Sept. 2
Simpson	Sept. 9
Buena Vista ■	Sept. 16
Wartburg ■	Sept. 23
Cornell College	Sept. 30
Loras	Oct. 7
Coe ■	Oct. 14
Dubuque	Oct. 28
William Penn	Nov. 4
Luther ■	Nov. 11

1999 RESULTS (6-4-0)
7	Buena Vista	17
68	Cornell College	13
15	Loras	18
21	Simpson	7
31	Luther	14
55	Dubuque	25
32	Coe	31
0	Central (Iowa)	14
38	William Penn	7
24	Wartburg	31
291		**177**

Nickname: Peacocks.
Stadium: Eischeid (1993), 3,500 capacity. Natural turf.
Colors: Blue & White.
Conference: Iowa Intercollegiate Athletic.
SID: Karla K. Gavin, 319-425-5307.
AD: To be named.

URSINUS
Collegeville, PA 19426 III

Coach: Paul Guenther, Ursinus 1994
Record: 3 Years, 17-15-0

2000 SCHEDULE
Lebanon Valley ■	Sept. 9
Frank. & Marsh.	Sept. 16
Western Md. ■	Sept. 23
Swarthmore	Sept. 30
Johns Hopkins ■	Oct. 7
Gettysburg	Oct. 14
Wooster	Oct. 21
Muhlenberg ■	Oct. 28
Kean ■	Nov. 4
Dickinson ■	Nov. 11

1999 RESULTS (9-1-0)
25	Lebanon Valley	7
27	Frank. & Marsh.	20
15	Western Md.	36
59	Swarthmore	0
20	Johns Hopkins	18
55	Gettysburg	35
16	Wilkes	10
35	Muhlenberg	23
48	Waynesburg	35
32	Dickinson	30
332		**214**

DIVISION III CHAMPIONSHIP
| 43 | Bri'water (Mass.) | 38 |
| 0 | Rowan | 55 |

Nickname: Bears.
Stadium: Patterson Field (1923), 2,500 capacity. Natural turf.
Colors: Red, Old Gold & Black.
Conference: Centennial.

SID: William J. Stiles, 610-409-3612.
AD: William E. Akin.

UTAH
Salt Lake City, UT 84112 .... I-A

Coach: Ron McBride, San Jose St. 1963
Record: 10 Years, 71-46-0

2000 SCHEDULE
Arizona ■	*Sept. 2
California	Sept. 9
Washington St. ■	*Sept. 16
Air Force ■	Sept. 23
Utah St.	Sept. 30
San Diego St. ■	*Oct. 14
Colorado St. ■	Oct. 21
New Mexico	Oct. 28
UNLV ■	Nov. 4
Wyoming	Nov. 11
Brigham Young ■	Nov. 24

1999 RESULTS (8-3-0)
27	Washington St.	7
38	Utah St.	18
52	UNLV	14
20	Boise St.	26
42	La.-Monroe	0
21	Air Force	15
38	San Diego St.	16
24	Colorado St.	31
29	Wyoming	43
52	New Mexico	7
20	Brigham Young	17
363		**194**

LAS VEGAS BOWL
| 17 | Fresno St. | 16 |

Nickname: Utes.
Stadium: Rice-Eccles (1927), 45,634 capacity. Natural turf.
Colors: Crimson & White.
Conference: Mountain West.
SID: Liz Abel, 801-581-3511.
AD: Christopher Hill.

UTAH ST.
Logan, UT 84322 .... I-A

Coach: Mick Dennehy, Montana 1973
Record: 6 Years, 49-25-0

2000 SCHEDULE
Texas Tech	*Sept. 2
Southern Utah ■	*Sept. 9
Arizona St.	*Sept. 23
Utah ■	Sept. 30
Brigham Young	*Oct. 6
North Texas	Oct. 14
Idaho ■	Oct. 21
Arkansas St. ■	Oct. 28
New Mexico St.	*Nov. 4
Boise St.	Nov. 11
Idaho St. ■	Nov. 18

1999 RESULTS (4-7-0)
7	Georgia	38
51	Stephen F. Austin	17
18	Utah	38
31	Brigham Young	34
20	Arkansas St.	14
0	Kansas St.	40
3	Idaho	31
27	Boise St.	33
6	New Mexico St.	14
37	Nevada	35
34	North Texas	7
234		**301**

Nickname: Aggies.
Stadium: E. L. Romney (1968), 30,257 capacity. Natural turf.
Colors: Navy Blue & White.
Conference: Big West.
SID: Mike Strauss, 801-797-1361.
AD: Rance Pugmire.

VALDOSTA ST.
Valdosta, GA 31698 II

Coach: Chris Hatcher, Valdosta St. 1995
(First year as head coach)

2000 SCHEDULE
Albany St. (Ga.)	*Aug. 26
Fort Valley St. ■	*Sept. 2
Southern Ark.	*Sept. 16
Central Ark. ■	*Sept. 23
Henderson St.	Sept. 30
Delta St. ■	Oct. 7
Harding	*Oct. 14
West Ala. ■	Oct. 21
North Ala.	Oct. 28
Ouachita Baptist ■	Nov. 4
West Ga.	*Nov. 11

1999 RESULTS (4-7-0)
18	Albany St. (Ga.)	6
13	Fort Valley St.	24
39	Henderson St.	3
6	Delta St.	9
14	Arkansas Tech	21
21	West Ala.	19
14	Southern Ark.	28
33	Central Ark.	20
31	Ark.-Monticello	35
28	North Ala.	31
16	West Ga.	23
233		**219**

Nickname: Blazers.
Stadium: Cleveland Field (1922), 11,500 capacity. Natural turf.
Colors: Red & Black.
Conference: Gulf South.
SID: Steve Roberts, 912-333-5890.
AD: Herb F. Reinhard III.

VALPARAISO
Valparaiso, IN 46383 .... I-AA

Coach: Tom Horne, Wis.-La Crosse 1976
Record: 14 Years, 60-82-2

2000 SCHEDULE
Tri-State	Sept. 2
Hope	*Sept. 9
St. Francis (Ind.)	Sept. 16
Austin Peay ■	Sept. 23
Morehead St. ■	Sept. 30
Drake	Oct. 7
Butler ■	Oct. 14
St. Joseph's (Ind.)	Oct. 21
San Diego	*Oct. 28
Dayton ■	Nov. 4
Aurora ■	Nov. 11

1999 RESULTS (9-2-0)
35	St. Francis (Ind.)	6
17	Robert Morris	13
2	Yale	48
27	Drake	17
38	Butler	20
31	Morehead St.	21
14	San Diego	7
10	Dayton	34
33	St. Joseph's (Ind.)	10
31	Aurora	0
52	Austin Peay	23
290		**199**

Nickname: Crusaders.
Stadium: Brown Field (1947), 5,000 capacity. Natural turf.
Colors: Brown & Gold.
Conference: Pioneer Football.
SID: Bill Rogers, 219-464-5232.
AD: William L. Steinbrecher.

VANDERBILT
Nashville, TN 37212 .... I-A

Coach: Woody Widenhofer, Missouri 1965
Record: 7 Years, 22-54-1

2000 SCHEDULE
Miami (Ohio) ■	*Sept. 2
Alabama	Sept. 9
Mississippi ■	Sept. 16
Duke ■	Sept. 23
Auburn	Sept. 30
Wake Forest	Oct. 7
Georgia	Oct. 14
South Carolina ■	Oct. 21
Florida	Nov. 4
Kentucky	Nov. 11
Tennessee	Nov. 25

1999 RESULTS (5-6-0)
17	Alabama	28
34	Northern Ill.	31
37	Mississippi	34
31	Duke	14
14	Mississippi St.	42
58	Citadel	0
17	Georgia	27
11	South Carolina	10
6	Florida	13
17	Kentucky	19
10	Tennessee	38
252		**256**

Nickname: Commodores.
Stadium: Vanderbilt Stadium (1981), 41,600 capacity. Natural turf.
Colors: Black & Gold.
Conference: Southeastern.
SID: Rod Williamson, 615-322-4121.
AD: William T. Turner.

VILLANOVA
Villanova, PA 19085 .... I-AA

Coach: Andy Talley, Southern Conn. St. 1967
Record: 20 Years, 128-78-2

2000 SCHEDULE
Rutgers	*Sept. 2
Millersville ■	Sept. 9
Norfolk St. ■	Sept. 16
Maine ■	Sept. 23
James Madison	Oct. 7
Northeastern	Oct. 14
New Hampshire ■	Oct. 21
Richmond ■	Oct. 28
Massachusetts	Nov. 4
William & Mary ■	Nov. 11
Delaware	Nov. 18

1999 RESULTS (7-4-0)
13	Air Force	37
35	Richmond	30
26	Massachusetts	21
34	Pennsylvania	6
20	James Madison	23
10	William & Mary	45
48	Connecticut	45
45	Northeastern	16
31	New Hampshire	28
21	Youngstown St.	28
51	Delaware	45
334		**324**

Nickname: Wildcats.
Stadium: Villanova (1927), 12,000 capacity. Artificial turf.
Colors: Blue & White.
Conference: Atlantic 10.
SID: Dean Kenefick, 610-519-4120.
AD: Tim Hofferth.

VIRGINIA
Charlottesville, VA 22903 .... I-A

Coach: George Welsh, Navy 1956
Record: 27 Years, 183-126-4

2000 SCHEDULE
Brigham Young	Sept. 2
Richmond ■	Sept. 9
Duke	Sept. 16
Clemson ■	Sept. 23
Wake Forest	Sept. 30
Maryland ■	Oct. 7
Florida St.	Oct. 21
North Carolina ■	Oct. 28
Georgia Tech	*Nov. 9
North Carolina St. ■	Nov. 18
Virginia Tech	Nov. 25

1999 RESULTS (7-4-0)
20	North Carolina	17
14	Clemson	33
35	Wake Forest	7
45	Brigham Young	40
7	Virginia Tech	31
17	Duke	24
47	North Carolina St.	26
10	Florida St.	35
45	Georgia Tech	38
50	Buffalo	21
34	Maryland	30
324		**302**

MICRONPC.COM BOWL
21	Illinois	63

Nickname: Cavaliers.
Stadium: Smith/Harrison/Scott (1931), 61,500 capacity. Natural turf.
Colors: Orange & Blue.
Conference: Atlantic Coast.
SID: Rich Murray, 804-982-5500.
AD: M. Terrance Holland.

VMI
Lexington, VA 24450 .... I-AA

Coach: Cal McCombs, Citadel 1967
Record: 1 Year, 1-10-0

2000 SCHEDULE
Duquesne ■	Sept. 2
William & Mary	Sept. 9
East Tenn. St.	Sept. 16
Furman ■	Sept. 23
Ga. Southern	Sept. 30
Wofford	Oct. 7
Chattanooga	*Oct. 14
Charleston So. ■	Oct. 21
Western Caro. ■	Oct. 28
Appalachian St.	Nov. 4
Citadel	Nov. 11

1999 RESULTS (1-10-0)
6	Richmond	42
15	Concord	14
17	East Tenn. St.	26
0	Furman	58
0	Ga. Southern	62
10	Wofford	55
0	Chattanooga	27
14	William & Mary	35
2	Western Caro.	40
7	Appalachian St.	34
6	Citadel	7
77		**400**

Nickname: Keydets.
Stadium: Alumni Field (1962), 10,000 capacity. Natural turf.
Colors: Red, White, Yellow.
Conference: Southern.
SID: Wade Branner, 703-464-7253.
AD: Donald T. White.

VIRGINIA ST.
Petersburg, VA 23806 II

Coach: Louis Anderson, Claflin 1961
Record: 9 Years, 56-36-0

2000 SCHEDULE
Norfolk St.	*Sept. 2
N.C. Central	Sept. 16
Savannah St. ■	*Sept. 23
Livingstone ■	Sept. 30
Elizabeth City St.	Oct. 7
Fayetteville St.	*Oct. 14
Winston-Salem ■	Oct. 21
Virginia Union	Oct. 28
Bowie St.	Nov. 4

1999 RESULTS (6-4-0)
7	Norfolk St.	19
27	Johnson Smith	6
35	N.C. Central	28
21	Savannah St.	31
17	Livingstone	0
50	Fayetteville St.	7
14	Winston-Salem	17
27	Virginia Union	31
56	Bowie St.	32
45	Elizabeth City St.	17
299		**188**

Nickname: Trojans.
Stadium: Rogers (1950), 13,500 capacity. Natural turf.
Colors: Orange & Navy Blue.
Conference: Central Intercollegiate Athletic Assn.
SID: Gregory C. Goings, 804-524-5028.
AD: Edward Cooper.

VIRGINIA TECH
Blacksburg, VA 24061 .... I-A

Coach: Frank Beamer, Virginia Tech 1969
Record: 19 Years, 130-83-4

2000 SCHEDULE
Georgia Tech ■	*Aug. 27
Akron ■	Sept. 2
East Caro.	*Sept. 7
Rutgers ■	Sept. 16
Boston College	Sept. 30
Temple ■	Oct. 7
West Virginia ■	*Oct. 12
Syracuse	Oct. 21
Pittsburgh ■	Oct. 28
Miami (Fla.)	Nov. 4
UCF	*Nov. 11
Virginia ■	Nov. 25

1999 RESULTS (11-0-0)
47	James Madison	0
31	UAB	10
31	Clemson	11
31	Virginia	7
58	Rutgers	20
62	Syracuse	0
30	Pittsburgh	17
22	West Virginia	20
43	Miami (Fla.)	10
62	Temple	7
38	Boston College	14
455		**116**

SUGAR BOWL
29	Florida St.	46

Nickname: Hokies.
Stadium: Lane (1965), 50,000 capacity. Natural turf.
Colors: Orange & Maroon.
Conference: Big East.
SID: Dave Smith, 540-231-6726.
AD: James C. Weaver.

VIRGINIA UNION
Richmond, VA 23220 II

Coach: Willard Bailey, Norfolk St. 1962
Record: 27 Years, 183-97-7

2000 SCHEDULE
Elizabeth City St.	*Sept. 2
Morehouse ■	Sept. 9
Livingstone [Roanoke, VA]	Sept. 16
Winston-Salem	*Sept. 23
Bowie St.	Sept. 30
Johnson Smith ■	Oct. 7
Gardner-Webb	Oct. 14
N.C. Central	Oct. 21
Virginia St. ■	Oct. 28
Fayetteville St.	Nov. 4

1999 RESULTS (8-2-0)
12	Liberty	21
41	Cheyney	12
24	Livingstone	6
0	Winston-Salem	17
39	Bowie St.	6
40	Elizabeth City St.	6
21	Norfolk St.	9
31	Virginia St.	27
49	Fayetteville St.	14
50	Johnson Smith	6
307		**124**

Nickname: Panthers.
Stadium: Hovey Field (NA), 10,000 capacity. Natural turf.
Colors: Steel & Maroon.
Conference: Central Intercollegiate Athletic Assn.
SID: Paul Williams, 804-342-1233.
AD: James F. Battle.

WABASH
Crawfordsville, IN 47933 III

Coach: Greg Carlson, Wis.-Oshkosh 1970
Record: 17 Years, 106-53-2

2000 SCHEDULE
Manchester	Sept. 9
Wheaton (Ill.)	Sept. 16
Wittenberg ■	Sept. 23
Oberlin ■	Sept. 30
Wooster	Oct. 7
Earlham	Oct. 14
Hiram	Oct. 21
Allegheny ■	Oct. 28
Denison ■	Nov. 4
DePauw ■	Nov. 11

1999 RESULTS (5-5-0)
6	Ohio Northern	38
20	Washington (Mo.)	24
34	Mt. St. Joseph	21
31	Anderson (Ind.)	13
27	Bluffton	7
23	Manchester	3
30	Wilmington (Ohio)	32
31	Franklin	21
18	Hanover	28
7	DePauw	21
227		**208**

Nickname: Little Giants.
Stadium: Little Giant (1967), 4,200 capacity. Natural turf.
Colors: Scarlet & White.
Conference: North Coast Athletic.
SID: Brent Harris, 317-361-6364.
AD: Vernon H. Mummert.

WAGNER
Staten Island, NY 10301 .... I-AA

Coach: Walt Hameline, Brockport St. 1975
Record: 19 Years, 141-56-2

2000 SCHEDULE
Monmouth ■	Sept. 9
Georgetown ■	Sept. 16
Albany (N.Y.)	*Sept. 23
Marist ■	Sept. 30
Stony Brook ■	Oct. 7
Central Conn. St.	Oct. 14
St. Francis (Pa.)	Oct. 21
Robert Morris ■	Oct. 28
St. John's (N.Y.) ■	Nov. 4
Jacksonville	Nov. 11
Sacred Heart	Nov. 18

1999 RESULTS (5-5-0)
24	Stony Brook	12
33	Sacred Heart	0
45	St. Francis (Pa.)	13
21	Robert Morris	23
21	Albany (N.Y.)	37
35	Central Conn. St.	16
17	Marist	20
14	Cornell	31
35	Monmouth	3
12	San Diego	31
257		**186**

Nickname: Seahawks.
Stadium: Wagner (1997), 3,300 capacity. Natural turf.
Colors: Green & White.
Conference: Northeast.
SID: Bob Balut, 718-390-3227.
AD: Walt Hameline.

WAKE FOREST
Winston-Salem, NC 27109 .... I-A

Coach: Jim Caldwell, Iowa 1977
Record: 7 Years, 24-54-0

2000 SCHEDULE
Appalachian St. ■	*Aug. 31
North Carolina ■	*Sept. 9
Clemson	Sept. 16
Virginia ■	Sept. 30
Vanderbilt ■	Oct. 7
Georgia Tech	Oct. 14
Maryland	Oct. 21
Duke ■	Nov. 4
Florida St. ■	Nov. 11
Navy	Nov. 18
North Carolina St.	Nov. 25

1999 RESULTS (6-5-0)
34	Army	15
7	Virginia	35
31	North Carolina St.	7
17	Rutgers	10
14	Maryland	17
10	Florida St.	33
47	UAB	3
3	Clemson	12
19	North Carolina	3
35	Duke	48
26	Georgia Tech	23
243		**206**

ALOHA CLASSIC
23	Arizona St.	3

Nickname: Demon Deacons.
Stadium: Groves (1968), 31,500 capacity. Natural turf.
Colors: Old Gold & Black.
Conference: Atlantic Coast.
SID: To be named, 910-759-5640.
AD: Ronald D. Wellman.

WARTBURG
Waverly, IA 50677 III

Coach: Rick Willis, Cornell College 1988
Record: 3 Years, 26-5-0

2000 SCHEDULE
Dubuque	Sept. 2
Cornell College ■	Sept. 9
William Penn	Sept. 16
Upper Iowa	Sept. 23
Buena Vista ■	Oct. 7
Luther ■	Oct. 14
Coe	Oct. 21
Simpson ■	Oct. 28
Central (Iowa)	Nov. 4
Loras ■	Nov. 11

1999 RESULTS (10-0-0)
51	William Penn	16
49	Buena Vista	27
56	Cornell College	13
30	Loras	19
42	Simpson	10
20	Luther	17
28	Dubuque	0
33	Coe	13
40	Central (Iowa)	23
31	Upper Iowa	24
380		**162**

DIVISION III CHAMPIONSHIP
14	Pacific Lutheran	49

Nickname: Knights.
Stadium: Schield (1956), 2,500 capacity. Natural turf.
Colors: Orange & Black.
Conference: Iowa Intercollegiate Athletic.
SID: Duane Schroeder, 319-352-8277.
AD: Gary Grace.

WASHBURN
Topeka, KS 66621 II

Coach: Tony DeMeo, Iona 1971
Record: 17 Years, 86-71-4

2000 SCHEDULE
Wis.-La Crosse ■	*Sept. 2
Lincoln (Mo.)	Sept. 9
Mo. Southern St.	*Sept. 16
Mo. Western St. ■	*Sept. 23
Central Mo. St.	Sept. 30
Mo.-Rolla	Oct. 7
Southwest Baptist ■	Oct. 14
Pittsburg St.	Oct. 21
Northwest Mo. St. ■	Oct. 28
Truman	Nov. 4
Emporia St. ■	Nov. 11

1999 RESULTS (6-5-0)
24	Wis.-La Crosse	21
17	Fort Hays St.	14
35	Mo. Southern St.	28
10	Mo. Western St.	42
18	Central Mo. St.	32
53	Mo.-Rolla	18
36	Southwest Baptist	0
8	Pittsburg St.	27
10	Northwest Mo. St.	35
52	Truman	18
20	Emporia St.	45
283		**280**

Nickname: Ichabods.
Stadium: Moore Bowl (1928), 7,200 capacity. Natural turf.
Colors: Yale Blue & White.
Conference: Mid-America Intercollegiate Athletic.
SID: Gene Cassell, 913-231-1010.
AD: Loren Ferré'.

WASHINGTON
Seattle, WA 98195 ....I-A

Coach: Rick Neuheisel, UCLA 1984
Record: 5 Years, 40-19-0

2000 SCHEDULE
Idaho ■	Sept. 2
Miami (Fla.) ■	Sept. 9
Colorado	Sept. 16
Oregon	Sept. 30
Oregon St. ■	*Oct. 7
Arizona St.	*Oct. 14
California ■	Oct. 21
Stanford	Oct. 28
Arizona ■	Nov. 4
UCLA ■	Nov. 11
Washington St.	Nov. 18

1999 RESULTS (7-4-0)
28	Brigham Young	35
21	Air Force	31
31	Colorado	24
34	Oregon	20
47	Oregon St.	21
7	Arizona St.	28
31	California	27
35	Stanford	30
33	Arizona	25
20	UCLA	23
24	Washington St.	14
311		**278**

HOLIDAY BOWL
20	Kansas St.	24

Nickname: Huskies.
Stadium: Husky (1920), 72,500 capacity. Artificial turf.
Colors: Purple & Gold.
Conference: Pacific-10.
SID: Jim Daves, 206-543-2230.
AD: Barbara A. Hedges.

WASH. & JEFF.
Washington, PA 15301 III

Coach: John Banaszak, Eastern Mich. 1975
Record: 1 Year, 9-3-0

2000 SCHEDULE
Allegheny	Sept. 9
Randolph-Macon ■	Sept. 16
Hanover	Sept. 23
Westminster (Pa.) ■	Sept. 30
Grove City	Oct. 7
Bethany (W.Va.)	Oct. 14
Waynesburg ■	Oct. 21
Thiel	Oct. 28
Malone ■	Nov. 4
Buffalo St.	Nov. 11

1999 RESULTS (8-2-0)
24	Emory & Henry	17
19	Allegheny	13
55	Randolph-Macon	28
13	Hanover	30
33	Cortland St.	28
33	Grove City	10
42	Bethany (W.Va.)	13
56	Waynesburg	28
21	Buffalo St.	40
51	Thiel	6
347		**213**

DIVISION III CHAMPIONSHIP
14	Lycoming	7
3	Hardin-Simmons	51

Nickname: Presidents.
Stadium: College Field (1958), 5,000 capacity. Natural turf.
Colors: Red & Black.
Conference: Presidents' Athletic.
SID: Jewel J. John, 412-223-6074.
AD: John L. Luckhardt.

WASH. & LEE
Lexington, VA 24450 III

Coach: Frank Miriello, East Stroudsburg 1967
Record: 5 Years, 23-25-1

2000 SCHEDULE
Johns Hopkins ■	Sept. 9
Guilford	Sept. 16
Centre	Sept. 23
Randolph-Macon ■	Sept. 30
Catholic	Oct. 7
Hampden-Sydney ■	Oct. 14
Sewanee	Oct. 21
Bridgewater (Va.)	Oct. 28
Emory & Henry ■	Nov. 4
Swarthmore	Nov. 11

1999 RESULTS (5-5-0)
14	Johns Hopkins	31
20	Guilford	22
23	Centre	17
23	Randolph-Macon	30
28	Davidson	35
24	Hampden-Sydney	12
31	Sewanee	28
44	Bridgewater (Va.)	38
21	Emory & Henry	23
40	Swarthmore	13
268		**249**

Nickname: Generals.
Stadium: Wilson Field (1930), 7,000 capacity. Natural turf.
Colors: Royal Blue & White.
Conference: Old Dominion Athletic.
SID: Brian Laubscher, 540-463-8676.
AD: Michael F. Walsh.

WASHINGTON (MO.)
St. Louis, MO 63130 III

Coach: Larry Kindbom, Kalamazoo 1974
Record: 17 Years, 98-70-1

2000 SCHEDULE
Westminster (Mo.) ■	*Sept. 2
Ill. Wesleyan	Sept. 9
Case Reserve ■	Sept. 16
Albion	Sept. 23
Rhodes	Sept. 30
Trinity (Tex.)	Oct. 7
Carnegie Mellon ■	*Oct. 14
Rochester	*Oct. 21
Chicago	Oct. 28
Colorado Col. ■	Nov. 4

1999 RESULTS (8-2-0)
25	Rose-Hulman	13
12	Wheaton (Ill.)	35
24	Wabash	20
42	Case Reserve	7
12	Rhodes	7
15	Trinity (Tex.)	25
41	Rochester	7
24	Carnegie Mellon	7
20	Chicago	3
23	Colorado Col.	0
238		**124**

DIVISION III CHAMPIONSHIP
21	Hardin-Simmons	28

Nickname: Bears.
Stadium: Francis Field (1904), 4,000 capacity. Natural turf.
Colors: Red & Green.
Conference: University Athletic Assoc.
SID: Keith Jenkins, 314-935-5077.
AD: John M. Schael.

WASHINGTON ST.
Pullman, WA 99164 ....I-A

Coach: Mike Price, Puget Sound 1969
Record: 19 Years, 105-110-0

2000 SCHEDULE
Stanford ■	*Sept. 2
Utah	*Sept. 16
Idaho ■	Sept. 23
California	Sept. 30
Boise St. ■	Oct. 7
Arizona	*Oct. 14
Arizona St. ■	Oct. 21
Oregon St.	Oct. 28
Oregon ■	Nov. 4
Southern California	Nov. 11
Washington ■	Nov. 18

1999 RESULTS (3-9-0)
7	Utah	27
17	Stanford	54
17	Idaho	28
24	Arizona	30
31	California	7
44	La.-Lafayette	0
21	Arizona St.	33
13	Oregon St.	27
10	Oregon	52
28	Southern California	31
14	Washington	24
22	Hawaii	14
248		**327**

Nickname: Cougars.
Stadium: Clarence D. Martin (1972), 37,600 capacity. Artificial turf.
Colors: Crimson & Gray.
Conference: Pacific-10.
SID: Rod Commons, 509-335-2684.
AD: Richard P. Dickson.

WAYNE ST. (MICH.)
Detroit, MI 48202 II

Coach: Steve Kazor, Westminster 1972
Record: 4 Years, 27-13-0

2000 SCHEDULE
Mercyhurst	Sept. 2
Ashland ■	Sept. 9
Ferris St.	Sept. 23
Findlay ■	Sept. 30
Northern Mich. ■	Oct. 7
Hillsdale	*Oct. 14
Saginaw Valley ■	Oct. 21

Indianapolis ....Oct. 28
Grand Valley St. ■ ....Nov. 4
Northwood ....Nov. 11

1999 RESULTS (0-11-0)

35	Mercyhurst	49
15	Findlay	39
33	Saginaw Valley	45
7	Ashland	46
24	Northwood	27
20	Ferris St.	62
19	Indianapolis	26
9	Hillsdale	24
10	Michigan Tech	22
14	Westminster (Pa.)	24
15	St. Joseph's (Ind.)	23
201		**387**

Nickname: Tartars.
Stadium: Wayne State (1968), 6,000 capacity. Natural turf.
Colors: Green & Gold.
Conference: Great Lakes Intercollegiate Athletic.
SID: Lisa McCoy, 313-577-7542.
AD: Bob V. Brennan.

WAYNE ST. (NEB.)
Wayne, NE 68787 II

Coach: Scott Hoffman, Nebraska 1978
Record: 4 Years, 16-23-0

2000 SCHEDULE

Neb.-Kearney ....*Aug. 31
South Dakota St. ....Sept. 9
Bemidji St. ■ ....Sept. 16
Winona St. ■ ....Sept. 23
Minn.-Crookston ....Sept. 30
Moorhead St. ■ ....Oct. 7
Concordia-St. Paul ....Oct. 14
Southwest St. ■ ....Oct. 21
Minn.-Duluth ....Oct. 28
Minn.-Morris ■ ....Nov. 4

1999 RESULTS (3-8-0)

17	Neb.-Kearney	59
31	South Dakota St.	59
38	Bemidji St.	52
28	Winona St.	42
35	Minn.-Crookston	28
25	Moorhead St.	31
39	Concordia-St. Paul	21
16	Southwest St.	44
19	Minn.-Duluth	31
70	Minn.-Morris	21
30	Northwestern Okla.	71
348		**459**

Nickname: Wildcats.
Stadium: Memorial (1931), 3,500 capacity. Natural turf.
Colors: Black & Gold.
Conference: Division II Independent.
SID: Kevin Ludwig, 403-375-7326.
AD: To be named.

WAYNESBURG
Waynesburg, PA 15370 III

Coach: Dan Baranik, Shippensburg 1984
Record: 6 Years, 26-28-0

2000 SCHEDULE

Marietta ■ ....Sept. 2
Denison ■ ....Sept. 9
Ohio Wesleyan ....Sept. 16
Averett ....Sept. 23
Bethany (W.Va.) ■ ....Sept. 30
Thiel ....Oct. 7
Grove City ■ ....Oct. 14
Wash. & Jeff. ....Oct. 21
Juniata ....Nov. 4
Westminster (Pa.) ....Nov. 11

1999 RESULTS (5-4-0)

28	Marietta	23
37	Manchester	39
50	Gannon	43
26	Bethany (W.Va.)	21
40	Thiel	7
24	Grove City	28
28	Wash. & Jeff.	56
35	Ursinus	48
48	Wm. Paterson	7
316		**272**

Nickname: Yellow Jackets.
Stadium: John F. Wiley (1904), 4,000 capacity. Natural turf.
Colors: Orange & Black.
Conference: Presidents' Athletic.
SID: Jessica Hajek, 412-852-3334.
AD: Rudy Marisa.

WEBER ST.
Ogden, UT 84408 ....I-AA

Coach: Jerry Graybeal, Eastern Wash. 1981
Record: 2 Years, 9-13-0

2000 SCHEDULE

Western St. (Colo.) ■ ....*Aug. 31
Toledo ....*Sept. 9
Montana St. ....Sept. 16
Eastern Wash. ■ ....*Sept. 23
Cal St. Sacramento ....*Sept. 30
Cal St. Northridge ■ ....*Oct. 5
Northern Ariz. ....Oct. 14
Portland St. ....Oct. 21
Idaho St. ....*Oct. 28
Western N.M. ■ ....Nov. 4
Montana ■ ....Nov. 11

1999 RESULTS (3-8-0)

33	Western St. (Colo.)	3
16	Wyoming	41
27	Idaho St.	24
22	Montana	81
52	Cal St. Sacramento	49
6	Montana St.	29
7	Southern Utah	39
14	Portland St.	31
28	Cal St. Northridge	30
19	Northern Ariz.	36
27	Eastern Wash.	30
251		**393**

Nickname: Wildcats.
Stadium: Wildcat (1966), 17,500 capacity. Natural turf.
Colors: Purple & White.
Conference: Big Sky.
SID: Brad Larsen, 801-626-6010.
AD: John W. Johnson.

WESLEY
Dover, DE 19901 III

Coach: Mike Drass, Mansfield 1983
Record: 7 Years, 50-20-1

2000 SCHEDULE

Rowan ....Sept. 9
Mount Ida ■ ....Sept. 16
Kean ....Sept. 23
Greensboro ....Sept. 30
Frostburg St. ....Oct. 7
Newport News ■ ....Oct. 14
Methodist ■ ....Oct. 21
Salisbury St. ....Oct. 28
Chowan ....Nov. 4
Ferrum ■ ....Nov. 11

1999 RESULTS (6-4-0)

6	Rowan	29
43	Mount Ida	6
19	Butler	34
35	Greensboro	21
17	Frostburg St.	42
48	Newport News	33
34	Methodist	20
14	Salisbury St.	7
40	Chowan	14
7	Ferrum	9
263		**215**

Nickname: Wolverines.
Stadium: Wolverine (1989), 2,000 capacity. Natural turf.
Colors: Navy Blue & White.
Conference: Atlantic Central Football.
SID: Jason Bowen, 302-736-2557.
AD: Steve D. Clark.

WESLEYAN (CONN.)
Middletown, CT 06459 III

Coach: Frank Hauser, Wesleyan 1979
Record: 8 Years, 36-28-0

2000 SCHEDULE

Tufts ....Sept. 23
Hamilton ■ ....Sept. 30
Colby ....Oct. 7
Bates ....Oct. 14
Amherst ■ ....Oct. 21
Bowdoin ■ ....Oct. 28
Williams ....Nov. 4
Trinity (Conn.) ■ ....Nov. 11

1999 RESULTS (5-3-0)

28	Middlebury	21
34	Hamilton	6
7	Colby	13
36	Bates	29
14	Amherst	28
35	Bowdoin	14
33	Williams	28
12	Trinity (Conn.)	26
199		**165**

Nickname: Cardinals.
Stadium: Andrus Field (1881), 8,000 capacity. Natural turf.
Colors: Red & Black.
Conference: NESCAC.
SID: Brian Katten, 203-685-2887.
AD: John S. Biddiscombe.

WEST ALA.
Livingston, AL 35470 II

Coach: Bobby Johns, Alabama 1968
Record: 3 Years, 8-23-0

2000 SCHEDULE

Stillman ....Sept. 2
Miles ....Sept. 9
Delta St. ■ ....Sept. 16
Ark.-Monticello ....*Sept. 23
Southern Ark. ■ ....Sept. 30
Arkansas Tech ....Oct. 7
West Ga. ■ ....Oct. 14
Valdosta St. ....Oct. 21
Ouachita Baptist ....Oct. 28
Harding ■ ....Nov. 4
North Ala. ■ ....Nov. 11

1999 RESULTS (1-10-0)

6	Belhaven	16
19	Harding	21
17	Arkansas Tech	32
28	Henderson St.	7
20	Delta St.	27
19	Valdosta St.	21
6	West Ga.	20
24	Southern Ark.	30
10	Central Ark.	26
17	Ark.-Monticello	23
33	North Ala.	51
199		**274**

Nickname: Tigers.
Stadium: Tiger (NA), 7,000 capacity. Natural turf.
Colors: Red, White & Black.
Conference: Gulf South.
SID: Kevin Graber, 205-652-3596.
AD: Curtis "Dee" Outlaw.

WEST CHESTER
West Chester, PA 19383 II

Coach: Rick Daniels, West Chester 1975
Record: 11 Years, 74-44-1

2000 SCHEDULE

New Haven ■ ....*Aug. 31

East Stroudsburg ■	*Sept. 9
UC Davis ■	Sept. 16
Delaware	*Sept. 23
Bloomsburg ■	*Sept. 30
Mansfield	Oct. 7
Kutztown	Oct. 14
Millersville ■	*Oct. 21
Edinboro ■	Oct. 28
Cheyney	Nov. 4
Clarion	Nov. 11

1999 RESULTS (7-3-0)
9	Indiana (Pa.)	12
10	Delaware	29
30	Shippensburg	48
49	East Stroudsburg	3
42	Mansfield	6
35	Bloomsburg	17
40	Millersville	35
62	Clarion	20
56	Cheyney	23
55	Kutztown	30
388		223

Nickname: Golden Rams.
Stadium: Farrell (1970), 7,500 capacity. Natural turf.
Colors: Purple & Gold.
Conference: Pennsylvania State Athletic.
SID: Tom Di Camillo, 610-436-3316.
AD: Edward Matejkovic.

WEST GA.
Carrollton, GA 30118 II

Coach: Glenn Spencer, Georgia Tech 1986
Record: 2 Years, 18-5-0

2000 SCHEDULE
Presbyterian ■	*Sept. 2
Henderson St. ■	*Sept. 16
Arkansas Tech ■	*Sept. 23
Ark.-Monticello	Sept. 30
Southern Ark. ■	*Oct. 7
West Ala.	Oct. 14
Ouachita Baptist	Oct. 21
Harding ■	Oct. 28
North Ala.	Nov. 4
Valdosta St. ■	*Nov. 11

1999 RESULTS (8-3-0)
40	Presbyterian	41
20	Ark.-Monticello	10
38	Central Ark.	14
24	Southern Ark.	29
34	Morehead St.	28
21	North Ala.	7
20	West Ala.	6
42	Delta St.	31
33	Henderson St.	13
23	Arkansas Tech	41
23	Valdosta St.	16
318		236

Nickname: Braves.
Stadium: Grisham (1966), 6,500 capacity. Natural turf.
Colors: Blue & Red.
Conference: Gulf South.
SID: Mitch Gray, 770-836-6542.
AD: Edward G. Murphy.

WEST LIBERTY ST.
West Liberty, WV 26074 II

Coach: Bob Eaton, Glenville St. 1978
Record: 10 Years, 46-53-1

2000 SCHEDULE
Virginia-Wise ■	Sept. 2
Walsh	Sept. 16
Westminster (Pa.) [Wheeling, WV]	*Sept. 23
West Virginia St.	Sept. 30
Concord	Oct. 7
West Va. Wesleyan ■	Oct. 14
Fairmont St.	Oct. 21
West Va. Tech	Oct. 28
Shepherd ■	Nov. 4
Glenville St. ■	Nov. 11

1999 RESULTS (6-4-0)
36	Mansfield	15
13	Virginia-Wise	7
6	Walsh	21
19	West Virginia St.	17
17	Concord	13
28	West Va. Wesleyan	3
19	Fairmont St.	29
27	West Va. Tech	10
7	Shepherd	56
34	Glenville St.	44
206		215

Nickname: Hilltoppers.
Stadium: Russek Field (1960), 4,000 capacity. Natural turf.
Colors: Gold & Black.
Conference: West Virginia Intercollegiate Athletic.
SID: Lynn Ullom, 304-336-8320.
AD: James W. Watson.

WEST TEX. A&M
Canyon, TX 79016 II

Coach: Stan McGarvey, William Jewell 1972
Record: 15 Years, 97-62-4

2000 SCHEDULE
Western N.M. ■	*Aug. 26
Midwestern St.	*Sept. 9
Western Wash.	Sept. 16
Northeastern St. ■	*Sept. 23
Angelo St. ■	*Sept. 30
Tarleton St.	*Oct. 7
Tex. A&M-Commerce ■	*Oct. 14
Texas A&M-Kingsville	*Oct. 21
East Central	Oct. 28
Eastern N.M. ■	Nov. 4
Abilene Christian	*Nov. 11

1999 RESULTS (3-8-0)
30	Okla. Panhandle	20
20	Central Ark.	27
20	Southwestern Okla.	25
24	Southeastern Okla.	31
7	Angelo St.	28
7	Tarleton St.	6
3	Tex. A&M-Commerce	9
14	Texas A&M-Kingsville	35
0	Midwestern St.	24
16	Eastern N.M.	24
21	Abilene Christian	9
162		238

Nickname: Buffaloes.
Stadium: Kimbrough (1959), 20,000 capacity. Natural turf.
Colors: Maroon & White.
Conference: Lone Star.
SID: Bill Kauffman, 806-656-2687.
AD: Ed Harris.

WEST VIRGINIA
Morgantown, WV 26506 .... I-A

Coach: Don Nehlen, Bowling Green 1958
Record: 29 Years, 195-123-8

2000 SCHEDULE
Boston College ■	Sept. 2
Maryland ■	Sept. 16
Miami (Fla.) ■	Sept. 23
Temple	*Sept. 28
Idaho ■	Oct. 7
Virginia Tech	*Oct. 12
Notre Dame ■	Oct. 21
Syracuse	Nov. 4
Rutgers	Nov. 11
East Caro. ■	Nov. 18
Pittsburgh	Nov. 24

1999 RESULTS (4-7-0)
23	East Caro.	30
43	Miami (Ohio)	27
0	Maryland	33
7	Syracuse	30
28	Navy	31
62	Rutgers	16
20	Temple	17
20	Miami (Fla.)	28
20	Virginia Tech	22
17	Boston College	34
52	Pittsburgh	21
292		289

Nickname: Mountaineers.
Stadium: Mountaineer Field (1980), 63,500 capacity. Artificial turf.
Colors: Old Gold & Blue.
Conference: Big East.
SID: Shelly Poe, 304-293-2821.
AD: Ed Pastilong.

WEST VIRGINIA ST.
Institute, WV 25112 II

Coach: Carl Lee, Marshall 1983
Record: 4 Years, 17-26-0

2000 SCHEDULE
Kentucky St.	Sept. 2
Wingate	Sept. 9
Charleston So.	Sept. 16
Bowie St. ■	Sept. 23
West Liberty St. ■	Sept. 30
West Va. Wesleyan	Oct. 7
West Va. Tech	Oct. 14
Shepherd ■	Oct. 21
Concord ■	Oct. 28
Glenville St.	Nov. 4
Fairmont St.	Nov. 11

1999 RESULTS (5-5-0)
35	West Va. Tech	0
14	Newberry	16
55	Wingate	14
17	West Liberty St.	19
7	West Va. Wesleyan	13
40	West Va. Tech	17
14	Shepherd	63
42	Concord	14
32	Glenville St.	24
20	Fairmont St.	31
276		211

Nickname: Yellow Jackets.
Stadium: Lakin Field (NA), 5,000 capacity. Natural turf.
Colors: Old Gold & Black.
Conference: West Virginia Intercollegiate Athletic.
SID: Sean McAndrews, 304-766-3238.
AD: S. Bryce Casto.

WEST VA. TECH
Montgomery, WV 25136 II

Coach: Mike Springston, West Va. Tech 1982
Record: 1 Year, 1-10-0

2000 SCHEDULE
Tusculum	Aug. 26
Illinois St.	*Aug. 31
Gannon	Sept. 16
Quincy	Sept. 23
Fairmont St.	Sept. 30
Shepherd ■	Oct. 7
West Virginia St. ■	Oct. 14
Glenville St.	Oct. 21
West Liberty St. ■	Oct. 28
West Va. Wesleyan	Nov. 4
Concord ■	Nov. 11

1999 RESULTS (1-10-0)
0	West Virginia St.	35
21	Frostburg St.	38
19	Virginia-Wise	49
0	East Tenn. St.	61
24	Fairmont St.	37
6	Shepherd	60
17	West Virginia St.	40
17	Glenville St.	46
10	West Liberty St.	27
6	West Va. Wesleyan	10
26	Concord	21
146		424

Nickname: Golden Bears.
Stadium: Martin Field (NA), 2,500 capacity. Artificial turf.
Colors: Blue & Gold.
Conference: West Virginia Intercollegiate Athletic.
SID: Russ Melvin Jr., 304-442-3085.
AD: Michael Neese.

WEST VA. WESLEYAN
Buckhannon, WV 26201 II

Coach: Bill Struble, West Va. Wesleyan 1976
Record: 17 Years, 77-92-0

2000 SCHEDULE
Slippery Rock ■	Sept. 9
Calif. (Pa.)	*Sept. 16
Newberry ■	Sept. 23
Glenville St. ■	Sept. 30
West Virginia St.	Oct. 7
West Liberty St.	Oct. 14
Concord ■	Oct. 21
Fairmont St.	Oct. 28
West Va. Tech ■	Nov. 4
Shepherd	Nov. 11

1999 RESULTS (2-8-0)
3	Slippery Rock	38
8	Calif. (Pa.)	42
0	Catawba	36
7	Glenville St.	17
13	West Virginia St.	7
3	West Liberty St.	28
7	Concord	20
26	Fairmont St.	55
10	West Va. Tech	6
3	Shepherd	55
80		304

Nickname: Bobcats.
Stadium: Cebe Ross Field (0000), 3,500 capacity. Natural turf.
Colors: Orange & Black.
Conference: West Virginia Intercollegiate Athletic.
SID: Peter Galarneau Jr., 304-473-8102.
AD: George A. Klebez.

WESTERN CARO.
Cullowhee, NC 28723 .... I-AA

Coach: Bill Bleil, NW Iowa 1981
Record: 3 Years, 12-21-0

2000 SCHEDULE
LSU	*Sept. 2
Lenoir-Rhyne ■	*Sept. 9
Citadel	*Sept. 16
East Tenn. St. ■	*Sept. 23
Furman	Sept. 30
Ga. Southern ■	*Oct. 7
Wofford	Oct. 14
Chattanooga	Oct. 21
VMI	Oct. 28
Appalachian St. ■	Nov. 11
Tennessee Tech ■	Nov. 18

1999 RESULTS (3-8-0)
59	Mars Hill	0
10	Maryland	51
10	East Tenn. St.	38
19	Furman	27
7	Ga. Southern	70
21	Wofford	35
28	Chattanooga	56
40	VMI	2
32	Samford	35
10	Appalachian St.	34
24	Citadel	17
260		365

Nickname: Catamounts.
Stadium: E.J. Whitmire (1974), 12,000 capacity. Artificial turf.
Colors: Purple & Gold.
Conference: Southern.
SID: Jody Jones, 704-227-7171.
AD: Jeff Compher.

WESTERN CONN. ST.
Danbury, CT 06810 III

Coach: Bob Surace, Princeton 1990
(First year as head coach)

2000 SCHEDULE
Marist	Sept. 2
Mount Ida	Sept. 9
New Jersey City ■	Sept. 16
Wm. Paterson	Sept. 23
Plymouth St. ■	Sept. 30
Springfield	*Oct. 6
Coast Guard	Oct. 14
Worcester Tech ■	Oct. 28
Merchant Marine ■	Nov. 4
Norwich ■	Nov. 11

1999 RESULTS (10-0-0)
50	Mass.-Dartmouth	18
28	New Jersey City	7
47	Wm. Paterson	7
12	Plymouth St.	9
56	Springfield	48
65	Coast Guard	14
27	Montclair St.	13
35	Worcester Tech	6
45	Merchant Marine	21
27	Norwich	17
392		160

DIVISION III CHAMPIONSHIP
24	Montclair St.	32

Nickname: Colonials.
Stadium: Midtown Campus Field (0000), 2,800 capacity. Artificial turf.
Colors: Blue & White.
Conference: Freedom Football.
SID: Scott Ames, 203-837-9014.
AD: Edward Farrington.

WESTERN ILL.
Macomb, IL 61455 .... I-AA

Coach: Don Patterson, Army 1973
Record: 1 Year, 7-4-0

2000 SCHEDULE
Missouri	*Sept. 2
Ball St.	Sept. 9
Sam Houston St. ■	Sept. 16
Nicholls St. ■	Sept. 23
Indiana St. ■	Sept. 30
Southern Ill.	Oct. 7
Southwest Mo. St.	Oct. 14
Youngstown St. ■	Oct. 21
Morgan St. ■	Oct. 28
Illinois St. ■	Nov. 4
Northern Iowa	*Nov. 18

1999 RESULTS (7-4-0)
27	Northern Ill.	21
77	Mississippi Val.	7
14	Nicholls St.	13
24	Youngstown St.	28
17	Southwest Mo. St.	27
20	Elon	14
68	Southern Ill.	27
36	Indiana St.	39
30	Illinois St.	38
46	Northern Iowa	27
24	Drake	0
383		241

Nickname: Leathernecks.
Stadium: Hanson Field (1948), 15,000 capacity. Natural turf.
Colors: Purple & Gold.
Conference: Gateway Football.
SID: Doug Smiley, 309-298-1133.
AD: Helen Smiley.

WESTERN KY.
Bowling Green, KY 42101 .... I-AA

Coach: Jack Harbaugh, Bowling Green 1961
Record: 16 Years, 85-86-3

2000 SCHEDULE
Tenn.-Martin ■	Sept. 9
Elon	Sept. 16
Southeast Mo. St.	*Sept. 23
Murray St.	*Sept. 30
Eastern Ky. ■	Oct. 7
Tennessee Tech ■	Oct. 14
Tennessee St.	Oct. 21
Eastern Ill. ■	Oct. 28
South Fla.	*Nov. 4
Indiana St. ■	Nov. 11
Southern Ill.	Nov. 18

1999 RESULTS (6-5-0)
34	Tenn.-Martin	10
55	Cumberland (Tenn.)	7
6	South Fla.	21
21	Southeast Mo. St.	10
21	Murray St.	15
10	Eastern Ky.	30
10	Tennessee Tech	23
21	Tennessee St.	28
38	Eastern Ill.	15
40	Indiana St.	34
14	Southern Ill.	52
270		245

Nickname: Hilltoppers.
Stadium: L.T. Smith (1968), 17,500 capacity. Natural turf.
Colors: Red & White.
Conference: Ohio Valley.
SID: Paul Just, 502-745-4298.
AD: Camden Wood Selig.

WESTERN MD.
Westminster, MD 21157 III

Coach: Tim Keating, Bethany (W. Va.) 1975
Record: 12 Years, 74-44-3

2000 SCHEDULE
Bridgewater (Va.) ■	Sept. 2
Randolph-Macon	Sept. 9
Gettysburg ■	Sept. 16
Ursinus	Sept. 23
Muhlenberg ■	Sept. 30
Dickinson	Oct. 14
Frank. & Marsh.	Oct. 21
Widener	Oct. 28
Swarthmore ■	Nov. 4
Johns Hopkins	Nov. 11

1999 RESULTS (10-0-0)
24	Bridgewater (Va.)	0
28	Randolph-Macon	7
44	Gettysburg	0
36	Ursinus	15
21	Muhlenberg	14
42	Dickinson	0
19	Frank. & Marsh.	0
57	Widener	20
41	Swarthmore	14
37	Johns Hopkins	7
349		77

DIVISION III CHAMPIONSHIP
20	Catholic	16
16	Trinity (Tex.)	20

Nickname: Green Terror.
Stadium: Scott S. Bair (1981), 4,000 capacity. Natural turf.
Colors: Green & Gold.
Conference: Centennial.
SID: To be named, 410-857-2291.
AD: James M. Smith.

WESTERN MICH.
Kalamazoo, MI 49008 .... I-A

Coach: Gary Darnell, Oklahoma St. 1970
Record: 7 Years, 28-45-0

2000 SCHEDULE
Wisconsin	*Aug. 31
Iowa	Sept. 9
Indiana St. ■	*Sept. 16
Toledo ■	*Sept. 23

Ohio ■	Sept. 30
Marshall	*Oct. 5
Northern Ill. ■	Oct. 21
Kent St.	Oct. 28
Ball St.	Nov. 4
Central Mich.	Nov. 11
Eastern Mich. ■	Nov. 18

1999 RESULTS (7-5-0)

26	Florida	55
46	Youngstown St.	28
34	Missouri	48
24	Northern Ill.	21
38	Central Mich.	16
40	Eastern Mich.	37
45	Buffalo	17
28	Ball St.	0
24	Akron	10
17	Marshall	31
21	Toledo	45
30	Marshall	34
373		342

Nickname: Broncos.
Stadium: Waldo (1939), 30,200 capacity. Natural turf.
Colors: Brown & Gold.
Conference: Mid-American.
SID: Daniel Jankowski, 616-387-4138.
AD: Kathy Beauregard.

WESTERN NEW ENG.
Springfield, MA 01119..................................III

Coach: Gerry Martin, Connecticut 1980
Record: 9 Years, 25-53-1

2000 SCHEDULE

Westfield St. ■	Sept. 9
Nichols ■	Sept. 16
Salve Regina	Sept. 23
Mass.-Boston ■	Sept. 30
Curry ■	Oct. 7
Mass.-Dartmouth	Oct. 14
Framingham St.	Oct. 21
MIT ■	Oct. 28
Fitchburg St. ■	Nov. 4

1999 RESULTS (3-7-0)

15	Mount Ida	36
28	Westfield St.	21
7	Nichols	19
9	Salve Regina	26
31	Mass.-Boston	15
22	Curry	30
6	Mass.-Dartmouth	34
20	Framingham St.	14
9	MIT	34
28	Fitchburg St.	43
175		272

Nickname: Golden Bears.
Stadium: WNEC (NA), 1,500 capacity. Natural turf.
Colors: Royal Blue & Gold.
Conference: New England Football.
SID: Gene Gumbs, 413-782-1227.
AD: Michael Theulen.

WESTERN N.M.
Silver City, NM 88061..................................II

Coach: Land Jacobsen, Central Okla. 1976
Record: 4 Years, 14-23-0

2000 SCHEDULE

West Tex. A&M	*Aug. 26
Eastern N.M.	*Sept. 2
Tarleton St.	*Sept. 9
Mesa St. ■	Sept. 16
N.M. Highlands ■	Sept. 23
Western Wash.	Oct. 7
Cal Poly	*Oct. 14
Fort Lewis ■	Oct. 21
Okla. Panhandle ■	Oct. 28
Weber St.	Nov. 4

1999 RESULTS (4-5-0)

27	Fort Lewis	20
13	Eastern N.M.	33
8	Montana St.	65
14	N.M. Highlands	7
47	Sul Ross St.	12
21	Western Wash.	49
36	Southeastern Okla.	46
17	Okla. Panhandle	20
21	Mesa St.	14
204		266

Nickname: Mustangs.
Stadium: Silver Sports Complex (1969), 2,000 capacity. Natural turf.
Colors: Purple & Gold.
Conference: Division II Independent.
SID: Jim Callender, 505-538-6220.
AD: Scott Woodard.

WESTERN ST. (COLO.)
Gunnison, CO 81231..................................II

Coach: Carl Iverson, Whitman 1962
Record: 16 Years, 106-54-3

2000 SCHEDULE

Weber St.	*Aug. 31
Northern Colo.	Sept. 9
Fort Lewis	Sept. 16
Mesa St. ■	Sept. 23
Okla. Panhandle ■	Sept. 30
N.M. Highlands ■	Oct. 7
Chadron St.	Oct. 14
Adams St.	Oct. 21
Fort Hays St. ■	Oct. 28
Colorado Mines ■	Nov. 4
Neb.-Kearney	Nov. 11

1999 RESULTS (5-6-0)

3	Weber St.	33
31	Northern Colo.	38
45	Mesa St.	10
43	Okla. Panhandle	0
38	N.M. Highlands	45
6	Chadron St.	10
24	Adams St.	21
3	Fort Hays St.	23
31	Colorado Mines	17
17	Neb.-Kearney	23
35	Fort Lewis	10
276		230

Nickname: Mountaineers.
Stadium: Mountaineer Bowl (1950), 2,400 capacity. Natural turf.
Colors: Crimson & Slate.
Conference: Rocky Mountain Athletic.
SID: Keith Hawkins, 303-943-2831.
AD: Greg Waggoner.

WESTERN WASH.
Bellingham, WA 98225..................................II

Coach: Rob Smith, Washington 1981
Record: 2 Years, 13-8-0

2000 SCHEDULE

Portland St.	Sept. 2
St. Mary's (Cal.)	Sept. 9
West Tex. A&M ■	Sept. 16
Western Mont. ■	Sept. 23
Central Wash.	Sept. 30
Western N.M. ■	Oct. 7
Western Ore.	Oct. 21
Simon Fraser ■	Oct. 28
Humboldt St. ■	Nov. 4
UC Davis ■	Nov. 11

1999 RESULTS (8-2-0)

28	Portland St.	48
45	Wis.-Whitewater	14
20	St. Mary's (Cal.)	7
49	Western N.M.	21
45	Simon Fraser	0
27	Central Wash.	7
26	Chadron St.	14
58	Humboldt St.	0
21	Western Ore.	20
24	UC Davis	55
343		186

24	Northeastern St.	27

Nickname: Vikings.
Stadium: Bellingham Civic (NA), 4,500 capacity. Natural turf.
Colors: Navy Blue, Silver & White.
Conference: Division II Independent.
SID: Paul Madison, 360-650-3108.
AD: Lynda Goodrich.

WESTFIELD ST.
Westfield, MA 01086..................................III

Coach: Steve Marino, Westfield St. 1971
Record: 10 Years, 45-52-1

2000 SCHEDULE

Western New Eng.	Sept. 9
Fitchburg St. ■	Sept. 16
Mass. Maritime	Sept. 23
Framingham St. ■	Sept. 30
Maine Maritime ■	Oct. 7
Bri'water (Mass.) ■	Oct. 14
Mass.-Boston	Oct. 21
Nichols ■	Oct. 28
Worcester St.	Nov. 4

1999 RESULTS (4-6-0)

15	Hartwick	27
21	Western New Eng.	28
20	Fitchburg St.	34
9	Mass. Maritime	14
31	Framingham St.	13
14	Maine Maritime	13
19	Bri'water (Mass.)	49
52	Mass.-Boston	14
13	Nichols	35
31	Worcester St.	26
225		253

Nickname: Owls.
Stadium: Alumni Field (1982), 4,800 capacity. Artificial turf.
Colors: Royal Blue & White.
Conference: New England Football.
SID: Mickey Curtis, 413-572-5433.
AD: Kenneth Magarian.

WESTMINSTER (MO.)
Fulton, MO 65251..................................III

Coach: John Welty, Benedictine 1977
Record: 1 Year, 8-2-0

2000 SCHEDULE

Washington (Mo.)	*Sept. 2
Concordia-St. Paul ■	Sept. 9
Greenville	Sept. 16
Ky. Wesleyan	Sept. 23
Blackburn ■	Sept. 30
Colorado Col.	Oct. 14
Thomas More ■	Oct. 21
Bethel (Tenn.)	Oct. 28
Southern Nazarene ■	Nov. 4
MacMurray ■	Nov. 11

1999 RESULTS (8-2-0)

56	Illinois Col.	36
45	Central Methodist	14
55	Greenville	27
35	Ky. Wesleyan	51
47	Maranatha Baptist	22
63	Blackburn	9
21	Northwestern (Minn.)	6
63	Colorado Col.	26
58	Bethel (Tenn.)	7
49	MacMurray	56
492		254

Nickname: Blue Jays.
Stadium: Priest Field (1906), 1,500 capacity. Natural turf.
Colors: Blue & White.
Conference: St. Louis Intercollegiate Athletic.
SID: Andrew Holmes, 573-592-5345.
AD: Terry Logue.

WESTMINSTER (PA.)
New Wilmington, PA 16172..................II

Coach: Jerry Schmitt, Westminster (Pa.) 1982
(First year as head coach)

2000 SCHEDULE
Walsh ■	Sept. 9
Geneva ■	Sept. 16
West Liberty St. [Wheeling, WV]	*Sept. 23
Wash. & Jeff.	Sept. 30
Bethany (W.Va.) ■	Oct. 7
Thiel	Oct. 14
Grove City	Oct. 21
Gannon ■	Oct. 28
Waynesburg ■	Nov. 11

1999 RESULTS (3-8-0)
0	Michigan Tech	10
6	Indianapolis	9
14	Northwood	45
17	Hillsdale	30
10	Ashland	24
30	Saginaw Valley	36
7	Mercyhurst	17
22	Findlay	19
52	Gannon	0
24	Wayne St. (Mich.)	14
27	Northern Mich.	33
209		**237**

Nickname: Titans.
Stadium: Harold Burry (NA), 4,500 capacity. Natural turf.
Colors: Navy Blue & White.
Conference: Great Lakes Intercollegiate Athletic.
SID: Joe Onderko, 724-946-6357.
AD: James E. Dafler.

WHEATON (ILL.)
Wheaton, IL 60187........................III

Coach: Mike Swider, Wheaton (Ill.) 1977
Record: 4 Years, 25-11-0

2000 SCHEDULE
St. Xavier	Sept. 9
Wabash ■	Sept. 16
Hope	Sept. 23
North Central ■	Sept. 30
Millikin	Oct. 7
Carthage ■	Oct. 14
Ill. Wesleyan ■	Oct. 21
Elmhurst	Oct. 28
North Park ■	Nov. 4
Augustana (Ill.)	Nov. 11

1999 RESULTS (7-2-0)
35	Washington (Mo.)	12
42	Anderson (Ind.)	3
49	North Central	13
30	Carthage	14
36	North Park	15
22	Ill. Wesleyan	20
23	Millikin	14
16	Elmhurst	22
19	Augustana (Ill.)	31
272		**144**

Nickname: Crusaders.
Stadium: McCully Field (1956), 7,000 capacity. Natural turf.
Colors: Orange & Blue.
Conference: College Conf. of Illinois. & Wisconsin.
SID: Brett Marhanka, 708-752-5747.
AD: Tony Ladd.

WHITTIER
Whittier, CA 90608.......................III

Coach: Bob Owens, La Verne 1971
Record: 4 Years, 13-23-0

2000 SCHEDULE
San Diego ■	*Sept. 9
Chapman	*Sept. 23
Menlo	Sept. 30
Linfield ■	*Oct. 7
Claremont-M-S	*Oct. 14
Occidental	Oct. 21
Cal Lutheran ■	Oct. 28
Redlands ■	*Nov. 4
La Verne ■	*Nov. 11

1999 RESULTS (0-9-0)
13	San Diego	40
0	La Verne	45
32	Menlo	45
12	Cal Lutheran	48
12	Pomona-Pitzer	33
13	Claremont-M-S	15
7	Chapman	44
3	Redlands	73
7	Occidental	17
99		**360**

Nickname: Poets.
Stadium: Memorial (NA), 7,000 capacity. Natural turf.
Colors: Purple & Gold.
Conference: Southern California Intercollegiate Athletic.
SID: Rock Carter, 310-907-4271.
AD: David A. Jacobs.

WHITWORTH
Spokane, WA 99251.....................III

Coach: John Tully, Azusa Pacific 1975
Record: 10 Years, 45-54-1

2000 SCHEDULE
Redlands	*Sept. 9
Chapman ■	Sept. 16
Pacific Lutheran ■	Sept. 23
Simon Fraser	Sept. 30
Willamette	Oct. 14
Puget Sound	Oct. 21
Eastern Ore. ■	Oct. 28
Linfield ■	Nov. 4
Lewis & Clark	Nov. 11

1999 RESULTS (5-5-0)
21	Menlo	24
33	Simon Fraser	19
28	Cal Lutheran	3
45	Puget Sound	12
7	Linfield	31
7	Pacific Lutheran	33
20	Azusa Pacific	41
16	Willamette	31
31	Eastern Ore.	28
52	Lewis & Clark	0
260		**222**

Nickname: Pirates.
Stadium: Pine Bowl (NA), 2,200 capacity. Natural turf.
Colors: Crimson & Black.
Conference: Northwest.
SID: Steve Flegel, 509-777-3239.
AD: Scott McQuilkin.

WIDENER
Chester, PA 19013........................III

Coach: Bill Zwaan, Delaware 1979
Record: 3 Years, 21-10-0

2000 SCHEDULE
FDU-Madison ■	Sept. 9
Lycoming ■	Sept. 16
Delaware Valley	Sept. 23
Moravian	Sept. 30
Albright ■	Oct. 7
Susquehanna ■	Oct. 14
King's (Pa.)	Oct. 21
Western Md. ■	Oct. 28
Lebanon Valley ■	Nov. 4
Juniata	Nov. 11

1999 RESULTS (6-4-0)
25	FDU-Madison	23
0	Lycoming	30
40	Delaware Valley	27
40	Moravian	14
35	Albright	27
7	Susquehanna	28
45	King's (Pa.)	14
20	Western Md.	57
32	Lebanon Valley	0
45	Juniata	59
289		**279**

Nickname: Pioneers.
Stadium: Leslie Quick Jr. (1994), 4,000 capacity. Natural turf.
Colors: Widener Blue & Gold.
Conference: Middle Atlantic.
SID: Susan Fumagalli, 610-499-4436.
AD: William A. Zwaan.

WILKES
Wilkes-Barre, PA 18766................III

Coach: Frank Sheptock, Bloomsburg 1986
Record: 4 Years, 24-16-0

2000 SCHEDULE
Albright	*Sept. 9
FDU-Madison	*Sept. 15
Juniata ■	Sept. 23
Susquehanna	Sept. 30
Delaware Valley ■	Oct. 7
Lycoming	Oct. 14
Ithaca	Oct. 21
Lebanon Valley ■	Oct. 28
Moravian ■	Nov. 4
King's (Pa.)	Nov. 11

1999 RESULTS (6-4-0)
36	Albright	15
32	FDU-Madison	19
21	Juniata	38
26	Susquehanna	0
54	Delaware Valley	0
15	Lycoming	20
10	Ursinus	16
27	Lebanon Valley	25
22	Moravian	28
30	King's (Pa.)	6
273		**167**

ECAC PLAYOFFS
27	FDU-Madison	6

Nickname: Colonels.
Stadium: Ralston Field (1965), 4,000 capacity. Natural turf.
Colors: Navy & Gold.
Conference: Middle Atlantic.
SID: John Seitzinger, 570-831-4777.
AD: Addy Malatesta.

WILLAMETTE
Salem, OR 97301.........................III

Coach: Mark Speckman, Azusa Pacific 1977
Record: 2 Years, 14-7-0

2000 SCHEDULE
Chapman	*Sept. 9
Trinity (Tex.)	*Sept. 16
Puget Sound ■	Sept. 23
Western Ore. ■	Sept. 30
Southern Ore. ■	Oct. 7
Whitworth	Oct. 14
Eastern Ore. ■	Oct. 21
Pacific Lutheran	Oct. 28
Lewis & Clark ■	Nov. 4
Linfield	Nov. 11

1999 RESULTS (7-3-0)
51	Colorado Col.	6
42	Chapman	13
3	Humboldt St.	9
24	Southern Ore.	38
29	Pacific Lutheran	20
7	Eastern Ore.	28
41	Puget Sound	14
31	Whitworth	16
42	Lewis & Clark	6
28	Linfield	7
298		**157**

DIVISION III CHAMPIONSHIP
24	Pacific Lutheran	28

Nickname: Bearcats.

Stadium: McCulloch (NA), 2,400 capacity. Natural turf.
Colors: Cardinal & Old Gold.
Conference: Northwest Conference.
SID: Cliff Voliva, 503-370-6110.
AD: William G. Trenbeath.

WILLIAM & MARY
Williamsburg, VA 23187 ....I-AA

Coach: Jimmye Laycock, William & Mary 1970
Record: 20 Years, 135-90-2

2000 SCHEDULE
Massachusetts	*Aug. 31
VMI ■	Sept. 9
Furman	*Sept. 16
UCF	*Sept. 23
Maine	*Sept. 30
Rhode Island ■	Oct. 7
Delaware ■	Oct. 14
James Madison	Oct. 21
Northeastern ■	Oct. 28
Villanova	Nov. 11
Richmond ■	Nov. 18

1999 RESULTS (6-5-0)
27	Delaware	34
9	North Carolina St.	38
6	Furman	52
42	Northeastern	30
45	Villanova	10
20	James Madison	30
35	VMI	14
37	Maine	13
24	Rhode Island	6
16	Massachusetts	25
31	Richmond	14
292		266

Nickname: Tribe.
Stadium: Walter Zable (1935), 13,279 capacity. Natural turf.
Colors: Green, Gold, Silver.
Conference: Atlantic 10.
SID: Pete Clawson, 804-221-3344.
AD: Edward C. Driscoll Jr.

WM. PATERSON
Wayne, NJ 07470 III

Coach: Larry Arico, Lehigh 1992
Record: 3 Years, 7-23-0

2000 SCHEDULE
Salisbury St.	Sept. 9
Col. of New Jersey	*Sept. 15
Western Conn. St. ■	Sept. 23
Kean ■	Sept. 30
FDU-Madison	Oct. 6
Montclair St.	*Oct. 14
Cortland St.	Oct. 21
Alfred ■	Oct. 28
Rowan	Nov. 4
New Jersey City ■	Nov. 11

1999 RESULTS (2-8-0)
38	Delaware Valley	33
0	Col. of New Jersey	28
7	Western Conn. St.	47
29	Kean	12
7	FDU-Madison	17
21	Montclair St.	41
7	Cortland St.	45
21	New Jersey City	33
0	Rowan	41
7	Waynesburg	48
137		345

Nickname: Pioneers.
Stadium: Wightman Field (0000), 2,000 capacity. Natural turf.
Colors: Orange & Black.
Conference: New Jersey Athletic.
SID: Joe Martinelli, 201-595-2705.
AD: Arthur Eason.

WILLIAM PENN
Oskaloosa, IA 52577 III

Coach: Tom Shea, Dakota St. 1972
Record: 15 Years, 97-55-3

2000 SCHEDULE
Coe ■	Sept. 2
Loras	Sept. 9
Wartburg ■	Sept. 16
Buena Vista	Sept. 30
Cornell College ■	Oct. 7
Dubuque	Oct. 14
Central (Iowa) ■	Oct. 21
Luther	Oct. 28
Upper Iowa ■	Nov. 4
Simpson	Nov. 11

1999 RESULTS (3-7-0)
16	Wartburg	51
14	Buena Vista	38
28	Cornell College	32
20	Loras	32
21	Simpson	30
28	Luther	22
30	Dubuque	23
35	Coe	21
7	Central (Iowa)	38
7	Upper Iowa	38
206		325

Nickname: The Statesmen.
Stadium: Community (NA), 5,000 capacity. Natural turf.
Colors: Navy Blue & Gold.
Conference: Iowa Intercollegiate Athletic.
SID: Connie J. Davis, 515-673-1046.
AD: Mike Laird.

WILLIAMS
Williamstown, MA 01267 III

Coach: Dick Farley, Boston U. 1968
Record: 13 Years, 88-13-3

2000 SCHEDULE
Colby ■	Sept. 23
Trinity (Conn.) ■	Sept. 30
Bates	Oct. 7
Middlebury ■	Oct. 14
Tufts	Oct. 21
Hamilton	Oct. 28
Wesleyan (Conn.) ■	Nov. 4
Amherst	Nov. 11

1999 RESULTS (7-1-0)
42	Bowdoin	0
17	Trinity (Conn.)	0
34	Bates	10
25	Middlebury	0
28	Tufts	21
42	Hamilton	13
28	Wesleyan (Conn.)	33
10	Amherst	7
226		84

Nickname: Ephs.
Stadium: Weston Field (1875), 10,000 capacity. Natural turf.
Colors: Purple.
Conference: NESCAC.
SID: Dick Quinn, 413-597-4982.
AD: Robert R. Peck.

WILMINGTON (OHIO)
Wilmington, OH 45177 III

Coach: Mike Wallace, Bowling Green 1968
Record: 9 Years, 36-51-1

2000 SCHEDULE
Alma	Sept. 9
Baldwin-Wallace ■	Sept. 16
Muskingum	*Sept. 23
Otterbein ■	Sept. 30
John Carroll	Oct. 7
Mount Union	Oct. 14
Heidelberg ■	Oct. 21
Ohio Northern ■	Oct. 28
Marietta	Nov. 4
Capital ■	Nov. 11

1999 RESULTS (9-1-0)
48	Urbana	17
41	Olivet	10
47	Adrian	21
45	Mt. St. Joseph	8
55	Franklin	6
15	Hanover	30
32	Wabash	30
39	Manchester	0
40	Anderson (Ind.)	23
31	Bluffton	28
393		173

Nickname: Quakers.
Stadium: Williams (1983), 3,250 capacity. Natural turf.
Colors: Green & White.
Conference: Heartland Collegiate Athletic.
SID: Marty Fuller, 513-382-6661.
AD: Terry A. Rupert.

WINGATE
Wingate, NC 28174 II

Coach: Bob Brush, Rutgers 1966
Record: 5 Years, 23-27-0

2000 SCHEDULE
Concord	Sept. 2
West Virginia St. ■	Sept. 9
Catawba	Sept. 16
Tusculum ■	Sept. 23
Liberty	*Sept. 30
Lenoir-Rhyne ■	Oct. 7
Newberry	Oct. 14
Presbyterian ■	Oct. 21
Mars Hill ■	Oct. 28
Carson-Newman	Nov. 4
Tenn.-Martin	Nov. 11

1999 RESULTS (3-8-0)
45	North Greenville	30
14	West Virginia St.	55
42	Newberry	39
7	Mars Hill	37
25	Gardner-Webb	35
15	Carson-Newman	64
21	Lenoir-Rhyne	28
38	Tusculum	14
35	Presbyterian	43
13	Catawba	54
11	Stephen F. Austin	73
266		472

Nickname: Bulldogs.
Stadium: Irwin Belk (NA), 3,000 capacity. Natural turf.
Colors: Navy Blue & Old Gold.
Conference: South Atlantic.
SID: David Sherwood, 704-233-8186.
AD: Beth L. Murray.

WINONA ST.
Winona, MN 55987 II

Coach: Tom Sawyer, Winona St. 1983
Record: 4 Years, 28-16-0

2000 SCHEDULE
Central Mo. St.	*Aug. 31
Wis.-La Crosse	*Sept. 9
Moorhead St. ■	Sept. 16
Wayne St. (Neb.)	Sept. 23
Minn.-Morris	Sept. 30
Minn.-Crookston ■	Oct. 7
Southwest St.	Oct. 14
Concordia-St. Paul ■	Oct. 21
Northern St.	Oct. 28
Minn.-Duluth ■	Nov. 4
Wis.-Stevens Point [Minneapolis, MN]	Nov. 11

1999 RESULTS (7-4-0)
24	Central Mo. St.	30
41	Wis.-La Crosse	22

21	Moorhead St.	17
42	Wayne St. (Neb.)	28
46	Minn.-Morris	6
61	Minn.-Crookston	35
13	Southwest St.	9
38	Concordia-St. Paul	12
34	Northern St.	37
17	Minn.-Duluth	21
20	Wis.-River Falls	29
357		**246**

Nickname: Warriors.
Stadium: Maxwell (NA), 3,500 capacity. Natural turf.
Colors: Purple & White.
Conference: Northern Sun Intercollegiate Athletic.
SID: Michael R. Herzberg, 507-457-5576.
AD: Larry Holstad.

WINSTON-SALEM
Winston-Salem, NC 27110 II

Coach: Kermit Blount, Winston-Salem 1980
Record: 7 Years, 31-29-3

2000 SCHEDULE
South Carolina St. .... *Sept. 2
Bowie St. ■ .... *Sept. 9
Hampton .... Sept. 16
Virginia Union ■ .... *Sept. 23
Fayetteville St. ■ .... *Sept. 30
Livingstone ■ .... Oct. 7
N.C. Central .... Oct. 14
Virginia St. .... Oct. 21
Johnson Smith .... Oct. 28
Elizabeth City St. .... Nov. 4

1999 RESULTS (8-3-0)
14	Catawba	17
7	N.C. A&T	20
17	Virginia Union	0
44	Fayetteville St.	0
34	Livingstone	0
20	N.C. Central	7
17	Virginia St.	14
25	Johnson Smith	6
21	Elizabeth City St.	6
23	Grambling	25
23	Tuskegee	7
245		**102**

Nickname: Rams.
Stadium: Bowman-Gray (1940), 18,000 capacity. Natural turf.
Colors: Scarlet & White.
Conference: Central Intercollegiate Athletic.
SID: Adrian Ferguson, 919-750-2143.
AD: Anne Little.

WISCONSIN
Madison, WI 53711 .... I-A

Coach: Barry Alvarez, Nebraska 1969
Record: 10 Years, 70-44-4

2000 SCHEDULE
Western Mich. ■ .... *Aug. 31
Oregon ■ .... Sept. 9
Cincinnati ■ .... Sept. 16
Northwestern ■ .... Sept. 23
Michigan .... Sept. 30
Ohio St. ■ .... Oct. 7
Michigan St. .... Oct. 14
Purdue ■ .... Oct. 21
Iowa .... Oct. 28
Minnesota ■ .... Nov. 4
Indiana .... Nov. 11
Hawaii .... *Nov. 25

1999 RESULTS (9-2-0)
49	Murray St.	10
50	Ball St.	10
12	Cincinnati	17
16	Michigan	21
42	Ohio St.	17
20	Minnesota	17
59	Indiana	0
40	Michigan St.	10
35	Northwestern	19

28	Purdue	21
41	Iowa	3
392		**145**

ROSE BOWL
| 17 | Stanford | 9 |

Nickname: Badgers.
Stadium: Camp Randall (1917), 76,129 capacity. Artificial turf.
Colors: Cardinal & White.
Conference: Big Ten.
SID: Steve Malchow, 608-262-1811.
AD: Pat Richter.

WIS.-EAU CLAIRE
Eau Claire, WI 54702 III

Coach: Todd Hoffner, Valley City St. 1989
Record: 1 Year, 2-8-0

2000 SCHEDULE
St. John's (Minn.) ■ .... *Sept. 2
Augsburg .... *Sept. 9
Wis.-Oshkosh ■ .... Sept. 23
Wis.-Platteville .... Sept. 30
Wis.-Stout .... Oct. 7
Wis.-River Falls ■ .... Oct. 14
Wis.-Whitewater ■ .... Oct. 21
Wis.-La Crosse .... Oct. 28
Wis.-Stevens Point ■ .... Nov. 4
Moorhead St. [Minneapolis, MN] .... *Nov. 11

1999 RESULTS (2-8-0)
19	Tiffin	21
28	St. John's (Minn.)	40
14	Wis.-Oshkosh	16
28	Wis.-Platteville	13
20	Wis.-Stout	22
34	Wis.-River Falls	38
14	Wis.-Whitewater	0
46	Wis.-La Crosse	49
30	Wis.-Stevens Point	31
20	Northern St.	27
253		**257**

Nickname: Blugolds.
Stadium: Carson Park (NA), 6,500 capacity. Natural turf.
Colors: Navy Blue & Old Gold.
Conference: Wisconsin Intercollegiate Athletic.
SID: Tim Petermann, 715-836-4184.
AD: Marilyn Skrivseth.

WIS.-LA CROSSE
La Crosse, WI 54601 III

Coach: Larry Terry, Wis.-La Crosse 1977
Record: 5 Years, 25-29-1

2000 SCHEDULE
Washburn .... *Sept. 2
Winona St. ■ .... *Sept. 9
Wis.-River Falls ■ .... *Sept. 23
Wis.-Whitewater .... Sept. 30
Wis.-Platteville ■ .... Oct. 7
Wis.-Stout .... Oct. 14
Wis.-Stevens Point .... Oct. 21
Wis.-Eau Claire ■ .... Oct. 28
Wis.-Oshkosh .... Nov. 4
Northern St. [Minneapolis, MN] .... *Nov. 11

1999 RESULTS (7-3-0)
21	Washburn	24
22	Winona St.	41
19	Wis.-River Falls	18
28	Wis.-Whitewater	14
14	Wis.-Platteville	27
42	Wis.-Stout	14
21	Wis.-Stevens Point	14
49	Wis.-Eau Claire	46
36	Wis.-Oshkosh	26
22	Minn.-Duluth	21
274		**245**

DIVISION III CHAMPIONSHIP
| 17 | Central (Iowa) | 38 |

Nickname: Eagles.
Stadium: Memorial (1924), 4,349 capacity. Natural turf.
Colors: Maroon & Gray.
Conference: Wisconsin Intercollegiate Athletic.
SID: Todd Clark, 608-785-8493.
AD: Joe R. Baker.

WIS.-OSHKOSH
Oshkosh, WI 54901 III

Coach: Phil Meyer
(First year as head coach)

2000 SCHEDULE
Southwest St. .... *Sept. 1
Wis.-River Falls ■ .... *Sept. 9
Wis.-Eau Claire .... Sept. 23
Wis.-Stevens Point .... Sept. 30
Wis.-Whitewater ■ .... Oct. 7
Wis.-Platteville ■ .... Oct. 14
Wis.-River Falls .... Oct. 21
Wis.-Stout .... Oct. 28
Wis.-La Crosse ■ .... Nov. 4
Minn.-Morris [Minneapolis, MN] .... *Nov. 10

1999 RESULTS (3-7-0)
24	St. Norbert	14
14	Wittenberg	28
16	Wis.-Eau Claire	14
3	Wis.-Stevens Point	22
20	Wis.-Whitewater	53
20	Wis.-Platteville	25
21	Wis.-River Falls	35
27	Wis.-Stout	17
26	Wis.-La Crosse	36
7	Moorhead St.	56
178		**300**

Nickname: Titans.
Stadium: Titan (1970), 9,800 capacity. Natural turf.
Colors: Black, Gold & White.
Conference: Wisconsin Intercollegiate Athletic.
SID: Kennan Timm, 414-424-0365.
AD: Allen F. Ackerman.

WIS.-PLATTEVILLE
Platteville, WI 53818 III

Coach: Mike Emendorfer, William Penn 1986
Record: 1 Year, 5-5-0

2000 SCHEDULE
Mt. Senario .... Sept. 9
Augustana (Ill.) ■ .... *Sept. 16
Wis.-Whitewater ■ .... Sept. 23
Wis.-Eau Claire ■ .... Sept. 30
Wis.-La Crosse .... Oct. 7
Wis.-Oshkosh .... Oct. 14
Wis.-Stout ■ .... Oct. 21
Wis.-Stevens Point .... Oct. 28
Wis.-River Falls ■ .... Nov. 4
Southwest St. [Minneapolis, MN] .... *Nov. 11

1999 RESULTS (5-5-0)
20	Lakeland	17
6	Augustana (Ill.)	31
20	Wis.-Whitewater	55
13	Wis.-Eau Claire	28
27	Wis.-La Crosse	14
25	Wis.-Oshkosh	20
14	Wis.-Stout	9
16	Wis.-Stevens Point	27
14	Wis.-River Falls	31
46	Minn.-Morris	15
201		**247**

Nickname: Pioneers.
Stadium: Ralph E. Davis Pioneer (1972), 10,000 capacity. Natural turf.
Colors: Blue & Orange.
Conference: Wisconsin Intercollegiate Athletic.
SID: Paul Erickson, 608-342-1574.
AD: Mark Molesworth.

WIS.-RIVER FALLS
River Falls, WI 54022 III

Coach: John O'Grady, Wis.-River Falls 1979
Record: 11 Years, 71-38-3

2000 SCHEDULE
Chadron St.	Sept. 2
Wis.-Oshkosh	*Sept. 9
Wis.-La Crosse	*Sept. 23
Wis.-Stout	Sept. 30
Wis.-Stevens Point ■	Oct. 7
Wis.-Eau Claire	Oct. 14
Wis.-Oshkosh ■	Oct. 21
Wis.-Whitewater ■	Oct. 28
Wis.-Platteville	Nov. 4
Bemidji St. [Minneapolis, MN]	*Nov. 10

1999 RESULTS (6-4-0)
17	St. Cloud St.	22
7	Augustana (S.D.)	21
18	Wis.-La Crosse	19
47	Wis.-Stout	0
19	Wis.-Stevens Point	21
38	Wis.-Eau Claire	34
35	Wis.-Oshkosh	21
23	Wis.-Whitewater	16
31	Wis.-Platteville	14
29	Winona St.	20
264		**188**

Nickname: Falcons.
Stadium: Ramer Field (1966), 4,800 capacity. Natural turf.
Colors: Red & White.
Conference: Wisconsin Intercollegiate Athletic.
SID: Jim Thies, 715-425-3846.
AD: Connie Foster.

WIS.-STEVENS POINT
Stevens Point, WI 54481 III

Coach: John Miech, Wis.-Stevens Point 1975
Record: 12 Years, 83-35-2

2000 SCHEDULE
Northern St. ■	*Sept. 9
Drake ■	Sept. 16
Wis.-Stout	Sept. 23
Wis.-Oshkosh ■	Sept. 30
Wis.-River Falls	Oct. 7
Wis.-Whitewater	Oct. 14
Wis.-La Crosse ■	Oct. 21
Wis.-Platteville ■	Oct. 28
Wis.-Eau Claire	Nov. 4
Winona St. [Minneapolis, MN]	Nov. 11

1999 RESULTS (9-2-0)
28	Northern St.	26
28	Drake	17
24	Wis.-Stout	20
22	Wis.-Oshkosh	3
21	Wis.-River Falls	19
23	Wis.-Whitewater	7
14	Wis.-La Crosse	21
27	Wis.-Platteville	16
31	Wis.-Eau Claire	30
35	Bemidji St.	23
10	St. John's (Minn.)	23
263		**205**

Nickname: Pointers.
Stadium: Goerke Field (1932), 4,000 capacity. Natural turf.
Colors: Purple & Gold.
Conference: Wisconsin Intercollegiate Athletic.
SID: Jim Strick, 715-346-2840.
AD: Frank O'Brien.

WIS.-STOUT
Menomonie, WI 54751 III

Coach: Ed Meierkort, Dakota Wesleyan 1981
Record: 7 Years, 26-44-0

2000 SCHEDULE
Lakeland	Sept. 2
Franklin	Sept. 9
Wis.-Stevens Point ■	Sept. 23
Wis.-River Falls	Sept. 30
Wis.-Eau Claire ■	Oct. 7
Wis.-La Crosse ■	Oct. 14
Wis.-Platteville	Oct. 21
Wis.-Oshkosh ■	Oct. 28
Wis.-Whitewater	Nov. 4
Minn.-Duluth [Minneapolis, MN]	*Nov. 11

1999 RESULTS (2-8-0)
48	Minn.-Morris	27
28	St. Ambrose	34
20	Wis.-Stevens Point	24
0	Wis.-River Falls	47
22	Wis.-Eau Claire	20
14	Wis.-La Crosse	42
9	Wis.-Platteville	14
17	Wis.-Oshkosh	27
14	Wis.-Whitewater	21
23	Southwest St.	43
195		**299**

Nickname: Blue Devils.
Stadium: Nelson Field (1936), 5,000 capacity. Natural turf.
Colors: Royal Blue & White.
Conference: Wisconsin Intercollegiate Athletic.
SID: Layne Pitt, 715-232-2275.
AD: Steve Terry.

WIS.-WHITEWATER
Whitewater, WI 53190 III

Coach: Bob Berezowitz, Wis.-Whitewater 1967
Record: 15 Years, 102-49-4

2000 SCHEDULE
Howard Payne ■	Sept. 2
Hardin-Simmons	Sept. 9
Lambuth ■	Sept. 16
Wis.-Platteville	Sept. 23
Wis.-La Crosse ■	Sept. 30
Wis.-Oshkosh	Oct. 7
Wis.-Stevens Point ■	Oct. 14
Wis.-Eau Claire	Oct. 21
Wis.-River Falls	Oct. 28
Wis.-Stout ■	Nov. 4

1999 RESULTS (3-7-0)
16	Lambuth	39
7	Hardin-Simmons	25
14	Western Wash.	45
55	Wis.-Platteville	20
14	Wis.-La Crosse	28
53	Wis.-Oshkosh	20
7	Wis.-Stevens Point	23
0	Wis.-Eau Claire	14
16	Wis.-River Falls	23
21	Wis.-Stout	14
203		**251**

Nickname: Warhawks.
Stadium: Warhawk (1970), 11,000 capacity. Natural turf.
Colors: Purple & White.
Conference: Wisconsin Intercollegiate Athletic.
SID: Tom Fick, 414-472-1147.
AD: Shawn Eichorst.

WITTENBERG
Springfield, OH 45501 III

Coach: Joe Fincham, Ohio 1988
Record: 4 Years, 40-4-0

2000 SCHEDULE
Urbana ■	*Sept. 2
Heidelberg	*Sept. 9
Alma ■	Sept. 16
Wabash	Sept. 23
Allegheny	Sept. 30
Denison ■	Oct. 7
Wooster ■	Oct. 14
Ohio Wesleyan	Oct. 21
Hiram ■	Oct. 28
Earlham ■	Nov. 4

1999 RESULTS (10-0-0)
26	Baldwin-Wallace	21
28	Wis.-Oshkosh	14
62	Earlham	6
56	St. Francis (Ill.)	7
42	Denison	7
20	Allegheny	17
49	Case Reserve	21
14	Ohio Wesleyan	0
48	Kenyon	3
28	Wooster	14
373		**110**

DIVISION III CHAMPIONSHIP
42	Alma	19
24	Ohio Northern	58

Nickname: Tigers.
Stadium: Edwards-Maurer (1994), 2,400 capacity. Artificial turf.
Colors: Red & White.
Conference: North Coast Athletic.
SID: Kristin Evans, 513-327-6115.
AD: Garnett Purnell.

WOFFORD
Spartanburg, SC 29303 .... I-AA

Coach: Mike Ayers, Georgetown (Ky.) 1974
Record: 15 Years, 81-82-2

2000 SCHEDULE
Lehigh ■	*Sept. 9
Ga. Southern	Sept. 16
Charleston So.	Sept. 23
Chattanooga ■	Sept. 30
VMI	Oct. 7
Western Caro. ■	Oct. 14
Appalachian St.	Oct. 21
Citadel ■	Oct. 28
East Tenn. St.	Nov. 4
Furman	Nov. 11
La.-Monroe	Nov. 18

1999 RESULTS (6-5-0)
14	Ga. Southern	55
42	Middle Tenn. St.	52
35	Charleston So.	13
41	Chattanooga	34
55	VMI	10
35	Western Caro.	21
20	Appalachian St.	21
47	Citadel	16
38	East Tenn. St.	14
3	Furman	30
34	La.-Lafayette	37
364		**303**

Nickname: Terriers.
Stadium: Gibbs (1996), 13,000 capacity. Natural turf.
Colors: Old Gold & Black.
Conference: Southern.
SID: Mark Cohen, 864-597-4093.
AD: David S. Wood.

WOOSTER
Wooster, OH 44691 III

Coach: Mike Schmitz, Bowling Green 1974
(First year as head coach)

2000 SCHEDULE
Kalamazoo	Sept. 9
Grove City ■	Sept. 16
Kenyon ■	Sept. 23
Ohio Wesleyan ■	Sept. 30
Wabash ■	Oct. 7
Wittenberg	Oct. 14
Ursinus ■	Oct. 21
Oberlin	Oct. 28
Allegheny ■	Nov. 4
Hiram	Nov. 11

1999 RESULTS (8-2-0)
31	Grove City	28
23	Kalamazoo	0
11	Ohio Wesleyan	14
45	Kenyon	8
13	Allegheny	10
71	Oberlin	0
46	Earlham	6
45	Denison	0

31	Case Reserve	27
14	Wittenberg	28
330		**121**

Nickname: Fighting Scots.
Stadium: John P. Papp (1991), 4,500 capacity. Natural turf.
Colors: Black & Old Gold.
Conference: North Coast Athletic.
SID: Hugh Howard, 330-263-2374.
AD: Robert Malekoff.

WORCESTER ST.
Worcester, MA 01602..................................III

Coach: Brien Cullen, Worcester St. 1977
Record: 15 Years, 81-62-0

2000 SCHEDULE
Worcester Tech ■	*Sept. 8
Bri'water (Mass.) ■	*Sept. 15
Fitchburg St.	Sept. 23
Salve Regina ■	Sept. 30
Mass. Maritime	Oct. 7
Framingham St. ■	Oct. 14
MIT	Oct. 21
Maine Maritime	Oct. 28
Westfield St. ■	Nov. 4

1999 RESULTS (1-9-0)
20	Worcester Tech	24
3	Mass.-Dartmouth	10
17	Bri'water (Mass.)	41
16	Fitchburg St.	25
7	Salve Regina	35
26	Mass. Maritime	27
27	Framingham St.	26
7	MIT	27
27	Maine Maritime	30
26	Westfield St.	31
176		**276**

Nickname: Lancers.
Stadium: John Coughlin Memorial (1976), 2,500 capacity. Artificial turf.
Colors: Royal Blue & Gold.
Conference: New England Football.
SID: Bruce Baker, 508-793-8128.
AD: Susan E. Chapman.

WORCESTER TECH
Worcester, MA 01609..................................III

Coach: Ed Zaloom, Cortland St. 1975
Record: 4 Years, 16-20-0

2000 SCHEDULE
Mass.-Lowell ■	*Sept. 1
Worcester St.	*Sept. 8
Union (N.Y.) ■	Sept. 16
Rensselaer	Sept. 23
Merchant Marine ■	Sept. 30
Norwich	Oct. 7
Springfield ■	*Oct. 21
Western Conn. St.	Oct. 28
Coast Guard ■	Nov. 4
Plymouth St.	Nov. 11

1999 RESULTS (5-4-0)
24	Worcester St.	20
7	Union (N.Y.)	3
27	Rensselaer	42
49	Merchant Marine	28
28	Norwich	25
17	Springfield	52
6	Western Conn. St.	35
27	Coast Guard	23
0	Plymouth St.	21
185		**249**

Nickname: Engineers.
Stadium: Alumni Field (1916), 2,800 capacity. Artificial turf.
Colors: Crimson & Gray.
Conference: Freedom Football.
SID: Steve Raczynski, 508-831-5328.
AD: Raymond R. Gilbert.

WYOMING
Laramie, WY 82071..................................I-A

Coach: Vic Koenning, Kansas St. 1982
(First year as head coach)

2000 SCHEDULE
Auburn	*Aug. 31
Texas A&M	*Sept. 9
Central Mich. ■	Sept. 16
Nevada ■	Sept. 23
New Mexico	*Sept. 30
San Diego St. ■	Oct. 7
Air Force ■	Oct. 14
UNLV	Oct. 21
Brigham Young	*Oct. 26
Utah ■	Nov. 11
Colorado St.	*Nov. 16

1999 RESULTS (7-4-0)
17	Tennessee	42
41	Weber St.	16
10	Air Force	7
28	Idaho	13
32	UNLV	35
38	La.-Monroe	20
13	Colorado St.	24
43	Utah	29
31	Brigham Young	17
42	New Mexico	28
7	San Diego St.	39
302		**270**

Nickname: Cowboys.
Stadium: War Memorial (1950), 33,500 capacity. Natural turf.
Colors: Brown & Yellow.
Conference: Mountain West.
SID: Kevin McKinney, 307-766-2256.
AD: Lee Moon.

YALE
New Haven, CT 06520..................................I-AA

Coach: Jack Siedlecki, Union (N.Y.) 1974
Record: 12 Years, 72-36-2

2000 SCHEDULE
Dayton ■	Sept. 16
Cornell	Sept. 23
Holy Cross ■	Sept. 30
Dartmouth	Oct. 7
Fordham	Oct. 14
Pennsylvania ■	Oct. 21
Columbia ■	Oct. 28
Brown	Nov. 4
Princeton ■	Nov. 11
Harvard	Nov. 18

1999 RESULTS (9-1-0)
24	Brown	25
48	Valparaiso	2
17	San Diego	6
34	Holy Cross	14
44	Dartmouth	3
41	Columbia	29
23	Pennsylvania	19
37	Cornell	20
23	Princeton	21
24	Harvard	21
315		**160**

Nickname: Elis, Bulldogs.
Stadium: Yale Bowl (1914), 60,000 capacity. Natural turf.
Colors: Yale Blue & White.
Conference: Ivy.
SID: Steve Conn, 203-432-1456.
AD: Thomas A. Beckett.

YOUNGSTOWN ST.
Youngstown, OH 44555..................................I-AA

Coach: Jim Tressel, Baldwin-Wallace 1975
Record: 14 Years, 126-54-2

2000 SCHEDULE
Slippery Rock ■	*Aug. 31
Edinboro ■	*Sept. 9
Kent St.	*Sept. 16
Southwest Mo. St.	*Sept. 30
Illinois St.	Oct. 7
Northern Iowa ■	Oct. 14
Western Ill.	Oct. 21
Indiana St. ■	Oct. 28
Hofstra ■	Nov. 4
Southern Ill. ■	Nov. 11
Cal Poly	Nov. 18

1999 RESULTS (9-2-0)
44	Slippery Rock	14
28	Western Mich.	46
13	Indiana (Pa.)	7
28	Western Ill.	24
31	Indiana St.	28
43	Southern Ill.	37
10	Cal Poly	7
29	Northern Iowa	20
28	Illinois St.	31
17	Southwest Mo. St.	14
28	Villanova	21
299		**249**

DIVISION I-AA CHAMPIONSHIP
30	Montana	27
41	N.C. A&T	3
27	Florida A&M	24
24	Ga. Southern	59

Nickname: Penguins.
Stadium: Arnold D. Stambaugh (1982), 20,630 capacity. Artificial turf.
Colors: Red & White.
Conference: Gateway Football.
SID: Rocco Gasparro, 216-742-3192.
AD: James P. Tressel.

2000 Divisions I-A and I-AA Schedules by Date

This listing by dates includes all 2000 season games involving Divisions I-A and I-AA teams, as of printing deadline.

Neutral sites, indicated by footnote numbers, are listed at the end of each date. Asterisks (*) before the visiting team indicate night games. **Game dates are subject to change.**

SATURDAY, AUGUST 26

HOME	OPPONENT
Florida St. [1]	*Brigham Young
Kansas St. [2]	Iowa
Louisiana Tech	*Mississippi Val.
Texas Tech	*New Mexico

[1] Jacksonville, FL
[2] Kansas City, MO

SUNDAY, AUGUST 27

HOME	OPPONENT
Penn St. [1]	Southern California
Virginia Tech	*Georgia Tech

[1] East Rutherford, NJ

THURSDAY, AUGUST 31

HOME	OPPONENT
Auburn	*Wyoming
Chattanooga	*Samford
Cumberland (Tenn.)	Austin Peay
Dayton	*Tiffin
Eastern Ky.	*Glenville St.
Illinois St.	*West Va. Tech
Indiana St.	*Eastern Ill.
Marshall	*Southeast Mo. St.
Massachusetts	*William & Mary
Miami (Fla.)	*McNeese St.
Murray St.	*Southern Ill.
Nicholls St.	*Central Ark.
North Texas	*Baylor
Northern Iowa	*Morningside
Northwestern	*Northern Ill.
San Diego St.	*Arizona St.
Southwest Tex. St.	*Midwestern St.
Stephen F. Austin	*Central Okla.
Tenn.-Martin	*Lambuth
Wake Forest	*Appalachian St.
Weber St.	*Western St. (Colo.)
Wisconsin	*Western Mich.
Youngstown St.	*Slippery Rock

SATURDAY, SEPTEMBER 2

HOME	OPPONENT
Air Force	Cal St. Northridge
Alabama A&M	*Troy St.
Arkansas [1]	*Southwest Mo. St.
Butler	St. Francis (Ind.)
Charleston So.	Guilford
Clemson	*Citadel
Colorado [2]	Colorado St.
Delaware St.	Florida A&M
Drake	McKendree
Duke	East Caro.
Eastern Mich.	*Connecticut
Florida	*Ball St.
Fordham	Towson
Furman	*Elon
Georgia	*Ga. Southern
Georgia Tech	*UCF
Grambling	*Alcorn St.
Hampton	New Hampshire
Howard [3]	Jackson St.
Illinois	Middle Tenn. St.
Iowa St.	Ohio
Jacksonville	Lenoir-Rhyne
James Madison	*Lock Haven
Kansas St.	*Louisiana Tech
LSU	*Western Caro.
La.-Lafayette	*Sam Houston St.
Liberty	*East Tenn. St.
Louisville	*Kentucky
Marist	Western Conn. St.
Memphis	Mississippi St.
Michigan	Bowling Green
Minnesota	La.-Monroe
Mississippi	Tulane
Mississippi Val.	*Ark.-Pine Bluff
Missouri	*Western Ill.
Montana	Hofstra
Navy	*Temple
Nebraska	San Jose St.
New Mexico	*Boise St.
Norfolk St.	*Virginia St.
North Carolina	Tulsa
North Carolina St.	*Arkansas St.
Northeastern	American Int'l
Northwestern St.	*Southern U.
Notre Dame	Texas A&M
Ohio St.	Fresno St.
Oklahoma	*UTEP
Oregon	Nevada
Oregon St.	Eastern Wash.
Penn St.	Toledo
Pittsburgh	Kent St.
Portland St.	Western Wash.
Prairie View [4]	*Texas Southern
Purdue	Central Mich.
Rhode Island	Delaware
Rice	*Houston
Richmond	*Bucknell
Robert Morris	Buffalo St.
Rutgers	*Villanova
Sacred Heart	*Assumption
San Diego	*Azusa Pacific
South Carolina	*New Mexico St.
South Carolina St.	*Benedict
South Fla.	Jacksonville St.
Southern Methodist	*Kansas
Southern Utah	*Fort Lewis
St. Francis (Pa.)	La Salle
St. Mary's (Cal.)	Cal St. Sacramento
Syracuse	Buffalo
Tennessee	*Southern Miss.
Tennessee St.	*Alabama St.
Texas Tech	*Utah St.
Tri-State	Valparaiso
UCLA	Alabama
Utah	*Arizona
VMI	Duquesne
Vanderbilt	*Miami (Ohio)
Virginia	Brigham Young
Virginia Tech	Akron
Washington	Idaho
Washington St.	*Stanford
West Virginia	Boston College

[1] Little Rock, AR
[2] Denver, CO
[3] Chicago, IL
[4] Houston, TX

SUNDAY, SEPTEMBER 3

HOME	OPPONENT
N.C. A&T [1]	*N.C. Central

[1] Raleigh, NC

MONDAY, SEPTEMBER 4

HOME	OPPONENT
Cincinnati	Army

THURSDAY, SEPTEMBER 7

HOME	OPPONENT
East Caro.	*Virginia Tech
Sam Houston St.	*Southeastern Okla.
Samford	*Murray St.
St. Peter's	*Marist
UAB	*Chattanooga

SATURDAY, SEPTEMBER 9

HOME	OPPONENT
Air Force	Brigham Young
Alabama	Vanderbilt
Alabama A&M	*Henderson St.
Alcorn St.	*Alabama St.
Appalachian St.	*Troy St.
Arizona	*Ohio St.
Ark.-Pine Bluff	*Southern U.
Army	Boston College
Austin Peay	*Catawba
Ball St.	Western Ill.
Bethune-Cookman	Norfolk St.
Boise St.	*Northern Iowa
Bowling Green	Pittsburgh
Cal St. Sacramento	*Cal Poly
California	Utah
Central Conn. St.	Frostburg St.
UCF	*Northwestern St.
Central Mich.	Akron
Cincinnati	Syracuse
Clemson	Missouri
Colorado St.	East Tenn. St.
Connecticut	*Colgate
Davidson	Jacksonville
Dayton	*Ohio Northern
Delaware	*Citadel
Eastern Ill.	*Ky. Wesleyan
Eastern Mich.	Miami (Ohio)
Eastern Wash.	*Western Ore.
Elon	*Delaware St.
Florida	*Middle Tenn. St.
Florida A&M	*Morgan St.
Fordham	Fairfield
Furman	*Newberry
Ga. Southern	*Johnson Smith
Georgetown	Holy Cross
Georgia Tech	*Florida St.
Hampton	Howard
Hawaii	*Portland St.
Hope	*Valparaiso
Idaho	Montana
Idaho St.	*Montana Tech
Indiana	North Carolina St.
Indiana St.	*Eastern Ky.
Iona	Canisius
Iowa	Western Mich.
Iowa St.	UNLV
Jackson St.	*Texas Southern
James Madison	*Liberty
Kentucky	South Fla.
LSU	*Houston
La Salle	Duquesne
Lafayette	Towson
Louisville	*Grambling
Maine	*Hofstra
Maryland	*Temple
Memphis	*La.-Monroe
Michigan	Rice
Michigan St.	Marshall
Minnesota	Ohio
Mississippi	*Auburn
Mississippi Val.	*Delta St.
Montana St.	Humboldt St.
Morehead St.	*Butler
N.C. A&T [1]	Tennessee St.
Nevada	TCU
New Hampshire	Rhode Island
New Mexico	*Oregon St.
Nicholls St.	*Jacksonville St.
Northeastern	Albany (N.Y.)
Northern Ariz.	Chadron St.
Northern Ill.	*Illinois St.
Northwestern	Duke
Notre Dame	Nebraska
Oklahoma	*Arkansas St.

HOME	OPPONENT
Penn St.	Louisiana Tech
Prairie View [2]	*McNeese St.
Presbyterian	Charleston So.
Purdue	Kent St.
Rutgers	*Buffalo
Sacred Heart	Bryant
San Diego St.	*Illinois
Siena	*Hartwick
South Carolina	*Georgia
South Carolina St.	Savannah St.
Southern California	Colorado
Southern Ill.	Southeast Mo. St.
Southwest Mo. St.	*Mo. Southern St.
Southwest Tex. St.	*Cal St. Northridge
St. Ambrose	*Drake
St. Francis (Pa.)	St. John's (N.Y.)
St. Mary's (Cal.)	Western Wash.
Stanford	*San Jose St.
Stephen F. Austin	*Tex. A&M-Commerce
Stony Brook	Southern Conn. St.
Tennessee Tech	*Harding
Texas	La.-Lafayette
Texas A&M	*Wyoming
Texas Tech	*North Texas
Toledo	*Weber St.
Tulsa	*Oklahoma St.
UCLA	Fresno St.
UTEP	*Southern Methodist
Utah St.	*Southern Utah
Villanova	Millersville
Virginia	Richmond
Wagner	Monmouth
Wake Forest	*North Carolina
Washington	Miami (Fla.)
Western Caro.	*Lenoir-Rhyne
Western Ky.	Tenn.-Martin
Whittier	*San Diego
William & Mary	VMI
Wisconsin	Oregon
Wofford	*Lehigh
Youngstown St.	*Edinboro

[1] Cincinnati, OH
[2] Houston, TX

THURSDAY, SEPTEMBER 14

HOME	OPPONENT
Brigham Young	*Mississippi St.
Samford	*Tenn.-Martin

SATURDAY, SEPTEMBER 16

HOME	OPPONENT
Akron	*UCF
Alabama	Southern Miss.
Alabama A&M	*Grambling
Alcorn St.	*Fort Valley St.
Arizona	*San Diego St.
Arizona St.	*Colorado St.
Arkansas [1]	*Boise St.
Arkansas St.	*Memphis
Auburn	*LSU
Baylor	Minnesota
Bethune-Cookman	Johnson Smith
Brown	San Diego
Bucknell	Cornell
Buffalo	*Connecticut
Butler	St. Francis (Pa.)
Cal St. Northridge	Northern Ariz.
Cal St. Sacramento	*Portland St.
Canisius	St. Peter's
Charleston So.	West Virginia St.
Chattanooga	Mississippi Val.
Citadel	*Western Caro.
Clemson	Wake Forest
Colorado	Washington
Columbia	*Fordham
Dartmouth	Colgate
Delaware St.	Fayetteville St.
Duke	Virginia
Duquesne	Fairfield
East Caro.	Tulane
East Tenn. St.	VMI

HOME	OPPONENT
Eastern Wash.	*Idaho St.
Elon	Western Ky.
Florida St.	North Carolina
Furman	*William & Mary
Ga. Southern	Wofford
Georgia Tech	Navy
Hampton	Winston-Salem
Harvard	Holy Cross
Hofstra	*Delaware
Houston	*Army
Humboldt St.	*St. Mary's (Cal.)
Illinois	California
Iona	La Salle
Iowa	Iowa St.
Jackson St. [2]	*Tennessee St.
Jacksonville	Tusculum
Kansas	*UAB
Kansas St.	*Ball St.
Kent St.	*Youngstown St.
Kentucky	Indiana
Kutztown	Siena
La.-Monroe	*Nicholls St.
Lafayette	Princeton
Lehigh	Pennsylvania
Liberty	*Gardner-Webb
Louisiana Tech	*Stephen F. Austin
Maine	*Howard
McNeese St.	*Southwest Mo. St.
Middle Tenn. St.	*Murray St.
Missouri	Michigan St.
Montana	Cal Poly
Montana St.	Weber St.
New Hampshire	Northeastern
New Mexico St.	*New Mexico
North Carolina St.	*Southern Methodist
Notre Dame	Purdue
Ohio	Tennessee Tech
Ohio St.	Miami (Ohio)
Oklahoma St.	*Southwest Tex. St.
Oregon	Idaho
Pittsburgh	Penn St.
Prairie View [3]	*Southern U.
Rice	*Tulsa
Richmond	Massachusetts
Robert Morris	Monmouth
Rowan	Albany (N.Y.)
Sacred Heart	Central Conn. St.
San Jose St.	*Southern Utah
Sewanee	Davidson
South Carolina	*Eastern Mich.
South Fla.	James Madison
Southeast Mo. St.	*Illinois St.
Southern Ill.	Northern Iowa
St. Francis (Ind.)	Valparaiso
Stanford	*Texas
Stony Brook	St. John's (N.Y.)
TCU	Northwestern
Temple	*Bowling Green
Tennessee	Florida
Tennessee St. [4]	*Jackson St.
Texas A&M	*UTEP
Texas Southern	*Lane
Texas Tech	*La.-Lafayette
Toledo	*Eastern Ill.
Towson	Morgan St.
Troy St.	Alabama St.
UCLA	Michigan
UNLV	*North Texas
Utah	*Washington St.
Vanderbilt	Mississippi
Villanova	Norfolk St.
Virginia Tech	Rutgers
Wagner	Georgetown
West Virginia	Maryland
Western Ill.	Sam Houston St.
Western Mich.	*Indiana St.
Wis.-Stevens Point	Drake
Wisconsin	Cincinnati
Wyoming	Central Mich.
Yale	Dayton

[1] Little Rock, AR
[2] Memphis, TN
[3] Houston, TX
[4] Memphis, TN

THURSDAY, SEPTEMBER 21

HOME	OPPONENT
Jacksonville St.	*Samford
North Carolina St.	*Georgia Tech

FRIDAY, SEPTEMBER 22

HOME	OPPONENT
St. John's (N.Y.)	*Sacred Heart
St. Peter's	*Pace

SATURDAY, SEPTEMBER 23

HOME	OPPONENT
Alabama St.	*Ark.-Pine Bluff
Albany (N.Y.)	*Wagner
Alcorn St.	*McNeese St.
Appalachian St.	Citadel
Arizona St.	*Utah St.
Arkansas	*Alabama
Army	Memphis
Auburn	*Northern Ill.
Baylor	*South Fla.
Boston College	Navy
Brigham Young	UNLV
Brown	Harvard
Bucknell	Columbia
Buffalo	*Bowling Green
UCF	*William & Mary
Central Mich.	Boise St.
Charleston So.	Wofford
Chattanooga	*Ga. Southern
Colgate	Fordham
Connecticut	Northeastern
Cornell	Yale
Davidson	Emory & Henry
Dayton	*Morehead St.
Delaware	*West Chester
Delaware St.	Liberty
Duquesne	Marist
East Caro.	Syracuse
Eastern Ky.	*Tennessee Tech
Florida	Kentucky
Florida A&M [1]	Tennessee St.
Florida St.	*Louisville
Fresno St.	California
Gannon	Canisius
Georgetown	Butler
Georgia	New Mexico St.
Hofstra	*Rhode Island
Holy Cross	Towson
Howard	Morgan St.
Idaho St.	*Cal St. Sacramento
Illinois	*Michigan
Indiana	Cincinnati
Iona	Montclair St.
Kansas	*Southern Ill.
Kansas St.	North Texas
LSU	*UAB
La Salle	Siena
La.-Lafayette	*Northwestern St.
Maryland	*Middle Tenn. St.
Massachusetts	New Haven
Miami (Ohio)	Kent St.
Michigan St.	Notre Dame
Mississippi Val.	*Grambling
Monmouth	Central Conn. St.
Montana St.	Cal Poly
Morris Brown	*Bethune-Cookman
Murray St.	*Indiana St.
N.C. A&T	*Elon
Nebraska	Iowa
New Hampshire	Dartmouth
New Mexico	*Northern Ariz.
North Carolina	Marshall
Northern Iowa	Stephen F. Austin
Ohio	Akron
Ohio St.	Penn St.
Oklahoma	Rice
Oklahoma St.	*Southern Miss.
Oregon	UCLA

2000 SCHEDULES BY DATE

HOME	OPPONENT
Oregon St.	San Diego St.
Pennsylvania	Lafayette
Pittsburgh	Rutgers
Prairie View	*Alabama A&M
Princeton	*Lehigh
Purdue	Minnesota
Sam Houston St.	*Texas A&M-Kingsville
San Diego	*Menlo
South Carolina	Mississippi St.
Southeast Mo. St.	*Western Ky.
Southern California	San Jose St.
Southern Methodist	*Tulane
Southern U.	Jackson St.
St. Francis (Pa.)	Stony Brook
St. Mary's (Cal.)	Central Wash.
TCU	*Arkansas St.
Temple	*Eastern Mich.
Tenn.-Martin	Eastern Ill.
Tennessee	*La.-Monroe
Tennessee St. [2]	Florida A&M
Texas	Houston
Tulsa	*Louisiana Tech
UTEP	*Hawaii
Utah	Air Force
VMI	Furman
Valparaiso	Austin Peay
Vanderbilt	Duke
Villanova	Maine
Virginia	Clemson
Washington St.	Idaho
Weber St.	*Eastern Wash.
West Virginia	Miami (Fla.)
Western Caro.	*East Tenn. St.
Western Ill.	Nicholls St.
Western Mich.	*Toledo
Wisconsin	Northwestern
Wyoming	Nevada
[1] Atlanta, GA	
[2] Atlanta, GA	

THURSDAY, SEPTEMBER 28

HOME	OPPONENT
Maryland	*Florida St.
Temple	*West Virginia

SATURDAY, SEPTEMBER 30

HOME	OPPONENT
Akron	*Miami (Ohio)
Alabama	South Carolina
Alabama A&M	Mississippi Val.
Arkansas	*Georgia
Arkansas St.	*Richmond
Auburn	Vanderbilt
Ball St.	Northern Ill.
Baylor	*Iowa St.
Boston College	Virginia Tech
Bucknell	Duquesne
Butler	Dayton
Cal St. Northridge	Idaho St.
Cal St. Sacramento	*Weber St.
California	Washington St.
Catholic	La Salle
Central Conn. St.	St. John's (N.Y.)
Citadel	South Carolina St.
Colorado	Kansas St.
Columbia	Princeton
Delaware	Northeastern
Delaware St.	Hampton
Drake	San Diego
Duke	Clemson
East Tenn. St.	*Appalachian St.
Eastern Ky.	*Southeast Mo. St.
Eastern Mich.	UCF
Elon	New Haven
Fairfield	Iona
Florida A&M	*Howard
Furman	Western Caro.
Ga. Southern	VMI
Georgetown	Fordham
Hawaii	*Tulsa

HOME	OPPONENT
Houston	*Southern Methodist
Idaho	*Montana St.
Indiana	Iowa
Jacksonville	Austin Peay
James Madison	New Hampshire
Kent St.	*Bowling Green
LSU	*Tennessee
La.-Monroe	*Southwest Tex. St.
Lafayette	Harvard
Lehigh	Cornell
Liberty	*Wingate
Louisville	Connecticut
Maine	*William & Mary
Marshall	*Buffalo
Massachusetts	Hofstra
Michigan	Wisconsin
Michigan St.	Northwestern
Minnesota	Illinois
Mississippi	*Kentucky
Mississippi St.	Florida
Monmouth	Sacred Heart
Morgan St.	Bethune-Cookman
Murray St.	*Western Ky.
N.C. A&T	*Norfolk St.
Navy	TCU
Nebraska	Missouri
Nevada	Colorado St.
New Mexico	*Wyoming
North Carolina	Georgia Tech
Northern Ariz.	Portland St.
Northern Iowa	Illinois St.
Northwestern St.	*Gardner-Webb
Oklahoma	Kansas
Oregon	Washington
Oregon St.	Southern California
Penn St.	Purdue
Pennsylvania	Dartmouth
Prairie View [1]	*Grambling
Rhode Island	Brown
Rutgers	*Miami (Fla.)
Samford	*Nicholls St.
San Jose St.	Rice
South Fla.	Troy St.
Southern Miss.	*Memphis
Southern U.	*Alabama St.
Southern Utah	*Cal Poly
Southwest Mo. St.	*Youngstown St.
St. Francis (Pa.)	Robert Morris
St. Peter's	*Siena
Stanford	Arizona
Stony Brook	Albany (N.Y.)
Syracuse	Brigham Young
Tennessee Tech	Tenn.-Martin
Texas	Oklahoma St.
Texas A&M	Texas Tech
Texas Southern	*Langston
Toledo	*Central Mich.
Towson	Colgate
Tulane	Cincinnati
UAB	La.-Lafayette
UC Davis	*St. Mary's (Cal.)
UCLA	*Arizona St.
UNLV	*Air Force
UTEP	*New Mexico St.
Utah St.	Utah
Valparaiso	Morehead St.
Wagner	Marist
Wake Forest	Virginia
Western Ill.	Indiana St.
Western Mich.	Ohio
Wofford	Chattanooga
Yale	Holy Cross
[1] Dallas, TX	

THURSDAY, OCTOBER 5

HOME	OPPONENT
Marshall	*Western Mich.
North Texas	*Samford
Rice	*Fresno St.
Weber St.	*Cal St. Northridge

FRIDAY, OCTOBER 6

HOME	OPPONENT
Brigham Young	*Utah St.

SATURDAY, OCTOBER 7

HOME	OPPONENT
Air Force	Navy
Alabama A&M	*Southern U.
Alabama St. [1]	Jackson St.
Albany (N.Y.)	St. Francis (Pa.)
Albion	Butler
Appalachian St.	Furman
Arizona St.	*California
Arkansas	*La.-Monroe
Austin Peay	*Dayton
Bethune-Cookman	Delaware St.
Boston College	Connecticut
Bowling Green	Akron
Cal Poly	*St. Mary's (Cal.)
Canisius	La Salle
Central Mich.	Kent St.
Charleston So.	Jacksonville
Cincinnati	Houston
Citadel	East Tenn. St.
Clemson	North Carolina St.
Colgate	Princeton
Colorado St.	New Mexico
Columbia	Lafayette
Dartmouth	Yale
Davidson	Morehead St.
Drake	Valparaiso
Eastern Ill.	Tennessee St.
Eastern Mich.	Toledo
Elon	Gardner-Webb
Florida	LSU
Florida A&M [2]	Grambling
Fordham	Brown
Georgetown	Bucknell
Georgia	Tennessee
Harvard	Cornell
Holy Cross	Pennsylvania
Idaho St.	*Northern Ariz.
Illinois St.	Youngstown St.
Indiana St.	Southwest Mo. St.
Iona	St. Peter's
Iowa	Michigan St.
Iowa St.	Nebraska
Jacksonville St.	Sam Houston St.
James Madison	Villanova
Kansas	Kansas St.
Kentucky	*South Carolina
C. W. Post	Monmouth
La.-Lafayette	Tulane
McNeese St.	*Stephen F. Austin
Memphis	*East Caro.
Miami (Fla.)	Florida St.
Miami (Ohio)	Ball St.
Middle Tenn. St.	*Louisiana Tech
Minnesota	Penn St.
Mississippi	Arkansas St.
Mississippi St.	Auburn
Missouri	Oklahoma St.
Montana	Cal St. Sacramento
Montana St.	Eastern Wash.
N.C. A&T	Morgan St.
New Mexico St.	*Army
Norfolk St.	South Carolina St.
Northeastern	Massachusetts
Northern Ill.	UCF
Northwestern	Indiana
Northwestern St.	*Troy St.
Notre Dame	Stanford
Ohio	*Buffalo
Oklahoma [3]	Texas
Portland St.	Hofstra
Prairie View	*Alcorn St.
Purdue	Michigan
Richmond	Delaware
Robert Morris	St. John's (N.Y.)
San Diego	Central Conn. St.
Siena	Fairfield

HOME	OPPONENT
Southern California	Arizona
Southern Ill.	Western Ill.
Southern Methodist	*San Jose St.
Southern Miss.	*South Fla.
Southwest Tex. St.	Nicholls St.
Syracuse	Pittsburgh
TCU	*Hawaii
Tenn.-Martin	Murray St.
Tennessee Tech	Southeast Mo. St.
Texas A&M	Colorado
Texas Southern	*Ark.-Pine Bluff
Texas Tech	*Baylor
Towson	Lehigh
Tulsa	*UTEP
UAB	Louisville
UNLV	*Nevada
VMI	Wofford
Virginia	Maryland
Virginia Tech	Temple
Wagner	Stony Brook
Wake Forest	Vanderbilt
Washington	*Oregon St.
Washington St.	Boise St.
West Virginia	Idaho
Western Caro.	*Ga. Southern
Western Ky.	Eastern Ky.
William & Mary	Rhode Island
Wisconsin	Ohio St.
Wyoming	San Diego St.

[1] Mobile, AL
[2] Indianapolis, IN
[3] Dallas, TX

THURSDAY, OCTOBER 12

HOME	OPPONENT
Virginia Tech	*West Virginia

FRIDAY, OCTOBER 13

HOME	OPPONENT
Hofstra	*Liberty
St. John's (N.Y.)	*Albany (N.Y.)

SATURDAY, OCTOBER 14

HOME	OPPONENT
Akron	*Northern Ill.
Alabama	Mississippi
Alcorn St.	Texas Southern
Arizona	*Washington St.
Arizona St.	*Washington
Austin Peay	Charleston So.
Ball St.	Eastern Mich.
Baylor	Texas A&M
Bethune-Cookman	*South Carolina St.
Boise St.	Eastern Wash.
Boston College	Syracuse
Bucknell	Lafayette
Cal Poly	*Western N.M.
Cal St. Northridge	Montana
Cal St. Sacramento	*Montana St.
California	UCLA
Central Conn. St.	Wagner
UCF	*Eastern Ky.
Chattanooga	*VMI
Clemson	Maryland
Colorado	Texas
Colorado St.	UNLV
Cornell	Colgate
Dartmouth	Holy Cross
Dayton	Robert Morris
Duquesne	Georgetown
East Caro.	Army
Eastern Ill.	Murray St.
Elon	Samford
Fairfield	St. Peter's
Florida	Auburn
Florida A&M	N.C. A&T
Florida St.	*Duke
Fordham	Yale
Fresno St.	Nevada

HOME	OPPONENT
Furman	Citadel
Ga. Southern	Appalachian St.
Georgia	Vanderbilt
Georgia Tech	Wake Forest
Grambling [1]	Ark.-Pine Bluff
Hampton	Norfolk St.
Harvard	Lehigh
Hawaii	*Southern Methodist
Idaho	*Arkansas St.
Illinois	Iowa
Indiana St.	Illinois St.
Jackson St.	*Mississippi Val.
Kansas St.	Oklahoma
Kent St.	Ohio
LSU	*Kentucky
Louisiana Tech	*La.-Lafayette
Louisville	Cincinnati
Marist	Iona
Massachusetts	Maine
McNeese St.	*Jacksonville St.
Miami (Ohio)	Bowling Green
Michigan	Indiana
Michigan St.	Wisconsin
Middle Tenn. St.	*La.-Monroe
Missouri	Kansas
Monmouth	St. Francis (Pa.)
Morris Brown	Alabama A&M
Navy [2]	Notre Dame
New Hampshire	Richmond
New Mexico St.	*Tulsa
Nicholls St.	Northwestern St.
North Carolina	North Carolina St.
North Texas	Utah St.
Northeastern	Villanova
Northern Ariz.	Weber St.
Northwestern	Purdue
Ohio St.	Minnesota
Oklahoma St.	Iowa St.
Oregon St.	Stanford
Pennsylvania	Columbia
Portland St.	Idaho St.
Prairie View	Alabama St.
Princeton	Brown
Rhode Island	James Madison
Rochester	Canisius
Rutgers	Temple
San Diego	*Davidson
San Diego St.	*Utah
San Jose St.	*UTEP
Savannah St.	Morgan St.
South Carolina	Arkansas
Southern California	Oregon
Southern Ill.	Drake
Southwest Mo. St.	Western Ill.
St. Mary's (Cal.)	Menlo
Stephen F. Austin	Sam Houston St.
Stony Brook	Sacred Heart
Tennessee	*Tenn.-Martin
Texas Tech	*Nebraska
Toledo	*Marshall
Towson	Howard
Troy St.	*Southwest Tex. St.
Tulane	Southern Miss.
UAB	Memphis
UC Davis	Southern Utah
Valparaiso	Butler
Western Ky.	Tennessee Tech
William & Mary	Delaware
Wofford	Western Caro.
Wyoming	Air Force
Youngstown St.	Northern Iowa

[1] Shreveport, LA
[2] Orlando, FL

THURSDAY, OCTOBER 19

HOME	OPPONENT
Louisville	*East Caro.

SATURDAY, OCTOBER 21

HOME	OPPONENT
Air Force	New Mexico

HOME	OPPONENT
Akron	*Connecticut
Alcorn St.	Southern U.
Appalachian St.	Wofford
Ark.-Pine Bluff	*Kentucky St.
Arkansas St.	New Mexico St.
Army	Tulane
Auburn	Louisiana Tech
Boise St.	North Texas
Bowling Green	*Eastern Mich.
Brigham Young	San Diego St.
Brown	Cornell
Buffalo	Ball St.
Butler	San Diego
Cal Poly	*UC Davis
Canisius	Siena
UCF	La.-Monroe
Citadel	Ga. Southern
Colgate	St. Mary's (Cal.)
Columbia	Dartmouth
Davidson	Randolph-Macon
Dayton	Drake
Delaware St.	Morgan St.
Duquesne	Iona
East Tenn. St.	*Furman
Eastern Wash.	Cal St. Sacramento
Florida St.	Virginia
Georgia Tech	Duke
Grambling	Jackson St.
Hofstra	Elon
Howard	N.C. A&T
Idaho St.	Southern Utah
Illinois St.	Prairie View
Indiana	Minnesota
Indiana St.	Northern Iowa
Iowa	Ohio St.
Iowa St.	Texas A&M
James Madison	William & Mary
Kansas	Colorado
Kansas St.	Texas Tech
Kentucky	*Georgia
Ky. Wesleyan	*Austin Peay
LSU	*Mississippi St.
La Salle	Shenandoah
Lafayette	Holy Cross
Lehigh	Bucknell
Marist	Georgetown
Marshall	Kent St.
Maryland	Wake Forest
Massachusetts	American Int'l
Memphis	*Houston
Michigan	Michigan St.
Monmouth	Stony Brook
Montana	Northern Ariz.
Montana St.	Cal St. Northridge
Navy	Rutgers
Nebraska	Baylor
Nevada	San Jose St.
Nicholls St.	*Stephen F. Austin
Norfolk St.	Florida A&M
North Carolina	Clemson
Northeastern	Rhode Island
Northwestern St.	McNeese St.
Ohio	Central Mich.
Oregon	*Arizona
Penn St.	Illinois
Pittsburgh	Boston College
Princeton	Harvard
Rice	Hawaii
Richmond	Maine
Robert Morris	Central Conn. St.
Sacred Heart	Albany (N.Y.)
Sam Houston St.	*Troy St.
Samford	Gardner-Webb
South Carolina St.	Hampton
South Fla.	*Liberty
Southeast Mo. St.	Murray St.
Southwest Mo. St.	Southern Ill.
Southwest Tex. St.	Jacksonville St.
St. Francis (Pa.)	Wagner
St. Joseph's (Ind.)	Valparaiso
St. Peter's	*St. John's (N.Y.)
Stanford	Southern California
Syracuse	Virginia Tech
Temple	Miami (Fla.)
Tenn.-Martin	Eastern Ky.

2000 SCHEDULES BY DATE

HOME	OPPONENT
Tennessee	Alabama
Tennessee St.	Western Ky.
Tennessee Tech	Eastern Ill.
Texas	Missouri
Texas Southern	*Mississippi Val.
Tulsa	*TCU
UAB	Middle Tenn. St.
UCLA	Oregon St.
UNLV	Wyoming
UTEP	*Fresno St.
Utah	Colorado St.
Utah St.	Idaho
VMI	Charleston So.
Vanderbilt	South Carolina
Villanova	New Hampshire
Virginia-Wise	Jacksonville
Washington	California
Washington St.	Arizona St.
Weber St.	Portland St.
West Virginia	Notre Dame
Western Caro.	Chattanooga
Western Ill.	Youngstown St.
Western Mich.	Northern Ill.
Wisconsin	Purdue
Yale	Pennsylvania

THURSDAY, OCTOBER 26

HOME	OPPONENT
Brigham Young	*Wyoming
Eastern Ky.	*Tennessee St.

SATURDAY, OCTOBER 28

HOME	OPPONENT
Akron	*Marshall
Alabama	UCF
Alabama A&M [1]	Alabama St.
Albany (N.Y.)	Central Conn. St.
Arizona	UCLA
Arizona St.	*Oregon
Ark.-Pine Bluff	*Jackson St.
Auburn	Arkansas
Austin Peay	Morehead St.
Boston College	Rutgers
Bucknell	Fordham
Cal Poly	Hofstra
Cal St. Northridge	Eastern Wash.
Central Mich.	Ball St.
Charleston So.	Elon
Chattanooga	Appalachian St.
Cincinnati	Miami (Ohio)
Clemson	Georgia Tech
Colgate	Lafayette
Colorado	Oklahoma St.
Connecticut	South Fla.
Cornell	Princeton
Dartmouth	Harvard
Dayton	St. Joseph's (Ind.)
Delaware	James Madison
Delaware St.	South Carolina St.
Drake	Butler
Duke	Maryland
East Caro.	UAB
Fairfield	Georgetown
Florida [2]	Georgia
Florida A&M	Hampton
Fresno St.	*Tulsa
Ga. Southern	East Tenn. St.
Georgia [3]	Florida
Hampden-Sydney	Davidson
Hawaii	*San Jose St.
Holy Cross	Lehigh
Houston	Southern Miss.
Howard	Norfolk St.
Idaho St.	*Weber St.
Illinois St.	Southern Ill.
Indiana [4]	*Penn St.
Iowa	Wisconsin
Iowa St.	Missouri
Jacksonville	Stony Brook
Jacksonville St.	Stephen F. Austin
Kansas	Texas Tech

HOME	OPPONENT
Kent St.	Western Mich.
La.-Lafayette	*North Texas
Liberty	Samford
Louisville	Tulane
Maine	Rhode Island
Marist	Canisius
Miami (Fla.)	Louisiana Tech
Michigan St.	Illinois
Minnesota	Northwestern
Mississippi	UNLV
Mississippi St.	Middle Tenn. St.
Mississippi Val.	Prairie View
Monmouth	Towson
Murray St.	Tennessee Tech
N.C. A&T	Bethune-Cookman
Navy	Toledo
New Hampshire	Massachusetts
New Mexico	Utah
New Mexico St.	*Boise St.
North Carolina St.	*Florida St.
Northern Ariz.	Montana St.
Northern Ill.	Buffalo
Northern Iowa	Southwest Mo. St.
Notre Dame	Air Force
Oklahoma	Nebraska
Oregon St.	Washington St.
Pennsylvania	Brown
Portland St.	Montana
Purdue	Ohio St.
Sacred Heart	Iona
Sam Houston St.	McNeese St.
San Diego	*Valparaiso
San Diego St.	Colorado St.
South Carolina	Tennessee
Southeast Mo. St.	*Tenn.-Martin
Southern California	California
Southern Methodist	*Nevada
Southern U.	*Morris Brown
Southern Utah	St. Mary's (Cal.)
Southwest Tex. St.	Northwestern St.
St. Anselm	Siena
St. John's (N.Y.)	La Salle
St. Peter's	Duquesne
Stanford	Washington
TCU	Rice
Texas	Baylor
Texas A&M	Kansas St.
Texas Southern	*Grambling
Troy St.	Nicholls St.
UC Davis	Cal St. Sacramento
Utah St.	Arkansas St.
VMI	Western Caro.
Villanova	Richmond
Virginia	North Carolina
Virginia Tech	Pittsburgh
Wagner	Robert Morris
Western Ill.	Morgan St.
Western Ky.	Eastern Ill.
William & Mary	Northeastern
Wofford	Citadel
Yale	Columbia
Youngstown St.	Indiana St.

[1] Birmingham, AL
[2] Jacksonville, FL
[3] Jacksonville, FL
[4] Indianapolis, IN

THURSDAY, NOVEMBER 2

HOME	OPPONENT
Colorado St.	*Brigham Young

SATURDAY, NOVEMBER 4

HOME	OPPONENT
Albany (N.Y.)	Monmouth
Alfred	Canisius
Appalachian St.	VMI
Arizona St.	*Southern California
Ark.-Pine Bluff	Prairie View
Arkansas	Mississippi
Arkansas St.	Boise St.
Army	Air Force

HOME	OPPONENT
Austin Peay	Virginia-Wise
Ball St.	Western Mich.
Baylor	Oklahoma
Boston College	Temple
Bowling Green	Marshall
Brown	Yale
Buffalo	Kent St.
Cal Poly	Northern Iowa
Cal St. Sacramento	*Cal St. Northridge
California	Oregon St.
Central Conn. St.	St. Francis (Pa.)
Cincinnati	UAB
Citadel	Chattanooga
Connecticut	Middle Tenn. St.
Cornell	Dartmouth
Davidson	Centre
Delaware	New Hampshire
Delaware St.	N.C. A&T
Drake	Jacksonville
East Tenn. St.	Wofford
Eastern Ill.	Southeast Mo. St.
Eastern Ky.	Murray St.
Eastern Mich.	Central Mich.
Eastern Wash.	Northern Ariz.
Elon	Liberty
Florida St.	*Clemson
Fordham	Lafayette
Fresno St.	Hawaii
Furman	Ga. Southern
Georgetown	Iona
Grambling	Alabama St.
Hampton	Bethune-Cookman
Harvard	Columbia
Holy Cross	Bucknell
Illinois	Indiana
Jackson St.	Alabama A&M
Jacksonville St.	Northwestern St.
James Madison	Maine
Kansas St.	Iowa St.
Kentucky	Mississippi St.
LSU	Alabama
La.-Monroe	*La.-Lafayette
Lehigh	Colgate
Louisiana Tech	*UCF
Marist	Fairfield
Maryland	North Carolina St.
Massachusetts	Villanova
McNeese St.	*Southwest Tex. St.
Memphis	Tennessee
Miami (Fla.)	Virginia Tech
Miami (Ohio)	Ohio
Mississippi Val.	Alcorn St.
Missouri	Colorado
Montana	Idaho St.
Montana St.	Portland St.
Morehead St.	Ky. Wesleyan
Morris Brown	Texas Southern
Nebraska	Kansas
Nevada	UTEP
New Mexico	San Diego St.
New Mexico St.	*Utah St.
Nicholls St.	*Sam Houston St.
Norfolk St.	Morgan St.
North Texas	Idaho
Northern Ill.	Toledo
Northwestern	Michigan
Ohio St.	Michigan St.
Oklahoma St.	Texas A&M
Penn St.	Iowa
Pittsburgh	North Carolina
Princeton	Pennsylvania
Quincy	Butler
Rhode Island	Richmond
Rice	Southern Methodist
Sacred Heart	Robert Morris
Samford	Charleston So.
San Jose St.	TCU
Siena	Duquesne
South Carolina St.	Howard
South Fla.	*Western Ky.
Southern Ill.	Indiana St.
Southern Miss.	Louisville
Southern U.	*Florida A&M
Southern Utah	Rocky Mountain
Southwest Mo. St.	Tenn.-Martin

HOME	OPPONENT
St. Mary's (Cal.)	Towson
St. Peter's	*La Salle
Stephen F. Austin	Troy St.
Tennessee Tech	Tennessee St.
Texas Tech	Texas
Tulane	Houston
UCLA	Stanford
Utah	UNLV
Valparaiso	Dayton
Vanderbilt	Florida
Wagner	St. John's (N.Y.)
Wake Forest	Duke
Washington	Arizona
Washington St.	Oregon
Weber St.	Western N.M.
West Virginia	Syracuse
Western Ill.	Illinois St.
Wisconsin	Minnesota
Youngstown St.	Hofstra

THURSDAY, NOVEMBER 9

HOME	OPPONENT
Georgia Tech	*Virginia
Tennessee Tech	*Samford

FRIDAY, NOVEMBER 10

HOME	OPPONENT
St. John's (N.Y.)	*Monmouth

SATURDAY, NOVEMBER 11

HOME	OPPONENT
Air Force	Colorado St.
Akron	*Buffalo
Alabama A&M	Alcorn St.
Alabama St.	Mississippi Val.
Arizona	*Oregon St.
Ark.-Pine Bluff	Lane
Arkansas St.	North Texas
Auburn	Georgia
Austin Peay	Davidson
Baylor	Missouri
Boise St.	Utah St.
Bowling Green	Ohio
Cal St. Northridge	Cal Poly
Central Conn. St.	Stony Brook
UCF	*Virginia Tech
Central Mich.	Western Mich.
Chattanooga	East Tenn. St.
Colgate	Holy Cross
Colorado	Iowa St.
Columbia	Cornell
Connecticut	Rhode Island
Dartmouth	Brown
Duquesne	Lafayette
East Caro.	Houston
Eastern Ky.	Kentucky St.
Eastern Mich.	Northern Ill.
Fairfield	Canisius
Florida	South Carolina
Ga. Southern	Elon
Georgetown	St. Peter's
Hampton	N.C. A&T
Hawaii	*Nevada
Howard	*Bethune-Cookman
Idaho	*New Mexico St.
Idaho St.	*Montana St.
Illinois	Ohio St.
Illinois St.	Eastern Ill.
Indiana	Wisconsin
Iona	Siena
Iowa	Northwestern
Jackson St.	New Haven
Jacksonville	Wagner
Kansas	Texas
Kansas St.	Nebraska
Kentucky	Vanderbilt
La Salle	Marist
La.-Lafayette	Jacksonville St.
La.-Monroe	*Louisiana Tech

HOME	OPPONENT
Lehigh	Fordham
Liberty	Charleston So.
Louisville	Army
Maine	Northeastern
Marshall	*Miami (Ohio)
Massachusetts	Delaware
Memphis	Cincinnati
Miami (Fla.)	Pittsburgh
Michigan	Penn St.
Michigan St.	Purdue
Middle Tenn. St.	South Fla.
Mississippi	LSU
Mississippi St.	Alabama
Murray St.	Tennessee St.
New Hampshire	Gardner-Webb
Norfolk St.	Delaware St.
North Carolina	Maryland
North Carolina St.	Duke
Northern Ariz.	Cal St. Sacramento
Northern Iowa	*Prairie View
Northwestern St.	Sam Houston St.
Notre Dame	Boston College
Oregon	California
Pennsylvania	Harvard
Portland St.	Eastern Wash.
Richmond	James Madison
Robert Morris	Albany (N.Y.)
Rutgers	West Virginia
San Diego	*Dayton
South Carolina St.	Morgan St.
Southern California	Washington St.
Southern Methodist	*Tulsa
Southern U.	*Texas Southern
Southern Utah	Morehead St.
Southwest Mo. St.	Southeast Mo. St.
Southwest Tex. St.	Stephen F. Austin
St. Francis (Pa.)	Sacred Heart
St. Mary's (Cal.)	Drake
Stanford	Arizona St.
TCU	Fresno St.
Temple	Syracuse
Tenn.-Martin	Wingate
Tennessee	Arkansas
Texas A&M	Oklahoma
Texas Tech	Oklahoma St.
Toledo	Ball St.
Towson	Bucknell
Troy St.	McNeese St.
Tulane	Navy
UAB	Southern Miss.
UNLV	New Mexico
UTEP	*Rice
VMI	Citadel
Valparaiso	Aurora
Villanova	William & Mary
Wake Forest	Florida St.
Washington	UCLA
Weber St.	Montana
Western Caro.	Appalachian St.
Western Ky.	Indiana St.
Wofford	Furman
Wyoming	Utah
Yale	Princeton
Youngstown St.	Southern Ill.

THURSDAY, NOVEMBER 16

HOME	OPPONENT
Colorado St.	*Wyoming

SATURDAY, NOVEMBER 18

HOME	OPPONENT
Air Force	San Diego St.
Alabama	Auburn
Appalachian St.	Liberty
Ark.-Pine Bluff	Alabama A&M
Army	UAB
Ball St.	Connecticut
Boise St.	Idaho
Brigham Young	New Mexico
Brown	Columbia
Bucknell	Colgate

HOME	OPPONENT
Buffalo	Miami (Ohio)
Cal Poly	Youngstown St.
California	Stanford
Canisius	Duquesne
Cincinnati	Southern Miss.
Clemson	South Carolina
Cornell	Pennsylvania
Davidson	Georgetown
Delaware	Villanova
Drake	Towson
Duke	North Carolina
East Tenn. St.	*Charleston So.
Eastern Ill.	Eastern Ky.
Florida St.	Florida
Fresno St.	Southern Methodist
Furman	Chattanooga
Georgia	Mississippi
Harvard	Yale
Hawaii	*Louisiana Tech
Hofstra	Albany (N.Y.)
Holy Cross	Fordham
Houston	Louisville
Howard	Delaware St.
Illinois St.	Southwest Mo. St.
Iona	St. John's (N.Y.)
Iowa St.	Kansas
Jackson St.	Alcorn St.
Jacksonville	Monmouth
Jacksonville St.	Troy St.
Kent St.	Akron
La Salle	Fairfield
La.-Monroe	Wofford
Lafayette	Lehigh
Maine	New Hampshire
Maryland	Georgia Tech
McNeese St.	*Nicholls St.
Middle Tenn. St.	La.-Lafayette
Minnesota	Iowa
Mississippi St.	Arkansas
Missouri	Kansas St.
Montana	Montana St.
Morgan St.	Hampton
N.C. A&T [1]	South Carolina St.
Navy	Wake Forest
Nevada	Rice
Norfolk St.[2]	Texas Southern
North Texas	New Mexico St.
Northeastern	James Madison
Northern Ariz.	Southern Utah
Northern Ill.	Central Mich.
Northern Iowa	*Western Ill.
Northwestern	Illinois
Ohio	Marshall
Ohio St.	Michigan
Oklahoma	Texas Tech
Oklahoma St.	Baylor
Oregon St.	Oregon
Penn St.	Michigan St.
Portland St.	Cal St. Northridge
Princeton	Dartmouth
Purdue	Indiana
Rhode Island	Massachusetts
Rutgers	Notre Dame
Sacred Heart	Wagner
Sam Houston St.	Southwest Tex. St.
Siena	Marist
South Fla.	Austin Peay
St. Peter's	*St. Francis (Pa.)
Stephen F. Austin	Northwestern St.
Stony Brook	Robert Morris
Syracuse	Miami (Fla.)
TCU	UTEP
Temple	Pittsburgh
Tennessee	Kentucky
Tennessee St.	Southeast Mo. St.
Tulane	Memphis
Tulsa	San Jose St.
UCLA	Southern California
Utah St.	Idaho St.
Virginia	North Carolina St.
Washington St.	Washington
West Virginia	East Caro.
Western Caro.	Tennessee Tech
Western Ky.	Southern Ill.
Western Mich.	Eastern Mich.

2000 SCHEDULES BY DATE

HOME	OPPONENT
William & Mary	Richmond

[1] Charlotte, NC
[2] San Diego, CA

WEDNESDAY, NOVEMBER 22

HOME	OPPONENT
Toledo	*Bowling Green

THURSDAY, NOVEMBER 23

HOME	OPPONENT
Alabama St.	Tuskegee
Mississippi	*Mississippi St.

FRIDAY, NOVEMBER 24

HOME	OPPONENT
Arizona	Arizona St.

HOME	OPPONENT
Arkansas [1]	LSU
Jacksonville [2]	*Fairfield
Nebraska	Colorado
Pittsburgh	West Virginia
Texas	Texas A&M
Utah	Brigham Young

[1] Little Rock, AR
[2] Orlando, FL

SATURDAY, NOVEMBER 25

HOME	OPPONENT
Georgia	Georgia Tech
Hawaii	*Wisconsin
Miami (Fla.)	Boston College
North Carolina St.	Wake Forest
Oklahoma St.	Oklahoma
San Diego St.	UNLV
San Jose St.	Fresno St.
Southern California	Notre Dame

HOME	OPPONENT
Southern Methodist	TCU
Southern Miss.	East Caro.
Syracuse	Rutgers
Tulsa	Nevada
Vanderbilt	Tennessee
Virginia Tech	Virginia

SATURDAY, DECEMBER 2

HOME	OPPONENT
Hawaii	*UNLV
Navy [1]	Army

[1] Baltimore, MD